GRADUATE STUDY IN
PSYCHOLOGY

2014

American
Psychological
Association

American Psychological Association
Washington, DC

Published by
American Psychological Association
750 First Street, NE
Washington, DC 20002

www.apa.org

Typeset by Cadmus Communications, Baltimore, MD

Printer: United Book Press, Inc., Baltimore, MD
Cover Designer: Naylor Design, Washington, DC

ISBN-13: 978-1-4338-1548-5
ISBN-10: 1-4338-1548-6
ISSN: 2160-9527
47th edition

To order
APA Order Department
P.O. Box 92984
Washington, DC 20090-2984
Tel: (800) 374-2721, Direct: (202) 336-5510
Fax: (202) 336-5502, TDD/TTY: (202) 336-6123
Online: www.apa.org/pubs/books/
E-mail: order@apa.org

Printed in the United States of America

Contents

Foreword

This is the 47th edition of a book prepared to assist individuals interested in graduate study in psychology. The current edition provides information for more than 600 graduate departments, programs, and schools of psychology in the United States and Canada. The information was obtained from questionnaires sent to graduate departments and schools of psychology and was provided voluntarily. The American Psychological Association (APA) is not responsible for the accuracy of the information reported.

The purpose of this publication is to provide an information service, offering in one book information about the majority of graduate programs in psychology. Inclusion in this publication does not signify APA approval or endorsement of a graduate program, nor should it be assumed that a listing of a program in *Graduate Study in Psychology* means that its graduates are automatically qualified to sit for licensure as psychologists or are eligible for positions requiring a psychology degree.

However, programs listed in this publication have agreed to the following quality assurance provisions:

1. They have agreed to honor April 15 as the date allowed for graduate applicants to accept or reject an offer of admission and financial assistance for fall matriculation. This date adheres to national policy guidelines as stated by the Council of Graduate Schools and the Council of Graduate Departments of Psychology.

2. They have satisfied the following criteria: The program offers a graduate degree and is sponsored by a public or private higher education institution accredited by one of six regional accrediting bodies recognized by the U.S. Secretary of Education, or, in the case of Canadian programs, the institution is publicly recognized by the Association of Universities and Colleges of Canada as a member in good standing, or the program indicates that it meets *all* of the following criteria:

    A. The graduate program, wherever it may be administratively housed, is publicly labeled as a psychology program in pertinent institutional catalogs and brochures.

    B. The psychology program stands as a recognizable, coherent organizational entity within the institution.

    C. There is an identifiable core of full-time psychology faculty.

    D. Psychologists have clear authority and primary responsibility for the academic core and specialty preparation, whether or not the program involves multiple administrative lines.

    E. There is an identifiable body of graduate students who are enrolled in the program for the attainment of the graduate degree offered.

    F. The program is an organized, integrated sequence of study designed by the psychology faculty responsible for the program.

    G. Programs leading to a doctoral degree require at least the equivalent of 3 full-time academic years of graduate study.

    H. Doctoral programs ensure appropriate breadth and depth of education and training in psychology as follows:

        1) Methodology and history, including systematic preparation in scientific standards and responsibilities, research design and methodology, quantitative methods (e.g., statistics, psychometric methods), and historical foundations in psychology.

        2) Foundations in psychology, including

            a. biological bases of behavior (e.g., physiological psychology, comparative psychology, neuropsychology, psychopharmacology);

            b. cognitive–affective bases of behavior (e.g., learning, memory, perception, cognition, thinking, motivation, emotion);

            c. social bases of behavior (e.g., social psychology; cultural, ethnic, and group processes; sex roles; organizational behavior); and

            d. individual differences (e.g., personality theory, human development, individual differences, abnormal psychology, psychology of women, psychology of persons with disabilities, psychology of the minority experience).

        3) Additional preparation in the program's area of specialization, to include

            a. knowledge and application of ethical principles and guidelines and standards as may apply to scientific and professional practice activities;

            b. supervised practicum and/or laboratory experiences appropriate to the area of practice, teaching, or research in psychology; and

            c. advanced preparation appropriate to the area of specialization.

This publication may not answer all questions you have about graduate education in psychology. Some questions you may want to direct to particular graduate departments, programs, or schools of psychology. *For more information about general policies and information related to graduate education, visit the APA Education website (http://www.apa.org/ed).*

Producing this annual publication involves the cooperation of many individuals each year. We wish to express appreciation to all graduate departments, programs, and schools that contributed information. We also wish to acknowledge the support and contributions by individuals in the Education Directorate, Internet Services, Publications and Databases, and the Center for Psychology Workforce Analysis and Research.

Caroline Cope, MA
Research Officer
Office of Graduate and Postgraduate Education and Training
Education Directorate
American Psychological Association

Considering Graduate Study

Psychology is a broad scientific discipline bridging the social and biological sciences. Psychology's applications include education and human development, health and human resilience, family and community relations, organizations and other work environments, engineering and technology, the arts and architecture, communications, and political and judiciary systems.

There are many types of graduate programs in psychology. Selecting a graduate program that is best for you requires thoughtful consideration. The American Psychological Association (APA) does not rank graduate programs in psychology. Rather, APA encourages selecting graduate programs based on the best match for you. Some programs focus on preparing students for an academic research career, while others focus on preparing students for applied research outside the university. Other programs prepare students to provide psychological services as licensed professional psychologists. Some programs offer professional development, in addition to a focus in psychology, to prepare students for a college teaching career. Psychology subfields of recent master's and doctoral graduates are illustrated in Figures 1 and 2.

Figure 1. Master's Degrees Awarded by Psychology Subfield: 2011–2012

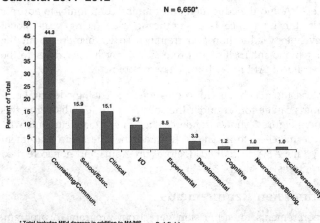

Source: *Graduate Study in Psychology, 2014 Edition* data. Prepared by the APA Office of Graduate and Postgraduate Education and Training.

Figure 2. Doctoral Degrees Awarded by Psychology Subfield: 2011–2012

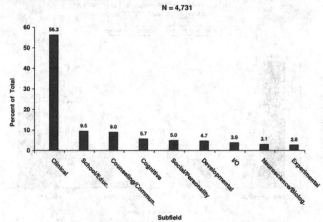

Source: *Graduate Study in Psychology, 2014 Edition* data. Prepared by the APA Office of Graduate and Postgraduate Education and Training.

Programs, Degrees, and Employment

Although employment in research, teaching, and human service positions is possible for those with a master's degree in psychology, the doctoral degree is considered the entry-level degree in psychology for the independent, licensed practice of psychology as a profession. The doctoral degree is the preferred degree for college and university faculty, and it has long been a requirement for faculty positions in research universities. For specific information about employment outcomes of a program's graduates, review the section entitled "Employment of Department Graduates" in each listing in this publication.

Figures 3 and 4 summarize the types of postdegree outcomes of graduates of master's and doctoral degree programs. Nearly one fourth of those awarded a baccalaureate degree in psychology

Figure 3. Employment and Outcomes of Master's Recipients: 2011–2012

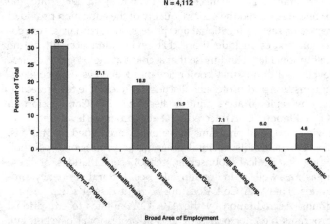

Source: *Graduate Study in Psychology, 2014 Edition* data. Prepared by the APA Office of Graduate and Postgraduate Education and Training.

Figure 4. Employment and Outcomes of Doctoral Recipients: 2011–2012

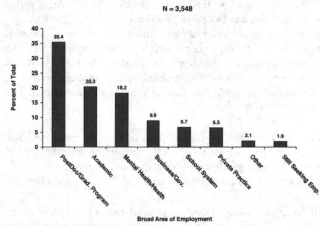

Source: *Graduate Study in Psychology, 2014 Edition* data. Prepared by the APA Office of Graduate and Postgraduate Education and Training.

continue in graduate or professional education in psychology or other fields.

Doctoral programs differ in the type of doctoral degree awarded. The two most common doctoral degrees are the PhD (Doctor of Philosophy) and the PsyD (Doctor of Psychology). Programs in colleges of education may offer the EdD (Doctor of Education) degree. The PhD is generally regarded as a research degree. Although many professional psychology programs award the PhD degree, especially those in university academic departments, these programs typically have an emphasis on research training integrated with applied or practice training. The PsyD is a professional degree in psychology (similar to the MD in medicine). Programs awarding the PsyD typically emphasize preparing their graduates for professional practice. About two thirds of all doctoral degrees in psychology are PhDs; of the degrees awarded in clinical psychology, about the same percentage receive PhDs as PsyDs. For more information about degrees, employment, and salaries in psychology, visit the APA Center for Workforce Studies website (http://www.apa.org/workforce).

Accreditation in Professional Psychology

Accreditation is the mechanism by which students and the public are assured the general quality of the education provided has met a set of educational and professional standards. Accreditation bodies include those that review and accredit at the institutional level and those that accredit at the program or area level. Institutions that confer advanced degrees (i.e., colleges, universities, and professional schools) are eligible for accreditation by regional accrediting bodies. The APA Commission on Accreditation (CoA) accredits at the program level and only reviews doctoral programs in regionally accredited institutions. The CoA accredits doctoral programs in professional psychology (e.g., clinical, counseling, school, combinations of these areas), as well as internship and postdoctoral residency programs. The APA CoA does not accredit master's degree programs. Accreditation by the APA CoA applies to educational programs (i.e., doctoral programs in professional psychology), not to individuals. The APA CoA is currently phasing out accreditation of programs in Canada. Beginning on September 1, 2015, the APA CoA will no longer accredit programs in Canada. This follows several years of discussion and is based on an agreement with the Canadian Psychological Association (CPA). The CPA has their own accreditation system for programs in Canada. Doctoral programs accredited by the APA or the CPA are required to make publicly available information about the education and training outcomes of their students so that prospective students can make informed decisions. Please refer to the section entitled "Accreditation Status" in a department's entry for the URL to locate the information for a specific program.

Graduation from an accredited institution or program does not guarantee employment or licensure for individuals, although being a graduate of an accredited program may facilitate such achievement and is required in some jurisdictions.

All programs listed in this publication are, at a minimum, situated in regionally accredited institutions. The doctoral programs that are APA-accredited are identified as such. For more informa-

tion and the most current lists of accredited programs, see the APA Office of Program Consultation and Accreditation website (http://www.apa.org/ed/accreditation).

Doctoral Internship Training in Professional Psychology

Doctoral programs that prepare their graduates for the professional practice of psychology, especially in health service provision, typically require a doctoral internship prior to the awarding of the doctorate. The doctoral internship consists of 1 year (or the equivalent) of full-time supervised practice training. The internship is completed in a professional service agency training program that is typically not affiliated with the student's graduate program. Internship programs vary widely in terms of the settings and populations served as well as their models of training. Students sometimes relocate geographically to complete their internships. All accredited internship programs select students through a nationwide computerized matching process that has a standardized application and fixed deadlines administered by the Association of Psychology Postdoctoral and Internship Centers (APPIC). For many years the number of available internships has not grown at the rate the number of students has, resulting in an imbalance in which large numbers of students do not successfully match to an internship (e.g., 17% in 2013). While efforts are underway by the APA and the education and training community to address this, the imbalance is a significant issue facing professional psychology education and training. To learn more about the match and internships in professional psychology, refer to the website of APPIC at http://www.appic.org.

Internship match rates for professional psychology doctoral programs can be found under the specific institution listing in this book. Figure 5 shows the percentage of graduate students who were matched to an internship and the internship placement type for APA-accredited doctoral programs and nonaccredited programs.

Admission Requirements

Requirements for admission vary from program to program. Some psychology programs may require significant undergradu-

Figure 5. Internship Placement by Program Type: 2011–2012

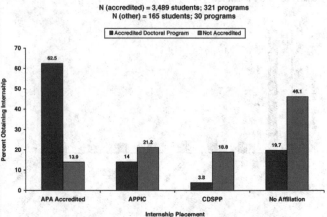

Source: *Graduate Study in Psychology, 2014 Edition* data. Prepared by the APA Office of Graduate and Postgraduate Education and Training.

ate coursework in psychology, often the equivalent of a major or minor, while others do not. Seventy percent of recent psychology PhD recipients have also received a bachelor's degree in psychology.

Of the graduate departments listed in this publication that offer master's degrees, 80% require the Graduate Record Examination (GRE) Verbal and Quantitative sections and 6% require the GRE-Subject (Psychology). Ninety-seven percent of the doctoral programs listed require the GRE-Verbal and Quantitative sections, 13% require the GRE-Subject (Psychology). If the programs in which you are interested require these standardized tests, you should take the GRE-V, GRE-Q, and GRE-Subject (Psychology) in time for the scores to be included with your application materials. (As of August 2011, the GRE General Test implemented a new scoring system with scores ranging from 130 to 170.) The scores below are reported on both the new and old (200 to 800 point) scales. The overall median GRE scores reported for applicants admitted to master's degree programs listed in this publication are GRE-Verbal: 154 (new)/510 (old); GRE-Quantative: 150 (new)/591 (old); and GRE-Subject: 682. The overall median GRE scores reported for applicants admitted to doctoral degree programs listed in this publication are GRE-Verbal: 158 (new)/577 (old); GRE-Quantative 154 (new)/668 (old); and GRE-Subject: 686.

Other criteria considered as admission factors may include previous research activities, work experience, relevant public service, extracurricular activities, letters of recommendation, statement of goals and objectives, an interview, a major or minor in psychology or a record of specific courses in psychology, and undergraduate GPA. Figure 6 shows the ratings of importance of these other admissions criteria by master's and doctoral programs listed in this publication. A rating of 3 indicates that the individual admissions criterion is considered to be of high importance, while a rating of 0 indicates that the admissions criterion holds no importance in a program's admissions process. The three admissions criteria rated as of highest importance for both master's and doctoral programs are letters of recommendation, a

statement of goals and interests, and undergraduate GPA. The overall median undergraduate GPA reported for applicants admitted to master's degree programs listed in this publication is 3.5, while that for doctoral programs is 3.63.

The number of graduate school applicants typically exceeds the number of student openings. The number of applications received by a program and the number of students accepted provide a sense of the expected competition when applying to a particular department, program, or school. Figure 7 shows the percentage of students admitted in relationship to the number of applications for psychology programs in different areas. For more information, review the section entitled "Student Applications/Admissions" for each of the programs of interest to you listed in this publication.

Application Information

An application to a department or program of study is a very important document. Always confirm (a) the deadline for filing the application, (b) what documents are required, and (c) who should receive the application. Include the required application fee.

Most graduate programs in psychology accept students only for fall admission. However, if you are interested in winter, spring, or summer admission, check the application information listed in this publication for the program to which you are applying. Information about application deadlines in this publication is listed in the section entitled "Application Information."

Time to Degree

Programs should be clear about the average number of years in full-time study (or part-time equivalent) required to complete the degree requirements. On average, graduate students take 6 years from entrance into a graduate program to complete the doctoral degree. Eighty percent of recent psychology PhD recipients also have master's degrees.

Figure 6. Mean Rating of Importance of Various Admissions Criteria

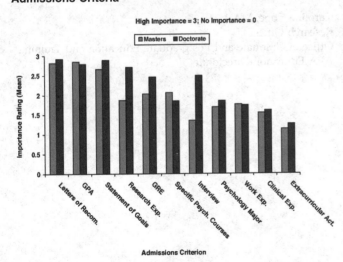

Source: *Graduate Study in Psychology, 2014 Edition* data. Prepared by the APA Office of Graduate and Postgraduate Education and Training.

Figure 7. Percentage of Applicants Admitted to Graduate Programs by Selected Psychology Subfield: 2011–2012

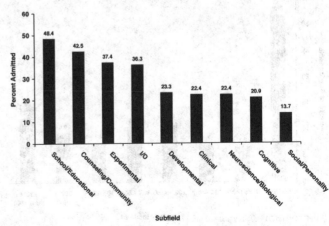

Source: *Graduate Study in Psychology, 2014 Edition* data. Prepared by the APA Office of Graduate and Postgraduate Education and Training.

Tuition and Financial Assistance

Graduate education can be expensive. Figure 8 shows the average in-state and out-of-state public university and private university tuition rates for master's and doctoral level programs in psychology.

Many students require loans to pay for their graduate education. The amount of debt incurred by doctoral students can be significant, as illustrated in Figure 9.

Financial assistance in various forms is available to students. You can apply for a fellowship, scholarship, assistantship, or another type of financial assistance. Many fellowships and scholarships are grants that do not require service to the department or university. Of departments and programs listed in this publication, 68% indicate that they offer some form of fellowship or scholarship to 1st-year students, and 67% indicate that they offer

some form of fellowship or scholarship to advanced students. Assistantships in teaching and research are also available in many programs. These are forms of employment for services in a department. Teaching assistantships may require teaching a class or assisting a professor by grading papers, acting as a laboratory assistant, or performing other such supporting work. Research assistants ordinarily work on research projects being conducted by program faculty. Among the departments and programs reporting for this publication, 76% indicate that they offer teaching and research assistantships to 1st-year students and 85% report offering teaching and research assistantships to advanced students.

The amount of work required for fellowships, assistantships, and traineeships is expressed in hours per week. Stipends are expressed in terms of total stipend for an academic year of 9 months. Students should inquire, when receiving an offer of financial assistance, as to the amount to be given in terms of tuition remission (not requiring the student to pay tuition) versus a stipend (actual cash in hand).

For information about tuition costs and the types of assistance offered by departments and programs, review the section entitled ''Financial Information/Assistance'' for the programs of interest listed in this publication. You can review information listed on the APA Education website (http://www.apa.org/ed/graduate) for information about scholarships, fellowships, grants, and other funding opportunities.

The summary information presented in this introduction is based on the responses provided by the graduate programs listed in this publication. This information is not exhaustive in that a number of graduate programs in the United States and Canada are not listed in this publication and not all programs listed provide complete information to all questions. For this reason, you should look closely at the information provided by a specific program of interest to you and not rely exclusively on the group averages presented in this introduction.

Catherine Grus, PhD
Deputy Executive Director
APA Education Directorate

Caroline Cope, MA
Research Officer
Office of Graduate and Postgraduate Education and Training
APA Education Directorate

Figure 8.   Median Tuition by Type of Institution/Residency: 2011–2012

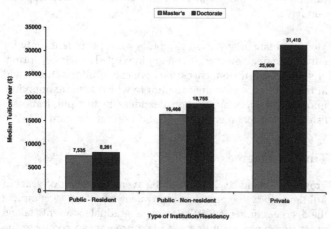

Source: *Graduate Study in Psychology, 2014 Edition* data. Prepared by the APA Office of Graduate and Postgraduate Education and Training.

Figure 9.   Graduate School Debt for Recent Doctorate Recipients: 2007

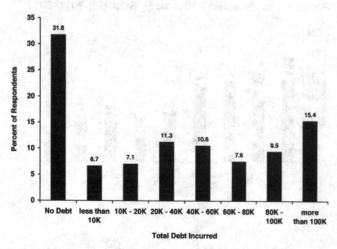

Source: *2007 Survey of Earned Doctorates*. Prepared by the APA Office Graduate and Postgraduate Education and Training.

Rules for Acceptance of Offers for Admission and Financial Aid

The Council of Graduate Schools has adopted the following policy that provides guidance to students and graduate programs regarding offers of financial support. The policy was adopted by the Council of Graduate Schools in 1965 and reaffirmed in 1992. It was endorsed by the Council of Graduate Departments of Psychology in 1981 and reaffirmed in 2000. Graduate programs and schools currently listed in the book have agreed to honor the policy. The policy reads as follows:

Acceptance of an offer of financial support (such as graduate scholarship, fellowship, traineeship, or assistantship) for the next academic year by a prospective or enrolled graduate student completes an agreement that both student and graduate school expect to honor. In that context, the conditions affecting such offers and their acceptance must be defined carefully and understood by all parties.

Students are under no obligation to respond to offers of financial support prior to April 15; earlier deadlines for acceptance of such offers violate the intent of this Resolution. In those instances in which the student accepts the offer before April 15 and subsequently desires to withdraw that acceptance, the student may submit in writing a resignation of the appointment at any time through April 15. However, an acceptance given or left in force after April 15 commits the student not to accept another offer without first obtaining a written release from the institution to which a commitment has been made. Similarly, an offer by an institution after April 15 is conditional on presentation by the student of the written release from any previously accepted offer. It is further agreed by the institutions and organizations subscribing to the above Resolution that a copy of this Resolution should accompany every scholarship, fellowship, traineeship, and assistantship offer.

Explanation of Program Listings

The following summarizes the information solicited from each program:

Contact Information

The name of the university or school, address, telephone number, fax number, e-mail, and World Wide Web address are provided. There may be more than one department in an institution that offers degrees in psychology, and if so, each department is listed separately.

Department Information

The year the department was established is provided, including the name of the department chairperson, and the number of full-time and part-time faculty members including information on the number of minority faculty employees.

Programs and Degrees Offered

This heading highlights the program areas in which degrees are offered by the department or school and includes the type of degree awarded and the number of degrees awarded.

APA Accreditation Status

Whether a department or school has a program accredited in clinical psychology, counseling psychology, school psychology, or combined professional–scientific psychology is noted. Because changes in accreditation status may occur after publication, please contact the APA Office of Program Consultation and Accreditation, or review the website (http://www.apa.org/ed/accreditation).

Student Applications/Admissions

This section includes information about the number of applications received by the individual program areas of departments and schools. Also listed are the number of applicants accepted into the program and the number of openings anticipated in the next year. In addition, the information reflects the median number of years required for a degree and the number of students enrolled who were dismissed or voluntarily withdrew from the program before completing their degree requirements.

Information on standardized test scores and other criteria considered during admission decisions are rated according to their importance.

This section also includes characteristics of students enrolled in the department or psychology program.

Financial Information/Assistance

Tuition figures per year and per academic unit are indicated. Note that some schools and institutions have different fee structures for doctoral and master's students. The words *non-state residents* are used by state universities that charge more for out-of-state residents than students who reside in the state. These fees should be used as rough guidelines and are subject to change.

Teaching assistantships, research assistantships, traineeships, or fellowships and scholarships are reported. The data for each type of assistance are listed for 1st-year and advanced students. The average amount awarded to each student and the average number of hours that must be worked each week are included in the listing. Contact information for financial assistance is also listed.

Information has been added by departments on those programs that require a professional internship of doctoral students prior to graduation. Information is included on the number of students who applied for an internship, the number who obtained an internship, and if the internship was paid or unpaid. In addition, the department was asked to indicate whether the student achieved an APA- or CPA-accredited internship, and if the internship was listed by the Association of Psychology Postdoctoral Internship Centers or by the Council of Directors of School Psychology Programs. Lastly, many departments provided additional information about the types of settings where students were located, the number of hours spent weekly at the internship site, and other information.

Employment of Department Graduates

This section provides information about employment activities of graduates. Data presented by departments or schools include information about master's and doctoral degree graduates, such as enrollment in psychology doctoral programs, and employment in academic positions, business, and government.

Additional Information

This section provides an opportunity for the department or school to present the orientation, objectives, and emphasis of the department or school. Information is also presented about the special facilities or resources offered by the school or institution.

Also included in this section are statements related to personal behavior and religious beliefs statements that are considered a condition for admission and retention with the program. All information in *Graduate Study in Psychology* is self-reported. In the interest of full disclosure to prospective students, therefore, departments, programs, or institutions by which they are governed that have a statement to this effect are requested to cite the statement or provide a Web site or address at which it can be found.

Application Information

This last section provides the addresses, deadlines, and fees for the submission of applications for each department or school.

2014

Graduate
Study
in
Psychology

Alabama, University of
Department of Psychology
College of Arts and Sciences
Box 870348
Tuscaloosa, AL 35487-0348
Telephone: (205) 348-1919
Fax: (205) 348-8648
E-mail: *mbhubbard@as.ua.edu*
Web: *http://psychology.ua.edu*

Department Information:
1937. Chairperson: Beverly E. Thorn. Number of faculty: total—full-time 32, part-time 1; women—full-time 16, part-time 1; total—minority—full-time 3; women minority—full-time 3.

Programs and Degrees Offered:
Listed in the following order: Program area, degree type (T if terminal Master's), number awarded 7/11–6/12. Clinical Psychology PhD (Doctor of Philosophy) 7, Cognitive Psychology PhD (Doctor of Philosophy) 4, Social Psychology PhD (Doctor of Philosophy) 1, Developmental Science PhD (Doctor of Philosophy) 0.

APA Accreditation: Clinical PhD (Doctor of Philosophy). Student Outcome Data Website: http://psychology.ua.edu/graduate-studies/clinical-psychology/.

Student Applications/Admissions:
Student Applications
Clinical Psychology PhD (Doctor of Philosophy)—Applications 2012–2013, 305. Total applicants accepted 2012–2013, 16. Number full-time enrolled (new admits only) 2012–2013, 11. Total enrolled 2012–2013 full-time, 65. Total enrolled 2012–2013 part-time, 1. Openings 2013–2014, 8. The median number of years required for completion of a degree in 2012–2013 were 6. The number of students enrolled full- and part-time who were dismissed or voluntarily withdrew from this program area in 2012–2013 were 0. *Cognitive Psychology PhD (Doctor of Philosophy)*—Applications 2012–2013, 10. Total applicants accepted 2012–2013, 2. Number full-time enrolled (new admits only) 2012–2013, 0. Total enrolled 2012–2013 full-time, 6. Total enrolled 2012–2013 part-time, 0. Openings 2013–2014, 2. The median number of years required for completion of a degree in 2012–2013 were 6. The number of students enrolled full- and part-time who were dismissed or voluntarily withdrew from this program area in 2012–2013 were 1. *Social Psychology PhD (Doctor of Philosophy)*—Applications 2012–2013, 40. Total applicants accepted 2012–2013, 5. Number full-time enrolled (new admits only) 2012–2013, 4. Number part-time enrolled (new admits only) 2012–2013, 0. Total enrolled 2012–2013 full-time, 17. Total enrolled 2012–2013 part-time, 0. Openings 2013–2014, 3. The median number of years required for completion of a degree in 2012–2013 were 6. The number of students enrolled full- and part-time who were dismissed or voluntarily withdrew from this program area in 2012–2013 were 2. *Developmental Science PhD (Doctor of Philosophy)*—Applications 2012–2013, 11. Total applicants accepted 2012–2013, 4. Number full-time enrolled (new admits only) 2012–2013, 3. Number part-time enrolled (new admits only) 2012–2013, 0. Total enrolled 2012–2013 full-time, 14. Total enrolled 2012–2013 part-time, 0. Openings 2013–2014, 2. The number of students enrolled full- and part-time who were dismissed or voluntarily withdrew from this program area in 2012–2013 were 0.

Scores: Entries appear in this order: required test or GPA, minimum score (if required), median score of students entering in 2012–2013. *Clinical Psychology PhD (Doctor of Philosophy):* GRE-V no minimum stated, 660, GRE-Q no minimum stated, 665, GRE-Analytical no minimum stated, 5.0, overall undergraduate GPA no minimum stated, 3.8; *Cognitive Psychology PhD (Doctor of Philosophy):* GRE-V no minimum stated, GRE-Q no minimum stated0, GRE-Analytical no minimum stated0, overall undergraduate GPA no minimum stated0; *Social Psychology PhD (Doctor of Philosophy):* GRE-V no minimum stated, 615, GRE-Q no minimum stated, 715, GRE-Analytical no minimum stated, 4.0, overall undergraduate GPA no minimum stated, 3.75; *Developmental Science PhD (Doctor of Philosophy):* GRE-V no minimum stated, 580, GRE-Q no minimum stated, 730, GRE-Analytical no minimum stated, 4.5, overall undergraduate GPA no minimum stated, 3.7.

Other Criteria: (importance of criteria rated low, medium, or high): GRE scores—high, research experience—high, work experience—low, extracurricular activity—low, clinically related public service—low, GPA—medium, letters of recommendation—high, interview—medium, statement of goals and objectives—high, undergraduate major in psychology—medium, specific undergraduate psychology courses taken—high, GRE Advanced Subject Test is preferred (but not required) for applicants to the Clinical Program. For additional information on admission requirements, go to http://psychology.ua.edu/graduate-studies/prospective-students/graduate-application-procedures/.

Student Characteristics: The following represents characteristics of students in 2012–2013 in all graduate psychology programs in the department: Female—full-time 75, part-time 1; Male—full-time 27, part-time 0; African American/Black—full-time 4, part-time 0; Hispanic/Latino(a)—full-time 5, part-time 0; Asian/Pacific Islander—full-time 6, part-time 0; American Indian/Alaska Native—full-time 2, part-time 0; Caucasian/White—full-time 85, part-time 1; Multi-ethnic—full-time 0, part-time 0; students subject to the Americans With Disabilities Act—full-time 0, part-time 0; Unknown ethnicity—full-time 0, part-time 0; International students who hold an F-1 or J-1 Visa—full-time 8, part-time 0.

Financial Information/Assistance:
Tuition for Full-Time Study: *Doctoral:* State residents: per academic year $9,200; Nonstate residents: per academic year $22,950. Tuition is subject to change. Additional fees are assessed to students beyond the costs of tuition for the following: course fee - $10.00 per hour; facility/technology fee - $9.00 per hour. See the following website for updates and changes in tuition costs: http://cost.ua.edu.

1

Financial Assistance:

First-Year Students: Teaching assistantships available for first year. Average amount paid per academic year: $13,392. Average number of hours worked per week: 20. Research assistantships available for first year. Average amount paid per academic year: $12,366. Average number of hours worked per week: 20. Fellowships and scholarships available for first year. Average amount paid per academic year: $15,000.

Advanced Students: Teaching assistantships available for advanced students. Average amount paid per academic year: $13,392. Average number of hours worked per week: 20. Research assistantships available for advanced students. Average amount paid per academic year: $12,366. Average number of hours worked per week: 20. Traineeships available for advanced students. Average amount paid per academic year: $12,366. Average number of hours worked per week: 20. Fellowships and scholarships available for advanced students. Average amount paid per academic year: $15,000.

Additional Information: Of all students currently enrolled full time, 99% benefited from one or more of the listed financial assistance programs. Application and information available online at: http://graduate.ua.edu/financial/.

Internships/Practica: Doctoral Degree (PhD Clinical Psychology): For those doctoral students for whom a professional psychology internship was required in this program prior to graduation, (8) students applied for an internship in 2011–2012, with (8) students obtaining an internship. Of those students who obtained an internship, (8) were paid internships. Of those students who obtained an internship, (7) students placed in APA/CPA accredited internships, (1) students placed in internships not APA/CPA accredited, but listed with the Association of Psychology Postdoctoral and Internship Programs (APPIC), (0) students placed in internships conforming to guidelines of the Council of Directors of School Psychology Programs (CDSPP), (0) students placed in internships that were not APA/CPA accredited, APPIC or CDSPP listed. There are a number of practica available to graduate students. Most doctoral students take PY695, a teaching internship, in which the student teaches an introductory psychology class under the supervision of a faculty member. Two semesters of basic psychotherapy practicum are required of every doctoral student in clinical psychology. In this practicum, students conduct psychotherapy with four to six clients in the Department's Psychological Clinic. Students complete approximately 100 hours of direct client contact to fulfill this requirement. After the basic psychotherapy practicum, doctoral clinical psychology students take either one or two (depending on specialty area) advanced practica in their area of specialization. Many of these practica are housed in community service agencies (e.g., state psychiatric hospital, community mental health center, University-operated treatment center for disturbed children). In addition to these formal practica, most doctoral students in the clinical program are financially supported at some time during their graduate school years through field placements in various community agencies. These students are supervised by either licensed psychologists employed by these agencies or by Department of Psychology clinical faculty. In addition to the intervention practica discussed above, all clinical doctoral students must take two of the three graduate psychological assessment courses offered. These courses have a significant practicum component, requiring approximately 5 administrations of commonly used psychological assessment instruments with Psychology Clinic clients.

Housing and Day Care: No on-campus housing is available. On-campus day care facilities are available. See the following website for more information: http://www.ches.ua.edu/departments/hd/childrensprogram/.

Employment of Department Graduates:

Master's Degree Graduates: Of those who graduated in the academic year 2011–2012, the following categories and numbers represent the postgraduate activities and employment of master's degree graduates: Enrolled in a postdoctoral residency/fellowship (n/a), employed in independent practice (n/a), total from the above (master's) (0).

Doctoral Degree Graduates: Of those who graduated in the academic year 2011–2012, the following categories and numbers represent the postgraduate activities and employment of doctoral degree graduates: Enrolled in a psychology doctoral program (n/a), enrolled in a postdoctoral residency/fellowship (7), employed in an academic position at a university (2), employed in an academic position at a 2-year/4-year college (1), employed in other positions at a higher education institution (1), employed in a hospital/medical center (1), total from the above (doctoral) (12).

Additional Information:

Orientation, Objectives, and Emphasis of Department: The University of Alabama doctoral program in psychology was founded in 1957 and trains students in clinical and experimental psychology. The clinical program has been continually accredited by the American Psychological Association since 1959. The department trains scientists and scientist–practitioners for a variety of roles: research, teaching, and applied practice. Both the clinical and the experimental programs strongly emphasize furthering psychology as a science. The clinical program has specialty areas in psychology-law, clinical-child, gerontology, and health and the experimental program has specialty areas in cognitive, social, and developmental. The social and developmental training areas involve exciting collaborations with other units on campus. The doctoral programs emphasize core knowledge in the social, cognitive, developmental, and biological aspects of behavior as well as methodological/statistical foundations. All students take additional courses designed to prepare them with the necessary knowledge and skills in their chosen specialty area. A further objective of the department is to promote independent scholarship and professional development. Coursework is supplemented by the active collaboration of faculty and students in ongoing research projects and clinical activities. The department maintains access to a wide range of settings in which students can refine their research and applied skills.

Special Facilities or Resources: The department is housed in a four-story building that it shares with the Department of Mathematics. It is directly connected to the University's Seebeck Computer Center. Facilities include faculty offices, student offices, classroom and seminar space, and research laboratories. Graduate students have access to microcomputers for research and word processing and videotaping capabilities for instruction and training. A major resource is the Psychology Clinic which recently moved to newly renovated space a short distance from the department offices. This clinic provides psychological assessment, referral, treatment planning, and direct intervention for a variety of clinical populations. The department's Child and Family Research Clinic serves as a specialized training and research laboratory and houses the departments Autism College Transition Program (UA-

ACTS). Both clinics include observation facilities. Also affiliated with the department is the brand new Child Development Research Center, which has research, office, and training space, and runs a state-of-the-art preschool where the department's Autism Clinic is located. Other affiliations on campus include the Center for Mental Health and Aging, the Institute for Social Science Research, the Brewer-Porch Childrens Center, the Student Counseling Center, and the University Medical Center. In the community, the department maintains research and clinical relationships with DCH Regional Medical Center, VA Medical Center, Bryce Hospital, Family Counseling Services, city and county school systems, Indian Rivers Mental Health Center, and the Taylor Hardin Forensic Medical Facility.

Information for Students With Physical Disabilities: See the following website for more information: http://ods.ua.edu.

Application Information:
Send to Office of the Graduate School, University of Alabama, Box 870118, Tuscaloosa, AL 35487-0118. Application available online. URL of online application: http://graduate.ua.edu/application/index.html. Students are admitted in the Fall, application deadline December 1. Deadline for applications to the clinical program is December 1; December 15 is the deadline for the cognitive, social, and developmental programs. The Graduate School requests that application material (application, statement of purpose, GRE scores, transcripts) arrive in their office no later than 6 weeks prior to the department deadlines. *Fee:* $50. Application fee is waived for McNair Scholars.

Alabama, University of, at Birmingham
Department of Psychology
Arts and Sciences
415 Campbell Hall
Birmingham, AL 35294-1170
Telephone: (205) 934-3850
Fax: (205) 975-6110
E-mail: *kball@uab.edu*
Web: *http://www.psy.uab.edu*

Department Information:
1969. Chairperson: Karlene Ball, PhD. Number of faculty: total—full-time 28, part-time 1; women—full-time 10; total—minority—full-time 5; women minority—full-time 1.

Programs and Degrees Offered:
Listed in the following order: Program area, degree type (T if terminal Master's), number awarded 7/11–6/12. Behavioral Neuroscience Psychology PhD (Doctor of Philosophy) 4, Lifespan Developmental Psychology PhD (Doctor of Philosophy) 6, Medical/Clinical Psychology PhD (Doctor of Philosophy) 6.

APA Accreditation: Clinical PhD (Doctor of Philosophy). Student Outcome Data Website: http://www.uab.edu/psychology/graduate/medical-psychology.

Student Applications/Admissions:
Student Applications
Behavioral Neuroscience Psychology PhD (Doctor of Philosophy)—Applications 2012–2013, 14. Total applicants accepted 2012–

2013, 6. Number full-time enrolled (new admits only) 2012–2013, 3. Total enrolled 2012–2013 full-time, 14. Total enrolled 2012–2013 part-time, 0. Openings 2013–2014, 5. The median number of years required for completion of a degree in 2012–2013 were 6. The number of students enrolled full- and part-time who were dismissed or voluntarily withdrew from this program area in 2012–2013 were 0. *Lifespan Developmental Psychology PhD (Doctor of Philosophy)*—Applications 2012–2013, 19. Total applicants accepted 2012–2013, 6. Number full-time enrolled (new admits only) 2012–2013, 6. Number part-time enrolled (new admits only) 2012–2013, 0. Total enrolled 2012–2013 full-time, 18. Total enrolled 2012–2013 part-time, 0. Openings 2013–2014, 4. The median number of years required for completion of a degree in 2012–2013 were 4. The number of students enrolled full- and part-time who were dismissed or voluntarily withdrew from this program area in 2012–2013 were 0. *Medical/Clinical Psychology PhD (Doctor of Philosophy)*—Applications 2012–2013, 192. Total applicants accepted 2012–2013, 14. Number full-time enrolled (new admits only) 2012–2013, 10. Number part-time enrolled (new admits only) 2012–2013, 0. Total enrolled 2012–2013 full-time, 41. Total enrolled 2012–2013 part-time, 0. Openings 2013–2014, 8. The median number of years required for completion of a degree in 2012–2013 were 6. The number of students enrolled full- and part-time who were dismissed or voluntarily withdrew from this program area in 2012–2013 were 1.

Scores: Entries appear in this order: required test or GPA, minimum score (if required), median score of students entering in 2012–2013. *Behavioral Neuroscience Psychology PhD (Doctor of Philosophy):* GRE-V no minimum stated, 155, GRE-Q no minimum stated, 155, GRE-Analytical no minimum stated, 4.5; *Lifespan Developmental Psychology PhD (Doctor of Philosophy):* GRE-V no minimum stated, 154, GRE-Q no minimum stated, 151, GRE-Analytical no minimum stated, 4.5, overall undergraduate GPA no minimum stated, 3.6; *Medical/Clinical Psychology PhD (Doctor of Philosophy):* GRE-V no minimum stated, 161, GRE-Q no minimum stated, 155, GRE-Analytical no minimum stated, 4.5, overall undergraduate GPA no minimum stated, 3.65.

Other Criteria: (importance of criteria rated low, medium, or high): GRE scores—high, research experience—high, work experience—low, extracurricular activity—low, clinically related public service—medium, GPA—high, letters of recommendation—medium, interview—medium, statement of goals and objectives—medium. For additional information on admission requirements, go to http://www.uab.edu/psychology/graduate.

Student Characteristics: The following represents characteristics of students in 2012–2013 in all graduate psychology programs in the department: Female—full-time 58, part-time 0; Male—full-time 15, part-time 0; African American/Black—full-time 3, part-time 0; Hispanic/Latino(a)—part-time 0; Asian/Pacific Islander—full-time 5, part-time 0; American Indian/Alaska Native—full-time 0, part-time 0; Caucasian/White—full-time 65, part-time 0; Multi-ethnic—part-time 0; students subject to the Americans With Disabilities Act—full-time 0, part-time 0; Unknown ethnicity—full-time 0, part-time 0; International students who hold an F-1 or J-1 Visa—full-time 2, part-time 0.

Financial Information/Assistance:

Tuition for Full-Time Study: *Doctoral:* State residents: per academic year $9,630, $335 per credit hour; . Tuition is subject to change. Additional fees are assessed to students beyond the costs of tuition for the following: lab. See the following website for updates and changes in tuition costs: https://www.uab.edu/students/current/paying-for-college/detailed-tuition-and-fees.

Financial Assistance:

First-Year Students: Fellowships and scholarships available for first year. Average amount paid per academic year: $20,000. Average number of hours worked per week: 0. Apply by December 6.

Advanced Students: Teaching assistantships available for advanced students. Average amount paid per academic year: $20,000. Average number of hours worked per week: 20. Research assistantships available for advanced students. Average amount paid per academic year: $20,000. Average number of hours worked per week: 20. Traineeships available for advanced students. Average amount paid per academic year: $20,000. Average number of hours worked per week: 20. Fellowships and scholarships available for advanced students. Average amount paid per academic year: $20,000. Average number of hours worked per week: 0.

Additional Information: Of all students currently enrolled full time, 100% benefited from one or more of the listed financial assistance programs.

Internships/Practica: Doctoral Degree (PhD Medical/Clinical Psychology): For those doctoral students for whom a professional psychology internship was required in this program prior to graduation, (10) students applied for an internship in 2011–2012, with (10) students obtaining an internship. Of those students who obtained an internship, (10) were paid internships. Of those students who obtained an internship, (10) students placed in APA/CPA accredited internships, (0) students placed in internships not APA/CPA accredited, but listed with the Association of Psychology Postdoctoral and Internship Programs (APPIC), (0) students placed in internships conforming to guidelines of the Council of Directors of School Psychology Programs (CDSPP), (0) students placed in internships that were not APA/CPA accredited, APPIC or CDSPP listed. Students in the Medical/Clinical Psychology program have opportunities for research and clinical practica across the UAB campus in the Departments of Psychology, Anesthesiology, Neurology, Pediatrics, Psychiatry, and Rehabilitation Medicine; as well as at the Center for Aging and the Sparks Center for Developmental and Learning Disorders. These opportunities also extend to adjacent health care facilities — the Birmingham VA Medical Center and Children's of Alabama — and to faculty in program-affiliated private practices.

Housing and Day Care: On-campus housing is available. See the following website for more information: https://www.uab.edu/students/housing. On-campus day care facilities are available. See the following website for more information: http://www.hrm.uab.edu/main/uabcdc/.

Employment of Department Graduates:

Master's Degree Graduates: Of those who graduated in the academic year 2011–2012, the following categories and numbers represent the postgraduate activities and employment of master's degree graduates: Enrolled in a postdoctoral residency/fellowship (n/a), employed in independent practice (n/a), total from the above (master's) (0).

Doctoral Degree Graduates: Of those who graduated in the academic year 2011–2012, the following categories and numbers represent the postgraduate activities and employment of doctoral degree graduates: Enrolled in a psychology doctoral program (n/a), enrolled in another graduate/professional program (1), enrolled in a postdoctoral residency/fellowship (7), employed in an academic position at a university (4), employed in other positions at a higher education institution (4), employed in a hospital/medical center (4), total from the above (doctoral) (20).

Additional Information:

Orientation, Objectives, and Emphasis of Department: The Department offers three doctoral programs: Clinical/Medical Psychology, Behavioral Neuroscience, and Developmental Psychology. Each program promotes rigorous scientific training for students pursuing basic or applied research careers. The programs are designed to produce scholars who will engage in independent research, clinical practice, and teaching. Medical / Clinical Psychology provides broad clinical training with an additional focus on behavioral and psychological factors in medical care and health. The Behavioral Neuroscience program provides individualized, interdisciplinary training for research on the biological bases of behavior. The Developmental program trains students to conduct research to discover and apply basic principles of developmental psychology across the lifespan in an interdisciplinary context. Students are exposed to the issues of development in its natural and social contexts, as well as in laboratories. Across the three programs, faculty research interests include: neuropsychology, psychophysiology, adult and developmental psychopathology, neuroimaging, sensation and perception, pain, spinal cord injury, control of movement, rehabilitation, aging, mental retardation/developmental disabilities, healthy aging, pediatric psychology, social ecology, cognitive development, caregiver and survivor issues, cancer, eating disorders, obesity, substance abuse, and psychopharmacology.

Special Facilities or Resources: The University of Alabama at Birmingham is a comprehensive, urban research university, recently ranked by U.S. News and World Report as the number one up-and-coming university in the country. The UAB Psychology Department, in the College of Arts and Sciences, ranks among the top 100 psychology departments in the U.S. by NSF in federal/research funding and the Clinical Psychology doctoral program was recently recognized as 10th in the nation for scholarly productivity. The UAB campus encompasses a 75-block area on Birmingham's Southside, offering all of the advantages of a university within a highly supportive city. Resources are available from the School of Medicine, Department of Physiological Optics, School of Public Health, Civitan International Research Center, Sparks Center for Developmental and Learning Disorders, Center for Aging, Department of Pediatrics, Department of Psychiatry and Behavioral Neurobiology, Neurobiology Research Center, School of Education, School of Nursing, Department of Computer and Information Sciences, University Hospital, a psychiatric hospital, and Children's Hospital. The Department boasts two faculty members at the rank of University Professor as recognized by The University of Alabama Board of Trustees.

Information for Students With Physical Disabilities: See the following website for more information: http://main.uab.edu/Sites/students/services/disability-support/.

Application Information:
Application available online. URL of online application: https://app.applyyourself.com/?id=uab-grad. Students are admitted in the Fall, application deadline November 30. Medical/Clinical - November 30; Developmental - December 6; BNS - January 15. *Fee:* $0. Waived for U.S. citizens; $60 international application fee.

Alabama, University of, at Huntsville
Department of Psychology
Liberal Arts
Morton Hall 335
Huntsville, AL 35899
Telephone: (256) 824-6191
Fax: (256) 824-6949
E-mail: *carpens@email.uah.edu*
Web: *http://www.uah.edu/la/departments/psychology*

Department Information:
1968. Chairperson: Jeffrey Neuschatz. Number of faculty: total—full-time 6; women—full-time 4; total—minority—full-time 1; women minority—full-time 1.

Programs and Degrees Offered:
Listed in the following order: Program area, degree type (T if terminal Master's), number awarded 7/11–6/12. General Experimental Psychology MA/MS (Master of Arts/Science) (T) 3, I/O Psychology Specialization MA/MS (Master of Arts/Science) (T) 0.

Student Applications/Admissions:
Student Applications
General Experimental Psychology MA/MS (Master of Arts/Science)—Applications 2012–2013, 15. Total applicants accepted 2012–2013, 8. Number full-time enrolled (new admits only) 2012–2013, 8. Number part-time enrolled (new admits only) 2012–2013, 0. Total enrolled 2012–2013 full-time, 11. Total enrolled 2012–2013 part-time, 0. Openings 2013–2014, 10. The median number of years required for completion of a degree in 2012–2013 were 2. The number of students enrolled full- and part-time who were dismissed or voluntarily withdrew from this program area in 2012–2013 were 0. *I/O Psychology Specialization MA/MS (Master of Arts/Science)*—Applications 2012–2013, 10. Total applicants accepted 2012–2013, 4. Number full-time enrolled (new admits only) 2012–2013, 4. Total enrolled 2012–2013 full-time, 4. The median number of years required for completion of a degree in 2012–2013 were 2. The number of students enrolled full- and part-time who were dismissed or voluntarily withdrew from this program area in 2012–2013 were 0.
Scores: Entries appear in this order: required test or GPA, minimum score (if required), median score of students entering

in 2012–2013. *General Experimental Psychology MA/MS (Master of Arts/Science):* GRE-V no minimum stated, GRE-Q no minimum stated, overall undergraduate GPA 3.00; *I/O Psychology Specialization MA/MS (Master of Arts/Science):* GRE-V 160, GRE-Q 160, overall undergraduate GPA no minimum stated, last 2 years GPA 3.25.
Other Criteria: (importance of criteria rated low, medium, or high): GRE scores—high, research experience—high, work experience—low, clinically related public service—low, GPA—high, letters of recommendation—high, interview—low, statement of goals and objectives—high, Empirical paper—high, undergraduate major in psychology—medium, specific undergraduate psychology courses taken—high. For additional information on admission requirements, go to http://www.uah.edu/la/departments/psychology/student-affairs/graduate-admissions.

Student Characteristics: The following represents characteristics of students in 2012–2013 in all graduate psychology programs in the department: Female—full-time 6, part-time 0; Male—full-time 5, part-time 0; African American/Black—full-time 0, part-time 0; Hispanic/Latino(a)—full-time 1, part-time 0; Asian/Pacific Islander—full-time 0, part-time 0; American Indian/Alaska Native—full-time 0, part-time 0; Caucasian/White—full-time 10, part-time 0; Multi-ethnic—full-time 0, part-time 0; students subject to the Americans With Disabilities Act—full-time 0, part-time 0; Unknown ethnicity—full-time 0, part-time 0; International students who hold an F-1 or J-1 Visa—full-time 1, part-time 0.

Financial Information/Assistance:
Tuition for Full-Time Study: *Master's:* State residents: per academic year $10,008, $556 per credit hour; Nonstate residents: per academic year $23,580, $1,310 per credit hour. Tuition is subject to change. See the following website for updates and changes in tuition costs: http://www.uah.edu/bursar/tuition.

Financial Assistance:
First-Year Students: Research assistantships available for first year. Average number of hours worked per week: 20. Apply by June 1. Fellowships and scholarships available for first year. Average number of hours worked per week: 0. Apply by June 1.
Advanced Students: Teaching assistantships available for advanced students. Average amount paid per academic year: $10,000. Average number of hours worked per week: 20. Apply by June 1. Research assistantships available for advanced students. Average amount paid per academic year: $10,000. Average number of hours worked per week: 20. Apply by June 1. Fellowships and scholarships available for advanced students. Average amount paid per academic year: $4,000. Average number of hours worked per week: 0. Apply by June 1.
Additional Information: Of all students currently enrolled full time, 90% benefited from one or more of the listed financial assistance programs. Application and information available online at: http://www.uah.edu/la/departments/psychology/student-affairs/financial-aid/graduate.

Internships/Practica: Master's Degree (MA/MS General Experimental Psychology): An internship experience, such as a final research project or "capstone" experience is required of graduates.

Master's Degree (MA/MS I/O Psychology Specialization): An internship experience, such as a final research project or "capstone" experience is required of graduates. Internships in academic student advising and in psychological test administration may be available for some students.

Housing and Day Care: On-campus housing is available. See the following website for more information: http://www.uah.edu/housing/. On-campus day care facilities are available.

Employment of Department Graduates:

Master's Degree Graduates: Of those who graduated in the academic year 2011–2012, the following categories and numbers represent the postgraduate activities and employment of master's degree graduates: Enrolled in a psychology doctoral program (2), enrolled in a postdoctoral residency/fellowship (n/a), employed in independent practice (n/a), other employment position (2), do not know (1), total from the above (master's) (5).

Doctoral Degree Graduates: Of those who graduated in the academic year 2011–2012, the following categories and numbers represent the postgraduate activities and employment of doctoral degree graduates: Enrolled in a psychology doctoral program (n/a), total from the above (doctoral) (0).

Additional Information:

Orientation, Objectives, and Emphasis of Department: The content of our program is directed toward the study of psychology as an intellectual and scientific pursuit, as contrasted with training directly applicable to counselor or psychologist licensure and practice. Specialization areas include applied psychology, social/personality, cognitive, developmental and biopsychological psychology. The program is designed for a small number of students who will work in close interaction with individual faculty members and with each other. Although there are a few structured courses that are required of all students, a substantial portion of the students' program focuses on individual readings, research and a thesis.

Special Facilities or Resources: Access to research facilities at NASA's-Marshall Space Flight Center is available via an existing Space Act Agreement. Students also have access to archives at the National Children's Advocacy Center. Some students work collaboratively with the scientists in the Center for Simulation and Modeling on the UAH campus.

Information for Students With Physical Disabilities: See the following website for more information: http://www.uah.edu/health-and-wellness/disability-support/welcome.

Application Information:

Send to Department Chair, Department of Psychology, Morton Hall 335, University of Alabama in Huntsville, Huntsville, AL 35899. Application available online. URL of online application: http://www.uah.edu/graduate/admissions/application. Students are admitted in the Fall, application deadline July 1; Spring, application deadline December 1; Summer, application deadline May 1. *Fee:* $40.

Auburn University

Department of Psychology
College of Liberal Arts
226 Thach Hall
Auburn University, AL 36849-5214
Telephone: (334) 844-4412
Fax: (334) 844-4447
E-mail: *bryangt@auburn.edu*
Web: *http://www.cla.auburn.edu/psychology/*

Department Information:

1948. Chairperson: Daniel Svyantek. Number of faculty: total—full-time 23, part-time 2; women—full-time 9, part-time 2; total—minority—full-time 5; women minority—full-time 2.

Programs and Degrees Offered:

Listed in the following order: Program area, degree type (T if terminal Master's), number awarded 7/11–6/12. Clinical Psychology PhD (Doctor of Philosophy) 3, Cognitive and Behavioral Sciences PhD (Doctor of Philosophy) 4, Industrial/Organizational Psychology PhD (Doctor of Philosophy) 1, Aba in Developmental Disabilities MA/MS (Master of Arts/Science) (T) 12.

APA Accreditation: Clinical PhD (Doctor of Philosophy). Student Outcome Data Website: http://www.cla.auburn.edu/psychology/clinical/full-disclosure/.

Student Applications/Admissions:

Student Applications

Clinical Psychology PhD (Doctor of Philosophy)—Applications 2012–2013, 264. Total applicants accepted 2012–2013, 10. Number full-time enrolled (new admits only) 2012–2013, 8. Number part-time enrolled (new admits only) 2012–2013, 0. Total enrolled 2012–2013 full-time, 40. Total enrolled 2012–2013 part-time, 0. Openings 2013–2014, 6. The median number of years required for completion of a degree in 2012–2013 were 6. The number of students enrolled full- and part-time who were dismissed or voluntarily withdrew from this program area in 2012–2013 were 0. *Cognitive and Behavioral Sciences PhD (Doctor of Philosophy)*—Applications 2012–2013, 31. Total applicants accepted 2012–2013, 9. Number full-time enrolled (new admits only) 2012–2013, 6. Number part-time enrolled (new admits only) 2012–2013, 0. Total enrolled 2012–2013 full-time, 24. Total enrolled 2012–2013 part-time, 0. Openings 2013–2014, 5. The median number of years required for completion of a degree in 2012–2013 were 5. The number of students enrolled full- and part-time who were dismissed or voluntarily withdrew from this program area in 2012–2013 were 0. *Industrial/Organizational Psychology PhD (Doctor of Philosophy)*—Applications 2012–2013, 66. Total applicants accepted 2012–2013, 5. Number full-time enrolled (new admits only) 2012–2013, 3. Number part-time enrolled (new admits only) 2012–2013, 0. Total enrolled 2012–2013 full-time, 21. Total enrolled 2012–2013 part-time, 0. Openings 2013–2014, 3. The median number of years required for completion of a degree in 2012–2013 were 6. The number of students enrolled full- and part-time who were dismissed or voluntarily withdrew from this program area in 2012–2013 were 0. *Aba in Developmental Disabilities MA/MS (Master of Arts/Science)*—Applications 2012–2013, 78. Total applicants accepted 2012–2013,

10. Number full-time enrolled (new admits only) 2012–2013, 8. Number part-time enrolled (new admits only) 2012–2013, 0. Total enrolled 2012–2013 full-time, 8. Total enrolled 2012–2013 part-time, 0. Openings 2013–2014, 10. The median number of years required for completion of a degree in 2012–2013 was 1. The number of students enrolled full- and part-time who were dismissed or voluntarily withdrew from this program area in 2012–2013 were 0.

Scores: Entries appear in this order: required test or GPA, minimum score (if required), median score of students entering in 2012–2013. *Clinical Psychology PhD (Doctor of Philosophy):* GRE-V no minimum stated, 153, GRE-Q no minimum stated, 154, GRE-Analytical no minimum stated, 5, overall undergraduate GPA no minimum stated, 3.6; *Cognitive and Behavioral Sciences PhD (Doctor of Philosophy):* GRE-V no minimum stated, 155, GRE-Q no minimum stated, 154, GRE-Analytical no minimum stated, 4.5, overall undergraduate GPA no minimum stated, 3.6; *Industrial/Organizational Psychology PhD (Doctor of Philosophy):* GRE-V 600, 155, GRE-Q 600, 155, GRE-Analytical no minimum stated, 4, overall undergraduate GPA 3.0, 3.8; *ABA in Developmental Disabilities MA/MS (Master of Arts/Science):* GRE-V no minimum stated, 156, GRE-Q no minimum stated, 150, GRE-Analytical no minimum stated, 4.0, overall undergraduate GPA no minimum stated, 3.65.

Other Criteria: (importance of criteria rated low, medium, or high): GRE scores—medium, research experience—high, work experience—medium, extracurricular activity—low, clinically related public service—medium, GPA—high, letters of recommendation—high, interview—high, statement of goals and objectives—medium, For I/O and CaBS programs, clinically related public service has less significance. For additional information on admission requirements, go to http://www.cla.auburn.edu/psychology/graduate-studies/.

Student Characteristics: The following represents characteristics of students in 2012–2013 in all graduate psychology programs in the department: Female—full-time 56, part-time 0; Male—full-time 37, part-time 0; African American/Black—full-time 7, part-time 0; Hispanic/Latino(a)—full-time 3, part-time 0; Asian/Pacific Islander—full-time 6, part-time 0; American Indian/Alaska Native—full-time 0, part-time 0; Caucasian/White—full-time 77, part-time 0; Multi-ethnic—full-time 0, part-time 0; students subject to the Americans With Disabilities Act—full-time 0, part-time 0; Unknown ethnicity—full-time 0, part-time 0; International students who hold an F-1 or J-1 Visa—full-time 3, part-time 0.

Financial Information/Assistance:

Tuition for Full-Time Study: *Master's:* State residents: per academic year $14,160, $437 per credit hour; Nonstate residents: per academic year $37,758, $1,311 per credit hour. *Doctoral:* State residents: per academic year $14,160, $437 per credit hour; Nonstate residents: per academic year $37,758, $1,311 per credit hour. Tuition is subject to change. See the following website for updates and changes in tuition costs: http://www.auburn.edu/administration/business_office/sfs/.

Financial Assistance:

First-Year Students: Teaching assistantships available for first year. Average amount paid per academic year: $12,600. Average number of hours worked per week: 13.

Advanced Students: Teaching assistantships available for advanced students. Average amount paid per academic year: $14,600. Average number of hours worked per week: 13. Research assistantships available for advanced students. Average amount paid per academic year: $14,600. Average number of hours worked per week: 13.

Additional Information: Of all students currently enrolled full time, 80% benefited from one or more of the listed financial assistance programs.

Internships/Practica: Doctoral Degree (PhD Clinical Psychology): For those doctoral students for whom a professional psychology internship was required in this program prior to graduation, (4) students applied for an internship in 2011–2012, with (4) students obtaining an internship. Of those students who obtained an internship, (4) were paid internships. Of those students who obtained an internship, (4) students placed in APA/CPA accredited internships, (0) students placed in internships not APA/CPA accredited, but listed with the Association of Psychology Postdoctoral and Internship Programs (APPIC), (0) students placed in internships conforming to guidelines of the Council of Directors of School Psychology Programs (CDSPP), (0) students placed in internships that were not APA/CPA accredited, APPIC or CDSPP listed. Master's Degree (MA/MS ABA in Developmental Disabilities): An internship experience, such as a final research project or "capstone" experience is required of graduates. Current practicum sites that offer assistantships for clinical graduate students are Auburn University Psychological Services Center, Auburn University Student Counseling Services, Mt. Meigs Adolescent Correctional Facility (Mt. Meigs, AL), Lee County Youth Development Center (Opelika, AL), Head Start Program of Lee County (Auburn and Opelika, AL), the Auburn University School of Pharmacy, the Auburn University College of Veterinary Medicine, UAB/Montgomery Internal Medicine/Family Medicine Residency Program (Montgomery, AL), the Central Alabama Veterans Health Care System, and other pediatric or mental health settings. Industrial/organizational psychology students receive paid practicum training at a number of area organizations, including Auburn University's Center for Governmental Services, Auburn University at Montgomery's Center for Business and Economic Development, and the Fort Benning Field Station of the Army Research Institute. I/O students may participate in consulting internship work before completing their doctoral work. CaBS students have participated in practica at the Army Research Institute. Students in the Master's program in Applied Behavior Analysis in Developmental Disabilities participate in an intensive practicum program that involves various sites serving individuals with developmental disabilities, including local public schools, the Little Tree Preschool, the Learning Tree Tallassee Campus, and Lee Co. Dept. of Human Resources.

Housing and Day Care: No on-campus housing is available. No on-campus day care facilities are available.

Employment of Department Graduates:

Master's Degree Graduates: Of those who graduated in the academic year 2011–2012, the following categories and numbers represent the postgraduate activities and employment of master's degree graduates: Enrolled in a postdoctoral residency/fellowship (n/a), employed in independent practice (n/a), employed in other positions at a higher education institution (1), employed in government agency (3), employed in a community mental health/counseling center (8), total from the above (master's) (12).

Doctoral Degree Graduates: Of those who graduated in the academic year 2011–2012, the following categories and numbers represent the postgraduate activities and employment of doctoral degree graduates: Enrolled in a psychology doctoral program (n/a), enrolled in a postdoctoral residency/fellowship (3), employed in an academic position at a 2-year/4-year college (2), employed in government agency (2), employed in a community mental health/counseling center (1), total from the above (doctoral) (8).

Additional Information:

Orientation, Objectives, and Emphasis of Department: Graduate education in Auburn's psychology program offers training in basic research and in the application of knowledge and theory to societal problems. Faculty are committed to the premise that inquiry, breadth, and respect for the research process and the application of behavioral science knowledge are valued elements in graduate education. Students work closely in laboratories with fellow students and faculty mentors. Students interested in applied work are provided with direct experience and supervision within community agencies and organizations where theory and technique can be practiced and refined. The Clinical Psychology training program applies a scientist–practitioner model that blends an empirical approach to knowledge within an experiential context. The Cognitive and Behavioral Sciences (CaBS) program provides training in Psychological Sciences. Top-notch animal and human laboratories are available in a number of settings. The Industrial/Organizational program emphasizes a scientist–practitioner approach in which research is used to improve both organizational effectiveness and the quality of work life of individual employees. The Applied Behavior Analysis in Developmental Disabilities program (Master's) trains students to provide evidence-based behavioral services to individuals with developmental disabilities and prepares students to qualify for certification by the Behavior Analyst Certification Board. This one-year program integrates foundational and specialized coursework with carefully designed practicum experiences.

Special Facilities or Resources: A substantial clinical psychology training grant from the State of Alabama, university teaching assistantships, a wide variety of contracts with community agencies, and faculty research contracts and grants have typically provided all doctoral psychology graduate students with financial support throughout their graduate careers. The department administers a multipurpose psychological services center in a renovated and newly furnished building. Relationships with extra-university agencies and organizations facilitate training in applied research. A relationship with the Auburn University MRI Research Center allows us access to an open-bore 3T MRI scanner and a whole-body 7T MRI scanner for cutting-edge research in neuroimaging and cognitive neuroscience.

Information for Students With Physical Disabilities: See the following website for more information: http://www.auburn.edu/disability.

Application Information:
Send to Thane Bryant, Department of Psychology, 226 Thach Hall, Auburn University, AL 36849-5214. Application available online. URL of online application: https://fp.auburn.edu/gradschl/gwaap/Default.aspx. Students are admitted in the Fall, application deadline December 1. Clinical PhD: December 1; I/O PhD and Cognitive and Behavioral Sciences PhD: January 15; Master's Concentration in Applied Behavior Analysis in Developmental Disabilities: February 1. *Fee:* $60.

Auburn University

Special Education, Rehabilitation, Counseling
College of Education
2084 Haley Center
Auburn University, AL 36849-5222
Telephone: (334) 844-7676
Fax: (334) 844-7677
E-mail: *ask0002@auburn.edu*
Web: *http://www.education.auburn.edu/academic_departments/serc/academicprograms/counpsych.html*

Department Information:
1965. Chairperson: Everett D. Martin. Number of faculty: total—full-time 21, part-time 1; women—full-time 15, part-time 1; total—minority—full-time 1, part-time 1; women minority—full-time 1, part-time 1; faculty subject to the Americans With Disabilities Act 1.

Programs and Degrees Offered:
Listed in the following order: Program area, degree type (T if terminal Master's), number awarded 7/11–6/12. Counseling Psychology PhD (Doctor of Philosophy) 6.

APA Accreditation: Counseling PhD (Doctor of Philosophy). Student Outcome Data Website: http://www.education.auburn.edu/academic_departments/serc/academicprograms/counpsych.html.

Student Applications/Admissions:
Student Applications
Counseling Psychology PhD (Doctor of Philosophy)—Applications 2012–2013, 100. Total applicants accepted 2012–2013, 7. Number full-time enrolled (new admits only) 2012–2013, 7. Number part-time enrolled (new admits only) 2012–2013, 0. Total enrolled 2012–2013 full-time, 35. Total enrolled 2012–2013 part-time, 0. Openings 2013–2014, 7. The number of students enrolled full- and part-time who were dismissed or voluntarily withdrew from this program area in 2012–2013 were 1.

Scores: Entries appear in this order: required test or GPA, minimum score (if required), median score of students entering in 2012–2013. *Counseling Psychology PhD (Doctor of Philosophy):* GRE-V no minimum stated, 530, GRE-Q no minimum stated, 655, GRE-Analytical no minimum stated, 4.25, overall undergraduate GPA no minimum stated, 3.7, last 2 years GPA no minimum stated, psychology GPA no minimum stated.

Other Criteria: (importance of criteria rated low, medium, or high): GRE scores—medium, research experience—high, work experience—medium, extracurricular activity—low, clinically related public service—medium, GPA—high, letters of recommendation—high, interview—high, statement of goals and objectives—high, undergraduate major in psychology—medium, specific undergraduate psychology courses Ttbaken—medium. For additional information on admission requirements, go to http://www.education.auburn.edu/academic_departments/serc/academicprograms/counpsych.html.

Student Characteristics: The following represents characteristics of students in 2012–2013 in all graduate psychology programs in the department: Female—full-time 29, part-time 0; Male—full-time 6, part-time 0; African American/Black—full-time 8, part-time 0; Hispanic/Latino(a)—full-time 0, part-time 0; Asian/Pacific Islander—full-time 1, part-time 0; American Indian/Alaska Native—full-time 0, part-time 0; Caucasian/White—full-time 26, part-time 0; Multi-ethnic—full-time 0, part-time 0; students subject to the Americans With Disabilities Act—full-time 0, part-time 0; Unknown ethnicity—full-time 0, part-time 0; International students who hold an F-1 or J-1 Visa—full-time 1, part-time 0.

Financial Information/Assistance:

Tuition for Full-Time Study: *Doctoral:* State residents: per academic year $11,799; Nonstate residents: per academic year $35,397. Tuition is subject to change. Additional fees are assessed to students beyond the costs of tuition for the following: Approximately $2400/yr. See the following website for updates and changes in tuition costs: http://www.auburn.edu/administration/business_office/sfs/.

Financial Assistance:

First-Year Students: Teaching assistantships available for first year. Average amount paid per academic year: $5,508. Average number of hours worked per week: 10. Apply by April 1. Research assistantships available for first year. Average amount paid per academic year: $5,508. Average number of hours worked per week: 10. Apply by April 1. Traineeships available for first year. Average amount paid per academic year: $5,508. Average number of hours worked per week: 12. Apply by April 1. Fellowships and scholarships available for first year. Average amount paid per academic year: $15,000. Average number of hours worked per week: 10.

Advanced Students: Teaching assistantships available for advanced students. Average amount paid per academic year: $5,508. Average number of hours worked per week: 10. Apply by April 1. Research assistantships available for advanced students. Average amount paid per academic year: $5,508. Average number of hours worked per week: 10. Apply by April 1. Traineeships available for advanced students. Average amount paid per academic year: $5,508. Average number of hours worked per week: 12. Apply by April 1. Fellowships and scholarships available for advanced students. Average amount paid per academic year: $5,508. Average number of hours worked per week: 10.

Additional Information: Of all students currently enrolled full time, 93% benefited from one or more of the listed financial assistance programs. Application and information available online at: http://www.grad.auburn.edu/cs/grad_assist_guide.html.

Internships/Practica: Doctoral Degree (PhD Counseling Psychology): For those doctoral students for whom a professional psychology internship was required in this program prior to graduation, (5) students applied for an internship in 2011–2012, with (3) students obtaining an internship. Of those students who obtained an internship, (3) were paid internships. Of those students who obtained an internship, (3) students placed in APA/CPA accredited internships, (0) students placed in internships not APA/CPA accredited, but listed with the Association of Psychology Postdoctoral and Internship Programs (APPIC), (0) students placed in internships conforming to guidelines of the Council of Directors of School Psychology Programs (CDSPP), (0) students placed in internships that were not APA/CPA accredited, APPIC or CDSPP listed. University counseling centers; community mental health centers; VAs; hospitals; community counseling agencies.

Housing and Day Care: On-campus housing is available. See the following website for more information: https://fp.auburn.edu/housing/. No on-campus day care facilities are available.

Employment of Department Graduates:

Master's Degree Graduates: Of those who graduated in the academic year 2011–2012, the following categories and numbers represent the postgraduate activities and employment of master's degree graduates: Enrolled in a postdoctoral residency/fellowship (n/a), employed in independent practice (n/a), total from the above (master's) (0).

Doctoral Degree Graduates: Of those who graduated in the academic year 2011–2012, the following categories and numbers represent the postgraduate activities and employment of doctoral degree graduates: Enrolled in a psychology doctoral program (n/a), enrolled in a postdoctoral residency/fellowship (1), employed in other positions at a higher education institution (3), employed in a community mental health/counseling center (1), total from the above (doctoral) (5).

Additional Information:

Orientation, Objectives, and Emphasis of Department: The Department offers the PhD in Counseling Psychology with masters and doctoral degrees in several other areas. The department values teaching, research, and outreach that contribute to the missions of the College and University. Further, the department seeks to foster a culture in which individual creativity and scholarship is reinforced and nurtured. Diversity is considered a core value in all that we do.

Special Facilities or Resources: Interdisciplinary community. University partnership serving underserved, rural minority communities devoted to education, research and service. We also partner with University Student Affairs, Career Services, Housing, and the Athletic Department.

Information for Students With Physical Disabilities: See the following website for more information: https://fp.auburn.edu/disability/.

Application Information:
Send to Counseling Psychology, 2084 Haley Center, Auburn University, AL 36849-5222. Application available online. URL of online application: http://www.grad.auburn.edu/. Students are admitted in the Fall, application deadline December 1. *Fee:* $60.

Jacksonville State University

Department of Psychology
College of Graduate Studies
700 Pelham Road, North
Jacksonville, AL 36265-1602
Telephone: (256) 782-5402
Fax: (256) 782-5637
E-mail: *pmkerchar@jsu.edu*
Web: *http://www.jsu.edu/psychology/*

Department Information:
1971. Chairperson: Paige McKerchar, PhD, BCBA-D. Number of faculty: total—full-time 6; women—full-time 2.

Programs and Degrees Offered:
Listed in the following order: Program area, degree type (T if terminal Master's), number awarded 7/11–6/12. Applied Psychology MA/MS (Master of Arts/Science) (T) 8.

Student Applications/Admissions:
Student Applications
Applied Psychology MA/MS (Master of Arts/Science)—Applications 2012–2013, 10. Total applicants accepted 2012–2013, 7. Number full-time enrolled (new admits only) 2012–2013, 5. Number part-time enrolled (new admits only) 2012–2013, 1. Total enrolled 2012–2013 full-time, 11. Total enrolled 2012–2013 part-time, 4. Openings 2013–2014, 12. The median number of years required for completion of a degree in 2012–2013 were 2. The number of students enrolled full- and part-time who were dismissed or voluntarily withdrew from this program area in 2012–2013 were 0.
Scores: Entries appear in this order: required test or GPA, minimum score (if required), median score of students entering in 2012–2013. *Applied Psychology MA/MS (Master of Arts/Science):* GRE-V no minimum stated, GRE-Q no minimum stated, GRE-Analytical no minimum stated, overall undergraduate GPA no minimum stated.
Other Criteria: (importance of criteria rated low, medium, or high): GRE scores—high, research experience—low, GPA—high, letters of recommendation—high, statement of goals and objectives—high, undergraduate major in psychology—low, specific undergraduate psychology courses taken—low. For additional information on admission requirements, go to http://www.jsu.edu/psychology/gradfaq.html.

Student Characteristics: The following represents characteristics of students in 2012–2013 in all graduate psychology programs in the department: Female—full-time 10, part-time 2; Male—full-time 1, part-time 2; African American/Black—full-time 1, part-time 0; Hispanic/Latino(a)—full-time 0, part-time 0; Asian/Pacific Islander—full-time 0, part-time 0; American Indian/Alaska Native—full-time 0, part-time 0; Caucasian/White—full-time 10, part-time 4; Multi-ethnic—full-time 0, part-time 0; students subject to the Americans With Disabilities Act—full-time 0, part-time 0; Unknown ethnicity—full-time 0, part-time 0; International students who hold an F-1 or J-1 Visa—full-time 0, part-time 0.

Financial Information/Assistance:
Tuition for Full-Time Study: *Master's:* State residents: per academic year $7,329, $349 per credit hour; Nonstate residents: per

academic year $14,658, $698 per credit hour. Tuition is subject to change. See the following website for updates and changes in tuition costs: http://www.jsu.edu/bursar/tuition.html.

Financial Assistance:
First-Year Students: No information provided.
Advanced Students: No information provided.
Additional Information: Of all students currently enrolled full time, 0% benefited from one or more of the listed financial assistance programs. Application and information available online at: http://www.jsu.edu/finaid/.

Internships/Practica: Applied Behavior Analysis practica are available in a variety of settings in which behavioral principles are used to improve human behavior. An Instructional Practicum is also available and allows outstanding students to gain teaching experience assisting a psychology professor.

Housing and Day Care: On-campus housing is available. See the following website for more information: http://www.jsu.edu/housing/index.html. On-campus day care facilities are available. See the following website for more information: http://www.jsu.edu/edprof/fcs/cdc.html.

Employment of Department Graduates:
Master's Degree Graduates: Of those who graduated in the academic year 2011–2012, the following categories and numbers represent the postgraduate activities and employment of master's degree graduates: Enrolled in a psychology doctoral program (1), enrolled in a postdoctoral residency/fellowship (n/a), employed in independent practice (n/a), still seeking employment (1), other employment position (7), total from the above (master's) (9).
Doctoral Degree Graduates: Of those who graduated in the academic year 2011–2012, the following categories and numbers represent the postgraduate activities and employment of doctoral degree graduates: Enrolled in a psychology doctoral program (n/a), total from the above (doctoral) (0).

Additional Information:
Orientation, Objectives, and Emphasis of Department: JSU's master's program in psychology offers instruction and training in the analysis of behavior. Students complete courses in the experimental analysis of behavior and applied behavior analysis. Courses in the experimental analysis of behavior teach students about basic functional relations between environmental events and behavior, whereas courses in applied behavior analysis train students in the application of those basic behavioral principles to human populations. Hands-on experience is available in our animal and human research facilities and local practicum sites. The program has a Behavior Analyst Certification Board (BACB)-approved course sequence.

Special Facilities or Resources: Special facilities include an animal room, a running room with 15 chambers, student offices, and a seminar computer room. A network of control computers (which were developed at JSU and used in many other universities) runs experiments and provides interactive graphical analyses.

Information for Students With Physical Disabilities: See the following website for more information: http://www.jsu.edu/dss/.

Application Information:
Send to Jacksonville State University, College of Graduate Studies, 700 Pelham Road North, Jacksonville, AL 36265-1602. Application available online. URL of online application: http://www.jsu.edu/graduate/grad_app.html. Students are admitted in the Fall, application deadline August 1. *Fee:* $30.

South Alabama, University of
Department of Psychology
Arts and Sciences
LSCB Room 326
Mobile, AL 36688
Telephone: (251) 460-6371
Fax: (251) 460-6320
E-mail: *lchriste@southalabama.edu*
Web: *http://www.southalabama.edu/psychology/*

Department Information:
1964. Chairperson: Larry Christensen. Number of faculty: total—full-time 15, part-time 12; women—full-time 6, part-time 6; minority—part-time 1.

Programs and Degrees Offered:
Listed in the following order: Program area, degree type (T if terminal Master's), number awarded 7/11–6/12. Experimental Psychology MA/MS (Master of Arts/Science) (T) 3, Clinical/Counseling Psychology PhD (Doctor of Philosophy) 0.

Student Applications/Admissions:
Student Applications
Experimental Psychology MA/MS (Master of Arts/Science)—Applications 2012–2013, 0. Total applicants accepted 2012–2013, 0. Number full-time enrolled (new admits only) 2012–2013, 0. Number part-time enrolled (new admits only) 2012–2013, 0. Total enrolled 2012–2013 full-time, 1. Total enrolled 2012–2013 part-time, 0. Openings 2013–2014, 3. The median number of years required for completion of a degree in 2012–2013 were 4. The number of students enrolled full- and part-time who were dismissed or voluntarily withdrew from this program area in 2012–2013 were 0. *Clinical/Counseling Psychology PhD (Doctor of Philosophy)*—Applications 2012–2013, 57. Total applicants accepted 2012–2013, 15. Number full-time enrolled (new admits only) 2012–2013, 13. Number part-time enrolled (new admits only) 2012–2013, 0. Total enrolled 2012–2013 full-time, 36. Total enrolled 2012–2013 part-time, 0. Openings 2013–2014, 7. The number of students enrolled full- and part-time who were dismissed or voluntarily withdrew from this program area in 2012–2013 were 1.
Scores: Entries appear in this order: required test or GPA, minimum score (if required), median score of students entering in 2012–2013. *Experimental Psychology MA/MS (Master of Arts/Science)*: GRE-V 460, 565, GRE-Q 630, 650, overall undergraduate GPA 3.20, 3.59, psychology GPA 3.29, 3.65; *Clinical/Counseling Psychology PhD (Doctor of Philosophy)*: GRE-V 146, 165, GRE-Q 140, 148, GRE-Analytical 3.0, 4.0, overall undergraduate GPA 2.80, 3.61, psychology GPA no minimum stated, Masters GPA 3.27, 4.00.
Other Criteria: (importance of criteria rated low, medium, or high): GRE scores—high, research experience—medium, work experience—low, extracurricular activity—low, clinically related public service—medium, GPA—high, letters of recommendation—high, interview—high, statement of goals and objectives—medium, undergraduate major in psychology—high, specific undergraduate psychology courses taken—high. For additional information on admission requirements, go to http://www.southalabama.edu/psychology/application.html.

Student Characteristics: The following represents characteristics of students in 2012–2013 in all graduate psychology programs in the department: Female—full-time 31, part-time 0; Male—full-time 6, part-time 0; African American/Black—full-time 1, part-time 0; Hispanic/Latino(a)—full-time 1, part-time 0; Asian/Pacific Islander—full-time 3, part-time 0; American Indian/Alaska Native—full-time 2, part-time 0; Caucasian/White—full-time 29, part-time 0; Multi-ethnic—full-time 1, part-time 0; students subject to the Americans With Disabilities Act—full-time 0, part-time 0; Unknown ethnicity—full-time 0, part-time 0; International students who hold an F-1 or J-1 Visa—full-time 0, part-time 0.

Financial Information/Assistance:
Tuition for Full-Time Study: *Master's:* State residents: per academic year $7,968, $332 per credit hour; Nonstate residents: per academic year $15,936, $664 per credit hour. *Doctoral:* State residents: per academic year $7,968, $332 per credit hour; Nonstate residents: per academic year $15,936, $664 per credit hour. Tuition is subject to change. Additional fees are assessed to students beyond the costs of tuition for the following: registration, student health, building, library, activity/athletic fee, transportation. See the following website for updates and changes in tuition costs: http://www.southalabama.edu/studentaccounting/tuition.html.

Financial Assistance:
First-Year Students: Research assistantships available for first year. Average amount paid per academic year: $9,000. Average number of hours worked per week: 20. Apply by December 15.
Advanced Students: Teaching assistantships available for advanced students. Average amount paid per academic year: $11,000. Average number of hours worked per week: 20. Apply by December 15. Research assistantships available for advanced students. Average amount paid per academic year: $11,000. Average number of hours worked per week: 20. Apply by December 15.
Additional Information: Of all students currently enrolled full time, 100% benefited from one or more of the listed financial assistance programs. Application and information available online at: http://www.southalabama.edu/psychology/application.html.

Internships/Practica: Doctoral Degree (PhD Clinical/Counseling Psychology): For those doctoral students for whom a professional psychology internship was required in this program prior to graduation, (6) students applied for an internship in 2011–2012, with (6) students obtaining an internship. Of those students who obtained an internship, (6) were paid internships. Of those students who obtained an internship, (5) students placed in APA/CPA accredited internships, (1) students placed in internships not APA/CPA accredited, but listed with the Association of Psychology Postdoctoral and Internship Programs (APPIC), (0) students placed in internships conforming to guidelines of the Council of Directors of School Psychology Programs (CDSPP), (0) students placed in internships that were not APA/CPA accredited, APPIC or CDSPP listed. Master's Degree (MA/MS Experimental Psychology): An internship experience, such as a final research project or "capstone" experience is required of graduates. Graduate students receive practical experience in the application of psychological assessment and treatment procedures in a variety of clinical settings. Emphasis is given to ethical and professional issues with intensive individual and group supervision. The Department of Psychology operates an outpatient teaching clinic where a variety of children and adults are seen for short-term assessment and treatment. External practicum placements are also available in a variety of community settings including a state mental hospital, a mental retardation facility and community substance abuse programs.

Housing and Day Care: On-campus housing is available. See the following website for more information: http://www. southalabama.edu/housing/. No on-campus day care facilities are available.

Employment of Department Graduates:

Master's Degree Graduates: Of those who graduated in the academic year 2011–2012, the following categories and numbers represent the postgraduate activities and employment of master's degree graduates: Enrolled in a psychology doctoral program (5), enrolled in a postdoctoral residency/fellowship (n/a), employed in independent practice (n/a), employed in business or industry (1), employed in a community mental health/counseling center (1), do not know (1), total from the above (master's) (8).

Doctoral Degree Graduates: Of those who graduated in the academic year 2011–2012, the following categories and numbers represent the postgraduate activities and employment of doctoral degree graduates: Enrolled in a psychology doctoral program (n/a), total from the above (doctoral) (0).

Additional Information:

Orientation, Objectives, and Emphasis of Department: The University of South Alabama offers a combined Clinical/Counseling Psychology (CCP) doctoral program of studies integrating the missions and philosophies of clinical and counseling psychology. The CCP program will train students to provide the most effective types of psychological treatment and, upon completion of the program of studies, students will have a set of competencies enabling them to work successfully with a variety of professionals for the purpose of health promotion and treatment of mental illness. Students will be trained in the asset-strength model traditionally associated with counseling psychology and to conduct research and provide treatment for serious psychopathology traditionally associated with clinical psychology. The University of South Alabama also offers a master's program in general experimental psychology. All students complete a core curriculum designed to provide them with knowledge of current theories, principles, and methods of experimental psychology. Courses for the experimental student are designed to provide more extensive information in research design and experimental methods as well as theoretical background related to the student's thesis research. The program is designed to provide students with the necessary theoretical and research background to pursue further graduate study, if they so choose. Graduate students receive individual attention and close supervision by departmental faculty.

Special Facilities or Resources: In addition to the Psychological Clinic, the Psychology Department has laboratory facilities for neuropsychological and behavioral research, and has access to both mainframe and personal computer facilities. An EEG/ERP laboratory is used for conducting research requiring the utilization of a dense array electrode cap. This laboratory is available for both faculty and graduate student research. A family interaction laboratory exists for studying parent-child interactions with the goal of enhancing parenting skills. A cognitive laboratory exists with the capability of studying linguistic enhancement. This laboratory also has an eye-tracking apparatus capable of being integrated into a variety of research projects. A social interaction laboratory exists to provide research into the dynamics of social interactions. A biofeedback laboratory exists for research into the treatment of issues such as headaches. A flight simulation laboratory exists for research into factors that influence flight safety.

Information for Students With Physical Disabilities: See the following website for more information: http://www. southalabama.edu/dss/.

Application Information:

Send to Director of Admission, 2500 Meisler Hall, University of South Alabama, Mobile, AL 36688-0002. Application available online. URL of online application: http://www.southalabama.edu/admissions/grad. html. Students are admitted in the Fall, application deadline December 15. *Fee:* $35.

Alaska Pacific University

Department of Counseling Psychology & Human Services
4101 University Drive
Anchorage, AK 99508
Telephone: (907) 564-8351
Fax: (907) 564-8396
E-mail: admissions@alaskapacific.edu
Web: http://www.alaskapacific.edu/academics/counseling-psychology-human-services/

Department Information:

1959. Chairperson: Dr. Dorothy Dunne. Number of faculty: total—full-time 8; women—full-time 5.

Programs and Degrees Offered:

Listed in the following order: Program area, degree type (T if terminal Master's), number awarded 7/11–6/12. Counseling Psychology MA/MS (Master of Arts/Science) (T) 18, Counseling Psychology PsyD (Doctor of Psychology) 0.

Student Applications/Admissions:

Student Applications

Counseling Psychology MA/MS (Master of Arts/Science)—Applications 2012–2013, 41. Total applicants accepted 2012–2013, 23. Number full-time enrolled (new admits only) 2012–2013, 15. Number part-time enrolled (new admits only) 2012–2013, 6. Total enrolled 2012–2013 full-time, 41. Total enrolled 2012–2013 part-time, 8. Openings 2013–2014, 20. The median number of years required for completion of a degree in 2012–2013 were 2. The number of students enrolled full- and part-time who were dismissed or voluntarily withdrew from this program area in 2012–2013 were 2. *Counseling Psychology PsyD (Doctor of Psychology)*—Applications 2012–2013, 322. Total applicants accepted 2012–2013, 10. Number full-time enrolled (new admits only) 2012–2013, 10. Number part-time enrolled (new admits only) 2012–2013, 0. Total enrolled 2012–2013 full-time, 10. Total enrolled 2012–2013 part-time, 0. Openings 2013–2014, 10. The median number of years required for completion of a degree in 2012–2013 were 3. The number of students enrolled full- and part-time who were dismissed or voluntarily withdrew from this program area in 2012–2013 were 0.

Scores: Entries appear in this order: required test or GPA, minimum score (if required), median score of students entering in 2012–2013. *Counseling Psychology PsyD (Doctor of Psychology):* Masters GPA no minimum stated.

Other Criteria: (importance of criteria rated low, medium, or high): research experience—low, work experience—medium, extracurricular activity—medium, clinically related public service—medium, GPA—medium, letters of recommendation—high, interview—high, statement of goals and objectives—high, MAT scores—medium, undergraduate major in psychology—low, specific undergraduate psychology courses taken—medium, MAT just used for the MSCP.

Student Characteristics: The following represents characteristics of students in 2012–2013 in all graduate psychology programs in the department: Female—full-time 49, part-time 4; Male—full-time 11, part-time 4; African American/Black—full-time 0, part-time 0; Hispanic/Latino(a)—full-time 0, part-time 0; Asian/Pacific Islander—full-time 0, part-time 0; American Indian/Alaska Native—full-time 0, part-time 0; Caucasian/White—full-time 0, part-time 0; Multi-ethnic—full-time 0, part-time 0; students subject to the Americans With Disabilities Act—full-time 0, part-time 0; Unknown ethnicity—full-time 60, part-time 8; International students who hold an F-1 or J-1 Visa—full-time 0, part-time 0.

Financial Information/Assistance:

Tuition for Full-Time Study: *Master's:* State residents: $630 per credit hour; Nonstate residents: $630 per credit hour. *Doctoral:* State residents: $845 per credit hour; Nonstate residents: $845 per credit hour. Tuition is subject to change. Tuition costs vary by program. See the following website for updates and changes in tuition costs: http://www.alaskapacific.edu/apply/financial-aid/cost-of-attendance/.

Financial Assistance:

First-Year Students: No information provided.

Advanced Students: Traineeships available for advanced students. Average number of hours worked per week: 20. Apply by March 15.

Additional Information: Of all students currently enrolled full time, 90% benefited from one or more of the listed financial assistance programs. Application and information available online at: http://www.alaskapacific.edu/apply/financial-aid/.

Internships/Practica: Master's Degree (MA/MS Counseling Psychology): An internship experience, such as a final research project or "capstone" experience is required of graduates. A significant part of a counselor's or psychologist's education occurs outside the classroom through practica and an internship experience. This is a unique opportunity for the student to begin applying theories and techniques of their classroom education as well as to focus their professional development in a specialized area of counseling. Internship opportunities are diverse in clientele and therapeutic context. In collaboration with the MSCP Director, PsyD Director, and faculty, students identify sites consistent with their needs. Past MSCP internship sites have included: Southcentral Counseling Center, Anchorage School District, McLaughlin Youth Center, Southcentral Foundation, Catholic Social Services, Alaska Native Medical Center, Alaska Human Services, Salvation Army Clitheroe Center, Life Quest, Alaska Children's Services, Abused Women's Aid in Crisis (AWAIC), Providence Hospital Breakthrough Program, North Star Hospital, and Valley Women's Resource Center.

Housing and Day Care: On-campus housing is available. See the following website for more information: http://www.alaskapacific. edu/explore-apu/student-life/housing/. No on-campus day care facilities are available.

Employment of Department Graduates:

Master's Degree Graduates: Of those who graduated in the academic year 2011–2012, the following categories and numbers represent the postgraduate activities and employment of master's degree graduates: Enrolled in a psychology doctoral program (1), enrolled in a postdoctoral residency/fellowship (n/a), employed in independent practice (n/a), employed in a professional position in a school system (2), employed in business or industry (1), employed in government agency (2), employed in a community mental health/counseling center (14), employed in a hospital/ medical center (3), total from the above (master's) (23).

Doctoral Degree Graduates: Of those who graduated in the academic year 2011–2012, the following categories and numbers represent the postgraduate activities and employment of doctoral degree graduates: Enrolled in a psychology doctoral program (n/a), total from the above (doctoral) (0).

Additional Information:

Orientation, Objectives, and Emphasis of Department: The Master of Science in Counseling Psychology Program (MSCP) and the Psychology Doctorate programs are selective, rigorous programs for the creative adult who plans to become a licensed professional counselor or licensed psychologist. The MSCP program is eclectic in theoretical orientation and committed to celebrating diversity within the range of professional mental health approaches and techniques. The MSCP program encourages students to explore and develop their own special interests within the field. The program integrates theory and practice. The MSCP program meets the educational requirements for licensure as a Licensed Professional Counselor with the State of Alaska and other states throughout the US. The Psy D program was designed for professional working in the field of mental health who desire further education or licensure as a psychologist. The program adheres to Alaska statutes and regulations for licensure and seeks to embrace recommendations for education promulgated by ASPPB and APA. The program is designed for students to be able to pursue individual areas of interests while completing required curriculum areas. The program allows for a Project Demonstrating Excellence in lieu of a required dissertation and includes required practice experiences and a 1500 hour internship.

Special Facilities or Resources: We have counseling facilities with a one-way mirrored window and current recording technologies for providing feedback and learning. We also have a library of various current psychological tests and materials.

Application Information:
Send to Graduate Admissions; Alaska Pacific University, 4101 University Drive, Anchorage, AK 99508. Application available online. URL of online application: http://www.alaskapacific.edu/apply/graduate/. Students are admitted in the Fall, application deadline February 1; Summer, application deadline February 1. MSCP students begin in the fall and complete 5 full semesters. PsyD students start in the summer semester and complete 9 semesters, three full years of study. *Fee:* $25. Application fee is waived if apply online.

Alaska, University of, Anchorage

MS in Clinical Psychology
College of Arts and Sciences
3211 Providence Drive
Anchorage, AK 99508
Telephone: (907) 786-4717
Fax: (907) 786-1790
E-mail: kjbrandenburg@uaa.alaska.edu
Web: http://www.uaa.alaska.edu/psych/masters/index.cfm

Department Information:
1967. Chairperson: Dr. Claudia Lampman. Number of faculty: total—full-time 3, part-time 3; women—full-time 2, part-time 1.

Programs and Degrees Offered:
Listed in the following order: Program area, degree type (T if terminal Master's), number awarded 7/11–6/12. Clinical Psychology MA/MS (Master of Arts/Science) (T) 10.

Student Applications/Admissions:

Student Applications

Clinical Psychology MA/MS (Master of Arts/Science)—Applications 2012–2013, 34. Total applicants accepted 2012–2013, 9. Number full-time enrolled (new admits only) 2012–2013, 9. Number part-time enrolled (new admits only) 2012–2013, 0. Total enrolled 2012–2013 full-time, 25. Total enrolled 2012–2013 part-time, 0. Openings 2013–2014, 12. The median number of years required for completion of a degree in 2012–2013 were 2. The number of students enrolled full- and part-time who were dismissed or voluntarily withdrew from this program area in 2012–2013 were 1.

Scores: Entries appear in this order: required test or GPA, minimum score (if required), median score of students entering in 2012–2013. *Clinical Psychology MA/MS (Master of Arts/Science):* overall undergraduate GPA 2.79, 3.26.

Other Criteria: (importance of criteria rated low, medium, or high): research experience—medium, work experience—high, extracurricular activity—medium, clinically related public service—high, GPA—high, letters of recommendation—high, interview—medium, statement of goals and objectives—high, undergraduate major in psychology—high, specific undergraduate psychology courses taken—high. For additional information on admission requirements, go to http://www.uaa.alaska.edu/psych/masters/admissions.cfm.

Student Characteristics: The following represents characteristics of students in 2012–2013 in all graduate psychology programs in the department: Female—full-time 21, part-time 0; Male—full-time 4, part-time 0; African American/Black—full-time 0, part-time 0; Hispanic/Latino(a)—full-time 1, part-time 0; Asian/Pacific Islander—full-time 1, part-time 0; American Indian/Alaska Native—full-time 2, part-time 0; Caucasian/White—full-time 21, part-time 0; Multi-ethnic—full-time 0, part-time 0; students subject to the Americans With Disabilities Act—full-time 1, part-time 0; Unknown ethnicity—full-time 0, part-time 0; International students who hold an F-1 or J-1 Visa—full-time 1, part-time 0.

Financial Information/Assistance:
Tuition for Full-Time Study: *Master's:* State residents: $383 per credit hour; Nonstate residents: $783 per credit hour. Tuition is

subject to change. Additional fees are assessed to students beyond the costs of tuition for the following: student life, student government, student media, student technology, network fee, concert fee. See the following website for updates and changes in tuition costs: http://www.uaa.alaska.edu/financialaid/costs.cfm.

Financial Assistance:

First-Year Students: Teaching assistantships available for first year. Average amount paid per academic year: $6,200. Average number of hours worked per week: 20. Apply by May 1. Research assistantships available for first year. Average amount paid per academic year: $6,200. Average number of hours worked per week: 20. Apply by May 15.

Advanced Students: Teaching assistantships available for advanced students. Average amount paid per academic year: $6,200. Average number of hours worked per week: 20. Apply by May 1. Research assistantships available for advanced students. Average amount paid per academic year: $6,200. Average number of hours worked per week: 20. Apply by May 15.

Additional Information: Of all students currently enrolled full time, 30% benefited from one or more of the listed financial assistance programs. Application and information available online at: http://www.uaa.alaska.edu/financialaid/.

Internships/Practica: Master's Degree (MA/MS Clinical Psychology): An internship experience, such as a final research project or "capstone" experience is required of graduates. The psychology department maintains an in-house mental health clinic, the Psychological Services Center, where graduate students gain initial hands-on supervised psychotherapy experience. There are a variety of community internships available after completion of the first supervised practicum. The availability of community internships changes from year to year but we attempt to match student interests and internship experiences.

Housing and Day Care: On-campus housing is available. See the following website for more information: http://www.uaa.alaska.edu/housing/. On-campus day care facilities are available. See the following website for more information: http://www.uaa.alaska.edu/childdevelopmentcenter/.

Employment of Department Graduates:

Master's Degree Graduates: Of those who graduated in the academic year 2011–2012, the following categories and numbers represent the postgraduate activities and employment of master's degree graduates: Enrolled in a psychology doctoral program (2), enrolled in a postdoctoral residency/fellowship (n/a), employed in independent practice (n/a), employed in a community mental health/counseling center (8), total from the above (master's) (10).

Doctoral Degree Graduates: Of those who graduated in the academic year 2011–2012, the following categories and numbers represent the postgraduate activities and employment of doctoral degree graduates: Enrolled in a psychology doctoral program (n/a), total from the above (doctoral) (0).

Additional Information:

Orientation, Objectives, and Emphasis of Department: The mission of the M.S. program is to provide quality training to graduate students interested in mental health careers in diverse communities. The training seeks to produce graduates who are practitioner-scientists prepared to address local behavioral health needs in a context that is culturally sensitive and community focused.

Special Facilities or Resources: Center for Behavioral Health Research and Services, Center for Human Development.

Information for Students With Physical Disabilities: See the following website for more information: http://www.uaa.alaska.edu/dss/.

Application Information:
Send to Ms Katie Brandenburg, Administrative Secretary, Psychology Department. Application available online. URL of online application: http://www.uaa.alaska.edu/admissions/index.cfm. Students are admitted in the Fall, application deadline April 1. *Fee:* $60.

Alaska, University of, Fairbanks/Anchorage

Department of Psychology/Joint PhD Program in Clinical-
  Community Psychology
UAF College of Liberal Arts/UAA College of Arts & Sciences
P.O. Box 756480/3211 Providence Drive
Fairbanks, AK 99775
Telephone: (907) 474-7012/786-1640
Fax: (907) 474-5781
E-mail: *aehauser@uaa.alaska.edu*
Web: *http://psyphd.alaska.edu*

Department Information:
1984. Program Directors: Drs. James M. Fitterling / David Webster. Number of faculty: total—full-time 9, part-time 10; women—full-time 3, part-time 6; total—minority—full-time 2; women minority—full-time 1.

Programs and Degrees Offered:
Listed in the following order: Program area, degree type (T if terminal Master's), number awarded 7/11–6/12. Clinical-Community Psychology PhD (Doctor of Philosophy) 4.

APA Accreditation: Clinical PhD (Doctor of Philosophy). Student Outcome Data Website: http://psyphd.alaska.edu/program outcomes.htm.

Student Applications/Admissions:

Student Applications

Clinical-Community Psychology PhD (Doctor of Philosophy)—Applications 2012–2013, 50. Total applicants accepted 2012–2013, 8. Number full-time enrolled (new admits only) 2012–2013, 8. Number part-time enrolled (new admits only) 2012–2013, 0. Total enrolled 2012–2013 full-time, 45. Total enrolled 2012–2013 part-time, 2. Openings 2013–2014, 8. The number of students enrolled full- and part-time who were dismissed or voluntarily withdrew from this program area in 2012–2013 were 0.

Scores: Entries appear in this order: required test or GPA, minimum score (if required), median score of students entering in 2012–2013. *Clinical-Community Psychology PhD (Doctor of Philosophy):* overall undergraduate GPA 3.0.

Other Criteria: (importance of criteria rated low, medium, or high): GRE scores—low, research experience—medium, work experience—medium, extracurricular activity—medium, clinically related public service—medium, GPA—medium, letters of recommendation—high, interview—high, statement of goals and objectives—high, rural/indigenous interest—medium, undergraduate major in psychology—low, specific undergraduate psychology courses taken—high. For additional information on admission requirements, go to http://psyphd.alaska.edu/admissions.htm.

Student Characteristics: The following represents characteristics of students in 2012–2013 in all graduate psychology programs in the department: Female—full-time 32, part-time 2; Male—full-time 13, part-time 0; African American/Black—full-time 1, part-time 0; Hispanic/Latino(a)—full-time 2, part-time 0; Asian/Pacific Islander—full-time 3, part-time 0; American Indian/Alaska Native—full-time 9, part-time 1; Caucasian/White—full-time 28, part-time 1; Multi-ethnic—full-time 2, part-time 0; students subject to the Americans With Disabilities Act—full-time 0, part-time 0; Unknown ethnicity—full-time 0, part-time 0; International students who hold an F-1 or J-1 Visa—full-time 1, part-time 0.

Financial Information/Assistance:

Tuition for Full-Time Study: *Doctoral:* State residents: per academic year $10,752, $383 per credit hour; Nonstate residents: per academic year $20,252, $783 per credit hour. Tuition is subject to change. See the following website for updates and changes in tuition costs: http://www.uaf.edu/finaid/costs/.

Financial Assistance:

First-Year Students: Teaching assistantships available for first year. Average amount paid per academic year: $26,322. Average number of hours worked per week: 20. Apply by February 1. Research assistantships available for first year. Average amount paid per academic year: $26,322. Average number of hours worked per week: 20. Apply by February 1.

Advanced Students: Teaching assistantships available for advanced students. Average amount paid per academic year: $28,900. Average number of hours worked per week: 20. Apply by February 1. Research assistantships available for advanced students. Average amount paid per academic year: $28,900. Average number of hours worked per week: 20. Apply by February 1.

Additional Information: Of all students currently enrolled full time, 100% benefited from one or more of the listed financial assistance programs. Application and information available online at: http://psyphd.alaska.edu/financial support.htm.

Internships/Practica: Doctoral Degree (PhD Clinical-Community Psychology): For those doctoral students for whom a professional psychology internship was required in this program prior to graduation, (4) students applied for an internship in 2011–2012, with (4) students obtaining an internship. Of those students who obtained an internship, (4) were paid internships. Of those students who obtained an internship, (0) students placed in APA/CPA accredited internships, (4) students placed in internships not APA/CPA accredited, but listed with the Association of Psychology Postdoctoral and Internship Programs (APPIC), (0) students placed in internships conforming to guidelines of the Council of Directors of School Psychology Programs (CDSPP), (0) students placed in internships that were not APA/CPA accredited, APPIC or CDSPP listed. Both campuses provide clinical practica through on-campus clinics and placements in local behavioral health centers. Community practica in a variety of community settings are also provided to all students. Internship placements in Alaska will also be available to students.

Housing and Day Care: On-campus housing is available. See the following website for more information: http://www.uaa.alaska.edu/housing/ AND http://www.uaf.edu/reslife/graduate-family-housing/. On-campus day care facilities are available. See the following website for more information: http://www.uaa.alaska.edu/childdevelopmentcenter/ AND http://www.tvc.uaf.edu/programs/BunnellHouse/.

Employment of Department Graduates:

Master's Degree Graduates: Of those who graduated in the academic year 2011–2012, the following categories and numbers represent the postgraduate activities and employment of master's degree graduates: Enrolled in a postdoctoral residency/fellowship (n/a), employed in independent practice (n/a), total from the above (master's) (0).

Doctoral Degree Graduates: Of those who graduated in the academic year 2011–2012, the following categories and numbers represent the postgraduate activities and employment of doctoral degree graduates: Enrolled in a psychology doctoral program (n/a), employed in a community mental health/counseling center (1), employed in a hospital/medical center (3), total from the above (doctoral) (4).

Additional Information:

Orientation, Objectives, and Emphasis of Department: The UAF-UAA PhD Program in Clinical-Community Psychology is a scientist–practitioner program in clinical psychology that seeks to educate scholars and clinicians, who have strong commitments to research, evaluation, clinical practice, and community-based action, solidly grounded in the cultural contexts of all affected stakeholders. The program integrates clinical, community, and cultural psychology with a focus on rural, indigenous issues and an applied emphasis on the integration of research and practice. Through combining the spirit of clinical and community psychology, the program promotes contextually-grounded and culturally appropriate research, evaluation, prevention, clinical service, community work, and social action, relevant to individuals, groups, families, and communities. The PhD Program in Clinical-Community Psychology with Rural, Indigenous Emphasis is a program jointly delivered and administered by the Departments of Psychology at the University of Alaska Fairbanks and the University of Alaska Anchorage. All program courses are co-taught across campuses via videoconference and all program components are delivered by faculty at both campuses. The program is designed such that the student experience is as similar as possible regardless of residence (Fairbanks or Anchorage).

Special Facilities or Resources: At UAF, the academic facilities available to graduate students include two high definition video classrooms, individual study areas, and clinical space in the Psychology Department Clinic, consisting of individual, family/group, child, and telehealth therapy rooms. Other facilities available to graduate students include a departmental lab and several university labs with PCs and Macs. UAF is an international center for research in the Arctic and the North. At UAA, the academic facilities available to graduate students include two high definition video classrooms, individual study areas, clinical space in the Psychological Service Center, consisting of individual, family/group, child, and telehealth therapy rooms, and the Consortium

Library, the major research library for southcentral Alaska. Research facilities available to graduate students include the Center for Behavioral Health Research and Services, a departmental laboratory and several university computer labs with PCs and Macs.

Information for Students With Physical Disabilities: See the following website for more information: http://www.uaa.alaska.edu/dss/ AND http://www.uaf.edu/disability/.

Application Information:
Send to David Webster, UAF Program Director, Psychology PhD Program, University of Alaska Fairbanks, P.O. Box 756480, Fairbanks, Alaska 99775-6480 AND James M. Fitterling, UAA Program Director, Psychology PhD Program, University of Alaska Anchorage, 3211 Providence Drive, SSB 303, Anchorage, Alaska 99508. Students are admitted in the Fall, application deadline February 1. *Fee:* $120.

Arizona School of Professional Psychology, Argosy University, Phoenix

Clinical Psychology
College of Psychology and Behavioral Science
Suite 150, 2233 West Dunlap Avenue
Phoenix, AZ 85021
Telephone: (602) 216-2600
Fax: (602) 216-1940
E-mail: *bbutaney@argosy.edu*
Web: *http://www.argosy.edu/phoenix-arizona/default.aspx*

Department Information:
1997. Chairperson: Bhupin Butaney, PhD. Number of faculty: total—full-time 14, part-time 1; women—full-time 8, part-time 1; total—minority—full-time 6, part-time 1; women minority—full-time 4, part-time 1.

Programs and Degrees Offered:
Listed in the following order: Program area, degree type (T if terminal Master's), number awarded 7/11–6/12. Clinical Psychology PsyD (Doctor of Psychology) 32.

APA Accreditation: Clinical PsyD (Doctor of Psychology). Student Outcome Data Website: http://www.argosy.edu/clinical-psychology/phoenix-arizona/psyd-programs-doctorate-degree-97112.aspx.

Student Applications/Admissions:
Student Applications
Clinical Psychology PsyD (Doctor of Psychology)—Applications 2012–2013, 101. Total applicants accepted 2012–2013, 23. Number full-time enrolled (new admits only) 2012–2013, 23. Total enrolled 2012–2013 full-time, 23. Openings 2013–2014, 30. The median number of years required for completion of a degree in 2012–2013 were 5. The number of students enrolled full- and part-time who were dismissed or voluntarily withdrew from this program area in 2012–2013 were 0.
Scores: Entries appear in this order: required test or GPA, minimum score (if required), median score of students entering in 2012–2013. *Clinical Psychology PsyD (Doctor of Psychology):* GRE-V no minimum stated, GRE-Q no minimum stated, overall undergraduate GPA 3.25, 3.42, Masters GPA 3.5, 3.5.
Other Criteria: (importance of criteria rated low, medium, or high): research experience—low, work experience—medium, extracurricular activity—medium, clinically related public service—medium, GPA—high, letters of recommendation—high, interview—high, statement of goals and objectives—high, undergraduate major in psychology—low, specific undergraduate psychology courses taken—medium. For additional information on admission requirements, go to http://www.argosy.edu/clinical-psychology/phoenix-arizona/psyd-programs-admissions-97143.aspx.

Student Characteristics: The following represents characteristics of students in 2012–2013 in all graduate psychology programs in the department: Female—full-time 19, part-time 1; Male—full-time 4, part-time 0; African American/Black—full-time 0, part-time 0; Hispanic/Latino(a)—full-time 3, part-time 0; Asian/Pacific Islander—full-time 0, part-time 0; American Indian/Alaska Native—full-time 0, part-time 0; Caucasian/White—full-time 19, part-time 0; Multi-ethnic—full-time 1, part-time 0; students subject to the Americans With Disabilities Act—full-time 1, part-time 0; Unknown ethnicity—full-time 0, part-time 0; International students who hold an F-1 or J-1 Visa—full-time 0, part-time 0.

Financial Information/Assistance:
Tuition for Full-Time Study: *Doctoral:* State residents: per academic year $33,698, $1,162 per credit hour; Nonstate residents: per academic year $33,698, $1,162 per credit hour. Tuition is subject to change. Additional fees are assessed to students beyond the costs of tuition for the following: Total $460 - technology fee, student activity fee, graduation fee, add/drop fee, testing kit fee. See the following website for updates and changes in tuition costs: http://www.argosy.edu/admissions/Default.aspx.

Financial Assistance:
First-Year Students: Teaching assistantships available for first year. Average number of hours worked per week: 10. Fellowships and scholarships available for first year.
Advanced Students: Teaching assistantships available for advanced students. Traineeships available for advanced students. Average amount paid per academic year: $20,000. Fellowships and scholarships available for advanced students.
Additional Information: Of all students currently enrolled full time, 10% benefited from one or more of the listed financial assistance programs. Application and information available online at: http://www.argosy.edu/clinical-psychology/phoenix-arizona/psyd-programs-admissions-97143.aspx.

Internships/Practica: Doctoral Degree (PsyD Clinical Psychology): For those doctoral students for whom a professional psychology internship was required in this program prior to graduation, (22) students applied for an internship in 2011–2012, with (20) students obtaining an internship. Of those students who obtained an internship, (20) were paid internships. Of those students who obtained an internship, (9) students placed in APA/CPA accredited internships, (10) students placed in internships not APA/CPA accredited, but listed with the Association of Psychology Postdoctoral and Internship Programs (APPIC), (0) students placed in internships conforming to guidelines of the Council of Directors of School Psychology Programs (CDSPP), (1) students placed in internships that were not APA/CPA accredited, APPIC or CDSPP listed. The School maintains an extensive clinical training network including public and private hospitals, community mental health agencies, private practices, substance abuse and rehabilitation agencies, correctional facilities, and the Indian Health Service.

Housing and Day Care: No on-campus housing is available. No on-campus day care facilities are available.

Employment of Department Graduates:
Master's Degree Graduates: Of those who graduated in the academic year 2011–2012, the following categories and numbers

represent the postgraduate activities and employment of master's degree graduates: Enrolled in a postdoctoral residency/fellowship (n/a), employed in independent practice (n/a), total from the above (master's) (0).

Doctoral Degree Graduates: Of those who graduated in the academic year 2011–2012, the following categories and numbers represent the postgraduate activities and employment of doctoral degree graduates: Enrolled in a psychology doctoral program (n/a), total from the above (doctoral) (0).

Additional Information:

Orientation, Objectives, and Emphasis of Department: The mission of Argosy University/Phoenix is to educate and train students in clinical psychology and to prepare students for successful practitioner careers. The curriculum integrates theory, training, research, and practice and prepares students to work with a wide range of populations in need of psychological services. Faculty are both scholars and practitioners and guide students through coursework and field experiences so that they might understand how formal knowledge and practice operate to inform and enrich each other. The School follows a generalist practitioner-scholar orientation, exposing students to a broad array of clinical theories and interventions. Sensitivity to diverse populations, populations with specific needs, and multicultural awareness are important components of the school's training model.

Application Information:

Send to Director of Admissions, Arizona School of Professional Psychology, Argosy University/Phoenix, 2233 West Dunlap Avenue, Phoenix, AZ 85018. Application available online. URL of online application: https://portal.argosy.edu/Applicant/ApplyOnline_Login. aspx. Students are admitted in the Fall, application deadline April 1; Spring, application deadline November 15. *Fee:* $50.

Arizona State University (2012 data)
Cognitive Science and Engineering (Applied Psychology)
College of Technology and Innovation
7271 East Sonoran Arroyo Mall
Mesa, AZ 85212
Telephone: (480) 727-1781
E-mail: *russ.branaghan@asu.edu*
Web: *http://technology.asu.edu/appliedpsych*

Department Information:

1996. Director of Graduate Programs: Russell Branaghan. Number of faculty: total—full-time 8, part-time 5; women—full-time 2, part-time 2; total—minority—full-time 2; women minority—full-time 1; faculty subject to the Americans With Disabilities Act 1.

Programs and Degrees Offered:

Listed in the following order: Program area, degree type (T if terminal Master's), number awarded 7/11–6/12. Applied Psychology MA/MS (Master of Arts/Science) (T) 6, Simulation, Modeling and Cognitive Science PhD (Doctor of Philosophy) 0.

Student Applications/Admissions:

Student Applications

Applied Psychology MA/MS (Master of Arts/Science)—Applications 2012–2013, 24. Total applicants accepted 2012–2013,

9. Number full-time enrolled (new admits only) 2012–2013, 5. Number part-time enrolled (new admits only) 2012–2013, 0. Total enrolled 2012–2013 full-time, 15. Openings 2013–2014, 5. The median number of years required for completion of a degree in 2012–2013 were 3. The number of students enrolled full- and part-time who were dismissed or voluntarily withdrew from this program area in 2012–2013 were 2. *Simulation, Modeling and Cognitive Science PhD (Doctor of Philosophy)*—Applications 2012–2013, 21. Total applicants accepted 2012–2013, 7. Number full-time enrolled (new admits only) 2012–2013, 7. Total enrolled 2012–2013 full-time, 7. Openings 2013–2014, 5. The number of students enrolled full- and part-time who were dismissed or voluntarily withdrew from this program area in 2012–2013 were 0.

Scores: Entries appear in this order: required test or GPA, minimum score (if required), median score of students entering in 2012–2013. *Applied Psychology MA/MS (Master of Arts/Science):* GRE-V 500, 625, GRE-Q 500, 630, overall undergraduate GPA 3.0, 3.5, last 2 years GPA 3.0, 3.5; *Simulation, Modeling and Cognitive Science PhD (Doctor of Philosophy):* GRE-V 500, 700, GRE-Q 500, 710, overall undergraduate GPA no minimum stated, last 2 years GPA 3.0, 3.5, psychology GPA 3.0, 3.7, Masters GPA 3.0, 3.7.

Other Criteria: (importance of criteria rated low, medium, or high): GRE scores—medium, research experience—high, work experience—low, extracurricular activity—low, GPA—medium, letters of recommendation—high, interview—low, statement of goals and objectives—medium, undergraduate major in psychology—low, specific undergraduate psychology courses taken—medium. For additional information on admission requirements, go to https://technology.asu.edu/degrees/GRTS/TSSMACSPHD.

Student Characteristics: The following represents characteristics of students in 2012–2013 in all graduate psychology programs in the department: Female—full-time 8, part-time 0; Male—full-time 14, part-time 0; African American/Black—full-time 0, part-time 0; Hispanic/Latino(a)—full-time 4, part-time 0; Asian/Pacific Islander—full-time 8, part-time 0; American Indian/Alaska Native—full-time 0, part-time 0; Caucasian/White—full-time 10, part-time 0; Multi-ethnic—full-time 0, part-time 0; students subject to the Americans With Disabilities Act—full-time 0, part-time 0; Unknown ethnicity—full-time 0, part-time 0; International students who hold an F-1 or J-1 Visa—full-time 5, part-time 0.

Financial Information/Assistance:

Tuition for Full-Time Study: Master's: State residents: $694 per credit hour; Nonstate residents: $993 per credit hour. *Doctoral:* State residents: $694 per credit hour; Nonstate residents: $993 per credit hour. Tuition is subject to change. See the following website for updates and changes in tuition costs: https://students.asu.edu/costs.

Financial Assistance:

First-Year Students: Teaching assistantships available for first year. Research assistantships available for first year.

Advanced Students: Teaching assistantships available for advanced students. Research assistantships available for advanced students.

Additional Information: Of all students currently enrolled full time, 90% benefited from one or more of the listed financial

assistance programs. Application and information available online at: http://graduate.asu.edu/financing.

Internships/Practica: Master's Degree (MA/MS Applied Psychology): An internship experience, such as a final research project or "capstone" experience is required of graduates. Students, especially MS students who anticipate going into industry, are encouraged to pursue internships in the summer and the school year. Previous interns have worked at Dell, Motorola, Intel, GoDaddy, Veteran's Health Administration, and Air Force Research Lab.

Housing and Day Care: No on-campus housing is available. On-campus day care facilities are available. See the following website for more information: http://www.asu.edu/studentaffairs/reslife/family/oncampus.htm.

Employment of Department Graduates:
Master's Degree Graduates: Of those who graduated in the academic year 2011–2012, the following categories and numbers represent the postgraduate activities and employment of master's degree graduates: Enrolled in a psychology doctoral program (2), enrolled in a postdoctoral residency/fellowship (n/a), employed in independent practice (n/a), employed in business or industry (3), employed in government agency (2), total from the above (master's) (7).
Doctoral Degree Graduates: Of those who graduated in the academic year 2011–2012, the following categories and numbers represent the postgraduate activities and employment of doctoral degree graduates: Enrolled in a psychology doctoral program (n/a), total from the above (doctoral) (0).

Additional Information:
Orientation, Objectives, and Emphasis of Department: Our MS program has a strong emphasis on cognitive human factors. Our PhD program integrates experimental psychology with methods in simulation and modeling. Simulation includes air traffic control, aviation, health care, driving, team training, uninhabited aeronautical vehicles, and the like.

Special Facilities or Resources: Outstanding laboratory facilities. Simulators for driving, flight, UAS, health care, team training, etc. Eye tracking facilities, large flight school, large airport across the street from the labs.

Information for Students With Physical Disabilities: See the following website for more information: http://www.asu.edu/studentaffairs/ed/drc/.

Application Information:
Send to Department Chair. Application available online. URL of online application: http://asu.edu/gradapp. Students are admitted in the Fall, application deadline January 31; Spring, application deadline September 15. *Fee:* $70.

Arizona State University
Counseling & Counseling Psychology
School of Letters & Sciences
Payne Hall 446, MC-0811
Tempe, AZ 85287-0811
Telephone: (480) 965-8733
Fax: (480) 965-7293
E-mail: *ccp@asu.edu*
Web: *https://sls.asu.edu/ccp*

Department Information:
1968. Faculty Head: Terence J. G. Tracey. Number of faculty: total—full-time 10, part-time 2; women—full-time 6; total—minority—full-time 2, part-time 1; women minority—full-time 1.

Programs and Degrees Offered:
Listed in the following order: Program area, degree type (T if terminal Master's), number awarded 7/11–6/12. Counseling Psychology PhD (Doctor of Philosophy) 3, Master Of Counseling Other 35.

APA Accreditation: Counseling PhD (Doctor of Philosophy).

Student Applications/Admissions:
Student Applications
Counseling Psychology PhD (Doctor of Philosophy)—Applications 2012–2013, 128. Total applicants accepted 2012–2013, 10. Number full-time enrolled (new admits only) 2012–2013, 6. Number part-time enrolled (new admits only) 2012–2013, 0. Total enrolled 2012–2013 full-time, 42. Total enrolled 2012–2013 part-time, 1. Openings 2013–2014, 7. The median number of years required for completion of a degree in 2012–2013 were 6. The number of students enrolled full- and part-time who were dismissed or voluntarily withdrew from this program area in 2012–2013 were 0. *Master Of Counseling Other*—Applications 2012–2013, 124. Total applicants accepted 2012–2013, 72. Number full-time enrolled (new admits only) 2012–2013, 40. Number part-time enrolled (new admits only) 2012–2013, 0. Total enrolled 2012–2013 full-time, 79. Total enrolled 2012–2013 part-time, 6. Openings 2013–2014, 45. The median number of years required for completion of a degree in 2012–2013 were 2. The number of students enrolled full- and part-time who were dismissed or voluntarily withdrew from this program area in 2012–2013 were 0.
Scores: Entries appear in this order: required test or GPA, minimum score (if required), median score of students entering in 2012–2013. *Counseling Psychology PhD (Doctor of Philosophy):* GRE-V 520, 560, GRE-Q 580, 600, last 2 years GPA 3.2, 3.5; *Master of Counseling Other:* GRE-V 500, 560, GRE-Q 500, 590, last 2 years GPA 3.0, 3.45.
Other Criteria: (importance of criteria rated low, medium, or high): GRE scores—medium, research experience—high, work experience—medium, extracurricular activity—low, clinically related public service—medium, GPA—medium, letters of recommendation—low, interview—medium, statement of goals and objectives—medium, undergraduate major in psychology—low, specific undergraduate psychology courses taken—low, Programs use the FRK index which combines GRE V+Q with undergraduate GPA. Minimum FRKs are set

by faculty admissions committees. For additional information on admission requirements, go to https://sls.asu.edu/ccp.

Student Characteristics: The following represents characteristics of students in 2012–2013 in all graduate psychology programs in the department: Female—full-time 91, part-time 6; Male—full-time 30, part-time 1; African American/Black—full-time 4, part-time 0; Hispanic/Latino(a)—full-time 24, part-time 1; Asian/Pacific Islander—full-time 6, part-time 0; American Indian/Alaska Native—full-time 5, part-time 0; Caucasian/White—full-time 81, part-time 6; Multi-ethnic—full-time 5, part-time 0; students subject to the Americans With Disabilities Act—full-time 1, part-time 0; Unknown ethnicity—full-time 2, part-time 0; International students who hold an F-1 or J-1 Visa—full-time 7, part-time 0.

Financial Information/Assistance:
Tuition for Full-Time Study: *Master's:* State residents: per academic year $10,222, $847 per credit hour; Nonstate residents: per academic year $24,346, $1,146 per credit hour. *Doctoral:* State residents: per academic year $10,222, $847 per credit hour; Nonstate residents: per academic year $24,346, $1,146 per credit hour. Tuition is subject to change. Additional fees are assessed to students beyond the costs of tuition for the following: MC program fee $300 per credit hour. See the following website for updates and changes in tuition costs: https://students.asu.edu/tuitionandbilling.

Financial Assistance:
First-Year Students: Teaching assistantships available for first year. Average amount paid per academic year: $12,685. Average number of hours worked per week: 20. Apply by April 15. Research assistantships available for first year. Average amount paid per academic year: $12,685. Average number of hours worked per week: 20. Apply by April 15. Fellowships and scholarships available for first year. Average amount paid per academic year: $17,000. Apply by March 1.
Advanced Students: Teaching assistantships available for advanced students. Average amount paid per academic year: $12,685. Average number of hours worked per week: 20. Apply by April 15. Research assistantships available for advanced students. Average amount paid per academic year: $12,685. Average number of hours worked per week: 20. Apply by April 15.
Additional Information: Of all students currently enrolled full time, 30% benefited from one or more of the listed financial assistance programs. Application and information available online at: http://graduate.asu.edu/financing.

Internships/Practica: Doctoral Degree (PhD Counseling Psychology): For those doctoral students for whom a professional psychology internship was required in this program prior to graduation, (8) students applied for an internship in 2011–2012, with (8) students obtaining an internship. Of those students who obtained an internship, (8) were paid internships. Of those students who obtained an internship, (8) students placed in APA/CPA accredited internships, (0) students placed in internships not APA/CPA accredited, but listed with the Association of Psychology Postdoctoral and Internship Programs (APPIC), (0) students placed in internships conforming to guidelines of the Council of Directors of School Psychology Programs (CDSPP), (0) students placed in internships that were not APA/CPA accredited, APPIC or CDSPP listed. Master's Degree (Other Master of Counseling):

An internship experience, such as a final research project or "capstone" experience is required of graduates. Our doctoral internships include APA-approved sites throughout the nation. Sites include university counseling centers, community mental health clinics, and hospitals. Practica for doctoral and master's students typically are local (the greater Phoenix area) and include university counseling centers, community mental health clinics, and hospitals.

Housing and Day Care: No on-campus housing is available. On-campus day care facilities are available. See the following website for more information: http://wc.asu.edu/resources/family-and-childcare-resources.

Employment of Department Graduates:
Master's Degree Graduates: Of those who graduated in the academic year 2011–2012, the following categories and numbers represent the postgraduate activities and employment of master's degree graduates: Enrolled in a psychology doctoral program (2), enrolled in another graduate/professional program (2), enrolled in a postdoctoral residency/fellowship (n/a), employed in independent practice (n/a), employed in an academic position at a 2-year/4-year college (3), employed in other positions at a higher education institution (1), employed in a professional position in a school system (7), employed in government agency (2), employed in a community mental health/counseling center (9), employed in a hospital/medical center (3), other employment position (2), do not know (4), total from the above (master's) (35).
Doctoral Degree Graduates: Of those who graduated in the academic year 2011–2012, the following categories and numbers represent the postgraduate activities and employment of doctoral degree graduates: Enrolled in a psychology doctoral program (n/a), employed in an academic position at a university (1), employed in other positions at a higher education institution (1), employed in a hospital/medical center (1), total from the above (doctoral) (3).

Additional Information:
Orientation, Objectives, and Emphasis of Department: The faculty adheres to a scientist–practitioner model across all areas. Counseling Psychology doctoral program is APA-accredited and Master's in Counseling is accredited by CACREP.

Special Facilities or Resources: The Counseling Training Center is a training facility for Master's and PhD-level counseling students. The center serves clients from both the university and the general public.

Information for Students With Physical Disabilities: See the following website for more information: http://www.asu.edu/studentaffairs/ed/drc/.

Application Information:
Application available online. URL of online application: http://asu.edu/gradapp. Students are admitted in the Fall, application deadline December 15. Counseling Psychology PhD deadline is December 15; Master of Counseling deadline is January 15. *Fee:* $70. Application Fee for International Students is $90.00.

Arizona State University

Department of Psychology
College of Liberal Arts and Sciences
Box 871104
Tempe, AZ 85287-1104
Telephone: (480) 965-7598
Fax: (480) 965-8544
E-mail: *laurie.chassin@asu.edu*
Web: *http://psychology.clas.asu.edu/*

Department Information:
1932. Chairperson: Keith Crnic. Number of faculty: total—full-time 46; women—full-time 16; total—minority—full-time 7; women minority—full-time 3; faculty subject to the Americans With Disabilities Act 1.

Programs and Degrees Offered:
Listed in the following order: Program area, degree type (T if terminal Master's), number awarded 7/11–6/12. Clinical Psychology PhD (Doctor of Philosophy) 7, Developmental Psychology PhD (Doctor of Philosophy) 1, Quantitative Psychology PhD (Doctor of Philosophy) 0, Social Psychology PhD (Doctor of Philosophy) 5, Behavioral Neuroscience PhD (Doctor of Philosophy) 1, Cognition, Action & Perception PhD (Doctor of Philosophy) 1, Law/Psychology PhD (Doctor of Philosophy) 0.

APA Accreditation: Clinical PhD (Doctor of Philosophy). Student Outcome Data Website: http://psychology.clas.asu.edu/clinical.

Student Applications/Admissions:
Student Applications
Clinical Psychology PhD (Doctor of Philosophy)—Applications 2012–2013, 256. Total applicants accepted 2012–2013, 6. Number full-time enrolled (new admits only) 2012–2013, 6. Total enrolled 2012–2013 full-time, 43. Total enrolled 2012–2013 part-time, 0. Openings 2013–2014, 6. The median number of years required for completion of a degree in 2012–2013 were 7. The number of students enrolled full- and part-time who were dismissed or voluntarily withdrew from this program area in 2012–2013 were 0. *Developmental Psychology PhD (Doctor of Philosophy)*—Applications 2012–2013, 24. Total applicants accepted 2012–2013, 2. Number full-time enrolled (new admits only) 2012–2013, 2. Number part-time enrolled (new admits only) 2012–2013, 0. Total enrolled 2012–2013 full-time, 10. Total enrolled 2012–2013 part-time, 0. Openings 2013–2014, 4. The median number of years required for completion of a degree in 2012–2013 were 7. The number of students enrolled full- and part-time who were dismissed or voluntarily withdrew from this program area in 2012–2013 were 1. *Quantitative Psychology PhD (Doctor of Philosophy)*—Applications 2012–2013, 33. Total applicants accepted 2012–2013, 3. Number full-time enrolled (new admits only) 2012–2013, 3. Number part-time enrolled (new admits only) 2012–2013, 0. Total enrolled 2012–2013 full-time, 14. Total enrolled 2012–2013 part-time, 0. Openings 2013–2014, 3. The number of students enrolled full- and part-time who were dismissed or

voluntarily withdrew from this program area in 2012–2013 were 0. *Social Psychology PhD (Doctor of Philosophy)*—Applications 2012–2013, 102. Total applicants accepted 2012–2013, 4. Number full-time enrolled (new admits only) 2012–2013, 4. Number part-time enrolled (new admits only) 2012–2013, 0. Total enrolled 2012–2013 full-time, 20. Total enrolled 2012–2013 part-time, 0. Openings 2013–2014, 4. The median number of years required for completion of a degree in 2012–2013 were 6. The number of students enrolled full- and part-time who were dismissed or voluntarily withdrew from this program area in 2012–2013 were 0. *Behavioral Neuroscience PhD (Doctor of Philosophy)*—Applications 2012–2013, 32. Total applicants accepted 2012–2013, 1. Number full-time enrolled (new admits only) 2012–2013, 1. Total enrolled 2012–2013 full-time, 17. Openings 2013–2014, 2. The median number of years required for completion of a degree in 2012–2013 were 5. The number of students enrolled full- and part-time who were dismissed or voluntarily withdrew from this program area in 2012–2013 were 0. *Cognition, Action & Perception PhD (Doctor of Philosophy)*—Applications 2012–2013, 24. Total applicants accepted 2012–2013, 2. Number full-time enrolled (new admits only) 2012–2013, 2. Total enrolled 2012–2013 full-time, 22. Openings 2013–2014, 4. The median number of years required for completion of a degree in 2012–2013 were 6. The number of students enrolled full- and part-time who were dismissed or voluntarily withdrew from this program area in 2012–2013 were 0. *Law/Psychology PhD (Doctor of Philosophy)*—Applications 2012–2013, 18. Total applicants accepted 2012–2013, 0. Number full-time enrolled (new admits only) 2012–2013, 0. Total enrolled 2012–2013 full-time, 4. The number of students enrolled full- and part-time who were dismissed or voluntarily withdrew from this program area in 2012–2013 were 0.

Scores: Entries appear in this order: required test or GPA, minimum score (if required), median score of students entering in 2012–2013. *Clinical Psychology PhD (Doctor of Philosophy)*: GRE-V no minimum stated, 625, GRE-Q no minimum stated, 688, GRE-Analytical no minimum stated, overall undergraduate GPA 3.0, 3.79; *Behavioral Neuroscience PhD (Doctor of Philosophy)*: overall undergraduate GPA 3.0.

Other Criteria: (importance of criteria rated low, medium, or high): GRE scores—medium, research experience—high, work experience—low, extracurricular activity—low, clinically related public service—medium, GPA—medium, letters of recommendation—high, interview—high, statement of goals and objectives—high. For additional information on admission requirements, go to http://psychology.clas.asu.edu/grad-admissions.

Student Characteristics: The following represents characteristics of students in 2012–2013 in all graduate psychology programs in the department: Female—full-time 83, part-time 0; Male—full-time 47, part-time 0; African American/Black—full-time 2, part-time 0; Hispanic/Latino(a)—full-time 11, part-time 0; Asian/Pacific Islander—full-time 18, part-time 0; American Indian/Alaska Native—full-time 3, part-time 0; Caucasian/White—full-time 96, part-time 0; Multi-ethnic—full-time 0, part-time 0; students subject to the Americans With Disabilities Act—full-time 0, part-time 0; Unknown ethnicity—full-time 0, part-time 0; International students who hold an F-1 or J-1 Visa—full-time 14, part-time 0.

Financial Information/Assistance:

Tuition for Full-Time Study: *Doctoral:* State residents: per academic year $10,100, $714 per credit hour; Nonstate residents: per academic year $25,066, $1,023 per credit hour. Tuition is subject to change. See the following website for updates and changes in tuition costs: https://students.asu.edu/tuition.

Financial Assistance:

First-Year Students: Teaching assistantships available for first year. Average amount paid per academic year: $14,300. Average number of hours worked per week: 20. Research assistantships available for first year. Average amount paid per academic year: $14,300. Average number of hours worked per week: 20. Fellowships and scholarships available for first year.

Advanced Students: Teaching assistantships available for advanced students. Average amount paid per academic year: $15,300. Average number of hours worked per week: 20. Research assistantships available for advanced students. Average amount paid per academic year: $15,300. Average number of hours worked per week: 20. Traineeships available for advanced students. Fellowships and scholarships available for advanced students.

Additional Information: Of all students currently enrolled full time, 100% benefited from one or more of the listed financial assistance programs. Application and information available online at: http://graduate.asu.edu/financing.

Internships/Practica: Doctoral Degree (PhD Clinical Psychology): For those doctoral students for whom a professional psychology internship was required in this program prior to graduation, (4) students applied for an internship in 2011–2012, with (4) students obtaining an internship. Of those students who obtained an internship, (4) were paid internships. Of those students who obtained an internship, (4) students placed in APA/CPA accredited internships, (0) students placed in internships not APA/CPA accredited, but listed with the Association of Psychology Postdoctoral and Internship Programs (APPIC), (0) students placed in internships conforming to guidelines of the Council of Directors of School Psychology Programs (CDSPP), (0) students placed in internships that were not APA/CPA accredited, APPIC or CDSPP listed. Doctoral clinical students complete practica in community agencies and in our in-house training clinic.

Housing and Day Care: No on-campus housing is available. On-campus day care facilities are available. See the following website for more information: http://www.asu.edu/studentaffairs/reslife/family/oncampus.htm.

Employment of Department Graduates:

Master's Degree Graduates: Of those who graduated in the academic year 2011–2012, the following categories and numbers represent the postgraduate activities and employment of master's degree graduates: Enrolled in a postdoctoral residency/fellowship (n/a), employed in independent practice (n/a), total from the above (master's) (0).

Doctoral Degree Graduates: Of those who graduated in the academic year 2011–2012, the following categories and numbers represent the postgraduate activities and employment of doctoral degree graduates: Enrolled in a psychology doctoral program (n/a), enrolled in a postdoctoral residency/fellowship (7), employed in an academic position at a university (4), employed in government agency (1), employed in a hospital/medical center (1), do not know (2), total from the above (doctoral) (15).

Additional Information:

Orientation, Objectives, and Emphasis of Department: The department seeks to instill in students knowledge, skills, and an appreciation of psychology as a science and as a profession. To do so, it offers undergraduate and graduate programs emphasizing theory, research, and applied practice. The department encourages a multiplicity of theoretical viewpoints and research interests. The behavioral neuroscience area emphasizes the neural bases of motor disorders, drug abuse and recovery of function following brain damage. The clinical program includes areas of emphasis in health psychology, child-clinical psychology, and community-prevention. Also offered are classes in psychopathology, prevention, assessment and psychotherapy. The cognitive systems area includes cognitive psychology, adaptive systems, learning, sensation and perception, and cognitive development. The developmental area includes coursework and research experience in the core areas of cognitive and social development. The quantitative area focuses on design, measurement, and statistical analysis issues that arise in diverse areas of psychological research. The social area emphasizes theoretical and laboratory skills combined with program evaluation and applied social psychology. New interdisciplinary training opportunities are available in Arts, Media, and Engineering and Law and Psychology.

Special Facilities or Resources: The department has the Child Study Laboratory for training and research in developmental psychology, including both normal and clinical groups, particularly of preschool age; the Clinical Psychology Center, whose clients represent a wide range of psychological disorders and are not limited to the university community; and the experimental laboratories, with exceptional computer facilities for the study of speech perception, neural networks, categorization, memory, sensory processes and learning. The clinical and social programs maintain continuing liaisons with a wide range of off-campus agencies for research applications of psychological theory and research. Our NIMH-funded Preventive Intervention Research Center provides a site for training in the design, implementation, and evaluation of preventative interventions. Quantitatively-oriented students receive methodological experience in large-scale research programs and in our statistical laboratory.

Information for Students With Physical Disabilities: See the following website for more information: http://www.asu.edu/studentaffairs/ed/drc/.

Application Information:

Send to Admissions Secretary, Department of Psychology, Arizona State University, P.O. Box 871104, Tempe, AZ 85287-1104. Application available online. URL of online application: http://asu.edu/gradapp. Students are admitted in the Fall, application deadline December 15. December 15 for Clinical, January 5 for all other programs. *Fee:* $70. $90 for international applicants.

Arizona State University

Program in Family and Human Development
T. Denny Sanford School of Social and Family Dynamics
P.O. Box 873701
Tempe, AZ 85287-3701
Telephone: (480) 965-6978
Fax: (480) 965-6779
E-mail: *email@ssfd.info*
Web: *http://thesanfordschool.clas.asu.edu/fhd*

Department Information:
Director: Richard Fabes. Number of faculty: total—full-time 55; women—full-time 35; total—minority—full-time 6; women minority—full-time 3.

Programs and Degrees Offered:
Listed in the following order: Program area, degree type (T if terminal Master's), number awarded 7/11–6/12. Family and Human Development PhD (Doctor of Philosophy).

Student Applications/Admissions:
Student Applications
Family and Human Development PhD (Doctor of Philosophy)—Number full-time enrolled (new admits only) 2012–2013, 8. Number part-time enrolled (new admits only) 2012–2013, 0. Total enrolled 2012–2013 full-time, 54. Total enrolled 2012–2013 part-time, 0. Openings 2013–2014, 13. The number of students enrolled full- and part-time who were dismissed or voluntarily withdrew from this program area in 2012–2013 were 0.
Scores: Entries appear in this order: required test or GPA, minimum score (if required), median score of students entering in 2012–2013. *Family and Human Development PhD (Doctor of Philosophy):* GRE-V no minimum stated, 566, GRE-Q no minimum stated, 650, GRE-Analytical no minimum stated, overall undergraduate GPA 3.0, 3.78, last 2 years GPA 3.0, Masters GPA 3.0.
Other Criteria: (importance of criteria rated low, medium, or high): GRE scores—high, research experience—high, work experience—medium, extracurricular activity—medium, GPA—high, letters of recommendation—high, interview—high, statement of goals and objectives—high, fit w/ available faculty—high, undergraduate major in psychology—low, specific undergraduate psychology courses taken—low. For additional information on admission requirements, go to http://thesanfordschool.clas.asu.edu/fhdadmissions.

Student Characteristics: The following represents characteristics of students in 2012–2013 in all graduate psychology programs in the department: Female—full-time 47, part-time 0; Male—full-time 7, part-time 0; African American/Black—full-time 1, part-time 0; Hispanic/Latino(a)—full-time 12, part-time 0; Asian/Pacific Islander—full-time 3, part-time 0; American Indian/Alaska Native—full-time 0, part-time 0; Caucasian/White—full-time 35, part-time 0; Multi-ethnic—full-time 0, part-time 0; students subject to the Americans With Disabilities Act—full-time 0, part-time 0; Unknown ethnicity—full-time 0, part-time 0; International students who hold an F-1 or J-1 Visa—full-time 0, part-time 0.

Financial Information/Assistance:
Tuition for Full-Time Study: *Doctoral:* State residents: $714 per credit hour; Nonstate residents: $1,023 per credit hour. Tuition is subject to change. Additional fees are assessed to students beyond the costs of tuition for the following: technology, health and wellness, program fees. See the following website for updates and changes in tuition costs: https://students.asu.edu/tuitionandfees.

Financial Assistance:
First-Year Students: Teaching assistantships available for first year. Average amount paid per academic year: $14,000. Average number of hours worked per week: 20. Research assistantships available for first year. Average amount paid per academic year: $14,000. Average number of hours worked per week: 20. Fellowships and scholarships available for first year. Average amount paid per academic year: $14,000. Average number of hours worked per week: 20.
Advanced Students: Teaching assistantships available for advanced students. Average amount paid per academic year: $17,500. Average number of hours worked per week: 20. Research assistantships available for advanced students. Average amount paid per academic year: $17,500. Average number of hours worked per week: 20. Fellowships and scholarships available for advanced students. Average amount paid per academic year: $17,500. Average number of hours worked per week: 20.
Additional Information: Of all students currently enrolled full time, 100% benefited from one or more of the listed financial assistance programs. Application and information available online at: http://thesanfordschool.clas.asu.edu/fhdfunding.

Housing and Day Care: No on-campus housing is available. On-campus day care facilities are available. See the following website for more information: http://www.asu.edu/studentaffairs/reslife/family/oncampus.htm.

Employment of Department Graduates:
Master's Degree Graduates: Of those who graduated in the academic year 2011–2012, the following categories and numbers represent the postgraduate activities and employment of master's degree graduates: Enrolled in a postdoctoral residency/fellowship (n/a), employed in independent practice (n/a), total from the above (master's) (0).
Doctoral Degree Graduates: Of those who graduated in the academic year 2011–2012, the following categories and numbers represent the postgraduate activities and employment of doctoral degree graduates: Enrolled in a psychology doctoral program (n/a), employed in an academic position at a university (4), total from the above (doctoral) (4).

Additional Information:
Orientation, Objectives, and Emphasis of Department: The doctoral degree program in Family and Human Development prepares researchers with a focus on social processes, family relationships, and infant, child, adolescent and emerging adult development. The doctoral program is designed for graduates to assume leadership roles as researchers and academicians in universities or other research-oriented settings, or as directors in public or privately funded mental health agencies, industry or government.

Information for Students With Physical Disabilities: See the following website for more information: http://www.asu.edu/studentaffairs/ed/drc/.

Application Information:
Application available online. URL of online application: http://asu. edu/gradapp. Students are admitted in the Fall, application deadline January 10. *Fee:* $70. Application fee is $90 USD for international students.

Arizona, The University of
Department of Psychology
College of Sciences
P.O. Box 210068
Tucson, AZ 85721
Telephone: (520) 621-7448
Fax: (520) 621-9306
E-mail: *glisky@u.arizona.edu*
Web: *http://psychology.arizona.edu/*

Department Information:
1914. Head: Elizabeth L. Glisky. Number of faculty: total—full-time 25, part-time 8; women—full-time 10, part-time 4; total—minority—full-time 3; women minority—full-time 2.

Programs and Degrees Offered:
Listed in the following order: Program area, degree type (T if terminal Master's), number awarded 7/11–6/12. Clinical Psychology PhD (Doctor of Philosophy) 5, Cognition and Neural Systems PhD (Doctor of Philosophy) 1, Ethology and Evolutionary Psychology PhD (Doctor of Philosophy) 1, Social Psychology PhD (Doctor of Philosophy) 3, General PhD (Doctor of Philosophy) 1, Psychology Policy and Law PhD (Doctor of Philosophy) 1.

APA Accreditation: Clinical PhD (Doctor of Philosophy). Student Outcome Data Website: http://psychology.arizona.edu/Clinical.

Student Applications/Admissions:
Student Applications
Clinical Psychology PhD (Doctor of Philosophy)—Applications 2012–2013, 248. Total applicants accepted 2012–2013, 6. Number full-time enrolled (new admits only) 2012–2013, 6. Number part-time enrolled (new admits only) 2012–2013, 0. Total enrolled 2012–2013 full-time, 41. Total enrolled 2012–2013 part-time, 0. Openings 2013–2014, 7. The median number of years required for completion of a degree in 2012–2013 were 6. The number of students enrolled full- and part-time who were dismissed or voluntarily withdrew from this program area in 2012–2013 were 0. *Cognition and Neural Systems PhD (Doctor of Philosophy)*—Applications 2012–2013, 73. Total applicants accepted 2012–2013, 5. Number full-time enrolled (new admits only) 2012–2013, 5. Total enrolled 2012–2013 full-time, 24. Total enrolled 2012–2013 part-time, 0. Openings 2013–2014, 7. The median number of years required for completion of a degree in 2012–2013 were 6. The number of students enrolled full- and part-time who were dismissed or voluntarily withdrew from this program area in 2012–2013 were 3. *Ethology and Evolutionary Psychology PhD (Doctor of Philosophy)*—Applications 2012–2013, 0. Total applicants accepted 2012–2013, 2. Number full-time enrolled (new admits only) 2012–2013, 2. Total enrolled 2012–2013 full-time, 7. Total enrolled 2012–2013 part-time, 0. The median number of years required for completion of a degree in 2012–2013

were 5. The number of students enrolled full- and part-time who were dismissed or voluntarily withdrew from this program area in 2012–2013 were 0. *Social Psychology PhD (Doctor of Philosophy)*—Applications 2012–2013, 53. Total applicants accepted 2012–2013, 4. Number full-time enrolled (new admits only) 2012–2013, 4. Total enrolled 2012–2013 full-time, 7. Total enrolled 2012–2013 part-time, 0. The median number of years required for completion of a degree in 2012–2013 were 5. The number of students enrolled full- and part-time who were dismissed or voluntarily withdrew from this program area in 2012–2013 were 0. *General PhD (Doctor of Philosophy)*—Applications 2012–2013, 0. Total applicants accepted 2012–2013, 0. Number full-time enrolled (new admits only) 2012–2013, 0. Total enrolled 2012–2013 full-time, 1. The median number of years required for completion of a degree in 2012–2013 were 10. The number of students enrolled full- and part-time who were dismissed or voluntarily withdrew from this program area in 2012–2013 were 0. *Psychology Policy and Law PhD (Doctor of Philosophy)*—Applications 2012–2013, 0. Total applicants accepted 2012–2013, 0. Number full-time enrolled (new admits only) 2012–2013, 0. Total enrolled 2012–2013 full-time, 3. Total enrolled 2012–2013 part-time, 1. The median number of years required for completion of a degree in 2012–2013 were 8. The number of students enrolled full- and part-time who were dismissed or voluntarily withdrew from this program area in 2012–2013 were 1.

Scores: Entries appear in this order: required test or GPA, minimum score (if required), median score of students entering in 2012–2013. *Clinical Psychology PhD (Doctor of Philosophy):* GRE-V no minimum stated, 580, GRE-Q no minimum stated, 660, GRE-Analytical no minimum stated, 4.5, GRE-Subject (Psychology) no minimum stated, 720, overall undergraduate GPA 3.0, 3.75; *Cognition and Neural Systems PhD (Doctor of Philosophy):* GRE-V no minimum stated, 620, GRE-Q no minimum stated, 740, GRE-Analytical no minimum stated, 4.5; *Ethology and Evolutionary Psychology PhD (Doctor of Philosophy):* GRE-V no minimum stated, 520, GRE-Q no minimum stated, 760; *Social Psychology PhD (Doctor of Philosophy):* GRE-V no minimum stated, 550, GRE-Q no minimum stated, 720, GRE-Analytical no minimum stated, 4.5, overall undergraduate GPA 3.00, 3.60; *General PhD (Doctor of Philosophy):* GRE-V no minimum stated, GRE-Q no minimum stated, GRE-Analytical no minimum stated, overall undergraduate GPA 3.00; *Psychology Policy and Law PhD (Doctor of Philosophy):* GRE-V no minimum stated, GRE-Q no minimum stated, GRE-Analytical no minimum stated, overall undergraduate GPA 3.00.

Other Criteria: (importance of criteria rated low, medium, or high): GRE scores—medium, research experience—high, work experience—low, extracurricular activity—low, clinically related public service—low, GPA—medium, letters of recommendation—high, interview—medium, statement of goals and objectives—high, undergraduate major in psychology—medium, specific undergraduate psychology courses taken—medium. For additional information on admission requirements, go to http://psychology.arizona.edu/InfoforPhDApplicants.

Student Characteristics: The following represents characteristics of students in 2012–2013 in all graduate psychology programs in the department: Female—full-time 51, part-time 0; Male—full-time 32, part-time 1; African American/Black—full-time 0, part-time 0; Hispanic/Latino(a)—full-time 12, part-time 0; Asian/Pacific Islander—full-time 7, part-time 0; American Indian/Alaska Native—full-time 2, part-time 0; Caucasian/White—full-time 58, part-time 1; Multi-ethnic—part-time 0; students subject to the Americans With Disabilities Act—full-time 0, part-time 0; Unknown ethnicity—full-time 4, part-time 0; International students who hold an F-1 or J-1 Visa—full-time 9, part-time 0.

Financial Information/Assistance:

Tuition for Full-Time Study: *Doctoral:* State residents: per academic year $10,202, $729 per credit hour; Nonstate residents: per academic year $25,710, $1,423 per credit hour. Tuition is subject to change. Additional fees are assessed to students beyond the costs of tuition for the following: Misc fees for all students range from $391.68-$467.68. See the following website for updates and changes in tuition costs: http://www.bursar.arizona.edu/students/fees/index.asp.

Financial Assistance:

First-Year Students: Teaching assistantships available for first year. Average amount paid per academic year: $14,500. Average number of hours worked per week: 20. Research assistantships available for first year. Average amount paid per academic year: $14,500. Average number of hours worked per week: 20. Traineeships available for first year. Average amount paid per academic year: $14,500. Average number of hours worked per week: 20. Fellowships and scholarships available for first year. Average amount paid per academic year: $10,000. Average number of hours worked per week: 10.

Advanced Students: Teaching assistantships available for advanced students. Average amount paid per academic year: $14,500. Average number of hours worked per week: 20. Research assistantships available for advanced students. Average amount paid per academic year: $14,500. Average number of hours worked per week: 20. Traineeships available for advanced students. Average amount paid per academic year: $14,500. Average number of hours worked per week: 20. Fellowships and scholarships available for advanced students. Average amount paid per academic year: $10,000. Average number of hours worked per week: 10.

Additional Information: Of all students currently enrolled full time, 95% benefited from one or more of the listed financial assistance programs. Application and information available online at: http://financialaid.arizona.edu/graduate-students.

Internships/Practica: Doctoral Degree (PhD Clinical Psychology): For those doctoral students for whom a professional psychology internship was required in this program prior to graduation, (6) students applied for an internship in 2011–2012, with (5) students obtaining an internship. Of those students who obtained an internship, (5) were paid internships. Of those students who obtained an internship, (5) students placed in APA/CPA accredited internships, (0) students placed in internships not APA/CPA accredited, but listed with the Association of Psychology Postdoctoral and Internship Programs (APPIC), (0) students placed in internships conforming to guidelines of the Council of Directors of School Psychology Programs (CDSPP), (0) students placed in internships that were not APA/CPA accredited, APPIC or CDSPP listed. Graduate students within the clinical program are required to do a 1-year internship. The University Medical Center medical school offers internship positions, although most of our students leave campus for the internship. All of the clinical students are placed in APA-accredited internships. Students also participate in various clinical externships and practica available

within the department as well as throughout the community as part of their graduate training.

Housing and Day Care: On-campus housing is available. See the following website for more information: http://www.life.arizona.edu/home/graduate-housing/graduate-housing-options. No on-campus day care facilities are available.

Employment of Department Graduates:

Master's Degree Graduates: Of those who graduated in the academic year 2011–2012, the following categories and numbers represent the postgraduate activities and employment of master's degree graduates: Enrolled in a postdoctoral residency/fellowship (n/a), employed in independent practice (n/a), total from the above (master's) (0).

Doctoral Degree Graduates: Of those who graduated in the academic year 2011–2012, the following categories and numbers represent the postgraduate activities and employment of doctoral degree graduates: Enrolled in a psychology doctoral program (n/a), enrolled in a postdoctoral residency/fellowship (8), employed in an academic position at a university (2), employed in a community mental health/counseling center (1), total from the above (doctoral) (11).

Additional Information:

Orientation, Objectives, and Emphasis of Department: The Psychology Department is within the School of Mind, Brain, and Behavior. Our objectives as a department are to contribute to the growth of knowledge about the mind and its workings, and the training of students to participate in this pursuit, as well as using this knowledge to benefit society. The department emphasizes research and training students headed toward both academic and research-related careers. Required courses provide breadth of coverage, but emphasis is on research within the area of specialization through independent work with individual faculty members. The interdisciplinary nature of the department within the School of Mind, Brain and Behavior fosters specialization in areas that cut across program boundaries and permits work with faculty members in other programs. The cognition and neural systems area emphasizes language, perception, attention, memory, aging, ensemble recording of neural activity, and human neuroimaging; the clinical area emphasizes clinical neuropsychology, psychotherapy research, sleep disorders, psychophysiology, and assessment; the social area emphasizes prejudice and stereotyping, cognitive dissonance, self-esteem, and motivational factors in thought and behavior; and the ethology and evolutionary area emphasizes quantitative ethology, invertebrate behavior and human behavioral ecology.

Special Facilities or Resources: The department has modern laboratories devoted to research in various areas of cognitive, clinical, neuroscientific, social, and comparative research. The department provides computing resources and technical assistance for teaching and research. There are a number of clinics within the department, bringing in patients associated with research projects on aging, sleep disorders, memory disorders, depression, and others. The department has ties with a number of other programs on campus, including the departments of Anatomy, Family and Community Medicine, Neurology, Ophthalmology, Pediatrics, Pharmacology, Physiology and Psychiatry in the College of Medicine, the departments of Ecology and Evolutionary Biology, Family Studies, Linguistics, Management and Policy,

Mathematics, Philosophy, Renewable and Natural Resources, Speech and Hearing Sciences, and Physics on the main campus, and interdisciplinary programs including Cognitive Science, Statistics, and Neuroscience. Most of the department's faculty members are holders of research grants, permitting a significant proportion of the graduate students to serve as research assistants at various times during their training.

Information for Students With Physical Disabilities: See the following website for more information: http://drc.arizona.edu/.

Application Information:
Send to The University of Arizona, Department of Psychology, Graduate Admissions, 1503 East University Boulevard, Room 334, P.O. Box 210068, Tucson, AZ 85721-0068. Application available online. URL of online application: https://apply.grad.arizona.edu/. Students are admitted in the Fall, application deadline December 15. *Fee:* $75.

Midwestern University (2012 data)
Clinical Psychology
College of Health Sciences
19555 North 59th Avenue
Glendale, AZ 85308
Telephone: (623) 572-3860
Fax: (623) 572-3830
E-mail: *phutch@midwestern.edu*
Web: *http://www.midwestern.edu*

Department Information:
2006. Program Director: Philinda Smith Hutchings, PhD, ABPP. Number of faculty: total—full-time 6, part-time 1; women—full-time 4, part-time 1; total—minority—full-time 2, part-time 1; women minority—full-time 1, part-time 1.

Programs and Degrees Offered:
Listed in the following order: Program area, degree type (T if terminal Master's), number awarded 7/11–6/12. Clinical Psychology PsyD (Doctor of Psychology) 0.

APA Accreditation: Clinical PsyD (Doctor of Psychology). Student Outcome Data Website: http://www.midwestern.edu/Programs_and_Admission/AZ_Clinical_Psychology/Student_Admissions_Outcomes_and_Other_Data.html.

Student Applications/Admissions:
Student Applications
Clinical Psychology PsyD (Doctor of Psychology)—Applications 2012–2013, 29. Total applicants accepted 2012–2013, 13. Number full-time enrolled (new admits only) 2012–2013, 12. Number part-time enrolled (new admits only) 2012–2013, 0. Total enrolled 2012–2013 full-time, 48. Total enrolled 2012–2013 part-time, 0. Openings 2013–2014, 17. The number of students enrolled full- and part-time who were dismissed or voluntarily withdrew from this program area in 2012–2013 were 3.
Scores: Entries appear in this order: required test or GPA, minimum score (if required), median score of students entering in 2012–2013. *Clinical Psychology PsyD (Doctor of Psychology):*

GRE-V no minimum stated, 465, GRE-Q no minimum stated, 540, overall undergraduate GPA 3.0, 3.28.
Other Criteria: (importance of criteria rated low, medium, or high): GRE scores—medium, research experience—low, work experience—medium, extracurricular activity—medium, clinically related public service—high, GPA—high, letters of recommendation—high, interview—high, statement of goals and objectives—high, undergraduate major in psychology—medium, specific undergraduate psychology courses taken—high. For additional information on admission requirements, go to http://www.midwestern.edu/Programs_and_Admission/AZ_Clinical_Psychology.html.

Student Characteristics: The following represents characteristics of students in 2012–2013 in all graduate psychology programs in the department: Female—full-time 37, part-time 0; Male—full-time 11, part-time 0; African American/Black—full-time 2, part-time 0; Hispanic/Latino(a)—full-time 3, part-time 0; Asian/Pacific Islander—full-time 2, part-time 0; American Indian/Alaska Native—full-time 0, part-time 0; Caucasian/White—full-time 38, part-time 0; Multi-ethnic—full-time 3, part-time 0; students subject to the Americans With Disabilities Act—full-time 2, part-time 0; Unknown ethnicity—full-time 0, part-time 0; International students who hold an F-1 or J-1 Visa—full-time 2, part-time 0.

Financial Information/Assistance:
Tuition for Full-Time Study: *Doctoral:* State residents: per academic year $26,087; Nonstate residents: per academic year $26,087. Additional fees are assessed to students beyond the costs of tuition for the following: Student services, disability insurance. See the following website for updates and changes in tuition costs: http://www.midwestern.edu/Programs_and_Admission/AZ_Clinical_Psychology.html.

Financial Assistance:
First-Year Students: Fellowships and scholarships available for first year. Apply by varies.
Advanced Students: Teaching assistantships available for advanced students. Apply by varies. Fellowships and scholarships available for advanced students.
Additional Information: Of all students currently enrolled full time, 25% benefited from one or more of the listed financial assistance programs. Application and information available online at: http://www.midwestern.edu/Programs_and_Admission/F.

Internships/Practica: Doctoral Degree (PsyD Clinical Psychology): For those doctoral students for whom a professional psychology internship was required in this program prior to graduation, (7) students applied for an internship in 2011–2012, with (7) students obtaining an internship. Of those students who obtained an internship, (7) were paid internships. Of those students who obtained an internship, (0) students placed in APA/CPA accredited internships, (5) students placed in internships not APA/CPA accredited, but listed with the Association of Psychology Postdoctoral and Internship Programs (APPIC), (0) students placed in internships conforming to guidelines of the Council of Directors of School Psychology Programs (CDSPP), (2) students placed in internships that were not APA/CPA accredited, APPIC or CDSPP listed. Students begin their clinical experiences with a clerkship in the first year of the program, which exposes them to clinical practice. The specific clinical focus of the experience varies according to the student's needs, interests, and availability of sites. Students complete a minimum of eight quarters of practicum in the second and third years, approximately 16 to 20 hours per week in a clinical setting. The practicum experiences in psychodiagnostics and psychotherapy total a minimum of 1,000 hours over two years. A variety of practicum sites are available, including Midwestern University's Clinic on campus. Internship is completed in the fourth year of the program, and may be completed at any APPIC-member internship site in the U.S. or Canada.

Housing and Day Care: On-campus housing is available. See the following website for more information: http://www.midwestern. edu/x731.xml. No on-campus day care facilities are available.

Employment of Department Graduates:

Master's Degree Graduates: Of those who graduated in the academic year 2011–2012, the following categories and numbers represent the postgraduate activities and employment of master's degree graduates: Enrolled in a postdoctoral residency/fellowship (n/a), employed in independent practice (n/a), total from the above (master's) (0).

Doctoral Degree Graduates: Of those who graduated in the academic year 2011–2012, the following categories and numbers represent the postgraduate activities and employment of doctoral degree graduates: Enrolled in a psychology doctoral program (n/a), enrolled in another graduate/professional program (0), enrolled in a postdoctoral residency/fellowship (0), employed in independent practice (0), employed in an academic position at a university (0), employed in an academic position at a 2-year/4-year college (0), employed in other positions at a higher education institution (0), employed in a professional position in a school system (0), employed in business or industry (0), employed in government agency (0), employed in a community mental health/counseling center (0), employed in a hospital/medical center (0), still seeking employment (0), not seeking employment (0), other employment position (0), do not know (0), total from the above (doctoral) (0).

Additional Information:

Orientation, Objectives, and Emphasis of Department: The clinical psychology program at Midwestern University offers generalist training in clinical psychology, with an emphasis on integrated healthcare, offering psychological services in primary care settings. Midwestern University provides an environment of collaborative training in the healthcare professions, so that as you pursue your studies, you will be surrounded by students of osteopathic medicine, pharmacy, podiatry, physician's assistance, nurse-anesthesia, occupational therapy, cardiovascular science/perfusion, dentistry, physical therapy, optometry and biomedical sciences. The program curriculum includes the foundations of psychological science and emphasizes professional skills in relationship, assessment, intervention, research and evaluation, consultation and education, management and supervision, and diversity. In three years of full-time academic coursework and practicum experiences, and one year of internship, students gain the knowledge, skill, and values to practice clinical psychology in primary care settings, hospitals, outpatient clinics, schools, and private practice. The knowledgeable and dedicated faculty members are accessible and available to students in small classes, seminars, and individually.

Special Facilities or Resources: MWU Clinic provides training for all clinical psychology students in integrated healthcare, consulting and training with medicine, pharmacy, optometry, podiatry, dentistry and other healthcare professions students.

Information for Students With Physical Disabilities: See the following website for more information: http://www.midwestern. edu/Glendale_AZ_Campus/Student_Services.html.

Application Information:
Send to Office of Admissions Midwestern University, 19555 North 59th Avenue, Glendale, AZ 85308. Application available online. URL of online application: http://www.midwestern.edu/Programs_and_ Admission/AZ_Clinical_Psychology/AdmissionApply.html. Students are admitted in the Fall, application deadline 8/1; Programs have rolling admissions. *Fee:* $50.

Northcentral University
School of Psychology
10000 East University Drive
Prescott Valley, AZ 86314
Telephone: (888) 327-2877
Fax: (928) 541-7817
E-mail: *rhaussmann@ncu.edu*
Web: *http://www.ncu.edu/northcentral-programs/schools/ behavioral-and-health-sciences*

Department Information:
1999. Dean: Robert Haussmann, PhD. Number of faculty: total—full-time 2, part-time 59; women—full-time 2, part-time 30; minority—part-time 15; women minority—part-time 7.

Programs and Degrees Offered:
Listed in the following order: Program area, degree type (T if terminal Master's), number awarded 7/11–6/12. Psychology MA/MS (Master of Arts/Science) 50, Psychology PhD (Doctor of Philosophy) 9.

Student Applications/Admissions:
Student Applications
Psychology MA/MS (Master of Arts/Science)—Applications 2012–2013, 692. Total applicants accepted 2012–2013, 411. Number full-time enrolled (new admits only) 2012–2013, 330. Number part-time enrolled (new admits only) 2012–2013, 0. Total enrolled 2012–2013 full-time, 597. Total enrolled 2012–2013 part-time, 0. The median number of years required for completion of a degree in 2012–2013 were 3. The number of students enrolled full- and part-time who were dismissed or voluntarily withdrew from this program area in 2012–2013 were 181. *Psychology PhD (Doctor of Philosophy)*—Applications 2012–2013, 720. Total applicants accepted 2012–2013, 529. Number full-time enrolled (new admits only) 2012–2013, 348. Number part-time enrolled (new admits only) 2012–2013, 0. Total enrolled 2012–2013 full-time, 1001. Total enrolled 2012–2013 part-time, 0. The median number of years required for completion of a degree in 2012–2013 were 5. The number of students enrolled full- and part-time who were dismissed or voluntarily withdrew from this program area in 2012–2013 were 236.

Other Criteria: (importance of criteria rated low, medium, or high): research experience—low, work experience—medium, extracurricular activity—low, clinically related public service—medium, GPA—low, letters of recommendation—low, interview—low, statement of goals and objectives—medium, undergraduate major in psychology—low, specific undergraduate psychology courses taken—low.

Student Characteristics: The following represents characteristics of students in 2012–2013 in all graduate psychology programs in the department: Female—full-time 1133, part-time 0; Male—full-time 465, part-time 0; African American/Black—full-time 76, part-time 0; Hispanic/Latino(a)—full-time 12, part-time 0; Asian/Pacific Islander—full-time 5, part-time 0; American Indian/Alaska Native—full-time 7, part-time 0; Caucasian/White—full-time 199, part-time 0; Multi-ethnic—full-time 0, part-time 0; students subject to the Americans With Disabilities Act—full-time 44, part-time 0; Unknown ethnicity—full-time 1299, part-time 0; International students who hold an F-1 or J-1 Visa—full-time 0, part-time 0.

Financial Information/Assistance:

Tuition for Full-Time Study: *Master's:* State residents: $708 per credit hour; Nonstate residents: $708 per credit hour. *Doctoral:* State residents: $845 per credit hour; Nonstate residents: $845 per credit hour. Tuition is subject to change. See the following website for updates and changes in tuition costs: http://www.ncu.edu/northcentral-global/tuition.

Financial Assistance:

First-Year Students: No information provided.
Advanced Students: No information provided.
Additional Information: Application and information available online at: http://www.ncu.edu/northcentral-admissions/financing.

Internships/Practica: Students may enroll in supervised practica.

Housing and Day Care: No on-campus housing is available. No on-campus day care facilities are available.

Employment of Department Graduates:

Master's Degree Graduates: Of those who graduated in the academic year 2011–2012, the following categories and numbers represent the postgraduate activities and employment of master's degree graduates: Enrolled in a psychology doctoral program (1), enrolled in a postdoctoral residency/fellowship (n/a), employed in independent practice (n/a), employed in an academic position at a university (4), employed in an academic position at a 2-year/4-year college (3), employed in a professional position in a school system (1), employed in business or industry (1), employed in government agency (7), employed in a community mental health/counseling center (3), employed in a hospital/medical center (1), still seeking employment (3), not seeking employment (2), other employment position (3), do not know (21), total from the above (master's) (50).

Doctoral Degree Graduates: Of those who graduated in the academic year 2011–2012, the following categories and numbers represent the postgraduate activities and employment of doctoral degree graduates: Enrolled in a psychology doctoral program (n/a), employed in an academic position at a university (2), employed in an academic position at a 2-year/4-year college (2), employed in other positions at a higher education institution (1), employed in business or industry (1), employed in government agency (1),

employed in a community mental health/counseling center (1), employed in a hospital/medical center (1), total from the above (doctoral) (9).

Additional Information:

Orientation, Objectives, and Emphasis of Department: The department emphasizes applications of psychology. All instruction is carried out via distance learning in which students and faculty mentors work together in one-on-one relationships. Students need to be highly motivated, independent, and conscientious.

Application Information:

Send to Northcentral University, Attn: Enrollment, 8667 Hartford Drive, Scottsdale, AZ 85255. Application available online. URL of online application: https://apply.ncu.edu/. Students are admitted in Programs have rolling admissions. *Fee:* $0.

Northern Arizona University

Department of Psychology
Social and Behavioral Sciences
NAU Box 15106
Flagstaff, AZ 86011
Telephone: (928) 523-3063
Fax: (928) 523-6777
E-mail: *heidi.wayment@nau.edu*
Web: *http://nau.edu/sbs/psych/*

Department Information:

1967. Chairperson: Heidi A. Wayment. Number of faculty: total—full-time 23; women—full-time 12; total—minority—full-time 1.

Programs and Degrees Offered:

Listed in the following order: Program area, degree type (T if terminal Master's), number awarded 7/11–6/12. Clinical Health Psychology MA/MS (Master of Arts/Science) (T) 1, Pre-Doctoral General Psychology MA/MS (Master of Arts/Science) (T) 4, Teaching Of Psychology MA/MS (Master of Arts/Science) (T) 0, Pre Doctoral Health Psychology MA/MS (Master of Arts/Science) (T) 3.

Student Applications/Admissions:

Student Applications

Clinical Health Psychology MA/MS (Master of Arts/Science)—Applications 2012–2013, 5. Total applicants accepted 2012–2013, 1. Number full-time enrolled (new admits only) 2012–2013, 1. Number part-time enrolled (new admits only) 2012–2013, 0. Total enrolled 2012–2013 full-time, 3. Total enrolled 2012–2013 part-time, 0. Openings 2013–2014, 2. The median number of years required for completion of a degree in 2012–2013 were 2. The number of students enrolled full- and part-time who were dismissed or voluntarily withdrew from this program area in 2012–2013 were 0. *Pre-Doctoral General Psychology MA/MS (Master of Arts/Science)*—Applications 2012–2013, 11. Total applicants accepted 2012–2013, 6. Number full-time enrolled (new admits only) 2012–2013, 6. Total enrolled 2012–2013 full-time, 11. Openings 2013–2014, 8. The median number of years required for completion of a degree in 2012–2013 were 2. The number of students enrolled full-

and part-time who were dismissed or voluntarily withdrew from this program area in 2012–2013 were 0. *Teaching Of Psychology MA/MS (Master of Arts/Science)*—Applications 2012–2013, 3. Total applicants accepted 2012–2013, 2. Number full-time enrolled (new admits only) 2012–2013, 1. Total enrolled 2012–2013 full-time, 3. Openings 2013–2014, 2. The median number of years required for completion of a degree in 2012–2013 were 2. The number of students enrolled full- and part-time who were dismissed or voluntarily withdrew from this program area in 2012–2013 were 1. *Pre Doctoral Health Psychology MA/MS (Master of Arts/Science)*—Applications 2012–2013, 16. Total applicants accepted 2012–2013, 9. Number full-time enrolled (new admits only) 2012–2013, 9. Total enrolled 2012–2013 full-time, 14. Openings 2013–2014, 6. The median number of years required for completion of a degree in 2012–2013 were 2. The number of students enrolled full- and part-time who were dismissed or voluntarily withdrew from this program area in 2012–2013 were 0.

Scores: Entries appear in this order: required test or GPA, minimum score (if required), median score of students entering in 2012–2013. *Clinical Health Psychology MA/MS (Master of Arts/Science):* GRE-V no minimum stated, 510, GRE-Q no minimum stated, 545, overall undergraduate GPA no minimum stated, 3.6, psychology GPA no minimum stated, 3.8; *Pre-Doctoral General Psychology MA/MS (Master of Arts/Science):* GRE-V no minimum stated, 470, GRE-Q no minimum stated, 580, overall undergraduate GPA no minimum stated, 3.5, psychology GPA no minimum stated, 3.6; *Teaching of Psychology MA/MS (Master of Arts/Science):* GRE-V no minimum stated, 550, GRE-Q no minimum stated, 625, overall undergraduate GPA no minimum stated, 3.5, psychology GPA no minimum stated, 4; *Pre Doctoral Health Psychology MA/MS (Master of Arts/Science):* GRE-V no minimum stated, 475, GRE-Q no minimum stated, 547, overall undergraduate GPA no minimum stated, 3.5, last 2 years GPA no minimum stated, psychology GPA no minimum stated, 3.7.

Other Criteria: (importance of criteria rated low, medium, or high): GRE scores—high, research experience—high, work experience—low, extracurricular activity—low, clinically related public service—low, GPA—high, letters of recommendation—high, interview—high, statement of goals and objectives—high, undergraduate major in psychology—low, specific undergraduate psychology courses taken—high, Clinically related public service used only for Clinical Health Psychology program. Work experience and extracurricular activity given somewhat higher importance for Clinical Health Psychology program. Phone interviews are conducted for selected applicants for the Clinical Health and Pre-doctoral training in Clinical Health Psychology. For additional information on admission requirements, go to http://nau.edu/SBS/Psych/Degrees-Programs/Graduate/.

Student Characteristics: The following represents characteristics of students in 2012–2013 in all graduate psychology programs in the department: Female—full-time 22, part-time 0; Male—full-time 10, part-time 1; African American/Black—full-time 0, part-time 0; Hispanic/Latino(a)—full-time 1, part-time 0; Asian/Pacific Islander—full-time 0, part-time 0; American Indian/Alaska Native—full-time 1, part-time 1; Caucasian/White—full-time 30, part-time 0; Multi-ethnic—full-time 0, part-time 0; students subject to the Americans With Disabilities Act—full-time 0, part-time 0; Unknown ethnicity—full-time 0, part-time 0; Interna-tional students who hold an F-1 or J-1 Visa—full-time 0, part-time 0.

Financial Information/Assistance:
Tuition for Full-Time Study: *Master's:* State residents: per academic year $8,344, $463 per credit hour; Nonstate residents: per academic year $19,438, $1,080 per credit hour. Tuition is subject to change. See the following website for updates and changes in tuition costs: http://nau.edu/SDAS/Tuition-Fees/.

Financial Assistance:
First-Year Students: Teaching assistantships available for first year. Average number of hours worked per week: 10. Apply by February 1. Research assistantships available for first year. Average number of hours worked per week: 10. Apply by February 1.

Advanced Students: Teaching assistantships available for advanced students. Average number of hours worked per week: 10. Research assistantships available for advanced students. Average number of hours worked per week: 10.

Additional Information: Of all students currently enrolled full time, 90% benefited from one or more of the listed financial assistance programs. Application and information available online at: http://nau.edu/FinAid/Graduate-Students/.

Internships/Practica: Master's Degree (MA/MS Clinical Health Psychology): An internship experience, such as a final research project or "capstone" experience is required of graduates. Master's Degree (MA/MS Pre-Doctoral General Psychology): An internship experience, such as a final research project or "capstone" experience is required of graduates. Master's Degree (MA/MS Teaching of Psychology): An internship experience, such as a final research project or "capstone" experience is required of graduates. Master's Degree (MA/MS Pre Doctoral Health Psychology): An internship experience, such as a final research project or "capstone" experience is required of graduates. Clinical Health and Pre-doctoral Clinical Health Psychology students are required to take two or three semesters of practicum in the department's Health Psychology Center. Our multipurpose training and service facility serves NAU students, faculty, and staff as well as community residents. In the Center, supervised graduate students in applied health psychology work to promote wellness and healthy lifestyles in adults and children through a variety of educational and treatment modalities. The Center offers programs on such topics as stress management, healthy eating and weight control, exercise, and smoking cessation, as well as group and individual interventions for these topics. The Center also provides psychological evaluation and behavioral management for health-related problems such as headaches, high blood pressure, cardiovascular disease, obesity, premenstrual syndrome, ulcers, diabetes, asthma, smoking, cancer, and chronic pain. Health Psychology students also are encouraged to take one or more semesters of fieldwork placement at a variety of agencies in the surrounding communities (including ethnic and rural communities). Pre-doctoral General Psychology students also may enroll in fieldwork placement. Teaching of Psychology students are required to enroll in a teaching practicum and teaching fieldwork.

Housing and Day Care: On-campus housing is available. See the following website for more information: http://home.nau.edu/reslife/. No on-campus day care facilities are available.

Employment of Department Graduates:

Master's Degree Graduates: Of those who graduated in the academic year 2011–2012, the following categories and numbers represent the postgraduate activities and employment of master's degree graduates: Enrolled in a psychology doctoral program (19), enrolled in a postdoctoral residency/fellowship (n/a), employed in independent practice (n/a), employed in an academic position at a university (1), employed in a hospital/medical center (2), other employment position (1), total from the above (master's) (23).

Doctoral Degree Graduates: Of those who graduated in the academic year 2011–2012, the following categories and numbers represent the postgraduate activities and employment of doctoral degree graduates: Enrolled in a psychology doctoral program (n/a), total from the above (doctoral) (0).

Additional Information:

Orientation, Objectives, and Emphasis of Department: The Psychology Department is committed to excellence in education at the graduate level, emphasizing teaching, scholarship, and service to the university and to the larger community. The department emphasizes theoretical foundations, empirical research, innovative curriculum, and practical hands-on applications of psychological knowledge. Four graduate programs are offered. First, the Pre-doctoral General Psychology Training program, which involves study of the theoretical and methodological foundations of general (clinical, cognitive, developmental, experimental, industrial/organizational, social, personality, neurosciences) psychology, is appropriate if you plan to pursue a doctoral degree or to conduct research and data management in a variety of settings. Second, the Pre-doctoral Clinical Health Psychology Training program, which involves study of the theoretical and methodological foundations of Clinical Health psychology, is appropriate if you plan to pursue a doctoral degree or to conduct research and data management in a variety of settings. Third, the Teaching of Psychology graduate program provides extensive training in the theoretical and methodological foundations of psychology and affords students a variety of teaching experiences and skills in face-to-face, web, and hybrid settings. This program prepares students to pursue a teaching career at the high school or community college level. Fourth, the Clinical Health Psychology program is appropriate if you plan to work in a master's-level position using skills related to the promotion of health and wellness and the prevention and treatment of illness.

Special Facilities or Resources: The Department of Psychology has over 1,500 square feet of clinic space dedicated to training in Health Psychology and a state-of-the-art psychophysiology/biofeedback laboratory. Other well-equipped research facilities are available in an adjunct building, and are assigned to faculty members engaged in research. A computer laboratory used for teaching purposes is also available for data collection. The department is housed in a modern building at the south end of the Flagstaff Mountain Campus. All teaching rooms are equipped with up-to-date technology.

Information for Students With Physical Disabilities: See the following website for more information: http://www4.nau.edu/dr/.

Application Information:
Send to Department of Psychology, Graduate Programs, Northern Arizona University, Box 15106, Flagstaff, AZ 86011. Application available online. URL of online application: https://www.applyweb.com/apply/northazg/. Students are admitted in the Fall, application deadline February 1. *Fee:* $50.

Northern Arizona University
Educational Psychology
College of Education
P.O. Box 5774
Flagstaff, AZ 86011
Telephone: (928) 523-7103
Fax: (928) 523-9284
E-mail: *kathy.bohan@nau.edu*
Web: *http://nau.edu/coe/ed-psych/*

Department Information:
1962. Chairperson: Kathy Bohan. Number of faculty: total—full-time 19; women—full-time 8; total—minority—full-time 2; women minority—full-time 1.

Programs and Degrees Offered:
Listed in the following order: Program area, degree type (T if terminal Master's), number awarded 7/11–6/12. Community Counseling MA/MS (Master of Arts/Science) (T) 25, School Counseling MEd (Education) 13, Student Affairs MEd (Education) 6, Counseling Psychology PhD (Doctor of Philosophy) 4, School Psychology PhD (Doctor of Philosophy) 3, Human Relations MEd (Education) 109, School Psychology EdS (School Psychology) 4.

Student Applications/Admissions:
Student Applications
Community Counseling MA/MS (Master of Arts/Science)—Applications 2012–2013, 70. Total applicants accepted 2012–2013, 38. Number full-time enrolled (new admits only) 2012–2013, 22. Number part-time enrolled (new admits only) 2012–2013, 3. Total enrolled 2012–2013 full-time, 73. Total enrolled 2012–2013 part-time, 25. Openings 2013–2014, 56. The median number of years required for completion of a degree in 2012–2013 were 2. *School Counseling MEd (Education)*—Applications 2012–2013, 13. Total applicants accepted 2012–2013, 10. Number full-time enrolled (new admits only) 2012–2013, 6. Number part-time enrolled (new admits only) 2012–2013, 4. Total enrolled 2012–2013 full-time, 41. Total enrolled 2012–2013 part-time, 65. Openings 2013–2014, 30. The median number of years required for completion of a degree in 2012–2013 were 2. The number of students enrolled full- and part-time who were dismissed or voluntarily withdrew from this program area in 2012–2013 were 0. *Student Affairs MEd (Education)*—Applications 2012–2013, 23. Total applicants accepted 2012–2013, 17. Number full-time enrolled (new admits only) 2012–2013, 10. Number part-time enrolled (new admits only) 2012–2013, 0. Total enrolled 2012–2013 full-time, 19. Total enrolled 2012–2013 part-time, 4. Openings 2013–2014, 10. The median number of years required for completion of a degree in 2012–2013 were 2. The number of students enrolled full- and part-time who were dismissed or voluntarily withdrew from this program area in 2012–2013 were 0. *Counseling Psychology PhD (Doctor of Philosophy)*—Applications 2012–2013, 12. Total applicants accepted 2012–

2013, 8. Number full-time enrolled (new admits only) 2012–2013, 6. Number part-time enrolled (new admits only) 2012–2013, 0. Total enrolled 2012–2013 full-time, 19. Total enrolled 2012–2013 part-time, 10. Openings 2013–2014, 6. The median number of years required for completion of a degree in 2012–2013 were 5. The number of students enrolled full- and part-time who were dismissed or voluntarily withdrew from this program area in 2012–2013 were 0. *School Psychology PhD (Doctor of Philosophy)*—Applications 2012–2013, 14. Total applicants accepted 2012–2013, 7. Number full-time enrolled (new admits only) 2012–2013, 4. Number part-time enrolled (new admits only) 2012–2013, 0. Total enrolled 2012–2013 full-time, 10. Total enrolled 2012–2013 part-time, 5. Openings 2013–2014, 5. The median number of years required for completion of a degree in 2012–2013 were 4. The number of students enrolled full- and part-time who were dismissed or voluntarily withdrew from this program area in 2012–2013 were 0. *Human Relations MEd (Education)*—Applications 2012–2013, 152. Total applicants accepted 2012–2013, 145. Number full-time enrolled (new admits only) 2012–2013, 63. Number part-time enrolled (new admits only) 2012–2013, 69. Total enrolled 2012–2013 full-time, 172. Total enrolled 2012–2013 part-time, 228. Openings 2013–2014, 200. The median number of years required for completion of a degree in 2012–2013 were 2. The number of students enrolled full- and part-time who were dismissed or voluntarily withdrew from this program area in 2012–2013 were 0. *School Psychology EdS (School Psychology)*—Applications 2012–2013, 29. Total applicants accepted 2012–2013, 17. Number full-time enrolled (new admits only) 2012–2013, 7. Number part-time enrolled (new admits only) 2012–2013, 0. Total enrolled 2012–2013 full-time, 49. Total enrolled 2012–2013 part-time, 27. Openings 2013–2014, 12. The median number of years required for completion of a degree in 2012–2013 were 2. The number of students enrolled full- and part-time who were dismissed or voluntarily withdrew from this program area in 2012–2013 were 0.

Scores: Entries appear in this order: required test or GPA, minimum score (if required), median score of students entering in 2012–2013. *Community Counseling MA/MS (Master of Arts/Science):* GRE-V no minimum stated, 156, GRE-Q no minimum stated, 149, overall undergraduate GPA no minimum stated, 3.63; *School Counseling MEd (Education):* GRE-V no minimum stated, 155, GRE-Q no minimum stated, 147, overall undergraduate GPA no minimum stated, 3.78; *Student Affairs MEd (Education):* GRE-V no minimum stated, 152, GRE-Q no minimum stated, 146, overall undergraduate GPA no minimum stated, 3.34; *Counseling Psychology PhD (Doctor of Philosophy):* GRE-V no minimum stated, 150, GRE-Q no minimum stated, 147, overall undergraduate GPA no minimum stated, 3.85; *School Psychology PhD (Doctor of Philosophy):* GRE-V no minimum stated, 157, GRE-Q no minimum stated, 148, overall undergraduate GPA no minimum stated, 3.91; *Human Relations MEd (Education):* overall undergraduate GPA 3.0, last 2 years GPA 3.0; *School Psychology EdS (School Psychology):* GRE-V no minimum stated, 148, GRE-Q no minimum stated, 142, overall undergraduate GPA no minimum stated, 3.45.

Other Criteria: (importance of criteria rated low, medium, or high): GRE scores—medium, research experience—low, work experience—medium, extracurricular activity—low, clinically related public service—low, GPA—medium, letters of recom-

mendation—medium, interview—low, statement of goals and objectives—high.

Student Characteristics: The following represents characteristics of students in 2012–2013 in all graduate psychology programs in the department: Female—full-time 410, part-time 401; Male—full-time 124, part-time 96; African American/Black—full-time 30, part-time 19; Hispanic/Latino(a)—full-time 94, part-time 104; Asian/Pacific Islander—full-time 4, part-time 6; American Indian/Alaska Native—full-time 44, part-time 19; Caucasian/White—full-time 344, part-time 331; Multi-ethnic—full-time 13, part-time 13; students subject to the Americans With Disabilities Act—full-time 0, part-time 0; Unknown ethnicity—full-time 0, part-time 3; International students who hold an F-1 or J-1 Visa—full-time 5, part-time 2.

Financial Information/Assistance:

Tuition for Full-Time Study: *Master's:* State residents: per academic year $7,560, $373 per credit hour; Nonstate residents: per academic year $18,654, $1,036 per credit hour. *Doctoral:* State residents: per academic year $7,560, $373 per credit hour; Nonstate residents: per academic year $18,654, $1,036 per credit hour. Tuition is subject to change. See the following website for updates and changes in tuition costs: http://nau.edu/SDAS/Tuition-Fees/.

Financial Assistance:

First-Year Students: Teaching assistantships available for first year. Average amount paid per academic year: $9,698. Average number of hours worked per week: 20. Apply by April 15. Research assistantships available for first year. Average amount paid per academic year: $9,698. Average number of hours worked per week: 20. Apply by April 15.

Advanced Students: Teaching assistantships available for advanced students. Average amount paid per academic year: $9,698. Average number of hours worked per week: 20. Apply by April 15. Research assistantships available for advanced students. Average amount paid per academic year: $9,698. Average number of hours worked per week: 20. Apply by April 15.

Additional Information: Application and information available online at: http://nau.edu/FinAid/Graduate-Students/.

Internships/Practica: Doctoral Degree (PhD Counseling Psychology): For those doctoral students for whom a professional psychology internship was required in this program prior to graduation, (4) students applied for an internship in 2011–2012, with (4) students obtaining an internship. Of those students who obtained an internship, (4) were paid internships. Of those students who obtained an internship, (1) students placed in APA/CPA accredited internships, (3) students placed in internships not APA/CPA accredited, but listed with the Association of Psychology Postdoctoral and Internship Programs (APPIC), (0) students placed in internships conforming to guidelines of the Council of Directors of School Psychology Programs (CDSPP), (0) students placed in internships that were not APA/CPA accredited, APPIC or CDSPP listed. Doctoral Degree (PhD School Psychology): For those doctoral students for whom a professional psychology internship was required in this program prior to graduation, (3) students applied for an internship in 2011–2012, with (3) students obtaining an internship. Of those students who obtained an internship, (3) were paid internships. Of those students who obtained an internship, (0) students placed in APA/CPA accredited internships, (0) students placed in internships not APA/CPA accredited, but listed with the Association of Psychology Postdoctoral and Internship Programs (APPIC), (3) students placed in internships conforming to guidelines of the Council of Directors of School Psychology Programs (CDSPP), (0) students placed in internships that were not APA/CPA accredited, APPIC or CDSPP listed. Master's Degree (MA/MS Community Counseling): An internship experience, such as a final research project or "capstone" experience is required of graduates. Master's Degree (Med Student Affairs): An internship experience, such as a final research project or "capstone" experience is required of graduates. Our programs are built on competency-based models and include closely supervised experiential practica and internship components. Some of these experiences are offered in NAU's Counseling Center and the Institute for Human Development; student service facilities; public-school settings; reservation schools and communities; rural settings; and community agencies. In addition, the College of Education houses a Skills Lab that includes comprehensive testing and curriculum libraries and a practicum facility that uses both recorded and direct live feedback in the supervision of students working with clients.

Housing and Day Care: On-campus housing is available. See the following website for more information: http://nau.edu/residence-life/. No on-campus day care facilities are available.

Employment of Department Graduates:

Master's Degree Graduates: Of those who graduated in the academic year 2011–2012, the following categories and numbers represent the postgraduate activities and employment of master's degree graduates: Enrolled in a postdoctoral residency/fellowship (n/a), employed in independent practice (n/a), total from the above (master's) (0).

Doctoral Degree Graduates: Of those who graduated in the academic year 2011–2012, the following categories and numbers represent the postgraduate activities and employment of doctoral degree graduates: Enrolled in a psychology doctoral program (n/a), total from the above (doctoral) (0).

Additional Information:

Orientation, Objectives, and Emphasis of Department: Because of the barriers to learning and living in our society, there is an increasing need for professionally trained counseling and school psychology personnel. Our graduate programs are based on a developmental, experiential training model that includes understanding theory, learning assessment and intervention skills, practicing skills in a supervised clinical setting, and performing skills in like settings. Integrated throughout our programs is a scientist–practitioner orientation that prepares students to ascertain the efficacy of assessment and intervention techniques.

Special Facilities or Resources: Students in School Psychology programs (EdS and PhD) complete portions of their practicum training at sites located on the Indian reservations and work with children and schools affiliated with the Navajo, Hopi and Supai tribes. The MA Counseling and the MEd School Counseling programs are also available at select sites in Arizona (i.e., Phoenix, Tucson, Kayenta, and Yuma). The MEd Human Relations program is an online 30 hr. program that does not lead to certification or licensure, but develops knowledge and skills in interpersonal, communication, critical thinking, research, and diversity awareness to assist individuals in careers in education, law enforcement, military, business, and other professions.

Information for Students With Physical Disabilities: See the following website for more information: http://www.nau.edu/dr/.

Application Information:
Application available online. URL of online application: http://www.applyweb.com/apply/northazg/. Students are admitted in the Fall, application deadline January 15; Spring, application deadline. PhD - Counseling Psychology and School Psychology - January 15. EdS + Certification in School Psychology, MA Community Counseling, MEd School Counseling - February 15. MA Student Affairs-March 15 and June 15. *Fee:* $65.

Arkansas, University of
Department of Psychology
J. William Fulbright College of Arts and Science
216 Memorial Hall
Fayetteville, AR 72701
Telephone: (479) 575-4256
Fax: (479) 575-3219
E-mail: *psycapp@uark.edu*
Web: *http://psyc.uark.edu/*

Department Information:
1926. Chairperson: Denise Beike. Number of faculty: total—full-time 22; women—full-time 9; total—minority—full-time 1; women minority—full-time 1; faculty subject to the Americans With Disabilities Act 1.

Programs and Degrees Offered:
Listed in the following order: Program area, degree type (T if terminal Master's), number awarded 7/11–6/12. Clinical Psychology PhD (Doctor of Philosophy) 5, Experimental Psychology PhD (Doctor of Philosophy) 3.

APA Accreditation: Clinical PhD (Doctor of Philosophy). Student Outcome Data Website: http://psyc.uark.edu/3455.php.

Student Applications/Admissions:
Student Applications
Clinical Psychology PhD (Doctor of Philosophy)—Applications 2012–2013, 148. Total applicants accepted 2012–2013, 6. Number full-time enrolled (new admits only) 2012–2013, 6. Total enrolled 2012–2013 full-time, 30. Total enrolled 2012–2013 part-time, 0. Openings 2013–2014, 6. The median number of years required for completion of a degree in 2012–2013 were 5. The number of students enrolled full- and part-time who were dismissed or voluntarily withdrew from this program area in 2012–2013 were 0. *Experimental Psychology PhD (Doctor of Philosophy)*—Applications 2012–2013, 34. Total applicants accepted 2012–2013, 3. Number full-time enrolled (new admits only) 2012–2013, 3. Total enrolled 2012–2013 full-time, 16. Total enrolled 2012–2013 part-time, 0. Openings 2013–2014, 4. The median number of years required for completion of a degree in 2012–2013 were 5. The number of students enrolled full- and part-time who were dismissed or voluntarily withdrew from this program area in 2012–2013 were 0.
Scores: Entries appear in this order: required test or GPA, minimum score (if required), median score of students entering in 2012–2013. *Clinical Psychology PhD (Doctor of Philosophy):* GRE-V no minimum stated, 556, GRE-Q no minimum stated, 639, overall undergraduate GPA no minimum stated, 3.62; *Experimental Psychology PhD (Doctor of Philosophy):* GRE-V no minimum stated, 560, GRE-Q no minimum stated, 630, GRE-Analytical no minimum stated, 4.5, overall undergraduate GPA no minimum stated, 3.7.
Other Criteria: (importance of criteria rated low, medium, or high): GRE scores—high, research experience—high, work experience—low, extracurricular activity—low, clinically related public service—low, GPA—high, letters of recommendation—high, interview—high, statement of goals and objectives—high, fit with faculty research—high, undergraduate major in psychology—medium, specific undergraduate psychology courses taken—low. For additional information on admission requirements, go to http://psyc.uark.edu/3452.php.

Student Characteristics: The following represents characteristics of students in 2012–2013 in all graduate psychology programs in the department: Female—full-time 29, part-time 0; Male—full-time 17, part-time 0; African American/Black—full-time 0, part-time 0; Hispanic/Latino(a)—full-time 2, part-time 0; Asian/Pacific Islander—full-time 0, part-time 0; American Indian/Alaska Native—full-time 0, part-time 0; Caucasian/White—full-time 41, part-time 0; Multi-ethnic—full-time 1, part-time 0; students subject to the Americans With Disabilities Act—full-time 0, part-time 0; Unknown ethnicity—full-time 2, part-time 0; International students who hold an F-1 or J-1 Visa—full-time 2, part-time 0.

Financial Information/Assistance:
Tuition for Full-Time Study: *Doctoral:* State residents: per academic year $8,140, $349 per credit hour; Nonstate residents: per academic year $20,650, $826 per credit hour. Tuition is subject to change. Additional fees are assessed to students beyond the costs of tuition for the following: health insurance (optional), student activity fees, technology fees. See the following website for updates and changes in tuition costs: http://treasurer.uark.edu/tuition.asp.

Financial Assistance:
First-Year Students: Teaching assistantships available for first year. Average amount paid per academic year: $9,700. Average number of hours worked per week: 20. Apply by December 1. Research assistantships available for first year. Average amount paid per academic year: $9,700. Average number of hours worked per week: 20. Apply by December 1. Fellowships and scholarships available for first year. Average amount paid per academic year: $20,000. Average number of hours worked per week: 20. Apply by December 1.
Advanced Students: Teaching assistantships available for advanced students. Average amount paid per academic year: $9,700. Average number of hours worked per week: 20. Research assistantships available for advanced students. Average amount paid per academic year: $9,700. Average number of hours worked per week: 20. Fellowships and scholarships available for advanced students. Average amount paid per academic year: $20,000. Average number of hours worked per week: 20.
Additional Information: Of all students currently enrolled full time, 100% benefited from one or more of the listed financial assistance programs. Application and information available online at: http://psyc.uark.edu/3453.php.

Internships/Practica: Doctoral Degree (PhD Clinical Psychology): For those doctoral students for whom a professional psychology internship was required in this program prior to graduation, (3) students applied for an internship in 2011–2012, with (2)

students obtaining an internship. Of those students who obtained an internship, (2) were paid internships. Of those students who obtained an internship, (2) students placed in APA/CPA accredited internships, (0) students placed in internships not APA/CPA accredited, but listed with the Association of Psychology Postdoctoral and Internship Programs (APPIC), (0) students placed in internships conforming to guidelines of the Council of Directors of School Psychology Programs (CDSPP), (0) students placed in internships that were not APA/CPA accredited, APPIC or CDSPP listed. Doctoral students in the Clinical Training Program have always been able to obtain high-quality, APA-accredited predoctoral internships. Additionally, our students have numerous mental health agency placement opportunities throughout their tenure with us. These clerkship placements include local community mental health centers, the University Health Service, inpatient psychiatric hospitals, and several facilities dealing with disabilities, neuropsychology, and other clinical specialties.

Housing and Day Care: On-campus housing is available. See the following website for more information: http://housing.uark.edu/. On-campus day care facilities are available. See the following website for more information: http://children.uark.edu/index.php.

Employment of Department Graduates:

Master's Degree Graduates: Of those who graduated in the academic year 2011–2012, the following categories and numbers represent the postgraduate activities and employment of master's degree graduates: Enrolled in a postdoctoral residency/fellowship (n/a), employed in independent practice (n/a), total from the above (master's) (0).

Doctoral Degree Graduates: Of those who graduated in the academic year 2011–2012, the following categories and numbers represent the postgraduate activities and employment of doctoral degree graduates: Enrolled in a psychology doctoral program (n/a), enrolled in a postdoctoral residency/fellowship (3), employed in an academic position at a 2-year/4-year college (4), total from the above (doctoral) (7).

Additional Information:

Orientation, Objectives, and Emphasis of Department: The PhD program in clinical psychology follows the scientist/practitioner model of training. Although some of our graduates obtain applied, direct service provision positions, our training curriculum is such that those students whose career aspirations have been directed toward academic and research positions also have been successful. The clinical training program is based on the premise that clinical psychologists should be skilled practitioners and mental health service providers as well as competent researchers. To facilitate these goals, we strive to maximize the match between the clinical and research interests of the faculty with those of the graduate students. The academic courses and clinical experiences are designed to promote development in both areas. The objective of the Clinical Training Program is to graduate clinical psychologists capable of applying psychological theory, research methodology, and clinical skills to complex clinical problems and diverse populations. The program is fully accredited by the American Psychological Association. The PhD program in experimental psychology provides students with a broad knowledge of psychology via a core curriculum, with a specialized training emphasis in our social and cognitive processes focus area via research team meetings, colloquia, and advanced seminars. Training in social, developmental and cognitive psychology within the focus area includes independent research experience and extensive, supervised classroom teaching experience. The program provides students with a thorough understanding of psychological principles and prepares them for careers as academics and researchers.

Special Facilities or Resources: The Department of Psychology is housed in Memorial Hall, a multilevel building with 58,000 square feet of office and research space for faculty and students. The building contains modern facilities for both human and small animal research, including specialized space for use with individuals and small groups of children and adults. The on-site Psychological Clinic is a state-of-the-art training and research facility dedicated to providing practicum and applied research experiences for clinical students. The clinic's treatment, testing, and research rooms are equipped with a closed-circuit videotaping system. Memorial Hall has comprehensive data analysis facilities, including personal computers networked to the University and internet. Finally, the department is the beneficiary of a generous bequest that established the Marie Wilson Howells Fund, which provides funding for thesis and dissertation research, numerous research assistantships, student travel, and departmental colloquia. The department also nominates qualified students for supplemental Doctoral Fellowships available through the Graduate School.

Information for Students With Physical Disabilities: See the following website for more information: http://cea.uark.edu/.

Application Information:
Send to Graduate Studies Secretary, Department of Psychology, 216 Memorial Hall, University of Arkansas, Fayetteville, AR 72701. Application available online. URL of online application: http://psyc.uark.edu/3452.php. Students are admitted in the Fall, application deadline December 1. The deadline for the Clinical Program is December 1. The deadline for the Experimental Program is January 1. *Fee:* $40. The Department will pay the Graduate School application fees for admitted students. International applicants must apply to the Graduate School and pay a $50 application fee.

Central Arkansas, University of
Department of Psychology and Counseling
Health and Behavioral Sciences
201 Donaghey Avenue
Conway, AR 72035-0001
Telephone: (501) 450-3193
Fax: (501) 450-5424
E-mail: *ArtG@uca.edu*
Web: *http://uca.edu/psychology*

Department Information:
1967. Chairperson: J. Arthur Gillaspy, Jr. Number of faculty: total—full-time 21, part-time 11; women—full-time 6, part-time 9; total—minority—full-time 3, part-time 5; women minority—full-time 2, part-time 4.

Programs and Degrees Offered:
Listed in the following order: Program area, degree type (T if terminal Master's), number awarded 7/11–6/12. School Psychology PhD (Doctor of Philosophy) 3, School Psychology MA/MS

(Master of Arts/Science) (T) 9, Counseling Psychology MA/MS (Master of Arts/Science) (T) 10, Community Counseling MA/MS (Master of Arts/Science) (T) 9, Counseling Psychology PhD (Doctor of Philosophy) 0.

APA Accreditation: School PhD (Doctor of Philosophy). Student Outcome Data Website: http://uca.edu/psychology/doc-school-psyc/.

Student Applications/Admissions:
Student Applications
School Psychology PhD (Doctor of Philosophy)—Applications 2012–2013, 9. Total applicants accepted 2012–2013, 2. Number full-time enrolled (new admits only) 2012–2013, 2. Number part-time enrolled (new admits only) 2012–2013, 0. Total enrolled 2012–2013 full-time, 10. Total enrolled 2012–2013 part-time, 4. Openings 2013–2014, 5. The median number of years required for completion of a degree in 2012–2013 were 5. The number of students enrolled full- and part-time who were dismissed or voluntarily withdrew from this program area in 2012–2013 were 1. *School Psychology MA/MS (Master of Arts/Science)*—Applications 2012–2013, 15. Total applicants accepted 2012–2013, 7. Number full-time enrolled (new admits only) 2012–2013, 7. Number part-time enrolled (new admits only) 2012–2013, 0. Total enrolled 2012–2013 full-time, 19. Total enrolled 2012–2013 part-time, 0. Openings 2013–2014, 8. The median number of years required for completion of a degree in 2012–2013 were 3. The number of students enrolled full- and part-time who were dismissed or voluntarily withdrew from this program area in 2012–2013 were 0. *Counseling Psychology MA/MS (Master of Arts/Science)*—Applications 2012–2013, 18. Total applicants accepted 2012–2013, 11. Number full-time enrolled (new admits only) 2012–2013, 10. Number part-time enrolled (new admits only) 2012–2013, 0. Total enrolled 2012–2013 full-time, 25. Total enrolled 2012–2013 part-time, 0. Openings 2013–2014, 12. The median number of years required for completion of a degree in 2012–2013 were 2. The number of students enrolled full- and part-time who were dismissed or voluntarily withdrew from this program area in 2012–2013 were 0. *Community Counseling MA/MS (Master of Arts/Science)*—Applications 2012–2013, 13. Total applicants accepted 2012–2013, 10. Number full-time enrolled (new admits only) 2012–2013, 10. Number part-time enrolled (new admits only) 2012–2013, 0. Total enrolled 2012–2013 full-time, 29. Total enrolled 2012–2013 part-time, 0. Openings 2013–2014, 15. The median number of years required for completion of a degree in 2012–2013 were 2. The number of students enrolled full- and part-time who were dismissed or voluntarily withdrew from this program area in 2012–2013 were 0. *Counseling Psychology PhD (Doctor of Philosophy)*—Applications 2012–2013, 11. Total applicants accepted 2012–2013, 4. Number full-time enrolled (new admits only) 2012–2013, 3. Number part-time enrolled (new admits only) 2012–2013, 0. Total enrolled 2012–2013 full-time, 16. Total enrolled 2012–2013 part-time, 0. Openings 2013–2014, 3. The median number of years required for completion of a degree in 2012–2013 were 5. The number of students enrolled full- and part-time who were dismissed or voluntarily withdrew from this program area in 2012–2013 were 0.
Scores: Entries appear in this order: required test or GPA, minimum score (if required), median score of students entering in 2012–2013. *School Psychology PhD (Doctor of Philosophy):*

GRE-V no minimum stated, 500, GRE-Q no minimum stated, 530, overall undergraduate GPA no minimum stated, 3.7; *School Psychology MA/MS (Master of Arts/Science):* GRE-V no minimum stated, 500, GRE-Q no minimum stated, 500, overall undergraduate GPA no minimum stated, 3.5; *Counseling Psychology MA/MS (Master of Arts/Science):* GRE-V no minimum stated, 530, GRE-Q no minimum stated, 525, overall undergraduate GPA no minimum stated, 3.5; *Community Counseling MA/MS (Master of Arts/Science):* GRE-V no minimum stated, 500, GRE-Q no minimum stated, 500, overall undergraduate GPA no minimum stated, 3.5; *Counseling Psychology PhD (Doctor of Philosophy):* GRE-V no minimum stated, 560, GRE-Q no minimum stated, 620, overall undergraduate GPA no minimum stated, 3.8.
Other Criteria: (importance of criteria rated low, medium, or high): GRE scores—medium, research experience—medium, work experience—low, extracurricular activity—low, clinically related public service—medium, GPA—high, letters of recommendation—medium, interview—high, statement of goals and objectives—high, undergraduate major in psychology—medium, specific undergraduate psychology courses taken—medium, Doctoral programs place greater emphasis on previous research experience.

Student Characteristics: The following represents characteristics of students in 2012–2013 in all graduate psychology programs in the department: Female—full-time 74, part-time 4; Male—full-time 25, part-time 0; African American/Black—full-time 11, part-time 0; Hispanic/Latino(a)—full-time 3, part-time 0; Asian/Pacific Islander—full-time 3, part-time 0; American Indian/Alaska Native—full-time 1, part-time 0; Caucasian/White—full-time 81, part-time 4; Multi-ethnic—full-time 0, part-time 0; students subject to the Americans With Disabilities Act—full-time 0, part-time 0; Unknown ethnicity—full-time 0, part-time 0; International students who hold an F-1 or J-1 Visa—full-time 1, part-time 0.

Financial Information/Assistance:
Tuition for Full-Time Study: *Master's:* State residents: $278 per credit hour; Nonstate residents: $503 per credit hour. *Doctoral:* State residents: $278 per credit hour; Nonstate residents: $503 per credit hour. Tuition is subject to change. See the following website for updates and changes in tuition costs: http://uca.edu/studentaccounts/tuition-fees/.

Financial Assistance:
   First-Year Students: Research assistantships available for first year. Average amount paid per academic year: $8,000. Average number of hours worked per week: 20.
   Advanced Students: Teaching assistantships available for advanced students. Average amount paid per academic year: $5,200. Average number of hours worked per week: 10. Research assistantships available for advanced students. Average amount paid per academic year: $8,000. Average number of hours worked per week: 20.
   Additional Information: Of all students currently enrolled full time, 80% benefited from one or more of the listed financial assistance programs. Application and information available online at: http://uca.edu/graduateschool/assistantships-and-other-aid/.

Internships/Practica: Doctoral Degree (PhD School Psychology): For those doctoral students for whom a professional psychology internship was required in this program prior to graduation, (2) students applied for an internship in 2011–2012, with (2) students obtaining an internship. Of those students who obtained an internship, (2) were paid internships. Of those students who obtained an internship, (0) students placed in APA/CPA accredited internships, (0) students placed in internships not APA/CPA accredited, but listed with the Association of Psychology Postdoctoral and Internship Programs (APPIC), (2) students placed in internships conforming to guidelines of the Council of Directors of School Psychology Programs (CDSPP), (0) students placed in internships that were not APA/CPA accredited, APPIC or CDSPP listed. Doctoral Degree (PhD Counseling Psychology): For those doctoral students for whom a professional psychology internship was required in this program prior to graduation, (2) students applied for an internship in 2011–2012, with (1) students obtaining an internship. Of those students who obtained an internship, (1) were paid internships. Of those students who obtained an internship, (1) students placed in APA/CPA accredited internships, (0) students placed in internships not APA/CPA accredited, but listed with the Association of Psychology Postdoctoral and Internship Programs (APPIC), (0) students placed in internships conforming to guidelines of the Council of Directors of School Psychology Programs (CDSPP), (0) students placed in internships that were not APA/CPA accredited, APPIC or CDSPP listed. Master's Degree (MA/MS School Psychology): An internship experience, such as a final research project or "capstone" experience is required of graduates. Master's Degree (MA/MS Counseling Psychology): An internship experience, such as a final research project or "capstone" experience is required of graduates. Master's Degree (MA/MS Community Counseling): An internship experience, such as a final research project or "capstone" experience is required of graduates. Students are placed in a wide-range of practica and internships depending on their program of study, career aspirations, and match between the site and our program objectives. Examples of placements include schools, community agencies, hospitals, residential homes, university counseling centers, and clinics.

Housing and Day Care: On-campus housing is available. See the following website for more information: http://www.uca.edu/housing/. On-campus day care facilities are available. See the following website for more information: http://uca.edu/childstudy/.

Employment of Department Graduates:

Master's Degree Graduates: Of those who graduated in the academic year 2011–2012, the following categories and numbers represent the postgraduate activities and employment of master's degree graduates: Enrolled in a psychology doctoral program (2), enrolled in a postdoctoral residency/fellowship (n/a), employed in independent practice (n/a), employed in a professional position in a school system (6), employed in a community mental health/counseling center (16), employed in a hospital/medical center (4), total from the above (master's) (28).

Doctoral Degree Graduates: Of those who graduated in the academic year 2011–2012, the following categories and numbers represent the postgraduate activities and employment of doctoral degree graduates: Enrolled in a psychology doctoral program (n/a), employed in a professional position in a school system (1), employed in a community mental health/counseling center (2), total from the above (doctoral) (3).

Additional Information:

Orientation, Objectives, and Emphasis of Department: The M.S. programs in Counseling Psychology, Community Counseling, and School Psychology are designed to serve as terminal degrees with professional employment opportunities or as a firm foundation for prospective doctoral candidates. Broad training is offered in the understanding of psychological theories, assessment, and mental health interventions to enable graduates to function successfully in a variety of mental health and educational settings. The PhD in School Psychology is grounded in the scientist–practitioner model of training. Strong emphasis is placed on child mental health promotion, primary prevention, and intervention with a broad range of community related problems involving children, families, and schools. The program is responsive to ongoing societal concerns and issues pertaining to children, families, and schools. It prepares its graduates to function in schools, clinics, community agencies, and hospitals. The Counseling Psychology Emphasis (leading to a PhD in School Psychology, Emphasis in Counseling Psychology) is structured as a counseling psychology program. The program of study is based on the scientist–practitioner model of training and emphasizes community mental health intervention and prevention services for clients with a wide variety of mental health problems. Graduates will be prepared to provide evidence-based assessment and treatment services and to conduct research in clinical and university settings. The department plans to seek APA accreditation of the Counseling Psychology Emphasis as a Counseling Psychology program within the next two years.

Special Facilities or Resources: The department has (a) a fully operational computer instruction/research room which can be used for onsite research purposes; (b) human and animal research labs; and (c) a multi-media computer system for research-related editing (e.g., self-modeling, therapy tapes). The department also operates the Psychology and Counseling Training Clinic that provides assessment services for the community.

Information for Students With Physical Disabilities: See the following website for more information: http://www.uca.edu/disability/.

Application Information:
Send to Director of Training, Department of Psychology & Counseling, Box 4915, University of Central Arkansas, Conway, AR 72035. Application available online. URL of online application: http://uca.edu/graduateschool/admission-process/. Students are admitted in the Fall, application deadline February 10. Deadline for doctoral programs is February 10; for the Master's programs the deadline is March 15. *Fee:* $25.

Alliant International University: Fresno
Programs in Clinical Psychology
California School of Professional Psychology
5130 East Clinton Way
Fresno, CA 93727
Telephone: (559) 253-2215
Fax: (559) 253-2267
E-mail: *mschwartz@alliant.edu*
Web: *http://www.alliant.edu/cspp/*

Department Information:
1973. Dean, California School of Professional Psychology: Morgan T. Sammons, PhD, ABPP. Number of faculty: total—full-time 13, part-time 14; women—full-time 4, part-time 6; total—minority—full-time 3, part-time 1.

Programs and Degrees Offered:
Listed in the following order: Program area, degree type (T if terminal Master's), number awarded 7/11–6/12. Clinical Psychology PsyD (Doctor of Psychology) 10, Clinical Psychology PhD (Doctor of Philosophy) 6.

APA Accreditation: On Probation PsyD (Doctor of Psychology). Student Outcome Data Website: http://www.alliant.edu/cspp/programs-degrees/clinical-psychology/clinical_psyd_fresno/. Clinical PhD (Doctor of Philosophy). Student Outcome Data Website: http://www.alliant.edu/cspp/programs-degrees/clinical-psychology/clinical_phd_fresno/index.php.

Student Applications/Admissions:
Student Applications
Clinical Psychology PsyD (Doctor of Psychology)—Applications 2012–2013, 39. Total applicants accepted 2012–2013, 15. Number full-time enrolled (new admits only) 2012–2013, 9. Number part-time enrolled (new admits only) 2012–2013, 0. Total enrolled 2012–2013 full-time, 43. Total enrolled 2012–2013 part-time, 12. Openings 2013–2014, 13. The median number of years required for completion of a degree in 2012–2013 were 4. The number of students enrolled full- and part-time who were dismissed or voluntarily withdrew from this program area in 2012–2013 were 0. *Clinical Psychology PhD (Doctor of Philosophy)*—Applications 2012–2013, 34. Total applicants accepted 2012–2013, 12. Number full-time enrolled (new admits only) 2012–2013, 10. Number part-time enrolled (new admits only) 2012–2013, 0. Total enrolled 2012–2013 full-time, 46. Total enrolled 2012–2013 part-time, 5. Openings 2013–2014, 12. The median number of years required for completion of a degree in 2012–2013 were 5. The number of students enrolled full- and part-time who were dismissed or voluntarily withdrew from this program area in 2012–2013 were 0.

Scores: Entries appear in this order: required test or GPA, minimum score (if required), median score of students entering in 2012–2013. *Clinical Psychology PsyD (Doctor of Psychology):* overall undergraduate GPA 3.0, 3.20, psychology GPA 3.0;

Clinical Psychology PhD (Doctor of Philosophy): overall undergraduate GPA 3.0, 3.12, psychology GPA 3.0.

Other Criteria: (importance of criteria rated low, medium, or high): research experience—medium, work experience—medium, extracurricular activity—low, clinically related public service—medium, GPA—high, letters of recommendation—high, interview—high, statement of goals and objectives—high, undergraduate major in psychology—medium, specific undergraduate psychology courses taken—medium. For additional information on admission requirements, go to http://www.alliant.edu/cspp/.

Student Characteristics: The following represents characteristics of students in 2012–2013 in all graduate psychology programs in the department: Female—full-time 66, part-time 11; Male—full-time 23, part-time 6; African American/Black—full-time 6, part-time 2; Hispanic/Latino(a)—full-time 18, part-time 1; Asian/Pacific Islander—full-time 6, part-time 1; American Indian/Alaska Native—full-time 0, part-time 0; Caucasian/White—full-time 39, part-time 10; Multi-ethnic—full-time 4, part-time 0; students subject to the Americans With Disabilities Act—full-time 1, part-time 2; Unknown ethnicity—full-time 16, part-time 3; International students who hold an F-1 or J-1 Visa—full-time 0, part-time 1.

Financial Information/Assistance:
Tuition for Full-Time Study: *Doctoral:* State residents: $1,030 per credit hour; Nonstate residents: $1,030 per credit hour. Tuition is subject to change. See the following website for updates and changes in tuition costs: http://www.alliant.edu/admissions/tuition.php.

Financial Assistance:
First-Year Students: Research assistantships available for first year. Average amount paid per academic year: $1,000. Average number of hours worked per week: 10. Fellowships and scholarships available for first year. Average amount paid per academic year: $5,000. Apply by December 15.

Advanced Students: Teaching assistantships available for advanced students. Average amount paid per academic year: $3,000. Average number of hours worked per week: 10. Research assistantships available for advanced students. Average amount paid per academic year: $1,000. Average number of hours worked per week: 10. Fellowships and scholarships available for advanced students. Average amount paid per academic year: $5,000. Apply by December 15.

Additional Information: Of all students currently enrolled full time, 56% benefited from one or more of the listed financial assistance programs. Application and information available online at: http://www.alliant.edu/admissions/financial-aid-scholarships/.

Internships/Practica: Doctoral Degree (PsyD Clinical Psychology): For those doctoral students for whom a professional psychology internship was required in this program prior to graduation, (13) students applied for an internship in 2011–2012, with (13) students obtaining an internship. Of those students who obtained an internship, (9) were paid internships. Of those students who obtained an internship, (4) students placed in APA/CPA accredited internships, (4) students placed in internships not APA/CPA accredited, but listed with the Association of Psychology Postdoctoral and Internship Programs (APPIC), (0) students placed in internships conforming to guidelines of the Council of Directors of School Psychology Programs (CDSPP), (5) students placed in internships that were not APA/CPA accredited, APPIC or CDSPP listed. Doctoral Degree (PhD Clinical Psychology): For those doctoral students for whom a professional psychology internship was required in this program prior to graduation, (6) students applied for an internship in 2011–2012, with (6) students obtaining an internship. Of those students who obtained an internship, (4) were paid internships. Of those students who obtained an internship, (3) students placed in APA/CPA accredited internships, (0) students placed in internships not APA/CPA accredited, but listed with the Association of Psychology Postdoctoral and Internship Programs (APPIC), (0) students placed in internships conforming to guidelines of the Council of Directors of School Psychology Programs (CDSPP), (3) students placed in internships that were not APA/CPA accredited, APPIC or CDSPP listed. The clinical psychology programs emphasize the integration of academic coursework and research with clinical practice. In order to integrate appropriate skills with material learned in the classroom, students participate in a professional training placement experience beginning in the first year. The settings where students complete the professional training requirements include community mental health centers, clinics, inpatient mental health facilities, medical settings, specialized service centers, rehabilitation programs, residential/day care programs, forensic/correctional facilities, and educational programs. Third year students will spend fifteen hours per week in a practicum either at CSPP's Psychological Services Center or at some other CSPP-approved agency. During their final year, clinical students complete a full year internship at an appropriate APA or APPIC internship. PhD students must also complete teaching practica.

Housing and Day Care: No on-campus housing is available. No on-campus day care facilities are available.

Employment of Department Graduates:

Master's Degree Graduates: Of those who graduated in the academic year 2011–2012, the following categories and numbers represent the postgraduate activities and employment of master's degree graduates: Enrolled in a postdoctoral residency/fellowship (n/a), employed in independent practice (n/a), total from the above (master's) (0).

Doctoral Degree Graduates: Of those who graduated in the academic year 2011–2012, the following categories and numbers represent the postgraduate activities and employment of doctoral degree graduates: Enrolled in a psychology doctoral program (n/a), total from the above (doctoral) (0).

Additional Information:

Orientation, Objectives, and Emphasis of Department: The clinical psychology PsyD program emphasizes training in clinical skills and clinical application of research knowledge and is designed for students who are interested in careers as practitioners, but it also includes a research component. The program is multisystemically or ecosystemically oriented and trains students to consider the role of diverse systems in creating and/or remedying individual and social problems. An empirical PsyD dissertation is required and may focus on program development and/or evaluation, test development, survey research or therapeutic outcomes. The clinical psychology PhD program puts equal weight on training in clinical, research, and teaching skills. The program is for students whose goal is an academic career in psychology. Emphasis areas are offered are: ecosystemic clinical child emphasis — trains students to work with infants, children, and adolescents, as well as with the adults in these clients' lives; health psychology emphasis — provides students with exposure to the expanding field of health psychology and behavioral medicine; forensic clinical psychology emphasis — prepares students to practice clinical psychology in a forensic environment.

Special Facilities or Resources: The Psychological Service Center serves the dual purpose of offering high quality psychological services to the community, particularly underserved segments, and continuing the tradition of education, training and service. The facility consists of eight therapy and two play therapy rooms, a large conference room, student work room, TV/monitor, and staff offices. The campus is also home to the Association for Play Therapy.

Information for Students With Physical Disabilities: See the following website for more information: http://www.alliant.edu/about-alliant/consumer-information-heoa/disability-services.

Application Information:
Send to Alliant International University, Admissions Processing Center, 10455 Pomerado Road, San Diego, CA 92131-1799. Application available online. URL of online application: https://my.alliant.edu/ICS/Prospective_Students/. Students are admitted in the Fall, application deadline December 15. The programs have a December 15 priority deadline in order to provide a response by April 1 for applicants who need a decision by that date. Programs accept and admit applicants on a space available basis after the priority deadline. *Fee:* $65. A limited number of application fee waivers are available for students with significant financial need.

Alliant International University: Fresno
Programs in Organizational Psychology
California School of Professional Psychology
5130 East Clinton Way
Fresno, CA 93727-2014
Telephone: (559) 253-2215
Fax: (559) 253-2267
E-mail: *mschwartz@alliant.edu*
Web: *http://www.alliant.edu/cspp/programs-degrees/organizational-psychology/*

Department Information:
1995. Dean, California School of Professional Psychology: Morgan T. Sammons, PhD, ABPP. Number of faculty: total—full-time 4, part-time 2; women—full-time 4, part-time 1.

Programs and Degrees Offered:
Listed in the following order: Program area, degree type (T if terminal Master's), number awarded 7/11–6/12. Organization Development PsyD (Doctor of Psychology) 9, Organizational Behavior MA/MS (Master of Arts/Science) (T) 2.

Student Applications/Admissions:

Student Applications

Organization Development PsyD (Doctor of Psychology)—Applications 2012–2013, 2. Total applicants accepted 2012–2013, 2. Number full-time enrolled (new admits only) 2012–2013, 0. Number part-time enrolled (new admits only) 2012–2013, 2. Total enrolled 2012–2013 full-time, 14. Total enrolled 2012–2013 part-time, 28. Openings 2013–2014, 3. The median number of years required for completion of a degree in 2012–2013 were 4. The number of students enrolled full- and part-time who were dismissed or voluntarily withdrew from this program area in 2012–2013 were 0. *Organizational Behavior MA/MS (Master of Arts/Science)*—Applications 2012–2013, 6. Total applicants accepted 2012–2013, 4. Number full-time enrolled (new admits only) 2012–2013, 0. Number part-time enrolled (new admits only) 2012–2013, 4. Total enrolled 2012–2013 full-time, 3. Total enrolled 2012–2013 part-time, 4. Openings 2013–2014, 3. The median number of years required for completion of a degree in 2012–2013 were 2. The number of students enrolled full- and part-time who were dismissed or voluntarily withdrew from this program area in 2012–2013 were 0.

Scores: Entries appear in this order: required test or GPA, minimum score (if required), median score of students entering in 2012–2013. *Organization Development PsyD (Doctor of Psychology):* overall undergraduate GPA 3.0, 3.20, psychology GPA 3.0; *Organizational Behavior MA/MS (Master of Arts/Science):* overall undergraduate GPA 3.0, 3.33, psychology GPA 3.0.

Other Criteria: (importance of criteria rated low, medium, or high): research experience—low, work experience—high, extracurricular activity—medium, GPA—high, letters of recommendation—high, interview—high, statement of goals and objectives—high, undergraduate major in psychology—low, specific undergraduate psychology courses taken—low. For additional information on admission requirements, go to http://www.alliant.edu/cspp/admissions/apply/op-app-req.php.

Student Characteristics: The following represents characteristics of students in 2012–2013 in all graduate psychology programs in the department: Female—full-time 14, part-time 22; Male—full-time 3, part-time 10; African American/Black—full-time 1, part-time 5; Hispanic/Latino(a)—full-time 4, part-time 5; Asian/Pacific Islander—full-time 1, part-time 3; American Indian/Alaska Native—full-time 0, part-time 2; Caucasian/White—full-time 7, part-time 14; Multi-ethnic—full-time 1, part-time 1; students subject to the Americans With Disabilities Act—full-time 0, part-time 1; Unknown ethnicity—full-time 3, part-time 2; International students who hold an F-1 or J-1 Visa—full-time 0, part-time 0.

Financial Information/Assistance:

Tuition for Full-Time Study: *Master's:* State residents: $760 per credit hour; Nonstate residents: $760 per credit hour. *Doctoral:* State residents: $1,030 per credit hour; Nonstate residents: $1,030 per credit hour. Tuition is subject to change. Tuition costs vary by program. See the following website for updates and changes in tuition costs: http://www.alliant.edu/admissions/tuition.php.

Financial Assistance:

First-Year Students: Research assistantships available for first year. Average amount paid per academic year: $1,000. Aver-

age number of hours worked per week: 10. Fellowships and scholarships available for first year. Average amount paid per academic year: $5,000. Apply by March 1.

Advanced Students: Teaching assistantships available for advanced students. Average amount paid per academic year: $3,000. Average number of hours worked per week: 10. Research assistantships available for advanced students. Average amount paid per academic year: $1,000. Average number of hours worked per week: 10. Fellowships and scholarships available for advanced students. Average amount paid per academic year: $5,000. Apply by March 1.

Additional Information: Of all students currently enrolled full time, 51% benefited from one or more of the listed financial assistance programs. Application and information available online at: http://www.alliant.edu/admissions/financial-aid-scholarships/.

Internships/Practica: Master's Degree (MA/MS Organizational Behavior): An internship experience, such as a final research project or "capstone" experience is required of graduates. The second and third years of the doctoral program involve a professional placement in organizational studies.

Housing and Day Care: No on-campus housing is available. No on-campus day care facilities are available.

Employment of Department Graduates:

Master's Degree Graduates: Of those who graduated in the academic year 2011–2012, the following categories and numbers represent the postgraduate activities and employment of master's degree graduates: Enrolled in a postdoctoral residency/fellowship (n/a), employed in independent practice (n/a), total from the above (master's) (0).

Doctoral Degree Graduates: Of those who graduated in the academic year 2011–2012, the following categories and numbers represent the postgraduate activities and employment of doctoral degree graduates: Enrolled in a psychology doctoral program (n/a), total from the above (doctoral) (0).

Additional Information:

Orientation, Objectives, and Emphasis of Department: The doctoral program prepares students for careers as consultants, leaders/managers, or faculty in community colleges or other academic institutions. The program is three years post-Master's and accessible to working adults. Students focus on the individual as a scholar-practitioner, themes and cultures of organizations, and practice in the global community. During the program they learn about managing change in complex organizations, examine and assess organizational procedures and processes, design interventions at the system/group/individual levels, and learn skills for OD consulting and conducting applied research. A PsyD project is a required part of the program. The PsyD program is accredited by the Organization Development Institute. The master's program is a two year program for working professionals and may be taken jointly with another doctoral program at Alliant in Fresno. The program has a practical curriculum related to management issues involving people and organizational processes.

Information for Students With Physical Disabilities: See the following website for more information: http://www.alliant.edu/about-alliant/consumer-information-heoa/disability-services.

Application Information:
Send to Alliant International University, Admissions Processing Center, 10455 Pomerado Road, San Diego CA 92131-1799. Application available online. URL of online application: https://my.alliant.edu/ICS/Prospective_Students/. Students are admitted in the Fall, application deadline March 1; Spring, application deadline October 1. Applications are due March 1 (priority deadline) for the Fall semester and October 1 (priority deadline) for the Spring semester. The program accepts applications and admits students on a space available basis after the priority deadlines. *Fee:* $65. A limited number of fee waivers are available to those with significant financial need.

Alliant International University: Irvine
Couple and Family Therapy Program
California School of Professional Psychology
Jamboree Building Center, 2855 Michelle Drive, Suite 300
Irvine, CA 92606
Telephone: (949) 812-7469
Fax: (949) 833-3507
E-mail: *mschwartz@alliant.edu*
Web: *http://www.alliant.edu/cspp/programs-degrees/couple-family-therapy/*

Department Information:
1973. Dean, California School of Professional Psychology: Morgan T. Sammons, PhD, ABPP. Number of faculty: total—full-time 9, part-time 15; women—full-time 3, part-time 11; total—minority—full-time 1, part-time 4; women minority—part-time 3.

Programs and Degrees Offered:
Listed in the following order: Program area, degree type (T if terminal Master's), number awarded 7/11–6/12. Marital and Family Therapy MA/MS (Master of Arts/Science) (T) 25, Marital and Family Therapy PsyD (Doctor of Psychology) 2.

Student Applications/Admissions:
Student Applications
Marital and Family Therapy MA/MS (Master of Arts/Science)—Applications 2012–2013, 68. Total applicants accepted 2012–2013, 40. Number full-time enrolled (new admits only) 2012–2013, 24. Number part-time enrolled (new admits only) 2012–2013, 1. Total enrolled 2012–2013 full-time, 49. Total enrolled 2012–2013 part-time, 4. Openings 2013–2014, 29. The median number of years required for completion of a degree in 2012–2013 were 2. The number of students enrolled full- and part-time who were dismissed or voluntarily withdrew from this program area in 2012–2013 were 1. Marital and Family Therapy PsyD (Doctor of Psychology)—Applications 2012–2013, 27. Total applicants accepted 2012–2013, 14. Number full-time enrolled (new admits only) 2012–2013, 8. Number part-time enrolled (new admits only) 2012–2013, 1. Total enrolled 2012–2013 full-time, 43. Total enrolled 2012–2013 part-time, 42. Openings 2013–2014, 6. The median number of years required for completion of a degree in 2012–2013 were 8. The number of students enrolled full- and part-time who were dismissed or voluntarily withdrew from this program area in 2012–2013 were 0.

Scores: Entries appear in this order: required test or GPA, minimum score (if required), median score of students entering in 2012–2013. *Marital and Family Therapy MA/MS (Master of Arts/Science):* overall undergraduate GPA 3.0, 3.04, psychology GPA 3.0; *Marital and Family Therapy PsyD (Doctor of Psychology):* overall undergraduate GPA 3.0, 3.00, psychology GPA 3.0.

Other Criteria: (importance of criteria rated low, medium, or high): research experience—medium, work experience—medium, extracurricular activity—low, clinically related public service—medium, GPA—high, letters of recommendation—high, interview—high, statement of goals and objectives—high, undergraduate major in psychology—medium, specific undergraduate psychology courses taken—medium. For additional information on admission requirements, go to http://www.alliant.edu/cspp/admissions/.

Student Characteristics: The following represents characteristics of students in 2012–2013 in all graduate psychology programs in the department: Female—full-time 80, part-time 37; Male—full-time 12, part-time 9; African American/Black—full-time 8, part-time 1; Hispanic/Latino(a)—full-time 10, part-time 6; Asian/Pacific Islander—full-time 8, part-time 8; American Indian/Alaska Native—full-time 1, part-time 1; Caucasian/White—full-time 41, part-time 22; Multi-ethnic—full-time 3, part-time 1; students subject to the Americans With Disabilities Act—full-time 0, part-time 0; Unknown ethnicity—full-time 21, part-time 7; International students who hold an F-1 or J-1 Visa—full-time 0, part-time 0.

Financial Information/Assistance:
Tuition for Full-Time Study: *Master's:* State residents: $1,030 per credit hour; Nonstate residents: $1,030 per credit hour. *Doctoral:* State residents: $1,030 per credit hour; Nonstate residents: $1,030 per credit hour. Tuition is subject to change. See the following website for updates and changes in tuition costs: http://www.alliant.edu/admissions/tuition.php.

Financial Assistance:
First-Year Students: Research assistantships available for first year. Average amount paid per academic year: $1,000. Average number of hours worked per week: 10. Fellowships and scholarships available for first year. Average amount paid per academic year: $2,500. Apply by January 15.

Advanced Students: Teaching assistantships available for advanced students. Average amount paid per academic year: $3,000. Average number of hours worked per week: 10. Research assistantships available for advanced students. Average amount paid per academic year: $1,000. Average number of hours worked per week: 10. Fellowships and scholarships available for advanced students. Average amount paid per academic year: $2,500. Apply by January 15.

Additional Information: Of all students currently enrolled full time, 58% benefited from one or more of the listed financial assistance programs. Application and information available online at: http://www.alliant.edu/admissions/financial-aid-scholarships/.

Internships/Practica: As part of the practicum experience, students complete 500 client contact hours, 250 of which must be with couples and families. Students receive at least 100 hours of individual and group supervision, 50 hours of which are based on direct observation, videotape, or audiotape. At least 25 of those hours must be videotape or direct observation. When students are ready to begin practicum, experienced faculty and staff assist students through each step in obtaining a field placement site approved by Alliant. While students are doing practicum training they are required to perform marriage and family therapy under a California state licensed, AAMFT-approved supervisor or the equivalent.

Housing and Day Care: No on-campus housing is available. No on-campus day care facilities are available.

Employment of Department Graduates:
Master's Degree Graduates: Of those who graduated in the academic year 2011–2012, the following categories and numbers represent the postgraduate activities and employment of master's degree graduates: Enrolled in a postdoctoral residency/fellowship (n/a), employed in independent practice (n/a), total from the above (master's) (0).
Doctoral Degree Graduates: Of those who graduated in the academic year 2011–2012, the following categories and numbers represent the postgraduate activities and employment of doctoral degree graduates: Enrolled in a psychology doctoral program (n/a), total from the above (doctoral) (0).

Additional Information:
Orientation, Objectives, and Emphasis of Department: The mission of the Couple and Family Therapy Program is to prepare graduate students who are skilled in the theory, research, and clinical practice of the field of Marriage and Family Therapy and can integrate individual and systemic therapeutic models in an international, multicultural environment. The Couple and Family Therapy (CFT) programs provide students with the essential training needed to pursue a career as a professional Marriage and Family Therapist (MFT). The Master of Arts in MFT allows students to be licensed as an MFT and the Doctor of Psychology (PsyD) in MFT prepares students with academic and research experience. Students who complete the MFT Master's at Alliant can apply all of their Master's degree coursework and practicum hours toward the doctoral program. The programs are accredited by COAMFTE.

Information for Students With Physical Disabilities: See the following website for more information: http://www.alliant.edu/about-alliant/consumer-information-heoa/disability-services.

Application Information:
Send to Alliant International University, Admissions Processing Center, 10455 Pomerado Road, San Diego, CA 92131-1799. Application available online. URL of online application: https://my.alliant.edu/ICS/Prospective_Students/. Students are admitted in the Fall, application deadline January 15. Applications for the Fall semester are due January 15 (priority deadline). Applications received after the priority deadline are accepted and admitted on a space-available basis. *Fee:* $65. A limited number of fee waivers are available for those with significant financial need.

Alliant International University: Irvine
Programs in Educational and School Psychology
Hufstedler School of Education
Jamboree Building Center, 2855 Michelle Drive, Suite 300
Irvine, CA 92606
Telephone: (949) 833-2651
Fax: (949) 833-3507
E-mail: *acarter@alliant.edu*
Web: *http://www.alliant.edu/hsoe/*

Department Information:
2002. Program Director: Donald Wofford, PsyD. Number of faculty: total—full-time 1, part-time 15; women—part-time 5.

Programs and Degrees Offered:
Listed in the following order: Program area, degree type (T if terminal Master's), number awarded 7/11–6/12. Educational Psychology PsyD (Doctor of Psychology) 7, School Psychology MA/MS (Master of Arts/Science) (T) 12.

Student Applications/Admissions:
Student Applications
Educational Psychology PsyD (Doctor of Psychology)—Applications 2012–2013, 6. Total applicants accepted 2012–2013, 6. Number full-time enrolled (new admits only) 2012–2013, 1. Number part-time enrolled (new admits only) 2012–2013, 4. Total enrolled 2012–2013 full-time, 1. Total enrolled 2012–2013 part-time, 13. Openings 2013–2014, 15. The median number of years required for completion of a degree in 2012–2013 were 3. The number of students enrolled full- and part-time who were dismissed or voluntarily withdrew from this program area in 2012–2013 were 0. *School Psychology MA/MS (Master of Arts/Science)*—Applications 2012–2013, 8. Total applicants accepted 2012–2013, 7. Number full-time enrolled (new admits only) 2012–2013, 4. Number part-time enrolled (new admits only) 2012–2013, 2. Total enrolled 2012–2013 full-time, 8. Total enrolled 2012–2013 part-time, 13. Openings 2013–2014, 18. The median number of years required for completion of a degree in 2012–2013 were 2. The number of students enrolled full- and part-time who were dismissed or voluntarily withdrew from this program area in 2012–2013 were 0.
Scores: Entries appear in this order: required test or GPA, minimum score (if required), median score of students entering in 2012–2013. *Educational Psychology PsyD (Doctor of Psychology)*: overall undergraduate GPA 3.0, 3.92, psychology GPA 3.0; *School Psychology MA/MS (Master of Arts/Science)*: overall undergraduate GPA 3.0, 3.0, psychology GPA 3.0.
Other Criteria: (importance of criteria rated low, medium, or high): research experience—medium, work experience—medium, extracurricular activity—low, clinically related public service—high, GPA—high, letters of recommendation—high, interview—high, statement of goals and objectives—high, Criteria differ by program and level. For additional information on admission requirements, go to http://www.alliant.edu/admissions/index.php.

Student Characteristics: The following represents characteristics of students in 2012–2013 in all graduate psychology programs in the department: Female—full-time 6, part-time 24; Male—full-

time 3, part-time 2; African American/Black—full-time 0, part-time 1; Hispanic/Latino(a)—full-time 1, part-time 6; Asian/Pacific Islander—full-time 1, part-time 4; American Indian/Alaska Native—full-time 0, part-time 0; Caucasian/White—full-time 5, part-time 10; Multi-ethnic—full-time 1, part-time 2; students subject to the Americans With Disabilities Act—full-time 0, part-time 0; Unknown ethnicity—full-time 1, part-time 3; International students who hold an F-1 or J-1 Visa—full-time 0, part-time 0.

Financial Information/Assistance:

Tuition for Full-Time Study: *Master's:* State residents: $580 per credit hour; Nonstate residents: $580 per credit hour. *Doctoral:* State residents: $935 per credit hour; Nonstate residents: $935 per credit hour. Tuition is subject to change. Tuition costs vary by program. See the following website for updates and changes in tuition costs: http://www.alliant.edu/admissions/tuition.php.

Financial Assistance:

First-Year Students: Research assistantships available for first year. Average amount paid per academic year: $1,000. Average number of hours worked per week: 10. Fellowships and scholarships available for first year. Average amount paid per academic year: $750. Apply by June 1.

Advanced Students: Teaching assistantships available for advanced students. Average amount paid per academic year: $3,000. Average number of hours worked per week: 10. Research assistantships available for advanced students. Average amount paid per academic year: $1,000. Average number of hours worked per week: 10. Fellowships and scholarships available for advanced students. Average amount paid per academic year: $750. Apply by April 1.

Additional Information: Of all students currently enrolled full time, 40% benefited from one or more of the listed financial assistance programs. Application and information available online at: http://www.alliant.edu/admissions/financial-aid-scholarships/.

Internships/Practica: Students in the master's program have practica tied to their coursework beginning in the first semester of their programs. Internships are required of students seeking a Pupil Personnel Services (PPS) credential post-masters or as part of the doctoral program in educational psychology. The 1200 required internship hours are completed at a public school district. Doctoral students interested in seeking clinical licensure must complete a separate psychology internship.

Housing and Day Care: No on-campus housing is available. No on-campus day care facilities are available.

Employment of Department Graduates:

Master's Degree Graduates: Of those who graduated in the academic year 2011–2012, the following categories and numbers represent the postgraduate activities and employment of master's degree graduates: Enrolled in a postdoctoral residency/fellowship (n/a), employed in independent practice (n/a), total from the above (master's) (0).

Doctoral Degree Graduates: Of those who graduated in the academic year 2011–2012, the following categories and numbers represent the postgraduate activities and employment of doctoral degree graduates: Enrolled in a psychology doctoral program (n/a), total from the above (doctoral) (0).

Additional Information:

Orientation, Objectives, and Emphasis of Department: Programs train students with the skills necessary to work with students, teachers, parents, and other school professionals in today's school environments. Curriculum includes professional skills, professional roles courses, applied research, and professional concepts. The master's degree program prepares students to gain the PPS (Pupil Personnel Services) credential that allows them to practice in California's schools. Students take afternoon, evening, and weekend classes and engage in fieldwork. At the doctoral level, students complete special focus area courses, examples of which include adolescent stress and coping, school culture and administration, pediatric psychology, infant and preschool mental health, child neuropsychology, and provision of services for children in alternative placement. Doctoral students also complete a PsyD project.

Information for Students With Physical Disabilities: See the following website for more information: http://www.alliant.edu/about-alliant/consumer-information-heoa/disability-services.

Application Information:
Send to Alliant International University, Admissions Processing Center, 10455 Pomerado Road, San Diego, CA 92131-1799. Application available online. URL of online application: https://my.alliant.edu/ICS/Prospective_Students/. Students are admitted in the Fall, application deadline June 1; Programs have rolling admissions. Fee: $65. A limited number of fee waivers are available to those with significant financial need.

Alliant International University: Los Angeles
Forensic Psychology Programs
California School of Forensic Studies
1000 South Fremont Avenue, Unit 5
Alhambra, CA 91803-1360
Telephone: (626) 270-3378
Fax: (626) 284-0550
E-mail: fshattuck@alliant.edu
Web: http://www.alliant.edu/csfs/index.php

Department Information:
1999. Interim Program Director: Tracy Fass, J.D., PhD. Number of faculty: total—full-time 7, part-time 3; women—full-time 6, part-time 2; total—minority—full-time 1.

Programs and Degrees Offered:
Listed in the following order: Program area, degree type (T if terminal Master's), number awarded 7/11–6/12. Forensic Psychology PsyD (Doctor of Psychology) 17.

Student Applications/Admissions:
Student Applications
Forensic Psychology PsyD (Doctor of Psychology)—Applications 2012–2013, 25. Total applicants accepted 2012–2013, 19. Number full-time enrolled (new admits only) 2012–2013, 10. Number part-time enrolled (new admits only) 2012–2013, 0. Total enrolled 2012–2013 full-time, 52. Total enrolled 2012–2013 part-time, 16. Openings 2013–2014, 25. The median number of years required for completion of a degree in 2012–

2013 were 4. The number of students enrolled full- and part-time who were dismissed or voluntarily withdrew from this program area in 2012–2013 were 2.

Scores: Entries appear in this order: required test or GPA, minimum score (if required), median score of students entering in 2012–2013. *Forensic Psychology PsyD (Doctor of Psychology):* overall undergraduate GPA 3.0, 3.21, psychology GPA 3.0.

Other Criteria: (importance of criteria rated low, medium, or high): research experience—medium, work experience—high, extracurricular activity—low, clinically related public service—high, GPA—high, letters of recommendation—high, interview—high, statement of goals and objectives—high. For additional information on admission requirements, go to http://www.alliant.edu/csfs/admissions/admissions-requirements.php.

Student Characteristics: The following represents characteristics of students in 2012–2013 in all graduate psychology programs in the department: Female—full-time 45, part-time 13; Male—full-time 7, part-time 3; African American/Black—full-time 4, part-time 0; Hispanic/Latino(a)—full-time 7, part-time 3; Asian/Pacific Islander—full-time 5, part-time 1; American Indian/Alaska Native—full-time 0, part-time 0; Caucasian/White—full-time 29, part-time 8; Multi-ethnic—full-time 3, part-time 0; students subject to the Americans With Disabilities Act—full-time 0, part-time 0; Unknown ethnicity—full-time 4, part-time 4; International students who hold an F-1 or J-1 Visa—full-time 0, part-time 0.

Financial Information/Assistance:

Tuition for Full-Time Study: *Doctoral:* State residents: $1,030 per credit hour; Nonstate residents: $1,030 per credit hour. Tuition is subject to change. See the following website for updates and changes in tuition costs: http://www.alliant.edu/admissions/tuition.php.

Financial Assistance:

First-Year Students: Research assistantships available for first year. Average amount paid per academic year: $1,000. Average number of hours worked per week: 10. Fellowships and scholarships available for first year. Average amount paid per academic year: $1,500. Apply by February 15.

Advanced Students: Teaching assistantships available for advanced students. Average amount paid per academic year: $3,000. Average number of hours worked per week: 20. Research assistantships available for advanced students. Average amount paid per academic year: $1,000. Average number of hours worked per week: 10. Fellowships and scholarships available for advanced students. Average amount paid per academic year: $1,500. Apply by February 15.

Additional Information: Of all students currently enrolled full time, 52% benefited from one or more of the listed financial assistance programs. Application and information available online at: http://www.alliant.edu/admissions/financial-aid-scholarships/.

Internships/Practica: Doctoral Degree (PsyD Forensic Psychology): For those doctoral students for whom a professional psychology internship was required in this program prior to graduation, (22) students applied for an internship in 2011–2012, with (22) students obtaining an internship. Of those students who obtained an internship, (7) were paid internships. Of those students who obtained an internship, (1) students placed in APA/CPA accred-

ited internships, (7) students placed in internships not APA/CPA accredited, but listed with the Association of Psychology Postdoctoral and Internship Programs (APPIC), (0) students placed in internships conforming to guidelines of the Council of Directors of School Psychology Programs (CDSPP), (14) students placed in internships that were not APA/CPA accredited, APPIC or CDSPP listed. Students are provided opportunities to apply the knowledge gained during their coursework through the first, second, and third year practica. Practicum placements are 10 to 20 hour weekly training commitments at one of CSFS's 20 Los Angeles-based community training partners, which include adult and youth correctional facilities, department of mental health agencies, and community organizations. Through these experiences, students are introduced to the role of clinical psychologists, exposed to a wide range of differing populations and mental health issues and are provided with direct experience in clinical interviewing, cognitive and personality assessment, as well as evidenced-informed and evidence-based treatment interventions. The program culminates in a 2,000-hour internship in students' fourth year of study that focuses upon clinical intervention, psychological assessment, professional development and lifelong learning, multicultural issues, professional ethics and standards, supervision and consultation and advocacy. During this experience, students work with increasing independence to apply the knowledge and skills gained during the preceding years, supporting future success as independent professional psychologists.

Housing and Day Care: No on-campus housing is available. No on-campus day care facilities are available.

Employment of Department Graduates:

Master's Degree Graduates: Of those who graduated in the academic year 2011–2012, the following categories and numbers represent the postgraduate activities and employment of master's degree graduates: Enrolled in a postdoctoral residency/fellowship (n/a), employed in independent practice (n/a), total from the above (master's) (0).

Doctoral Degree Graduates: Of those who graduated in the academic year 2011–2012, the following categories and numbers represent the postgraduate activities and employment of doctoral degree graduates: Enrolled in a psychology doctoral program (n/a), total from the above (doctoral) (0).

Additional Information:

Orientation, Objectives, and Emphasis of Department: The California School of Forensic Studies Clinical Forensic Psychology PsyD program employs a practitioner-scholar model of education to support students to acquire core clinical competencies. The program is for students who have an interest in pursuing forensic post-doctoral training, practice in forensic settings — such as in correctional facilities or forensic mental health hospitals — and/or pursuing private practice conducting forensic assessment or mandated treatment. The Clinical Forensic Psychology program supports the development of competency in foundational clinical areas, including professionalism, reflective practice/self-assessment/self-care, scientific knowledge and practice, relationships, individual and cultural diversity awareness, ethical legal standards, interdisciplinary systems, assessment, intervention, supervision and advocacy. The program also supports the development of fundamental competencies appropriate to the practice of clinical psychology in forensic-specific contexts, with an emphasis on specialty ethical guidelines, forensic assessment and mandated intervention/treatment.

Information for Students With Physical Disabilities: See the following website for more information: http://www.alliant.edu/about-alliant/consumer-information-heoa/disability-services.

Application Information:
Send to Alliant International University, Admissions Processing Center, 10455 Pomerado Road, San Diego, CA 92131-1799. Application available online. URL of online application: https://my.alliant.edu/ICS/Prospective_Students/. Students are admitted in the Fall, application deadline January; Programs have rolling admissions. Applicants wishing notification by April 1 should submit their applications in January. However, applications are welcomed on a rolling basis and will be processed on a space available basis. *Fee:* $65. A limited number of fee waivers are available for those with significant financial need.

Alliant International University: Los Angeles
Programs in Clinical Psychology and Couple and Family Therapy
California School of Professional Psychology
1000 South Fremont Avenue, Unit 5
Alhambra, CA 91803-1360
Telephone: (626) 270-3315
Fax: (626) 284-0550
E-mail: *mschwartz@alliant.edu*
Web: *http://www.alliant.edu/cspp/*

Department Information:
1970. Dean, California School of Professional Psychology: Morgan T. Sammons, PhD, ABPP. Number of faculty: total—full-time 41, part-time 32; women—full-time 19, part-time 19; total—minority—full-time 7, part-time 5; women minority—full-time 4, part-time 3.

Programs and Degrees Offered:
Listed in the following order: Program area, degree type (T if terminal Master's), number awarded 7/11–6/12. Clinical Psychology PsyD (Doctor of Psychology) 46, Clinical Psychology PhD (Doctor of Philosophy) 25, Marital and Family Therapy MA/MS (Master of Arts/Science) (T) 15, Marital and Family Therapy PsyD (Doctor of Psychology) 0, Psychology MA/MS (Master of Arts/Science) (T) 0.

APA Accreditation: Clinical PsyD (Doctor of Psychology). Student Outcome Data Website: http://www.alliant.edu/cspp/programs-degrees/clinical-psychology/clinical_psyd_los-angeles/index.php. Clinical PhD (Doctor of Philosophy). Student Outcome Data Website: http://www.alliant.edu/cspp/programs-degrees/clinical-psychology/phd-la.php.

Student Applications/Admissions:
Student Applications
Clinical Psychology PsyD (Doctor of Psychology)—Applications 2012–2013, 255. Total applicants accepted 2012–2013, 87. Number full-time enrolled (new admits only) 2012–2013, 48. Number part-time enrolled (new admits only) 2012–2013, 3.

Total enrolled 2012–2013 full-time, 202. Total enrolled 2012–2013 part-time, 26. Openings 2013–2014, 45. The median number of years required for completion of a degree in 2012–2013 were 4. The number of students enrolled full- and part-time who were dismissed or voluntarily withdrew from this program area in 2012–2013 were 0. *Clinical Psychology PhD (Doctor of Philosophy)*—Applications 2012–2013, 97. Total applicants accepted 2012–2013, 43. Number full-time enrolled (new admits only) 2012–2013, 24. Number part-time enrolled (new admits only) 2012–2013, 0. Total enrolled 2012–2013 full-time, 116. Total enrolled 2012–2013 part-time, 18. Openings 2013–2014, 25. The median number of years required for completion of a degree in 2012–2013 were 5. The number of students enrolled full- and part-time who were dismissed or voluntarily withdrew from this program area in 2012–2013 were 2. *Marital and Family Therapy MA/MS (Master of Arts/Science)*—Applications 2012–2013, 64. Total applicants accepted 2012–2013, 25. Number full-time enrolled (new admits only) 2012–2013, 13. Number part-time enrolled (new admits only) 2012–2013, 1. Total enrolled 2012–2013 full-time, 25. Total enrolled 2012–2013 part-time, 4. Openings 2013–2014, 15. The median number of years required for completion of a degree in 2012–2013 were 2. The number of students enrolled full- and part-time who were dismissed or voluntarily withdrew from this program area in 2012–2013 were 1. *Marital and Family Therapy PsyD (Doctor of Psychology)*—Applications 2012–2013, 27. Total applicants accepted 2012–2013, 15. Number full-time enrolled (new admits only) 2012–2013, 11. Number part-time enrolled (new admits only) 2012–2013, 0. Total enrolled 2012–2013 full-time, 12. Total enrolled 2012–2013 part-time, 0. Openings 2013–2014, 8. The number of students enrolled full- and part-time who were dismissed or voluntarily withdrew from this program area in 2012–2013 were 0. *Psychology MA/MS (Master of Arts/Science)*—Applications 2012–2013, 0. Total applicants accepted 2012–2013, 0. Number full-time enrolled (new admits only) 2012–2013, 0. Number part-time enrolled (new admits only) 2012–2013, 0. Openings 2013–2014, 10. The number of students enrolled full- and part-time who were dismissed or voluntarily withdrew from this program area in 2012–2013 were 0.

Scores: Entries appear in this order: required test or GPA, minimum score (if required), median score of students entering in 2012–2013. *Clinical Psychology PsyD (Doctor of Psychology):* overall undergraduate GPA 3.0, 3.33, psychology GPA 3.0; *Clinical Psychology PhD (Doctor of Philosophy):* overall undergraduate GPA 3.0, 3.24, psychology GPA 3.0; *Marital and Family Therapy MA/MS (Master of Arts/Science):* overall undergraduate GPA 3.0, 3.16, psychology GPA 3.0; *Psychology MA/MS (Master of Arts/Science):* overall undergraduate GPA 3.0, psychology GPA 3.0.

Other Criteria: (importance of criteria rated low, medium, or high): research experience—medium, work experience—medium, extracurricular activity—low, clinically related public service—medium, GPA—high, letters of recommendation—high, interview—high, statement of goals and objectives—high, undergraduate major in psychology—medium, specific undergraduate psychology courses taken—medium. For additional information on admission requirements, go to http://www.alliant.edu/cspp.

Student Characteristics: The following represents characteristics of students in 2012–2013 in all graduate psychology programs in

the department: Female—full-time 273, part-time 43; Male—full-time 82, part-time 5; African American/Black—full-time 25, part-time 2; Hispanic/Latino(a)—full-time 46, part-time 7; Asian/Pacific Islander—full-time 39, part-time 7; American Indian/Alaska Native—full-time 2, part-time 0; Caucasian/White—full-time 166, part-time 17; Multi-ethnic—full-time 15, part-time 5; students subject to the Americans With Disabilities Act—full-time 1, part-time 0; Unknown ethnicity—full-time 62, part-time 10; International students who hold an F-1 or J-1 Visa—full-time 7, part-time 1.

Financial Information/Assistance:

Tuition for Full-Time Study: *Master's:* State residents: $1,030 per credit hour; Nonstate residents: $1,030 per credit hour. *Doctoral:* State residents: $1,030 per credit hour; Nonstate residents: $1,030 per credit hour. Tuition is subject to change. See the following website for updates and changes in tuition costs: http://www.alliant.edu/admissions/tuition.php.

Financial Assistance:

First-Year Students: Research assistantships available for first year. Average amount paid per academic year: $1,000. Average number of hours worked per week: 10. Fellowships and scholarships available for first year. Average amount paid per academic year: $5,000. Apply by December 15.

Advanced Students: Teaching assistantships available for advanced students. Average amount paid per academic year: $3,000. Average number of hours worked per week: 10. Research assistantships available for advanced students. Average amount paid per academic year: $1,000. Average number of hours worked per week: 10. Fellowships and scholarships available for advanced students. Average amount paid per academic year: $5,000. Apply by December 15.

Additional Information: Of all students currently enrolled full time, 57% benefited from one or more of the listed financial assistance programs. Application and information available online at: http://www.alliant.edu/admissions/financial-aid-scholarships/.

Internships/Practica: Doctoral Degree (PsyD Clinical Psychology): For those doctoral students for whom a professional psychology internship was required in this program prior to graduation, (99) students applied for an internship in 2011–2012, with (99) students obtaining an internship. Of those students who obtained an internship, (19) were paid internships. Of those students who obtained an internship, (1) students placed in APA/CPA accredited internships, (3) students placed in internships not APA/CPA accredited, but listed with the Association of Psychology Postdoctoral and Internship Programs (APPIC), (0) students placed in internships conforming to guidelines of the Council of Directors of School Psychology Programs (CDSPP), (95) students placed in internships that were not APA/CPA accredited, APPIC or CDSPP listed. Doctoral Degree (PhD Clinical Psychology): For those doctoral students for whom a professional psychology internship was required in this program prior to graduation, (41) students applied for an internship in 2011–2012, with (40) students obtaining an internship. Of those students who obtained an internship, (13) were paid internships. Of those students who obtained an internship, (4) students placed in APA/CPA accredited internships, (3) students placed in internships not APA/CPA accredited, but listed with the Association of Psychology Postdoctoral and Internship Programs (APPIC), (0) students placed in internships conforming to guidelines of the Council of

Directors of School Psychology Programs (CDSPP), (33) students placed in internships that were not APA/CPA accredited, APPIC or CDSPP listed. Master's Degree (MA/MS Psychology): An internship experience, such as a final research project or "capstone" experience is required of graduates. All students engage in practica and internships. Clinical psychology students complete 2000 predoctoral internship hours as part of their programs. The majority of the professional training sites are within 40 miles of the campus. These agencies serve a diverse range of individuals across ethnicity, culture, religion, and sexual orientation. These sites provide excellent training, offering a variety of theoretical orientations related to children, adolescents, adults, families and the elderly. Students who wish to pursue full-time internships are encouraged to make applications throughout the country. Couple and Family Therapy students complete 500 client contact hours, 250 of which must be with couples and families. Students receive at least 100 hours of individual and group supervision, 50 hours of which are based on direct observation, videotape, or audiotape. At least 25 of those hours must be videotape or direct observation. When students are ready to begin practicum, experienced faculty and staff assist students through each step in obtaining a field placement site approved by Alliant. While students are doing practicum training they are required to perform marriage and family therapy under a California state licensed, AAMFT-approved supervisor or the equivalent. The Master's program in Psychology, with an emphasis on marriage and family therapy and art therapy requires students to complete two traineeships for a minimum of 700 hours of supervised art therapy practicum/traineeship hours, out of which 350 are direct client contact hours. This requirement meets the Board of Behavior Science in California practicum requirements experience which must be completed at an approved training agency prior to degree completion. This requirement also meets the pre-graduation requirements for Art Therapy Registration (ATR). Students receive assistance with field placement, providing students with a valuable link to community resources, clinical training opportunities, and professional organizations.

Housing and Day Care: No on-campus housing is available. No on-campus day care facilities are available.

Employment of Department Graduates:

Master's Degree Graduates: Of those who graduated in the academic year 2011–2012, the following categories and numbers represent the postgraduate activities and employment of master's degree graduates: Enrolled in a postdoctoral residency/fellowship (n/a), employed in independent practice (n/a), total from the above (master's) (0).

Doctoral Degree Graduates: Of those who graduated in the academic year 2011–2012, the following categories and numbers represent the postgraduate activities and employment of doctoral degree graduates: Enrolled in a psychology doctoral program (n/a), total from the above (doctoral) (0).

Additional Information:

Orientation, Objectives, and Emphasis of Department: The clinical psychology PsyD and PhD programs at the California School of Professional Psychology prepare students to function as multifaceted clinical psychologists through a curriculum based on an integration of psychological theory, research, and practice. Students develop competencies in seven areas: clinical health psychology; interpersonal/relationship; assessment; multifaceted multimodal intervention; research and evaluation; consultation/ teaching; management/supervision/training; and quality assurance. The PsyD program is a practitioner program where candidates gain relatively greater mastery in assessment, intervention, and management/supervision. The PhD program is a based on a scholar-practitioner model where practice and scholarship receive equal emphasis and includes the following guiding principles: the generation and application of knowledge must occur with an awareness of the sociocultural and sociopolitical contexts of mental health and mental illness; scholarship and practice must not only build upon existing literature but also maintain relevance to the diverse elements in our society and assume the challenges of attending to the complex social issues associated with psychological functioning; and methods of research and intervention must be appropriate to the culture in which they are conducted. Practicum and internship experiences are integrated throughout the programs. Students have the opportunity to choose a curricular emphasis in clinical health psychology, multicultural community clinical, or family and couple clinical psychology. The mission of the Couple and Family Therapy Program is to prepare graduate students who are skilled in the theory, research, and clinical practice of the field of Marriage and Family Therapy and can integrate individual and systemic therapeutic models in an international, multicultural environment. The Couple and Family Therapy (CFT) programs provide students with the essential training needed to pursue a career as a professional Marriage and Family Therapist (MFT). The Master of Arts in MFT allows students to be licensed as an MFT and the Doctor of Psychology (PsyD) in MFT prepares students with academic and research experience. Students who complete the MFT Master's at Alliant can apply all of their Master's degree coursework and practicum hours toward the doctoral program. The programs are accredited by COAMFTE. The Master's program in Psychology, with an emphasis on marriage and family therapy and art therapy, is taught in a hybrid model that combines classroom courses in Los Angeles with online instruction. The program prepares students for professional careers with expertise in non-verbal expressive modes of therapy, specifically art therapy. The program provides students with an interdisciplinary education, which builds upon relational therapy models and art psychotherapy practices, and draws from interpersonal neurobiology theory, clinical neuroscience research and fine arts heritage. This program meets the educational standards and licensure requirements for both the MFT and LPCC license in California and most other states. The program also meets the Art Therapy Credentialing Board requirements for registration and Board Certification as an Art Therapist.

Special Facilities or Resources: The Psychological Services Center (PSC) is charged with the mission of developing professional training, research, and consultation opportunities for CSPP faculty and students, while providing services to a variety of public/ private agencies. It is committed to developing effective and innovative service strategies and resources that address the needs of a wide range of clients; with a particular focus on ethnically diverse, underserved populations. As a center "without walls," the PSC is the administrative umbrella for two major community-based programs: the Children, Youth, and Family Consortium and the School Court Accountability Project. These projects are designed to provide hands-on research, consulting, and clinical experience for students and to enhance the critically needed services to school-aged youth within the court system and school-aged populations. These programs enable participating CSPP fac-

ulty, staff, students, alumni/ae, and external consultant associates to provide services few other institutions can offer. Students also receive unique training and supervision that prepares them for critically needed roles as community advocates and leaders.

Information for Students With Physical Disabilities: See the following website for more information: http://www.alliant.edu/ about-alliant/consumer-information-heoa/disability-services.

Application Information:
Send to Alliant International University, Admissions Processing Center, 10455 Pomerado Road, San Diego, CA 92131-1799. Application available online. URL of online application: https://my.alliant.edu/ ICS/Prospective_Students/. Students are admitted in the Fall, application deadline December 15. The Clinical Psychology programs have a December 15 priority deadline in order to provide a response by April 1 for applicants who need a decision by that date. The CFT programs have a January 15 priority deadline for the Fall semester. Programs accept applications and admit students on a space-available basis after any stated deadlines. *Fee:* $65. A limited number of application fee waivers are available for students with significant financial need.

Alliant International University: Los Angeles
Programs in Educational and School Psychology
Hufstedler School of Education
1000 South Fremont Avenue, Unit 5
Alhambra, CA 91803-1360
Telephone: (626) 284-2777
Fax: (626) 284-0550
E-mail: *acarter@alliant.edu*
Web: *http://www.alliant.edu/hsoe/index.php*

Department Information:
1999. Program Director: Carlton W. Parks, Jr. PhD. Number of faculty: total—full-time 2, part-time 6; women—part-time 3; total—minority—full-time 1, part-time 2; women minority—part-time 1.

Programs and Degrees Offered:
Listed in the following order: Program area, degree type (T if terminal Master's), number awarded 7/11–6/12. School Psychology MA/MS (Master of Arts/Science) (T) 5, Educational Psychology PsyD (Doctor of Psychology) 5.

Student Applications/Admissions:
Student Applications
School Psychology MA/MS (Master of Arts/Science)—Applications 2012–2013, 3. Total applicants accepted 2012–2013, 2. Number full-time enrolled (new admits only) 2012–2013, 0. Number part-time enrolled (new admits only) 2012–2013, 0. Total enrolled 2012–2013 full-time, 8. Total enrolled 2012–2013 part-time, 2. Openings 2013–2014, 18. The median number of years required for completion of a degree in 2012–2013 were 2. The number of students enrolled full- and part-time who were dismissed or voluntarily withdrew from this program area in 2012–2013 were 0. *Educational Psychology PsyD (Doctor of Psychology)*—Applications 2012–2013, 2. Total applicants accepted 2012–2013, 2. Number full-time enrolled (new

admits only) 2012–2013, 0. Number part-time enrolled (new admits only) 2012–2013, 2. Total enrolled 2012–2013 full-time, 8. Total enrolled 2012–2013 part-time, 11. Openings 2013–2014, 10. The median number of years required for completion of a degree in 2012–2013 were 3. The number of students enrolled full- and part-time who were dismissed or voluntarily withdrew from this program area in 2012–2013 were 0.

Scores: Entries appear in this order: required test or GPA, minimum score (if required), median score of students entering in 2012–2013. *School Psychology MA/MS (Master of Arts/Science):* overall undergraduate GPA 3.0, psychology GPA 3.0; *Educational Psychology PsyD (Doctor of Psychology):* overall undergraduate GPA 3.0, 3.75, psychology GPA 3.0.

Other Criteria: (importance of criteria rated low, medium, or high): research experience—medium, work experience—high, extracurricular activity—low, clinically related public service—high, GPA—high, letters of recommendation—high, interview—high, statement of goals and objectives—high, Criteria differ by program and level. For additional information on admission requirements, go to http://www.alliant.edu/hsoe/hsoe-admissions/index.php.

Student Characteristics: The following represents characteristics of students in 2012–2013 in all graduate psychology programs in the department: Female—full-time 14, part-time 13; Male—full-time 2, part-time 0; African American/Black—full-time 3, part-time 4; Hispanic/Latino(a)—full-time 1, part-time 3; Asian/Pacific Islander—full-time 2, part-time 0; American Indian/Alaska Native—full-time 1, part-time 0; Caucasian/White—full-time 1, part-time 5; Multi-ethnic—full-time 4, part-time 0; students subject to the Americans With Disabilities Act—full-time 0, part-time 0; Unknown ethnicity—full-time 4, part-time 1; International students who hold an F-1 or J-1 Visa—full-time 0, part-time 0.

Financial Information/Assistance:

Tuition for Full-Time Study: *Master's:* State residents: $580 per credit hour; Nonstate residents: $580 per credit hour. *Doctoral:* State residents: $935 per credit hour; Nonstate residents: $935 per credit hour. Tuition is subject to change. Tuition costs vary by program. See the following website for updates and changes in tuition costs: http://www.alliant.edu/admissions/tuition.php.

Financial Assistance:

First-Year Students: Research assistantships available for first year. Average amount paid per academic year: $1,000. Average number of hours worked per week: 10. Fellowships and scholarships available for first year. Average amount paid per academic year: $1,500. Apply by June 1.

Advanced Students: Teaching assistantships available for advanced students. Average amount paid per academic year: $3,000. Average number of hours worked per week: 10. Research assistantships available for advanced students. Average amount paid per academic year: $1,000. Average number of hours worked per week: 10. Fellowships and scholarships available for advanced students. Average amount paid per academic year: $1,500. Apply by April 1.

Additional Information: Of all students currently enrolled full time, 40% benefited from one or more of the listed financial assistance programs. Application and information available online at: http://www.alliant.edu/admissions/financial-aid-scholarships/.

Internships/Practica: Students in the master's program have practica tied to their coursework beginning in the first semester of their programs. Internships are required of any students seeking the Pupil Personnel Services (PPS) credential post-masters or as part of the doctoral program in educational psychology. The 1200 internship hours are completed at a public school district. Those in the doctoral program who are interested in clinical licensure must complete a separate psychology internship.

Housing and Day Care: No on-campus housing is available. No on-campus day care facilities are available.

Employment of Department Graduates:

Master's Degree Graduates: Of those who graduated in the academic year 2011–2012, the following categories and numbers represent the postgraduate activities and employment of master's degree graduates: Enrolled in a postdoctoral residency/fellowship (n/a), employed in independent practice (n/a), total from the above (master's) (0).

Doctoral Degree Graduates: Of those who graduated in the academic year 2011–2012, the following categories and numbers represent the postgraduate activities and employment of doctoral degree graduates: Enrolled in a psychology doctoral program (n/a), total from the above (doctoral) (0).

Additional Information:

Orientation, Objectives, and Emphasis of Department: Programs train students with the skills necessary to work with students, teachers, parents, and other school professionals in today's school environments. The curriculum includes professional skills, professional roles courses, applied research, and professional concepts. The master's degree program prepares students to gain the PPS (Pupil Personnel Services) credential that allow them to practice in California's schools. Students take afternoon, evening and weekend classes and engage in fieldwork. At the doctoral level, students complete special focus area courses, examples of which include adolescent stress and coping, school culture and administration, pediatric psychology, infant and preschool mental health, child neuropsychology, and provision of services for children in alternative placement. Doctoral students also complete a PsyD project.

Information for Students With Physical Disabilities: See the following website for more information: http://www.alliant.edu/about-alliant/consumer-information-heoa/disability-services.

Application Information:
Send to Alliant International University, Admissions Processing Center, 10455 Pomerado Road, San Diego, CA 93121-1799. Application available online. URL of online application: https://my.alliant.edu/ICS/Prospective_Students/. Students are admitted in the Fall, application deadline June 1; Programs have rolling admissions. *Fee:* $65. A limited number of fee waivers are available for those with significant financial need.

Alliant International University: Los Angeles
Programs in Organizational Psychology
California School of Professional Psychology
1000 South Fremont Avenue, Unit 5
Alhambra, CA 91803-1360
Telephone: (626) 270-3315
Fax: (626) 284-0550
E-mail: *mschwartz@alliant.edu*
Web: *http://www.alliant.edu/cspp/programs-degrees/
organizational-psychology/*

Department Information:
1981. Dean, California School of Professional Psychology: Morgan T. Sammons, PhD, ABPP. Number of faculty: total—full-time 5, part-time 2; women—full-time 1.

Programs and Degrees Offered:
Listed in the following order: Program area, degree type (T if terminal Master's), number awarded 7/11–6/12. Industrial/Organizational Psychology PhD (Doctor of Philosophy) 4, Industrial/Organizational Psychology MA/MS (Master of Arts/Science) (T) 11.

Student Applications/Admissions:
Student Applications
Industrial/Organizational Psychology PhD (Doctor of Philosophy)—Applications 2012–2013, 12. Total applicants accepted 2012–2013, 11. Number full-time enrolled (new admits only) 2012–2013, 6. Number part-time enrolled (new admits only) 2012–2013, 1. Total enrolled 2012–2013 full-time, 21. Total enrolled 2012–2013 part-time, 26. Openings 2013–2014, 8. The median number of years required for completion of a degree in 2012–2013 were 4. The number of students enrolled full- and part-time who were dismissed or voluntarily withdrew from this program area in 2012–2013 were 0. *Industrial/Organizational Psychology MA/MS (Master of Arts/Science)*—Applications 2012–2013, 12. Total applicants accepted 2012–2013, 5. Number full-time enrolled (new admits only) 2012–2013, 4. Number part-time enrolled (new admits only) 2012–2013, 0. Total enrolled 2012–2013 full-time, 6. Total enrolled 2012–2013 part-time, 3. Openings 2013–2014, 5. The median number of years required for completion of a degree in 2012–2013 were 2. The number of students enrolled full- and part-time who were dismissed or voluntarily withdrew from this program area in 2012–2013 were 0.
Scores: Entries appear in this order: required test or GPA, minimum score (if required), median score of students entering in 2012–2013. *Industrial/Organizational Psychology PhD (Doctor of Philosophy):* overall undergraduate GPA 3.0, 3.19, psychology GPA 3.0; *Industrial/Organizational Psychology MA/MS (Master of Arts/Science):* overall undergraduate GPA 3.0, 3.00, psychology GPA 3.0.
Other Criteria: (importance of criteria rated low, medium, or high): research experience—high, work experience—high, extracurricular activity—low, clinically related public service—low, GPA—high, letters of recommendation—high, interview—high, statement of goals and objectives—high, undergraduate major in psychology—low, specific undergraduate psychology courses taken—low, Criteria vary by program. For

additional information on admission requirements, go to http://www.alliant.edu/cspp/admissions/apply/op-app-req.php.

Student Characteristics: The following represents characteristics of students in 2012–2013 in all graduate psychology programs in the department: Female—full-time 16, part-time 20; Male—full-time 11, part-time 9; African American/Black—full-time 1, part-time 4; Hispanic/Latino(a)—full-time 3, part-time 2; Asian/Pacific Islander—full-time 3, part-time 3; American Indian/Alaska Native—full-time 0, part-time 0; Caucasian/White—full-time 14, part-time 12; Multi-ethnic—full-time 2, part-time 1; students subject to the Americans With Disabilities Act—full-time 0, part-time 1; Unknown ethnicity—full-time 4, part-time 7; International students who hold an F-1 or J-1 Visa—full-time 1, part-time 1.

Financial Information/Assistance:
Tuition for Full-Time Study: *Master's:* State residents: $1,030 per credit hour; Nonstate residents: $1,030 per credit hour. *Doctoral:* State residents: $1,030 per credit hour; Nonstate residents: $1,030 per credit hour. Tuition is subject to change. See the following website for updates and changes in tuition costs: http://www.alliant.edu/admissions/tuition.php.

Financial Assistance:
First-Year Students: Research assistantships available for first year. Average amount paid per academic year: $1,000. Average number of hours worked per week: 10. Fellowships and scholarships available for first year. Average amount paid per academic year: $5,000. Apply by March 1.
Advanced Students: Teaching assistantships available for advanced students. Average amount paid per academic year: $3,000. Average number of hours worked per week: 10. Research assistantships available for advanced students. Average amount paid per academic year: $1,000. Average number of hours worked per week: 10. Fellowships and scholarships available for advanced students. Average amount paid per academic year: $5,000. Apply by March 1.
Additional Information: Of all students currently enrolled full time, 53% benefited from one or more of the listed financial assistance programs. Application and information available online at: http://www.alliant.edu/admissions/financial-aid-scholarships/.

Internships/Practica: Doctoral students may begin their practical training though the Center for Innovation and Change, working with faculty on pro bono consulting projects. A doctoral level field placement/internship is completed typically in the fourth year. Students spend 8-40 hours per week in a corporate, business, governmental, or non-profit setting. The majority of these are local to the student's campus; a few are outside the area, and are usually identified as part of a student's own career development interests. Students in the organizational psychology master's program have a one semester practicum in organizational studies.

Housing and Day Care: No on-campus housing is available. No on-campus day care facilities are available.

Employment of Department Graduates:
Master's Degree Graduates: Of those who graduated in the academic year 2011–2012, the following categories and numbers represent the postgraduate activities and employment of master's degree graduates: Enrolled in a postdoctoral residency/fellowship

(n/a), employed in independent practice (n/a), total from the above (master's) (0).

Doctoral Degree Graduates: Of those who graduated in the academic year 2011–2012, the following categories and numbers represent the postgraduate activities and employment of doctoral degree graduates: Enrolled in a psychology doctoral program (n/a), total from the above (doctoral) (0).

Additional Information:

Orientation, Objectives, and Emphasis of Department: The doctoral program is based on the philosophy that the foundations of effective organizational change are science-based, especially the science of human behavior in work settings. The program is designed to address both sides of the consultant/client relationship. The program integrates a strong foundation in the behavioral and organizational sciences; an understanding of intrapersonal and self-reflective approaches for examining human behavior; knowledge of interpersonal dynamics and political processes in professional practice, organizational interventions and consultant-clients relations; and professional experiential training. Graduates are prepared for careers in a wide variety of practice areas including management consulting, organizational assessment and design, human resources development, organizational development, diversity training and change management. The master's degree program is for those seeking preparation to begin or continue careers in organizational leadership and management. Some master's students are seeking an academic foundation for future doctoral work. Students in the programs are hired in the field as early as the first year of the program. Doctoral students find employment in such companies as Disney, JPL, City of Hope, IBM Business Consulting Services, and Korn Ferry International.

Special Facilities or Resources: At the Center for Innovation and Change in Los Angeles, graduate students apply what they are learning in the classroom by providing consulting services to non-profit organizations. Through the Center, first and second year students form consulting teams that provide pro bono service to clients in the Los Angeles area. Each consulting team works with a faculty supervisor. Thus students get practical training beginning early on in their programs.

Information for Students With Physical Disabilities: See the following website for more information: http://www.alliant.edu/about-alliant/consumer-information-heoa/disability-services.

Application Information:
Send to Alliant International University, Admissions Processing Center, 10455 Pomerado Road, San Diego, CA 92131-1799. Application available online. URL of online application: https://my.alliant.edu/ICS/Prospective_Students/. Students are admitted in the Fall, application deadline March 1; Spring, application deadline October 1. Applications are due March 1 (priority deadline) for the Fall semester and October 1 (priority deadline) for the Spring semester. The program accepts applications and admits students on a space available basis after the priority deadlines. *Fee:* $65. A limited number of fee waivers are available to those with significant financial need.

Alliant International University: Sacramento
Forensic Psychology Program
California School of Forensic Studies
2030 West El Camino Avenue, Suite 200
Sacramento, CA 95833
Telephone: (916) 565-2955
Fax: (916) 565-2959
E-mail: *brianevans@alliant.edu*
Web: *http://www.alliant.edu/csfs/index.php*

Department Information:
2008. Interim Program Director: Marion Chiurazzi, PsyD. Number of faculty: total—full-time 2, part-time 8; women—full-time 1, part-time 3; minority—part-time 1.

Programs and Degrees Offered:
Listed in the following order: Program area, degree type (T if terminal Master's), number awarded 7/11–6/12. Forensic Psychology PsyD (Doctor of Psychology) 0.

Student Applications/Admissions:
Student Applications

Forensic Psychology PsyD (Doctor of Psychology)—Applications 2012–2013, 18. Total applicants accepted 2012–2013, 15. Number full-time enrolled (new admits only) 2012–2013, 11. Number part-time enrolled (new admits only) 2012–2013, 0. Total enrolled 2012–2013 full-time, 35. Total enrolled 2012–2013 part-time, 11. Openings 2013–2014, 15. The number of students enrolled full- and part-time who were dismissed or voluntarily withdrew from this program area in 2012–2013 were 1.

Scores: Entries appear in this order: required test or GPA, minimum score (if required), median score of students entering in 2012–2013. *Forensic Psychology PsyD (Doctor of Psychology):* overall undergraduate GPA 3.0, 3.12, psychology GPA 3.0.

Other Criteria: (importance of criteria rated low, medium, or high): research experience—medium, work experience—high, extracurricular activity—low, clinically related public service—high, GPA—high, letters of recommendation—high, interview—high, statement of goals and objectives—high. For additional information on admission requirements, go to http://www.alliant.edu/csfs/admissions/admissions-requirements.php.

Student Characteristics: The following represents characteristics of students in 2012–2013 in all graduate psychology programs in the department: Female—full-time 30, part-time 9; Male—full-time 5, part-time 2; African American/Black—full-time 5, part-time 1; Hispanic/Latino(a)—full-time 6, part-time 3; Asian/Pacific Islander—full-time 3, part-time 0; American Indian/Alaska Native—full-time 0, part-time 0; Caucasian/White—full-time 15, part-time 7; Multi-ethnic—full-time 3, part-time 0; students subject to the Americans With Disabilities Act—full-time 1, part-

AMERICAN PSYCHOLOGICAL ASSOCIATION

Affiliate Membership Application

Students | High School Teachers | Community College Teachers | International

Please complete the required information below. Return your completed application with payment to:
American Psychological Association, Service Center/Membership, 750 First Street, NE, Washington, DC 20002-4242

Applicant Information

Please print clearly or type.

Name (First/Middle/Last)_____

Contact Address _____

_____

City _____

State/Province/Country_____ Zip/Postal/Country Code _____

Phone (_____) _____ Fax (_____) _____

► E-mail_____

Add phone (include area/ country code), e-mail and school or institution.

► Name of School or Institution _____

► ☐ Your contact information will be listed in the APA Membership Directory. If you wish to publish <u>only your name</u> in the directory, please check here.

Membership Category

Please check the affiliate type that best describes you. See reverse side for requirements.

Student: ☐ Graduate $56.00*   ☐ Undergraduate $35.00
Required ☐ Undergraduate with APAGS Membership $56.00*   ☐ High School $35.00
☐ Please check here if you attend a community college
*Includes membership in the American Psychological Association of Graduate Students (APAGS) and a subscription to *gradPSYCH*

Optional ☐ Graduate Student Fee to join the APA Practice Organization (APAPO): $20
☐ Graduate Student Fee to join the Education Advocacy Trust (EdAT): $20

Teacher: ☐ High School $50.00   ☐ Community College $50.00

International: ☐ Psychologists residing outside the U.S. or Canada $50.00 *Required:* Name of your national psychological association of which you are a member; or give highest degree in psychology; include date, institution, and major field of study:

_____

_____

For Students Only

All <u>U.S.</u> graduate and undergraduate student applicants <u>must</u> complete sections A, B, and C.

Ⓐ Licensure/Ethics
If the graduate degree for which you are currently enrolled is a health service provider subfield (i.e., clinical, child clinical, counseling, school, geropsychology or health), do you intend to seek licensure/certification by a state or provincial board of psychologist examiners for the independent practice of psychology?
☐ Yes, within the next year   ☐ Yes, eventually   ☐ No
☐ N/A, already licensed for the independent practice of psychology

Ⓑ Have you at any time been convicted of a felony, sanctioned by any professional ethics body, licensing board, or other regulatory body or by any professional or scientific organization? ☐ No ☐ Yes *If yes, please provide an explanation on a separate sheet of paper.*

In submitting this application, I subscribe to and will support the objectives of the American Psychological Association as set forth in Article 1 of the Bylaws, and the Ethical Principles of Psychologists and Code of Conduct, as adopted by the Association, and I affirm that the statements made in this application correctly represent my qualifications for election, and understand that if they do not, my affiliation may be voided.

The Ethical Principles of Psychologists and Code of Conduct is available on APA's Website at http://www.apa.org/ethics/. The Bylaws are available at http://www.apa.org/about/governance/. Copies of these documents are also available upon request.

All students must sign section C. **Ⓒ** Signature _____ Date _____

Additional Information

The following items are <u>voluntary</u> and are used for research purposes only.

☐ Male   ☐ Female   ☐ Transgender   Date of birth (MM/DD/YY) _____

What is your race/ethnicity? *(Mark all that apply)*
☐ American Indian or Alaska Native   ☐ Hispanic/Latino(a)   ☐ African American/Black
☐ Caucasian/White   ☐ Asian or Pacific Islander   ☐ Other (Specify)_____

Payment Method

Applications will not be processed without payment. All payments must be drawn on a U.S. bank in U.S. dollars.

APA membership is based on the calendar year (January–December). See membership requirements on reverse side.

I am paying my total of $_____ by:
☐ Check or money order Check #_____ payable to the American Psychological Association
☐ American Express   ☐ MasterCard   ☐ Visa

Account Number _____ Expiration Date_____

Cardholder Name_____

Credit Card Billing Address _____

City/State/ZIP/Country/Country Code _____

Daytime Telephone Number (_____)_____

Signature of Credit Card Holder (Required) _____

GS13

AMERICAN
PSYCHOLOGICAL
ASSOCIATION

Affiliate Membership Requirements Summary

Student requirements: High school, undergraduate and graduate students taking courses in psychology can become APA student affiliates. Graduate student affiliates are automatically enrolled in the American Psychological Association of Graduate Students (APAGS). Undergraduate affiliates may choose to join APAGS by paying the same rate as graduate students. Students must have a doctoral degree in psychology or a related field from a regionally accredited graduate or professional school (or a school that achieved such accreditation within 5 years of the awarding of your doctoral degree, or a school of similar standing outside of the United States) to become a full **Member** of APA.

Teacher requirements: Teachers of psychology in high schools, junior colleges and community colleges qualify as APA teacher affiliates. High school teacher affiliates are automatically members of Teachers of Psychology in Secondary Schools (TOPSS), an APA organization. Community college teacher affiliates receive membership in Psychology Teachers at Community Colleges (PT@CC), also an APA organization.

Psychologists residing in countries other than the United States or Canada: May become APA international affiliates by providing required documentation indicating membership in your country's national psychology organization or evidence of appropriate qualifications. Psychologists in developing world or transition economy countries may contact APA to receive a nominal discount off their dues.

Complete membership requirements: Are available from APA's Service Center/Membership (see below for contact information).

Dues: Payment must accompany application. Applications without payment can not be processed. Payment must be made in United States dollars, drawn on a U.S. bank. Forms of payment include credit card, bank check and money order (contact APA for other forms of payment). APA affiliate dues (stated on the front of this application) are substantially discounted, over 75% off 2013 full member rates.

Graduate Student Fee to join the APA Practice Organization (APAPO): After joining APAGS ($56), graduate student affiliates who are are interested in health and mental health services have the option to also join APAPO. Declining to join APAPO does not affect your status as a student affiliate of APA. For information about APAPO and benefits of membership visit http://www.apapracticecentral.org.

Graduate Student Fee to join the Education Advocacy Trust (EdAT): After joining APAGS ($56), graduate students affiliates have the option to also join EdAT. Declining to join EdAT does not affect your status as a student affiliate of APA. For more information about EdAT visit http://www.apaedat.org.

Membership term: APA membership is based on the calendar year (January–December). If your application is approved in September through December of the current year, your membership (including your subscriptions to the *Monitor on Psychology* and the *American Psychologist*) will automatically be extended to the end of the following year.

Standard inclusions: All APA affiliates receive a subscription to the *Monitor on Psychology* (11 issues*). Student affiliates and teacher affiliates also receive a subscription to *American Psychologist* (9 issues*). APAGS members receive a subscription to *gradPSYCH* (4 issues*).

Membership also includes substantial discounts (up to 60%) on various APA publications and electronic products. A detailed list of publications will be sent to you upon acceptance of your application.

Delivery of products and services: Allow 3–4 weeks for the processing of your application and 6–8 weeks for the initial delivery of your APA publications. International orders are sent via surface mail and may take longer.

APA Member and Affiliate Directory: Upon your acceptance, your contact information will be automatically included in the official directory, which is a main source of member-to-member communication. To publish <u>only your name</u> in the directory, please check the appropriate box on the front of this application.

For questions or additional information:

Service Center/Membership: 1(202) 336-5580; 1(800) 374-2721 (within the U.S. and Canada); or TDD/TTY: 1(202) 336-6123; Fax: 1(202) 336-5568, Email: membership@apa.org; Web: http://www.apa.org

Return your completed application to: American Psychological Association, Service Center/Membership, 750 First Street, NE, Washington, DC 20002-4242

*$6 of APA dues is allocated toward the *Monitor on Psychology* subscription and $12 of APA dues is allocated toward the *American Psychologist* subscription. If you receive *gradPSYCH*, $3 of APA dues is allocated toward the subscription.

time 0; Unknown ethnicity—full-time 3, part-time 0; International students who hold an F-1 or J-1 Visa—full-time 0, part-time 0.

Financial Information/Assistance:

Tuition for Full-Time Study: *Doctoral:* State residents: $1,030 per credit hour; Nonstate residents: $1,030 per credit hour. Tuition is subject to change. See the following website for updates and changes in tuition costs: http://www.alliant.edu/admissions/tuition.php.

Financial Assistance:

First-Year Students: Research assistantships available for first year. Average amount paid per academic year: $1,000. Average number of hours worked per week: 10. Fellowships and scholarships available for first year. Average amount paid per academic year: $1,500. Apply by February 15.

Advanced Students: Teaching assistantships available for advanced students. Average amount paid per academic year: $3,000. Average number of hours worked per week: 20. Research assistantships available for advanced students. Average amount paid per academic year: $1,000. Average number of hours worked per week: 10. Fellowships and scholarships available for advanced students. Average amount paid per academic year: $1,500. Apply by February 15.

Additional Information: Application and information available online at: http://www.alliant.edu/admissions/financial-aid-scholarships/.

Internships/Practica: Doctoral Degree (PsyD Forensic Psychology): For those doctoral students for whom a professional psychology internship was required in this program prior to graduation, (9) students applied for an internship in 2011–2012, with (9) students obtaining an internship. Of those students who obtained an internship, (8) were paid internships. Of those students who obtained an internship, (1) students placed in APA/CPA accredited internships, (4) students placed in internships not APA/CPA accredited, but listed with the Association of Psychology Postdoctoral and Internship Programs (APPIC), (0) students placed in internships conforming to guidelines of the Council of Directors of School Psychology Programs (CDSPP), (4) students placed in internships that were not APA/CPA accredited, APPIC or CDSPP listed. Students are provided opportunities to apply the knowledge gained during their coursework through the first, second, and third year practica. Practicum placements are 10 to 20 hour weekly training commitments at one of CSFS's community training partners, which include adult and youth correctional facilities, department of mental health agencies, and community organizations. Through these experiences, students are introduced to the role of clinical psychologists, exposed to a wide range of differing populations and mental health issues and are provided with direct experience in clinical interviewing, cognitive and personality assessment, as well as evidenced-informed and evidence-based treatment interventions. The program culminates in a 2,000-hour internship in students' fourth year of study that focuses upon clinical intervention, psychological assessment, professional development and lifelong learning, multicultural issues, professional ethics and standards, supervision and consultation and advocacy. During this experience, students work with increasing independence to apply the knowl-

edge and skills gained during the preceding years, supporting future success as independent professional psychologists.

Housing and Day Care: No on-campus housing is available. No on-campus day care facilities are available.

Employment of Department Graduates:

Master's Degree Graduates: Of those who graduated in the academic year 2011–2012, the following categories and numbers represent the postgraduate activities and employment of master's degree graduates: Enrolled in a postdoctoral residency/fellowship (n/a), employed in independent practice (n/a), total from the above (master's) (0).

Doctoral Degree Graduates: Of those who graduated in the academic year 2011–2012, the following categories and numbers represent the postgraduate activities and employment of doctoral degree graduates: Enrolled in a psychology doctoral program (n/a), total from the above (doctoral) (0).

Additional Information:

Orientation, Objectives, and Emphasis of Department: The California School of Forensic Studies Clinical Forensic Psychology PsyD program employs a practitioner-scholar model of education to support students to acquire core clinical competencies. The program is for students who have an interest in pursuing forensic post-doctoral training, practice in forensic settings — such as in correctional facilities or forensic mental health hospitals — and/or pursuing private practice conducting forensic assessment or mandated treatment. The Clinical Forensic Psychology program supports the development of competency in foundational clinical areas, including professionalism, reflective practice/self-assessment/self-care, scientific knowledge and practice, relationships, individual and cultural diversity awareness, ethical legal standards, interdisciplinary systems, assessment, intervention, supervision and advocacy. The program also supports the development of fundamental competencies appropriate to the practice of clinical psychology in forensic-specific contexts, with an emphasis on specialty ethical guidelines, forensic assessment and mandated intervention/treatment.

Information for Students With Physical Disabilities: See the following website for more information: http://www.alliant.edu/about-alliant/consumer-information-heoa/disability-services.

Application Information:

Send to Alliant International University, Admissions Processing Center, 10455 Pomerado Road, San Diego, CA 92131-1799. Application available online. URL of online application: https://my.alliant.edu/ICS/Prospective_Students/. Students are admitted in the Fall, application deadline January; Programs have rolling admissions. Applicants wishing notification by April 1 should submit their applications in January. However, applications are welcomed on a rolling basis and will be processed on a space available basis. *Fee:* $65. A limited number of fee waivers are available for those with significant financial need. Please contact the Director of Admissions for details.

Alliant International University: Sacramento
Programs in Clinical Psychology and Couple and Family
  Therapy
California School of Professional Psychology
2030 West El Camino Avenue, Suite 200
Sacramento, CA 95833
Telephone: (916) 561-3230
Fax: (916) 565-2959
E-mail: *mschwartz@alliant.edu*
Web: *http://www.alliant.edu/cspp/index.php*

Department Information:
1999. Dean, California School of Professional Psychology: Morgan
T. Sammons, PhD, ABPP. Number of faculty: total—full-time
16, part-time 24; women—full-time 6, part-time 15; total—minority—full-time 4, part-time 3; women minority—part-time 2.

Programs and Degrees Offered:
Listed in the following order: Program area, degree type (T if
terminal Master's), number awarded 7/11–6/12. Marital and Family Therapy MA/MS (Master of Arts/Science) (T) 18, Marital
and Family Therapy PsyD (Doctor of Psychology) 1, Clinical
Psychology PsyD (Doctor of Psychology) 4.

APA Accreditation: On Probation PsyD (Doctor of Psychology). Student Outcome Data Website: http://www.alliant.edu/cspp/programs-
degrees/clinical-psychology/clinical_psyd_sacramento/.

Student Applications/Admissions:
Student Applications
  Marital and Family Therapy MA/MS (Master of Arts/Science)—
Applications 2012–2013, 33. Total applicants accepted 2012–
2013, 22. Number full-time enrolled (new admits only) 2012–
2013, 16. Number part-time enrolled (new admits only) 2012–
2013, 0. Total enrolled 2012–2013 full-time, 29. Total enrolled
2012–2013 part-time, 4. Openings 2013–2014, 20. The median
number of years required for completion of a degree in 2012–
2013 were 2. The number of students enrolled full- and part-
time who were dismissed or voluntarily withdrew from this
program area in 2012–2013 were 0. *Marital and Family Therapy
PsyD (Doctor of Psychology)*—Applications 2012–2013, 12.
Total applicants accepted 2012–2013, 8. Number full-time
enrolled (new admits only) 2012–2013, 3. Number part-time
enrolled (new admits only) 2012–2013, 1. Total enrolled
2012–2013 full-time, 19. Total enrolled 2012–2013 part-time,
13. Openings 2013–2014, 5. The median number of years
required for completion of a degree in 2012–2013 were 4. The
number of students enrolled full- and part-time who were
dismissed or voluntarily withdrew from this program area in
2012–2013 were 0. *Clinical Psychology PsyD (Doctor of Psychology)*—Applications 2012–2013, 72. Total applicants accepted
2012–2013, 16. Number full-time enrolled (new admits only)
2012–2013, 8. Number part-time enrolled (new admits only)
2012–2013, 1. Total enrolled 2012–2013 full-time, 49. Total
enrolled 2012–2013 part-time, 21. Openings 2013–2014, 15.
The median number of years required for completion of a
degree in 2012–2013 were 4. The number of students enrolled
full- and part-time who were dismissed or voluntarily withdrew
from this program area in 2012–2013 were 1.

Scores: Entries appear in this order: required test or GPA,
minimum score (if required), median score of students entering
in 2012–2013. *Marital and Family Therapy MA/MS (Master of
Arts/Science)*: overall undergraduate GPA 3.0, 3.09, psychology GPA 3.0; *Marital and Family Therapy PsyD (Doctor of
Psychology)*: overall undergraduate GPA 3.0, 3.00, psychology
GPA 3.0; *Clinical Psychology PsyD (Doctor of Psychology)*: overall undergraduate GPA 3.0, 3.15, psychology GPA 3.0.
Other Criteria: (importance of criteria rated low, medium,
or high): research experience—medium, work experience—
medium, extracurricular activity—low, clinically related public service—medium, GPA—high, letters of recommendation—medium, interview—high, statement of goals and objectives—high, undergraduate major in psychology—medium,
specific undergraduate psychology courses taken—medium.
For additional information on admission requirements, go to
http://www.alliant.edu/cspp/.

Student Characteristics: The following represents characteristics
of students in 2012–2013 in all graduate psychology programs in
the department: Female—full-time 74, part-time 31; Male—full-
time 23, part-time 7; African American/Black—full-time 10, part-
time 2; Hispanic/Latino(a)—full-time 5, part-time 2; Asian/Pa-
cific Islander—full-time 8, part-time 5; American Indian/Alaska
Native—full-time 0, part-time 0; Caucasian/White—full-time 57,
part-time 24; Multi-ethnic—full-time 6, part-time 3; students
subject to the Americans With Disabilities Act—full-time 2, part-
time 0; Unknown ethnicity—full-time 11, part-time 2; International students who hold an F-1 or J-1 Visa—full-time 0, part-
time 0.

Financial Information/Assistance:
Tuition for Full-Time Study: *Master's:* State residents: $1,030
per credit hour; Nonstate residents: $1,030 per credit hour. *Doc-
toral:* State residents: $1,030 per credit hour; Nonstate residents:
$1,030 per credit hour. Tuition is subject to change. See the
following website for updates and changes in tuition costs: http://
www.alliant.edu/admissions/tuition.php.

Financial Assistance:
  First-Year Students: Fellowships and scholarships available
for first year. Average amount paid per academic year: $5,000.
Apply by December 15.
  Advanced Students: Teaching assistantships available for
advanced students. Average amount paid per academic year:
$3,000. Average number of hours worked per week: 10. Research
assistantships available for advanced students. Average amount
paid per academic year: $1,000. Average number of hours worked
per week: 10. Fellowships and scholarships available for advanced
students. Average amount paid per academic year: $5,000. Apply
by December 15.
  Additional Information: Of all students currently enrolled
full time, 65% benefited from one or more of the listed financial
assistance programs. Application and information available online
at: http://www.alliant.edu/admissions/financial-aid-scholarships/.

Internships/Practica: Doctoral Degree (PsyD Clinical Psychology): For those doctoral students for whom a professional psychology internship was required in this program prior to graduation,
(28) students applied for an internship in 2011–2012, with (24)
students obtaining an internship. Of those students who obtained
an internship, (17) were paid internships. Of those students who

obtained an internship, (2) students placed in APA/CPA accredited internships, (9) students placed in internships not APA/CPA accredited, but listed with the Association of Psychology Postdoctoral and Internship Programs (APPIC), (0) students placed in internships conforming to guidelines of the Council of Directors of School Psychology Programs (CDSPP), (13) students placed in internships that were not APA/CPA accredited, APPIC or CDSPP listed. The clinical psychology program emphasizes the integration of academic coursework and research with clinical practice. In order to integrate appropriate skills with material learned in the classroom, students participate in a professional training placement experience beginning in the first year. The settings where students complete the professional training requirements include community mental health centers, clinics, inpatient mental health facilities, medical settings, specialized service centers, rehabilitation programs, residential/day care programs, forensic/correctional facilities, and educational programs. During their final year, clinical students complete an appropriate APA, APPIC, or CAPIC internship. As part of the practicum for the CFT program experience, students complete 500 client contact hours, 250 of which must be with couples and families. Students receive at least 100 hours of individual and group supervision, 50 hours of which are based on direct observation, videotape, or audiotape. At least 25 of those hours must be videotaped or direct observation. When students are ready to begin practicum, experienced faculty and staff assist students through each step in obtaining a field placement site approved by Alliant. While students are doing practicum training they are required to perform marriage and family therapy under a California state licensed, AAMFT-approved supervisor or the equivalent.

Housing and Day Care: No on-campus housing is available. No on-campus day care facilities are available.

Employment of Department Graduates:
Master's Degree Graduates: Of those who graduated in the academic year 2011–2012, the following categories and numbers represent the postgraduate activities and employment of master's degree graduates: Enrolled in a postdoctoral residency/fellowship (n/a), employed in independent practice (n/a), total from the above (master's) (0).
Doctoral Degree Graduates: Of those who graduated in the academic year 2011–2012, the following categories and numbers represent the postgraduate activities and employment of doctoral degree graduates: Enrolled in a psychology doctoral program (n/a), total from the above (doctoral) (0).

Additional Information:
Orientation, Objectives, and Emphasis of Department: The clinical psychology PsyD program emphasizes training in clinical skills and clinical application of research knowledge and is designed for students who are interested in careers as practitioners but it also includes a research component. The program is multisystemically or ecosystemically oriented and trains students to consider the role of diverse systems in creating and/or remedying individual and social problems. An empirical PsyD dissertation is required and may focus on program development and/or evaluation, test development, survey research or therapeutic outcomes. The mission of the Couple and Family Therapy Program is to prepare graduate students who are skilled in the theory, research, and clinical practice of the field of Marriage and Family Therapy and can integrate individual and systemic therapeutic models in an

international, multicultural environment. The Couple and Family Therapy (CFT) programs provide students with the essential training needed to pursue a career as a professional Marriage and Family Therapist (MFT). The Master of Arts in MFT allows students to be licensed as an MFT and the Doctor of Psychology (PsyD) in MFT prepares students with academic and research experience. Students who complete the MFT Master's at Alliant can apply all of their Master's degree coursework and practicum hours toward the doctoral program. The programs are accredited by COAMFTE.

Information for Students With Physical Disabilities: See the following website for more information: http://www.alliant.edu/about-alliant/consumer-information-heoa/disability-services.

Application Information:
Send to Alliant International University Admissions Processing Center, 10455 Pomerado Road, San Diego, CA 92131-1799. Application available online. URL of online application: https://my.alliant.edu/ICS/Prospective_Students/. Students are admitted in the Fall, application deadline December 15. The Clinical Psychology programs have a December 15 priority deadline in order to provide a response by April 1 for applicants who need a decision by that date. The CFT programs have a January 15 priority deadline for the Fall semester. Programs accept applications and admit students on a space available basis after any stated deadlines. *Fee:* $65. A limited number of fee waivers are available for those with significant financial need.

Alliant International University: San Diego
Forensic Psychology Programs
California School of Forensic Studies
10455 Pomerado Road
San Diego, CA 92131
Telephone: (858) 635-4772
Fax: (858) 635-4739
E-mail: *avarnes@alliant.edu*
Web: *http://www.alliant.edu/csfs/index.php*

Department Information:
2008. Interim Progam Director: Glenn Scott Lipson, PhD. Number of faculty: total—full-time 3, part-time 7; women—part-time 5.

Programs and Degrees Offered:
Listed in the following order: Program area, degree type (T if terminal Master's), number awarded 7/11–6/12. Forensic Psychology PsyD (Doctor of Psychology) 1.

Student Applications/Admissions:
Student Applications
Forensic Psychology PsyD (Doctor of Psychology)—Applications 2012–2013, 32. Total applicants accepted 2012–2013, 27. Number full-time enrolled (new admits only) 2012–2013, 9. Number part-time enrolled (new admits only) 2012–2013, 0. Total enrolled 2012–2013 full-time, 59. Total enrolled 2012–2013 part-time, 10. Openings 2013–2014, 25. The median number of years required for completion of a degree in 2012–2013 were 5. The number of students enrolled full- and part-

time who were dismissed or voluntarily withdrew from this program area in 2012–2013 were 0.

Scores: Entries appear in this order: required test or GPA, minimum score (if required), median score of students entering in 2012–2013. *Forensic Psychology PsyD (Doctor of Psychology):* overall undergraduate GPA 3.0, 3.22, psychology GPA 3.0, Masters GPA 3.0, 3.00.

Other Criteria: (importance of criteria rated low, medium, or high): research experience—medium, work experience—high, extracurricular activity—low, clinically related public service—high, GPA—high, letters of recommendation—high, interview—high, statement of goals and objectives—high. For additional information on admission requirements, go to http://www.alliant.edu/csfs/admissions/admissions-requirements.php.

Student Characteristics: The following represents characteristics of students in 2012–2013 in all graduate psychology programs in the department: Female—full-time 50, part-time 6; Male—full-time 9, part-time 4; African American/Black—full-time 3, part-time 0; Hispanic/Latino(a)—full-time 7, part-time 0; Asian/Pacific Islander—full-time 6, part-time 0; American Indian/Alaska Native—full-time 0, part-time 0; Caucasian/White—full-time 36, part-time 8; Multi-ethnic—full-time 3, part-time 0; students subject to the Americans With Disabilities Act—full-time 1, part-time 0; Unknown ethnicity—full-time 4, part-time 2; International students who hold an F-1 or J-1 Visa—full-time 0, part-time 0.

Financial Information/Assistance:

Tuition for Full-Time Study: *Doctoral:* State residents: $1,030 per credit hour; Nonstate residents: $1,030 per credit hour. Tuition is subject to change. See the following website for updates and changes in tuition costs: http://www.alliant.edu/admissions/tuition.php.

Financial Assistance:

First-Year Students: Research assistantships available for first year. Average amount paid per academic year: $1,000. Average number of hours worked per week: 10. Fellowships and scholarships available for first year. Average amount paid per academic year: $1,500. Apply by February 15.

Advanced Students: Teaching assistantships available for advanced students. Average amount paid per academic year: $3,000. Average number of hours worked per week: 20. Research assistantships available for advanced students. Average amount paid per academic year: $1,000. Average number of hours worked per week: 10. Fellowships and scholarships available for advanced students. Average amount paid per academic year: $1,500. Apply by February 15.

Additional Information: Application and information available online at: http://www.alliant.edu/admissions/financial-aid-scholarships/.

Internships/Practica: Doctoral Degree (PsyD Forensic Psychology): For those doctoral students for whom a professional psychology internship was required in this program prior to graduation, (8) students applied for an internship in 2011–2012, with (8) students obtaining an internship. Of those students who obtained an internship, (5) were paid internships. Of those students who obtained an internship, (0) students placed in APA/CPA accredited internships, (5) students placed in internships not APA/

CPA accredited, but listed with the Association of Psychology Postdoctoral and Internship Programs (APPIC), (0) students placed in internships conforming to guidelines of the Council of Directors of School Psychology Programs (CDSPP), (3) students placed in internships that were not APA/CPA accredited, APPIC or CDSPP listed. Students are provided opportunities to apply the knowledge gained during their coursework through the first, second, and third year practica. Practicum placements are 10 to 20 hour weekly training commitments at one of CSFS's community training partners, which include adult and youth correctional facilities, department of mental health agencies, and community organizations. Through these experiences, students are introduced to the role of clinical psychologists, exposed to a wide range of differing populations and mental health issues and are provided with direct experience in clinical interviewing, cognitive and personality assessment, as well as evidenced-informed and evidence-based treatment interventions. The program culminates in a 2,000-hour internship in students' fourth year of study that focuses upon clinical intervention, psychological assessment, professional development and lifelong learning, multicultural issues, professional ethics and standards, supervision and consultation and advocacy. During this experience, students work with increasing independence to apply the knowledge and skills gained during the preceding years, supporting future success as independent professional psychologists.

Housing and Day Care: On-campus housing is available. See the following website for more information: http://www.alliant.edu/locations/san-diego-campus/housing-dining.php. No on-campus day care facilities are available.

Employment of Department Graduates:

Master's Degree Graduates: Of those who graduated in the academic year 2011–2012, the following categories and numbers represent the postgraduate activities and employment of master's degree graduates: Enrolled in a postdoctoral residency/fellowship (n/a), employed in independent practice (n/a), total from the above (master's) (0).

Doctoral Degree Graduates: Of those who graduated in the academic year 2011–2012, the following categories and numbers represent the postgraduate activities and employment of doctoral degree graduates: Enrolled in a psychology doctoral program (n/a), total from the above (doctoral) (0).

Additional Information:

Orientation, Objectives, and Emphasis of Department: The California School of Forensic Studies Clinical Forensic Psychology PsyD program employs a practitioner-scholar model of education to support students to acquire core clinical competencies. The program is for students who have an interest in pursuing forensic post-doctoral training, practice in forensic settings — such as in correctional facilities or forensic mental health hospitals — and/or pursuing private practice conducting forensic assessment or mandated treatment. The Clinical Forensic Psychology program supports the development of competency in foundational clinical areas, including professionalism, reflective practice/self-assessment/self-care, scientific knowledge and practice, relationships, individual and cultural diversity awareness, ethical legal standards, interdisciplinary systems, assessment, intervention, supervision and advocacy. The program also supports the development of fundamental competencies appropriate to the practice of clinical psychology in forensic-specific contexts, with an emphasis on specialty ethical guidelines, forensic assessment and mandated intervention/treatment.

Information for Students With Physical Disabilities: See the following website for more information: http://www.alliant.edu/about-alliant/consumer-information-heoa/disability-services.

Application Information:

Send to Alliant International University, Admissions Processing Center, 10455 Pomerado Road, San Diego, CA 92131-1799. Application available online. URL of online application: https://my.alliant.edu/ICS/Prospective_Students/. Students are admitted in the Fall, application deadline January; Programs have rolling admissions. Applicants wishing notification by April 1 should submit their applications in January, however, applications are welcomed on a rolling basis and will be processed on a space available basis. *Fee:* $65. A limited number of fee waivers are available for those with significant financial need.

Alliant International University: San Diego
Programs in Clinical Psychology and Couple and Family
  Therapy
California School of Professional Psychology
10455 Pomerado Road
San Diego, CA 92131-1799
Telephone: (858) 635-4820
Fax: (858) 635-4739
E-mail: *mschwartz@alliant.edu*
Web: *http://www.alliant.edu/cspp/*

Department Information:

1972. Dean, California School of Professional Psychology: Morgan T. Sammons, PhD, ABPP. Number of faculty: total—full-time 42, part-time 60; women—full-time 17, part-time 30; total—minority—full-time 5, part-time 4; women minority—full-time 2, part-time 2.

Programs and Degrees Offered:

Listed in the following order: Program area, degree type (T if terminal Master's), number awarded 7/11–6/12. Clinical Psychology PhD (Doctor of Philosophy) 41, Clinical Psychology PsyD (Doctor of Psychology) 40, Clinical Psychology Respecialization Diploma 0, Marital and Family Therapy MA/MS (Master of Arts/Science) (T) 42, Marital and Family Therapy PsyD (Doctor of Psychology) 2.

APA Accreditation: Clinical PhD (Doctor of Philosophy). Student Outcome Data Website: http://www.alliant.edu/cspp/programs-degrees/clinical-psychology/clinical_phd_san-diego/index.php. Clinical PsyD (Doctor of Psychology). Student Outcome Data Website: http://www.alliant.edu/cspp/programs-degrees/clinical-psychology/psyd-sandiego.php.

Student Applications/Admissions:

Student Applications

Clinical Psychology PhD (Doctor of Philosophy)—Applications 2012–2013, 93. Total applicants accepted 2012–2013, 40. Number full-time enrolled (new admits only) 2012–2013, 22. Number part-time enrolled (new admits only) 2012–2013, 0.

Total enrolled 2012–2013 full-time, 118. Total enrolled 2012–2013 part-time, 83. Openings 2013–2014, 25. The median number of years required for completion of a degree in 2012–2013 were 6. The number of students enrolled full- and part-time who were dismissed or voluntarily withdrew from this program area in 2012–2013 were 1. *Clinical Psychology PsyD (Doctor of Psychology)*—Applications 2012–2013, 186. Total applicants accepted 2012–2013, 67. Number full-time enrolled (new admits only) 2012–2013, 38. Number part-time enrolled (new admits only) 2012–2013, 0. Total enrolled 2012–2013 full-time, 143. Total enrolled 2012–2013 part-time, 91. Openings 2013–2014, 42. The median number of years required for completion of a degree in 2012–2013 were 6. The number of students enrolled full- and part-time who were dismissed or voluntarily withdrew from this program area in 2012–2013 were 1. *Clinical Psychology Respecialization Diploma*—Applications 2012–2013, 0. Total applicants accepted 2012–2013, 0. Number full-time enrolled (new admits only) 2012–2013, 0. Number part-time enrolled (new admits only) 2012–2013, 0. Total enrolled 2012–2013 full-time, 1. Total enrolled 2012–2013 part-time, 0. Openings 2013–2014, 1. The number of students enrolled full- and part-time who were dismissed or voluntarily withdrew from this program area in 2012–2013 were 0. *Marital and Family Therapy MA/MS (Master of Arts/Science)*—Applications 2012–2013, 102. Total applicants accepted 2012–2013, 64. Number full-time enrolled (new admits only) 2012–2013, 38. Number part-time enrolled (new admits only) 2012–2013, 4. Total enrolled 2012–2013 full-time, 74. Total enrolled 2012–2013 part-time, 17. Openings 2013–2014, 40. The median number of years required for completion of a degree in 2012–2013 were 2. The number of students enrolled full- and part-time who were dismissed or voluntarily withdrew from this program area in 2012–2013 were 1. *Marital and Family Therapy PsyD (Doctor of Psychology)*—Applications 2012–2013, 30. Total applicants accepted 2012–2013, 13. Number full-time enrolled (new admits only) 2012–2013, 5. Number part-time enrolled (new admits only) 2012–2013, 2. Total enrolled 2012–2013 full-time, 28. Total enrolled 2012–2013 part-time, 41. Openings 2013–2014, 10. The median number of years required for completion of a degree in 2012–2013 were 6. The number of students enrolled full- and part-time who were dismissed or voluntarily withdrew from this program area in 2012–2013 were 1.

Scores: Entries appear in this order: required test or GPA, minimum score (if required), median score of students entering in 2012–2013. *Clinical Psychology PhD (Doctor of Philosophy):* overall undergraduate GPA 3.0, 3.44, psychology GPA 3.0; *Clinical Psychology PsyD (Doctor of Psychology):* overall undergraduate GPA 3.0, 3.38, psychology GPA 3.0, Masters GPA 3.0, 3.79; *Clinical Psychology Respecialization Diploma:* overall undergraduate GPA 3.0, psychology GPA 3.0; *Marital and Family Therapy MA/MS (Master of Arts/Science):* overall undergraduate GPA 3.0, 3.14, psychology GPA 3.0; *Marital and Family Therapy PsyD (Doctor of Psychology):* overall undergraduate GPA 3.0, 3.00, psychology GPA 3.0.

Other Criteria: (importance of criteria rated low, medium, or high): research experience—medium, work experience—medium, extracurricular activity—low, clinically related public service—medium, GPA—high, letters of recommendation—medium, interview—high, statement of goals and objectives—high, undergraduate major in psychology—medium, specific undergraduate psychology courses taken—medium.

For additional information on admission requirements, go to http://www.alliant.edu/cspp.

Student Characteristics: The following represents characteristics of students in 2012–2013 in all graduate psychology programs in the department: Female—full-time 294, part-time 192; Male—full-time 70, part-time 40; African American/Black—full-time 12, part-time 13; Hispanic/Latino(a)—full-time 36, part-time 29; Asian/Pacific Islander—full-time 28, part-time 21; American Indian/Alaska Native—full-time 3, part-time 4; Caucasian/White—full-time 217, part-time 138; Multi-ethnic—full-time 12, part-time 5; students subject to the Americans With Disabilities Act—full-time 8, part-time 3; Unknown ethnicity—full-time 56, part-time 22; International students who hold an F-1 or J-1 Visa—full-time 4, part-time 2.

Financial Information/Assistance:

Tuition for Full-Time Study: *Master's:* State residents: $1,030 per credit hour; Nonstate residents: $1,030 per credit hour. *Doctoral:* State residents: $1,030 per credit hour; Nonstate residents: $1,030 per credit hour. Tuition is subject to change. See the following website for updates and changes in tuition costs: http://www.alliant.edu/admissions/tuition.php.

Financial Assistance:

First-Year Students: Research assistantships available for first year. Average amount paid per academic year: $1,000. Average number of hours worked per week: 10. Fellowships and scholarships available for first year. Average amount paid per academic year: $5,000. Apply by December 15.

Advanced Students: Teaching assistantships available for advanced students. Average amount paid per academic year: $3,000. Average number of hours worked per week: 10. Research assistantships available for advanced students. Average amount paid per academic year: $1,000. Average number of hours worked per week: 10. Fellowships and scholarships available for advanced students. Average amount paid per academic year: $5,000. Apply by December 15.

Additional Information: Of all students currently enrolled full time, 62% benefited from one or more of the listed financial assistance programs. Application and information available online at: http://www.alliant.edu/admissions/financial-aid-scholarships/.

Internships/Practica: Doctoral Degree (PhD Clinical Psychology): For those doctoral students for whom a professional psychology internship was required in this program prior to graduation, (28) students applied for an internship in 2011–2012, with (22) students obtaining an internship. Of those students who obtained an internship, (18) were paid internships. Of those students who obtained an internship, (6) students placed in APA/CPA accredited internships, (1) students placed in internships not APA/CPA accredited, but listed with the Association of Psychology Postdoctoral and Internship Programs (APPIC), (0) students placed in internships conforming to guidelines of the Council of Directors of School Psychology Programs (CDSPP), (15) students placed in internships that were not APA/CPA accredited, APPIC or CDSPP listed. Doctoral Degree (PsyD Clinical Psychology): For those doctoral students for whom a professional psychology internship was required in this program prior to graduation, (52) students applied for an internship in 2011–2012, with (50) students obtaining an internship. Of those students who obtained an internship, (31) were paid internships. Of those students who

obtained an internship, (6) students placed in APA/CPA accredited internships, (3) students placed in internships not APA/CPA accredited, but listed with the Association of Psychology Postdoctoral and Internship Programs (APPIC), (0) students placed in internships conforming to guidelines of the Council of Directors of School Psychology Programs (CDSPP), (41) students placed in internships that were not APA/CPA accredited, APPIC or CDSPP listed. Clinical psychology doctoral students receive practicum and internship experience at more than 80 agencies which meet the requirements for licensure set by the California Board of Psychology. Assignments to these agencies result from an application process conducted by year level, with third, fourth, and fifth year students receiving priority for licensable placements. The option of doing an APA-accredited full-time internship in the fourth or fifth years (depending on the program and year level requirements) is available and encouraged. Couple and family therapy students complete a required practicum including 500 client contact hours, 250 of which must be with couples and families. Students receive at least 100 hours of individual and group supervision, 50 hours of which are based on direct observation, videotape, or audiotape. At least 25 of those hours must be videotape or direct observation. While students are doing practicum training, they are required to perform marriage and family therapy under a California state-licensed, AAMFT-approved supervisor or the equivalent. CFT doctoral students complete a predoctoral internship.

Housing and Day Care: On-campus housing is available. See the following website for more information: http://www.alliant.edu/locations/san-diego-campus/housing-dining.php. No on-campus day care facilities are available.

Employment of Department Graduates:

Master's Degree Graduates: Of those who graduated in the academic year 2011–2012, the following categories and numbers represent the postgraduate activities and employment of master's degree graduates: Enrolled in a postdoctoral residency/fellowship (n/a), employed in independent practice (n/a), total from the above (master's) (0).

Doctoral Degree Graduates: Of those who graduated in the academic year 2011–2012, the following categories and numbers represent the postgraduate activities and employment of doctoral degree graduates: Enrolled in a psychology doctoral program (n/a), total from the above (doctoral) (0).

Additional Information:

Orientation, Objectives, and Emphasis of Department: The California School of Professional Psychology (CSPP) at Alliant International University offers comprehensive PhD and PsyD programs of instruction in professional psychology with an emphasis on doctoral training in clinical psychology in which academic requirements are integrated with supervised field experience. Students are evaluated by instructors and field supervisors on the basis of their performance and participation throughout the year. Theory, personal growth, professional skill, humanities, investigatory skills courses, and field experience are designed to stimulate the graduate toward a scholarly as well as a professional contribution to society. Elective areas of emphasis in health psychology (PhD only), family and child psychology, clinical forensic psychology, psychodynamic, multicultural and international, and integrative psychology (PsyD only) are available within the clinical programs. Students in CSPP's Couple and Family Therapy MA and PsyD programs are trained to treat individuals, couples, and families with relational mental health issues from a systemic perspective. Skills are developed in mental health assessment, diagnosis, and treatment of individuals and relationship systems. The PsyD is based on the scholar-practitioner model; both degrees are offered in a format for working professionals. The CFT programs are accredited by COAMFTE.

Special Facilities or Resources: The Center for Applied Behavioral Services (CABS) is a multi-service and training center. The Center incorporates the expertise of CSPP faculty in the delivery of direct services and in modeling specific techniques of treatment and service for practicum students and interns. This is currently accomplished through an array of clinical and community services which are directed by faculty members.

Information for Students With Physical Disabilities: See the following website for more information: http://www.alliant.edu/about-alliant/consumer-information-heoa/disability-services.

Application Information:
Send to Alliant International University, Admissions Processing Center, 10455 Pomerado Road, San Diego, CA 92131-1799. Application available online. URL of online application: https://my.alliant.edu/ICS/Prospective_Students/. Students are admitted in the Fall, application deadline December 15. The Clinical Psychology programs have a December 15 priority deadline in order to provide a response by April 1 for applicants who need a decision by that date. The CFT programs have a January 15 priority deadline for the Fall semester. Programs accept applications and admit students on a space available basis after any stated deadlines. *Fee:* $65. A limited number of fee waivers are available for those with significant financial need.

Alliant International University: San Diego
Programs in Educational and School Psychology
Hufstedler School of Education
10455 Pomerado Road
San Diego, CA 92131-1799
Telephone: (858) 635-4772
Fax: (858) 635-4739
E-mail: acarter@alliant.edu
Web: http://www.alliant.edu/hsoe/index.php

Department Information:
2002. Program Director: Steven Fisher, PsyD. Number of faculty: total—full-time 2, part-time 15; women—part-time 8; total—minority—full-time 1, part-time 2; women minority—part-time 2.

Programs and Degrees Offered:
Listed in the following order: Program area, degree type (T if terminal Master's), number awarded 7/11–6/12. Educational Psychology PsyD (Doctor of Psychology) 9, School Psychology MA/MS (Master of Arts/Science) (T) 18.

Student Applications/Admissions:
Student Applications
Educational Psychology PsyD (Doctor of Psychology)—Applications 2012–2013, 3. Total applicants accepted 2012–2013, 3.

Number full-time enrolled (new admits only) 2012–2013, 0. Number part-time enrolled (new admits only) 2012–2013, 1. Openings 2013–2014, 15. The median number of years required for completion of a degree in 2012–2013 were 3. The number of students enrolled full- and part-time who were dismissed or voluntarily withdrew from this program area in 2012–2013 were 0. *School Psychology MA/MS (Master of Arts/Science)*—Applications 2012–2013, 17. Total applicants accepted 2012–2013, 14. Number full-time enrolled (new admits only) 2012–2013, 10. Number part-time enrolled (new admits only) 2012–2013, 0. Total enrolled 2012–2013 full-time, 18. Total enrolled 2012–2013 part-time, 14. Openings 2013–2014, 18. The median number of years required for completion of a degree in 2012–2013 were 2. The number of students enrolled full- and part-time who were dismissed or voluntarily withdrew from this program area in 2012–2013 were 0.
Scores: Entries appear in this order: required test or GPA, minimum score (if required), median score of students entering in 2012–2013. *Educational Psychology PsyD (Doctor of Psychology):* overall undergraduate GPA 3.0, 3.63, psychology GPA 3.0; *School Psychology MA/MS (Master of Arts/Science):* overall undergraduate GPA 3.0, 3.00, psychology GPA 3.0.
Other Criteria: (importance of criteria rated low, medium, or high): research experience—medium, work experience—medium, extracurricular activity—low, clinically related public service—high, GPA—high, letters of recommendation—high, interview—high, statement of goals and objectives—high, Criteria differ by program and level. For additional information on admission requirements, go to http://www.alliant.edu/hsoe/hsoe-admissions/index.php.

Student Characteristics: The following represents characteristics of students in 2012–2013 in all graduate psychology programs in the department: Female—full-time 17, part-time 22; Male—full-time 1, part-time 2; African American/Black—full-time 2, part-time 3; Hispanic/Latino(a)—full-time 5, part-time 5; Asian/Pacific Islander—full-time 0, part-time 0; American Indian/Alaska Native—full-time 0, part-time 1; Caucasian/White—full-time 8, part-time 13; Multi-ethnic—full-time 0, part-time 1; students subject to the Americans With Disabilities Act—full-time 0, part-time 0; Unknown ethnicity—full-time 3, part-time 1; International students who hold an F-1 or J-1 Visa—full-time 0, part-time 0.

Financial Information/Assistance:
Tuition for Full-Time Study: *Master's:* State residents: $580 per credit hour; Nonstate residents: $580 per credit hour. *Doctoral:* State residents: $935 per credit hour; Nonstate residents: $935 per credit hour. Tuition is subject to change. Tuition costs vary by program. See the following website for updates and changes in tuition costs: http://www.alliant.edu/admissions/tuition.php.

Financial Assistance:
First-Year Students: Research assistantships available for first year. Average amount paid per academic year: $1,000. Average number of hours worked per week: 10. Fellowships and scholarships available for first year. Average amount paid per academic year: $750. Apply by June 1.
Advanced Students: Teaching assistantships available for advanced students. Average amount paid per academic year: $3,000. Average number of hours worked per week: 10. Research assistantships available for advanced students. Average amount

paid per academic year: $1,000. Average number of hours worked per week: 10. Fellowships and scholarships available for advanced students. Average amount paid per academic year: $750. Apply by April 1.

Additional Information: Of all students currently enrolled full time, 40% benefited from one or more of the listed financial assistance programs. Application and information available online at: http://www.alliant.edu/admissions/financial-aid-scholarships/.

Internships/Practica: Students in the master's program have practica tied to their coursework beginning in the first semester of their programs. Internships are required of students seeking a Pupil Personnel Services (PPS) credential post-masters or as part of the doctoral program in educational psychology. The 1200 required internship hours are completed at a public school district. Doctoral students interested in seeking clinical licensure must complete a separate psychology internship.

Housing and Day Care: On-campus housing is available. See the following website for more information: http://www.alliant.edu/locations/san-diego-campus/housing-dining.php. No on-campus day care facilities are available.

Employment of Department Graduates:

Master's Degree Graduates: Of those who graduated in the academic year 2011–2012, the following categories and numbers represent the postgraduate activities and employment of master's degree graduates: Enrolled in a postdoctoral residency/fellowship (n/a), employed in independent practice (n/a), total from the above (master's) (0).

Doctoral Degree Graduates: Of those who graduated in the academic year 2011–2012, the following categories and numbers represent the postgraduate activities and employment of doctoral degree graduates: Enrolled in a psychology doctoral program (n/a), total from the above (doctoral) (0).

Additional Information:

Orientation, Objectives, and Emphasis of Department: Programs train students with the skills necessary to work with students, teachers, parents, and other school professionals in today's school environments. Curriculum includes professional skills, professional roles courses, applied research, and professional concepts. The master's degree program prepares students to gain the PPS (Pupil Personnel Services) credential that allows them to practice in California's schools. Students take afternoon, evening, and weekend classes and engage in fieldwork. At the doctoral level, students complete special focus area courses, examples of which include adolescent stress and coping, school culture and administration, pediatric psychology, infant and preschool mental health, child neuropsychology, and provision of services for children in alternative placement. Doctoral students also complete a PsyD project.

Special Facilities or Resources: The Graduate School of Education at the San Diego campus houses the World Council of Curriculum and Instruction.

Information for Students With Physical Disabilities: See the following website for more information: http://www.alliant.edu/about-alliant/consumer-information-heoa/disability-services.

Application Information:

Send to Alliant International University, Admissions Processing Center, 10455 Pomerado Road, San Diego, CA 92131-1799. Application available online. URL of online application: https://my.alliant.edu/ICS/Prospective_Students/. Students are admitted in the Fall, application deadline June 1; Programs have rolling admissions. *Fee:* $65. A limited number of fee waivers are available for those with significant financial need.

Alliant International University: San Diego
Programs in Organizational Psychology
California School of Professional Psychology
10455 Pomerado Road
San Diego, CA 92121-1799
Telephone: (858) 635-4820
Fax: (858) 635-4739
E-mail: *mschwartz@alliant.edu*
Web: *http://www.alliant.edu/cspp/programs-degrees/organizational-psychology/*

Department Information:

1981. Dean, California School of Professional Psychology: Morgan T. Sammons, PhD, ABPP. Number of faculty: total—full-time 6, part-time 6; women—part-time 1.

Programs and Degrees Offered:

Listed in the following order: Program area, degree type (T if terminal Master's), number awarded 7/11–6/12. Industrial/Organizational Psychology PhD (Doctor of Philosophy) 3, Consulting Psychology PhD (Doctor of Philosophy) 2, Industrial/Organizational Psychology MA/MS (Master of Arts/Science) (T) 7.

Student Applications/Admissions:

Student Applications

Industrial/Organizational Psychology PhD (Doctor of Philosophy)—Applications 2012–2013, 7. Total applicants accepted 2012–2013, 4. Number full-time enrolled (new admits only) 2012–2013, 2. Number part-time enrolled (new admits only) 2012–2013, 1. Total enrolled 2012–2013 full-time, 11. Total enrolled 2012–2013 part-time, 25. Openings 2013–2014, 7. The median number of years required for completion of a degree in 2012–2013 were 7. The number of students enrolled full- and part-time who were dismissed or voluntarily withdrew from this program area in 2012–2013 were 0. *Consulting Psychology PhD (Doctor of Philosophy)*—Applications 2012–2013, 3. Total applicants accepted 2012–2013, 1. Number full-time enrolled (new admits only) 2012–2013, 1. Number part-time enrolled (new admits only) 2012–2013, 0. Total enrolled 2012–2013 full-time, 8. Total enrolled 2012–2013 part-time, 15. Openings 2013–2014, 2. The median number of years required for completion of a degree in 2012–2013 were 7. The number of students enrolled full- and part-time who were dismissed or voluntarily withdrew from this program area in 2012–2013 were 0. *Industrial/Organizational Psychology MA/MS (Master of Arts/Science)*—Applications 2012–2013, 18. Total applicants accepted 2012–2013, 13. Number full-time enrolled (new admits only) 2012–2013, 3. Number part-time enrolled (new admits only) 2012–2013, 3. Total enrolled 2012–2013 full-time, 10. Total enrolled 2012–2013 part-time, 6. Openings

2013–2014, 10. The median number of years required for completion of a degree in 2012–2013 were 2. The number of students enrolled full- and part-time who were dismissed or voluntarily withdrew from this program area in 2012–2013 were 1.

Scores: Entries appear in this order: required test or GPA, minimum score (if required), median score of students entering in 2012–2013. *Industrial/Organizational Psychology PhD (Doctor of Philosophy):* overall undergraduate GPA 3.0, 3.45, psychology GPA 3.0, 3.48; *Consulting Psychology PhD (Doctor of Philosophy):* overall undergraduate GPA 3.0, 3.45, psychology GPA 3.0; *Industrial/Organizational Psychology MA/MS (Master of Arts/Science):* overall undergraduate GPA 3.0, 3.28, psychology GPA 3.0.

Other Criteria: (importance of criteria rated low, medium, or high): research experience—high, work experience—medium, extracurricular activity—low, clinically related public service—low, GPA—high, letters of recommendation—high, interview—high, statement of goals and objectives—high, undergraduate major in psychology—low, specific undergraduate psychology courses taken—low, Criteria vary by program. Research experience is more important for doctoral applicants; work experience is more important for some master's programs. For additional information on admission requirements, go to http://www.alliant.edu/cspp/.

Student Characteristics: The following represents characteristics of students in 2012–2013 in all graduate psychology programs in the department: Female—full-time 16, part-time 28; Male—full-time 13, part-time 18; African American/Black—full-time 3, part-time 5; Hispanic/Latino(a)—full-time 2, part-time 3; Asian/Pacific Islander—full-time 2, part-time 3; American Indian/Alaska Native—full-time 0, part-time 1; Caucasian/White—full-time 20, part-time 19; Multi-ethnic—full-time 1, part-time 2; students subject to the Americans With Disabilities Act—full-time 0, part-time 1; Unknown ethnicity—full-time 1, part-time 13; International students who hold an F-1 or J-1 Visa—full-time 0, part-time 1.

Financial Information/Assistance:

Tuition for Full-Time Study: *Master's:* State residents: $1,030 per credit hour; Nonstate residents: $1,030 per credit hour. *Doctoral:* State residents: $1,030 per credit hour; Nonstate residents: $1,030 per credit hour. Tuition is subject to change. See the following website for updates and changes in tuition costs: http://www.alliant.edu/admissions/tuition.php.

Financial Assistance:

First-Year Students: Research assistantships available for first year. Average amount paid per academic year: $1,000. Average number of hours worked per week: 10. Fellowships and scholarships available for first year. Average amount paid per academic year: $5,000. Apply by March 1.

Advanced Students: Teaching assistantships available for advanced students. Average amount paid per academic year: $3,000. Average number of hours worked per week: 10. Research assistantships available for advanced students. Average amount paid per academic year: $1,000. Average number of hours worked per week: 10. Fellowships and scholarships available for advanced students. Average amount paid per academic year: $5,000. Apply by March 1.

Additional Information: Of all students currently enrolled full time, 51% benefited from one or more of the listed financial assistance programs. Application and information available online at: http://www.alliant.edu/admissions/financial-aid-scholarships/.

Internships/Practica: Doctoral students participate in two half-time internships in the third and fourth years of the program; this allows for the integration of professional training with courses, seminars and research. Consulting psychology doctoral students' internships have an individual/group focus in the third year and systemwide interventions focus in the fourth year. Master's students in I/O psychology have a one-semester practicum in the last term of their programs. The majority of these internships are local to the students' campus.

Housing and Day Care: On-campus housing is available. See the following website for more information: http://www.alliant.edu/locations/san-diego-campus/housing-dining.php. No on-campus day care facilities are available.

Employment of Department Graduates:

Master's Degree Graduates: Of those who graduated in the academic year 2011–2012, the following categories and numbers represent the postgraduate activities and employment of master's degree graduates: Enrolled in a postdoctoral residency/fellowship (n/a), employed in independent practice (n/a), total from the above (master's) (0).

Doctoral Degree Graduates: Of those who graduated in the academic year 2011–2012, the following categories and numbers represent the postgraduate activities and employment of doctoral degree graduates: Enrolled in a psychology doctoral program (n/a), total from the above (doctoral) (0).

Additional Information:

Orientation, Objectives, and Emphasis of Department: The consulting psychology doctoral program combines individual, group, organization and systemic consultation skills to produce specialists in the psychological aspects of organizational consulting. The individual focus includes career assessment and executive coaching; the group focus includes team building and assisting dysfunctional work groups; the organizational/systemic focus includes the understanding, diagnosis and intervention with organizational systems. The industrial-organizational doctoral program is patterned after the doctoral-level training guidelines prepared by the Education and Training Committee of the Society for Industrial and Organizational Psychology (Division 14 of the APA). The programs emphasize personnel selections, work motivation, design of compensation systems, measurement and productivity. Master's programs lead to careers as internal consultants within organizations or other master's-level or entry-level careers in organizations and provide foundations for further study if desired. These programs stress leadership, management, and organizational skills. Some master's programs are structured specifically for working professionals.

Special Facilities or Resources: The Organizational Consulting Center (OCC) provides students with opportunities to participate with faculty and OCC associates on consulting projects during their programs.

Application Information:

Send to Alliant International University, Admissions Processing Center, 10455 Pomerado Road, San Diego, CA 92121-1799. Application available online. URL of online application: https://my.alliant.edu/ICS/Prospective_Students/. Students are admitted in the Fall, application deadline March 1; Spring, application deadline October 1; Programs have rolling admissions. Applications are due March 1 (priority deadline) for the Fall semester and October 1 (priority deadline) for the Spring semester. The program accepts applications and admits students on a space available basis after the priority deadlines. *Fee:* $65. A limited number of fee waivers are available to those with significant financial need.

Alliant International University: San Francisco
Programs in Clinical Psychology, Clinical Counseling,
  Couple & Family Therapy, and Clinical Psychopharmacology
California School of Professional Psychology
One Beach Street, Suite 100
San Francisco, CA 94133-1221
Telephone: (415) 955-2146
Fax: (415) 955-2179
E-mail: *mschwartz@alliant.edu*
Web: *http://www.alliant.edu/cspp/*

Department Information:

1969. Dean, California School of Professional Psychology: Morgan T. Sammons, PhD, ABPP. Number of faculty: total—full-time 39, part-time 41; women—full-time 17, part-time 21; total—minority—full-time 3, part-time 7; women minority—full-time 1, part-time 4; faculty subject to the Americans With Disabilities Act 2.

Programs and Degrees Offered:

Listed in the following order: Program area, degree type (T if terminal Master's), number awarded 7/11–6/12. Clinical Psychology PsyD (Doctor of Psychology) 41, Clinical Psychology PhD (Doctor of Philosophy) 27, Clinical Psychology Respecialization Diploma 1, Clinical Counseling MA/MS (Master of Arts/Science) (T) 0, Clinical Psychopharmacology MA/MS (Master of Arts/Science) (T) 9, Marital and Family Therapy MA/MS (Master of Arts/Science) (T) 0.

APA Accreditation: Clinical PsyD (Doctor of Psychology). Student Outcome Data Website: http://www.alliant.edu/cspp/programs-degrees/clinical-psychology/psyd-sanfrancisco.php. Clinical PhD (Doctor of Philosophy). Student Outcome Data Website: http://www.alliant.edu/cspp/programs-degrees/clinical-psychology/phd-sanfrancisco.php.

Student Applications/Admissions:

Student Applications

Clinical Psychology PsyD (Doctor of Psychology)—Applications 2012–2013, 210. Total applicants accepted 2012–2013, 114. Number full-time enrolled (new admits only) 2012–2013, 51. Number part-time enrolled (new admits only) 2012–2013, 0. Total enrolled 2012–2013 full-time, 233. Total enrolled 2012–2013 part-time, 68. Openings 2013–2014, 45. The median number of years required for completion of a degree in 2012–2013 were 5. The number of students enrolled full- and part-time who were dismissed or voluntarily withdrew from this program area in 2012–2013 were 0. *Clinical Psychology PhD (Doctor of Philosophy)*—Applications 2012–2013, 82. Total

applicants accepted 2012–2013, 49. Number full-time enrolled (new admits only) 2012–2013, 24. Number part-time enrolled (new admits only) 2012–2013, 2. Total enrolled 2012–2013 full-time, 103. Total enrolled 2012–2013 part-time, 29. Openings 2013–2014, 25. The median number of years required for completion of a degree in 2012–2013 were 6. The number of students enrolled full- and part-time who were dismissed or voluntarily withdrew from this program area in 2012–2013 were 2. *Clinical Psychology Respecialization Diploma*—Applications 2012–2013, 3. Total applicants accepted 2012–2013, 2. Number full-time enrolled (new admits only) 2012–2013, 0. Number part-time enrolled (new admits only) 2012–2013, 0. Total enrolled 2012–2013 full-time, 3. Total enrolled 2012–2013 part-time, 1. Openings 2013–2014, 1. The median number of years required for completion of a degree in 2012–2013 were 3. The number of students enrolled full- and part-time who were dismissed or voluntarily withdrew from this program area in 2012–2013 were 0. *Clinical Counseling MA/MS (Master of Arts/Science)*—Applications 2012–2013, 32. Total applicants accepted 2012–2013, 22. Number full-time enrolled (new admits only) 2012–2013, 11. Number part-time enrolled (new admits only) 2012–2013, 1. Total enrolled 2012–2013 full-time, 22. Total enrolled 2012–2013 part-time, 2. Openings 2013–2014, 12. The number of students enrolled full- and part-time who were dismissed or voluntarily withdrew from this program area in 2012–2013 were 0. *Clinical Psychopharmacology MA/MS (Master of Arts/Science)*—Applications 2012–2013, 28. Total applicants accepted 2012–2013, 26. Number full-time enrolled (new admits only) 2012–2013, 0. Number part-time enrolled (new admits only) 2012–2013, 26. Openings 2013–2014, 25. The median number of years required for completion of a degree in 2012–2013 were 3. The number of students enrolled full- and part-time who were dismissed or voluntarily withdrew from this program area in 2012–2013 were 0. *Marital and Family Therapy MA/MS (Master of Arts/Science)*—Applications 2012–2013, 0. Total applicants accepted 2012–2013, 0. Number full-time enrolled (new admits only) 2012–2013, 0. Number part-time enrolled (new admits only) 2012–2013, 0. Openings 2013–2014, 12. The number of students enrolled full- and part-time who were dismissed or voluntarily withdrew from this program area in 2012–2013 were 0.

Scores: Entries appear in this order: required test or GPA, minimum score (if required), median score of students entering in 2012–2013. *Clinical Psychology PsyD (Doctor of Psychology):* overall undergraduate GPA 3.0, 3.44, psychology GPA 3.0; *Clinical Psychology PhD (Doctor of Philosophy):* overall undergraduate GPA 3.0, 3.22, psychology GPA 3.0; *Clinical Psychology Respecialization Diploma:* overall undergraduate GPA 3.0, psychology GPA no minimum stated; *Marital and Family Therapy MA/MS (Master of Arts/Science):* overall undergraduate GPA 3.0, psychology GPA 3.0.

Other Criteria: (importance of criteria rated low, medium, or high): research experience—high, work experience—high, extracurricular activity—low, clinically related public service—high, GPA—high, letters of recommendation—high, interview—high, statement of goals and objectives—high, undergraduate major in psychology—medium, specific undergraduate psychology courses taken—medium. For additional information on admission requirements, go to http://www.alliant.edu/cspp/.

Student Characteristics: The following represents characteristics of students in 2012–2013 in all graduate psychology programs in the department: Female—full-time 276, part-time 104; Male—full-time 85, part-time 51; African American/Black—full-time 13, part-time 12; Hispanic/Latino(a)—full-time 24, part-time 16; Asian/Pacific Islander—full-time 48, part-time 19; American Indian/Alaska Native—full-time 3, part-time 1; Caucasian/White—full-time 203, part-time 87; Multi-ethnic—full-time 21, part-time 8; students subject to the Americans With Disabilities Act—full-time 12, part-time 2; Unknown ethnicity—full-time 49, part-time 12; International students who hold an F-1 or J-1 Visa—full-time 15, part-time 0.

Financial Information/Assistance:

Tuition for Full-Time Study: *Master's:* State residents: $1,030 per credit hour; Nonstate residents: $1,030 per credit hour. *Doctoral:* State residents: $1,030 per credit hour; Nonstate residents: $1,030 per credit hour. Tuition is subject to change. See the following website for updates and changes in tuition costs: http://www.alliant.edu/admissions/tuition.php.

Financial Assistance:

First-Year Students: Research assistantships available for first year. Average amount paid per academic year: $1,500. Average number of hours worked per week: 10. Fellowships and scholarships available for first year. Average amount paid per academic year: $5,000. Apply by December 15.

Advanced Students: Teaching assistantships available for advanced students. Average amount paid per academic year: $3,000. Average number of hours worked per week: 10. Research assistantships available for advanced students. Average amount paid per academic year: $1,000. Average number of hours worked per week: 10. Fellowships and scholarships available for advanced students. Average amount paid per academic year: $5,000. Apply by December 15.

Additional Information: Of all students currently enrolled full time, 58% benefited from one or more of the listed financial assistance programs. Application and information available online at: http://www.alliant.edu/admissions/financial-aid-scholarships/.

Internships/Practica: Doctoral Degree (PsyD Clinical Psychology): For those doctoral students for whom a professional psychology internship was required in this program prior to graduation, (73) students applied for an internship in 2011–2012, with (62) students obtaining an internship. Of those students who obtained an internship, (44) were paid internships. Of those students who obtained an internship, (14) students placed in APA/CPA accredited internships, (13) students placed in internships not APA/CPA accredited, but listed with the Association of Psychology Postdoctoral and Internship Programs (APPIC), (0) students placed in internships conforming to guidelines of the Council of Directors of School Psychology Programs (CDSPP), (35) students placed in internships that were not APA/CPA accredited, APPIC or CDSPP listed. Doctoral Degree (PhD Clinical Psychology): For those doctoral students for whom a professional psychology internship was required in this program prior to graduation, (25) students applied for an internship in 2011–2012, with (22) students obtaining an internship. Of those students who obtained an internship, (18) were paid internships. Of those students who obtained an internship, (9) students placed in APA/CPA accredited internships, (4) students placed in internships not APA/CPA accredited, but listed with the Association of Psychology

Postdoctoral and Internship Programs (APPIC), (0) students placed in internships conforming to guidelines of the Council of Directors of School Psychology Programs (CDSPP), (9) students placed in internships that were not APA/CPA accredited, APPIC or CDSPP listed. Master's Degree (MA/MS Clinical Counseling): An internship experience, such as a final research project or "capstone" experience is required of graduates. During the first three years of the PsyD program and during the second and third years of the PhD program, students are engaged in field practica 8-16 hours per week. All students get experience working with adults, children/adolescents, and persons with severe mental illness as well as more moderate forms of dysfunction. The tremendous ethnic/racial diversity of the San Francisco Bay Area insures that all students get exposure to working with clients from a variety of cultural groups. Practica are selected and approved by CSPP based on the quality of training and supervision provided for the students. They include community mental health centers, neuropsychology clinics, hospitals, child guidance clinics, college counseling centers, forensic settings, couple and family therapy agencies, residential treatment centers, infant/toddler mental health programs, corporate settings, and school programs for children and adolescents. Students begin the required internship in the fourth year (PsyD program) or the fifth year (PhD program). Full-time internship options include APA-accredited or APPIC-member training programs pursued through the national selection process, or local internship programs approved by the California Psychology Internship Council (CAPIC). Students have the option of completing the internship requirement in two years of half-time experience. Clinical Counseling students conduct a minimum of 700 hours of direct and indirect supervised clinical experience counseling individuals, families or groups. The CFT practicum program includes 500 hours of direct client contact.

Housing and Day Care: No on-campus housing is available. No on-campus day care facilities are available.

Employment of Department Graduates:

Master's Degree Graduates: Of those who graduated in the academic year 2011–2012, the following categories and numbers represent the postgraduate activities and employment of master's degree graduates: Enrolled in a postdoctoral residency/fellowship (n/a), employed in independent practice (n/a), total from the above (master's) (0).

Doctoral Degree Graduates: Of those who graduated in the academic year 2011–2012, the following categories and numbers represent the postgraduate activities and employment of doctoral degree graduates: Enrolled in a psychology doctoral program (n/a), total from the above (doctoral) (0).

Additional Information:

Orientation, Objectives, and Emphasis of Department: CSPP's clinical psychology programs combine supervised field experiences with study of psychological theory, clinical techniques, and applied research. The PsyD is a practitioner-oriented program. The PhD provides a balance of clinical and research training and is intended for students who expect independent research, teaching, and scholarship to be a significant part of their professional careers in addition to clinical work. In addition to the usual offerings, special training opportunities are available in five areas: family-child-adolescent psychology, health psychology, multicultural-community psychology, psychodynamic psychology, and gender studies (including psychology of women and men, and lesbian, gay, bisexual and transgender issues). The PsyD program also offers an intensive child and family track (focusing on child assessment, child therapy, and family therapy), a forensic family/ child track (focusing on child abuse, child custody, delinquency, and family court services), and a social justice track (focusing on mental health services to historically underserved and culturally diverse populations). Students in the PsyD tracks are required to complete a specific sequence of courses, a dissertation, and an internship related to their track's focus. Other students in the PhD and PsyD programs can take many of these same training experiences on an elective basis. Multicultural/diversity issues are infused throughout the entire curriculum. Three major theoretical orientations are strongly represented in the program: cognitive-behavioral, family systems, and psychodynamic. The CSPP Master's program in Clinical Counseling trains students to provide competent professional therapeutic services in a variety of settings. Our program is designed in accordance with the educational requirements of the Board of Behavioral Sciences of California; graduates are positioned to pursue the Licensed Professional Clinical Counselor (LPCC) license in most states. Students in the CSPP Master's program in Couple & Family Therapy are trained to treat individuals, couples, and families with relational mental health issues from a systemic perspective. Skills are developed in mental health assessment, diagnosis, and treatment of individuals and relationship systems. The CFT program is accredited by COAMFTE.

Special Facilities or Resources: Students can elect to receive supervised clinical experience through CSPP's Psychological Services Center (PSC)—a community mental health clinic that serves children, adults, couples, and families. The PSC enables faculty to model professional service delivery and to directly supervise and evaluate students' clinical work. Clinical services provided at the PSC include psychodiagnostic assessment and individual, couple, family, and group psychotherapy. The PSC has both Adult-Clinical and Child/Family-Clinical training programs. The Rockway Institute works to counter antigay prejudice and inform public policies affecting lesbian, gay, bisexual, and transgender (LGBT) people. The primary goals of the Institute are to convey accurate scientific and professional information about LGBT issues to the media, legislatures and the courts, and conduct research relevant to LGBT public policy questions in the areas of family relations, education, healthcare, social services, and the workplace. Computer labs are available to students and are fully equipped with SPSS and other statistical programs for research purposes. Designated space is available on campus for research activities (such as data collection) and the library is equipped with the major searchable databases for the research literature in psychology and related areas. The campus occupies approximately 31,000 square feet of space in an historic building near the San Francisco waterfront across from Pier 39.

Information for Students With Physical Disabilities: See the following website for more information: http://www.alliant.edu/ about-alliant/consumer-information-heoa/disability-services.

Application Information:
Send to Alliant International University, Admissions Processing Center, 10455 Pomerado Road, San Diego, CA 92131. Application available online. URL of online application: https://my.alliant.edu/ICS/ Prospective_Students/. Students are admitted in the Fall, application deadline December 15. The Clinical Psychology programs have a December 15 priority deadline in order to provide a response by April 1 for applicants who need a decision by that date. The Clinical Counseling program has a June 1 priority deadline for the Fall semester. The CFT program has a January 15 priority deadline for the Fall Semester. Applications submitted after priority deadlines are reviewed and applicants are admitted on a space-available basis. *Fee:* $65. A limited number of fee waivers are available for those with significant financial need.

Alliant International University: San Francisco
Programs in Educational and School Psychology
Hufstedler School of Education
One Beach Street, Suite 100
San Francisco, CA 94133-1221
Telephone: (415) 955-2100
Fax: (415) 955-2179
E-mail: *acarter@alliant.edu*
Web: *http://www.alliant.edu/hsoe/index.php*

Department Information:
2002. Interim Program Director: Steven Fisher, PsyD. Number of faculty: total—full-time 3, part-time 8; women—full-time 1, part-time 6; total—minority—full-time 2, part-time 1; women minority—full-time 1.

Programs and Degrees Offered:
Listed in the following order: Program area, degree type (T if terminal Master's), number awarded 7/11–6/12. School Psychology MA/MS (Master of Arts/Science) (T) 3, Educational Psychology PsyD (Doctor of Psychology) 5.

Student Applications/Admissions:
Student Applications
School Psychology MA/MS (Master of Arts/Science)—Applications 2012–2013, 8. Total applicants accepted 2012–2013, 6. Number full-time enrolled (new admits only) 2012–2013, 4. Number part-time enrolled (new admits only) 2012–2013, 1. Total enrolled 2012–2013 full-time, 10. Total enrolled 2012–2013 part-time, 6. Openings 2013–2014, 15. The median number of years required for completion of a degree in 2012–2013 were 2. The number of students enrolled full- and part-time who were dismissed or voluntarily withdrew from this program area in 2012–2013 were 1. *Educational Psychology PsyD (Doctor of Psychology)*—Applications 2012–2013, 4. Total applicants accepted 2012–2013, 3. Number full-time enrolled (new admits only) 2012–2013, 3. Number part-time enrolled (new admits only) 2012–2013, 0. Total enrolled 2012–2013 full-time, 6. Total enrolled 2012–2013 part-time, 6. Openings 2013–2014, 5. The median number of years required for completion of a degree in 2012–2013 were 3. The number of students enrolled full- and part-time who were dismissed or voluntarily withdrew from this program area in 2012–2013 were 0.

Scores: Entries appear in this order: required test or GPA, minimum score (if required), median score of students entering in 2012–2013. *School Psychology MA/MS (Master of Arts/Science):* overall undergraduate GPA 3.0, 3.26, psychology GPA 3.0; *Educational Psychology PsyD (Doctor of Psychology):* overall undergraduate GPA 3.0, 3.50, psychology GPA 3.0.

Other Criteria: (importance of criteria rated low, medium, or high): research experience—medium, work experience—high, extracurricular activity—low, clinically related public service—high, GPA—high, letters of recommendation—high, interview—high, statement of goals and objectives—high, Criteria differ for master's and doctoral programs. For additional information on admission requirements, go to http://www.alliant.edu/hsoe/hsoe-admissions/index.php.

Student Characteristics: The following represents characteristics of students in 2012–2013 in all graduate psychology programs in the department: Female—full-time 15, part-time 9; Male—full-time 1, part-time 3; African American/Black—full-time 1, part-time 0; Hispanic/Latino(a)—full-time 1, part-time 1; Asian/Pacific Islander—full-time 4, part-time 0; American Indian/Alaska Native—full-time 0, part-time 0; Caucasian/White—full-time 7, part-time 9; Multi-ethnic—full-time 2, part-time 0; students subject to the Americans With Disabilities Act—full-time 0, part-time 0; Unknown ethnicity—full-time 1, part-time 2; International students who hold an F-1 or J-1 Visa—full-time 1, part-time 0.

Financial Information/Assistance:

Tuition for Full-Time Study: *Master's:* State residents: $580 per credit hour; Nonstate residents: $580 per credit hour. *Doctoral:* State residents: $935 per credit hour; Nonstate residents: $935 per credit hour. Tuition is subject to change. See the following website for updates and changes in tuition costs: http://www.alliant.edu/admissions/tuition.php.

Financial Assistance:

First-Year Students: Research assistantships available for first year. Average amount paid per academic year: $1,000. Average number of hours worked per week: 10. Fellowships and scholarships available for first year. Average amount paid per academic year: $750. Apply by June 1.

Advanced Students: Teaching assistantships available for advanced students. Average amount paid per academic year: $3,000. Average number of hours worked per week: 10. Research assistantships available for advanced students. Average amount paid per academic year: $1,000. Average number of hours worked per week: 10. Fellowships and scholarships available for advanced students. Average amount paid per academic year: $750. Apply by April 1.

Additional Information: Of all students currently enrolled full time, 40% benefited from one or more of the listed financial assistance programs. Application and information available online at: http://www.alliant.edu/admissions/financial-aid-scholarships/.

Internships/Practica: Students in the master's program have practica tied to their coursework beginning in the first semester of their programs. Internships are required of any students seeking a Pupil Personnel Services (PPS) credential post-masters or as part of the doctoral program in educational psychology. The 1200 internships hours are completed at a public school district. Those in the doctoral program who are interested in clinical licensure must complete a separate psychology internship.

Housing and Day Care: No on-campus housing is available. No on-campus day care facilities are available.

Employment of Department Graduates:

Master's Degree Graduates: Of those who graduated in the academic year 2011–2012, the following categories and numbers represent the postgraduate activities and employment of master's degree graduates: Enrolled in a postdoctoral residency/fellowship (n/a), employed in independent practice (n/a), total from the above (master's) (0).

Doctoral Degree Graduates: Of those who graduated in the academic year 2011–2012, the following categories and numbers represent the postgraduate activities and employment of doctoral degree graduates: Enrolled in a psychology doctoral program (n/a), total from the above (doctoral) (0).

Additional Information:

Orientation, Objectives, and Emphasis of Department: Programs train students with the skills necessary to work with students, teachers, parents, and other school professionals in today's school environments. The curriculum includes professional skills, professional roles courses, applied research, and professional concepts. The master's degree program prepares students to gain the PPS (Pupil Personnel Services) credential that allows them to practice in California's schools. Students take afternoon, evening and weekend classes and engage in fieldwork. At the doctoral level, students complete special focus area courses, examples of which include adolescent stress and coping, school culture and administration, pediatric psychology, infant and preschool mental health, child neuropsychology, and provision of services for children in alternative placement. Doctoral students also complete a PsyD project.

Information for Students With Physical Disabilities: See the following website for more information: http://www.alliant.edu/about-alliant/consumer-information-heoa/disability-services.

Application Information:
Send to Alliant International University, Admissions Processing Center, 10455 Pomerado Road, San Diego, CA 92131-1799. Application available online. URL of online application: https://my.alliant.edu/ICS/Prospective_Students/. Students are admitted in the Fall, application deadline June 1; Programs have rolling admissions. *Fee:* $65. A limited number of fee waivers are available for those with significant financial need.

Alliant International University: San Francisco
Programs in Organizational Psychology
California School of Professional Psychology
One Beach Street, Suite 100
San Francisco, CA 94133-1221
Telephone: (415) 955-2146
Fax: (415) 955-2179
E-mail: mschwartz@alliant.edu
Web: http://www.alliant.edu/cspp/programs-degrees/organizational-psychology/

Department Information:
1983. Dean, California School of Professional Psychology: Morgan T. Sammons, PhD, ABPP. Number of faculty: total—full-time 6, part-time 3; women—full-time 5.

Programs and Degrees Offered:
Listed in the following order: Program area, degree type (T if terminal Master's), number awarded 7/11–6/12. Organizational Psychology PhD (Doctor of Philosophy) 3, Organizational Psychology MA/MS (Master of Arts/Science) (T) 5.

Student Applications/Admissions:
Student Applications
Organizational Psychology PhD (Doctor of Philosophy)—Applications 2012–2013, 3. Total applicants accepted 2012–2013, 3. Number full-time enrolled (new admits only) 2012–2013, 2. Number part-time enrolled (new admits only) 2012–2013, 1. Total enrolled 2012–2013 full-time, 18. Total enrolled 2012–2013 part-time, 21. Openings 2013–2014, 3. The median number of years required for completion of a degree in 2012–2013 were 5. The number of students enrolled full- and part-time who were dismissed or voluntarily withdrew from this program area in 2012–2013 were 0. *Organizational Psychology MA/MS (Master of Arts/Science)*—Applications 2012–2013, 3. Total applicants accepted 2012–2013, 3. Number full-time enrolled (new admits only) 2012–2013, 3. Number part-time enrolled (new admits only) 2012–2013, 0. Total enrolled 2012–2013 full-time, 6. Total enrolled 2012–2013 part-time, 1. Openings 2013–2014, 7. The median number of years required for completion of a degree in 2012–2013 were 2. The number of students enrolled full- and part-time who were dismissed or voluntarily withdrew from this program area in 2012–2013 were 0.
Scores: Entries appear in this order: required test or GPA, minimum score (if required), median score of students entering in 2012–2013. *Organizational Psychology PhD (Doctor of Philosophy):* overall undergraduate GPA 3.0, 3.00, psychology GPA 3.0; *Organizational Psychology MA/MS (Master of Arts/Science):* overall undergraduate GPA 3.0, 3.27, psychology GPA 3.0.
Other Criteria: (importance of criteria rated low, medium, or high): research experience—high, work experience—high, extracurricular activity—low, clinically related public service—low, GPA—high, letters of recommendation—high, interview—high, statement of goals and objectives—high, undergraduate major in psychology—low, specific undergraduate psychology courses taken—low, Admission criteria vary by program and program level. For additional information on admission requirements, go to http://www.alliant.edu/cspp.

Student Characteristics: The following represents characteristics of students in 2012–2013 in all graduate psychology programs in the department: Female—full-time 14, part-time 18; Male—full-time 10, part-time 4; African American/Black—full-time 2, part-time 4; Hispanic/Latino(a)—full-time 1, part-time 0; Asian/Pacific Islander—full-time 3, part-time 4; American Indian/Alaska Native—full-time 0, part-time 0; Caucasian/White—full-time 16, part-time 11; Multi-ethnic—full-time 0, part-time 1; students subject to the Americans With Disabilities Act—full-time 0, part-time 0; Unknown ethnicity—full-time 2, part-time 2; International students who hold an F-1 or J-1 Visa—full-time 3, part-time 0.

Financial Information/Assistance:
Tuition for Full-Time Study: *Master's:* State residents: $1,030 per credit hour; Nonstate residents: $1,030 per credit hour. *Doctoral:* State residents: $1,030 per credit hour; Nonstate residents: $1,030 per credit hour. Tuition is subject to change. See the following website for updates and changes in tuition costs: http://www.alliant.edu/admissions/tuition.php.

Financial Assistance:
First-Year Students: Research assistantships available for first year. Average amount paid per academic year: $1,000. Average number of hours worked per week: 10. Fellowships and scholarships available for first year. Average amount paid per academic year: $5,000. Apply by March 1.
Advanced Students: Teaching assistantships available for advanced students. Average amount paid per academic year: $3,000. Average number of hours worked per week: 10. Research assistantships available for advanced students. Average amount paid per academic year: $1,000. Average number of hours worked per week: 10. Fellowships and scholarships available for advanced students. Average amount paid per academic year: $5,000. Apply by March 1.
Additional Information: Of all students currently enrolled full time, 53% benefited from one or more of the listed financial assistance programs. Application and information available online at: http://www.alliant.edu/admissions/financial-aid-scholarships/.

Internships/Practica: Organizational doctoral students develop skills through practical training experiences during the third and fourth years of the program. Students usually devote 8-40 hours per week to field placement assignments. Some training sites are local to the student's campus location; occasionally students find internships at out-of-area or out-of-state sites that meet their professional training needs. Placements are available in a variety of settings including consulting firms, major corporations, government agencies, healthcare organizations, and non-profit agencies. Students in the master's programs have a one semester applied experience with supervision.

Housing and Day Care: No on-campus housing is available. No on-campus day care facilities are available.

Employment of Department Graduates:
Master's Degree Graduates: Of those who graduated in the academic year 2011–2012, the following categories and numbers represent the postgraduate activities and employment of master's degree graduates: Enrolled in a postdoctoral residency/fellowship (n/a), employed in independent practice (n/a), total from the above (master's) (0).
Doctoral Degree Graduates: Of those who graduated in the academic year 2011–2012, the following categories and numbers represent the postgraduate activities and employment of doctoral degree graduates: Enrolled in a psychology doctoral program (n/a), total from the above (doctoral) (0).

Additional Information:
Orientation, Objectives, and Emphasis of Department: Doctoral students gain exposure to three core areas of study: organizational theory, grounded in the behavioral sciences; quantitative and qualitative research methods; and professional practice skill development. The program focuses on research and practice in organizational consulting at the individual, team, and system levels; collaborative strategic change; organizational culture and leadership; multicultural competence; executive coaching and mentoring; and organizational innovation, creativity and knowledge management. Programs are structured so students can attend at a moderated pace — this allows students to continue working while in

their programs. The Organizational Psychology master's program is a 46-unit program that can be completed in two years on a full-time basis, or three to four years on a part-time basis. Courses are offered in the late afternoons and evenings to accommodate working adults. In addition, some classes combine more intensive weekend sessions with weekly scheduled classes. The curriculum includes a full semester applied field work project under faculty supervision. This program is also a good option for students who think they may want to continue on to the doctoral degree but are not yet ready to commit to doctoral-length training.

Special Facilities or Resources: The Organizational Consulting Center (OCC) provides students with opportunities to participate with faculty and OCC associates on consulting projects during their program.

Information for Students With Physical Disabilities: See the following website for more information: http://www.alliant.edu/about-alliant/consumer-information-heoa/disability-services.

Application Information:
Send to Alliant International University, Admissions Processing Center, 10455 Pomerado Road, San Diego, CA 92131-1799. Application available online. URL of online application: https://my.alliant.edu/ICS/Prospective_Students/. Students are admitted in the Fall, application deadline March 1; Spring, application deadline October 1; Programs have rolling admissions. Applications are due March 1 (priority deadline) for the Fall semester and October 1 (priority deadline) for the Spring semester. The program accepts applications and admits students on a space available basis after the priority deadlines. *Fee:* $65. A limited number of fee waivers are available for those with significant financial need.

American School of Professional Psychology at Argosy University/San Francisco Bay Area
Clinical Psychology
College of Psychology and Behavioral Sciences
1005 Atlantic Avenue
Alameda, CA 94501
Telephone: (510) 217-4700
Fax: (510) 217-4800
E-mail: rperl@argosy.edu
Web: http://www.argosy.edu

Department Information:
1999. Program Chair: Robert Perl, PsyD. Number of faculty: total—full-time 11, part-time 4; women—full-time 6, part-time 2; total—minority—full-time 4; women minority—full-time 1; faculty subject to the Americans With Disabilities Act 2.

Programs and Degrees Offered:
Listed in the following order: Program area, degree type (T if terminal Master's), number awarded 7/11–6/12. Clinical Psychology MA/MS (Master of Arts/Science) (T) 4, Clinical Psychology PsyD (Doctor of Psychology) 67.

APA Accreditation: On Probation PsyD (Doctor of Psychology). Student Outcome Data Website: http://www.argosy.edu/documents/psydinfo/SanFranciscoBayArea-psyd-outcomes.pdf.

Student Applications/Admissions:
Student Applications
Clinical Psychology MA/MS (Master of Arts/Science)—Number full-time enrolled (new admits only) 2012–2013, 0. Number part-time enrolled (new admits only) 2012–2013, 0. Total enrolled 2012–2013 full-time, 8. Total enrolled 2012–2013 part-time, 0. Openings 2013–2014, 5. The median number of years required for completion of a degree in 2012–2013 were 2. The number of students enrolled full- and part-time who were dismissed or voluntarily withdrew from this program area in 2012–2013 were 1. *Clinical Psychology PsyD (Doctor of Psychology)*—Applications 2012–2013, 44. Total applicants accepted 2012–2013, 10. Number full-time enrolled (new admits only) 2012–2013, 4. Total enrolled 2012–2013 full-time, 160. Openings 2013–2014, 15. The median number of years required for completion of a degree in 2012–2013 were 4. The number of students enrolled full- and part-time who were dismissed or voluntarily withdrew from this program area in 2012–2013 were 3.
Scores: Entries appear in this order: required test or GPA, minimum score (if required), median score of students entering in 2012–2013. *Clinical Psychology MA/MS (Master of Arts/Science):* overall undergraduate GPA 3.00; *Clinical Psychology PsyD (Doctor of Psychology):* GRE-V no minimum stated, GRE-Q no minimum stated, GRE-Analytical no minimum stated, overall undergraduate GPA 3.25.
Other Criteria: (importance of criteria rated low, medium, or high): GRE scores—medium, research experience—medium, work experience—medium, extracurricular activity—medium, clinically related public service—high, GPA—high, letters of recommendation—high, interview—high, statement of goals and objectives—high, undergraduate major in psychology—medium, specific undergraduate psychology courses taken—high.

Student Characteristics: The following represents characteristics of students in 2012–2013 in all graduate psychology programs in the department: Female—full-time 132, part-time 0; Male—full-time 36, part-time 0; African American/Black—full-time 36, part-time 0; Hispanic/Latino(a)—full-time 21, part-time 0; Asian/Pacific Islander—full-time 42, part-time 0; American Indian/Alaska Native—full-time 1, part-time 0; Caucasian/White—full-time 58, part-time 0; Multi-ethnic—full-time 10, part-time 0; students subject to the Americans With Disabilities Act—full-time 22, part-time 0; Unknown ethnicity—full-time 0, part-time 0; International students who hold an F-1 or J-1 Visa—full-time 15, part-time 0.

Financial Information/Assistance:
Tuition for Full-Time Study: *Master's:* State residents: $1,162 per credit hour; Nonstate residents: $1,162 per credit hour. *Doctoral:* State residents: $1,162 per credit hour; Nonstate residents: $1,162 per credit hour. Tuition is subject to change. Additional fees are assessed to students beyond the costs of tuition for the following: professional liability insurance, student activity fee, technology fee. See the following website for updates and changes in tuition costs: http://www.argosy.edu/admissions/default.aspx.

Financial Assistance:
First-Year Students: Teaching assistantships available for first year. Average amount paid per academic year: $25,000. Fel-

lowships and scholarships available for first year. Average amount paid per academic year: $11,000.

Advanced Students: Teaching assistantships available for advanced students. Average amount paid per academic year: $25,000. Average number of hours worked per week: 5. Research assistantships available for advanced students. Traineeships available for advanced students. Fellowships and scholarships available for advanced students. Average amount paid per academic year: $11,000.

Additional Information: Of all students currently enrolled full time, 90% benefited from one or more of the listed financial assistance programs. Application and information available online at: http://www.argosy.edu/financial-aid/Default.aspx.

Internships/Practica: Doctoral Degree (PsyD Clinical Psychology): For those doctoral students for whom a professional psychology internship was required in this program prior to graduation, (43) students applied for an internship in 2011–2012, with (42) students obtaining an internship. Of those students who obtained an internship, (33) were paid internships. Of those students who obtained an internship, (3) students placed in APA/CPA accredited internships, (10) students placed in internships not APA/CPA accredited, but listed with the Association of Psychology Postdoctoral and Internship Programs (APPIC), (0) students placed in internships conforming to guidelines of the Council of Directors of School Psychology Programs (CDSPP), (29) students placed in internships that were not APA/CPA accredited, APPIC or CDSPP listed. Master's Degree (MA/MS Clinical Psychology): An internship experience, such as a final research project or "capstone" experience is required of graduates. PsyD students are encouraged to choose the internship experience that best meets their long term training goals. Students in our PsyD program are strongly encouraged to apply to APA internships, though APPIC and CAPIC (California Psychology Internship Council) internships are also available. Students to have the option of applying to either a full-time or a half-time internship, but full-time is expected of most students. Practicum opportunities are organized through BAPIC or through our own in-house practicum program, which focuses on assessment practice. Students are required to complete 3 years of practicum prior to internship in the PsyD program and one year of practicum in the MA program. Argosy University SFBA's database of approved San Francisco Bay Area practicum sites includes community mental health centers, consortia, state, community and private psychiatric hospitals, medical and trauma centers, university counseling centers, schools, correctional facilities, residential treatment programs, independent and group practices, and corporate settings. Some sites serve the general population while others service specific populations (e.g., children, adolescents, geriatrics, particular ethnic or racial groups, criminal offenders, etc) or clinical problems (e.g., chemical dependency, eating disorders, medical and psychiatric rehabilitation, etc). Students are required to seek a combination of practicum placements that will provide a breadth of experience including working with severely disordered clients, children or adolescents, and adults. The Training Department works throughout the year to maintain positive relationships with existing sites and to affiliate itself with new sites throughout the Bay Area. Argosy University SFBA strongly encourages students to complete their training in settings that provide opportunities to work with diverse populations. It is essential that students learn to work with people who are different from themselves (e.g. race, ethnicity, disability, sexual orientation, etc.) in a supervised setting where they can learn the skills, knowledge and attitudes necessary to practice as a competent clinician.

Housing and Day Care: No on-campus housing is available. No on-campus day care facilities are available.

Employment of Department Graduates:

Master's Degree Graduates: Of those who graduated in the academic year 2011–2012, the following categories and numbers represent the postgraduate activities and employment of master's degree graduates: Enrolled in a postdoctoral residency/fellowship (n/a), employed in independent practice (n/a), total from the above (master's) (0).

Doctoral Degree Graduates: Of those who graduated in the academic year 2011–2012, the following categories and numbers represent the postgraduate activities and employment of doctoral degree graduates: Enrolled in a psychology doctoral program (n/a), total from the above (doctoral) (0).

Additional Information:

Orientation, Objectives, and Emphasis of Department: The Doctor of Psychology (PsyD) in Clinical Psychology program has been designed to educate and train students so that they will be able to function effectively as clinical psychologists. To ensure that students are adequately prepared, the curriculum is designed to provide for the meaningful integration of psychological science, theory, and clinical practice. The clinical psychology program is designed to emphasize the development of knowledge, skills and attitudes essential in the training of professional psychologists who are committed to the ethical provision of quality, evidence based services. The program follows a practitioner-scholar model and is based on the competencies developed by the National Council of Schools and Programs in Professional Psychology (NCSPP). The curriculum is designed to provide students with a broad array of theoretical perspectives in preparation for the general practice of clinical psychology. Required courses expose students to assessment and intervention strategies that are based on psychodynamic, cognitive, and experiential approaches. As a group, the program faculty is also representative of this diversity. Rather than being immersed in a single theoretical perspective, students are encouraged to consider these alternative perspectives, to critically evaluate the full range of theories and associated practices, and to be able to apply multiple theoretical perspectives to clinical issues.

Special Facilities or Resources: Our program emphasizes a specialized hands-on clinical training through our Intensive Clinical Training facility. Through the Intensive Clinical Training series, students work directly with clients referred from the community while being observed by a team through a one-way mirror. The team consists of the instructor and/or clinical assistant and fellow students who participate in pre and post-therapy sessions in which they provide input and feedback about the therapeutic process. Each client session is guided by the instructor/assistant who, through the use of a microphone, provides clinical guidance and interventions directly to the student therapist through an earpiece worn by the student. As the session progresses, the instructor/assistant educates the team about the dynamics of the therapist/

client interaction and the treatment approach. Students may participate on three levels: 1) as a clinical observer and a member of the team; 2) as a student therapist working directly with clients, and 3) as a clinical assistant in concert with our Supervision/Consultation course. Our program also houses a community assessment clinic that serves as a practicum and internship site for students, or as an opportunity for supplemental assessment experience.

Application Information:

Send to Admissions Department, Argosy University, San Francisco Bay Area, 1005 Atlantic Avenue, Alameda, CA 94501. Application available online. URL of online application: https://portal.argosy.edu/Applicant/ApplyOnline_Login.aspx. Students are admitted in the Fall, application deadline January 15; Programs have rolling admissions. January 15 priority deadline for Fall, May 15 or later depending on space availability. Rolling Admissions depending on availability. *Fee:* $50.

Antioch University Santa Barbara (2012 data)

Graduate Psychology
602 Anacapa Street
Santa Barbara, CA 93101
Telephone: (805) 962-8179
Fax: (805) 962-4786
E-mail: *Blipinski@antioch.edu*
Web: *http://www.antiochsb.edu*

Department Information:

1977. Chairperson: Barbara Lipinski, PhD, J.D. Number of faculty: total—full-time 6, part-time 24; women—full-time 3, part-time 13; total—minority—full-time 1, part-time 13; women minority—part-time 5; faculty subject to the Americans With Disabilities Act 2.

Programs and Degrees Offered:

Listed in the following order: Program area, degree type (T if terminal Master's), number awarded 7/11–6/12. Clinical Psychology PsyD (Doctor of Psychology) 4.

Student Applications/Admissions:

Student Applications

Clinical Psychology PsyD (Doctor of Psychology)—Applications 2012–2013, 48. Total applicants accepted 2012–2013, 15. Number full-time enrolled (new admits only) 2012–2013, 15. Number part-time enrolled (new admits only) 2012–2013, 0. Total enrolled 2012–2013 full-time, 60. Total enrolled 2012–2013 part-time, 12. Openings 2013–2014, 15. The median number of years required for completion of a degree in 2012–2013 were 4. The number of students enrolled full- and part-time who were dismissed or voluntarily withdrew from this program area in 2012–2013 were 3.

Scores: Entries appear in this order: required test or GPA, minimum score (if required), median score of students entering in 2012–2013. *Clinical Psychology PsyD (Doctor of Psychology):* overall undergraduate GPA no minimum stated, last 2 years GPA no minimum stated, psychology GPA no minimum stated, Masters GPA no minimum stated.

Other Criteria: (importance of criteria rated low, medium, or high): GRE scores—low, research experience—low, work experience—medium, extracurricular activity—low, clinically related public service—high, GPA—medium, letters of recommendation—high, interview—high, statement of goals and objectives—high, writing sample—high, undergraduate major in psychology—medium, specific undergraduate psychology courses taken—low, The doctoral program requires two essays that are used to assess analytic and critical thinking. These are heavily weighted.

Student Characteristics: The following represents characteristics of students in 2012–2013 in all graduate psychology programs in the department: Female—full-time 46, part-time 7; Male—full-time 14, part-time 5; African American/Black—full-time 6, part-time 1; Hispanic/Latino(a)—full-time 12, part-time 1; Asian/Pacific Islander—full-time 3, part-time 1; American Indian/Alaska Native—full-time 2, part-time 0; Caucasian/White—full-time 34, part-time 7; Multi-ethnic—full-time 3, part-time 2; students subject to the Americans With Disabilities Act—full-time 3, part-time 0; Unknown ethnicity—full-time 0, part-time 0; International students who hold an F-1 or J-1 Visa—full-time 0, part-time 0.

Financial Information/Assistance:

Tuition for Full-Time Study: *Doctoral:* State residents: per academic year $21,915, $732 per credit hour; Nonstate residents: per academic year $21,915, $732 per credit hour. Tuition is subject to change. Additional fees are assessed to students beyond the costs of tuition for the following: Testing supplies, practicum and materials fee, professional liability insurance, technology fee. Tuition costs vary by program. See the following website for updates and changes in tuition costs: http://www.antiochsb.edu/financial-aid/tuition/.

Financial Assistance:

First-Year Students: Fellowships and scholarships available for first year.

Advanced Students: Teaching assistantships available for advanced students. Research assistantships available for advanced students. Traineeships available for advanced students. Fellowships and scholarships available for advanced students.

Additional Information: Of all students currently enrolled full time, 10% benefited from one or more of the listed financial assistance programs.

Internships/Practica: Doctoral Degree (PsyD Clinical Psychology): For those doctoral students for whom a professional psychology internship was required in this program prior to graduation, (15) students applied for an internship in 2011–2012, with (15) students obtaining an internship. Of those students who obtained an internship, (5) were paid internships. Of those students who obtained an internship, (0) students placed in APA/CPA accredited internships, (3) students placed in internships not APA/CPA accredited, but listed with the Association of Psychology Postdoctoral and Internship Programs (APPIC), (0) students placed in internships conforming to guidelines of the Council of Directors of School Psychology Programs (CDSPP), (12) students placed in internships that were not APA/CPA accredited, APPIC or CDSPP listed. Practica are available in a variety of settings such as community agencies, schools, hospitals, and mental health clinics, in Santa Barbara, San Luis Obispo, Los Angeles and

Ventura Counties. Doctoral candidates apply for full time internships through the national APPIC Match and through the CAPIC (California Psychology Internship Council) Match. Our applicants for internship have obtained APPIC member internships, APA accredited internships, and CAPIC member internships.

Housing and Day Care: No on-campus housing is available. No on-campus day care facilities are available.

Employment of Department Graduates:

Master's Degree Graduates: Of those who graduated in the academic year 2011–2012, the following categories and numbers represent the postgraduate activities and employment of master's degree graduates: Enrolled in a postdoctoral residency/fellowship (n/a), employed in independent practice (n/a), total from the above (master's) (0).

Doctoral Degree Graduates: Of those who graduated in the academic year 2011–2012, the following categories and numbers represent the postgraduate activities and employment of doctoral degree graduates: Enrolled in a psychology doctoral program (n/a), enrolled in a postdoctoral residency/fellowship (2), employed in government agency (2), total from the above (doctoral) (4).

Additional Information:

Orientation, Objectives, and Emphasis of Department: The Doctoral Program in Clinical Psychology at Antioch University Santa Barbara is a practitioner-scholar Doctor of Psychology (PsyD) Program. In addition to rigorous training in the broad and general scientific bases of psychology as well as the academic discipline and profession of clinical psychology, the curriculum integrates systemic, social justice, and multicultural perspectives with an emphasis in family psychology. Family forensic psychology coursework is offered for advanced students with training in assessing children and families, child custody evaluation, mediation and conflict resolution, family violence, forensic psychology, and expert witness testimony. Our practitioner-scholar program prepares students in a sequential fashion over the course of four years culminating in the full time internship in the fifth year. Students contribute to the base of research in professional psychology through their applied dissertations. Applicants may seek enrollment post bachelor's degree or post master's degree. Students entering with an earned master's degree in psychology, with equivalent courses, are given advanced standing and begin the program as second year students.

Special Facilities or Resources: Faculty are practicing professionals in their respective areas of expertise. Core faculty are engaged in a variety of research projects (according to their professional interests) which provide an opportunity for research assistantships for financial aid-eligible students.

Application Information:
Send to Admissions Office, Antioch University Santa Barbara, 602 Anacapa Street, Santa Barbara, CA 93101. Application available online. Students are admitted in the Fall, application deadline January 31. Priority admission for applicants meeting the January 31st deadline. *Fee:* $60. Fee may be waived in circumstances of financial need and when applicants attend a regularly scheduled information session about the PsyD program.

Argosy University/Orange County
Psychology
School of Psychology and Behavioral Sciences
601 South Lewis
Orange, CA 92868
Telephone: (714) 620-3701
Fax: (714) 620-3804
E-mail: *gbruss@argosy.edu*
Web: *http://www.argosy.edu*

Department Information:
2001. Program Chair, Clinical Psychology: Gary Bruss, PhD. Number of faculty: total—full-time 10, part-time 1; women—full-time 4; total—minority—full-time 5; women minority—full-time 4.

Programs and Degrees Offered:
Listed in the following order: Program area, degree type (T if terminal Master's), number awarded 7/11–6/12. Clinical Psychology PsyD (Doctor of Psychology) 16, Counseling Psychology EdD (Doctor of Education), Counseling Psychology MA/MS (Master of Arts/Science) (T), Clinical Psychology MA/MS (Master of Arts/Science) (T) 10, Forensic Psychology MA/MS (Master of Arts/Science) (T) 0.

APA Accreditation: Clinical PsyD (Doctor of Psychology). Student Outcome Data Website: http://www.argosy.edu/clinical-psychology/orange-county-california/psyd-programs-doctorate-degree-67912.aspx.

Student Applications/Admissions:

Student Applications

Clinical Psychology PsyD (Doctor of Psychology)—Applications 2012–2013, 137. Total applicants accepted 2012–2013, 40. Number full-time enrolled (new admits only) 2012–2013, 16. Number part-time enrolled (new admits only) 2012–2013, 0. Total enrolled 2012–2013 full-time, 134. Total enrolled 2012–2013 part-time, 0. Openings 2013–2014, 30. The median number of years required for completion of a degree in 2012–2013 were 5. The number of students enrolled full- and part-time who were dismissed or voluntarily withdrew from this program area in 2012–2013 were 4. *Counseling Psychology EdD (Doctor of Education)*—The median number of years required for completion of a degree in 2012–2013 were 4. *Counseling Psychology MA/MS (Master of Arts/Science)*—Openings 2013–2014, 40. *Clinical Psychology MA/MS (Master of Arts/Science)*—Applications 2012–2013, 17. Total applicants accepted 2012–2013, 9. Number full-time enrolled (new admits only) 2012–2013, 4. Number part-time enrolled (new admits only) 2012–2013, 0. Total enrolled 2012–2013 full-time, 12. Total enrolled 2012–2013 part-time, 0. Openings 2013–2014, 15. The median number of years required for completion of a degree in 2012–2013 were 2. The number of students enrolled full- and part-time who were dismissed or voluntarily withdrew from this program area in 2012–2013 were 0. *Forensic Psychology MA/MS (Master of Arts/Science)*—The median number of years required for completion of a degree in 2012–2013 were 2.

Scores: Entries appear in this order: required test or GPA, minimum score (if required), median score of students entering in 2012–2013. *Clinical Psychology PsyD (Doctor of Psychology):* GRE-V no minimum stated, GRE-Q no minimum stated, overall undergraduate GPA 3.25, 3.62, Masters GPA 3.5, 3.84; *Clinical Psychology MA/MS (Master of Arts/Science)*: overall undergraduate GPA 3.00, last 2 years GPA 3.00.

Other Criteria: (importance of criteria rated low, medium, or high): GRE scores—medium, research experience—medium, work experience—medium, extracurricular activity—medium, clinically related public service—medium, GPA—high, letters of recommendation—high, interview—high, statement of goals and objectives—high, undergraduate major in psychology—medium, specific undergraduate psychology courses taken—high, High emphasis on work experience for doctoral programs, although outstanding presentation in areas related to GPA, recommendation letters, interview, and personal statement can offset a deficit in work experience. Letters of recommendation from work, prior training, and/or academic references are expected for all programs. Emphasis on both clinical and academic references for doctoral applicants. For additional information on admission requirements, go to http://argosy.edu/clinical-psychology/orange-county-california/psyd-programs-admissions-67943.aspx.

Student Characteristics: The following represents characteristics of students in 2012–2013 in all graduate psychology programs in the department: Female—full-time 128, part-time 0; Male—full-time 30, part-time 0; African American/Black—full-time 6, part-time 0; Hispanic/Latino(a)—full-time 10, part-time 0; Asian/Pacific Islander—full-time 19, part-time 0; American Indian/Alaska Native—full-time 0, part-time 0; Caucasian/White—full-time 113, part-time 0; Multi-ethnic—full-time 8, part-time 0; students subject to the Americans With Disabilities Act—full-time 8, part-time 0; Unknown ethnicity—full-time 4, part-time 0; International students who hold an F-1 or J-1 Visa—full-time 3, part-time 0.

Financial Information/Assistance:

Tuition for Full-Time Study: *Master's:* State residents: $666 per credit hour; Nonstate residents: $666 per credit hour. *Doctoral:* State residents: $871 per credit hour; Nonstate residents: $871 per credit hour. Tuition is subject to change. Tuition costs vary by program. See the following website for updates and changes in tuition costs: http://www.argosy.edu/admissions/Default.aspx. Higher tuition cost for this program: Clinical Programs: MA, PsyD=$1107 per credit hour.

Financial Assistance:

First-Year Students: Teaching assistantships available for first year. Average amount paid per academic year: $1,000. Average number of hours worked per week: 6. Fellowships and scholarships available for first year. Average amount paid per academic year: $9,450.

Advanced Students: Teaching assistantships available for advanced students. Average amount paid per academic year: $1,000. Average number of hours worked per week: 6. Fellowships and scholarships available for advanced students. Average amount paid per academic year: $8,000.

Additional Information: Application and information available online at: http://www.argosy.edu/financial-aid/Default.aspx.

Internships/Practica: Doctoral Degree (PsyD Clinical Psychology): For those doctoral students for whom a professional psychology internship was required in this program prior to graduation, (26) students applied for an internship in 2011–2012, with (25)

students obtaining an internship. Of those students who obtained an internship, (23) were paid internships. Of those students who obtained an internship, (14) students placed in APA/CPA accredited internships, (8) students placed in internships not APA/CPA accredited, but listed with the Association of Psychology Postdoctoral and Internship Programs (APPIC), (0) students placed in internships conforming to guidelines of the Council of Directors of School Psychology Programs (CDSPP), (3) students placed in internships that were not APA/CPA accredited, APPIC or CDSPP listed. Master's Degree (MA/MS Clinical Psychology): An internship experience, such as a final research project or "capstone" experience is required of graduates. The specific clinical focus of the practicum varies according to the student's program, training needs, professional interests and goals, and the availability of practicum sites. MA Counseling and Clinical practica focus on training students in couples/family counseling and therapy skills. The PsyD Clinical Psychology practica provide one year of psychodiagnostic assessment training and one year of therapy training. Students are also required to complete a third year of practicum training in either therapy or psychodiagnostic assessment, or a combination thereof. The program is committed to finding a wide range of practicum sites to provide many options for student professional exposure and development.

Housing and Day Care: No on-campus housing is available. No on-campus day care facilities are available.

Employment of Department Graduates:

Master's Degree Graduates: Of those who graduated in the academic year 2011–2012, the following categories and numbers represent the postgraduate activities and employment of master's degree graduates: Enrolled in a postdoctoral residency/fellowship (n/a), employed in independent practice (n/a), total from the above (master's) (0).

Doctoral Degree Graduates: Of those who graduated in the academic year 2011–2012, the following categories and numbers represent the postgraduate activities and employment of doctoral degree graduates: Enrolled in a psychology doctoral program (n/a), total from the above (doctoral) (0).

Additional Information:

Orientation, Objectives, and Emphasis of Department: The graduate programs in psychology are designed to educate and train practitioners, with an additional emphasis on scholarly training in the doctoral programs. Courses and fieldwork experiences embrace multiple theoretical and intervention approaches, and a range of psychodiagnostic techniques (in the clinical programs), all of which are designed to serve a wide and diverse range of populations. Two PsyD concentrations are available in Forensic Psychology and in Child/Adolescent Psychology. Students are taught by faculty with strong teaching and practitioner skills, with a strong focus on developing students with the fundamental clinical, counseling and relevant scholarly competencies required to pursue careers in psychology. Courses in applied and academic areas are considered to be critical in the development of practitioners with the skills to develop, innovate, implement, and assess delivery of services to clientele in clinical, counseling, and educational types of settings.

Special Facilities or Resources: The campus has its own psychology clinic that is utilized for both clinical and research purposes.

Application Information:
Send to Director of Admissions, c/o Argosy University/Orange County, 601 South Lewis Street, Orange, CA 92868. Application available online. URL of online application: http://www.argosy.edu/admissions/Default.aspx. Students are admitted in the Fall, application deadline January 15; Spring, application deadline October 15; Summer, application deadline March 30. We offer a year around rolling admissions process for both the EdD-CP and MACP programs, with admissions points for Fall, Spring, and Summer semesters. PsyD and MA Clinical applicant deadlines are January 15 for fall admission only, with a May 15 deadline if spaces are available. *Fee:* $50.

Azusa Pacific University

Department of Graduate Psychology
School of Behavioral and Applied Sciences
901 East Alosta, P.O. Box 7000
Azusa, CA 91702-7000
Telephone: (626) 815-5008
Fax: (626) 815-5015
E-mail: *mlhoward@apu.edu*
Web: *http://www.apu.edu/bas/graduatepsychology/*

Department Information:
1976. Chairperson: Marjorie Graham-Howard, PhD. Number of faculty: total—full-time 17, part-time 1; women—full-time 9; total—minority—full-time 3, part-time 1; women minority—full-time 1.

Programs and Degrees Offered:
Listed in the following order: Program area, degree type (T if terminal Master's), number awarded 7/11–6/12. Clinical Psychology MA/MS (Master of Arts/Science) (T) 74, Clinical Psychology PsyD (Doctor of Psychology) 27.

APA Accreditation: Clinical PsyD (Doctor of Psychology). Student Outcome Data Website: http://www.apu.edu/bas/graduatepsychology/psyd/.

Student Applications/Admissions:
Student Applications
Clinical Psychology MA/MS (Master of Arts/Science)—Applications 2012–2013, 278. Total applicants accepted 2012–2013, 158. Number full-time enrolled (new admits only) 2012–2013, 56. Number part-time enrolled (new admits only) 2012–2013, 52. Total enrolled 2012–2013 full-time, 181. Total enrolled 2012–2013 part-time, 106. Openings 2013–2014, 140. The median number of years required for completion of a degree in 2012–2013 were 3. The number of students enrolled full- and part-time who were dismissed or voluntarily withdrew from this program area in 2012–2013 were 19. *Clinical Psychology PsyD (Doctor of Psychology)*—Applications 2012–2013, 182. Total applicants accepted 2012–2013, 47. Number full-time enrolled (new admits only) 2012–2013, 26. Number part-time enrolled (new admits only) 2012–2013, 0. Total enrolled 2012–2013 full-time, 76. Total enrolled 2012–2013 part-time, 41. Openings 2013–2014, 28. The median number of years required for completion of a degree in 2012–2013 were 4. The number of students enrolled full- and part-time who were

dismissed or voluntarily withdrew from this program area in 2012–2013 were 3.
Scores: Entries appear in this order: required test or GPA, minimum score (if required), median score of students entering in 2012–2013. *Clinical Psychology MA/MS (Master of Arts/Science)*: overall undergraduate GPA 2.7, 3.3; *Clinical Psychology PsyD (Doctor of Psychology)*: GRE-V 500, 500, GRE-Q 500, 600, GRE-Analytical 4.0, 4.5, overall undergraduate GPA 3.0, 3.4, Masters GPA 3.5, 3.9.
Other Criteria: (importance of criteria rated low, medium, or high): GRE scores—medium, research experience—medium, work experience—medium, extracurricular activity—medium, clinically related public service—medium, GPA—high, letters of recommendation—high, interview—high, statement of goals and objectives—high, undergraduate major in psychology—medium, specific undergraduate psychology courses taken—low, No GRE scores required for MA; Work experience of medium importance for MA; Research experience of medium importance for MA; Clinically Related Public Service low for MA; Specific undergraduate psychology courses taken medium weight for MA. For additional information on admission requirements, go to http://www.apu.edu/bas/graduatepsychology/.

Student Characteristics: The following represents characteristics of students in 2012–2013 in all graduate psychology programs in the department: Female—full-time 228, part-time 108; Male—full-time 55, part-time 40; African American/Black—full-time 16, part-time 6; Hispanic/Latino(a)—full-time 54, part-time 36; Asian/Pacific Islander—full-time 17, part-time 16; American Indian/Alaska Native—full-time 0, part-time 0; Caucasian/White—full-time 147, part-time 70; Multi-ethnic—full-time 3, part-time 0; students subject to the Americans With Disabilities Act—full-time 1, part-time 0; Unknown ethnicity—full-time 46, part-time 20; International students who hold an F-1 or J-1 Visa—full-time 4, part-time 2.

Financial Information/Assistance:
Tuition for Full-Time Study: *Master's:* State residents: $625 per credit hour; Nonstate residents: $625 per credit hour. *Doctoral:* State residents: $879 per credit hour; Nonstate residents: $879 per credit hour. Tuition is subject to change. Tuition costs vary by program. See the following website for updates and changes in tuition costs: http://www.apu.edu/graduatecenter/sfs/costs/tuition/.

Financial Assistance:
First-Year Students: Teaching assistantships available for first year. Average amount paid per academic year: $6,250. Average number of hours worked per week: 15. Apply by April 15. Research assistantships available for first year. Average amount paid per academic year: $6,250. Average number of hours worked per week: 15. Apply by April 15.
Advanced Students: Teaching assistantships available for advanced students. Average amount paid per academic year: $6,250. Average number of hours worked per week: 15. Apply by April 15. Research assistantships available for advanced students. Average amount paid per academic year: $6,250. Average number of hours worked per week: 15. Apply by April 15.
Additional Information: Of all students currently enrolled full time, 7% benefited from one or more of the listed financial

assistance programs. Application and information available online at: http://www.apu.edu/graduatecenter/sfs/financialaid/.

Internships/Practica: Doctoral Degree (PsyD Clinical Psychology): For those doctoral students for whom a professional psychology internship was required in this program prior to graduation, (25) students applied for an internship in 2011–2012, with (21) students obtaining an internship. Of those students who obtained an internship, (21) were paid internships. Of those students who obtained an internship, (15) students placed in APA/CPA accredited internships, (4) students placed in internships not APA/CPA accredited, but listed with the Association of Psychology Postdoctoral and Internship Programs (APPIC), (0) students placed in internships conforming to guidelines of the Council of Directors of School Psychology Programs (CDSPP), (2) students placed in internships that were not APA/CPA accredited, APPIC or CDSPP listed. PsyD students are required to complete 6 semesters of practicum experience. These experiences are gained in placements throughout Los Angeles, Orange, and San Bernardino Counties which provide diverse clinical and multicultural experiences. The Community Counseling Center at Azusa Pacific University provides clinical training for Masters level and Doctoral level students and serves as an outreach to the diverse area surrounding APU. A sequence of clinical practicum courses is offered simultaneously with the field placement experience. All doctoral students are required to complete one full year of psychology internship. APU places interns in a variety of sites (must be APA approved or those meeting APPIC standards) across the country. Students enrolled in the MA Program in Clinical Psychology complete a clinical training sequence that meets all requirements for future licensure as a Marriage and Family Therapist (MFT) in the state of California. Students complete 225 hours of direct client contact in diverse, multi-cultural settings, such as community counseling centers, domestic violence clinics, and schools. Students receive training in individual, marital, and group therapy and exposure to treatments that have been demonstrated to be effective with specific problems. A sequence of clinical placement courses is offered simultaneously with the field placement experience.

Housing and Day Care: No on-campus housing is available. No on-campus day care facilities are available.

Employment of Department Graduates:

Master's Degree Graduates: Of those who graduated in the academic year 2011–2012, the following categories and numbers represent the postgraduate activities and employment of master's degree graduates: Enrolled in a psychology doctoral program (2), enrolled in a postdoctoral residency/fellowship (n/a), employed in independent practice (n/a), employed in a professional position in a school system (1), employed in business or industry (1), employed in government agency (1), employed in a community mental health/counseling center (15), employed in a hospital/medical center (1), still seeking employment (2), not seeking employment (2), other employment position (6), do not know (43), total from the above (master's) (74).

Doctoral Degree Graduates: Of those who graduated in the academic year 2011–2012, the following categories and numbers represent the postgraduate activities and employment of doctoral degree graduates: Enrolled in a psychology doctoral program (n/a), enrolled in a postdoctoral residency/fellowship (2), employed in independent practice (3), employed in an academic position at

a 2-year/4-year college (1), employed in other positions at a higher education institution (3), employed in business or industry (2), employed in government agency (1), do not know (15), total from the above (doctoral) (27).

Additional Information:

Orientation, Objectives, and Emphasis of Department: The PsyD in Clinical Psychology with an emphasis in Family Psychology (APA-accredited) prepares students for the practice of professional psychology. The program adheres to a practitioner-scholar model of training and emphasizes development of the core competencies in clinical psychology adopted by the National Council of Schools and Programs of Professional Psychology. The program requires completion of a rigorous sequence of courses in the science and practice of psychology. Requirements include three years of clinical training, successful demonstration of clinical competency through examination, completion of a clinical dissertation, and a predoctoral internship. Pre-specialty education in family psychology and an emphasis in interdisciplinary studies, relating psychology to ethics, theology, and philosophy, are included. The program was designed to be consistent with the requirements of the Guidelines and Principles for Accreditation of Programs in Professional Psychology (APA, 1996). The MA in Clinical Psychology with an emphasis in Marriage and Family Therapy meets requirements for California MFT licensure. Concepts of individual psychology are integrated with interpersonal and ecological concepts of systems theory. Goals include cultivating the examined life, fostering theoretical mastery, developing practical clinical skills, encouraging clinically integrative strategies, and preparing psychotherapists to work in a culturally diverse world.

Special Facilities or Resources: All students have access to the APA PsycINFO database and all APA journals full-text online as part of their student library privileges. The Darling Library provides an attractive and functional set of resources for the APU PsyD and MA. The library is technology-friendly and includes the Ahmanson Information Technology Center, an area with 75 computer desks. Each computer is wired into the university system for Internet and library catalog system searches. PsycINFO, as well as over 100 additional licensed databases, are available for student literature and subject searches. Eight "scholar rooms" were designed as a part of the Darling Graduate Library to be used for conducting research and writing. Doctoral students in the dissertation phase of their program are given priority in the reservation of these rooms. There are also several conference rooms in the Darling Library that may be reserved for student study groups or research teams. The Department of Graduate Psychology runs the Community Counseling Center (CCC) which offers a range of psychological services to residents of the local and surrounding communities. The CCC is also a viable mental health resource for both undergraduate and graduate students enrolled at Azusa Pacific University, with a significant number of annual referrals obtained from the University Counseling Center. The CCC further contracts to provide services to the Azusa Unified School District, Walnut Valley Unified School District, and a domestic violence shelter as well as other entities based in the community. The CCC currently trains 60 MA and PsyD graduate students and has provided data for doctoral dissertations.

Information for Students With Physical Disabilities: See the following website for more information: http://www.apu.edu/lec/disabilities/.

Application Information:
Send to Azusa Pacific University, Graduate Admissions, 901 East Alosta, P.O. Box 7000, Azusa, CA 91702-7000. Application available online. URL of online application: http://www.apu.edu/apply/grad/. Students are admitted in the Fall, application deadline January 15; Spring, application deadline October 1. Application deadline for the PsyD program is January 15. Application deadlines for MA are as follows: Fall deadline is March 1 and Spring deadline is October 1. *Fee:* $45. $65 International Application Fee.

Biola University
Rosemead School of Psychology
13800 Biola Avenue
La Mirada, CA 90639
Telephone: (562) 903-4867
Fax: (562) 903-4864
E-mail: *tamara.anderson@biola.edu*
Web: *http://www.rosemead.edu/*

Department Information:
1941. Associate Dean and Director of Doctoral Programs: Tamara L. Anderson, PhD. Number of faculty: total—full-time 22, part-time 5; women—full-time 12, part-time 2; total—minority—full-time 5, part-time 2; women minority—full-time 4, part-time 1.

Programs and Degrees Offered:
Listed in the following order: Program area, degree type (T if terminal Master's), number awarded 7/11–6/12. Clinical Psychology PsyD (Doctor of Psychology) 7, Clinical Psychology PhD (Doctor of Philosophy) 6.

APA Accreditation: Clinical PsyD (Doctor of Psychology). Student Outcome Data Website: http://www.rosemead.edu/programs/. Clinical PhD (Doctor of Philosophy). Student Outcome Data Website: http://www.rosemead.edu/programs/.

Student Applications/Admissions:
Student Applications
Clinical Psychology PsyD (Doctor of Psychology)—Applications 2012–2013, 157. Total applicants accepted 2012–2013, 30. Number full-time enrolled (new admits only) 2012–2013, 14. Number part-time enrolled (new admits only) 2012–2013, 0. Total enrolled 2012–2013 full-time, 78. Total enrolled 2012–2013 part-time, 0. Openings 2013–2014, 18. The median number of years required for completion of a degree in 2012–2013 were 5. The number of students enrolled full- and part-time who were dismissed or voluntarily withdrew from this program area in 2012–2013 were 2. *Clinical Psychology PhD (Doctor of Philosophy)*—Applications 2012–2013, 105. Total applicants accepted 2012–2013, 15. Number full-time enrolled (new admits only) 2012–2013, 10. Number part-time enrolled (new admits only) 2012–2013, 0. Total enrolled 2012–2013 full-time, 53. Total enrolled 2012–2013 part-time, 1. Openings 2013–2014, 8. The median number of years required for completion of a degree in 2012–2013 were 6. The number of students enrolled full- and part-time who were dismissed or voluntarily withdrew from this program area in 2012–2013 were 0.

Scores: Entries appear in this order: required test or GPA, minimum score (if required), median score of students entering in 2012–2013. *Clinical Psychology PsyD (Doctor of Psychology):* GRE-V 500, 540, GRE-Q 500, 620, overall undergraduate GPA 3.0, 3.59, last 2 years GPA no minimum stated, psychology GPA no minimum stated, Masters GPA 3.0, 3.65; *Clinical Psychology PhD (Doctor of Philosophy):* GRE-V 500, 580, GRE-Q 500, 680, overall undergraduate GPA 3.0, 3.56, last 2 years GPA no minimum stated, psychology GPA no minimum stated, Masters GPA 3.0, 3.89.

Other Criteria: (importance of criteria rated low, medium, or high): GRE scores—high, research experience—medium, work experience—low, extracurricular activity—low, clinically related public service—medium, GPA—high, letters of recommendation—high, interview—high, statement of goals and objectives—medium, essays—high, undergraduate major in psychology—medium, specific undergraduate psychology courses taken—high. For additional information on admission requirements, go to http://www.rosemead.edu/admissions/requirements/.

Student Characteristics: The following represents characteristics of students in 2012–2013 in all graduate psychology programs in the department: Female—full-time 78, part-time 1; Male—full-time 53, part-time 0; African American/Black—full-time 5, part-time 0; Hispanic/Latino(a)—full-time 12, part-time 0; Asian/Pacific Islander—full-time 24, part-time 0; American Indian/Alaska Native—full-time 1, part-time 0; Caucasian/White—full-time 83, part-time 1; Multi-ethnic—full-time 6, part-time 0; students subject to the Americans With Disabilities Act—full-time 0, part-time 0; Unknown ethnicity—full-time 0, part-time 0; International students who hold an F-1 or J-1 Visa—full-time 8, part-time 0.

Financial Information/Assistance:
Tuition for Full-Time Study: *Doctoral:* State residents: per academic year $22,408, $934 per credit hour; Nonstate residents: per academic year $22,408, $934 per credit hour. Tuition is subject to change. Additional fees are assessed to students beyond the costs of tuition for the following: professional growth fees. See the following website for updates and changes in tuition costs: http://www.rosemead.edu/tuition-financial-aid/tuition-and-fees/.

Financial Assistance:
First-Year Students: Teaching assistantships available for first year. Average amount paid per academic year: $1,688. Average number of hours worked per week: 5. Fellowships and scholarships available for first year. Average amount paid per academic year: $2,500.

Advanced Students: Teaching assistantships available for advanced students. Average amount paid per academic year: $2,025. Average number of hours worked per week: 6. Apply by April 1. Fellowships and scholarships available for advanced students. Average amount paid per academic year: $3,576. Apply by April 13.

Additional Information: Of all students currently enrolled full time, 89% benefited from one or more of the listed financial assistance programs. Application and information available online at: http://rosemead.edu/tuition-financial-aid/financial-aid/.

Internships/Practica: Doctoral Degree (PsyD Clinical Psychology): For those doctoral students for whom a professional psychology internship was required in this program prior to graduation, (12) students applied for an internship in 2011–2012, with (11) students obtaining an internship. Of those students who obtained an internship, (11) were paid internships. Of those students who obtained an internship, (7) students placed in APA/CPA accredited internships, (4) students placed in internships not APA/CPA accredited, but listed with the Association of Psychology Postdoctoral and Internship Programs (APPIC), (0) students placed in internships conforming to guidelines of the Council of Directors of School Psychology Programs (CDSPP), (0) students placed in internships that were not APA/CPA accredited, APPIC or CDSPP listed. Doctoral Degree (PhD Clinical Psychology): For those doctoral students for whom a professional psychology internship was required in this program prior to graduation, (8) students applied for an internship in 2011–2012, with (8) students obtaining an internship. Of those students who obtained an internship, (8) were paid internships. Of those students who obtained an internship, (6) students placed in APA/CPA accredited internships, (2) students placed in internships not APA/CPA accredited, but listed with the Association of Psychology Postdoctoral and Internship Programs (APPIC), (0) students placed in internships conforming to guidelines of the Council of Directors of School Psychology Programs (CDSPP), (0) students placed in internships that were not APA/CPA accredited, APPIC or CDSPP listed. The location of Biola University in La Mirada, California allows students access to multiple and diverse practicum and internship training sites throughout the five very large and culturally diverse counties. Given this prime location, Rosemead enjoys over sixty practicum training sites that include community mental health clinics, several university counseling centers, VA, and other medical centers. Overall, students will complete more than 2,000 hours of practicum and internship before they graduate; ensuring students are well equipped to enter the mental health community.

Housing and Day Care: On-campus housing is available. See the following website for more information: http://rosemead.edu/about/student-life/housing/. No on-campus day care facilities are available.

Employment of Department Graduates:
Master's Degree Graduates: Of those who graduated in the academic year 2011–2012, the following categories and numbers represent the postgraduate activities and employment of master's degree graduates: Enrolled in a postdoctoral residency/fellowship (n/a), employed in independent practice (n/a), total from the above (master's) (0).
Doctoral Degree Graduates: Of those who graduated in the academic year 2011–2012, the following categories and numbers represent the postgraduate activities and employment of doctoral degree graduates: Enrolled in a psychology doctoral program (n/a), enrolled in a postdoctoral residency/fellowship (6), employed in independent practice (3), employed in an academic position at a university (2), employed in other positions at a higher education

institution (1), employed in business or industry (1), employed in government agency (1), employed in a community mental health/counseling center (3), still seeking employment (1), total from the above (doctoral) (18).

Additional Information:
Orientation, Objectives, and Emphasis of Department: The historical theoretical orientation at Rosemead has been psychodynamic, and that model continues to be a cornerstone of training students to become excellent psychologists who provide high-quality psychotherapy services. The programs are based on the scholar-practitioner (PhD) and practitioner-scholar (PsyD) model of training in professional psychology. The substantive area is clinical psychology, and graduates are prepared to pursue postdoctoral training and become licensed to practice as clinical psychologists. The model of training leads to the formation of educational goals, which in turn lead to objectives and competencies. The goals, objectives, and competencies form a hierarchical educational structure that is stated in terms of student outcomes with increasing specificity for the competencies. The curriculum, including clinical training and required experiences, is designed to facilitate this educational structure. Achievement of program competencies is expected of all graduates.

Personal Behavior Statement: http://biola.edu/grad/downloads/applications/rosemead_application.pdf.

Special Facilities or Resources: Rosemead is housed on the Biola University campus. This campus is a 100-acre undergraduate and graduate campus, which for 20 years has been ranked by U.S. News & World Report as a National University. The Carnegie Foundation also lists Biola University as a Doctoral Research University. Rose Hall houses all psychology faculty and includes 25 offices, 4 therapy/research rooms equipped with one-way mirrors, videotape equipment, seminar, conference, and classrooms, the testing room and administrative staff space, the Rosemead Student Lounge, as well as a room specifically equipped for family/child therapy and outfitted with toys. Also available in Rose Hall are two research labs. One is devoted to Neuro-feedback research, and the other houses twelve computers, a discussion area, and media equipment for presentations. Biola Counseling Center is located just off the edge of campus and is housed in a professional building. BCC services the university undergraduates, graduate students, faculty and staff, as well as the community at large. BCC serves as a training clinic for our doctoral students and includes 20 consulting rooms (2 of which are fully stocked play therapy rooms), videotape equipment, one-way mirrors, computers for test scoring, and a large seminar room for student trainings and meetings.

Information for Students With Physical Disabilities: See the following website for more information: http://studentlife.biola.edu/academics/learning-center/disability.

Application Information:
Send to Office of Graduate Admissions, Biola University, Rosemead School of Psychology, 13800 Biola Avenue, La Mirada, CA 90639. Application available online. URL of online application: http://www.rosemead.edu/admissions/apply-now/. Students are admitted in the Fall, application deadline January 15. *Fee:* $55.

California Lutheran University

Graduate Psychology Department MC 4250
60 West Olsen Road
Thousand Oaks, CA 91360-2787
Telephone: (805) 493-3528
Fax: (805) 493-3388
E-mail: *mpuopolo@clunet.edu*
Web: *http://www.callutheran.edu/admission/psychology.php*

Department Information:

1959. Director, Graduate Programs in Psychology: Mindy Puopolo, PsyD. Number of faculty: total—full-time 12, part-time 27; women—full-time 4, part-time 18; total—minority—full-time 3, part-time 5; women minority—full-time 1, part-time 4.

Programs and Degrees Offered:

Listed in the following order: Program area, degree type (T if terminal Master's), number awarded 7/11–6/12. Clinical MA/MS (Master of Arts/Science) (T) 15, Marital and Family Therapy MA/MS (Master of Arts/Science) (T) 51, Clinical Psychology PsyD (Doctor of Psychology) 0.

Student Applications/Admissions:

Student Applications

Clinical MA/MS (Master of Arts/Science)—Applications 2012–2013, 59. Total applicants accepted 2012–2013, 36. Number full-time enrolled (new admits only) 2012–2013, 15. Number part-time enrolled (new admits only) 2012–2013, 2. Total enrolled 2012–2013 full-time, 35. Total enrolled 2012–2013 part-time, 6. Openings 2013–2014, 17. The median number of years required for completion of a degree in 2012–2013 were 2. The number of students enrolled full- and part-time who were dismissed or voluntarily withdrew from this program area in 2012–2013 were 1. *Marital and Family Therapy MA/MS (Master of Arts/Science)*—Applications 2012–2013, 143. Total applicants accepted 2012–2013, 101. Number full-time enrolled (new admits only) 2012–2013, 58. Number part-time enrolled (new admits only) 2012–2013, 1. Total enrolled 2012–2013 full-time, 118. Total enrolled 2012–2013 part-time, 17. Openings 2013–2014, 60. The median number of years required for completion of a degree in 2012–2013 were 2. The number of students enrolled full- and part-time who were dismissed or voluntarily withdrew from this program area in 2012–2013 were 1. *Clinical Psychology PsyD (Doctor of Psychology)*—Applications 2012–2013, 34. Total applicants accepted 2012–2013, 28. Number full-time enrolled (new admits only) 2012–2013, 15. Number part-time enrolled (new admits only) 2012–2013, 0. Total enrolled 2012–2013 full-time, 47. Total enrolled 2012–2013 part-time, 0. Openings 2013–2014, 17. The median number of years required for completion of a degree in 2012–2013 were 5. The number of students enrolled full- and part-time who were dismissed or voluntarily withdrew from this program area in 2012–2013 were 2.

Scores: Entries appear in this order: required test or GPA, minimum score (if required), median score of students entering in 2012–2013. *Clinical MA/MS (Master of Arts/Science):* last 2 years GPA 3.0; *Marital and Family Therapy MA/MS (Master of Arts/Science):* last 2 years GPA 3.0; *Clinical Psychology PsyD (Doctor of Psychology):* GRE-V no minimum stated, GRE-Q no minimum stated, GRE-Analytical no minimum stated, GRE-Subject (Psychology) no minimum stated, overall undergraduate GPA 3.0.

Other Criteria: (importance of criteria rated low, medium, or high): GRE scores—medium, research experience—medium, work experience—medium, extracurricular activity—low, clinically related public service—medium, GPA—high, letters of recommendation—medium, interview—high, statement of goals and objectives—high, undergraduate major in psychology—medium, specific undergraduate psychology courses taken—high, The PsyD in Clinical Psychology requires GRE scores as well as statements regarding previous research and practice experience. The Master's programs require either a minimum 3.0 GPA in upper division courses or GRE scores.

Student Characteristics: The following represents characteristics of students in 2012–2013 in all graduate psychology programs in the department: Female—full-time 177, part-time 20; Male—full-time 23, part-time 3; African American/Black—full-time 6, part-time 1; Hispanic/Latino(a)—full-time 39, part-time 8; Asian/Pacific Islander—full-time 11, part-time 0; American Indian/Alaska Native—full-time 1, part-time 0; Caucasian/White—full-time 114, part-time 11; Multi-ethnic—full-time 13, part-time 0; students subject to the Americans With Disabilities Act—full-time 6, part-time 6; Unknown ethnicity—full-time 16, part-time 3; International students who hold an F-1 or J-1 Visa—full-time 7, part-time 1.

Financial Information/Assistance:

Tuition for Full-Time Study: *Master's:* State residents: $625 per credit hour; Nonstate residents: $625 per credit hour. *Doctoral:* State residents: $875 per credit hour; Nonstate residents: $875 per credit hour. Tuition is subject to change. Additional fees are assessed to students beyond the costs of tuition for the following: practicum fee; assessment lab fee; competency exam fee. See the following website for updates and changes in tuition costs: http://www.callutheran.edu/student_accounts/tuition/.

Financial Assistance:

First-Year Students: Teaching assistantships available for first year. Average amount paid per academic year: $1,200. Average number of hours worked per week: 5. Apply by August 15. Research assistantships available for first year. Average amount paid per academic year: $1,200. Average number of hours worked per week: 5. Apply by August 15.

Advanced Students: Teaching assistantships available for advanced students. Average amount paid per academic year: $1,750. Average number of hours worked per week: 5. Apply by May 1. Research assistantships available for advanced students. Average amount paid per academic year: $1,750. Average number of hours worked per week: 5. Apply by May 1. Fellowships and scholarships available for advanced students. Average amount paid per academic year: $2,000. Average number of hours worked per week: 0.

Additional Information: Of all students currently enrolled full time, 44% benefited from one or more of the listed financial assistance programs. Application and information available online at: http://www.callutheran.edu/financial_aid/.

Internships/Practica: Master's Degree (MA/MS Clinical): An internship experience, such as a final research project or "capstone" experience is required of graduates. Master's Degree (MA/MS Marital and Family Therapy): An internship experience, such as a final research project or "capstone" experience is required of graduates. The Graduate Psychology Programs at CLU provide training through two Community Counseling and Parent Child Study Centers. Both centers offer low cost therapy services to the community. In addition, each center provides state-of-the-art counseling facilities including video and audio recording capabilities, two-way observation windows, play therapy rooms and a professional staff. Individual supervision, group supervision, case conference, staff training, peer support, and sharing of learning experiences in an atmosphere designed to facilitate growth as a therapist create exceptional training opportunities. The PsyD Program in Clinical Psychology requires three years of practicum experience and a one year full-time internship. The first year of practicum experience is completed at one of CLU's Counseling Centers. Practicum students have opportunities to work with individuals, couples, families and groups. A special feature of the Counseling Psychology Marital and Family Therapy Program is a 12-month practicum placement in the University's Community Counseling Services Center. Students may also choose an external practicum in a local community agency. Approximately 500 hours applicable to the California licensing requirement can be obtained through the MFT practicum experience.

Housing and Day Care: On-campus housing is available. See the following website for more information: http://www.callutheran. edu/student_life/res_life/graduate_housing.php. On-campus day care facilities are available. See the following website for more information: http://www.callutheran.edu/ecc/.

Employment of Department Graduates:

Master's Degree Graduates: Of those who graduated in the academic year 2011–2012, the following categories and numbers represent the postgraduate activities and employment of master's degree graduates: Enrolled in a postdoctoral residency/fellowship (n/a), employed in independent practice (n/a), total from the above (master's) (0).

Doctoral Degree Graduates: Of those who graduated in the academic year 2011–2012, the following categories and numbers represent the postgraduate activities and employment of doctoral degree graduates: Enrolled in a psychology doctoral program (n/a), total from the above (doctoral) (0).

Additional Information:

Orientation, Objectives, and Emphasis of Department: California Lutheran University's Doctor of Psychology (PsyD) degree in Clinical Psychology is a five-year program that integrates theoretical and practical approaches to prepare graduates for careers as licensed clinical psychologists. The program provides students with a broad perspective of psychology and explores the role of research in clinical practice. The program is accredited by the Western Association of Schools and Colleges (WASC), one of six regional accrediting associations in the United States. The curriculum includes six core courses that provide an in-depth developmental examination of major diagnostic categories, as well as areas of emphasis in research and practical skill development. The Master of Science degree in Clinical Psychology provides both a scientific and practitioner foundation in addition to providing excellent preparation for application to doctoral programs.

The Master of Science Degree in Counseling Psychology prepares the student to become a professional Marital and Family Therapist (MFT). The program is designed to meet all academic requirements for the state license in marriage and family therapy, administered by the California Board of Behavioral Sciences.

Special Facilities or Resources: In addition to the two Community Counseling and Parent Child Study Centers, CLU is in the process of completing a new Social and Behavioral Science Building complete with lab space and research facilities. The graduate programs in psychology also benefit from close relationships with local mental health agencies, both private and public.

Information for Students With Physical Disabilities: See the following website for more information: http://www.callutheran. edu/car/.

Application Information:
Send to Julius Munyantwali, Graduate Admission Counselor, 60 West Olsen Road, Thousand Oaks, CA 91360. Application available online. URL of online application: http://www.callutheran.edu/admission/ graduate/apply/. Students are admitted in the Fall, application deadline January 15. *Fee:* $75. Fee is $75 for PsyD and $50 for MFT/Clinical. Candidates who attend the regularly scheduled Information Meetings are eligible for an application fee waiver.

California Polytechnic State University
Psychology and Child Development
Liberal Arts
1 Grand Avenue, Building 47-24
San Luis Obispo, CA 93407
Telephone: (805) 756-2456
Fax: (805) 756-1134
E-mail: *escanu@calpoly.edu*
Web: *http://psycd.calpoly.edu/*

Department Information:
1969. Chairperson: Gary D. Laver. Number of faculty: total—full-time 18, part-time 14; women—full-time 13, part-time 8; total—minority—full-time 5, part-time 2; women minority—full-time 4, part-time 1; faculty subject to the Americans With Disabilities Act 1.

Programs and Degrees Offered:
Listed in the following order: Program area, degree type (T if terminal Master's), number awarded 7/11–6/12. Counseling Marriage and Family MA/MS (Master of Arts/Science) (T) 15.

Student Applications/Admissions:
Student Applications
Counseling Marriage and Family MA/MS (Master of Arts/Science)—Applications 2012–2013, 71. Total applicants accepted 2012–2013, 15. Number full-time enrolled (new admits only) 2012–2013, 12. Number part-time enrolled (new admits only) 2012–2013, 0. Total enrolled 2012–2013 full-time, 28. Total enrolled 2012–2013 part-time, 8. Openings 2013–2014, 20. The median number of years required for completion of a degree in 2012–2013 were 3. The number of students enrolled

full- and part-time who were dismissed or voluntarily withdrew from this program area in 2012–2013 were 1.

Scores: Entries appear in this order: required test or GPA, minimum score (if required), median score of students entering in 2012–2013. *Counseling Marriage and Family MA/MS (Master of Arts/Science):* GRE-V no minimum stated, 153, GRE-Q no minimum stated, 148, GRE-Analytical no minimum stated, 3.8, last 2 years GPA no minimum stated, 3.36.

Other Criteria: (importance of criteria rated low, medium, or high): GRE scores—medium, research experience—low, work experience—high, extracurricular activity—low, clinically related public service—high, GPA—medium, letters of recommendation—high, interview—high, statement of goals and objectives—high, undergraduate major in psychology—low, specific undergraduate psychology courses taken—low. For additional information on admission requirements, go to http://psycd.calpoly.edu/graduate/psychology.asp?pid=3.

Student Characteristics: The following represents characteristics of students in 2012–2013 in all graduate psychology programs in the department: Female—full-time 23, part-time 6; Male—full-time 5, part-time 2; African American/Black—full-time 0, part-time 0; Hispanic/Latino(a)—full-time 5, part-time 0; Asian/Pacific Islander—full-time 1, part-time 0; American Indian/Alaska Native—full-time 0, part-time 0; Caucasian/White—full-time 20, part-time 7; Multi-ethnic—full-time 2, part-time 0; students subject to the Americans With Disabilities Act—full-time 0, part-time 0; Unknown ethnicity—full-time 0, part-time 1; International students who hold an F-1 or J-1 Visa—full-time 0, part-time 0.

Financial Information/Assistance:

Tuition for Full-Time Study: *Master's:* State residents: per academic year $9,459; Nonstate residents: per academic year $20,619. Tuition is subject to change. See the following website for updates and changes in tuition costs: http://www.afd.calpoly.edu/fees/index.asp.

Financial Assistance:

First-Year Students: No information provided.

Advanced Students: No information provided.

Additional Information: Of all students currently enrolled full time, 0% benefited from one or more of the listed financial assistance programs. Application and information available online at: http://financialaid.calpoly.edu/.

Internships/Practica: Master's Degree (MA/MS Counseling Marriage and Family): An internship experience, such as a final research project or "capstone" experience is required of graduates. Cal Poly's MS in Psychology offers numerous well-supervised clinical practica and traineeships in a variety of public and private non-profit agencies. Training sites are selected based on their ability to provide: 1) quality supervision by a state-qualified licensed clinician; 2) assessment, diagnostic, and treatment experience with a wide variety of psychiatric disorders; 3) training in various treatment modalities, i.e., individual, couple, family, and group; and 4) exposure to a range of clients that represent the diversity of the community.

Housing and Day Care: On-campus housing is available. See the following website for more information: http://www.housing.calpoly.edu/. On-campus day care facilities are available. See the following website for more information: http://www.asi.calpoly.edu/childrens_center.

Employment of Department Graduates:

Master's Degree Graduates: Of those who graduated in the academic year 2011–2012, the following categories and numbers represent the postgraduate activities and employment of master's degree graduates: Enrolled in a postdoctoral residency/fellowship (n/a), employed in independent practice (n/a), total from the above (master's) (0).

Doctoral Degree Graduates: Of those who graduated in the academic year 2011–2012, the following categories and numbers represent the postgraduate activities and employment of doctoral degree graduates: Enrolled in a psychology doctoral program (n/a), total from the above (doctoral) (0).

Additional Information:

Orientation, Objectives, and Emphasis of Department: The M.S. in Psychology is designed for persons who desire to practice in the field of clinical/counseling psychology. The program's mission is to provide the state of California with highly competent master's-level practitioners who are academically and clinically prepared to counsel individuals, couples, families, and groups in a multicultural society. The program fulfills the educational requirements for the state of California's Marriage and Family Therapist (MFT) License. Its mission is also to provide students who want to proceed on to doctoral programs in clinical or counseling psychology with sound research skills, thesis experience, and clinical intervention training. Graduates find career opportunities in public agencies such as County Mental Health and Departments of Social Services as well as in private non-profit and private practice agencies. Ten to twenty percent of graduates go on to doctoral programs in clinical or counseling psychology.

Special Facilities or Resources: Closely supervised, on-campus practicum experiences leading to challenging traineeships in diverse community agencies are the cornerstone of Cal Poly's preparation for the future clinician. The program hosts and operates a community counseling services clinic with three counseling offices and an observation room that provides direct viewing through one-way mirrors and remotely controlled video equipment. Cal Poly's MS in Psychology is a clinically intensive program where on-campus practicum experience prepares students for community traineeship, and both training requirements position students nicely for community internships once they've graduated.

Information for Students With Physical Disabilities: See the following website for more information: http://drc.calpoly.edu/.

Application Information:

Send to Admissions Office, California Polytechnic State University, San Luis Obispo, CA 93407. Application available online. URL of online application: http://www.csumentor.edu/AdmissionApp/grad_apply.asp. Students are admitted in the Fall, application deadline December 1. Portfolio deadline is January 1. *Fee:* $55.

California State Polytechnic University-Pomona

Psychology & Sociology Department
College of Letters, Arts, and Social Sciences
3801 West Temple Avenue
Pomona, CA 91768
Telephone: (909) 869-3888
Fax: (909) 869-4930
E-mail: jsmio@csupomona.edu
Web: http://www.class.csupomona.edu/bhs/masters-in-psychology

Department Information:
1978. Director of M.S. in Psychology Program: Jeffery Scott Mio. Number of faculty: total—full-time 14, part-time 8; women—full-time 9, part-time 6; total—minority—full-time 4, part-time 2; women minority—full-time 3, part-time 1.

Programs and Degrees Offered:
Listed in the following order: Program area, degree type (T if terminal Master's), number awarded 7/11–6/12. Psychology MA/MS (Master of Arts/Science) (T) 12.

Student Applications/Admissions:
Student Applications

Psychology MA/MS (Master of Arts/Science)—Applications 2012–2013, 125. Total applicants accepted 2012–2013, 14. Number full-time enrolled (new admits only) 2012–2013, 14. Number part-time enrolled (new admits only) 2012–2013, 0. Total enrolled 2012–2013 full-time, 28. Total enrolled 2012–2013 part-time, 2. Openings 2013–2014, 16. The median number of years required for completion of a degree in 2012–2013 were 2. The number of students enrolled full- and part-time who were dismissed or voluntarily withdrew from this program area in 2012–2013 were 1.

Scores: Entries appear in this order: required test or GPA, minimum score (if required), median score of students entering in 2012–2013. *Psychology MA/MS (Master of Arts/Science):* overall undergraduate GPA 3.0, 3.7, last 2 years GPA 3.0, 3.7, psychology GPA 3.0, 3.7.

Other Criteria: (importance of criteria rated low, medium, or high): GPA—high, letters of recommendation—high, interview—medium, statement of goals and objectives—high, undergraduate major in psychology—medium, specific undergraduate psychology courses taken—medium. For additional information on admission requirements, go to http://www.class.csupomona.edu/bhs/psy/psy-master.html.

Student Characteristics: The following represents characteristics of students in 2012–2013 in all graduate psychology programs in the department: Female—full-time 21, part-time 1; Male—full-time 7, part-time 0; African American/Black—full-time 0, part-time 0; Hispanic/Latino(a)—full-time 7, part-time 1; Asian/Pacific Islander—full-time 4, part-time 0; American Indian/Alaska Native—full-time 0, part-time 0; Caucasian/White—full-time 14, part-time 1; Multi-ethnic—full-time 3, part-time 0; students subject to the Americans With Disabilities Act—full-time 0, part-time 0; Unknown ethnicity—full-time 0, part-time 0; International students who hold an F-1 or J-1 Visa—full-time 0, part-time 0.

Financial Information/Assistance:
Tuition for Full-Time Study: *Master's:* State residents: per academic year $5,800; Nonstate residents: per academic year $16,456. Tuition is subject to change. See the following website for updates and changes in tuition costs: http://cpp4me.csupomona.edu/cost-resources/tuition-costs.html.

Financial Assistance:
First-Year Students: No information provided.
Advanced Students: Fellowships and scholarships available for advanced students. Average amount paid per academic year: $1,000. Apply by March 2.
Additional Information: Of all students currently enrolled full time, 4% benefited from one or more of the listed financial assistance programs. Application and information available online at: http://dsa.csupomona.edu/financial_aid/.

Internships/Practica: Master's Degree (MA/MS Psychology): An internship experience, such as a final research project or "capstone" experience is required of graduates. This is an MFT program, so we require students to complete traineeships as per BBS requirements.

Housing and Day Care: On-campus housing is available. See the following website for more information: http://dsa.csupomona.edu/uhs/. On-campus day care facilities are available. See the following website for more information: http://dsa.csupomona.edu/childrenscenter/.

Employment of Department Graduates:
Master's Degree Graduates: Of those who graduated in the academic year 2011–2012, the following categories and numbers represent the postgraduate activities and employment of master's degree graduates: Enrolled in a postdoctoral residency/fellowship (n/a), employed in independent practice (n/a), employed in a community mental health/counseling center (12), total from the above (master's) (12).

Doctoral Degree Graduates: Of those who graduated in the academic year 2011–2012, the following categories and numbers represent the postgraduate activities and employment of doctoral degree graduates: Enrolled in a psychology doctoral program (n/a), total from the above (doctoral) (0).

Additional Information:
Orientation, Objectives, and Emphasis of Department: General marital and family orientation; eclectic.

Information for Students With Physical Disabilities: See the following website for more information: http://dsa.csupomona.edu/drc/.

Application Information:
Send to Graduate Admissions, Psychology & Sociology Department, 3801 West Temple Avenue, Pomona, CA 91768. Application available online. URL of online application: http://csumentor.edu. Students are admitted in the Fall, application deadline April 1. Deadline for international students: March 1. *Fee:* $55.

California State University, Dominguez Hills

Department of Psychology
Natural and Behavioral Sciences
1000 East Victoria Street
Carson, CA 90747
Telephone: (310) 243-3427
Fax: (310) 516-3642
E-mail: *kmason@csudh.edu*
Web: *http://www.nbs.csudh.edu/psychology*

Department Information:
1969. Coordinator, M.A in Psychology Program: Karen I. Wilson, PhD. Number of faculty: total—full-time 10, part-time 16; women—full-time 6, part-time 8; total—minority—full-time 7, part-time 6; women minority—full-time 5, part-time 3.

Programs and Degrees Offered:
Listed in the following order: Program area, degree type (T if terminal Master's), number awarded 7/11–6/12. Clinical Psychology MA/MS (Master of Arts/Science) (T) 15, Health Psychology MA/MS (Master of Arts/Science) (T) 0.

Student Applications/Admissions:
Student Applications
Clinical Psychology MA/MS (Master of Arts/Science)—Applications 2012–2013, 72. Total applicants accepted 2012–2013, 21. Number full-time enrolled (new admits only) 2012–2013, 21. Number part-time enrolled (new admits only) 2012–2013, 0. Total enrolled 2012–2013 full-time, 46. Total enrolled 2012–2013 part-time, 21. Openings 2013–2014, 20. The median number of years required for completion of a degree in 2012–2013 were 2. The number of students enrolled full- and part-time who were dismissed or voluntarily withdrew from this program area in 2012–2013 were 0. *Health Psychology MA/MS (Master of Arts/Science)*—Applications 2012–2013, 2. Total applicants accepted 2012–2013, 1. Number full-time enrolled (new admits only) 2012–2013, 1. Total enrolled 2012–2013 full-time, 1. Openings 2013–2014, 5. The number of students enrolled full- and part-time who were dismissed or voluntarily withdrew from this program area in 2012–2013 were 0.
Scores: Entries appear in this order: required test or GPA, minimum score (if required), median score of students entering in 2012–2013. *Clinical Psychology MA/MS (Master of Arts/Science):* GRE-V no minimum stated, GRE-Q no minimum stated, last 2 years GPA 3.0; *Health Psychology MA/MS (Master of Arts/Science):* GRE-V no minimum stated, GRE-Q no minimum stated, GRE-Analytical no minimum stated, overall undergraduate GPA no minimum stated, last 2 years GPA no minimum stated, psychology GPA no minimum stated.
Other Criteria: (importance of criteria rated low, medium, or high): GRE scores—medium, research experience—medium, work experience—low, clinically related public service—medium, GPA—high, letters of recommendation—high, interview—low, statement of goals and objectives—high. For additional information on admission requirements, go to http://www.nbs.csudh.edu/psychology/ma.htm.

Student Characteristics: The following represents characteristics of students in 2012–2013 in all graduate psychology programs in the department: Female—full-time 35, part-time 15; Male—full-time 12, part-time 6; African American/Black—full-time 6, part-time 3; Hispanic/Latino(a)—full-time 12, part-time 4; Asian/Pacific Islander—full-time 5, part-time 0; American Indian/Alaska Native—full-time 0, part-time 0; Caucasian/White—full-time 20, part-time 10; Multi-ethnic—full-time 0, part-time 0; students subject to the Americans With Disabilities Act—full-time 0, part-time 1; Unknown ethnicity—full-time 8, part-time 0; International students who hold an F-1 or J-1 Visa—full-time 0, part-time 1.

Financial Information/Assistance:
Tuition for Full-Time Study: *Master's:* State residents: per academic year $6,738; Nonstate residents: per academic year $13,434. Tuition is subject to change. Additional fees are assessed to students beyond the costs of tuition for the following: $618/academic year. See the following website for updates and changes in tuition costs: http://www.csudh.edu/admfin/accounting_services_sfs.shtml.

Financial Assistance:
First-Year Students: Fellowships and scholarships available for first year. Average amount paid per academic year: $2,000. Apply by March.
Advanced Students: Teaching assistantships available for advanced students. Fellowships and scholarships available for advanced students. Average amount paid per academic year: $2,000. Apply by March.
Additional Information: Of all students currently enrolled full time, 12% benefited from one or more of the listed financial assistance programs.

Internships/Practica: Master's Degree (MA/MS Clinical Psychology): An internship experience, such as a final research project or "capstone" experience is required of graduates. Master's Degree (MA/MS Health Psychology): An internship experience, such as a final research project or "capstone" experience is required of graduates. The Master of Arts in Psychology offers 550 supervised hours of practicum experience in a variety of settings.

Housing and Day Care: On-campus housing is available. See the following website for more information: http://www3.csudh.edu/student-affairs/housing/. On-campus day care facilities are available. See the following website for more information: http://www2.csudh.edu/asi/cdc/.

Employment of Department Graduates:
Master's Degree Graduates: Of those who graduated in the academic year 2011–2012, the following categories and numbers represent the postgraduate activities and employment of master's degree graduates: Enrolled in a psychology doctoral program (5), enrolled in another graduate/professional program (1), enrolled in a postdoctoral residency/fellowship (n/a), employed in independent practice (n/a), do not know (9), total from the above (master's) (15).
Doctoral Degree Graduates: Of those who graduated in the academic year 2011–2012, the following categories and numbers represent the postgraduate activities and employment of doctoral degree graduates: Enrolled in a psychology doctoral program (n/a), total from the above (doctoral) (0).

Additional Information:

Orientation, Objectives, and Emphasis of Department: The Clinical Psychology Master of Arts Program provides you with a solid academic background in clinical psychology as it is applied within a community mental health framework. This program prepares you for a career in counseling, teaching and research in community settings, which includes public or private agencies. Eighteen units of additional coursework prepare you for practice as a marriage and family therapist. Our graduates are successful in gaining admission to and graduating from the doctoral programs of their choice.

Special Facilities or Resources: Special resources include laboratory facilities.

Information for Students With Physical Disabilities: See the following website for more information: http://www3.csudh.edu/student-affairs/dss/.

Application Information:

Send to Department of Psychology, California State University, Dominguez Hills, 1000 East Victoria Street, Carson, CA 90747. Application available online. URL of online application: http://www3.csudh.edu/student-affairs/ois/graduate-students/. Students are admitted in the Fall, application deadline March 1. *Fee:* $55.

California State University, Fresno
Psychology
College of Science and Mathematics
2576 East San Ramon, Suite 11
Fresno, CA 93740
Telephone: (559) 278-2691
Fax: (559) 278-7910
E-mail: *llachs@csufresno.edu*
Web: *http://www.fresnostate.edu/csm/psych/*

Department Information:

1927. Chairperson: Constance Jones. Number of faculty: total—full-time 17, part-time 15; women—full-time 8, part-time 7; total—minority—full-time 1, part-time 2; women minority—full-time 1, part-time 1.

Programs and Degrees Offered:

Listed in the following order: Program area, degree type (T if terminal Master's), number awarded 7/11–6/12. General Experimental Psychology MA/MS (Master of Arts/Science) (T) 8, Applied Behavior Analysis MA/MS (Master of Arts/Science) (T) 3, School Psychology EdS (School Psychology) 9.

Student Applications/Admissions:

Student Applications

General Experimental Psychology MA/MS (Master of Arts/Science)—Applications 2012–2013, 24. Total applicants accepted 2012–2013, 10. Number full-time enrolled (new admits only) 2012–2013, 10. Total enrolled 2012–2013 full-time, 14. Openings 2013–2014, 10. The median number of years required for completion of a degree in 2012–2013 were 2. The number of students enrolled full- and part-time who were dismissed or voluntarily withdrew from this program area in 2012–2013 were 0. *Applied Behavior Analysis MA/MS (Master of Arts/Science)*—Applications 2012–2013, 29. Total applicants accepted 2012–2013, 10. Number full-time enrolled (new admits only) 2012–2013, 9. Total enrolled 2012–2013 full-time, 22. Openings 2013–2014, 10. The median number of years required for completion of a degree in 2012–2013 were 3. The number of students enrolled full- and part-time who were dismissed or voluntarily withdrew from this program area in 2012–2013 were 2. *School Psychology EdS (School Psychology)*—Applications 2012–2013, 23. Total applicants accepted 2012–2013, 10. Number full-time enrolled (new admits only) 2012–2013, 10. Total enrolled 2012–2013 full-time, 28. Openings 2013–2014, 10. The median number of years required for completion of a degree in 2012–2013 were 3. The number of students enrolled full- and part-time who were dismissed or voluntarily withdrew from this program area in 2012–2013 were 0.

Scores: Entries appear in this order: required test or GPA, minimum score (if required), median score of students entering in 2012–2013. *General Experimental Psychology MA/MS (Master of Arts/Science):* GRE-V no minimum stated, GRE-Q no minimum stated, GRE-Analytical no minimum stated, overall undergraduate GPA 3.0, last 2 years GPA no minimum stated, psychology GPA 3.0; *Applied Behavior Analysis MA/MS (Master of Arts/Science):* GRE-V no minimum stated, GRE-Q no minimum stated, GRE-Analytical no minimum stated, overall undergraduate GPA 3.0, last 2 years GPA no minimum stated, psychology GPA 3.0; *School Psychology EdS (School Psychology):* GRE-V no minimum stated, GRE-Q no minimum stated, GRE-Analytical no minimum stated, overall undergraduate GPA 3.0, last 2 years GPA no minimum stated, psychology GPA 3.0.

Other Criteria: (importance of criteria rated low, medium, or high): GRE scores—low, research experience—medium, work experience—low, extracurricular activity—low, clinically related public service—low, GPA—medium, letters of recommendation—high, interview—medium, statement of goals and objectives—high, undergraduate major in psychology—medium, specific undergraduate psychology courses taken—medium. For additional information on admission requirements, go to http://www.fresnostate.edu/csm/psych/graduate/requirements/.

Student Characteristics: The following represents characteristics of students in 2012–2013 in all graduate psychology programs in the department: Female—full-time 29, part-time 0; Male—full-time 25, part-time 0; African American/Black—full-time 0, part-time 0; Hispanic/Latino(a)—full-time 23, part-time 0; Asian/Pacific Islander—full-time 5, part-time 0; American Indian/Alaska Native—full-time 0, part-time 0; Caucasian/White—full-time 23, part-time 0; Multi-ethnic—full-time 2, part-time 0; students subject to the Americans With Disabilities Act—full-time 0, part-time 0; Unknown ethnicity—full-time 0, part-time 0; International students who hold an F-1 or J-1 Visa—full-time 0, part-time 0.

Financial Information/Assistance:

Tuition for Full-Time Study: *Master's:* State residents: per academic year $7,540; Nonstate residents: per academic year $16,840. Tuition is subject to change. See the following website for updates and changes in tuition costs: http://www.fresnostate.edu/catoffice/current/fees.html.

Financial Assistance:

First-Year Students: Teaching assistantships available for first year. Average amount paid per academic year: $8,000. Average number of hours worked per week: 10. Apply by March 1. Fellowships and scholarships available for first year. Apply by November.

Advanced Students: Teaching assistantships available for advanced students. Average amount paid per academic year: $8,000. Average number of hours worked per week: 10. Apply by March 1. Fellowships and scholarships available for advanced students. Apply by November.

Additional Information: Application and information available online at: http://www.fresnostate.edu/studentaffairs/financialaid/.

Internships/Practica: Master's Degree (MA/MS General Experimental Psychology): An internship experience, such as a final research project or "capstone" experience is required of graduates. Master's Degree (MA/MS Applied Behavior Analysis): An internship experience, such as a final research project or "capstone" experience is required of graduates. EdS program students are required to complete 500 hours of practicum and 1200 hours of internship.

Housing and Day Care: On-campus housing is available. See the following website for more information: http://www.universitycourtyard.org/. On-campus day care facilities are available. See the following website for more information: http://www.fresnostate.edu/academics/pfc/.

Employment of Department Graduates:

Master's Degree Graduates: Of those who graduated in the academic year 2011–2012, the following categories and numbers represent the postgraduate activities and employment of master's degree graduates: Enrolled in a postdoctoral residency/fellowship (n/a), employed in independent practice (n/a), total from the above (master's) (0).

Doctoral Degree Graduates: Of those who graduated in the academic year 2011–2012, the following categories and numbers represent the postgraduate activities and employment of doctoral degree graduates: Enrolled in a psychology doctoral program (n/a), total from the above (doctoral) (0).

Additional Information:

Orientation, Objectives, and Emphasis of Department: The Master of Arts and Education Specialist degrees in psychology are designed to provide students with a broad background in psychology while allowing them opportunities to pursue areas of special interest. Fulfillment of the requirements for either degree prepares the student for positions in related community service, public institutions, college teaching, or research or for entrance into PhD programs in psychology.

Special Facilities or Resources: Extensive computer facilities and test library available.

Information for Students With Physical Disabilities: See the following website for more information: http://www.fresnostate.edu/studentaffairs/ssd/.

Application Information:

Application available online. URL of online application: http://www.fresnostate.edu/csm/psych/graduate/application/. Students are admitted in the Fall, application deadline January 15. *Fee:* $55.

California State University, Fullerton

Department of Psychology
Humanities and Social Sciences
P.O. Box 6846
Fullerton, CA 92834-6846
Telephone: (657) 278-3589
Fax: (657) 278-7134
E-mail: *kkarlson@fullerton.edu*
Web: *http://hss.fullerton.edu/psychology/graduate.asp*

Department Information:

1957. Chairperson: Jack Mearns. Number of faculty: total—full-time 28, part-time 48; women—full-time 18, part-time 33; total—minority—full-time 6, part-time 10; women minority—full-time 4, part-time 7.

Programs and Degrees Offered:

Listed in the following order: Program area, degree type (T if terminal Master's), number awarded 7/11–6/12. Clinical Psychology MA/MS (Master of Arts/Science) (T), Psychological Research MA/MS (Master of Arts/Science) (T).

Student Applications/Admissions:

Student Applications

Clinical Psychology MA/MS (Master of Arts/Science)—Total applicants accepted 2012–2013, 20. Number full-time enrolled (new admits only) 2012–2013, 20. Number part-time enrolled (new admits only) 2012–2013, 0. Total enrolled 2012–2013 full-time, 20. Openings 2013–2014, 20. The number of students enrolled full- and part-time who were dismissed or voluntarily withdrew from this program area in 2012–2013 were 1. *Psychological Research MA/MS (Master of Arts/Science)*—Applications 2012–2013, 80. Total applicants accepted 2012–2013, 18. Number full-time enrolled (new admits only) 2012–2013, 18. Number part-time enrolled (new admits only) 2012–2013, 0. Total enrolled 2012–2013 part-time, 7. Openings 2013–2014, 20. The median number of years required for completion of a degree in 2012–2013 were 2. The number of students enrolled full- and part-time who were dismissed or voluntarily withdrew from this program area in 2012–2013 were 1.

Scores: Entries appear in this order: required test or GPA, minimum score (if required), median score of students entering in 2012–2013. *Clinical Psychology MA/MS (Master of Arts/Science):* GRE-V no minimum stated, 151, GRE-Q no minimum stated, 148, GRE-Subject (Psychology) no minimum stated, 580, overall undergraduate GPA no minimum stated, 3.5, last 2 years GPA no minimum stated, psychology GPA 3.0, 3.47; *Psychological Research MA/MS (Master of Arts/Science):* GRE-V no minimum stated, 154, GRE-Q no minimum stated, 148, GRE-Subject (Psychology) no minimum stated, 600, overall undergraduate GPA no minimum stated, 3.5, last 2 years GPA no minimum stated, psychology GPA 3.0, 3.5.

Other Criteria: (importance of criteria rated low, medium, or high): GRE scores—high, research experience—high, clinically related public service—high, GPA—high, letters of recommendation—high, interview—high, statement of goals and objectives—high, specific undergraduate psychology courses taken—high, The Master of Science Program requires an interview. There is no interview required for the Master of Arts Program. For additional information on admission requirements, go to http://hss.fullerton.edu/psychology/graduate.asp.

Student Characteristics: The following represents characteristics of students in 2012–2013 in all graduate psychology programs in the department: Female—full-time 38, part-time 30; Male—full-time 23, part-time 6; African American/Black—full-time 0, part-time 0; Hispanic/Latino(a)—full-time 12, part-time 5; Asian/Pacific Islander—full-time 7, part-time 7; American Indian/Alaska Native—full-time 0, part-time 0; Caucasian/White—full-time 0, part-time 0; Multi-ethnic—full-time 1, part-time 0; students subject to the Americans With Disabilities Act—full-time 0, part-time 0; Unknown ethnicity—full-time 2, part-time 0; International students who hold an F-1 or J-1 Visa—full-time 2, part-time 1.

Financial Information/Assistance:
Financial Assistance:
First-Year Students: No information provided.
Advanced Students: No information provided.
Additional Information: Of all students currently enrolled full time, 0% benefited from one or more of the listed financial assistance programs. Application and information available online at: http://hss.fullerton.edu/psychology/financialaid.asp.

Internships/Practica: Master's Degree (MA/MS Clinical Psychology): An internship experience, such as a final research project or "capstone" experience is required of graduates. Master's Degree (MA/MS Psychological Research): An internship experience, such as a final research project or "capstone" experience is required of graduates. A majority of the internships are done in agencies which do family therapy and substance abuse prevention and treatment. Many are community mental health centers. Most internships have live and videotape supervision. Students have done internships in schools, policy psychology, county clinics, and inpatient settings as well. Most agencies combine clinical and community work and serve low income and minority populations. Internship sites must meet California Board of Behavioral Sciences licensure requirements for supervision. Students enroll in Fieldwork classes on campus, in addition to their on-site supervision. Fieldwork classes entail additional consultation about cases and review of videos of students' therapy sessions.

Housing and Day Care: On-campus housing is available. See the following website for more information: http://www.fullerton.edu/housing/. On-campus day care facilities are available. See the following website for more information: http://asi.fullerton.edu/cc/index.asp.

Employment of Department Graduates:
Master's Degree Graduates: Of those who graduated in the academic year 2011–2012, the following categories and numbers represent the postgraduate activities and employment of master's degree graduates: Enrolled in a postdoctoral residency/fellowship (n/a), employed in independent practice (n/a), total from the above (master's) (0).
Doctoral Degree Graduates: Of those who graduated in the academic year 2011–2012, the following categories and numbers represent the postgraduate activities and employment of doctoral degree graduates: Enrolled in a psychology doctoral program (n/a), total from the above (doctoral) (0).

Additional Information:
Orientation, Objectives, and Emphasis of Department: The MA program provides advanced coursework and research training in core areas of psychology. Completion of the MA can facilitate application to PhD programs in psychology and provides skills important to careers in education, the health professions, and industry. The MS program in clinical psychology is intended to prepare students for work in a variety of mental health settings, and the program contains coursework relevant for the MFT and LPCC licenses in California. The program is also designed to prepare students for PhD work in both academic and professional schools of clinical psychology.

Special Facilities or Resources: The department has laboratories for research in cognitive psychology, conditioning, perception, biopsychology, social psychology, psychological testing, and developmental psychology. The department also has extensive computer facilities, including a lab dedicated to grad student use.

Information for Students With Physical Disabilities: See the following website for more information: http://www.fullerton.edu/dss/.

Application Information:
Send to Graduate Office, Department of Psychology, California State Fullerton, P.O. Box 6846 (H-830M), Fullerton CA 92834-6846. Application available online. URL of online application: http://www.fullerton.edu/graduate/prospectivestudents/application.asp. Students are admitted in the Fall, application deadline March 1. *Fee:* $55. The fee waiver process is built into CSU Mentor (on line application). Only California residents are eligible.

California State University, Long Beach
Department of Psychology
College of Liberal Arts
1250 Bellflower Boulevard
Long Beach, CA 90840-0901
Telephone: (562) 985-5000
E-mail: *psygrad@csulb.edu*
Web: *http://www.csulb.edu/colleges/cla/departments/psychology/*

Department Information:
1949. Chairperson: Kenneth F. Green. Number of faculty: total—full-time 27, part-time 37; women—full-time 11, part-time 28; total—minority—full-time 8, part-time 10; women minority—full-time 6, part-time 7.

Programs and Degrees Offered:
Listed in the following order: Program area, degree type (T if terminal Master's), number awarded 7/11–6/12. Psychological Re-

search MA/MS (Master of Arts/Science) (T) 6, Industrial/Organizational Psychology MA/MS (Master of Arts/Science) (T) 6, Human Factors MA/MS (Master of Arts/Science) (T) 5.

Student Applications/Admissions:

Student Applications

Psychological Research MA/MS (Master of Arts/Science)—Applications 2012–2013, 66. Total applicants accepted 2012–2013, 18. Number full-time enrolled (new admits only) 2012–2013, 7. Number part-time enrolled (new admits only) 2012–2013, 3. Total enrolled 2012–2013 full-time, 12. Total enrolled 2012–2013 part-time, 15. Openings 2013–2014, 25. The median number of years required for completion of a degree in 2012–2013 were 2. The number of students enrolled full- and part-time who were dismissed or voluntarily withdrew from this program area in 2012–2013 were 0. *Industrial/Organizational Psychology MA/MS (Master of Arts/Science)*—Applications 2012–2013, 88. Total applicants accepted 2012–2013, 8. Number full-time enrolled (new admits only) 2012–2013, 8. Number part-time enrolled (new admits only) 2012–2013, 0. Total enrolled 2012–2013 full-time, 16. Total enrolled 2012–2013 part-time, 2. Openings 2013–2014, 10. The median number of years required for completion of a degree in 2012–2013 were 2. The number of students enrolled full- and part-time who were dismissed or voluntarily withdrew from this program area in 2012–2013 were 0. *Human Factors MA/MS (Master of Arts/Science)*—Applications 2012–2013, 24. Total applicants accepted 2012–2013, 13. Number full-time enrolled (new admits only) 2012–2013, 6. Number part-time enrolled (new admits only) 2012–2013, 1. Total enrolled 2012–2013 full-time, 12. Total enrolled 2012–2013 part-time, 4. Openings 2013–2014, 15. The median number of years required for completion of a degree in 2012–2013 were 2. The number of students enrolled full- and part-time who were dismissed or voluntarily withdrew from this program area in 2012–2013 were 0.

Scores: Entries appear in this order: required test or GPA, minimum score (if required), median score of students entering in 2012–2013. *Psychological Research MA/MS (Master of Arts/Science):* GRE-V no minimum stated, 155, GRE-Q no minimum stated, 151, GRE-Analytical no minimum stated, 4.42, last 2 years GPA no minimum stated, 3.65, psychology GPA no minimum stated, 3.64; *Industrial/Organizational Psychology MA/MS (Master of Arts/Science):* GRE-V no minimum stated, 155, GRE-Q no minimum stated, 153, GRE-Analytical no minimum stated, 4.40, last 2 years GPA no minimum stated, 3.78, psychology GPA no minimum stated, 3.87; *Human Factors MA/MS (Master of Arts/Science):* GRE-V no minimum stated, 155, GRE-Q no minimum stated, 151, GRE-Analytical no minimum stated, 4.23, last 2 years GPA no minimum stated, 3.71, psychology GPA no minimum stated, 3.68.

Other Criteria: (importance of criteria rated low, medium, or high): GRE scores—high, research experience—high, work experience—low, extracurricular activity—low, GPA—high, letters of recommendation—high, statement of goals and objectives—high, undergraduate major in psychology—medium, specific undergraduate psychology courses taken—high. For additional information on admission requirements, go to http://www.csulb.edu/colleges/cla/departments/psychology/graduate-application/.

Student Characteristics: The following represents characteristics of students in 2012–2013 in all graduate psychology programs in the department: Female—full-time 18, part-time 10; Male—full-time 22, part-time 11; African American/Black—full-time 1, part-time 3; Hispanic/Latino(a)—full-time 9, part-time 4; Asian/Pacific Islander—full-time 8, part-time 4; American Indian/Alaska Native—full-time 1, part-time 0; Caucasian/White—full-time 21, part-time 9; Multi-ethnic—full-time 0, part-time 1; students subject to the Americans With Disabilities Act—full-time 0, part-time 0; Unknown ethnicity—full-time 0, part-time 0; International students who hold an F-1 or J-1 Visa—full-time 1, part-time 0.

Financial Information/Assistance:

Tuition for Full-Time Study: *Master's:* State residents: per academic year $7,506; Nonstate residents: per academic year $14,202. Tuition is subject to change. See the following website for updates and changes in tuition costs: http://www.csulb.edu/depts/enrollment/registration/fees_basics.html.

Financial Assistance:

First-Year Students: Research assistantships available for first year. Average amount paid per academic year: $5,500. Average number of hours worked per week: 10. Apply by April 15. Fellowships and scholarships available for first year. Average amount paid per academic year: $2,500. Apply by March 1.

Advanced Students: Research assistantships available for advanced students. Average amount paid per academic year: $5,500. Average number of hours worked per week: 10. Apply by April 15. Fellowships and scholarships available for advanced students. Average amount paid per academic year: $2,500. Apply by March 1.

Additional Information: Of all students currently enrolled full time, 49% benefited from one or more of the listed financial assistance programs. Application and information available online at: http://www.csulb.edu/colleges/cla/departments/psychology/financial-sources/.

Internships/Practica: Master's Degree (MA/MS Psychological Research): An internship experience, such as a final research project or "capstone" experience is required of graduates. Master's Degree (MA/MS Industrial/Organizational Psychology): An internship experience, such as a final research project or "capstone" experience is required of graduates. Master's Degree (MA/MS Human Factors): An internship experience, such as a final research project or "capstone" experience is required of graduates. Graduate assistantship positions provide teaching, computer, and internship experiences to selected students in all the master's programs. Available teaching assignments include assistance to the introductory and intermediate statistics, psychological assessment, critical thinking, program evaluation, computer applications, and research methods courses. In addition to the aforementioned paid departmental positions, volunteer and/or externally funded research positions can be arranged with individual faculty members. Such research opportunities are often available in the physiological, cognition, language, human factors, language acquisition, and social psychology laboratories. Various internships in outside industrial and organizational settings are options for second-year MSIO students. Internships are available through Boeing, NASA and CUDA for MSHF students.

Housing and Day Care: On-campus housing is available. See the following website for more information: http://www.csulb.edu/divisions/students/housing/. On-campus day care facilities are available. See the following website for more information: http://www.csulb.edu/divisions/students/asi/cdc/index.html.

Employment of Department Graduates:

Master's Degree Graduates: Of those who graduated in the academic year 2011–2012, the following categories and numbers represent the postgraduate activities and employment of master's degree graduates: Enrolled in a postdoctoral residency/fellowship (n/a), employed in independent practice (n/a), total from the above (master's) (0).

Doctoral Degree Graduates: Of those who graduated in the academic year 2011–2012, the following categories and numbers represent the postgraduate activities and employment of doctoral degree graduates: Enrolled in a psychology doctoral program (n/a), total from the above (doctoral) (0).

Additional Information:

Orientation, Objectives, and Emphasis of Department: California State University Long Beach has three master's programs in psychology. The Master of Science in Psychology, Option in Human Factors (MSHF) prepares students to apply knowledge of psychology to the design of jobs, information systems, consumer products, workplaces and equipment in order to improve user performance, safety and comfort. Students acquire a background in the core areas of experimental psychology, research design and methodology, human factors, computer applications and applied research methods. The Master of Arts in Psychology, Option in Psychological Research (MAPR) prepares students for doctoral work in any psychology field or for master's-level research or teaching positions. Core seminars include cognition, learning, physiological and sensory psychology, social, personality, and developmental psychology, and quantitative methods. MAPR graduates who apply to doctoral programs have high acceptance rates with financial support. The Master of Science in Psychology, Option in Industrial and Organizational Psychology (MSIO) offers preparation for careers for which a background in industrial/organizational psychology is essential. These fields include personnel, organizational development, industrial relations, employee training, and marketing research.

Special Facilities or Resources: The Psychology Department is housed in a building that has wide and varied research facilities, including computer rooms and laboratories in clinical, developmental, human factors, industrial-organizational, behavioral neuroscience, social, and other areas of psychology. Computer facilities include many current software packages. The behavioral neuroscience area has access to a staffed university animal facility. For research in applied (e.g., community, health, industrial-organizational) and experimental (e.g., behavioral neuroscience, social) studies in psychology, there are many research suites and a test materials center. These facilities, located in the psychology building, are for research and training in interviewing, assessment, program and treatment evaluation, behavioral observation, collection and analysis of biological samples, and intervention strategies for hard-to-reach populations. Computer facilities are central to research in decision analysis, human-computer interface, statistical theory, assessment, and computer-aided instruction. Human factors labs include state-of-the-art air traffic control simulators (CHAAT - Center for Human Factors and Advanced Aeronautics Technologies), computerized tools for usability analyses (CUDA - Center for Usability Design and Accessibility), eye and motion tracking systems, and other computerized systems for research and

analysis. Our diversified facilities also accommodate research in managing diversity in the workplace and other topics in industrial/organizational psychology. Wifi is available throughout the campus.

Information for Students With Physical Disabilities: See the following website for more information: http://www.csulb.edu/divisions/students/dss.

Application Information:

Send to Psychology Graduate Office, 1250 Bellflower Boulevard, Long Beach, CA 90840-0901. Application available online. URL of online application: http://www.csulb.edu/depts/enrollment/admissions/graduate_programs.html. Students are admitted in the Fall, application deadline December 1. *Fee:* $55.

California State University, Northridge

Department of Psychology
Social and Behavioral Sciences
18111 Nordhoff Street
Northridge, CA 91330-8255
Telephone: (818) 677-2827
Fax: (818) 677-2829
E-mail: *carrie.saetermoe@csun.edu*
Web: *http://www.csun.edu/psychology*

Department Information:

1958. Chairperson: Carrie Saetermoe. Number of faculty: total—full-time 21, part-time 24; women—full-time 12, part-time 10; total—minority—full-time 7, part-time 3; women minority—full-time 6, part-time 1; faculty subject to the Americans With Disabilities Act 2.

Programs and Degrees Offered:

Listed in the following order: Program area, degree type (T if terminal Master's), number awarded 7/11–6/12. Clinical Psychology MA/MS (Master of Arts/Science) (T) 17, General Experimental Psychology MA/MS (Master of Arts/Science) (T) 13, Behavioral Clinical Psychology MA/MS (Master of Arts/Science) (T) 0.

Student Applications/Admissions:

Student Applications

Clinical Psychology MA/MS (Master of Arts/Science)—Applications 2012–2013, 57. Total applicants accepted 2012–2013, 17. Number full-time enrolled (new admits only) 2012–2013, 17. Number part-time enrolled (new admits only) 2012–2013, 0. Total enrolled 2012–2013 full-time, 38. Total enrolled 2012–2013 part-time, 0. Openings 2013–2014, 15. The median number of years required for completion of a degree in 2012–2013 were 2. The number of students enrolled full- and part-time who were dismissed or voluntarily withdrew from this program area in 2012–2013 were 0. *General Experimental Psychology MA/MS (Master of Arts/Science)*—Applications 2012–2013, 50. Total applicants accepted 2012–2013, 15. Number full-time enrolled (new admits only) 2012–2013, 15. Number part-time enrolled (new admits only) 2012–2013, 0. Total enrolled 2012–2013 full-time, 30. Total enrolled 2012–2013 part-time, 0. Openings 2013–2014, 15. The median number of years required for completion of a degree in 2012–2013 were 2. The number of students enrolled full- and part-time who were dismissed or voluntarily withdrew from this program area in 2012–2013 were 2. *Behavioral Clinical Psychology MA/ MS (Master of Arts/Science)*—Applications 2012–2013, 100. Total applicants accepted 2012–2013, 30. Number full-time enrolled (new admits only) 2012–2013, 28. Total enrolled 2012–2013 full-time, 58. Openings 2013–2014, 35. The median number of years required for completion of a degree in 2012–2013 were 2. The number of students enrolled full- and part-time who were dismissed or voluntarily withdrew from this program area in 2012–2013 were 2.

Scores: Entries appear in this order: required test or GPA, minimum score (if required), median score of students entering in 2012–2013. *Clinical Psychology MA/MS (Master of Arts/ Science):* GRE-V no minimum stated, GRE-Q no minimum stated, GRE-Analytical no minimum stated, GRE-Subject (Psychology) no minimum stated; *General Experimental Psychology MA/MS (Master of Arts/Science):* GRE-V no minimum stated, GRE-Q no minimum stated, GRE-Analytical no minimum stated; *Behavioral Clinical Psychology MA/MS (Master of Arts/Science):* GRE-V no minimum stated, GRE-Q no minimum stated, GRE-Analytical no minimum stated, overall undergraduate GPA 3.0, 3.3, last 2 years GPA 3.0, 3.3, psychology GPA 3.0, 3.3.

Other Criteria: (importance of criteria rated low, medium, or high): GRE scores—medium, research experience—high, work experience—medium, extracurricular activity—medium, clinically related public service—high, GPA—medium, letters of recommendation—high, interview—medium, statement of goals and objectives—high, undergraduate major in psychology—medium, specific undergraduate psychology courses taken—medium, Clinically Related Public Services is rated HIGH by the Clinical option; low relevance for the General Experimental option. Interviews are required by the Clinical and Behavioral Clinical options, either in-person (preferred) or via telephone (if necessary due to geographical restrictions). For additional information on admission requirements, go to https://www.csun.edu/grip/graduatestudies/admissions.html.

Student Characteristics: The following represents characteristics of students in 2012–2013 in all graduate psychology programs in the department: Female—full-time 102, part-time 0; Male—full-time 32, part-time 0; African American/Black—full-time 4, part-time 0; Hispanic/Latino(a)—full-time 11, part-time 0; Asian/Pacific Islander—full-time 11, part-time 0; American Indian/Alaska Native—full-time 0, part-time 0; Caucasian/White—full-time 12, part-time 0; Multi-ethnic—full-time 18, part-time 0; students subject to the Americans With Disabilities Act—full-time 2, part-time 0; Unknown ethnicity—full-time 78, part-time 0; International students who hold an F-1 or J-1 Visa—full-time 3, part-time 0.

Financial Information/Assistance:
Tuition for Full-Time Study: *Master's:* State residents: per academic year $7,770; Nonstate residents: per academic year $17,744. Tuition is subject to change. Tuition costs vary by program. See the following website for updates and changes in tuition costs: http://www.csun.edu/financialaid/basics/cost.php. Higher tuition cost for this program: Behavioral Clinical Program: $23,310 (~$630 a unit; 37 units) + Practica.

Financial Assistance:
First-Year Students: No information provided.
Advanced Students: Teaching assistantships available for advanced students. Apply by March 13.
Additional Information: Application and information available online at: http://www.csun.edu/grip/graduatestudies/sfo/.

Internships/Practica: Master's Degree (MA/MS Behavioral Clinical Psychology): An internship experience, such as a final research project or "capstone" experience is required of graduates. Graduate students in applied fields have available an array of practicum experiences in the area. Direct clinical practicum experience is required of the Clinical students, who receive supervised training in three campus clinics specializing in Parent Child Interaction Training, Child and Adolescent Diagnostic Assessment, and Cognitive-Behavioral Psychotherapy. In addition, clinical internships are available in many community sites including the University Counseling Services and local mental health care facilities. General Experimental students work with departmental faculty as well as with those at neighboring universities. The Behavioral Clinical Psychology (BCP) graduate program offers practica and internships in community, school, clinics, and in-home settings. The purpose of the CSUN practicum program is to offer BCP students access to high quality supervised experiences during which students apply the skills acquired in their educational coursework.

Housing and Day Care: On-campus housing is available. See the following website for more information: http://housing.csun.edu. On-campus day care facilities are available. See the following website for more information: http://www.csunas.org/childrenscenter/.

Employment of Department Graduates:
Master's Degree Graduates: Of those who graduated in the academic year 2011–2012, the following categories and numbers represent the postgraduate activities and employment of master's degree graduates: Enrolled in a psychology doctoral program (15), enrolled in another graduate/professional program (5), enrolled in a postdoctoral residency/fellowship (n/a), employed in independent practice (n/a), other employment position (3), do not know (5), total from the above (master's) (28).
Doctoral Degree Graduates: Of those who graduated in the academic year 2011–2012, the following categories and numbers represent the postgraduate activities and employment of doctoral degree graduates: Enrolled in a psychology doctoral program (n/a), total from the above (doctoral) (0).

Additional Information:
Orientation, Objectives, and Emphasis of Department: The Department of Psychology has, as a primary goal, the assurance that students receive a strong theoretical foundation as well as rigorous methodological and statistical coursework. In addition, all students must complete a project or a thesis in order to display their knowledge of their content area and their methodological sophistication. The General Experimental and Clinical programs emphasize the basic research and content knowledge required to enhance students' opportunities for entry into doctoral programs. The Behavioral Clinical Program (BCP) is a 2-year program during which students can obtain their MA degree and complete the Behavior Analyst Certification Board (BACB) coursework

requirements to be able to practice as behavior analysts and/or pursue PhD programs in behavior analysis.

Special Facilities or Resources: Some professors have federal or private grants that employ graduate students as research assistants. In addition, we have laboratories in Physiological Psychology (NeuroScan, BioPac), computer applications for Cognitive Psychology, multiple childcare sites for observation of children, and extensive research space. We also have a state-of-the-art Statistics Laboratory that can be used for data analysis for theses or projects.

Information for Students With Physical Disabilities: See the following website for more information: http://www.csun.edu/cod/.

Application Information:
Send to Psychology Graduate Office, California State University Northridge, 18111 Nordhoff Street, Northridge, CA 91330-8255. URL of online application: http://www.csumentor.edu/admissionapp/grad_apply.asp. Students are admitted in the Fall, application deadline February 1. Deadline for Clinical Psychology program is February 1; for Behavioral Clinical Psychology program February 22; for General Experimental Psychology March 1. *Fee:* $55.

California State University, Sacramento
Psychology
Social Sciences and Interdisciplinary Studies
6000 J Street
Sacramento, CA 95819-6007
Telephone: (916) 278-6254
Fax: (916) 278-6820
E-mail: *mendriga@csus.edu*
Web: *http://www.csus.edu/psyc/*

Department Information:
1947. Chairperson: Marya C. Endriga, PhD. Number of faculty: total—full-time 18, part-time 16; women—full-time 10, part-time 13; total—minority—full-time 6, part-time 5; women minority—full-time 2, part-time 5.

Programs and Degrees Offered:
Listed in the following order: Program area, degree type (T if terminal Master's), number awarded 7/11–6/12. Master Of Arts in Psychology MA/MS (Master of Arts/Science) (T) 18.

Student Applications/Admissions:
Student Applications
Master Of Arts in Psychology MA/MS (Master of Arts/Science)—Applications 2012–2013, 105. Total applicants accepted 2012–2013, 21. Number full-time enrolled (new admits only) 2012–2013, 17. Total enrolled 2012–2013 full-time, 76. Openings 2013–2014, 20. The median number of years required for completion of a degree in 2012–2013 were 4. The number of students enrolled full- and part-time who were dismissed or voluntarily withdrew from this program area in 2012–2013 were 6.
Scores: Entries appear in this order: required test or GPA, minimum score (if required), median score of students entering

in 2012–2013. *Master of Arts in Psychology MA/MS (Master of Arts/Science):* GRE-V no minimum stated, 152, GRE-Q no minimum stated, 149, GRE-Analytical no minimum stated, 4, GRE-Subject (Psychology) no minimum stated, 610, last 2 years GPA 2.5.
Other Criteria: (importance of criteria rated low, medium, or high): GRE scores—high, research experience—high, work experience—low, GPA—high, letters of recommendation—high, statement of goals and objectives—medium, undergraduate major in psychology—medium, specific undergraduate psychology courses taken—high. For additional information on admission requirements, go to http://www.csus.edu/psyc/graduate/Application-Materials.html.

Student Characteristics: The following represents characteristics of students in 2012–2013 in all graduate psychology programs in the department: Female—full-time 63, part-time 0; Male—full-time 21, part-time 0; African American/Black—full-time 5, part-time 0; Hispanic/Latino(a)—full-time 13, part-time 0; Asian/Pacific Islander—full-time 7, part-time 0; American Indian/Alaska Native—full-time 2, part-time 0; Caucasian/White—full-time 44, part-time 0; Multi-ethnic—full-time 5, part-time 0; Unknown ethnicity—full-time 4, part-time 0; International students who hold an F-1 or J-1 Visa—full-time 4, part-time 0.

Financial Information/Assistance:
Tuition for Full-Time Study: *Master's:* State residents: per academic year $6,738; Nonstate residents: per academic year $14,202. Tuition is subject to change. Additional fees are assessed to students beyond the costs of tuition for the following: athletics, student union, health facilities. See the following website for updates and changes in tuition costs: http://www.csus.edu/schedule/Fall2012Spring2013/fees.html#reg.

Financial Assistance:
First-Year Students: Traineeships available for first year.
Advanced Students: Teaching assistantships available for advanced students. Traineeships available for advanced students.
Additional Information: Of all students currently enrolled full time, 20% benefited from one or more of the listed financial assistance programs.

Internships/Practica: Master's Degree (MA/MS Master of Arts in Psychology): An internship experience, such as a final research project or "capstone" experience is required of graduates. Internships and practica are available for ABA and I/O students through local community agencies and state and county government departments.

Housing and Day Care: On-campus housing is available. See the following website for more information: http://www.csus.edu/housing/. On-campus day care facilities are available. See the following website for more information: http://www.asi.csus.edu/programs/childrens-center/.

Employment of Department Graduates:
Master's Degree Graduates: Of those who graduated in the academic year 2011–2012, the following categories and numbers represent the postgraduate activities and employment of master's degree graduates: Enrolled in a psychology doctoral program (3), enrolled in a postdoctoral residency/fellowship (n/a), employed in independent practice (n/a), employed in government agency

(3), employed in a community mental health/counseling center (4), total from the above (master's) (10).

Doctoral Degree Graduates: Of those who graduated in the academic year 2011–2012, the following categories and numbers represent the postgraduate activities and employment of doctoral degree graduates: Enrolled in a psychology doctoral program (n/a), total from the above (doctoral) (0).

Additional Information:

Orientation, Objectives, and Emphasis of Department: Our mission is to educate, research, and practice in the field of Psychology with dedication and enthusiasm. We facilitate students' intellectual and personal growth. We prepare students for graduate studies, the workforce, managing citizenship responsibilities and life demands. We advance the many areas of our discipline through active and creative scholarship. We serve diverse communities through meaningful collaborations with people and organizations. Through teaching, scholarship, and service we promote human equity, health and well-being, effective functioning, and respect for diversity.

Special Facilities or Resources: Department has a vivarium (rats), neuroscience labs, clinic facilities (for ABA, faculty research), after-school program for children with autism, trainee placements with community ABA programs, research opportunities with state government departments.

Information for Students With Physical Disabilities: See the following website for more information: http://www.csus.edu/sswd/.

Application Information:

Send to Psychology Department, CSU Sacramento. Application available online. URL of online application: http://www.csuMentor.edu. Students are admitted in the Fall, application deadline February 1. *Fee:* $55.

California State University, San Marcos
Master of Arts in General Experimental Psychology
College of Humanities, Arts, Behavioral, & Social Sciences
333 South Twin Oaks Valley Road
San Marcos, CA 92096
Telephone: (760) 750-4102
Fax: (760) 750-3418
E-mail: *smohseni@csusm.edu*
Web: *http://www.csusm.edu/psychology/*

Department Information:

1989. Chairperson: Miriam Schustack. Number of faculty: total—full-time 14, part-time 23; women—full-time 10, part-time 20; total—minority—full-time 3, part-time 1; women minority—full-time 1.

Programs and Degrees Offered:

Listed in the following order: Program area, degree type (T if terminal Master's), number awarded 7/11–6/12. General Experimental Psychology MA/MS (Master of Arts/Science) (T) 5.

Student Applications/Admissions:
Student Applications

General Experimental Psychology MA/MS (*Master of Arts/Science*)—Applications 2012–2013, 60. Total applicants accepted 2012–2013, 18. Number full-time enrolled (new admits only) 2012–2013, 11. Number part-time enrolled (new admits only) 2012–2013, 0. Total enrolled 2012–2013 full-time, 25. Total enrolled 2012–2013 part-time, 6. Openings 2013–2014, 12. The median number of years required for completion of a degree in 2012–2013 were 2. The number of students enrolled full- and part-time who were dismissed or voluntarily withdrew from this program area in 2012–2013 were 0.

Scores: Entries appear in this order: required test or GPA, minimum score (if required), median score of students entering in 2012–2013. *General Experimental Psychology MA/MS (Master of Arts/Science):* GRE-V no minimum stated, GRE-Q no minimum stated, GRE-Analytical no minimum stated, overall undergraduate GPA 2.5, last 2 years GPA no minimum stated, psychology GPA no minimum stated.

Other Criteria: (importance of criteria rated low, medium, or high): GRE scores—medium, research experience—high, work experience—low, extracurricular activity—low, GPA—high, letters of recommendation—high, statement of goals and objectives—high, undergraduate major in psychology—high, specific undergraduate psychology courses taken—medium. For additional information on admission requirements, go to http://www.csusm.edu/psychology/maprogram/index.html.

Student Characteristics: The following represents characteristics of students in 2012–2013 in all graduate psychology programs in the department: Female—full-time 19, part-time 5; Male—full-time 6, part-time 1; African American/Black—full-time 1, part-time 1; Hispanic/Latino(a)—full-time 6, part-time 2; Asian/Pacific Islander—full-time 1, part-time 0; American Indian/Alaska Native—full-time 0, part-time 0; Caucasian/White—full-time 14, part-time 3; Multi-ethnic—full-time 2, part-time 0; students subject to the Americans With Disabilities Act—full-time 0, part-time 0; Unknown ethnicity—full-time 1, part-time 0; International students who hold an F-1 or J-1 Visa—full-time 0, part-time 0.

Financial Information/Assistance:
Tuition for Full-Time Study: *Master's:* State residents: per academic year $8,066; Nonstate residents: per academic year $14,762. Tuition is subject to change. See the following website for updates and changes in tuition costs: http://www.csusm.edu/schedule/spring_2013/fees_and_charges.html.

Financial Assistance:

First-Year Students: Teaching assistantships available for first year. Average amount paid per academic year: $1,900. Average number of hours worked per week: 5. Research assistantships available for first year. Fellowships and scholarships available for first year.

Advanced Students: Teaching assistantships available for advanced students. Average amount paid per academic year: $1,900. Average number of hours worked per week: 5. Research

assistantships available for advanced students. Fellowships and scholarships available for advanced students.

Additional Information: Of all students currently enrolled full time, 90% benefited from one or more of the listed financial assistance programs. Application and information available online at: http://www.csusm.edu/finaid/.

Internships/Practica: Master's Degree (MA/MS General Experimental Psychology): An internship experience, such as a final research project or "capstone" experience is required of graduates. All students take a course in the Teaching of Psychology and are individually responsible for break-out groups from the Introduction to Psychology class.

Housing and Day Care: On-campus housing is available. See the following website for more information: http://www.csusm.edu/housing/. On-campus day care facilities are available. See the following website for more information: http://www.csusm.edu/ccf/.

Employment of Department Graduates:

Master's Degree Graduates: Of those who graduated in the academic year 2011–2012, the following categories and numbers represent the postgraduate activities and employment of master's degree graduates: Enrolled in a psychology doctoral program (5), enrolled in a postdoctoral residency/fellowship (n/a), employed in independent practice (n/a), total from the above (master's) (5).

Doctoral Degree Graduates: Of those who graduated in the academic year 2011–2012, the following categories and numbers represent the postgraduate activities and employment of doctoral degree graduates: Enrolled in a psychology doctoral program (n/a), total from the above (doctoral) (0).

Additional Information:

Orientation, Objectives, and Emphasis of Department: Our Master of Arts degree is designed to accommodate students with a range of goals. The active research programs of our faculty, and our recognition of psychology as a scientific enterprise, provide graduate students with the intensive research training and course work in primary content areas that are central to preparation for more advanced graduate work. Likewise, students who have aspirations for careers in community college teaching, community service, or business and industry, benefit from our program's emphasis on critical thinking, research methods, and advanced course work.

Special Facilities or Resources: In addition to well-equipped classrooms and research space campus-wide, the Psychology Department offers high quality research facilities in the Social and Behavioral Sciences building, which opened in Fall 2011. This building includes a new vivarium, and observational and experimental research rooms designed with the research programs of our faculty and their students in mind.

Information for Students With Physical Disabilities: See the following website for more information: http://www.csusm.edu/dss/.

Application Information:
Send to Administrative Coordinator, Department of Psychology, CSU San Marcos, San Marcos, CA 92096. Application available online. URL of online application: http://www.csusm.edu/gsr/graduatestudies/future-applynow.html. Students are admitted in the Fall, application deadline February 1. *Fee:* $55.

California, University of, Berkeley
Psychology Department
Letters & Sciences
3210 Tolman Hall
Berkeley, CA 94720-1650
Telephone: (510) 642-1382
Fax: (510) 642-5293
E-mail: *psychgradinfo@berkeley.edu*
Web: *http://psychology.berkeley.edu/*

Department Information:
1921. Chairperson: Richard Ivry. Number of faculty: total—full-time 35; women—full-time 16; total—minority—full-time 8; women minority—full-time 4; faculty subject to the Americans With Disabilities Act 1.

Programs and Degrees Offered:
Listed in the following order: Program area, degree type (T if terminal Master's), number awarded 7/11–6/12. Cognition, Brain, and Behavior PhD (Doctor of Philosophy) 4, Social/Personality Psychology PhD (Doctor of Philosophy) 6, Change, Plasticity, and Development PhD (Doctor of Philosophy) 4, Clinical Science PhD (Doctor of Philosophy) 4, Behavioral Neuroscience PhD (Doctor of Philosophy) 1.

APA Accreditation: Clinical PhD (Doctor of Philosophy). Student Outcome Data Website: http://psychology.berkeley.edu/research/clinical-science.

Student Applications/Admissions:
Student Applications
Cognition, Brain, and Behavior PhD (Doctor of Philosophy)—Applications 2012–2013, 146. Total applicants accepted 2012–2013, 8. Number full-time enrolled (new admits only) 2012–2013, 5. Number part-time enrolled (new admits only) 2012–2013, 0. Total enrolled 2012–2013 full-time, 31. Total enrolled 2012–2013 part-time, 0. Openings 2013–2014, 8. The median number of years required for completion of a degree in 2012–2013 were 6. The number of students enrolled full- and part-time who were dismissed or voluntarily withdrew from this program area in 2012–2013 were 0. *Social/Personality Psychology PhD (Doctor of Philosophy)*—Applications 2012–2013, 200. Total applicants accepted 2012–2013, 11. Number full-time enrolled (new admits only) 2012–2013, 6. Number part-time enrolled (new admits only) 2012–2013, 0. Total enrolled 2012–2013 full-time, 24. Total enrolled 2012–2013 part-time, 0. Openings 2013–2014, 6. The median number of years required for completion of a degree in 2012–2013 were 6. The number of students enrolled full- and part-time who

were dismissed or voluntarily withdrew from this program area in 2012–2013 were 0. *Change, Plasticity, and Development PhD (Doctor of Philosophy)*—Applications 2012–2013, 42. Total applicants accepted 2012–2013, 3. Number full-time enrolled (new admits only) 2012–2013, 1. Total enrolled 2012–2013 full-time, 11. Openings 2013–2014, 4. The median number of years required for completion of a degree in 2012–2013 were 5. The number of students enrolled full- and part-time who were dismissed or voluntarily withdrew from this program area in 2012–2013 were 0. *Clinical Science PhD (Doctor of Philosophy)*—Applications 2012–2013, 365. Total applicants accepted 2012–2013, 9. Number full-time enrolled (new admits only) 2012–2013, 3. Number part-time enrolled (new admits only) 2012–2013, 0. Total enrolled 2012–2013 full-time, 37. Total enrolled 2012–2013 part-time, 0. Openings 2013–2014, 7. The median number of years required for completion of a degree in 2012–2013 were 7. The number of students enrolled full- and part-time who were dismissed or voluntarily withdrew from this program area in 2012–2013 were 0. *Behavioral Neuroscience PhD (Doctor of Philosophy)*—Applications 2012–2013, 14. Total applicants accepted 2012–2013, 0. Number full-time enrolled (new admits only) 2012–2013, 0. Total enrolled 2012–2013 full-time, 4. Total enrolled 2012–2013 part-time, 0. Openings 2013–2014, 1. The median number of years required for completion of a degree in 2012–2013 were 5. The number of students enrolled full- and part-time who were dismissed or voluntarily withdrew from this program area in 2012–2013 were 0.

Scores: Entries appear in this order: required test or GPA, minimum score (if required), median score of students entering in 2012–2013. *Cognition, Brain, and Behavior PhD (Doctor of Philosophy)*: GRE-V no minimum stated, 618, GRE-Q no minimum stated, 700, GRE-Analytical no minimum stated, 3.7, overall undergraduate GPA 3.0, 3.55, last 2 years GPA 3.0, 3.86; *Social/Personality Psychology PhD (Doctor of Philosophy)*: GRE-V no minimum stated, 547, GRE-Q no minimum stated, 737, GRE-Analytical no minimum stated, 4.0, overall undergraduate GPA 3.0, 3.84, last 2 years GPA 3.0, 3.69; *Change, Plasticity, and Development PhD (Doctor of Philosophy)*: GRE-V no minimum stated, 750, GRE-Q no minimum stated, 765, GRE-Analytical no minimum stated, 5.25, overall undergraduate GPA 3.0, 3.77, last 2 years GPA 3.0, 3.8; *Clinical Science PhD (Doctor of Philosophy)*: GRE-V no minimum stated, 632, GRE-Q no minimum stated, 700, GRE-Analytical no minimum stated, 4.7, overall undergraduate GPA 3.0, 3.67, last 2 years GPA 3.0, 3.88; *Behavioral Neuroscience PhD (Doctor of Philosophy)*: GRE-V no minimum stated, 633, GRE-Q no minimum stated, 683, GRE-Analytical no minimum stated, 4.5, overall undergraduate GPA 3.0, 3.6, last 2 years GPA 3.0, 3.85.

Other Criteria: (importance of criteria rated low, medium, or high): GRE scores—medium, research experience—high, work experience—high, extracurricular activity—medium, clinically related public service—high, GPA—medium, letters of recommendation—high, interview—high, statement of goals and objectives—high, interest in fac research—high, undergraduate major in psychology—medium, specific undergraduate psychology courses taken—medium, Clinical Science places heavier emphasis on clinical experience. For additional information on admission requirements, go to http://psychology.berkeley.edu/graduate-program/application-process-and-requirements.

Student Characteristics: The following represents characteristics of students in 2012–2013 in all graduate psychology programs in the department: Female—full-time 69, part-time 0; Male—full-time 38, part-time 0; African American/Black—full-time 6, part-time 0; Hispanic/Latino(a)—full-time 10, part-time 0; Asian/Pacific Islander—full-time 17, part-time 0; American Indian/Alaska Native—full-time 1, part-time 0; Caucasian/White—full-time 66, part-time 0; Multi-ethnic—full-time 7, part-time 0; students subject to the Americans With Disabilities Act—full-time 0, part-time 0; Unknown ethnicity—full-time 0, part-time 0; International students who hold an F-1 or J-1 Visa—full-time 8, part-time 0.

Financial Information/Assistance:

Tuition for Full-Time Study: *Doctoral:* State residents: per academic year $14,498; Nonstate residents: per academic year $29,600. Tuition is subject to change. See the following website for updates and changes in tuition costs: http://registrar.berkeley.edu/current_students/registration_enrollment/feesched.html.

Financial Assistance:

First-Year Students: Teaching assistantships available for first year. Average amount paid per academic year: $17,656. Average number of hours worked per week: 20. Research assistantships available for first year. Average amount paid per academic year: $19,160. Average number of hours worked per week: 20. Fellowships and scholarships available for first year. Average amount paid per academic year: $26,000. Apply by November 30.

Advanced Students: Teaching assistantships available for advanced students. Average amount paid per academic year: $18,610. Average number of hours worked per week: 20. Research assistantships available for advanced students. Average amount paid per academic year: $19,160. Average number of hours worked per week: 20. Fellowships and scholarships available for advanced students. Average amount paid per academic year: $24,000.

Additional Information: Of all students currently enrolled full time, 95% benefited from one or more of the listed financial assistance programs. Application and information available online at: http://students.berkeley.edu/finaid/graduates/index.htm.

Internships/Practica: Doctoral Degree (PhD Clinical Science): For those doctoral students for whom a professional psychology internship was required in this program prior to graduation, (3) students applied for an internship in 2011–2012, with (2) students obtaining an internship. Of those students who obtained an internship, (2) were paid internships. Of those students who obtained an internship, (2) students placed in APA/CPA accredited internships, (0) students placed in internships not APA/CPA accredited, but listed with the Association of Psychology Postdoctoral and Internship Programs (APPIC), (0) students placed in internships conforming to guidelines of the Council of Directors of School Psychology Programs (CDSPP), (0) students placed in internships that were not APA/CPA accredited, APPIC or CDSPP listed. The sole practicum experience on-site is the Psychology Clinic, a pre-internship site for 2nd and 3rd year students in the Clinical Science program. A community clinic, operating on a sliding scale basis, for individuals and families in the Bay Area, the Clinic offers assessment, individual therapy, couples therapy, child/family therapy, and consultations.

Housing and Day Care: On-campus housing is available. See the following website for more information: http://www.housing.berkeley.edu/. On-campus day care facilities are available. See the following website for more information: http://www.housing.berkeley.edu/child/families/.

Employment of Department Graduates:

Master's Degree Graduates: Of those who graduated in the academic year 2011–2012, the following categories and numbers represent the postgraduate activities and employment of master's degree graduates: Enrolled in a postdoctoral residency/fellowship (n/a), employed in independent practice (n/a), total from the above (master's) (0).

Doctoral Degree Graduates: Of those who graduated in the academic year 2011–2012, the following categories and numbers represent the postgraduate activities and employment of doctoral degree graduates: Enrolled in a psychology doctoral program (n/a), total from the above (doctoral) (0).

Additional Information:

Orientation, Objectives, and Emphasis of Department: The goal of the graduate program in Psychology at Berkeley is to produce scholar-researchers with sufficient breadth to retain perspective on the field of psychology and sufficient depth to permit successful independent and significant research. The members of the Department have organized themselves into five graduate training areas. These areas reflect a sense of intellectual community among the faculty and correspond, in general, with traditional designations in the field. However, each graduate training area has a distinctive stamp placed upon it by the faculty and students that make up the program. The majority of our students enter graduate training and fulfill the requirements established by the five existent training areas. These requirements vary from area to area but always involve a combination of courses, seminars, and supervised independent research. Students are also encouraged to take courses outside the Psychology Department, using the unique faculty strengths found on the Berkeley campus to enrich their graduate training.

Special Facilities or Resources: The Department of Psychology is housed in Tolman Hall, a building shared with the Graduate School of Education. A library devoted to books and journals in psychology and education is maintained on the second floor of this building. The main office of the Psychology Department, as well as faculty and teaching assistant offices are on the third floor of Tolman Hall. Research rooms for carrying out a variety of studies with human subjects are on the basement, ground, fourth, and fifth floors. The basement also houses a human audition laboratory and an electronics shop. The Institute of Human Development is housed on the first floor of Tolman Hall, the Psychology Clinic on the second floor, and the Institute of Personality and Social Research on the fourth floor. The remaining research units—the Institute for Cognitive and Brain Sciences, the Field Station for the Study of Behavior, Ecology and Reproduction, the Institute of Business and Employee Relations, the Helen Wills Neuroscience Institute, the Henry H. Wheeler Center for Brain Imaging, and the Northwest Animal Facility—are located elsewhere on campus and in the adjacent areas.

Information for Students With Physical Disabilities: See the following website for more information: http://dsp.berkeley.edu/.

Application Information:
Send to Graduate Admissions, University of California, Berkeley, Department of Psychology, 3210 Tolman Hall, Berkeley, CA 94720-1652. Application available online. URL of online application: http://www.grad.berkeley.edu/prospective/index.shtml. Students are admitted in the Fall, application deadline November 30. *Fee:* $80. $100 fee for international applicants.

California, University of, Berkeley
School Psychology Program
Graduate School of Education
4511 Tolman Hall
Berkeley, CA 94720-1670
Telephone: (510) 642-7581
Fax: (510) 642-3555
E-mail: *frankc@berkeley.edu*
Web: *http://dev.gse.pantheon.berkeley.edu/cognition-development/school-psychology*

Department Information:
1966. Program Director: Frank C. Worrell. Number of faculty: total—full-time 2, part-time 7; women—full-time 1, part-time 5; total—minority—full-time 1.

Programs and Degrees Offered:
Listed in the following order: Program area, degree type (T if terminal Master's), number awarded 7/11–6/12. School Psychology PhD (Doctor of Philosophy) 3.

APA Accreditation: School PhD (Doctor of Philosophy). Student Outcome Data Website: http://gse3.berkeley.edu/program/SP/html/admissions.html.

Student Applications/Admissions:

Student Applications

School Psychology PhD (Doctor of Philosophy)—Applications 2012–2013, 59. Total applicants accepted 2012–2013, 8. Number full-time enrolled (new admits only) 2012–2013, 6. Total enrolled 2012–2013 full-time, 32. Openings 2013–2014, 7. The median number of years required for completion of a degree in 2012–2013 were 6. The number of students enrolled full- and part-time who were dismissed or voluntarily withdrew from this program area in 2012–2013 were 0.

Scores: Entries appear in this order: required test or GPA, minimum score (if required), median score of students entering in 2012–2013. *School Psychology PhD (Doctor of Philosophy):* GRE-V no minimum stated, GRE-Q no minimum stated, overall undergraduate GPA no minimum stated.

Other Criteria: (importance of criteria rated low, medium, or high): GRE scores—high, research experience—high, work experience—medium, extracurricular activity—medium, clinically related public service—medium, GPA—high, letters of recommendation—high, interview—high, statement of goals and objectives—high, undergraduate major in psychology—medium, specific undergraduate psychology courses taken—medium. For additional information on admission requirements, go to http://gse3.berkeley.edu/program/SP/html/admissions.html.

Student Characteristics: The following represents characteristics of students in 2012–2013 in all graduate psychology programs in the department: Female—full-time 24, part-time 0; Male—full-time 8, part-time 0; African American/Black—full-time 4, part-time 0; Hispanic/Latino(a)—full-time 3, part-time 0; Asian/Pacific Islander—full-time 3, part-time 0; American Indian/Alaska Native—full-time 0, part-time 0; Caucasian/White—full-time 21, part-time 0; Multi-ethnic—full-time 1, part-time 0; students subject to the Americans With Disabilities Act—full-time 0, part-time 0; Unknown ethnicity—full-time 0, part-time 0; International students who hold an F-1 or J-1 Visa—full-time 2, part-time 0.

Financial Information/Assistance:

Tuition for Full-Time Study: *Doctoral:* State residents: per academic year $15,339; Nonstate residents: per academic year $30,441. Tuition is subject to change. See the following website for updates and changes in tuition costs: http://registrar.berkeley.edu/Registration/feesched.html.

Financial Assistance:

First-Year Students: Teaching assistantships available for first year. Average amount paid per academic year: $17,655. Average number of hours worked per week: 20. Research assistantships available for first year. Average amount paid per academic year: $16,698. Average number of hours worked per week: 20. Fellowships and scholarships available for first year. Average amount paid per academic year: $23,050. Apply by December 1.

Advanced Students: Teaching assistantships available for advanced students. Average amount paid per academic year: $19,535. Average number of hours worked per week: 20. Research assistantships available for advanced students. Average amount paid per academic year: $19,956. Average number of hours worked per week: 20. Fellowships and scholarships available for advanced students. Average amount paid per academic year: $14,250. Apply by March 1.

Additional Information: Of all students currently enrolled full time, 80% benefited from one or more of the listed financial assistance programs. Application and information available online at: http://dev.gse.pantheon.berkeley.edu/fees-and-financial-support.

Internships/Practica: Doctoral Degree (PhD School Psychology): For those doctoral students for whom a professional psychology internship was required in this program prior to graduation, (8) students applied for an internship in 2011–2012, with (8) students obtaining an internship. Of those students who obtained an internship, (6) were paid internships. Of those students who obtained an internship, (0) students placed in APA/CPA accredited internships, (0) students placed in internships not APA/CPA accredited, but listed with the Association of Psychology Postdoctoral and Internship Programs (APPIC), (8) students placed in internships conforming to guidelines of the Council of Directors of School Psychology Programs (CDSPP), (0) students placed in internships that were not APA/CPA accredited, APPIC or CDSPP listed. Students on school-based internships are usually paid on the basis of school-district schedule for half to three quarter time, usually from $13,000-$17,000/school year.

Housing and Day Care: On-campus housing is available. See the following website for more information: http://www.housing.berkeley.edu/livingatcal/graduatestudents.html. On-campus day care facilities are available. See the following website for more information: http://www.housing.berkeley.edu/child/families/.

Employment of Department Graduates:
Master's Degree Graduates: Of those who graduated in the academic year 2011–2012, the following categories and numbers represent the postgraduate activities and employment of master's degree graduates: Enrolled in a postdoctoral residency/fellowship (n/a), employed in independent practice (n/a), total from the above (master's) (0).
Doctoral Degree Graduates: Of those who graduated in the academic year 2011–2012, the following categories and numbers represent the postgraduate activities and employment of doctoral degree graduates: Enrolled in a psychology doctoral program (n/a), employed in a professional position in a school system (3), total from the above (doctoral) (3).

Additional Information:
Orientation, Objectives, and Emphasis of Department: The school psychology program is a doctoral program within the cognition and development area. The program emphasizes the scientist-professional model of school psychological services, linking strong preparation in theory and research to applications in the professional context of schools and school systems. Through the thoughtful application of knowledge and skills, school psychologists work together with teachers and other school professionals to clarify and resolve problems regarding the educational and mental health needs of children in classrooms. Working as consultants and collaborators, school psychologists help others to accommodate the social systems of schools to the individual differences of students, with the ultimate goal of promoting academic and social development. Graduate work within the program is supervised by professors from the Departments of Education and Psychology. Students fulfill all requirements for the academic PhD in human development, with additional coursework representing professional preparation for the specialty practice of school psychology. The program is accredited by APA.

Special Facilities or Resources: The school psychology program is based at the University of California, Berkeley, which is a major research university in a large metropolitan area of the country. Students have access to faculty research and university resources in countless topics and areas of specialization. The university and department sponsor numerous colloquia, speakers, and visiting lecturers from around the world throughout the year. Both intellectual and cultural resources abound. Ongoing research programs of faculty offer students opportunities to engage in applications of psychology to educational problems during their first three years of the program and in their dissertation research.

Information for Students With Physical Disabilities: See the following website for more information: http://dsp.berkeley.edu.

Application Information:
Send to Admission Office, Graduate School of Education. Application available online. URL of online application: http://www.grad.berkeley.edu/admissions/index.shtml. Students are admitted in the Fall, application deadline December 1. *Fee:* $80.

California, University of, Davis
Department of Psychology
College of Letters and Science
One Shields Avenue
Davis, CA 95616-8686
Telephone: (530) 752-9362
Fax: (530) 752-2087
E-mail: *klbales@ucdavis.edu*
Web: *http://psychology.ucdavis.edu*

Department Information:
1957. Chairperson: Paul Hastings. Number of faculty: total—full-time 39; women—full-time 15; total—minority—full-time 7; women minority—full-time 3.

Programs and Degrees Offered:
Listed in the following order: Program area, degree type (T if terminal Master's), number awarded 7/11–6/12. Developmental Psychology PhD (Doctor of Philosophy) 5, Social/Personality Psychology PhD (Doctor of Philosophy) 2, Quantitative Psychology PhD (Doctor of Philosophy) 1, Biological Psychology PhD (Doctor of Philosophy) 2, Perception, Cognition and Cognitive Neuroscience PhD (Doctor of Philosophy) 3.

Student Applications/Admissions:
Student Applications

Developmental Psychology PhD (Doctor of Philosophy)—Applications 2012–2013, 72. Total applicants accepted 2012–2013, 8. Number full-time enrolled (new admits only) 2012–2013, 4. Number part-time enrolled (new admits only) 2012–2013, 0. Total enrolled 2012–2013 full-time, 26. Total enrolled 2012–2013 part-time, 0. Openings 2013–2014, 4. The median number of years required for completion of a degree in 2012–2013 were 5. The number of students enrolled full- and part-time who were dismissed or voluntarily withdrew from this program area in 2012–2013 were 1. *Social/Personality Psychology PhD (Doctor of Philosophy)*—Applications 2012–2013, 163. Total applicants accepted 2012–2013, 5. Number full-time enrolled (new admits only) 2012–2013, 3. Number part-time enrolled (new admits only) 2012–2013, 0. Total enrolled 2012–2013 full-time, 26. Total enrolled 2012–2013 part-time, 0. Openings 2013–2014, 4. The median number of years required for completion of a degree in 2012–2013 were 5. The number of students enrolled full- and part-time who were dismissed or voluntarily withdrew from this program area in 2012–2013 were 1. *Quantitative Psychology PhD (Doctor of Philosophy)*—Applications 2012–2013, 21. Total applicants accepted 2012–2013, 6. Number full-time enrolled (new admits only) 2012–2013, 1. Total enrolled 2012–2013 full-time, 8. Openings 2013–2014, 4. The median number of years required for completion of a degree in 2012–2013 were 5. The number of students enrolled full- and part-time who were dismissed or voluntarily withdrew from this program area in 2012–2013 were 0. *Biological Psychology PhD (Doctor of Philosophy)*—Applications 2012–2013, 131. Total applicants accepted 2012–2013, 13. Number full-time enrolled (new admits only) 2012–2013, 6. Total enrolled 2012–2013 full-time, 25. Openings 2013–2014, 4. The median number of years required for completion of a degree in 2012–2013 were 6. The number of students enrolled full- and part-time who were dismissed or

voluntarily withdrew from this program area in 2012–2013 were 2. *Perception, Cognition and Cognitive Neuroscience PhD (Doctor of Philosophy)*—Applications 2012–2013, 131. Total applicants accepted 2012–2013, 13. Number full-time enrolled (new admits only) 2012–2013, 4. Total enrolled 2012–2013 full-time, 28. Openings 2013–2014, 4. The median number of years required for completion of a degree in 2012–2013 were 5.

Scores: Entries appear in this order: required test or GPA, minimum score (if required), median score of students entering in 2012–2013. *Developmental Psychology PhD (Doctor of Philosophy):* GRE-V no minimum stated, GRE-Q no minimum stated, GRE-Analytical no minimum stated, overall undergraduate GPA 3.0; *Social/Personality Psychology PhD (Doctor of Philosophy):* GRE-V no minimum stated, GRE-Q no minimum stated, GRE-Analytical no minimum stated, overall undergraduate GPA 3.0; *Quantitative Psychology PhD (Doctor of Philosophy):* GRE-V no minimum stated, GRE-Q no minimum stated, GRE-Analytical no minimum stated, overall undergraduate GPA 3.0; *Biological Psychology PhD (Doctor of Philosophy):* GRE-V no minimum stated, GRE-Q no minimum stated, GRE-Analytical no minimum stated, overall undergraduate GPA 3.0; *Perception, Cognition and Cognitive Neuroscience PhD (Doctor of Philosophy):* GRE-V no minimum stated, GRE-Q no minimum stated, GRE-Analytical no minimum stated, overall undergraduate GPA 3.0.

Other Criteria: (importance of criteria rated low, medium, or high): GRE scores—high, research experience—high, work experience—low, extracurricular activity—low, GPA—high, letters of recommendation—high, interview—high, statement of goals and objectives—high, undergraduate major in psychology—medium, specific undergraduate psychology courses taken—medium. For additional information on admission requirements, go to http://psychology.ucdavis.edu/graduate/.

Student Characteristics: The following represents characteristics of students in 2012–2013 in all graduate psychology programs in the department: Female—full-time 55, part-time 0; Male—full-time 39, part-time 0; African American/Black—part-time 0; Hispanic/Latino(a)—full-time 7, part-time 0; Asian/Pacific Islander—full-time 20, part-time 0; American Indian/Alaska Native—full-time 2, part-time 0; Caucasian/White—full-time 50, part-time 0; Multi-ethnic—full-time 5, part-time 0; students subject to the Americans With Disabilities Act—full-time 1, part-time 0; Unknown ethnicity—full-time 10, part-time 0; International students who hold an F-1 or J-1 Visa—full-time 6, part-time 0.

Financial Information/Assistance:
Tuition for Full-Time Study: *Doctoral:* State residents: per academic year $15,387; Nonstate residents: per academic year $30,489. Tuition is subject to change. See the following website for updates and changes in tuition costs: http://budget.ucdavis.edu/studentfees.

Financial Assistance:
First-Year Students: Teaching assistantships available for first year. Average amount paid per academic year: $17,655. Average number of hours worked per week: 20. Research assistantships available for first year. Average amount paid per academic year: $16,168. Average number of hours worked per week: 20. Fellow-

ships and scholarships available for first year. Average amount paid per academic year: $31,500. Apply by January 15.

Advanced Students: Teaching assistantships available for advanced students. Average amount paid per academic year: $17,655. Average number of hours worked per week: 20. Research assistantships available for advanced students. Average amount paid per academic year: $17,463. Average number of hours worked per week: 20. Fellowships and scholarships available for advanced students. Average amount paid per academic year: $35,000. Apply by January 15.

Additional Information: Of all students currently enrolled full time, 100% benefited from one or more of the listed financial assistance programs. Application and information available online at: http://psychology.ucdavis.edu/graduate/?link=11.

Housing and Day Care: On-campus housing is available. See the following website for more information: http://www.housing.ucdavis.edu. On-campus day care facilities are available. See the following website for more information: http://www.hr.ucdavis.edu/worklife-wellness/Life/childcare/on-campus-childcare.

Employment of Department Graduates:

Master's Degree Graduates: Of those who graduated in the academic year 2011–2012, the following categories and numbers represent the postgraduate activities and employment of master's degree graduates: Enrolled in a postdoctoral residency/fellowship (n/a), employed in independent practice (n/a), total from the above (master's) (0).

Doctoral Degree Graduates: Of those who graduated in the academic year 2011–2012, the following categories and numbers represent the postgraduate activities and employment of doctoral degree graduates: Enrolled in a psychology doctoral program (n/a), enrolled in a postdoctoral residency/fellowship (4), employed in an academic position at a university (1), employed in an academic position at a 2-year/4-year college (3), employed in business or industry (1), do not know (2), total from the above (doctoral) (11).

Additional Information:

Orientation, Objectives, and Emphasis of Department: The department places strong emphasis on empirical research in five broad areas: (1) biological psychology (e.g., animal behavior, primatology, hormones and behavior, brain bases of social attachments, behavioral neuroscience); (2) perception, cognition, and cognitive neuroscience (e.g., memory, attention, language, consciousness); (3) personality, social psychology, and social neuroscience (e.g., emotions, attitudes, prejudice, close relationships, cultural psychology, psychology of religion, brain bases of personality traits); (4) developmental psychology (cognitive, affective, and social development, personality development, effects of child abuse, brain bases of developmental disorders); and (5) quantitative psychology (e.g., psychometrics, multivariate statistics, hierarchical linear models, statistical models used in areas as diverse as neuroscience and longitudinal developmental research). Weekly colloquia in these five areas provide students with opportunities to hear about new research and present their own ideas and findings. Each student selects a three-person faculty advisory committee, which guides and evaluates the student's progress through the program. Major exams are tailored to each student by his or her advisory committee. Every faculty member has an active lab, permitting students to learn about anything from cellular recording and brain imaging to behavioral studies of development,

perception, cognition, language, emotion, and both individual and social behavior, in both humans and nonhuman animals.

Special Facilities or Resources: The Psychology Department, which contains numerous state-of-the art laboratories, computer facilities, and a survey research facility, overlaps with several other major research centers on campus: California National Primate Research Center, a Center for Neuroscience, a Center for Mind and Brain, and the M.I.N.D. Institute for research on developmental disorders. Departmental faculty members participate in campus-wide graduate groups in psychology, human development, animal behavior, neuroscience, and other fields, and in a cross-university Bay Area Affective Sciences Training Program. The university includes a medical school, a veterinary school, a business school, and a law school, as well as exceptionally strong programs in all of the biological and social sciences. The Department of Psychology offers graduate students an education that is intellectually exciting, personally challenging, and very forward-looking, one that prepares new teacher-scientist-scholars to advance the study of mind, brain, and behavior.

Information for Students With Physical Disabilities: See the following website for more information: http://sdc.ucdavis.edu/.

Application Information:
Send to Graduate Program Coordinator, Psychology Department, University of California, One Shields Avenue, Davis, CA 95616-8686. Application available online. URL of online application: http://gradstudies.ucdavis.edu/prospective/apply_online.cfm. Students are admitted in the Fall, application deadline December 1. *Fee:* $80.

California, University of, Davis
Human Development Graduate Group
Agricultural and Environmental Sciences
One Shields Avenue
Davis, CA 95616-8523
Telephone: (530) 754-4109
Fax: (530) 752-5660
E-mail: *jagouine@ucdavis.edu*
Web: *http://humandevelopment.ucdavis.edu*

Department Information:
1971. Chairperson: Katherine Conger. Number of faculty: total—full-time 44; women—full-time 27.

Programs and Degrees Offered:
Listed in the following order: Program area, degree type (T if terminal Master's), number awarded 7/11–6/12. Child Development MA/MS (Master of Arts/Science) (T) 0, Human Development PhD (Doctor of Philosophy) 9.

Student Applications/Admissions:
Student Applications
Child Development MA/MS (Master of Arts/Science)—Applications 2012–2013, 22. Total applicants accepted 2012–2013, 5. Number full-time enrolled (new admits only) 2012–2013, 4. Total enrolled 2012–2013 full-time, 9. Total enrolled 2012–2013 part-time, 0. Openings 2013–2014, 3. The median num-

ber of years required for completion of a degree in 2012–2013 were 2. The number of students enrolled full- and part-time who were dismissed or voluntarily withdrew from this program area in 2012–2013 were 0. *Human Development PhD (Doctor of Philosophy)*—Applications 2012–2013, 25. Total applicants accepted 2012–2013, 10. Number full-time enrolled (new admits only) 2012–2013, 6. Total enrolled 2012–2013 full-time, 34. Total enrolled 2012–2013 part-time, 1. Openings 2013–2014, 6. The median number of years required for completion of a degree in 2012–2013 were 5. The number of students enrolled full- and part-time who were dismissed or voluntarily withdrew from this program area in 2012–2013 were 1.

Scores: Entries appear in this order: required test or GPA, minimum score (if required), median score of students entering in 2012–2013. *Child Development MA/MS (Master of Arts/ Science):* GRE-V no minimum stated, GRE-Q no minimum stated, GRE-Analytical no minimum stated, overall undergraduate GPA 3.0; *Human Development PhD (Doctor of Philosophy):* GRE-V no minimum stated, GRE-Q no minimum stated, GRE-Analytical no minimum stated, overall undergraduate GPA 3.0.

Other Criteria: (importance of criteria rated low, medium, or high): GRE scores—high, research experience—high, work experience—high, extracurricular activity—low, clinically related public service—low, GPA—high, letters of recommendation—high, statement of goals and objectives—high, undergraduate major in psychology—medium, specific undergraduate psychology courses taken—high, For the Human Development PhD, we require a writing sample/paper. This can be an MS thesis but more often it is a past publication where the applicant is considered a major author.

Student Characteristics: The following represents characteristics of students in 2012–2013 in all graduate psychology programs in the department: Female—full-time 36, part-time 0; Male—full-time 7, part-time 1; African American/Black—full-time 0, part-time 0; Hispanic/Latino(a)—full-time 4, part-time 0; Asian/Pacific Islander—full-time 8, part-time 0; American Indian/Alaska Native—full-time 1, part-time 0; Caucasian/White—full-time 29, part-time 1; Multi-ethnic—full-time 0, part-time 0; students subject to the Americans With Disabilities Act—full-time 0, part-time 0; Unknown ethnicity—full-time 1, part-time 0; International students who hold an F-1 or J-1 Visa—full-time 2, part-time 0.

Financial Information/Assistance:

Tuition for Full-Time Study: *Master's:* State residents: per academic year $15,272; Nonstate residents: per academic year $30,374. *Doctoral:* State residents: per academic year $15,272; Nonstate residents: per academic year $30,374. Tuition is subject to change. See the following website for updates and changes in tuition costs: http://budget.ucdavis.edu/studentfees/.

Financial Assistance:

First-Year Students: Teaching assistantships available for first year. Average number of hours worked per week: 20. Apply by December 15. Research assistantships available for first year. Average number of hours worked per week: 20. Apply by December 15. Fellowships and scholarships available for first year. Apply by December 15.

Advanced Students: Teaching assistantships available for advanced students. Average number of hours worked per week: 20. Research assistantships available for advanced students. Average number of hours worked per week: 20. Fellowships and scholarships available for advanced students.

Additional Information: Of all students currently enrolled full time, 90% benefited from one or more of the listed financial assistance programs. Application and information available online at: http://gradstudies.ucdavis.edu/ssupport/index.html.

Internships/Practica: Master's Degree (MA/MS Child Development): An internship experience, such as a final research project or "capstone" experience is required of graduates. For Child Development MS students: application of learning and development theories to interaction with children six months to five years at the Center for Child and Family Studies; field studies with children and adolescents; study of children's affective, cognitive and social development within the context of family/school environments, hospitals, and foster group homes; Child Life internships through the University of California Davis Medical Center; internships through the 4-H Center for Youth Development, including 4-H and CE-sponsored out-of-school childcare; the M.I.N.D. Institute, etc.

Housing and Day Care: On-campus housing is available. See the following website for more information: http://www.housing.ucdavis.edu/prospective/. On-campus day care facilities are available. See the following website for more information: http://catalog.ucdavis.edu/student/childcare.html.

Employment of Department Graduates:

Master's Degree Graduates: Of those who graduated in the academic year 2011–2012, the following categories and numbers represent the postgraduate activities and employment of master's degree graduates: Enrolled in a postdoctoral residency/fellowship (n/a), employed in independent practice (n/a), total from the above (master's) (0).

Doctoral Degree Graduates: Of those who graduated in the academic year 2011–2012, the following categories and numbers represent the postgraduate activities and employment of doctoral degree graduates: Enrolled in a psychology doctoral program (n/a), enrolled in a postdoctoral residency/fellowship (2), employed in an academic position at a university (3), employed in an academic position at a 2-year/4-year college (1), employed in other positions at a higher education institution (1), employed in business or industry (1), employed in a hospital/medical center (1), total from the above (doctoral) (9).

Additional Information:

Orientation, Objectives, and Emphasis of Department: Both the Child Development MS and Human Development PhD are offered by a graduate group which is interdisciplinary in nature, with a core faculty housed in the Department of Human Ecology and other graduate faculty housed in education, law, medicine, psychiatry, the M.I.N.D. Institute and psychology. Child Development MS students will be prepared to teach at the community college level in developmental psychology, to do applied/evaluation research, or pursue higher degrees. The Human Development PhD students will be prepared to teach at the University level and do basic or applied research in lifespan, cognitive, and social-emotional development from an interdisciplinary perspective with an appreciation of the contexts of development (family, school, health, social-cultural, and social policy).

Special Facilities or Resources: Center for Child and Family Studies, Infant Sleep Lab, Parent and Child Lab, Center for Neuroscience, Center for Youth Development, Cooperative Research and Extension Services for Schools, M.I.N.D. Institute. Extensive community placements in education and social welfare.

Information for Students With Physical Disabilities: See the following website for more information: http://sdc.ucdavis.edu.

Application Information:
Send to Graduate Program Coordinator, Human Development Graduate Group, University of California Davis, One Shields Avenue, Davis, CA 95616. Application available online. URL of online application: http://www.gradstudies.ucdavis.edu/prospective/applicationlanding. html. Students are admitted in the Fall, application deadline December 15. December 15 - Priority Deadline (to be considered for admission and funding), March 1 - Final Deadline (to be considered for admission only). *Fee:* $80. $80 fee for U.S. citizens and permanent residents, $100 fee for citizens of other countries.

California, University of, Irvine
Department of Cognitive Sciences
School of Social Sciences
2201 Social & Behavioral Sciences Gateway Building
Irvine, CA 92697-5100
Telephone: (949) 824-3771
Fax: (949) 824-2307
E-mail: *cogsci@uci.edu*
Web: *http://www.cogsci.uci.edu/*

Department Information:
1986. Chairperson: Ramesh Srinivasan. Number of faculty: total—full-time 29, part-time 4; women—full-time 11, part-time 2; total—minority—full-time 2, part-time 1.

Programs and Degrees Offered:
Listed in the following order: Program area, degree type (T if terminal Master's), number awarded 7/11–6/12. Cognitive Science PhD (Doctor of Philosophy) 6.

Student Applications/Admissions:
Student Applications
Cognitive Science PhD (Doctor of Philosophy)—Applications 2012–2013, 110. Total applicants accepted 2012–2013, 9. Number full-time enrolled (new admits only) 2012–2013, 9. Total enrolled 2012–2013 full-time, 57. Total enrolled 2012–2013 part-time, 0. Openings 2013–2014, 10. The median number of years required for completion of a degree in 2012–2013 were 5. The number of students enrolled full- and part-time who were dismissed or voluntarily withdrew from this program area in 2012–2013 were 0.
Scores: Entries appear in this order: required test or GPA, minimum score (if required), median score of students entering in 2012–2013. *Cognitive Science PhD (Doctor of Philosophy):* GRE-V no minimum stated, GRE-Q no minimum stated.

Other Criteria: (importance of criteria rated low, medium, or high): GRE scores—high, research experience—high, work experience—low, GPA—medium, letters of recommendation—high, interview—high, statement of goals and objectives—high. For additional information on admission requirements, go to http://www.cogsci.uci.edu/cs_graduateprogram.

Student Characteristics: The following represents characteristics of students in 2012–2013 in all graduate psychology programs in the department: Female—full-time 20, part-time 0; Male—full-time 37, part-time 0; African American/Black—full-time 0, part-time 0; Hispanic/Latino(a)—full-time 3, part-time 0; Asian/Pacific Islander—full-time 7, part-time 0; American Indian/Alaska Native—full-time 0, part-time 0; Caucasian/White—full-time 34, part-time 0; Multi-ethnic—full-time 1, part-time 0; students subject to the Americans With Disabilities Act—full-time 0, part-time 0; Unknown ethnicity—full-time 12, part-time 0; International students who hold an F-1 or J-1 Visa—full-time 3, part-time 0.

Financial Information/Assistance:
Tuition for Full-Time Study: *Doctoral:* State residents: per academic year $15,049; Nonstate residents: per academic year $30,151. Tuition is subject to change. See the following website for updates and changes in tuition costs: http://www.reg.uci. edu/fees/.

Financial Assistance:
First-Year Students: Teaching assistantships available for first year. Average amount paid per academic year: $17,309. Average number of hours worked per week: 20. Apply by April 15. Research assistantships available for first year. Average amount paid per academic year: $14,967. Average number of hours worked per week: 20. Apply by April 15. Fellowships and scholarships available for first year. Apply by April 15.
Advanced Students: Teaching assistantships available for advanced students. Average amount paid per academic year: $17,309. Average number of hours worked per week: 20. Research assistantships available for advanced students. Average amount paid per academic year: $19,956. Average number of hours worked per week: 20. Fellowships and scholarships available for advanced students.
Additional Information: Of all students currently enrolled full time, 99% benefited from one or more of the listed financial assistance programs. Application and information available online at: http://www.grad.uci.edu/funding/index.html.

Housing and Day Care: On-campus housing is available. See the following website for more information: http://www.housing.uci. edu. On-campus day care facilities are available. See the following website for more information: http://www.childcare.uci.edu.

Employment of Department Graduates:
Master's Degree Graduates: Of those who graduated in the academic year 2011–2012, the following categories and numbers represent the postgraduate activities and employment of master's degree graduates: Enrolled in a postdoctoral residency/fellowship (n/a), employed in independent practice (n/a), total from the above (master's) (0).
Doctoral Degree Graduates: Of those who graduated in the academic year 2011–2012, the following categories and numbers represent the postgraduate activities and employment of doctoral

degree graduates: Enrolled in a psychology doctoral program (n/a), enrolled in a postdoctoral residency/fellowship (3), employed in an academic position at a 2-year/4-year college (1), do not know (1), total from the above (doctoral) (5).

Additional Information:

Orientation, Objectives, and Emphasis of Department: Cognitive science is a new multidisciplinary field, built around modern computational and neuroscience capabilities. UC Irvine provides the perfect modern environment for research training, as the youngest member of 61 premier research institutions in the Association of American Universities, and the best U.S. university under fifty years old according to the Times Higher Education rankings. The Department of Cognitive Sciences at UC Irvine has a tradition of excellence in quantitative approaches to understanding the brain, perception, cognition and behavior. The department maintains its historic strengths in mathematical psychology, and has seen them expand to include computational approaches to studying cognition. The department has also grown a strong and broad research program and graduate concentration in cognitive neuroscience, with expertise ranging from language and memory to brain-computer interfaces. The department continues to specialize in vision and auditory research, and has newer research areas in the language sciences, cognitive development, and cognitive robotics.

Special Facilities or Resources: The facilities of the Department of Cognitive Sciences are housed in four buildings with teaching labs, lecture rooms, and instructional computing equipment. Its research laboratories are on the technological forefront and highly computerized. A research-dedicated 4.0T whole body MR Imaging/Spectroscopy System supports research in cognitive neuroscience.

Information for Students With Physical Disabilities: See the following website for more information: http://www.disability.uci.edu/.

Application Information:
Send to Graduate Program, Department of Cognitive Sciences, 3151 Social Science Plaza, University of California, Irvine, CA 92697-5100. Application available online. URL of online application: http://www.grad.uci.edu/admissions/applying-to-uci/index.html. Students are admitted in the Fall, application deadline December 15. *Fee:* $80.

California, University of, Irvine
Psychology and Social Behavior
School of Social Ecology
4201 Social & Behavioral Sciences Gateway
Irvine, CA 92697-7085
Telephone: (949) 824-5574
Fax: (949) 824-3002
E-mail: *eobryant@uci.edu*
Web: *http://psb.soceco.uci.edu/*

Department Information:
Chairperson: Linda Levine. Number of faculty: total—full-time 24; women—full-time 16; total—minority—full-time 1.

Programs and Degrees Offered:
Listed in the following order: Program area, degree type (T if terminal Master's), number awarded 7/11–6/12. Psychology & Social Behavior PhD (Doctor of Philosophy).

Student Applications/Admissions:
Student Applications
Psychology & Social Behavior PhD (Doctor of Philosophy)—Number full-time enrolled (new admits only) 2012–2013, 11. Number part-time enrolled (new admits only) 2012–2013, 0. Total enrolled 2012–2013 full-time, 57. Total enrolled 2012–2013 part-time, 0.
Scores: Entries appear in this order: required test or GPA, minimum score (if required), median score of students entering in 2012–2013. *Psychology & Social Behavior PhD (Doctor of Philosophy):* GRE-V no minimum stated, GRE-Q no minimum stated, overall undergraduate GPA no minimum stated, 3.7.
Other Criteria: (importance of criteria rated low, medium, or high): GRE scores—high, research experience—high, work experience—low, extracurricular activity—low, clinically related public service—low, GPA—medium, letters of recommendation—high, interview—high, statement of goals and objectives—high, undergraduate major in psychology—medium, specific undergraduate psychology courses taken—medium. For additional information on admission requirements, go to http://psb.soceco.uci.edu/pages/admissions.

Student Characteristics: The following represents characteristics of students in 2012–2013 in all graduate psychology programs in the department: Female—full-time 39, part-time 0; Male—full-time 18, part-time 0; African American/Black—full-time 2, part-time 0; Hispanic/Latino(a)—full-time 1, part-time 0; Asian/Pacific Islander—full-time 11, part-time 0; American Indian/Alaska Native—full-time 0, part-time 0; Caucasian/White—full-time 42, part-time 0; Multi-ethnic—full-time 1, part-time 0; students subject to the Americans With Disabilities Act—full-time 0, part-time 0; Unknown ethnicity—full-time 0, part-time 0; International students who hold an F-1 or J-1 Visa—full-time 0, part-time 0.

Financial Information/Assistance:
Tuition for Full-Time Study: Doctoral: State residents: per academic year $15,102; Nonstate residents: per academic year $30,151. Tuition is subject to change. See the following website for updates and changes in tuition costs: http://www.reg.uci.edu/fees/.

Financial Assistance:
First-Year Students: Teaching assistantships available for first year. Average amount paid per academic year: $17,600. Average number of hours worked per week: 20. Research assistantships available for first year. Average amount paid per academic year: $17,600. Average number of hours worked per week: 20. Fellowships and scholarships available for first year. Average amount paid per academic year: $17,600. Average number of hours worked per week: 0.
Advanced Students: Teaching assistantships available for advanced students. Average amount paid per academic year: $17,600. Research assistantships available for advanced students. Average amount paid per academic year: $17,600. Fellowships and scholarships available for advanced students. Average amount paid per academic year: $17,600.

Additional Information: Of all students currently enrolled full time, 100% benefited from one or more of the listed financial assistance programs. Application and information available online at: http://www.grad.uci.edu/funding/index.html.

Internships/Practica: The school places a strong emphasis on training in conducting research that has both theoretical and practical applications. The school maintains a list of community agencies where students may seek various forms of research involvement.

Housing and Day Care: On-campus housing is available. See the following website for more information: http://www.housing.uci.edu/. On-campus day care facilities are available. See the following website for more information: http://www.childcare.uci.edu/.

Employment of Department Graduates:

Master's Degree Graduates: Of those who graduated in the academic year 2011–2012, the following categories and numbers represent the postgraduate activities and employment of master's degree graduates: Enrolled in a postdoctoral residency/fellowship (n/a), employed in independent practice (n/a), total from the above (master's) (0).

Doctoral Degree Graduates: Of those who graduated in the academic year 2011–2012, the following categories and numbers represent the postgraduate activities and employment of doctoral degree graduates: Enrolled in a psychology doctoral program (n/a), total from the above (doctoral) (0).

Additional Information:

Orientation, Objectives, and Emphasis of Department: The Department of Psychology and Social Behavior is united by an overarching interest in human adaptation in various sociocultural and developmental contexts. The department has emphases in four areas (Health Psychology, Developmental Psychology, Social and Personality Psychology, and Psychopathology and Behavioral Disorders). The multidisciplinary faculty, whose training is mainly in social developmental, clinical, and community psychology, examines human health, well-being, and the ways in which individuals respond and adjust to changing circumstances over the lifespan. Faculty interests include stress and coping, cognitive and biobehavioral processes in health behavior, subjective well-being, cognition and emotion, social development and developmental transitions across the lifespan, cultural influences on cognition and behavior, psychology and law, aging and health, and societal problems such as violence and unemployment.

Special Facilities or Resources: In-house laboratories, including the Consortium for Integrative Health Studies, the Family Studies Lab, the Development in Cultural Contexts Lab, and the Health Psychology Lab, provide graduate students with direct access to state-of-the-art facilities and opportunities for research training. In addition, the department maintains strong ties with psychologists at other campuses in the area, include UC-Los Angeles, UC-Riverside, and UC-San Diego (each approximately one hour away), and the UCI College of Medicine. For example, we participate in the Consortium on Families and Human Development, a joint undertaking of faculty members and graduate students at UCLA, UCR, UCI, and the University of Southern California. Selected students participate as predoctoral fellows in the Department's NIMH Training Program, and opportunities continually

arise for all students to become involved in many ongoing faculty research projects.

Information for Students With Physical Disabilities: See the following website for more information: http://www.disability.uci.edu/.

Application Information:

Send to Graduate Admissions, Psychology & Social Behavior, 4201 Social & Behavioral Sciences Gateway, Irvine, CA 92697-7085. Application available online. URL of online application: http://www.grad.uci.edu/admissions/applying-to-uci/index.html. Students are admitted in the Fall, application deadline December 1. *Fee:* $80. Students may apply for need-based fee waiver.

California, University of, Los Angeles

Department of Psychology
Letters and Science
405 Hilgard Avenue
Los Angeles, CA 90095-1563
Telephone: (310) 825-2617
Fax: (310) 206-5895
E-mail: *gradadm@psych.ucla.edu*
Web: *http://www.psych.ucla.edu*

Department Information:

1937. Chairperson: Bruce Baker. Number of faculty: total—full-time 68; women—full-time 29; total—minority—full-time 17; women minority—full-time 10.

Programs and Degrees Offered:

Listed in the following order: Program area, degree type (T if terminal Master's), number awarded 7/11–6/12. Behavioral Neuroscience PhD (Doctor of Philosophy) 5, Clinical Psychology PhD (Doctor of Philosophy) 11, Cognitive Psychology PhD (Doctor of Philosophy) 3, Developmental Psychology PhD (Doctor of Philosophy) 3, Learning and Behavior PhD (Doctor of Philosophy) 0, Quantitative Psychology PhD (Doctor of Philosophy) 3, Social Psychology PhD (Doctor of Philosophy) 7, Health Psychology PhD (Doctor of Philosophy) 0.

APA Accreditation: Clinical PhD (Doctor of Philosophy). Student Outcome Data Website: http://www.psych.ucla.edu/graduate/prospective-students/clinical-student-data.

Student Applications/Admissions:

Student Applications

Behavioral Neuroscience PhD (Doctor of Philosophy)—Applications 2012–2013, 60. Total applicants accepted 2012–2013, 4. Number full-time enrolled (new admits only) 2012–2013, 2. Number part-time enrolled (new admits only) 2012–2013, 0. Total enrolled 2012–2013 full-time, 17. Total enrolled 2012–2013 part-time, 0. Openings 2013–2014, 3. The median number of years required for completion of a degree in 2012–2013 were 6. The number of students enrolled full- and part-time who were dismissed or voluntarily withdrew from this program area in 2012–2013 were 0. *Clinical Psychology PhD (Doctor of Philosophy)*—Applications 2012–2013, 409. Total applicants accepted 2012–2013, 17. Number full-time enrolled (new admits only) 2012–2013, 13. Number part-time enrolled (new admits only) 2012–2013, 0. Total enrolled 2012–2013 full-time, 75. Total enrolled 2012–2013 part-time, 0. Openings 2013–2014, 12. The median number of years required for completion of a degree in 2012–2013 were 6. The number of students enrolled full- and part-time who were dismissed or voluntarily withdrew from this program area in 2012–2013 were 0. *Cognitive Psychology PhD (Doctor of Philosophy)*—Applications 2012–2013, 94. Total applicants accepted 2012–2013, 6. Number full-time enrolled (new admits only) 2012–2013, 6. Total enrolled 2012–2013 full-time, 33. Total enrolled 2012–2013 part-time, 0. Openings 2013–2014, 6. The median number of years required for completion of a degree in 2012–2013 were 6. The number of students enrolled full- and part-time who were dismissed or voluntarily withdrew from this program area in 2012–2013 were 0. *Developmental Psychology PhD (Doctor of Philosophy)*—Applications 2012–2013, 81. Total applicants accepted 2012–2013, 5. Number full-time enrolled (new admits only) 2012–2013, 5. Total enrolled 2012–2013 full-time, 27. Total enrolled 2012–2013 part-time, 0. Openings 2013–2014, 6. The median number of years required for completion of a degree in 2012–2013 were 6. The number of students enrolled full- and part-time who were dismissed or voluntarily withdrew from this program area in 2012–2013 were 0. *Learning and Behavior PhD (Doctor of Philosophy)*—Applications 2012–2013, 9. Total applicants accepted 2012–2013, 1. Number full-time enrolled (new admits only) 2012–2013, 2. Total enrolled 2012–2013 full-time, 5. Total enrolled 2012–2013 part-time, 0. Openings 2013–2014, 2. The number of students enrolled full- and part-time who were dismissed or voluntarily withdrew from this program area in 2012–2013 were 3. *Quantitative Psychology PhD (Doctor of Philosophy)*—Applications 2012–2013, 33. Total applicants accepted 2012–2013, 2. Number full-time enrolled (new admits only) 2012–2013, 1. Total enrolled 2012–2013 full-time, 9. Total enrolled 2012–2013 part-time, 0. Openings 2013–2014, 2. The median number of years required for completion of a degree in 2012–2013 were 6. The number of students enrolled full- and part-time who were dismissed or voluntarily withdrew from this program area in 2012–2013 were 0. *Social Psychology PhD (Doctor of Philosophy)*—Applications 2012–2013, 183. Total applicants accepted 2012–2013, 4. Number full-time enrolled (new admits only) 2012–2013, 7. Total enrolled 2012–2013 full-time, 32. Total enrolled 2012–2013 part-time, 0. Openings 2013–2014, 4. The median number of years required for completion of a degree in 2012–2013 were 6. The number of students enrolled full- and part-time who were dismissed or voluntarily withdrew from this program area in 2012–2013 were 0. *Health Psychology PhD (Doctor of Philosophy)*—Applications 2012–2013, 46. Total applicants accepted 2012–2013, 4. Number full-time enrolled (new admits only) 2012–2013, 2. Number part-time enrolled (new admits only) 2012–2013, 0. Total enrolled 2012–2013 full-time, 12. Total enrolled 2012–2013 part-time, 0. Openings 2013–2014, 3. The number of students enrolled full- and part-time who were dismissed or voluntarily withdrew from this program area in 2012–2013 were 0.

Scores: Entries appear in this order: required test or GPA, minimum score (if required), median score of students entering in 2012–2013. *Behavioral Neuroscience PhD (Doctor of Philosophy)*: GRE-V no minimum stated, GRE-Q no minimum stated, GRE-Analytical no minimum stated, overall undergraduate GPA no minimum stated; *Clinical Psychology PhD (Doctor of Philosophy)*: GRE-V no minimum stated, 166, GRE-Q no minimum stated, 162, GRE-Analytical no minimum stated, 5.0, GRE-Subject (Psychology) no minimum stated, overall undergraduate GPA no minimum stated, 3.79; *Cognitive Psychology PhD (Doctor of Philosophy)*: GRE-V no minimum stated, GRE-Q no minimum stated, GRE-Analytical no minimum stated, overall undergraduate GPA no minimum stated; *Developmental Psychology PhD (Doctor of Philosophy)*: GRE-V no minimum stated, GRE-Q no minimum stated, GRE-Analytical no minimum stated, overall undergraduate GPA no minimum stated; *Learning and Behavior PhD (Doctor of Philosophy)*: GRE-V no minimum stated, GRE-Q no minimum stated, GRE-Analytical no minimum stated, overall undergraduate GPA no minimum stated; *Quantitative Psychology PhD (Doctor of Philosophy)*: GRE-V no minimum stated, GRE-Q no minimum stated, GRE-Analytical no minimum stated, overall undergraduate GPA no minimum stated; *Social Psychology PhD (Doctor of Philosophy)*: GRE-V no minimum stated, GRE-Q no minimum stated, GRE-Analytical no minimum stated, overall undergraduate GPA no minimum stated; *Health Psychology PhD (Doctor of Philosophy)*: GRE-V no minimum stated, GRE-Q no minimum stated, GRE-Analytical no minimum stated, overall undergraduate GPA no minimum stated.

Other Criteria: (importance of criteria rated low, medium, or high): GRE scores—high, research experience—high, work experience—medium, extracurricular activity—medium, clinically related public service—medium, GPA—high, letters of recommendation—high, interview—high, statement of goals and objectives—high, The Clinical, Developmental, Health, and Social areas also require an interview as part of their admissions process. After an initial screening of applications, the areas invite selected candidates to an on-campus interview. For additional information on admission requirements, go to http://www.psych.ucla.edu/graduate/prospective-students/preparation.

Student Characteristics: The following represents characteristics of students in 2012–2013 in all graduate psychology programs in the department: Female—full-time 150, part-time 0; Male—full-time 60, part-time 0; African American/Black—full-time 6, part-time 0; Hispanic/Latino(a)—full-time 13, part-time 0; Asian/Pacific Islander—full-time 31, part-time 0; American Indian/Alaska Native—full-time 0, part-time 0; Caucasian/White—full-time 154, part-time 0; Multi-ethnic—full-time 6, part-time 0; students subject to the Americans With Disabilities Act—full-time 0, part-time 0; Unknown ethnicity—full-time 0, part-time 0; International students who hold an F-1 or J-1 Visa—full-time 5, part-time 0.

Financial Information/Assistance:

Tuition for Full-Time Study: *Doctoral:* State residents: per academic year $14,809; Nonstate residents: per academic year $29,911. Tuition is subject to change. See the following website for updates and changes in tuition costs: http://www.registrar.ucla.edu/fees/.

Financial Assistance:

First-Year Students: Teaching assistantships available for first year. Average amount paid per academic year: $16,632. Average number of hours worked per week: 20. Research assistantships

available for first year. Average amount paid per academic year: $13,104. Average number of hours worked per week: 20. Traineeships available for first year. Average amount paid per academic year: $22,000. Average number of hours worked per week: 0. Fellowships and scholarships available for first year. Average amount paid per academic year: $22,000. Average number of hours worked per week: 0. Apply by December 1.

Advanced Students: Teaching assistantships available for advanced students. Average amount paid per academic year: $18,569. Average number of hours worked per week: 20. Research assistantships available for advanced students. Average amount paid per academic year: $16,740. Average number of hours worked per week: 20. Traineeships available for advanced students. Average amount paid per academic year: $20,000. Average number of hours worked per week: 0. Fellowships and scholarships available for advanced students. Average amount paid per academic year: $20,000. Average number of hours worked per week: 0. Apply by varies.

Additional Information: Of all students currently enrolled full time, 100% benefited from one or more of the listed financial assistance programs. Application and information available online at: http://www.psych.ucla.edu/graduate/prospective-students/fellowships-other-support.

Internships/Practica: Doctoral Degree (PhD Clinical Psychology): For those doctoral students for whom a professional psychology internship was required in this program prior to graduation, (16) students applied for an internship in 2011–2012, with (15) students obtaining an internship. Of those students who obtained an internship, (15) were paid internships. Of those students who obtained an internship, (15) students placed in APA/CPA accredited internships, (0) students placed in internships not APA/CPA accredited, but listed with the Association of Psychology Postdoctoral and Internship Programs (APPIC), (0) students placed in internships conforming to guidelines of the Council of Directors of School Psychology Programs (CDSPP), (0) students placed in internships that were not APA/CPA accredited, APPIC or CDSPP listed. VA Hospitals; San Fernando Valley Child Guidance Center; St. John's Child Development Center; Neuropsychiatric Institute/UCLA; UCLA Student Psych Services.

Housing and Day Care: On-campus housing is available. See the following website for more information: http://www.housing.ucla.edu. On-campus day care facilities are available. See the following website for more information: http://map.ais.ucla.edu/go/1002117.

Employment of Department Graduates:

Master's Degree Graduates: Of those who graduated in the academic year 2011–2012, the following categories and numbers represent the postgraduate activities and employment of master's degree graduates: Enrolled in a postdoctoral residency/fellowship (n/a), employed in independent practice (n/a), total from the above (master's) (0).

Doctoral Degree Graduates: Of those who graduated in the academic year 2011–2012, the following categories and numbers represent the postgraduate activities and employment of doctoral degree graduates: Enrolled in a psychology doctoral program (n/a), enrolled in a postdoctoral residency/fellowship (17), employed in an academic position at a university (5), employed in an academic position at a 2-year/4-year college (1), employed in other positions at a higher education institution (2), employed in business or industry (2), other employment position (2), do not know (2), total from the above (doctoral) (31).

Additional Information:

Orientation, Objectives, and Emphasis of Department: Rigorous scientific training is the foundation of the PhD program. The graduate curriculum focuses on the usage of systematic methods of investigation to understand and quantify general principles of human behavior, pathology, cognition and emotion. More specifically, the department includes such research clusters as psychobiology and the brain; child-clinical and developmental psychology; adult psychopathology and family dynamics; cognition and memory; health, community, and political psychology; minority mental health; social cognition and intergroup relations; quantitative; and learning and behavior. In all these areas, the department's central aim is to train researchers dedicated to expanding the scientific knowledge upon which the discipline of psychology rests. This orientation also applies to the clinical program; while it offers excellent clinical training, its emphasis is on training researchers rather than private practitioners. In sum, the graduate training is designed to prepare research psychologists for careers in academic and applied settings—as college and university instructors; for leadership roles in community, government, and business organizations; and as professional research psychologists.

Special Facilities or Resources: The department is one of the largest on campus. Our three-connected buildings (known collectively as Franz Hall) provide ample space (over 120,000 square feet) for psychological research. Laboratory facilities are of the highest quality. Precision equipment is available for electro-physiological stimulation and recording, magnetic resonance imaging (MRI), and for all major areas of sensory study. Specially designed laboratories exist for studies of group behavior and naturalistic observation. An extensive vivarium contains facilities for physiological animal studies. Computing facilities are leading-edge at all levels, from microcomputers to supercomputer clusters. The department also houses the Psychology Clinic, a training and research center for psychotherapy and diagnostics. Other resources include the Fernald Child Study Center (a research facility committed to investigating childhood behavioral disorders); the National Research Center for Asian American Mental Health; the California Self-Help Center; and the Center for Computer-Based Behavioral Studies. Departmental affiliations with the Brain Research Institute, the University Elementary School, the Neuropsychiatric Institute, and the local Veterans Administration also provide year-round research opportunities.

Information for Students With Physical Disabilities: See the following website for more information: http://www.osd.ucla.edu/.

Application Information:
Send to Graduate Admissions Advisor, Psychology Department, 405 Hilgard Avenue, 1285 Franz Hall, Los Angeles, CA 90095-1563. Application available online. URL of online application: http://www.gdnet.ucla.edu/gasaa/admissions/applicat.htm. Students are admitted in the Fall, application deadline December 1. *Fee:* $80.

California, University of, Merced

Psychological Sciences
Social Sciences, Humanities, and Arts
5200 North Lake Road
Merced, CA 95343
Telephone: (209) 228-2260
Fax: (209) 228-4390
E-mail: *jwallander@ucmerced.edu*
Web: *http://psychology.ucmerced.edu*

Department Information:
2007. Chairperson: Jeff Gilger. Number of faculty: total—full-time 12, part-time 4; women—full-time 6, part-time 1; total—minority—full-time 1; women minority—full-time 1.

Programs and Degrees Offered:
Listed in the following order: Program area, degree type (T if terminal Master's), number awarded 7/11–6/12. Developmental Psychology PhD (Doctor of Philosophy) 1, Health Psychology PhD (Doctor of Philosophy) 0, Quantitative Psychology PhD (Doctor of Philosophy) 1.

Student Applications/Admissions:
Student Applications
Developmental Psychology PhD (Doctor of Philosophy)—Applications 2012–2013, 20. Total applicants accepted 2012–2013, 4. Number full-time enrolled (new admits only) 2012–2013, 5. Number part-time enrolled (new admits only) 2012–2013, 0. Total enrolled 2012–2013 full-time, 9. Total enrolled 2012–2013 part-time, 0. Openings 2013–2014, 4. The median number of years required for completion of a degree in 2012–2013 were 6. The number of students enrolled full- and part-time who were dismissed or voluntarily withdrew from this program area in 2012–2013 were 0. *Health Psychology PhD (Doctor of Philosophy)*—Applications 2012–2013, 20. Total applicants accepted 2012–2013, 7. Number full-time enrolled (new admits only) 2012–2013, 3. Number part-time enrolled (new admits only) 2012–2013, 0. Total enrolled 2012–2013 full-time, 13. Total enrolled 2012–2013 part-time, 0. Openings 2013–2014, 5. The number of students enrolled full- and part-time who were dismissed or voluntarily withdrew from this program area in 2012–2013 were 0. *Quantitative Psychology PhD (Doctor of Philosophy)*—Applications 2012–2013, 8. Total applicants accepted 2012–2013, 3. Number full-time enrolled (new admits only) 2012–2013, 2. Number part-time enrolled (new admits only) 2012–2013, 0. Total enrolled 2012–2013 full-time, 5. Total enrolled 2012–2013 part-time, 0. Openings 2013–2014, 3. The median number of years required for completion of a degree in 2012–2013 were 5. The number of students enrolled full- and part-time who were dismissed or voluntarily withdrew from this program area in 2012–2013 were 0.
Scores: Entries appear in this order: required test or GPA, minimum score (if required), median score of students entering in 2012–2013. *Developmental Psychology PhD (Doctor of Philosophy):* GRE-V 400, 415, GRE-Q 550, 675, GRE-Analytical 3, 4.5, overall undergraduate GPA 3.70, 3.83; *Health Psychology PhD (Doctor of Philosophy):* GRE-V 520, 620, GRE-Q 620,

670, GRE-Analytical 4, 4, overall undergraduate GPA 3.24, 3.50; *Quantitative Psychology PhD (Doctor of Philosophy):* GRE-V 440, 480, GRE-Q 630, 665, GRE-Analytical 4, 4, overall undergraduate GPA 3.75, 3.78.
Other Criteria: (importance of criteria rated low, medium, or high): GRE scores—medium, research experience—high, work experience—low, extracurricular activity—low, clinically related public service—low, GPA—high, letters of recommendation—medium, statement of goals and objectives—high, undergraduate major in psychology—medium, specific undergraduate psychology courses taken—low, Admission decisions are based on a combination of factors, including academic degrees and records, the statement of purpose, letters of recommendation, test scores, and relevant experience. We also consider the appropriateness of applicant's goals to the degree program in which you are interested and to the research interests of the program's faculty. In addition, consideration may be given to how your background and life experience would contribute significantly to an educationally beneficial blend of students.

Student Characteristics: The following represents characteristics of students in 2012–2013 in all graduate psychology programs in the department: Female—full-time 14, part-time 0; Male—full-time 13, part-time 0; African American/Black—full-time 3, part-time 0; Hispanic/Latino(a)—full-time 3, part-time 0; Asian/Pacific Islander—full-time 0, part-time 0; American Indian/Alaska Native—full-time 1, part-time 0; Caucasian/White—full-time 20, part-time 0; Multi-ethnic—full-time 0, part-time 0; students subject to the Americans With Disabilities Act—full-time 0, part-time 0; Unknown ethnicity—full-time 0, part-time 0; International students who hold an F-1 or J-1 Visa—full-time 1, part-time 0.

Financial Information/Assistance:
Tuition for Full-Time Study: *Doctoral:* State residents: per academic year $11,220; Nonstate residents: per academic year $27,322. Tuition is subject to change. Additional fees are assessed to students beyond the costs of tuition for the following: student services and health insurance. See the following website for updates and changes in tuition costs: http://graduatedivision.ucmerced.edu/financial-support.

Financial Assistance:
First-Year Students: Teaching assistantships available for first year. Average amount paid per academic year: $17,000. Average number of hours worked per week: 15. Research assistantships available for first year. Average amount paid per academic year: $17,000. Average number of hours worked per week: 15. Fellowships and scholarships available for first year. Average amount paid per academic year: $17,000. Average number of hours worked per week: 0.
Advanced Students: Teaching assistantships available for advanced students. Average amount paid per academic year: $19,000. Average number of hours worked per week: 20. Research assistantships available for advanced students. Average amount paid per academic year: $19,000. Average number of hours worked per week: 20. Fellowships and scholarships available for advanced students. Average amount paid per academic year: $19,000. Average number of hours worked per week: 20.

Additional Information: Of all students currently enrolled full time, 100% benefited from one or more of the listed financial assistance programs. Application and information available online at: http://graduatedivision.ucmerced.edu/financial-support.

Housing and Day Care: No on-campus housing is available. On-campus day care facilities are available. See the following website for more information: http://ecec.ucmerced.edu/welcome/.

Employment of Department Graduates:

Master's Degree Graduates: Of those who graduated in the academic year 2011–2012, the following categories and numbers represent the postgraduate activities and employment of master's degree graduates: Enrolled in a postdoctoral residency/fellowship (n/a), employed in independent practice (n/a), total from the above (master's) (0).

Doctoral Degree Graduates: Of those who graduated in the academic year 2011–2012, the following categories and numbers represent the postgraduate activities and employment of doctoral degree graduates: Enrolled in a psychology doctoral program (n/a), enrolled in a postdoctoral residency/fellowship (2), not seeking employment (1), total from the above (doctoral) (3).

Additional Information:

Orientation, Objectives, and Emphasis of Department: UC Merced is the first research university built in the U.S. this century, and is one of the 10 campuses making up the premiere research university system of University of California. Our graduate training started in 2006, and is growing rapidly in developmental, health, and quantitative psychology. New psychology faculty are added every year. We are highly research-oriented, and do not offer any clinical training. We place priority on graduate students who desire a research career, but welcome applications from students with other aspirations as well. We employ a mentor model where a graduate student works closely with one faculty member (sometimes two) in his/her research program over the course of completing the program.

Special Facilities or Resources: We moved into the new Social Sciences and Management building in fall 2011, which has purpose-built psychology labs and views towards the Sierra Nevada mountains. Most students are assigned work space in this building. Relevant to those with health psychology interests is the Health Sciences Research Institute led by psychology faculty.

Information for Students With Physical Disabilities: See the following website for more information: http://disability.ucmerced.edu/.

Application Information:
Send to University of California, Merced, Attn: Graduate Division Application, 5200 North Lake Road, Suite KL 227, Merced, CA 95343. Application available online. URL of online application: http://graduatedivision.ucmerced.edu/prospective-students/how-apply. Students are admitted in the Fall, application deadline January 15. Early applications by December 1 receive special consideration for certain fellowships. We will accept late applications and consider for admission if space in incoming cohort is available. *Fee:* $80. International student application fee is $100.

California, University of, Riverside

Department of Psychology
College of Humanities, Arts & Social Sciences
Psychology Building
Riverside, CA 92521-0426
Telephone: (951) 827-6306
Fax: (951) 827-3985
E-mail: *dianne.fewkes@ucr.edu*
Web: *http://www.psych.ucr.edu*

Department Information:
1962. Chairperson: Glenn Stanley. Number of faculty: total—full-time 28; women—full-time 13; total—minority—full-time 4; women minority—full-time 2.

Programs and Degrees Offered:
Listed in the following order: Program area, degree type (T if terminal Master's), number awarded 7/11–6/12. Cognitive Psychology PhD (Doctor of Philosophy) 1, Developmental Psychology PhD (Doctor of Philosophy) 4, Social/Personality Psychology PhD (Doctor of Philosophy) 5, Systems Neuroscience PhD (Doctor of Philosophy) 1.

Student Applications/Admissions:
Student Applications

Cognitive Psychology PhD (Doctor of Philosophy)—Applications 2012–2013, 20. Total applicants accepted 2012–2013, 5. Number full-time enrolled (new admits only) 2012–2013, 0. Total enrolled 2012–2013 full-time, 18. Total enrolled 2012–2013 part-time, 0. Openings 2013–2014, 5. The median number of years required for completion of a degree in 2012–2013 were 5. The number of students enrolled full- and part-time who were dismissed or voluntarily withdrew from this program area in 2012–2013 were 1. *Developmental Psychology PhD (Doctor of Philosophy)*—Applications 2012–2013, 40. Total applicants accepted 2012–2013, 6. Number full-time enrolled (new admits only) 2012–2013, 4. Total enrolled 2012–2013 full-time, 23. Total enrolled 2012–2013 part-time, 0. Openings 2013–2014, 5. The median number of years required for completion of a degree in 2012–2013 were 5. The number of students enrolled full- and part-time who were dismissed or voluntarily withdrew from this program area in 2012–2013 were 0. *Social/Personality Psychology PhD (Doctor of Philosophy)*—Applications 2012–2013, 64. Total applicants accepted 2012–2013, 12. Number full-time enrolled (new admits only) 2012–2013, 6. Total enrolled 2012–2013 full-time, 29. Total enrolled 2012–2013 part-time, 0. Openings 2013–2014, 5. The median number of years required for completion of a degree in 2012–2013 were 5. The number of students enrolled full- and part-time who were dismissed or voluntarily withdrew from this program area in 2012–2013 were 1. *Systems Neuroscience PhD (Doctor of Philosophy)*—Applications 2012–2013, 5. Total applicants accepted 2012–2013, 3. Number full-time enrolled (new admits only) 2012–2013, 1. Total enrolled 2012–2013 full-time, 6. Total enrolled 2012–2013 part-time, 0. Openings 2013–2014, 3. The median number of years required for completion of a degree in 2012–2013 were 5. The number of students enrolled full- and part-time who were dismissed or voluntarily withdrew from this program area in 2012–2013 were 0.

Scores: Entries appear in this order: required test or GPA, minimum score (if required), median score of students entering in 2012–2013. *Cognitive Psychology PhD (Doctor of Philosophy):* GRE-V no minimum stated, GRE-Q no minimum stated, last 2 years GPA no minimum stated; *Developmental Psychology PhD (Doctor of Philosophy):* GRE-V no minimum stated, GRE-Q no minimum stated, last 2 years GPA no minimum stated; *Social/Personality Psychology PhD (Doctor of Philosophy):* GRE-V no minimum stated, GRE-Q no minimum stated, last 2 years GPA no minimum stated; *Systems Neuroscience PhD (Doctor of Philosophy):* GRE-V no minimum stated, GRE-Q no minimum stated, last 2 years GPA no minimum stated.

Other Criteria: (importance of criteria rated low, medium, or high): GRE scores—medium, research experience—high, work experience—low, extracurricular activity—low, GPA—medium, letters of recommendation—high, interview—high, statement of goals and objectives—high. For additional information on admission requirements, go to http://www.psych.ucr.edu/grad/admissions.html.

Student Characteristics: The following represents characteristics of students in 2012–2013 in all graduate psychology programs in the department: Female—full-time 53, part-time 0; Male—full-time 23, part-time 0; African American/Black—full-time 5, part-time 0; Hispanic/Latino(a)—full-time 6, part-time 0; Asian/Pacific Islander—full-time 6, part-time 0; American Indian/Alaska Native—full-time 0, part-time 0; Caucasian/White—full-time 59, part-time 0; Multi-ethnic—full-time 0, part-time 0; students subject to the Americans With Disabilities Act—full-time 0, part-time 0; Unknown ethnicity—full-time 0, part-time 0; International students who hold an F-1 or J-1 Visa—full-time 0, part-time 0.

Financial Information/Assistance:

Tuition for Full-Time Study: Doctoral: State residents: per academic year $13,485; Nonstate residents: per academic year $28,587. Tuition is subject to change. See the following website for updates and changes in tuition costs: http://graduate.ucr.edu/fees_fellowship.html.

Financial Assistance:

First-Year Students: Teaching assistantships available for first year. Average amount paid per academic year: $16,314. Average number of hours worked per week: 20. Apply by January 2. Research assistantships available for first year. Average amount paid per academic year: $16,314. Average number of hours worked per week: 20. Apply by January 2. Fellowships and scholarships available for first year. Average amount paid per academic year: $17,000. Average number of hours worked per week: 0. Apply by January 2.

Advanced Students: Teaching assistantships available for advanced students. Average amount paid per academic year: $16,637. Average number of hours worked per week: 20. Apply by January 2. Research assistantships available for advanced students. Average amount paid per academic year: $19,542. Average number of hours worked per week: 20. Apply by January 2.

Additional Information: Of all students currently enrolled full time, 100% benefited from one or more of the listed financial assistance programs. Application and information available online at: http://www.psych.ucr.edu/grad/admissions.html.

Housing and Day Care: On-campus housing is available. See the following website for more information: http://housing.ucr.edu/.

On-campus day care facilities are available. See the following website for more information: http://cdc.ucr.edu.

Employment of Department Graduates:

Master's Degree Graduates: Of those who graduated in the academic year 2011–2012, the following categories and numbers represent the postgraduate activities and employment of master's degree graduates: Enrolled in a postdoctoral residency/fellowship (n/a), employed in independent practice (n/a), total from the above (master's) (0).

Doctoral Degree Graduates: Of those who graduated in the academic year 2011–2012, the following categories and numbers represent the postgraduate activities and employment of doctoral degree graduates: Enrolled in a psychology doctoral program (n/a), enrolled in another graduate/professional program (1), enrolled in a postdoctoral residency/fellowship (2), employed in an academic position at a university (2), employed in an academic position at a 2-year/4-year college (2), employed in business or industry (1), total from the above (doctoral) (8).

Additional Information:

Orientation, Objectives, and Emphasis of Department: The orientation is toward theoretical and research training. Objectives are to provide the appropriate theoretical, quantitative, and methodological background to enable graduates of the program to engage in high-quality research. Additionally, training and experience in university-level teaching are provided. We also offer a minor in quantitative psychology which may be completed by any student in the PhD program in Psychology regardless of main area of interest. A concentration in health psychology is also offered in the social and developmental areas. The cognitive area has a strong concentration in cognitive modeling.

Special Facilities or Resources: The Psychology Department has recently moved into a new building built specifically for the department. The department has equipment and support systems to help students conduct research in all aspects of behavior. The neuroscience laboratories are equipped with the latest instrumentation for hormonal assays, extracellular and intracellular electrophysiology, and microscopic analysis of neuronal morphology. Research in the cognitive area incorporates computer-assisted experimental control for most any kind of reaction time experiment and has facilities for video and speech digitization and infrared eye-tracking. The developmental faculty have laboratory facilities to study parents and children, have access to the campus day-care center for studies that involve toddlers and preschool children, and have been very successful in conducting research in a culturally diverse local school system. The developmental faculty all participate in the Center for Family Studies, an interdisciplinary center. The social/personality psychology labs support research in social perception, nonverbal communication, health psychology, emotional expression, and attribution processes using audiovisual laboratories and observation rooms. Direct, free access is available to PsycInfo, PubMed, and many other online journals and databases.

Information for Students With Physical Disabilities: See the following website for more information: http://specialservices.ucr.edu/.

Application Information:

Send to Graduate Admissions, Psychology Department, University of California, Riverside, Riverside, CA 92521. Application available online. URL of online application: http://graduate.ucr.edu/grad_admissions.html. Students are admitted in the Fall, application deadline December 5. *Fee:* $80.

California, University of, San Diego

Department of Psychology
9500 Gilman Drive #0109
La Jolla, CA 92093-0109
Telephone: (858) 534-3002
Fax: (858) 534-2324
E-mail: *psycphdinfo@ucsd.edu*
Web: *http://psychology.ucsd.edu/*

Department Information:
1965. Chairperson: Victor S. Ferreira. Number of faculty: total—full-time 31; women—full-time 5; total—minority—full-time 2.

Programs and Degrees Offered:
Listed in the following order: Program area, degree type (T if terminal Master's), number awarded 7/11–6/12. Experimental Psychology PhD (Doctor of Philosophy) 14.

Student Applications/Admissions:
Student Applications
Experimental Psychology PhD (Doctor of Philosophy)—Applications 2012–2013, 296. Total applicants accepted 2012–2013, 18. Number full-time enrolled (new admits only) 2012–2013, 5. Total enrolled 2012–2013 full-time, 57. Total enrolled 2012–2013 part-time, 0. Openings 2013–2014, 14. The median number of years required for completion of a degree in 2012–2013 were 6. The number of students enrolled full- and part-time who were dismissed or voluntarily withdrew from this program area in 2012–2013 were 3.
Scores: Entries appear in this order: required test or GPA, minimum score (if required), median score of students entering in 2012–2013. *Experimental Psychology PhD (Doctor of Philosophy):* GRE-V 156, 159, GRE-Q 155, 159, overall undergraduate GPA 3.22, 3.7.
Other Criteria: (importance of criteria rated low, medium, or high): GRE scores—high, research experience—high, work experience—medium, extracurricular activity—low, clinically related public service—low, GPA—high, letters of recommendation—high, interview—high, statement of goals and objectives—high, undergraduate major in psychology—medium, specific undergraduate psychology courses taken—medium. For additional information on admission requirements, go to http://psychology.ucsd.edu/graduate-program/prospective-students/admissions.html.

Student Characteristics: The following represents characteristics of students in 2012–2013 in all graduate psychology programs in the department: Female—full-time 36, part-time 0; Male—full-time 21, part-time 0; African American/Black—full-time 1, part-time 0; Hispanic/Latino(a)—full-time 0, part-time 0; Asian/Pacific Islander—full-time 4, part-time 0; American Indian/Alaska Native—full-time 1, part-time 0; Caucasian/White—full-time 49, part-time 0; Multi-ethnic—full-time 2, part-time 0; students subject to the Americans With Disabilities Act—full-time 1, part-time 0; Unknown ethnicity—full-time 0, part-time 0; International students who hold an F-1 or J-1 Visa—full-time 1, part-time 0.

Financial Information/Assistance:
Tuition for Full-Time Study: *Doctoral:* State residents: per academic year $14,515; Nonstate residents: per academic year $29,617. Tuition is subject to change. See the following website for updates and changes in tuition costs: http://ogs.ucsd.edu/financial-support/graduate-tuition-fees.html.

Financial Assistance:
First-Year Students: Teaching assistantships available for first year. Average amount paid per academic year: $13,284. Average number of hours worked per week: 20. Fellowships and scholarships available for first year. Average amount paid per academic year: $9,216.
Advanced Students: Teaching assistantships available for advanced students. Average amount paid per academic year: $17,936. Average number of hours worked per week: 20. Research assistantships available for advanced students. Average amount paid per academic year: $17,936. Average number of hours worked per week: 20. Fellowships and scholarships available for advanced students. Average amount paid per academic year: $4,564.
Additional Information: Of all students currently enrolled full time, 100% benefited from one or more of the listed financial assistance programs. Application and information available online at: http://psychology.ucsd.edu/graduate-program/prospective-students/financial-support.html.

Housing and Day Care: On-campus housing is available. See the following website for more information: http://hdh.ucsd.edu/arch/gradhousing.asp. On-campus day care facilities are available. See the following website for more information: http://blink.ucsd.edu/HR/services/support/child/.

Employment of Department Graduates:
Master's Degree Graduates: Of those who graduated in the academic year 2011–2012, the following categories and numbers represent the postgraduate activities and employment of master's degree graduates: Enrolled in a postdoctoral residency/fellowship (n/a), employed in independent practice (n/a), total from the above (master's) (0).
Doctoral Degree Graduates: Of those who graduated in the academic year 2011–2012, the following categories and numbers represent the postgraduate activities and employment of doctoral degree graduates: Enrolled in a psychology doctoral program (n/a), enrolled in a postdoctoral residency/fellowship (10), employed in an academic position at a university (2), employed in business or industry (1), employed in a hospital/medical center (1), total from the above (doctoral) (14).

Additional Information:
Orientation, Objectives, and Emphasis of Department: The Department of Psychology at the University of California, San Diego provides advanced training in research in most aspects of experimental psychology. Modern laboratories and an attractive physical setting combine with a distinguished faculty, both within the Department of Psychology and in supporting disciplines, to provide research opportunities and training at the frontiers of psychological science. The graduate training program emphasizes and supports individual research, starting with the first year of study.

Special Facilities or Resources: The Department shares research space and facilities with the Center for Brain and Cognition. Within the joint facilities, there are two computing facilities, a computational laboratory, visual and auditory laboratories, social psychology laboratories, cognitive laboratories, developmental laboratories, a clinic for autistic children, animal facilities, and extensive contacts with hospitals, industry, and the legal system. In addition to the numerous impressive libraries on campus, the Department also keeps a large selection of literature within our Mandler Library. Collaborative research is carried out with members of the Departments of Linguistics, Cognitive Science, Computer Science and Engineering, Sociology, Music, Ophthalmology, Neurosciences, members of the UCSD School of Medicine, Scripps Clinic and Research Foundation, and with the Salk Institute for Biological Studies and the Neurosciences Institute. The Scripps Institution of Oceanography, located on campus, provides facilities in neurosciences as does the School of Medicine.

Information for Students With Physical Disabilities: See the following website for more information: http://disabilities.ucsd.edu.

Application Information:
Send to Graduate Admission, Department of Psychology-0109, University of California-San Diego, La Jolla, CA 92093. Application available online. URL of online application: https://gradapply.ucsd.edu/. Students are admitted in the Fall, application deadline December 2. *Fee:* $80. U.S. citizens and permanent residents only may request a waiver of the application fee. All fee waivers are granted provisionally. Applicants must provide supporting information and documentation to finalize the waiver. Waivers are provided to applicants in the following situations: applicants who are currently receiving need-based financial assistance from an undergraduate or graduate institution; applicants who are able to demonstrate financial hardship; applicants who are participating in selected federal, state and private graduate school preparation programs. Application fee is $100 for international applicants.

California, University of, Santa Barbara
Counseling, Clinical, and School Psychology
Gevirtz Graduate School of Education
Education Building 275
Santa Barbara, CA 93106-9490
Telephone: (805) 893-3375
Fax: (805) 893-7762
E-mail: *ccspapp@education.ucsb.edu*
Web: *http://education.ucsb.edu/Graduate-Studies/CCSP/
   CCSP-home.html*

Department Information:
1965. Chairperson: Merith Cosden. Number of faculty: total—full-time 14; women—full-time 7; total—minority—full-time 3; women minority—full-time 2.

Programs and Degrees Offered:
Listed in the following order: Program area, degree type (T if terminal Master's), number awarded 7/11–6/12. Counseling/Clinical/School PhD (Doctor of Philosophy) 11, School Psychology MEd (Education) 4.

APA Accreditation: Combination PhD (Doctor of Philosophy). Student Outcome Data Website: http://education.ucsb.edu/Graduate-Studies/CCSP/CCSP-home.html.

Student Applications/Admissions:
Student Applications
  Counseling/Clinical/School PhD (Doctor of Philosophy)—Applications 2012–2013, 344. Total applicants accepted 2012–2013, 27. Number full-time enrolled (new admits only) 2012–2013, 16. Number part-time enrolled (new admits only) 2012–2013, 0. Total enrolled 2012–2013 full-time, 72. Total enrolled 2012–2013 part-time, 0. Openings 2013–2014, 16. The median number of years required for completion of a degree in 2012–2013 were 5. The number of students enrolled full- and part-time who were dismissed or voluntarily withdrew from this program area in 2012–2013 were 2. *School Psychology MEd (Education)*—Applications 2012–2013, 26. Total applicants accepted 2012–2013, 5. Number full-time enrolled (new admits only) 2012–2013, 3. Number part-time enrolled (new admits only) 2012–2013, 0. Total enrolled 2012–2013 full-time, 9. Total enrolled 2012–2013 part-time, 0. Openings 2013–2014, 4. The median number of years required for completion of a degree in 2012–2013 were 3. The number of students enrolled full- and part-time who were dismissed or voluntarily withdrew from this program area in 2012–2013 were 0.
Scores: Entries appear in this order: required test or GPA, minimum score (if required), median score of students entering in 2012–2013. *Counseling/Clinical/School PhD (Doctor of Philosophy):* GRE-V no minimum stated, 580, GRE-Q no minimum stated, 650, GRE-Analytical no minimum stated, 5.0, overall undergraduate GPA 3.40, 3.66; *School Psychology MEd (Education):* GRE-V no minimum stated, 580, GRE-Q no minimum stated, 640, GRE-Analytical no minimum stated, 5.0, overall undergraduate GPA 3.46, 3.58.
Other Criteria: (importance of criteria rated low, medium, or high): GRE scores—medium, research experience—high, work experience—medium, extracurricular activity—medium, clinically related public service—medium, GPA—medium, letters of recommendation—medium, interview—high, statement of goals and objectives—high, undergraduate major in psychology—medium, specific undergraduate psychology courses taken—medium. For additional information on admission requirements, go to http://education.ucsb.edu/Graduate-Studies/CCSP/prospective-students/how-to-apply-checklist.htm.

Student Characteristics: The following represents characteristics of students in 2012–2013 in all graduate psychology programs in the department: Female—full-time 68, part-time 0; Male—full-time 13, part-time 0; African American/Black—full-time 3, part-time 0; Hispanic/Latino(a)—full-time 18, part-time 0; Asian/Pacific Islander—full-time 6, part-time 0; American Indian/Alaska Native—full-time 0, part-time 0; Caucasian/White—full-time 44, part-time 0; Multi-ethnic—full-time 0, part-time 0; students subject to the Americans With Disabilities Act—full-time 4, part-time 0; Unknown ethnicity—full-time 10, part-time 0; International students who hold an F-1 or J-1 Visa—full-time 5, part-time 0.

Financial Information/Assistance:
Tuition for Full-Time Study: *Master's:* State residents: per academic year $15,499; Nonstate residents: per academic year

$30,600. *Doctoral:* State residents: per academic year $15,499; Nonstate residents: per academic year $30,600. Tuition is subject to change. See the following website for updates and changes in tuition costs: http://registrar.sa.ucsb.edu/feechart.aspx.

Financial Assistance:

First-Year Students: Teaching assistantships available for first year. Average amount paid per academic year: $14,000. Average number of hours worked per week: 10. Research assistantships available for first year. Average amount paid per academic year: $13,000. Average number of hours worked per week: 10. Fellowships and scholarships available for first year. Average amount paid per academic year: $20,000. Average number of hours worked per week: 0.

Advanced Students: Teaching assistantships available for advanced students. Average amount paid per academic year: $14,000. Average number of hours worked per week: 10. Research assistantships available for advanced students. Average amount paid per academic year: $13,000. Average number of hours worked per week: 10. Fellowships and scholarships available for advanced students. Average amount paid per academic year: $20,000. Average number of hours worked per week: 0.

Additional Information: Of all students currently enrolled full time, 95% benefited from one or more of the listed financial assistance programs. Application and information available online at: http://education.ucsb.edu/Graduate-Studies/Student-Services/prospective-students/financial-aid.htm.

Internships/Practica: Doctoral Degree (PhD Counseling/Clinical/School): For those doctoral students for whom a professional psychology internship was required in this program prior to graduation, (14) students applied for an internship in 2011–2012, with (13) students obtaining an internship. Of those students who obtained an internship, (13) were paid internships. Of those students who obtained an internship, (13) students placed in APA/CPA accredited internships, (0) students placed in internships not APA/CPA accredited, but listed with the Association of Psychology Postdoctoral and Internship Programs (APPIC), (0) students placed in internships conforming to guidelines of the Council of Directors of School Psychology Programs (CDSPP), (0) students placed in internships that were not APA/CPA accredited, APPIC or CDSPP listed. During their first years in the program, students receive practicum experience in the Hosford Counseling and Psychological Services Clinic on campus, a sliding scale agency which serves adults, children, and families from the community. Advanced students receive experience as supervisors in the clinic. Students in the clinical emphasis have external practica in community-based settings, including an agency that serves families and children exposed to violence, a local hospital, and programs associated with county alcohol, drug and mental health services. Students in the counseling emphasis have external practica at UCSB's Counseling and Career Services centers. Students in the school emphasis have external practica in the schools. All doctoral students apply for predoctoral internships at APA-accredited sites across the country and participate in the APPIC match. The school psychology MEd students receive their degree in two years and have a third year of school internship for their credential.

Housing and Day Care: On-campus housing is available. See the following website for more information: http://www.housing.ucsb.edu/. On-campus day care facilities are available. See the following website for more information: http://childrenscenter.sa.ucsb.edu/.

Employment of Department Graduates:

Master's Degree Graduates: Of those who graduated in the academic year 2011–2012, the following categories and numbers represent the postgraduate activities and employment of master's degree graduates: Enrolled in a postdoctoral residency/fellowship (n/a), employed in independent practice (n/a), employed in a professional position in a school system (4), total from the above (master's) (4).

Doctoral Degree Graduates: Of those who graduated in the academic year 2011–2012, the following categories and numbers represent the postgraduate activities and employment of doctoral degree graduates: Enrolled in a psychology doctoral program (n/a), enrolled in a postdoctoral residency/fellowship (6), employed in an academic position at a university (2), employed in other positions at a higher education institution (1), employed in a community mental health/counseling center (2), total from the above (doctoral) (11).

Additional Information:

Orientation, Objectives, and Emphasis of Department: The primary goals of the combined psychology program are to prepare graduates who will (a) conduct research and teach in university settings and (b) assume leadership roles in the academic community and in the helping professions. The Department recently moved to the new Education Building on campus with state-of-the-art instructional equipment and technologically-enhanced clinics. The doctoral program is fully accredited in counseling, clinical and school psychology.

Special Facilities or Resources: The UCSB Combined Psychology Program houses several training clinics: the Hosford Clinic serves community clients and is equipped with state-of-the-art equipment for recording, reviewing, editing, and live monitoring of assessment and counseling sessions; the Psychology Assessment Center provides psychological assessment services for the measurement of disorders that affect psychological, emotional, academic, and occupational functioning; and the Koegel Autism Center provides training in evidence-based practices for children with an autism spectrum disorder. Faculty have research labs in their areas of interest.

Information for Students With Physical Disabilities: See the following website for more information: http://dsp.sa.ucsb.edu/.

Application Information:
Send to Student Affairs Office, Gevirtz Graduate School of Education, Building 275, Room 4100, University of California Santa Barbara, Santa Barbara, CA 93106-9490. Application available online. URL of online application: https://www.graddiv.ucsb.edu/eapp/. Students are admitted in the Fall, application deadline November 15. *Fee:* $80. Application fee is $80 for U.S. students and $100 for international students.

California, University of, Santa Cruz

Psychology Department
273 Social Sciences 2
Santa Cruz, CA 95064
Telephone: (831) 459-4932
Fax: (831) 459-3519
E-mail: hmhender@ucsc.edu
Web: http://psych.ucsc.edu/

Department Information:

1965. Chairperson: Heather Bullock. Number of faculty: total—full-time 25; women—full-time 14; total—minority—full-time 8; women minority—full-time 6.

Programs and Degrees Offered:

Listed in the following order: Program area, degree type (T if terminal Master's), number awarded 7/11–6/12. Developmental Psychology PhD (Doctor of Philosophy) 3, Social Psychology PhD (Doctor of Philosophy) 1, Cognitive Psychology PhD (Doctor of Philosophy) 3.

Student Applications/Admissions:

Student Applications

Developmental Psychology PhD (Doctor of Philosophy)—Applications 2012–2013, 50. Total applicants accepted 2012–2013, 6. Number full-time enrolled (new admits only) 2012–2013, 3. Total enrolled 2012–2013 full-time, 21. Openings 2013–2014, 5. The median number of years required for completion of a degree in 2012–2013 were 6. The number of students enrolled full- and part-time who were dismissed or voluntarily withdrew from this program area in 2012–2013 were 0. *Social Psychology PhD (Doctor of Philosophy)*—Applications 2012–2013, 85. Total applicants accepted 2012–2013, 10. Number full-time enrolled (new admits only) 2012–2013, 2. Total enrolled 2012–2013 full-time, 23. Total enrolled 2012–2013 part-time, 1. Openings 2013–2014, 5. The median number of years required for completion of a degree in 2012–2013 were 7. The number of students enrolled full- and part-time who were dismissed or voluntarily withdrew from this program area in 2012–2013 were 0. *Cognitive Psychology PhD (Doctor of Philosophy)*—Applications 2012–2013, 54. Total applicants accepted 2012–2013, 10. Number full-time enrolled (new admits only) 2012–2013, 3. Total enrolled 2012–2013 full-time, 20. Openings 2013–2014, 5. The median number of years required for completion of a degree in 2012–2013 were 6. The number of students enrolled full- and part-time who were dismissed or voluntarily withdrew from this program area in 2012–2013 were 3.

Scores: Entries appear in this order: required test or GPA, minimum score (if required), median score of students entering in 2012–2013. *Developmental Psychology PhD (Doctor of Philosophy):* GRE-V no minimum stated, 620, GRE-Q no minimum stated, 620, GRE-Analytical no minimum stated, 5, overall undergraduate GPA no minimum stated, 3.70; *Social Psychology PhD (Doctor of Philosophy):* GRE-V no minimum stated, 590, GRE-Q no minimum stated, 590, GRE-Analytical no minimum stated, 4.5, overall undergraduate GPA no minimum stated, 3.50; *Cognitive Psychology PhD (Doctor of Philosophy):* GRE-V no minimum stated, 650, GRE-Q no minimum stated, 710, GRE-Analytical no minimum stated, 4.5, overall undergraduate GPA no minimum stated, 3.65.

Other Criteria: (importance of criteria rated low, medium, or high): GRE scores—high, research experience—high, work experience—medium, extracurricular activity—medium, GPA—high, letters of recommendation—high, statement of goals and objectives—high, undergraduate major in psychology—low, specific undergraduate psychology courses taken—medium. For additional information on admission requirements, go to http://psychology.ucsc.edu/graduate/admission/index.html.

Student Characteristics: The following represents characteristics of students in 2012–2013 in all graduate psychology programs in the department: Female—full-time 48, part-time 1; Male—full-time 16, part-time 0; African American/Black—full-time 2, part-time 0; Hispanic/Latino(a)—full-time 12, part-time 1; Asian/Pacific Islander—full-time 8, part-time 0; American Indian/Alaska Native—full-time 2, part-time 0; Caucasian/White—full-time 29, part-time 0; Multi-ethnic—full-time 3, part-time 0; students subject to the Americans With Disabilities Act—full-time 0, part-time 0; Unknown ethnicity—full-time 8, part-time 0; International students who hold an F-1 or J-1 Visa—full-time 0, part-time 0.

Financial Information/Assistance:

Tuition for Full-Time Study: *Doctoral:* State residents: per academic year $16,174; Nonstate residents: per academic year $31,276. Tuition is subject to change. See the following website for updates and changes in tuition costs: http://reg.ucsc.edu/Fees/fees.html#gradFees.

Financial Assistance:

First-Year Students: Teaching assistantships available for first year. Average number of hours worked per week: 20. Research assistantships available for first year. Average number of hours worked per week: 20. Fellowships and scholarships available for first year. Apply by December 15.

Advanced Students: Teaching assistantships available for advanced students. Average number of hours worked per week: 20. Research assistantships available for advanced students. Average number of hours worked per week: 20.

Additional Information: Of all students currently enrolled full time, 95% benefited from one or more of the listed financial assistance programs. Application and information available online at: http://graddiv.ucsc.edu/financial-aid/.

Housing and Day Care: On-campus housing is available. See the following website for more information: http://housing.ucsc.edu/gradhsg/index.html. On-campus day care facilities are available. See the following website for more information: http://childcare.ucsc.edu/index.html.

Employment of Department Graduates:

Master's Degree Graduates: Of those who graduated in the academic year 2011–2012, the following categories and numbers represent the postgraduate activities and employment of master's degree graduates: Enrolled in a postdoctoral residency/fellowship (n/a), employed in independent practice (n/a), total from the above (master's) (0).

Doctoral Degree Graduates: Of those who graduated in the academic year 2011–2012, the following categories and numbers represent the postgraduate activities and employment of doctoral degree graduates: Enrolled in a psychology doctoral program (n/a), enrolled in a postdoctoral residency/fellowship (1), employed in an academic position at a university (4), employed in government agency (1), other employment position (1), total from the above (doctoral) (7).

Additional Information:

Orientation, Objectives, and Emphasis of Department: The Psychology Department at UC Santa Cruz offers a PhD degree with areas of specialization in cognitive, developmental, and social psychology. The program does not offer courses, training, or supervision in counseling or clinical psychology. Students are not admitted to pursue only a Master's degree. However, students may be awarded a Master's degree as part of their studies for the PhD Students are prepared for research, teaching, and administrative positions in colleges and universities, as well as positions in schools, government, and other public and private organizations. The PhD is a research degree. Students are required to demonstrate the ability to carry through to completion rigorous empirical research and to be active in research throughout their graduate career. Course requirements establish a foundation for critical evaluation of research literature and the design of conceptually important empirical research. To support students in achieving these goals, each student must be associated with one of the faculty, who serves as academic advisor and research sponsor. The program requires full-time enrollment.

Special Facilities or Resources: The department provides training to prepare the student for academic and applied settings. Graduate students have the use of a variety of research facilities, including a number of computer-controlled experimental laboratories. Electronic equipment is available to allow the generation of sophisticated written and pictorial vision displays, musical sequences, and synthesized and visual speech patterns. There are observational facilities for developmental psychological research and a discourse analysis lab. A bilingual survey unit is under development which will utilize public opinion survey technology to study significant public policy, legal, and political issues that are critical to California's emerging majority population. Research opportunities exist with diverse sample groups in both laboratory and natural settings. The department has collaborative relationships with the National Center for Research on Cultural Diversity, Second Language Learning, and the Bilingual Research Center.

Information for Students With Physical Disabilities: See the following website for more information: http://drc.ucsc.edu/.

Application Information:
Send to UC Santa Cruz, Graduate Application Processing, 1156 High Street, Santa Cruz, CA 95064. Application available online. URL of online application: http://graddiv.ucsc.edu/prospective-students/. Students are admitted in the Fall, application deadline December 15. *Fee:* $80. Fee waivers for cases of hardship are available to U.S. citizens and permanent residents only.

Claremont Graduate University

Graduate Department of Psychology
School of Behavioral and Organizational Sciences
123 East Eighth Street
Claremont, CA 91711-3955
Telephone: (909) 621-8084
Fax: (909) 621-8905
E-mail: *Stewart.Donaldson@cgu.edu*
Web: *http://www.cgu.edu/pages/154.asp*

Department Information:
1926. Dean: Stewart I. Donaldson. Number of faculty: total—full-time 15, part-time 60; women—full-time 7, part-time 29; total—minority—full-time 5, part-time 14; women minority—full-time 3, part-time 7.

Programs and Degrees Offered:
Listed in the following order: Program area, degree type (T if terminal Master's), number awarded 7/11–6/12. Applied Social Psych/Evaluation Co-Concentration MA/MS (Master of Arts/Science) (T) 4, Cognitive Psychology/Evaluation Co-Concentration MA/MS (Master of Arts/Science) (T) 1, Organizational/Evaluation Co-Concentration MA/MS (Master of Arts/Science) (T) 12, Human Resources Design MA/MS (Master of Arts/Science) (T) 21, Positive Organizational Psych/Evaluation Co-Concen MA/MS (Master of Arts/Science) (T) 10, Applied Cognitive Psychology PhD (Doctor of Philosophy) 2, Applied Social Psychology PhD (Doctor of Philosophy) 12, Evaluation and Applied Research Methods PhD (Doctor of Philosophy) 0, Organizational Behavior PhD (Doctor of Philosophy) 3, Health Behavior Research/Evaluation MA/MS (Master of Arts/Science) (T) 0, Positive Developmental Psychology PhD (Doctor of Philosophy) 0, Positive Organizational Psychology PhD (Doctor of Philosophy) 0, Positive Developmental Psych/Evaluation Co-Concen MA/MS (Master of Arts/Science) (T) 5.

Student Applications/Admissions:
Student Applications
Applied Social Psych/Evaluation Co-Concentration MA/MS (Master of Arts/Science)—Applications 2012–2013, 28. Number full-time enrolled (new admits only) 2012–2013, 8. Total enrolled 2012–2013 full-time, 13. Total enrolled 2012–2013 part-time, 2. Openings 2013–2014, 9. The median number of years required for completion of a degree in 2012–2013 were 2. The number of students enrolled full- and part-time who were dismissed or voluntarily withdrew from this program area in 2012–2013 were 0. *Cognitive Psychology/Evaluation Co-Concentration MA/MS (Master of Arts/Science)*—Applications 2012–2013, 14. Number full-time enrolled (new admits only) 2012–2013, 2. Total enrolled 2012–2013 full-time, 3. Total enrolled 2012–2013 part-time, 0. Openings 2013–2014, 3. The median number of years required for completion of a degree in 2012–2013 were 2. The number of students enrolled full- and part-time who were dismissed or voluntarily withdrew from this program area in 2012–2013 were 0. *Organizational/Evaluation Co-Concentration MA/MS (Master of Arts/Science)*—Applications 2012–2013, 42. Number full-time enrolled (new admits only) 2012–2013, 9. Number part-time enrolled (new admits only) 2012–2013, 0. Total enrolled 2012–2013 full-time, 19. Total enrolled 2012–2013 part-time,

3. Openings 2013–2014, 10. The median number of years required for completion of a degree in 2012–2013 were 2. The number of students enrolled full- and part-time who were dismissed or voluntarily withdrew from this program area in 2012–2013 were 0. *Human Resources Design MA/MS (Master of Arts/Science)*—Applications 2012–2013, 53. Number full-time enrolled (new admits only) 2012–2013, 5. Number part-time enrolled (new admits only) 2012–2013, 3. Total enrolled 2012–2013 full-time, 10. Total enrolled 2012–2013 part-time, 11. Openings 2013–2014, 20. The median number of years required for completion of a degree in 2012–2013 were 2. The number of students enrolled full- and part-time who were dismissed or voluntarily withdrew from this program area in 2012–2013 were 0. *Positive Organizational Psych/Evaluation Co-Concen MA/MS (Master of Arts/Science)*—Applications 2012–2013, 40. Number full-time enrolled (new admits only) 2012–2013, 9. Number part-time enrolled (new admits only) 2012–2013, 1. Total enrolled 2012–2013 full-time, 14. Total enrolled 2012–2013 part-time, 3. Openings 2013–2014, 6. The median number of years required for completion of a degree in 2012–2013 were 2. *Applied Cognitive Psychology PhD (Doctor of Philosophy)*—Applications 2012–2013, 21. Number full-time enrolled (new admits only) 2012–2013, 4. Total enrolled 2012–2013 full-time, 21. Total enrolled 2012–2013 part-time, 5. Openings 2013–2014, 6. The median number of years required for completion of a degree in 2012–2013 were 7. The number of students enrolled full- and part-time who were dismissed or voluntarily withdrew from this program area in 2012–2013 were 0. *Applied Social Psychology PhD (Doctor of Philosophy)*—Applications 2012–2013, 33. Number full-time enrolled (new admits only) 2012–2013, 11. Number part-time enrolled (new admits only) 2012–2013, 1. Total enrolled 2012–2013 full-time, 52. Total enrolled 2012–2013 part-time, 8. Openings 2013–2014, 9. The median number of years required for completion of a degree in 2012–2013 were 6. The number of students enrolled full- and part-time who were dismissed or voluntarily withdrew from this program area in 2012–2013 were 0. *Evaluation and Applied Research Methods PhD (Doctor of Philosophy)*—Applications 2012–2013, 14. Number full-time enrolled (new admits only) 2012–2013, 1. Number part-time enrolled (new admits only) 2012–2013, 1. Total enrolled 2012–2013 full-time, 12. Total enrolled 2012–2013 part-time, 6. Openings 2013–2014, 6. The median number of years required for completion of a degree in 2012–2013 were 6. The number of students enrolled full- and part-time who were dismissed or voluntarily withdrew from this program area in 2012–2013 were 0. *Organizational Behavior PhD (Doctor of Philosophy)*—Applications 2012–2013, 20. Number full-time enrolled (new admits only) 2012–2013, 2. Total enrolled 2012–2013 full-time, 18. Total enrolled 2012–2013 part-time, 7. Openings 2013–2014, 4. The median number of years required for completion of a degree in 2012–2013 were 7. The number of students enrolled full- and part-time who were dismissed or voluntarily withdrew from this program area in 2012–2013 were 0. *Health Behavior Research/Evaluation MA/MS (Master of Arts/Science)*—Applications 2012–2013, 6. Number full-time enrolled (new admits only) 2012–2013, 3. Total enrolled 2012–2013 full-time, 5. Total enrolled 2012–2013 part-time, 1. Openings 2013–2014, 5. The median number of years required for completion of a degree in 2012–2013 were 2. The number of students enrolled full- and part-time who were dismissed or voluntarily withdrew from this program

area in 2012–2013 were 0. *Positive Developmental Psychology PhD (Doctor of Philosophy)*—Applications 2012–2013, 39. Number full-time enrolled (new admits only) 2012–2013, 7. Total enrolled 2012–2013 full-time, 24. Total enrolled 2012–2013 part-time, 7. Openings 2013–2014, 6. *Positive Organizational Psychology PhD (Doctor of Philosophy)*—Applications 2012–2013, 19. Number full-time enrolled (new admits only) 2012–2013, 4. Total enrolled 2012–2013 full-time, 8. Total enrolled 2012–2013 part-time, 3. Openings 2013–2014, 3. *Positive Developmental Psych/Evaluation Co-Concen MA/MS (Master of Arts/Science)*—Applications 2012–2013, 51. Number full-time enrolled (new admits only) 2012–2013, 7. Number part-time enrolled (new admits only) 2012–2013, 1. Total enrolled 2012–2013 full-time, 10. Total enrolled 2012–2013 part-time, 2. Openings 2013–2014, 3. The median number of years required for completion of a degree in 2012–2013 were 2.

Scores: Entries appear in this order: required test or GPA, minimum score (if required), median score of students entering in 2012–2013. *Applied Social Psych/Evaluation Co-Concentration MA/MS (Master of Arts/Science):* GRE-V no minimum stated, 515, GRE-Q no minimum stated, 632, GRE-Analytical no minimum stated, 4.47, overall undergraduate GPA no minimum stated; *Cognitive Psychology/Evaluation Co-Concentration MA/MS (Master of Arts/Science):* GRE-V no minimum stated, 490, GRE-Q no minimum stated, 700, GRE-Analytical no minimum stated, 4.47, overall undergraduate GPA no minimum stated; *Organizational/Evaluation Co-Concentration MA/MS (Master of Arts/Science):* GRE-V no minimum stated, 533, GRE-Q no minimum stated, 661, GRE-Analytical no minimum stated, 4.47, overall undergraduate GPA no minimum stated; *Human Resources Design MA/MS (Master of Arts/Science):* GRE-V no minimum stated, 422, GRE-Q no minimum stated, 503; *Positive Organizational Psych/Evaluation Co-Concen MA/MS (Master of Arts/Science):* GRE-V no minimum stated, 534, GRE-Q no minimum stated, 647, GRE-Analytical no minimum stated, 4.47, overall undergraduate GPA no minimum stated; *Applied Cognitive Psychology PhD (Doctor of Philosophy):* GRE-V no minimum stated, 514, GRE-Q no minimum stated, 612, GRE-Analytical no minimum stated, 4.92, overall undergraduate GPA no minimum stated; *Applied Social Psychology PhD (Doctor of Philosophy):* GRE-V no minimum stated, 554, GRE-Q no minimum stated, 639, GRE-Analytical no minimum stated, 4.67, overall undergraduate GPA no minimum stated; *Evaluation and Applied Research Methods PhD (Doctor of Philosophy):* GRE-V no minimum stated, 565, GRE-Q no minimum stated, 619, GRE-Analytical no minimum stated, 4.5, overall undergraduate GPA no minimum stated; *Organizational Behavior PhD (Doctor of Philosophy):* GRE-V no minimum stated, 544, GRE-Q no minimum stated, 651, GRE-Analytical no minimum stated, 4.75, overall undergraduate GPA no minimum stated; *Health Behavior Research/Evaluation MA/MS (Master of Arts/Science):* GRE-V no minimum stated, 436, GRE-Q no minimum stated, 544, GRE-Analytical no minimum stated, 4.47, overall undergraduate GPA no minimum stated; *Positive Developmental Psychology PhD (Doctor of Philosophy):* GRE-V no minimum stated, 552, GRE-Q no minimum stated, 665, GRE-Analytical no minimum stated, 4.5, overall undergraduate GPA no minimum stated; *Positive Organizational Psychology PhD (Doctor of Philosophy):* GRE-V no minimum stated, 629, GRE-Q no minimum stated, 679, GRE-Analytical no minimum stated, 4.75, overall undergraduate GPA no minimum stated; *Positive Developmental Psych/Evaluation Co-Concen MA/*

MS (*Master of Arts/Science*): GRE-V no minimum stated, 516, GRE-Q no minimum stated, 565, GRE-Analytical no minimum stated, 4.47, overall undergraduate GPA no minimum stated.

Other Criteria: (importance of criteria rated low, medium, or high): GRE scores—high, research experience—medium, work experience—medium, extracurricular activity—medium, GPA—high, letters of recommendation—high, statement of goals and objectives—high, undergraduate major in psychology—medium, specific undergraduate psychology courses taken—medium, HRD program does not require research experience but emphasizes work experience more strongly. For additional information on admission requirements, go to http://www.cgu.edu/pages/502.asp.

Student Characteristics: The following represents characteristics of students in 2012–2013 in all graduate psychology programs in the department: Female—full-time 159, part-time 27; Male—full-time 94, part-time 34; African American/Black—full-time 10, part-time 6; Hispanic/Latino(a)—full-time 21, part-time 5; Asian/Pacific Islander—full-time 21, part-time 6; American Indian/Alaska Native—full-time 2, part-time 0; Caucasian/White—full-time 136, part-time 34; Multi-ethnic—full-time 8, part-time 3; students subject to the Americans With Disabilities Act—full-time 0, part-time 0; Unknown ethnicity—full-time 18, part-time 2; International students who hold an F-1 or J-1 Visa—full-time 23, part-time 16.

Financial Information/Assistance:

Tuition for Full-Time Study: *Master's:* State residents: per academic year $31,645, $1,581 per credit hour; Nonstate residents: per academic year $31,645, $1,581 per credit hour. *Doctoral:* State residents: per academic year $18,187, $1,581 per credit hour; Nonstate residents: per academic year $18,187, $1,581 per credit hour. Tuition is subject to change. See the following website for updates and changes in tuition costs: http://www.cgu.edu/pages/312.asp.

Financial Assistance:

First-Year Students: Teaching assistantships available for first year. Average amount paid per academic year: $5,200. Average number of hours worked per week: 10. Research assistantships available for first year. Average amount paid per academic year: $5,200. Average number of hours worked per week: 12. Fellowships and scholarships available for first year. Average amount paid per academic year: $8,761. Apply by January 15.

Advanced Students: Teaching assistantships available for advanced students. Average amount paid per academic year: $5,200. Average number of hours worked per week: 10. Research assistantships available for advanced students. Average amount paid per academic year: $5,200. Average number of hours worked per week: 12. Fellowships and scholarships available for advanced students. Average amount paid per academic year: $8,761. Apply by January 15.

Additional Information: Of all students currently enrolled full time, 100% benefited from one or more of the listed financial assistance programs. Application and information available online at: http://www.cgu.edu/pages/1003.asp.

Internships/Practica: Research and consulting internships are available and encouraged for all students. Appropriate settings and roles are arranged according to the interests of individual students within the wide range of opportunities available in a large urban area. Typical settings include social service agencies; business and industrial organizations; hospitals, clinics, and mental health agencies; schools; governmental and regulatory agencies; and nonacademic research institutions, as well as numerous onsite research institutes.

Housing and Day Care: On-campus housing is available. See the following website for more information: http://www.cgu.edu/pages/1156.asp. On-campus day care facilities are available.

Employment of Department Graduates:

Master's Degree Graduates: Of those who graduated in the academic year 2011–2012, the following categories and numbers represent the postgraduate activities and employment of master's degree graduates: Enrolled in another graduate/professional program (1), enrolled in a postdoctoral residency/fellowship (n/a), employed in independent practice (n/a), employed in an academic position at a university (1), employed in an academic position at a 2-year/4-year college (1), employed in other positions at a higher education institution (1), employed in a professional position in a school system (3), employed in business or industry (2), employed in a community mental health/counseling center (2), employed in a hospital/medical center (1), other employment position (1), total from the above (master's) (13).

Doctoral Degree Graduates: Of those who graduated in the academic year 2011–2012, the following categories and numbers represent the postgraduate activities and employment of doctoral degree graduates: Enrolled in a psychology doctoral program (n/a), enrolled in a postdoctoral residency/fellowship (4), employed in an academic position at a university (2), employed in an academic position at a 2-year/4-year college (3), employed in other positions at a higher education institution (2), employed in a professional position in a school system (1), employed in business or industry (3), employed in a community mental health/counseling center (2), employed in a hospital/medical center (2), other employment position (3), total from the above (doctoral) (22).

Additional Information:

Orientation, Objectives, and Emphasis of Department: The program emphasizes contemporary human problems and social issues, and the organizations and systems involved in such issues, as well as on basic substantive research in social, organizational, developmental, and cognitive psychology and health behavior. Unusual specialty opportunities are available in positive psychology, organizational behavior, applied cognitive psychology, applied social psychology, health psychology, and program evaluation research. The program offers preparation for careers in public service and business and industry as well as teaching and research. Research, theory, and practice are stressed in such policy and program areas as organizations and work; human social and physical environments; social service systems; psychological effects of educational computer technology; health and mental health systems; crime, delinquency, and law; and aging and life span education. Many opportunities are available for research, consulting, and field experiences in these and related areas. Strong emphasis is given to training in a broad range of research methodologies, from naturalistic observation to experimental design, with special attention to field research methods. Seminars, tutorials, independent research, individualized student program plans, practical field experience, and close advisory and collaborative relations with the faculty are designed to foster clarifications of individual goals, intellectual and professional growth, self-pacing, and attractive career opportunities.

Special Facilities or Resources: The school is equipped with labs for social, developmental, identity, health, positive psychology, and cognitive research, supplies and equipment for field research, a student lounge, and department library. The computer facilities are excellent, conveniently located, and include a wide variety of application programs. The department cooperates in overseeing research institutes for student-faculty grant or contract research, focusing on major problems of organizational and program evaluation research as well as research on social issues. Claremont Graduate University is a free-standing graduate institution within the context of the Claremont University Consortium of five colleges, the Graduate University, and the Keck Graduate Institute. This context allows the department to concentrate exclusively on graduate education in a relaxed, intimate context while enjoying the resources of a major university. In addition to the full-time graduate psychology faculty, there are more than 40 full-time faculty members from the undergraduate Claremont Colleges who participate in the graduate program and who are available to students for research, advising, and instruction. Resources from other programs within the Graduate University are also available to psychology students, in such areas as public policy, education, information sciences, business administration, executive management, economics, and government. The nearby Los Angeles basin is a major urban area that offers rich and varied opportunities for interesting research, field placements and internships, part-time employment, and career development.

Application Information:
Send to Admissions Office, McManus Hall 131, Claremont Graduate University, Claremont, CA 91711. Application available online. URL of online application: http://www.cgu.edu/pages/431.asp. Students are admitted in the Fall, application deadline January 15; Spring, application deadline November 15; Programs have rolling admissions. The Human Resources Design M.S. program accepts applications throughout the year on a space-available basis. *Fee:* $70.

Fuller Theological Seminary
Department of Clinical Psychology
School of Psychology
180 North Oakland Avenue
Pasadena, CA 91101
Telephone: (626) 584-5500
Fax: (626) 584-9630
E-mail: *clements@fuller.edu*
Web: *http://www.fuller.edu/sop/*

Department Information:
1965. Chairperson: Mari L. Clements, PhD Number of faculty: total—full-time 16, part-time 3; women—full-time 7, part-time 2; total—minority—full-time 5, part-time 2; women minority—full-time 3, part-time 1.

Programs and Degrees Offered:
Listed in the following order: Program area, degree type (T if terminal Master's), number awarded 7/11–6/12. Clinical Psychol-

ogy PhD (Doctor of Philosophy) 24, Clinical Psychology PsyD (Doctor of Psychology) 17.

APA Accreditation: Clinical PhD (Doctor of Philosophy). Student Outcome Data Website: http://www.fuller.edu/academics/school-of-psychology/department-of-clinical-psychology/doctor-of-philosophy.aspx. Clinical PsyD (Doctor of Psychology). Student Outcome Data Website: http://www.fuller.edu/academics/school-of-psychology/department-of-clinical-psychology/doctor-of-psychology.aspx.

Student Applications/Admissions:
Student Applications
Clinical Psychology PhD (Doctor of Philosophy)—Applications 2012–2013, 62. Total applicants accepted 2012–2013, 45. Number full-time enrolled (new admits only) 2012–2013, 24. Number part-time enrolled (new admits only) 2012–2013, 0. Total enrolled 2012–2013 full-time, 159. Total enrolled 2012–2013 part-time, 0. Openings 2013–2014, 18. The median number of years required for completion of a degree in 2012–2013 were 6. The number of students enrolled full- and part-time who were dismissed or voluntarily withdrew from this program area in 2012–2013 were 1. *Clinical Psychology PsyD (Doctor of Psychology)*—Applications 2012–2013, 54. Total applicants accepted 2012–2013, 28. Number full-time enrolled (new admits only) 2012–2013, 10. Number part-time enrolled (new admits only) 2012–2013, 0. Total enrolled 2012–2013 full-time, 86. Total enrolled 2012–2013 part-time, 0. Openings 2013–2014, 18. The median number of years required for completion of a degree in 2012–2013 were 6. The number of students enrolled full- and part-time who were dismissed or voluntarily withdrew from this program area in 2012–2013 were 1.

Scores: Entries appear in this order: required test or GPA, minimum score (if required), median score of students entering in 2012–2013. *Clinical Psychology PhD (Doctor of Philosophy):* GRE-V no minimum stated, 530, GRE-Q no minimum stated, 580, GRE-Analytical no minimum stated, 4.5, psychology GPA 3.17, 3.69; *Clinical Psychology PsyD (Doctor of Psychology):* GRE-V no minimum stated, 530, GRE-Q no minimum stated, 620, GRE-Analytical no minimum stated, 4, psychology GPA no minimum stated, 3.69.

Other Criteria: (importance of criteria rated low, medium, or high): GRE scores—high, research experience—high, work experience—medium, extracurricular activity—medium, clinically related public service—medium, GPA—high, letters of recommendation—high, interview—high, statement of goals and objectives—high, integration experience—high, undergraduate major in psychology—low, specific undergraduate psychology courses taken—high, Research experience is less important for PsyD candidates than for PhD candidates. For additional information on admission requirements, go to http://www.fuller.edu/Admissions/Admission-Requirements-Clinical-Psychology.aspx.

Student Characteristics: The following represents characteristics of students in 2012–2013 in all graduate psychology programs in the department: Female—full-time 154, part-time 0; Male—full-time 91, part-time 0; African American/Black—full-time 23, part-time 0; Hispanic/Latino(a)—full-time 15, part-time 0; Asian/Pacific Islander—full-time 41, part-time 0; American Indian/Alaska Native—full-time 1, part-time 0; Caucasian/White—full-time 152, part-time 0; Multi-ethnic—full-time 8, part-time 0; students subject to the Americans With Disabilities Act—full-time 7, part-time 0; Unknown ethnicity—full-time 5, part-time 0; International students who hold an F-1 or J-1 Visa—full-time 12, part-time 0.

Financial Information/Assistance:

Tuition for Full-Time Study: *Doctoral:* State residents: per academic year $37,500, $625 per credit hour; Nonstate residents: per academic year $37,500, $625 per credit hour. Tuition is subject to change. Additional fees are assessed to students beyond the costs of tuition for the following: $36/quarter All Seminary Council (student government) fee, $50 new student fee. See the following website for updates and changes in tuition costs: http://www.fuller.edu/admissions/tuition-and-fees.aspx.

Financial Assistance:

First-Year Students: Research assistantships available for first year. Average amount paid per academic year: $10,000. Average number of hours worked per week: 10. Apply by December 15. Traineeships available for first year. Average amount paid per academic year: $3,500. Average number of hours worked per week: 0. Apply by December 15. Fellowships and scholarships available for first year. Average amount paid per academic year: $5,000. Average number of hours worked per week: 0. Apply by December 15.

Advanced Students: Teaching assistantships available for advanced students. Average amount paid per academic year: $3,000. Average number of hours worked per week: 10. Research assistantships available for advanced students. Average amount paid per academic year: $15,000. Average number of hours worked per week: 15. Traineeships available for advanced students. Average amount paid per academic year: $10,000. Average number of hours worked per week: 10. Fellowships and scholarships available for advanced students. Average amount paid per academic year: $3,000. Average number of hours worked per week: 15.

Additional Information: Of all students currently enrolled full time, 90% benefited from one or more of the listed financial assistance programs. Application and information available online at: http://fuller.edu/sfs/.

Internships/Practica: Doctoral Degree (PhD Clinical Psychology): For those doctoral students for whom a professional psychology internship was required in this program prior to graduation, (27) students applied for an internship in 2011–2012, with (23) students obtaining an internship. Of those students who obtained an internship, (21) were paid internships. Of those students who obtained an internship, (14) students placed in APA/CPA accredited internships, (7) students placed in internships not APA/CPA accredited, but listed with the Association of Psychology Postdoctoral and Internship Programs (APPIC), (0) students placed in internships conforming to guidelines of the Council of Directors of School Psychology Programs (CDSPP), (2) students placed in internships that were not APA/CPA accredited, APPIC or CDSPP listed. Doctoral Degree (PsyD Clinical Psychology): For those doctoral students for whom a professional psychology internship was required in this program prior to graduation, (19) students applied for an internship in 2011–2012, with (16) students obtaining an internship. Of those students who obtained an internship, (13) were paid internships. Of those students who obtained an internship, (6) students placed in APA/CPA accredited internships, (5) students placed in internships not APA/CPA accredited, but listed with the Association of Psychology

Postdoctoral and Internship Programs (APPIC), (0) students placed in internships conforming to guidelines of the Council of Directors of School Psychology Programs (CDSPP), (5) students placed in internships that were not APA/CPA accredited, APPIC or CDSPP listed. Students are placed in field training sites throughout their program including 2 years of practicum, 1 year of assessment clerkship, 1 year of pre-internship (PhD only) and a 1-year full-time clinical internship. Students are placed at Fuller Psychological and Family Services clinic as well as in over 80 sites throughout the L.A. metropolitan area. Because of our location, students are exposed to multiple methods of service delivery as well as to diverse ethnic, clinical, and age populations. Students obtain internships throughout the U.S. and Canada.

Housing and Day Care: On-campus housing is available. See the following website for more information: http://fuller.edu/housing/. No on-campus day care facilities are available.

Employment of Department Graduates:

Master's Degree Graduates: Of those who graduated in the academic year 2011–2012, the following categories and numbers represent the postgraduate activities and employment of master's degree graduates: Enrolled in a postdoctoral residency/fellowship (n/a), employed in independent practice (n/a), total from the above (master's) (0).

Doctoral Degree Graduates: Of those who graduated in the academic year 2011–2012, the following categories and numbers represent the postgraduate activities and employment of doctoral degree graduates: Enrolled in a psychology doctoral program (n/a), enrolled in a postdoctoral residency/fellowship (25), employed in independent practice (2), employed in an academic position at a university (3), employed in government agency (1), employed in a community mental health/counseling center (2), employed in a hospital/medical center (7), still seeking employment (1), total from the above (doctoral) (41).

Additional Information:

Orientation, Objectives, and Emphasis of Department: The purpose of the Graduate School of Psychology is to prepare a distinctive kind of clinical psychologist: men and women whose understanding and action are deeply informed by both psychology and the Christian faith. It is based on the conviction that the coupling of Christian understanding with refined clinical and research skills will produce a psychologist with a special ability to help persons of faith on their journeys to wholeness. The school has adopted the scientist–practitioner model for its PhD program and the clinical scientist model for its PsyD program.

Special Facilities or Resources: The Lee Edward Travis Research Institute (TRI) in the School of Psychology at Fuller Theological Seminary is committed to fostering interdisciplinary research into the relationships between social systems, environmental situations, personality, mental and affective states, biological processes, and spiritual and religious states and practices. Fuller Psychological & Family Services clinic provides assistance to individuals, couples, and families, including services to children and adolescents. Psychological interventions are offered for adjustment disorders, anxiety, depression, stress management, abuse and domestic violence, and physical conditions affected by psychological factors. Student trainees may be placed in the clinic for practicum, clerkship or pre-internship.

Application Information:

Send to Office of Admissions, Fuller Theological Seminary, 135 North Oakland Avenue, Pasadena, CA 91182. Application available online. URL of online application: http://www.fuller.edu/admissions/Apply-Online-Landing-Page.aspx. Students are admitted in the Fall, application deadline December 15. We have three application deadlines. Early admissions is November 5, Regular is December 15, Final is January 10. Fee: $75. Fee is waived for early admission. Online application fee is $50 for Regular admissions deadline and $75 for Final admissions deadline.

Golden Gate University

Psychology
536 Mission Street
San Francisco, CA 94005
Telephone: (800) 442-7000
E-mail: info@ggu.edu
Web: http://www.ggu.edu/programs/psychology/master-of-arts-in-psychology

Department Information:

1997. Chairperson: Kit Yarrow. Number of faculty: total—full-time 2, part-time 23; women—full-time 1, part-time 11; minority—part-time 3; women minority—part-time 1.

Programs and Degrees Offered:

Listed in the following order: Program area, degree type (T if terminal Master's), number awarded 7/11–6/12. Marriage and Family Therapy MA/MS (Master of Arts/Science) (T) 25, Industrial/Organizational Psychology MA/MS (Master of Arts/Science) (T) 12, Industrial-Organizational Psychology/Mft MA/MS (Master of Arts/Science) (T) 7.

Student Applications/Admissions:

Student Applications

Marriage and Family Therapy MA/MS (Master of Arts/Science)—Applications 2012–2013, 90. Total applicants accepted 2012–2013, 80. Number full-time enrolled (new admits only) 2012–2013, 10. Number part-time enrolled (new admits only) 2012–2013, 30. Total enrolled 2012–2013 full-time, 15. Total enrolled 2012–2013 part-time, 50. Openings 2013–2014, 50. The median number of years required for completion of a degree in 2012–2013 were 2. The number of students enrolled full- and part-time who were dismissed or voluntarily withdrew from this program area in 2012–2013 were 2. Industrial/Organizational Psychology MA/MS (Master of Arts/Science)—Applications 2012–2013, 25. Total applicants accepted 2012–2013, 25. Number full-time enrolled (new admits only) 2012–2013, 2. Number part-time enrolled (new admits only) 2012–2013, 18. Total enrolled 2012–2013 full-time, 2. Total enrolled 2012–2013 part-time, 18. Openings 2013–2014, 25. The median number of years required for completion of a degree in 2012–2013 was 1. The number of students enrolled full- and part-time who were dismissed or voluntarily withdrew from this program area in 2012–2013 were 0. Industrial-Organizational Psychology/Mft MA/MS (Master of Arts/Science)—Applications 2012–2013, 8. Total applicants accepted 2012–2013, 8. Number full-time enrolled (new admits only) 2012–2013, 8. Number part-time enrolled (new admits only) 2012–2013, 2. Total enrolled 2012–2013 full-time, 8. Total enrolled 2012–2013 part-time, 2. Openings 2013–2014, 10. The median number of years required for completion of a degree in 2012–2013 were 2. The number of students enrolled full- and part-time who were dismissed or voluntarily withdrew from this program area in 2012–2013 were 0.

Scores: Entries appear in this order: required test or GPA, minimum score (if required), median score of students entering in 2012–2013. Marriage and Family Therapy MA/MS (Master of Arts/Science): overall undergraduate GPA no minimum stated; Industrial/Organizational Psychology MA/MS (Master of Arts/Science): overall undergraduate GPA no minimum stated; Industrial-Organizational Psychology/MFT MA/MS (Master of Arts/Science): overall undergraduate GPA no minimum stated.

Other Criteria: (importance of criteria rated low, medium, or high): work experience—medium, extracurricular activity—low, clinically related public service—low, GPA—high, letters of recommendation—low, interview—low, statement of goals and objectives—high, undergraduate major in psychology—low. For additional information on admission requirements, go to http://www.ggu.edu/graduate/enrollment/admission-requirements.

Student Characteristics: The following represents characteristics of students in 2012–2013 in all graduate psychology programs in the department: Female—full-time 20, part-time 60; Male—full-time 5, part-time 10; African American/Black—full-time 3, part-time 5; Hispanic/Latino(a)—full-time 0, part-time 5; Asian/Pacific Islander—full-time 12, part-time 2; American Indian/Alaska Native—full-time 0, part-time 0; Caucasian/White—full-time 8, part-time 49; Multi-ethnic—full-time 1, part-time 5; students subject to the Americans With Disabilities Act—full-time 1, part-time 0; Unknown ethnicity—full-time 1, part-time 4; International students who hold an F-1 or J-1 Visa—full-time 12, part-time 0.

Financial Information/Assistance:

Tuition for Full-Time Study: Master's: State residents: $810 per credit hour; Nonstate residents: $810 per credit hour. Tuition is subject to change. See the following website for updates and changes in tuition costs: http://www.ggu.edu/enrollment/tuition-and-fees/tuition.

Financial Assistance:

First-Year Students: Fellowships and scholarships available for first year.

Advanced Students: Fellowships and scholarships available for advanced students.

Additional Information: Of all students currently enrolled full time, 50% benefited from one or more of the listed financial assistance programs. Application and information available online at: http://www.ggu.edu/enrollment/financial-aid.

Internships/Practica: Master's Degree (MA/MS Marriage and Family Therapy): An internship experience, such as a final research project or "capstone" experience is required of graduates. Master's Degree (MA/MS Industrial-Organizational Psychology/MFT): An internship experience, such as a final research project or "capstone" experience is required of graduates. Golden Gate University has relationships with over 80 San Francisco Bay Area clinics and agencies that provide clinical traineeships for our students and alumni. Located in a vigorous business community,

Golden Gate University also assists Industrial/Organizational students with internship opportunities in businesses ranging from consulting to technology and in government organizations.

Housing and Day Care: No on-campus housing is available. No on-campus day care facilities are available.

Employment of Department Graduates:
Master's Degree Graduates: Of those who graduated in the academic year 2011–2012, the following categories and numbers represent the postgraduate activities and employment of master's degree graduates: Enrolled in a psychology doctoral program (3), enrolled in a postdoctoral residency/fellowship (n/a), employed in independent practice (n/a), employed in a professional position in a school system (2), employed in business or industry (13), employed in government agency (1), employed in a community mental health/counseling center (30), employed in a hospital/medical center (2), total from the above (master's) (51).
Doctoral Degree Graduates: Of those who graduated in the academic year 2011–2012, the following categories and numbers represent the postgraduate activities and employment of doctoral degree graduates: Enrolled in a psychology doctoral program (n/a), total from the above (doctoral) (0).

Additional Information:
Orientation, Objectives, and Emphasis of Department: Golden Gate University offers applied psychology degrees for students wishing to begin or enhance a career where they can make a difference in society. Concentrations prepare students for a range of careers from licensed clinical therapists to organizational consultants. Certificates in conflict resolution may be combined with degrees.

Application Information:
Send to Admissions, Golden Gate University, 536 Mission Street, San Francisco, CA 94005. Application available online. URL of online application: http://www.ggu.edu/admission/applydegree.do?type=G. Students are admitted in the Fall, application deadline June 1; Spring, application deadline October 1; Summer, application deadline February 1. *Fee:* $70.

Humboldt State University
Department of Psychology
College of Professional Studies
1 Harpst Street
Arcata, CA 95521
Telephone: (707) 826-5264
Fax: (707) 826-4993
E-mail: *kees@humboldt.edu*
Web: *http://www.humboldt.edu/psychology*

Department Information:
1964. Chairperson: Gregg Gold, PhD. Number of faculty: total—full-time 9, part-time 8; women—full-time 3, part-time 5.

Programs and Degrees Offered:
Listed in the following order: Program area, degree type (T if terminal Master's), number awarded 7/11–6/12. Academic Re-

search MA/MS (Master of Arts/Science) (T) 5, Counseling MA/MS (Master of Arts/Science) (T) 8, School Psychology MA/MS (Master of Arts/Science) (T) 11.

Student Applications/Admissions:
Student Applications
Academic Research MA/MS (Master of Arts/Science)—Applications 2012–2013, 14. Total applicants accepted 2012–2013, 9. Number full-time enrolled (new admits only) 2012–2013, 12. Number part-time enrolled (new admits only) 2012–2013, 0. Total enrolled 2012–2013 full-time, 18. Total enrolled 2012–2013 part-time, 0. Openings 2013–2014, 14. The median number of years required for completion of a degree in 2012–2013 were 2. The number of students enrolled full- and part-time who were dismissed or voluntarily withdrew from this program area in 2012–2013 were 0. *Counseling MA/MS (Master of Arts/Science)*—Applications 2012–2013, 22. Total applicants accepted 2012–2013, 13. Number full-time enrolled (new admits only) 2012–2013, 8. Number part-time enrolled (new admits only) 2012–2013, 0. Total enrolled 2012–2013 full-time, 19. Openings 2013–2014, 12. The median number of years required for completion of a degree in 2012–2013 were 3. The number of students enrolled full- and part-time who were dismissed or voluntarily withdrew from this program area in 2012–2013 were 1. *School Psychology MA/MS (Master of Arts/Science)*—Applications 2012–2013, 24. Total applicants accepted 2012–2013, 12. Number full-time enrolled (new admits only) 2012–2013, 12. Number part-time enrolled (new admits only) 2012–2013, 0. Total enrolled 2012–2013 full-time, 19. Openings 2013–2014, 10. The median number of years required for completion of a degree in 2012–2013 were 3. The number of students enrolled full- and part-time who were dismissed or voluntarily withdrew from this program area in 2012–2013 were 0.
Scores: Entries appear in this order: required test or GPA, minimum score (if required), median score of students entering in 2012–2013. *Academic Research MA/MS (Master of Arts/Science):* overall undergraduate GPA 3.25, psychology GPA 3.25; *Counseling MA/MS (Master of Arts/Science):* GRE-V no minimum stated, GRE-Q no minimum stated, GRE-Analytical no minimum stated, overall undergraduate GPA 3.0; *School Psychology MA/MS (Master of Arts/Science):* overall undergraduate GPA 3.0.
Other Criteria: (importance of criteria rated low, medium, or high): GRE scores—low, research experience—medium, work experience—medium, extracurricular activity—medium, clinically related public service—medium, GPA—high, letters of recommendation—high, interview—medium, statement of goals and objectives—high, undergraduate major in psychology—low, An interview is required for Counseling and School Psychology; research experience is important for Academic Research; clinically related public service or work experience is highly important for Counseling and School Psychology; school/child related work experience highly important for School Psychology. For additional information on admission requirements, go to http://www.humboldt.edu/psychology/grad/gradhome.htm.

Student Characteristics: The following represents characteristics of students in 2012–2013 in all graduate psychology programs in the department: Female—full-time 36, part-time 0; Male—full-time 20, part-time 0; African American/Black—full-time 1, part-

time 0; Hispanic/Latino(a)—full-time 6, part-time 0; Asian/Pacific Islander—full-time 5, part-time 0; American Indian/Alaska Native—full-time 0, part-time 0; Caucasian/White—full-time 36, part-time 0; Multi-ethnic—full-time 6, part-time 0; students subject to the Americans With Disabilities Act—full-time 0, part-time 0; Unknown ethnicity—full-time 2, part-time 0; International students who hold an F-1 or J-1 Visa—full-time 0, part-time 0.

Financial Information/Assistance:

Tuition for Full-Time Study: *Master's:* State residents: per academic year $8,396; Nonstate residents: per academic year $21,044. Tuition is subject to change. See the following website for updates and changes in tuition costs: http://www.humboldt.edu/studentfinancial/tuition_fees.html.

Financial Assistance:

First-Year Students: Fellowships and scholarships available for first year. Average amount paid per academic year: $4,000.

Advanced Students: Fellowships and scholarships available for advanced students.

Additional Information: Of all students currently enrolled full time, 0% benefited from one or more of the listed financial assistance programs. Application and information available online at: http://www.humboldt.edu/finaid/.

Internships/Practica: Master's Degree (MA/MS Academic Research): An internship experience, such as a final research project or "capstone" experience is required of graduates. Master's Degree (MA/MS Counseling): An internship experience, such as a final research project or "capstone" experience is required of graduates. Master's Degree (MA/MS School Psychology): An internship experience, such as a final research project or "capstone" experience is required of graduates. School Psychology internships (paid) are required of all students seeking the School Psychology credential. Counseling MA students are provided the opportunity to do fieldwork/practica in the department's community counseling clinic, as well as in several local mental health agencies.

Housing and Day Care: On-campus housing is available. See the following website for more information: http://www.humboldt.edu/housing/. On-campus day care facilities are available. See the following website for more information: http://www.humboldt.edu/childrencenter/.

Employment of Department Graduates:

Master's Degree Graduates: Of those who graduated in the academic year 2011–2012, the following categories and numbers represent the postgraduate activities and employment of master's degree graduates: Enrolled in a psychology doctoral program (4), enrolled in a postdoctoral residency/fellowship (n/a), employed in independent practice (n/a), employed in an academic position at a university (4), employed in an academic position at a 2-year/4-year college (2), employed in a professional position in a school system (15), employed in government agency (1), employed in a community mental health/counseling center (6), total from the above (master's) (32).

Doctoral Degree Graduates: Of those who graduated in the academic year 2011–2012, the following categories and numbers represent the postgraduate activities and employment of doctoral degree graduates: Enrolled in a psychology doctoral program (n/a), total from the above (doctoral) (0).

Additional Information:

Orientation, Objectives, and Emphasis of Department: The objectives of our department are to provide students with an understanding of principles and theories concerning human behavior and to the processes by which such information is obtained; to provide quality professional graduate education for students working toward California School Psychologist credentials, Marriage and Family Therapist licenses and other specialized occupational fields; and to provide a flexibility in our offerings that responds to changing societal agenda and student needs. Our Academic Research Master's program provides specializations in the following areas: Developmental Psychopathology, Biological Psychology, and Social and Environmental Psychology. Students should select one of these areas when they apply to the program.

Special Facilities or Resources: The department has an on-campus clinic staffed by MA counseling students, an electronic equipment shop, a lab with biofeedback and EEG equipment, a lab equipped for research on motion sickness, observation and research access to an on-campus demonstration nursery school, a test library, and a computer laboratory. Our new Behavioral and Social Sciences Building provides exceptional research, instruction, faculty and student space for the Department of Psychology.

Information for Students With Physical Disabilities: See the following website for more information: http://www.humboldt.edu/disability/.

Application Information:

Send to Office of Admissions, Humboldt State University, Arcata, CA 95521. Application available online. URL of online application: http://www.humboldt.edu/gradprograms/future-students. Students are admitted in the Fall, application deadline February 1. With all programs, we will accept applications until we accept a full cohort. *Fee:* $55.

John F. Kennedy University
College of Graduate and Professional Studies
100 Ellinwood Way
Pleasant Hill, CA 94523
Telephone: (925) 969-3400
Fax: (925) 969-3401
E-mail: *rfassinger@jfku.edu*
Web: *http://www.jfku.edu/Programs-and-Courses/College-of-Graduate-Professional-Studies.html*

Department Information:

1965. Dean: Ruth Fassinger, PhD. Number of faculty: total—full-time 22, part-time 220; women—full-time 12, part-time 152; total—minority—full-time 13, part-time 34; women minority—full-time 9, part-time 22; faculty subject to the Americans With Disabilities Act 2.

Programs and Degrees Offered:

Listed in the following order: Program area, degree type (T if terminal Master's), number awarded 7/11–6/12. Counseling Psychology MA/MS (Master of Arts/Science) (T) 83, Clinical Psychology PsyD (Doctor of Psychology) 26, Sport Psychology MA/

MS (Master of Arts/Science) (T) 21, Counseling Psychology (Holistic) MA/MS (Master of Arts/Science) (T) 54.

APA Accreditation: On Probation PsyD (Doctor of Psychology).

Student Applications/Admissions:

Student Applications

Counseling Psychology MA/MS (Master of Arts/Science)—Applications 2012–2013, 165. Total applicants accepted 2012–2013, 102. Number full-time enrolled (new admits only) 2012–2013, 55. Number part-time enrolled (new admits only) 2012–2013, 9. Total enrolled 2012–2013 full-time, 150. Total enrolled 2012–2013 part-time, 161. The median number of years required for completion of a degree in 2012–2013 were 3. The number of students enrolled full- and part-time who were dismissed or voluntarily withdrew from this program area in 2012–2013 were 8. *Clinical Psychology PsyD (Doctor of Psychology)*—Applications 2012–2013, 142. Total applicants accepted 2012–2013, 64. Number full-time enrolled (new admits only) 2012–2013, 29. Number part-time enrolled (new admits only) 2012–2013, 1. Total enrolled 2012–2013 full-time, 103. Total enrolled 2012–2013 part-time, 33. Openings 2013–2014, 30. The median number of years required for completion of a degree in 2012–2013 were 5. The number of students enrolled full- and part-time who were dismissed or voluntarily withdrew from this program area in 2012–2013 were 5. *Sport Psychology MA/MS (Master of Arts/Science)*—Applications 2012–2013, 57. Total applicants accepted 2012–2013, 31. Number full-time enrolled (new admits only) 2012–2013, 20. Number part-time enrolled (new admits only) 2012–2013, 2. Total enrolled 2012–2013 full-time, 43. Total enrolled 2012–2013 part-time, 53. Openings 2013–2014, 25. The median number of years required for completion of a degree in 2012–2013 were 3. The number of students enrolled full- and part-time who were dismissed or voluntarily withdrew from this program area in 2012–2013 were 7. *Counseling Psychology (Holistic) MA/MS (Master of Arts/Science)*—Applications 2012–2013, 104. Total applicants accepted 2012–2013, 69. Number full-time enrolled (new admits only) 2012–2013, 17. Number part-time enrolled (new admits only) 2012–2013, 26. Total enrolled 2012–2013 full-time, 85. Total enrolled 2012–2013 part-time, 197. The median number of years required for completion of a degree in 2012–2013 were 3. The number of students enrolled full- and part-time who were dismissed or voluntarily withdrew from this program area in 2012–2013 were 8.

Scores: Entries appear in this order: required test or GPA, minimum score (if required), median score of students entering in 2012–2013. *Counseling Psychology MA/MS (Master of Arts/Science):* overall undergraduate GPA 3.0; *Clinical Psychology PsyD (Doctor of Psychology):* overall undergraduate GPA 3.0; *Sport Psychology MA/MS (Master of Arts/Science):* overall undergraduate GPA 3.0; *Counseling Psychology (Holistic) MA/MS (Master of Arts/Science):* overall undergraduate GPA 3.0.

Other Criteria: (importance of criteria rated low, medium, or high): research experience—low, work experience—medium, extracurricular activity—medium, clinically related public service—high, GPA—medium, letters of recommendation—high, interview—high, statement of goals and objectives—high, undergraduate major in psychology—medium, specific undergraduate psychology courses taken—low, The quality of writing and GPA are highly important to the PsyD program when evaluating applicants. The MA programs put a strong emphasis on the personal statement of goals and objectives and experience in public/social service. The Sport Psychology program looks for a strong personal statement and solid GPA for admission.

Student Characteristics: The following represents characteristics of students in 2012–2013 in all graduate psychology programs in the department: Female—full-time 303, part-time 346; Male—full-time 78, part-time 98; African American/Black—full-time 37, part-time 31; Hispanic/Latino(a)—full-time 19, part-time 38; Asian/Pacific Islander—full-time 28, part-time 36; American Indian/Alaska Native—full-time 5, part-time 5; Caucasian/White—full-time 208, part-time 215; Multi-ethnic—full-time 16, part-time 7; students subject to the Americans With Disabilities Act—full-time 15, part-time 26; Unknown ethnicity—full-time 68, part-time 112; International students who hold an F-1 or J-1 Visa—full-time 0, part-time 1.

Financial Information/Assistance:

Tuition for Full-Time Study: *Master's:* State residents: $615 per credit hour; Nonstate residents: $615 per credit hour. *Doctoral:* State residents: $730 per credit hour; Nonstate residents: $730 per credit hour. Tuition is subject to change. Additional fees are assessed to students beyond the costs of tuition for the following: internship, comprehensive exams, student services, technology. See the following website for updates and changes in tuition costs: http://www.jfku.edu/Admissions/Tuition-and-Fees.html.

Financial Assistance:

First-Year Students: No information provided.

Advanced Students: No information provided.

Additional Information: Of all students currently enrolled full time, 0% benefited from one or more of the listed financial assistance programs. Application and information available online at: http://www.jfku.edu/Admissions/Financial-Aid.html.

Internships/Practica: Doctoral Degree (PsyD Clinical Psychology): For those doctoral students for whom a professional psychology internship was required in this program prior to graduation, (24) students applied for an internship in 2011–2012, with (21) students obtaining an internship. Of those students who obtained an internship, (17) were paid internships. Of those students who obtained an internship, (3) students placed in APA/CPA accredited internships, (9) students placed in internships not APA/CPA accredited, but listed with the Association of Psychology Postdoctoral and Internship Programs (APPIC), (0) students placed in internships conforming to guidelines of the Council of Directors of School Psychology Programs (CDSPP), (9) students placed in internships that were not APA/CPA accredited, APPIC or CDSPP listed. Master's Degree (MA/MS Counseling Psychology): An internship experience, such as a final research project or "capstone" experience is required of graduates. Master's Degree (MA/MS Sport Psychology): An internship experience, such as a final research project or "capstone" experience is required of graduates. Master's Degree (MA/MS Counseling Psychology (Holistic)): An internship experience, such as a final research project or "capstone" experience is required of graduates. John F. Kennedy University has three community counseling centers, each located near one of our three campuses, which provide state-of-the-art supervision for students and thousands of hours of low-fee counseling each year. Additionally, approximately 150 external fieldwork sites, monitored by our faculty, are available in the surrounding counties. Students in the MA Counseling Psychology programs and the PsyD program accumulate hours toward their respective licenses at both the community counseling centers and the external sites. The MA in Sport Psychology program and Expressive Arts specialization offer summer camps for incarcerated youth, youth sport teams and children which also serve as additional field placement sites for graduate students. In addition, the Sport Psychology program offers internship experiences for all onsite and online students.

Housing and Day Care: No on-campus housing is available. No on-campus day care facilities are available.

Employment of Department Graduates:

Master's Degree Graduates: Of those who graduated in the academic year 2011–2012, the following categories and numbers represent the postgraduate activities and employment of master's degree graduates: Enrolled in a postdoctoral residency/fellowship (n/a), employed in independent practice (n/a), total from the above (master's) (0).

Doctoral Degree Graduates: Of those who graduated in the academic year 2011–2012, the following categories and numbers represent the postgraduate activities and employment of doctoral degree graduates: Enrolled in a psychology doctoral program (n/a), total from the above (doctoral) (0).

Additional Information:

Orientation, Objectives, and Emphasis of Department: Our Graduate Psychology programs provide an academic environment that is rigorous, supportive, and transformative. Students are offered an array of opportunities to develop the knowledge, skills, and understanding needed to reach their potential. We are committed to active learning and community service, and are guided by a commitment to traditionally underserved populations. Our graduate-level degree and certificate programs provide a solid foundation in the theoretical bases of the field of study, opportunities for specialized study, and an abundance of supervised internships and other types of field studies. The Doctor of Psychology (PsyD) program follows the practitioner-scholar model providing an educational and training program in clinical psychology at the doctoral level. The Sport Psychology program is an innovative program that integrates the core elements of performance enhancement, counseling skills, and sport science. Students may also enroll in the Dual MA/PsyD degree program and receive both the MA in Sports Psychology and the PsyD in Clinical Psychology. The Counseling Psychology program offers specializations in Marriage and Family Therapy and Professional Clinical Counseling. Our Holistic Counseling Psychology program adds a perspective that integrates body, mind, spirit and culture into its curriculum with four areas of study; Transpersonal, Somatic, Holistic, and Expressive Arts.

Special Facilities or Resources: As noted, the John F. Kennedy University community counseling centers serve a broad-based clientele throughout the surrounding communities. The programs in the school are actively engaged in community service. For example, the Sport Psychology program is an active participant in the Life Enhancement Through Athletic and Academic Participation (LEAP) in numerous Bay Area schools. The Expressive Arts specialization in the Counseling Psychology MA program works with elementary school children from a variety of sites.

Information for Students With Physical Disabilities: See the following website for more information: http://www.jfku.edu/Student-Service/Student-Services.html.

Application Information:
Send to Admissions Office, John F. Kennedy University, 100 Ellinwood Way, Pleasant Hill, CA 94523-4817. Application available online. URL of online application: http://www.jfku.edu/Admissions/Apply-to-JFK-University.html. Students are admitted in the Fall, application deadline January 16; Spring, application deadline; Programs have rolling admissions. January 16 for Psy.D (Fall admissions only). MA Counseling Programs take new students in Fall and Spring. The MA Sport Psychology program takes new students each quarter. The Counseling Psychology and Counseling Psychology-Holistic Programs admit each term. *Fee:* $65. $65 for MA Programs, $90 for PsyD Program.

La Verne, University of
Psychology Department
Arts and Sciences
1950 Third Street
La Verne, CA 91750
Telephone: (909) 593-3511, ext. 4414
Fax: (909) 392-2745
E-mail: *jkernes@laverne.edu*
Web: *http://sites.laverne.edu/psychology/psyd-program/*

Department Information:
1968. PsyD Program Chair: Jerry L. Kernes, PhD. Number of faculty: total—full-time 9, part-time 2; women—full-time 6, part-time 1; total—minority—full-time 5, part-time 1; women minority—full-time 4, part-time 1.

Programs and Degrees Offered:
Listed in the following order: Program area, degree type (T if terminal Master's), number awarded 7/11–6/12. Clinical Psychology PsyD (Doctor of Psychology) 14.

APA Accreditation: Clinical PsyD (Doctor of Psychology). Student Outcome Data Website: http://sites.laverne.edu/psychology/psyd-program/.

Student Applications/Admissions:
Student Applications
Clinical Psychology PsyD (Doctor of Psychology)—Applications 2012–2013, 137. Total applicants accepted 2012–2013, 38. Number full-time enrolled (new admits only) 2012–2013, 20. Number part-time enrolled (new admits only) 2012–2013, 0. Total enrolled 2012–2013 full-time, 106. Openings 2013–2014, 14. The median number of years required for completion of a degree in 2012–2013 were 5. The number of students enrolled full- and part-time who were dismissed or voluntarily withdrew from this program area in 2012–2013 were 4.
Scores: Entries appear in this order: required test or GPA, minimum score (if required), median score of students entering in 2012–2013. *Clinical Psychology PsyD (Doctor of Psychology):* GRE-V no minimum stated, GRE-Q no minimum stated, GRE-Analytical no minimum stated, GRE-Subject (Psychology) no minimum stated, overall undergraduate GPA no minimum stated.

Other Criteria: (importance of criteria rated low, medium, or high): GRE scores—medium, research experience—high, work experience—high, extracurricular activity—medium, clinically related public service—high, GPA—high, letters of recommendation—high, interview—high, statement of goals and objectives—high, undergraduate major in psychology—high, specific undergraduate psychology courses taken—high. For additional information on admission requirements, go to http://sites.laverne.edu/psychology/psyd-program/admissions/.

Student Characteristics: The following represents characteristics of students in 2012–2013 in all graduate psychology programs in the department: Female—full-time 90, part-time 0; Male—full-time 16, part-time 0; African American/Black—full-time 12, part-time 0; Hispanic/Latino(a)—full-time 31, part-time 0; Asian/Pacific Islander—full-time 11, part-time 0; American Indian/Alaska Native—full-time 0, part-time 0; Caucasian/White—full-time 43, part-time 0; Multi-ethnic—full-time 7, part-time 0; students subject to the Americans With Disabilities Act—full-time 1, part-time 0; Unknown ethnicity—full-time 2, part-time 0; International students who hold an F-1 or J-1 Visa—full-time 0, part-time 0.

Financial Information/Assistance:

Tuition for Full-Time Study: *Doctoral:* State residents: $885 per credit hour; Nonstate residents: $885 per credit hour. Tuition is subject to change. See the following website for updates and changes in tuition costs: http://laverne.edu/tuition/graduate/.

Financial Assistance:

First-Year Students: No information provided.

Advanced Students: Teaching assistantships available for advanced students. Average amount paid per academic year: $4,000. Average number of hours worked per week: 8. Apply by June. Research assistantships available for advanced students. Average amount paid per academic year: $4,000. Average number of hours worked per week: 8. Apply by June. Traineeships available for advanced students. Average amount paid per academic year: $4,000. Average number of hours worked per week: 20. Apply by March.

Additional Information: Of all students currently enrolled full time, 20% benefited from one or more of the listed financial assistance programs. Application and information available online at: http://sites.laverne.edu/financial-aid/.

Internships/Practica: Doctoral Degree (PsyD Clinical Psychology): For those doctoral students for whom a professional psychology internship was required in this program prior to graduation, (16) students applied for an internship in 2011–2012, with (10) students obtaining an internship. Of those students who obtained an internship, (9) were paid internships. Of those students who obtained an internship, (7) students placed in APA/CPA accredited internships, (1) students placed in internships not APA/CPA accredited, but listed with the Association of Psychology Postdoctoral and Internship Programs (APPIC), (0) students placed in internships conforming to guidelines of the Council of Directors of School Psychology Programs (CDSPP), (2) students placed in internships that were not APA/CPA accredited, APPIC or CDSPP listed. The PsyD program includes required supervised practica in the second and third years of the program, with an optional fourth year practicum available. A minimum of 1500 hours of clinical practicum activities are required for the PsyD

The culminating predoctoral internship in the fifth and final year of the program consists of an additional 1500 clinical hours, which is typically completed as a one-year full-time internship. While most students follow this track, a two-year half-time internship option is available. The PsyD program participates in a regional consortium of program and training site directors for doctoral programs, and is a doctoral program member of CAPIC and NCSPP. The Psychology department has an extensive network of practicum, fieldwork, and internship sites with mental health and educational settings throughout the Southern California area.

Housing and Day Care: On-campus housing is available. See the following website for more information: http://sites.laverne.edu/housing/. On-campus day care facilities are available. See the following website for more information: http://www.fairplexcdc.org/.

Employment of Department Graduates:

Master's Degree Graduates: Of those who graduated in the academic year 2011–2012, the following categories and numbers represent the postgraduate activities and employment of master's degree graduates: Enrolled in a postdoctoral residency/fellowship (n/a), employed in independent practice (n/a), total from the above (master's) (0).

Doctoral Degree Graduates: Of those who graduated in the academic year 2011–2012, the following categories and numbers represent the postgraduate activities and employment of doctoral degree graduates: Enrolled in a psychology doctoral program (n/a), enrolled in a postdoctoral residency/fellowship (14), total from the above (doctoral) (14).

Additional Information:

Orientation, Objectives, and Emphasis of Department: The clinical faculty consists of psychologists whose theoretical orientations include psychodynamic, humanist, cognitive-behavioral, and multicultural, and who are clinically active in a range of clinical settings and populations. Faculty research interests include topics such as multiculturalism, psychotherapy outcome research, racial identity and acculturation, child and family development, positive psychology, moral development and decision making, and violence and victimization. The curriculum of the PsyD program is anchored in a multi-cultural perspective and involves a multi-disciplinary faculty who are actively involved in clinical and research activities. The PsyD program meets all predoctoral requirements for California psychology licensure. Students proceed through the program in a cohort model, taking all but elective courses together with their entering group. This fosters a high level of cooperation among students. Student-faculty ratios are relatively small, resulting in multiple opportunities for mentoring by faculty and for student-faculty collaboration.

Special Facilities or Resources: Students have access to a wide network of local and regional clinical, research and library facilities in the metropolitan Los Angeles and Southern California area.

Information for Students With Physical Disabilities: See the following website for more information: http://laverne.edu/students/students-with-disabilities/.

Application Information:
Send to Graduate Admissions, 1950 Third Street, University of La Verne, La Verne, CA 91750. Application available online. URL of

online application: http://laverne.edu/admission/applyapply2/. Students are admitted in the Fall, application deadline December 1. *Fee:* $75.

Loma Linda University

Department of Psychology
School of Behavioral Health
11130 Anderson Street, Suite 106
Loma Linda, CA 92350
Telephone: (909) 558-8577
Fax: (909) 558-0971
E-mail: *sLane@llu.edu*
Web: *http://www.llu.edu/behavioral-health/psychology*

Department Information:

1994. Chairperson: Louis E Jenkins, PhD, ABPP. Number of faculty: total—full-time 12, part-time 1; women—full-time 4, part-time 1; total—minority—full-time 4; women minority—full-time 1.

Programs and Degrees Offered:

Listed in the following order: Program area, degree type (T if terminal Master's), number awarded 7/11–6/12. Clinical Psychology PhD (Doctor of Philosophy) 5, Clinical Psychology PsyD (Doctor of Psychology) 8.

APA Accreditation: Clinical PhD (Doctor of Philosophy). Student Outcome Data Website: http://www.llu.edu/behavioral-health/psychology/programs/phd.page?. Clinical PsyD (Doctor of Psychology). Student Outcome Data Website: http://www.llu.edu/behavioral-health/psychology/programs/psyd.page?.

Student Applications/Admissions:

Student Applications

Clinical Psychology PhD (Doctor of Philosophy)—Applications 2012–2013, 90. Total applicants accepted 2012–2013, 11. Number full-time enrolled (new admits only) 2012–2013, 11. Number part-time enrolled (new admits only) 2012–2013, 0. Total enrolled 2012–2013 full-time, 64. Total enrolled 2012–2013 part-time, 0. Openings 2013–2014, 10. The median number of years required for completion of a degree in 2012–2013 were 7. The number of students enrolled full- and part-time who were dismissed or voluntarily withdrew from this program area in 2012–2013 were 0. *Clinical Psychology PsyD (Doctor of Psychology)*—Applications 2012–2013, 80. Total applicants accepted 2012–2013, 11. Number full-time enrolled (new admits only) 2012–2013, 11. Number part-time enrolled (new admits only) 2012–2013, 0. Total enrolled 2012–2013 full-time, 52. Total enrolled 2012–2013 part-time, 0. Openings 2013–2014, 20. The median number of years required for completion of a degree in 2012–2013 were 5. The number of students enrolled full- and part-time who were dismissed or voluntarily withdrew from this program area in 2012–2013 were 1.

Scores: Entries appear in this order: required test or GPA, minimum score (if required), median score of students entering in 2012–2013. *Clinical Psychology PhD (Doctor of Philosophy):* GRE-V 148, 151, GRE-Q 148, 151, GRE-Analytical 3.5, 4.0, overall undergraduate GPA 3.0, 3.43; *Clinical Psychology PsyD*

(Doctor of Psychology): GRE-V 148, 153, GRE-Q 148, 152, GRE-Analytical 3.5, 4.5, overall undergraduate GPA 3.0, 3.31, last 2 years GPA 3.0, 3.41.

Other Criteria: (importance of criteria rated low, medium, or high): GRE scores—high, research experience—high, work experience—medium, extracurricular activity—medium, clinically related public service—high, GPA—high, letters of recommendation—high, interview—high, statement of goals and objectives—high, undergraduate major in psychology—high, specific undergraduate psychology courses taken—high, For PhD applicants, research experience is highly desirable. For PsyD applicants, clinically-related experience is highly desirable. For additional information on admission requirements, go to http://www.llu.edu/behavioral-health/psychology/programs/howtoapply.page?.

Student Characteristics: The following represents characteristics of students in 2012–2013 in all graduate psychology programs in the department: Female—full-time 84, part-time 0; Male—full-time 32, part-time 0; African American/Black—full-time 9, part-time 0; Hispanic/Latino(a)—full-time 8, part-time 0; Asian/Pacific Islander—full-time 26, part-time 0; American Indian/Alaska Native—full-time 0, part-time 0; Caucasian/White—full-time 71, part-time 0; Multi-ethnic—full-time 2, part-time 0; students subject to the Americans With Disabilities Act—full-time 2, part-time 0; Unknown ethnicity—full-time 0, part-time 0; International students who hold an F-1 or J-1 Visa—full-time 0, part-time 0.

Financial Information/Assistance:

Tuition for Full-Time Study: *Doctoral:* State residents: per academic year $33,024; Nonstate residents: per academic year $33,024. Tuition is subject to change. Additional fees are assessed to students beyond the costs of tuition for the following: $837.00 (enrollment fee, lab fees and parking fee).

Financial Assistance:

First-Year Students: Research assistantships available for first year. Average amount paid per academic year: $4,500. Average number of hours worked per week: 5.

Advanced Students: Teaching assistantships available for advanced students. Average amount paid per academic year: $2,000. Average number of hours worked per week: 7. Research assistantships available for advanced students. Average amount paid per academic year: $7,000. Average number of hours worked per week: 10.

Additional Information: Of all students currently enrolled full time, 35% benefited from one or more of the listed financial assistance programs. Application and information available online at: http://www.llu.edu/central/ssweb/finaid/.

Internships/Practica: Doctoral Degree (PhD Clinical Psychology): For those doctoral students for whom a professional psychology internship was required in this program prior to graduation, (12) students applied for an internship in 2011–2012, with (10) students obtaining an internship. Of those students who obtained an internship, (10) were paid internships. Of those students who obtained an internship, (10) students placed in APA/CPA accredited internships, (0) students placed in internships not APA/CPA accredited, but listed with the Association of Psychology Postdoctoral and Internship Programs (APPIC), (0) students placed in internships conforming to guidelines of the Council of

Directors of School Psychology Programs (CDSPP), (0) students placed in internships that were not APA/CPA accredited, APPIC or CDSPP listed. Doctoral Degree (PsyD Clinical Psychology): For those doctoral students for whom a professional psychology internship was required in this program prior to graduation, (11) students applied for an internship in 2011–2012, with (6) students obtaining an internship. Of those students who obtained an internship, (6) were paid internships. Of those students who obtained an internship, (5) students placed in APA/CPA accredited internships, (1) students placed in internships not APA/CPA accredited, but listed with the Association of Psychology Postdoctoral and Internship Programs (APPIC), (0) students placed in internships conforming to guidelines of the Council of Directors of School Psychology Programs (CDSPP), (0) students placed in internships that were not APA/CPA accredited, APPIC or CDSPP listed. Second-year practicum experiences are obtained in the departmental clinic and in a satellite clinic which reaches a previously underserved area of the City of San Bernardino. Other department training experiences include the LLU Pediatrics Department population. Second-year practicum students may also receive some supervised clinical training in area public and private school settings. The external practicum (20 hours per week, normally in the third year of the program) is entirely off the departmental campus. Students are expected to accumulate 950 to 1000 hours of supervised experience while on external practicum, with an absolute minimum of 250 hours being spent in direct service experiences with patients. External practicum students are presently placed in five settings: 1) The Rehabilitation Unit of the Loma Linda University Medical Center; 2) The San Bernardino County Department of Mental Health; 3) the Casa Colina Hospital for Rehabilitative Medicine; 4) LLU Department of Family Medicine-Primary Care; and 5) Local Indian Reservation. A full-year (40 hours per week) of internship is required with sites available across the country. All acceptable internship sites must meet the criteria for membership in the Association of Psychology Postdoctoral and Internship Centers.

Housing and Day Care: On-campus housing is available. See the following website for more information: http://www.llu.edu/central/housing/. On-campus day care facilities are available.

Employment of Department Graduates:

Master's Degree Graduates: Of those who graduated in the academic year 2011–2012, the following categories and numbers represent the postgraduate activities and employment of master's degree graduates: Enrolled in a postdoctoral residency/fellowship (n/a), employed in independent practice (n/a), total from the above (master's) (0).

Doctoral Degree Graduates: Of those who graduated in the academic year 2011–2012, the following categories and numbers represent the postgraduate activities and employment of doctoral degree graduates: Enrolled in a psychology doctoral program (n/a), enrolled in a postdoctoral residency/fellowship (11), employed in a community mental health/counseling center (1), total from the above (doctoral) (12).

Additional Information:

Orientation, Objectives, and Emphasis of Department: Doctoral training at Loma Linda University takes place within the context of a holistic approach to human health and welfare. The university motto 'To make man whole' takes in every aspect of being human—the physical, psychological, spiritual, and social. Building

on a university tradition of health sciences research, training, and service, the doctoral programs in the department offer a combination of traditional and innovative training opportunities. The PhD in clinical psychology follows the traditional scientist–practitioner model and emphasizes research and clinical training. The PsyD is oriented toward clinical practice with emphasis on the understanding and application of the principles and research of psychological science.

Special Facilities or Resources: As a health sciences university, Loma Linda provides an ideal environment with resources for research and clinical training in such areas as health psychology/behavioral medicine and the delivery of health services. LLU Medical Center has nearly 900 beds, is staffed by more than 5000 people, and is the "flagship" of a system including hundreds of health care institutions around the world. In addition, a number of institutions in the area, such as the LLU Behavioral Medicine Center, Jerry L. Pettis VA Hospital, Patton State Hospital, and the San Bernardino County Mental Health Department represent numerous opportunities for research and clinical training in psychology.

Application Information:
Send to Loma Linda University, School of Behavioral Health, Office of Admissions, 11065 Campus Street Suite 217 (Griggs Hall), Loma Linda, CA 92350. Application available online. URL of online application: http://www.llu.edu/central/apply/. Students are admitted in the Fall, application deadline December 31. *Fee:* $75.

Mount St. Mary's College (2012 data)
Graduate Psychology
10 Chester Place
Los Angeles, CA 90007
Telephone: (213) 477-2650
E-mail: *gtravis@msmc.la.edu*
Web: *http://www.msmc.la.edu*

Department Information:
Director: Gregory Travis, PhD. Number of faculty: total—full-time 2, part-time 12; women—full-time 1, part-time 7; minority—part-time 7; women minority—part-time 5.

Programs and Degrees Offered:
Listed in the following order: Program area, degree type (T if terminal Master's), number awarded 7/11–6/12. Marriage/Family Therapy MA/MS (Master of Arts/Science) (T) 5, General Counseling Psychology MA/MS (Master of Arts/Science) (T) 0, Mental Health Administration MA/MS (Master of Arts/Science) (T) 0.

Student Applications/Admissions:
Student Applications
Marriage/Family Therapy MA/MS (Master of Arts/Science)—Applications 2012–2013, 46. Total applicants accepted 2012–2013, 39. Number full-time enrolled (new admits only) 2012–2013, 35. Total enrolled 2012–2013 full-time, 90. Total enrolled 2012–2013 part-time, 10. Openings 2013–2014, 35. The median number of years required for completion of a degree in 2012–2013 were 2. The number of students enrolled full- and part-time who were dismissed or voluntarily withdrew from

this program area in 2012–2013 were 5. *General Counseling Psychology MA/MS (Master of Arts/Science)*—Applications 2012–2013, 8. Total applicants accepted 2012–2013, 6. Number full-time enrolled (new admits only) 2012–2013, 6. Total enrolled 2012–2013 full-time, 10. Openings 2013–2014, 10. The median number of years required for completion of a degree in 2012–2013 were 2. The number of students enrolled full- and part-time who were dismissed or voluntarily withdrew from this program area in 2012–2013 were 0. *Mental Health Administration MA/MS (Master of Arts/Science)*—Applications 2012–2013, 4. Total applicants accepted 2012–2013, 2. Number full-time enrolled (new admits only) 2012–2013, 2. Total enrolled 2012–2013 full-time, 2. Openings 2013–2014, 5. The median number of years required for completion of a degree in 2012–2013 were 2. The number of students enrolled full- and part-time who were dismissed or voluntarily withdrew from this program area in 2012–2013 were 0.

Scores: Entries appear in this order: required test or GPA, minimum score (if required), median score of students entering in 2012–2013. *Marriage/Family Therapy MA/MS (Master of Arts/Science):* overall undergraduate GPA 3.0; *General Counseling Psychology MA/MS (Master of Arts/Science):* overall undergraduate GPA 3.0; *Mental Health Administration MA/MS (Master of Arts/Science):* overall undergraduate GPA 3.0.

Other Criteria: (importance of criteria rated low, medium, or high): work experience—high, extracurricular activity—low, clinically related public service—high, GPA—medium, letters of recommendation—high, interview—high, statement of goals and objectives—high, undergraduate major in psychology—low, Only MFT uses clinically related work experience.

Student Characteristics: The following represents characteristics of students in 2012–2013 in all graduate psychology programs in the department: Female—full-time 90, part-time 8; Male—full-time 12, part-time 2; African American/Black—full-time 10, part-time 1; Hispanic/Latino(a)—full-time 63, part-time 7; Asian/Pacific Islander—full-time 5, part-time 0; American Indian/Alaska Native—full-time 1, part-time 0; Caucasian/White—full-time 23, part-time 2; Multi-ethnic—full-time 0, part-time 0; students subject to the Americans With Disabilities Act—full-time 0, part-time 0; Unknown ethnicity—full-time 0, part-time 0; International students who hold an F-1 or J-1 Visa—full-time 4, part-time 0.

Financial Information/Assistance:
Tuition for Full-Time Study: *Master's:* State residents: $730 per credit hour; Nonstate residents: $730 per credit hour.

Financial Assistance:
First-Year Students: No information provided.
Advanced Students: Fellowships and scholarships available for advanced students.
Additional Information: Of all students currently enrolled full time, 25% benefited from one or more of the listed financial assistance programs.

Internships/Practica: Master's Degree (MA/MS Marriage/Family Therapy): An internship experience, such as a final research project or "capstone" experience is required of graduates. Master's Degree (MA/MS General Counseling Psychology): An internship experience, such as a final research project or "capstone" experience is required of graduates. Master's Degree (MA/MS Mental Health Administration): An internship experience, such as a final research project or "capstone" experience is required of graduates.

Housing and Day Care: No on-campus housing is available. No on-campus day care facilities are available.

Employment of Department Graduates:
Master's Degree Graduates: Of those who graduated in the academic year 2011–2012, the following categories and numbers represent the postgraduate activities and employment of master's degree graduates: Enrolled in a postdoctoral residency/fellowship (n/a), employed in independent practice (n/a), total from the above (master's) (0).
Doctoral Degree Graduates: Of those who graduated in the academic year 2011–2012, the following categories and numbers represent the postgraduate activities and employment of doctoral degree graduates: Enrolled in a psychology doctoral program (n/a), total from the above (doctoral) (0).

Application Information:
Send to Graduate Admissions, Mount St. Mary's College, 10 Chester Place, Los Angeles, CA 90007. Application available online. URL of online application: http://www.msmc.la.edu/graduate-programs/application-procedures.asp. Students are admitted in the Fall, application deadline June 30. *Fee:* $50. Fee waived if attend program Info Session.

Pacific, University of the
Department of Psychology
3601 Pacific Avenue
Stockton, CA 95211
Telephone: (209) 946-2133
Fax: (209) 946-2454
E-mail: ckohn@pacific.edu
Web: http://www.pacific.edu/Academics/Schools-and-Colleges/College-of-the-Pacific/Academics/Departments-and-Programs/Psychology.html

Department Information:
1960. Chairperson: Scott Jensen, PhD. Number of faculty: total—full-time 7; women—full-time 3.

Programs and Degrees Offered:
Listed in the following order: Program area, degree type (T if terminal Master's), number awarded 7/11–6/12. Behavior Analysis / Doctoral Preparation MA/MS (Master of Arts/Science) (T) 1.

Student Applications/Admissions:
Student Applications
Behavior Analysis / Doctoral Preparation MA/MS (Master of Arts/Science)—Applications 2012–2013, 34. Total applicants accepted 2012–2013, 7. Number full-time enrolled (new admits only) 2012–2013, 7. Number part-time enrolled (new admits only) 2012–2013, 0. Total enrolled 2012–2013 full-time, 6. Total enrolled 2012–2013 part-time, 3. Openings 2013–2014, 8. The median number of years required for completion of a degree in 2012–2013 were 3. The number of

students enrolled full- and part-time who were dismissed or voluntarily withdrew from this program area in 2012–2013 were 1.

Scores: Entries appear in this order: required test or GPA, minimum score (if required), median score of students entering in 2012–2013. *Behavior Analysis / Doctoral Preparation MA/MS (Master of Arts/Science):* GRE-V no minimum stated, 155, GRE-Q no minimum stated, 152, overall undergraduate GPA 3.0, 3.4, last 2 years GPA 3.0, psychology GPA 3.0.

Other Criteria: (importance of criteria rated low, medium, or high): GRE scores—medium, research experience—high, work experience—low, clinically related public service—low, GPA—high, letters of recommendation—high, statement of goals and objectives—high, applied experience—medium, undergraduate major in psychology—medium, specific undergraduate psychology courses taken—medium, Applicants planning to take the BACB exam should have some relevant course work and research in behavior analysis.

Student Characteristics: The following represents characteristics of students in 2012–2013 in all graduate psychology programs in the department: Female—full-time 11, part-time 4; Male—full-time 3, part-time 1; African American/Black—full-time 0, part-time 0; Hispanic/Latino(a)—full-time 1, part-time 0; Asian/Pacific Islander—full-time 2, part-time 0; American Indian/Alaska Native—full-time 0, part-time 0; Caucasian/White—full-time 7, part-time 5; Multi-ethnic—full-time 3, part-time 0; students subject to the Americans With Disabilities Act—full-time 0, part-time 0; Unknown ethnicity—full-time 1, part-time 0; International students who hold an F-1 or J-1 Visa—full-time 0, part-time 0.

Financial Information/Assistance:

Tuition for Full-Time Study: *Master's:* State residents: per academic year $17,885, $1,118 per credit hour; Nonstate residents: per academic year $17,885, $1,118 per credit hour. Tuition is subject to change. See the following website for updates and changes in tuition costs: http://www.pacific.edu/Campus-Life/Student-Services/Student-Accounts/Stockton-Tuition-and-Fees.html.

Financial Assistance:

First-Year Students: Teaching assistantships available for first year. Average amount paid per academic year: $10,700. Average number of hours worked per week: 20. Apply by February 15. Traineeships available for first year. Average amount paid per academic year: $12,400. Average number of hours worked per week: 20. Apply by February 15.

Advanced Students: Teaching assistantships available for advanced students. Average amount paid per academic year: $10,700. Average number of hours worked per week: 20. Apply by February 15. Traineeships available for advanced students. Average amount paid per academic year: $12,400. Average number of hours worked per week: 20. Apply by February 15.

Additional Information: Of all students currently enrolled full time, 100% benefited from one or more of the listed financial assistance programs. Application and information available online at: http://www.pacific.edu/Academics/Schools-and-Colleges/College-of-the-Pacific/Academics/Departments-and-Programs/Psychology/Academics/Graduate-Program/Financial-Assistance.html.

Internships/Practica: Master's Degree (MA/MS Behavior Analysis / Doctoral Preparation): An internship experience, such as a final research project or "capstone" experience is required of graduates. The department directs the Community Re-entry Program (contracted directly with the local county), which provides a wide range of behaviorally-based programs to assist the mentally disabled/ill in becoming independent. This program provides half-time employment for eight graduate students per year. Students interested in developmental disabilities can work with the Behavioral Instructional Service (in cooperation with Valley Mountain Regional Center, which serves these clients), and part-time employment is available with this program. We also have contracts with several outside agencies at which students can obtain practicum experience, including the Stockton Unified School District (ABA assessment and interventions for school problem behaviors) and BEST (early ABA interventions with children diagnosed with autism).

Housing and Day Care: On-campus housing is available. See the following website for more information: http://www.pacific.edu/Campus-Life/Housing-and-Facilities.html. No on-campus day care facilities are available.

Employment of Department Graduates:

Master's Degree Graduates: Of those who graduated in the academic year 2011–2012, the following categories and numbers represent the postgraduate activities and employment of master's degree graduates: Enrolled in a psychology doctoral program (1), enrolled in a postdoctoral residency/fellowship (n/a), employed in independent practice (n/a), total from the above (master's) (1).

Doctoral Degree Graduates: Of those who graduated in the academic year 2011–2012, the following categories and numbers represent the postgraduate activities and employment of doctoral degree graduates: Enrolled in a psychology doctoral program (n/a), total from the above (doctoral) (0).

Additional Information:

Orientation, Objectives, and Emphasis of Department: The Psychology Department offers a program of graduate study leading to the MA degree in Psychology. Students accepted into our program plan to complete their MA degree and sit for the BCBA exam and/or plan to apply to doctoral programs in behavior analysis or clinical/counseling psychology with a behavioral focus. We do not offer an MFT or a Counseling MA. The overall program focus includes: a wide variety of applied experience in a number of different settings; intensive involvement in designing, conducting, and evaluating research; coursework in theoretical and research foundations of applied behavior analysis and behavior theory; and commitment to the development of student potential by active, supportive, involved faculty.

Special Facilities or Resources: The department provides office space for faculty and graduate students, computing equipment, and video equipment for research projects. Applied research projects are also conducted in community settings (e.g. schools, medical settings). The Community Re-entry Program and Valley Mountain Regional Center also provide rich opportunities for research in community settings.

Information for Students With Physical Disabilities: See the following website for more information: http://www.pacific.edu/Campus-Life/Student-Services.html.

Application Information:
Send to Dean of the Graduate School, University of the Pacific, 3601 Pacific Avenue, Stockton, CA 95211. Application available online. URL of online application: https://www.applyweb.com/apply/uopg/menu.html. Students are admitted in the Fall, application deadline February 15. Although the deadline for applications is February 15th, on occasion we accept late applications. However, applying after the deadline decreases an applicant's chances to receive funding. *Fee:* $75.

Pacifica Graduate Institute (2012 data)

PhD in Clinical Psychology with emphasis in Depth
  Psychology
Department of Psychology
249 Lambert Road
Carpinteria, CA 93013
Telephone: (805) 969-3626 ext. 305
Fax: (805) 879-7391
E-mail: *admissions @pacifica.edu*
Web: *http://www.pacifica.edu/*

Department Information:
1989. Chairperson: James L. Broderick, PhD. Number of faculty: total—full-time 12, part-time 37; women—full-time 2, part-time 21; total—minority—full-time 1, part-time 3; women minority—part-time 2.

Programs and Degrees Offered:
Listed in the following order: Program area, degree type (T if terminal Master's), number awarded 7/11–6/12. Clinical Psychology PhD (Doctor of Philosophy).

Student Applications/Admissions:
  Student Applications
  Clinical Psychology PhD (Doctor of Philosophy)—
  Other Criteria: (importance of criteria rated low, medium, or high): research experience—medium, work experience—medium, extracurricular activity—medium, clinically related public service—medium, GPA—high, letters of recommendation—high, interview—high, statement of goals and objectives—high, Writing ability—high, undergraduate major in psychology—high, specific undergraduate psychology courses taken—high. For additional information on admission requirements, go to http://www.pacifica.edu/admissions.html.

  Student Characteristics: The following represents characteristics of students in 2012–2013 in all graduate psychology programs in the department: Female—full-time 0, part-time 0; Male—full-time 0, part-time 0; African American/Black—full-time 0, part-time 0; Hispanic/Latino(a)—full-time 0, part-time 0; Asian/Pacific Islander—full-time 0, part-time 0; American Indian/Alaska Native—full-time 0, part-time 0; Caucasian/White—full-time 0, part-time 0; Multi-ethnic—full-time 0, part-time 0; students subject to the Americans With Disabilities Act—full-time 0, part-time 0; Unknown ethnicity—full-time 0, part-time 0; International students who hold an F-1 or J-1 Visa—full-time 0, part-time 0.

Financial Information/Assistance:
  Tuition for Full-Time Study: Doctoral: State residents: per academic year $24,100. Tuition is subject to change. See the follow-ing website for updates and changes in tuition costs: http://www.pacifica.edu/admissions_fee_schedule.html.

Financial Assistance:
  First-Year Students: Fellowships and scholarships available for first year. Average amount paid per academic year: $1,500. Apply by August 1.
  Advanced Students: No information provided.
  Additional Information: Of all students currently enrolled full time, 55% benefited from one or more of the listed financial assistance programs.

Internships/Practica: The practicum sites are to serve as laboratory settings that allow students the opportunity for mastering the fundamental skills and knowledge being taught in the introductory courses in psychopathology, assessment, and intervention. The internship experience follows from both this practicum experience and the successful completion of three core practicum courses. Internship training requires more responsibility on the part of the students, with interns viewed as junior colleagues who perform, under supervision, all the duties of staff psychologists. The internship years are designed to prepare the students for the assumption of an autonomous professional role by allowing for the participation in the full repertoire of activities in which psychologists engage. Interns are expected to refine and to coordinate the skills acquired in the first three years of practica training, as well as to acquire new skills that are specifically related to supervision, care management, decision making, and treatment team leadership.

Housing and Day Care: On-campus housing is available.

Employment of Department Graduates:
  Master's Degree Graduates: Of those who graduated in the academic year 2011–2012, the following categories and numbers represent the postgraduate activities and employment of master's degree graduates: Enrolled in a postdoctoral residency/fellowship (n/a), employed in independent practice (n/a), total from the above (master's) (0).
  Doctoral Degree Graduates: Of those who graduated in the academic year 2011–2012, the following categories and numbers represent the postgraduate activities and employment of doctoral degree graduates: Enrolled in a psychology doctoral program (n/a), total from the above (doctoral) (0).

Additional Information:
  Orientation, Objectives, and Emphasis of Department: The course of study in the Clinical Psychology Program at Pacifica Graduate Institute is designed to provide foundational coursework in clinical psychology. This program seeks to educate scholar-practitioners skilled in quantitative, qualitative, and mixed research methods, and to apply their research skills to improve clinical outcomes. The program also exposes students to advanced training and education in the depth psychological tradition. The Clinical Psychology Program at Pacifica honors the full complexity of psychological life in a diverse society. The educational mission of this program is to provide clinical training and foster research framed in the traditions of both clinical and depth psychology. The program seeks to fulfill this purpose by creating an educational setting which nourishes respect for cultural diversity and individual differences, and an academic community which

fosters a spirit of inquiry and dialogue in an intellectually challenging academic environment.

Information for Students With Physical Disabilities: See the following website for more information: http://www.pacifica.edu/Disability-Services.aspx.

Application Information:

Send to Department of Admissions. Application available online. URL of online application: http://www.pacifica.edu. Students are admitted in the Fall, application deadline Availability; Winter, application deadline; Spring, application deadline; Summer, application deadline. June 30th for applications, August 1st for scholarships. *Fee:* $75.

Palo Alto University
Master's Programs
1791 Arastradero Road
Palo Alto, CA 94304
Telephone: (800) 818-6136
Fax: (650) 433-3888
E-mail: *admissions@paloaltou.edu*
Web: *http://www.paloaltou.edu/content/academics*

Department Information:

2000. Director - Master's Programs: Dr. Denise Daniels. Number of faculty: total—full-time 3, part-time 34; women—full-time 2, part-time 20; total—minority—full-time 1, part-time 4; women minority—full-time 1, part-time 3.

Programs and Degrees Offered:

Listed in the following order: Program area, degree type (T if terminal Master's), number awarded 7/11–6/12. Counseling Psychology MA/MS (Master of Arts/Science) (T) 2, Counseling MA/MS (Master of Arts/Science) (T) 0, Psychology MA/MS (Master of Arts/Science) (T).

Student Applications/Admissions:

Student Applications

Counseling Psychology MA/MS (Master of Arts/Science)—Applications 2012–2013, 55. Total applicants accepted 2012–2013, 52. Number full-time enrolled (new admits only) 2012–2013, 23. Number part-time enrolled (new admits only) 2012–2013, 2. Total enrolled 2012–2013 full-time, 69. Total enrolled 2012–2013 part-time, 6. Openings 2013–2014, 40. The median number of years required for completion of a degree in 2012–2013 were 3. The number of students enrolled full- and part-time who were dismissed or voluntarily withdrew from this program area in 2012–2013 were 0. *Counseling MA/MS (Master of Arts/Science)*—Applications 2012–2013, 48. Total applicants accepted 2012–2013, 35. Number full-time enrolled (new admits only) 2012–2013, 22. Number part-time enrolled (new admits only) 2012–2013, 3. Total enrolled 2012–2013 full-time, 22. Total enrolled 2012–2013 part-time, 3. Openings 2013–2014, 50. The number of students enrolled full- and part-time who were dismissed or voluntarily withdrew from

this program area in 2012–2013 were 0. *Psychology MA/MS (Master of Arts/Science)*—Applications 2012–2013, 60. Total applicants accepted 2012–2013, 40. Number full-time enrolled (new admits only) 2012–2013, 0. Number part-time enrolled (new admits only) 2012–2013, 33. Openings 2013–2014, 30. The median number of years required for completion of a degree in 2012–2013 were 2. The number of students enrolled full- and part-time who were dismissed or voluntarily withdrew from this program area in 2012–2013 were 2.

Scores: Entries appear in this order: required test or GPA, minimum score (if required), median score of students entering in 2012–2013. *Counseling Psychology MA/MS (Master of Arts/Science):* overall undergraduate GPA 3.0; *Counseling MA/MS (Master of Arts/Science):* overall undergraduate GPA 3.0; *Psychology MA/MS (Master of Arts/Science):* overall undergraduate GPA 3.3.

Other Criteria: (importance of criteria rated low, medium, or high): research experience—low, work experience—high, extracurricular activity—high, clinically related public service—high, GPA—high, letters of recommendation—high, interview—high, statement of goals and objectives—high, undergraduate major in psychology—medium, specific undergraduate psychology courses taken—medium, Counseling programs focus more strongly on clinical potential, while the general psychology program focuses more strongly on academic performance and research experience. For additional information on admission requirements, go to http://www.paloaltou.edu/department/admissions.

Student Characteristics: The following represents characteristics of students in 2012–2013 in all graduate psychology programs in the department: Female—full-time 115, part-time 7; Male—full-time 21, part-time 2; African American/Black—full-time 8, part-time 0; Hispanic/Latino(a)—full-time 18, part-time 0; Asian/Pacific Islander—full-time 10, part-time 0; American Indian/Alaska Native—full-time 1, part-time 0; Caucasian/White—full-time 59, part-time 0; Multi-ethnic—full-time 1, part-time 0; students subject to the Americans With Disabilities Act—full-time 2, part-time 0; Unknown ethnicity—full-time 39, part-time 9; International students who hold an F-1 or J-1 Visa—full-time 0, part-time 0.

Financial Information/Assistance:

Tuition for Full-Time Study: *Master's:* State residents: per academic year $17,169, $428 per credit hour; Nonstate residents: per academic year $17,169, $428 per credit hour. Tuition costs vary by program. See the following website for updates and changes in tuition costs: http://www.paloaltou.edu/department/admissions/tuition-fees.

Financial Assistance:

First-Year Students: No information provided.

Advanced Students: Teaching assistantships available for advanced students. Traineeships available for advanced students.

Additional Information: Application and information available online at: http://www.paloaltou.edu/department/financial-aid.

Internships/Practica: Master's Degree (MA/MS Counseling Psychology): An internship experience, such as a final research project or "capstone" experience is required of graduates. Master's Degree (MA/MS Counseling): An internship experience, such as a final research project or "capstone" experience is required of graduates. The MA programs require a practicum during the second year of the programs. The department offers students support with networking and applying for practicum placements.

Housing and Day Care: No on-campus housing is available. No on-campus day care facilities are available.

Employment of Department Graduates:
Master's Degree Graduates: Of those who graduated in the academic year 2011–2012, the following categories and numbers represent the postgraduate activities and employment of master's degree graduates: Enrolled in a postdoctoral residency/fellowship (n/a), employed in independent practice (n/a), total from the above (master's) (0).
Doctoral Degree Graduates: Of those who graduated in the academic year 2011–2012, the following categories and numbers represent the postgraduate activities and employment of doctoral degree graduates: Enrolled in a psychology doctoral program (n/a), total from the above (doctoral) (0).

Additional Information:
Orientation, Objectives, and Emphasis of Department: The master's programs department exists to train master's-level researchers and clinicians in preparation for clinical and counseling work, further academic study, and other related careers.

Special Facilities or Resources: PAU offers an annual research forum and a network of many community mental health agencies throughout the greater Bay Area and Monterey Bay area.

Information for Students With Physical Disabilities: See the following website for more information: http://www.paloaltou.edu/student-services/disability.

Application Information:
Send to Palo Alto University, Office of Admissions, 1791 Arastradero Road, Palo Alto, CA 94304. Application available online. URL of online application: https://my.paloaltou.edu/ICS/Admissions/Graduate_Applicants.jnz. Students are admitted in the Fall, application deadline August 1; Winter, application deadline November 1. Winter admission only for counseling programs. *Fee:* $40.

Palo Alto University
PGSP - Stanford PsyD Consortium
1791 Arastradero Road
Palo Alto, CA 94304
Telephone: (800) 818-6136
Fax: (650) 433-3888
E-mail: *admissions@paloaltou.edu*
Web: *http://www.paloaltou.edu/ program_stanford_psyd_home.php*

Department Information:
2002. Director of Clinical Training: Kimberly Hill, PhD. Number of faculty: total—full-time 15, part-time 33; women—full-time 9, part-time 25; total—minority—full-time 1, part-time 6; women minority—full-time 1, part-time 4.

Programs and Degrees Offered:
Listed in the following order: Program area, degree type (T if terminal Master's), number awarded 7/11–6/12. Clinical Psychology PsyD (Doctor of Psychology) 17.

APA Accreditation: Clinical PsyD (Doctor of Psychology). Student Outcome Data Website: http://www.paloaltou.edu/program_stanford_psyd_home.php.

Student Applications/Admissions:
Student Applications
Clinical Psychology PsyD (Doctor of Psychology)—Applications 2012–2013, 290. Total applicants accepted 2012–2013, 57. Number full-time enrolled (new admits only) 2012–2013, 31. Number part-time enrolled (new admits only) 2012–2013, 0. Total enrolled 2012–2013 full-time, 173. Total enrolled 2012–2013 part-time, 0. Openings 2013–2014, 30. The median number of years required for completion of a degree in 2012–2013 were 5. The number of students enrolled full- and part-time who were dismissed or voluntarily withdrew from this program area in 2012–2013 were 1.
Scores: Entries appear in this order: required test or GPA, minimum score (if required), median score of students entering in 2012–2013. *Clinical Psychology PsyD (Doctor of Psychology):* GRE-V no minimum stated, 602, GRE-Q no minimum stated, 668, GRE-Analytical no minimum stated, 4.9, overall undergraduate GPA no minimum stated, 3.56.
Other Criteria: (importance of criteria rated low, medium, or high): GRE scores—medium, research experience—medium, work experience—high, extracurricular activity—medium, clinically related public service—high, GPA—high, letters of recommendation—high, interview—high, statement of goals and objectives—high, undergraduate major in psychology—low, specific undergraduate psychology courses taken—low. For additional information on admission requirements, go to http://www.paloaltou.edu/pgsp-stanford-psyd-consortium/admissions-req.

Student Characteristics: The following represents characteristics of students in 2012–2013 in all graduate psychology programs in the department: Female—full-time 145, part-time 0; Male—full-time 28, part-time 0; African American/Black—full-time 1, part-time 0; Hispanic/Latino(a)—full-time 10, part-time 0; Asian/Pacific Islander—full-time 28, part-time 0; American Indian/Alaska Native—full-time 1, part-time 0; Caucasian/White—full-time 98, part-time 0; Multi-ethnic—full-time 0, part-time 0; students subject to the Americans With Disabilities Act—full-time 6, part-time 0; Unknown ethnicity—full-time 35, part-time 0; International students who hold an F-1 or J-1 Visa—full-time 3, part-time 0.

Financial Information/Assistance:
Tuition for Full-Time Study: *Doctoral:* State residents: per academic year $41,256; Nonstate residents: per academic year $41,256. Tuition is subject to change. See the following website for updates and changes in tuition costs: http://www.paloaltou.edu/department/admissions/tuition-fees.

Financial Assistance:

First-Year Students: Research assistantships available for first year. Average amount paid per academic year: $1,000. Average number of hours worked per week: 5. Fellowships and scholarships available for first year. Average amount paid per academic year: $4,000. Apply by January 15.

Advanced Students: Teaching assistantships available for advanced students. Average amount paid per academic year: $3,000. Average number of hours worked per week: 6. Research assistantships available for advanced students. Average amount paid per academic year: $1,000. Average number of hours worked per week: 5. Fellowships and scholarships available for advanced students. Average amount paid per academic year: $4,000.

Additional Information: Application and information available online at: http://www.paloaltou.edu/department/financial-aid.

Internships/Practica: Doctoral Degree (PsyD Clinical Psychology): For those doctoral students for whom a professional psychology internship was required in this program prior to graduation, (28) students applied for an internship in 2011–2012, with (26) students obtaining an internship. Of those students who obtained an internship, (26) were paid internships. Of those students who obtained an internship, (23) students placed in APA/CPA accredited internships, (3) students placed in internships not APA/CPA accredited, but listed with the Association of Psychology Postdoctoral and Internship Programs (APPIC), (0) students placed in internships conforming to guidelines of the Council of Directors of School Psychology Programs (CDSPP), (0) students placed in internships that were not APA/CPA accredited, APPIC or CDSPP listed. The PGSP-Stanford Consortium provides students with experiences that are sequenced with increasing amounts of time spent in clinical work during each year of graduate training, with a total of approximately 2,000 clinical hours obtained prior to internship. In year 1, students begin Supplemental Clinical Practica in the Stanford Psychiatry Department. In year two, students complete formal practica in captive training sites such as the PAU Gronowski Center, the Palo Alto VA, Stanford Inpatient Hospital, Stanford Pain Clinic, Stanford Faculty and Staff Help Center, and the Stanford East Palo Alto Academy (adolescents). In years 3 and 4, students have many varied practica options spanning theoretical orientations, settings, populations, and locations across the Bay Area. At present there are approximately 40 approved practicum sites to which 3rd and 4th year students may apply including UCSF neuropsych, Santa Clara University College Counseling, Kaiser Permanente (child and adult), Children's Hospital Oakland, San Francisco VA, and the Palo Alto VA. In the fifth year, students are required to complete a 2,000-hour external APA-Accredited predoctoral internship.

Housing and Day Care: No on-campus housing is available. No on-campus day care facilities are available.

Employment of Department Graduates:

Master's Degree Graduates: Of those who graduated in the academic year 2011–2012, the following categories and numbers represent the postgraduate activities and employment of master's degree graduates: Enrolled in a postdoctoral residency/fellowship (n/a), employed in independent practice (n/a), total from the above (master's) (0).

Doctoral Degree Graduates: Of those who graduated in the academic year 2011–2012, the following categories and numbers represent the postgraduate activities and employment of doctoral degree graduates: Enrolled in a psychology doctoral program (n/a), enrolled in a postdoctoral residency/fellowship (6), employed in a community mental health/counseling center (2), employed in a hospital/medical center (4), not seeking employment (2), do not know (3), total from the above (doctoral) (17).

Additional Information:

Orientation, Objectives, and Emphasis of Department: The PGSP-Stanford PsyD Consortium is a practitioner-scholar program intended for individuals seeking careers devoted primarily to the direct delivery of clinical psychological services. The program provides a generalist education in clinical psychology, relegating the pursuit of more specialized training to students' later postdoctoral education. The Consortium training model emphasizes evidenced-based practice, and the priority we assign to evidenced-based practice is matched by our commitment to promote students' broad and general understanding of science and to foster students' ability to critically evaluate scientific theories, methods, and conclusions. As might be expected of an interdisciplinary faculty drawn from a medical school and an academic psychology department, the program takes a bio-psycho-social approach to psychology, striving for a balanced, integrated, contemporary understanding of the biological, social and psychological factors affecting human behavior. Thus, students' competent understanding of science and scientific methods represents a critical priority of the Consortium educational program.

Special Facilities or Resources: The PGSP-Stanford PsyD Consortium at Palo Alto University draws upon nationally renowned faculty and resources from the Pacific Graduate School of Psychology and the Stanford University School of Medicine's Department of Psychiatry and Behavioral Sciences. Among the unique features of the PGSP-Stanford Consortium is the context in which students are trained. In addition to its research and teaching facilities, the Stanford University Department of Psychiatry and Behavioral Sciences is the home of the largest clinic at the Stanford University Medical Center. Over 40,000 patient visits per year are completed at the Department of Psychiatry. The mission of the Stanford clinics involves the care of a wide variety of patients with diagnoses that span the spectrum from mood and anxiety disorders, to personality disorders, as well as bipolar disorder and schizophrenia. The majority of faculty who teach clinical courses also provide direct clinical care. Thus, instructors bring a fresh and vital perspective to their teaching. Almost all students elect to complete supplemental practica in the context of applied clinical research projects at the Stanford Psychiatry Department.

Information for Students With Physical Disabilities: See the following website for more information: http://www.paloaltou.edu/student-services/disability.

Application Information:
Send to PGSP-Stanford PsyD Consortium, Palo Alto University, Admissions Office, 1791 Arastradero Road, Palo Alto, CA 94304. Application available online. URL of online application: https://my.paloaltou.edu/ICS/Admissions/Graduate_Applicants.jnz. Students are admitted in the Fall, application deadline January 3. We also have an Early Consideration deadline of December 1. *Fee:* $50.

Palo Alto University

PhD Clinical Psychology Program
1791 Arastradero Road
Palo Alto, CA 94304
Telephone: (800) 818-6136
Fax: (650) 433-3888
E-mail: *admissions@paloaltou.edu*
Web: *http://www.paloaltou.edu/phd-clinical-psychology*

Department Information:
1975. Director of Clinical Training: Dr. Robert Russell. Number of faculty: total—full-time 26, part-time 18; women—full-time 17, part-time 10; total—minority—full-time 9, part-time 1; women minority—full-time 6.

Programs and Degrees Offered:
Listed in the following order: Program area, degree type (T if terminal Master's), number awarded 7/11–6/12. Clinical Psychology PhD (Doctor of Philosophy) 34.

APA Accreditation: Clinical PhD (Doctor of Philosophy). Student Outcome Data Website: http://www.paloaltou.edu/phd-clinical-psychology.

Student Applications/Admissions:
Student Applications
Clinical Psychology PhD (Doctor of Philosophy)—Applications 2012–2013, 236. Total applicants accepted 2012–2013, 161. Number full-time enrolled (new admits only) 2012–2013, 74. Number part-time enrolled (new admits only) 2012–2013, 0. Total enrolled 2012–2013 full-time, 470. Total enrolled 2012–2013 part-time, 0. Openings 2013–2014, 75. The median number of years required for completion of a degree in 2012–2013 were 6. The number of students enrolled full- and part-time who were dismissed or voluntarily withdrew from this program area in 2012–2013 were 10.
Scores: Entries appear in this order: required test or GPA, minimum score (if required), median score of students entering in 2012–2013. *Clinical Psychology PhD (Doctor of Philosophy):* GRE-V no minimum stated, 528, GRE-Q no minimum stated, 611, GRE-Analytical no minimum stated, 4.1, overall undergraduate GPA no minimum stated, 3.27, last 2 years GPA no minimum stated, psychology GPA no minimum stated, Masters GPA no minimum stated.
Other Criteria: (importance of criteria rated low, medium, or high): GRE scores—high, research experience—medium, work experience—medium, extracurricular activity—medium, clinically related public service—medium, GPA—high, letters of recommendation—high, interview—medium, statement of goals and objectives—medium. For additional information on admission requirements, go to http://www.paloaltou.edu/phd-clinical-psychology/admissionsreq.

Student Characteristics: The following represents characteristics of students in 2012–2013 in all graduate psychology programs in the department: Female—full-time 370, part-time 0; Male—full-time 100, part-time 0; African American/Black—full-time 21, part-time 0; Hispanic/Latino(a)—full-time 32, part-time 0; Asian/Pacific Islander—full-time 84, part-time 0; American Indian/Alaska Native—full-time 5, part-time 0; Caucasian/White—full-time 244, part-time 0; Multi-ethnic—full-time 1, part-time 0; students subject to the Americans With Disabilities Act—full-time 37, part-time 0; Unknown ethnicity—full-time 83, part-time 0; International students who hold an F-1 or J-1 Visa—full-time 20, part-time 0.

Financial Information/Assistance:
Tuition for Full-Time Study: *Doctoral:* State residents: per academic year $43,803; Nonstate residents: per academic year $43,803. Tuition is subject to change. See the following website for updates and changes in tuition costs: http://www.paloaltou.edu/department/admissions/tuition-fees.

Financial Assistance:
First-Year Students: Fellowships and scholarships available for first year. Average amount paid per academic year: $5,000. Apply by January 15.
Advanced Students: Teaching assistantships available for advanced students. Average amount paid per academic year: $3,000. Average number of hours worked per week: 25. Research assistantships available for advanced students. Average amount paid per academic year: $4,000. Average number of hours worked per week: 30. Fellowships and scholarships available for advanced students. Average amount paid per academic year: $5,000.
Additional Information: Application and information available online at: http://www.paloaltou.edu/financial-aid/veterans-benefits.

Internships/Practica: Doctoral Degree (PhD Clinical Psychology): For those doctoral students for whom a professional psychology internship was required in this program prior to graduation, (82) students applied for an internship in 2011–2012, with (72) students obtaining an internship. Of those students who obtained an internship, (61) were paid internships. Of those students who obtained an internship, (45) students placed in APA/CPA accredited internships, (9) students placed in internships not APA/CPA accredited, but listed with the Association of Psychology Postdoctoral and Internship Programs (APPIC), (0) students placed in internships conforming to guidelines of the Council of Directors of School Psychology Programs (CDSPP), (18) students placed in internships that were not APA/CPA accredited, APPIC or CDSPP listed. All students take their second year of practicum in our Kurt and Barbara Gronowski Clinic and the third and fourth years in local agencies. All students are expected to complete an APA-accredited, APPIC or CAPIC-approved internship.

Housing and Day Care: No on-campus housing is available. No on-campus day care facilities are available.

Employment of Department Graduates:
Master's Degree Graduates: Of those who graduated in the academic year 2011–2012, the following categories and numbers represent the postgraduate activities and employment of master's degree graduates: Enrolled in a postdoctoral residency/fellowship (n/a), employed in independent practice (n/a), total from the above (master's) (0).
Doctoral Degree Graduates: Of those who graduated in the academic year 2011–2012, the following categories and numbers represent the postgraduate activities and employment of doctoral degree graduates: Enrolled in a psychology doctoral program (n/a), enrolled in a postdoctoral residency/fellowship (6), other employ-

ment position (1), do not know (27), total from the above (doctoral) (34).

Additional Information:

Orientation, Objectives, and Emphasis of Department: Palo Alto University, formerly Pacific Graduate School of Psychology, is a university offering doctoral degrees in clinical psychology to students from diverse backgrounds. The program is designed to integrate academic work, research, and clinical experiences at every level of the student's training. All students must develop a thorough understanding of a systematic body of knowledge that comprises the current field of psychology. They are expected to carry out an independent investigation that makes an original contribution to scientific knowledge in psychology and to demonstrate excellence in the application of specific clinical skills. PAU considers this integration of scholarship, research, and practical experience the best training model for preparing psychologists to meet the highest standards of scholarly research and community service. Graduates are expected to enter the community at large prepared to do research, practice, and teach in culturally and professionally diverse settings.

Special Facilities or Resources: PAU's setting as a free-standing graduate school of psychology is much enhanced by our San Francisco Bay Area location. We provide students with access to local university libraries (e.g., Stanford, UC Berkeley). The range of clinical experience available to students is inexhaustible. All faculty have active research programs in which students participate. Furthermore, PAU has a close relationship with local VA MC's.

Information for Students With Physical Disabilities: See the following website for more information: http://www.paloaltou.edu/student-services/disability.

Application Information:

Send to Office of Admissions, Palo Alto University, 1791 Arastradero Road, Palo Alto, CA. 94304. Application available online. URL of online application: https://my.paloaltou.edu/ICS/Admissions/Graduate_Applicants.jnz. Students are admitted in the Fall, application deadline January 15; Programs have rolling admissions. Rolling Admission, however application is due January 15 for those who want to be considered for a PGSP fellowship. *Fee:* $50.

Pepperdine University (2012 data)
Psychology Division
Graduate School of Education and Psychology
6100 Center Drive, 5th Floor
Los Angeles, CA 90045
Telephone: (310) 568-5600
Fax: (310) 568-5755
E-mail: *mapsych@pepperdine.edu*
Web: *http://gsep.pepperdine.edu/*

Department Information:

1951. Associate Dean of Psychology: Dr. Robert A. de Mayo. Number of faculty: total—full-time 32, part-time 66; women—full-time 17, part-time 39; total—minority—full-time 14, part-

time 14; women minority—full-time 10, part-time 6; faculty subject to the Americans With Disabilities Act 1.

Programs and Degrees Offered:

Listed in the following order: Program area, degree type (T if terminal Master's), number awarded 7/11–6/12. Psychology MA/MS (Master of Arts/Science) 47, Clinical Psychology PsyD (Doctor of Psychology) 41, Clinical Psychology Mft Emphasis - Evening Format MA/MS (Master of Arts/Science) 159, Clinical Psychology Mft Emphasis - Day Format MA/MS (Master of Arts/Science) 105.

APA Accreditation: Clinical PsyD (Doctor of Psychology). Student Outcome Data Website: http://gsep.pepperdine.edu/doctorate-clinical-psychology/.

Student Applications/Admissions:

Student Applications

Psychology MA/MS (Master of Arts/Science)—Applications 2012–2013, 144. Total applicants accepted 2012–2013, 112. Number full-time enrolled (new admits only) 2012–2013, 88. Total enrolled 2012–2013 full-time, 205. Openings 2013–2014, 70. The median number of years required for completion of a degree in 2012–2013 were 2. *Clinical Psychology PsyD (Doctor of Psychology)*—Applications 2012–2013, 162. Total applicants accepted 2012–2013, 31. Number full-time enrolled (new admits only) 2012–2013, 28. Total enrolled 2012–2013 full-time, 141. Openings 2013–2014, 26. The median number of years required for completion of a degree in 2012–2013 were 4. *Clinical Psychology Mft Emphasis - Evening Format MA/MS (Master of Arts/Science)*—Applications 2012–2013, 394. Total applicants accepted 2012–2013, 302. Number full-time enrolled (new admits only) 2012–2013, 245. Total enrolled 2012–2013 full-time, 546. Openings 2013–2014, 280. The median number of years required for completion of a degree in 2012–2013 were 2. *Clinical Psychology Mft Emphasis - Day Format MA/MS (Master of Arts/Science)*—Applications 2012–2013, 205. Total applicants accepted 2012–2013, 74. Number full-time enrolled (new admits only) 2012–2013, 44. Total enrolled 2012–2013 full-time, 86. Openings 2013–2014, 44. The median number of years required for completion of a degree in 2012–2013 were 2.

Scores: Entries appear in this order: required test or GPA, minimum score (if required), median score of students entering in 2012–2013. *Psychology MA/MS (Master of Arts/Science):* GRE-V no minimum stated, 471, GRE-Q no minimum stated, 592, GRE-Analytical no minimum stated, 4.1, overall undergraduate GPA no minimum stated, 3.31; *Clinical Psychology PsyD (Doctor of Psychology):* GRE-V no minimum stated, 568, GRE-Q no minimum stated, 620, GRE-Analytical no minimum stated, 4.8, overall undergraduate GPA no minimum stated, 3.46, Masters GPA no minimum stated, 3.84; *Clinical Psychology MFT Emphasis - Evening Format MA/MS (Master of Arts/Science):* GRE-V no minimum stated, 452, GRE-Q no minimum stated, 505, GRE-Analytical no minimum stated, 3.8, overall undergraduate GPA no minimum stated, 3.2; *Clinical Psychology MFT Emphasis - Day Format MA/MS (Master of Arts/Science):* GRE-V no minimum stated, 499, GRE-Q no minimum stated, 582, GRE-Analytical no minimum stated, 4.3, overall undergraduate GPA no minimum stated, 3.39.

Other Criteria: (importance of criteria rated low, medium, or high): GRE scores—high, research experience—high, work

experience—medium, extracurricular activity—medium, clinically related public service—high, GPA—high, letters of recommendation—high, interview—low, statement of goals and objectives—high, undergraduate major in psychology—high, specific undergraduate psychology courses taken—high, The above admissions criteria are based upon admission into the Master of Arts in Clinical Psychology with an Emphasis in Marriage and Family Therapy (MFT) program. The criteria vary for both the Master of Arts in Psychology and Doctorate in Clinical Psychology (PsyD) programs. For additional information on admission requirements, go to http://gsep.pepperdine.edu/admission/.

Student Characteristics: The following represents characteristics of students in 2012–2013 in all graduate psychology programs in the department: Female—full-time 801, part-time 4; Male—full-time 157, part-time 2; African American/Black—full-time 80, part-time 1; Hispanic/Latino(a)—full-time 122, part-time 1; Asian/Pacific Islander—full-time 96, part-time 0; American Indian/Alaska Native—full-time 10, part-time 0; Caucasian/White—full-time 405, part-time 4; Multi-ethnic—full-time 218, part-time 0; students subject to the Americans With Disabilities Act—full-time 0, part-time 0; Unknown ethnicity—full-time 27, part-time 0; International students who hold an F-1 or J-1 Visa—full-time 0, part-time 0.

Financial Information/Assistance:

Tuition for Full-Time Study: *Master's:* State residents: $982 per credit hour; Nonstate residents: $982 per credit hour. *Doctoral:* State residents: $1,236 per credit hour; Nonstate residents: $1,236 per credit hour. Additional fees are assessed to students beyond the costs of tuition for the following: PsyD graduate association fee $45. See the following website for updates and changes in tuition costs: http://gsep.pepperdine.edu/financial-aid/cost/. Higher tuition cost for this program: MA in Clinical Psychology, MFT Day Format, full-time program, $1236 per credit hour.

Financial Assistance:

First-Year Students: Teaching assistantships available for first year. Research assistantships available for first year. Fellowships and scholarships available for first year.

Advanced Students: Teaching assistantships available for advanced students. Research assistantships available for advanced students. Fellowships and scholarships available for advanced students.

Additional Information: Of all students currently enrolled full time, 83% benefited from one or more of the listed financial assistance programs. Application and information available online at: http://gsep.pepperdine.edu/financial-aid/.

Internships/Practica: Doctoral Degree (PsyD Clinical Psychology): For those doctoral students for whom a professional psychology internship was required in this program prior to graduation, (26) students applied for an internship in 2011–2012, with (25) students obtaining an internship. Of those students who obtained an internship, (23) were paid internships. Of those students who obtained an internship, (16) students placed in APA/CPA accredited internships, (7) students placed in internships not APA/CPA accredited, but listed with the Association of Psychology Postdoctoral and Internship Programs (APPIC), (0) students placed in internships conforming to guidelines of the Council of Directors of School Psychology Programs (CDSPP), (2) students placed in internships that were not APA/CPA accredited, APPIC or CDSPP listed. Students in the PsyD and MA in Clinical Psychology programs complete practicum requirements at Pepperdine clinics or affiliated agencies in the community. PsyD students complete predoctoral internships in approved agencies. Pepperdine clinical training staff assist students in locating training positions.

Housing and Day Care: On-campus housing is available. See the following website for more information: http://gsep.pepperdine.edu/student-services/housing/. No on-campus day care facilities are available.

Employment of Department Graduates:

Master's Degree Graduates: Of those who graduated in the academic year 2011–2012, the following categories and numbers represent the postgraduate activities and employment of master's degree graduates: Enrolled in a psychology doctoral program (83), enrolled in a postdoctoral residency/fellowship (n/a), employed in independent practice (n/a), employed in an academic position at a university (1), employed in other positions at a higher education institution (20), employed in a professional position in a school system (5), employed in business or industry (13), employed in a community mental health/counseling center (58), employed in a hospital/medical center (1), still seeking employment (112), not seeking employment (46), other employment position (16), do not know (144), total from the above (master's) (499).

Doctoral Degree Graduates: Of those who graduated in the academic year 2011–2012, the following categories and numbers represent the postgraduate activities and employment of doctoral degree graduates: Enrolled in a psychology doctoral program (n/a), enrolled in a postdoctoral residency/fellowship (6), employed in independent practice (6), employed in other positions at a higher education institution (5), employed in government agency (1), employed in a community mental health/counseling center (9), employed in a hospital/medical center (1), still seeking employment (5), not seeking employment (13), do not know (22), total from the above (doctoral) (68).

Additional Information:

Orientation, Objectives, and Emphasis of Department: The psychology degree programs are designed to provide the student with a theoretical and practical understanding of the principles of psychology within the framework of a strong clinical emphasis. Courses present various aspects of the art and science of psychology as it is applied to the understanding of human behavior and to the prevention, diagnosis, and treatment of mental and emotional problems. The MA in psychology serves as the prerequisite for the PsyD degree, or for students seeking human services positions in community agencies and organizations. The MA in Clinical Psychology provides the academic preparation for the Marriage and Family Therapy license. The PsyD program subscribes to a practitioner-scholar model of training.

Special Facilities or Resources: The Master of Arts in Psychology and Clinical Psychology programs at Pepperdine University are offered at four campuses throughout Southern California. Computer laboratories and libraries are available at all four campuses. Psychology clinics are located at the West Los Angeles Graduate Campus, the Irvine Graduate Campus and the Encino Graduate Campus, as well as a student counseling center on the Malibu Campus.

Information for Students With Physical Disabilities: See the following website for more information: http://www.pepperdine.edu/disabilityservices/.

Application Information:
Application available online. URL of online application: http://gsep.pepperdine.edu/admission/application/. Students are admitted in the Fall, application deadline June 1; Spring, application deadline October 1; Summer, application deadline February 1. Above listed application deadlines pertain to the Master's in Psychology and Master's in Clinical Psychology with an Emphasis in Marriage and Family Therapy (MFT) Evening Format programs only. The application deadline for the PsyD in Clinical Psychology program is November 16 (priority) and January 4 (final). The application deadline for the Master's in Clinical Psychology with an Emphasis in Marriage and Family Therapy (MFT) Day Format is February 1. The PsyD and Master's in Clinical Psychology-Day Format programs admit one time each year for the fall term. *Fee:* $55.

San Diego State University
Department of Psychology
College of Sciences
5500 Campanile Drive
San Diego, CA 92182-4611
Telephone: (619) 594-5359
Fax: (619) 594-1332
E-mail: *mcrawfor@sciences.sdsu.edu*
Web: *http://www.psychology.sdsu.edu/*

Department Information:
1947. Chairperson: Georg Matt. Number of faculty: total—full-time 40, part-time 20; women—full-time 22, part-time 10; total—minority—full-time 5, part-time 3; women minority—full-time 3, part-time 3.

Programs and Degrees Offered:
Listed in the following order: Program area, degree type (T if terminal Master's), number awarded 7/11–6/12. Psychology MA/MS (Master of Arts/Science) 33, Applied Psychology MA/MS (Master of Arts/Science) (T) 6.

Student Applications/Admissions:
Student Applications
Psychology MA/MS (Master of Arts/Science)—Applications 2012–2013, 99. Total applicants accepted 2012–2013, 64. Number full-time enrolled (new admits only) 2012–2013, 22. Number part-time enrolled (new admits only) 2012–2013, 0. Total enrolled 2012–2013 full-time, 26. Total enrolled 2012–2013 part-time, 0. Openings 2013–2014, 24. The median number of years required for completion of a degree in 2012–2013 were 2. The number of students enrolled full- and part-time who were dismissed or voluntarily withdrew from this program area in 2012–2013 were 1. *Applied Psychology MA/MS (Master of Arts/Science)*—Applications 2012–2013, 20. Total applicants accepted 2012–2013, 5. Number full-time enrolled (new admits only) 2012–2013, 4. Number part-time enrolled (new admits only) 2012–2013, 0. Total enrolled 2012–2013 full-time, 20. Openings 2013–2014, 6. The median number of years required for completion of a degree in 2012–2013 were

2. The number of students enrolled full- and part-time who were dismissed or voluntarily withdrew from this program area in 2012–2013 were 0.
Other Criteria: (importance of criteria rated low, medium, or high): GRE scores—high, research experience—high, work experience—medium, extracurricular activity—low, clinically related public service—low, GPA—high, letters of recommendation—high, interview—high, statement of goals and objectives—high, undergraduate major in psychology—medium, specific undergraduate psychology courses taken—medium, Work experience is viewed more closely by the Applied Psychology (MS) faculty than by the MA faculty. Research experience is particularly important in the MA program as this is a predoctoral program. For additional information on admission requirements, go to http://www.psychology.sdsu.edu/graduate/masters-programs/prospective-students/application-procedures.

Student Characteristics: The following represents characteristics of students in 2012–2013 in all graduate psychology programs in the department: Female—full-time 33, part-time 0; Male—full-time 17, part-time 0; African American/Black—full-time 4, part-time 0; Hispanic/Latino(a)—full-time 12, part-time 0; Asian/Pacific Islander—full-time 12, part-time 0; American Indian/Alaska Native—full-time 0, part-time 0; Caucasian/White—full-time 43, part-time 0; Multi-ethnic—full-time 2, part-time 0; students subject to the Americans With Disabilities Act—full-time 0, part-time 0; Unknown ethnicity—full-time 6, part-time 0; International students who hold an F-1 or J-1 Visa—full-time 2, part-time 0.

Financial Information/Assistance:
Tuition for Full-Time Study: *Master's:* State residents: per academic year $7,844; Nonstate residents: per academic year $14,540. Tuition is subject to change. See the following website for updates and changes in tuition costs: http://bfa.sdsu.edu/fm/co/sfs/registration.html.

Financial Assistance:
First-Year Students: Teaching assistantships available for first year. Average amount paid per academic year: $12,198. Average number of hours worked per week: 20. Apply by December 15. Research assistantships available for first year. Average amount paid per academic year: $12,198. Average number of hours worked per week: 20. Apply by December 15.
Advanced Students: Teaching assistantships available for advanced students. Average amount paid per academic year: $12,198. Average number of hours worked per week: 20. Apply by December 15. Research assistantships available for advanced students. Average amount paid per academic year: $12,198. Average number of hours worked per week: 20. Apply by December 15.
Additional Information: Of all students currently enrolled full time, 85% benefited from one or more of the listed financial assistance programs. Application and information available online at: http://gra.sdsu.edu/grad/finsupport.html.

Internships/Practica: An essential component of graduate training in Applied Psychology is an internship experience that provides students with an opportunity to apply their classroom training and acquire new skills in a field setting. Interns are placed in a variety of settings, such as community-based organizations, consulting firms, city and county organizations, education, hospitality, high tech and private industry. Through the internship experience students also develop close contacts with other psychologists and practitioners working in their field. Internships are normally undertaken during the summer following the first year in the program and during the fall semester of the second year.

Housing and Day Care: On-campus housing is available. See the following website for more information: http://housing.sdsu.edu/housing/. On-campus day care facilities are available. See the following website for more information: http://childcare.sdsu.edu/.

Employment of Department Graduates:

Master's Degree Graduates: Of those who graduated in the academic year 2011–2012, the following categories and numbers represent the postgraduate activities and employment of master's degree graduates: Enrolled in a psychology doctoral program (17), enrolled in another graduate/professional program (2), enrolled in a postdoctoral residency/fellowship (n/a), employed in independent practice (n/a), employed in an academic position at a 2-year/4-year college (1), employed in other positions at a higher education institution (4), employed in business or industry (6), employed in a community mental health/counseling center (1), employed in a hospital/medical center (1), still seeking employment (1), not seeking employment (4), do not know (3), total from the above (master's) (40).

Doctoral Degree Graduates: Of those who graduated in the academic year 2011–2012, the following categories and numbers represent the postgraduate activities and employment of doctoral degree graduates: Enrolled in a psychology doctoral program (n/a), total from the above (doctoral) (0).

Additional Information:

Orientation, Objectives, and Emphasis of Department: The MA degree program provides graduate level studies and preparation for PhD programs in several areas. It is particularly appropriate for students who need advanced work to strengthen their profiles for application to PhD programs, or for those wishing to explore graduate-level work before committing to PhD training. Areas of emphasis within the MA are: Behavioral Psychology, Social Psychology, Physical and or Mental Health Psychology, Social Psychology, Developmental Psychology, and Learning/Cognition Psychology. Our research-oriented program does not offer instruction in technical skills (e.g., intelligence testing) and does not have a counseling practicum or provide opportunities for development of clinical skills. Students gain valuable research experience, which may involve working with humans in non-clinical areas. Upon admission to the program students are assigned a faculty research mentor who guides them through the research process leading to the thesis. Students take core classes in the major areas of psychology and electives in their areas of specialization. The M.S. Degree program in Applied Psychology has emphases in Program Evaluation and Industrial/Organizational Psychology. Students are prepared for professional careers in the public and private sectors or for doctoral-level training in Applied Psychology. All M.S. students take core courses in statistics and measurement and complete an internship.

Special Facilities or Resources: The following research labs welcome master's students: Anxiety and Depression in Children/Adolescents; Stereotype Threat, Aging/Dementia, Active Living/Healthy Eating; Alcohol Research; Behavioral Teratology; Brain Development Imaging; Categorical Distortions; Child Language/Emotion; Child and Adolescent Mental Health; Cognitive Development; Culture, Work Values/Organizational Behavior; Generational Differences; Child Abuse/Neglect; Health Outcomes; Intergroup Relations; Life-Span Human Senses; Measurement and Evaluation; Minority Community Health Intervention; Organizational Leadership/Citizenship; Organizational Research; Personality Assessment/Psychometrics; Personality Measurement Binge Drinking/intervention; Family Library Use/Lifelong Learning; Social Support and Education on Health/Well Being of People with Chronic Diseases; Psychosocial Factors in Coronary Heart Disease; Language/Cognitive Studies; Psychosocial, Chronic Illness adjustment; Smoking; Social Development; Social Influence and Group Dynamics; Social Rejection; Stress/Coping; and Activity for Adolescent Girls. Students may conduct research at Children's Hospital, where several faculty members have their offices. Other resources include a community psychology clinic, the Center for Behavioral and Community Health Studies, Center for Behavioral Teratology, and the Center for Research in Mathematics and Science Education. Also available is an exchange program with the University of Mannheim, Germany. Students can choose to spend a semester or a year attending classes in Mannheim, and graduate students from Mannheim can spend a semester or a year taking classes here.

Information for Students With Physical Disabilities: See the following website for more information: http://www.sa.sdsu.edu/sds/index.html.

Application Information:
Send to Master's Programs Admissions Coordinator, Department of Psychology, San Diego State University, 5500 Campanile Drive, San Diego, CA 92182-4611. Application available online. URL of online application: https://app.applyyourself.com/AYApplicantLogin/ApplicantConnectLogin.asp?id=sdsu-grad. Students are admitted in the Fall, application deadline December 15. *Fee:* $55.

San Diego State University/University of California, San Diego Joint Doctoral Program in Clinical Psychology
SDSU Department of Psychology/UCSD Department of Psychiatry
SDSU: College of Sciences UCSD: School of Medicine
6363 Alvarado Court, Suite #103
San Diego, CA 92120-4913
Telephone: (619) 594-2246
Fax: (619) 594-6780
E-mail: PsycJDP@mail.sdsu.edu
Web: http://www.psychology.sdsu.edu/doctoral

Department Information:
1985. Co-Directors: Elizabeth Klonoff, PhD, Robert Heaton, PhD. Number of faculty: total—full-time 43, part-time 71; women—full-time 19, part-time 32; total—minority—full-time 2, part-time 7; women minority—full-time 1, part-time 3; faculty subject to the Americans With Disabilities Act 2.

Programs and Degrees Offered:
Listed in the following order: Program area, degree type (T if terminal Master's), number awarded 7/11–6/12. Clinical Psychology PhD (Doctor of Philosophy) 11.

APA Accreditation: Clinical PhD (Doctor of Philosophy). Student Outcome Data Website: http://www.psychology.sdsu.edu/doctoral/Demographics.html.

Student Applications/Admissions:

Student Applications

Clinical Psychology PhD (Doctor of Philosophy)—Applications 2012–2013, 476. Total applicants accepted 2012–2013, 15. Number full-time enrolled (new admits only) 2012–2013, 12. Number part-time enrolled (new admits only) 2012–2013, 0. Total enrolled 2012–2013 full-time, 73. Total enrolled 2012–2013 part-time, 0. Openings 2013–2014, 15. The median number of years required for completion of a degree in 2012–2013 were 6. The number of students enrolled full- and part-time who were dismissed or voluntarily withdrew from this program area in 2012–2013 were 0.

Scores: Entries appear in this order: required test or GPA, minimum score (if required), median score of students entering in 2012–2013. *Clinical Psychology PhD (Doctor of Philosophy):* GRE-V 540, 675, GRE-Q 570, 725, GRE-Subject (Psychology) 700, 740, overall undergraduate GPA 3.09, 3.79, psychology GPA no minimum stated, Masters GPA no minimum stated.

Other Criteria: (importance of criteria rated low, medium, or high): GRE scores—medium, research experience—high, work experience—low, clinically related public service—medium, GPA—high, letters of recommendation—high, interview—high, statement of goals and objectives—high, undergraduate major in psychology—medium, specific undergraduate psychology courses taken—medium. For additional information on admission requirements, go to http://www.psychology.sdsu.edu/doctoral/instructions.html.

Student Characteristics: The following represents characteristics of students in 2012–2013 in all graduate psychology programs in the department: Female—full-time 63, part-time 0; Male—full-time 10, part-time 0; African American/Black—full-time 1, part-time 0; Hispanic/Latino(a)—full-time 7, part-time 0; Asian/Pacific Islander—full-time 7, part-time 0; American Indian/Alaska Native—full-time 2, part-time 0; Caucasian/White—full-time 52, part-time 0; Multi-ethnic—full-time 4, part-time 0; students subject to the Americans With Disabilities Act—full-time 2, part-time 0; Unknown ethnicity—full-time 0, part-time 0; International students who hold an F-1 or J-1 Visa—full-time 6, part-time 0.

Financial Information/Assistance:

Tuition for Full-Time Study: *Doctoral:* State residents: per academic year $8,032; Nonstate residents: per academic year $14,728. Tuition is subject to change. See the following website for updates and changes in tuition costs: http://arweb.sdsu.edu/es/admissions/costs.html.

Financial Assistance:

First-Year Students: Research assistantships available for first year. Average amount paid per academic year: $18,000. Average number of hours worked per week: 20. Fellowships and scholarships available for first year. Average amount paid per academic year: $18,000. Average number of hours worked per week: 20.

Advanced Students: Teaching assistantships available for advanced students. Average amount paid per academic year: $18,000. Average number of hours worked per week: 20. Research assistantships available for advanced students. Average amount paid per academic year: $18,000. Average number of hours worked per week: 20. Fellowships and scholarships available for advanced students. Average amount paid per academic year: $18,000. Average number of hours worked per week: 20.

Additional Information: Of all students currently enrolled full time, 100% benefited from one or more of the listed financial assistance programs.

Internships/Practica: Doctoral Degree (PhD Clinical Psychology): For those doctoral students for whom a professional psychology internship was required in this program prior to graduation, (12) students applied for an internship in 2011–2012, with (11) students obtaining an internship. Of those students who obtained an internship, (11) were paid internships. Of those students who obtained an internship, (11) students placed in APA/CPA accredited internships, (0) students placed in internships not APA/CPA accredited, but listed with the Association of Psychology Postdoctoral and Internship Programs (APPIC), (0) students placed in internships conforming to guidelines of the Council of Directors of School Psychology Programs (CDSPP), (0) students placed in internships that were not APA/CPA accredited, APPIC or CDSPP listed. SDSU: Primary placement for all students in their second year is the Psychology Clinic. Students are taught general clinical skills. Therapy sessions are routinely videotaped for review in intensive weekly supervision session. UCSD: VA Outpatient Clinic: psychiatric outpatients—assessment and individual and group therapy. VA Medical Center: psychiatric inpatients—assessment, individual and group therapy. UCSD Outpatient Psychiatric Clinic: psychiatric outpatients—neuropsychological assessment and individual and group therapy. UCSD Medical Center: assessment and therapy of all types. All practicum placements are assigned for one full year beginning in the student's second year.

Housing and Day Care: On-campus housing is available. See the following website for more information: http://housing.sdsu.edu/housing/. On-campus day care facilities are available. See the following website for more information: http://childcare.sdsu.edu/.

Employment of Department Graduates:

Master's Degree Graduates: Of those who graduated in the academic year 2011–2012, the following categories and numbers represent the postgraduate activities and employment of master's degree graduates: Enrolled in a postdoctoral residency/fellowship (n/a), employed in independent practice (n/a), total from the above (master's) (0).

Doctoral Degree Graduates: Of those who graduated in the academic year 2011–2012, the following categories and numbers represent the postgraduate activities and employment of doctoral degree graduates: Enrolled in a psychology doctoral program (n/a), enrolled in a postdoctoral residency/fellowship (11), total from the above (doctoral) (11).

Additional Information:

Orientation, Objectives, and Emphasis of Department: Our PhD program is a cooperative venture of an academic Department of Psychology (SDSU) and a medical school Department of Psychiatry (UCSD). This partnership between two different departments in two universities provides unusual opportunities for interdisciplinary research. We currently offer concentrations in behavioral medicine, neuropsychology, and experimental psychopathology. The scientist–practitioner model on which the program is based involves a strong commitment to research as well as clinical training. The program aims to prepare students for leadership roles in academic and research settings. Our program is designed as a 5-year curriculum with a core of classroom instruction followed by apprenticeship training in specialty areas with appropriate seminars and tutorials. Clinical experiences are integrated with formal instruction throughout.

Special Facilities or Resources: The UCSD Department of Psychiatry, through the medical school, UCSD hospitals, and the VA Medical Center, has available all of the modern research and clinical facilities consistent with the School of Medicine's ranking among the top ten in the country in biomedical research. These include specialty laboratories (e.g., sleep labs), access to clinical trials, supercomputing facilities, and state-of-the-art neurochemical and biochemical laboratory facilities. Qualified students interested in MRI studies have access to a number of fully-supported imagers. At SDSU, the Department of Psychology has a state-of-the-art video-equipped therapy training complex, as well as experiment rooms, equipment (e.g. computerized test administration capabilities), and supplies available for research, including computerized physiological assessment and biofeedback laboratories. Animal research can be conducted on campus, where small animals are housed in a modern vivarium staffed with a veterinarian. SDSU faculty also supervise research on more exotic species at Sea World and the San Diego Zoo. The College of Sciences maintains a completely equipped electronics shop, a wood shop, a metal shop, and computer support facilities with several high end UNIX servers, all staffed with full-time technicians. Collaborative relationships with faculty in the Graduate School of Public Health allow access to resources there as well.

Information for Students With Physical Disabilities: See the following website for more information: http://www.sa.sdsu.edu/sds/.

Application Information:

Application available online. URL of online application: https://app.applyyourself.com/AYApplicantLogin/ApplicantConnectLogin.asp?id=sdsu-grad. Students are admitted in the Fall, application deadline December 1. *Fee:* $55.

San Francisco State University
Psychology
Science & Engineering
1600 Holloway Avenue
San Francisco, CA 94132
Telephone: (415) 338-2167
Fax: (415) 338-2398
E-mail: *psych@sfsu.edu*
Web: *http://psychology.sfsu.edu*

Department Information:

1923. Chairperson: Jeffrey Cookston. Number of faculty: total—full-time 20, part-time 13; women—full-time 11, part-time 8; total—minority—full-time 9, part-time 4; women minority—full-time 6, part-time 2; faculty subject to the Americans With Disabilities Act 1.

Programs and Degrees Offered:

Listed in the following order: Program area, degree type (T if terminal Master's), number awarded 7/11–6/12. Clinical Psychology MA/MS (Master of Arts/Science) (T) 10, Developmental Psychology MA/MS (Master of Arts/Science) (T) 11, Industrial/Organizational Psychology MA/MS (Master of Arts/Science) (T) 10, Mind Brain and Behavior MA/MS (Master of Arts/Science) (T), School Psychology MA/MS (Master of Arts/Science) (T) 10, Social Psychology MA/MS (Master of Arts/Science) (T) 9.

Student Applications/Admissions:
Student Applications

Clinical Psychology MA/MS (Master of Arts/Science)—Applications 2012–2013, 158. Total applicants accepted 2012–2013, 8. Number full-time enrolled (new admits only) 2012–2013, 8. Total enrolled 2012–2013 full-time, 16. Openings 2013–2014, 8. The median number of years required for completion of a degree in 2012–2013 were 2. The number of students enrolled full- and part-time who were dismissed or voluntarily withdrew from this program area in 2012–2013 were 0. *Developmental Psychology MA/MS (Master of Arts/Science)*—Applications 2012–2013, 31. Total applicants accepted 2012–2013, 9. Number full-time enrolled (new admits only) 2012–2013, 6. Total enrolled 2012–2013 full-time, 14. Openings 2013–2014, 9. The median number of years required for completion of a degree in 2012–2013 were 2. The number of students enrolled full- and part-time who were dismissed or voluntarily withdrew from this program area in 2012–2013 were 0. *Industrial/Organizational Psychology MA/MS (Master of Arts/Science)*—Applications 2012–2013, 79. Total applicants accepted 2012–2013, 10. Number full-time enrolled (new admits only) 2012–2013, 6. Total enrolled 2012–2013 full-time, 15. Openings 2013–2014, 10. The median number of years required for completion of a degree in 2012–2013 were 2. The number of students enrolled full- and part-time who were dismissed or voluntarily withdrew from this program area in 2012–2013 were 0. *Mind Brain and Behavior MA/MS (Master of Arts/Science)*—Applications 2012–2013, 62. Total applicants accepted 2012–2013, 19. Number full-time enrolled (new admits only) 2012–2013, 10. Openings 2013–2014, 12. The median number of years required for completion of a degree in 2012–2013 were 2. The number of students enrolled full- and part-time who were dismissed or voluntarily withdrew from this program area in 2012–2013 were 0. *School Psychology MA/MS (Master of Arts/Science)*—Applications 2012–2013, 36. Total applicants accepted 2012–2013, 11. Number full-time enrolled (new admits only) 2012–2013, 8. Total enrolled 2012–2013 full-time, 8. Openings 2013–2014, 8. The median number of years required for completion of a degree in 2012–2013 were 3. The number of students enrolled full- and part-time who were dismissed or voluntarily withdrew from this program area in 2012–2013 were 0. *Social Psychology MA/MS (Master of Arts/Science)*—Applications 2012–2013, 36. Total applicants accepted 2012–2013, 11. Number full-time enrolled (new admits only) 2012–2013, 10. Total enrolled 2012–2013 full-time, 21. Openings 2013–2014, 10. The median number of years required for completion of a degree in 2012–2013 were 2. The number of students enrolled full- and part-time who were dismissed or voluntarily withdrew from this program area in 2012–2013 were 0.

Scores: Entries appear in this order: required test or GPA, minimum score (if required), median score of students entering

in 2012–2013. *Clinical Psychology MA/MS (Master of Arts/Science)*: GRE-V no minimum stated, GRE-Q no minimum stated, GRE-Analytical no minimum stated, overall undergraduate GPA 3.0, last 2 years GPA 3.0, psychology GPA 3.0; *Developmental Psychology MA/MS (Master of Arts/Science)*: GRE-V no minimum stated, GRE-Q no minimum stated, GRE-Analytical no minimum stated, overall undergraduate GPA 3.0, last 2 years GPA 3.0, psychology GPA 3.0; *Industrial/Organizational Psychology MA/MS (Master of Arts/Science)*: GRE-V no minimum stated, GRE-Q no minimum stated, GRE-Analytical no minimum stated, overall undergraduate GPA 3.0, last 2 years GPA 3.0, psychology GPA 3.0; *Mind Brain and Behavior MA/MS (Master of Arts/Science)*: GRE-V no minimum stated, GRE-Q no minimum stated, GRE-Analytical no minimum stated, overall undergraduate GPA 3.0, last 2 years GPA 3.0, psychology GPA 3.0; *School Psychology MA/MS (Master of Arts/Science)*: GRE-V no minimum stated, GRE-Q no minimum stated, GRE-Analytical no minimum stated, overall undergraduate GPA 3.0, last 2 years GPA 3.0, psychology GPA 3.0; *Social Psychology MA/MS (Master of Arts/Science)*: GRE-V no minimum stated, GRE-Q no minimum stated, GRE-Analytical no minimum stated, overall undergraduate GPA 3.0, last 2 years GPA 3.0, psychology GPA 3.0.

Other Criteria: (importance of criteria rated low, medium, or high): GRE scores—medium, research experience—high, work experience—medium, extracurricular activity—low, clinically related public service—high, GPA—high, letters of recommendation—high, interview—high, statement of goals and objectives—high, undergraduate major in psychology—medium, specific undergraduate psychology courses taken—medium, Requirements vary from program to program. For additional information on admission requirements, go to http://psychology.sfsu.edu/graduate/application.html.

Student Characteristics: The following represents characteristics of students in 2012–2013 in all graduate psychology programs in the department: Female—full-time 45, part-time 0; Male—full-time 29, part-time 0; African American/Black—full-time 3, part-time 0; Hispanic/Latino(a)—full-time 5, part-time 0; Asian/Pacific Islander—full-time 6, part-time 0; American Indian/Alaska Native—full-time 0, part-time 0; Caucasian/White—full-time 50, part-time 0; Multi-ethnic—full-time 10, part-time 0; students subject to the Americans With Disabilities Act—full-time 0, part-time 0; Unknown ethnicity—full-time 0, part-time 0; International students who hold an F-1 or J-1 Visa—full-time 5, part-time 0.

Financial Information/Assistance:

Tuition for Full-Time Study: *Master's:* State residents: per academic year $7,542; Nonstate residents: per academic year $14,982. Tuition is subject to change. See the following website for updates and changes in tuition costs: http://www.sfsu.edu/prospect/costs/fees.html.

Financial Assistance:

First-Year Students: Teaching assistantships available for first year. Fellowships and scholarships available for first year.

Advanced Students: Teaching assistantships available for advanced students. Fellowships and scholarships available for advanced students.

Additional Information: Of all students currently enrolled full time, 30% benefited from one or more of the listed financial assistance programs. Application and information available online at: http://www.sfsu.edu/~finaid/scholarships/.

Internships/Practica: Master's Degree (MA/MS Clinical Psychology): An internship experience, such as a final research project or "capstone" experience is required of graduates. Master's Degree (MA/MS Developmental Psychology): An internship experience, such as a final research project or "capstone" experience is required of graduates. Master's Degree (MA/MS Industrial/Organizational Psychology): An internship experience, such as a final research project or "capstone" experience is required of graduates. Master's Degree (MA/MS Mind Brain and Behavior): An internship experience, such as a final research project or "capstone" experience is required of graduates. Master's Degree (MA/MS School Psychology): An internship experience, such as a final research project or "capstone" experience is required of graduates. Master's Degree (MA/MS Social Psychology): An internship experience, such as a final research project or "capstone" experience is required of graduates. For clinical students, practicum in the first year is provided in the Psychology Clinic and at sites in San Francisco dealing with children and adolescents. Second year internships are located in mental health settings throughout the San Francisco Bay area. For I/O students, an internship is required during the 2nd year of study. Students are placed in various work organizations throughout the San Francisco Bay area. Students enrolled in the School Psychology program are placed in a first year school-based practicum by the program. Students apply for and are placed in schools throughout the San Francisco bay area in their second year. Students are required to complete a 3rd year paid internship.

Housing and Day Care: On-campus housing is available. See the following website for more information: http://www.sfsu.edu/~housing/. On-campus day care facilities are available. See the following website for more information: http://childrenscampus.sfsu.edu/.

Employment of Department Graduates:

Master's Degree Graduates: Of those who graduated in the academic year 2011–2012, the following categories and numbers represent the postgraduate activities and employment of master's degree graduates: Enrolled in a psychology doctoral program (23), enrolled in another graduate/professional program (7), enrolled in a postdoctoral residency/fellowship (n/a), employed in independent practice (n/a), employed in an academic position at a university (3), employed in an academic position at a 2-year/4-year college (1), employed in other positions at a higher education institution (1), employed in a professional position in a school system (3), employed in business or industry (7), employed in government agency (2), employed in a community mental health/counseling center (7), employed in a hospital/medical center (4), still seeking employment (2), not seeking employment (5), other employment position (1), do not know (8), total from the above (master's) (74).

Doctoral Degree Graduates: Of those who graduated in the academic year 2011–2012, the following categories and numbers represent the postgraduate activities and employment of doctoral degree graduates: Enrolled in a psychology doctoral program (n/a), total from the above (doctoral) (0).

Additional Information:

Orientation, Objectives, and Emphasis of Department: Clinical: The theoretical orientation of the Clinical program is based on psychodynamic theory within a family and community systems framework. The Clinical program emphasizes training in psychotherapy and applied clinical experience. Developmental: The Developmental program takes a life span approach. Research and courses emphasize family systems, attachment, social, cognitive and emotional development, and the development of diverse populations. Training is provided on developmental research methods. Industrial/Organizational: The Industrial/Organizational MS program has a science-practice approach to work place issues. The program prepares graduates for professional work in business, industry, and government and for continuing education in I/O psychology. Mind, Brain and Behavior: This program takes a basic scientific research approach, including the study of physiological issues. Prepares students for MA level careers and doctoral study. School: The School Psychology program emphasizes, within a cultural context, developmental and psychodynamic theories with an applied interpersonal relations and family systems approach. Social: The Social psychology program, oriented toward research and applications in the public interest, prepares students for MA level careers and doctoral study with training in both qualitative and quantitative methods.

Special Facilities or Resources: Each full time faculty member in the department has an active research lab in which students are active and essential members. There is a Psychology Clinic within the Psychology department which is a training facility for Clinical graduate students. The Clinic attracts clients within San Francisco State University and from the larger San Francisco bay area.

Information for Students With Physical Disabilities: See the following website for more information: http://www.sfsu.edu/~dprc/.

Application Information:
Send to Graduate Program Secretary, Department of Psychology, San Francisco State University, 1600 Holloway Avenue, EP 301, San Francisco, CA 94132. Application available online. URL of online application: http://www.sfsu.edu/~gradstdy/domestic-application-submission.htm. Students are admitted in the Fall, application deadline February 1. *Fee:* $55.

San Jose State University
Department of Psychology
Social Sciences
One Washington Square
San Jose, CA 95192-0120
Telephone: (408) 924-5600
Fax: (408) 924-5605
E-mail: *psychology@sjsu.edu*
Web: *http://www.sjsu.edu/psych/*

Department Information:
1944. Chairperson: Dr. Ron Rogers. Number of faculty: total—full-time 23, part-time 33; women—full-time 12, part-time 19; total—minority—full-time 6, part-time 10; women minority—

full-time 4, part-time 5; faculty subject to the Americans With Disabilities Act 1.

Programs and Degrees Offered:
Listed in the following order: Program area, degree type (T if terminal Master's), number awarded 7/11–6/12. Experimental Psychology MA/MS (Master of Arts/Science) (T) 5, Industrial/Organizational Psychology MA/MS (Master of Arts/Science) (T) 7.

Student Applications/Admissions:
Student Applications

Experimental Psychology MA/MS (Master of Arts/Science)—Applications 2012–2013, 32. Total applicants accepted 2012–2013, 17. Number full-time enrolled (new admits only) 2012–2013, 12. Number part-time enrolled (new admits only) 2012–2013, 0. Total enrolled 2012–2013 full-time, 12. Total enrolled 2012–2013 part-time, 0. Openings 2013–2014, 11. The median number of years required for completion of a degree in 2012–2013 were 2. The number of students enrolled full- and part-time who were dismissed or voluntarily withdrew from this program area in 2012–2013 were 1. *Industrial/Organizational Psychology MA/MS (Master of Arts/Science)*—Applications 2012–2013, 45. Total applicants accepted 2012–2013, 13. Number full-time enrolled (new admits only) 2012–2013, 12. Number part-time enrolled (new admits only) 2012–2013, 0. Total enrolled 2012–2013 full-time, 12. Total enrolled 2012–2013 part-time, 0. Openings 2013–2014, 15. The median number of years required for completion of a degree in 2012–2013 were 3. The number of students enrolled full- and part-time who were dismissed or voluntarily withdrew from this program area in 2012–2013 were 1.

Scores: Entries appear in this order: required test or GPA, minimum score (if required), median score of students entering in 2012–2013. *Experimental Psychology MA/MS (Master of Arts/Science):* GRE-V no minimum stated, GRE-Q no minimum stated, last 2 years GPA 3.0, psychology GPA 3.0; *Industrial/Organizational Psychology MA/MS (Master of Arts/Science):* GRE-V no minimum stated, GRE-Q no minimum stated, last 2 years GPA 3.0, psychology GPA 3.0.

Other Criteria: (importance of criteria rated low, medium, or high): Clinical Program has specific course requirements for admission and requires minimum 1 year of applied clinical experience and 100 hours. Admission criteria vary by program. For additional information on admission requirements, go to http://www.sjsu.edu/psych/Graduates/experimentalpsych/maEligible.html.

Student Characteristics: The following represents characteristics of students in 2012–2013 in all graduate psychology programs in the department: Female—full-time 47, part-time 0; Male—full-time 16, part-time 0; African American/Black—full-time 1, part-time 0; Hispanic/Latino(a)—full-time 3, part-time 0; Asian/Pacific Islander—full-time 5, part-time 0; American Indian/Alaska Native—full-time 0, part-time 0; Caucasian/White—full-time 0, part-time 0; Multi-ethnic—full-time 2, part-time 0; students subject to the Americans With Disabilities Act—full-time 0, part-time 0; Unknown ethnicity—full-time 0, part-time 0; International students who hold an F-1 or J-1 Visa—full-time 0, part-time 0.

Financial Information/Assistance:
Tuition for Full-Time Study: *Master's:* State residents: per academic year $6,612; Nonstate residents: per academic year $17,772.

Tuition is subject to change. See the following website for updates and changes in tuition costs: http://www.sjsu.edu/bursar/fees_due_dates/tuition_fees/index.html.

Financial Assistance:
First-Year Students: Teaching assistantships available for first year. Research assistantships available for first year. Fellowships and scholarships available for first year.

Advanced Students: Teaching assistantships available for advanced students. Research assistantships available for advanced students. Fellowships and scholarships available for advanced students.

Additional Information: Application and information available online at: http://www.sjsu.edu/faso/.

Internships/Practica: An internship is required for students in the Industrial/Organizational Psychology program. The program coordinator works with each student to determine the student's interests and helps find a placement site for each student. Some students in the Experimental Program are offered internships at NASA/Ames Research Center.

Housing and Day Care: On-campus housing is available. See the following website for more information: http://housing.sjsu.edu/. On-campus day care facilities are available. See the following website for more information: http://as.sjsu.edu/ascdc/.

Employment of Department Graduates:
Master's Degree Graduates: Of those who graduated in the academic year 2011–2012, the following categories and numbers represent the postgraduate activities and employment of master's degree graduates: Enrolled in a psychology doctoral program (4), enrolled in a postdoctoral residency/fellowship (n/a), employed in independent practice (n/a), employed in business or industry (3), employed in government agency (4), employed in a community mental health/counseling center (10), total from the above (master's) (21).

Doctoral Degree Graduates: Of those who graduated in the academic year 2011–2012, the following categories and numbers represent the postgraduate activities and employment of doctoral degree graduates: Enrolled in a psychology doctoral program (n/a), total from the above (doctoral) (0).

Additional Information:
Orientation, Objectives, and Emphasis of Department: The mission of the University is to enrich the lives of its students, to transmit knowledge to its students along with the necessary skills for applying it in the service of our society, and to expand the base of knowledge through research and scholarship. It emphasizes the following goals for both undergraduate and graduate students: in-depth knowledge of a major field of study; broad understanding of the sciences, social sciences, humanities, and the arts; skills in communication and in critical inquiry; multi-cultural and global perspectives gained through intellectual and social exchange with people of diverse economic and ethnic backgrounds; and active participation in professional, artistic, and ethnic communities, responsible citizenship and an understanding of ethical choices inherent in human development.

Special Facilities or Resources: The department maintains a variety of facilities and support staff to enhance instruction and research. For biological and cognitive research and instruction, the department has a number of laboratories and specialized laboratory equipment on campus, and lab technicians are available to construct additional equipment. For work in clinical and counseling psychology, the department has a Psychology Clinic consisting of therapy rooms and adjoining observation rooms equipped with audio and video equipment. These rooms are also available to individuals working in other areas, such as developmental, personality, and social psychology. In addition, students interested in counseling-related activities have access to a number of off-campus organizations. Three computer laboratories containing microcomputers and terminals hooked up to minicomputers and mainframes are available for students. These labs have extensive software, and computer consultants are on call to help with software and hardware problems, design and interpretation of statistical analyses, and computer exercises. There is a child care center on campus.

Information for Students With Physical Disabilities: See the following website for more information: http://www.sjsu.edu/drc/.

Application Information:
Send to Program Coordinator. Application available online. URL of online application: http://www.sjsu.edu/gape/prospective_students/. Students are admitted in the Fall, application deadline February 1. *Fee:* $55.

Santa Clara University
Department of Counseling Psychology
School of Education and Counseling Psychology
500 El Camino Real - Loyola Hall 140
Santa Clara, CA 95053-0201
Telephone: (408) 551-1603
Fax: (408) 554-2392
E-mail: *sbabbel@scu.edu*
Web: *http://www.scu.edu/ecppm/*

Department Information:
1964. Chairperson: Jerrold Lee Shapiro, PhD. Number of faculty: total—full-time 12, part-time 27; women—full-time 5, part-time 19; total—minority—full-time 1, part-time 9; women minority—full-time 1, part-time 8; faculty subject to the Americans With Disabilities Act 10.

Programs and Degrees Offered:
Listed in the following order: Program area, degree type (T if terminal Master's), number awarded 7/11–6/12. Counseling Psychology MA/MS (Master of Arts/Science) (T) 70, Counseling MA/MS (Master of Arts/Science) (T) 10.

Student Applications/Admissions:
Student Applications
Counseling Psychology MA/MS (Master of Arts/Science)—Applications 2012–2013, 165. Total applicants accepted 2012–2013, 91. Number full-time enrolled (new admits only) 2012–2013, 32. Number part-time enrolled (new admits only) 2012–2013, 44. Total enrolled 2012–2013 full-time, 88. Total enrolled 2012–2013 part-time, 166. Openings 2013–2014, 70. The median number of years required for completion of a degree in 2012–2013 were 3. The number of students enrolled

full- and part-time who were dismissed or voluntarily withdrew from this program area in 2012–2013 were 12. *Counseling MA/MS (Master of Arts/Science)*—Applications 2012–2013, 21. Total applicants accepted 2012–2013, 16. Number full-time enrolled (new admits only) 2012–2013, 6. Number part-time enrolled (new admits only) 2012–2013, 8. Total enrolled 2012–2013 full-time, 20. Total enrolled 2012–2013 part-time, 25. Openings 2013–2014, 20. The median number of years required for completion of a degree in 2012–2013 were 3. The number of students enrolled full- and part-time who were dismissed or voluntarily withdrew from this program area in 2012–2013 were 1.

Scores: Entries appear in this order: required test or GPA, minimum score (if required), median score of students entering in 2012–2013. *Counseling MA/MS (Master of Arts/Science)*: GRE-Analytical no minimum stated.

Other Criteria: (importance of criteria rated low, medium, or high): research experience—low, work experience—medium, extracurricular activity—medium, clinically related public service—high, GPA—medium, letters of recommendation—medium, statement of goals and objectives—high. For additional information on admission requirements, go to http://www.scu.edu/ecp/admissions/requirements/index.cfm.

Student Characteristics: The following represents characteristics of students in 2012–2013 in all graduate psychology programs in the department: Female—full-time 42, part-time 195; Male—full-time 8, part-time 38; African American/Black—full-time 4, part-time 6; Hispanic/Latino(a)—full-time 8, part-time 45; Asian/Pacific Islander—full-time 7, part-time 38; American Indian/Alaska Native—full-time 1, part-time 1; Caucasian/White—full-time 23, part-time 104; Multi-ethnic—full-time 2, part-time 6; students subject to the Americans With Disabilities Act—full-time 2, part-time 3; Unknown ethnicity—full-time 5, part-time 33; International students who hold an F-1 or J-1 Visa—full-time 7, part-time 4.

Financial Information/Assistance:

Tuition for Full-Time Study: *Master's:* State residents: $497 per credit hour; Nonstate residents: $497 per credit hour. Tuition is subject to change. Additional fees are assessed to students beyond the costs of tuition for the following: lab fees. See the following website for updates and changes in tuition costs: http://www.scu.edu/ecp/admissions/quickfacts/index.cfm.

Financial Assistance:

First-Year Students: Teaching assistantships available for first year. Average amount paid per academic year: $1,350. Average number of hours worked per week: 3. Research assistantships available for first year. Average amount paid per academic year: $600. Average number of hours worked per week: 6. Fellowships and scholarships available for first year. Average amount paid per academic year: $1,400. Average number of hours worked per week: 0.

Advanced Students: Teaching assistantships available for advanced students. Average amount paid per academic year: $1,350. Average number of hours worked per week: 3. Research assistantships available for advanced students. Average amount paid per academic year: $600. Average number of hours worked per week: 6. Fellowships and scholarships available for advanced students. Average amount paid per academic year: $1,400. Average number of hours worked per week: 0.

Additional Information: Of all students currently enrolled full time, 20% benefited from one or more of the listed financial assistance programs. Application and information available online at: http://www.scu.edu/ecp/admissions/financialaid/.

Internships/Practica: Master's Degree (MA/MS Counseling Psychology): An internship experience, such as a final research project or "capstone" experience is required of graduates. Master's Degree (MA/MS Counseling): An internship experience, such as a final research project or "capstone" experience is required of graduates. Supervised counseling experience designed specifically to meet California MFT and LPCC licensing requirements are required. Students will participate in weekly seminars for consultation and discussion with a licensed supervisor on such topics as case management and evaluation, referral procedures, ethical practices, professional and client interaction, confidential communication, and interprofessional ethical considerations.

Housing and Day Care: On-campus housing is available. See the following website for more information: http://www.scu.edu/housing/. On-campus day care facilities are available. See the following website for more information: http://www.scu.edu/koc/.

Employment of Department Graduates:

Master's Degree Graduates: Of those who graduated in the academic year 2011–2012, the following categories and numbers represent the postgraduate activities and employment of master's degree graduates: Enrolled in a psychology doctoral program (5), enrolled in another graduate/professional program (1), enrolled in a postdoctoral residency/fellowship (n/a), employed in independent practice (n/a), employed in an academic position at a 2-year/4-year college (2), employed in other positions at a higher education institution (5), employed in a professional position in a school system (7), employed in business or industry (4), employed in government agency (2), employed in a community mental health/counseling center (8), employed in a hospital/medical center (1), other employment position (6), do not know (47), total from the above (master's) (88).

Doctoral Degree Graduates: Of those who graduated in the academic year 2011–2012, the following categories and numbers represent the postgraduate activities and employment of doctoral degree graduates: Enrolled in a psychology doctoral program (n/a), total from the above (doctoral) (0).

Additional Information:

Orientation, Objectives, and Emphasis of Department: Santa Clara University's graduate programs in counseling and counseling psychology are offered through the School of Education and Counseling Psychology. Programs lead to the Master of Arts in Counseling or the Master of Arts in Counseling Psychology, with the option of an emphasis in Health Psychology, Latino Counseling and Correctional Psychology. All of the Counseling Psychology (90-unit) programs prepare students for MFT licensure and/or the LPCC licensure through the California Board of Behavioral Sciences (BBS). The LPCC is more portable across the United States. Santa Clara is accredited by the Western Association of Schools and Colleges and is approved by the Board of Behavioral Science, Department of Consumer Affairs (California) to prepare students for MFT and LPCC licensure. The faculty represent a diverse set of clinical theories and perspectives, and students gain a broad exposure to a range of theories and practical applications in counseling.

Special Facilities or Resources: Santa Clara University is located in the heart of Silicon Valley, with close connection to major business and academic resources in this area. The University has a complete complement of facilities including an excellent library, theatre, museum and state of the art physical fitness center. The University has a dedication to educating the whole person and includes Centers of Distinction which explore diversity, ethics and the interface of technology and society.

Information for Students With Physical Disabilities: See the following website for more information: http://www.scu.edu/studentlife/disabilities/.

Application Information:
Send to Graduate Admissions, School of ECP, Loyola Hall, Santa Clara University, 500 El Camino Real, Santa Clara, CA 95053-0201. Application available online. URL of online application: https://www.scu.edu/apply/edcp/handler.cfm?event=home. Students are admitted in the Fall, application deadline May 24; Winter, application deadline November 15; Spring, application deadline March 8; Summer, application deadline May 24. *Fee:* $50.

Sonoma State University
Counseling MA
Social Sciences
1801 East Cotati Avenue
Rohnert Park, CA 94928
Telephone: (707) 664-2544
Fax: (707) 664-2038
E-mail: *stephanie.wilkinson@sonoma.edu*
Web: *http://www.sonoma.edu/counseling/*

Department Information:
1979. Chairperson: Maureen Buckley, Ph. D. Number of faculty: total—full-time 5, part-time 13; women—full-time 3, part-time 10; total—minority—full-time 2, part-time 2; women minority—full-time 2, part-time 2.

Programs and Degrees Offered:
Listed in the following order: Program area, degree type (T if terminal Master's), number awarded 7/11–6/12. Clinical Mental Health Counseling (Mft & Lpcc) MA/MS (Master of Arts/Science) (T) 24, School Counseling (Pps) MA/MS (Master of Arts/Science) (T) 12.

Student Applications/Admissions:
Student Applications
Clinical Mental Health Counseling (Mft & Lpcc) MA/MS (Master of Arts/Science)—Applications 2012–2013, 111. Total applicants accepted 2012–2013, 24. Number full-time enrolled (new admits only) 2012–2013, 22. Number part-time enrolled (new admits only) 2012–2013, 2. Total enrolled 2012–2013 full-time, 46. Total enrolled 2012–2013 part-time, 6. Openings 2013–2014, 24. The median number of years required for completion of a degree in 2012–2013 were 2. The number of students enrolled full- and part-time who were dismissed or voluntarily withdrew from this program area in 2012–2013 were 1. *School Counseling (Pps) MA/MS (Master of Arts/Science)*—Applications 2012–2013, 26. Total applicants accepted

2012–2013, 12. Number full-time enrolled (new admits only) 2012–2013, 10. Number part-time enrolled (new admits only) 2012–2013, 2. Total enrolled 2012–2013 full-time, 19. Total enrolled 2012–2013 part-time, 5. Openings 2013–2014, 12. The median number of years required for completion of a degree in 2012–2013 were 2. The number of students enrolled full- and part-time who were dismissed or voluntarily withdrew from this program area in 2012–2013 were 0.

Scores: Entries appear in this order: required test or GPA, minimum score (if required), median score of students entering in 2012–2013. *Clinical Mental Health Counseling (MFT & LPCC) MA/MS (Master of Arts/Science):* overall undergraduate GPA 3.0, 3.3; *School Counseling (PPS) MA/MS (Master of Arts/Science):* overall undergraduate GPA 3.0, 3.4.

Other Criteria: (importance of criteria rated low, medium, or high): work experience—high, clinically related public service—high, GPA—high, letters of recommendation—high, interview—high, statement of goals and objectives—high, undergraduate major in psychology—medium, specific undergraduate psychology courses taken—high. For additional information on admission requirements, go to http://www.sonoma.edu/counseling/application-process.htm.

Student Characteristics: The following represents characteristics of students in 2012–2013 in all graduate psychology programs in the department: Female—full-time 60, part-time 7; Male—full-time 7, part-time 1; African American/Black—full-time 1, part-time 0; Hispanic/Latino(a)—full-time 20, part-time 0; Asian/Pacific Islander—full-time 0, part-time 0; American Indian/Alaska Native—full-time 0, part-time 0; Caucasian/White—full-time 52, part-time 5; Multi-ethnic—full-time 0, part-time 0; students subject to the Americans With Disabilities Act—full-time 0, part-time 0; Unknown ethnicity—full-time 0, part-time 0; International students who hold an F-1 or J-1 Visa—full-time 0, part-time 0.

Financial Information/Assistance:
Tuition for Full-Time Study: *Master's:* State residents: per academic year $8,782; Nonstate residents: per academic year $13,246. Tuition is subject to change. Additional fees are assessed to students beyond the costs of tuition for the following: Course fee for assessment materials. See the following website for updates and changes in tuition costs: http://www.sonoma.edu/registration/fees.

Financial Assistance:
First-Year Students: Fellowships and scholarships available for first year.

Advanced Students: Fellowships and scholarships available for advanced students.

Additional Information: Of all students currently enrolled full time, 39% benefited from one or more of the listed financial assistance programs. Application and information available online at: http://www.sonoma.edu/FinAid/.

Internships/Practica: Master's Degree (MA/MS Clinical Mental Health Counseling (MFT & LPCC)): An internship experience, such as a final research project or "capstone" experience is required of graduates. Master's Degree (MA/MS School Counseling (PPS)): An internship experience, such as a final research project or "capstone" experience is required of graduates. All students complete a 100 hour practicum and a 600 hour internship in relevant settings.

Housing and Day Care: No on-campus housing is available. On-campus day care facilities are available. See the following website for more information: http://www.sonoma.edu/tcs/.

Employment of Department Graduates:

Master's Degree Graduates: Of those who graduated in the academic year 2011–2012, the following categories and numbers represent the postgraduate activities and employment of master's degree graduates: Enrolled in a postdoctoral residency/fellowship (n/a), employed in independent practice (n/a), employed in a community mental health/counseling center (7), still seeking employment (3), other employment position (25), total from the above (master's) (35).

Doctoral Degree Graduates: Of those who graduated in the academic year 2011–2012, the following categories and numbers represent the postgraduate activities and employment of doctoral degree graduates: Enrolled in a psychology doctoral program (n/a), total from the above (doctoral) (0).

Additional Information:

Orientation, Objectives, and Emphasis of Department: The 60-unit graduate program in counseling (nationally accredited through CACREP, affiliated with the American Counseling Association) prepares students for entry into the profession of counseling or student personnel services. The marriage and family therapy (MFT) program prepares students for licensure as MFTs in California; the School Counseling students obtain a Pupil Personnel Services credential. The program relies heavily on interpersonal skill training and field experience, beginning during the first semester and culminating with an intensive supervised internship in some aspect of counseling, permitting the integration of theoretical constructs and research appraisal with practical application during the second year. The department is prepared to assist students in obtaining field placements relevant to their projected professional goals. These placements include, but are not limited to, family service agencies, mental health clinics, counseling centers, public schools, community colleges, and college-level student counseling centers. Special characteristics of the program include the following: early involvement in actual counseling settings; development of a core of knowledge and experience in both individual and group counseling theory and practice; encouragement in the maintenance and development of individual counseling styles; and commitment to self-exploration and personal growth through participation in peer counseling, individual counseling, and group experiences. This aspect of the program is seen as crucial to the development of counseling skills and is given special consideration by the faculty as part of its evaluation of student readiness to undertake internship responsibilities.

Special Facilities or Resources: The Department maintains 7 rooms of counseling training facility space with audio and video recording capabilities.

Information for Students With Physical Disabilities: See the following website for more information: http://www.sonoma.edu/dss/.

Application Information:
Application available online. URL of online application: http://www.sonoma.edu/admissions/gs/. Students are admitted in the Fall, application deadline January 31. *Fee:* $25.

Southern California, University of
Department of Psychology
College of Letters, Arts and Sciences
University Park - SGM 501
Los Angeles, CA 90089-1061
Telephone: (213) 740-2203
Fax: (213) 746-9082
E-mail: *itakarag@usc.edu*
Web: *http://dornsife.usc.edu/psyc/*

Department Information:
1929. Chairperson: Margaret Gatz. Number of faculty: total—full-time 34; women—full-time 12; total—minority—full-time 3.

Programs and Degrees Offered:
Listed in the following order: Program area, degree type (T if terminal Master's), number awarded 7/11–6/12. Brain and Cognitive Sciences PhD (Doctor of Philosophy) 5, Clinical Science PhD (Doctor of Philosophy) 8, Developmental Psychology PhD (Doctor of Philosophy) 2, Quantitative Methods PhD (Doctor of Philosophy) 3, Social Psychology PhD (Doctor of Philosophy) 2.

APA Accreditation: Clinical PhD (Doctor of Philosophy). Student Outcome Data Website: http://dornsife.usc.edu/psyc/student-admissions-outcomes/.

Student Applications/Admissions:
Student Applications

Brain and Cognitive Sciences PhD (Doctor of Philosophy)—Applications 2012–2013, 75. Total applicants accepted 2012–2013, 7. Number full-time enrolled (new admits only) 2012–2013, 3. Total enrolled 2012–2013 full-time, 22. Total enrolled 2012–2013 part-time, 0. Openings 2013–2014, 4. The median number of years required for completion of a degree in 2012–2013 were 6. The number of students enrolled full- and part-time who were dismissed or voluntarily withdrew from this program area in 2012–2013 were 0. *Clinical Science PhD (Doctor of Philosophy)*—Applications 2012–2013, 396. Total applicants accepted 2012–2013, 8. Number full-time enrolled (new admits only) 2012–2013, 4. Total enrolled 2012–2013 full-time, 36. Openings 2013–2014, 5. The median number of years required for completion of a degree in 2012–2013 were 7. The number of students enrolled full- and part-time who were dismissed or voluntarily withdrew from this program area in 2012–2013 were 1. *Developmental Psychology PhD (Doctor of Philosophy)*—Applications 2012–2013, 42. Total applicants accepted 2012–2013, 2. Number full-time enrolled (new admits only) 2012–2013, 1. Total enrolled 2012–2013 full-time, 6. Total enrolled 2012–2013 part-time, 0. Openings 2013–2014, 1. The median number of years required for completion of a degree in 2012–2013 were 5. The number of students enrolled full- and part-time who were dismissed or voluntarily withdrew from this program area in 2012–2013 were 0. *Quantitative Methods PhD (Doctor of Philosophy)*—Applications 2012–2013, 16. Total applicants accepted 2012–2013, 3. Number full-time enrolled (new admits only) 2012–2013, 2. Total enrolled 2012–2013 full-time, 9. Total enrolled 2012–2013 part-time, 0. Openings 2013–2014, 2. The number of students enrolled full- and part-time who were dismissed or voluntarily withdrew from this program area in 2012–2013 were 0. *Social Psychology PhD (Doctor of Philosophy)*—Applications 2012–2013, 88. Total applicants accepted 2012–2013, 2. Number full-time enrolled (new admits only) 2012–2013, 1. Total enrolled 2012–2013 full-time, 8. Total enrolled 2012–2013 part-time, 0. Openings 2013–2014, 2. The median number of years required for completion of a degree in 2012–2013 were 7. The number of students enrolled full- and part-time who were dismissed or voluntarily withdrew from this program area in 2012–2013 were 0.

Scores: Entries appear in this order: required test or GPA, minimum score (if required), median score of students entering in 2012–2013. *Brain and Cognitive Sciences PhD (Doctor of Philosophy)*: GRE-V no minimum stated, 163, GRE-Q 146, 164, GRE-Analytical no minimum stated, 4.5; *Clinical Science PhD (Doctor of Philosophy)*: GRE-V no minimum stated, 165, GRE-Q 146, 158, GRE-Analytical no minimum stated, 5.0; *Developmental Psychology PhD (Doctor of Philosophy)*: GRE-V no minimum stated, 166, GRE-Q 156, 153, GRE-Analytical no minimum stated; *Quantitative Methods PhD (Doctor of Philosophy)*: GRE-V no minimum stated, 157, GRE-Q 146, 161, GRE-Analytical no minimum stated, 4.5; *Social Psychology PhD (Doctor of Philosophy)*: GRE-V no minimum stated, 164, GRE-Q 146, 156, GRE-Analytical no minimum stated, 5.

Other Criteria: (importance of criteria rated low, medium, or high): GRE scores—high, research experience—high, work experience—medium, extracurricular activity—low, clinically related public service—medium, GPA—high, letters of recommendation—high, statement of goals and objectives—high, Interview and clinically related public service are very important for the Clinical Science program but less so for other areas. For additional information on admission requirements, go to http://dornsife.usc.edu/psyc/admissions/.

Student Characteristics: The following represents characteristics of students in 2012–2013 in all graduate psychology programs in the department: Female—full-time 54, part-time 0; Male—full-time 27, part-time 0; African American/Black—full-time 4, part-time 0; Hispanic/Latino(a)—full-time 9, part-time 0; Asian/Pacific Islander—full-time 15, part-time 0; American Indian/Alaska Native—full-time 0, part-time 0; Caucasian/White—full-time 37, part-time 0; Multi-ethnic—full-time 0, part-time 0; students subject to the Americans With Disabilities Act—full-time 0, part-time 0; Unknown ethnicity—full-time 0, part-time 0; International students who hold an F-1 or J-1 Visa—full-time 16, part-time 0.

Financial Information/Assistance:
Tuition for Full-Time Study: *Doctoral:* State residents: per academic year $35,352, $1,473 per credit hour; Nonstate residents: per academic year $35,352, $1,473 per credit hour. Tuition is subject to change. Additional fees are assessed to students beyond the costs of tuition for the following: One time orientation fee of $35 ($150 for non-domestic) + other fees (of about $60) per semester. See the following website for updates and changes in tuition costs: http://web-app.usc.edu/soc/.

Financial Assistance:
First-Year Students: Teaching assistantships available for first year. Average amount paid per academic year: $23,000. Average number of hours worked per week: 20. Research assistantships available for first year. Average amount paid per academic year: $23,000. Average number of hours worked per week: 20. Traineeships available for first year. Average amount paid per academic year: $23,000. Average number of hours worked per week: 0. Fellowships and scholarships available for first year. Average amount paid per academic year: $23,000. Average number of hours worked per week: 0.

Advanced Students: Teaching assistantships available for advanced students. Average amount paid per academic year: $20,250. Average number of hours worked per week: 20. Research assistantships available for advanced students. Average amount paid per academic year: $20,250. Average number of hours worked per week: 20. Traineeships available for advanced students. Average amount paid per academic year: $22,032. Average number of hours worked per week: 0. Fellowships and scholarships available for advanced students. Average amount paid per academic year: $23,000. Average number of hours worked per week: 0.

Additional Information: Of all students currently enrolled full time, 93% benefited from one or more of the listed financial assistance programs. Application and information available online at: http://dornsife.usc.edu/psyc/financial-aid/.

Internships/Practica: Doctoral Degree (PhD Clinical Science): For those doctoral students for whom a professional psychology internship was required in this program prior to graduation, (4) students applied for an internship in 2011–2012, with (4) students obtaining an internship. Of those students who obtained an internship, (4) were paid internships. Of those students who obtained an internship, (4) students placed in APA/CPA accredited internships, (0) students placed in internships not APA/CPA accredited, but listed with the Association of Psychology Postdoctoral and Internship Programs (APPIC), (0) students placed in internships conforming to guidelines of the Council of Directors of School Psychology Programs (CDSPP), (0) students placed in internships that were not APA/CPA accredited, APPIC or CDSPP listed. Students in the clinical psychology area take at least six semesters of clinical didactic practica, each of which involves instruction and supervised clinical service provision. Students receive both group and individual supervision of their cases. The first year practicum focus on clinical interviewing and formal assessment. In the second and third year, students take practica based on their interests and specialty track. Practica are offered in general adult psychotherapy, psychotherapy with older adults, and child/family psychotherapy. After admission to doctoral candidacy, all students must complete a one-year, APA approved clinical internship for which students separately apply at the time.

Housing and Day Care: On-campus housing is available. See the following website for more information: http://housing.usc.edu/.

On-campus day care facilities are available. See the following website for more information: http://www.cclc.com/center/ca/upc-child-development-center; http://www.cclc.com/center/ca/hsc-child-development-center.

Employment of Department Graduates:

Master's Degree Graduates: Of those who graduated in the academic year 2011–2012, the following categories and numbers represent the postgraduate activities and employment of master's degree graduates: Enrolled in a postdoctoral residency/fellowship (n/a), employed in independent practice (n/a), total from the above (master's) (0).

Doctoral Degree Graduates: Of those who graduated in the academic year 2011–2012, the following categories and numbers represent the postgraduate activities and employment of doctoral degree graduates: Enrolled in a psychology doctoral program (n/a), enrolled in a postdoctoral residency/fellowship (7), employed in an academic position at a university (2), still seeking employment (1), total from the above (doctoral) (10).

Additional Information:

Orientation, Objectives, and Emphasis of Department: Graduate training in psychology prepares students for careers in research and teaching, as well as in empirically-oriented applied settings including health service, business, or other sectors. In addition to completing the required coursework, students in all specialty areas engage in empirical research throughout graduate study. Areas of specialization include: brain & cognitive science, clinical science, developmental psychology, quantitative methods, and social psychology. The clinical program—which is accredited by both APA and the Psychological Clinical Science Accreditation System (PCSAS)—offers formal tracks in clinical-aging and child and family and a PhD/M.P.H. dual degree.

Special Facilities or Resources: We are housed in the upper six floors of a 10-story building, which provides the department ample laboratory and office space. Most graduate students and faculty have offices and labs in the building. The department has state-of-the-art research facilities, including the Dana & David Dornsife Cognitive Neuroscience Imaging Center located in an adjacent building. A shared, communal social behavior laboratory of testing rooms and equipment is available for use by all faculty and students who are doing behavioral research. The clinical science program offers clinical services to the community through the on-campus Psychology Services Center.

Information for Students With Physical Disabilities: See the following website for more information: http://sait.usc.edu/academicsupport/centerprograms/dsp/home_index.html.

Application Information:
Send to Irene Takaragawa, Graduate Advisor, Department of Psychology/SGM 508, University of Southern California, Los Angeles, CA 90089-1061. Application available online. URL of online application: http://www.usc.edu/admission/graduate/apply/. Students are admitted in the Fall, application deadline December 1. *Fee:* $85. Indicate in online application that financial hardship waiver is requested. Applicant must also submit to the Office of Graduate and International Admissions the most current financial aid statement from current/last school of enrollment.

Southern California, University of, Keck School of Medicine
Department of Preventive Medicine, Division of Health Behavior Research
USC Health Science Building, 2001 North Soto Street, 3rd Floor
Los Angeles, CA 90032
Telephone: (323) 442-8299
E-mail: *barovich@usc.edu*
Web: *http://ipr.usc.edu/hbrphd*

Department Information:
1984. Director: Mary Ann Pentz. Number of faculty: total—full-time 18; women—full-time 12; total—minority—full-time 4; women minority—full-time 2.

Programs and Degrees Offered:
Listed in the following order: Program area, degree type (T if terminal Master's), number awarded 7/11–6/12. Health Behavior Research PhD (Doctor of Philosophy) 2.

Student Applications/Admissions:
Student Applications
Health Behavior Research PhD (Doctor of Philosophy)—Applications 2012–2013, 25. Total applicants accepted 2012–2013, 5. Number full-time enrolled (new admits only) 2012–2013, 5. Number part-time enrolled (new admits only) 2012–2013, 0. Total enrolled 2012–2013 full-time, 26. Total enrolled 2012–2013 part-time, 0. Openings 2013–2014, 5. The median number of years required for completion of a degree in 2012–2013 were 4. The number of students enrolled full- and part-time who were dismissed or voluntarily withdrew from this program area in 2012–2013 were 0.

Scores: Entries appear in this order: required test or GPA, minimum score (if required), median score of students entering in 2012–2013. *Health Behavior Research PhD (Doctor of Philosophy):* GRE-V 480, 550, GRE-Q 670, 760, overall undergraduate GPA 2.81, 3.26, Masters GPA 3.35, 3.55.

Other Criteria: (importance of criteria rated low, medium, or high): GRE scores—high, research experience—medium, work experience—medium, extracurricular activity—low, GPA—high, letters of recommendation—high, interview—medium, statement of goals and objectives—high, undergraduate major in psychology—low, Students are invited to interview, in-person or on the phone, but interviews are not required. (They are helpful, however.). For additional information on admission requirements, go to http://phdhbr.usc.edu.

Student Characteristics: The following represents characteristics of students in 2012–2013 in all graduate psychology programs in the department: Female—full-time 18, part-time 0; Male—full-time 8, part-time 0; African American/Black—full-time 0, part-time 0; Hispanic/Latino(a)—full-time 2, part-time 0; Asian/Pacific Islander—full-time 7, part-time 0; American Indian/Alaska Native—full-time 1, part-time 0; Caucasian/White—full-time 14, part-time 0; Multi-ethnic—full-time 0, part-time 0; students subject to the Americans With Disabilities Act—full-time 0, part-time 0; Unknown ethnicity—full-time 0, part-time 0; International students who hold an F-1 or J-1 Visa—full-time 2, part-time 0.

Financial Information/Assistance:

Tuition for Full-Time Study: *Doctoral:* State residents: per academic year $21,378, $1,527 per credit hour; Nonstate residents: per academic year $21,378, $1,527 per credit hour. Additional fees are assessed to students beyond the costs of tuition for the following: programming, student services, and Norman Topping fee: currently $147 per academic year.

Financial Assistance:

First-Year Students: Teaching assistantships available for first year. Average amount paid per academic year: $22,500. Average number of hours worked per week: 20. Apply by December 1. Research assistantships available for first year. Average amount paid per academic year: $22,500. Average number of hours worked per week: 20. Apply by December 1. Fellowships and scholarships available for first year. Average amount paid per academic year: $22,500. Average number of hours worked per week: 20. Apply by December 1.

Advanced Students: Teaching assistantships available for advanced students. Average amount paid per academic year: $22,500. Average number of hours worked per week: 20. Research assistantships available for advanced students. Average amount paid per academic year: $22,500. Average number of hours worked per week: 20. Traineeships available for advanced students. Average amount paid per academic year: $22,500. Average number of hours worked per week: 20. Apply by June 1. Fellowships and scholarships available for advanced students. Average amount paid per academic year: $22,500. Average number of hours worked per week: 20. Apply by March 1.

Additional Information: Of all students currently enrolled full time, 100% benefited from one or more of the listed financial assistance programs. Application and information available online at: http://www.usc.edu/schools/GraduateSchool/current_fellowships.html.

Housing and Day Care: On-campus housing is available. See the following website for more information: http://housing.usc.edu/. On-campus day care facilities are available. See the following website for more information: http://www.usc.edu/dept/hr/childcare/.

Employment of Department Graduates:

Master's Degree Graduates: Of those who graduated in the academic year 2011–2012, the following categories and numbers represent the postgraduate activities and employment of master's degree graduates: Enrolled in a postdoctoral residency/fellowship (n/a), employed in independent practice (n/a), total from the above (master's) (0).

Doctoral Degree Graduates: Of those who graduated in the academic year 2011–2012, the following categories and numbers represent the postgraduate activities and employment of doctoral degree graduates: Enrolled in a psychology doctoral program (n/a), enrolled in a postdoctoral residency/fellowship (2), total from the above (doctoral) (2).

Additional Information:

Orientation, Objectives, and Emphasis of Department: The University of Southern California (USC) School of Medicine, Department of Preventive Medicine, Division of Health Behavior Research, offers a doctorate in health behavior research (HBR), providing academic and research training for students interested in pursuing career opportunities in the field of health promotion and disease prevention research. The specific objective of the program is to train exceptional researchers and scholars in the multidisciplinary field of health behavior research who will apply this knowledge creatively to the goal of primary and secondary prevention of disease. Students receive well-rounded training that encompasses theory and methods from many allied fields, including communication, psychology, preventive medicine, statistics, social network analysis, public/global health, and epidemiology. Students receive research experience participating in projects conducted through the USC Institute for Health Promotion and Disease Prevention Research (IPR). Required core courses: foundations of health behavior, data analysis, behavioral epidemiology, biological basis of disease, basic theory and strategies in prevention, basic theories and strategies for compliance/adaptation, health behavior research methods, and research seminar in health behavior. In addition to core course requirements, the curriculum includes content courses from the Department of Preventive Medicine's Divisions of Biostatistics and Epidemiology.

Special Facilities or Resources: Faculty and other researchers at IPR are recognized leaders in community-based approaches to health promotion and disease prevention. The research at IPR integrates the scientific perspectives of epidemiology, the behavioral sciences, biology, communication, and policy research in disease etiology and prevention. IPR enjoys research collaborations in 10 schools and 35 departments within USC and with noted researchers and public health leaders in leading universities across the U.S., Europe, Latin America, and Asia. IPR's faculty and researchers are world leaders in school- and community-based prevention, tobacco control, and cancer control and epidemiology; prevention of drug abuse, childhood obesity, and cardiovascular disease; promotion of improvements in nutrition and physical activity; research examining health disparities; and health communication campaigns for chronic disease prevention. A new focus has been on developing health and wellness interventions for childhood cancer survivors. Students are also trained in transdisciplinary approaches to research.

Information for Students With Physical Disabilities: See the following website for more information: http://sait.usc.edu/academicsupport/centerprograms/dsp/home_index.html.

Application Information:

Application available online. URL of online application: http://www.usc.edu/admission/graduate/apply/index.html. Students are admitted in the Fall, application deadline December 1. *Fee:* $85.

Stanford University

Department of Psychology
Humanities & Sciences
450 Serra Mall, Jordan Hall, Building 420
Stanford, CA 94305-2130
Telephone: (650) 725-2400
Fax: (650) 725-5699
E-mail: *psych-info@lists.stanford.edu*
Web: *https://psychology.stanford.edu/*

Department Information:

1892. Chairperson: Ian H. Gotlib. Number of faculty: total—full-time 29; women—full-time 10; total—minority—full-time 4; women minority—full-time 2.

Programs and Degrees Offered:

Listed in the following order: Program area, degree type (T if terminal Master's), number awarded 7/11–6/12. Cognitive Psychology PhD (Doctor of Philosophy) 3, Social Psychology PhD (Doctor of Philosophy) 3, Neuroscience PhD (Doctor of Philosophy) 3, Developmental Psychology PhD (Doctor of Philosophy) 1, Affective Science PhD (Doctor of Philosophy) 4.

Student Applications/Admissions:

Student Applications

Cognitive Psychology PhD (Doctor of Philosophy)—Applications 2012–2013, 79. Total applicants accepted 2012–2013, 5. Number full-time enrolled (new admits only) 2012–2013, 3. Number part-time enrolled (new admits only) 2012–2013, 0. Total enrolled 2012–2013 full-time, 12. Total enrolled 2012–2013 part-time, 0. Openings 2013–2014, 3. The median number of years required for completion of a degree in 2012–2013 were 5. The number of students enrolled full- and part-time who were dismissed or voluntarily withdrew from this program area in 2012–2013 were 0. *Social Psychology PhD (Doctor of Philosophy)*—Applications 2012–2013, 130. Total applicants accepted 2012–2013, 5. Number full-time enrolled (new admits only) 2012–2013, 2. Number part-time enrolled (new admits only) 2012–2013, 0. Total enrolled 2012–2013 full-time, 18. Total enrolled 2012–2013 part-time, 0. Openings 2013–2014, 4. The median number of years required for completion of a degree in 2012–2013 were 5. The number of students enrolled full- and part-time who were dismissed or voluntarily withdrew from this program area in 2012–2013 were 0. *Neuroscience PhD (Doctor of Philosophy)*—Applications 2012–2013, 22. Total applicants accepted 2012–2013, 5. Number full-time enrolled (new admits only) 2012–2013, 1. Number part-time enrolled (new admits only) 2012–2013, 0. Total enrolled 2012–2013 full-time, 11. Total enrolled 2012–2013 part-time, 0. Openings 2013–2014, 3. The median number of years required for completion of a degree in 2012–2013 were 5. The number of students enrolled full- and part-time who were dismissed or voluntarily withdrew from this program area in 2012–2013 were 0. *Developmental Psychology PhD (Doctor of Philosophy)*—Applications 2012–2013, 36. Total applicants accepted 2012–2013, 3. Number full-time enrolled (new admits only) 2012–2013, 3. Number part-time enrolled (new admits only) 2012–2013, 0. Total enrolled 2012–2013 full-time, 11. Total enrolled 2012–2013 part-time, 0. Openings 2013–2014, 3. The median number of years required for completion of a degree in 2012–

2013 were 5. The number of students enrolled full- and part-time who were dismissed or voluntarily withdrew from this program area in 2012–2013 were 0. *Affective Science PhD (Doctor of Philosophy)*—Applications 2012–2013, 101. Total applicants accepted 2012–2013, 4. Number full-time enrolled (new admits only) 2012–2013, 4. Openings 2013–2014, 4. The median number of years required for completion of a degree in 2012–2013 were 5.

Other Criteria: (importance of criteria rated low, medium, or high): GRE scores—high, research experience—high, work experience—low, extracurricular activity—low, clinically related public service—low, GPA—high, letters of recommendation—high, interview—high, statement of goals and objectives—high, undergraduate major in psychology—low, specific undergraduate psychology courses taken—low. For additional information on admission requirements, go to https://psychology.stanford.edu/graduate_admissions.html.

Student Characteristics: The following represents characteristics of students in 2012–2013 in all graduate psychology programs in the department: Female—full-time 44, part-time 0; Male—full-time 26, part-time 0; African American/Black—full-time 3, part-time 0; Hispanic/Latino(a)—full-time 5, part-time 0; Asian/Pacific Islander—full-time 8, part-time 0; American Indian/Alaska Native—full-time 0, part-time 0; Caucasian/White—full-time 32, part-time 0; Multi-ethnic—full-time 0, part-time 0; students subject to the Americans With Disabilities Act—full-time 0, part-time 0; Unknown ethnicity—full-time 9, part-time 0; International students who hold an F-1 or J-1 Visa—full-time 13, part-time 0.

Financial Information/Assistance:

Tuition for Full-Time Study: *Doctoral:* State residents: per academic year $41,250; Nonstate residents: per academic year $41,250. Tuition is subject to change.

Financial Assistance:

First-Year Students: Teaching assistantships available for first year. Average amount paid per academic year: $30,000. Average number of hours worked per week: 20. Research assistantships available for first year. Average amount paid per academic year: $30,000. Average number of hours worked per week: 20. Traineeships available for first year. Average amount paid per academic year: $30,000. Average number of hours worked per week: 20. Fellowships and scholarships available for first year. Average amount paid per academic year: $30,000. Average number of hours worked per week: 20.

Advanced Students: Teaching assistantships available for advanced students. Average amount paid per academic year: $30,000. Average number of hours worked per week: 20. Research assistantships available for advanced students. Average amount paid per academic year: $30,000. Average number of hours worked per week: 20. Traineeships available for advanced students. Average amount paid per academic year: $30,000. Average number of hours worked per week: 20. Fellowships and scholarships available for advanced students. Average amount paid per academic year: $30,000. Average number of hours worked per week: 20.

Additional Information: Of all students currently enrolled full time, 95% benefited from one or more of the listed financial assistance programs. Application and information available online at: http://www.stanford.edu/dept/finaid/grad/.

Housing and Day Care: On-campus housing is available. See the following website for more information: http://studenthousing. stanford.edu/. On-campus day care facilities are available. See the following website for more information: http://www.stanford.edu/ dept/worklife/cgi-bin/drupal/childcareresources/.

Employment of Department Graduates:
Master's Degree Graduates: Of those who graduated in the academic year 2011–2012, the following categories and numbers represent the postgraduate activities and employment of master's degree graduates: Enrolled in a postdoctoral residency/fellowship (n/a), employed in independent practice (n/a), total from the above (master's) (0).
Doctoral Degree Graduates: Of those who graduated in the academic year 2011–2012, the following categories and numbers represent the postgraduate activities and employment of doctoral degree graduates: Enrolled in a psychology doctoral program (n/a), total from the above (doctoral) (0).

Additional Information:

Special Facilities or Resources: The department comprises facilities and personnel housed in Jordan Hall, where it maintains extensive laboratory and shop facilities, supervised by specialized technical assistants. These facilities include laboratories for behavioral and neural (fMRI, EEG, and TMS) research. Most of the laboratories are equipped with computer terminals linked directly to the university's computer center. Others are equipped with their own computers. In addition, the department has its own computer and a computer programmer on the psychology staff. The department maintains a nursery school close to the married students' housing area. This provides a laboratory for child observation, for training in nursery school practice, and for research.

Information for Students With Physical Disabilities: See the following website for more information: http://studentaffairs. stanford.edu/oae.

Application Information:
Application available online. URL of online application: http:// studentaffairs.stanford.edu/gradadmissions. Students are admitted in the Fall, application deadline November 20. *Fee:* $125.

Wright Institute (2012 data)
Graduate School of Psychology
2728 Durant Avenue
Berkeley, CA 94704
Telephone: (510) 841-9230
Fax: (510) 841-0167
E-mail: *info@wi.edu*
Web: *http://www.wi.edu*

Department Information:
1969. Dean: Charles Alexander, PhD. Number of faculty: total—full-time 12, part-time 47; women—full-time 10, part-time 20; total—minority—full-time 5, part-time 6; women minority—full-time 5, part-time 5.

Programs and Degrees Offered:
Listed in the following order: Program area, degree type (T if terminal Master's), number awarded 7/11–6/12. Clinical Psychology PsyD (Doctor of Psychology) 66.

APA Accreditation: Clinical PsyD (Doctor of Psychology). Student Outcome Data Website: www.wi.edu/psyd-outcomes.

Student Applications/Admissions:
Student Applications
Clinical Psychology PsyD (Doctor of Psychology)—Applications 2012–2013, 335. Total applicants accepted 2012–2013, 131. Number full-time enrolled (new admits only) 2012–2013, 62. Number part-time enrolled (new admits only) 2012–2013, 0. Total enrolled 2012–2013 full-time, 336. Total enrolled 2012–2013 part-time, 0. Openings 2013–2014, 58. The median number of years required for completion of a degree in 2012–2013 were 5. The number of students enrolled full- and part-time who were dismissed or voluntarily withdrew from this program area in 2012–2013 were 3.
Scores: Entries appear in this order: required test or GPA, minimum score (if required), median score of students entering in 2012–2013. *Clinical Psychology PsyD (Doctor of Psychology):* GRE-V no minimum stated, GRE-Q no minimum stated, GRE-Analytical no minimum stated, overall undergraduate GPA 3.0, 3.35.
Other Criteria: (importance of criteria rated low, medium, or high): GRE scores—medium, research experience—medium, work experience—medium, extracurricular activity—medium, clinically related public service—high, GPA—high, letters of recommendation—high, interview—high, statement of goals and objectives—high, undergraduate major in psychology—medium, specific undergraduate psychology courses taken—high. For additional information on admission requirements, go to http://www.wi.edu/admission-psyd-info.

Student Characteristics: The following represents characteristics of students in 2012–2013 in all graduate psychology programs in the department: Female—full-time 232, part-time 0; Male—full-time 104, part-time 0; African American/Black—full-time 14, part-time 0; Hispanic/Latino(a)—full-time 26, part-time 0; Asian/ Pacific Islander—full-time 37, part-time 0; American Indian/ Alaska Native—full-time 3, part-time 0; Caucasian/White—full-time 232, part-time 0; Multi-ethnic—full-time 20, part-time 0; students subject to the Americans With Disabilities Act—full-time 7, part-time 0; Unknown ethnicity—full-time 4, part-time 0; International students who hold an F-1 or J-1 Visa—full-time 4, part-time 0.

Financial Information/Assistance:
Tuition for Full-Time Study: *Doctoral:* State residents: per academic year $28,100; Nonstate residents: per academic year $28,100. Tuition is subject to change. See the following website for updates and changes in tuition costs: http://www.wi.edu/psyd-tuition-financial-aid.

Financial Assistance:
First-Year Students: Research assistantships available for first year. Average amount paid per academic year: $1,900. Average number of hours worked per week: 5.

Advanced Students: Teaching assistantships available for advanced students. Average amount paid per academic year: $2,400. Average number of hours worked per week: 5. Research assistantships available for advanced students. Average amount paid per academic year: $2,200. Average number of hours worked per week: 5. Fellowships and scholarships available for advanced students. Average amount paid per academic year: $2,200. Apply by December 9.

Additional Information: Of all students currently enrolled full time, 45% benefited from one or more of the listed financial assistance programs. Application and information available online at: www.wi.edu/psyd-tuition-financial-aid.

Internships/Practica: Doctoral Degree (PsyD Clinical Psychology): For those doctoral students for whom a professional psychology internship was required in this program prior to graduation, (78) students applied for an internship in 2011–2012, with (72) students obtaining an internship. Of those students who obtained an internship, (50) were paid internships. Of those students who obtained an internship, (24) students placed in APA/CPA accredited internships, (5) students placed in internships not APA/CPA accredited, but listed with the Association of Psychology Postdoctoral and Internship Programs (APPIC), (0) students placed in internships conforming to guidelines of the Council of Directors of School Psychology Programs (CDSPP), (43) students placed in internships that were not APA/CPA accredited, APPIC or CDSPP listed. Through three years of practicum plus the internship, the Institute's field training program prepares students to integrate the knowledge base of psychology with clinical experience while working in a variety of roles. Beginning with the first-year practicum, students work with a range of clinical populations, treatment modalities, and train in a variety of clinical settings serving the ethno-culturally diverse populations of the San Francisco Bay Area. The Field Placement Office (FPO) operates a large clinical services program (see below) thus easing the placement process significantly and furnishes extensive support to students in the practicum and internship application process. Our internship match rate meets the national rate for those students from the Wright Institute applying nationally for APA internships. Our students are valued by the most well-regarded internship sites in the Bay Area and throughout the nation. The Bay Area also has an established community of internship agencies as part of the California Psychology Internship Council (CAPIC). California licensing recognizes as a formal internship a program that is accredited by the APA or that's a member of APPIC or CAPIC. Because many students are established residents of the Bay Area, the Wright Institute approves internships at APPIC and CAPIC member programs.

Housing and Day Care: No on-campus housing is available. No on-campus day care facilities are available.

Employment of Department Graduates:

Master's Degree Graduates: Of those who graduated in the academic year 2011–2012, the following categories and numbers represent the postgraduate activities and employment of master's degree graduates: Enrolled in a psychology doctoral program (0), enrolled in a postdoctoral residency/fellowship (n/a), employed in independent practice (n/a), total from the above (master's) (0).

Doctoral Degree Graduates: Of those who graduated in the academic year 2011–2012, the following categories and numbers represent the postgraduate activities and employment of doctoral degree graduates: Enrolled in a psychology doctoral program (n/a), enrolled in another graduate/professional program (0), enrolled in a postdoctoral residency/fellowship (31), employed in independent practice (11), employed in an academic position at a university (0), employed in an academic position at a 2-year/4-year college (0), employed in other positions at a higher education institution (1), employed in a professional position in a school system (1), employed in business or industry (0), employed in government agency (1), employed in a community mental health/counseling center (7), employed in a hospital/medical center (3), still seeking employment (5), not seeking employment (1), other employment position (3), do not know (2), total from the above (doctoral) (66).

Additional Information:

Orientation, Objectives, and Emphasis of Department: The Wright Institute teaches the scientific knowledge base of clinical psychology, preparing students to think rigorously and critically. Students learn to apply critical thinking skills to three fundamental areas: clinical theory and research, understanding of the self in social context, and appreciation of the interaction between clinician and client. Students are exposed to a number of clinical orientations. This includes a strong emphasis on the multicultural dimensions of learning to become a clinical psychologist. Students learn to formulate and address clinical problems by examining the lenses through which they filter experience. Coursework is integrated yearly with rigorous practical experience, providing for the systematic, progressive acquisition of skills and knowledge. Students actively participate in professional seminars over the full three years of residency. Weekly, three-hour small-group seminars provide mentoring and a rich forum for developing and integrating theory, technique, and reflective judgment. Practica and internship consolidate the applied aspects of scientific knowledge. Education about the multiple roles of the psychologist "clinician, supervisor, consultant, advocate, etc." prepares students for working in fulfilling ways amid the changing realities of the healthcare field. We expect our graduates to become excellent clinicians and also to assume roles in which they can exhibit clinical leadership.

Special Facilities or Resources: The Wright Institute has traditional low fee psychotherapy and assessment clinics as well as innovative programs in schools and primary care facilities. The Institute's psychodynamically oriented clinic has been in operation for over 35 years, and the Institute also operates clinics focusing on evidence-based treatment and addiction recovery. The Wright Institute's School-Based Collaboration program enables students to work with students, teachers and parents in communities challenged by violence, discrimination and poverty. Our approach is to tackle the severe non-academic barriers to learning by viewing the school community as a whole, and collaborating to identify key needs and deliver relevant services. In the Institute's Integrated Health Psychology Training Program interns and practicum students learn primary care health psychology and perform as part of a multidisciplinary team, addressing the lifestyle and behavioral components contributing to poor health, and treating the co-occurring psychological disorders many patients experience. Through these clinics and programs, the Institute educates students to apply psychological knowledge and skills, not just to work with the problems and dysfunctions of underserved populations, but also to appreciate and cultivate those populations' strengths and aspirations. In so doing our students build a deeper multicultural perspective grounded in their own developing experience.

Application Information:
Send to Admissions Director, The Wright Institute, 2728 Durant Avenue, Berkeley, CA 94704. Application available online. URL of online application: www.wi.edu/admission-apply-online. Students are admitted in the Fall, application deadline January 15. *Fee:* $50.

Colorado State University

Department of Psychology
Natural Sciences
200 West Lake Street, 1876 Campus Delivery
Fort Collins, CO 80523-1876
Telephone: (970) 491-6363
Fax: (970) 491-1032
E-mail: *kurt.kraiger@colostate.edu*
Web: *http://www.colostate.edu/Depts/Psychology/*

Department Information:

1962. Chairperson: Kurt Kraiger. Number of faculty: total—full-time 27; women—full-time 16; total—minority—full-time 3; women minority—full-time 1.

Programs and Degrees Offered:

Listed in the following order: Program area, degree type (T if terminal Master's), number awarded 7/11–6/12. Counseling Psychology PhD (Doctor of Philosophy) 7, Industrial/Organizational Psychology PhD (Doctor of Philosophy) 2, Cognitive Psychology PhD (Doctor of Philosophy) 3, Applied Social Psychology PhD (Doctor of Philosophy) 3, Cognitive Neuroscience PhD (Doctor of Philosophy) 1.

APA Accreditation: Counseling PhD (Doctor of Philosophy). Student Outcome Data Website: http://www.colostate.edu/Depts/Psychology/counseling/FAQ.shtml.

Student Applications/Admissions:

Student Applications

Counseling Psychology PhD (Doctor of Philosophy)—Applications 2012–2013, 292. Total applicants accepted 2012–2013, 8. Number full-time enrolled (new admits only) 2012–2013, 8. Number part-time enrolled (new admits only) 2012–2013, 0. Total enrolled 2012–2013 full-time, 35. Total enrolled 2012–2013 part-time, 0. Openings 2013–2014, 5. The median number of years required for completion of a degree in 2012–2013 were 5. The number of students enrolled full- and part-time who were dismissed or voluntarily withdrew from this program area in 2012–2013 were 0. *Industrial/Organizational Psychology PhD (Doctor of Philosophy)*—Applications 2012–2013, 69. Total applicants accepted 2012–2013, 4. Number full-time enrolled (new admits only) 2012–2013, 3. Number part-time enrolled (new admits only) 2012–2013, 0. Total enrolled 2012–2013 full-time, 27. Total enrolled 2012–2013 part-time, 0. Openings 2013–2014, 5. The median number of years required for completion of a degree in 2012–2013 were 6. The number of students enrolled full- and part-time who were dismissed or voluntarily withdrew from this program area in 2012–2013 were 0. *Cognitive Psychology PhD (Doctor of Philosophy)*—Applications 2012–2013, 50. Total applicants accepted 2012–2013, 3. Number full-time enrolled (new admits only) 2012–2013, 3. Number part-time enrolled (new admits only) 2012–2013, 0. Total enrolled 2012–2013 full-time, 12. Total enrolled 2012–2013 part-time, 0. Openings 2013–2014, 2. The median number of years required for completion of a degree

in 2012–2013 were 6. The number of students enrolled full- and part-time who were dismissed or voluntarily withdrew from this program area in 2012–2013 were 0. *Applied Social Psychology PhD (Doctor of Philosophy)*—Applications 2012–2013, 49. Total applicants accepted 2012–2013, 3. Number full-time enrolled (new admits only) 2012–2013, 3. Number part-time enrolled (new admits only) 2012–2013, 0. Total enrolled 2012–2013 full-time, 15. Total enrolled 2012–2013 part-time, 0. Openings 2013–2014, 2. The median number of years required for completion of a degree in 2012–2013 were 6. The number of students enrolled full- and part-time who were dismissed or voluntarily withdrew from this program area in 2012–2013 were 0. *Cognitive Neuroscience PhD (Doctor of Philosophy)*—Applications 2012–2013, 28. Total applicants accepted 2012–2013, 1. Number full-time enrolled (new admits only) 2012–2013, 1. Number part-time enrolled (new admits only) 2012–2013, 0. Total enrolled 2012–2013 full-time, 9. Total enrolled 2012–2013 part-time, 0. Openings 2013–2014, 2. The median number of years required for completion of a degree in 2012–2013 were 5. The number of students enrolled full- and part-time who were dismissed or voluntarily withdrew from this program area in 2012–2013 were 0.

Scores: Entries appear in this order: required test or GPA, minimum score (if required), median score of students entering in 2012–2013. *Counseling Psychology PhD (Doctor of Philosophy):* GRE-V 500, GRE-Q 560, overall undergraduate GPA 3.6; *Industrial/Organizational Psychology PhD (Doctor of Philosophy):* GRE-V 500, GRE-Q 560, overall undergraduate GPA 3.6; *Cognitive Psychology PhD (Doctor of Philosophy):* GRE-V 500, GRE-Q 560, overall undergraduate GPA 3.6; *Applied Social Psychology PhD (Doctor of Philosophy):* GRE-V 500, GRE-Q 560, overall undergraduate GPA 3.6; *Cognitive Neuroscience PhD (Doctor of Philosophy):* GRE-V 500, GRE-Q 560, overall undergraduate GPA 3.6.

Other Criteria: (importance of criteria rated low, medium, or high): GRE scores—medium, research experience—high, work experience—medium, extracurricular activity—medium, clinically related public service—medium, GPA—high, letters of recommendation—high, statement of goals and objectives—high, undergraduate major in psychology—low, specific undergraduate psychology courses taken—medium, Scientific writing sample required by Applied Social and Industrial/Organizational Programs; optional for Cognitive and Cognitive Neuroscience. For additional information on admission requirements, go to http://www.colostate.edu/Depts/Psychology/apply.shtml.

Student Characteristics: The following represents characteristics of students in 2012–2013 in all graduate psychology programs in the department: Female—full-time 70, part-time 0; Male—full-time 28, part-time 0; African American/Black—full-time 2, part-time 0; Hispanic/Latino(a)—full-time 9, part-time 0; Asian/Pacific Islander—full-time 4, part-time 0; American Indian/Alaska Native—full-time 1, part-time 0; Caucasian/White—full-time 78, part-time 0; Multi-ethnic—full-time 4, part-time 0; students subject to the Americans With Disabilities Act—full-time 0, part-time 0; Unknown ethnicity—full-time 0, part-time 0; Interna-

tional students who hold an F-1 or J-1 Visa—full-time 4, part-time 0.

Financial Information/Assistance:

Tuition for Full-Time Study: *Doctoral:* State residents: per academic year $8,391, $466 per credit hour; Nonstate residents: per academic year $20,571, $1,142 per credit hour. Tuition is subject to change. Additional fees are assessed to students beyond the costs of tuition for the following: General Fees - $41.82, University Technology Fee - $20, University Facility Fee - $15/credit hour. See the following website for updates and changes in tuition costs: http://registrar.colostate.edu/tuition-fees.

Financial Assistance:

First-Year Students: Teaching assistantships available for first year. Average amount paid per academic year: $12,700. Average number of hours worked per week: 20. Research assistantships available for first year. Average amount paid per academic year: $12,700. Average number of hours worked per week: 20. Fellowships and scholarships available for first year. Average amount paid per academic year: $14,400. Average number of hours worked per week: 0.

Advanced Students: Teaching assistantships available for advanced students. Average amount paid per academic year: $13,029. Average number of hours worked per week: 20. Research assistantships available for advanced students. Average amount paid per academic year: $13,029. Average number of hours worked per week: 20. Traineeships available for advanced students. Fellowships and scholarships available for advanced students. Average amount paid per academic year: $0. Average number of hours worked per week: 0.

Additional Information: Of all students currently enrolled full time, 89% benefited from one or more of the listed financial assistance programs. Application and information available online at: http://graduateschool.colostate.edu/financial-resources/.

Internships/Practica: Doctoral Degree (PhD Counseling Psychology): For those doctoral students for whom a professional psychology internship was required in this program prior to graduation, (7) students applied for an internship in 2011–2012, with (7) students obtaining an internship. Of those students who obtained an internship, (7) were paid internships. Of those students who obtained an internship, (7) students placed in APA/CPA accredited internships, (0) students placed in internships not APA/CPA accredited, but listed with the Association of Psychology Postdoctoral and Internship Programs (APPIC), (0) students placed in internships conforming to guidelines of the Council of Directors of School Psychology Programs (CDSPP), (0) students placed in internships that were not APA/CPA accredited, APPIC or CDSPP listed. There are a number of related practica for counseling students throughout Northern Colorado. The following are examples: neuropsychology, local community college, primary health care, and school districts. Industrial/Organizational students consult with a variety of businesses throughout the state including: United Airlines, HP, Sun Systems, IBM, microbreweries and hospitals. The Tri Ethnic Center for Prevention Research (TEC) and the Colorado Injury Control Research Center (CICRC) are a part of the department. The Institute of Applied Prevention Research was designated a Center of Research and Scholarly Excellence by the University in 2008.

Housing and Day Care: On-campus housing is available. See the following website for more information: http://www.housing. colostate.edu/index.htm. On-campus day care facilities are available. See the following website for more information: http://www. hdfs.cahs.colostate.edu/centers_outreach/ecc/general.aspx.

Employment of Department Graduates:

Master's Degree Graduates: Of those who graduated in the academic year 2011–2012, the following categories and numbers represent the postgraduate activities and employment of master's degree graduates: Enrolled in a postdoctoral residency/fellowship (n/a), employed in independent practice (n/a), total from the above (master's) (0).

Doctoral Degree Graduates: Of those who graduated in the academic year 2011–2012, the following categories and numbers represent the postgraduate activities and employment of doctoral degree graduates: Enrolled in a psychology doctoral program (n/a), enrolled in a postdoctoral residency/fellowship (3), employed in an academic position at a university (1), employed in an academic position at a 2-year/4-year college (1), employed in other positions at a higher education institution (3), employed in business or industry (2), employed in government agency (2), employed in a community mental health/counseling center (2), employed in a hospital/medical center (1), do not know (1), total from the above (doctoral) (16).

Additional Information:

Orientation, Objectives, and Emphasis of Department: Colorado State University offers graduate training leading to the MS and PhD degrees in applied social, cognitive, cognitive neuroscience, counseling, and industrial/organizational psychology. A core program of study is required of all students in the first years of graduate work to insure a broad and thorough grounding in psychology. Graduate students in applied social, cognitive and cognitive neuroscience areas take positions in academic, research, or government agencies. Industrial/Organizational has opportunities for students to have experiences in selection techniques, occupational health psychology, assessment centers, organizational climate and structure, and consultation. Counseling students are trained in academic and applied skills with opportunities in behavior therapy, group techniques, assessment, outreach, consultation, and supervision. Emphasis is on diversity and breadth. In addition to the adult specialty, a program is available that will lead to a PhD in counseling psychology with advanced courses that deal with children and adolescents.

Special Facilities or Resources: The Tri Ethnic Center for Prevention Research, a NIDA, CDC and Justice Department funded research center, focuses on adolescent issues such as substance use, violence, rural issues, and culturally appropriate prevention strategies. The CICR is currently in year 2 of a 5 year second cycle of funding by the CDC and the National Center for Injury Prevention and Control. CICR's focus is to address the prevention and control of injuries among rural and under-served populations. The Institute for Applied Prevention Research (IAPR), which is a Diversity Program of Research and Scholarly Excellence, is the umbrella group for a number of centers including Tri-Ethnic, CICRC, CFERT and CoAMP.

Information for Students With Physical Disabilities: See the following website for more information: http://www.rds. colostate.edu/.

Application Information:
Send to Graduate Admissions Committee, Department of Psychology, Colorado State University, 1876 Campus Delivery, Fort Collins, CO 80526-1876. Application available online. URL of online application: http://graduateschool.colostate.edu/prospective-students/apply/index. aspx. Students are admitted in the Fall, application deadline December 1. Counseling and Industrial/Organizational - December 1 application deadline Applied Social, Cognitive, and Cognitive Neuroscience- January 15 application deadline. *Fee:* $50. Fee is waived for McNair, Fulbright, Peace Corps, Project 1000.

Colorado, University of, Boulder
Department of Psychology and Neuroscience
Arts and Sciences
Muenzinger D244, UCB 345
Boulder, CO 80309-0345
Telephone: (303) 492-8662
Fax: (303) 492-2967
E-mail: *info@psych.colorado.edu*
Web: *http://psych.colorado.edu*

Department Information:
1910. Chairperson: Theresa Hernandez. Number of faculty: total—full-time 39, part-time 1; women—full-time 13, part-time 1; total—minority—full-time 9; women minority—full-time 6.

Programs and Degrees Offered:
Listed in the following order: Program area, degree type (T if terminal Master's), number awarded 7/11–6/12. Behavioral Genetics PhD (Doctor of Philosophy) 1, Behavioral Neuroscience PhD (Doctor of Philosophy) 1, Clinical Psychology PhD (Doctor of Philosophy) 2, Cognitive Psychology PhD (Doctor of Philosophy) 3, Social Psychology PhD (Doctor of Philosophy) 3.

APA Accreditation: Clinical PhD (Doctor of Philosophy). Student Outcome Data Website: http://psych.colorado.edu/~clinical/.

Student Applications/Admissions:
Student Applications
Behavioral Genetics PhD (Doctor of Philosophy)—Applications 2012–2013, 14. Total applicants accepted 2012–2013, 0. Number full-time enrolled (new admits only) 2012–2013, 0. Number part-time enrolled (new admits only) 2012–2013, 0. Total enrolled 2012–2013 full-time, 10. Total enrolled 2012–2013 part-time, 0. Openings 2013–2014, 2. The median number of years required for completion of a degree in 2012–2013 were 5. The number of students enrolled full- and part-time who were dismissed or voluntarily withdrew from this program area in 2012–2013 were 0. *Behavioral Neuroscience PhD (Doctor of Philosophy)*—Applications 2012–2013, 110. Total applicants accepted 2012–2013, 2. Number full-time enrolled (new admits only) 2012–2013, 2. Total enrolled 2012–2013 full-time, 18. Total enrolled 2012–2013 part-time, 0. Openings 2013–2014, 3. The median number of years required for completion of a degree in 2012–2013 were 5. The number of students enrolled full- and part-time who were dismissed or voluntarily withdrew from this program area in 2012–2013 were 1. *Clinical Psychology PhD (Doctor of Philosophy)*—Applications 2012–2013, 206. Total applicants accepted 2012–

2013, 6. Number full-time enrolled (new admits only) 2012–2013, 4. Total enrolled 2012–2013 full-time, 22. Total enrolled 2012–2013 part-time, 0. Openings 2013–2014, 4. The number of students enrolled full- and part-time who were dismissed or voluntarily withdrew from this program area in 2012–2013 were 1. *Cognitive Psychology PhD (Doctor of Philosophy)*—Applications 2012–2013, 138. Total applicants accepted 2012–2013, 8. Number full-time enrolled (new admits only) 2012–2013, 3. Total enrolled 2012–2013 full-time, 24. Openings 2013–2014, 4. The median number of years required for completion of a degree in 2012–2013 were 5. The number of students enrolled full- and part-time who were dismissed or voluntarily withdrew from this program area in 2012–2013 were 1. *Social Psychology PhD (Doctor of Philosophy)*—Applications 2012–2013, 116. Total applicants accepted 2012–2013, 5. Number full-time enrolled (new admits only) 2012–2013, 4. Total enrolled 2012–2013 full-time, 14. Total enrolled 2012–2013 part-time, 0. Openings 2013–2014, 4. The median number of years required for completion of a degree in 2012–2013 were 5. The number of students enrolled full- and part-time who were dismissed or voluntarily withdrew from this program area in 2012–2013 were 0.

Scores: Entries appear in this order: required test or GPA, minimum score (if required), median score of students entering in 2012–2013. *Clinical Psychology PhD (Doctor of Philosophy):* GRE-V no minimum stated, 555, GRE-Q no minimum stated, 630.

Other Criteria: (importance of criteria rated low, medium, or high): GRE scores—high, research experience—high, work experience—medium, extracurricular activity—medium, clinically related public service—medium, GPA—high, letters of recommendation—high, interview—high, statement of goals and objectives—high, undergraduate major in psychology—high, Clinical work experience is only relevant in clinical program. Research experience is critical to admissions to all programs. Undergraduate major or equivalent coursework in psychology required for clinical program and recommended for social program. For additional information on admission requirements, go to http://psych.colorado.edu/grad-appinfo.html.

Student Characteristics: The following represents characteristics of students in 2012–2013 in all graduate psychology programs in the department: Female—full-time 54, part-time 0; Male—full-time 38, part-time 0; African American/Black—full-time 0, part-time 0; Hispanic/Latino(a)—full-time 4, part-time 0; Asian/Pacific Islander—full-time 4, part-time 0; American Indian/Alaska Native—full-time 1, part-time 0; Caucasian/White—full-time 82, part-time 0; Multi-ethnic—full-time 1, part-time 0; students subject to the Americans With Disabilities Act—full-time 1, part-time 0; Unknown ethnicity—full-time 0, part-time 0; International students who hold an F-1 or J-1 Visa—full-time 2, part-time 0.

Financial Information/Assistance:
Tuition for Full-Time Study: *Doctoral:* State residents: per academic year $9,738; Nonstate residents: per academic year $26,208. Tuition is subject to change. See the following website for updates and changes in tuition costs: http://bursar.colorado.edu/tuition-fees/tuition-and-fees-rate-sheets/.

Financial Assistance:

First-Year Students: Teaching assistantships available for first year. Average amount paid per academic year: $16,373. Average number of hours worked per week: 20. Research assistantships available for first year. Average amount paid per academic year: $16,373. Average number of hours worked per week: 20. Traineeships available for first year. Average amount paid per academic year: $20,000. Average number of hours worked per week: 20. Fellowships and scholarships available for first year.

Advanced Students: Teaching assistantships available for advanced students. Average amount paid per academic year: $16,373. Average number of hours worked per week: 20. Research assistantships available for advanced students. Average amount paid per academic year: $17,604. Average number of hours worked per week: 20. Traineeships available for advanced students. Average amount paid per academic year: $20,000. Average number of hours worked per week: 20. Fellowships and scholarships available for advanced students.

Additional Information: Of all students currently enrolled full time, 100% benefited from one or more of the listed financial assistance programs.

Internships/Practica: Doctoral Degree (PhD Clinical Psychology): For those doctoral students for whom a professional psychology internship was required in this program prior to graduation, (7) students applied for an internship in 2011–2012, with (6) students obtaining an internship. Of those students who obtained an internship, (6) were paid internships. Of those students who obtained an internship, (6) students placed in APA/CPA accredited internships, (0) students placed in internships not APA/CPA accredited, but listed with the Association of Psychology Postdoctoral and Internship Programs (APPIC), (0) students placed in internships conforming to guidelines of the Council of Directors of School Psychology Programs (CDSPP), (0) students placed in internships that were not APA/CPA accredited, APPIC or CDSPP listed.

Housing and Day Care: On-campus housing is available. See the following website for more information: http://housing.colorado.edu/residences/graduate-family. On-campus day care facilities are available. See the following website for more information: https://childcare.colorado.edu/.

Employment of Department Graduates:

Master's Degree Graduates: Of those who graduated in the academic year 2011–2012, the following categories and numbers represent the postgraduate activities and employment of master's degree graduates: Enrolled in a postdoctoral residency/fellowship (n/a), employed in independent practice (n/a), total from the above (master's) (0).

Doctoral Degree Graduates: Of those who graduated in the academic year 2011–2012, the following categories and numbers represent the postgraduate activities and employment of doctoral degree graduates: Enrolled in a psychology doctoral program (n/a), enrolled in a postdoctoral residency/fellowship (8), employed in business or industry (2), total from the above (doctoral) (10).

Additional Information:

Orientation, Objectives, and Emphasis of Department: Our emphasis is on training graduate students who have the capability to advance knowledge in the field, and who are committed to applying their knowledge. We emphasize rigorous training in both the theory and methods of psychological research.

Special Facilities or Resources: The Department of Psychology & Neuroscience is housed in a large six-story building that contains space for offices, a clinic and research laboratories. There are extensive research facilities available to students, both in individual laboratories and from the department generally. The department has excellent laboratory facilities for human and animal research. The animal care facilities include those for mice, rats, and bullfrogs. The various labs in the department have access to state-of-the-art hardware, including fluorescent and confocal microscopy capability, CCD video camera for image analysis, and real time PCR optogenetics capabilities as well as various behavioral research setups. We have a new human imaging facility based on a Siemens 3T MRI imager that enables state-of-the-art cognitive neuroscience experiments. In terms of computing facilities, the department provides centralized facilities for departmental mailing lists, data analysis, model development and simulation, and many common computing tasks. The computing facility also has extensive support for development of and running real-time computer-controlled experiments. The facilities of the Institute of Behavioral Genetics, the Institute of Behavioral Science, the Institute of Cognitive Science and the Center for Neuroscience are available to students. Each of these institutes has its own laboratory space and specialized computer facilities.

Information for Students With Physical Disabilities: See the following website for more information: http://disabilityservices.colorado.edu/.

Application Information:
Application available online. URL of online application: http://www.colorado.edu/admissions/graduate/apply. Students are admitted in the Fall, application deadline December 1. *Fee:* $50. $70 international application fee.

Colorado, University of, Colorado Springs
Department of Psychology
Letters, Arts, and Sciences
1420 Austin Bluffs Parkway, P.O. Box 7150
Colorado Springs, CO 80933-7150
Telephone: (719) 255-4500
Fax: (719) 255-4166
E-mail: *ddubois@uccs.edu*
Web: *http://www.uccs.edu/psych*

Department Information:
1965. Chairperson: Dr. Edie Greene. Number of faculty: total—full-time 16, part-time 4; women—full-time 8, part-time 2; total—minority—full-time 1, part-time 1; women minority—full-time 1, part-time 1.

Programs and Degrees Offered:
Listed in the following order: Program area, degree type (T if terminal Master's), number awarded 7/11–6/12. Clinical Psychology MA/MS (Master of Arts/Science) (T) 5, Clinical Psychology PhD (Doctor of Philosophy) 2, Psychological Science MA/MS (Master of Arts/Science) (T) 6.

APA Accreditation: Clinical PhD (Doctor of Philosophy). Student Outcome Data Website: http://www.uccs.edu/psych/graduate-program/phd-program.html.

Student Applications/Admissions:

Student Applications

Clinical Psychology MA/MS (Master of Arts/Science)—Applications 2012–2013, 76. Total applicants accepted 2012–2013, 17. Number full-time enrolled (new admits only) 2012–2013, 6. Number part-time enrolled (new admits only) 2012–2013, 0. Total enrolled 2012–2013 full-time, 24. Total enrolled 2012–2013 part-time, 0. Openings 2013–2014, 12. The median number of years required for completion of a degree in 2012–2013 were 2. The number of students enrolled full- and part-time who were dismissed or voluntarily withdrew from this program area in 2012–2013 were 0. *Clinical Psychology PhD (Doctor of Philosophy)*—Applications 2012–2013, 73. Total applicants accepted 2012–2013, 7. Number full-time enrolled (new admits only) 2012–2013, 5. Total enrolled 2012–2013 full-time, 16. Total enrolled 2012–2013 part-time, 0. Openings 2013–2014, 3. The median number of years required for completion of a degree in 2012–2013 were 5. The number of students enrolled full- and part-time who were dismissed or voluntarily withdrew from this program area in 2012–2013 were 0. *Psychological Science MA/MS (Master of Arts/Science)*—Applications 2012–2013, 29. Total applicants accepted 2012–2013, 15. Number full-time enrolled (new admits only) 2012–2013, 7. Number part-time enrolled (new admits only) 2012–2013, 0. Total enrolled 2012–2013 full-time, 23. Total enrolled 2012–2013 part-time, 0. Openings 2013–2014, 7. The median number of years required for completion of a degree in 2012–2013 were 2. The number of students enrolled full- and part-time who were dismissed or voluntarily withdrew from this program area in 2012–2013 were 0.

Scores: Entries appear in this order: required test or GPA, minimum score (if required), median score of students entering in 2012–2013. *Clinical Psychology MA/MS (Master of Arts/Science):* GRE-V no minimum stated, 159, GRE-Q no minimum stated, 152, GRE-Analytical no minimum stated, 4.5, overall undergraduate GPA no minimum stated, 3.56, psychology GPA no minimum stated; *Clinical Psychology PhD (Doctor of Philosophy):* GRE-V no minimum stated, 159, GRE-Q no minimum stated, 154, GRE-Analytical no minimum stated, 5.0, overall undergraduate GPA no minimum stated, 3.75; *Psychological Science MA/MS (Master of Arts/Science):* GRE-V no minimum stated, 155, GRE-Q no minimum stated, 151, GRE-Analytical no minimum stated, 4.0, overall undergraduate GPA no minimum stated, 3.56, psychology GPA no minimum stated.

Other Criteria: (importance of criteria rated low, medium, or high): GRE scores—high, research experience—medium, work experience—low, extracurricular activity—medium, clinically related public service—medium, GPA—medium, letters of recommendation—medium, interview—medium, statement of goals and objectives—medium, undergraduate major in psychology—medium, specific undergraduate psychology courses taken—medium, For the Psychological Science MA program, clinically related public service is not required. Interviews are only for applicants to the doctoral program. MA applicants do not need to complete an interview as part of the application process.

Student Characteristics: The following represents characteristics of students in 2012–2013 in all graduate psychology programs in the department: Female—full-time 47, part-time 0; Male—full-time 16, part-time 0; African American/Black—full-time 2, part-time 0; Hispanic/Latino(a)—full-time 2, part-time 0; Asian/Pacific Islander—full-time 5, part-time 0; American Indian/Alaska Native—full-time 0, part-time 0; Caucasian/White—full-time 54, part-time 0; Multi-ethnic—full-time 0, part-time 0; students subject to the Americans With Disabilities Act—full-time 0, part-time 0; Unknown ethnicity—full-time 0, part-time 0; International students who hold an F-1 or J-1 Visa—full-time 2, part-time 0.

Financial Information/Assistance:

Tuition for Full-Time Study: *Master's:* State residents: $581 per credit hour; Nonstate residents: $1,056 per credit hour. *Doctoral:* State residents: $655 per credit hour; Nonstate residents: $1,122 per credit hour. Tuition is subject to change. Additional fees are assessed to students beyond the costs of tuition for the following: University set fees; psychology program fee. Tuition costs vary by program. See the following website for updates and changes in tuition costs: http://www.uccs.edu/bursar/estimate-your-total-bill.html.

Financial Assistance:

First-Year Students: Teaching assistantships available for first year. Average amount paid per academic year: $3,600. Average number of hours worked per week: 7. Apply by March 1. Research assistantships available for first year. Average amount paid per academic year: $5,000. Average number of hours worked per week: 10. Apply by March 1. Fellowships and scholarships available for first year. Average amount paid per academic year: $3,000. Apply by March 1.

Advanced Students: Teaching assistantships available for advanced students. Average amount paid per academic year: $3,600. Average number of hours worked per week: 7. Apply by March 1. Research assistantships available for advanced students. Average amount paid per academic year: $5,000. Average number of hours worked per week: 10. Apply by March 1. Traineeships available for advanced students. Average amount paid per academic year: $20,000. Fellowships and scholarships available for advanced students. Average amount paid per academic year: $3,000. Apply by March 1.

Additional Information: Of all students currently enrolled full time, 65% benefited from one or more of the listed financial assistance programs. Application and information available online at: http://www.uccs.edu/~finaid/.

Internships/Practica: Doctoral Degree (PhD Clinical Psychology): For those doctoral students for whom a professional psychology internship was required in this program prior to graduation, (7) students applied for an internship in 2011–2012, with (7) students obtaining an internship. Of those students who obtained an internship, (7) were paid internships. Of those students who obtained an internship, (7) students placed in APA/CPA accredited internships, (0) students placed in internships not APA/CPA accredited, but listed with the Association of Psychology Postdoctoral and Internship Programs (APPIC), (0) students placed in internships conforming to guidelines of the Council of Directors of School Psychology Programs (CDSPP), (0) students placed in internships that were not APA/CPA accredited, APPIC or CDSPP listed. Master's Degree (MA/MS Clinical Psychology):

An internship experience, such as a final research project or "capstone" experience is required of graduates. Master's Degree (MA/MS Psychological Science): An internship experience, such as a final research project or "capstone" experience is required of graduates. Required practicum experiences for MA Clinical and PhD Clinical are completed at the departmental CU Aging Center, the CU Counseling Center, or in community placements under licensed supervision (e.g., school settings, community health centers, state mental health facility, domestic violence center, inpatient psychiatric hospital). The goal of these experiences is to expose students to clinical settings, to roles of clinical psychologists, and to begin the development of clinical skills.

Housing and Day Care: On-campus housing is available. See the following website for more information: http://www.uccs.edu/residence/index.html. On-campus day care facilities are available. See the following website for more information: http://www.uccs.edu/~fdc/.

Employment of Department Graduates:
Master's Degree Graduates: Of those who graduated in the academic year 2011–2012, the following categories and numbers represent the postgraduate activities and employment of master's degree graduates: Enrolled in a postdoctoral residency/fellowship (n/a), employed in independent practice (n/a), total from the above (master's) (0).
Doctoral Degree Graduates: Of those who graduated in the academic year 2011–2012, the following categories and numbers represent the postgraduate activities and employment of doctoral degree graduates: Enrolled in a psychology doctoral program (n/a), total from the above (doctoral) (0).

Additional Information:
Orientation, Objectives, and Emphasis of Department: The MA program places special emphasis in general areas of applied clinical practice and general experimental psychology. The MA training will enable a student to prepare for a doctoral program, teach in community colleges, work under a licensed psychologist in private and public agencies, work in university counseling centers, or work as a researcher in a variety of organizations. A research thesis is required of all students. There is a broad range of faculty research interests including: aging (e.g., psychopathology and psychological treatment of older adults, family dynamics, self-concept development, memory, cognition, and personality), social psychology, psychology and the law, personality, program evaluation, prevention of child abuse, adolescent psychology and psychological trauma. There are optional tracks for Psychology and Law, Trauma Psychology, Cognitive Psychology, or Developmental Psychology for Masters Students. Please see our Web site for additional information. The accredited clinical PhD program has an emphasis in geropsychology.

Special Facilities or Resources: Research facilities include clinical training laboratories with observational capabilities, laboratories for individual and small group research, and a psychophysiological laboratory. Columbine Hall houses a 50-station computer lab that is available for general use. The CU Aging Center, administered through the Psychology Department, is a community-based nonprofit mental health clinic designed to serve the mental health needs of older adults and their families. The mission of the Center is to provide state-of-the-art psychological assessment and treatment services to older persons and their families, to study psychological aging processes, and to train students in clinical psychology and related disciplines.

Information for Students With Physical Disabilities: See the following website for more information: http://www.uccs.edu/~dservice/.

Application Information:
Send to David DuBois, Program Assistant. Application available online. URL of online application: http://www.uccs.edu/gradschl/admissions.html. Students are admitted in the Fall, application deadline January 1. *Fee:* $60. International Application Fee: $75.

Colorado, University of, Denver
Department of Psychology
College of Liberal Arts and Sciences
Campus Box 173, P.O. Box 173364
Denver, CO 80217-3364
Telephone: (303) 556-8565
Fax: (303) 556-3520
E-mail: *anne.beard@ucdenver.edu*
Web: *http://www.ucdenver.edu/academics/colleges/CLAS/Departments/psychology/Pages/Psychology.aspx*

Department Information:
1960. Chairperson: Peter Kaplan, PhD. Number of faculty: total—full-time 19, part-time 2; women—full-time 11, part-time 1; total—minority—full-time 3; women minority—full-time 2.

Programs and Degrees Offered:
Listed in the following order: Program area, degree type (T if terminal Master's), number awarded 7/11–6/12. Clinical Health Psychology PhD (Doctor of Philosophy).

Student Applications/Admissions:
Student Applications
Clinical Health Psychology PhD (Doctor of Philosophy)—Applications 2012–2013, 94. Total applicants accepted 2012–2013, 6. Number full-time enrolled (new admits only) 2012–2013, 6. Total enrolled 2012–2013 full-time, 20. Openings 2013–2014, 5. The number of students enrolled full- and part-time who were dismissed or voluntarily withdrew from this program area in 2012–2013 were 2.
Scores: Entries appear in this order: required test or GPA, minimum score (if required), median score of students entering in 2012–2013. *Clinical Health Psychology PhD (Doctor of Philosophy):* GRE-V 470, 590, GRE-Q 550, 680, overall undergraduate GPA 3.02, 3.80, last 2 years GPA no minimum stated, 3.90.
Other Criteria: (importance of criteria rated low, medium, or high): GRE scores—high, research experience—high, work experience—medium, extracurricular activity—low, clinically related public service—low, GPA—high, letters of recommendation—high, interview—high, statement of goals and objectives—high, undergraduate major in psychology—low, specific undergraduate psychology courses taken—medium.

Student Characteristics: The following represents characteristics of students in 2012–2013 in all graduate psychology programs in

the department: Female—full-time 16, part-time 0; Male—full-time 4, part-time 0; African American/Black—full-time 0, part-time 0; Hispanic/Latino(a)—full-time 1, part-time 0; Asian/Pacific Islander—full-time 2, part-time 0; American Indian/Alaska Native—full-time 0, part-time 0; Caucasian/White—full-time 15, part-time 0; Multi-ethnic—full-time 2, part-time 0; students subject to the Americans With Disabilities Act—full-time 0, part-time 0; Unknown ethnicity—full-time 0, part-time 0; International students who hold an F-1 or J-1 Visa—full-time 0, part-time 0.

Financial Information/Assistance:

Tuition for Full-Time Study: *Doctoral:* State residents: per academic year $8,936, $355 per credit hour; Nonstate residents: per academic year $26,800, $1,055 per credit hour. Tuition is subject to change. Additional fees are assessed to students beyond the costs of tuition for the following: transportation, technology, student services, etc. See the following website for updates and changes in tuition costs: http://www.ucdenver.edu/student-services/resources/CostsAndFinancing.

Financial Assistance:

First-Year Students: Teaching assistantships available for first year. Average amount paid per academic year: $15,000. Average number of hours worked per week: 20. Research assistantships available for first year. Average amount paid per academic year: $15,000. Average number of hours worked per week: 20. Fellowships and scholarships available for first year. Average amount paid per academic year: $15,000.

Advanced Students: Teaching assistantships available for advanced students. Average amount paid per academic year: $15,000. Average number of hours worked per week: 20. Research assistantships available for advanced students. Average amount paid per academic year: $15,000. Average number of hours worked per week: 20. Fellowships and scholarships available for advanced students. Average amount paid per academic year: $15,000.

Additional Information: Of all students currently enrolled full time, 100% benefited from one or more of the listed financial assistance programs. Application and information available online at: http://www.ucdenver.edu/academics/colleges/CLAS/Departments/psychology/Programs/PhD/Pages/Costs-Student-Funding.aspx.

Internships/Practica: Doctoral Degree (PhD Clinical Health Psychology): For those doctoral students for whom a professional psychology internship was required in this program prior to graduation, (3) students applied for an internship in 2011–2012, with (1) students obtaining an internship. Of those students who obtained an internship, (1) were paid internships. Of those students who obtained an internship, (1) students placed in APA/CPA accredited internships, (0) students placed in internships not APA/CPA accredited, but listed with the Association of Psychology Postdoctoral and Internship Programs (APPIC), (0) students placed in internships conforming to guidelines of the Council of Directors of School Psychology Programs (CDSPP), (0) students placed in internships that were not APA/CPA accredited, APPIC or CDSPP listed. Clinical practica are widely available at several community agencies. Past students have completed practica at local hospitals, mental health centers, residential treatment centers, and the division of corrections. All field placements must be approved by the program director in advance.

Housing and Day Care: On-campus housing is available. See the following website for more information: http://www.ucdenver.edu/life/services/housing/Pages/default.aspx. On-campus day care facilities are available. See the following website for more information: http://www.tivoli.org/earlylearning/index.html.

Employment of Department Graduates:

Master's Degree Graduates: Of those who graduated in the academic year 2011–2012, the following categories and numbers represent the postgraduate activities and employment of master's degree graduates: Enrolled in a postdoctoral residency/fellowship (n/a), employed in independent practice (n/a), total from the above (master's) (0).

Doctoral Degree Graduates: Of those who graduated in the academic year 2011–2012, the following categories and numbers represent the postgraduate activities and employment of doctoral degree graduates: Enrolled in a psychology doctoral program (n/a), total from the above (doctoral) (0).

Additional Information:

Orientation, Objectives, and Emphasis of Department: The Clinical Health Psychology programs adheres to the scientist–practitioner model, and training emphasizes the contribution of research to the understanding, treatment, and prevention of human problems, and the application of knowledge that is grounded in scientific evidence. Students are trained to work within the community to use psychological tools and techniques to promote health, prevent and treat illness, and improve the health care system. In addition to coursework, students acquire expertise in research by completing a master's thesis and doctoral dissertation, and demonstrate competence in clinical assessment and intervention through a clinical competency examination along with several applied practicum experiences and a predoctoral internship. The program will apply for accreditation by the APA as a Clinical PhD as soon as allowable by APA rules.

Special Facilities or Resources: In July 2004, the University of Colorado, Downtown Denver Campus (our campus) merged with the University of Colorado Health Sciences Center. There are numerous possibilities for research collaborations with faculty at the Health Sciences Center (renamed Anschutz Medical Campus) in addition to the faculty members in our own department. There are also several affiliated institutions (e.g., AMC Cancer Research Center, The Children's Hospital and Kempe Center, Denver Health Medical Center, National Jewish Health, and the VA) in the area that provide additional opportunities for research collaborations and applied clinical work.

Information for Students With Physical Disabilities: See the following website for more information: http://www.ucdenver.edu/disabilityresources.

Application Information:

Send to Graduate School; University of Colorado Denver; Campus Box 163; 1380 Lawrence Street, Suite 1250; PO Box 173364; Denver, CO 80217-3364. Application available online. URL of online application: http://www.ucdenver.edu/admissions/doctoral/Pages/index.aspx. Students are admitted in the Fall, application deadline December 15. *Fee:* $50. International student application fee: $75.00.

Denver, University of (2012 data)
Child, Family, and School Psychology Program
Morgridge College of Education
1999 East Evans Avenue
Denver, CO 80208
Telephone: (303) 871-2112
Fax: (303) 871-4456
E-mail: *nora.mcpherson@du.edu*
Web: *http://www.du.edu/education/programs/cfsp/index.html*

Department Information:
2003. Program Coordinator: Cynthia Hazel, PhD. Number of faculty: total—full-time 5; women—full-time 5.

Programs and Degrees Offered:
Listed in the following order: Program area, degree type (T if terminal Master's), number awarded 7/11–6/12. Child, Family and School Psychology MA/MS (Master of Arts/Science) (T) 2, Child, Family and School Psychology EdS (School Psychology) 7, Child, Family and School Psychology PhD (Doctor of Philosophy) 2.

Student Applications/Admissions:
Student Applications
Child, Family and School Psychology MA/MS (Master of Arts/ Science)—Applications 2012–2013, 3. Total applicants accepted 2012–2013, 0. Number full-time enrolled (new admits only) 2012–2013, 0. Number part-time enrolled (new admits only) 2012–2013, 0. Total enrolled 2012–2013 full-time, 2. Total enrolled 2012–2013 part-time, 0. Openings 2013–2014, 4. The median number of years required for completion of a degree in 2012–2013 were 2. The number of students enrolled full- and part-time who were dismissed or voluntarily withdrew from this program area in 2012–2013 were 0. *Child, Family and School Psychology EdS (School Psychology)*—Applications 2012–2013, 47. Total applicants accepted 2012–2013, 39. Number full-time enrolled (new admits only) 2012–2013, 15. Number part-time enrolled (new admits only) 2012–2013, 1. Total enrolled 2012–2013 full-time, 45. Total enrolled 2012–2013 part-time, 1. Openings 2013–2014, 14. The median number of years required for completion of a degree in 2012–2013 were 4. The number of students enrolled full- and part-time who were dismissed or voluntarily withdrew from this program area in 2012–2013 were 0. *Child, Family and School Psychology PhD (Doctor of Philosophy)*—Applications 2012–2013, 12. Total applicants accepted 2012–2013, 10. Number full-time enrolled (new admits only) 2012–2013, 2. Number part-time enrolled (new admits only) 2012–2013, 0. Total enrolled 2012–2013 full-time, 13. Total enrolled 2012–2013 part-time, 5. Openings 2013–2014, 3. The median number of years required for completion of a degree in 2012–2013 were 5. The number of students enrolled full- and part-time who were dismissed or voluntarily withdrew from this program area in 2012–2013 were 0.
Other Criteria: (importance of criteria rated low, medium, or high): GRE scores—medium, research experience—medium, work experience—medium, extracurricular activity—medium, clinically related public service—medium, GPA—medium, letters of recommendation—high, interview—high, statement of goals and objectives—high, undergraduate major in psychol-

ogy—low, specific undergraduate psychology courses taken— low. For additional information on admission requirements, go to http://www.du.edu/education/calls/admission.html.

Student Characteristics: The following represents characteristics of students in 2012–2013 in all graduate psychology programs in the department: Female—full-time 52, part-time 6; Male—full-time 7, part-time 1; African American/Black—full-time 0, part-time 0; Hispanic/Latino(a)—full-time 7, part-time 0; Asian/Pacific Islander—full-time 1, part-time 1; American Indian/Alaska Native—full-time 0, part-time 0; Caucasian/White—full-time 51, part-time 6; Multi-ethnic—full-time 0, part-time 0; students subject to the Americans With Disabilities Act—full-time 0, part-time 0; Unknown ethnicity—full-time 0, part-time 0; International students who hold an F-1 or J-1 Visa—full-time 0, part-time 0.

Financial Information/Assistance:
Tuition for Full-Time Study: *Master's:* State residents: $1,026 per credit hour; Nonstate residents: $1,026 per credit hour. *Doctoral:* State residents: $1,026 per credit hour; Nonstate residents: $1,026 per credit hour. Tuition is subject to change. Additional fees are assessed to students beyond the costs of tuition for the following: Technology Fee of $4 per credit hour. Lab fees for certain classes. See the following website for updates and changes in tuition costs: http://www.du.edu/registrar.

Financial Assistance:
First-Year Students: Research assistantships available for first year. Traineeships available for first year. Fellowships and scholarships available for first year.
Advanced Students: Teaching assistantships available for advanced students. Research assistantships available for advanced students. Traineeships available for advanced students. Fellowships and scholarships available for advanced students.
Additional Information: Of all students currently enrolled full time, 95% benefited from one or more of the listed financial assistance programs. Application and information available online at: http://www.du.edu/education/calls/financial-aid/index.html.

Internships/Practica: Doctoral Degree (PhD Child, Family and School Psychology): For those doctoral students for whom a professional psychology internship was required in this program prior to graduation, (1) students applied for an internship in 2011–2012, with (1) students obtaining an internship. Of those students who obtained an internship, (1) were paid internships. Of those students who obtained an internship, (0) students placed in APA/ CPA accredited internships, (0) students placed in internships not APA/CPA accredited, but listed with the Association of Psychology Postdoctoral and Internship Programs (APPIC), (1) students placed in internships conforming to guidelines of the Council of Directors of School Psychology Programs (CDSPP), (0) students placed in internships that were not APA/CPA accredited, APPIC or CDSPP listed. Master's Degree (MA/MS Child, Family and School Psychology): An internship experience, such as a final research project or "capstone" experience is required of graduates. Integrated and well supervised field experiences taken during coursework and as independent placement courses are an integral part of the training of future school psychologists and child and family professionals. Such experiences in total provide opportunities for students to build and reflect upon professional roles and competencies and to master critical professional skills. Field coursework experiences are designed as a developmental Chain of Relevant Experiences (CoRE) where students progress from being Critical Observers, to Directed Participants, to Active Contributors, and ultimately to become Independent Practitioners. Although the structure and content of our field courses differ across degree programs, all students complete practica. EdS and PhD School Psychology Licensure students also complete a 1200-hour (EdS) or 1500-hour (PhD) internship, which can occur over one full year or two consecutive years. Our programmatic field-based coursework includes training and practice in the following: comprehensive assessment of developmental strengths and weaknesses; direct and preventative interventions within home, school, and community settings; communication and collaboration with families and children with diverse life experiences; individual, group, and family crisis counseling; interdisciplinary and transdisciplinary team collaboration in school and community settings; delivery of in-service trainings and presentations; system-wide program evaluation, research, and intervention; applications of emergent technology.

Housing and Day Care: On-campus housing is available. See the following website for more information: http://www.du.edu/housing/. On-campus day care facilities are available.

Employment of Department Graduates:

Master's Degree Graduates: Of those who graduated in the academic year 2011–2012, the following categories and numbers represent the postgraduate activities and employment of master's degree graduates: Enrolled in a psychology doctoral program (0), enrolled in another graduate/professional program (1), enrolled in a postdoctoral residency/fellowship (n/a), employed in independent practice (n/a), employed in an academic position at a university (0), employed in an academic position at a 2-year/4-year college (0), employed in other positions at a higher education institution (0), employed in a professional position in a school system (8), employed in business or industry (0), employed in government agency (0), employed in a community mental health/counseling center (0), employed in a hospital/medical center (0), still seeking employment (0), not seeking employment (0), other employment position (0), do not know (0), total from the above (master's) (9).

Doctoral Degree Graduates: Of those who graduated in the academic year 2011–2012, the following categories and numbers represent the postgraduate activities and employment of doctoral degree graduates: Enrolled in a psychology doctoral program (n/a), enrolled in another graduate/professional program (0), enrolled in a postdoctoral residency/fellowship (0), employed in independent practice (0), employed in an academic position at a university (0), employed in an academic position at a 2-year/4-year college (0), employed in other positions at a higher education institution (0), employed in a professional position in a school system (2), employed in business or industry (0), employed in government agency (0), employed in a community mental health/counseling center (0), employed in a hospital/medical center (0), still seeking employment (0), not seeking employment (0), other employment position (0), do not know (0), total from the above (doctoral) (2).

Additional Information:

Orientation, Objectives, and Emphasis of Department: The Child, Family, & School Psychology (CFSP) program, which stresses serving children in the context of their families and communities, teaches students about psychological factors that influ-

ence human development and learning. Students can be prepared for licensure as school psychologists through the National Association of School Psychologists (NASP) approved EdS degree program or the doctoral program; or for professional careers in a broad range of educational, medical, research, or treatment-oriented service systems serving children from birth through age 21. The program offers a distinctive opportunity to interested students to develop a specialization in early childhood development. The curriculum emphasizes strategies for supporting and intervening with children and families with diverse needs, as well as policy development, research, and program development and evaluation. The CFSP Program provides students expanded career options in schools and the community. As a student in this program, you will have the opportunity to work in a range of educational, medical, research, or treatment-oriented service systems at the local, state and national levels. You will also acquire a broad base of information about typical and atypical development, learning, and biological and environmental contexts that affect these areas. You'll gain an expertise in a wide array of diagnostic, assessment, prevention, intervention, consultation, evaluation and research methods that reinforce expertise within a concentration/area of study.

Special Facilities or Resources: The Child, Family, and School Psychology program resides in a recently constructed technology-rich building, Katherine A. Ruffatto Hall. Our new building provides teleconferencing capabilities, smart classrooms, interactive whiteboards, and a state-of-the-art space dedicated to the Counseling and Educational Services Clinic where students work with community clients. In addition, the Fisher Early Learning Center provides a wide range of supervised opportunities for our students including research, training, and practice with young children and their families.

Information for Students With Physical Disabilities: See the following website for more information: http://www.du.edu/disability/.

Application Information:
Send to Morgridge College of Education Office of Admissions, 1999 East Evans Avenue, Denver, CO 80208. Application available online. URL of online application: http://www.du.edu/education/calls/admission.html. Students are admitted in the Fall, application deadline January 1st. *Fee:* $60.

Denver, University of
Counseling Psychology
Morgridge College of Education
2450 South Vine Street
Denver, CO 80208
Telephone: (303) 871-2509
Fax: (303) 871-4456
E-mail: *psherry@du.edu*
Web: *http://www.du.edu/education/programs/cnp/*

Department Information:
1978. Program Chair: Ruth Chu-Lien Caho. Number of faculty: total—full-time 8, part-time 2; women—full-time 5; total—minority—full-time 4; women minority—full-time 3.

Programs and Degrees Offered:
Listed in the following order: Program area, degree type (T if terminal Master's), number awarded 7/11–6/12. Counseling MA/MS (Master of Arts/Science) (T) 25, Counseling Psychology PhD (Doctor of Philosophy) 6.

APA Accreditation: Counseling PhD (Doctor of Philosophy). Student Outcome Data Website: http://www.du.edu/education/programs/cnp/phd/index.html.

Student Applications/Admissions:
Student Applications
Counseling MA/MS (Master of Arts/Science)—Applications 2012–2013, 125. Total applicants accepted 2012–2013, 80. Number full-time enrolled (new admits only) 2012–2013, 39. Number part-time enrolled (new admits only) 2012–2013, 1. Total enrolled 2012–2013 full-time, 40. Total enrolled 2012–2013 part-time, 1. Openings 2013–2014, 40. The median number of years required for completion of a degree in 2012–2013 were 2. The number of students enrolled full- and part-time who were dismissed or voluntarily withdrew from this program area in 2012–2013 were 1. *Counseling Psychology PhD (Doctor of Philosophy)*—Applications 2012–2013, 135. Total applicants accepted 2012–2013, 12. Number full-time enrolled (new admits only) 2012–2013, 8. Number part-time enrolled (new admits only) 2012–2013, 0. Total enrolled 2012–2013 full-time, 41. Total enrolled 2012–2013 part-time, 0. Openings 2013–2014, 8. The median number of years required for completion of a degree in 2012–2013 were 5. The number of students enrolled full- and part-time who were dismissed or voluntarily withdrew from this program area in 2012–2013 were 0.
Scores: Entries appear in this order: required test or GPA, minimum score (if required), median score of students entering in 2012–2013. *Counseling MA/MS (Master of Arts/Science):* GRE-V 450, 490, GRE-Q 450, 570, GRE-Analytical 3.0, 4.5, overall undergraduate GPA 2.0, 3.6; *Counseling Psychology PhD (Doctor of Philosophy):* GRE-V 450, 530, GRE-Q 450, 640, GRE-Analytical 3.0, 4.5, overall undergraduate GPA 3.07, 3.6.
Other Criteria: (importance of criteria rated low, medium, or high): GRE scores—medium, research experience—high, work experience—high, extracurricular activity—low, clinically related public service—medium, GPA—high, letters of recommendation—high, interview—high, statement of goals and objectives—high, undergraduate major in psychology—medium, specific undergraduate psychology courses taken—low.

Student Characteristics: The following represents characteristics of students in 2012–2013 in all graduate psychology programs in the department: Female—full-time 77, part-time 0; Male—full-time 19, part-time 0; African American/Black—full-time 1, part-time 0; Hispanic/Latino(a)—full-time 11, part-time 0; Asian/Pacific Islander—full-time 6, part-time 0; American Indian/Alaska Native—full-time 0, part-time 0; Caucasian/White—full-time 74, part-time 0; Multi-ethnic—full-time 4, part-time 0; students subject to the Americans With Disabilities Act—full-time 1, part-time 0; Unknown ethnicity—full-time 0, part-time 0; International students who hold an F-1 or J-1 Visa—full-time 8, part-time 0.

Financial Information/Assistance:
Tuition for Full-Time Study: *Master's:* State residents: $1,062 per credit hour; Nonstate residents: $1,062 per credit hour. *Doctoral:* State residents: $1,062 per credit hour; Nonstate residents: $1,062 per credit hour. Tuition is subject to change. Additional fees are assessed to students beyond the costs of tuition for the following: technology fee of $4 per credit hour. See the following website for updates and changes in tuition costs: http://www.du.edu/registrar/regbill/reg_tuitionfees.html.

Financial Assistance:
First-Year Students: Teaching assistantships available for first year. Average amount paid per academic year: $5,000. Average number of hours worked per week: 10. Apply by April 1. Research assistantships available for first year. Average amount paid per academic year: $5,000. Average number of hours worked per week: 10. Apply by April 1. Fellowships and scholarships available for first year. Average number of hours worked per week: 0.
Advanced Students: Teaching assistantships available for advanced students. Average amount paid per academic year: $5,000. Average number of hours worked per week: 10. Apply by April 1. Research assistantships available for advanced students. Average number of hours worked per week: 10. Apply by April 1. Fellowships and scholarships available for advanced students. Average amount paid per academic year: $5,000. Average number of hours worked per week: 0. Apply by April 1.
Additional Information: Of all students currently enrolled full time, 90% benefited from one or more of the listed financial assistance programs. Application and information available online at: http://www.du.edu/education/calls/financial-aid/index.html.

Internships/Practica: Doctoral Degree (PhD Counseling Psychology): For those doctoral students for whom a professional psychology internship was required in this program prior to graduation, (9) students applied for an internship in 2011–2012, with (8) students obtaining an internship. Of those students who obtained an internship, (8) were paid internships. Of those students who obtained an internship, (8) students placed in APA/CPA accredited internships, (0) students placed in internships not APA/CPA accredited, but listed with the Association of Psychology Postdoctoral and Internship Programs (APPIC), (0) students placed in internships conforming to guidelines of the Council of Directors of School Psychology Programs (CDSPP), (0) students placed in internships that were not APA/CPA accredited, APPIC or CDSPP listed. Master's Degree (MA/MS Counseling): An internship experience, such as a final research project or "capstone" experience is required of graduates. Both Doctoral and Master's student complete practica and internship as well as hours in a campus clinic. Most practica and internships are off campus. Doctoral students must complete APA-approved internships (exceptions made in unusual circumstances). Doctoral students have opportunities to complete advanced practica in variety of settings including college counseling centers, hospitals and mental health agencies. MA students complete practica and internships at Denver area sites including adolescent treatment facilities, mental health centers, women's crisis centers, schools, etc.

Housing and Day Care: On-campus housing is available. See the following website for more information: http://www.du.edu/housing/. On-campus day care facilities are available. See the following website for more information: http://www.du.edu/fisher/index.html.

Employment of Department Graduates:

Master's Degree Graduates: Of those who graduated in the academic year 2011–2012, the following categories and numbers represent the postgraduate activities and employment of master's degree graduates: Enrolled in a psychology doctoral program (7), enrolled in another graduate/professional program (2), enrolled in a postdoctoral residency/fellowship (n/a), employed in independent practice (n/a), employed in other positions at a higher education institution (1), employed in a community mental health/counseling center (4), employed in a hospital/medical center (1), still seeking employment (1), do not know (16), total from the above (master's) (32).

Doctoral Degree Graduates: Of those who graduated in the academic year 2011–2012, the following categories and numbers represent the postgraduate activities and employment of doctoral degree graduates: Enrolled in a psychology doctoral program (n/a), enrolled in a postdoctoral residency/fellowship (6), employed in an academic position at a university (1), employed in an academic position at a 2-year/4-year college (1), employed in government agency (2), employed in a community mental health/counseling center (1), employed in a hospital/medical center (2), total from the above (doctoral) (13).

Additional Information:

Orientation, Objectives, and Emphasis of Department: As a graduate student in the Counseling Psychology program, you'll develop the skills necessary to become an effective practitioner, researcher, and/or leader in your field. Our goal is to develop professionals who are insightful and self-reflective, who are innovative risk takers and superior critical thinkers. Our highly selective doctoral program is accredited by the American Psychological Association and is well known for providing access to high quality internships for our students. We want our students not only to demonstrate accurate and current knowledge, but to have expertise related to the many issues confronting society and to have the skills to create effective strategies and approaches to address these challenges. To work professionally in counseling psychology at the master's or doctoral level, you will need a strong background in the practice of counseling and psychotherapy, as well as knowledge of the scientific foundations of psychology in order to evaluate and think critically about your practice.

Special Facilities or Resources: PhD students are required to complete a minor in one of two APA-approved clinical psychology programs on campus. Microcomputers and video equipment are available for use in conjunction with coursework. An in-house clinic is available. Students are required to spend one evening a week for two quarters in the clinic. Intensive supervision is provided.

Information for Students With Physical Disabilities: See the following website for more information: http://www.du.edu/studentlife/disability/dsp/index.html.

Application Information:
Send to Graduate Studies, Office of Admission, 2199 South University Boulevard, Denver, CO 80208-0302. Application available online. URL of online application: http://www.du.edu/education/calls/admission.html. Students are admitted in the Fall, application deadline

December 15. Master's Degree in Counseling application deadline is January 15. For the Doctorate in Counseling Psychology, the deadline is December 15. *Fee: $65.*

Denver, University of
Department of Psychology
Frontier Hall, 2155 South Race Street
Denver, CO 80208
Telephone: (303) 871-3803
Fax: (303) 871-4747
E-mail: *daniel.mcintosh@du.edu*
Web: *http://www.du.edu/psychology*

Department Information:
1952. Chairperson: Daniel N. McIntosh. Number of faculty: total—full-time 18, part-time 2; women—full-time 7, part-time 2; total—minority—full-time 3, part-time 1; women minority—full-time 1, part-time 1.

Programs and Degrees Offered:
Listed in the following order: Program area, degree type (T if terminal Master's), number awarded 7/11–6/12. Clinical Child Psychology PhD (Doctor of Philosophy) 4, Developmental Psychology PhD (Doctor of Philosophy) 1, Social Psychology PhD (Doctor of Philosophy) 2, Cognitive Psychology PhD (Doctor of Philosophy) 1, Developmental Cognitive Neuroscience PhD (Doctor of Philosophy) 5, Affective Science PhD (Doctor of Philosophy) 2.

APA Accreditation: Clinical PhD (Doctor of Philosophy). Student Outcome Data Website: http://www.du.edu/psychology/research/child_clinical_breakdown.htm.

Student Applications/Admissions:
Student Applications

Clinical Child Psychology PhD (Doctor of Philosophy)—Applications 2012–2013, 290. Total applicants accepted 2012–2013, 10. Number full-time enrolled (new admits only) 2012–2013, 4. Total enrolled 2012–2013 full-time, 33. Total enrolled 2012–2013 part-time, 0. Openings 2013–2014, 4. The median number of years required for completion of a degree in 2012–2013 were 6. The number of students enrolled full- and part-time who were dismissed or voluntarily withdrew from this program area in 2012–2013 were 0. *Developmental Psychology PhD (Doctor of Philosophy)*—Applications 2012–2013, 26. Total applicants accepted 2012–2013, 2. Number full-time enrolled (new admits only) 2012–2013, 2. Total enrolled 2012–2013 full-time, 6. Total enrolled 2012–2013 part-time, 0. Openings 2013–2014, 2. The median number of years required for completion of a degree in 2012–2013 were 6. The number of students enrolled full- and part-time who were dismissed or voluntarily withdrew from this program area in 2012–2013 were 0. *Social Psychology PhD (Doctor of Philosophy)*—Applications 2012–2013, 42. Total applicants accepted 2012–2013, 2. Number full-time enrolled (new admits only) 2012–2013, 1. Total enrolled 2012–2013 full-time, 5. Openings 2013–2014, 2. The median number of years required for completion of a degree in 2012–2013 were 6. The number of students enrolled full- and part-time who were dismissed or voluntarily withdrew from this program area in 2012–2013 were 2. *Cognitive Psychology PhD (Doctor of Philosophy)*—Applications 2012–2013, 26. Total applicants accepted 2012–2013, 1. Number full-time enrolled (new admits only) 2012–2013, 0. Total enrolled 2012–2013 full-time, 4. Openings 2013–2014, 2. The median number of years required for completion of a degree in 2012–2013 were 6. The number of students enrolled full- and part-time who were dismissed or voluntarily withdrew from this program area in 2012–2013 were 0. *Developmental Cognitive Neuroscience PhD (Doctor of Philosophy)*—Applications 2012–2013, 80. Total applicants accepted 2012–2013, 7. Number full-time enrolled (new admits only) 2012–2013, 5. Total enrolled 2012–2013 full-time, 24. Openings 2013–2014, 4. The median number of years required for completion of a degree in 2012–2013 were 6. The number of students enrolled full- and part-time who were dismissed or voluntarily withdrew from this program area in 2012–2013 were 0. *Affective Science PhD (Doctor of Philosophy)*—Applications 2012–2013, 42. Total applicants accepted 2012–2013, 2. Number full-time enrolled (new admits only) 2012–2013, 1. Total enrolled 2012–2013 full-time, 5. Openings 2013–2014, 2. The median number of years required for completion of a degree in 2012–2013 were 6. The number of students enrolled full- and part-time who were dismissed or voluntarily withdrew from this program area in 2012–2013 were 2.

Scores: Entries appear in this order: required test or GPA, minimum score (if required), median score of students entering in 2012–2013. *Clinical Child Psychology PhD (Doctor of Philosophy)*: GRE-V no minimum stated, 600, GRE-Q no minimum stated, 750, GRE-Analytical no minimum stated, 4.75; *Developmental Psychology PhD (Doctor of Philosophy)*: GRE-V no minimum stated, 675, GRE-Q no minimum stated, 775, GRE-Analytical no minimum stated, 5.0, overall undergraduate GPA no minimum stated, 3.69; *Social Psychology PhD (Doctor of Philosophy)*: GRE-V no minimum stated, 550, GRE-Q no minimum stated, 690, GRE-Analytical no minimum stated, 5; *Cognitive Psychology PhD (Doctor of Philosophy)*: GRE-V no minimum stated, 570, GRE-Q no minimum stated, 660, GRE-Analytical no minimum stated, 5.0; *Developmental Cognitive Neuroscience PhD (Doctor of Philosophy)*: GRE-V no minimum stated, 640, GRE-Q no minimum stated, 750, GRE-Analytical no minimum stated, 5.5; *Affective Science PhD (Doctor of Philosophy)*: GRE-V no minimum stated, 550, GRE-Q no minimum stated, 690, GRE-Analytical no minimum stated, 4.0, overall undergraduate GPA no minimum stated, 4.0.

Other Criteria: (importance of criteria rated low, medium, or high): GRE scores—high, research experience—high, work experience—medium, extracurricular activity—medium, clinically related public service—high, GPA—high, letters of recommendation—high, interview—high, statement of goals and objectives—high. For additional information on admission requirements, go to http://www.du.edu/psychology/graduate/admission.htm.

Student Characteristics: The following represents characteristics of students in 2012–2013 in all graduate psychology programs in the department: Female—full-time 48, part-time 0; Male—full-time 3, part-time 0; African American/Black—full-time 2, part-time 0; Hispanic/Latino(a)—full-time 3, part-time 0; Asian/Pacific Islander—full-time 8, part-time 0; American Indian/Alaska Native—full-time 0, part-time 0; Caucasian/White—full-time 37, part-time 0; Multi-ethnic—full-time 1, part-time 0; students sub-

ject to the Americans With Disabilities Act—full-time 0, part-time 0; Unknown ethnicity—full-time 0, part-time 0; International students who hold an F-1 or J-1 Visa—full-time 5, part-time 0.

Financial Information/Assistance:
Tuition for Full-Time Study: *Doctoral:* State residents: per academic year $33,120, $1,104 per credit hour; Nonstate residents: per academic year $33,120, $1,104 per credit hour. See the following website for updates and changes in tuition costs: http://www.du.edu/registrar/regbill/reg_tuitionrates.html.

Financial Assistance:
First-Year Students: Teaching assistantships available for first year. Average amount paid per academic year: $20,000. Average number of hours worked per week: 20. Research assistantships available for first year. Average amount paid per academic year: $20,000. Average number of hours worked per week: 20.

Advanced Students: Teaching assistantships available for advanced students. Average amount paid per academic year: $20,000. Average number of hours worked per week: 20. Research assistantships available for advanced students. Average amount paid per academic year: $20,000. Average number of hours worked per week: 20.

Additional Information: Of all students currently enrolled full time, 100% benefited from one or more of the listed financial assistance programs. Application and information available online at: http://www.du.edu/psychology/graduate/student_support.htm.

Internships/Practica: Doctoral Degree (PhD Clinical Child Psychology): For those doctoral students for whom a professional psychology internship was required in this program prior to graduation, (6) students applied for an internship in 2011–2012, with (6) students obtaining an internship. Of those students who obtained an internship, (6) were paid internships. Of those students who obtained an internship, (6) students placed in APA/CPA accredited internships, (0) students placed in internships not APA/CPA accredited, but listed with the Association of Psychology Postdoctoral and Internship Programs (APPIC), (0) students placed in internships conforming to guidelines of the Council of Directors of School Psychology Programs (CDSPP), (0) students placed in internships that were not APA/CPA accredited, APPIC or CDSPP listed. The department offers two clinical training facilities: the Child and Family Clinic and the Developmental Neuropsychology Clinic. The Child and Family Clinic provides training in assessment and psychotherapy with children, families, and adults. The Neuropsychology Clinic provides specialized training in assessment of learning disorders, mainly in school-age children. Thus, a considerable amount of clinical training is provided within our Department by faculty supervisors, ensuring that each clinical student is solidly grounded in both assessment and treatment. Clinical students also typically do externships in the community, at sites such as local hospitals, day treatment programs, and other community agencies. Graduate students who are not in clinical can also get experience with patient populations either by internships in the neuropsychology clinic or through research in labs that study developmental disorders.

Housing and Day Care: On-campus housing is available. See the following website for more information: http://www.du.edu/housing/apartments/. On-campus day care facilities are available.

See the following website for more information: http://www.du.edu/fisher/.

Employment of Department Graduates:

Master's Degree Graduates: Of those who graduated in the academic year 2011–2012, the following categories and numbers represent the postgraduate activities and employment of master's degree graduates: Enrolled in a postdoctoral residency/fellowship (n/a), employed in independent practice (n/a), total from the above (master's) (0).

Doctoral Degree Graduates: Of those who graduated in the academic year 2011–2012, the following categories and numbers represent the postgraduate activities and employment of doctoral degree graduates: Enrolled in a psychology doctoral program (n/a), enrolled in a postdoctoral residency/fellowship (4), employed in an academic position at a 2-year/4-year college (2), employed in business or industry (1), employed in a hospital/medical center (1), total from the above (doctoral) (8).

Additional Information:

Orientation, Objectives, and Emphasis of Department: Programs are oriented toward training students to pursue careers in research, teaching, and professional practice. They include Affective Science, Clinical Child, Cognitive, Developmental, and Social, as well as Developmental Cognitive Neuroscience, a program open to students in any of the other programs, and that fosters an interdisciplinary approach to cognitive, affective, and social neuroscience. The department has one of the few APA-accredited child clinical programs, and has been ranked very highly in past rankings by the American Psychological Society for publication impact. We value inclusive excellence and recognize that the success of our department and university depends on including a rich diversity of constituents. The department offers close collaborative relationships between faculty and students, with an emphasis on individualized tutorial relationships. The department's atmosphere encourages collaboration and offers students the freedom to seek out and work with multiple faculty members as fits the student's evolving interests. Our students are successful in publishing in prestigious journals, in winning predoctoral grants, and obtaining their first choice for clinical internships. Situated at the foot of the Rocky Mountains, Denver combines urban culture with readily accessible skiing, hiking, and biking in a climate that has over 300 days of sunshine.

Special Facilities or Resources: Our labs are custom-designed for the kinds of research conducted in our department. They include the Center for Marital and Family Studies, the Relationship Center, the Developmental Neuropsychology Center, the Cognitive Neuroscience Lab, the Reading & Language Lab, the Emotion Regulation Lab, the Center for Infant Development, the Center for Research on Family Stress, the Perception/Action Lab, the Emotion and Coping Lab, the Traumatic Stress Studies Lab, the Mechanisms of Cognitive Control Lab, the Affective Neuroscience Lab, the Social Perception and Attitudes Lab, the Child Health and Development Lab and the Neurodevelopmental Research Program. Labs are equipped with computers for controlling the presentation of stimuli and the collection of data. Some labs include equipment to measure EDA, ECG, and EMG. The Perception-Action Lab employs eye movement recording methods in children and adults. The Child Health Development Lab is equipped with a modified wet lab for processing saliva samples including a -80 freezer for storage. The Neurodevelopmental Research program is set up to collect and process biological samples including blood and saliva from pregnant women, infants and children. In addition, we have a host of conventional laboratory rooms with one-way observation windows and up-to-date audio and video recording equipment. Finally, we are closely partnered with the neuroimaging facilities at the University of Colorado Health Sciences Center and a genotyping facility at the Institute for Behavioral Genetics at UC-Boulder. The neuroimaging facilities allow us to conduct fMRI and MEG studies. Genotype data allows us to test directly genetic effects on behavior. In addition to research laboratories, the department also maintains its own clinical training facility, the Child Study Center, and houses the Neuropsychology Clinic. Research subjects are available from undergraduate classes, and from nearby schools and the university daycare center, and local hospitals and rehab centers for patients with neuropsychological disorders.

Information for Students With Physical Disabilities: See the following website for more information: http://www.du.edu/studentlife/disability/dsp/index.html.

Application Information:
Send to Graduate Studies Office, University of Denver, 2199 S. University Blvd, Denver, CO 80208. Application available online. URL of online application: http://www.du.edu/apply/graduates/applicationrequirements.html. Students are admitted in the Fall, application deadline December 1. *Fee:* $65.

Denver, University of
Graduate School of Professional Psychology
2460 South Vine Street
Denver, CO 80210
Telephone: (303) 871-3736
Fax: (303) 871-7656
E-mail: *gsppinfo@du.edu*
Web: *http://www.du.edu/gspp/*

Department Information:
1976. Dean: Dr. Shelly Smith-Acuña. Number of faculty: total—full-time 14, part-time 5; women—full-time 7, part-time 3; total—minority—full-time 3, part-time 1; women minority—full-time 1, part-time 1.

Programs and Degrees Offered:
Listed in the following order: Program area, degree type (T if terminal Master's), number awarded 7/11–6/12. Clinical Psychology PsyD (Doctor of Psychology) 23, Forensic Psychology MA/MS (Master of Arts/Science) (T) 25, International Disaster Psychology MA/MS (Master of Arts/Science) (T) 17, Sport and Performance Psychology MA/MS (Master of Arts/Science) (T) 25.

APA Accreditation: Clinical PsyD (Doctor of Psychology). Student Outcome Data Website: http://www.du.edu/gspp/degree-programs/clinical-psychology/overview/program-statistics.html.

Student Applications/Admissions:
Student Applications
Clinical Psychology PsyD (Doctor of Psychology)—Applications 2012–2013, 450. Total applicants accepted 2012–2013, 75.

Number full-time enrolled (new admits only) 2012–2013, 40. Total enrolled 2012–2013 full-time, 131. Total enrolled 2012–2013 part-time, 0. Openings 2013–2014, 35. The median number of years required for completion of a degree in 2012–2013 were 4. The number of students enrolled full- and part-time who were dismissed or voluntarily withdrew from this program area in 2012–2013 were 3. *Forensic Psychology MA/MS (Master of Arts/Science)*—Applications 2012–2013, 87. Total applicants accepted 2012–2013, 44. Number full-time enrolled (new admits only) 2012–2013, 23. Total enrolled 2012–2013 full-time, 48. Total enrolled 2012–2013 part-time, 0. Openings 2013–2014, 25. The median number of years required for completion of a degree in 2012–2013 were 2. The number of students enrolled full- and part-time who were dismissed or voluntarily withdrew from this program area in 2012–2013 were 0. *International Disaster Psychology MA/MS (Master of Arts/Science)*—Applications 2012–2013, 46. Total applicants accepted 2012–2013, 25. Number full-time enrolled (new admits only) 2012–2013, 17. Total enrolled 2012–2013 full-time, 33. Openings 2013–2014, 15. The median number of years required for completion of a degree in 2012–2013 were 2. The number of students enrolled full- and part-time who were dismissed or voluntarily withdrew from this program area in 2012–2013 were 0. *Sport and Performance Psychology MA/MS (Master of Arts/Science)*—Applications 2012–2013, 102. Total applicants accepted 2012–2013, 56. Number full-time enrolled (new admits only) 2012–2013, 21. Total enrolled 2012–2013 full-time, 43. Openings 2013–2014, 25. The median number of years required for completion of a degree in 2012–2013 were 2. The number of students enrolled full- and part-time who were dismissed or voluntarily withdrew from this program area in 2012–2013 were 0.

Scores: Entries appear in this order: required test or GPA, minimum score (if required), median score of students entering in 2012–2013. *Clinical Psychology PsyD (Doctor of Psychology):* GRE-V no minimum stated, 158, GRE-Q no minimum stated, 153, GRE-Analytical no minimum stated, 4.3, overall undergraduate GPA no minimum stated; *Forensic Psychology MA/MS (Master of Arts/Science):* GRE-V no minimum stated, GRE-Q no minimum stated, GRE-Analytical no minimum stated; *International Disaster Psychology MA/MS (Master of Arts/Science):* GRE-V no minimum stated, GRE-Q no minimum stated, GRE-Analytical no minimum stated; *Sport and Performance Psychology MA/MS (Master of Arts/Science):* GRE-V no minimum stated, GRE-Q no minimum stated, GRE-Analytical no minimum stated.

Other Criteria: (importance of criteria rated low, medium, or high): GRE scores—high, research experience—medium, work experience—high, extracurricular activity—high, clinically related public service—high, GPA—high, letters of recommendation—high, interview—high, statement of goals and objectives—high, required essay responses—high. For additional information on admission requirements, go to http://www.du.edu/gspp/admissions/application-faq.html.

Student Characteristics: The following represents characteristics of students in 2012–2013 in all graduate psychology programs in the department: Female—full-time 209, part-time 0; Male—full-time 46, part-time 0; African American/Black—full-time 8, part-time 0; Hispanic/Latino(a)—full-time 8, part-time 0; Asian/Pacific Islander—full-time 11, part-time 0; American Indian/Alaska Native—full-time 3, part-time 0; Caucasian/White—full-time

193, part-time 0; Multi-ethnic—full-time 7, part-time 0; students subject to the Americans With Disabilities Act—full-time 0, part-time 0; Unknown ethnicity—full-time 25, part-time 0; International students who hold an F-1 or J-1 Visa—full-time 0, part-time 0.

Financial Information/Assistance:
Tuition for Full-Time Study: *Master's:* State residents: per academic year $39,744, $1,104 per credit hour; Nonstate residents: per academic year $38,232, $1,104 per credit hour. *Doctoral:* State residents: per academic year $52,992, $1,104 per credit hour; Nonstate residents: per academic year $52,992, $1,104 per credit hour. Tuition is subject to change. See the following website for updates and changes in tuition costs: http://www.du.edu/financialaid/graduate/cost.html.

Financial Assistance:
First-Year Students: Research assistantships available for first year. Average amount paid per academic year: $5,000. Fellowships and scholarships available for first year. Average amount paid per academic year: $5,000.

Advanced Students: Research assistantships available for advanced students. Average amount paid per academic year: $2,500.

Additional Information: Of all students currently enrolled full time, 45% benefited from one or more of the listed financial assistance programs. Application and information available online at: http://www.du.edu/financialaid/graduate/index.html.

Internships/Practica: Doctoral Degree (PsyD Clinical Psychology): For those doctoral students for whom a professional psychology internship was required in this program prior to graduation, (40) students applied for an internship in 2011–2012, with (37) students obtaining an internship. Of those students who obtained an internship, (37) were paid internships. Of those students who obtained an internship, (37) students placed in APA/CPA accredited internships, (0) students placed in internships not APA/CPA accredited, but listed with the Association of Psychology Postdoctoral and Internship Programs (APPIC), (0) students placed in internships conforming to guidelines of the Council of Directors of School Psychology Programs (CDSPP), (0) students placed in internships that were not APA/CPA accredited, APPIC or CDSPP listed. Master's Degree (MA/MS Forensic Psychology): An internship experience, such as a final research project or "capstone" experience is required of graduates. Master's Degree (MA/MS International Disaster Psychology): An internship experience, such as a final research project or "capstone" experience is required of graduates. Master's Degree (MA/MS Sport and Performance Psychology): An internship experience, such as a final research project or "capstone" experience is required of graduates. In addition to participation in the APPIC internship match, the GSPP offers an exclusive consortium of APA-accredited internship sites for which appropriate students may apply.

Housing and Day Care: On-campus housing is available. See the following website for more information: http://www.du.edu/live/housing.html. On-campus day care facilities are available. See the following website for more information: http://www.du.edu/childcare/.

Employment of Department Graduates:

Master's Degree Graduates: Of those who graduated in the academic year 2011–2012, the following categories and numbers represent the postgraduate activities and employment of master's degree graduates: Enrolled in a postdoctoral residency/fellowship (n/a), employed in independent practice (n/a), total from the above (master's) (0).

Doctoral Degree Graduates: Of those who graduated in the academic year 2011–2012, the following categories and numbers represent the postgraduate activities and employment of doctoral degree graduates: Enrolled in a psychology doctoral program (n/a), total from the above (doctoral) (0).

Additional Information:

Orientation, Objectives, and Emphasis of Department: The Graduate School of Professional Psychology focuses on scientifically-based training for applied professional work rather than on the more traditional academic-scientific approach to clinical training. In addition to the basic clinical curriculum, special emphases are available in several areas. Our students should have a probing, questioning stance toward human problems and, therefore, should be: (1) knowledgeable about intra- and interpersonal theories, including assessment and intervention; (2) conversant with relevant issues and techniques in research; (3) sensitive to self and to interpersonal interactions as primary clinical tools; (4) skilled in assessing and effectively intervening in human problems; (5) able to assess effectiveness of outcomes; and (6) aware of current professional and ethical issues. To these ends the programs focus on major social and psychological theories; research training directed toward the consumer rather than the producer of research; technical knowledge of assessment; and intervention in problems involving individuals, families, groups, and institutional systems. Strong emphasis is placed on practicum training. There are no requirements for empirical research output. The Master's degree in Forensic Psychology supplements graduate-level clinical training with course work and practicum experiences in the legal, criminal justice, and law enforcement systems. The Master's degree in International Disaster Psychology supplements graduate-level clinical training with coursework and practicum experiences in trauma, community building, and international field experience.

Special Facilities or Resources: The program offers its own in-house community psychological services center, and varied opportunities are available in many community facilities for the required practicum experiences.

Information for Students With Physical Disabilities: See the following website for more information: http://www.du.edu/studentlife/disability/.

Application Information:

Application available online. URL of online application: http://www.du.edu/apply/graduates/applicationrequirements.html. Students are admitted in the Fall, application deadline December 4. Deadline is December 4 for PsyD program and January 3 for Master's programs. *Fee:* $65.

Northern Colorado, University of
Department of Counseling Psychology
College of Education and Behavioral Sciences
501 20th Street, Box 131
Greeley, CO 80639
Telephone: (970) 351-2731
Fax: (970) 351-2625
E-mail: *diane.greenshields@unco.edu*
Web: *http://www.unco.edu/cebs/counspsych/*

Department Information:

1911. Coordinator and Director of Training: Lia Softas-Nall. Number of faculty: total—full-time 5; women—full-time 2; total—minority—full-time 1; women minority—full-time 1.

Programs and Degrees Offered:

Listed in the following order: Program area, degree type (T if terminal Master's), number awarded 7/11–6/12. Counseling Psychology PhD (Doctor of Philosophy) 5.

APA Accreditation: Counseling PhD (Doctor of Philosophy). Student Outcome Data Website: http://www.unco.edu/cebs/counspsych/studentData.html.

Student Applications/Admissions:

Student Applications

Counseling Psychology PhD (Doctor of Philosophy)—Applications 2012–2013, 147. Total applicants accepted 2012–2013, 7. Number full-time enrolled (new admits only) 2012–2013, 7. Total enrolled 2012–2013 full-time, 35. Openings 2013–2014, 7. The median number of years required for completion of a degree in 2012–2013 were 6. The number of students enrolled full- and part-time who were dismissed or voluntarily withdrew from this program area in 2012–2013 were 0.

Scores: Entries appear in this order: required test or GPA, minimum score (if required), median score of students entering in 2012–2013. *Counseling Psychology PhD (Doctor of Philosophy):* GRE-V 450, 550, GRE-Q 450, 600, GRE-Analytical 3.5, overall undergraduate GPA 3.0, 3.79, last 2 years GPA 3.0, 3.79, Masters GPA 3.0, 3.81.

Other Criteria: (importance of criteria rated low, medium, or high): GRE scores—high, research experience—high, work experience—medium, extracurricular activity—low, clinically related public service—medium, GPA—high, letters of recommendation—high, interview—high, statement of goals and objectives—high, undergraduate major in psychology—medium, specific undergraduate psychology courses taken—low. For additional information on admission requirements, go to http://www.unco.edu/cebs/counspsych/prospective.html.

Student Characteristics: The following represents characteristics of students in 2012–2013 in all graduate psychology programs in the department: Female—full-time 26, part-time 0; Male—full-time 9, part-time 0; African American/Black—full-time 3, part-time 0; Hispanic/Latino(a)—full-time 2, part-time 0; Asian/Pacific Islander—full-time 2, part-time 0; American Indian/Alaska Native—full-time 0, part-time 0; Caucasian/White—full-time 28, part-time 0; Multi-ethnic—full-time 0, part-time 0; students subject to the Americans With Disabilities Act—full-time 1, part-time 0; Unknown ethnicity—full-time 0, part-time 0; Interna-

tional students who hold an F-1 or J-1 Visa—full-time 3, part-time 0.

Financial Information/Assistance:

Tuition for Full-Time Study: *Doctoral:* State residents: per academic year $9,666, $537 per credit hour; Nonstate residents: per academic year $20,754, $1,153 per credit hour. Tuition is subject to change. Additional fees are assessed to students beyond the costs of tuition for the following: Total student fees $63.24/credit hour. Other fees for practica and assessment classes may apply. See the following website for updates and changes in tuition costs: http://www.unco.edu/costs/.

Financial Assistance:

First-Year Students: Research assistantships available for first year. Average amount paid per academic year: $7,705. Average number of hours worked per week: 10. Apply by April 15. Fellowships and scholarships available for first year. Average amount paid per academic year: $1,500. Apply by April 15.

Advanced Students: Teaching assistantships available for advanced students. Average amount paid per academic year: $7,705. Average number of hours worked per week: 10. Research assistantships available for advanced students. Average amount paid per academic year: $7,705. Average number of hours worked per week: 10. Fellowships and scholarships available for advanced students. Average amount paid per academic year: $1,500.

Additional Information: Of all students currently enrolled full time, 85% benefited from one or more of the listed financial assistance programs. Application and information available online at: http://www.unco.edu/cebs/counspsych/cost.html.

Internships/Practica: Doctoral Degree (PhD Counseling Psychology): For those doctoral students for whom a professional psychology internship was required in this program prior to graduation, (8) students applied for an internship in 2011–2012, with (5) students obtaining an internship. Of those students who obtained an internship, (5) were paid internships. Of those students who obtained an internship, (5) students placed in APA/CPA accredited internships, (0) students placed in internships not APA/CPA accredited, but listed with the Association of Psychology Postdoctoral and Internship Programs (APPIC), (0) students placed in internships conforming to guidelines of the Council of Directors of School Psychology Programs (CDSPP), (0) students placed in internships that were not APA/CPA accredited, APPIC or CDSPP listed. Doctoral practica in individual, couples and family, and group take place within our in-house clinic. After their second year students may complete external practica in counseling centers, VAs, community agencies and other agencies. Students are required to do an APA accredited internship.

Housing and Day Care: On-campus housing is available. See the following website for more information: http://www.unco.edu/housing/. No on-campus day care facilities are available.

Employment of Department Graduates:

Master's Degree Graduates: Of those who graduated in the academic year 2011–2012, the following categories and numbers represent the postgraduate activities and employment of master's degree graduates: Enrolled in a postdoctoral residency/fellowship (n/a), employed in independent practice (n/a), total from the above (master's) (0).

Doctoral Degree Graduates: Of those who graduated in the academic year 2011–2012, the following categories and numbers represent the postgraduate activities and employment of doctoral degree graduates: Enrolled in a psychology doctoral program (n/a), enrolled in a postdoctoral residency/fellowship (1), employed in independent practice (3), employed in an academic position at a university (1), employed in other positions at a higher education institution (1), employed in a community mental health/counseling center (4), total from the above (doctoral) (10).

Additional Information:

Orientation, Objectives, and Emphasis of Department: The Counseling Psychology PhD program's educational philosophy is based on the Scientist-Practitioner, or Boulder model. Our program places emphasis on both training clinicians to work with diverse populations, and becoming producers and consumers of research. The faculty view doctoral training as a developmental process in which, through course sequencing and mentoring relationships, students move from a learner role to one of increasing independence and responsibility.

Special Facilities or Resources: The Department has an in house clinic with one way mirror observation capabilities and all sessions can be videorecorded and comments from licensed supervisors can be dubbed onto the video. This facility is built around a central observation area, from which eight counseling rooms, one testing room, two family therapy rooms, one group therapy room, and three play therapy rooms radiate. A Diagnostic Materials Library has an excellent collection of current assessment instruments. The main university library has provided excellent support for the counseling psychology program. Many journals can be retrieved online and from the student's home. Additionally, funding is available for purchasing tests listed in the Mental Measurements Yearbook.

Information for Students With Physical Disabilities: See the following website for more information: http://www.unco.edu/dss.

Application Information:

Send to The Graduate School, University of Northern Colorado, 501 20th Street, Campus Box 135, Greeley, CO 80639. Application available online. URL of online application: http://www.unco.edu/grad/admissions/howtoapply.html. Students are admitted in the Fall, application deadline December 1. *Fee:* $50.

Northern Colorado, University of
School Psychology
Education and Behavioral Sciences
501 20th Street, McKee 248
Greeley, CO 80639
Telephone: (970) 351-2731
Fax: (970) 351-2625
E-mail: *robyn.hess@unco.edu*
Web: *http://www.unco.edu/cebs/SchoolPsych/*

Department Information:

2010. Chairperson: Robyn Hess. Number of faculty: total—full-time 5; women—full-time 3.

Programs and Degrees Offered:
Listed in the following order: Program area, degree type (T if terminal Master's), number awarded 7/11–6/12. School Psychology PhD (Doctor of Philosophy) 4, School Psychology EdS (School Psychology) 6.

APA Accreditation: On Probation PhD (Doctor of Philosophy). Student Outcome Data Website: http://www.unco.edu/cebs/SchoolPsych/phd_psychology/phd_desc.html.

Student Applications/Admissions:

Student Applications

School Psychology PhD (Doctor of Philosophy)—Applications 2012–2013, 20. Total applicants accepted 2012–2013, 12. Number full-time enrolled (new admits only) 2012–2013, 8. Number part-time enrolled (new admits only) 2012–2013, 0. Total enrolled 2012–2013 full-time, 31. Total enrolled 2012–2013 part-time, 10. Openings 2013–2014, 7. The median number of years required for completion of a degree in 2012–2013 were 6. The number of students enrolled full- and part-time who were dismissed or voluntarily withdrew from this program area in 2012–2013 were 0. *School Psychology EdS (School Psychology)*—Applications 2012–2013, 23. Total applicants accepted 2012–2013, 17. Number full-time enrolled (new admits only) 2012–2013, 3. Number part-time enrolled (new admits only) 2012–2013, 0. Total enrolled 2012–2013 full-time, 34. Total enrolled 2012–2013 part-time, 1. Openings 2013–2014, 8. The median number of years required for completion of a degree in 2012–2013 were 3. The number of students enrolled full- and part-time who were dismissed or voluntarily withdrew from this program area in 2012–2013 were 0.

Scores: Entries appear in this order: required test or GPA, minimum score (if required), median score of students entering in 2012–2013. *School Psychology PhD (Doctor of Philosophy):* GRE-V 140, 530, GRE-Q 146, 555, GRE-Analytical 3.5, 4.0, last 2 years GPA 3.0, 3.64; *School Psychology EdS (School Psychology):* GRE-V 140, 440, GRE-Q 146, 510, overall undergraduate GPA 3.0, 3.52.

Other Criteria: (importance of criteria rated low, medium, or high): GRE scores—medium, research experience—medium, work experience—low, extracurricular activity—low, clinically related public service—low, GPA—medium, letters of recommendation—medium, interview—high, statement of goals and objectives—high, These criteria vary between the PhD and EdS. For the PhD, there is a greater emphasis on GREs and research experience. The interview only applies to the PhD program. For additional information on admission requirements, go to http://www.unco.edu/cebs/SchoolPsych/admissions.html.

Student Characteristics: The following represents characteristics of students in 2012–2013 in all graduate psychology programs in the department: Female—full-time 54, part-time 8; Male—full-time 11, part-time 3; African American/Black—full-time 1, part-time 1; Hispanic/Latino(a)—full-time 5, part-time 1; Asian/Pacific Islander—full-time 3, part-time 0; American Indian/Alaska Native—full-time 0, part-time 0; Caucasian/White—full-time 56, part-time 9; Multi-ethnic—full-time 0, part-time 0; students subject to the Americans With Disabilities Act—full-time 1, part-time 0; Unknown ethnicity—full-time 0, part-time 0; International students who hold an F-1 or J-1 Visa—full-time 1, part-time 0.

Financial Information/Assistance:
Tuition for Full-Time Study: *Master's:* State residents: per academic year $11,502, $426 per credit hour; Nonstate residents: per academic year $26,406, $978 per credit hour. *Doctoral:* State residents: per academic year $14,499, $537 per credit hour; Nonstate residents: per academic year $31,131, $1,153 per credit hour. Tuition is subject to change. Additional fees are assessed to students beyond the costs of tuition for the following: Estimated fees per year: $1707. See the following website for updates and changes in tuition costs: http://www.unco.edu/grad/funding/index.html.

Financial Assistance:

First-Year Students: Research assistantships available for first year. Average amount paid per academic year: $8,653. Average number of hours worked per week: 11. Apply by April 15. Fellowships and scholarships available for first year. Average amount paid per academic year: $1,000. Average number of hours worked per week: 0. Apply by June 1.

Advanced Students: Research assistantships available for advanced students. Average amount paid per academic year: $8,653. Average number of hours worked per week: 10. Apply by April 15. Fellowships and scholarships available for advanced students. Average amount paid per academic year: $1,000. Average number of hours worked per week: 0. Apply by June 1.

Additional Information: Of all students currently enrolled full time, 27% benefited from one or more of the listed financial assistance programs. Application and information available online at: http://www.unco.edu/grad/funding/assistantships.html.

Internships/Practica: Doctoral Degree (PhD School Psychology): For those doctoral students for whom a professional psychology internship was required in this program prior to graduation, (4) students applied for an internship in 2011–2012, with (4) students obtaining an internship. Of those students who obtained an internship, (4) were paid internships. Of those students who obtained an internship, (0) students placed in APA/CPA accredited internships, (0) students placed in internships not APA/CPA accredited, but listed with the Association of Psychology Postdoctoral and Internship Programs (APPIC), (0) students placed in internships conforming to guidelines of the Council of Directors of School Psychology Programs (CDSPP), (4) students placed in internships that were not APA/CPA accredited, APPIC or CDSPP listed. All students are required to complete numerous practicum courses prior to graduation. Each course is designed to provide hands-on experience related to skills-based competencies. Students will accrue an estimated 635-710 hours of practicum training prior to internship. Elective practica may be taken in the areas of couples and family counseling, neuropsychology, consultation, and play therapy. Requirements for the School Psychology Internship include at least 1500 hours of supervised experience at the PhD level with supervision from a licensed psychologist/licensed school psychologist. The internship in School Psychology is intended to be an opportunity for students to progressively assume the professional role of a School Psychologist with supervision. The School Psychology internship will include experiences with a variety of populations from early childhood through high school in the areas of: direct and indirect interventions, child advocacy, program development and evaluation, and assessment and diagnosis from Child Find to staffing. It is highly recommended that students apply for an APA Internship through APPIC.

Housing and Day Care: On-campus housing is available. See the following website for more information: http://www.unco.edu/housing/Grad_Students/index.html. No on-campus day care facilities are available.

Employment of Department Graduates:

Master's Degree Graduates: Of those who graduated in the academic year 2011–2012, the following categories and numbers represent the postgraduate activities and employment of master's degree graduates: Enrolled in a postdoctoral residency/fellowship (n/a), employed in independent practice (n/a), employed in a professional position in a school system (6), total from the above (master's) (6).

Doctoral Degree Graduates: Of those who graduated in the academic year 2011–2012, the following categories and numbers represent the postgraduate activities and employment of doctoral degree graduates: Enrolled in a psychology doctoral program (n/a), employed in a professional position in a school system (4), total from the above (doctoral) (4).

Additional Information:

Orientation, Objectives, and Emphasis of Department: The program's training philosophy is based on the scientist–practitioner model. Our goal is to develop professionals who are able to apply psychological and educational principles to improve the psychosocial environments of children (ages birth-21) and their families. Attention is directed toward the development of skills in the assessment of the intellectual, emotional, and social development of children; planning and implementing direct academic and social/emotional interventions with a focus on evidence-based and culturally sensitive practice; and providing individual and systems consultation within schools and the larger community. Foundational aspects of psychological practice, including human learning, development, relevant law, ethical principles and professional practice provide a basis upon which skills in assessment and intervention are built. The faculty believe strongly in the importance of science informing practice and vice versa. As such, we stress the importance of an evidence base for psychological practices, as well as measurement of outcomes in all aspects of practice.

Special Facilities or Resources: The Diagnostic Materials Library (DML) is a library for the exclusive use of school psychology and counseling students and faculty. It contains tests, protocols, textbooks, and other materials that are needed for selected courses. Currently the DML has well over 100 different tests, and there are multiple copies of major academic, cognitive, neuropsychological, behavioral, and personality instruments.

Information for Students With Physical Disabilities: See the following website for more information: http://www.unco.edu/dss/.

Application Information:
Send to Graduate School and International Admissions, University of Northern Colorado, 501 20th Street, Campus Box 135, Greeley, CO 80639. Application available online. URL of online application: http://www.unco.edu/grad/admissions/applying.html. Students are admitted in the Fall, application deadline December 15. *Fee:* $50.

Central Connecticut State University
Department of Psychological Science
1615 Stanley Street
New Britain, CT 06050-4010
Telephone: (860) 832-3100
Fax: (860) 832-3123
E-mail: *bowman@ccsu.edu*
Web: *http://www.ccsu.edu/page.cfm?p=1785*

Department Information:
1967. Chairperson: Dr. Laura Bowman. Number of faculty: total—full-time 22, part-time 19; women—full-time 13, part-time 9; total—minority—full-time 3, part-time 2; women minority—full-time 2, part-time 1.

Programs and Degrees Offered:
Listed in the following order: Program area, degree type (T if terminal Master's), number awarded 7/11–6/12. Community Psychology MA/MS (Master of Arts/Science) (T) 2, General Psychology MA/MS (Master of Arts/Science) (T) 2, Health Psychology MA/MS (Master of Arts/Science) (T) 1.

Student Applications/Admissions:
Student Applications
Community Psychology MA/MS (Master of Arts/Science)—Applications 2012–2013, 9. Total applicants accepted 2012–2013, 4. Number full-time enrolled (new admits only) 2012–2013, 1. Number part-time enrolled (new admits only) 2012–2013, 1. Total enrolled 2012–2013 full-time, 3. Total enrolled 2012–2013 part-time, 5. Openings 2013–2014, 5. The median number of years required for completion of a degree in 2012–2013 were 8. The number of students enrolled full- and part-time who were dismissed or voluntarily withdrew from this program area in 2012–2013 were 0. *General Psychology MA/MS (Master of Arts/Science)*—Applications 2012–2013, 32. Total applicants accepted 2012–2013, 11. Number full-time enrolled (new admits only) 2012–2013, 1. Number part-time enrolled (new admits only) 2012–2013, 2. Total enrolled 2012–2013 full-time, 26. Total enrolled 2012–2013 part-time, 27. Openings 2013–2014, 10. *Health Psychology MA/MS (Master of Arts/Science)*—Applications 2012–2013, 14. Total applicants accepted 2012–2013, 7. Number full-time enrolled (new admits only) 2012–2013, 6. Number part-time enrolled (new admits only) 2012–2013, 1. Total enrolled 2012–2013 full-time, 13. Total enrolled 2012–2013 part-time, 11. Openings 2013–2014, 7.

Scores: Entries appear in this order: required test or GPA, minimum score (if required), median score of students entering in 2012–2013. *Community Psychology MA/MS (Master of Arts/Science):* overall undergraduate GPA 2.75, psychology GPA 3.0; *General Psychology MA/MS (Master of Arts/Science):* overall undergraduate GPA 2.75, psychology GPA 3.0; *Health Psychology MA/MS (Master of Arts/Science):* overall undergraduate GPA 2.75, psychology GPA 3.0.

Other Criteria: (importance of criteria rated low, medium, or high): research experience—medium, work experience—medium, extracurricular activity—low, clinically related public service—medium, GPA—high, letters of recommendation—high, statement of goals and objectives—high, undergraduate major in psychology—low, specific undergraduate psychology courses taken—medium. For additional information on admission requirements, go to http://www.ccsu.edu/page.cfm?p=2303.

Student Characteristics: The following represents characteristics of students in 2012–2013 in all graduate psychology programs in the department: Female—full-time 30, part-time 34; Male—full-time 12, part-time 9; African American/Black—full-time 0, part-time 4; Hispanic/Latino(a)—full-time 5, part-time 3; Asian/Pacific Islander—full-time 1, part-time 1; American Indian/Alaska Native—full-time 0, part-time 0; Caucasian/White—full-time 32, part-time 33; Multi-ethnic—full-time 2, part-time 1; students subject to the Americans With Disabilities Act—full-time 0, part-time 0; Unknown ethnicity—full-time 0, part-time 1; International students who hold an F-1 or J-1 Visa—full-time 2, part-time 0.

Financial Information/Assistance:
Tuition for Full-Time Study: *Master's:* State residents: per academic year $9,307, $498 per credit hour; Nonstate residents: per academic year $20,290, $510 per credit hour. Tuition is subject to change. See the following website for updates and changes in tuition costs: http://www.ccsu.edu/page.cfm?p=768.

Financial Assistance:
First-Year Students: Teaching assistantships available for first year. Average amount paid per academic year: $2,700. Average number of hours worked per week: 10.

Advanced Students: Teaching assistantships available for advanced students. Average amount paid per academic year: $2,700. Average number of hours worked per week: 10.

Additional Information: Of all students currently enrolled full time, 7% benefited from one or more of the listed financial assistance programs. Application and information available online at: http://www.ccsu.edu/page.cfm?p=1186.

Internships/Practica: Master's Degree (MA/MS Community Psychology): An internship experience, such as a final research project or "capstone" experience is required of graduates. Master's Degree (MA/MS General Psychology): An internship experience, such as a final research project or "capstone" experience is required of graduates. Master's Degree (MA/MS Health Psychology): An internship experience, such as a final research project or "capstone" experience is required of graduates. We offer a variety of internships. For students in the community specialization, there are internships in prevention-oriented community programs dealing with substance abuse, teen pregnancy, etc. We also offer internships in developmental and counseling areas.

Housing and Day Care: On-campus housing is available. See the following website for more information: http://www.ccsu.edu/page.cfm?p=2595. On-campus day care facilities are available. See the following website for more information: http://www.ccsu.edu/page.cfm?p=403.

Employment of Department Graduates:
  Master's Degree Graduates: Of those who graduated in the academic year 2011–2012, the following categories and numbers represent the postgraduate activities and employment of master's degree graduates: Enrolled in a postdoctoral residency/fellowship (n/a), employed in independent practice (n/a), total from the above (master's) (0).
  Doctoral Degree Graduates: Of those who graduated in the academic year 2011–2012, the following categories and numbers represent the postgraduate activities and employment of doctoral degree graduates: Enrolled in a psychology doctoral program (n/a), total from the above (doctoral) (0).

Additional Information:
  Orientation, Objectives, and Emphasis of Department: The Department of Psychological Science includes 20 faculty members whose interests cover a wide range of psychological areas. Collectively, the orientation of the department is toward applied areas (clinical, community, health, applied, developmental), with generally little emphasis on animal learning/behavior. The specialization in community psychology focuses heavily on primary prevention. The general specialization is intended to expose students to a broad range of applied areas in psychology, while the one in health psychology prepares students for careers in the field of health psychology. The three specializations have a strong research emphasis.

  Special Facilities or Resources: The Department of Psychological Science has limited space available for human experimental research. The department has a computer laboratory, and the university has very good computer facilities available for student use. Students may also work on applied research projects with faculty through the Institute for Municipal and Regional Policy at the University.

  Information for Students With Physical Disabilities: See the following website for more information: http://www.ccsu.edu/page.cfm?p=3639.

Application Information:
Send to Office of Graduate Admissions, Central CT State University, 1615 Stanley Street, New Britain, CT 06050-4010. Application available online. URL of online application: https://www.applyweb.com/apply/ccsu/menu.html. Students are admitted in the Fall, application deadline May 1; Spring, application deadline November 1. *Fee:* $50.

Connecticut, University of
Department of Psychology
College of Liberal Arts and Sciences
406 Babbidge Road, Unit 1020
Storrs, CT 06269-1020
Telephone: (860) 486-3515
Fax: (860) 486-2760
E-mail: *Jackie.Soroka@uconn.edu*
Web: *http://psychology.uconn.edu*

Department Information:
  1939. Head: James A. Green. Number of faculty: total—full-time 57, part-time 4; women—full-time 27, part-time 2; total—minority—full-time 10, part-time 2; women minority—full-time 4, part-time 1.

Programs and Degrees Offered:
  Listed in the following order: Program area, degree type (T if terminal Master's), number awarded 7/11–6/12. Behavioral Neuroscience PhD (Doctor of Philosophy) 8, Developmental Psychology PhD (Doctor of Philosophy) 1, Clinical Psychology PhD (Doctor of Philosophy) 3, Perception, Action, Cognition PhD (Doctor of Philosophy) 5, Industrial/Organizational Psychology PhD (Doctor of Philosophy) 7, Social Psychology PhD (Doctor of Philosophy) 7.

APA Accreditation: Clinical PhD (Doctor of Philosophy). Student Outcome Data Website: http://psychology.uconn.edu/academics/graduate/phd_clinical.html.

Student Applications/Admissions:
  Student Applications
  Behavioral Neuroscience PhD (Doctor of Philosophy)—Applications 2012–2013, 38. Total applicants accepted 2012–2013, 4. Number full-time enrolled (new admits only) 2012–2013, 3. Number part-time enrolled (new admits only) 2012–2013, 0. Total enrolled 2012–2013 full-time, 18. Total enrolled 2012–2013 part-time, 0. Openings 2013–2014, 3. The median number of years required for completion of a degree in 2012–2013 were 6. The number of students enrolled full- and part-time who were dismissed or voluntarily withdrew from this program area in 2012–2013 were 0. *Developmental Psychology PhD (Doctor of Philosophy)*—Applications 2012–2013, 23. Total applicants accepted 2012–2013, 4. Number full-time enrolled (new admits only) 2012–2013, 4. Number part-time enrolled (new admits only) 2012–2013, 0. Total enrolled 2012–2013 full-time, 19. Total enrolled 2012–2013 part-time, 0. Openings 2013–2014, 4. The median number of years required for completion of a degree in 2012–2013 were 6. The number of students enrolled full- and part-time who were dismissed or voluntarily withdrew from this program area in 2012–2013 were 0. *Clinical Psychology PhD (Doctor of Philosophy)*—Applications 2012–2013, 441. Total applicants accepted 2012–2013, 12. Number full-time enrolled (new admits only) 2012–2013, 9. Number part-time enrolled (new admits only) 2012–2013, 0. Total enrolled 2012–2013 full-time, 55. Total enrolled 2012–2013 part-time, 0. Openings 2013–2014, 10. The median number of years required for completion of a degree in 2012–2013 were 6. The number of students enrolled full- and part-time who were dismissed or voluntarily withdrew from this program area in 2012–2013 were 0. *Perception, Action, Cognition PhD (Doctor of Philosophy)*—Applications 2012–2013, 31. Total applicants accepted 2012–2013, 8. Number full-time enrolled (new admits only) 2012–2013, 5. Number part-time enrolled (new admits only) 2012–2013, 0. Total enrolled 2012–2013 full-time, 27. Total enrolled 2012–2013 part-time, 2. Openings 2013–2014, 5. The median number of years required for completion of a degree in 2012–2013 were 7. The number of students enrolled full- and part-time who were dismissed or voluntarily withdrew from this program area in 2012–2013 were 0. *Industrial/Organizational Psychology PhD (Doctor of Philosophy)*—Applications 2012–2013, 64. Total applicants accepted 2012–2013, 5. Number full-time enrolled (new admits only) 2012–2013, 4. Number part-time enrolled (new admits only) 2012–2013, 0. Total enrolled 2012–2013

full-time, 23. Total enrolled 2012–2013 part-time, 0. Openings 2013–2014, 5. The median number of years required for completion of a degree in 2012–2013 were 6. The number of students enrolled full- and part-time who were dismissed or voluntarily withdrew from this program area in 2012–2013 were 0. *Social Psychology PhD (Doctor of Philosophy)*—Applications 2012–2013, 82. Total applicants accepted 2012–2013, 8. Number full-time enrolled (new admits only) 2012–2013, 4. Number part-time enrolled (new admits only) 2012–2013, 0. Total enrolled 2012–2013 full-time, 21. Total enrolled 2012–2013 part-time, 0. Openings 2013–2014, 8. The median number of years required for completion of a degree in 2012–2013 were 5. The number of students enrolled full- and part-time who were dismissed or voluntarily withdrew from this program area in 2012–2013 were 1.

Scores: Entries appear in this order: required test or GPA, minimum score (if required), median score of students entering in 2012–2013. *Behavioral Neuroscience PhD (Doctor of Philosophy)*: GRE-V no minimum stated, GRE-Q no minimum stated, GRE-Analytical no minimum stated; *Developmental Psychology PhD (Doctor of Philosophy)*: GRE-V no minimum stated, GRE-Q no minimum stated, GRE-Analytical no minimum stated; *Clinical Psychology PhD (Doctor of Philosophy)*: GRE-V no minimum stated, 161, GRE-Q no minimum stated, 162, GRE-Analytical no minimum stated, 5.5; *Perception, Action, Cognition PhD (Doctor of Philosophy)*: GRE-V no minimum stated, GRE-Q no minimum stated, GRE-Analytical no minimum stated; *Industrial/Organizational Psychology PhD (Doctor of Philosophy)*: GRE-V no minimum stated, GRE-Q no minimum stated, GRE-Analytical no minimum stated; *Social Psychology PhD (Doctor of Philosophy)*: GRE-V no minimum stated, GRE-Q no minimum stated, GRE-Analytical no minimum stated.

Other Criteria: (importance of criteria rated low, medium, or high): GRE scores—medium, research experience—high, work experience—low, clinically related public service—low, GPA—medium, letters of recommendation—high, interview—medium, statement of goals and objectives—high, The Clinical Division interviews applicants, by invitation only. The clinical interviews are considered to be high in importance of criteria used for offering admission. The Behavioral Neuroscience Division may interview by invitation or by applicant request, however interviews are not required. The Developmental, Perception, Action, and Cognition, Industrial/Organizational, and Social divisions do not interview applicants as part of the admissions process. For additional information on admission requirements, go to http://www.psychology.uconn. edu/academics/graduate/graduate_program.html.

Student Characteristics: The following represents characteristics of students in 2012–2013 in all graduate psychology programs in the department: Female—full-time 114, part-time 0; Male—full-time 49, part-time 2; African American/Black—full-time 4, part-time 1; Hispanic/Latino(a)—full-time 15, part-time 0; Asian/Pacific Islander—full-time 32, part-time 0; American Indian/Alaska Native—full-time 0, part-time 0; Caucasian/White—full-time 102, part-time 1; Multi-ethnic—full-time 0, part-time 0; students subject to the Americans With Disabilities Act—full-time 1, part-time 0; Unknown ethnicity—full-time 10, part-time 0; International students who hold an F-1 or J-1 Visa—full-time 26, part-time 0.

Financial Information/Assistance:

Tuition for Full-Time Study: *Doctoral:* State residents: per academic year $10,782, $568 per credit hour; Nonstate residents: per academic year $27,990, $1,474 per credit hour. Tuition is subject to change. Additional fees are assessed to students beyond the costs of tuition for the following: gen. univ., infrastructure, matriculation, tech., student acct., transit, student union. See the following website for updates and changes in tuition costs: http://bursar. uconn.edu/tuit_grad_current.html.

Financial Assistance:

First-Year Students: Teaching assistantships available for first year. Average amount paid per academic year: $14,538. Average number of hours worked per week: 15. Research assistantships available for first year. Average amount paid per academic year: $14,538. Average number of hours worked per week: 15. Traineeships available for first year. Average amount paid per academic year: $26,016. Fellowships and scholarships available for first year. Average amount paid per academic year: $2,600. Average number of hours worked per week: 0.

Advanced Students: Teaching assistantships available for advanced students. Average amount paid per academic year: $17,007. Average number of hours worked per week: 15. Research assistantships available for advanced students. Average amount paid per academic year: $17,007. Average number of hours worked per week: 15. Traineeships available for advanced students. Average amount paid per academic year: $26,016. Fellowships and scholarships available for advanced students. Average amount paid per academic year: $2,600. Average number of hours worked per week: 0.

Additional Information: Of all students currently enrolled full time, 93% benefited from one or more of the listed financial assistance programs. Application and information available online at: http://www.psychology.uconn.edu/academics/graduate/graduate_program.html.

Internships/Practica: Doctoral Degree (PhD Clinical Psychology): For those doctoral students for whom a professional psychology internship was required in this program prior to graduation, (12) students applied for an internship in 2011–2012, with (10) students obtaining an internship. Of those students who obtained an internship, (10) were paid internships. Of those students who obtained an internship, (9) students placed in APA/CPA accredited internships, (1) students placed in internships not APA/CPA accredited, but listed with the Association of Psychology Postdoctoral and Internship Programs (APPIC), (0) students placed in internships conforming to guidelines of the Council of Directors of School Psychology Programs (CDSPP), (0) students placed in internships that were not APA/CPA accredited, APPIC or CDSPP listed.

Housing and Day Care: On-campus housing is available. See the following website for more information: http://www.reslife.uconn. edu/graduate_housing.html. On-campus day care facilities are available. See the following website for more information: http:// www.childlabs.uconn.edu.

Employment of Department Graduates:

Master's Degree Graduates: Of those who graduated in the academic year 2011–2012, the following categories and numbers represent the postgraduate activities and employment of master's degree graduates: Enrolled in a postdoctoral residency/fellowship

(n/a), employed in independent practice (n/a), total from the above (master's) (0).

Doctoral Degree Graduates: Of those who graduated in the academic year 2011–2012, the following categories and numbers represent the postgraduate activities and employment of doctoral degree graduates: Enrolled in a psychology doctoral program (n/a), enrolled in a postdoctoral residency/fellowship (17), employed in an academic position at a university (4), employed in an academic position at a 2-year/4-year college (2), employed in business or industry (4), employed in government agency (2), do not know (2), total from the above (doctoral) (31).

Additional Information:

Orientation, Objectives, and Emphasis of Department: The department is focused on a dual mission of pursuing excellence in both research and teaching, while not losing sight of its broader mission to engage in meaningful outreach. The department is comprised of six divisions, each of which offers doctoral training in one or more areas of concentration as follows: (1) Behavioral Neuroscience (biopsychology, neuroscience); (2) Clinical Psychology; (3) Developmental Psychology; (4) Perception, Action, Cognition (ecological psychology, language and cognition); (5) Industrial/Organizational Psychology; and (6) Social Psychology. Interdivisional areas of strength, and targets for future growth, include (a) quantitative research methods, (b) health psychology, (c) cognitive science, (d) neuropsychology, and (e) developmental psychopathology. The pursuit of new knowledge (i.e., discovery through research) is the dominant emphasis of the department. This emphasis relies heavily on the interactive contributions from faculty, graduate students, and undergraduate students. In addition, the department's Graduate Student Teacher Training Program provides multiple, mentored teaching experiences for graduate students interested in pursuing a career that combines research with teaching. Despite these varied emphases and endeavors, the department continues to maintain a collegial and supportive atmosphere where individual contributions are both recognized and rewarded.

Special Facilities or Resources: Multiple facilities, resources, and opportunities for research and training endeavors are not only available, but also are encouraged, fostered, and strongly supported by the department. These opportunities include existing and strong research collaborations with the University of Connecticut Health Center, with Haskins Laboratories in New Haven, with the Olin Neuropsychiatry Research Center at the Institute of Living in Hartford, and with a wide variety of research and internship opportunities available at multiple industries, hospitals, mental institutions, and school systems located in Connecticut. In addition, the department makes available and encourages research and training opportunities with units located within the department and/or within the University, including the Center for Health Intervention and Prevention, the Psychological Services Clinic (PSC), the Industrial Psychology Applications Center (IPAC), and the Center for the Ecological Study of Perception and Action (CESPA). Collectively, these collaborative relationships provide graduate students with a myriad of opportunities to pursue their research and training experience objectives.

Information for Students With Physical Disabilities: See the following website for more information: http://www.csd.uconn.edu.

Application Information:
Send to University of Connecticut, Graduate School, 438 Whitney Road Ext., Unit 1152, Storrs, CT 06269-1152. Application available online. URL of online application: https://app.applyyourself.com/?id=uconngrad. Students are admitted in the Fall, application deadline December 1. Clinical Psychology program deadline: December 1st; Social Psychology and Industrial/Organizational Psychology programs deadline: December 15th; Behavioral Neuroscience, Developmental Psychology, and Perception, Action, Cognition programs deadline: January 1st. *Fee:* $75.

Connecticut, University of (2012 data)
School Psychology Program
NEAG School of Education
249 Glenbrook Road, Unit 2064
Storrs, CT 06269-2064
Telephone: (860) 486-4031
Fax: (860) 486-0180
E-mail: *thomas.kehle@uconn.edu*
Web: *http://www.education.uconn.edu/departments/epsy/*

Department Information:
1960. Director, School Psychology Program: Thomas J. Kehle. Number of faculty: total—full-time 4, part-time 1; women—full-time 3, part-time 1.

Programs and Degrees Offered:
Listed in the following order: Program area, degree type (T if terminal Master's), number awarded 7/11–6/12. School Psychology PhD (Doctor of Philosophy) 3, School Psychology MA/MS (Master of Arts/Science) 6.

APA Accreditation: School PhD (Doctor of Philosophy).

Student Applications/Admissions:
Student Applications

School Psychology PhD (Doctor of Philosophy)—Applications 2012–2013, 38. Total applicants accepted 2012–2013, 16. Number full-time enrolled (new admits only) 2012–2013, 8. Number part-time enrolled (new admits only) 2012–2013, 0. Total enrolled 2012–2013 full-time, 29. Total enrolled 2012–2013 part-time, 2. Openings 2013–2014, 6. The median number of years required for completion of a degree in 2012–2013 were 5. The number of students enrolled full- and part-time who were dismissed or voluntarily withdrew from this program area in 2012–2013 were 0. *School Psychology MA/MS (Master of Arts/Science)*—Applications 2012–2013, 47. Total applicants accepted 2012–2013, 11. Number full-time enrolled (new admits only) 2012–2013, 6. Number part-time enrolled (new admits only) 2012–2013, 0. Total enrolled 2012–2013 full-time, 22. Total enrolled 2012–2013 part-time, 0. Openings 2013–2014, 6. The median number of years required for completion of a degree in 2012–2013 were 3. The number of students enrolled full- and part-time who were dismissed or voluntarily withdrew from this program area in 2012–2013 were 0.

Scores: Entries appear in this order: required test or GPA, minimum score (if required), median score of students entering in 2012–2013. *School Psychology PhD (Doctor of Philosophy):*

GRE-V 500, 618, GRE-Q 500, 658, overall undergraduate GPA 3.0, 3.8; *School Psychology MA/MS (Master of Arts/Science)*: GRE-V 500, 589, GRE-Q 500, 650, overall undergraduate GPA 3.0, 3.7.

Other Criteria: (importance of criteria rated low, medium, or high): GRE scores—high, research experience—medium, work experience—medium, extracurricular activity—low, clinically related public service—low, GPA—medium, letters of recommendation—high, interview—high, statement of goals and objectives—high, undergraduate major in psychology—low, specific undergraduate psychology courses taken—low.

Student Characteristics: The following represents characteristics of students in 2012–2013 in all graduate psychology programs in the department: Female—full-time 38, part-time 2; Male—full-time 11, part-time 0; African American/Black—full-time 2, part-time 0; Hispanic/Latino(a)—full-time 3, part-time 0; Asian/Pacific Islander—full-time 2, part-time 0; American Indian/Alaska Native—full-time 0, part-time 0; Caucasian/White—full-time 38, part-time 2; Multi-ethnic—full-time 0, part-time 0; students subject to the Americans With Disabilities Act—full-time 0, part-time 0; Unknown ethnicity—full-time 0, part-time 0; International students who hold an F-1 or J-1 Visa—full-time 1, part-time 0.

Financial Information/Assistance:
Tuition for Full-Time Study: *Master's:* State residents: per academic year $9,972, $530 per credit hour; Nonstate residents: per academic year $25,884, $1,410 per credit hour. *Doctoral:* State residents: per academic year $9,972, $530 per credit hour; Nonstate residents: per academic year $25,834, $1,410 per credit hour. Additional fees are assessed to students beyond the costs of tuition for the following: General University, Infrastructure/Maintenance, Graduate Matriculation, Activity, Transit. See the following website for updates and changes in tuition costs: http://bursar.uconn.edu/tuit_grad_current.html.

Financial Assistance:
First-Year Students: Research assistantships available for first year. Average amount paid per academic year: $19,098. Average number of hours worked per week: 20. Apply by September 1.
Advanced Students: Research assistantships available for advanced students. Average amount paid per academic year: $22,342. Average number of hours worked per week: 20. Apply by September 1.
Additional Information: Of all students currently enrolled full time, 90% benefited from one or more of the listed financial assistance programs. Application and information available online at: http://grad.uconn.edu/funding_resources.html.

Internships/Practica: Doctoral Degree (PhD School Psychology): For those doctoral students for whom a professional psychology internship was required in this program prior to graduation, (7) students applied for an internship in 2011–2012, with (7) students obtaining an internship. Of those students who obtained an internship, (7) were paid internships. Of those students who obtained an internship, (0) students placed in APA/CPA accredited internships, (0) students placed in internships not APA/CPA accredited, but listed with the Association of Psychology Postdoctoral and Internship Programs (APPIC), (7) students placed in internships conforming to guidelines of the Council of Directors of School Psychology Programs (CDSPP), (0) students placed in internships that were not APA/CPA accredited, APPIC or CDSPP listed. There are a number of practicum and internship placement opportunities for school psychology students at the University of Connecticut, affiliated sites, and school districts. The overwhelming majority of internship placements are paid, as are many of the practicum placements.

Housing and Day Care: On-campus housing is available. See the following website for more information: http://www.reslife.uconn.edu/. On-campus day care facilities are available. See the following website for more information: http://childlabs.uconn.edu/.

Employment of Department Graduates:
Master's Degree Graduates: Of those who graduated in the academic year 2011–2012, the following categories and numbers represent the postgraduate activities and employment of master's degree graduates: Enrolled in a psychology doctoral program (1), enrolled in a postdoctoral residency/fellowship (n/a), employed in independent practice (n/a), employed in an academic position at a university (1), employed in a professional position in a school system (3), total from the above (master's) (5).
Doctoral Degree Graduates: Of those who graduated in the academic year 2011–2012, the following categories and numbers represent the postgraduate activities and employment of doctoral degree graduates: Enrolled in a psychology doctoral program (n/a), total from the above (doctoral) (0).

Additional Information:
Orientation, Objectives, and Emphasis of Department: The Department of Educational Psychology sponsors master of arts/sixth-year and doctor of philosophy programs in school psychology. The programs are an integrated and organized preparation of psychologists whose primary professional interests involve children, families, and the educational process. The programs adhere to the scientist–practitioner model of training that assumes the effective practice of school psychology is based on knowledge gained from established methods of scientific inquiry. The faculty are committed to a learning environment that stresses an organized and explicit curriculum with clear expectations. In addition, the programs are designed to acquaint students with the diversity of theories and practices of school psychology, allowing students sufficient intellectual freedom to experiment with different delivery systems and various theoretical bases. The atmosphere is intended to foster informal student-faculty interactions, critical debate, and respect for theoretical diversity of practice, thus creating a more intense and exciting learning experience. It is believed that such a philosophy encourages and reinforces students' creativity and intellectual risk taking that are fundamental in the further development of the professional practice of school psychology.

Special Facilities or Resources: Research space, equipment and/or opportunities exist in the following center/labs: Center for Behavioral and Educational Research; The National Research Center for Gifted and Talented; The Pappanikou Special Education Center; University Program for Students with Learning Disabilities; The University of Connecticut Educational Microcomputing Laboratory; and The Hartford Professional Development Academy.

Information for Students With Physical Disabilities: See the following website for more information: http://www.csd.uconn.edu/index.html.

Application Information:

Send to Graduate Admissions, Room 108, Whetten Center Box U-6A, 438 Whitney Road Ext, Storrs, CT 06269-1006. Application available online. URL of online application: http://grad.uconn.edu/online.html. Students are admitted in the Fall, application deadline December 1. Fee: $75. $55 for electronic application; $75 for paper application.

Hartford, University of

Department of Psychology
Arts & Sciences
200 Bloomfield Avenue, East Hall
West Hartford, CT 06117
Telephone: (860) 768-4544
Fax: (860) 768-5292
E-mail: *jpowell@hartford.edu*
Web: *http://www.hartford.edu/A_and_S/departments/psychology/*

Department Information:

1957. Chairperson: Jack Powell, PhD; Mala Matacin, PhD. Number of faculty: total—full-time 22, part-time 13; women—full-time 13, part-time 8; total—minority—full-time 2, part-time 1; women minority—full-time 2, part-time 1.

Programs and Degrees Offered:

Listed in the following order: Program area, degree type (T if terminal Master's), number awarded 7/11–6/12. Clinical Practices in Psychology MA/MS (Master of Arts/Science) (T) 10, General Psychology MA/MS (Master of Arts/Science) (T) 6, School Psychology MA/MS (Master of Arts/Science) (T) 21, Organizational Psychology MA/MS (Master of Arts/Science) (T) 10.

Student Applications/Admissions:

Student Applications

Clinical Practices in Psychology MA/MS (Master of Arts/Science)—Applications 2012–2013, 59. Total applicants accepted 2012–2013, 34. Number full-time enrolled (new admits only) 2012–2013, 10. Number part-time enrolled (new admits only) 2012–2013, 1. Total enrolled 2012–2013 full-time, 25. Total enrolled 2012–2013 part-time, 1. Openings 2013–2014, 12. The median number of years required for completion of a degree in 2012–2013 were 2. The number of students enrolled full- and part-time who were dismissed or voluntarily withdrew from this program area in 2012–2013 were 0. *General Psychology MA/MS (Master of Arts/Science)*—Applications 2012–2013, 18. Total applicants accepted 2012–2013, 12. Number full-time enrolled (new admits only) 2012–2013, 3. Number part-time enrolled (new admits only) 2012–2013, 1. Total enrolled 2012–2013 full-time, 7. Total enrolled 2012–2013 part-time, 4. Openings 2013–2014, 5. The median number of years required for completion of a degree in 2012–2013 were 3. The number of students enrolled full- and part-time who were dismissed or voluntarily withdrew from this program area in 2012–2013 were 0. *School Psychology MA/MS (Master of Arts/Science)*—Applications 2012–2013, 28. Total applicants accepted 2012–2013, 16. Number full-time enrolled (new admits only) 2012–2013, 10. Number part-time enrolled (new admits only) 2012–2013, 0. Total enrolled 2012–2013 full-time, 32. Total enrolled 2012–2013 part-time, 0. Openings 2013–2014, 12. The median number of years required for completion of a degree in 2012–2013 were 3. The number of students enrolled full- and part-time who were dismissed or voluntarily withdrew from this program area in 2012–2013 were 0. *Organizational Psychology MA/MS (Master of Arts/Science)*—Applications 2012–2013, 38. Total applicants accepted 2012–2013, 16. Number full-time enrolled (new admits only) 2012–2013, 2. Number part-time enrolled (new admits only) 2012–2013, 8. Total enrolled 2012–2013 full-time, 2. Total enrolled 2012–2013 part-time, 25. Openings 2013–2014, 12. The median number of years required for completion of a degree in 2012–2013 were 4. The number of students enrolled full- and part-time who were dismissed or voluntarily withdrew from this program area in 2012–2013 were 0.

Scores: Entries appear in this order: required test or GPA, minimum score (if required), median score of students entering in 2012–2013. *Clinical Practices in Psychology MA/MS (Master of Arts/Science):* GRE-V no minimum stated, 555, GRE-Q no minimum stated, 540, GRE-Analytical no minimum stated, 4.0, GRE-Subject (Psychology) no minimum stated, 590, overall undergraduate GPA no minimum stated, 3.45; *General Psychology MA/MS (Master of Arts/Science):* GRE-V no minimum stated, 500, GRE-Q no minimum stated, 610, GRE-Analytical no minimum stated, 4.5, GRE-Subject (Psychology) no minimum stated, 530, overall undergraduate GPA no minimum stated, 3.5; *School Psychology MA/MS (Master of Arts/Science):* GRE-V no minimum stated, 150, GRE-Q no minimum stated, 149, GRE-Analytical no minimum stated, 4.5, GRE-Subject (Psychology) no minimum stated, 490, overall undergraduate GPA no minimum stated, 3.45; *Organizational Psychology MA/MS (Master of Arts/Science):* GRE-V no minimum stated, 510, GRE-Q no minimum stated, 610, GRE-Analytical no minimum stated, 4.0, overall undergraduate GPA no minimum stated, 3.35.

Other Criteria: (importance of criteria rated low, medium, or high): GRE scores—medium, research experience—medium, work experience—medium, extracurricular activity—low, GPA—high, letters of recommendation—high, interview—high, statement of goals and objectives—medium, Only the school psychology program requires an interview.

Student Characteristics: The following represents characteristics of students in 2012–2013 in all graduate psychology programs in the department: Female—full-time 56, part-time 23; Male—full-time 10, part-time 7; African American/Black—full-time 5, part-time 3; Hispanic/Latino(a)—full-time 4, part-time 3; Asian/Pacific Islander—full-time 4, part-time 3; American Indian/Alaska Native—full-time 0, part-time 0; Caucasian/White—full-time 50, part-time 19; Multi-ethnic—full-time 2, part-time 0; students subject to the Americans With Disabilities Act—full-time 1, part-time 0; Unknown ethnicity—full-time 1, part-time 2; International students who hold an F-1 or J-1 Visa—full-time 1, part-time 0.

Financial Information/Assistance:

Tuition for Full-Time Study: *Master's:* State residents: $485 per credit hour; Nonstate residents: $485 per credit hour. Tuition is subject to change. Additional fees are assessed to students beyond the costs of tuition for the following: registration fee, technology fee. See the following website for updates and changes in tuition costs: http://www.hartford.edu/aboutuofh/ finance_administration/financial_affairs/bursar/tuition/.

Financial Assistance:

First-Year Students: Teaching assistantships available for first year. Average amount paid per academic year: $2,550. Average number of hours worked per week: 8. Research assistantships available for first year. Average amount paid per academic year: $2,550. Average number of hours worked per week: 8.

Advanced Students: Teaching assistantships available for advanced students. Average amount paid per academic year: $2,550. Average number of hours worked per week: 8. Research assistantships available for advanced students. Average amount paid per academic year: $2,550. Average number of hours worked per week: 8.

Additional Information: Of all students currently enrolled full time, 28% benefited from one or more of the listed financial assistance programs. Application and information available online at: http://admission.hartford.edu/finaid/.

Internships/Practica: Master's Degree (MA/MS Clinical Practices in Psychology): An internship experience, such as a final research project or "capstone" experience is required of graduates. Master's Degree (MA/MS General Psychology): An internship experience, such as a final research project or "capstone" experience is required of graduates. Master's Degree (MA/MS School Psychology): An internship experience, such as a final research project or "capstone" experience is required of graduates. Master's Degree (MA/MS Organizational Psychology): An internship experience, such as a final research project or "capstone" experience is required of graduates. All Clinical Practices in Psychology students are assigned a half-time practicum in the second year of their academic program. The assignments for practica include mental health clinics, in- and out-patient services in hospitals, community centers, schools, and correctional institutions. Students are supervised both on-site by professional psychologists and at the University by the faculty. All School Psychology students are assigned a half-time practicum in their second year in a school setting and a full-time internship in their third year. Students are supervised by school psychologists on site and at the University by the faculty. Organizational Psychology students have an option of a one-semester practicum or capstone project, and General Psychology students have an option of a two-semester, half-time practicum at a facility in an area relevant to the student's training or a thesis.

Housing and Day Care: On-campus housing is available. See the following website for more information: http://www.hartford.edu/ res_life/. No on-campus day care facilities are available.

Employment of Department Graduates:

Master's Degree Graduates: Of those who graduated in the academic year 2011–2012, the following categories and numbers represent the postgraduate activities and employment of master's degree graduates: Enrolled in a postdoctoral residency/fellowship (n/a), employed in independent practice (n/a), total from the above (master's) (0).

Doctoral Degree Graduates: Of those who graduated in the academic year 2011–2012, the following categories and numbers represent the postgraduate activities and employment of doctoral degree graduates: Enrolled in a psychology doctoral program (n/a), total from the above (doctoral) (0).

Additional Information:

Orientation, Objectives, and Emphasis of Department: The Department of Psychology at the University of Hartford is strongly student-centered and committed to engaging students in the understanding of behavior, cognition, emotion, and social interaction. Major emphasis is placed on the development of critical thinking and analytical skills so students become adept at formulating meaningful questions, implementing strategies to enhance growth and development, and solving problems of individual and group behavior. Students are encouraged to understand, appreciate, and embrace diversity and the need for community involvement. The Department promotes self-awareness and life-long learning aimed at developing well-rounded, resourceful, ethical, competent, and compassionate graduates at all levels of education.

Special Facilities or Resources: In addition to mock therapy observational studios, located within the Department of Psychology, there are research labs dedicated to the study of stress management, pain management, and attachment. Numerous community organizations are available for student internships and practica.

Information for Students With Physical Disabilities: See the following website for more information: http://www.hartford.edu/ academics/disability_services.aspx.

Application Information:
Send to Center for Graduate and Adult Academic Services, University of Hartford, 200 Bloomfield Avenue, West Hartford, CT 06117. Application available online. URL of online application: http://www. hartford.edu/graduate/. Students are admitted in the Fall, application deadline February 15; Spring, application deadline November 1. Only the General Psychology program admits students in the spring. *Fee:* $50.

Hartford, University of
Department of Psychology: Graduate Institute of Professional Psychology
Arts and Sciences
200 Bloomfield Avenue
West Hartford, CT 06117-1599
Telephone: (860) 768-4778
Fax: (860) 768-4814
E-mail: *viereck@hartford.edu*
Web: *http://uhaweb.hartford.edu/gipppsyd/*

Department Information:
1957. Chairperson: Jack Powell, PhD / Mala Matacin, PhD. Number of faculty: total—full-time 22, part-time 15; women—full-time 13, part-time 6; total—minority—full-time 2, part-time 3; women minority—full-time 2, part-time 1.

Programs and Degrees Offered:
Listed in the following order: Program area, degree type (T if terminal Master's), number awarded 7/11–6/12. Clinical Psychology PsyD (Doctor of Psychology) 17.

APA Accreditation: Clinical PsyD (Doctor of Psychology). Student Outcome Data Website: http://uhaweb.hartford.edu/gipppsyd/ PROGRAM-DATA.html.

Student Applications/Admissions:

Student Applications

Clinical Psychology PsyD (Doctor of Psychology)—Applications 2012–2013, 213. Total applicants accepted 2012–2013, 55. Number full-time enrolled (new admits only) 2012–2013, 23. Number part-time enrolled (new admits only) 2012–2013, 0. Total enrolled 2012–2013 full-time, 148. Total enrolled 2012–2013 part-time, 0. Openings 2013–2014, 24. The median number of years required for completion of a degree in 2012–2013 were 6. The number of students enrolled full- and part-time who were dismissed or voluntarily withdrew from this program area in 2012–2013 were 2.

Scores: Entries appear in this order: required test or GPA, minimum score (if required), median score of students entering in 2012–2013. *Clinical Psychology PsyD (Doctor of Psychology):* GRE-V no minimum stated, 157, GRE-Q no minimum stated, 153, GRE-Analytical no minimum stated, 4.5, GRE-Subject (Psychology) no minimum stated, 635, overall undergraduate GPA no minimum stated, 3.64.

Other Criteria: (importance of criteria rated low, medium, or high): GRE scores—medium, research experience—medium, work experience—medium, extracurricular activity—low, clinically related public service—medium, GPA—high, letters of recommendation—high, interview—high, statement of goals and objectives—high, undergraduate major in psychology—medium, specific undergraduate psychology courses taken—medium. For additional information on admission requirements, go to http://uhaweb.hartford.edu/gipppsyd/AdmissionReq.html.

Student Characteristics: The following represents characteristics of students in 2012–2013 in all graduate psychology programs in the department: Female—full-time 120, part-time 0; Male—full-time 28, part-time 0; African American/Black—full-time 5, part-time 0; Hispanic/Latino(a)—full-time 12, part-time 0; Asian/Pacific Islander—full-time 7, part-time 0; American Indian/Alaska Native—full-time 0, part-time 0; Caucasian/White—full-time 117, part-time 0; Multi-ethnic—full-time 7, part-time 0; students subject to the Americans With Disabilities Act—full-time 1, part-time 0; Unknown ethnicity—full-time 0, part-time 0; International students who hold an F-1 or J-1 Visa—full-time 4, part-time 0.

Financial Information/Assistance:

Tuition for Full-Time Study: *Doctoral:* State residents: per academic year $23,578, $975 per credit hour; Nonstate residents: per academic year $23,578, $975 per credit hour. Tuition is subject to change. Additional fees are assessed to students beyond the costs of tuition for the following: registration fee, technology fee. See the following website for updates and changes in tuition costs: http://www.hartford.edu/aboutuofh/finance_administration/financial_affairs/bursar/tuition/.

Financial Assistance:

First-Year Students: Research assistantships available for first year. Average amount paid per academic year: $3,100. Average number of hours worked per week: 6. Fellowships and scholarships available for first year. Average amount paid per academic year: $4,000. Average number of hours worked per week: 0.

Advanced Students: Teaching assistantships available for advanced students. Average amount paid per academic year: $6,200. Average number of hours worked per week: 12. Research assistantships available for advanced students. Average amount paid per academic year: $3,100. Average number of hours worked per week: 6. Fellowships and scholarships available for advanced students. Average amount paid per academic year: $4,000.

Additional Information: Of all students currently enrolled full time, 61% benefited from one or more of the listed financial assistance programs. Application and information available online at: http://www.hartford.edu/graduate/FinancialAid.aspx.

Internships/Practica: Doctoral Degree (PsyD Clinical Psychology): For those doctoral students for whom a professional psychology internship was required in this program prior to graduation, (31) students applied for an internship in 2011–2012, with (23) students obtaining an internship. Of those students who obtained an internship, (21) were paid internships. Of those students who obtained an internship, (17) students placed in APA/CPA accredited internships, (4) students placed in internships not APA/CPA accredited, but listed with the Association of Psychology Postdoctoral and Internship Programs (APPIC), (0) students placed in internships conforming to guidelines of the Council of Directors of School Psychology Programs (CDSPP), (2) students placed in internships that were not APA/CPA accredited, APPIC or CDSPP listed. Our practicum network is extensive (approximately 100 sites in 4 states) and includes child, adolescent, and adult placements. Students generally get their first or second choice of sites. Practicum placement is coordinated with Professional Practice Seminar (2nd year) and Case Conference Seminar (3rd year) to insure students' clinical training needs are being met. Emphasis is placed upon the concept of "self-in-role" learning.

Housing and Day Care: On-campus housing is available. See the following website for more information: http://www.hartford.edu/res_life/. No on-campus day care facilities are available.

Employment of Department Graduates:

Master's Degree Graduates: Of those who graduated in the academic year 2011–2012, the following categories and numbers represent the postgraduate activities and employment of master's degree graduates: Enrolled in a postdoctoral residency/fellowship (n/a), employed in independent practice (n/a), total from the above (master's) (0).

Doctoral Degree Graduates: Of those who graduated in the academic year 2011–2012, the following categories and numbers represent the postgraduate activities and employment of doctoral degree graduates: Enrolled in a psychology doctoral program (n/a), enrolled in a postdoctoral residency/fellowship (5), employed in independent practice (1), employed in other positions at a higher education institution (2), employed in government agency (1), employed in a community mental health/counseling center (4), employed in a hospital/medical center (2), not seeking employment (1), do not know (10), total from the above (doctoral) (26).

Additional Information:

Orientation, Objectives, and Emphasis of Department: The primary mission of the program is to prepare students for effective functioning in the multiple roles they will need to fill as practicing psychologists in these rapidly changing times. The program also espouses the principle of affirmative diversity, defined as upholding the fundamental values of human differences and the belief that respect for individual and cultural differences enhances and increases the quality of educational and interpersonal experiences.

Special Facilities or Resources: The Graduate Institute offers a Child and Adolescent Proficiency Track. The goal of the track is to allow students to develop not only broad clinical skills, but also strong therapeutic, assessment, and program development skills in working specifically with children, adolescents, and families.

Information for Students With Physical Disabilities: See the following website for more information: http://www.hartford.edu/support/desc.asp?id=9.

Application Information:
Send to Center for Graduate and Adult Academic Services, Computer Center, Room 231, University of Hartford, 200 Bloomfield Avenue, West Hartford, CT 06117. Application available online. URL of online application: http://banweb.hartford.edu/. Students are admitted in the Fall, application deadline December 2. *Fee:* $50.

New Haven, University of
Graduate Psychology
College of Arts and Sciences
300 Boston Post Road
West Haven, CT 06516
Telephone: (203) 932-7339
Fax: (203) 931-6032
E-mail: *ssidle@newhaven.edu*
Web: *http://www.newhaven.edu/4488/psych/*

Department Information:
1972. Chairperson: Stuart Sidle PhD. Number of faculty: total—full-time 15, part-time 17; women—full-time 7, part-time 12; total—minority—full-time 2, part-time 5; women minority—full-time 1, part-time 3.

Programs and Degrees Offered:
Listed in the following order: Program area, degree type (T if terminal Master's), number awarded 7/11–6/12. Industrial/Organizational Psychology MA/MS (Master of Arts/Science) (T) 45, Community Psychology MA/MS (Master of Arts/Science) 15.

Student Applications/Admissions:
Student Applications
Industrial/Organizational Psychology MA/MS (Master of Arts/Science)—Applications 2012–2013, 140. Total applicants accepted 2012–2013, 112. Number full-time enrolled (new admits only) 2012–2013, 47. Number part-time enrolled (new admits only) 2012–2013, 26. Total enrolled 2012–2013 full-time, 75. Total enrolled 2012–2013 part-time, 35. Openings 2013–2014, 39. The median number of years required for completion of a degree in 2012–2013 were 2. The number of students enrolled full- and part-time who were dismissed or voluntarily withdrew from this program area in 2012–2013 were 4. *Community Psychology MA/MS (Master of Arts/Science)*—Applications 2012–2013, 30. Total applicants accepted 2012–2013, 22. Number full-time enrolled (new admits only) 2012–2013, 11. Number part-time enrolled (new admits only) 2012–2013, 6. Total enrolled 2012–2013 full-time, 32. Total enrolled 2012–2013 part-time, 6. Openings 2013–2014, 25.

The median number of years required for completion of a degree in 2012–2013 were 2.
Scores: Entries appear in this order: required test or GPA, minimum score (if required), median score of students entering in 2012–2013. *Industrial/Organizational Psychology MA/MS (Master of Arts/Science):* overall undergraduate GPA 2.8, 3.4, last 2 years GPA 3.0, 3.5; *Community Psychology MA/MS (Master of Arts/Science):* overall undergraduate GPA 2.8, 3.5, last 2 years GPA 3.0, 3.5.
Other Criteria: (importance of criteria rated low, medium, or high): research experience—medium, work experience—medium, extracurricular activity—medium, clinically related public service—low, GPA—high, letters of recommendation—high, statement of goals and objectives—high, undergraduate major in psychology—low, specific undergraduate psychology courses taken—medium.

Student Characteristics: The following represents characteristics of students in 2012–2013 in all graduate psychology programs in the department: Female—full-time 81, part-time 30; Male—full-time 28, part-time 11; African American/Black—full-time 11, part-time 5; Hispanic/Latino(a)—full-time 5, part-time 2; Asian/Pacific Islander—full-time 8, part-time 1; American Indian/Alaska Native—full-time 0, part-time 0; Caucasian/White—full-time 59, part-time 25; Multi-ethnic—full-time 2, part-time 7; students subject to the Americans With Disabilities Act—full-time 0, part-time 0; Unknown ethnicity—full-time 26, part-time 0; International students who hold an F-1 or J-1 Visa—full-time 11, part-time 0.

Financial Information/Assistance:
Tuition for Full-Time Study: *Master's:* State residents: $750 per credit hour; Nonstate residents: $750 per credit hour. Tuition is subject to change. See the following website for updates and changes in tuition costs: http://www.newhaven.edu/academics/169211/.

Financial Assistance:
First-Year Students: Teaching assistantships available for first year. Average number of hours worked per week: 15. Research assistantships available for first year. Average number of hours worked per week: 15.

Advanced Students: Teaching assistantships available for advanced students. Research assistantships available for advanced students.

Additional Information: Of all students currently enrolled full time, 70% benefited from one or more of the listed financial assistance programs. Application and information available online at: http://www.newhaven.edu/admissions/gradadmissions/4931/.

Internships/Practica: Most of the full time students complete an internship which allows the student to acquire special skills through coordinating formal coursework with an internship or practicum in an organizational setting. The internship gives the student with limited work experience the opportunity to work in cooperating organizations or consulting firms. We have longstanding relationships with a wide variety of business organizations that seek our students as interns.

Housing and Day Care: No on-campus housing is available. No on-campus day care facilities are available.

Employment of Department Graduates:

Master's Degree Graduates: Of those who graduated in the academic year 2011–2012, the following categories and numbers represent the postgraduate activities and employment of master's degree graduates: Enrolled in a psychology doctoral program (2), enrolled in another graduate/professional program (1), enrolled in a postdoctoral residency/fellowship (n/a), employed in independent practice (n/a), employed in other positions at a higher education institution (2), employed in business or industry (44), employed in government agency (8), employed in a community mental health/counseling center (6), employed in a hospital/medical center (2), do not know (1), total from the above (master's) (66).

Doctoral Degree Graduates: Of those who graduated in the academic year 2011–2012, the following categories and numbers represent the postgraduate activities and employment of doctoral degree graduates: Enrolled in a psychology doctoral program (n/a), total from the above (doctoral) (0).

Additional Information:

Orientation, Objectives, and Emphasis of Department: The primary goal of the Master of Arts in Industrial and Organizational Psychology program is to provide students with the knowledge and experience necessary to improve the satisfaction and productivity of people at work. Graduates obtain challenging and rewarding positions in public and private corporations, consulting firms, and government agencies. Even though our program has a strong applied/career orientation we have been quite successful in providing those students who wish to pursue doctoral study with a strong research foundation.

Information for Students With Physical Disabilities: See the following website for more information: http://www.newhaven.edu/10569/.

Application Information:
Send to Graduate Admissions, 300 Boston Post Road, University of New Haven, West Haven, CT 06516. Application available online. URL of online application: http://www.newhaven.edu/admissions/gradadmissions/15164/. Programs have rolling admissions. *Fee:* $50.

Southern Connecticut State University
Department of Psychology
501 Crescent Street
New Haven, CT 06515
Telephone: (203) 392-6868
Fax: (203) 392-6805
E-mail: *hauseltw1@southernct.edu*
Web: *http://www.southernct.edu/psychology/*

Department Information:
1893. Graduate Coordinator: W.J. Hauselt. Number of faculty: total—full-time 20, part-time 4; women—full-time 13, part-time 2.

Programs and Degrees Offered:
Listed in the following order: Program area, degree type (T if terminal Master's), number awarded 7/11–6/12. General Psychology MA/MS (Master of Arts/Science) (T) 24.

Student Applications/Admissions:
Student Applications

General Psychology MA/MS (Master of Arts/Science)—Applications 2012–2013, 61. Total applicants accepted 2012–2013, 27. Number full-time enrolled (new admits only) 2012–2013, 10. Number part-time enrolled (new admits only) 2012–2013, 6. Total enrolled 2012–2013 full-time, 16. Total enrolled 2012–2013 part-time, 8. Openings 2013–2014, 18. The median number of years required for completion of a degree in 2012–2013 were 2. The number of students enrolled full- and part-time who were dismissed or voluntarily withdrew from this program area in 2012–2013 were 0.

Scores: Entries appear in this order: required test or GPA, minimum score (if required), median score of students entering in 2012–2013. *General Psychology MA/MS (Master of Arts/Science):* GRE-V no minimum stated, GRE-Q no minimum stated, GRE-Analytical no minimum stated, overall undergraduate GPA 3.0, psychology GPA 3.0.

Other Criteria: (importance of criteria rated low, medium, or high): GRE scores—medium, research experience—low, work experience—low, extracurricular activity—low, GPA—high, letters of recommendation—high, statement of goals and objectives—high, undergraduate major in psychology—low, specific undergraduate psychology courses taken—high. For additional information on admission requirements, go to http://www.southernct.edu/psychology/graduate/.

Student Characteristics: The following represents characteristics of students in 2012–2013 in all graduate psychology programs in the department: Female—full-time 10, part-time 5; Male—full-time 6, part-time 3; African American/Black—full-time 0, part-time 0; Hispanic/Latino(a)—full-time 0, part-time 0; Asian/Pacific Islander—full-time 0, part-time 0; American Indian/Alaska Native—full-time 0, part-time 0; Caucasian/White—full-time 0, part-time 0; Multi-ethnic—full-time 0, part-time 0; students subject to the Americans With Disabilities Act—full-time 0, part-time 0; Unknown ethnicity—full-time 16, part-time 8; International students who hold an F-1 or J-1 Visa—full-time 0, part-time 0.

Financial Information/Assistance:

Tuition for Full-Time Study: *Master's:* State residents: per academic year $9,477, $594 per credit hour; Nonstate residents: per academic year $20,460, $616 per credit hour. Tuition is subject to change. See the following website for updates and changes in tuition costs: http://www.southernct.edu/bursar/tuitionfees/.

Financial Assistance:

First-Year Students: Teaching assistantships available for first year. Average amount paid per academic year: $9,600. Average number of hours worked per week: 20. Apply by May 1.

Advanced Students: Teaching assistantships available for advanced students. Average amount paid per academic year: $9,600. Average number of hours worked per week: 20. Apply by May 1.

Additional Information: Of all students currently enrolled full time, 10% benefited from one or more of the listed financial assistance programs. Application and information available online at: http://www.southernct.edu/financialaid/.

Internships/Practica: Master's Degree (MA/MS General Psychology): An internship experience, such as a final research project or "capstone" experience is required of graduates. With departmental permission, advanced MA students may arrange a one- or two-semester clinical or research internship (3 credits for one semester; 6 credits for two semesters). These are not available to students in their first semester. The internship is not required.

Housing and Day Care: On-campus housing is available. See the following website for more information: http://www.southernct.edu/residencelife/. No on-campus day care facilities are available.

Employment of Department Graduates:

Master's Degree Graduates: Of those who graduated in the academic year 2011–2012, the following categories and numbers represent the postgraduate activities and employment of master's degree graduates: Enrolled in a psychology doctoral program (4), enrolled in another graduate/professional program (5), enrolled in a postdoctoral residency/fellowship (n/a), employed in independent practice (n/a), employed in a professional position in a school system (1), employed in business or industry (3), employed in a community mental health/counseling center (6), employed in a hospital/medical center (1), do not know (4), total from the above (master's) (24).

Doctoral Degree Graduates: Of those who graduated in the academic year 2011–2012, the following categories and numbers represent the postgraduate activities and employment of doctoral degree graduates: Enrolled in a psychology doctoral program (n/a), total from the above (doctoral) (0).

Additional Information:

Orientation, Objectives, and Emphasis of Department: This research-based academic program is designed to develop creative, problem-solving skills that graduates can apply to a variety of clinical, industrial, and educational settings. Leading to a Master of Arts degree, this program is flexible enough to be completed on either a full- or part-time basis, meeting the needs of a wide range of candidates. For potential doctoral candidates who can enter neither a PhD nor a PsyD program at the present time, this program may provide the basis for later acceptance into a doctoral program. For those who are already working in clinical, educational, or industrial settings, it offers updating and credentials. In addition, this program provides ideal training for people who want to explore their personal interest in careers related to psychology. High school teachers may use the program to prepare themselves to teach psychology in addition to their current certification. The program emphasizes faculty advisement to help tailor the program to the needs of each individual student. With advisement, it may be completed in one year.

Information for Students With Physical Disabilities: See the following website for more information: http://www.southernct.edu/drc/.

Application Information:
Send to School of Graduate Studies, Southern Connecticut State University, New Haven, CT 06515. Application available online. URL of online application: http://www.southernct.edu/grad/admissions/graduateapplication/. Students are admitted in the Fall, application deadline June 1; Spring, application deadline November 1. *Fee:* $50.

Yale University
Department of Psychology
P.O. Box 208205
New Haven, CT 06520-8205
Telephone: (203) 432-4518
Fax: (203) 432-7172
E-mail: *lauretta.olivi@yale.edu*
Web: *http://psychology.yale.edu/*

Department Information:
1928. Chairperson: Marcia Johnson. Number of faculty: total—full-time 25; women—full-time 11; total—minority—full-time 3; women minority—full-time 2.

Programs and Degrees Offered:
Listed in the following order: Program area, degree type (T if terminal Master's), number awarded 7/11–6/12. Neuroscience PhD (Doctor of Philosophy) 3, Clinical Psychology PhD (Doctor of Philosophy) 5, Cognitive Psychology PhD (Doctor of Philosophy) 0, Developmental Psychology PhD (Doctor of Philosophy) 2, Social/Personality Psychology PhD (Doctor of Philosophy) 3.

APA Accreditation: Clinical PhD (Doctor of Philosophy).

Student Applications/Admissions:

Student Applications

Neuroscience PhD (Doctor of Philosophy)—Applications 2012–2013, 35. Total applicants accepted 2012–2013, 1. Number full-time enrolled (new admits only) 2012–2013, 1. Number part-time enrolled (new admits only) 2012–2013, 0. Total enrolled 2012–2013 full-time, 6. Total enrolled 2012–2013 part-time, 0. The median number of years required for completion of a degree in 2012–2013 were 6. The number of students enrolled full- and part-time who were dismissed or voluntarily withdrew from this program area in 2012–2013 were 0. *Clinical Psychology PhD (Doctor of Philosophy)*—Applications 2012–2013, 362. Total applicants accepted 2012–2013, 6. Number full-time enrolled (new admits only) 2012–2013, 5. Number part-time enrolled (new admits only) 2012–2013, 0. Total enrolled 2012–2013 full-time, 21. Total enrolled 2012–2013 part-time, 0. Openings 2013–2014, 5. The median number of years required for completion of a degree in 2012–2013 were 6. The number of students enrolled full- and part-time who were dismissed or voluntarily withdrew from this program area in 2012–2013 were 0. *Cognitive Psychology PhD (Doctor of Philosophy)*—Applications 2012–2013, 88. Total applicants accepted 2012–2013, 6. Number full-time enrolled (new admits only) 2012–2013, 3. Number part-time enrolled (new admits only) 2012–2013, 0. Total enrolled 2012–2013 full-time, 16. Total enrolled 2012–2013 part-time, 0. Openings 2013–2014, 5. The number of students enrolled full- and part-time who were dismissed or voluntarily withdrew from this program area in 2012–2013 were 0. *Developmental Psychology PhD (Doctor of Philosophy)*—Applications 2012–2013, 65. Total applicants accepted 2012–2013, 2. Number full-time enrolled (new admits only) 2012–2013, 2. Number part-time enrolled (new admits only) 2012–2013, 0. Total enrolled 2012–2013 full-time, 16. Total enrolled 2012–2013 part-time, 0. Openings 2013–2014, 7. The median number of years required for completion of a degree in 2012–2013 were 5. The number of students enrolled full- and part-time who were dismissed or voluntarily withdrew from this program area in 2012–2013 were 1. *Social/Personality Psychology PhD (Doctor of Philosophy)*—Applications 2012–2013, 164. Total applicants accepted 2012–2013, 8. Number full-time enrolled (new admits only) 2012–2013, 3. Number part-time enrolled (new admits only) 2012–2013, 0. Total enrolled 2012–2013 full-time, 16. Total enrolled 2012–2013 part-time, 0. Openings 2013–2014, 6. The median number of years required for completion of a degree in 2012–2013 were 5. The number of students enrolled full- and part-time who were dismissed or voluntarily withdrew from this program area in 2012–2013 were 0.

Scores: Entries appear in this order: required test or GPA, minimum score (if required), median score of students entering in 2012–2013. *Neuroscience PhD (Doctor of Philosophy)*: GRE-V no minimum stated, GRE-Q no minimum stated, GRE-Analytical no minimum stated, overall undergraduate GPA no minimum stated, last 2 years GPA no minimum stated, psychology GPA no minimum stated, Masters GPA no minimum stated; *Clinical Psychology PhD (Doctor of Philosophy)*: GRE-V no minimum stated, GRE-Q no minimum stated, GRE-Analytical no minimum stated, overall undergraduate GPA no minimum stated, last 2 years GPA no minimum stated, psychology GPA no minimum stated, Masters GPA no minimum stated; *Cognitive Psychology PhD (Doctor of Philosophy)*: GRE-V no minimum stated, GRE-Q no minimum stated, GRE-Analytical no minimum stated, overall undergraduate GPA no minimum stated, last 2 years GPA no minimum stated, psychology GPA no minimum stated, Masters GPA no minimum stated; *Developmental Psychology PhD (Doctor of Philosophy)*: GRE-V no minimum stated, GRE-Q no minimum stated, GRE-Analytical no minimum stated, overall undergraduate GPA no minimum stated, last 2 years GPA no minimum stated, psychology GPA no minimum stated, Masters GPA no minimum stated; *Social/Personality Psychology PhD (Doctor of Philosophy)*: GRE-V no minimum stated, GRE-Q no minimum stated, GRE-Analytical no minimum stated, overall undergraduate GPA no minimum stated, last 2 years GPA no minimum stated, psychology GPA no minimum stated, Masters GPA no minimum stated.

Other Criteria: (importance of criteria rated low, medium, or high): GRE scores—high, research experience—high, work experience—low, extracurricular activity—low, clinically related public service—low, GPA—high, letters of recommendation—high, interview—medium, statement of goals and objectives—high, undergraduate major in psychology—medium, specific undergraduate psychology courses taken—medium. For additional information on admission requirements, go to http://psychology.yale.edu/brochure/applying-admission.

Student Characteristics: The following represents characteristics of students in 2012–2013 in all graduate psychology programs in the department: Female—full-time 57, part-time 0; Male—full-time 18, part-time 0; African American/Black—full-time 2, part-time 0; Hispanic/Latino(a)—full-time 6, part-time 0; Asian/Pacific Islander—full-time 7, part-time 0; American Indian/Alaska Native—full-time 0, part-time 0; Caucasian/White—full-time 50, part-time 0; Multi-ethnic—full-time 10, part-time 0; students subject to the Americans With Disabilities Act—full-time 1, part-time 0; Unknown ethnicity—full-time 0, part-time 0; International students who hold an F-1 or J-1 Visa—full-time 4, part-time 0.

Financial Information/Assistance:
Tuition for Full-Time Study: *Doctoral:* State residents: per academic year $35,500; Nonstate residents: per academic year $35,500. Tuition is subject to change. See the following website for updates and changes in tuition costs: http://www.yale.edu/graduateschool/financial/costs.html.

Financial Assistance:
First-Year Students: No information provided.

Advanced Students: Teaching assistantships available for advanced students. Average amount paid per academic year: $16,000. Average number of hours worked per week: 15. Apply by June 30. Research assistantships available for advanced students. Average number of hours worked per week: 10. Traineeships available for advanced students. Fellowships and scholarships available for advanced students.

Additional Information: Of all students currently enrolled full time, 100% benefited from one or more of the listed financial assistance programs. Application and information available online at: http://www.yale.edu/graduateschool/financial/.

Internships/Practica: Doctoral Degree (PhD Clinical Psychology): For those doctoral students for whom a professional psychology internship was required in this program prior to graduation, (1) students applied for an internship in 2011–2012, with (1) students obtaining an internship. Of those students who obtained an internship, (1) were paid internships. Of those students who obtained an internship, (1) students placed in APA/CPA accredited internships, (0) students placed in internships not APA/CPA accredited, but listed with the Association of Psychology Postdoctoral and Internship Programs (APPIC), (0) students placed in internships conforming to guidelines of the Council of Directors of School Psychology Programs (CDSPP), (0) students placed in internships that were not APA/CPA accredited, APPIC or CDSPP listed. Students are required to assist in teaching an average of 10-15 hours per week in their second, third, and fourth years as part of their educational program. Local facilities for predoctoral internships are the Veterans Administration Center in West Haven, Yale Psychological Services Clinic, the Yale Child Study Center, and Yale Department of Psychiatry, with placement in the Connecticut Mental Health Center, Yale-New Haven Hospital, or the Yale Psychiatric Institute. Also, internships are arranged in accredited facilities throughout the United States.

Housing and Day Care: On-campus housing is available. See the following website for more information: http://gradhousing.yale.edu/. On-campus day care facilities are available. See the following website for more information: http://www.yale.edu/hronline/worklife/ccd.html.

Employment of Department Graduates:
Master's Degree Graduates: Of those who graduated in the academic year 2011–2012, the following categories and numbers represent the postgraduate activities and employment of master's degree graduates: Enrolled in a postdoctoral residency/fellowship (n/a), employed in independent practice (n/a), total from the above (master's) (0).

Doctoral Degree Graduates: Of those who graduated in the academic year 2011–2012, the following categories and numbers represent the postgraduate activities and employment of doctoral degree graduates: Enrolled in a psychology doctoral program (n/a), enrolled in another graduate/professional program (1), enrolled in a postdoctoral residency/fellowship (7), employed in business or industry (2), not seeking employment (1), do not know (1), total from the above (doctoral) (12).

Additional Information:

Orientation, Objectives, and Emphasis of Department: The chief goal of graduate education in psychology at Yale University is the training of research workers in academic and other settings who will broaden the basic scientific knowledge on which the discipline of psychology rests. Major emphasis is given to preparation for research; a definite effort is made to give students a background for teaching. The concentration of doctoral training on research and teaching is consistent with a variety of career objectives in addition to traditional academics. The department believes that rigorous and balanced exposure to basic psychology is the best preparation for research careers. The first important aspect of graduate training is advanced study of general psychology, including methods and psychological theory. The second is specialized training within a subfield. Third, the student is encouraged to take advantage of opportunities for wider training emphasizing research rather than practice. For the clinical area, research and practica are strongly integrated. Training is geared to the expectation that the majority of students will have research careers.

Special Facilities or Resources: Facilities available as adjuncts to research and teaching include The Yale Capuchin Cognition Lab, The Yale Parenting Center and Child Conduct Clinic, The Rudd Center for Food Policy and Obesity, and the Yale Anxiety and Mood Disorders Clinic. Other facilities include special rooms equipped for observation, intercommunication, and recording as required for clinical supervision or testing or for interview training and research. Also available to our students is an fMRI facility in the Yale University School of Medicine.

Information for Students With Physical Disabilities: See the following website for more information: http://www.yale.edu/rod/.

Application Information:

Send to Graduate School, Yale University, Office of Admissions, P.O. Box 208323, New Haven, CT 06520-8323. Application available online. URL of online application: http://www.yale.edu/graduateschool/admissions/application.html. Students are admitted in the Fall, application deadline December 15. *Fee:* $100.

Delaware, University of
Department of Psychology
College of Arts and Science
108 Wolf Hall
Newark, DE 19716
Telephone: (302) 831-2271
Fax: (302) 831-6393
E-mail: *gderr@psych.udel.edu*
Web: *http://www.psych.udel.edu/graduate/index.asp*

Department Information:

1946. Chairperson: Gregory A. Miller. Number of faculty: total—full-time 36; women—full-time 15; total—minority—full-time 7; women minority—full-time 3; faculty subject to the Americans With Disabilities Act 2.

Programs and Degrees Offered:

Listed in the following order: Program area, degree type (T if terminal Master's), number awarded 7/11–6/12. Clinical Science PhD (Doctor of Philosophy) 5, Behavioral Neuroscience PhD (Doctor of Philosophy) 1, Social Psychology PhD (Doctor of Philosophy) 3, Cognitive Psychology PhD (Doctor of Philosophy) 1.

APA Accreditation: Clinical PhD (Doctor of Philosophy). Student Outcome Data Website: http://www.psych.udel.edu/graduate/detail/student_admissions_outcomes_and_other_data/.

Student Applications/Admissions:

Student Applications

Clinical Science PhD (Doctor of Philosophy)—Applications 2012–2013, 266. Total applicants accepted 2012–2013, 17. Number full-time enrolled (new admits only) 2012–2013, 9. Number part-time enrolled (new admits only) 2012–2013, 0. Total enrolled 2012–2013 full-time, 31. Total enrolled 2012–2013 part-time, 0. Openings 2013–2014, 2. The median number of years required for completion of a degree in 2012–2013 were 6. The number of students enrolled full- and part-time who were dismissed or voluntarily withdrew from this program area in 2012–2013 were 0. *Behavioral Neuroscience PhD (Doctor of Philosophy)*—Applications 2012–2013, 30. Total applicants accepted 2012–2013, 7. Number full-time enrolled (new admits only) 2012–2013, 5. Number part-time enrolled (new admits only) 2012–2013, 0. Total enrolled 2012–2013 full-time, 13. Total enrolled 2012–2013 part-time, 0. Openings 2013–2014, 4. The median number of years required for completion of a degree in 2012–2013 were 6. The number of students enrolled full- and part-time who were dismissed or voluntarily withdrew from this program area in 2012–2013 were 0. *Social Psychology PhD (Doctor of Philosophy)*—Applications 2012–2013, 45. Total applicants accepted 2012–2013, 3. Number full-time enrolled (new admits only) 2012–2013, 2. Number part-time enrolled (new admits only) 2012–2013, 0. Total enrolled 2012–2013 full-time, 8. Total enrolled 2012–2013 part-time, 0. Openings 2013–2014, 1. The median number of years required for completion of a degree in 2012–2013

were 5. The number of students enrolled full- and part-time who were dismissed or voluntarily withdrew from this program area in 2012–2013 were 0. *Cognitive Psychology PhD (Doctor of Philosophy)*—Applications 2012–2013, 26. Total applicants accepted 2012–2013, 0. Number full-time enrolled (new admits only) 2012–2013, 0. Number part-time enrolled (new admits only) 2012–2013, 0. Total enrolled 2012–2013 full-time, 7. Total enrolled 2012–2013 part-time, 0. Openings 2013–2014, 6. The median number of years required for completion of a degree in 2012–2013 were 5. The number of students enrolled full- and part-time who were dismissed or voluntarily withdrew from this program area in 2012–2013 were 0.

Scores: Entries appear in this order: required test or GPA, minimum score (if required), median score of students entering in 2012–2013. *Clinical Science PhD (Doctor of Philosophy):* GRE-V no minimum stated, 630, GRE-Q no minimum stated, 710, GRE-Analytical no minimum stated, 5.0, overall undergraduate GPA no minimum stated, 3.68.

Other Criteria: (importance of criteria rated low, medium, or high): GRE scores—high, research experience—medium, work experience—low, extracurricular activity—low, clinically related public service—medium, GPA—high, letters of recommendation—high, interview—high, statement of goals and objectives—high, In the behavioral neuroscience, cognitive and social areas, GRE scores are emphasized less and research experience is emphasized more relative to the clinical area. For additional information on admission requirements, go to http://www.psych.udel.edu/graduate/detail/category/prospective_graduate_students/.

Student Characteristics: The following represents characteristics of students in 2012–2013 in all graduate psychology programs in the department: Female—full-time 43, part-time 0; Male—full-time 16, part-time 0; African American/Black—full-time 4, part-time 0; Hispanic/Latino(a)—full-time 2, part-time 0; Asian/Pacific Islander—full-time 7, part-time 0; American Indian/Alaska Native—full-time 0, part-time 0; Caucasian/White—full-time 46, part-time 0; Multi-ethnic—full-time 0, part-time 0; students subject to the Americans With Disabilities Act—full-time 1, part-time 0; Unknown ethnicity—full-time 0, part-time 0; International students who hold an F-1 or J-1 Visa—full-time 5, part-time 0.

Financial Information/Assistance:

Tuition for Full-Time Study: *Doctoral:* State residents: per academic year $27,240, $1,513 per credit hour; Nonstate residents: per academic year $27,240, $1,513 per credit hour. Tuition is subject to change. Additional fees are assessed to students beyond the costs of tuition for the following: student health fees and student service center fees. See the following website for updates and changes in tuition costs: http://www.udel.edu/finaid/index.html?rates.

Financial Assistance:

First-Year Students: Teaching assistantships available for first year. Average amount paid per academic year: $16,500. Average number of hours worked per week: 20. Apply by January 7.

Research assistantships available for first year. Average amount paid per academic year: $16,500. Average number of hours worked per week: 20. Apply by January 7. Fellowships and scholarships available for first year. Average amount paid per academic year: $16,500. Average number of hours worked per week: 20. Apply by January 7.

Advanced Students: Teaching assistantships available for advanced students. Average amount paid per academic year: $16,500. Average number of hours worked per week: 20. Research assistantships available for advanced students. Average amount paid per academic year: $16,500. Average number of hours worked per week: 20. Traineeships available for advanced students. Average amount paid per academic year: $23,717. Apply by October 1. Fellowships and scholarships available for advanced students. Average amount paid per academic year: $16,500. Average number of hours worked per week: 20.

Additional Information: Of all students currently enrolled full time, 100% benefited from one or more of the listed financial assistance programs. Application and information available online at: http://www.udel.edu/gradoffice/financial/index.html.

Internships/Practica: Doctoral Degree (PhD Clinical Science): For those doctoral students for whom a professional psychology internship was required in this program prior to graduation, (5) students applied for an internship in 2011–2012, with (4) students obtaining an internship. Of those students who obtained an internship, (3) were paid internships. Of those students who obtained an internship, (3) students placed in APA/CPA accredited internships, (0) students placed in internships not APA/CPA accredited, but listed with the Association of Psychology Postdoctoral and Internship Programs (APPIC), (0) students placed in internships conforming to guidelines of the Council of Directors of School Psychology Programs (CDSPP), (1) students placed in internships that were not APA/CPA accredited, APPIC or CDSPP listed. A wide range of external practicum experiences are available for Clinical Science graduate students in their third year and beyond. In their first two years, students in the Clinical Science Program are supervised by our faculty in our Psychological Services Training Center.

Housing and Day Care: On-campus housing is available. See the following website for more information: http://www.udel.edu/reslife/. On-campus day care facilities are available. See the following website for more information: http://www.udel.edu/hr/childcare.html.

Employment of Department Graduates:

Master's Degree Graduates: Of those who graduated in the academic year 2011–2012, the following categories and numbers represent the postgraduate activities and employment of master's degree graduates: Enrolled in a postdoctoral residency/fellowship (n/a), employed in independent practice (n/a), total from the above (master's) (0).

Doctoral Degree Graduates: Of those who graduated in the academic year 2011–2012, the following categories and numbers represent the postgraduate activities and employment of doctoral degree graduates: Enrolled in a psychology doctoral program (n/a), enrolled in a postdoctoral residency/fellowship (6), employed in an academic position at a university (1), employed in government agency (1), employed in a hospital/medical center (2), total from the above (doctoral) (10).

Additional Information:

Orientation, Objectives, and Emphasis of Department: The department fosters a scientific approach to all areas of psychology. The training is organized around Behavioral Neuroscience, Clinical Science, Cognitive, and Social Areas, as well as an integrative developmental focus that cuts across Areas. The goal of this training is to prepare students to function as scientists and teachers in academic, applied, and clinical settings. Students in the Clinical Science program are additionally trained for full competence in independent practice, although that career path is not the goal of the program. Major current research interests in these areas: (1) Behavioral Neuroscience: neuroanatomy, developmental psychobiology, psychopharmacology, and neurobiology of learning; (2) Clinical Science: development, evaluation, and dissemination of intervention/prevention programs for adults, adolescents, and children; basic research on effects of poverty, peer relations, intimate relationships, and brain mechanisms and psychophysiology of psychopathology; (3) Cognitive: attention, pattern recognition, psycholinguistics, visual information processing, memory, and cognitive development; (4) Social: intergroup relations, effects of being the victim of prejudice, social neuroscience, behavior in situations of social interdependence, and cultural and cross-cultural psychology. The PhD programs are flexible and encourage students to develop unique interests. The Department has strengths in early experience and developmental processes, spatial cognition, and brain plasticity during development and learning.

Special Facilities or Resources: The University Mills (Linux) Community Cluster provides exceptional processing capacity. The Department of Psychology is also well equipped to handle departmental computing needs with a large assortment of Windows, Linux, and Macintosh computers and servers. Graduate students will find strong laboratory resources appropriate to their scientific and computing needs. Department laboratories are well equipped for the online control of experiments for human and animal subjects as well as for data analysis and modeling. Laboratories are equipped with video, acoustic, behavioral and physiological recording systems as appropriate. The Department also operates the Psychological Services Training Center for practicum training and research in clinical psychology.

Information for Students With Physical Disabilities: See the following website for more information: http://www.udel.edu/DSS/.

Application Information:
Send to The Office of Graduate Studies, 234 Hullihen Hall, University of Delaware, Newark, DE 19716. Application available online. URL of online application: http://www.udel.edu/gradoffice/apply/. Students are admitted in the Fall, application deadline January 7. *Fee:* $75. The fee may be waived or deferred by the Department of Psychology.

American University
Department of Psychology
College of Arts and Sciences
321 Asbury, 4400 Massachusetts Avenue, NW
Washington, DC 20016-8062
Telephone: (202) 885-1710
Fax: (202) 885-1023
E-mail: *psychology@american.edu*
Web: *http://www.american.edu/cas/psychology*

Department Information:
1929. Chairperson: Anthony L. Riley. Number of faculty: total—full-time 24; women—full-time 8; total—minority—full-time 3; women minority—full-time 2.

Programs and Degrees Offered:
Listed in the following order: Program area, degree type (T if terminal Master's), number awarded 7/11–6/12. Behavior, Cognition and Neuroscience (Bcan) PhD (Doctor of Philosophy) 4, Clinical Psychology PhD (Doctor of Philosophy) 9, General Psychology MA/MS (Master of Arts/Science) (T) 20.

APA Accreditation: Clinical PhD (Doctor of Philosophy). Student Outcome Data Website: http://www.american.edu/cas/psychology/clinical/index.cfm.

Student Applications/Admissions:
Student Applications
Behavior, Cognition and Neuroscience (Bcan) PhD (Doctor of Philosophy)—Applications 2012–2013, 39. Total applicants accepted 2012–2013, 6. Number full-time enrolled (new admits only) 2012–2013, 5. Number part-time enrolled (new admits only) 2012–2013, 0. Total enrolled 2012–2013 full-time, 31. Total enrolled 2012–2013 part-time, 0. Openings 2013–2014, 6. The median number of years required for completion of a degree in 2012–2013 were 5. The number of students enrolled full- and part-time who were dismissed or voluntarily withdrew from this program area in 2012–2013 were 1. *Clinical Psychology PhD (Doctor of Philosophy)*—Applications 2012–2013, 227. Total applicants accepted 2012–2013, 8. Number full-time enrolled (new admits only) 2012–2013, 6. Number part-time enrolled (new admits only) 2012–2013, 0. Total enrolled 2012–2013 full-time, 38. Total enrolled 2012–2013 part-time, 0. Openings 2013–2014, 6. The median number of years required for completion of a degree in 2012–2013 were 7. The number of students enrolled full- and part-time who were dismissed or voluntarily withdrew from this program area in 2012–2013 were 3. *General Psychology MA/MS (Master of Arts/Science)*—Applications 2012–2013, 193. Total applicants accepted 2012–2013, 40. Number full-time enrolled (new admits only) 2012–2013, 24. Number part-time enrolled (new admits only) 2012–2013, 0. Total enrolled 2012–2013 full-time, 28.

Total enrolled 2012–2013 part-time, 17. Openings 2013–2014, 25. The median number of years required for completion of a degree in 2012–2013 were 2. The number of students enrolled full- and part-time who were dismissed or voluntarily withdrew from this program area in 2012–2013 were 0.

Scores: Entries appear in this order: required test or GPA, minimum score (if required), median score of students entering in 2012–2013. *Behavior, Cognition and Neuroscience (BCAN) PhD (Doctor of Philosophy):* GRE-V 160, 160, GRE-Q 155, 155, GRE-Analytical 4.3, 4.5, GRE-Subject (Psychology) no minimum stated, 690, overall undergraduate GPA 3.63, 3.4; *Clinical Psychology PhD (Doctor of Philosophy):* GRE-V 165, 165, GRE-Q 157, 158, GRE-Analytical 4, 4.5, GRE-Subject (Psychology) 693, 700, overall undergraduate GPA 3.66, 3.78; *General Psychology MA/MS (Master of Arts/Science):* GRE-V 160, 160, GRE-Q 154, 155, GRE-Analytical 4.1, 4, overall undergraduate GPA 3.50, 3.54.

Other Criteria: (importance of criteria rated low, medium, or high): GRE scores—high, research experience—high, work experience—medium, clinically related public service—low, GPA—high, letters of recommendation—high, interview—high, statement of goals and objectives—high, undergraduate major in psychology—medium, specific undergraduate psychology courses taken—medium, Clinically related public service not required for Behavior, Cognition, and Neuroscience program. For additional information on admission requirements, go to http://www.american.edu/cas/psychology/.

Student Characteristics: The following represents characteristics of students in 2012–2013 in all graduate psychology programs in the department: Female—full-time 80, part-time 14; Male—full-time 17, part-time 3; African American/Black—full-time 5, part-time 0; Hispanic/Latino(a)—full-time 2, part-time 0; Asian/Pacific Islander—full-time 6, part-time 2; American Indian/Alaska Native—full-time 0, part-time 0; Caucasian/White—full-time 53, part-time 7; Multi-ethnic—full-time 2, part-time 2; students subject to the Americans With Disabilities Act—full-time 0, part-time 0; Unknown ethnicity—full-time 29, part-time 6; International students who hold an F-1 or J-1 Visa—full-time 0, part-time 4.

Financial Information/Assistance:
Tuition for Full-Time Study: *Master's:* State residents: $1,440 per credit hour; Nonstate residents: $1,440 per credit hour. *Doctoral:* State residents: $1,440 per credit hour; Nonstate residents: $1,440 per credit hour. Tuition is subject to change. See the following website for updates and changes in tuition costs: http://www.american.edu/provost/registrar/registration/tuition.cfm.

Financial Assistance:
First-Year Students: Teaching assistantships available for first year. Average amount paid per academic year: $19,200. Average number of hours worked per week: 20. Apply by December 1.

Advanced Students: Teaching assistantships available for advanced students. Average amount paid per academic year: $19,200. Average number of hours worked per week: 20. Apply by December 1.

Additional Information: Of all students currently enrolled full time, 75% benefited from one or more of the listed financial assistance programs. Application and information available online at: http://www.american.edu/cas/admissions/finance.cfm.

Internships/Practica: Doctoral Degree (PhD Clinical Psychology): For those doctoral students for whom a professional psychology internship was required in this program prior to graduation, (10) students applied for an internship in 2011–2012, with (9) students obtaining an internship. Of those students who obtained an internship, (9) were paid internships. Of those students who obtained an internship, (9) students placed in APA/CPA accredited internships, (0) students placed in internships not APA/CPA accredited, but listed with the Association of Psychology Postdoctoral and Internship Programs (APPIC), (0) students placed in internships conforming to guidelines of the Council of Directors of School Psychology Programs (CDSPP), (0) students placed in internships that were not APA/CPA accredited, APPIC or CDSPP listed. The greater Washington, DC metropolitan area provides a wealth of applied and research resources to complement our students' work in the classroom and faculty laboratories. These include the university's Counseling Center, local hospitals (Children's, St. Elizabeth's, Walter Reed, Georgetown University, National Rehabilitation), the Kennedy Institute, Gallaudet University, the NIH (NIMH, NINDS, NIA, NCI), the National Zoo, and the national offices of many agencies (e.g., APA, APS, NAMI). Field work and short-term externships are available in many city, county, and private organizations, such as the Alexandria, VA Community Mental Health Center, the Montgomery County, MD Department of Addiction, Victim, and Mental Health Services, and the DC Rape Crisis Center. MA and PhD students can also earn degree credit while obtaining practical experience working in the private sector with autistic children, teaching self-management skills, or volunteering at shelters for battered women or the homeless. Many of these positions sometimes can provide funding. Clinical students participate in Rogerian, cognitive-behavioral, and psychodynamic therapy practica.

Housing and Day Care: No on-campus housing is available. On-campus day care facilities are available. See the following website for more information: http://www.american.edu/hr/cdc.cfm.

Employment of Department Graduates:

Master's Degree Graduates: Of those who graduated in the academic year 2011–2012, the following categories and numbers represent the postgraduate activities and employment of master's degree graduates: Enrolled in a psychology doctoral program (8), enrolled in another graduate/professional program (2), enrolled in a postdoctoral residency/fellowship (n/a), employed in independent practice (n/a), employed in business or industry (2), employed in a community mental health/counseling center (1), employed in a hospital/medical center (1), do not know (6), total from the above (master's) (20).

Doctoral Degree Graduates: Of those who graduated in the academic year 2011–2012, the following categories and numbers represent the postgraduate activities and employment of doctoral degree graduates: Enrolled in a psychology doctoral program (n/a), enrolled in a postdoctoral residency/fellowship (4), employed in independent practice (2), employed in an academic position at a university (2), employed in government agency (1), employed in a community mental health/counseling center (3), still seeking employment (1), total from the above (doctoral) (13).

Additional Information:

Orientation, Objectives, and Emphasis of Department: The psychology department of American University offers three graduate programs. These are two separate PhD programs in clinical psychology and in behavior, cognition and neuroscience. The MA program has tracks in general, personality/social, and biological/experimental psychology. The doctoral program in clinical psychology trains psychologists to do therapy, assessment, research, university teaching, and consultation. The theoretical orientation is eclectic and follows the Boulder scientist–practitioner model. The doctoral program in behavioral neuroscience/experimental psychology involves intensive training in both pure and applied research settings. Students can work in laboratories exploring conditioning and learning, the experimental analysis of behavior, cognition and memory, physiological psychology, neuropsychology, and neuropharmacology. Study at the master's level provides the basis for further doctoral-level work and prepares students for immediate employment in a variety of careers including clinical-medical research, teaching, counseling and policy formulation, law enforcement, and government work. Our graduate students are expected to be professional, ethical, committed, full-time members of our psychology community.

Special Facilities or Resources: Fifteen well-equipped laboratories investigate conditioning and learning, clinical and experimental neuropsychology, human cognition and memory, neuropharmacology, physiological psychology, rodent olfaction, social behavior, psychopathology, depression, anxiety disorders, emotion, eating disorders, parent-child interaction, addictive behavior, child development, and various other issues in applied and experimental psychology. In addition, students train in the Department's cognitive behavioral training clinic. Close working relationships with laboratories at the National Institutes of Health, the Walter Reed Army Institutes of Research, and Georgetown University's Hospital and School of Medicine allow additional training opportunities. The Washington Research Library Consortium (WRLC) provides access to six local college and university libraries in addition to AU's Bender Library, the National Library of Medicine, and the Library of Congress. AU's computing center supports IBM, Macintosh, and UNIX systems, has dial-in access, and maintains fifteen computing labs. EagleNet, a campus-wide network service runs on Novell Netware 4.x and 5.0. Applications include WordPerfect, Quattro Pro, Presentations, Paradox, SAS, SPSS, Photoshop, Netscape, and e-mail as well as many Internet applications and services.

Information for Students With Physical Disabilities: See the following website for more information: http://www.american.edu/ocl/dss/.

Application Information:
Send to College of Arts and Sciences, American University, Battelle-Tompkins, Terrace 27, 4400 Massachusetts Avenue, NW, Washington, DC 20016-8107. Application available online. URL of online application: http://www.american.edu/cas/admissions/apply.cfm. Students are admitted in the Fall, application deadline December 1. Deadlines: Clinical, December 1; Behavior, Cognition and Neuroscience,

January 1; MA, March 1. *Fee:* $50. Application fee is $80.00 if a paper application is used.

Gallaudet University

Department of Psychology
College of Liberal Arts, Sciences & Technologies
800 Florida Avenue, NE
Washington, DC 20002
Telephone: (202) 651-5540
Fax: (202) 651-5747
E-mail: *irene.leigh@gallaudet.edu*
Web: *http://www.gallaudet.edu/psychology.html*

Department Information:

1954. Chairperson: Dennis B. Galvan, PhD. Number of faculty: total—full-time 15, part-time 5; women—full-time 10, part-time 4; total—minority—full-time 3, part-time 1; women minority—full-time 2, part-time 1; faculty subject to the Americans With Disabilities Act 5.

Programs and Degrees Offered:

Listed in the following order: Program area, degree type (T if terminal Master's), number awarded 7/11–6/12. Clinical Psychology PhD (Doctor of Philosophy) 6, Specialist in School Psychology Other 2.

APA Accreditation: Clinical PhD (Doctor of Philosophy). Student Outcome Data Website: http://www.gallaudet.edu/Psychology/ Graduate_Programs/PhD_Clinical_Psychology/Student_Admissions_ Outcomes_and_Other_Data.html.

Student Applications/Admissions:

Student Applications

Clinical Psychology PhD (Doctor of Philosophy)—Applications 2012–2013, 30. Total applicants accepted 2012–2013, 8. Number full-time enrolled (new admits only) 2012–2013, 6. Number part-time enrolled (new admits only) 2012–2013, 0. Total enrolled 2012–2013 full-time, 30. Total enrolled 2012–2013 part-time, 5. Openings 2013–2014, 7. The median number of years required for completion of a degree in 2012–2013 were 6. The number of students enrolled full- and part-time who were dismissed or voluntarily withdrew from this program area in 2012–2013 were 2. *Specialist in School Psychology Other*—Applications 2012–2013, 15. Total applicants accepted 2012–2013, 7. Number full-time enrolled (new admits only) 2012–2013, 7. Number part-time enrolled (new admits only) 2012–2013, 0. Total enrolled 2012–2013 full-time, 14. Total enrolled 2012–2013 part-time, 0. Openings 2013–2014, 7. The median number of years required for completion of a degree in 2012–2013 were 3. The number of students enrolled full- and part-time who were dismissed or voluntarily withdrew from this program area in 2012–2013 were 0.

Scores: Entries appear in this order: required test or GPA, minimum score (if required), median score of students entering in 2012–2013. *Clinical Psychology PhD (Doctor of Philosophy):* GRE-V no minimum stated, 154, GRE-Q no minimum stated, 150, GRE-Analytical no minimum stated, 4, overall undergraduate GPA no minimum stated, 3.59; *Specialist in School Psychology Other:* GRE-V no minimum stated, 395, GRE-Q

no minimum stated, 495, GRE-Analytical no minimum stated, 3, overall undergraduate GPA 3.0, 3.65.

Other Criteria: (importance of criteria rated low, medium, or high): GRE scores—medium, research experience—high, work experience—medium, extracurricular activity—medium, clinically related public service—medium, GPA—medium, letters of recommendation—medium, interview—high, statement of goals and objectives—high, undergraduate major in psychology—high, specific undergraduate psychology courses taken—high, Students with little experience with deaf people or sign language may be required to take sign language (ASL) courses prior to enrolling. Prior research experience and clinically related public service are rated high for clinical psychology doctoral program admissions and medium for school psychology admissions. GPA is rated high for the School Psychology program and medium for the doctoral program. Interview is low for School Psychology and high for the doctoral program. For additional information on admission requirements, go to http://www.gallaudet.edu/GSPP/Graduate_ School/Graduate_Admissions/Application_Information. html.

Student Characteristics: The following represents characteristics of students in 2012–2013 in all graduate psychology programs in the department: Female—full-time 36, part-time 6; Male—full-time 7, part-time 2; African American/Black—full-time 4, part-time 1; Hispanic/Latino(a)—full-time 4, part-time 1; Asian/Pacific Islander—full-time 0, part-time 0; American Indian/Alaska Native—full-time 0, part-time 0; Caucasian/White—full-time 35, part-time 6; Multi-ethnic—full-time 1, part-time 0; students subject to the Americans With Disabilities Act—full-time 10, part-time 4; Unknown ethnicity—full-time 0, part-time 0; International students who hold an F-1 or J-1 Visa—full-time 3, part-time 0.

Financial Information/Assistance:

Tuition for Full-Time Study: *Master's:* State residents: per academic year $13,956, $760 per credit hour; Nonstate residents: per academic year $13,956, $760 per credit hour. *Doctoral:* State residents: per academic year $13,956, $760 per credit hour; Nonstate residents: per academic year $13,956, $760 per credit hour. Tuition is subject to change. Additional fees are assessed to students beyond the costs of tuition for the following: unit fee, room/ board, health insurance and services. See the following website for updates and changes in tuition costs: http://www.gallaudet. edu/finance_office.html. Higher tuition cost for this program: International students pay higher tuition; higher for nondeveloping than developing countries.

Financial Assistance:

First-Year Students: Teaching assistantships available for first year. Average amount paid per academic year: $4,500. Average number of hours worked per week: 10. Research assistantships available for first year. Average amount paid per academic year: $4,500. Average number of hours worked per week: 10. Fellowships and scholarships available for first year. Average amount paid per academic year: $12,000. Average number of hours worked per week: 10.

Advanced Students: Teaching assistantships available for advanced students. Average amount paid per academic year: $4,500. Average number of hours worked per week: 10. Research assistantships available for advanced students. Average amount

paid per academic year: $4,500. Average number of hours worked per week: 10. Fellowships and scholarships available for advanced students. Average amount paid per academic year: $12,000. Average number of hours worked per week: 10.

Additional Information: Of all students currently enrolled full time, 90% benefited from one or more of the listed financial assistance programs. Application and information available online at: http://www.gallaudet.edu/financial_aid.html.

Internships/Practica: Doctoral Degree (PhD Clinical Psychology): For those doctoral students for whom a professional psychology internship was required in this program prior to graduation, (6) students applied for an internship in 2011–2012, with (3) students obtaining an internship. Of those students who obtained an internship, (3) were paid internships. Of those students who obtained an internship, (2) students placed in APA/CPA accredited internships, (1) students placed in internships not APA/CPA accredited, but listed with the Association of Psychology Postdoctoral and Internship Programs (APPIC), (0) students placed in internships conforming to guidelines of the Council of Directors of School Psychology Programs (CDSPP), (0) students placed in internships that were not APA/CPA accredited, APPIC or CDSPP listed. Students in the School Psychology specialist program (which includes the MA as a non-terminal degree), begin with a practicum experience in their first semester, visiting and observing school programs as part of their Introduction to School Psychology course. During their second semester they are involved in Practicum I (3 credit course), which involves closely supervised practicum doing cognitive assessments of deaf and hearing children (if appropriate) at laboratory schools on campus and a D.C. neighborhood school. Practicum II (3 credits) is taken the third semester and requires two full days per week for a minimum of 14 weeks in which they work with a school psychologist in the Washington Metropolitan area doing comprehensive assessments, and some counseling if opportunities are available, and observation on a limited basis during their fourth semester (an option). The third year (semesters 5 and 6) are spent in a full-time internship in a school program approved by the program. These internships are typically located in both residential schools for the deaf as well as public school systems serving main streamed deaf youngsters. Internship sites are located in all parts of the United States. Students in the Clinical Psychology doctoral program begin practicum in their second year, conducting psychological assessments and psychotherapy at the Gallaudet University Mental Health Center. Advanced students can apply for any of the more than 80 externships available in the Washington, DC area. These externships allow students to work with a wide variety of settings and populations in assessment, psychotherapy, and other psychological interventions. Experiences with both deaf and hearing clients are available. A full-time, one-year doctoral level internship (typically in an APA-accredited internship program) is required.

Housing and Day Care: On-campus housing is available. See the following website for more information: http://www.gallaudet.edu/x12270.xml. On-campus day care facilities are available. See the following website for more information: http://www.gallaudet.edu/cdc.html.

Employment of Department Graduates:

Master's Degree Graduates: Of those who graduated in the academic year 2011–2012, the following categories and numbers represent the postgraduate activities and employment of master's degree graduates: Enrolled in a postdoctoral residency/fellowship (n/a), employed in independent practice (n/a), employed in a professional position in a school system (2), total from the above (master's) (2).

Doctoral Degree Graduates: Of those who graduated in the academic year 2011–2012, the following categories and numbers represent the postgraduate activities and employment of doctoral degree graduates: Enrolled in a psychology doctoral program (n/a), enrolled in a postdoctoral residency/fellowship (2), employed in an academic position at a university (1), employed in a community mental health/counseling center (1), employed in a hospital/medical center (1), still seeking employment (1), total from the above (doctoral) (6).

Additional Information:

Orientation, Objectives, and Emphasis of Department: The Psychology Department at Gallaudet University offers graduate programs in school psychology and clinical psychology. The school psychology program awards a nonterminal Master of Arts degree in developmental psychology followed by a Specialist in School Psychology degree with specialization in deafness. The clinical psychology program is a scholar-practitioner model PhD program, and trains generalist clinical psychologists to work with deaf, hard-of-hearing, and hearing populations. The school psychology program is both NCATE/NASP and NASDTEC-approved, and leads to certification as a school psychologist in the District of Columbia and approximately 24 states with reciprocity of certification. The full-time, three-year program requires completion of at least 72 graduate semester hours, including a one-year internship. The APA-accredited clinical psychology doctoral program is a five-year program providing balanced training in research and clinical skills with a variety of age groups, including deaf and hard-of-hearing children, adults, and older adults. The fifth year is designed as a full-time clinical psychology internship. A research-based dissertation is required.

Special Facilities or Resources: Gallaudet University is an internationally recognized center for research and training in areas related to deafness. With a diverse student body of approximately 1,800, the university trains deaf, hard-of-hearing, and hearing students in a variety of fields at the bachelor, master's, and doctoral levels. Gallaudet programs are located on historic Kendall Green, in northeast Washington, DC near the U.S. Capitol, the Library of Congress, and the Smithsonian Institute. Also located on the campus are the Gallaudet University Mental Health Center, the Kendall Demonstration Elementary School, the Model Secondary School for the Deaf, the Gallaudet Research Institute, the Kellogg Conference Center, and the Gallaudet Library, which contains the largest collection of references on deafness in the world. Gallaudet faculty, including both deaf and hearing individuals, possess a unique combination of scholarly activity in their respective disciplines and experience with deaf clients and research on deafness. The University is committed to a working model of a bilingual (American Sign Language and English), multicultural community, where deaf, hard-of-hearing, and hearing people can work together without communication barriers.

Information for Students With Physical Disabilities: See the following website for more information: http://www.gallaudet.edu/Office_for_Students_with_Disabilities.html.

Application Information:
Send to Office of Graduate Admissions, Gallaudet University, 800 Florida Avenue NE, Washington, DC 20002. Application available online. URL of online application: http://www.gallaudet.edu/ GradAdmissions.xml. Students are admitted in the Fall, application deadline February 1. *Fee:* $50. Waived for McNair Scholars.

George Washington University
Department of Organizational Sciences and Communication
  I/O Psychology Program
Columbian College of Arts and Sciences
600 21st Street NW, #201
Washington, DC 20052
Telephone: (202) 994-1875
Fax: (202) 994-1881
E-mail: *orgsci@gwu.edu*
Web: *http://departments.columbian.gwu.edu/orgsci/*

Department Information:
2005. Chairperson: Clay Warren. Number of faculty: total—full-time 10, part-time 2; women—full-time 7, part-time 1; total—minority—full-time 2; women minority—full-time 2.

Programs and Degrees Offered:
Listed in the following order: Program area, degree type (T if terminal Master's), number awarded 7/11–6/12. Industrial/Organizational Psychology PhD (Doctor of Philosophy) 5.

Student Applications/Admissions:
Student Applications
Industrial/Organizational Psychology PhD (Doctor of Philosophy)—Applications 2012–2013, 100. Total applicants accepted 2012–2013, 3. Number full-time enrolled (new admits only) 2012–2013, 3. Number part-time enrolled (new admits only) 2012–2013, 0. Total enrolled 2012–2013 full-time, 16. Total enrolled 2012–2013 part-time, 0. Openings 2013–2014, 2. The median number of years required for completion of a degree in 2012–2013 were 5. The number of students enrolled full- and part-time who were dismissed or voluntarily withdrew from this program area in 2012–2013 were 0.
Scores: Entries appear in this order: required test or GPA, minimum score (if required), median score of students entering in 2012–2013. *Industrial/Organizational Psychology PhD (Doctor of Philosophy)*: GRE-V 500, 640, GRE-Q 500, 760, GRE-Analytical 3.5, 4.5, overall undergraduate GPA 3.0, 3.5.
Other Criteria: (importance of criteria rated low, medium, or high): GRE scores—high, research experience—high, work experience—low, extracurricular activity—low, GPA—high, letters of recommendation—high, interview—high, statement of goals and objectives—high, undergraduate major in psychology—medium, specific undergraduate psychology courses taken—medium. For additional information on admission requirements, go to http://departments.columbian.gwu.edu/ orgsci/academics/io-psychology/admissions.

Student Characteristics: The following represents characteristics of students in 2012–2013 in all graduate psychology programs in the department stunt: Female—full-time 11, part-time 0; Male—full-time 5, part-time 0; African American/Black—full-time 0, part-time 0; Hispanic/Latino(a)—full-time 0, part-time 0; Asian/Pacific Islander—full-time 0, part-time 0; American Indian/Alaska Native—full-time 0, part-time 0; Caucasian/White—full-time 16, part-time 0; Multi-ethnic—full-time 0, part-time 0; students subject to the Americans With Disabilities Act—full-time 0, part-time 0; Unknown ethnicity—full-time 0, part-time 0; International students who hold an F-1 or J-1 Visa—full-time 0, part-time 0.

Financial Information/Assistance:
Tuition for Full-Time Study: *Doctoral:* State residents: $1,340 per credit hour; Nonstate residents: $1,340 per credit hour. Tuition is subject to change. See the following website for updates and changes in tuition costs: http://www.gwu.edu/tuition-and-fees.

Financial Assistance:
First-Year Students: Teaching assistantships available for first year. Average amount paid per academic year: $5,000. Average number of hours worked per week: 20. Apply by December 15. Research assistantships available for first year. Average amount paid per academic year: $5,000. Average number of hours worked per week: 20. Apply by December 15. Fellowships and scholarships available for first year. Average amount paid per academic year: $8,000. Average number of hours worked per week: 0. Apply by December 15.
Advanced Students: Teaching assistantships available for advanced students. Average amount paid per academic year: $5,000. Average number of hours worked per week: 20. Research assistantships available for advanced students. Average amount paid per academic year: $5,000. Average number of hours worked per week: 20. Fellowships and scholarships available for advanced students. Average amount paid per academic year: $8,000. Average number of hours worked per week: 0.
Additional Information: Of all students currently enrolled full time, 50% benefited from one or more of the listed financial assistance programs. Application and information available online at: http://graduate.admissions.gwu.edu/financial-assistance.

Internships/Practica: Internships and applied work experiences are available at a wide variety of organizations including in the government, private practice, the military, corporate, educational and non-profit sectors.

Housing and Day Care: On-campus housing is available. See the following website for more information: http://living.gwu.edu/ halls/graduatehousing/. No on-campus day care facilities are available.

Employment of Department Graduates:
Master's Degree Graduates: Of those who graduated in the academic year 2011–2012, the following categories and numbers represent the postgraduate activities and employment of master's degree graduates: Enrolled in a postdoctoral residency/fellowship (n/a), employed in independent practice (n/a), total from the above (master's) (0).
Doctoral Degree Graduates: Of those who graduated in the academic year 2011–2012, the following categories and numbers represent the postgraduate activities and employment of doctoral degree graduates: Enrolled in a psychology doctoral program (n/a), employed in independent practice (1), employed in business or

industry (2), employed in government agency (2), total from the above (doctoral) (5).

Additional Information:

Orientation, Objectives, and Emphasis of Department: The Department of Organizational Sciences and Communication is an interdisciplinary unit that builds on a broad range of disciplines including organizational management, psychology, communication, economics, and statistics. The Industrial/Organizational (I/O) Psychology Doctoral Program offers graduate training in areas such as personnel selection, training and development, work motivation, leadership, work teams, and organizational development. The program of study is designed in accordance with guidelines established by the Society for Industrial and Organizational Psychology (SIOP; Division 14, APA).

Information for Students With Physical Disabilities: See the following website for more information: http://gwired.gwu.edu/dss.

Application Information:

Application available online. URL of online application: http://columbian.gwu.edu/graduate/admissions/applyforadmission. Students are admitted in the Fall, application deadline December 15. *Fee:* $75.

George Washington University

Department of Psychology
Columbian College of Arts and Sciences
2125 G Street, NW
Washington, DC 20052
Telephone: (202) 994-6320
Fax: (202) 994-1602
E-mail: *pjp@gwu.edu*
Web: *http://departments.columbian.gwu.edu/psychology/*

Department Information:

1922. Chairperson: Paul Poppen. Number of faculty: total—full-time 24, part-time 2; women—full-time 14, part-time 2; total—minority—full-time 9; women minority—full-time 7.

Programs and Degrees Offered:

Listed in the following order: Program area, degree type (T if terminal Master's), number awarded 7/11–6/12. Applied Social Psychology PhD (Doctor of Philosophy) 1, Clinical Psychology PhD (Doctor of Philosophy) 3, Cognitive Neuroscience PhD (Doctor of Philosophy) 3.

APA Accreditation: Clinical PhD (Doctor of Philosophy). Student Outcome Data Website: http://departments.columbian.gwu.edu/psychology/graduate/clinical.

Student Applications/Admissions:

Student Applications

Applied Social Psychology PhD (Doctor of Philosophy)—Applications 2012–2013, 70. Total applicants accepted 2012–2013, 2. Number full-time enrolled (new admits only) 2012–2013, 2. Number part-time enrolled (new admits only) 2012–2013, 0. Total enrolled 2012–2013 full-time, 9. Total enrolled 2012–2013 part-time, 0. Openings 2013–2014, 3. The median num-

ber of years required for completion of a degree in 2012–2013 were 5. *Clinical Psychology PhD (Doctor of Philosophy)*—Applications 2012–2013, 300. Total applicants accepted 2012–2013, 5. Number full-time enrolled (new admits only) 2012–2013, 5. Number part-time enrolled (new admits only) 2012–2013, 0. Total enrolled 2012–2013 full-time, 31. Total enrolled 2012–2013 part-time, 0. Openings 2013–2014, 6. The median number of years required for completion of a degree in 2012–2013 were 6. The number of students enrolled full- and part-time who were dismissed or voluntarily withdrew from this program area in 2012–2013 were 0. *Cognitive Neuroscience PhD (Doctor of Philosophy)*—Applications 2012–2013, 40. Total applicants accepted 2012–2013, 3. Number full-time enrolled (new admits only) 2012–2013, 3. Total enrolled 2012–2013 full-time, 9. Total enrolled 2012–2013 part-time, 0. Openings 2013–2014, 3. The median number of years required for completion of a degree in 2012–2013 were 5.

Scores: Entries appear in this order: required test or GPA, minimum score (if required), median score of students entering in 2012–2013. *Applied Social Psychology PhD (Doctor of Philosophy):* GRE-V no minimum stated, 600, GRE-Q no minimum stated, 650, GRE-Analytical no minimum stated, 650, overall undergraduate GPA no minimum stated, 3.65; *Clinical Psychology PhD (Doctor of Philosophy):* GRE-V no minimum stated, 600, GRE-Q no minimum stated, 650, GRE-Analytical no minimum stated, overall undergraduate GPA no minimum stated, 3.70; *Cognitive Neuroscience PhD (Doctor of Philosophy):* GRE-V no minimum stated, 660, GRE-Q no minimum stated, 680, GRE-Analytical no minimum stated, overall undergraduate GPA no minimum stated, 3.50.

Other Criteria: (importance of criteria rated low, medium, or high): GRE scores—medium, research experience—high, work experience—medium, extracurricular activity—medium, clinically related public service—medium, GPA—high, letters of recommendation—medium, interview—high, statement of goals and objectives—high, undergraduate major in psychology—low, specific undergraduate psychology courses taken—medium, Interview & Clinical Public Service apply to Clinical program. For additional information on admission requirements, go to http://departments.columbian.gwu.edu/psychology/graduate/apply.

Student Characteristics: The following represents characteristics of students in 2012–2013 in all graduate psychology programs in the department: Female—full-time 40, part-time 0; Male—full-time 9, part-time 0; African American/Black—full-time 7, part-time 0; Hispanic/Latino(a)—full-time 9, part-time 0; Asian/Pacific Islander—full-time 4, part-time 0; American Indian/Alaska Native—full-time 0, part-time 0; Caucasian/White—full-time 29, part-time 0; Multi-ethnic—full-time 0, part-time 0; students subject to the Americans With Disabilities Act—full-time 0, part-time 0; Unknown ethnicity—full-time 0, part-time 0; International students who hold an F-1 or J-1 Visa—full-time 2, part-time 0.

Financial Information/Assistance:

Tuition for Full-Time Study: *Doctoral:* State residents: per academic year $24,000, $1,333 per credit hour; Nonstate residents: per academic year $24,000, $1,333 per credit hour. Tuition is subject to change. See the following website for updates and changes in tuition costs: http://graduate.admissions.gwu.edu/tuition-fees.

Financial Assistance:

First-Year Students: Teaching assistantships available for first year. Average amount paid per academic year: $22,000. Average number of hours worked per week: 20. Research assistantships available for first year. Average amount paid per academic year: $22,000. Average number of hours worked per week: 20. Fellowships and scholarships available for first year. Average amount paid per academic year: $25,000.

Advanced Students: Teaching assistantships available for advanced students. Average amount paid per academic year: $22,000. Average number of hours worked per week: 20. Research assistantships available for advanced students. Average amount paid per academic year: $22,000. Average number of hours worked per week: 20. Fellowships and scholarships available for advanced students. Average amount paid per academic year: $25,000.

Additional Information: Of all students currently enrolled full time, 100% benefited from one or more of the listed financial assistance programs. Application and information available online at: http://departments.columbian.gwu.edu/psychology/graduate/financialaid.

Internships/Practica: Doctoral Degree (PhD Clinical Psychology): For those doctoral students for whom a professional psychology internship was required in this program prior to graduation, (5) students applied for an internship in 2011–2012, with (5) students obtaining an internship. Of those students who obtained an internship, (5) were paid internships. Of those students who obtained an internship, (4) students placed in APA/CPA accredited internships, (0) students placed in internships not APA/CPA accredited, but listed with the Association of Psychology Postdoctoral and Internship Programs (APPIC), (0) students placed in internships conforming to guidelines of the Council of Directors of School Psychology Programs (CDSPP), (1) students placed in internships that were not APA/CPA accredited, APPIC or CDSPP listed. There is a wide variety of placements available in the DC Metro area. Placements are a required part of training in the clinical program.

Housing and Day Care: On-campus housing is available. See the following website for more information: http://living.gwu.edu/halls/graduatehousing. On-campus day care facilities are available. See the following website for more information: http://gradlife.gwu.edu/gradlife/information2/WashingtonDCResourcesandInformation/Family/Daycare/.

Employment of Department Graduates:

Master's Degree Graduates: Of those who graduated in the academic year 2011–2012, the following categories and numbers represent the postgraduate activities and employment of master's degree graduates: Enrolled in a postdoctoral residency/fellowship (n/a), employed in independent practice (n/a), total from the above (master's) (0).

Doctoral Degree Graduates: Of those who graduated in the academic year 2011–2012, the following categories and numbers represent the postgraduate activities and employment of doctoral degree graduates: Enrolled in a psychology doctoral program (n/a), enrolled in a postdoctoral residency/fellowship (3), employed in an academic position at a 2-year/4-year college (1), employed in government agency (2), total from the above (doctoral) (6).

Additional Information:

Orientation, Objectives, and Emphasis of Department: The department provides training in the basic science of psychology for each of its graduate programs. Specialized training is offered in three program areas: applied social, clinical, and cognitive neuropsychology. The applied social program focuses on theory and methods of addressing current social problems such as in health care, education, and the prevention of high risk social behaviors. The clinical program is an APA-approved program emphasizing both the basic science and applied aspects of clinical psychology. The focus of the program is health promotion and disease prevention in diverse urban communities. The cognitive neuroscience program focuses on cognition, learning, and memory with emphasis on the psychobiological determinants of these functions. The training in each program addresses both scientific and professional objectives. Students are trained for careers in academic institutions, applied research, and professional practice.

Special Facilities or Resources: We have excellent on-campus computer facilities; laboratories for child study, group studies, cognitive testing and small animal research. There is convenient access to staff, libraries, and facilities at national health and mental health institutes (NIH) and to mental health training centers for clinical students.

Information for Students With Physical Disabilities: See the following website for more information: http://gwired.gwu.edu/dss.

Application Information:
Send to Graduate School, CCAS, George Washington University, Washington, DC 20052. Application available online. URL of online application: http://graduate.admissions.gwu.edu/. Students are admitted in the Fall, application deadline December 1. Cognitive Neuroscience and Applied Social Psychology deadline is January 5. *Fee:* $65.

George Washington University
Professional Psychology Program
The George Washington University
1922 F Street NW, Suite 130
Washington, DC 20052
Telephone: (202) 994-4929
Fax: (202) 994-4800
E-mail: *psyd@gwu.edu*
Web: *http://programs.columbian.gwu.edu/psyd/*

Department Information:
1996. Program Director: Loring J. Ingraham, PhD. Number of faculty: total—full-time 4, part-time 8; women—full-time 1, part-time 4; total—minority—full-time 2; women minority—full-time 1; faculty subject to the Americans With Disabilities Act 1.

Programs and Degrees Offered:
Listed in the following order: Program area, degree type (T if terminal Master's), number awarded 7/11–6/12. Clinical Psychology PsyD (Doctor of Psychology) 23, Forensic Psychology MA/MS (Master of Arts/Science) (T) 0.

APA Accreditation: Clinical PsyD (Doctor of Psychology). Student Outcome Data Website: http://programs.columbian.gwu.edu/psyd/program-statistics.

Student Applications/Admissions:

Student Applications

Clinical Psychology PsyD (Doctor of Psychology)—Applications 2012–2013, 424. Total applicants accepted 2012–2013, 49. Number full-time enrolled (new admits only) 2012–2013, 28. Number part-time enrolled (new admits only) 2012–2013, 0. Total enrolled 2012–2013 full-time, 80. Total enrolled 2012–2013 part-time, 59. Openings 2013–2014, 30. The median number of years required for completion of a degree in 2012–2013 were 4. The number of students enrolled full- and part-time who were dismissed or voluntarily withdrew from this program area in 2012–2013 were 0. *Forensic Psychology MA/MS (Master of Arts/Science)*—Applications 2012–2013, 129. Total applicants accepted 2012–2013, 52. Number full-time enrolled (new admits only) 2012–2013, 19. Number part-time enrolled (new admits only) 2012–2013, 8. Total enrolled 2012–2013 full-time, 19. Total enrolled 2012–2013 part-time, 8. Openings 2013–2014, 60. The number of students enrolled full- and part-time who were dismissed or voluntarily withdrew from this program area in 2012–2013 were 2.

Scores: Entries appear in this order: required test or GPA, minimum score (if required), median score of students entering in 2012–2013. *Clinical Psychology PsyD (Doctor of Psychology):* GRE-V no minimum stated, 159, GRE-Q no minimum stated, 158, GRE-Analytical no minimum stated, 4.5, overall undergraduate GPA no minimum stated, 3.48; *Forensic Psychology MA/MS (Master of Arts/Science):* GRE-V no minimum stated, 155, GRE-Q no minimum stated, 162, GRE-Analytical no minimum stated, 4.41, overall undergraduate GPA no minimum stated, 3.39.

Other Criteria: (importance of criteria rated low, medium, or high): GRE scores—medium, research experience—medium, work experience—medium, extracurricular activity—medium, clinically related public service—medium, GPA—high, letters of recommendation—high, interview—high, statement of goals and objectives—high, integrity and motivation—high, undergraduate major in psychology—medium, specific undergraduate psychology courses taken—medium, The Forensic Psychology program's admission criteria are different for the following: -Undergraduate Major in Psychology: Low; -Specific Undergraduate psychology courses taken: Low. For additional information on admission requirements, go to http://programs.columbian.gwu.edu/psyd/program/apply.

Student Characteristics: The following represents characteristics of students in 2012–2013 in all graduate psychology programs in the department: Female—full-time 79, part-time 54; Male—full-time 20, part-time 13; African American/Black—full-time 7, part-time 5; Hispanic/Latino(a)—full-time 4, part-time 3; Asian/Pacific Islander—full-time 7, part-time 6; American Indian/Alaska Native—full-time 1, part-time 0; Caucasian/White—full-time 80, part-time 51; Multi-ethnic—full-time 0, part-time 0; students subject to the Americans With Disabilities Act—full-time 0, part-time 0; Unknown ethnicity—full-time 0, part-time 2; International students who hold an F-1 or J-1 Visa—full-time 0, part-time 0.

Financial Information/Assistance:

Tuition for Full-Time Study: *Master's:* State residents: $980 per credit hour; Nonstate residents: $980 per credit hour. *Doctoral:* State residents: $1,310 per credit hour; Nonstate residents: $1,310 per credit hour. Tuition is subject to change. See the following website for updates and changes in tuition costs: http://www.gwu.edu/tuition-and-fees.

Financial Assistance:

First-Year Students: Research assistantships available for first year. Average amount paid per academic year: $3,000. Average number of hours worked per week: 10. Fellowships and scholarships available for first year.

Advanced Students: Fellowships and scholarships available for advanced students.

Additional Information: Of all students currently enrolled full time, 15% benefited from one or more of the listed financial assistance programs. Application and information available online at: http://gwired.gwu.edu/finaid-g/Forms/.

Internships/Practica: Doctoral Degree (PsyD Clinical Psychology): For those doctoral students for whom a professional psychology internship was required in this program prior to graduation, (36) students applied for an internship in 2011–2012, with (30) students obtaining an internship. Of those students who obtained an internship, (28) were paid internships. Of those students who obtained an internship, (17) students placed in APA/CPA accredited internships, (10) students placed in internships not APA/CPA accredited, but listed with the Association of Psychology Postdoctoral and Internship Programs (APPIC), (0) students placed in internships conforming to guidelines of the Council of Directors of School Psychology Programs (CDSPP), (3) students placed in internships that were not APA/CPA accredited, APPIC or CDSPP listed. Master's Degree (MA/MS Forensic Psychology): An internship experience, such as a final research project or "capstone" experience is required of graduates. Professional Psychology program students participate in practica during every term of enrollment. The practicum component, the core experiential learning element of the PsyD program, provides doctoral candidates with the opportunity to integrate theory and practice. During their first year, students are immersed in the basics of psychological assessment and introduced to the psychodynamic approaches to psychotherapy. First-year doctoral students receive hands-on experience administering, scoring, interpreting, and writing reports involving both cognitive and personality assessments. Towards the end of the first year and after the first course in psychodynamic psychotherapy, students begin their supervised experience in conducting psychotherapy in our Center Clinic. In the second year of training, students serve as student clinical externs at the Center Clinic. Rising third-year students have the option of either continuing their training in the Clinic or pursuing an extramural externship outside the Clinic. Additionally, students begin a one-year internship (or a two-year internship, each year at least half time) early in the third year of full time study, after comprehensive exams. The Forensic Psychology program offers externship training, tailored to a student's professional interest, at a law enforcement agency, treatment site, correctional institution, public defender's office, prosecutor's office, or other similar setting.

Housing and Day Care: On-campus housing is available. See the following website for more information: http://living.gwu.edu/halls/graduatehousing/. No on-campus day care facilities are available.

Employment of Department Graduates:

Master's Degree Graduates: Of those who graduated in the academic year 2011–2012, the following categories and numbers

represent the postgraduate activities and employment of master's degree graduates: Enrolled in a postdoctoral residency/fellowship (n/a), employed in independent practice (n/a), total from the above (master's) (0).

Doctoral Degree Graduates: Of those who graduated in the academic year 2011–2012, the following categories and numbers represent the postgraduate activities and employment of doctoral degree graduates: Enrolled in a psychology doctoral program (n/a), enrolled in a postdoctoral residency/fellowship (5), employed in independent practice (5), employed in a community mental health/counseling center (3), still seeking employment (1), other employment position (1), do not know (8), total from the above (doctoral) (23).

Additional Information:

Orientation, Objectives, and Emphasis of Department: The mission of the PsyD Program is to graduate practitioner-scholar professional psychologists who are exceptionally skilled as local clinical scientists in using a psychodynamic framework for the assessment and treatment of psychopathology. Our graduates know the clinical research methods necessary for new discoveries and base their professional practice in ongoing critical consumption of relevant research. We value openness, curiosity, diversity, tolerance, beneficence, humility, methodological ability and professional ethics in the discovery and equitable provision of effective clinical services. The Program also offers a MA in Forensic Psychology. The MA addresses the nation's critical need for criminal profilers, competency experts, psychological evaluators, counselors, and related positions, to help solve crimes and prevent future criminal behavior. Potential employers include agencies involved in homeland security, federal and state law enforcement, correctional systems, and organizations that provide services to criminal offenders and their victims.

Special Facilities or Resources: The Professional Psychology program houses a Center Clinic, which provides mental health services to adults, adolescents, and children in the Washington, DC area who may otherwise not have access to needed care. These services include individual, couples, family, and group psychotherapy, as well as psychological assessment. Patients may also be referred for a psychiatric consultation through a partnership with the University's Department of Psychiatry and Behavioral Science. The Clinic also contributes to local community service agencies (such as public and charter schools, homeless shelters and addiction recovery programs) by providing needed consultation, assessment and therapeutic services free of charge. The Clinic is staffed by PsyD candidates who are supervised by licensed, highly-experienced professionals. All PsyD candidates are required to complete a Clinic externship during their second year of training.

Information for Students With Physical Disabilities: See the following website for more information: http://gwired.gwu.edu/dss.

Application Information:
Send to Columbian College of Arts and Sciences, Graduate Admissions Office, The George Washington University, 801 22nd Street NW, Phillips Hall, Room 107, Washington, DC 20052. Application available online. URL of online application: http://programs.columbian.gwu.edu/psyd/program/apply. Students are admitted in the Fall, application deadline December 1. *Fee:* $75.

Georgetown University
Department of Psychology
Georgetown College
Box 571001, White Gravenor Hall 306
Washington, DC 20057
Telephone: (202) 687-4042
Fax: (202) 687-6050
E-mail: *psychology@georgetown.edu*
Web: *http://psychology.georgetown.edu/*

Department Information:
1970. Chairperson: James Lamiell. Number of faculty: total—full-time 16; women—full-time 10.

Programs and Degrees Offered:
Listed in the following order: Program area, degree type (T if terminal Master's), number awarded 7/11–6/12. Human Development and Public Policy PhD (Doctor of Philosophy) 2, Lifespan Cognitive Neuroscience PhD (Doctor of Philosophy) 2.

Student Applications/Admissions:
Student Applications

Human Development and Public Policy PhD (Doctor of Philosophy)—Applications 2012–2013, 49. Total applicants accepted 2012–2013, 0. Number full-time enrolled (new admits only) 2012–2013, 0. Number part-time enrolled (new admits only) 2012–2013, 0. Total enrolled 2012–2013 full-time, 10. Total enrolled 2012–2013 part-time, 0. Openings 2013–2014, 2. The median number of years required for completion of a degree in 2012–2013 were 5. The number of students enrolled full- and part-time who were dismissed or voluntarily withdrew from this program area in 2012–2013 were 0. *Lifespan Cognitive Neuroscience PhD (Doctor of Philosophy)*—Applications 2012–2013, 34. Total applicants accepted 2012–2013, 2. Number full-time enrolled (new admits only) 2012–2013, 2. Number part-time enrolled (new admits only) 2012–2013, 0. Total enrolled 2012–2013 full-time, 5. Total enrolled 2012–2013 part-time, 0. Openings 2013–2014, 2. The median number of years required for completion of a degree in 2012–2013 were 5. The number of students enrolled full- and part-time who were dismissed or voluntarily withdrew from this program area in 2012–2013 were 0.

Scores: Entries appear in this order: required test or GPA, minimum score (if required), median score of students entering in 2012–2013. *Human Development and Public Policy PhD (Doctor of Philosophy):* GRE-V no minimum stated, GRE-Q no minimum stated, overall undergraduate GPA no minimum stated; *Lifespan Cognitive Neuroscience PhD (Doctor of Philosophy):* GRE-V no minimum stated, GRE-Q no minimum stated, overall undergraduate GPA no minimum stated.

Other Criteria: (importance of criteria rated low, medium, or high): GRE scores—high, research experience—high, work experience—low, extracurricular activity—low, clinically related public service—low, GPA—high, letters of recommendation—high, interview—high, statement of goals and objectives—high. For additional information on admission requirements, go to http://psychology.georgetown.edu/graduate/admissions/.

Student Characteristics: The following represents characteristics of students in 2012–2013 in all graduate psychology programs in the department: Female—full-time 15, part-time 0; Male—full-time 2, part-time 0; African American/Black—full-time 0, part-time 0; Hispanic/Latino(a)—full-time 1, part-time 0; Asian/Pacific Islander—full-time 1, part-time 0; American Indian/Alaska Native—full-time 0, part-time 0; Caucasian/White—full-time 14, part-time 0; Multi-ethnic—full-time 1, part-time 0; students subject to the Americans With Disabilities Act—full-time 0, part-time 0; Unknown ethnicity—full-time 0, part-time 0; International students who hold an F-1 or J-1 Visa—full-time 1, part-time 0.

Financial Information/Assistance:

Tuition for Full-Time Study: *Doctoral:* State residents: per academic year $44,408; Nonstate residents: per academic year $44,408. Tuition is subject to change. Additional fees are assessed to students beyond the costs of tuition for the following: health insurance, athletic access fee. See the following website for updates and changes in tuition costs: http://finaid.georgetown.edu/cost-of-attendance/graduate/.

Financial Assistance:

First-Year Students: Teaching assistantships available for first year. Average amount paid per academic year: $22,000. Average number of hours worked per week: 15.

Advanced Students: Teaching assistantships available for advanced students. Average amount paid per academic year: $22,000. Average number of hours worked per week: 15.

Additional Information: Of all students currently enrolled full time, 100% benefited from one or more of the listed financial assistance programs. Application and information available online at: http://psychology.georgetown.edu/graduate/admissions/financial-support/.

Housing and Day Care: No on-campus housing is available. On-campus day care facilities are available. See the following website for more information: http://www3.georgetown.edu/hr/hoya_kids/index.html.

Employment of Department Graduates:

Master's Degree Graduates: Of those who graduated in the academic year 2011–2012, the following categories and numbers represent the postgraduate activities and employment of master's degree graduates: Enrolled in a postdoctoral residency/fellowship (n/a), employed in independent practice (n/a), total from the above (master's) (0).

Doctoral Degree Graduates: Of those who graduated in the academic year 2011–2012, the following categories and numbers represent the postgraduate activities and employment of doctoral degree graduates: Enrolled in a psychology doctoral program (n/a), employed in government agency (2), total from the above (doctoral) (2).

Additional Information:

Orientation, Objectives, and Emphasis of Department: We are an intellectually diverse community of scholars engaged in research addressing both basic psychological processes and social issues. We strive for excellence in our scholarship and teaching, and we seek to cultivate in our students a dedication to the highest standards in their endeavors. We are committed to collaboration within and across disciplinary lines and to sustaining professional links with relevant local, national, and global organizations.

Special Facilities or Resources: Graduate students have office space in a graduate student suite or faculty laboratory space. They enter a rich interdisciplinary community in which psychology graduate students take courses with graduate students from public policy, neuroscience, linguistics, and other related disciplines. The Psychology Department has an observational laboratory facility as well as faculty laboratories investigating cognitive and developmental issues. The department also maintains the Georgetown Research Volunteer Project, a university-funded, Web-based facility for recruiting research participants across the lifespan. The Medical Center, which is immediately adjacent to the Main Campus, contains the Center for Functional and Molecular Imaging, affording the opportunity to conduct research using fMRI and other state-of-the-art neuroimaging technology.

Information for Students With Physical Disabilities: See the following website for more information: http://academicsupport.georgetown.edu/disability/.

Application Information:

Send to Georgetown Graduate School of Arts and Sciences. Application available online. URL of online application: http://grad.georgetown.edu/admissions/. Students are admitted in the Fall, application deadline December 1. *Fee:* $80.

Barry University

Department of Psychology
College of Arts and Sciences
11300 NE 2nd Avenue
Miami Shores, FL 33161
Telephone: (305) 899-3270
Fax: (305) 899-3279
E-mail: *fmuscarella@mail.barry.edu*
Web: *http://www.barry.edu/psychologyclinical/*

Department Information:

1978. Chairperson: Frank Muscarella, PhD. Number of faculty: total—full-time 8, part-time 7; women—full-time 3, part-time 4; total—minority—full-time 3, part-time 2; women minority—full-time 2, part-time 1.

Programs and Degrees Offered:

Listed in the following order: Program area, degree type (T if terminal Master's), number awarded 7/11–6/12. Clinical Psychology MA/MS (Master of Arts/Science) (T) 4.

Student Applications/Admissions:

Student Applications

Clinical Psychology MA/MS (Master of Arts/Science)—Applications 2012–2013, 61. Total applicants accepted 2012–2013, 16. Number full-time enrolled (new admits only) 2012–2013, 5. Number part-time enrolled (new admits only) 2012–2013, 0. Total enrolled 2012–2013 full-time, 19. Total enrolled 2012–2013 part-time, 6. Openings 2013–2014, 15. The median number of years required for completion of a degree in 2012–2013 were 2. The number of students enrolled full- and part-time who were dismissed or voluntarily withdrew from this program area in 2012–2013 were 3.

Other Criteria: (importance of criteria rated low, medium, or high): GRE scores—medium, research experience—medium, work experience—medium, extracurricular activity—low, clinically related public service—medium, GPA—high, letters of recommendation—high, statement of goals and objectives—high, undergraduate major in psychology—medium, specific undergraduate psychology courses taken—high. For additional information on admission requirements, go to http://www.barry.edu/clinical-psychology/admissions/admission-requirements.html.

Student Characteristics: The following represents characteristics of students in 2012–2013 in all graduate psychology programs in the department: Female—full-time 13, part-time 6; Male—full-time 6, part-time 0; African American/Black—full-time 2, part-time 0; Hispanic/Latino(a)—full-time 4, part-time 2; Asian/Pacific Islander—full-time 0, part-time 0; American Indian/Alaska Native—full-time 0, part-time 0; Caucasian/White—full-time 8, part-time 4; Multi-ethnic—full-time 0, part-time 0; students subject to the Americans With Disabilities Act—full-time 0, part-time 0; Unknown ethnicity—full-time 5, part-time 0; International students who hold an F-1 or J-1 Visa—full-time 5, part-time 0.

Financial Information/Assistance:

Tuition for Full-Time Study: Master's: State residents: $935 per credit hour; Nonstate residents: $935 per credit hour. Tuition is subject to change. See the following website for updates and changes in tuition costs: http://www.barry.edu/clinical-psychology/admissions/tuition-fees.html.

Financial Assistance:

First-Year Students: Teaching assistantships available for first year. Average amount paid per academic year: $4,215. Average number of hours worked per week: 14. Apply by April 30.

Advanced Students: Teaching assistantships available for advanced students. Average amount paid per academic year: $4,215. Average number of hours worked per week: 14. Apply by April 30.

Additional Information: Of all students currently enrolled full time, 12% benefited from one or more of the listed financial assistance programs. Application and information available online at: http://www.barry.edu/clinical-psychology/financial-aid/.

Internships/Practica: Master's Degree (MA/MS Clinical Psychology): An internship experience, such as a final research project or "capstone" experience is required of graduates. All students enrolled in the M.S. in Clinical Psychology program must complete a one-semester practicum. Students in the 60-credit program must also complete a two-semester full-time clinical internship. Because Barry University is located in a large, multi-cultural metropolitan area, the program is able to offer more than the usual number and variety of settings for the internship experience. Sites include but are not limited to community mental health centers, assessment centers (primarily for the assessment of children), psychiatric hospitals, addiction treatment programs, nursing homes, and prison settings. Supervision is provided both at the site and by a clinical supervisor on campus.

Housing and Day Care: No on-campus housing is available. No on-campus day care facilities are available.

Employment of Department Graduates:

Master's Degree Graduates: Of those who graduated in the academic year 2011–2012, the following categories and numbers represent the postgraduate activities and employment of master's degree graduates: Enrolled in a psychology doctoral program (2), enrolled in another graduate/professional program (1), enrolled in a postdoctoral residency/fellowship (n/a), employed in independent practice (n/a), employed in a community mental health/counseling center (1), total from the above (master's) (4).

Doctoral Degree Graduates: Of those who graduated in the academic year 2011–2012, the following categories and numbers represent the postgraduate activities and employment of doctoral degree graduates: Enrolled in a psychology doctoral program (n/a), total from the above (doctoral) (0).

Additional Information:

Orientation, Objectives, and Emphasis of Department: In the M.S. Program in Clinical Psychology, students are expected to achieve competence in theory, assessment, therapy, and research. All clinical psychology students complete a thesis and a practicum.

The 36-credit option, a 2-year program, is designed for students who want to go directly into a doctoral program. Students who complete the 3-year, 60-credit program meet licensure requirements for the Mental Health Counselor in Florida. In the third year these students complete a full-time internship.

Special Facilities or Resources: The psychology department is normally composed of 8 full-time faculty members. Classes are small, and the students are given individual attention and supervision.

Information for Students With Physical Disabilities: See the following website for more information: http://www.barry.edu/disability-services/.

Application Information:
Send to Office of Enrollment Services, Barry University, 11300 NE 2nd Avenue, Miami FL 33161. Application available online. URL of online application: http://www.barry.edu/future-students/graduate/admissions/. Students are admitted in the Fall, application deadline February 15. Deadline is February 15 with review continuing as long as space is available. *Fee:* $30.

Central Florida, University of
Department of Psychology
College of Sciences
P.O. Box 161390
Orlando, FL 32816-1390
Telephone: (407) 823-3576
Fax: (407) 823-5862
E-mail: *psyinfo@ucf.edu*
Web: *http://psychology.cos.ucf.edu/*

Department Information:
1968. Chairperson: Jeffrey E. Cassisi, PhD. Number of faculty: total—full-time 49; women—full-time 21; total—minority—full-time 5; women minority—full-time 1; faculty subject to the Americans With Disabilities Act 1.

Programs and Degrees Offered:
Listed in the following order: Program area, degree type (T if terminal Master's), number awarded 7/11–6/12. Clinical Psychology MA/MS (Master of Arts/Science) (T) 15, Industrial/Organizational Psychology MA/MS (Master of Arts/Science) (T) 21, Applied Experimental and Human Factors PhD (Doctor of Philosophy) 8, Clinical Psychology PhD (Doctor of Philosophy) 1, Industrial/Organizational Psychology PhD (Doctor of Philosophy) 4.

APA Accreditation: Clinical PhD (Doctor of Philosophy). Student Outcome Data Website: http://psychology.cos.ucf.edu/graduate/ph-d-clinical/.

Student Applications/Admissions:
Student Applications
Clinical Psychology MA/MS (Master of Arts/Science)—Applications 2012–2013, 129. Total applicants accepted 2012–2013, 20. Number full-time enrolled (new admits only) 2012–2013,

16. Total enrolled 2012–2013 full-time, 30. Openings 2013–2014, 16. The median number of years required for completion of a degree in 2012–2013 were 2. The number of students enrolled full- and part-time who were dismissed or voluntarily withdrew from this program area in 2012–2013 were 0. *Industrial/Organizational Psychology MA/MS (Master of Arts/Science)*—Applications 2012–2013, 88. Total applicants accepted 2012–2013, 14. Number full-time enrolled (new admits only) 2012–2013, 12. Total enrolled 2012–2013 full-time, 29. Openings 2013–2014, 14. The median number of years required for completion of a degree in 2012–2013 were 2. The number of students enrolled full- and part-time who were dismissed or voluntarily withdrew from this program area in 2012–2013 were 0. *Applied Experimental and Human Factors PhD (Doctor of Philosophy)*—Applications 2012–2013, 45. Total applicants accepted 2012–2013, 11. Number full-time enrolled (new admits only) 2012–2013, 10. Number part-time enrolled (new admits only) 2012–2013, 0. Total enrolled 2012–2013 full-time, 54. Total enrolled 2012–2013 part-time, 0. Openings 2013–2014, 8. The median number of years required for completion of a degree in 2012–2013 were 6. The number of students enrolled full- and part-time who were dismissed or voluntarily withdrew from this program area in 2012–2013 were 0. *Clinical Psychology PhD (Doctor of Philosophy)*—Applications 2012–2013, 214. Total applicants accepted 2012–2013, 4. Number full-time enrolled (new admits only) 2012–2013, 4. Number part-time enrolled (new admits only) 2012–2013, 0. Total enrolled 2012–2013 full-time, 39. Total enrolled 2012–2013 part-time, 0. Openings 2013–2014, 8. The median number of years required for completion of a degree in 2012–2013 were 7. The number of students enrolled full- and part-time who were dismissed or voluntarily withdrew from this program area in 2012–2013 were 2. *Industrial/Organizational Psychology PhD (Doctor of Philosophy)*—Applications 2012–2013, 70. Total applicants accepted 2012–2013, 5. Number full-time enrolled (new admits only) 2012–2013, 5. Number part-time enrolled (new admits only) 2012–2013, 0. Total enrolled 2012–2013 full-time, 34. Total enrolled 2012–2013 part-time, 0. Openings 2013–2014, 6. The median number of years required for completion of a degree in 2012–2013 were 5. The number of students enrolled full- and part-time who were dismissed or voluntarily withdrew from this program area in 2012–2013 were 0.

Scores: Entries appear in this order: required test or GPA, minimum score (if required), median score of students entering in 2012–2013. *Industrial/Organizational Psychology MA/MS (Master of Arts/Science):* GRE-V 500, GRE-Q 500, overall undergraduate GPA 3.0; *Applied Experimental and Human Factors PhD (Doctor of Philosophy):* GRE-V 500, GRE-Q 500, overall undergraduate GPA 3.0, last 2 years GPA no minimum stated, psychology GPA no minimum stated, Masters GPA 3.0; *Clinical Psychology PhD (Doctor of Philosophy):* GRE-V 152, 157, GRE-Q 151, 157, overall undergraduate GPA 2.8, 3.2; *Industrial/Organizational Psychology PhD (Doctor of Philosophy):* GRE-V 500, 650, GRE-Q 640, 720, overall undergraduate GPA 3.7, 3.8, last 2 years GPA no minimum stated, psychology GPA no minimum stated.

Other Criteria: (importance of criteria rated low, medium, or high): GRE scores—high, research experience—high, work experience—low, extracurricular activity—medium, clinically related public service—medium, GPA—high, letters of recommendation—high, interview—high, statement of goals and objectives—high, undergraduate major in psychology—low, specific undergraduate psychology courses taken—medium, Criteria vary by program.

Student Characteristics: The following represents characteristics of students in 2012–2013 in all graduate psychology programs in the department: Female—full-time 117, part-time 0; Male—full-time 70, part-time 0; African American/Black—full-time 10, part-time 0; Hispanic/Latino(a)—full-time 16, part-time 0; Asian/Pacific Islander—full-time 10, part-time 0; American Indian/Alaska Native—full-time 3, part-time 0; Caucasian/White—full-time 140, part-time 0; Multi-ethnic—full-time 0, part-time 0; students subject to the Americans With Disabilities Act—full-time 2, part-time 0; Unknown ethnicity—full-time 8, part-time 0; International students who hold an F-1 or J-1 Visa—full-time 4, part-time 0.

Financial Information/Assistance:

Tuition for Full-Time Study: *Master's:* State residents: $288 per credit hour; Nonstate residents: $1,043 per credit hour. *Doctoral:* State residents: per academic year $7,758, $288 per credit hour; Nonstate residents: per academic year $28,897, $1,043 per credit hour. Tuition is subject to change. Additional fees are assessed to students beyond the costs of tuition for the following: additional fees are up to $100 depending on course. See the following website for updates and changes in tuition costs: http://tuitionfees.smca.ucf.edu/.

Financial Assistance:

First-Year Students: Teaching assistantships available for first year. Average amount paid per academic year: $10,000. Average number of hours worked per week: 20. Research assistantships available for first year. Average amount paid per academic year: $15,000. Average number of hours worked per week: 20. Fellowships and scholarships available for first year. Average amount paid per academic year: $13,500. Average number of hours worked per week: 20.

Advanced Students: Teaching assistantships available for advanced students. Average amount paid per academic year: $10,000. Average number of hours worked per week: 20. Research assistantships available for advanced students. Average amount paid per academic year: $15,000. Average number of hours worked per week: 20. Fellowships and scholarships available for advanced students. Average amount paid per academic year: $13,500. Average number of hours worked per week: 20.

Additional Information: Of all students currently enrolled full time, 90% benefited from one or more of the listed financial assistance programs. Application and information available online at: http://www.admissions.graduate.ucf.edu/funding/.

Internships/Practica: Doctoral Degree (PhD Clinical Psychology): For those doctoral students for whom a professional psychology internship was required in this program prior to graduation, (5) students applied for an internship in 2011–2012, with (5) students obtaining an internship. Of those students who obtained an internship, (5) were paid internships. Of those students who obtained an internship, (5) students placed in APA/CPA accredited internships, (0) students placed in internships not APA/CPA accredited, but listed with the Association of Psychology Postdoctoral and Internship Programs (APPIC), (0) students placed in internships conforming to guidelines of the Council of Directors of School Psychology Programs (CDSPP), (0) students placed in internships that were not APA/CPA accredited, APPIC or CDSPP listed. Master's Degree (MA/MS Clinical Psychology): An internship experience, such as a final research project or "capstone" experience is required of graduates. Master's Degree (MA/MS Industrial/Organizational Psychology): An internship experience, such as a final research project or "capstone" experience is required of graduates. Clinical: Internships for clinical masters students exist in community mental health centers and other agencies throughout Central Florida. Doctoral students complete their practica in our on-campus clinic as well as in a variety of community based clinical agencies. Human Factors: Human Factors students complete internships in a variety of government, business, and industry settings. Industrial/Organizational: I/O master's students complete practica placements in a variety of government, business and industry settings. Doctoral students complete an internship in a variety of business, industry and government settings.

Housing and Day Care: On-campus housing is available. See the following website for more information: http://www.housing.ucf.edu/. On-campus day care facilities are available. See the following website for more information: http://csc.sdes.ucf.edu/.

Employment of Department Graduates:

Master's Degree Graduates: Of those who graduated in the academic year 2011–2012, the following categories and numbers represent the postgraduate activities and employment of master's degree graduates: Enrolled in a psychology doctoral program (6), enrolled in another graduate/professional program (1), enrolled in a postdoctoral residency/fellowship (n/a), employed in independent practice (n/a), employed in other positions at a higher education institution (1), employed in business or industry (10), employed in government agency (5), employed in a community mental health/counseling center (12), employed in a hospital/medical center (1), still seeking employment (3), do not know (4), total from the above (master's) (43).

Doctoral Degree Graduates: Of those who graduated in the academic year 2011–2012, the following categories and numbers represent the postgraduate activities and employment of doctoral degree graduates: Enrolled in a psychology doctoral program (n/a), employed in an academic position at a university (7), employed in business or industry (14), employed in government agency (2), employed in a hospital/medical center (3), total from the above (doctoral) (26).

Additional Information:

Orientation, Objectives, and Emphasis of Department: The PhD program in clinical psychology is an APA accredited program, designed for individuals seeking a research oriented career in the field of clinical psychology. The program also emphasizes training in consultation, teaching, supervision, and the design/evaluation of mental health programs. The MA program in clinical psychology has major emphases in assessment and evaluation skills; intervention, counseling, and psychotherapy skills; and an academic foundation in research methods. The program is designed to provide training and preparation for persons desiring to deliver clinical services at the master's level through community agencies. Graduates of this program meet the educational requirements for the mental health counselor state license. The MS program in Industrial/Organizational psychology has major emphases in selection and training of employees, applied theories of organizational behavior, job satisfaction, test theory and construction; assessment center technology, statistics and experimental design. I/O students receive training in the 21 competence areas detailed by Division 14 of the APA. The PhD program in applied experimental human factors is patterned on the scientist–practitioner model of the APA. It adheres to the guidelines for education and training established by the committee for Education and Training of APA's Division 21 (Applied Experimental and Engineering Psychology). The Applied Experimental and Human Factors program is accredited by the Educational Committee of the Human Factors and Ergonomics Society. Concentration areas include human-computer interaction, human performance, and human factors in simulation and training.

Special Facilities or Resources: The department's facilities and resources include extensive videotape capability, an intelligence and personality testing library, a statistics library, computer facilities within the department and in the computer center, a counseling and testing center, a creative school for children, and a communicative disorders clinic. Doctoral students have use of specialized equipment in the department-based Human Visual Performance Laboratory and Team Performance Laboratory. The clinical program has extensive ties to a number of community agencies for practica and internships as well as an on-site clinic.

Information for Students With Physical Disabilities: See the following website for more information: http://sds.sdes.ucf.edu/.

Application Information:

Send to University of Central Florida, Department of Psychology-ATTN: Graduate Admissions, P.O. Box 161390, Orlando, FL 32816-1390. Application available online. URL of online application: http://www.students.graduate.ucf.edu/gradonlineapp/. Students are admitted in the Fall, application deadline December 15. The Clinical PhD application deadline is December 1. *Fee:* $30.

Florida Atlantic University (2012 data)
Psychology
Charles E. Schmidt College of Science
777 Glades Road, P.O. Box 3091
Boca Raton, FL 33431-0991
Telephone: (561) 297-3360
Fax: (561) 297-2160
E-mail: laursen@fau.edu
Web: http://www.psy.fau.edu

Department Information:
1965. Chairperson: David L. Wolgin. Number of faculty: total—full-time 28; women—full-time 7; total—minority—full-time 2; women minority—full-time 1.

Programs and Degrees Offered:
Listed in the following order: Program area, degree type (T if terminal Master's), number awarded 7/11–6/12. General-Experimental Psychology MA/MS (Master of Arts/Science) (T) 10, Experimental Psychology PhD (Doctor of Philosophy) 4.

Student Applications/Admissions:
Student Applications
General-Experimental Psychology MA/MS (Master of Arts/Science)—Applications 2012–2013, 75. Total applicants accepted 2012–2013, 30. Number full-time enrolled (new admits only) 2012–2013, 10. Number part-time enrolled (new admits only) 2012–2013, 0. Total enrolled 2012–2013 full-time, 37. Total enrolled 2012–2013 part-time, 5. Openings 2013–2014, 20. The median number of years required for completion of a degree in 2012–2013 were 2. The number of students enrolled full- and part-time who were dismissed or voluntarily withdrew from this program area in 2012–2013 were 5. *Experimental Psychology PhD (Doctor of Philosophy)*—Applications 2012–2013, 54. Total applicants accepted 2012–2013, 17. Number full-time enrolled (new admits only) 2012–2013, 10. Number part-time enrolled (new admits only) 2012–2013, 0. Total enrolled 2012–2013 full-time, 24. Total enrolled 2012–2013 part-time, 8. Openings 2013–2014, 10. The median number of years required for completion of a degree in 2012–2013 were 5. The number of students enrolled full- and part-time who were dismissed or voluntarily withdrew from this program area in 2012–2013 were 2.

Scores: Entries appear in this order: required test or GPA, minimum score (if required), median score of students entering in 2012–2013. *General-Experimental Psychology MA/MS (Master of Arts/Science)*: GRE-V 150, GRE-Q 150, last 2 years GPA 3.0; *Experimental Psychology PhD (Doctor of Philosophy)*: GRE-V 153, 159, GRE-Q 152, 157, last 2 years GPA 3.0.

Other Criteria: (importance of criteria rated low, medium, or high): GRE scores—high, research experience—high, clinically related public service—low, GPA—high, letters of recommendation—high, statement of goals and objectives—high, undergraduate major in psychology—medium, specific undergraduate psychology courses taken—low.

Student Characteristics: The following represents characteristics of students in 2012–2013 in all graduate psychology programs in the department: Female—full-time 34, part-time 8; Male—full-time 27, part-time 5; African American/Black—full-time 2, part-time 1; Hispanic/Latino(a)—full-time 6, part-time 0; Asian/Pacific Islander—full-time 3, part-time 0; American Indian/Alaska Native—full-time 0, part-time 0; Caucasian/White—full-time 50, part-time 12; Multi-ethnic—full-time 0, part-time 0; students subject to the Americans With Disabilities Act—full-time 0, part-time 0; Unknown ethnicity—full-time 0, part-time 0; International students who hold an F-1 or J-1 Visa—full-time 5, part-time 0.

Financial Information/Assistance:
Tuition for Full-Time Study: *Master's:* State residents: $343 per credit hour; Nonstate residents: $997 per credit hour. *Doctoral:* State residents: $343 per credit hour; Nonstate residents: $997 per credit hour. Tuition is subject to change. See the following website for updates and changes in tuition costs: http://www.fau.edu/controller/student_information/tuition_breakdown.php.

Financial Assistance:
First-Year Students: Teaching assistantships available for first year. Average amount paid per academic year: $20,050. Average number of hours worked per week: 20. Apply by August 1. Research assistantships available for first year. Average amount paid per academic year: $20,050. Average number of hours worked per week: 20. Apply by August 1. Fellowships and scholarships available for first year. Average amount paid per academic year: $25,000. Average number of hours worked per week: 20. Apply by January 1.

Advanced Students: Teaching assistantships available for advanced students. Average amount paid per academic year: $20,050. Average number of hours worked per week: 20. Apply by August 1. Research assistantships available for advanced students. Average amount paid per academic year: $20,050. Average number of hours worked per week: 20. Apply by August 1. Fellowships and scholarships available for advanced students. Average amount paid per academic year: $25,000. Average number of hours worked per week: 20. Apply by January 1.

Additional Information: Of all students currently enrolled full time, 100% benefited from one or more of the listed financial assistance programs. Application and information available online.

Housing and Day Care: On-campus housing is available. See the following website for more information: http://www.fau.edu/housing/. On-campus day care facilities are available. See the following website for more information: http://www.coe.fau.edu/erccd/.

Employment of Department Graduates:

Master's Degree Graduates: Of those who graduated in the academic year 2011–2012, the following categories and numbers represent the postgraduate activities and employment of master's degree graduates: Enrolled in a psychology doctoral program (8), enrolled in another graduate/professional program (4), enrolled in a postdoctoral residency/fellowship (n/a), employed in independent practice (n/a), employed in business or industry (2), employed in government agency (1), employed in a community mental health/counseling center (2), employed in a hospital/medical center (1), do not know (2), total from the above (master's) (20).

Doctoral Degree Graduates: Of those who graduated in the academic year 2011–2012, the following categories and numbers represent the postgraduate activities and employment of doctoral degree graduates: Enrolled in a psychology doctoral program (n/a), enrolled in a postdoctoral residency/fellowship (2), employed in an academic position at a university (0), employed in an academic position at a 2-year/4-year college (2), employed in a professional position in a school system (0), do not know (0), total from the above (doctoral) (4).

Additional Information:

Orientation, Objectives, and Emphasis of Department: The PhD program emphasizes research in several areas of experimental psychology. Students may select courses and conduct research in five areas: cognitive psychology, developmental psychology, evolutionary psychology, psychobiology/neuroscience, and social/personality psychology. Current research by faculty includes psycholinguistics, sentence processing, visual perception, and speech production and perception; the role of parent and peer relationships in individual adaptation; the relation between tool use and style of play in preschool children; mental synchronization in social interaction; neural mechanisms in recovery of function from brain damage, psychopharmacology, and nonlinear dynamics of brain and behavior; the use of traits to predict behavior, sex differences in mating, domestic violence, and the dynamics of social influence. The MA program is designed to prepare students

for entry into doctoral-level programs in all areas of psychology. Research in developmental psychology uses a campus laboratory school for children in kindergarten through the eighth grade. Research in social/personality psychology uses laboratories with video and online computer facilities. The cognitive psychology laboratories include testing rooms with a network of PCs for online control of experiments in perception, learning, language, and cognition. The EEG laboratory includes an acoustic isolation chamber and a variety of amplifying and recording systems.

Special Facilities or Resources: Faculty in the Department of Psychology collaborate with scholars at the FAU Center for Complex Systems and Brain Sciences, the Max Planck Florida Institute, and the Torrey Pines Institute for Molecular Studies.

Information for Students With Physical Disabilities: See the following website for more information: http://osd.fau.edu/.

Application Information:
Application available online. URL of online application: http://www.psy.fau.edu/graduate/onlineAppform/graduate/application.html. Students are admitted in the Fall, application deadline January 15. PhD Application Deadline January 15 MA Application Deadline May 1. *Fee:* $30.

Florida Institute of Technology
School of Psychology
College of Psychology and Liberal Arts
150 West University Boulevard
Melbourne, FL 32901-6988
Telephone: (321) 674-8104
Fax: (321) 674-7105
E-mail: *mkenkel@fit.edu*
Web: *http://cpla.fit.edu/psych/*

Department Information:
1978. Dean, College of Psychology and Liberal Arts: Mary Beth Kenkel. Number of faculty: total—full-time 34, part-time 4; women—full-time 18, part-time 1; total—minority—full-time 4; women minority—full-time 3; faculty subject to the Americans With Disabilities Act 2.

Programs and Degrees Offered:
Listed in the following order: Program area, degree type (T if terminal Master's), number awarded 7/11–6/12. Applied Behavior Analysis MA/MS (Master of Arts/Science) (T) 19, Clinical Psychology PsyD (Doctor of Psychology) 13, Industrial/Organizational Psychology MA/MS (Master of Arts/Science) (T) 17, Industrial/Organizational Psychology PhD (Doctor of Philosophy) 3, Organizational Behavior Management MA/MS (Master of Arts/Science) (T) 4, Applied Behavior Analysis PhD (Doctor of Philosophy) 2, Applied Behavior Analysis and Org Behavior MA/MS (Master of Arts/Science) (T) 3.

APA Accreditation: Clinical PsyD (Doctor of Psychology). Student Outcome Data Website: http://cpla.fit.edu/clinical/outcomes.php.

Student Applications/Admissions:

Student Applications

Applied Behavior Analysis MA/MS (Master of Arts/Science)—Applications 2012–2013, 99. Total applicants accepted 2012–2013, 64. Number full-time enrolled (new admits only) 2012–2013, 20. Number part-time enrolled (new admits only) 2012–2013, 0. Total enrolled 2012–2013 full-time, 52. Total enrolled 2012–2013 part-time, 0. Openings 2013–2014, 30. The median number of years required for completion of a degree in 2012–2013 were 2. The number of students enrolled full- and part-time who were dismissed or voluntarily withdrew from this program area in 2012–2013 were 1. *Clinical Psychology PsyD (Doctor of Psychology)*—Applications 2012–2013, 155. Total applicants accepted 2012–2013, 44. Number full-time enrolled (new admits only) 2012–2013, 19. Number part-time enrolled (new admits only) 2012–2013, 0. Total enrolled 2012–2013 full-time, 99. Total enrolled 2012–2013 part-time, 3. Openings 2013–2014, 22. The median number of years required for completion of a degree in 2012–2013 were 5. The number of students enrolled full- and part-time who were dismissed or voluntarily withdrew from this program area in 2012–2013 were 2. *Industrial/Organizational Psychology MA/MS (Master of Arts/Science)*—Applications 2012–2013, 88. Total applicants accepted 2012–2013, 29. Number full-time enrolled (new admits only) 2012–2013, 10. Number part-time enrolled (new admits only) 2012–2013, 0. Total enrolled 2012–2013 full-time, 27. Total enrolled 2012–2013 part-time, 1. Openings 2013–2014, 8. The median number of years required for completion of a degree in 2012–2013 were 2. The number of students enrolled full- and part-time who were dismissed or voluntarily withdrew from this program area in 2012–2013 were 1. *Industrial/Organizational Psychology PhD (Doctor of Philosophy)*—Applications 2012–2013, 48. Total applicants accepted 2012–2013, 15. Number full-time enrolled (new admits only) 2012–2013, 7. Number part-time enrolled (new admits only) 2012–2013, 0. Total enrolled 2012–2013 full-time, 33. Total enrolled 2012–2013 part-time, 2. Openings 2013–2014, 4. The median number of years required for completion of a degree in 2012–2013 were 5. The number of students enrolled full- and part-time who were dismissed or voluntarily withdrew from this program area in 2012–2013 were 1. *Organizational Behavior Management MA/MS (Master of Arts/Science)*—Applications 2012–2013, 7. Total applicants accepted 2012–2013, 2. Number full-time enrolled (new admits only) 2012–2013, 2. Number part-time enrolled (new admits only) 2012–2013, 0. Total enrolled 2012–2013 full-time, 3. Total enrolled 2012–2013 part-time, 0. Openings 2013–2014, 7. The median number of years required for completion of a degree in 2012–2013 were 3. The number of students enrolled full- and part-time who were dismissed or voluntarily withdrew from this program area in 2012–2013 were 0. *Applied Behavior Analysis PhD (Doctor of Philosophy)*—Applications 2012–2013, 18. Total applicants accepted 2012–2013, 3. Number full-time enrolled (new admits only) 2012–2013, 3. Number part-time enrolled (new admits only) 2012–2013, 0. Total enrolled 2012–2013 full-time, 10. Total enrolled 2012–2013 part-time, 0. Openings

2013–2014, 4. The median number of years required for completion of a degree in 2012–2013 were 2. The number of students enrolled full- and part-time who were dismissed or voluntarily withdrew from this program area in 2012–2013 were 0. *Applied Behavior Analysis and Org Behavior MA/MS (Master of Arts/Science)*—Applications 2012–2013, 15. Total applicants accepted 2012–2013, 14. Number full-time enrolled (new admits only) 2012–2013, 4. Number part-time enrolled (new admits only) 2012–2013, 0. Total enrolled 2012–2013 full-time, 17. Total enrolled 2012–2013 part-time, 1. Openings 2013–2014, 7. The median number of years required for completion of a degree in 2012–2013 were 3. The number of students enrolled full- and part-time who were dismissed or voluntarily withdrew from this program area in 2012–2013 were 0.

Scores: Entries appear in this order: required test or GPA, minimum score (if required), median score of students entering in 2012–2013. *Applied Behavior Analysis MA/MS (Master of Arts/Science):* GRE-V no minimum stated, 149, GRE-Q no minimum stated, 143, GRE-Analytical no minimum stated, 4.0, overall undergraduate GPA 3.0, 3.43, last 2 years GPA no minimum stated, 3.75, psychology GPA no minimum stated, 3.61; *Clinical Psychology PsyD (Doctor of Psychology):* GRE-V no minimum stated, 154, GRE-Q no minimum stated, 149, GRE-Analytical no minimum stated, 4.0, overall undergraduate GPA 3.0, 3.6, last 2 years GPA no minimum stated, 3.75, psychology GPA no minimum stated, 3.8, Masters GPA 3.2, 3.9; *Industrial/Organizational Psychology MA/MS (Master of Arts/Science):* GRE-V no minimum stated, 153, GRE-Q no minimum stated, 152, GRE-Analytical no minimum stated, 4.0, overall undergraduate GPA 3.0, 3.67, last 2 years GPA no minimum stated, 3.72, psychology GPA no minimum stated, 3.76; *Industrial/Organizational Psychology PhD (Doctor of Philosophy):* GRE-V no minimum stated, 155, GRE-Q no minimum stated, 155, GRE-Analytical no minimum stated, 4.25, overall undergraduate GPA 3.0, 3.77, last 2 years GPA no minimum stated, 3.72, psychology GPA no minimum stated, 3.9, Masters GPA 3.26, 3.94; *Organizational Behavior Management MA/MS (Master of Arts/Science):* GRE-V no minimum stated, 150, GRE-Q no minimum stated, 152, GRE-Analytical no minimum stated, 4.0, overall undergraduate GPA 3.0, 3.68, last 2 years GPA no minimum stated, 3.57, psychology GPA no minimum stated, 3.68; *Applied Behavior Analysis PhD (Doctor of Philosophy):* GRE-V no minimum stated, 430, GRE-Q no minimum stated, 630, GRE-Analytical no minimum stated, 4.0, overall undergraduate GPA 3.0, 3.65, last 2 years GPA no minimum stated, 3.9, psychology GPA no minimum stated, 3.8, Masters GPA 3.2, 4.0; *Applied Behavior Analysis and Org Behavior MA/MS (Master of Arts/Science):* GRE-V no minimum stated, 154, GRE-Q no minimum stated, 149, GRE-Analytical no minimum stated, 4.0, overall undergraduate GPA 3.0, 3.5, last 2 years GPA no minimum stated, 3.73, psychology GPA no minimum stated, 3.7.

Other Criteria: (importance of criteria rated low, medium, or high): GRE scores—medium, research experience—medium, work experience—high, extracurricular activity—medium, clinically related public service—high, GPA—high, letters of recommendation—high, interview—medium, statement of goals and objectives—medium, undergraduate major in psychology—medium, specific undergraduate psychology courses taken—medium. For additional information on admission requirements, go to http://cpla.fit.edu/psych/.

Student Characteristics: The following represents characteristics of students in 2012–2013 in all graduate psychology programs in the department: Female—full-time 193, part-time 2; Male—full-time 48, part-time 5; African American/Black—full-time 10, part-time 0; Hispanic/Latino(a)—full-time 20, part-time 1; Asian/Pacific Islander—full-time 12, part-time 0; American Indian/Alaska Native—full-time 0, part-time 0; Caucasian/White—full-time 188, part-time 6; Multi-ethnic—full-time 5, part-time 0; students subject to the Americans With Disabilities Act—full-time 1, part-time 0; Unknown ethnicity—full-time 6, part-time 0; International students who hold an F-1 or J-1 Visa—full-time 19, part-time 0.

Financial Information/Assistance:

Tuition for Full-Time Study: *Master's:* State residents: $1,123 per credit hour; Nonstate residents: $1,123 per credit hour. *Doctoral:* State residents: per academic year $30,321, $1,123 per credit hour; Nonstate residents: per academic year $30,321, $1,123 per credit hour. Tuition is subject to change. Tuition costs vary by program. See the following website for updates and changes in tuition costs: http://www.fit.edu/registrar/registration/tuitionchrgs.php. Higher tuition cost for this program: PsyD program charges a flat $30,321 yearly tuition.

Financial Assistance:

First-Year Students: Fellowships and scholarships available for first year. Average amount paid per academic year: $6,000. Apply by June 1.

Advanced Students: Teaching assistantships available for advanced students. Average amount paid per academic year: $8,000. Average number of hours worked per week: 15. Apply by March 15. Research assistantships available for advanced students. Average amount paid per academic year: $4,000. Average number of hours worked per week: 5. Apply by March 15. Fellowships and scholarships available for advanced students. Average amount paid per academic year: $4,000. Average number of hours worked per week: 20. Apply by June 1.

Additional Information: Of all students currently enrolled full time, 43% benefited from one or more of the listed financial assistance programs. Application and information available online at: http://www.fit.edu/grad-programs/gsa/.

Internships/Practica: Doctoral Degree (PsyD Clinical Psychology): For those doctoral students for whom a professional psychology internship was required in this program prior to graduation, (23) students applied for an internship in 2011–2012, with (22) students obtaining an internship. Of those students who obtained an internship, (22) were paid internships. Of those students who obtained an internship, (20) students placed in APA/CPA accredited internships, (2) students placed in internships not APA/CPA accredited, but listed with the Association of Psychology Postdoctoral and Internship Programs (APPIC), (0) students placed in internships conforming to guidelines of the Council of Directors of School Psychology Programs (CDSPP), (0) students placed in internships that were not APA/CPA accredited, APPIC or CDSPP listed. Master's Degree (MA/MS Applied Behavior Analysis): An internship experience, such as a final research project or "capstone" experience is required of graduates. Master's Degree (MA/MS Organizational Behavior Management): An internship experience, such as a final research project or "capstone" experience is required of graduates. Master's Degree (MA/MS Applied Behavior Analysis and Org Behavior): An internship

experience, such as a final research project or "capstone" experience is required of graduates. Students in the PsyD program complete a sequence of three or more separate practicum placements prior to internship. These include Florida Tech's Community Psychological Services Center and options at other outpatient and inpatient facilities. Inpatient sites include adult psychiatric hospitals, rehabilitation hospitals, child and adolescent inpatient units, and behavioral medicine units within a medical hospital and prison setting. Outpatient sites include mental health centers, private practice settings, VA outpatient clinics, primary care clinics, and neuropsychological practices. Students gain experience in assessment and treatment of individuals, groups, couples, and families, in consultation and psychoeducational presentations. Treatment specialties include neuropsychology, aging, sexual abuse, domestic violence, PTSD, and behavioral health. The I/O program has ties to local business. Students are placed in a wide range of practicum sites including county and federal departments, aerospace and electronics industries, financial institutions, health care organizations, and management consulting firms. The Applied Behavior Analysis program has practicum opportunities at Florida Tech's Scott Center for Autism Treatment, as well as other agencies working with children with developmental disabilities, serious emotional and behavioral disorders and autism. Students receive on-site supervision as well as ancillary supervision by program faculty. The Organizational Behavior Management (OBM) program has internships with local businesses and national consulting firms.

Housing and Day Care: On-campus housing is available. See the following website for more information: http://www.fit.edu/housing/. No on-campus day care facilities are available.

Employment of Department Graduates:

Master's Degree Graduates: Of those who graduated in the academic year 2011–2012, the following categories and numbers represent the postgraduate activities and employment of master's degree graduates: Enrolled in a psychology doctoral program (13), enrolled in another graduate/professional program (1), enrolled in a postdoctoral residency/fellowship (n/a), employed in independent practice (n/a), employed in business or industry (24), still seeking employment (2), do not know (3), total from the above (master's) (43).

Doctoral Degree Graduates: Of those who graduated in the academic year 2011–2012, the following categories and numbers represent the postgraduate activities and employment of doctoral degree graduates: Enrolled in a psychology doctoral program (n/a), enrolled in a postdoctoral residency/fellowship (4), employed in independent practice (3), employed in other positions at a higher education institution (1), employed in a professional position in a school system (1), employed in business or industry (4), employed in a hospital/medical center (4), other employment position (1), total from the above (doctoral) (18).

Additional Information:

Orientation, Objectives, and Emphasis of Department: The School of Psychology at Florida Institute of Technology offers an MS and PhD in Industrial/Organizational (I/O) Psychology, MS and PhD in Behavior Analysis, MS in Organizational Behavior Management, and PsyD in Clinical Psychology. The clinical PsyD program trains students based on a practitioner/scientist model focused on development of clinical skills. The program incorporates multiple theoretical orientations and has emphases in neuropsychology, integrated behavioral health psychology, child and family therapy, and forensic psychology. In the I/O Psychology program, students are trained in the scientist/practitioner framework in the core I/O content areas of personnel testing and selection, performance appraisal, motivation and emotion at work, and group and team processes. Students also gain skills in advanced statistics and research methods in order to conduct organizational research. The program prepares graduates for a wide variety of careers in consulting and academics. The master's program in Behavioral Psychology offers degrees in Applied Behavior Analysis (ABA) and Organizational Behavior Management. The program prepares graduates for employment as Board Certified Behavior Analysts in a variety of clinical settings and as consultants in business/industry. Upon graduation, students from the ABA program meet all the educational and supervised practicum requirements to seek certification as a BCBA. The ABA PhD prepares students for teaching, research, supervision and management careers.

Special Facilities or Resources: The facilities of the School of Psychology include offices, classrooms, research labs and computer labs in the new (2012) Florida Tech Commons facility. Additionally the Scott Center houses all the clinical services operations of the School. It includes autism treatment facilities and general psychological services. A separate Neuropsychology Lab and cogniton applied research lab are also available. The University's Academic Computing Services-Microcenter provides computers and software, media conversion, digital graphics assistance, and professional editing of theses and papers for publication. The Scott Center includes early intervention rooms, observation rooms, and group and individual treatment rooms. Additionally, students receive training and conduct research in several community service programs operated by the School of Psychology. These include the Center for Organizational Effectiveness, a campus-based I/O consulting and research organization; East Central Florida Memory Clinic, which through a contract with Holmes Regional Medical Center serves individuals with memory disorders by providing memory screenings, case management, education, wellness and support groups; and the Family Learning Program, which offers psychological assessment and treatment to child victims of sexual abuse and their family members.

Information for Students With Physical Disabilities: See the following website for more information: http://www.fit.edu/asc/disabilities.php.

Application Information:
Send to Florida Institute of Technology, Office of Graduate Admissions, 150 West University Boulevard, Melbourne, FL 32901. Application available online. URL of online application: http://www.fit.edu/grad/apply. Students are admitted in the Fall, application deadline January 15. PsyD deadline is January 15. Industrial/Organizational Psychology MS & PhD deadline is January 15. ABA-PhD deadline is January 15 and the ABA/OBM/ABA & OBM-MS deadline is February 15. *Fee:* $60. Application fee is $60 for doctoral programs and $50 for Master's programs.

Florida International University

Psychology
Arts and Sciences
11200 SW 8th Street
Miami, FL 33199
Telephone: (305) 348-2881
Fax: (305) 348-3879
E-mail: *wpelham@fiu.edu*
Web: *http://psychology.fiu.edu/*

Department Information:
1972. Chairperson: William Pelham. Number of faculty: total—full-time 36; women—full-time 19; total—minority—full-time 4; women minority—full-time 2.

Programs and Degrees Offered:
Listed in the following order: Program area, degree type (T if terminal Master's), number awarded 7/11–6/12. Developmental Science PhD (Doctor of Philosophy) 6, Industrial/Organizational Psychology PhD (Doctor of Philosophy) 2, Legal Psychology PhD (Doctor of Philosophy) 0, Counseling Psychology MA/MS (Master of Arts/Science) (T) 5, Behavior Analysis MA/MS (Master of Arts/Science) (T) 0, Clinical Science PhD (Doctor of Philosophy) 0.

Student Applications/Admissions:
Student Applications
Developmental Science PhD (Doctor of Philosophy)—Applications 2012–2013, 21. Total applicants accepted 2012–2013, 14. Number full-time enrolled (new admits only) 2012–2013, 6. Total enrolled 2012–2013 full-time, 32. Openings 2013–2014, 7. The median number of years required for completion of a degree in 2012–2013 were 6. The number of students enrolled full- and part-time who were dismissed or voluntarily withdrew from this program area in 2012–2013 were 1. *Industrial/Organizational Psychology PhD (Doctor of Philosophy)*—Applications 2012–2013, 38. Total applicants accepted 2012–2013, 12. Number full-time enrolled (new admits only) 2012–2013, 3. Total enrolled 2012–2013 full-time, 21. Openings 2013–2014, 3. The median number of years required for completion of a degree in 2012–2013 were 8. The number of students enrolled full- and part-time who were dismissed or voluntarily withdrew from this program area in 2012–2013 were 1. *Legal Psychology PhD (Doctor of Philosophy)*—Applications 2012–2013, 31. Total applicants accepted 2012–2013, 6. Number full-time enrolled (new admits only) 2012–2013, 2. Total enrolled 2012–2013 full-time, 17. Openings 2013–2014, 3. The number of students enrolled full- and part-time who were dismissed or voluntarily withdrew from this program area in 2012–2013 were 0. *Counseling Psychology MA/MS (Master of Arts/Science)*—Applications 2012–2013, 97. Total applicants accepted 2012–2013, 32. Number full-time enrolled (new admits only) 2012–2013, 25. Total enrolled 2012–2013 full-time, 55. Openings 2013–2014, 25. The median number of years required for completion of a degree in 2012–2013 were 2. The number of students enrolled full- and part-time who were dismissed or voluntarily withdrew from this program area in 2012–2013 were 0. *Behavior Analysis MA/MS (Master of Arts/Science)*—Applications 2012–2013, 33. Total applicants accepted 2012–2013, 16. Number full-time enrolled (new

admits only) 2012–2013, 9. Total enrolled 2012–2013 full-time, 21. The number of students enrolled full- and part-time who were dismissed or voluntarily withdrew from this program area in 2012–2013 were 1. *Clinical Science PhD (Doctor of Philosophy)*—Applications 2012–2013, 63. Total applicants accepted 2012–2013, 5. Number full-time enrolled (new admits only) 2012–2013, 5. Total enrolled 2012–2013 full-time, 19. Openings 2013–2014, 5. The number of students enrolled full- and part-time who were dismissed or voluntarily withdrew from this program area in 2012–2013 were 0.

Scores: Entries appear in this order: required test or GPA, minimum score (if required), median score of students entering in 2012–2013. *Developmental Science PhD (Doctor of Philosophy):* GRE-V no minimum stated, 520, GRE-Q no minimum stated, 605, last 2 years GPA 3.0, 3.70; *Industrial/Organizational Psychology PhD (Doctor of Philosophy):* GRE-V no minimum stated, 546, GRE-Q no minimum stated, 642, last 2 years GPA 3.0, 3.58; *Legal Psychology PhD (Doctor of Philosophy):* GRE-V no minimum stated, 525, GRE-Q no minimum stated, 595, last 2 years GPA 3.0, 3.58; *Counseling Psychology MA/MS (Master of Arts/Science):* GRE-V no minimum stated, 523, GRE-Q no minimum stated, 560, last 2 years GPA 3.0, 3.45; *Behavior Analysis MA/MS (Master of Arts/Science):* GRE-V no minimum stated, 414, GRE-Q no minimum stated, 444, last 2 years GPA 3.0, 3.27; *Clinical Science PhD (Doctor of Philosophy):* GRE-V no minimum stated, 490, GRE-Q no minimum stated, 580, last 2 years GPA 3.0, 3.67.

Other Criteria: (importance of criteria rated low, medium, or high): GRE scores—high, research experience—high, work experience—medium, extracurricular activity—low, clinically related public service—low, GPA—high, letters of recommendation—high, statement of goals and objectives—high, undergraduate major in psychology—medium, specific undergraduate psychology courses taken—low. For additional information on admission requirements, go to http://psychology.fiu.edu/graduate-programs/prospective-grad-students/.

Student Characteristics: The following represents characteristics of students in 2012–2013 in all graduate psychology programs in the department: Female—full-time 116, part-time 0; Male—full-time 49, part-time 0; African American/Black—full-time 8, part-time 0; Hispanic/Latino(a)—full-time 63, part-time 0; Asian/Pacific Islander—full-time 1, part-time 0; American Indian/Alaska Native—full-time 0, part-time 0; Caucasian/White—full-time 87, part-time 0; Multi-ethnic—part-time 0; students subject to the Americans With Disabilities Act—full-time 0, part-time 0; Unknown ethnicity—full-time 6, part-time 0; International students who hold an F-1 or J-1 Visa—full-time 3, part-time 0.

Financial Information/Assistance:

Tuition for Full-Time Study: *Master's:* State residents: per academic year $10,128, $422 per credit hour; Nonstate residents: per academic year $22,224, $926 per credit hour. *Doctoral:* State residents: per academic year $10,128, $422 per credit hour; Nonstate residents: per academic year $22,224, $926 per credit hour. Tuition is subject to change. See the following website for updates and changes in tuition costs: http://finaid.fiu.edu/index.php?id=1572. Higher tuition cost for this program: Counseling Psychology.

Financial Assistance:

First-Year Students: Teaching assistantships available for first year. Average amount paid per academic year: $19,194. Aver-

age number of hours worked per week: 20. Apply by December 15. Research assistantships available for first year. Average amount paid per academic year: $19,194. Average number of hours worked per week: 20. Apply by December 15. Fellowships and scholarships available for first year. Average amount paid per academic year: $30,000. Average number of hours worked per week: 20. Apply by December 15.

Advanced Students: Teaching assistantships available for advanced students. Average amount paid per academic year: $19,194. Average number of hours worked per week: 20. Apply by December 15. Research assistantships available for advanced students. Average amount paid per academic year: $19,194. Average number of hours worked per week: 20. Apply by December 15. Fellowships and scholarships available for advanced students. Average amount paid per academic year: $30,000. Average number of hours worked per week: 20. Apply by December 15.

Additional Information: Of all students currently enrolled full time, 50% benefited from one or more of the listed financial assistance programs. Application and information available online at: http://psychology.fiu.edu/graduate-programs/graduate-funding/.

Internships/Practica: Doctoral Degree (PhD Clinical Science): For those doctoral students for whom a professional psychology internship was required in this program prior to graduation, (0) students applied for an internship in 2011–2012, with (0) students obtaining an internship. Of those students who obtained an internship, (0) were paid internships. Of those students who obtained an internship, (0) students placed in APA/CPA accredited internships, (0) students placed in internships not APA/CPA accredited, but listed with the Association of Psychology Postdoctoral and Internship Programs (APPIC), (0) students placed in internships conforming to guidelines of the Council of Directors of School Psychology Programs (CDSPP), (0) students placed in internships that were not APA/CPA accredited, APPIC or CDSPP listed. Master's Degree (MA/MS Counseling Psychology): An internship experience, such as a final research project or "capstone" experience is required of graduates.

Housing and Day Care: On-campus housing is available. See the following website for more information: http://www.housing.fiu.edu/. On-campus day care facilities are available. See the following website for more information: http://children.fiu.edu/overview.html.

Employment of Department Graduates:

Master's Degree Graduates: Of those who graduated in the academic year 2011–2012, the following categories and numbers represent the postgraduate activities and employment of master's degree graduates: Enrolled in a postdoctoral residency/fellowship (n/a), employed in independent practice (n/a), total from the above (master's) (0).

Doctoral Degree Graduates: Of those who graduated in the academic year 2011–2012, the following categories and numbers represent the postgraduate activities and employment of doctoral degree graduates: Enrolled in a psychology doctoral program (n/a), total from the above (doctoral) (0).

Additional Information:

Orientation, Objectives, and Emphasis of Department: The mission of the Department of Psychology at Florida International University is to create new knowledge about human behavior, apply what is known to improve the human condition, and educate and train students. Our graduate programs are designed to foster a commitment both to basic research and application as an integral part of the student's specialty area.

Information for Students With Physical Disabilities: See the following website for more information: http://drc.fiu.edu/.

Application Information:
Send to Graduate Studies Admissions Committee, Department of Psychology, Florida International University, DM 256, Miami, FL 33199. Application available online. URL of online application: http://gradschool.fiu.edu/admissions.html. Students are admitted in the Fall, application deadline December 15. Master's in Behavior Analysis is February 15th and Master's in Counseling is March 1st. *Fee:* $30.

Florida State University
Department of Psychology
Arts & Sciences
1107 West Call Street, P.O. Box 3064301
Tallahassee, FL 32306-4301
Telephone: (850) 644-2499
Fax: (850) 644-7739
E-mail: *plant@psy.fsu.edu*
Web: *http://www.psy.fsu.edu*

Department Information:
1918. Chairperson: Jeanette Taylor. Number of faculty: total—full-time 43; women—full-time 18; total—minority—full-time 4; women minority—full-time 1.

Programs and Degrees Offered:
Listed in the following order: Program area, degree type (T if terminal Master's), number awarded 7/11–6/12. Cognitive Psychology PhD (Doctor of Philosophy) 5, Clinical Psychology PhD (Doctor of Philosophy) 9, Neuroscience PhD (Doctor of Philosophy) 5, Applied Behavior Analysis MA/MS (Master of Arts/Science) (T) 16, Developmental Psychology PhD (Doctor of Philosophy) 0, Social Psychology PhD (Doctor of Philosophy) 1.

APA Accreditation: Clinical PhD (Doctor of Philosophy). Student Outcome Data Website: http://www.psy.fsu.edu/clinical/studata.htm.

Student Applications/Admissions:
Student Applications
Cognitive Psychology PhD (Doctor of Philosophy)—Applications 2012–2013, 40. Total applicants accepted 2012–2013, 5. Number full-time enrolled (new admits only) 2012–2013, 3. Total enrolled 2012–2013 full-time, 19. Total enrolled 2012–2013 part-time, 1. Openings 2013–2014, 6. The median number of years required for completion of a degree in 2012–2013 were 6. The number of students enrolled full- and part-time who were dismissed or voluntarily withdrew from this program area in 2012–2013 were 0. *Clinical Psychology PhD (Doctor of Philosophy)*—Applications 2012–2013, 333. Total applicants accepted 2012–2013, 17. Number full-time enrolled (new admits only) 2012–2013, 9. Number part-time enrolled (new admits only) 2012–2013, 0. Total enrolled 2012–2013 full-time, 52.

Total enrolled 2012–2013 part-time, 5. Openings 2013–2014, 10. The median number of years required for completion of a degree in 2012–2013 were 6. The number of students enrolled full- and part-time who were dismissed or voluntarily withdrew from this program area in 2012–2013 were 2. *Neuroscience PhD (Doctor of Philosophy)*—Applications 2012–2013, 36. Total applicants accepted 2012–2013, 7. Number full-time enrolled (new admits only) 2012–2013, 2. Total enrolled 2012–2013 full-time, 24. Openings 2013–2014, 6. The median number of years required for completion of a degree in 2012–2013 were 7. The number of students enrolled full- and part-time who were dismissed or voluntarily withdrew from this program area in 2012–2013 were 3. *Applied Behavior Analysis MA/MS (Master of Arts/Science)*—Applications 2012–2013, 70. Total applicants accepted 2012–2013, 26. Number full-time enrolled (new admits only) 2012–2013, 17. Total enrolled 2012–2013 full-time, 36. Total enrolled 2012–2013 part-time, 0. Openings 2013–2014, 16. The median number of years required for completion of a degree in 2012–2013 were 2. *Developmental Psychology PhD (Doctor of Philosophy)*—Applications 2012–2013, 29. Total applicants accepted 2012–2013, 2. Number full-time enrolled (new admits only) 2012–2013, 1. Total enrolled 2012–2013 full-time, 12. Total enrolled 2012–2013 part-time, 2. Openings 2013–2014, 4. The median number of years required for completion of a degree in 2012–2013 were 4. The number of students enrolled full- and part-time who were dismissed or voluntarily withdrew from this program area in 2012–2013 were 2. *Social Psychology PhD (Doctor of Philosophy)*—Applications 2012–2013, 130. Total applicants accepted 2012–2013, 6. Number full-time enrolled (new admits only) 2012–2013, 4. Total enrolled 2012–2013 full-time, 23. Total enrolled 2012–2013 part-time, 2. Openings 2013–2014, 6. The median number of years required for completion of a degree in 2012–2013 were 6. The number of students enrolled full- and part-time who were dismissed or voluntarily withdrew from this program area in 2012–2013 were 1.

Scores: Entries appear in this order: required test or GPA, minimum score (if required), median score of students entering in 2012–2013. *Cognitive Psychology PhD (Doctor of Philosophy):* GRE-V 500, 550, GRE-Q 500, 700; *Clinical Psychology PhD (Doctor of Philosophy):* GRE-V 550, 640, GRE-Q 550, 730; *Neuroscience PhD (Doctor of Philosophy):* GRE-V 500, 640, GRE-Q 500, 750, last 2 years GPA 3.0, 3.7; *Applied Behavior Analysis MA/MS (Master of Arts/Science):* GRE-V 500, GRE-Q 500, 580; *Developmental Psychology PhD (Doctor of Philosophy):* GRE-V 500, 500, GRE-Q 500, 670, last 2 years GPA 3.0, 3.8; *Social Psychology PhD (Doctor of Philosophy):* GRE-V 550, 650, GRE-Q 550, 760, last 2 years GPA 3.0, 3.8.

Other Criteria: (importance of criteria rated low, medium, or high): GRE scores—high, research experience—high, work experience—low, extracurricular activity—low, clinically related public service—low, GPA—high, letters of recommendation—high, interview—medium, statement of goals and objectives—high, match w/ faculty interest—high, undergraduate major in psychology—medium, specific undergraduate psychology courses taken—medium, Research experience is not an important factor for admission to the Applied Behavior Analysis master's program; work or volunteer experience in behavior analysis is of high importance for this program. For additional information on admission requirements, go to http://www.psy.fsu.edu/grad.prog/over.html.

Student Characteristics: The following represents characteristics of students in 2012–2013 in all graduate psychology programs in the department: Female—full-time 110, part-time 8; Male—full-time 56, part-time 2; African American/Black—full-time 6, part-time 0; Hispanic/Latino(a)—full-time 10, part-time 0; Asian/Pacific Islander—full-time 8, part-time 0; American Indian/Alaska Native—part-time 0; Caucasian/White—full-time 138, part-time 10; Multi-ethnic—full-time 3, part-time 0; students subject to the Americans With Disabilities Act—full-time 0, part-time 0; Unknown ethnicity—full-time 1, part-time 0; International students who hold an F-1 or J-1 Visa—full-time 5, part-time 0.

Financial Information/Assistance:

Tuition for Full-Time Study: *Master's:* State residents: per academic year $8,604, $478 per credit hour; Nonstate residents: per academic year $19,962, $1,109 per credit hour. *Doctoral:* State residents: per academic year $8,604, $478 per credit hour; Nonstate residents: per academic year $19,962, $1,109 per credit hour. Tuition is subject to change. See the following website for updates and changes in tuition costs: http://controller.vpfa.fsu.edu/Student-Financial-Services/SFS-For-Students/Tuition-Rates.

Financial Assistance:

First-Year Students: Teaching assistantships available for first year. Average amount paid per academic year: $16,500. Average number of hours worked per week: 16. Research assistantships available for first year. Average amount paid per academic year: $20,000. Average number of hours worked per week: 20. Traineeships available for first year. Average amount paid per academic year: $22,000. Average number of hours worked per week: 20. Fellowships and scholarships available for first year. Average amount paid per academic year: $20,000. Average number of hours worked per week: 0.

Advanced Students: Teaching assistantships available for advanced students. Average amount paid per academic year: $16,500. Average number of hours worked per week: 16. Research assistantships available for advanced students. Average amount paid per academic year: $20,000. Average number of hours worked per week: 20. Traineeships available for advanced students. Average amount paid per academic year: $22,000. Average number of hours worked per week: 20. Fellowships and scholarships available for advanced students. Average amount paid per academic year: $20,000. Average number of hours worked per week: 0.

Additional Information: Of all students currently enrolled full time, 100% benefited from one or more of the listed financial assistance programs. Application and information available online at: http://www.psy.fsu.edu/grad.prog/financial.html.

Internships/Practica: Doctoral Degree (PhD Clinical Psychology): For those doctoral students for whom a professional psychology internship was required in this program prior to graduation, (4) students applied for an internship in 2011–2012, with (4) students obtaining an internship. Of those students who obtained an internship, (4) were paid internships. Of those students who obtained an internship, (4) students placed in APA/CPA accredited internships, (0) students placed in internships not APA/CPA accredited, but listed with the Association of Psychology Postdoctoral and Internship Programs (APPIC), (0) students placed in internships conforming to guidelines of the Council of Directors of School Psychology Programs (CDSPP), (0) students placed in internships that were not APA/CPA accredited, APPIC or CDSPP listed. Master's Degree (MA/MS Applied Behavior Analysis): An internship experience, such as a final research project or "capstone" experience is required of graduates. Community facilities provide a multitude of settings for practicum placements for clinical students and for master's students in applied behavior analysis. Clinical students receive a stipend and tuition waivers for their practicum work in the community as well as excellent supervised experience and opportunities for research. Practicum settings for clinical students include an inpatient psychiatric hospital, a comprehensive evaluation center for children, a juvenile treatment program, forensic facilities, and other agencies in the community. Clinical psychology students complete a required unpaid practicum at our nationally recognized on-campus Psychology Clinic during the second and typically third year of study. The clinic provides empirically-based assessment and therapy services to adults, children, and families in the north Florida region. Psychology faculty provides supervision. The clinical program culminates in a required one-year internship in an APA-approved facility. Clinical students from the FSU program have, over the years, been highly successful in obtaining excellent internships throughout the country. Applied Behavior Analysis master's students have diverse practicum sites from which to choose, including public schools, family homes, residential treatment facilities, businesses, consulting firms, and state agencies. Stipends and tuition waivers are available for many of the applied behavior analysis practicum settings.

Housing and Day Care: On-campus housing is available. See the following website for more information: http://www.housing.fsu.edu/. On-campus day care facilities are available. See the following website for more information: http://www.childcare.fsu.edu/.

Employment of Department Graduates:

Master's Degree Graduates: Of those who graduated in the academic year 2011–2012, the following categories and numbers represent the postgraduate activities and employment of master's degree graduates: Enrolled in a postdoctoral residency/fellowship (n/a), employed in independent practice (n/a), employed in a community mental health/counseling center (15), do not know (1), total from the above (master's) (16).

Doctoral Degree Graduates: Of those who graduated in the academic year 2011–2012, the following categories and numbers represent the postgraduate activities and employment of doctoral degree graduates: Enrolled in a psychology doctoral program (n/a), enrolled in a postdoctoral residency/fellowship (9), employed in an academic position at a university (7), employed in government agency (1), employed in a hospital/medical center (1), not seeking employment (1), other employment position (1), total from the above (doctoral) (20).

Additional Information:

Orientation, Objectives, and Emphasis of Department: This is a scientifically-oriented department with over $6 million in annual grant funding. The Clinical Psychology program promotes a scientifically-based approach to understanding, assessing, and ameliorating cognitive, emotional, behavioral, and health problems. Integrative training in clinical science and clinical service delivery is provided. Cognitive Psychology students develop research and analytical skills while learning to coordinate basic research with theory development and application. Current research includes expert performance, skill acquisition, reading, memory, attention, language processing, and cognitive aging. Students in the Developmental Psychology program conduct basic and applied research. A developmental perspective is interdisciplinary; consequently members of the developmental faculty routinely hold appointments in one of our other doctoral programs. The Social Psychology program provides students with in-depth training in personality and social psychology, focusing on basic and applied research. Current research areas include the self, prejudice and stereotyping, romantic relationships, health psychology, and evolutionary perspectives on various topics. The interdisciplinary Neuroscience program offers students broad training in brain and behavior research. Areas of emphasis include sensory processes, neural development and plasticity, behavioral and molecular genetics, regulation of energy balance and hormonal control of behavior. The terminal master's program in Applied Behavior Analysis focuses on analyzing and modifying behavior using well-established principles of learning.

Special Facilities or Resources: The department's technical staff and support facilities are some of the best in the country. Fully staffed and equipped electronic and machine shops support faculty and graduate student research. Highly trained staff provides assistance in graphic arts, photography, instrument and computer software design, and electronic communication services. A neurosurgical operating room and a neurohistological laboratory are available. Faculty and students have available to them workstations offering human eyetracking and brain wave and psychophysiological recording, among others. A molecular neuroscience laboratory provides equipment and training for studies of gene cloning and gene expression, as well as techniques to measure levels of hormones and neurotransmitters. The Clinical program administers an in-department outpatient clinic that offers empirically-based assessment and therapy services to members of the Tallahassee and surrounding communities. The department has been recognized by the APA for innovative practices in graduate education in psychology. This recognition was for the in-department clinic, which is a full-fledged clinical research laboratory. Based on research and case studies conducted at the clinic, faculty and students have published many books and peer-reviewed articles. The department and clinic are housed in a new, state-of-the-art building.

Information for Students With Physical Disabilities: See the following website for more information: http://www.disabilitycenter.fsu.edu/.

Application Information:
Send to Graduate Program, Department of Psychology, Florida State University, 1107 West Call Street, P.O. Box 3064301, Tallahassee, FL 32306-4301. Application available online. URL of online application: https://admissions.fsu.edu/gradapp/. Students are admitted in the Fall, application deadline December 2. The application deadline is December 2 for Clinical Psychology and Neuroscience; December 16 for Social Psychology and Cognitive; and January 13 for Developmental Psychology. The Applied Behavior Analysis application deadline is January 15. *Fee:* $30.

Florida State University
Psychological and Counseling Services (PCS)
Education
306 Stone Building
Tallahassee, FL 32306-4453
Telephone: (850) 644-4592
Fax: (850) 644-8776
E-mail: *spfeiffer@fsu.edu*
Web: *http://coe.fsu.edu/EPLS*

Department Information:
2002. Director of Clinical Training: Steven Pfeiffer. Number of faculty: total—full-time 9; women—full-time 5; total—minority—full-time 1; faculty subject to the Americans With Disabilities Act 1.

Programs and Degrees Offered:
Listed in the following order: Program area, degree type (T if terminal Master's), number awarded 7/11–6/12. Combined Counseling and School Psychology PhD (Doctor of Philosophy) 8, Mental Health Counseling MA/MS (Master of Arts/Science) (T) 12, School Psychology EdS (School Psychology) 12, Career Counseling MA/MS (Master of Arts/Science) (T) 6.

APA Accreditation: Combination PhD (Doctor of Philosophy).

Student Applications/Admissions:
Student Applications
Combined Counseling and School Psychology PhD (Doctor of Philosophy)—Applications 2012–2013, 95. Total applicants accepted 2012–2013, 12. Number full-time enrolled (new admits only) 2012–2013, 12. Number part-time enrolled (new admits only) 2012–2013, 0. Total enrolled 2012–2013 full-time, 48. Total enrolled 2012–2013 part-time, 0. Openings 2013–2014, 10. The median number of years required for completion of a degree in 2012–2013 were 6. The number of students enrolled full- and part-time who were dismissed or voluntarily withdrew from this program area in 2012–2013 were 1. *Mental Health Counseling MA/MS (Master of Arts/Science)*—Applications 2012–2013, 53. Total applicants accepted 2012–2013, 33. Number full-time enrolled (new admits only) 2012–2013, 17. Number part-time enrolled (new admits only) 2012–2013, 0. Total enrolled 2012–2013 full-time, 33. Total enrolled 2012–2013 part-time, 0. Openings 2013–2014, 18. The median number of years required for completion of a degree in 2012–2013 were 2. The number of students enrolled full- and part-time who were dismissed or voluntarily withdrew from this program area in 2012–2013 were 0. *School Psychology EdS (School Psychology)*—Applications 2012–2013, 80. Total applicants accepted 2012–2013, 14. Number full-time enrolled (new admits only) 2012–2013, 9. Number part-time enrolled (new admits only) 2012–2013, 0. Total enrolled 2012–2013 full-time, 37. Total enrolled 2012–2013 part-time, 0. Openings 2013–2014, 14. The median number of years required for completion of a degree in 2012–2013 were 3. The number of students enrolled full- and part-time who were dismissed or voluntarily withdrew from this program area in 2012–2013 were 1. *Career Counseling MA/MS (Master of Arts/Science)*—Applications 2012–2013, 16. Total applicants accepted 2012–2013, 7. Number full-time enrolled (new admits only) 2012–2013, 4. Total enrolled

2012–2013 full-time, 10. Openings 2013–2014, 6. The median number of years required for completion of a degree in 2012–2013 were 2. The number of students enrolled full- and part-time who were dismissed or voluntarily withdrew from this program area in 2012–2013 were 0.

Scores: Entries appear in this order: required test or GPA, minimum score (if required), median score of students entering in 2012–2013. *Combined Counseling and School Psychology PhD (Doctor of Philosophy):* GRE-V 500, 575, GRE-Q 500, 620, overall undergraduate GPA 3.0, 3.5, last 2 years GPA 3.2, 3.6; *Mental Health Counseling MA/MS (Master of Arts/Science):* GRE-V 500, GRE-Q 500, 620, overall undergraduate GPA 3.0, 3.5, last 2 years GPA 3.0, 3.5; *School Psychology EdS (School Psychology):* GRE-V 500, 510, GRE-Q 500, 620, overall undergraduate GPA 3.0, 3.5, last 2 years GPA 3.0, 3.6; *Career Counseling MA/MS (Master of Arts/Science):* GRE-V 500, 520, GRE-Q 500, 580, overall undergraduate GPA 3.0, 3.5, last 2 years GPA 3.2, 3.7.

Other Criteria: (importance of criteria rated low, medium, or high): GRE scores—high, research experience—medium, work experience—medium, extracurricular activity—low, clinically related public service—medium, GPA—high, letters of recommendation—high, interview—high, statement of goals and objectives—high, undergraduate major in psychology—low, specific undergraduate psychology courses taken—low, Research experience and high interest highly valued among successful applicants to the APA-accredited doctoral program in combined psychology. For additional information on admission requirements, go to http://coe.fsu.edu/Admissions-Scholarships/Graduate-Admissions.

Student Characteristics: The following represents characteristics of students in 2012–2013 in all graduate psychology programs in the department: Female—full-time 100, part-time 0; Male—full-time 41, part-time 0; African American/Black—full-time 10, part-time 0; Hispanic/Latino(a)—full-time 8, part-time 0; Asian/Pacific Islander—full-time 6, part-time 0; American Indian/Alaska Native—full-time 0, part-time 0; Caucasian/White—full-time 117, part-time 0; Multi-ethnic—full-time 0, part-time 0; students subject to the Americans With Disabilities Act—full-time 6, part-time 0; Unknown ethnicity—full-time 0, part-time 0; International students who hold an F-1 or J-1 Visa—full-time 3, part-time 0.

Financial Information/Assistance:

Tuition for Full-Time Study: *Master's:* State residents: per academic year $10,500, $350 per credit hour; Nonstate residents: per academic year $28,560, $952 per credit hour. *Doctoral:* State residents: per academic year $10,500, $350 per credit hour; Nonstate residents: per academic year $28,560, $952 per credit hour. Tuition is subject to change. See the following website for updates and changes in tuition costs: http://controller.vpfa.fsu.edu/Student-Financial-Services/SFS-For-Students/Tuition-Rates.

Financial Assistance:

First-Year Students: Teaching assistantships available for first year. Average amount paid per academic year: $3,800. Average number of hours worked per week: 10. Research assistantships available for first year. Average amount paid per academic year: $3,500. Average number of hours worked per week: 10. Fellowships and scholarships available for first year. Average amount

paid per academic year: $6,300. Average number of hours worked per week: 10. Apply by January 3.

Advanced Students: Teaching assistantships available for advanced students. Average amount paid per academic year: $3,800. Average number of hours worked per week: 10. Research assistantships available for advanced students. Average amount paid per academic year: $3,500. Average number of hours worked per week: 10. Fellowships and scholarships available for advanced students. Average amount paid per academic year: $6,300. Average number of hours worked per week: 10. Apply by January 3.

Additional Information: Of all students currently enrolled full time, 60% benefited from one or more of the listed financial assistance programs. Application and information available online at: http://gradschool.fsu.edu/Funding-Awards.

Internships/Practica: Doctoral Degree (PhD Combined Counseling and School Psychology): For those doctoral students for whom a professional psychology internship was required in this program prior to graduation, (8) students applied for an internship in 2011–2012, with (8) students obtaining an internship. Of those students who obtained an internship, (8) were paid internships. Of those students who obtained an internship, (7) students placed in APA/CPA accredited internships, (0) students placed in internships not APA/CPA accredited, but listed with the Association of Psychology Postdoctoral and Internship Programs (APPIC), (1) students placed in internships conforming to guidelines of the Council of Directors of School Psychology Programs (CDSPP), (0) students placed in internships that were not APA/CPA accredited, APPIC or CDSPP listed. Master's Degree (MA/MS Mental Health Counseling): An internship experience, such as a final research project or "capstone" experience is required of graduates. Master's Degree (MA/MS Career Counseling): An internship experience, such as a final research project or "capstone" experience is required of graduates. The program offers both on-campus and off-campus practicum experiences; on-campus clinical practica include a mental health clinic serving clients from the community; adult learning disability clinic serving college students and the community; student career counseling center; multidisciplinary center serving K-12 students from a number of school districts; university student counseling center, student disability resource center. Off-campus practica include a wide range of mental health, psychiatric, educational, and behavioral healthcare agencies and private practice settings.

Housing and Day Care: On-campus housing is available. See the following website for more information: http://housing.fsu.edu/Graduate-Family-Housing. On-campus day care facilities are available. See the following website for more information: http://www.childcare.fsu.edu/.

Employment of Department Graduates:

Master's Degree Graduates: Of those who graduated in the academic year 2011–2012, the following categories and numbers represent the postgraduate activities and employment of master's degree graduates: Enrolled in a psychology doctoral program (5), enrolled in another graduate/professional program (2), enrolled in a postdoctoral residency/fellowship (n/a), employed in independent practice (n/a), employed in other positions at a higher education institution (1), employed in a professional position in a school system (12), employed in business or industry (1), employed in government agency (3), other employment position (6), do not know (5), total from the above (master's) (35).

Doctoral Degree Graduates: Of those who graduated in the academic year 2011–2012, the following categories and numbers represent the postgraduate activities and employment of doctoral degree graduates: Enrolled in a psychology doctoral program (n/a), enrolled in a postdoctoral residency/fellowship (4), employed in independent practice (3), employed in an academic position at a university (2), employed in a professional position in a school system (1), employed in a community mental health/counseling center (1), employed in a hospital/medical center (2), total from the above (doctoral) (13).

Additional Information:

Orientation, Objectives, and Emphasis of Department: The Combined Doctoral Program in Counseling Psychology and School Psychology is fully accredited by the American Psychological Association. This unique program allows students to acquire knowledge and skills necessary for leadership positions in the practice of counseling psychology and school psychology in a variety of academic and applied settings. Students acquire basic competency in counseling psychology and school psychology, and advanced expertise in either counseling psychology or school psychology. The program prepares graduates for national certification and state licensure. Within the combined program, all students share a common core of experience in research and practice in counseling psychology and school psychology (70% shared coursework/practica); students also are afforded the opportunity to concentrate in counseling psychology or school psychology (a few students decide to concentrate in both). The Combined Program embraces a scientist–practitioner model consistent with the mission of Florida State, a Research I University. The program faculty enjoy diverse research and clinical interests, providing students with a range of opportunities for professional development in the areas of mental health counseling, school psychology, career counseling, rehabilitation counseling, addictions counseling, prevention and early intervention, wellness, and psychology of the gifted. The program has graduated a number of alumni who have distinguished themselves and is among the top programs nationwide in terms of graduates' success passing the EPPP exam for state licensure.

Special Facilities or Resources: The program uses the following clinic facilities for the development of assessment, counseling and consultation skills: (1) The Human Services Center is a mental health training clinic that provides counseling services at no cost to residents of Tallahassee and surrounding communities. This center offers counseling for a wide range of mental health and psychiatric problems, social skill training, anger management, relationship counseling, family counseling, and personal growth and development. The center works with the juvenile justice system in providing services to court-referred cases. (2) The Adult Learning and Evaluation Center is a referral source for FSU, our other two local colleges, FAMU and TCC, and the community. It serves to assist adults in identifying ADHD, learning disabilities and related problems that may compromise the attainment of educational and career progress. It offers students practica and assistantships in psychological assessment and consultation. (3) The Career Center is located in the Dunlap Success Center and is one of the most technologically-advanced career facilities in the nation. The Career Center provides opportunities for practica and internships as well as for student employment opportunities as career advisors. This Center serves as many as 6000 students per year with a variety of career concerns from choice of major

to job placement. The philosophy is one of a full-service career center that is able to address not only presenting career concerns but related mental health issues as well.

Information for Students With Physical Disabilities: See the following website for more information: http://www.disabilitycenter.fsu.edu/.

Application Information:
Send to Admissions Committee, Psychological and Counseling Services, Florida State University, Stone Building, Tallahassee, FL 32306-4453. Application available online. URL of online application: https://admissions.fsu.edu/gradapp/. Students are admitted in the Fall, application deadline January 15. Master's Deadlines: February 1 for School Psych and Mental Health Counseling; April 1 for Career Counseling. *Fee:* $30.

Florida, University of
Department of Clinical and Health Psychology
Public Health and Health Professions
Box 100165 HSC
Gainesville, FL 32610-0165
Telephone: (352) 273-6455
Fax: (352) 273-6530
E-mail: *progasstchp@phhp.ufl.edu*
Web: *http://chp.phhp.ufl.edu/*

Department Information:
1953. Chairperson: William W. Latimer. Number of faculty: total—full-time 25, part-time 1; women—full-time 10, part-time 1; total—minority—full-time 4; women minority—full-time 2.

Programs and Degrees Offered:
Listed in the following order: Program area, degree type (T if terminal Master's), number awarded 7/11–6/12. Clinical Psychology PhD (Doctor of Philosophy) 15.

APA Accreditation: Clinical PhD (Doctor of Philosophy). Student Outcome Data Website: http://chp.phhp.ufl.edu/academics/doctoral-in-clinical-psychology/student-admissions-outcomes-and-other-data/.

Student Applications/Admissions:
Student Applications

Clinical Psychology PhD (Doctor of Philosophy)—Applications 2012–2013, 357. Total applicants accepted 2012–2013, 25. Number full-time enrolled (new admits only) 2012–2013, 17. Number part-time enrolled (new admits only) 2012–2013, 0. Total enrolled 2012–2013 full-time, 83. Total enrolled 2012–2013 part-time, 0. Openings 2013–2014, 15. The median number of years required for completion of a degree in 2012–2013 were 6. The number of students enrolled full- and part-time who were dismissed or voluntarily withdrew from this program area in 2012–2013 were 1.

Scores: Entries appear in this order: required test or GPA, minimum score (if required), median score of students entering in 2012–2013. *Clinical Psychology PhD (Doctor of Philosophy):* GRE-V no minimum stated, 600, GRE-Q no minimum stated, 690, GRE-Analytical no minimum stated, 4.8, overall undergraduate GPA no minimum stated, 3.74.

Other Criteria: (importance of criteria rated low, medium, or high): GRE scores—medium, research experience—high, work experience—medium, extracurricular activity—medium, clinically related public service—high, GPA—medium, letters of recommendation—high, interview—high, statement of goals and objectives—high, undergraduate major in psychology—medium, specific undergraduate psychology courses taken—medium. For additional information on admission requirements, go to http://chp.phhp.ufl.edu/academics/doctoral-in-clinical-psychology/apply-to-the-program/.

Student Characteristics: The following represents characteristics of students in 2012–2013 in all graduate psychology programs in the department: Female—full-time 59, part-time 0; Male—full-time 24, part-time 0; African American/Black—full-time 4, part-time 0; Hispanic/Latino(a)—full-time 8, part-time 0; Asian/Pacific Islander—full-time 5, part-time 0; American Indian/Alaska Native—full-time 0, part-time 0; Caucasian/White—full-time 63, part-time 0; Multi-ethnic—full-time 3, part-time 0; students subject to the Americans With Disabilities Act—full-time 2, part-time 0; Unknown ethnicity—full-time 0, part-time 0; International students who hold an F-1 or J-1 Visa—full-time 2, part-time 0.

Financial Information/Assistance:

Tuition for Full-Time Study: *Doctoral:* State residents: per academic year $12,590, $525 per credit hour; Nonstate residents: per academic year $29,984, $1,218 per credit hour. Tuition is subject to change. See the following website for updates and changes in tuition costs: http://www.fa.ufl.edu/bursar/current-students/.

Financial Assistance:

First-Year Students: Research assistantships available for first year. Average amount paid per academic year: $18,000. Average number of hours worked per week: 20. Apply by December 1. Fellowships and scholarships available for first year. Average amount paid per academic year: $20,000. Average number of hours worked per week: 20. Apply by December 1.

Advanced Students: Teaching assistantships available for advanced students. Average amount paid per academic year: $15,000. Average number of hours worked per week: 20. Research assistantships available for advanced students. Average amount paid per academic year: $18,000. Average number of hours worked per week: 20. Fellowships and scholarships available for advanced students. Average amount paid per academic year: $20,000.

Additional Information: Of all students currently enrolled full time, 99% benefited from one or more of the listed financial assistance programs. Application and information available online at: http://chp.phhp.ufl.edu/academics/doctoral-in-clinical-psychology/financial-aid/.

Internships/Practica: Doctoral Degree (PhD Clinical Psychology): For those doctoral students for whom a professional psychology internship was required in this program prior to graduation, (18) students applied for an internship in 2011–2012, with (14) students obtaining an internship. Of those students who obtained an internship, (14) were paid internships. Of those students who obtained an internship, (14) students placed in APA/CPA accredited internships, (0) students placed in internships not APA/CPA accredited, but listed with the Association of Psychology Postdoctoral and Internship Programs (APPIC), (0) students placed in internships conforming to guidelines of the Council of

Directors of School Psychology Programs (CDSPP), (0) students placed in internships that were not APA/CPA accredited, APPIC or CDSPP listed. The Department of Clinical and Health Psychology operates a Psychology Clinic which is part of Shands Hospital within the University of Florida Health Science Center. This clinic provides consultation, assessment, and intervention services to medical-surgical inpatients and outpatients, as well as community patients with emotional and behavioral problems. Major services include clinical health psychology, child/pediatric psychology and clinical neuropsychology.

Housing and Day Care: On-campus housing is available. See the following website for more information: http://www.housing.ufl.edu/gfh/. On-campus day care facilities are available. See the following website for more information: http://www.babygator.ufl.edu/.

Employment of Department Graduates:

Master's Degree Graduates: Of those who graduated in the academic year 2011–2012, the following categories and numbers represent the postgraduate activities and employment of master's degree graduates: Enrolled in a postdoctoral residency/fellowship (n/a), employed in independent practice (n/a), total from the above (master's) (0).

Doctoral Degree Graduates: Of those who graduated in the academic year 2011–2012, the following categories and numbers represent the postgraduate activities and employment of doctoral degree graduates: Enrolled in a psychology doctoral program (n/a), enrolled in a postdoctoral residency/fellowship (12), employed in business or industry (1), employed in a hospital/medical center (1), still seeking employment (1), total from the above (doctoral) (15).

Additional Information:

Orientation, Objectives, and Emphasis of Department: The program is designed to train doctoral-level professional psychologists in the scientist–practitioner model through the development of broad clinical skills and competencies, through mastery of broad areas of knowledge in psychology and clinical psychology, and through demonstrated competencies in contributing to that knowledge by research. Within these program objectives particular emphases can be identified: clinical health psychology, clinical neuropsychology and clinical child/pediatric psychology. Courses, practica, conferences, committees, supervision, and settings are designed to augment each emphasis.

Special Facilities or Resources: The Department and its parent College, the College of Public Health and Health Professions, is housed in a modern building that contains faculty offices, student work spaces, and state-of-the-art classroom facilities. In addition, department faculty currently occupy several thousand square feet of laboratory space for clinical and basic research. The Department is particularly strong in instrumentation and methodology for clinical research in pediatric and clinical child psychology, health psychology, and neuropsychology. Psychophysiological and neuroimaging capabilities are present and utilized by many faculty. The clinical psychology program uses the extensive resources of the campus and community. Sites utilized for clinical training include the department's Psychology Clinic, university student health services, the university counseling center; and the VA Medical Center in Gainesville. Agencies and centers throughout the state and nation are also available, principally for internship training for students. The use of these varied resources is consonant with the program objectives. The trainee is directly involved with a broad range of clinical and health problems, professionals, agencies, and settings.

Information for Students With Physical Disabilities: See the following website for more information: http://www.dso.ufl.edu/drc/.

Application Information:
Send to Graduate Admissions, Department of Clinical and Health Psychology, Box 100165 HSC, University of Florida, Gainesville, FL 32610-0165. Application available online. URL of online application: http://www.admissions.ufl.edu/prospectivegraduate.html. Students are admitted in the Fall, application deadline December 1. *Fee:* $30.

Florida, University of
Department of Psychology
Liberal Arts and Sciences
P.O. Box 112250
Gainesville, FL 32611-2250
Telephone: (352) 392-0601
Fax: (352) 392-7985
E-mail: *psyinfo@ufl.edu*
Web: *http://www.psych.ufl.edu*

Department Information:
1947. Chairperson: Neil Rowland. Number of faculty: total—full-time 30; women—full-time 13; total—minority—full-time 2; women minority—full-time 1.

Programs and Degrees Offered:
Listed in the following order: Program area, degree type (T if terminal Master's), number awarded 7/11–6/12. Behavior Analysis PhD (Doctor of Philosophy) 6, Counseling Psychology PhD (Doctor of Philosophy) 8, Developmental Psychology PhD (Doctor of Philosophy) 0, Social Psychology PhD (Doctor of Philosophy) 2, Behavioral and Cognitive Neuroscience PhD (Doctor of Philosophy) 3.

APA Accreditation: Counseling PhD (Doctor of Philosophy). Student Outcome Data Website: http://www.psych.ufl.edu/index.php/counselingpsychology.

Student Applications/Admissions:
Student Applications
Behavior Analysis PhD (Doctor of Philosophy)—Applications 2012–2013, 40. Total applicants accepted 2012–2013, 4. Number full-time enrolled (new admits only) 2012–2013, 4. Number part-time enrolled (new admits only) 2012–2013, 0. Total enrolled 2012–2013 full-time, 29. Total enrolled 2012–2013 part-time, 0. Openings 2013–2014, 6. The median number of years required for completion of a degree in 2012–2013 were 5. The number of students enrolled full- and part-time who were dismissed or voluntarily withdrew from this program area in 2012–2013 were 0. *Counseling Psychology PhD (Doctor of Philosophy)*—Applications 2012–2013, 150. Total applicants accepted 2012–2013, 6. Number full-time enrolled (new

admits only) 2012–2013, 6. Number part-time enrolled (new admits only) 2012–2013, 0. Total enrolled 2012–2013 full-time, 45. Total enrolled 2012–2013 part-time, 0. Openings 2013–2014, 6. The median number of years required for completion of a degree in 2012–2013 were 6. The number of students enrolled full- and part-time who were dismissed or voluntarily withdrew from this program area in 2012–2013 were 0. *Developmental Psychology PhD (Doctor of Philosophy)*—Applications 2012–2013, 26. Total applicants accepted 2012–2013, 10. Number full-time enrolled (new admits only) 2012–2013, 5. Number part-time enrolled (new admits only) 2012–2013, 0. Total enrolled 2012–2013 full-time, 17. Total enrolled 2012–2013 part-time, 0. Openings 2013–2014, 3. The number of students enrolled full- and part-time who were dismissed or voluntarily withdrew from this program area in 2012–2013 were 1. *Social Psychology PhD (Doctor of Philosophy)*—Applications 2012–2013, 55. Total applicants accepted 2012–2013, 1. Number full-time enrolled (new admits only) 2012–2013, 1. Number part-time enrolled (new admits only) 2012–2013, 0. Total enrolled 2012–2013 full-time, 9. Total enrolled 2012–2013 part-time, 0. Openings 2013–2014, 2. The median number of years required for completion of a degree in 2012–2013 were 4. The number of students enrolled full- and part-time who were dismissed or voluntarily withdrew from this program area in 2012–2013 were 0. *Behavioral and Cognitive Neuroscience PhD (Doctor of Philosophy)*—Applications 2012–2013, 35. Total applicants accepted 2012–2013, 3. Number full-time enrolled (new admits only) 2012–2013, 3. Number part-time enrolled (new admits only) 2012–2013, 0. Total enrolled 2012–2013 full-time, 15. Total enrolled 2012–2013 part-time, 0. Openings 2013–2014, 5. The median number of years required for completion of a degree in 2012–2013 were 6. The number of students enrolled full- and part-time who were dismissed or voluntarily withdrew from this program area in 2012–2013 were 0.

Scores: Entries appear in this order: required test or GPA, minimum score (if required), median score of students entering in 2012–2013. *Behavior Analysis PhD (Doctor of Philosophy):* GRE-V no minimum stated, 158, GRE-Q no minimum stated, 160, overall undergraduate GPA no minimum stated, 3.39; *Counseling Psychology PhD (Doctor of Philosophy):* GRE-V no minimum stated, 164, GRE-Q no minimum stated, 152, overall undergraduate GPA no minimum stated, 3.52; *Developmental Psychology PhD (Doctor of Philosophy):* GRE-V no minimum stated, 159, GRE-Q no minimum stated, 148, overall undergraduate GPA no minimum stated, 3.50; *Social Psychology PhD (Doctor of Philosophy):* GRE-V no minimum stated, 158, GRE-Q no minimum stated, 155, overall undergraduate GPA no minimum stated, last 2 years GPA no minimum stated, 3.8; *Behavioral and Cognitive Neuroscience PhD (Doctor of Philosophy):* GRE-V no minimum stated, 160, GRE-Q no minimum stated, 151, overall undergraduate GPA no minimum stated, 3.90.

Other Criteria: (importance of criteria rated low, medium, or high): GRE scores—medium, research experience—high, work experience—low, extracurricular activity—medium, clinically related public service—medium, GPA—medium, letters of recommendation—medium, interview—high, statement of goals and objectives—high, match w/ faculty interest—high, undergraduate major in psychology—medium, specific undergraduate psychology courses taken—medium, Only the Counseling Psychology program requires clinically related experience. Weight given to these criteria varies from program to program. Some programs do not conduct interviews every year. For additional information on admission requirements, go to http://www.psych.ufl.edu/index.php/pg-admissions.

Student Characteristics: The following represents characteristics of students in 2012–2013 in all graduate psychology programs in the department: Female—full-time 81, part-time 0; Male—full-time 29, part-time 0; African American/Black—full-time 2, part-time 0; Hispanic/Latino(a)—full-time 7, part-time 0; Asian/Pacific Islander—full-time 9, part-time 0; American Indian/Alaska Native—full-time 1, part-time 0; Caucasian/White—full-time 77, part-time 0; Multi-ethnic—full-time 5, part-time 0; students subject to the Americans With Disabilities Act—full-time 0, part-time 0; Unknown ethnicity—full-time 9, part-time 0; International students who hold an F-1 or J-1 Visa—full-time 8, part-time 0.

Financial Information/Assistance:
Tuition for Full-Time Study: *Doctoral:* State residents: per academic year $10,776, $449 per credit hour; Nonstate residents: per academic year $28,152, $1,173 per credit hour. Tuition is subject to change. Additional fees are assessed to students beyond the costs of tuition for the following: Fees are $75 per credit hour. See the following website for updates and changes in tuition costs: http://www.fa.ufl.edu/bursar/current-students/.

Financial Assistance:
First-Year Students: Teaching assistantships available for first year. Average amount paid per academic year: $15,500. Average number of hours worked per week: 14. Apply by December 10. Research assistantships available for first year. Average amount paid per academic year: $15,500. Average number of hours worked per week: 14. Apply by December 10. Fellowships and scholarships available for first year. Average amount paid per academic year: $20,000. Average number of hours worked per week: 16. Apply by December 10.

Advanced Students: Teaching assistantships available for advanced students. Average amount paid per academic year: $16,000. Average number of hours worked per week: 16. Research assistantships available for advanced students. Average amount paid per academic year: $16,000. Average number of hours worked per week: 16. Fellowships and scholarships available for advanced students. Average amount paid per academic year: $20,000. Average number of hours worked per week: 16.

Additional Information: Of all students currently enrolled full time, 98% benefited from one or more of the listed financial assistance programs. Application and information available online at: http://www.psych.ufl.edu/index.php/pg-financial.

Internships/Practica: Doctoral Degree (PhD Counseling Psychology): For those doctoral students for whom a professional psychology internship was required in this program prior to graduation, (7) students applied for an internship in 2011–2012, with (7) students obtaining an internship. Of those students who obtained an internship, (7) were paid internships. Of those students who obtained an internship, (7) students placed in APA/CPA accredited internships, (0) students placed in internships not APA/CPA accredited, but listed with the Association of Psychology Postdoctoral and Internship Programs (APPIC), (0) students placed in internships conforming to guidelines of the Council of Directors of School Psychology Programs (CDSPP), (0) students

placed in internships that were not APA/CPA accredited, APPIC or CDSPP listed. University Counseling and Wellness Center, Family Practice Medical Group, Meridian Behavioral Healthcare, Alachua County Crisis Center, VA Medical Center, North Florida Treatment and Evaluation Center, and Northeast Florida State Hospital.

Housing and Day Care: On-campus housing is available. See the following website for more information: http://www.housing.ufl.edu/gfh/choices/. On-campus day care facilities are available. See the following website for more information: http://www.babygator.ufl.edu/.

Employment of Department Graduates:
Master's Degree Graduates: Of those who graduated in the academic year 2011–2012, the following categories and numbers represent the postgraduate activities and employment of master's degree graduates: Enrolled in a postdoctoral residency/fellowship (n/a), employed in independent practice (n/a), total from the above (master's) (0).
Doctoral Degree Graduates: Of those who graduated in the academic year 2011–2012, the following categories and numbers represent the postgraduate activities and employment of doctoral degree graduates: Enrolled in a psychology doctoral program (n/a), enrolled in a postdoctoral residency/fellowship (7), employed in independent practice (2), employed in an academic position at a university (2), employed in an academic position at a 2-year/4-year college (1), employed in other positions at a higher education institution (1), employed in business or industry (1), employed in government agency (1), employed in a community mental health/counseling center (2), employed in a hospital/medical center (2), still seeking employment (2), other employment position (2), do not know (4), total from the above (doctoral) (27).

Additional Information:
Orientation, Objectives, and Emphasis of Department: The graduate program in psychology at the University of Florida is designed for those planning careers as researchers, teacher-scholars, and scientist–practitioners in psychology. In addition to specialized training in one or more areas, a core program of theories, methods, and research in general psychology insures that each student will be well prepared in the basic areas of psychology. The primary goal of the department is educating scientists who will help advance psychology as a science through teaching, research, and professional practice. Because the University of Florida is a broad spectrum university, including almost all the major academic departments as well as professional schools on a single campus, a unique atmosphere exists for the evolution of the general program and the development of personal programs of study. Each student also receives training in at least one of the areas of specialization including counseling psychology, developmental, behavior analysis, behavioral and cognitive neuroscience, and social. One of the fundamental goals of the doctoral program is to engage the student as early as possible in the area of interest while ensuring a sound background of knowledge of theory, methodology, and major content areas so that maximum integration may be achieved. All students participate in ongoing aspects of the academic community such as teaching, research, field experience, and professional activities. Seminars are offered in techniques of teaching accompanied by supervised undergraduate teaching. Continuous research experience is required. The department participates in a number of interdisciplinary programs in-

cluding sensory studies, neurobiological sciences, and aging training.

Special Facilities or Resources: Special facilities in the department include laboratories in developmental (child, adolescent, aging), experimental analysis of behavior, cognitive and information processing, perception, behavioral neuroscience, and social; a vivarium; a statistical computation laboratory; a laboratory in neuropsychology and developmental learning disabilities; and the Computing Center.

Information for Students With Physical Disabilities: See the following website for more information: http://www.dso.ufl.edu/drc/.

Application Information:
Send to Graduate Program Assistant, P.O. Box 112250, Psychology, University of Florida, Gainesville, FL 32611-2250. Application available online. URL of online application: http://www.admissions.ufl.edu/start.html. Students are admitted in the Fall, application deadline December 10. *Fee:* $30.

Miami, University of
Department of Educational & Psychological Studies/Area of
   Counseling Psychology
Education
P.O. Box 248065
Coral Gables, FL 33124-2040
Telephone: (305) 284-3001
Fax: (305) 284-3003
E-mail: *l.buki@miami.edu*
Web: *http://www.education.miami.edu/department/
   departments.asp?Department_ID=2*

Department Information:
1967. Chairperson: M. Guerda Nicolas, PhD. Number of faculty: total—full-time 8, part-time 10; women—full-time 3, part-time 6; total—minority—full-time 4, part-time 4; women minority—full-time 3, part-time 3.

Programs and Degrees Offered:
Listed in the following order: Program area, degree type (T if terminal Master's), number awarded 7/11–6/12. Counseling Psychology PhD (Doctor of Philosophy) 6, Marriage and Family Therapy MA/MS (Master of Arts/Science) (T) 7, Mental Health Counseling MA/MS (Master of Arts/Science) (T) 7, Counseling and Research MA/MS (Master of Arts/Science) (T) 1.

APA Accreditation: Counseling PhD (Doctor of Philosophy). Student Outcome Data Website: http://www.education.miami.edu/program/programs.asp?Program_ID=47.

Student Applications/Admissions:
Student Applications
Counseling Psychology PhD (Doctor of Philosophy)—Applications 2012–2013, 155. Total applicants accepted 2012–2013, 7. Number full-time enrolled (new admits only) 2012–2013, 5. Number part-time enrolled (new admits only) 2012–2013, 0.

Total enrolled 2012–2013 full-time, 30. Total enrolled 2012–2013 part-time, 1. Openings 2013–2014, 6. The median number of years required for completion of a degree in 2012–2013 were 5. The number of students enrolled full- and part-time who were dismissed or voluntarily withdrew from this program area in 2012–2013 were 0. *Marriage and Family Therapy MA/MS (Master of Arts/Science)*—Applications 2012–2013, 23. Total applicants accepted 2012–2013, 14. Number full-time enrolled (new admits only) 2012–2013, 5. Number part-time enrolled (new admits only) 2012–2013, 0. Total enrolled 2012–2013 full-time, 18. Total enrolled 2012–2013 part-time, 3. Openings 2013–2014, 10. The median number of years required for completion of a degree in 2012–2013 were 3. The number of students enrolled full- and part-time who were dismissed or voluntarily withdrew from this program area in 2012–2013 were 2. *Mental Health Counseling MA/MS (Master of Arts/Science)*—Applications 2012–2013, 88. Total applicants accepted 2012–2013, 37. Number full-time enrolled (new admits only) 2012–2013, 17. Number part-time enrolled (new admits only) 2012–2013, 0. Total enrolled 2012–2013 full-time, 32. Total enrolled 2012–2013 part-time, 0. Openings 2013–2014, 15. The median number of years required for completion of a degree in 2012–2013 were 4. The number of students enrolled full- and part-time who were dismissed or voluntarily withdrew from this program area in 2012–2013 were 1. *Counseling and Research MA/MS (Master of Arts/Science)*—Applications 2012–2013, 19. Total applicants accepted 2012–2013, 11. Number full-time enrolled (new admits only) 2012–2013, 1. Number part-time enrolled (new admits only) 2012–2013, 0. Total enrolled 2012–2013 full-time, 5. Total enrolled 2012–2013 part-time, 1. Openings 2013–2014, 5. The median number of years required for completion of a degree in 2012–2013 were 3. The number of students enrolled full- and part-time who were dismissed or voluntarily withdrew from this program area in 2012–2013 were 0.

Scores: Entries appear in this order: required test or GPA, minimum score (if required), median score of students entering in 2012–2013. *Counseling Psychology PhD (Doctor of Philosophy)*: GRE-V 500, 600, GRE-Q 510, 680, GRE-Analytical 4.0, 5.5, overall undergraduate GPA 2.94, 3.59, last 2 years GPA no minimum stated, psychology GPA no minimum stated, Masters GPA 3.48, 3.93; *Marriage and Family Therapy MA/MS (Master of Arts/Science)*: GRE-V 400, 491, GRE-Q 400, 648, GRE-Analytical 4, 4, overall undergraduate GPA 3.0, 3.5; *Mental Health Counseling MA/MS (Master of Arts/Science)*: GRE-V 400, 534, GRE-Q 400, 551, GRE-Analytical 4, 4, overall undergraduate GPA 3.0, 3.4; *Counseling and Research MA/MS (Master of Arts/Science)*: GRE-V 400, 537, GRE-Q 400, 613, GRE-Analytical 4, 4, overall undergraduate GPA 3.0, 3.4.

Other Criteria: (importance of criteria rated low, medium, or high): GRE scores—medium, research experience—high, work experience—medium, extracurricular activity—low, clinically related public service—medium, GPA—high, letters of recommendation—high, interview—high, statement of goals and objectives—high, undergraduate major in psychology—medium, specific undergraduate psychology courses taken—low.

Student Characteristics: The following represents characteristics of students in 2012–2013 in all graduate psychology programs in the department: Female—full-time 21, part-time 1; Male—full-

time 9, part-time 0; African American/Black—full-time 4, part-time 0; Hispanic/Latino(a)—full-time 4, part-time 1; Asian/Pacific Islander—full-time 1, part-time 0; American Indian/Alaska Native—full-time 0, part-time 0; Caucasian/White—full-time 20, part-time 0; Multi-ethnic—full-time 1, part-time 0; students subject to the Americans With Disabilities Act—full-time 0, part-time 0; Unknown ethnicity—full-time 0, part-time 0; International students who hold an F-1 or J-1 Visa—full-time 3, part-time 0.

Financial Information/Assistance:

Tuition for Full-Time Study: *Master's:* State residents: $1,600 per credit hour; Nonstate residents: $1,600 per credit hour. *Doctoral:* State residents: $1,600 per credit hour; Nonstate residents: $1,600 per credit hour. See the following website for updates and changes in tuition costs: http://www.miami.edu/gs/index.php/graduate_school/costs_and_financial_aid/tuition_and_fee_rates/.

Financial Assistance:

First-Year Students: Teaching assistantships available for first year. Average amount paid per academic year: $18,900. Average number of hours worked per week: 20. Apply by January 2. Research assistantships available for first year. Average amount paid per academic year: $18,900. Average number of hours worked per week: 20. Apply by January 2. Fellowships and scholarships available for first year. Average amount paid per academic year: $25,000. Average number of hours worked per week: 0. Apply by January 2.

Advanced Students: Teaching assistantships available for advanced students. Average amount paid per academic year: $18,900. Average number of hours worked per week: 20. Apply by April 15. Research assistantships available for advanced students. Average amount paid per academic year: $18,900. Average number of hours worked per week: 20. Apply by April 15. Fellowships and scholarships available for advanced students. Average amount paid per academic year: $28,900. Average number of hours worked per week: 0. Apply by February 1.

Additional Information: Of all students currently enrolled full time, 100% benefited from one or more of the listed financial assistance programs. Application and information available online at: http://www.education.miami.edu/ProgramReq/ProgramRep.asp?ID=1&PgmID=47.

Internships/Practica: Doctoral Degree (PhD Counseling Psychology): For those doctoral students for whom a professional psychology internship was required in this program prior to graduation, (4) students applied for an internship in 2011–2012, with (4) students obtaining an internship. Of those students who obtained an internship, (4) were paid internships. Of those students who obtained an internship, (4) students placed in APA/CPA accredited internships, (0) students placed in internships not APA/CPA accredited, but listed with the Association of Psychology Postdoctoral and Internship Programs (APPIC), (0) students placed in internships conforming to guidelines of the Council of Directors of School Psychology Programs (CDSPP), (0) students placed in internships that were not APA/CPA accredited, APPIC or CDSPP listed. Master's Degree (MA/MS Marriage and Family Therapy): An internship experience, such as a final research project or "capstone" experience is required of graduates. Master's Degree (MA/MS Mental Health Counseling): An internship experience, such as a final research project or "capstone" experience is required of graduates. Master's Degree (MA/MS Counseling and Research): An internship experience, such as a final research project or "capstone" experience is required of graduates. Doctoral students complete two academic years of practicum: the first year in our on-campus training clinic and the second year in an agency or hospital setting located in the community. Program faculty supervise the practicum through weekly one-to-one meetings and group supervision meetings. Therapeutic modalities in these placements include individual, couple, and group therapies. The off-campus placement is tailored to the student's career goals. Many students also complete an optional advanced practicum in their third year with placements tailored to their career goals. Placements include university counseling centers, psychiatric facilities, VA hospitals, behavioral medicine settings, correctional facilities, and schools among others.

Housing and Day Care: On-campus housing is available. On-campus day care facilities are available.

Employment of Department Graduates:

Master's Degree Graduates: Of those who graduated in the academic year 2011–2012, the following categories and numbers represent the postgraduate activities and employment of master's degree graduates: Enrolled in a psychology doctoral program (5), enrolled in another graduate/professional program (0), enrolled in a postdoctoral residency/fellowship (n/a), employed in independent practice (n/a), other employment position (8), do not know (2), total from the above (master's) (15).

Doctoral Degree Graduates: Of those who graduated in the academic year 2011–2012, the following categories and numbers represent the postgraduate activities and employment of doctoral degree graduates: Enrolled in a psychology doctoral program (n/a), enrolled in a postdoctoral residency/fellowship (2), employed in independent practice (0), employed in an academic position at a university (1), employed in other positions at a higher education institution (1), employed in a community mental health/counseling center (0), employed in a hospital/medical center (2), total from the above (doctoral) (6).

Additional Information:

Orientation, Objectives, and Emphasis of Department: Multicultural competence, health psychology, and family/community intervention are foci in the doctoral program that is designed to educate counseling psychologists following the scientist–practitioner model to prepare individuals who will contribute to knowledge in psychology through research and scholarship and who will be highly skilled, multiculturally competent clinicians. A sequence of research experiences is required as well as at least four semesters of supervised practicum and a full-year internship. In addition to coursework in the psychological foundations, requirements include the study of human development and personality (including career development), theories of therapy and the change process, therapeutic methodologies, and psychological assessment.

Special Facilities or Resources: The Institute for Individual and Family Counseling, an on-campus clinic, is used as the primary practicum site. It is equipped with facilities for audio, video, and live supervision. The multi-cultural clientele of the Institute and the other agencies and schools in the Miami area are available for practica and fieldwork. Computer laboratories are available to students in the department. A microcomputer laboratory is available to all students in the department. In addition, an assessment laboratory is an integral part of assessment training in the program.

Information for Students With Physical Disabilities: See the following website for more information: http://www.umarc.miami.edu/arc/ODS.html.

Application Information:
Send to Coordinator of Graduate Studies, School of Education, University of Miami, P.O. Box 248065, Coral Gables, FL 33124. Application available online. URL of online application: https://www.applyweb.com/aw?mgred/. Students are admitted in the Fall, application deadline December 10. December 10 deadline is for Doctoral program applicants. August 1 deadline is for master's degree applicants. *Fee:* $50.

Miami, University of
Department of Psychology
College of Arts & Sciences
P.O. Box 248185
Coral Gables, FL 33124
Telephone: (305) 284-2814
Fax: (305) 284-8469
E-mail: *rwellens@miami.edu*
Web: *http://www.psy.miami.edu*

Department Information:
1937. Chairperson: A. Rodney Wellens. Number of faculty: total—full-time 36; women—full-time 22; total—minority—full-time 5; women minority—full-time 5.

Programs and Degrees Offered:
Listed in the following order: Program area, degree type (T if terminal Master's), number awarded 7/11–6/12. Developmental Psychology PhD (Doctor of Philosophy) 0, Behavioral Neuroscience PhD (Doctor of Philosophy) 0, Clinical Psychology PhD (Doctor of Philosophy) 14.

APA Accreditation: Clinical PhD (Doctor of Philosophy). Student Outcome Data Website: http://www.psy.miami.edu/graduate/clinical_training/.

Student Applications/Admissions:
Student Applications
Developmental Psychology PhD (Doctor of Philosophy)—Applications 2012–2013, 29. Total applicants accepted 2012–2013, 4. Number full-time enrolled (new admits only) 2012–2013, 2. Number part-time enrolled (new admits only) 2012–2013, 0. Total enrolled 2012–2013 full-time, 10. Total enrolled 2012–2013 part-time, 0. Openings 2013–2014, 4. The median number of years required for completion of a degree in 2012–2013 were 6. The number of students enrolled full- and part-time who were dismissed or voluntarily withdrew from this program area in 2012–2013 were 0. *Behavioral Neuroscience PhD (Doctor of Philosophy)*—Applications 2012–2013, 21. Total applicants accepted 2012–2013, 1. Number full-time enrolled (new admits only) 2012–2013, 1. Number part-time enrolled (new admits only) 2012–2013, 0. Total enrolled 2012–2013 full-time, 5. Total enrolled 2012–2013 part-time, 0. Openings

2013–2014, 1. The median number of years required for completion of a degree in 2012–2013 were 5. The number of students enrolled full- and part-time who were dismissed or voluntarily withdrew from this program area in 2012–2013 were 0. *Clinical Psychology PhD (Doctor of Philosophy)*—Applications 2012–2013, 494. Total applicants accepted 2012–2013, 18. Number full-time enrolled (new admits only) 2012–2013, 12. Number part-time enrolled (new admits only) 2012–2013, 0. Total enrolled 2012–2013 full-time, 69. Total enrolled 2012–2013 part-time, 0. Openings 2013–2014, 14. The median number of years required for completion of a degree in 2012–2013 were 6. The number of students enrolled full- and part-time who were dismissed or voluntarily withdrew from this program area in 2012–2013 were 0.

Scores: Entries appear in this order: required test or GPA, minimum score (if required), median score of students entering in 2012–2013. *Developmental Psychology PhD (Doctor of Philosophy):* GRE-V no minimum stated, GRE-Q no minimum stated, GRE-Analytical no minimum stated, overall undergraduate GPA no minimum stated; *Behavioral Neuroscience PhD (Doctor of Philosophy):* GRE-V no minimum stated, GRE-Q no minimum stated, GRE-Analytical no minimum stated, overall undergraduate GPA no minimum stated; *Clinical Psychology PhD (Doctor of Philosophy):* GRE-V no minimum stated, 620, GRE-Q no minimum stated, 740, GRE-Analytical no minimum stated, overall undergraduate GPA no minimum stated, 3.6.

Other Criteria: (importance of criteria rated low, medium, or high): GRE scores—high, research experience—high, work experience—medium, extracurricular activity—medium, clinically related public service—medium, GPA—high, letters of recommendation—high, interview—high, statement of goals and objectives—high, undergraduate major in psychology—medium, specific undergraduate psychology courses taken—medium, Clinically related public service not weighted for non-clinical programs. For additional information on admission requirements, go to http://www.psy.miami.edu/graduate/admissions.phtml.

Student Characteristics: The following represents characteristics of students in 2012–2013 in all graduate psychology programs in the department: Female—full-time 69, part-time 0; Male—full-time 15, part-time 0; African American/Black—full-time 6, part-time 0; Hispanic/Latino(a)—full-time 13, part-time 0; Asian/Pacific Islander—full-time 7, part-time 0; American Indian/Alaska Native—full-time 0, part-time 0; Caucasian/White—full-time 55, part-time 0; Multi-ethnic—full-time 2, part-time 0; students subject to the Americans With Disabilities Act—full-time 0, part-time 0; Unknown ethnicity—full-time 1, part-time 0; International students who hold an F-1 or J-1 Visa—full-time 2, part-time 0.

Financial Information/Assistance:
Tuition for Full-Time Study: *Doctoral:* State residents: per academic year $38,060, $1,730 per credit hour; Nonstate residents: per academic year $38,060, $1,730 per credit hour. Additional fees are assessed to students beyond the costs of tuition for the following: student activity fee. See the following website for updates and changes in tuition costs: http://www.miami.edu/gs/index.php/graduate_school/costs_and_financial_aid/tuition_and_fee_rates/.

Financial Assistance:

First-Year Students: Teaching assistantships available for first year. Average amount paid per academic year: $20,000. Average number of hours worked per week: 15. Apply by December 1. Research assistantships available for first year. Average amount paid per academic year: $22,660. Average number of hours worked per week: 20. Apply by December 1. Traineeships available for first year. Average amount paid per academic year: $22,660. Average number of hours worked per week: 15. Apply by December 1. Fellowships and scholarships available for first year. Average amount paid per academic year: $25,000. Average number of hours worked per week: 0. Apply by December 1.

Advanced Students: Teaching assistantships available for advanced students. Average amount paid per academic year: $20,000. Average number of hours worked per week: 15. Research assistantships available for advanced students. Average amount paid per academic year: $22,660. Average number of hours worked per week: 20. Traineeships available for advanced students. Average amount paid per academic year: $22,660. Average number of hours worked per week: 15. Fellowships and scholarships available for advanced students. Average amount paid per academic year: $25,000. Average number of hours worked per week: 0.

Additional Information: Of all students currently enrolled full time, 100% benefited from one or more of the listed financial assistance programs. Application and information available online at: http://www.psy.miami.edu/graduate/financing.phtml.

Internships/Practica: Doctoral Degree (PhD Clinical Psychology): For those doctoral students for whom a professional psychology internship was required in this program prior to graduation, (12) students applied for an internship in 2011–2012, with (12) students obtaining an internship. Of those students who obtained an internship, (12) were paid internships. Of those students who obtained an internship, (12) students placed in APA/CPA accredited internships, (0) students placed in internships not APA/CPA accredited, but listed with the Association of Psychology Postdoctoral and Internship Programs (APPIC), (0) students placed in internships conforming to guidelines of the Council of Directors of School Psychology Programs (CDSPP), (0) students placed in internships that were not APA/CPA accredited, APPIC or CDSPP listed. Practicum sites are available for students enrolled in our APA-accredited clinical program on the Coral Gables campus, Medical School campus and throughout Miami-Dade County. The department's Psychological Services Center represents a primary site for students developing skills in psychological assessment and empirically-based interventions. Additional specialty practica are located in the Department of Pediatrics at the Medical School, the Veterans Administration Medical Center and various clinics throughout Miami-Dade County.

Housing and Day Care: No on-campus housing is available. On-campus day care facilities are available. See the following website for more information: http://www.umcanterbury.com/.

Employment of Department Graduates:

Master's Degree Graduates: Of those who graduated in the academic year 2011–2012, the following categories and numbers represent the postgraduate activities and employment of master's degree graduates: Enrolled in a postdoctoral residency/fellowship (n/a), employed in independent practice (n/a), total from the above (master's) (0).

Doctoral Degree Graduates: Of those who graduated in the academic year 2011–2012, the following categories and numbers represent the postgraduate activities and employment of doctoral degree graduates: Enrolled in a psychology doctoral program (n/a), enrolled in a postdoctoral residency/fellowship (7), employed in independent practice (2), employed in an academic position at a university (1), employed in a community mental health/counseling center (1), employed in a hospital/medical center (1), do not know (2), total from the above (doctoral) (14).

Additional Information:

Orientation, Objectives, and Emphasis of Department: The Department of Psychology's mission is to acquire, advance, and disseminate knowledge within the psychological and biobehavioral sciences. The Department seeks a balance among several academic endeavors including: basic scientific research, applied research, undergraduate teaching, graduate teaching, professional training, and community service. The department offers courses leading to the degree of Doctor of Philosophy. The Clinical Psychology program, with tracks in adult, child, pediatric health, and health, uses a scientist–practitioner model of training with somewhat greater emphasis on the clinical science component. A mentor-model method of research training is employed. Prospective students in psychology are admitted to graduate study within the Adult, Child, or Health Divisions. The Adult Division houses the adult clinical track that includes a focus on personality-social psychology in addition to adult psychopathology and treatment. The Child Division houses the clinical child and pediatric health tracks of the clinical program and also the developmental program. The Health Division houses the health clinical track and the behavioral neuroscience and evolutionary psychology program. All students teach at least one undergraduate course as part of their graduate training. Students are supported via training grants, fellowships, teaching assistantships and research assistantships.

Special Facilities or Resources: The Psychological Services Center serves as a community-based mental health training clinic for clinical students. The Behavioral Medicine Research Building provides excellent research facilities for students in behavioral neuroscience and health psychology. The Behavioral Medicine Research Center located at the UM Miller School of Medicine Clinical Research Building provides state-of-the-art facilities for research in psychoneuroimmunology. The Linda Ray Intervention Center and the Center for Autism and Related Disabilities provide excellent research opportunities for students in our child programs. Faculty research is supported by more than $15 million yearly in federal and state funding. The department resides in a new state-of-the-art research and teaching facility constructed for its use in 2003. A new research fMRI facility is under construction and scheduled to open in 2013.

Information for Students With Physical Disabilities: See the following website for more information: http://www.miami.edu/index.php/academic_resource_center/disability_services.

Application Information:
Send to Graduate Admissions, Department of Psychology, 5665 Ponce de Leon Boulevard, 5th Floor, Coral Gables, FL 33146. Application available online. URL of online application: http://www.applyweb.com/aw?mgrpsy. Students are admitted in the Fall, application deadline December 1. *Fee:* $65.

North Florida, University of
Psychology/Masters of General Psychology
College of Arts and Sciences
1 UNF Drive
Jacksonville, FL 32224
Telephone: (904) 620-2807
Fax: (904) 620-3814
E-mail: *llange@unf.edu*
Web: *http://www.unf.edu/coas/psychology/*
Master_of_Arts_in_General_Psychology.aspx

Department Information:
Chairperson: Michael P. Toglia. Number of faculty: total—full-time 27, part-time 13; women—full-time 14, part-time 6; total—minority—full-time 2; women minority—full-time 1.

Programs and Degrees Offered:
Listed in the following order: Program area, degree type (T if terminal Master's), number awarded 7/11–6/12. General Psychology MA/MS (Master of Arts/Science) (T) 10.

Student Applications/Admissions:
Student Applications
General Psychology MA/MS (Master of Arts/Science)—Applications 2012–2013, 74. Total applicants accepted 2012–2013, 18. Number full-time enrolled (new admits only) 2012–2013, 18. Number part-time enrolled (new admits only) 2012–2013, 0. Total enrolled 2012–2013 full-time, 32. Total enrolled 2012–2013 part-time, 0. Openings 2013–2014, 15. The median number of years required for completion of a degree in 2012–2013 were 2. The number of students enrolled full- and part-time who were dismissed or voluntarily withdrew from this program area in 2012–2013 were 1.
Scores: Entries appear in this order: required test or GPA, minimum score (if required), median score of students entering in 2012–2013. *General Psychology MA/MS (Master of Arts/Science):* GRE-V no minimum stated, GRE-Q no minimum stated, GRE-Analytical no minimum stated, overall undergraduate GPA 3.0.
Other Criteria: (importance of criteria rated low, medium, or high): For additional information on admission requirements, go to http://www.unf.edu/coas/psychology/Master_of_Arts_in_General_Psychology.aspx.

Student Characteristics: The following represents characteristics of students in 2012–2013 in all graduate psychology programs in the department: Female—full-time 20, part-time 0; Male—full-time 12, part-time 0; African American/Black—full-time 1, part-time 0; Hispanic/Latino(a)—full-time 2, part-time 0; Asian/Pacific Islander—full-time 2, part-time 0; American Indian/Alaska Native—full-time 0, part-time 0; Caucasian/White—full-time 27, part-time 0; Multi-ethnic—full-time 0, part-time 0; students subject to the Americans With Disabilities Act—full-time 0, part-time 0; Unknown ethnicity—full-time 0, part-time 0; International students who hold an F-1 or J-1 Visa—full-time 0, part-time 0.

Financial Information/Assistance:
Tuition for Full-Time Study: *Master's:* State residents: per academic year $9,661, $483 per credit hour; Nonstate residents: per academic year $20,819, $1,040 per credit hour. Tuition is subject to change. See the following website for updates and changes in tuition costs: http://www.unf.edu/tuition/.

Financial Assistance:
First-Year Students: Fellowships and scholarships available for first year.
Advanced Students: Teaching assistantships available for advanced students. Fellowships and scholarships available for advanced students.
Additional Information: Application and information available online at: http://www.unf.edu/graduateschool/prospective/funding/Scholarships.aspx.

Internships/Practica: Master's Degree (MA/MS General Psychology): An internship experience, such as a final research project or "capstone" experience is required of graduates.

Housing and Day Care: On-campus housing is available. See the following website for more information: http://www.unf.edu/housing/. On-campus day care facilities are available. See the following website for more information: http://www.unf.edu/cdrc/.

Employment of Department Graduates:
Master's Degree Graduates: Of those who graduated in the academic year 2011–2012, the following categories and numbers represent the postgraduate activities and employment of master's degree graduates: Enrolled in a psychology doctoral program (2), enrolled in another graduate/professional program (2), enrolled in a postdoctoral residency/fellowship (n/a), employed in independent practice (n/a), employed in an academic position at a university (2), employed in an academic position at a 2-year/4-year college (1), employed in other positions at a higher education institution (2), still seeking employment (1), total from the above (master's) (10).
Doctoral Degree Graduates: Of those who graduated in the academic year 2011–2012, the following categories and numbers represent the postgraduate activities and employment of doctoral degree graduates: Enrolled in a psychology doctoral program (n/a), total from the above (doctoral) (0).

Additional Information:
Orientation, Objectives, and Emphasis of Department: The Master of Arts in General Psychology (MAGP) is broad-based and research oriented. This program supplies the critical skills and knowledge for educational and occupational advancement in psychology. The program centers around a core curriculum of statistics, research design, substantive areas of psychology, and a research-based thesis. Students tailor their sequence of courses and research to: pursue further graduate work at universities that offer the PhD in psychology; find employment that requires masters-level expertise in applied psychology; or work as human factors and evaluation research specialists in government, community agencies and industry.

Special Facilities or Resources: Graduate library, research laboratories for all full-time faculty members and their lab members, shared lab space for larger research projects, community connections department, and Animal Behavior Laboratory.

Information for Students With Physical Disabilities: See the following website for more information: http://www.unf.edu/drc/.

Application Information:
Send to UNF Graduate School. Application available online. URL of online application: http://www.unf.edu/admissions/applynow/. Students are admitted in the Fall, application deadline June 1. *Fee:* $30.

Nova Southeastern University (2012 data)
Center for Psychological Studies
3301 College Avenue
Fort Lauderdale, FL 33314
Telephone: (954) 262-5700
Fax: (954) 262-3859
E-mail: *karol@nsu.nova.edu*
Web: *http://www.cps.nova.edu*

Department Information:
1967. Dean: Karen S. Grosby, Ed.D. Number of faculty: total—full-time 41, part-time 118; women—full-time 15, part-time 60; total—minority—full-time 10, part-time 21; women minority—full-time 7, part-time 14; faculty subject to the Americans With Disabilities Act 1.

Programs and Degrees Offered:
Listed in the following order: Program area, degree type (T if terminal Master's), number awarded 7/11–6/12. Clinical Psychology PhD (Doctor of Philosophy) 20, Clinical Psychology PsyD (Doctor of Psychology) 91, Mental Health Counseling MA/MS (Master of Arts/Science) (T) 147, Clinical Psychopharmacology MA/MS (Master of Arts/Science) (T) 6, School Counseling MA/MS (Master of Arts/Science) (T) 56, School Psychology Other 28, Counseling MA/MS (Master of Arts/Science) (T) 50, General Psychology MA/MS (Master of Arts/Science) (T) 0, School Psychology PsyD (Doctor of Psychology) 0.

APA Accreditation: Clinical PhD (Doctor of Philosophy). Clinical PsyD (Doctor of Psychology).

Student Applications/Admissions:
Student Applications
Clinical Psychology PhD (Doctor of Philosophy)—Applications 2012–2013, 235. Total applicants accepted 2012–2013, 14. Number full-time enrolled (new admits only) 2012–2013, 10. Number part-time enrolled (new admits only) 2012–2013, 0. Total enrolled 2012–2013 full-time, 71. Total enrolled 2012–2013 part-time, 0. Openings 2013–2014, 9. The median number of years required for completion of a degree in 2012–2013 were 5. The number of students enrolled full- and part-time who were dismissed or voluntarily withdrew from this program area in 2012–2013 were 1. *Clinical Psychology PsyD (Doctor of Psychology)*—Applications 2012–2013, 359. Total applicants accepted 2012–2013, 143. Number full-time enrolled (new admits only) 2012–2013, 82. Number part-time enrolled (new admits only) 2012–2013, 0. Total enrolled 2012–2013 full-time, 392. Total enrolled 2012–2013 part-time, 0. Openings 2013–2014, 82. The median number of years required for completion of a degree in 2012–2013 were 5. The number of students enrolled full- and part-time who were dismissed or voluntarily withdrew from this program area in 2012–2013 were 9. *Mental Health Counseling MA/MS (Master of Arts/Science)*—Applications 2012–2013, 544. Total applicants ac-cepted 2012–2013, 245. Number full-time enrolled (new admits only) 2012–2013, 65. Total enrolled 2012–2013 full-time, 540. Openings 2013–2014, 175. The median number of years required for completion of a degree in 2012–2013 were 3. The number of students enrolled full- and part-time who were dismissed or voluntarily withdrew from this program area in 2012–2013 were 6. *Clinical Psychopharmacology MA/MS (Master of Arts/Science)*—Applications 2012–2013, 0. Total applicants accepted 2012–2013, 0. Number full-time enrolled (new admits only) 2012–2013, 0. Number part-time enrolled (new admits only) 2012–2013, 0. Total enrolled 2012–2013 full-time, 11. Total enrolled 2012–2013 part-time, 0. The median number of years required for completion of a degree in 2012–2013 were 2. The number of students enrolled full- and part-time who were dismissed or voluntarily withdrew from this program area in 2012–2013 were 7. *School Counseling MA/MS (Master of Arts/Science)*—Applications 2012–2013, 60. Total applicants accepted 2012–2013, 35. Number full-time enrolled (new admits only) 2012–2013, 19. Number part-time enrolled (new admits only) 2012–2013, 0. Total enrolled 2012–2013 full-time, 107. Openings 2013–2014, 60. The median number of years required for completion of a degree in 2012–2013 were 2. The number of students enrolled full- and part-time who were dismissed or voluntarily withdrew from this program area in 2012–2013 were 1. *School Psychology Other*—Applications 2012–2013, 36. Total applicants accepted 2012–2013, 21. Number full-time enrolled (new admits only) 2012–2013, 19. Number part-time enrolled (new admits only) 2012–2013, 0. Total enrolled 2012–2013 full-time, 81. Total enrolled 2012–2013 part-time, 0. Openings 2013–2014, 82. The median number of years required for completion of a degree in 2012–2013 were 4. The number of students enrolled full- and part-time who were dismissed or voluntarily withdrew from this program area in 2012–2013 were 5. *Counseling MA/MS (Master of Arts/Science)*—Applications 2012–2013, 407. Total applicants accepted 2012–2013, 258. Number full-time enrolled (new admits only) 2012–2013, 154. Number part-time enrolled (new admits only) 2012–2013, 0. Total enrolled 2012–2013 full-time, 449. Total enrolled 2012–2013 part-time, 0. Openings 2013–2014, 175. The median number of years required for completion of a degree in 2012–2013 were 2. The number of students enrolled full- and part-time who were dismissed or voluntarily withdrew from this program area in 2012–2013 were 50. *General Psychology MA/MS (Master of Arts/Science)*—Applications 2012–2013, 143. Total applicants accepted 2012–2013, 90. Number full-time enrolled (new admits only) 2012–2013, 43. Total enrolled 2012–2013 full-time, 66. Openings 2013–2014, 30. The median number of years required for completion of a degree in 2012–2013 were 2. The number of students enrolled full- and part-time who were dismissed or voluntarily withdrew from this program area in 2012–2013 were 3. *School Psychology PsyD (Doctor of Psychology)*—Applications 2012–2013, 41. Total applicants accepted 2012–2013, 20. Number full-time enrolled (new admits only) 2012–2013, 13. Total enrolled 2012–2013 full-time, 13. Openings 2013–2014, 15. The median number of years required for completion of a degree in 2012–2013 were 4. The number of students enrolled full- and part-time who were dismissed or voluntarily withdrew from this program area in 2012–2013 were 2.

Scores: Entries appear in this order: required test or GPA, minimum score (if required), median score of students entering in 2012–2013. *Clinical Psychology PhD (Doctor of Philosophy):* GRE-V no minimum stated, 570, GRE-Q no minimum stated, 640, GRE-Analytical no minimum stated, 4.0, overall undergraduate GPA no minimum stated, 3.4; *Clinical Psychology PsyD (Doctor of Psychology):* GRE-V no minimum stated, 510, GRE-Q no minimum stated, 580, GRE-Analytical no minimum stated, 4.0, overall undergraduate GPA no minimum stated, 3.5; *School Psychology Other:* GRE-V 500, GRE-Q 500, GRE-Analytical 4, overall undergraduate GPA 3.0; *School Psychology PsyD (Doctor of Psychology):* GRE-V 500, GRE-Q 500, GRE-Analytical 4, overall undergraduate GPA 3.0.

Other Criteria: (importance of criteria rated low, medium, or high): GRE scores—high, work experience—medium, extracurricular activity—low, clinically related public service—medium, GPA—high, letters of recommendation—high, interview—high, statement of goals and objectives—high, undergraduate major in psychology—high, The importance of research is high for the PhD program; Undergraduate major in psychology is highly recommended for the PhD and PsyD programs. For additional information on admission requirements, go to http://cps.nova.edu/.

Student Characteristics: The following represents characteristics of students in 2012–2013 in all graduate psychology programs in the department: Female—full-time 1507, part-time 0; Male—full-time 223, part-time 0; African American/Black—full-time 265, part-time 0; Hispanic/Latino(a)—full-time 421, part-time 0; Asian/Pacific Islander—full-time 40, part-time 0; American Indian/Alaska Native—full-time 2, part-time 0; Caucasian/White—full-time 802, part-time 0; Multi-ethnic—full-time 28, part-time 0; students subject to the Americans With Disabilities Act—full-time 43, part-time 0; Unknown ethnicity—full-time 172, part-time 0; International students who hold an F-1 or J-1 Visa—full-time 22, part-time 0.

Financial Information/Assistance:

Tuition for Full-Time Study: *Master's:* State residents: $580 per credit hour; Nonstate residents: $580 per credit hour. *Doctoral:* State residents: $890 per credit hour; Nonstate residents: $890 per credit hour. Tuition is subject to change. Additional fees are assessed to students beyond the costs of tuition for the following: online counseling program: one-time fee of $750 for practicum. Tuition costs vary by program. Higher tuition cost for this program: Specialist in School Psychology - $640 per credit hour.

Financial Assistance:

First-Year Students: Research assistantships available for first year. Average amount paid per academic year: $5,600. Average number of hours worked per week: 15.

Advanced Students: Teaching assistantships available for advanced students. Average amount paid per academic year: $2,000. Average number of hours worked per week: 6. Research assistantships available for advanced students. Average amount paid per academic year: $5,600. Average number of hours worked per week: 15. Traineeships available for advanced students. Average amount paid per academic year: $5,800. Average number of hours worked per week: 15. Fellowships and scholarships available for advanced students.

Additional Information: Of all students currently enrolled full time, 12% benefited from one or more of the listed financial assistance programs.

Internships/Practica: Doctoral Degree (PhD Clinical Psychology): For those doctoral students for whom a professional psychology internship was required in this program prior to graduation, (23) students applied for an internship in 2011–2012, with (22) students obtaining an internship. Of those students who obtained an internship, (22) were paid internships. Of those students who obtained an internship, (13) students placed in APA/CPA accredited internships, (9) students placed in internships not APA/CPA accredited, but listed with the Association of Psychology Postdoctoral and Internship Programs (APPIC), (0) students placed in internships conforming to guidelines of the Council of Directors of School Psychology Programs (CDSPP), (0) students placed in internships that were not APA/CPA accredited, APPIC or CDSPP listed. Master's Degree (MA/MS Mental Health Counseling): An internship experience, such as a final research project or "capstone" experience is required of graduates. Master's Degree (MA/MS School Counseling): An internship experience, such as a final research project or "capstone" experience is required of graduates. Master's Degree (MA/MS General Psychology): An internship experience, such as a final research project or "capstone" experience is required of graduates. Accredited by the American Psychological Association, the Psychology Services Center Internship Program offers doctoral candidates in psychology the opportunity to develop professionally, to enhance their ability to use scholarly research for informed practice, to develop proficiency in psychological assessment and psychotherapeutic intervention, and to acquire basic competence in the provision of supervision and consultation. In addition, the Center for Psychological Studies sponsors the Consortium Internship Program (APPIC member) that provides internship experiences in hospital and other settings within the South Florida Community. In addition to the extensive practicum placements available in the community, practicum opportunities for more than 100 students are provided through various CPS faculty supervised applied-research clinical programs located within the NSU Psychology Services Center. Areas of research include ADHD, alcohol and substance abuse, anxiety treatment, child and adolescent traumatic stress, clinical biofeedback, interpersonal violence, neuropsychological assessment, older adults, school psychology assessment and testing, the seriously emotionally disturbed, and trauma resolution integration.

Housing and Day Care: On-campus housing is available. On-campus day care facilities are available.

Employment of Department Graduates:

Master's Degree Graduates: Of those who graduated in the academic year 2011–2012, the following categories and numbers represent the postgraduate activities and employment of master's degree graduates: Enrolled in a psychology doctoral program (1), enrolled in a postdoctoral residency/fellowship (n/a), employed in independent practice (n/a), employed in a professional position in a school system (56), employed in government agency (0), employed in a community mental health/counseling center (4), employed in a hospital/medical center (2), do not know (85), total from the above (master's) (148).

Doctoral Degree Graduates: Of those who graduated in the academic year 2011–2012, the following categories and numbers represent the postgraduate activities and employment of doctoral degree graduates: Enrolled in a psychology doctoral program (n/a), enrolled in a postdoctoral residency/fellowship (67), employed in independent practice (0), employed in a professional position in a school system (1), employed in government agency (2), employed in a community mental health/counseling center (3), employed in a hospital/medical center (0), do not know (9), total from the above (doctoral) (82).

Additional Information:

Orientation, Objectives, and Emphasis of Department: The Center for Psychological Studies (CPS) is committed to providing the highest quality educational experience to future psychologists and counseling professionals. These training experiences provide individuals with a sophisticated understanding of psychological research and the delivery of the highest-quality mental health care. Through the intimate interplay between CPS academic programs and the Nova Southeastern University (NSU) Psychology Services Center, learning becomes rooted in real problems, and research activities attempt to find answers to extant concerns. The center offers master's programs in counseling, mental health counseling, school counseling, general psychology, and forensic psychology, specialist (PsyS) and doctoral (PsyD) programs in school psychology, and two APA-accredited doctoral programs in clinical psychology. The doctor of psychology (PsyD) program provides emphasis on training professionals to do service while the doctor of philosophy (PhD) program provides greater emphasis on applied research. In response to changes in health care delivery and the profession of psychology, the center developed concentrations at the doctoral level. Concentrations/tracks based on the existing PsyD and PhD curriculum are available in the areas of Clinical Neuropsychology, Clinical Health Psychology, Forensic Psychology, Psychodynamic Psychology, Psychology of Long-Term Mental Illness, Multicultural/diversity, and Child, Adolescent and Family.

Special Facilities or Resources: The Center for Psychological Studies is housed in the Maltz Psychology Building, a 65,000 square-foot facility that includes classrooms with state-of-the-art computer technology, a microcomputer lab with 30 multimedia computers connected to major databases and the Internet, study carrels, lounges and meeting rooms, and the Psychology Services Center where there are therapy rooms with audio and video monitoring capability, play-therapy rooms, and workstations for practicum students assigned to faculty specialty clinical programs. As a university-based professional school, CPS provides access to the NSU 325,000 square-foot Library, Research and Information Technology Center, as well as NSU's Schools of Law, Business and Systemic Studies, the colleges of its Health Professions Division (Medicine, Dentistry, Pharmacy, Allied Health, and Optometry), and its Family and School Center.

Information for Students With Physical Disabilities: See the following website for more information: http://www.nova.edu/disabilityservices/.

Application Information:
Send to Enrollment Processing Services, Attn: Center for Psychological Studies, P.O. Box 299000, Fort Lauderdale, FL 33329-9905. URL of online application: http://www.cps.nova.edu/. Students are admitted in the Fall, application deadline January 8**; Winter, application deadline; Summer, application deadline. **Applications for the doctoral programs are accepted only for the Fall; the deadline is January 8. Application deadlines for master's and school psychology programs vary by site. *Fee:* $50.

Nova Southeastern University
Master of Science in Experimental Psychology
Farquhar College of Arts and Sciences
3301 College Avenue
Fort Lauderdale, FL 33314-7796
Telephone: (954) 262-7941
Fax: (954) 262-3760
E-mail: scheydjr@nova.edu
Web: http://www.fcas.nova.edu/programs/graduate/
experimental_psychology/index.cfm

Department Information:
1985. Asst. Director, Division of Social and Behavioral Sciences: Dr. Glenn Scheyd. Number of faculty: total—full-time 18; women—full-time 9; total—minority—full-time 8; women minority—full-time 6.

Programs and Degrees Offered:
Listed in the following order: Program area, degree type (T if terminal Master's), number awarded 7/11–6/12. Experimental Psychology MA/MS (Master of Arts/Science) (T) 0.

Student Applications/Admissions:
Student Applications
Experimental Psychology MA/MS (Master of Arts/Science)—Applications 2012–2013, 10. Total applicants accepted 2012–2013, 9. Number full-time enrolled (new admits only) 2012–2013, 8. Number part-time enrolled (new admits only) 2012–2013, 0. Total enrolled 2012–2013 full-time, 13. Total enrolled 2012–2013 part-time, 0. Openings 2013–2014, 10. The number of students enrolled full- and part-time who were dismissed or voluntarily withdrew from this program area in 2012–2013 were 1.

Scores: Entries appear in this order: required test or GPA, minimum score (if required), median score of students entering in 2012–2013. *Experimental Psychology MA/MS (Master of Arts/Science):* GRE-V no minimum stated, GRE-Q no minimum stated.

Other Criteria: (importance of criteria rated low, medium, or high): GRE scores—medium, research experience—high, work experience—low, extracurricular activity—low, clinically related public service—low, GPA—high, letters of recommendation—high, interview—low, statement of goals and objectives—high, undergraduate major in psychology—medium, specific undergraduate psychology courses taken—medium. For additional information on admission requirements, go to http://www.fcas.nova.edu/programs/graduate/experimental_psychology/apply.cfm.

Student Characteristics: The following represents characteristics of students in 2012–2013 in all graduate psychology programs in the department: Female—full-time 13, part-time 0; Male—full-time 0, part-time 0; African American/Black—full-time 0, part-time 0; Hispanic/Latino(a)—full-time 2, part-time 0; Asian/Pacific Islander—full-time 3, part-time 0; American Indian/Alaska Native—full-time 0, part-time 0; Caucasian/White—full-time 7, part-time 0; Multi-ethnic—full-time 1, part-time 0; students subject to the Americans With Disabilities Act—full-time 0, part-time 0; Unknown ethnicity—full-time 0, part-time 0; Interna-

tional students who hold an F-1 or J-1 Visa—full-time 2, part-time 0.

Financial Information/Assistance:

Tuition for Full-Time Study: *Master's:* State residents: $580 per credit hour; Nonstate residents: $580 per credit hour. Tuition is subject to change. See the following website for updates and changes in tuition costs: http://www.fcas.nova.edu/services/tuition/cost.cfm.

Financial Assistance:

First-Year Students: Fellowships and scholarships available for first year.

Advanced Students: Fellowships and scholarships available for advanced students.

Additional Information: Application and information available online at: http://www.fcas.nova.edu/services/tuition/index.cfm.

Internships/Practica: Master's Degree (MA/MS Experimental Psychology): An internship experience, such as a final research project or "capstone" experience is required of graduates.

Housing and Day Care: On-campus housing is available. See the following website for more information: http://www.nova.edu/reslife/. No on-campus day care facilities are available.

Employment of Department Graduates:

Master's Degree Graduates: Of those who graduated in the academic year 2011–2012, the following categories and numbers represent the postgraduate activities and employment of master's degree graduates: Enrolled in a postdoctoral residency/fellowship (n/a), employed in independent practice (n/a), total from the above (master's) (0).

Doctoral Degree Graduates: Of those who graduated in the academic year 2011–2012, the following categories and numbers represent the postgraduate activities and employment of doctoral degree graduates: Enrolled in a psychology doctoral program (n/a), total from the above (doctoral) (0).

Additional Information:

Orientation, Objectives, and Emphasis of Department: The Master of Science in Experimental Psychology degree program provides students with a strong academic foundation in the theories and concepts of experimental psychology. Through focused coursework and the experience of mentored independent research, students are equipped with comprehensive skills in scientific inquiry and research methodology. These skills may prepare students for admission into a doctoral program in psychology or for career opportunities that include teaching and research in industrial, government, private consulting, health care, and community settings.

Information for Students With Physical Disabilities: See the following website for more information: http://www.nova.edu/disabilityservices/.

Application Information:

Send to Nova Southeastern University, Enrollment Processing Services, Farquhar College of Arts and Sciences, P.O. Box 299000, Fort Lauderdale, FL 33329-9905. Application available online. URL of online application: http://www.nova.edu/apply/index.html. Students are admitted in the Fall, application deadline June 1. *Fee:* $50.

South Florida, University of

Department of Psychological and Social Foundations
College of Education
EDU 105
Tampa, FL 33620-7750
Telephone: (813) 974-4614
Fax: (813) 974-5814
E-mail: *batsche@usf.edu*
Web: *http://www.coedu.usf.edu/schoolpsych/*

Department Information:

1970. Chairperson: Sherman Dorn, PhD. Number of faculty: total—full-time 22; women—full-time 13; total—minority—full-time 8; women minority—full-time 3.

Programs and Degrees Offered:

Listed in the following order: Program area, degree type (T if terminal Master's), number awarded 7/11–6/12. School Psychology PhD (Doctor of Philosophy) 7, School Psychology EdS (School Psychology) 2.

APA Accreditation: School PhD (Doctor of Philosophy). Student Outcome Data Website: http://www.coedu.usf.edu/schoolpsych/Program/program_outcomes.htm.

Student Applications/Admissions:

Student Applications

School Psychology PhD (Doctor of Philosophy)—Applications 2012–2013, 44. Total applicants accepted 2012–2013, 10. Number full-time enrolled (new admits only) 2012–2013, 6. Number part-time enrolled (new admits only) 2012–2013, 0. Total enrolled 2012–2013 full-time, 40. Total enrolled 2012–2013 part-time, 0. Openings 2013–2014, 6. The median number of years required for completion of a degree in 2012–2013 were 5. The number of students enrolled full- and part-time who were dismissed or voluntarily withdrew from this program area in 2012–2013 were 0. *School Psychology EdS (School Psychology)*—Applications 2012–2013, 39. Total applicants accepted 2012–2013, 4. Number full-time enrolled (new admits only) 2012–2013, 2. Number part-time enrolled (new admits only) 2012–2013, 0. Total enrolled 2012–2013 full-time, 9. Total enrolled 2012–2013 part-time, 0. Openings 2013–2014, 3. The median number of years required for completion of a degree in 2012–2013 were 3. The number of students enrolled full- and part-time who were dismissed or voluntarily withdrew from this program area in 2012–2013 were 0.

Scores: Entries appear in this order: required test or GPA, minimum score (if required), median score of students entering in 2012–2013. *School Psychology PhD (Doctor of Philosophy):* GRE-V no minimum stated, 540, GRE-Q no minimum stated, 615, GRE-Analytical no minimum stated, 4.0, overall undergraduate GPA no minimum stated, 3.8, last 2 years GPA no minimum stated, 3.9, Masters GPA no minimum stated, 4.0; *School Psychology EdS (School Psychology):* GRE-V no minimum stated, 540, GRE-Q no minimum stated, 595, GRE-Analytical no minimum stated. Overall undergraduate GPA no minimum stated, 4.0.

Other Criteria: (importance of criteria rated low, medium, or high): GRE scores—medium, research experience—high, work experience—medium, extracurricular activity—low, clinically related public service—medium, GPA—high, letters of recommendation—high, interview—high, statement of goals and objectives—high, writing sample—high, undergraduate major in psychology—medium, specific undergraduate psychology courses taken—high. For additional information on admission requirements, go to http://www.coedu.usf.edu/schoolpsych/Program/program_admissions.htm.

Student Characteristics: The following represents characteristics of students in 2012–2013 in all graduate psychology programs in the department: Female—full-time 38, part-time 0; Male—full-time 11, part-time 0; African American/Black—full-time 6, part-time 0; Hispanic/Latino(a)—full-time 4, part-time 0; Asian/Pacific Islander—full-time 3, part-time 0; American Indian/Alaska Native—full-time 0, part-time 0; Caucasian/White—full-time 36, part-time 0; Multi-ethnic—full-time 0, part-time 0; students subject to the Americans With Disabilities Act—full-time 0, part-time 0; Unknown ethnicity—full-time 0, part-time 0; International students who hold an F-1 or J-1 Visa—full-time 4, part-time 0.

Financial Information/Assistance:

Tuition for Full-Time Study: *Master's:* State residents: per academic year $12,078, $366 per credit hour; Nonstate residents: per academic year $25,608, $776 per credit hour. *Doctoral:* State residents: per academic year $12,078, $366 per credit hour; Nonstate residents: per academic year $25,608, $776 per credit hour. Tuition is subject to change. Additional fees are assessed to students beyond the costs of tuition for the following: athletic fees, service fees, technology fees, and student union fees. See the following website for updates and changes in tuition costs: http://usfweb2.usf.edu/uco/cashaccounting/tuition.asp.

Financial Assistance:

First-Year Students: Research assistantships available for first year. Average amount paid per academic year: $10,250. Average number of hours worked per week: 20. Apply by May 1. Fellowships and scholarships available for first year. Average amount paid per academic year: $10,250. Average number of hours worked per week: 0. Apply by February 15.

Advanced Students: Teaching assistantships available for advanced students. Average amount paid per academic year: $10,250. Average number of hours worked per week: 20. Apply by May 1. Research assistantships available for advanced students. Average amount paid per academic year: $10,250. Average number of hours worked per week: 20. Apply by May 1. Fellowships and scholarships available for advanced students. Average amount paid per academic year: $10,000. Average number of hours worked per week: 0. Apply by February 15.

Additional Information: Of all students currently enrolled full time, 100% benefited from one or more of the listed financial assistance programs. Application and information available online at: http://www.coedu.usf.edu/schoolpsych/Financial_Aid/financial_aid.htm.

Internships/Practica: Doctoral Degree (PhD School Psychology): For those doctoral students for whom a professional psychology internship was required in this program prior to graduation, (6) students applied for an internship in 2011–2012, with (6) students obtaining an internship. Of those students who obtained an internship, (6) were paid internships. Of those students who obtained an internship, (1) students placed in APA/CPA accredited internships, (0) students placed in internships not APA/CPA accredited, but listed with the Association of Psychology Postdoctoral and Internship Programs (APPIC), (5) students placed in internships conforming to guidelines of the Council of Directors of School Psychology Programs (CDSPP), (0) students placed in internships that were not APA/CPA accredited, APPIC or CDSPP listed. Our practica and internships integrate home, school, and community service programs for students at risk for educational failure and their families, including students with disabilities. We focus especially on the priorities of researching and promoting effective educational and mental health practices for all children, youth and their families. All doctoral students participate in practica during the first three years of the program. Practicum settings include schools (public, charter, alternative), hospital settings, research settings, university-affiliated agencies (e.g., USF Dept. of Pediatrics, Florida Mental Health Institute) and special programs (e.g., Early Intervention Program). Doctoral students participate in approximately 1000 hours of practicum prior to internship. All doctoral students complete a 2000-hour predoctoral internship in an APA-accredited/APPIC site or one that meets the APA/APPIC criteria.

Housing and Day Care: On-campus housing is available. See the following website for more information: http://www.housing.usf.edu/. On-campus day care facilities are available. See the following website for more information: http://child-care-preschool.brighthorizons.com/FL/Tampa/usf/; http://www.coedu.usf.edu/main/auxiliary/pcl/.

Employment of Department Graduates:

Master's Degree Graduates: Of those who graduated in the academic year 2011–2012, the following categories and numbers represent the postgraduate activities and employment of master's degree graduates: Enrolled in a psychology doctoral program (6), enrolled in a postdoctoral residency/fellowship (n/a), employed in independent practice (n/a), total from the above (master's) (6).

Doctoral Degree Graduates: Of those who graduated in the academic year 2011–2012, the following categories and numbers represent the postgraduate activities and employment of doctoral degree graduates: Enrolled in a psychology doctoral program (n/a), enrolled in a postdoctoral residency/fellowship (1), employed in independent practice (1), employed in other positions at a higher education institution (1), employed in a professional position in a school system (3), not seeking employment (1), total from the above (doctoral) (7).

Additional Information:

Orientation, Objectives, and Emphasis of Department: Thorough admissions procedures result in the selection of outstanding students. This makes possible a faculty commitment to do everything possible to guide each student to a high level of professional competence. The curriculum is well organized and explicit such that students are always aware of program expectations and their progress in relation to these expectations. The student body is kept small, resulting in greater student-faculty contact than would otherwise be possible. Skills of practice are developed through non-threatening apprenticeship networks established with local school systems. This model encourages students to assist several professors and practicing school psychologists throughout their training. The notion here is to provide positive environments, containing rich feedback, in which competent psychological skills develop. We emphasize a scientist–practitioner model representing primarily a cognitive-behavioral orientation. Further, we support comprehensive school psychology, including consultation, prevention, intervention, and program evaluation.

Special Facilities or Resources: The University of South Florida is a comprehensive Research I (FL) and Doctoral/Research Universities-Extensive (Carnegie) university that has over 45,000 students on a 1,700 acre campus 10 miles northeast of downtown Tampa, a city of over 350,000 people. Amongst its faculty, the School Psychology Program has one APA Fellow, two past presidents of the National Association of School Psychologists, the past-president of the Council of Directors of School Psychology Programs, the 2009 recipient of the APA Division 16 Lightner Witmer Award, and faculty who have received over $40 million in federal and state grants over the past years. Students collaborate with professors and researchers in the program, the College of Education, Departments of Psychology and Psychiatry, the Florida Mental Health Institute, the Department of Pediatrics, Shriner's Hospital, Tampa General and St. Joseph's hospitals, the Florida Department of Education and other settings. The program is housed in a new College of Education physical plant that has the latest fiber optic based technology, clinical and research observation areas, and strong technology support. Strong links exist with community schools and agencies.

Information for Students With Physical Disabilities: See the following website for more information: http://www.sds.usf.edu/.

Application Information:
Send to Linda Raffaele Mendez, Coordinator of Admissions, School Psychology Program, EDU 105, University of South Florida, Tampa, FL 33620-7750. Application available online. URL of online application: https://secure.vzcollegeapp.com/usf/. Students are admitted in the Fall, application deadline January 1. *Fee:* $30.

South Florida, University of
Department of Psychology
Arts and Sciences
4202 East Fowler Avenue, PCD 4118G
Tampa, FL 33620-7200
Telephone: (813) 974-2492
Fax: (813) 974-4617
E-mail: *lpierce@usf.edu*
Web: *http://psychology.usf.edu/*

Department Information:
1964. Chairperson: Toru Shimizu. Number of faculty: total—full-time 37; women—full-time 16; total—minority—full-time 3; women minority—full-time 2.

Programs and Degrees Offered:
Listed in the following order: Program area, degree type (T if terminal Master's), number awarded 7/11–6/12. Clinical Psychology PhD (Doctor of Philosophy) 8, Cognition, Neuroscience,

and Social Psychology PhD (Doctor of Philosophy) 5, Industrial/Organizational Psychology PhD (Doctor of Philosophy) 10.

APA Accreditation: Clinical PhD (Doctor of Philosophy). Student Outcome Data Website: http://psychology.usf.edu/grad/studentstat/.

Student Applications/Admissions:
Student Applications
Clinical Psychology PhD (Doctor of Philosophy)—Applications 2012–2013, 306. Total applicants accepted 2012–2013, 11. Number full-time enrolled (new admits only) 2012–2013, 7. Number part-time enrolled (new admits only) 2012–2013, 0. Total enrolled 2012–2013 full-time, 55. Total enrolled 2012–2013 part-time, 0. Openings 2013–2014, 6. The median number of years required for completion of a degree in 2012–2013 were 8. The number of students enrolled full- and part-time who were dismissed or voluntarily withdrew from this program area in 2012–2013 were 0. *Cognition, Neuroscience, and Social Psychology PhD (Doctor of Philosophy)*—Applications 2012–2013, 107. Total applicants accepted 2012–2013, 9. Number full-time enrolled (new admits only) 2012–2013, 6. Number part-time enrolled (new admits only) 2012–2013, 0. Total enrolled 2012–2013 full-time, 29. Total enrolled 2012–2013 part-time, 0. Openings 2013–2014, 6. The median number of years required for completion of a degree in 2012–2013 were 6. The number of students enrolled full- and part-time who were dismissed or voluntarily withdrew from this program area in 2012–2013 were 0. *Industrial/Organizational Psychology PhD (Doctor of Philosophy)*—Applications 2012–2013, 136. Total applicants accepted 2012–2013, 14. Number full-time enrolled (new admits only) 2012–2013, 5. Number part-time enrolled (new admits only) 2012–2013, 0. Total enrolled 2012–2013 full-time, 35. Total enrolled 2012–2013 part-time, 0. Openings 2013–2014, 6. The median number of years required for completion of a degree in 2012–2013 were 6. The number of students enrolled full- and part-time who were dismissed or voluntarily withdrew from this program area in 2012–2013 were 2.

Scores: Entries appear in this order: required test or GPA, minimum score (if required), median score of students entering in 2012–2013. *Clinical Psychology PhD (Doctor of Philosophy)*: GRE-V 152, 164, GRE-Q 152, 155, GRE-Analytical no minimum stated, last 2 years GPA 3.40, 3.89; *Cognition, Neuroscience, and Social Psychology PhD (Doctor of Philosophy)*: GRE-V 152, 155, GRE-Q 152, 152, GRE-Analytical no minimum stated, last 2 years GPA 3.4, 3.90; *Industrial/Organizational Psychology PhD (Doctor of Philosophy)*: GRE-V 152, 162, GRE-Q 152, 160, GRE-Analytical no minimum stated, last 2 years GPA 3.4, 3.92.

Other Criteria: (importance of criteria rated low, medium, or high): GRE scores—high, research experience—high, work experience—low, clinically related public service—low, GPA—high, letters of recommendation—high, interview—medium, statement of goals and objectives—high. For additional information on admission requirements, go to http://psychology.usf.edu/grad/admission/adminreq/.

Student Characteristics: The following represents characteristics of students in 2012–2013 in all graduate psychology programs in the department: Female—full-time 71, part-time 0; Male—full-time 48, part-time 0; African American/Black—full-time 4, part-time 0; Hispanic/Latino(a)—full-time 8, part-time 0; Asian/Pa-

cific Islander—full-time 21, part-time 0; American Indian/Alaska Native—full-time 0, part-time 0; Caucasian/White—full-time 86, part-time 0; Multi-ethnic—full-time 0, part-time 0; students subject to the Americans With Disabilities Act—full-time 2, part-time 0; Unknown ethnicity—full-time 0, part-time 0; International students who hold an F-1 or J-1 Visa—full-time 16, part-time 0.

Financial Information/Assistance:

Tuition for Full-Time Study: *Doctoral:* State residents: per academic year $7,740, $430 per credit hour; Nonstate residents: per academic year $15,390, $855 per credit hour. Tuition is subject to change. Additional fees are assessed to students beyond the costs of tuition for the following: $37 flat fees, $10 bank card fee, $35 one-time orientation fee, technology fee (varies). See the following website for updates and changes in tuition costs: http:// usfweb2.usf.edu/uco/cashaccounting/tuition.asp.

Financial Assistance:

First-Year Students: Teaching assistantships available for first year. Average amount paid per academic year: $14,500. Average number of hours worked per week: 20. Research assistantships available for first year. Average amount paid per academic year: $14,500. Average number of hours worked per week: 20. Fellowships and scholarships available for first year. Average amount paid per academic year: $20,000. Average number of hours worked per week: 10.

Advanced Students: Teaching assistantships available for advanced students. Average amount paid per academic year: $14,500. Average number of hours worked per week: 20. Research assistantships available for advanced students. Average amount paid per academic year: $14,500. Average number of hours worked per week: 20. Fellowships and scholarships available for advanced students. Average amount paid per academic year: $20,000. Average number of hours worked per week: 10.

Additional Information: Of all students currently enrolled full time, 77% benefited from one or more of the listed financial assistance programs. Application and information available online at: http://usfweb2.usf.edu/finaid/.

Internships/Practica: Doctoral Degree (PhD Clinical Psychology): For those doctoral students for whom a professional psychology internship was required in this program prior to graduation, (9) students applied for an internship in 2011–2012, with (8) students obtaining an internship. Of those students who obtained an internship, (8) were paid internships. Of those students who obtained an internship, (8) students placed in APA/CPA accredited internships, (0) students placed in internships not APA/ CPA accredited, but listed with the Association of Psychology Postdoctoral and Internship Programs (APPIC), (0) students placed in internships conforming to guidelines of the Council of Directors of School Psychology Programs (CDSPP), (0) students placed in internships that were not APA/CPA accredited, APPIC or CDSPP listed. The Clinical Program operates its own Psychology Clinic within the Psychology Department, providing opportunities for practical training in clinical assessment and clinical psychological interventions. Students are active in the Psychology Clinic throughout their training. Clinical core faculty provide most of the supervision of Clinic cases. The Clinical Psychology Program is fortunate to have a unique cluster of campus and community training facilities available for student placement. For example, we have student placements at or near such campus

facilities as the USF Florida Mental Health Research Institute, the USF Counseling Center for Human Development, the Moffitt Cancer Center and Research Institute and the Tampa Veterans Administration Hospital as well as carefully selected community agencies. Students in the Industrial/Organizational Program are required to complete a predoctoral internship. Placements are made in numerous governmental, corporate and consulting firms both locally and nationally. Recent placements have included the cities of Tampa and Clearwater, GTE, Tampa Electric Company, Personnel Decisions Research Institute, Personnel Decisions, Inc., Florida Power and USF&G.

Housing and Day Care: On-campus housing is available. See the following website for more information: http://www.housing.usf. edu/. On-campus day care facilities are available. See the following website for more information: http://child-care-preschool. brighthorizons.com/FL/Tampa/usf/, http://www.coedu.usf.edu/ main/auxiliary/pcl/.

Employment of Department Graduates:

Master's Degree Graduates: Of those who graduated in the academic year 2011–2012, the following categories and numbers represent the postgraduate activities and employment of master's degree graduates: Enrolled in a postdoctoral residency/fellowship (n/a), employed in independent practice (n/a), total from the above (master's) (0).

Doctoral Degree Graduates: Of those who graduated in the academic year 2011–2012, the following categories and numbers represent the postgraduate activities and employment of doctoral degree graduates: Enrolled in a psychology doctoral program (n/a), enrolled in a postdoctoral residency/fellowship (6), employed in an academic position at a university (3), employed in an academic position at a 2-year/4-year college (1), employed in a professional position in a school system (2), employed in business or industry (6), employed in government agency (1), employed in a hospital/ medical center (2), still seeking employment (1), do not know (1), total from the above (doctoral) (23).

Additional Information:

Orientation, Objectives, and Emphasis of Department: The department attempts to educate graduate students to a high level of proficiency in research and in practice. The department expects its doctoral students to be of such quality as to take their place at major institutions of learning if they choose academic careers and to assume roles of responsibility and importance if they choose professional careers. The doctoral program in clinical psychology provides broad-based professional and research training to prepare students for careers in a variety of applied, research, and teaching settings. The doctoral program in cognition, neuroscience, and social psychology prepares students for research careers in both applied and academic environments. This program also offers an interdisciplinary degree in Speech, Language, and Hearing Science in conjunction with the Department of Communication Sciences and Disorders. The doctoral program in industrial/organizational psychology provides professional and research training to prepare students for careers in industrial, governmental, academic, and related organizational settings.

Special Facilities or Resources: The Psychology Department houses state-of-the-art facilities and equipment. There is research space for faculty, graduate, and advanced undergraduate students, including a large vivarium. An open-use lab has been equipped with computer terminals that access the mainframe computer on campus. The University Computer Center is available. The Psychological Services Center is operated as the department's facility for clinical practicum work. A state-of-the-art video system permits supervisory capabilities for clinical practica.

Information for Students With Physical Disabilities: See the following website for more information: http://www.sds.usf.edu/.

Application Information:
Send to Department of Psychology, University of South Florida, 4202 East Fowler Avenue, PCD4118G, Attn: Graduate Admissions Coordinator, Tampa, FL 33620-7200. Application available online. URL of online application: http://www.grad.usf.edu/graduate-admissions.php. Students are admitted in the Fall, application deadline December 1. Clinical deadline is December 1. CNS and Industrial/Organizational deadline is January 2. *Fee:* $30. Fee waiver available for McNair Scholars Program, FAMU Feeder Program, RISE Program, USTAR-MARC Program. Application Fee Waiver Verification Request Form submission required prior to application submission.

West Florida, The University of
School of Psychological and Behavioral Sciences
College of Arts and Sciences
11000 University Parkway
Pensacola, FL 32514-5751
Telephone: (850) 474-2363
Fax: (850) 857-6060
E-mail: *psych@uwf.edu*
Web: *http://uwf.edu/spbs*

Department Information:
1967. Director: Steven J.Kass. Number of faculty: total—full-time 14; women—full-time 8; total—minority—full-time 1; women minority—full-time 1.

Programs and Degrees Offered:
Listed in the following order: Program area, degree type (T if terminal Master's), number awarded 7/11–6/12. Counseling Psychology MA/MS (Master of Arts/Science) (T) 13, Applied Experimental MA/MS (Master of Arts/Science) (T) 13, Industrial/Organizational Psychology MA/MS (Master of Arts/Science) (T) 17.

Student Applications/Admissions:
Student Applications
Counseling Psychology MA/MS (Master of Arts/Science)—Applications 2012–2013, 39. Total applicants accepted 2012–2013, 18. Number full-time enrolled (new admits only) 2012–2013, 12. Total enrolled 2012–2013 full-time, 38. Total enrolled 2012–2013 part-time, 11. Openings 2013–2014, 15. The median number of years required for completion of a degree in 2012–2013 were 3. The number of students enrolled full- and part-time who were dismissed or voluntarily withdrew from this program area in 2012–2013 were 9. Applied Experimental MA/MS (Master of Arts/Science)—Applications 2012–2013, 17. Total applicants accepted 2012–2013, 11. Number full-time enrolled (new admits only) 2012–2013, 10. Total enrolled 2012–2013 full-time, 21. Total enrolled 2012–2013 part-time,

11. Openings 2013–2014, 15. The median number of years required for completion of a degree in 2012–2013 were 2. The number of students enrolled full- and part-time who were dismissed or voluntarily withdrew from this program area in 2012–2013 were 3. Industrial/Organizational Psychology MA/MS (Master of Arts/Science)—Applications 2012–2013, 58. Total applicants accepted 2012–2013, 33. Number full-time enrolled (new admits only) 2012–2013, 9. Total enrolled 2012–2013 full-time, 20. Total enrolled 2012–2013 part-time, 11. Openings 2013–2014, 18. The median number of years required for completion of a degree in 2012–2013 were 2. The number of students enrolled full- and part-time who were dismissed or voluntarily withdrew from this program area in 2012–2013 were 1.

Scores: Entries appear in this order: required test or GPA, minimum score (if required), median score of students entering in 2012–2013. Counseling Psychology MA/MS (Master of Arts/Science): GRE-V no minimum stated, 155, GRE-Q no minimum stated, 148, last 2 years GPA 3.0, 3.55; Applied Experimental MA/MS (Master of Arts/Science): GRE-V no minimum stated, 157, GRE-Q no minimum stated, 152, last 2 years GPA 3.0, 3.45; Industrial/Organizational Psychology MA/MS (Master of Arts/Science): GRE-V no minimum stated, 153, GRE-Q no minimum stated, 150, last 2 years GPA 3.0, 3.44.

Other Criteria: (importance of criteria rated low, medium, or high): GRE scores—high, research experience—medium, work experience—medium, extracurricular activity—medium, clinically related public service—medium, GPA—high, letters of recommendation—high, interview—high, statement of goals and objectives—high, undergraduate major in psychology—high, specific undergraduate psychology courses taken—high, Counseling applicants are required to complete an interview. For additional information on admission requirements, go to http://uwf.edu/spbs/how-to-apply/.

Student Characteristics: The following represents characteristics of students in 2012–2013 in all graduate psychology programs in the department: Female—full-time 57, part-time 21; Male—full-time 22, part-time 12; African American/Black—full-time 4, part-time 1; Hispanic/Latino(a)—full-time 7, part-time 1; Asian/Pacific Islander—full-time 1, part-time 2; American Indian/Alaska Native—full-time 0, part-time 0; Caucasian/White—full-time 64, part-time 28; Multi-ethnic—full-time 3, part-time 1; students subject to the Americans With Disabilities Act—full-time 0, part-time 0; Unknown ethnicity—full-time 0, part-time 0; International students who hold an F-1 or J-1 Visa—full-time 0, part-time 0.

Financial Information/Assistance:
Tuition for Full-Time Study: *Master's:* State residents: $353 per credit hour; Nonstate residents: $1,013 per credit hour. Tuition is subject to change. See the following website for updates and changes in tuition costs: http://catalog.uwf.edu/graduate/tuitionandfees/.

Financial Assistance:
First-Year Students: Research assistantships available for first year. Average amount paid per academic year: $3,760. Average number of hours worked per week: 10. Apply by April 15. Fellowships and scholarships available for first year. Average amount paid per academic year: $2,000. Apply by April 15.

Advanced Students: Teaching assistantships available for advanced students. Average amount paid per academic year: $3,760. Average number of hours worked per week: 10. Apply by April 15. Research assistantships available for advanced students. Average amount paid per academic year: $3,760. Average number of hours worked per week: 10. Apply by April 15. Fellowships and scholarships available for advanced students. Average amount paid per academic year: $750. Apply by April 15.

Additional Information: Of all students currently enrolled full time, 65% benefited from one or more of the listed financial assistance programs. Application and information available online at: http://uwf.edu/finaid/.

Internships/Practica: Master's Degree (MA/MS Counseling Psychology): An internship experience, such as a final research project or "capstone" experience is required of graduates. Master's Degree (MA/MS Applied Experimental): An internship experience, such as a final research project or "capstone" experience is required of graduates. Master's Degree (MA/MS Industrial/Organizational Psychology): An internship experience, such as a final research project or "capstone" experience is required of graduates. Master's students may elect either the thesis or 600-hour internship (850-hour for mental health counseling licensure) option. Faculty assist in finding suitable placements in field settings under qualified supervision. The student also prepares a portfolio demonstrating mastery of several specific competencies and includes an integrative paper reflecting on professional development. Practica (required for counseling students, optional for other students) are completed earlier in the program and involve more limited applied experience and closer supervision by faculty. Internship placements for counseling students include a variety of local mental health agencies providing inpatient, outpatient and community outreach services. Internship placements for industrial/organizational students include a variety of business and healthcare settings.

Housing and Day Care: On-campus housing is available. See the following website for more information: http://uwf.edu/housing/. On-campus day care facilities are available. See the following website for more information: http://uwf.edu/childdev.

Employment of Department Graduates:
Master's Degree Graduates: Of those who graduated in the academic year 2011–2012, the following categories and numbers represent the postgraduate activities and employment of master's degree graduates: Enrolled in a psychology doctoral program (3), enrolled in a postdoctoral residency/fellowship (n/a), employed in independent practice (n/a), employed in other positions at a higher education institution (2), employed in business or industry (4), employed in government agency (5), employed in a community mental health/counseling center (3), other employment position (2), total from the above (master's) (19).

Doctoral Degree Graduates: Of those who graduated in the academic year 2011–2012, the following categories and numbers represent the postgraduate activities and employment of doctoral degree graduates: Enrolled in a psychology doctoral program (n/a), total from the above (doctoral) (0).

Additional Information:
Orientation, Objectives, and Emphasis of Department: The school is a member of the Council of Applied Master's Programs in Psychology and is committed to the philosophy of training with a foundation in general psychology (individual, social, biological, and learned bases of behavior) as the basis for training in application of psychology. Applied students receive significant supervised field experience. The school mission is preparation of master's level practitioners and preparation of students for doctoral work as well. The programs in Counseling Psychology and Industrial/Organizational Psychology are accredited by the Master's in Psychology Accreditation Council (MPAC). The school also offers a certificate in Health Psychology. The Counseling Psychology program offers a 60-hour option with coursework comparable to requirements for licensure as a Mental Health Counselor in Florida.

Special Facilities or Resources: The school is housed in a modern, 22,000 sq. ft. building with excellent research facilities, including a Neurocognition lab with a 128 channel Neuroscan ESI System. The University of West Florida Center for Applied Psychology (CAP) is a consulting group within the School of Psychological and Behavioral Sciences aimed at optimizing human performance across the lifespan in educational, health, and workplace contexts. The University of West Florida Center on Aging is also housed within the School of Psychological and Behavioral Sciences and its mission is to improve the quality of life of aging adults through the application of science to address challenges associated with aging and to promote healthy aging, with an emphasis on prevention. Other University resources include the Institute for Business and Economic Research and the Institute for Human and Machine Cognition. We have links with CMHCs and local health/mental health professionals and organizations. Community resources include three major hospitals and a large Naval training facility. The school hosts student chapters of Psi Chi, Society for Human Resource Management (SHRM), and Student Psychological Association.

Information for Students With Physical Disabilities: See the following website for more information: http://uwf.edu/sdrc/.

Application Information:
Send to School of Psychological and Behavioral Sciences-Graduate Admissions, University of West Florida, 11000 University Parkway, Pensacola, FL 32514-5751. Application available online. URL of online application: http://uwf.edu/graduate/apply_online_now.html. Students are admitted in the Fall, application deadline February 1; Summer, application deadline February 1. *Fee:* $30.

Augusta State University (2012 data)

Department of Psychology
2500 Walton Way
Augusta, GA 30904-2200
Telephone: (706) 737-1694
Fax: (706) 737-1538
E-mail: jgriffin34@aug.edu
Web: http://www.aug.edu/psychology/

Department Information:

1963. Chairperson: Dr. Sabina Widner. Number of faculty: total—full-time 12; women—full-time 8.

Programs and Degrees Offered:

Listed in the following order: Program area, degree type (T if terminal Master's), number awarded 7/11–6/12. Clinical/Counseling Psychology MA/MS (Master of Arts/Science) (T) 8, Applied Experimental Psychology MA/MS (Master of Arts/Science) (T) 2, Experimental (General) MA/MS (Master of Arts/Science) (T) 0.

Student Applications/Admissions:

Student Applications

Clinical/Counseling Psychology MA/MS (Master of Arts/Science)—Applications 2012–2013, 69. Total applicants accepted 2012–2013, 20. Number full-time enrolled (new admits only) 2012–2013, 13. Number part-time enrolled (new admits only) 2012–2013, 0. Total enrolled 2012–2013 full-time, 30. Total enrolled 2012–2013 part-time, 0. Openings 2013–2014, 14. The median number of years required for completion of a degree in 2012–2013 were 2. The number of students enrolled full- and part-time who were dismissed or voluntarily withdrew from this program area in 2012–2013 were 1. *Applied Experimental Psychology MA/MS (Master of Arts/Science)*—Applications 2012–2013, 19. Total applicants accepted 2012–2013, 6. Number full-time enrolled (new admits only) 2012–2013, 6. Number part-time enrolled (new admits only) 2012–2013, 0. Total enrolled 2012–2013 full-time, 13. Total enrolled 2012–2013 part-time, 0. Openings 2013–2014, 6. The median number of years required for completion of a degree in 2012–2013 were 2. The number of students enrolled full- and part-time who were dismissed or voluntarily withdrew from this program area in 2012–2013 were 0. *Experimental (General) MA/MS (Master of Arts/Science)*—Applications 2012–2013, 11. Total applicants accepted 2012–2013, 5. Number full-time enrolled (new admits only) 2012–2013, 2. Total enrolled 2012–2013 full-time, 8.

Scores: Entries appear in this order: required test or GPA, minimum score (if required), median score of students entering in 2012–2013. *Clinical/Counseling Psychology MA/MS (Master of Arts/Science):* GRE-V no minimum stated, GRE-Q no minimum stated, GRE-Analytical no minimum stated, overall undergraduate GPA no minimum stated; *Applied Experimental Psychology MA/MS (Master of Arts/Science):* GRE-V 400, GRE-Q 400, GRE-Analytical 3.5, overall undergraduate GPA 3.0.

Other Criteria: (importance of criteria rated low, medium, or high): GRE scores—medium, research experience—medium, work experience—medium, extracurricular activity—low, clinically related public service—low, GPA—high, letters of recommendation—high, statement of goals and objectives—high, undergraduate major in psychology—medium, specific undergraduate psychology courses taken—high.

Student Characteristics: The following represents characteristics of students in 2012–2013 in all graduate psychology programs in the department: Female—full-time 34, part-time 0; Male—full-time 7, part-time 0; African American/Black—full-time 1, part-time 0; Hispanic/Latino(a)—full-time 2, part-time 0; Asian/Pacific Islander—full-time 5, part-time 0; American Indian/Alaska Native—full-time 0, part-time 0; Caucasian/White—full-time 33, part-time 0; Multi-ethnic—full-time 0, part-time 0; students subject to the Americans With Disabilities Act—full-time 0, part-time 0; Unknown ethnicity—full-time 0, part-time 0; International students who hold an F-1 or J-1 Visa—full-time 1, part-time 0.

Financial Information/Assistance:

Tuition for Full-Time Study: *Master's:* State residents: per academic year $6,885, $165 per credit hour; Nonstate residents: per academic year $21,045, $701 per credit hour. Tuition is subject to change. Additional fees are assessed to students beyond the costs of tuition for the following: Student services, student center, athletic, transportation, technology, and institutional fees.

Financial Assistance:

First-Year Students: Teaching assistantships available for first year. Average amount paid per academic year: $7,500. Average number of hours worked per week: 10. Research assistantships available for first year. Average amount paid per academic year: $7,500. Average number of hours worked per week: 10.

Advanced Students: Teaching assistantships available for advanced students. Average amount paid per academic year: $7,500. Average number of hours worked per week: 10. Apply by May 1. Research assistantships available for advanced students. Average amount paid per academic year: $7,500. Average number of hours worked per week: 10. Apply by May 1.

Additional Information: Of all students currently enrolled full time, 80% benefited from one or more of the listed financial assistance programs. Application and information available online at: http://www.aug.edu/psychology/assistantships.html.

Internships/Practica: Master's Degree (MA/MS Clinical/Counseling Psychology): An internship experience, such as a final research project or "capstone" experience is required of graduates. Master's Degree (MA/MS Experimental (General)): An internship experience, such as a final research project or "capstone" experience is required of graduates. Institutions that provide unique opportunities for fieldwork and internship experiences include two Veterans Administration hospitals, a regional psychiatric hospital, the Georgia Health Sciences University, Gracewood State School and Hospital, Dwight David Eisenhower Medical Center, and various other agencies. Internships are also available in business, education and private practice settings.

Housing and Day Care: On-campus housing is available. See the following website for more information: http://www.aug.edu/housing. No on-campus day care facilities are available.

Employment of Department Graduates:

Master's Degree Graduates: Of those who graduated in the academic year 2011–2012, the following categories and numbers represent the postgraduate activities and employment of master's degree graduates: Enrolled in a psychology doctoral program (1), enrolled in a postdoctoral residency/fellowship (n/a), employed in independent practice (n/a), employed in a hospital/medical center (3), do not know (4), total from the above (master's) (8).

Doctoral Degree Graduates: Of those who graduated in the academic year 2011–2012, the following categories and numbers represent the postgraduate activities and employment of doctoral degree graduates: Enrolled in a psychology doctoral program (n/a), employed in independent practice (1), total from the above (doctoral) (1).

Additional Information:

Orientation, Objectives, and Emphasis of Department: Augusta State University offers three tracks at the masters level: clinical/counseling, general experimental, and applied experimental. The clinical/counseling track is MPAC accredited and meets the educational requirements for the LPC license in Georgia. Coursework is offered in psychological assessments, individual and group psychotherapies, research methods, and foundation psychology courses. The Augusta area provides a wealth of clinical and research internship experiences including placements at the Augusta VAMC, the Medical College of Georgia, and Eisenhower Army Hospital. The general experimental track is geared toward preparing students for doctoral level work. A thesis is required. Those who pursue the applied experimental track seek to work after the master's degree in a research, teaching, or business field. The applied experimental track requires internship experiences in lieu of a thesis. Most students finish the degree in 5 semesters or two years.

Special Facilities or Resources: The department maintains an active human and animal research laboratory and a clinical facility with videotaping and closed circuit television capabilities, and the university provides easy access to advanced computer resources. Students and faculty additionally engage in collaborative research at the Georgia Health Sciences University and Veterans Medical Center. Social and developmental labs are available for teaching and research.

Information for Students With Physical Disabilities: See the following website for more information: http://www.aug.edu/testing_and_disability_services/.

Application Information:
Send to Director of Graduate Studies, Department of Psychology, 2500 Walton Way, Augusta State University, Augusta, GA 30904-2200. Application available online. URL of online application: http://www.aug.edu/psychology/gradadmissions.html. Students are admitted in the Fall, application deadline May 1. *Fee:* $30.

Brenau University

Psychology/MS in Clinical Counseling Psychology
College of Health and Science
500 Washington Street
Gainesville, GA 30501
Telephone: (770) 534-6225
E-mail: *gbauman@brenau.edu*
Web: *http://www.brenau.edu/shs/psychology*

Department Information:
1999. Chairperson: Dr. Julie Battle. Number of faculty: total—full-time 5, part-time 2; women—full-time 4, part-time 1; total—minority—full-time 1; women minority—full-time 1.

Programs and Degrees Offered:
Listed in the following order: Program area, degree type (T if terminal Master's), number awarded 7/11–6/12. Clinical Counseling Psychology MA/MS (Master of Arts/Science) (T) 11.

Student Applications/Admissions:

Student Applications

Clinical Counseling Psychology MA/MS (Master of Arts/Science)—Applications 2012–2013, 45. Total applicants accepted 2012–2013, 25. Number full-time enrolled (new admits only) 2012–2013, 20. Number part-time enrolled (new admits only) 2012–2013, 5. Total enrolled 2012–2013 full-time, 44. Total enrolled 2012–2013 part-time, 10. Openings 2013–2014, 24. The median number of years required for completion of a degree in 2012–2013 were 2. The number of students enrolled full- and part-time who were dismissed or voluntarily withdrew from this program area in 2012–2013 were 5.

Scores: Entries appear in this order: required test or GPA, minimum score (if required), median score of students entering in 2012–2013. *Clinical Counseling Psychology MA/MS (Master of Arts/Science):* GRE-V 145, 150, GRE-Q 140, 145, overall undergraduate GPA 2.75, 3.00.

Other Criteria: (importance of criteria rated low, medium, or high): GRE scores—medium, research experience—medium, work experience—medium, extracurricular activity—medium, clinically related public service—medium, GPA—medium, letters of recommendation—medium, interview—medium, statement of goals and objectives—medium, undergraduate major in psychology—medium, specific undergraduate psychology courses taken—medium. For additional information on admission requirements, go to http://www.brenau.edu/mpsy-prospective-students/.

Student Characteristics: The following represents characteristics of students in 2012–2013 in all graduate psychology programs in the department: Female—full-time 40, part-time 10; Male—full-time 4, part-time 0; African American/Black—full-time 9, part-time 2; Hispanic/Latino(a)—full-time 3, part-time 0; Asian/Pacific Islander—full-time 0, part-time 0; American Indian/Alaska Native—full-time 0, part-time 1; Caucasian/White—full-time 31, part-time 7; Multi-ethnic—full-time 1, part-time 0; students subject to the Americans With Disabilities Act—full-time 0, part-time 0; Unknown ethnicity—full-time 0, part-time 0; International students who hold an F-1 or J-1 Visa—full-time 0, part-time 0.

Financial Information/Assistance:

Tuition for Full-Time Study: *Master's:* State residents: per academic year $14,000, $490 per credit hour; Nonstate residents: per academic year $14,000, $490 per credit hour. See the following website for updates and changes in tuition costs: http://www.brenau.edu/about/offices-and-resources/tuition-fees-and-accounting-office/.

Financial Assistance:

First-Year Students: No information provided.

Advanced Students: Teaching assistantships available for advanced students. Average amount paid per academic year: $10,000. Average number of hours worked per week: 20.

Additional Information: Of all students currently enrolled full time, 15% benefited from one or more of the listed financial assistance programs. Application and information available online at: http://www.brenau.edu/admissions/pay-for-school/.

Internships/Practica: Master's Degree (MA/MS Clinical Counseling Psychology): An internship experience, such as a final research project or "capstone" experience is required of graduates. Faculty and students will work together to set up practicum site placements. It is the student's responsibility to research available sites and determine his/her top three choices for placement. If a student wishes to receive practicum experience at a placement that has not been approved by the faculty, the student is responsible for providing faculty with the needed information for the approval of that site. The student must turn in his/her top three choices for placement, using the practicum pre-registration approval form, by the end of the semester preceding placement. The faculty member overseeing practicum placement will review student preferences, contact potential placement sites, and attempt to match students to placement sites. In the case that there are more students interested in a practicum site than there are openings at that practicum site, the students may be required to set up interviews with their potential supervisors at the site. Following the interviews, the site supervisor will report back to the faculty member who will make the final decision about placement.

Housing and Day Care: No on-campus housing is available. On-campus day care facilities are available. See the following website for more information: http://www.brenau.edu/about/child-development-center/.

Employment of Department Graduates:

Master's Degree Graduates: Of those who graduated in the academic year 2011–2012, the following categories and numbers represent the postgraduate activities and employment of master's degree graduates: Enrolled in a postdoctoral residency/fellowship (n/a), employed in independent practice (n/a), total from the above (master's) (0).

Doctoral Degree Graduates: Of those who graduated in the academic year 2011–2012, the following categories and numbers represent the postgraduate activities and employment of doctoral degree graduates: Enrolled in a psychology doctoral program (n/a), total from the above (doctoral) (0).

Additional Information:

Orientation, Objectives, and Emphasis of Department: The M.S. program in Clinical Counseling Psychology is committed to excellence in preparing students for work in a wide variety of clinical, counseling, assessment, and research settings. Our mission is to provide an education founded in the scientist–practitioner model, which will lead to competency in applied clinical/counseling work as well as to an understanding of the importance of ongoing research into the effectiveness of our work and an ability to competently carry out research. Furthermore, the mission of the program is to provide an education that fosters personal growth, promotes reflection about practice, cultivates compassion and sensitivity in the therapeutic approach, encourages community responsibility and global understanding, and leads to intellectual and professional competence. The program provides coursework and practicum/internship experiences which emphasize the application of theories of human development, psychopathology, and behavior change to psychosocial problems of a diverse clientele seeking mental health services. The program provides a basis in general psychological principles, therapeutic principles, a framework of research methodology, evaluation and statistics as well as applied work with these skills through the thesis requirement, and applied work in the area of clinical counseling psychology including the theory and practice of therapy, psychological assessment, ethics and professional identity, and social and cultural diversity. The program includes 57 hours of course work with the option of completing an additional 6 hours of coursework in a specialty area. Part of the coursework involves completing an applied research thesis, and part of the coursework involves gaining 700 hours of applied practica and internship experiences. Graduates are eligible to sit for the National Counselor's Exam (NCE). Passing of the exam in conjunction with program requirements and additional supervised experience support eligibility for licensure as Licensed Professional Counselor (LPC).

Application Information:

Send to Admissions, Attention: Michelle Leavell, Brenau University, 500 Washington Street, Gainesville, GA 30501. Application available online. URL of online application: http://www.brenau.edu/apply/. Students are admitted in the Fall, application deadline March 1; Spring, application deadline October 1. *Fee:* $35.

Emory University
Department of Psychology
36 Eagle Row
Atlanta, GA 30322
Telephone: (404) 727-7438
Fax: (404) 727-0372
E-mail: *paula.mitchell@emory.edu*
Web: *http://www.psychology.emory.edu/*

Department Information:

1945. Chairperson: Harold Gouzoules. Number of faculty: total—full-time 35; women—full-time 15; total—minority—full-time 1.

Programs and Degrees Offered:

Listed in the following order: Program area, degree type (T if terminal Master's), number awarded 7/11–6/12. Clinical Psychology PhD (Doctor of Philosophy) 8, Cognition & Development PhD (Doctor of Philosophy) 3, Neuroscience & Animal Behavior PhD (Doctor of Philosophy) 5.

APA Accreditation: Clinical PhD (Doctor of Philosophy). Student Outcome Data Website: http://www.psychology.emory.edu/clinical/admission.html.

Student Applications/Admissions:

Student Applications

Clinical Psychology PhD (Doctor of Philosophy)—Applications 2012–2013, 384. Total applicants accepted 2012–2013, 10. Number full-time enrolled (new admits only) 2012–2013, 6. Number part-time enrolled (new admits only) 2012–2013, 0. Total enrolled 2012–2013 full-time, 31. Total enrolled 2012–2013 part-time, 0. Openings 2013–2014, 6. The median number of years required for completion of a degree in 2012–2013 were 6. The number of students enrolled full- and part-time who were dismissed or voluntarily withdrew from this program area in 2012–2013 were 0. *Cognition & Development PhD (Doctor of Philosophy)*—Applications 2012–2013, 75. Total applicants accepted 2012–2013, 5. Number full-time enrolled (new admits only) 2012–2013, 5. Total enrolled 2012–2013 full-time, 24. Total enrolled 2012–2013 part-time, 0. Openings 2013–2014, 5. The median number of years required for completion of a degree in 2012–2013 were 6. The number of students enrolled full- and part-time who were dismissed or voluntarily withdrew from this program area in 2012–2013 were 1. *Neuroscience & Animal Behavior PhD (Doctor of Philosophy)*—Applications 2012–2013, 80. Total applicants accepted 2012–2013, 7. Number full-time enrolled (new admits only) 2012–2013, 5. Number part-time enrolled (new admits only) 2012–2013, 0. Total enrolled 2012–2013 full-time, 15. Total enrolled 2012–2013 part-time, 0. Openings 2013–2014, 5. The median number of years required for completion of a degree in 2012–2013 were 6. The number of students enrolled full- and part-time who were dismissed or voluntarily withdrew from this program area in 2012–2013 were 1.

Scores: Entries appear in this order: required test or GPA, minimum score (if required), median score of students entering in 2012–2013. *Clinical Psychology PhD (Doctor of Philosophy):* GRE-V 600, GRE-Q 600, GRE-Analytical 5.0, overall undergraduate GPA 3.5, Masters GPA no minimum stated; *Cognition & Development PhD (Doctor of Philosophy):* GRE-V 550, GRE-Q 650, GRE-Analytical 5.0, overall undergraduate GPA 3.5, Masters GPA no minimum stated; *Neuroscience & Animal Behavior PhD (Doctor of Philosophy):* GRE-V 600, GRE-Q 600, GRE-Analytical 5.0, overall undergraduate GPA 3.5, Masters GPA no minimum stated.

Other Criteria: (importance of criteria rated low, medium, or high): GRE scores—high, research experience—high, work experience—medium, extracurricular activity—low, clinically related public service—medium, GPA—high, letters of recommendation—high, interview—high, statement of goals and objectives—high, faculty research match—high, undergraduate major in psychology—medium, specific undergraduate psychology courses taken—medium, Clinically related public service is less pertinent to the Cognition & Development and the Neuroscience & Animal Behavior programs. For additional information on admission requirements, go to http://www.psychology.emory.edu/graduate/admission.html.

Student Characteristics: The following represents characteristics of students in 2012–2013 in all graduate psychology programs in the department: Female—full-time 54, part-time 0; Male—full-time 16, part-time 0; African American/Black—full-time 7, part-time 0; Hispanic/Latino(a)—full-time 1, part-time 0; Asian/Pacific Islander—full-time 9, part-time 0; American Indian/Alaska Native—full-time 0, part-time 0; Caucasian/White—full-time 53, part-time 0; Multi-ethnic—full-time 0, part-time 0; students subject to the Americans With Disabilities Act—full-time 0, part-time 0; Unknown ethnicity—full-time 0, part-time 0; International students who hold an F-1 or J-1 Visa—full-time 4, part-time 0.

Financial Information/Assistance:

Tuition for Full-Time Study: *Doctoral:* State residents: per academic year $50,539; Nonstate residents: per academic year $50,539. Tuition is subject to change. Additional fees are assessed to students beyond the costs of tuition for the following: health insurance, computing fee, mental health fee, athletic fee, activity fee. See the following website for updates and changes in tuition costs: http://www.gs.emory.edu/financial_support/tuition.html.

Financial Assistance:

First-Year Students: Teaching assistantships available for first year. Average amount paid per academic year: $250. Average number of hours worked per week: 10. Fellowships and scholarships available for first year. Average amount paid per academic year: $23,000. Average number of hours worked per week: 10. Apply by February.

Advanced Students: Teaching assistantships available for advanced students. Average amount paid per academic year: $24,000. Average number of hours worked per week: 10. Apply by December. Fellowships and scholarships available for advanced students. Average amount paid per academic year: $23,000. Average number of hours worked per week: 10. Apply by February.

Additional Information: Of all students currently enrolled full time, 100% benefited from one or more of the listed financial assistance programs. Application and information available online at: http://www.gs.emory.edu/financial_support/index.html.

Internships/Practica: Doctoral Degree (PhD Clinical Psychology): For those doctoral students for whom a professional psychology internship was required in this program prior to graduation, (2) students applied for an internship in 2011–2012, with (2) students obtaining an internship. Of those students who obtained an internship, (2) were paid internships. Of those students who obtained an internship, (2) students placed in APA/CPA accredited internships, (0) students placed in internships not APA/CPA accredited, but listed with the Association of Psychology Postdoctoral and Internship Programs (APPIC), (0) students placed in internships conforming to guidelines of the Council of Directors of School Psychology Programs (CDSPP), (0) students placed in internships that were not APA/CPA accredited, APPIC or CDSPP listed. .

Housing and Day Care: On-campus housing is available. See the following website for more information: http://www.emory.edu/HOUSING/GRAD/gradhouse.html. On-campus day care facilities are available. See the following website for more information: http://www.emory.edu/HOUSING/CLAIRMONT/child.html.

Employment of Department Graduates:

Master's Degree Graduates: Of those who graduated in the academic year 2011–2012, the following categories and numbers represent the postgraduate activities and employment of master's degree graduates: Enrolled in a postdoctoral residency/fellowship (n/a), employed in independent practice (n/a), total from the above (master's) (0).

Doctoral Degree Graduates: Of those who graduated in the academic year 2011–2012, the following categories and numbers represent the postgraduate activities and employment of doctoral degree graduates: Enrolled in a psychology doctoral program (n/a), enrolled in a postdoctoral residency/fellowship (12), employed in an academic position at a university (2), employed in a community mental health/counseling center (2), total from the above (doctoral) (16).

Additional Information:

Orientation, Objectives, and Emphasis of Department: The primary emphasis of our clinical curriculum is to provide students with the knowledge and skills they need to function as productive clinical researchers in psychology. This requires a basic understanding of the determinants of human behavior, including biological, psychological, and social factors, and a strong background in research design and quantitative methods. The program in cognition and development at Emory is committed to the principle that cognition and its development are best studied together. The research interests of the faculty span a wide range, and are reflected in our graduate courses, which include memory, emotion, language, perception, and concepts and categories. The program in neuroscience and animal behavior approaches topics within the areas of neuroscience, physiological psychology, acquired behavior, and ethology as a unified entity. Thus, the emphasis is on behavior as a biological phenomenon. Research in neuroscience and physiological psychology explores brain-behavior relationships; research on acquired behavior studies the ongoing and evolutionary factors influenced in individual adaptations; and ethological studies are concerned with understanding how animals function in their natural environment.

Special Facilities or Resources: The department has affiliations with the Emory Medical School, Yerkes National Primate Center, and the Center for Behavioral Neuroscience. In addition, faculty and students from many of the universities in the Atlanta area meet formally and informally to discuss common research interests.

Information for Students With Physical Disabilities: See the following website for more information: http://www.ods.emory. edu/.

Application Information:

Send to Mrs. Paula Mitchell, Academic Degree Program Coordinator, Department of Psychology, Emory University, 36 Eagle Row, Suite 276, Atlanta, GA 30322. Application available online. URL of online application: https://www.applyweb.com/apply/emorylgs/. Students are admitted in the Fall, application deadline December 1. Clinical: December 1; Cognition and Development: January 3; Neuroscience and Animal Behavior: January 3. *Fee:* $75.

Georgia Institute of Technology
School of Psychology
College of Sciences
654 Cherry Street
Atlanta, GA 30332-0170
Telephone: (404) 894-0886
Fax: (404) 894-8905
E-mail: *psych@gatech.edu*
Web: *http://www.psychology.gatech.edu/*

Department Information:

1959. Chairperson: Dr. Howard Weiss. Number of faculty: total—full-time 24, part-time 1; women—full-time 5, part-time 1; total—minority—full-time 2; women minority—full-time 1.

Programs and Degrees Offered:

Listed in the following order: Program area, degree type (T if terminal Master's), number awarded 7/11–6/12. Cognition and Brain Science PhD (Doctor of Philosophy), Cognitive Aging PhD (Doctor of Philosophy), Engineering Psychology PhD (Doctor of Philosophy), Industrial/Organizational Psychology PhD (Doctor of Philosophy), Quantitative Psychology PhD (Doctor of Philosophy).

Student Applications/Admissions:

Student Applications

Cognition and Brain Science PhD (Doctor of Philosophy)—Cognitive Aging PhD (Doctor of Philosophy)—Engineering Psychology PhD (Doctor of Philosophy)—Industrial/Organizational Psychology PhD (Doctor of Philosophy)—Quantitative Psychology PhD (Doctor of Philosophy)—

Other Criteria: (importance of criteria rated low, medium, or high): GRE scores—high, research experience—medium, work experience—medium, extracurricular activity—low, GPA—high, letters of recommendation—high, interview—medium, statement of goals and objectives—high, undergraduate major in psychology—medium, specific undergraduate psychology courses taken—medium. For additional information on admission requirements, go to http://www.psychology. gatech.edu/graduate/prospectivestudents/ prospectivestudents_ar.php.

Student Characteristics: The following represents characteristics of students in 2012–2013 in all graduate psychology programs in the department: Female—full-time 44, part-time 0; Male—full-time 43, part-time 0; African American/Black—full-time 3, part-time 0; Hispanic/Latino(a)—full-time 2, part-time 0; Asian/Pacific Islander—full-time 12, part-time 0; American Indian/Alaska Native—full-time 0, part-time 0; Caucasian/White—full-time 65, part-time 0; Multi-ethnic—full-time 0, part-time 0; students subject to the Americans With Disabilities Act—full-time 1, part-time 0; Unknown ethnicity—full-time 5, part-time 0; International students who hold an F-1 or J-1 Visa—full-time 15, part-time 0.

Financial Information/Assistance:

Tuition for Full-Time Study: *Doctoral:* State residents: $417 per credit hour; Nonstate residents: $1,120 per credit hour. Tuition is subject to change. Additional fees are assessed to students beyond the costs of tuition for the following: Transportation, health, technology, activity fees. See the following website for updates and changes in tuition costs: http://bursar.gatech.edu/tuiandfee.php.

Financial Assistance:

First-Year Students: Teaching assistantships available for first year. Average amount paid per academic year: $16,445. Average number of hours worked per week: 20. Apply by December 15. Research assistantships available for first year. Average amount paid per academic year: $16,445. Average number of hours worked per week: 20. Apply by December 15. Traineeships available for first year. Fellowships and scholarships available for first year.

Advanced Students: Teaching assistantships available for advanced students. Average amount paid per academic year: $16,445. Average number of hours worked per week: 20. Research assistantships available for advanced students. Average amount paid per academic year: $16,445. Average number of hours worked per week: 20. Fellowships and scholarships available for advanced students.

Additional Information: Of all students currently enrolled full time, 90% benefited from one or more of the listed financial assistance programs. Application and information available online at: http://psychology.gatech.edu/graduate/prospectivestudents/prospectivestudents_fa.php.

Internships/Practica: Internships are available for Industrial/Organizational and Engineering Psychology doctoral students in local corporations.

Housing and Day Care: On-campus housing is available. See the following website for more information: http://housing.gatech.edu/. On-campus day care facilities are available. See the following website for more information: http://www.ohr.gatech.edu/worklife/childcare.

Employment of Department Graduates:

Master's Degree Graduates: Of those who graduated in the academic year 2011–2012, the following categories and numbers represent the postgraduate activities and employment of master's degree graduates: Enrolled in a psychology doctoral program (6), enrolled in another graduate/professional program (1), enrolled in a postdoctoral residency/fellowship (n/a), employed in independent practice (n/a), total from the above (master's) (7).

Doctoral Degree Graduates: Of those who graduated in the academic year 2011–2012, the following categories and numbers represent the postgraduate activities and employment of doctoral degree graduates: Enrolled in a psychology doctoral program (n/a), enrolled in a postdoctoral residency/fellowship (5), employed in an academic position at a university (4), employed in business or industry (3), employed in government agency (1), total from the above (doctoral) (13).

Additional Information:

Orientation, Objectives, and Emphasis of Department: Programs are offered leading to the PhD degrees with five areas of specialization: Engineering, Cognition and Brain Science, Cognitive Aging, Industrial/Organizational, and Quantitative Psychology. Each program of study involves intensive exposure to the experimental and theoretical foundations of psychology with a strong emphasis on quantitative methods. It is the basic philosophy of the faculty that the student is trained as a psychologist first and a specialist second. Individual initiative in research and study is strongly encouraged and supported by close faculty-student contact.

Special Facilities or Resources: New fMRI machine and brain center.

Information for Students With Physical Disabilities: See the following website for more information: http://www.adapts.gatech.edu/.

Application Information:
Application available online. URL of online application: http://www.gradadmiss.gatech.edu/apply/apply_now.php. Students are admitted in the Fall, application deadline December 15. *Fee:* $50.

Georgia School of Professional Psychology at Argosy University, Atlanta
Clinical Psychology
College of Psychology and Behavioral Sciences
980 Hammond Drive, Building 2, Suite 100
Atlanta, GA 30328
Telephone: (888) 671-4777
Fax: (770) 671-0476
E-mail: *tcbrown@argosy.edu*
Web: *http://www.argosy.edu*

Department Information:
1990. Chairperson: Timothy C. Brown, PhD. Number of faculty: total—full-time 12, part-time 1; women—full-time 9; total—minority—full-time 2; women minority—full-time 2.

Programs and Degrees Offered:
Listed in the following order: Program area, degree type (T if terminal Master's), number awarded 7/11–6/12. Clinical Psychology MA/MS (Master of Arts/Science) (T) 6, Clinical Psychology PsyD (Doctor of Psychology) 42.

APA Accreditation: Clinical PsyD (Doctor of Psychology). Student Outcome Data Website: http://www.argosy.edu/clinical-psychology/atlanta-georgia/psyd-programs-doctorate-degree-57712.aspx.

Student Applications/Admissions:
Student Applications
Clinical Psychology MA/MS (Master of Arts/Science)—Applications 2012–2013, 6. Total applicants accepted 2012–2013, 4. Number full-time enrolled (new admits only) 2012–2013, 2. Number part-time enrolled (new admits only) 2012–2013, 0. Total enrolled 2012–2013 full-time, 7. Total enrolled 2012–2013 part-time, 1. Openings 2013–2014, 10. The median number of years required for completion of a degree in 2012–2013 were 2. The number of students enrolled full- and part-time who were dismissed or voluntarily withdrew from this program area in 2012–2013 were 0. *Clinical Psychology PsyD (Doctor of Psychology)*—Applications 2012–2013, 45. Total applicants accepted 2012–2013, 10. Number full-time enrolled (new

admits only) 2012–2013, 8. Number part-time enrolled (new admits only) 2012–2013, 0. Total enrolled 2012–2013 full-time, 109. Total enrolled 2012–2013 part-time, 0. Openings 2013–2014, 20. The median number of years required for completion of a degree in 2012–2013 were 6. The number of students enrolled full- and part-time who were dismissed or voluntarily withdrew from this program area in 2012–2013 were 1.

Scores: Entries appear in this order: required test or GPA, minimum score (if required), median score of students entering in 2012–2013. *Clinical Psychology MA/MS (Master of Arts/ Science):* overall undergraduate GPA 3.0; *Clinical Psychology PsyD (Doctor of Psychology):* GRE-V no minimum stated, GRE-Q no minimum stated, GRE-Analytical no minimum stated, overall undergraduate GPA 3.25, 3.55.

Other Criteria: (importance of criteria rated low, medium, or high): GRE scores—medium, research experience—medium, work experience—high, extracurricular activity—medium, clinically related public service—high, GPA—high, letters of recommendation—high, interview—high, statement of goals and objectives—high, undergraduate major in psychology—medium, specific undergraduate psychology courses taken—high. For additional information on admission requirements, go to http://www.argosy.edu/clinical-psychology/atlanta-georgia/psyd-programs-admissions-57743.aspx.

Student Characteristics: The following represents characteristics of students in 2012–2013 in all graduate psychology programs in the department: Female—full-time 93, part-time 1; Male—full-time 23, part-time 0; African American/Black—full-time 29, part-time 0; Hispanic/Latino(a)—full-time 4, part-time 0; Asian/Pacific Islander—full-time 0, part-time 0; American Indian/Alaska Native—full-time 0, part-time 0; Caucasian/White—full-time 80, part-time 1; Multi-ethnic—full-time 3, part-time 0; students subject to the Americans With Disabilities Act—full-time 6, part-time 0; Unknown ethnicity—full-time 0, part-time 0; International students who hold an F-1 or J-1 Visa—full-time 2, part-time 0.

Financial Information/Assistance:

Tuition for Full-Time Study: *Master's:* State residents: $1,162 per credit hour; Nonstate residents: $1,162 per credit hour. *Doctoral:* State residents: $1,162 per credit hour; Nonstate residents: $1,162 per credit hour. Tuition is subject to change. Additional fees are assessed to students beyond the costs of tuition for the following: technology fee: $15/credit hour; student activity fee: $25 annually. See the following website for updates and changes in tuition costs: http://www.argosy.edu/admissions/.

Financial Assistance:

First-Year Students: Research assistantships available for first year. Average amount paid per academic year: $750. Average number of hours worked per week: 5. Fellowships and scholarships available for first year. Average amount paid per academic year: $5,000. Average number of hours worked per week: 0. Apply by June 30.

Advanced Students: Teaching assistantships available for advanced students. Average amount paid per academic year: $1,050. Average number of hours worked per week: 7. Apply by September 1. Research assistantships available for advanced students. Average amount paid per academic year: $750. Average number of hours worked per week: 5. Fellowships and scholarships available for advanced students. Average amount paid per academic year: $5,000. Average number of hours worked per week: 0. Apply by June 30.

Additional Information: Of all students currently enrolled full time, 35% benefited from one or more of the listed financial assistance programs. Application and information available online at: http://www.argosy.edu/financial-aid/Default.aspx.

Internships/Practica: Doctoral Degree (PsyD Clinical Psychology): For those doctoral students for whom a professional psychology internship was required in this program prior to graduation, (23) students applied for an internship in 2011–2012, with (18) students obtaining an internship. Of those students who obtained an internship, (18) were paid internships. Of those students who obtained an internship, (10) students placed in APA/CPA accredited internships, (8) students placed in internships not APA/CPA accredited, but listed with the Association of Psychology Postdoctoral and Internship Programs (APPIC), (0) students placed in internships conforming to guidelines of the Council of Directors of School Psychology Programs (CDSPP), (0) students placed in internships that were not APA/CPA accredited, APPIC or CDSPP listed. Master's Degree (MA/MS Clinical Psychology): An internship experience, such as a final research project or "capstone" experience is required of graduates. Our PsyD students program advances through a sequence of clinical training experiences that are progressively more challenging. The first year of our two-year practicum training sequence focuses upon developing students' knowledge and skills in assessment, testing, and diagnosis. Students' second year of practicum training focuses upon developing their knowledge base and skills in providing therapeutic interventions that are grounded in clinical theory and evidence-based practice. Most PsyD students participate in a third year of advanced practicum training, allowing them to specialize further in areas consistent with their interests. GSPP maintains longstanding practicum training relationships with local psychologists, agencies, and facilities—including local and regional medical centers, inpatient psychiatric facilities, specialty clinics, the VA Medical Center, college and university counseling centers, correctional facilities, children's hospitals, neuro-rehabilitation centers, and private practitioners. On practicum, students spend 16-20 hours per week providing services to clients in an agency, program, or professional practice that is formally affiliated with the program. Practicum students receive on-site supervision from licensed psychologists and other mental healthcare providers. During each practicum placement, students must also enroll in a weekly practicum seminar led by a faculty member on-campus, who offers didactic training and opportunities for case consultation.

Housing and Day Care: No on-campus housing is available. No on-campus day care facilities are available.

Employment of Department Graduates:

Master's Degree Graduates: Of those who graduated in the academic year 2011–2012, the following categories and numbers represent the postgraduate activities and employment of master's degree graduates: Enrolled in a postdoctoral residency/fellowship (n/a), employed in independent practice (n/a), total from the above (master's) (0).

Doctoral Degree Graduates: Of those who graduated in the academic year 2011–2012, the following categories and numbers represent the postgraduate activities and employment of doctoral degree graduates: Enrolled in a psychology doctoral program (n/a), enrolled in a postdoctoral residency/fellowship (15), employed in independent practice (7), employed in an academic position at a university (1), employed in other positions at a higher education institution (5), employed in government agency (3), employed in a community mental health/counseling center (2), employed in a hospital/medical center (1), other employment position (2), do not know (6), total from the above (doctoral) (42).

Additional Information:

Orientation, Objectives, and Emphasis of Department: The PsyD program at the Georgia School of Professional Psychology at Argosy University, Atlanta follows the practitioner-scholar model of clinical training. We are devoted to preparing students to practice as clinical psychologists. The core element of our doctoral program is a solid foundation in the discipline of psychology. Our practitioner training is firmly grounded in the theoretical constructs and empirical findings of psychology. The faculty at GSPP represent a wide range of clinical interests and theoretical orientations. No particular approach to clinical practice dominates the program, so that students engage in a theoretically rich and diverse training experience. The PsyD program is comprised of a 98-credit hour curriculum that can be completed over a five-year period, including the internship year. Our program is designed to provide students with well-rounded generalist training in clinical psychology. We believe this generalist approach is critically important given the growing emphasis on accountability, evidence-based practice, working in multidisciplinary settings, and flexibility in adapting to newly emerging roles. The PsyD program also offers elective courses and clinical training in four concentration areas: general adult clinical, child and family psychology, neuropsychology/geropsychology, and health psychology. Our MA program focuses upon preparing students for doctoral study in professional psychology.

Special Facilities or Resources: Our students engage in collaborative research with behavioral healthcare agencies in the metro-Atlanta area. GSPP also maintains archival data and therapy session recordings from the Vanderbilt University Center for Psychotherapy Research, which was directed by Dr. Hans Strupp until his retirement. Under the direction of Dr. Jeff Binder, this valuable resource provides both psychotherapy training and research opportunities for our students and faculty. Students in our neuropsychology concentration have participated in ongoing neuropsychological test development research with Dr. Nick De-Filippis, who also holds a multinational pharmaceutical research grant involving neuropsychological assessment.

Application Information:

Send to Office of Admissions, GSPP at Argosy University, Atlanta, 980 Hammond Drive, Building 2, Suite 100, Atlanta, GA 30328. Application available online. URL of online application: http://www.argosy.edu/admissions/. Students are admitted in the Fall, application deadline February 1. *Fee:* $50.

Georgia Southern University
Department of Psychology
College of Liberal Arts and Social Sciences
P.O. Box 8041
Statesboro, GA 30460-8041
Telephone: (912) 478-5539
Fax: (912) 478-0751
E-mail: *mnielsen@georgiasouthern.edu*
Web: *http://class.georgiasouthern.edu/psychology/*

Department Information:

1967. Chairperson: Dr. Michael Nielsen. Number of faculty: total—full-time 17; women—full-time 7.

Programs and Degrees Offered:

Listed in the following order: Program area, degree type (T if terminal Master's), number awarded 7/11–6/12. Psychology MA/MS (Master of Arts/Science) (T) 13, Clinical Psychology PsyD (Doctor of Psychology) 0.

Student Applications/Admissions:

Student Applications

Psychology MA/MS (Master of Arts/Science)—Applications 2012–2013, 18. Total applicants accepted 2012–2013, 12. Number full-time enrolled (new admits only) 2012–2013, 12. Number part-time enrolled (new admits only) 2012–2013, 0. Total enrolled 2012–2013 full-time, 20. Total enrolled 2012–2013 part-time, 0. Openings 2013–2014, 12. The median number of years required for completion of a degree in 2012–2013 were 2. The number of students enrolled full- and part-time who were dismissed or voluntarily withdrew from this program area in 2012–2013 were 0. *Clinical Psychology PsyD (Doctor of Psychology)*—Applications 2012–2013, 29. Total applicants accepted 2012–2013, 8. Number full-time enrolled (new admits only) 2012–2013, 8. Number part-time enrolled (new admits only) 2012–2013, 0. Total enrolled 2012–2013 full-time, 32. Total enrolled 2012–2013 part-time, 1. Openings 2013–2014, 8. The number of students enrolled full- and part-time who were dismissed or voluntarily withdrew from this program area in 2012–2013 were 0.

Scores: Entries appear in this order: required test or GPA, minimum score (if required), median score of students entering in 2012–2013. *Psychology MA/MS (Master of Arts/Science):* GRE-V no minimum stated, 157., GRE-Q no minimum stated, 150, overall undergraduate GPA 3.0; *Clinical Psychology PsyD (Doctor of Psychology):* GRE-V no minimum stated, 505, GRE-Q no minimum stated, 595, overall undergraduate GPA no minimum stated, 3.44.

Other Criteria: (importance of criteria rated low, medium, or high): GRE scores—high, research experience—medium, work experience—medium, extracurricular activity—low, clinically related public service—medium, GPA—high, letters of recommendation—medium, interview—high, statement of goals and objectives—high, undergraduate major in psychology—low, specific undergraduate psychology courses taken—high, MS: GRE, grades, research experience all important. Psy.D: GRE, grades, statement, interview most important. For additional information on admission requirements, go to http://class.georgiasouthern.edu/psychology/.

Student Characteristics: The following represents characteristics of students in 2012–2013 in all graduate psychology programs in the department: Female—full-time 32, part-time 1; Male—full-time 20, part-time 0; African American/Black—full-time 4, part-time 0; Hispanic/Latino(a)—full-time 0, part-time 0; Asian/Pacific Islander—full-time 1, part-time 0; American Indian/Alaska Native—full-time 0, part-time 0; Caucasian/White—full-time 45, part-time 1; Multi-ethnic—full-time 0, part-time 0; students subject to the Americans With Disabilities Act—full-time 1, part-time 0; Unknown ethnicity—full-time 2, part-time 0; International students who hold an F-1 or J-1 Visa—full-time 0, part-time 0.

Financial Information/Assistance:

Tuition for Full-Time Study: Master's: State residents: per academic year $4,734, $263 per credit hour; Nonstate residents: per academic year $20,354, $1,049 per credit hour. *Doctoral:* State residents: per academic year $7,101, $263 per credit hour; Nonstate residents: per academic year $28,323, $1,049 per credit hour. Tuition is subject to change. Additional fees are assessed to students beyond the costs of tuition for the following: technology, health insurance, activity, transit, athletics. See the following website for updates and changes in tuition costs: http://services.georgiasouthern.edu/bursar/tuitionandfees/main.htm.

Financial Assistance:

First-Year Students: Research assistantships available for first year. Average amount paid per academic year: $6,850. Average number of hours worked per week: 20. Apply by April 15.

Advanced Students: Teaching assistantships available for advanced students. Average amount paid per academic year: $12,000. Average number of hours worked per week: 20. Research assistantships available for advanced students. Average amount paid per academic year: $7,200. Average number of hours worked per week: 20. Apply by April 15.

Additional Information: Of all students currently enrolled full time, 42% benefited from one or more of the listed financial assistance programs. Application and information available online at: http://em.georgiasouthern.edu/finaid/.

Internships/Practica: Doctoral Degree (PsyD Clinical Psychology): For those doctoral students for whom a professional psychology internship was required in this program prior to graduation, (4) students applied for an internship in 2011–2012, with (3) students obtaining an internship. Of those students who obtained an internship, (3) were paid internships. Of those students who obtained an internship, (0) students placed in APA/CPA accredited internships, (3) students placed in internships not APA/CPA accredited, but listed with the Association of Psychology Postdoctoral and Internship Programs (APPIC), (0) students placed in internships conforming to guidelines of the Council of Directors of School Psychology Programs (CDSPP), (0) students placed in internships that were not APA/CPA accredited, APPIC or CDSPP listed. Master's Degree (MA/MS Psychology): An internship experience, such as a final research project or "capstone" experience is required of graduates. Clinical students engage in practica in their 2nd - 4th years. Sites include the department's clinic, which serves a range of community members, the campus counseling center serving students, and a variety of sites in surrounding communities.

Housing and Day Care: On-campus housing is available. See the following website for more information: http://gsuhousing.com/. On-campus day care facilities are available. See the following website for more information: http://chhs.georgiasouthern.edu/she/cdc/.

Employment of Department Graduates:

Master's Degree Graduates: Of those who graduated in the academic year 2011–2012, the following categories and numbers represent the postgraduate activities and employment of master's degree graduates: Enrolled in a psychology doctoral program (4), enrolled in another graduate/professional program (5), enrolled in a postdoctoral residency/fellowship (n/a), employed in independent practice (n/a), employed in other positions at a higher education institution (1), employed in government agency (1), do not know (2), total from the above (master's) (13).

Doctoral Degree Graduates: Of those who graduated in the academic year 2011–2012, the following categories and numbers represent the postgraduate activities and employment of doctoral degree graduates: Enrolled in a psychology doctoral program (n/a), total from the above (doctoral) (0).

Additional Information:

Orientation, Objectives, and Emphasis of Department: The MS program focuses on general psychology and prepares students for doctoral study in any area of psychology. The program consists of coursework and supervised research in traditional areas of interest such as social, developmental, learning, cognitive, physiological, and industrial/organizational and has a thesis requirement. The PsyD program in clinical psychology is new (beginning Fall 2007) and follows the practitioner/scholar model of training. The program is 5 years (including internship) and is consistent with the guidelines for accreditation set forth by the APA (although is not yet accredited). It has been granted 'designated' status by the National Register of Health Care Providers. The program emphasizes training in psychotherapy and assessment with individuals in rural settings.

Special Facilities or Resources: The department is housed in a newly remodeled building, with research laboratories in a variety of subdisciplines in psychology (social, cognitive, physiological). The department also hosts a community psychology clinic, where students in the clinical program are supervised in seeing adults from the Statesboro community and surrounding rural areas.

Information for Students With Physical Disabilities: See the following website for more information: http://students.georgiasouthern.edu/disability/.

Application Information:

Send to Office of Graduate Admissions, Georgia Southern University, P.O. Box 8113, Statesboro, GA 30460-8113. Application available online. URL of online application: http://cogs.georgiasouthern.edu/gradadmin/applytogradschool. Students are admitted in the Fall, application deadline January 15. PsyD applications are due January 15. MS priority deadline: February 15, final deadline: July 1. *Fee:* $50.

Georgia State University

Counseling and Psychological Services
College of Education
P.O. Box 3980
Atlanta, GA 30302-3980
Telephone: (404) 413-8010
Fax: (404) 413-8013
E-mail: *bdew@gsu.edu*
Web: *http://education.gsu.edu/CPS/index.htm*

Department Information:

1968. Chairperson: Dr. Brian J. Dew. Number of faculty: total—full-time 16, part-time 1; women—full-time 6; total—minority—full-time 3; women minority—full-time 2.

Programs and Degrees Offered:

Listed in the following order: Program area, degree type (T if terminal Master's), number awarded 7/11–6/12. Counseling Psychology PhD (Doctor of Philosophy) 4, School Psychology PhD (Doctor of Philosophy) 5, Counselor Education and Practice PhD (Doctor of Philosophy) 4, School Psychology EdS (School Psychology) 13, School Counseling MEd (Education) 19, Mental Health Counseling MA/MS (Master of Arts/Science) (T) 38.

APA Accreditation: Counseling PhD (Doctor of Philosophy). Student Outcome Data Website: http://education.gsu.edu/CPS/4502.html. School PhD (Doctor of Philosophy). Student Outcome Data Website: http://education.gsu.edu/CPS/4962.html.

Student Applications/Admissions:

Student Applications

Counseling Psychology PhD (Doctor of Philosophy)—Applications 2012–2013, 86. Total applicants accepted 2012–2013, 7. Number full-time enrolled (new admits only) 2012–2013, 4. Number part-time enrolled (new admits only) 2012–2013, 0. Total enrolled 2012–2013 full-time, 17. Openings 2013–2014, 4. The median number of years required for completion of a degree in 2012–2013 were 4. The number of students enrolled full- and part-time who were dismissed or voluntarily withdrew from this program area in 2012–2013 were 1. *School Psychology PhD (Doctor of Philosophy)*—Applications 2012–2013, 31. Total applicants accepted 2012–2013, 5. Number full-time enrolled (new admits only) 2012–2013, 4. Total enrolled 2012–2013 full-time, 14. Openings 2013–2014, 4. The median number of years required for completion of a degree in 2012–2013 were 4. The number of students enrolled full- and part-time who were dismissed or voluntarily withdrew from this program area in 2012–2013 were 1. *Counselor Education and Practice PhD (Doctor of Philosophy)*—Applications 2012–2013, 19. Total applicants accepted 2012–2013, 4. Number full-time enrolled (new admits only) 2012–2013, 3. Number part-time enrolled (new admits only) 2012–2013, 0. Total enrolled 2012–2013 full-time, 14. Total enrolled 2012–2013 part-time, 0. Openings 2013–2014, 4. The median number of years required for completion of a degree in 2012–2013 were 4. The number of students enrolled full- and part-time who were dismissed or voluntarily withdrew from this program area

in 2012–2013 were 0. *School Psychology EdS (School Psychology)*—Applications 2012–2013, 53. Total applicants accepted 2012–2013, 20. Number full-time enrolled (new admits only) 2012–2013, 7. Number part-time enrolled (new admits only) 2012–2013, 0. Total enrolled 2012–2013 full-time, 16. Total enrolled 2012–2013 part-time, 0. Openings 2013–2014, 12. The median number of years required for completion of a degree in 2012–2013 were 2. The number of students enrolled full- and part-time who were dismissed or voluntarily withdrew from this program area in 2012–2013 were 1. *School Counseling MEd (Education)*—Applications 2012–2013, 53. Total applicants accepted 2012–2013, 20. Number full-time enrolled (new admits only) 2012–2013, 15. Number part-time enrolled (new admits only) 2012–2013, 0. Total enrolled 2012–2013 full-time, 34. Openings 2013–2014, 23. The median number of years required for completion of a degree in 2012–2013 were 2. The number of students enrolled full- and part-time who were dismissed or voluntarily withdrew from this program area in 2012–2013 were 2. *Mental Health Counseling MA/MS (Master of Arts/Science)*—Applications 2012–2013, 152. Total applicants accepted 2012–2013, 29. Number full-time enrolled (new admits only) 2012–2013, 23. Number part-time enrolled (new admits only) 2012–2013, 0. Total enrolled 2012–2013 full-time, 58. Total enrolled 2012–2013 part-time, 0. Openings 2013–2014, 30. The median number of years required for completion of a degree in 2012–2013 were 2. The number of students enrolled full- and part-time who were dismissed or voluntarily withdrew from this program area in 2012–2013 were 0.

Scores: Entries appear in this order: required test or GPA, minimum score (if required), median score of students entering in 2012–2013. *Counseling Psychology PhD (Doctor of Philosophy):* GRE-V no minimum stated, 582, GRE-Q no minimum stated, 530, overall undergraduate GPA 3.3, 3.92, last 2 years GPA no minimum stated, psychology GPA no minimum stated, Masters GPA no minimum stated; *School Psychology PhD (Doctor of Philosophy):* GRE-V no minimum stated, 154, GRE-Q no minimum stated, 155, GRE-Analytical no minimum stated, GRE-Subject (Psychology) no minimum stated, overall undergraduate GPA 3.3, 3.61, last 2 years GPA no minimum stated, psychology GPA no minimum stated, Masters GPA no minimum stated; *Counselor Education and Practice PhD (Doctor of Philosophy):* GRE-V no minimum stated, 151, GRE-Q no minimum stated, 155, overall undergraduate GPA no minimum stated, 3.91; *School Psychology EdS (School Psychology):* GRE-V no minimum stated, 152, GRE-Q no minimum stated, 151, overall undergraduate GPA no minimum stated, 3.55, last 2 years GPA no minimum stated; *School Counseling MEd (Education):* GRE-V no minimum stated, 153, GRE-Q no minimum stated, 150, overall undergraduate GPA 2.5, 3.45; *Mental Health Counseling MA/MS (Master of Arts/Science):* GRE-V no minimum stated, 154, GRE-Q no minimum stated, 145, overall undergraduate GPA no minimum stated, 3.32.

Other Criteria: (importance of criteria rated low, medium, or high): GRE scores—high, research experience—high, work experience—medium, extracurricular activity—high, clinically related public service—medium, GPA—high, letters of recommendation—high, interview—high, statement of goals and objectives—high, undergraduate major in psychology—medium, specific undergraduate psychology courses taken—

high. For additional information on admission requirements, go to http://education.gsu.edu/oaa/3997.html.

Student Characteristics: The following represents characteristics of students in 2012–2013 in all graduate psychology programs in the department: Female—full-time 72, part-time 40; Male—full-time 23, part-time 12; African American/Black—full-time 6, part-time 4; Hispanic/Latino(a)—full-time 3, part-time 3; Asian/Pacific Islander—full-time 3, part-time 3; American Indian/Alaska Native—full-time 2, part-time 1; Caucasian/White—full-time 81, part-time 41; Multi-ethnic—full-time 0, part-time 0; students subject to the Americans With Disabilities Act—full-time 0, part-time 0; Unknown ethnicity—full-time 0, part-time 0; International students who hold an F-1 or J-1 Visa—full-time 0, part-time 0.

Financial Information/Assistance:
Tuition for Full-Time Study: *Master's:* State residents: per academic year $8,064, $336 per credit hour; Nonstate residents: per academic year $28,800, $1,200 per credit hour. *Doctoral:* State residents: per academic year $8,064, $336 per credit hour; Nonstate residents: per academic year $28,800, $1,200 per credit hour. Tuition is subject to change. See the following website for updates and changes in tuition costs: http://www.gsu.edu/studentaccounts/tuition_and_fees.html.

Financial Assistance:
First-Year Students: Teaching assistantships available for first year. Research assistantships available for first year. Traineeships available for first year. Fellowships and scholarships available for first year.
Advanced Students: Teaching assistantships available for advanced students. Research assistantships available for advanced students. Traineeships available for advanced students. Fellowships and scholarships available for advanced students.
Additional Information: Of all students currently enrolled full time, 40% benefited from one or more of the listed financial assistance programs. Application and information available online at: http://www.gsu.edu/financialaid/.

Internships/Practica: Doctoral Degree (PhD Counseling Psychology): For those doctoral students for whom a professional psychology internship was required in this program prior to graduation, (10) students applied for an internship in 2011–2012, with (10) students obtaining an internship. Of those students who obtained an internship, (10) were paid internships. Of those students who obtained an internship, (10) students placed in APA/CPA accredited internships, (0) students placed in internships not APA/CPA accredited, but listed with the Association of Psychology Postdoctoral and Internship Programs (APPIC), (0) students placed in internships conforming to guidelines of the Council of Directors of School Psychology Programs (CDSPP), (0) students placed in internships that were not APA/CPA accredited, APPIC or CDSPP listed. Doctoral Degree (PhD School Psychology): For those doctoral students for whom a professional psychology internship was required in this program prior to graduation, (7) students applied for an internship in 2011–2012, with (6) students obtaining an internship. Of those students who obtained an internship, (6) were paid internships. Of those students who obtained an internship, (3) students placed in APA/CPA accredited internships, (2) students placed in internships not APA/CPA accredited, but listed with the Association of Psychology Postdoctoral and Internship Programs (APPIC), (0) students placed in internships conforming to guidelines of the Council of Directors of School Psychology Programs (CDSPP), (1) students placed in internships that were not APA/CPA accredited, APPIC or CDSPP listed. Master's Degree (MA/MS Mental Health Counseling): An internship experience, such as a final research project or "capstone" experience is required of graduates.

Housing and Day Care: On-campus housing is available. See the following website for more information: http://www.gsu.edu/housing/. On-campus day care facilities are available. See the following website for more information: http://education.gsu.edu/cdc/index.htm.

Employment of Department Graduates:
Master's Degree Graduates: Of those who graduated in the academic year 2011–2012, the following categories and numbers represent the postgraduate activities and employment of master's degree graduates: Enrolled in a postdoctoral residency/fellowship (n/a), employed in independent practice (n/a), total from the above (master's) (0).
Doctoral Degree Graduates: Of those who graduated in the academic year 2011–2012, the following categories and numbers represent the postgraduate activities and employment of doctoral degree graduates: Enrolled in a psychology doctoral program (n/a), total from the above (doctoral) (0).

Additional Information:
Orientation, Objectives, and Emphasis of Department: Based on our commitment to diversity, advocacy and the belief that change is possible, the mission of the Department of Counseling and Psychological Services is to prepare competent professionals in counseling and psychological services to contribute to the body of knowledge that undergirds these professions and to provide service to the profession and the community. The CPS department prepares students for employment in settings such as rehabilitation clinics, public and private schools, correction agencies, colleges and universities, and mental health facilities. A concerted effort is devoted to providing students with the knowledge and skills to work successfully in these particular environments.

Information for Students With Physical Disabilities: See the following website for more information: http://www.gsu.edu/disability/.

Application Information:
Send to Georgia State University, Office of Academic Assistance, College of Education, 30 Pryor Street, Suite 300, Atlanta, GA 30303. Application available online. URL of online application: http://education.gsu.edu/oaa/4427.html. Students are admitted in the Fall, application deadline November 15; Summer, application deadline December 1. School Psychology PhD deadline is November 15; Counseling Psychology PhD, Counselor Education PhD, and School Psychology EdS is December 1; Mental Health Counseling MS is February 1. School Counseling MEd deadline is December 1 for a summer start. *Fee:* $50.

Georgia State University

Department of Psychology
College of Arts and Sciences
P.O. Box 5010
Atlanta, GA 30302-5010
Telephone: (404) 413-6200
Fax: (404) 413-6207
E-mail: *GradAdmissions@langate.gsu.edu*
Web: *http://www2.gsu.edu/~wwwpsy/*

Department Information:

1955. Chairperson: Lisa Armistead. Number of faculty: total—full-time 36; women—full-time 20; total—minority—full-time 6; women minority—full-time 3.

Programs and Degrees Offered:

Listed in the following order: Program area, degree type (T if terminal Master's), number awarded 7/11–6/12. Clinical Psychology PhD (Doctor of Philosophy) 2, Community Psychology PhD (Doctor of Philosophy) 5, Developmental Psychology PhD (Doctor of Philosophy) 0, Neuropsychology and Behavioral Neurosciences PhD (Doctor of Philosophy) 0, Coginitive Sciences Psychology PhD (Doctor of Philosophy) 0.

APA Accreditation: Clinical PhD (Doctor of Philosophy). Student Outcome Data Website: http://www2.gsu.edu/~wwwpsy/clinical.html.

Student Applications/Admissions:

Student Applications

Clinical Psychology PhD (Doctor of Philosophy)—Applications 2012–2013, 507. Total applicants accepted 2012–2013, 20. Number full-time enrolled (new admits only) 2012–2013, 11. Total enrolled 2012–2013 full-time, 59. Total enrolled 2012–2013 part-time, 0. Openings 2013–2014, 10. The median number of years required for completion of a degree in 2012–2013 were 8. The number of students enrolled full- and part-time who were dismissed or voluntarily withdrew from this program area in 2012–2013 were 2. *Community Psychology PhD (Doctor of Philosophy)*—Applications 2012–2013, 50. Total applicants accepted 2012–2013, 11. Number full-time enrolled (new admits only) 2012–2013, 4. Number part-time enrolled (new admits only) 2012–2013, 0. Total enrolled 2012–2013 full-time, 13. Total enrolled 2012–2013 part-time, 0. Openings 2013–2014, 4. The median number of years required for completion of a degree in 2012–2013 were 6. The number of students enrolled full- and part-time who were dismissed or voluntarily withdrew from this program area in 2012–2013 were 1. *Developmental Psychology PhD (Doctor of Philosophy)*—Applications 2012–2013, 31. Total applicants accepted 2012–2013, 10. Number full-time enrolled (new admits only) 2012–2013, 6. Number part-time enrolled (new admits only) 2012–2013, 0. Total enrolled 2012–2013 full-time, 17. Total enrolled 2012–2013 part-time, 0. Openings 2013–2014, 4. The number of students enrolled full- and part-time who were dismissed or voluntarily withdrew from this program area in 2012–2013 were 1. *Neuropsychology and Behavioral Neurosciences PhD (Doctor of Philosophy)*—Applications 2012–2013, 31. Total applicants accepted 2012–2013, 0. Number full-time enrolled (new admits only) 2012–2013, 0. Number part-time enrolled (new admits only) 2012–2013, 0. Total enrolled 2012–2013 full-time, 1. Total enrolled 2012–2013 part-time, 0. Openings 2013–2014, 2. The number of students enrolled full- and part-time who were dismissed or voluntarily withdrew from this program area in 2012–2013 were 0. *Coginitive Sciences Psychology PhD (Doctor of Philosophy)*—Applications 2012–2013, 33. Total applicants accepted 2012–2013, 9. Number full-time enrolled (new admits only) 2012–2013, 4. Number part-time enrolled (new admits only) 2012–2013, 0. Total enrolled 2012–2013 full-time, 16. Total enrolled 2012–2013 part-time, 0. Openings 2013–2014, 4. The number of students enrolled full- and part-time who were dismissed or voluntarily withdrew from this program area in 2012–2013 were 0.

Scores: Entries appear in this order: required test or GPA, minimum score (if required), median score of students entering in 2012–2013. *Clinical Psychology PhD (Doctor of Philosophy):* GRE-V no minimum stated, 159, GRE-Q no minimum stated, 156, overall undergraduate GPA no minimum stated, 3.78.

Other Criteria: (importance of criteria rated low, medium, or high): GRE scores—high, research experience—high, work experience—medium, extracurricular activity—low, clinically related public service—medium, GPA—high, letters of recommendation—high, interview—high, statement of goals and objectives—high, undergraduate major in psychology—medium, specific undergraduate psychology courses taken—high. For additional information on admission requirements, go to http://www2.gsu.edu/~wwwpsy/8582.html.

Student Characteristics: The following represents characteristics of students in 2012–2013 in all graduate psychology programs in the department: Female—full-time 86, part-time 0; Male—full-time 20, part-time 0; African American/Black—full-time 13, part-time 0; Hispanic/Latino(a)—full-time 4, part-time 0; Asian/Pacific Islander—full-time 9, part-time 0; American Indian/Alaska Native—full-time 0, part-time 0; Caucasian/White—full-time 66, part-time 0; Multi-ethnic—full-time 2, part-time 0; students subject to the Americans With Disabilities Act—full-time 0, part-time 0; Unknown ethnicity—full-time 12, part-time 0; International students who hold an F-1 or J-1 Visa—full-time 5, part-time 0.

Financial Information/Assistance:

Tuition for Full-Time Study: *Doctoral:* State residents: per academic year $8,064, $336 per credit hour; Nonstate residents: per academic year $28,800, $1,200 per credit hour. Tuition is subject to change. See the following website for updates and changes in tuition costs: http://www.gsu.edu/studentaccounts/tuition_and_fees.html.

Financial Assistance:

First-Year Students: Teaching assistantships available for first year. Average amount paid per academic year: $15,000. Average number of hours worked per week: 20. Research assistantships available for first year. Average amount paid per academic year: $15,000. Average number of hours worked per week: 20. Fellowships and scholarships available for first year. Average amount paid per academic year: $21,000.

Advanced Students: Teaching assistantships available for advanced students. Average amount paid per academic year: $18,000. Average number of hours worked per week: 20. Research assistantships available for advanced students. Average amount paid per academic year: $18,000. Average number of hours worked per week: 20. Fellowships and scholarships available for advanced students. Average amount paid per academic year: $21,000.

Additional Information: Of all students currently enrolled full time, 95% benefited from one or more of the listed financial assistance programs. Application and information available online at: http://www2.gsu.edu/~wwwpsy/8584.html.

Internships/Practica: Doctoral Degree (PhD Clinical Psychology): For those doctoral students for whom a professional psychology internship was required in this program prior to graduation, (6) students applied for an internship in 2011–2012, with (6) students obtaining an internship. Of those students who obtained an internship, (6) were paid internships. Of those students who obtained an internship, (6) students placed in APA/CPA accredited internships, (0) students placed in internships not APA/CPA accredited, but listed with the Association of Psychology Postdoctoral and Internship Programs (APPIC), (0) students placed in internships conforming to guidelines of the Council of Directors of School Psychology Programs (CDSPP), (0) students placed in internships that were not APA/CPA accredited, APPIC or CDSPP listed. Practicum experiences are an important component of the clinical training program. Supervised therapy and assessment practica are available in a variety of settings. For clinical students, one source of training is the Psychology Clinic which is located within the department. It provides services to students and members of the community in a variety of modalities, including assessment, individual therapy, group therapy, and family therapy. Another facility within the department is the Regent's Center for Learning Disorders, which offers comprehensive psychoeducational assessments to students and members of the community. Student clinicians are the primary providers of services in both of these clinics. In addition, there are numerous off-campus settings that offer supervised practicum experiences in a variety of areas including health psychology, neuropsychological assessment, personality assessment, psychiatric emergency room services, day treatment programs, etc. Many of these practica are available at Grady Memorial Hospital, a major metropolitan full-service facility located two blocks from the center of campus. Community students likewise do practica at various community based organizations. Often this research takes the form of needs assessment, program development, and program evaluation.

Housing and Day Care: On-campus housing is available. See the following website for more information: http://www.gsu.edu/housing/. On-campus day care facilities are available. See the following website for more information: http://education.gsu.edu/cdc/.

Employment of Department Graduates:
Master's Degree Graduates: Of those who graduated in the academic year 2011–2012, the following categories and numbers represent the postgraduate activities and employment of master's degree graduates: Enrolled in a postdoctoral residency/fellowship (n/a), employed in independent practice (n/a), total from the above (master's) (0).
Doctoral Degree Graduates: Of those who graduated in the academic year 2011–2012, the following categories and numbers represent the postgraduate activities and employment of doctoral degree graduates: Enrolled in a psychology doctoral program (n/a), total from the above (doctoral) (0).

Additional Information:
Orientation, Objectives, and Emphasis of Department: The department is eclectic, and many philosophical perspectives and research interests are represented. The policy of the department is to promote the personal and professional development of students. This includes the discovery of individual interests and goals, the growth of independent scholarship and research skills, the mastery of fundamental psychological knowledge and methodology, and the development of various professional skills (e.g., clinical skills, community intervention).

Special Facilities or Resources: The facilities of the department permit work in cognition, development, neuroscience + neuropsychology, learning, infant behavior, sensation and perception, motivation, aging, social psychology, assessment, individual, group and family therapy, behavior therapy, and community psychology. Students may work with both human and nonhuman populations. Human populations include all age ranges and a variety of ethnic and socioeconomic backgrounds. Nonhuman populations include a variety of rodent and nonhuman primates.

Information for Students With Physical Disabilities: See the following website for more information: http://www.gsu.edu/disability/.

Application Information:
Send to Office of Graduate Studies, College of Arts and Sciences, Georgia State University, P.O. Box 3993, Atlanta, GA 30302-3993. Application available online. URL of online application: http://www.cas.gsu.edu/grad_admission.html. Students are admitted in the Fall, application deadline December 1. The following programs have an application deadline of December 1: Clinical, Neuropsychology and Behavioral Neuroscience, Cognitive. The following programs have an application deadline of January 5: Community, Developmental. *Fee:* $50.

Georgia, University of
Department of Counseling and Human Development Services
College of Education
402 Aderhold Hall
Athens, GA 30602
Telephone: (706) 542-1812
Fax: (706) 542-4130
E-mail: *edelgado@uga.edu*
Web: *http://www.coe.uga.edu/chds/*

Department Information:
1946. Department Head: Diane L. Cooper. Number of faculty: total—full-time 26, part-time 2; women—full-time 16, part-time 1; total—minority—full-time 7, part-time 2; women minority—full-time 3, part-time 1.

Programs and Degrees Offered:
Listed in the following order: Program area, degree type (T if terminal Master's), number awarded 7/11–6/12. Counseling Psychology PhD (Doctor of Philosophy) 10.

APA Accreditation: Counseling PhD (Doctor of Philosophy). Student Outcome Data Website: http://www.coe.uga.edu/chds/academic-programs/counseling-psychology/ph-d/outcomes-other-data/.

Student Applications/Admissions:

Student Applications

Counseling Psychology PhD (Doctor of Philosophy)—Applications 2012–2013, 90. Total applicants accepted 2012–2013, 25. Number full-time enrolled (new admits only) 2012–2013, 16. Number part-time enrolled (new admits only) 2012–2013, 0. Total enrolled 2012–2013 full-time, 64. Total enrolled 2012–2013 part-time, 1. Openings 2013–2014, 10. The median number of years required for completion of a degree in 2012–2013 were 4. The number of students enrolled full- and part-time who were dismissed or voluntarily withdrew from this program area in 2012–2013 were 1.

Scores: Entries appear in this order: required test or GPA, minimum score (if required), median score of students entering in 2012–2013. *Counseling Psychology PhD (Doctor of Philosophy):* GRE-V no minimum stated, GRE-Q no minimum stated, GRE-Analytical no minimum stated, overall undergraduate GPA no minimum stated, Masters GPA no minimum stated.

Other Criteria: (importance of criteria rated low, medium, or high): GRE scores—medium, research experience—high, work experience—high, extracurricular activity—low, clinically related public service—medium, GPA—medium, letters of recommendation—high, interview—high, statement of goals and objectives—high, undergraduate major in psychology—low. For additional information on admission requirements, go to http://www.coe.uga.edu/chds/academic-programs/counseling-psychology/ph-d/admissions/.

Student Characteristics: The following represents characteristics of students in 2012–2013 in all graduate psychology programs in the department: Female—full-time 53, part-time 0; Male—full-time 11, part-time 1; African American/Black—full-time 23, part-time 1; Hispanic/Latino(a)—full-time 3, part-time 0; Asian/Pacific Islander—full-time 3, part-time 0; American Indian/Alaska Native—full-time 0, part-time 0; Caucasian/White—full-time 35, part-time 0; Multi-ethnic—full-time 0, part-time 0; students subject to the Americans With Disabilities Act—full-time 0, part-time 0; Unknown ethnicity—full-time 0, part-time 0; International students who hold an F-1 or J-1 Visa—full-time 3, part-time 0.

Financial Information/Assistance:

Tuition for Full-Time Study: *Doctoral:* State residents: per academic year $9,390; Nonstate residents: per academic year $24,090. Tuition is subject to change. See the following website for updates and changes in tuition costs: https://busfin1.busfin.uga.edu/bursar/schedule.cfm.

Financial Assistance:

First-Year Students: Teaching assistantships available for first year. Average amount paid per academic year: $11,515. Average number of hours worked per week: 13. Apply by December 1. Research assistantships available for first year. Average amount paid per academic year: $11,515. Average number of hours worked per week: 13. Apply by December 1.

Advanced Students: Teaching assistantships available for advanced students. Average amount paid per academic year: $11,515. Average number of hours worked per week: 13. Apply by December 1. Research assistantships available for advanced students. Average amount paid per academic year: $11,515. Average number of hours worked per week: 13. Apply by December 1.

Additional Information: Of all students currently enrolled full time, 100% benefited from one or more of the listed financial assistance programs. Application and information available online at: http://www.coe.uga.edu/chds/about/graduate-assistantship-opportunities/.

Internships/Practica: Doctoral Degree (PhD Counseling Psychology): For those doctoral students for whom a professional psychology internship was required in this program prior to graduation, (9) students applied for an internship in 2011–2012, with (7) students obtaining an internship. Of those students who obtained an internship, (7) were paid internships. Of those students who obtained an internship, (7) students placed in APA/CPA accredited internships, (0) students placed in internships not APA/CPA accredited, but listed with the Association of Psychology Postdoctoral and Internship Programs (APPIC), (0) students placed in internships conforming to guidelines of the Council of Directors of School Psychology Programs (CDSPP), (0) students placed in internships that were not APA/CPA accredited, APPIC or CDSPP listed. Practicum opportunities are provided at one of three sites: the Juvenile Counseling and Assessment Program (JCAP), the Counseling and Personal Evaluation Center (department clinic) and Counseling Psychological Services (the university counseling center). Advanced practica are available in the area and in Atlanta at Georgia Tech, Emory University, Morehouse College, Kennesaw State University, and the Atlanta VA.

Housing and Day Care: On-campus housing is available. See the following website for more information: http://housing.uga.edu/. On-campus day care facilities are available. See the following website for more information: http://www.fcs.uga.edu/cfd/cdl/.

Employment of Department Graduates:

Master's Degree Graduates: Of those who graduated in the academic year 2011–2012, the following categories and numbers represent the postgraduate activities and employment of master's degree graduates: Enrolled in a postdoctoral residency/fellowship (n/a), employed in independent practice (n/a), total from the above (master's) (0).

Doctoral Degree Graduates: Of those who graduated in the academic year 2011–2012, the following categories and numbers represent the postgraduate activities and employment of doctoral degree graduates: Enrolled in a psychology doctoral program (n/a), enrolled in a postdoctoral residency/fellowship (4), employed in an academic position at a university (2), employed in other positions at a higher education institution (1), employed in government agency (1), still seeking employment (2), total from the above (doctoral) (10).

Additional Information:

Orientation, Objectives, and Emphasis of Department: The goal of the program is to educate students in the scientist–practitioner model of training in professional counseling psychology. The program focuses on professional competency development in three areas: teaching, research, and clinical service. The theoretical orientations of faculty members vary widely including representatives of most major schools of thought. The broad emphases of the program include developmental perspectives, cultural diversity perspectives, cognitive-behavioral approaches, and psychodynamic therapies.

Special Facilities or Resources: The University, the College, and the Department separately and collectively offer a number of services and fully-equipped facilities to assist students in conducting academic inquiry, including special computer labs, research assistance centers, and major libraries.

Information for Students With Physical Disabilities: See the following website for more information: http://drc.uga.edu/.

Application Information:

Send to Admissions Committee, Department of Counseling and Human Development Services, University of Georgia, 402 Aderhold Hall, Athens, GA 30602. Application available online. URL of online application: https://www.applyweb.com/apply/ugagrad/. Students are admitted in the Fall, application deadline December 1. *Fee:* $75.

Georgia, University of
Department of Psychology
Franklin College of Arts and Sciences
Athens, GA 30602-3013
Telephone: (706) 542-2174
Fax: (706) 542-3275
E-mail: *bhammond@uga.edu*
Web: *http://psychology.uga.edu/*

Department Information:

1921. Chairperson: W. Keith Campbell. Number of faculty: total—full-time 36, part-time 7; women—full-time 12, part-time 3; total—minority—full-time 1; women minority—full-time 1.

Programs and Degrees Offered:

Listed in the following order: Program area, degree type (T if terminal Master's), number awarded 7/11–6/12. Clinical Psychology PhD (Doctor of Philosophy) 2, Industrial/Organizational Psychology PhD (Doctor of Philosophy) 1, Behavioral and Brain Sciences PhD (Doctor of Philosophy) 2.

APA Accreditation: Clinical PhD (Doctor of Philosophy). Student Outcome Data Website: http://psychology.uga.edu/graduate/programs/clinical/info.php.

Student Applications/Admissions:
Student Applications

Clinical Psychology PhD (Doctor of Philosophy)—Applications 2012–2013, 273. Total applicants accepted 2012–2013, 16. Number full-time enrolled (new admits only) 2012–2013, 4. Total enrolled 2012–2013 full-time, 31. Total enrolled 2012–2013 part-time, 8. Openings 2013–2014, 6. The median number of years required for completion of a degree in 2012–2013 were 5. The number of students enrolled full- and part-time who were dismissed or voluntarily withdrew from this program area in 2012–2013 were 1. *Industrial/Organizational Psychology PhD (Doctor of Philosophy)*—Applications 2012–2013, 63. Total applicants accepted 2012–2013, 10. Number full-time enrolled (new admits only) 2012–2013, 6. Total enrolled 2012–2013 full-time, 28. Total enrolled 2012–2013 part-time, 7. Openings 2013–2014, 5. The median number of years required for completion of a degree in 2012–2013 were 5. The number of students enrolled full- and part-time who were dismissed or voluntarily withdrew from this program area in 2012–2013

were 1. *Behavioral and Brain Sciences PhD (Doctor of Philosophy)*—Applications 2012–2013, 50. Total applicants accepted 2012–2013, 12. Number full-time enrolled (new admits only) 2012–2013, 7. Total enrolled 2012–2013 full-time, 45. Total enrolled 2012–2013 part-time, 2. Openings 2013–2014, 10. The median number of years required for completion of a degree in 2012–2013 were 5. The number of students enrolled full- and part-time who were dismissed or voluntarily withdrew from this program area in 2012–2013 were 1.

Scores: Entries appear in this order: required test or GPA, minimum score (if required), median score of students entering in 2012–2013. *Clinical Psychology PhD (Doctor of Philosophy):* GRE-V no minimum stated, 650, GRE-Q no minimum stated, 740, GRE-Analytical no minimum stated, overall undergraduate GPA 3.0, 3.71; *Industrial/Organizational Psychology PhD (Doctor of Philosophy):* GRE-V no minimum stated, 540, GRE-Q no minimum stated, 650, GRE-Analytical no minimum stated, overall undergraduate GPA 3.25, 3.62; *Behavioral and Brain Sciences PhD (Doctor of Philosophy):* GRE-V no minimum stated, 590, GRE-Q no minimum stated, 680, GRE-Analytical no minimum stated, 4.5, overall undergraduate GPA 3.0, 3.79.

Other Criteria: (importance of criteria rated low, medium, or high): GRE scores—medium, research experience—high, work experience—high, extracurricular activity—medium, clinically related public service—medium, GPA—medium, letters of recommendation—medium, interview—medium, statement of goals and objectives—high, Interviews are required by Clinical but occur for all programs. For additional information on admission requirements, go to http://psychology.uga.edu/graduate/general_information.php.

Student Characteristics: The following represents characteristics of students in 2012–2013 in all graduate psychology programs in the department: Female—full-time 75, part-time 14; Male—full-time 29, part-time 3; African American/Black—full-time 5, part-time 0; Hispanic/Latino(a)—full-time 2, part-time 1; Asian/Pacific Islander—full-time 9, part-time 0; American Indian/Alaska Native—full-time 1, part-time 0; Caucasian/White—full-time 84, part-time 16; Multi-ethnic—full-time 2, part-time 0; students subject to the Americans With Disabilities Act—full-time 0, part-time 0; Unknown ethnicity—full-time 1, part-time 0; International students who hold an F-1 or J-1 Visa—full-time 8, part-time 0.

Financial Information/Assistance:
Tuition for Full-Time Study: *Doctoral:* State residents: per academic year $7,400, $309 per credit hour; Nonstate residents: per academic year $22,400, $934 per credit hour. Tuition is subject to change. Additional fees are assessed to students beyond the costs of tuition for the following: transportation, activity, athletic, health, facilities, tech, institutional. See the following website for updates and changes in tuition costs: http://www.reg.uga.edu/tuition.

Financial Assistance:

First-Year Students: Teaching assistantships available for first year. Average amount paid per academic year: $14,270. Average number of hours worked per week: 17. Research assistantships available for first year. Average amount paid per academic year: $14,270. Average number of hours worked per week: 17. Fellowships and scholarships available for first year. Average amount paid per academic year: $17,112. Average number of hours worked per week: 16.

Advanced Students: Teaching assistantships available for advanced students. Average amount paid per academic year: $15,226. Average number of hours worked per week: 17. Research assistantships available for advanced students. Average amount paid per academic year: $15,226. Average number of hours worked per week: 17. Fellowships and scholarships available for advanced students. Average amount paid per academic year: $17,112. Average number of hours worked per week: 16.

Additional Information: Of all students currently enrolled full time, 100% benefited from one or more of the listed financial assistance programs. Application and information available online at: http://psychology.uga.edu/graduate/funding.php.

Internships/Practica: Doctoral Degree (PhD Clinical Psychology): For those doctoral students for whom a professional psychology internship was required in this program prior to graduation, (4) students applied for an internship in 2011–2012, with (4) students obtaining an internship. Of those students who obtained an internship, (4) were paid internships. Of those students who obtained an internship, (4) students placed in APA/CPA accredited internships, (0) students placed in internships not APA/CPA accredited, but listed with the Association of Psychology Postdoctoral and Internship Programs (APPIC), (0) students placed in internships conforming to guidelines of the Council of Directors of School Psychology Programs (CDSPP), (0) students placed in internships that were not APA/CPA accredited, APPIC or CDSPP listed.

Housing and Day Care: On-campus housing is available. See the following website for more information: http://housing.uga.edu/family-graduate. On-campus day care facilities are available. See the following website for more information: http://www.fcs.uga.edu/cfd/cdl/; http://universitychildcarecenter.uga.edu/.

Employment of Department Graduates:
Master's Degree Graduates: Of those who graduated in the academic year 2011–2012, the following categories and numbers represent the postgraduate activities and employment of master's degree graduates: Enrolled in a postdoctoral residency/fellowship (n/a), employed in independent practice (n/a), total from the above (master's) (0).
Doctoral Degree Graduates: Of those who graduated in the academic year 2011–2012, the following categories and numbers represent the postgraduate activities and employment of doctoral degree graduates: Enrolled in a psychology doctoral program (n/a), enrolled in a postdoctoral residency/fellowship (2), employed in an academic position at a university (2), other employment position (1), total from the above (doctoral) (5).

Additional Information:
Orientation, Objectives, and Emphasis of Department: Our emphasis is on research and the basic science aspects of psychology with a focus on doctoral education. A few state and private facilities provide internships. We have a cooperative liaison with several mental health facilities in the region as well as at other universities.

Special Facilities or Resources: Facilities include the Regents Center for Learning Disabilities, the Institute for Behavioral Research, the Psychology Clinic and the Vision Sciences Laboratory. We recently opened a new center (9000 square feet) for bioimaging which contains equipment for high-density EEG, MEG, MRI and fMRI. We are also part of the Biomedical and Health Sciences Institute which focuses on neurosciences and biomedical applications.

Information for Students With Physical Disabilities: See the following website for more information: http://drc.uga.edu/.

Application Information:
Send to Department of Psychology c/o Graduate Coordinator, University of Georgia, Athens, GA 30602-3013. Application available online. URL of online application: https://www.applyweb.com/apply/ugagrad/. Students are admitted in the Fall, application deadline December 1. *Fee:* $75. Fee for international applicants is $100.

Georgia, University of
School Psychology Program
Education
325 Aderhold Hall
Athens, GA 30602-7143
Telephone: (706) 542-4110
Fax: (706) 542-4240
E-mail: *reschly@uga.edu*
Web: *http://www.coe.uga.edu/epit/spy/*

Department Information:
1968. Program Coordinator: Amy L. Reschly. Number of faculty: total—full-time 3, part-time 2; women—full-time 2, part-time 2.

Programs and Degrees Offered:
Listed in the following order: Program area, degree type (T if terminal Master's), number awarded 7/11–6/12. School Psychology PhD (Doctor of Philosophy) 4.

APA Accreditation: School PhD (Doctor of Philosophy).

Student Applications/Admissions:
Student Applications
School Psychology PhD (Doctor of Philosophy)—Applications 2012–2013, 42. Total applicants accepted 2012–2013, 19. Number full-time enrolled (new admits only) 2012–2013, 6. Number part-time enrolled (new admits only) 2012–2013, 0. Total enrolled 2012–2013 full-time, 25. Total enrolled 2012–2013 part-time, 0. Openings 2013–2014, 5. The median number of years required for completion of a degree in 2012–2013 were 6. The number of students enrolled full- and part-time who were dismissed or voluntarily withdrew from this program area in 2012–2013 were 1.
Scores: Entries appear in this order: required test or GPA, minimum score (if required), median score of students entering in 2012–2013. *School Psychology PhD (Doctor of Philosophy):* GRE-V no minimum stated, 158, GRE-Q no minimum stated, 153, overall undergraduate GPA no minimum stated, 3.5, Masters GPA no minimum stated.

Other Criteria: (importance of criteria rated low, medium, or high): GRE scores—medium, research experience—high, work experience—low, extracurricular activity—low, clinically related public service—medium, GPA—high, letters of recommendation—high, interview—medium, statement of goals and objectives—medium, undergraduate major in psychology—low, specific undergraduate psychology courses taken—low.

Student Characteristics: The following represents characteristics of students in 2012–2013 in all graduate psychology programs in the department: Female—full-time 18, part-time 0; Male—full-time 7, part-time 0; African American/Black—full-time 3, part-time 0; Hispanic/Latino(a)—full-time 1, part-time 0; Asian/Pacific Islander—full-time 2, part-time 0; American Indian/Alaska Native—full-time 0, part-time 0; Caucasian/White—full-time 19, part-time 0; Multi-ethnic—full-time 0, part-time 0; students subject to the Americans With Disabilities Act—full-time 0, part-time 0; Unknown ethnicity—full-time 0, part-time 0; International students who hold an F-1 or J-1 Visa—full-time 0, part-time 0.

Financial Information/Assistance:
Tuition for Full-Time Study: *Doctoral:* State residents: $309 per credit hour; Nonstate residents: $934 per credit hour. Tuition is subject to change. See the following website for updates and changes in tuition costs: http://www.reg.uga.edu/tuition.

Financial Assistance:
First-Year Students: Teaching assistantships available for first year. Average amount paid per academic year: $12,623. Average number of hours worked per week: 13. Apply by March 1. Research assistantships available for first year. Average amount paid per academic year: $12,623. Average number of hours worked per week: 13. Apply by March 1. Fellowships and scholarships available for first year. Average amount paid per academic year: $12,623. Average number of hours worked per week: 13.

Advanced Students: Teaching assistantships available for advanced students. Average amount paid per academic year: $13,643. Average number of hours worked per week: 13. Apply by February 1. Research assistantships available for advanced students. Average amount paid per academic year: $13,643. Average number of hours worked per week: 13. Apply by February 1. Fellowships and scholarships available for advanced students. Average amount paid per academic year: $13,643.

Additional Information: Of all students currently enrolled full time, 100% benefited from one or more of the listed financial assistance programs. Application and information available online at: http://gradschool.uga.edu/financial/.

Internships/Practica: Doctoral Degree (PhD School Psychology): For those doctoral students for whom a professional psychology internship was required in this program prior to graduation, (4) students applied for an internship in 2011–2012, with (4) students obtaining an internship. Of those students who obtained an internship, (3) were paid internships. Of those students who obtained an internship, (3) students placed in APA/CPA accredited internships, (0) students placed in internships not APA/CPA accredited, but listed with the Association of Psychology Postdoctoral and Internship Programs (APPIC), (1) students placed in internships conforming to guidelines of the Council of Directors of School Psychology Programs (CDSPP), (0) students placed in internships that were not APA/CPA accredited, APPIC or CDSPP listed.

Housing and Day Care: On-campus housing is available. See the following website for more information: http://housing.uga.edu/family-graduate. On-campus day care facilities are available. See the following website for more information: http://universitychildcarecenter.uga.edu/ AND http://www.fcs.uga.edu/cfd/cdl/.

Employment of Department Graduates:
Master's Degree Graduates: Of those who graduated in the academic year 2011–2012, the following categories and numbers represent the postgraduate activities and employment of master's degree graduates: Enrolled in a postdoctoral residency/fellowship (n/a), employed in independent practice (n/a), total from the above (master's) (0).
Doctoral Degree Graduates: Of those who graduated in the academic year 2011–2012, the following categories and numbers represent the postgraduate activities and employment of doctoral degree graduates: Enrolled in a psychology doctoral program (n/a), employed in a professional position in a school system (2), employed in a hospital/medical center (1), total from the above (doctoral) (3).

Additional Information:
Orientation, Objectives, and Emphasis of Department: The PhD program in school psychology trains research-oriented school psychologists for work in educational settings, hospitals, clinics, and universities in which they can provide leadership in applied practice, research and teaching. The school psychology program follows the scientist–practitioner model, and emphasizes human development, developmental psychopathology, and the central core elements of training.

Special Facilities or Resources: Special facilities and resources include access to a superior computer center, decentralized computational equipment, a major research library, and faculty members who are extraordinarily accessible to students. The department is strongly committed to affirmative action and fair treatment. Despite the suburban setting (a small urban area of 75,000 over an hour from Atlanta), we attract ethnic minority as well as out-of-state and out-of-region students and faculty. NASP and APA requirements and full accreditation from APA and NCATE form the foundation of our programs.

Information for Students With Physical Disabilities: See the following website for more information: http://drc.uga.edu/.

Application Information:
Send to Graduate Admissions Office, Graduate Studies Building, The University of Georgia, Athens, GA 30602. URL of online application: https://www.applyweb.com/apply/ugagrad/. Students are admitted in the Fall, application deadline December 15. *Fee:* $75.

Mercer University School of Medicine
Psychiatry & Behavioral Sciences/Clinical Medical Psychology
  Program
School of Medicine
Psychiatry & Behavioral Sciences Building, 655 First Street
Macon, GA 31201
Telephone: (478) 301-5339
Fax: (478) 301-5337
E-mail: hobbs_sa@mercer.edu
Web: http://medicine.mercer.edu/admissions/psychology/

Department Information:
1985. Program Director, Clinical Medical Psychology: Steven
A. Hobbs. Number of faculty: total—full-time 5, part-time 3;
women—full-time 1, part-time 1; total—minority—full-time 1;
women minority—full-time 1.

Programs and Degrees Offered:
Listed in the following order: Program area, degree type (T if
terminal Master's), number awarded 7/11–6/12. Clinical Medical
Psychology PhD (Doctor of Philosophy) 0.

Student Applications/Admissions:
Student Applications
Clinical Medical Psychology PhD (Doctor of Philosophy)—Applications 2012–2013, 0. Total applicants accepted 2012–2013,
0. Number full-time enrolled (new admits only) 2012–2013,
14. Number part-time enrolled (new admits only) 2012–2013,
0. Total enrolled 2012–2013 full-time, 14. Total enrolled
2012–2013 part-time, 0. Openings 2013–2014, 12. The number of students enrolled full- and part-time who were dismissed
or voluntarily withdrew from this program area in 2012–2013
were 0.
Scores: Entries appear in this order: required test or GPA,
minimum score (if required), median score of students entering
in 2012–2013. *Clinical Medical Psychology PhD (Doctor of Philosophy):* GRE-V 490, 530, GRE-Q 510, 635, GRE-Analytical
3.5, 4.5, overall undergraduate GPA 3.0, 3.6, last 2 years GPA
3.3, psychology GPA 3.3.
Other Criteria: (importance of criteria rated low, medium,
or high): GRE scores—medium, research experience—high,
work experience—medium, extracurricular activity—low,
clinically related public service—medium, GPA—high, letters
of recommendation—high, interview—high, statement of
goals and objectives—high, undergraduate major in psychology—high, specific undergraduate psychology courses taken—
high. For additional information on admission requirements,
go to http://medicine.mercer.edu/admissions/psychology/
admissions/.

Student Characteristics: The following represents characteristics
of students in 2012–2013 in all graduate psychology programs in
the department: Female—full-time 14, part-time 0; Male—full-
time 0, part-time 0; African American/Black—full-time 1, part-
time 0; Hispanic/Latino(a)—full-time 2, part-time 0; Asian/Pa-
cific Islander—full-time 0, part-time 0; American Indian/Alaska
Native—full-time 0, part-time 0; Caucasian/White—full-time 11,
part-time 0; Multi-ethnic—full-time 0, part-time 0; students subject to the Americans With Disabilities Act—full-time 0, part-
time 0; Unknown ethnicity—full-time 0, part-time 0; Interna-

tional students who hold an F-1 or J-1 Visa—full-time 0, part-
time 0.

Financial Information/Assistance:
Tuition for Full-Time Study: *Doctoral:* State residents: $940 per
credit hour; Nonstate residents: $940 per credit hour. Tuition is
subject to change. Additional fees are assessed to students beyond
the costs of tuition for the following: Technology fee $150 per se-
mester; health insurance $545 per semester if student has no cover-
age. See the following website for updates and changes in tuition
costs: https://bursar.mercer.edu/macon/cost-of-attendance/.

Financial Assistance:
First-Year Students: Research assistantships available for
first year. Traineeships available for first year.
Advanced Students: Research assistantships available for
advanced students. Average amount paid per academic year:
$12,000. Average number of hours worked per week: 20. Trainee-
ships available for advanced students. Average amount paid per
academic year: $8,000. Average number of hours worked per
week: 12.
Additional Information: Of all students currently enrolled
full time, 50% benefited from one or more of the listed financial
assistance programs. Application and information available online
at: http://medicine.mercer.edu/student-services/financial-aid/.

Internships/Practica: Practicum training opportunities have
been developed in varied healthcare settings in Macon and the
surrounding area. These include the Departments of Family Medicine, Internal Medicine, Pediatrics, Obstetrics/Gynecology, and
Psychiatry within the School of Medicine and in Mercer's affiliated teaching hospital, the Medical Center of Central Georgia.
The School of Medicine's Psychological Assessment Center and
the University Counseling & Psychological Services Center also
serve as practicum sites on the Macon campus.

Housing and Day Care: On-campus housing is available. See
the following website for more information: http://studentaffairs.
mercer.edu/housing/. No on-campus day care facilities are
available.

Employment of Department Graduates:
Master's Degree Graduates: Of those who graduated in the
academic year 2011–2012, the following categories and numbers
represent the postgraduate activities and employment of master's
degree graduates: Enrolled in a postdoctoral residency/fellowship
(n/a), employed in independent practice (n/a), total from the
above (master's) (0).
Doctoral Degree Graduates: Of those who graduated in the academic year 2011–2012, the following categories and numbers
represent the postgraduate activities and employment of doctoral
degree graduates: Enrolled in a psychology doctoral program (n/a),
total from the above (doctoral) (0).

Additional Information:
Orientation, Objectives, and Emphasis of Department: The interface between psychology, health, and disease represents the
focus of the PhD program in Clinical Medical Psychology at
Mercer University School of Medicine. The Clinical Medical
Psychology program began in 2012 with the mission of training
its graduates to apply clinical and research skills in an integrated,
biopsychosocial approach to healthcare. The program endeavors

to produce psychologists with training aligned with a national public policy steadily moving toward embracing an integrated, primary care-oriented health care delivery system. This role is consistent with the overall mission of Mercer University's School of Medicine: To educate physicians and health professionals to meet the primary care and healthcare needs of rural and medically underserved areas of Georgia. The program follows the scientist–practitioner approach (Boulder model) to clinical training as well as guidelines and principles set forth by the APA Commission on Accreditation. Coursework consistent with a traditional clinical psychology curriculum is augmented by a focus on medical aspects of healthcare and training in concert with physicians and allied healthcare professionals throughout the Mercer University School of Medicine. Beyond required courses, students may select coursework in one of three areas of concentration: adult health psychology, neuropsychology/geropsychology, and pediatric psychology.

Special Facilities or Resources: Operating within the Department of Psychiatry and Behavioral Sciences, the Clinical Medical Psychology Program has access to facilities and resources available in the School of Medicine as well as in other Schools on Mercer University's Macon campus. It has close ties with the Department of Psychology in the College of Liberal Arts as well as other graduate training programs (e.g., Family Therapy, Public Health) in the School of Medicine.

Information for Students With Physical Disabilities: See the following website for more information: http://studentaffairs.mercer.edu/disabilityservices/.

Application Information:

Send to Office of Admissions, Mercer University School of Medicine, 1550 College Street, Macon GA 31207. Application available online. URL of online application: https://www.applyweb.com/apply/mercermp/. Students are admitted in the Fall, application deadline March 15. *Fee:* $50. $150.00 application fee for international applicants.

West Georgia, University of
Department of Psychology
Arts and Sciences
1600 Maple Street
Carrollton, GA 30118
Telephone: (678) 839-6510
Fax: (678) 839-0611
E-mail: *drice@westga.edu*
Web: *http://www.westga.edu/psydept/*

Department Information:

1967. Professor and Chair: Donadrian L. Rice. Number of faculty: total—full-time 16, part-time 2; women—full-time 6, part-time 2; total—minority—full-time 2; women minority—full-time 1.

Programs and Degrees Offered:

Listed in the following order: Program area, degree type (T if terminal Master's), number awarded 7/11–6/12. Humanistic/Transpersonal Psychology MA/MS (Master of Arts/Science) (T) 11, Consciousness and Society PhD (Doctor of Philosophy) 1.

Student Applications/Admissions:
Student Applications

Humanistic/Transpersonal Psychology MA/MS (Master of Arts/Science)—Applications 2012–2013, 42. Total applicants accepted 2012–2013, 20. Number full-time enrolled (new admits only) 2012–2013, 20. Number part-time enrolled (new admits only) 2012–2013, 0. Total enrolled 2012–2013 full-time, 60. Total enrolled 2012–2013 part-time, 0. Openings 2013–2014, 20. The median number of years required for completion of a degree in 2012–2013 were 3. The number of students enrolled full- and part-time who were dismissed or voluntarily withdrew from this program area in 2012–2013 were 0. *Consciousness and Society PhD (Doctor of Philosophy)*—Applications 2012–2013, 57. Total applicants accepted 2012–2013, 10. Number full-time enrolled (new admits only) 2012–2013, 10. Number part-time enrolled (new admits only) 2012–2013, 0. Total enrolled 2012–2013 full-time, 30. Total enrolled 2012–2013 part-time, 0. Openings 2013–2014, 10. The median number of years required for completion of a degree in 2012–2013 were 4. The number of students enrolled full- and part-time who were dismissed or voluntarily withdrew from this program area in 2012–2013 were 0.

Scores: Entries appear in this order: required test or GPA, minimum score (if required), median score of students entering in 2012–2013. *Humanistic/Transpersonal Psychology MA/MS (Master of Arts/Science):* GRE-V 450, GRE-Q 450, overall undergraduate GPA 2.5; *Consciousness and Society PhD (Doctor of Philosophy):* GRE-V 500, 675, GRE-Q 500, 636, overall undergraduate GPA 3.5.

Other Criteria: (importance of criteria rated low, medium, or high): GRE scores—medium, research experience—high, work experience—high, extracurricular activity—medium, clinically related public service—high, GPA—high, letters of recommendation—high, interview—high, statement of goals and objectives—high, undergraduate major in psychology—medium, specific undergraduate psychology courses taken—high, All candidates for all programs are interviewed.

Student Characteristics: The following represents characteristics of students in 2012–2013 in all graduate psychology programs in the department: Female—full-time 50, part-time 0; Male—full-time 40, part-time 0; African American/Black—full-time 5, part-time 0; Hispanic/Latino(a)—full-time 4, part-time 0; Asian/Pacific Islander—full-time 2, part-time 0; American Indian/Alaska Native—full-time 0, part-time 0; Caucasian/White—full-time 79, part-time 0; Multi-ethnic—full-time 0, part-time 0; students subject to the Americans With Disabilities Act—part-time 0; Unknown ethnicity—full-time 0, part-time 0; International students who hold an F-1 or J-1 Visa—full-time 2, part-time 0.

Financial Information/Assistance:

Tuition for Full-Time Study: *Master's:* State residents: $187 per credit hour; Nonstate residents: $745 per credit hour. *Doctoral:* State residents: $256 per credit hour; Nonstate residents: $1,022 per credit hour. Tuition is subject to change. Tuition costs vary by program. See the following website for updates and changes in tuition costs: http://www.westga.edu/bursar/index_19747.php.

Financial Assistance:

First-Year Students: Teaching assistantships available for first year. Research assistantships available for first year. Average amount paid per academic year: $3,000. Average number of hours worked per week: 13.

Advanced Students: No information provided.

Additional Information: Of all students currently enrolled full time, 25% benefited from one or more of the listed financial assistance programs. Application and information available online at: http://www.westga.edu/financialAid/index_18816.php.

Internships/Practica: Master's Degree (MA/MS Humanistic/ Transpersonal Psychology): An internship experience, such as a final research project or "capstone" experience is required of graduates. Internships are available at local facilities.

Housing and Day Care: No on-campus housing is available. On-campus day care facilities are available.

Employment of Department Graduates:

Master's Degree Graduates: Of those who graduated in the academic year 2011–2012, the following categories and numbers represent the postgraduate activities and employment of master's degree graduates: Enrolled in a psychology doctoral program (3), enrolled in another graduate/professional program (13), enrolled in a postdoctoral residency/fellowship (n/a), employed in independent practice (n/a), employed in an academic position at a university (5), employed in an academic position at a 2-year/4-year college (2), employed in other positions at a higher education institution (4), employed in a community mental health/counseling center (2), other employment position (6), total from the above (master's) (35).

Doctoral Degree Graduates: Of those who graduated in the academic year 2011–2012, the following categories and numbers represent the postgraduate activities and employment of doctoral degree graduates: Enrolled in a psychology doctoral program (n/a), total from the above (doctoral) (0).

Additional Information:

Orientation, Objectives, and Emphasis of Department: The department is a pioneer of humanistic-transpersonal psychology. It differs from other programs in that it goes beyond conventional subjects and approaches a holistic and integrative understanding of human experience. Alongside demanding academic work, student growth and personal awareness are inherent to this venture since such reflection is considered an important factor in human understanding. Individual programs are designed according to personal needs and interests; the overall atmosphere is communal, encouraging personal and intellectual dialogue and encounter. Most conventional topic areas are taught. Beyond these are areas almost uniquely explorable in a program such as this: the horizons of consciousness through such vantages as Eastern and transpersonal psychologies, hermeneutics, existential and phenomenological psychologies, and critical psychology. Specific areas include women's studies; aesthetic and sacred experience; myths, dreams, and symbols; and creativity. Areas of applied interest are viewed as correlates of the learning process: skill courses related to human services, prevention and community psychology, counseling psychology, Cross-cultural psychology, organizational development, and growth therapies. The department offers training in qualitative and traditional methodologies of research. Practicum and internship experience along with individual research and reading are highly encouraged for those who can profit from these. Interest areas include human science research; parapsychology; transpersonal and Eastern psychologies; counseling, clinical, community, and organizational development; and psychology in the classroom.

Special Facilities or Resources: Special resources include large library holdings in the areas of humanistic, parapsychology, transpersonal, philosophical, and Asian psychology. The library holds papers of Sidney M. Jourard, Edith Weiskoff-Joelsen and the Psychical Research Foundation Library. The department hosts major conferences, and faculty are associated with several journals and newsletters exploring orientation areas.

Information for Students With Physical Disabilities: See the following website for more information: http://www.westga.edu/counseling/index_8884.php.

Application Information:
Send to Graduate Coordinator, Department of Psychology, University of West Georgia, Carrollton, GA 30118. Application available online. URL of online application: http://www.westga.edu/gradstudies/apply-now.php. Students are admitted in the Fall, application deadline January 10; Spring, application deadline November 15; Summer, application deadline May 15. Enrollment for PhD program in Fall only. *Fee:* $40.

Argosy University, Hawaii

Hawaii School of Professional Psychology at Argosy
  University, Hawaii
College of Psychology and Behavioral Sciences
1001 Bishop Street, Suite 400
Honolulu, HI 96813
Telephone: (808) 536-5555
Fax: (808) 536-5505
E-mail: *momizo@argosy.edu*
Web: *http://www.argosy.edu/locations/hawaii/*

Department Information:

1994. Chairperson: Michael M. Omizo, PhD. Number of faculty: total—full-time 10, part-time 1; women—full-time 3, part-time 1; total—minority—full-time 8, part-time 1; women minority—full-time 3, part-time 1; faculty subject to the Americans With Disabilities Act 3.

Programs and Degrees Offered:

Listed in the following order: Program area, degree type (T if terminal Master's), number awarded 7/11–6/12. Clinical Psychology PsyD (Doctor of Psychology) 26, Clinical Psychology MA/MS (Master of Arts/Science) (T) 14.

APA Accreditation: Clinical PsyD (Doctor of Psychology). Student Outcome Data Website: http://www.argosy.edu/clinical-psychology/honolulu-hawaii/psyd-programs-doctorate-degree-62712.aspx.

Student Applications/Admissions:

Student Applications

Clinical Psychology PsyD (Doctor of Psychology)—Applications 2012–2013, 95. Total applicants accepted 2012–2013, 23. Number full-time enrolled (new admits only) 2012–2013, 22. Number part-time enrolled (new admits only) 2012–2013, 0. Total enrolled 2012–2013 full-time, 159. Total enrolled 2012–2013 part-time, 12. Openings 2013–2014, 20. The median number of years required for completion of a degree in 2012–2013 were 6. The number of students enrolled full- and part-time who were dismissed or voluntarily withdrew from this program area in 2012–2013 were 4. *Clinical Psychology MA/MS (Master of Arts/Science)*—Applications 2012–2013, 17. Total applicants accepted 2012–2013, 2. Number full-time enrolled (new admits only) 2012–2013, 2. Number part-time enrolled (new admits only) 2012–2013, 0. Total enrolled 2012–2013 full-time, 7. Total enrolled 2012–2013 part-time, 1. Openings 2013–2014, 10. The median number of years required for completion of a degree in 2012–2013 were 2. The number of students enrolled full- and part-time who were dismissed or voluntarily withdrew from this program area in 2012–2013 were 0.

Scores: Entries appear in this order: required test or GPA, minimum score (if required), median score of students entering in 2012–2013. *Clinical Psychology PsyD (Doctor of Psychology):* overall undergraduate GPA 3.25, 3.59, Masters GPA 3.50, 3.83; *Clinical Psychology MA/MS (Master of Arts/Science):* overall undergraduate GPA 3.12, 3.25.

Other Criteria: (importance of criteria rated low, medium, or high): GRE scores—medium, research experience—medium, work experience—medium, extracurricular activity—medium, clinically related public service—medium, GPA—high, letters of recommendation—high, interview—high, statement of goals and objectives—high, relevant experience—medium, undergraduate major in psychology—high, specific undergraduate psychology courses taken—high. For additional information on admission requirements, go to http://www.argosy.edu/clinical-psychology/honolulu-hawaii/psyd-programs-admissions-62743.aspx.

Student Characteristics: The following represents characteristics of students in 2012–2013 in all graduate psychology programs in the department: Female—full-time 137, part-time 10; Male—full-time 34, part-time 7; African American/Black—full-time 7, part-time 3; Hispanic/Latino(a)—full-time 4, part-time 1; Asian/Pacific Islander—full-time 66, part-time 8; American Indian/Alaska Native—full-time 3, part-time 1; Caucasian/White—full-time 76, part-time 4; Multi-ethnic—full-time 5, part-time 0; students subject to the Americans With Disabilities Act—full-time 0, part-time 0; Unknown ethnicity—full-time 10, part-time 0; International students who hold an F-1 or J-1 Visa—full-time 4, part-time 0.

Financial Information/Assistance:

Tuition for Full-Time Study: *Master's:* State residents: $1,197 per credit hour; Nonstate residents: $1,197 per credit hour. *Doctoral:* State residents: $1,197 per credit hour; Nonstate residents: $1,197 per credit hour. Tuition is subject to change. See the following website for updates and changes in tuition costs: http://www.argosy.edu/admissions/Default.aspx.

Financial Assistance:

First-Year Students: Fellowships and scholarships available for first year. Average amount paid per academic year: $25,000. Apply by August 15.

Advanced Students: Teaching assistantships available for advanced students. Average amount paid per academic year: $1,200. Average number of hours worked per week: 15. Fellowships and scholarships available for advanced students. Average amount paid per academic year: $3,000.

Additional Information: Of all students currently enrolled full time, 15% benefited from one or more of the listed financial assistance programs. Application and information available online at: http://www.argosy.edu/financial-aid/Default.aspx.

Internships/Practica: Doctoral Degree (PsyD Clinical Psychology): For those doctoral students for whom a professional psychology internship was required in this program prior to graduation, (31) students applied for an internship in 2011–2012, with (26) students obtaining an internship. Of those students who obtained an internship, (25) were paid internships. Of those students who obtained an internship, (8) students placed in APA/CPA accredited internships, (18) students placed in internships not APA/CPA accredited, but listed with the Association of Psychology Postdoctoral and Internship Programs (APPIC), (0) students placed in internships conforming to guidelines of the Council of

Directors of School Psychology Programs (CDSPP), (0) students placed in internships that were not APA/CPA accredited, APPIC or CDSPP listed. Master's Degree (MA/MS Clinical Psychology): An internship experience, such as a final research project or "capstone" experience is required of graduates. Students in the Master of Arts in Clinical Psychology program are required to complete a one year intervention practicum which also includes a seminar for three semesters. They need to be at their sites from 20 to 25 hours a week totaling 720 hours a year and be supervised by licensed professionals. Sites that are available include hospitals, schools, community agencies, private agencies, and counseling centers. They may work with children, adolescents, and adults who have psychiatric problems, medical conditions, personal issues, and learning disabilities. Students in the Doctor of Psychology program are required to complete a Diagnostic Practicum and an Intervention Practicum. Each is for a year and includes a seminar. Students spend between 20-25 hours a week totaling 720 hours a year being supervised by a licensed psychologist. Typical sites include military installations, hospitals, higher education counseling centers, non-profit community agencies, schools, private agencies, psychologists in private practice, and agencies in rural communities. Clients include the elderly, substance abusers, patients with medical conditions, military personnel and families, children/students in schools, and college students. Some students also enroll in Advanced Practicum. Students are also required to complete a one-year internship which may include any of the above mentioned sites and populations.

Housing and Day Care: No on-campus housing is available. No on-campus day care facilities are available.

Employment of Department Graduates:

Master's Degree Graduates: Of those who graduated in the academic year 2011–2012, the following categories and numbers represent the postgraduate activities and employment of master's degree graduates: Enrolled in a psychology doctoral program (4), enrolled in a postdoctoral residency/fellowship (n/a), employed in independent practice (n/a), total from the above (master's) (4). *Doctoral Degree Graduates:* Of those who graduated in the academic year 2011–2012, the following categories and numbers represent the postgraduate activities and employment of doctoral degree graduates: Enrolled in a psychology doctoral program (n/a), enrolled in a postdoctoral residency/fellowship (15), employed in independent practice (3), employed in government agency (2), employed in a community mental health/counseling center (1), do not know (7), total from the above (doctoral) (28).

Additional Information:

Orientation, Objectives, and Emphasis of Department: The Clinical Program has been accredited by the American Psychological Association (APA) since 1998. It proudly employs the practitioner-scholar and Local Clinical Scientist models of training, both of which emphasize educating and training doctoral students to become clinicians and practitioners. A driving goal of the program is to prepare students to serve diverse populations. As such, it is comprised of diverse faculty members who devote part of their time to the practice of psychology and have various areas of expertise. The program is designed to educate and train students to function effectively as clinical psychologists. Specific goals include the preparation of practitioners of psychology who: (1)

ethically deliver diagnostic and therapeutic services effectively to diverse populations; (2) understand the scientific foundations of psychology; (3) operate in the expanding roles of psychology; (4) demonstrate their knowledge of and competence in addressing the needs, values, and experiences of people from diverse, marginalized, or underserved subpopulations during relevant courses and practicum; and (5) evaluate and use the existing and evolving body of knowledge and methods in the practice and science of psychology to enhance applications of psychology.

Application Information:
Send to Admissions, Hawaii School of Professional Psychology, Argosy University Hawaii, 1001 Bishop Street, Suite 400, Honolulu, HI 96813. Application available online. URL of online application: http://www.argosy.edu/admissions/Default.aspx. Students are admitted in the Fall, application deadline January 15. *Fee:* $50.

Hawaii, University of
Department of Educational Psychology
College of Education
1776 University Avenue
Honolulu, HI 96822-2463
Telephone: (808) 956-4300
Fax: (808) 956-6615
E-mail: *msalzman@hawaii.edu*
Web: *https://coe.hawaii.edu/academics/educational-psychology*

Department Information:
1961. Chairperson: Michael Salzman. Number of faculty: total—full-time 9, part-time 1; women—full-time 8; total—minority—full-time 5; women minority—full-time 5.

Programs and Degrees Offered:
Listed in the following order: Program area, degree type (T if terminal Master's), number awarded 7/11–6/12. Educational Psychology MEd (Education) 10, Educational Psychology PhD (Doctor of Philosophy) 3.

Student Applications/Admissions:
Student Applications
Educational Psychology MEd (Education)—Applications 2012–2013, 34. Total applicants accepted 2012–2013, 19. Number full-time enrolled (new admits only) 2012–2013, 3. Number part-time enrolled (new admits only) 2012–2013, 4. Total enrolled 2012–2013 full-time, 9. Total enrolled 2012–2013 part-time, 18. The median number of years required for completion of a degree in 2012–2013 were 2. The number of students enrolled full- and part-time who were dismissed or voluntarily withdrew from this program area in 2012–2013 were 1. *Educational Psychology PhD (Doctor of Philosophy)*—Applications 2012–2013, 16. Total applicants accepted 2012–2013, 8. Number full-time enrolled (new admits only) 2012–2013, 3. Number part-time enrolled (new admits only) 2012–2013, 5. Total enrolled 2012–2013 full-time, 13. Total enrolled 2012–2013 part-time, 15. Openings 2013–2014, 68. The median number of years required for completion of a degree in

2012–2013 were 6. The number of students enrolled full- and part-time who were dismissed or voluntarily withdrew from this program area in 2012–2013 were 0.

Scores: Entries appear in this order: required test or GPA, minimum score (if required), median score of students entering in 2012–2013. *Educational Psychology PhD (Doctor of Philosophy):* GRE-V no minimum stated, 520, GRE-Q no minimum stated, 630, GRE-Analytical no minimum stated, 4.5, overall undergraduate GPA no minimum stated, 3.69.

Other Criteria: (importance of criteria rated low, medium, or high): GRE scores—medium, research experience—medium, work experience—medium, extracurricular activity—low, GPA—high, letters of recommendation—high, statement of goals and objectives—high, Criteria above pertain to the PhD program. The MEd program does not require the GRE or research experience. For additional information on admission requirements, go to https://coe.hawaii.edu/academics/educational-psychology.

Student Characteristics: The following represents characteristics of students in 2012–2013 in all graduate psychology programs in the department: Female—full-time 17, part-time 20; Male—full-time 7, part-time 10; African American/Black—full-time 0, part-time 0; Hispanic/Latino(a)—full-time 0, part-time 0; Asian/Pacific Islander—full-time 12, part-time 15; American Indian/Alaska Native—full-time 0, part-time 0; Caucasian/White—full-time 12, part-time 12; Multi-ethnic—full-time 0, part-time 3; students subject to the Americans With Disabilities Act—full-time 0, part-time 0; Unknown ethnicity—full-time 0, part-time 0; International students who hold an F-1 or J-1 Visa—full-time 7, part-time 0.

Financial Information/Assistance:

Tuition for Full-Time Study: *Master's:* State residents: per academic year $11,592, $483 per credit hour; Nonstate residents: per academic year $28,152, $1,173 per credit hour. *Doctoral:* State residents: per academic year $11,592, $483 per credit hour; Nonstate residents: per academic year $28,152, $1,173 per credit hour. Tuition is subject to change. See the following website for updates and changes in tuition costs: http://www.hawaii.edu/admissions/tuition.html.

Financial Assistance:

First-Year Students: Fellowships and scholarships available for first year. Average amount paid per academic year: $800.

Advanced Students: Fellowships and scholarships available for advanced students. Average amount paid per academic year: $800.

Additional Information: Of all students currently enrolled full time, 15% benefited from one or more of the listed financial assistance programs. Application and information available online at: http://manoa.hawaii.edu/graduate/content/financial-support.

Internships/Practica: Research and teaching internships are highly recommended for doctoral students; however, financial support continues to be very limited.

Housing and Day Care: On-campus housing is available. See the following website for more information: http://manoa.hawaii.edu/housing/familygrad. On-campus day care facilities are available. See the following website for more information: http://www.hawaii.edu/childrenscenter/.

Employment of Department Graduates:

Master's Degree Graduates: Of those who graduated in the academic year 2011–2012, the following categories and numbers represent the postgraduate activities and employment of master's degree graduates: Enrolled in a postdoctoral residency/fellowship (n/a), employed in independent practice (n/a), employed in an academic position at a university (1), employed in a professional position in a school system (6), employed in business or industry (2), do not know (1), total from the above (master's) (10).

Doctoral Degree Graduates: Of those who graduated in the academic year 2011–2012, the following categories and numbers represent the postgraduate activities and employment of doctoral degree graduates: Enrolled in a psychology doctoral program (n/a), employed in an academic position at a 2-year/4-year college (1), employed in a professional position in a school system (1), employed in business or industry (1), total from the above (doctoral) (3).

Additional Information:

Orientation, Objectives, and Emphasis of Department: The primary objective of graduate training is the development of competent educators and scholars in the discipline of Educational Psychology. Therefore, the faculty seeks students with research interests and abilities, independence of thought, and a willingness to actively participate in both formal and informal teaching and learning experiences. The students' efforts may be directed toward the attainment of the MEd or the PhD degree. Members of the faculty share a commitment to a model of graduate education that is humanistic and inquiry oriented. An extensive core of quantitative coursework—measurement, statistics, and research methodology—underlies most programs of study, especially at the doctoral level. In addition, core courses in human learning and development give the student a contextual framework within which inquiry methodologies are applied. The small size of the department ensures a high level of interaction among students and faculty in and out of class. Working closely with the faculty, each student creates a degree plan uniquely suited to his or her academic goals. Interdisciplinary study is particularly encouraged.

Special Facilities or Resources: The college's Curriculum Research and Development Group can afford opportunities for involvement in a wide variety of educational research and program evaluation activities, many of which are centered in the K-12 laboratory school on campus.

Information for Students With Physical Disabilities: See the following website for more information: http://www.hawaii.edu/kokua/.

Application Information:

Send to Department of Educational Psychology, College of Education, 1776 University Avenue, Honolulu, HI 96822. Application available online. URL of online application: http://apply.hawaii.edu/. Students are admitted in the Fall, application deadline February 1; Spring, application deadline September 1. PhD program has Fall admission only. *Fee:* $100.

Hawaii, University of, Manoa

Department of Psychology
College of Social Sciences
Sakamaki Hall, 2530 Dole Street
Honolulu, HI 96822-2294
Telephone: (808) 956-8414
Fax: (808) 956-4700
E-mail: *gradpsy@hawaii.edu*
Web: *http://www.psychology.hawaii.edu/*

Department Information:

1939. Chairperson: Ashley E. Maynard, PhD. Number of faculty: total—full-time 24; women—full-time 11; total—minority—full-time 5; women minority—full-time 1.

Programs and Degrees Offered:

Listed in the following order: Program area, degree type (T if terminal Master's), number awarded 7/11–6/12. Behavioral Neuroscience PhD (Doctor of Philosophy) 1, Clinical Psychology PhD (Doctor of Philosophy) 11, Community and Cultural Psychology PhD (Doctor of Philosophy) 1, Developmental Psychology PhD (Doctor of Philosophy) 1, Experimental Psychopathology PhD (Doctor of Philosophy) 0, Social-Personality Psychology PhD (Doctor of Philosophy) 3, Cognition PhD (Doctor of Philosophy) 1.

APA Accreditation: Clinical PhD (Doctor of Philosophy). Student Outcome Data Website: http://www.psychology.hawaii.edu/concentrations/clinical-psychology.html.

Student Applications/Admissions:

Student Applications

Behavioral Neuroscience PhD (Doctor of Philosophy)—Applications 2012–2013, 11. Total applicants accepted 2012–2013, 0. Number full-time enrolled (new admits only) 2012–2013, 0. Total enrolled 2012–2013 full-time, 3. Total enrolled 2012–2013 part-time, 0. Openings 2013–2014, 1. The number of students enrolled full- and part-time who were dismissed or voluntarily withdrew from this program area in 2012–2013 were 0. *Clinical Psychology PhD (Doctor of Philosophy)*—Applications 2012–2013, 127. Total applicants accepted 2012–2013, 10. Number full-time enrolled (new admits only) 2012–2013, 5. Number part-time enrolled (new admits only) 2012–2013, 0. Total enrolled 2012–2013 full-time, 40. Total enrolled 2012–2013 part-time, 0. Openings 2013–2014, 6. The median number of years required for completion of a degree in 2012–2013 were 6. The number of students enrolled full- and part-time who were dismissed or voluntarily withdrew from this program area in 2012–2013 were 0. *Community and Cultural Psychology PhD (Doctor of Philosophy)*—Applications 2012–2013, 28. Total applicants accepted 2012–2013, 3. Number full-time enrolled (new admits only) 2012–2013, 1. Total enrolled 2012–2013 full-time, 12. Total enrolled 2012–2013 part-time, 0. Openings 2013–2014, 2. The median number of years required for completion of a degree in 2012–2013 were 5. The number of students enrolled full- and part-time who were dismissed or voluntarily withdrew from this program area in 2012–2013 were 0. *Developmental Psychology PhD (Doctor of* *Philosophy)*—Applications 2012–2013, 8. Total applicants accepted 2012–2013, 0. Number full-time enrolled (new admits only) 2012–2013, 0. Total enrolled 2012–2013 full-time, 4. Total enrolled 2012–2013 part-time, 0. Openings 2013–2014, 2. The number of students enrolled full- and part-time who were dismissed or voluntarily withdrew from this program area in 2012–2013 were 0. *Experimental Psychopathology PhD (Doctor of Philosophy)*—Applications 2012–2013, 3. Total applicants accepted 2012–2013, 1. Number full-time enrolled (new admits only) 2012–2013, 1. Total enrolled 2012–2013 full-time, 4. Total enrolled 2012–2013 part-time, 0. Openings 2013–2014, 1. The number of students enrolled full- and part-time who were dismissed or voluntarily withdrew from this program area in 2012–2013 were 0. *Social-Personality Psychology PhD (Doctor of Philosophy)*—Applications 2012–2013, 37. Total applicants accepted 2012–2013, 1. Number full-time enrolled (new admits only) 2012–2013, 1. Total enrolled 2012–2013 full-time, 12. Total enrolled 2012–2013 part-time, 0. Openings 2013–2014, 2. The number of students enrolled full- and part-time who were dismissed or voluntarily withdrew from this program area in 2012–2013 were 1. *Cognition PhD (Doctor of Philosophy)*—Applications 2012–2013, 7. Total applicants accepted 2012–2013, 0. Number full-time enrolled (new admits only) 2012–2013, 0. Total enrolled 2012–2013 full-time, 10. Total enrolled 2012–2013 part-time, 0. Openings 2013–2014, 2. The number of students enrolled full- and part-time who were dismissed or voluntarily withdrew from this program area in 2012–2013 were 0.

Scores: Entries appear in this order: required test or GPA, minimum score (if required), median score of students entering in 2012–2013. *Behavioral Neuroscience PhD (Doctor of Philosophy):* GRE-V no minimum stated, GRE-Q no minimum stated, GRE-Analytical no minimum stated, overall undergraduate GPA no minimum stated, Masters GPA no minimum stated; *Clinical Psychology PhD (Doctor of Philosophy):* GRE-V no minimum stated, 163, GRE-Q no minimum stated, 154, GRE-Analytical no minimum stated, 4, overall undergraduate GPA no minimum stated, 3.57, Masters GPA no minimum stated; *Community and Cultural Psychology PhD (Doctor of Philosophy):* GRE-V no minimum stated, GRE-Q no minimum stated, GRE-Analytical no minimum stated, overall undergraduate GPA no minimum stated, Masters GPA no minimum stated; *Developmental Psychology PhD (Doctor of Philosophy):* GRE-V no minimum stated, GRE-Q no minimum stated, GRE-Analytical no minimum stated, overall undergraduate GPA no minimum stated, Masters GPA no minimum stated; *Experimental Psychopathology PhD (Doctor of Philosophy):* GRE-V no minimum stated, GRE-Q no minimum stated, GRE-Analytical no minimum stated, overall undergraduate GPA no minimum stated, Masters GPA no minimum stated; *Social-Personality Psychology PhD (Doctor of Philosophy):* GRE-V no minimum stated, GRE-Q no minimum stated, GRE-Analytical no minimum stated, overall undergraduate GPA no minimum stated, Masters GPA no minimum stated; *Cognition PhD (Doctor of Philosophy):* GRE-V no minimum stated, GRE-Q no minimum stated, GRE-Analytical no minimum stated, overall undergraduate GPA no minimum stated, Masters GPA no minimum stated.

Other Criteria: (importance of criteria rated low, medium, or high): GRE scores—high, research experience—high, work experience—low, extracurricular activity—low, clinically related public service—low, GPA—high, letters of recommendation—high, statement of goals and objectives—high, undergraduate major in psychology—low. For additional information on admission requirements, go to http://www.psychology.hawaii.edu/graduate/application.html.

Student Characteristics: The following represents characteristics of students in 2012–2013 in all graduate psychology programs in the department: Female—full-time 60, part-time 0; Male—full-time 26, part-time 0; African American/Black—full-time 0, part-time 0; Hispanic/Latino(a)—full-time 3, part-time 0; Asian/Pacific Islander—full-time 24, part-time 0; American Indian/Alaska Native—full-time 1, part-time 0; Caucasian/White—full-time 48, part-time 0; Multi-ethnic—full-time 8, part-time 0; students subject to the Americans With Disabilities Act—full-time 0, part-time 0; Unknown ethnicity—full-time 2, part-time 0; International students who hold an F-1 or J-1 Visa—full-time 13, part-time 0.

Financial Information/Assistance:

Tuition for Full-Time Study: *Master's:* State residents: per academic year $12,336, $514 per credit hour; Nonstate residents: per academic year $29,880, $1,245 per credit hour. *Doctoral:* State residents: per academic year $12,336, $514 per credit hour; Nonstate residents: per academic year $29,880, $1,245 per credit hour. Tuition is subject to change. See the following website for updates and changes in tuition costs: http://www.catalog.hawaii.edu/tuitionfees/tuition.htm.

Financial Assistance:

First-Year Students: Teaching assistantships available for first year. Average amount paid per academic year: $17,496. Average number of hours worked per week: 20. Apply by December 1. Research assistantships available for first year. Average amount paid per academic year: $17,496. Average number of hours worked per week: 20. Apply by December 1.

Advanced Students: Teaching assistantships available for advanced students. Average amount paid per academic year: $18,198. Average number of hours worked per week: 20. Apply by January 1. Research assistantships available for advanced students. Average amount paid per academic year: $18,198. Average number of hours worked per week: 20. Apply by January 1.

Additional Information: Of all students currently enrolled full time, 33% benefited from one or more of the listed financial assistance programs. Application and information available online at: http://www.catalog.hawaii.edu/tuitionfees/gradassistants.htm.

Internships/Practica: Doctoral Degree (PhD Clinical Psychology): For those doctoral students for whom a professional psychology internship was required in this program prior to graduation, (7) students applied for an internship in 2011–2012, with (4) students obtaining an internship. Of those students who obtained an internship, (4) were paid internships. Of those students who obtained an internship, (4) students placed in APA/CPA accredited internships, (0) students placed in internships not APA/CPA accredited, but listed with the Association of Psychology Postdoctoral and Internship Programs (APPIC), (0) students placed in internships conforming to guidelines of the Council of Directors of School Psychology Programs (CDSPP), (0) students

placed in internships that were not APA/CPA accredited, APPIC or CDSPP listed. A minimum of 2 years of practica (18 to 20 hours per week) are required for all 2nd through 4th year graduate students in the Clinical Studies program. A variety of sites are available throughout the state and most include stipend support (average $14,000 per academic year). Sites include the department's Cognitive Behavior Therapy Clinic, community mental health outpatient centers, VA (including PTSD specialty clinics), mental health hospitals, child mental health institutions, UH counseling center, and state supported work with the seriously mentally disabled population.

Housing and Day Care: On-campus housing is available. See the following website for more information: http://manoa.hawaii.edu/housing/. On-campus day care facilities are available. See the following website for more information: http://www.hawaii.edu/childrenscenter/.

Employment of Department Graduates:

Master's Degree Graduates: Of those who graduated in the academic year 2011–2012, the following categories and numbers represent the postgraduate activities and employment of master's degree graduates: Enrolled in a postdoctoral residency/fellowship (n/a), employed in independent practice (n/a), total from the above (master's) (0).

Doctoral Degree Graduates: Of those who graduated in the academic year 2011–2012, the following categories and numbers represent the postgraduate activities and employment of doctoral degree graduates: Enrolled in a psychology doctoral program (n/a), enrolled in a postdoctoral residency/fellowship (11), employed in an academic position at a university (2), employed in business or industry (2), employed in a community mental health/counseling center (1), other employment position (2), total from the above (doctoral) (18).

Additional Information:

Orientation, Objectives, and Emphasis of Department: The Department of Psychology's orientation is best characterized as a synthesis of biological, behavioral, social, cognitive and developmental areas, with an overriding emphasis on empiricism (i.e., the study of psychological phenomena based on sound research findings). The graduate concentrations in clinical, developmental, community and cultural, behavioral neuroscience, experimental psychopathology, social-personality, and cognition emphasize the development of research skills and knowledge that are applicable to a wide range of academic and applied settings. The clinical program adheres to the scientist–practitioner model of training, wherein research and clinical skills are equally emphasized. Research opportunities in all graduate concentrations are available. The faculty is particularly interested in admitting students who are interested in pursuing academically related careers.

Special Facilities or Resources: The Psychology Department is mainly housed in Sakamaki Hall. Sakamaki Hall is devoted to facilities for office space, research, and teaching in psychology. Faculty members have specialized laboratories for research, including equipment to support cognitive, social and developmental work. Graduate students are assigned shared office space in Saka-maki Hall and have access to most departmental facilities. The computing facilities in the department and university are of a high standard, and the campus has good wireless internet coverage. Opportunities for study and research also exist elsewhere at the university and in the community. These include the Pacific Biosci-ences Research Center, the John A. Burns School of Medicine, the Center for Disability Studies, the Hawaii State Hospital at Kaneohe, Leahi Hospital, the State Departments of Health and Education, and the Osher Lifelong Learning Institute. Beyond the physical facilities available to the department is the unusual opportunity for research provided by the unique social and envi-ronmental structure of Hawaii. An important dimension is also provided by the East-West Center for Cultural Interchange, which provides fellowships for Asian and U.S. students and for senior scholars from mainland and foreign universities.

Information for Students With Physical Disabilities: See the following website for more information: http://www.hawaii.edu/kokua/.

Application Information:
Send to Graduate Admissions, Department of Psychology, University of Hawaii at Manoa, Sakamaki Hall C400, 2530 Dole Street, Honolulu, Hawaii 96822. Application available online. URL of online applica-tion: http://manoa.hawaii.edu/graduate/content/submitting-your-application. Students are admitted in the Fall, application deadline December 1. *Fee:* $100.

Idaho State University

Department of Psychology
Arts and Sciences
921 South 8th Avenue, Stop 8112
Pocatello, ID 83209-8112
Telephone: (208) 282-2462
Fax: (208) 282-4832
E-mail: *lyncshan@isu.edu*
Web: *http://www.isu.edu/psych*

Department Information:

1968. Chairperson: Shannon Lynch. Number of faculty: total—full-time 13, part-time 16; women—full-time 9, part-time 7; total—minority—full-time 2, part-time 2; women minority—full-time 2; faculty subject to the Americans With Disabilities Act 2.

Programs and Degrees Offered:

Listed in the following order: Program area, degree type (T if terminal Master's), number awarded 7/11–6/12. Clinical Psychology PhD (Doctor of Philosophy) 7, General Experimental Psychology PhD (Doctor of Philosophy) 0.

APA Accreditation: Clinical PhD (Doctor of Philosophy). Student Outcome Data Website: http://www.isu.edu/psych/clinicalprogram.shtml.

Student Applications/Admissions:

Student Applications

Clinical Psychology PhD (Doctor of Philosophy)—Applications 2012–2013, 60. Total applicants accepted 2012–2013, 9. Number full-time enrolled (new admits only) 2012–2013, 6. Number part-time enrolled (new admits only) 2012–2013, 0. Total enrolled 2012–2013 full-time, 26. Total enrolled 2012–2013 part-time, 2. Openings 2013–2014, 6. The median number of years required for completion of a degree in 2012–2013 were 5. The number of students enrolled full- and part-time who were dismissed or voluntarily withdrew from this program area in 2012–2013 were 1. *General Experimental Psychology PhD (Doctor of Philosophy)*—Applications 2012–2013, 20. Total applicants accepted 2012–2013, 6. Number full-time enrolled (new admits only) 2012–2013, 3. Number part-time enrolled (new admits only) 2012–2013, 0. Total enrolled 2012–2013 full-time, 6. Total enrolled 2012–2013 part-time, 0. Openings 2013–2014, 6. The number of students enrolled full- and part-time who were dismissed or voluntarily withdrew from this program area in 2012–2013 were 0.

Scores: Entries appear in this order: required test or GPA, minimum score (if required), median score of students entering in 2012–2013. *Clinical Psychology PhD (Doctor of Philosophy)*: GRE-V no minimum stated, 161, GRE-Q no minimum stated, 155, GRE-Analytical no minimum stated, 5.0, last 2 years GPA 3.0, 3.8; *General Experimental Psychology PhD (Doctor of Philosophy)*: GRE-V no minimum stated, 157, GRE-Q no minimum stated, 150, GRE-Analytical no minimum stated, 4.4, overall undergraduate GPA no minimum stated, last 2 years GPA 3.0, 3.64.

Other Criteria: (importance of criteria rated low, medium, or high): GRE scores—medium, research experience—high, work experience—low, extracurricular activity—low, clinically related public service—medium, GPA—medium, letters of recommendation—medium, interview—medium, statement of goals and objectives—high, undergraduate major in psychology—high, specific undergraduate psychology courses taken—medium, For the experimental doctoral program, clinically related public service is not relevant. For additional information on admission requirements, go to http://www.isu.edu/psych/apply.shtml.

Student Characteristics: The following represents characteristics of students in 2012–2013 in all graduate psychology programs in the department: Female—full-time 20, part-time 2; Male—full-time 12, part-time 0; African American/Black—full-time 0, part-time 0; Hispanic/Latino(a)—full-time 0, part-time 0; Asian/Pacific Islander—full-time 4, part-time 0; American Indian/Alaska Native—full-time 0, part-time 0; Caucasian/White—full-time 28, part-time 2; Multi-ethnic—full-time 0, part-time 0; students subject to the Americans With Disabilities Act—full-time 1, part-time 0; Unknown ethnicity—full-time 0, part-time 0; International students who hold an F-1 or J-1 Visa—full-time 3, part-time 0.

Financial Information/Assistance:

Tuition for Full-Time Study: *Doctoral:* State residents: per academic year $7,150, $358 per credit hour; Nonstate residents: per academic year $18,950, $548 per credit hour. Tuition is subject to change. Additional fees are assessed to students beyond the costs of tuition for the following: $925 health insurance premium per semester, unless waived by proof of insurance. See the following website for updates and changes in tuition costs: http://www.isu.edu/finserv/costinfo.shtml.

Financial Assistance:

First-Year Students: Teaching assistantships available for first year. Average amount paid per academic year: $12,524. Average number of hours worked per week: 20. Apply by March 1. Traineeships available for first year. Average amount paid per academic year: $6,900. Average number of hours worked per week: 15. Apply by March 1.

Advanced Students: Teaching assistantships available for advanced students. Average amount paid per academic year: $12,524. Average number of hours worked per week: 20. Apply by March 1. Traineeships available for advanced students. Average amount paid per academic year: $11,385. Average number of hours worked per week: 15. Apply by March 1.

Additional Information: Of all students currently enrolled full time, 100% benefited from one or more of the listed financial assistance programs. Application and information available online at: http://www.isu.edu/psych/apply.shtml.

Internships/Practica: Doctoral Degree (PhD Clinical Psychology): For those doctoral students for whom a professional psychology internship was required in this program prior to graduation, (5) students applied for an internship in 2011–2012, with (5) students obtaining an internship. Of those students who obtained

an internship, (4) were paid internships. Of those students who obtained an internship, (4) students placed in APA/CPA accredited internships, (0) students placed in internships not APA/CPA accredited, but listed with the Association of Psychology Postdoctoral and Internship Programs (APPIC), (0) students placed in internships conforming to guidelines of the Council of Directors of School Psychology Programs (CDSPP), (1) students placed in internships that were not APA/CPA accredited, APPIC or CDSPP listed. Master's Degree (PhD General Experimental Psychology): An internship experience, such as a final research project or "capstone" experience is required of graduates. First and second year students complete practica in the ISU Psychology Clinic under the supervision of clinical faculty. Third and fourth year students often participate in community practica and/or clinical externships under the supervision of licensed psychologists employed by local mental health providers/agencies. One semester on the ISU Interdisciplinary Evaluation Team is also required during the 4th year. Currently, 7 clinical externship sites provide stipends and supervised practice in applied settings; 8 sites provide community practica.

Housing and Day Care: On-campus housing is available. See the following website for more information: http://www.isu.edu/housing/. On-campus day care facilities are available. See the following website for more information: http://www.isu.edu/earlylc/.

Employment of Department Graduates:
  Master's Degree Graduates: Of those who graduated in the academic year 2011–2012, the following categories and numbers represent the postgraduate activities and employment of master's degree graduates: Enrolled in a postdoctoral residency/fellowship (n/a), employed in independent practice (n/a), total from the above (master's) (0).
  Doctoral Degree Graduates: Of those who graduated in the academic year 2011–2012, the following categories and numbers represent the postgraduate activities and employment of doctoral degree graduates: Enrolled in a psychology doctoral program (n/a), enrolled in a postdoctoral residency/fellowship (3), employed in other positions at a higher education institution (1), employed in government agency (1), employed in a community mental health/counseling center (1), employed in a hospital/medical center (1), total from the above (doctoral) (7).

Additional Information:
  Orientation, Objectives, and Emphasis of Department: The doctoral program in experimental psychology matriculated its second class in fall 2012. Its mission is to provide educational and research training across core areas of psychological science: cognition, developmental, learning, physiology, personality, social, and sensation/perception. Four program objectives are defined: research knowledge & expertise; breadth of knowledge & integration across core areas; methodology and analysis; and communication skills. The mission of the clinical doctoral program is to train competent clinical psychologists who can apply and adapt general conceptual and technical skills in diverse regional and professional settings. A scientist–practitioner training model has been adopted. Five objectives are defined: research knowledge & skill; professional knowledge & skill; integration of science & practice; professional identification & ethical practice; and appreciation & knowledge of individual & cultural differences.

Special Facilities or Resources: The Psychology Department has office and laboratory space for all faculty. The ISU Psychology Clinic, housed in the same building, provides four individual therapy rooms, two child/family rooms, two testing rooms, and a group therapy room, all equipped with observation systems and videotape capabilities. Computer access is available in offices, in the department, the clinic, and a university center located nearby. The university maintains an animal colony at which two Psychology faculty members conduct and supervise research, an Office of Sponsored Programs (grant assistance), and an instructional technical resource center (website assistance).

Information for Students With Physical Disabilities: See the following website for more information: http://www.isu.edu/ada4isu/.

Application Information:
Send to Admissions Committee, 921 South 8th Avenue, Stop 8112, Idaho State University, Pocatello, ID 83209-8112. Application available online. URL of online application: http://apply.isu.edu/. Students are admitted in the Fall, application deadline December 1. Fee: $55.

Idaho, University of
Department of Psychology and Communication Studies
College of Letters, Arts, and Social Sciences
University of Idaho, MS 3043
Moscow, ID 83844-3043
Telephone: (208) 885-6324
Fax: (208) 885-7710
E-mail: *seanm@uidaho.edu*
Web: *http://www.uidaho.edu/class/psychcomm*

Department Information:
  Chairperson: Traci Craig. Number of faculty: total—full-time 12; women—full-time 2.

Programs and Degrees Offered:
  Listed in the following order: Program area, degree type (T if terminal Master's), number awarded 7/11–6/12. General Experimental Psychology MA/MS (Master of Arts/Science) (T) 1, Human Factors MA/MS (Master of Arts/Science) (T) 4, Neuroscience PhD (Doctor of Philosophy) 0.

Student Applications/Admissions:
  Student Applications
  General Experimental Psychology MA/MS (Master of Arts/Science)—Applications 2012–2013, 1. Total applicants accepted 2012–2013, 1. Number full-time enrolled (new admits only) 2012–2013, 1. Number part-time enrolled (new admits only) 2012–2013, 0. Total enrolled 2012–2013 full-time, 2. Total enrolled 2012–2013 part-time, 1. Openings 2013–2014, 1. The median number of years required for completion of a degree in 2012–2013 were 2. The number of students enrolled full- and part-time who were dismissed or voluntarily withdrew from this program area in 2012–2013 were 0. *Human Factors MA/MS (Master of Arts/Science)*—Applications 2012–2013, 21. Total applicants accepted 2012–2013, 15. Number full-time enrolled (new admits only) 2012–2013, 7. Number part-time enrolled (new admits only) 2012–2013, 0. Total enrolled

2012–2013 full-time, 12. Total enrolled 2012–2013 part-time, 9. Openings 2013–2014, 8. The median number of years required for completion of a degree in 2012–2013 were 2. The number of students enrolled full- and part-time who were dismissed or voluntarily withdrew from this program area in 2012–2013 were 0. *Neuroscience PhD (Doctor of Philosophy)*— Applications 2012–2013, 1. Total applicants accepted 2012–2013, 0. Number full-time enrolled (new admits only) 2012–2013, 0. Number part-time enrolled (new admits only) 2012–2013, 0. Total enrolled 2012–2013 full-time, 1. Total enrolled 2012–2013 part-time, 1. Openings 2013–2014, 1. The median number of years required for completion of a degree in 2012–2013 were 5. The number of students enrolled full- and part-time who were dismissed or voluntarily withdrew from this program area in 2012–2013 were 0.

Scores: Entries appear in this order: required test or GPA, minimum score (if required), median score of students entering in 2012–2013. *General Experimental Psychology MA/MS (Master of Arts/Science):* GRE-V no minimum stated, GRE-Q no minimum stated, overall undergraduate GPA 3.0; *Human Factors MA/MS (Master of Arts/Science):* GRE-V no minimum stated, GRE-Q no minimum stated, overall undergraduate GPA 3.0; *Neuroscience PhD (Doctor of Philosophy):* GRE-V no minimum stated, GRE-Q no minimum stated, GRE-Analytical 4.0, overall undergraduate GPA 3.0.

Other Criteria: (importance of criteria rated low, medium, or high): GRE scores—high, research experience—high, work experience—medium, extracurricular activity—low, GPA—high, letters of recommendation—high, statement of goals and objectives—high, undergraduate major in psychology—low, specific undergraduate psychology courses taken—low, Work experience is more important for Human Factors candidates than for General Experimental candidates. For additional information on admission requirements, go to http://www.uidaho.edu/class/psychcomm/graduate.

Student Characteristics: The following represents characteristics of students in 2012–2013 in all graduate psychology programs in the department: Female—full-time 6, part-time 3; Male—full-time 9, part-time 8; African American/Black—full-time 0, part-time 0; Hispanic/Latino(a)—full-time 0, part-time 0; Asian/Pacific Islander—full-time 0, part-time 0; American Indian/Alaska Native—full-time 0, part-time 0; Caucasian/White—full-time 13, part-time 8; Multi-ethnic—full-time 1, part-time 0; students subject to the Americans With Disabilities Act—full-time 0, part-time 0; Unknown ethnicity—full-time 1, part-time 3; International students who hold an F-1 or J-1 Visa—full-time 1, part-time 0.

Financial Information/Assistance:

Tuition for Full-Time Study: *Master's:* State residents: per academic year $7,162; Nonstate residents: per academic year $19,950. Tuition is subject to change. See the following website for updates and changes in tuition costs: http://www.uidaho.edu/cogs/finances/costofattendance.

Financial Assistance:

First-Year Students: Teaching assistantships available for first year. Average amount paid per academic year: $10,000. Average number of hours worked per week: 20. Apply by February 15. Research assistantships available for first year. Average amount

paid per academic year: $10,000. Average number of hours worked per week: 20. Apply by February 15.

Advanced Students: Teaching assistantships available for advanced students. Average amount paid per academic year: $11,000. Average number of hours worked per week: 20. Apply by February 15. Research assistantships available for advanced students. Average amount paid per academic year: $11,000. Average number of hours worked per week: 20. Apply by February 15.

Additional Information: Of all students currently enrolled full time, 100% benefited from one or more of the listed financial assistance programs. Application and information available online at: http://www.uidaho.edu/cogs/finances/costofattendance.

Internships/Practica: A few internships are available locally through the university (e.g., usability testing, web analytics). Other internships are regularly available throughout the northwest region (e.g., at Idaho National Laboratory).

Housing and Day Care: On-campus housing is available. See the following website for more information: http://www.uidaho.edu/universityhousing. On-campus day care facilities are available. See the following website for more information: http://www.uidaho.edu/studentaffairs/childrens-center.

Employment of Department Graduates:

Master's Degree Graduates: Of those who graduated in the academic year 2011–2012, the following categories and numbers represent the postgraduate activities and employment of master's degree graduates: Enrolled in a psychology doctoral program (2), enrolled in another graduate/professional program (1), enrolled in a postdoctoral residency/fellowship (n/a), employed in independent practice (n/a), employed in an academic position at a university (1), employed in an academic position at a 2-year/4-year college (1), employed in other positions at a higher education institution (1), employed in business or industry (5), employed in government agency (1), employed in a community mental health/counseling center (2), other employment position (2), total from the above (master's) (16).

Doctoral Degree Graduates: Of those who graduated in the academic year 2011–2012, the following categories and numbers represent the postgraduate activities and employment of doctoral degree graduates: Enrolled in a psychology doctoral program (n/a), total from the above (doctoral) (0).

Additional Information:

Orientation, Objectives, and Emphasis of Department: In the Land Grant tradition of providing a "practical education," the Department of Psychology and Communication Studies at the University of Idaho offers the MS degree in experimental psychology with an emphasis in Human Factors psychology (human technology interaction, ergonomics, human performance). The program emphasizes developing knowledge and skills germane to a professional position, but also provides students with the foundation for further graduate study. Thus, students are helped to develop analytical and problem solving skills that will serve them well in whatever they choose to do after graduation. The department is small, but is able to address the broad needs of its students through working relationships with various other units on campus (e.g., College of Engineering) and Washington State University's Department of Psychology (only 9 miles away). Student placement figures show that our graduates have been very successful in obtaining positions in technical industries. The Department also offers the MS in Psychology degree to off-campus students by making all required courses available through distance education (e.g., online courses, streaming video). The department will consider, and occasionally admits, students for a general experimental MS; general experimental students typically use the program to prepare for admission to doctoral programs elsewhere. The department also hosts doctoral students who are enrolled in the university's interdisciplinary PhD program in Neuroscience.

Special Facilities or Resources: The department provides over 3000 square feet of research space. Labs are equipped with cutting-edge technology (e.g., driving and flight simulators, immersive virtual reality displays, multiple graphics workstations, eye- and head-tracking technology, six web cameras with a quad multiplexer to allow for simultaneous recording of four camera views simultaneously). Research opportunities are available at remote sites, such as the Motion Analysis Lab at Shriners Hospital in Spokane, WA.

Information for Students With Physical Disabilities: See the following website for more information: http://www.uidaho.edu/studentaffairs/asap/dss.

Application Information:
Send to Graduate Admissions, University of Idaho, 875 Perimeter Drive MS 3019, Moscow, ID 83844-3019. Application available online. URL of online application: http://www.uidaho.edu/graduateadmissions/applynow/apply. Students are admitted in the Fall, application deadline February 15. Applications will be considered after the deadline, but availability of funding declines with passage of time. *Fee:* $60. Online- $60 domestic applicants, $70 international applicants. Paper- $85 domestic and international applicants.

Adler School of Professional Psychology

Department of Clinical Psychology
17 North Dearborn Street
Chicago, IL 60602-4310
Telephone: (312) 662-4100
Fax: (312) 662-4199
E-mail: dkatz@adler.edu
Web: http://www.adler.edu

Department Information:

1952. Chair, Clinical Psychology Department: David Katz, PhD, ABPP. Number of faculty: total—full-time 25, part-time 1; women—full-time 14; total—minority—full-time 12; women minority—full-time 8.

Programs and Degrees Offered:

Listed in the following order: Program area, degree type (T if terminal Master's), number awarded 7/11–6/12. Clinical Psychology PsyD (Doctor of Psychology) 56.

APA Accreditation: Clinical PsyD (Doctor of Psychology). Student Outcome Data Website: http://www.adler.edu/page/programs/chicago/doctor-of-psychology-in-clinical-psychology/student-admissions—outcome-data.

Student Applications/Admissions:

Student Applications

Clinical Psychology PsyD (Doctor of Psychology)—Applications 2012–2013, 514. Total applicants accepted 2012–2013, 223. Number full-time enrolled (new admits only) 2012–2013, 110. Total enrolled 2012–2013 full-time, 458. Openings 2013–2014, 110. The median number of years required for completion of a degree in 2012–2013 were 5.

Scores: Entries appear in this order: required test or GPA, minimum score (if required), median score of students entering in 2012–2013. *Clinical Psychology PsyD (Doctor of Psychology):* overall undergraduate GPA no minimum stated, 3.34, Masters GPA no minimum stated, 3.80.

Other Criteria: (importance of criteria rated low, medium, or high): GRE scores—high, research experience—medium, work experience—medium, extracurricular activity—medium, clinically related public service—high, GPA—high, letters of recommendation—high, interview—high, statement of goals and objectives—high, interest in mission—high, undergraduate major in psychology—medium, specific undergraduate psychology courses taken—medium. For additional information on admission requirements, go to http://www.adler.edu/page/campuses/chicago/admission/admission-requirements.

Student Characteristics: The following represents characteristics of students in 2012–2013 in all graduate psychology programs in the department: Female—full-time 354, part-time 0; Male—full-time 104, part-time 0; African American/Black—full-time 48, part-time 0; Hispanic/Latino(a)—full-time 36, part-time 0; Asian/Pacific Islander—full-time 26, part-time 0; American Indian/Alaska Native—full-time 2, part-time 0; Caucasian/White—full-

time 298, part-time 0; Multi-ethnic—part-time 0; students subject to the Americans With Disabilities Act—full-time 15, part-time 0; Unknown ethnicity—full-time 48, part-time 0; International students who hold an F-1 or J-1 Visa—full-time 23, part-time 0.

Financial Information/Assistance:

Tuition for Full-Time Study: *Doctoral:* State residents: per academic year $34,800, $1,160 per credit hour; Nonstate residents: per academic year $34,800, $1,160 per credit hour. Tuition is subject to change. Additional fees are assessed to students beyond the costs of tuition for the following: student services fee, lab fee, professional liability insurances fee, UPass (for full time students). See the following website for updates and changes in tuition costs: http://www.adler.edu/page/campuses/chicago/student-services/tuition—fees.

Financial Assistance:

First-Year Students: Teaching assistantships available for first year. Average amount paid per academic year: $3,101. Average number of hours worked per week: 6. Research assistantships available for first year. Average amount paid per academic year: $3,101. Average number of hours worked per week: 6. Fellowships and scholarships available for first year. Average amount paid per academic year: $10,000.

Advanced Students: Teaching assistantships available for advanced students. Average amount paid per academic year: $3,101. Average number of hours worked per week: 6. Research assistantships available for advanced students. Average amount paid per academic year: $3,101. Average number of hours worked per week: 6. Fellowships and scholarships available for advanced students. Average amount paid per academic year: $5,000. Apply by May 15.

Additional Information: Of all students currently enrolled full time, 13% benefited from one or more of the listed financial assistance programs.

Internships/Practica: Doctoral Degree (PsyD Clinical Psychology): For those doctoral students for whom a professional psychology internship was required in this program prior to graduation, (80) students applied for an internship in 2011–2012, with (67) students obtaining an internship. Of those students who obtained an internship, (67) were paid internships. Of those students who obtained an internship, (35) students placed in APA/CPA accredited internships, (29) students placed in internships not APA/CPA accredited, but listed with the Association of Psychology Postdoctoral and Internship Programs (APPIC), (0) students placed in internships conforming to guidelines of the Council of Directors of School Psychology Programs (CDSPP), (3) students placed in internships that were not APA/CPA accredited, APPIC or CDSPP listed. Practicum training is a core component of the educational experience at the Adler School. Students are required to undertake a Community Service Practicum, designed to provide practical application of the principles of socially responsible practice central to the training model. Students also engage in assessment, intervention, and advanced practicum experiences prior to their internship training. The training department works diligently to match student interests and skills with available training venues, and our affiliation with large, regional social service organizations, such as Heartland Alliance, provide students with a wide array of opportunities to work with diverse and traditionally underserved populations in settings ranging from correctional facilities to family service agencies. The Adler Community Health Services, comprised of several mental and general healthcare settings, offers training to practicum students as well as an APA-accredited internship site. The Training Department works to prepare students for the internship application process and Adler School students have enjoyed considerable success in matching for APA-accredited and APPIC-affiliated internships. Training is guided by an emphasis on evidence-based practice and the principles of social responsibility and justice.

Housing and Day Care: No on-campus housing is available. No on-campus day care facilities are available.

Employment of Department Graduates:
Master's Degree Graduates: Of those who graduated in the academic year 2011–2012, the following categories and numbers represent the postgraduate activities and employment of master's degree graduates: Enrolled in a postdoctoral residency/fellowship (n/a), employed in independent practice (n/a), total from the above (master's) (0).
Doctoral Degree Graduates: Of those who graduated in the academic year 2011–2012, the following categories and numbers represent the postgraduate activities and employment of doctoral degree graduates: Enrolled in a psychology doctoral program (n/a), total from the above (doctoral) (0).

Additional Information:
Orientation, Objectives, and Emphasis of Department: Established in 1952, the Adler School follows in the tradition of Alfred Adler, founder of community psychology. Adlerian theory, especially its emphasis on social responsibility and justice, forms the theoretical basis for training across programs, and as a platform for exposure to a broad array of theoretical approaches. A core principle common to the programs at Adler School is the incorporation of socially responsible practice in didactic, seminar and applied training experiences. In addition to Adlerian psychotherapy, students in the doctoral program are able to obtain training in a variety of theoretical approaches, including cognitive-behavioral, humanistic, psychodynamic and group therapies. In addition, concentrations in specialty areas, such as primary care, trauma-related intervention, child and adolescent treatment and clinical neuropsychology are available. Doctoral program graduates often go on to serve their communities as clinicians, advocates, researchers and policy makers. Students learn to think critically, understand and utilize the available evidence in making informed clinical decisions and incorporate what Adler referred to as Social Interest in all their professional endeavors.

Special Facilities or Resources: Our new facility offers state-of-the-art and accessible computer, classroom, lab and common area facilities located in the heart of downtown Chicago. The Adler Institutes for Social Justice (Institute on Social Exclusion, Institute on Public Safety and Social Justice, and LGBTQ Mental Health and Inclusion Center) sponsor national conferences of interest in the areas of social responsibility and public health. In addition, their affiliations with major community organizations provide students at all levels of training with opportunities for practicum and internship training with culturally diverse and traditionally underserved groups. These placements provide a

practical application of the principles of social justice and responsibility that form the core of the training experience at the Adler School. The library offers a vast array of electronic journal and print holdings, made more extensive by institutional lending agreements and consortium affiliations. In addition, the library boasts a large collection of the works of both Alfred Adler and the school's founder, Rudolf Dreikurs. The Institutional Review Board is federally registered and the school possesses a Federal Wide Assurance certificate, facilitating efforts to secure extramural funding for research and educational programming.

Application Information:
Send to Office of Admissions, 17 North Dearborn Street, 15th Floor, Chicago, IL 60602. Application available online. URL of online application: http://www.adler.edu/page/campuses/chicago/admission. Students are admitted in the Fall, application deadline February 15. PsyD priority deadline is February 15 for Fall semester. *Fee:* $50. Fee is waived for McNair Scholars.

Benedictine University
Graduate Department of Clinical Psychology
College of Liberal Arts
5700 College Road
Lisle, IL 60532
Telephone: (630) 829-6230
Fax: (630) 829-6231
E-mail: *jbooth@ben.edu*
Web: *http://www.ben.edu*

Department Information:
1967. Chairperson: James K. Crissman. Number of faculty: total—full-time 4, part-time 7; women—full-time 2, part-time 5; total—minority—full-time 1, part-time 1; women minority—part-time 1.

Programs and Degrees Offered:
Listed in the following order: Program area, degree type (T if terminal Master's), number awarded 7/11–6/12. Clinical Psychology MA/MS (Master of Arts/Science) (T) 20.

Student Applications/Admissions:
Student Applications
Clinical Psychology MA/MS (Master of Arts/Science)—Applications 2012–2013, 30. Total applicants accepted 2012–2013, 19. Number full-time enrolled (new admits only) 2012–2013, 10. Number part-time enrolled (new admits only) 2012–2013, 9. Total enrolled 2012–2013 full-time, 35. Total enrolled 2012–2013 part-time, 45. Openings 2013–2014, 30. The median number of years required for completion of a degree in 2012–2013 were 2. The number of students enrolled full- and part-time who were dismissed or voluntarily withdrew from this program area in 2012–2013 were 2.
Other Criteria: (importance of criteria rated low, medium, or high): GRE scores—medium, research experience—low, work experience—medium, extracurricular activity—medium, clinically related public service—high, GPA—medium, letters of recommendation—high, interview—high, statement of goals and objectives—high, undergraduate major in psychology—low, specific undergraduate psychology courses taken—medium. For additional information on admission requirements,

go to http://www.ben.edu/future_students/graduate/Admission-Requirements.cfm.

Student Characteristics: The following represents characteristics of students in 2012–2013 in all graduate psychology programs in the department: Female—full-time 11, part-time 51; Male—full-time 5, part-time 3; African American/Black—full-time 2, part-time 4; Hispanic/Latino(a)—full-time 4, part-time 1; Asian/Pacific Islander—full-time 2, part-time 0; American Indian/Alaska Native—full-time 0, part-time 0; Caucasian/White—full-time 8, part-time 0; Multi-ethnic—full-time 0, part-time 0; students subject to the Americans With Disabilities Act—full-time 1, part-time 1; Unknown ethnicity—full-time 0, part-time 0; International students who hold an F-1 or J-1 Visa—full-time 0, part-time 0.

Financial Information/Assistance:

Tuition for Full-Time Study: *Master's:* State residents: $570 per credit hour; Nonstate residents: $570 per credit hour. Tuition is subject to change. See the following website for updates and changes in tuition costs: http://www.ben.edu/future_students/graduate/tuition_fees.cfm.

Financial Assistance:

First-Year Students: No information provided.

Advanced Students: No information provided.

Additional Information: Of all students currently enrolled full time, 0% benefited from one or more of the listed financial assistance programs. Application and information available online at: http://www.ben.edu/future_students/graduate/financial_aid.cfm.

Internships/Practica: Master's Degree (MA/MS Clinical Psychology): An internship experience, such as a final research project or "capstone" experience is required of graduates. The program has established relationships with over 100 mental health agencies, in-patient, out-patient, and social service agencies in the Chicago metropolitan area.

Housing and Day Care: On-campus housing is available. See the following website for more information: http://www.ben.edu/student_life/reslife/residence_halls/founders.cfm. No on-campus day care facilities are available.

Employment of Department Graduates:

Master's Degree Graduates: Of those who graduated in the academic year 2011–2012, the following categories and numbers represent the postgraduate activities and employment of master's degree graduates: Enrolled in a psychology doctoral program (3), enrolled in a postdoctoral residency/fellowship (n/a), employed in independent practice (n/a), total from the above (master's) (3). **Doctoral Degree Graduates:** Of those who graduated in the academic year 2011–2012, the following categories and numbers represent the postgraduate activities and employment of doctoral degree graduates: Enrolled in a psychology doctoral program (n/a), total from the above (doctoral) (0).

Additional Information:

Orientation, Objectives, and Emphasis of Department: Our program is a rigorous one, offering two clinical internship experiences that more than meet the number of hours required for state licensure. Our program has a curriculum in place that satisfies all Licensed Clinical Professional Counselor (LCPC) licensure requirements. To date, more than 90% of our alumni have successfully passed the licensure exam. Our program is approved by the Illinois Department of Professional Regulation.

Special Facilities or Resources: The department has lab space provided for role play and audio and video taping. The building has a beautiful new library and teaching facilities.

Information for Students With Physical Disabilities: See the following website for more information: http://www.ben.edu/springfield/student-life/rc/disability.cfm.

Application Information:

Send to Graduate Admissions, Benedictine University, 5700 College Road, Lisle, IL 60532. Application available online. URL of online application: http://www.ben.edu/future_students/apply-online.cfm. Programs have rolling admissions. *Fee:* $40.

Chicago, University of
Department of Psychology
5848 South University Avenue
Chicago, IL 60637
Telephone: (773) 702-8861
Fax: (773) 702-0886
E-mail: *mhalpern@uchicago.edu*
Web: *http://psychology.uchicago.edu/*

Department Information:

1893. Chairperson: Susan Levine. Number of faculty: total—full-time 21; women—full-time 11.

Programs and Degrees Offered:

Listed in the following order: Program area, degree type (T if terminal Master's), number awarded 7/11–6/12. Developmental Psychology PhD (Doctor of Philosophy) 2, Social Psychology PhD (Doctor of Philosophy) 2, Integrative Neuroscience PhD (Doctor of Philosophy) 3, Cognition Program PhD (Doctor of Philosophy) 7.

Student Applications/Admissions:

Student Applications

Developmental Psychology PhD (Doctor of Philosophy)—Applications 2012–2013, 51. Total applicants accepted 2012–2013, 3. Number full-time enrolled (new admits only) 2012–2013, 1. Number part-time enrolled (new admits only) 2012–2013, 0. Total enrolled 2012–2013 full-time, 17. Total enrolled 2012–2013 part-time, 0. Openings 2013–2014, 3. The median number of years required for completion of a degree in 2012–2013 were 6. The number of students enrolled full- and part-time who were dismissed or voluntarily withdrew from this program area in 2012–2013 were 0. *Social Psychology PhD (Doctor of Philosophy)*—Applications 2012–2013, 124. Total applicants accepted 2012–2013, 3. Number full-time enrolled (new admits only) 2012–2013, 0. Number part-time enrolled (new admits only) 2012–2013, 0. Total enrolled 2012–2013 full-time, 11. Total enrolled 2012–2013 part-time, 0. Openings 2013–2014, 2. The median number of years required for completion of a degree in 2012–2013 were 6. The number of students enrolled full- and part-time who were dismissed or voluntarily withdrew from this program area in 2012–2013 were 0. *Integrative Neuroscience PhD (Doctor of Philosophy)*—Applications 2012–2013, 108. Total applicants accepted 2012–2013, 7. Number full-time enrolled (new admits only) 2012–2013, 6. Number part-time enrolled (new admits only) 2012–2013, 0. Total enrolled 2012–2013 full-time, 15. Total enrolled 2012–2013 part-time, 0. Openings 2013–2014, 3. The median number of years required for completion of a degree in 2012–2013 were 5. The number of students enrolled full- and part-time who were dismissed or voluntarily withdrew from this program area in 2012–2013 were 0. *Cognition Program PhD (Doctor of Philosophy)*—Applications 2012–2013, 61. Total applicants accepted 2012–2013, 3. Number full-time enrolled (new admits only) 2012–2013, 2. Number part-time enrolled (new admits only) 2012–2013, 0. Total enrolled 2012–2013 full-time, 12. Total enrolled 2012–2013 part-time, 0. Openings 2013–2014, 3. The median number of years required for completion of a degree in 2012–2013 were 6. The number of students enrolled full- and part-time who were dismissed or voluntarily withdrew from this program area in 2012–2013 were 0.

Scores: Entries appear in this order: required test or GPA, minimum score (if required), median score of students entering in 2012–2013. *Developmental Psychology PhD (Doctor of Philosophy):* GRE-V no minimum stated, GRE-Q no minimum stated, GRE-Analytical no minimum stated, overall undergraduate GPA no minimum stated, last 2 years GPA no minimum stated; *Social Psychology PhD (Doctor of Philosophy):* GRE-V no minimum stated, GRE-Q no minimum stated, GRE-Analytical no minimum stated, overall undergraduate GPA no minimum stated, last 2 years GPA no minimum stated; *Integrative Neuroscience PhD (Doctor of Philosophy):* GRE-V no minimum stated, GRE-Q no minimum stated, GRE-Analytical no minimum stated, overall undergraduate GPA no minimum stated, last 2 years GPA no minimum stated; *Cognition Program PhD (Doctor of Philosophy):* GRE-V no minimum stated, GRE-Q no minimum stated, GRE-Analytical no minimum stated, overall undergraduate GPA no minimum stated, last 2 years GPA no minimum stated.

Other Criteria: (importance of criteria rated low, medium, or high): GRE scores—high, research experience—high, work experience—low, extracurricular activity—low, GPA—high, letters of recommendation—high, interview—high, statement of goals and objectives—high, undergraduate major in psychology—medium, specific undergraduate psychology courses taken—medium, Some science background is helpful for the Integrative Neuroscience program. For additional information on admission requirements, go to http://psychology.uchicago.edu/academics/doctoral/admissions/.

Student Characteristics: The following represents characteristics of students in 2012–2013 in all graduate psychology programs in the department: Female—full-time 35, part-time 0; Male—full-time 20, part-time 0; African American/Black—full-time 1, part-time 0; Hispanic/Latino(a)—full-time 6, part-time 0; Asian/Pacific Islander—full-time 11, part-time 0; American Indian/Alaska Native—full-time 1, part-time 0; Caucasian/White—full-time 36, part-time 0; Multi-ethnic—full-time 0, part-time 0; students subject to the Americans With Disabilities Act—full-time 0, part-time 0; Unknown ethnicity—full-time 0, part-time 0; Interna-

tional students who hold an F-1 or J-1 Visa—full-time 12, part-time 0.

Financial Information/Assistance:
Tuition for Full-Time Study: *Doctoral:* State residents: per academic year $45,900; Nonstate residents: per academic year $45,900. Tuition is subject to change. Additional fees are assessed to students beyond the costs of tuition for the following: An activity fee and a health and wellness fee. See the following website for updates and changes in tuition costs: http://bursar.uchicago.edu/students.html.

Financial Assistance:
First-Year Students: Fellowships and scholarships available for first year. Average amount paid per academic year: $22,000. Apply by December 10.

Advanced Students: Teaching assistantships available for advanced students. Average amount paid per academic year: $3,000. Research assistantships available for advanced students. Fellowships and scholarships available for advanced students. Average amount paid per academic year: $22,000.

Additional Information: Of all students currently enrolled full time, 95% benefited from one or more of the listed financial assistance programs. Application and information available online at: http://gradfinancing.uchicago.edu/.

Housing and Day Care: On-campus housing is available. See the following website for more information: http://rp.uchicago.edu/graduate_housing/. No on-campus day care facilities are available.

Employment of Department Graduates:
Master's Degree Graduates: Of those who graduated in the academic year 2011–2012, the following categories and numbers represent the postgraduate activities and employment of master's degree graduates: Enrolled in a postdoctoral residency/fellowship (n/a), employed in independent practice (n/a), total from the above (master's) (0).

Doctoral Degree Graduates: Of those who graduated in the academic year 2011–2012, the following categories and numbers represent the postgraduate activities and employment of doctoral degree graduates: Enrolled in a psychology doctoral program (n/a), enrolled in a postdoctoral residency/fellowship (8), employed in an academic position at a university (1), employed in business or industry (2), still seeking employment (3), total from the above (doctoral) (14).

Additional Information:
Orientation, Objectives, and Emphasis of Department: The Department of Psychology at the University of Chicago has been for a century a leading center of scholarship, research and teaching in psychology and related fields. The Department is organized into specialized programs that reflect the contemporary state of the discipline as well as the wide-ranging interests of its own faculty. The four areas are: the Cognition Program, the Developmental Psychology Program, the Integrative Neuroscience Program, and the Social Psychology Program. The interdisciplinary character of the University is further reflected in the close connections the Department of Psychology maintains with other departments in the University.

Special Facilities or Resources: Facilities include a Laboratory for Conceptual Psychology, an Audio Visual Laboratory, an Early

Childhood Initiative, Institute for Mind and Biology, Center for Cognitive and Social Neuroscience, Spatial Intelligence and Learning Center, Language Development Project, and The Arete Initiative.

Information for Students With Physical Disabilities: See the following website for more information: http://disabilities.uchicago.edu/.

Application Information:

Send to Social Science Division, Office of Admissions, Foster Hall 105, 1130 East 59th Street, University of Chicago, Chicago, IL 60637. Application available online. URL of online application: https://grad-application.uchicago.edu/. Students are admitted in the Fall, application deadline December 10. *Fee:* $65.

DePaul University
Department of Psychology
College of Science and Health
2219 North Kenmore - Room 420
Chicago, IL 60614
Telephone: (773) 325-7887
Fax: (773) 325-7888
E-mail: *bdelucca@depaul.edu*
Web: *http://csh.depaul.edu/academics/graduate/psychology/Pages/default.aspx*

Department Information:

1936. Chairperson: Susan D. McMahon, PhD. Number of faculty: total—full-time 35, part-time 4; women—full-time 21, part-time 2; total—minority—full-time 8; women minority—full-time 6.

Programs and Degrees Offered:

Listed in the following order: Program area, degree type (T if terminal Master's), number awarded 7/11–6/12. Clinical Psychology PhD (Doctor of Philosophy) 7, Experimental Psychology PhD (Doctor of Philosophy) 1, Industrial/Organizational Psychology PhD (Doctor of Philosophy) 1, Community Psychology PhD (Doctor of Philosophy) 1, General Psychology MA/MS (Master of Arts/Science) (T) 1.

APA Accreditation:

Clinical PhD (Doctor of Philosophy). Student Outcome Data Website: http://csh.depaul.edu/academics/graduate/clinical-psychology-ma-phd/Pages/clinical-data.aspx.

Student Applications/Admissions:

Student Applications

Clinical Psychology PhD (Doctor of Philosophy)—Applications 2012–2013, 431. Total applicants accepted 2012–2013, 7. Number full-time enrolled (new admits only) 2012–2013, 7. Number part-time enrolled (new admits only) 2012–2013, 0. Total enrolled 2012–2013 full-time, 43. Total enrolled 2012–2013 part-time, 0. Openings 2013–2014, 6. The median number of years required for completion of a degree in 2012–2013 were 8. The number of students enrolled full- and part-time who were dismissed or voluntarily withdrew from this program area in 2012–2013 were 0. *Experimental Psychology PhD (Doctor of Philosophy)*—Applications 2012–2013, 68. Total applicants

accepted 2012–2013, 3. Number full-time enrolled (new admits only) 2012–2013, 3. Number part-time enrolled (new admits only) 2012–2013, 0. Total enrolled 2012–2013 full-time, 16. Total enrolled 2012–2013 part-time, 0. Openings 2013–2014, 4. The median number of years required for completion of a degree in 2012–2013 were 7. The number of students enrolled full- and part-time who were dismissed or voluntarily withdrew from this program area in 2012–2013 were 0. *Industrial/Organizational Psychology PhD (Doctor of Philosophy)*—Applications 2012–2013, 74. Total applicants accepted 2012–2013, 3. Number full-time enrolled (new admits only) 2012–2013, 3. Number part-time enrolled (new admits only) 2012–2013, 0. Total enrolled 2012–2013 full-time, 21. Total enrolled 2012–2013 part-time, 0. Openings 2013–2014, 3. The median number of years required for completion of a degree in 2012–2013 were 6. The number of students enrolled full- and part-time who were dismissed or voluntarily withdrew from this program area in 2012–2013 were 1. *Community Psychology PhD (Doctor of Philosophy)*—Applications 2012–2013, 44. Total applicants accepted 2012–2013, 3. Number full-time enrolled (new admits only) 2012–2013, 3. Number part-time enrolled (new admits only) 2012–2013, 0. Total enrolled 2012–2013 full-time, 20. Total enrolled 2012–2013 part-time, 0. Openings 2013–2014, 3. The median number of years required for completion of a degree in 2012–2013 were 6. The number of students enrolled full- and part-time who were dismissed or voluntarily withdrew from this program area in 2012–2013 were 0. *General Psychology MA/MS (Master of Arts/Science)*—Applications 2012–2013, 86. Total applicants accepted 2012–2013, 8. Number full-time enrolled (new admits only) 2012–2013, 8. Number part-time enrolled (new admits only) 2012–2013, 0. Total enrolled 2012–2013 full-time, 20. Total enrolled 2012–2013 part-time, 0. Openings 2013–2014, 5. The median number of years required for completion of a degree in 2012–2013 were 2. The number of students enrolled full- and part-time who were dismissed or voluntarily withdrew from this program area in 2012–2013 were 0.

Scores: Entries appear in this order: required test or GPA, minimum score (if required), median score of students entering in 2012–2013. *Clinical Psychology PhD (Doctor of Philosophy):* GRE-V no minimum stated, GRE-Q no minimum stated, GRE-Analytical no minimum stated, overall undergraduate GPA no minimum stated, Masters GPA no minimum stated; *Experimental Psychology PhD (Doctor of Philosophy):* GRE-V no minimum stated, GRE-Q no minimum stated, GRE-Analytical no minimum stated, overall undergraduate GPA no minimum stated, Masters GPA no minimum stated; *Industrial/Organizational Psychology PhD (Doctor of Philosophy):* GRE-V no minimum stated, GRE-Q no minimum stated, GRE-Analytical no minimum stated, overall undergraduate GPA no minimum stated, psychology GPA no minimum stated, Masters GPA no minimum stated; *Community Psychology PhD (Doctor of Philosophy):* GRE-V no minimum stated, GRE-Q no minimum stated, GRE-Analytical no minimum stated, overall undergraduate GPA no minimum stated, Masters GPA no minimum stated; *General Psychology MA/MS (Master of Arts/Science):* GRE-V no minimum stated, GRE-Q no minimum stated, GRE-Analytical no minimum stated, overall undergraduate GPA no minimum stated, psychology GPA no minimum stated.

Other Criteria: (importance of criteria rated low, medium, or high): GRE scores—high, research experience—high, work experience—medium, extracurricular activity—medium, clinically related public service—medium, GPA—high, letters of recommendation—high, interview—high, statement of goals and objectives—high, specific undergraduate psychology courses taken—high, Clinically related public service is not applicable for the Community, Experimental, I/O, or General MS programs. Only the Clinical and Community programs require interviews. For additional information on admission requirements, go to http://www.depaul.edu/admission-and-aid/types-of-admission/graduate-student/Pages/psychology.aspx.

Student Characteristics: The following represents characteristics of students in 2012–2013 in all graduate psychology programs in the department: Female—full-time 83, part-time 0; Male—full-time 37, part-time 0; African American/Black—full-time 21, part-time 0; Hispanic/Latino(a)—full-time 11, part-time 0; Asian/Pacific Islander—full-time 10, part-time 0; American Indian/Alaska Native—full-time 1, part-time 0; Caucasian/White—full-time 73, part-time 0; Multi-ethnic—full-time 4, part-time 0; students subject to the Americans With Disabilities Act—full-time 0, part-time 0; Unknown ethnicity—full-time 0, part-time 0; International students who hold an F-1 or J-1 Visa—full-time 3, part-time 0.

Financial Information/Assistance:

Tuition for Full-Time Study: *Master's:* State residents: per academic year $22,680, $630 per credit hour; Nonstate residents: per academic year $22,680, $630 per credit hour. *Doctoral:* State residents: per academic year $22,680, $630 per credit hour; Nonstate residents: per academic year $22,680, $630 per credit hour. Tuition is subject to change. See the following website for updates and changes in tuition costs: http://www.depaul.edu/admission-and-aid/tuition/Pages/default.aspx.

Financial Assistance:

First-Year Students: Teaching assistantships available for first year. Average amount paid per academic year: $16,000. Average number of hours worked per week: 22. Research assistantships available for first year. Average amount paid per academic year: $16,000. Average number of hours worked per week: 22.

Advanced Students: Teaching assistantships available for advanced students. Average amount paid per academic year: $16,000. Average number of hours worked per week: 22. Research assistantships available for advanced students. Average amount paid per academic year: $16,000. Average number of hours worked per week: 22. Traineeships available for advanced students. Average amount paid per academic year: $16,000. Average number of hours worked per week: 22.

Additional Information: Of all students currently enrolled full time, 100% benefited from one or more of the listed financial assistance programs. Application and information available online at: http://www.depaul.edu/admission-and-aid/financial-aid/.

Internships/Practica: Doctoral Degree (PhD Clinical Psychology): For those doctoral students for whom a professional psychology internship was required in this program prior to graduation, (9) students applied for an internship in 2011–2012, with (8)

students obtaining an internship. Of those students who obtained an internship, (8) were paid internships. Of those students who obtained an internship, (8) students placed in APA/CPA accredited internships, (0) students placed in internships not APA/CPA accredited, but listed with the Association of Psychology Postdoctoral and Internship Programs (APPIC), (0) students placed in internships conforming to guidelines of the Council of Directors of School Psychology Programs (CDSPP), (0) students placed in internships that were not APA/CPA accredited, APPIC or CDSPP listed. All of our clinical students are required to take a practicum course every quarter in their second and third years. Though DePaul does not have an internship program, our students fulfill their internship requirement at top facilities in Chicago and across the nation.

Housing and Day Care: On-campus housing is available. See the following website for more information: http://housing.depaul.edu/. No on-campus day care facilities are available.

Employment of Department Graduates:

Master's Degree Graduates: Of those who graduated in the academic year 2011–2012, the following categories and numbers represent the postgraduate activities and employment of master's degree graduates: Enrolled in a postdoctoral residency/fellowship (n/a), employed in independent practice (n/a), do not know (1), total from the above (master's) (1).

Doctoral Degree Graduates: Of those who graduated in the academic year 2011–2012, the following categories and numbers represent the postgraduate activities and employment of doctoral degree graduates: Enrolled in a psychology doctoral program (n/a), enrolled in a postdoctoral residency/fellowship (3), employed in an academic position at a university (2), employed in an academic position at a 2-year/4-year college (1), do not know (3), total from the above (doctoral) (9).

Additional Information:

Orientation, Objectives, and Emphasis of Department: In addition to several common training experiences, the Clinical program has two areas of emphasis, or tracks: Community and Child. The Community track focuses on prevention, consultation, program development, empowerment, and health promotion, rather than traditional treatment. The Child track emphasizes training in developmental psychopathology, in the development of efficacious treatments for low income African-American and Latino families, and the delivery of services for youth living in urban settings, including schools and community mental health centers. Applicants select an area of emphasis and are admitted to one of the two tracks. The two areas of emphasis are complementary to one another. Most of the research and training conducted in the Community track is focused on children, adolescents, and families, and the training received in the Child track is informed by Community principles (e.g., prevention, empowerment, health promotion). The educational philosophy of the Department of Psychology is based upon a recognition of three components of modern psychology. The first of these is academic: the accumulated body of knowledge and theory relevant to the many areas of psychological study. The second is research: the methodologies and skills whereby the science of psychology is advanced. The third is application: the use of psychology for individuals and society. A major function of the graduate curriculum in psychology is to bring to the student an awareness of the real unity of psychological study and practice, despite apparent diversity. The student must come to appreciate the fact that psychology is both a pure science and an applied science, and that these aspects are not mutually exclusive. This educational philosophy underlies all programs within the department. Each seeks to incorporate the three interrelated components of psychology at the graduate and professional levels; hence each program contains an academic, a research, and an applied component. It is the emphasis given to each component that is distinctive for each of our graduate programs. Students are strongly encouraged to work with faculty in research and tutorial settings. Doctoral candidates are given opportunities to gain teaching experience. Many students work in applied or research settings in the metropolitan Chicago area so that they can apply their graduate education to practical settings. Our Experimental program has three tracks: Cognitive, Developmental, and Social Psychology. Students specialize in one of these areas, but are free to change areas during their graduate careers or to work with faculty in multiple areas.

Special Facilities or Resources: Extensive facilities are available to support the graduate programs and research projects. We have state-of-the-art classrooms and computer facilities. The university also has a new library, recreation center, athletic facility, and student center. The Family and Community Services (FCS) Center, which is located in the same building as the psychology department, serves approximately 150,000 people. Our clinical students gain their initial practicum experiences in the Family and Community Services (FCS) Center. In addition, the center serves as a venue for community and applied research. The university has prominent law and business colleges, which are well reputed in the Midwestern business community and provide work opportunities for our experimental and industrial/organizational students. The department maintains an active network of our PhD graduates to help in obtaining jobs. There are many educational opportunities in this area, including colloquia, lectures, and regional and national organizations and conferences. We have an active graduate student organization that maintains contact with graduate students from other universities, providing opportunities to share educational experiences and recreational activities.

Information for Students With Physical Disabilities: See the following website for more information: http://studentaffairs. depaul.edu/plus/index.asp.

Application Information:
Send to Office of Graduate Admissions, RE: Graduate Psychology Program, 2400 North Sheffield, Chicago, IL 60614-3504. Application available online. URL of online application: http://www.depaul.edu/ apply. Students are admitted in the Fall, application deadline December 1. Clinical Child and Clinical Community—December 1; Community—December 5; Industrial/Organizational—January 5; Experimental—February 1; General (MS)—May 1. *Fee:* $40. A student in need of financial aid may request a waiver of the application fee by submitting a personal letter requesting this consideration, a letter from the financial aid office of the institution attended outlining need, and official copies of financial aid transcripts. These materials must be sent with the other application materials.

Eastern Illinois University (2012 data)
Department of Psychology
College of Sciences
Charleston, IL 61920
Telephone: (217) 581-2127
Fax: (217) 581-6764
E-mail: *ahailemariam@eiu.edu; wallan@eiu.edu*
Web: *http://www.eiu.edu/~psych/*

Department Information:
1963. Chairperson: John Mace. Number of faculty: total—full-time 19; women—full-time 7; total—minority—full-time 4; women minority—full-time 3.

Programs and Degrees Offered:
Listed in the following order: Program area, degree type (T if terminal Master's), number awarded 7/11–6/12. Clinical Psychology MA/MS (Master of Arts/Science) (T) 12, School Psychology Other 8.

Student Applications/Admissions:
Student Applications
Clinical Psychology MA/MS (Master of Arts/Science)—Applications 2012–2013, 44. Total applicants accepted 2012–2013, 22. Number full-time enrolled (new admits only) 2012–2013, 11. Total enrolled 2012–2013 full-time, 22. Total enrolled 2012–2013 part-time, 1. Openings 2013–2014, 10. The median number of years required for completion of a degree in 2012–2013 were 2. The number of students enrolled full- and part-time who were dismissed or voluntarily withdrew from this program area in 2012–2013 were 0. *School Psychology Other*—Applications 2012–2013, 40. Total applicants accepted 2012–2013, 18. Number full-time enrolled (new admits only) 2012–2013, 8. Number part-time enrolled (new admits only) 2012–2013, 0. Total enrolled 2012–2013 full-time, 21. Total enrolled 2012–2013 part-time, 0. Openings 2013–2014, 12. The median number of years required for completion of a degree in 2012–2013 were 3. The number of students enrolled full- and part-time who were dismissed or voluntarily withdrew from this program area in 2012–2013 were 1.
Scores: Entries appear in this order: required test or GPA, minimum score (if required), median score of students entering in 2012–2013. *Clinical Psychology MA/MS (Master of Arts/ Science):* GRE-V no minimum stated, 540, GRE-Q no minimum stated, 600, overall undergraduate GPA 3.00, 3.52, last 2 years GPA no minimum stated, 3.5, psychology GPA 3.25, 3.61; *School Psychology Other:* GRE-V no minimum stated, 500, GRE-Q no minimum stated, 630, GRE-Analytical no minimum stated, 4.5, overall undergraduate GPA 3.25, 3.61, psychology GPA no minimum stated, 3.9.
Other Criteria: (importance of criteria rated low, medium, or high): GRE scores—high, research experience—medium, work experience—medium, extracurricular activity—medium, clinically related public service—medium, GPA—high, letters of recommendation—high, interview—low, statement of goals and objectives—high, undergraduate major in psychology—medium, specific undergraduate psychology courses taken—medium.

Student Characteristics: The following represents characteristics of students in 2012–2013 in all graduate psychology programs in the department: Female—full-time 30, part-time 1; Male—full-time 12, part-time 0; African American/Black—full-time 0, part-time 0; Hispanic/Latino(a)—full-time 2, part-time 0; Asian/Pacific Islander—full-time 3, part-time 0; American Indian/Alaska Native—full-time 0, part-time 0; Caucasian/White—full-time 37, part-time 1; Multi-ethnic—full-time 1, part-time 0; students subject to the Americans With Disabilities Act—full-time 0, part-time 0; Unknown ethnicity—full-time 0, part-time 0; International students who hold an F-1 or J-1 Visa—full-time 2, part-time 0.

Financial Information/Assistance:

Tuition for Full-Time Study: *Master's:* State residents: $239 per credit hour; Nonstate residents: $717 per credit hour. Additional fees are assessed to students beyond the costs of tuition for the following: assessment courses.

Financial Assistance:

First-Year Students: Research assistantships available for first year. Average amount paid per academic year: $7,740. Average number of hours worked per week: 18. Apply by February 15.

Advanced Students: Research assistantships available for advanced students. Average amount paid per academic year: $7,740. Average number of hours worked per week: 18. Apply by February 15.

Additional Information: Of all students currently enrolled full time, 90% benefited from one or more of the listed financial assistance programs. Application and information available online at: http://www.eiu.edu/~finaid/.

Internships/Practica: Master's Degree (MA/MS Clinical Psychology): An internship experience, such as a final research project or "capstone" experience is required of graduates. A summer practicum and two-semester clinical internship in the second year of graduate study are required for the Master of Arts degree. The practicum and internship include a weekly seminar emphasizing treatment planning, ethical practice and case management, and requires 700 hours total of supervised clinical practice in an approved community agency setting with regular on-campus clinical supervision coordinated with on-site supervision provided by an approved agency supervisor. During the two years of on-campus study required by the school psychology program, students participate in three practica. First-semester students complete a school-based practicum which is designed to orient them to the workings of the public education system. During the first semester of the second year students participate in an assessment practicum centered in the on-campus psychological assessment center. A field-based component of this practicum allows students to also complete assessment activities in a public school setting. During their last semester on campus students participate in a field-based practicum devoted to enhancing counseling and consultation skills.

Housing and Day Care: On-campus housing is available. See the following website for more information: http://www.eiu.edu/~housing/. No on-campus day care facilities are available.

Employment of Department Graduates:

Master's Degree Graduates: Of those who graduated in the academic year 2011–2012, the following categories and numbers represent the postgraduate activities and employment of master's degree graduates: Enrolled in a psychology doctoral program (3), enrolled in another graduate/professional program (1), enrolled in a postdoctoral residency/fellowship (n/a), employed in independent practice (n/a), employed in an academic position at a university (0), employed in an academic position at a 2-year/4-year college (0), employed in other positions at a higher education institution (0), employed in a professional position in a school system (8), employed in a community mental health/counseling center (7), employed in a hospital/medical center (0), still seeking employment (2), other employment position (2), total from the above (master's) (23).

Doctoral Degree Graduates: Of those who graduated in the academic year 2011–2012, the following categories and numbers represent the postgraduate activities and employment of doctoral degree graduates: Enrolled in a psychology doctoral program (n/a), total from the above (doctoral) (0).

Additional Information:

Orientation, Objectives, and Emphasis of Department: The Master of Arts degree in Clinical Psychology at Eastern Illinois University is designed to provide graduate training with a solid foundation in the science and practice of clinical psychology. The program is a terminal master's degree training experience, which is approved by the Council of Applied Master's Programs in Psychology. The emphases highlight training and instruction in psychological interventions and therapy, assessment, and research. EIU graduates in Clinical Psychology possess a combination of skills in assessment, data management and analysis that uniquely position them amongst other master's level practitioners when it comes to assisting mental health organizations to meet the increasing demands of accurate evaluation, current, state-of-the-art programming, timely treatment protocols and accountability. The clinical psychology program also provides solid preparation for further graduate study. The purpose of the school psychology program is to prepare students to deliver high quality services to students, parents, and professional personnel in public school settings. The program offers a generalist curriculum designed to allow students to develop the flexibility to practice in varied settings. Particular emphasis is placed on assessment, consultation, behavior management, and counseling. The importance of applied experiences is stressed.

Special Facilities or Resources: The Department of Psychology has a computer/statistics lab, as well as faculty directed research labs, one currently in use as a setting for an NIH grant. Training facilities include a three room suite used as a Psychology Assessment Center with one-way-mirror viewing for testing and interviews and video taping facilities. A further Clinical/Observation research suite, with video and one-way mirror equipment is available for clinical training and supervised community services. Both applied programs enjoy viable cooperative agreements with a number of area educational, correctional and mental health agencies which serve as training and practicum sites for graduate clinical experiences in addition to the internship sites.

Information for Students With Physical Disabilities: See the following website for more information: http://www.eiu.edu/~disablty/.

Application Information:
Send to Psychology Department, Eastern Illinois University, Charleston, IL 61920. Application available online. URL of online application: http://castle.eiu.edu/psych. Students are admitted in the Fall, application deadline February 15. *Fee:* $30.

Illinois Institute of Technology
College of Psychology
3105 South Dearborn, LS-252
Chicago, IL 60616
Telephone: (312) 567-3500
Fax: (312) 567-3493
E-mail: *morriss@iit.edu*
Web: *http://www.iit.edu/psych/*

Department Information:
1929. Chairperson: Scott B. Morris. Number of faculty: total—full-time 21, part-time 12; women—full-time 10, part-time 6; total—minority—full-time 3, part-time 2; women minority—full-time 2, part-time 2; faculty subject to the Americans With Disabilities Act 7.

Programs and Degrees Offered:
Listed in the following order: Program area, degree type (T if terminal Master's), number awarded 7/11–6/12. Clinical Psychology PhD (Doctor of Philosophy) 13, Industrial/Organizational Psychology PhD (Doctor of Philosophy) 0, Personnel and Human Resources Development MA/MS (Master of Arts/Science) (T) 13, Rehabilitation PhD (Doctor of Philosophy) 0, Rehabilitation Counseling MA/MS (Master of Arts/Science) (T) 12.

APA Accreditation: Clinical PhD (Doctor of Philosophy). Student Outcome Data Website: http://www.iit.edu/psych/admission/graduate/clinical/admissions_internship_acceptance_tables.shtml.

Student Applications/Admissions:
Student Applications
Clinical Psychology PhD (Doctor of Philosophy)—Applications 2012–2013, 136. Total applicants accepted 2012–2013, 25. Number full-time enrolled (new admits only) 2012–2013, 13. Number part-time enrolled (new admits only) 2012–2013, 0. Total enrolled 2012–2013 full-time, 92. Total enrolled 2012–2013 part-time, 0. Openings 2013–2014, 13. The median number of years required for completion of a degree in 2012–2013 were 7. The number of students enrolled full- and part-time who were dismissed or voluntarily withdrew from this program area in 2012–2013 were 0. *Industrial/Organizational Psychology PhD (Doctor of Philosophy)*—Applications 2012–2013, 70. Total applicants accepted 2012–2013, 26. Number full-time enrolled (new admits only) 2012–2013, 9. Number part-time enrolled (new admits only) 2012–2013, 0. Total enrolled 2012–2013 full-time, 68. Total enrolled 2012–2013 part-time, 0. Openings 2013–2014, 9. The median number of years required for completion of a degree in 2012–2013 were 10. The number of students enrolled full- and part-time who were

dismissed or voluntarily withdrew from this program area in 2012–2013 were 2. *Personnel and Human Resources Development MA/MS (Master of Arts/Science)*—Applications 2012–2013, 58. Total applicants accepted 2012–2013, 29. Number full-time enrolled (new admits only) 2012–2013, 8. Number part-time enrolled (new admits only) 2012–2013, 0. Total enrolled 2012–2013 full-time, 12. Total enrolled 2012–2013 part-time, 0. Openings 2013–2014, 10. The number of students enrolled full- and part-time who were dismissed or voluntarily withdrew from this program area in 2012–2013 were 2. *Rehabilitation PhD (Doctor of Philosophy)*—Applications 2012–2013, 2. Total applicants accepted 2012–2013, 0. Number full-time enrolled (new admits only) 2012–2013, 0. Number part-time enrolled (new admits only) 2012–2013, 0. Total enrolled 2012–2013 full-time, 4. Total enrolled 2012–2013 part-time, 0. Openings 2013–2014, 1. The number of students enrolled full- and part-time who were dismissed or voluntarily withdrew from this program area in 2012–2013 were 0. *Rehabilitation Counseling MA/MS (Master of Arts/Science)*—Applications 2012–2013, 36. Total applicants accepted 2012–2013, 12. Number full-time enrolled (new admits only) 2012–2013, 12. Number part-time enrolled (new admits only) 2012–2013, 0. Total enrolled 2012–2013 full-time, 40. Total enrolled 2012–2013 part-time, 0. Openings 2013–2014, 15. The median number of years required for completion of a degree in 2012–2013 were 2. The number of students enrolled full- and part-time who were dismissed or voluntarily withdrew from this program area in 2012–2013 were 0.

Scores: Entries appear in this order: required test or GPA, minimum score (if required), median score of students entering in 2012–2013. *Clinical Psychology PhD (Doctor of Philosophy):* GRE-V 152, GRE-Q 152, GRE-Analytical no minimum stated, overall undergraduate GPA 3.46; *Industrial/Organizational Psychology PhD (Doctor of Philosophy):* GRE-V 152, GRE-Q 152, overall undergraduate GPA 3.2; *Personnel and Human Resources Development MA/MS (Master of Arts/Science):* GRE-V no minimum stated, GRE-Q no minimum stated, GRE-Analytical no minimum stated, overall undergraduate GPA no minimum stated; *Rehabilitation PhD (Doctor of Philosophy):* GRE-V no minimum stated, GRE-Q no minimum stated.

Other Criteria: (importance of criteria rated low, medium, or high): GRE scores—high, research experience—high, work experience—high, extracurricular activity—low, clinically related public service—medium, GPA—high, letters of recommendation—high, interview—high, statement of goals and objectives—high, GPA and GRE are less important for MS programs; MS in rehabilitation does not require the GRE. For additional information on admission requirements, go to http://www.iit.edu/psych/admission/graduate/.

Student Characteristics: The following represents characteristics of students in 2012–2013 in all graduate psychology programs in the department: Female—full-time 166, part-time 0; Male—full-time 65, part-time 0; African American/Black—full-time 5, part-time 0; Hispanic/Latino(a)—full-time 9, part-time 0; Asian/Pacific Islander—full-time 26, part-time 0; American Indian/Alaska Native—full-time 0, part-time 0; Caucasian/White—full-time 115, part-time 0; Multi-ethnic—full-time 0, part-time 0; students subject to the Americans With Disabilities Act—full-time 7, part-

time 0; Unknown ethnicity—full-time 76, part-time 0; International students who hold an F-1 or J-1 Visa—full-time 15, part-time 0.

Financial Information/Assistance:

Tuition for Full-Time Study: *Master's:* State residents: $1,204 per credit hour; Nonstate residents: $1,204 per credit hour. *Doctoral:* State residents: $1,204 per credit hour; Nonstate residents: $1,204 per credit hour. Tuition is subject to change. Tuition costs vary by program. See the following website for updates and changes in tuition costs: http://www.iit.edu/psych/admission/graduate/deadlines_and_costs.shtml. Higher tuition cost for this program: Clinical Psychology program charges $36,480/year.

Financial Assistance:

First-Year Students: Teaching assistantships available for first year. Average amount paid per academic year: $0. Average number of hours worked per week: 0. Research assistantships available for first year. Average amount paid per academic year: $0. Average number of hours worked per week: 0. Traineeships available for first year. Average amount paid per academic year: $0. Average number of hours worked per week: 0. Fellowships and scholarships available for first year. Average amount paid per academic year: $0. Average number of hours worked per week: 0.

Advanced Students: Teaching assistantships available for advanced students. Average amount paid per academic year: $5,000. Average number of hours worked per week: 10. Research assistantships available for advanced students. Average amount paid per academic year: $2,250. Average number of hours worked per week: 10. Traineeships available for advanced students. Average amount paid per academic year: $615. Average number of hours worked per week: 0. Fellowships and scholarships available for advanced students. Average amount paid per academic year: $0. Average number of hours worked per week: 0.

Additional Information: Of all students currently enrolled full time, 55% benefited from one or more of the listed financial assistance programs. Application and information available online at: http://www.iit.edu/psych/admission/graduate/financial_aid.shtml.

Internships/Practica: Doctoral Degree (PhD Clinical Psychology): For those doctoral students for whom a professional psychology internship was required in this program prior to graduation, (15) students applied for an internship in 2011–2012, with (13) students obtaining an internship. Of those students who obtained an internship, (13) were paid internships. Of those students who obtained an internship, (13) students placed in APA/CPA accredited internships, (0) students placed in internships not APA/CPA accredited, but listed with the Association of Psychology Postdoctoral and Internship Programs (APPIC), (0) students placed in internships conforming to guidelines of the Council of Directors of School Psychology Programs (CDSPP), (0) students placed in internships that were not APA/CPA accredited, APPIC or CDSPP listed. Master's Degree (MA/MS Personnel and Human Resources Development): An internship experience, such as a final research project or "capstone" experience is required of graduates. Master's Degree (MA/MS Rehabilitation Counseling): An internship experience, such as a final research project or "capstone" experience is required of graduates. All students are required to complete fieldwork internships and practica. Experiences vary by program. As one of the largest cities in the United States, Chicago provides access to diverse practicum and internship sites.

Housing and Day Care: On-campus housing is available. See the following website for more information: http://www.iit.edu/housing/. No on-campus day care facilities are available.

Employment of Department Graduates:

Master's Degree Graduates: Of those who graduated in the academic year 2011–2012, the following categories and numbers represent the postgraduate activities and employment of master's degree graduates: Enrolled in a postdoctoral residency/fellowship (n/a), employed in independent practice (n/a), total from the above (master's) (0).

Doctoral Degree Graduates: Of those who graduated in the academic year 2011–2012, the following categories and numbers represent the postgraduate activities and employment of doctoral degree graduates: Enrolled in a psychology doctoral program (n/a), total from the above (doctoral) (0).

Additional Information:

Orientation, Objectives, and Emphasis of Department: The primary emphasis in the Department is on a scientist–practitioner model of training. Our APA-approved clinical psychology program offers intensive clinical and research training with an emphasis on a cognitive theoretical framework, community involvement, and exposure to under-served populations. The MS in rehabilitation counseling prepares students to function as rehabilitation counselors for disabled persons. The PhD program in rehabilitation psychology prepares students for careers in rehabilitation education, research, and the practice of rehabilitation psychology. Our industrial/organizational program provides a solid scientific background as well as knowledge and expertise in personnel selection, evaluation, training and development, motivation, and organizational behavior.

Special Facilities or Resources: Facilities include laboratories for human behavior studies, psychophysiological research, infant and maternal attachment, and a testing and interviewing laboratory with attached one-way viewing rooms. Equipment includes programming equipment for learning studies, specialized computer facilities, and videotaping and other audiovisual equipment. There are graduate student offices, a testing library of assessment equipment, and a student lounge. The Disabilities Resource Center is housed within psychology. The department offers professional consulting services through the Center for Research and Service.

Information for Students With Physical Disabilities: See the following website for more information: http://www.iit.edu/cdr/.

Application Information:

Send to Department of Psychology, Attention: Admissions, Illinois Institute of Technology, 3105 South Dearborn, Suite 252, Chicago, IL 60616-3793. Application available online. URL of online application: http://www.iit.edu/psych/admission/graduate/apply.shtml. Students are admitted in the Fall, application deadline January 15. Clinical deadline is January 15, I/O and PHRD deadline is February 15, Rehabilitation deadline is March 15. *Fee:* $55.

Illinois School of Professional Psychology at Argosy University, Chicago

Clinical Psychology
225 North Michigan, Suite 1300
Chicago, IL 60601
Telephone: (312) 777-7600
Fax: (312) 777-7625
E-mail: aslobig@argosy.edu
Web: http://www.argosy.edu/isppchicago

Department Information:

1976. Dean of the Clinical Psychology Programs: Annemarie Slobig. Number of faculty: total—full-time 24, part-time 4; women—full-time 12, part-time 1; total—minority—full-time 6; women minority—full-time 2.

Programs and Degrees Offered:

Listed in the following order: Program area, degree type (T if terminal Master's), number awarded 7/11–6/12. Clinical Psychology PsyD (Doctor of Psychology) 67.

APA Accreditation: Clinical PsyD (Doctor of Psychology). Student Outcome Data Website: http://www.argosy.edu/clinical-psychology/chicago-illinois/psyd-programs-doctorate-degree-56812.aspx.

Student Applications/Admissions:

Student Applications

Clinical Psychology PsyD (Doctor of Psychology)—Applications 2012–2013, 194. Total applicants accepted 2012–2013, 40. Number full-time enrolled (new admits only) 2012–2013, 21. Number part-time enrolled (new admits only) 2012–2013, 0. Total enrolled 2012–2013 full-time, 321. Total enrolled 2012–2013 part-time, 16. Openings 2013–2014, 26. The median number of years required for completion of a degree in 2012–2013 were 5. The number of students enrolled full- and part-time who were dismissed or voluntarily withdrew from this program area in 2012–2013 were 9.

Scores: Entries appear in this order: required test or GPA, minimum score (if required), median score of students entering in 2012–2013. *Clinical Psychology PsyD (Doctor of Psychology):* GRE-V no minimum stated, GRE-Q no minimum stated, overall undergraduate GPA 3.25, Masters GPA 3.5.

Other Criteria: (importance of criteria rated low, medium, or high): GRE scores—low, research experience—medium, work experience—high, extracurricular activity—medium, clinically related public service—high, GPA—high, letters of recommendation—high, interview—high, statement of goals and objectives—high, undergraduate major in psychology—low, specific undergraduate psychology courses taken—low. For additional information on admission requirements, go to http://www.argosy.edu/clinical-psychology/chicago-illinois/psyd-programs-admissions-56843.aspx.

Student Characteristics: The following represents characteristics of students in 2012–2013 in all graduate psychology programs in the department: Female—full-time 245, part-time 14; Male—full-time 76, part-time 2; African American/Black—full-time 49, part-time 2; Hispanic/Latino(a)—full-time 21, part-time 2; Asian/Pacific Islander—full-time 21, part-time 1; American Indian/Alaska Native—full-time 1, part-time 0; Caucasian/White—full-time 212, part-time 9; Multi-ethnic—full-time 7, part-time 1; students subject to the Americans With Disabilities Act—full-time 11, part-time 0; Unknown ethnicity—full-time 10, part-time 1; International students who hold an F-1 or J-1 Visa—full-time 6, part-time 0.

Financial Information/Assistance:

Tuition for Full-Time Study: *Doctoral:* State residents: per academic year $22,775, $1,162 per credit hour; Nonstate residents: per academic year $22,775, $1,162 per credit hour. Tuition is subject to change. Additional fees are assessed to students beyond the costs of tuition for the following: testing kit fee, technology fee. See the following website for updates and changes in tuition costs: http://www.argosy.edu/admissions/Default.aspx.

Financial Assistance:

First-Year Students: Teaching assistantships available for first year. Average amount paid per academic year: $3,300. Average number of hours worked per week: 5. Apply by September 14. Fellowships and scholarships available for first year. Average amount paid per academic year: $27,000. Average number of hours worked per week: 0. Apply by January 15.

Advanced Students: Teaching assistantships available for advanced students. Average amount paid per academic year: $3,300. Average number of hours worked per week: 5. Apply by September 14. Fellowships and scholarships available for advanced students. Average amount paid per academic year: $5,000. Average number of hours worked per week: 10. Apply by April 24.

Additional Information: Of all students currently enrolled full time, 7% benefited from one or more of the listed financial assistance programs. Application and information available online at: www.argosy.edu.

Internships/Practica: Doctoral Degree (PsyD Clinical Psychology): For those doctoral students for whom a professional psychology internship was required in this program prior to graduation, (66) students applied for an internship in 2011–2012, with (58) students obtaining an internship. Of those students who obtained an internship, (54) were paid internships. Of those students who obtained an internship, (22) students placed in APA/CPA accredited internships, (28) students placed in internships not APA/CPA accredited, but listed with the Association of Psychology Postdoctoral and Internship Programs (APPIC), (0) students placed in internships conforming to guidelines of the Council of Directors of School Psychology Programs (CDSPP), (8) students placed in internships that were not APA/CPA accredited, APPIC or CDSPP listed. Master's Degree (PsyD Clinical Psychology): An internship experience, such as a final research project or "capstone" experience is required of graduates. The School approves and monitors over 200 practicum sites and assists students in locating and applying for internships across the country and in Canada. Both practicum and internship sites offer a wide range of training populations and approaches to students in the programs.

Housing and Day Care: No on-campus housing is available. No on-campus day care facilities are available.

Employment of Department Graduates:

Master's Degree Graduates: Of those who graduated in the academic year 2011–2012, the following categories and numbers represent the postgraduate activities and employment of master's

degree graduates: Enrolled in a postdoctoral residency/fellowship (n/a), employed in independent practice (n/a), total from the above (master's) (0).

Doctoral Degree Graduates: Of those who graduated in the academic year 2011–2012, the following categories and numbers represent the postgraduate activities and employment of doctoral degree graduates: Enrolled in a psychology doctoral program (n/a), enrolled in a postdoctoral residency/fellowship (27), employed in independent practice (8), employed in an academic position at a university (1), employed in a professional position in a school system (1), employed in a community mental health/counseling center (9), employed in a hospital/medical center (3), still seeking employment (1), not seeking employment (1), total from the above (doctoral) (51).

Additional Information:
Orientation, Objectives, and Emphasis of Department: The Illinois School of Professional Psychology at Argosy University, Chicago prepares students for contemporary practice through a clinically focused curriculum, taught by practitioner-scholar faculty, with a strong commitment to quality teaching and supervision. The current curricula have been structured to provide students with the fundamental knowledge and skills in psychological assessment and psychotherapy necessary to work with a wide range of traditional clinical populations. In addition, the required curricula include courses and perspectives designed to prepare students for emerging populations from diverse backgrounds and contemporary practice approaches now addressed by clinical psychology. PsyD students may satisfy basic requirements that address the learning of fundamental knowledge and competencies in intervention, assessment, population diversity, and professional practice areas through elective clusters that also provide choices that may conform to their individualized professional goals. As part of the commitment to providing both general and concentrated education and training for doctoral students, the PsyD program offers nine minors, or optional areas of elective choices for students wishing to focus their predoctoral studies in particular areas.

Special Facilities or Resources: The Illinois School of Professional Psychology at Argosy University, Chicago offers predoctoral minors which support students' interests in the following areas: Child/Adolescent Psychology, Health Psychology, Family Psychology, Forensic Psychology, Psychoanalytic Psychology, Client-Centered and Experiential Psychology, Diversity and Multicultural Psychology, Cognitive Behavioral Therapy and Neuropsychology. The Psychological Services Center on campus offers clinical psychology students the opportunity to train in our in-house assessment and therapy clinic. The Center is also the hub or our APPIC-approved internship consortium, which provides captive internship training opportunities for ISPP students in a number of clinical settings in the Chicagoland area. The School has over 200 practicum sites available for student training in agencies, schools, clinics, hospitals, and practice organizations. The program has a rich tradition of experiential learning through its personal and professional development course including a first year off-campus retreat in Lake Geneva, Wisconsin. Each year students have opportunities to study abroad by taking classes offered in an intensive format for 10-14 days in a foreign country.

Application Information:
Send to Admissions Department, Argosy University, Chicago Campus, 225 North Michigan, Suite 1300, Chicago, IL 60601. Application available online. URL of online application: https://portal.argosy.edu/Applicant/ApplyOnline_Login.aspx. Students are admitted in the Fall, application deadline January 15. *Fee:* $50.

Illinois School of Professional Psychology at Argosy University, Schaumburg
Clinical Psychology
Psychology and Behavioral Sciences
999 North Plaza Drive, Suite 111
Schaumburg, IL 60173
Telephone: (847) 969-4900
Fax: (847) 969-4999
E-mail: *jwasner@argosy.edu*
Web: *http://www.argosy.edu*

Department Information:
1994. Dean, ISPP and Chair, Clinical Psychology: Jim Wasner, PhD Number of faculty: total—full-time 18, part-time 12; women—full-time 10, part-time 7; total—minority—full-time 3; women minority—full-time 3; faculty subject to the Americans With Disabilities Act 1.

Programs and Degrees Offered:
Listed in the following order: Program area, degree type (T if terminal Master's), number awarded 7/11–6/12. Clinical Psychology MA/MS (Master of Arts/Science) (T) 14, Clinical Psychology PsyD (Doctor of Psychology) 29.

APA Accreditation: Clinical PsyD (Doctor of Psychology). Student Outcome Data Website: http://www.argosy.edu/clinical-psychology/schaumburg-illinois/psyd-programs-doctorate-degree-79712.aspx.

Student Applications/Admissions:
Student Applications
Clinical Psychology MA/MS (Master of Arts/Science)—Applications 2012–2013, 36. Total applicants accepted 2012–2013, 12. Number full-time enrolled (new admits only) 2012–2013, 10. Number part-time enrolled (new admits only) 2012–2013, 0. Total enrolled 2012–2013 full-time, 26. Total enrolled 2012–2013 part-time, 4. Openings 2013–2014, 10. The median number of years required for completion of a degree in 2012–2013 were 2. The number of students enrolled full- and part-time who were dismissed or voluntarily withdrew from this program area in 2012–2013 were 1. *Clinical Psychology PsyD (Doctor of Psychology)*—Applications 2012–2013, 66. Total applicants accepted 2012–2013, 26. Number full-time enrolled (new admits only) 2012–2013, 20. Number part-time enrolled (new admits only) 2012–2013, 0. Total enrolled 2012–2013 full-time, 166. Total enrolled 2012–2013 part-time, 28. Openings 2013–2014, 30. The median number of years required for completion of a degree in 2012–2013 were 5. The number of students enrolled full- and part-time who were dismissed or voluntarily withdrew from this program area in 2012–2013 were 2.
Scores: Entries appear in this order: required test or GPA, minimum score (if required), median score of students entering in 2012–2013. *Clinical Psychology PsyD (Doctor of Psychology):* GRE-V no minimum stated, GRE-Q no minimum stated.

Other Criteria: (importance of criteria rated low, medium, or high): GRE scores—medium, research experience—medium, work experience—medium, extracurricular activity—low, clinically related public service—medium, GPA—high, letters of recommendation—high, interview—high, statement of goals and objectives—high, undergraduate major in psychology—medium, specific undergraduate psychology courses taken—high. For additional information on admission requirements, go to http://www.argosy.edu/clinical-psychology/schaumburg-illinois/psyd-programs-admissions-79743.aspx.

Student Characteristics: The following represents characteristics of students in 2012–2013 in all graduate psychology programs in the department: Female—full-time 157, part-time 27; Male—full-time 35, part-time 5; African American/Black—full-time 13, part-time 6; Hispanic/Latino(a)—full-time 10, part-time 1; Asian/Pacific Islander—full-time 11, part-time 1; American Indian/Alaska Native—full-time 0, part-time 0; Caucasian/White—full-time 148, part-time 24; Multi-ethnic—full-time 3, part-time 0; students subject to the Americans With Disabilities Act—full-time 12, part-time 0; Unknown ethnicity—full-time 7, part-time 0; International students who hold an F-1 or J-1 Visa—full-time 3, part-time 0.

Financial Information/Assistance:

Tuition for Full-Time Study: *Master's:* State residents: per academic year $29,050, $1,162 per credit hour; Nonstate residents: per academic year $29,050, $1,162 per credit hour. *Doctoral:* State residents: per academic year $28,469, $1,162 per credit hour; Nonstate residents: per academic year $28,469, $1,162 per credit hour. Tuition is subject to change. See the following website for updates and changes in tuition costs: http://www.argosy.edu/admissions/Default.aspx.

Financial Assistance:

First-Year Students: Teaching assistantships available for first year. Average amount paid per academic year: $2,500. Average number of hours worked per week: 5. Fellowships and scholarships available for first year. Average amount paid per academic year: $6,000.

Advanced Students: Teaching assistantships available for advanced students. Average amount paid per academic year: $2,500. Average number of hours worked per week: 5. Fellowships and scholarships available for advanced students. Average amount paid per academic year: $3,000.

Additional Information: Of all students currently enrolled full time, 18% benefited from one or more of the listed financial assistance programs. Application and information available online at: http://www.argosy.edu/financial-aid/Default.aspx.

Internships/Practica: Doctoral Degree (PsyD Clinical Psychology): For those doctoral students for whom a professional psychology internship was required in this program prior to graduation, (36) students applied for an internship in 2011–2012, with (32) students obtaining an internship. Of those students who obtained an internship, (31) were paid internships. Of those students who obtained an internship, (7) students placed in APA/CPA accredited internships, (23) students placed in internships not APA/CPA accredited, but listed with the Association of Psychology Postdoctoral and Internship Programs (APPIC), (0) students placed in internships conforming to guidelines of the Council of Directors of School Psychology Programs (CDSPP), (2) students placed in internships that were not APA/CPA accredited, APPIC or CDSPP listed. Clinical field training is a required component of all programs at the Illinois School of Professional Psychology at Argosy University, Schaumburg, and is a direct outgrowth of the practitioner emphasis of professional psychology. The school provides advisement and assistance in placing students in a wide variety of clinical sites, including hospitals, schools, mental health facilities, treatment centers, and non-profit and social service agencies. The MA in clinical psychology requires a minimum of 750 hours of practicum experience. The PsyD program includes two years of basic practicum experience, including separate practica for diagnosis and assessment, and psychotherapy, with a minimum of 800 hours per year; there is an additional year of advanced practicum (minimum 600 hours). Clinical field training culminates with a final one-year, full-time clinical predoctoral internship. In addition to nationwide internship opportunities, our program has developed its own internship consortium, the Northwest Suburban Internship Consortium (NSIC), which is exclusively for our students.

Housing and Day Care: No on-campus housing is available. No on-campus day care facilities are available.

Employment of Department Graduates:

Master's Degree Graduates: Of those who graduated in the academic year 2011–2012, the following categories and numbers represent the postgraduate activities and employment of master's degree graduates: Enrolled in a psychology doctoral program (4), enrolled in a postdoctoral residency/fellowship (n/a), employed in independent practice (n/a), employed in government agency (1), employed in a community mental health/counseling center (3), employed in a hospital/medical center (2), other employment position (1), do not know (3), total from the above (master's) (14).

Doctoral Degree Graduates: Of those who graduated in the academic year 2011–2012, the following categories and numbers represent the postgraduate activities and employment of doctoral degree graduates: Enrolled in a psychology doctoral program (n/a), enrolled in a postdoctoral residency/fellowship (23), employed in independent practice (3), employed in government agency (1), employed in a community mental health/counseling center (1), not seeking employment (1), total from the above (doctoral) (29).

Additional Information:

Orientation, Objectives, and Emphasis of Department: The primary purpose of the Clinical Psychology program of the Illinois School of Professional Psychology at Argosy University, Schaumburg is to educate and train students in the major aspects of clinical practice and prepare students for careers as practitioners. To ensure that students are prepared adequately, the curriculum integrates theory, training, research, and practice in preparing students to work with a wide range of populations in need of psychological services. Faculty are both scholars and practitioners and guide students through coursework and field experiences so that they might learn the work involved in professional psychology and understand how formal knowledge and practice operate to inform and enrich each other. The emphasis of the school is a scholar/practitioner orientation, with faculty skilled in all major theories of assessment and intervention. Working closely with faculty, students are provided with exposure to a variety of diagnostic and therapeutic approaches. Sensitivity to diverse populations, populations with specific needs, and multicultural issues are important components of all programs. The program also has emphasis areas and concentrations in neuropsychology (listed in APA Div. 40), forensic psychology, neuropsychology, clinical health psychology and child and family psychology.

Special Facilities or Resources: The Illinois School of Professional Psychology at Argosy University, Schaumburg has core faculty with extensive experience and training in the following areas: neuropsychology, forensic psychology, clinical health and rehabilitation psychology, substance abuse and addictive disorders, clinical hypnosis, multiculturalism and diversity issues, including sexual orientation and gender issues, severe psychopathology, sleep disorders, eating disorders and self-injury, multiple models of psychotherapy including (child and family therapy, cognitive behavioral therapy, group therapy, client-centered and experiential therapies, emotion focused therapy and psychodynamic therapies.) Faculty members actively encourage student involvement in research projects as a means of fostering mentoring relationships. The program also has recently offered the PsyD Scholar Fellowship for selective and exceptional students which pay 25% of the tuition for the entire program. The program also offers full reimbursement of the cost of EPPP licensing preparation by AATBS for all graduating students.

Application Information:
Send to Tina Boing, Senior Director of Admissions, 999 North Plaza Drive, Suite 111, Schaumburg, Illinois 60173. Application available online. URL of online application: https://portal.argosy.edu/Applicant/ApplyOnline_Login.aspx. Students are admitted in the Fall, application deadline May 15; Spring, application deadline November 15; Programs have rolling admissions. Deadlines may be extended dependent upon space availability. *Fee:* $50.

Illinois State University
Department of Psychology
College of Arts and Sciences
Campus Box 4620
Normal, IL 61790-4620
Telephone: (309) 438-8701
Fax: (309) 438-5789
E-mail: *psygrad@ilstu.edu*
Web: *http://psychology.illinoisstate.edu/grad/index.shtml*

Department Information:
1966. Chairperson: J. Scott Jordan, PhD. Number of faculty: total—full-time 34, part-time 6; women—full-time 13, part-time 4; total—minority—full-time 3; women minority—full-time 1; faculty subject to the Americans With Disabilities Act 1.

Programs and Degrees Offered:
Listed in the following order: Program area, degree type (T if terminal Master's), number awarded 7/11–6/12. Clinical-Counseling Psychology MA/MS (Master of Arts/Science) (T) 12, Developmental Psychology MA/MS (Master of Arts/Science) (T) 0, Cognitive & Behavioral Sciences MA/MS (Master of Arts/Science) (T) 5, School Psychology PhD (Doctor of Philosophy) 6, Quantitative Psychology MA/MS (Master of Arts/Science) (T) 2, Industrial/Organizational-Social Psychology MA/MS (Master of Arts/Science) (T) 2, Specialist in School Psychology Other 8.

APA Accreditation: School PhD (Doctor of Philosophy). Student Outcome Data Website: http://psychology.illinoisstate.edu/school/docdata.shtml.

Student Applications/Admissions:
Student Applications
Clinical-Counseling Psychology MA/MS (*Master of Arts/Science*)—Applications 2012–2013, 81. Total applicants accepted 2012–2013, 18. Number full-time enrolled (new admits only) 2012–2013, 12. Number part-time enrolled (new admits only) 2012–2013, 0. Total enrolled 2012–2013 full-time, 24. Total enrolled 2012–2013 part-time, 6. Openings 2013–2014, 13. The median number of years required for completion of a degree in 2012–2013 were 3. The number of students enrolled full- and part-time who were dismissed or voluntarily withdrew from this program area in 2012–2013 were 0. *Developmental Psychology MA/MS (Master of Arts/Science)*—Applications 2012–2013, 15. Total applicants accepted 2012–2013, 4. Number full-time enrolled (new admits only) 2012–2013, 0. Number part-time enrolled (new admits only) 2012–2013, 1. Total enrolled 2012–2013 full-time, 4. Total enrolled 2012–2013 part-time, 4. Openings 2013–2014, 3. The number of students enrolled full- and part-time who were dismissed or voluntarily withdrew from this program area in 2012–2013 were 0. *Cognitive & Behavioral Sciences MA/MS (Master of Arts/Science)*—Applications 2012–2013, 8. Total applicants accepted 2012–2013, 8. Number full-time enrolled (new admits only) 2012–2013, 3. Number part-time enrolled (new admits only) 2012–2013, 1. Total enrolled 2012–2013 full-time, 5. Total enrolled 2012–2013 part-time, 6. Openings 2013–2014, 5. The median number of years required for completion of a degree in 2012–2013 were 3. The number of students enrolled full- and part-time who were dismissed or voluntarily withdrew from this program area in 2012–2013 were 0. *School Psychology PhD (Doctor of Philosophy)*—Applications 2012–2013, 15. Total applicants accepted 2012–2013, 8. Number full-time enrolled (new admits only) 2012–2013, 5. Number part-time enrolled (new admits only) 2012–2013, 0. Total enrolled 2012–2013 full-time, 23. Total enrolled 2012–2013 part-time, 13. Openings 2013–2014, 7. The median number of years required for completion of a degree in 2012–2013 were 7. The number of students enrolled full- and part-time who were dismissed or voluntarily withdrew from this program area in 2012–2013 were 0. *Quantitative Psychology MA/MS (Master of Arts/Science)*—Applications 2012–2013, 12. Total applicants accepted 2012–2013, 2. Number full-time enrolled (new admits only) 2012–2013, 1. Number part-time enrolled (new admits only) 2012–2013, 0. Total enrolled 2012–2013 full-time, 3. Total enrolled 2012–2013 part-time, 4. Openings 2013–2014, 4. The median number of years required for completion of a degree in 2012–2013 were 4. The number of students enrolled full- and part-time who were dismissed or voluntarily withdrew from this program area in 2012–2013 were 0. *Industrial/Organizational-Social Psychology MA/MS (Master of Arts/Science)*—Applications 2012–2013, 30. Total applicants accepted 2012–2013, 17. Number full-time enrolled (new admits only) 2012–2013, 4. Number part-time enrolled (new admits only) 2012–2013, 0. Total enrolled 2012–2013 full-time, 9. Total enrolled 2012–2013 part-time, 14. Openings 2013–2014, 5. The median number of years required for completion of a degree in 2012–2013 were 3. The number of students enrolled full- and part-time who were dismissed or voluntarily withdrew from this

program area in 2012–2013 were 4. *Specialist in School Psychology Other*—Applications 2012–2013, 51. Total applicants accepted 2012–2013, 8. Number full-time enrolled (new admits only) 2012–2013, 7. Number part-time enrolled (new admits only) 2012–2013, 0. Total enrolled 2012–2013 full-time, 12. Total enrolled 2012–2013 part-time, 5. Openings 2013–2014, 5. The median number of years required for completion of a degree in 2012–2013 were 4. The number of students enrolled full- and part-time who were dismissed or voluntarily withdrew from this program area in 2012–2013 were 0.

Scores: Entries appear in this order: required test or GPA, minimum score (if required), median score of students entering in 2012–2013. *Clinical-Counseling Psychology MA/MS (Master of Arts/Science)*: GRE-V no minimum stated, 155, GRE-Q no minimum stated, 150, GRE-Analytical no minimum stated, 4.25, overall undergraduate GPA no minimum stated, 3.74, last 2 years GPA 3.0, 3.93, psychology GPA no minimum stated, 3.76; *Developmental Psychology MA/MS (Master of Arts/Science)*: GRE-V no minimum stated, GRE-Q no minimum stated, GRE-Analytical no minimum stated, overall undergraduate GPA no minimum stated, last 2 years GPA 3.0, psychology GPA no minimum stated; *Cognitive & Behavioral Sciences MA/MS (Master of Arts/Science)*: GRE-V no minimum stated, 154, GRE-Q no minimum stated, 152, GRE-Analytical no minimum stated, 4.13, overall undergraduate GPA no minimum stated, 3.57, last 2 years GPA 3.0, 3.59, psychology GPA no minimum stated, 3.57; *School Psychology PhD (Doctor of Philosophy)*: GRE-V no minimum stated, 153, GRE-Q no minimum stated, 148, GRE-Analytical no minimum stated, 4.50, overall undergraduate GPA no minimum stated, 3.76, last 2 years GPA 3.0, 3.83, psychology GPA no minimum stated, 3.83; *Quantitative Psychology MA/MS (Master of Arts/Science)*: GRE-V no minimum stated, GRE-Q no minimum stated, GRE-Analytical no minimum stated, overall undergraduate GPA no minimum stated, last 2 years GPA 3.0, psychology GPA no minimum stated; *Industrial/Organizational-Social Psychology MA/MS (Master of Arts/Science)*: GRE-V no minimum stated, 160, GRE-Q no minimum stated, 161, GRE-Analytical no minimum stated, 4.50, overall undergraduate GPA no minimum stated, 3.38, last 2 years GPA 3.0, 3.56, psychology GPA no minimum stated, 3.61; *Specialist in School Psychology Other*: GRE-V no minimum stated, 154, GRE-Q no minimum stated, 152, GRE-Analytical no minimum stated, 4.43, overall undergraduate GPA no minimum stated, 3.84, last 2 years GPA 3.0, 3.92, psychology GPA no minimum stated, 3.33.

Other Criteria: (importance of criteria rated low, medium, or high): GRE scores—high, research experience—high, work experience—medium, extracurricular activity—medium, clinically related public service—medium, GPA—high, letters of recommendation—high, interview—high, statement of goals and objectives—medium, undergraduate major in psychology—medium, specific undergraduate psychology courses taken—medium, On-campus interview required for doctoral program in school psychology applicants. Interview by invitation in person (preferred) or by phone for master's program applicants. An interview is not offered for specialist program in school psychology applicants. The Clinical-Counseling Psychology Program identifies clinically-related public service as a high criteria for admission. For additional information on admission requirements, go to http://psychology.illinoisstate.edu/grad/application/index.shtml.

Student Characteristics: The following represents characteristics of students in 2012–2013 in all graduate psychology programs in the department: Female—full-time 58, part-time 33; Male—full-time 22, part-time 19; African American/Black—full-time 3, part-time 2; Hispanic/Latino(a)—full-time 4, part-time 0; Asian/Pacific Islander—full-time 2, part-time 2; American Indian/Alaska Native—full-time 1, part-time 0; Caucasian/White—full-time 66, part-time 47; Multi-ethnic—full-time 4, part-time 0; students subject to the Americans With Disabilities Act—full-time 0, part-time 0; Unknown ethnicity—full-time 0, part-time 1; International students who hold an F-1 or J-1 Visa—full-time 0, part-time 0.

Financial Information/Assistance:

Tuition for Full-Time Study: *Master's:* State residents: per academic year $7,392, $308 per credit hour; Nonstate residents: per academic year $15,336, $639 per credit hour. *Doctoral:* State residents: per academic year $7,392, $308 per credit hour; Nonstate residents: per academic year $15,336, $639 per credit hour. Tuition is subject to change. Additional fees are assessed to students beyond the costs of tuition for the following: general fees; student insurance (may be waived with proof of other coverage). See the following website for updates and changes in tuition costs: http://studentaccounts.illinoisstate.edu/tuition/graduate.shtml.

Financial Assistance:

First-Year Students: Teaching assistantships available for first year. Average amount paid per academic year: $3,825. Average number of hours worked per week: 10. Research assistantships available for first year. Average amount paid per academic year: $3,825. Average number of hours worked per week: 10. Traineeships available for first year. Average amount paid per academic year: $5,067. Average number of hours worked per week: 10. Fellowships and scholarships available for first year. Average amount paid per academic year: $4,100. Average number of hours worked per week: 0.

Advanced Students: Teaching assistantships available for advanced students. Average amount paid per academic year: $5,625. Average number of hours worked per week: 10. Research assistantships available for advanced students. Average amount paid per academic year: $5,625. Average number of hours worked per week: 10. Traineeships available for advanced students. Average amount paid per academic year: $6,756. Average number of hours worked per week: 10.

Additional Information: Of all students currently enrolled full time, 94% benefited from one or more of the listed financial assistance programs. Application and information available online at: http://psychology.illinoisstate.edu/grad/financial.shtml.

Internships/Practica: Doctoral Degree (PhD School Psychology): For those doctoral students for whom a professional psychology internship was required in this program prior to graduation, (7) students applied for an internship in 2011–2012, with (7) students obtaining an internship. Of those students who obtained an internship, (6) were paid internships. Of those students who obtained an internship, (6) students placed in APA/CPA accredited internships, (0) students placed in internships not APA/CPA accredited, but listed with the Association of Psychology Postdoctoral and Internship Programs (APPIC), (1) students placed in internships conforming to guidelines of the Council of Directors of School Psychology Programs (CDSPP), (0) students placed in internships that were not APA/CPA accredited, APPIC or

CDSPP listed. Master's Degree (MA/MS Clinical-Counseling Psychology): An internship experience, such as a final research project or "capstone" experience is required of graduates. Master's Degree (MA/MS Developmental Psychology): An internship experience, such as a final research project or "capstone" experience is required of graduates. Master's Degree (MA/MS Cognitive & Behavioral Sciences): An internship experience, such as a final research project or "capstone" experience is required of graduates. Master's Degree (MA/MS Quantitative Psychology): An internship experience, such as a final research project or "capstone" experience is required of graduates. Master's Degree (MA/MS Industrial/Organizational-Social Psychology): An internship experience, such as a final research project or "capstone" experience is required of graduates. Students in the clinical-counseling psychology master's degree program complete a one-year paid practicum that provides an extensive supervised experience at mental health agencies in the surrounding communities. Students in the school psychology specialist and doctoral degree programs participate during their first year in supervised practica in public and private schools in the local community, Head Start centers, and at the University's Psychological Services Center. Full-time one-year paid professional practice internships are required for students in the specialist and doctoral programs in school psychology.

Housing and Day Care: On-campus housing is available. See the following website for more information: http://www.housing.ilstu. edu/. On-campus day care facilities are available. See the following website for more information: http://childcarecenter.illinoisstate. edu/.

Employment of Department Graduates:
Master's Degree Graduates: Of those who graduated in the academic year 2011–2012, the following categories and numbers represent the postgraduate activities and employment of master's degree graduates: Enrolled in a psychology doctoral program (7), enrolled in a postdoctoral residency/fellowship (n/a), employed in independent practice (n/a), employed in an academic position at a university (1), employed in a professional position in a school system (7), employed in business or industry (3), employed in government agency (1), employed in a community mental health/counseling center (7), employed in a hospital/medical center (1), not seeking employment (1), do not know (1), total from the above (master's) (29).
Doctoral Degree Graduates: Of those who graduated in the academic year 2011–2012, the following categories and numbers represent the postgraduate activities and employment of doctoral degree graduates: Enrolled in a psychology doctoral program (n/a), enrolled in another graduate/professional program (1), employed in independent practice (2), employed in other positions at a higher education institution (3), total from the above (doctoral) (6).

Additional Information:
Orientation, Objectives, and Emphasis of Department: The department provides training in professional areas supplemented by options in cognitive and behavioral sciences, clinical-counseling, developmental, industrial/organizational-social, quantitative, and school psychology. Training in these professional areas takes advantage of the teaching and career experience of the department faculty in human service settings, schools, and industry so that instruction is both practical and theoretical. Graduate study includes a master's thesis or clinical competency project, an applied research apprenticeship for the specialist program in school psychology, or a doctoral dissertation. The doctoral program in school psychology also requires a comprehensive examination.

Special Facilities or Resources: The department has a dedicated computer lab and, human subject and animal laboratories. The department sponsors the Psychological Services Center (PSC) where graduate clinicians and faculty supervisors provide assessment and work closely with referred children, adolescents, and their families from the community and college-age students. PSC services are provided at the Center, at a home, or at a local school. For the clinical-counseling psychology program, several local community agencies (hospitals, mental health centers, rehabilitation centers, etc.) provide a full-year practicum, where students receive practical experience and training by professionals in the field. A school psychology program faculty member manages and graduate trainees staff The Autism Place, an affiliate of The Autism Program of Illinois, which is a network of resources for Autism Spectrum Disorders and an infrastructure of provider networks to help Illinois families.

Information for Students With Physical Disabilities: See the following website for more information: http://disabilityconcerns. illinoisstate.edu/.

Application Information:
Send to Illinois State University, Department of Psychology, Graduate Programs Office, Campus Box 4620, Normal, IL 61790-4620. Application available online. URL of online application: http://admissions. illinoisstate.edu/apply/. Students are admitted in the Fall, application deadline November 15. Application deadline for the doctoral program in school psychology is November 15, for the specialist program in school psychology is December 1, for all of the master's programs is December 15. *Fee:* $40. Fee waiver based on documented financial need, veteran service (active duty for one year or more), McNair, Project 1000, and Fulbright Scholarship applicants.

Illinois, University of, Chicago
Department of Educational Psychology
Education (MC 147)
1040 West Harrison Street
Chicago, IL 60607-7133
Telephone: (312) 996-5580
Fax: (312) 996-5651
E-mail: missv@uic.edu
Web: http://education.uic.edu/academics/departments/418-department-of-educational-psychology

---

Department Information:
2008. Chairperson: Kimberly Lawless. Number of faculty: total—full-time 10, part-time 2; women—full-time 7, part-time 2; total—minority—full-time 4; women minority—full-time 3.

Programs and Degrees Offered:

Listed in the following order: Program area, degree type (T if terminal Master's), number awarded 7/11–6/12. Educational Psychology PhD (Doctor of Philosophy) 3, Measurement, Evaluation, Statistics, & Assm't MEd (Education) 9, Youth Development MEd (Education) 17.

Student Applications/Admissions:

Student Applications

Educational Psychology PhD (Doctor of Philosophy)—Applications 2012–2013, 16. Total applicants accepted 2012–2013, 11. Number full-time enrolled (new admits only) 2012–2013, 3. Number part-time enrolled (new admits only) 2012–2013, 2. Total enrolled 2012–2013 full-time, 11. Total enrolled 2012–2013 part-time, 27. Openings 2013–2014, 7. The median number of years required for completion of a degree in 2012–2013 were 6. The number of students enrolled full- and part-time who were dismissed or voluntarily withdrew from this program area in 2012–2013 were 0. *Measurement, Evaluation, Statistics, & Assm't MEd (Education)*—Applications 2012–2013, 10. Total applicants accepted 2012–2013, 9. Number full-time enrolled (new admits only) 2012–2013, 1. Number part-time enrolled (new admits only) 2012–2013, 5. Total enrolled 2012–2013 full-time, 5. Total enrolled 2012–2013 part-time, 24. Openings 2013–2014, 14. The median number of years required for completion of a degree in 2012–2013 were 2. The number of students enrolled full- and part-time who were dismissed or voluntarily withdrew from this program area in 2012–2013 were 0. *Youth Development MEd (Education)*—Applications 2012–2013, 34. Total applicants accepted 2012–2013, 17. Number full-time enrolled (new admits only) 2012–2013, 0. Number part-time enrolled (new admits only) 2012–2013, 14. Total enrolled 2012–2013 full-time, 3. Total enrolled 2012–2013 part-time, 27. Openings 2013–2014, 18. The median number of years required for completion of a degree in 2012–2013 were 2. The number of students enrolled full- and part-time who were dismissed or voluntarily withdrew from this program area in 2012–2013 were 0.

Scores: Entries appear in this order: required test or GPA, minimum score (if required), median score of students entering in 2012–2013. *Educational Psychology PhD (Doctor of Philosophy):* GRE-V 150, 156, GRE-Q 150, 160, overall undergraduate GPA 3.00, 3.6, Masters GPA 3.00, 3.8; *Measurement, Evaluation, Statistics, & Assm't MEd (Education):* GRE-V 150, 153, GRE-Q 150, 160, overall undergraduate GPA 3.00, 3.5; *Youth Development MEd (Education):* overall undergraduate GPA 3.0, 3.5.

Other Criteria: (importance of criteria rated low, medium, or high): GRE scores—medium, research experience—medium, work experience—low, extracurricular activity—medium, clinically related public service—medium, GPA—medium, letters of recommendation—medium, statement of goals and objectives—high, match w/ college mission—high, undergraduate major in psychology—low, specific undergraduate psychology courses taken—low, For students seeking enrollment in the MESA concentration for the PhD Program and the MESA MEd programs, more emphasis is placed on GRE scores and research experience. Students applying to the MESA concentration for the PhD program are expected to have earned a Master's degree in one or more of the relevant areas. For students seeking admission to the MEd in Youth Development, no GRE or other test scores are required. Instead, students must demonstrate more direct involvement in youth development activities. For additional information on admission requirements, go to http://education.uic.edu/prospective-students/admissions-graduate-programs.

Student Characteristics: The following represents characteristics of students in 2012–2013 in all graduate psychology programs in the department: Female—full-time 15, part-time 54; Male—full-time 4, part-time 24; African American/Black—full-time 5, part-time 21; Hispanic/Latino(a)—full-time 1, part-time 10; Asian/Pacific Islander—full-time 3, part-time 7; American Indian/Alaska Native—full-time 0, part-time 0; Caucasian/White—full-time 10, part-time 36; Multi-ethnic—full-time 0, part-time 2; students subject to the Americans With Disabilities Act—full-time 0, part-time 0; Unknown ethnicity—full-time 0, part-time 2; International students who hold an F-1 or J-1 Visa—full-time 1, part-time 0.

Financial Information/Assistance:

Tuition for Full-Time Study: *Master's:* State residents: per academic year $10,882; Nonstate residents: per academic year $22,880. *Doctoral:* State residents: per academic year $10,882; Nonstate residents: per academic year $22,880. Tuition is subject to change. Additional fees are assessed to students beyond the costs of tuition for the following: $1,853.00 for services and academic facilities maintenance. See the following website for updates and changes in tuition costs: http://www.uic.edu/depts/oar/grad/tuition_grad.html.

Financial Assistance:

First-Year Students: Teaching assistantships available for first year. Average amount paid per academic year: $14,525. Average number of hours worked per week: 10. Research assistantships available for first year. Average amount paid per academic year: $29,050. Average number of hours worked per week: 20. Fellowships and scholarships available for first year. Average amount paid per academic year: $49,733.

Advanced Students: Teaching assistantships available for advanced students. Average amount paid per academic year: $14,525. Average number of hours worked per week: 10. Research assistantships available for advanced students. Average amount paid per academic year: $29,050. Average number of hours worked per week: 20. Fellowships and scholarships available for advanced students. Average amount paid per academic year: $49,733.

Additional Information: Of all students currently enrolled full time, 10% benefited from one or more of the listed financial assistance programs. Application and information available online at: http://education.uic.edu/prospective-students/financial-aid.

Internships/Practica: Our students in the Youth Development MEd program complete 6 hours of fieldwork that is negotiated with their program advisor and enroll in courses designed to help them maximize the benefits of those experiences.

Housing and Day Care: On-campus housing is available. See the following website for more information: http://www.housing.uic.edu/. On-campus day care facilities are available. See the following website for more information: http://www.uic.edu/depts/children/.

Employment of Department Graduates:

Master's Degree Graduates: Of those who graduated in the academic year 2011–2012, the following categories and numbers represent the postgraduate activities and employment of master's degree graduates: Enrolled in a postdoctoral residency/fellowship (n/a), employed in independent practice (n/a), total from the above (master's) (0).

Doctoral Degree Graduates: Of those who graduated in the academic year 2011–2012, the following categories and numbers represent the postgraduate activities and employment of doctoral degree graduates: Enrolled in a psychology doctoral program (n/a), enrolled in a postdoctoral residency/fellowship (1), employed in other positions at a higher education institution (2), employed in a professional position in a school system (1), total from the above (doctoral) (4).

Additional Information:

Orientation, Objectives, and Emphasis of Department: The Department of Educational Psychology is internationally known for its rigorous degree programs, esteemed faculty, and commitment to urban education and test fairness. Our work focuses on understanding how children's ethnicity, culture, class, and gender impact their development and learning, and we are dedicated to developing and applying fair approaches of measurement, statistics, and evaluation to support such efforts. Our research is guided by our commitment to understand what it means to be both a teacher and a learner in an urban context such as Chicago. We research how children's homes, schools, and communities, along with media, contribute to students' learning in various collaborative instructional and play activities. We seek to understand how children construct notions of morality, fairness, and gender, and how they develop resilience in the face of enduring economic difficulties. As part of this endeavor, we seek to contribute to basic scientific understanding of cognition and cognitive development. We strive to advance knowledge in research methodology to address our research questions in a fair manner.

Special Facilities or Resources: UIC is a Research Intensive university and has all the resources that allow for that designation. Our department also has a laboratory that allows faculty and students to obtain measurement, evaluation, statistical, and assessment consulting services as these are used in research.

Information for Students With Physical Disabilities: See the following website for more information: http://www.uic.edu/depts/oaa/disability_resources/index.html.

Application Information:

Application available online. URL of online application: http://education.uic.edu/prospective-students/apply. Students are admitted in the Fall, application deadline January 1; Spring, application deadline October 1. Deadline of March 15 for Fall admission to Youth Development and MESA programs. October 1 for Spring admission to the MESA face-to-face program and May 15 for Fall admission to the MESA online program. *Fee:* $60.

Illinois, University of, Chicago
Department of Psychology (M/C 285)
Liberal Arts and Sciences
1007 West Harrison Street
Chicago, IL 60607-7137
Telephone: (312) 996-2434
Fax: (312) 413-4122
E-mail: *pschinfo@uic.edu*
Web: *http://home.psch.uic.edu/*

Department Information:

1965. Interim Head: Michael Ragozzino. Number of faculty: total—full-time 31, part-time 19; women—full-time 15, part-time 10; total—minority—full-time 5, part-time 3; women minority—full-time 5, part-time 1.

Programs and Degrees Offered:

Listed in the following order: Program area, degree type (T if terminal Master's), number awarded 7/11–6/12. Social and Personality Psychology PhD (Doctor of Philosophy) 1, Behavioral Neuroscience PhD (Doctor of Philosophy) 1, Clinical Psychology PhD (Doctor of Philosophy) 5, Cognitive Psychology PhD (Doctor of Philosophy) 1, Community and Prevention Research PhD (Doctor of Philosophy) 4.

APA Accreditation: Clinical PhD (Doctor of Philosophy). Student Outcome Data Website: http://portal.psch.uic.edu/Clinical/characteristics.aspx.

Student Applications/Admissions:

Student Applications

Social and Personality Psychology PhD (Doctor of Philosophy)— Applications 2012–2013, 78. Total applicants accepted 2012–2013, 4. Number full-time enrolled (new admits only) 2012–2013, 2. Total enrolled 2012–2013 full-time, 12. Openings 2013–2014, 3. The median number of years required for completion of a degree in 2012–2013 were 6. The number of students enrolled full- and part-time who were dismissed or voluntarily withdrew from this program area in 2012–2013 were 0. *Behavioral Neuroscience PhD (Doctor of Philosophy)*— Applications 2012–2013, 25. Total applicants accepted 2012–2013, 1. Number full-time enrolled (new admits only) 2012–2013, 1. Number part-time enrolled (new admits only) 2012–2013, 0. Total enrolled 2012–2013 full-time, 10. Total enrolled 2012–2013 part-time, 0. Openings 2013–2014, 2. The median number of years required for completion of a degree in 2012–2013 were 11. The number of students enrolled full- and part-time who were dismissed or voluntarily withdrew from this program area in 2012–2013 were 0. *Clinical Psychology PhD (Doctor of Philosophy)*—Applications 2012–2013, 452. Total applicants accepted 2012–2013, 9. Number full-time enrolled (new admits only) 2012–2013, 5. Total enrolled 2012–2013 full-time, 41. Openings 2013–2014, 5. The median number of years required for completion of a degree in 2012–2013 were 7. The number of students enrolled full- and part-time who were dismissed or voluntarily withdrew from this program area in 2012–2013 were 0. *Cognitive Psychology PhD (Doctor of Philosophy)*—Applications 2012–2013, 43. Total applicants accepted 2012–2013, 2. Number full-time enrolled (new admits only) 2012–2013, 1. Total enrolled 2012–2013 full-time, 19. Openings 2013–2014, 4. The median number of years required for completion of a degree in 2012–2013 were 7. The number of students enrolled full- and part-time who were dismissed or voluntarily withdrew from this program area in 2012–2013 were 3. *Community and Prevention Research PhD (Doctor of Philosophy)*—Applications 2012–2013, 43. Total applicants accepted 2012–2013, 5. Number full-time enrolled (new admits only) 2012–2013, 3. Total enrolled 2012–2013 full-time, 25. Openings 2013–2014, 3. The median number of years required for completion of a degree in 2012–2013 were 8. The number of students enrolled full- and part-time who were dismissed or voluntarily withdrew from this program area in 2012–2013 were 0.

Scores: Entries appear in this order: required test or GPA, minimum score (if required), median score of students entering in 2012–2013. *Social and Personality Psychology PhD (Doctor of Philosophy)*: GRE-V no minimum stated, 157, GRE-Q no minimum stated, 159, GRE-Analytical no minimum stated, 4.0, last 2 years GPA 3.2; *Behavioral Neuroscience PhD (Doctor of Philosophy)*: GRE-V no minimum stated, 157, GRE-Q no minimum stated, 153, GRE-Analytical no minimum stated, 5.5, last 2 years GPA 3.2; *Clinical Psychology PhD (Doctor of Philosophy)*: GRE-V no minimum stated, 610, GRE-Q no minimum stated, 730, GRE-Analytical no minimum stated, 5, last 2 years GPA 3.2; *Cognitive Psychology PhD (Doctor of Philosophy)*: GRE-V no minimum stated, 700, GRE-Q no minimum stated, 600, GRE-Analytical no minimum stated, 4.5, last 2 years GPA 3.2; *Community and Prevention Research PhD (Doctor of Philosophy)*: GRE-V no minimum stated, 159, GRE-Q no minimum stated, 155, GRE-Analytical no minimum stated, 5, last 2 years GPA 3.2.

Other Criteria: (importance of criteria rated low, medium, or high): GRE scores—medium, research experience—high, work experience—medium, extracurricular activity—medium, clinically related public service—low, GPA—high, letters of recommendation—high, interview—high, statement of goals and objectives—high, fit with faculty research—high, undergraduate major in psychology—medium, specific undergraduate psychology courses taken—medium. For additional information on admission requirements, go to http://portal.psch.uic.edu/Prospective/application.aspx.

Student Characteristics: The following represents characteristics of students in 2012–2013 in all graduate psychology programs in the department: Female—full-time 71, part-time 0; Male—full-time 36, part-time 0; African American/Black—full-time 10, part-time 0; Hispanic/Latino(a)—full-time 6, part-time 0; Asian/Pacific Islander—full-time 7, part-time 0; American Indian/Alaska Native—full-time 0, part-time 0; Caucasian/White—full-time 83, part-time 0; Multi-ethnic—full-time 0, part-time 0; students subject to the Americans With Disabilities Act—full-time 0, part-time 0; Unknown ethnicity—full-time 1, part-time 0; International students who hold an F-1 or J-1 Visa—full-time 4, part-time 0.

Financial Information/Assistance:

Tuition for Full-Time Study: *Doctoral:* State residents: per academic year $11,066; Nonstate residents: per academic year

$23,064. Tuition is subject to change. See the following website for updates and changes in tuition costs: http://www.uic.edu/depts/oar/grad/tuition_grad.html.

Financial Assistance:

First-Year Students: Teaching assistantships available for first year. Average amount paid per academic year: $14,708. Average number of hours worked per week: 20. Apply by December 15. Research assistantships available for first year. Average amount paid per academic year: $14,708. Average number of hours worked per week: 20. Apply by December 15. Fellowships and scholarships available for first year. Average amount paid per academic year: $20,600. Average number of hours worked per week: 0. Apply by December 15.

Advanced Students: Teaching assistantships available for advanced students. Average amount paid per academic year: $14,708. Average number of hours worked per week: 20. Research assistantships available for advanced students. Average amount paid per academic year: $14,708. Average number of hours worked per week: 20. Fellowships and scholarships available for advanced students. Average amount paid per academic year: $25,000. Average number of hours worked per week: 0.

Additional Information: Of all students currently enrolled full time, 100% benefited from one or more of the listed financial assistance programs.

Internships/Practica: Doctoral Degree (PhD Clinical Psychology): For those doctoral students for whom a professional psychology internship was required in this program prior to graduation, (6) students applied for an internship in 2011–2012, with (6) students obtaining an internship. Of those students who obtained an internship, (6) were paid internships. Of those students who obtained an internship, (6) students placed in APA/CPA accredited internships, (0) students placed in internships not APA/CPA accredited, but listed with the Association of Psychology Postdoctoral and Internship Programs (APPIC), (0) students placed in internships conforming to guidelines of the Council of Directors of School Psychology Programs (CDSPP), (0) students placed in internships that were not APA/CPA accredited, APPIC or CDSPP listed. Access to a wide variety of practicum and research sites is available to advanced students. These include the UIC Counseling Service, Cook County Hospital, Rush-Presbyterian-St. Luke's Medical Center, the Institute for Juvenile Research, the Institute on Disabilities and Human Development, several Veterans Administration hospitals and mental health clinics, schools, and diverse community agencies throughout the Chicago area, in addition to our own Office of Applied Psychology.

Housing and Day Care: On-campus housing is available. See the following website for more information: http://www.housing.uic.edu/. On-campus day care facilities are available. See the following website for more information: http://www.uic.edu/depts/children/.

Employment of Department Graduates:

Master's Degree Graduates: Of those who graduated in the academic year 2011–2012, the following categories and numbers represent the postgraduate activities and employment of master's

degree graduates: Enrolled in a postdoctoral residency/fellowship (n/a), employed in independent practice (n/a), total from the above (master's) (0).

Doctoral Degree Graduates: Of those who graduated in the academic year 2011–2012, the following categories and numbers represent the postgraduate activities and employment of doctoral degree graduates: Enrolled in a psychology doctoral program (n/a), enrolled in a postdoctoral residency/fellowship (9), employed in an academic position at a university (4), employed in an academic position at a 2-year/4-year college (1), total from the above (doctoral) (14).

Additional Information:

Orientation, Objectives, and Emphasis of Department: The goal of the psychology department's doctoral program is to educate scholars and researchers who will contribute to the growth of psychological knowledge, whether they work in academic, applied, or policy settings. Within the framework of satisfying the requirements of a major division and a minor, the department encourages students in consultation with their advisors to construct programs individually tailored to their research interests. The psychology department has more than 30 faculty and over 100 graduate students. It has 5 major divisions: behavioral neuroscience, clinical, cognitive, community and prevention research, and social and personality. It has a psychology and law minor, a statistics, methods and measurement minor and an interdepartmental specialization in neuroscience. We have close collaborations with the Institute for Juvenile Research, the Institute for Disabilities and Human Development, the School of Public Health, the Center for Urban Educational Research and Development, the Center for the Study of Learning, Instruction and Teacher Development, the Center for Literacy, and the Institute of Government and Public Affairs. These partnerships provide students and faculty with an interest in interdisciplinary research an opportunity to work with scholars from diverse fields.

Special Facilities or Resources: The department is located in the Behavioral Sciences Building, a fully equipped facility designed to serve the needs of the behavioral and social sciences. Physical facilities include seminar rooms, animal laboratories, human research labs, clinical observation rooms with one-way observational windows and video-recording and biofeedback equipment, a well-equipped electronics and mechanics shop with an on-staff engineer, a department library, the Office of Applied Psychological Services which coordinates clinical and community interventions, the Office of Social Science Research which provides research support, and faculty-student lounge. The Department maintains its own computer lab, in which personal computer workstations connected to a mainframe and standalone PCs (MS-DOS based and Macintosh) are offered for student use. The department also offers wireless internet access.

Information for Students With Physical Disabilities: See the following website for more information: http://www.uic.edu/depts/oaa/disability_resources/.

Application Information:

Application available online. URL of online application: http://www.uic.edu/depts/oar/grad/apply_grad.html. Students are admitted in the Fall, application deadline December 15. *Fee:* $60. McNair application fee waivers.

Illinois, University of, Urbana–Champaign
Department of Educational Psychology
College of Education
210 Education Building
1310 South Sixth Street
Champaign, IL 61820
Telephone: (217) 333-2245
Fax: (217) 244-7620
E-mail: *edpsy@illinois.edu*
Web: *http://education.illinois.edu/edpsy/*

Department Information:

1962. Chairperson: Jose P. Mestre. Number of faculty: total—full-time 18, part-time 2; women—full-time 7, part-time 2; total—minority—full-time 4, part-time 1; women minority—full-time 1, part-time 1; faculty subject to the Americans With Disabilities Act 1.

Programs and Degrees Offered:

Listed in the following order: Program area, degree type (T if terminal Master's), number awarded 7/11–6/12. Counseling Psychology PhD (Doctor of Philosophy) 2, Child Development PhD (Doctor of Philosophy) 2, Measurement and Evaluation (Queries) PhD (Doctor of Philosophy) 3, Cognitive Science Of Teaching and Learning (Cstl) PhD (Doctor of Philosophy) 7, Evidence Based Decision Making MEd (Education) 0.

APA Accreditation: Counseling PhD (Doctor of Philosophy). Student Outcome Data Website: http://education.illinois.edu/edpsy/areasofstudy/counseling/counselingstatistics.

Student Applications/Admissions:

Student Applications

Counseling Psychology PhD (Doctor of Philosophy)—Applications 2012–2013, 83. Total applicants accepted 2012–2013, 4. Number full-time enrolled (new admits only) 2012–2013, 4. Number part-time enrolled (new admits only) 2012–2013, 0. Total enrolled 2012–2013 full-time, 17. Total enrolled 2012–2013 part-time, 0. Openings 2013–2014, 4. The median number of years required for completion of a degree in 2012–2013 were 7. The number of students enrolled full- and part-time who were dismissed or voluntarily withdrew from this program area in 2012–2013 were 0. *Child Development PhD (Doctor of Philosophy)*—Applications 2012–2013, 14. Total applicants accepted 2012–2013, 1. Number full-time enrolled (new admits only) 2012–2013, 0. Number part-time enrolled (new admits only) 2012–2013, 0. Total enrolled 2012–2013 full-time, 11. Total enrolled 2012–2013 part-time, 0. Openings 2013–2014, 2. The median number of years required for completion of a degree in 2012–2013 were 7. The number of students enrolled full- and part-time who were dismissed or voluntarily withdrew from this program area in 2012–2013 were 0. *Measurement and Evaluation (Queries) PhD (Doctor of Philosophy)*—Applications 2012–2013, 26. Total applicants accepted 2012–2013, 7. Number full-time enrolled (new admits only) 2012–2013, 3. Number part-time enrolled (new admits only) 2012–2013, 0. Total enrolled 2012–2013 full-time, 23. Total enrolled 2012–2013 part-time, 0. Openings 2013–2014, 6. The median number of years required for completion of a degree in 2012–2013 were 9. The number of students enrolled full- and part-time who were dismissed or voluntarily withdrew from this program area in 2012–2013 were 0. *Cognitive Science Of Teaching and Learning (Cstl) PhD (Doctor of Philosophy)*—Applications 2012–2013, 14. Total applicants accepted 2012–2013, 5. Number full-time enrolled (new admits only) 2012–2013, 3. Number part-time enrolled (new admits only) 2012–2013, 0. Total enrolled 2012–2013 full-time, 23. Total enrolled 2012–2013 part-time, 0. Openings 2013–2014, 4. The median number of years required for completion of a degree in 2012–2013 were 6. The number of students enrolled full- and part-time who were dismissed or voluntarily withdrew from this program area in 2012–2013 were 0. *Evidence Based Decision Making MEd (Education)*—Applications 2012–2013, 0. Total applicants accepted 2012–2013, 0. Number part-time enrolled (new admits only) 2012–2013, 0. Openings 2013–2014, 25. The number of students enrolled full- and part-time who were dismissed or voluntarily withdrew from this program area in 2012–2013 were 0.

Scores: Entries appear in this order: required test or GPA, minimum score (if required), median score of students entering in 2012–2013. *Counseling Psychology PhD (Doctor of Philosophy):* GRE-V 540, 690, GRE-Q 600, 700, last 2 years GPA 3.44, 3.57, Masters GPA 3.57, 3.76; *Child Development PhD (Doctor of Philosophy):* GRE-V 390, 575, GRE-Q 560, 715, last 2 years GPA 3.2, 3.84, Masters GPA 4, 4; *Measurement and Evaluation (Queries) PhD (Doctor of Philosophy):* GRE-V 330, 455, GRE-Q 590, 695, last 2 years GPA 3.3, 3.58, Masters GPA 3.6, 3.7; *Cognitive Science of Teaching and Learning (CSTL) PhD (Doctor of Philosophy):* GRE-V 470, 560, GRE-Q 400, 765, last 2 years GPA 3.52, 3.6, Masters GPA 3.96, 3.98; *Evidence Based Decision Making MEd (Education):* last 2 years GPA no minimum stated.

Other Criteria: (importance of criteria rated low, medium, or high): GRE scores—medium, research experience—high, work experience—medium, extracurricular activity—low, clinically related public service—medium, GPA—medium, letters of recommendation—high, interview—low, statement of goals and objectives—high, research interests—high, undergraduate major in psychology—medium, specific undergraduate psychology courses taken—medium, GRE scores and research experience are not required or evaluated for EBDM applicants. For additional information on admission requirements, go to http://education.illinois.edu/edpsy/howtoapply.html.

Student Characteristics: The following represents characteristics of students in 2012–2013 in all graduate psychology programs in the department: Female—full-time 56, part-time 0; Male—full-time 18, part-time 0; African American/Black—full-time 7, part-time 0; Hispanic/Latino(a)—full-time 9, part-time 0; Asian/Pacific Islander—full-time 30, part-time 0; American Indian/Alaska Native—full-time 0, part-time 0; Caucasian/White—full-time 26, part-time 0; Multi-ethnic—full-time 0, part-time 0; students subject to the Americans With Disabilities Act—full-time 0, part-time 0; Unknown ethnicity—full-time 2, part-time 0; International students who hold an F-1 or J-1 Visa—full-time 33, part-time 0.

Financial Information/Assistance:

Tuition for Full-Time Study: *Doctoral:* State residents: per academic year $11,626; Nonstate residents: per academic year $25,118. Tuition is subject to change. See the following website for updates and changes in tuition costs: http://registrar.illinois.edu/financial/tuition.html.

Financial Assistance:

First-Year Students: Teaching assistantships available for first year. Average amount paid per academic year: $15,415. Average number of hours worked per week: 20. Research assistantships available for first year. Average amount paid per academic year: $15,415. Average number of hours worked per week: 20. Traineeships available for first year. Fellowships and scholarships available for first year.

Advanced Students: Teaching assistantships available for advanced students. Average amount paid per academic year: $15,415. Average number of hours worked per week: 20. Research assistantships available for advanced students. Average amount paid per academic year: $15,415. Average number of hours worked per week: 20. Traineeships available for advanced students. Fellowships and scholarships available for advanced students.

Additional Information: Of all students currently enrolled full time, 90% benefited from one or more of the listed financial assistance programs. Application and information available online at: http://education.illinois.edu/edpsy/financialaid.

Internships/Practica: Doctoral Degree (PhD Counseling Psychology): For those doctoral students for whom a professional psychology internship was required in this program prior to graduation, (5) students applied for an internship in 2011–2012, with (4) students obtaining an internship. Of those students who obtained an internship, (4) were paid internships. Of those students who obtained an internship, (4) students placed in APA/CPA accredited internships, (0) students placed in internships not APA/CPA accredited, but listed with the Association of Psychology Postdoctoral and Internship Programs (APPIC), (0) students placed in internships conforming to guidelines of the Council of Directors of School Psychology Programs (CDSPP), (0) students placed in internships that were not APA/CPA accredited, APPIC or CDSPP listed. The Counseling Psychology Division offers a variety of practica in University and community settings. Within the university, students work in agencies such as the Counseling Center, Career Center, McKinley Health Center, and the Disability Resources and Education Services Center at the University of Illinois and the Counseling Center at Illinois State University. Within the community, students work at the Psychological Services Center, the Champaign County Mental Health Center, Carle Clinic (a multi-specialty medical center), Veterans Administration Medical Center, and Cunningham Children's Home. Supervision is provided by on-site supervisors and by faculty members. Each Counseling Psychology doctoral student is required to complete a year long, full-time predoctoral internship approved by APPIC, or the equivalent. Typical internship sites include university counseling centers, hospitals/VA medical centers, child/adolescent treatment programs, and community mental health agencies.

Housing and Day Care: On-campus housing is available. See the following website for more information: http://www.housing.illinois.edu/. On-campus day care facilities are available. See the following website for more information: http://cdl.illinois.edu/.

Employment of Department Graduates:

Master's Degree Graduates: Of those who graduated in the academic year 2011–2012, the following categories and numbers

represent the postgraduate activities and employment of master's degree graduates: Enrolled in a postdoctoral residency/fellowship (n/a), employed in independent practice (n/a), total from the above (master's) (0).

Doctoral Degree Graduates: Of those who graduated in the academic year 2011–2012, the following categories and numbers represent the postgraduate activities and employment of doctoral degree graduates: Enrolled in a psychology doctoral program (n/a), enrolled in a postdoctoral residency/fellowship (3), employed in an academic position at a university (4), employed in an academic position at a 2-year/4-year college (1), employed in other positions at a higher education institution (2), employed in business or industry (2), employed in government agency (1), do not know (1), total from the above (doctoral) (14).

Additional Information:

Orientation, Objectives, and Emphasis of Department: The Department of Educational Psychology has been a leader in placing students as university/college professors, researchers, professional psychologists, and administrators in educational, private and government settings. The Department is composed of four divisions, each with a with distinctive program of doctoral study: (1) Counseling Psychology, offering an APA-accredited program, in which students are trained in the scientist–practitioner model from a multicultural perspective; (2) Child Development, focused on the development of children and adolescents, especially as it is relevant to education and educationally relevant outcomes; (3) Studies in Interpretive, Statistical, Measurement, and Evaluative Methodologies for Education (QUERIES), focused on developing and applying new methodologies in educational measurement, statistics, research design, and evaluation; and (4) the Cognitive Science of Teaching and Learning (CSTL), which is concerned with the study of basic processes in learning, cognition, and language understanding, and the principles through which learning is optimized in diverse contexts across the life span, among individuals who vary with respect to abilities, interests, and goals.

Special Facilities or Resources: The Department of Educational Psychology is under the purview of the College of Education, rated one of the nation's top education colleges, with research and support facilities that include the Children's Research Center, Bureau of Educational Research, Office of Educational Technology, Adult Learning Lab (with eyetracking equipment), Center for the Study of Reading, and classrooms for video demonstration, telecommunications, and computer-based education. Faculty research is funded by the National Science Foundation, National Institutes of Health, Centers for Disease Control, Institute of Educational Sciences, WT Grant Foundation, and the Spencer Foundation. The University of Illinois offers a rich academic environment with top-ranked Departments of Psychology, Computer Science, Engineering, and Speech Communication, as well as the 3rd largest academic library system in the U.S., ranking only behind Harvard and Yale. There are also strong programs in Cognitive Neuroscience (Brain and Cognition Program), Human and Community Development, Gender and Women's Studies, Afro-American Studies and Research, and a Center for Latin American and Caribbean Studies. Research and support facilities on campus include Beckman Institute for Advanced Science and Technology, Statistical Laboratory for Educational and Psychological Measurement, Language Learning Lab, Survey Research Laboratory, and Illinois Statistical Office (consulting services).

Information for Students With Physical Disabilities: See the following website for more information: http://www.disability.illinois.edu/.

Application Information:
Send to Admissions, Department of Educational Psychology, 226 Education, 1310 South Sixth Street, Champaign, IL 61820. Application available online. URL of online application: http://www.grad.uiuc.edu/admissions/apply/. Students are admitted in the Fall, application deadline December 1. *Fee:* $70. International applicant fee $90.

Illinois, University of, Urbana–Champaign
Department of Human and Community Development
Agricultural, Consumer and Environmental Sciences
274 Bevier Hall, MC-180
Urbana, IL 61801
Telephone: (217) 333-3790
Fax: (217) 244-7877
E-mail: *roswald@illinois.edu*
Web: *http://hcd.illinois.edu/*

Department Information:
1996. Department Head: Robert Hughes, Jr., PhD. Number of faculty: total—full-time 19; women—full-time 13; total—minority—full-time 4; women minority—full-time 3; faculty subject to the Americans With Disabilities Act 1.

Programs and Degrees Offered:
Listed in the following order: Program area, degree type (T if terminal Master's), number awarded 7/11–6/12. Human Development and Family Studies PhD (Doctor of Philosophy) 4.

Student Applications/Admissions:
Student Applications
Human Development and Family Studies PhD (Doctor of Philosophy)—Applications 2012–2013, 32. Total applicants accepted 2012–2013, 13. Number full-time enrolled (new admits only) 2012–2013, 6. Number part-time enrolled (new admits only) 2012–2013, 0. Total enrolled 2012–2013 full-time, 27. Total enrolled 2012–2013 part-time, 0. Openings 2013–2014, 10. The median number of years required for completion of a degree in 2012–2013 were 6. The number of students enrolled full- and part-time who were dismissed or voluntarily withdrew from this program area in 2012–2013 were 1.
Scores: Entries appear in this order: required test or GPA, minimum score (if required), median score of students entering in 2012–2013. *Human Development and Family Studies PhD (Doctor of Philosophy):* GRE-V 156, 156, GRE-Q 146, 151, GRE-Analytical 4.5, 4.5, last 2 years GPA 3.0, 3.8.
Other Criteria: (importance of criteria rated low, medium, or high): GRE scores—medium, research experience—high, GPA—medium, letters of recommendation—high, statement of goals and objectives—high, fit with HCD—high. For additional information on admission requirements, go to http://hcd.illinois.edu/student_information/graduate/grad_hdfs.html.

Student Characteristics: The following represents characteristics of students in 2012–2013 in all graduate psychology programs in

the department: Female—full-time 22, part-time 0; Male—full-time 5, part-time 0; African American/Black—full-time 2, part-time 0; Hispanic/Latino(a)—full-time 4, part-time 0; Asian/Pacific Islander—full-time 4, part-time 0; American Indian/Alaska Native—full-time 0, part-time 0; Caucasian/White—full-time 16, part-time 0; Multi-ethnic—full-time 1, part-time 0; students subject to the Americans With Disabilities Act—full-time 0, part-time 0; Unknown ethnicity—full-time 0, part-time 0; International students who hold an F-1 or J-1 Visa—full-time 1, part-time 0.

Financial Information/Assistance:

Tuition for Full-Time Study: *Master's:* State residents: per academic year $12,000; Nonstate residents: per academic year $27,000. *Doctoral:* State residents: per academic year $12,000; Nonstate residents: per academic year $27,000. Tuition is subject to change. See the following website for updates and changes in tuition costs: http://www.registrar.illinois.edu/financial/tuition.html.

Financial Assistance:

First-Year Students: Teaching assistantships available for first year. Average amount paid per academic year: $15,190. Average number of hours worked per week: 20. Research assistantships available for first year. Average amount paid per academic year: $15,190. Average number of hours worked per week: 20. Fellowships and scholarships available for first year. Average amount paid per academic year: $17,500. Average number of hours worked per week: 0.

Advanced Students: Teaching assistantships available for advanced students. Average amount paid per academic year: $15,190. Average number of hours worked per week: 20. Research assistantships available for advanced students. Average amount paid per academic year: $15,190. Average number of hours worked per week: 20. Fellowships and scholarships available for advanced students. Average amount paid per academic year: $20,000. Average number of hours worked per week: 0.

Additional Information: Of all students currently enrolled full time, 100% benefited from one or more of the listed financial assistance programs. Application and information available online at: http://www.grad.illinois.edu/funding-jobs.

Internships/Practica: Doctoral students with the applied option complete at least one semester-long internship, usually within a human services setting.

Housing and Day Care: On-campus housing is available. See the following website for more information: http://www.housing.illinois.edu/. On-campus day care facilities are available. See the following website for more information: http://cdl.illinois.edu/.

Employment of Department Graduates:

Master's Degree Graduates: Of those who graduated in the academic year 2011–2012, the following categories and numbers represent the postgraduate activities and employment of master's degree graduates: Enrolled in a postdoctoral residency/fellowship (n/a), employed in independent practice (n/a), total from the above (master's) (0).

Doctoral Degree Graduates: Of those who graduated in the academic year 2011–2012, the following categories and numbers represent the postgraduate activities and employment of doctoral degree graduates: Enrolled in a psychology doctoral program (n/a), enrolled in a postdoctoral residency/fellowship (1), employed in an academic position at a university (2), employed in other positions at a higher education institution (1), total from the above (doctoral) (4).

Additional Information:

Orientation, Objectives, and Emphasis of Department: Our Human Development and Family Studies doctoral program focuses on the positive development and resilience of children, youth, and families within everyday life contexts. Emphases include the social and emotional development of children and youth; parent-child and sibling relationships; and racial, ethnic, and sexual orientation diversity. All topics are studied within specific settings. Faculty have expertise in both qualitative and quantitative research. Students may choose an applied supporting option in program development, evaluation, and outreach.

Special Facilities or Resources: Our department includes two laboratory preschool facilities, a childcare resource and referral service, a lab for community and economic development, and the Family Resiliency Center.

Information for Students With Physical Disabilities: See the following website for more information: http://www.disability.illinois.edu/.

Application Information:

Send to Graduate Secretary, 274 Bevier Hall, 905 South Goodwin, Urbana, IL 61801. Application available online. URL of online application: http://www.grad.illinois.edu/admissions/apply. Students are admitted in the Fall, application deadline January 15. *Fee:* $70. $90 for international applicants.

Illinois, University of, Urbana–Champaign
Department of Psychology
Liberal Arts & Sciences
Psychology Building, 603 East Daniel Street
Champaign, IL 61820
Telephone: (217) 333-2169
Fax: (217) 244-5876
E-mail: *garnsey@illinois.edu*
Web: *http://www.psychology.illinois.edu/*

Department Information:

1904. Professor and Head: David E. Irwin. Number of faculty: total—full-time 48, part-time 6; women—full-time 18, part-time 2; total—minority—full-time 8, part-time 3; women minority—full-time 3, part-time 2.

Programs and Degrees Offered:

Listed in the following order: Program area, degree type (T if terminal Master's), number awarded 7/11–6/12. Applied Measurement MA/MS (Master of Arts/Science) (T) 0, Applied Personnel MA/MS (Master of Arts/Science) (T) 0, Behavioral Neuroscience PhD (Doctor of Philosophy) 2, Clinical/Community Psychology PhD (Doctor of Philosophy) 7, Cognitive Psychology PhD (Doctor of Philosophy) 3, Developmental Psychology PhD (Doctor of Philosophy) 1, Quantitative Psychology PhD (Doctor of Philosophy) 0, Cognitive Neuroscience PhD (Doctor of Philosophy) 3, Visual Cognition & Human Performance PhD (Doctor of Philosophy) 1, Social-Personality PhD (Doctor of Philosophy) 6, Industrial/Organizational Psychology PhD (Doctor of Philosophy) 5.

APA Accreditation: Clinical PhD (Doctor of Philosophy). Student Outcome Data Website: http://www.psychology.illinois.edu/about/divisions/clinicalcommunity/.

Student Applications/Admissions:

Student Applications

Applied Measurement MA/MS (Master of Arts/Science)—Applications 2012–2013, 9. Total applicants accepted 2012–2013, 0. Number full-time enrolled (new admits only) 2012–2013, 0. Number part-time enrolled (new admits only) 2012–2013, 0. The number of students enrolled full- and part-time who were dismissed or voluntarily withdrew from this program area in 2012–2013 were 0. *Applied Personnel MA/MS (Master of Arts/Science)*—Applications 2012–2013, 19. Total applicants accepted 2012–2013, 0. Number full-time enrolled (new admits only) 2012–2013, 0. The number of students enrolled full- and part-time who were dismissed or voluntarily withdrew from this program area in 2012–2013 were 0. *Behavioral Neuroscience PhD (Doctor of Philosophy)*—Applications 2012–2013, 11. Total applicants accepted 2012–2013, 3. Number full-time enrolled (new admits only) 2012–2013, 1. Number part-time enrolled (new admits only) 2012–2013, 0. Total enrolled 2012–2013 full-time, 6. Total enrolled 2012–2013 part-time, 0. Openings 2013–2014, 10. The median number of years required for completion of a degree in 2012–2013 were 6. The number of students enrolled full- and part-time who were dismissed or voluntarily withdrew from this program area in 2012–2013 were 0. *Clinical/Community Psychology PhD (Doctor of Philosophy)*—Applications 2012–2013, 194. Total applicants accepted 2012–2013, 14. Number full-time enrolled (new admits only) 2012–2013, 8. Number part-time enrolled (new admits only) 2012–2013, 0. Total enrolled 2012–2013 full-time, 30. Total enrolled 2012–2013 part-time, 0. Openings 2013–2014, 16. The median number of years required for completion of a degree in 2012–2013 were 7. The number of students enrolled full- and part-time who were dismissed or voluntarily withdrew from this program area in 2012–2013 were 0. *Cognitive Psychology PhD (Doctor of Philosophy)*—Applications 2012–2013, 38. Total applicants accepted 2012–2013, 11. Number full-time enrolled (new admits only) 2012–2013, 6. Number part-time enrolled (new admits only) 2012–2013, 0. Total enrolled 2012–2013 full-time, 20. Total enrolled 2012–2013 part-time, 0. Openings 2013–2014, 10. The median number of years required for completion of a degree in 2012–2013 were 6. The number of students enrolled full- and part-time who were dismissed or voluntarily withdrew from this program area in 2012–2013 were 0. *Developmental Psychology PhD (Doctor of Philosophy)*—Applications 2012–2013, 46. Total applicants accepted 2012–2013, 8. Number full-time enrolled (new admits only) 2012–2013, 3. Number part-time enrolled (new admits only) 2012–2013, 0. Total enrolled 2012–2013 full-time, 15. Total enrolled 2012–2013 part-time, 0. Openings 2013–2014, 14. The median number of years required for completion of a degree in 2012–2013 were 6. The number of students enrolled full- and part-time who were

dismissed or voluntarily withdrew from this program area in 2012–2013 were 1. *Quantitative Psychology PhD (Doctor of Philosophy)*—Applications 2012–2013, 20. Total applicants accepted 2012–2013, 2. Number full-time enrolled (new admits only) 2012–2013, 1. Number part-time enrolled (new admits only) 2012–2013, 0. Total enrolled 2012–2013 full-time, 9. Total enrolled 2012–2013 part-time, 0. Openings 2013–2014, 6. The number of students enrolled full- and part-time who were dismissed or voluntarily withdrew from this program area in 2012–2013 were 0. *Cognitive Neuroscience PhD (Doctor of Philosophy)*—Applications 2012–2013, 44. Total applicants accepted 2012–2013, 8. Number full-time enrolled (new admits only) 2012–2013, 3. Number part-time enrolled (new admits only) 2012–2013, 0. Total enrolled 2012–2013 full-time, 16. Total enrolled 2012–2013 part-time, 0. Openings 2013–2014, 14. The median number of years required for completion of a degree in 2012–2013 were 6. The number of students enrolled full- and part-time who were dismissed or voluntarily withdrew from this program area in 2012–2013 were 0. *Visual Cognition & Human Performance PhD (Doctor of Philosophy)*—Applications 2012–2013, 17. Total applicants accepted 2012–2013, 4. Number full-time enrolled (new admits only) 2012–2013, 1. Number part-time enrolled (new admits only) 2012–2013, 0. Total enrolled 2012–2013 full-time, 13. Total enrolled 2012–2013 part-time, 0. Openings 2013–2014, 12. The median number of years required for completion of a degree in 2012–2013 were 5. The number of students enrolled full- and part-time who were dismissed or voluntarily withdrew from this program area in 2012–2013 were 0. *Social-Personality PhD (Doctor of Philosophy)*—Applications 2012–2013, 104. Total applicants accepted 2012–2013, 7. Number full-time enrolled (new admits only) 2012–2013, 3. Number part-time enrolled (new admits only) 2012–2013, 0. Total enrolled 2012–2013 full-time, 13. Total enrolled 2012–2013 part-time, 0. Openings 2013–2014, 14. The median number of years required for completion of a degree in 2012–2013 were 6. The number of students enrolled full- and part-time who were dismissed or voluntarily withdrew from this program area in 2012–2013 were 2. *Industrial/Organizational Psychology PhD (Doctor of Philosophy)*—Applications 2012–2013, 67. Total applicants accepted 2012–2013, 8. Number full-time enrolled (new admits only) 2012–2013, 2. Number part-time enrolled (new admits only) 2012–2013, 0. Total enrolled 2012–2013 full-time, 12. Total enrolled 2012–2013 part-time, 0. Openings 2013–2014, 12. The median number of years required for completion of a degree in 2012–2013 were 6. The number of students enrolled full- and part-time who were dismissed or voluntarily withdrew from this program area in 2012–2013 were 0.

Scores: Entries appear in this order: required test or GPA, minimum score (if required), median score of students entering in 2012–2013. *Applied Measurement MA/MS (Master of Arts/Science):* GRE-V no minimum stated, 600, GRE-Q no minimum stated, 700, overall undergraduate GPA 3.0, 3.5; *Applied Personnel MA/MS (Master of Arts/Science):* GRE-V no minimum stated, 600, GRE-Q no minimum stated, 700, overall undergraduate GPA 3.0, 3.5; *Behavioral Neuroscience PhD (Doctor of Philosophy):* GRE-V no minimum stated, 163, GRE-Q no minimum stated, 164, overall undergraduate GPA 3.0, 3.25; *Clinical/Community Psychology PhD (Doctor of Philosophy):* GRE-V no minimum stated, 164, GRE-Q no minimum stated, 158, overall undergraduate GPA 3.0, 3.69; *Cognitive Psychology PhD (Doctor of Philosophy):* GRE-V no minimum stated, 164, GRE-Q no minimum stated, 159, overall undergraduate GPA 3.0, 3.84; *Developmental Psychology PhD (Doctor of Philosophy):* GRE-V no minimum stated, 160, GRE-Q no minimum stated, 156, overall undergraduate GPA 3.0, 3.76; *Quantitative Psychology PhD (Doctor of Philosophy):* GRE-V no minimum stated, 164, GRE-Q no minimum stated, 165, overall undergraduate GPA 3.0, 3.83; *Cognitive Neuroscience PhD (Doctor of Philosophy):* GRE-V no minimum stated, 163, GRE-Q no minimum stated, 158, overall undergraduate GPA 3.0, 3.82; *Visual Cognition & Human Performance PhD (Doctor of Philosophy):* GRE-V no minimum stated, 162, GRE-Q no minimum stated, 157, overall undergraduate GPA 3.0, 3.41; *Social-Personality PhD (Doctor of Philosophy):* GRE-V no minimum stated, 165, GRE-Q no minimum stated, 163, overall undergraduate GPA 3.0, 3.88; *Industrial/Organizational Psychology PhD (Doctor of Philosophy):* GRE-V no minimum stated, 160, GRE-Q no minimum stated, 159, overall undergraduate GPA 3.0, 3.02.

Other Criteria: (importance of criteria rated low, medium, or high): GRE scores—high, research experience—high, work experience—medium, clinically related public service—high, GPA—high, letters of recommendation—high, interview—high, statement of goals and objectives—high. For additional information on admission requirements, go to http://www. psychology.illinois.edu/graduate/apply/.

Student Characteristics: The following represents characteristics of students in 2012–2013 in all graduate psychology programs in the department: Female—full-time 85, part-time 0; Male—full-time 49, part-time 0; African American/Black—full-time 6, part-time 0; Hispanic/Latino(a)—full-time 4, part-time 0; Asian/Pacific Islander—full-time 43, part-time 0; American Indian/Alaska Native—full-time 0, part-time 0; Caucasian/White—full-time 77, part-time 0; Multi-ethnic—full-time 4, part-time 0; students subject to the Americans With Disabilities Act—full-time 1, part-time 0; Unknown ethnicity—full-time 0, part-time 0; International students who hold an F-1 or J-1 Visa—full-time 37, part-time 0.

Financial Information/Assistance:

Tuition for Full-Time Study: *Master's:* State residents: per academic year $11,432; Nonstate residents: per academic year $24,698. *Doctoral:* State residents: per academic year $11,432; Nonstate residents: per academic year $24,698. Tuition is subject to change. See the following website for updates and changes in tuition costs: http://registrar.illinois.edu/financial/tuition.html.

Financial Assistance:

First-Year Students: Teaching assistantships available for first year. Average amount paid per academic year: $17,084. Average number of hours worked per week: 20. Apply by December 10. Research assistantships available for first year. Average amount paid per academic year: $17,084. Average number of hours worked per week: 20. Apply by December 10. Traineeships available for first year. Average amount paid per academic year: $22,032. Apply by December 10. Fellowships and scholarships available for first year. Average amount paid per academic year: $17,084. Apply by December 10.

Advanced Students: Teaching assistantships available for advanced students. Average amount paid per academic year: $17,084. Average number of hours worked per week: 20. Research assistantships available for advanced students. Average amount paid per academic year: $17,084. Average number of hours worked per week: 20. Traineeships available for advanced students. Average amount paid per academic year: $22,032. Fellowships and scholarships available for advanced students. Average amount paid per academic year: $17,084.

Additional Information: Of all students currently enrolled full time, 100% benefited from one or more of the listed financial assistance programs. Application and information available online at: http://www.psychology.illinois.edu/graduate/FinancialAid-Prospective.htm.

Internships/Practica: Doctoral Degree (PhD Clinical/Community Psychology): For those doctoral students for whom a professional psychology internship was required in this program prior to graduation, (7) students applied for an internship in 2011–2012, with (5) students obtaining an internship. Of those students who obtained an internship, (4) were paid internships. Of those students who obtained an internship, (4) students placed in APA/CPA accredited internships, (0) students placed in internships not APA/CPA accredited, but listed with the Association of Psychology Postdoctoral and Internship Programs (APPIC), (0) students placed in internships conforming to guidelines of the Council of Directors of School Psychology Programs (CDSPP), (1) students placed in internships that were not APA/CPA accredited, APPIC or CDSPP listed. Laboratories in Clinical Psychology—Intensive practice in techniques of clinical assessment and behavior modification with emphasis on recent innovations; small sections of the course formed according to the specialized interests of students and staff.

Housing and Day Care: On-campus housing is available. See the following website for more information: http://www.housing. illinois.edu/Future/Graduate.aspx. On-campus day care facilities are available. See the following website for more information: http://www.cdl.uiuc.edu.

Employment of Department Graduates:

Master's Degree Graduates: Of those who graduated in the academic year 2011–2012, the following categories and numbers represent the postgraduate activities and employment of master's degree graduates: Enrolled in a postdoctoral residency/fellowship (n/a), employed in independent practice (n/a), total from the above (master's) (0).

Doctoral Degree Graduates: Of those who graduated in the academic year 2011–2012, the following categories and numbers represent the postgraduate activities and employment of doctoral degree graduates: Enrolled in a psychology doctoral program (n/a), enrolled in a postdoctoral residency/fellowship (11), employed in an academic position at a university (10), employed in business or industry (5), do not know (2), total from the above (doctoral) (28).

Additional Information:

Orientation, Objectives, and Emphasis of Department: The department trains students at the doctoral level for basic research in all areas. Students are admitted in one of the nine divisions:

behavioral neuroscience, clinical/community, cognitive, cognitive neuroscience, developmental, quantitative, social-personality, industrial-organizational, and visual cognition & human performance. Interactions with faculty in other divisions are quite common; interdisciplinary training is encouraged. Applied research training is offered in measurement and personnel psychology. There is a strong emphasis on individualized training programs in an apprenticeship model. Each student's program is tailored to his or her research interests. Wide opportunities exist for students to participate in ongoing research programs. Students are encouraged to develop their own programs of research.

Special Facilities or Resources: The department has extensive laboratory facilities in all areas, including behavioral neuroscience/biological psychology. Excellent departmental and university computer facilities are readily available to graduate students. Most faculty laboratories are computerized. The department maintains computer servers that support data storage and management and communication between laboratories and campus computers. There are very advanced facilities for research in all areas, including psychophysiology, cognitive psychology, neurochemistry, and neuroanatomy. A first-rate animal colony is maintained by the department. There is an excellent machine shop and a fine electronics shop. Programs are coordinated with other campus departments and institutes, including life sciences, communication, labor, education, and child study.

Information for Students With Physical Disabilities: See the following website for more information: http://www.disability.illinois.edu/.

Application Information:
Send to Graduate Student Affairs Office, 307 Psychology Building, 603 East Daniel Street, Champaign, IL 61820. Application available online. URL of online application: https://app.applyyourself.com/?id=uiuc-grad. Students are admitted in the Fall, application deadline December 10. *Fee:* $70. The fee for an international application is $90.00.

Lewis University
Department of Psychology
One University Parkway
Romeoville, IL 60446
Telephone: (815) 836-5594
Fax: (815) 836-5032
E-mail: *Helmka@lewisu.edu*
Web: *http://www.lewisu.edu/academics/grad-psychology/index.htm*

Department Information:
1993. Director of Graduate Programs in Psychology: Katherine Helm. Number of faculty: total—full-time 17, part-time 5; women—full-time 11, part-time 1; total—minority—full-time 4; women minority—full-time 3.

Programs and Degrees Offered:
Listed in the following order: Program area, degree type (T if terminal Master's), number awarded 7/11–6/12. School Counseling MA/MS (Master of Arts/Science) (T) 93, Clinical Mental Health Counseling MA/MS (Master of Arts/Science) (T) 35.

Student Applications/Admissions:
Student Applications
School Counseling MA/MS (Master of Arts/Science)—Applications 2012–2013, 98. Total applicants accepted 2012–2013, 76. Number full-time enrolled (new admits only) 2012–2013, 78. Number part-time enrolled (new admits only) 2012–2013, 155. Total enrolled 2012–2013 full-time, 97. Total enrolled 2012–2013 part-time, 122. Openings 2013–2014, 40. The median number of years required for completion of a degree in 2012–2013 were 2. The number of students enrolled full- and part-time who were dismissed or voluntarily withdrew from this program area in 2012–2013 were 16. *Clinical Mental Health Counseling MA/MS (Master of Arts/Science)*—Applications 2012–2013, 63. Total applicants accepted 2012–2013, 60. Number full-time enrolled (new admits only) 2012–2013, 14. Number part-time enrolled (new admits only) 2012–2013, 42. Total enrolled 2012–2013 full-time, 16. Total enrolled 2012–2013 part-time, 92. Openings 2013–2014, 45. The median number of years required for completion of a degree in 2012–2013 were 3. The number of students enrolled full- and part-time who were dismissed or voluntarily withdrew from this program area in 2012–2013 were 9.

Other Criteria: (importance of criteria rated low, medium, or high): research experience—low, work experience—high, extracurricular activity—medium, clinically related public service—high, GPA—high, letters of recommendation—high, statement of goals and objectives—high, undergraduate major in psychology—medium, specific undergraduate psychology courses taken—medium, The counseling psychology program requires that applicants have taken 15 hours of undergraduate psychology courses prior to being considered for the program. The school counseling program is a joint program in Psychology and Education. There are no prerequisite psychology courses for this program. Before being admitted to the program student must pass the TAP test (taken through the State of Illinois). For additional information on admission requirements, go to http://www.lewisu.edu/admissions/graduate/howtoapply.htm.

Student Characteristics: The following represents characteristics of students in 2012–2013 in all graduate psychology programs in the department: Female—full-time 93, part-time 172; Male—full-time 8, part-time 32; African American/Black—full-time 0, part-time 35; Hispanic/Latino(a)—full-time 0, part-time 14; Asian/Pacific Islander—full-time 0, part-time 8; American Indian/Alaska Native—full-time 0, part-time 0; Caucasian/White—full-time 70, part-time 90; Multi-ethnic—full-time 0, part-time 9; students subject to the Americans With Disabilities Act—full-time 6, part-time 2; Unknown ethnicity—full-time 19, part-time 49; International students who hold an F-1 or J-1 Visa—full-time 0, part-time 0.

Financial Information/Assistance:
Tuition for Full-Time Study: *Master's:* State residents: per academic year $16,640, $740 per credit hour; Nonstate residents: per academic year $16,640, $740 per credit hour. Tuition is subject to change. Tuition costs vary by program. See the following website for updates and changes in tuition costs: http://www.lewisu.edu/welcome/offices/business/bursar/tuitionrates.htm.

Financial Assistance:

First-Year Students: Research assistantships available for first year. Average amount paid per academic year: $8,880. Average number of hours worked per week: 15.

Advanced Students: Research assistantships available for advanced students. Average amount paid per academic year: $8,880. Average number of hours worked per week: 15.

Additional Information: Of all students currently enrolled full time, 1% benefited from one or more of the listed financial assistance programs. Application and information available online at: http://www.lewisu.edu/admissions/finaid/index.htm.

Internships/Practica: Master's Degree (MA/MS Clinical Mental Health Counseling): An internship experience, such as a final research project or "capstone" experience is required of graduates. Numerous practicum and internship sites available in the community.

Housing and Day Care: No on-campus housing is available. No on-campus day care facilities are available.

Employment of Department Graduates:

Master's Degree Graduates: Of those who graduated in the academic year 2011–2012, the following categories and numbers represent the postgraduate activities and employment of master's degree graduates: Enrolled in a postdoctoral residency/fellowship (n/a), employed in independent practice (n/a), total from the above (master's) (0).

Doctoral Degree Graduates: Of those who graduated in the academic year 2011–2012, the following categories and numbers represent the postgraduate activities and employment of doctoral degree graduates: Enrolled in a psychology doctoral program (n/a), total from the above (doctoral) (0).

Additional Information:

Orientation, Objectives, and Emphasis of Department: The program in Clinical Mental Health Counseling is oriented toward individuals who have some experience or great interest in mental health, behavioral, social service or educational interventions or assessment. It is designed primarily as part-time with courses offered primarily in the evenings and on occasional weekends. The Program has two sub-specialty areas: 1. Clinical Mental Health Counseling; 2. Child and Adolescent Clinical Mental Health Counseling. There is a second program in School Counseling that is designed for those individuals who want to work in the public or private school systems. The School Counseling program has several sites including the main campus and Tinley Park. Students may be required to submit to a criminal background check. Admission to the school counseling now requires that all students pass the State of Illinois TAP prior to being admitted to the program.

Application Information:

Send to Graduate Program Director, Department of Psychology, Lewis University, One University Parkway, Romeoville, IL 60446. Application available online. URL of online application: https://www.selectlewis.org/grad. Programs have rolling admissions. *Fee:* $40. Need based waiver.

Loyola University of Chicago

Counseling Psychology
School of Education
820 North Michigan Avenue
Chicago, IL 60611
Telephone: (312) 915-7403
Fax: (312) 915-6660
E-mail: *athoma9@luc.edu*
Web: *http://www.luc.edu/education/*

Department Information:

1969. Graduate Program Director: Anita Jones Thomas. Number of faculty: total—full-time 5, part-time 10; women—full-time 4, part-time 3; total—minority—full-time 3, part-time 4; women minority—full-time 3, part-time 2.

Programs and Degrees Offered:

Listed in the following order: Program area, degree type (T if terminal Master's), number awarded 7/11–6/12. Counseling Psychology PhD (Doctor of Philosophy) 6, Community Counseling MA/MS (Master of Arts/Science) (T) 9, School Counseling MEd (Education) 18, Clinical Mental Health Counseling EdS (School Psychology) 0, Community Counseling MEd (Education) 12.

APA Accreditation: Counseling PhD (Doctor of Philosophy). Student Outcome Data Website: http://www.luc.edu/education/programs/cpsy-phd_quality_indicators.shtml.

Student Applications/Admissions:

Student Applications

Counseling Psychology PhD (Doctor of Philosophy)—Applications 2012–2013, 54. Total applicants accepted 2012–2013, 4. Number full-time enrolled (new admits only) 2012–2013, 4. Number part-time enrolled (new admits only) 2012–2013, 0. Total enrolled 2012–2013 full-time, 20. Total enrolled 2012–2013 part-time, 0. Openings 2013–2014, 4. The median number of years required for completion of a degree in 2012–2013 were 6. The number of students enrolled full- and part-time who were dismissed or voluntarily withdrew from this program area in 2012–2013 were 0. *Community Counseling MA/MS (Master of Arts/Science)*—Applications 2012–2013, 48. Total applicants accepted 2012–2013, 34. Number full-time enrolled (new admits only) 2012–2013, 8. Number part-time enrolled (new admits only) 2012–2013, 0. Total enrolled 2012–2013 full-time, 16. Total enrolled 2012–2013 part-time, 0. Openings 2013–2014, 30. The median number of years required for completion of a degree in 2012–2013 were 2. The number of students enrolled full- and part-time who were dismissed or voluntarily withdrew from this program area in 2012–2013 were 0. *School Counseling MEd (Education)*—Applications 2012–2013, 38. Total applicants accepted 2012–2013, 31. Number full-time enrolled (new admits only) 2012–2013, 7. Number part-time enrolled (new admits only) 2012–2013, 0. Total enrolled 2012–2013 full-time, 16. Total enrolled 2012–2013 part-time, 2. Openings 2013–2014, 30. The median number of years required for completion of a degree in 2012–2013 were 2. The number of students enrolled full- and part-time who were dismissed or voluntarily withdrew from this program area in 2012–2013 were 0. *Clinical Mental Health Counseling EdS (School Psychology)*—Applications 2012–2013, 18. Total applicants accepted 2012–2013, 7. Number full-time enrolled (new admits only) 2012–2013, 0. Number part-time enrolled (new admits only) 2012–2013, 0. Total enrolled 2012–2013 full-time, 3. Total enrolled 2012–2013 part-time, 0. Openings 2013–2014, 15. The number of students enrolled full- and part-time who were dismissed or voluntarily withdrew from this program area in 2012–2013 were 0. *Community Counseling MEd (Education)*—Applications 2012–2013, 16. Total applicants accepted 2012–2013, 11. Number full-time enrolled (new admits only) 2012–2013, 7. Number part-time enrolled (new admits only) 2012–2013, 0. Total enrolled 2012–2013 full-time, 13. Total enrolled 2012–2013 part-time, 0. Openings 2013–2014, 30. The median number of years required for completion of a degree in 2012–2013 were 2. The number of students enrolled full- and part-time who were dismissed or voluntarily withdrew from this program area in 2012–2013 were 0.

Scores: Entries appear in this order: required test or GPA, minimum score (if required), median score of students entering in 2012–2013. *Counseling Psychology PhD (Doctor of Philosophy):* GRE-V 550, 600, GRE-Q 550, 600, GRE-Analytical 4.5, 5.0, GRE-Subject (Psychology) 550, 550, overall undergraduate GPA 3.5, 3.5, last 2 years GPA 3.0, 3.0, Masters GPA 3.5, 3.5; *Community Counseling MA/MS (Master of Arts/Science):* GRE-V 500, 550, GRE-Q 500, 550, GRE-Analytical 4.0, 4.5, overall undergraduate GPA 3.0, 3.0, last 2 years GPA 3.0, 3.0; *School Counseling MEd (Education):* GRE-V 500, 550, GRE-Q 500, 550, GRE-Analytical 4.5, 5.0, overall undergraduate GPA 3.0, 3.0, last 2 years GPA 3.0, 3.0; *Clinical Mental Health Counseling EdS (School Psychology):* GRE-V 550, 600, GRE-Q 550, 600, GRE-Analytical 4.0, 4.5, overall undergraduate GPA 3.0, 3.5, last 2 years GPA 3.0, 3.0; *Community Counseling MEd (Education):* GRE-V 500, 550, GRE-Q 500, 550, GRE-Analytical 4.0, 4.5, overall undergraduate GPA 3.0, 3.5, last 2 years GPA 3.0, 3.5.

Other Criteria: (importance of criteria rated low, medium, or high): GRE scores—medium, research experience—high, work experience—medium, clinically related public service—high, GPA—medium, letters of recommendation—high, interview—high, statement of goals and objectives—high, match w/ faculty interest—high, undergraduate major in psychology—medium, specific undergraduate psychology courses taken—low, These are for the PhD program in Counseling Psychology. For additional information on admission requirements, go to http://www.luc.edu/education/applicationinfo.shtml.

Student Characteristics: The following represents characteristics of students in 2012–2013 in all graduate psychology programs in the department: Female—full-time 56, part-time 1; Male—full-time 12, part-time 1; African American/Black—full-time 9, part-time 1; Hispanic/Latino(a)—full-time 4, part-time 0; Asian/Pacific Islander—full-time 3, part-time 0; American Indian/Alaska Native—full-time 0, part-time 0; Caucasian/White—full-time 51, part-time 1; Multi-ethnic—full-time 1, part-time 0; students subject to the Americans With Disabilities Act—full-time 0, part-time 0; Unknown ethnicity—full-time 0, part-time 0; International students who hold an F-1 or J-1 Visa—full-time 0, part-time 0.

Financial Information/Assistance:
Tuition for Full-Time Study: *Master's:* State residents: $930 per credit hour; Nonstate residents: $930 per credit hour. *Doctoral:* State residents: $930 per credit hour; Nonstate residents: $930 per credit hour. Tuition is subject to change. Additional fees are assessed to students beyond the costs of tuition for the following: student development fee, technology fee, course management fee, matriculation fee. See the following website for updates and changes in tuition costs: http://www.luc.edu/bursar/tuition.shtml.

Financial Assistance:
First-Year Students: Teaching assistantships available for first year. Average amount paid per academic year: $14,000. Average number of hours worked per week: 20. Apply by December 1. Research assistantships available for first year. Average amount paid per academic year: $14,000. Average number of hours worked per week: 20. Apply by December 1. Fellowships and scholarships available for first year. Average amount paid per academic year: $16,000. Average number of hours worked per week: 0.

Advanced Students: Teaching assistantships available for advanced students. Average amount paid per academic year: $14,000. Average number of hours worked per week: 20. Apply by December 1. Research assistantships available for advanced students. Average amount paid per academic year: $14,000. Average number of hours worked per week: 20. Apply by December 1. Fellowships and scholarships available for advanced students. Average amount paid per academic year: $16,000. Average number of hours worked per week: 0.

Additional Information: Of all students currently enrolled full time, 25% benefited from one or more of the listed financial assistance programs. Application and information available online at: http://luc.edu/finaid/grad_checklist.shtml.

Internships/Practica: Doctoral Degree (PhD Counseling Psychology): For those doctoral students for whom a professional psychology internship was required in this program prior to graduation, (3) students applied for an internship in 2011–2012, with (3) students obtaining an internship. Of those students who obtained an internship, (3) were paid internships. Of those students who obtained an internship, (3) students placed in APA/CPA accredited internships, (0) students placed in internships not APA/CPA accredited, but listed with the Association of Psychology Postdoctoral and Internship Programs (APPIC), (0) students placed in internships conforming to guidelines of the Council of Directors of School Psychology Programs (CDSPP), (0) students placed in internships that were not APA/CPA accredited, APPIC or CDSPP listed. Master's Degree (MA/MS Community Counseling): An internship experience, such as a final research project or "capstone" experience is required of graduates. Internships and practica are available at many excellent training facilities in the greater Chicagoland area, including university counseling centers, hospitals, VA centers, and mental health clinics. There are both therapy-oriented and diagnostic/assessment-oriented practica. Most practicum sites serve a diverse clientele.

Housing and Day Care: On-campus housing is available. See the following website for more information: http://www.luc.edu/wtcl/living/gradhousing/. No on-campus day care facilities are available.

Employment of Department Graduates:
Master's Degree Graduates: Of those who graduated in the academic year 2011–2012, the following categories and numbers represent the postgraduate activities and employment of master's degree graduates: Enrolled in a psychology doctoral program (5),

enrolled in a postdoctoral residency/fellowship (n/a), employed in independent practice (n/a), employed in a professional position in a school system (10), employed in business or industry (1), total from the above (master's) (16).

Doctoral Degree Graduates: Of those who graduated in the academic year 2011–2012, the following categories and numbers represent the postgraduate activities and employment of doctoral degree graduates: Enrolled in a psychology doctoral program (n/a), enrolled in a postdoctoral residency/fellowship (5), employed in an academic position at a university (1), employed in a community mental health/counseling center (2), employed in a hospital/medical center (2), total from the above (doctoral) (10).

Additional Information:

Orientation, Objectives, and Emphasis of Department: The PhD program, accredited by the APA, is based on the scientist–practitioner model of graduate education and emphasizes the interdependence of science and practice. Doctoral students are provided opportunities to collaborate with faculty in terms of research, prevention/intervention, and teaching activities from the first year of enrollment. Faculty research concentrates in three areas: multicultural psychology, preventive psychology, and vocational psychology. Applicant interest in one of these three areas is a major admission criterion since students are expected to apprentice themselves with a faculty member throughout their tenure in the program. Regardless of the field of interest, each student is exposed to the scientist–practitioner model. Graduates are prepared for teaching, research, and professional practice.

Special Facilities or Resources: The school has excellent library and research facilities and computer resources available to students.

Information for Students With Physical Disabilities: See the following website for more information: http://www.luc.edu/sswd/index.shtml.

Application Information:
Send to Graduate & Professional Enrollment Management, Loyola University Chicago, Lewis Towers, 8th Floor, 820 North Michigan Avenue, Chicago, IL 60611. Application available online. URL of online application: http://www.luc.edu/education/applicationinfo.shtml. Students are admitted in the Fall, application deadline December 1. Master's programs in School and Community Counseling have an application deadline of January 1. *Fee:* $50. Waived if application is submitted on line.

Loyola University of Chicago
Department of Psychology
Arts and Sciences
1032 West Sheridan Road
Chicago, IL 60660
Telephone: (773) 508-3001
Fax: (773) 508-8713
E-mail: *jlarson4@luc.edu*
Web: *http://www.luc.edu/psychology/*

Department Information:
1930. Chairperson: James R. Larson, Jr., PhD. Number of faculty: total—full-time 30, part-time 8; women—full-time 16, part-time 3; total—minority—full-time 4, part-time 1; women minority—full-time 2, part-time 1.

Programs and Degrees Offered:
Listed in the following order: Program area, degree type (T if terminal Master's), number awarded 7/11–6/12. Developmental Psychology PhD (Doctor of Philosophy) 2, Social Psychology PhD (Doctor of Philosophy) 5, Clinical Psychology PhD (Doctor of Philosophy) 5, Applied Social Psychology MA/MS (Master of Arts/Science) (T) 5.

APA Accreditation: Clinical PhD (Doctor of Philosophy). Student Outcome Data Website: http://www.luc.edu/psychology/studentadmissionsoutcomesandotherdata/.

Student Applications/Admissions:
Student Applications

Developmental Psychology PhD (Doctor of Philosophy)—Applications 2012–2013, 18. Total applicants accepted 2012–2013, 2. Number full-time enrolled (new admits only) 2012–2013, 2. Number part-time enrolled (new admits only) 2012–2013, 0. Total enrolled 2012–2013 full-time, 12. Total enrolled 2012–2013 part-time, 0. Openings 2013–2014, 2. The median number of years required for completion of a degree in 2012–2013 were 5. The number of students enrolled full- and part-time who were dismissed or voluntarily withdrew from this program area in 2012–2013 were 0. *Social Psychology PhD (Doctor of Philosophy)*—Applications 2012–2013, 50. Total applicants accepted 2012–2013, 5. Number full-time enrolled (new admits only) 2012–2013, 3. Number part-time enrolled (new admits only) 2012–2013, 0. Total enrolled 2012–2013 full-time, 20. Total enrolled 2012–2013 part-time, 0. Openings 2013–2014, 3. The median number of years required for completion of a degree in 2012–2013 were 6. The number of students enrolled full- and part-time who were dismissed or voluntarily withdrew from this program area in 2012–2013 were 0. *Clinical Psychology PhD (Doctor of Philosophy)*—Applications 2012–2013, 288. Total applicants accepted 2012–2013, 10. Number full-time enrolled (new admits only) 2012–2013, 6. Number part-time enrolled (new admits only) 2012–2013, 0. Total enrolled 2012–2013 full-time, 36. Total enrolled 2012–2013 part-time, 0. Openings 2013–2014, 6. The median number of years required for completion of a degree in 2012–2013 were 6. The number of students enrolled full- and part-time who were dismissed or voluntarily withdrew from this program area in 2012–2013 were 2. *Applied Social Psychology MA/MS (Master of Arts/Science)*—Applications 2012–2013, 33. Total applicants accepted 2012–2013, 8. Number full-time enrolled (new admits only) 2012–2013, 4. Total enrolled 2012–2013 full-time, 9. Total enrolled 2012–2013 part-time, 0. Openings 2013–2014, 4. The median number of years required for completion of a degree in 2012–2013 were 2. The number of students enrolled full- and part-time who were dismissed or voluntarily withdrew from this program area in 2012–2013 were 0.

Scores: Entries appear in this order: required test or GPA, minimum score (if required), median score of students entering in 2012–2013. *Developmental Psychology PhD (Doctor of Philosophy):* GRE-V no minimum stated, 560, GRE-Q no minimum stated, 670, GRE-Analytical 4.0, 4.5, GRE-Subject (Psychology) no minimum stated, overall undergraduate GPA no minimum stated, 3.34, last 2 years GPA no minimum stated, 3.8, psychology GPA no minimum stated, 3.7; *Social Psychology PhD (Doctor of Philosophy)*: GRE-V no minimum stated, 670, GRE-Q no minimum stated, 700, GRE-Analytical no minimum stated, 4.0; *Clinical Psychology PhD (Doctor of Philosophy)*: GRE-V no minimum stated, 675, GRE-Q no minimum stated, 720, GRE-Analytical no minimum stated, GRE-Subject (Psychology) no minimum stated, overall undergraduate GPA no minimum stated, 3.80; *Applied Social Psychology MA/MS (Master of Arts/Science)*: GRE-V no minimum stated, 630, GRE-Q no minimum stated, 700, GRE-Analytical no minimum stated, 4.0, overall undergraduate GPA no minimum stated.

Other Criteria: (importance of criteria rated low, medium, or high): GRE scores—high, research experience—high, work experience—low, extracurricular activity—low, clinically related public service—medium, GPA—high, letters of recommendation—high, interview—high, statement of goals and objectives—high, Only the Clinical program requires an interview and clinically related public service. Arranging an interview is strongly recommended (but not required) for the Developmental and Social Psychology programs. For additional information on admission requirements, go to http://www.luc.edu/psychology/academics_graduate.shtml.

Student Characteristics: The following represents characteristics of students in 2012–2013 in all graduate psychology programs in the department: Female—full-time 66, part-time 0; Male—full-time 11, part-time 0; African American/Black—full-time 9, part-time 0; Hispanic/Latino(a)—full-time 7, part-time 0; Asian/Pacific Islander—full-time 5, part-time 0; American Indian/Alaska Native—full-time 1, part-time 0; Caucasian/White—full-time 54, part-time 0; Multi-ethnic—full-time 1, part-time 0; students subject to the Americans With Disabilities Act—full-time 0, part-time 0; Unknown ethnicity—full-time 0, part-time 0; International students who hold an F-1 or J-1 Visa—full-time 1, part-time 0.

Financial Information/Assistance:
Tuition for Full-Time Study: *Master's*: State residents: per academic year $16,290, $905 per credit hour; Nonstate residents: per academic year $16,290, $905 per credit hour. *Doctoral*: State residents: per academic year $19,005, $905 per credit hour; Nonstate residents: per academic year $19,005, $905 per credit hour. Tuition is subject to change. See the following website for updates and changes in tuition costs: http://www.luc.edu/bursar/tuition.shtml.

Financial Assistance:
First-Year Students: Research assistantships available for first year. Average amount paid per academic year: $18,000. Average number of hours worked per week: 20. Apply by December 1.

Advanced Students: Teaching assistantships available for advanced students. Average amount paid per academic year: $18,000. Average number of hours worked per week: 20. Apply by March 1. Research assistantships available for advanced students. Average amount paid per academic year: $18,000. Average number of hours worked per week: 20. Apply by March 1.

Additional Information: Of all students currently enrolled full time, 80% benefited from one or more of the listed financial assistance programs. Application and information available online at: http://www.luc.edu/finaid/.

Internships/Practica: Doctoral Degree (PhD Clinical Psychology): For those doctoral students for whom a professional psychology internship was required in this program prior to graduation, (6) students applied for an internship in 2011–2012, with (6) students obtaining an internship. Of those students who obtained an internship, (6) were paid internships. Of those students who obtained an internship, (6) students placed in APA/CPA accredited internships, (0) students placed in internships not APA/CPA accredited, but listed with the Association of Psychology Postdoctoral and Internship Programs (APPIC), (0) students placed in internships conforming to guidelines of the Council of Directors of School Psychology Programs (CDSPP), (0) students placed in internships that were not APA/CPA accredited, APPIC or CDSPP listed. Externship experiences are available for clinical psychology students through our in-house Training Clinic at the Wellness Center. In addition, numerous externship training opportunities are available throughout the Chicago metropolitan area and clinical students apply nationally for APA-accredited internships. Students in the doctoral applied social psychology program serve a 1000-hour planning, research and evaluation internship during their third year, while students in the developmental program complete a 250-hour internship. These positions are usually found in health-related, governmental, and research organizations in the Chicago area.

Housing and Day Care: On-campus housing is available. See the following website for more information: http://www.luc.edu/reslife/. On-campus day care facilities are available. See the following website for more information: http://www.luc.edu/preschool/.

Employment of Department Graduates:
Master's Degree Graduates: Of those who graduated in the academic year 2011–2012, the following categories and numbers represent the postgraduate activities and employment of master's degree graduates: Enrolled in a psychology doctoral program (3), enrolled in a postdoctoral residency/fellowship (n/a), employed in independent practice (n/a), employed in business or industry (3), total from the above (master's) (6).

Doctoral Degree Graduates: Of those who graduated in the academic year 2011–2012, the following categories and numbers represent the postgraduate activities and employment of doctoral degree graduates: Enrolled in a psychology doctoral program (n/a), enrolled in a postdoctoral residency/fellowship (8), employed in an academic position at a 2-year/4-year college (4), employed in a professional position in a school system (1), employed in government agency (1), employed in a community mental health/counseling center (1), total from the above (doctoral) (15).

Additional Information:
Orientation, Objectives, and Emphasis of Department: Graduate study is organized into three areas: clinical, developmental, and social. All programs offer the PhD; only the social program offers a terminal MA in applied social psychology. The clinical program emphasizes the scientist–practitioner model, with students receiving extensive training in both areas. Students may specialize in work with children or adults. The developmental program provides training for students wishing to pursue the study of human development, particularly among infants, children, and adolescents. Cognition, social, gender role, and personality development are covered. The social psychology program includes training in both basic and applied social psychology. The emphasis in the applied program is on developing social psychologists who are capable of conducting applied research on the planning, evaluating, and modification of social programs in the areas of law and

criminal justice, educational systems, health and/or community services, and organizational behavior.

Special Facilities or Resources: Excellent libraries and computer support are available. Departmental facilities include specialized laboratories for audition, vision, and neurophysiology research; a general purpose laboratory for sensory processes; suites of research and observation rooms for clinical research; observation and videotaping rooms and equipment; an extensive psychological test library; a psychophysiology and biofeedback laboratory; and computer facilities.

Information for Students With Physical Disabilities: See the following website for more information: http://www.luc.edu/sswd/.

Application Information:
Send to Department of Psychology, Loyola University Chicago, 1032 West Sheridan Road, Chicago, IL 60660. Application available online. URL of online application: https://gpem.luc.edu/apply/. Students are admitted in the Fall, application deadline December 1. Deadline for clinical program is December 1; deadline for developmental and social programs is January 15. *Fee:* $40. No application fee for online application submissions.

Midwestern University
Clinical Psychology Program
College of Health Sciences
555 31st Street
Downers Grove, IL 60515
Telephone: (630) 515-7650
Fax: (630) 515-7655
E-mail: *afreem@midwestern.edu*
Web: *http://www.midwestern.edu/programs-and-admission/il-clinical-psychology.html*

Department Information:
2002. Executive Program Director: Arthur Freeman, Ed.D.,Sc.D. Number of faculty: total—full-time 9, part-time 7; women—full-time 6, part-time 5; total—minority—full-time 1; women minority—full-time 1.

Programs and Degrees Offered:
Listed in the following order: Program area, degree type (T if terminal Master's), number awarded 7/11–6/12. Clinical Psychology PsyD (Doctor of Psychology) 21.

Student Applications/Admissions:
Student Applications
Clinical Psychology PsyD (Doctor of Psychology)—Applications 2012–2013, 86. Total applicants accepted 2012–2013, 39. Number full-time enrolled (new admits only) 2012–2013, 20. Number part-time enrolled (new admits only) 2012–2013, 0. Total enrolled 2012–2013 full-time, 82. Openings 2013–2014, 22. The median number of years required for completion of a degree in 2012–2013 were 4. The number of students enrolled full- and part-time who were dismissed or voluntarily withdrew from this program area in 2012–2013 were 2.
Scores: Entries appear in this order: required test or GPA, minimum score (if required), median score of students entering

in 2012–2013. *Clinical Psychology PsyD (Doctor of Psychology):* GRE-V no minimum stated, GRE-Q no minimum stated, GRE-Analytical no minimum stated, overall undergraduate GPA 3.0.
Other Criteria: (importance of criteria rated low, medium, or high): GRE scores—medium, research experience—medium, work experience—medium, extracurricular activity—medium, clinically related public service—high, GPA—high, letters of recommendation—high, interview—high, statement of goals and objectives—medium, health care experience—medium, undergraduate major in psychology—medium, specific undergraduate psychology courses taken—low. For additional information on admission requirements, go to http://www.midwestern.edu/programs-and-admission/il-clinical-psychology/admissionapply.html.

Student Characteristics: The following represents characteristics of students in 2012–2013 in all graduate psychology programs in the department: Female—full-time 65, part-time 0; Male—full-time 17, part-time 0; African American/Black—full-time 3, part-time 0; Hispanic/Latino(a)—full-time 4, part-time 0; Asian/Pacific Islander—full-time 15, part-time 0; American Indian/Alaska Native—full-time 0, part-time 0; Caucasian/White—full-time 60, part-time 0; Multi-ethnic—full-time 0, part-time 0; students subject to the Americans With Disabilities Act—full-time 0, part-time 0; Unknown ethnicity—full-time 0, part-time 0; International students who hold an F-1 or J-1 Visa—full-time 0, part-time 0.

Financial Information/Assistance:
Tuition for Full-Time Study: *Doctoral:* State residents: per academic year $25,740, $485 per credit hour; Nonstate residents: per academic year $25,740, $485 per credit hour. Tuition is subject to change. Additional fees are assessed to students beyond the costs of tuition for the following: $255 for testing material fee. See the following website for updates and changes in tuition costs: http://www.midwestern.edu/programs-and-admission/student-financial-services/budgets.html.

Financial Assistance:
First-Year Students: No information provided.
Advanced Students: No information provided.
Additional Information: Of all students currently enrolled full time, 0% benefited from one or more of the listed financial assistance programs. Application and information available online at: http://www.midwestern.edu/programs-and-admission/student-financial-services.html.

Internships/Practica: Doctoral Degree (PsyD Clinical Psychology): For those doctoral students for whom a professional psychology internship was required in this program prior to graduation, (15) students applied for an internship in 2011–2012, with (15) students obtaining an internship. Of those students who obtained an internship, (15) were paid internships. Of those students who obtained an internship, (1) students placed in APA/CPA accredited internships, (14) students placed in internships not APA/CPA accredited, but listed with the Association of Psychology Postdoctoral and Internship Programs (APPIC), (0) students placed in internships conforming to guidelines of the Council of Directors of School Psychology Programs (CDSPP), (0) students placed in internships that were not APA/CPA accredited, APPIC or CDSPP listed. Students participate in clerkships during their first year under the supervision of program core faculty. These are clinical experiences at various direct service sites. A diagnostic practicum is completed in the second year and is followed with a therapy practicum. The fourth year of study consists of a full-time internship. Students may opt for an advanced practicum in their third year while postponing internship into the next year. Students are given individualized attention to help secure appropriate clinical training experiences in practica and internship. Midwestern University has numerous affiliation agreements with clinical sites throughout the metropolitan area of Chicago.

Housing and Day Care: On-campus housing is available. See the following website for more information: http://www.midwestern.edu/downers-grove-il-campus/housing.html. No on-campus day care facilities are available.

Employment of Department Graduates:
Master's Degree Graduates: Of those who graduated in the academic year 2011–2012, the following categories and numbers represent the postgraduate activities and employment of master's degree graduates: Enrolled in a postdoctoral residency/fellowship (n/a), employed in independent practice (n/a), total from the above (master's) (0).
Doctoral Degree Graduates: Of those who graduated in the academic year 2011–2012, the following categories and numbers represent the postgraduate activities and employment of doctoral degree graduates: Enrolled in a psychology doctoral program (n/a), enrolled in a postdoctoral residency/fellowship (12), employed in a professional position in a school system (1), employed in government agency (2), employed in a community mental health/counseling center (2), still seeking employment (2), do not know (2), total from the above (doctoral) (21).

Additional Information:
Orientation, Objectives, and Emphasis of Department: The program follows a practitioner-scholar model of training entry-level mental health professionals with an eclectic focus who can serve a diverse population. The training model adheres to a competency approach in the development of knowledge, skills, and attitudes related to the practice of clinical psychology. Students are systematically evaluated in the development of competency areas including relationship, assessment, intervention, professionalism, diversity, management and supervision, consultation and education, and research and evaluation. The program emphasizes first-year supervised clinical experiences to produce a foundation for later clinical training. The program provides an individualized mentoring experience for its students.

Special Facilities or Resources: The clinical psychology program has the full support of the resources available from the Midwestern University Osteopathic Medical School and School of Pharmacy, including research scientists and practicing clinicians. The program is housed on a large wooded campus with numerous buildings and research facilities including a state-of-the-art library. The majority of the physical resources have been constructed or remodeled in the past three years.

Application Information:
Send to Executive Program Director. Application available online. URL of online application: https://online.midwestern.edu/public/initapp.cgi?prog=ADCP. Programs have rolling admissions. *Fee:* $50.

Northern Illinois University
Department of Psychology
College of Liberal Arts and Sciences
DeKalb, IL 60115-2892
Telephone: (815) 753-0372
Fax: (815) 753-8088
E-mail: *mholliday@niu.edu*
Web: *http://www.niu.edu/psyc/*

Department Information:
1959. Chairperson: Greg Waas. Number of faculty: total—full-time 30; women—full-time 18; total—minority—full-time 2.

Programs and Degrees Offered:
Listed in the following order: Program area, degree type (T if terminal Master's), number awarded 7/11–6/12. Clinical Psychology PhD (Doctor of Philosophy) 7, Neuroscience and Behavior PhD (Doctor of Philosophy) 1, Social-Industrial/Organizational Psychology PhD (Doctor of Philosophy) 9, Cognitive Psychology PhD (Doctor of Philosophy) 0, Developmental Psychology PhD (Doctor of Philosophy) 0, School Psychology PhD (Doctor of Philosophy) 0.

APA Accreditation: Clinical PhD (Doctor of Philosophy). Student Outcome Data Website: http://www.niu.edu/psyc/graduate/clinical/admissions.shtml. School PhD (Doctor of Philosophy). Student Outcome Data Website: http://www.niu.edu/psyc/graduate/school/outcomes.shtml.

Student Applications/Admissions:
Student Applications
Clinical Psychology PhD (Doctor of Philosophy)—Applications 2012–2013, 235. Total applicants accepted 2012–2013, 14. Number full-time enrolled (new admits only) 2012–2013, 7. Number part-time enrolled (new admits only) 2012–2013, 0. Total enrolled 2012–2013 full-time, 45. Total enrolled 2012–2013 part-time, 2. Openings 2013–2014, 8. The median number of years required for completion of a degree in 2012–2013 were 8. The number of students enrolled full- and part-time who were dismissed or voluntarily withdrew from this program area in 2012–2013 were 0. *Neuroscience and Behavior PhD (Doctor of Philosophy)*—Applications 2012–2013, 18. Total applicants accepted 2012–2013, 5. Number full-time enrolled (new admits only) 2012–2013, 2. Total enrolled 2012–2013 full-time, 7. Total enrolled 2012–2013 part-time, 0. Openings 2013–2014, 2. The median number of years required for completion of a degree in 2012–2013 were 5. The number of students enrolled full- and part-time who were dismissed or voluntarily withdrew from this program area in 2012–2013 were 0. *Social-Industrial/Organizational Psychology PhD (Doctor of Philosophy)*—Applications 2012–2013, 80. Total applicants accepted 2012–2013, 10. Number full-time enrolled (new admits only) 2012–2013, 5. Total enrolled 2012–2013 full-time, 26. Total enrolled 2012–2013 part-time, 8. Openings 2013–2014, 6. The median number of years required for completion of a degree in 2012–2013 were 7. The number of students enrolled full- and part-time who were dismissed or voluntarily withdrew from this program area in 2012–2013 were 0. *Cognitive Psychology PhD (Doctor of Philosophy)*—Applications 2012–2013, 14. Total applicants accepted 2012–

2013, 3. Number full-time enrolled (new admits only) 2012–2013, 2. Total enrolled 2012–2013 full-time, 12. Total enrolled 2012–2013 part-time, 0. Openings 2013–2014, 2. The number of students enrolled full- and part-time who were dismissed or voluntarily withdrew from this program area in 2012–2013 were 0. *Developmental Psychology PhD (Doctor of Philosophy)*— Applications 2012–2013, 15. Total applicants accepted 2012–2013, 4. Number full-time enrolled (new admits only) 2012–2013, 2. Total enrolled 2012–2013 full-time, 8. Total enrolled 2012–2013 part-time, 0. Openings 2013–2014, 2. The number of students enrolled full- and part-time who were dismissed or voluntarily withdrew from this program area in 2012–2013 were 1. *School Psychology PhD (Doctor of Philosophy)*—Applications 2012–2013, 21. Total applicants accepted 2012–2013, 1. Number full-time enrolled (new admits only) 2012–2013, 1. Total enrolled 2012–2013 full-time, 15. Total enrolled 2012–2013 part-time, 4. Openings 2013–2014, 6. The number of students enrolled full- and part-time who were dismissed or voluntarily withdrew from this program area in 2012–2013 were 0.

Scores: Entries appear in this order: required test or GPA, minimum score (if required), median score of students entering in 2012–2013. *Clinical Psychology PhD (Doctor of Philosophy):* GRE-V no minimum stated, 160, GRE-Q no minimum stated, 156, overall undergraduate GPA 3.0, 3.74; *Social-Industrial/Organizational Psychology PhD (Doctor of Philosophy):* GRE-V no minimum stated, GRE-Q no minimum stated, GRE-Analytical no minimum stated, overall undergraduate GPA no minimum stated, Masters GPA no minimum stated; *School Psychology PhD (Doctor of Philosophy):* GRE-V no minimum stated, 160, GRE-Q no minimum stated, 148, GRE-Analytical no minimum stated, 4.0, overall undergraduate GPA no minimum stated, 3.43.

Other Criteria: (importance of criteria rated low, medium, or high): GRE scores—high, research experience—high, work experience—low, extracurricular activity—low, clinically related public service—low, GPA—high, letters of recommendation—high, interview—medium, statement of goals and objectives—high, Clinical and School programs interview students; other programs generally do not. For additional information on admission requirements, go to http://www.niu.edu/psyc/graduate/admissions/index.shtml.

Student Characteristics: The following represents characteristics of students in 2012–2013 in all graduate psychology programs in the department: Female—full-time 76, part-time 9; Male—full-time 37, part-time 5; African American/Black—full-time 6, part-time 0; Hispanic/Latino(a)—full-time 7, part-time 0; Asian/Pacific Islander—full-time 3, part-time 0; American Indian/Alaska Native—full-time 2, part-time 0; Caucasian/White—full-time 94, part-time 14; Multi-ethnic—full-time 1, part-time 0; students subject to the Americans With Disabilities Act—full-time 0, part-time 0; Unknown ethnicity—full-time 0, part-time 0; International students who hold an F-1 or J-1 Visa—full-time 5, part-time 0.

Financial Information/Assistance:
Tuition for Full-Time Study: *Master's:* State residents: $335 per credit hour; Nonstate residents: $671 per credit hour. *Doctoral:* State residents: $335 per credit hour; Nonstate residents: $671 per credit hour. Tuition is subject to change. Additional fees are assessed to students beyond the costs of tuition for the following:

General university student fees. See the following website for updates and changes in tuition costs: http://www.niu.edu/bursar/tuition/graduate.shtml.

Financial Assistance:
First-Year Students: Teaching assistantships available for first year. Average amount paid per academic year: $12,350. Average number of hours worked per week: 20. Research assistantships available for first year. Average amount paid per academic year: $12,350. Average number of hours worked per week: 20. Traineeships available for first year. Average amount paid per academic year: $12,350. Average number of hours worked per week: 20. Fellowships and scholarships available for first year.

Advanced Students: Teaching assistantships available for advanced students. Average amount paid per academic year: $12,350. Average number of hours worked per week: 20. Research assistantships available for advanced students. Average amount paid per academic year: $12,350. Average number of hours worked per week: 20. Traineeships available for advanced students. Average amount paid per academic year: $12,350. Average number of hours worked per week: 20. Fellowships and scholarships available for advanced students.

Additional Information: Of all students currently enrolled full time, 89% benefited from one or more of the listed financial assistance programs. Application and information available online at: http://www.niu.edu/psyc/graduate/admissions/financial.shtml.

Internships/Practica: Doctoral Degree (PhD Clinical Psychology): For those doctoral students for whom a professional psychology internship was required in this program prior to graduation, (6) students applied for an internship in 2011–2012, with (3) students obtaining an internship. Of those students who obtained an internship, (3) were paid internships. Of those students who obtained an internship, (3) students placed in APA/CPA accredited internships, (0) students placed in internships not APA/CPA accredited, but listed with the Association of Psychology Postdoctoral and Internship Programs (APPIC), (0) students placed in internships conforming to guidelines of the Council of Directors of School Psychology Programs (CDSPP), (0) students placed in internships that were not APA/CPA accredited, APPIC or CDSPP listed. Doctoral Degree (PhD School Psychology): For those doctoral students for whom a professional psychology internship was required in this program prior to graduation, (2) students applied for an internship in 2011–2012, with (2) students obtaining an internship. Of those students who obtained an internship, (2) were paid internships. Of those students who obtained an internship, (2) students placed in APA/CPA accredited internships, (0) students placed in internships not APA/CPA accredited, but listed with the Association of Psychology Postdoctoral and Internship Programs (APPIC), (0) students placed in internships conforming to guidelines of the Council of Directors of School Psychology Programs (CDSPP), (0) students placed in internships that were not APA/CPA accredited, APPIC or CDSPP listed. Clinical and school psychology students will undertake internsips. Clinical students also are required to take at least five semesters of clinical practicum in the in-house training clinic during the first three years of training as well as two semesters of an advanced clinical practicum at external placements.

Housing and Day Care: On-campus housing is available. See the following website for more information: http://www.niu.edu/housing/housing/grad_students.shtml. On-campus day care facilities are available. See the following website for more information: http://www.niu.edu/ccc/.

Employment of Department Graduates:

Master's Degree Graduates: Of those who graduated in the academic year 2011–2012, the following categories and numbers represent the postgraduate activities and employment of master's degree graduates: Enrolled in a postdoctoral residency/fellowship (n/a), employed in independent practice (n/a), total from the above (master's) (0).

Doctoral Degree Graduates: Of those who graduated in the academic year 2011–2012, the following categories and numbers represent the postgraduate activities and employment of doctoral degree graduates: Enrolled in a psychology doctoral program (n/a), enrolled in a postdoctoral residency/fellowship (3), employed in government agency (1), employed in a community mental health/counseling center (1), employed in a hospital/medical center (2), total from the above (doctoral) (7).

Additional Information:

Orientation, Objectives, and Emphasis of Department: The PhD program in psychology is designed to prepare graduate students to function in a variety of settings including academic institutions, which emphasize research and/or teaching, non-academic institutions, which emphasize research on mental health, human factors, or skill acquisition, and various consultative modalities, which emphasize practitioner applications and the delivery of human services. Doctorates are awarded in six specialty areas: APA-accredited programs in clinical psychology and school psychology (NASP-approved); cognitive/instructional; developmental; neuroscience and behavior; and social and industrial/organizational psychology. Students are equipped to conduct sophisticated, theoretically-based empirical research and to teach at the graduate or undergraduate level. In addition to academic placements, students can also find suitable employment as applied researchers or service practitioners in a variety of mental health (clinical), educational (instructional, developmental, school), physical health (neuroscience), or business (social and industrial/organizational) settings. The overall goal of the graduate program is to produce doctoral graduates who appreciate and are deeply committed to the study of psychological processes and behavior, who are familiar with fundamental knowledge in the field, and who are well-trained in methodology and modern techniques of data analysis.

Special Facilities or Resources: The department has a modern psychology building with offices for faculty, staff, and graduate students; classrooms; shops; a six-story research wing with research equipment, including computers and direct access to the university computer and Internet applications; and a Psychological Services Center for practicum training in clinical psychology.

Information for Students With Physical Disabilities: See the following website for more information: http://niu.edu/disability/.

Application Information:

Send to The Graduate School, Altgeld Hall, Northern Illinois University, DeKalb, IL 60115-2864. Application available online. URL of online application: http://www.niu.edu/grad/apply/degree_seeking.shtml. Students are admitted in the Fall, application deadline December 1. December 1 deadline for Clinical applicants. December 15 deadline for School. January 15 deadline for Social/Industrial Organiza-

tional and Neuroscience and Behavior. February 1 deadline for Cognitive/Instructional and Developmental. *Fee:* $40.

Northwestern University
Counseling Psychology
618 Library Place
Evanston, IL 60201
Telephone: (847) 733-4300
Fax: (847) 733-0390
E-mail: *counseling-psychology@northwestern.edu*
Web: *http://www.family-institute.org/education/ counselingpsychology*

Department Information:

Director of Counseling Psychology: Francesca G. Giordano, PhD. Number of faculty: total—full-time 3, part-time 17; women—full-time 3, part-time 12; total—minority—full-time 1, part-time 1; women minority—full-time 1, part-time 1.

Programs and Degrees Offered:

Listed in the following order: Program area, degree type (T if terminal Master's), number awarded 7/11–6/12. Counseling Psychology MA/MS (Master of Arts/Science) (T) 24.

Student Applications/Admissions:

Student Applications

Counseling Psychology MA/MS (Master of Arts/Science)—Number full-time enrolled (new admits only) 2012–2013, 26. Number part-time enrolled (new admits only) 2012–2013, 0. Total enrolled 2012–2013 full-time, 57. Total enrolled 2012–2013 part-time, 0.

Scores: Entries appear in this order: required test or GPA, minimum score (if required), median score of students entering in 2012–2013. *Counseling Psychology MA/MS (Master of Arts/Science):* GRE-V no minimum stated, GRE-Q no minimum stated, GRE-Analytical no minimum stated, overall undergraduate GPA no minimum stated.

Other Criteria: (importance of criteria rated low, medium, or high): GRE scores—medium, work experience—medium, extracurricular activity—low, clinically related public service—high, GPA—medium, letters of recommendation—high, interview—low, statement of goals and objectives—high, undergraduate major in psychology—high, specific undergraduate psychology courses taken—high. For additional information on admission requirements, go to http://www.family-institute.org/academics-alumni/counseling-psychology/admissions.

Student Characteristics: The following represents characteristics of students in 2012–2013 in all graduate psychology programs in the department: Female—full-time 49, part-time 0; Male—full-time 8, part-time 0; African American/Black—full-time 4, part-time 0; Hispanic/Latino(a)—full-time 5, part-time 0; Asian/Pacific Islander—full-time 3, part-time 0; American Indian/Alaska Native—full-time 2, part-time 0; Caucasian/White—full-time 43, part-time 0; Multi-ethnic—full-time 0, part-time 0; students subject to the Americans With Disabilities Act—full-time 0, part-time 0; Unknown ethnicity—full-time 0, part-time 0; Interna-

tional students who hold an F-1 or J-1 Visa—full-time 1, part-time 0.

Financial Information/Assistance:

Tuition for Full-Time Study: *Master's:* State residents: per academic year $43,380; Nonstate residents: per academic year $43,380. Tuition is subject to change. See the following website for updates and changes in tuition costs: http://www.northwestern.edu/sfs/tuition/t_grad_s_tuition.html.

Financial Assistance:

First-Year Students: No information provided.

Advanced Students: Teaching assistantships available for advanced students.

Additional Information: Application and information available online at: http://www.tgs.northwestern.edu/financial-aid/.

Internships/Practica: Master's Degree (MA/MS Counseling Psychology): An internship experience, such as a final research project or "capstone" experience is required of graduates. Fieldwork activity follows a developmental model consisting of a sequence of 9 to 12 month training experiences of increasing complexity and responsibility. Each training experience is designed to accommodate the student's particular level of professional development: pre-practica familiarize students with the basic features and broad outlines of mental health service delivery; practica serve primarily to introduce students to professional setting and clinical roles, and expose them to supervision and the supervisory relationship; and externships emphasize the expansion and refinement of clinical skills and behaviors specifically according to the student's identified goals, competencies and training needs. To optimize and personalize the clinical experience, each student is carefully matched with a quality field training setting and clinical supervisor every year, and the training process is closely monitored throughout the student's academic tenure. In addition, a distinctive feature of the program is the Preceptor Model of Clinical Training. The model embodies the program's strong belief in the importance of individualizing and personalizing the clinical training process: every Supervised Practicum student is assigned to a Backhome Preceptor, an experienced clinical practitioner who serves as a coach and mentor to facilitate the emergence of basic skills and professional identity development during the early phases of the training process specifically in concordance with the student's own personal attributes and characteristics.

Housing and Day Care: On-campus housing is available. See the following website for more information: http://www.northwestern.edu/gradhousing/. No on-campus day care facilities are available.

Employment of Department Graduates:

Master's Degree Graduates: Of those who graduated in the academic year 2011–2012, the following categories and numbers represent the postgraduate activities and employment of master's degree graduates: Enrolled in a postdoctoral residency/fellowship (n/a), employed in independent practice (n/a), total from the above (master's) (0).

Doctoral Degree Graduates: Of those who graduated in the academic year 2011–2012, the following categories and numbers represent the postgraduate activities and employment of doctoral degree graduates: Enrolled in a psychology doctoral program (n/a), total from the above (doctoral) (0).

Additional Information:

Orientation, Objectives, and Emphasis of Department: The Master of Arts in Counseling Psychology is dedicated to the cutting edge preparation of counseling psychologists. There are four pillars that create the foundation of the counseling psychology program. The program is influenced by the theoretical and intellectual traditions of both the Counseling Psychology field and the Counseling field. Additionally, the program has a unique training context as it is housed within the Family Institute at Northwestern University. The theoretical coursework from the counseling psychology tradition embraces a psychodynamic influence in its emphasis on the centrality of the therapeutic relationship as well as the emphasis on the importance of self-reflection and the person of the therapist. Students are encouraged to become practitioner-scholars by engaging a wide variety of research and scholarly projects and professional presentations. A counseling approach is infused throughout the coursework by reflecting issues of culture, ethics, and counselor identity. Counselors-in-training are intensely supervised as they work with clients at every step of their training process.

Information for Students With Physical Disabilities: See the following website for more information: http://www.northwestern.edu/disability/.

Application Information:

Application available online. URL of online application: https://app.applyyourself.com/?id=wu-grad. Students are admitted in the Fall, application deadline March 1. Early Decision December 31, Regular Decision March 1, Late Admissions April 30. *Fee:* $75.

Northwestern University
Department of Psychology
102 Swift Hall, 2029 Sheridan Road
Evanston, IL 60208-2710
Telephone: (847) 491-5190
Fax: (847) 491-7859
E-mail: *f-sales@northwestern.edu*
Web: *http://www.wcas.northwestern.edu/psych/*

Department Information:

1909. Chairperson: Dan P. McAdams. Number of faculty: total—full-time 37, part-time 1; women—full-time 12, part-time 1; total—minority—full-time 5; women minority—full-time 4.

Programs and Degrees Offered:

Listed in the following order: Program area, degree type (T if terminal Master's), number awarded 7/11–6/12. Clinical Psychology PhD (Doctor of Philosophy) 0, Cognitive Psychology PhD (Doctor of Philosophy) 2, Personality Psychology PhD (Doctor of Philosophy) 0, Brain, Behavior, and Cognition PhD (Doctor of Philosophy) 1, Social Psychology PhD (Doctor of Philosophy) 0.

APA Accreditation: Clinical PhD (Doctor of Philosophy). Student Outcome Data Website: http://www.wcas.northwestern.edu/psych/program_areas/clinical/ClinicalStudentOutcomes.htm.

Student Applications/Admissions:

Student Applications

Clinical Psychology PhD (Doctor of Philosophy)—Applications 2012–2013, 86. Total applicants accepted 2012–2013, 6. Number full-time enrolled (new admits only) 2012–2013, 2. Number part-time enrolled (new admits only) 2012–2013, 0. Total enrolled 2012–2013 full-time, 13. Total enrolled 2012–2013 part-time, 0. Openings 2013–2014, 2. The median number of years required for completion of a degree in 2012–2013 were 6. The number of students enrolled full- and part-time who were dismissed or voluntarily withdrew from this program area in 2012–2013 were 0. Cognitive Psychology PhD (Doctor of Philosophy)—Applications 2012–2013, 54. Total applicants accepted 2012–2013, 9. Number full-time enrolled (new admits only) 2012–2013, 7. Number part-time enrolled (new admits only) 2012–2013, 0. Total enrolled 2012–2013 full-time, 22. Total enrolled 2012–2013 part-time, 0. Openings 2013–2014, 3. The median number of years required for completion of a degree in 2012–2013 were 5. The number of students enrolled full- and part-time who were dismissed or voluntarily withdrew from this program area in 2012–2013 were 0. Personality Psychology PhD (Doctor of Philosophy)—Applications 2012–2013, 17. Total applicants accepted 2012–2013, 3. Number full-time enrolled (new admits only) 2012–2013, 3. Number part-time enrolled (new admits only) 2012–2013, 0. Total enrolled 2012–2013 full-time, 5. Total enrolled 2012–2013 part-time, 0. The median number of years required for completion of a degree in 2012–2013 were 5. The number of students enrolled full- and part-time who were dismissed or voluntarily withdrew from this program area in 2012–2013 were 0. Brain, Behavior, and Cognition PhD (Doctor of Philosophy)—Applications 2012–2013, 64. Total applicants accepted 2012–2013, 6. Number full-time enrolled (new admits only) 2012–2013, 5. Number part-time enrolled (new admits only) 2012–2013, 0. Total enrolled 2012–2013 full-time, 15. Total enrolled 2012–2013 part-time, 0. Openings 2013–2014, 2. The median number of years required for completion of a degree in 2012–2013 were 5. The number of students enrolled full- and part-time who were dismissed or voluntarily withdrew from this program area in 2012–2013 were 1. Social Psychology PhD (Doctor of Philosophy)—Applications 2012–2013, 148. Total applicants accepted 2012–2013, 5. Number full-time enrolled (new admits only) 2012–2013, 2. Number part-time enrolled (new admits only) 2012–2013, 0. Total enrolled 2012–2013 full-time, 15. Total enrolled 2012–2013 part-time, 0. The median number of years required for completion of a degree in 2012–2013 were 5. The number of students enrolled full- and part-time who were dismissed or voluntarily withdrew from this program area in 2012–2013 were 1.

Other Criteria: (importance of criteria rated low, medium, or high): GRE scores—high, research experience—high, GPA—high, letters of recommendation—medium, interview—medium, statement of goals and objectives—medium, undergraduate major in psychology—medium, specific undergraduate psychology courses taken—low. For additional information on admission requirements, go to http://www.wcas.northwestern.edu/psych/graduate_studies/prospective_students/.

Student Characteristics: The following represents characteristics of students in 2012–2013 in all graduate psychology programs in the department: Female—full-time 57, part-time 0; Male—full-time 31, part-time 0; African American/Black—full-time 7, part-time 0; Hispanic/Latino(a)—full-time 4, part-time 0; Asian/Pacific Islander—full-time 11, part-time 0; American Indian/Alaska Native—full-time 2, part-time 0; Caucasian/White—full-time 63, part-time 0; Multi-ethnic—full-time 1, part-time 0; students subject to the Americans With Disabilities Act—full-time 0, part-time 0; Unknown ethnicity—full-time 0, part-time 0; International students who hold an F-1 or J-1 Visa—full-time 5, part-time 0.

Financial Information/Assistance:

Tuition for Full-Time Study: Doctoral: State residents: per academic year $57,840; Nonstate residents: per academic year $57,840. Tuition is subject to change. See the following website for updates and changes in tuition costs: http://www.northwestern.edu/sfs/tuition/.

Financial Assistance:

First-Year Students: Fellowships and scholarships available for first year. Average amount paid per academic year: $21,876. Apply by December 1.

Advanced Students: Teaching assistantships available for advanced students. Average amount paid per academic year: $16,920. Average number of hours worked per week: 10. Research assistantships available for advanced students. Average amount paid per academic year: $16,920. Fellowships and scholarships available for advanced students. Average amount paid per academic year: $21,876.

Additional Information: Of all students currently enrolled full time, 100% benefited from one or more of the listed financial assistance programs. Application and information available online at: http://www.wcas.northwestern.edu/psych/graduate_studies/fellowship_and_funding/.

Internships/Practica: Doctoral Degree (PhD Clinical Psychology): For those doctoral students for whom a professional psychology internship was required in this program prior to graduation, (4) students applied for an internship in 2011–2012, with (4) students obtaining an internship. Of those students who obtained an internship, (4) were paid internships. Of those students who obtained an internship, (4) students placed in APA/CPA accredited internships, (0) students placed in internships not APA/CPA accredited, but listed with the Association of Psychology Postdoctoral and Internship Programs (APPIC), (0) students placed in internships conforming to guidelines of the Council of Directors of School Psychology Programs (CDSPP), (0) students placed in internships that were not APA/CPA accredited, APPIC or CDSPP listed. A variety of internships in community settings are available.

Housing and Day Care: On-campus housing is available. See the following website for more information: http://www.northwestern.edu/gradhousing/. No on-campus day care facilities are available.

Employment of Department Graduates:

Master's Degree Graduates: Of those who graduated in the academic year 2011–2012, the following categories and numbers represent the postgraduate activities and employment of master's degree graduates: Enrolled in a postdoctoral residency/fellowship (n/a), employed in independent practice (n/a), total from the above (master's) (0).

Doctoral Degree Graduates: Of those who graduated in the academic year 2011–2012, the following categories and numbers represent the postgraduate activities and employment of doctoral degree graduates: Enrolled in a psychology doctoral program (n/a), total from the above (doctoral) (0).

Additional Information:

Orientation, Objectives, and Emphasis of Department: The faculty in each graduate area has designed programs tailored to the needs of students in that area. Whatever a student's field of interest, the department tries to produce doctoral students with a strong research orientation. Administrative barriers between areas are permeable; most faculty members take an active part in the instruction and research programs of more than one interest area. A significant population of postdoctoral fellows enhances the informal professional education of graduate students. In addition, all graduate students are given opportunities for teaching. Teaching is independent of type of financial aid.

Information for Students With Physical Disabilities: See the following website for more information: http://www.northwestern. edu/disability/.

Application Information:

Send to Florence Sales, Graduate Admissions Coordinator, 102 Swift Hall, Department of Psychology, Northwestern University, 2029 Sheridan Road, Evanston, IL 60208-2710. Application available online. URL of online application: https://app.applyyourself.com/?id=wu-grad. Students are admitted in the Fall, application deadline December 1. *Fee:* $75.

Northwestern University Feinberg School of Medicine

Department of Psychiatry and Behavioral Sciences, Division of Psychology

Abbott Hall, Suite 1205, 710 North Lake Shore Drive

Chicago, IL 60611

Telephone: (312) 908-8262

Fax: (312) 908-5070

E-mail: *clinpsych@northwestern.edu*

Web: *http://www.clinpsych.northwestern.edu/doctoral-program-in-clinical-psychology/*

Department Information:

1970. Chief: Mark A. Reinecke, PhD Number of faculty: total—full-time 23, part-time 35; women—full-time 12, part-time 23; total—minority—full-time 1, part-time 1; women minority—part-time 1.

Programs and Degrees Offered:

Listed in the following order: Program area, degree type (T if terminal Master's), number awarded 7/11–6/12. Clinical Psychology PhD (Doctor of Philosophy) 4.

APA Accreditation: Clinical PhD (Doctor of Philosophy). Student Outcome Data Website: http://www.clinpsych.northwestern.edu/doctoral-program-in-clinical-psychology/student-admissions-outcomes-and-other-data/.

Student Applications/Admissions:

Student Applications

Clinical Psychology PhD (Doctor of Philosophy)—Applications 2012–2013, 356. Total applicants accepted 2012–2013, 14. Number full-time enrolled (new admits only) 2012–2013, 8. Number part-time enrolled (new admits only) 2012–2013, 0. Total enrolled 2012–2013 full-time, 40. Total enrolled 2012–2013 part-time, 0. Openings 2013–2014, 8. The median number of years required for completion of a degree in 2012–2013 were 7. The number of students enrolled full- and part-time who were dismissed or voluntarily withdrew from this program area in 2012–2013 were 0.

Scores: Entries appear in this order: required test or GPA, minimum score (if required), median score of students entering in 2012–2013. *Clinical Psychology PhD (Doctor of Philosophy):* GRE-V no minimum stated, 637, GRE-Q no minimum stated, 717, GRE-Analytical no minimum stated, 4.9, overall undergraduate GPA no minimum stated, 3.62.

Other Criteria: (importance of criteria rated low, medium, or high): GRE scores—medium, research experience—high, work experience—medium, clinically related public service—low, GPA—high, letters of recommendation—high, interview—high, statement of goals and objectives—high, undergraduate major in psychology—low, specific undergraduate psychology courses taken—low.

Student Characteristics: The following represents characteristics of students in 2012–2013 in all graduate psychology programs in the department: Female—full-time 36, part-time 0; Male—full-time 4, part-time 0; African American/Black—full-time 1, part-time 0; Hispanic/Latino(a)—full-time 1, part-time 0; Asian/Pacific Islander—full-time 5, part-time 0; American Indian/Alaska Native—full-time 0, part-time 0; Caucasian/White—full-time 33, part-time 0; Multi-ethnic—full-time 0, part-time 0; students subject to the Americans With Disabilities Act—full-time 0, part-time 0; Unknown ethnicity—full-time 0, part-time 0; International students who hold an F-1 or J-1 Visa—full-time 1, part-time 0.

Financial Information/Assistance:

Tuition for Full-Time Study: *Doctoral:* State residents: per academic year $43,380; Nonstate residents: per academic year $43,380. Tuition is subject to change. See the following website for updates and changes in tuition costs: http://www.tgs.northwestern.edu/financial-aid/Information/tuition-fees/index.html.

Financial Assistance:

First-Year Students: Research assistantships available for first year. Average amount paid per academic year: $22,428. Average number of hours worked per week: 24. Fellowships and scholarships available for first year.

Advanced Students: Research assistantships available for advanced students. Average amount paid per academic year: $22,428. Average number of hours worked per week: 24. Fellowships and scholarships available for advanced students.

Additional Information: Of all students currently enrolled full time, 100% benefited from one or more of the listed financial assistance programs. Application and information available online at: http://psychiatry.northwestern.edu/education/psychology-program/doctoral-program-in-clinical-psychology/tuitionfinancial-aid/.

Internships/Practica: Doctoral Degree (PhD Clinical Psychology): For those doctoral students for whom a professional psychology internship was required in this program prior to graduation, (5) students applied for an internship in 2011–2012, with (5) students obtaining an internship. Of those students who obtained an internship, (5) were paid internships. Of those students who obtained an internship, (5) students placed in APA/CPA accredited internships, (0) students placed in internships not APA/CPA accredited, but listed with the Association of Psychology Postdoctoral and Internship Programs (APPIC), (0) students placed in internships conforming to guidelines of the Council of Directors of School Psychology Programs (CDSPP), (0) students placed in internships that were not APA/CPA accredited, APPIC or CDSPP listed. Doctoral students generally have guaranteed practicum placements in their second and third year of the program. Practicum placements for second year students typically include Northwestern Memorial Hospital's (NMH) Stone Mental Health Center, Lurie Children's Hospital's Diagnostic/Neuropsychological Testing practicum, and the Neurobehavior and Memory Health Clinic at Northwestern University. Placements for third year students typically include Illinois Masonic Hospital, Cook County Hospital (John H. Stroger Jr. Hospital), the Counseling Services Department at the School of the Art Institute of Chicago, Jessie Brown VA, Lurie Children's Hospital's Child and Adolescent Psychiatry Outpatient Services, NMH's Inpatient Neuropsychological Consultation Service, Northwestern University Behavioral Medicine Practicum, University of Chicago Medical Center, and University of Illinois at Chicago. Examples of internship placements in the last three years include Children's National Hospital, University of California San Diego School of Medicine and VA Consortium, Packard Children's Hospital/Stanford University School of Medicine, Rush University Medical Center, Kennedy Krieger Institute/Johns Hopkins University School of Medicine, VA New Jersey Health Care System, University of Minnesota Medical School, Edward Hines Jr. VA Hospital, University of Tennessee Professional Psychology Internship Consortium, and Brown University's Alpert Medical School.

Housing and Day Care: No on-campus housing is available. On-campus day care facilities are available. See the following website for more information: http://www.tgs.northwestern.edu/graduate-life/student-parents/index.html.

Employment of Department Graduates:
Master's Degree Graduates: Of those who graduated in the academic year 2011–2012, the following categories and numbers represent the postgraduate activities and employment of master's degree graduates: Enrolled in a postdoctoral residency/fellowship (n/a), employed in independent practice (n/a), total from the above (master's) (0).
Doctoral Degree Graduates: Of those who graduated in the academic year 2011–2012, the following categories and numbers represent the postgraduate activities and employment of doctoral degree graduates: Enrolled in a psychology doctoral program (n/a), enrolled in a postdoctoral residency/fellowship (3), employed in a community mental health/counseling center (1), total from the above (doctoral) (4).

Additional Information:
Orientation, Objectives, and Emphasis of Department: The goal of our doctoral program is to train clinical psychologists who excel as scientist–practitioners and are competitive for positions in academic medical centers and similar healthcare centers. The program takes advantage of its placement within the Department of Psychiatry and Behavioral Sciences at the Feinberg School of Medicine by offering a true balance of research and clinical training. This unique setting provides opportunities for translational research and practice that span molecular to social models of disease, and epidemiologic to clinical and neuroimaging methodologies. Our program prepares students for research and clinical careers in academic medical centers and other health care settings. Preparation is provided through core and emphasis-specific curricula, intensive research mentoring and training, and at least three years of clinical practica. Milestones include a research qualifying paper, a clinical qualifying exam, an empirical dissertation with original research, and an APA-approved clinical internship. A Master's of Science in Clinical Psychology is available as part of the program. The program is committed to an evidence-based clinical model that provides intensive supervision and training to develop skills in assessment, diagnosis, and treatment. Research labs are organized into four emphases: Behavioral Medicine, Neuropsychology & Behavioral Neuroscience, Policy, and Psychopathology & Treatment. Clinical training is organized into 4 emphases: Adult Clinical, Behavioral Medicine, Clinical Child & Adolescent, and Clinical Neuropsychology.

Special Facilities or Resources: The doctoral program is located within a premier academic medical center and has access to numerous academic and research facilities, such as neuroimaging facilities (e.g., NU's Center for Translational Imaging), genomic services (e.g., NU's Genomics Core), and neuromodulation devices (e.g., Transcranial Magnetic Stimulation). Students in our program have full access to the world-class academic resources associated with Northwestern University, as well resources specific to the Feinberg School of Medicine, such as the Galter Health Sciences Library, the Learning Resources Center, and the Biostatistics Collaboration Center.

Information for Students With Physical Disabilities: See the following website for more information: http://www.northwestern.edu/disability/.

Application Information:
Application available online. URL of online application: https://app.applyyourself.com/?id—wu-grad. Students are admitted in the Fall, application deadline November 15. *Fee:* $75.

Roosevelt University
Department of Psychology
Arts and Sciences
430 South Michigan Avenue
Chicago, IL 60605-1394
Telephone: (312) 341-3760
Fax: (312) 341-6362
E-mail: *jchoca@roosevelt.edu*
Web: *http://www.roosevelt.edu/CAS/Programs/Psychology.aspx*

Department Information:
1945. Chairperson: Dr. James Choca. Number of faculty: total—full-time 24, part-time 39; women—full-time 12, part-time 23;

total—minority—full-time 3, part-time 4; women minority—full-time 2, part-time 4; faculty subject to the Americans With Disabilities Act 2.

Programs and Degrees Offered:

Listed in the following order: Program area, degree type (T if terminal Master's), number awarded 7/11–6/12. Clinical Psychology MA/MS (Master of Arts/Science) (T) 11, Industrial/Organizational Psychology MA/MS (Master of Arts/Science) (T) 31, Clinical Professional Psychology MA/MS (Master of Arts/Science) (T) 47, Clinical Psychology PsyD (Doctor of Psychology) 16, Industrial/Organizational Psychology PhD (Doctor of Philosophy) 0, Clinical Psychology (Counseling Practice) MA/MS (Master of Arts/Science) (T) 0.

APA Accreditation: Clinical PsyD (Doctor of Psychology). Student Outcome Data Website: http://www.roosevelt.edu/CAS/Programs/Psychology/PsyD.aspx.

Student Applications/Admissions:

Student Applications

Clinical Psychology MA/MS (Master of Arts/Science)—Applications 2012–2013, 49. Total applicants accepted 2012–2013, 27. Number full-time enrolled (new admits only) 2012–2013, 10. Number part-time enrolled (new admits only) 2012–2013, 3. Total enrolled 2012–2013 full-time, 14. Total enrolled 2012–2013 part-time, 8. Openings 2013–2014, 20. The median number of years required for completion of a degree in 2012–2013 were 3. The number of students enrolled full- and part-time who were dismissed or voluntarily withdrew from this program area in 2012–2013 were 0. *Industrial/Organizational Psychology MA/MS (Master of Arts/Science)*—Applications 2012–2013, 70. Total applicants accepted 2012–2013, 52. Number full-time enrolled (new admits only) 2012–2013, 16. Number part-time enrolled (new admits only) 2012–2013, 3. Total enrolled 2012–2013 full-time, 29. Total enrolled 2012–2013 part-time, 33. Openings 2013–2014, 25. The median number of years required for completion of a degree in 2012–2013 were 2. The number of students enrolled full- and part-time who were dismissed or voluntarily withdrew from this program area in 2012–2013 were 0. *Clinical Professional Psychology MA/MS (Master of Arts/Science)*—Applications 2012–2013, 201. Total applicants accepted 2012–2013, 153. Number full-time enrolled (new admits only) 2012–2013, 60. Number part-time enrolled (new admits only) 2012–2013, 14. Total enrolled 2012–2013 full-time, 144. Total enrolled 2012–2013 part-time, 82. The median number of years required for completion of a degree in 2012–2013 were 3. The number of students enrolled full- and part-time who were dismissed or voluntarily withdrew from this program area in 2012–2013 were 2. *Clinical Psychology PsyD (Doctor of Psychology)*—Applications 2012–2013, 207. Total applicants accepted 2012–2013, 37. Number full-time enrolled (new admits only) 2012–2013, 20. Number part-time enrolled (new admits only) 2012–2013, 0. Total enrolled 2012–2013 full-time, 71. Total enrolled 2012–2013 part-time, 28. Openings 2013–2014, 20. The median number of years required for completion of a degree in 2012–2013 were 5. The number of students enrolled full- and part-time who were dismissed or voluntarily withdrew from this program area in 2012–2013 were 3. *Industrial/Organizational Psychology PhD (Doctor of Philosophy)*—Applications 2012–2013, 19. Total applicants accepted 2012–2013, 6. Number

full-time enrolled (new admits only) 2012–2013, 5. Number part-time enrolled (new admits only) 2012–2013, 0. Total enrolled 2012–2013 full-time, 5. Total enrolled 2012–2013 part-time, 0. Openings 2013–2014, 8. The number of students enrolled full- and part-time who were dismissed or voluntarily withdrew from this program area in 2012–2013 were 0. *Clinical Psychology (Counseling Practice) MA/MS (Master of Arts/Science)*—Applications 2012–2013, 81. Total applicants accepted 2012–2013, 51. Number full-time enrolled (new admits only) 2012–2013, 24. Number part-time enrolled (new admits only) 2012–2013, 9. Total enrolled 2012–2013 full-time, 40. Total enrolled 2012–2013 part-time, 14. Openings 2013–2014, 90. The number of students enrolled full- and part-time who were dismissed or voluntarily withdrew from this program area in 2012–2013 were 1.

Scores: Entries appear in this order: required test or GPA, minimum score (if required), median score of students entering in 2012–2013. *Clinical Psychology MA/MS (Master of Arts/Science)*: overall undergraduate GPA 3.0, 3.4, last 2 years GPA 3.0, 3.5, psychology GPA 3.0, 3.5; *Industrial/Organizational Psychology MA/MS (Master of Arts/Science)*: GRE-V no minimum stated, 151, GRE-Q no minimum stated, 151, GRE-Analytical no minimum stated, 4, overall undergraduate GPA 3.0; *Clinical Professional Psychology MA/MS (Master of Arts/Science)*: overall undergraduate GPA 3.0, last 2 years GPA 3.0, 3.50, psychology GPA 3.0; *Clinical Psychology PsyD (Doctor of Psychology)*: GRE-V 150, GRE-Q 149, GRE-Analytical 4.0, overall undergraduate GPA 3.25; *Industrial/Organizational Psychology PhD (Doctor of Philosophy)*: GRE-V no minimum stated, 155, GRE-Q no minimum stated, 155, GRE-Analytical no minimum stated, 4, overall undergraduate GPA no minimum stated, 3.62; *Clinical Psychology (Counseling Practice) MA/MS (Master of Arts/Science)*: overall undergraduate GPA 3.0, 3.4, last 2 years GPA 3.0, 3.5, psychology GPA 3.0, 3.6.

Other Criteria: (importance of criteria rated low, medium, or high): GRE scores—high, research experience—medium, work experience—medium, extracurricular activity—low, clinically related public service—medium, GPA—high, letters of recommendation—medium, interview—high, statement of goals and objectives—medium, undergraduate major in psychology—medium, specific undergraduate psychology courses taken—medium, Ratings are shown for the PsyD program. The Clinical MA program matches the criteria above except it has a high rating for the Statement of Goals and Objectives. For additional information on admission requirements, go to http://www.roosevelt.edu/Admission/Graduate.

Student Characteristics: The following represents characteristics of students in 2012–2013 in all graduate psychology programs in the department: Female—full-time 240, part-time 124; Male—full-time 63, part-time 41; African American/Black—full-time 38, part-time 36; Hispanic/Latino(a)—full-time 34, part-time 14; Asian/Pacific Islander—full-time 19, part-time 5; American Indian/Alaska Native—full-time 1, part-time 0; Caucasian/White—full-time 193, part-time 98; Multi-ethnic—full-time 13, part-time 3; students subject to the Americans With Disabilities Act—full-time 2, part-time 1; Unknown ethnicity—full-time 5, part-time 9; International students who hold an F-1 or J-1 Visa—full-time 10, part-time 2.

Financial Information/Assistance:

Tuition for Full-Time Study: *Master's*: State residents: per academic year $17,850; Nonstate residents: per academic year

$17,850. *Doctoral:* State residents: per academic year $18,360; Nonstate residents: per academic year $18,360. Tuition is subject to change. Tuition costs vary by program. See the following website for updates and changes in tuition costs: http://www.roosevelt.edu/TuitionAndFees.aspx. Higher tuition cost for this program: PsyD: $21,930.

Financial Assistance:

First-Year Students: Research assistantships available for first year. Average amount paid per academic year: $5,200. Average number of hours worked per week: 17. Apply by March 1. Fellowships and scholarships available for first year. Average amount paid per academic year: $3,000. Average number of hours worked per week: 0.

Advanced Students: Research assistantships available for advanced students. Average amount paid per academic year: $5,200. Average number of hours worked per week: 17. Apply by March 1. Fellowships and scholarships available for advanced students. Average amount paid per academic year: $3,000. Apply by March 1.

Additional Information: Of all students currently enrolled full time, 25% benefited from one or more of the listed financial assistance programs. Application and information available online at: http://www.roosevelt.edu/FinancialAid/InfoPages/Graduate.aspx.

Internships/Practica: Doctoral Degree (PsyD Clinical Psychology): For those doctoral students for whom a professional psychology internship was required in this program prior to graduation, (15) students applied for an internship in 2011–2012, with (15) students obtaining an internship. Of those students who obtained an internship, (15) were paid internships. Of those students who obtained an internship, (14) students placed in APA/CPA accredited internships, (1) students placed in internships not APA/CPA accredited, but listed with the Association of Psychology Postdoctoral and Internship Programs (APPIC), (0) students placed in internships conforming to guidelines of the Council of Directors of School Psychology Programs (CDSPP), (0) students placed in internships that were not APA/CPA accredited, APPIC or CDSPP listed. Master's Degree (MA/MS Clinical Psychology): An internship experience, such as a final research project or "capstone" experience is required of graduates. Master's Degree (MA/MS Industrial/Organizational Psychology): An internship experience, such as a final research project or "capstone" experience is required of graduates. Master's Degree (MA/MS Clinical Professional Psychology): An internship experience, such as a final research project or "capstone" experience is required of graduates. Master's Degree (MA/MS Clinical Psychology (Counseling Practice)): An internship experience, such as a final research project or "capstone" experience is required of graduates. Students in our clinical programs have available over 250 sites in the greater Chicago area for practicum experience. We have a full-time Director of Training to assist students with this process. I/O, Clinical MA, and PsyD students have ample opportunities for training; I/O students nearly always obtain paid practicum experience.

Housing and Day Care: On-campus housing is available. See the following website for more information: http://www.roosevelt.edu/ResidenceLife.aspx. On-campus day care facilities are available. See the following website for more information: http://www.roosevelt.edu/Schaumburg/About/Childcare.aspx.

Employment of Department Graduates:

Master's Degree Graduates: Of those who graduated in the academic year 2011–2012, the following categories and numbers represent the postgraduate activities and employment of master's degree graduates: Enrolled in a postdoctoral residency/fellowship (n/a), employed in independent practice (n/a), total from the above (master's) (0).

Doctoral Degree Graduates: Of those who graduated in the academic year 2011–2012, the following categories and numbers represent the postgraduate activities and employment of doctoral degree graduates: Enrolled in a psychology doctoral program (n/a), enrolled in a postdoctoral residency/fellowship (7), employed in independent practice (1), employed in a community mental health/counseling center (6), employed in a hospital/medical center (2), total from the above (doctoral) (16).

Additional Information:

Orientation, Objectives, and Emphasis of Department: Roosevelt University was founded over 65 years ago, in 1945, on the principles of social justice and equal educational access for all qualified students. A primary goal of the Department of Psychology is to prepare students to work effectively with diverse cultures in metropolitan settings. Our new PhD program in I/O Psychology is based on the scientist–practitioner model of professional training and stresses the importance of apprenticeship, emphasizing working closely with faculty on research and applied projects outside of the classroom. The PsyD program, established in 1996, was the first university-based clinical PsyD program in Illinois. This program is designed to provide generalist training in all facets of clinical practice, in preparation for post-doctoral specialization of the student's choice. At the MA level, we currently have an I/O Psychology, and two Clinical Psychology programs which offer streamlined and personally tailored predoctoral training designed to help qualified students enter PhD or PsyD programs, including our own. The Clinical Psychology (Counseling Practice) program prepares students to apply for the professional counselor license in Illinois and other states. Approximately 85% of our graduates who have applied to doctoral programs have been accepted. We prepare students for professional employment in mental health and I/O careers.

Special Facilities or Resources: The Department of Psychology has an exceptional faculty who are actively involved in applied research and clinical practice, supplemented by a large and highly trained adjunct faculty similarly involved in clinical, forensic, and experimental work. In addition to the extensive Roosevelt library and other facilities, there is access to clinical, research, computer, and library facilities of major Chicago universities, hospitals, and clinics. Volunteer research assistantships are available to qualified students interested in doing publishable research. A major resource is the urban location with varied employment, educational, and cultural opportunities. The Stress Institute offers training in the Comprehensive Stress Management and Meditation/Mindfulness System for students and health professionals in clinical or I/O psychology, pastoral counseling, social work, counseling, nursing and rehabilitation. The Children and Family Studies Initiative allows students to train for the clinical treatment of children and families. The I/O Psychology Consulting Center aligns students with real-world experiences in the form of applied projects and internships with business, non-profit, government and educational organizations. The Instructor Development Program prepares PsyD students to teach undergraduate courses during the last 2 years of doctoral training.

Information for Students With Physical Disabilities: See the following website for more information: http://www.roosevelt.edu/StudentServices/Disability.

Application Information:

Send to Roosevelt University, Office of Admission, 1400 North Roosevelt Boulevard, Schaumburg, IL 60173. Application available online. URL of online application: http://www.roosevelt.edu/apply. Students are admitted in the Fall, application deadline December 15; Spring, application deadline November 1. PsyD program deadline is December 15 for fall admission only. Clinical MA Programs deadlines: Spring - November 1; Fall - February 1 (priority) and May 1 (final). I/O MA Program has Fall, Spring and Summer rolling admissions. I/O PhD Program deadline: February 15 (Fall admission only). *Fee:* $25.

Rosalind Franklin University of Medicine and Science

Department of Psychology
College of Health Professions
3333 Green Bay Road
North Chicago, IL 60064
Telephone: (847) 578-3305
Fax: (847) 578-8758
E-mail: *arthur.cantos@rosalindfranklin.edu*
Web: *http://www.rosalindfranklin.edu/chp/psychology.aspx*

Department Information:

1977. Chairperson: John Calamari, PhD. Number of faculty: total—full-time 8, part-time 1; women—full-time 2; total—minority—full-time 1.

Programs and Degrees Offered:

Listed in the following order: Program area, degree type (T if terminal Master's), number awarded 7/11–6/12. Clinical Psychology PhD (Doctor of Philosophy) 6, Clinical Counseling Psychology MA/MS (Master of Arts/Science) (T) 14.

APA Accreditation: Clinical PhD (Doctor of Philosophy). Student Outcome Data Website: http://www.rosalindfranklin.edu/chp/psychology/Doctorate/StudentData.aspx.

Student Applications/Admissions:

Student Applications

Clinical Psychology PhD (Doctor of Philosophy)—Applications 2012–2013, 91. Total applicants accepted 2012–2013, 14. Number full-time enrolled (new admits only) 2012–2013, 9. Total enrolled 2012–2013 full-time, 58. Openings 2013–2014, 7. The median number of years required for completion of a degree in 2012–2013 were 7. The number of students enrolled full- and part-time who were dismissed or voluntarily withdrew from this program area in 2012–2013 were 0. *Clinical Counseling Psychology MA/MS (Master of Arts/Science)*—Applications 2012–2013, 35. Total applicants accepted 2012–2013, 17. Number full-time enrolled (new admits only) 2012–2013, 17. Number part-time enrolled (new admits only) 2012–2013, 0.

Total enrolled 2012–2013 full-time, 38. Total enrolled 2012–2013 part-time, 2. Openings 2013–2014, 17. The median number of years required for completion of a degree in 2012–2013 were 2. The number of students enrolled full- and part-time who were dismissed or voluntarily withdrew from this program area in 2012–2013 were 0.

Scores: Entries appear in this order: required test or GPA, minimum score (if required), median score of students entering in 2012–2013. *Clinical Psychology PhD (Doctor of Philosophy):* GRE-V 600, GRE-Q 600, GRE-Analytical 4.5, last 2 years GPA 3.2; *Clinical Counseling Psychology MA/MS (Master of Arts/Science):* overall undergraduate GPA no minimum stated, last 2 years GPA 3.0.

Other Criteria: (importance of criteria rated low, medium, or high): GRE scores—medium, research experience—high, work experience—low, extracurricular activity—medium, clinically related public service—medium, GPA—high, letters of recommendation—high, interview—high, statement of goals and objectives—high. For additional information on admission requirements, go to http://www.rosalindfranklin.edu/Degreeprograms/ClinicalPsychology/apply.aspx.

Student Characteristics: The following represents characteristics of students in 2012–2013 in all graduate psychology programs in the department: Female—full-time 81, part-time 2; Male—full-time 15, part-time 0; African American/Black—full-time 5, part-time 0; Hispanic/Latino(a)—full-time 4, part-time 0; Asian/Pacific Islander—full-time 8, part-time 0; American Indian/Alaska Native—part-time 1; Caucasian/White—full-time 77, part-time 1; Multi-ethnic—full-time 0, part-time 0; students subject to the Americans With Disabilities Act—full-time 0, part-time 0; Unknown ethnicity—full-time 2, part-time 0; International students who hold an F-1 or J-1 Visa—full-time 0, part-time 0.

Financial Information/Assistance:

Tuition for Full-Time Study: *Master's:* State residents: per academic year $25,637; Nonstate residents: per academic year $25,637. *Doctoral:* State residents: per academic year $25,637; Nonstate residents: per academic year $25,637. Tuition is subject to change.

Financial Assistance:

First-Year Students: Research assistantships available for first year. Average number of hours worked per week: 10. Fellowships and scholarships available for first year.

Advanced Students: Teaching assistantships available for advanced students. Research assistantships available for advanced students. Average number of hours worked per week: 10. Traineeships available for advanced students. Average number of hours worked per week: 10. Fellowships and scholarships available for advanced students. Average number of hours worked per week: 10.

Additional Information: Of all students currently enrolled full time, 69% benefited from one or more of the listed financial assistance programs. Application and information available online at: http://www.rosalindfranklin.edu/prospectivestudents/StudentFinancialServices/financialaid.aspx.

Internships/Practica: Doctoral Degree (PhD Clinical Psychology): For those doctoral students for whom a professional psychology internship was required in this program prior to graduation, (8) students applied for an internship in 2011–2012, with (5) students obtaining an internship. Of those students who obtained

an internship, (5) were paid internships. Of those students who obtained an internship, (5) students placed in APA/CPA accredited internships, (0) students placed in internships not APA/CPA accredited, but listed with the Association of Psychology Postdoctoral and Internship Programs (APPIC), (0) students placed in internships conforming to guidelines of the Council of Directors of School Psychology Programs (CDSPP), (0) students placed in internships that were not APA/CPA accredited, APPIC or CDSPP listed. Master's Degree (MA/MS Clinical Counseling Psychology): An internship experience, such as a final research project or "capstone" experience is required of graduates. The Department enjoys formal relationships with many of the major clinical, health and neuropsychology facilities in the catchment area from Chicago to the south and Milwaukee to the north. These include both inpatient and outpatient facilities. Thus, students have the opportunity to obtain experience and clinical training with a diverse range of clinical populations and socioeconomic strata. Our students also receive training in our In-House free primary care mental health clinic, Healthy Families, serving the vulnerable and underserved/uninsured in northern Lake County, Illinois.

Housing and Day Care: On-campus housing is available. See the following website for more information: http://www.rosalindfranklin.edu/prospectivestudents/studenthousing.aspx. No on-campus day care facilities are available.

Employment of Department Graduates:

Master's Degree Graduates: Of those who graduated in the academic year 2011–2012, the following categories and numbers represent the postgraduate activities and employment of master's degree graduates: Enrolled in a psychology doctoral program (1), enrolled in a postdoctoral residency/fellowship (n/a), employed in independent practice (n/a), employed in government agency (1), employed in a community mental health/counseling center (7), do not know (3), total from the above (master's) (12).

Doctoral Degree Graduates: Of those who graduated in the academic year 2011–2012, the following categories and numbers represent the postgraduate activities and employment of doctoral degree graduates: Enrolled in a psychology doctoral program (n/a), enrolled in a postdoctoral residency/fellowship (5), other employment position (1), total from the above (doctoral) (6).

Additional Information:

Orientation, Objectives, and Emphasis of Department: The Department of Psychology offers an APA-approved program leading to the PhD degree in clinical psychology. Within the context of the general clinical training program, students select a specialty emphasis in clinical neuropsychology, psychopathology or health/behavioral medicine. The program provides students with intensive training in the methods and theories of clinical practice with emphasis in these specialty areas. Research is a vital part of the program and students work closely with professors throughout their training. Research topics include biopsychosocial issues associated with various medical illnesses (e.g., cancer, diabetes, heart disease), aging, psychopathology (e.g., schizophrenia, OCD, psychopathy; intimate partner violence), and neuropsychological features of various clinical populations (e.g., epilepsy, head injury, multiple sclerosis, AIDS, Alzheimer's disease, dementia, stroke). Subject populations range in age from childhood through adulthood and include those with physical and psychiatric disorders. The Department subscribes to the philosophy that a clinical psychologist is knowledgeable in formulating and solving scientific problems, and skilled in formulating clinical problems and applying empirically supported interventions. To this end, core courses are organized as integrated theory-research-practice units with a problem solving orientation. Our goal is to graduate clinical psychologists who are highly trained, clinically effective, and able to contribute to the continuing development of the profession as practitioners, teachers, and researchers.

Special Facilities or Resources: Research facilities within the Department include an Experimental Neuropsychology Lab, Clinical Health Psychophysiology Lab, Neuroimaging Laboratory, and a Behavioral Therapy Lab. There are ongoing research programs in arthritis, oncology, diabetes, blood pressure regulation, epilepsy, anxiety disorders, schizophrenia, psychopathy, aging and dementia and intimate partner violence. Collaborative research opportunities are also ongoing with a number of community and academic institutions in the area and include projects using MRI and fMRI to study higher order cognitive processes.

Information for Students With Physical Disabilities: See the following website for more information: http://www.rosalindfranklin.edu/campuslife/disabilities.aspx.

Application Information:
Send to Rosalind Franklin University of Medicine and Science, CHP Admissions Office, 3333 Green Bay Road, North Chicago, IL 60064. Students are admitted in the Fall, application deadline December 1. *Fee:* $50.

Southern Illinois University Carbondale
Department of Psychology
College of Liberal Arts
Life Science Building II, Room 281
Carbondale, IL 62901
Telephone: (618) 453-3564
Fax: (618) 453-3563
E-mail: *benrodii@siu.edu*
Web: *http://www.psychology.siu.edu*

Department Information:
1948. Chairperson: Benjamin Rodriguez. Number of faculty: total—full-time 22, part-time 2; women—full-time 10, part-time 2; total—minority—full-time 3; women minority—full-time 3.

Programs and Degrees Offered:
Listed in the following order: Program area, degree type (T if terminal Master's), number awarded 7/11–6/12. Clinical Psychology PhD (Doctor of Philosophy) 3, Counseling Psychology PhD (Doctor of Philosophy) 5, Applied Psychology PhD (Doctor of Philosophy) 0, Brain and Cognitive Sciences PhD (Doctor of Philosophy) 2.

APA Accreditation: Clinical PhD (Doctor of Philosophy). Counseling PhD (Doctor of Philosophy).

Student Applications/Admissions:
Student Applications
Clinical Psychology PhD (Doctor of Philosophy)—Applications 2012–2013, 130. Total applicants accepted 2012–2013, 10.

Number full-time enrolled (new admits only) 2012–2013, 7. Total enrolled 2012–2013 full-time, 31. Total enrolled 2012–2013 part-time, 0. Openings 2013–2014, 6. The median number of years required for completion of a degree in 2012–2013 were 6. The number of students enrolled full- and part-time who were dismissed or voluntarily withdrew from this program area in 2012–2013 were 0. *Counseling Psychology PhD (Doctor of Philosophy)*—Applications 2012–2013, 78. Total applicants accepted 2012–2013, 10. Number full-time enrolled (new admits only) 2012–2013, 4. Total enrolled 2012–2013 full-time, 20. Openings 2013–2014, 5. The median number of years required for completion of a degree in 2012–2013 were 5. The number of students enrolled full- and part-time who were dismissed or voluntarily withdrew from this program area in 2012–2013 were 0. *Applied Psychology PhD (Doctor of Philosophy)*—Applications 2012–2013, 19. Total applicants accepted 2012–2013, 6. Number full-time enrolled (new admits only) 2012–2013, 3. Number part-time enrolled (new admits only) 2012–2013, 0. Total enrolled 2012–2013 full-time, 16. Total enrolled 2012–2013 part-time, 0. Openings 2013–2014, 3. The median number of years required for completion of a degree in 2012–2013 were 6. The number of students enrolled full- and part-time who were dismissed or voluntarily withdrew from this program area in 2012–2013 were 0. *Brain and Cognitive Sciences PhD (Doctor of Philosophy)*—Applications 2012–2013, 25. Total applicants accepted 2012–2013, 8. Number full-time enrolled (new admits only) 2012–2013, 3. Total enrolled 2012–2013 full-time, 20. Openings 2013–2014, 3. The median number of years required for completion of a degree in 2012–2013 were 5. The number of students enrolled full- and part-time who were dismissed or voluntarily withdrew from this program area in 2012–2013 were 1.

Scores: Entries appear in this order: required test or GPA, minimum score (if required), median score of students entering in 2012–2013. *Clinical Psychology PhD (Doctor of Philosophy):* GRE-V no minimum stated, GRE-Q no minimum stated, overall undergraduate GPA no minimum stated, last 2 years GPA no minimum stated, psychology GPA no minimum stated; *Counseling Psychology PhD (Doctor of Philosophy):* GRE-V no minimum stated, GRE-Q no minimum stated, overall undergraduate GPA no minimum stated, last 2 years GPA no minimum stated, psychology GPA no minimum stated; *Applied Psychology PhD (Doctor of Philosophy):* GRE-V no minimum stated, GRE-Q no minimum stated, overall undergraduate GPA no minimum stated, last 2 years GPA no minimum stated, psychology GPA no minimum stated; *Brain and Cognitive Sciences PhD (Doctor of Philosophy):* GRE-V no minimum stated, GRE-Q no minimum stated, overall undergraduate GPA no minimum stated, last 2 years GPA no minimum stated, psychology GPA no minimum stated.

Other Criteria: (importance of criteria rated low, medium, or high): GRE scores—medium, research experience—high, work experience—medium, extracurricular activity—medium, clinically related public service—medium, GPA—medium, letters of recommendation—high, interview—low, statement of goals and objectives—high, undergraduate major in psychology—medium, specific undergraduate psychology courses taken—medium, Some variation across programs. Clinical/work experiences relevant to programs are important. For additional information on admission requirements, go to http://www.psychology.siu.edu.

Student Characteristics: The following represents characteristics of students in 2012–2013 in all graduate psychology programs in the department: Female—full-time 48, part-time 0; Male—full-time 39, part-time 0; African American/Black—full-time 8, part-time 0; Hispanic/Latino(a)—full-time 0, part-time 0; Asian/Pacific Islander—full-time 9, part-time 0; American Indian/Alaska Native—full-time 0, part-time 0; Caucasian/White—full-time 68, part-time 0; Multi-ethnic—full-time 2, part-time 0; students subject to the Americans With Disabilities Act—full-time 1, part-time 0; Unknown ethnicity—full-time 0, part-time 0; International students who hold an F-1 or J-1 Visa—full-time 7, part-time 0.

Financial Information/Assistance:

Tuition for Full-Time Study: *Master's:* State residents: per academic year $7,872, $328 per credit hour; Nonstate residents: per academic year $19,680, $820 per credit hour. *Doctoral:* State residents: per academic year $7,872, $328 per credit hour; Nonstate residents: per academic year $19,680, $820 per credit hour. Tuition is subject to change. Additional fees are assessed to students beyond the costs of tuition for the following: Health care and activity fees, approximately $1550 per semester. See the following website for updates and changes in tuition costs: http://www.gradschool.siuc.edu.

Financial Assistance:

First-Year Students: Teaching assistantships available for first year. Average amount paid per academic year: $12,060. Average number of hours worked per week: 20. Research assistantships available for first year. Average amount paid per academic year: $12,060. Average number of hours worked per week: 20. Traineeships available for first year. Average amount paid per academic year: $12,060. Average number of hours worked per week: 20. Fellowships and scholarships available for first year. Average amount paid per academic year: $12,060. Average number of hours worked per week: 20.

Advanced Students: Teaching assistantships available for advanced students. Average amount paid per academic year: $13,518. Average number of hours worked per week: 20. Research assistantships available for advanced students. Average amount paid per academic year: $13,518. Average number of hours worked per week: 20. Traineeships available for advanced students. Average amount paid per academic year: $13,518. Average number of hours worked per week: 20. Fellowships and scholarships available for advanced students. Average amount paid per academic year: $13,518. Average number of hours worked per week: 20.

Additional Information: Of all students currently enrolled full time, 100% benefited from one or more of the listed financial assistance programs.

Internships/Practica: Doctoral Degree (PhD Clinical Psychology): For those doctoral students for whom a professional psychology internship was required in this program prior to graduation, (5) students applied for an internship in 2011–2012, with (4) students obtaining an internship. Of those students who obtained an internship, (4) were paid internships. Of those students who obtained an internship, (4) students placed in APA/CPA accredited internships, (0) students placed in internships not APA/CPA accredited, but listed with the Association of Psychology Postdoctoral and Internship Programs (APPIC), (0) students placed in internships conforming to guidelines of the Council of Directors of School Psychology Programs (CDSPP), (0) students placed in internships that were not APA/CPA accredited, APPIC or CDSPP listed. Doctoral Degree (PhD Counseling Psychology): For those doctoral students for whom a professional psychology internship was required in this program prior to graduation, (4) students applied for an internship in 2011–2012, with (4) students obtaining an internship. Of those students who obtained an internship, (4) were paid internships. Of those students who obtained an internship, (4) students placed in APA/CPA accredited internships, (0) students placed in internships not APA/CPA accredited, but listed with the Association of Psychology Postdoctoral and Internship Programs (APPIC), (0) students placed in internships conforming to guidelines of the Council of Directors of School Psychology Programs (CDSPP), (0) students placed in internships that were not APA/CPA accredited, APPIC or CDSPP listed. A variety of practica and field experiences are available at a department Career Development & Resource Clinic, a university Clinical Center, campus Counseling Center, campus Health Service, Applied Research Consultants, and various local mental health centers, hospitals, and human service agencies.

Housing and Day Care: On-campus housing is available. See the following website for more information: http://www.housing.siu.edu/. On-campus day care facilities are available.

Employment of Department Graduates:

Master's Degree Graduates: Of those who graduated in the academic year 2011–2012, the following categories and numbers represent the postgraduate activities and employment of master's degree graduates: Enrolled in a postdoctoral residency/fellowship (n/a), employed in independent practice (n/a), total from the above (master's) (0).

Doctoral Degree Graduates: Of those who graduated in the academic year 2011–2012, the following categories and numbers represent the postgraduate activities and employment of doctoral degree graduates: Enrolled in a psychology doctoral program (n/a), enrolled in a postdoctoral residency/fellowship (1), employed in independent practice (0), employed in an academic position at a university (1), employed in other positions at a higher education institution (1), employed in government agency (1), employed in a community mental health/counseling center (3), employed in a hospital/medical center (3), do not know (1), total from the above (doctoral) (11).

Additional Information:

Orientation, Objectives, and Emphasis of Department: The department maintains a collaborative learning environment that is responsive to student needs, that promotes professional development, and that sustains high academic standards. In all programs the student selects courses from a rich curriculum that promotes mastery of core material while allowing the pursuit of particular interests. A favorable student-faculty ratio permits close supervision of students, whether in student research, clinical/applied practica, or training assignments that provide graduated experience in research, teaching, and service as a complement to formal coursework. Such training serves to expose students to many of the activities in which they will be engaged after receiving their degrees.

Special Facilities or Resources: The department is located in a building with extensive laboratory facilities for human and animal research available to all students. Additional facilities include a clinic and a counseling center for practicum and research experiences.

Application Information:

Send to Psychology Graduate Admissions, SIUC, Mailcode 6502, Carbondale, IL 62901-6502. Application available online. URL of online application: http://www.psychology.siu.edu. Students are admitted in the Fall, application deadline Clinical: December 1 Counseling: December 1 Applied Psychology: February 1 Brain and Cognitive Sciences: February 1. *Fee:* $50. Students experiencing significant financial need may apply for waiver.

Southern Illinois University Edwardsville
Department of Psychology
Box 1121
Edwardsville, IL 62026-1121
Telephone: (618) 650-2202
Fax: (618) 650-5087
E-mail: *prose@siue.edu*
Web: *http://www.siue.edu/education/psychology/graduate/*

Department Information:

1964. Chairperson: Paul Rose. Number of faculty: total—full-time 20, part-time 5; women—full-time 10, part-time 4; total—minority—full-time 2; women minority—full-time 1; faculty subject to the Americans With Disabilities Act 2.

Programs and Degrees Offered:

Listed in the following order: Program area, degree type (T if terminal Master's), number awarded 7/11–6/12. School Psychology EdS (School Psychology) 8, Clinical-Adult Psychology MA/MS (Master of Arts/Science) (T) 11, Industrial/Organizational Psychology MA/MS (Master of Arts/Science) (T) 9, Clinical Child and School Psychology MA/MS (Master of Arts/Science) (T) 15.

Student Applications/Admissions:

Student Applications

School Psychology EdS (School Psychology)—Applications 2012–2013, 12. Total applicants accepted 2012–2013, 6. Number full-time enrolled (new admits only) 2012–2013, 6. Number part-time enrolled (new admits only) 2012–2013, 0. Total enrolled 2012–2013 full-time, 12. Total enrolled 2012–2013 part-time, 0. Openings 2013–2014, 10. The median number of years required for completion of a degree in 2012–2013 were 2. The number of students enrolled full- and part-time who were dismissed or voluntarily withdrew from this program area in 2012–2013 were 0. *Clinical-Adult Psychology MA/MS (Master of Arts/Science)*—Applications 2012–2013, 40. Total applicants accepted 2012–2013, 16. Number full-time enrolled (new admits only) 2012–2013, 10. Number part-time enrolled (new admits only) 2012–2013, 0. Total enrolled 2012–2013 full-time, 23. Total enrolled 2012–2013 part-time, 0. Openings 2013–2014, 10. The median number of years required for completion of a degree in 2012–2013 were 2. The number of students enrolled full- and part-time who were dismissed or voluntarily withdrew from this program area in 2012–2013 were 0. *Industrial/Organizational Psychology MA/MS (Master of Arts/Science)*—Applications 2012–2013, 40. Total applicants accepted 2012–2013, 15. Number full-time enrolled (new admits only) 2012–2013, 10. Number part-time enrolled (new admits only) 2012–2013, 0. Total enrolled 2012–2013 full-time, 25. Total enrolled 2012–2013 part-time, 0. Openings 2013–2014, 10. The median number of years required for completion of a degree in 2012–2013 were 2. The number of students enrolled full- and part-time who were dismissed or voluntarily withdrew from this program area in 2012–2013 were 0. *Clinical Child and School Psychology MA/MS (Master of Arts/Science)*—Applications 2012–2013, 65. Total applicants accepted 2012–2013, 16. Number full-time enrolled (new admits only) 2012–2013, 10. Number part-time enrolled (new admits only) 2012–2013, 0. Total enrolled 2012–2013 full-time, 20. Total enrolled 2012–2013 part-time, 0. Openings 2013–2014, 10. The median number of years required for completion of a degree in 2012–2013 were 2. The number of students enrolled full- and part-time who were dismissed or voluntarily withdrew from this program area in 2012–2013 were 2.

Scores: Entries appear in this order: required test or GPA, minimum score (if required), median score of students entering in 2012–2013. *School Psychology EdS (School Psychology):* GRE-V no minimum stated, GRE-Q no minimum stated, GRE-Analytical no minimum stated, overall undergraduate GPA no minimum stated; *Clinical-Adult Psychology MA/MS (Master of Arts/Science):* GRE-V no minimum stated, GRE-Q no minimum stated, GRE-Analytical no minimum stated; *Industrial/Organizational Psychology MA/MS (Master of Arts/Science):* GRE-V no minimum stated, GRE-Q no minimum stated, GRE-Analytical no minimum stated, overall undergraduate GPA no minimum stated; *Clinical Child and School Psychology MA/MS (Master of Arts/Science):* GRE-V no minimum stated, GRE-Q no minimum stated, GRE-Analytical no minimum stated, overall undergraduate GPA no minimum stated.

Other Criteria: (importance of criteria rated low, medium, or high): GRE scores—medium, research experience—high, work experience—medium, extracurricular activity—medium, clinically related public service—medium, GPA—high, letters of recommendation—high, interview—high, statement of goals and objectives—high, undergraduate major in psychology—medium, specific undergraduate psychology courses taken—high. For additional information on admission requirements, go to http://www.siue.edu/education/psychology/graduate/apinfo.shtml.

Student Characteristics: The following represents characteristics of students in 2012–2013 in all graduate psychology programs in the department: Female—full-time 60, part-time 0; Male—full-time 20, part-time 0; African American/Black—full-time 4, part-time 0; Hispanic/Latino(a)—full-time 3, part-time 0; Asian/Pacific Islander—full-time 2, part-time 0; American Indian/Alaska Native—full-time 0, part-time 0; Caucasian/White—full-time 71, part-time 0; Multi-ethnic—full-time 0, part-time 0; students subject to the Americans With Disabilities Act—full-time 1, part-time 0; Unknown ethnicity—full-time 0, part-time 0; International students who hold an F-1 or J-1 Visa—full-time 1, part-time 0.

Financial Information/Assistance:

Tuition for Full-Time Study: *Master's:* State residents: per academic year $8,292, $691 per credit hour; Nonstate residents: per academic year $18,046, $1,504 per credit hour. Tuition is subject to change. See the following website for updates and changes in tuition costs: http://www.siue.edu/apply/tuition/.

Financial Assistance:

First-Year Students: Research assistantships available for first year. Average amount paid per academic year: $3,555. Average number of hours worked per week: 10. Apply by March 1. Fellowships and scholarships available for first year. Average amount paid per academic year: $7,425. Average number of hours worked per week: 0. Apply by January 15.

Advanced Students: Research assistantships available for advanced students. Average amount paid per academic year: $3,825. Average number of hours worked per week: 10. Apply by March 1.

Additional Information: Of all students currently enrolled full time, 80% benefited from one or more of the listed financial assistance programs. Application and information available online at: http://www.siue.edu/education/psychology/graduate/.

Internships/Practica: Master's Degree (MA/MS Clinical-Adult Psychology): An internship experience, such as a final research project or "capstone" experience is required of graduates. Master's Degree (MA/MS Industrial/Organizational Psychology): An internship experience, such as a final research project or "capstone" experience is required of graduates. Master's Degree (MA/MS Clinical Child and School Psychology): An internship experience, such as a final research project or "capstone" experience is required of graduates. All graduate programs require several credit hours of supervised practicum experience in appropriate professional settings. The Specialist Degree Program also requires a 10-hour-per-week paid internship.

Housing and Day Care: On-campus housing is available. See the following website for more information: http://www.siue.edu/housing/. On-campus day care facilities are available. See the following website for more information: http://www.siue.edu/earlychildhood/.

Employment of Department Graduates:

Master's Degree Graduates: Of those who graduated in the academic year 2011–2012, the following categories and numbers represent the postgraduate activities and employment of master's degree graduates: Enrolled in a psychology doctoral program (3), enrolled in a postdoctoral residency/fellowship (n/a), employed in independent practice (n/a), employed in an academic position at a university (2), employed in a professional position in a school system (9), employed in business or industry (9), employed in government agency (2), employed in a community mental health/counseling center (4), employed in a hospital/medical center (3), total from the above (master's) (32).

Doctoral Degree Graduates: Of those who graduated in the academic year 2011–2012, the following categories and numbers represent the postgraduate activities and employment of doctoral degree graduates: Enrolled in a psychology doctoral program (n/a), total from the above (doctoral) (0).

Additional Information:

Orientation, Objectives, and Emphasis of Department: The department, faculty and students have won several awards for teaching excellence, educational outcomes, academic excellence and community contribution. The department is generally eclectic in orientation. Students in each specialization are provided with training that is balanced between scientific and applied orientations.

Special Facilities or Resources: The psychology department houses faculty offices, classrooms, and approximately 10,000 square feet of laboratory space. Sophisticated resources are available, including videotaping equipment, computers and software for data analysis, books containing the full text of thousands of psychological measures and online data collection and discussion tools.

Information for Students With Physical Disabilities: See the following website for more information: http://www.siue.edu/dss/.

Application Information:

Send to Attention: Graduate Records Secretary, Psychology Department, Box 1121, Edwardsville, IL 62026. Application available online. URL of online application: http://www.siue.edu/graduatestudents/apply/. Students are admitted in the Fall, application deadline February 1. *Fee:* $30.

The Chicago School of Professional Psychology
Professional School
325 North Wells
Chicago, IL 60654
Telephone: (800) 721-8072
E-mail: *admissions@thechicagoschool.edu*
Web: *http://www.thechicagoschool.edu*

Department Information:

1979. President: Michele Nealon-Woods. Number of faculty: total—full-time 73, part-time 246; women—full-time 42, part-time 161; total—minority—full-time 19, part-time 25; women minority—full-time 12, part-time 14.

Programs and Degrees Offered:

Listed in the following order: Program area, degree type (T if terminal Master's), number awarded 7/11–6/12. Clinical Psychology PsyD (Doctor of Psychology) 62, Industrial/Organizational Psychology MA/MS (Master of Arts/Science) (T) 177, Forensic Psychology MA/MS (Master of Arts/Science) (T) 145, Clinical Psychology (Applied Behavior Analysis) MA/MS (Master of Arts/Science) (T) 48, Clinical Psychology (Counseling) MA/MS (Master of Arts/Science) (T) 137, Business Psychology PsyD (Doctor of Psychology) 9, School Psychology EdS (School Psychology) 46, Board Certified Behavior Analyst Respecialization Respecialization Diploma 53, Applied Behavior Analysis PhD (Doctor of Philosophy), Applied Forensics Certificate Other 54, Applied Industrial/Organizational Certificate Other 17, General Psychology MA/MS (Master of Arts/Science) (T) 157, Organizational Leadership PhD (Doctor of Philosophy), International Psychology PhD (Doctor of Philosophy) 2, Clinical Psychology (Marital and Family Therapy) MA/MS (Master of Arts/Science) (T) 103, Marital and Family Therapy PsyD (Doctor of Psychology), Psychology PsyD (Doctor of Psychology) 24, Clinical Forensic Psychology PsyD (Doctor of Psychology), Child and Adolescent Psychology Certificate Other 13, Consumer Psychology Certificate Other 5, Leadership in Healthcare Professions Certificate Other 1, Organizational Effectiveness Certificate Other 1, Work-

place Diversity Certificate Other 3, School Psychology EdD (Doctor of Education), Counselor Ed & Supervision PhD (Doctor of Philosophy), Somatic Psychology MA/MS (Master of Arts/Science), Somatic Psychology PhD (Doctor of Philosophy), Applied Clinical Psychology PsyD (Doctor of Psychology), Clinical Psychology (Child and Adolescent) PsyD (Doctor of Psychology) 11.

APA Accreditation: Clinical PsyD (Doctor of Psychology). Student Outcome Data Website: http://www.thechicagoschool.edu/Chicago/Our_Programs/PsyD_in_Clinical_Psychology.

Student Applications/Admissions:
Student Applications

Clinical Psychology PsyD (Doctor of Psychology)—Number full-time enrolled (new admits only) 2012–2013, 104. Number part-time enrolled (new admits only) 2012–2013, 0. Total enrolled 2012–2013 full-time, 375. Total enrolled 2012–2013 part-time, 231. The median number of years required for completion of a degree in 2012–2013 were 5. *Industrial/Organizational Psychology MA/MS (Master of Arts/Science)*—Number full-time enrolled (new admits only) 2012–2013, 112. Number part-time enrolled (new admits only) 2012–2013, 27. Total enrolled 2012–2013 full-time, 287. Total enrolled 2012–2013 part-time, 92. *Forensic Psychology MA/MS (Master of Arts/Science)*—Number full-time enrolled (new admits only) 2012–2013, 193. Number part-time enrolled (new admits only) 2012–2013, 26. Total enrolled 2012–2013 full-time, 423. Total enrolled 2012–2013 part-time, 105. *Clinical Psychology (Applied Behavior Analysis) MA/MS (Master of Arts/Science)*—Number full-time enrolled (new admits only) 2012–2013, 92. Number part-time enrolled (new admits only) 2012–2013, 18. Total enrolled 2012–2013 full-time, 168. Total enrolled 2012–2013 part-time, 97. *Clinical Psychology (Counseling) MA/MS (Master of Arts/Science)*—Number full-time enrolled (new admits only) 2012–2013, 150. Number part-time enrolled (new admits only) 2012–2013, 85. Total enrolled 2012–2013 full-time, 368. Total enrolled 2012–2013 part-time, 165. *Business Psychology PsyD (Doctor of Psychology)*—Number full-time enrolled (new admits only) 2012–2013, 4. Number part-time enrolled (new admits only) 2012–2013, 49. Total enrolled 2012–2013 full-time, 18. Total enrolled 2012–2013 part-time, 160. *School Psychology EdS (School Psychology)*—Number full-time enrolled (new admits only) 2012–2013, 30. Number part-time enrolled (new admits only) 2012–2013, 12. Total enrolled 2012–2013 full-time, 80. Total enrolled 2012–2013 part-time, 81. *Board Certified Behavior Analyst Respecialization Respecialization Diploma*—Number full-time enrolled (new admits only) 2012–2013, 0. Number part-time enrolled (new admits only) 2012–2013, 77. Total enrolled 2012–2013 full-time, 16. Total enrolled 2012–2013 part-time, 141. *Applied Behavior Analysis PhD (Doctor of Philosophy)*—Number full-time enrolled (new admits only) 2012–2013, 15. Number part-time enrolled (new admits only) 2012–2013, 3. Total enrolled 2012–2013 full-time, 40. Total enrolled 2012–2013 part-time, 62. *Applied Forensics Certificate Other*—Number full-time enrolled (new admits only) 2012–2013, 0. Number part-time enrolled (new admits only) 2012–2013, 0. *Applied Industrial/Organizational Certificate Other*—Number full-time enrolled (new admits only) 2012–2013, 0. Number part-time enrolled (new admits only) 2012–2013, 33. *General Psychology MA/MS (Master of Arts/Science)*—Number full-time enrolled (new admits only) 2012–2013, 23.

Number part-time enrolled (new admits only) 2012–2013, 151. Total enrolled 2012–2013 full-time, 59. Total enrolled 2012–2013 part-time, 437. *Organizational Leadership PhD (Doctor of Philosophy)*—Number full-time enrolled (new admits only) 2012–2013, 1. Number part-time enrolled (new admits only) 2012–2013, 73. Total enrolled 2012–2013 full-time, 10. Total enrolled 2012–2013 part-time, 199. *International Psychology PhD (Doctor of Philosophy)*—Number full-time enrolled (new admits only) 2012–2013, 5. Number part-time enrolled (new admits only) 2012–2013, 72. Total enrolled 2012–2013 full-time, 30. Total enrolled 2012–2013 part-time, 189. *Clinical Psychology (Marital and Family Therapy) MA/MS (Master of Arts/Science)*—Number full-time enrolled (new admits only) 2012–2013, 1. Number part-time enrolled (new admits only) 2012–2013, 81. Total enrolled 2012–2013 full-time, 37. Total enrolled 2012–2013 part-time, 193. *Marital and Family Therapy PsyD (Doctor of Psychology)*—Number full-time enrolled (new admits only) 2012–2013, 17. Number part-time enrolled (new admits only) 2012–2013, 20. Total enrolled 2012–2013 full-time, 17. Total enrolled 2012–2013 part-time, 44. *Psychology PsyD (Doctor of Psychology)*—Number full-time enrolled (new admits only) 2012–2013, 0. Number part-time enrolled (new admits only) 2012–2013, 0. *Clinical Forensic Psychology PsyD (Doctor of Psychology)*—Number full-time enrolled (new admits only) 2012–2013, 47. Number part-time enrolled (new admits only) 2012–2013, 18. Total enrolled 2012–2013 full-time, 155. Total enrolled 2012–2013 part-time, 82. *Child and Adolescent Psychology Certificate Other*—Number full-time enrolled (new admits only) 2012–2013, 0. Number part-time enrolled (new admits only) 2012–2013, 23. Total enrolled 2012–2013 full-time, 1. Total enrolled 2012–2013 part-time, 25. *Consumer Psychology Certificate Other*—Number full-time enrolled (new admits only) 2012–2013, 0. Number part-time enrolled (new admits only) 2012–2013, 0. *Leadership in Healthcare Professions Certificate Other*—Number full-time enrolled (new admits only) 2012–2013, 0. Number part-time enrolled (new admits only) 2012–2013, 0. *Organizational Effectiveness Certificate Other*—Number full-time enrolled (new admits only) 2012–2013, 0. Number part-time enrolled (new admits only) 2012–2013, 0. *Workplace Diversity Certificate Other*—Number full-time enrolled (new admits only) 2012–2013, 0. Number part-time enrolled (new admits only) 2012–2013, 0. *School Psychology EdD (Doctor of Education)*—Number full-time enrolled (new admits only) 2012–2013, 0. Number part-time enrolled (new admits only) 2012–2013, 0. *Counselor Ed & Supervision PhD (Doctor of Philosophy)*—Number full-time enrolled (new admits only) 2012–2013, 11. Number part-time enrolled (new admits only) 2012–2013, 0. Total enrolled 2012–2013 full-time, 11. Total enrolled 2012–2013 part-time, 0. *Somatic Psychology MA/MS (Master of Arts/Science)*—Number full-time enrolled (new admits only) 2012–2013, 0. Number part-time enrolled (new admits only) 2012–2013, 0. Total enrolled 2012–2013 full-time, 1. Total enrolled 2012–2013 part-time, 17. *Somatic Psychology PhD (Doctor of Philosophy)*—Number full-time enrolled (new admits only) 2012–2013, 0. Number part-time enrolled (new admits only) 2012–2013, 0. Total enrolled 2012–2013 full-time, 5. Total enrolled 2012–2013 part-time, 51. *Applied Clinical Psychology PsyD (Doctor of Psychology)*—Number full-time enrolled (new admits only) 2012–2013, 87. Number part-time enrolled (new admits only) 2012–2013, 8. Total enrolled 2012–2013 full-time, 102. Total enrolled 2012–2013 part-time, 143. *Clinical Psychology (Child and Adolescent) PsyD (Doctor of Psychology)*—Number full-time enrolled (new admits only) 2012–2013, 23. Number part-time enrolled (new admits only) 2012–2013, 0. Total enrolled 2012–2013 full-time, 68. Total enrolled 2012–2013 part-time, 42.

Scores: Entries appear in this order: required test or GPA, minimum score (if required), median score of students entering in 2012–2013. *Clinical Psychology PsyD (Doctor of Psychology)*: GRE-V no minimum stated, GRE-Q no minimum stated; *Applied Behavior Analysis PhD (Doctor of Philosophy)*: GRE-V no minimum stated, GRE-Q no minimum stated.

Other Criteria: (importance of criteria rated low, medium, or high): GRE scores—medium, research experience—medium, work experience—medium, extracurricular activity—low, clinically related public service—medium, GPA—high, letters of recommendation—medium, interview—high, statement of goals and objectives—medium, undergraduate major in psychology—low, specific undergraduate psychology courses taken—low, The criteria listed above is summary of all programs. Please note the weighing may vary by program. Interviews are required and by invitation for select programs. For additional information on admission requirements, go to http://www.thechicagoschool.edu/Chicago/Admissions/Get_to_Know_Us.

Student Characteristics: The following represents characteristics of students in 2012–2013 in all graduate psychology programs in the department: Female—full-time 1852, part-time 2108; Male—full-time 419, part-time 587; African American/Black—full-time 366, part-time 560; Hispanic/Latino(a)—full-time 271, part-time 311; Asian/Pacific Islander—full-time 119, part-time 136; American Indian/Alaska Native—full-time 15, part-time 11; Caucasian/White—full-time 1299, part-time 1349; Multi-ethnic—full-time 48, part-time 43; students subject to the Americans With Disabilities Act—full-time 0, part-time 0; Unknown ethnicity—full-time 90, part-time 204; International students who hold an F-1 or J-1 Visa—full-time 63, part-time 81.

Financial Information/Assistance:

Tuition for Full-Time Study: *Master's*: State residents: $982 per credit hour; Nonstate residents: $982 per credit hour. *Doctoral*: State residents: $1,223 per credit hour; Nonstate residents: $1,223 per credit hour. Tuition is subject to change. Additional fees are assessed to students beyond the costs of tuition for the following: technology, institutional services, registration, eCollege. Tuition costs vary by program. See the following website for updates and changes in tuition costs: http://www.thechicagoschool.edu/Home/Admissions/Costs_Financial_Aid/Tuition_and_Fees.

Financial Assistance:

First-Year Students: Teaching assistantships available for first year. Average amount paid per academic year: $6,000. Average number of hours worked per week: 20. Research assistantships available for first year. Average amount paid per academic year: $6,000. Average number of hours worked per week: 20. Fellowships and scholarships available for first year. Average amount paid per academic year: $10,000. Average number of hours worked per week: 10. Apply by April 1.

Advanced Students: Teaching assistantships available for advanced students. Average amount paid per academic year: $6,000. Average number of hours worked per week: 20. Research assistantships available for advanced students. Average amount

paid per academic year: $6,000. Average number of hours worked per week: 20. Fellowships and scholarships available for advanced students. Average amount paid per academic year: $10,000. Average number of hours worked per week: 10. Apply by April 1.

Additional Information: Of all students currently enrolled full time, 60% benefited from one or more of the listed financial assistance programs. Application and information available online at: http://www.thechicagoschool.edu/Chicago/Admissions/Costs_and_Financial_Aid/Funding_Your_Education.

Internships/Practica: Doctoral Degree (PsyD Clinical Psychology): For those doctoral students for whom a professional psychology internship was required in this program prior to graduation, (62) students applied for an internship in 2011–2012, with (61) students obtaining an internship. Of those students who obtained an internship, (54) were paid internships. Of those students who obtained an internship, (24) students placed in APA/CPA accredited internships, (26) students placed in internships not APA/CPA accredited, but listed with the Association of Psychology Postdoctoral and Internship Programs (APPIC), (0) students placed in internships conforming to guidelines of the Council of Directors of School Psychology Programs (CDSPP), (11) students placed in internships that were not APA/CPA accredited, APPIC or CDSPP listed. Master's Degree (MA/MS Industrial/Organizational Psychology): An internship experience, such as a final research project or "capstone" experience is required of graduates. Master's Degree (MA/MS Forensic Psychology): An internship experience, such as a final research project or "capstone" experience is required of graduates. Master's Degree (MA/MS Clinical Psychology (Applied Behavior Analysis)): An internship experience, such as a final research project or "capstone" experience is required of graduates. Master's Degree (MA/MS Clinical Psychology (Counseling)): An internship experience, such as a final research project or "capstone" experience is required of graduates. Currently there are over 500 assessment and therapy practicum sites in the city and surrounding area at which our students train.

Housing and Day Care: No on-campus housing is available. No on-campus day care facilities are available.

Employment of Department Graduates:
Master's Degree Graduates: Of those who graduated in the academic year 2011–2012, the following categories and numbers represent the postgraduate activities and employment of master's degree graduates: Enrolled in a postdoctoral residency/fellowship (n/a), employed in independent practice (n/a), total from the above (master's) (0).
Doctoral Degree Graduates: Of those who graduated in the academic year 2011–2012, the following categories and numbers represent the postgraduate activities and employment of doctoral degree graduates: Enrolled in a psychology doctoral program (n/a), total from the above (doctoral) (0).

Additional Information:
Orientation, Objectives, and Emphasis of Department: The Chicago School educates students to be competent practitioners by providing curricula that emphasize both a broad knowledge of the scientific and theoretical bases of psychology and the ability to apply that knowledge to specific employment situations. A student-centered environment, with personal advising and supervision provide opportunities for deepening awareness, knowledge, and skills. The programs are designed to integrate the study of cultural and individual differences and their impact in clinical and work settings. The professional and ethical development of the student is of foremost concern throughout the educational program.

Special Facilities or Resources: The Chicago School offers experiential learning opportunities at the Center for Multicultural and Diversity Studies, the Center for International Studies, the Center for Latino Mental Health, the Forensic Center, and the Platt Retail Institute. The Naomi Ruth Cohen Institute for Mental Health Education at The Chicago School (TCSPP) continues to offer an annual predoctoral fellowship to a TCSPP student. The mission of the Cohen Institute is to overcome the stigma associated with mental illness through culturally competent community outreach and educational programming.

Information for Students With Physical Disabilities: See the following website for more information: http://www.thechicagoschool.edu/content.cfm/disability_accommodations.

Application Information:
Send to Admission Operations, c/o The Chicago School of Professional Psychology, 350 N Orleans St, Suite 1050, Chicago, IL 60654-1822. Application available online. URL of online application: http://www.thechicagoschool.edu/Apply. Students are admitted in the Fall, application deadline February 15; Spring, application deadline December 7; Summer, application deadline February 15. *Fall Early consideration deadline for PsyD in Clinical Psychology program is December 15. Early consideration deadline for PsyD in Business Psychology, Clinical Forensic Psychology, Applied Behavior Analysis, EdS in School Psychology, all MA programs, and Latino Mental Health Certificate is February 15. General consideration deadline for PsyD in Clinical Psychology program is February 15. General consideration deadline for PsyD in Business Psychology, EdS in School Psychology and all MA programs is April 1. *Fee:* $50. McNair Scholars are eligible for an application fee waiver.

Western Illinois University
Department of Psychology
Arts and Sciences
Waggoner Hall
Macomb, IL 61455
Telephone: (309) 298-1919
Fax: (309) 298-3265
E-mail: *cj-kreps@wiu.edu*
Web: *http://www.wiu.edu/cas/psychology/*

Department Information:
1960. Interim Chair: Dr. Karen Sears. Number of faculty: total—full-time 28, part-time 4; women—full-time 13, part-time 3; total—minority—full-time 2; women minority—full-time 1.

Programs and Degrees Offered:
Listed in the following order: Program area, degree type (T if terminal Master's), number awarded 7/11–6/12. Clinical/Community Mental Health MA/MS (Master of Arts/Science) (T) 6, General Experimental Psychology MA/MS (Master of Arts/Science) (T) 10, Specialist in School Psychology Other 6.

Student Applications/Admissions:

Student Applications

Clinical/Community Mental Health MA/MS (Master of Arts/ Science)—Applications 2012–2013, 36. Total applicants accepted 2012–2013, 6. Number full-time enrolled (new admits only) 2012–2013, 6. Number part-time enrolled (new admits only) 2012–2013, 0. Total enrolled 2012–2013 full-time, 20. Total enrolled 2012–2013 part-time, 0. Openings 2013–2014, 6. The median number of years required for completion of a degree in 2012–2013 were 3. The number of students enrolled full- and part-time who were dismissed or voluntarily withdrew from this program area in 2012–2013 were 0. General Experimental Psychology MA/MS (Master of Arts/Science)—Applications 2012–2013, 17. Total applicants accepted 2012–2013, 10. Number full-time enrolled (new admits only) 2012–2013, 10. Number part-time enrolled (new admits only) 2012–2013, 0. Total enrolled 2012–2013 full-time, 26. Total enrolled 2012–2013 part-time, 0. Openings 2013–2014, 10. The median number of years required for completion of a degree in 2012–2013 were 2. The number of students enrolled full- and part-time who were dismissed or voluntarily withdrew from this program area in 2012–2013 were 0. Specialist in School Psychology Other—Applications 2012–2013, 32. Total applicants accepted 2012–2013, 8. Number full-time enrolled (new admits only) 2012–2013, 8. Number part-time enrolled (new admits only) 2012–2013, 0. Total enrolled 2012–2013 full-time, 23. Total enrolled 2012–2013 part-time, 0. Openings 2013–2014, 12. The median number of years required for completion of a degree in 2012–2013 were 3. The number of students enrolled full- and part-time who were dismissed or voluntarily withdrew from this program area in 2012–2013 were 1.

Scores: Entries appear in this order: required test or GPA, minimum score (if required), median score of students entering in 2012–2013. Clinical/Community Mental Health MA/MS (Master of Arts/Science): GRE-V 500, 530, GRE-Q 500, 500, GRE-Analytical 4.0, 4.30, last 2 years GPA 2.75, psychology GPA 2.75, 3.64; General Experimental Psychology MA/MS (Master of Arts/Science): GRE-V 500, GRE-Q 500, GRE-Analytical 4.0, overall undergraduate GPA 2.75, last 2 years GPA 2.75, psychology GPA 2.75; Specialist in School Psychology Other: GRE-V 500, GRE-Q 500, GRE-Analytical 4.0, overall undergraduate GPA 2.75, last 2 years GPA 2.75, psychology GPA 2.75.

Other Criteria: (importance of criteria rated low, medium, or high): GRE scores—high, research experience—medium, work experience—medium, extracurricular activity—medium, clinically related public service—medium, GPA—high, letters of recommendation—high, statement of goals and objectives—high, undergraduate major in psychology—medium, specific undergraduate psychology courses taken—high. For additional information on admission requirements, go to http://wiu.edu/cas/psychology/gradadmission.php.

Student Characteristics: The following represents characteristics of students in 2012–2013 in all graduate psychology programs in the department: Female—full-time 43, part-time 0; Male—full-time 26, part-time 0; African American/Black—full-time 2, part-time 0; Hispanic/Latino(a)—full-time 0, part-time 0; Asian/Pacific Islander—full-time 1, part-time 0; American Indian/Alaska Native—full-time 0, part-time 0; Caucasian/White—full-time 64, part-time 0; Multi-ethnic—full-time 2, part-time 0; students subject to the Americans With Disabilities Act—full-time 0, part-

time 0; Unknown ethnicity—full-time 0, part-time 0; International students who hold an F-1 or J-1 Visa—full-time 3, part-time 0.

Financial Information/Assistance:

Tuition for Full-Time Study: Master's: State residents: per academic year $7,068, $294 per credit hour; Nonstate residents: per academic year $14,136, $589 per credit hour. Tuition is subject to change. See the following website for updates and changes in tuition costs: http://www.wiu.edu/vpas/business_services/tuition/.

Financial Assistance:

First-Year Students: Teaching assistantships available for first year. Average amount paid per academic year: $5,032. Average number of hours worked per week: 13. Apply by February 1. Research assistantships available for first year. Average amount paid per academic year: $5,032. Average number of hours worked per week: 13. Apply by February 1.

Advanced Students: Teaching assistantships available for advanced students. Average amount paid per academic year: $5,032. Average number of hours worked per week: 13. Apply by February 1. Research assistantships available for advanced students. Average amount paid per academic year: $5,032. Average number of hours worked per week: 13. Apply by February 1.

Additional Information: Of all students currently enrolled full time, 90% benefited from one or more of the listed financial assistance programs. Application and information available online at: http://www.wiu.edu/graduate_studies/catalog/costs_and_financial_assistance/.

Internships/Practica: Master's Degree (MA/MS Clinical/Community Mental Health): An internship experience, such as a final research project or "capstone" experience is required of graduates. Master's Degree (MA/MS General Experimental Psychology): An internship experience, such as a final research project or "capstone" experience is required of graduates. The Clinical/Community Mental Health program includes a four semester practicum sequence of intensive, supervised work in the department's Psychology Clinic. An internship for which postgraduate credit is given prepares students for jobs in clinical psychology. Practicum work in community schools and the department's psychoeducational clinic under faculty supervision is required throughout both years of the School Psychology program, and a paid internship for which postgraduate credit is given prepares students for certification in Illinois.

Housing and Day Care: On-campus housing is available. See the following website for more information: http://www.wiu.edu/student_services/housing/. On-campus day care facilities are available. See the following website for more information: http://www.wiu.edu/coehs/preschool/.

Employment of Department Graduates:

Master's Degree Graduates: Of those who graduated in the academic year 2011–2012, the following categories and numbers represent the postgraduate activities and employment of master's degree graduates: Enrolled in a psychology doctoral program (3), enrolled in a postdoctoral residency/fellowship (n/a), employed in independent practice (n/a), employed in an academic position at a university (4), employed in other positions at a higher education institution (1), employed in a professional position in a school system (6), employed in government agency (1), employed in a community mental health/counseling center (6), employed in a hospital/medical center (1), total from the above (master's) (22). *Doctoral Degree Graduates:* Of those who graduated in the academic year 2011–2012, the following categories and numbers represent the postgraduate activities and employment of doctoral degree graduates: Enrolled in a psychology doctoral program (n/a), total from the above (doctoral) (0).

Additional Information:

Orientation, Objectives, and Emphasis of Department: The psychology department offers master's degrees in Clinical/Community Mental Health (C/CMH) and General Experimental Psychology, and a Specialist Degree in School Ssychology. C/CMH-MS and School-Specialist degrees are three year programs with the third year consisting of a paid internship. The emphasis in the Clin/CMH program is to prepare students to assume professional responsibilities in outpatient mental health settings. Central to the program is the practicum experience offered through the University Psychology Clinic. Graduates of the Clin/CMH program have found employment in a variety of mental health agencies, with over 90 percent of all graduates currently employed in mental health positions. Students in the general psychology program engage in one to two years of course work in psychology. The opportunity to specialize in industrial/organizational, social, developmental, or experimental psychology is available within the general psychology program. Many students completing the general program have been admitted to PhD programs in psychology. Students in the school psychology program acquire an academic background in psychology and a practical awareness of public school systems. During the first year of the program, students are placed in elementary schools for practical experience, and during their second year, students work in the university psychoeducational clinic. Graduates of the program have had no difficulty finding employment as school psychologists following their internships. Many have also pursued doctoral training.

Special Facilities or Resources: The Department of Psychology is housed in a large modern structure providing facilities for teaching, clinical training, and human and animal research. The department has 55 rooms, including regular classrooms, seminar rooms, observation rooms, small experimental cubicles, and neuroscience labs. Computers are available throughout the department and campus. The department operates a psychology clinic for community referrals, which aids in clinical training, and a psychoeducational clinic for training in school psychology.

Information for Students With Physical Disabilities: See the following website for more information: http://www.wiu.edu/student_services/disability_resource_center/.

Application Information:

Send to School of Graduate Studies, Western Illinois University, #1 University Circle, 116 Sherman Hall, Macomb, IL 61455. Application available online. URL of online application: https://app.applyyourself.com/?id=wiug. Students are admitted in the Fall, application deadline February 1; Spring, application deadline December 1. Spring and Fall admission pertains to the MS in General Experimental program. The School Psychology and Clinical/Community Mental Health programs take Fall semester admission only. *Fee:* $30.

Wheaton College

Department of Psychology
501 College Avenue
Wheaton, IL 60187-5593
Telephone: (630) 752-5762
Fax: (630) 752-7033
E-mail: *ted.kahn@wheaton.edu*
Web: *http://www.wheaton.edu/academics/departments/psychology*

Department Information:

1979. Associate Dean: Terri S. Watson, PsyD. Number of faculty: total—full-time 20, part-time 4; women—full-time 9, part-time 2; total—minority—full-time 2, part-time 1; women minority—full-time 1, part-time 1.

Programs and Degrees Offered:

Listed in the following order: Program area, degree type (T if terminal Master's), number awarded 7/11–6/12. Clinical Psychology MA/MS (Master of Arts/Science) (T) 28, Clinical Psychology PsyD (Doctor of Psychology) 22, Counseling Ministries MA/MS (Master of Arts/Science) (T) 3, Marriage and Family Therapy MA/MS (Master of Arts/Science) (T) 0, Clinical Mental Health Counseling MA/MS (Master of Arts/Science) (T) 0.

APA Accreditation: Clinical PsyD (Doctor of Psychology). Student Outcome Data Website: http://www.wheaton.edu/Academics/Departments/Psychology/Graduate-Programs/Student-Admissions-Outcomes-and-Other-Data.

Student Applications/Admissions:

Student Applications

Clinical Psychology MA/MS (Master of Arts/Science)—Applications 2012–2013, 80. Total applicants accepted 2012–2013, 49. Number full-time enrolled (new admits only) 2012–2013, 28. Number part-time enrolled (new admits only) 2012–2013, 0. Total enrolled 2012–2013 full-time, 64. Total enrolled 2012–2013 part-time, 2. The median number of years required for completion of a degree in 2012–2013 were 2. The number of students enrolled full- and part-time who were dismissed or voluntarily withdrew from this program area in 2012–2013 were 0. *Clinical Psychology PsyD (Doctor of Psychology)*—Applications 2012–2013, 77. Total applicants accepted 2012–2013, 27. Number full-time enrolled (new admits only) 2012–2013, 19. Number part-time enrolled (new admits only) 2012–2013, 0. Total enrolled 2012–2013 full-time, 104. Total enrolled 2012–2013 part-time, 15. Openings 2013–2014, 20. The median number of years required for completion of a degree in 2012–2013 were 6. The number of students enrolled full- and part-time who were dismissed or voluntarily withdrew from this program area in 2012–2013 were 4. *Counseling Ministries MA/MS (Master of Arts/Science)*—Applications 2012–2013, 14. Total applicants accepted 2012–2013, 4. Number full-time enrolled (new admits only) 2012–2013, 2. Number part-time enrolled (new admits only) 2012–2013, 0. Total enrolled 2012–2013 full-time, 2. Total enrolled 2012–2013 part-time, 1. Openings 2013–2014, 5. The median number of years required for completion of a degree in 2012–2013 were 2. The number of students enrolled full- and part-time who were dismissed or voluntarily withdrew from this program area in

2012–2013 were 0. *Marriage and Family Therapy MA/MS (Master of Arts/Science)*—Applications 2012–2013, 33. Total applicants accepted 2012–2013, 21. Number full-time enrolled (new admits only) 2012–2013, 18. Number part-time enrolled (new admits only) 2012–2013, 0. Openings 2013–2014, 23. The number of students enrolled full- and part-time who were dismissed or voluntarily withdrew from this program area in 2012–2013 were 0. *Clinical Mental Health Counseling MA/MS (Master of Arts/Science)*—Applications 2012–2013, 0. Total applicants accepted 2012–2013, 0. Number full-time enrolled (new admits only) 2012–2013, 0. Number part-time enrolled (new admits only) 2012–2013, 0. Openings 2013–2014, 23. The number of students enrolled full- and part-time who were dismissed or voluntarily withdrew from this program area in 2012–2013 were 0.

Scores: Entries appear in this order: required test or GPA, minimum score (if required), median score of students entering in 2012–2013. *Clinical Psychology MA/MS (Master of Arts/Science):* GRE-V no minimum stated, GRE-Q no minimum stated, GRE-Analytical no minimum stated, overall undergraduate GPA 3.0; *Clinical Psychology PsyD (Doctor of Psychology):* GRE-V 150, GRE-Q 150, GRE-Analytical no minimum stated, overall undergraduate GPA 3.0, Masters GPA no minimum stated; *Counseling Ministries MA/MS (Master of Arts/Science):* GRE-V no minimum stated, GRE-Q no minimum stated, GRE-Analytical no minimum stated, overall undergraduate GPA 2.75; *Marriage and Family Therapy MA/MS (Master of Arts/Science):* GRE-V no minimum stated, GRE-Q no minimum stated, GRE-Analytical no minimum stated, overall undergraduate GPA 3.0; *Clinical Mental Health Counseling MA/MS (Master of Arts/Science):* GRE-V no minimum stated, GRE-Q no minimum stated, GRE-Analytical no minimum stated, overall undergraduate GPA 3.0.

Other Criteria: (importance of criteria rated low, medium, or high): GRE scores—medium, research experience—medium, work experience—medium, extracurricular activity—medium, clinically related public service—medium, GPA—medium, letters of recommendation—high, interview—high, statement of goals and objectives—high, undergraduate major in psychology—low, specific undergraduate psychology courses taken—high, PsyD Program conducts applicant interviews. MA Programs work with application packages only. For additional information on admission requirements, go to http://www.wheaton.edu/Admissions-and-Aid/Graduate/Admission-Requirements.

Student Characteristics: The following represents characteristics of students in 2012–2013 in all graduate psychology programs in the department: Female—full-time 122, part-time 16; Male—full-time 48, part-time 2; African American/Black—full-time 11, part-time 0; Hispanic/Latino(a)—full-time 9, part-time 1; Asian/Pacific Islander—full-time 21, part-time 3; American Indian/Alaska Native—full-time 0, part-time 0; Caucasian/White—full-time 128, part-time 14; Multi-ethnic—full-time 0, part-time 0; students subject to the Americans With Disabilities Act—full-time 1, part-time 0; Unknown ethnicity—full-time 1, part-time 0; International students who hold an F-1 or J-1 Visa—full-time 7, part-time 1.

Financial Information/Assistance:

Tuition for Full-Time Study: *Master's:* State residents: per academic year $17,160, $715 per credit hour; Nonstate residents: per academic year $17,160, $715 per credit hour. *Doctoral:* State residents: per academic year $27,300, $910 per credit hour; Nonstate residents: per academic year $27,300, $910 per credit hour. Tuition is subject to change. Tuition costs vary by program. See the following website for updates and changes in tuition costs: http://www.wheaton.edu/Admissions-and-Aid/Graduate/Tuition-and-Fees.

Financial Assistance:

First-Year Students: Teaching assistantships available for first year. Average amount paid per academic year: $4,700. Average number of hours worked per week: 8. Fellowships and scholarships available for first year. Average amount paid per academic year: $6,000. Average number of hours worked per week: 0.

Advanced Students: Teaching assistantships available for advanced students. Average amount paid per academic year: $5,500. Average number of hours worked per week: 10. Research assistantships available for advanced students. Average amount paid per academic year: $5,500. Average number of hours worked per week: 10. Fellowships and scholarships available for advanced students. Average amount paid per academic year: $6,000. Average number of hours worked per week: 0.

Additional Information: Of all students currently enrolled full time, 80% benefited from one or more of the listed financial assistance programs. Application and information available online at: http://www.wheaton.edu/Admissions-and-Aid/Financial-Aid/Graduate-Students.

Internships/Practica: Doctoral Degree (PsyD Clinical Psychology): For those doctoral students for whom a professional psychology internship was required in this program prior to graduation, (16) students applied for an internship in 2011–2012, with (11) students obtaining an internship. Of those students who obtained an internship, (11) were paid internships. Of those students who obtained an internship, (10) students placed in APA/CPA accredited internships, (1) students placed in internships not APA/CPA accredited, but listed with the Association of Psychology Postdoctoral and Internship Programs (APPIC), (0) students placed in internships conforming to guidelines of the Council of Directors of School Psychology Programs (CDSPP), (0) students placed in internships that were not APA/CPA accredited, APPIC or CDSPP listed. Master's Degree (MA/MS Clinical Psychology): An internship experience, such as a final research project or "capstone" experience is required of graduates. Master's Degree (MA/MS Counseling Ministries): An internship experience, such as a final research project or "capstone" experience is required of graduates. Master's Degree (MA/MS Marriage and Family Therapy): An internship experience, such as a final research project or "capstone" experience is required of graduates. Master's Degree (MA/MS Clinical Mental Health Counseling): An internship experience, such as a final research project or "capstone" experience is required of graduates. The Graduate Psychology Programs have liaisons with over 90 agencies in the Chicago and suburban area with facility types ranging from hospitals, clinics, community agencies, residential, and correctional facilities. The MA Program requires 600 on-site hours and the PsyD requires a minimum of 1200 hours. Faculty are involved through professional development groups while students are placed in field assignments.

Housing and Day Care: On-campus housing is available. See the following website for more information: http://www.wheaton.edu/

Academics/Graduate-School/Graduate-Student-Services/ Housing. No on-campus day care facilities are available.

Employment of Department Graduates:

Master's Degree Graduates: Of those who graduated in the academic year 2011–2012, the following categories and numbers represent the postgraduate activities and employment of master's degree graduates: Enrolled in a postdoctoral residency/fellowship (n/a), employed in independent practice (n/a), employed in other positions at a higher education institution (3), employed in a community mental health/counseling center (10), employed in a hospital/medical center (4), still seeking employment (2), not seeking employment (1), other employment position (1), do not know (7), total from the above (master's) (28).

Doctoral Degree Graduates: Of those who graduated in the academic year 2011–2012, the following categories and numbers represent the postgraduate activities and employment of doctoral degree graduates: Enrolled in a psychology doctoral program (n/a), enrolled in a postdoctoral residency/fellowship (8), employed in independent practice (4), employed in an academic position at a university (1), employed in government agency (5), employed in a community mental health/counseling center (2), employed in a hospital/medical center (3), total from the above (doctoral) (23).

Additional Information:

Orientation, Objectives, and Emphasis of Department: The doctoral program aims to produce competent scholar-practitioners in clinical psychology who will understand professional practice as service. The primary emphasis of the MA programs is the professional preparation of the master's level therapist for employment in clinical settings; a secondary objective is the preparation of selected students for doctoral studies. The departmental orientation is eclectic, with students exposed to the theory, research, and practical clinical skills of the major clinical models in use today. A pre-eminent concern of all faculty is the interface of psychological theory and practice with Christian faith. Thus, students also take coursework in the theory and practice of integrating psychology and Christian faith, and coursework in theology/biblical studies. Students are encouraged to participate in a growth-oriented group therapy experience or an individual therapy experience. The objectives of the department are to produce mature, capable Master's and doctoral-level clinicians who are well grounded in clinical theory and the essentials of professional practice, and who responsibly and capably relate their Christian faith and professional interests.

Personal Behavior Statement: http://www.wheaton.edu/About-Wheaton/Community-Covenant.

Special Facilities or Resources: The PsyD Program has its own computer lab/reading room for research and study. The Psychology Department also has a state-of-the-art child development lab equipped with Noldus XT. Many students work with faculty research projects and most faculty have separate lab space within the department. Opportunities exist for professional conference presentations and involvement in international projects.

Information for Students With Physical Disabilities: See the following website for more information: http://www.wheaton.edu/external-links/Disabilities-Services.

Application Information:

Send to Graduate Admissions Office, Wheaton College, 501 College Avenue, Wheaton, IL, 60187. Application available online. URL of online application: http://www.wheaton.edu/Admissions-and-Aid/Graduate/Apply-Now. Students are admitted in the Fall, application deadline December 15. December 15 deadline PsyD, March 1 deadline for Master's programs. *Fee:* $50. $50 PsyD application fee; $30 application fee for all MA programs.

Ball State University

Department of Counseling Psychology and Guidance Services
Teachers College
Teachers College, Room 605
Muncie, IN 47306-0585
Telephone: (765) 285-8040
Fax: (765) 285-2067
E-mail: *sbowman@bsu.edu*
Web: *http://www.bsu.edu/counselingpsychology/*

Department Information:

1967. Chairperson: Sharon L. Bowman. Number of faculty: total—full-time 11; women—full-time 6; total—minority—full-time 3; women minority—full-time 2.

Programs and Degrees Offered:

Listed in the following order: Program area, degree type (T if terminal Master's), number awarded 7/11–6/12. Social Psychology MA/MS (Master of Arts/Science) (T) 7, Counseling MA/MS (Master of Arts/Science) (T) 40, Counseling Psychology PhD (Doctor of Philosophy) 9.

APA Accreditation: Counseling PhD (Doctor of Philosophy). Student Outcome Data Website: http://www.bsu.edu/counselingpsychology/phdcounpsych/.

Student Applications/Admissions:

Student Applications

Social Psychology MA/MS (Master of Arts/Science)—Applications 2012–2013, 20. Total applicants accepted 2012–2013, 13. Number full-time enrolled (new admits only) 2012–2013, 10. Total enrolled 2012–2013 full-time, 20. Total enrolled 2012–2013 part-time, 1. Openings 2013–2014, 10. The median number of years required for completion of a degree in 2012–2013 were 2. The number of students enrolled full- and part-time who were dismissed or voluntarily withdrew from this program area in 2012–2013 were 0. *Counseling MA/MS (Master of Arts/Science)*—Applications 2012–2013, 90. Total applicants accepted 2012–2013, 65. Number full-time enrolled (new admits only) 2012–2013, 51. Number part-time enrolled (new admits only) 2012–2013, 5. Total enrolled 2012–2013 full-time, 122. Total enrolled 2012–2013 part-time, 18. Openings 2013–2014, 43. The median number of years required for completion of a degree in 2012–2013 were 2. The number of students enrolled full- and part-time who were dismissed or voluntarily withdrew from this program area in 2012–2013 were 2. *Counseling Psychology PhD (Doctor of Philosophy)*—Applications 2012–2013, 110. Total applicants accepted 2012–2013, 14. Number full-time enrolled (new admits only) 2012–2013, 10. Total enrolled 2012–2013 full-time, 40. Total enrolled 2012–2013 part-time, 11. Openings 2013–2014, 10. The median number of years required for completion of a degree in 2012–2013 were 5. The number of students enrolled full- and part-time who were dismissed or voluntarily withdrew from this program area in 2012–2013 were 1.

Scores: Entries appear in this order: required test or GPA, minimum score (if required), median score of students entering in 2012–2013. *Social Psychology MA/MS (Master of Arts/Science):* GRE-V 490, GRE-Q 490, overall undergraduate GPA 3.5; *Counseling MA/MS (Master of Arts/Science):* GRE-V 480, GRE-Q 500, overall undergraduate GPA no minimum stated, 3.6; *Counseling Psychology PhD (Doctor of Philosophy):* GRE-V 500, GRE-Q 500, overall undergraduate GPA 3.5.

Other Criteria: (importance of criteria rated low, medium, or high): GRE scores—high, research experience—high, work experience—high, extracurricular activity—medium, clinically related public service—medium, GPA—high, letters of recommendation—high, interview—medium, statement of goals and objectives—high, diversity interest—high, undergraduate major in psychology—low, Interview is a requirement for the Doctoral program, not the Master's programs.

Student Characteristics: The following represents characteristics of students in 2012–2013 in all graduate psychology programs in the department: Female—full-time 140, part-time 20; Male—full-time 42, part-time 9; African American/Black—full-time 1, part-time 0; Hispanic/Latino(a)—full-time 1, part-time 0; Asian/Pacific Islander—full-time 10, part-time 0; American Indian/Alaska Native—full-time 1, part-time 0; Caucasian/White—full-time 164, part-time 20; Multi-ethnic—full-time 2, part-time 0; students subject to the Americans With Disabilities Act—full-time 1, part-time 0; Unknown ethnicity—full-time 3, part-time 9; International students who hold an F-1 or J-1 Visa—full-time 12, part-time 0.

Financial Information/Assistance:

Tuition for Full-Time Study: *Master's:* State residents: per academic year $7,666; Nonstate residents: per academic year $19,114. *Doctoral:* State residents: per academic year $7,666; Nonstate residents: per academic year $19,114. Tuition is subject to change. Additional fees are assessed to students beyond the costs of tuition for the following: health center, technology, recreation center fees. See the following website for updates and changes in tuition costs: https://cms.bsu.edu/admissions/tuitionandfees/graduate.

Financial Assistance:

First-Year Students: Teaching assistantships available for first year. Average amount paid per academic year: $10,364. Average number of hours worked per week: 20. Apply by December 15. Research assistantships available for first year. Average amount paid per academic year: $10,364. Average number of hours worked per week: 20. Apply by December 15.

Advanced Students: Teaching assistantships available for advanced students. Average amount paid per academic year: $10,364. Average number of hours worked per week: 20. Apply by March 1. Research assistantships available for advanced students. Average amount paid per academic year: $10,364. Average number of hours worked per week: 20. Apply by March 1. Traineeships available for advanced students. Average amount paid per academic year: $10,364. Average number of hours worked per week: 20. Apply by March 1.

Additional Information: Of all students currently enrolled full time, 70% benefited from one or more of the listed financial assistance programs.

Internships/Practica: Doctoral Degree (PhD Counseling Psychology): For those doctoral students for whom a professional psychology internship was required in this program prior to graduation, (12) students applied for an internship in 2011–2012, with (10) students obtaining an internship. Of those students who obtained an internship, (10) were paid internships. Of those students who obtained an internship, (9) students placed in APA/CPA accredited internships, (0) students placed in internships not APA/CPA accredited, but listed with the Association of Psychology Postdoctoral and Internship Programs (APPIC), (0) students placed in internships conforming to guidelines of the Council of Directors of School Psychology Programs (CDSPP), (1) students placed in internships that were not APA/CPA accredited, APPIC or CDSPP listed. Master's Degree (MA/MS Counseling): An internship experience, such as a final research project or "capstone" experience is required of graduates. The department operates a practicum clinic that serves the surrounding community on a low-cost basis. All counseling master's students and doctoral students are required to complete at least one practicum in this clinic. Other practicum opportunities are available at the university counseling center, a local elementary school, and the nearby medical hospital. Master's students are required to complete an internship prior to graduation. The Master's Internship Director maintains a listing of available sites and assists students in identifying and securing such a site. Most of these sites are unpaid, although a few are paying sites. Doctoral students typically seek APA-approved predoctoral internship sites. There is one such site on campus, in the university's counseling center. Although that site does not guarantee a slot to students from this program, usually one CPSY student a year is matched there.

Housing and Day Care: On-campus housing is available. See the following website for more information: http://cms.bsu.edu/CampusLife/Housing.aspx. On-campus day care facilities are available. See the following website for more information: http://cms.bsu.edu/Academics/CentersandInstitutes/ChildStudyCenter.aspx.

Employment of Department Graduates:

Master's Degree Graduates: Of those who graduated in the academic year 2011–2012, the following categories and numbers represent the postgraduate activities and employment of master's degree graduates: Enrolled in a psychology doctoral program (10), enrolled in another graduate/professional program (1), enrolled in a postdoctoral residency/fellowship (n/a), employed in independent practice (n/a), employed in other positions at a higher education institution (1), employed in a professional position in a school system (9), employed in government agency (3), employed in a community mental health/counseling center (7), employed in a hospital/medical center (1), other employment position (4), do not know (4), total from the above (master's) (40).

Doctoral Degree Graduates: Of those who graduated in the academic year 2011–2012, the following categories and numbers represent the postgraduate activities and employment of doctoral degree graduates: Enrolled in a psychology doctoral program (n/a), enrolled in a postdoctoral residency/fellowship (1), employed in independent practice (1), employed in an academic position at a 2-year/4-year college (2), employed in other positions at a higher education institution (3), employed in government agency (2), not seeking employment (0), total from the above (doctoral) (9).

Additional Information:

Orientation, Objectives, and Emphasis of Department: The objective of the master's counseling programs is to prepare effective counselors by providing students with a common professional core of courses and experiences. The faculty is committed to keeping abreast of trends, skills, and knowledge and to modifying the program to prepare students for their profession. Students will be able to practice in a variety of settings using therapeutic, preventive, or developmental counseling approaches. The counseling programs also prepare students for doctoral study in counseling psychology. The program goals are to develop an atmosphere conducive to inquiry, creativity, and learning and to the discovery of new knowledge through research, counseling, and interactive involvement between students and faculty. The master's program in social psychology provides a conceptual background for those pursuing careers in education, counseling, criminology, personnel work, etc. and prepares students for entry into doctoral programs in social psychology. The doctoral program is designed to broaden students' knowledge beyond the master's degree. The rigorous program includes a sound theoretical basis, a substantial experiential component, a research component, and a variety of assistantship assignments. A basic core of courses stresses competence in the social, psychological, biological, cognitive, and affective bases of behavior. The counseling psychology PhD program is structured within a scientist-professional model of training.

Special Facilities or Resources: Departmental instructional and research facilities are exceptional. The facilities of the department occupy the sixth floor of the Teachers College building. The department operates an outpatient counseling clinic that serves as the training facility for all counseling graduate students. The clinic includes ten practicum rooms, an observation corridor, several group observation rooms, and digital taping of sessions. The clinic serves clients from Muncie and surrounding communities as well as Ball State faculty/staff. The university operates a separate state-of-the-art counseling center that serves as a training site for a select number of graduate students from the department. The campus is wireless, and offers state-of-the-art emerging media access.

Information for Students With Physical Disabilities: See the following website for more information: http://www.bsu.edu/dsd.

Application Information:
Send to Graduate Admissions Coordinator, Department of Counseling Psychology and Guidance Services, Ball State University, Muncie, Indiana 47306. Application available online. URL of online application: http://www.bsu.edu/webapps/gradapplication/. Students are admitted in the Fall, application deadline December 1. Doctoral program - December 1. Master's programs deadlines are February 1 and June 15 for fall admission. Counseling (Rehabilitation track) has rolling admissions. *Fee:* $50. International applicants will pay $40 to apply through the Rinker Center for International Programs.

Ball State University
Department of Psychological Science
Sciences and Humanities
Muncie, IN 47306-0520
Telephone: (765) 285-1690
Fax: (765) 285-1702
E-mail: *kpickel@bsu.edu*
Web: *http://cms.bsu.edu/academics/collegesanddepartments/
psychology*

Department Information:
1968. Chairperson: Bernie Whitley. Number of faculty: total—full-time 20; women—full-time 8; total—minority—full-time 1; women minority—full-time 1; faculty subject to the Americans With Disabilities Act 2.

Programs and Degrees Offered:
Listed in the following order: Program area, degree type (T if terminal Master's), number awarded 7/11–6/12. Clinical Psychology MA/MS (Master of Arts/Science) (T) 7, Cognitive and Social Processes MA/MS (Master of Arts/Science) (T) 5.

Student Applications/Admissions:
Student Applications

Clinical Psychology MA/MS (Master of Arts/Science)—Applications 2012–2013, 60. Total applicants accepted 2012–2013, 8. Number full-time enrolled (new admits only) 2012–2013, 8. Number part-time enrolled (new admits only) 2012–2013, 0. Total enrolled 2012–2013 full-time, 15. Total enrolled 2012–2013 part-time, 2. Openings 2013–2014, 8. The median number of years required for completion of a degree in 2012–2013 were 2. The number of students enrolled full- and part-time who were dismissed or voluntarily withdrew from this program area in 2012–2013 were 0. *Cognitive and Social Processes MA/MS (Master of Arts/Science)*—Applications 2012–2013, 25. Total applicants accepted 2012–2013, 8. Number full-time enrolled (new admits only) 2012–2013, 6. Number part-time enrolled (new admits only) 2012–2013, 0. Total enrolled 2012–2013 full-time, 11. Total enrolled 2012–2013 part-time, 2. Openings 2013–2014, 8. The median number of years required for completion of a degree in 2012–2013 were 2. The number of students enrolled full- and part-time who were dismissed or voluntarily withdrew from this program area in 2012–2013 were 0.

Scores: Entries appear in this order: required test or GPA, minimum score (if required), median score of students entering in 2012–2013. *Clinical Psychology MA/MS (Master of Arts/Science)*: GRE-V no minimum stated, 156, GRE-Q no minimum stated, 149, GRE-Analytical no minimum stated, 4.75, overall undergraduate GPA 2.75, 3.57, last 2 years GPA no minimum stated, psychology GPA no minimum stated; *Cognitive and Social Processes MA/MS (Master of Arts/Science)*: GRE-V no minimum stated, 156, GRE-Q no minimum stated, 151, GRE-Analytical no minimum stated, 4.3, GRE-Subject (Psychology) no minimum stated, overall undergraduate GPA 2.75, 3.70, last 2 years GPA no minimum stated, psychology GPA no minimum stated.

Other Criteria: (importance of criteria rated low, medium, or high): GRE scores—high, research experience—high, work experience—medium, extracurricular activity—low, clinically related public service—medium, GPA—high, letters of recommendation—high, statement of goals and objectives—high, Fit w/ faculty interests—high, undergraduate major in psychology—low, specific undergraduate psychology courses taken—low, Clinical experience not important for Cognitive/Social Processes program. For additional information on admission requirements, go to http://www.bsu.edu/psysc/masters/.

Student Characteristics: The following represents characteristics of students in 2012–2013 in all graduate psychology programs in the department: Female—full-time 19, part-time 2; Male—full-time 7, part-time 2; African American/Black—full-time 1, part-time 0; Hispanic/Latino(a)—full-time 1, part-time 0; Asian/Pacific Islander—full-time 2, part-time 0; American Indian/Alaska Native—full-time 0, part-time 0; Caucasian/White—full-time 22, part-time 4; Multi-ethnic—full-time 0, part-time 0; students subject to the Americans With Disabilities Act—full-time 0, part-time 0; Unknown ethnicity—full-time 0, part-time 0; International students who hold an F-1 or J-1 Visa—full-time 2, part-time 0.

Financial Information/Assistance:
Tuition for Full-Time Study: *Master's:* State residents: per academic year $7,666; Nonstate residents: per academic year $19,114. Tuition is subject to change. Additional fees are assessed to students beyond the costs of tuition for the following: technology, recreation, health center. See the following website for updates and changes in tuition costs: http://cms.bsu.edu/admissions/tuitionandfees/graduate.

Financial Assistance:
First-Year Students: Teaching assistantships available for first year. Average amount paid per academic year: $8,902. Average number of hours worked per week: 20. Apply by March 1. Research assistantships available for first year. Average amount paid per academic year: $8,902. Average number of hours worked per week: 20. Apply by March 1. Fellowships and scholarships available for first year. Average amount paid per academic year: $8,902. Average number of hours worked per week: 0. Apply by March 1.

Advanced Students: Teaching assistantships available for advanced students. Average amount paid per academic year: $8,902. Average number of hours worked per week: 20. Research assistantships available for advanced students. Average amount paid per academic year: $8,902. Average number of hours worked per week: 20. Fellowships and scholarships available for advanced students. Average amount paid per academic year: $8,902. Average number of hours worked per week: 0.

Additional Information: Of all students currently enrolled full time, 92% benefited from one or more of the listed financial assistance programs. Application and information available online at: http://www.bsu.edu/psysc/masters/.

Internships/Practica: Master's Degree (MA/MS Clinical Psychology): An internship experience, such as a final research project or "capstone" experience is required of graduates. Internships for clinical students are available in various settings serving adult or adolescent clients. Cognitive/social students may complete internships to gain specialized training or research opportunities.

Housing and Day Care: On-campus housing is available. See the following website for more information: http://cms.bsu.edu/

CampusLife/Housing.aspx. No on-campus day care facilities are available.

Employment of Department Graduates:

Master's Degree Graduates: Of those who graduated in the academic year 2011–2012, the following categories and numbers represent the postgraduate activities and employment of master's degree graduates: Enrolled in a postdoctoral residency/fellowship (n/a), employed in independent practice (n/a), total from the above (master's) (0).

Doctoral Degree Graduates: Of those who graduated in the academic year 2011–2012, the following categories and numbers represent the postgraduate activities and employment of doctoral degree graduates: Enrolled in a psychology doctoral program (n/a), total from the above (doctoral) (0).

Additional Information:

Orientation, Objectives, and Emphasis of Department: Our Clinical Psychology program is a two-year, 48-credit hour program based on the scientist–practitioner model. Our Cognitive and Social Processes program is a two-year, 43-credit hour program that provides students with intensive training in cognitive and social psychology, research methods, and statistics. We admit a limited number of new students per year, which allows our faculty to work closely with students in terms of providing instruction and research opportunities. Our primary goal is to prepare students for doctoral study.

Special Facilities or Resources: Students have access to university and departmental computers and a wireless network. The department maintains space for faculty and student research. Internal grants are available for student research and travel.

Information for Students With Physical Disabilities: See the following website for more information: http://www.bsu.edu/dsd/.

Application Information:

Send to Kerri Pickel, PhD, Director of Graduate Studies, Department of Psychological Science, Ball State University, Muncie, IN 47306-0520. Application available online. URL of online application: https://www.bsu.edu/webapps/gradapplication/. Students are admitted in the Fall, application deadline March 1. *Fee*: $50. Fee is waived for McNair Scholars.

Ball State University
Educational Psychology
Teachers College
Room 505
Muncie, IN 47306
Telephone: (765) 285-8500
Fax: (765) 285-3653
E-mail: *spaulson@bsu.edu*
Web: *http://www.bsu.edu/edpsych*

Department Information:

1968. Chairperson: Dr. Sharon Paulson. Number of faculty: total—full-time 20; women—full-time 12; total—minority—full-time 4; women minority—full-time 3.

Programs and Degrees Offered:

Listed in the following order: Program area, degree type (T if terminal Master's), number awarded 7/11–6/12. School Psychology EdS (School Psychology) 7, Educational Psychology PhD (Doctor of Philosophy) 3, School Psychology PhD (Doctor of Philosophy) 10.

APA Accreditation: School PhD (Doctor of Philosophy). Student Outcome Data Website: http://cms.bsu.edu/Academics/CollegesandDepartments/Teachers/Departments/EdPsychology/Academic/SchoolPsych/Academics/PhDtrack.aspx.

Student Applications/Admissions:

Student Applications

School Psychology EdS (School Psychology)—Applications 2012–2013, 22. Total applicants accepted 2012–2013, 5. Number full-time enrolled (new admits only) 2012–2013, 4. Number part-time enrolled (new admits only) 2012–2013, 0. Total enrolled 2012–2013 full-time, 18. Total enrolled 2012–2013 part-time, 0. Openings 2013–2014, 6. The median number of years required for completion of a degree in 2012–2013 were 3. The number of students enrolled full- and part-time who were dismissed or voluntarily withdrew from this program area in 2012–2013 were 0. *Educational Psychology PhD (Doctor of Philosophy)*—Applications 2012–2013, 12. Total applicants accepted 2012–2013, 8. Number full-time enrolled (new admits only) 2012–2013, 4. Number part-time enrolled (new admits only) 2012–2013, 0. Total enrolled 2012–2013 full-time, 19. Total enrolled 2012–2013 part-time, 0. Openings 2013–2014, 8. The median number of years required for completion of a degree in 2012–2013 were 4. The number of students enrolled full- and part-time who were dismissed or voluntarily withdrew from this program area in 2012–2013 were 0. *School Psychology PhD (Doctor of Philosophy)*—Applications 2012–2013, 22. Total applicants accepted 2012–2013, 7. Number full-time enrolled (new admits only) 2012–2013, 6. Number part-time enrolled (new admits only) 2012–2013, 0. Total enrolled 2012–2013 full-time, 34. Total enrolled 2012–2013 part-time, 0. Openings 2013–2014, 10. The median number of years required for completion of a degree in 2012–2013 were 6. The number of students enrolled full- and part-time who were dismissed or voluntarily withdrew from this program area in 2012–2013 were 0.

Scores: Entries appear in this order: required test or GPA, minimum score (if required), median score of students entering in 2012–2013. *School Psychology EdS (School Psychology)*: GRE-V no minimum stated, 520, GRE-Q no minimum stated, 630, GRE-Analytical no minimum stated, 4.5, overall undergraduate GPA no minimum stated, 3.78; *Educational Psychology PhD (Doctor of Philosophy)*: GRE-V no minimum stated, 547, GRE-Q no minimum stated, 663, GRE-Analytical no minimum stated, 4.0, overall undergraduate GPA no minimum stated, 3.63, Masters GPA no minimum stated, 3.89; *School Psychology PhD (Doctor of Philosophy)*: GRE-V no minimum stated, 531, GRE-Q no minimum stated, 659, GRE-Analytical no minimum stated, 4.1, overall undergraduate GPA no minimum stated, 3.73, Masters GPA no minimum stated, 3.74.

Other Criteria: (importance of criteria rated low, medium, or high): GRE scores—high, research experience—medium, work experience—low, extracurricular activity—low, clinically related public service—low, GPA—high, letters of recommendation—high, interview—high, statement of goals and objectives—high, undergraduate major in psychology—low.

Student Characteristics: The following represents characteristics of students in 2012–2013 in all graduate psychology programs in the department: Female—full-time 52, part-time 0; Male—full-time 19, part-time 0; African American/Black—full-time 2, part-time 0; Hispanic/Latino(a)—full-time 1, part-time 0; Asian/Pacific Islander—full-time 5, part-time 0; American Indian/Alaska Native—full-time 0, part-time 0; Caucasian/White—full-time 63, part-time 0; Multi-ethnic—full-time 0, part-time 0; students subject to the Americans With Disabilities Act—full-time 0, part-time 0; Unknown ethnicity—full-time 0, part-time 0; International students who hold an F-1 or J-1 Visa—full-time 5, part-time 0.

Financial Information/Assistance:

Tuition for Full-Time Study: *Master's:* State residents: per academic year $8,328, $299 per credit hour; Nonstate residents: per academic year $19,776, $506 per credit hour. *Doctoral:* State residents: per academic year $8,328, $299 per credit hour; Nonstate residents: per academic year $19,776, $506 per credit hour. Tuition is subject to change. Additional fees are assessed to students beyond the costs of tuition for the following: health and technology. See the following website for updates and changes in tuition costs: http://cms.bsu.edu/admissions/tuitionandfees/graduate.

Financial Assistance:

First-Year Students: Research assistantships available for first year. Average amount paid per academic year: $8,850. Average number of hours worked per week: 20. Apply by January 1. Fellowships and scholarships available for first year. Average amount paid per academic year: $11,850. Average number of hours worked per week: 20. Apply by January 1.

Advanced Students: Teaching assistantships available for advanced students. Average amount paid per academic year: $11,450. Average number of hours worked per week: 20. Apply by January 1. Research assistantships available for advanced students. Average amount paid per academic year: $11,450. Average number of hours worked per week: 20. Apply by January 1. Traineeships available for advanced students. Average amount paid per academic year: $11,450. Average number of hours worked per week: 20. Apply by January 1. Fellowships and scholarships available for advanced students. Average amount paid per academic year: $14,450. Average number of hours worked per week: 20. Apply by January 1.

Additional Information: Of all students currently enrolled full time, 100% benefited from one or more of the listed financial assistance programs. Application and information available online at: http://cms.bsu.edu/Academics/CollegesandDepartments/GradSchool/EmploymentandGraduateAssistantships.aspx.

Internships/Practica: Doctoral Degree (PhD School Psychology): For those doctoral students for whom a professional psychology internship was required in this program prior to graduation, (7) students applied for an internship in 2011–2012, with (7) students obtaining an internship. Of those students who obtained an internship, (7) were paid internships. Of those students who obtained an internship, (1) students placed in APA/CPA accredited internships, (1) students placed in internships not APA/CPA accredited, but listed with the Association of Psychology Postdoc-

toral and Internship Programs (APPIC), (5) students placed in internships conforming to guidelines of the Council of Directors of School Psychology Programs (CDSPP), (0) students placed in internships that were not APA/CPA accredited, APPIC or CDSPP listed. The total minimum number of practicum hours required of all PhD in School Psychology students is 550. Of the 550 hours, at least 200 hours must involve direct service and 100 hours must be met under formally scheduled supervision. Doctoral students complete practicum in two settings: The Muncie Community Schools (Primary) and the Psychoeducational, Diagnostic, and Intervention Clinic (PDIC). The BSU School Psychology Internship Consortium provides internship opportunities for students. The consortium is listed in the Council of Directors of School Psychology Programs Internship Directory and meets the same internship requirements as APPIC members. The program maintains complete control and oversight of the internship ensuring the quality of the internships. Each intern must have at least two licensed psychologists as supervisors, attend weekly group supervision, participate in weekly seminars, and complete at least 2000 hours of internship over no less than 12 months. In addition, each intern is required to receive no less than two hours of individual, face-to-face, supervision from a licensed psychologist each week and two hours of group supervision each week.

Housing and Day Care: On-campus housing is available. See the following website for more information: http://cms.bsu.edu/campuslife/housing.aspx. On-campus day care facilities are available. See the following website for more information: http://www.bsu.edu/fcs/csc.

Employment of Department Graduates:

Master's Degree Graduates: Of those who graduated in the academic year 2011–2012, the following categories and numbers represent the postgraduate activities and employment of master's degree graduates: Enrolled in a postdoctoral residency/fellowship (n/a), employed in independent practice (n/a), employed in a professional position in a school system (7), total from the above (master's) (7).

Doctoral Degree Graduates: Of those who graduated in the academic year 2011–2012, the following categories and numbers represent the postgraduate activities and employment of doctoral degree graduates: Enrolled in a psychology doctoral program (n/a), enrolled in a postdoctoral residency/fellowship (2), employed in an academic position at a university (4), employed in a professional position in a school system (3), do not know (4), total from the above (doctoral) (13).

Additional Information:

Orientation, Objectives, and Emphasis of Department: The mission of the professional education program at Ball State University is to prepare engaged educational experts who are sensitive and responsive to the contextual bases of teaching, learning, and development. The Department of Educational Psychology offers an APA-accredited program in School Psychology as well as a PhD program in Educational Psychology an a NASP-approved EdS program in School Psychology.

Special Facilities or Resources: For more than 20 years, the Ball State University Psychoeducational Diagnostic Intervention Clinic has conducted psychological and educational assessments of individuals of any age, gender, or race. The Clinic also provides training for MA, EdS, and PhD students in school psychology.

The Neuropsychology Laboratory was established in 1984 as a research and teaching facility of the Department of Educational Psychology. The laboratory also serves the larger community by assessment of, and remedial planning for, people with neurologic disorders. The Neuropsychology Laboratory provides support for neuropschology courses offered through the Department of Educational Psychology's cognate specialization in neuropsychology. The laboratory is also a site for internships in the school psychology doctoral program.

Information for Students With Physical Disabilities: See the following website for more information: http://www.bsu.edu/dsd/.

Application Information:
Send to Graduate Admissions Specialist. URL of online application: https://www.bsu.edu/webapps/gradapplication/. Students are admitted in the Fall, application deadline January 1. PhD in Educational Psychology = February 15. *Fee:* $50.

Indiana State University
Department of Communication Disorders & Counseling, School, & Educational Psychology
Education
Bayh College of Education
Terre Haute, IN 47809
Telephone: (812) 237-2870
Fax: (812) 237-2729
E-mail: *Sandie.Edwards@indstate.edu*
Web: *http://coe.indstate.edu/cdcsep/counseling/*

Department Information:
1968. Chairperson: Linda Sperry. Number of faculty: total—full-time 4, part-time 3; women—full-time 4, part-time 3.

Programs and Degrees Offered:
Listed in the following order: Program area, degree type (T if terminal Master's), number awarded 7/11–6/12. Counseling Psychology PhD (Doctor of Philosophy) 8, Clinical Mental Health Counseling MA/MS (Master of Arts/Science) 27.

APA Accreditation: Counseling PhD (Doctor of Philosophy). Student Outcome Data Website: http://coe.indstate.edu/cdcsep/counseling/counselingpsychphd.htm.

Student Applications/Admissions:
Student Applications
Counseling Psychology PhD (Doctor of Philosophy)—Applications 2012–2013, 0. Total applicants accepted 2012–2013, 0. Number full-time enrolled (new admits only) 2012–2013, 0. Number part-time enrolled (new admits only) 2012–2013, 0. Total enrolled 2012–2013 full-time, 4. Total enrolled 2012–2013 part-time, 5. The median number of years required for completion of a degree in 2012–2013 were 5. The number of students enrolled full- and part-time who were dismissed or voluntarily withdrew from this program area in 2012–2013 were 0. *Clinical Mental Health Counseling MA/MS (Master of Arts/Science)*—Applications 2012–2013, 42. Total applicants accepted 2012–2013, 13. Number full-time enrolled (new

admits only) 2012–2013, 11. Number part-time enrolled (new admits only) 2012–2013, 2. Total enrolled 2012–2013 full-time, 8. Total enrolled 2012–2013 part-time, 1. Openings 2013–2014, 15. The median number of years required for completion of a degree in 2012–2013 were 2. The number of students enrolled full- and part-time who were dismissed or voluntarily withdrew from this program area in 2012–2013 were 1.

Scores: Entries appear in this order: required test or GPA, minimum score (if required), median score of students entering in 2012–2013. *Counseling Psychology PhD (Doctor of Philosophy):* GRE-V 500, GRE-Q 500, overall undergraduate GPA 2.5, Masters GPA 3.5; *Clinical Mental Health Counseling MA/MS (Master of Arts/Science):* GRE-V 450, GRE-Q 450, GRE-Analytical no minimum stated, overall undergraduate GPA 2.75.

Other Criteria: (importance of criteria rated low, medium, or high): GRE scores—medium, research experience—medium, work experience—high, extracurricular activity—medium, clinically related public service—high, GPA—medium, letters of recommendation—high, interview—high, statement of goals and objectives—high. For additional information on admission requirements, go to http://coe.indstate.edu/cdcsep/counseling/mhapplication.htm.

Student Characteristics: The following represents characteristics of students in 2012–2013 in all graduate psychology programs in the department: Female—full-time 18, part-time 6; Male—full-time 4, part-time 2; African American/Black—full-time 1, part-time 5; Hispanic/Latino(a)—full-time 0, part-time 1; Asian/Pacific Islander—full-time 0, part-time 0; American Indian/Alaska Native—full-time 0, part-time 0; Caucasian/White—full-time 21, part-time 2; Multi-ethnic—full-time 0, part-time 0; students subject to the Americans With Disabilities Act—full-time 0, part-time 0; Unknown ethnicity—full-time 0, part-time 0; International students who hold an F-1 or J-1 Visa—part-time 0.

Financial Information/Assistance:
Tuition for Full-Time Study: *Master's:* State residents: per academic year $6,588, $366 per credit hour; Nonstate residents: per academic year $12,942, $719 per credit hour. Tuition is subject to change. See the following website for updates and changes in tuition costs: http://www.indstate.edu/gradexpress/fees.htm.

Financial Assistance:
First-Year Students: Teaching assistantships available for first year. Average amount paid per academic year: $6,112. Average number of hours worked per week: 15. Apply by March 1. Research assistantships available for first year. Average amount paid per academic year: $6,112. Average number of hours worked per week: 15. Apply by April 15.
Advanced Students: No information provided.
Additional Information: Of all students currently enrolled full time, 50% benefited from one or more of the listed financial assistance programs. Application and information available online at: http://coe.indstate.edu/cdcsep/counseling/mhassistantships.htm.

Internships/Practica: Doctoral Degree (PhD Counseling Psychology): For those doctoral students for whom a professional psychology internship was required in this program prior to graduation, (4) students applied for an internship in 2011–2012, with (4) students obtaining an internship. Of those students who obtained an internship, (4) were paid internships. Of those students who obtained an internship, (4) students placed in APA/CPA accredited internships, (0) students placed in internships not APA/CPA accredited, but listed with the Association of Psychology Postdoctoral and Internship Programs (APPIC), (0) students placed in internships conforming to guidelines of the Council of Directors of School Psychology Programs (CDSPP), (0) students placed in internships that were not APA/CPA accredited, APPIC or CDSPP listed. Master's Degree (MA/MS Clinical Mental Health Counseling): An internship experience, such as a final research project or "capstone" experience is required of graduates. Training settings include public and special-need schools, community mental health centers, family service centers, alcohol and substance abuse treatment facilities, college and university counseling centers, psychiatric hospitals, state correctional facilities, and specialized juvenile treatment centers.

Housing and Day Care: On-campus housing is available. See the following website for more information: http://www.indstate.edu/reslife/. On-campus day care facilities are available. See the following website for more information: http://www.indstate.edu/ecec/.

Employment of Department Graduates:

Master's Degree Graduates: Of those who graduated in the academic year 2011–2012, the following categories and numbers represent the postgraduate activities and employment of master's degree graduates: Enrolled in a psychology doctoral program (2), enrolled in another graduate/professional program (1), enrolled in a postdoctoral residency/fellowship (n/a), employed in independent practice (n/a), employed in government agency (1), employed in a community mental health/counseling center (3), do not know (6), total from the above (master's) (13).

Doctoral Degree Graduates: Of those who graduated in the academic year 2011–2012, the following categories and numbers represent the postgraduate activities and employment of doctoral degree graduates: Enrolled in a psychology doctoral program (n/a), enrolled in a postdoctoral residency/fellowship (1), employed in other positions at a higher education institution (2), employed in government agency (1), employed in a community mental health/counseling center (4), total from the above (doctoral) (8).

Additional Information:

Orientation, Objectives, and Emphasis of Department: The Counseling Psychology program is designed to prepare professional psychologists, through a scientist-professional model of training, for general practice in a variety of practice, service, and educational settings. These setting may include colleges and universities, mental health centers, medical care facilities, government agencies, private practice settings, and the private corporate sector. The program is seen as an area of applied psychology that helps individuals solve problems by making more effective use of their resources. Toward this end, training and research focus on facilitating the personal, interpersonal, educational, and vocational development of individuals, as well as enhancing the environments in which they live. Attention is focused on individual clients' personal and social assets and strengths as well their sociopsychological liabilities and weaknesses. The program emphasizes human development, personalized assessment, and planned problem-solving, while de-emphasizing dichotomies such as sick vs. well and abnormal vs. normal. Our program allows flexibility for students to pursue personal career goals through

focused electives, independent study, and specialized training experiences in practica, fieldwork, assistantship assignments, teaching, research, and community and university work experiences. Faculty members represent a broad range of professional and research interests, theoretical perspectives, and treatment modalities. The Counseling Psychology PhD program is currently inactive and is not accepting new applications.

Special Facilities or Resources: The counseling psychology training area is housed in the Bayh College of Education. This area provides faculty and student offices and a departmental clinic (individual and group therapy rooms, videotaping equipment with observation rooms, and a career and testing laboratory). Also available in the building are research stations, microcomputer labs, a statistics laboratory, a psychological evaluation library, testing rooms, and an instructional resource center.

Information for Students With Physical Disabilities: See the following website for more information: http://www.indstate.edu/cfss/programs/dss/.

Application Information:
Send to Sandie Edwards, Bayh College of Education 226E, CMHC Program, Indiana State University, Terre Haute, IN 47809. Application available online. URL of online application: http://www.indstate.edu/graduate/apply.htm. Students are admitted in the Summer, application deadline February 1. *Fee:* $35.

Indiana State University
Department of Communication Disorders, Counseling, School, and Educational Psychology
College of Education
Terre Haute, IN 47809
Telephone: (812) 237-2880
Fax: (812) 237-2729
E-mail: *patricia.snyder@indstate.edu*
Web: *http://coe.indstate.edu/cdcsep/*

Department Information:
1981. Chairperson: Linda L. Sperry, Ph. D. Number of faculty: total—full-time 8, part-time 5; women—full-time 7, part-time 3; total—minority—full-time 2; women minority—full-time 2.

Programs and Degrees Offered:
Listed in the following order: Program area, degree type (T if terminal Master's), number awarded 7/11–6/12. School Psychology PhD (Doctor of Philosophy) 3, School Psychology MEd (Education) 7, School Psychology EdS (School Psychology) 7.

APA Accreditation: School PhD (Doctor of Philosophy). Student Outcome Data Website: http://coe.indstate.edu/cdcsep/edpsych/phdstudentdata.htm.

Student Applications/Admissions:

Student Applications

School Psychology PhD (Doctor of Philosophy)—Applications 2012–2013, 10. Total applicants accepted 2012–2013, 4. Number full-time enrolled (new admits only) 2012–2013, 4. Number part-time enrolled (new admits only) 2012–2013, 0. Total enrolled 2012–2013 full-time, 18. Total enrolled 2012–2013 part-time, 0. Openings 2013–2014, 8. The median number of years required for completion of a degree in 2012–2013 were 6. The number of students enrolled full- and part-time who were dismissed or voluntarily withdrew from this program area in 2012–2013 were 0. *School Psychology MEd (Education)*— Applications 2012–2013, 7. Total applicants accepted 2012–2013, 6. Number full-time enrolled (new admits only) 2012–2013, 6. Number part-time enrolled (new admits only) 2012–2013, 0. Total enrolled 2012–2013 full-time, 6. Total enrolled 2012–2013 part-time, 0. Openings 2013–2014, 8. The median number of years required for completion of a degree in 2012–2013 were 2. The number of students enrolled full- and part-time who were dismissed or voluntarily withdrew from this program area in 2012–2013 were 0. *School Psychology EdS (School Psychology)*—Applications 2012–2013, 8. Total applicants accepted 2012–2013, 3. Number full-time enrolled (new admits only) 2012–2013, 3. Number part-time enrolled (new admits only) 2012–2013, 0. Total enrolled 2012–2013 full-time, 17. Total enrolled 2012–2013 part-time, 2. Openings 2013–2014, 12. The median number of years required for completion of a degree in 2012–2013 were 3. The number of students enrolled full- and part-time who were dismissed or voluntarily withdrew from this program area in 2012–2013 were 0.

Scores: Entries appear in this order: required test or GPA, minimum score (if required), median score of students entering in 2012–2013. *School Psychology PhD (Doctor of Philosophy):* GRE-V no minimum stated, GRE-Q no minimum stated, GRE-Analytical no minimum stated, overall undergraduate GPA 2.7; *School Psychology MEd (Education):* GRE-V 450, GRE-Q 450, GRE-Analytical no minimum stated, overall undergraduate GPA 2.5; *School Psychology EdS (School Psychology):* GRE-V no minimum stated, GRE-Q no minimum stated, GRE-Analytical no minimum stated, overall undergraduate GPA 2.7.

Other Criteria: (importance of criteria rated low, medium, or high): GRE scores—medium, research experience—medium, work experience—medium, extracurricular activity—high, clinically related public service—high, GPA—high, letters of recommendation—high, interview—high, statement of goals and objectives—high, vita—high, undergraduate major in psychology—medium, specific undergraduate psychology courses taken—medium. For additional information on admission requirements, go to http://coe.indstate.edu/cdcsep/edpsych/admission.htm.

Student Characteristics: The following represents characteristics of students in 2012–2013 in all graduate psychology programs in the department: Female—full-time 34, part-time 2; Male—full-time 7, part-time 0; African American/Black—full-time 5, part-time 0; Hispanic/Latino(a)—full-time 0, part-time 0; Asian/Pacific Islander—full-time 1, part-time 1; American Indian/Alaska Native—full-time 0, part-time 0; Caucasian/White—full-time 34, part-time 1; Multi-ethnic—full-time 1, part-time 0; students subject to the Americans With Disabilities Act—full-time 0, part-time 0; Unknown ethnicity—full-time 0, part-time 0; International students who hold an F-1 or J-1 Visa—full-time 0, part-time 0.

Financial Information/Assistance:
Tuition for Full-Time Study: *Master's:* State residents: per academic year $6,588, $366 per credit hour; Nonstate residents: per academic year $12,942, $719 per credit hour. *Doctoral:* State residents: per academic year $6,588, $366 per credit hour; Nonstate residents: per academic year $12,942, $719 per credit hour. Tuition is subject to change. See the following website for updates and changes in tuition costs: http://www.indstate.edu/gradexpress/fees.htm.

Financial Assistance:
First-Year Students: Teaching assistantships available for first year. Average amount paid per academic year: $6,112. Average number of hours worked per week: 15. Apply by March 1. Research assistantships available for first year. Average amount paid per academic year: $6,112. Average number of hours worked per week: 15. Apply by March 1. Fellowships and scholarships available for first year. Average amount paid per academic year: $6,112. Average number of hours worked per week: 15. Apply by March 1.

Advanced Students: Teaching assistantships available for advanced students. Average amount paid per academic year: $8,475. Average number of hours worked per week: 15. Apply by March 1. Research assistantships available for advanced students. Average amount paid per academic year: $8,475. Average number of hours worked per week: 15. Apply by March 1. Fellowships and scholarships available for advanced students. Average amount paid per academic year: $8,475. Average number of hours worked per week: 15. Apply by March 1.

Additional Information: Of all students currently enrolled full time, 100% benefited from one or more of the listed financial assistance programs. Application and information available online at: http://www.indstate.edu/finaid/graduate/.

Internships/Practica: Doctoral Degree (PhD School Psychology): For those doctoral students for whom a professional psychology internship was required in this program prior to graduation, (2) students applied for an internship in 2011–2012, with (2) students obtaining an internship. Of those students who obtained an internship, (2) were paid internships. Of those students who obtained an internship, (0) students placed in APA/CPA accredited internships, (0) students placed in internships not APA/CPA accredited, but listed with the Association of Psychology Postdoctoral and Internship Programs (APPIC), (1) students placed in internships conforming to guidelines of the Council of Directors of School Psychology Programs (CDSPP), (1) students placed in internships that were not APA/CPA accredited, APPIC or CDSPP listed. Students in all programs are required to complete a minimum of 160 direct contact hours each semester in which they are enrolled in the program. Practicum experiences include observation, consultation, assessment, counseling and intervention with diverse populations ranging from preschool-aged to school-aged students, as well as with college students, parents, teachers, and other professionals. Practicum sites include public school settings, the Porter School Psychology Clinic, ISU ADHD Clinic, the READ Clinic as well as agencies such as Gibault, Inc. and Riley Children's Hospital. PhD students have the opportunity to complete advanced practicum requirements in school or clinical settings in order to gain additional experiences and to foster increasing autonomy. Final experiences include a 1200+ hour school-based internship for EdS students and a 1500+ hour predoctoral internship in clinic and/or school settings for PhD students. Predoctoral internship sites include public school settings, hospitals and mental health agencies.

Housing and Day Care: On-campus housing is available. See the following website for more information: http://www.indstate.edu/reslife/. On-campus day care facilities are available. See the following website for more information: http://web.indstate.edu/ecec/.

Employment of Department Graduates:

Master's Degree Graduates: Of those who graduated in the academic year 2011–2012, the following categories and numbers represent the postgraduate activities and employment of master's degree graduates: Enrolled in another graduate/professional program (7), enrolled in a postdoctoral residency/fellowship (n/a), employed in independent practice (n/a), total from the above (master's) (7).

Doctoral Degree Graduates: Of those who graduated in the academic year 2011–2012, the following categories and numbers represent the postgraduate activities and employment of doctoral degree graduates: Enrolled in a psychology doctoral program (n/a), employed in a professional position in a school system (3), total from the above (doctoral) (3).

Additional Information:

Orientation, Objectives, and Emphasis of Department: The PhD program in Guidance and Psychological Services, Specialization in School Psychology follows a scholar-practitioner model which serves as a foundation upon which program goals and objectives are based. The mission of the program is to prepare professional school psychologists as scholar-practitioners with a broad cognitive behavioral orientation through a program that is research-based, theory-driven, school-focused, and experiential in nature.

Special Facilities or Resources: The program has a university-based clinic that provides psychological and educational services to children, youth, and families. The clinic includes programs specifically designed to serve children, adolescents, and college students. The clinic is part of an interdisciplinary clinic that also includes the communication disorders and counseling programs. This interdisciplinary clinic provides an opportunity for students to work collaboratively and provide integrated, comprehensive services to clients.

Information for Students With Physical Disabilities: See the following website for more information: http://www.indstate.edu/cfss/programs/dss/index.htm.

Application Information:
Send to Leah Nellis, Director of School Psychology Training Program, Bayh College of Education, Room 302D, Indiana State University, Terre Haute, IN 47809. Application available online. URL of online application: http://www.indstate.edu/graduate/degree.htm. Students are admitted in the Fall, application deadline December 15. *Fee:* $35.

Indiana University
Department of Counseling and Educational Psychology
School of Education
201 North Rose Avenue
Bloomington, IN 47405-1006
Telephone: (812) 856-8300
Fax: (812) 856-8333
E-mail: *gdelands@indiana.edu*
Web: *http://education.indiana.edu/cep*

Department Information:
1948. Chairperson: Ginette Delandshere, PhD. Number of faculty: total—full-time 31, part-time 17; women—full-time 14, part-time 12; total—minority—full-time 5; women minority—full-time 2.

Programs and Degrees Offered:
Listed in the following order: Program area, degree type (T if terminal Master's), number awarded 7/11–6/12. Counseling Psychology PhD (Doctor of Philosophy) 7, Educational Psychology PhD (Doctor of Philosophy) 8, School Psychology PhD (Doctor of Philosophy) 4, School Psychology EdS (School Psychology) 4, Educational Psychology MA/MS (Master of Arts/Science) 0.

APA Accreditation: Counseling PhD (Doctor of Philosophy). School PhD (Doctor of Philosophy).

Student Applications/Admissions:
Student Applications
Counseling Psychology PhD (Doctor of Philosophy)—Applications 2012–2013, 107. Total applicants accepted 2012–2013, 12. Number full-time enrolled (new admits only) 2012–2013, 7. Total enrolled 2012–2013 full-time, 46. Total enrolled 2012–2013 part-time, 0. Openings 2013–2014, 9. The median number of years required for completion of a degree in 2012–2013 were 6. The number of students enrolled full- and part-time who were dismissed or voluntarily withdrew from this program area in 2012–2013 were 1. *Educational Psychology PhD (Doctor of Philosophy)*—Applications 2012–2013, 45. Total applicants accepted 2012–2013, 25. Number full-time enrolled (new admits only) 2012–2013, 17. Total enrolled 2012–2013 full-time, 71. Total enrolled 2012–2013 part-time, 0. Openings 2013–2014, 20. The median number of years required for completion of a degree in 2012–2013 were 6. The number of students enrolled full- and part-time who were dismissed or voluntarily withdrew from this program area in 2012–2013 were 2. *School Psychology PhD (Doctor of Philosophy)*—Applications 2012–2013, 37. Total applicants accepted 2012–2013, 25. Number full-time enrolled (new admits only) 2012–2013, 10. Total enrolled 2012–2013 full-time, 40. Total enrolled 2012–2013 part-time, 0. Openings 2013–2014, 8. The median number of years required for completion of a degree in 2012–2013 were 5. The number of students enrolled full- and part-time who were dismissed or voluntarily withdrew from this program area in 2012–2013 were 3. *School Psychology EdS (School Psychology)*—Applications 2012–2013, 41. Total applicants accepted 2012–2013, 23. Number full-time enrolled

(new admits only) 2012–2013, 4. Total enrolled 2012–2013 full-time, 14. Openings 2013–2014, 10. The median number of years required for completion of a degree in 2012–2013 were 3. The number of students enrolled full- and part-time who were dismissed or voluntarily withdrew from this program area in 2012–2013 were 1. *Educational Psychology MA/MS (Master of Arts/Science)*—Applications 2012–2013, 18. Total applicants accepted 2012–2013, 4. Number full-time enrolled (new admits only) 2012–2013, 0. Total enrolled 2012–2013 full-time, 7. Openings 2013–2014, 8. The number of students enrolled full- and part-time who were dismissed or voluntarily withdrew from this program area in 2012–2013 were 0.

Scores: Entries appear in this order: required test or GPA, minimum score (if required), median score of students entering in 2012–2013. *Counseling Psychology PhD (Doctor of Philosophy):* GRE-V no minimum stated, 157, GRE-Q no minimum stated, 149, GRE-Analytical no minimum stated, 4, overall undergraduate GPA no minimum stated, 3.38, Masters GPA no minimum stated, 3.8; *Educational Psychology PhD (Doctor of Philosophy):* GRE-V no minimum stated, 504, GRE-Q no minimum stated, 605, GRE-Analytical no minimum stated, 4., overall undergraduate GPA no minimum stated, 3.53, Masters GPA no minimum stated, 3.89; *School Psychology PhD (Doctor of Philosophy):* GRE-V no minimum stated, 157, GRE-Q no minimum stated, 153, GRE-Analytical no minimum stated, 4.5, overall undergraduate GPA no minimum stated, 3.51; *Educational Psychology MA/MS (Master of Arts/Science):* GRE-V no minimum stated, 154, GRE-Q no minimum stated, 152, GRE-Analytical no minimum stated, 4.4, overall undergraduate GPA no minimum stated, 3.36.

Other Criteria: (importance of criteria rated low, medium, or high): GRE scores—high, research experience—medium, work experience—medium, extracurricular activity—medium, clinically related public service—medium, GPA—high, letters of recommendation—high, interview—high, statement of goals and objectives—high, Personal interviews are required for applicants to the PhD programs. GRE scores are interpreted differently for domestic and international applicants. For additional information on admission requirements, go to https://education.indiana.edu/graduate/apply/index.html.

Student Characteristics: The following represents characteristics of students in 2012–2013 in all graduate psychology programs in the department: Female—full-time 135, part-time 0; Male—full-time 43, part-time 0; African American/Black—full-time 17, part-time 0; Hispanic/Latino(a)—full-time 17, part-time 0; Asian/Pacific Islander—full-time 25, part-time 0; American Indian/Alaska Native—full-time 0, part-time 0; Caucasian/White—full-time 99, part-time 0; Multi-ethnic—full-time 0, part-time 0; students subject to the Americans With Disabilities Act—full-time 0, part-time 0; Unknown ethnicity—full-time 20, part-time 0; International students who hold an F-1 or J-1 Visa—full-time 23, part-time 0.

Financial Information/Assistance:

Tuition for Full-Time Study: *Master's:* State residents: $397 per credit hour; Nonstate residents: $1,155 per credit hour. *Doctoral:* State residents: $352 per credit hour; Nonstate residents: $1,026 per credit hour. Tuition is subject to change. See the following website for updates and changes in tuition costs: http://bursar.indiana.edu/fee_schedule.php.

Financial Assistance:

First-Year Students: Teaching assistantships available for first year. Average amount paid per academic year: $15,225. Average number of hours worked per week: 18. Research assistantships available for first year. Average amount paid per academic year: $12,795. Average number of hours worked per week: 18. Fellowships and scholarships available for first year. Average amount paid per academic year: $16,000. Average number of hours worked per week: 18.

Advanced Students: Teaching assistantships available for advanced students. Average amount paid per academic year: $15,225. Average number of hours worked per week: 18. Research assistantships available for advanced students. Average amount paid per academic year: $12,795. Average number of hours worked per week: 18. Fellowships and scholarships available for advanced students. Average amount paid per academic year: $16,000. Average number of hours worked per week: 18.

Additional Information: Of all students currently enrolled full time, 50% benefited from one or more of the listed financial assistance programs. Application and information available online at: https://education.indiana.edu/graduate/cost-aid/index.html.

Internships/Practica: Doctoral Degree (PhD Counseling Psychology): For those doctoral students for whom a professional psychology internship was required in this program prior to graduation, (6) students applied for an internship in 2011–2012, with (6) students obtaining an internship. Of those students who obtained an internship, (6) were paid internships. Of those students who obtained an internship, (4) students placed in APA/CPA accredited internships, (0) students placed in internships not APA/CPA accredited, but listed with the Association of Psychology Postdoctoral and Internship Programs (APPIC), (0) students placed in internships conforming to guidelines of the Council of Directors of School Psychology Programs (CDSPP), (2) students placed in internships that were not APA/CPA accredited, APPIC or CDSPP listed. Doctoral Degree (PhD School Psychology): For those doctoral students for whom a professional psychology internship was required in this program prior to graduation, (4) students applied for an internship in 2011–2012, with (4) students obtaining an internship. Of those students who obtained an internship, (4) were paid internships. Of those students who obtained an internship, (3) students placed in APA/CPA accredited internships, (0) students placed in internships not APA/CPA accredited, but listed with the Association of Psychology Postdoctoral and Internship Programs (APPIC), (0) students placed in internships conforming to guidelines of the Council of Directors of School Psychology Programs (CDSPP), (1) students placed in internships that were not APA/CPA accredited, APPIC or CDSPP listed. All counseling and school psychology students must take both practica and internships.

Housing and Day Care: On-campus housing is available. See the following website for more information: http://www.rps.indiana.edu/index.cfml. On-campus day care facilities are available. See the following website for more information: http://www.childcare.indiana.edu/.

Employment of Department Graduates:

Master's Degree Graduates: Of those who graduated in the academic year 2011–2012, the following categories and numbers represent the postgraduate activities and employment of master's degree graduates: Enrolled in a postdoctoral residency/fellowship (n/a), employed in independent practice (n/a), total from the above (master's) (0).

Doctoral Degree Graduates: Of those who graduated in the academic year 2011–2012, the following categories and numbers represent the postgraduate activities and employment of doctoral degree graduates: Enrolled in a psychology doctoral program (n/a), enrolled in a postdoctoral residency/fellowship (2), employed in independent practice (1), employed in an academic position at a university (2), employed in an academic position at a 2-year/4-year college (1), employed in other positions at a higher education institution (4), employed in a professional position in a school system (1), employed in a community mental health/counseling center (1), total from the above (doctoral) (12).

Additional Information:

Orientation, Objectives, and Emphasis of Department: The Department has multiple missions, but at the heart of our enterprise is a community of scholars working to contribute solutions to the problems faced by children, adolescents, and adults in the context of contemporary education. Additionally, the counseling psychology program promotes a broad range of interventions designed to facilitate the maximal adjustment of individuals. Faculty, staff and students share a commitment to open-mindedness and to social justice. We recognize the complex and dynamic nature of the social fabric and welcome qualified students of all ethnic, racial, national, religious, gender, social class, sexual, political, and philosophic orientations. Faculty and students collaboratively investigate numerous facets of child and adolescent development, creativity, learning, metacognition, aging, semiotics, and inquiry methodologies. Our programs require an understanding of both quantitative and qualitative research paradigms. We ascribe to the scientist–practitioner model for preparing professional psychologists. Our graduates work in various research and practice settings; universities, public schools, state departments of education, mental health centers, hospitals, and corporations.

Special Facilities or Resources: Special facilities include the Institute for Child Study, Center for Human Growth, Center for Evaluation and Education Policy, Center for Adolescent & Family Studies, Center for Research on Learning & Technology, and the Indiana Institute on Disability and Community.

Information for Students With Physical Disabilities: See the following website for more information: http://studentaffairs.iub.edu/dss/.

Application Information:

Send to Office of Graduate Studies, Room 2100, W.W. Wright Education Building, 201 North Rose Avenue, Bloomington, IN 47405-1005. Application available online. URL of online application: http://graduate.indiana.edu/admissions.php. Students are admitted in the Fall, application deadline December 1. *Fee:* $55. Application fee of $65 for international students.

Indiana University
Department of Psychological and Brain Sciences
College of Arts and Sciences
1101 East 10th Street
Bloomington, IN 47405
Telephone: (812) 856-2409
E-mail: *psychgrd@indiana.edu*
Web: *http://psych.indiana.edu/*

Department Information:

1919. Chairperson: Dr. William Hetrick. Number of faculty: total—full-time 52; women—full-time 14; total—minority—full-time 2; women minority—full-time 2; faculty subject to the Americans With Disabilities Act 1.

Programs and Degrees Offered:

Listed in the following order: Program area, degree type (T if terminal Master's), number awarded 7/11–6/12. Clinical Science PhD (Doctor of Philosophy) 2, Cognitive Neuroscience PhD (Doctor of Philosophy) 0, Cognitive Psychology PhD (Doctor of Philosophy) 2, Mechanisms Of Behavior PhD (Doctor of Philosophy) 0, Developmental Psychology PhD (Doctor of Philosophy) 2, Social Psychology PhD (Doctor of Philosophy) 1, Molecular Systems Neuroscience PhD (Doctor of Philosophy) 0, Biology/Behavior/Neuroscience PhD (Doctor of Philosophy) 3.

APA Accreditation: Clinical PhD (Doctor of Philosophy). Student Outcome Data Website: http://psych.indiana.edu/clinical.php.

Student Applications/Admissions:
Student Applications

Clinical Science PhD (Doctor of Philosophy)—Applications 2012–2013, 160. Total applicants accepted 2012–2013, 5. Number full-time enrolled (new admits only) 2012–2013, 2. Total enrolled 2012–2013 full-time, 17. The median number of years required for completion of a degree in 2012–2013 were 7. The number of students enrolled full- and part-time who were dismissed or voluntarily withdrew from this program area in 2012–2013 were 0. *Cognitive Neuroscience PhD (Doctor of Philosophy)*—Applications 2012–2013, 31. Total applicants accepted 2012–2013, 4. Number full-time enrolled (new admits only) 2012–2013, 3. Number part-time enrolled (new admits only) 2012–2013, 0. Total enrolled 2012–2013 full-time, 14. Total enrolled 2012–2013 part-time, 0. The number of students enrolled full- and part-time who were dismissed or voluntarily withdrew from this program area in 2012–2013 were 0. *Cognitive Psychology PhD (Doctor of Philosophy)*—Applications 2012–2013, 47. Total applicants accepted 2012–2013, 5. Number full-time enrolled (new admits only) 2012–2013, 2. Number part-time enrolled (new admits only) 2012–2013, 0. Total enrolled 2012–2013 full-time, 28. Total enrolled 2012–2013 part-time, 0. The median number of years required for completion of a degree in 2012–2013 were 6. The number of students enrolled full- and part-time who were dismissed or voluntarily withdrew from this program area in 2012–2013 were 1. *Mechanisms Of Behavior PhD (Doctor of Philosophy)*—

Applications 2012–2013, 16. Total applicants accepted 2012–2013, 3. Number full-time enrolled (new admits only) 2012–2013, 1. Number part-time enrolled (new admits only) 2012–2013, 0. Total enrolled 2012–2013 full-time, 5. Total enrolled 2012–2013 part-time, 0. The number of students enrolled full- and part-time who were dismissed or voluntarily withdrew from this program area in 2012–2013 were 0. *Developmental Psychology PhD (Doctor of Philosophy)*—Applications 2012–2013, 20. Total applicants accepted 2012–2013, 1. Number full-time enrolled (new admits only) 2012–2013, 0. Number part-time enrolled (new admits only) 2012–2013, 0. Total enrolled 2012–2013 full-time, 9. Total enrolled 2012–2013 part-time, 0. The median number of years required for completion of a degree in 2012–2013 were 5. The number of students enrolled full- and part-time who were dismissed or voluntarily withdrew from this program area in 2012–2013 were 0. *Social Psychology PhD (Doctor of Philosophy)*—Applications 2012–2013, 51. Total applicants accepted 2012–2013, 4. Number full-time enrolled (new admits only) 2012–2013, 3. Number part-time enrolled (new admits only) 2012–2013, 0. Total enrolled 2012–2013 full-time, 13. Total enrolled 2012–2013 part-time, 0. The median number of years required for completion of a degree in 2012–2013 were 5. *Molecular Systems Neuroscience PhD (Doctor of Philosophy)*—Applications 2012–2013, 17. Total applicants accepted 2012–2013, 3. Number full-time enrolled (new admits only) 2012–2013, 2. Number part-time enrolled (new admits only) 2012–2013, 0. Total enrolled 2012–2013 full-time, 4. *Biology/Behavior/Neuroscience PhD (Doctor of Philosophy)*—Applications 2012–2013, 0. Total applicants accepted 2012–2013, 0. Number full-time enrolled (new admits only) 2012–2013, 0. Number part-time enrolled (new admits only) 2012–2013, 0. Total enrolled 2012–2013 full-time, 5. Total enrolled 2012–2013 part-time, 0. The median number of years required for completion of a degree in 2012–2013 were 6. The number of students enrolled full- and part-time who were dismissed or voluntarily withdrew from this program area in 2012–2013 were 0.

Scores: Entries appear in this order: required test or GPA, minimum score (if required), median score of students entering in 2012–2013. *Clinical Science PhD (Doctor of Philosophy):* GRE-V no minimum stated, GRE-Q no minimum stated, GRE-Analytical no minimum stated; *Cognitive Neuroscience PhD (Doctor of Philosophy):* GRE-V no minimum stated, GRE-Q no minimum stated, GRE-Analytical no minimum stated; *Cognitive Psychology PhD (Doctor of Philosophy):* GRE-V no minimum stated, GRE-Q no minimum stated, GRE-Analytical no minimum stated; *Mechanisms of Behavior PhD (Doctor of Philosophy):* GRE-V no minimum stated, GRE-Q no minimum stated, GRE-Analytical no minimum stated; *Developmental Psychology PhD (Doctor of Philosophy):* GRE-V no minimum stated, GRE-Q no minimum stated, GRE-Analytical no minimum stated; *Social Psychology PhD (Doctor of Philosophy):* GRE-V no minimum stated, GRE-Q no minimum stated, GRE-Analytical no minimum stated; *Molecular Systems Neuroscience PhD (Doctor of Philosophy):* GRE-V no minimum stated, GRE-Q no minimum stated, GRE-Analytical no minimum stated; *Biology/Behavior/Neuroscience PhD (Doctor of Philosophy):* GRE-V no minimum stated, GRE-Q no minimum stated, GRE-Analytical no minimum stated.

Other Criteria: (importance of criteria rated low, medium, or high): GRE scores—high, research experience—high, GPA—high, letters of recommendation—high, interview—medium, statement of goals and objectives—medium, undergraduate major in psychology—medium. For additional information on admission requirements, go to http://psych.indiana.edu/grad_admissions.php.

Student Characteristics: The following represents characteristics of students in 2012–2013 in all graduate psychology programs in the department: Female—full-time 54, part-time 0; Male—full-time 38, part-time 0; African American/Black—full-time 4, part-time 0; Hispanic/Latino(a)—full-time 7, part-time 0; Asian/Pacific Islander—full-time 6, part-time 0; American Indian/Alaska Native—full-time 0, part-time 0; Caucasian/White—full-time 60, part-time 0; Multi-ethnic—full-time 0, part-time 0; students subject to the Americans With Disabilities Act—full-time 1, part-time 0; Unknown ethnicity—full-time 15, part-time 0; International students who hold an F-1 or J-1 Visa—full-time 13, part-time 0.

Financial Information/Assistance:

Tuition for Full-Time Study: *Doctoral:* State residents: per academic year $7,725, $321 per credit hour; Nonstate residents: per academic year $22,512, $938 per credit hour. Tuition is subject to change. Additional fees are assessed to students beyond the costs of tuition for the following: activity, health, technology, transportation, repair. See the following website for updates and changes in tuition costs: http://bursar.indiana.edu/fee_schedule.php.

Financial Assistance:

First-Year Students: Teaching assistantships available for first year. Average amount paid per academic year: $22,500. Average number of hours worked per week: 20. Research assistantships available for first year. Average amount paid per academic year: $22,500. Average number of hours worked per week: 20. Fellowships and scholarships available for first year. Average amount paid per academic year: $22,500. Average number of hours worked per week: 0.

Advanced Students: Teaching assistantships available for advanced students. Average amount paid per academic year: $22,500. Average number of hours worked per week: 20. Research assistantships available for advanced students. Average amount paid per academic year: $22,500. Average number of hours worked per week: 20. Fellowships and scholarships available for advanced students. Average amount paid per academic year: $22,500.

Additional Information: Of all students currently enrolled full time, 100% benefited from one or more of the listed financial assistance programs.

Internships/Practica: Doctoral Degree (PhD Clinical Science): For those doctoral students for whom a professional psychology internship was required in this program prior to graduation, (5) students applied for an internship in 2011–2012, with (3) students obtaining an internship. Of those students who obtained an internship, (3) were paid internships. Of those students who obtained an internship, (3) students placed in APA/CPA accredited internships, (0) students placed in internships not APA/CPA accredited, but listed with the Association of Psychology Postdoctoral and Internship Programs (APPIC), (0) students placed in internships conforming to guidelines of the Council of Directors of School Psychology Programs (CDSPP), (0) students placed in internships that were not APA/CPA accredited, APPIC or CDSPP listed. .

Housing and Day Care: On-campus housing is available. See the following website for more information: http://rps.indiana.edu/index.cfml. On-campus day care facilities are available. See the following website for more information: http://www.childcare.indiana.edu/.

Employment of Department Graduates:

Master's Degree Graduates: Of those who graduated in the academic year 2011–2012, the following categories and numbers represent the postgraduate activities and employment of master's degree graduates: Enrolled in a postdoctoral residency/fellowship (n/a), employed in independent practice (n/a), total from the above (master's) (0).

Doctoral Degree Graduates: Of those who graduated in the academic year 2011–2012, the following categories and numbers represent the postgraduate activities and employment of doctoral degree graduates: Enrolled in a psychology doctoral program (n/a), enrolled in a postdoctoral residency/fellowship (2), employed in an academic position at a university (6), do not know (2), total from the above (doctoral) (10).

Additional Information:

Orientation, Objectives, and Emphasis of Department: The mission of the Department of Psychological and Brain Sciences is to lead scientific advances through state-of-the-art experimentation and theory with the goal of understanding how the entire brain-behavior system works, from molecular neuroscience to cognition to the social behavior of groups. Through the application of cutting-edge discoveries to real world problems, through the training of the next generation of scientists, and through training citizens who will apply their knowledge in many fields from medicine to industry to public service, the department accepts the responsibility to translate scientific knowledge into practical solutions for problems that impact human lives.

Special Facilities or Resources: The Department of Psychological and Brain Sciences is home to the IU Imaging Research Facility. The facility houses a 3T Siemens Magnetom Trio whole body system, used for magnetic resonance imaging (MRI) or functional MRI (fMRI), a noninvasive method for studying patterns of brain activity during mental operations. The facility gives our students the opportunity to be part of research labs doing MRI and fMRI studies and to take classes with the MRI scientists.

Information for Students With Physical Disabilities: See the following website for more information: http://studentaffairs.iub.edu/dss/.

Application Information:

Send to Indiana University, Graduate Admissions, Psychological and Brain Sciences, 1101 E. 10th Street, Bloomington, IN 47405-7007. Application available online. URL of online application: http://www.indiana.edu/~grdschl/admissions.php. Students are admitted in the Fall, application deadline December 1. *Fee:* $60.

Indiana University–Purdue University Indianapolis
Department of Psychology
School of Science
402 North Blackford Street, LD 124
Indianapolis, IN 46202-3275
Telephone: (317) 274-6945
Fax: (317) 274-6756
E-mail: *gradpsy@iupui.edu*
Web: *http://psych.iupui.edu*

Department Information:
1969. Chairperson: Peggy Stockdale. Number of faculty: total—full-time 26; women—full-time 14.

Programs and Degrees Offered:
Listed in the following order: Program area, degree type (T if terminal Master's), number awarded 7/11–6/12. Industrial/Organizational Psychology MA/MS (Master of Arts/Science) (T) 3, Clinical Psychology PhD (Doctor of Philosophy) 3, Psychobiology PhD (Doctor of Philosophy) 3.

APA Accreditation: Clinical PhD (Doctor of Philosophy). Student Outcome Data Website: http://psych.iupui.edu/graduate/degrees/phd-clinical.

Student Applications/Admissions:
Student Applications
Industrial/Organizational Psychology MA/MS (Master of Arts/Science)—Applications 2012–2013, 69. Total applicants accepted 2012–2013, 5. Number full-time enrolled (new admits only) 2012–2013, 5. Number part-time enrolled (new admits only) 2012–2013, 0. Total enrolled 2012–2013 full-time, 10. Total enrolled 2012–2013 part-time, 0. Openings 2013–2014, 5. The median number of years required for completion of a degree in 2012–2013 were 2. The number of students enrolled full- and part-time who were dismissed or voluntarily withdrew from this program area in 2012–2013 were 0. *Clinical Psychology PhD (Doctor of Philosophy)*—Applications 2012–2013, 68. Total applicants accepted 2012–2013, 10. Number full-time enrolled (new admits only) 2012–2013, 6. Number part-time enrolled (new admits only) 2012–2013, 0. Total enrolled 2012–2013 full-time, 25. Total enrolled 2012–2013 part-time, 0. Openings 2013–2014, 7. The median number of years required for completion of a degree in 2012–2013 were 5. The number of students enrolled full- and part-time who were dismissed or voluntarily withdrew from this program area in 2012–2013 were 1. *Psychobiology PhD (Doctor of Philosophy)*—Applications 2012–2013, 10. Total applicants accepted 2012–2013, 1. Number full-time enrolled (new admits only) 2012–2013, 0. Total enrolled 2012–2013 full-time, 15. Total enrolled 2012–2013 part-time, 0. Openings 2013–2014, 3. The median number of years required for completion of a degree in 2012–2013 were 6. The number of students enrolled full- and part-time who were dismissed or voluntarily withdrew from this program area in 2012–2013 were 2.

Scores: Entries appear in this order: required test or GPA, minimum score (if required), median score of students entering in 2012–2013. *Industrial/Organizational Psychology MA/MS (Master of Arts/Science):* GRE-V 151, 149, GRE-Q 149, 151, GRE-Analytical 3.5, 4, overall undergraduate GPA 3.36, 3.71; *Clinical Psychology PhD (Doctor of Philosophy):* GRE-V 158, 159, GRE-Q 151, 156, GRE-Analytical 3.5, 4, GRE-Subject (Psychology) 530, 690, overall undergraduate GPA 3.2, 3.63; *Psychobiology PhD (Doctor of Philosophy):* GRE-V 155, 157, GRE-Q 152, 153, GRE-Analytical 4, 4, overall undergraduate GPA 3, 3.21.

Other Criteria: (importance of criteria rated low, medium, or high): GRE scores—high, research experience—high, work experience—low, GPA—high, letters of recommendation—high, interview—high, statement of goals and objectives—high, undergraduate major in psychology—medium, specific undergraduate psychology courses taken—medium. For additional information on admission requirements, go to http://psych.iupui.edu/graduate/admissions.

Student Characteristics: The following represents characteristics of students in 2012–2013 in all graduate psychology programs in the department: Female—full-time 37, part-time 0; Male—full-time 13, part-time 0; African American/Black—full-time 4, part-time 0; Hispanic/Latino(a)—full-time 2, part-time 0; Asian/Pacific Islander—full-time 4, part-time 0; American Indian/Alaska Native—full-time 0, part-time 0; Caucasian/White—full-time 40, part-time 0; Multi-ethnic—full-time 0, part-time 0; students subject to the Americans With Disabilities Act—full-time 0, part-time 0; Unknown ethnicity—full-time 0, part-time 0; International students who hold an F-1 or J-1 Visa—full-time 2, part-time 0.

Financial Information/Assistance:

Tuition for Full-Time Study: *Master's:* State residents: $345 per credit hour; Nonstate residents: $1,007 per credit hour. *Doctoral:* State residents: $345 per credit hour; Nonstate residents: $1,007 per credit hour. Tuition is subject to change. Additional fees are assessed to students beyond the costs of tuition for the following: recreational fee, graduate fee and technology fee. Tuition costs vary by program. See the following website for updates and changes in tuition costs: http://bursar.iupui.edu/apps/costestimator.aspx.

Financial Assistance:

First-Year Students: Teaching assistantships available for first year. Average amount paid per academic year: $14,000. Average number of hours worked per week: 20. Research assistantships available for first year. Average amount paid per academic year: $14,000. Average number of hours worked per week: 20. Fellowships and scholarships available for first year. Average amount paid per academic year: $22,000. Average number of hours worked per week: 0.

Advanced Students: Teaching assistantships available for advanced students. Average amount paid per academic year: $14,000. Average number of hours worked per week: 20. Research assistantships available for advanced students. Average amount paid per academic year: $14,000. Average number of hours worked per week: 20. Fellowships and scholarships available for advanced students. Average amount paid per academic year: $14,000. Average number of hours worked per week: 0.

Additional Information: Of all students currently enrolled full time, 95% benefited from one or more of the listed financial assistance programs. Application and information available online at: http://psych.iupui.edu/graduate/financial-support.

Internships/Practica: Doctoral Degree (PhD Clinical Psychology): For those doctoral students for whom a professional psychology internship was required in this program prior to graduation, (4) students applied for an internship in 2011–2012, with (4) students obtaining an internship. Of those students who obtained an internship, (4) were paid internships. Of those students who obtained an internship, (4) students placed in APA/CPA accredited internships, (0) students placed in internships not APA/CPA accredited, but listed with the Association of Psychology Postdoctoral and Internship Programs (APPIC), (0) students placed in internships conforming to guidelines of the Council of Directors of School Psychology Programs (CDSPP), (0) students placed in internships that were not APA/CPA accredited, APPIC or CDSPP listed. Clinical practicum sites are located at IUPUI and within the Indianapolis area, and involve supervised clinical training individually tailored for each student. A practicum coordinator, the site supervisor, and the student develop specific contracts that emphasize education and the acquisition of clinical skills and knowledge, rather than experience per se. These contractual activities and goals are monitored and evaluated at the end of each placement. Practicum opportunities are varied and numerous and include many different types of clinical settings with different clinical populations. On-site supervisors are psychologists. General practicum sites include a university counseling center and several psychiatric clinics. More advanced settings can be categorized as 1) Behavioral Medicine/Health Psychology; or 2) Severe Mental Illness/Psychiatric Rehabilitation. The I/O Master's program offers opportunities to achieve applied experience in business settings. Students have the opportunity to sign up for practicum in the spring of their second year. Students are typically placed in an organization for one 8-hour day each week of the semester. Paid summer internships (15-20 hours per week) in the community are also available.

Housing and Day Care: On-campus housing is available. See the following website for more information: http://life.iupui.edu/housing/. On-campus day care facilities are available. See the following website for more information: http://www.childcare.iupui.edu/.

Employment of Department Graduates:

Master's Degree Graduates: Of those who graduated in the academic year 2011–2012, the following categories and numbers represent the postgraduate activities and employment of master's degree graduates: Enrolled in a psychology doctoral program (2), enrolled in a postdoctoral residency/fellowship (n/a), employed in independent practice (n/a), employed in business or industry (1), total from the above (master's) (3).

Doctoral Degree Graduates: Of those who graduated in the academic year 2011–2012, the following categories and numbers represent the postgraduate activities and employment of doctoral degree graduates: Enrolled in a psychology doctoral program (n/a), enrolled in a postdoctoral residency/fellowship (4), employed in an academic position at a university (1), total from the above (doctoral) (5).

Additional Information:

Orientation, Objectives, and Emphasis of Department: Graduate education is offered at the PhD level in Clinical Psychology and Psychobiology of Addictions. The APA-Accredited Clinical program follows the scientist–practitioner model. A rigorous academic and research education is combined with supervised practical training. The clinical program provides specialization in behavioral medicine/health psychology, and severe mental illness/psychiatric rehabilitation. The PhD program in the psychobiological bases of addictions emphasizes the core content areas of psychology along with specialization in psychobiology and animal models of addiction. Research, scholarship, and close faculty-student mentor relationships are viewed as integral training elements within both programs. Graduate training at the MS level is designed to provide students with theory and practice that will enable them to apply psychological techniques and findings to subsequent jobs. All students are required to take departmental methods courses and then specific area core courses and electives. The MS degree areas are applied in focus and science-based, and this reflects the interests and orientation of the faculty.

Special Facilities or Resources: IUPUI is a unique urban university campus with 27,000 students enrolled in 235 degree programs at the undergraduate and graduate level. The campus includes schools of law, dentistry, and medicine, among others, along with undergraduate programs in the arts, humanities, and science. In addition, there are over 75 research institutes, centers, laboratories and specialized programs. The Department of Psychology at IUPUI occupies teaching and research facilities in a modern science building in the heart of campus. Facilities include a 4000-square foot space and self-contained area devoted to faculty and graduate student basic animal research in experimental psychology and psychobiology. Many of the research rooms are equipped for online computer recording to one of the faculty offices. Laboratories for human research, research rooms, and teaching laboratories are separately located on the first floor of the building. The Psychology Department maintains ties with the faculty and programs in other schools within IUPUI, including the School of Nursing, and the Departments of Psychiatry, Adolescent Medicine, and Neurology. The clinical program provides an unusually rich array of practicum opportunities in behavioral medicine/health psychology and psychiatric rehabilitation.

Information for Students With Physical Disabilities: See the following website for more information: http://aes.iupui.edu/.

Application Information:

Send to Heather Sissons,Office Manager and Graduate Coordinator, IUPUI, Department of Psychology, LD124, 402 North Blackford Street, Indianapolis, IN 46202-3275. Application available online. URL of online application: http://psych.iupui.edu/graduate/admissions/application. Students are admitted in the Fall, application deadline December 1. Clinical PhD deadline is December 1. Psychobiology application deadline is January 1. Industrial/Organizational application deadline is February 1. *Fee:* $60.

Indianapolis, University of
Graduate Psychology Program
School of Psychological Sciences
1400 East Hanna Avenue GH 109
Indianapolis, IN 46227
Telephone: (317) 788-3353
Fax: (317) 788-2120
E-mail: *psychology@uindy.edu*
Web: *http://psych.uindy.edu/*

Department Information:

1994. Dean/Director of Graduate Programs: Richard Holigrocki, PhD/David Downing, PsyD, ABPP. Number of faculty: total—full-time 16, part-time 3; women—full-time 8, part-time 1; total—minority—full-time 1; faculty subject to the Americans With Disabilities Act 1.

Programs and Degrees Offered:

Listed in the following order: Program area, degree type (T if terminal Master's), number awarded 7/11–6/12. Clinical Psychology MA/MS (Master of Arts/Science) 20, Clinical Psychology PsyD (Doctor of Psychology) 21, Mental Health Counseling MA/MS (Master of Arts/Science) (T) 13.

APA Accreditation: Clinical PsyD (Doctor of Psychology). Student Outcome Data Website: http://psych.uindy.edu/outcomes.php.

Student Applications/Admissions:

Student Applications

Clinical Psychology MA/MS (Master of Arts/Science)—Applications 2012–2013, 90. Total applicants accepted 2012–2013, 26. Number full-time enrolled (new admits only) 2012–2013, 13. Number part-time enrolled (new admits only) 2012–2013, 0. Total enrolled 2012–2013 full-time, 15. Total enrolled 2012–2013 part-time, 0. Openings 2013–2014, 6. The median number of years required for completion of a degree in 2012–2013 were 2. The number of students enrolled full- and part-time who were dismissed or voluntarily withdrew from this program area in 2012–2013 were 0. *Clinical Psychology PsyD (Doctor of Psychology)*—Applications 2012–2013, 229. Total applicants accepted 2012–2013, 44. Number full-time enrolled (new admits only) 2012–2013, 28. Number part-time enrolled (new admits only) 2012–2013, 0. Total enrolled 2012–2013 full-time, 121. Total enrolled 2012–2013 part-time, 14. Openings 2013–2014, 20. The median number of years required for completion of a degree in 2012–2013 were 5. The number of students enrolled full- and part-time who were dismissed or voluntarily withdrew from this program area in 2012–2013 were 1. *Mental Health Counseling MA/MS (Master of Arts/Science)*—Applications 2012–2013, 88. Total applicants accepted 2012–2013, 24. Number full-time enrolled (new admits only) 2012–2013, 10. Number part-time enrolled (new admits only) 2012–2013, 0. Total enrolled 2012–2013 full-time, 25. Total enrolled 2012–2013 part-time, 1. Openings 2013–2014, 19. The median number of years required for completion of a degree in 2012–2013 were 2. The number of students enrolled full- and part-time who were dismissed or voluntarily withdrew from this program area in 2012–2013 were 1.

Scores: Entries appear in this order: required test or GPA, minimum score (if required), median score of students entering

in 2012–2013. *Clinical Psychology MA/MS (Master of Arts/ Science)*: GRE-V 153, 153, GRE-Q 144, 148, GRE-Analytical 4.0, 4.2, overall undergraduate GPA 3.0, 3.45; *Clinical Psychology PsyD (Doctor of Psychology)*: GRE-V 153, 157, GRE-Q 144, 153, GRE-Analytical 4.0, 4.63, overall undergraduate GPA 3.0, 3.74; *Mental Health Counseling MA/MS (Master of Arts/Science)*: GRE-V 153, 153, GRE-Q 144, 148, GRE-Analytical 4.0, 4.2, overall undergraduate GPA 3.0, 3.45.

Other Criteria: (importance of criteria rated low, medium, or high): GRE scores—high, research experience—medium, work experience—medium, extracurricular activity—low, clinically related public service—medium, GPA—high, letters of recommendation—high, interview—high, statement of goals and objectives—medium, 18 credits in psychology—high. For additional information on admission requirements, go to http://psych.uindy.edu/psydapply.php.

Student Characteristics: The following represents characteristics of students in 2012–2013 in all graduate psychology programs in the department: Female—full-time 135, part-time 13; Male—full-time 26, part-time 2; African American/Black—full-time 3, part-time 0; Hispanic/Latino(a)—full-time 5, part-time 1; Asian/Pacific Islander—full-time 10, part-time 2; American Indian/Alaska Native—full-time 0, part-time 0; Caucasian/White—full-time 141, part-time 12; Multi-ethnic—full-time 2, part-time 0; students subject to the Americans With Disabilities Act—full-time 5, part-time 1; Unknown ethnicity—full-time 0, part-time 0; International students who hold an F-1 or J-1 Visa—full-time 5, part-time 2.

Financial Information/Assistance:

Tuition for Full-Time Study: *Master's:* State residents: $760 per credit hour; Nonstate residents: $760 per credit hour. *Doctoral:* State residents: $760 per credit hour; Nonstate residents: $760 per credit hour. Tuition is subject to change. Additional fees are assessed to students beyond the costs of tuition for the following: lab fees for some classes. See the following website for updates and changes in tuition costs: http://psych.uindy.edu/tuifinaidpsyd.php.

Financial Assistance:

First-Year Students: Teaching assistantships available for first year. Average amount paid per academic year: $0. Average number of hours worked per week: 11. Apply by January 10. Research assistantships available for first year. Average amount paid per academic year: $0. Average number of hours worked per week: 11. Apply by January 10. Fellowships and scholarships available for first year. Average amount paid per academic year: $0. Average number of hours worked per week: 0. Apply by January 10.

Advanced Students: Teaching assistantships available for advanced students. Average amount paid per academic year: $0. Average number of hours worked per week: 11. Research assistantships available for advanced students. Average amount paid per academic year: $0. Average number of hours worked per week: 11. Fellowships and scholarships available for advanced students. Average amount paid per academic year: $0. Average number of hours worked per week: 0.

Additional Information: Of all students currently enrolled full time, 30% benefited from one or more of the listed financial assistance programs. Application and information available online at: http://psych.uindy.edu/tuifinaidpsyd.php.

Internships/Practica: Doctoral Degree (PsyD Clinical Psychology): For those doctoral students for whom a professional psychology internship was required in this program prior to graduation, (26) students applied for an internship in 2011–2012, with (22) students obtaining an internship. Of those students who obtained an internship, (22) were paid internships. Of those students who obtained an internship, (12) students placed in APA/CPA accredited internships, (10) students placed in internships not APA/CPA accredited, but listed with the Association of Psychology Postdoctoral and Internship Programs (APPIC), (0) students placed in internships conforming to guidelines of the Council of Directors of School Psychology Programs (CDSPP), (0) students placed in internships that were not APA/CPA accredited, APPIC or CDSPP listed. Master's Degree (MA/MS Mental Health Counseling): An internship experience, such as a final research project or "capstone" experience is required of graduates. There are numerous clinical practicum experiences available for both master's and doctoral students. In 2011-2012 there are 43 clinical practicum sites, with 96 openings for doctoral or master's students. The number of practicum openings exceeds the number of applicants ensuring that all students receive placements. Clinical psychology master's students (CP) obtain a minimum of 225 hours of supervised clinical practicum experience, clinical psychology mental health counseling students (MHC) require 1000 hours of supervised clinical practicum experience and doctoral students receive a minimum of 1200 hours of supervised clinical practicum experience. Practica are available at numerous settings, including medical centers, local community hospitals, university counseling centers, forensic settings, private practice placements, schools, social service agencies, and mental health centers. At these placements, students gain supervised experience in clinical assessment and testing, psychotherapy, collaboration and consultation with interdisciplinary teams, program development and evaluation, treatment planning and case management, and participation in development and delivery of services to professional staff. In addition to mainstream psychological services, practicum students have opportunities to obtain specific training in forensics, psychodiagnostic assessment, neuropsychology, health psychology, pain, substance abuse/dependence, eating disorders, developmental disabilities, and HIV/AIDS. All doctoral practica are supervised by licensed, doctoral level psychologists and all master's practica are supervised by licensed, master's level mental health professionals. In conjunction with practica, students enroll in a professional practice seminar that addresses a wide variety of issues that confront mental health professionals and students. Doctoral students must also complete a 2000-hour internship. The Director of Clinical Training develops training sites, assists students in their placement and ensures the quality of practicum and internship training.

Housing and Day Care: No on-campus housing is available. On-campus day care facilities are available.

Employment of Department Graduates:

Master's Degree Graduates: Of those who graduated in the academic year 2011–2012, the following categories and numbers represent the postgraduate activities and employment of master's degree graduates: Enrolled in a psychology doctoral program (20), enrolled in another graduate/professional program (1), enrolled in a postdoctoral residency/fellowship (n/a), employed in independent practice (n/a), employed in business or industry (1), employed in a community mental health/counseling center (5), other employment position (1), do not know (5), total from the above (master's) (33).

Doctoral Degree Graduates: Of those who graduated in the academic year 2011–2012, the following categories and numbers represent the postgraduate activities and employment of doctoral degree graduates: Enrolled in a psychology doctoral program (n/a), employed in independent practice (6), employed in an academic position at a university (1), employed in other positions at a higher education institution (2), employed in a hospital/medical center (2), other employment position (4), do not know (6), total from the above (doctoral) (21).

Additional Information:

Orientation, Objectives, and Emphasis of Department: The doctoral program in clinical psychology at the University of Indianapolis is based on a practitioner-scholar model of training. The focus of the program is on preparing individuals to aid in the prevention and treatment of human problems, as well as the enhancement of human functioning and potential. The program trains students in the general, integrative practice of professional psychology through a broad-based exposure to a variety of psychological approaches and modalities. These include in-depth coursework in the theories and psychotherapies associated with psychoanalytical, humanistic-existential, cognitive-behavioral, systems and multi-cultural paradigms. The program is committed to sensitizing students to working with diverse, under-served populations. Students develop the capacity for thinking in a systematic and disciplined manner about clinical cases, evaluating theories and intervention strategies, case conceptualization, diagnoses, problem solving, and the exercise of ethical professional judgment. They learn to translate psychological science into clinical practice, judiciously consider various sources of data and weigh evidence from multiple sources, evaluate and modify beliefs based upon evidence, be outcome-oriented, and consider alternative viewpoints and perspectives. Scholarship, including scientific inquiry and research is seen as a necessary methodology and discipline for the development of critical thinking, and the foundations of design and statistics are well enough in place to permit professional activity in these areas. In addition, the program offers advanced training in three clinical emphasis areas: health psychology/behavioral medicine, childhood and adolescent psychology and adult psychopathology and psychotherapy. The program offers a master's degree with four tracks: foundational, research, mental health counseling, and mental health counseling and addictions counseling. Each track meets specific academic and career goals. Factors to consider include an interest for future admission to a doctoral program in psychology; to work as a researcher; or to work as a licensed counselor. Additional considerations in choosing a track include: working with specific populations, including children, adolescents, and persons affected by addictions. The faculty believe that education is most effective when the relationship between students and faculty is characterized by mutual respect, responsibility, and dedication to excellence. The program is founded on a deep and abiding respect for diversity in individuals, the ethical practice of psychology, and a commitment to service to others. These core values are reflected in the selection of students, the coursework and training experiences offered, and the faculty who serve as role models and mentors.

Special Facilities or Resources: Specialized training facilities include several clinical therapy labs designed for supervised assessment, testing, and therapy, and for videotaping of clinical sessions utilized in feedback and instruction. The Large Groups Lab includes interconnected classrooms used for videotaping and monitoring of experiential group or class exercises, psychoeducational programs, and other large group activities. Individualized Study and Research Labs equipped with computers are available for research projects, classroom assignments, and personal study. Computer facilities in the School of Psychological Sciences and throughout the university allow access to the internet, a full range of statistical and office software and library holdings. Wireless internet is available throughout the university and all psychology classrooms are equipped with large flatscreen monitors readied for notebook display. In addition, the capability of conducting direct, online literature searches using a variety of databases (e.g., PsycBOOKS, PsycINFO (with PsycARTICLES), PsycEXTRA, MedLine, PEP) is available. The library subscribes to the major psychology journals and contains the latest publications in the field of clinical psychology. The School has a separate graduate psychology study area in which students meet to confer about class assignments, have group study sessions, practice presentations, or just relax between classes. The School also has an on-site Psychological Services Center, which offers treatment services to community residents including underserved and marginalized patients on a sliding fee scale. Students receive applied training experience at the Center while conducting intake assessments or providing therapeutic services.

Information for Students With Physical Disabilities: See the following website for more information: http://www.uindy.edu/ssd/.

Application Information:
Send to University of Indianapolis, School of Psychological Sciences, Director of Communication and Information Systems, 1400 East Hanna Avenue GH 109, Indianapolis, IN 46227. Application available online. URL of online application: https://app.applyyourself.com/?id=uindy. Students are admitted in the Fall, application deadline January 10. January 10 PsyD deadline; February 25 MA deadline. *Fee:* $55.

Notre Dame, University of
Department of Psychology
Arts & Letters
118 Haggar Hall
Notre Dame, IN 46556
Telephone: (574) 631-6650
Fax: (574) 631-8883
E-mail: *James.Brockmole@nd.edu*
Web: *http://psychology.nd.edu/*

Department Information:
1965. Chairperson: Daniel K. Lapsley. Number of faculty: total—full-time 44; women—full-time 20; total—minority—full-time 9; women minority—full-time 4.

Programs and Degrees Offered:
Listed in the following order: Program area, degree type (T if terminal Master's), number awarded 7/11–6/12. Cognition, Brain, and Behavior PhD (Doctor of Philosophy) 2, Clinical Psychology PhD (Doctor of Philosophy) 5, Developmental Psychology PhD

(Doctor of Philosophy) 2, Quantitative Psychology PhD (Doctor of Philosophy) 0.

APA Accreditation: Clinical PhD (Doctor of Philosophy). Student Outcome Data Website: http://psychology.nd.edu/graduate-programs/clinical-program/accreditation-data-outcome/.

Student Applications/Admissions:

Student Applications

Cognition, Brain, and Behavior PhD (Doctor of Philosophy)—Applications 2012–2013, 47. Total applicants accepted 2012–2013, 6. Number full-time enrolled (new admits only) 2012–2013, 6. Total enrolled 2012–2013 full-time, 17. Openings 2013–2014, 4. The median number of years required for completion of a degree in 2012–2013 were 6. The number of students enrolled full- and part-time who were dismissed or voluntarily withdrew from this program area in 2012–2013 were 2. *Clinical Psychology PhD (Doctor of Philosophy)*—Applications 2012–2013, 280. Total applicants accepted 2012–2013, 7. Number full-time enrolled (new admits only) 2012–2013, 4. Total enrolled 2012–2013 full-time, 22. Openings 2013–2014, 4. The median number of years required for completion of a degree in 2012–2013 were 6. The number of students enrolled full- and part-time who were dismissed or voluntarily withdrew from this program area in 2012–2013 were 1. *Developmental Psychology PhD (Doctor of Philosophy)*—Applications 2012–2013, 50. Total applicants accepted 2012–2013, 2. Number full-time enrolled (new admits only) 2012–2013, 2. Total enrolled 2012–2013 full-time, 18. Openings 2013–2014, 4. The median number of years required for completion of a degree in 2012–2013 were 5. The number of students enrolled full- and part-time who were dismissed or voluntarily withdrew from this program area in 2012–2013 were 0. *Quantitative Psychology PhD (Doctor of Philosophy)*—Applications 2012–2013, 31. Total applicants accepted 2012–2013, 5. Number full-time enrolled (new admits only) 2012–2013, 5. Number part-time enrolled (new admits only) 2012–2013, 0. Total enrolled 2012–2013 full-time, 16. Total enrolled 2012–2013 part-time, 0. Openings 2013–2014, 3. The number of students enrolled full- and part-time who were dismissed or voluntarily withdrew from this program area in 2012–2013 were 0.

Scores: Entries appear in this order: required test or GPA, minimum score (if required), median score of students entering in 2012–2013. *Cognition, Brain, and Behavior PhD (Doctor of Philosophy)*: GRE-V no minimum stated, 550, GRE-Q no minimum stated, 540, GRE-Analytical no minimum stated, 5, overall undergraduate GPA no minimum stated, 3.84; *Clinical Psychology PhD (Doctor of Philosophy)*: GRE-V no minimum stated, GRE-Q no minimum stated, GRE-Analytical no minimum stated, overall undergraduate GPA no minimum stated, 3.93; *Developmental Psychology PhD (Doctor of Philosophy)*: GRE-V no minimum stated, 84, GRE-Q no minimum stated, 85, GRE-Analytical no minimum stated, 4.75, overall undergraduate GPA no minimum stated, 3.64; *Quantitative Psychology PhD (Doctor of Philosophy)*: GRE-V no minimum stated, 75, GRE-Q no minimum stated, 88, GRE-Analytical no minimum stated, 72, overall undergraduate GPA no minimum stated, 3.73.

Other Criteria: (importance of criteria rated low, medium, or high): GRE scores—high, research experience—high, work experience—low, extracurricular activity—low, clinically re-

lated public service—low, GPA—high, letters of recommendation—high, interview—medium, statement of goals and objectives—high, undergraduate major in psychology—high, specific undergraduate psychology courses taken—medium. For additional information on admission requirements, go to http://psychology.nd.edu/graduate-programs/admission-and-financial-support/.

Student Characteristics: The following represents characteristics of students in 2012–2013 in all graduate psychology programs in the department: Female—full-time 48, part-time 0; Male—full-time 25, part-time 0; African American/Black—full-time 0, part-time 0; Hispanic/Latino(a)—full-time 4, part-time 0; Asian/Pacific Islander—full-time 11, part-time 0; American Indian/Alaska Native—full-time 0, part-time 0; Caucasian/White—full-time 56, part-time 0; Multi-ethnic—full-time 2, part-time 0; students subject to the Americans With Disabilities Act—full-time 0, part-time 0; Unknown ethnicity—full-time 0, part-time 0; International students who hold an F-1 or J-1 Visa—full-time 0, part-time 0.

Financial Information/Assistance:

Tuition for Full-Time Study: *Doctoral:* State residents: per academic year $44,380; Nonstate residents: per academic year $44,380. Tuition is subject to change. See the following website for updates and changes in tuition costs: http://studentaccounts.nd.edu/rates/rates_graduate.shtml.

Financial Assistance:

First-Year Students: Teaching assistantships available for first year. Average amount paid per academic year: $18,450. Research assistantships available for first year. Average amount paid per academic year: $18,450. Fellowships and scholarships available for first year. Average amount paid per academic year: $26,000.

Advanced Students: Teaching assistantships available for advanced students. Average amount paid per academic year: $18,450. Research assistantships available for advanced students. Average amount paid per academic year: $18,450. Fellowships and scholarships available for advanced students. Average amount paid per academic year: $26,000.

Additional Information: Of all students currently enrolled full time, 100% benefited from one or more of the listed financial assistance programs. Application and information available online at: http://graduateschool.nd.edu/admissions/financial-support/.

Internships/Practica: Doctoral Degree (PhD Clinical Psychology): For those doctoral students for whom a professional psychology internship was required in this program prior to graduation, (1) students applied for an internship in 2011–2012, with (1) students obtaining an internship. Of those students who obtained an internship, (1) were paid internships. Of those students who obtained an internship, (1) students placed in APA/CPA accredited internships, (0) students placed in internships not APA/CPA accredited, but listed with the Association of Psychology Postdoctoral and Internship Programs (APPIC), (0) students placed in internships conforming to guidelines of the Council of Directors of School Psychology Programs (CDSPP), (0) students placed in internships that were not APA/CPA accredited, APPIC or CDSPP listed. All students in the APA-accredited clinical program receive practicum placements at local training sites. Opportunities include the University Counseling Center as well as a variety of practicum placements in agencies and institutions in the South Bend community. The University Counseling Center also houses an APA-accredited internship. Advanced students in the clinical program are eligible to apply.

Housing and Day Care: On-campus housing is available. See the following website for more information: http://housing.nd.edu/graduate/. On-campus day care facilities are available. See the following website for more information: http://www3.nd.edu/~ecdcnd/.

Employment of Department Graduates:
Master's Degree Graduates: Of those who graduated in the academic year 2011–2012, the following categories and numbers represent the postgraduate activities and employment of master's degree graduates: Enrolled in a postdoctoral residency/fellowship (n/a), employed in independent practice (n/a), total from the above (master's) (0).
Doctoral Degree Graduates: Of those who graduated in the academic year 2011–2012, the following categories and numbers represent the postgraduate activities and employment of doctoral degree graduates: Enrolled in a psychology doctoral program (n/a), enrolled in a postdoctoral residency/fellowship (5), employed in an academic position at a university (2), employed in business or industry (2), employed in a community mental health/counseling center (1), other employment position (1), do not know (2), total from the above (doctoral) (13).

Additional Information:
Orientation, Objectives, and Emphasis of Department: The Department of Psychology at the University of Notre Dame is committed to excellence in psychological science and its applications. To realize this commitment a major focus is upon developing knowledge and expertise in the increasingly sophisticated methodology of the discipline. With this methodological core as its major emphasis and integrating link, the department has emphasized four content areas: clinical, cognitive, developmental and quantitative psychology. In the context of the mores of the academy, the faculty of each content area organize and coordinate work in the three domains of research, graduate education and undergraduate education. Using our methodological understandings as a base, we strive to find intellectual common ground among the content areas within our department and other disciplines throughout the social sciences and the academy.

Special Facilities or Resources: We are involved in the development of innovative science and practice experiences for undergraduate and graduate students in the local community. Currently, many faculty have excellent relationships with community groups (e.g., the local schools, hospitals, Madison Center, Logan Center, Center for the Homeless, Head Start). Many faculty conduct research with undergraduate and graduate students in these settings. Over and above these research activities, many students volunteer in these agencies. Finally, clinical psychology graduate students receive supervision to work in Madison Center, Family and Children's Center, Michiana EAP, Oaklawn, St. Joseph Medical Center, and the Center for the Homeless and, in a new initiative, postdoctoral positions exist in the Multicultural Research Institute.

Information for Students With Physical Disabilities: See the following website for more information: http://disabilityservices.nd.edu/.

Application Information:
Send to Graduate Admissions, The Graduate School, University of Notre Dame, Notre Dame, IN 46556. Application available online. URL of online application: https://app.applyyourself.com/?id–d-grad. Students are admitted in the Fall, application deadline December 1. *Fee:* $75.

Purdue University
Department of Educational Studies
Counseling Psychology
College of Education
100 North University Street
West Lafayette, IN 47907
Telephone: (765) 494-0837
Fax: (765) 496-1228
E-mail: *servaty@purdue.edu*
Web: *http://www.edst.purdue.edu/counseling_psychology/*

Department Information:
1995. Training Director: Heather Servaty-Seib, PhD. Number of faculty: total—full-time 4; women—full-time 3; total—minority—full-time 1; women minority—full-time 1.

Programs and Degrees Offered:
Listed in the following order: Program area, degree type (T if terminal Master's), number awarded 7/11–6/12. Counseling Psychology PhD (Doctor of Philosophy) 2.

APA Accreditation: Counseling PhD (Doctor of Philosophy). Student Outcome Data Website: http://www.edst.purdue.edu/counseling_psychology/student_admissions_outcomes.html.

Student Applications/Admissions:
Student Applications
Counseling Psychology PhD (Doctor of Philosophy)—Applications 2012–2013, 51. Total applicants accepted 2012–2013, 10. Number full-time enrolled (new admits only) 2012–2013, 5. Number part-time enrolled (new admits only) 2012–2013, 0. Total enrolled 2012–2013 full-time, 31. Openings 2013–2014, 6. The median number of years required for completion of a degree in 2012–2013 were 6. The number of students enrolled full- and part-time who were dismissed or voluntarily withdrew from this program area in 2012–2013 were 0.
Scores: Entries appear in this order: required test or GPA, minimum score (if required), median score of students entering in 2012–2013. *Counseling Psychology PhD (Doctor of Philosophy):* GRE-V 500, GRE-Q 500, GRE-Analytical 3.5, overall undergraduate GPA 3.5, Masters GPA 3.5.
Other Criteria: (importance of criteria rated low, medium, or high): GRE scores—high, research experience—high, work experience—medium, extracurricular activity—medium, clinically related public service—high, GPA—high, letters of recommendation—high, interview—high, statement of goals and objectives—high, undergraduate major in psychology—medium, specific undergraduate psychology courses taken—medium. For additional information on admission requirements, go to http://www.edst.purdue.edu/counseling_psychology/admissions/index.html.

Student Characteristics: The following represents characteristics of students in 2012–2013 in all graduate psychology programs in the department: Female—full-time 23, part-time 0; Male—full-time 8, part-time 0; African American/Black—full-time 5, part-time 0; Hispanic/Latino(a)—full-time 1, part-time 0; Asian/Pacific Islander—full-time 6, part-time 0; American Indian/Alaska Native—full-time 0, part-time 0; Caucasian/White—full-time 16, part-time 0; Multi-ethnic—full-time 1, part-time 0; students subject to the Americans With Disabilities Act—full-time 3, part-time 0; Unknown ethnicity—full-time 0, part-time 0; International students who hold an F-1 or J-1 Visa—full-time 4, part-time 0.

Financial Information/Assistance:

Tuition for Full-Time Study: *Doctoral:* State residents: per academic year $9,900; Nonstate residents: per academic year $28,702. Tuition is subject to change. Additional fees are assessed to students beyond the costs of tuition for the following: assessment course fees, technology fees, student fitness and wellness fees. See the following website for updates and changes in tuition costs: http://www.purdue.edu/bursar/tuition/fees_wl.html.

Financial Assistance:

First-Year Students: Teaching assistantships available for first year. Average amount paid per academic year: $14,200. Average number of hours worked per week: 20. Research assistantships available for first year. Average amount paid per academic year: $14,200. Average number of hours worked per week: 20. Fellowships and scholarships available for first year. Average amount paid per academic year: $17,040. Average number of hours worked per week: 20. Apply by January 27.

Advanced Students: Teaching assistantships available for advanced students. Average amount paid per academic year: $14,200. Average number of hours worked per week: 20. Research assistantships available for advanced students. Average amount paid per academic year: $14,200. Average number of hours worked per week: 20.

Additional Information: Of all students currently enrolled full time, 97% benefited from one or more of the listed financial assistance programs. Application and information available online at: http://www.gradschool.purdue.edu/funding/.

Internships/Practica: Doctoral Degree (PhD Counseling Psychology): For those doctoral students for whom a professional psychology internship was required in this program prior to graduation, (4) students applied for an internship in 2011–2012, with (4) students obtaining an internship. Of those students who obtained an internship, (4) were paid internships. Of those students who obtained an internship, (4) students placed in APA/CPA accredited internships, (0) students placed in internships not APA/CPA accredited, but listed with the Association of Psychology Postdoctoral and Internship Programs (APPIC), (0) students placed in internships conforming to guidelines of the Council of Directors of School Psychology Programs (CDSPP), (0) students placed in internships that were not APA/CPA accredited, APPIC or CDSPP listed. Students get practicum and internship placements at community mental health agencies, veterans affairs hospitals, college counseling centers, psychiatric and medical hospitals, prisons and group psychological practices.

Housing and Day Care: On-campus housing is available. See the following website for more information: http://www.housing. purdue.edu/. On-campus day care facilities are available. See the following website for more information: http://www.purdue.edu/hr/Benefits/childcare/campus.html.

Employment of Department Graduates:

Master's Degree Graduates: Of those who graduated in the academic year 2011–2012, the following categories and numbers represent the postgraduate activities and employment of master's degree graduates: Enrolled in a postdoctoral residency/fellowship (n/a), employed in independent practice (n/a), total from the above (master's) (0).

Doctoral Degree Graduates: Of those who graduated in the academic year 2011–2012, the following categories and numbers represent the postgraduate activities and employment of doctoral degree graduates: Enrolled in a psychology doctoral program (n/a), employed in a community mental health/counseling center (2), total from the above (doctoral) (2).

Additional Information:

Orientation, Objectives, and Emphasis of Department: The counseling psychology program provides training in line with specific training goals. The first goal is to train scientist–practitioners in inquiry skills for use in advancing knowledge of psychology. The second goal is to train scientist–practitioners in inquiry skills for use in psychological conceptualization, diagnosis, intervention, and other counseling professional services to clients and consumers resulting from a sound theoretical and research knowledge base. The third goal is to develop scientist–practitioners who demonstrate ethical and professional behavior consistent with the standards of counseling psychology. Finally, the fourth goal is to prepare scientist–practitioners who can provide competent services that are responsive to individual and cultural differences in a multicultural environment.

Special Facilities or Resources: The Purdue Counseling and Guidance Center (PCGC) is the counseling service and training facility for the College of Education on the Purdue University campus. Students in their second year of training in the counseling psychology program provide counseling under the supervision of a faculty member to clients who are either college students or community members. To facilitate the counselors' training, all sessions are recorded. Recordings are used to help counselors provide competent and effective services. These recordings are used for counselor development and supervision purposes only, are kept confidential, and are then erased. Given these guidelines, individuals who seek counseling at the Counseling and Guidance Center understand and agree to these standards.

Information for Students With Physical Disabilities: See the following website for more information: http://www.purdue.edu/odos/drc/.

Application Information:

Send to Purdue University, Office of Graduate Studies, BRNG, Room 6104, 100 North University Street, West Lafayette, IN 47907. Application available online. URL of online application: https://app.applyyourself.com/?id=purduegrad. Students are admitted in the Fall, application deadline December 15. *Fee:* $60. Fee for international applicants is $75.

Purdue University

Department of Psychological Sciences
College of Health and Human Sciences
701 Third Street
West Lafayette, IN 47906-2004
Telephone: (765) 494-6067
Fax: (765) 496-1264
E-mail: *nobrien@psych.purdue.edu*
Web: *http://www.purdue.edu/hhs/psy/*

Department Information:
1954. Professor and Head: Christopher R. Agnew. Number of faculty: total—full-time 41, part-time 1; women—full-time 13; total—minority—full-time 3; women minority—full-time 2.

Programs and Degrees Offered:
Listed in the following order: Program area, degree type (T if terminal Master's), number awarded 7/11–6/12. Clinical Psychology PhD (Doctor of Philosophy) 3, Cognitive Psychology PhD (Doctor of Philosophy) 1, Industrial/Organizational Psychology PhD (Doctor of Philosophy) 2, Behavioral Neuroscience PhD (Doctor of Philosophy) 1, Mathematical and Computational Cognitive Science PhD (Doctor of Philosophy) 0, Social Psychology PhD (Doctor of Philosophy) 1, Developmental PhD (Doctor of Philosophy) 0, Learning & Memory PhD (Doctor of Philosophy) 0.

APA Accreditation: Clinical PhD (Doctor of Philosophy). Student Outcome Data Website: http://www.purdue.edu/hhs/psy/graduate/research_training_areas/clinical_psychology/index.php.

Student Applications/Admissions:
Student Applications
Clinical Psychology PhD (Doctor of Philosophy)—Applications 2012–2013, 174. Total applicants accepted 2012–2013, 6. Number full-time enrolled (new admits only) 2012–2013, 3. Number part-time enrolled (new admits only) 2012–2013, 0. Total enrolled 2012–2013 full-time, 11. Total enrolled 2012–2013 part-time, 0. Openings 2013–2014, 4. The median number of years required for completion of a degree in 2012–2013 were 5. The number of students enrolled full- and part-time who were dismissed or voluntarily withdrew from this program area in 2012–2013 were 0. *Cognitive Psychology PhD (Doctor of Philosophy)*—Applications 2012–2013, 39. Total applicants accepted 2012–2013, 4. Number full-time enrolled (new admits only) 2012–2013, 3. Number part-time enrolled (new admits only) 2012–2013, 0. Total enrolled 2012–2013 full-time, 13. Total enrolled 2012–2013 part-time, 0. Openings 2013–2014, 1. The median number of years required for completion of a degree in 2012–2013 were 5. The number of students enrolled full- and part-time who were dismissed or voluntarily withdrew from this program area in 2012–2013 were 0. *Industrial/Organizational Psychology PhD (Doctor of Philosophy)*—Applications 2012–2013, 74. Total applicants accepted 2012–2013, 5. Number full-time enrolled (new admits only) 2012–2013, 0. Number part-time enrolled (new admits only) 2012–2013, 0. Total enrolled 2012–2013 full-time, 6. Total enrolled 2012–2013 part-time, 0. Openings 2013–2014, 4. The median number of years required for completion of a degree in 2012–2013 were 5. The number of students enrolled

full- and part-time who were dismissed or voluntarily withdrew from this program area in 2012–2013 were 0. *Behavioral Neuroscience PhD (Doctor of Philosophy)*—Applications 2012–2013, 14. Total applicants accepted 2012–2013, 3. Number full-time enrolled (new admits only) 2012–2013, 2. Number part-time enrolled (new admits only) 2012–2013, 0. Total enrolled 2012–2013 full-time, 10. Total enrolled 2012–2013 part-time, 0. Openings 2013–2014, 2. The median number of years required for completion of a degree in 2012–2013 were 5. The number of students enrolled full- and part-time who were dismissed or voluntarily withdrew from this program area in 2012–2013 were 2. *Mathematical and Computational Cognitive Science PhD (Doctor of Philosophy)*—Applications 2012–2013, 3. Total applicants accepted 2012–2013, 0. Number full-time enrolled (new admits only) 2012–2013, 0. Number part-time enrolled (new admits only) 2012–2013, 0. Total enrolled 2012–2013 full-time, 7. Total enrolled 2012–2013 part-time, 0. Openings 2013–2014, 2. The number of students enrolled full- and part-time who were dismissed or voluntarily withdrew from this program area in 2012–2013 were 0. *Social Psychology PhD (Doctor of Philosophy)*—Applications 2012–2013, 82. Total applicants accepted 2012–2013, 5. Number full-time enrolled (new admits only) 2012–2013, 2. Number part-time enrolled (new admits only) 2012–2013, 0. Total enrolled 2012–2013 full-time, 17. Total enrolled 2012–2013 part-time, 0. Openings 2013–2014, 4. The median number of years required for completion of a degree in 2012–2013 were 5. The number of students enrolled full- and part-time who were dismissed or voluntarily withdrew from this program area in 2012–2013 were 0. *Developmental PhD (Doctor of Philosophy)*—Applications 2012–2013, 0. Total applicants accepted 2012–2013, 0. Number full-time enrolled (new admits only) 2012–2013, 0. Total enrolled 2012–2013 full-time, 2. The number of students enrolled full- and part-time who were dismissed or voluntarily withdrew from this program area in 2012–2013 were 0. *Learning & Memory PhD (Doctor of Philosophy)*—Applications 2012–2013, 1. Total applicants accepted 2012–2013, 0. Number full-time enrolled (new admits only) 2012–2013, 0. Total enrolled 2012–2013 full-time, 2. The number of students enrolled full- and part-time who were dismissed or voluntarily withdrew from this program area in 2012–2013 were 0.
Scores: Entries appear in this order: required test or GPA, minimum score (if required), median score of students entering in 2012–2013. *Clinical Psychology PhD (Doctor of Philosophy):* GRE-V no minimum stated, 559, GRE-Q no minimum stated, 645, GRE-Analytical no minimum stated, 4.4, overall undergraduate GPA 3.0, 3.62; *Cognitive Psychology PhD (Doctor of Philosophy):* GRE-V no minimum stated, 561, GRE-Q no minimum stated, 697, GRE-Analytical no minimum stated, 4.1, overall undergraduate GPA 3.0, 3.42; *Industrial/Organizational Psychology PhD (Doctor of Philosophy):* GRE-V no minimum stated, 670, GRE-Q no minimum stated, 730, GRE-Analytical no minimum stated, 5.0, overall undergraduate GPA 3.0, 3.54; *Behavioral Neuroscience PhD (Doctor of Philosophy):* GRE-V no minimum stated, 537, GRE-Q no minimum stated, 648, GRE-Analytical no minimum stated, 4.1, overall undergraduate GPA 3.0, 3.40; *Mathematical and Computational Cognitive Science PhD (Doctor of Philosophy):* GRE-V no minimum stated, 544, GRE-Q no minimum stated, 763, GRE-Analytical no minimum stated, 4.6, overall undergraduate GPA 3.0, 3.13; *Social Psychology PhD (Doctor of Philosophy):* GRE-V no minimum stated, 555, GRE-Q no minimum stated, 665, GRE-

Analytical no minimum stated, 4.3, overall undergraduate GPA 3.0, 3.51; *Developmental PhD (Doctor of Philosophy):* GRE-V no minimum stated, GRE-Q no minimum stated, GRE-Analytical no minimum stated, overall undergraduate GPA 3.00, 3.50.

Other Criteria: (importance of criteria rated low, medium, or high): GRE scores—high, research experience—medium, work experience—low, extracurricular activity—low, clinically related public service—medium, GPA—high, letters of recommendation—high, interview—high, statement of goals and objectives—high, undergraduate major in psychology—medium, specific undergraduate psychology courses taken—low, Not all areas hold formal interviews. Clinically related public service is important if you are applying to the clinical program. For additional information on admission requirements, go to http://www.purdue.edu/hhs/psy/graduate/prospective_students/applications_admissions.php.

Student Characteristics: The following represents characteristics of students in 2012–2013 in all graduate psychology programs in the department: Female—full-time 49, part-time 0; Male—full-time 19, part-time 0; African American/Black—full-time 1, part-time 0; Hispanic/Latino(a)—full-time 1, part-time 0; Asian/Pacific Islander—full-time 13, part-time 0; American Indian/Alaska Native—full-time 1, part-time 0; Caucasian/White—full-time 52, part-time 0; Multi-ethnic—full-time 0, part-time 0; students subject to the Americans With Disabilities Act—full-time 0, part-time 0; Unknown ethnicity—full-time 0, part-time 0; International students who hold an F-1 or J-1 Visa—full-time 16, part-time 0.

Financial Information/Assistance:

Tuition for Full-Time Study: *Doctoral:* State residents: per academic year $9,900, $346 per credit hour; Nonstate residents: per academic year $28,702, $948 per credit hour. Tuition is subject to change. Additional fees are assessed to students beyond the costs of tuition for the following: International Student Fee: $80 per semester. See the following website for updates and changes in tuition costs: http://www.purdue.edu/bursar/tuition/fees_wl.html.

Financial Assistance:

First-Year Students: Teaching assistantships available for first year. Average amount paid per academic year: $15,000. Average number of hours worked per week: 20. Apply by December 3. Research assistantships available for first year. Average amount paid per academic year: $15,000. Average number of hours worked per week: 20. Apply by December 3. Fellowships and scholarships available for first year. Average amount paid per academic year: $17,000. Apply by December 3.

Advanced Students: Teaching assistantships available for advanced students. Average amount paid per academic year: $16,000. Average number of hours worked per week: 20. Research assistantships available for advanced students. Average amount paid per academic year: $16,000. Average number of hours worked per week: 20. Fellowships and scholarships available for advanced students. Average amount paid per academic year: $17,000.

Additional Information: Of all students currently enrolled full time, 90% benefited from one or more of the listed financial assistance programs. Application and information available online at: http://www.purdue.edu/hhs/psy/graduate/current_students/financial_support.php.

Internships/Practica: Doctoral Degree (PhD Clinical Psychology): For those doctoral students for whom a professional psychology internship was required in this program prior to graduation, (3) students applied for an internship in 2011–2012, with (3) students obtaining an internship. Of those students who obtained an internship, (3) were paid internships. Of those students who obtained an internship, (3) students placed in APA/CPA accredited internships, (0) students placed in internships not APA/CPA accredited, but listed with the Association of Psychology Postdoctoral and Internship Programs (APPIC), (0) students placed in internships conforming to guidelines of the Council of Directors of School Psychology Programs (CDSPP), (0) students placed in internships that were not APA/CPA accredited, APPIC or CDSPP listed. After the first year requirements, clinical psychology students enroll in clinical practica carried out in the Purdue Psychology Treatment and Research Clinics. Practica include providing services for anxiety disorders, depression, personality disorders, Attention Deficit Hyperactivity Disorder, and oppositional disorders. Practicum training emphasizes use of empirically corroborated interventions for particular problems. A year-long clinical internship is required in order to complete training.

Housing and Day Care: On-campus housing is available. See the following website for more information: http://www.housing.purdue.edu. On-campus day care facilities are available. See the following website for more information: http://www.purdue.edu/hr/Benefits/childcare/campus.html.

Employment of Department Graduates:

Master's Degree Graduates: Of those who graduated in the academic year 2011–2012, the following categories and numbers represent the postgraduate activities and employment of master's degree graduates: Enrolled in a postdoctoral residency/fellowship (n/a), employed in independent practice (n/a), total from the above (master's) (0).

Doctoral Degree Graduates: Of those who graduated in the academic year 2011–2012, the following categories and numbers represent the postgraduate activities and employment of doctoral degree graduates: Enrolled in a psychology doctoral program (n/a), employed in an academic position at a university (8), total from the above (doctoral) (8).

Additional Information:

Orientation, Objectives, and Emphasis of Department: The dominant emphasis of the department is a commitment to research and scholarship as the major core of graduate education. All programs are structured so that students become involved in research activities almost immediately upon beginning their graduate education, and this involvement is expected to continue throughout an individual's entire graduate career.

Special Facilities or Resources: Excellent research facilities are available in many areas, including more than 35 computer-controlled laboratories.

Information for Students With Physical Disabilities: See the following website for more information: http://www.purdue.edu/odos/drc/.

Application Information:
Send to Nancy O'Brien, Psychological Sciences, Purdue University, 701 Third Street, West Lafayette, IN 47906-2004. Application avail-

able online. URL of online application: http://www.gradschool.purdue.edu/admissions. Students are admitted in the Fall, application deadline December 3. *Fee:* $60. Application fee for International applicants is $75.

Saint Francis, University of
Psychology and Counseling
School of Professional Studies
2701 Spring Street
Fort Wayne, IN 46808
Telephone: (260) 399-7700 ext 8425
Fax: (260) 399-8170
E-mail: *jbrinkman@sf.edu*
Web: *http://www.sf.edu/psychology*

Department Information:
1971. Chairperson: John Brinkman, PhD. Number of faculty: total—full-time 5, part-time 4; women—full-time 1, part-time 3.

Programs and Degrees Offered:
Listed in the following order: Program area, degree type (T if terminal Master's), number awarded 7/11–6/12. Clinical Mental Health Counseling MA/MS (Master of Arts/Science) (T) 6, Psychology MA/MS (Master of Arts/Science) (T) 2, Pastoral Counseling MA/MS (Master of Arts/Science) 1, Advanced Certificate in Pastoral Counseling Other 0, School Counseling MEd (Education) 10, Rehabilitation Counseling MA/MS (Master of Arts/Science) (T) 0.

Student Applications/Admissions:
Student Applications
Clinical Mental Health Counseling MA/MS (Master of Arts/Science)—Applications 2012–2013, 16. Total applicants accepted 2012–2013, 15. Number full-time enrolled (new admits only) 2012–2013, 9. Number part-time enrolled (new admits only) 2012–2013, 6. Total enrolled 2012–2013 full-time, 29. Total enrolled 2012–2013 part-time, 19. Openings 2013–2014, 15. The median number of years required for completion of a degree in 2012–2013 were 3. The number of students enrolled full- and part-time who were dismissed or voluntarily withdrew from this program area in 2012–2013 were 0. *Psychology MA/MS (Master of Arts/Science)*—Applications 2012–2013, 2. Total applicants accepted 2012–2013, 2. Number full-time enrolled (new admits only) 2012–2013, 0. Number part-time enrolled (new admits only) 2012–2013, 2. Total enrolled 2012–2013 full-time, 13. Total enrolled 2012–2013 part-time, 4. Openings 2013–2014, 10. The median number of years required for completion of a degree in 2012–2013 were 2. The number of students enrolled full- and part-time who were dismissed or voluntarily withdrew from this program area in 2012–2013 were 0. *Pastoral Counseling MA/MS (Master of Arts/Science)*—Applications 2012–2013, 1. Total applicants accepted 2012–2013, 1. Number full-time enrolled (new admits only) 2012–2013, 0. Number part-time enrolled (new admits only) 2012–2013, 0. Openings 2013–2014, 8. The median number of years required for completion of a degree in 2012–2013 were 2. The number of students enrolled full- and part-time who were dismissed or voluntarily withdrew from this program area in 2012–2013 were 0. *Advanced Certificate in Pastoral Counseling Other*—Applications 2012–2013, 0. Total applicants accepted 2012–2013, 0. Number full-time enrolled (new admits only) 2012–2013, 0. Number part-time enrolled (new admits only) 2012–2013, 0. Openings 2013–2014, 10. The median number of years required for completion of a degree in 2012–2013 were 2. The number of students enrolled full- and part-time who were dismissed or voluntarily withdrew from this program area in 2012–2013 were 0. *School Counseling MEd (Education)*—Applications 2012–2013, 5. Total applicants accepted 2012–2013, 5. Number full-time enrolled (new admits only) 2012–2013, 2. Number part-time enrolled (new admits only) 2012–2013, 3. Total enrolled 2012–2013 full-time, 12. Total enrolled 2012–2013 part-time, 9. Openings 2013–2014, 10. The median number of years required for completion of a degree in 2012–2013 were 2. The number of students enrolled full- and part-time who were dismissed or voluntarily withdrew from this program area in 2012–2013 were 0. *Rehabilitation Counseling MA/MS (Master of Arts/Science)*—Applications 2012–2013, 6. Total applicants accepted 2012–2013, 6. Number full-time enrolled (new admits only) 2012–2013, 3. Number part-time enrolled (new admits only) 2012–2013, 3. Total enrolled 2012–2013 full-time, 3. Total enrolled 2012–2013 part-time, 3. Openings 2013–2014, 10. The number of students enrolled full- and part-time who were dismissed or voluntarily withdrew from this program area in 2012–2013 were 0.

Scores: Entries appear in this order: required test or GPA, minimum score (if required), median score of students entering in 2012–2013. *Clinical Mental Health Counseling MA/MS (Master of Arts/Science)*: overall undergraduate GPA 3.0; *Psychology MA/MS (Master of Arts/Science)*: overall undergraduate GPA 3.0; *Pastoral Counseling MA/MS (Master of Arts/Science)*: overall undergraduate GPA 3.0; *School Counseling MEd (Education)*: GRE-V no minimum stated, GRE-Q no minimum stated, overall undergraduate GPA 3.0; *Rehabilitation Counseling MA/MS (Master of Arts/Science)*: overall undergraduate GPA 3.00.
Other Criteria: (importance of criteria rated low, medium, or high): GRE scores—medium, research experience—medium, work experience—high, extracurricular activity—low, clinically related public service—high, GPA—high, letters of recommendation—high, interview—high, statement of goals and objectives—high, undergraduate major in psychology—high, specific undergraduate psychology courses taken—high. For additional information on admission requirements, go to http://www.sf.edu/sf/graduate-studies/admissions/entrance-requirements.

Student Characteristics: The following represents characteristics of students in 2012–2013 in all graduate psychology programs in the department: Female—full-time 48, part-time 22; Male—full-time 9, part-time 15; African American/Black—full-time 4, part-time 5; Hispanic/Latino(a)—full-time 1, part-time 3; Asian/Pacific Islander—full-time 1, part-time 0; American Indian/Alaska Native—full-time 0, part-time 0; Caucasian/White—full-time 49, part-time 25; Multi-ethnic—full-time 2, part-time 4; students subject to the Americans With Disabilities Act—full-time 3, part-time 0; Unknown ethnicity—full-time 0, part-time 0; International students who hold an F-1 or J-1 Visa—full-time 0, part-time 0.

Financial Information/Assistance:
Tuition for Full-Time Study: *Master's:* State residents: $805 per credit hour; Nonstate residents: $805 per credit hour. Tuition is

subject to change. See the following website for updates and changes in tuition costs: http://www.sf.edu/sf/graduate-studies/financial-aid/tuition.

Financial Assistance:

First-Year Students: Teaching assistantships available for first year. Average amount paid per academic year: $0. Average number of hours worked per week: 10. Apply by June 30.

Advanced Students: Teaching assistantships available for advanced students. Average amount paid per academic year: $0. Average number of hours worked per week: 10. Apply by June 30.

Additional Information: Of all students currently enrolled full time, 30% benefited from one or more of the listed financial assistance programs. Application and information available online at: http://www.sf.edu/sf/graduate/financial-aid.

Internships/Practica: Master's Degree (MA/MS Clinical Mental Health Counseling): An internship experience, such as a final research project or "capstone" experience is required of graduates. Master's Degree (MA/MS Rehabilitation Counseling): An internship experience, such as a final research project or "capstone" experience is required of graduates. General Psychology students can elect to do a practicum experience. This experience would be 150 clock hours (10 hours/week) of supervised practical field experience tailored to the individual needs/interests of the students. Students choosing to have a practicum experience have an on-site supervisor who helps define, mentor, and direct the student's activities. Students also have 15 hours of supervision on campus. This experience is designed to give students an opportunity to integrate formal education with work experience. Mental Health Counseling (MS) has required practicum and internship sequence: Practicum: 1 semester-100 hours/60 face-to-face client contact hours. Internship: 1 or 2 semesters - 600 hours/240 face-to-face client contact hours. Advanced Internship: 1 semester-300 hours/120 face-to-face client contact hours. MSEd School Counseling students complete a 105-hour practicum and non-teacher licensed candidates complete a 600-hour, two-semester internship.

Housing and Day Care: No on-campus housing is available. No on-campus day care facilities are available.

Employment of Department Graduates:

Master's Degree Graduates: Of those who graduated in the academic year 2011–2012, the following categories and numbers represent the postgraduate activities and employment of master's degree graduates: Enrolled in a psychology doctoral program (1), enrolled in a postdoctoral residency/fellowship (n/a), employed in independent practice (n/a), employed in a professional position in a school system (14), employed in business or industry (1), employed in a community mental health/counseling center (6), total from the above (master's) (22).

Doctoral Degree Graduates: Of those who graduated in the academic year 2011–2012, the following categories and numbers represent the postgraduate activities and employment of doctoral degree graduates: Enrolled in a psychology doctoral program (n/a), total from the above (doctoral) (0).

Additional Information:

Orientation, Objectives, and Emphasis of Department: The MS in Psychology Program is designed for people who are either interested in preparation for doctoral work, or furthering their professional careers through a greater understanding of basic psychological principles. The primary goal of the program is to give students a solid, graduate-level grounding in psychology. This program emphasizes a mastery of psychological fundamentals, i.e., theories and research methods, areas of specialization (development, social, abnormal behavior, physiological data, personality development and behavior management techniques). The program of study leading to the MS Degree in Mental Health Counseling is designed to prepare persons to function as Licensed Mental Health Counselors (LMHC) in health care residential, private practice, community agency, governmental, business, and industrial settings. To successfully complete the M.S. in Mental Health Counseling, students will: 1. Demonstrate ability to analyze, synthesize, and critique in a scholarly manner academic subject matter, professional journal articles, and other professional resources. Students will demonstrate ability to write coherently and professionally according to the Publication Manual of the American Psychological Association (4th edition) standards. 2. Promote and adhere to the standards/guidelines for ethical and professional conduct in all classroom and field experiences (i.e., American Counseling Association's Ethical Standards for Mental Health Professionals, and the American Psychological Association's Ethical Principles), as well as legal mandates regarding the practice of their profession. 3. Demonstrate an ability to synthesize, evaluate, and articulate broad knowledge of counseling theories and approaches. This will include the ability to apply scientific and measurement principles to the study of psychology. 4. Develop a capacity to communicate respect, empathy, and unconditional positive regard toward others, including demonstration of a tolerant, non-judgmental attitude toward different ethnic/cultural heritage, value orientations, and lifestyles. 5. Recognize and effectively conceptualize the special needs of persons with varying mental, adjustment, developmental and/or chemical dependence disorders. Students will recognize the need for, request, and benefit from consultation and supervision when practicing in areas of insufficient competence. 6. Demonstrate competence to counsel/interview using basic listening and influencing skills in one-to-one, marital, family, and group counseling modalities. 7. Be prepared to seek employment as a Licensed Mental Health Counselor, enter a program of additional education/training, and/or seek other appropriate certifications. The M.S. in Pastoral Counseling program is designed for active members of the clergy with a minimum of a Bachelor's degree from an accredited college. The program consists of three parts: a core of clinical courses (18 hours) in psychology, a foundation in Pastoral Counseling (27 hours) and elective courses (6 hours). Upon completion of nine additional credits, Master's degree students can qualify to take the examination for licensure as a Licensed Professional Counselor. The Advanced Certificate in Pastoral Counseling is available for licensed mental health professionals, such as licensed clinical social workers, licensed mental health counselors, licensed marriage and family therapists, and licensed psychologists. The certificate program includes six courses (18 hours): Pastoral Theological Methods, History of Pastoral Care and Counseling, Pastoral Diagnosis, Franciscan Intellectual and Spiritual Tradition, Spirituality and Spiritual Formation and Pastoral Care Specialist Training.

Information for Students With Physical Disabilities: See the following website for more information: http://www.sf.edu/sf/studentservices/academics/disability.

Application Information:
Send to Office of Admissions, Trinity Hall, Room 110A, University of Saint Francis, 2701 Spring Street, Fort Wayne, IN 46808. Application available online. URL of online application: http://www.sf.edu/sf/graduate-studies/admissions/apply-online. Programs have rolling admissions. *Fee:* $20. Application fee waived if applicant applies online.

Valparaiso University
Department of Psychology
1001 Campus Drive South
Valparaiso, IN 46383
Telephone: (219) 464-5440
Fax: (219) 464-6878
E-mail: *David.Simpson@valpo.edu*
Web: *http://www.valpo.edu/psychology/graduate/index.php*

Department Information:
Chairperson: Daniel Arkkelin, PhD. Number of faculty: total—full-time 10, part-time 5; women—full-time 5, part-time 3; minority—part-time 1; women minority—part-time 1.

Programs and Degrees Offered:
Listed in the following order: Program area, degree type (T if terminal Master's), number awarded 7/11–6/12. Clinical Mental Health Counseling MA/MS (Master of Arts/Science) (T) 15.

Student Applications/Admissions:
Student Applications
Clinical Mental Health Counseling MA/MS (Master of Arts/Science)—Applications 2012–2013, 57. Total applicants accepted 2012–2013, 20. Number full-time enrolled (new admits only) 2012–2013, 32. Number part-time enrolled (new admits only) 2012–2013, 2. Total enrolled 2012–2013 full-time, 55. Total enrolled 2012–2013 part-time, 24. Openings 2013–2014, 20. The median number of years required for completion of a degree in 2012–2013 were 2. The number of students enrolled full- and part-time who were dismissed or voluntarily withdrew from this program area in 2012–2013 were 1.
Scores: Entries appear in this order: required test or GPA, minimum score (if required), median score of students entering in 2012–2013. *Clinical Mental Health Counseling MA/MS (Master of Arts/Science):* overall undergraduate GPA 3.0, 3.6.
Other Criteria: (importance of criteria rated low, medium, or high): research experience—low, work experience—medium, extracurricular activity—low, clinically related public service—medium, GPA—high, letters of recommendation—high, interview—high, statement of goals and objectives—high, resume—low, undergraduate major in psychology—low, specific undergraduate psychology courses taken—medium. For additional information on admission requirements, go to http://www.valpo.edu/psychology/graduate/prospective-grad-students.php.

Student Characteristics: The following represents characteristics of students in 2012–2013 in all graduate psychology programs in the department: Female—full-time 45, part-time 19; Male—full-time 10, part-time 5; African American/Black—full-time 0, part-time 5; Hispanic/Latino(a)—full-time 7, part-time 2; Asian/Pacific Islander—full-time 3, part-time 0; American Indian/Alaska Native—full-time 0, part-time 0; Caucasian/White—full-time 40, part-time 16; Multi-ethnic—full-time 3, part-time 0; students subject to the Americans With Disabilities Act—full-time 0, part-time 0; Unknown ethnicity—full-time 2, part-time 1; International students who hold an F-1 or J-1 Visa—full-time 2, part-time 0.

Financial Information/Assistance:
Tuition for Full-Time Study: *Master's:* State residents: $560 per credit hour; Nonstate residents: $560 per credit hour. Tuition is subject to change. Additional fees are assessed to students beyond the costs of tuition for the following: administrative/graduate student fees. See the following website for updates and changes in tuition costs: http://www.valpo.edu/grad/prospective/tuition.php.

Financial Assistance:
First-Year Students: Teaching assistantships available for first year. Research assistantships available for first year. Fellowships and scholarships available for first year.
Advanced Students: Teaching assistantships available for advanced students. Research assistantships available for advanced students.
Additional Information: Of all students currently enrolled full time, 75% benefited from one or more of the listed financial assistance programs. Application and information available online at: http://www.valpo.edu/grad/prospective/scholarshipintern.php.

Internships/Practica: Master's Degree (MA/MS Clinical Mental Health Counseling): An internship experience, such as a final research project or "capstone" experience is required of graduates. Numerous practicum and internship sites are available in the Northwest Indiana region and our proximity to Chicago and southern Michigan provides additional clinical training opportunities for our students. Clinical/experiential training is perhaps the single most important element of a counseling training program. The knowledge, skills, and attitudes acquired through academic coursework may be severely tested by the demands of real world counseling situations. Students are mentored through the process by both faculty and supervisors from each training site.

Housing and Day Care: No on-campus housing is available. No on-campus day care facilities are available.

Employment of Department Graduates:
Master's Degree Graduates: Of those who graduated in the academic year 2011–2012, the following categories and numbers represent the postgraduate activities and employment of master's degree graduates: Enrolled in a postdoctoral residency/fellowship (n/a), employed in independent practice (n/a), total from the above (master's) (0).
Doctoral Degree Graduates: Of those who graduated in the academic year 2011–2012, the following categories and numbers represent the postgraduate activities and employment of doctoral degree graduates: Enrolled in a psychology doctoral program (n/a), total from the above (doctoral) (0).

Additional Information:
Orientation, Objectives, and Emphasis of Department: The Clinical Mental Health Counseling program at Valparaiso Uni-

versity serves as an ethical and professional point of entry for individuals from diverse populations interested in acquiring the requisite skills associated with becoming a licensed professional counselor. The CMHC program emphasizes the development of professional identity, awareness of cultural diversity and spirituality, and basic counselor competencies. It is the mission of the Clinical Mental Health Counseling program faculty to prepare counselors who will ethically promote the well-being of individuals, families, mental health organizations and communities located in metropolitan, rural and global settings.

Information for Students With Physical Disabilities: See the following website for more information: http://www.valpo.edu/disabilityss/.

Application Information:
Send to Valparaiso University, Graduate School, 1700 Chapel Drive, Kretzmann Hall, Room 114, Valparaiso, IN 46383. Application available online. URL of online application: http://www.valpo.edu/grad/apply. Students are admitted in the Fall, application deadline March 1. *Fee:* $30. $50.00 for international applicants.

Iowa State University

Department of Psychology
Liberal Arts & Sciences
Lagomarcino Hall
Ames, IA 50011-3180
Telephone: (515) 294-1743
Fax: (515) 294-6424
E-mail: *stapleto@iastate.edu*
Web: *http://www.psychology.iastate.edu/*

Department Information:

1924. Chairperson: Carolyn Cutrona, PhD. Number of faculty: total—full-time 27, part-time 2; women—full-time 10, part-time 2; total—minority—full-time 3, part-time 1; women minority—full-time 1.

Programs and Degrees Offered:

Listed in the following order: Program area, degree type (T if terminal Master's), number awarded 7/11–6/12. Counseling Psychology PhD (Doctor of Philosophy) 9, Social Psychology PhD (Doctor of Philosophy) 9, Cognitive Psychology PhD (Doctor of Philosophy) 4, Quantiative Certificate Other 2.

APA Accreditation: Counseling PhD (Doctor of Philosophy). Student Outcome Data Website: http://counseling.psych.iastate.edu/data.

Student Applications/Admissions:

Student Applications

Counseling Psychology PhD (Doctor of Philosophy)—Applications 2012–2013, 116. Total applicants accepted 2012–2013, 5. Number full-time enrolled (new admits only) 2012–2013, 5. Number part-time enrolled (new admits only) 2012–2013, 0. Total enrolled 2012–2013 full-time, 25. Total enrolled 2012–2013 part-time, 0. Openings 2013–2014, 5. The median number of years required for completion of a degree in 2012–2013 were 6. The number of students enrolled full- and part-time who were dismissed or voluntarily withdrew from this program area in 2012–2013 were 0. *Social Psychology PhD (Doctor of Philosophy)*—Applications 2012–2013, 46. Total applicants accepted 2012–2013, 4. Number full-time enrolled (new admits only) 2012–2013, 4. Number part-time enrolled (new admits only) 2012–2013, 0. Total enrolled 2012–2013 full-time, 16. Total enrolled 2012–2013 part-time, 0. Openings 2013–2014, 3. The median number of years required for completion of a degree in 2012–2013 were 5. The number of students enrolled full- and part-time who were dismissed or voluntarily withdrew from this program area in 2012–2013 were 0. *Cognitive Psychology PhD (Doctor of Philosophy)*—Applications 2012–2013, 30. Total applicants accepted 2012–2013, 4. Number full-time enrolled (new admits only) 2012–2013, 4. Number part-time enrolled (new admits only) 2012–2013, 0. Total enrolled 2012–2013 full-time, 9. Total enrolled 2012–2013 part-time,

0. Openings 2013–2014, 2. The median number of years required for completion of a degree in 2012–2013 were 5. The number of students enrolled full- and part-time who were dismissed or voluntarily withdrew from this program area in 2012–2013 were 0. *Quantiative Certificate Other*—Applications 2012–2013, 9. Total applicants accepted 2012–2013, 9. Number full-time enrolled (new admits only) 2012–2013, 9. Total enrolled 2012–2013 full-time, 9. Openings 2013–2014, 15. The median number of years required for completion of a degree in 2012–2013 were 2. The number of students enrolled full- and part-time who were dismissed or voluntarily withdrew from this program area in 2012–2013 were 0.

Scores: Entries appear in this order: required test or GPA, minimum score (if required), median score of students entering in 2012–2013. *Counseling Psychology PhD (Doctor of Philosophy):* GRE-V 490, 560, GRE-Q 720, 740, GRE-Analytical 3.5, 4.5, GRE-Subject (Psychology) 700, 700, overall undergraduate GPA 3.0, 3.56, last 2 years GPA 3.33, 3.58, psychology GPA 3.0, 3.66, Masters GPA no minimum stated; *Social Psychology PhD (Doctor of Philosophy):* GRE-V 500, 570, GRE-Q 620, 680, GRE-Analytical 4.25, 4.25, overall undergraduate GPA 3.10, 3.15, last 2 years GPA 3.20, 3.45, psychology GPA 3.20, 3.51; *Cognitive Psychology PhD (Doctor of Philosophy):* GRE-V 520, 555, GRE-Q 490, 690, GRE-Analytical 3.50, 4.5, overall undergraduate GPA 3.16, 3.6, last 2 years GPA 3.16, 3.78, psychology GPA 3.70, 3.90, Masters GPA no minimum stated.

Other Criteria: (importance of criteria rated low, medium, or high): GRE scores—high, research experience—high, work experience—low, extracurricular activity—low, clinically related public service—low, GPA—high, letters of recommendation—high, interview—high, statement of goals and objectives—high, fit with faculty research—high, undergraduate major in psychology—medium, specific undergraduate psychology courses taken—medium, Interviews important for Counseling area, less so for Social and Cognitive. Clinically related service or work is more important in Counseling than in the other areas. For additional information on admission requirements, go to http://www.psychology.iastate.edu/index.php?id=29.

Student Characteristics: The following represents characteristics of students in 2012–2013 in all graduate psychology programs in the department: Female—full-time 39, part-time 0; Male—full-time 20, part-time 0; African American/Black—full-time 2, part-time 0; Hispanic/Latino(a)—full-time 2, part-time 0; Asian/Pacific Islander—full-time 3, part-time 0; American Indian/Alaska Native—full-time 0, part-time 0; Caucasian/White—full-time 52, part-time 0; Multi-ethnic—full-time 0, part-time 0; students subject to the Americans With Disabilities Act—full-time 0, part-time 0; Unknown ethnicity—full-time 0, part-time 0; International students who hold an F-1 or J-1 Visa—full-time 9, part-time 0.

Financial Information/Assistance:

Tuition for Full-Time Study: *Doctoral:* State residents: per academic year $7,848; Nonstate residents: per academic year $20,158.

Tuition is subject to change. Additional fees are assessed to students beyond the costs of tuition for the following: activity, student fees assessed, Approximately $400/year. See the following website for updates and changes in tuition costs: http://www.registrar.iastate.edu//fees/.

Financial Assistance:

First-Year Students: Teaching assistantships available for first year. Average amount paid per academic year: $14,400. Average number of hours worked per week: 20. Apply by January 2. Research assistantships available for first year. Average amount paid per academic year: $14,400. Average number of hours worked per week: 20. Apply by January 2. Fellowships and scholarships available for first year. Average amount paid per academic year: $14,400. Average number of hours worked per week: 20. Apply by January 2.

Advanced Students: Teaching assistantships available for advanced students. Average amount paid per academic year: $14,400. Average number of hours worked per week: 20. Research assistantships available for advanced students. Average amount paid per academic year: $14,400. Average number of hours worked per week: 20.

Additional Information: Of all students currently enrolled full time, 100% benefited from one or more of the listed financial assistance programs. Application and information available online at: http://www.psychology.iastate.edu/index.php?id=28.

Internships/Practica: Doctoral Degree (PhD Counseling Psychology): For those doctoral students for whom a professional psychology internship was required in this program prior to graduation, (3) students applied for an internship in 2011–2012, with (3) students obtaining an internship. Of those students who obtained an internship, (3) were paid internships. Of those students who obtained an internship, (3) students placed in APA/CPA accredited internships, (0) students placed in internships not APA/CPA accredited, but listed with the Association of Psychology Postdoctoral and Internship Programs (APPIC), (0) students placed in internships conforming to guidelines of the Council of Directors of School Psychology Programs (CDSPP), (0) students placed in internships that were not APA/CPA accredited, APPIC or CDSPP listed. Sequential, progressive practica provide students in our professional programs with individually supervised applied training in their specialty area. All supervision is provided by appropriately certified/licensed faculty and adjuncts in a range of settings, including university counseling centers, major hospitals, outpatient clinics, child and adolescent treatment centers, correctional facilities, and the public school system. Based on such practicum experience and their academic training, ISU students compete successfully for select predoctoral internships across the country.

Housing and Day Care: On-campus housing is available. See the following website for more information: http://www.housing.iastate.edu/. On-campus day care facilities are available. See the following website for more information: http://www.hrs.iastate.edu/hrs/node/137.

Employment of Department Graduates:

Master's Degree Graduates: Of those who graduated in the academic year 2011–2012, the following categories and numbers represent the postgraduate activities and employment of master's degree graduates: Enrolled in a postdoctoral residency/fellowship (n/a), employed in independent practice (n/a), total from the above (master's) (0).

Doctoral Degree Graduates: Of those who graduated in the academic year 2011–2012, the following categories and numbers represent the postgraduate activities and employment of doctoral degree graduates: Enrolled in a psychology doctoral program (n/a), enrolled in a postdoctoral residency/fellowship (1), employed in independent practice (1), employed in an academic position at a university (1), employed in an academic position at a 2-year/4-year college (3), employed in a community mental health/counseling center (2), still seeking employment (1), total from the above (doctoral) (9).

Additional Information:

Orientation, Objectives, and Emphasis of Department: Graduate programs emphasize the acquisition of a broad base of knowledge in psychology as well as concentration on the content and methodological skills requisite to performance in teaching, research, and applied activities. A strong research orientation is evident in all areas of the department, with involvement in research being required of all doctoral students throughout their graduate studies. Curriculum requirements for the degrees are based on a core course system, which is designed to enable students to tailor a program best suited to their particular objectives. Subsequent courses, seminars, research, and applied experiences are determined by the student and his or her graduate advisory committee. Additionally, teaching experience is available to all doctoral students, and extensive supervised practicum experience is required of students in the applied programs.

Special Facilities or Resources: The department maintains the full array of physical facilities and equipment required for behavioral research. Observational and videotaping facilities are available for research and applied training. The department maintains a microcomputer lab, and the university maintains a superior computation center. We are currently completing an eye-tracking lab for faculty and student use. Statistical consulting is also available from faculty jointly appointed with the Statistics Department and the Behavioral and Survey Research Center.

Information for Students With Physical Disabilities: See the following website for more information: http://www.dso.iastate.edu/dr/.

Application Information:

Send to Iowa State University, Graduate Admissions, Department of Psychology, W112 Lagomarcino, Ames, IA 50011. Application available online. URL of online application: https://www.admissions.iastate.edu/apply/online/. Students are admitted in the Fall, application deadline December 15. Counseling application deadline is December 15; Social and Cognitive deadline is now January 2. *Fee:* $40. $90 fee for international application. Application fee is waived only for McNair scholars.

Iowa State University

Human Development & Family Studies
Human Sciences
2330 Palmer
Ames, IA 50011-4380
Telephone: (515) 294-6321
Fax: (515) 294-2502
E-mail: *hdfs-grad-adm@iastate.edu*
Web: *http://www.hdfs.hs.iastate.edu/*

Department Information:

Chairperson: Gong-Soog Hong.

Programs and Degrees Offered:

Listed in the following order: Program area, degree type (T if terminal Master's), number awarded 7/11–6/12. Human Development and Family Studies MA/MS (Master of Arts/Science) (T), Human Development and Family Studies PhD (Doctor of Philosophy).

Student Applications/Admissions:

Student Applications

Human Development and Family Studies MA/MS (Master of Arts/Science)—Human Development and Family Studies PhD (Doctor of Philosophy)—

Scores: Entries appear in this order: required test or GPA, minimum score (if required), median score of students entering in 2012–2013. *Human Development and Family Studies MA/MS (Master of Arts/Science):* GRE-V no minimum stated, GRE-Q no minimum stated, GRE-Analytical no minimum stated, overall undergraduate GPA no minimum stated; *Human Development and Family Studies PhD (Doctor of Philosophy):* GRE-V no minimum stated, GRE-Q no minimum stated, GRE-Analytical no minimum stated, overall undergraduate GPA no minimum stated, Masters GPA no minimum stated.

Other Criteria: (importance of criteria rated low, medium, or high): GRE scores—medium, research experience—medium, work experience—medium, extracurricular activity—low, clinically related public service—low, GPA—medium, letters of recommendation—high, statement of goals and objectives—medium. For additional information on admission requirements, go to http://www.hdfs.hs.iastate.edu/graduate/apply/.

Student Characteristics: The following represents characteristics of students in 2012–2013 in all graduate psychology programs in the department: Female—full-time 47, part-time 0; Male—full-time 11, part-time 0; African American/Black—full-time 3, part-time 0; Hispanic/Latino(a)—full-time 2, part-time 0; Asian/Pacific Islander—full-time 4, part-time 0; American Indian/Alaska Native—full-time 35, part-time 0; Caucasian/White—full-time 11, part-time 0; Multi-ethnic—full-time 3, part-time 0; students subject to the Americans With Disabilities Act—full-time 0, part-time 0; Unknown ethnicity—full-time 0, part-time 0; International students who hold an F-1 or J-1 Visa—full-time 0, part-time 0.

Financial Information/Assistance:

Tuition for Full-Time Study: *Master's:* State residents: per academic year $7,756, $430 per credit hour; Nonstate residents: per academic year $19,696, $1,091 per credit hour. *Doctoral:* State residents: per academic year $7,756, $430 per credit hour; Nonstate residents: per academic year $19,696, $1,091 per credit hour. Tuition is subject to change. Additional fees are assessed to students beyond the costs of tuition for the following: Activity, Services, Building & Recreation Fee; Health Facility Fee, Health Fee; Technology Fee. See the following website for updates and changes in tuition costs: http://www.registrar.iastate.edu/fees/.

Financial Assistance:

First-Year Students: Teaching assistantships available for first year. Average amount paid per academic year: $13,500. Average number of hours worked per week: 20. Apply by January 15. Research assistantships available for first year. Average amount paid per academic year: $13,500. Average number of hours worked per week: 20. Apply by January 15. Fellowships and scholarships available for first year. Apply by February 1.

Advanced Students: Teaching assistantships available for advanced students. Average amount paid per academic year: $13,500. Average number of hours worked per week: 20. Apply by February 10. Research assistantships available for advanced students. Average amount paid per academic year: $13,500. Average number of hours worked per week: 20. Apply by February 10. Fellowships and scholarships available for advanced students. Apply by March 1.

Additional Information: Of all students currently enrolled full time, 100% benefited from one or more of the listed financial assistance programs. Application and information available online at: http://www.hs.iastate.edu/current-students/scholarships/.

Internships/Practica: Master's Degree (MA/MS Human Development and Family Studies): An internship experience, such as a final research project or "capstone" experience is required of graduates.

Housing and Day Care: On-campus housing is available. See the following website for more information: http://www.housing.iastate.edu/. On-campus day care facilities are available. See the following website for more information: http://www.hrs.iastate.edu/hrs/node/137.

Employment of Department Graduates:

Master's Degree Graduates: Of those who graduated in the academic year 2011–2012, the following categories and numbers represent the postgraduate activities and employment of master's degree graduates: Enrolled in a postdoctoral residency/fellowship (n/a), employed in independent practice (n/a), employed in government agency (1), employed in a community mental health/counseling center (10), other employment position (4), total from the above (master's) (15).

Doctoral Degree Graduates: Of those who graduated in the academic year 2011–2012, the following categories and numbers represent the postgraduate activities and employment of doctoral degree graduates: Enrolled in a psychology doctoral program (n/a),

employed in an academic position at a university (2), employed in government agency (1), employed in a community mental health/counseling center (0), total from the above (doctoral) (3).

Additional Information:
Orientation, Objectives, and Emphasis of Department: The mission of the Department of Human Development and Family Studies is to have a positive impact on the quality of life for individuals and families across the lifespan, as well as for schools and communities through research, teaching, extension/outreach, and service. The Department of Human Development and Family Studies offers multidisciplinary educational programs covering a range of human sciences and services related to children and families. Research in the department is focused on three signature areas: early development, care and education; family policy and practice; and lifespan development. Graduates have been successful nationally and internationally in obtaining teaching, research, and service positions in research institutes, human service agencies, and colleges and universities, including the cooperative extension service.

Special Facilities or Resources: Human Development and Family Studies is committed to making a positive impact on the quality of life for individuals and families across the lifespan. Our outreach and engagement programs include: HDFS Family Extension, Iowa State University Child Development Lab, and Financial Counseling Clinic.

Information for Students With Physical Disabilities: See the following website for more information: http://www.dso.iastate.edu/dr/.

Application Information:
Application available online. URL of online application: http://www.admissions.iastate.edu/apply/graduate.php. Students are admitted in the Fall, application deadline January 15. *Fee:* $40. $90 application fee for International Applicants.

Iowa, University of
Department of Psychological and Quantitative Foundations
College of Education
361 Lindquist Center
Iowa City, IA 52242
Telephone: (319) 335-5578
Fax: (319) 335-6145
E-mail: *janet-ervin@uiowa.edu*
Web: *http://www.education.uiowa.edu/pq*

Department Information:
Chairperson: Timothy Ansley. Number of faculty: total—full-time 16, part-time 8; women—full-time 9, part-time 1; total—minority—full-time 3; women minority—full-time 2.

Programs and Degrees Offered:
Listed in the following order: Program area, degree type (T if terminal Master's), number awarded 7/11–6/12. Educational Psychology PhD (Doctor of Philosophy) 5, Educational Measurement and Statistics MA/MS (Master of Arts/Science) 8, Educational

Measurement and Statistics PhD (Doctor of Philosophy) 9, School Psychology PhD (Doctor of Philosophy) 6, Counseling Psychology PhD (Doctor of Philosophy) 5.

APA Accreditation: School PhD (Doctor of Philosophy). Student Outcome Data Website: http://www.education.uiowa.edu/pq/schpsych/program/Programoverview/program-statistics.aspx. Counseling PhD (Doctor of Philosophy). Student Outcome Data Website: http://www.education.uiowa.edu/pq/counspsy/outcomes.aspx.

Student Applications/Admissions:
Student Applications
Educational Psychology PhD (Doctor of Philosophy)—Applications 2012–2013, 16. Total applicants accepted 2012–2013, 5. Number full-time enrolled (new admits only) 2012–2013, 5. Number part-time enrolled (new admits only) 2012–2013, 0. Total enrolled 2012–2013 full-time, 31. Total enrolled 2012–2013 part-time, 0. Openings 2013–2014, 15. The number of students enrolled full- and part-time who were dismissed or voluntarily withdrew from this program area in 2012–2013 were 0. *Educational Measurement and Statistics MA/MS (Master of Arts/Science)*—Applications 2012–2013, 19. Total applicants accepted 2012–2013, 12. Number full-time enrolled (new admits only) 2012–2013, 12. Number part-time enrolled (new admits only) 2012–2013, 0. Total enrolled 2012–2013 full-time, 34. Total enrolled 2012–2013 part-time, 0. Openings 2013–2014, 15. The median number of years required for completion of a degree in 2012–2013 were 3. The number of students enrolled full- and part-time who were dismissed or voluntarily withdrew from this program area in 2012–2013 were 0. *Educational Measurement and Statistics PhD (Doctor of Philosophy)*—Applications 2012–2013, 15. Total applicants accepted 2012–2013, 12. Number full-time enrolled (new admits only) 2012–2013, 12. Number part-time enrolled (new admits only) 2012–2013, 0. Total enrolled 2012–2013 full-time, 61. Total enrolled 2012–2013 part-time, 0. Openings 2013–2014, 15. The median number of years required for completion of a degree in 2012–2013 were 4. The number of students enrolled full- and part-time who were dismissed or voluntarily withdrew from this program area in 2012–2013 were 0. *School Psychology PhD (Doctor of Philosophy)*—Applications 2012–2013, 37. Total applicants accepted 2012–2013, 9. Number full-time enrolled (new admits only) 2012–2013, 9. Total enrolled 2012–2013 full-time, 55. Total enrolled 2012–2013 part-time, 0. Openings 2013–2014, 15. The median number of years required for completion of a degree in 2012–2013 were 5. *Counseling Psychology PhD (Doctor of Philosophy)*—Applications 2012–2013, 72. Total applicants accepted 2012–2013, 10. Number full-time enrolled (new admits only) 2012–2013, 10. Number part-time enrolled (new admits only) 2012–2013, 0. Total enrolled 2012–2013 full-time, 63. Total enrolled 2012–2013 part-time, 0. Openings 2013–2014, 10. The median number of years required for completion of a degree in 2012–2013 were 5. The number of students enrolled full- and part-time who were dismissed or voluntarily withdrew from this program area in 2012–2013 were 0.
Scores: Entries appear in this order: required test or GPA, minimum score (if required), median score of students entering in 2012–2013. *Educational Psychology PhD (Doctor of Philosophy):* GRE-V no minimum stated, GRE-Q no minimum stated, overall undergraduate GPA 3.0; *Educational Measurement and Statistics MA/MS (Master of Arts/Science):* GRE-V no minimum

stated, GRE-Q no minimum stated, overall undergraduate GPA no minimum stated; *Educational Measurement and Statistics PhD (Doctor of Philosophy)*: GRE-V no minimum stated, GRE-Q no minimum stated, overall undergraduate GPA no minimum stated; *School Psychology PhD (Doctor of Philosophy)*: GRE-V no minimum stated, GRE-Q no minimum stated, overall undergraduate GPA no minimum stated; *Counseling Psychology PhD (Doctor of Philosophy)*: GRE-V no minimum stated, GRE-Q no minimum stated, overall undergraduate GPA 3.0, Masters GPA 3.5.

Other Criteria: (importance of criteria rated low, medium, or high): GRE scores—high, research experience—high, work experience—medium, extracurricular activity—low, clinically related public service—high, GPA—high, letters of recommendation—high, interview—medium, statement of goals and objectives—high, undergraduate major in psychology—low, specific undergraduate psychology courses taken—low.

Student Characteristics: The following represents characteristics of students in 2012–2013 in all graduate psychology programs in the department: Female—full-time 165, part-time 0; Male—full-time 79, part-time 0; African American/Black—full-time 18, part-time 0; Hispanic/Latino(a)—full-time 7, part-time 0; Asian/Pacific Islander—full-time 4, part-time 0; American Indian/Alaska Native—full-time 0, part-time 0; Caucasian/White—full-time 116, part-time 0; Multi-ethnic—full-time 0, part-time 0; students subject to the Americans With Disabilities Act—full-time 0, part-time 0; Unknown ethnicity—full-time 0, part-time 0; International students who hold an F-1 or J-1 Visa—full-time 99, part-time 0.

Financial Information/Assistance:

Tuition for Full-Time Study: *Master's:* State residents: per academic year $7,523; Nonstate residents: per academic year $21,900. *Doctoral:* State residents: per academic year $7,523; Nonstate residents: per academic year $21,900. See the following website for updates and changes in tuition costs: http://www.registrar.uiowa.edu/TuitionandFees/tabid/93/Default.aspx.

Financial Assistance:

First-Year Students: Research assistantships available for first year. Average amount paid per academic year: $17,230. Average number of hours worked per week: 20. Apply by April 1.

Advanced Students: Research assistantships available for advanced students. Average amount paid per academic year: $17,230. Average number of hours worked per week: 20. Apply by April 1. Fellowships and scholarships available for advanced students. Average amount paid per academic year: $17,230. Average number of hours worked per week: 20.

Additional Information: Of all students currently enrolled full time, 5% benefited from one or more of the listed financial assistance programs. Application and information available online at: http://grad.admissions.uiowa.edu/finances.

Internships/Practica: Doctoral Degree (PhD School Psychology): For those doctoral students for whom a professional psychology internship was required in this program prior to graduation, (1) students applied for an internship in 2011–2012, with (1) students obtaining an internship. Of those students who obtained an internship, (1) were paid internships. Of those students who obtained an internship, (1) students placed in APA/CPA accredited internships, (0) students placed in internships not APA/CPA accredited, but listed with the Association of Psychology Postdoctoral and Internship Programs (APPIC), (0) students placed in internships conforming to guidelines of the Council of Directors of School Psychology Programs (CDSPP), (0) students placed in internships that were not APA/CPA accredited, APPIC or CDSPP listed. Doctoral Degree (PhD Counseling Psychology): For those doctoral students for whom a professional psychology internship was required in this program prior to graduation, (4) students applied for an internship in 2011–2012, with (4) students obtaining an internship. Of those students who obtained an internship, (4) were paid internships. Of those students who obtained an internship, (4) students placed in APA/CPA accredited internships, (0) students placed in internships not APA/CPA accredited, but listed with the Association of Psychology Postdoctoral and Internship Programs (APPIC), (0) students placed in internships conforming to guidelines of the Council of Directors of School Psychology Programs (CDSPP), (0) students placed in internships that were not APA/CPA accredited, APPIC or CDSPP listed. There are multiple practicum sites at a variety of agencies, (e.g., university counseling centers, VA medical centers, community mental health centers). In the educational psychology program, formal internship and practicum experiences are not available for MA students, although some students do find paid positions as teaching or research assistants in fields in which they have prior experience. At the PhD level, most students are supported by half-time fellowships or assistantships. In a research-oriented program, these paid positions serve the purpose of an internship or fellowship. In the school psychology program, practica are available in the public schools, The University of Iowa Hospitals and Clinics (Department of Pediatrics, Psychiatry and Neurology), the Berlin-Blank National Center for Gifted, located in the College of Education, The Wendell Johnson Speech and Hearing Clinic at the University of Iowa, and in local mental health agencies.

Housing and Day Care: On-campus housing is available. See the following website for more information: http://housing.uiowa.edu/departments/univapts/. On-campus day care facilities are available. See the following website for more information: http://www.uiowa.edu/hr/famserv/childcare/index.html.

Employment of Department Graduates:

Master's Degree Graduates: Of those who graduated in the academic year 2011–2012, the following categories and numbers represent the postgraduate activities and employment of master's degree graduates: Enrolled in a psychology doctoral program (9), enrolled in a postdoctoral residency/fellowship (n/a), employed in independent practice (n/a), still seeking employment (1), do not know (2), total from the above (master's) (12).

Doctoral Degree Graduates: Of those who graduated in the academic year 2011–2012, the following categories and numbers represent the postgraduate activities and employment of doctoral degree graduates: Enrolled in a psychology doctoral program (n/a), enrolled in a postdoctoral residency/fellowship (2), employed in independent practice (3), employed in an academic position at a university (5), employed in other positions at a higher education institution (4), employed in a professional position in a school system (3), employed in business or industry (3), employed in government agency (1), employed in a community mental health/counseling center (2), employed in a hospital/medical center (2), total from the above (doctoral) (25).

Additional Information:

Orientation, Objectives, and Emphasis of Department: The counseling psychology program endorses a scientist–practitioner model and expects students to be competent researchers and practitioners at the completion of their program. At the PhD level, the educational psychology program at the University of Iowa is designed to provide students with strong grounding in the psychology of learning and instruction. Students are encouraged to become proficient in both quantitative and qualitative research methods with an emphasis on the former. The study of individual differences is one program emphasis. At the MA level, the program provides a broad introduction to educational psychology and flexible accommodation of individual students' interest in diverse areas such as instructional technology, reading acquisition and program evaluation. The doctoral program in school psychology is committed to training professional psychologists who are knowledgeable about providing services to children in school, medical and mental health settings. The students will possess expertise in addressing children's social/emotional needs and learning processes. The program's curriculum has been developed to reflect consideration of multicultural issues within psychological theory, research and professional development. The program strives to produce psychologists who are competent in working in a variety of settings with children/adolescents with a wide array of problems and be able to provide a wide range of psychological services to children and the adults in their lives.

Special Facilities or Resources: The University of Iowa Hospitals and Clinics provide multiple research opportunities. Outstanding computer facilities exist on the campus. Students in the educational psychology program frequently make use of two important resources of the University of Iowa College of Education. The Iowa Testing Programs, creator of the Iowa Tests of Basic Skills and the Iowa Tests of Educational Development, are housed here. Students have access to test databases for research and may work with faculty or research assistantships supported by the Iowa Measurement Research Foundation. The Berlin/Blank International Center for Gifted Education also provides opportunities for research, teaching, and counseling experiences as well as assistantship support. All of the above settings are open to students in the school psychology program for applied research and have existing data available to students as do American College Testing and National Computer Systems, located in Iowa City, IA.

Information for Students With Physical Disabilities: See the following website for more information: http://www.uiowa.edu/homepage/diversity/disability.html.

Application Information:
Send to Susan Cline, Student Services Admissions, College of Education, N310 Lindquist Center, Iowa City, IA 52242. Application available online. URL of online application: http://grad.admissions.uiowa.edu/apply. Students are admitted in the Fall, application deadline December 1; Spring, application deadline September 1. For students admitted in the Fall, application deadlines are: MA: May 1-Measurement and Statistics, January 1-Educational Psychology; PhD: January 1-Educational Psychology, March 1-Measurement and Statistics, December 1-Counseling Psychology, January 1-School Psychology. For students admitted in the Spring, deadlines are: MA November 1-Measurement and Statistics; PhD September 1-Measurement and Statistics. *Fee:* $50.

Iowa, University of
Department of Psychology
Liberal Arts and Sciences
11 Seashore Hall East
Iowa City, IA 52242-1407
Telephone: (319) 335-2406
Fax: (319) 335-0191
E-mail: *alan-christensen@uiowa.edu*
Web: *http://www.psychology.uiowa.edu*

Department Information:
1887. Chairperson: Jodie Plumert. Number of faculty: total—full-time 31, part-time 5; women—full-time 10, part-time 2; total—minority—full-time 2; women minority—full-time 1.

Programs and Degrees Offered:
Listed in the following order: Program area, degree type (T if terminal Master's), number awarded 7/11–6/12. Behavioral and Cognitive Neuroscience PhD (Doctor of Philosophy) 2, Clinical Psychology PhD (Doctor of Philosophy) 7, Cognition and Perception PhD (Doctor of Philosophy) 3, Developmental Science PhD (Doctor of Philosophy) 1, Social Psychology PhD (Doctor of Philosophy) 1, Health Psychology PhD (Doctor of Philosophy) 0.

APA Accreditation: Clinical PhD (Doctor of Philosophy). Student Outcome Data Website: http://www.psychology.uiowa.edu/research/clinical_admissions_outcomes.

Student Applications/Admissions:
Student Applications
Behavioral and Cognitive Neuroscience PhD (Doctor of Philosophy)—Applications 2012–2013, 27. Total applicants accepted 2012–2013, 7. Number full-time enrolled (new admits only) 2012–2013, 4. Number part-time enrolled (new admits only) 2012–2013, 0. Total enrolled 2012–2013 full-time, 15. Total enrolled 2012–2013 part-time, 0. Openings 2013–2014, 3. The median number of years required for completion of a degree in 2012–2013 were 6. The number of students enrolled full- and part-time who were dismissed or voluntarily withdrew from this program area in 2012–2013 were 0. *Clinical Psychology PhD (Doctor of Philosophy)*—Applications 2012–2013, 143. Total applicants accepted 2012–2013, 7. Number full-time enrolled (new admits only) 2012–2013, 6. Number part-time enrolled (new admits only) 2012–2013, 0. Total enrolled 2012–2013 full-time, 36. Total enrolled 2012–2013 part-time, 0. Openings 2013–2014, 5. The median number of years required for completion of a degree in 2012–2013 were 7. The number of students enrolled full- and part-time who were dismissed or voluntarily withdrew from this program area in 2012–2013 were 0. *Cognition and Perception PhD (Doctor of Philosophy)*—Applications 2012–2013, 36. Total applicants accepted 2012–2013, 3. Number full-time enrolled (new admits only) 2012–2013, 1. Number part-time enrolled (new admits only) 2012–2013, 0. Total enrolled 2012–2013 full-time, 16. Total enrolled 2012–2013 part-time, 0. Openings 2013–2014, 3. The median number of years required for completion of a degree in 2012–2013 were 6. The number of students enrolled full- and part-time who were dismissed or voluntarily withdrew from this program area in 2012–2013 were 1. *Developmental Science PhD (Doctor of Philosophy)*—Applications 2012–2013,

13. Total applicants accepted 2012–2013, 3. Number full-time enrolled (new admits only) 2012–2013, 2. Number part-time enrolled (new admits only) 2012–2013, 0. Total enrolled 2012–2013 full-time, 9. Total enrolled 2012–2013 part-time, 0. Openings 2013–2014, 3. The median number of years required for completion of a degree in 2012–2013 were 6. The number of students enrolled full- and part-time who were dismissed or voluntarily withdrew from this program area in 2012–2013 were 0. *Social Psychology PhD (Doctor of Philosophy)*—Applications 2012–2013, 51. Total applicants accepted 2012–2013, 0. Number full-time enrolled (new admits only) 2012–2013, 0. Number part-time enrolled (new admits only) 2012–2013, 0. Total enrolled 2012–2013 full-time, 8. Total enrolled 2012–2013 part-time, 0. Openings 2013–2014, 1. The median number of years required for completion of a degree in 2012–2013 were 6. The number of students enrolled full- and part-time who were dismissed or voluntarily withdrew from this program area in 2012–2013 were 0. *Health Psychology PhD (Doctor of Philosophy)*—Applications 2012–2013, 18. Total applicants accepted 2012–2013, 3. Number full-time enrolled (new admits only) 2012–2013, 0. Number part-time enrolled (new admits only) 2012–2013, 0. Total enrolled 2012–2013 full-time, 2. Total enrolled 2012–2013 part-time, 0. Openings 2013–2014, 1. The number of students enrolled full- and part-time who were dismissed or voluntarily withdrew from this program area in 2012–2013 were 0.

Scores: Entries appear in this order: required test or GPA, minimum score (if required), median score of students entering in 2012–2013. *Behavioral and Cognitive Neuroscience PhD (Doctor of Philosophy):* GRE-V no minimum stated, GRE-Q no minimum stated, GRE-Analytical no minimum stated, overall undergraduate GPA no minimum stated; *Clinical Psychology PhD (Doctor of Philosophy):* GRE-V no minimum stated, 610, GRE-Q no minimum stated, 690, GRE-Analytical no minimum stated, 5.0, overall undergraduate GPA no minimum stated, 3.78; *Cognition and Perception PhD (Doctor of Philosophy):* GRE-V no minimum stated, GRE-Q no minimum stated, GRE-Analytical no minimum stated, overall undergraduate GPA no minimum stated; *Developmental Science PhD (Doctor of Philosophy):* GRE-V no minimum stated, GRE-Q no minimum stated, GRE-Analytical no minimum stated, overall undergraduate GPA no minimum stated; *Social Psychology PhD (Doctor of Philosophy):* GRE-V no minimum stated, GRE-Q no minimum stated, GRE-Analytical no minimum stated, overall undergraduate GPA no minimum stated; *Health Psychology PhD (Doctor of Philosophy):* GRE-V no minimum stated, GRE-Q no minimum stated, GRE-Analytical no minimum stated, overall undergraduate GPA no minimum stated.

Other Criteria: (importance of criteria rated low, medium, or high): GRE scores—high, research experience—high, work experience—low, extracurricular activity—low, clinically related public service—medium, GPA—high, letters of recommendation—high, interview—high, statement of goals and objectives—high, undergraduate major in psychology—low, specific undergraduate psychology courses taken—low. For additional information on admission requirements, go to http://www.psychology.uiowa.edu/phd_application.html.

Student Characteristics: The following represents characteristics of students in 2012–2013 in all graduate psychology programs in the department: Female—full-time 59, part-time 0; Male—full-time 27, part-time 0; African American/Black—full-time 2, part-time 0; Hispanic/Latino(a)—full-time 10, part-time 0; Asian/Pacific Islander—full-time 8, part-time 0; American Indian/Alaska Native—full-time 0, part-time 0; Caucasian/White—full-time 66, part-time 0; Multi-ethnic—full-time 0, part-time 0; students subject to the Americans With Disabilities Act—full-time 0, part-time 0; Unknown ethnicity—full-time 0, part-time 0; International students who hold an F-1 or J-1 Visa—full-time 9, part-time 0.

Financial Information/Assistance:

Tuition for Full-Time Study: *Doctoral:* State residents: per academic year $7,900; Nonstate residents: per academic year $24,064. Tuition is subject to change. Additional fees are assessed to students beyond the costs of tuition for the following: additional student fees of $950 per academic year. See the following website for updates and changes in tuition costs: http://www.registrar.uiowa.edu/TuitionandFees/TuitionandFeeTables/tabid/95/Default.aspx.

Financial Assistance:

First-Year Students: Teaching assistantships available for first year. Average amount paid per academic year: $21,181. Average number of hours worked per week: 20. Research assistantships available for first year. Average amount paid per academic year: $21,181. Average number of hours worked per week: 20. Fellowships and scholarships available for first year. Average amount paid per academic year: $24,000. Average number of hours worked per week: 0.

Advanced Students: Teaching assistantships available for advanced students. Average amount paid per academic year: $21,181. Average number of hours worked per week: 20. Research assistantships available for advanced students. Average amount paid per academic year: $21,181. Average number of hours worked per week: 20. Fellowships and scholarships available for advanced students. Average amount paid per academic year: $24,000. Average number of hours worked per week: 0.

Additional Information: Of all students currently enrolled full time, 100% benefited from one or more of the listed financial assistance programs. Application and information available online at: http://www.grad.uiowa.edu/financing-your-education.

Internships/Practica: Doctoral Degree (PhD Clinical Psychology): For those doctoral students for whom a professional psychology internship was required in this program prior to graduation, (1) students applied for an internship in 2011–2012, with (1) students obtaining an internship. Of those students who obtained an internship, (1) were paid internships. Of those students who obtained an internship, (1) students placed in APA/CPA accredited internships, (0) students placed in internships not APA/CPA accredited, but listed with the Association of Psychology Postdoctoral and Internship Programs (APPIC), (0) students placed in internships conforming to guidelines of the Council of Directors of School Psychology Programs (CDSPP), (0) students placed in internships that were not APA/CPA accredited, APPIC or CDSPP listed. Students in our Clinical Psychology program participate in clinical assessment and treatment practica at our department-run clinic (the Carl E. Seashore Psychology Training Clinic) and in clinics run by departments such as Psychiatry and Neurology at the University of Iowa Hospitals and Clinics.

Housing and Day Care: On-campus housing is available. See the following website for more information: http://housing.uiowa.

edu/. On-campus day care facilities are available. See the following website for more information: http://www.uiowa.edu/hr/famserv/childcare/.

Employment of Department Graduates:

Master's Degree Graduates: Of those who graduated in the academic year 2011–2012, the following categories and numbers represent the postgraduate activities and employment of master's degree graduates: Enrolled in a postdoctoral residency/fellowship (n/a), employed in independent practice (n/a), total from the above (master's) (0).

Doctoral Degree Graduates: Of those who graduated in the academic year 2011–2012, the following categories and numbers represent the postgraduate activities and employment of doctoral degree graduates: Enrolled in a psychology doctoral program (n/a), enrolled in a postdoctoral residency/fellowship (8), employed in an academic position at a university (5), employed in a community mental health/counseling center (1), total from the above (doctoral) (14).

Additional Information:

Orientation, Objectives, and Emphasis of Department: The mission of the PhD program is to produce professional scholars who contribute significantly to the advancement of scientific psychological knowledge and who can effectively teach students about the science of psychology. Some of these scholars are also prepared to deliver psychological services. Our goal is to produce PhDs who have developed world-class programs of research, who have published extensively, and who have both broad and deep knowledge. Graduate training is organized into six broad training areas: Behavioral & Cognitive Neuroscience, Clinical Psychology, Cognition & Perception, Developmental Science, Health Psychology, and Personality & Social Psychology. The training programs are flexible, and there is considerable overlap and interaction among students and faculty in all areas, leading to an exciting intellectual environment. Students in good standing receive full support for at least five years. The student-faculty ratio remains quite low, usually less than 2 to 1. The department has been successful in establishing strong ties with other campus units such as Psychiatry, Neurology, the law school, and the business school. Through these associations, one may study such topics as the law and psychology, aging, consumer behavior, and neuroscience.

Special Facilities or Resources: The Kenneth W. Spence Laboratories of Psychology and adjoining space in Seashore Hall and Stuit Hall include automated data acquisition and analysis systems, extensive computing facilities, observation suites with remote audiovisual control and recording equipment, multiple animal facilities, several surgeries, a histology laboratory, soundproof chambers, closed-circuit TV systems, electrophysiological recording rooms, conditioning laboratories, the Carl E. Seashore Psychology Training Clinic, and well-equipped electronic, mechanical, woodworking, and computer shops. Well over half of the departmental laboratories have been extensively renovated or created anew within the past 5 years. In addition, many resources are available through collaboration with colleagues at the university hospital, the Iowa Veterans Administration Hospital, community service centers, and the Colleges of Medicine, Nursing, Dentistry, Engineering, Business, Education, and Law.

Information for Students With Physical Disabilities: See the following website for more information: http://www.uiowa.edu/~sds/.

Application Information:
Send to Graduate Admissions Office, 11 Seashore Hall E. Application available online. URL of online application: http://grad.admissions.uiowa.edu/apply. Students are admitted in the Fall, application deadline December 15. *Fee:* $60. $100 for international applicants.

Northern Iowa, University of
Department of Psychology
Social and Behavioral Sciences
334 Baker Hall
Cedar Falls, IA 50614-0505
Telephone: (319) 273-2303
Fax: (319) 273-6188
E-mail: *harton@uni.edu*
Web: *http://www.uni.edu/csbs/psych/psychology-graduate-program*

Department Information:
1968. Head: Carolyn Hildebrandt. Number of faculty: total—full-time 18, part-time 3; women—full-time 8, part-time 3; total—minority—full-time 1, part-time 1; women minority—full-time 1, part-time 1.

Programs and Degrees Offered:
Listed in the following order: Program area, degree type (T if terminal Master's), number awarded 7/11–6/12. Social Psychology MA/MS (Master of Arts/Science) (T) 2, Clinical Science MA/MS (Master of Arts/Science) (T) 10, Individualized Study MA/MS (Master of Arts/Science) 0.

Student Applications/Admissions:
Student Applications

Social Psychology MA/MS (Master of Arts/Science)—Applications 2012–2013, 23. Total applicants accepted 2012–2013, 9. Number full-time enrolled (new admits only) 2012–2013, 5. Number part-time enrolled (new admits only) 2012–2013, 0. Total enrolled 2012–2013 full-time, 9. Total enrolled 2012–2013 part-time, 0. Openings 2013–2014, 4. The median number of years required for completion of a degree in 2012–2013 were 2. The number of students enrolled full- and part-time who were dismissed or voluntarily withdrew from this program area in 2012–2013 were 2. *Clinical Science MA/MS (Master of Arts/Science)*—Applications 2012–2013, 40. Total applicants accepted 2012–2013, 11. Number full-time enrolled (new admits only) 2012–2013, 8. Number part-time enrolled (new admits only) 2012–2013, 0. Total enrolled 2012–2013 full-time, 13. Total enrolled 2012–2013 part-time, 0. Openings 2013–2014, 4. The median number of years required for completion of a degree in 2012–2013 were 2. The number of students enrolled full- and part-time who were dismissed or voluntarily withdrew from this program area in 2012–2013 were 1. *Individualized Study MA/MS (Master of Arts/Science)*—Applications 2012–2013, 1. Total applicants accepted 2012–2013, 0. Number full-time enrolled (new admits only) 2012–2013, 0. Number part-time enrolled (new admits only) 2012–2013, 0. Total enrolled 2012–2013 full-time, 2. Total enrolled 2012–2013 part-time, 1. Openings 2013–2014, 1. The median number of years required for completion of a degree in 2012–2013 were 2. The number of students enrolled full- and part-time who were dismissed or voluntarily withdrew from this program area in 2012–2013 were 0.

Scores: Entries appear in this order: required test or GPA, minimum score (if required), median score of students entering in 2012–2013. *Social Psychology MA/MS (Master of Arts/Science):* GRE-V no minimum stated, 158, GRE-Q no minimum stated, 151, GRE-Analytical no minimum stated, 4.5, overall undergraduate GPA 3, 3.71; *Clinical Science MA/MS (Master of Arts/Science):* GRE-V no minimum stated, 155, GRE-Q no minimum stated, 149, GRE-Analytical no minimum stated, 4, overall undergraduate GPA 3.0, 3.59; *Individualized Study MA/MS (Master of Arts/Science):* GRE-V no minimum stated, GRE-Q no minimum stated, GRE-Analytical no minimum stated, overall undergraduate GPA 3.0.

Other Criteria: (importance of criteria rated low, medium, or high): GRE scores—high, research experience—high, work experience—low, extracurricular activity—low, clinically related public service—medium, GPA—high, letters of recommendation—high, interview—medium, statement of goals and objectives—high, undergraduate major in psychology—high, specific undergraduate psychology courses taken—medium, Clinically Related Public Service is important only for the clinical science emphasis. For additional information on admission requirements, go to http://www.uni.edu/csbs/psych/application-procedure.

Student Characteristics: The following represents characteristics of students in 2012–2013 in all graduate psychology programs in the department: Female—full-time 18, part-time 0; Male—full-time 6, part-time 1; African American/Black—full-time 1, part-time 0; Hispanic/Latino(a)—full-time 0, part-time 0; Asian/Pacific Islander—full-time 0, part-time 0; American Indian/Alaska Native—full-time 2, part-time 0; Caucasian/White—full-time 20, part-time 1; Multi-ethnic—full-time 1, part-time 0; students subject to the Americans With Disabilities Act—full-time 0, part-time 0; Unknown ethnicity—full-time 0, part-time 0; International students who hold an F-1 or J-1 Visa—full-time 1, part-time 0.

Financial Information/Assistance:

Tuition for Full-Time Study: *Master's:* State residents: per academic year $7,756; Nonstate residents: per academic year $17,026. Tuition is subject to change. Additional fees are assessed to students beyond the costs of tuition for the following: health, technology, recreation, etc. See the following website for updates and changes in tuition costs: http://www.uni.edu/tuition/.

Financial Assistance:

First-Year Students: Teaching assistantships available for first year. Average amount paid per academic year: $4,694. Average number of hours worked per week: 10. Apply by February 1. Research assistantships available for first year. Average amount paid per academic year: $4,694. Average number of hours worked per week: 10. Apply by February 1. Traineeships available for first year. Average number of hours worked per week: 10. Apply by February 1. Fellowships and scholarships available for first year. Average amount paid per academic year: $3,878. Average number of hours worked per week: 0. Apply by February 1.

Advanced Students: Teaching assistantships available for advanced students. Average amount paid per academic year: $4,694. Average number of hours worked per week: 10. Apply by February 1. Research assistantships available for advanced stu-

dents. Average amount paid per academic year: $4,694. Average number of hours worked per week: 10. Apply by February 1. Traineeships available for advanced students. Average number of hours worked per week: 10. Apply by February 1. Fellowships and scholarships available for advanced students. Average amount paid per academic year: $3,878. Average number of hours worked per week: 0. Apply by February 1.

Additional Information: Of all students currently enrolled full time, 100% benefited from one or more of the listed financial assistance programs. Application and information available online at: http://www.grad.uni.edu/assistantships.

Internships/Practica: Master's Degree (MA/MS Social Psychology): An internship experience, such as a final research project or "capstone" experience is required of graduates. Master's Degree (MA/MS Clinical Science): An internship experience, such as a final research project or "capstone" experience is required of graduates. A variety of practicum sites are available for second year students in the clinical science emphasis. Clinical practicum sites have included the University Counseling Center, the State Psychiatric Hospital, correctional facilities, private hospitals, educational settings, and community-based agencies. Students in the social emphasis conduct independent first-year research projects under faculty supervision and present these research projects at regional and national professional conferences.

Housing and Day Care: On-campus housing is available. See the following website for more information: http://www.uni.edu/dor/. On-campus day care facilities are available. See the following website for more information: http://www.uni.edu/cdc/.

Employment of Department Graduates:

Master's Degree Graduates: Of those who graduated in the academic year 2011–2012, the following categories and numbers represent the postgraduate activities and employment of master's degree graduates: Enrolled in a psychology doctoral program (3), enrolled in a postdoctoral residency/fellowship (n/a), employed in independent practice (n/a), employed in an academic position at a 2-year/4-year college (1), employed in other positions at a higher education institution (2), employed in business or industry (2), employed in government agency (1), employed in a community mental health/counseling center (1), employed in a hospital/medical center (1), not seeking employment (1), do not know (3), total from the above (master's) (15).

Doctoral Degree Graduates: Of those who graduated in the academic year 2011–2012, the following categories and numbers represent the postgraduate activities and employment of doctoral degree graduates: Enrolled in a psychology doctoral program (n/a), total from the above (doctoral) (0).

Additional Information:

Orientation, Objectives, and Emphasis of Department: The MA program in General Psychology provides a strong empirical, research-based approach to the study of human behavior. Students may select one of two emphases: a) clinical science; or b) social psychology. They may also choose to complete an individualized study program in conjunction with a faculty mentor. The objectives of the program are: a) to develop skills in research methodology; b) to gain knowledge of basic areas of scientific psychology; and c) to obtain competence in research and/or clinical skills. The clinical science emphasis is designed for those who wish to either obtain doctoral degrees in clinical or counseling psychology or become master's-level providers of services operating in clinical settings under appropriate supervision. These students also pursue research-related careers. The social emphasis is designed for students who wish to pursue doctoral degrees in social psychology or master's-level research or teaching positions. Admissions to the I/O program have been suspended until further notice.

Special Facilities or Resources: The department provides laboratory space for research with human participants; access to community facilities and populations for applied research; 24/7 access to computers for graduate students; and office space for graduate students. We are affiliated with a center for social research and students have access to psychiatric, work, and community populations for research projects.

Information for Students With Physical Disabilities: See the following website for more information: http://www.uni.edu/disability/.

Application Information:
Send to Helen C. Harton, PhD, Graduate Coordinator, Department of Psychology, University of Northern Iowa, Cedar Falls, IA 50614-0505. Application available online. URL of online application: http://www.uni.edu/admissions/apply. Students are admitted in the Fall, application deadline February 1. For full consideration, applications should be received by February 1, although applications will be considered if received by April 30 as space permits. *Fee:* $50. Application fee for international students is $70.

Emporia State University

Department of Psychology
The Teachers College
1200 Commercial Street
Emporia, KS 66801-5087
Telephone: (620) 341-5317
Fax: (620) 341-5801
E-mail: *psych@emporia.edu*
Web: *http://www.emporia.edu/psych*

Department Information:
1932. Chairperson: Brian W. Schrader. Number of faculty: total—full-time 8, part-time 1; women—full-time 3.

Programs and Degrees Offered:
Listed in the following order: Program area, degree type (T if terminal Master's), number awarded 7/11–6/12. Experimental Psychology MA/MS (Master of Arts/Science) (T) 3, School Psychology EdS (School Psychology) 6, Clinical Psychology MA/MS (Master of Arts/Science) (T) 9, Industrial/Organizational Psychology MA/MS (Master of Arts/Science) (T) 8.

Student Applications/Admissions:

Student Applications

Experimental Psychology MA/MS (Master of Arts/Science)—Applications 2012–2013, 7. Total applicants accepted 2012–2013, 6. Number full-time enrolled (new admits only) 2012–2013, 4. Number part-time enrolled (new admits only) 2012–2013, 0. Total enrolled 2012–2013 full-time, 4. Total enrolled 2012–2013 part-time, 0. Openings 2013–2014, 15. The median number of years required for completion of a degree in 2012–2013 were 2. The number of students enrolled full- and part-time who were dismissed or voluntarily withdrew from this program area in 2012–2013 were 0. *School Psychology EdS (School Psychology)*—Applications 2012–2013, 12. Total applicants accepted 2012–2013, 10. Number full-time enrolled (new admits only) 2012–2013, 8. Number part-time enrolled (new admits only) 2012–2013, 0. Total enrolled 2012–2013 full-time, 15. Total enrolled 2012–2013 part-time, 6. Openings 2013–2014, 15. The median number of years required for completion of a degree in 2012–2013 were 3. The number of students enrolled full- and part-time who were dismissed or voluntarily withdrew from this program area in 2012–2013 were 0. *Clinical Psychology MA/MS (Master of Arts/Science)*—Applications 2012–2013, 14. Total applicants accepted 2012–2013, 10. Number full-time enrolled (new admits only) 2012–2013, 7. Total enrolled 2012–2013 full-time, 18. Total enrolled 2012–2013 part-time, 2. Openings 2013–2014, 15. The median number of years required for completion of a degree in 2012–2013 were 2. *Industrial/Organizational Psychology MA/MS (Master of Arts/Science)*—Applications 2012–2013, 14. Total applicants accepted 2012–2013, 12. Number full-time enrolled (new admits only) 2012–2013, 7. Number part-time enrolled (new admits only) 2012–2013, 0. Total enrolled 2012–2013 full-time, 27. Total enrolled 2012–2013 part-time, 5. Openings 2013–2014, 15. The median number of years required for completion of a degree in 2012–2013 were 2. The number of students enrolled full- and part-time who were dismissed or voluntarily withdrew from this program area in 2012–2013 were 0.

Scores: Entries appear in this order: required test or GPA, minimum score (if required), median score of students entering in 2012–2013. *Experimental Psychology MA/MS (Master of Arts/Science):* GRE-V no minimum stated, GRE-Q no minimum stated, overall undergraduate GPA 3.00, last 2 years GPA 3.25; *School Psychology EdS (School Psychology):* GRE-V no minimum stated, GRE-Q no minimum stated, overall undergraduate GPA 3.00; *Clinical Psychology MA/MS (Master of Arts/Science):* GRE-V no minimum stated, GRE-Q no minimum stated, overall undergraduate GPA 3.00, last 2 years GPA 3.25, psychology GPA 3.0; *Industrial/Organizational Psychology MA/MS (Master of Arts/Science):* GRE-V no minimum stated, GRE-Q no minimum stated, overall undergraduate GPA 3.00.

Other Criteria: (importance of criteria rated low, medium, or high): GRE scores—medium, research experience—medium, work experience—medium, extracurricular activity—medium, clinically related public service—low, GPA—high, letters of recommendation—high, statement of goals and objectives—medium, undergraduate major in psychology—medium, specific undergraduate psychology courses taken—low. For additional information on admission requirements, go to http://www.emporia.edu/psych/graduate-programs/.

Student Characteristics: The following represents characteristics of students in 2012–2013 in all graduate psychology programs in the department: Female—full-time 48, part-time 12; Male—full-time 25, part-time 8; African American/Black—full-time 10, part-time 0; Hispanic/Latino(a)—full-time 4, part-time 0; Asian/Pacific Islander—full-time 2, part-time 0; American Indian/Alaska Native—full-time 0, part-time 0; Caucasian/White—full-time 51, part-time 0; Multi-ethnic—full-time 6, part-time 0; students subject to the Americans With Disabilities Act—full-time 1, part-time 0; Unknown ethnicity—full-time 0, part-time 0; International students who hold an F-1 or J-1 Visa—full-time 0, part-time 0.

Financial Information/Assistance:

Tuition for Full-Time Study: *Master's:* State residents: $207 per credit hour; Nonstate residents: $643 per credit hour. Tuition is subject to change. See the following website for updates and changes in tuition costs: http://www.emporia.edu/busaff/student-information/tuition-and-waivers.html.

Financial Assistance:

First-Year Students: Teaching assistantships available for first year. Average amount paid per academic year: $7,150. Average number of hours worked per week: 20. Apply by March 15. Research assistantships available for first year. Average amount paid per academic year: $7,150. Average number of hours worked per week: 20. Apply by March 15. Fellowships and scholarships available for first year. Average amount paid per academic year: $300.

Advanced Students: Teaching assistantships available for advanced students. Average amount paid per academic year:

$7,150. Average number of hours worked per week: 20. Apply by March 15. Research assistantships available for advanced students. Average amount paid per academic year: $7,150. Average number of hours worked per week: 20. Apply by March 15. Fellowships and scholarships available for advanced students. Average amount paid per academic year: $500.

Additional Information: Of all students currently enrolled full time, 50% benefited from one or more of the listed financial assistance programs. Application and information available online at: http://www.emporia.edu/grad/financial/.

Internships/Practica: Master's Degree (MA/MS Clinical Psychology): An internship experience, such as a final research project or "capstone" experience is required of graduates. Master's Degree (MA/MS Industrial/Organizational Psychology): An internship experience, such as a final research project or "capstone" experience is required of graduates. For Clinical students, internship is 750 clock hours in a mental health setting supervised by a PhD psychologist. For I/O students, the internship is 300 clock hours in a business setting performing I/O-related tasks. For Experimental students, the internship is defined as experiences working in a laboratory setting. School Psychology students do semester internships/practica in the schools. In addition, there is a one-year, paid, post-EdS internship for School Psychology.

Housing and Day Care: On-campus housing is available. See the following website for more information: http://www.emporia.edu/reslife/. On-campus day care facilities are available. See the following website for more information: http://www.emporia.edu/teach/cece/.

Employment of Department Graduates:

Master's Degree Graduates: Of those who graduated in the academic year 2011–2012, the following categories and numbers represent the postgraduate activities and employment of master's degree graduates: Enrolled in a psychology doctoral program (3), enrolled in another graduate/professional program (1), enrolled in a postdoctoral residency/fellowship (n/a), employed in independent practice (n/a), employed in an academic position at a university (1), employed in an academic position at a 2-year/4-year college (1), employed in a professional position in a school system (6), employed in business or industry (8), employed in government agency (2), employed in a community mental health/counseling center (7), employed in a hospital/medical center (1), still seeking employment (1), do not know (2), total from the above (master's) (33).

Doctoral Degree Graduates: Of those who graduated in the academic year 2011–2012, the following categories and numbers represent the postgraduate activities and employment of doctoral degree graduates: Enrolled in a psychology doctoral program (n/a), total from the above (doctoral) (0).

Additional Information:

Orientation, Objectives, and Emphasis of Department: Emporia State offers the Master of Science degree in general experimental psychology, clinical psychology, and industrial/organizational psychology. Additionally, students may pursue the EdS degree in school psychology.

Special Facilities or Resources: In 2012, all classrooms in the Department of Psychology were upgraded with multimedia technology. Facilities include cognitive, animal behavior, and physio-logical psychology laboratories; a complete animal vivarium; suites of rooms for administration of psychological tests and observation of testing or clinical and counseling sessions; and microprocessors and mainframe computer facilities. The computers and animal lab have been periodically updated every three years.

Information for Students With Physical Disabilities: See the following website for more information: http://www.emporia.edu/disability/.

Application Information:
Send to Dean of Graduate Studies and Research, Campus Box 4003, Emporia State University, 1200 Commercial Street, Emporia, KS 66801. Application available online. URL of online application: http://www.emporia.edu/grad/admissions/. Students are admitted in the Fall, application deadline March 1; Spring, application deadline October 1. Most programs have continuous admission/enrollment but the application deadline dates give the student the optimal opportunity for financial aid, etc. *Fee:* $40.

Fort Hays State University
Department of Psychology
600 Park Street
Hays, KS 67601-4099
Telephone: (785) 628-4405
Fax: (785) 628-5861
E-mail: *jmbondsraacke@fhsu.edu*
Web: *http://www.fhsu.edu/psych/*

Department Information:
1929. Chairperson: Jennifer Bonds-Raacke. Number of faculty: total—full-time 8, part-time 1; women—full-time 6, part-time 1; total—minority—full-time 1; women minority—full-time 1.

Programs and Degrees Offered:
Listed in the following order: Program area, degree type (T if terminal Master's), number awarded 7/11–6/12. Applied Clinical Psychology MA/MS (Master of Arts/Science) (T) 5, General Psychology MA/MS (Master of Arts/Science) (T) 0, School Psychology MA/MS (Master of Arts/Science) (T) 12, School Psychology EdS (School Psychology) 11.

Student Applications/Admissions:
Student Applications
Applied Clinical Psychology MA/MS *(Master of Arts/Science)*— Applications 2012–2013, 12. Total applicants accepted 2012–2013, 12. Number full-time enrolled (new admits only) 2012–2013, 7. Number part-time enrolled (new admits only) 2012–2013, 0. Total enrolled 2012–2013 full-time, 19. Total enrolled 2012–2013 part-time, 0. Openings 2013–2014, 7. The median number of years required for completion of a degree in 2012–2013 were 2. The number of students enrolled full- and part-time who were dismissed or voluntarily withdrew from this program area in 2012–2013 were 0. *General Psychology MA/MS (Master of Arts/Science)*—Applications 2012–2013, 5. Total applicants accepted 2012–2013, 2. Number full-time enrolled (new admits only) 2012–2013, 0. Number part-time enrolled (new admits only) 2012–2013, 0. Total enrolled 2012–2013 full-time, 4. Total enrolled 2012–2013 part-time, 0. Openings

2013–2014, 4. The number of students enrolled full- and part-time who were dismissed or voluntarily withdrew from this program area in 2012–2013 were 0. *School Psychology MA/MS (Master of Arts/Science)*—Applications 2012–2013, 16. Total applicants accepted 2012–2013, 12. Number full-time enrolled (new admits only) 2012–2013, 2. Number part-time enrolled (new admits only) 2012–2013, 10. Total enrolled 2012–2013 full-time, 2. Total enrolled 2012–2013 part-time, 10. Openings 2013–2014, 7. The median number of years required for completion of a degree in 2012–2013 were 2. The number of students enrolled full- and part-time who were dismissed or voluntarily withdrew from this program area in 2012–2013 were 0. *School Psychology EdS (School Psychology)*—Applications 2012–2013, 13. Total applicants accepted 2012–2013, 11. Number full-time enrolled (new admits only) 2012–2013, 5. Number part-time enrolled (new admits only) 2012–2013, 6. Total enrolled 2012–2013 full-time, 9. Total enrolled 2012–2013 part-time, 7. Openings 2013–2014, 4. The median number of years required for completion of a degree in 2012–2013 were 2.

Scores: Entries appear in this order: required test or GPA, minimum score (if required), median score of students entering in 2012–2013. *Applied Clinical Psychology MA/MS (Master of Arts/Science):* GRE-V no minimum stated, GRE-Q no minimum stated, overall undergraduate GPA 3.0, last 2 years GPA 3.0, psychology GPA 3.0; *General Psychology MA/MS (Master of Arts/Science):* GRE-V no minimum stated, GRE-Q no minimum stated, overall undergraduate GPA 3.0, last 2 years GPA 3.0, psychology GPA 3.0; *School Psychology MA/MS (Master of Arts/Science):* GRE-V no minimum stated, GRE-Q no minimum stated, overall undergraduate GPA 3.0, last 2 years GPA 3.0, psychology GPA 3.0; *School Psychology EdS (School Psychology):* GRE-V no minimum stated, GRE-Q no minimum stated, overall undergraduate GPA 3.0.

Other Criteria: (importance of criteria rated low, medium, or high): GRE scores—medium, research experience—medium, work experience—medium, extracurricular activity—medium, clinically related public service—medium, GPA—high, letters of recommendation—high, interview—medium, statement of goals and objectives—high, undergraduate major in psychology—medium, specific undergraduate psychology courses taken—medium. For additional information on admission requirements, go to http://www.fhsu.edu/psych/graduate-studies/.

Student Characteristics: The following represents characteristics of students in 2012–2013 in all graduate psychology programs in the department: Female—full-time 25, part-time 15; Male—full-time 9, part-time 2; African American/Black—full-time 2, part-time 1; Hispanic/Latino(a)—full-time 0, part-time 0; Asian/Pacific Islander—full-time 1, part-time 0; American Indian/Alaska Native—full-time 0, part-time 0; Caucasian/White—full-time 30, part-time 15; Multi-ethnic—full-time 1, part-time 0; students subject to the Americans With Disabilities Act—full-time 0, part-time 0; Unknown ethnicity—full-time 0, part-time 1; International students who hold an F-1 or J-1 Visa—full-time 1, part-time 0.

Financial Information/Assistance:

Tuition for Full-Time Study: *Master's:* State residents: $194 per credit hour; Nonstate residents: $493 per credit hour. Tuition is subject to change. See the following website for updates and

changes in tuition costs: http://www.fhsu.edu/academic/gradschl/tuition/.

Financial Assistance:

First-Year Students: Teaching assistantships available for first year. Apply by March 15.

Advanced Students: Teaching assistantships available for advanced students. Average amount paid per academic year: $3,500. Average number of hours worked per week: 9. Apply by March 15. Fellowships and scholarships available for advanced students. Average amount paid per academic year: $200. Apply by February 15.

Additional Information: Of all students currently enrolled full time, 70% benefited from one or more of the listed financial assistance programs. Application and information available online at: http://www.fhsu.edu/academic/gradschl/Graduate-Assistantships/.

Internships/Practica: Master's Degree (MA/MS Applied Clinical Psychology): An internship experience, such as a final research project or "capstone" experience is required of graduates. Master's Degree (MA/MS General Psychology): An internship experience, such as a final research project or "capstone" experience is required of graduates. All students in the applied psychology programs (clinical, school) are required to take a practicum in their specialty area. Students in the clinical psychology program receive initial practicum experience in the Kelly Center (an on-campus psychological services center), and then are required to complete an internship at a regional mental health agency or other approved agency. Students in the school psychology program receive initial practicum experience in a school district. School psychology graduates are also required to complete one year of paid, supervised post-EdS internship before being recommended for full Licensure (certification). Students in the general psychology program have the opportunity to take apprenticeships concentrating on the teaching of psychology.

Housing and Day Care: On-campus housing is available. See the following website for more information: http://www.fhsu.edu/reslife/. On-campus day care facilities are available. See the following website for more information: http://www.fhsu.edu/tigertots/.

Employment of Department Graduates:

Master's Degree Graduates: Of those who graduated in the academic year 2011–2012, the following categories and numbers represent the postgraduate activities and employment of master's degree graduates: Enrolled in another graduate/professional program (11), enrolled in a postdoctoral residency/fellowship (n/a), employed in independent practice (n/a), employed in an academic position at a university (1), employed in a professional position in a school system (11), employed in a community mental health/counseling center (1), do not know (3), total from the above (master's) (27).

Doctoral Degree Graduates: Of those who graduated in the academic year 2011–2012, the following categories and numbers represent the postgraduate activities and employment of doctoral degree graduates: Enrolled in a psychology doctoral program (n/a), total from the above (doctoral) (0).

Additional Information:

Orientation, Objectives, and Emphasis of Department: The department emphasizes a research approach to the understanding of behavior. We strive to provide basic empirical and theoretical foundations of psychology to prepare the student for doctoral study, for teaching, or for employment in a service or professional agency. The school program offers broad preparation for students in both psychology and education and includes training as a consultant to work with educators and parents as well as with children. The clinical program emphasizes the preparation of rural mental health workers, although many graduates go on to doctoral programs. The general program is intended to prepare the student for doctoral study.

Special Facilities or Resources: The Department of Psychology now occupies a newly remodeled building in the center of campus. Some of the new facilities in this building include: a 25-machine computer facility with separate spaces for individualized research and full Internet connections; testing and observation rooms for children, adults, and small groups; separate research and teaching labs for the major areas of psychology; and several seminar rooms. We are located adjacent to the student psychological services center. There is an active social organization for psychology graduate students. All students at the university have free remote Internet access.

Information for Students With Physical Disabilities: See the following website for more information: http://www.fhsu.edu/disability/.

Application Information:
Send to Dean of the Graduate School, Fort Hays State University, 600 Park Street, Hays, KS 67601-4099. Application available online. URL of online application: https://secure.fhsu.edu/Admissions/ApplyToGradSchool.aspx. Programs have rolling admissions. Deadline for financial aid is March 1. *Fee:* $35.

Kansas State University
Department of Psychological Sciences
College of Arts and Sciences
492 Bluemont Hall
1100 Mid-Campus Drive
Manhattan, KS 66506-5302
Telephone: (785) 532-6850
Fax: (785) 532-5401
E-mail: *psych@ksu.edu*
Web: *http://www.k-state.edu/psych*

Department Information:
1951. Head: Michael Young. Number of faculty: total—full-time 15, part-time 2; women—full-time 4, part-time 2; total—minority—full-time 1; women minority—full-time 1.

Programs and Degrees Offered:
Listed in the following order: Program area, degree type (T if terminal Master's), number awarded 7/11–6/12. Animal Learning/Behavioral Neuroscience PhD (Doctor of Philosophy) 1, Cognitive and Human Factors PhD (Doctor of Philosophy) 3, Social/Personality Psychology PhD (Doctor of Philosophy) 3, Industrial/

Organizational Psychology PhD (Doctor of Philosophy) 1, Industrial/Organizational (Distance) MA/MS (Master of Arts/Science) (T) 10, Occupational Health Psychology Other 3.

Student Applications/Admissions:
Student Applications
Animal Learning/Behavioral Neuroscience PhD (Doctor of Philosophy)—Applications 2012–2013, 10. Total applicants accepted 2012–2013, 3. Number full-time enrolled (new admits only) 2012–2013, 0. Number part-time enrolled (new admits only) 2012–2013, 0. Total enrolled 2012–2013 full-time, 6. Total enrolled 2012–2013 part-time, 0. Openings 2013–2014, 2. The median number of years required for completion of a degree in 2012–2013 were 5. The number of students enrolled full- and part-time who were dismissed or voluntarily withdrew from this program area in 2012–2013 were 0. *Cognitive and Human Factors PhD (Doctor of Philosophy)*—Applications 2012–2013, 25. Total applicants accepted 2012–2013, 5. Number full-time enrolled (new admits only) 2012–2013, 5. Number part-time enrolled (new admits only) 2012–2013, 0. Total enrolled 2012–2013 full-time, 10. Total enrolled 2012–2013 part-time, 0. Openings 2013–2014, 1. The median number of years required for completion of a degree in 2012–2013 were 5. The number of students enrolled full- and part-time who were dismissed or voluntarily withdrew from this program area in 2012–2013 were 0. *Social/Personality Psychology PhD (Doctor of Philosophy)*—Applications 2012–2013, 40. Total applicants accepted 2012–2013, 2. Number full-time enrolled (new admits only) 2012–2013, 2. Total enrolled 2012–2013 full-time, 15. Openings 2013–2014, 1. The median number of years required for completion of a degree in 2012–2013 were 5. The number of students enrolled full- and part-time who were dismissed or voluntarily withdrew from this program area in 2012–2013 were 0. *Industrial/Organizational Psychology PhD (Doctor of Philosophy)*—Applications 2012–2013, 40. Total applicants accepted 2012–2013, 3. Number full-time enrolled (new admits only) 2012–2013, 3. Number part-time enrolled (new admits only) 2012–2013, 0. Total enrolled 2012–2013 full-time, 10. Total enrolled 2012–2013 part-time, 0. Openings 2013–2014, 2. The median number of years required for completion of a degree in 2012–2013 were 5. The number of students enrolled full- and part-time who were dismissed or voluntarily withdrew from this program area in 2012–2013 were 0. *Industrial/Organizational (Distance) MA/MS (Master of Arts/Science)*—Applications 2012–2013, 30. Total applicants accepted 2012–2013, 10. Number part-time enrolled (new admits only) 2012–2013, 12. Total enrolled 2012–2013 part-time, 25. Openings 2013–2014, 10. The median number of years required for completion of a degree in 2012–2013 were 2. The number of students enrolled full- and part-time who were dismissed or voluntarily withdrew from this program area in 2012–2013 were 0. *Occupational Health Psychology Other*—Applications 2012–2013, 5. Total applicants accepted 2012–2013, 4. Number part-time enrolled (new admits only) 2012–2013, 4. Total enrolled 2012–2013 part-time, 6. Openings 2013–2014, 10. The median number of years required for completion of a degree in 2012–2013 were 2. The number of students enrolled full- and part-time who were dismissed or voluntarily withdrew from this program area in 2012–2013 were 1.

Scores: Entries appear in this order: required test or GPA, minimum score (if required), median score of students entering

in 2012–2013. *Cognitive and Human Factors PhD (Doctor of Philosophy)*: overall undergraduate GPA 3.0; *Industrial/Organizational (Distance) MA/MS (Master of Arts/Science)*: overall undergraduate GPA 3.0.

Other Criteria: (importance of criteria rated low, medium, or high): GRE scores—high, research experience—high, work experience—low, extracurricular activity—low, clinically related public service—low, GPA—high, letters of recommendation—high, statement of goals and objectives—high, undergraduate major in psychology—high, specific undergraduate psychology courses taken—medium. For additional information on admission requirements, go to http://www.k-state.edu/psych/graduate/application/procedures.html.

Student Characteristics: The following represents characteristics of students in 2012–2013 in all graduate psychology programs in the department: Female—full-time 20, part-time 15; Male—full-time 25, part-time 10; African American/Black—full-time 1, part-time 1; Hispanic/Latino(a)—full-time 2, part-time 2; Asian/Pacific Islander—full-time 2, part-time 0; American Indian/Alaska Native—full-time 0, part-time 0; Caucasian/White—full-time 39, part-time 7; Multi-ethnic—full-time 1, part-time 0; students subject to the Americans With Disabilities Act—full-time 0, part-time 0; Unknown ethnicity—full-time 0, part-time 0; International students who hold an F-1 or J-1 Visa—full-time 1, part-time 0.

Financial Information/Assistance:

Tuition for Full-Time Study: *Master's:* State residents: $327 per credit hour; Nonstate residents: $738 per credit hour. *Doctoral:* State residents: $327 per credit hour; Nonstate residents: $738 per credit hour. Tuition is subject to change. See the following website for updates and changes in tuition costs: http://www.k-state.edu/finsvcs/cashiers/tuitionfeesinfo.html.

Financial Assistance:

First-Year Students: Teaching assistantships available for first year. Average amount paid per academic year: $10,437. Average number of hours worked per week: 20. Apply by January 15. Research assistantships available for first year. Average amount paid per academic year: $15,900. Average number of hours worked per week: 20. Apply by January 15.

Advanced Students: Teaching assistantships available for advanced students. Average amount paid per academic year: $10,437. Average number of hours worked per week: 20. Research assistantships available for advanced students. Average amount paid per academic year: $15,900. Average number of hours worked per week: 20.

Additional Information: Of all students currently enrolled full time, 85% benefited from one or more of the listed financial assistance programs. Application and information available online at: http://www.k-state.edu/psych/graduate/application/financial.html.

Internships/Practica: Arrangements for internships in human factors/applied experimental and industrial/organizational psychology vary widely and are made on an individual basis.

Housing and Day Care: On-campus housing is available. See the following website for more information: http://housing.k-state.edu/living-options/apartments/. On-campus day care facilities are available. See the following website for more information: http://www.k-state.edu/ccd/.

Employment of Department Graduates:

Master's Degree Graduates: Of those who graduated in the academic year 2011–2012, the following categories and numbers represent the postgraduate activities and employment of master's degree graduates: Enrolled in a psychology doctoral program (5), enrolled in a postdoctoral residency/fellowship (n/a), employed in independent practice (n/a), employed in an academic position at a university (1), employed in an academic position at a 2-year/4-year college (1), employed in other positions at a higher education institution (1), employed in a professional position in a school system (1), employed in business or industry (1), employed in government agency (1), total from the above (master's) (11).

Doctoral Degree Graduates: Of those who graduated in the academic year 2011–2012, the following categories and numbers represent the postgraduate activities and employment of doctoral degree graduates: Enrolled in a psychology doctoral program (n/a), enrolled in another graduate/professional program (1), enrolled in a postdoctoral residency/fellowship (1), employed in independent practice (1), employed in an academic position at a university (1), employed in an academic position at a 2-year/4-year college (1), employed in other positions at a higher education institution (1), employed in a professional position in a school system (1), employed in business or industry (1), employed in government agency (1), total from the above (doctoral) (9).

Additional Information:

Orientation, Objectives, and Emphasis of Department: Both teaching and research are heavily emphasized. Training prepares students for a variety of positions, including teaching and research positions in colleges and universities. Students have also assumed research and evaluative positions in hospitals, clinics, governmental agencies, and industry.

Special Facilities or Resources: The department has rooms for individual and group research; several computer laboratories and remote terminal access to mainframe computers; a photographic darkroom; one-way observation facilities; an electrically shielded, light-tight, sound-deadened room for auditory and visual research; laboratories for behavioral research with animals; surgical and histological facilities; and colony rooms.

Information for Students With Physical Disabilities: See the following website for more information: http://www.k-state.edu/dss/.

Application Information:

Send to Graduate Admissions, Department of Psychology, 492 Bluemont Hall, 1100 Mid-campus Drive, Kansas State University, Manhattan, KS 66506-5302. Application available online. URL of online application: https://www.k-state.edu/admit/apply/applynow.html?type=grad. Students are admitted in the Fall, application deadline January 15. Applicants for the Distance Master's Program in Industrial/Organizational Psychology should apply online at http://www.k-state.edu/psych/graduate/distance/iomasters.html. The deadline for applications is April 30th. *Fee:* $50. International applicants must pay a $75 application fee.

Kansas, University of

Department of Applied Behavioral Science
College of Liberal Arts and Sciences
1000 Sunnyside Avenue
Lawrence, KS 66045-7555
Telephone: (785) 864-4840
Fax: (785) 864-5202
E-mail: *absc@ku.edu*
Web: *http://www.absc.ku.edu/*

Department Information:
1964. Chairperson: Edward K. Morris. Number of faculty: total—full-time 18; women—full-time 8; total—minority—full-time 2; women minority—full-time 2; faculty subject to the Americans With Disabilities Act 1.

Programs and Degrees Offered:
Listed in the following order: Program area, degree type (T if terminal Master's), number awarded 7/11–6/12. Behavioral Psychology PhD (Doctor of Philosophy) 8, Applied Behavioral Science MA/MS (Master of Arts/Science) 3.

Student Applications/Admissions:
Student Applications

Behavioral Psychology PhD (Doctor of Philosophy)—Applications 2012–2013, 55. Total applicants accepted 2012–2013, 6. Number full-time enrolled (new admits only) 2012–2013, 6. Total enrolled 2012–2013 full-time, 55. Openings 2013–2014, 8. The median number of years required for completion of a degree in 2012–2013 were 6. The number of students enrolled full- and part-time who were dismissed or voluntarily withdrew from this program area in 2012–2013 were 0. *Applied Behavioral Science MA/MS (Master of Arts/Science)*—Applications 2012–2013, 6. Total applicants accepted 2012–2013, 2. Number full-time enrolled (new admits only) 2012–2013, 0. Total enrolled 2012–2013 full-time, 6. Openings 2013–2014, 2. The median number of years required for completion of a degree in 2012–2013 were 3. The number of students enrolled full- and part-time who were dismissed or voluntarily withdrew from this program area in 2012–2013 were 0.

Other Criteria: (importance of criteria rated low, medium, or high): GRE scores—medium, research experience—high, work experience—high, extracurricular activity—low, clinically related public service—medium, GPA—high, letters of recommendation—high, interview—high, statement of goals and objectives—high, undergraduate major in psychology—medium, specific undergraduate psychology courses taken—low, Applicants designate individual faculty members whom they want as advisors. Only those faculty members review the applications and make their admission decisions. For additional information on admission requirements, go to http://www.absc.ku.edu/graduate/prospective.shtml.

Student Characteristics: The following represents characteristics of students in 2012–2013 in all graduate psychology programs in the department: Female—full-time 43, part-time 0; Male—full-time 18, part-time 0; African American/Black—full-time 4, part-time 0; Hispanic/Latino(a)—full-time 2, part-time 0; Asian/Pacific Islander—full-time 1, part-time 0; American Indian/Alaska Native—full-time 1, part-time 0; Caucasian/White—full-time 51,

part-time 0; Multi-ethnic—full-time 2, part-time 0; students subject to the Americans With Disabilities Act—full-time 3, part-time 0; Unknown ethnicity—full-time 0, part-time 0; International students who hold an F-1 or J-1 Visa—full-time 4, part-time 0.

Financial Information/Assistance:
Tuition for Full-Time Study: *Master's:* State residents: $330 per credit hour; Nonstate residents: $771 per credit hour. *Doctoral:* State residents: $330 per credit hour; Nonstate residents: $771 per credit hour. Tuition is subject to change. Additional fees are assessed to students beyond the costs of tuition for the following: student services. Tuition costs vary by program. See the following website for updates and changes in tuition costs: http://affordability.ku.edu/cs/index.shtml.

Financial Assistance:
First-Year Students: Teaching assistantships available for first year. Apply by December 15. Research assistantships available for first year. Apply by December 15. Traineeships available for first year. Apply by December 15. Fellowships and scholarships available for first year. Apply by December 15.

Advanced Students: Teaching assistantships available for advanced students. Research assistantships available for advanced students. Traineeships available for advanced students. Fellowships and scholarships available for advanced students.

Additional Information: Of all students currently enrolled full time, 80% benefited from one or more of the listed financial assistance programs. Application and information available online at: http://www.graduate.ku.edu/funding-opportunities.

Internships/Practica: A wide variety of research settings and practicum sites are available to graduate students. They include: Behavioral Pediatrics; Center for Independent Living; Center for the Study of Mental Retardation and Related Problems; Child and Family Research Center; Community Programs for Adults with Mental Retardation; Edna A. Hill Child Development Center; Experimental Analysis of Behavior Laboratories; Performance Management Laboratory; Family Enhancement Project; Gerontology Center; Juniper Gardens Project; Research on Children with Retardation; Schiefelbusch Institute for Life Span Studies; Work Group on Health Promotion and Community Development.

Housing and Day Care: On-campus housing is available. See the following website for more information: http://www.housing.ku.edu/. On-campus day care facilities are available. See the following website for more information: http://www.hilltop.ku.edu/.

Employment of Department Graduates:
Master's Degree Graduates: Of those who graduated in the academic year 2011–2012, the following categories and numbers represent the postgraduate activities and employment of master's degree graduates: Enrolled in a psychology doctoral program (1), enrolled in a postdoctoral residency/fellowship (n/a), employed in independent practice (n/a), employed in a professional position in a school system (1), do not know (1), total from the above (master's) (3).
Doctoral Degree Graduates: Of those who graduated in the academic year 2011–2012, the following categories and numbers represent the postgraduate activities and employment of doctoral degree graduates: Enrolled in a psychology doctoral program (n/a),

enrolled in a postdoctoral residency/fellowship (1), employed in an academic position at a university (3), total from the above (doctoral) (4).

Additional Information:

Orientation, Objectives, and Emphasis of Department: The primary purpose of the program is to train students in basic and applied research in behavior analysis. It features emphases in applied behavior analysis, early childhood, developmental disabilities, organizational behavior management, community health and development, the experimental analysis of human and animal behavior, conceptual issues in behavior analysis, independent living, and rehabilitation. Throughout the PhD training sequence, students work closely as junior colleagues with a faculty adviser and a research group. Although students typically work with one faculty adviser, they are free to select a different adviser if their interests change during the course of their training. Students participate in research throughout their graduate careers in an individualized, intensive program. As a result, most students complete more research projects than those required for the degree.

Special Facilities or Resources: A wide range of research settings are available to graduate students. Populations and settings include both typically developing and disabled infants, toddlers, preschool children, elementary school settings, adolescents, adults, and elders. In addition, the department has an animal laboratory facility.

Information for Students With Physical Disabilities: See the following website for more information: http://www.disability.ku.edu/.

Application Information:

Send to Graduate Admissions, University of Kansas, Applied Behavioral Science, 1000 Sunnyside Avenue, 4001 Dole, Lawrence KS 66047. Application available online. URL of online application: https://www.applyweb.com/apply/kugrad/. Students are admitted in the Fall, application deadline December 15. *Fee:* $55.

Kansas, University of
Department of Psychology
College of Liberal Arts and Sciences
426 Fraser Hall
1415 Jayhawk Boulevard
Lawrence, KS 66045-7556
Telephone: (785) 864-4195
Fax: (785) 864-5696
E-mail: *psycgrad@ku.edu*
Web: *http://psych.ku.edu/*

Department Information:
1916. Chairperson: Ruth Ann Atchley. Number of faculty: total—full-time 24, part-time 12; women—full-time 10, part-time 5; total—minority—full-time 2, part-time 1; women minority—full-time 1, part-time 1.

Programs and Degrees Offered:
Listed in the following order: Program area, degree type (T if terminal Master's), number awarded 7/11–6/12. Clinical Psychol-

ogy PhD (Doctor of Philosophy) 8, Cognitive Psychology PhD (Doctor of Philosophy) 3, Quantitative Psychology PhD (Doctor of Philosophy) 3, Social Psychology PhD (Doctor of Philosophy) 5, Developmental Psychology PhD (Doctor of Philosophy) 1.

APA Accreditation: Clinical PhD (Doctor of Philosophy). Student Outcome Data Website: http://psych.ku.edu/clinical/.

Student Applications/Admissions:
Student Applications

Clinical Psychology PhD (Doctor of Philosophy)—Applications 2012–2013, 118. Total applicants accepted 2012–2013, 7. Number full-time enrolled (new admits only) 2012–2013, 4. Number part-time enrolled (new admits only) 2012–2013, 0. Total enrolled 2012–2013 full-time, 41. Total enrolled 2012–2013 part-time, 0. Openings 2013–2014, 6. The median number of years required for completion of a degree in 2012–2013 were 6. The number of students enrolled full- and part-time who were dismissed or voluntarily withdrew from this program area in 2012–2013 were 0. *Cognitive Psychology PhD (Doctor of Philosophy)*—Applications 2012–2013, 17. Total applicants accepted 2012–2013, 3. Number full-time enrolled (new admits only) 2012–2013, 3. Total enrolled 2012–2013 full-time, 15. Total enrolled 2012–2013 part-time, 0. Openings 2013–2014, 3. The median number of years required for completion of a degree in 2012–2013 were 6. The number of students enrolled full- and part-time who were dismissed or voluntarily withdrew from this program area in 2012–2013 were 2. *Quantitative Psychology PhD (Doctor of Philosophy)*—Applications 2012–2013, 21. Total applicants accepted 2012–2013, 9. Number full-time enrolled (new admits only) 2012–2013, 3. Total enrolled 2012–2013 full-time, 18. Total enrolled 2012–2013 part-time, 0. Openings 2013–2014, 5. The median number of years required for completion of a degree in 2012–2013 were 6. The number of students enrolled full- and part-time who were dismissed or voluntarily withdrew from this program area in 2012–2013 were 0. *Social Psychology PhD (Doctor of Philosophy)*—Applications 2012–2013, 76. Total applicants accepted 2012–2013, 10. Number full-time enrolled (new admits only) 2012–2013, 3. Total enrolled 2012–2013 full-time, 21. Total enrolled 2012–2013 part-time, 0. Openings 2013–2014, 5. The median number of years required for completion of a degree in 2012–2013 were 6. The number of students enrolled full- and part-time who were dismissed or voluntarily withdrew from this program area in 2012–2013 were 3. *Developmental Psychology PhD (Doctor of Philosophy)*—Applications 2012–2013, 17. Total applicants accepted 2012–2013, 1. Number full-time enrolled (new admits only) 2012–2013, 0. Total enrolled 2012–2013 full-time, 4. Openings 2013–2014, 2. The median number of years required for completion of a degree in 2012–2013 were 6. The number of students enrolled full- and part-time who were dismissed or voluntarily withdrew from this program area in 2012–2013 were 0.

Scores: Entries appear in this order: required test or GPA, minimum score (if required), median score of students entering in 2012–2013. *Clinical Psychology PhD (Doctor of Philosophy):* GRE-V no minimum stated, 598, GRE-Q no minimum stated, 638, GRE-Analytical no minimum stated, 4.80, overall undergraduate GPA 3.0, 3.68.

Other Criteria: (importance of criteria rated low, medium, or high): GRE scores—high, research experience—high, work

experience—medium, extracurricular activity—low, clinically related public service—medium, GPA—high, letters of recommendation—high, interview—high, statement of goals and objectives—high, undergraduate major in psychology—medium, specific undergraduate psychology courses taken—medium, Writing sample for Clinical programs only. For additional information on admission requirements, go to http://psych.ku.edu/academics/graduate/apply/.

Student Characteristics: The following represents characteristics of students in 2012–2013 in all graduate psychology programs in the department: Female—full-time 65, part-time 0; Male—full-time 34, part-time 0; African American/Black—full-time 3, part-time 0; Hispanic/Latino(a)—full-time 2, part-time 0; Asian/Pacific Islander—full-time 11, part-time 0; American Indian/Alaska Native—full-time 0, part-time 0; Caucasian/White—full-time 67, part-time 0; Multi-ethnic—full-time 2, part-time 0; students subject to the Americans With Disabilities Act—full-time 2, part-time 0; Unknown ethnicity—full-time 14, part-time 0; International students who hold an F-1 or J-1 Visa—full-time 14, part-time 0.

Financial Information/Assistance:

Tuition for Full-Time Study: *Doctoral:* State residents: $329 per credit hour; Nonstate residents: $771 per credit hour. Tuition is subject to change. See the following website for updates and changes in tuition costs: http://affordability.ku.edu/cs/index.shtml.

Financial Assistance:

First-Year Students: Teaching assistantships available for first year. Average amount paid per academic year: $13,005. Average number of hours worked per week: 20. Apply by December 1. Research assistantships available for first year. Average amount paid per academic year: $12,980. Average number of hours worked per week: 20. Apply by December 1. Fellowships and scholarships available for first year. Apply by December 1.

Advanced Students: Teaching assistantships available for advanced students. Average amount paid per academic year: $13,359. Average number of hours worked per week: 20. Research assistantships available for advanced students. Average amount paid per academic year: $13,600. Average number of hours worked per week: 20. Fellowships and scholarships available for advanced students. Average number of hours worked per week: 0.

Additional Information: Of all students currently enrolled full time, 92% benefited from one or more of the listed financial assistance programs.

Internships/Practica: Doctoral Degree (PhD Clinical Psychology): For those doctoral students for whom a professional psychology internship was required in this program prior to graduation, (4) students applied for an internship in 2011–2012, with (4) students obtaining an internship. Of those students who obtained an internship, (4) were paid internships. Of those students who obtained an internship, (4) students placed in APA/CPA accredited internships, (0) students placed in internships not APA/CPA accredited, but listed with the Association of Psychology Postdoctoral and Internship Programs (APPIC), (0) students placed in internships conforming to guidelines of the Council of

Directors of School Psychology Programs (CDSPP), (0) students placed in internships that were not APA/CPA accredited, APPIC or CDSPP listed.

Housing and Day Care: On-campus housing is available. See the following website for more information: http://www.housing.ku.edu/. On-campus day care facilities are available. See the following website for more information: http://www.hilltop.ku.edu/.

Employment of Department Graduates:

Master's Degree Graduates: Of those who graduated in the academic year 2011–2012, the following categories and numbers represent the postgraduate activities and employment of master's degree graduates: Enrolled in a postdoctoral residency/fellowship (n/a), employed in independent practice (n/a), total from the above (master's) (0).

Doctoral Degree Graduates: Of those who graduated in the academic year 2011–2012, the following categories and numbers represent the postgraduate activities and employment of doctoral degree graduates: Enrolled in a psychology doctoral program (n/a), enrolled in a postdoctoral residency/fellowship (8), employed in an academic position at a university (5), other employment position (2), do not know (4), total from the above (doctoral) (19).

Additional Information:

Orientation, Objectives, and Emphasis of Department: With 36 faculty, the department offers a wide range of opportunities for the study and treatment of human psychological and behavioral functioning. Students develop skills in statistics, research methods, and specific content areas with basic and applied emphases, with the flexibility to tailor programs to individual students' needs. Students in all programs (Clinical, Developmental, Quantitative, Cognitive or Social) may also complete coursework toward a minor in quantitative psychology.

Special Facilities or Resources: The department has well-equipped computer labs and access to university mainframe computers. Clinical and research support facilities include an on-site clinic with a test resource library, individual and group therapy rooms, and play and psychodrama rooms. Specialized research facilities include interview rooms with audio and video capacities, psychophysiological and stress laboratories, ERP facilities, eye-movement monitoring laboratories, and an anechoic chamber. The Kansas University Medical Center houses the Hoglund Brain Imaging Center, a state-of-the-art facility with fMRI and MEG laboratories.

Information for Students With Physical Disabilities: See the following website for more information: http://www.disability.ku.edu/.

Application Information:

Send to The University of Kansas, Graduate School, 1450 Jayhawk Boulevard, Room 313, Lawrence, KS 66045-7535. Application available online. URL of online application: http://www.graduate.ku.edu/apply. Students are admitted in the Fall, application deadline December 1. *Fee:* $55. $65 for international applicants.

Kansas, University of
Psychology and Research in Education
School of Education
Joseph R. Pearson Hall, 1122 West Campus Road, Room 621
Lawrence, KS 66045-3101
Telephone: (785) 864-3931
Fax: (785) 864-3820
E-mail: *preadmit@ku.edu*
Web: *http://pre.soe.ku.edu/*

Department Information:

1955. Chairperson: Steven W. Lee, PhD. Number of faculty: total—full-time 14, part-time 7; women—full-time 4, part-time 5; total—minority—full-time 1, part-time 1; women minority—full-time 1, part-time 1.

Programs and Degrees Offered:

Listed in the following order: Program area, degree type (T if terminal Master's), number awarded 7/11–6/12. School Psychology PhD (Doctor of Philosophy) 3, Counseling Psychology MA/MS (Master of Arts/Science) (T) 18, Educational Psychology and Research PhD (Doctor of Philosophy) 2, Educational Psychology and Research MEd (Education) 2, Counseling Psychology PhD (Doctor of Philosophy) 4, School Psychology EdS (School Psychology) 9.

APA Accreditation: School PhD (Doctor of Philosophy). Student Outcome Data Website: http://soe.ku.edu/pre/academics/psy/doctorate/. Counseling PhD (Doctor of Philosophy). Student Outcome Data Website: http://pre.soe.ku.edu/academics/cpsy/doctorate.

Student Applications/Admissions:

Student Applications

School Psychology PhD (Doctor of Philosophy)—Applications 2012–2013, 10. Total applicants accepted 2012–2013, 8. Number full-time enrolled (new admits only) 2012–2013, 2. Number part-time enrolled (new admits only) 2012–2013, 0. Total enrolled 2012–2013 full-time, 18. Total enrolled 2012–2013 part-time, 0. Openings 2013–2014, 5. The median number of years required for completion of a degree in 2012–2013 were 5. The number of students enrolled full- and part-time who were dismissed or voluntarily withdrew from this program area in 2012–2013 were 0. *Counseling Psychology MA/MS (Master of Arts/Science)*—Applications 2012–2013, 54. Total applicants accepted 2012–2013, 23. Number full-time enrolled (new admits only) 2012–2013, 12. Number part-time enrolled (new admits only) 2012–2013, 0. Total enrolled 2012–2013 full-time, 34. Total enrolled 2012–2013 part-time, 0. Openings 2013–2014, 15. The median number of years required for completion of a degree in 2012–2013 were 3. The number of students enrolled full- and part-time who were dismissed or voluntarily withdrew from this program area in 2012–2013 were 0. *Educational Psychology and Research PhD (Doctor of Philosophy)*—Applications 2012–2013, 14. Total applicants accepted 2012–2013, 9. Number full-time enrolled (new admits only) 2012–2013, 7. Number part-time enrolled (new admits only) 2012–2013, 0. Total enrolled 2012–2013 full-time, 33.

Total enrolled 2012–2013 part-time, 0. Openings 2013–2014, 4. The median number of years required for completion of a degree in 2012–2013 were 4. The number of students enrolled full- and part-time who were dismissed or voluntarily withdrew from this program area in 2012–2013 were 0. *Educational Psychology and Research MEd (Education)*—Applications 2012–2013, 17. Total applicants accepted 2012–2013, 6. Number full-time enrolled (new admits only) 2012–2013, 4. Number part-time enrolled (new admits only) 2012–2013, 0. Total enrolled 2012–2013 full-time, 11. Total enrolled 2012–2013 part-time, 0. Openings 2013–2014, 1. The median number of years required for completion of a degree in 2012–2013 were 2. The number of students enrolled full- and part-time who were dismissed or voluntarily withdrew from this program area in 2012–2013 were 0. *Counseling Psychology PhD (Doctor of Philosophy)*—Applications 2012–2013, 47. Total applicants accepted 2012–2013, 13. Number full-time enrolled (new admits only) 2012–2013, 12. Number part-time enrolled (new admits only) 2012–2013, 0. Total enrolled 2012–2013 full-time, 30. Total enrolled 2012–2013 part-time, 0. Openings 2013–2014, 8. The median number of years required for completion of a degree in 2012–2013 were 5. The number of students enrolled full- and part-time who were dismissed or voluntarily withdrew from this program area in 2012–2013 were 1. *School Psychology EdS (School Psychology)*—Applications 2012–2013, 9. Total applicants accepted 2012–2013, 7. Number full-time enrolled (new admits only) 2012–2013, 3. Total enrolled 2012–2013 full-time, 15. Openings 2013–2014, 8. The median number of years required for completion of a degree in 2012–2013 were 3. The number of students enrolled full- and part-time who were dismissed or voluntarily withdrew from this program area in 2012–2013 were 0.

Scores: Entries appear in this order: required test or GPA, minimum score (if required), median score of students entering in 2012–2013. *School Psychology PhD (Doctor of Philosophy):* GRE-V no minimum stated, 156, GRE-Q no minimum stated, 152, GRE-Analytical no minimum stated, 4.5; *Counseling Psychology PhD (Doctor of Philosophy):* GRE-V no minimum stated, 153, GRE-Q no minimum stated, 145, GRE-Analytical no minimum stated, 4.5, overall undergraduate GPA no minimum stated, 3.65; *School Psychology EdS (School Psychology):* GRE-V no minimum stated, 156, GRE-Q no minimum stated, 149, GRE-Analytical no minimum stated, 4.

Other Criteria: (importance of criteria rated low, medium, or high): GRE scores—high, research experience—medium, work experience—medium, extracurricular activity—low, clinically related public service—low, GPA—high, letters of recommendation—high, interview—high, statement of goals and objectives—high, The admission criteria above are for applicants to the Counseling Psychology PhD program. The admission criteria for applicants to the School Psychology PhD program are: GRE/MAT scores-HIGH; research experience-HIGH; work experience-MEDIUM; extracurricular activity-LOW; clinically related public service-HIGH; UGPA-HIGH; letters of recommendation-HIGH; statement of goals and objectives-HIGH. For additional information on admission requirements, go to http://pre.soe.ku.edu/admission.

Student Characteristics: The following represents characteristics of students in 2012–2013 in all graduate psychology programs in the department: Female—full-time 96, part-time 0; Male—full-time 45, part-time 0; African American/Black—full-time 5, part-

time 0; Hispanic/Latino(a)—full-time 0, part-time 0; Asian/Pacific Islander—full-time 5, part-time 0; American Indian/Alaska Native—full-time 0, part-time 0; Caucasian/White—full-time 96, part-time 0; Multi-ethnic—full-time 8, part-time 0; students subject to the Americans With Disabilities Act—full-time 0, part-time 0; Unknown ethnicity—full-time 27, part-time 0; International students who hold an F-1 or J-1 Visa—full-time 28, part-time 0.

Financial Information/Assistance:

Tuition for Full-Time Study: *Master's:* State residents: $329 per credit hour; Nonstate residents: $771 per credit hour. *Doctoral:* State residents: $329 per credit hour; Nonstate residents: $771 per credit hour. Tuition is subject to change. Additional fees are assessed to students beyond the costs of tuition for the following: campus fees- $74.00/credit hour if fewer than 5 hrs or $444.00 if over 5 credit hours. See the following website for updates and changes in tuition costs: http://www.registrar.ku.edu/tuition-and-fees. Higher tuition cost for this program: The School of Education has a differential tuition fee of $22.55 per credit hour.

Financial Assistance:

First-Year Students: Teaching assistantships available for first year. Average amount paid per academic year: $7,800. Average number of hours worked per week: 12. Apply by March 15. Research assistantships available for first year. Average amount paid per academic year: $7,000. Average number of hours worked per week: 12. Fellowships and scholarships available for first year.

Advanced Students: Teaching assistantships available for advanced students. Average amount paid per academic year: $8,200. Average number of hours worked per week: 12. Apply by March 15. Research assistantships available for advanced students. Average amount paid per academic year: $13,000. Average number of hours worked per week: 20. Fellowships and scholarships available for advanced students.

Additional Information: Of all students currently enrolled full time, 80% benefited from one or more of the listed financial assistance programs. Application and information available online at: http://www.soe.ku.edu/scholarships/.

Internships/Practica: Doctoral Degree (PhD School Psychology): For those doctoral students for whom a professional psychology internship was required in this program prior to graduation, (1) students applied for an internship in 2011–2012, with (1) students obtaining an internship. Of those students who obtained an internship, (1) were paid internships. Of those students who obtained an internship, (0) students placed in APA/CPA accredited internships, (0) students placed in internships not APA/CPA accredited, but listed with the Association of Psychology Postdoctoral and Internship Programs (APPIC), (1) students placed in internships conforming to guidelines of the Council of Directors of School Psychology Programs (CDSPP), (0) students placed in internships that were not APA/CPA accredited, APPIC or CDSPP listed. Doctoral Degree (PhD Counseling Psychology): For those doctoral students for whom a professional psychology internship was required in this program prior to graduation, (9) students applied for an internship in 2011–2012, with (9) students

obtaining an internship. Of those students who obtained an internship, (9) were paid internships. Of those students who obtained an internship, (9) students placed in APA/CPA accredited internships, (0) students placed in internships not APA/CPA accredited, but listed with the Association of Psychology Postdoctoral and Internship Programs (APPIC), (0) students placed in internships conforming to guidelines of the Council of Directors of School Psychology Programs (CDSPP), (0) students placed in internships that were not APA/CPA accredited, APPIC or CDSPP listed. The Counseling Psychology and School Psychology programs require practicum and/or internship courses as part of the degree requirements. Additionally, PRE graduate students enroll in field experience, seminars, and specific PRE courses to obtain additional training with special populations and/or psychological testing procedures. Counseling Psychology doctoral students must participate in three semesters of practicum and one full year of internship. Both master's and doctoral students in the Counseling Psychology programs complete their practica in a variety of local applied settings. Our doctoral students in Counseling Psychology have been successful in obtaining APA-accredited internships in university counseling centers, veterans' administration medical centers, community mental health centers, and other human service agencies. Students in the School Psychology EdS program devote a full year to a school psychology internship. These students obtain internships in a variety of elementary, secondary, and special needs school settings throughout the country. Individuals obtaining their doctoral degree in School Psychology are required to participate in a second full year of internship.

Housing and Day Care: On-campus housing is available. See the following website for more information: http://housing.ku.edu/you-belong-here/apartments-and-towers/. On-campus day care facilities are available. See the following website for more information: http://www.hilltop.ku.edu/.

Employment of Department Graduates:

Master's Degree Graduates: Of those who graduated in the academic year 2011–2012, the following categories and numbers represent the postgraduate activities and employment of master's degree graduates: Enrolled in a postdoctoral residency/fellowship (n/a), employed in independent practice (n/a), employed in a professional position in a school system (3), total from the above (master's) (3).

Doctoral Degree Graduates: Of those who graduated in the academic year 2011–2012, the following categories and numbers represent the postgraduate activities and employment of doctoral degree graduates: Enrolled in a psychology doctoral program (n/a), enrolled in a postdoctoral residency/fellowship (2), employed in an academic position at a university (1), employed in a community mental health/counseling center (1), employed in a hospital/medical center (3), total from the above (doctoral) (7).

Additional Information:

Orientation, Objectives, and Emphasis of Department: Psychology and Research in Education offers graduate degrees in three distinct areas. The doctoral programs in Counseling Psychology and School Psychology are APA accredited. The EdS and PhD degrees in School Psychology are NASP accredited. Counseling Psychology trains professionals to possess the generalist skills to function in a wide array of work settings. This program is strongly committed to the training of scientist–practitioners focused on facilitating the personal, social, educational, and vocational development of individuals. School Psychology endorses the training model of the psychoeducational consultant with multifaceted skills drawn from psychology and education to assist children toward greater realization of their potential. The psychoeducational consultant is vitally concerned with enhancing teacher effectiveness, creating a positive classroom environment for children, and influencing educational thought within the school system. The Educational Psychology and Research Program offers instruction in two tracks. The objectives of the program are to prepare students to become faculty members, researchers, and measurement specialists. Students may focus on (a) development and learning, or (b) research, evaluation, measurement, and statistics. Graduate study includes experiences in designing, conducting, and evaluating research and field experiences in a variety of settings.

Special Facilities or Resources: Students have employment and/or research opportunities with diverse populations in a variety of settings, including university-related facilities and public/private schools. KU's Multicultural Resource Center seeks to reshape notions of education, research, and public service to include a multicultural focus. The America Reads Challenge, Institute of Educational Research and Public Service, Center for Educational Testing and Evaluation, Center for Research on Learning, and the Center for Psychoeducational Services are under the umbrella of KU's School of Education. The Center for Psychoeducational Services serves the needs of local schools and community members while offering excellent training opportunities for School Psychology and Counseling Psychology students. Graduate students may work with preschool, school-age children and their families, and college students from the local area. KU's Life Span Institute has numerous programs such as the Juniper Gardens Children's Project, Beach Center on Disability, Research and Training Center on Independent Living, Gerontology Center, and the Work Group for Community Health and Development. The School of Education provides extensive media and internet technology in its state-of-the-art facility, Joseph R. Pearson Hall. Students have access to mediated classrooms and laboratories, instructional and assessment libraries, audio visual resources, and computer labs.

Information for Students With Physical Disabilities: See the following website for more information: http://www.disability.ku.edu/.

Application Information:
Send to KU Psychology and Research in Education, Admissions Committee, 1122 West Campus Road, Room 621 JRP, Lawrence, KS 66045-3101. Application available online. URL of online application: http://graduate.ku.edu/apply. Students are admitted in the Fall, application deadline December 15. Application deadlines for PhD programs in Counseling Psychology and School Psychology as well as EdS in School Psychology are December 15. Deadline for MS in Counseling Psychology is January 1. Applications for the MS.Ed. and PhD in Educational Psychology and Research are reviewed at any time, however, students interested in applying for a Graduate Teaching Assistantship should have application materials in by January 15. *Fee:* $55. $65 for the online international application.

Pittsburg State University
Department of Psychology and Counseling
College of Education
207 Whitesitt Hall, 1701 South Broadway
Pittsburg, KS 66762-7551
Telephone: (620) 235-4523
Fax: (620) 235-6102
E-mail: *dhurford@pittstate.edu*
Web: *http://www.pittstate.edu/department/psychology/*

Department Information:
1929. Chairperson: David P. Hurford. Number of faculty: total—full-time 15; women—full-time 8.

Programs and Degrees Offered:
Listed in the following order: Program area, degree type (T if terminal Master's), number awarded 7/11–6/12. Clinical Psychology MA/MS (Master of Arts/Science) (T) 6, General Psychology MA/MS (Master of Arts/Science) (T) 9, School Psychology EdS (School Psychology) 9, School Counseling MA/MS (Master of Arts/Science) (T) 3, Clinical Mental Health Counseling MA/MS (Master of Arts/Science) (T) 9.

Student Applications/Admissions:
Student Applications
Clinical Psychology MA/MS (Master of Arts/Science)—Applications 2012–2013, 31. Total applicants accepted 2012–2013, 12. Number full-time enrolled (new admits only) 2012–2013, 10. Total enrolled 2012–2013 full-time, 12. Openings 2013–2014, 10. *General Psychology MA/MS (Master of Arts/Science)*—Applications 2012–2013, 16. Total applicants accepted 2012–2013, 14. Number full-time enrolled (new admits only) 2012–2013, 10. Total enrolled 2012–2013 full-time, 11. Openings 2013–2014, 12. *School Psychology EdS (School Psychology)*—Applications 2012–2013, 7. Total applicants accepted 2012–2013, 7. Number full-time enrolled (new admits only) 2012–2013, 7. Total enrolled 2012–2013 full-time, 18. Total enrolled 2012–2013 part-time, 4. Openings 2013–2014, 10. *School Counseling MA/MS (Master of Arts/Science)*—Applications 2012–2013, 14. Total applicants accepted 2012–2013, 14. Number full-time enrolled (new admits only) 2012–2013, 5. Number part-time enrolled (new admits only) 2012–2013, 3. Total enrolled 2012–2013 full-time, 14. Total enrolled 2012–2013 part-time, 16. Openings 2013–2014, 10. *Clinical Mental Health Counseling MA/MS (Master of Arts/Science)*—Applications 2012–2013, 30. Total applicants accepted 2012–2013, 24. Number full-time enrolled (new admits only) 2012–2013, 12. Number part-time enrolled (new admits only) 2012–2013, 12. The median number of years required for completion of a degree in 2012–2013 were 2.
Scores: Entries appear in this order: required test or GPA, minimum score (if required), median score of students entering in 2012–2013. *Clinical Psychology MA/MS (Master of Arts/Science):* GRE-V 146, GRE-Q 141, GRE-Analytical 3.5, overall undergraduate GPA 3.0; *General Psychology MA/MS (Master of Arts/Science):* GRE-V 146, GRE-Q 141, GRE-Analytical 3.5, overall undergraduate GPA 3.0; *School Psychology EdS (School Psychology):* GRE-V 146, GRE-Q 141, GRE-Analytical 3.5, overall undergraduate GPA 3.0; *School Counseling MA/MS (Master of Arts/Science):* GRE-V 146, GRE-Q 141, GRE-

Analytical 3.5, overall undergraduate GPA 3.0; *Clinical Mental Health Counseling MA/MS (Master of Arts/Science)*: GRE-V 146, GRE-Q 141, GRE-Analytical 3.5, overall undergraduate GPA 3.0.

Other Criteria: (importance of criteria rated low, medium, or high): GRE scores—high, research experience—medium, work experience—high, extracurricular activity—low, clinically related public service—medium, GPA—high, letters of recommendation—high, interview—medium, statement of goals and objectives—high. For additional information on admission requirements, go to http://www.pittstate.edu/department/psychology/application-materials.dot.

Student Characteristics: The following represents characteristics of students in 2012–2013 in all graduate psychology programs in the department: Female—full-time 22, part-time 24; Male—full-time 15, part-time 12; African American/Black—full-time 3, part-time 1; Hispanic/Latino(a)—full-time 2, part-time 0; Asian/Pacific Islander—full-time 6, part-time 0; American Indian/Alaska Native—full-time 2, part-time 1; Caucasian/White—full-time 0, part-time 0; Multi-ethnic—full-time 0, part-time 0; students subject to the Americans With Disabilities Act—full-time 0, part-time 0; Unknown ethnicity—full-time 0, part-time 0; International students who hold an F-1 or J-1 Visa—full-time 0, part-time 0.

Financial Information/Assistance:

Tuition for Full-Time Study: *Master's:* State residents: per academic year $6,164, $261 per credit hour; Nonstate residents: per academic year $14,518, $609 per credit hour. Tuition is subject to change. See the following website for updates and changes in tuition costs: http://www.pittstate.edu/office/registrar/fees.dot.

Financial Assistance:

First-Year Students: Teaching assistantships available for first year. Average amount paid per academic year: $5,000. Average number of hours worked per week: 20. Apply by March 1.

Advanced Students: Teaching assistantships available for advanced students. Average amount paid per academic year: $5,000. Average number of hours worked per week: 20. Apply by March 1.

Additional Information: Of all students currently enrolled full time, 5% benefited from one or more of the listed financial assistance programs. Application and information available online at: http://www.pittstate.edu/office/financial_aid/index.dot.

Internships/Practica: Master's Degree (MA/MS School Counseling): An internship experience, such as a final research project or "capstone" experience is required of graduates. Master's Degree (MA/MS Clinical Mental Health Counseling): An internship experience, such as a final research project or "capstone" experience is required of graduates. All M.S. and EdS practitioner programs include a 3-8 semester hour (150-400 clock hour) practicum sequence and a 4-32 semester hour (600-1200 clock hour) internship at a site appropriate to the specialty, and under the supervision of faculty and site supervisors. The internship in school psychology is post-degree, and is typically a paid internship. Some internships in other programs are also paid. All internships meet guidelines of the professional association or accrediting body of the specialty (i.e., CACREP, MPAC, NASP).

Housing and Day Care: On-campus housing is available. See the following website for more information: http://www.pittstate.edu/office/housing/. No on-campus day care facilities are available.

Employment of Department Graduates:

Master's Degree Graduates: Of those who graduated in the academic year 2011–2012, the following categories and numbers represent the postgraduate activities and employment of master's degree graduates: Enrolled in a psychology doctoral program (2), enrolled in another graduate/professional program (3), enrolled in a postdoctoral residency/fellowship (n/a), employed in independent practice (n/a), employed in an academic position at a university (1), employed in an academic position at a 2-year/4-year college (2), employed in a professional position in a school system (20), employed in a community mental health/counseling center (16), employed in a hospital/medical center (2), still seeking employment (2), other employment position (3), total from the above (master's) (51).

Doctoral Degree Graduates: Of those who graduated in the academic year 2011–2012, the following categories and numbers represent the postgraduate activities and employment of doctoral degree graduates: Enrolled in a psychology doctoral program (n/a), total from the above (doctoral) (0).

Additional Information:

Orientation, Objectives, and Emphasis of Department: The Department of Psychology and Counseling uses an interdisciplinary model to provide broad-based training, understanding and appreciation of the specialties that we represent. The major objective of the department is to prepare graduates with knowledge in scientific foundations and practical applied skills to function as mental health service providers or to pursue study at the doctoral level. Faculty in the department represent a diverse collection of theoretical backgrounds in scientific and applied psychology. All faculty teach coursework in each program area, providing students with the opportunity to learn multidisciplinary approaches and models. The emphasis in the department is on integrated, cross-disciplinary studies within a close faculty-student colleague model that promotes frequent contact and close supervision, aimed at developing practitioner skills. The department is pleased to have the first accredited master's degree program in clinical psychology in the nation (MPAC accreditation received in May 1997), and enjoys CACREP accreditation of the master's degree program in clinical mental health counseling. The department also enjoys NCATE accreditation of the M.S. Degree program in school counseling and the EdS Degree program in school psychology.

Special Facilities or Resources: The department has counseling and psychotherapy training facilities equipped with one-way mirrors and audio and video taping equipment. Microcomputer laboratories with network capacity, word processing, and SAS and SPSS software are available in the department. The university library, in addition to a large book collection, currently maintains over 150 periodical subscriptions in psychology. The department operates the Center for Human Services, an on-campus training, research, and service facility, which includes University Testing Services, a family counseling center, an adult assessment center, the Center for Assessment and Remediation of Reading Difficulties, the Attention Deficit/Hyperactivity Disorder Neurofeedback Diagnostic and Treatment Center, and the Welfare to Work Assessment Center. The department has a close working relationship with local hospitals and mental health facilities, and is a constituent member of the regional community service coalition.

Information for Students With Physical Disabilities: See the following website for more information: http://www.pittstate.edu/office/eoaa/disability-services/.

Application Information:

Send to Chairperson, Department of Psychology and Counseling, Pittsburg State University, 1701 South Broadway, Pittsburg, KS 66762-7551. Application available online. URL of online application: http://www.pittstate.edu/office/graduate/. Students are admitted in the Fall, application deadline March 1; Spring, application deadline October 1; Summer, application deadline March 1. Applications for the M.S. in Clinical Psychology are normally accepted for Fall admission. Applications will be considered for Spring admission, but please note that this will extend the student's program of study by one semester. *Fee:* $40.

Washburn University

Department of Psychology
1700 SW College Avenue
Topeka, KS 66621
Telephone: (785) 670-1564
Fax: (785) 670-1239
E-mail: *dave.provorse@washburn.edu*
Web: *http://www.washburn.edu/academics/college-schools/arts-sciences/departments/psychology/*

Department Information:

1940. Chairperson: Dave Provorse. Number of faculty: total—full-time 9; women—full-time 5.

Programs and Degrees Offered:

Listed in the following order: Program area, degree type (T if terminal Master's), number awarded 7/11–6/12. Clinical MA/MS (Master of Arts/Science) (T) 6.

Student Applications/Admissions:

Student Applications

Clinical MA/MS (Master of Arts/Science)—Applications 2012–2013, 18. Total applicants accepted 2012–2013, 11. Number full-time enrolled (new admits only) 2012–2013, 7. Total enrolled 2012–2013 full-time, 22. Total enrolled 2012–2013 part-time, 3. Openings 2013–2014, 12. The median number of years required for completion of a degree in 2012–2013 were 3. The number of students enrolled full- and part-time who were dismissed or voluntarily withdrew from this program area in 2012–2013 were 1.

Scores: Entries appear in this order: required test or GPA, minimum score (if required), median score of students entering in 2012–2013. *Clinical MA/MS (Master of Arts/Science):* GRE-V no minimum stated, GRE-Q no minimum stated, overall undergraduate GPA no minimum stated, last 2 years GPA no minimum stated, psychology GPA no minimum stated.

Other Criteria: (importance of criteria rated low, medium, or high): GRE scores—medium, research experience—medium, work experience—low, extracurricular activity—medium, clinically related public service—medium, GPA—high, letters of recommendation—high, statement of goals and objec-

tives—medium, undergraduate major in psychology—medium, specific undergraduate psychology courses taken—high. For additional information on admission requirements, go to http://www.washburn.edu/academics/college-schools/arts-sciences/graduate/psychology/application.html.

Student Characteristics: The following represents characteristics of students in 2012–2013 in all graduate psychology programs in the department: Female—full-time 16, part-time 1; Male—full-time 6, part-time 2; African American/Black—part-time 0; Hispanic/Latino(a)—full-time 2, part-time 1; Asian/Pacific Islander—full-time 0, part-time 0; American Indian/Alaska Native—part-time 1; Caucasian/White—full-time 20, part-time 1; Multi-ethnic—full-time 0, part-time 0; students subject to the Americans With Disabilities Act—full-time 0, part-time 0; Unknown ethnicity—full-time 0, part-time 0; International students who hold an F-1 or J-1 Visa—part-time 0.

Financial Information/Assistance:

Tuition for Full-Time Study: Master's: State residents: per academic year $5,018, $309 per credit hour; Nonstate residents: per academic year $12,600, $630 per credit hour. Tuition is subject to change. See the following website for updates and changes in tuition costs: http://www.washburn.edu/current-students/business-office/tuition-fees.html.

Financial Assistance:

First-Year Students: Teaching assistantships available for first year. Average amount paid per academic year: $3,500. Average number of hours worked per week: 10. Apply by March 15. Research assistantships available for first year. Average amount paid per academic year: $1,500. Average number of hours worked per week: 5. Apply by August 15.

Advanced Students: Teaching assistantships available for advanced students. Average amount paid per academic year: $4,000. Average number of hours worked per week: 10. Apply by May 15. Traineeships available for advanced students. Average amount paid per academic year: $5,400. Average number of hours worked per week: 20. Apply by August 1.

Additional Information: Of all students currently enrolled full time, 50% benefited from one or more of the listed financial assistance programs. Application and information available online at: http://www.washburn.edu/academics/college-schools/arts-sciences/graduate/psychology/financial-aid.html.

Internships/Practica: Master's Degree (MA/MS Clinical): An internship experience, such as a final research project or "capstone" experience is required of graduates. Psychological services are offered to the community through a clinic staffed by graduate students enrolled in practica and supervised by licensed doctoral level faculty. Services offered focus on remediation of anxiety and depression, and psychological assessment of learning disorders and ADHD. Student therapists practice skills of diagnostic interviewing, and integrating interview information with personality and intelligence testing into the formulation of a DSM-IV-TR diagnosis. Under the close supervision of a faculty clinical psychologist, they use this information to conceptualize etiologies and develop and deliver therapeutic treatment options. The therapy processes implemented reflect several theoretical orientations, including Motivational Interviewing, Interpersonal Process, Cognitive/Behavioral and Brief approaches. Issues of suicide, cross-cultural sensitivity, and individual therapist development are also addressed. An internship consisting of 750 supervised hours over an academic year is required of each student prior to graduation. This requirement is met by working twenty hours per week at an assigned site and meeting three hours weekly in a classroom setting. Both on-site and university-based supervisors are available to the student throughout the internship. The types of experiences provided student interns include: provision of individual adult and child therapy; cofacilitation of group therapy; psychological testing/assessment; and involvement in multidisciplinary treatment teams.

Housing and Day Care: On-campus housing is available. See the following website for more information: http://www.washburn. edu/campus-life/housing-dining/index.html. No on-campus day care facilities are available.

Employment of Department Graduates:

Master's Degree Graduates: Of those who graduated in the academic year 2011–2012, the following categories and numbers represent the postgraduate activities and employment of master's degree graduates: Enrolled in a postdoctoral residency/fellowship (n/a), employed in independent practice (n/a), employed in other positions at a higher education institution (1), employed in a community mental health/counseling center (5), total from the above (master's) (6).

Doctoral Degree Graduates: Of those who graduated in the academic year 2011–2012, the following categories and numbers represent the postgraduate activities and employment of doctoral degree graduates: Enrolled in a psychology doctoral program (n/a), total from the above (doctoral) (0).

Additional Information:

Orientation, Objectives, and Emphasis of Department: Training is designed to establish a strong foundation in the content, methods and applications of psychology. Students obtain experience and skills in research, psychological assessment and individual and group therapy. Clinical training reflects an emphasis on empirically supported treatments and an integrative blend of humanistic, cognitive/behavioral, interpersonal process and brief therapies. The MA program is designed to prepare students for the pursuit of a doctoral degree in psychology, or for future employment as providers of psychological services in community mental health centers, hospitals, correctional settings and other social service agencies and clinics that require master's level training. Students with special interests in children, rural or sport psychology, or correctional and prison settings have the opportunity to pursue such interests in their thesis research and/or internship placement.

Special Facilities or Resources: The psychology department, housed with other departments in a modern building, has well-equipped laboratories available for human experimentation. These facilities also include observation areas designed for the direct supervision of psychotherapy and psychological testing. The psychology department provides access to computer hardware and software resources. Thesis research can be conducted by accessing participants from the undergraduate subject pool, or in a wide array of community-based agencies.

Information for Students With Physical Disabilities: See the following website for more information: http://www.washburn. edu/disability-services/index.html.

Application Information:
Send to Department of Psychology, Washburn University, Topeka, KS 66621. Application available online. URL of online application: http://www.washburn.edu/academics/college-schools/arts-sciences/ graduate/psychology/application.html. Students are admitted in the Fall, application deadline March 15; Spring, application deadline December 1. *Fee:* $0.

Wichita State University
Department of Psychology
Fairmount College of Liberal Arts and Sciences
1845 Fairmount
Wichita, KS 67260-0034
Telephone: (316) 978-3170
Fax: (316) 978-3086
E-mail: *alex.chaparro@wichita.edu*
Web: *http://psychology.wichita.edu*

Department Information:
1948. Chairperson: Alex Chaparro. Number of faculty: total—full-time 13, part-time 1; women—full-time 2, part-time 1; total—minority—full-time 3; women minority—full-time 1.

Programs and Degrees Offered:
Listed in the following order: Program area, degree type (T if terminal Master's), number awarded 7/11–6/12. Clinical Psychology PhD (Doctor of Philosophy) 6, Human Factors PhD (Doctor of Philosophy) 4, Community Psychology PhD (Doctor of Philosophy) 6.

APA Accreditation: Clinical PhD (Doctor of Philosophy). Student Outcome Data Website: http://webs.wichita.edu/?u=psychology&p=/ graduate/clinical/clinicalphd/.

Student Applications/Admissions:
Student Applications

Clinical Psychology PhD (Doctor of Philosophy)—Applications 2012–2013, 54. Total applicants accepted 2012–2013, 10. Number full-time enrolled (new admits only) 2012–2013, 4. Total enrolled 2012–2013 full-time, 25. Total enrolled 2012–2013 part-time, 0. Openings 2013–2014, 4. The median number of years required for completion of a degree in 2012–2013 were 5. The number of students enrolled full- and part-time who were dismissed or voluntarily withdrew from this program area in 2012–2013 were 0. *Human Factors PhD (Doctor of Philosophy)*—Applications 2012–2013, 18. Total applicants accepted 2012–2013, 7. Number full-time enrolled (new admits only) 2012–2013, 5. Total enrolled 2012–2013 full-time, 26. Total enrolled 2012–2013 part-time, 0. Openings 2013–2014, 4. The median number of years required for completion of a degree in 2012–2013 were 5. The number of students enrolled full- and part-time who were dismissed or voluntarily withdrew from this program area in 2012–2013 were 1. *Community Psychology PhD (Doctor of Philosophy)*—Applications 2012–2013, 18. Total applicants accepted 2012–2013, 12. Number full-time enrolled (new admits only) 2012–2013, 5. Total enrolled 2012–2013 full-time, 22. Total enrolled 2012–2013 part-time, 0. Openings 2013–2014, 4. The median number of years required for completion of a degree in 2012–2013 were 4. The number of students enrolled full- and part-time who were dismissed or voluntarily withdrew from this program area in 2012–2013 were 4.

Scores: Entries appear in this order: required test or GPA, minimum score (if required), median score of students entering in 2012–2013. *Clinical Psychology PhD (Doctor of Philosophy):* GRE-V no minimum stated, 540, GRE-Q no minimum stated, 620, last 2 years GPA 3.00, 3.81, Masters GPA 3.25; *Human Factors PhD (Doctor of Philosophy):* GRE-V no minimum stated, 480, GRE-Q no minimum stated, 590, last 2 years GPA 3.0, 3.57, Masters GPA 3.25; *Community Psychology PhD (Doctor of Philosophy):* GRE-V no minimum stated, 510, GRE-Q no minimum stated, 520, last 2 years GPA 3.00, 3.86, Masters GPA 3.25.

Other Criteria: (importance of criteria rated low, medium, or high): GRE scores—medium, research experience—high, work experience—medium, clinically related public service—medium, GPA—high, letters of recommendation—medium, interview—medium, statement of goals and objectives—high, undergraduate major in psychology—low, specific undergraduate psychology courses taken—low. For additional information on admission requirements, go to http://webs.wichita.edu/?u=psychology&p=/application/gradapplication/.

Student Characteristics: The following represents characteristics of students in 2012–2013 in all graduate psychology programs in the department: Female—full-time 48, part-time 0; Male—full-time 25, part-time 0; African American/Black—full-time 4, part-time 0; Hispanic/Latino(a)—full-time 5, part-time 0; Asian/Pacific Islander—full-time 7, part-time 0; American Indian/Alaska Native—full-time 0, part-time 0; Caucasian/White—full-time 47, part-time 0; Multi-ethnic—full-time 3, part-time 0; students subject to the Americans With Disabilities Act—full-time 0, part-time 0; Unknown ethnicity—full-time 7, part-time 0; International students who hold an F-1 or J-1 Visa—full-time 0, part-time 0.

Financial Information/Assistance:

Tuition for Full-Time Study: *Doctoral:* State residents: per academic year $5,184, $234 per credit hour; Nonstate residents: per academic year $14,424, $618 per credit hour. Tuition is subject to change. Additional fees are assessed to students beyond the costs of tuition for the following: student fees, facility fee, registration fee. See the following website for updates and changes in tuition costs: http://www.wichita.edu/tuitionfees.

Financial Assistance:

First-Year Students: Teaching assistantships available for first year. Average amount paid per academic year: $6,864. Average number of hours worked per week: 20. Research assistantships available for first year. Average amount paid per academic year: $10,000. Average number of hours worked per week: 20.

Advanced Students: Teaching assistantships available for advanced students. Average amount paid per academic year: $7,912. Average number of hours worked per week: 20. Research assistantships available for advanced students. Average amount paid per academic year: $10,000. Average number of hours worked per week: 20.

Additional Information: Of all students currently enrolled full time, 70% benefited from one or more of the listed financial assistance programs. Application and information available online at: http://webs.wichita.edu/?u=finaid_graduate&p=/index.

Internships/Practica: Doctoral Degree (PhD Clinical Psychology): For those doctoral students for whom a professional psychology internship was required in this program prior to graduation, (5) students applied for an internship in 2011–2012, with (4) students obtaining an internship. Of those students who obtained an internship, (4) were paid internships. Of those students who obtained an internship, (4) students placed in APA/CPA accredited internships, (0) students placed in internships not APA/CPA accredited, but listed with the Association of Psychology Postdoctoral and Internship Programs (APPIC), (0) students placed in internships conforming to guidelines of the Council of Directors of School Psychology Programs (CDSPP), (0) students placed in internships that were not APA/CPA accredited, APPIC or CDSPP listed. An important aspect of the Human Factors program is its requirement that all students complete an internship. The internship is designed to provide students with practical experience integrating their education in real-world situations. The internships have included positions with the FAA, Google, Bell Laboratories, IBM, Microsoft, and other similar settings. These placements have often led to post-PhD employment opportunities. In the Clinical and Community programs, practicum opportunities, most of them funded, are available in on-campus training facilities and community agencies. Settings include the Psychology Clinic and the Counseling and Testing Center, both at Wichita State University, the Sedgwick County Department of Mental Health, Head Start, and various community-based projects. Students in the Clinical program are required to complete one year of internship experience towards the end of their graduate studies.

Housing and Day Care: On-campus housing is available. See the following website for more information: http://www.wichita.edu/thisis/studentlife/campus_housing.asp. On-campus day care facilities are available. See the following website for more information: http://www.wichita.edu/childdevelopmentcenter.

Employment of Department Graduates:

Master's Degree Graduates: Of those who graduated in the academic year 2011–2012, the following categories and numbers represent the postgraduate activities and employment of master's degree graduates: Enrolled in a postdoctoral residency/fellowship (n/a), employed in independent practice (n/a), total from the above (master's) (0).

Doctoral Degree Graduates: Of those who graduated in the academic year 2011–2012, the following categories and numbers represent the postgraduate activities and employment of doctoral degree graduates: Enrolled in a psychology doctoral program (n/a), employed in an academic position at a university (3), employed in an academic position at a 2-year/4-year college (1), employed in other positions at a higher education institution (1), employed in business or industry (2), employed in a community mental health/counseling center (1), employed in a hospital/medical center (2), do not know (2), total from the above (doctoral) (12).

Additional Information:

Orientation, Objectives, and Emphasis of Department: The Psychology Department, open to various theoretical orientations, emphasizes research in its three programs. The Human Factors program is accredited by the Education Committee of the Human Factors and Ergonomics Society. This program provides students with wide exposure to research, training, practice, and literature in the field of Human Factors, as well as to issues in the wider context of basic and applied experimental psychology. Current human factors research involves cognitive functioning, aging, development, human-computer interactions, aerospace issues, perception, attention, vision, and driving related issues, especially with the elderly. The APA-accredited Clinical program seeks to integrate community and clinical psychology. The goal of the program is to educate and license students to be competent clinical psychologists who conceptualize, research, intervene, and treat problems at the individual, group, organizational and societal levels. Special areas of interest and research include parent-child interaction, treatment and prevention of depression, treatment and prevention of delinquency, adolescent health and development, and assessment of personality and psychopathology. The Community program seeks to educate students in Community Psychology with an emphasis on assessing and solving problems at the group, organizational and societal levels. Special areas of research and practice include: adolescent health and development, self-help groups, voluntary and paid helping relationships especially with the elderly, animal welfare, and treatment and prevention of delinquency. All three programs have an applied research focus.

Special Facilities or Resources: The department is located in Jabara Hall and maintains fully equipped laboratories. Currently active research groups include the Software Usability Research Lab, Perception & Attention Lab, Visual Psychophysics Lab, Decision Making Research Lab, Child & Family Research Center, Personality Research Lab, and Quantitative Modeling Lab. Our computer facilities are state-of-the-art and are available to students for coursework and research. The department also has access to the National Institute for Aviation Research, the Social Science Research Laboratory, and the University Computing Center. The Psychology Clinic, which is part of the psychology department, provides outpatient services via individual, group, and family modalities. The clinic has facilities for individual and group research. The statewide Center for Community Support & Research, with a computerized database and an 800 number, also operates out of the psychology department. Faculty maintain working relationships with a number of governmental and community agencies which facilitate student involvement in community practice and research. The agencies include the public school system, the Sedgwick County Department of Mental Health, and COMCARE, among others.

Information for Students With Physical Disabilities: See the following website for more information: http://webs.wichita.edu/dss.

Application Information:
Send to Graduate Coordinator, Psychology Department. URL of online application: http://webs.wichita.edu/?u=apply&p=/OnlineApplication Gateway. Students are admitted in the Fall, application deadline January 15. *Fee:* $50. International Students $65.

Eastern Kentucky University

Department of Psychology
Arts and Sciences
Cammack 127
Richmond, KY 40475
Telephone: (859) 622-1105
Fax: (859) 622-5871
E-mail: *robert.brubaker@eku.edu*
Web: *http://www.psychology.eku.edu*

Department Information:

1967. Chairperson: Robert G. Brubaker. Number of faculty: total—full-time 22, part-time 17; women—full-time 11, part-time 12; total—minority—full-time 2, part-time 1; women minority—full-time 2; faculty subject to the Americans With Disabilities Act 1.

Programs and Degrees Offered:

Listed in the following order: Program area, degree type (T if terminal Master's), number awarded 7/11–6/12. Clinical Psychology MA/MS (Master of Arts/Science) (T) 14, Industrial/Organizational Psychology MA/MS (Master of Arts/Science) (T) 4, School Psychology EdS (School Psychology) 8, General Psychology MA/MS (Master of Arts/Science) (T) 2.

Student Applications/Admissions:

Student Applications

Clinical Psychology MA/MS (Master of Arts/Science)—Applications 2012–2013, 66. Total applicants accepted 2012–2013, 12. Number full-time enrolled (new admits only) 2012–2013, 14. Total enrolled 2012–2013 full-time, 28. Openings 2013–2014, 12. The median number of years required for completion of a degree in 2012–2013 were 2. The number of students enrolled full- and part-time who were dismissed or voluntarily withdrew from this program area in 2012–2013 were 0. *Industrial/Organizational Psychology MA/MS (Master of Arts/Science)*—Applications 2012–2013, 30. Total applicants accepted 2012–2013, 15. Number full-time enrolled (new admits only) 2012–2013, 6. Number part-time enrolled (new admits only) 2012–2013, 0. Total enrolled 2012–2013 full-time, 11. Total enrolled 2012–2013 part-time, 0. Openings 2013–2014, 8. The median number of years required for completion of a degree in 2012–2013 were 2. The number of students enrolled full- and part-time who were dismissed or voluntarily withdrew from this program area in 2012–2013 were 0. *School Psychology EdS (School Psychology)*—Applications 2012–2013, 19. Total applicants accepted 2012–2013, 7. Number full-time enrolled (new admits only) 2012–2013, 4. Number part-time enrolled (new admits only) 2012–2013, 0. Total enrolled 2012–2013 full-time, 24. Total enrolled 2012–2013 part-time, 0. Openings 2013–2014, 10. The median number of years required for completion of a degree in 2012–2013 were 3. The number of students enrolled full- and part-time who were dismissed or voluntarily withdrew from this program area in 2012–2013 were 0. *General Psychology MA/MS (Master of Arts/Science)*—Applications 2012–2013, 6. Total applicants accepted 2012–

2013, 4. Number full-time enrolled (new admits only) 2012–2013, 4. Total enrolled 2012–2013 full-time, 8. Openings 2013–2014, 4. The median number of years required for completion of a degree in 2012–2013 were 2. The number of students enrolled full- and part-time who were dismissed or voluntarily withdrew from this program area in 2012–2013 were 0.

Scores: Entries appear in this order: required test or GPA, minimum score (if required), median score of students entering in 2012–2013. *Clinical Psychology MA/MS (Master of Arts/Science):* GRE-V no minimum stated, 550, GRE-Q no minimum stated, 490, overall undergraduate GPA no minimum stated, 3.4, last 2 years GPA no minimum stated, 3.6, psychology GPA no minimum stated, 3.7; *Industrial/Organizational Psychology MA/MS (Master of Arts/Science):* GRE-V 149, 151, GRE-Q 144, 149, overall undergraduate GPA 2.5, 3.4, last 2 years GPA 2.75, 3.6, psychology GPA no minimum stated, 3.6; *School Psychology EdS (School Psychology):* GRE-V no minimum stated, 152, GRE-Q no minimum stated, 147, overall undergraduate GPA no minimum stated, 3.49, last 2 years GPA no minimum stated, 3.5, psychology GPA no minimum stated, 3.7; *General Psychology MA/MS (Master of Arts/Science):* GRE-V 153, GRE-Q 144, overall undergraduate GPA 3.0, 3.4, last 2 years GPA no minimum stated, 3.5, psychology GPA no minimum stated, 3.6.

Other Criteria: (importance of criteria rated low, medium, or high): GRE scores—medium, research experience—medium, work experience—medium, extracurricular activity—low, clinically related public service—high, GPA—medium, letters of recommendation—high, statement of goals and objectives—high, undergraduate major in psychology—medium, specific undergraduate psychology courses taken—medium. For additional information on admission requirements, go to http://psychology.eku.edu/application-admission-graduate-studies.

Student Characteristics: The following represents characteristics of students in 2012–2013 in all graduate psychology programs in the department: Female—full-time 63, part-time 2; Male—full-time 8, part-time 0; African American/Black—full-time 3, part-time 0; Hispanic/Latino(a)—full-time 0, part-time 0; Asian/Pacific Islander—full-time 0, part-time 0; American Indian/Alaska Native—full-time 0, part-time 0; Caucasian/White—full-time 68, part-time 2; Multi-ethnic—full-time 0, part-time 0; students subject to the Americans With Disabilities Act—full-time 0, part-time 0; Unknown ethnicity—full-time 0, part-time 0; International students who hold an F-1 or J-1 Visa—full-time 0, part-time 0.

Financial Information/Assistance:

Tuition for Full-Time Study: *Master's:* State residents: $440 per credit hour; Nonstate residents: $770 per credit hour. Tuition is subject to change. See the following website for updates and changes in tuition costs: http://gradschool.eku.edu/graduate-tuition.

Financial Assistance:

First-Year Students: Research assistantships available for first year. Average amount paid per academic year: $5,280. Average number of hours worked per week: 10. Apply by March 15.

Advanced Students: Research assistantships available for advanced students. Average amount paid per academic year: $5,280. Average number of hours worked per week: 10. Apply by May 1.

Additional Information: Of all students currently enrolled full time, 80% benefited from one or more of the listed financial assistance programs. Application and information available online at: http://gradschool.eku.edu/assistantships-awards.

Internships/Practica: Master's Degree (MA/MS Clinical Psychology): An internship experience, such as a final research project or "capstone" experience is required of graduates. Master's Degree (MA/MS General Psychology): An internship experience, such as a final research project or "capstone" experience is required of graduates. A variety of field placements are available within easy commuting distance from Richmond. Practicum sites have included private psychiatric and VA hospitals, the University counseling center, a residential treatment facility for children, alcohol and drug abuse treatment programs, and several adult and child outpatient mental health centers. Students also gain experience working in the EKU Psychology Clinic, an outpatient mental health facility operated by the Department. School psychology students can choose from a variety of public and private elementary and secondary schools. Students have completed internships in Kentucky as well as many other states. Students in the I/O program work on practicum projects with various for-profit and non-profit organizations in the region.

Housing and Day Care: On-campus housing is available. See the following website for more information: http://housing.eku.edu/. No on-campus day care facilities are available.

Employment of Department Graduates:

Master's Degree Graduates: Of those who graduated in the academic year 2011–2012, the following categories and numbers represent the postgraduate activities and employment of master's degree graduates: Enrolled in a psychology doctoral program (5), enrolled in a postdoctoral residency/fellowship (n/a), employed in independent practice (n/a), employed in an academic position at a university (1), employed in other positions at a higher education institution (1), employed in a professional position in a school system (10), employed in business or industry (2), employed in government agency (1), employed in a community mental health/counseling center (8), still seeking employment (1), not seeking employment (2), other employment position (1), total from the above (master's) (32).

Doctoral Degree Graduates: Of those who graduated in the academic year 2011–2012, the following categories and numbers represent the postgraduate activities and employment of doctoral degree graduates: Enrolled in a psychology doctoral program (n/a), total from the above (doctoral) (0).

Additional Information:

Orientation, Objectives, and Emphasis of Department: The MS program in clinical psychology is designed to train professional psychologists to work in clinics, hospitals, or other agencies, or to continue on to doctoral training. In the clinical program, approximately one-third of the course hours are devoted to theory and research, one-third to clinical skills training, and one-third to practicum and internship placements in the community. The clinical program also offers specialized training and experience serving individuals with autism spectrum disorders leading to an Autism Spectrum Disorder Certificate. The clinical program meets the curriculum standards required for membership in the Council of Applied Master's Programs in Psychology and is accredited nationally by the Master's Program Accreditation Council. The Psy.S. program in school psychology is designed to train professional psychologists to work in schools and school-related agencies. The program involves 71 graduate hours including internship, is NASP and NCATE-accredited and meets Kentucky certification requirements. The I/O program is designed to meet the education and training guidelines established by the Society for Industrial and Organizational Psychology. The scientist–practitioner I/O program prepares students to work in organizations and/or pursue a doctoral degree. Degree requirements include intensive required courses and electives, and practicum. Research opportunities are available in all programs, and all programs prepare students for doctoral study. The M.S. in General Psychology program offers a flexible curriculum designed to prepare students for further graduate study in psychology or for a variety of non-applied career options.

Special Facilities or Resources: Laboratories include several multipurpose rooms. The clinical training facility includes a group therapy room, individual therapy rooms, a testing room, and a play therapy room. All rooms have two-way mirror viewing and videotape facilities. The department operates a psychology training clinic providing outpatient services to the community, with its primary mission the training of students.

Information for Students With Physical Disabilities: See the following website for more information: http://disabilities.eku.edu/.

Application Information:
Send to Graduate School, Eastern Kentucky University, 521 Lancaster Avenue, Richmond, KY 40475. Application available online. URL of online application: http://gradschool.eku.edu/apply/. Students are admitted in the Fall, application deadline March 15. Applications received after March 15 are considered on a space-available basis. *Fee:* $35.

Kentucky, University of

Department of Educational, School, and Counseling
  Psychology
Education
Dickey Hall, Room 237
Lexington, KY 40506-0017
Telephone: (859) 257-7881
Fax: (859) 257-5662
E-mail: *keisha.love@uky.edu*
Web: *http://education.uky.edu/EDP*

Department Information:
1968. Chairperson: Keisha Love. Number of faculty: total—full-time 15; women—full-time 6; total—minority—full-time 4; women minority—full-time 2.

Programs and Degrees Offered:

Listed in the following order: Program area, degree type (T if terminal Master's), number awarded 7/11–6/12. Counseling Psychology MA/MS (Master of Arts/Science) 8, Educational Psychology MA/MS (Master of Arts/Science) (T) 1, Counseling Psychology PhD (Doctor of Philosophy) 3, Educational Psychology PhD (Doctor of Philosophy) 1, School Psychology PhD (Doctor of Philosophy) 2, School Psychology EdS (School Psychology) 7, Counseling Psychology EdS (School Psychology) 3.

APA Accreditation: Counseling PhD (Doctor of Philosophy). Student Outcome Data Website: http://education.uky.edu/EDP/content/counseling-psych-full-disclosure. School PhD (Doctor of Philosophy). Student Outcome Data Website: http://education.uky.edu/EDP/content/school-psych-admissions-outcomes-data.

Student Applications/Admissions:

Student Applications

Counseling Psychology MA/MS (Master of Arts/Science)—Applications 2012–2013, 65. Total applicants accepted 2012–2013, 28. Number full-time enrolled (new admits only) 2012–2013, 14. Number part-time enrolled (new admits only) 2012–2013, 0. Total enrolled 2012–2013 full-time, 28. Total enrolled 2012–2013 part-time, 0. Openings 2013–2014, 15. The median number of years required for completion of a degree in 2012–2013 were 2. The number of students enrolled full- and part-time who were dismissed or voluntarily withdrew from this program area in 2012–2013 were 0. *Educational Psychology MA/MS (Master of Arts/Science)*—Applications 2012–2013, 9. Total applicants accepted 2012–2013, 3. Number full-time enrolled (new admits only) 2012–2013, 2. Number part-time enrolled (new admits only) 2012–2013, 0. Total enrolled 2012–2013 full-time, 4. Total enrolled 2012–2013 part-time, 0. Openings 2013–2014, 5. The median number of years required for completion of a degree in 2012–2013 were 2. The number of students enrolled full- and part-time who were dismissed or voluntarily withdrew from this program area in 2012–2013 were 0. *Counseling Psychology PhD (Doctor of Philosophy)*—Applications 2012–2013, 75. Total applicants accepted 2012–2013, 13. Number full-time enrolled (new admits only) 2012–2013, 8. Number part-time enrolled (new admits only) 2012–2013, 0. Total enrolled 2012–2013 full-time, 34. Total enrolled 2012–2013 part-time, 0. Openings 2013–2014, 9. The median number of years required for completion of a degree in 2012–2013 were 7. The number of students enrolled full- and part-time who were dismissed or voluntarily withdrew from this program area in 2012–2013 were 0. *Educational Psychology PhD (Doctor of Philosophy)*—Applications 2012–2013, 6. Total applicants accepted 2012–2013, 3. Number full-time enrolled (new admits only) 2012–2013, 3. Number part-time enrolled (new admits only) 2012–2013, 0. Total enrolled 2012–2013 full-time, 20. Total enrolled 2012–2013 part-time, 0. Openings 2013–2014, 5. The median number of years required for completion of a degree in 2012–2013 were 7. The number of students enrolled full- and part-time who were dismissed or voluntarily withdrew from this program area in 2012–2013 were 0. *School Psychology PhD (Doctor of Philosophy)*—Applications 2012–2013, 15. Total applicants accepted 2012–2013, 13. Number full-time enrolled (new admits only) 2012–2013, 4. Number part-time enrolled (new admits only) 2012–2013, 0. Total enrolled 2012–2013 full-time, 33. Total enrolled 2012–2013 part-time, 9. Openings 2013–2014, 7. The median number of years required for completion of a degree in 2012–2013 were 8. The number of students enrolled full- and part-time who were dismissed or voluntarily withdrew from this program area in 2012–2013 were 0. *School Psychology EdS (School Psychology)*—Applications 2012–2013, 43. Total applicants accepted 2012–2013, 9. Number full-time enrolled (new admits only) 2012–2013, 4. Number part-time enrolled (new admits only) 2012–2013, 0. Total enrolled 2012–2013 full-time, 20. Total enrolled 2012–2013 part-time, 0. Openings 2013–2014, 10. The median number of years required for completion of a degree in 2012–2013 were 2. The number of students enrolled full- and part-time who were dismissed or voluntarily withdrew from this program area in 2012–2013 were 0. *Counseling Psychology EdS (School Psychology)*—Applications 2012–2013, 10. Total applicants accepted 2012–2013, 7. Number full-time enrolled (new admits only) 2012–2013, 7. Total enrolled 2012–2013 full-time, 13. Openings 2013–2014, 6. The median number of years required for completion of a degree in 2012–2013 were 2. The number of students enrolled full- and part-time who were dismissed or voluntarily withdrew from this program area in 2012–2013 were 0.

Scores: Entries appear in this order: required test or GPA, minimum score (if required), median score of students entering in 2012–2013. *Counseling Psychology MA/MS (Master of Arts/Science):* GRE-V no minimum stated, GRE-Q no minimum stated, GRE-Analytical no minimum stated, overall undergraduate GPA no minimum stated; *Educational Psychology MA/MS (Master of Arts/Science):* GRE-V no minimum stated, GRE-Q no minimum stated, GRE-Analytical no minimum stated, overall undergraduate GPA no minimum stated; *Counseling Psychology PhD (Doctor of Philosophy):* GRE-V no minimum stated, GRE-Q no minimum stated, GRE-Analytical no minimum stated, overall undergraduate GPA no minimum stated, Masters GPA no minimum stated; *Educational Psychology PhD (Doctor of Philosophy):* GRE-V no minimum stated, GRE-Q no minimum stated, GRE-Analytical no minimum stated, overall undergraduate GPA no minimum stated, Masters GPA no minimum stated; *School Psychology PhD (Doctor of Philosophy):* GRE-V no minimum stated, GRE-Q no minimum stated, GRE-Analytical no minimum stated, overall undergraduate GPA no minimum stated, Masters GPA no minimum stated; *School Psychology EdS (School Psychology):* GRE-V no minimum stated, GRE-Q no minimum stated, GRE-Analytical no minimum stated, overall undergraduate GPA no minimum stated; *Counseling Psychology EdS (School Psychology):* GRE-V no minimum stated, GRE-Q no minimum stated, GRE-Analytical no minimum stated, overall undergraduate GPA no minimum stated.

Other Criteria: (importance of criteria rated low, medium, or high): GRE scores—medium, research experience—high, work experience—medium, extracurricular activity—medium, clinically related public service—high, GPA—medium, letters of recommendation—high, interview—high, statement of goals and objectives—high, Research experience and statement of goals are the highest priority for Educational Psychology programs. Work experiences and clinically related service are more important for School and Counseling programs. For additional information on admission requirements, go to http://education.uky.edu/EDP.

Student Characteristics: The following represents characteristics of students in 2012–2013 in all graduate psychology programs in

the department: Female—full-time 120, part-time 0; Male—full-time 32, part-time 0; African American/Black—full-time 19, part-time 0; Hispanic/Latino(a)—full-time 4, part-time 0; Asian/Pacific Islander—full-time 7, part-time 0; American Indian/Alaska Native—full-time 1, part-time 0; Caucasian/White—full-time 109, part-time 0; Multi-ethnic—full-time 5, part-time 0; students subject to the Americans With Disabilities Act—full-time 0, part-time 0; Unknown ethnicity—full-time 5, part-time 0; International students who hold an F-1 or J-1 Visa—full-time 2, part-time 0.

Financial Information/Assistance:

Tuition for Full-Time Study: *Master's:* State residents: per academic year $10,458, $552 per credit hour; Nonstate residents: per academic year $21,546, $1,168 per credit hour. *Doctoral:* State residents: per academic year $10,458, $552 per credit hour; Nonstate residents: per academic year $21,546, $1,168 per credit hour. Tuition is subject to change. See the following website for updates and changes in tuition costs: http://www.uky.edu/Registrar/feesgen.htm.

Financial Assistance:

First-Year Students: Teaching assistantships available for first year. Average amount paid per academic year: $11,724. Average number of hours worked per week: 20. Research assistantships available for first year. Average amount paid per academic year: $12,874. Average number of hours worked per week: 20.

Advanced Students: Teaching assistantships available for advanced students. Average amount paid per academic year: $11,724. Average number of hours worked per week: 20. Research assistantships available for advanced students. Average amount paid per academic year: $12,874. Average number of hours worked per week: 20.

Additional Information: Of all students currently enrolled full time, 60% benefited from one or more of the listed financial assistance programs. Application and information available online at: http://education.uky.edu/AcadServ/content/scholarships.

Internships/Practica: Doctoral Degree (PhD Counseling Psychology): For those doctoral students for whom a professional psychology internship was required in this program prior to graduation, (8) students applied for an internship in 2011–2012, with (4) students obtaining an internship. Of those students who obtained an internship, (4) were paid internships. Of those students who obtained an internship, (4) students placed in APA/CPA accredited internships, (0) students placed in internships not APA/CPA accredited, but listed with the Association of Psychology Postdoctoral and Internship Programs (APPIC), (0) students placed in internships conforming to guidelines of the Council of Directors of School Psychology Programs (CDSPP), (0) students placed in internships that were not APA/CPA accredited, APPIC or CDSPP listed. Doctoral Degree (PhD School Psychology): For those doctoral students for whom a professional psychology internship was required in this program prior to graduation, (1) students applied for an internship in 2011–2012, with (1) students obtaining an internship. Of those students who obtained an internship, (1) were paid internships. Of those students who obtained an internship, (1) students placed in APA/CPA accredited internships, (0) students placed in internships not APA/CPA accredited, but listed with the Association of Psychology Postdoctoral and Internship Programs (APPIC), (0) students placed in internships conforming to guidelines of the Council of Directors

of School Psychology Programs (CDSPP), (0) students placed in internships that were not APA/CPA accredited, APPIC or CDSPP listed. Master's Degree (MA/MS Educational Psychology): An internship experience, such as a final research project or "capstone" experience is required of graduates.

Housing and Day Care: On-campus housing is available. See the following website for more information: http://www.uky.edu/Housing/graduate/index.html. On-campus day care facilities are available. See the following website for more information: http://www.uky.edu/HR/WorkLife/childcare.html.

Employment of Department Graduates:

Master's Degree Graduates: Of those who graduated in the academic year 2011–2012, the following categories and numbers represent the postgraduate activities and employment of master's degree graduates: Enrolled in a psychology doctoral program (9), enrolled in another graduate/professional program (3), enrolled in a postdoctoral residency/fellowship (n/a), employed in independent practice (n/a), employed in other positions at a higher education institution (2), employed in a professional position in a school system (4), employed in business or industry (1), employed in government agency (2), employed in a community mental health/counseling center (4), total from the above (master's) (25).

Doctoral Degree Graduates: Of those who graduated in the academic year 2011–2012, the following categories and numbers represent the postgraduate activities and employment of doctoral degree graduates: Enrolled in a psychology doctoral program (n/a), enrolled in a postdoctoral residency/fellowship (1), employed in independent practice (1), employed in an academic position at a university (6), employed in an academic position at a 2-year/4-year college (6), employed in other positions at a higher education institution (3), employed in a professional position in a school system (1), employed in government agency (2), employed in a community mental health/counseling center (2), total from the above (doctoral) (22).

Additional Information:

Orientation, Objectives, and Emphasis of Department: Three programs are housed within the department: counseling psychology, educational psychology, and school psychology. The program faculties in counseling psychology and in school psychology are committed to the scientist–practitioner model for professional training, while educational psychology faculty emphasize the researcher-teacher model. A strong emphasis has been placed upon the psychology core for all professional training. Because we are a graduate department with a professional emphasis, a high premium is placed on professional writing skills throughout—from admissions to course papers to final projects (theses and dissertations) in all programs. Counseling faculty research interests focus upon cultural diversity and social justice, counseling issues for sexual minorities, family processes, experiential therapies, and rape awareness. The school psychology faculty research interests focus upon evaluation and assessment, positive mental health outcomes, literacy and social development in young children, and direct interventions. The educational psychology faculty research interests include motivation in educational settings, cardiovascular stress in minority children, culture and socialization in relation to cognition, engagement in risky behaviors, and sleep deprivation. Students in each program are encouraged to establish mentoring relationships with their major professor by the beginning of their second semester. The counseling faculty intends to prepare professionals for diverse settings, e.g., colleges and universities, research facilities, hospitals, regional mental health centers, and private practice. The school psychology faculty aims to prepare scientist–practitioners who will function in school and university settings, in mental health consortia, and in private practice. The educational psychology faculty prepares graduates for research and teaching careers within higher education and applied research settings.

Special Facilities or Resources: The University of Kentucky is located on the western edge of Appalachia, which provides students with the opportunity to interact with a rich and varied American culture. The uniqueness of this potential client and research pool allows our students to examine attributes of the bridge between old, rural America and the future, more technological America. Microcomputer facilities are available within the department and within the college for student use in word processing, model development, simulation and evaluation, and data analysis. The university provides all the facilities and resources expected of a major research institution (e.g., extensive libraries, computer facilities, research environment, and medical center).

Information for Students With Physical Disabilities: See the following website for more information: http://www.uky.edu/StudentAffairs/DisabilityResourceCenter/.

Application Information:
Application available online. URL of online application: http://www.research.uky.edu/gs/ProspectiveStudents/Admission.html. Students are admitted in the Fall, application deadline December 1. December 1 deadline for PhD; February 15 deadline for Master's and EdS programs. *Fee:* $65. $75 International.

Kentucky, University of
Department of Psychology
Arts and Sciences
Kastle Hall
Lexington, KY 40506-0044
Telephone: (859) 257-9640
Fax: (859) 323-1979
E-mail: *psychology@uky.edu*
Web: *http://psychology.as.uky.edu/*

Department Information:
1917. Chairperson: Robert Lorch, PhD. Number of faculty: total—full-time 35; women—full-time 14; total—minority—full-time 5; women minority—full-time 3; faculty subject to the Americans With Disabilities Act 1.

Programs and Degrees Offered:
Listed in the following order: Program area, degree type (T if terminal Master's), number awarded 7/11–6/12. Clinical Psychology PhD (Doctor of Philosophy) 4, Experimental Psychology PhD (Doctor of Philosophy) 6.

APA Accreditation: Clinical PhD (Doctor of Philosophy). Student Outcome Data Website: http://psychology.as.uky.edu/clinical-psychology.

Student Applications/Admissions:
Student Applications
Clinical Psychology PhD (Doctor of Philosophy)—Applications 2012–2013, 171. Total applicants accepted 2012–2013, 9. Number full-time enrolled (new admits only) 2012–2013, 9. Number part-time enrolled (new admits only) 2012–2013, 0. Total enrolled 2012–2013 full-time, 42. Total enrolled 2012–2013 part-time, 0. Openings 2013–2014, 5. The median number of years required for completion of a degree in 2012–2013 were 6. The number of students enrolled full- and part-time who were dismissed or voluntarily withdrew from this program area in 2012–2013 were 1. *Experimental Psychology PhD (Doctor of Philosophy)*—Applications 2012–2013, 126. Total applicants accepted 2012–2013, 13. Number full-time enrolled (new admits only) 2012–2013, 13. Total enrolled 2012–2013 full-time, 44. Total enrolled 2012–2013 part-time, 0. Openings 2013–2014, 6. The median number of years required for completion of a degree in 2012–2013 were 5. The number of students enrolled full- and part-time who were dismissed or voluntarily withdrew from this program area in 2012–2013 were 3.

Scores: Entries appear in this order: required test or GPA, minimum score (if required), median score of students entering in 2012–2013. *Clinical Psychology PhD (Doctor of Philosophy):* GRE-V no minimum stated, 562, GRE-Q no minimum stated, 659, GRE-Analytical no minimum stated, 4.67, overall undergraduate GPA no minimum stated, 3.67, psychology GPA no minimum stated, Masters GPA no minimum stated, 3.65; *Experimental Psychology PhD (Doctor of Philosophy):* GRE-V no minimum stated, 517, GRE-Q no minimum stated, 632, GRE-Analytical no minimum stated, 4.17, overall undergraduate GPA no minimum stated, 3.54, psychology GPA no minimum stated, Masters GPA no minimum stated, 3.75.

Other Criteria: (importance of criteria rated low, medium, or high): GRE scores—high, research experience—high, work experience—medium, extracurricular activity—low, clinically related public service—medium, GPA—high, letters of recommendation—high, interview—high, statement of goals and objectives—high, knowl. of mentor's work—high, undergraduate major in psychology—medium, specific undergraduate psychology courses taken—medium. For additional information on admission requirements, go to http://psychology.as.uky.edu/psych-application-info.

Student Characteristics: The following represents characteristics of students in 2012–2013 in all graduate psychology programs in the department: Female—full-time 63, part-time 0; Male—full-time 23, part-time 0; African American/Black—full-time 5, part-time 0; Hispanic/Latino(a)—full-time 2, part-time 0; Asian/Pacific Islander—full-time 3, part-time 0; American Indian/Alaska Native—full-time 0, part-time 0; Caucasian/White—full-time 76, part-time 0; Multi-ethnic—full-time 0, part-time 0; students subject to the Americans With Disabilities Act—full-time 0, part-time 0; Unknown ethnicity—full-time 0, part-time 0; International students who hold an F-1 or J-1 Visa—full-time 2, part-time 0.

Financial Information/Assistance:
Tuition for Full-Time Study: *Doctoral:* State residents: per academic year $10,458, $552 per credit hour; Nonstate residents: per academic year $21,546, $1,168 per credit hour. Tuition is subject to change. Additional fees are assessed to students beyond the

costs of tuition for the following: Health fee/Recreation fee: total of approximately $500 per semester. See the following website for updates and changes in tuition costs: http://www.uky.edu/registrar/tuition-fees.

Financial Assistance:

First-Year Students: Teaching assistantships available for first year. Average amount paid per academic year: $14,400. Average number of hours worked per week: 20. Research assistantships available for first year. Average amount paid per academic year: $14,400. Average number of hours worked per week: 20. Fellowships and scholarships available for first year. Average amount paid per academic year: $14,000.

Advanced Students: Teaching assistantships available for advanced students. Average amount paid per academic year: $14,400. Average number of hours worked per week: 20. Research assistantships available for advanced students. Average amount paid per academic year: $14,400. Average number of hours worked per week: 20. Fellowships and scholarships available for advanced students. Average amount paid per academic year: $14,400.

Additional Information: Of all students currently enrolled full time, 99% benefited from one or more of the listed financial assistance programs. Application and information available online at: http://www.research.uky.edu/gs/StudentFunding/funding.html.

Internships/Practica: Doctoral Degree (PhD Clinical Psychology): For those doctoral students for whom a professional psychology internship was required in this program prior to graduation, (8) students applied for an internship in 2011–2012, with (8) students obtaining an internship. Of those students who obtained an internship, (8) were paid internships. Of those students who obtained an internship, (8) students placed in APA/CPA accredited internships, (0) students placed in internships not APA/CPA accredited, but listed with the Association of Psychology Postdoctoral and Internship Programs (APPIC), (0) students placed in internships conforming to guidelines of the Council of Directors of School Psychology Programs (CDSPP), (0) students placed in internships that were not APA/CPA accredited, APPIC or CDSPP listed. .

Housing and Day Care: On-campus housing is available. See the following website for more information: http://www.uky.edu/Housing/graduate/. On-campus day care facilities are available. See the following website for more information: http://www.uky.edu/HR/WorkLife/childcare.html.

Employment of Department Graduates:

Master's Degree Graduates: Of those who graduated in the academic year 2011–2012, the following categories and numbers represent the postgraduate activities and employment of master's degree graduates: Enrolled in a postdoctoral residency/fellowship (n/a), employed in independent practice (n/a), total from the above (master's) (0).

Doctoral Degree Graduates: Of those who graduated in the academic year 2011–2012, the following categories and numbers represent the postgraduate activities and employment of doctoral degree graduates: Enrolled in a psychology doctoral program (n/a), enrolled in a postdoctoral residency/fellowship (3), employed in an academic position at a university (1), total from the above (doctoral) (4).

Additional Information:

Orientation, Objectives, and Emphasis of Department: The goals of the doctoral program depend partly upon the specific program area in which a student enrolls. The program in Clinical Psychology follows the Clinical Science training model. All students are actively engaged in research throughout their graduate training, and the program views the scientific method as the appropriate basis for clinical psychology. Beginning in the second year of study, each student also receives extensive clinical experience via placements in mental or behavioral health settings. Graduates of the program are prepared to pursue an academic career or to be a practitioner. Students in the program receive broad exposure to the major theoretical perspectives influencing clinical psychology. Students in the program in Experimental Psychology, with concentrations in cognitive, developmental, social, animal learning and behavioral neuroscience, are trained as research scientists. They are exposed to the important theoretical perspectives and research paradigms of their respective areas. There is considerable latitude for individuals to define their specific programs of study. Graduates are prepared to pursue an academic career or a research position in an applied setting. All students complete a Master's thesis, written and oral doctoral qualifying examinations, and a dissertation demonstrating accomplishment in independent research.

Special Facilities or Resources: The psychology department occupies its own three-story building located by the computer center and main campus library. Kastle Hall houses faculty and student offices, classrooms, and research space. Research facilities in the building include animal laboratories for behavioral and physiological research; observation rooms with one-way mirrors; extensive video equipment; and microcomputer equipped rooms for cognitive research. Two additional buildings on campus are available for behavioral research. Current faculty have collaborative arrangements with several facilities on campus, including the neuropsychology laboratories in the Department of Neurology; the Oro-Facial Pain Clinic in the College of Dentistry; the Central Animal Research Facility; and the Sanders-Brown Center on Aging. The department maintains a large undergraduate subject pool. Clinical training facilities are excellent and include a departmental clinic housed in a separate building and clinical placement arrangements with a variety of mental and behavioral health facilities in Lexington.

Information for Students With Physical Disabilities: See the following website for more information: http://www.uky.edu/StudentAffairs/DisabilityResourceCenter/.

Application Information:
Send to Office of Research and Graduate Studies, Department of Psychology, University of Kentucky, 106B Kastle Hall, Lexington, KY 40506-0044. Application available online. URL of online application: http://www.research.uky.edu/gs/ProspectiveStudents/Admission.html. Students are admitted in the Fall, application deadline December 2. *Fee:* $65. International Fee: $75.00.

Louisville, University of
Department of Educational & Counseling Psychology,
 Counseling, and College Student Personnel
College of Education & Human Development
1905 South 1st Street
Louisville, KY 40292
Telephone: (502) 852-6884
Fax: (502) 852-0629
E-mail: *m.leach@louisville.edu*
Web: *http://louisville.edu/education/departments/ecpy*

Department Information:
1999. Chairperson: Dr. Jason Osborne. Number of faculty: total—full-time 5; women—full-time 1; total—minority—full-time 1.

Programs and Degrees Offered:
Listed in the following order: Program area, degree type (T if terminal Master's), number awarded 7/11–6/12. Counseling and Personnel Services PhD (Doctor of Philosophy) 8.

APA Accreditation: Counseling PhD (Doctor of Philosophy). Student Outcome Data Website: http://louisville.edu/education/degrees/phd-cps-cp.

Student Applications/Admissions:
Student Applications
Counseling and Personnel Services PhD (Doctor of Philosophy)—Applications 2012–2013, 99. Total applicants accepted 2012–2013, 7. Number full-time enrolled (new admits only) 2012–2013, 7. Number part-time enrolled (new admits only) 2012–2013, 0. Total enrolled 2012–2013 full-time, 36. Total enrolled 2012–2013 part-time, 2. Openings 2013–2014, 7. The median number of years required for completion of a degree in 2012–2013 were 4. The number of students enrolled full- and part-time who were dismissed or voluntarily withdrew from this program area in 2012–2013 were 0.
Scores: Entries appear in this order: required test or GPA, minimum score (if required), median score of students entering in 2012–2013. *Counseling and Personnel Services PhD (Doctor of Philosophy):* GRE-V 500, 610, GRE-Q 500, 710, GRE-Analytical 4.0, 4.5, overall undergraduate GPA 3.0, 3.5.
Other Criteria: (importance of criteria rated low, medium, or high): GRE scores—high, research experience—high, work experience—medium, extracurricular activity—low, clinically related public service—low, GPA—high, letters of recommendation—high, interview—high, statement of goals and objectives—high, undergraduate major in psychology—medium, specific undergraduate psychology courses taken—medium. For additional information on admission requirements, go to http://louisville.edu/education/degrees/phd-cps-cp.

Student Characteristics: The following represents characteristics of students in 2012–2013 in all graduate psychology programs in the department: Female—full-time 24, part-time 2; Male—full-time 12, part-time 0; African American/Black—full-time 1, part-time 0; Hispanic/Latino(a)—full-time 0, part-time 0; Asian/Pacific Islander—full-time 3, part-time 0; American Indian/Alaska Native—full-time 0, part-time 0; Caucasian/White—full-time 32, part-time 2; Multi-ethnic—full-time 0, part-time 0; students subject to the Americans With Disabilities Act—full-time 0, part-time 0; Unknown ethnicity—full-time 0, part-time 0; International students who hold an F-1 or J-1 Visa—full-time 2, part-time 0.

Financial Information/Assistance:
Tuition for Full-Time Study: *Doctoral:* State residents: per academic year $13,700, $571 per credit hour; Nonstate residents: per academic year $28,506, $1,188 per credit hour. Tuition is subject to change. See the following website for updates and changes in tuition costs: http://louisville.edu/finance/bursar/tuition.

Financial Assistance:
First-Year Students: Teaching assistantships available for first year. Average amount paid per academic year: $18,000. Average number of hours worked per week: 20. Apply by January 15. Research assistantships available for first year. Average amount paid per academic year: $18,000. Average number of hours worked per week: 20. Apply by January 15. Fellowships and scholarships available for first year. Average amount paid per academic year: $18,000. Average number of hours worked per week: 0. Apply by January 15.

Advanced Students: Teaching assistantships available for advanced students. Average amount paid per academic year: $18,000. Apply by January 15. Research assistantships available for advanced students. Average amount paid per academic year: $18,000. Apply by January 15. Fellowships and scholarships available for advanced students. Average amount paid per academic year: $18,000. Apply by January 15.

Additional Information: Of all students currently enrolled full time, 100% benefited from one or more of the listed financial assistance programs. Application and information available online at: http://louisville.edu/education/financialaid.

Internships/Practica: Doctoral Degree (PhD Counseling and Personnel Services): For those doctoral students for whom a professional psychology internship was required in this program prior to graduation, (2) students applied for an internship in 2011–2012, with (2) students obtaining an internship. Of those students who obtained an internship, (2) were paid internships. Of those students who obtained an internship, (2) students placed in APA/CPA accredited internships, (0) students placed in internships not APA/CPA accredited, but listed with the Association of Psychology Postdoctoral and Internship Programs (APPIC), (0) students placed in internships conforming to guidelines of the Council of Directors of School Psychology Programs (CDSPP), (0) students placed in internships that were not APA/CPA accredited, APPIC or CDSPP listed. Due to the wide variety of practicum placement sites in the city and surrounding area prior to internship, students accept internship positions in counseling centers, hospitals, community mental health centers, and VAs. Our community sites include the same, which is a strength of our program.

Housing and Day Care: On-campus housing is available. See the following website for more information: http://louisville.edu/housing/. On-campus day care facilities are available. See the following website for more information: http://louisville.edu/education/elc.

Employment of Department Graduates:

Master's Degree Graduates: Of those who graduated in the academic year 2011–2012, the following categories and numbers represent the postgraduate activities and employment of master's degree graduates: Enrolled in a postdoctoral residency/fellowship (n/a), employed in independent practice (n/a), total from the above (master's) (0).

Doctoral Degree Graduates: Of those who graduated in the academic year 2011–2012, the following categories and numbers represent the postgraduate activities and employment of doctoral degree graduates: Enrolled in a psychology doctoral program (n/a), employed in an academic position at a university (1), employed in a community mental health/counseling center (4), employed in a hospital/medical center (3), total from the above (doctoral) (8).

Additional Information:

Orientation, Objectives, and Emphasis of Department: The Counseling Psychology PhD Program adheres to a scientist–practitioner model and we strive to be balanced in each area. Students have a wide variety of applied settings from which to engage in counseling work, many consistent with the mission of an urban university. We tend to focus on applied work with adults. Our faculty emphasize cognitive-behavioral, psychodynamic, and interpersonal models in conjunction with multicultural and feminist approaches. Our research foci include diversity, microaggressions, LGBTQ issues, prevention of depression in adolescents, interpersonal relationships, forgiveness, suicide, religion and spirituality, vocational issues, international counseling, and gender issues. Faculty emphasize student collaboration on research projects and most students have a publication prior to graduation. Our Doctoral Student Organization is very active and engages in projects within and outside the department.

Special Facilities or Resources: Students have opportunities to collect research data at a variety of sites in the city. Depending on the faculty member with whom you work there may be opportunities in the department. General research space is available in the department. A research lab is housed in the college. Ample computers and training opportunities are available in the college and university.

Information for Students With Physical Disabilities: See the following website for more information: http://louisville.edu/disability.

Application Information:
Send to Graduate Admissions Office, University of Louisville, Houchens Room 6, Louisville, KY 40292-0001. Application available online. URL of online application: https://graduate.louisville.edu/apply. Students are admitted in the Fall, application deadline December 1. *Fee:* $60.

Louisville, University of
Psychological and Brain Sciences
Arts and Sciences
317 Life Sciences Building
Louisville, KY 40292
Telephone: (502) 852-6775
Fax: (502) 852-8904
E-mail: smeeks@louisville.edu
Web: http://www.louisville.edu/psychology/

Department Information:
1963. Chairperson: Suzanne Meeks. Number of faculty: total—full-time 26, part-time 6; women—full-time 11, part-time 4; total—minority—full-time 4; women minority—full-time 2; faculty subject to the Americans With Disabilities Act 1.

Programs and Degrees Offered:
Listed in the following order: Program area, degree type (T if terminal Master's), number awarded 7/11–6/12. Clinical Psychology PhD (Doctor of Philosophy) 5, Experimental Psychology PhD (Doctor of Philosophy) 6.

APA Accreditation: Clinical PhD (Doctor of Philosophy). Student Outcome Data Website: http://louisville.edu/psychology/doctorate/clinical-psychology/program-statistics.html.

Student Applications/Admissions:
Student Applications

Clinical Psychology PhD (Doctor of Philosophy)—Applications 2012–2013, 154. Total applicants accepted 2012–2013, 12. Number full-time enrolled (new admits only) 2012–2013, 10. Number part-time enrolled (new admits only) 2012–2013, 0. Total enrolled 2012–2013 full-time, 42. Total enrolled 2012–2013 part-time, 0. Openings 2013–2014, 6. The median number of years required for completion of a degree in 2012–2013 were 6. The number of students enrolled full- and part-time who were dismissed or voluntarily withdrew from this program area in 2012–2013 were 0. *Experimental Psychology PhD (Doctor of Philosophy)*—Applications 2012–2013, 22. Total applicants accepted 2012–2013, 6. Number full-time enrolled (new admits only) 2012–2013, 4. Number part-time enrolled (new admits only) 2012–2013, 0. Total enrolled 2012–2013 full-time, 26. Total enrolled 2012–2013 part-time, 0. Openings 2013–2014, 5. The median number of years required for completion of a degree in 2012–2013 were 8. The number of students enrolled full- and part-time who were dismissed or voluntarily withdrew from this program area in 2012–2013 were 2.

Scores: Entries appear in this order: required test or GPA, minimum score (if required), median score of students entering in 2012–2013. *Clinical Psychology PhD (Doctor of Philosophy):* GRE-V 550, 590, GRE-Q 550, 690, overall undergraduate GPA 3.0, 3.88; *Experimental Psychology PhD (Doctor of Philosophy):* GRE-V 550, 555, GRE-Q 550, 690, overall undergraduate GPA 3.0, 3.49, last 2 years GPA 3.0, 3.85.

Other Criteria: (importance of criteria rated low, medium, or high): GRE scores—high, research experience—high, work experience—high, extracurricular activity—high, clinically related public service—high, GPA—high, letters of recommendation—high, interview—high, statement of goals and objectives—high, undergraduate major in psychology—medium, specific undergraduate psychology courses taken—medium, Experimental Psychology PhD does not require clinically related public service.

Student Characteristics: The following represents characteristics of students in 2012–2013 in all graduate psychology programs in the department: Female—full-time 44, part-time 0; Male—full-time 24, part-time 0; African American/Black—full-time 5, part-time 0; Hispanic/Latino(a)—full-time 1, part-time 0; Asian/Pacific Islander—full-time 5, part-time 0; American Indian/Alaska Native—full-time 0, part-time 0; Caucasian/White—full-time 57, part-time 0; Multi-ethnic—part-time 0; students subject to the Americans With Disabilities Act—full-time 0, part-time 0; Unknown ethnicity—full-time 0, part-time 0; International students who hold an F-1 or J-1 Visa—full-time 5, part-time 0.

Financial Information/Assistance:

Tuition for Full-Time Study: *Doctoral:* State residents: per academic year $13,700, $571 per credit hour; Nonstate residents: per academic year $28,506, $1,188 per credit hour. Tuition is subject to change. See the following website for updates and changes in tuition costs: http://louisville.edu/finance/bursar/tuition.

Financial Assistance:

First-Year Students: Teaching assistantships available for first year. Average amount paid per academic year: $22,000. Average number of hours worked per week: 20. Apply by December 1. Research assistantships available for first year. Average amount paid per academic year: $22,000. Average number of hours worked per week: 20. Apply by December 1. Fellowships and scholarships available for first year. Average amount paid per academic year: $22,000. Average number of hours worked per week: 0. Apply by December 1.

Advanced Students: Teaching assistantships available for advanced students. Average amount paid per academic year: $22,000. Average number of hours worked per week: 20. Apply by December 1. Research assistantships available for advanced students. Average amount paid per academic year: $22,000. Average number of hours worked per week: 20. Apply by December 1. Traineeships available for advanced students. Average number of hours worked per week: 0. Fellowships and scholarships available for advanced students. Average amount paid per academic year: $22,000. Average number of hours worked per week: 0. Apply by December 1.

Additional Information: Of all students currently enrolled full time, 65% benefited from one or more of the listed financial assistance programs. Application and information available online at: https://graduate.louisville.edu/sigs/financial-support.html.

Internships/Practica: Doctoral Degree (PhD Clinical Psychology): For those doctoral students for whom a professional psychology internship was required in this program prior to graduation, (7) students applied for an internship in 2011–2012, with (7) students obtaining an internship. Of those students who obtained an internship, (7) were paid internships. Of those students who obtained an internship, (7) students placed in APA/CPA accredited internships, (0) students placed in internships not APA/CPA accredited, but listed with the Association of Psychology Postdoctoral and Internship Programs (APPIC), (0) students placed in internships conforming to guidelines of the Council of Directors of School Psychology Programs (CDSPP), (0) students placed in internships that were not APA/CPA accredited, APPIC or CDSPP listed. Most practicum experience takes place in our in-house Psychological Services Center. Paid and unpaid practica are available in community and government agencies. These vary from year to year, but include Central State Hospital, private practices, and the Departments of Psychiatry and Behavioral Sciences, Anesthesiology, and Family Medicine.

Housing and Day Care: On-campus housing is available. See the following website for more information: http://louisville.edu/housing/. On-campus day care facilities are available. See the following website for more information: http://louisville.edu/education/elc/.

Employment of Department Graduates:

Master's Degree Graduates: Of those who graduated in the academic year 2011–2012, the following categories and numbers represent the postgraduate activities and employment of master's degree graduates: Enrolled in a postdoctoral residency/fellowship (n/a), employed in independent practice (n/a), total from the above (master's) (0).

Doctoral Degree Graduates: Of those who graduated in the academic year 2011–2012, the following categories and numbers represent the postgraduate activities and employment of doctoral degree graduates: Enrolled in a psychology doctoral program (n/a), enrolled in another graduate/professional program (1), enrolled in a postdoctoral residency/fellowship (3), employed in independent practice (1), employed in an academic position at a university (1), employed in business or industry (1), employed in government agency (2), employed in a hospital/medical center (1), do not know (1), total from the above (doctoral) (11).

Additional Information:

Orientation, Objectives, and Emphasis of Department: The Clinical Psychology PhD program adheres to a scientist–practitioner model and is designed to provide training in research, psychological assessment, psychological intervention, and legal and professional issues. Faculty research foci are in health psychology, geropsychology and psychopathology. Clinical emphasis includes interpersonal and cognitive-behavioral approaches. The Experimental Psychology PhD program offers a flexible curriculum tailored to the individual student's interests while providing extensive training in the core processes of psychology, research methodology, and data analysis. Research is an integral component of the Experimental Psychology PhD, thus students begin working in their mentor's laboratory when they arrive on campus. Faculty research interests are varied, but fall into the following areas of strength: Cognitive Science, Developmental Science, Neuroscience, and Vision & Hearing Sciences. Recent graduates are pursuing careers in academic and non-academic fields in numerous settings, including universities and colleges, industry, government and private consulting organizations.

Special Facilities or Resources: Departmental facilities include modern laboratories and a Psychological Services Center. The University Computing resources are available from departmental stations via a campus-wide network. Additional training opportunities are available through such facilities as the Department of Psychiatry and Behavioral Sciences, the Child Evaluation Center, Central State Hospital, and other community agencies.

Information for Students With Physical Disabilities: See the following website for more information: http://louisville.edu/disability/.

Application Information:
Send to Graduate Admissions Office, University of Louisville, Houchens Room 6, Louisville, KY 40292-0001. Application available online. URL of online application: https://graduate.louisville.edu/apply. Students are admitted in the Fall, application deadline December 1. *Fee:* $50.

Morehead State University
Department of Psychology
Science & Technology
414 Reed Hall
Morehead, KY 40351
Telephone: (606) 783-2981
Fax: (606) 783-5077
E-mail: *g.corso@moreheadstate.edu*
Web: *http://www.moreheadstate.edu/psych*

Department Information:
1968. Chairperson: Gregory M. Corso. Number of faculty: total—full-time 9, part-time 3; women—full-time 4, part-time 2; total—minority—full-time 1; women minority—full-time 1.

Programs and Degrees Offered:
Listed in the following order: Program area, degree type (T if terminal Master's), number awarded 7/11–6/12. Clinical/Counseling Psychology MA/MS (Master of Arts/Science) (T) 11, General Experimental Psychology MA/MS (Master of Arts/Science) (T) 0.

Student Applications/Admissions:
Student Applications
Clinical/Counseling Psychology MA/MS (Master of Arts/Science)—Applications 2012–2013, 31. Number full-time enrolled (new admits only) 2012–2013, 13. Number part-time enrolled (new admits only) 2012–2013, 0. Total enrolled 2012–2013 full-time, 30. Total enrolled 2012–2013 part-time, 0. Openings 2013–2014, 14. The median number of years required for completion of a degree in 2012–2013 were 2. The number of students enrolled full- and part-time who were dismissed or voluntarily withdrew from this program area in 2012–2013 were 1. *General Experimental Psychology MA/MS (Master of Arts/Science)*—Applications 2012–2013, 5. Total applicants accepted 2012–2013, 1. Number full-time enrolled (new admits only) 2012–2013, 1. Number part-time enrolled (new admits only) 2012–2013, 0. Total enrolled 2012–2013 full-time, 1. Openings 2013–2014, 15. The median number of years required for completion of a degree in 2012–2013 were 2. The number of students enrolled full- and part-time who were dismissed or voluntarily withdrew from this program area in 2012–2013 were 0.
Scores: Entries appear in this order: required test or GPA, minimum score (if required), median score of students entering in 2012–2013. *Clinical/Counseling Psychology MA/MS (Master of Arts/Science):* GRE-V 143, 151, GRE-Q 137, 144, overall undergraduate GPA 2.8, 3.42; *General Experimental Psychology*

MA/MS (Master of Arts/Science): GRE-V 146, 151, GRE-Q 143, 147, overall undergraduate GPA 2.5, 3.4.
Other Criteria: (importance of criteria rated low, medium, or high): GRE scores—medium, research experience—medium, work experience—low, extracurricular activity—low, clinically related public service—low, GPA—medium, letters of recommendation—medium, interview—high, statement of goals and objectives—medium, undergraduate major in psychology—medium, specific undergraduate psychology courses taken—medium, Interview is High for the Clinical Program. Not used for the Experimental Program.

Student Characteristics: The following represents characteristics of students in 2012–2013 in all graduate psychology programs in the department: Female—full-time 26, part-time 0; Male—full-time 5, part-time 0; African American/Black—full-time 1, part-time 0; Hispanic/Latino(a)—full-time 2, part-time 0; Asian/Pacific Islander—full-time 3, part-time 0; American Indian/Alaska Native—full-time 0, part-time 0; Caucasian/White—full-time 24, part-time 1; Multi-ethnic—full-time 1, part-time 0; students subject to the Americans With Disabilities Act—full-time 0, part-time 0; Unknown ethnicity—full-time 0, part-time 0; International students who hold an F-1 or J-1 Visa—full-time 2, part-time 0.

Financial Information/Assistance:
Tuition for Full-Time Study: *Master's:* State residents: $414 per credit hour; Nonstate residents: $1,035 per credit hour. Tuition is subject to change. Additional fees are assessed to students beyond the costs of tuition for the following: laboratory fees for some courses. See the following website for updates and changes in tuition costs: http://www.moreheadstate.edu/bestvalue.

Financial Assistance:
First-Year Students: Teaching assistantships available for first year. Average amount paid per academic year: $10,000. Average number of hours worked per week: 20. Research assistantships available for first year. Average amount paid per academic year: $10,000. Average number of hours worked per week: 20.
Advanced Students: Teaching assistantships available for advanced students. Average amount paid per academic year: $10,000. Average number of hours worked per week: 20. Research assistantships available for advanced students. Average amount paid per academic year: $10,000. Average number of hours worked per week: 20.
Additional Information: Of all students currently enrolled full time, 100% benefited from one or more of the listed financial assistance programs. Application and information available online at: http://www.moreheadstate.edu/ga/.

Internships/Practica: Master's Degree (MA/MS Clinical/Counseling Psychology): An internship experience, such as a final research project or "capstone" experience is required of graduates. Master's Degree (MA/MS General Experimental Psychology): An internship experience, such as a final research project or "capstone" experience is required of graduates. The Department of Psychology maintains clinical affiliation agreements with a number of mental health agencies/facilities in Kentucky and in several other states. Internship and practicum placement sites include community mental health centers, outpatient clinics, hospitals, schools, juvenile justice facilities, and correctional settings.

Housing and Day Care: On-campus housing is available. See the following website for more information: http://www.moreheadstate.edu/housing/. No on-campus day care facilities are available.

Employment of Department Graduates:

Master's Degree Graduates: Of those who graduated in the academic year 2011–2012, the following categories and numbers represent the postgraduate activities and employment of master's degree graduates: Enrolled in a psychology doctoral program (1), enrolled in a postdoctoral residency/fellowship (n/a), employed in independent practice (n/a), employed in an academic position at a 2-year/4-year college (2), employed in a community mental health/counseling center (8), employed in a hospital/medical center (1), total from the above (master's) (12).

Doctoral Degree Graduates: Of those who graduated in the academic year 2011–2012, the following categories and numbers represent the postgraduate activities and employment of doctoral degree graduates: Enrolled in a psychology doctoral program (n/a), total from the above (doctoral) (0).

Additional Information:

Orientation, Objectives, and Emphasis of Department: The clinical and counseling programs are designed primarily to train Master's level psychologists to practice in a variety of settings, and lead to certification in many states. However, approximately 30% of our students also enter doctoral level programs upon graduation. The scientist–practitioner model is emphasized in the program, with primary emphasis on acquisition of applied clinical skills and knowledge of the general field of psychology. Consequently, competencies in critical analysis of theories, experimental design, and quantitative data analysis are expected. Clinical and counseling students are encouraged to conduct or participate in ongoing research in the department. Students interested in pursuing doctoral level training are encouraged to complete a thesis. The purpose of the general/experimental master's program is primarily to prepare students for entry into doctoral programs. Students and faculty are involved in research in several areas including cognitive, perception, animal learning and motivation, psychopharmacology, neurophysiology, developmental, social, and personality.

Special Facilities or Resources: The psychology program provides excellent laboratory facilities for the study of human and animal behavior. Faculty/student research programs often are funded through both intra- and extramural grants. The department maintains several microcomputer laboratories, and offers training in SPSS. Most accepted students are supported by graduate assistantships. Financial assistance for paper presentations at professional conferences is normally available.

Information for Students With Physical Disabilities: See the following website for more information: http://www2.moreheadstate.edu/disability/.

Application Information:

Send to Graduate Office, Morehead State University, 701 Ginger Hall, Morehead, KY 40351. Application available online. URL of online application: http://www.moreheadstate.edu/apply/. Students are admitted in the Fall, application deadline March 1. Preference will be given to applications received by March 1. Admissions continue through June 15. *Fee:* $30.

Northern Kentucky University

Department of Psychological Science
Arts & Sciences
Nunn Drive
Highland Heights, KY 41099
Telephone: (859) 572-5310
Fax: (859) 572-6085
E-mail: *msio@nku.edu*
Web: *http://msio.nku.edu*

Department Information:

1968. Chairperson: Jeffrey Smith. Number of faculty: total—full-time 21, part-time 16; women—full-time 11, part-time 13; total—minority—full-time 2, part-time 1; women minority—full-time 2, part-time 1.

Programs and Degrees Offered:

Listed in the following order: Program area, degree type (T if terminal Master's), number awarded 7/11–6/12. Industrial/Organizational Psychology MA/MS (Master of Arts/Science) (T) 12.

Student Applications/Admissions:

Student Applications

Industrial/Organizational Psychology MA/MS (*Master of Arts/Science*)—Applications 2012–2013, 47. Total applicants accepted 2012–2013, 19. Number full-time enrolled (new admits only) 2012–2013, 7. Number part-time enrolled (new admits only) 2012–2013, 10. Total enrolled 2012–2013 full-time, 11. Total enrolled 2012–2013 part-time, 30. Openings 2013–2014, 15. The median number of years required for completion of a degree in 2012–2013 were 3. The number of students enrolled full- and part-time who were dismissed or voluntarily withdrew from this program area in 2012–2013 were 3.

Scores: Entries appear in this order: required test or GPA, minimum score (if required), median score of students entering in 2012–2013. Industrial/Organizational Psychology MA/MS (*Master of Arts/Science*): GRE-V 150, 150, GRE-Q 144, 146, GRE-Analytical 3.5, 4.0, overall undergraduate GPA 3.0, 3.53, last 2 years GPA 3.0, 3.57.

Other Criteria: (importance of criteria rated low, medium, or high): GRE scores—high, research experience—medium, work experience—medium, extracurricular activity—low, GPA—high, letters of recommendation—medium, statement of goals and objectives—high, statistics course—high, undergraduate major in psychology—medium, specific undergraduate psychology courses taken—high.

Student Characteristics: The following represents characteristics of students in 2012–2013 in all graduate psychology programs in the department: Female—full-time 10, part-time 19; Male—full-time 1, part-time 11; African American/Black—full-time 2, part-time 5; Hispanic/Latino(a)—full-time 1, part-time 0; Asian/Pacific Islander—full-time 0, part-time 0; American Indian/Alaska Native—full-time 0, part-time 0; Caucasian/White—full-time 8, part-time 25; Multi-ethnic—full-time 0, part-time 0; students subject to the Americans With Disabilities Act—full-time 0, part-time 0; Unknown ethnicity—full-time 0, part-time 0; International students who hold an F-1 or J-1 Visa—full-time 0, part-time 0.

Financial Information/Assistance:

Tuition for Full-Time Study: *Master's:* State residents: $452 per credit hour; Nonstate residents: $765 per credit hour. Tuition is subject to change. See the following website for updates and changes in tuition costs: http://bursar.nku.edu/tuition.html.

Financial Assistance:

First-Year Students: Teaching assistantships available for first year. Average number of hours worked per week: 18. Apply by March 1. Research assistantships available for first year. Average number of hours worked per week: 18. Apply by March 1.

Advanced Students: Teaching assistantships available for advanced students. Average number of hours worked per week: 18. Apply by March 1. Research assistantships available for advanced students. Average number of hours worked per week: 18. Apply by March 1.

Additional Information: Of all students currently enrolled full time, 20% benefited from one or more of the listed financial assistance programs. Application and information available online at: http://gradschool.nku.edu/ProspectiveStudents/financing.html.

Internships/Practica: Master's Degree (MA/MS Industrial/Organizational Psychology): An internship experience, such as a final research project or "capstone" experience is required of graduates. Applied professional experience is gained through internships, which are competitive in nature and become available depending on sponsor funding, and through community engagement projects that allow graduate students to apply their accumulated professional knowledge, statistical skills, and analytic abilities within a consulting framework to challenges confronting regional non-for-profit organizations.

Housing and Day Care: On-campus housing is available. See the following website for more information: http://housing.nku.edu/. On-campus day care facilities are available. See the following website for more information: http://earlychildhood.nku.edu/.

Employment of Department Graduates:

Master's Degree Graduates: Of those who graduated in the academic year 2011–2012, the following categories and numbers represent the postgraduate activities and employment of master's degree graduates: Enrolled in a postdoctoral residency/fellowship (n/a), employed in independent practice (n/a), employed in business or industry (6), employed in government agency (1), employed in a hospital/medical center (1), still seeking employment (1), do not know (1), total from the above (master's) (10).

Doctoral Degree Graduates: Of those who graduated in the academic year 2011–2012, the following categories and numbers represent the postgraduate activities and employment of doctoral degree graduates: Enrolled in a psychology doctoral program (n/a), total from the above (doctoral) (0).

Additional Information:

Orientation, Objectives, and Emphasis of Department: The Department of Psychological Science at Northern Kentucky University embodies a rigorous, comprehensive, and evidence-based approach to the application of empirical science and research in psychology. The graduate program in Industrial and Organizational Psychology reflects this empirical orientation in developing the critical professional competencies identified by the Society for Industrial and Organizational Psychology as essential for prac-

tice and research in I/O psychology. To ensure that the program reflects contemporary trends, an advisory board comprised of I/O psychologists and representatives of major organizations in the greater Cincinnati region provides guidance. Graduate students are encouraged to conduct independent study, practicum, or thesis research with faculty on topics of interest throughout the program. Graduate seminars are presented by four fulltime graduate faculty holding doctoral degrees in I/O or applied social psychology, supplemented by adjunct faculty holding advanced degrees accompanied by specialized knowledge or relevant experience.

Special Facilities or Resources: The Department of Psychological Science employs two digitally equipped instructional computer labs equipped with 24 and 30 new Dell personal computers and 6 Apple Macintosh computers for statistics, research methods, and psychometrics seminars. Three additional laboratories are available for graduate student use: a suite of four rooms equipped with 16 Apple Macintosh computers and office; a computer lab equipped with eight Dell desktop computers; and a survey research lab equipped with eight Dell laptop computers. All computer labs are hardwired or linked to the campus wireless network. The Steely Library at NKU subscribes to most major research databases including PsycArticles (all APA journals), PsycInfo (APA articles, texts, and books), and Psychology and Behavioral Science Collection (575 journals) through EBSCO Host, and participates in national, regional, and state interlibrary loan systems. The Information Systems group at NKU provides lifetime email accounts to graduate students, and operates a contemporary, professional information management system with full access to the internet from remote (home) log in, including home access to SPSS with full content.

Information for Students With Physical Disabilities: See the following website for more information: http://disability.nku.edu/.

Application Information:
Send to Office of Graduate Programs, LAC 302, Northern Kentucky University, 1 Nunn Drive, Highland Heights, KY 41099. Application available online. URL of online application: http://www.nku.edu/apply/applygrad.html. Students are admitted in the Fall, application deadline August 1; Spring, application deadline December 1; Summer, application deadline May 1. *Fee:* $40.

Spalding University
School of Professional Psychology
College of Health and Natural Sciences
845 South Third Street
Louisville, KY 40203
Telephone: (502) 585-7127
Fax: (502) 585-7159
E-mail: *esimpson@spalding.edu*
Web: *http://www.spalding.edu/psychology*

Department Information:
1952. Chairperson: Steven Katsikas, PhD. Number of faculty: total—full-time 13, part-time 10; women—full-time 6, part-time 5; total—minority—full-time 2, part-time 1; women minority—full-time 1, part-time 1.

Programs and Degrees Offered:

Listed in the following order: Program area, degree type (T if terminal Master's), number awarded 7/11–6/12. Clinical Psychology PsyD (Doctor of Psychology) 16.

APA Accreditation: Clinical PsyD (Doctor of Psychology). Student Outcome Data Website: http://spalding.edu/academics/psychology/psy-d-student-admissions-outcomes-and-other-data-c-20/.

Student Applications/Admissions:

Student Applications

Clinical Psychology PsyD (Doctor of Psychology)—Applications 2012–2013, 122. Total applicants accepted 2012–2013, 59. Number full-time enrolled (new admits only) 2012–2013, 32. Number part-time enrolled (new admits only) 2012–2013, 0. Total enrolled 2012–2013 full-time, 146. Total enrolled 2012–2013 part-time, 21. Openings 2013–2014, 30. The median number of years required for completion of a degree in 2012–2013 were 5. The number of students enrolled full- and part-time who were dismissed or voluntarily withdrew from this program area in 2012–2013 were 3.

Scores: Entries appear in this order: required test or GPA, minimum score (if required), median score of students entering in 2012–2013. *Clinical Psychology PsyD (Doctor of Psychology):* GRE-V no minimum stated, 152, GRE-Q no minimum stated, 147, GRE-Analytical no minimum stated, 4, overall undergraduate GPA no minimum stated, 3.5.

Other Criteria: (importance of criteria rated low, medium, or high): GRE scores—medium, research experience—medium, work experience—medium, extracurricular activity—medium, clinically related public service—medium, GPA—medium, letters of recommendation—medium, interview—medium, statement of goals and objectives—medium, undergraduate major in psychology—low, specific undergraduate psychology courses taken—low. For additional information on admission requirements, go to http://spalding.edu/academics/psychology/about-the-psy-d-program/how-to-apply/.

Student Characteristics: The following represents characteristics of students in 2012–2013 in all graduate psychology programs in the department: Female—full-time 113, part-time 11; Male—full-time 33, part-time 10; African American/Black—full-time 4, part-time 0; Hispanic/Latino(a)—full-time 5, part-time 1; Asian/Pacific Islander—full-time 7, part-time 1; American Indian/Alaska Native—full-time 3, part-time 0; Caucasian/White—full-time 125, part-time 19; Multi-ethnic—full-time 2, part-time 0; students subject to the Americans With Disabilities Act—full-time 1, part-time 0; Unknown ethnicity—full-time 0, part-time 0; International students who hold an F-1 or J-1 Visa—full-time 4, part-time 0.

Financial Information/Assistance:

Tuition for Full-Time Study: *Doctoral:* State residents: per academic year $25,500, $895 per credit hour; Nonstate residents: per academic year $25,500, $895 per credit hour. Tuition is subject to change. See the following website for updates and changes in tuition costs: http://spalding.edu/admissions/tuition-and-fees/.

Financial Assistance:

First-Year Students: Research assistantships available for first year. Average amount paid per academic year: $4,945. Average number of hours worked per week: 10. Apply by March 1. Fellowships and scholarships available for first year. Average amount paid per academic year: $8,441. Average number of hours worked per week: 0. Apply by October 1.

Advanced Students: Research assistantships available for advanced students. Average amount paid per academic year: $6,010. Average number of hours worked per week: 10. Apply by March 1. Fellowships and scholarships available for advanced students. Average amount paid per academic year: $8,441. Average number of hours worked per week: 0. Apply by October 1.

Additional Information: Of all students currently enrolled full time, 62% benefited from one or more of the listed financial assistance programs. Application and information available online at: http://spalding.edu/financial-aid/.

Internships/Practica: Doctoral Degree (PsyD Clinical Psychology): For those doctoral students for whom a professional psychology internship was required in this program prior to graduation, (23) students applied for an internship in 2011–2012, with (22) students obtaining an internship. Of those students who obtained an internship, (22) were paid internships. Of those students who obtained an internship, (17) students placed in APA/CPA accredited internships, (0) students placed in internships not APA/CPA accredited, but listed with the Association of Psychology Postdoctoral and Internship Programs (APPIC), (0) students placed in internships conforming to guidelines of the Council of Directors of School Psychology Programs (CDSPP), (5) students placed in internships that were not APA/CPA accredited, APPIC or CDSPP listed. The Graduate Practicum Program has been designed to give students the opportunity to take their classroom learning into diverse, real-world settings. Over the course of four years, students learn to excel in assessment and evidence based psychotherapy, and begin to learn the practice of supervision. With over 60 community sites as practicum partners, students are afforded both a breadth of experience, to develop strong generalist skills, and a depth of experience in a chosen emphasis area. Practicum opportunities are available at such sites as university counseling centers, community agencies, rape crisis centers, inpatient psychiatric and VA hospitals, private practices, schools, and prisons. Further, focused learning opportunities are offered in such areas as behavioral medicine, corrections, pediatrics, neuropsychological assessment, addiction treatment and trauma recovery. Each year, the faculty review the placement preferences and training needs of each student and work diligently to make the best matches possible. Further, faculty are dedicated to ensuring students have the resources and support they need to be effective with their clients. To this end, each student each year is supervised by a site and a university supervisor, both licensed psychologists. The SOPP takes great pride in training professional, competent, ethical psychologists.

Housing and Day Care: On-campus housing is available. See the following website for more information: http://spalding.edu/student-life/housing-and-residence-life/. No on-campus day care facilities are available.

Employment of Department Graduates:

Master's Degree Graduates: Of those who graduated in the academic year 2011–2012, the following categories and numbers represent the postgraduate activities and employment of master's degree graduates: Enrolled in a postdoctoral residency/fellowship (n/a), employed in independent practice (n/a), total from the above (master's) (0).

Doctoral Degree Graduates: Of those who graduated in the academic year 2011–2012, the following categories and numbers represent the postgraduate activities and employment of doctoral degree graduates: Enrolled in a psychology doctoral program (n/a), enrolled in a postdoctoral residency/fellowship (1), employed in independent practice (4), employed in an academic position at a 2-year/4-year college (1), employed in other positions at a higher education institution (1), employed in government agency (6), employed in a community mental health/counseling center (3), total from the above (doctoral) (16).

Additional Information:

Orientation, Objectives, and Emphasis of Department: The Spalding University School of Professional Psychology is dedicated to providing generalist training in clinical psychology based upon scientific principles, grounded in evidence-based practice, and offered in a collaborative and cooperative setting. Furthermore, to train competent professionals to function in a complex and diverse society, the program emphasizes critical thinking, ethical decision-making, and the promotion of social justice. The School of Professional Psychology uses the Scholar-Practitioner Model to train students as local clinical scientists (Stricker & Trierweiler, 1995). The curriculum is based on a biopsychosocial approach to understanding human functioning. In addition, doctoral training is organized according to professional competencies set forth by the National Council of Schools of Professional Psychology (NCSPP). Current competencies include: Intervention, Assessment, Research and Evaluation, Relationship, Diversity, and Supervision/Consultation. The faculty share the belief that the most effective approach to training in professional psychology is one of cooperation and mutual support. As such, good relationship skills, compassion and sensitivity to ethical standards are values in our program.

Special Facilities or Resources: The faculty have various areas of expertise and interest and form research and discussion groups around these areas of interest. Current Research and Interest Groups (RIGs) include: a Health Psychology RIG, a Violence Prevention RIG, a Spirituality and Religion RIG, an Ibogaine Treatment Outcome RIG, two forensic-focused RIGs, a Child/Adolescent/Family RIG, a RIG focused on stereotypes and implicit biases, and a RIG focused on sports performance. The RIGs are constantly evolving based on student and faculty interests. Because we are a professional training program, research is conducted in applied settings. Students and faculty collaborate with other universities, medical centers and specialty clinics in conducting clinical research. Students also actively participate in state, regional and national conferences in the presentation of these projects. Students are encouraged to select dissertation and other research projects based on their own desires as well as the interests of the faculty.

Information for Students With Physical Disabilities: See the following website for more information: http://blog.spalding.edu/arc/accessibility-services/.

Application Information:
Send to Administrative Coordinator, School of Professional Psychology, 845 South Third Street, Louisville, KY 40203. Students are admitted in the Fall, application deadline January 15. *Fee:* $30.

Western Kentucky University (2012 data)

Department of Psychology
College of Education and Behavioral Sciences
1906 College Heights Boulevard #21030
Bowling Green, KY 42104-1030
Telephone: (270) 745-2696
Fax: (270) 745-6934
E-mail: *psych@wku.edu*
Web: *http://www.wku.edu/psychology/*

Department Information:
1931. Chairperson: Steven J. Haggbloom. Number of faculty: total—full-time 30, part-time 1; women—full-time 17; total—minority—full-time 4; women minority—full-time 4.

Programs and Degrees Offered:
Listed in the following order: Program area, degree type (T if terminal Master's), number awarded 7/11–6/12. Clinical Psychology MA/MS (Master of Arts/Science) (T) 9, Industrial/Organizational Psychology MA/MS (Master of Arts/Science) (T) 6, Psychological Science MA/MS (Master of Arts/Science) 4, School Psychology EdS (School Psychology) 12.

Student Applications/Admissions:

Student Applications

Clinical Psychology MA/MS (Master of Arts/Science)—Applications 2012–2013, 45. Total applicants accepted 2012–2013, 27. Number full-time enrolled (new admits only) 2012–2013, 13. Number part-time enrolled (new admits only) 2012–2013, 0. Total enrolled 2012–2013 full-time, 24. Total enrolled 2012–2013 part-time, 0. Openings 2013–2014, 10. The median number of years required for completion of a degree in 2012–2013 were 3. The number of students enrolled full- and part-time who were dismissed or voluntarily withdrew from this program area in 2012–2013 were 0. *Industrial/Organizational Psychology MA/MS (Master of Arts/Science)*—Applications 2012–2013, 30. Total applicants accepted 2012–2013, 9. Number full-time enrolled (new admits only) 2012–2013, 6. Number part-time enrolled (new admits only) 2012–2013, 0. Total enrolled 2012–2013 full-time, 12. Total enrolled 2012–2013 part-time, 0. Openings 2013–2014, 10. The median number of years required for completion of a degree in 2012–2013 were 2. The number of students enrolled full- and part-time who were dismissed or voluntarily withdrew from this program area in 2012–2013 were 0. *Psychological Science MA/MS (Master of Arts/Science)*—Applications 2012–2013, 13. Total applicants accepted 2012–2013, 11. Number full-time enrolled (new admits only) 2012–2013, 7. Number part-time enrolled (new admits only) 2012–2013, 0. Total enrolled 2012–2013 full-time, 12. Total enrolled 2012–2013 part-time, 0. Openings 2013–2014, 10. The median number of years required for completion of a degree in 2012–2013 were 2. The number of students enrolled full- and part-time who were dismissed or voluntarily withdrew from this program area in 2012–2013 were 0. *School Psychology EdS (School Psychology)*—Applications 2012–2013, 20. Total applicants accepted 2012–2013, 9. Number full-time enrolled (new admits only) 2012–2013, 6. Number part-time enrolled (new admits only) 2012–2013, 0. Total enrolled 2012–2013 full-time, 19. Total enrolled 2012–2013 part-time, 0. Openings 2013–2014, 10. The median number of years required for completion of a degree in 2012–2013 were 3. The number of students enrolled full- and part-time who were dismissed or voluntarily withdrew from this program area in 2012–2013 were 1.

Scores: Entries appear in this order: required test or GPA, minimum score (if required), median score of students entering in 2012–2013. *Clinical Psychology MA/MS (Master of Arts/Science):* GRE-V 139, 152, GRE-Q 139, 146, GRE-Analytical 3.5, 4, overall undergraduate GPA 2.75, 3.42, psychology GPA 3.00, 3.56; *Industrial/Organizational Psychology MA/MS (Master of Arts/Science):* GRE-V 139, 154, GRE-Q 139, 148, GRE-Analytical 3.5, 4.0, overall undergraduate GPA 2.75, 3.4, psychology GPA 3.00; *Psychological Science MA/MS (Master of Arts/Science):* GRE-V 139, 149, GRE-Q 139, 153, GRE-Analytical 3.5, 4.0, overall undergraduate GPA 2.75, 3.5, psychology GPA 3.00, 3.7; *School Psychology EdS (School Psychology):* GRE-V 139, 149, GRE-Q 139, 147, GRE-Analytical 3.5, 4.0, overall undergraduate GPA 2.75, 3.56.

Other Criteria: (importance of criteria rated low, medium, or high): GRE scores—high, research experience—medium, work experience—low, extracurricular activity—low, clinically related public service—low, GPA—high, letters of recommendation—high, interview—medium, statement of goals and objectives—medium, undergraduate major in psychology—medium, specific undergraduate psychology courses taken—low, The psychological science program may place greater emphasis on research experience. For additional information on admission requirements, go to http://www.wku.edu/psychology/programs/graduate/index.php.

Student Characteristics: The following represents characteristics of students in 2012–2013 in all graduate psychology programs in the department: Female—full-time 37, part-time 0; Male—full-time 30, part-time 0; African American/Black—full-time 2, part-time 0; Hispanic/Latino(a)—full-time 0, part-time 0; Asian/Pacific Islander—full-time 1, part-time 0; American Indian/Alaska Native—full-time 0, part-time 0; Caucasian/White—full-time 64, part-time 0; Multi-ethnic—full-time 0, part-time 0; students subject to the Americans With Disabilities Act—full-time 0, part-time 0; Unknown ethnicity—full-time 0, part-time 0; International students who hold an F-1 or J-1 Visa—full-time 0, part-time 0.

Financial Information/Assistance:

Tuition for Full-Time Study: *Master's:* State residents: $445 per credit hour; Nonstate residents: $489 per credit hour. Tuition is subject to change. See the following website for updates and changes in tuition costs: http://www.wku.edu/bursar/tuition_fees_current.php.

Financial Assistance:

First-Year Students: Teaching assistantships available for first year. Average amount paid per academic year: $1,200. Average number of hours worked per week: 20. Apply by March 1. Research assistantships available for first year. Average amount paid per academic year: $8,000. Average number of hours worked per week: 20. Apply by March 1.

Advanced Students: No information provided.

Additional Information: Of all students currently enrolled full time, 95% benefited from one or more of the listed financial assistance programs. Application and information available online at: http://www.wku.edu/graduate/aid/ga/.

Internships/Practica: Master's Degree (MA/MS Clinical Psychology): An internship experience, such as a final research project or "capstone" experience is required of graduates. Master's Degree (MA/MS Industrial/Organizational Psychology): An internship experience, such as a final research project or "capstone" experience is required of graduates. Clinical students complete a practicum experience with a local institution in the second year. School psychology students complete an assessment practicum experience in the Psychology Department training clinic in the first year, and have a one day per week practicum experience in the schools in the second year. The third year of the program consists of a minimum 1200 hour full-time internship in the schools.

Housing and Day Care: On-campus housing is available. See the following website for more information: http://www.wku.edu/housing/. On-campus day care facilities are available. See the following website for more information: http://www.wku.edu/ccc/.

Employment of Department Graduates:

Master's Degree Graduates: Of those who graduated in the academic year 2011–2012, the following categories and numbers represent the postgraduate activities and employment of master's degree graduates: Enrolled in a psychology doctoral program (6), enrolled in a postdoctoral residency/fellowship (n/a), employed in independent practice (n/a), employed in an academic position at a university (1), employed in business or industry (3), employed in government agency (2), employed in a community mental health/counseling center (1), employed in a hospital/medical center (1), still seeking employment (1), other employment position (4), do not know (2), total from the above (master's) (21).

Doctoral Degree Graduates: Of those who graduated in the academic year 2011–2012, the following categories and numbers represent the postgraduate activities and employment of doctoral degree graduates: Enrolled in a psychology doctoral program (n/a), total from the above (doctoral) (0).

Additional Information:

Orientation, Objectives, and Emphasis of Department: The Psychological Science program is designed to give students the quantitative and research skills needed for success in a PhD program. It has focus areas in cognitive, developmental, and biobehavioral psychology. The clinical program prepares graduates to work as master's level practitioners and for entry into a doctoral program. The school psychology program emphasizes the applied practice of psychology in the schools.

Special Facilities or Resources: The Department is located in a new building as of January, 2011, Gary Ransdell Hall. The building has a large clinic space shared with two other programs and considerable research lab space. Additional psychology lab space is located in Tate Page Hall. The Department recently acquired EEG/ERP/eye tracking equipment.

Information for Students With Physical Disabilities: See the following website for more information: http://www.wku.edu/sds/.

Application Information:
Application available online. URL of online application: http://www.wku.edu/graduate/prospective_students/admission/degree_instructions.php. Students are admitted in the Fall, application deadline March 1. *Fee:* $40. $40.00 domestic, $75.00 for international students.

Louisiana State University
Department of Psychology
College of Humanities and Social Sciences
236 Audubon Hall
Baton Rouge, LA 70803
Telephone: (225) 578-4120
Fax: (225) 578-4125
E-mail: narnol1@lsu.edu
Web: http://www.lsu.edu/psychology/

Department Information:
1908. Chairperson: Robert C. Mathews, PhD. Number of faculty: total—full-time 21; women—full-time 9.

Programs and Degrees Offered:
Listed in the following order: Program area, degree type (T if terminal Master's), number awarded 7/11–6/12. Clinical Psychology PhD (Doctor of Philosophy) 15, Cognitive and Developmental Psychology PhD (Doctor of Philosophy) 2, Biological Psychology PhD (Doctor of Philosophy) 0, Industrial/Organizational Psychology PhD (Doctor of Philosophy) 1, School Psychology PhD (Doctor of Philosophy) 6.

APA Accreditation: Clinical PhD (Doctor of Philosophy). Student Outcome Data Website: http://www.lsu.edu/psychology/specialty_clinical.html. School PhD (Doctor of Philosophy). Student Outcome Data Website: http://www.lsu.edu/psychology/specialty_school.html.

Student Applications/Admissions:

Student Applications ·

Clinical Psychology PhD (Doctor of Philosophy)—Applications 2012–2013, 166. Total applicants accepted 2012–2013, 15. Number full-time enrolled (new admits only) 2012–2013, 10. Total enrolled 2012–2013 full-time, 62. Openings 2013–2014, 8. The median number of years required for completion of a degree in 2012–2013 were 6. The number of students enrolled full- and part-time who were dismissed or voluntarily withdrew from this program area in 2012–2013 were 1. *Cognitive and Developmental Psychology PhD (Doctor of Philosophy)*—Applications 2012–2013, 27. Total applicants accepted 2012–2013, 6. Number full-time enrolled (new admits only) 2012–2013, 3. Number part-time enrolled (new admits only) 2012–2013, 0. Total enrolled 2012–2013 full-time, 17. Total enrolled 2012–2013 part-time, 0. Openings 2013–2014, 3. The median number of years required for completion of a degree in 2012–2013 were 6. The number of students enrolled full- and part-time who were dismissed or voluntarily withdrew from this program area in 2012–2013 were 0. *Biological Psychology PhD (Doctor of Philosophy)*—Applications 2012–2013, 11. Total applicants accepted 2012–2013, 0. Number full-time enrolled (new admits only) 2012–2013, 0. Total enrolled 2012–2013 full-time, 2. The number of students enrolled full- and part-time who were dismissed or voluntarily withdrew from this program area in 2012–2013 were 0. *Industrial/Organizational Psychology PhD (Doctor of Philosophy)*—Applications 2012–2013, 29. Total applicants accepted 2012–2013, 0. Number full-time enrolled (new admits only) 2012–2013, 0. Total enrolled 2012–2013 full-time, 4. The median number of years required for completion of a degree in 2012–2013 were 4. The number of students enrolled full- and part-time who were dismissed or voluntarily withdrew from this program area in 2012–2013 were 0. *School Psychology PhD (Doctor of Philosophy)*—Applications 2012–2013, 22. Total applicants accepted 2012–2013, 3. Number full-time enrolled (new admits only) 2012–2013, 3. Total enrolled 2012–2013 full-time, 22. Openings 2013–2014, 4. The median number of years required for completion of a degree in 2012–2013 were 5. The number of students enrolled full- and part-time who were dismissed or voluntarily withdrew from this program area in 2012–2013 were 4.

Scores: Entries appear in this order: required test or GPA, minimum score (if required), median score of students entering in 2012–2013. *Clinical Psychology PhD (Doctor of Philosophy):* GRE-V 151, 158, GRE-Q 147, 152, GRE-Analytical 3.5, 4.5, overall undergraduate GPA 3.39, 3.61, Masters GPA 3.37, 3.87; *Cognitive and Developmental Psychology PhD (Doctor of Philosophy):* GRE-V 154, 155, GRE-Q 147, 147, GRE-Analytical 3.5, 4.5, overall undergraduate GPA 3.20, 3.77, Masters GPA no minimum stated; *Biological Psychology PhD (Doctor of Philosophy):* GRE-V 570, 575, GRE-Q 620, 625, GRE-Analytical 4.0, 4.25, overall undergraduate GPA 3.27, 3.5, Masters GPA no minimum stated; *Industrial/Organizational Psychology PhD (Doctor of Philosophy):* GRE-V 520, 630, GRE-Q 580, 630, GRE-Analytical 3.5, 4.5, overall undergraduate GPA 3.06, 3.69, Masters GPA 3.64, 3.82; *School Psychology PhD (Doctor of Philosophy):* GRE-V 152, 156, GRE-Q 152, 151, GRE-Analytical 4.0, 4.0, overall undergraduate GPA 3.47, 3.5, Masters GPA 3.88, 3.88.

Other Criteria: (importance of criteria rated low, medium, or high): GRE scores—high, research experience—high, work experience—low, extracurricular activity—low, clinically related public service—low, GPA—high, letters of recommendation—high, interview—medium, statement of goals and objectives—high, undergraduate major in psychology—medium, specific undergraduate psychology courses taken—high. For additional information on admission requirements, go to http://www.lsu.edu/psychology/prospectivestudents.html.

Student Characteristics: The following represents characteristics of students in 2012–2013 in all graduate psychology programs in the department: Female—full-time 78, part-time 0; Male—full-time 29, part-time 0; African American/Black—full-time 3, part-time 0; Hispanic/Latino(a)—full-time 3, part-time 0; Asian/Pacific Islander—full-time 3, part-time 0; American Indian/Alaska Native—full-time 2, part-time 0; Caucasian/White—full-time 94, part-time 0; Multi-ethnic—full-time 2, part-time 0; students subject to the Americans With Disabilities Act—full-time 0, part-time 0; Unknown ethnicity—full-time 0, part-time 0; International students who hold an F-1 or J-1 Visa—full-time 3, part-time 0.

Financial Information/Assistance:
Tuition for Full-Time Study: *Doctoral:* State residents: per academic year $5,888; Nonstate residents: per academic year $21,280. Tuition is subject to change. Additional fees are assessed to stu-

dents beyond the costs of tuition for the following: Operational fees, technology fee, etc., of roughly $1200 per year. See the following website for updates and changes in tuition costs: http://www.bgtplan.lsu.edu/fees.htm.

Financial Assistance:

First-Year Students: Teaching assistantships available for first year. Average amount paid per academic year: $10,500. Average number of hours worked per week: 20. Apply by December 1. Research assistantships available for first year. Average amount paid per academic year: $16,000. Average number of hours worked per week: 20. Apply by December 1.

Advanced Students: Teaching assistantships available for advanced students. Average amount paid per academic year: $10,500. Average number of hours worked per week: 20. Research assistantships available for advanced students. Average amount paid per academic year: $16,000. Average number of hours worked per week: 20.

Additional Information: Of all students currently enrolled full time, 99% benefited from one or more of the listed financial assistance programs. Application and information available online at: http://www.lsu.edu/psychology/financial.html.

Internships/Practica: Doctoral Degree (PhD Clinical Psychology): For those doctoral students for whom a professional psychology internship was required in this program prior to graduation, (12) students applied for an internship in 2011–2012, with (12) students obtaining an internship. Of those students who obtained an internship, (12) were paid internships. Of those students who obtained an internship, (12) students placed in APA/CPA accredited internships, (0) students placed in internships not APA/CPA accredited, but listed with the Association of Psychology Postdoctoral and Internship Programs (APPIC), (0) students placed in internships conforming to guidelines of the Council of Directors of School Psychology Programs (CDSPP), (0) students placed in internships that were not APA/CPA accredited, APPIC or CDSPP listed. Doctoral Degree (PhD School Psychology): For those doctoral students for whom a professional psychology internship was required in this program prior to graduation, (3) students applied for an internship in 2011–2012, with (3) students obtaining an internship. Of those students who obtained an internship, (3) were paid internships. Of those students who obtained an internship, (3) students placed in APA/CPA accredited internships, (0) students placed in internships not APA/CPA accredited, but listed with the Association of Psychology Postdoctoral and Internship Programs (APPIC), (0) students placed in internships conforming to guidelines of the Council of Directors of School Psychology Programs (CDSPP), (0) students placed in internships that were not APA/CPA accredited, APPIC or CDSPP listed. Internships and practica are primarily used in the clinical and school programs. Examples of practicum sites include: LSU Department of Psychology, Psychological Services Center, Baton Rouge Health Center & Substance Abuse Clinic, Earl K. Long Hospital, LSU Medical School Unit, Pennington Biomedical Research Center, Pinecrest Developmental Center and Northshore Supports and Services Center. Recent internship sites include: Kennedy Krieger Institute at Johns Hopkins University School of Medicine, Baltimore, MD; Nebraska Internship Consortium in Professional Psychology, Lincoln, NE; Baylor College of Medicine, Houston, TX; University of Florida, Gainesville, FL; and Brown University Clinical Psychology Training Consortium, Providence, RI.

Housing and Day Care: On-campus housing is available. See the following website for more information: http://www.lsu.edu/housing. On-campus day care facilities are available. See the following website for more information: http://www.lsu.edu/childcare.

Employment of Department Graduates:

Master's Degree Graduates: Of those who graduated in the academic year 2011–2012, the following categories and numbers represent the postgraduate activities and employment of master's degree graduates: Enrolled in a postdoctoral residency/fellowship (n/a), employed in independent practice (n/a), total from the above (master's) (0).

Doctoral Degree Graduates: Of those who graduated in the academic year 2011–2012, the following categories and numbers represent the postgraduate activities and employment of doctoral degree graduates: Enrolled in a psychology doctoral program (n/a), enrolled in a postdoctoral residency/fellowship (1), employed in an academic position at a university (2), employed in a professional position in a school system (3), employed in business or industry (1), employed in a community mental health/counseling center (2), employed in a hospital/medical center (9), do not know (6), total from the above (doctoral) (24).

Additional Information:

Orientation, Objectives, and Emphasis of Department: The Department of Psychology at Louisiana State University is committed to the view that psychology is both a science and a profession, and it regards all areas of specialization as interdependent. All graduate students, regardless of intended area of specialization, receive broad training to develop the research skills needed to make scholarly contributions to the discipline of psychology throughout their subsequent careers. A student interested in only professional application without regard to research will not be comfortable in the graduate training program in this department. Both faculty and students in psychology recognize, however, that the model of the psychologist as a practitioner is a legitimate one. Those students whose main interest is in research are encouraged to develop familiarity with clinical, industrial, developmental or educational settings as potential research environments. Our program of graduate education reflects an emphasis on research and on professional aspects of psychology.

Special Facilities or Resources: The department occupies a centrally located building designed specifically to accommodate our program. Audubon Hall houses faculty offices, instructional space, office space for graduate students, and facilities for a wide array of research. The department also has a Psychological Services Center that provides training for our students and mental health services to the community.

Information for Students With Physical Disabilities: See the following website for more information: http://disability.lsu.edu/.

Application Information:
Send to Admissions Secretary, LSU Department of Psychology, 236 Audubon Hall, Baton Rouge, LA 70803. Application available online. URL of online application: http://www.lsu.edu/gradapply. Students are admitted in the Fall, application deadline December 1. *Fee:* $50.

Louisiana State University Shreveport

Department of Psychology
School of Human Sciences
One University Place
Shreveport, LA 71115
Telephone: (318) 797-5044
Fax: (318) 798-4171
E-mail: *Gary.Jones@LSUS.edu*
Web: *http://www.lsus.edu/ehd/psyc/*

Department Information:

1967. Chairperson: Gary E. Jones, PhD Number of faculty: total—full-time 12; women—full-time 6; total—minority—full-time 1.

Programs and Degrees Offered:

Listed in the following order: Program area, degree type (T if terminal Master's), number awarded 7/11–6/12. School Psychology Other 6, Counseling Psychology MA/MS (Master of Arts/Science) (T) 14.

Student Applications/Admissions:

Student Applications

School Psychology Other—Applications 2012–2013, 12. Total applicants accepted 2012–2013, 8. Number full-time enrolled (new admits only) 2012–2013, 5. Number part-time enrolled (new admits only) 2012–2013, 0. Total enrolled 2012–2013 full-time, 15. Total enrolled 2012–2013 part-time, 1. Openings 2013–2014, 10. The median number of years required for completion of a degree in 2012–2013 were 3. The number of students enrolled full- and part-time who were dismissed or voluntarily withdrew from this program area in 2012–2013 were 4. *Counseling Psychology MA/MS (Master of Arts/Science)*—Applications 2012–2013, 36. Total applicants accepted 2012–2013, 14. Number full-time enrolled (new admits only) 2012–2013, 10. Number part-time enrolled (new admits only) 2012–2013, 4. Total enrolled 2012–2013 full-time, 40. Total enrolled 2012–2013 part-time, 8. Openings 2013–2014, 20. The median number of years required for completion of a degree in 2012–2013 were 2. The number of students enrolled full- and part-time who were dismissed or voluntarily withdrew from this program area in 2012–2013 were 3.

Scores: Entries appear in this order: required test or GPA, minimum score (if required), median score of students entering in 2012–2013. *School Psychology Other:* GRE-V 144, 153, GRE-Q 144, 147, overall undergraduate GPA 2.5, 3.47; *Counseling Psychology MA/MS (Master of Arts/Science):* GRE-V 144, 146, GRE-Q 144, 142, overall undergraduate GPA 2.5, 3.03.

Other Criteria: (importance of criteria rated low, medium, or high): GRE scores—medium, research experience—low, work experience—low, extracurricular activity—low, clinically related public service—low, GPA—high, letters of recommendation—high, interview—high, statement of goals and objectives—high, undergraduate major in psychology—medium, specific undergraduate psychology courses taken—medium.

Student Characteristics: The following represents characteristics of students in 2012–2013 in all graduate psychology programs in the department: Female—full-time 61, part-time 18; Male—full-time 20, part-time 2; African American/Black—full-time 4, part-time 3; Hispanic/Latino(a)—full-time 1, part-time 2; Asian/Pacific Islander—full-time 0, part-time 1; American Indian/Alaska Native—full-time 0, part-time 0; Caucasian/White—full-time 73, part-time 13; Multi-ethnic—full-time 3, part-time 0; students subject to the Americans With Disabilities Act—full-time 2, part-time 0; Unknown ethnicity—full-time 0, part-time 0; International students who hold an F-1 or J-1 Visa—full-time 0, part-time 0.

Financial Information/Assistance:

Tuition for Full-Time Study: *Master's:* State residents: per academic year $6,006, $250 per credit hour; Nonstate residents: per academic year $14,565, $607 per credit hour. Tuition is subject to change. See the following website for updates and changes in tuition costs: http://www.lsus.edu/offices-and-services/accounting-services/tuition-and-fee-schedule.

Financial Assistance:

First-Year Students: Research assistantships available for first year. Average amount paid per academic year: $5,000. Average number of hours worked per week: 20. Apply by June 1.

Advanced Students: Research assistantships available for advanced students. Average amount paid per academic year: $5,000. Average number of hours worked per week: 20. Apply by June 1.

Additional Information: Of all students currently enrolled full time, 5% benefited from one or more of the listed financial assistance programs. Application and information available online at: http://www.lsus.edu/academics/graduate-studies/financial-assistance.

Internships/Practica: Master's Degree (MA/MS Counseling Psychology): An internship experience, such as a final research project or "capstone" experience is required of graduates. Practica for our Specialist degree students are carried out in surrounding parishes which have cooperative agreements with the university for training purposes. There are two distinct practicum experiences for our students. The first involves an observational practicum required during the Introduction to School Psychology course. The second occurs during Psych 754-a formal 200-plus hour practicum that is done in cooperating parishes with field school psychologist supervisors. All students must complete an appropriate internship to qualify for State certification. These internships meet state certification requirements. Students in the MSCP program also are also required to serve community-based supervised practicum experiences, in addition to a two semester internship experience supervised by an LPC or other appropriate mental health professional acceptable to the program. These internships currently meet LPC licensure requirements. Also, note the caution on the near universal requirement for a full legal background check prior to placement in community or school settings.

Housing and Day Care: On-campus housing is available. See the following website for more information: http://www.lsus.edu/

student-life/housing. No on-campus day care facilities are available.

Employment of Department Graduates:

Master's Degree Graduates: Of those who graduated in the academic year 2011–2012, the following categories and numbers represent the postgraduate activities and employment of master's degree graduates: Enrolled in a postdoctoral residency/fellowship (n/a), employed in independent practice (n/a), employed in government agency (4), employed in a community mental health/counseling center (7), employed in a hospital/medical center (2), not seeking employment (1), do not know (1), total from the above (master's) (15).

Doctoral Degree Graduates: Of those who graduated in the academic year 2011–2012, the following categories and numbers represent the postgraduate activities and employment of doctoral degree graduates: Enrolled in a psychology doctoral program (n/a), total from the above (doctoral) (0).

Additional Information:

Orientation, Objectives, and Emphasis of Department: The LSUS School Psychology Program curriculum is aligned with the training standards recommended by the National Association of School Psychologists (NASP), and the program is fully accredited. The primary focus of training is to develop fluency in data-based problem solving across both academic and behavior domains, and the overarching framework is a tiered model of service delivery based on student response to intervention (RTI). The program features three practicum experiences prior to a culminating 1200-hour internship in a public school setting. In the MSCP program, students are offered a curriculum that will lead to licensure as a professional counselor with a 48 credit hour program. Louisiana requires a 48 hour program while many other states require 60 hours, and students are easily able to take a full 60 hours, if desired. The program follows a practitioner-scientist model of training. There are a limited number of competitive graduate assistantships available for both programs.

Special Facilities or Resources: The Master's in Counseling Psychology and Specialist in School Psychology have state-of-the-art audio/video equipment for counseling and intervention techniques and skills, all housed in the psychology clinic and Department.

Information for Students With Physical Disabilities: See the following website for more information: http://www.lsus.edu/sdcc/services4disabilities/index.asp.

Application Information:

Send to Department Chair, Department of Psychology, Louisiana State University Shreveport, 1 University Place, Shreveport, LA 71115. Application available online. URL of online application: http://www.lsus.edu/admissions-and-financial-aid/graduate-admissions. Students are admitted in the Fall, application deadline May 31; Spring, application deadline October 31; Summer, application deadline March 31. Note, at this time, SSP program applications are due one month (30 days) later than the dates above. *Fee:* $10.

Louisiana, University of, Lafayette

Department of Psychology
Liberal Arts
P.O. Box 43131 UL-Lafayette Station
Lafayette, LA 70504-3131
Telephone: (337) 482-6597
Fax: (337) 482-6587
E-mail: *csm5689@louisiana.edu*
Web: *http://psychology.louisiana.edu/*

Department Information:

1970. Department Head: Cheryl S. Lynch. Number of faculty: total—full-time 16, part-time 2; women—full-time 9, part-time 1; total—minority—full-time 3; women minority—full-time 2.

Programs and Degrees Offered:

Listed in the following order: Program area, degree type (T if terminal Master's), number awarded 7/11–6/12. Psychology MA/MS (Master of Arts/Science) (T) 10.

Student Applications/Admissions:

Student Applications

Psychology MA/MS (Master of Arts/Science)—Applications 2012–2013, 56. Total applicants accepted 2012–2013, 24. Number full-time enrolled (new admits only) 2012–2013, 16. Number part-time enrolled (new admits only) 2012–2013, 2. Total enrolled 2012–2013 full-time, 29. Total enrolled 2012–2013 part-time, 12. Openings 2013–2014, 15. The median number of years required for completion of a degree in 2012–2013 were 4. The number of students enrolled full- and part-time who were dismissed or voluntarily withdrew from this program area in 2012–2013 were 3.

Scores: Entries appear in this order: required test or GPA, minimum score (if required), median score of students entering in 2012–2013. *Psychology MA/MS (Master of Arts/Science):* GRE-V 148, GRE-Q 147, overall undergraduate GPA 3.0, last 2 years GPA 3.0, psychology GPA 3.0.

Other Criteria: (importance of criteria rated low, medium, or high): GRE scores—medium, research experience—medium, work experience—medium, extracurricular activity—low, clinically related public service—medium, GPA—medium, letters of recommendation—high, interview—high, statement of goals and objectives—medium, The applied track requires an interview, which may take place via phone. For additional information on admission requirements, go to http://psychology.louisiana.edu/programs/gr-degrees.shtml.

Student Characteristics: The following represents characteristics of students in 2012–2013 in all graduate psychology programs in the department: Female—full-time 23, part-time 8; Male—full-time 6, part-time 4; African American/Black—full-time 1, part-time 3; Hispanic/Latino(a)—full-time 0, part-time 0; Asian/Pacific Islander—full-time 0, part-time 0; American Indian/Alaska Native—full-time 0, part-time 0; Caucasian/White—full-time 28, part-time 9; Multi-ethnic—full-time 0, part-time 0; students subject to the Americans With Disabilities Act—full-time 0, part-time 0; Unknown ethnicity—full-time 0, part-time 0; International students who hold an F-1 or J-1 Visa—full-time 2, part-time 0.

Financial Information/Assistance:

Tuition for Full-Time Study: *Master's:* State residents: per academic year $6,100; Nonstate residents: per academic year $14,934. Tuition is subject to change. See the following website for updates and changes in tuition costs: http://bursar.louisiana.edu/.

Financial Assistance:

First-Year Students: Teaching assistantships available for first year. Average amount paid per academic year: $7,500. Average number of hours worked per week: 15. Apply by April 12.

Advanced Students: Teaching assistantships available for advanced students. Average amount paid per academic year: $7,500. Average number of hours worked per week: 15. Apply by April 12.

Additional Information: Of all students currently enrolled full time, 27% benefited from one or more of the listed financial assistance programs. Application and information available online at: http://gradschool.ucs.louisiana.edu/?q=content/money-matters.

Internships/Practica: Master's Degree (MA/MS Psychology): An internship experience, such as a final research project or "capstone" experience is required of graduates. Internships for master's students in the applied option are available at the Community Mental Health Center, local psychiatric and rehabilitation hospitals and facilities, private agencies and practices, and at the University Counseling and Testing Center.

Housing and Day Care: On-campus housing is available. See the following website for more information: http://housing.louisiana.edu/. On-campus day care facilities are available. See the following website for more information: http://www.louisiana.edu/Student/ChildDev/.

Employment of Department Graduates:

Master's Degree Graduates: Of those who graduated in the academic year 2011–2012, the following categories and numbers represent the postgraduate activities and employment of master's degree graduates: Enrolled in a psychology doctoral program (2), enrolled in another graduate/professional program (2), enrolled in a postdoctoral residency/fellowship (n/a), employed in independent practice (n/a), employed in other positions at a higher education institution (2), do not know (4), total from the above (master's) (10).

Doctoral Degree Graduates: Of those who graduated in the academic year 2011–2012, the following categories and numbers represent the postgraduate activities and employment of doctoral degree graduates: Enrolled in a psychology doctoral program (n/a), total from the above (doctoral) (0).

Additional Information:

Orientation, Objectives, and Emphasis of Department: The Department of Psychology at the University of Louisiana at Lafayette strives to promote the study of psychology as a science, as a profession, and as a means of promoting human welfare. A master's program is offered with options in general experimental or applied psychology. After obtaining their degree, students may pursue the doctorate at other universities. Applied program students who just seek a terminal master's have found employment in the locality working for private and public agencies.

Special Facilities or Resources: The Psychology Department houses a computer laboratory for cognitive and social research. Computer assisted instruction is available for several courses. Major physiological research is conducted at the nearby primate center, The New Iberia Research Center. An additional smaller physiological laboratory is housed in the Psychology Department. The University of Louisiana at Lafayette has excellent computer facilities.

Information for Students With Physical Disabilities: See the following website for more information: http://disability.louisiana.edu/.

Application Information:

Send to Graduate School Director, Martin Hall, PO Box 44610, University of Louisiana at Lafayette, Lafayette, LA 70504. Application available online. URL of online application: http://gradschool.ucs.louisiana.edu/. Students are admitted in the Fall, application deadline June 30; Spring, application deadline November 30; Summer, application deadline April 30. Fellowships have a deadline of February 15; applicants seeking an assistantship ought to have all materials in by the start of April (for the Fall semester). Applicants for the Applied Track are normally admitted only in the Fall semester. *Fee:* $25. For international students, the fee is $30.

Louisiana, University of, Monroe (2012 data)
Department of Psychology
University of Louisiana—Monroe
700 University Avenue
Monroe, LA 71209
Telephone: (318) 342-1330
Fax: (318) 342-1352
E-mail: *williamson@ulm.edu*
Web: *http://www.ulm.edu/psychology/*

Department Information:

1965. Head: David Williamson. Number of faculty: total—full-time 8, part-time 3; women—full-time 2, part-time 1; total—minority—full-time 1, part-time 1; women minority—full-time 1, part-time 1.

Programs and Degrees Offered:

Listed in the following order: Program area, degree type (T if terminal Master's), number awarded 7/11–6/12. Experimental Psychology MA/MS (Master of Arts/Science) (T) 1, Psychometrics MA/MS (Master of Arts/Science) 5, Forensic Psychology MA/MS (Master of Arts/Science) (T) 0.

Student Applications/Admissions:

Student Applications

Experimental Psychology MA/MS (Master of Arts/Science)—Applications 2012–2013, 8. Total applicants accepted 2012–2013, 6. Number full-time enrolled (new admits only) 2012–2013, 4. Total enrolled 2012–2013 full-time, 5. Openings 2013–2014, 15. The median number of years required for completion of a degree in 2012–2013 were 2. *Psychometrics MA/MS (Master of Arts/Science)*—Applications 2012–2013, 9. Total applicants accepted 2012–2013, 7. Number full-time enrolled (new admits only) 2012–2013, 5. Total enrolled 2012–2013 full-time, 18. Openings 2013–2014, 15. The median number of years required for completion of a degree in

2012–2013 were 2. *Forensic Psychology MA/MS (Master of Arts/Science)*—Applications 2012–2013, 3. Total applicants accepted 2012–2013, 3. Number full-time enrolled (new admits only) 2012–2013, 3. Total enrolled 2012–2013 full-time, 3. The median number of years required for completion of a degree in 2012–2013 were 2.

Scores: Entries appear in this order: required test or GPA, minimum score (if required), median score of students entering in 2012–2013. *Experimental Psychology MA/MS (Master of Arts/Science):* GRE-V 450, GRE-Q 450, overall undergraduate GPA 2.75; *Psychometrics MA/MS (Master of Arts/Science):* GRE-V 450, GRE-Q 450, overall undergraduate GPA 2.75; *Forensic Psychology MA/MS (Master of Arts/Science):* GRE-V 450, GRE-Q 450.

Other Criteria: (importance of criteria rated low, medium, or high): GRE scores—high, research experience—medium, work experience—medium, extracurricular activity—low, clinically related public service—medium, GPA—high, letters of recommendation—high.

Student Characteristics: The following represents characteristics of students in 2012–2013 in all graduate psychology programs in the department: Female—full-time 16, part-time 0; Male—full-time 10, part-time 0; African American/Black—full-time 8, part-time 0; Hispanic/Latino(a)—full-time 0, part-time 0; Asian/Pacific Islander—full-time 1, part-time 0; American Indian/Alaska Native—full-time 0, part-time 0; Caucasian/White—full-time 17, part-time 0; Multi-ethnic—full-time 0, part-time 0; students subject to the Americans With Disabilities Act—full-time 0, part-time 0; Unknown ethnicity—full-time 0, part-time 0; International students who hold an F-1 or J-1 Visa—full-time 0, part-time 0.

Financial Information/Assistance:
Tuition for Full-Time Study: *Master's:* State residents: per academic year $5,060; Nonstate residents: per academic year $13,000. See the following website for updates and changes in tuition costs: http://www.ulm.edu/controller/sas/.

Financial Assistance:
First-Year Students: Research assistantships available for first year. Average amount paid per academic year: $5,000. Average number of hours worked per week: 20.

Advanced Students: Research assistantships available for advanced students. Average amount paid per academic year: $5,000.

Additional Information: Of all students currently enrolled full time, 40% benefited from one or more of the listed financial assistance programs.

Internships/Practica: Master's Degree (MA/MS Experimental Psychology): An internship experience, such as a final research project or "capstone" experience is required of graduates. Master's Degree (MA/MS Forensic Psychology): An internship experience, such as a final research project or "capstone" experience is required of graduates. Practica and internships are not required but encouraged for the psychometric concentration of the MS program.

Housing and Day Care: On-campus housing is available. See the following website for more information: http://www.ulm.edu/reslife/. On-campus day care facilities are available. See the following website for more information: http://www.ulm.edu/cdc/.

Employment of Department Graduates:
Master's Degree Graduates: Of those who graduated in the academic year 2011–2012, the following categories and numbers represent the postgraduate activities and employment of master's degree graduates: Enrolled in a psychology doctoral program (1), enrolled in another graduate/professional program (1), enrolled in a postdoctoral residency/fellowship (n/a), employed in independent practice (n/a), employed in an academic position at a university (1), employed in government agency (1), employed in a community mental health/counseling center (1), other employment position (1), total from the above (master's) (6).

Doctoral Degree Graduates: Of those who graduated in the academic year 2011–2012, the following categories and numbers represent the postgraduate activities and employment of doctoral degree graduates: Enrolled in a psychology doctoral program (n/a), total from the above (doctoral) (0).

Additional Information:
Orientation, Objectives, and Emphasis of Department: Three areas of concentration are available in the MS program. The general-experimental option focuses upon the basic science areas of psychology. The psychometric (preclinical) option is structured for those whose primary interest is employment in mental health or related settings. A new concentration in Forensic Psychology has been created. All programs require a comprehensive examination and an option of a thesis or research project in conjunction with an internship or grant application.

Special Facilities or Resources: A psychological services center includes a test library and special rooms. The department also has a computer room with 16 PCs with printer for general student use.

Application Information:
Send to Graduate School University of Louisiana-Monroe 700 University Avenue Monroe, LA 71209. Application available online. URL of online application: http://www.ulm.edu/gradschool/admis.html. Programs have rolling admissions. *Fee:* $20.

New Orleans, University of
Department of Psychology
College of Science
2001 Geology and Psychology Building
New Orleans, LA 70148
Telephone: (504) 280-6291
Fax: (504) 280-6049
E-mail: *lscarame@uno.edu*
Web: *http://psyc.uno.edu/*

Department Information:
1982. Chairperson: Paul Frick. Number of faculty: total—full-time 10; women—full-time 5; faculty subject to the Americans With Disabilities Act 1.

Programs and Degrees Offered:
Listed in the following order: Program area, degree type (T if terminal Master's), number awarded 7/11–6/12. Applied Developmental Psychology PhD (Doctor of Philosophy) 1, Applied Biopsychology PhD (Doctor of Philosophy) 2.

Student Applications/Admissions:

Student Applications

Applied Developmental Psychology PhD (Doctor of Philosophy)—Applications 2012–2013, 28. Total applicants accepted 2012–2013, 3. Number full-time enrolled (new admits only) 2012–2013, 3. Number part-time enrolled (new admits only) 2012–2013, 0. Total enrolled 2012–2013 full-time, 19. Total enrolled 2012–2013 part-time, 0. Openings 2013–2014, 4. The median number of years required for completion of a degree in 2012–2013 were 4. The number of students enrolled full- and part-time who were dismissed or voluntarily withdrew from this program area in 2012–2013 were 0. *Applied Biopsychology PhD (Doctor of Philosophy)*—Applications 2012–2013, 10. Total applicants accepted 2012–2013, 4. Number full-time enrolled (new admits only) 2012–2013, 4. Number part-time enrolled (new admits only) 2012–2013, 0. Total enrolled 2012–2013 full-time, 11. Total enrolled 2012–2013 part-time, 0. Openings 2013–2014, 3. The median number of years required for completion of a degree in 2012–2013 were 5. The number of students enrolled full- and part-time who were dismissed or voluntarily withdrew from this program area in 2012–2013 were 2.

Scores: Entries appear in this order: required test or GPA, minimum score (if required), median score of students entering in 2012–2013. *Applied Developmental Psychology PhD (Doctor of Philosophy)*: GRE-V no minimum stated, 155, GRE-Q no minimum stated, 151, overall undergraduate GPA no minimum stated, 3.47; *Applied Biopsychology PhD (Doctor of Philosophy)*: GRE-V no minimum stated, 152, GRE-Q no minimum stated, 149, overall undergraduate GPA no minimum stated, 3.5.

Other Criteria: (importance of criteria rated low, medium, or high): GRE scores—high, research experience—high, work experience—low, extracurricular activity—low, clinically related public service—medium, GPA—high, letters of recommendation—high, interview—medium, statement of goals and objectives—high, undergraduate major in psychology—medium, specific undergraduate psychology courses taken—high. For additional information on admission requirements, go to http://psyc.uno.edu/ApplicationInfo.html.

Student Characteristics: The following represents characteristics of students in 2012–2013 in all graduate psychology programs in the department: Female—full-time 19, part-time 0; Male—full-time 11, part-time 0; African American/Black—full-time 0, part-time 0; Hispanic/Latino(a)—full-time 1, part-time 0; Asian/Pacific Islander—full-time 2, part-time 0; American Indian/Alaska Native—full-time 0, part-time 0; Caucasian/White—full-time 26, part-time 0; Multi-ethnic—full-time 1, part-time 0; students subject to the Americans With Disabilities Act—full-time 0, part-time 0; Unknown ethnicity—full-time 0, part-time 0; International students who hold an F-1 or J-1 Visa—full-time 2, part-time 0.

Financial Information/Assistance:

Tuition for Full-Time Study: *Doctoral:* State residents: per academic year $5,164; Nonstate residents: per academic year $12,012. Tuition is subject to change. Additional fees are assessed to students beyond the costs of tuition for the following: graduate enhancement fee, technology fee. See the following website for updates and changes in tuition costs: http://www.uno.edu/bursar/TuitionFees/gradfees.aspx.

Financial Assistance:

First-Year Students: Teaching assistantships available for first year. Average amount paid per academic year: $9,750. Average number of hours worked per week: 20. Research assistantships available for first year. Average amount paid per academic year: $11,000. Average number of hours worked per week: 20. Fellowships and scholarships available for first year. Average amount paid per academic year: $15,000.

Advanced Students: Teaching assistantships available for advanced students. Average amount paid per academic year: $10,339. Average number of hours worked per week: 20. Research assistantships available for advanced students. Average amount paid per academic year: $12,421. Average number of hours worked per week: 20. Fellowships and scholarships available for advanced students. Average amount paid per academic year: $1,537.

Additional Information: Of all students currently enrolled full time, 100% benefited from one or more of the listed financial assistance programs. Application and information available online at: http://www.uno.edu/grad/FinancialResources.aspx.

Internships/Practica: Students in both applied specialties are required to complete 12 semester hours of practicum for the doctoral degree. There are a wide array of practicum experiences available and student's choice of practicum is based on his or her specific career objectives.

Housing and Day Care: On-campus housing is available. See the following website for more information: http://www.uno.edu/housing/. On-campus day care facilities are available. See the following website for more information: http://www.uno.edu/coehd/ChildrensCenter/index.aspx.

Employment of Department Graduates:

Master's Degree Graduates: Of those who graduated in the academic year 2011–2012, the following categories and numbers represent the postgraduate activities and employment of master's degree graduates: Enrolled in a postdoctoral residency/fellowship (n/a), employed in independent practice (n/a), total from the above (master's) (0).

Doctoral Degree Graduates: Of those who graduated in the academic year 2011–2012, the following categories and numbers represent the postgraduate activities and employment of doctoral degree graduates: Enrolled in a psychology doctoral program (n/a), enrolled in a postdoctoral residency/fellowship (1), employed in an academic position at a university (1), employed in government agency (1), total from the above (doctoral) (3).

Additional Information:

Orientation, Objectives, and Emphasis of Department: The University of New Orleans, Department of Psychology offers a PhD program with specializations in applied biopsychology and applied developmental psychology. The program was established in 1980 in response to a growing need for persons who are thoroughly trained in the basic content areas of human development or biopsychology, and who are able to translate that knowledge into practical applications. Both specialties emphasize research and service delivery in applied contexts. The applied developmental program has chosen to focus its training in the area of developmental psychopathology. Graduates are trained to work in a variety of settings where they can advance programmatic research focused on understanding psychopathological conditions from a developmental perspective and where they can make practical applications from this research (e.g., design and implement innovative prevention programs, or develop assessments for at-risk children). Similarly, the applied biopsychology program has chosen to focus its training in the area of the biological bases of psychopathology. Graduates are trained to work in a variety of settings where they can advance programmatic research focused on understanding psychopathological conditions from a biological and neuroscience perspective and where they can make practical applications from this research (e.g., test pharmacological treatments for psychological disorders; development of neurological, psychophysiological, or other biological tests for psychological disorders).

Information for Students With Physical Disabilities: See the following website for more information: http://www.ods.uno.edu/.

Application Information:
Send to Graduate Coordinator, Department of Psychology, 2001 Geology & Psychology Building, New Orleans, LA 70148. Application available online. URL of online application: http://www.uno.edu/admissions/apply/. Students are admitted in the Fall, application deadline February 1. *Fee:* $50.

Southeastern Louisiana University
Department of Psychology
Arts, Humanities, and Social Sciences
SLU 10831
Hammond, LA 70402
Telephone: (985) 549-2154
Fax: (985) 549-3892
E-mail: *pvarnado@selu.edu*
Web: *http://www.selu.edu/acad_research/depts/psyc/grad_degree/index.html*

Department Information:
Interim Department Head: Susan Coats. Number of faculty: total—full-time 9, part-time 5; women—full-time 5, part-time 4.

Programs and Degrees Offered:
Listed in the following order: Program area, degree type (T if terminal Master's), number awarded 7/11–6/12. General Psychology MA/MS (Master of Arts/Science) (T) 5, Industrial/Organizational Psychology MA/MS (Master of Arts/Science) (T) 0.

Student Applications/Admissions:
Student Applications
General Psychology MA/MS (Master of Arts/Science)—Applications 2012–2013, 40. Total applicants accepted 2012–2013, 12. Number full-time enrolled (new admits only) 2012–2013, 10. Number part-time enrolled (new admits only) 2012–2013, 0. Total enrolled 2012–2013 full-time, 18. Total enrolled 2012–2013 part-time, 6. Openings 2013–2014, 10. The median number of years required for completion of a degree in 2012–2013 were 2. The number of students enrolled full- and part-time who were dismissed or voluntarily withdrew from this program area in 2012–2013 were 3. *Industrial/Organizational Psychology MA/MS (Master of Arts/Science)*—Applications 2012–2013, 5. Total applicants accepted 2012–2013, 2. Number full-time enrolled (new admits only) 2012–2013, 2. Num-ber part-time enrolled (new admits only) 2012–2013, 0. Total enrolled 2012–2013 full-time, 3. Total enrolled 2012–2013 part-time, 2. Openings 2013–2014, 8. The number of students enrolled full- and part-time who were dismissed or voluntarily withdrew from this program area in 2012–2013 were 0.

Scores: Entries appear in this order: required test or GPA, minimum score (if required), median score of students entering in 2012–2013. *General Psychology MA/MS (Master of Arts/Science):* GRE-V no minimum stated, GRE-Q no minimum stated, overall undergraduate GPA 2.5, psychology GPA 2.5; *Industrial/Organizational Psychology MA/MS (Master of Arts/Science):* GRE-V no minimum stated, GRE-Q no minimum stated, overall undergraduate GPA 2.5, psychology GPA 2.5.

Other Criteria: (importance of criteria rated low, medium, or high): GRE scores—high, research experience—high, work experience—low, extracurricular activity—low, clinically related public service—low, GPA—high, letters of recommendation—high, statement of goals and objectives—medium, specific undergraduate psychology courses taken—medium. For additional information on admission requirements, go to http://www.selu.edu/acad_research/depts/psyc/grad_degree/app_procedure/.

Student Characteristics: The following represents characteristics of students in 2012–2013 in all graduate psychology programs in the department: Female—full-time 17, part-time 8; Male—full-time 4, part-time 0; African American/Black—full-time 0, part-time 1; Hispanic/Latino(a)—full-time 0, part-time 0; Asian/Pacific Islander—full-time 1, part-time 0; American Indian/Alaska Native—full-time 0, part-time 0; Caucasian/White—full-time 20, part-time 7; Multi-ethnic—full-time 0, part-time 0; students subject to the Americans With Disabilities Act—full-time 0, part-time 1; Unknown ethnicity—full-time 0, part-time 0; International students who hold an F-1 or J-1 Visa—full-time 0, part-time 0.

Financial Information/Assistance:
Tuition for Full-Time Study: *Master's:* State residents: per academic year $5,768; Nonstate residents: per academic year $10,858. Tuition is subject to change. See the following website for updates and changes in tuition costs: http://www.selu.edu/future_students/scholar_finaid/tuition_fees/index.html.

Financial Assistance:
First-Year Students: Research assistantships available for first year. Average amount paid per academic year: $9,000. Average number of hours worked per week: 20. Apply by March 15. Fellowships and scholarships available for first year. Average amount paid per academic year: $12,500. Average number of hours worked per week: 0. Apply by March 15.

Advanced Students: Research assistantships available for advanced students. Average amount paid per academic year: $9,000. Average number of hours worked per week: 20. Apply by March 15. Fellowships and scholarships available for advanced students. Average amount paid per academic year: $12,500. Average number of hours worked per week: 0. Apply by March 15.

Additional Information: Of all students currently enrolled full time, 45% benefited from one or more of the listed financial assistance programs.

Internships/Practica: Master's Degree (MA/MS General Psychology): An internship experience, such as a final research project or "capstone" experience is required of graduates. Master's Degree (MA/MS Industrial/Organizational Psychology): An internship experience, such as a final research project or "capstone" experience is required of graduates. Practica are available in clinical, counseling, and business (for I/O concentration) settings.

Housing and Day Care: On-campus housing is available. See the following website for more information: http://www.selu.edu/admin/housing/. No on-campus day care facilities are available.

Employment of Department Graduates:

Master's Degree Graduates: Of those who graduated in the academic year 2011–2012, the following categories and numbers represent the postgraduate activities and employment of master's degree graduates: Enrolled in a psychology doctoral program (3), enrolled in a postdoctoral residency/fellowship (n/a), employed in independent practice (n/a), employed in other positions at a higher education institution (1), other employment position (1), total from the above (master's) (5).

Doctoral Degree Graduates: Of those who graduated in the academic year 2011–2012, the following categories and numbers represent the postgraduate activities and employment of doctoral degree graduates: Enrolled in a psychology doctoral program (n/a), total from the above (doctoral) (0).

Additional Information:

Orientation, Objectives, and Emphasis of Department: The purposes of offering graduate study in the Department of Psychology are to prepare the student for a PhD program in Psychology through a Master of Arts degree program providing knowledge and research skills, and to provide students not intending to pursue a PhD degree with a variety of courses that will help prepare them for paraprofessional positions. We are a general psychology program intent on preparing students for doctoral level work. We also offer an Industrial/Organizational concentration for students interested in entering the business professions following graduation with their master's degree. Our program has maintained a strong rate of placement (75-90%) into doctoral programs over the last 7 years.

Special Facilities or Resources: The department has three 5-room laboratory suites for conducting research with humans. There are about 40 microcomputers and 7 printers in the department, about half of which are in a microcomputer laboratory. Statistical packages, such as SPSS, are available on the microcomputers and (via departmental terminal) on the university's mainframe computers.

Information for Students With Physical Disabilities: See the following website for more information: http://www.selu.edu/admin/ds/.

Application Information:

Send to Paula Varnado-Sullivan, PhD, SLU Box 10831, Hammond, LA 70402. Application available online. URL of online application: https://www.selu.edu/future_students/apply/grad_students/. Students are admitted in the Fall, application deadline March 15; Spring, application deadline October 15. *Fee:* $20.

Tulane University

Department of Psychology
School of Science and Engineering
2007 Stern Hall
New Orleans, LA 70118
Telephone: (504) 865-5331
Fax: (504) 862-8744
E-mail: *ruscher@tulane.edu*
Web: *http://tulane.edu/sse/psyc/*

Department Information:
1911. Chairperson: Stacy L. Overstreet. Number of faculty: total—full-time 22; women—full-time 12; total—minority—full-time 5; women minority—full-time 2.

Programs and Degrees Offered:
Listed in the following order: Program area, degree type (T if terminal Master's), number awarded 7/11–6/12. Social Psychology PhD (Doctor of Philosophy) 1, School Psychology PhD (Doctor of Philosophy) 4, Developmental Psychology PhD (Doctor of Philosophy) 2, Cognitive/Behavioral Neuroscience PhD (Doctor of Philosophy) 0.

APA Accreditation: School PhD (Doctor of Philosophy). Student Outcome Data Website: http://psych.tulane.edu/graduate/School/Aboutourprogram.Outcomes.htm.

Student Applications/Admissions:
Student Applications

Social Psychology PhD (Doctor of Philosophy)—Applications 2012–2013, 40. Total applicants accepted 2012–2013, 0. Number full-time enrolled (new admits only) 2012–2013, 0. Total enrolled 2012–2013 full-time, 9. Total enrolled 2012–2013 part-time, 0. Openings 2013–2014, 3. The median number of years required for completion of a degree in 2012–2013 were 5. The number of students enrolled full- and part-time who were dismissed or voluntarily withdrew from this program area in 2012–2013 were 0. *School Psychology PhD (Doctor of Philosophy)*—Applications 2012–2013, 40. Total applicants accepted 2012–2013, 8. Number full-time enrolled (new admits only) 2012–2013, 6. Total enrolled 2012–2013 full-time, 26. Total enrolled 2012–2013 part-time, 0. Openings 2013–2014, 3. The median number of years required for completion of a degree in 2012–2013 were 6. The number of students enrolled full- and part-time who were dismissed or voluntarily withdrew from this program area in 2012–2013 were 0. *Developmental Psychology PhD (Doctor of Philosophy)*—Applications 2012–2013, 15. Total applicants accepted 2012–2013, 1. Number full-time enrolled (new admits only) 2012–2013, 1. Total enrolled 2012–2013 full-time, 3. Total enrolled 2012–2013 part-time, 0. Openings 2013–2014, 1. The median number of years required for completion of a degree in 2012–2013 were 7. The number of students enrolled full- and part-time who were dismissed or voluntarily withdrew from this program area in 2012–2013 were 0. *Cognitive/Behavioral Neuroscience PhD (Doctor of Philosophy)*—Applications 2012–2013, 30. Total applicants accepted 2012–2013, 1. Number full-time enrolled (new admits only) 2012–2013, 1. Total enrolled 2012–2013 full-time, 7. Openings 2013–2014, 3. The number of students enrolled full- and part-time who were dismissed or voluntarily withdrew from this program area in 2012–2013 were 1.

Scores: Entries appear in this order: required test or GPA, minimum score (if required), median score of students entering in 2012–2013. *Social Psychology PhD (Doctor of Philosophy):* GRE-V no minimum stated, GRE-Q no minimum stated; *School Psychology PhD (Doctor of Philosophy):* GRE-V no minimum stated, GRE-Q no minimum stated; *Developmental Psychology PhD (Doctor of Philosophy):* GRE-V no minimum stated, GRE-Q no minimum stated; *Cognitive/Behavioral Neuroscience PhD (Doctor of Philosophy):* GRE-V no minimum stated, GRE-Q no minimum stated.

Other Criteria: (importance of criteria rated low, medium, or high): GRE scores—high, research experience—high, work experience—low, extracurricular activity—low, clinically related public service—medium, GPA—high, letters of recommendation—high, interview—high, statement of goals and objectives—medium, undergraduate major in psychology—medium, specific undergraduate psychology courses taken—medium, Clinical experience and interview important for school psychology. Relevant work experience can be looked upon favorably in other programs (e.g. statistical consulting; market research). For additional information on admission requirements, go to http://tulane.edu/sse/psyc/academics/graduate/phd-programs/admission.cfm.

Student Characteristics: The following represents characteristics of students in 2012–2013 in all graduate psychology programs in the department: Female—full-time 35, part-time 0; Male—full-time 10, part-time 0; African American/Black—full-time 5, part-time 0; Hispanic/Latino(a)—full-time 0, part-time 0; Asian/Pacific Islander—full-time 4, part-time 0; American Indian/Alaska Native—full-time 0, part-time 0; Caucasian/White—full-time 36, part-time 0; Multi-ethnic—full-time 0, part-time 0; students subject to the Americans With Disabilities Act—full-time 0, part-time 0; Unknown ethnicity—full-time 0, part-time 0; International students who hold an F-1 or J-1 Visa—full-time 3, part-time 0.

Financial Information/Assistance:

Tuition for Full-Time Study: *Doctoral:* State residents: per academic year $43,300; Nonstate residents: per academic year $43,300. Tuition is subject to change. See the following website for updates and changes in tuition costs: http://pandora.tcs.tulane.edu/acctrec/tuition.asp.

Financial Assistance:

First-Year Students: Teaching assistantships available for first year. Average amount paid per academic year: $18,135. Average number of hours worked per week: 12. Apply by December 15. Research assistantships available for first year. Average amount paid per academic year: $18,135. Average number of hours worked per week: 12. Apply by December 15. Fellowships and scholarships available for first year. Average amount paid per academic year: $22,000. Average number of hours worked per week: 12. Apply by December 15.

Advanced Students: Teaching assistantships available for advanced students. Average amount paid per academic year: $18,135. Average number of hours worked per week: 12. Research assistantships available for advanced students. Average amount paid per academic year: $18,135. Average number of hours worked per week: 12. Fellowships and scholarships available for advanced students. Average amount paid per academic year: $22,000. Average number of hours worked per week: 12.

Additional Information: Of all students currently enrolled full time, 100% benefited from one or more of the listed financial assistance programs. Application and information available online at: http://tulane.edu/financialaid/.

Internships/Practica: Doctoral Degree (PhD School Psychology): For those doctoral students for whom a professional psychology internship was required in this program prior to graduation, (1) students applied for an internship in 2011–2012, with (0) students obtaining an internship. Of those students who obtained an internship, (0) were paid internships. Of those students who obtained an internship, (0) students placed in APA/CPA accredited internships, (0) students placed in internships not APA/CPA accredited, but listed with the Association of Psychology Postdoctoral and Internship Programs (APPIC), (0) students placed in internships conforming to guidelines of the Council of Directors of School Psychology Programs (CDSPP), (0) students placed in internships that were not APA/CPA accredited, APPIC or CDSPP listed. Practicum opportunities are available in psychoeducational assessment, school consultation, family-school intervention, and cognitive-behavioral assessment and intervention.

Housing and Day Care: On-campus housing is available. See the following website for more information: http://tulane.edu/studentaffairs/housing/grad/. On-campus day care facilities are available. See the following website for more information: http://tulane.edu/childdevelopmentctrs/.

Employment of Department Graduates:

Master's Degree Graduates: Of those who graduated in the academic year 2011–2012, the following categories and numbers represent the postgraduate activities and employment of master's degree graduates: Enrolled in a postdoctoral residency/fellowship (n/a), employed in independent practice (n/a), total from the above (master's) (0).

Doctoral Degree Graduates: Of those who graduated in the academic year 2011–2012, the following categories and numbers represent the postgraduate activities and employment of doctoral degree graduates: Enrolled in a psychology doctoral program (n/a), employed in an academic position at a university (2), employed in other positions at a higher education institution (2), employed in a professional position in a school system (2), do not know (1), total from the above (doctoral) (7).

Additional Information:

Orientation, Objectives, and Emphasis of Department: Tulane's Department of Psychology offers the PhD in cognitive/behavioral neuroscience, developmental psychology, school psychology (APA-accredited program) and social psychology. The Department does not offer programs in clinical or counseling psychology. All students are expected to articulate an individualized plan of study by the end of the first year of training, a plan developed in consultation with an advisor and a committee of faculty members. Our two broad areas of substantive focus are development (e.g., infant, childhood, adolescence, cognitive aging and neuroscience) and culture & context (e.g., minority youth, stereotyping, ecological systems). Students are required to complete empirical studies for the master's thesis and the dissertation, and are expected to carry out additional research while in training. The APA-accredited program in school psychology, which emphasizes ecological systems and normal developmental processes, will take a minimum of four years to complete, and an additional year-long internship.

Special Facilities or Resources: The department has research laboratories and computer resources to facilitate research efforts requiring special equipment or space, including physiological, social, sensory, comparative, cognitive, and developmental psychology and human and animal learning. The Newcomb Children's Center, the Hebert facilities at Riverside for natural observation of animals, the laboratories of the Delta Primate Center, and the Audubon Zoological Gardens are available as research sites. There are also opportunities for research in the New Orleans area in organizations and industries, in public and private schools, and in hospitals and other settings serving children.

Information for Students With Physical Disabilities: See the following website for more information: http://tulane.edu/studentaffairs/disability/.

Application Information:
Send to Dean of the School of Science and Engineering, Tulane University, New Orleans, LA 70118. Application available online. URL of online application: https://app.applyyourself.com/?id=tulane-g. Students are admitted in the Fall, application deadline December 15. *Fee:* $0.

Maine, University of
Department of Psychology
Liberal Arts and Sciences
5742 Little Hall
Orono, ME 04469-5742
Telephone: (207) 581-2030
Fax: (207) 581-6128
E-mail: *michael.robbins@umit.maine.edu*
Web: *http://www.umaine.edu/psychology/*

Department Information:
1926. Chairperson: Michael A. Robbins. Number of faculty: total—full-time 15, part-time 3; women—full-time 6, part-time 1; total—minority—full-time 1; women minority—full-time 1.

Programs and Degrees Offered:
Listed in the following order: Program area, degree type (T if terminal Master's), number awarded 7/11–6/12. Clinical Psychology PhD (Doctor of Philosophy) 3, Developmental Psychology PhD (Doctor of Philosophy) 0, Psychological Sciences MA/MS (Master of Arts/Science) 2, Psychological Sciences PhD (Doctor of Philosophy) 0.

APA Accreditation:
Clinical PhD (Doctor of Philosophy). Student Outcome Data Website: http://www.umaine.edu/psychology/clinicalprogram/.

Student Applications/Admissions:
Student Applications
Clinical Psychology PhD (Doctor of Philosophy)—Applications 2012–2013, 139. Total applicants accepted 2012–2013, 6. Number full-time enrolled (new admits only) 2012–2013, 3. Number part-time enrolled (new admits only) 2012–2013, 0. Total enrolled 2012–2013 full-time, 23. Total enrolled 2012–2013 part-time, 0. Openings 2013–2014, 4. The median number of years required for completion of a degree in 2012–2013 were 7. The number of students enrolled full- and part-time who were dismissed or voluntarily withdrew from this program area in 2012–2013 were 1. *Developmental Psychology PhD (Doctor of Philosophy)*—Applications 2012–2013, 7. Total applicants accepted 2012–2013, 1. Number full-time enrolled (new admits only) 2012–2013, 1. Total enrolled 2012–2013 full-time, 3. Total enrolled 2012–2013 part-time, 0. The number of students enrolled full- and part-time who were dismissed or voluntarily withdrew from this program area in 2012–2013 were 0. *Psychological Sciences MA/MS (Master of Arts/Science)*—Applications 2012–2013, 7. Total applicants accepted 2012–2013, 0. Number full-time enrolled (new admits only) 2012–2013, 0. Total enrolled 2012–2013 full-time, 1. Total enrolled 2012–2013 part-time, 0. The median number of years required for completion of a degree in 2012–2013 were 3. The number of students enrolled full- and part-time who were dismissed or voluntarily withdrew from this program area in 2012–2013 were 0. *Psychological Sciences PhD (Doctor of Philosophy)*—Applications 2012–2013, 21. Total applicants accepted 2012–2013, 2. Number full-time enrolled (new admits only) 2012–2013, 2. Total enrolled 2012–2013 full-time, 11. Openings 2013–2014, 1. The number of students enrolled full- and part-time who were dismissed or voluntarily withdrew from this program area in 2012–2013 were 1.

Scores: Entries appear in this order: required test or GPA, minimum score (if required), median score of students entering in 2012–2013. *Clinical Psychology PhD (Doctor of Philosophy):* GRE-V no minimum stated, 540, GRE-Q no minimum stated, 680, overall undergraduate GPA no minimum stated, 3.64; *Developmental Psychology PhD (Doctor of Philosophy):* GRE-V no minimum stated, 390, GRE-Q no minimum stated, 560, overall undergraduate GPA no minimum stated; *Psychological Sciences PhD (Doctor of Philosophy):* GRE-V no minimum stated, 160, GRE-Q no minimum stated, 158, overall undergraduate GPA no minimum stated, 3.60.

Other Criteria: (importance of criteria rated low, medium, or high): GRE scores—medium, research experience—high, work experience—low, extracurricular activity—low, clinically related public service—medium, GPA—high, letters of recommendation—high, interview—high, statement of goals and objectives—high, undergraduate major in psychology—low, specific undergraduate psychology courses taken—low. For additional information on admission requirements, go to http://umaine.edu/psychology/graduate-program/.

Student Characteristics: The following represents characteristics of students in 2012–2013 in all graduate psychology programs in the department: Female—full-time 25, part-time 0; Male—full-time 13, part-time 0; African American/Black—full-time 0, part-time 0; Hispanic/Latino(a)—full-time 0, part-time 0; Asian/Pacific Islander—full-time 1, part-time 0; American Indian/Alaska Native—full-time 0, part-time 0; Caucasian/White—full-time 37, part-time 0; Multi-ethnic—full-time 0, part-time 0; students subject to the Americans With Disabilities Act—full-time 0, part-time 0; Unknown ethnicity—full-time 0, part-time 0; International students who hold an F-1 or J-1 Visa—full-time 1, part-time 0.

Financial Information/Assistance:
Tuition for Full-Time Study: *Master's:* State residents: $418 per credit hour; Nonstate residents: $1,259 per credit hour. *Doctoral:* State residents: per academic year $7,524, $418 per credit hour; Nonstate residents: per academic year $22,662, $1,202 per credit hour. Tuition is subject to change. Additional fees are assessed to students beyond the costs of tuition for the following: $238 for 1-5 credits; $554 for 6-11 credits; unified fee and recreation center fee. See the following website for updates and changes in tuition costs: http://umaine.edu/bursar/tuition-and-fees/.

Financial Assistance:
First-Year Students: Teaching assistantships available for first year. Average amount paid per academic year: $14,100. Average number of hours worked per week: 14. Research assistantships available for first year. Average amount paid per academic year: $15,100. Average number of hours worked per week: 20.

Advanced Students: Teaching assistantships available for advanced students. Average amount paid per academic year: $14,100. Average number of hours worked per week: 14. Research

assistantships available for advanced students. Average amount paid per academic year: $15,100. Average number of hours worked per week: 20. Traineeships available for advanced students. Average number of hours worked per week: 12. Fellowships and scholarships available for advanced students. Average number of hours worked per week: 0.

Additional Information: Of all students currently enrolled full time, 78% benefited from one or more of the listed financial assistance programs. Application and information available online at: http://www.umaine.edu/graduate/prospectivestudents/financialawardsandassistance.

Internships/Practica: Doctoral Degree (PhD Clinical Psychology): For those doctoral students for whom a professional psychology internship was required in this program prior to graduation, (4) students applied for an internship in 2011–2012, with (4) students obtaining an internship. Of those students who obtained an internship, (4) were paid internships. Of those students who obtained an internship, (3) students placed in APA/CPA accredited internships, (0) students placed in internships not APA/CPA accredited, but listed with the Association of Psychology Postdoctoral and Internship Programs (APPIC), (0) students placed in internships conforming to guidelines of the Council of Directors of School Psychology Programs (CDSPP), (1) students placed in internships that were not APA/CPA accredited, APPIC or CDSPP listed. Several settings are used for practicum training: The Psychological Services Center housed within the department, Penobscot Job Corps, Kennebec Valley Mental Health Center, Penquis CAPS Head Start, School Administrative District #4, #68, KidsPeace New England.

Housing and Day Care: On-campus housing is available. See the following website for more information: http://umaine.edu/housing/graduate-housing/. On-campus day care facilities are available. See the following website for more information: http://umaine.edu/cntsp/childcare/.

Employment of Department Graduates:

Master's Degree Graduates: Of those who graduated in the academic year 2011–2012, the following categories and numbers represent the postgraduate activities and employment of master's degree graduates: Enrolled in a postdoctoral residency/fellowship (n/a), employed in independent practice (n/a), total from the above (master's) (0).

Doctoral Degree Graduates: Of those who graduated in the academic year 2011–2012, the following categories and numbers represent the postgraduate activities and employment of doctoral degree graduates: Enrolled in a psychology doctoral program (n/a), enrolled in a postdoctoral residency/fellowship (3), total from the above (doctoral) (3).

Additional Information:

Orientation, Objectives, and Emphasis of Department: The department believes that the best graduate education involves close working relationships between the faculty and the student. Thus, a high faculty-to-student ratio and small class sizes characterize the department. In addition, incoming students are selected to work with a faculty research mentor. There are also opportunities for individualized study and experience in directed readings, research, and teaching. A faculty committee, selected to represent the student's interests, will assist the student in planning an appropriate graduate program.

Special Facilities or Resources: Psychophysiological, perception, EEG laboratories; animal research laboratory; on-site practicum training center; department-run preschool.

Information for Students With Physical Disabilities: See the following website for more information: http://umaine.edu/disability/.

Application Information:
Send to Graduate School, 5782 Winslow Hall, University of Maine, Orono, ME 04469-5782. Application available online. URL of online application: https://www.umaine.edu/graduate/application/pages/login.php. Students are admitted in the Fall, application deadline December 31. *Fee:* $50.

Baltimore, University of
Division of Applied Behavioral Sciences
Yale Gordon College of Arts and Sciences
1420 North Charles Street
Baltimore, MD 21201-5779
Telephone: (410) 837-5310
Fax: (410) 837-4059
E-mail: *eljohnson@ubalt.edu*
Web: *http://www.ubalt.edu/cas/graduate-programs-and-certificates/degree-programs/applied-psychology/*

Department Information:
1970. Acting Chair: Jonathan Shorr, PhD. Number of faculty: total—full-time 8; women—full-time 4; total—minority—full-time 1.

Programs and Degrees Offered:
Listed in the following order: Program area, degree type (T if terminal Master's), number awarded 7/11–6/12. Counseling Psychology MA/MS (Master of Arts/Science) (T) 17, Industrial/Organizational Psychology MA/MS (Master of Arts/Science) (T) 9, Certificate in Professional Counseling Studies Other 7.

Student Applications/Admissions:
Student Applications
Counseling Psychology MA/MS (Master of Arts/Science)—Applications 2012–2013, 82. Total applicants accepted 2012–2013, 64. Number full-time enrolled (new admits only) 2012–2013, 22. Number part-time enrolled (new admits only) 2012–2013, 16. Total enrolled 2012–2013 full-time, 41. Total enrolled 2012–2013 part-time, 36. Openings 2013–2014, 25. The median number of years required for completion of a degree in 2012–2013 were 4. The number of students enrolled full- and part-time who were dismissed or voluntarily withdrew from this program area in 2012–2013 were 2. *Industrial/Organizational Psychology MA/MS (Master of Arts/Science)*—Number full-time enrolled (new admits only) 2012–2013, 15. Number part-time enrolled (new admits only) 2012–2013, 0. Total enrolled 2012–2013 full-time, 6. Total enrolled 2012–2013 part-time, 12. Openings 2013–2014, 25. The median number of years required for completion of a degree in 2012–2013 were 2. The number of students enrolled full- and part-time who were dismissed or voluntarily withdrew from this program area in 2012–2013 were 0. *Certificate in Professional Counseling Studies Other*—Applications 2012–2013, 10. Total applicants accepted 2012–2013, 10. Number full-time enrolled (new admits only) 2012–2013, 1. Number part-time enrolled (new admits only) 2012–2013, 11. Total enrolled 2012–2013 full-time, 5. Total enrolled 2012–2013 part-time, 15. Openings 2013–2014, 20. The median number of years required for completion of a degree in 2012–2013 was 1. The number of students enrolled full- and part-time who were dismissed or voluntarily withdrew from this program area in 2012–2013 were 0.
Scores: Entries appear in this order: required test or GPA, minimum score (if required), median score of students entering in 2012–2013. *Counseling Psychology MA/MS (Master of Arts/Science)*: GRE-V no minimum stated, 440, GRE-Q no minimum stated, 530, GRE-Analytical no minimum stated, 4.0, overall undergraduate GPA 3.0; *Industrial/Organizational Psychology MA/MS (Master of Arts/Science)*: GRE-V no minimum stated, 440, GRE-Q no minimum stated, 535, overall undergraduate GPA 3.0.
Other Criteria: (importance of criteria rated low, medium, or high): GRE scores—medium, research experience—low, work experience—low, GPA—high, letters of recommendation—high, statement of goals and objectives—medium, undergraduate major in psychology—medium, specific undergraduate psychology courses taken—low. For additional information on admission requirements, go to http://www.ubalt.edu/cas/graduate-programs-and-certificates/degree-programs/applied-psychology/.

Student Characteristics: The following represents characteristics of students in 2012–2013 in all graduate psychology programs in the department: Female—full-time 44, part-time 45; Male—full-time 18, part-time 12; African American/Black—full-time 14, part-time 17; Hispanic/Latino(a)—full-time 2, part-time 1; Asian/Pacific Islander—full-time 1, part-time 0; American Indian/Alaska Native—full-time 0, part-time 0; Caucasian/White—full-time 38, part-time 33; Multi-ethnic—full-time 5, part-time 1; students subject to the Americans With Disabilities Act—full-time 0, part-time 0; Unknown ethnicity—full-time 2, part-time 5; International students who hold an F-1 or J-1 Visa—full-time 0, part-time 0.

Financial Information/Assistance:
Tuition for Full-Time Study: *Master's:* State residents: per academic year $12,574, $618 per credit hour; Nonstate residents: per academic year $17,528, $896 per credit hour. Tuition is subject to change. See the following website for updates and changes in tuition costs: http://www.ubalt.edu/admission/tuition-and-fees/index.cfm.

Financial Assistance:
First-Year Students: Research assistantships available for first year. Average amount paid per academic year: $4,260. Average number of hours worked per week: 20. Apply by March 15.
Advanced Students: Research assistantships available for advanced students. Average amount paid per academic year: $4,260. Average number of hours worked per week: 20. Apply by March 15.
Additional Information: Of all students currently enrolled full time, 3% benefited from one or more of the listed financial assistance programs. Application and information available online at: http://www.ubalt.edu/admission/graduate/financial-aid/.

Internships/Practica: The Baltimore/Washington Metropolitan area provides a wide range of settings for paid and unpaid practicum and internships. The academic and site supervisors work closely with the intern to insure a quality experience.

Housing and Day Care: On-campus housing is available. See the following website for more information: http://www.ubalt.edu/

campus-life/housing/. No on-campus day care facilities are available.

Employment of Department Graduates:

Master's Degree Graduates: Of those who graduated in the academic year 2011–2012, the following categories and numbers represent the postgraduate activities and employment of master's degree graduates: Enrolled in a postdoctoral residency/fellowship (n/a), employed in independent practice (n/a), total from the above (master's) (0).

Doctoral Degree Graduates: Of those who graduated in the academic year 2011–2012, the following categories and numbers represent the postgraduate activities and employment of doctoral degree graduates: Enrolled in a psychology doctoral program (n/a), total from the above (doctoral) (0).

Additional Information:

Orientation, Objectives, and Emphasis of Department: The Division of Applied Behavioral Sciences has a practitioner-oriented faculty of applied psychologists and researchers.

Special Facilities or Resources: Four different university labs and 100% of our classrooms provide Internet access, MS Office, and SPSS for students and faculty members. The Wagman Psychology Lab provides space for computer based testing and assessment.

Information for Students With Physical Disabilities: See the following website for more information: http://www.ubalt.edu/campus-life/center-for-educational-access/index.cfm.

Application Information:
Send to Office of Graduate Admissions, University of Baltimore, 1420 North Charles Street, Baltimore, MD 21201-5779. Application available online. URL of online application: http://www2.ubalt.edu/admission/apply-now/index.cfm. Students are admitted in the Fall, application deadline July 1; Spring, application deadline December 1. *Fee:* $40.

Frostburg State University
MS in Counseling Psychology Program
College of Liberal Arts and Sciences
Department of Psychology, 101 Braddock Road
Frostburg, MD 21532
Telephone: (301) 687-4446
Fax: (301) 687-7418
E-mail: *mpmurtagh@frostburg.edu*
Web: *http://www.frostburg.edu/dept/psyc/graduate-information/*

Department Information:
1977. Graduate Coordinator: Michael Murtagh. Number of faculty: total—full-time 5, part-time 2; women—full-time 2, part-time 1; total—minority—full-time 1; women minority—full-time 1.

Programs and Degrees Offered:
Listed in the following order: Program area, degree type (T if terminal Master's), number awarded 7/11–6/12. Counseling Psychology MA/MS (Master of Arts/Science) (T) 13.

Student Applications/Admissions:
Student Applications
Counseling Psychology MA/MS (Master of Arts/Science)—Applications 2012–2013, 40. Total applicants accepted 2012–2013, 12. Number full-time enrolled (new admits only) 2012–2013, 9. Number part-time enrolled (new admits only) 2012–2013, 2. Total enrolled 2012–2013 full-time, 26. Total enrolled 2012–2013 part-time, 4. Openings 2013–2014, 14. The median number of years required for completion of a degree in 2012–2013 were 3. The number of students enrolled full- and part-time who were dismissed or voluntarily withdrew from this program area in 2012–2013 were 0.

Scores: Entries appear in this order: required test or GPA, minimum score (if required), median score of students entering in 2012–2013. *Counseling Psychology MA/MS (Master of Arts/Science):* overall undergraduate GPA 3.00.

Other Criteria: (importance of criteria rated low, medium, or high): GRE scores—low, research experience—low, work experience—high, extracurricular activity—low, clinically related public service—high, GPA—high, letters of recommendation—medium, interview—high, statement of goals and objectives—medium, people skills—high, undergraduate major in psychology—medium, specific undergraduate psychology courses taken—medium. For additional information on admission requirements, go to http://www.frostburg.edu/dept/psyc/graduate-information/admissions/.

Student Characteristics: The following represents characteristics of students in 2012–2013 in all graduate psychology programs in the department: Female—full-time 25, part-time 2; Male—full-time 1, part-time 2; African American/Black—full-time 4, part-time 1; Hispanic/Latino(a)—full-time 2, part-time 0; Asian/Pacific Islander—full-time 0, part-time 0; American Indian/Alaska Native—full-time 0, part-time 0; Caucasian/White—full-time 20, part-time 3; Multi-ethnic—full-time 0, part-time 0; students subject to the Americans With Disabilities Act—full-time 0, part-time 0; Unknown ethnicity—full-time 0, part-time 0; International students who hold an F-1 or J-1 Visa—full-time 2, part-time 0.

Financial Information/Assistance:
Tuition for Full-Time Study: *Master's:* State residents: $327 per credit hour; Nonstate residents: $420 per credit hour. Tuition is subject to change. Additional fees are assessed to students beyond the costs of tuition for the following: $92.00 fees per credit hour. See the following website for updates and changes in tuition costs: http://www.frostburg.edu/ungrad/expense/.

Financial Assistance:
First-Year Students: Teaching assistantships available for first year. Average amount paid per academic year: $5,000. Average number of hours worked per week: 20. Apply by March 15. Research assistantships available for first year. Average amount paid per academic year: $5,000. Average number of hours worked per week: 20. Apply by March 15. Fellowships and scholarships available for first year. Average amount paid per academic year: $6,500. Average number of hours worked per week: 20. Apply by March 15.

Advanced Students: Teaching assistantships available for advanced students. Average amount paid per academic year: $5,000. Average number of hours worked per week: 20. Apply by March 15. Research assistantships available for advanced students.

Average amount paid per academic year: $5,000. Average number of hours worked per week: 20. Apply by March 15. Fellowships and scholarships available for advanced students. Average amount paid per academic year: $6,500. Average number of hours worked per week: 20. Apply by March 15.

Additional Information: Of all students currently enrolled full time, 37% benefited from one or more of the listed financial assistance programs. Application and information available online at: http://www.frostburg.edu/grad/ga.htm.

Internships/Practica: Master's Degree (MA/MS Counseling Psychology): An internship experience, such as a final research project or "capstone" experience is required of graduates. An extensive, two semester internship experience is required which facilitates students' receptivity to supervisory feedback, enhances self-awareness, and provides a setting in which the transition from student to professional is accomplished. In addition to on-site supervision, students participate in individual and group supervision with FSU faculty. Past graduate internship sites for the M.S. Counseling Psychology program have included: outpatient community mental health (the most frequent internship setting); college counseling; inpatient psychiatric; inpatient and outpatient addictions; family services; K-12 psychological assessment and alternative classroom and after school care programs; community health advocacy and counseling; criminal justice system; nursing homes; hospital-based crisis services; hospice; and domestic violence programs. Students construct their internship experiences in order to meet training goals they formulate. Students electing to complete graduate emphasis programs in Addictions Counseling Psychology and Child and Family Counseling Psychology must complete at least 150 hours of direct services in settings consistent with the certificate program's focus. Internship experiences, in addition to at least four academic semesters of study, prepare graduates for positions as mental health counselors, marriage and family counselors, crisis counselors, drug and alcohol counselors, community health specialists, and for supervisory positions in a variety of settings.

Housing and Day Care: On-campus housing is available. See the following website for more information: http://www.frostburg.edu/clife/reslife/. On-campus day care facilities are available. See the following website for more information: http://www.frostburg.edu/childrenscenter/.

Employment of Department Graduates:
Master's Degree Graduates: Of those who graduated in the academic year 2011–2012, the following categories and numbers represent the postgraduate activities and employment of master's degree graduates: Enrolled in a postdoctoral residency/fellowship (n/a), employed in independent practice (n/a), total from the above (master's) (0).
Doctoral Degree Graduates: Of those who graduated in the academic year 2011–2012, the following categories and numbers represent the postgraduate activities and employment of doctoral degree graduates: Enrolled in a psychology doctoral program (n/a), total from the above (doctoral) (0).

Additional Information:
Orientation, Objectives, and Emphasis of Department: Providing training in professional psychology at the Master's level, FSU's program is designed for those pursuing further study in science-based counseling psychology. Our theoretical perspective is integrative, including cognitive-behavioral, motivational interviewing, family systems, developmental, multicultural, humanistic, and brief therapies. We emphasize training in empirically-supported treatments for children, adolescents, families and adults. Students develop counseling skills through learning about self, client, counselor-client relationships, and the importance of cultural contexts. Considerable attention is given not only to development of professional skills but also to personal development and multicultural awareness. These emphases reflect our belief that an effective counselor is one who is self-aware and receptive to consultation. For continuing study at the doctoral level, experience and knowledge gained in this program provide a firm foundation. Optional research opportunities prepare students for advanced graduate study in psychology. Two emphasis programs provide specialized training in Addictions Counseling Psychology and Child and Family Counseling Psychology. These can be completed within the three-year program of study, as well as courses required for licensure. All National Counselor Exam course areas are offered, and FSU offers this exam. The Master's in Psychology Accreditation Council accredits this program.

Special Facilities or Resources: Resources include specially designed counseling practice rooms for individual and group counseling. Two-way mirrors with adjacent observation rooms are available for supervision. Audiotaping and videotaping resources are available for faculty and student use. In addition, students' case conceptualization write-ups and all previous internship papers are available for restricted use by students.

Information for Students With Physical Disabilities: See the following website for more information: http://www.frostburg.edu/clife/dss/.

Application Information:
Send to Office of Graduate Services, 101 Braddock Road, Frostburg State University, Frostburg, MD 21532. Application available online. URL of online application: http://www.frostburg.edu/grad/apply.htm. Students are admitted in the Fall, application deadline February 1. *Fee:* $30.

Johns Hopkins University
Psychological and Brain Sciences
School of Arts and Sciences
3400 North Charles Street, Ames Hall 204
Baltimore, MD 21218
Telephone: (410) 516-6175
Fax: (410) 516-4478
E-mail: *pbs@jhu.edu*
Web: *http://pbs.jhu.edu*

Department Information:
1883. Acting Chairperson: Dr. Susan Courtney. Number of faculty: total—full-time 12, part-time 8; women—full-time 4, part-time 1; faculty subject to the Americans With Disabilities Act 1.

Programs and Degrees Offered:
Listed in the following order: Program area, degree type (T if terminal Master's), number awarded 7/11–6/12. Biopsychology PhD (Doctor of Philosophy) 1, Cognitive PhD (Doctor of Philoso-

phy) 0, Cognitive Neuroscience PhD (Doctor of Philosophy) 2, Developmental PhD (Doctor of Philosophy) 0.

Student Applications/Admissions:

Student Applications

Biopsychology PhD (Doctor of Philosophy)—Applications 2012–2013, 20. Total applicants accepted 2012–2013, 0. Number full-time enrolled (new admits only) 2012–2013, 0. Total enrolled 2012–2013 full-time, 6. The median number of years required for completion of a degree in 2012–2013 were 5. *Cognitive PhD (Doctor of Philosophy)*—Applications 2012–2013, 19. Total applicants accepted 2012–2013, 2. Number full-time enrolled (new admits only) 2012–2013, 2. Total enrolled 2012–2013 full-time, 8. The median number of years required for completion of a degree in 2012–2013 were 5. *Cognitive Neuroscience PhD (Doctor of Philosophy)*—Applications 2012–2013, 68. Total applicants accepted 2012–2013, 9. Number full-time enrolled (new admits only) 2012–2013, 4. Total enrolled 2012–2013 full-time, 15. The median number of years required for completion of a degree in 2012–2013 were 5. *Developmental PhD (Doctor of Philosophy)*—Applications 2012–2013, 13. Total applicants accepted 2012–2013, 1. Number full-time enrolled (new admits only) 2012–2013, 1. Total enrolled 2012–2013 full-time, 2. The median number of years required for completion of a degree in 2012–2013 were 5.

Other Criteria: (importance of criteria rated low, medium, or high): GRE scores—high, research experience—high, work experience—medium, extracurricular activity—low, clinically related public service—low, GPA—high, letters of recommendation—high, interview—high, statement of goals and objectives—high, sample of work—medium, undergraduate major in psychology—medium, specific undergraduate psychology courses taken—low. For additional information on admission requirements, go to http://pbs.jhu.edu/graduate/phdprog.html.

Student Characteristics: The following represents characteristics of students in 2012–2013 in all graduate psychology programs in the department: Female—full-time 13, part-time 0; Male—full-time 18, part-time 0; African American/Black—full-time 2, part-time 0; Hispanic/Latino(a)—full-time 1, part-time 0; Asian/Pacific Islander—full-time 9, part-time 0; American Indian/Alaska Native—full-time 0, part-time 0; Caucasian/White—full-time 14, part-time 0; Multi-ethnic—full-time 4, part-time 0; students subject to the Americans With Disabilities Act—full-time 0, part-time 0; Unknown ethnicity—full-time 1, part-time 0; International students who hold an F-1 or J-1 Visa—full-time 11, part-time 0.

Financial Information/Assistance:

Tuition for Full-Time Study: *Doctoral:* State residents: per academic year $45,595; Nonstate residents: per academic year $45,595. Tuition is subject to change. See the following website for updates and changes in tuition costs: http://grad.jhu.edu/admissions/cost-financial-aid/index.php.

Financial Assistance:

First-Year Students: Teaching assistantships available for first year. Research assistantships available for first year.

Advanced Students: Teaching assistantships available for advanced students. Research assistantships available for advanced students.

Additional Information: Of all students currently enrolled full time, 100% benefited from one or more of the listed financial assistance programs. Application and information available online at: http://pbs.jhu.edu/graduate/financial-support.

Housing and Day Care: No on-campus housing is available. No on-campus day care facilities are available.

Employment of Department Graduates:

Master's Degree Graduates: Of those who graduated in the academic year 2011–2012, the following categories and numbers represent the postgraduate activities and employment of master's degree graduates: Enrolled in a postdoctoral residency/fellowship (n/a), employed in independent practice (n/a), total from the above (master's) (0).

Doctoral Degree Graduates: Of those who graduated in the academic year 2011–2012, the following categories and numbers represent the postgraduate activities and employment of doctoral degree graduates: Enrolled in a psychology doctoral program (n/a), enrolled in a postdoctoral residency/fellowship (3), total from the above (doctoral) (3).

Additional Information:

Orientation, Objectives, and Emphasis of Department: The graduate program in psychology at The Johns Hopkins University emphasizes research training, stressing the application of basic research methodology to theoretical problems in psychology. Students are actively engaged in research projects within the first semester. There is a low student/faculty ratio; students work closely with their advisors. Courses, seminars, and research activities provide training so that students will emerge as independent investigators who can embark on successful research careers in psychology. Courses cover fundamental issues in experimental design and analysis, and provide a broad background in all the major areas of psychology. Advanced seminars deal with topics of current interest in various specific areas. The department has programs in cognitive psychology (including perceptual and cognitive development), cognitive neuroscience, quantitative psychology, and biopsychology.

Special Facilities or Resources: Each faculty member in the Department of Psychology maintains a laboratory for conducting research. The psychology building was recently renovated, and the research space is both excellent and plentiful. Every lab contains multiple microcomputer systems for experimentation, analysis, and word processing; most machines are connected via a local-area network to one another and to the Internet. In addition, individual laboratories contain special-purpose equipment designed for the research carried out there. Laboratories in cognition, for example, include high-resolution display devices for experiments in visual. Quantitative psychology laboratories include UNIX work stations for computational analysis and simulation studies. Biopsychology laboratories have facilities for animal surgery, histology, electrophysiological recording of single units and evoked potentials, analysis of neurotransmitters through assays and high-pressure liquid chromatography, bioacoustics, and for general behavioral testing.

Information for Students With Physical Disabilities: See the following website for more information: http://web.jhu.edu/disabilities.

Application Information:
Send to Johns Hopkins University, Graduate Affairs & Admissions, 3400 North Charles Street, Shriver Hall 28, Baltimore MD 21218. Application available online. URL of online application: https://app. applyyourself.com/?id=jhu-grad. Students are admitted in the Fall, application deadline December 15. *Fee:* $75.

Loyola University Maryland
Department of Psychology
4501 North Charles Street
Baltimore, MD 21210
Telephone: (410) 617-2175
Fax: (410) 617-5341
E-mail: *tpmartino@loyola.edu*
Web: *http://www.loyola.edu/academic/psychology.aspx*

Department Information:
1968. Chairperson: Dr. Beth A. Kotchick. Number of faculty: total—full-time 22, part-time 12; women—full-time 13, part-time 7; total—minority—full-time 6; women minority—full-time 6; faculty subject to the Americans With Disabilities Act 1.

Programs and Degrees Offered:
Listed in the following order: Program area, degree type (T if terminal Master's), number awarded 7/11–6/12. Clinical Psychology MA/MS (Master of Arts/Science) (T) 29, Counseling Psychology MA/MS (Master of Arts/Science) (T) 37, Clinical Psychology PsyD (Doctor of Psychology) 15.

APA Accreditation: Clinical PsyD (Doctor of Psychology). Student Outcome Data Website: http://www.loyola.edu/academic/psychology/programs/doctorate/admissions-outcomes.aspx.

Student Applications/Admissions:
Student Applications
Clinical Psychology MA/MS (Master of Arts/Science)—Applications 2012–2013, 192. Total applicants accepted 2012–2013, 121. Number full-time enrolled (new admits only) 2012–2013, 39. Number part-time enrolled (new admits only) 2012–2013, 5. Total enrolled 2012–2013 full-time, 99. Total enrolled 2012–2013 part-time, 15. Openings 2013–2014, 40. The median number of years required for completion of a degree in 2012–2013 were 2. The number of students enrolled full- and part-time who were dismissed or voluntarily withdrew from this program area in 2012–2013 were 5. *Counseling Psychology MA/MS (Master of Arts/Science)*—Applications 2012–2013, 128. Total applicants accepted 2012–2013, 86. Number full-time enrolled (new admits only) 2012–2013, 28. Number part-time enrolled (new admits only) 2012–2013, 2. Total enrolled 2012–2013 full-time, 62. Total enrolled 2012–2013 part-time, 7. Openings 2013–2014, 40. The median number of years required for completion of a degree in 2012–2013 were 2. The number of students enrolled full- and part-time who were dismissed or voluntarily withdrew from this program area in 2012–2013 were 3. *Clinical Psychology PsyD (Doctor of Psychology)*—Applications 2012–2013, 325. Total applicants accepted 2012–2013, 22. Number full-time enrolled (new admits only) 2012–2013, 15. Total enrolled 2012–2013 full-time, 76. Openings 2013–2014, 15. The median number of years re-

quired for completion of a degree in 2012–2013 were 4. The number of students enrolled full- and part-time who were dismissed or voluntarily withdrew from this program area in 2012–2013 were 0.

Scores: Entries appear in this order: required test or GPA, minimum score (if required), median score of students entering in 2012–2013. *Clinical Psychology MA/MS (Master of Arts/Science):* GRE-V no minimum stated, 155, GRE-Q no minimum stated, 152, GRE-Analytical no minimum stated, 4.5, overall undergraduate GPA 3.0; *Counseling Psychology MA/MS (Master of Arts/Science):* GRE-V no minimum stated, 155, GRE-Q no minimum stated, 153, GRE-Analytical no minimum stated, 4.5, overall undergraduate GPA 3.0, 3.4; *Clinical Psychology PsyD (Doctor of Psychology):* GRE-V no minimum stated, 158, GRE-Q no minimum stated, 152, GRE-Analytical no minimum stated, 4.4, overall undergraduate GPA 3.0, 3.7.

Other Criteria: (importance of criteria rated low, medium, or high): GRE scores—high, research experience—high, work experience—high, extracurricular activity—high, clinically related public service—high, GPA—high, letters of recommendation—high, interview—high, statement of goals and objectives—high, undergraduate major in psychology—medium, specific undergraduate psychology courses taken—high, Interviews by invitation only for PsyD program. No interview for Master's programs. For additional information on admission requirements, go to http://www.loyola.edu/loyola-college/graduate/psychology-reqs.html.

Student Characteristics: The following represents characteristics of students in 2012–2013 in all graduate psychology programs in the department: Female—full-time 192, part-time 16; Male—full-time 45, part-time 6; African American/Black—full-time 21, part-time 1; Hispanic/Latino(a)—full-time 11, part-time 0; Asian/Pacific Islander—full-time 16, part-time 0; American Indian/Alaska Native—full-time 3, part-time 0; Caucasian/White—full-time 162, part-time 21; Multi-ethnic—full-time 3, part-time 0; students subject to the Americans With Disabilities Act—full-time 0, part-time 0; Unknown ethnicity—full-time 11, part-time 0; International students who hold an F-1 or J-1 Visa—full-time 4, part-time 0.

Financial Information/Assistance:
Tuition for Full-Time Study: *Master's:* State residents: $725 per credit hour; Nonstate residents: $725 per credit hour. *Doctoral:* State residents: per academic year $28,562; Nonstate residents: per academic year $28,562. Tuition is subject to change. Tuition costs vary by program. See the following website for updates and changes in tuition costs: http://www.loyola.edu/department/financialservices/studentaccounts/tuition/graduatefees.aspx.

Financial Assistance:
First-Year Students: No information provided.
Advanced Students: Teaching assistantships available for advanced students. Average amount paid per academic year: $1,600. Average number of hours worked per week: 10. Research assistantships available for advanced students. Average amount paid per academic year: $1,600. Average number of hours worked per week: 10. Fellowships and scholarships available for advanced students.

Additional Information: Of all students currently enrolled full time, 45% benefited from one or more of the listed financial assistance programs. Application and information available online at: http://www.loyola.edu/department/hr/studentemployment. aspx.

Internships/Practica: Doctoral Degree (PsyD Clinical Psychology): For those doctoral students for whom a professional psychology internship was required in this program prior to graduation, (14) students applied for an internship in 2011–2012, with (13) students obtaining an internship. Of those students who obtained an internship, (13) were paid internships. Of those students who obtained an internship, (11) students placed in APA/CPA accredited internships, (2) students placed in internships not APA/CPA accredited, but listed with the Association of Psychology Postdoctoral and Internship Programs (APPIC), (0) students placed in internships conforming to guidelines of the Council of Directors of School Psychology Programs (CDSPP), (0) students placed in internships that were not APA/CPA accredited, APPIC or CDSPP listed. Master's Degree (MA/MS Clinical Psychology): An internship experience, such as a final research project or "capstone" experience is required of graduates. Master's Degree (MA/MS Counseling Psychology): An internship experience, such as a final research project or "capstone" experience is required of graduates. The MS program, Practitioner Track requires 300 hours of externship experience. The MS program, Thesis Track requires 150 hours of externship experience. Students are able to choose from a wide variety of sites approved by the Department. The PsyD program incorporates field placement training throughout the curriculum; a minimum of 1,260 hours of field training is required. The final (fifth) year of the PsyD program is a full-time internship.

Housing and Day Care: No on-campus housing is available. No on-campus day care facilities are available.

Employment of Department Graduates:

Master's Degree Graduates: Of those who graduated in the academic year 2011–2012, the following categories and numbers represent the postgraduate activities and employment of master's degree graduates: Enrolled in a psychology doctoral program (6), enrolled in another graduate/professional program (7), enrolled in a postdoctoral residency/fellowship (n/a), employed in independent practice (n/a), other employment position (3), do not know (51), total from the above (master's) (67).

Doctoral Degree Graduates: Of those who graduated in the academic year 2011–2012, the following categories and numbers represent the postgraduate activities and employment of doctoral degree graduates: Enrolled in a psychology doctoral program (n/a), enrolled in a postdoctoral residency/fellowship (15), total from the above (doctoral) (15).

Additional Information:

Orientation, Objectives, and Emphasis of Department: The Master's programs in Clinical and Counseling Psychology at Loyola University Maryland provides training to individuals who wish to promote mental health in individuals, families, organizations, and communities through careers in direct service, leadership, research, and education. We strive to provide a learning environment that facilitates the development of skills in critical thinking, scholarship, assessment and intervention, and that is grounded in an appreciation for both psychological science and human diversity. The goals of the PsyD program in Clinical Psychology are based on the scholar-professional model of training, designed to train autonomous practitioners of professional psy-chology who will deliver mental health services and lead others in service to the general public in diverse settings.

Special Facilities or Resources: Departmental facilities include the Loyola Clinic, a health psychology/behavioral medicine laboratory, audiovisual recording facilities, assessment and therapy training rooms, and a student lounge. Students have access to a campus-wide computer system, including SPSS and SAS software. All graduate students have telephone voicemail and e-mail addresses. Advanced doctoral students are provided with individual workstations with computers.

Information for Students With Physical Disabilities: See the following website for more information: http://www.loyola.edu/department/dss.aspx.

Application Information:
Send to Office of Graduate Admissions, Loyola University Maryland, 2034 Greenspring Drive, Suite 80, Timonium, MD 21093. Application available online. URL of online application: http://www.loyola.edu/loyola-college/graduate/psychology-apply.html. Students are admitted in the Fall, application deadline December 1. Deadline for MS in Clinical or Counseling Psychology is March 1. *Fee:* $50.

Maryland, University of
Department of Counseling, Higher Education, and Special Education
College of Education
3214 Benjamin Building
College Park, MD 20742
Telephone: (301) 405-2858
Fax: (301) 405-9995
E-mail: *cscott18@umd.edu*
Web: *http://www.education.umd.edu/CHSE/*

Department Information:
2011. Interim Chair: Robert Lent. Number of faculty: total—full-time 52, part-time 26; women—full-time 35, part-time 21; total—minority—full-time 11, part-time 5; women minority—full-time 6, part-time 3.

Programs and Degrees Offered:
Listed in the following order: Program area, degree type (T if terminal Master's), number awarded 7/11–6/12. Counseling Psychology PhD (Doctor of Philosophy) 4, School Psychology PhD (Doctor of Philosophy) 3.

APA Accreditation: Counseling PhD (Doctor of Philosophy). Student Outcome Data Website: www.bsos.umd.edu/psyc/counseling/admissionsoutcomesdata.html. School PhD (Doctor of Philosophy). Student Outcome Data Website: http://www.education.umd.edu/CHSE/academics/specialization/schoolPsychology.html.

Student Applications/Admissions:
Student Applications
   Counseling Psychology PhD (Doctor of Philosophy)—Applications 2012–2013, 283. Total applicants accepted 2012–2013, 5. Number full-time enrolled (new admits only) 2012–2013,

5. Number part-time enrolled (new admits only) 2012–2013, 0. Total enrolled 2012–2013 full-time, 36. Total enrolled 2012–2013 part-time, 2. Openings 2013–2014, 7. The median number of years required for completion of a degree in 2012–2013 were 6. The number of students enrolled full- and part-time who were dismissed or voluntarily withdrew from this program area in 2012–2013 were 1. *School Psychology PhD (Doctor of Philosophy)*—Applications 2012–2013, 63. Total applicants accepted 2012–2013, 8. Number full-time enrolled (new admits only) 2012–2013, 3. Number part-time enrolled (new admits only) 2012–2013, 0. Total enrolled 2012–2013 full-time, 16. Total enrolled 2012–2013 part-time, 11. Openings 2013–2014, 4. The median number of years required for completion of a degree in 2012–2013 were 7. The number of students enrolled full- and part-time who were dismissed or voluntarily withdrew from this program area in 2012–2013 were 1.

Scores: Entries appear in this order: required test or GPA, minimum score (if required), median score of students entering in 2012–2013. *Counseling Psychology PhD (Doctor of Philosophy):* GRE-V 153, 163, GRE-Q 151, 158, GRE-Analytical 4.00, 5.00, overall undergraduate GPA 3.00, 3.82, Masters GPA 3.51, 3.90; *School Psychology PhD (Doctor of Philosophy):* GRE-V 160, 162, GRE-Q 144, 151, GRE-Analytical 4.0, 5.0, overall undergraduate GPA 3.60, 3.79, Masters GPA 3.89, 3.89.

Other Criteria: (importance of criteria rated low, medium, or high): GRE scores—medium, research experience—high, work experience—medium, extracurricular activity—medium, clinically related public service—low, GPA—high, letters of recommendation—high, interview—high, statement of goals and objectives—high, undergraduate major in psychology—medium, specific undergraduate psychology courses taken—medium. For additional information on admission requirements, go to http://www.education.umd.edu/CHSE/admissions/admission_criteria/.

Student Characteristics: The following represents characteristics of students in 2012–2013 in all graduate psychology programs in the department: Female—full-time 41, part-time 11; Male—full-time 11, part-time 2; African American/Black—full-time 3, part-time 4; Hispanic/Latino(a)—full-time 2, part-time 0; Asian/Pacific Islander—full-time 13, part-time 1; American Indian/Alaska Native—full-time 0, part-time 0; Caucasian/White—full-time 33, part-time 7; Multi-ethnic—full-time 1, part-time 1; students subject to the Americans With Disabilities Act—full-time 1, part-time 0; Unknown ethnicity—full-time 0, part-time 0; International students who hold an F-1 or J-1 Visa—full-time 2, part-time 1.

Financial Information/Assistance:

Tuition for Full-Time Study: *Doctoral:* State residents: per academic year $11,020, $551 per credit hour; Nonstate residents: per academic year $23,760, $1,188 per credit hour. Tuition is subject to change. Additional fees are assessed to students beyond the costs of tuition for the following: various fees total $1,383 per year. See the following website for updates and changes in tuition costs: http://bursar.umd.edu/t_grd1213.php.

Financial Assistance:

First-Year Students: Research assistantships available for first year. Average amount paid per academic year: $19,500. Average number of hours worked per week: 20. Fellowships and scholarships available for first year. Average amount paid per academic year: $18,000.

Advanced Students: Teaching assistantships available for advanced students. Average amount paid per academic year: $20,795. Average number of hours worked per week: 20. Research assistantships available for advanced students. Average amount paid per academic year: $20,795. Average number of hours worked per week: 20.

Additional Information: Of all students currently enrolled full time, 100% benefited from one or more of the listed financial assistance programs. Application and information available online at: http://www.education.umd.edu/CHSE/admissions/finance/.

Internships/Practica: Doctoral Degree (PhD Counseling Psychology): For those doctoral students for whom a professional psychology internship was required in this program prior to graduation, (7) students applied for an internship in 2011–2012, with (6) students obtaining an internship. Of those students who obtained an internship, (6) were paid internships. Of those students who obtained an internship, (6) students placed in APA/CPA accredited internships, (0) students placed in internships not APA/CPA accredited, but listed with the Association of Psychology Postdoctoral and Internship Programs (APPIC), (0) students placed in internships conforming to guidelines of the Council of Directors of School Psychology Programs (CDSPP), (0) students placed in internships that were not APA/CPA accredited, APPIC or CDSPP listed. Doctoral Degree (PhD School Psychology): For those doctoral students for whom a professional psychology internship was required in this program prior to graduation, (2) students applied for an internship in 2011–2012, with (2) students obtaining an internship. Of those students who obtained an internship, (2) were paid internships. Of those students who obtained an internship, (0) students placed in APA/CPA accredited internships, (0) students placed in internships not APA/CPA accredited, but listed with the Association of Psychology Postdoctoral and Internship Programs (APPIC), (2) students placed in internships conforming to guidelines of the Council of Directors of School Psychology Programs (CDSPP), (0) students placed in internships that were not APA/CPA accredited, APPIC or CDSPP listed. The Washington DC area offers an abundance of training settings which supplement our on-campus training facilities. A number of practica are offered at the University of Maryland Counseling Center. In addition, other practica and externships are offered at schools, community agencies, medical centers, and other counseling centers. Counseling Psychology students all complete APA-accredited internships. In order to maximize school-based training, students in the School Psychology program may complete internships that conform to CDSPP guidelines or those that are APA-accredited.

Housing and Day Care: No on-campus housing is available. On-campus day care facilities are available. See the following website for more information: http://www.education.umd.edu/EDHD/CYC/.

Employment of Department Graduates:

Master's Degree Graduates: Of those who graduated in the academic year 2011–2012, the following categories and numbers represent the postgraduate activities and employment of master's degree graduates: Enrolled in a postdoctoral residency/fellowship (n/a), employed in independent practice (n/a), total from the above (master's) (0).

Doctoral Degree Graduates: Of those who graduated in the academic year 2011–2012, the following categories and numbers represent the postgraduate activities and employment of doctoral degree graduates: Enrolled in a psychology doctoral program (n/a), enrolled in a postdoctoral residency/fellowship (3), employed in independent practice (1), employed in a professional position in a school system (3), total from the above (doctoral) (7).

Additional Information:

Orientation, Objectives, and Emphasis of Department: Both the Counseling Psychology and School Psychology programs espouse the scientist–practitioner model of training. These programs enable students to become psychologists who are trained in general psychology, have expertise in conducting research on a wide range of psychological topics, and are highly competent in providing effective assessment and intervention services from a variety of theoretical perspectives. The Counseling Psychology program is administered collaboratively by the Counseling Psychology, School Psychology and Counselor Education Department, and the Psychology Department.

Special Facilities or Resources: Observation/training facilities and access to extensive library facilities both on and off campus (e.g., NIH Library of Medicine, Library of Congress).

Information for Students With Physical Disabilities: See the following website for more information: http://www.counseling. umd.edu/DSS/.

Application Information:
Application available online. URL of online application: http://www. gradschool.umd.edu/welcome/apply_now.html. Students are admitted in the Fall, application deadline December 1. *Fee:* $75.

Maryland, University of
Department of Human Development and Quantitative
  Methodology
College of Education
3304 Benjamin Building
College Park, MD 20742
Telephone: (301) 405-2827
Fax: (301) 405-2891
E-mail: *mkillen@umd.edu*
Web: *http://www.education.umd.edu/EDHD*

Department Information:
1947. Interim Chair: Nathan Fox. Number of faculty: total—full-time 20; women—full-time 11; total—minority—full-time 4; women minority—full-time 4.

Programs and Degrees Offered:
Listed in the following order: Program area, degree type (T if terminal Master's), number awarded 7/11–6/12. Developmental Science PhD (Doctor of Philosophy) 8, Educational Psychology PhD (Doctor of Philosophy) 5.

Student Applications/Admissions:
Student Applications
   Developmental Science PhD (Doctor of Philosophy)—Applications 2012–2013, 40. Total applicants accepted 2012–2013,

11. Number full-time enrolled (new admits only) 2012–2013, 5. Total enrolled 2012–2013 full-time, 32. Openings 2013–2014, 10. The median number of years required for completion of a degree in 2012–2013 were 5. The number of students enrolled full- and part-time who were dismissed or voluntarily withdrew from this program area in 2012–2013 were 1. *Educational Psychology PhD (Doctor of Philosophy)*—Applications 2012–2013, 30. Total applicants accepted 2012–2013, 10. Number full-time enrolled (new admits only) 2012–2013, 6. Number part-time enrolled (new admits only) 2012–2013, 0. Total enrolled 2012–2013 full-time, 39. Total enrolled 2012–2013 part-time, 0. Openings 2013–2014, 10. The median number of years required for completion of a degree in 2012–2013 were 5. The number of students enrolled full- and part-time who were dismissed or voluntarily withdrew from this program area in 2012–2013 were 0.

Scores: Entries appear in this order: required test or GPA, minimum score (if required), median score of students entering in 2012–2013. *Developmental Science PhD (Doctor of Philosophy):* GRE-V no minimum stated, GRE-Q no minimum stated, GRE-Analytical no minimum stated, overall undergraduate GPA 3.0, Masters GPA 3.0; *Educational Psychology PhD (Doctor of Philosophy):* GRE-V no minimum stated, GRE-Q no minimum stated, GRE-Analytical no minimum stated, overall undergraduate GPA 3.0, Masters GPA 3.5.

Other Criteria: (importance of criteria rated low, medium, or high): GRE scores—high, research experience—high, work experience—medium, clinically related public service—medium, GPA—medium, letters of recommendation—high, interview—medium, statement of goals and objectives—high, undergraduate major in psychology—high, specific undergraduate psychology courses taken—medium. For additional information on admission requirements, go to http://www. education.umd.edu/EDHD/index.php.

Student Characteristics: The following represents characteristics of students in 2012–2013 in all graduate psychology programs in the department: Female—full-time 53, part-time 17; Male—full-time 5, part-time 10; African American/Black—full-time 6, part-time 2; Hispanic/Latino(a)—full-time 5, part-time 1; Asian/Pacific Islander—full-time 11, part-time 2; American Indian/Alaska Native—full-time 0, part-time 0; Caucasian/White—full-time 36, part-time 22; Multi-ethnic—full-time 0, part-time 0; students subject to the Americans With Disabilities Act—full-time 1, part-time 0; Unknown ethnicity—full-time 0, part-time 0; International students who hold an F-1 or J-1 Visa—full-time 10, part-time 0.

Financial Information/Assistance:
Tuition for Full-Time Study: *Master's:* State residents: $471 per credit hour; Nonstate residents: $1,016 per credit hour. *Doctoral:* State residents: $471 per credit hour; Nonstate residents: $1,016 per credit hour. Tuition is subject to change. Additional fees are assessed to students beyond the costs of tuition for the following: Campus activities fees. See the following website for updates and changes in tuition costs: http://www.umd.edu/bursar/.

Financial Assistance:
   First-Year Students: Research assistantships available for first year. Average amount paid per academic year: $15,000. Average number of hours worked per week: 20. Apply by December 15. Fellowships and scholarships available for first year. Average

amount paid per academic year: $15,000. Average number of hours worked per week: 20. Apply by December 15.

Advanced Students: Teaching assistantships available for advanced students. Average amount paid per academic year: $15,000. Average number of hours worked per week: 20. Research assistantships available for advanced students. Average amount paid per academic year: $15,000. Average number of hours worked per week: 20. Traineeships available for advanced students. Average amount paid per academic year: $15,000. Average number of hours worked per week: 20. Fellowships and scholarships available for advanced students. Average amount paid per academic year: $15,000. Average number of hours worked per week: 20.

Additional Information: Of all students currently enrolled full time, 85% benefited from one or more of the listed financial assistance programs.

Housing and Day Care: No on-campus housing is available. On-campus day care facilities are available. See the following website for more information: http://www.education.umd.edu/EDHD/CYC/.

Employment of Department Graduates:

Master's Degree Graduates: Of those who graduated in the academic year 2011–2012, the following categories and numbers represent the postgraduate activities and employment of master's degree graduates: Enrolled in a psychology doctoral program (0), enrolled in another graduate/professional program (0), enrolled in a postdoctoral residency/fellowship (n/a), employed in independent practice (n/a), total from the above (master's) (0).

Doctoral Degree Graduates: Of those who graduated in the academic year 2011–2012, the following categories and numbers represent the postgraduate activities and employment of doctoral degree graduates: Enrolled in a psychology doctoral program (n/a), enrolled in a postdoctoral residency/fellowship (3), employed in independent practice (1), employed in an academic position at a university (1), employed in an academic position at a 2-year/4-year college (0), employed in other positions at a higher education institution (1), employed in a professional position in a school system (15), employed in business or industry (0), employed in government agency (0), employed in a community mental health/counseling center (0), employed in a hospital/medical center (2), other employment position (1), do not know (3), total from the above (doctoral) (27).

Additional Information:

Orientation, Objectives, and Emphasis of Department: The Department of Human Development provides an academic environment with characteristics consistent with a culture of scholars model, which is reflected by the mentor-based apprenticeship model of graduate training. The program is designed for the training of graduate students who are preparing for careers as research scientists, college professors, educators and policy makers informed by research. Included in this area of training are two specializations: 1) Developmental Science, and 2) Educational Psychology. The Developmental Sciences specialization is designed to train students in the areas of social, cognitive, emotional, moral, and biological aspects of human development in normal and clinical populations. Research topics within Developmental Science include peer relationships, parent-child relationships, attachment, neuroscience, emotional development, social-cognitive development, moral development, motivation, social goals, intergroup relationships, prejudice, father involvement, early childhood pol-

icy, and cultural influences on development. The specialization in Educational Psychology is designed to mentor students in the areas of cognitive, social, motivational, emotional, and neurobiological aspects of learning and human development. Research topics within Educational Psychology include reading, literacy, parent-child discourse, motivation, civic engagement, social goals, domain of knowledge expertise, learning, and bilingualism. Collaborative research opportunities are available at universities and the NIH in the Washington, D.C. metropolitan area.

Special Facilities or Resources: The Center for Young Children is a university research laboratory school affiliated with the Department of Human Development, which provides on-site research and training opportunities. The Center for Children, Relationships and Culture facilitates national and international collaborative research through hosting visiting scholars as well as coordinating a weekly colloquium series. The Department of Human Development hosts the Institute for Child Study which has a 55-year history of translating research and theory into practice. There are a number of dedicated research laboratories in the department for conducting research with infants, children, and adolescents, both onsite as well as in the regional school systems.

Application Information:

Send to The University of Maryland, Enrollment Services Operations, 0130 Mitchell Building, College Park, MD 20742. Application available online. URL of online application: www.gradschool.umd.edu/gss/admission.html. Students are admitted in the Fall, application deadline December 15*; Spring, application deadline October 1. *IMPORTANT: Deadline for financial aid consideration (e.g., fellowships) is December 15 for domestic students for Fall admissions. For international students the application deadline for Spring admissions is June 1. *Fee:* $60.

Maryland, University of
Department of Psychology
College of Behavioral and Social Sciences
Biology–Psychology Building
College Park, MD 20742-4411
Telephone: (301) 405-5865
Fax: (301) 314-9566
E-mail: *cgorham@umd.edu*
Web: *http://psychology.umd.edu/*

Department Information:
1937. Chairperson: Jack Blanchard. Number of faculty: total—full-time 40; women—full-time 15; total—minority—full-time 4; women minority—full-time 1.

Programs and Degrees Offered:
Listed in the following order: Program area, degree type (T if terminal Master's), number awarded 7/11–6/12. Clinical Psychology PhD (Doctor of Philosophy) 4, Developmental Psychology PhD (Doctor of Philosophy) 1, Counseling Psychology PhD (Doctor of Philosophy) 2, Cognitive and Neural Systems PhD (Doctor of Philosophy) 0, Social Decision and Organizational Sciences PhD (Doctor of Philosophy) 2.

APA Accreditation: Clinical PhD (Doctor of Philosophy). Student Outcome Data Website: http://marylandclinicalpsychology.tumblr.com/Data. Counseling PhD (Doctor of Philosophy). Student Outcome Data Website: http://www.bsos.umd.edu/psyc/counseling/admissions outcomesdata.html.

Student Applications/Admissions:

Student Applications

Clinical Psychology PhD (Doctor of Philosophy)—Applications 2012–2013, 319. Total applicants accepted 2012–2013, 15. Number full-time enrolled (new admits only) 2012–2013, 8. Total enrolled 2012–2013 full-time, 23. Total enrolled 2012–2013 part-time, 0. Openings 2013–2014, 6. The median number of years required for completion of a degree in 2012–2013 were 6. The number of students enrolled full- and part-time who were dismissed or voluntarily withdrew from this program area in 2012–2013 were 1. *Developmental Psychology PhD (Doctor of Philosophy)*—Applications 2012–2013, 32. Total applicants accepted 2012–2013, 6. Number full-time enrolled (new admits only) 2012–2013, 3. Total enrolled 2012–2013 full-time, 8. Total enrolled 2012–2013 part-time, 0. Openings 2013–2014, 3. The median number of years required for completion of a degree in 2012–2013 were 5. The number of students enrolled full- and part-time who were dismissed or voluntarily withdrew from this program area in 2012–2013 were 0. *Counseling Psychology PhD (Doctor of Philosophy)*—Applications 2012–2013, 204. Total applicants accepted 2012–2013, 5. Number full-time enrolled (new admits only) 2012–2013, 4. Total enrolled 2012–2013 full-time, 21. Openings 2013–2014, 3. The median number of years required for completion of a degree in 2012–2013 were 6. The number of students enrolled full- and part-time who were dismissed or voluntarily withdrew from this program area in 2012–2013 were 0. *Cognitive and Neural Systems PhD (Doctor of Philosophy)*—Applications 2012–2013, 51. Total applicants accepted 2012–2013, 4. Number full-time enrolled (new admits only) 2012–2013, 1. Total enrolled 2012–2013 full-time, 2. Openings 2013–2014, 3. The median number of years required for completion of a degree in 2012–2013 were 5. The number of students enrolled full- and part-time who were dismissed or voluntarily withdrew from this program area in 2012–2013 were 0. *Social Decision and Organizational Sciences PhD (Doctor of Philosophy)*—Applications 2012–2013, 175. Total applicants accepted 2012–2013, 9. Number full-time enrolled (new admits only) 2012–2013, 3. Total enrolled 2012–2013 full-time, 20. Openings 2013–2014, 5. The median number of years required for completion of a degree in 2012–2013 were 5. The number of students enrolled full- and part-time who were dismissed or voluntarily withdrew from this program area in 2012–2013 were 0.

Scores: Entries appear in this order: required test or GPA, minimum score (if required), median score of students entering in 2012–2013. *Clinical Psychology PhD (Doctor of Philosophy):* GRE-V no minimum stated, 590, GRE-Q no minimum stated, 695, GRE-Analytical no minimum stated, overall undergraduate GPA no minimum stated, 3.71, psychology GPA no minimum stated, Masters GPA no minimum stated; *Developmental Psychology PhD (Doctor of Philosophy):* GRE-V no minimum stated, GRE-Q no minimum stated, GRE-Analytical no minimum stated, overall undergraduate GPA no minimum stated, psychology GPA no minimum stated, Masters GPA no minimum stated; *Counseling Psychology PhD (Doctor of Philosophy):* GRE-V no minimum stated, GRE-Q no minimum stated, GRE-Analytical no minimum stated, overall undergraduate GPA no minimum stated, psychology GPA no minimum stated, Masters GPA no minimum stated; *Cognitive and Neural Systems PhD (Doctor of Philosophy):* GRE-V no minimum stated, GRE-Q no minimum stated, GRE-Analytical no minimum stated, overall undergraduate GPA no minimum stated, psychology GPA no minimum stated, Masters GPA no minimum stated; *Social Decision and Organizational Sciences PhD (Doctor of Philosophy):* GRE-V no minimum stated, GRE-Q no minimum stated, GRE-Analytical no minimum stated, overall undergraduate GPA no minimum stated, psychology GPA no minimum stated, Masters GPA no minimum stated.

Other Criteria: (importance of criteria rated low, medium, or high): GRE scores—high, research experience—high, work experience—low, extracurricular activity—low, clinically related public service—low, GPA—high, letters of recommendation—high, interview—high, statement of goals and objectives—high, undergraduate major in psychology—medium, specific undergraduate psychology courses taken—medium. For additional information on admission requirements, go to http://psychology.umd.edu/grad/apply.html.

Student Characteristics: The following represents characteristics of students in 2012–2013 in all graduate psychology programs in the department: Female—full-time 61, part-time 0; Male—full-time 13, part-time 0; African American/Black—full-time 5, part-time 0; Hispanic/Latino(a)—full-time 4, part-time 0; Asian/Pacific Islander—full-time 8, part-time 0; American Indian/Alaska Native—full-time 0, part-time 0; Caucasian/White—full-time 45, part-time 0; Multi-ethnic—full-time 0, part-time 0; students subject to the Americans With Disabilities Act—full-time 0, part-time 0; Unknown ethnicity—full-time 12, part-time 0; International students who hold an F-1 or J-1 Visa—full-time 12, part-time 0.

Financial Information/Assistance:

Tuition for Full-Time Study: *Doctoral:* State residents: $551 per credit hour; Nonstate residents: $1,582 per credit hour. Tuition is subject to change. Additional fees are assessed to students beyond the costs of tuition for the following: technology, shuttle bus, athletic, recreation. See the following website for updates and changes in tuition costs: http://bursar.umd.edu/Tuitionfees.php.

Financial Assistance:

First-Year Students: Teaching assistantships available for first year. Average amount paid per academic year: $16,586. Average number of hours worked per week: 20. Research assistantships available for first year. Average amount paid per academic year: $16,586. Average number of hours worked per week: 20. Fellowships and scholarships available for first year. Average amount paid per academic year: $21,000. Average number of hours worked per week: 20.

Advanced Students: Teaching assistantships available for advanced students. Average amount paid per academic year: $18,637. Average number of hours worked per week: 20. Research assistantships available for advanced students. Average amount paid per academic year: $18,637. Average number of hours worked per week: 20. Fellowships and scholarships available for advanced students.

Additional Information: Of all students currently enrolled full time, 100% benefited from one or more of the listed financial

assistance programs. Application and information available online at: http://psychology.umd.edu/grad/financial.html.

Internships/Practica: Doctoral Degree (PhD Clinical Psychology): For those doctoral students for whom a professional psychology internship was required in this program prior to graduation, (2) students applied for an internship in 2011–2012, with (2) students obtaining an internship. Of those students who obtained an internship, (2) were paid internships. Of those students who obtained an internship, (2) students placed in APA/CPA accredited internships, (0) students placed in internships not APA/CPA accredited, but listed with the Association of Psychology Postdoctoral and Internship Programs (APPIC), (0) students placed in internships conforming to guidelines of the Council of Directors of School Psychology Programs (CDSPP), (0) students placed in internships that were not APA/CPA accredited, APPIC or CDSPP listed. Doctoral Degree (PhD Counseling Psychology): For those doctoral students for whom a professional psychology internship was required in this program prior to graduation, (2) students applied for an internship in 2011–2012, with (2) students obtaining an internship. Of those students who obtained an internship, (2) were paid internships. Of those students who obtained an internship, (2) students placed in APA/CPA accredited internships, (0) students placed in internships not APA/CPA accredited, but listed with the Association of Psychology Postdoctoral and Internship Programs (APPIC), (0) students placed in internships conforming to guidelines of the Council of Directors of School Psychology Programs (CDSPP), (0) students placed in internships that were not APA/CPA accredited, APPIC or CDSPP listed. The specialty areas have established collaborative relationships with several federal and community agencies and hospitals as well as with businesses and consulting firms, where it is possible for students to arrange for research, practicum and internship placement. These opportunities are available for Clinical and Counseling students at the National Institutes of Health, Veteran's Administration clinics and hospitals in Washington, DC, Baltimore Perry Point, Coatesville, Martinsburg, Kecoughton, and a number of others within a hundred-mile radius of the University. Experiences include a wide range of research activities, as well as psychodiagnostic work, psychotherapy, and work within drug and alcohol abuse clinics. Various other hospitals, clinics and research facilities in the Washington, DC and Baltimore metropolitan area are also available. Industrial/Organizational students also have opportunities for practitioner experiences in organizations such as the U.S. Office of Personnel Management, GEICO, Bell Atlantic, and various consulting firms. The metropolitan area also has many psychologists who can provide students with excellent opportunities for collaboration and/or consultation.

Housing and Day Care: No on-campus housing is available. On-campus day care facilities are available. See the following website for more information: http://www.education.umd.edu/EDHD/CYC/.

Employment of Department Graduates:

Master's Degree Graduates: Of those who graduated in the academic year 2011–2012, the following categories and numbers represent the postgraduate activities and employment of master's degree graduates: Enrolled in a postdoctoral residency/fellowship (n/a), employed in independent practice (n/a), total from the above (master's) (0).

Doctoral Degree Graduates: Of those who graduated in the academic year 2011–2012, the following categories and numbers represent the postgraduate activities and employment of doctoral degree graduates: Enrolled in a psychology doctoral program (n/a), enrolled in a postdoctoral residency/fellowship (5), employed in an academic position at a university (6), employed in an academic position at a 2-year/4-year college (6), employed in other positions at a higher education institution (1), employed in business or industry (3), employed in government agency (1), other employment position (2), total from the above (doctoral) (24).

Additional Information:

Orientation, Objectives, and Emphasis of Department: The department offers a full-time graduate program with an emphasis on intensive individual training made possible by a 3-to-1 student/faculty ratio. All students are expected to participate in a variety of relevant experiences that, in addition to coursework and research training, can include practicum experiences, field training, and teaching. The department offers a variety of programs described in the admissions brochure as well as other emphases that cut across the various specialties. All programs have a strong research emphasis with programs in clinical, counseling, and industrial advocating the scientist–practitioner model.

Special Facilities or Resources: The Department of Psychology has all of the advantages of a large state university, and also has advantages offered by the many resources available in the metropolitan Washington-Baltimore area. The University is approximately 15 miles from the center of Washington, DC and is in close proximity to a number of libraries and state and federal agencies. Students are able to benefit from the excellent additional library resources of the community, such as the Library of Congress, National Library of Medicine, and the National Archives (which is located on the UMCP campus). The building in which the Department is housed was designed by the faculty to incorporate research and educational facilities for all specialty areas. The building contains special centers for research, with acoustical centers, observational units, video equipment, computer facilities, surgical facilities, and radio frequency shielding. Departmental laboratories are well equipped for research in animal behavior, audition, biopsychology, cognition, coordinated motor control, counseling, industrial/organizational psychology, learning, lifespan development, psycholinguistics, psychotherapy, social psychology, and vision.

Information for Students With Physical Disabilities: See the following website for more information: http://www.counseling.umd.edu/DSS/.

Application Information:
Send to University of Maryland College Park, Enrollment Services Operations, Graduate Admission, Room 0130 Mitchell Building, College Park, MD 20742. Application available online. URL of online application: http://www.gradschool.umd.edu/welcome/apply_now.html. Students are admitted in the Fall, application deadline December 1. *Fee:* $75.

Maryland, University of, Baltimore County

Department of Psychology
Arts and Sciences
1000 Hilltop Circle
Baltimore, MD 21250
Telephone: (410) 455-2567
Fax: (410) 455-1055
E-mail: *psycdept@umbc.edu*
Web: *http://www.umbc.edu/psyc/index.html*

Department Information:

1966. Chairperson: Linda Baker, PhD. Number of faculty: total—full-time 30, part-time 11; women—full-time 15, part-time 4; total—minority—full-time 5; women minority—full-time 3; faculty subject to the Americans With Disabilities Act 1.

Programs and Degrees Offered:

Listed in the following order: Program area, degree type (T if terminal Master's), number awarded 7/11–6/12. Applied Behavior Analysis MA/MS (Master of Arts/Science) (T) 8, Applied Developmental Psychology PhD (Doctor of Philosophy) 3, Human Services Psychology PhD (Doctor of Philosophy) 6.

APA Accreditation: Clinical PhD (Doctor of Philosophy). Student Outcome Data Website: http://www.umbc.edu/psyc/hsp_clinical.html.

Student Applications/Admissions:

Student Applications

Applied Behavior Analysis MA/MS (Master of Arts/Science)—Applications 2012–2013, 83. Total applicants accepted 2012–2013, 16. Number full-time enrolled (new admits only) 2012–2013, 14. Number part-time enrolled (new admits only) 2012–2013, 0. Total enrolled 2012–2013 full-time, 26. Total enrolled 2012–2013 part-time, 0. Openings 2013–2014, 15. The median number of years required for completion of a degree in 2012–2013 were 2. The number of students enrolled full- and part-time who were dismissed or voluntarily withdrew from this program area in 2012–2013 were 2. *Applied Developmental Psychology PhD (Doctor of Philosophy)*—Applications 2012–2013, 28. Total applicants accepted 2012–2013, 2. Number full-time enrolled (new admits only) 2012–2013, 2. Number part-time enrolled (new admits only) 2012–2013, 0. Total enrolled 2012–2013 full-time, 28. Total enrolled 2012–2013 part-time, 0. Openings 2013–2014, 6. The median number of years required for completion of a degree in 2012–2013 were 8. The number of students enrolled full- and part-time who were dismissed or voluntarily withdrew from this program area in 2012–2013 were 0. *Human Services Psychology PhD (Doctor of Philosophy)*—Applications 2012–2013, 120. Total applicants accepted 2012–2013, 28. Number full-time enrolled (new admits only) 2012–2013, 13. Number part-time enrolled (new admits only) 2012–2013, 0. Total enrolled 2012–2013 full-time, 70. Total enrolled 2012–2013 part-time, 0. Openings 2013–2014, 12. The median number of years required for completion of a degree in 2012–2013 were 7. The number of students enrolled full- and part-time who were dismissed or voluntarily withdrew from this program area in 2012–2013 were 0.

Scores: Entries appear in this order: required test or GPA, minimum score (if required), median score of students entering in 2012–2013. *Applied Behavior Analysis MA/MS (Master of Arts/Science):* GRE-V no minimum stated, GRE-Q no minimum stated, GRE-Analytical no minimum stated, overall undergraduate GPA no minimum stated; *Applied Developmental Psychology PhD (Doctor of Philosophy):* GRE-V no minimum stated, GRE-Q no minimum stated, GRE-Analytical no minimum stated, overall undergraduate GPA 3.0; *Human Services Psychology PhD (Doctor of Philosophy):* GRE-V no minimum stated, GRE-Q no minimum stated, GRE-Analytical no minimum stated, GRE-Subject (Psychology) no minimum stated, overall undergraduate GPA 3.0, Masters GPA no minimum stated.

Other Criteria: (importance of criteria rated low, medium, or high): GRE scores—high, research experience—high, work experience—medium, extracurricular activity—medium, clinically related public service—medium, GPA—high, letters of recommendation—high, interview—high, statement of goals and objectives—high, undergraduate major in psychology—medium, specific undergraduate psychology courses taken—low, ADP puts less weight (low) on clinical service than does HSP.

Student Characteristics: The following represents characteristics of students in 2012–2013 in all graduate psychology programs in the department: Female—full-time 105, part-time 0; Male—full-time 19, part-time 0; African American/Black—full-time 13, part-time 0; Hispanic/Latino(a)—full-time 2, part-time 0; Asian/Pacific Islander—full-time 14, part-time 0; American Indian/Alaska Native—full-time 0, part-time 0; Caucasian/White—full-time 87, part-time 0; Multi-ethnic—full-time 7, part-time 0; students subject to the Americans With Disabilities Act—full-time 0, part-time 0; Unknown ethnicity—full-time 1, part-time 0; International students who hold an F-1 or J-1 Visa—full-time 0, part-time 0.

Financial Information/Assistance:

Tuition for Full-Time Study: *Master's:* State residents: $510 per credit hour; Nonstate residents: $844 per credit hour. *Doctoral:* State residents: $510 per credit hour; Nonstate residents: $844 per credit hour. Tuition is subject to change. See the following website for updates and changes in tuition costs: http://www.umbc.edu/gradschool/funding/tuition_fees.html.

Financial Assistance:

First-Year Students: Teaching assistantships available for first year. Average amount paid per academic year: $15,450. Average number of hours worked per week: 20. Research assistantships available for first year. Average amount paid per academic year: $15,450. Average number of hours worked per week: 20.

Advanced Students: Teaching assistantships available for advanced students. Average amount paid per academic year: $15,450. Average number of hours worked per week: 20. Research assistantships available for advanced students. Average amount paid per academic year: $15,450. Average number of hours worked per week: 20.

Additional Information: Of all students currently enrolled full time, 80% benefited from one or more of the listed financial assistance programs. Application and information available online at: http://www.umbc.edu/gradschool/funding/opps.html.

Internships/Practica: Doctoral Degree (PhD Human Services Psychology): For those doctoral students for whom a professional psychology internship was required in this program prior to graduation, (10) students applied for an internship in 2011–2012, with (10) students obtaining an internship. Of those students who obtained an internship, (10) were paid internships. Of those students who obtained an internship, (10) students placed in APA/CPA accredited internships, (0) students placed in internships not APA/CPA accredited, but listed with the Association of Psychology Postdoctoral and Internship Programs (APPIC), (0) students placed in internships conforming to guidelines of the Council of Directors of School Psychology Programs (CDSPP), (0) students placed in internships that were not APA/CPA accredited, APPIC or CDSPP listed. Master's Degree (MA/MS Applied Behavior Analysis): An internship experience, such as a final research project or "capstone" experience is required of graduates. Course-linked practica provide students with a focused experience in the application of the skills and knowledge presented in the associated course. The course instructor is responsible for arranging these practica. Beyond the course-linked practica, students in the HSP and ADP programs are required to take a minimum of six additional credits of practicum, usually in their second and third years. These practica, in various clinical, research, and human services settings, are intended to give students a broader and more integrative experience in the application of the skills and knowledge that they have acquired in the various courses they have taken.

Housing and Day Care: On-campus housing is available. See the following website for more information: http://www.umbc.edu/reslife/communities/waa.php. On-campus day care facilities are available.

Employment of Department Graduates:

Master's Degree Graduates: Of those who graduated in the academic year 2011–2012, the following categories and numbers represent the postgraduate activities and employment of master's degree graduates: Enrolled in a postdoctoral residency/fellowship (n/a), employed in independent practice (n/a), total from the above (master's) (0).

Doctoral Degree Graduates: Of those who graduated in the academic year 2011–2012, the following categories and numbers represent the postgraduate activities and employment of doctoral degree graduates: Enrolled in a psychology doctoral program (n/a), enrolled in a postdoctoral residency/fellowship (8), employed in an academic position at a university (2), employed in a community mental health/counseling center (2), employed in a hospital/medical center (3), other employment position (2), total from the above (doctoral) (17).

Additional Information:

Orientation, Objectives, and Emphasis of Department: UMBC Psychology is committed to a scientist–practitioner model and emphasizes science with an applied psychological research focus. The department uses a biopsychosocial interactive framework as the foundation for exploring various problems and issues in psychology. Two doctoral graduate programs are housed in the department: Applied Developmental Psychology (ADP) and Human Services Psychology (HSP). The ADP program has three concentrations: Early Development/Early Intervention, Socioemotional Development of Children, and Educational Contexts of Development; students can affiliate flexibly with one or more concentrations. The ADP program is accredited by the ASPPB/National Register of Health Service Providers in Psychology. The

HSP program consists of three subprograms—community/social, behavioral medicine, and an APA-approved clinical subprogram. Many HSP students take cross-area training in clinical/behavioral medicine or clinical/community areas. There is also a Master's program in Applied Behavior Analysis, housed at UMBC and in collaboration with the Kennedy Krieger Institute. Faculty represent a broad range of theoretical perspectives and maintain active research programs. The psychology department has many collaborative relationships for research and clinical and practical training opportunities with institutions in the Baltimore-Washington corridor.

Special Facilities or Resources: The Psychology Department at UMBC has numerous faculty research laboratories on campus in close proximity to faculty offices. Laboratories include equipment for psychological assessment, videotaping and coding, and observation as well as an animal laboratory. The department has access to several large computer laboratories on campus and has a small computer laboratory for graduate students. Through collaborative arrangements with the medical school and other University of Maryland System facilities, and Kennedy Krieger Institute, graduate students have access to different patient populations and opportunities for community based projects.

Information for Students With Physical Disabilities: See the following website for more information: http://www.umbc.edu/sss/.

Application Information:
Send to Dean of Graduate School, 1000 Hilltop Circle, Baltimore, MD 21250. Application available online. URL of online application: http://www.umbc.edu/gradschool/admissions/apply.html. Students are admitted in the Fall, application deadline December 1. Applied Behavior Analysis Master's program deadline is February 1. Doctoral program in Applied Developmental Psychology is January 9. *Fee:* $50.

Towson University
Department of Psychology
8000 York Road
Towson, MD 21252
Telephone: (410) 704-3080
Fax: (410) 704-3800
E-mail: cjohnson@towson.edu
Web: http://www.towson.edu/psychology/

Department Information:
1965. Chairperson: Craig T. Johnson, PhD. Number of faculty: total—full-time 41, part-time 44; women—full-time 25, part-time 23; total—minority—full-time 4, part-time 3; women minority—full-time 4, part-time 2.

Programs and Degrees Offered:
Listed in the following order: Program area, degree type (T if terminal Master's), number awarded 7/11–6/12. Clinical Psychology MA/MS (Master of Arts/Science) (T) 8, Counseling Psychology MA/MS (Master of Arts/Science) (T) 10, Experimental Psychology MA/MS (Master of Arts/Science) (T) 14, School Psychology MA/MS (Master of Arts/Science) 14, Human Resource Development MA/MS (Master of Arts/Science) 40.

Student Applications/Admissions:

Student Applications

Clinical Psychology MA/MS (Master of Arts/Science)—Applications 2012–2013, 88. Total applicants accepted 2012–2013, 14. Number full-time enrolled (new admits only) 2012–2013, 13. Number part-time enrolled (new admits only) 2012–2013, 0. Total enrolled 2012–2013 full-time, 26. Total enrolled 2012–2013 part-time, 2. Openings 2013–2014, 15. The median number of years required for completion of a degree in 2012–2013 were 2. The number of students enrolled full- and part-time who were dismissed or voluntarily withdrew from this program area in 2012–2013 were 2. Counseling Psychology MA/MS (Master of Arts/Science)—Applications 2012–2013, 120. Total applicants accepted 2012–2013, 21. Number full-time enrolled (new admits only) 2012–2013, 16. Number part-time enrolled (new admits only) 2012–2013, 0. Total enrolled 2012–2013 full-time, 32. Total enrolled 2012–2013 part-time, 3. Openings 2013–2014, 18. The median number of years required for completion of a degree in 2012–2013 were 2. The number of students enrolled full- and part-time who were dismissed or voluntarily withdrew from this program area in 2012–2013 were 0. Experimental Psychology MA/MS (Master of Arts/Science)—Applications 2012–2013, 48. Total applicants accepted 2012–2013, 24. Number full-time enrolled (new admits only) 2012–2013, 12. Number part-time enrolled (new admits only) 2012–2013, 2. Total enrolled 2012–2013 full-time, 22. Total enrolled 2012–2013 part-time, 11. Openings 2013–2014, 14. The median number of years required for completion of a degree in 2012–2013 were 2. The number of students enrolled full- and part-time who were dismissed or voluntarily withdrew from this program area in 2012–2013 were 0. School Psychology MA/MS (Master of Arts/Science)—Applications 2012–2013, 58. Total applicants accepted 2012–2013, 14. Number full-time enrolled (new admits only) 2012–2013, 13. Number part-time enrolled (new admits only) 2012–2013, 0. Total enrolled 2012–2013 full-time, 39. Total enrolled 2012–2013 part-time, 0. Openings 2013–2014, 14. The median number of years required for completion of a degree in 2012–2013 were 3. The number of students enrolled full- and part-time who were dismissed or voluntarily withdrew from this program area in 2012–2013 were 1. Human Resource Development MA/MS (Master of Arts/Science)—Applications 2012–2013, 115. Total applicants accepted 2012–2013, 45. Number full-time enrolled (new admits only) 2012–2013, 0. Number part-time enrolled (new admits only) 2012–2013, 45. Openings 2013–2014, 50. The median number of years required for completion of a degree in 2012–2013 were 2. The number of students enrolled full- and part-time who were dismissed or voluntarily withdrew from this program area in 2012–2013 were 8.

Scores: Entries appear in this order: required test or GPA, minimum score (if required), median score of students entering in 2012–2013. Clinical Psychology MA/MS (Master of Arts/Science): GRE-V 153, 156, GRE-Q 144, 151, GRE-Analytical 4.0, 4.5, overall undergraduate GPA 3.0, 3.6, last 2 years GPA 3.0; Counseling Psychology MA/MS (Master of Arts/Science): GRE-V 146, 150, GRE-Q 140, 144, GRE-Analytical 4, 4, overall undergraduate GPA 3.0, 3.5, last 2 years GPA 3.0, 3.6; Experimental Psychology MA/MS (Master of Arts/Science): overall undergraduate GPA 2.8, 3.5; School Psychology MA/MS (Master of Arts/Science): GRE-V 146, GRE-Q 146, GRE-Analytical 4.0, 4.5, overall undergraduate GPA 3.2, 3.53; Human Resource Development MA/MS (Master of Arts/Science): overall undergraduate GPA 2.8, 3.3.

Other Criteria: (importance of criteria rated low, medium, or high): GRE scores—medium, research experience—medium, work experience—medium, clinically related public service—medium, GPA—high, letters of recommendation—high, interview—high, statement of goals and objectives—medium, specific undergraduate psychology courses taken—medium, Clinically related public service or experience, letters of recommendation and interview are all used by the clinical, counseling, and school psychology programs. Research experience is very important for the experimental program and clinical program. Counseling, clinical, experimental, and school psychology also use a letter of intent and consider it very important. The clinical program considers GRE scores very important for making initial decisions about whom to interview for admission. The HRD program does not require GRE, but does rely heavily on both GPA and work experience, along with an Application Essay; some applicants may be asked to interview. The experimental program does not require GRE scores.

Student Characteristics: The following represents characteristics of students in 2012–2013 in all graduate psychology programs in the department: Female—full-time 57, part-time 0; Male—full-time 11, part-time 2; African American/Black—full-time 14, part-time 40; Hispanic/Latino(a)—full-time 0, part-time 6; Asian/Pacific Islander—full-time 2, part-time 1; American Indian/Alaska Native—full-time 0, part-time 0; Caucasian/White—full-time 102, part-time 108; Multi-ethnic—full-time 0, part-time 0; students subject to the Americans With Disabilities Act—full-time 3, part-time 0; Unknown ethnicity—full-time 0, part-time 0; International students who hold an F-1 or J-1 Visa—full-time 6, part-time 0.

Financial Information/Assistance:

Tuition for Full-Time Study: *Master's:* State residents: $446 per credit hour; Nonstate residents: $832 per credit hour. Tuition is not available at this time. Tuition is subject to change. Additional fees are assessed to students beyond the costs of tuition for the following: technology fees: $7 per credit with a $80 cap per term. See the following website for updates and changes in tuition costs: http://www.towson.edu/adminfinance/fiscalplanning/bursar/tuitionandfees/.

Financial Assistance:

First-Year Students: Teaching assistantships available for first year. Average amount paid per academic year: $4,000. Average number of hours worked per week: 10. Research assistantships available for first year. Average amount paid per academic year: $5,000. Average number of hours worked per week: 20.

Advanced Students: Teaching assistantships available for advanced students. Average amount paid per academic year: $4,000. Average number of hours worked per week: 10. Research assistantships available for advanced students. Average amount paid per academic year: $5,000. Average number of hours worked per week: 20.

Additional Information: Of all students currently enrolled full time, 25% benefited from one or more of the listed financial assistance programs. Application and information available online at: http://www.towson.edu/provost/provost/graduatestudies/assistantships/index.asp.

Internships/Practica: Master's Degree (MA/MS Clinical Psychology): An internship experience, such as a final research project or "capstone" experience is required of graduates. Master's Degree (MA/MS Counseling Psychology): An internship experience, such as a final research project or "capstone" experience is required of graduates. Master's Degree (MA/MS Experimental Psychology): An internship experience, such as a final research project or "capstone" experience is required of graduates. School Psychology students are required to complete two 150-hour practica over two consecutive semesters in a local school system. The program culminates in a 1200-hour internship that is to be completed full-time over one year or part-time over two consecutive years. At least 50% of the 1200 hours must be completed in a public school system; however most students complete all hours in public schools. Students in clinical psychology complete a required 500 hour, nine-month internship. Students may elect to complete a clinical or research internship depending upon their personal and professional goals. Students on clinical internships provide supervised psychological services to clients in an off-campus mental health setting. Students on research internships will assist an experienced scientist in conducting clinical trials research. Counseling students are required to complete a 240-hour practicum and a 300-hour internship over two semesters. Students are placed in community mental health centers, college counseling centers, drug and alcohol rehabilitation agencies, domestic violence centers, and other mental health service agencies. A limited number of graduate assistantships are available for students in the experimental psychology program. The HRD program requires graduates to have field work experience in order to graduate. For those not already working in HR, students can complete an internship or practicum for 3 credit hours near the end of their studies.

Housing and Day Care: No on-campus housing is available. On-campus day care facilities are available. See the following website for more information: http://www.towson.edu/daycare/.

Employment of Department Graduates:

Master's Degree Graduates: Of those who graduated in the academic year 2011–2012, the following categories and numbers represent the postgraduate activities and employment of master's degree graduates: Enrolled in a psychology doctoral program (12), enrolled in another graduate/professional program (6), enrolled in a postdoctoral residency/fellowship (n/a), employed in independent practice (n/a), employed in other positions at a higher education institution (5), employed in a professional position in a school system (14), employed in business or industry (34), employed in government agency (8), employed in a community mental health/counseling center (21), employed in a hospital/medical center (10), other employment position (8), do not know (16), total from the above (master's) (134).

Doctoral Degree Graduates: Of those who graduated in the academic year 2011–2012, the following categories and numbers represent the postgraduate activities and employment of doctoral degree graduates: Enrolled in a psychology doctoral program (n/a), total from the above (doctoral) (0).

Additional Information:

Orientation, Objectives, and Emphasis of Department: The experimental psychology program is designed to prepare students for subsequent enrollment in PhD programs or for research jobs in industrial, government, private consulting, or hospital settings.

Students receive comprehensive instruction in research design, statistical methods (both univariate and multivariate), computer applications (for both data collection and analysis), and take a series of courses in specialized areas of psychology (biological, cognitive, and social psychology). Students collaborate on research with faculty mentors and complete an empirical thesis. The Clinical concentration is ideally suited to meet the needs of individuals who want to provide clinical services that are informed by science, want to work as master's-level psychometricians or behavioral specialists, want to work as research or clinical staff on applied research studies, or are considering pursuing doctoral training in clinical psychology. The program curriculum provides comprehensive and hands-on training in personality and intellectual assessment, diagnosis, state-of-the-art and empirically-supported treatment, as well as research methods and statistics. Opportunities are also available for students to work on research projects under the direct supervision of a faculty member. In addition to completing a research thesis, students may also have the opportunity, depending on the faculty member, to assist in developing research conference presentations and manuscripts for publication. The Counseling Psychology program trains students to facilitate personal, educational, and vocational adjustment across the lifespan. The program offers a practitioner track and a research track from which degree candidates choose. Graduates of the program may go on to meet the requirements of the Licensed Clinical Professional Counselor, pursue a doctoral degree, and/or find employment in a wide variety of counseling agencies. The School Psychology program is fully approved by the National Association of School Psychologists (NASP) and trains graduate students to become school psychologists. The program emphasizes consultation and early intervention. It is unique in its close relationship with its surrounding urban and suburban communities, which welcome Towson's school psychology students in both practicum and internship settings. The program offers a single 63-credit degree: the Master of Arts in Psychology with a concentration in School Psychology and the Certificate of Advanced Study (CAS) in School Psychology. The mission of the Towson University HRD Professional Track MS Graduate Degree program is to equip students with the knowledge, skills and abilities needed to assume and perform successfully professional, managerial and administrative positions in various domains of Human Resources practices through the use of well-organized and implemented classroom-based, online and hybrid instructional events by a highly-qualified faculty for students and employers in the greater Baltimore regional area. It is a 36-credit hour program, and is ideally suited for people looking to enter the human resources profession, for current practitioners seeking to expand their knowledge and expertise, as well as for mid-career professionals wanting to improve their practice and advancement opportunities. Students can specialize in human resource development, human resource management, or organization development and change.

Special Facilities or Resources: The new Liberal Arts building houses laboratories for histology and computer analysis as well as specialized space for clinical/counseling training as well as the conduct of research in learning/motivation, physiological, comparative, cognitive, social, developmental, and general experimental psychology. Additionally, because of the popularity of the undergraduate Psychology major, there are many students willing to participate in research studies.

Information for Students With Physical Disabilities: See the following website for more information: http://www.towson.edu/dss/.

Application Information:

Send to Graduate School, Towson University, Towson, MD 21252. Application available online. URL of online application: http://grad.towson.edu/apply/applynow.asp. Students are admitted in the Fall, application deadline January 15; Spring, application deadline September 30. Clinical, Counseling, Experimental, and School admit for the Fall only with an application deadline of January 15. HRD has a May 15 deadline for Fall admission (early admission deadline is April 1) and a September 30 deadline for Spring admission. Human Resource Development has rolling admission. *Fee:* $45. Fee is $45 for online applications and $50 for paper applications.

Uniformed Services University of the Health Sciences
Medical and Clinical Psychology
F Edward Hebert School of Medicine
4301 Jones Bridge Road
Bethesda, MD 20814
Telephone: (301) 295-9669
Fax: (301) 295-3034
E-mail: *tricia.crum@usuhs.edu*
Web: *http://www.usuhs.mil/mps/*

Department Information:

1977. Chairperson: David S. Krantz, PhD. Number of faculty: total—full-time 9; women—full-time 4; total—minority—full-time 1; women minority—full-time 1.

Programs and Degrees Offered:

Listed in the following order: Program area, degree type (T if terminal Master's), number awarded 7/11–6/12. Medical Psychology PhD (Doctor of Philosophy) 0, Clinical Psychology PhD (Doctor of Philosophy) 2, Medical Psychology (Clinical Track) PhD (Doctor of Philosophy) 0.

APA Accreditation: Clinical PhD (Doctor of Philosophy). Clinical PhD (Doctor of Philosophy).

Student Applications/Admissions:
Student Applications

Medical Psychology PhD (Doctor of Philosophy)—Applications 2012–2013, 3. Total applicants accepted 2012–2013, 2. Number full-time enrolled (new admits only) 2012–2013, 0. Number part-time enrolled (new admits only) 2012–2013, 0. Total enrolled 2012–2013 full-time, 4. Total enrolled 2012–2013 part-time, 0. Openings 2013–2014, 3. The median number of years required for completion of a degree in 2012–2013 were 6. The number of students enrolled full- and part-time who were dismissed or voluntarily withdrew from this program area in 2012–2013 were 0. *Clinical Psychology PhD (Doctor of Philosophy)*—Applications 2012–2013, 132. Total applicants accepted 2012–2013, 6. Number full-time enrolled (new admits only) 2012–2013, 6. Number part-time enrolled (new admits only) 2012–2013, 0. Total enrolled 2012–2013 full-time, 30. Total enrolled 2012–2013 part-time, 0. Openings 2013–2014,

6. The median number of years required for completion of a degree in 2012–2013 were 5. The number of students enrolled full- and part-time who were dismissed or voluntarily withdrew from this program area in 2012–2013 were 1. *Medical Psychology (Clinical Track) PhD (Doctor of Philosophy)*—Applications 2012–2013, 101. Total applicants accepted 2012–2013, 3. Number full-time enrolled (new admits only) 2012–2013, 3. Number part-time enrolled (new admits only) 2012–2013, 0. Total enrolled 2012–2013 full-time, 15. Total enrolled 2012–2013 part-time, 0. Openings 2013–2014, 3. The median number of years required for completion of a degree in 2012–2013 were 6. The number of students enrolled full- and part-time who were dismissed or voluntarily withdrew from this program area in 2012–2013 were 0.

Scores: Entries appear in this order: required test or GPA, minimum score (if required), median score of students entering in 2012–2013. *Medical Psychology PhD (Doctor of Philosophy):* GRE-V 550, 600, GRE-Q 550, 600, GRE-Analytical 4.5, 5, overall undergraduate GPA 3.2, 3.5; *Clinical Psychology PhD (Doctor of Philosophy):* GRE-V 550, 600, GRE-Q 550, 600, GRE-Analytical 4.5, 5, overall undergraduate GPA 3.2, 3.5; *Medical Psychology (Clinical Track) PhD (Doctor of Philosophy):* GRE-V 550, 600, GRE-Q 550, 600, GRE-Analytical 4.5, 5, overall undergraduate GPA 3.2, 3.5, Masters GPA no minimum stated.

Other Criteria: (importance of criteria rated low, medium, or high): GRE scores—high, research experience—high, work experience—low, extracurricular activity—low, clinically related public service—medium, GPA—high, letters of recommendation—high, interview—high, statement of goals and objectives—high, undergraduate major in psychology—medium, specific undergraduate psychology courses taken—medium. For additional information on admission requirements, go to http://www.usuhs.mil/mps/.

Student Characteristics: The following represents characteristics of students in 2012–2013 in all graduate psychology programs in the department: Female—full-time 37, part-time 0; Male—full-time 12, part-time 0; African American/Black—full-time 4, part-time 0; Hispanic/Latino(a)—full-time 1, part-time 0; Asian/Pacific Islander—full-time 2, part-time 0; American Indian/Alaska Native—full-time 0, part-time 0; Caucasian/White—full-time 41, part-time 0; Multi-ethnic—full-time 1, part-time 0; students subject to the Americans With Disabilities Act—full-time 0, part-time 0; Unknown ethnicity—full-time 0, part-time 0; International students who hold an F-1 or J-1 Visa—full-time 1, part-time 0.

Financial Information/Assistance:
Tuition for Full-Time Study: *Doctoral:* State residents: per academic year $0; Nonstate residents: per academic year $0.

Financial Assistance:

First-Year Students: Traineeships available for first year. Average amount paid per academic year: $26,000. Average number of hours worked per week: 20. Fellowships and scholarships available for first year. Average amount paid per academic year: $31,000. Average number of hours worked per week: 20.

Advanced Students: Teaching assistantships available for advanced students. Average amount paid per academic year: $26,000. Average number of hours worked per week: 20. Research assistantships available for advanced students. Average amount

paid per academic year: $26,000. Average number of hours worked per week: 20. Traineeships available for advanced students. Average amount paid per academic year: $26,000. Average number of hours worked per week: 20. Fellowships and scholarships available for advanced students. Average amount paid per academic year: $31,000. Average number of hours worked per week: 20.

Additional Information: Of all students currently enrolled full time, 100% benefited from one or more of the listed financial assistance programs.

Internships/Practica: Doctoral Degree (PhD Clinical Psychology): For those doctoral students for whom a professional psychology internship was required in this program prior to graduation, (5) students applied for an internship in 2011–2012, with (5) students obtaining an internship. Of those students who obtained an internship, (5) were paid internships. Of those students who obtained an internship, (4) students placed in APA/CPA accredited internships, (1) students placed in internships not APA/CPA accredited, but listed with the Association of Psychology Postdoctoral and Internship Programs (APPIC), (0) students placed in internships conforming to guidelines of the Council of Directors of School Psychology Programs (CDSPP), (0) students placed in internships that were not APA/CPA accredited, APPIC or CDSPP listed. Doctoral Degree (PhD Medical Psychology (Clinical Track)): For those doctoral students for whom a professional psychology internship was required in this program prior to graduation, (1) students applied for an internship in 2011–2012, with (1) students obtaining an internship. Of those students who obtained an internship, (1) were paid internships. Of those students who obtained an internship, (1) students placed in APA/CPA accredited internships, (0) students placed in internships not APA/CPA accredited, but listed with the Association of Psychology Postdoctoral and Internship Programs (APPIC), (0) students placed in internships conforming to guidelines of the Council of Directors of School Psychology Programs (CDSPP), (0) students placed in internships that were not APA/CPA accredited, APPIC or CDSPP listed. Military Clinical Psychology and Clinical/Medical Psychology students complete the 12-month internship during the fifth and final year of the program within an APA-approved military or civilian clinical psychology training program. Practicum training occurs during the Fall, Winter, and Spring quarters of the second, third and fourth years. Students work at practicum sites at local facilities for 6 to 10 hours per week.

Housing and Day Care: No on-campus housing is available. No on-campus day care facilities are available.

Employment of Department Graduates:

Master's Degree Graduates: Of those who graduated in the academic year 2011–2012, the following categories and numbers represent the postgraduate activities and employment of master's degree graduates: Enrolled in a postdoctoral residency/fellowship (n/a), employed in independent practice (n/a), total from the above (master's) (0).

Doctoral Degree Graduates: Of those who graduated in the academic year 2011–2012, the following categories and numbers represent the postgraduate activities and employment of doctoral degree graduates: Enrolled in a psychology doctoral program (n/a), employed in a hospital/medical center (2), total from the above (doctoral) (2).

Additional Information:

Orientation, Objectives, and Emphasis of Department: The Department's educational programs provide a background in general psychological principles. Two content areas are emphasized: Health Psychology and Clinical Psychology. Educational and research activities focus on the application of principles and methods of scientific psychology relevant to physical and mental health. The Department is set in a School of Medicine and has an interdisciplinary focus. A Clinical Psychology program for uniformed military personnel and a Medical Psychology clinical track for civilians are APA-accredited and follow the scientist'-practitioner model. A research/academic program in Medical Psychology encompasses the fields of Health Psychology and Behavioral Medicine. The Department provides many research opportunities for students in the graduate programs and opportunities for mentorship because of the active and varied research programs conducted by the full-time faculty. Research opportunities available for students all involve the study of behavioral, psychological and biobehavioral factors in physical and mental health. In addition, several faculty in the Department participate in an NIH-funded predoctoral and postdoctoral training programs in cardiovascular behavioral medicine.

Special Facilities or Resources: The Department has office space, laboratory space for human and animal experimentation, multiple psychophysiology laboratories, and a biochemistry laboratory. There is access to classrooms, conference rooms, an excellent library, a computer center, audiovisual support, teaching hospitals, and a laboratory animal facility that is accredited by the Association for the Assessment and Accreditation of Laboratory Animal Care (AAALAC). The Bethesda campus of the National Institutes of Health, including the National Library of Medicine, is within walking distance from USUHS. The NIH is a resource for lecture series, specialized courses, funding information, and research collaborations. The major military training hospitals also are nearby, as are all the social and cultural offerings of Washington, D.C.

Application Information:
Send to Eleanor Metcalf, PhD, Associate Dean for Graduate Education, USUHS, 4301 Jones Bridge Road, Bethesda, MD 20814-4799. Application available online. URL of online application: http://www.usuhs.mil/graded/application.html. Students are admitted in the Fall, application deadline January 1. *Fee:* $0.

American International College
Department of Graduate Psychology
1000 State Street
Springfield, MA 01109
Telephone: (800) 242-3142
Fax: (413) 737-2803
E-mail: *john.defrancesco@aic.edu*
Web: *http://www.aic.edu/academics/aes/*

Department Information:
1979. Chairperson: John J. DeFrancesco, PhD. Number of faculty: total—full-time 3, part-time 7; women—full-time 1, part-time 4.

Programs and Degrees Offered:
Listed in the following order: Program area, degree type (T if terminal Master's), number awarded 7/11–6/12. Clinical Psychology MA/MS (Master of Arts/Science) (T) 12, Educational Psychology MA/MS (Master of Arts/Science) 2, Educational Psychology EdD (Doctor of Education) 8, Forensic Psychology MA/MS (Master of Arts/Science) (T) 7.

Student Applications/Admissions:
Student Applications

Clinical Psychology MA/MS (Master of Arts/Science)—Applications 2012–2013, 53. Total applicants accepted 2012–2013, 28. Number full-time enrolled (new admits only) 2012–2013, 20. Number part-time enrolled (new admits only) 2012–2013, 6. Total enrolled 2012–2013 full-time, 45. Total enrolled 2012–2013 part-time, 35. Openings 2013–2014, 20. The median number of years required for completion of a degree in 2012–2013 were 3. *Educational Psychology MA/MS (Master of Arts/Science)*—Applications 2012–2013, 2. Total applicants accepted 2012–2013, 2. Number full-time enrolled (new admits only) 2012–2013, 2. Number part-time enrolled (new admits only) 2012–2013, 0. Total enrolled 2012–2013 full-time, 2. Total enrolled 2012–2013 part-time, 0. Openings 2013–2014, 10. The median number of years required for completion of a degree in 2012–2013 were 2. The number of students enrolled full- and part-time who were dismissed or voluntarily withdrew from this program area in 2012–2013 were 0. *Educational Psychology EdD (Doctor of Education)*—Applications 2012–2013, 16. Total applicants accepted 2012–2013, 9. Number full-time enrolled (new admits only) 2012–2013, 7. Number part-time enrolled (new admits only) 2012–2013, 2. Total enrolled 2012–2013 full-time, 25. Total enrolled 2012–2013 part-time, 14. Openings 2013–2014, 15. The median number of years required for completion of a degree in 2012–2013 were 5. The number of students enrolled full- and part-time who were dismissed or voluntarily withdrew from this program area in 2012–2013 were 1. *Forensic Psychology MA/MS (Master of Arts/Science)*—Applications 2012–2013, 27. Total applicants accepted 2012–2013, 12. Number full-time enrolled (new admits only) 2012–2013, 7. Number part-time enrolled (new admits only) 2012–2013, 5. Total enrolled 2012–2013 full-time, 13. Total enrolled 2012–2013 part-time, 10. Openings 2013–2014, 20. The median number of years

required for completion of a degree in 2012–2013 were 2. The number of students enrolled full- and part-time who were dismissed or voluntarily withdrew from this program area in 2012–2013 were 1.

Scores: Entries appear in this order: required test or GPA, minimum score (if required), median score of students entering in 2012–2013. *Clinical Psychology MA/MS (Master of Arts/Science):* overall undergraduate GPA 2.75, 3.25; *Educational Psychology MA/MS (Master of Arts/Science):* overall undergraduate GPA 3.25, 3.50; *Educational Psychology EdD (Doctor of Education):* GRE-V no minimum stated, GRE-Q no minimum stated, overall undergraduate GPA 3.25, 3.59, Masters GPA 3.25, 3.50; *Forensic Psychology MA/MS (Master of Arts/Science):* overall undergraduate GPA 2.75, 3.00.

Other Criteria: (importance of criteria rated low, medium, or high): GRE scores—medium, research experience—high, work experience—high, extracurricular activity—high, clinically related public service—high, GPA—high, letters of recommendation—high, interview—high, statement of goals and objectives—high, undergraduate major in psychology—medium, specific undergraduate psychology courses taken—medium, GRE optional for Doctoral Program.

Student Characteristics: The following represents characteristics of students in 2012–2013 in all graduate psychology programs in the department: Female—full-time 76, part-time 37; Male—full-time 20, part-time 8; African American/Black—full-time 25, part-time 2; Hispanic/Latino(a)—full-time 20, part-time 2; Asian/Pacific Islander—full-time 2, part-time 2; American Indian/Alaska Native—full-time 0, part-time 0; Caucasian/White—full-time 49, part-time 39; Multi-ethnic—full-time 0, part-time 0; students subject to the Americans With Disabilities Act—full-time 1, part-time 0; Unknown ethnicity—full-time 0, part-time 0; International students who hold an F-1 or J-1 Visa—full-time 2, part-time 0.

Financial Information/Assistance:
Tuition for Full-Time Study: *Master's:* State residents: $759 per credit hour; Nonstate residents: $759 per credit hour. *Doctoral:* State residents: $759 per credit hour; Nonstate residents: $759 per credit hour. Tuition is subject to change. See the following website for updates and changes in tuition costs: http://www.aic.edu/admissions/graduate/costs.

Financial Assistance:
First-Year Students: Research assistantships available for first year. Average number of hours worked per week: 15. Apply by April 1. Fellowships and scholarships available for first year. Average number of hours worked per week: 15. Apply by April 1.

Advanced Students: Teaching assistantships available for advanced students. Average number of hours worked per week: 15. Apply by April 1. Research assistantships available for advanced students. Average number of hours worked per week: 15. Apply by April 1. Fellowships and scholarships available for advanced students. Average number of hours worked per week: 15. Apply by April 1.

Additional Information: Of all students currently enrolled full time, 15% benefited from one or more of the listed financial

assistance programs. Application and information available online at: http://www.aic.edu/admissions/graduate/ga.

Internships/Practica: Doctoral Degree (EdD Educational Psychology): For those doctoral students for whom a professional psychology internship was required in this program prior to graduation, (4) students applied for an internship in 2011–2012, with (4) students obtaining an internship. Of those students who obtained an internship, (1) were paid internships. Of those students who obtained an internship, (0) students placed in APA/CPA accredited internships, (0) students placed in internships not APA/CPA accredited, but listed with the Association of Psychology Postdoctoral and Internship Programs (APPIC), (0) students placed in internships conforming to guidelines of the Council of Directors of School Psychology Programs (CDSPP), (4) students placed in internships that were not APA/CPA accredited, APPIC or CDSPP listed. Master's Degree (MA/MS Clinical Psychology): An internship experience, such as a final research project or "capstone" experience is required of graduates. Master's Degree (MA/MS Forensic Psychology): An internship experience, such as a final research project or "capstone" experience is required of graduates. Internships and practica are secured at various institutions and facilities throughout the area.

Housing and Day Care: No on-campus housing is available. No on-campus day care facilities are available.

Employment of Department Graduates:

Master's Degree Graduates: Of those who graduated in the academic year 2011–2012, the following categories and numbers represent the postgraduate activities and employment of master's degree graduates: Enrolled in a postdoctoral residency/fellowship (n/a), employed in independent practice (n/a), total from the above (master's) (0).

Doctoral Degree Graduates: Of those who graduated in the academic year 2011–2012, the following categories and numbers represent the postgraduate activities and employment of doctoral degree graduates: Enrolled in a psychology doctoral program (n/a), total from the above (doctoral) (0).

Additional Information:

Orientation, Objectives, and Emphasis of Department: All graduate programs are based on a balanced scientific/practitioner model that emphasizes the interrelatedness of theory, research, and practice. Our focus is to develop competent, ethical, and self-aware professionals who can function effectively in a diverse, global, and increasingly interdependent world. Graduates of the MA Program in Clinical Psychology are eligible for master's level licensure. Graduates of the Ed.D. Program in Educational Psychology who are interested in seeking certification or licensure will generally meet academic, experiential, and other requirements depending upon the type of certification/license sought, however, each state or jurisdiction may have additional requirements. For specific information, the state or provisional certification/licensing board should be contacted.

Special Facilities or Resources: Curtis Blake Child Development Center.

Application Information:

Send to Graduate Admissions Office, American International College, 1000 State Street, Springfield, MA 01109. Application available on-line. URL of online application: http://www.aic.edu/admissions/graduate/apply. Students are admitted in the Programs have rolling admissions. *Fee:* $50.

Assumption College
Division of Counseling Psychology
500 Salisbury Street
Worcester, MA 01609-1296
Telephone: (508) 767-7390
Fax: (508) 767-7263
E-mail: *doerfler@assumption.edu*
Web: *http://graduate.assumption.edu/counseling-psychology/masterofarts*

Department Information:
1962. Program Director: Leonard A. Doerfler. Number of faculty: total—full-time 7, part-time 8; women—full-time 3, part-time 4.

Programs and Degrees Offered:
Listed in the following order: Program area, degree type (T if terminal Master's), number awarded 7/11–6/12. Counseling Psychology MA/MS (Master of Arts/Science) (T) 24.

Student Applications/Admissions:
Student Applications
Counseling Psychology MA/MS (Master of Arts/Science)—Applications 2012–2013, 110. Total applicants accepted 2012–2013, 75. Number full-time enrolled (new admits only) 2012–2013, 47. Number part-time enrolled (new admits only) 2012–2013, 5. Total enrolled 2012–2013 full-time, 94. Total enrolled 2012–2013 part-time, 15. Openings 2013–2014, 45. The median number of years required for completion of a degree in 2012–2013 were 2. The number of students enrolled full- and part-time who were dismissed or voluntarily withdrew from this program area in 2012–2013 were 5.

Scores: Entries appear in this order: required test or GPA, minimum score (if required), median score of students entering in 2012–2013. Counseling Psychology MA/MS (Master of Arts/Science): overall undergraduate GPA 3.0, 3.4, last 2 years GPA 3.0, 3.4, psychology GPA 3.0, 3.5.

Other Criteria: (importance of criteria rated low, medium, or high): research experience—low, work experience—medium, extracurricular activity—low, clinically related public service—medium, GPA—high, letters of recommendation—high, statement of goals and objectives—medium, undergraduate major in psychology—medium, specific undergraduate psychology courses taken—high. For additional information on admission requirements, go to http://graduate.assumption.edu/counseling-psychology/admission.

Student Characteristics: The following represents characteristics of students in 2012–2013 in all graduate psychology programs in the department: Female—full-time 55, part-time 36; Male—full-time 10, part-time 7; African American/Black—full-time 2, part-time 3; Hispanic/Latino(a)—full-time 4, part-time 0; Asian/Pacific Islander—full-time 1, part-time 1; American Indian/Alaska Native—full-time 0, part-time 0; Caucasian/White—full-time 49, part-time 34; Multi-ethnic—full-time 0, part-time 0; students subject to the Americans With Disabilities Act—full-time 5, part-

time 0; Unknown ethnicity—full-time 0, part-time 0; International students who hold an F-1 or J-1 Visa—full-time 2, part-time 1.

Financial Information/Assistance:
Tuition for Full-Time Study: *Master's:* State residents: $543 per credit hour; Nonstate residents: $543 per credit hour. Tuition is subject to change. See the following website for updates and changes in tuition costs: http://graduate.assumption.edu/financial-aid/graduate-tuition-financial-aid.

Financial Assistance:
First-Year Students: Fellowships and scholarships available for first year. Apply by March 1.
Advanced Students: Fellowships and scholarships available for advanced students. Apply by March 1.
Additional Information: Of all students currently enrolled full time, 10% benefited from one or more of the listed financial assistance programs. Application and information available online at: http://graduate.assumption.edu/financial-aid/graduate-tuition-financial-aid.

Internships/Practica: Practicum and internship placements are available in a wide range of community settings. Students can elect to work in outpatient/community, college counseling centers, substance abuse, inpatient, residential, and correctional settings. Opportunities to work with children, adolescents, adults, and families are available. The department maintains a close working relationship with the University of Massachusetts Medical Center, McLean Hospital/Harvard Medical School, and other mental health training agencies; students attend clinical case conferences, workshops, and lectures at these agencies. Students often receive training in innovative treatment models like home-based, brief problem-focused, or cognitive-behavioral treatments.

Housing and Day Care: No on-campus housing is available. No on-campus day care facilities are available.

Employment of Department Graduates:
Master's Degree Graduates: Of those who graduated in the academic year 2011–2012, the following categories and numbers represent the postgraduate activities and employment of master's degree graduates: Enrolled in a psychology doctoral program (1), enrolled in a postdoctoral residency/fellowship (n/a), employed in independent practice (n/a), employed in a professional position in a school system (2), employed in a community mental health/counseling center (21), total from the above (master's) (24).
Doctoral Degree Graduates: Of those who graduated in the academic year 2011–2012, the following categories and numbers represent the postgraduate activities and employment of doctoral degree graduates: Enrolled in a psychology doctoral program (n/a), total from the above (doctoral) (0).

Additional Information:
Orientation, Objectives, and Emphasis of Department: The program is organized to prepare students for entrance into doctoral programs in clinical and counseling psychology and for master's degree entry-level positions in a variety of mental health and related social service settings. Students are given conceptual preparation in a variety of theoretical positions in clinical and counseling psychology. A number of skill courses in counseling, testing, and research are an integral part of the program at both the entry and advanced levels. The goal of the program is to produce master's level psychologists who show conceptual versatility in theory and practice and depth of preparation in one of several special areas of counseling work. The student takes classes in areas such as personality theory, abnormal psychology, child development, counseling, advanced therapeutic procedure, measurement and research. Outside of class the student gains applied experience in clinical practice in the one-semester practicum and two-semester internship.

Special Facilities or Resources: Special facilities on campus include a well-equipped media center and an observation laboratory. Students also have access to in-service training at a local medical school, agencies, and hospitals. The college is located within commuting distance of Boston training facilities. College libraries in Worcester operate on a consortium basis. Programs of study are available on campus in the summer.

Information for Students With Physical Disabilities: See the following website for more information: http://www.assumption.edu/academics/resources/disabilityservices.

Application Information:
Send to Dean of Graduate Studies, Graduate Office, Assumption College, 500 Salisbury Street, Worcester, MA 01609-1296. Application available online. URL of online application: http://graduate.assumption.edu/admissions/graduate-application. Students are admitted in the Fall, application deadline February 15; Spring, application deadline October 1; Summer, application deadline January 15. *Fee:* $30.

Boston College
Department of Counseling, Developmental, and Educational
  Psychology
Lynch School of Education
309 Campion Hall
Chestnut Hill, MA 02467
Telephone: (617) 552-4710
Fax: (617) 552-1981
E-mail: *lykes@bc.edu*
Web: *http://www.bc.edu/schools/lsoe/academics/departments/cdep.html*

Department Information:
1950. Chairperson: M. Brinton Lykes, PhD Number of faculty: total—full-time 20, part-time 2; women—full-time 14, part-time 2; total—minority—full-time 4; women minority—full-time 3.

Programs and Degrees Offered:

Listed in the following order: Program area, degree type (T if terminal Master's), number awarded 7/11–6/12. School Counseling MA/MS (Master of Arts/Science) (T) 14, Counseling Psychology PhD (Doctor of Philosophy) 8, Mental Health Counseling MA/MS (Master of Arts/Science) (T) 64, Applied Developmental and Educational Psychology MA/MS (Master of Arts/Science) 25, Applied Developmental and Educational Psychology PhD (Doctor of Philosophy) 4.

APA Accreditation: Counseling PhD (Doctor of Philosophy). Student Outcome Data Website: http://www.bc.edu/content/bc/schools/lsoe/academics/departments/cdep/graduate/counsel/Publicdata.html.

Student Applications/Admissions:

Student Applications

School Counseling MA/MS (Master of Arts/Science)—Applications 2012–2013, 82. Total applicants accepted 2012–2013, 57. Number full-time enrolled (new admits only) 2012–2013, 20. Number part-time enrolled (new admits only) 2012–2013, 2. Total enrolled 2012–2013 full-time, 36. Total enrolled 2012–2013 part-time, 7. Openings 2013–2014, 25. The median number of years required for completion of a degree in 2012–2013 were 2. The number of students enrolled full- and part-time who were dismissed or voluntarily withdrew from this program area in 2012–2013 were 0. Counseling Psychology PhD (Doctor of Philosophy)—Applications 2012–2013, 293. Total applicants accepted 2012–2013, 6. Number full-time enrolled (new admits only) 2012–2013, 6. Number part-time enrolled (new admits only) 2012–2013, 0. Total enrolled 2012–2013 full-time, 38. Total enrolled 2012–2013 part-time, 2. Openings 2013–2014, 7. The median number of years required for completion of a degree in 2012–2013 were 6. The number of students enrolled full- and part-time who were dismissed or voluntarily withdrew from this program area in 2012–2013 were 0. Mental Health Counseling MA/MS (Master of Arts/Science)—Applications 2012–2013, 260. Total applicants accepted 2012–2013, 211. Number full-time enrolled (new admits only) 2012–2013, 69. Number part-time enrolled (new admits only) 2012–2013, 0. Total enrolled 2012–2013 full-time, 144. Total enrolled 2012–2013 part-time, 1. Openings 2013–2014, 70. The median number of years required for completion of a degree in 2012–2013 were 2. The number of students enrolled full- and part-time who were dismissed or voluntarily withdrew from this program area in 2012–2013 were 0. Applied Developmental and Educational Psychology MA/MS (Master of Arts/Science)—Applications 2012–2013, 103. Total applicants accepted 2012–2013, 71. Number full-time enrolled (new admits only) 2012–2013, 18. Number part-time enrolled (new admits only) 2012–2013, 4. Total enrolled 2012–2013 full-time, 22. Total enrolled 2012–2013 part-time, 8. Openings 2013–2014, 35. The median number of years required for completion of a degree in 2012–2013 were 2. The number of students enrolled full- and part-time who were dismissed or voluntarily withdrew from this program area in 2012–2013 were 0. Applied Developmental and Educational Psychology PhD (Doctor of Philosophy)—Applications 2012–2013, 71. Total applicants accepted 2012–2013, 3. Number full-time enrolled (new admits only) 2012–2013, 3. Number part-time enrolled (new admits only) 2012–2013, 0. Total enrolled 2012–2013 full-time, 19. Total enrolled 2012–2013 part-time, 0. Openings 2013–2014, 5. The median number of years required for completion of a degree in 2012–2013 were 4. The number of students enrolled full- and part-time who were dismissed or voluntarily withdrew from this program area in 2012–2013 were 0.

Scores: Entries appear in this order: required test or GPA, minimum score (if required), median score of students entering in 2012–2013. School Counseling MA/MS (Master of Arts/Science): GRE-V 410, 480, GRE-Q 370, 580, GRE-Analytical 3.0, 4.5, overall undergraduate GPA 2.77, 3.62; Counseling Psychology PhD (Doctor of Philosophy): GRE-V 490, 550, GRE-Q 580, 690, GRE-Analytical 3.5, 5.0, overall undergraduate GPA 3.3, 3.67, Masters GPA 3.9, 3.95; Mental Health Counseling MA/MS (Master of Arts/Science): GRE-V 330, 540, GRE-Q 370, 600, GRE-Analytical 3, 4.5, overall undergraduate GPA 3, 3.59; Applied Developmental and Educational Psychology MA/MS (Master of Arts/Science): GRE-V 290, 485, GRE-Q 440, 655, GRE-Analytical 3, 4, overall undergraduate GPA 3.0, 3.6; Applied Developmental and Educational Psychology PhD (Doctor of Philosophy): GRE-V 570, 645, GRE-Q 640, 750, GRE-Analytical 5.0, 5.3, overall undergraduate GPA 3.6, 3.84, Masters GPA 3.9, 3.95.

Other Criteria: (importance of criteria rated low, medium, or high): GRE scores—medium, research experience—high, work experience—medium, extracurricular activity—low, clinically related public service—high, GPA—high, letters of recommendation—high, interview—high, statement of goals and objectives—high, social justice commitment—high, undergraduate major in psychology—low, specific undergraduate psychology courses taken—low, For developmental programs, clinically related public service is low. For counseling programs, social justice commitment is high. For additional information on admission requirements, go to http://www.bc.edu/schools/lsoe/gradadmission/applying/requirements.html.

Student Characteristics: The following represents characteristics of students in 2012–2013 in all graduate psychology programs in the department: Female—full-time 221, part-time 15; Male—full-time 38, part-time 3; African American/Black—full-time 22, part-time 1; Hispanic/Latino(a)—full-time 14, part-time 1; Asian/Pacific Islander—full-time 21, part-time 0; American Indian/Alaska Native—full-time 0, part-time 0; Caucasian/White—full-time 151, part-time 11; Multi-ethnic—full-time 5, part-time 0; students subject to the Americans With Disabilities Act—full-time 3, part-time 0; Unknown ethnicity—full-time 46, part-time 5; International students who hold an F-1 or J-1 Visa—full-time 29, part-time 3.

Financial Information/Assistance:

Tuition for Full-Time Study: Master's: State residents: $1,166 per credit hour; Nonstate residents: $1,166 per credit hour. Doctoral: State residents: $1,166 per credit hour; Nonstate residents: $1,166 per credit hour. Tuition is subject to change. See the following website for updates and changes in tuition costs: http://www.bc.edu/offices/stserv/financial/tuitionandfees.html.

Financial Assistance:

First-Year Students: Research assistantships available for first year. Average amount paid per academic year: $17,000. Average number of hours worked per week: 20.

Advanced Students: Teaching assistantships available for advanced students. Average amount paid per academic year: $17,000. Average number of hours worked per week: 20. Research assistantships available for advanced students. Average amount paid per academic year: $17,000. Average number of hours worked per week: 20.

Additional Information: Of all students currently enrolled full time, 80% benefited from one or more of the listed financial assistance programs. Application and information available online at: http://www.bc.edu/schools/lsoe/gradadmission/funding.

Internships/Practica: Doctoral Degree (PhD Counseling Psychology): For those doctoral students for whom a professional psychology internship was required in this program prior to graduation, (5) students applied for an internship in 2011–2012, with (4) students obtaining an internship. Of those students who obtained an internship, (4) were paid internships. Of those students who obtained an internship, (4) students placed in APA/CPA accredited internships, (0) students placed in internships not APA/CPA accredited, but listed with the Association of Psychology Postdoctoral and Internship Programs (APPIC), (0) students placed in internships conforming to guidelines of the Council of Directors of School Psychology Programs (CDSPP), (0) students placed in internships that were not APA/CPA accredited, APPIC or CDSPP listed. Master's Degree (MA/MS Mental Health Counseling): An internship experience, such as a final research project or "capstone" experience is required of graduates. Doctoral students in Counseling Psychology complete two advanced practica in community mental health agencies, schools, clinics, hospitals, and college counseling centers. They also complete a one year predoctoral internship. Master's students in mental health and school counseling work with the Master's Program Coordinator to identify internships that meet requirements for mental health licensure or school counselor certification. Master's students in the Applied Developmental and Educational Psychology program can complete a non-required internship and Doctoral students in the Applied Developmental and Educational Psychology program must complete a required internship.

Housing and Day Care: No on-campus housing is available. On-campus day care facilities are available. See the following website for more information: http://www.bc.edu/offices/hr/employees/all-cc-docs.html.

Employment of Department Graduates:
Master's Degree Graduates: Of those who graduated in the academic year 2011–2012, the following categories and numbers represent the postgraduate activities and employment of master's degree graduates: Enrolled in a postdoctoral residency/fellowship (n/a), employed in independent practice (n/a), total from the above (master's) (0).
Doctoral Degree Graduates: Of those who graduated in the academic year 2011–2012, the following categories and numbers represent the postgraduate activities and employment of doctoral degree graduates: Enrolled in a psychology doctoral program (n/a), enrolled in a postdoctoral residency/fellowship (6), employed in independent practice (1), employed in an academic position at a university (1), employed in a hospital/medical center (1), still seeking employment (1), not seeking employment (1), do not know (1), total from the above (doctoral) (12).

Additional Information:
Orientation, Objectives, and Emphasis of Department: The Programs in Counseling, Developmental and Educational Psychology emphasize a foundation in developmental theory, research skills, and a commitment to preparing professionals to work in public practice, public service, academic or research institutions. The counseling psychology doctoral program espouses a scientist–practitioner model and provides broad-based training with special attention to group and individual counseling processes, theory and skill in research and assessment, and understanding individual development within a social context. Master's counseling students specialize in mental health counseling or school counseling. The program in Applied Developmental and Educational Psychology focuses on application and draws on psychology, educational and community programs, and engages public policies to enhance the development of individuals and their key institutional contexts-schools, families, and work settings- across the life span. Faculty research interests include psychotherapy, process and outcome, career and moral development, individual differences in cognitive and affective development including developmental disabilities, influence of gender role strain on the well-being of men, Asian-American and Latino mental health, racial identity, marital and community violence, marital satisfaction, and prevention and intervention for promoting positive development among youth.

Special Facilities or Resources: Boston College offers ample student access to computing facilities (Alpha mainframe, Macintosh and PCs) at no charge to students. The Educational Resource Center houses current psychological assessment kits and computerized instructional software. The Thomas P. O'Neill Library is fully automated with all major computerized databases. Through the consortium, students may cross-register in courses in other greater Boston universities (Boston University, Brandeis, and Tufts). The career center provides comprehensive resources and information regarding career planning and placement. The Institute for the Study and Promotion of Race and Culture (ISPRC), under the direction of Dr. Janet E. Helms, promotes the assets and addresses the societal conflicts associated with race or culture in theory and research, mental health practice, education, business, and society at large. The Center for Human Rights and International Justice at Boston College addresses the increasingly interdisciplinary needs of human rights work. Through multidisciplinary training programs, applied research, and the interaction of scholars with practitioners, the Center aims to nurture a new generation of scholars and practitioners in the United States and abroad who draw upon the strengths of many disciplines and the wisdom of rigorous ethical training in the attainment of human rights and international justice.

Information for Students With Physical Disabilities: See the following website for more information: http://www.bc.edu/offices/dos/disabilityservices.html.

Application Information:
Send to Boston College, LSOE, Data Processing Center, P.O. Box 226, Randolph, MA 02368-9998. Application available online. URL of online application: http://www.bc.edu/schools/lsoe/gradadmission/applying.html. Students are admitted in the Fall, application deadline December 1. Counseling MA programs January 1; Counseling PhD December 1. Developmental PhD January 1. Developmental MA January 1. *Fee:* $65.

Boston College
Department of Psychology
College of Arts and Sciences
140 Commonwealth Avenue, McGuinn 300
Chestnut Hill, MA 02467
Telephone: (617) 552-4100
Fax: (617) 552-0523
E-mail: *psychoffice@bc.edu*
Web: *http://www.bc.edu/psychology*

Department Information:
1950. Chairperson: Ellen Winner. Number of faculty: total—full-time 21, part-time 5; women—full-time 11, part-time 5; total—minority—full-time 3; women minority—full-time 2.

Programs and Degrees Offered:
Listed in the following order: Program area, degree type (T if terminal Master's), number awarded 7/11–6/12. Cognitive Neuroscience PhD (Doctor of Philosophy) 1, Social Psychology PhD (Doctor of Philosophy) 1, Developmental Psychology PhD (Doctor of Philosophy) 1, Behavioral Neuroscience PhD (Doctor of Philosophy) 0, Quantitative Psychology PhD (Doctor of Philosophy).

Student Applications/Admissions:
Student Applications
Cognitive Neuroscience PhD (Doctor of Philosophy)—Applications 2012–2013, 91. Total applicants accepted 2012–2013, 2. Number full-time enrolled (new admits only) 2012–2013, 3. Total enrolled 2012–2013 full-time, 5. The median number of years required for completion of a degree in 2012–2013 were 5. *Social Psychology PhD (Doctor of Philosophy)*—Applications 2012–2013, 103. Total applicants accepted 2012–2013, 3. Number full-time enrolled (new admits only) 2012–2013, 1. Total enrolled 2012–2013 full-time, 4. *Developmental Psychology PhD (Doctor of Philosophy)*—Applications 2012–2013, 73. Total applicants accepted 2012–2013, 1. Number full-time enrolled (new admits only) 2012–2013, 1. Total enrolled 2012–2013 full-time, 6. The median number of years required for completion of a degree in 2012–2013 were 5. *Behavioral Neuroscience PhD (Doctor of Philosophy)*—Applications 2012–2013, 38. Total applicants accepted 2012–2013, 2. Number full-time enrolled (new admits only) 2012–2013, 2. Total enrolled 2012–2013 full-time, 6. The median number of years required for completion of a degree in 2012–2013 were 5. *Quantitative Psychology PhD (Doctor of Philosophy)*—Applications 2012–2013, 10. Total applicants accepted 2012–2013, 0. Number full-time enrolled (new admits only) 2012–2013, 0.
Scores: Entries appear in this order: required test or GPA, minimum score (if required), median score of students entering in 2012–2013. *Cognitive Neuroscience PhD (Doctor of Philosophy)*: GRE-V no minimum stated, GRE-Q no minimum stated, GRE-Analytical no minimum stated, overall undergraduate GPA no minimum stated; *Social Psychology PhD (Doctor of Philosophy)*: GRE-V no minimum stated, GRE-Q no minimum stated, GRE-Analytical no minimum stated, overall undergraduate GPA no minimum stated, Masters GPA no minimum stated; *Developmental Psychology PhD (Doctor of Philosophy)*: GRE-V no minimum stated, GRE-Q no minimum stated, GRE-Analytical no minimum stated, overall undergraduate

GPA no minimum stated, Masters GPA no minimum stated; *Behavioral Neuroscience PhD (Doctor of Philosophy)*: GRE-V no minimum stated, GRE-Q no minimum stated, GRE-Analytical no minimum stated, overall undergraduate GPA no minimum stated, Masters GPA no minimum stated; *Quantitative Psychology PhD (Doctor of Philosophy)*: GRE-V no minimum stated, GRE-Q no minimum stated, GRE-Analytical no minimum stated, overall undergraduate GPA no minimum stated, Masters GPA no minimum stated.
Other Criteria: (importance of criteria rated low, medium, or high): GRE scores—high, research experience—high, work experience—low, extracurricular activity—low, clinically related public service—low, GPA—high, letters of recommendation—high, interview—high, statement of goals and objectives—high, undergraduate major in psychology—medium, specific undergraduate psychology courses taken—medium. For additional information on admission requirements, go to http://www.bc.edu/schools/cas/psych/graduate.html.

Student Characteristics: The following represents characteristics of students in 2012–2013 in all graduate psychology programs in the department: Female—full-time 13, part-time 0; Male—full-time 8, part-time 0; African American/Black—full-time 0, part-time 0; Hispanic/Latino(a)—full-time 0, part-time 0; Asian/Pacific Islander—full-time 3, part-time 0; American Indian/Alaska Native—full-time 0, part-time 0; Caucasian/White—full-time 18, part-time 0; Multi-ethnic—full-time 0, part-time 0; students subject to the Americans With Disabilities Act—full-time 0, part-time 0; Unknown ethnicity—full-time 0, part-time 0; International students who hold an F-1 or J-1 Visa—full-time 4, part-time 0.

Financial Information/Assistance:
Tuition for Full-Time Study: *Doctoral:* State residents: $1,292 per credit hour; Nonstate residents: $1,292 per credit hour. Tuition is subject to change. See the following website for updates and changes in tuition costs: http://www.bc.edu/offices/stserv/financial/tuitionandfees.html.

Financial Assistance:
First-Year Students: Teaching assistantships available for first year. Average amount paid per academic year: $21,000. Average number of hours worked per week: 20. Apply by December 15. Fellowships and scholarships available for first year.
Advanced Students: Teaching assistantships available for advanced students. Average amount paid per academic year: $21,000. Average number of hours worked per week: 20. Apply by December 15. Fellowships and scholarships available for advanced students.
Additional Information: Of all students currently enrolled full time, 100% benefited from one or more of the listed financial assistance programs. Application and information available online at: http://www.bc.edu/content/bc/schools/gsas/admissions/financial-aid.html.

Housing and Day Care: No on-campus housing is available. On-campus day care facilities are available. See the following website for more information: http://www.bc.edu/content/bc/offices/hr/employees/all-cc-docs.html.

Employment of Department Graduates:
Master's Degree Graduates: Of those who graduated in the academic year 2011–2012, the following categories and numbers

represent the postgraduate activities and employment of master's degree graduates: Enrolled in a postdoctoral residency/fellowship (n/a), employed in independent practice (n/a), total from the above (master's) (0).

Doctoral Degree Graduates: Of those who graduated in the academic year 2011–2012, the following categories and numbers represent the postgraduate activities and employment of doctoral degree graduates: Enrolled in a psychology doctoral program (n/a), enrolled in a postdoctoral residency/fellowship (3), total from the above (doctoral) (3).

Additional Information:

Orientation, Objectives, and Emphasis of Department: We emphasize rigorous research and a close working relationship between student and professor.

Special Facilities or Resources: Individual faculty maintain separate research laboratories. There is a shared psychophysiology lab. An animal lab facility contains two components: an animal facility and research laboratory space. The animal facility includes small animal housing and behavioral testing rooms, a surgery suite, and special procedure rooms equipped with hoods. The animal research space includes a (1) microscopy suite, (2) dark room, (3) data analysis room, and (4) 3 research labs/wet labs equipped with hoods, sinks, and workspace.

Information for Students With Physical Disabilities: See the following website for more information: http://www.bc.edu/disability.

Application Information:

Application available online. URL of online application: http://www.bc.edu/schools/gsas/admissions/howtoapply.html. Students are admitted in the Fall, application deadline December 15. *Fee:* $75.

Boston University (2012 data)
Department of Psychology
64 Cummington Street
Boston, MA 02215
Telephone: (617) 353-2580
Fax: (617) 353-6933
E-mail: *mlyons@bu.edu*
Web: *http://www.bu.edu/psych*

Department Information:
1935. Chairperson: Michael Lyons. Number of faculty: total—full-time 32, part-time 2; women—full-time 16, part-time 1; minority—part-time 1.

Programs and Degrees Offered:
Listed in the following order: Program area, degree type (T if terminal Master's), number awarded 7/11–6/12. Brain, Behavior, and Cognition PhD (Doctor of Philosophy) 0, Clinical Psychology PhD (Doctor of Philosophy) 8, General Psychology MA/MS (Master of Arts/Science) (T) 38, Developmental Science PhD (Doctor of Philosophy) 1.

APA Accreditation: Clinical PhD (Doctor of Philosophy). Student Outcome Data Website: http://www.bu.edu/psych/graduate/clinical/.

Student Applications/Admissions:
Student Applications
Brain, Behavior, and Cognition PhD (Doctor of Philosophy)—Applications 2012–2013, 75. Total applicants accepted 2012–2013, 5. Number full-time enrolled (new admits only) 2012–2013, 5. Number part-time enrolled (new admits only) 2012–2013, 0. Total enrolled 2012–2013 full-time, 17. Total enrolled 2012–2013 part-time, 1. Openings 2013–2014, 4. The median number of years required for completion of a degree in 2012–2013 were 5. The number of students enrolled full- and part-time who were dismissed or voluntarily withdrew from this program area in 2012–2013 were 0. *Clinical Psychology PhD (Doctor of Philosophy)*—Applications 2012–2013, 632. Total applicants accepted 2012–2013, 8. Number full-time enrolled (new admits only) 2012–2013, 5. Number part-time enrolled (new admits only) 2012–2013, 0. Total enrolled 2012–2013 full-time, 55. Total enrolled 2012–2013 part-time, 2. Openings 2013–2014, 8. The median number of years required for completion of a degree in 2012–2013 were 6. The number of students enrolled full- and part-time who were dismissed or voluntarily withdrew from this program area in 2012–2013 were 0. *General Psychology MA/MS (Master of Arts/Science)*—Applications 2012–2013, 229. Total applicants accepted 2012–2013, 98. Number full-time enrolled (new admits only) 2012–2013, 29. Number part-time enrolled (new admits only) 2012–2013, 4. Total enrolled 2012–2013 full-time, 35. Total enrolled 2012–2013 part-time, 10. Openings 2013–2014, 35. The median number of years required for completion of a degree in 2012–2013 was 1. The number of students enrolled full- and part-time who were dismissed or voluntarily withdrew from this program area in 2012–2013 were 0. *Developmental Science PhD (Doctor of Philosophy)*—Applications 2012–2013, 62. Total applicants accepted 2012–2013, 6. Number full-time enrolled (new admits only) 2012–2013, 2. Number part-time enrolled (new admits only) 2012–2013, 0. Total enrolled 2012–2013 full-time, 10. Total enrolled 2012–2013 part-time, 1. Openings 2013–2014, 4. The median number of years required for completion of a degree in 2012–2013 were 5. The number of students enrolled full- and part-time who were dismissed or voluntarily withdrew from this program area in 2012–2013 were 0.

Scores: Entries appear in this order: required test or GPA, minimum score (if required), median score of students entering in 2012–2013. *Brain, Behavior, and Cognition PhD (Doctor of Philosophy)*: GRE-V no minimum stated, 640, GRE-Q no minimum stated, 750, GRE-Analytical no minimum stated, overall undergraduate GPA no minimum stated, last 2 years GPA no minimum stated, psychology GPA no minimum stated, Masters GPA no minimum stated; *Clinical Psychology PhD (Doctor of Philosophy)*: GRE-V no minimum stated, 610, GRE-Q no minimum stated, 670, GRE-Analytical no minimum stated, overall undergraduate GPA no minimum stated, 3.7, last 2 years GPA no minimum stated, psychology GPA no minimum stated, Masters GPA no minimum stated; *General Psychology MA/MS (Master of Arts/Science)*: GRE-V no minimum stated, GRE-Q no minimum stated, GRE-Analytical no minimum stated, overall undergraduate GPA no minimum stated, last 2 years GPA no minimum stated, psychology GPA no minimum stated; *Developmental Science PhD (Doctor of Philosophy)*: GRE-V no minimum stated, 565, GRE-Q no minimum stated, 625, GRE-Analytical no minimum stated, overall undergraduate GPA no minimum stated, last 2 years GPA no minimum stated, psychology GPA no minimum stated, Masters GPA no minimum stated.

Other Criteria: (importance of criteria rated low, medium, or high): GRE scores—high, research experience—high, work experience—low, extracurricular activity—low, clinically related public service—high, GPA—high, letters of recommendation—high, interview—high, statement of goals and objectives—high. For additional information on admission requirements, go to http://www.bu.edu/psych/graduate/prospective/.

Student Characteristics: The following represents characteristics of students in 2012–2013 in all graduate psychology programs in the department: Female—full-time 94, part-time 10; Male—full-time 23, part-time 4; African American/Black—full-time 7, part-time 1; Hispanic/Latino(a)—full-time 3, part-time 0; Asian/Pacific Islander—full-time 23, part-time 0; American Indian/Alaska Native—full-time 0, part-time 0; Caucasian/White—full-time 81, part-time 12; Multi-ethnic—full-time 1, part-time 0; students subject to the Americans With Disabilities Act—full-time 0, part-time 0; Unknown ethnicity—full-time 2, part-time 1; International students who hold an F-1 or J-1 Visa—full-time 11, part-time 0.

Financial Information/Assistance:

Tuition for Full-Time Study: *Master's:* State residents: per academic year $41,050, $1,276 per credit hour; Nonstate residents: per academic year $41,050, $1,276 per credit hour. *Doctoral:* State residents: per academic year $41,050, $1,276 per credit hour; Nonstate residents: per academic year $41,050, $1,276 per credit hour. See the following website for updates and changes in tuition costs: http://www.bu.edu/cas/admissions/graduate/aid/.

Financial Assistance:

First-Year Students: Teaching assistantships available for first year. Average amount paid per academic year: $19,300. Average number of hours worked per week: 20. Research assistantships available for first year. Average amount paid per academic year: $28,950. Average number of hours worked per week: 20. Fellowships and scholarships available for first year. Average amount paid per academic year: $19,300. Average number of hours worked per week: 0.

Advanced Students: Teaching assistantships available for advanced students. Average amount paid per academic year: $19,300. Average number of hours worked per week: 20. Research assistantships available for advanced students. Average amount paid per academic year: $28,950. Average number of hours worked per week: 20. Traineeships available for advanced students. Average amount paid per academic year: $19,300. Average number of hours worked per week: 20.

Additional Information: Of all students currently enrolled full time, 81% benefited from one or more of the listed financial assistance programs. Application and information available online at: http://www.bu.edu/cas/admissions/graduate/aid/.

Internships/Practica: Doctoral Degree (PhD Clinical Psychology): For those doctoral students for whom a professional psychology internship was required in this program prior to graduation, (8) students applied for an internship in 2011–2012, with (8) students obtaining an internship. Of those students who obtained an internship, (8) were paid internships. Of those students who obtained an internship, (8) students placed in APA/CPA accredited internships, (0) students placed in internships not APA/

CPA accredited, but listed with the Association of Psychology Postdoctoral and Internship Programs (APPIC), (0) students placed in internships conforming to guidelines of the Council of Directors of School Psychology Programs (CDSPP), (0) students placed in internships that were not APA/CPA accredited, APPIC or CDSPP listed.

Housing and Day Care: No on-campus housing is available. No on-campus day care facilities are available.

Employment of Department Graduates:

Master's Degree Graduates: Of those who graduated in the academic year 2011–2012, the following categories and numbers represent the postgraduate activities and employment of master's degree graduates: Enrolled in a postdoctoral residency/fellowship (n/a), employed in independent practice (n/a), total from the above (master's) (0).

Doctoral Degree Graduates: Of those who graduated in the academic year 2011–2012, the following categories and numbers represent the postgraduate activities and employment of doctoral degree graduates: Enrolled in a psychology doctoral program (n/a), total from the above (doctoral) (0).

Additional Information:

Orientation, Objectives, and Emphasis of Department: The department offers specialized training leading to the PhD degree in three areas of concentration: clinical; brain, behavior, and cognition; and development science. The PhD degree in psychology is awarded to students of scholarly competence as reflected by course achievement and by performance on written and oral examinations and of research competence as reflected by student's skillful application and communication of knowledge in the area of specialization. Breadth is encouraged within psychology and in related social, behavioral, and biological sciences, but it is also expected that the student will engage in intensive and penetrating study of a specialized area of the field.

Special Facilities or Resources: Laboratories for research pursuits in animal behavior, behavior disorders, child development, cognition, neurophysiology, molecular biology and psychopharmacology add to the department's facilities. The Center for Anxiety and Related Disorders (CARD), a nationally recognized clinical research and treatment center, is a recent addition to the department and allows students to engage in a variety of ongoing research projects and receive training in focused clinical interventions. In addition, the Boston area is fortunate to have a number of nationally known hospitals, counseling centers, and community mental health centers directly affiliated with our clinical program where students have opportunities to gain experience in a variety of clinical settings with different client populations. The New England Regional Primate Center, which is supported by the National Institutes of Health, is also available to Boston University faculty and students.

Information for Students With Physical Disabilities: See the following website for more information: http://www.bu.edu/disability/.

Application Information:

Application available online. URL of online application: http://www.bu.edu/cas/admissions/graduate/apply/. Students are admitted in the Fall, application deadline December 1. The application deadline for the

MA-only program is May 15. Applications will be reviewed beginning March 1. *Fee:* $70.

Boston University (2012 data)

Division of Graduate Medical Sciences, Program in Mental Health Counseling and Behavioral Medicine
School of Medicine
72 East Concord Street, Robinson Building, Suite B-2903
Boston, MA 02118
Telephone: (617) 414-2320
Fax: (617) 414-2323
E-mail: *nicey@bu.edu*
Web: *http://www.bumc.bu.edu/mhbm*

Department Information:

2001. Chairperson: Stephen Brady, PhD. Number of faculty: total—full-time 4, part-time 11; women—full-time 2, part-time 7; total—minority—full-time 2, part-time 2; women minority—full-time 1, part-time 1.

Programs and Degrees Offered:

Listed in the following order: Program area, degree type (T if terminal Master's), number awarded 7/11–6/12. Mental Health Counseling and Behavioral Medicine MA/MS (Master of Arts/Science) (T) 28.

Student Applications/Admissions:

Student Applications

Mental Health Counseling and Behavioral Medicine MA/MS (Master of Arts/Science)—Applications 2012–2013, 81. Total applicants accepted 2012–2013, 38. Number full-time enrolled (new admits only) 2012–2013, 36. Number part-time enrolled (new admits only) 2012–2013, 0. Total enrolled 2012–2013 full-time, 54. Total enrolled 2012–2013 part-time, 0. Openings 2013–2014, 30. The median number of years required for completion of a degree in 2012–2013 were 2. The number of students enrolled full- and part-time who were dismissed or voluntarily withdrew from this program area in 2012–2013 were 1.

Other Criteria: (importance of criteria rated low, medium, or high): GRE scores—medium, research experience—medium, work experience—medium, extracurricular activity—medium, clinically related public service—medium, GPA—medium, letters of recommendation—high, interview—high, statement of goals and objectives—high. For additional information on admission requirements, go to http://www.bumc.bu.edu/mhbm.

Student Characteristics: The following represents characteristics of students in 2012–2013 in all graduate psychology programs in the department: Female—full-time 55, part-time 0; Male—full-time 5, part-time 0; African American/Black—full-time 4, part-time 0; Hispanic/Latino(a)—full-time 0, part-time 0; Asian/Pacific Islander—full-time 6, part-time 0; American Indian/Alaska Native—full-time 2, part-time 0; Caucasian/White—full-time 48, part-time 0; Multi-ethnic—full-time 0, part-time 0; students subject to the Americans With Disabilities Act—full-time 0, part-time 0; Unknown ethnicity—full-time 0, part-time 0; Interna-

tional students who hold an F-1 or J-1 Visa—full-time 4, part-time 0.

Financial Information/Assistance:

Tuition for Full-Time Study: *Master's:* State residents: per academic year $40,848, $1,276 per credit hour; Nonstate residents: per academic year $40,848, $1,276 per credit hour. Tuition is subject to change.

Financial Assistance:

First-Year Students: No information provided.
Advanced Students: No information provided.
Additional Information: No information provided.

Internships/Practica: Completion of the Masters in Mental Health Counseling and Behavioral Medicine program prepares students for independent licensure as a Mental Health Counselor (LMHC). Our students are primarily trained to conduct clinical practice with urban multicultural underserved populations. Our clinical training program includes curricula in mental health, behavioral medicine, and neuroscience offered in an urban hospital and medical school environment. The coursework is intended to prepare students to provide clinical services to a range of individuals in diversified settings. More specifically, students are trained to perform brief forms of assessment and psychotherapeutic interventions in medical and behavioral health care settings. We offer clinical training opportunities in diverse settings such as psychiatric emergency department services, child, adolescent, and adult outpatient psychiatric clinics, medical and psychiatric inpatient services, adolescent substance abuse treatment centers, college counseling centers, and community mental health clinics. Our practicum program is a 16 hour a week commitment over the course of one semester and our internship training is a 24 hour a week commitment over the course of an academic year. At the completion of the Program students will have accumulated approximately 1,000 hours of clinical training.

Housing and Day Care: On-campus housing is available. No on-campus day care facilities are available.

Employment of Department Graduates:

Master's Degree Graduates: Of those who graduated in the academic year 2011–2012, the following categories and numbers represent the postgraduate activities and employment of master's degree graduates: Enrolled in a postdoctoral residency/fellowship (n/a), employed in independent practice (n/a), total from the above (master's) (0).

Doctoral Degree Graduates: Of those who graduated in the academic year 2011–2012, the following categories and numbers represent the postgraduate activities and employment of doctoral degree graduates: Enrolled in a psychology doctoral program (n/a), total from the above (doctoral) (0).

Additional Information:

Orientation, Objectives, and Emphasis of Department: The Mental Health Counseling and Behavioral Medicine Program is the first of its kind in the United States, as it is located within a School of Medicine. Our program curriculum blends scholarship, practical experience and an appreciation of the scientific bases of assessment and treatments for behavioral and neurological disorders. Our objective is to provide Master's level counselors with a strong foundation in psychopathology and psychotherapeutic intervention, as well as a background in behavioral medicine and neuroscience. Our primary focus is the development of professional counselors with the skills to develop as scholars, teachers, researchers and clinicians. Our program fills a major gap in the delivery of mental health services in health care settings and to patients with healthcare concerns. Students have a unique opportunity to work with outstanding mentors in psychology, psychiatry, neuroscience and medicine. Graduates of the program assume positions in a variety of settings, including community mental health centers, college/university settings, clinical research settings, and government facilities. Approximately one-half of our students pursue doctoral level training either immediately upon graduation or soon thereafter.

Special Facilities or Resources: Because the program is housed within the Boston University School of Medicine and is part of Boston University, our students and faculty have access to a wide variety of academic and medical resources. Although not a required part of students' experiences in the program, many of our students collaborate in clinical research activities, which are always a part of our campus. Students also engage in a wide variety of clinical experiences. Books, journals, and access to computerized literature searches currently are available in the Alumni Medical Library at BUSM. This full service medical library contains most relevant publications for students in a mental health related program. On the Charles River Campus, the Charles Mugar Library is available for any students who wish further supplementary readings in the behavioral and social sciences. As a member of the Boston Library Consortium, Boston University students have access to additional library collections through inter-library loans. Overall, the library resources available to these students are excellent and do not require additional acquisitions. The current Mental Health Counseling and Behavioral Medicine Program occupies a newly renovated space with approximately 1,200 square feet for its administrative and core faculty office space.

Application Information:
Application available online. URL of online application: www.bumc.bu.edu/mhbm. Programs have rolling admissions. *Fee:* $75.

Brandeis University
Department of Psychology
College of Arts & Sciences
415 South Street, Mail Stop 62
Waltham, MA 02454-9110
Telephone: (781) 736-3300
Fax: (781) 736-3291
E-mail: *gnat@brandeis.edu*
Web: *http://www.brandeis.edu/departments/psych*

Department Information:
1948. Chairperson: Prof. Paul DiZio. Number of faculty: total—full-time 18, part-time 1; women—full-time 7; total—minority—full-time 1; women minority—full-time 1.

Programs and Degrees Offered:
Listed in the following order: Program area, degree type (T if terminal Master's), number awarded 7/11–6/12. General Psychol-

ogy MA/MS (Master of Arts/Science) (T) 10, Psychology PhD (Doctor of Philosophy) 4.

Student Applications/Admissions:
Student Applications
General Psychology MA/MS (Master of Arts/Science)—Applications 2012–2013, 97. Total applicants accepted 2012–2013, 12. Number full-time enrolled (new admits only) 2012–2013, 12. Number part-time enrolled (new admits only) 2012–2013, 0. Total enrolled 2012–2013 full-time, 24. Total enrolled 2012–2013 part-time, 0. Openings 2013–2014, 15. The median number of years required for completion of a degree in 2012–2013 was 1. The number of students enrolled full- and part-time who were dismissed or voluntarily withdrew from this program area in 2012–2013 were 0. *Psychology PhD (Doctor of Philosophy)*—Applications 2012–2013, 98. Total applicants accepted 2012–2013, 6. Number full-time enrolled (new admits only) 2012–2013, 6. Number part-time enrolled (new admits only) 2012–2013, 0. Total enrolled 2012–2013 full-time, 27. Total enrolled 2012–2013 part-time, 1. Openings 2013–2014, 6. The median number of years required for completion of a degree in 2012–2013 were 6. The number of students enrolled full- and part-time who were dismissed or voluntarily withdrew from this program area in 2012–2013 were 1.

Scores: Entries appear in this order: required test or GPA, minimum score (if required), median score of students entering in 2012–2013. *General Psychology MA/MS (Master of Arts/Science):* GRE-V no minimum stated, 161, GRE-Q no minimum stated, 153, GRE-Analytical no minimum stated, 4.5, overall undergraduate GPA no minimum stated, 3.43; *Psychology PhD (Doctor of Philosophy):* GRE-V no minimum stated, 161, GRE-Q no minimum stated, 154, GRE-Analytical no minimum stated, 4.5, overall undergraduate GPA no minimum stated, 3.61.

Other Criteria: (importance of criteria rated low, medium, or high): GRE scores—high, research experience—high, work experience—medium, extracurricular activity—low, clinically related public service—low, GPA—high, letters of recommendation—high, interview—high, statement of goals and objectives—high, undergraduate major in psychology—medium, specific undergraduate psychology courses taken—medium. For additional information on admission requirements, go to http://www.brandeis.edu/gsas/programs/psychology.html.

Student Characteristics: The following represents characteristics of students in 2012–2013 in all graduate psychology programs in the department: Female—full-time 37, part-time 0; Male—full-time 15, part-time 1; African American/Black—full-time 3, part-time 0; Hispanic/Latino(a)—full-time 2, part-time 0; Asian/Pacific Islander—full-time 1, part-time 0; American Indian/Alaska Native—full-time 0, part-time 0; Caucasian/White—full-time 32, part-time 0; Multi-ethnic—full-time 0, part-time 0; students subject to the Americans With Disabilities Act—full-time 0, part-time 0; Unknown ethnicity—full-time 0, part-time 0; International students who hold an F-1 or J-1 Visa—full-time 14, part-time 1.

Financial Information/Assistance:
Tuition for Full-Time Study: *Master's:* State residents: per academic year $42,094, $1,318 per credit hour; Nonstate residents: per academic year $42,094, $1,318 per credit hour. *Doctoral:* State

residents: per academic year $42,094, $1,318 per credit hour; Nonstate residents: per academic year $42,094, $1,318 per credit hour. Tuition is subject to change. Additional fees are assessed to students beyond the costs of tuition for the following: health insurance. See the following website for updates and changes in tuition costs: http://www.brandeis.edu/gsas/financing/cost.html.

Financial Assistance:

First-Year Students: Fellowships and scholarships available for first year. Average amount paid per academic year: $20,400. Apply by December 1.

Advanced Students: Fellowships and scholarships available for advanced students. Average amount paid per academic year: $20,400.

Additional Information: Of all students currently enrolled full time, 100% benefited from one or more of the listed financial assistance programs. Application and information available online at: http://www.brandeis.edu/gsas/financing/.

Internships/Practica: Master's Degree (MA/MS General Psychology): An internship experience, such as a final research project or "capstone" experience is required of graduates.

Housing and Day Care: No on-campus housing is available. On-campus day care facilities are available. See the following website for more information: http://www.brandeis.edu/lemberg/.

Employment of Department Graduates:

Master's Degree Graduates: Of those who graduated in the academic year 2011–2012, the following categories and numbers represent the postgraduate activities and employment of master's degree graduates: Enrolled in a psychology doctoral program (3), enrolled in a postdoctoral residency/fellowship (n/a), employed in independent practice (n/a), employed in business or industry (2), other employment position (1), total from the above (master's) (6).

Doctoral Degree Graduates: Of those who graduated in the academic year 2011–2012, the following categories and numbers represent the postgraduate activities and employment of doctoral degree graduates: Enrolled in a psychology doctoral program (n/a), enrolled in another graduate/professional program (1), employed in an academic position at a university (1), employed in an academic position at a 2-year/4-year college (1), do not know (1), total from the above (doctoral) (4).

Additional Information:

Orientation, Objectives, and Emphasis of Department: The goal of the PhD program is to develop excellent researchers and teachers who will become leaders in psychological science. From the start of graduate study, research activity is emphasized. The program helps students develop an area of research specialization, and gives them opportunities to work in one of two general areas: social/developmental psychology or cognitive neuroscience. In both areas, dissertation supervisors are leaders in the following areas: motor control, visual perception, taste physiology and psychophysics, memory, learning, aggression, emotion, personality and cognition in adulthood and old age, social relations and health, stereotypes, and nonverbal communication.

Special Facilities or Resources: Laboratories in the Psychology Department are well-equipped for research on memory, speech recognition, psycholinguistics, visual psychophysics, visual per-

ception, motor control, and spatial orientation, including a NASA-sponsored laboratory for research on human spatial orientation in unusual gravitational environments. Social and developmental psychology laboratories include one-way observation rooms, videorecording and eye-tracking apparatus. There are also opportunities for social neuroscience research through a collaborative grant with the MGH-NMR center. Child development research is facilitated by cooperative relations with the Lemberg Children's Center on the Brandeis campus; applied social research is facilitated by cooperative relations with the Brandeis University Florence Heller Graduate School for Advanced Studies in Social Welfare and the Graduate School of International Economics and Finance. Research on cognitive aging is supported by a training grant from the National Institute on Aging. A special feature of the aging program is an interest in the interaction of cognitive, social and personality factors in healthy aging. The psychology department also participates in an interdisciplinary neuroscience program at the Volen National Center for Complex Systems located on the Brandeis Campus.

Information for Students With Physical Disabilities: See the following website for more information: http://www.brandeis.edu/acserv/disabilities/.

Application Information:
Send to Graduate School of Arts & Sciences, Brandeis University, 415 South Street, MS-031, Waltham, MA 02454-9110. Application available online. URL of online application: http://www.brandeis.edu/gsas/apply/. Students are admitted in the Fall, application deadline December 1. The deadline for fall admission to the PhD program is December 1st. Applications for the Master's program are accepted on a continuous basis with rolling admission. Review of Master's applications will begin January 15 and continue until the incoming class is filled. *Fee:* $75. Application fee waived for McNair Fellows.

Bridgewater State University
Department of Psychology
College of Humanities and Social Science
91 Burrill Avenue
Bridgewater, MA 02035
Telephone: (508) 531-1769
Fax: (508) 531-1761
E-mail: *jcalicchia@bridgew.edu*
Web: *http://www.bridgew.edu/psychology/*

Department Information:
1958. Graduate Program Coordinator: John A Calicchia, PhD. Number of faculty: total—full-time 19, part-time 2; women—full-time 13; total—minority—full-time 1.

Programs and Degrees Offered:
Listed in the following order: Program area, degree type (T if terminal Master's), number awarded 7/11–6/12. Clinical Psychology MA/MS (Master of Arts/Science) (T) 21.

Student Applications/Admissions:
Student Applications
Clinical Psychology MA/MS (Master of Arts/Science)—Applications 2012–2013, 34. Total applicants accepted 2012–2013,

14. Number full-time enrolled (new admits only) 2012–2013, 7. Number part-time enrolled (new admits only) 2012–2013, 7. Total enrolled 2012–2013 full-time, 18. Total enrolled 2012–2013 part-time, 15. Openings 2013–2014, 18. The median number of years required for completion of a degree in 2012–2013 were 3. The number of students enrolled full- and part-time who were dismissed or voluntarily withdrew from this program area in 2012–2013 were 3.

Scores: Entries appear in this order: required test or GPA, minimum score (if required), median score of students entering in 2012–2013. *Clinical Psychology MA/MS (Master of Arts/Science):* GRE-V 145, 152, GRE-Q 141, 147, overall undergraduate GPA 2.8, 3.4.

Other Criteria: (importance of criteria rated low, medium, or high): GRE scores—medium, research experience—low, work experience—high, extracurricular activity—low, clinically related public service—high, GPA—high, letters of recommendation—high, interview—high, statement of goals and objectives—high, undergraduate major in psychology—high, specific undergraduate psychology courses taken—medium.

Student Characteristics: The following represents characteristics of students in 2012–2013 in all graduate psychology programs in the department: Female—full-time 15, part-time 12; Male—full-time 3, part-time 3; African American/Black—full-time 1, part-time 1; Hispanic/Latino(a)—full-time 0, part-time 0; Asian/Pacific Islander—full-time 1, part-time 0; American Indian/Alaska Native—full-time 0, part-time 0; Caucasian/White—full-time 16, part-time 14; Multi-ethnic—full-time 0, part-time 0; students subject to the Americans With Disabilities Act—full-time 1, part-time 0; Unknown ethnicity—full-time 0, part-time 0; International students who hold an F-1 or J-1 Visa—full-time 1, part-time 0.

Financial Information/Assistance:

Tuition for Full-Time Study: *Master's:* State residents: per academic year $6,518, $362 per credit hour; Nonstate residents: per academic year $6,518, $362 per credit hour. Tuition is subject to change. See the following website for updates and changes in tuition costs: http://www.bridgew.edu/StudentAccounts/costsofattending.cfm.

Financial Assistance:

First-Year Students: Teaching assistantships available for first year. Average amount paid per academic year: $6,500. Average number of hours worked per week: 20. Apply by March 15. Research assistantships available for first year. Average amount paid per academic year: $4,200. Average number of hours worked per week: 10. Apply by March 15. Fellowships and scholarships available for first year. Average amount paid per academic year: $500. Average number of hours worked per week: 0. Apply by March 15.

Advanced Students: No information provided.

Additional Information: Of all students currently enrolled full time, 12% benefited from one or more of the listed financial assistance programs. Application and information available online at: http://www.bridgew.edu/CoGS/assistantshipfellowship.cfm.

Internships/Practica: All graduate students are required to engage in both clinical practicum and internship for a total of 3 to 5 semesters. Students will work closely with their advisors to select an appropriate placement that meets their intended career goals. The practicum and internship fieldwork allows graduate students to continue their training and extend their services to individuals, families, and groups within the community. A variety of both inpatient and outpatient sites are available to graduate students including (but not limited to) community agencies, hospital settings, school settings, and substance abuse settings.

Housing and Day Care: No on-campus housing is available. On-campus day care facilities are available. See the following website for more information: http://www.bridgew.edu/childrenscenter/.

Employment of Department Graduates:

Master's Degree Graduates: Of those who graduated in the academic year 2011–2012, the following categories and numbers represent the postgraduate activities and employment of master's degree graduates: Enrolled in a psychology doctoral program (2), enrolled in a postdoctoral residency/fellowship (n/a), employed in independent practice (n/a), employed in an academic position at a university (1), employed in an academic position at a 2-year/4-year college (1), employed in a community mental health/counseling center (22), employed in a hospital/medical center (3), total from the above (master's) (29).

Doctoral Degree Graduates: Of those who graduated in the academic year 2011–2012, the following categories and numbers represent the postgraduate activities and employment of doctoral degree graduates: Enrolled in a psychology doctoral program (n/a), total from the above (doctoral) (0).

Additional Information:

Orientation, Objectives, and Emphasis of Department: The mission of the Master's program in Clinical Psychology is to prepare students to become mental health professionals who can contribute to a diverse society grounded in a framework of professional ethics and personal responsibility. The faculty seeks to provide a high quality and rigorous academic experience that facilitates the development of clinical skills through intensive engagement and experiential learning of both theory and techniques. Moreover, the program seeks to provide students with an empirical theoretical base from scientific psychology and high quality clinical skills which will enable each student to begin a life time of clinical work, consultation and/or teaching. Students graduating from the program, who attain additional supervision hours, are eligible to become Licensed Mental Health Counselors (LMHC) in the state of Massachusetts and to employ the clinical techniques and knowledge of the profession to improve individual, group, and systemic problems.

Special Facilities or Resources: A psychology department research lab is available that provides a standardized, distraction-free testing environment, continuous oversight, and ongoing participation tracking. The psychology department research lab provides a location for graduate students to conduct their research studies and review and analyze their data.

Information for Students With Physical Disabilities: See the following website for more information: http://www.bridgew.edu/AAC/Disability_Resources.cfm.

Application Information:

Send to Bridgewater State University, College of Graduate Studies, Graduate Admissions, 10 Shaw Road, Bridgewater, MA 02325. Application available online. URL of online application: http://www.

bridgew.edu/CoGS/gradadmissions.cfm. Students are admitted in the Fall, application deadline March 15. *Fee:* $50.

Harvard University

Department of Psychology
33 Kirkland Street
Cambridge, MA 02138
Telephone: (617) 495-3800
E-mail: *cir@wjh.harvard.edu*
Web: *http://www.wjh.harvard.edu/psych/*

Department Information:

1936. Chairperson: Ken Nakayama. Number of faculty: total—full-time 25, part-time 63; women—full-time 9, part-time 7; total—minority—full-time 5, part-time 3; women minority—full-time 2, part-time 2.

Programs and Degrees Offered:

Listed in the following order: Program area, degree type (T if terminal Master's), number awarded 7/11–6/12. Clinical Psychology PhD (Doctor of Philosophy) 4, Cognition, Brain, and Behavior PhD (Doctor of Philosophy) 3, Developmental Psychology PhD (Doctor of Philosophy) 4, Social Psychology PhD (Doctor of Philosophy) 2, Common Curriculum PhD (Doctor of Philosophy) 0.

APA Accreditation: Clinical PhD (Doctor of Philosophy).

Student Applications/Admissions:

Student Applications

Clinical Psychology PhD (Doctor of Philosophy)—Applications 2012–2013, 304. Total applicants accepted 2012–2013, 6. Number full-time enrolled (new admits only) 2012–2013, 6. Number part-time enrolled (new admits only) 2012–2013, 0. Total enrolled 2012–2013 full-time, 23. Total enrolled 2012–2013 part-time, 0. Openings 2013–2014, 3. The median number of years required for completion of a degree in 2012–2013 were 6. The number of students enrolled full- and part-time who were dismissed or voluntarily withdrew from this program area in 2012–2013 were 0. *Cognition, Brain, and Behavior PhD (Doctor of Philosophy)*—Applications 2012–2013, 0. Total applicants accepted 2012–2013, 0. Number full-time enrolled (new admits only) 2012–2013, 0. Number part-time enrolled (new admits only) 2012–2013, 0. Total enrolled 2012–2013 full-time, 5. Total enrolled 2012–2013 part-time, 0. The median number of years required for completion of a degree in 2012–2013 were 5. The number of students enrolled full- and part-time who were dismissed or voluntarily withdrew from this program area in 2012–2013 were 0. *Developmental Psychology PhD (Doctor of Philosophy)*—Applications 2012–2013, 0. Total applicants accepted 2012–2013, 0. Number full-time enrolled (new admits only) 2012–2013, 0. Number part-time enrolled (new admits only) 2012–2013, 0. Total enrolled 2012–2013 full-time, 2. Total enrolled 2012–2013 part-time, 0. The median number of years required for completion of a degree in 2012–2013 were 6. The number of students enrolled full- and part-time who were dismissed or voluntarily withdrew from this program area in 2012–2013 were 0. *Social Psychology PhD (Doctor of Philosophy)*—Applications 2012–2013, 0. Total

applicants accepted 2012–2013, 0. Number full-time enrolled (new admits only) 2012–2013, 0. Number part-time enrolled (new admits only) 2012–2013, 0. The median number of years required for completion of a degree in 2012–2013 were 6. The number of students enrolled full- and part-time who were dismissed or voluntarily withdrew from this program area in 2012–2013 were 0. *Common Curriculum PhD (Doctor of Philosophy)*—Applications 2012–2013, 315. Total applicants accepted 2012–2013, 11. Number full-time enrolled (new admits only) 2012–2013, 9. Total enrolled 2012–2013 full-time, 50. Openings 2013–2014, 10. The number of students enrolled full- and part-time who were dismissed or voluntarily withdrew from this program area in 2012–2013 were 0.

Scores: Entries appear in this order: required test or GPA, minimum score (if required), median score of students entering in 2012–2013. *Clinical Psychology PhD (Doctor of Philosophy):* GRE-V 630, 668, GRE-Q 680, 740, GRE-Analytical 4.5, 4.83; *Common Curriculum PhD (Doctor of Philosophy):* GRE-V no minimum stated, GRE-Q no minimum stated, GRE-Analytical 3.5, 4.83.

Other Criteria: (importance of criteria rated low, medium, or high): GRE scores—high, research experience—high, work experience—high, extracurricular activity—low, clinically related public service—medium, GPA—high, letters of recommendation—high, interview—high, statement of goals and objectives—high, undergraduate major in psychology—medium, specific undergraduate psychology courses taken—medium.

Student Characteristics: The following represents characteristics of students in 2012–2013 in all graduate psychology programs in the department: Female—full-time 47, part-time 0; Male—full-time 33, part-time 0; African American/Black—full-time 2, part-time 0; Hispanic/Latino(a)—full-time 1, part-time 0; Asian/Pacific Islander—full-time 13, part-time 0; American Indian/Alaska Native—full-time 0, part-time 0; Caucasian/White—full-time 62, part-time 0; Multi-ethnic—full-time 2, part-time 0; students subject to the Americans With Disabilities Act—full-time 1, part-time 0; Unknown ethnicity—full-time 0, part-time 0; International students who hold an F-1 or J-1 Visa—full-time 18, part-time 0.

Financial Information/Assistance:

Tuition for Full-Time Study: *Doctoral:* State residents: per academic year $40,674; Nonstate residents: per academic year $40,674. Tuition is subject to change. See the following website for updates and changes in tuition costs: http://www.gsas.harvard.edu/prospective_students/costs_tuition_and_fees.php. Higher tuition cost for this program: Tuition is highest in first two years.

Financial Assistance:

First-Year Students: Research assistantships available for first year. Fellowships and scholarships available for first year. Average amount paid per academic year: $29,424. Apply by December 15.

Advanced Students: Teaching assistantships available for advanced students. Average amount paid per academic year: $29,424. Average number of hours worked per week: 20. Apply by May 1. Research assistantships available for advanced students. Average amount paid per academic year: $29,424. Average number of hours worked per week: 20. Fellowships and scholarships available for advanced students. Average amount paid per academic year: $29,424.

Additional Information: Of all students currently enrolled full time, 95% benefited from one or more of the listed financial assistance programs. Application and information available online at: http://www.gsas.harvard.edu/current_students/financial_aid.php.

Internships/Practica: Doctoral Degree (PhD Clinical Psychology): For those doctoral students for whom a professional psychology internship was required in this program prior to graduation, (4) students applied for an internship in 2011–2012, with (4) students obtaining an internship. Of those students who obtained an internship, (4) were paid internships. Of those students who obtained an internship, (4) students placed in APA/CPA accredited internships, (0) students placed in internships not APA/CPA accredited, but listed with the Association of Psychology Postdoctoral and Internship Programs (APPIC), (0) students placed in internships conforming to guidelines of the Council of Directors of School Psychology Programs (CDSPP), (0) students placed in internships that were not APA/CPA accredited, APPIC or CDSPP listed. Students in the clinical program will have predoctoral practicum placements in a local Harvard-affiliated hospital. Students are required to have defended their thesis prospectus, and are strongly encouraged to collect most of the data prior to departing for internship, but the thesis project need not be completed before beginning the internship. Clinical internship applicants use the APPIC system.

Housing and Day Care: On-campus housing is available. See the following website for more information: http://www.gsas.harvard.edu/current_students/housing.php. On-campus day care facilities are available. See the following website for more information: http://www.childcare.harvard.edu/.

Employment of Department Graduates:

Master's Degree Graduates: Of those who graduated in the academic year 2011–2012, the following categories and numbers represent the postgraduate activities and employment of master's degree graduates: Enrolled in a postdoctoral residency/fellowship (n/a), employed in independent practice (n/a), total from the above (master's) (0).

Doctoral Degree Graduates: Of those who graduated in the academic year 2011–2012, the following categories and numbers represent the postgraduate activities and employment of doctoral degree graduates: Enrolled in a psychology doctoral program (n/a), enrolled in a postdoctoral residency/fellowship (12), employed in an academic position at a university (1), total from the above (doctoral) (13).

Additional Information:

Orientation, Objectives, and Emphasis of Department: The psychology department is divided into two main curricula: an APA-accredited clinical science program, and a common curriculum covering all other areas. The aim of the program is to train students for careers in psychological research and teaching. These careers are mainly in academia. The emphasis of the program is heavily on research training; in addition to a small number of required courses, students do a first-year research project, a second-year research project, and the doctoral dissertation. Students take a major examination or intense seminar(s) in their major specialty fields. Since most students prepare for academic careers, there are ample opportunities to serve as teaching fellows.

Special Facilities or Resources: The department is well equipped with facilities for conducting research. Faculty are the recipients of many grants in various areas of psychology, and graduate students play an essential role in the conduct of most of this research. William James Hall houses a well-staffed computer lab to serve faculty and students. Students are given offices, the use of laboratory space, and a sum of money for research support. The department encourages interdisciplinary study, and students have the benefit of taking courses and working with the faculty at other Harvard graduate schools (Education, Medical School, Public Health, etc.) and at MIT. The Cambridge and Boston areas are well endowed with research facilities and hospitals that offer resources, such as MRI equipment, to students.

Information for Students With Physical Disabilities: See the following website for more information: http://www.fas.harvard.edu/~aeo/.

Application Information:
Send to Harvard University, Office of Admissions, The Graduate School of Arts and Sciences, P.O. Box 9129, Cambridge, MA 02238-9129. Application available online. URL of online application: http://www.gsas.harvard.edu/apply. Students are admitted in the Fall, application deadline December 15. *Fee:* $105. Requests for waivers should be submitted in writing to the Graduate School of Arts and Sciences Admissions Office.

Massachusetts School of Professional Psychology
Professional School
One Wells Avenue
Newton, MA 02459
Telephone: (617) 327-6777
Fax: (617) 327-4447
E-mail: *admissions@mspp.edu*
Web: *http://www.mspp.edu*

Department Information:
1974. President: Nicholas A. Covino, PsyD.

Programs and Degrees Offered:
Listed in the following order: Program area, degree type (T if terminal Master's), number awarded 7/11–6/12. Clinical Psychology PsyD (Doctor of Psychology) 44, Respecialization in Clinical Psychology Respecialization Diploma, School Psychology MA/MS (Master of Arts/Science) (T) 13, Forensic and Counseling Psychology MA/MS (Master of Arts/Science) (T) 15, Counseling Psychology MA/MS (Master of Arts/Science) (T) 24, Organizational Psychology MA/MS (Master of Arts/Science) (T) 13, School Psychology PsyD (Doctor of Psychology) 0, Higher Education Student Personnel Administration MA/MS (Master of Arts/Science) (T) 0, Counseling Psychology and Primary Care MA/MS (Master of Arts/Science) (T) 0, Counseling Psychology and Global Mental Health MA/MS (Master of Arts/Science) 0, Counseling Psychology and Community Mental Health MA/MS (Master of Arts/Science) (T) 0, Media Psychology MA/MS (Master of Arts/Science) (T) 0, Leadership Psychology PsyD (Doctor of Psychology) 0.

APA Accreditation: Clinical PsyD (Doctor of Psychology). Student Outcome Data Website: http://www.mspp.edu/academics/degree-programs/psyd/outcomes.php.

Student Applications/Admissions:

Student Applications

Clinical Psychology PsyD (Doctor of Psychology)—Applications 2012–2013, 470. Total applicants accepted 2012–2013, 200. Number full-time enrolled (new admits only) 2012–2013, 96. Number part-time enrolled (new admits only) 2012–2013, 1. Total enrolled 2012–2013 full-time, 357. Total enrolled 2012–2013 part-time, 3. Openings 2013–2014, 100. The median number of years required for completion of a degree in 2012–2013 were 4. The number of students enrolled full- and part-time who were dismissed or voluntarily withdrew from this program area in 2012–2013 were 8. *Respecialization in Clinical Psychology Respecialization Diploma*—Applications 2012–2013, 3. Total applicants accepted 2012–2013, 3. Number full-time enrolled (new admits only) 2012–2013, 3. Number part-time enrolled (new admits only) 2012–2013, 0. Total enrolled 2012–2013 full-time, 5. Total enrolled 2012–2013 part-time, 0. The median number of years required for completion of a degree in 2012–2013 were 3. The number of students enrolled full- and part-time who were dismissed or voluntarily withdrew from this program area in 2012–2013 were 0. *School Psychology MA/MS (Master of Arts/Science)*—Applications 2012–2013, 67. Total applicants accepted 2012–2013, 25. Number full-time enrolled (new admits only) 2012–2013, 12. Total enrolled 2012–2013 full-time, 32. Openings 2013–2014, 16. The median number of years required for completion of a degree in 2012–2013 were 3. The number of students enrolled full- and part-time who were dismissed or voluntarily withdrew from this program area in 2012–2013 were 0. *Forensic and Counseling Psychology MA/MS (Master of Arts/Science)*—Applications 2012–2013, 62. Total applicants accepted 2012–2013, 34. Number full-time enrolled (new admits only) 2012–2013, 19. Number part-time enrolled (new admits only) 2012–2013, 4. Total enrolled 2012–2013 full-time, 35. Total enrolled 2012–2013 part-time, 5. Openings 2013–2014, 25. The median number of years required for completion of a degree in 2012–2013 were 2. The number of students enrolled full- and part-time who were dismissed or voluntarily withdrew from this program area in 2012–2013 were 2. *Counseling Psychology MA/MS (Master of Arts/Science)*—Applications 2012–2013, 119. Total applicants accepted 2012–2013, 58. Number full-time enrolled (new admits only) 2012–2013, 30. Number part-time enrolled (new admits only) 2012–2013, 7. Total enrolled 2012–2013 full-time, 74. Total enrolled 2012–2013 part-time, 12. Openings 2013–2014, 45. The median number of years required for completion of a degree in 2012–2013 were 2. The number of students enrolled full- and part-time who were dismissed or voluntarily withdrew from this program area in 2012–2013 were 6. *Organizational Psychology MA/MS (Master of Arts/Science)*—Applications 2012–2013, 35. Total applicants accepted 2012–2013, 21. Number full-time enrolled (new admits only) 2012–2013, 19. Total enrolled 2012–2013 full-time, 19. Openings 2013–2014, 20. The median number of years required for completion of a degree in 2012–2013 was 1. The number of students enrolled full- and part-time who were dismissed or voluntarily withdrew from this program area in 2012–2013 were 1. *School Psychology PsyD (Doctor of Psychology)*—Applications 2012–2013, 17. Total applicants accepted 2012–2013, 10. Number full-time enrolled (new admits only) 2012–2013, 8. Total enrolled 2012–2013 full-time, 29. Openings 2013–2014, 8. The median number of years required for completion of a degree in 2012–2013 were 4. The number of students enrolled full- and part-time who were dismissed or voluntarily withdrew from this program area in 2012–2013 were 0. *Higher Education Student Personnel Administration MA/MS (Master of Arts/Science)*—Total applicants accepted 2012–2013, 12. Number full-time enrolled (new admits only) 2012–2013, 12. Total enrolled 2012–2013 full-time, 12. Openings 2013–2014, 15. The number of students enrolled full- and part-time who were dismissed or voluntarily withdrew from this program area in 2012–2013 were 1. *Counseling Psychology and Primary Care MA/MS (Master of Arts/Science)*—Applications 2012–2013, 18. Total applicants accepted 2012–2013, 9. Number full-time enrolled (new admits only) 2012–2013, 8. Number part-time enrolled (new admits only) 2012–2013, 0. Total enrolled 2012–2013 full-time, 8. Total enrolled 2012–2013 part-time, 0. Openings 2013–2014, 16. The number of students enrolled full- and part-time who were dismissed or voluntarily withdrew from this program area in 2012–2013 were 1. *Counseling Psychology and Global Mental Health MA/MS (Master of Arts/Science)*—Applications 2012–2013, 15. Total applicants accepted 2012–2013, 5. Number full-time enrolled (new admits only) 2012–2013, 4. Number part-time enrolled (new admits only) 2012–2013, 0. Total enrolled 2012–2013 full-time, 4. Total enrolled 2012–2013 part-time, 0. Openings 2013–2014, 12. The number of students enrolled full- and part-time who were dismissed or voluntarily withdrew from this program area in 2012–2013 were 0. *Counseling Psychology and Community Mental Health MA/MS (Master of Arts/Science)*—Applications 2012–2013, 6. Total applicants accepted 2012–2013, 6. Number full-time enrolled (new admits only) 2012–2013, 6. Number part-time enrolled (new admits only) 2012–2013, 0. Total enrolled 2012–2013 full-time, 13. Total enrolled 2012–2013 part-time, 0. Openings 2013–2014, 12. The number of students enrolled full- and part-time who were dismissed or voluntarily withdrew from this program area in 2012–2013 were 0. *Media Psychology MA/MS (Master of Arts/Science)*—Applications 2012–2013, 7. Total applicants accepted 2012–2013, 6. Number full-time enrolled (new admits only) 2012–2013, 6. Total enrolled 2012–2013 full-time, 6. Openings 2013–2014, 10. The median number of years required for completion of a degree in 2012–2013 was 1. The number of students enrolled full- and part-time who were dismissed or voluntarily withdrew from this program area in 2012–2013 were 0. *Leadership Psychology PsyD (Doctor of Psychology)*—Applications 2012–2013, 11. Total applicants accepted 2012–2013, 8. Number full-time enrolled (new admits only) 2012–2013, 7. Number part-time enrolled (new admits only) 2012–2013, 1. Total enrolled 2012–2013 full-time, 7. Total enrolled 2012–2013 part-time, 1. Openings 2013–2014, 10. The median number of years required for completion of a degree in 2012–2013 were 4. The number of students enrolled full- and part-time who were dismissed or voluntarily withdrew from this program area in 2012–2013 were 1.

Scores: Entries appear in this order: required test or GPA, minimum score (if required), median score of students entering in 2012–2013. *Clinical Psychology PsyD (Doctor of Psychology)*: GRE-V no minimum stated, GRE-Q no minimum stated, GRE-Analytical no minimum stated, overall undergraduate GPA no minimum stated; *Forensic and Counseling Psychology MA/MS (Master of Arts/Science)*: overall undergraduate GPA 3.0; *Counseling Psychology MA/MS (Master of Arts/Science)*: overall undergraduate GPA 3.00; *School Psychology PsyD (Doctor of Psychology)*: GRE-V no minimum stated, GRE-Q no minimum stated, GRE-Analytical no minimum stated; *Counseling Psychology and Primary Care MA/MS (Master of Arts/Science)*: overall undergraduate GPA 3.0; *Counseling Psychology and Global Mental Health MA/MS (Master of Arts/Science)*: overall undergraduate GPA 3.0; *Counseling Psychology and Community Mental Health MA/MS (Master of Arts/Science)*: overall undergraduate GPA 3.0; *Leadership Psychology PsyD (Doctor of Psychology)*: GRE-V no minimum stated, GRE-Q no minimum stated, GRE-Analytical no minimum stated, overall undergraduate GPA 3.0, Masters GPA 3.0.

Other Criteria: (importance of criteria rated low, medium, or high): GRE scores—medium, research experience—low, work experience—medium, extracurricular activity—high, clinically related public service—high, GPA—high, letters of recommendation—high, interview—high, statement of goals and objectives—high, community service—medium, undergraduate major in psychology—medium, specific undergraduate psychology courses taken—high. For additional information on admission requirements, go to http://www.mspp.edu/admissions/apply/.

Student Characteristics: The following represents characteristics of students in 2012–2013 in all graduate psychology programs in the department: Female—full-time 385, part-time 90; Male—full-time 125, part-time 31; African American/Black—full-time 20, part-time 3; Hispanic/Latino(a)—full-time 28, part-time 6; Asian/Pacific Islander—full-time 20, part-time 4; American Indian/Alaska Native—full-time 2, part-time 0; Caucasian/White—full-time 374, part-time 89; Multi-ethnic—full-time 1, part-time 0; students subject to the Americans With Disabilities Act—full-time 15, part-time 1; Unknown ethnicity—full-time 65, part-time 19; International students who hold an F-1 or J-1 Visa—full-time 7, part-time 0.

Financial Information/Assistance:

Tuition for Full-Time Study: *Master's:* State residents: per academic year $36,160, $1,130 per credit hour; Nonstate residents: per academic year $36,160, $1,130 per credit hour. *Doctoral:* State residents: per academic year $36,160, $1,130 per credit hour; Nonstate residents: per academic year $36,160, $1,130 per credit hour. Tuition is subject to change. See the following website for updates and changes in tuition costs: http://www.mspp.edu/admissions/tuition.php.

Financial Assistance:

First-Year Students: Research assistantships available for first year. Average amount paid per academic year: $4,200. Average number of hours worked per week: 8. Fellowships and scholarships available for first year. Average amount paid per academic year: $2,500. Apply by February 14.

Advanced Students: Teaching assistantships available for advanced students. Average amount paid per academic year: $2,500. Research assistantships available for advanced students. Average amount paid per academic year: $4,200. Average number of hours worked per week: 8. Fellowships and scholarships available for advanced students. Average amount paid per academic year: $2,500. Apply by April 16.

Additional Information: Of all students currently enrolled full time, 43% benefited from one or more of the listed financial assistance programs. Application and information available online at: http://www.mspp.edu/admissions/financial-aid/.

Internships/Practica: Doctoral Degree (PsyD Clinical Psychology): For those doctoral students for whom a professional psychology internship was required in this program prior to graduation, (144) students applied for an internship in 2011–2012, with (142) students obtaining an internship. Of those students who obtained an internship, (20) were paid internships. Of those students who obtained an internship, (17) students placed in APA/CPA accredited internships, (0) students placed in internships not APA/CPA accredited, but listed with the Association of Psychology Postdoctoral and Internship Programs (APPIC), (0) students placed in internships conforming to guidelines of the Council of Directors of School Psychology Programs (CDSPP), (125) students placed in internships that were not APA/CPA accredited, APPIC or CDSPP listed. Doctoral Degree (PsyD School Psychology): For those doctoral students for whom a professional psychology internship was required in this program prior to graduation, (8) students applied for an internship in 2011–2012, with (8) students obtaining an internship. Of those students who obtained an internship, (2) were paid internships. Of those students who obtained an internship, (0) students placed in APA/CPA accredited internships, (2) students placed in internships not APA/CPA accredited, but listed with the Association of Psychology Postdoctoral and Internship Programs (APPIC), (6) students placed in internships conforming to guidelines of the Council of Directors of School Psychology Programs (CDSPP), (0) students placed in internships that were not APA/CPA accredited, APPIC or CDSPP listed. Master's Degree (MA/MS School Psychology): An internship experience, such as a final research project or "capstone" experience is required of graduates. Master's Degree (MA/MS Forensic and Counseling Psychology): An internship experience, such as a final research project or "capstone" experience is required of graduates. Master's Degree (MA/MS Counseling Psychology): An internship experience, such as a final research project or "capstone" experience is required of graduates. Master's Degree (MA/MS Organizational Psychology): An internship experience, such as a final research project or "capstone" experience is required of graduates. Master's Degree (MA/MS Counseling Psychology and Primary Care): An internship experience, such as a final research project or "capstone" experience is required of graduates. Master's Degree (MA/MS Counseling Psychology and Community Mental Health): An internship experience, such as a final research project or "capstone" experience is required of graduates. Master's Degree (MA/MS Media Psychology): An internship experience, such as a final research project or "capstone" experience is required of graduates. Field placements are an integral part of the program throughout the duration of the program. The practicum and internship experiences are integrated with the curriculum and individual's educational needs at each level of the program. Over 200 training sites are available in the greater Boston area including hospitals, mental health centers, court clinics, and other agencies offering mental health services. They provide students the opportunity to work with varied populations, life span issues, theoretical orientations, and treatment modalities in the context of supervised training. The large number of qualified agencies included in our training network enable students the option of applying for full or half-time APA-approved internships or securing suitable, high quality, local internships.

Housing and Day Care: No on-campus housing is available. No on-campus day care facilities are available.

Employment of Department Graduates:

Master's Degree Graduates: Of those who graduated in the academic year 2011–2012, the following categories and numbers represent the postgraduate activities and employment of master's degree graduates: Enrolled in a psychology doctoral program (15), enrolled in a postdoctoral residency/fellowship (n/a), employed in independent practice (n/a), employed in a community mental health/counseling center (24), do not know (43), total from the above (master's) (82).

Doctoral Degree Graduates: Of those who graduated in the academic year 2011–2012, the following categories and numbers represent the postgraduate activities and employment of doctoral degree graduates: Enrolled in a psychology doctoral program (n/a), enrolled in another graduate/professional program (1), employed in independent practice (23), employed in an academic position at a university (6), employed in an academic position at a 2-year/4-year college (4), employed in other positions at a higher education institution (6), employed in a professional position in a school system (3), employed in business or industry (1), employed in a community mental health/counseling center (15), employed in a hospital/medical center (11), still seeking employment (1), not seeking employment (1), other employment position (7), total from the above (doctoral) (79).

Additional Information:

Orientation, Objectives, and Emphasis of Department: MSPP strives to be a preeminent school of psychology that integrates rigorous academic instruction with extensive field education and close attention to professional development. We assume an ongoing social responsibility to create programs to educate specialists of many disciplines to meet the evolving mental health needs of society.

Special Facilities or Resources: MSPP moved into a newly renovated state-of-the-art facility this past academic year. Learning technology and our facilities are top notch.

Information for Students With Physical Disabilities: See the following website for more information: http://www.mspp.edu/student-life/student-disability-policy.php.

Application Information:

Send to Admissions Office, MSPP, One Wells Avenue, Newton, MA 02459. Application available online. URL of online application: http://www.mspp.edu/admissions/apply/. Students are admitted in the Fall, application deadline January 17; Programs have rolling admissions. Applications received after the deadline will be considered on a space-available basis. *Fee:* $50.

Massachusetts, University of
Department of Psychology
Tobin Hall
Amherst, MA 01003
Telephone: (413) 545-2383
Fax: (413) 545-0996
E-mail: *lisbell@psych.umass.edu*
Web: *http://www.psych.umass.edu/*

Department Information:
1947. Chairperson: Melinda Novak. Number of faculty: total—full-time 39; women—full-time 22; total—minority—full-time 2; women minority—full-time 1; faculty subject to the Americans With Disabilities Act 1.

Programs and Degrees Offered:
Listed in the following order: Program area, degree type (T if terminal Master's), number awarded 7/11–6/12. Clinical Psychology PhD (Doctor of Philosophy) 4, Cognitive Psychology PhD (Doctor of Philosophy) 2, Developmental Science PhD (Doctor of Philosophy) 1, Social Psychology PhD (Doctor of Philosophy) 3, Psychology Of Peace and The Prevention Of Violence PhD (Doctor of Philosophy) 1.

APA Accreditation: Clinical PhD (Doctor of Philosophy). Student Outcome Data Website: http://www.psych.umass.edu/research_and_training/areas_of_training_and_research/clinical_psychology/program-statistics/.

Student Applications/Admissions:
Student Applications

Clinical Psychology PhD (Doctor of Philosophy)—Applications 2012–2013, 285. Total applicants accepted 2012–2013, 7. Number full-time enrolled (new admits only) 2012–2013, 4. Total enrolled 2012–2013 full-time, 29. Total enrolled 2012–2013 part-time, 0. Openings 2013–2014, 3. The median number of years required for completion of a degree in 2012–2013 were 5. The number of students enrolled full- and part-time who were dismissed or voluntarily withdrew from this program area in 2012–2013 were 0. *Cognitive Psychology PhD (Doctor of Philosophy)*—Applications 2012–2013, 65. Total applicants accepted 2012–2013, 4. Number full-time enrolled (new admits only) 2012–2013, 1. Total enrolled 2012–2013 full-time, 10. Total enrolled 2012–2013 part-time, 0. Openings 2013–2014, 3. The median number of years required for completion of a degree in 2012–2013 were 5. The number of students enrolled full- and part-time who were dismissed or voluntarily withdrew from this program area in 2012–2013 were 0. *Developmental Science PhD (Doctor of Philosophy)*—Applications 2012–2013, 46. Total applicants accepted 2012–2013, 3. Number full-time enrolled (new admits only) 2012–2013, 2. Total enrolled 2012–2013 full-time, 10. Total enrolled 2012–2013 part-time, 0. Openings 2013–2014, 2. The median number of years required for completion of a degree in 2012–2013 were 5. The number of students enrolled full- and part-time who were dismissed or voluntarily withdrew from this program area in 2012–2013 were 0. *Social Psychology PhD*

(Doctor of Philosophy)—Applications 2012–2013, 103. Total applicants accepted 2012–2013, 8. Number full-time enrolled (new admits only) 2012–2013, 2. Number part-time enrolled (new admits only) 2012–2013, 0. Total enrolled 2012–2013 full-time, 12. Total enrolled 2012–2013 part-time, 0. Openings 2013–2014, 4. The median number of years required for completion of a degree in 2012–2013 were 5. The number of students enrolled full- and part-time who were dismissed or voluntarily withdrew from this program area in 2012–2013 were 0. *Psychology Of Peace and The Prevention Of Violence PhD (Doctor of Philosophy)*—Applications 2012–2013, 23. Total applicants accepted 2012–2013, 2. Number full-time enrolled (new admits only) 2012–2013, 2. Number part-time enrolled (new admits only) 2012–2013, 0. Total enrolled 2012–2013 full-time, 7. Total enrolled 2012–2013 part-time, 0. Openings 2013–2014, 2. The median number of years required for completion of a degree in 2012–2013 were 5. The number of students enrolled full- and part-time who were dismissed or voluntarily withdrew from this program area in 2012–2013 were 0.

Scores: Entries appear in this order: required test or GPA, minimum score (if required), median score of students entering in 2012–2013. *Clinical Psychology PhD (Doctor of Philosophy)*: GRE-V 550, 580, GRE-Q 620, 650, GRE-Analytical 4.5, 4.5, overall undergraduate GPA 3.2, 3.9; *Cognitive Psychology PhD (Doctor of Philosophy)*: GRE-V no minimum stated, GRE-Q no minimum stated, GRE-Analytical no minimum stated, overall undergraduate GPA no minimum stated; *Developmental Science PhD (Doctor of Philosophy)*: GRE-V no minimum stated, GRE-Q no minimum stated, GRE-Analytical no minimum stated, overall undergraduate GPA no minimum stated; *Social Psychology PhD (Doctor of Philosophy)*: GRE-V no minimum stated, 650, GRE-Q no minimum stated, 650, GRE-Analytical no minimum stated, overall undergraduate GPA no minimum stated, 3.5; *Psychology of Peace and the Prevention of Violence PhD (Doctor of Philosophy)*: GRE-V no minimum stated, GRE-Q no minimum stated, GRE-Analytical no minimum stated, overall undergraduate GPA no minimum stated.

Other Criteria: (importance of criteria rated low, medium, or high): GRE scores—high, research experience—high, work experience—low, clinically related public service—low, GPA—high, letters of recommendation—high, interview—medium, statement of goals and objectives—medium, undergraduate major in psychology—medium, specific undergraduate psychology courses taken—medium, Only clinical requires an interview. Clinically related public service also is a criterion (low) in admission to clinical. Undergraduate major in psychology and specific undergraduate courses will be weighed differently depending on division. For additional information on admission requirements, go to http://www.psych.umass.edu/graduate/program_application/.

Student Characteristics: The following represents characteristics of students in 2012–2013 in all graduate psychology programs in the department: Female—full-time 52, part-time 0; Male—full-time 15, part-time 0; African American/Black—full-time 3, part-time 0; Hispanic/Latino(a)—full-time 3, part-time 0; Asian/Pacific Islander—full-time 6, part-time 0; American Indian/Alaska Native—full-time 0, part-time 0; Caucasian/White—full-time 54, part-time 0; Multi-ethnic—full-time 0, part-time 0; students subject to the Americans With Disabilities Act—full-time 0, part-time 0; Unknown ethnicity—full-time 0, part-time 0; International students who hold an F-1 or J-1 Visa—full-time 5, part-time 0.

Financial Information/Assistance:

Tuition for Full-Time Study: *Doctoral:* State residents: per academic year $12,318; Nonstate residents: per academic year $23,652. Tuition is subject to change. See the following website for updates and changes in tuition costs: http://www.umass.edu/bursar.

Financial Assistance:

First-Year Students: Teaching assistantships available for first year. Average amount paid per academic year: $16,712. Average number of hours worked per week: 20. Research assistantships available for first year. Average amount paid per academic year: $16,712. Average number of hours worked per week: 20. Traineeships available for first year. Average amount paid per academic year: $16,712. Average number of hours worked per week: 20. Fellowships and scholarships available for first year. Average amount paid per academic year: $16,000. Average number of hours worked per week: 0.

Advanced Students: Teaching assistantships available for advanced students. Average amount paid per academic year: $16,712. Average number of hours worked per week: 20. Research assistantships available for advanced students. Average amount paid per academic year: $16,712. Average number of hours worked per week: 20. Traineeships available for advanced students. Average amount paid per academic year: $16,712. Average number of hours worked per week: 20. Fellowships and scholarships available for advanced students. Average amount paid per academic year: $16,000. Average number of hours worked per week: 0.

Additional Information: Of all students currently enrolled full time, 100% benefited from one or more of the listed financial assistance programs. Application and information available online at: http://www.psych.umass.edu/graduate/financial_support_and_expenses/.

Internships/Practica: Doctoral Degree (PhD Clinical Psychology): For those doctoral students for whom a professional psychology internship was required in this program prior to graduation, (7) students applied for an internship in 2011–2012, with (6) students obtaining an internship. Of those students who obtained an internship, (6) were paid internships. Of those students who obtained an internship, (5) students placed in APA/CPA accredited internships, (0) students placed in internships not APA/CPA accredited, but listed with the Association of Psychology Postdoctoral and Internship Programs (APPIC), (0) students placed in internships conforming to guidelines of the Council of Directors of School Psychology Programs (CDSPP), (1) students placed in internships that were not APA/CPA accredited, APPIC or CDSPP listed. Clinical students must complete an APA-approved clinical internship. None of these required internships are offered by our program.

Housing and Day Care: On-campus housing is available. See the following website for more information: http://www.housing.umass.edu. On-campus day care facilities are available. See the following website for more information: http://www.umass.edu/ofr/education.php.

Employment of Department Graduates:

Master's Degree Graduates: Of those who graduated in the academic year 2011–2012, the following categories and numbers represent the postgraduate activities and employment of master's degree graduates: Enrolled in a postdoctoral residency/fellowship (n/a), employed in independent practice (n/a), total from the above (master's) (0).

Doctoral Degree Graduates: Of those who graduated in the academic year 2011–2012, the following categories and numbers represent the postgraduate activities and employment of doctoral degree graduates: Enrolled in a psychology doctoral program (n/a), enrolled in a postdoctoral residency/fellowship (6), employed in an academic position at a university (1), employed in an academic position at a 2-year/4-year college (2), employed in business or industry (1), do not know (2), total from the above (doctoral) (12).

Additional Information:

Orientation, Objectives, and Emphasis of Department: The psychology program is designed to develop research scholars, college teachers, and scientific/professional psychologists in the five areas listed. Individual student programs combine basic courses and seminars in a variety of specialized areas, research experience, and practica in both on- and off-campus settings. In addition, the social area has begun a new specialization in the Psychology of Peace and Prevention of Violence. Students with applied interests, such as clinical and developmental, have ample opportunity for in-depth practical experience.

Special Facilities or Resources: The Department has specialized laboratory facilities, including biochemistry, eyetracking, video data analysis, and other laboratories. It maintains its own clinic for research, clinical training, and service to the community. It provides students with access to microcomputers and to the VAX mainframes at University Computing Services. Departmental facilities and faculty are supplemented by the University's participation in Five-College programs (with Amherst, Hampshire, Mount Holyoke, and Smith Colleges) and by cooperation with other University departments including Computer and Information Science, Industrial Engineering, Education, Linguistics, Sociology, and Biology. The University of Massachusetts also offers a separate PhD program in neuroscience and behavior. Many of the students in this program receive the bulk of their training in the Psychology Department and work primarily with Psychology faculty.

Information for Students With Physical Disabilities: See the following website for more information: http://www.umass.edu/disability/.

Application Information:

Send to Graduate Admissions Office, Goodell Building, University of Massachusetts, Amherst, MA 01003. Application available online. URL of online application: http://www.umass.edu/gradschool/. Students are admitted in the Fall, application deadline December 1. December 1 for Clinical; January 2 for all other programs. *Fee:* $75. Application fee can be waived if GRE fees were waived.

Massachusetts, University of, Boston
Counseling and School Psychology
College of Education and Human Development
100 Morrissey Boulevard
Boston, MA 02125-3393
Telephone: (617) 287-7602
Fax: (617) 287-7667
E-mail: *sharon.lamb@umb.edu*
Web: *http://www.umb.edu/academics/cehd/counseling/*

Department Information:

1982. Chairperson: Sharon Lamb. Number of faculty: total—full-time 15, part-time 34; women—full-time 10, part-time 21; total—minority—full-time 2, part-time 4; women minority—full-time 1, part-time 3.

Programs and Degrees Offered:

Listed in the following order: Program area, degree type (T if terminal Master's), number awarded 7/11–6/12. School Psychology EdS (School Psychology) 29, Mental Health Counseling MA/MS (Master of Arts/Science) (T) 35, School Counseling MA/MS (Master of Arts/Science) (T) 35, Family Therapy MA/MS (Master of Arts/Science) (T) 14, Counseling Psychology PhD (Doctor of Philosophy) 0, School Psychology PhD (Doctor of Philosophy).

Student Applications/Admissions:

Student Applications

School Psychology EdS (School Psychology)—Applications 2012–2013, 81. Total applicants accepted 2012–2013, 35. Number full-time enrolled (new admits only) 2012–2013, 14. Number part-time enrolled (new admits only) 2012–2013, 2. Total enrolled 2012–2013 full-time, 39. Total enrolled 2012–2013 part-time, 7. Openings 2013–2014, 18. The median number of years required for completion of a degree in 2012–2013 were 2. The number of students enrolled full- and part-time who were dismissed or voluntarily withdrew from this program area in 2012–2013 were 1. *Mental Health Counseling MA/MS (Master of Arts/Science)*—Applications 2012–2013, 147. Total applicants accepted 2012–2013, 60. Number full-time enrolled (new admits only) 2012–2013, 25. Number part-time enrolled (new admits only) 2012–2013, 4. Total enrolled 2012–2013 full-time, 57. Total enrolled 2012–2013 part-time, 6. Openings 2013–2014, 30. The median number of years required for completion of a degree in 2012–2013 were 2. The number of students enrolled full- and part-time who were dismissed or voluntarily withdrew from this program area in 2012–2013 were 1. *School Counseling MA/MS (Master of Arts/Science)*—Applications 2012–2013, 80. Total applicants accepted 2012–2013, 48. Number full-time enrolled (new admits only) 2012–2013, 33. Number part-time enrolled (new admits only) 2012–2013, 10. Total enrolled 2012–2013 full-time, 83. Total enrolled 2012–2013 part-time, 17. Openings 2013–2014, 24. The median number of years required for completion of a degree in 2012–2013 were 2. *Family Therapy MA/MS (Master of Arts/Science)*—Applications 2012–2013, 54. Total applicants accepted 2012–2013, 26. Number full-time enrolled (new admits only) 2012–2013, 10. Number part-time enrolled (new admits only) 2012–2013, 3. Total enrolled 2012–2013 full-time, 27. Total enrolled 2012–2013 part-time, 11. Openings 2013–2014,

20. The median number of years required for completion of a degree in 2012–2013 were 3. The number of students enrolled full- and part-time who were dismissed or voluntarily withdrew from this program area in 2012–2013 were 0. *Counseling Psychology PhD (Doctor of Philosophy)*—Applications 2012–2013, 47. Total applicants accepted 2012–2013, 6. Number full-time enrolled (new admits only) 2012–2013, 6. Total enrolled 2012–2013 full-time, 6. Openings 2013–2014, 4. *School Psychology PhD (Doctor of Philosophy)*—Applications 2012–2013, 20. Total applicants accepted 2012–2013, 4. Number full-time enrolled (new admits only) 2012–2013, 4. Total enrolled 2012–2013 full-time, 4. Openings 2013–2014, 4.

Scores: Entries appear in this order: required test or GPA, minimum score (if required), median score of students entering in 2012–2013. *School Psychology EdS (School Psychology):* GRE-V no minimum stated, GRE-Q no minimum stated, GRE-Analytical no minimum stated, overall undergraduate GPA 3.0; *Mental Health Counseling MA/MS (Master of Arts/Science):* GRE-V no minimum stated, GRE-Q no minimum stated, GRE-Analytical no minimum stated, overall undergraduate GPA 3.0, last 2 years GPA no minimum stated, psychology GPA no minimum stated; *School Counseling MA/MS (Master of Arts/Science):* GRE-V no minimum stated, GRE-Q no minimum stated, GRE-Analytical no minimum stated, overall undergraduate GPA 3.0; *Family Therapy MA/MS (Master of Arts/Science):* GRE-V no minimum stated, GRE-Q no minimum stated, GRE-Analytical no minimum stated, overall undergraduate GPA 3.0, psychology GPA no minimum stated; *Counseling Psychology PhD (Doctor of Philosophy):* GRE-V no minimum stated, 161, GRE-Q no minimum stated, 154, GRE-Analytical no minimum stated, 4.5, overall undergraduate GPA no minimum stated, 3.58, psychology GPA no minimum stated, Masters GPA no minimum stated, 3.95; *School Psychology PhD (Doctor of Philosophy):* GRE-V no minimum stated, 153, GRE-Q no minimum stated, 147, GRE-Analytical no minimum stated, 4.0, overall undergraduate GPA no minimum stated, 3.9, Masters GPA no minimum stated, 3.92.

Other Criteria: (importance of criteria rated low, medium, or high): GRE scores—medium, research experience—medium, work experience—medium, extracurricular activity—low, clinically related public service—medium, GPA—medium, letters of recommendation—high, interview—high, statement of goals and objectives—high, undergraduate major in psychology—low, specific undergraduate psychology courses taken—medium, For the PhD program research experience is very important. It is helpful for obtaining a Graduate Assistantship for the Masters' programs but not essential. GRE Scores and a high GPA are also more important for the PhD program than for the Master's programs. For additional information on admission requirements, go to http://www.umb.edu/academics/cehd/counseling/admissions.

Student Characteristics: The following represents characteristics of students in 2012–2013 in all graduate psychology programs in the department: Female—full-time 213, part-time 47; Male—full-time 30, part-time 9; African American/Black—full-time 13, part-time 4; Hispanic/Latino(a)—full-time 7, part-time 6; Asian/Pacific Islander—full-time 10, part-time 3; American Indian/Alaska Native—full-time 0, part-time 1; Caucasian/White—full-time 217, part-time 35; Multi-ethnic—full-time 0, part-time 0; students subject to the Americans With Disabilities Act—full-time 7, part-time 0; Unknown ethnicity—full-time 0, part-time 0; International students who hold an F-1 or J-1 Visa—full-time 12, part-time 0.

Financial Information/Assistance:
Tuition for Full-Time Study: *Master's:* State residents: per academic year $12,875; Nonstate residents: per academic year $24,941. Tuition is subject to change. See the following website for updates and changes in tuition costs: http://www.umb.edu/bursar/tuition_and_fees.

Financial Assistance:
First-Year Students: Teaching assistantships available for first year. Average amount paid per academic year: $3,587. Average number of hours worked per week: 4. Research assistantships available for first year. Average amount paid per academic year: $3,587. Average number of hours worked per week: 4.

Advanced Students: Teaching assistantships available for advanced students. Average amount paid per academic year: $7,000. Average number of hours worked per week: 9. Research assistantships available for advanced students. Average amount paid per academic year: $3,587. Average number of hours worked per week: 4.

Additional Information: Of all students currently enrolled full time, 10% benefited from one or more of the listed financial assistance programs. Application and information available online at: http://www.umb.edu/admissions/financial_aid_scholarships/grad_aid.

Internships/Practica: Master's Degree (MA/MS Mental Health Counseling): An internship experience, such as a final research project or "capstone" experience is required of graduates. Master's Degree (MA/MS School Counseling): An internship experience, such as a final research project or "capstone" experience is required of graduates. Master's Degree (MA/MS Family Therapy): An internship experience, such as a final research project or "capstone" experience is required of graduates. The department maintains collaborative partnerships with a number of Greater Boston area schools, mental health clinics, rehabilitation centers, and other facilities which provide practicum and internship sites for students.

Housing and Day Care: No on-campus housing is available. On-campus day care facilities are available. See the following website for more information: http://www.umb.edu/life_on_campus/elc.

Employment of Department Graduates:
Master's Degree Graduates: Of those who graduated in the academic year 2011–2012, the following categories and numbers represent the postgraduate activities and employment of master's degree graduates: Enrolled in a postdoctoral residency/fellowship (n/a), employed in independent practice (n/a), total from the above (master's) (0).
Doctoral Degree Graduates: Of those who graduated in the academic year 2011–2012, the following categories and numbers represent the postgraduate activities and employment of doctoral degree graduates: Enrolled in a psychology doctoral program (n/a), total from the above (doctoral) (0).

Additional Information:
Orientation, Objectives, and Emphasis of Department: The Department and our programs are committed to the preparation of highly qualified professionals who will seek to promote maximum

growth and development of individuals (children, adolescents, and adults) with whom they work. This is accomplished through a carefully planned curriculum which includes the following: interdisciplinary and multidisciplinary approaches; theory linked to practice; a practitioner-scientist approach; self awareness and self-exploration activities; opportunities to learn and demonstrate respect for others; and socialization into the role of the profession. We value respect for the social foundations and cultural diversity of others and promote opportunities for students to learn how others construct their world. We emphasize to our students to focus on the assets and coping abilities of the people with whom they work rather than focusing on deficits. Additionally, we encourage the promotion of preventative services, which maximize individual functioning. Our programs are grounded in a systematic eclectic philosophical orientation, which includes: systemic theory; social constructionism; cognitive behavioral; psychodynamic; and person-centered approaches.

Special Facilities or Resources: We work in collaboration and have partnerships with the Mass Rehabilitation Commission, the Institute of Community Inclusion, and several school districts. Our students often find Graduate Assistantships outside of our department which come with full tuition remission and partial fee reductions. We also offer research opportunities with tuition remission and partial fee reductions to incoming students.

Information for Students With Physical Disabilities: See the following website for more information: http://www.rosscenter. umb.edu/.

Application Information:
Send to Graduate Admissions, University of Massachusetts Boston, 100 Morrissey Boulevard, Boston, MA 02125. Application available online. URL of online application: http://www.umb.edu/admissions/graduate/apply/. Students are admitted in the Fall, application deadline December 1. Application deadline for PhD in Counseling and School Psychology is December 1. Deadline for EdS School Psychology program is January 2. Deadline is February 1 for School Counseling, Mental Health Counseling, and Family Therapy. Deadline for Rehabilitation Counseling is June 1. *Fee:* $40. $40 application fee for Massachusetts residents, $60 for non-residents.

Massachusetts, University of, Boston
Department of Psychology
College of Liberal Arts
Harbor Campus, 100 Morrissey Boulevard
Boston, MA 02125
Telephone: (617) 287-6350
Fax: (617) 287-6336
E-mail: *jane.adams@umb.edu*
Web: *http://www.umb.edu/academics/cla/psychology/*

Department Information:
1967. Chairperson: Jane Adams. Number of faculty: total—full-time 24; women—full-time 17; total—minority—full-time 6; women minority—full-time 4.

Programs and Degrees Offered:
Listed in the following order: Program area, degree type (T if terminal Master's), number awarded 7/11–6/12. Clinical Psychol-

ogy PhD (Doctor of Philosophy) 10, Developmental Brain Sciences PhD (Doctor of Philosophy) 0.

APA Accreditation: Clinical PhD (Doctor of Philosophy). Student Outcome Data Website: http://www.umb.edu/academics/cla/psychology/grad/cp/full_disclosure/.

Student Applications/Admissions:
Student Applications
Clinical Psychology PhD (Doctor of Philosophy)—Applications 2012–2013, 368. Total applicants accepted 2012–2013, 12. Number full-time enrolled (new admits only) 2012–2013, 8. Total enrolled 2012–2013 full-time, 55. Openings 2013–2014, 8. The median number of years required for completion of a degree in 2012–2013 were 6. The number of students enrolled full- and part-time who were dismissed or voluntarily withdrew from this program area in 2012–2013 were 0. *Developmental Brain Sciences PhD (Doctor of Philosophy)*—Applications 2012–2013, 32. Total applicants accepted 2012–2013, 5. Number full-time enrolled (new admits only) 2012–2013, 5. Number part-time enrolled (new admits only) 2012–2013, 0. Total enrolled 2012–2013 full-time, 5. Total enrolled 2012–2013 part-time, 0. Openings 2013–2014, 5. The number of students enrolled full- and part-time who were dismissed or voluntarily withdrew from this program area in 2012–2013 were 0.
Scores: Entries appear in this order: required test or GPA, minimum score (if required), median score of students entering in 2012–2013. *Clinical Psychology PhD (Doctor of Philosophy):* GRE-V no minimum stated, 163, GRE-Q no minimum stated, 155, GRE-Analytical no minimum stated, 4.5, GRE-Subject (Psychology) no minimum stated, 705, overall undergraduate GPA no minimum stated, 3.75, last 2 years GPA no minimum stated, 3.86, psychology GPA no minimum stated, 3.84, Masters GPA no minimum stated, 4.0; *Developmental Brain Sciences PhD (Doctor of Philosophy):* GRE-V no minimum stated, 157, GRE-Q no minimum stated, 148, GRE-Analytical no minimum stated, 4, overall undergraduate GPA no minimum stated, 3.3, last 2 years GPA no minimum stated, 3.5, psychology GPA no minimum stated, 3.4, Masters GPA no minimum stated, 3.7.
Other Criteria: (importance of criteria rated low, medium, or high): GRE scores—medium, research experience—high, work experience—high, extracurricular activity—medium, clinically related public service—high, GPA—high, letters of recommendation—high, interview—high, statement of goals and objectives—high, undergraduate major in psychology—medium, specific undergraduate psychology courses taken—medium, The admissions criteria are different for the Developmental Brain Sciences program. Work experience and clinically related public service are rated low for them instead of high. For additional information on admission requirements, go to http://www.umb.edu/academics/cla/psychology/grad.

Student Characteristics: The following represents characteristics of students in 2012–2013 in all graduate psychology programs in the department: Female—full-time 50, part-time 0; Male—full-time 10, part-time 0; African American/Black—full-time 6, part-time 0; Hispanic/Latino(a)—full-time 11, part-time 0; Asian/Pacific Islander—full-time 9, part-time 0; American Indian/Alaska Native—full-time 0, part-time 0; Caucasian/White—full-time 31, part-time 0; Multi-ethnic—full-time 3, part-time 0; students subject to the Americans With Disabilities Act—full-time 0, part-

time 0; Unknown ethnicity—full-time 0, part-time 0; International students who hold an F-1 or J-1 Visa—full-time 6, part-time 0.

Financial Information/Assistance:

Tuition for Full-Time Study: *Doctoral:* State residents: per academic year $15,546; Nonstate residents: per academic year $28,204. Tuition is subject to change. See the following website for updates and changes in tuition costs: http://www.umb.edu/bursar/tuition_and_fees.

Financial Assistance:

First-Year Students: Teaching assistantships available for first year. Average amount paid per academic year: $15,908. Average number of hours worked per week: 20. Research assistantships available for first year. Average amount paid per academic year: $15,908. Average number of hours worked per week: 20. Fellowships and scholarships available for first year. Average amount paid per academic year: $15,908.

Advanced Students: Teaching assistantships available for advanced students. Average amount paid per academic year: $17,256. Research assistantships available for advanced students. Average amount paid per academic year: $17,256. Traineeships available for advanced students. Average amount paid per academic year: $24,000. Fellowships and scholarships available for advanced students. Average amount paid per academic year: $22,000.

Additional Information: Of all students currently enrolled full time, 93% benefited from one or more of the listed financial assistance programs. Application and information available online at: http://www.umb.edu/academics/cla/psychology/grad/cp/cp_funding_opportunities/.

Internships/Practica: Doctoral Degree (PhD Clinical Psychology): For those doctoral students for whom a professional psychology internship was required in this program prior to graduation, (11) students applied for an internship in 2011–2012, with (11) students obtaining an internship. Of those students who obtained an internship, (11) were paid internships. Of those students who obtained an internship, (11) students placed in APA/CPA accredited internships, (0) students placed in internships not APA/CPA accredited, but listed with the Association of Psychology Postdoctoral and Internship Programs (APPIC), (0) students placed in internships conforming to guidelines of the Council of Directors of School Psychology Programs (CDSPP), (0) students placed in internships that were not APA/CPA accredited, APPIC or CDSPP listed. In the Clinical PhD program, students do a 15 hour per week clinical practicum in the University Counseling Center in their second year. They obtain supervised clinical experience doing intake evaluations, short-term dynamic and cognitive behavioral therapy, and some group and couples treatment. Students also do an 18-20 hour per week clinical practicum in a training hospital or community health center in their third year. Examples of external practica include: Cambridge Hospital, Children's Hospital, McLean Hospital, the Brookline Center, South Cove Health Center, and Chelsea Memorial Health Center. These agencies all serve a significant number of low income and ethnic minority clients. Students get supervised clinical training in testing and assessment and a range of psychotherapeutic interventions with children, adolescents, and adults at their external practica. Students do a full-time APA approved clinical internship in their fifth year.

Housing and Day Care: No on-campus housing is available. No on-campus day care facilities are available.

Employment of Department Graduates:

Master's Degree Graduates: Of those who graduated in the academic year 2011–2012, the following categories and numbers represent the postgraduate activities and employment of master's degree graduates: Enrolled in a postdoctoral residency/fellowship (n/a), employed in independent practice (n/a), total from the above (master's) (0).

Doctoral Degree Graduates: Of those who graduated in the academic year 2011–2012, the following categories and numbers represent the postgraduate activities and employment of doctoral degree graduates: Enrolled in a psychology doctoral program (n/a), enrolled in a postdoctoral residency/fellowship (8), employed in independent practice (1), employed in government agency (1), total from the above (doctoral) (10).

Additional Information:

Orientation, Objectives, and Emphasis of Department: The Psychology Department offers two PhD programs. APA accredited, the PhD program in Clinical Psychology adopts the scientist–practitioner model, integrating research and clinical training. This program prepares academics, researchers, and clinicians who have a strong theoretical background in scientific psychology and essential skills in both research and clinical practice. This program prepares students to serve underserved populations by ensuring that they are knowledgeable and skilled in developmentally and culturally competent research and clinical practice. Graduates translate basic psychological knowledge into practical applications to meet the needs of individuals from diverse economic, age, racial, and sociocultural groups. Graduates are qualified to take the Massachusetts Licensing Examination for clinical psychologists and to work in academic, research, and clinical settings. The PhD program in Developmental and Brain Sciences is research-intensive, focused on understanding cognition, perception, and behavior when underlying neural and hormonal mechanisms are developing. Research ranges from cognitive development and psychophysics to neuroendocrinology and behavioral genetics. Students may specialize in Cognitive or Behavioral Neuroscience. All DBS students receive training in methods (dry and wet lab skills, advanced statistics, MATLAB) and multiple levels of investigation including psychophysical and neuropsychological evaluation, functional brain imaging (NIRS, ERP), and neuropharmacological, molecular/cellular, and (epi-)genetic approaches.

Special Facilities or Resources: For both PhD programs, the Psychology Department's research laboratories support a wide range of research and teaching functions. There are several rooms equipped with one-way mirrors and audio and visual recording equipment that can be used for clinical, social, and developmental research. Human laboratories employ various technologies such as eye-tracking, ERP, and NIRS. Animal laboratories are equipped for research on behavior, genetics, and physiology. The department's laboratory facilities also include woodworking and electronic shops. A technical staff provides programming, electronic, and other related support to the faculty and students. Students in the Clinical program have access to the facilities of other research centers at the university, including the Center for Survey Research, the Center for the Study of Social Acceptance, the William Monroe Trotter Institute for the Study of Black Culture, and the William Joiner Center for the Study of War and Social

Consequences. DBS students and faculty may work in collaboration with colleagues and laboratories in Clinical Psychology, Biology, and Computer Science. DBS students currently receive a stipend of $24,000 per academic year.

Information for Students With Physical Disabilities: See the following website for more information: http://www.umb.edu/academics/vpass/disability/.

Application Information:
Send to Graduate Admissions, University of Massachusetts Boston, 100 Morrissey Boulevard, Boston, MA 02125. Application available online. URL of online application: http://www.umb.edu/admissions/grad/apply. Students are admitted in the Fall, application deadline December 1. *Fee:* $60. McNair Scholars.

Massachusetts, University of, Dartmouth

Psychology Department
College of Arts & Sciences
285 Old Westport Road
North Dartmouth, MA 02747-2300
Telephone: (508) 999-8380
Fax: (508) 999-9169
E-mail: *bhaimson@umassd.edu*
Web: *http://www.umassd.edu/cas/psychology/*

Department Information:
1962. Chairperson: Barry Haimson. Number of faculty: total—full-time 18, part-time 6; women—full-time 10, part-time 3.

Programs and Degrees Offered:
Listed in the following order: Program area, degree type (T if terminal Master's), number awarded 7/11–6/12. Clinical Psychology MA/MS (Master of Arts/Science) (T) 12, Research MA/MS (Master of Arts/Science) (T) 6, Applied Behavior Analysis MA/MS (Master of Arts/Science) (T) 2, Applied Behavior Analysis Certificate Other 3.

Student Applications/Admissions:
Student Applications
Clinical Psychology MA/MS (Master of Arts/Science)—Applications 2012–2013, 68. Total applicants accepted 2012–2013, 25. Number full-time enrolled (new admits only) 2012–2013, 15. Number part-time enrolled (new admits only) 2012–2013, 0. Total enrolled 2012–2013 full-time, 43. Total enrolled 2012–2013 part-time, 0. Openings 2013–2014, 15. The median number of years required for completion of a degree in 2012–2013 were 3. The number of students enrolled full- and part-time who were dismissed or voluntarily withdrew from this program area in 2012–2013 were 1. *Research MA/MS (Master of Arts/Science)*—Applications 2012–2013, 12. Total applicants accepted 2012–2013, 8. Number full-time enrolled (new admits only) 2012–2013, 2. Number part-time enrolled (new admits only) 2012–2013, 0. Total enrolled 2012–2013 full-time, 10. Total enrolled 2012–2013 part-time, 0. Openings 2013–2014, 9. The median number of years required for completion of a degree in 2012–2013 were 2. The number of students enrolled full- and part-time who were dismissed or voluntarily withdrew from this program area in 2012–2013

were 1. *Applied Behavior Analysis MA/MS (Master of Arts/Science)*—Applications 2012–2013, 15. Total applicants accepted 2012–2013, 10. Number full-time enrolled (new admits only) 2012–2013, 8. Number part-time enrolled (new admits only) 2012–2013, 2. Total enrolled 2012–2013 full-time, 20. Total enrolled 2012–2013 part-time, 5. Openings 2013–2014, 18. The median number of years required for completion of a degree in 2012–2013 were 3. The number of students enrolled full- and part-time who were dismissed or voluntarily withdrew from this program area in 2012–2013 were 0. *Applied Behavior Analysis Certificate Other*—Applications 2012–2013, 6. Total applicants accepted 2012–2013, 5. Number full-time enrolled (new admits only) 2012–2013, 0. Number part-time enrolled (new admits only) 2012–2013, 5. Openings 2013–2014, 10. The median number of years required for completion of a degree in 2012–2013 were 2. The number of students enrolled full- and part-time who were dismissed or voluntarily withdrew from this program area in 2012–2013 were 0.

Scores: Entries appear in this order: required test or GPA, minimum score (if required), median score of students entering in 2012–2013. *Clinical Psychology MA/MS (Master of Arts/Science):* overall undergraduate GPA 2.80; *Research MA/MS (Master of Arts/Science):* GRE-V no minimum stated, GRE-Q no minimum stated, GRE-Analytical no minimum stated; *Applied Behavior Analysis MA/MS (Master of Arts/Science):* GRE-V no minimum stated, GRE-Q no minimum stated, GRE-Analytical no minimum stated, overall undergraduate GPA 3.0.

Other Criteria: (importance of criteria rated low, medium, or high): GRE scores—medium, research experience—medium, work experience—high, clinically related public service—high, GPA—medium, letters of recommendation—high, interview—high, statement of goals and objectives—high, These criteria vary across options. The Research track does not require work experience or clinical services. The clinical and ABA tracks do not require research experience. Interview is important for clinical track. For additional information on admission requirements, go to http://www.umassd.edu/cas/psychology/graduateprograms/.

Student Characteristics: The following represents characteristics of students in 2012–2013 in all graduate psychology programs in the department: Female—full-time 12, part-time 12; Male—full-time 61, part-time 8; Caucasian/White—full-time 0, part-time 0; students subject to the Americans With Disabilities Act—full-time 0, part-time 0; Unknown ethnicity—full-time 73, part-time 20; International students who hold an F-1 or J-1 Visa—full-time 0, part-time 0.

Financial Information/Assistance:
Tuition for Full-Time Study: *Master's:* State residents: per academic year $9,741; Nonstate residents: per academic year $16,464. Tuition is subject to change. Additional fees are assessed to students beyond the costs of tuition for the following: athletic fee, student fee, campus center, health. Tuition costs vary by program. See the following website for updates and changes in tuition costs: http://www1.umassd.edu/graduate/tuition/welcome.cfm.

Financial Assistance:
First-Year Students: Teaching assistantships available for first year. Average amount paid per academic year: $6,000. Average number of hours worked per week: 10. Research assistantships

available for first year. Average amount paid per academic year: $12,000. Average number of hours worked per week: 20.

Advanced Students: Teaching assistantships available for advanced students. Average amount paid per academic year: $6,000. Average number of hours worked per week: 10. Research assistantships available for advanced students. Average amount paid per academic year: $12,000. Average number of hours worked per week: 20.

Additional Information: Of all students currently enrolled full time, 21% benefited from one or more of the listed financial assistance programs. Application and information available online at: http://www.umassd.edu/cas/psychology/graduateprograms/financialaid/.

Internships/Practica: Master's Degree (MA/MS Clinical Psychology): An internship experience, such as a final research project or "capstone" experience is required of graduates. Master's Degree (MA/MS Research): An internship experience, such as a final research project or "capstone" experience is required of graduates. Master's Degree (MA/MS Applied Behavior Analysis): An internship experience, such as a final research project or "capstone" experience is required of graduates. We have a wide variety of internship and practicum experiences available for clinical students. Field experiences are tailored to specific student needs. In addition, we can recommend a number of paid internships for students in the ABA track.

Housing and Day Care: On-campus housing is available. See the following website for more information: http://www.umassd.edu/housing. No on-campus day care facilities are available.

Employment of Department Graduates:

Master's Degree Graduates: Of those who graduated in the academic year 2011–2012, the following categories and numbers represent the postgraduate activities and employment of master's degree graduates: Enrolled in a psychology doctoral program (1), enrolled in another graduate/professional program (1), enrolled in a postdoctoral residency/fellowship (n/a), employed in independent practice (n/a), employed in business or industry (2), employed in a community mental health/counseling center (1), do not know (1), total from the above (master's) (6).

Doctoral Degree Graduates: Of those who graduated in the academic year 2011–2012, the following categories and numbers represent the postgraduate activities and employment of doctoral degree graduates: Enrolled in a psychology doctoral program (n/a), total from the above (doctoral) (0).

Additional Information:

Orientation, Objectives, and Emphasis of Department: The research track of the MA program in psychology is designed to prepare students for doctoral work in psychology and related fields, including cognitive science. The program combines coursework in basic areas of psychology with the opportunity to do collaborative research with faculty members. Students have considerable flexibility to tailor their programs to their individual needs. The outstanding feature of this program is the opportunity for close interaction between faculty and students, both in the classroom and in the laboratory, because of the low student/faculty ratio. The objectives of the Clinical track are: to train competent MA-level clinicians; to provide students with applied research and problem-solving skills; to provide students with a broad exposure to a variety of therapy modalities; to provide students with extensive

experiential learning opportunities, practica, internships and intensive supervision; and to prepare students to be Licensed Mental Health Counselors. The ABA MA track is designed to prepare students to sit for the BCBA (Board Certified Behavior Analyst) exam administered by the Behavior Analyst Certification Board (BACB). The ABA certificate program is designed to prepare individuals with Master's degrees in other areas and appropriate internship experience to sit for the BCBA exam. All ABA specific courses have been approved by the BACB.

Special Facilities or Resources: Our ABA MA track and certificate programs are currently offered in collaboration with Evergreen Center and Beacon Services. The Evergreen Center is a residential school serving children with severe developmental disabilities. Beacon Services provides ABA consulting services to schools and families with children requiring behavioral support. Students may also receive field work experience at other ABA sites in the area. The department has two Event-Related Potential (ERP) laboratories as well as behavioral testing laboratories.

Information for Students With Physical Disabilities: See the following website for more information: http://www.umassd.edu/dss/.

Application Information:
Send to Office of Graduate Studies. Application available online. URL of online application: http://www1.umassd.edu/graduate/prospects/programselect.cfm. Students are admitted in the Fall, application deadline March 31; Spring, application deadline December 10. April 15 for Fall admission to Research, March 31 for Clinical. August 15 for fall admissions for ABA; December 28 for Spring admission for ABA. ABA program is the only program that admits students in the spring. *Fee:* $60.

Massachusetts, University of, Lowell
Department of Psychology
Fine Arts, Humanities, & Social Sciences
113 Wilder Street, Suite 300
Lowell, MA 01854-3059
Telephone: (978) 934-3950
Fax: (978) 934-3074
E-mail: *csp@uml.edu and asp@uml.edu*
Web: *http://www.uml.edu/FAHSS/Psychology/Graduate/ default.aspx*

Department Information:
1980. Chairperson: Richard Siegel. Number of faculty: total—full-time 26, part-time 3; women—full-time 19, part-time 2; total—minority—full-time 6; women minority—full-time 4.

Programs and Degrees Offered:
Listed in the following order: Program area, degree type (T if terminal Master's), number awarded 7/11–6/12. Community Social Psychology MA/MS (Master of Arts/Science) (T) 15, Autism Studies MA/MS (Master of Arts/Science) (T).

Student Applications/Admissions:
Student Applications
Community Social Psychology MA/MS (*Master of Arts/Science*)—Applications 2012–2013, 25. Total applicants accepted

2012–2013, 20. Number full-time enrolled (new admits only) 2012–2013, 16. Number part-time enrolled (new admits only) 2012–2013, 3. Total enrolled 2012–2013 full-time, 30. Total enrolled 2012–2013 part-time, 10. Openings 2013–2014, 20. The median number of years required for completion of a degree in 2012–2013 were 2. The number of students enrolled full- and part-time who were dismissed or voluntarily withdrew from this program area in 2012–2013 were 1. *Autism Studies MA/MS (Master of Arts/Science)*—Total applicants accepted 2012–2013, 13. Number full-time enrolled (new admits only) 2012–2013, 8. Number part-time enrolled (new admits only) 2012–2013, 2. Total enrolled 2012–2013 full-time, 8. Total enrolled 2012–2013 part-time, 2. Openings 2013–2014, 14. The number of students enrolled full- and part-time who were dismissed or voluntarily withdrew from this program area in 2012–2013 were 0.

Other Criteria: (importance of criteria rated low, medium, or high): GRE scores—medium, research experience—medium, work experience—high, extracurricular activity—low, clinically related public service—medium, GPA—high, letters of recommendation—high, statement of goals and objectives—high, undergraduate major in psychology—medium, specific undergraduate psychology courses taken—low.

Student Characteristics: The following represents characteristics of students in 2012–2013 in all graduate psychology programs in the department: Female—full-time 33, part-time 9; Male—full-time 5, part-time 3; African American/Black—full-time 6, part-time 1; Hispanic/Latino(a)—full-time 2, part-time 1; Asian/Pacific Islander—full-time 2, part-time 4; American Indian/Alaska Native—full-time 0, part-time 0; Caucasian/White—full-time 28, part-time 6; Multi-ethnic—full-time 0, part-time 0; students subject to the Americans With Disabilities Act—full-time 1, part-time 0; Unknown ethnicity—full-time 0, part-time 0; International students who hold an F-1 or J-1 Visa—full-time 6, part-time 0.

Financial Information/Assistance:
Tuition for Full-Time Study: *Master's:* State residents: per academic year $11,229, $624 per credit hour; Nonstate residents: per academic year $20,774, $1,154 per credit hour. Tuition is subject to change. See the following website for updates and changes in tuition costs: http://www.uml.edu/Tuition-fees/Tuition-Costs/default.aspx. Higher tuition cost for this program: online graduate courses cost more.

Financial Assistance:
First-Year Students: Teaching assistantships available for first year. Average amount paid per academic year: $4,500. Average number of hours worked per week: 10.
Advanced Students: Teaching assistantships available for advanced students. Average amount paid per academic year: $4,500. Average number of hours worked per week: 10.
Additional Information: Of all students currently enrolled full time, 30% benefited from one or more of the listed financial assistance programs. Application and information available online at: http://www.uml.edu/FinancialAid/info-for/graduate/default.aspx.

Internships/Practica: Master's Degree (MA/MS Community Social Psychology): An internship experience, such as a final research project or "capstone" experience is required of graduates. For CSP students, there is a one-year practicum requirement of 10 to 12 hours a week. Settings vary but much of the fieldwork takes place directly in Lowell, MA, perhaps the most culturally diverse mid-size city in the United States, located just 25 miles from Boston. For ASP students, there is a two-semester practicum requirement of 27 hours per week in a school or agency that applies behavioral intervention methods with individuals on the autism spectrum. Students can also opt to complete an independent fieldwork experience, but all students meet together as a class to share their experiences.

Housing and Day Care: On-campus housing is available. See the following website for more information: http://www.uml.edu/student-services/reslife/default.aspx. No on-campus day care facilities are available.

Employment of Department Graduates:
Master's Degree Graduates: Of those who graduated in the academic year 2011–2012, the following categories and numbers represent the postgraduate activities and employment of master's degree graduates: Enrolled in a psychology doctoral program (2), enrolled in another graduate/professional program (1), enrolled in a postdoctoral residency/fellowship (n/a), employed in independent practice (n/a), employed in an academic position at a university (2), employed in an academic position at a 2-year/4-year college (3), employed in a professional position in a school system (1), employed in business or industry (4), employed in government agency (2), still seeking employment (2), other employment position (3), do not know (1), total from the above (master's) (21). *Doctoral Degree Graduates:* Of those who graduated in the academic year 2011–2012, the following categories and numbers represent the postgraduate activities and employment of doctoral degree graduates: Enrolled in a psychology doctoral program (n/a), total from the above (doctoral) (0).

Additional Information:
Orientation, Objectives, and Emphasis of Department: The Psychology Department offers two master's-level graduate programs: the Community Social Psychology (CSP) program and the Autism Studies program (ASP). The faculty and students of both programs share a commitment to social justice and the empowerment of all individuals and communities. The CSP program focuses on applying tested psychological knowledge to strengthen community life and to increase individual and community well-being. The ASP provides students with a full appreciation of autism from behavioral, developmental and community perspectives, as well as fully preparing graduates for national Board Certified Behavior Analyst (BCBA)® certification. Our department goal is to produce graduates with the analytic, creative and practical skills needed to design and implement programs and services that will facilitate positive changes within and across communities ' changes that will empower all people to reach their full potential and empower social organizations, public and private, to be more responsive to human needs. The CSP program is a 36-credit master's degree program, providing multiple opportunities for hands-on classroom experiences, community field study, independent learning, and interdisciplinary collaboration. Students admitted to CSP will work and learn together with nationally recognized faculty, community leaders, and talented students from highly diverse backgrounds. The ASP is a 42-credit master's degree program that blends online courses with face-to-face instruction. Students admitted to ASP are provided with exceptional, supervised practicum experience working directly with children with

autism, as well as opportunities for interdisciplinary collaboration and independent research. CSP graduates are prepared for leadership positions in government, health and human services, and community and educational organizations in a variety of professional roles and capacities. Many also proceed on toward doctoral degrees. ASP graduates will have met all the education and training requirements that will allow them to sit for the national certification exam to become Board Certified Behavior Analysts (BCBAs). As BCBAs, they will be able to work with schools and other agencies to design and implement effective interventions for children with autism spectrum disorders and supervise other direct service providers, including those who aspire to become board certified. They will also be able to conduct research that could lead to new and effective interventions.

Special Facilities or Resources: Special facilities and resources consist of a graduate student lounge/computer lab, grant-related technical services from the Office of Research Administration, numerous research centers such as the Center for Family, Work and Community and the Center for Women and Work, and a unique multi-ethnic urban setting in a mid-sized city accessible to Boston.

Information for Students With Physical Disabilities: See the following website for more information: http://www.uml.edu/student-services/disability/default.aspx.

Application Information:
Send to Office of Graduate School Admissions, 820 Broadway Street, Lowell, MA 01854-5104. Application available online. URL of online application: http://www.uml.edu/Grad/Process/default.aspx. Students are admitted in the Fall, application deadline March 1; Programs have rolling admissions. The Autism Studies program accepts applications for Fall semester only, and the application deadline is March 1. The Community Social Psychology program accepts and acts on applications year-round. Most of our students start our program in the Fall semester, and this is recommended given the timing and sequence of required courses. *Fee:* $50.

Northeastern University
Department of Counseling & Applied Educational Psychology
Bouve College of Health Sciences
360 Huntington Avenue, 404 INV
Boston, MA 02115
Telephone: (617) 373-2485
Fax: (617) 373-8892
E-mail: *caep@neu.edu*
Web: *http://www.northeastern.edu/bouve/caep/index.html*

Department Information:
1983. Chair: Emanuel Mason, Ed.D. Number of faculty: total—full-time 17, part-time 33; women—full-time 10, part-time 23; total—minority—full-time 6, part-time 3; women minority—full-time 4, part-time 3; faculty subject to the Americans With Disabilities Act 2.

Programs and Degrees Offered:
Listed in the following order: Program area, degree type (T if terminal Master's), number awarded 7/11–6/12. Combined Counseling/School Psychology PhD (Doctor of Philosophy) 8, College Student Development & Counseling MA/MS (Master of Arts/Science) (T) 25, Counseling Psychology MA/MS (Master of Arts/Science) (T) 16, School Counseling MA/MS (Master of Arts/Science) (T) 12, Early Intervention Other 5, School Psychology EdS (School Psychology) 23, School Psychology MA/MS (Master of Arts/Science) (T) 23, Counseling Psychology PhD (Doctor of Philosophy) 0, School Psychology PhD (Doctor of Philosophy) 0.

APA Accreditation: Combination PhD (Doctor of Philosophy).

Student Applications/Admissions:
Student Applications
Combined Counseling/School Psychology PhD (Doctor of Philosophy)—Applications 2012–2013, 0. Total applicants accepted 2012–2013, 0. Number full-time enrolled (new admits only) 2012–2013, 0. Number part-time enrolled (new admits only) 2012–2013, 0. Total enrolled 2012–2013 full-time, 53. Total enrolled 2012–2013 part-time, 0. The median number of years required for completion of a degree in 2012–2013 were 6. The number of students enrolled full- and part-time who were dismissed or voluntarily withdrew from this program area in 2012–2013 were 2. *College Student Development & Counseling MA/MS (Master of Arts/Science)*—Applications 2012–2013, 49. Total applicants accepted 2012–2013, 39. Number full-time enrolled (new admits only) 2012–2013, 21. Number part-time enrolled (new admits only) 2012–2013, 1. Total enrolled 2012–2013 full-time, 46. Total enrolled 2012–2013 part-time, 2. Openings 2013–2014, 26. The median number of years required for completion of a degree in 2012–2013 were 2. The number of students enrolled full- and part-time who were dismissed or voluntarily withdrew from this program area in 2012–2013 were 0. *Counseling Psychology MA/MS (Master of Arts/Science)*—Applications 2012–2013, 282. Total applicants accepted 2012–2013, 57. Number full-time enrolled (new admits only) 2012–2013, 13. Number part-time enrolled (new admits only) 2012–2013, 5. Total enrolled 2012–2013 full-time, 33. Total enrolled 2012–2013 part-time, 5. Openings 2013–2014, 20. The median number of years required for completion of a degree in 2012–2013 were 2. The number of students enrolled full- and part-time who were dismissed or voluntarily withdrew from this program area in 2012–2013 were 0. *School Counseling MA/MS (Master of Arts/Science)*—Applications 2012–2013, 26. Total applicants accepted 2012–2013, 26. Number full-time enrolled (new admits only) 2012–2013, 13. Number part-time enrolled (new admits only) 2012–2013, 2. Total enrolled 2012–2013 full-time, 32. Total enrolled 2012–2013 part-time, 2. Openings 2013–2014, 20. The median number of years required for completion of a degree in 2012–2013 were 2. The number of students enrolled full- and part-time who were dismissed or voluntarily withdrew from this program area in 2012–2013 were 0. *Early Intervention Other*—Applications 2012–2013, 16. Total applicants accepted 2012–2013, 11. Number full-time enrolled (new admits only) 2012–2013, 1. Number part-time enrolled (new admits only) 2012–2013, 10. Total enrolled 2012–2013 full-time, 2. Total enrolled 2012–2013 part-time, 33. Openings 2013–2014, 10. The median number of years required for completion of a degree in 2012–2013 were 2. The number of students enrolled full- and part-time who were dismissed or voluntarily withdrew from this program area in 2012–2013 were 0. *School Psychology EdS (School Psychology)*—Applications 2012–2013, 114. Total

applicants accepted 2012–2013, 67. Number full-time enrolled (new admits only) 2012–2013, 17. Total enrolled 2012–2013 full-time, 36. Openings 2013–2014, 20. The median number of years required for completion of a degree in 2012–2013 were 3. *School Psychology MA/MS (Master of Arts/Science)*— Applications 2012–2013, 48. Total applicants accepted 2012–2013, 48. Number full-time enrolled (new admits only) 2012–2013, 17. Number part-time enrolled (new admits only) 2012–2013, 0. Total enrolled 2012–2013 full-time, 36. Total enrolled 2012–2013 part-time, 0. Openings 2013–2014, 20. The median number of years required for completion of a degree in 2012–2013 were 2. The number of students enrolled full- and part-time who were dismissed or voluntarily withdrew from this program area in 2012–2013 were 0. *Counseling Psychology PhD (Doctor of Philosophy)*—Applications 2012–2013, 38. Total applicants accepted 2012–2013, 10. Number full-time enrolled (new admits only) 2012–2013, 5. Number part-time enrolled (new admits only) 2012–2013, 0. Total enrolled 2012–2013 full-time, 17. Total enrolled 2012–2013 part-time, 0. Openings 2013–2014, 3. The number of students enrolled full- and part-time who were dismissed or voluntarily withdrew from this program area in 2012–2013 were 0. *School Psychology PhD (Doctor of Philosophy)*—Applications 2012–2013, 35. Total applicants accepted 2012–2013, 6. Number full-time enrolled (new admits only) 2012–2013, 4. Number part-time enrolled (new admits only) 2012–2013, 0. Total enrolled 2012–2013 full-time, 10. Total enrolled 2012–2013 part-time, 0. Openings 2013–2014, 3. The median number of years required for completion of a degree in 2012–2013 were 6. The number of students enrolled full- and part-time who were dismissed or voluntarily withdrew from this program area in 2012–2013 were 0.

Scores: Entries appear in this order: required test or GPA, minimum score (if required), median score of students entering in 2012–2013. *College Student Development & Counseling MA/MS (Master of Arts/Science)*: GRE-V 158, 483, GRE-Q 154, 532, GRE-Analytical 3.5, 4.1; *Counseling Psychology MA/MS (Master of Arts/Science)*: GRE-V 360, 435, GRE-Q 370, 486, GRE-Analytical 3, 4.0; *School Counseling MA/MS (Master of Arts/Science)*: GRE-V no minimum stated, 530, GRE-Q no minimum stated, 520, GRE-Analytical no minimum stated, 4, overall undergraduate GPA 3.0, 3.65; *Early Intervention Other*: overall undergraduate GPA 3.0; *School Psychology EdS (School Psychology)*: GRE-V no minimum stated, GRE-Q no minimum stated, GRE-Analytical no minimum stated, overall undergraduate GPA no minimum stated; *Counseling Psychology PhD (Doctor of Philosophy)*: GRE-V 500, 600, GRE-Q 500, 600, GRE-Analytical 3.5, 4, overall undergraduate GPA 3.5, 3.8; *School Psychology PhD (Doctor of Philosophy)*: GRE-V no minimum stated, GRE-Q no minimum stated, GRE-Analytical no minimum stated, overall undergraduate GPA no minimum stated.

Other Criteria: (importance of criteria rated low, medium, or high): GRE scores—medium, research experience—medium, work experience—high, extracurricular activity—medium, clinically related public service—high, GPA—medium, letters of recommendation—high, interview—high, statement of goals and objectives—high.

Student Characteristics: The following represents characteristics of students in 2012–2013 in all graduate psychology programs in the department: Female—full-time 158, part-time 31; Male—full-

time 35, part-time 7; African American/Black—full-time 8, part-time 3; Hispanic/Latino(a)—full-time 11, part-time 2; Asian/Pacific Islander—full-time 5, part-time 1; American Indian/Alaska Native—full-time 0, part-time 0; Caucasian/White—full-time 83, part-time 20; Multi-ethnic—full-time 2, part-time 0; students subject to the Americans With Disabilities Act—full-time 0, part-time 0; Unknown ethnicity—full-time 76, part-time 12; International students who hold an F-1 or J-1 Visa—full-time 8, part-time 0.

Financial Information/Assistance:
Tuition for Full-Time Study: *Master's:* State residents: $1,135 per credit hour; Nonstate residents: $1,135 per credit hour. *Doctoral:* State residents: $1,135 per credit hour; Nonstate residents: $1,135 per credit hour. Tuition is subject to change. See the following website for updates and changes in tuition costs: http://www.northeastern.edu/financialaid/studentaccounts/tuition.html.

Financial Assistance:
   First-Year Students: Teaching assistantships available for first year. Average amount paid per academic year: $15,360. Average number of hours worked per week: 20. Research assistantships available for first year. Average amount paid per academic year: $15,360. Average number of hours worked per week: 20. Fellowships and scholarships available for first year. Average amount paid per academic year: $0. Average number of hours worked per week: 0.

   Advanced Students: Teaching assistantships available for advanced students. Average amount paid per academic year: $15,360. Average number of hours worked per week: 20. Research assistantships available for advanced students. Average amount paid per academic year: $15,360. Average number of hours worked per week: 20. Fellowships and scholarships available for advanced students. Average amount paid per academic year: $0. Average number of hours worked per week: 0.

   Additional Information: Of all students currently enrolled full time, 10% benefited from one or more of the listed financial assistance programs.

Internships/Practica: Doctoral Degree (PhD Combined Counseling/School Psychology): For those doctoral students for whom a professional psychology internship was required in this program prior to graduation, (6) students applied for an internship in 2011–2012, with (5) students obtaining an internship. Of those students who obtained an internship, (5) were paid internships. Of those students who obtained an internship, (5) students placed in APA/CPA accredited internships, (0) students placed in internships not APA/CPA accredited, but listed with the Association of Psychology Postdoctoral and Internship Programs (APPIC), (0) students placed in internships conforming to guidelines of the Council of Directors of School Psychology Programs (CDSPP), (0) students placed in internships that were not APA/CPA accredited, APPIC or CDSPP listed. Master's Degree (MA/MS College Student Development & Counseling): An internship experience, such as a final research project or "capstone" experience is required of graduates. Master's Degree (MA/MS Counseling Psychology): An internship experience, such as a final research project or "capstone" experience is required of graduates. Master's Degree (MA/MS School Counseling): An internship experience, such as a final research project or "capstone" experience is required of graduates. Master's Degree (MA/MS School Psychology): An internship experience, such as a final research project or "capstone" experience is required of graduates. Internship and field placement sites are varied depending on the program and specialization. Sites are in the Boston metropolitan area and include some of the most desirable and prestigious settings in the field.

Housing and Day Care: On-campus housing is available. See the following website for more information: http://www.northeastern. edu/reslife/. On-campus day care facilities are available.

Employment of Department Graduates:

Master's Degree Graduates: Of those who graduated in the academic year 2011–2012, the following categories and numbers represent the postgraduate activities and employment of master's degree graduates: Enrolled in a postdoctoral residency/fellowship (n/a), employed in independent practice (n/a), total from the above (master's) (0).

Doctoral Degree Graduates: Of those who graduated in the academic year 2011–2012, the following categories and numbers represent the postgraduate activities and employment of doctoral degree graduates: Enrolled in a psychology doctoral program (n/a), total from the above (doctoral) (0).

Additional Information:

Orientation, Objectives, and Emphasis of Department: Philosophically, the school and counseling psychology programs are based on an ecological model. This model focuses on the contexts in which people and their environments intersect, including individuals' families, groups, cultures, and social, political, and economic institutions. Thus, the ecological model includes individual and interpersonal relationships along with their interactive physical and sociocultural environments. It employs a general systems perspective to understand the mutually reciprocal interactions of all of these elements. Central to this theoretical stance are assumptions of interdependence, circular and multilevel influence and causality, and interactive identities. Issues of gender, status, and culture are given special emphasis as well as the developmental stages of the individual, family, or group. The ecological model is large enough and sufficiently comprehensive to allow for teaching and using other models such as psychodynamic, behaviorist, and humanistic, as they help to explain behavior and phenomena in individuals, families, and groups. This allows faculty and students to teach, understand, and use many explanations of human activities. This ecological orientation provides the lenses through which students study psychological and counseling theory and research. In their varied fieldwork settings, students have the opportunity to translate this orientation into practice.

Special Facilities or Resources: Northeastern University, one of the largest private universities in the country, is located in Boston, a center of academic excellence and psychological research. There are numerous opportunities for diverse experiences, such as placements specializing in neuropsychology, early intervention, and sexual abuse. The campus is in the Back Bay, an area with a large student population and rich cultural opportunities. The Snell Library, one of the most advanced college libraries in the Boston area, provides access for students not only to its large psychology and education collections, but also to media and microcomputer centers and an extensive global academic computer networking system. Northeastern students also have privileges at the other Boston area research libraries.

Information for Students With Physical Disabilities: See the following website for more information: http://www.drc.neu.edu/.

Application Information:
Send to Graduate Admissions, Bouve College of Health Sciences, 123 Beharakis Health Science Building, Boston, MA 02115. Application available online. URL of online application: http://www.northeastern. edu/graduate/apply_now/. Students are admitted in the Fall, application deadline December 1; Spring, application deadline December 12; Programs have rolling admissions. MS Counseling Psychology - January 15, fall admission only; MS/CAGS School Psychology - January 15, fall admission only; MS School Counseling - August 1 fall; December 12 spring; PhD School Psychology - December 1, fall admission only; PhD Counseling Psychology - January 5, fall admission only. *Fee:* $50.

Northeastern University
Department of Psychology
College of Science
125 Nightingale Hall
Boston, MA 02115
Telephone: (617) 373-3076
Fax: (617) 373-8714
E-mail: *j.miller@neu.edu*
Web: *http://www.northeastern.edu/psychology/*

Department Information:
1966. Chairperson: Joanne L. Miller. Number of faculty: total—full-time 22; women—full-time 8; total—minority—full-time 3; women minority—full-time 2.

Programs and Degrees Offered:
Listed in the following order: Program area, degree type (T if terminal Master's), number awarded 7/11–6/12. Cognition PhD (Doctor of Philosophy) 3, Behavioral Neuroscience PhD (Doctor of Philosophy) 0, Social/Personality Psychology PhD (Doctor of Philosophy) 0, Perception PhD (Doctor of Philosophy) 0.

Student Applications/Admissions:
Student Applications
Cognition PhD (Doctor of Philosophy)—Applications 2012–2013, 26. Total applicants accepted 2012–2013, 2. Number full-time enrolled (new admits only) 2012–2013, 2. Number part-time enrolled (new admits only) 2012–2013, 0. Total enrolled 2012–2013 full-time, 8. Total enrolled 2012–2013 part-time, 0. Openings 2013–2014, 2. The median number of years required for completion of a degree in 2012–2013 were 5. The number of students enrolled full- and part-time who were dismissed or voluntarily withdrew from this program area in 2012–2013 were 2. *Behavioral Neuroscience PhD (Doctor of Philosophy)*—Applications 2012–2013, 41. Total applicants accepted 2012–2013, 1. Number full-time enrolled (new admits only) 2012–2013, 1. Number part-time enrolled (new admits only) 2012–2013, 0. Total enrolled 2012–2013 full-time, 4. Total enrolled 2012–2013 part-time, 0. Openings 2013–2014, 2. The number of students enrolled full- and part-time who were dismissed or voluntarily withdrew from this program area in 2012–2013 were 0. *Social/Personality Psychology PhD (Doctor of Philosophy)*—Applications 2012–2013, 113. Total applicants accepted 2012–2013, 5. Number full-time

enrolled (new admits only) 2012–2013, 4. Number part-time enrolled (new admits only) 2012–2013, 0. Total enrolled 2012–2013 full-time, 15. Total enrolled 2012–2013 part-time, 0. Openings 2013–2014, 2. The number of students enrolled full- and part-time who were dismissed or voluntarily withdrew from this program area in 2012–2013 were 0. *Perception PhD (Doctor of Philosophy)*—Applications 2012–2013, 13. Total applicants accepted 2012–2013, 0. Number full-time enrolled (new admits only) 2012–2013, 0. Number part-time enrolled (new admits only) 2012–2013, 0. Total enrolled 2012–2013 full-time, 4. Total enrolled 2012–2013 part-time, 0. The number of students enrolled full- and part-time who were dismissed or voluntarily withdrew from this program area in 2012–2013 were 0.

Scores: Entries appear in this order: required test or GPA, minimum score (if required), median score of students entering in 2012–2013. *Cognition PhD (Doctor of Philosophy):* GRE-V no minimum stated, GRE-Q no minimum stated; *Behavioral Neuroscience PhD (Doctor of Philosophy):* GRE-V no minimum stated, GRE-Q no minimum stated; *Social/Personality Psychology PhD (Doctor of Philosophy):* GRE-V no minimum stated, GRE-Q no minimum stated; *Perception PhD (Doctor of Philosophy):* GRE-V no minimum stated, GRE-Q no minimum stated.

Other Criteria: (importance of criteria rated low, medium, or high): GRE scores—high, research experience—high, work experience—low, GPA—high, letters of recommendation—high, interview—high, statement of goals and objectives—high, undergraduate major in psychology—low, specific undergraduate psychology courses taken—low. For additional information on admission requirements, go to http://www.northeastern.edu/cos/future-students/college-of-science-graduate-school/admissions/.

Student Characteristics: The following represents characteristics of students in 2012–2013 in all graduate psychology programs in the department: Female—full-time 18, part-time 0; Male—full-time 13, part-time 0; African American/Black—full-time 1, part-time 0; Hispanic/Latino(a)—full-time 0, part-time 0; Asian/Pacific Islander—full-time 6, part-time 0; American Indian/Alaska Native—full-time 0, part-time 0; Caucasian/White—full-time 24, part-time 0; Multi-ethnic—full-time 0, part-time 0; students subject to the Americans With Disabilities Act—full-time 0, part-time 0; Unknown ethnicity—full-time 0, part-time 0; International students who hold an F-1 or J-1 Visa—full-time 8, part-time 0.

Financial Information/Assistance:

Tuition for Full-Time Study: *Doctoral:* State residents: $1,175 per credit hour; Nonstate residents: $1,175 per credit hour. Tuition is subject to change. See the following website for updates and changes in tuition costs: http://www.northeastern.edu/financialaid/studentaccounts/tuition.html.

Financial Assistance:

First-Year Students: Teaching assistantships available for first year. Average amount paid per academic year: $27,900. Average number of hours worked per week: 20. Apply by January 1. Research assistantships available for first year. Average amount paid per academic year: $27,900. Average number of hours worked per week: 20. Apply by January 1.

Advanced Students: Teaching assistantships available for advanced students. Average amount paid per academic year:

$27,900. Average number of hours worked per week: 20. Apply by January 1. Research assistantships available for advanced students. Average amount paid per academic year: $27,900. Average number of hours worked per week: 20. Apply by January 1.

Additional Information: Of all students currently enrolled full time, 100% benefited from one or more of the listed financial assistance programs. Application and information available online at: http://www.northeastern.edu/cos/future-students/college-of-science-graduate-school/financial-awards/.

Housing and Day Care: No on-campus housing is available. On-campus day care facilities are available. See the following website for more information: http://www.northeastern.edu/hrm/benefits/work-life/index.html.

Employment of Department Graduates:

Master's Degree Graduates: Of those who graduated in the academic year 2011–2012, the following categories and numbers represent the postgraduate activities and employment of master's degree graduates: Enrolled in a postdoctoral residency/fellowship (n/a), employed in independent practice (n/a), total from the above (master's) (0).

Doctoral Degree Graduates: Of those who graduated in the academic year 2011–2012, the following categories and numbers represent the postgraduate activities and employment of doctoral degree graduates: Enrolled in a psychology doctoral program (n/a), enrolled in a postdoctoral residency/fellowship (2), employed in an academic position at a university (1), total from the above (doctoral) (3).

Additional Information:

Orientation, Objectives, and Emphasis of Department: The PhD program aims to train students to undertake basic, translational, and interdisciplinary research involving the following areas: behavioral neuroscience; perception; cognition; and social/personality. Students may expect to collaborate with faculty in conducting research in state-of-the-art laboratories. The doctoral program also provides opportunities to gain teaching experience. The program does not provide training in clinical/counseling psychology.

Special Facilities or Resources: The department has a wide range of research laboratories containing state-of-the-art facilities in the following main areas: behavioral neuroscience; perception; cognition; and social/personality. These facilities include an array of computer systems used for subject testing, data acquisition and analysis, computational modeling, and graphics, as well as numerous special-purpose systems, such as eye-trackers, histology facilities, multiple electrode EEG, small animal fMRI, and speech processing systems. In addition, laboratory resources outside the department are available to students through the collaborative network the department maintains with other institutions in the Boston/Cambridge area.

Information for Students With Physical Disabilities: See the following website for more information: http://www.northeastern.edu/drc/.

Application Information:

Application available online. URL of online application: http://www.northeastern.edu/graduate/prospective-students/admissions/. Students are admitted in the Fall, application deadline January 1. *Fee:* $50.

Salem State University

Psychology Department
352 Lafayette Street
Salem, MA 01970
Telephone: (978) 542-6354
Fax: (978) 542-6834
E-mail: patrice.miller@salemstate.edu
Web: http://www.salemstate.edu/academics/schools/2635.php

Department Information:

Chairperson: Patricia Markunas. Number of faculty: total— part-time 31; women—part-time 17; minority—part-time 2; women minority—part-time 1.

Programs and Degrees Offered:

Listed in the following order: Program area, degree type (T if terminal Master's), number awarded 7/11–6/12. Counseling and Psychological Services MA/MS (Master of Arts/Science) (T) 21, Industrial/Organizational Psychology MA/MS (Master of Arts/Science) (T) 5, Advanced Prof Certificate in Behavior Analysis Other 0.

Student Applications/Admissions:

Student Applications

Counseling and Psychological Services MA/MS (Master of Arts/Science)—Applications 2012–2013, 40. Total applicants accepted 2012–2013, 25. Total enrolled 2012–2013 full-time, 23. Total enrolled 2012–2013 part-time, 56. Openings 2013–2014, 35. The median number of years required for completion of a degree in 2012–2013 were 2. The number of students enrolled full- and part-time who were dismissed or voluntarily withdrew from this program area in 2012–2013 were 0. Industrial/Organizational Psychology MA/MS (Master of Arts/Science)—Applications 2012–2013, 17. Total applicants accepted 2012–2013, 14. Total enrolled 2012–2013 full-time, 3. Total enrolled 2012–2013 part-time, 23. Openings 2013–2014, 15. The median number of years required for completion of a degree in 2012–2013 were 2. The number of students enrolled full- and part-time who were dismissed or voluntarily withdrew from this program area in 2012–2013 were 0. Advanced Prof Certificate in Behavior Analysis Other—Applications 2012–2013, 5. Total applicants accepted 2012–2013, 4. Number full-time enrolled (new admits only) 2012–2013, 1. Number part-time enrolled (new admits only) 2012–2013, 3. Total enrolled 2012–2013 full-time, 1. Total enrolled 2012–2013 part-time, 3. Openings 2013–2014, 12. The median number of years required for completion of a degree in 2012–2013 was 1. The number of students enrolled full- and part-time who were dismissed or voluntarily withdrew from this program area in 2012–2013 were 0.

Scores: Entries appear in this order: required test or GPA, minimum score (if required), median score of students entering in 2012–2013. Counseling and Psychological Services MA/MS (Master of Arts/Science): GRE-V 450, GRE-Q 450, GRE-Analytical 4, overall undergraduate GPA 2.6, psychology GPA 2.7; Industrial/Organizational Psychology MA/MS (Master of Arts/Science): GRE-V 450, GRE-Q 450, GRE-Analytical 4, overall undergraduate GPA 2.6, psychology GPA 2.7; Advanced Prof Certificate in Behavior Analysis Other: overall undergraduate GPA 3.00.

Other Criteria: (importance of criteria rated low, medium, or high): GRE scores—high, research experience—medium, work experience—high, extracurricular activity—medium, clinically related public service—high, GPA—high, letters of recommendation—high, statement of goals and objectives—high, undergraduate major in psychology—medium, specific undergraduate psychology courses taken—high, Research experience is likely more heavily weighted in the Industrial/Organizational MS Program; clinically-related work experience or internships are more heavily weighted for the Counseling and Psychological Services MS Program. The Advanced Certificate in Behavior Analysis requires a Master's degree in a related field. For additional information on admission requirements, go to http://www.salemstate.edu/admissions/10887.php.

Student Characteristics: The following represents characteristics of students in 2012–2013 in all graduate psychology programs in the department: Female—full-time 21, part-time 63; Male—full-time 5, part-time 16; African American/Black—full-time 0, part-time 4; Hispanic/Latino(a)—full-time 0, part-time 5; Asian/Pacific Islander—full-time 0, part-time 1; American Indian/Alaska Native—full-time 0, part-time 0; Caucasian/White—full-time 26, part-time 69; Multi-ethnic—full-time 0, part-time 0; students subject to the Americans With Disabilities Act—full-time 0, part-time 0; Unknown ethnicity—full-time 0, part-time 0; International students who hold an F-1 or J-1 Visa—full-time 0, part-time 0.

Financial Information/Assistance:

Tuition for Full-Time Study: Master's: State residents: per academic year $7,560; Nonstate residents: per academic year $9,720. Tuition is subject to change. See the following website for updates and changes in tuition costs: http://www.salemstate.edu/admissions/tuition.php.

Financial Assistance:

First-Year Students: Research assistantships available for first year. Average amount paid per academic year: $2,880. Average number of hours worked per week: 10. Apply by March 1.

Advanced Students: Research assistantships available for advanced students. Average amount paid per academic year: $2,880. Average number of hours worked per week: 10. Apply by March 1.

Additional Information: Of all students currently enrolled full time, 15% benefited from one or more of the listed financial assistance programs. Application and information available online at: http://www.salemstate.edu/admissions/1363.php.

Internships/Practica: Master's Degree (MA/MS Counseling and Psychological Services): An internship experience, such as a final research project or "capstone" experience is required of graduates. Master's Degree (MA/MS Industrial/Organizational Psychology): An internship experience, such as a final research project or "capstone" experience is required of graduates. Students in the M.S. Program in Counseling and Psychological Services complete a 3 semester (700 hour-minimum) practicum and internship sequence in a community agency, hospital unit or other setting. Site choice is made jointly by student and faculty. Students in the Industrial/Organizational M.S. Program complete a one-semester internship at an organization that is chosen to best satisfy their training and career goals.

Housing and Day Care: No on-campus housing is available. On-campus day care facilities are available. See the following website for more information: http://www.salemstate.edu/3600.php.

Employment of Department Graduates:

Master's Degree Graduates: Of those who graduated in the academic year 2011–2012, the following categories and numbers represent the postgraduate activities and employment of master's degree graduates: Enrolled in a postdoctoral residency/fellowship (n/a), employed in independent practice (n/a), employed in a professional position in a school system (2), employed in business or industry (5), employed in a community mental health/counseling center (17), employed in a hospital/medical center (1), total from the above (master's) (25).

Doctoral Degree Graduates: Of those who graduated in the academic year 2011–2012, the following categories and numbers represent the postgraduate activities and employment of doctoral degree graduates: Enrolled in a psychology doctoral program (n/a), total from the above (doctoral) (0).

Additional Information:

Orientation, Objectives, and Emphasis of Department: We offer flexible and individualized programs of study for adults, many of whom are working part-time. Our programs offer an attractive combination of faculty who practice or work in the areas being taught and rigorously trained Psychology Department faculty.

Special Facilities or Resources: We have close and longstanding relationships with a large variety of counseling sites, and for profit and non-profit organizations, particularly in the surrounding communities on the North Shore of Boston. This is of great benefit to both programs.

Information for Students With Physical Disabilities: See the following website for more information: http://www.salemstate.edu/3719.php.

Application Information:

Application available online. URL of online application: http://www.salemstate.edu/admissions/10814.php. Students are admitted in the Fall, application deadline May 1; Spring, application deadline October 1; Summer, application deadline February 1. *Fee:* $50.

Suffolk University

Department of Psychology
College of Arts and Sciences
41 Temple Street
Boston, MA 02114
Telephone: (617) 573-8293
Fax: (617) 367-2924
E-mail: *phd@suffolk.edu*
Web: *http://www.suffolk.edu/psychology*

Department Information:

1968. Department Chairperson: Gary Fireman. Number of faculty: total—full-time 17, part-time 2; women—full-time 9, part-time 5; total—minority—full-time 3; women minority—full-time 3.

Programs and Degrees Offered:

Listed in the following order: Program area, degree type (T if terminal Master's), number awarded 7/11–6/12. Clinical Psychology PhD (Doctor of Philosophy) 12, Clinical Psychology Respecialization Respecialization Diploma 0, Mental Health Counseling MA/MS (Master of Arts/Science) (T), School Counseling MA/MS (Master of Arts/Science) (T) 17.

APA Accreditation: Clinical PhD (Doctor of Philosophy). Student Outcome Data Website: http://www2.suffolk.edu/college/10531.html.

Student Applications/Admissions:

Student Applications

Clinical Psychology PhD (Doctor of Philosophy)—Applications 2012–2013, 340. Total applicants accepted 2012–2013, 15. Number full-time enrolled (new admits only) 2012–2013, 8. Number part-time enrolled (new admits only) 2012–2013, 0. Total enrolled 2012–2013 full-time, 69. Total enrolled 2012–2013 part-time, 0. Openings 2013–2014, 10. The median number of years required for completion of a degree in 2012–2013 were 8. The number of students enrolled full- and part-time who were dismissed or voluntarily withdrew from this program area in 2012–2013 were 0. *Clinical Psychology Respecialization Respecialization Diploma*—Applications 2012–2013, 6. Total applicants accepted 2012–2013, 1. Number full-time enrolled (new admits only) 2012–2013, 1. Number part-time enrolled (new admits only) 2012–2013, 0. Total enrolled 2012–2013 full-time, 6. Total enrolled 2012–2013 part-time, 0. Openings 2013–2014, 1. The number of students enrolled full- and part-time who were dismissed or voluntarily withdrew from this program area in 2012–2013 were 0. *Mental Health Counseling MA/MS (Master of Arts/Science)*—Number full-time enrolled (new admits only) 2012–2013, 11. Number part-time enrolled (new admits only) 2012–2013, 2. *School Counseling MA/MS (Master of Arts/Science)*—Applications 2012–2013, 42. Total applicants accepted 2012–2013, 27. Number full-time enrolled (new admits only) 2012–2013, 8. Number part-time enrolled (new admits only) 2012–2013, 4. Openings 2013–2014, 17. The median number of years required for completion of a degree in 2012–2013 were 2. The number of students enrolled full- and part-time who were dismissed or voluntarily withdrew from this program area in 2012–2013 were 0.

Scores: Entries appear in this order: required test or GPA, minimum score (if required), median score of students entering in 2012–2013. *Clinical Psychology PhD (Doctor of Philosophy):* GRE-V no minimum stated, 158, GRE-Q no minimum stated, 152, GRE-Analytical no minimum stated, 4.8, overall undergraduate GPA no minimum stated, 3.7.

Other Criteria: (importance of criteria rated low, medium, or high): GRE scores—medium, research experience—high, work experience—medium, extracurricular activity—low, clinically related public service—medium, GPA—high, letters of recommendation—high, interview—high, statement of goals and objectives—high, research mentor match—high, undergraduate major in psychology—high, specific undergraduate psychology courses taken—medium. For additional information on admission requirements, go to http://www2.suffolk.edu/college/12093.html.

Student Characteristics: The following represents characteristics of students in 2012–2013 in all graduate psychology programs in the department: Female—full-time 66, part-time 0; Male—full-

time 9, part-time 0; African American/Black—full-time 4, part-time 0; Hispanic/Latino(a)—full-time 8, part-time 0; Asian/Pacific Islander—full-time 6, part-time 0; American Indian/Alaska Native—full-time 0, part-time 0; Caucasian/White—full-time 48, part-time 0; Multi-ethnic—full-time 0, part-time 0; students subject to the Americans With Disabilities Act—full-time 0, part-time 1; Unknown ethnicity—full-time 9, part-time 0; International students who hold an F-1 or J-1 Visa—full-time 2, part-time 0.

Financial Information/Assistance:

Tuition for Full-Time Study: *Doctoral:* State residents: per academic year $32,570, $1,356 per credit hour; Nonstate residents: per academic year $32,570, $1,356 per credit hour. Tuition is subject to change. See the following website for updates and changes in tuition costs: http://www2.suffolk.edu/college/41230.html.

Financial Assistance:

First-Year Students: Research assistantships available for first year. Average amount paid per academic year: $4,800. Average number of hours worked per week: 10. Apply by April 1. Fellowships and scholarships available for first year. Average amount paid per academic year: $22,608. Average number of hours worked per week: 15. Apply by April 1.

Advanced Students: Research assistantships available for advanced students. Average amount paid per academic year: $4,800. Average number of hours worked per week: 10. Apply by April 1. Fellowships and scholarships available for advanced students. Average amount paid per academic year: $23,803. Average number of hours worked per week: 15. Apply by April 1.

Additional Information: Of all students currently enrolled full time, 75% benefited from one or more of the listed financial assistance programs. Application and information available online at: http://www2.suffolk.edu/college/24767.html.

Internships/Practica: Doctoral Degree (PhD Clinical Psychology): For those doctoral students for whom a professional psychology internship was required in this program prior to graduation, (20) students applied for an internship in 2011–2012, with (20) students obtaining an internship. Of those students who obtained an internship, (20) were paid internships. Of those students who obtained an internship, (19) students placed in APA/CPA accredited internships, (1) students placed in internships not APA/CPA accredited, but listed with the Association of Psychology Postdoctoral and Internship Programs (APPIC), (0) students placed in internships conforming to guidelines of the Council of Directors of School Psychology Programs (CDSPP), (0) students placed in internships that were not APA/CPA accredited, APPIC or CDSPP listed. Master's Degree (MA/MS Mental Health Counseling): An internship experience, such as a final research project or "capstone" experience is required of graduates. Master's Degree (MA/MS School Counseling): An internship experience, such as a final research project or "capstone" experience is required of graduates. The student's individualized clinical training program, which begins the fall of their second year under the supervision of doctoral level psychologists, is carefully overseen by the Coordinator and Director of Clinical Training. All students are required to complete at least two years of practicum training, though most elect to do an optional third year. Students are placed with partner sites (medical centers, psychiatric hospitals, community mental health clinics, university counseling centers, and school psychol-

ogy centers) in the greater Boston area committed to providing quality supervision and training consistent with our scientist–practitioner model. Students concurrently take two year-long practicum courses which serve to: 1) integrate the external practicum and didactic experience, and 2) provide knowledge regarding professional standards and ethics, diversity, treatment and assessment processes and outcomes, consultation and supervision. Students who opt to pursue an additional year of clinical training are supported in their efforts to obtain a training experience consistent with their emerging areas of interest. Students receive a total of 3-5 hours a week, on average, of individual and group supervision during each of their three years of training. A limited number of pre-practicum training experiences are also available to students during their first year in the program.

Housing and Day Care: No on-campus housing is available. No on-campus day care facilities are available.

Employment of Department Graduates:

Master's Degree Graduates: Of those who graduated in the academic year 2011–2012, the following categories and numbers represent the postgraduate activities and employment of master's degree graduates: Enrolled in a postdoctoral residency/fellowship (n/a), employed in independent practice (n/a), employed in other positions at a higher education institution (2), employed in a professional position in a school system (9), employed in business or industry (6), total from the above (master's) (17).

Doctoral Degree Graduates: Of those who graduated in the academic year 2011–2012, the following categories and numbers represent the postgraduate activities and employment of doctoral degree graduates: Enrolled in a psychology doctoral program (n/a), enrolled in a postdoctoral residency/fellowship (3), employed in independent practice (2), employed in an academic position at a 2-year/4-year college (1), employed in business or industry (1), employed in a hospital/medical center (2), other employment position (1), do not know (2), total from the above (doctoral) (12).

Additional Information:

Orientation, Objectives, and Emphasis of Department: Suffolk University's PhD program in clinical psychology is based on the philosophy that clinical practice should be grounded in scientific knowledge and that scientific research should be informed by and relevant to clinical practice. The program's orientation is that of understanding the processes underlying adaptation and maladaptation within a cultural and biopsychosocial frame, thus throughout all aspects of training the program encourages an awareness of and respect for diversity. Our faculty approach intervention and psychotherapy from a variety of perspectives including developmental, psychodynamic, systemic, behavioral, cognitive-behavioral, humanistic and integrative/eclectic. Our intent is to enable students to take a creative, empirical, and ethical approach to diagnostic and therapeutic problems among diverse populations; to critically evaluate and contribute to the evolving body of scholarly literature in the science and practice of psychology; and to integrate the clinical, theoretical, and scientific foundations of psychology. Our program adheres to a generalist model of clinical training, although we also offer concentrated experiences in neuropsychology and child clinical psychology. Across all aspects of our training program we strive to train our students to be knowledgeable about and able to conduct culturally competent clinical practice and research. Implications of this framework include the recognition that: (a) knowledge of a breadth of psychological subdisciplines such as neuropsychology, developmental psychology, cultural psychology, is required to effectively work within the clinical developmental model; (b) professional psychologists can complement the roles of natural contexts such as families, relationships, schools, and workplaces in fostering development; and (c) psychological pain and conflict can be understood as indicative of a continuum of ongoing life span transformational processes, which include what is typically labeled normal development as well as the development or manifestation of psychopathology. Thus, the program emphasizes that clinical problems are best understood in the context of knowledge about normal and optimal development over the lifespan. The program strives to develop student competencies necessary for successfully working in a range of clinical, educational, research, organizational, and public policy settings. Throughout core content and applied areas of training, the program encourages awareness of and respect for diversity of culture, language, national origin, race, gender, age, disability, religious beliefs, sexual orientation, lifestyle, and other individual differences. The program combines a strong theoretical and research background (in both quantitative and qualitative methodologies) with preparation to deliver high-quality psychological services to children, adolescents, and adults.

Special Facilities or Resources: The department has a variety of laboratory spaces available for general use by faculty and doctoral students, and core graduate faculty all have dedicated laboratory space with software/hardware accessed by their graduate student teams. Special equipment includes psychophysiological equipment (skin conductance), sleep study equipment, dedicated work stations with brain image analysis software (anatomic and functional images acquired off-site), SPSS software licensed for AMOS (complex statistical modeling software), one-way mirrors for observation of structured clinical interviews and treatment sessions, and video recording equipment. A portion of research occurs off-site with our research collaborators in the clinical, medical and scholastic institutions of the Boston area. There are two computer labs for graduate student use within the department in addition to larger computer labs throughout the university; all provide access to SPSS, the Internet, and the extensive Sawyer Library electronic databases. Our test library has copies of 231 current psychological tests and measures. Graduate students receive interlibrary loan and online document delivery privileges and have access to most of the academic libraries in the Boston area.

Information for Students With Physical Disabilities: See the following website for more information: http://www.suffolk.edu/campuslife/1316.php.

Application Information:
Send to Office of Graduate Admissions, Suffolk University, 8 Ashburton Place, Boston, MA 02108. Application available online. URL of online application: https://app.applyyourself.com/?id=suffolk-g. Students are admitted in the Fall, application deadline December 1; Programs have rolling admissions. The M.S. programs in School Counseling and Mental Health Counseling have rolling admissions. The PhD program in Clinical Psychology has a single yearly admissions cycle with applications due December 1st. *Fee:* $50.

Tufts University
Department of Education; School Psychology Program
Graduate School of Arts and Sciences
Paige Hall
Medford, MA 02155
Telephone: (617) 627-2390
Fax: (617) 627-3901
E-mail: *steven.luz-alterman@tufts.edu*
Web: *http://ase.tufts.edu/education/programs/schoolPsych/*

Department Information:
1910. Co-Director, School Psychology Program: Steven Luz-Alterman. Number of faculty: total—full-time 4, part-time 10; women—full-time 2, part-time 6; total—minority—full-time 1, part-time 2; women minority—part-time 1.

Programs and Degrees Offered:
Listed in the following order: Program area, degree type (T if terminal Master's), number awarded 7/11–6/12. School Psychology EdS (School Psychology) 16.

Student Applications/Admissions:
Student Applications
School Psychology EdS (School Psychology)—Applications 2012–2013, 75. Total applicants accepted 2012–2013, 30. Number full-time enrolled (new admits only) 2012–2013, 16. Number part-time enrolled (new admits only) 2012–2013, 0. Total enrolled 2012–2013 full-time, 55. Total enrolled 2012–2013 part-time, 0. Openings 2013–2014, 16. The median number of years required for completion of a degree in 2012–2013 were 3. The number of students enrolled full- and part-time who were dismissed or voluntarily withdrew from this program area in 2012–2013 were 0.

Scores: Entries appear in this order: required test or GPA, minimum score (if required), median score of students entering in 2012–2013. *School Psychology EdS (School Psychology):* GRE-V 150, GRE-Q 150, GRE-Analytical 4.5, overall undergraduate GPA 3.0.

Other Criteria: (importance of criteria rated low, medium, or high): GRE scores—low, research experience—medium, work experience—high, extracurricular activity—medium, clinically related public service—high, GPA—medium, letters of recommendation—high, interview—high, statement of goals and objectives—high, multicultural interest—high, undergraduate major in psychology—low, specific undergraduate psychology courses taken—medium. For additional information on admission requirements, go to http://gradstudy.tufts.edu/admissions/howtoapply.htm.

Student Characteristics: The following represents characteristics of students in 2012–2013 in all graduate psychology programs in the department: Female—full-time 50, part-time 0; Male—full-time 5, part-time 0; African American/Black—full-time 1, part-time 0; Hispanic/Latino(a)—full-time 3, part-time 0; Asian/Pacific Islander—full-time 5, part-time 0; American Indian/Alaska Native—full-time 1, part-time 0; Caucasian/White—full-time 44, part-time 0; Multi-ethnic—full-time 1, part-time 0; students subject to the Americans With Disabilities Act—full-time 0, part-time 0; Unknown ethnicity—full-time 0, part-time 0; Interna-

tional students who hold an F-1 or J-1 Visa—full-time 0, part-time 0.

Financial Information/Assistance:

Tuition for Full-Time Study: *Master's:* State residents: per academic year $36,428; Nonstate residents: per academic year $36,428. See the following website for updates and changes in tuition costs: http://gradstudy.tufts.edu/admissions/expensesfinaid/.

Financial Assistance:

First-Year Students: Teaching assistantships available for first year. Average amount paid per academic year: $1,500. Average number of hours worked per week: 4. Apply by September 1. Research assistantships available for first year. Average amount paid per academic year: $1,500. Average number of hours worked per week: 4. Apply by September 1. Fellowships and scholarships available for first year. Average amount paid per academic year: $14,600. Apply by January 15.

Advanced Students: Teaching assistantships available for advanced students. Average amount paid per academic year: $1,500. Average number of hours worked per week: 4. Apply by September 1. Research assistantships available for advanced students. Average amount paid per academic year: $1,500. Average number of hours worked per week: 4. Apply by September 1. Fellowships and scholarships available for advanced students. Average amount paid per academic year: $14,600. Apply by April 15.

Additional Information: Of all students currently enrolled full time, 90% benefited from one or more of the listed financial assistance programs. Application and information available online at: http://ase.tufts.edu/education/admissions/.

Internships/Practica: Students complete a school-based pre-practicum experience of 150 hours during their first year and a school-based practicum of 600 hours during their second year. Students complete a 1200-hour internship during their third year. This may be completed through 600 hours in a school setting and 600 hours in a clinical setting, or all 1200 hours in a school setting. Internship sites must be approved by the program faculty and may be pursued anywhere in the United States, or abroad if the site is approved by the faculty and appropriate supervision is provided.

Housing and Day Care: On-campus housing is available. See the following website for more information: http://ase.tufts.edu/reslife/housing/graduate.asp. On-campus day care facilities are available. See the following website for more information: http://ase.tufts.edu/tedcc/.

Employment of Department Graduates:

Master's Degree Graduates: Of those who graduated in the academic year 2011–2012, the following categories and numbers represent the postgraduate activities and employment of master's degree graduates: Enrolled in a postdoctoral residency/fellowship (n/a), employed in independent practice (n/a), employed in a professional position in a school system (16), total from the above (master's) (16).

Doctoral Degree Graduates: Of those who graduated in the academic year 2011–2012, the following categories and numbers represent the postgraduate activities and employment of doctoral degree graduates: Enrolled in a psychology doctoral program (n/a), total from the above (doctoral) (0).

Additional Information:

Orientation, Objectives, and Emphasis of Department: Our mission is to prepare highly effective, culturally competent problem solvers ready to serve all children in general public education and children with disabilities. We are committed to preparing professional school psychologists who will work effectively with children from racially, ethnically, and linguistically diverse backgrounds in a variety of settings. These include urban, urban-rim, suburban, and rural communities. Providing high quality services in urban and urban-rim schools is a program priority. We seek a diverse cohort of students who think critically and are prepared to engage issues of social justice and cultural and linguistic diversity as they are reproduced in our schools.

Special Facilities or Resources: Tufts offers the resources of a major research university with the campus atmosphere of a small liberal arts college. Several courses of interest are offered through the Eliot-Pearson Department of Child Development. Tufts students may also cross-register for courses at several other Boston area universities at no additional charge through a consortium arrangement. We have a variety of urban, urban rim, and suburban field sites, including affiliations with Children's Hospital and the Step UP Program in Boston. Limited internship stipends are available for practice in urban sites.

Information for Students With Physical Disabilities: See the following website for more information: http://uss.tufts.edu/arc/disability/.

Application Information:

Send to Office of Graduate and Professional Studies, Tufts University, Ballou Hall, Medford, MA 02155. Application available online. URL of online application: http://gradstudy.tufts.edu/admissions/howtoapply.htm. Students are admitted in the Fall, application deadline January 15. *Fee:* $75.

Tufts University

Department of Psychology
Psychology Building, 490 Boston Avenue
Medford, MA 02155
Telephone: (617) 627-3523
Fax: (617) 627-3181
E-mail: *cynthia.goddard@tufts.edu*
Web: *http://ase.tufts.edu/psychology/*

Department Information:

Chairperson: Lisa Shin. Number of faculty: total—full-time 18; women—full-time 8; total—minority—full-time 3; women minority—full-time 1.

Programs and Degrees Offered:

Listed in the following order: Program area, degree type (T if terminal Master's), number awarded 7/11–6/12. General Experimental Psychology PhD (Doctor of Philosophy) 8.

Student Applications/Admissions:

Student Applications

General Experimental Psychology PhD (Doctor of Philosophy)— Applications 2012–2013, 155. Total applicants accepted

2012–2013, 12. Number full-time enrolled (new admits only) 2012–2013, 8. Total enrolled 2012–2013 full-time, 41. Openings 2013–2014, 8. The median number of years required for completion of a degree in 2012–2013 were 6. The number of students enrolled full- and part-time who were dismissed or voluntarily withdrew from this program area in 2012–2013 were 1.

Scores: Entries appear in this order: required test or GPA, minimum score (if required), median score of students entering in 2012–2013. *General Experimental Psychology PhD (Doctor of Philosophy):* GRE-V no minimum stated, GRE-Q no minimum stated, overall undergraduate GPA no minimum stated, last 2 years GPA no minimum stated.

Other Criteria: (importance of criteria rated low, medium, or high): GRE scores—medium, research experience—high, work experience—medium, extracurricular activity—low, GPA—medium, letters of recommendation—medium, interview—medium, statement of goals and objectives—high, research fit—high, undergraduate major in psychology—medium, specific undergraduate psychology courses taken—medium. For additional information on admission requirements, go to http://ase.tufts.edu/psychology/gradProspectives.htm.

Student Characteristics: The following represents characteristics of students in 2012–2013 in all graduate psychology programs in the department: Female—full-time 23, part-time 0; Male—full-time 18, part-time 0; African American/Black—full-time 2, part-time 0; Hispanic/Latino(a)—full-time 2, part-time 0; Asian/Pacific Islander—full-time 7, part-time 0; American Indian/Alaska Native—full-time 0, part-time 0; Caucasian/White—full-time 27, part-time 0; Multi-ethnic—full-time 3, part-time 0; students subject to the Americans With Disabilities Act—full-time 0, part-time 0; Unknown ethnicity—full-time 0, part-time 0; International students who hold an F-1 or J-1 Visa—full-time 8, part-time 0.

Financial Information/Assistance:

Tuition for Full-Time Study: *Doctoral:* State residents: per academic year $25,714; Nonstate residents: per academic year $25,714. See the following website for updates and changes in tuition costs: http://gradstudy.tufts.edu/admissions/expensesfinaid/tuitionArtsSciences.htm.

Financial Assistance:

First-Year Students: Teaching assistantships available for first year. Average amount paid per academic year: $20,900. Average number of hours worked per week: 20. Research assistantships available for first year. Average amount paid per academic year: $20,900. Average number of hours worked per week: 20.

Advanced Students: Teaching assistantships available for advanced students. Average amount paid per academic year: $20,900. Average number of hours worked per week: 20. Research assistantships available for advanced students. Average amount paid per academic year: $20,900. Average number of hours worked per week: 20.

Additional Information: Of all students currently enrolled full time, 100% benefited from one or more of the listed financial assistance programs. Application and information available online at: http://gradstudy.tufts.edu/admissions/expensesFinAid/.

Housing and Day Care: No on-campus housing is available. On-campus day care facilities are available. See the following website

for more information: http://ase.tufts.edu/tedcc/ AND http://ase.tufts.edu/epcs/.

Employment of Department Graduates:

Master's Degree Graduates: Of those who graduated in the academic year 2011–2012, the following categories and numbers represent the postgraduate activities and employment of master's degree graduates: Enrolled in a postdoctoral residency/fellowship (n/a), employed in independent practice (n/a), total from the above (master's) (0).

Doctoral Degree Graduates: Of those who graduated in the academic year 2011–2012, the following categories and numbers represent the postgraduate activities and employment of doctoral degree graduates: Enrolled in a psychology doctoral program (n/a), enrolled in a postdoctoral residency/fellowship (4), employed in an academic position at a university (2), employed in an academic position at a 2-year/4-year college (1), employed in other positions at a higher education institution (1), still seeking employment (1), total from the above (doctoral) (9).

Additional Information:

Orientation, Objectives, and Emphasis of Department: The Department of Psychology offers a graduate program in experimental psychology, with specializations in cognition, neuroscience, psychopathology, developmental, and social psychology. The program is designed to produce broadly trained graduates who are prepared for careers in teaching, research, or applied psychology. The department does not offer clinical training. Accepted applicants generally possess a substantial college background in psychology, including familiarity with fundamental statistical concepts and research design. The university is a PhD track program although completion of an MS is required as an integral part of the program. Students who already possess a master's degree may be admitted to the PhD program if a sufficient number of credits are acceptable for transfer and a thesis has been done. Areas of faculty research include infant perception, memory processes, animal cognition and learning, neural and hormonal control of animal sexual behavior, psychopharmacology, event-related brain potentials, neuropsychology of language processes, nutrition and behavior, experimental psychopathology, emotion, human factors, decision making, spatial cognition, psychology and law, and the social psychology of prejudicial attitudes. All graduate students participate in supervised research and/or teaching activities each semester. The department provides laboratory space and equipment for many kinds of research, and facilities are available for the behavioral and physiological study of humans and experimental animals. The Cognitive Science PhD program emphasizes interdisciplinary training, emphasizing competencies in experimental design, computation, statistics, and topic areas related to the students research interests.

Special Facilities or Resources: The Department has relatively new research facilities for both human and animal research in areas of cognition, cognitive neuroscience, biopsychology, neuroscience, and social psychology.

Information for Students With Physical Disabilities: See the following website for more information: http://uss.tufts.edu/arc/disability/.

Application Information:

Application available online. URL of online application: http://gradstudy.tufts.edu/admissions/howtoapply.htm. Students are admitted in the Fall, application deadline December 15. *Fee:* $75.

Tufts University (2012 data)

Eliot-Pearson Department of Child Development
105 College Avenue
Medford, MA 02155
Telephone: (617) 627-3355
Fax: (617) 627-3503
E-mail: *jayanthi.mistry@tufts.edu*
Web: *http://ase.tufts.edu/epcd/*

Department Information:

1964. Chairperson: Jayanthi Mistry. Number of faculty: total—full-time 16, part-time 14; women—full-time 13, part-time 12; total—minority—full-time 3, part-time 1; women minority—full-time 2.

Programs and Degrees Offered:

Listed in the following order: Program area, degree type (T if terminal Master's), number awarded 7/11–6/12. Child Development (Thesis) MA/MS (Master of Arts/Science) (T) 7, Child Development MA/MS (Master of Arts/Science) (T) 36, Child Development PhD (Doctor of Philosophy) 8.

Student Applications/Admissions:

Student Applications

Child Development (Thesis) MA/MS (Master of Arts/Science)—Applications 2012–2013, 0. Total applicants accepted 2012–2013, 0. Number full-time enrolled (new admits only) 2012–2013, 0. Number part-time enrolled (new admits only) 2012–2013, 0. Total enrolled 2012–2013 full-time, 5. Total enrolled 2012–2013 part-time, 1. Openings 2013–2014, 2. The median number of years required for completion of a degree in 2012–2013 were 2. The number of students enrolled full- and part-time who were dismissed or voluntarily withdrew from this program area in 2012–2013 were 0. *Child Development MA/MS (Master of Arts/Science)*—Applications 2012–2013, 82. Total applicants accepted 2012–2013, 45. Number full-time enrolled (new admits only) 2012–2013, 27. Number part-time enrolled (new admits only) 2012–2013, 3. Total enrolled 2012–2013 full-time, 71. Total enrolled 2012–2013 part-time, 11. Openings 2013–2014, 45. The median number of years required for completion of a degree in 2012–2013 were 2. The number of students enrolled full- and part-time who were dismissed or voluntarily withdrew from this program area in 2012–2013 were 0. *Child Development PhD (Doctor of Philosophy)*—Applications 2012–2013, 49. Total applicants accepted 2012–2013, 13. Number full-time enrolled (new admits only) 2012–2013, 5. Number part-time enrolled (new admits only) 2012–2013, 0. Total enrolled 2012–2013 full-time, 37. Total enrolled 2012–2013 part-time, 0. Openings 2013–2014, 4. The median number of years required for completion of a degree in 2012–2013 were 5. The number of students enrolled full- and part-time who were dismissed or voluntarily withdrew from this program area in 2012–2013 were 1.

Scores: Entries appear in this order: required test or GPA, minimum score (if required), median score of students entering in 2012–2013. *Child Development (Thesis) MA/MS (Master of Arts/Science)*: GRE-V no minimum stated, GRE-Q no minimum stated, overall undergraduate GPA no minimum stated, last 2 years GPA no minimum stated; *Child Development MA/MS (Master of Arts/Science)*: GRE-V no minimum stated, GRE-Q no minimum stated, overall undergraduate GPA no minimum stated, last 2 years GPA no minimum stated; *Child Development PhD (Doctor of Philosophy)*: GRE-V no minimum stated, GRE-Q no minimum stated, overall undergraduate GPA no minimum stated, last 2 years GPA no minimum stated.

Other Criteria: (importance of criteria rated low, medium, or high): GRE scores—medium, research experience—low, work experience—high, extracurricular activity—low, clinically related public service—low, GPA—high, letters of recommendation—high, statement of goals and objectives—medium, undergraduate major in psychology—low, specific undergraduate psychology courses taken—low, The Criteria filled in above is for consideration to our MA programs. The Criteria for application to our PhD program is as follows: GRE: high Research Exp: high Work Exp: high Extracurricular: low Clinically Related Public Serv: low GPA: high Letters of Rec: high Interview: low Statement of Goals/Obj: high UG major psych: medium Spec UG courses: medium.

Student Characteristics: The following represents characteristics of students in 2012–2013 in all graduate psychology programs in the department: Female—full-time 103, part-time 12; Male—full-time 10, part-time 0; African American/Black—full-time 9, part-time 0; Hispanic/Latino(a)—full-time 7, part-time 1; Asian/Pacific Islander—full-time 14, part-time 0; American Indian/Alaska Native—full-time 0, part-time 0; Caucasian/White—full-time 68, part-time 10; Multi-ethnic—full-time 0, part-time 0; students subject to the Americans With Disabilities Act—full-time 0, part-time 0; Unknown ethnicity—full-time 2, part-time 1; International students who hold an F-1 or J-1 Visa—full-time 13, part-time 0.

Financial Information/Assistance:

Tuition for Full-Time Study: *Master's:* State residents: per academic year $42,856; Nonstate residents: per academic year $42,856. *Doctoral:* State residents: per academic year $25,714; Nonstate residents: per academic year $25,714. Tuition is subject to change. Tuition costs vary by program. See the following website for updates and changes in tuition costs: http://gradstudy.tufts.edu/admissions/expensesfinaid/tuitionartssciences.htm.

Financial Assistance:

First-Year Students: Teaching assistantships available for first year. Average amount paid per academic year: $18,387. Average number of hours worked per week: 20. Research assistantships available for first year. Average amount paid per academic year: $18,387. Average number of hours worked per week: 20. Fellowships and scholarships available for first year.

Advanced Students: Teaching assistantships available for advanced students. Average amount paid per academic year: $18,387. Average number of hours worked per week: 20. Research assistantships available for advanced students. Average amount paid per academic year: $18,387. Average number of hours worked per week: 20. Fellowships and scholarships available for advanced students.

Additional Information: Of all students currently enrolled full time, 70% benefited from one or more of the listed financial assistance programs. Application and information available online at: http://ase.tufts.edu/epcd/programsGradFinAid.asp.

Internships/Practica: Master's Degree (MA/MS Child Development (Thesis)): An internship experience, such as a final research project or "capstone" experience is required of graduates. Master's Degree (MA/MS Child Development): An internship experience, such as a final research project or "capstone" experience is required of graduates. MA students engage in semester-long internship in applied settings such as hospitals, after-school centers, arts programs, policy centers, museums. PhD students engage in full-time 1-semester or half time full-year applied and research internships in varied settings.

Housing and Day Care: On-campus housing is available. On-campus day care facilities are available.

Additional Information:

Orientation, Objectives, and Emphasis of Department: The department prepares students for a variety of careers that have, as their common prerequisite, a comprehensive understanding of children and their development. Students receive a foundation in psychological theory and research concerning the social, emotional, intellectual, linguistic, and physiological growth of children. Course material is complemented with progressively more involved practica encompassing observations and work with children in a wide variety of applied and research settings. The major aim of the program is to train people who can translate their knowledge about development into effective strategies for working with and on behalf of children. We believe that a background in child development is the best possible preparation for teaching and administrative careers in schools, children's advocacy and mental health agencies, hospitals, after-school programs, daycare centers, arts programs, museums, the media, government agencies concerned with the rights and welfare of children, and related fields. There is considerable room for flexibility in the program. Also, students may chose from a rich variety of elective courses that touch upon such diverse topics as child advocacy, the arts and children's development, children and technology, arts and social activism, and children's literature.

Special Facilities or Resources: The department is housed in a complex of buildings on the Medford campus. The main building contains faculty and staff offices, class meeting rooms, and a library. Another building houses the Eliot-Pearson Children's School, which serves normal and special-needs children aged 2 to 6. The school has observation booths for student use. The department is also associated with the Tufts Educational Day Care Center. Students may work, as well as observe, in all of these settings. Both facilities are integrated into faculty research and research training for graduate students.

Application Information:

Send to Office of Graduate Studies Tufts University, Ballou Hall, Medford, MA 02155. Application available online. URL of online application: https://apply.embark.com/Grad/Tufts/grad/. Students are admitted in the Fall, application deadline December 15. *Fee:* $75. The application fee is waived only for current Tufts undergraduates and graduate students, students in Tufts certificate programs, Project 1000 applicants, and IRT and McNair Scholars. No other fee waivers are considered.

Central Michigan University
Department of Psychology
Humanities and Social and Behavioral Sciences
Sloan Hall
Mt. Pleasant, MI 48859
Telephone: (989) 774-3001
Fax: (989) 774-2553
E-mail: hough1ba@cmich.edu
Web: http://www.chsbs.cmich.edu/psychology

Department Information:
1965. Chairperson: Hajime Otani. Number of faculty: total—full-time 39, part-time 5; women—full-time 13, part-time 2; total—minority—full-time 6; women minority—full-time 3.

Programs and Degrees Offered:
Listed in the following order: Program area, degree type (T if terminal Master's), number awarded 7/11–6/12. Clinical Psychology PhD (Doctor of Philosophy) 8, Experimental Psychology PhD (Doctor of Philosophy) 4, General Psychology MA/MS (Master of Arts/Science) (T) 3, School Psychology PhD (Doctor of Philosophy) 5, Industrial/Organizational Psychology MA/MS (Master of Arts/Science) (T) 5, Industrial/Organizational Psychology PhD (Doctor of Philosophy) 5, Specialist in School Psychology Other 3.

APA Accreditation: Clinical PhD (Doctor of Philosophy). School PhD (Doctor of Philosophy).

Student Applications/Admissions:
Student Applications
Clinical Psychology PhD (Doctor of Philosophy)—Applications 2012–2013, 150. Total applicants accepted 2012–2013, 6. Number full-time enrolled (new admits only) 2012–2013, 6. Total enrolled 2012–2013 full-time, 37. Total enrolled 2012–2013 part-time, 0. Openings 2013–2014, 5. The median number of years required for completion of a degree in 2012–2013 were 5. The number of students enrolled full- and part-time who were dismissed or voluntarily withdrew from this program area in 2012–2013 were 0. Experimental Psychology PhD (Doctor of Philosophy)—Applications 2012–2013, 20. Total applicants accepted 2012–2013, 5. Number full-time enrolled (new admits only) 2012–2013, 5. Total enrolled 2012–2013 full-time, 18. Total enrolled 2012–2013 part-time, 0. Openings 2013–2014, 3. The median number of years required for completion of a degree in 2012–2013 were 6. The number of students enrolled full- and part-time who were dismissed or voluntarily withdrew from this program area in 2012–2013 were 1. General Psychology MA/MS (Master of Arts/Science)—Applications 2012–2013, 11. Total applicants accepted 2012–2013, 2. Number full-time enrolled (new admits only) 2012–2013, 2. Total enrolled 2012–2013 full-time, 18. Total enrolled 2012–2013 part-time, 0. Openings 2013–2014, 2. The median number of years required for completion of a degree in 2012–2013 were 3. The number of students enrolled full- and part-time who were dismissed or voluntarily withdrew from this program area in 2012–2013 were 1. School Psychology PhD (Doctor of Philosophy)—Applications 2012–2013, 22. Total applicants accepted 2012–2013, 9. Number full-time enrolled (new admits only) 2012–2013, 2. Total enrolled 2012–2013 full-time, 20. Openings 2013–2014, 3. The median number of years required for completion of a degree in 2012–2013 were 5. Industrial/Organizational Psychology MA/MS (Master of Arts/Science)—Applications 2012–2013, 25. Total applicants accepted 2012–2013, 2. Number full-time enrolled (new admits only) 2012–2013, 2. Total enrolled 2012–2013 full-time, 4. Openings 2013–2014, 1. The median number of years required for completion of a degree in 2012–2013 were 4. The number of students enrolled full- and part-time who were dismissed or voluntarily withdrew from this program area in 2012–2013 were 0. Industrial/Organizational Psychology PhD (Doctor of Philosophy)—Applications 2012–2013, 34. Total applicants accepted 2012–2013, 5. Number full-time enrolled (new admits only) 2012–2013, 5. Total enrolled 2012–2013 full-time, 37. Openings 2013–2014, 3. The median number of years required for completion of a degree in 2012–2013 were 6. Specialist in School Psychology Other—Applications 2012–2013, 24. Total applicants accepted 2012–2013, 5. Number full-time enrolled (new admits only) 2012–2013, 4. Total enrolled 2012–2013 full-time, 20. The median number of years required for completion of a degree in 2012–2013 were 4. The number of students enrolled full- and part-time who were dismissed or voluntarily withdrew from this program area in 2012–2013 were 2.

Scores: Entries appear in this order: required test or GPA, minimum score (if required), median score of students entering in 2012–2013. Clinical Psychology PhD (Doctor of Philosophy): GRE-V no minimum stated, 163, GRE-Q no minimum stated, 163, GRE-Analytical no minimum stated, 4.75, GRE-Subject (Psychology) no minimum stated, 700, overall undergraduate GPA no minimum stated, 3.91; Experimental Psychology PhD (Doctor of Philosophy): GRE-V no minimum stated, 576, GRE-Q no minimum stated, 670, GRE-Analytical no minimum stated, overall undergraduate GPA no minimum stated, 3.56; General Psychology MA/MS (Master of Arts/Science): GRE-V no minimum stated, 490, GRE-Q no minimum stated, 650, GRE-Analytical no minimum stated, overall undergraduate GPA no minimum stated, 3.27; School Psychology PhD (Doctor of Philosophy): GRE-V no minimum stated, 158, GRE-Q no minimum stated, 151, GRE-Analytical no minimum stated, 4.25, overall undergraduate GPA no minimum stated, 3.80; Industrial/Organizational Psychology MA/MS (Master of Arts/Science): GRE-V no minimum stated, 157, GRE-Q no minimum stated, 152, GRE-Analytical no minimum stated, overall undergraduate GPA no minimum stated, 3.66; Industrial/Organizational Psychology PhD (Doctor of Philosophy): GRE-V no minimum stated, 157, GRE-Q no minimum stated, 154, GRE-Analytical no minimum stated, overall undergraduate GPA no minimum stated, 3.63; Specialist in School Psychology Other: GRE-V no minimum stated, 157, GRE-Q no minimum stated, 153, GRE-Analytical no minimum stated, 4.5, overall undergraduate GPA no minimum stated, 3.54.

Other Criteria: (importance of criteria rated low, medium, or high): GRE scores—medium, research experience—high, work experience—medium, extracurricular activity—low, clinically related public service—medium, GPA—high, letters of recommendation—high, statement of goals and objectives—high.

Student Characteristics: The following represents characteristics of students in 2012–2013 in all graduate psychology programs in the department: Female—full-time 91, part-time 0; Male—full-time 63, part-time 0; African American/Black—full-time 2, part-time 0; Hispanic/Latino(a)—full-time 2, part-time 0; Asian/Pacific Islander—full-time 8, part-time 0; American Indian/Alaska Native—full-time 1, part-time 0; Caucasian/White—full-time 132, part-time 0; Multi-ethnic—full-time 0, part-time 0; students subject to the Americans With Disabilities Act—full-time 0, part-time 0; Unknown ethnicity—full-time 11, part-time 0; International students who hold an F-1 or J-1 Visa—full-time 8, part-time 0.

Financial Information/Assistance:

Tuition for Full-Time Study: *Master's:* State residents: $467 per credit hour; Nonstate residents: $766 per credit hour. *Doctoral:* State residents: $548 per credit hour; Nonstate residents: $850 per credit hour. Tuition is subject to change. See the following website for updates and changes in tuition costs: http://www.cmich.edu/registrar_office/RegistrarRegistration/Pages/Tuition_and_Fee_Schedule.aspx.

Financial Assistance:

First-Year Students: Research assistantships available for first year. Average amount paid per academic year: $10,500. Average number of hours worked per week: 20. Apply by February 6. Fellowships and scholarships available for first year. Average amount paid per academic year: $10,500. Average number of hours worked per week: 24. Apply by February 6.

Advanced Students: Teaching assistantships available for advanced students. Average amount paid per academic year: $12,850. Average number of hours worked per week: 20. Apply by February 6. Research assistantships available for advanced students. Average amount paid per academic year: $12,850. Average number of hours worked per week: 20. Apply by February 6. Fellowships and scholarships available for advanced students. Average amount paid per academic year: $12,850. Average number of hours worked per week: 24. Apply by February 6.

Additional Information: Of all students currently enrolled full time, 57% benefited from one or more of the listed financial assistance programs. Application and information available online at: http://go.cmich.edu/financial_information/OfficeofScholarshipsandFinancialAid/.

Internships/Practica: Doctoral Degree (PhD Clinical Psychology): For those doctoral students for whom a professional psychology internship was required in this program prior to graduation, (7) students applied for an internship in 2011–2012, with (6) students obtaining an internship. Of those students who obtained an internship, (6) were paid internships. Of those students who obtained an internship, (6) students placed in APA/CPA accredited internships, (0) students placed in internships not APA/CPA accredited, but listed with the Association of Psychology Postdoctoral and Internship Programs (APPIC), (0) students placed in internships conforming to guidelines of the Council of Directors of School Psychology Programs (CDSPP), (0) students placed in internships that were not APA/CPA accredited, APPIC

or CDSPP listed. Doctoral Degree (PhD School Psychology): For those doctoral students for whom a professional psychology internship was required in this program prior to graduation, (2) students applied for an internship in 2011–2012, with (2) students obtaining an internship. Of those students who obtained an internship, (2) were paid internships. Of those students who obtained an internship, (2) students placed in APA/CPA accredited internships, (0) students placed in internships not APA/CPA accredited, but listed with the Association of Psychology Postdoctoral and Internship Programs (APPIC), (0) students placed in internships conforming to guidelines of the Council of Directors of School Psychology Programs (CDSPP), (0) students placed in internships that were not APA/CPA accredited, APPIC or CDSPP listed. Master's Degree (MA/MS General Psychology): An internship experience, such as a final research project or "capstone" experience is required of graduates. Master's Degree (MA/MS Industrial/Organizational Psychology): An internship experience, such as a final research project or "capstone" experience is required of graduates. Most practica and internships are arranged through agencies and schools outside the University. However, practicum experiences are available through the Department's Psychological Training and Consultation Center. Second-year clinical students routinely have their first practicum at the Center.

Housing and Day Care: On-campus housing is available. See the following website for more information: http://www.reslife.cmich.edu/. No on-campus day care facilities are available.

Employment of Department Graduates:

Master's Degree Graduates: Of those who graduated in the academic year 2011–2012, the following categories and numbers represent the postgraduate activities and employment of master's degree graduates: Enrolled in a postdoctoral residency/fellowship (n/a), employed in independent practice (n/a), total from the above (master's) (0).

Doctoral Degree Graduates: Of those who graduated in the academic year 2011–2012, the following categories and numbers represent the postgraduate activities and employment of doctoral degree graduates: Enrolled in a psychology doctoral program (n/a), total from the above (doctoral) (0).

Additional Information:

Orientation, Objectives, and Emphasis of Department: Specialization is possible in the areas of clinical, applied experimental, industrial/organizational, and school psychology. There is also a general/experimental MS program with emphasis on foundations, statistics, methodology, and research, which is designed to prepare students for doctoral training or research positions in the public or private sectors. The clinical program follows a practitioner-scientist model, focusing on training for applied settings. The industrial/organizational program is oriented toward training students for careers in research, university, or business settings. The school program prepares school psychologists to provide consultation, intervention, and diagnostic services to schools and school children. The program meets Michigan requirements for certification.

Special Facilities or Resources: Space is reserved for student research with human subjects. Special equipment permits studies in learning, cognition, human factors, psychophysiology, neuropsychology, and perception. Computer laboratories are available, one specifically designated for clinical and school students. All computer labs have direct email and Internet access, as well as statistical and research software. The Psychology Training and Consultation Center provides training, research, and service functions. In a separate building, space is devoted to animal research and teaching of behavioral neuroscience and experimental behavior analysis. The behavioral neuroscience laboratory contains a fully equipped surgical/histological suite, behavioral testing area and equipment, and a data analysis room including microscopes and an image analysis system. The experimental analysis laboratory is equipped with automated operant chambers for both birds and rodents. A Life-Span Development Research Center has been established in the Department.

Information for Students With Physical Disabilities: See the following website for more information: http://www.cmich.edu/student-disability/.

Application Information:
Send to Psychology Department, Sloan Hall, Central Michigan University, Mt. Pleasant, MI 48859. Application available online. URL of online application: https://apply.cmich.edu/. Students are admitted in the Fall, application deadline December 15. Clinical deadline is December 15, Industrial/Organizational deadline is January 1, School deadline is January 15, and Experimental program deadline is February 1. *Fee:* $35.

Detroit Mercy, University of
Psychology Department
College of Liberal Arts and Education
4001 West McNichols
Detroit, MI 48221
Telephone: (313) 578-0392
Fax: (313) 578-0507
E-mail: *slowiklh@udmercy.edu*
Web: *http://liberalarts.udmercy.edu/programs/depts/psychology/graduate/index.htm*

Department Information:
1962. Chairperson: Linda Haynes Slowik, PhD. Number of faculty: total—full-time 16; women—full-time 12; total—minority—full-time 2; women minority—full-time 1; faculty subject to the Americans With Disabilities Act 1.

Programs and Degrees Offered:
Listed in the following order: Program area, degree type (T if terminal Master's), number awarded 7/11–6/12. Clinical Psychology MA/MS (Master of Arts/Science) 13, Industrial/Organizational Psychology MA/MS (Master of Arts/Science) (T) 4, Clinical Psychology PhD (Doctor of Philosophy) 3, School Psychology Other 6.

APA Accreditation: Clinical PhD (Doctor of Philosophy). Student Outcome Data Website: http://liberalarts.udmercy.edu/programs/depts/psychology/graduate/pycphd/disclosure/.

Student Applications/Admissions:
Student Applications
   Clinical Psychology MA/MS (Master of Arts/Science)—Applications 2012–2013, 52. Total applicants accepted 2012–2013, 14. Openings 2013–2014, 14. The median number of years required for completion of a degree in 2012–2013 were 2. The number of students enrolled full- and part-time who were dismissed or voluntarily withdrew from this program area in 2012–2013 were 0. *Industrial/Organizational Psychology MA/MS (Master of Arts/Science)*—Applications 2012–2013, 24. Total applicants accepted 2012–2013, 6. Number full-time enrolled (new admits only) 2012–2013, 4. Number part-time enrolled (new admits only) 2012–2013, 2. Total enrolled 2012–2013 full-time, 8. Total enrolled 2012–2013 part-time, 4. Openings 2013–2014, 10. The median number of years required for completion of a degree in 2012–2013 were 2. The number of students enrolled full- and part-time who were dismissed or voluntarily withdrew from this program area in 2012–2013 were 0. *Clinical Psychology PhD (Doctor of Philosophy)*—Applications 2012–2013, 75. Total applicants accepted 2012–2013, 8. Number full-time enrolled (new admits only) 2012–2013, 8. Number part-time enrolled (new admits only) 2012–2013, 0. Total enrolled 2012–2013 full-time, 54. Total enrolled 2012–2013 part-time, 0. Openings 2013–2014, 8. The median number of years required for completion of a degree in 2012–2013 were 6. The number of students enrolled full- and part-time who were dismissed or voluntarily withdrew from this program area in 2012–2013 were 0. *School Psychology Other*—Applications 2012–2013, 13. Total applicants accepted 2012–2013, 6. Number full-time enrolled (new admits only) 2012–2013, 6. Number part-time enrolled (new admits only) 2012–2013, 0. Total enrolled 2012–2013 full-time, 18. Total enrolled 2012–2013 part-time, 0. Openings 2013–2014, 8. The median number of years required for completion of a degree in 2012–2013 were 3. The number of students enrolled full- and part-time who were dismissed or voluntarily withdrew from this program area in 2012–2013 were 0.

Scores: Entries appear in this order: required test or GPA, minimum score (if required), median score of students entering in 2012–2013. *Clinical Psychology MA/MS (Master of Arts/Science)*: GRE-V no minimum stated, GRE-Q no minimum stated, overall undergraduate GPA 3.0; *Industrial/Organizational Psychology MA/MS (Master of Arts/Science)*: overall undergraduate GPA 3.0, 3.65, psychology GPA 3.0; *Clinical Psychology PhD (Doctor of Philosophy)*: GRE-V no minimum stated, 510, GRE-Q no minimum stated, 590, overall undergraduate GPA no minimum stated, 3.65; *School Psychology Other*: GRE-V no minimum stated, GRE-Q no minimum stated, overall undergraduate GPA 3.0.

Other Criteria: (importance of criteria rated low, medium, or high): GRE scores—high, research experience—high, work experience—low, extracurricular activity—low, clinically related public service—medium, GPA—high, letters of recommendation—high, interview—high, statement of goals and objectives—high, fit with UDM mission—medium, undergraduate major in psychology—medium, specific undergraduate psychology courses taken—medium, Evidence of academic capability is evaluated by considering GPA and GRE scores, and letters of recommendations, together. Work experience is highly valuable for the I/O Masters program, and important for the Clinical PhD as well, although lack thereof is also understandable and considered in the broader context. In all programs, the statement of Goals and Objectives is very important as evidence of written communication skills and degree of fit with program. The University of Detroit Mercy also places high value on evidence of fit with the University Mission, which emphasizes social justice. For additional information on admission requirements, go to http://liberalarts.udmercy.edu/programs/depts/psychology/graduate/index.htm.

Student Characteristics: The following represents characteristics of students in 2012–2013 in all graduate psychology programs in the department: Female—full-time 51, part-time 3; Male—full-time 31, part-time 1; African American/Black—full-time 21, part-time 2; Hispanic/Latino(a)—full-time 3, part-time 0; Asian/Pacific Islander—full-time 2, part-time 0; American Indian/Alaska Native—full-time 0, part-time 0; Caucasian/White—full-time 52, part-time 2; Multi-ethnic—full-time 2, part-time 0; students subject to the Americans With Disabilities Act—full-time 0, part-time 0; Unknown ethnicity—full-time 2, part-time 0; International students who hold an F-1 or J-1 Visa—full-time 2, part-time 0.

Financial Information/Assistance:
Financial Assistance:
First-Year Students: Teaching assistantships available for first year. Average number of hours worked per week: 20. Research assistantships available for first year. Average number of hours worked per week: 20.
Advanced Students: Teaching assistantships available for advanced students. Research assistantships available for advanced students.
Additional Information: Of all students currently enrolled full time, 90% benefited from one or more of the listed financial assistance programs.

Internships/Practica: Doctoral Degree (PhD Clinical Psychology): For those doctoral students for whom a professional psychology internship was required in this program prior to graduation, (8) students applied for an internship in 2011–2012, with (7) students obtaining an internship. Of those students who obtained an internship, (7) were paid internships. Of those students who obtained an internship, (7) students placed in APA/CPA accredited internships, (0) students placed in internships not APA/CPA accredited, but listed with the Association of Psychology Postdoctoral and Internship Programs (APPIC), (0) students placed in internships conforming to guidelines of the Council of Directors of School Psychology Programs (CDSPP), (0) students placed in internships that were not APA/CPA accredited, APPIC or CDSPP listed. Master's Degree (MA/MS Industrial/Organizational Psychology): An internship experience, such as a final research project or "capstone" experience is required of graduates. Internships or practica are a part of all four graduate programs, but specifics vary according to the program.

Housing and Day Care: On-campus housing is available. See the following website for more information: http://www.udmercy.edu/reslife/index.htm. No on-campus day care facilities are available.

Additional Information:
Orientation, Objectives, and Emphasis of Department: Our doctoral program in Clinical Psychology offers training in the psychodynamic tradition in the context of modern applications, and broad training in main areas of psychology. The School Specialist degree emphasizes cognitive and behavioral orientations. The School Specialist program is now fully accredited by the National Association of School Psychologists (NASP). The Masters in Clinical Psychology prepares students for licensure in the State of Michigan, and emphasizes cognitive orientation. The Industrial/Organizational Psychology Masters degree provides generalist training with special emphasis on quantitative applications.

Special Facilities or Resources: The Psychology Department has an on-campus Psychology Clinic in which Doctoral students begin their training. This clinic helps to meet the needs of the local urban community.

Information for Students With Physical Disabilities: See the following website for more information: http://www.udmercy.edu/uas/disability-support/index.htm.

Application Information:
Application available online. Students are admitted in the Fall, application deadline June 15; Winter, application deadline October 15; Summer, application deadline March 15; Programs have rolling admissions. Only Industrial/Organizational Psychology program has rolling admissions. Other dates are as follows: Clinical Doctoral program: January 1. Clinical Master's program: March 31. School Psychology Specialist program: March 15. *Fee:* $0. Students who are accepted will be asked to make a $200 deposit that will subsequently be credited to tuition costs.

Eastern Michigan University
Department of Psychology
College of Arts and Sciences
341 Science Complex
Ypsilanti, MI 48197
Telephone: (734) 487-1155
Fax: (734) 487-6553
E-mail: *cfreedman@emich.edu*
Web: *http://www.emich.edu/psychology*

Department Information:
1962. Department Head: Carol Freedman-Doan. Number of faculty: total—full-time 19; women—full-time 10; total—minority—full-time 3; women minority—full-time 2.

Programs and Degrees Offered:
Listed in the following order: Program area, degree type (T if terminal Master's), number awarded 7/11–6/12. General Clinical Psychology MA/MS (Master of Arts/Science) (T) 14, Clinical Behavioral Psychology MA/MS (Master of Arts/Science) (T) 10, General Experimental Psychology MA/MS (Master of Arts/Science) (T) 1, Clinical Psychology PhD (Doctor of Philosophy) 6.

APA Accreditation: Clinical PhD (Doctor of Philosophy). Student Outcome Data Website: http://www.emich.edu/psychology/phd_clinicalpsych.php.

Student Applications/Admissions:
Student Applications
General Clinical Psychology MA/MS (Master of Arts/Science)— Applications 2012–2013, 71. Total applicants accepted 2012–2013, 16. Number full-time enrolled (new admits only) 2012–2013, 12. Number part-time enrolled (new admits only) 2012–2013, 0. Total enrolled 2012–2013 full-time, 24. Total enrolled

2012–2013 part-time, 3. Openings 2013–2014, 12. The median number of years required for completion of a degree in 2012–2013 were 2. The number of students enrolled full- and part-time who were dismissed or voluntarily withdrew from this program area in 2012–2013 were 0. *Clinical Behavioral Psychology MA/MS (Master of Arts/Science)*—Applications 2012–2013, 41. Total applicants accepted 2012–2013, 12. Number full-time enrolled (new admits only) 2012–2013, 10. Number part-time enrolled (new admits only) 2012–2013, 2. Total enrolled 2012–2013 full-time, 20. Total enrolled 2012–2013 part-time, 8. Openings 2013–2014, 12. The median number of years required for completion of a degree in 2012–2013 were 3. The number of students enrolled full- and part-time who were dismissed or voluntarily withdrew from this program area in 2012–2013 were 1. *General Experimental Psychology MA/MS (Master of Arts/Science)*—Applications 2012–2013, 10. Total applicants accepted 2012–2013, 4. Number full-time enrolled (new admits only) 2012–2013, 3. Number part-time enrolled (new admits only) 2012–2013, 1. Total enrolled 2012–2013 full-time, 4. Total enrolled 2012–2013 part-time, 5. Openings 2013–2014, 3. The median number of years required for completion of a degree in 2012–2013 were 2. The number of students enrolled full- and part-time who were dismissed or voluntarily withdrew from this program area in 2012–2013 were 0. *Clinical Psychology PhD (Doctor of Philosophy)*—Applications 2012–2013, 144. Total applicants accepted 2012–2013, 10. Number full-time enrolled (new admits only) 2012–2013, 8. Number part-time enrolled (new admits only) 2012–2013, 0. Total enrolled 2012–2013 full-time, 46. Total enrolled 2012–2013 part-time, 0. Openings 2013–2014, 8. The median number of years required for completion of a degree in 2012–2013 were 6. The number of students enrolled full- and part-time who were dismissed or voluntarily withdrew from this program area in 2012–2013 were 1.

Scores: Entries appear in this order: required test or GPA, minimum score (if required), median score of students entering in 2012–2013. *General Clinical Psychology MA/MS (Master of Arts/Science):* GRE-V 150, GRE-Q 150, GRE-Analytical 4.0, overall undergraduate GPA 3.0; *Clinical Behavioral Psychology MA/MS (Master of Arts/Science):* GRE-V 150, GRE-Q 150, GRE-Analytical 4.0, overall undergraduate GPA 3.0, last 2 years GPA 3.0, psychology GPA 3.0; *General Experimental Psychology MA/MS (Master of Arts/Science):* GRE-V 150, GRE-Q 150, GRE-Analytical 4.0, overall undergraduate GPA 3.0; *Clinical Psychology PhD (Doctor of Philosophy):* GRE-V 150, 156, GRE-Q 150, 154, GRE-Analytical 4.0, 4.70, overall undergraduate GPA 3.0, 3.65, last 2 years GPA 3.0, psychology GPA 3.0.

Other Criteria: (importance of criteria rated low, medium, or high): GRE scores—high, research experience—medium, work experience—low, extracurricular activity—low, clinically related public service—medium, GPA—high, letters of recommendation—medium, interview—high, statement of goals and objectives—high, fit with faculty research—high, undergraduate major in psychology—medium, specific undergraduate psychology courses taken—medium.

Student Characteristics: The following represents characteristics of students in 2012–2013 in all graduate psychology programs in the department: Female—full-time 76, part-time 11; Male—full-time 18, part-time 5; African American/Black—full-time 3, part-time 0; Hispanic/Latino(a)—full-time 4, part-time 0; Asian/Pa-

cific Islander—full-time 6, part-time 1; American Indian/Alaska Native—full-time 1, part-time 0; Caucasian/White—full-time 80, part-time 15; Multi-ethnic—full-time 0, part-time 0; students subject to the Americans With Disabilities Act—full-time 0, part-time 0; Unknown ethnicity—full-time 0, part-time 0; International students who hold an F-1 or J-1 Visa—full-time 5, part-time 0.

Financial Information/Assistance:

Tuition for Full-Time Study: *Master's:* State residents: $449 per credit hour; Nonstate residents: $885 per credit hour. *Doctoral:* State residents: $516 per credit hour; Nonstate residents: $997 per credit hour. Tuition is subject to change. Additional fees are assessed to students beyond the costs of tuition for the following: general fee, tech fee, student union fee, program fee, assessment lab fees. Tuition costs vary by program. See the following website for updates and changes in tuition costs: http://www.emich.edu/graduate/admissions/tuition.php.

Financial Assistance:

First-Year Students: Teaching assistantships available for first year. Average amount paid per academic year: $9,200. Average number of hours worked per week: 20. Apply by February 1. Fellowships and scholarships available for first year. Average amount paid per academic year: $16,500. Average number of hours worked per week: 20. Apply by December 1.

Advanced Students: Research assistantships available for advanced students. Average amount paid per academic year: $9,200. Average number of hours worked per week: 20. Apply by February 1. Fellowships and scholarships available for advanced students. Average amount paid per academic year: $16,500. Average number of hours worked per week: 20. Apply by December 1.

Additional Information: Of all students currently enrolled full time, 45% benefited from one or more of the listed financial assistance programs. Application and information available online at: http://www.emich.edu/graduate/students/ga/index.php.

Internships/Practica: Doctoral Degree (PhD Clinical Psychology): For those doctoral students for whom a professional psychology internship was required in this program prior to graduation, (8) students applied for an internship in 2011–2012, with (8) students obtaining an internship. Of those students who obtained an internship, (8) were paid internships. Of those students who obtained an internship, (8) students placed in APA/CPA accredited internships, (0) students placed in internships not APA/CPA accredited, but listed with the Association of Psychology Postdoctoral and Internship Programs (APPIC), (0) students placed in internships conforming to guidelines of the Council of Directors of School Psychology Programs (CDSPP), (0) students placed in internships that were not APA/CPA accredited, APPIC or CDSPP listed. Master's Degree (MA/MS General Experimental Psychology): An internship experience, such as a final research project or "capstone" experience is required of graduates. Practicum settings (unpaid) are available in the surrounding community for clinical and clinical behavioral students. In addition, the university offers mental health services involving practicum experiences at both the campus Snow Health Center and the EMU Psychology Clinic. Both terminal MS and PhD programs require sufficient practicum hours to meet the State of Michigan requirements for the Limited License in Psychology (LLP).

Housing and Day Care: On-campus housing is available. See the following website for more information: http://www.emich.edu/

housing/housingEMU.php. On-campus day care facilities are available. See the following website for more information: http://www.emich.edu/childrensinstitute/.

Employment of Department Graduates:

Master's Degree Graduates: Of those who graduated in the academic year 2011–2012, the following categories and numbers represent the postgraduate activities and employment of master's degree graduates: Enrolled in a postdoctoral residency/fellowship (n/a), employed in independent practice (n/a), total from the above (master's) (0).

Doctoral Degree Graduates: Of those who graduated in the academic year 2011–2012, the following categories and numbers represent the postgraduate activities and employment of doctoral degree graduates: Enrolled in a psychology doctoral program (n/a), enrolled in a postdoctoral residency/fellowship (7), employed in independent practice (3), employed in other positions at a higher education institution (2), employed in government agency (2), employed in a hospital/medical center (4), total from the above (doctoral) (18).

Additional Information:

Orientation, Objectives, and Emphasis of Department: The Psychology Department offers three terminal Master's degree programs and courses in several orientations, including behavioral, social, insight, developmental, and physiological. Within the two Master's clinical programs, the major emphases are on psychological assessment (General Clinical Program) and behavioral treatment (Clinical Behavioral Program). Within each program there are a wide variety of theoretical, applied, and research interests. The goal of the Clinical and Clinical Behavioral programs is to give students the background to immediately begin work in clinical treatment settings or to prepare them for entry into doctoral programs, as matches students' educational objectives. The emphasis of the Master's in General Experimental Psychology is to prepare students for entry into higher level study in psychology or as researchers in applied/research settings. Because psychology is considered a natural science at Eastern Michigan University, there is also an emphasis on basing clinical practice on research findings. Theses, although optional in the clinical master's programs, are expected to be research based. The PhD program in Clinical Psychology is designed to give advanced training in the supervision of mental health professionals in mental health care settings. The entry requirements for this program are more stringent than those of our Master's programs with a more competitive applicant pool. The PhD offers specialization in general clinical or behavioral psychology, a terminal Master's degree en route, and a full four-year doctoral fellowship which covers tuition and fees plus an annual stipend.

Special Facilities or Resources: The faculty, which consists of approximately 20 full-time members with PhDs and varying number of part-time lecturers, is eclectic in orientation with a wide variety of interests and professional backgrounds. Research interests and publication record of the faculty include psychological test construction and validation, basic behavioral research with humans and non-humans, the history of psychology, applied behavior analysis, physiological psychology, behavioral medicine, PTSD, child and adolescent development, and many more. Student enrollment is intentionally kept low in order to provide the students with ample opportunities to develop close working relationships with the faculty. Students regularly present at regional, national, and international conventions, as well as co-author published papers with faculty. The facilities of the Psychology Department are located in the Mark Jefferson Science Complex and in the Psychology Clinic at 611 West Cross. The department features a state-of-the-art computer laboratory, IEEE 802.11 (AirPort) wireless networking capabilities, human and animal research facilities, seminar rooms, a clinic with one-way observation capabilities, a university library less than one minute away on foot, and other equipment and supplies needed for advanced study.

Information for Students With Physical Disabilities: See the following website for more information: http://www.emich.edu/drc/.

Application Information:

Send to Department of Psychology, Graduate Admissions Committee, 341 Science Complex, Eastern Michigan University, Ypsilanti, MI 48197. Application available online. URL of online application: http://www.emich.edu/graduate/admissions/. Students are admitted in the Fall, application deadline December 1. The deadline for PhD applications is December 1. The application deadline for the MS programs is February 1. *Fee:* $25. Applications that are submitted electronically involve a fee of $25. If the applicant mails in a paper Graduate Admission application, the fee is $35.

Michigan School of Professional Psychology

26811 Orchard Lake Road
Farmington Hills, MI 48334
Telephone: (248) 476-1122
Fax: (248) 476-1125
E-mail: *aming@mispp.edu*
Web: *http://www.mispp.edu/*

Department Information:

1980. President: Diane Blau, PhD Number of faculty: total—full-time 9, part-time 29; women—full-time 4, part-time 20; minority—part-time 4; women minority—part-time 4.

Programs and Degrees Offered:

Listed in the following order: Program area, degree type (T if terminal Master's), number awarded 7/11–6/12. Clinical Psychology PsyD (Doctor of Psychology) 13, Clinical Psychology MA/MS (Master of Arts/Science) (T) 32.

Student Applications/Admissions:

Student Applications

Clinical Psychology PsyD (Doctor of Psychology)—Applications 2012–2013, 37. Total applicants accepted 2012–2013, 20. Number full-time enrolled (new admits only) 2012–2013, 18. Number part-time enrolled (new admits only) 2012–2013, 0. Total enrolled 2012–2013 full-time, 60. Total enrolled 2012–2013 part-time, 20. Openings 2013–2014, 18. The median number of years required for completion of a degree in 2012–2013 were 4. The number of students enrolled full- and part-time who were dismissed or voluntarily withdrew from this program area in 2012–2013 were 2. *Clinical Psychology MA/MS (Master of Arts/Science)*—Applications 2012–2013, 121. Total applicants accepted 2012–2013, 81. Number full-time enrolled (new admits only) 2012–2013, 40. Number part-time enrolled (new admits only) 2012–2013, 23. Total enrolled 2012–2013 full-time, 38. Total enrolled 2012–2013 part-time, 47. Openings 2013–2014, 60. The median number of years required for completion of a degree in 2012–2013 was 1. The number of students enrolled full- and part-time who were dismissed or voluntarily withdrew from this program area in 2012–2013 were 2.

Scores: Entries appear in this order: required test or GPA, minimum score (if required), median score of students entering in 2012–2013. *Clinical Psychology PsyD (Doctor of Psychology):* overall undergraduate GPA 2.5, 3.0, Masters GPA 3.25, 3.5; *Clinical Psychology MA/MS (Master of Arts/Science):* overall undergraduate GPA 2.5, 3.0.

Other Criteria: (importance of criteria rated low, medium, or high): research experience—low, work experience—high, extracurricular activity—low, clinically related public service—medium, GPA—high, letters of recommendation—high, interview—high, statement of goals and objectives—high, undergraduate major in psychology—medium, specific undergraduate psychology courses taken—medium.

Student Characteristics: The following represents characteristics of students in 2012–2013 in all graduate psychology programs in the department: Female—full-time 76, part-time 59; Male—full-time 20, part-time 10; African American/Black—full-time 9, part-time 10; Hispanic/Latino(a)—full-time 2, part-time 0; Asian/Pacific Islander—full-time 4, part-time 2; American Indian/Alaska Native—full-time 1, part-time 0; Caucasian/White—full-time 79, part-time 56; Multi-ethnic—full-time 0, part-time 0; students subject to the Americans With Disabilities Act—full-time 2, part-time 1; Unknown ethnicity—full-time 0, part-time 0; International students who hold an F-1 or J-1 Visa—full-time 1, part-time 0.

Financial Information/Assistance:

Tuition for Full-Time Study: *Master's:* State residents: per academic year $27,200, $544 per credit hour; Nonstate residents: per academic year $27,200, $544 per credit hour. *Doctoral:* State residents: per academic year $26,200, $678 per credit hour; Nonstate residents: per academic year $26,200, $678 per credit hour. Tuition is subject to change. Additional fees are assessed to students beyond the costs of tuition for the following: technology, testing, electronic resources, dissertation, supervision. Tuition costs vary by program. See the following website for updates and changes in tuition costs: http://www.mispp.edu/index.php?option=com_content&task=view&id=115&Itemid=487.

Financial Assistance:

First-Year Students: No information provided.

Advanced Students: Teaching assistantships available for advanced students. Average amount paid per academic year: $12,000. Average number of hours worked per week: 20.

Additional Information: Of all students currently enrolled full time, 95% benefited from one or more of the listed financial assistance programs. Application and information available online at: http://www.mispp.edu/index.php?option=com_content&task=view&id=124&Itemid=1015.

Internships/Practica: Doctoral Degree (PsyD Clinical Psychology): For those doctoral students for whom a professional psychology internship was required in this program prior to graduation, (14) students applied for an internship in 2011–2012, with (14) students obtaining an internship. Of those students who obtained an internship, (13) were paid internships. Of those students who obtained an internship, (0) students placed in APA/CPA accredited internships, (2) students placed in internships not APA/CPA accredited, but listed with the Association of Psychology Postdoctoral and Internship Programs (APPIC), (0) students placed in internships conforming to guidelines of the Council of Directors of School Psychology Programs (CDSPP), (12) students placed in internships that were not APA/CPA accredited, APPIC or CDSPP listed. Master's Degree (MA/MS Clinical Psychology): An internship experience, such as a final research project or "capstone" experience is required of graduates. Master of Arts students complete a 500 hour practicum. Doctoral students complete a 500 hour practicum and a 2,000 hour internship.

Housing and Day Care: No on-campus housing is available. No on-campus day care facilities are available.

Employment of Department Graduates:

Master's Degree Graduates: Of those who graduated in the academic year 2011–2012, the following categories and numbers represent the postgraduate activities and employment of master's degree graduates: Enrolled in a postdoctoral residency/fellowship (n/a), employed in independent practice (n/a), total from the above (master's) (0).

Doctoral Degree Graduates: Of those who graduated in the academic year 2011–2012, the following categories and numbers represent the postgraduate activities and employment of doctoral degree graduates: Enrolled in a psychology doctoral program (n/a), total from the above (doctoral) (0).

Additional Information:

Orientation, Objectives, and Emphasis of Department: The mission of the Michigan School of Professional Psychology is to educate and train individuals to become reflective practitioner-scholars with the competencies necessary to serve diverse populations as professional psychologists and psychotherapists.

Application Information:

Send to Amanda Ming, MBA, Admissions & Recruitment Coordinator, Michigan School of Professional Psychology, 26811 Orchard Lake Road, Farmington Hills, MI 48334. Application available online. URL of online application: http://www.mispp.edu/index.php?option=com_content&task=view&id=114&Itemid=481. Students are admitted in the Programs have rolling admissions. *Fee:* $75.

Michigan State University
Counseling, Educational Psychology, and Special Education/
 School Psychology Program
College of Education
620 Farm Lane, Room 435 Erickson Hall
East Lansing, MI 49201
Telephone: (517) 432-0843
Fax: (517) 353-6393
E-mail: *carlsoj@msu.edu*
Web: *http://www.educ.msu.edu/cepse/schoolpsychology/*

Department Information:
 1981. Chairperson: Richard S. Prawat. Number of faculty: total—
 full-time 5; women—full-time 4; total—minority—full-time 2;
 women minority—full-time 2.

Programs and Degrees Offered:
 Listed in the following order: Program area, degree type (T if
 terminal Master's), number awarded 7/11–6/12. School Psychology PhD (Doctor of Philosophy) 5.

APA Accreditation: School PhD (Doctor of Philosophy). Student
Outcome Data Website: http://www.educ.msu.edu/cepse/
SchoolPsychology/student-data.asp.

Student Applications/Admissions:
 Student Applications
 School Psychology PhD (Doctor of Philosophy)—Applications
 2012–2013, 44. Total applicants accepted 2012–2013, 8. Number full-time enrolled (new admits only) 2012–2013, 8. Number part-time enrolled (new admits only) 2012–2013, 0. Total
 enrolled 2012–2013 full-time, 44. Total enrolled 2012–2013
 part-time, 0. Openings 2013–2014, 8. The median number of
 years required for completion of a degree in 2012–2013 were
 5. The number of students enrolled full- and part-time who
 were dismissed or voluntarily withdrew from this program area
 in 2012–2013 were 0.
 Scores: Entries appear in this order: required test or GPA,
 minimum score (if required), median score of students entering
 in 2012–2013. *School Psychology PhD (Doctor of Philosophy):*
 GRE-V 152, 155, GRE-Q 152, 156, GRE-Analytical 3.5, 4.0,
 overall undergraduate GPA 3.5, 3.66.
 Other Criteria: (importance of criteria rated low, medium, or
 high): GRE scores—high, research experience—high, work
 experience—medium, extracurricular activity—medium, clinically related public service—medium, GPA—high, letters of
 recommendation—high, interview—high, statement of goals
 and objectives—high, writing sample—medium, undergraduate major in psychology—medium, specific undergraduate psychology courses taken—medium. For additional information
 on admission requirements, go to http://www.educ.msu.edu/
 cepse/appforms.asp.

Student Characteristics: The following represents characteristics
 of students in 2012–2013 in all graduate psychology programs in
 the department: Female—full-time 45, part-time 0; Male—full-
 time 8, part-time 0; African American/Black—full-time 4, part-

time 0; Hispanic/Latino(a)—full-time 0, part-time 0; Asian/Pa-
cific Islander—full-time 1, part-time 0; American Indian/Alaska
Native—full-time 3, part-time 0; Caucasian/White—full-time 45,
part-time 0; Multi-ethnic—full-time 0, part-time 0; students subject to the Americans With Disabilities Act—full-time 0, part-
time 0; Unknown ethnicity—full-time 0, part-time 0; International students who hold an F-1 or J-1 Visa—full-time 0, part-
time 0.

Financial Information/Assistance:
 Tuition for Full-Time Study: *Doctoral:* State residents: $597 per
 credit hour; Nonstate residents: $1,173 per credit hour. Tuition
 is subject to change. See the following website for updates
 and changes in tuition costs: http://www.ctlr.msu.edu/
 CoStudentAccounts/Tuition_Fees_MainMenu.aspx.

Financial Assistance:
 First-Year Students: Teaching assistantships available for
 first year. Average amount paid per academic year: $13,923. Aver-
 age number of hours worked per week: 20. Apply by March 15.
 Research assistantships available for first year. Average amount
 paid per academic year: $13,923. Average number of hours worked
 per week: 20. Apply by March 15.
 Advanced Students: Teaching assistantships available for
 advanced students. Average amount paid per academic year:
 $16,185. Average number of hours worked per week: 20. Apply by
 March 15. Research assistantships available for advanced students.
 Average amount paid per academic year: $16,185. Average num-
 ber of hours worked per week: 20. Apply by March 15.
 Additional Information: Of all students currently enrolled full
 time, 100% benefited from one or more of the listed financial assistance programs. Application and information available online at:
 http://education.msu.edu/cepse/SchoolPsychology/financial.asp.

Internships/Practica: Doctoral Degree (PhD School Psychology):
For those doctoral students for whom a professional psychology
internship was required in this program prior to graduation, (6)
students applied for an internship in 2011–2012, with (6) students
obtaining an internship. Of those students who obtained an internship, (6) were paid internships. Of those students who obtained an internship, (4) students placed in APA/CPA accredited
internships, (0) students placed in internships not APA/CPA
accredited, but listed with the Association of Psychology Postdoctoral and Internship Programs (APPIC), (2) students placed in
internships conforming to guidelines of the Council of Directors
of School Psychology Programs (CDSPP), (0) students placed in
internships that were not APA/CPA accredited, APPIC or
CDSPP listed. Practica are completed in school districts and
community-based mental health settings such as hospitals and
clinics where school-aged children receive psychological services.
Internships are completed all over the country.

Housing and Day Care: On-campus housing is available. See the
following website for more information: http://www.liveon.msu.
edu/. On-campus day care facilities are available. See the following
website for more information: http://scdc.msu.edu/; http://hdfs.
msu.edu/cdl/.

Employment of Department Graduates:

Master's Degree Graduates: Of those who graduated in the academic year 2011–2012, the following categories and numbers represent the postgraduate activities and employment of master's degree graduates: Enrolled in a postdoctoral residency/fellowship (n/a), employed in independent practice (n/a), total from the above (master's) (0).

Doctoral Degree Graduates: Of those who graduated in the academic year 2011–2012, the following categories and numbers represent the postgraduate activities and employment of doctoral degree graduates: Enrolled in a psychology doctoral program (n/a), employed in an academic position at a university (1), employed in a professional position in a school system (2), employed in a community mental health/counseling center (2), total from the above (doctoral) (5).

Additional Information:

Orientation, Objectives, and Emphasis of Department: The MSU School Psychology program prepares school psychologists to work with educators, children, youth, and families to promote individuals' learning and development particularly in relation to schooling. Our vision for training and practice in school psychology is informed by the standards of the profession including the Specialty Definition of School Psychology by APA Division 16 and the Blueprint for School Psychology published by NASP. Our vision emanates from a set of four goals that define our program: Foundational Knowledge: To prepare future psychologists with foundational knowledge in psychological aspects of behavior; Professional Practice: To prepare future psychologists with the skills necessary for competent delivery of mental health services to school-aged children; Research and Inquiry: To prepare future psychologists who effectively consume, produce, and disseminate research; and Professional Conduct: To prepare future psychologists who effectively collaborate with others in the delivery of services according to ethical and legal guidelines. The fundamental goal of the MSU School Psychology program is to prepare school psychologists as data-based, system-wide problem-solvers in the educational domain who work with learners of all ages. Our goal for the doctoral program is to prepare psychologists for a wide range of practice that is consistent with contemporary models of school psychological services.

Special Facilities or Resources: The College of Education has been ranked as one of the leading universities in the country. The facilities and support for learning are exceptional.

Information for Students With Physical Disabilities: See the following website for more information: https://www.rcpd.msu.edu/.

Application Information:

Send to Admissions Secretary, Michigan State University, College of Education, CEPSE Department, 620 Farm Lane, Room 447 Erickson Hall, East Lansing, MI 48824. Application available online. URL of online application: http://grad.msu.edu/apply/. Students are admitted in the Fall, application deadline December 1. *Fee:* $50.

Michigan State University
Department of Psychology
Social Science
240E Psychology Building
East Lansing, MI 48824-1116
Telephone: (517) 353-5258
Fax: (517) 432-2476
E-mail: *psygrad@msu.edu*
Web: *http://psychology.msu.edu*

Department Information:

1946. Chairperson: Juli Wade. Number of faculty: total—full-time 55; women—full-time 27; total—minority—full-time 12; women minority—full-time 7.

Programs and Degrees Offered:

Listed in the following order: Program area, degree type (T if terminal Master's), number awarded 7/11–6/12. Behavioral Neuroscience PhD (Doctor of Philosophy) 1, Clinical Psychology PhD (Doctor of Philosophy) 2, Ecological/Community Psychology PhD (Doctor of Philosophy) 2, Organizational Psychology PhD (Doctor of Philosophy) 6, Cognition & Cognitive Neuroscience PhD (Doctor of Philosophy), Social/Personality Psychology PhD (Doctor of Philosophy).

APA Accreditation: Clinical PhD (Doctor of Philosophy). Student Outcome Data Website: http://psychology.msu.edu/Clinical/Disclosure.aspx.

Student Applications/Admissions:

Student Applications

Behavioral Neuroscience PhD (Doctor of Philosophy)—Applications 2012–2013, 9. Total applicants accepted 2012–2013, 2. Total enrolled 2012–2013 full-time, 18. Total enrolled 2012–2013 part-time, 0. Openings 2013–2014, 2. The median number of years required for completion of a degree in 2012–2013 were 6. The number of students enrolled full- and part-time who were dismissed or voluntarily withdrew from this program area in 2012–2013 were 0. *Clinical Psychology PhD (Doctor of Philosophy)*—Applications 2012–2013, 145. Total applicants accepted 2012–2013, 9. Number full-time enrolled (new admits only) 2012–2013, 4. Total enrolled 2012–2013 full-time, 55. Total enrolled 2012–2013 part-time, 0. Openings 2013–2014, 5. The median number of years required for completion of a degree in 2012–2013 were 6. The number of students enrolled full- and part-time who were dismissed or voluntarily withdrew from this program area in 2012–2013 were 0. *Ecological/Community Psychology PhD (Doctor of Philosophy)*—Applications 2012–2013, 21. Total applicants accepted 2012–2013, 5. Number full-time enrolled (new admits only) 2012–2013, 5. Total enrolled 2012–2013 full-time, 27. Total enrolled 2012–2013 part-time, 0. Openings 2013–2014, 5. The median number of years required for completion of a degree in 2012–2013 were 6. The number of students enrolled full- and part-time who were dismissed or voluntarily withdrew from this program area in 2012–2013 were 0. *Organizational Psychology PhD (Doctor of Philosophy)*—Applications 2012–2013, 70. Total applicants accepted 2012–2013, 5. Number full-time enrolled (new admits only) 2012–2013, 5. Total enrolled 2012–2013 full-time, 27. Total enrolled 2012–2013 part-time, 0. Openings 2013–2014, 5. The median number of years required for completion of a degree in 2012–2013 were 5. The number of students enrolled full- and part-time who were dismissed or voluntarily withdrew from this program area in 2012–2013 were 0. *Cognition & Cognitive Neuroscience PhD (Doctor of Philosophy)*—Applications 2012–2013, 29. Total applicants accepted 2012–2013, 5. Openings 2013–2014, 5. The median number of years required for completion of a degree in 2012–2013 were 6. The number of students enrolled full- and part-time who were dismissed or voluntarily withdrew from this program area in 2012–2013 were 0. *Social/Personality Psychology PhD (Doctor of Philosophy)*—Applications 2012–2013, 42. Total applicants accepted 2012–2013, 5. Total enrolled 2012–2013 full-time, 11. Total enrolled 2012–2013 part-time, 0. Openings 2013–2014, 5. The median number of years required for completion of a degree in 2012–2013 were 6. The number of students enrolled full- and part-time who were dismissed or voluntarily withdrew from this program area in 2012–2013 were 0.

Scores: Entries appear in this order: required test or GPA, minimum score (if required), median score of students entering in 2012–2013. *Behavioral Neuroscience PhD (Doctor of Philosophy):* GRE-V no minimum stated, GRE-Q no minimum stated, GRE-Analytical no minimum stated; *Clinical Psychology PhD (Doctor of Philosophy):* GRE-V no minimum stated, 610, GRE-Q no minimum stated, 690, GRE-Analytical no minimum stated, GRE-Subject (Psychology) no minimum stated, 670, overall undergraduate GPA no minimum stated, 3.72; *Ecological/Community Psychology PhD (Doctor of Philosophy):* GRE-V no minimum stated, GRE-Q no minimum stated, GRE-Analytical no minimum stated, overall undergraduate GPA no minimum stated, last 2 years GPA no minimum stated, psychology GPA no minimum stated, Masters GPA no minimum stated; *Organizational Psychology PhD (Doctor of Philosophy):* GRE-V no minimum stated, GRE-Q no minimum stated, GRE-Analytical no minimum stated, GRE-Subject (Psychology) no minimum stated, overall undergraduate GPA no minimum stated, psychology GPA no minimum stated; *Cognition & Cognitive Neuroscience PhD (Doctor of Philosophy):* GRE-V no minimum stated, GRE-Q no minimum stated, GRE-Analytical no minimum stated, GRE-Subject (Psychology) no minimum stated; *Social/Personality Psychology PhD (Doctor of Philosophy):* GRE-V no minimum stated, GRE-Q no minimum stated, GRE-Analytical no minimum stated, GRE-Subject (Psychology) no minimum stated, overall undergraduate GPA no minimum stated, psychology GPA no minimum stated.

Other Criteria: (importance of criteria rated low, medium, or high): GRE scores—high, research experience—high, work experience—medium, extracurricular activity—medium, GPA—high, letters of recommendation—high, interview—high, statement of goals and objectives—high, undergraduate major in psychology—medium, specific undergraduate psychology courses taken—medium, Extra curricular, public service and clinical activities are important for applicants to the clinical and ecological/community programs. For additional information on admission requirements, go to http://psychology.msu.edu/GraduateProgram/Standards.aspx.

Student Characteristics: The following represents characteristics of students in 2012–2013 in all graduate psychology programs in the department: Female—full-time 73, part-time 23; Male—full-time 30, part-time 12; African American/Black—full-time 5, part-time 0; Hispanic/Latino(a)—full-time 2, part-time 0; Asian/Pacific Islander—full-time 3, part-time 0; American Indian/Alaska Native—full-time 0, part-time 0; Caucasian/White—full-time 0, part-time 0; Multi-ethnic—full-time 0, part-time 0; students subject to the Americans With Disabilities Act—full-time 0, part-time 0; Unknown ethnicity—full-time 0, part-time 0; International students who hold an F-1 or J-1 Visa—full-time 0, part-time 0.

Financial Information/Assistance:

Tuition for Full-Time Study: *Doctoral:* State residents: $597 per credit hour; Nonstate residents: $1,173 per credit hour. Tuition is subject to change. See the following website for updates and changes in tuition costs: http://www.ctlr.msu.edu/COStudentAccounts/.

Financial Assistance:

First-Year Students: Teaching assistantships available for first year. Average amount paid per academic year: $20,752. Average number of hours worked per week: 20. Apply by December 1. Research assistantships available for first year. Average amount paid per academic year: $20,752. Average number of hours worked per week: 20. Apply by December 1. Fellowships and scholarships available for first year. Average amount paid per academic year: $25,000. Average number of hours worked per week: 0. Apply by December 1.

Advanced Students: Teaching assistantships available for advanced students. Average amount paid per academic year: $20,752. Average number of hours worked per week: 20. Research assistantships available for advanced students. Average amount paid per academic year: $20,752. Average number of hours worked per week: 20. Fellowships and scholarships available for advanced students. Average amount paid per academic year: $20,752.

Additional Information: Of all students currently enrolled full time, 95% benefited from one or more of the listed financial assistance programs. Application and information available online at: http://www.finaid.msu.edu/grad.asp.

Internships/Practica: Doctoral Degree (PhD Clinical Psychology): For those doctoral students for whom a professional psychology internship was required in this program prior to graduation, (5) students applied for an internship in 2011–2012, with (5) students obtaining an internship. Of those students who obtained an internship, (5) were paid internships. Of those students who obtained an internship, (5) students placed in APA/CPA accredited internships, (0) students placed in internships not APA/CPA accredited, but listed with the Association of Psychology Postdoctoral and Internship Programs (APPIC), (0) students placed in internships conforming to guidelines of the Council of Directors of School Psychology Programs (CDSPP), (0) students placed in internships that were not APA/CPA accredited, APPIC or CDSPP listed. Clinical practica provided by the clinical program at the department's Psychological Clinic.

Housing and Day Care: On-campus housing is available. See the following website for more information: http://www.liveon.msu.edu/. On-campus day care facilities are available. See the following website for more information: http://scdc.msu.edu/; http://hdfs.msu.edu/cdl/.

Employment of Department Graduates:

Master's Degree Graduates: Of those who graduated in the academic year 2011–2012, the following categories and numbers

represent the postgraduate activities and employment of master's degree graduates: Enrolled in a postdoctoral residency/fellowship (n/a), employed in independent practice (n/a), total from the above (master's) (0).

Doctoral Degree Graduates: Of those who graduated in the academic year 2011–2012, the following categories and numbers represent the postgraduate activities and employment of doctoral degree graduates: Enrolled in a psychology doctoral program (n/a), total from the above (doctoral) (0).

Additional Information:

Orientation, Objectives, and Emphasis of Department: The main objective of our programs is to train researchers who will engage in the generation and application of knowledge in a wide range of areas in psychology.

Special Facilities or Resources: Facilities include the Psychological Clinic for the clinical program, which includes playrooms equipped for audio and video recording, testing equipment, computer-based record keeping system, and neuropsychological assessment lab. The Neuroscience-Biological Psychology Laboratories include research animal facilities, computers, light and electron-microscopy, histology and endocrinology labs. The Vision Research Laboratory, Cognitive Processes Laboratories, Eye-Movement Lab, and Speech Processing Lab provide automated facilities for conducting research in cognitive science. Additional observational labs equipped with video remote control equipment, one-way windows, and automated data recording equipment are available. Computer labs are available within the department and across campus.

Information for Students With Physical Disabilities: See the following website for more information: https://www.rcpd.msu.edu/.

Application Information:

Application available online. URL of online application: http://grad.msu.edu/apply/. Students are admitted in the Fall, application deadline December 1. *Fee:* $50.

Michigan, University of
Combined Program in Education and Psychology
1406 School of Education, 610 East University Avenue
Ann Arbor, MI 48109-1259
Telephone: (734) 647-0626
Fax: (734) 615-2164
E-mail: *cpep@umich.edu*
Web: *http://www.soe.umich.edu/academics/doctoral_programs/ep/*

Department Information:

1956. Chairperson: Robert Jagers. Number of faculty: total—part-time 16; women—part-time 8; minority—part-time 5; women minority—part-time 4.

Programs and Degrees Offered:

Listed in the following order: Program area, degree type (T if terminal Master's), number awarded 7/11–6/12. Education and Psychology PhD (Doctor of Philosophy) 1.

Student Applications/Admissions:
Student Applications

Education and Psychology PhD (Doctor of Philosophy)—Applications 2012–2013, 88. Total applicants accepted 2012–2013, 12. Number full-time enrolled (new admits only) 2012–2013, 7. Number part-time enrolled (new admits only) 2012–2013, 0. Total enrolled 2012–2013 full-time, 39. Total enrolled 2012–2013 part-time, 0. Openings 2013–2014, 6. The median number of years required for completion of a degree in 2012–2013 were 6. The number of students enrolled full- and part-time who were dismissed or voluntarily withdrew from this program area in 2012–2013 were 2.

Scores: Entries appear in this order: required test or GPA, minimum score (if required), median score of students entering in 2012–2013. *Education and Psychology PhD (Doctor of Philosophy):* GRE-V no minimum stated, 610, GRE-Q no minimum stated, 666, GRE-Analytical no minimum stated, 4.1, overall undergraduate GPA no minimum stated, 3.6.

Other Criteria: (importance of criteria rated low, medium, or high): GRE scores—medium, research experience—high, work experience—medium, extracurricular activity—medium, clinically related public service—low, GPA—medium, letters of recommendation—high, interview—high, statement of goals and objectives—high, teaching/education—medium, undergraduate major in psychology—low, specific undergraduate psychology courses taken—low. For additional information on admission requirements, go to http://www.soe.umich.edu/academics/doctoral_programs/ep/ep_applying/.

Student Characteristics: The following represents characteristics of students in 2012–2013 in all graduate psychology programs in the department: Female—full-time 29, part-time 0; Male—full-time 10, part-time 0; African American/Black—full-time 11, part-time 0; Hispanic/Latino(a)—full-time 2, part-time 0; Asian/Pacific Islander—full-time 2, part-time 0; American Indian/Alaska Native—full-time 0, part-time 0; Caucasian/White—full-time 12, part-time 0; Multi-ethnic—full-time 4, part-time 0; students subject to the Americans With Disabilities Act—full-time 1, part-time 0; Unknown ethnicity—full-time 8, part-time 0; International students who hold an F-1 or J-1 Visa—full-time 7, part-time 0.

Financial Information/Assistance:

Tuition for Full-Time Study: *Doctoral:* State residents: per academic year $19,240; Nonstate residents: per academic year $38,882. Tuition is subject to change. See the following website for updates and changes in tuition costs: http://ro.umich.edu/tuition/.

Financial Assistance:

First-Year Students: Research assistantships available for first year. Average amount paid per academic year: $27,285. Average number of hours worked per week: 20. Apply by December 1. Fellowships and scholarships available for first year. Average amount paid per academic year: $24,000. Average number of hours worked per week: 20. Apply by December 1.

Advanced Students: Teaching assistantships available for advanced students. Average amount paid per academic year: $27,351. Average number of hours worked per week: 20. Research assistantships available for advanced students. Average amount paid per academic year: $27,285. Average number of hours worked per week: 20. Fellowships and scholarships available for advanced students. Average amount paid per academic year: $24,000. Average number of hours worked per week: 20.

Additional Information: Of all students currently enrolled full time, 98% benefited from one or more of the listed financial assistance programs. Application and information available online at: http://www.soe.umich.edu/academics/doctoral_programs/ep/ep_funding/.

Housing and Day Care: On-campus housing is available. See the following website for more information: http://www.housing. umich.edu. On-campus day care facilities are available. See the following website for more information: http://hr.umich.edu/childcare/.

Employment of Department Graduates:

Master's Degree Graduates: Of those who graduated in the academic year 2011–2012, the following categories and numbers represent the postgraduate activities and employment of master's degree graduates: Enrolled in a postdoctoral residency/fellowship (n/a), employed in independent practice (n/a), total from the above (master's) (0).

Doctoral Degree Graduates: Of those who graduated in the academic year 2011–2012, the following categories and numbers represent the postgraduate activities and employment of doctoral degree graduates: Enrolled in a psychology doctoral program (n/a), employed in business or industry (1), total from the above (doctoral) (1).

Additional Information:

Orientation, Objectives, and Emphasis of Department: The Combined Program in Education and Psychology focuses on research training in instructional psychology, broadly defined. Students are trained to study educational issues and do research in educational settings, on significant educational problems related to learning. There are currently four main research foci: 1) human development in context of schools, families, and communities; 2) cognitive and learning sciences; 3) motivation and self-regulated learning; 4) resilience and development. Faculty affiliated with the program have ongoing research programs on various important issues. These include projects on children's cognitive development and reading skills, children's achievement motivation, socialization in the schools, how computers are changing the ways in which children learn, and learning and achievement of ethnically diverse students. Students in the program work with faculty on these projects and learn to design projects in their own areas of interest. They take courses taught by faculty members in the program, and also courses taught by faculty in the Psychology Department and the School of Education. Because the department is an independent interdepartmental unit, students have the unique opportunity to work with faculty in both the Psychology Department and the School of Education, in addition to the faculty directly affiliated with the program. Graduates are well prepared for teaching and research careers in academic and non-academic settings. We are not a School Psychology or a Counseling Psychology program.

Special Facilities or Resources: The University of Michigan is blessed with an extensive scientific-scholarly community of psychologists that is virtually unique in breadth, diversity, and quality. Because of the close collaborative relationships that have evolved over the years, graduate and postgraduate students have the opportunity to learn and work in a wide variety of well-

developed specialty centers. These include: the Center for Human Growth and Development, the Center for Research on Learning and Teaching, the Center for Research on Women and Gender, the Human Performance Center, the Institute of Gerontology, the Institute for Social Research (i.e., Survey Research Center, Research Center for Group Dynamics, Center for Political Studies), the NASA Center of Excellence in Man-Systems Research, the Cognitive Science and Machine Intelligence Laboratory, the Human Factors Division of the University of Michigan Transportation Research Institute, the Kresge Hearing Research Institute, the Neuroscience Laboratory, the Evolution and Human Behavior Program, the Children's Center, the Vision Research Laboratory, and the Women's Studies Program. In addition to these resources, the Michigan campus also offers an unusually diverse series of stimulating colloquium and seminar presentations, involving both local and visiting speakers, that contributes significantly to the available opportunities for professional growth and development.

Information for Students With Physical Disabilities: See the following website for more information: http://ssd.umich.edu/.

Application Information:
Send to Department Chair. Application available online. URL of online application: http://www.rackham.umich.edu/admissions/. Students are admitted in the Fall, application deadline December 1. *Fee:* $65. $75 for non-U.S. citizens.

Michigan, University of
Department of Psychology
Literature, Science & Arts
530 Church Street, 1343 East Hall
Ann Arbor, MI 48109-1043
Telephone: (734) 764-2580
Fax: (734) 615-7584
E-mail: *psych.saa@umich.edu*
Web: *http://www.lsa.umich.edu/psych/grad/*

Department Information:
1929. Chairperson: Robert Sellers. Number of faculty: total—full-time 62, part-time 26; women—full-time 27, part-time 17; total—minority—full-time 18, part-time 5; women minority—full-time 9, part-time 3.

Programs and Degrees Offered:
Listed in the following order: Program area, degree type (T if terminal Master's), number awarded 7/11–6/12. Biopsychology PhD (Doctor of Philosophy) 1, Cognition and Cognitive Neuroscience PhD (Doctor of Philosophy) 5, Developmental Psychology PhD (Doctor of Philosophy) 5, Social Psychology PhD (Doctor of Philosophy) 6, Personality and Social Contexts PhD (Doctor of Philosophy) 2, Clinical Science PhD (Doctor of Philosophy) 6.

APA Accreditation: Clinical PhD (Doctor of Philosophy). Student Outcome Data Website: http://www.lsa.umich.edu/psych/areas/clinical/students/student_admissions.asp.

Student Applications/Admissions:
Student Applications
Biopsychology PhD *(Doctor of Philosophy)*—Applications 2012–2013, 46. Total applicants accepted 2012–2013, 5. Number

full-time enrolled (new admits only) 2012–2013, 3. Total enrolled 2012–2013 full-time, 16. Openings 2013–2014, 3. The median number of years required for completion of a degree in 2012–2013 were 5. The number of students enrolled full- and part-time who were dismissed or voluntarily withdrew from this program area in 2012–2013 were 0. *Cognition and Cognitive Neuroscience PhD (Doctor of Philosophy)*—Applications 2012–2013, 100. Total applicants accepted 2012–2013, 6. Number full-time enrolled (new admits only) 2012–2013, 2. Total enrolled 2012–2013 full-time, 16. Openings 2013–2014, 3. The median number of years required for completion of a degree in 2012–2013 were 5. The number of students enrolled full- and part-time who were dismissed or voluntarily withdrew from this program area in 2012–2013 were 0. *Developmental Psychology PhD (Doctor of Philosophy)*—Applications 2012–2013, 89. Total applicants accepted 2012–2013, 10. Number full-time enrolled (new admits only) 2012–2013, 5. Total enrolled 2012–2013 full-time, 24. Openings 2013–2014, 3. The median number of years required for completion of a degree in 2012–2013 were 5. The number of students enrolled full- and part-time who were dismissed or voluntarily withdrew from this program area in 2012–2013 were 0. *Social Psychology PhD (Doctor of Philosophy)*—Applications 2012–2013, 177. Total applicants accepted 2012–2013, 6. Number full-time enrolled (new admits only) 2012–2013, 2. Total enrolled 2012–2013 full-time, 22. Openings 2013–2014, 3. The median number of years required for completion of a degree in 2012–2013 were 5. The number of students enrolled full- and part-time who were dismissed or voluntarily withdrew from this program area in 2012–2013 were 0. *Personality and Social Contexts PhD (Doctor of Philosophy)*—Applications 2012–2013, 52. Total applicants accepted 2012–2013, 4. Number full-time enrolled (new admits only) 2012–2013, 4. Number part-time enrolled (new admits only) 2012–2013, 0. Total enrolled 2012–2013 full-time, 13. Total enrolled 2012–2013 part-time, 0. Openings 2013–2014, 3. The median number of years required for completion of a degree in 2012–2013 were 5. The number of students enrolled full- and part-time who were dismissed or voluntarily withdrew from this program area in 2012–2013 were 0. *Clinical Science PhD (Doctor of Philosophy)*—Applications 2012–2013, 297. Total applicants accepted 2012–2013, 5. Number full-time enrolled (new admits only) 2012–2013, 4. Total enrolled 2012–2013 full-time, 29. Openings 2013–2014, 3. The median number of years required for completion of a degree in 2012–2013 were 5. The number of students enrolled full- and part-time who were dismissed or voluntarily withdrew from this program area in 2012–2013 were 0.

Scores: Entries appear in this order: required test or GPA, minimum score (if required), median score of students entering in 2012–2013. *Biopsychology PhD (Doctor of Philosophy)*: GRE-V no minimum stated, 615, GRE-Q no minimum stated, 560, GRE-Analytical no minimum stated, 4.5, overall undergraduate GPA no minimum stated, 3.6; *Cognition and Cognitive Neuroscience PhD (Doctor of Philosophy)*: GRE-V no minimum stated, 690, GRE-Q no minimum stated, 720, GRE-Analytical no minimum stated, 4.25, overall undergraduate GPA no minimum stated, 3.62; *Developmental Psychology PhD (Doctor of Philosophy)*: GRE-V no minimum stated, 510, GRE-Q no minimum stated, 557, GRE-Analytical no minimum stated, 4.7, overall undergraduate GPA no minimum stated, 3.1; *Social Psychology PhD (Doctor of Philosophy)*: GRE-V no minimum

stated, 735, GRE-Q no minimum stated, 735, GRE-Analytical no minimum stated, 4.5, overall undergraduate GPA no minimum stated, 3.84; *Personality and Social Contexts PhD (Doctor of Philosophy)*: GRE-V no minimum stated, 657, GRE-Q no minimum stated, 737, GRE-Analytical no minimum stated, 4.33, overall undergraduate GPA no minimum stated, 3.68; *Clinical Science PhD (Doctor of Philosophy)*: GRE-V no minimum stated, 588, GRE-Q no minimum stated, 638, overall undergraduate GPA no minimum stated, 3.8.

Other Criteria: (importance of criteria rated low, medium, or high): GRE scores—medium, research experience—high, work experience—high, extracurricular activity—low, clinically related public service—low, GPA—medium, letters of recommendation—high, interview—high, statement of goals and objectives—high, undergraduate major in psychology—medium, specific undergraduate psychology courses taken—low. For additional information on admission requirements, go to http://www.lsa.umich.edu/psych/grad/prospective/.

Student Characteristics: The following represents characteristics of students in 2012–2013 in all graduate psychology programs in the department: Female—full-time 83, part-time 0; Male—full-time 36, part-time 0; African American/Black—full-time 17, part-time 0; Hispanic/Latino(a)—full-time 17, part-time 0; Asian/Pacific Islander—full-time 24, part-time 0; American Indian/Alaska Native—full-time 1, part-time 0; Caucasian/White—full-time 58, part-time 0; Multi-ethnic—part-time 0; students subject to the Americans With Disabilities Act—full-time 0, part-time 0; Unknown ethnicity—full-time 2, part-time 0; International students who hold an F-1 or J-1 Visa—full-time 12, part-time 0.

Financial Information/Assistance:

Tuition for Full-Time Study: *Doctoral:* State residents: per academic year $19,240; Nonstate residents: per academic year $39,076. Tuition is subject to change. See the following website for updates and changes in tuition costs: http://ro.umich.edu/tuition/.

Financial Assistance:

First-Year Students: Fellowships and scholarships available for first year. Average amount paid per academic year: $19,800. Average number of hours worked per week: 20. Apply by December 1.

Advanced Students: Teaching assistantships available for advanced students. Average amount paid per academic year: $23,634. Average number of hours worked per week: 20. Apply by December 1. Research assistantships available for advanced students. Average amount paid per academic year: $27,345. Average number of hours worked per week: 20. Apply by December 1. Fellowships and scholarships available for advanced students. Average amount paid per academic year: $19,800. Average number of hours worked per week: 20. Apply by December 1.

Additional Information: Of all students currently enrolled full time, 100% benefited from one or more of the listed financial assistance programs. Application and information available online at: http://www.lsa.umich.edu/psych/grad/prospective/financial-aid/.

Internships/Practica: Doctoral Degree (PhD Clinical Science): For those doctoral students for whom a professional psychology internship was required in this program prior to graduation, (6) students applied for an internship in 2011–2012, with (6) students obtaining an internship. Of those students who obtained an internship, (6) were paid internships. Of those students who obtained an internship, (6) students placed in APA/CPA accredited internships, (0) students placed in internships not APA/CPA accredited, but listed with the Association of Psychology Postdoctoral and Internship Programs (APPIC), (0) students placed in internships conforming to guidelines of the Council of Directors of School Psychology Programs (CDSPP), (0) students placed in internships that were not APA/CPA accredited, APPIC or CDSPP listed. Students in the clinical area begin practica [e.g., psychological testing] during their first year and continue the practicum experience in the second year [usually in local agencies] on a 6-8 hour a week basis. During the same two year period students are engaged in their Master's level research project. Students begin full-time clinical work [internships] usually in their fifth year of training.

Housing and Day Care: On-campus housing is available. See the following website for more information: http://www.housing.umich.edu. On-campus day care facilities are available. See the following website for more information: http://www.hr.umich.edu/childcare/.

Employment of Department Graduates:

Master's Degree Graduates: Of those who graduated in the academic year 2011–2012, the following categories and numbers represent the postgraduate activities and employment of master's degree graduates: Enrolled in a postdoctoral residency/fellowship (n/a), employed in independent practice (n/a), total from the above (master's) (0).

Doctoral Degree Graduates: Of those who graduated in the academic year 2011–2012, the following categories and numbers represent the postgraduate activities and employment of doctoral degree graduates: Enrolled in a psychology doctoral program (n/a), enrolled in another graduate/professional program (1), enrolled in a postdoctoral residency/fellowship (17), employed in an academic position at a university (10), employed in business or industry (1), employed in government agency (1), still seeking employment (1), do not know (1), total from the above (doctoral) (32).

Additional Information:

Orientation, Objectives, and Emphasis of Department: The Department of Psychology is committed to a broad mission of excellence in research, teaching, and apprenticeship: to create new scientific knowledge about psychological processes through first-rate scholarship; to teach innovative courses and engage students in our research and service activities; and to maintain our record of outstanding graduate training that produces tomorrow's leading researchers. We strive to accomplish these goals as a large, diverse and interdisciplinary community of scholars.

Special Facilities or Resources: The University of Michigan provides a rich environment for graduate studies. The faculty in both education and psychology are internationally known for their scholarly productivity, and so students receive excellent training in how to conduct educational research. Faculty in the Psychology Department have ties to school officials in Ann Arbor and the greater Detroit area, which means students receive ample opportunities to work on many different kinds of educational projects. Students can take advantage of the university's excellent library and computer facilities, both of which are among the best in the country. A distinct advantage of the program is that it is interdepartmental in the graduate school with full resources and faculty available from the Psychology Department, the School of Education, the School of Social Work, and the Women's Studies Department. The department has close collaborative relationships with the Center for Human Growth and Development, the Center for Research on Learning and Teaching, the Center for Research on Women and Gender, the Human Performance Center, the Institute of Gerontology, the Institute for Social Research, the Cognitive Science and Machine Intelligence Laboratory, the Evolution and Human Behavior Program, and the Children's Center.

Information for Students With Physical Disabilities: See the following website for more information: http://ssd.umich.edu/.

Application Information:
Send to Graduate Admissions, Rackham Graduate School, 915 East Washington, Ann Arbor, MI 48109-1070. Application available online. URL of online application: http://www.rackham.umich.edu/admissions/. Students are admitted in the Fall, application deadline December 1. *Fee:* $65. $75 for International Applications.

Michigan, University of, Dearborn
Master of Science in Psychology
College of Arts, Sciences, and Letters
4901 Evergreen Road
Dearborn, MI 48128
Telephone: (313) 593-5520
Fax: (313) 583-6358
E-mail: *chatkoff@umd.umich.edu*
Web: *http://www.casl.umd.umich.edu/psychology*

Department Information:
1959. Chairperson: Nancy Wrobel. Number of faculty: total—full-time 32, part-time 23; women—full-time 15, part-time 10; total—minority—full-time 6, part-time 3; women minority—full-time 3, part-time 3.

Programs and Degrees Offered:
Listed in the following order: Program area, degree type (T if terminal Master's), number awarded 7/11–6/12. Clinical Health Psychology MA/MS (Master of Arts/Science) (T), Health Psychology MA/MS (Master of Arts/Science) (T).

Student Applications/Admissions:
Student Applications
Clinical Health Psychology MA/MS (Master of Arts/Science)—Openings 2013–2014, 12. *Health Psychology MA/MS (Master of Arts/Science)*—Openings 2013–2014, 8.
Scores: Entries appear in this order: required test or GPA, minimum score (if required), median score of students entering in 2012–2013. *Clinical Health Psychology MA/MS (Master of Arts/Science):* GRE-V no minimum stated, GRE-Q no minimum stated, overall undergraduate GPA 3.0; *Health Psychology MA/MS (Master of Arts/Science):* GRE-V no minimum stated, GRE-Q no minimum stated, overall undergraduate GPA 3.0.
Other Criteria: (importance of criteria rated low, medium, or high): GRE scores—high, research experience—low, work experience—low, extracurricular activity—low, clinically related public service—low, GPA—high, letters of recommenda-

tion—high, statement of goals and objectives—high, undergraduate major in psychology—high, specific undergraduate psychology courses taken—high. For additional information on admission requirements, go to http://www.casl.umd.umich.edu/685267/.

Student Characteristics: The following represents characteristics of students in 2012–2013 in all graduate psychology programs in the department: Female—full-time 0, part-time 0; Male—full-time 0, part-time 0; African American/Black—full-time 0, part-time 0; Hispanic/Latino(a)—full-time 0, part-time 0; Asian/Pacific Islander—full-time 0, part-time 0; American Indian/Alaska Native—full-time 0, part-time 0; Caucasian/White—full-time 0, part-time 0; Multi-ethnic—full-time 0, part-time 0; students subject to the Americans With Disabilities Act—full-time 0, part-time 0; Unknown ethnicity—full-time 0, part-time 0; International students who hold an F-1 or J-1 Visa—full-time 0, part-time 0.

Financial Information/Assistance:
Tuition for Full-Time Study: *Master's:* State residents: $575 per credit hour; Nonstate residents: $1,093 per credit hour. Tuition is subject to change. See the following website for updates and changes in tuition costs: http://www.umd.umich.edu/rr_tuition-fees-2012-2013/.

Financial Assistance:
First-Year Students: No information provided.
Advanced Students: No information provided.
Additional Information: Application and information available online at: http://www.umd.umich.edu/financialaid/.

Internships/Practica: Master's Degree (MA/MS Clinical Health Psychology): An internship experience, such as a final research project or "capstone" experience is required of graduates. Master's Degree (MA/MS Health Psychology): An internship experience, such as a final research project or "capstone" experience is required of graduates. Students in the Clinical Health Psychology track will undertake practicum training. In practicum, students will attend a weekly class to discuss cases as well as work in a clinical setting approximately 20 hours each week. A variety of placement opportunities are available. Students will meet with the practicum coordinator the semester prior to beginning practicum to discuss practicum sites and locations of interest to the student. Every effort will be made to provide an opportunity for the student to interview at a practicum site within their interest and within a reasonable distance from the students' home. A total of six credit hours will be devoted to practicum over the course of two semesters. 250 hours will be logged each semester, providing the student with 500 hours total clinical experience.

Housing and Day Care: No on-campus housing is available. On-campus day care facilities are available. See the following website for more information: http://www.umd.umich.edu/ecec/.

Employment of Department Graduates:
Master's Degree Graduates: Of those who graduated in the academic year 2011–2012, the following categories and numbers represent the postgraduate activities and employment of master's degree graduates: Enrolled in a postdoctoral residency/fellowship (n/a), employed in independent practice (n/a), total from the above (master's) (0).

Doctoral Degree Graduates: Of those who graduated in the academic year 2011–2012, the following categories and numbers represent the postgraduate activities and employment of doctoral degree graduates: Enrolled in a psychology doctoral program (n/a), total from the above (doctoral) (0).

Additional Information:
Orientation, Objectives, and Emphasis of Department: The Behavioral Sciences Department at the University of Michigan-Dearborn offers a Masters of Science (MS) in Psychology in two specializations. The Master of Science in Clinical Health Psychology program trains mental health care providers to work in primary care settings, as well as more traditional clinical psychology settings. This track provides the coursework necessary to fulfill the state of Michigan requirements for the Limited License in Psychology. The Master of Science in Health Psychology program provides intense research training and is suited for students who wish to continue on to doctoral programs.

Information for Students With Physical Disabilities: See the following website for more information: http://www.umd.umich.edu/cs_disability/.

Application Information:
Send to Master of Science in Psychology, CASL Graduate Programs, 4901 Evergreen Road, 2200 SSB, Dearborn, MI 48128. Application available online. URL of online application: http://www.casl.umd.umich.edu/695757/. Students are admitted in the Fall, application deadline March 15. *Fee:* $60. Application fee is $75 for non-U.S. citizens.

Northern Michigan University
Psychology Department
Arts and Sciences
1401 Presque Isle Avenue
Marquette, MI 49855
Telephone: (906) 227-2935
Fax: (906) 227-2954
E-mail: *psych@nmu.edu*
Web: *http://psychology.nmu.edu/*

Department Information:
Head: Paul Andronis. Number of faculty: total—full-time 11; women—full-time 5.

Programs and Degrees Offered:
Listed in the following order: Program area, degree type (T if terminal Master's), number awarded 7/11–6/12. Training, Development and Performance Improvement MA/MS (Master of Arts/Science) (T), General Psychology MA/MS (Master of Arts/Science) (T).

Student Applications/Admissions:
Student Applications
Training, Development and Performance Improvement MA/MS (Master of Arts/Science)—General Psychology MA/MS (Master of Arts/Science)—
Scores: Entries appear in this order: required test or GPA, minimum score (if required), median score of students entering

in 2012–2013. *Training, Development and Performance Improvement MA/MS (Master of Arts/Science):* overall undergraduate GPA no minimum stated; *General Psychology MA/MS (Master of Arts/Science):* overall undergraduate GPA 3.0.

Other Criteria: (importance of criteria rated low, medium, or high): research experience—medium, work experience—low, extracurricular activity—low, GPA—medium, letters of recommendation—medium, statement of goals and objectives—high, undergraduate major in psychology—medium, specific undergraduate psychology courses taken—low. For additional information on admission requirements, go to http://www.nmu.edu/graduatestudies/node/45.

Student Characteristics: The following represents characteristics of students in 2012–2013 in all graduate psychology programs in the department: Female—full-time 37, part-time 0; Male—full-time 35, part-time 0; African American/Black—full-time 2, part-time 0; Hispanic/Latino(a)—full-time 0, part-time 0; Asian/Pacific Islander—full-time 0, part-time 0; American Indian/Alaska Native—full-time 3, part-time 0; Caucasian/White—full-time 66, part-time 0; Multi-ethnic—full-time 1, part-time 0; students subject to the Americans With Disabilities Act—full-time 0, part-time 0; Unknown ethnicity—full-time 0, part-time 0; International students who hold an F-1 or J-1 Visa—full-time 0, part-time 0.

Financial Information/Assistance:

Tuition for Full-Time Study: *Master's:* State residents: per academic year $7,213, $410 per credit hour; Nonstate residents: per academic year $10,101, $591 per credit hour. Tuition is subject to change. See the following website for updates and changes in tuition costs: http://www.nmu.edu/node/46.

Financial Assistance:

First-Year Students: Teaching assistantships available for first year. Apply by May 1.

Advanced Students: Teaching assistantships available for advanced students. Apply by May 1.

Additional Information: Application and information available online at: http://www.nmu.edu/graduatestudies/node/53.

Internships/Practica: Master's Degree (MA/MS Training, Development and Performance Improvement): An internship experience, such as a final research project or "capstone" experience is required of graduates. Master's Degree (MA/MS General Psychology): An internship experience, such as a final research project or "capstone" experience is required of graduates.

Housing and Day Care: On-campus housing is available. No on-campus day care facilities are available.

Employment of Department Graduates:

Master's Degree Graduates: Of those who graduated in the academic year 2011–2012, the following categories and numbers represent the postgraduate activities and employment of master's degree graduates: Enrolled in a postdoctoral residency/fellowship (n/a), employed in independent practice (n/a), total from the above (master's) (0).

Doctoral Degree Graduates: Of those who graduated in the academic year 2011–2012, the following categories and numbers represent the postgraduate activities and employment of doctoral degree graduates: Enrolled in a psychology doctoral program (n/a), total from the above (doctoral) (0).

Additional Information:

Orientation, Objectives, and Emphasis of Department: The Experimental Psychology program prepares students for doctoral programs and/or positions that require the master's degree. The MS degree in Psychology at NMU provides (a) intensive student-initiated research training in a variety of areas of experimental psychology, (b) the statistical and methodological knowledge required to examine basic or applied issues and to function as an applied psychologist and (c) an appreciation of the scientific basis of all fields of psychology. The Training, Development and Performance Improvement program provides a special emphasis on planned organizational change. The program prepares professionals to function as effective leaders of successful teams in private or public agencies and organizations. Graduates of the program will be able to create and lead learning and performance improvement efforts that contribute to organizational achievement, and employ action research to identify and solve organizational problems related to the effective use of human resources.

Special Facilities or Resources: The Psychology Department houses active laboratories for human and animal research. These laboratories include an EEG, extensive animal behavioral equipment, and a confocal laser-scanning microscope.

Information for Students With Physical Disabilities: See the following website for more information: http://www.nmu.edu/disabilityservices/.

Application Information:

Send to Department Head, Psychology Department, Northern Michigan University, 1401 Presque Isle Avenue, Marquette, MI 49855. Application available online. URL of online application: https://www.nmu.edu/applications/grad_application.shtml. Students are admitted in the Programs have rolling admissions. *Fee:* $50.

Oakland University

Department of Psychology
College of Arts and Sciences
2200 North Squirrel Road
Rochester, MI 48309
Telephone: (248) 370-2300
Fax: (248) 370-4612
E-mail: *zeiglerh@oakland.edu*
Web: *http://www.oakland.edu/psychology*

Department Information:

1957. Chairperson: Todd Shackelford. Number of faculty: total—full-time 16, part-time 11; women—full-time 9, part-time 9; total—minority—full-time 2, part-time 1; women minority—full-time 2, part-time 1.

Programs and Degrees Offered:

Listed in the following order: Program area, degree type (T if terminal Master's), number awarded 7/11–6/12. Experimental Psychology MA/MS (Master of Arts/Science) (T) 0, Experimental Psychology PhD (Doctor of Philosophy) 0.

Student Applications/Admissions:

Student Applications

Experimental Psychology MA/MS (Master of Arts/Science)—Applications 2012–2013, 42. Total applicants accepted 2012–2013, 12. Number full-time enrolled (new admits only) 2012–2013, 10. Total enrolled 2012–2013 full-time, 10. Openings 2013–2014, 12. The number of students enrolled full- and part-time who were dismissed or voluntarily withdrew from this program area in 2012–2013 were 2. *Experimental Psychology PhD (Doctor of Philosophy)*—Applications 2012–2013, 60. Total applicants accepted 2012–2013, 4. Number full-time enrolled (new admits only) 2012–2013, 4. Number part-time enrolled (new admits only) 2012–2013, 0. Total enrolled 2012–2013 full-time, 4. Total enrolled 2012–2013 part-time, 0. Openings 2013–2014, 4. The number of students enrolled full- and part-time who were dismissed or voluntarily withdrew from this program area in 2012–2013 were 0.

Other Criteria: (importance of criteria rated low, medium, or high): GRE scores—high, research experience—high, GPA—high, letters of recommendation—high, interview—high, statement of goals and objectives—high, undergraduate major in psychology—high. For additional information on admission requirements, go to http://www.oakland.edu/psychology/grad/admissions.

Student Characteristics: The following represents characteristics of students in 2012–2013 in all graduate psychology programs in the department: Female—full-time 7, part-time 0; Male—full-time 7, part-time 0; African American/Black—full-time 0, part-time 0; Hispanic/Latino(a)—full-time 1, part-time 0; Asian/Pacific Islander—full-time 1, part-time 0; American Indian/Alaska Native—full-time 0, part-time 0; Caucasian/White—full-time 12, part-time 0; Multi-ethnic—full-time 0, part-time 0; students subject to the Americans With Disabilities Act—full-time 0, part-time 0; Unknown ethnicity—full-time 0, part-time 0; International students who hold an F-1 or J-1 Visa—full-time 1, part-time 0.

Financial Information/Assistance:

Tuition for Full-Time Study: *Master's:* State residents: $595 per credit hour; Nonstate residents: $1,027 per credit hour. *Doctoral:* State residents: $595 per credit hour; Nonstate residents: $1,027 per credit hour. Tuition is subject to change. See the following website for updates and changes in tuition costs: http://www.oakland.edu/costs.

Financial Assistance:

First-Year Students: Teaching assistantships available for first year. Average amount paid per academic year: $14,000. Average number of hours worked per week: 20.

Advanced Students: Teaching assistantships available for advanced students. Average amount paid per academic year: $14,000. Average number of hours worked per week: 20.

Additional Information: Of all students currently enrolled full time, 100% benefited from one or more of the listed financial assistance programs. Application and information available online at: http://www.oakland.edu/financialaid/grad.

Internships/Practica: Master's Degree (MA/MS Experimental Psychology): An internship experience, such as a final research project or "capstone" experience is required of graduates.

Housing and Day Care: No on-campus housing is available. On-campus day care facilities are available. See the following website for more information: http://www.oakland.edu/lowry/.

Employment of Department Graduates:

Master's Degree Graduates: Of those who graduated in the academic year 2011–2012, the following categories and numbers represent the postgraduate activities and employment of master's degree graduates: Enrolled in a postdoctoral residency/fellowship (n/a), employed in independent practice (n/a), total from the above (master's) (0).

Doctoral Degree Graduates: Of those who graduated in the academic year 2011–2012, the following categories and numbers represent the postgraduate activities and employment of doctoral degree graduates: Enrolled in a psychology doctoral program (n/a), total from the above (doctoral) (0).

Additional Information:

Orientation, Objectives, and Emphasis of Department: Our graduate programs are intended to provide graduate students with the knowledge, skills, and experiences necessary to become successful consumers and producers of psychological science. Psychology is a broad discipline that interfaces with the biological and social sciences and our programs are organized around two concentrations that together encapsulate the breadth of psychological science: (1) Biological and Basic Processes and (2) Social and Behavioral Processes. These concentrations represent two broad areas that focus on phenomena from different orientations in moderately overlapping but distinguishable content areas. Students seeking the M.S. degree will be broadly exposed to the content and methods in both concentrations. Students seeking the PhD degree will have similar broad exposure to both concentrations which will be extended by an intensive inquiry specialized in one concentration. As a result, students in the PhD degree program will apply for admission in one concentration (either the Biological and Basic Processes concentration or the Social and Behavioral Processes concentration) whereas students in the M.S. degree program will be required to distribute their course work across these concentrations.

Information for Students With Physical Disabilities: See the following website for more information: http://www.oakland.edu/dss.

Application Information:

Send to Oakland University, Graduate Admissions, 511 O'Dowd Hall, Rochester, MI 48309-4401. Application available online. URL of online application: http://www.oakland.edu/grad/apply/. Students are admitted in the Fall, application deadline January 15. *Fee:* $0.

Wayne State University

Department of Psychology
College of Liberal Arts and Sciences
5057 Woodward Avenue, 7th Floor
Detroit, MI 48202
Telephone: (313) 577-2800
Fax: (313) 577-7636
E-mail: *aallen@wayne.edu*
Web: *http://www.psych.wayne.edu*

Department Information:

1923. Chairperson: R. Douglas Whitman. Number of faculty: total—full-time 37, part-time 8; women—full-time 13, part-time 4; total—minority—full-time 1; women minority—full-time 1; faculty subject to the Americans With Disabilities Act 1.

Programs and Degrees Offered:

Listed in the following order: Program area, degree type (T if terminal Master's), number awarded 7/11–6/12. Clinical Psychology PhD (Doctor of Philosophy) 7, Behavioral and Cognitive Neuroscience PhD (Doctor of Philosophy) 1, Industrial/Organizational Psychology PhD (Doctor of Philosophy) 6, Cognitive, Developmental & Social Psychology PhD (Doctor of Philosophy) 4, Industrial/Organizational Psychology MA/MS (Master of Arts/Science) (T) 10.

APA Accreditation: Clinical PhD (Doctor of Philosophy). Student Outcome Data Website: http://clasweb.clas.wayne.edu/psychology/ClinicalPsychology.

Student Applications/Admissions:

Student Applications

Clinical Psychology PhD (Doctor of Philosophy)—Applications 2012–2013, 193. Total applicants accepted 2012–2013, 15. Number full-time enrolled (new admits only) 2012–2013, 11. Total enrolled 2012–2013 full-time, 62. Openings 2013–2014, 8. The median number of years required for completion of a degree in 2012–2013 were 7. The number of students enrolled full- and part-time who were dismissed or voluntarily withdrew from this program area in 2012–2013 were 0. *Behavioral and Cognitive Neuroscience PhD (Doctor of Philosophy)*—Applications 2012–2013, 27. Total applicants accepted 2012–2013, 6. Number full-time enrolled (new admits only) 2012–2013, 3. Total enrolled 2012–2013 full-time, 14. Openings 2013–2014, 4. The number of students enrolled full- and part-time who were dismissed or voluntarily withdrew from this program area in 2012–2013 were 1. *Industrial/Organizational Psychology PhD (Doctor of Philosophy)*—Applications 2012–2013, 41. Total applicants accepted 2012–2013, 14. Number full-time enrolled (new admits only) 2012–2013, 4. Total enrolled 2012–2013 full-time, 20. Openings 2013–2014, 5. The median number of years required for completion of a degree in 2012–2013 were 5. The number of students enrolled full- and part-time who were dismissed or voluntarily withdrew from this program area in 2012–2013 were 1. *Cognitive, Developmental & Social Psychology PhD (Doctor of Philosophy)*—Applications 2012–2013, 34. Total applicants accepted 2012–2013, 11. Number full-time enrolled (new admits only) 2012–2013, 6. Total enrolled 2012–2013 full-time, 27. Openings 2013–2014, 4. The median number of years required for completion of a degree

in 2012–2013 were 5. The number of students enrolled full- and part-time who were dismissed or voluntarily withdrew from this program area in 2012–2013 were 0. *Industrial/Organizational Psychology MA/MS (Master of Arts/Science)*—Applications 2012–2013, 30. Total applicants accepted 2012–2013, 20. Number full-time enrolled (new admits only) 2012–2013, 0. Number part-time enrolled (new admits only) 2012–2013, 6. Total enrolled 2012–2013 part-time, 18. Openings 2013–2014, 15. The median number of years required for completion of a degree in 2012–2013 were 2. The number of students enrolled full- and part-time who were dismissed or voluntarily withdrew from this program area in 2012–2013 were 0.

Scores: Entries appear in this order: required test or GPA, minimum score (if required), median score of students entering in 2012–2013. *Clinical Psychology PhD (Doctor of Philosophy):* GRE-V no minimum stated, 580, GRE-Q no minimum stated, 700, GRE-Analytical no minimum stated, 5, overall undergraduate GPA 3.0, 3.76; *Behavioral and Cognitive Neuroscience PhD (Doctor of Philosophy):* GRE-V no minimum stated, GRE-Q no minimum stated, GRE-Analytical no minimum stated, overall undergraduate GPA 3.0; *Industrial/Organizational Psychology PhD (Doctor of Philosophy):* GRE-V no minimum stated, GRE-Q no minimum stated, overall undergraduate GPA 3.0; *Cognitive, Developmental & Social Psychology PhD (Doctor of Philosophy):* GRE-V no minimum stated, GRE-Q no minimum stated, GRE-Analytical no minimum stated, overall undergraduate GPA 3.0; *Industrial/Organizational Psychology MA/MS (Master of Arts/Science):* GRE-V no minimum stated, GRE-Q no minimum stated, GRE-Analytical no minimum stated, overall undergraduate GPA 3.0.

Other Criteria: (importance of criteria rated low, medium, or high): GRE scores—high, research experience—high, work experience—medium, extracurricular activity—low, clinically related public service—medium, GPA—high, letters of recommendation—high, interview—high, statement of goals and objectives—high, undergraduate major in psychology—medium, specific undergraduate psychology courses taken—high. For additional information on admission requirements, go to http://clasweb.clas.wayne.edu/psychology/DoctoralAdmissionRequirements.

Student Characteristics: The following represents characteristics of students in 2012–2013 in all graduate psychology programs in the department: Female—full-time 85, part-time 13; Male—full-time 38, part-time 10; African American/Black—full-time 8, part-time 1; Hispanic/Latino(a)—full-time 3, part-time 0; Asian/Pacific Islander—full-time 16, part-time 4; American Indian/Alaska Native—full-time 2, part-time 0; Caucasian/White—full-time 94, part-time 11; Multi-ethnic—full-time 0, part-time 0; students subject to the Americans With Disabilities Act—full-time 0, part-time 0; Unknown ethnicity—full-time 0, part-time 7; International students who hold an F-1 or J-1 Visa—full-time 9, part-time 4.

Financial Information/Assistance:

Tuition for Full-Time Study: *Master's:* State residents: $533 per credit hour; Nonstate residents: $1,177 per credit hour. *Doctoral:* State residents: $533 per credit hour; Nonstate residents: $1,177 per credit hour. Tuition is subject to change. Additional fees are assessed to students beyond the costs of tuition for the following: omnibus credit hour fee: $39.75, registration fee: $181.45, fitness center fee: $25.00. See the following website for updates and changes in tuition costs: http://reg.wayne.edu/students/tuition.php.

Financial Assistance:

First-Year Students: Teaching assistantships available for first year. Average amount paid per academic year: $16,508. Average number of hours worked per week: 20. Research assistantships available for first year. Average amount paid per academic year: $16,508. Average number of hours worked per week: 20. Traineeships available for first year. Average amount paid per academic year: $16,508. Average number of hours worked per week: 20. Fellowships and scholarships available for first year. Average amount paid per academic year: $16,508. Average number of hours worked per week: 20.

Advanced Students: Teaching assistantships available for advanced students. Average amount paid per academic year: $16,508. Average number of hours worked per week: 20. Research assistantships available for advanced students. Average amount paid per academic year: $16,508. Average number of hours worked per week: 20. Traineeships available for advanced students. Average amount paid per academic year: $16,508. Average number of hours worked per week: 20. Fellowships and scholarships available for advanced students. Average amount paid per academic year: $16,508. Average number of hours worked per week: 20.

Additional Information: Of all students currently enrolled full time, 80% benefited from one or more of the listed financial assistance programs. Application and information available online at: http://clasweb.clas.wayne.edu/psychology/FinancialAid.

Internships/Practica: Doctoral Degree (PhD Clinical Psychology): For those doctoral students for whom a professional psychology internship was required in this program prior to graduation, (6) students applied for an internship in 2011–2012, with (6) students obtaining an internship. Of those students who obtained an internship, (6) were paid internships. Of those students who obtained an internship, (6) students placed in APA/CPA accredited internships, (0) students placed in internships not APA/CPA accredited, but listed with the Association of Psychology Postdoctoral and Internship Programs (APPIC), (0) students placed in internships conforming to guidelines of the Council of Directors of School Psychology Programs (CDSPP), (0) students placed in internships that were not APA/CPA accredited, APPIC or CDSPP listed. The clinical program has a required 500-hour assessment practicum and a 500-hour therapy practicum at our in-house training clinic. We also have a network of approximately 25 external placements, supervised by psychologists, at a range of clinical settings, which our graduate students attend in years 3, 4, and / or 5. All clinical students are expected to complete a full-year predoctoral, APA-accredited internship.

Housing and Day Care: On-campus housing is available. See the following website for more information: http://housing.wayne.edu/. On-campus day care facilities are available. See the following website for more information: http://mpsi.wayne.edu/education/ecc.php.

Employment of Department Graduates:

Master's Degree Graduates: Of those who graduated in the academic year 2011–2012, the following categories and numbers represent the postgraduate activities and employment of master's degree graduates: Enrolled in a postdoctoral residency/fellowship (n/a), employed in independent practice (n/a), total from the above (master's) (0).

Doctoral Degree Graduates: Of those who graduated in the academic year 2011–2012, the following categories and numbers represent the postgraduate activities and employment of doctoral degree graduates: Enrolled in a psychology doctoral program (n/a), total from the above (doctoral) (0).

Additional Information:

Orientation, Objectives, and Emphasis of Department: This department strives to select graduate students with a strong educational background and outstanding potential and to train them to be knowledgeable, ethical practitioners and research scholars in their chosen areas. Program admission is limited to persons planning to obtain the doctoral degree. Initial broad training is followed by specialized training.

Special Facilities or Resources: The behavioral and cognitive neuroscience area participates in the university neuroscience program. Excellent laboratory facilities are available in neurobiology, neuropharmacology, psychopharmacology, neuropsychology, and ethology. Several faculty in behavioral and cognitive neuroscience and other areas in the department work in the area of substance abuse. The clinical program emphasizes psychotherapy, community mental health, diagnostics, alcohol abuse issues, neuropsychology, and child and geropsychology. Clinical practice and research experience are obtained in a variety of clinical placements and in our own clinic. The cognitive program emphasizes cognition theory and its application to applied problems. The developmental area emphasizes life-span studies and is affiliated with the Institute of Gerontology. The social psychology program has both basic and applied research emphases. Well-equipped laboratories in the department and at the Merrill-Palmer Institute, which is affiliated with the department, are available for cognitive, social, and developmental research. In addition, social psychology uses its urban setting to carry out field studies. The industrial/organizational area emphasizes organizational psychology, personnel research, and field placements. Excellent computer facilities and libraries support research in all areas.

Information for Students With Physical Disabilities: See the following website for more information: http://studentdisability.wayne.edu/.

Application Information:
Send to Graduate Office, Psychology Department, WSU, 5057 Woodward Avenue, 7th Floor, Detroit, MI 48202. Application available online. URL of online application: https://cardinal.wayne.edu/apply/gr.php. Students are admitted in the Fall, application deadline December 15. I/O Master's Program: Fall Term: Domestic Students Apply by June 1; Canadian and International Students Apply by May 1. Winter Term: Domestic Students Apply by October 1; Canadian and International Students Apply by Sept. 1. Spring/Summer Term: Domestic Students Apply by February 1; Canadian and International Students Apply by January 1. Doctoral Programs Deadline: December 15. *Fee:* $50.

Wayne State University

Division of Theoretical and Behavioral Foundations-
  Educational Psychology
College of Education
Detroit, MI 48202
Telephone: (313) 557-1614
Fax: (313) 577-5235
E-mail: *s.b.hillman@wayne.edu*
Web: *http://coe.wayne.edu/tbf/edp/index.php*

Department Information:

1957. Chairperson: Stephen B. Hillman. Number of faculty: total—full-time 7, part-time 12; women—full-time 4, part-time 8; total—minority—full-time 1, part-time 1; women minority—full-time 1.

Programs and Degrees Offered:

Listed in the following order: Program area, degree type (T if terminal Master's), number awarded 7/11–6/12. School Psychology PhD (Doctor of Philosophy) 7, School and Community Psychology MA/MS (Master of Arts/Science) (T) 14, Counseling Psychology MA/MS (Master of Arts/Science) (T) 11, Learning and Instruction Sciences PhD (Doctor of Philosophy) 0.

Student Applications/Admissions:

Student Applications

School Psychology PhD (Doctor of Philosophy)—Applications 2012–2013, 15. Total applicants accepted 2012–2013, 7. Number full-time enrolled (new admits only) 2012–2013, 7. Number part-time enrolled (new admits only) 2012–2013, 0. Total enrolled 2012–2013 full-time, 7. Total enrolled 2012–2013 part-time, 24. Openings 2013–2014, 10. The median number of years required for completion of a degree in 2012–2013 were 7. The number of students enrolled full- and part-time who were dismissed or voluntarily withdrew from this program area in 2012–2013 were 0. *School and Community Psychology MA/MS (Master of Arts/Science)*—Applications 2012–2013, 38. Total applicants accepted 2012–2013, 14. Number full-time enrolled (new admits only) 2012–2013, 14. Total enrolled 2012–2013 full-time, 26. Total enrolled 2012–2013 part-time, 12. Openings 2013–2014, 14. The median number of years required for completion of a degree in 2012–2013 were 2. The number of students enrolled full- and part-time who were dismissed or voluntarily withdrew from this program area in 2012–2013 were 0. *Counseling Psychology MA/MS (Master of Arts/Science)*—Applications 2012–2013, 29. Total applicants accepted 2012–2013, 12. Number full-time enrolled (new admits only) 2012–2013, 12. Total enrolled 2012–2013 full-time, 31. Openings 2013–2014, 14. The median number of years required for completion of a degree in 2012–2013 were 2. The number of students enrolled full- and part-time who were dismissed or voluntarily withdrew from this program area in 2012–2013 were 0. *Learning and Instruction Sciences PhD (Doctor of Philosophy)*—Applications 2012–2013, 6. Total applicants accepted 2012–2013, 2. Number full-time enrolled (new admits only) 2012–2013, 2. Total enrolled 2012–2013 full-time, 2. Openings 2013–2014, 5. The median number of years required for completion of a degree in 2012–2013 were 7. The number of students enrolled full- and part-time who were dismissed or voluntarily withdrew from this program area in 2012–2013 were 0.

Scores: Entries appear in this order: required test or GPA, minimum score (if required), median score of students entering in 2012–2013. *School Psychology PhD (Doctor of Philosophy):* GRE-V no minimum stated, GRE-Q no minimum stated, GRE-Analytical no minimum stated, overall undergraduate GPA no minimum stated, last 2 years GPA no minimum stated, psychology GPA no minimum stated, Masters GPA 3.5; *School and Community Psychology MA/MS (Master of Arts/Science):* GRE-V no minimum stated, GRE-Q no minimum stated, GRE-Analytical no minimum stated, overall undergraduate GPA 3.0, last 2 years GPA no minimum stated, psychology GPA no minimum stated; *Counseling Psychology MA/MS (Master of Arts/Science):* GRE-V no minimum stated, GRE-Q no minimum stated, GRE-Analytical no minimum stated, overall undergraduate GPA no minimum stated, last 2 years GPA no minimum stated, psychology GPA no minimum stated; *Learning and Instruction Sciences PhD (Doctor of Philosophy):* GRE-V no minimum stated, GRE-Q no minimum stated, GRE-Analytical no minimum stated, overall undergraduate GPA no minimum stated, last 2 years GPA no minimum stated, psychology GPA no minimum stated, Masters GPA no minimum stated.

Other Criteria: (importance of criteria rated low, medium, or high): GRE scores—medium, research experience—medium, work experience—medium, extracurricular activity—medium, clinically related public service—medium, GPA—high, letters of recommendation—high, interview—high, statement of goals and objectives—high, undergraduate major in psychology—medium, specific undergraduate psychology courses taken—low. For additional information on admission requirements, go to http://coe.wayne.edu/tbf/edp/index.php.

Student Characteristics: The following represents characteristics of students in 2012–2013 in all graduate psychology programs in the department: Female—full-time 31, part-time 43; Male—part-time 12; African American/Black—full-time 0, part-time 7; Hispanic/Latino(a)—full-time 0, part-time 0; Asian/Pacific Islander—full-time 0, part-time 0; American Indian/Alaska Native—full-time 0, part-time 0; Caucasian/White—full-time 0, part-time 54; Multi-ethnic—full-time 0, part-time 0; students subject to the Americans With Disabilities Act—full-time 0, part-time 0; Unknown ethnicity—full-time 0, part-time 0; International students who hold an F-1 or J-1 Visa—full-time 0, part-time 0.

Financial Information/Assistance:

Tuition for Full-Time Study: *Master's:* State residents: per academic year $14,144, $533 per credit hour; Nonstate residents: per academic year $28,242, $1,177 per credit hour. *Doctoral:* State residents: per academic year $14,144, $533 per credit hour; Nonstate residents: per academic year $28,242, $1,177 per credit hour. Tuition is subject to change. Additional fees are assessed to students beyond the costs of tuition for the following: testing materials. Tuition costs vary by program. See the following website for updates and changes in tuition costs: http://reg.wayne.edu/students/tuition.php.

Financial Assistance:

First-Year Students: Fellowships and scholarships available for first year. Apply by March 1.

Advanced Students: Fellowships and scholarships available for advanced students. Apply by March 1.

Additional Information: Of all students currently enrolled full time, 30% benefited from one or more of the listed financial assistance programs. Application and information available online at: http://coe.wayne.edu/scholarships.php.

Internships/Practica: Doctoral Degree (PhD School Psychology): For those doctoral students for whom a professional psychology internship was required in this program prior to graduation, (0) students applied for an internship in 2011–2012, with (0) students obtaining an internship. Of those students who obtained an internship, (0) were paid internships. Of those students who obtained an internship, (0) students placed in APA/CPA accredited internships, (0) students placed in internships not APA/CPA accredited, but listed with the Association of Psychology Postdoctoral and Internship Programs (APPIC), (0) students placed in internships conforming to guidelines of the Council of Directors of School Psychology Programs (CDSPP), (0) students placed in internships that were not APA/CPA accredited, APPIC or CDSPP listed. Master's Degree (MA/MS School and Community Psychology): An internship experience, such as a final research project or "capstone" experience is required of graduates. Master's Degree (MA/MS Counseling Psychology): An internship experience, such as a final research project or "capstone" experience is required of graduates.

Housing and Day Care: On-campus housing is available. See the following website for more information: http://housing.wayne.edu/. On-campus day care facilities are available. See the following website for more information: http://coe.wayne.edu/ted/ece/ecc/overview.php; http://mpsi.wayne.edu/education/ecc.php.

Employment of Department Graduates:

Master's Degree Graduates: Of those who graduated in the academic year 2011–2012, the following categories and numbers represent the postgraduate activities and employment of master's degree graduates: Enrolled in a psychology doctoral program (5), enrolled in a postdoctoral residency/fellowship (n/a), employed in independent practice (n/a), employed in a professional position in a school system (12), employed in a community mental health/counseling center (4), total from the above (master's) (21).

Doctoral Degree Graduates: Of those who graduated in the academic year 2011–2012, the following categories and numbers represent the postgraduate activities and employment of doctoral degree graduates: Enrolled in a psychology doctoral program (n/a), employed in independent practice (2), employed in a professional position in a school system (6), total from the above (doctoral) (8).

Additional Information:

Orientation, Objectives, and Emphasis of Department: The department offers MA programs in School and Community Psychology and Counseling Psychology, and PhD programs in Educational Psychology with concentrations in School Psychology and Learning and Instruction Sciences. The program orientations are eclectic, using the scientific-practitioner model, with emphasis on application of theory at the master's degree level and on theoretical issues at the PhD level.

Information for Students With Physical Disabilities: See the following website for more information: http://studentdisability.wayne.edu/.

Application Information:
Send to Department Chair. URL of online application: http://gradschool.wayne.edu/future/grad-admission.php. Students are admitted in the Fall, application deadline February 15. *Fee:* $50.

Western Michigan University
Counselor Education & Counseling Psychology
College of Education
3102 Sangren Hall, WMU, 1903 West Michigan Avenue
Kalamazoo, MI 49008-5226
Telephone: (269) 387-5100
Fax: (269) 387-5090
E-mail: *patrick.munley@wmich.edu*
Web: *http://www.wmich.edu/cecp/*

Department Information:
1970. Chairperson: Patrick H. Munley. Number of faculty: total—full-time 17, part-time 16; women—full-time 8, part-time 6; total—minority—full-time 5, part-time 6; women minority—full-time 2, part-time 5; faculty subject to the Americans With Disabilities Act 1.

Programs and Degrees Offered:
Listed in the following order: Program area, degree type (T if terminal Master's), number awarded 7/11–6/12. Counseling Psychology MA/MS (Master of Arts/Science) (T) 34, Counseling Psychology PhD (Doctor of Philosophy) 7.

APA Accreditation: Counseling PhD (Doctor of Philosophy). Student Outcome Data Website: http://www.wmich.edu/cecp/academics/doctoral/outcomes.html.

Student Applications/Admissions:
Student Applications
Counseling Psychology MA/MS (Master of Arts/Science)—Applications 2012–2013, 95. Total applicants accepted 2012–2013, 62. Number full-time enrolled (new admits only) 2012–2013, 58. Number part-time enrolled (new admits only) 2012–2013, 4. Total enrolled 2012–2013 full-time, 133. Total enrolled 2012–2013 part-time, 55. Openings 2013–2014, 55. The number of students enrolled full- and part-time who were dismissed or voluntarily withdrew from this program area in 2012–2013 were 8. *Counseling Psychology PhD (Doctor of Philosophy)*—Applications 2012–2013, 62. Total applicants accepted 2012–2013, 6. Number full-time enrolled (new admits only) 2012–2013, 6. Number part-time enrolled (new admits only) 2012–2013, 0. Total enrolled 2012–2013 full-time, 40. Total enrolled 2012–2013 part-time, 16. Openings 2013–2014, 8. The median number of years required for completion of a degree in 2012–2013 were 7. The number of students enrolled full- and part-time who were dismissed or voluntarily withdrew from this program area in 2012–2013 were 0.
Scores: Entries appear in this order: required test or GPA, minimum score (if required), median score of students entering in 2012–2013. *Counseling Psychology PhD (Doctor of Philosophy):* GRE-V no minimum stated, GRE-Q no minimum stated, GRE-Analytical no minimum stated, overall undergraduate GPA no minimum stated, psychology GPA no minimum stated, Masters GPA no minimum stated.

Other Criteria: (importance of criteria rated low, medium, or high): GRE scores—medium, research experience—medium, work experience—medium, extracurricular activity—medium, clinically related public service—low, GPA—high, letters of recommendation—high, interview—high, statement of goals and objectives—high, multicultural awareness—high, undergraduate major in psychology—medium, specific undergraduate psychology courses taken—low, There is no GRE requirement for the masters degree in Counseling Psychology. For additional information on admission requirements, go to http://www.wmich.edu/cecp/academics/admission/index.html.

Student Characteristics: The following represents characteristics of students in 2012–2013 in all graduate psychology programs in the department: Female—full-time 131, part-time 54; Male—full-time 42, part-time 17; African American/Black—full-time 20, part-time 17; Hispanic/Latino(a)—full-time 9, part-time 4; Asian/Pacific Islander—full-time 3, part-time 2; American Indian/Alaska Native—full-time 2, part-time 2; Caucasian/White—full-time 131, part-time 43; Multi-ethnic—full-time 5, part-time 2; students subject to the Americans With Disabilities Act—full-time 0, part-time 0; Unknown ethnicity—full-time 3, part-time 1; International students who hold an F-1 or J-1 Visa—full-time 3, part-time 1.

Financial Information/Assistance:

Tuition for Full-Time Study: *Master's:* State residents: per academic year $11,496, $479 per credit hour; Nonstate residents: per academic year $24,360, $1,015 per credit hour. *Doctoral:* State residents: per academic year $11,496, $479 per credit hour; Nonstate residents: per academic year $24,360, $1,015 per credit hour. Tuition is subject to change. See the following website for updates and changes in tuition costs: http://www.wmich.edu/registrar/tuition.

Financial Assistance:

First-Year Students: Teaching assistantships available for first year. Average amount paid per academic year: $18,800. Average number of hours worked per week: 20. Apply by February 15. Research assistantships available for first year. Average amount paid per academic year: $18,800. Average number of hours worked per week: 20. Apply by February 15. Fellowships and scholarships available for first year. Average amount paid per academic year: $10,400. Average number of hours worked per week: 10. Apply by February 15.

Advanced Students: Teaching assistantships available for advanced students. Average amount paid per academic year: $18,800. Average number of hours worked per week: 20. Apply by February 15. Research assistantships available for advanced students. Average amount paid per academic year: $18,800. Average number of hours worked per week: 20. Apply by February 15. Fellowships and scholarships available for advanced students.

Additional Information: Of all students currently enrolled full time, 95% benefited from one or more of the listed financial assistance programs. Application and information available online at: http://www.wmich.edu/cecp/scholarships/index.html.

Internships/Practica: Doctoral Degree (PhD Counseling Psychology): For those doctoral students for whom a professional psychology internship was required in this program prior to graduation, (9) students applied for an internship in 2011–2012, with (9) students obtaining an internship. Of those students who obtained an internship, (9) were paid internships. Of those students who obtained an internship, (8) students placed in APA/CPA accredited internships, (1) students placed in internships not APA/CPA accredited, but listed with the Association of Psychology Postdoctoral and Internship Programs (APPIC), (0) students placed in internships conforming to guidelines of the Council of Directors of School Psychology Programs (CDSPP), (0) students placed in internships that were not APA/CPA accredited, APPIC or CDSPP listed. Master's Degree (MA/MS Counseling Psychology): An internship experience, such as a final research project or "capstone" experience is required of graduates. Master's level practica are available in a wide range of settings. Doctoral practica are also available in hospitals, clinics, university counseling centers, etc.

Housing and Day Care: On-campus housing is available. See the following website for more information: http://www.wmich.edu/housing/. On-campus day care facilities are available. See the following website for more information: http://www.wmich.edu/childrensplace/index.html.

Employment of Department Graduates:

Master's Degree Graduates: Of those who graduated in the academic year 2011–2012, the following categories and numbers represent the postgraduate activities and employment of master's degree graduates: Enrolled in a postdoctoral residency/fellowship (n/a), employed in independent practice (n/a), total from the above (master's) (0).

Doctoral Degree Graduates: Of those who graduated in the academic year 2011–2012, the following categories and numbers represent the postgraduate activities and employment of doctoral degree graduates: Enrolled in a psychology doctoral program (n/a), employed in an academic position at a university (1), employed in government agency (1), employed in a community mental health/counseling center (4), employed in a hospital/medical center (1), total from the above (doctoral) (7).

Additional Information:

Orientation, Objectives, and Emphasis of Department: The department prepares professional counseling psychologists at the master's and doctoral levels. The counseling psychology doctoral program's philosophy holds that theory, research, and practice are interdependent and complementary. The curriculum and practical experiences are designed to ensure professional competency in all three dimensions and facilitate their integration. Program graduates are typically employed in a variety of settings including academic departments, university counseling centers, community mental health agencies, hospitals, and independent practices. The curriculum was developed by the Counseling Psychology faculty and is based on guidelines and principles of the American Psychological Association (APA) for accreditation of professional psychology programs. Requirements include course work in the basic scientific core of psychology including research design and statistics, the biological bases of behavior, cognitive-affective bases of behavior, social bases of behavior, individual behavior and human development, and the history and systems of psychology. Requirements also involve course work in the specialization of Counseling Psychology including professional issues and ethics in counseling psychology, counseling theory and practice, consultation, supervision, vocational psychology, intellectual and personality assessment, supervised practica, and an emphasis in multicultural counseling psychology. Students are able to pursue specialty interests in Counseling Psychology through elective courses and other adjunctive experiences (e.g. involvement in faculty research, individual or group clinical supervision, etc). In addition to course work and practica, students are required to successfully complete comprehensive examinations, a supervised APA approved predoctoral internship, and a dissertation that is psychologically focused. The student's doctoral chair and committee, along with the Counseling Psychology Training Committee, are responsible for helping the student develop a program of study and for monitoring the student's progress through the program.

Special Facilities or Resources: The department's primary training facility is the Center for Counseling and Psychological Services, which includes interview rooms, two group/family therapy rooms, and a seminar room; it is equipped with audio and video recording systems and provides for observation and telephone supervision. The department also maintains a comparable training clinic at the Graduate Center in Grand Rapids, Michigan. A wide variety of regional resources, including community clinics, schools, hospitals, and private clinics, are available to students.

Information for Students With Physical Disabilities: See the following website for more information: http://www.wmich.edu/disabilityservices/.

Application Information:
Send to Department of Counselor Education & Counseling Psychology, 1903 West Michigan Avenue, WMU, Kalamazoo, MI 49008-5226. Application available online. URL of online application: http://www.wmich.edu/apply/graduate/application.html. Students are admitted in the Fall, application deadline December 10; Spring, application deadline September 15. The application deadline for PhD admissions is December 10. Application deadlines for MA admission are January 15 for summer admission, May 15 for fall admission, and September 15 for spring admission. *Fee:* $40.

Argosy University, Twin Cities

Minnesota School of Professional Psychology
College of Psychology and Behavioral Sciences
1515 Central Parkway
Eagan, MN 55123
Telephone: (651) 286-7953
Fax: (651) 846-3380
E-mail: kkile@argosy.edu
Web: *http://www.argosy.edu/clinical-psychology/twin-cities-minnesota/psyd-programs-doctorate-degree-181612.aspx*

Department Information:

1988. Chairperson: Donna Johnson, PhD Number of faculty: total—full-time 12, part-time 2; women—full-time 4, part-time 2; total—minority—full-time 3, part-time 1; women minority—full-time 2, part-time 1.

Programs and Degrees Offered:

Listed in the following order: Program area, degree type (T if terminal Master's), number awarded 7/11–6/12. Clinical Psychology PsyD (Doctor of Psychology) 44.

APA Accreditation: Clinical PsyD (Doctor of Psychology). Student Outcome Data Website: http://www.argosy.edu/clinical-psychology/twin-cities-minnesota/psyd-programs-doctorate-degree-181612.aspx.

Student Applications/Admissions:

Student Applications

Clinical Psychology PsyD (Doctor of Psychology)—Applications 2012–2013, 88. Total applicants accepted 2012–2013, 26. Number full-time enrolled (new admits only) 2012–2013, 19. Number part-time enrolled (new admits only) 2012–2013, 0. Total enrolled 2012–2013 full-time, 182. Total enrolled 2012–2013 part-time, 0. Openings 2013–2014, 30. The median number of years required for completion of a degree in 2012–2013 were 6. The number of students enrolled full- and part-time who were dismissed or voluntarily withdrew from this program area in 2012–2013 were 9.

Scores: Entries appear in this order: required test or GPA, minimum score (if required), median score of students entering in 2012–2013. *Clinical Psychology PsyD (Doctor of Psychology):* GRE-V no minimum stated, GRE-Q no minimum stated, overall undergraduate GPA 3.25, Masters GPA 3.5.

Other Criteria: (importance of criteria rated low, medium, or high): GRE scores—low, research experience—low, work experience—high, extracurricular activity—medium, clinically related public service—medium, GPA—high, letters of recommendation—high, interview—high, statement of goals and objectives—medium, undergraduate major in psychology—medium, specific undergraduate psychology courses taken—low. For additional information on admission requirements, go to http://www.argosy.edu/admissions/Default.aspx.

Student Characteristics: The following represents characteristics of students in 2012–2013 in all graduate psychology programs in the department: Female—full-time 130, part-time 0; Male—full-time 52, part-time 0; African American/Black—full-time 6, part-time 0; Hispanic/Latino(a)—full-time 5, part-time 0; Asian/Pacific Islander—full-time 8, part-time 0; American Indian/Alaska Native—full-time 0, part-time 0; Caucasian/White—full-time 158, part-time 0; Multi-ethnic—full-time 2, part-time 0; students subject to the Americans With Disabilities Act—full-time 0, part-time 0; Unknown ethnicity—full-time 3, part-time 0; International students who hold an F-1 or J-1 Visa—full-time 0, part-time 0.

Financial Information/Assistance:

Tuition for Full-Time Study: *Doctoral:* State residents: per academic year $37,184, $1,162 per credit hour; Nonstate residents: per academic year $37,184, $1,162 per credit hour. Tuition is subject to change. Additional fees are assessed to students beyond the costs of tuition for the following: Program Fees: $3,077; Books and Digital Resources: $3,103. See the following website for updates and changes in tuition costs: http://www.argosy.edu/admissions/Default.aspx.

Financial Assistance:

First-Year Students: Fellowships and scholarships available for first year. Average amount paid per academic year: $3,000. Average number of hours worked per week: 0. Apply by September 1.

Advanced Students: Teaching assistantships available for advanced students. Average amount paid per academic year: $2,880. Average number of hours worked per week: 8. Apply by September 1. Research assistantships available for advanced students. Average amount paid per academic year: $2,880. Average number of hours worked per week: 8. Apply by September 1. Fellowships and scholarships available for advanced students. Average amount paid per academic year: $3,000. Apply by February 14.

Additional Information: Of all students currently enrolled full time, 14% benefited from one or more of the listed financial assistance programs. Application and information available online at: http://www.argosy.edu/financial-aid/.

Internships/Practica: Doctoral Degree (PsyD Clinical Psychology): For those doctoral students for whom a professional psychology internship was required in this program prior to graduation, (52) students applied for an internship in 2011–2012, with (48) students obtaining an internship. Of those students who obtained an internship, (40) were paid internships. Of those students who obtained an internship, (9) students placed in APA/CPA accredited internships, (25) students placed in internships not APA/CPA accredited, but listed with the Association of Psychology Postdoctoral and Internship Programs (APPIC), (0) students placed in internships conforming to guidelines of the Council of Directors of School Psychology Programs (CDSPP), (14) students placed in internships that were not APA/CPA accredited, APPIC or CDSPP listed. The Minneapolis/St. Paul Metropolitan Internship Consortium is affiliated with the program and accepts only Argosy University, Twin Cities students. Currently five agencies are members of the consortium: Relate Counseling Center, Ramsey County Mental Health Center, Fraser Child & Family Center, Riverwood Centers and Argosy University Student Counseling Services.

Housing and Day Care: No on-campus housing is available. No on-campus day care facilities are available.

Employment of Department Graduates:

Master's Degree Graduates: Of those who graduated in the academic year 2011–2012, the following categories and numbers represent the postgraduate activities and employment of master's degree graduates: Enrolled in a postdoctoral residency/fellowship (n/a), employed in independent practice (n/a), total from the above (master's) (0).

Doctoral Degree Graduates: Of those who graduated in the academic year 2011–2012, the following categories and numbers represent the postgraduate activities and employment of doctoral degree graduates: Enrolled in a psychology doctoral program (n/a), total from the above (doctoral) (0).

Additional Information:

Orientation, Objectives, and Emphasis of Department: The Clinical Psychology PsyD program at the Minnesota School of Professional Psychology at Argosy University, Twin Cities, emphasizes the development of knowledge, skills, and attitudes essential in the formation of professional psychologists who are committed to the ethical provision of quality services. To prepare students for entry-level practice as clinical psychologists, the doctoral program teaches: (1) knowledge in the history and systems of psychology; the theoretical and empirical foundations of clinical psychology, including the developmental, biopsychosocial, cognitive, and affective bases of behavior; and, the scientific methodology which serves as the foundation for empirically-based clinical practice; (2) skills in the identification, assessment, and diagnosis of clinical concerns; problem remediation and application of empirically-supported intervention procedures; and, the critical review of empirical literature and objective evaluation of clinical outcomes; (3) attitudes consistent with the ethical principles governing professional clinical practice, including concern for client welfare and respect for client diversity; and (4) skills in interpersonal functioning and the development of therapeutic relationships in a clinical setting.

Special Facilities or Resources: The program staffs the University's Student Counseling Center, providing both practicum and internship opportunities for our students.

Application Information:
Send to Admissions, Argosy University, Twin Cities, 1515 Central Parkway, Eagan, MN 55121. Application available online. URL of online application: https://portal.argosy.edu/Applicant/ApplyOnline_Login.aspx. Students are admitted in the Fall, application deadline February 1. *Fee:* $50.

Metropolitan State University
Psychology, MA in Psychology Program
College of Professional Studies
1450 Energy Park Drive
St. Paul, MN 55108-5218
Telephone: (651) 999-5814
Fax: (651) 999-5803
E-mail: *august.hoffman@metrostate.edu*
Web: *http://www.metrostate.edu/msweb/explore/gradstudies/masters/psych/*

Department Information:
1990. Chairperson: Gary Starr. Number of faculty: total—full-time 11, part-time 38; women—full-time 6, part-time 33; total—minority—full-time 2, part-time 7; women minority—full-time 1, part-time 6.

Programs and Degrees Offered:
Listed in the following order: Program area, degree type (T if terminal Master's), number awarded 7/11–6/12. Psychology MA/MS (Master of Arts/Science) (T) 2.

Student Applications/Admissions:
Student Applications
Psychology MA/MS (Master of Arts/Science)—Applications 2012–2013, 24. Total applicants accepted 2012–2013, 16. Number full-time enrolled (new admits only) 2012–2013, 2. Number part-time enrolled (new admits only) 2012–2013, 5. Total enrolled 2012–2013 full-time, 8. Total enrolled 2012–2013 part-time, 16. Openings 2013–2014, 15. The median number of years required for completion of a degree in 2012–2013 were 4. The number of students enrolled full- and part-time who were dismissed or voluntarily withdrew from this program area in 2012–2013 were 1.

Scores: Entries appear in this order: required test or GPA, minimum score (if required), median score of students entering in 2012–2013. Psychology MA/MS (Master of Arts/Science): overall undergraduate GPA 3.00.

Other Criteria: (importance of criteria rated low, medium, or high): research experience—medium, work experience—high, extracurricular activity—medium, GPA—high, letters of recommendation—high, interview—high, statement of goals and objectives—high, community-based work—high, undergraduate major in psychology—medium, specific undergraduate psychology courses taken—medium. For additional information on admission requirements, go to http://www.metrostate.edu/msweb/explore/gradstudies/masters/psych/applying.html.

Student Characteristics: The following represents characteristics of students in 2012–2013 in all graduate psychology programs in the department: Female—full-time 12, part-time 10; Male—full-time 2, part-time 3; African American/Black—full-time 4, part-time 2; Hispanic/Latino(a)—full-time 0, part-time 0; Asian/Pacific Islander—full-time 1, part-time 0; American Indian/Alaska Native—full-time 0, part-time 1; Caucasian/White—full-time 9, part-time 10; Multi-ethnic—full-time 0, part-time 0; students subject to the Americans With Disabilities Act—full-time 0, part-time 0; Unknown ethnicity—full-time 0, part-time 0; International students who hold an F-1 or J-1 Visa—full-time 0, part-time 0.

Financial Information/Assistance:

Tuition for Full-Time Study: *Master's:* State residents: $327 per credit hour; Nonstate residents: $654 per credit hour. Tuition is subject to change. See the following website for updates and changes in tuition costs: http://www.metrostate.edu/msweb/pathway/tuition/costs.html.

Financial Assistance:

First-Year Students: No information provided.
Advanced Students: No information provided.
Additional Information: Of all students currently enrolled full time, 0% benefited from one or more of the listed financial assistance programs. Application and information available online at: http://www.metrostate.edu/aid/index.html.

Internships/Practica: Master's Degree (MA/MS Psychology): An internship experience, such as a final research project or "capstone" experience is required of graduates. Community-based practica are arranged in consultation with the student and their faculty advisor. Practica are developed and implemented in cooperation with Metropolitan State University's Center for Community Based Learning.

Housing and Day Care: No on-campus housing is available. No on-campus day care facilities are available.

Employment of Department Graduates:

Master's Degree Graduates: Of those who graduated in the academic year 2011–2012, the following categories and numbers represent the postgraduate activities and employment of master's degree graduates: Enrolled in another graduate/professional program (2), enrolled in a postdoctoral residency/fellowship (n/a), employed in independent practice (n/a), employed in other positions at a higher education institution (1), employed in a professional position in a school system (1), employed in business or industry (2), not seeking employment (1), other employment position (4), total from the above (master's) (11).
Doctoral Degree Graduates: Of those who graduated in the academic year 2011–2012, the following categories and numbers represent the postgraduate activities and employment of doctoral degree graduates: Enrolled in a psychology doctoral program (n/a), total from the above (doctoral) (0).

Additional Information:

Orientation, Objectives, and Emphasis of Department: The Master of Arts in Psychology Program emphasizes the application of psychology in the form of community-based interventions that are rooted in the wisdom and work of members of each community. It is an innovative program, rooted in a community psychology model, in which students learn to combine theory, research, and practice to achieve positive social and community change. Prevention (rather than treatment) is a primary focus along with empowerment, health promotion, community organizing and community development.

Special Facilities or Resources: The graduate division in psychology at Metropolitan State now provides opportunities for students to participate in a variety of community service activities that supplement their graduate academic work experiences (i.e., community gardening programs, volunteer services within the community).

Information for Students With Physical Disabilities: See the following website for more information: http://www.metrostate.edu/msweb/pathway/academic_success/disability/.

Application Information:
Send to MA Psychology Program Coordinator; 1450 Energy Park Drive, St. Paul, MN 55108-5218. Application available online. URL of online application: http://www.metrostate.edu/msweb/apply/index.html. Students are admitted in the Fall, application deadline March 1; Spring, application deadline September 1. If openings remain, applications might be considered in the order received until as late as June 1. *Fee:* $20.

Minnesota State University—Mankato
Department of Psychology
AH 23
Mankato, MN 56001
Telephone: (507) 389-2724
Fax: (507) 389-5831
E-mail: *carol.seifert@mnsu.edu*
Web: *http://www.mnsu.edu/psych/*

Department Information:
1964. Chairperson: Rosemary Krawczyk. Number of faculty: total—full-time 17, part-time 2; women—full-time 10, part-time 1; total—minority—full-time 3; women minority—full-time 1; faculty subject to the Americans With Disabilities Act 1.

Programs and Degrees Offered:
Listed in the following order: Program area, degree type (T if terminal Master's), number awarded 7/11–6/12. Industrial/Organizational Psychology MA/MS (Master of Arts/Science) (T) 10, School Psychology PsyD (Doctor of Psychology) 0, Clinical Psychology MA/MS (Master of Arts/Science) (T) 10.

Student Applications/Admissions:
Student Applications
Industrial/Organizational Psychology MA/MS (Master of Arts/Science)—Applications 2012–2013, 68. Total applicants accepted 2012–2013, 18. Number full-time enrolled (new admits only) 2012–2013, 10. Number part-time enrolled (new admits only) 2012–2013, 0. Total enrolled 2012–2013 full-time, 22. Total enrolled 2012–2013 part-time, 0. Openings 2013–2014, 10. The median number of years required for completion of a degree in 2012–2013 were 2. The number of students enrolled full- and part-time who were dismissed or voluntarily withdrew from this program area in 2012–2013 were 0. *School Psychology PsyD (Doctor of Psychology)*—Applications 2012–2013, 16. Total applicants accepted 2012–2013, 8. Number full-time enrolled (new admits only) 2012–2013, 5. Number part-time enrolled (new admits only) 2012–2013, 0. Total enrolled 2012–2013 full-time, 21. Total enrolled 2012–2013 part-time, 0. Openings 2013–2014, 6. The number of students enrolled full- and part-time who were dismissed or voluntarily withdrew from this program area in 2012–2013 were 1. *Clinical Psychology MA/MS (Master of Arts/Science)*—Applications 2012–2013, 55. Total applicants accepted 2012–2013, 20. Number full-time enrolled (new admits only) 2012–2013, 8. Number part-time enrolled (new admits only) 2012–2013, 0. Total enrolled

2012–2013 full-time, 16. Total enrolled 2012–2013 part-time, 0. Openings 2013–2014, 10. The median number of years required for completion of a degree in 2012–2013 were 2. The number of students enrolled full- and part-time who were dismissed or voluntarily withdrew from this program area in 2012–2013 were 1.

Scores: Entries appear in this order: required test or GPA, minimum score (if required), median score of students entering in 2012–2013. *Industrial/Organizational Psychology MA/MS (Master of Arts/Science):* GRE-V 150, 154, GRE-Q 150, 162, overall undergraduate GPA 3.0, 3.4; *School Psychology PsyD (Doctor of Psychology):* GRE-V 153, 156, GRE-Q 144, 147; *Clinical Psychology MA/MS (Master of Arts/Science):* GRE-V 150, GRE-Q 150, GRE-Analytical 3.0, overall undergraduate GPA no minimum stated, last 2 years GPA no minimum stated, psychology GPA no minimum stated.

Other Criteria: (importance of criteria rated low, medium, or high): GRE scores—high, research experience—high, work experience—low, extracurricular activity—low, clinically related public service—medium, GPA—medium, letters of recommendation—high, interview—medium, statement of goals and objectives—medium, undergraduate major in psychology—high, specific undergraduate psychology courses taken—medium.

Student Characteristics: The following represents characteristics of students in 2012–2013 in all graduate psychology programs in the department: Female—full-time 41, part-time 0; Male—full-time 18, part-time 0; African American/Black—full-time 1, part-time 0; Hispanic/Latino(a)—full-time 1, part-time 0; Asian/Pacific Islander—full-time 5, part-time 0; American Indian/Alaska Native—full-time 0, part-time 0; Caucasian/White—full-time 51, part-time 0; Multi-ethnic—full-time 1, part-time 0; students subject to the Americans With Disabilities Act—full-time 0, part-time 0; Unknown ethnicity—full-time 0, part-time 0; International students who hold an F-1 or J-1 Visa—full-time 3, part-time 0.

Financial Information/Assistance:

Tuition for Full-Time Study: *Master's:* State residents: $381 per credit hour; Nonstate residents: $381 per credit hour. *Doctoral:* State residents: $537 per credit hour; Nonstate residents: $537 per credit hour. Tuition is subject to change. See the following website for updates and changes in tuition costs: http://www.mnsu.edu/campushub/tuition_fees/.

Financial Assistance:

First-Year Students: Teaching assistantships available for first year. Average amount paid per academic year: $4,500. Average number of hours worked per week: 10. Apply by March 15. Research assistantships available for first year. Average amount paid per academic year: $4,500. Average number of hours worked per week: 10. Apply by March 15.

Advanced Students: Teaching assistantships available for advanced students. Average amount paid per academic year: $4,500. Average number of hours worked per week: 10. Apply by March 15. Research assistantships available for advanced students. Average amount paid per academic year: $4,500. Average number of hours worked per week: 10. Apply by March 15.

Additional Information: Of all students currently enrolled full time, 50% benefited from one or more of the listed financial assistance programs. Application and information available online at: http://www.mnsu.edu/campushub/programs/.

Internships/Practica: Doctoral Degree (PsyD School Psychology): For those doctoral students for whom a professional psychology internship was required in this program prior to graduation, (5) students applied for an internship in 2011–2012, with (5) students obtaining an internship. Of those students who obtained an internship, (5) were paid internships. Of those students who obtained an internship, (0) students placed in APA/CPA accredited internships, (0) students placed in internships not APA/CPA accredited, but listed with the Association of Psychology Postdoctoral and Internship Programs (APPIC), (5) students placed in internships conforming to guidelines of the Council of Directors of School Psychology Programs (CDSPP), (0) students placed in internships that were not APA/CPA accredited, APPIC or CDSPP listed. Master's Degree (MA/MS Industrial/Organizational Psychology): An internship experience, such as a final research project or "capstone" experience is required of graduates. Master's Degree (MA/MS Clinical Psychology): An internship experience, such as a final research project or "capstone" experience is required of graduates. A variety of clinical practica are available to our clinical students. Sites have included the Mayo Clinic, The Munroe-Meyer Institute, Minneapolis VA Hospital and local Adult, Child & Family Services Clinic. I-O internship sites include 360 Solutions (TX), atrain (Germany), Augsburg Press (Mpls), Bersin & Associates (CA), Cargill (Mpls), Center for Rural Policy Development (St. Peter), City of Austin (TX), County of Orange (CA), Hogan Assessments (OK), Kenexa (Mpls), Land's End (WI), and Questar Consulting (Mpls). PsyD practicum sites include those in local school districts and a program in Belize. PsyD students are placed in internship sites in school districts across the state of Minnesota.

Housing and Day Care: On-campus housing is available. See the following website for more information: http://www.mnsu.edu/reslife/. On-campus day care facilities are available. See the following website for more information: http://ed.mnsu.edu/tch/.

Employment of Department Graduates:

Master's Degree Graduates: Of those who graduated in the academic year 2011–2012, the following categories and numbers represent the postgraduate activities and employment of master's degree graduates: Enrolled in a psychology doctoral program (6), enrolled in a postdoctoral residency/fellowship (n/a), employed in independent practice (n/a), employed in business or industry (10), employed in a community mental health/counseling center (1), other employment position (2), do not know (1), total from the above (master's) (20).

Doctoral Degree Graduates: Of those who graduated in the academic year 2011–2012, the following categories and numbers represent the postgraduate activities and employment of doctoral degree graduates: Enrolled in a psychology doctoral program (n/a), total from the above (doctoral) (0).

Additional Information:

Orientation, Objectives, and Emphasis of Department: The school psychology doctoral program emphasizes data-based decision-making, multiculturalism, mental health, and prevention. Graduates will be prepared to pursue certification and licensure at state and national levels. The clinical program is a research-based, predoctoral program with a strong behavioral emphasis.

The goal of the I/O program is to provide broad theoretical and technical training for individuals who will function as human resource professionals or who will go on to doctoral programs in I/O psychology.

Special Facilities or Resources: I-O faculty have research partnerships with major organizations such as U.S. Air Force Department of Special Investigations, JVM South Africa Mining, Catalyst Rx, U.S. Security Associates, and the National Pork Board, to name a few. Clinical faculty maintain professional relationships with Mayo Health System and with area schools. The Clinical Psychology program also runs an assessment clinic. The PsyD program maintains many active partnerships with local and regional school districts.

Information for Students With Physical Disabilities: See the following website for more information: http://www.mnsu.edu/dso/.

Application Information:
Send to Department of Psychology, AH 23, Minnesota State University, Mankato, Mankato, MN 56001. Application available online. URL of online application: https://secure.mnsu.edu/GSR/GAApp/Default.aspx. Students are admitted in the Fall, application deadline January 15. Application deadline for School Psychology PsyD program: January 15. Deadline for Clinical Psychology Program: February 15. Deadline for I/O Psychology Program: March 1. *Fee:* $40.

Minnesota State University—Moorhead
School Psychology Program
Social and Natural Sciences
1104 7th Avenue S
Moorhead, MN 56563
Telephone: (218) 477-2802
Fax: (218) 477-2602
E-mail: *schpsych@mnstate.edu*
Web: *http://web.mnstate.edu/gradpsyc*

Department Information:
1970. Program Director: Olivia Melroe. Number of faculty: total—full-time 11; women—full-time 8; total—minority—full-time 1.

Programs and Degrees Offered:
Listed in the following order: Program area, degree type (T if terminal Master's), number awarded 7/11–6/12. School Psychology EdS (School Psychology) 12.

Student Applications/Admissions:
Student Applications
School Psychology EdS (School Psychology)—Applications 2012–2013, 36. Total applicants accepted 2012–2013, 15. Number full-time enrolled (new admits only) 2012–2013, 10. Number part-time enrolled (new admits only) 2012–2013, 0. Total enrolled 2012–2013 full-time, 31. Total enrolled 2012–2013 part-time, 0. Openings 2013–2014, 12. The median number

of years required for completion of a degree in 2012–2013 were 3. The number of students enrolled full- and part-time who were dismissed or voluntarily withdrew from this program area in 2012–2013 were 1.

Scores: Entries appear in this order: required test or GPA, minimum score (if required), median score of students entering in 2012–2013. School Psychology EdS (School Psychology): GRE-V 150, 151, GRE-Q 142, 148, overall undergraduate GPA 3.0, 3.40.

Other Criteria: (importance of criteria rated low, medium, or high): GRE scores—high, research experience—medium, work experience—medium, extracurricular activity—medium, clinically related public service—low, GPA—high, letters of recommendation—high, interview—low, statement of goals and objectives—high, undergraduate major in psychology—medium, specific undergraduate psychology courses taken—medium. For additional information on admission requirements, go to http://web.mnstate.edu/gradpsyc/admissions.cfm.

Student Characteristics: The following represents characteristics of students in 2012–2013 in all graduate psychology programs in the department: Female—full-time 22, part-time 0; Male—full-time 9, part-time 0; African American/Black—full-time 0, part-time 0; Hispanic/Latino(a)—full-time 0, part-time 0; Asian/Pacific Islander—full-time 0, part-time 0; American Indian/Alaska Native—full-time 1, part-time 0; Caucasian/White—full-time 29, part-time 0; Multi-ethnic—full-time 0, part-time 0; students subject to the Americans With Disabilities Act—full-time 1, part-time 0; Unknown ethnicity—full-time 0, part-time 0; International students who hold an F-1 or J-1 Visa—full-time 0, part-time 0.

Financial Information/Assistance:
Tuition for Full-Time Study: Master's: State residents: per academic year $10,200, $425 per credit hour; Nonstate residents: per academic year $20,400, $850 per credit hour. Tuition is subject to change. Additional fees are assessed to students beyond the costs of tuition for the following: minimal basic university activity, health, etc. fees. See the following website for updates and changes in tuition costs: http://www.mnstate.edu/businessoffice/rates.aspx.

Financial Assistance:
First-Year Students: Research assistantships available for first year. Average amount paid per academic year: $1,900. Average number of hours worked per week: 5. Apply by May 15.

Advanced Students: Teaching assistantships available for advanced students. Average amount paid per academic year: $2,500. Average number of hours worked per week: 6. Apply by May 15. Research assistantships available for advanced students. Average amount paid per academic year: $2,500. Average number of hours worked per week: 6. Apply by May 15.

Additional Information: Of all students currently enrolled full time, 90% benefited from one or more of the listed financial assistance programs. Application and information available online at: http://www.mnstate.edu/graduate/finaid.aspx.

Internships/Practica: Field-based practica in both first and second years of study provide hands-on experience to students. Practica are supervised by local educators and school psychologists and are coordinated with on-campus course work so students can apply concepts and techniques learned in class. A 1200-hour internship during the third year of study serves as a capstone experience for the student's training. Internships are usually positions within school districts or special education cooperatives in the tri-state area, however students have completed internships in sites across the country.

Housing and Day Care: On-campus housing is available. See the following website for more information: http://www.mnstate.edu/housing/. On-campus day care facilities are available. See the following website for more information: http://www.mnstate.edu/childcare/.

Employment of Department Graduates:

Master's Degree Graduates: Of those who graduated in the academic year 2011–2012, the following categories and numbers represent the postgraduate activities and employment of master's degree graduates: Enrolled in a postdoctoral residency/fellowship (n/a), employed in independent practice (n/a), employed in a professional position in a school system (12), total from the above (master's) (12).

Doctoral Degree Graduates: Of those who graduated in the academic year 2011–2012, the following categories and numbers represent the postgraduate activities and employment of doctoral degree graduates: Enrolled in a psychology doctoral program (n/a), total from the above (doctoral) (0).

Additional Information:

Orientation, Objectives, and Emphasis of Department: Our goal is to provide the training necessary for our graduates to be skilled problem solvers in dealing with the needs of children, families, and others involved in the learning enterprise. Within a scientist–practitioner model and integrative perspective, the program's primary focus is on educating specialist-level professionals capable of working effectively in educational agencies and in collaboration with other human services providers. Our graduates are highly regarded by the schools and agencies within which they work because of their knowledge of current best practices in the field and because of their skills as team members.

Special Facilities or Resources: Our faculty work closely with local schools and reservations to promote opportunities for diverse practica and research experiences in two states.

Information for Students With Physical Disabilities: See the following website for more information: http://web.mnstate.edu/disability/.

Application Information:
Send to Graduate Studies Office, Minnesota State University Moorhead, 1104 7th Avenue South, Moorhead, Minnesota 56563. Application available online. URL of online application: http://www.mnstate.edu/graduate/apply.aspx. Students are admitted in the Fall, application deadline February 15. Applications will be accepted after February 15 if space is available. *Fee:* $20.

Minnesota, University of
Department of Educational Psychology: Counseling and Student Personnel; School Psychology
Education and Human Development
178 Pillsbury Drive Southeast, 206 Burton Hall
Minneapolis, MN 55455
Telephone: (612) 624-1698
Fax: (612) 624-8241
E-mail: *shupp@umn.edu*
Web: *http://www.education.umn.edu/EdPsych*

Department Information:
1947. Chairperson: Susan Hupp. Number of faculty: total—full-time 34; women—full-time 15; total—minority—full-time 8; women minority—full-time 4; faculty subject to the Americans With Disabilities Act 1.

Programs and Degrees Offered:
Listed in the following order: Program area, degree type (T if terminal Master's), number awarded 7/11–6/12. Counseling and Student Personnel MA/MS (Master of Arts/Science) (T) 33, School Psychology PhD (Doctor of Philosophy) 6, Counseling and Student Personnel PhD (Doctor of Philosophy) 4, School Psychology EdS (School Psychology) 6.

APA Accreditation: School PhD (Doctor of Philosophy). Student Outcome Data Website: http://www.cehd.umn.edu/EdPsych/Programs/SchoolPsych/outcomes.html. Counseling PhD (Doctor of Philosophy). Student Outcome Data Website: http://www.cehd.umn.edu/edpsych/Programs/CSPP/outcomes.html.

Student Applications/Admissions:

Student Applications

Counseling and Student Personnel MA/MS (Master of Arts/Science)—Applications 2012–2013, 138. Total applicants accepted 2012–2013, 68. Number full-time enrolled (new admits only) 2012–2013, 38. Number part-time enrolled (new admits only) 2012–2013, 0. Total enrolled 2012–2013 full-time, 70. Total enrolled 2012–2013 part-time, 0. Openings 2013–2014, 35. The median number of years required for completion of a degree in 2012–2013 were 2. The number of students enrolled full- and part-time who were dismissed or voluntarily withdrew from this program area in 2012–2013 were 1. *School Psychology PhD (Doctor of Philosophy)*—Applications 2012–2013, 29. Total applicants accepted 2012–2013, 11. Number full-time enrolled (new admits only) 2012–2013, 9. Number part-time enrolled (new admits only) 2012–2013, 0. Total enrolled 2012–2013 full-time, 49. Total enrolled 2012–2013 part-time, 0. Openings 2013–2014, 8. The median number of years required for completion of a degree in 2012–2013 were 7. The number of students enrolled full- and part-time who were dismissed or voluntarily withdrew from this program area in 2012–2013 were 1. *Counseling and Student Personnel PhD (Doctor of Philosophy)*—Applications 2012–2013, 74. Total applicants accepted 2012–2013, 10. Number full-time enrolled (new admits only) 2012–2013, 5. Number part-time enrolled (new admits only) 2012–2013, 0. Total enrolled 2012–2013 full-time, 37. Total enrolled 2012–2013 part-time, 0. The median number of years required for completion of a degree in 2012–2013 were 7. The number of students enrolled full-

and part-time who were dismissed or voluntarily withdrew from this program area in 2012–2013 were 1. *School Psychology EdS (School Psychology)*—Applications 2012–2013, 27. Total applicants accepted 2012–2013, 6. Number full-time enrolled (new admits only) 2012–2013, 6. Number part-time enrolled (new admits only) 2012–2013, 0. Total enrolled 2012–2013 full-time, 18. Total enrolled 2012–2013 part-time, 0. Openings 2013–2014, 7. The median number of years required for completion of a degree in 2012–2013 were 3. The number of students enrolled full- and part-time who were dismissed or voluntarily withdrew from this program area in 2012–2013 were 0.

Scores: Entries appear in this order: required test or GPA, minimum score (if required), median score of students entering in 2012–2013. *Counseling and Student Personnel MA/MS (Master of Arts/Science)*: GRE-V no minimum stated, 510, GRE-Q no minimum stated, 680, GRE-Analytical no minimum stated, 4.5, overall undergraduate GPA 3.0, 3.71; *School Psychology PhD (Doctor of Philosophy)*: GRE-V no minimum stated, 159, GRE-Q no minimum stated, 156, overall undergraduate GPA no minimum stated, 3.69; *Counseling and Student Personnel PhD (Doctor of Philosophy)*: GRE-V 350, 538, GRE-Q 400, 634, GRE-Analytical 3.5, 4.72, overall undergraduate GPA 3.1, 3.88; *School Psychology EdS (School Psychology)*: GRE-V no minimum stated, 160., GRE-Q no minimum stated, 159, overall undergraduate GPA no minimum stated, 3.66.

Other Criteria: (importance of criteria rated low, medium, or high): GRE scores—high, research experience—medium, work experience—medium, extracurricular activity—medium, clinically related public service—low, GPA—medium, letters of recommendation—high, interview—high, statement of goals and objectives—high. For additional information on admission requirements, go to http://www.cehd.umn.edu/EdPsych/.

Student Characteristics: The following represents characteristics of students in 2012–2013 in all graduate psychology programs in the department: Female—full-time 162, part-time 15; Male—full-time 63, part-time 5; African American/Black—full-time 8, part-time 2; Hispanic/Latino(a)—full-time 8, part-time 0; Asian/Pacific Islander—full-time 13, part-time 1; American Indian/Alaska Native—full-time 2, part-time 0; Caucasian/White—full-time 149, part-time 14; Multi-ethnic—full-time 5, part-time 1; students subject to the Americans With Disabilities Act—full-time 0, part-time 0; Unknown ethnicity—full-time 3, part-time 0; International students who hold an F-1 or J-1 Visa—full-time 37, part-time 2.

Financial Information/Assistance:

Tuition for Full-Time Study: *Master's:* State residents: per academic year $14,570, $1,214 per credit hour; Nonstate residents: per academic year $22,320, $1,860 per credit hour. *Doctoral:* State residents: per academic year $14,570, $1,214 per credit hour; Nonstate residents: per academic year $22,320, $1,860 per credit hour. Tuition is subject to change. See the following website for updates and changes in tuition costs: http://onestop.umn.edu/finances/costs_and_tuition/index.html.

Financial Assistance:

First-Year Students: Teaching assistantships available for first year. Average amount paid per academic year: $6,661. Average number of hours worked per week: 10. Apply by December

1. Research assistantships available for first year. Average amount paid per academic year: $6,661. Average number of hours worked per week: 10. Apply by December 1. Fellowships and scholarships available for first year. Average amount paid per academic year: $22,500. Average number of hours worked per week: 0. Apply by December 1.

Advanced Students: Teaching assistantships available for advanced students. Average amount paid per academic year: $6,661. Average number of hours worked per week: 10. Apply by December 1. Research assistantships available for advanced students. Average amount paid per academic year: $6,661. Average number of hours worked per week: 10. Apply by December 1. Fellowships and scholarships available for advanced students. Average amount paid per academic year: $22,500. Average number of hours worked per week: 0. Apply by December 1.

Additional Information: Of all students currently enrolled full time, 60% benefited from one or more of the listed financial assistance programs. Application and information available online at: http://www.grad.umn.edu/admissions/funding/index.html.

Internships/Practica: Doctoral Degree (PhD School Psychology): For those doctoral students for whom a professional psychology internship was required in this program prior to graduation, (9) students applied for an internship in 2011–2012, with (9) students obtaining an internship. Of those students who obtained an internship, (9) were paid internships. Of those students who obtained an internship, (1) students placed in APA/CPA accredited internships, (0) students placed in internships not APA/CPA accredited, but listed with the Association of Psychology Postdoctoral and Internship Programs (APPIC), (0) students placed in internships conforming to guidelines of the Council of Directors of School Psychology Programs (CDSPP), (8) students placed in internships that were not APA/CPA accredited, APPIC or CDSPP listed. Doctoral Degree (PhD Counseling and Student Personnel): For those doctoral students for whom a professional psychology internship was required in this program prior to graduation, (7) students applied for an internship in 2011–2012, with (7) students obtaining an internship. Of those students who obtained an internship, (7) were paid internships. Of those students who obtained an internship, (7) students placed in APA/CPA accredited internships, (0) students placed in internships not APA/CPA accredited, but listed with the Association of Psychology Postdoctoral and Internship Programs (APPIC), (0) students placed in internships conforming to guidelines of the Council of Directors of School Psychology Programs (CDSPP), (0) students placed in internships that were not APA/CPA accredited, APPIC or CDSPP listed. Counseling and Student Personnel Psychology MA students complete an academic year practicum in the second year with a focus on community counseling, school counseling or college student development. The practicum consists of direct work with clients/students, individual supervision on-site and an academic seminar at the university. PhD students complete one or more practica and then a year-long internship. Some students stay in the Twin Cities for the internship; others go nationally. School Psychology Doctoral students have three tiers of applied training. Tier 1 - Year-long practicum tied to assessment coursework followed by a second year of practicum tied to intervention coursework. Most of these experiences occur in metro area schools. Tier 2 - Formal school practicum under the supervision of a school psychologist in Twin Cities area schools. In addition, doctoral students complete a community/clinical practicum. These practica occur in a wide variety of settings including mental health and community agencies such as Indian Health Board, Washburn Child Guidance Center, Community University Health Care Center, and Fraser Child and Family and Center. Tier 3 - Internship. The majority of students complete their year-long internships in public schools settings, although some have found internships in settings that are a collaboration of community and educational settings. In one setting, interns work as part of a mental health and educational team providing school-based services to identified students with emotional and behavioral disorders.

Housing and Day Care: On-campus housing is available. See the following website for more information: http://www.housing.umn. edu/graduate. On-campus day care facilities are available. See the following website for more information: http://www.sphc.umn. edu/childcare.html.

Employment of Department Graduates:

Master's Degree Graduates: Of those who graduated in the academic year 2011–2012, the following categories and numbers represent the postgraduate activities and employment of master's degree graduates: Enrolled in a psychology doctoral program (8), enrolled in another graduate/professional program (1), enrolled in a postdoctoral residency/fellowship (n/a), employed in independent practice (n/a), employed in other positions at a higher education institution (5), employed in a professional position in a school system (14), employed in government agency (1), employed in a community mental health/counseling center (2), do not know (9), total from the above (master's) (40).

Doctoral Degree Graduates: Of those who graduated in the academic year 2011–2012, the following categories and numbers represent the postgraduate activities and employment of doctoral degree graduates: Enrolled in a psychology doctoral program (n/a), enrolled in a postdoctoral residency/fellowship (1), employed in an academic position at a university (1), employed in other positions at a higher education institution (3), employed in a professional position in a school system (1), employed in government agency (2), employed in a community mental health/counseling center (1), do not know (2), total from the above (doctoral) (11).

Additional Information:

Orientation, Objectives, and Emphasis of Department: Counseling and Student Personnel Psychology is intended to provide a fundamental body of knowledge and skills to prepare counselors and counseling psychologists for work in a variety of settings—counseling and human development, career development, staff development, and student personnel work. While the focus is primarily on facilitating human development in educational settings, it is possible for individuals to prepare for community and agency settings as well. The faculty is committed to addressing current social issues such as diversity concerns and adolescent well-being. The CSPP program is designed for a select group of individuals with a demonstrated capacity for leadership and a commitment in the human services. School Psychology: The range of the school psychologist's impact includes, but is not limited to, the application of theory and research in the psychosocial development and learning of children and youth, social interaction processes, prevention and competence enhancement strategies, instructional intervention and program development, and delivery of mental health services. Our major training goal is to prepare school psychologists for roles within higher education and school systems. Competencies needed include knowledge in developmental psychology, personality and learning theory, and social psychology; assessing individual and systems needs; generating and implementing prevention programs and intervention strategies; collaborative consultation; diversity; and evaluating and redesigning programs. Training modalities include a variety of seminars and independent study projects. A wide range of community resources are available to facilitate goals of the program.

Special Facilities or Resources: Our graduate program is located within a major research university where many research projects are ongoing. The program is also located within a state—Minnesota—and major metropolitan area—the Twin Cities—that are known for innovations in human services. The result is that both the research climate and the practice climate are good ones for students. CSPP: The department has some flexibility in the design of student programs. Excellent facilities for research opportunities exist throughout the university. There is a time-shared instructional computing laboratory with batch and online computer facilities available for student use; and free access to the central university computer. Students may borrow laptops, video cameras, LCD projectors, audiorecorders, overheads, and VCRs. Students record counseling role-play sessions in a state-of-the-art digital counseling laboratory. School Psychology: Two job files (academic and professional service positions) exist. School Psychology Resources houses journals, books, and intervention and assessment materials. This collection supplements the Psychology Department Journal Seminar Room (for psychology majors) and the Florence Goodenough Reading Room (for child psychology majors), the University Psychology and Educational Library with its specialized computer search facilities, and the extensive University libraries system with holdings numbering approximately 3.5 million volumes. School psychology also maintains a collection of standardized, individual, and group psychometric tests, measures, and protocols which can be borrowed for coursework use.

Information for Students With Physical Disabilities: See the following website for more information: https://diversity.umn.edu/disability/.

Application Information:

Application available online. URL of online application: http://www.grad.umn.edu/admissions/. Students are admitted in the Fall, application deadline November 15. Our CSPP MA program deadline is January 15. *Fee:* $75. The fee for international students is $95.

Minnesota, University of
Department of Psychology
N218 Elliott Hall, 75 East River Road
Minneapolis, MN 55455
Telephone: (612) 625-4042
Fax: (612) 626-2079
E-mail: *psyapply@umn.edu*
Web: *http://www.psych.umn.edu*

Department Information:
1919. Chairperson: Monica Lunciana. Number of faculty: total—full-time 44, part-time 35; women—full-time 10, part-time 15; total—minority—full-time 7, part-time 2; women minority—full-

time 3, part-time 2; faculty subject to the Americans With Disabilities Act 1.

Programs and Degrees Offered:
Listed in the following order: Program area, degree type (T if terminal Master's), number awarded 7/11–6/12. Biological Psychopathology PhD (Doctor of Philosophy) 1, Clinical Science & Psychopathology Research PhD (Doctor of Philosophy) 3, Cognitive and Brain Sciences PhD (Doctor of Philosophy) 8, Counseling Psychology PhD (Doctor of Philosophy) 3, Personality, Individual Diff. & Behav. Genetics PhD (Doctor of Philosophy) 0, Industrial/Organizational Psychology PhD (Doctor of Philosophy) 4, Quantitative/Psychometric Methods PhD (Doctor of Philosophy) 0, Social Psychology PhD (Doctor of Philosophy) 5.

APA Accreditation: Clinical PhD (Doctor of Philosophy). Student Outcome Data Website: http://www.psych.umn.edu/research/areas/clinical/. Counseling PhD (Doctor of Philosophy). Student Outcome Data Website: http://www.psych.umn.edu/research/areas/counseling/.

Student Applications/Admissions:
Student Applications
Biological Psychopathology PhD (Doctor of Philosophy)—Applications 2012–2013, 9. Total applicants accepted 2012–2013, 1. Number full-time enrolled (new admits only) 2012–2013, 1. Number part-time enrolled (new admits only) 2012–2013, 0. Total enrolled 2012–2013 full-time, 4. Total enrolled 2012–2013 part-time, 0. Openings 2013–2014, 1. The median number of years required for completion of a degree in 2012–2013 were 5. The number of students enrolled full- and part-time who were dismissed or voluntarily withdrew from this program area in 2012–2013 were 0. *Clinical Science & Psychopathology Research PhD (Doctor of Philosophy)*—Applications 2012–2013, 146. Total applicants accepted 2012–2013, 4. Number full-time enrolled (new admits only) 2012–2013, 5. Number part-time enrolled (new admits only) 2012–2013, 0. Total enrolled 2012–2013 full-time, 20. Total enrolled 2012–2013 part-time, 0. Openings 2013–2014, 4. The median number of years required for completion of a degree in 2012–2013 were 6. The number of students enrolled full- and part-time who were dismissed or voluntarily withdrew from this program area in 2012–2013 were 1. *Cognitive and Brain Sciences PhD (Doctor of Philosophy)*—Applications 2012–2013, 65. Total applicants accepted 2012–2013, 5. Number full-time enrolled (new admits only) 2012–2013, 4. Number part-time enrolled (new admits only) 2012–2013, 0. Total enrolled 2012–2013 full-time, 22. Total enrolled 2012–2013 part-time, 0. Openings 2013–2014, 7. The median number of years required for completion of a degree in 2012–2013 were 7. The number of students enrolled full- and part-time who were dismissed or voluntarily withdrew from this program area in 2012–2013 were 0. *Counseling Psychology PhD (Doctor of Philosophy)*—Applications 2012–2013, 109. Total applicants accepted 2012–2013, 4. Number full-time enrolled (new admits only) 2012–2013, 4. Number part-time enrolled (new admits only) 2012–2013, 0. Total enrolled 2012–2013 full-time, 21. Total enrolled 2012–2013 part-time, 0. Openings 2013–2014, 3. The median number of years required for completion of a degree in 2012–2013 were 6. The number of students enrolled full- and part-time who were dismissed or voluntarily withdrew from this program area in 2012–2013 were 0. *Personality, Individual Diff. & Behav. Genetics PhD (Doctor of Philosophy)*—Applica-

tions 2012–2013, 21. Total applicants accepted 2012–2013, 3. Number full-time enrolled (new admits only) 2012–2013, 2. Number part-time enrolled (new admits only) 2012–2013, 0. Total enrolled 2012–2013 full-time, 10. Total enrolled 2012–2013 part-time, 0. Openings 2013–2014, 1. The number of students enrolled full- and part-time who were dismissed or voluntarily withdrew from this program area in 2012–2013 were 0. *Industrial/Organizational Psychology PhD (Doctor of Philosophy)*—Applications 2012–2013, 46. Total applicants accepted 2012–2013, 6. Number full-time enrolled (new admits only) 2012–2013, 5. Number part-time enrolled (new admits only) 2012–2013, 0. Total enrolled 2012–2013 full-time, 22. Total enrolled 2012–2013 part-time, 0. Openings 2013–2014, 3. The median number of years required for completion of a degree in 2012–2013 were 5. The number of students enrolled full- and part-time who were dismissed or voluntarily withdrew from this program area in 2012–2013 were 0. *Quantitative/Psychometric Methods PhD (Doctor of Philosophy)*—Applications 2012–2013, 18. Total applicants accepted 2012–2013, 3. Number full-time enrolled (new admits only) 2012–2013, 1. Number part-time enrolled (new admits only) 2012–2013, 0. Total enrolled 2012–2013 full-time, 8. Total enrolled 2012–2013 part-time, 0. Openings 2013–2014, 2. The number of students enrolled full- and part-time who were dismissed or voluntarily withdrew from this program area in 2012–2013 were 0. *Social Psychology PhD (Doctor of Philosophy)*—Applications 2012–2013, 97. Total applicants accepted 2012–2013, 6. Number full-time enrolled (new admits only) 2012–2013, 2. Number part-time enrolled (new admits only) 2012–2013, 0. Total enrolled 2012–2013 full-time, 21. Total enrolled 2012–2013 part-time, 0. Openings 2013–2014, 4. The median number of years required for completion of a degree in 2012–2013 were 7. The number of students enrolled full- and part-time who were dismissed or voluntarily withdrew from this program area in 2012–2013 were 0.

Scores: Entries appear in this order: required test or GPA, minimum score (if required), median score of students entering in 2012–2013. *Clinical Science & Psychopathology Research PhD (Doctor of Philosophy)*: GRE-V no minimum stated, GRE-Q no minimum stated; *Counseling Psychology PhD (Doctor of Philosophy)*: GRE-V no minimum stated, GRE-Q no minimum stated.

Other Criteria: (importance of criteria rated low, medium, or high): GRE scores—high, research experience—high, work experience—medium, extracurricular activity—medium, clinically related public service—medium, GPA—high, letters of recommendation—high, interview—high, statement of goals and objectives—high. For additional information on admission requirements, go to http://www.psych.umn.edu/grad/applying.html.

Student Characteristics: The following represents characteristics of students in 2012–2013 in all graduate psychology programs in the department: Female—full-time 83, part-time 0; Male—full-time 53, part-time 0; African American/Black—full-time 2, part-time 0; Hispanic/Latino(a)—full-time 2, part-time 0; Asian/Pacific Islander—full-time 19, part-time 0; American Indian/Alaska Native—full-time 2, part-time 0; Caucasian/White—full-time 97, part-time 0; Multi-ethnic—full-time 2, part-time 0; students subject to the Americans With Disabilities Act—full-time 1, part-time 0; Unknown ethnicity—full-time 12, part-time 0; Interna-

tional students who hold an F-1 or J-1 Visa—full-time 22, part-time 0.

Financial Information/Assistance:

Tuition for Full-Time Study: *Doctoral:* State residents: per academic year $14,570, $1,214 per credit hour; Nonstate residents: per academic year $22,320, $1,860 per credit hour. Tuition is subject to change. Additional fees are assessed to students beyond the costs of tuition for the following: Student services fee of $368.29/semester; CLA fee of $155/semester. See the following website for updates and changes in tuition costs: http://onestop. umn.edu/finances/costs_and_tuition/index.html.

Financial Assistance:

First-Year Students: Teaching assistantships available for first year. Average amount paid per academic year: $13,985. Average number of hours worked per week: 20. Apply by December 1. Research assistantships available for first year. Average amount paid per academic year: $13,985. Average number of hours worked per week: 20. Apply by December 1. Traineeships available for first year. Average number of hours worked per week: 0. Apply by December 1. Fellowships and scholarships available for first year. Average amount paid per academic year: $22,500. Average number of hours worked per week: 0. Apply by December 1.

Advanced Students: Teaching assistantships available for advanced students. Average amount paid per academic year: $13,985. Average number of hours worked per week: 20. Research assistantships available for advanced students. Average amount paid per academic year: $13,985. Average number of hours worked per week: 20. Traineeships available for advanced students. Average amount paid per academic year: $20,788. Average number of hours worked per week: 0. Fellowships and scholarships available for advanced students. Average amount paid per academic year: $23,924. Average number of hours worked per week: 0.

Additional Information: Of all students currently enrolled full time, 87% benefited from one or more of the listed financial assistance programs. Application and information available online at: http://www.psych.umn.edu/grad/finsup.html.

Internships/Practica: Doctoral Degree (PhD Clinical Science & Psychopathology Research): For those doctoral students for whom a professional psychology internship was required in this program prior to graduation, (3) students applied for an internship in 2011–2012, with (3) students obtaining an internship. Of those students who obtained an internship, (3) were paid internships. Of those students who obtained an internship, (3) students placed in APA/CPA accredited internships, (0) students placed in internships not APA/CPA accredited, but listed with the Association of Psychology Postdoctoral and Internship Programs (AP-PIC), (0) students placed in internships conforming to guidelines of the Council of Directors of School Psychology Programs (CDSPP), (0) students placed in internships that were not APA/CPA accredited, APPIC or CDSPP listed. Doctoral Degree (PhD Counseling Psychology): For those doctoral students for whom a professional psychology internship was required in this program prior to graduation, (6) students applied for an internship in 2011–2012, with (6) students obtaining an internship. Of those students who obtained an internship, (6) were paid internships. Of those students who obtained an internship, (6) students placed in APA/CPA accredited internships, (0) students placed in internships not APA/CPA accredited, but listed with the Association of Psychology Postdoctoral and Internship Programs (AP-

PIC), (0) students placed in internships conforming to guidelines of the Council of Directors of School Psychology Programs (CDSPP), (0) students placed in internships that were not APA/CPA accredited, APPIC or CDSPP listed. Internships are available at the university hospitals, the department's Vocational Assessment Clinic, the University Counseling and Consulting Services, the Veterans Administration, and several other governmental and private agencies throughout the area.

Housing and Day Care: On-campus housing is available. See the following website for more information: http://www.housing.umn. edu/index.html. On-campus day care facilities are available. See the following website for more information: http://www.cehd. umn.edu/ChildDevelopmentCenter/; http://www.cehd.umn.edu/ ICD/LabSchool/default.asp.

Employment of Department Graduates:

Master's Degree Graduates: Of those who graduated in the academic year 2011–2012, the following categories and numbers represent the postgraduate activities and employment of master's degree graduates: Enrolled in a postdoctoral residency/fellowship (n/a), employed in independent practice (n/a), total from the above (master's) (0).

Doctoral Degree Graduates: Of those who graduated in the academic year 2011–2012, the following categories and numbers represent the postgraduate activities and employment of doctoral degree graduates: Enrolled in a psychology doctoral program (n/a), enrolled in a postdoctoral residency/fellowship (5), employed in an academic position at a university (8), employed in an academic position at a 2-year/4-year college (1), employed in business or industry (5), employed in a community mental health/counseling center (1), employed in a hospital/medical center (3), other employment position (1), total from the above (doctoral) (24).

Additional Information:

Orientation, Objectives, and Emphasis of Department: Minnesota has a broad range of areas of specialization in the department, which cannot be described in detail here. In general, the overall goal is to train the people who will become leaders in their chosen area of specialization. Consequently, the graduate training programs in the department are oriented first to the training of skilled researchers and teachers in psychology, and then to the training of specialists and practitioners. The PhD programs in Clinical Science and Psychopathology Research, Counseling, and School Psychology are accredited by APA. Department faculty also participate in independent degree programs in neuroscience and cognitive science. The Department of Psychology and the Institute of Child Development offer a training program in child clinical psychology focused on the study of psychopathology in the context of development.

Special Facilities or Resources: The department offers extensive laboratory and computer facilities, a wide variety of resources and collaborative relationships both on and off campus, and several federally funded research projects. For example, three research centers are headquartered in the Department: Center for Cognitive Sciences, Center for the Study of Political Psychology, and the Center for the Study of the Individual and Society. Other research centers with which the faculty are involved are located in Neuroscience, Radiology, Epidemiology, and Public Health. We have adjunct faculty at the University of Minnesota Counseling and Consulting Services, Carlson School of Management,

Institute of Child Development, and Department of Educational Psychology; and in the VA Medical Center, Hennepin County Medical Center (Minneapolis), Ramsey Medical Center (St. Paul), and Personnel Decisions International (Minneapolis).

Information for Students With Physical Disabilities: See the following website for more information: https://diversity.umn.edu/disability/.

Application Information:
Application available online. URL of online application: http://www.grad.umn.edu/admissions/. Students are admitted in the Fall, application deadline December 1. *Fee:* $75. $95 for international applicants.

Minnesota, University of
Institute of Child Development
College of Education and Human Development
51 East River Road
Minneapolis, MN 55455
Telephone: (612) 624-0526
Fax: (612) 624-6373
E-mail: *icd@umn.edu*
Web: *http://www.cehd.umn.edu/icd/*

Department Information:
1925. Director: Megan Gunnar. Number of faculty: total—full-time 18; women—full-time 9; total—minority—full-time 1; women minority—full-time 1.

Programs and Degrees Offered:
Listed in the following order: Program area, degree type (T if terminal Master's), number awarded 7/11–6/12. Child Psychology PhD (Doctor of Philosophy) 4, Child/Clinical Psychology PhD (Doctor of Philosophy) 4.

Student Applications/Admissions:
Student Applications
Child Psychology PhD (Doctor of Philosophy)—Applications 2012–2013, 53. Total applicants accepted 2012–2013, 10. Number full-time enrolled (new admits only) 2012–2013, 5. Total enrolled 2012–2013 full-time, 28. Total enrolled 2012–2013 part-time, 0. Openings 2013–2014, 4. The median number of years required for completion of a degree in 2012–2013 were 6. The number of students enrolled full- and part-time who were dismissed or voluntarily withdrew from this program area in 2012–2013 were 0. *Child/Clinical Psychology PhD (Doctor of Philosophy)*—Applications 2012–2013, 85. Total applicants accepted 2012–2013, 4. Number full-time enrolled (new admits only) 2012–2013, 4. Total enrolled 2012–2013 full-time, 22. Total enrolled 2012–2013 part-time, 0. Openings 2013–2014, 3. The median number of years required for completion of a degree in 2012–2013 were 6. The number of students enrolled full- and part-time who were dismissed or voluntarily withdrew from this program area in 2012–2013 were 0.

Scores: Entries appear in this order: required test or GPA, minimum score (if required), median score of students entering in 2012–2013. *Child Psychology PhD (Doctor of Philosophy):* GRE-V no minimum stated, 160, GRE-Q no minimum stated, 156, GRE-Analytical no minimum stated, 4.50, overall undergraduate GPA no minimum stated, 3.60; *Child/Clinical Psychology PhD (Doctor of Philosophy):* GRE-V no minimum stated, 161, GRE-Q no minimum stated, 155, GRE-Analytical no minimum stated, 4.50, overall undergraduate GPA no minimum stated, 3.69.

Other Criteria: (importance of criteria rated low, medium, or high): GRE scores—medium, research experience—high, work experience—low, extracurricular activity—low, clinically related public service—low, GPA—high, letters of recommendation—high, statement of goals and objectives—high, Clinically related public service rated low for joint child/clinical program. For additional information on admission requirements, go to http://www.cehd.umn.edu/icd/futurestudents/cpsy/graduate/.

Student Characteristics: The following represents characteristics of students in 2012–2013 in all graduate psychology programs in the department: Female—full-time 42, part-time 0; Male—full-time 8, part-time 0; African American/Black—full-time 0, part-time 0; Hispanic/Latino(a)—full-time 4, part-time 0; Asian/Pacific Islander—full-time 6, part-time 0; American Indian/Alaska Native—full-time 0, part-time 0; Caucasian/White—full-time 40, part-time 0; Multi-ethnic—full-time 0, part-time 0; students subject to the Americans With Disabilities Act—full-time 2, part-time 0; Unknown ethnicity—full-time 0, part-time 0; International students who hold an F-1 or J-1 Visa—full-time 6, part-time 0.

Financial Information/Assistance:
Tuition for Full-Time Study: *Doctoral:* State residents: per academic year $14,570, $1,214 per credit hour; Nonstate residents: per academic year $22,320, $1,860 per credit hour. Tuition is subject to change. See the following website for updates and changes in tuition costs: http://onestop.umn.edu/finances/costs_and_tuition/index.html.

Financial Assistance:
First-Year Students: Teaching assistantships available for first year. Average amount paid per academic year: $14,377. Average number of hours worked per week: 20. Research assistantships available for first year. Average amount paid per academic year: $14,377. Average number of hours worked per week: 20. Fellowships and scholarships available for first year. Average amount paid per academic year: $22,500.

Advanced Students: Teaching assistantships available for advanced students. Average amount paid per academic year: $14,377. Average number of hours worked per week: 20. Research assistantships available for advanced students. Average amount paid per academic year: $14,377. Average number of hours worked per week: 20. Traineeships available for advanced students. Average amount paid per academic year: $22,032. Fellowships and scholarships available for advanced students. Average amount paid per academic year: $22,500.

Additional Information: Of all students currently enrolled full time, 100% benefited from one or more of the listed financial assistance programs. Application and information available online at: http://www.grad.umn.edu/admissions/funding/index.html.

Internships/Practica: Clinical practica and internships are available within the local community to Developmental Psychopathology and Clinical Science students and are offered through the

APA-accredited Clinical Science and Psychopathology area of the Psychology Department.

Housing and Day Care: On-campus housing is available. See the following website for more information: http://www.housing.umn. edu/graduate/. On-campus day care facilities are available. See the following website for more information: http://www.cehd. umn.edu/ChildDevelopmentCenter/.

Employment of Department Graduates:

Master's Degree Graduates: Of those who graduated in the academic year 2011–2012, the following categories and numbers represent the postgraduate activities and employment of master's degree graduates: Enrolled in a postdoctoral residency/fellowship (n/a), employed in independent practice (n/a), total from the above (master's) (0).

Doctoral Degree Graduates: Of those who graduated in the academic year 2011–2012, the following categories and numbers represent the postgraduate activities and employment of doctoral degree graduates: Enrolled in a psychology doctoral program (n/a), enrolled in a postdoctoral residency/fellowship (1), employed in an academic position at a university (2), employed in an academic position at a 2-year/4-year college (2), employed in other positions at a higher education institution (2), employed in a hospital/medical center (1), total from the above (doctoral) (8).

Additional Information:

Orientation, Objectives, and Emphasis of Department: The Institute program emphasizes training for research and academic careers. The program offers a diversity of substantive and methodological approaches. In the core program, special strengths are in infancy, personality and social development, perception, cognitive processes, language development, biological bases of development, and developmental neuroscience. Formal clinical training is available through the Developmental Psychopathology and Clinical Science (DPCS) joint program. Formal minor programs are offered in Neuroscience, Cognitive Science, Prevention Science and Interpersonal Relationships Research. Special training is also available through affiliations with the Center for Cognitive Sciences, the Center for Neurobehavioral Development, the Center for Early Education and Development, the Center for Personalized Prevention Research, the Human Capital Research Collaborative, and the Consortium on Children, Youth, and Families.

Special Facilities or Resources: Physical and research facilities include an office for every student plus exclusive use of a laptop computer during the program, a reference room with more than 4,500 volumes and 4 computers, twenty-five experiment rooms, and a laboratory nursery school. In addition, state-of-the-art research facilities and interdisciplinary collaborations facilitate cutting-edge neuroscience research in the areas of cognitive, behavioral, and social/emotional development. Onsite facilities include both high density (128 channels) and low density (32 channels) electrophysiological recording equipment and eyetracking equipment. Facilities at the Center for Neurobehavioral Development (opened in 2001) include autonomic and electrophysiological laboratories equipped with functional magnetic resonance imaging (fMRI) and event-related potential (ERP) equipment; audiovisual systems for online data collection, videotaping, presentations, and training; research suites, computer workroom, library/conference room; and subject exam rooms and family waiting/play rooms. At the Center for Magnetic Resonance Research, structural and functional MRI equipment is available.

Information for Students With Physical Disabilities: See the following website for more information: https://diversity.umn.edu/disability/.

Application Information:
Application available online. URL of online application: http://www.grad.umn.edu/admissions/. Students are admitted in the Fall, application deadline December 1. *Fee:* $75. $95 for international applicants.

Saint Mary's University of Minnesota
Counseling and Psychological Services
School of Graduate Studies
2500 Park Avenue
Minneapolis, MN 55404
Telephone: (612) 728-5113
Fax: (612) 728-5121
E-mail: *chuck@smumn.edu*
Web: *http://www.smumn.edu/graduate-home/areas-of-study/graduate-school-of-health-human-services*

Department Information:
1982. Program Director: Christina Huck, PhD, L.P. Number of faculty: total—full-time 2, part-time 82; women—full-time 2, part-time 42; minority—part-time 6; women minority—part-time 4.

Programs and Degrees Offered:
Listed in the following order: Program area, degree type (T if terminal Master's), number awarded 7/11–6/12. Counseling and Psychological Services MA/MS (Master of Arts/Science) (T) 54, Marriage and Family Therapy MA/MS (Master of Arts/Science) (T) 65, Marriage and Family Therapy Certificate Other 4.

Student Applications/Admissions:
Student Applications
Counseling and Psychological Services MA/MS (Master of Arts/Science)—Applications 2012–2013, 234. Total applicants accepted 2012–2013, 234. Number full-time enrolled (new admits only) 2012–2013, 110. Number part-time enrolled (new admits only) 2012–2013, 24. Total enrolled 2012–2013 full-time, 300. Total enrolled 2012–2013 part-time, 219. *Marriage and Family Therapy MA/MS (Master of Arts/Science)*—Applications 2012–2013, 123. Total applicants accepted 2012–2013, 121. Number full-time enrolled (new admits only) 2012–2013, 84. Number part-time enrolled (new admits only) 2012–2013, 17. Total enrolled 2012–2013 full-time, 373. Total enrolled 2012–2013 part-time, 87. *Marriage and Family Therapy Certificate Other*—Applications 2012–2013, 45. Total applicants accepted 2012–2013, 45. Number full-time enrolled (new admits only) 2012–2013, 3. Number part-time enrolled (new admits only) 2012–2013, 4. Total enrolled 2012–2013 full-time, 13. Total enrolled 2012–2013 part-time, 14.

Scores: Entries appear in this order: required test or GPA, minimum score (if required), median score of students entering in 2012–2013. *Counseling and Psychological Services MA/MS (Master of Arts/Science):* overall undergraduate GPA 2.75;

Marriage and Family Therapy MA/MS (Master of Arts/Science): overall undergraduate GPA 2.75.

Other Criteria: (importance of criteria rated low, medium, or high): research experience—medium, work experience—high, extracurricular activity—medium, clinically related public service—high, GPA—high, letters of recommendation—high, interview—high, statement of goals and objectives—high, undergraduate major in psychology—medium. For additional information on admission requirements, go to http://www.smumn.edu/graduate-home/admission.

Student Characteristics: The following represents characteristics of students in 2012–2013 in all graduate psychology programs in the department: Female—full-time 588, part-time 271; Male—full-time 98, part-time 49; African American/Black—full-time 25, part-time 29; Hispanic/Latino(a)—full-time 16, part-time 9; Asian/Pacific Islander—full-time 22, part-time 5; American Indian/Alaska Native—full-time 1, part-time 1; Caucasian/White—full-time 413, part-time 191; Multi-ethnic—full-time 8, part-time 3; students subject to the Americans With Disabilities Act—full-time 2, part-time 7; Unknown ethnicity—full-time 201, part-time 82; International students who hold an F-1 or J-1 Visa—full-time 9, part-time 3.

Financial Information/Assistance:
Tuition for Full-Time Study: *Master's:* State residents: $400 per credit hour; Nonstate residents: $400 per credit hour. See the following website for updates and changes in tuition costs: http://www.smumn.edu/graduate-home/tuition-financial-aid/tuition-fees.

Financial Assistance:
  First-Year Students: Fellowships and scholarships available for first year.
  Advanced Students: Fellowships and scholarships available for advanced students.
  Additional Information: Of all students currently enrolled full time, 1% benefited from one or more of the listed financial assistance programs. Application and information available online at: http://www.smumn.edu/graduate-home/tuition-financial-aid.

Internships/Practica: Master's Degree (MA/MS Counseling and Psychological Services): An internship experience, such as a final research project or "capstone" experience is required of graduates. Master's Degree (MA/MS Marriage and Family Therapy): An internship experience, such as a final research project or "capstone" experience is required of graduates. A wide variety of practicum sites are available for students.

Housing and Day Care: No on-campus housing is available. No on-campus day care facilities are available.

Employment of Department Graduates:
Master's Degree Graduates: Of those who graduated in the academic year 2011–2012, the following categories and numbers represent the postgraduate activities and employment of master's degree graduates: Enrolled in a postdoctoral residency/fellowship (n/a), employed in independent practice (n/a), total from the above (master's) (0).
Doctoral Degree Graduates: Of those who graduated in the academic year 2011–2012, the following categories and numbers represent the postgraduate activities and employment of doctoral degree graduates: Enrolled in a psychology doctoral program (n/a), total from the above (doctoral) (0).

Additional Information:
Orientation, Objectives, and Emphasis of Department: The Master of Arts Program in Counseling and Psychological Services prepares graduates for professional work in counseling, psychotherapy, and other psychological services. It is designed to enhance the student's understanding of the complex nature of human behavior and social interaction, and to develop tools for assessing human problems and assisting individuals in developing greater understanding and acceptance of themselves and their relationships with others. The program is designed to meet the educational requirements for Minnesota licensure for Licensed Professional Counselors. Additional coursework is available for those seeking Minnesota licensure for Licensed Professional Clinical Counselors. The Counseling and Psychological Services program is offered in Rochester, MN, as well as in Minneapolis.

Special Facilities or Resources: The majority of our faculty are adjunct (part-time) instructors with doctorates who are practicing in the field. They bring a wealth of real-world experience to their teaching and possess strong academic credentials. Since our emphasis is on applied psychological competence, we consider the backgrounds of these practitioner-scholars to be a major strength of the program.

Application Information:
Send to Admissions, Saint Mary's University of Minnesota, 2500 Park Avenue, Minneapolis, MN 55404. Application available online. URL of online application: https://orion.smumn.edu/application/submit.php. Programs have rolling admissions. Deadlines are somewhat flexible. Recommend applying 3 months before the start of the semester. *Fee:* $25.

St. Cloud State University
Department of Psychology
Social Sciences
720 4th Avenue South
Saint Cloud, MN 56301
Telephone: (320) 308-4157
Fax: (320) 308-3098
E-mail: *dsprotolipac@stcloudstate.edu*
Web: *http://www.stcloudstate.edu/psychology/io/*

Department Information:
  1963. Chairperson: Dr. Joseph Melcher. Number of faculty: total—full-time 12, part-time 9; women—full-time 7, part-time 5; total—minority—full-time 1; women minority—full-time 1.

Programs and Degrees Offered:
  Listed in the following order: Program area, degree type (T if terminal Master's), number awarded 7/11–6/12. Industrial/Organizational Psychology MA/MS (Master of Arts/Science) (T) 5.

Student Applications/Admissions:
  Student Applications
  Industrial/Organizational Psychology MA/MS (Master of Arts/Science)—Applications 2012–2013, 36. Total applicants ac-

cepted 2012–2013, 16. Number full-time enrolled (new admits only) 2012–2013, 9. Number part-time enrolled (new admits only) 2012–2013, 0. Total enrolled 2012–2013 full-time, 16. Total enrolled 2012–2013 part-time, 0. Openings 2013–2014, 10. The median number of years required for completion of a degree in 2012–2013 were 2. The number of students enrolled full- and part-time who were dismissed or voluntarily withdrew from this program area in 2012–2013 were 0.

Scores: Entries appear in this order: required test or GPA, minimum score (if required), median score of students entering in 2012–2013. *Industrial/Organizational Psychology MA/MS (Master of Arts/Science):* GRE-V 152, GRE-Q 144, overall undergraduate GPA 2.75, last 2 years GPA 2.75.

Other Criteria: (importance of criteria rated low, medium, or high): GRE scores—high, research experience—medium, work experience—medium, extracurricular activity—low, GPA—high, letters of recommendation—medium, statement of goals and objectives—medium. For additional information on admission requirements, go to http://www.stcloudstate.edu/psychology/io/application/default.asp.

Student Characteristics: The following represents characteristics of students in 2012–2013 in all graduate psychology programs in the department: Female—full-time 8, part-time 0; Male—full-time 8, part-time 0; African American/Black—full-time 0, part-time 0; Hispanic/Latino(a)—full-time 0, part-time 0; Asian/Pacific Islander—full-time 1, part-time 0; American Indian/Alaska Native—full-time 0, part-time 0; Caucasian/White—full-time 15, part-time 0; Multi-ethnic—full-time 0, part-time 0; students subject to the Americans With Disabilities Act—full-time 0, part-time 0; Unknown ethnicity—full-time 0, part-time 0; International students who hold an F-1 or J-1 Visa—full-time 1, part-time 0.

Financial Information/Assistance:

Tuition for Full-Time Study: *Master's:* State residents: $337 per credit hour; Nonstate residents: $521 per credit hour. Tuition is subject to change. See the following website for updates and changes in tuition costs: http://www.stcloudstate.edu/billing/tuition/.

Financial Assistance:

First-Year Students: Teaching assistantships available for first year. Average amount paid per academic year: $5,000. Average number of hours worked per week: 10. Research assistantships available for first year. Average amount paid per academic year: $5,000. Average number of hours worked per week: 10. Fellowships and scholarships available for first year.

Advanced Students: Teaching assistantships available for advanced students. Average amount paid per academic year: $5,000. Average number of hours worked per week: 10. Research assistantships available for advanced students. Average amount paid per academic year: $5,000. Average number of hours worked per week: 10. Fellowships and scholarships available for advanced students.

Additional Information: Of all students currently enrolled full time, 75% benefited from one or more of the listed financial assistance programs. Application and information available online at: http://www.stcloudstate.edu/gradadmissions/financing-your-education/default.aspx.

Internships/Practica: Students pursuing the Master's Degree in Industrial-Organizational Psychology have the option of complet-

ing either a practicum/internship or a thesis. The practicum/internship option is designed for students planning to seek employment upon completion of their degree. The thesis option is designed for students planning to seek a doctoral degree in Industrial-Organizational Psychology.

Housing and Day Care: On-campus housing is available. See the following website for more information: http://www.stcloudstate.edu/reslife/. On-campus day care facilities are available. See the following website for more information: http://www.stcloudstate.edu/childcare/.

Employment of Department Graduates:

Master's Degree Graduates: Of those who graduated in the academic year 2011–2012, the following categories and numbers represent the postgraduate activities and employment of master's degree graduates: Enrolled in a postdoctoral residency/fellowship (n/a), employed in independent practice (n/a), employed in business or industry (5), total from the above (master's) (5).

Doctoral Degree Graduates: Of those who graduated in the academic year 2011–2012, the following categories and numbers represent the postgraduate activities and employment of doctoral degree graduates: Enrolled in a psychology doctoral program (n/a), total from the above (doctoral) (0).

Additional Information:

Orientation, Objectives, and Emphasis of Department: The St. Cloud State University Department of Psychology is dedicated to providing students with a quality graduate education. The Industrial-Organizational Psychology Master's Degree Program is designed to provide graduate students with the knowledge and skills that will prepare them for jobs in consulting, business, and government, or to continue their education. The curriculum reflects a commitment to the scientist–practitioner model of graduate education in psychology by including training in the theoretical and empirical bases of industrial-organizational psychology and in the application of these perspectives to work settings. Following the recommendations of the Society for Industrial-Organizational Psychology for master's level education, students' graduate experience will include: (a) training in the core areas of industrial-organizational psychology, including personnel selection, training and organizational development, criterion development, and organizational theory, (b) a firm foundation in psychological theory, research methods, statistics, and psychometrics, and (c) the opportunity to obtain both research experience and applied experience while completing their education.

Special Facilities or Resources: The St. Cloud State University Psychology Department has a dedicated psychology laboratory facility (new space established in 1999). It has 10 rooms for individual and group testing. The lab has networked computers and a laser printer. Activities that take place in this lab include: faculty and student research, meetings of student organizations, research seminars, and classroom demonstrations.

Information for Students With Physical Disabilities: See the following website for more information: http://www.stcloudstate.edu/sds/.

Application Information:

Send to School of Graduate Studies, 121 Administrative Services, St. Cloud State University, 720-4th Avenue South, St. Cloud, MN 56301.

Application available online. URL of online application: http://www.stcloudstate.edu/gradadmissions/application/default.aspx. Students are admitted in the Fall, application deadline February 15. *Fee:* $35.

St. Thomas, University of
Graduate School of Professional Psychology
College of Education, Leadership and Counseling
1000 La Salle Avenue, MOH 217
Minneapolis, MN 55403-2005
Telephone: (651) 962-4650
Fax: (651) 962-4651
E-mail: *gradpsych@stthomas.edu*
Web: *http://www.stthomas.edu/celc/*

Department Information:
1960. Associate Dean: Chris Vye. Number of faculty: total—full-time 10, part-time 19; women—full-time 5, part-time 8; total—minority—full-time 2, part-time 1; women minority—full-time 1.

Programs and Degrees Offered:
Listed in the following order: Program area, degree type (T if terminal Master's), number awarded 7/11–6/12. Counseling MA/MS (Master of Arts/Science) (T) 69, Counseling Psychology PsyD (Doctor of Psychology) 22.

APA Accreditation: Counseling PsyD (Doctor of Psychology). Student Outcome Data Website: http://www.stthomas.edu/celc/academics/counselingpsychologydoctorate/.

Student Applications/Admissions:
Student Applications
Counseling MA/MS (Master of Arts/Science)—Applications 2012–2013, 133. Total applicants accepted 2012–2013, 66. Number full-time enrolled (new admits only) 2012–2013, 53. Number part-time enrolled (new admits only) 2012–2013, 0. Total enrolled 2012–2013 full-time, 54. Total enrolled 2012–2013 part-time, 89. Openings 2013–2014, 60. The median number of years required for completion of a degree in 2012–2013 were 3. The number of students enrolled full- and part-time who were dismissed or voluntarily withdrew from this program area in 2012–2013 were 5. *Counseling Psychology PsyD (Doctor of Psychology)*—Applications 2012–2013, 53. Total applicants accepted 2012–2013, 14. Number full-time enrolled (new admits only) 2012–2013, 14. Number part-time enrolled (new admits only) 2012–2013, 0. Total enrolled 2012–2013 full-time, 56. Total enrolled 2012–2013 part-time, 9. Openings 2013–2014, 16. The median number of years required for completion of a degree in 2012–2013 were 4. The number of students enrolled full- and part-time who were dismissed or voluntarily withdrew from this program area in 2012–2013 were 0.
Scores: Entries appear in this order: required test or GPA, minimum score (if required), median score of students entering in 2012–2013. *Counseling MA/MS (Master of Arts/Science):* GRE-V no minimum stated, GRE-Q no minimum stated, GRE-Analytical no minimum stated, overall undergraduate GPA no minimum stated; *Counseling Psychology PsyD (Doctor of Psychology):* GRE-V no minimum stated, GRE-Q no mini-

mum stated, GRE-Analytical no minimum stated, overall undergraduate GPA no minimum stated.
Other Criteria: (importance of criteria rated low, medium, or high): GRE scores—medium, research experience—low, work experience—high, extracurricular activity—low, clinically related public service—high, GPA—high, letters of recommendation—high, interview—high, statement of goals and objectives—high, writing sample—medium, undergraduate major in psychology—medium, specific undergraduate psychology courses taken—medium, The writing sample is only mandatory for the PsyD admission. For additional information on admission requirements, go to http://www.stthomas.edu/celc/admission/.

Student Characteristics: The following represents characteristics of students in 2012–2013 in all graduate psychology programs in the department: Female—full-time 160, part-time 0; Male—full-time 49, part-time 0; African American/Black—full-time 6, part-time 0; Hispanic/Latino(a)—full-time 6, part-time 0; Asian/Pacific Islander—full-time 14, part-time 0; American Indian/Alaska Native—full-time 0, part-time 0; Caucasian/White—full-time 170, part-time 0; Multi-ethnic—full-time 7, part-time 0; students subject to the Americans With Disabilities Act—full-time 0, part-time 0; Unknown ethnicity—full-time 1, part-time 0; International students who hold an F-1 or J-1 Visa—full-time 5, part-time 0.

Financial Information/Assistance:
Tuition for Full-Time Study: *Master's:* State residents: $731 per credit hour; Nonstate residents: $731 per credit hour. *Doctoral:* State residents: $962 per credit hour; Nonstate residents: $962 per credit hour. Tuition is subject to change. See the following website for updates and changes in tuition costs: http://www.stthomas.edu/celc/admission/tuitionfees/.

Financial Assistance:
First-Year Students: Research assistantships available for first year. Average amount paid per academic year: $3,000. Average number of hours worked per week: 6. Apply by August 1. Fellowships and scholarships available for first year. Apply by August 1.
Advanced Students: Research assistantships available for advanced students. Average amount paid per academic year: $3,000. Average number of hours worked per week: 6. Apply by August 1. Fellowships and scholarships available for advanced students. Apply by August 1.
Additional Information: Of all students currently enrolled full time, 1% benefited from one or more of the listed financial assistance programs. Application and information available online at: http://www.stthomas.edu/financialaid/graduate/.

Internships/Practica: Doctoral Degree (PsyD Counseling Psychology): For those doctoral students for whom a professional psychology internship was required in this program prior to graduation, (14) students applied for an internship in 2011–2012, with (13) students obtaining an internship. Of those students who obtained an internship, (13) were paid internships. Of those students who obtained an internship, (7) students placed in APA/CPA accredited internships, (4) students placed in internships not APA/CPA accredited, but listed with the Association of Psychology Postdoctoral and Internship Programs (APPIC), (0) students placed in internships conforming to guidelines of the

Council of Directors of School Psychology Programs (CDSPP), (2) students placed in internships that were not APA/CPA accredited, APPIC or CDSPP listed. Master's and doctoral students have available a wide variety of practica and internships in the surrounding community in the Twin Cities area. Application is competitive and supported by the practicum coordinator at UST. Students also participate in predoctoral internships locally and across the country. Recent sites have included community mental health centers, regional hospitals, VA medical centers, residential chemical dependency centers, career and vocational services, college/university counseling and career centers, vocational rehabilitation programs, employee assistance counseling programs, health maintenance organizations, MN state hospitals, and the MN state prison system.

Housing and Day Care: No on-campus housing is available. On-campus day care facilities are available. See the following website for more information: http://www.stthomas.edu/childdevelopment/.

Employment of Department Graduates:
Master's Degree Graduates: Of those who graduated in the academic year 2011–2012, the following categories and numbers represent the postgraduate activities and employment of master's degree graduates: Enrolled in a psychology doctoral program (3), enrolled in a postdoctoral residency/fellowship (n/a), employed in independent practice (n/a), employed in other positions at a higher education institution (2), employed in a community mental health/counseling center (6), total from the above (master's) (11).
Doctoral Degree Graduates: Of those who graduated in the academic year 2011–2012, the following categories and numbers represent the postgraduate activities and employment of doctoral degree graduates: Enrolled in a psychology doctoral program (n/a), employed in an academic position at a university (1), employed in a community mental health/counseling center (4), other employment position (2), do not know (2), total from the above (doctoral) (9).

Additional Information:
Orientation, Objectives, and Emphasis of Department: The Graduate School of Professional Psychology is dedicated to the development of general practitioners who will make ethical, professional, and creative contributions to their communities and their profession. The programs strive toward leadership in emphasizing a practitioner focus with adult learners. Teaching, scholarship, and service are responsive to diverse perspectives, a blend of practical and reflective inquiry, and social needs. The PsyD is accredited by the APA.

Special Facilities or Resources: UST has developed the Inter-Professional Center (IPC) which is an inter-professional clinic involving counseling psychology, social work and law. This unique center provides free counseling and legal services to underserved populations in the Minneapolis/St. Paul vicinity. This is a practicum and predoctoral internship option for our students.

Information for Students With Physical Disabilities: See the following website for more information: http://www.stthomas.edu/enhancementprog/.

Application Information:
Send to Admissions, Graduate School of Professional Psychology, University of St. Thomas, 1000 LaSalle Avenue, MOH 217, Minneapolis, MN 55403. Application available online. URL of online application: http://www.stthomas.edu/celc/admission/. Students are admitted in the Fall, application deadline January 5; Spring, application deadline October 15. Application deadline for PsyD - January 5. Application deadline for MA - February 5 (Fall), October 15 (Spring). *Fee:* $50. Prospective students may attend an information session to receive a waiver code for the application fee.

Walden University (2012 data)
School of Psychology
College of Social and Behavioral Sciences
155 Fifth Avenue South
Minneapolis, MN 55401
Telephone: (800) 925-3368 X2431
Fax: (612) 338-5092
E-mail: *marilyn.powell@waldenu.edu*
Web: *http://www.waldenu.edu*

Department Information:
1996. Associate Dean: Marilyn Powell, PhD. Number of faculty: total—full-time 34; women—full-time 20; total—minority—full-time 6; women minority—full-time 5.

Programs and Degrees Offered:
Listed in the following order: Program area, degree type (T if terminal Master's), number awarded 7/11–6/12. Clinical Psychology PhD (Doctor of Philosophy), Counseling Psychology PhD (Doctor of Philosophy), Organizational Psychology PhD (Doctor of Philosophy), General Psychology PhD (Doctor of Philosophy), Health Psychology PhD (Doctor of Philosophy).

Student Applications/Admissions:
Student Applications
Clinical Psychology PhD (Doctor of Philosophy)—Counseling Psychology PhD (Doctor of Philosophy)—Organizational Psychology PhD (Doctor of Philosophy)—General Psychology PhD (Doctor of Philosophy)—Health Psychology PhD (Doctor of Philosophy)— **Other Criteria:** (importance of criteria rated low, medium, or high): research experience—medium, work experience—medium, clinically related public service—low, GPA—high, letters of recommendation—medium, statement of goals and objectives—medium, undergraduate major in psychology—medium, specific undergraduate psychology courses taken—medium.

Student Characteristics: The following represents characteristics of students in 2012–2013 in all graduate psychology programs in the department: Caucasian/White—full-time 0, part-time 0; Unknown ethnicity—full-time 0, part-time 0.

Financial Information/Assistance:
Tuition for Full-Time Study: *Master's:* State residents: $410 per credit hour; Nonstate residents: $410 per credit hour. *Doctoral:* State residents: $495 per credit hour; Nonstate residents: $495 per credit hour. Tuition is subject to change. Additional fees are assessed to students beyond the costs of tuition for the following:

Technology and PhD residency fees. Tuition costs vary by program.

Financial Assistance:

First-Year Students: No information provided.

Advanced Students: Research assistantships available for advanced students. Average amount paid per academic year: $6,000. Average number of hours worked per week: 10. Apply by varies. Fellowships and scholarships available for advanced students. Apply by varies.

Additional Information: Of all students currently enrolled full time, 0% benefited from one or more of the listed financial assistance programs.

Internships/Practica: Our field placement coordinators work with students to arrange for practicum and internship sites. We do not at this time have available internship or practicum sites.

Housing and Day Care: No on-campus housing is available. No on-campus day care facilities are available.

Employment of Department Graduates:

Master's Degree Graduates: Of those who graduated in the academic year 2011–2012, the following categories and numbers represent the postgraduate activities and employment of master's degree graduates: Enrolled in a postdoctoral residency/fellowship (n/a), employed in independent practice (n/a), total from the above (master's) (0).

Doctoral Degree Graduates: Of those who graduated in the academic year 2011–2012, the following categories and numbers represent the postgraduate activities and employment of doctoral degree graduates: Enrolled in a psychology doctoral program (n/a), total from the above (doctoral) (0).

Additional Information:

Orientation, Objectives, and Emphasis of Department: The School of Psychology envisions creating a community of competent and ethical professionals with strong critical thinking skills and the ability to work in a diverse, global community. We envision our graduates to have a commitment to social justice and social change through the inquiry, discovery, and application of their knowledge and skills, thereby positively influencing human experiences throughout the world.

Application Information:

Send to Office of Student Enrollment Walden University, 650 S. Exeter Street, Baltimore, MD 21202 USA. Application available online. URL of online application: http://www.waldenu.edu/. Students are admitted in the Fall, application deadline August 15; Winter, application deadline November 15; Spring, application deadline February 15; Summer, application deadline May 15; Programs have rolling admissions. *Fee:* $50.

Mississippi State University
Department of Counseling and Educational Psychology
College of Education
P.O. Box 9727
Mississippi State, MS 39762-5670
Telephone: (662) 325-3426
Fax: (662) 325-3263
E-mail: *cdh@colled.msstate.edu*
Web: *http://www.cep.msstate.edu/*

Department Information:
1954. Department Head: Dr. Daniel Wong. Number of faculty: total—full-time 18, part-time 12; women—full-time 13, part-time 5; total—minority—full-time 4, part-time 1; women minority—full-time 3, part-time 1; faculty subject to the Americans With Disabilities Act 2.

Programs and Degrees Offered:
Listed in the following order: Program area, degree type (T if terminal Master's), number awarded 7/11–6/12. School Psychology PhD (Doctor of Philosophy) 0, School Psychology EdS (School Psychology) 1, Educational Psychology MA/MS (Master of Arts/Science) (T) 0.

APA Accreditation: School PhD (Doctor of Philosophy). Student Outcome Data Website: http://schoolpsych.msstate.edu/schoolpsych/Home_Page.html.

Student Applications/Admissions:
Student Applications
School Psychology PhD (Doctor of Philosophy)—Applications 2012–2013, 16. Total applicants accepted 2012–2013, 9. Number full-time enrolled (new admits only) 2012–2013, 5. Number part-time enrolled (new admits only) 2012–2013, 0. Total enrolled 2012–2013 full-time, 18. Total enrolled 2012–2013 part-time, 10. Openings 2013–2014, 6. The number of students enrolled full- and part-time who were dismissed or voluntarily withdrew from this program area in 2012–2013 were 1. *School Psychology EdS (School Psychology)*—Applications 2012–2013, 11. Total applicants accepted 2012–2013, 6. Number full-time enrolled (new admits only) 2012–2013, 4. Total enrolled 2012–2013 full-time, 12. Total enrolled 2012–2013 part-time, 0. Openings 2013–2014, 7. The median number of years required for completion of a degree in 2012–2013 were 4. The number of students enrolled full- and part-time who were dismissed or voluntarily withdrew from this program area in 2012–2013 were 0. *Educational Psychology MA/MS (Master of Arts/Science)*—Applications 2012–2013, 7. Total applicants accepted 2012–2013, 6. Number full-time enrolled (new admits only) 2012–2013, 5. Number part-time enrolled (new admits only) 2012–2013, 0. Total enrolled 2012–2013 full-time, 13. Total enrolled 2012–2013 part-time, 2. Openings 2013–2014, 4. The number of students enrolled full- and part-time who were dismissed or voluntarily withdrew from this program area in 2012–2013 were 0.

Scores: Entries appear in this order: required test or GPA, minimum score (if required), median score of students entering in 2012–2013. *School Psychology PhD (Doctor of Philosophy):* GRE-V no minimum stated, 154, GRE-Q no minimum stated, 156, GRE-Analytical no minimum stated, 3.58, overall undergraduate GPA 2.75, 3.64; *School Psychology EdS (School Psychology):* GRE-V no minimum stated, 151, GRE-Q no minimum stated, 146, GRE-Analytical no minimum stated, 4.25, overall undergraduate GPA 2.75, 3.60; *Educational Psychology MA/MS (Master of Arts/Science):* GRE-V no minimum stated, GRE-Q no minimum stated, GRE-Analytical no minimum stated, overall undergraduate GPA 2.75.

Other Criteria: (importance of criteria rated low, medium, or high): GRE scores—high, research experience—high, work experience—high, extracurricular activity—low, clinically related public service—low, GPA—high, letters of recommendation—high, interview—high, statement of goals and objectives—high, undergraduate major in psychology—low, specific undergraduate psychology courses taken—high.

Student Characteristics: The following represents characteristics of students in 2012–2013 in all graduate psychology programs in the department: Female—full-time 34, part-time 11; Male—full-time 9, part-time 1; African American/Black—full-time 5, part-time 3; Hispanic/Latino(a)—full-time 0, part-time 0; Asian/Pacific Islander—full-time 5, part-time 0; American Indian/Alaska Native—full-time 0, part-time 0; Caucasian/White—full-time 33, part-time 7; Multi-ethnic—full-time 0, part-time 0; students subject to the Americans With Disabilities Act—full-time 1, part-time 1; Unknown ethnicity—full-time 0, part-time 2; International students who hold an F-1 or J-1 Visa—full-time 0, part-time 2.

Financial Information/Assistance:
Tuition for Full-Time Study: *Master's:* State residents: per academic year $6,264, $348 per credit hour; Nonstate residents: per academic year $15,828, $879 per credit hour. *Doctoral:* State residents: per academic year $6,264, $348 per credit hour; Nonstate residents: per academic year $15,828, $879 per credit hour. Tuition is subject to change. Additional fees are assessed to students beyond the costs of tuition for the following: assessment laboratory fees are assessed for specific courses. See the following website for updates and changes in tuition costs: http://www.grad.msstate.edu/prospective/tuition/.

Financial Assistance:
First-Year Students: Teaching assistantships available for first year. Average amount paid per academic year: $15,000. Average number of hours worked per week: 20. Research assistantships available for first year. Average amount paid per academic year: $15,000. Average number of hours worked per week: 20. Traineeships available for first year. Average amount paid per academic year: $15,000. Average number of hours worked per week: 20.

Advanced Students: Teaching assistantships available for advanced students. Average amount paid per academic year: $15,000. Average number of hours worked per week: 20. Research assistantships available for advanced students. Average amount paid per academic year: $15,000. Average number of hours worked per week: 20. Traineeships available for advanced students. Average amount paid per academic year: $15,000. Average number of hours worked per week: 20.

Additional Information: Of all students currently enrolled full time, 75% benefited from one or more of the listed financial assistance programs. Application and information available online at: http://www.grad.msstate.edu/financial/.

Internships/Practica: Doctoral Degree (PhD School Psychology): For those doctoral students for whom a professional psychology internship was required in this program prior to graduation, (4) students applied for an internship in 2011–2012, with (4) students obtaining an internship. Of those students who obtained an internship, (4) were paid internships. Of those students who obtained an internship, (2) students placed in APA/CPA accredited internships, (1) students placed in internships not APA/CPA accredited, but listed with the Association of Psychology Postdoctoral and Internship Programs (APPIC), (1) students placed in internships conforming to guidelines of the Council of Directors of School Psychology Programs (CDSPP), (0) students placed in internships that were not APA/CPA accredited, APPIC or CDSPP listed. The School Psychology program offers students numerous practicum and internship opportunities. Most practica are coordinated with local school districts. Some externships have also been coordinated with medical centers/hospitals and/or mental health or community counseling centers both within and outside of the state. Doctoral students are strongly encouraged to seek APA-accredited predoctoral internships.

Housing and Day Care: On-campus housing is available. See the following website for more information: http://www.housing.msstate.edu/. On-campus day care facilities are available. See the following website for more information: http://www.humansci.msstate.edu/cdfsc/.

Employment of Department Graduates:
Master's Degree Graduates: Of those who graduated in the academic year 2011–2012, the following categories and numbers represent the postgraduate activities and employment of master's degree graduates: Enrolled in a postdoctoral residency/fellowship (n/a), employed in independent practice (n/a), employed in a professional position in a school system (1), total from the above (master's) (1).
Doctoral Degree Graduates: Of those who graduated in the academic year 2011–2012, the following categories and numbers represent the postgraduate activities and employment of doctoral degree graduates: Enrolled in a psychology doctoral program (n/a), total from the above (doctoral) (0).

Additional Information:
Orientation, Objectives, and Emphasis of Department: Our psychology graduate programs are designed primarily to help develop and train competent and ethical psychologists in the areas of school psychology and educational psychology. The school psychology program is based on a scientist–practitioner model and trains students to implement empirically-based assessment, consultation, and intervention techniques. The flexibility of these offerings gives the student the option of functioning as an educational or school psychologist in a variety of settings, thereby enhancing employment opportunities.

Special Facilities or Resources: The Educational and School Psychology faculty maintain close working relationships with faculty in other programs and departments such as Counseling, Psychology and Special Education. Such relationships afford students the opportunity to work closely with diverse faculty members with various human services backgrounds. Moreover, students are encouraged to work closely with their faculty on various creative projects and research. Additional opportunities exist at the Rehabilitation Research and Training Center on Blindness and Low Vision, the Bureau of Educational Research and Evaluation, and the Research and Curriculum Unit for Vocational-Technical Education, Social Science Research Center, Child Development Center, and T.K. Martin Center for Technology and Disability, all of which are connected with Mississippi State University.

Information for Students With Physical Disabilities: See the following website for more information: http://www.sss.msstate.edu/.

Application Information:
Send to Mississippi State University, Office of the Graduate School, P.O. Box G, Mississippi State, MS 39762-5507. Application available online. URL of online application: http://www.grad.msstate.edu/prospective/. Students are admitted in the Fall, application deadline January 15. *Fee:* $60.

Mississippi State University (2012 data)
Department of Psychology
Arts and Sciences
P.O. Drawer 6161
Mississippi State, MS 39762
Telephone: (662) 325-3202
Fax: (662) 325-7212
E-mail: *deakin@psychology.msstate.edu*
Web: *http://psychology.msstate.edu*

Department Information:
1966. Department Head: Mitchell Berman. Number of faculty: total—full-time 19, part-time 4; women—full-time 6, part-time 4.

Programs and Degrees Offered:
Listed in the following order: Program area, degree type (T if terminal Master's), number awarded 7/11–6/12. Clinical Psychology MA/MS (Master of Arts/Science) (T) 16, Experimental Psychology MA/MS (Master of Arts/Science) (T) 2, Cognitive Science PhD (Doctor of Philosophy) 2.

Student Applications/Admissions:
Student Applications
Clinical Psychology MA/MS (Master of Arts/Science)—Applications 2012–2013, 30. Total applicants accepted 2012–2013, 15. Number full-time enrolled (new admits only) 2012–2013, 7. Number part-time enrolled (new admits only) 2012–2013, 0. Total enrolled 2012–2013 full-time, 14. Total enrolled 2012–2013 part-time, 1. Openings 2013–2014, 10. The median number of years required for completion of a degree in 2012–2013 were 2. The number of students enrolled full- and part-time who were dismissed or voluntarily withdrew from this program area in 2012–2013 were 1. *Experimental Psychology MA/MS (Master of Arts/Science)*—Applications 2012–2013, 14. Total applicants accepted 2012–2013, 9. Number full-time enrolled

(new admits only) 2012–2013, 9. Number part-time enrolled (new admits only) 2012–2013, 0. Total enrolled 2012–2013 full-time, 13. Total enrolled 2012–2013 part-time, 4. Openings 2013–2014, 4. The median number of years required for completion of a degree in 2012–2013 were 3. The number of students enrolled full- and part-time who were dismissed or voluntarily withdrew from this program area in 2012–2013 were 1. *Cognitive Science PhD (Doctor of Philosophy)*—Applications 2012–2013, 17. Total applicants accepted 2012–2013, 7. Number full-time enrolled (new admits only) 2012–2013, 4. Number part-time enrolled (new admits only) 2012–2013, 0. Total enrolled 2012–2013 full-time, 10. Total enrolled 2012–2013 part-time, 1. Openings 2013–2014, 3. The median number of years required for completion of a degree in 2012–2013 were 8. The number of students enrolled full- and part-time who were dismissed or voluntarily withdrew from this program area in 2012–2013 were 0.

Scores: Entries appear in this order: required test or GPA, minimum score (if required), median score of students entering in 2012–2013. *Clinical Psychology MA/MS (Master of Arts/Science):* GRE-V no minimum stated, 480, GRE-Q no minimum stated, 560, GRE-Analytical no minimum stated, 4.0, overall undergraduate GPA no minimum stated, last 2 years GPA no minimum stated, 3.6, psychology GPA no minimum stated; *Experimental Psychology MA/MS (Master of Arts/Science):* GRE-V no minimum stated, 440, GRE-Q no minimum stated, 560, GRE-Analytical no minimum stated, 4.0, overall undergraduate GPA no minimum stated, last 2 years GPA no minimum stated, 3.5, psychology GPA no minimum stated; *Cognitive Science PhD (Doctor of Philosophy):* GRE-V no minimum stated, 550, GRE-Q no minimum stated, 640, GRE-Analytical no minimum stated, 4.0, overall undergraduate GPA no minimum stated, last 2 years GPA no minimum stated, 3.6, psychology GPA no minimum stated, Masters GPA no minimum stated.

Other Criteria: (importance of criteria rated low, medium, or high): GRE scores—medium, research experience—high, work experience—medium, extracurricular activity—low, clinically related public service—medium, GPA—high, letters of recommendation—high, interview—low, statement of goals and objectives—high, undergraduate major in psychology—medium, specific undergraduate psychology courses taken—medium, The clinically related public service would be relevant for applicants to the master's program (clinical concentration). Computer-related experience is relevant to the Cognitive PhD program. Interviews are not required for any program. For additional information on admission requirements, go to http://www.psychology.msstate.edu.

Student Characteristics: The following represents characteristics of students in 2012–2013 in all graduate psychology programs in the department: Female—full-time 25, part-time 3; Male—full-time 12, part-time 3; African American/Black—full-time 1, part-time 0; Hispanic/Latino(a)—full-time 0, part-time 0; Asian/Pacific Islander—full-time 2, part-time 1; American Indian/Alaska Native—full-time 0, part-time 0; Caucasian/White—full-time 34, part-time 5; Multi-ethnic—full-time 0, part-time 0; students subject to the Americans With Disabilities Act—full-time 0, part-time 0; Unknown ethnicity—full-time 0, part-time 0; International students who hold an F-1 or J-1 Visa—full-time 4, part-time 0.

Financial Information/Assistance:

Tuition for Full-Time Study: *Master's:* State residents: per academic year $5,460, $303 per credit hour; Nonstate residents: per academic year $13,801, $767 per credit hour. *Doctoral:* State residents: per academic year $5,460, $303 per credit hour; Nonstate residents: per academic year $13,801, $767 per credit hour. Tuition is subject to change. See the following website for updates and changes in tuition costs: http://www.grad.msstate.edu/prospective/tuition/.

Financial Assistance:

First-Year Students: Teaching assistantships available for first year. Average number of hours worked per week: 20. Research assistantships available for first year. Average number of hours worked per week: 20.

Advanced Students: Teaching assistantships available for advanced students. Average amount paid per academic year: $11,950. Average number of hours worked per week: 20. Research assistantships available for advanced students. Average amount paid per academic year: $11,950. Average number of hours worked per week: 20. Traineeships available for advanced students. Average number of hours worked per week: 20.

Additional Information: Of all students currently enrolled full time, 84% benefited from one or more of the listed financial assistance programs.

Internships/Practica: Master's Degree (MA/MS Clinical Psychology): An internship experience, such as a final research project or "capstone" experience is required of graduates. Master's Degree (MA/MS Experimental Psychology): An internship experience, such as a final research project or "capstone" experience is required of graduates. Students in the clinical-emphasis program complete two 300 clock-hour practicum courses. These practica occur in a variety of settings (including public and private psychiatric hospitals and mental retardation facilities and community mental health centers) and can be completed in other states with prior approval from the program faculty. Students are exposed to diverse client populations (e.g., in- and outpatient children and adults with varied diagnoses and ethnic backgrounds).

Housing and Day Care: On-campus housing is available. See the following website for more information: http://www.housing.msstate.edu/. On-campus day care facilities are available. See the following website for more information: http://earlychildhood.msstate.edu.

Employment of Department Graduates:

Master's Degree Graduates: Of those who graduated in the academic year 2011–2012, the following categories and numbers represent the postgraduate activities and employment of master's degree graduates: Enrolled in a psychology doctoral program (3), enrolled in another graduate/professional program (0), enrolled in a postdoctoral residency/fellowship (n/a), employed in independent practice (n/a), employed in an academic position at a university (1), employed in government agency (1), employed in a community mental health/counseling center (2), other employment position (5), total from the above (master's) (12).

Doctoral Degree Graduates: Of those who graduated in the academic year 2011–2012, the following categories and numbers represent the postgraduate activities and employment of doctoral degree graduates: Enrolled in a psychology doctoral program (n/a), employed in other positions at a higher education institution

(0), employed in government agency (1), total from the above (doctoral) (1).

Additional Information:

Orientation, Objectives, and Emphasis of Department: Currently we offer both an MS and a PhD degree through different programs. Our master's degree programs offer concentrations in either experimental or clinical psychology. The clinical masters program is accredited by the Master's in Psychology Accreditation Council (MPAC). Our PhD program awards a degree in Applied Cognitive Science through an interdisciplinary program housed in the Psychology Department but operated in cooperation with the Computer Science Department, the Industrial Engineering Department, and other units on campus.

Special Facilities or Resources: The department houses a state-of-the-art computer lab for human subject data collection. Faculty laboratories include extensive computer labs for data collection, eye trackers, high-speed servers, and fast network access. Other research equipment, including a f-MRI, are available through connections to other facilities, both on-campus and off. Clinical students have research/training opportunities in the on-site Psychology Training Clinic and in several off-campus practicum placements.

Information for Students With Physical Disabilities: See the following website for more information: http://www.sss.msstate.edu/.

Application Information:
Application available online. URL of online application: http://www.grad.msstate.edu/prospective/admissions/domestic. Students are admitted in the Fall, application deadline January 15; Spring, application deadline November 1. The application deadline for the Cognitive Science PhD program is January 15. The deadline for application to the Master's Degree with an emphasis programs in Clinical is February 1st and with an emphasis in Experimental Psychology is March 15. *Fee:* $60. Application fee subject to change.

Mississippi, University of
Department of Psychology
Liberal Arts
205 Peabody Hall
University, MS 38677
Telephone: (662) 915-7383
Fax: (662) 915-5398
E-mail: *psych@olemiss.edu*
Web: *http://www.olemiss.edu/depts/psychology*

Department Information:
1932. Chairperson: Michael T. Allen. Number of faculty: total—full-time 21, part-time 3; women—full-time 9, part-time 2; total—minority—full-time 2; women minority—full-time 1.

Programs and Degrees Offered:
Listed in the following order: Program area, degree type (T if terminal Master's), number awarded 7/11–6/12. Clinical Psychology PhD (Doctor of Philosophy) 1, Experimental Psychology PhD (Doctor of Philosophy) 1.

APA Accreditation: Clinical PhD (Doctor of Philosophy). Student Outcome Data Website: http://www.olemiss.edu/depts/psychology/grad/clinical/disc_data.html.

Student Applications/Admissions:
Student Applications
Clinical Psychology PhD (Doctor of Philosophy)—Applications 2012–2013, 120. Total applicants accepted 2012–2013, 8. Number full-time enrolled (new admits only) 2012–2013, 5. Number part-time enrolled (new admits only) 2012–2013, 0. Total enrolled 2012–2013 full-time, 55. Total enrolled 2012–2013 part-time, 0. Openings 2013–2014, 6. The median number of years required for completion of a degree in 2012–2013 were 7. The number of students enrolled full- and part-time who were dismissed or voluntarily withdrew from this program area in 2012–2013 were 0. *Experimental Psychology PhD (Doctor of Philosophy)*—Applications 2012–2013, 20. Total applicants accepted 2012–2013, 7. Number full-time enrolled (new admits only) 2012–2013, 2. Number part-time enrolled (new admits only) 2012–2013, 0. Total enrolled 2012–2013 full-time, 13. Total enrolled 2012–2013 part-time, 0. Openings 2013–2014, 5. The median number of years required for completion of a degree in 2012–2013 were 6. The number of students enrolled full- and part-time who were dismissed or voluntarily withdrew from this program area in 2012–2013 were 1.

Scores: Entries appear in this order: required test or GPA, minimum score (if required), median score of students entering in 2012–2013. *Clinical Psychology PhD (Doctor of Philosophy):* GRE-V no minimum stated, 156, GRE-Q no minimum stated, 152, GRE-Analytical no minimum stated.

Other Criteria: (importance of criteria rated low, medium, or high): GRE scores—medium, research experience—high, work experience—medium, extracurricular activity—medium, clinically related public service—medium, GPA—medium, letters of recommendation—high, interview—high, statement of goals and objectives—high, undergraduate major in psychology—high, specific undergraduate psychology courses taken—medium.

Student Characteristics: The following represents characteristics of students in 2012–2013 in all graduate psychology programs in the department: Female—full-time 48, part-time 0; Male—full-time 20, part-time 0; African American/Black—full-time 7, part-time 0; Hispanic/Latino(a)—full-time 3, part-time 0; Asian/Pacific Islander—full-time 3, part-time 0; American Indian/Alaska Native—full-time 1, part-time 0; Caucasian/White—full-time 54, part-time 0; Multi-ethnic—full-time 0, part-time 0; students subject to the Americans With Disabilities Act—full-time 0, part-time 0; Unknown ethnicity—full-time 0, part-time 0; International students who hold an F-1 or J-1 Visa—full-time 0, part-time 0.

Financial Information/Assistance:
Tuition for Full-Time Study: *Doctoral:* State residents: per academic year $6,282; Nonstate residents: per academic year $16,264. Tuition is subject to change. See the following website for updates and changes in tuition costs: http://www.olemiss.edu/depts/bursar/estimator.html.

Financial Assistance:
First-Year Students: Teaching assistantships available for first year. Average amount paid per academic year: $7,200. Aver-

age number of hours worked per week: 10. Apply by December 1. Research assistantships available for first year. Average amount paid per academic year: $7,200. Average number of hours worked per week: 10. Apply by December 1.

Advanced Students: Teaching assistantships available for advanced students. Average amount paid per academic year: $7,200. Average number of hours worked per week: 10. Apply by December 1. Research assistantships available for advanced students. Average amount paid per academic year: $5,000. Average number of hours worked per week: 10. Apply by December 1. Traineeships available for advanced students. Average amount paid per academic year: $8,000. Average number of hours worked per week: 20. Apply by December 1. Fellowships and scholarships available for advanced students. Average amount paid per academic year: $3,000. Apply by December 1.

Additional Information: Of all students currently enrolled full time, 95% benefited from one or more of the listed financial assistance programs. Application and information available online at: http://www.olemiss.edu/depts/graduate_school/financial_aid.html.

Internships/Practica: Doctoral Degree (PhD Clinical Psychology): For those doctoral students for whom a professional psychology internship was required in this program prior to graduation, (6) students applied for an internship in 2011–2012, with (4) students obtaining an internship. Of those students who obtained an internship, (4) were paid internships. Of those students who obtained an internship, (4) students placed in APA/CPA accredited internships, (0) students placed in internships not APA/CPA accredited, but listed with the Association of Psychology Postdoctoral and Internship Programs (APPIC), (0) students placed in internships conforming to guidelines of the Council of Directors of School Psychology Programs (CDSPP), (0) students placed in internships that were not APA/CPA accredited, APPIC or CDSPP listed. Practica or field placements are available for clinical students beginning in the second year of the program. Students serve as therapists on practicum teams in our in-house clinic for a minimum of three years under the direct supervision of the members of our clinical faculty, all of whom are licensed psychologists. After students have demonstrated a minimum level of competence in the clinic, they are allowed to apply for practicum positions at field placement agencies in the community where they are supervised by licensed practitioners who are employed by the field placement agency. In recent years, students have completed field placements at Community Mental Health Centers in Oxford and Tupelo; North Mississippi Regional Center in Oxford; North Mississippi Medical Center in Tupelo; St. Jude Children's Research Hospital in Memphis, and others. Students are assisted and advised by faculty in choosing field placements most appropriate to their individual career goals.

Housing and Day Care: On-campus housing is available. See the following website for more information: http://www.olemiss.edu/depts/stu_housing/. On-campus day care facilities are available. See the following website for more information: http://education.olemiss.edu/willieprice/.

Employment of Department Graduates:

Master's Degree Graduates: Of those who graduated in the academic year 2011–2012, the following categories and numbers represent the postgraduate activities and employment of master's degree graduates: Enrolled in a postdoctoral residency/fellowship (n/a), employed in independent practice (n/a), total from the above (master's) (0).

Doctoral Degree Graduates: Of those who graduated in the academic year 2011–2012, the following categories and numbers represent the postgraduate activities and employment of doctoral degree graduates: Enrolled in a psychology doctoral program (n/a), enrolled in a postdoctoral residency/fellowship (1), employed in an academic position at a 2-year/4-year college (1), total from the above (doctoral) (2).

Additional Information:

Orientation, Objectives, and Emphasis of Department: The Department of Psychology offers programs of study in clinical and experimental psychology leading to the Doctor of Philosophy degree. The clinical program, which is fully accredited by the American Psychological Association, ordinarily requires five years beyond the bachelor's level to complete. Four of the five years are devoted to coursework and research, and the remaining year entails a clinical internship at an APA-approved training site. Requirements for the master's degree are also fulfilled during this period; however, the MA is considered to be a step in the doctoral training. The clinical program adheres to the scientist–practitioner model and emphasizes an empirical approach to clinical practice. A social learning or behavioral approach characterizes the clinical training offered. The experimental program is designed to prepare psychologists for careers in teaching and research. Specific programs include Behavioral Neuroscience, Cognitive Psychology, and Social Psychology. Students entering the experimental program are assigned a faculty mentor (major professor) whose research interests match their training goals. All students are required to engage in significant research projects.

Special Facilities or Resources: Most of the department's offices and laboratories are housed in the George Peabody Building. State-of-the-art facilities for animal research are available in a new centralized animal facility on campus. The psychology clinic is in Kinard Hall on campus which provides for a more professional office environment and better client accessibility. The psychology clinic includes multipurpose rooms for evaluation, consultation, and therapy and observation rooms equipped with one-way mirrors and videotape equipment. The department offers computer-based laboratories for psychopharmacology, psychophysiology, operant conditioning, and behavioral toxicology. The department has close ties with the pharmacy and law schools (located on the Oxford campus) and with the medical school in Jackson.

Information for Students With Physical Disabilities: See the following website for more information: http://www.olemiss.edu/depts/sds/.

Application Information:
Send to Admissions Chairperson. Application available online. URL of online application: http://www.olemiss.edu/depts/graduate_school/applynow.html. Students are admitted in the Fall, application deadline December 1. *Fee:* $40.

Central Missouri, University of
Department of Psychological Science
College of Health, Science, and Technology
Lovinger 1111
Warrensburg, MO 64093
Telephone: (660) 543-4185
Fax: (660) 543-8505
E-mail: *kreiner@ucmo.edu*
Web: *http://www.ucmo.edu/psychology/*

Department Information:
Chairperson: David Kreiner. Number of faculty: total—full-time 8, part-time 12; women—full-time 2, part-time 7; total—minority—full-time 2, part-time 2; women minority—full-time 1, part-time 1.

Programs and Degrees Offered:
Listed in the following order: Program area, degree type (T if terminal Master's), number awarded 7/11–6/12. Psychology MA/MS (Master of Arts/Science) (T) 7.

Student Applications/Admissions:
Student Applications
Psychology MA/MS (Master of Arts/Science)—Applications 2012–2013, 24. Total applicants accepted 2012–2013, 13. Number full-time enrolled (new admits only) 2012–2013, 8. Number part-time enrolled (new admits only) 2012–2013, 0. Total enrolled 2012–2013 full-time, 10. Total enrolled 2012–2013 part-time, 1. Openings 2013–2014, 15. The median number of years required for completion of a degree in 2012–2013 were 4. The number of students enrolled full- and part-time who were dismissed or voluntarily withdrew from this program area in 2012–2013 were 0.
Scores: Entries appear in this order: required test or GPA, minimum score (if required), median score of students entering in 2012–2013. *Psychology MA/MS (Master of Arts/Science):* GRE-V no minimum stated, 470, GRE-Q no minimum stated, 530, GRE-Analytical no minimum stated, 3.5, psychology GPA 3.0.
Other Criteria: (importance of criteria rated low, medium, or high): GRE scores—medium, research experience—medium, work experience—low, extracurricular activity—medium, clinically related public service—low, GPA—high, letters of recommendation—medium, statement of goals and objectives—high, undergraduate major in psychology—low, specific undergraduate psychology courses taken—high. For additional information on admission requirements, go to http://www.ucmo.edu/psychology/grad/admit.cfm.

Student Characteristics: The following represents characteristics of students in 2012–2013 in all graduate psychology programs in the department: Female—full-time 7, part-time 1; Male—full-time 3, part-time 0; African American/Black—full-time 1, part-time 0; Hispanic/Latino(a)—full-time 1, part-time 0; Asian/Pacific Islander—full-time 1, part-time 0; American Indian/Alaska Native—full-time 0, part-time 0; Caucasian/White—full-time 5,

part-time 1; Multi-ethnic—full-time 0, part-time 0; students subject to the Americans With Disabilities Act—full-time 0, part-time 0; Unknown ethnicity—full-time 2, part-time 0; International students who hold an F-1 or J-1 Visa—full-time 4, part-time 0.

Financial Information/Assistance:
Tuition for Full-Time Study: *Master's:* State residents: $271 per credit hour; Nonstate residents: $543 per credit hour. Tuition is subject to change. Additional fees are assessed to students beyond the costs of tuition for the following: athletics, facilities, student activity, student rec center, technology, union. See the following website for updates and changes in tuition costs: http://www.ucmo.edu/sfs/.

Financial Assistance:
First-Year Students: Teaching assistantships available for first year. Average amount paid per academic year: $7,500. Average number of hours worked per week: 20. Fellowships and scholarships available for first year. Apply by March 1.
Advanced Students: Teaching assistantships available for advanced students. Average amount paid per academic year: $7,500. Average number of hours worked per week: 20. Fellowships and scholarships available for advanced students. Apply by March 1.
Additional Information: Of all students currently enrolled full time, 46% benefited from one or more of the listed financial assistance programs. Application and information available online at: http://www.ucmo.edu/graduate/support/.

Internships/Practica: Master's Degree (MA/MS Psychology): An internship experience, such as a final research project or "capstone" experience is required of graduates.

Housing and Day Care: On-campus housing is available. See the following website for more information: http://www.ucmo.edu/housing/. On-campus day care facilities are available. See the following website for more information: http://www.ucmo.edu/childcare/ and http://www.ucmo.edu/ecel/about/lab.cfm.

Employment of Department Graduates:
Master's Degree Graduates: Of those who graduated in the academic year 2011–2012, the following categories and numbers represent the postgraduate activities and employment of master's degree graduates: Enrolled in a psychology doctoral program (2), enrolled in a postdoctoral residency/fellowship (n/a), employed in independent practice (n/a), employed in business or industry (2), employed in government agency (1), do not know (2), total from the above (master's) (7).
Doctoral Degree Graduates: Of those who graduated in the academic year 2011–2012, the following categories and numbers represent the postgraduate activities and employment of doctoral degree graduates: Enrolled in a psychology doctoral program (n/a), total from the above (doctoral) (0).

Additional Information:
Orientation, Objectives, and Emphasis of Department: The emphasis of the Psychology master's degree program is predoctoral

preparation. It is ideal for students who wish to improve their research skills, co-author articles and presentations with faculty, engage in professional networking, and expand their knowledge of psychology prior to applying or reapplying to PhD programs. The program also prepares students for employment that utilizes acquired psychological knowledge and skills.

Special Facilities or Resources: Behavioral Medicine and Biofeedback Laboratory; Neurocognition Laboratory; Eyetracking Laboratory; Experimental Psychology Laboratory; Virtual Reality Laboratory; Social Issues and Assessment of Learning Laboratory.

Information for Students With Physical Disabilities: See the following website for more information: http://www.ucmo.edu/access/.

Application Information:
Send to School of Graduate and Extended Studies, Ward Edwards 1800, Warrensburg, MO 64093. Application available online. URL of online application: https://www.ucmo.edu/graduate/admission/apply/secure/. Programs have rolling admissions. *Fee:* $30.

Missouri State University
Psychology Department
Health and Human Services
901 South National Avenue
Springfield, MO 65897
Telephone: (417) 836-5797
Fax: (417) 836-8330
E-mail: *hollyrobison@missouristate.edu*
Web: *http://psychology.missouristate.edu*

Department Information:
1967. Head: Timothy Daugherty. Number of faculty: total—full-time 29, part-time 24; women—full-time 14, part-time 13; total—minority—full-time 1, part-time 1; women minority—full-time 1.

Programs and Degrees Offered:
Listed in the following order: Program area, degree type (T if terminal Master's), number awarded 7/11–6/12. Clinical Psychology MA/MS (Master of Arts/Science) (T) 8, Experimental Psychology MA/MS (Master of Arts/Science) (T) 1, Industrial/Organizational Psychology MA/MS (Master of Arts/Science) (T) 12, Child Forensic Certificate Other 4.

Student Applications/Admissions:
Student Applications
Clinical Psychology MA/MS (Master of Arts/Science)—Applications 2012–2013, 56. Total applicants accepted 2012–2013, 9. Number full-time enrolled (new admits only) 2012–2013, 9. Number part-time enrolled (new admits only) 2012–2013, 0. Total enrolled 2012–2013 full-time, 17. Total enrolled 2012–2013 part-time, 1. Openings 2013–2014, 9. The median number of years required for completion of a degree in 2012–2013 were 2. The number of students enrolled full- and part-time who were dismissed or voluntarily withdrew from this program area in 2012–2013 were 1. *Experimental Psychology MA/MS (Master of Arts/Science)*—Applications 2012–2013, 8. Total

applicants accepted 2012–2013, 5. Number full-time enrolled (new admits only) 2012–2013, 5. Number part-time enrolled (new admits only) 2012–2013, 0. Total enrolled 2012–2013 full-time, 6. Total enrolled 2012–2013 part-time, 0. Openings 2013–2014, 6. The median number of years required for completion of a degree in 2012–2013 were 2. The number of students enrolled full- and part-time who were dismissed or voluntarily withdrew from this program area in 2012–2013 were 0. *Industrial/Organizational Psychology MA/MS (Master of Arts/Science)*—Applications 2012–2013, 58. Total applicants accepted 2012–2013, 23. Number full-time enrolled (new admits only) 2012–2013, 12. Number part-time enrolled (new admits only) 2012–2013, 0. Total enrolled 2012–2013 full-time, 22. Total enrolled 2012–2013 part-time, 0. Openings 2013–2014, 12. The median number of years required for completion of a degree in 2012–2013 were 2. The number of students enrolled full- and part-time who were dismissed or voluntarily withdrew from this program area in 2012–2013 were 0. *Child Forensic Certificate Other*—Applications 2012–2013, 9. Total applicants accepted 2012–2013, 9. Number part-time enrolled (new admits only) 2012–2013, 12. Total enrolled 2012–2013 part-time, 12. The median number of years required for completion of a degree in 2012–2013 was 1. The number of students enrolled full- and part-time who were dismissed or voluntarily withdrew from this program area in 2012–2013 were 1.

Scores: Entries appear in this order: required test or GPA, minimum score (if required), median score of students entering in 2012–2013. *Experimental Psychology MA/MS (Master of Arts/Science):* GRE-V 151, 155, GRE-Q 142, 151, overall undergraduate GPA 3.0, 3.66, psychology GPA 3.25; *Industrial/Organizational Psychology MA/MS (Master of Arts/Science):* GRE-V 151, 154, GRE-Q 142, 149.

Other Criteria: (importance of criteria rated low, medium, or high): GRE scores—medium, research experience—high, work experience—medium, extracurricular activity—medium, clinically related public service—high, GPA—high, letters of recommendation—high, statement of goals and objectives—high, undergraduate major in psychology—high, specific undergraduate psychology courses taken—high.

Student Characteristics: The following represents characteristics of students in 2012–2013 in all graduate psychology programs in the department: Female—full-time 24, part-time 12; Male—full-time 21, part-time 1; African American/Black—full-time 0, part-time 0; Hispanic/Latino(a)—full-time 3, part-time 0; Asian/Pacific Islander—full-time 3, part-time 0; American Indian/Alaska Native—full-time 0, part-time 0; Caucasian/White—full-time 23, part-time 0; Multi-ethnic—full-time 4, part-time 0; students subject to the Americans With Disabilities Act—full-time 1, part-time 0; Unknown ethnicity—full-time 12, part-time 13; International students who hold an F-1 or J-1 Visa—full-time 0, part-time 0.

Financial Information/Assistance:
Tuition for Full-Time Study: *Master's:* State residents: per academic year $5,808, $242 per credit hour; Nonstate residents: per academic year $11,616, $484 per credit hour. Tuition is subject to change. Additional fees are assessed to students beyond the costs of tuition for the following: student services fees, supplemental course fees vary. See the following website for updates and

changes in tuition costs: http://www.missouristate.edu/registrar/costs.htm.

Financial Assistance:

First-Year Students: Research assistantships available for first year. Average amount paid per academic year: $8,160. Average number of hours worked per week: 20. Apply by July.

Advanced Students: Teaching assistantships available for advanced students. Average amount paid per academic year: $8,160. Average number of hours worked per week: 20. Apply by March. Research assistantships available for advanced students. Average amount paid per academic year: $8,160. Average number of hours worked per week: 20. Apply by July.

Additional Information: Of all students currently enrolled full time, 90% benefited from one or more of the listed financial assistance programs. Application and information available online at: http://graduate.missouristate.edu/assistantship.htm.

Internships/Practica:

Master's Degree (MA/MS Clinical Psychology): An internship experience, such as a final research project or "capstone" experience is required of graduates. Master's Degree (MA/MS Experimental Psychology): An internship experience, such as a final research project or "capstone" experience is required of graduates. Master's Degree (MA/MS Industrial/Organizational Psychology): An internship experience, such as a final research project or "capstone" experience is required of graduates. Clinical - students must complete two 175 contact hour practica. Placements are in a variety of mental health settings. Students who choose a non-thesis option must complete an additional 175 contact hour internship. Experimental - practicum experience is acquired through basic laboratory research work tailored specifically to the graduate student's research area of interest. The goal of the practicum is for the student to develop or acquire competence in various research methods and behavioral/cognitive measurement skills that will prepare the student for later doctoral work.

Housing and Day Care:

On-campus housing is available. See the following website for more information: http://reslife.missouristate.edu/. On-campus day care facilities are available. See the following website for more information: http://education.missouristate.edu/cdc/.

Employment of Department Graduates:

Master's Degree Graduates: Of those who graduated in the academic year 2011–2012, the following categories and numbers represent the postgraduate activities and employment of master's degree graduates: Enrolled in a psychology doctoral program (4), enrolled in another graduate/professional program (2), enrolled in a postdoctoral residency/fellowship (n/a), employed in independent practice (n/a), employed in an academic position at a university (1), employed in other positions at a higher education institution (1), employed in business or industry (6), employed in government agency (3), employed in a community mental health/counseling center (1), employed in a hospital/medical center (1), still seeking employment (1), total from the above (master's) (20).

Doctoral Degree Graduates: Of those who graduated in the academic year 2011–2012, the following categories and numbers represent the postgraduate activities and employment of doctoral degree graduates: Enrolled in a psychology doctoral program (n/a), total from the above (doctoral) (0).

Additional Information:

Orientation, Objectives, and Emphasis of Department: We are an eclectic department of 28 full-time faculty serving over 700 undergraduate majors. The faculty have diverse research interests including clinical, I/O, forensic, human learning, language, motivation, human skills, and memory. The department operates the Learning Diagnostic Clinic for diagnosis and remediation of special populations, as well as limited therapy for other psychological disorders.

Special Facilities or Resources: The department has 14 separate labs that serve the Experimental, Clinical, and Industrial-Organizational tracks. The experimental track has three research labs that provide the means and opportunity for graduate students to conduct basic research. These include: 1) the Infant Perception Laboratory housing computer hardware and software to accommodate basic research in visual scanning and psycho-physiological testing; 2) the Implicit and Explicit Motivation Research Lab, which is designed to conduct research in automatic processing and to conduct Structural Equation Modeling and HLM analyses; and 3) the Cognitive Strategies Research Lab provides a facility to test and design stimulus materials to conduct applied memory research. Other laboratories support research focusing on cognition, gender issues, life-span development, motivation, body image, and sport psychology, and provide labs to all students regardless of their track. The department also has excellent computer support facilities in all labs. The department oversees the Learning Diagnostic Clinic that supports student learning and University ADA compliance. The clinic provides an excellent training facility for our clinical graduate students. Faculty in the department provide direct service to faculty and students throughout the College through the RSTATS Institute, which employs graduate student assistants in research and analysis consultation.

Information for Students With Physical Disabilities: See the following website for more information: http://www.missouristate.edu/disability/.

Application Information:

Send to Academic Administrative Assistant, Psychology Department, 901 South National Avenue, Hill 101, Springfield, MO 65897. Application available online. URL of online application: http://www.missouristate.edu/futurestudents/applynow.aspx. Students are admitted in the Fall, application deadline February 15. We will accept applications up to June 1 if all openings in each track aren't filled. *Fee:* $35. $50 application fee for all International Students.

Missouri Western State University
Psychology
Liberal Arts and Sciences
4525 Downs Drive
St. Joseph, MO 64507
Telephone: (816) 271-4444
E-mail: *cronk@missouriwestern.edu*
Web: *http://www.missouriwestern.edu/psychology/*

Department Information:

1969. Chairperson: Brian Cronk. Number of faculty: total—full-time 8; women—full-time 4.

Programs and Degrees Offered:

Listed in the following order: Program area, degree type (T if terminal Master's), number awarded 7/11–6/12. Human Factors and Usability Testing MA/MS (Master of Arts/Science) (T) 2.

Student Applications/Admissions:

Student Applications

Human Factors and Usability Testing MA/MS (Master of Arts/Science)—Applications 2012–2013, 12. Total applicants accepted 2012–2013, 2. Number full-time enrolled (new admits only) 2012–2013, 2. Total enrolled 2012–2013 full-time, 4. Openings 2013–2014, 4. The median number of years required for completion of a degree in 2012–2013 were 2. The number of students enrolled full- and part-time who were dismissed or voluntarily withdrew from this program area in 2012–2013 were 0.

Scores: Entries appear in this order: required test or GPA, minimum score (if required), median score of students entering in 2012–2013. *Human Factors and Usability Testing MA/MS (Master of Arts/Science):* GRE-V 400, 490, GRE-Q 450, 670, overall undergraduate GPA 2.75, 3.5.

Other Criteria: (importance of criteria rated low, medium, or high): GRE scores—medium, research experience—medium, work experience—medium, extracurricular activity—low, clinically related public service—low, GPA—medium, letters of recommendation—medium, interview—low, statement of goals and objectives—medium. For additional information on admission requirements, go to http://www.missouriwestern.edu/psychology/humanfactorsapplication.asp.

Student Characteristics: The following represents characteristics of students in 2012–2013 in all graduate psychology programs in the department: Female—full-time 2, part-time 0; Male—full-time 2, part-time 0; African American/Black—full-time 0, part-time 0; Hispanic/Latino(a)—full-time 1, part-time 0; Asian/Pacific Islander—full-time 0, part-time 0; American Indian/Alaska Native—full-time 0, part-time 0; Caucasian/White—full-time 3, part-time 0; Multi-ethnic—full-time 0, part-time 0; students subject to the Americans With Disabilities Act—full-time 0, part-time 0; Unknown ethnicity—full-time 0, part-time 0; International students who hold an F-1 or J-1 Visa—full-time 1, part-time 0.

Financial Information/Assistance:

Tuition for Full-Time Study: *Master's:* State residents: per academic year $5,000, $310 per credit hour; Nonstate residents: per academic year $10,000, $568 per credit hour. Tuition is subject to change. See the following website for updates and changes in tuition costs: http://www.missouriwestern.edu/graduate/financing.php.

Financial Assistance:

First-Year Students: Fellowships and scholarships available for first year. Apply by March 15.

Advanced Students: Teaching assistantships available for advanced students. Research assistantships available for advanced students.

Additional Information: Of all students currently enrolled full time, 100% benefited from one or more of the listed financial assistance programs. Application and information available online at: http://www.missouriwestern.edu/graduate/financing.php.

Internships/Practica: Master's Degree (MA/MS Human Factors and Usability Testing): An internship experience, such as a final research project or "capstone" experience is required of graduates.

Housing and Day Care: No on-campus housing is available. On-campus day care facilities are available. See the following website for more information: http://www.missouriwestern.edu/ykids/.

Employment of Department Graduates:

Master's Degree Graduates: Of those who graduated in the academic year 2011–2012, the following categories and numbers represent the postgraduate activities and employment of master's degree graduates: Enrolled in a postdoctoral residency/fellowship (n/a), employed in independent practice (n/a), employed in business or industry (2), total from the above (master's) (2).

Doctoral Degree Graduates: Of those who graduated in the academic year 2011–2012, the following categories and numbers represent the postgraduate activities and employment of doctoral degree graduates: Enrolled in a psychology doctoral program (n/a), total from the above (doctoral) (0).

Additional Information:

Orientation, Objectives, and Emphasis of Department: Our graduate program combines business and human factors education. We produce students who are able to understand the complex interactions between humans and computing devices. The program highlights the major areas necessary for developing products within a competitive industry environment. The ultimate goal of human factors professionals is to create and transform interactive devices into systems that will make everyone's lives a little easier, safer and more enjoyable.

Information for Students With Physical Disabilities: See the following website for more information: http://www.missouriwestern.edu/ds/.

Application Information:

Application available online. URL of online application: https://www-sec.missouriwestern.edu/admissions/app/. Students are admitted in the Fall, application deadline July 15. *Fee:* $15.

Missouri, University of
Department of Psychological Sciences
College of Arts and Science
210 McAlester Hall
Columbia, MO 65211
Telephone: (573) 882-0838
Fax: (573) 882-7710
E-mail: *gradpsych@missouri.edu*
Web: *http://psychology.missouri.edu/*

Department Information:

1900. Chairperson: Moshe Naveh-Benjamin. Number of faculty: total—full-time 47, part-time 3; women—full-time 18, part-time 3; total—minority—full-time 2; women minority—full-time 2.

Programs and Degrees Offered:

Listed in the following order: Program area, degree type (T if terminal Master's), number awarded 7/11–6/12. Clinical Psychol-

ogy PhD (Doctor of Philosophy) 1, Cognition and Neuroscience PhD (Doctor of Philosophy) 2, Social/Personality Psychology PhD (Doctor of Philosophy) 4, Quantitative Psychology PhD (Doctor of Philosophy) 2, Developmental Psychology PhD (Doctor of Philosophy) 0, Joint Child Clinical/Developmental PhD (Doctor of Philosophy) 0.

APA Accreditation: Clinical PhD (Doctor of Philosophy). Student Outcome Data Website: http://psychology.missouri.edu/clinical.

Student Applications/Admissions:

Student Applications

Clinical Psychology PhD (Doctor of Philosophy)—Applications 2012–2013, 186. Total applicants accepted 2012–2013, 10. Number full-time enrolled (new admits only) 2012–2013, 5. Number part-time enrolled (new admits only) 2012–2013, 0. Total enrolled 2012–2013 full-time, 36. Total enrolled 2012–2013 part-time, 0. Openings 2013–2014, 10. The median number of years required for completion of a degree in 2012–2013 were 7. The number of students enrolled full- and part-time who were dismissed or voluntarily withdrew from this program area in 2012–2013 were 0. *Cognition and Neuroscience PhD (Doctor of Philosophy)*—Applications 2012–2013, 24. Total applicants accepted 2012–2013, 2. Number full-time enrolled (new admits only) 2012–2013, 2. Total enrolled 2012–2013 full-time, 21. Total enrolled 2012–2013 part-time, 0. Openings 2013–2014, 7. The median number of years required for completion of a degree in 2012–2013 were 6. The number of students enrolled full- and part-time who were dismissed or voluntarily withdrew from this program area in 2012–2013 were 0. *Social/Personality Psychology PhD (Doctor of Philosophy)*—Applications 2012–2013, 60. Total applicants accepted 2012–2013, 4. Number full-time enrolled (new admits only) 2012–2013, 4. Number part-time enrolled (new admits only) 2012–2013, 0. Total enrolled 2012–2013 full-time, 13. Total enrolled 2012–2013 part-time, 0. Openings 2013–2014, 4. The median number of years required for completion of a degree in 2012–2013 were 6. The number of students enrolled full- and part-time who were dismissed or voluntarily withdrew from this program area in 2012–2013 were 0. *Quantitative Psychology PhD (Doctor of Philosophy)*—Applications 2012–2013, 9. Total applicants accepted 2012–2013, 3. Number full-time enrolled (new admits only) 2012–2013, 1. Number part-time enrolled (new admits only) 2012–2013, 0. Total enrolled 2012–2013 full-time, 6. Total enrolled 2012–2013 part-time, 0. Openings 2013–2014, 5. The median number of years required for completion of a degree in 2012–2013 were 7. The number of students enrolled full- and part-time who were dismissed or voluntarily withdrew from this program area in 2012–2013 were 0. *Developmental Psychology PhD (Doctor of Philosophy)*—Applications 2012–2013, 16. Total applicants accepted 2012–2013, 2. Number full-time enrolled (new admits only) 2012–2013, 0. Total enrolled 2012–2013 full-time, 9. Openings 2013–2014, 3. The number of students enrolled full- and part-time who were dismissed or voluntarily withdrew from this program area in 2012–2013 were 0. *Joint Child Clinical/Developmental PhD (Doctor of Philosophy)*—Applications 2012–2013, 0. Total applicants accepted 2012–2013, 0. Number full-time enrolled (new admits only) 2012–2013, 0. Total enrolled 2012–2013 full-time, 5. The number of students enrolled full- and part-time who were dismissed or voluntarily withdrew from this program area in 2012–2013 were 0.

Scores: Entries appear in this order: required test or GPA, minimum score (if required), median score of students entering in 2012–2013. *Clinical Psychology PhD (Doctor of Philosophy):* GRE-V 159, 163, GRE-Q 148, 155, overall undergraduate GPA 3.22, 3.53.

Other Criteria: (importance of criteria rated low, medium, or high): GRE scores—high, research experience—high, work experience—low, extracurricular activity—low, clinically related public service—low, GPA—medium, letters of recommendation—medium, interview—high, statement of goals and objectives—high, undergraduate major in psychology—medium, specific undergraduate psychology courses taken—low. For additional information on admission requirements, go to http://psychology.missouri.edu/apply-gen.

Student Characteristics: The following represents characteristics of students in 2012–2013 in all graduate psychology programs in the department: Female—full-time 49, part-time 0; Male—full-time 41, part-time 0; African American/Black—full-time 3, part-time 0; Hispanic/Latino(a)—full-time 3, part-time 0; Asian/Pacific Islander—full-time 12, part-time 0; American Indian/Alaska Native—full-time 0, part-time 0; Caucasian/White—full-time 69, part-time 0; Multi-ethnic—full-time 0, part-time 0; students subject to the Americans With Disabilities Act—full-time 0, part-time 0; Unknown ethnicity—full-time 3, part-time 0; International students who hold an F-1 or J-1 Visa—full-time 15, part-time 0.

Financial Information/Assistance:

Tuition for Full-Time Study: *Doctoral:* State residents: $336 per credit hour; Nonstate residents: $868 per credit hour. Tuition is subject to change. Additional fees are assessed to students beyond the costs of tuition for the following: information technology, student activity, recreation facility, health. See the following website for updates and changes in tuition costs: http://cashiers.missouri.edu/costs/index.html.

Financial Assistance:

First-Year Students: Teaching assistantships available for first year. Average amount paid per academic year: $15,165. Average number of hours worked per week: 20. Research assistantships available for first year. Average amount paid per academic year: $15,165. Average number of hours worked per week: 20. Fellowships and scholarships available for first year. Average amount paid per academic year: $15,165.

Advanced Students: Teaching assistantships available for advanced students. Average amount paid per academic year: $15,939. Average number of hours worked per week: 20. Research assistantships available for advanced students. Average amount paid per academic year: $15,939. Average number of hours worked per week: 20. Traineeships available for advanced students. Fellowships and scholarships available for advanced students. Average amount paid per academic year: $15,939.

Additional Information: Of all students currently enrolled full time, 100% benefited from one or more of the listed financial assistance programs. Application and information available online at: http://psychology.missouri.edu/grad-financial.

Internships/Practica: Doctoral Degree (PhD Clinical Psychology): For those doctoral students for whom a professional psychology internship was required in this program prior to graduation, (5) students applied for an internship in 2011–2012, with (5) students obtaining an internship. Of those students who obtained an internship, (5) were paid internships. Of those students who obtained an internship, (4) students placed in APA/CPA accredited internships, (1) students placed in internships not APA/CPA accredited, but listed with the Association of Psychology Postdoctoral and Internship Programs (APPIC), (0) students placed in internships conforming to guidelines of the Council of Directors of School Psychology Programs (CDSPP), (0) students placed in internships that were not APA/CPA accredited, APPIC or CDSPP listed. Doctoral Degree (PhD Joint Child Clinical/Developmental): For those doctoral students for whom a professional psychology internship was required in this program prior to graduation, (2) students applied for an internship in 2011–2012, with (2) students obtaining an internship. Of those students who obtained an internship, (2) were paid internships. Of those students who obtained an internship, (2) students placed in APA/CPA accredited internships, (0) students placed in internships not APA/CPA accredited, but listed with the Association of Psychology Postdoctoral and Internship Programs (APPIC), (0) students placed in internships conforming to guidelines of the Council of Directors of School Psychology Programs (CDSPP), (0) students placed in internships that were not APA/CPA accredited, APPIC or CDSPP listed.

Housing and Day Care: No on-campus housing is available. On-campus day care facilities are available. See the following website for more information: http://www.studentparentcenter.missouri.edu/.

Employment of Department Graduates:

Master's Degree Graduates: Of those who graduated in the academic year 2011–2012, the following categories and numbers represent the postgraduate activities and employment of master's degree graduates: Enrolled in a postdoctoral residency/fellowship (n/a), employed in independent practice (n/a), total from the above (master's) (0).

Doctoral Degree Graduates: Of those who graduated in the academic year 2011–2012, the following categories and numbers represent the postgraduate activities and employment of doctoral degree graduates: Enrolled in a psychology doctoral program (n/a), enrolled in a postdoctoral residency/fellowship (1), employed in an academic position at a university (3), employed in other positions at a higher education institution (3), employed in a community mental health/counseling center (1), other employment position (1), total from the above (doctoral) (9).

Additional Information:

Orientation, Objectives, and Emphasis of Department: The Department's mission is defined through research, graduate and undergraduate education, and service. The Department contributes to the theoretical and empirical body of knowledge in the discipline of psychology through research and other scholarly activities, trains graduate students to become contributors to psychology as scientists, disseminates the most current knowledge to students through high quality teaching at both the undergraduate and graduate level, and contributes through community, state, and professional service activities. The clinical program is fully accredited by the American Psychological Association and is a charter member of the Academy of Psychological Clinical Science.

Special Facilities or Resources: The department has the following special facilities or resources: a psychology research facility, a Brain Imaging Center, a psychological clinic, a medical school, a VA hospital, Mid-Missouri Mental Health Center, a counseling center, human experimental laboratories, and a university central computer system and departmental computers.

Information for Students With Physical Disabilities: See the following website for more information: http://disabilityservices.missouri.edu.

Application Information:
Application available online. URL of online application: https://app.applyyourself.com/?id=umc-grad. Students are admitted in the Fall, application deadline December 1. *Fee:* $55. The graduate school application fee for non-resident international students is $75.

Missouri, University of, Columbia
Department of Educational, School and Counseling
 Psychology
College of Education
16 Hill Hall
Columbia, MO 65211
Telephone: (573) 882-7731
Fax: (573) 884-5989
E-mail: *WedmanJ@missouri.edu*
Web: *http://education.missouri.edu/ESCP/*

Department Information:
1953. Chairperson: John Wedman. Number of faculty: total—full-time 24, part-time 2; women—full-time 10, part-time 1; total—minority—full-time 7, part-time 1; women minority—full-time 3, part-time 1; faculty subject to the Americans With Disabilities Act 1.

Programs and Degrees Offered:
Listed in the following order: Program area, degree type (T if terminal Master's), number awarded 7/11–6/12. Counseling Psychology PhD (Doctor of Philosophy) 7, Counseling Psychology EdS (School Psychology) 1, Counseling Psychology MEd (Education) 27, Educational Psychology PhD (Doctor of Philosophy) 0, Educational Psychology MEd (Education) 0, Educational Psychology MA/MS (Master of Arts/Science) (T) 0, School Psychology PhD (Doctor of Philosophy) 4, School Psychology EdS (School Psychology) 5, School Psychology MA/MS (Master of Arts/Science) 10.

APA Accreditation: Counseling PhD (Doctor of Philosophy). Student Outcome Data Website: http://education.missouri.edu/ESCP/program_areas/counseling_psychology/Admissions_Outcomes.php. School PhD (Doctor of Philosophy). Student Outcome Data Website: http://education.missouri.edu/ESCP/program_areas/school_psychology/index.php.

Student Applications/Admissions:
Student Applications
Counseling Psychology PhD (Doctor of Philosophy)—Applications 2012–2013, 143. Total applicants accepted 2012–2013, 9. Number full-time enrolled (new admits only) 2012–2013, 7. Number part-time enrolled (new admits only) 2012–2013, 0.

Total enrolled 2012–2013 full-time, 41. Total enrolled 2012–2013 part-time, 0. Openings 2013–2014, 9. The median number of years required for completion of a degree in 2012–2013 were 7. The number of students enrolled full- and part-time who were dismissed or voluntarily withdrew from this program area in 2012–2013 were 1. *Counseling Psychology EdS (School Psychology)*—Applications 2012–2013, 2. Total applicants accepted 2012–2013, 2. Number full-time enrolled (new admits only) 2012–2013, 2. Number part-time enrolled (new admits only) 2012–2013, 0. Total enrolled 2012–2013 full-time, 2. Total enrolled 2012–2013 part-time, 0. Openings 2013–2014, 1. The median number of years required for completion of a degree in 2012–2013 were 2. The number of students enrolled full- and part-time who were dismissed or voluntarily withdrew from this program area in 2012–2013 were 0. *Counseling Psychology MEd (Education)*—Applications 2012–2013, 65. Total applicants accepted 2012–2013, 35. Number full-time enrolled (new admits only) 2012–2013, 34. Number part-time enrolled (new admits only) 2012–2013, 0. Total enrolled 2012–2013 full-time, 100. Total enrolled 2012–2013 part-time, 0. Openings 2013–2014, 28. The median number of years required for completion of a degree in 2012–2013 were 2. The number of students enrolled full- and part-time who were dismissed or voluntarily withdrew from this program area in 2012–2013 were 0. *Educational Psychology PhD (Doctor of Philosophy)*—Applications 2012–2013, 11. Total applicants accepted 2012–2013, 8. Number full-time enrolled (new admits only) 2012–2013, 3. Total enrolled 2012–2013 full-time, 20. Total enrolled 2012–2013 part-time, 0. Openings 2013–2014, 6. The median number of years required for completion of a degree in 2012–2013 were 3. The number of students enrolled full- and part-time who were dismissed or voluntarily withdrew from this program area in 2012–2013 were 0. *Educational Psychology MEd (Education)*—Applications 2012–2013, 6. Total applicants accepted 2012–2013, 3. Number full-time enrolled (new admits only) 2012–2013, 1. Total enrolled 2012–2013 full-time, 3. The median number of years required for completion of a degree in 2012–2013 were 2. The number of students enrolled full- and part-time who were dismissed or voluntarily withdrew from this program area in 2012–2013 were 0. *Educational Psychology MA/MS (Master of Arts/Science)*—Applications 2012–2013, 6. Total applicants accepted 2012–2013, 5. Number full-time enrolled (new admits only) 2012–2013, 0. Number part-time enrolled (new admits only) 2012–2013, 0. Total enrolled 2012–2013 full-time, 3. Total enrolled 2012–2013 part-time, 0. Openings 2013–2014, 3. The median number of years required for completion of a degree in 2012–2013 were 2. The number of students enrolled full- and part-time who were dismissed or voluntarily withdrew from this program area in 2012–2013 were 0. *School Psychology PhD (Doctor of Philosophy)*—Applications 2012–2013, 11. Total applicants accepted 2012–2013, 4. Number full-time enrolled (new admits only) 2012–2013, 3. Number part-time enrolled (new admits only) 2012–2013, 0. Total enrolled 2012–2013 full-time, 25. Total enrolled 2012–2013 part-time, 0. Openings 2013–2014, 6. The median number of years required for completion of a degree in 2012–2013 were 6. The number of students enrolled full- and part-time who were dismissed or voluntarily withdrew from this program area in 2012–2013 were 1. *School Psychology EdS (School Psychology)*—Applications 2012–2013, 7. Total applicants accepted 2012–2013, 5. Number full-time enrolled (new admits only) 2012–2013, 4. Number part-time enrolled (new admits only) 2012–2013, 0. Total enrolled 2012–2013 full-time, 15. Total enrolled 2012–2013 part-time, 0. Openings 2013–2014, 5. The median number of years required for completion of a degree in 2012–2013 were 6. The number of students enrolled full- and part-time who were dismissed or voluntarily withdrew from this program area in 2012–2013 were 0. *School Psychology MA/MS (Master of Arts/Science)*—Applications 2012–2013, 0. Total applicants accepted 2012–2013, 0. Number full-time enrolled (new admits only) 2012–2013, 0. The median number of years required for completion of a degree in 2012–2013 were 4. The number of students enrolled full- and part-time who were dismissed or voluntarily withdrew from this program area in 2012–2013 were 0.

Scores: Entries appear in this order: required test or GPA, minimum score (if required), median score of students entering in 2012–2013. *Counseling Psychology PhD (Doctor of Philosophy):* GRE-V no minimum stated, 152, GRE-Q no minimum stated, 149, GRE-Analytical 3.0, 4.0, overall undergraduate GPA 3.0, 3.5, last 2 years GPA 3.0, 3.6, Masters GPA 3.0, 3.7; *Counseling Psychology EdS (School Psychology):* GRE-V no minimum stated, 150, GRE-Q no minimum stated, 160, GRE-Analytical no minimum stated, 4.0, overall undergraduate GPA no minimum stated, 3.8, last 2 years GPA no minimum stated, 3.8; *Counseling Psychology MEd (Education):* GRE-V no minimum stated, 151, GRE-Q no minimum stated, 145, GRE-Analytical no minimum stated, 3.5, overall undergraduate GPA no minimum stated, 3.3, last 2 years GPA no minimum stated, 3.4; *Educational Psychology PhD (Doctor of Philosophy):* GRE-V no minimum stated, 152, GRE-Q no minimum stated, 163, GRE-Analytical no minimum stated, 3.5, overall undergraduate GPA no minimum stated, 3.5, last 2 years GPA no minimum stated, 3.5, Masters GPA no minimum stated; *Educational Psychology MEd (Education):* GRE-V 500, GRE-Q 500, GRE-Analytical 3.0, overall undergraduate GPA 3.0, last 2 years GPA 3.0; *Educational Psychology MA/MS (Master of Arts/Science):* GRE-V no minimum stated, 152, GRE-Q no minimum stated, 163, GRE-Analytical no minimum stated, 3.5, overall undergraduate GPA no minimum stated, last 2 years GPA no minimum stated, 3.6; *School Psychology PhD (Doctor of Philosophy):* GRE-V no minimum stated, 155, GRE-Q no minimum stated, 149, GRE-Analytical no minimum stated, 4.5, overall undergraduate GPA no minimum stated, 4.0, last 2 years GPA no minimum stated, Masters GPA no minimum stated; *School Psychology EdS (School Psychology):* GRE-V no minimum stated, 150, GRE-Q no minimum stated, 143, GRE-Analytical no minimum stated, 4.5, overall undergraduate GPA no minimum stated, 3.3, last 2 years GPA no minimum stated; *School Psychology MA/MS (Master of Arts/Science):* GRE-V no minimum stated, GRE-Q no minimum stated, GRE-Analytical no minimum stated, overall undergraduate GPA no minimum stated, last 2 years GPA no minimum stated.

Other Criteria: (importance of criteria rated low, medium, or high): GRE scores—medium, research experience—high, work experience—medium, extracurricular activity—medium, clinically related public service—medium, GPA—high, letters of recommendation—high, interview—high, statement of goals and objectives—high. For additional information on admission requirements, go to http://education.missouri.edu/ESCP/prospective_students/application_materials.php.

Student Characteristics: The following represents characteristics of students in 2012–2013 in all graduate psychology programs in the department: Female—full-time 151, part-time 0; Male—full-time 58, part-time 0; African American/Black—full-time 15, part-time 0; Hispanic/Latino(a)—full-time 7, part-time 0; Asian/Pacific Islander—full-time 1, part-time 0; American Indian/Alaska Native—full-time 1, part-time 0; Caucasian/White—full-time 137, part-time 0; Multi-ethnic—full-time 0, part-time 0; students subject to the Americans With Disabilities Act—full-time 1, part-time 0; Unknown ethnicity—full-time 0, part-time 0; International students who hold an F-1 or J-1 Visa—full-time 48, part-time 0.

Financial Information/Assistance:

Tuition for Full-Time Study: *Master's:* State residents: $336 per credit hour; Nonstate residents: $868 per credit hour. *Doctoral:* State residents: $336 per credit hour; Nonstate residents: $868 per credit hour. Tuition is subject to change. See the following website for updates and changes in tuition costs: http://cashiers. missouri.edu/costs/index.html.

Financial Assistance:

First-Year Students: Teaching assistantships available for first year. Average amount paid per academic year: $5,100. Average number of hours worked per week: 10. Apply by December 1. Research assistantships available for first year. Average amount paid per academic year: $5,100. Average number of hours worked per week: 10. Apply by December 1. Fellowships and scholarships available for first year. Average amount paid per academic year: $10,000. Apply by February 10.

Advanced Students: Teaching assistantships available for advanced students. Average amount paid per academic year: $5,100. Average number of hours worked per week: 10. Apply by April 1. Research assistantships available for advanced students. Fellowships and scholarships available for advanced students.

Additional Information: Of all students currently enrolled full time, 70% benefited from one or more of the listed financial assistance programs. Application and information available online at: http://education.missouri.edu/ESCP/prospective_students/ financial_assistance/financial_assistance.php.

Internships/Practica: Doctoral Degree (PhD Counseling Psychology): For those doctoral students for whom a professional psychology internship was required in this program prior to graduation, (4) students applied for an internship in 2011–2012, with (4) students obtaining an internship. Of those students who obtained an internship, (4) were paid internships. Of those students who obtained an internship, (4) students placed in APA/CPA accredited internships, (0) students placed in internships not APA/CPA accredited, but listed with the Association of Psychology Postdoctoral and Internship Programs (APPIC), (0) students placed in internships conforming to guidelines of the Council of Directors of School Psychology Programs (CDSPP), (0) students placed in internships that were not APA/CPA accredited, APPIC or CDSPP listed. Doctoral Degree (PhD School Psychology): For those doctoral students for whom a professional psychology internship was required in this program prior to graduation, (6) students applied for an internship in 2011–2012, with (6) students obtaining an internship. Of those students who obtained an internship, (6) were paid internships. Of those students who obtained an internship, (6) students placed in APA/CPA accredited internships, (0) students placed in internships not APA/CPA accredited, but listed with the Association of Psychology Postdoctoral and Internship Programs (APPIC), (0) students placed in internships conforming to guidelines of the Council of Directors of School Psychology Programs (CDSPP), (0) students placed in internships that were not APA/CPA accredited, APPIC or CDSPP listed. Internships are available in counseling psychology: VA hospitals, rehabilitation centers, mental health centers, university student counseling services; in school psychology: public schools, schools of medicine; and in school counseling: public schools.

Housing and Day Care: On-campus housing is available. See the following website for more information: http://reslife.missouri. edu/. No on-campus day care facilities are available.

Employment of Department Graduates:

Master's Degree Graduates: Of those who graduated in the academic year 2011–2012, the following categories and numbers represent the postgraduate activities and employment of master's degree graduates: Enrolled in a psychology doctoral program (14), enrolled in a postdoctoral residency/fellowship (n/a), employed in independent practice (n/a), employed in a professional position in a school system (4), total from the above (master's) (18).

Doctoral Degree Graduates: Of those who graduated in the academic year 2011–2012, the following categories and numbers represent the postgraduate activities and employment of doctoral degree graduates: Enrolled in a psychology doctoral program (n/a), enrolled in a postdoctoral residency/fellowship (1), employed in an academic position at a university (3), employed in other positions at a higher education institution (6), employed in a professional position in a school system (1), employed in government agency (1), employed in a hospital/medical center (2), total from the above (doctoral) (14).

Additional Information:

Orientation, Objectives, and Emphasis of Department: The goals of the department include the preparation of students in the professional specialties of counseling, school and educational psychology, school counseling and student personnel work, and the conduct of research on the applications of psychological knowledge to counseling and educational settings. The department emphasizes general psychological foundations, assessment, career development, counselor training and supervision, group processes, and research on counseling processes and psychological measurement and assessment. The theoretical orientation of the faculty is eclectic.

Special Facilities or Resources: Individual and group counseling and psychological assessment training facilities are available in the department, the College of Education and the department's assessment and consultation clinic, and on campus in the Student Counseling Center. Access to computer services is available across the campus.

Information for Students With Physical Disabilities: See the following website for more information: http://disabilityservices. missouri.edu/.

Application Information:
Send to Graduate Secretary, 9 Hill Hall, University of Missouri, Educational, School and Counseling Psychology, Columbia, MO 65211. URL of online application: https://app.applyyourself.com/?id=umc-

grad. Students are admitted in the Fall, application deadline December 1. December 1 for Counseling Psychology PhD and School Psychology. January 15 for Educational Psychology PhD and MA/MEd. *Fee:* $55. International applicants pay a $75 admissions fee.

Missouri, University of, Kansas City

Department of Psychology
5030 Cherry Street, Room 324
Kansas City, MO 64110
Telephone: (816) 235-1318
Fax: (816) 235-1062
E-mail: *psychology@umkc.edu*
Web: *http://cas.umkc.edu/Psychology/*

Department Information:

1940. Chairperson: Jennifer Lundgren, PhD. Number of faculty: total—full-time 15; women—full-time 12; total—minority—full-time 2; women minority—full-time 1.

Programs and Degrees Offered:

Listed in the following order: Program area, degree type (T if terminal Master's), number awarded 7/11–6/12. Clinical Psychology PhD (Doctor of Philosophy) 3, Experimental Health Psychology PhD (Doctor of Philosophy) 0.

APA Accreditation: Clinical PhD (Doctor of Philosophy). Student Outcome Data Website: http://cas.umkc.edu/psychology/GCPhD.asp.

Student Applications/Admissions:

Student Applications

Clinical Psychology PhD (Doctor of Philosophy)—Applications 2012–2013, 83. Total applicants accepted 2012–2013, 4. Number full-time enrolled (new admits only) 2012–2013, 4. Number part-time enrolled (new admits only) 2012–2013, 0. Total enrolled 2012–2013 full-time, 28. Total enrolled 2012–2013 part-time, 0. Openings 2013–2014, 4. The median number of years required for completion of a degree in 2012–2013 were 6. The number of students enrolled full- and part-time who were dismissed or voluntarily withdrew from this program area in 2012–2013 were 0. *Experimental Health Psychology PhD (Doctor of Philosophy)*—Applications 2012–2013, 5. Total applicants accepted 2012–2013, 2. Number full-time enrolled (new admits only) 2012–2013, 2. Number part-time enrolled (new admits only) 2012–2013, 0. Total enrolled 2012–2013 full-time, 2. Total enrolled 2012–2013 part-time, 0. Openings 2013–2014, 2. The number of students enrolled full- and part-time who were dismissed or voluntarily withdrew from this program area in 2012–2013 were 0.

Scores: Entries appear in this order: required test or GPA, minimum score (if required), median score of students entering in 2012–2013. *Clinical Psychology PhD (Doctor of Philosophy):* GRE-V no minimum stated, 500, GRE-Q no minimum stated, 645, GRE-Analytical no minimum stated, 4.0, overall undergraduate GPA no minimum stated, 3.41; *Experimental Health Psychology PhD (Doctor of Philosophy):* GRE-V no minimum stated, 159, GRE-Q no minimum stated, 153, GRE-Analytical no minimum stated, 4.5.

Other Criteria: (importance of criteria rated low, medium, or high): GRE scores—high, research experience—high, work experience—medium, extracurricular activity—low, clinically related public service—medium, GPA—high, letters of recommendation—high, interview—high, statement of goals and objectives—high, undergraduate major in psychology—medium, specific undergraduate psychology courses taken—high.

Student Characteristics: The following represents characteristics of students in 2012–2013 in all graduate psychology programs in the department: Female—full-time 24, part-time 0; Male—full-time 9, part-time 0; African American/Black—full-time 1, part-time 0; Hispanic/Latino(a)—full-time 5, part-time 0; Asian/Pacific Islander—full-time 1, part-time 0; American Indian/Alaska Native—full-time 0, part-time 0; Caucasian/White—full-time 26, part-time 0; Multi-ethnic—full-time 0, part-time 0; students subject to the Americans With Disabilities Act—full-time 0, part-time 0; Unknown ethnicity—full-time 0, part-time 0; International students who hold an F-1 or J-1 Visa—full-time 0, part-time 0.

Financial Information/Assistance:

Tuition for Full-Time Study: *Doctoral:* State residents: $332 per credit hour; Nonstate residents: $857 per credit hour. Tuition is subject to change. Additional fees are assessed to students beyond the costs of tuition for the following: technology, student health, rec center. See the following website for updates and changes in tuition costs: http://www.umkc.edu/adminfinance/finance/cashiers/.

Financial Assistance:

First-Year Students: Teaching assistantships available for first year. Average amount paid per academic year: $9,000. Average number of hours worked per week: 20. Research assistantships available for first year. Average amount paid per academic year: $9,000. Average number of hours worked per week: 20. Fellowships and scholarships available for first year.

Advanced Students: Teaching assistantships available for advanced students. Average amount paid per academic year: $9,000. Average number of hours worked per week: 20. Research assistantships available for advanced students. Average amount paid per academic year: $9,000. Average number of hours worked per week: 20. Fellowships and scholarships available for advanced students.

Additional Information: Of all students currently enrolled full time, 100% benefited from one or more of the listed financial assistance programs. Application and information available online at: http://www.sfa.umkc.edu/.

Internships/Practica: Doctoral Degree (PhD Clinical Psychology): For those doctoral students for whom a professional psychology internship was required in this program prior to graduation, (6) students applied for an internship in 2011–2012, with (6) students obtaining an internship. Of those students who obtained an internship, (6) were paid internships. Of those students who obtained an internship, (6) students placed in APA/CPA accredited internships, (0) students placed in internships not APA/CPA accredited, but listed with the Association of Psychology Postdoctoral and Internship Programs (APPIC), (0) students placed in internships conforming to guidelines of the Council of Directors of School Psychology Programs (CDSPP), (0) students placed in internships that were not APA/CPA accredited, APPIC or CDSPP listed. With a population of over 1.5 million, Kansas City offers numerous practicum and research opportunities. A wide range of formal community practicum opportunities are offered to Clinical Psychology PhD students including placements at community agencies, medical centers, and other applied settings. Clinical psychology students are required to enroll in six semesters of practicum during which they are involved in many different types of clinical experiences, ranging from supervised work in specialized health care programs to more general outpatient settings for psychotherapy and psychological assessment. Basic clinical practica include training in general mental health assessment and treatment areas such as crisis intervention, depression screening, personnel and disability evaluations, and treatment of adjustment problems, depression, and anxiety disorders. Advanced training opportunities are available in the assessment and treatment of obesity and eating disorders, smoking and other substance abuse, and chronic pain. In the fifth year of study, students are required to complete a one-year clinical internship.

Housing and Day Care: On-campus housing is available. See the following website for more information: http://www.umkc.edu/housing/. On-campus day care facilities are available. See the following website for more information: http://education.umkc.edu/berkley/.

Employment of Department Graduates:
Master's Degree Graduates: Of those who graduated in the academic year 2011–2012, the following categories and numbers represent the postgraduate activities and employment of master's degree graduates: Enrolled in a postdoctoral residency/fellowship (n/a), employed in independent practice (n/a), total from the above (master's) (0).
Doctoral Degree Graduates: Of those who graduated in the academic year 2011–2012, the following categories and numbers represent the postgraduate activities and employment of doctoral degree graduates: Enrolled in a psychology doctoral program (n/a), enrolled in a postdoctoral residency/fellowship (4), employed in government agency (1), total from the above (doctoral) (5).

Additional Information:
Orientation, Objectives, and Emphasis of Department: The psychology program integrates clinical and epidemiological research with the health and life sciences. The department seeks to enhance the public health, broadly defined, through rigorous training of students (education mission); provide an accessible resource for the integration of behavioral sciences and health research and healthcare (service mission); develop knowledge and enhance health outcomes through empirical research (research and evaluation mission); and incorporate integrity and respect for human and intellectual diversity in all our activities (human mission).

Information for Students With Physical Disabilities: See the following website for more information: http://www.umkc.edu/disability/.

Application Information:
Send to UMKC, Department of Psychology, 5030 Cherry Street, Room 324, Kansas City, MO 64110. Application available online. URL of online application: http://www.umkc.edu/apply/grad.asp. Students are admitted in the Fall, application deadline December 5. *Fee:* $35.

Missouri, University of, Kansas City
Division of Counseling and Educational Psychology
School of Education
5100 Rockhill Road, 215, School of Education
Kansas City, MO 64110
Telephone: (816) 235-2722
Fax: (816) 235-5270
E-mail: *umkccep@umkc.edu*
Web: *http://education.umkc.edu/cep/*

Department Information:
Chairperson: Nancy L. Murdock, PhD. Number of faculty: total—full-time 9; women—full-time 8; total—minority—full-time 3; women minority—full-time 3.

Programs and Degrees Offered:
Listed in the following order: Program area, degree type (T if terminal Master's), number awarded 7/11–6/12. Counseling Psychology PhD (Doctor of Philosophy) 4, Counseling and Guidance EdS (School Psychology) 2, Counseling and Guidance MA/MS (Master of Arts/Science) (T) 25.

APA Accreditation: Counseling PhD (Doctor of Philosophy). Student Outcome Data Website: http://education.umkc.edu/cep/PhD/PhDdata.html.

Student Applications/Admissions:
Student Applications
Counseling Psychology PhD (Doctor of Philosophy)—Applications 2012–2013, 93. Total applicants accepted 2012–2013, 7. Number full-time enrolled (new admits only) 2012–2013, 7. Number part-time enrolled (new admits only) 2012–2013, 0. Total enrolled 2012–2013 full-time, 40. Total enrolled 2012–2013 part-time, 0. Openings 2013–2014, 7. The median number of years required for completion of a degree in 2012–2013 were 6. The number of students enrolled full- and part-time who were dismissed or voluntarily withdrew from this program area in 2012–2013 were 1. *Counseling and Guidance EdS (School Psychology)*—Applications 2012–2013, 19. Total applicants accepted 2012–2013, 9. Number full-time enrolled (new admits only) 2012–2013, 0. Number part-time enrolled (new admits only) 2012–2013, 8. The median number of years required for completion of a degree in 2012–2013 were 2. The number of students enrolled full- and part-time who were dismissed or voluntarily withdrew from this program area in 2012–2013 were 3. *Counseling and Guidance MA/MS (Master of Arts/Science)*—Applications 2012–2013, 117. Total applicants accepted 2012–2013, 78. Number full-time enrolled (new admits only) 2012–2013, 26. Number part-time enrolled (new admits only) 2012–2013, 11. Total enrolled 2012–2013 full-time, 65. Total enrolled 2012–2013 part-time, 83. The median number of years required for completion of a degree in 2012–2013 were 3. The number of students enrolled full- and part-time who were dismissed or voluntarily withdrew from this program area in 2012–2013 were 10.
Scores: Entries appear in this order: required test or GPA, minimum score (if required), median score of students entering in 2012–2013. *Counseling Psychology PhD (Doctor of Philosophy):* GRE-V no minimum stated, 622, GRE-Q no minimum stated, 644, GRE-Analytical no minimum stated, 4.5, overall

undergraduate GPA 3.0, 3.65, last 2 years GPA 3.25, Masters GPA no minimum stated, 3.98; *Counseling and Guidance EdS (School Psychology):* GRE-V no minimum stated, 146, GRE-Q no minimum stated, 144, GRE-Analytical no minimum stated, 4; *Counseling and Guidance MA/MS (Master of Arts/ Science):* GRE-V no minimum stated, 151, GRE-Q no minimum stated, 144, GRE-Analytical no minimum stated, 4.0, overall undergraduate GPA 2.75, 3.25.

Other Criteria: (importance of criteria rated low, medium, or high): GRE scores—medium, research experience—high, work experience—medium, extracurricular activity—medium, clinically related public service—medium, GPA—medium, letters of recommendation—high, interview—high, statement of goals and objectives—high, research interests—medium, undergraduate major in psychology—medium, specific undergraduate psychology courses taken—medium, Undergraduate psychology courses are not required for the MA programs but are for the PhD program, unless the student has a graduate degree in counseling or similar field. For additional information on admission requirements, go to http://education.umkc.edu/cep/.

Student Characteristics: The following represents characteristics of students in 2012–2013 in all graduate psychology programs in the department: Female—full-time 79, part-time 82; Male—full-time 26, part-time 13; African American/Black—full-time 10, part-time 9; Hispanic/Latino(a)—full-time 3, part-time 6; Asian/ Pacific Islander—full-time 4, part-time 3; American Indian/ Alaska Native—full-time 0, part-time 0; Caucasian/White—full-time 79, part-time 61; Multi-ethnic—full-time 1, part-time 0; students subject to the Americans With Disabilities Act—full-time 1, part-time 2; Unknown ethnicity—full-time 8, part-time 16; International students who hold an F-1 or J-1 Visa—full-time 4, part-time 1.

Financial Information/Assistance:

Tuition for Full-Time Study: *Doctoral:* State residents: per academic year $6,934, $322 per credit hour; Nonstate residents: per academic year $16,378, $856 per credit hour. Tuition is subject to change. See the following website for updates and changes in tuition costs: http://www.umkc.edu/adminfinance/finance/cashiers/default.asp.

Financial Assistance:

First-Year Students: Teaching assistantships available for first year. Average amount paid per academic year: $12,000. Average number of hours worked per week: 20. Research assistantships available for first year. Average amount paid per academic year: $12,000. Average number of hours worked per week: 20. Fellowships and scholarships available for first year. Apply by February 1.

Advanced Students: Teaching assistantships available for advanced students. Average amount paid per academic year: $12,000. Average number of hours worked per week: 20. Research assistantships available for advanced students. Average amount paid per academic year: $12,000. Average number of hours worked per week: 20. Fellowships and scholarships available for advanced students. Apply by February 1.

Additional Information: Of all students currently enrolled full time, 88% benefited from one or more of the listed financial assistance programs. Application and information available online at: http://sgs.umkc.edu/scholarships-financial-assistance/index.asp.

Internships/Practica: Doctoral Degree (PhD Counseling Psychology): For those doctoral students for whom a professional psychology internship was required in this program prior to graduation, (6) students applied for an internship in 2011–2012, with (5) students obtaining an internship. Of those students who obtained an internship, (5) were paid internships. Of those students who obtained an internship, (5) students placed in APA/CPA accredited internships, (0) students placed in internships not APA/CPA accredited, but listed with the Association of Psychology Postdoctoral and Internship Programs (APPIC), (0) students placed in internships conforming to guidelines of the Council of Directors of School Psychology Programs (CDSPP), (0) students placed in internships that were not APA/CPA accredited, APPIC or CDSPP listed. Master's Degree (MA/MS Counseling and Guidance): An internship experience, such as a final research project or "capstone" experience is required of graduates. All programs offer a wide range of practicum and internship placements. The Division of Counseling and Educational Psychology operates the Community Counseling and Assessment Services, an in-house training facility serving individuals, couples, and families in the surrounding community. Advanced practica are also available in a variety of agencies including local community mental health centers, counseling centers, Veterans Affairs Hospitals, and other local service provision agencies.

Housing and Day Care: On-campus housing is available. See the following website for more information: http://www.umkc.edu/housing/. No on-campus day care facilities are available.

Employment of Department Graduates:

Master's Degree Graduates: Of those who graduated in the academic year 2011–2012, the following categories and numbers represent the postgraduate activities and employment of master's degree graduates: Enrolled in a psychology doctoral program (1), enrolled in a postdoctoral residency/fellowship (n/a), employed in independent practice (n/a), employed in a professional position in a school system (14), employed in a community mental health/counseling center (4), other employment position (1), do not know (8), total from the above (master's) (28).

Doctoral Degree Graduates: Of those who graduated in the academic year 2011–2012, the following categories and numbers represent the postgraduate activities and employment of doctoral degree graduates: Enrolled in a psychology doctoral program (n/a), employed in other positions at a higher education institution (1), employed in government agency (1), employed in a community mental health/counseling center (4), total from the above (doctoral) (6).

Additional Information:

Orientation, Objectives, and Emphasis of Department: Consistent with the University of Missouri-Kansas City's (UMKC) urban mission, the UMKC counseling psychology program emphasizes cultural and individual diversity within a scientist–practitioner model. Our program model is intended to educate ethical and flexible professionals who can work in a variety of settings relying on the underlying philosophies of counseling psychology and the scientist–practitioner model. This diverse faculty is committed to educating future counseling psychologists to improve the welfare of individuals and communities through scholarship and applied interventions. Our model consists of four components: A. The program faculty encourages students to develop primary identification with the core values of counseling psychology, such as respect for cultural and individual diversity, scientific foundation for all activities, developmental models of human growth, education and prevention, and career/vocational development. B. The UMKC counseling psychology program emphasizes a scientist–practitioner model. This model stipulates that students are informed about and contribute to scientific knowledge, and are committed to life-long learning. Further, students' practice activities are informed by research and a scientific attitude, and all professional activities are approached and critically evaluated with an ethical, multicultural, and professional mindset. C. The UMKC counseling psychology program trains students to work effectively and ethically with diverse clients, using interventions based on theory and informed by science. D. The UMKC counseling psychology program follows a developmental model in which the integration of science and practice is emphasized throughout the program. Early and progressive training is provided in research, culminating in professionals who can design, conduct, and evaluate research relevant to the field of psychology. Similarly, early and progressive training in practice activity is emphasized.

Information for Students With Physical Disabilities: See the following website for more information: http://www.umkc.edu/disability/.

Application Information:

Send to Division of Counseling & Educational Psychology, Counseling Psychology Program, University of Missouri-Kansas City, ED 215, 5100 Rockhill Road, Kansas City, MO 64110. URL of online application: http://www.umkc.edu/apply/grad.asp. Students are admitted in the Fall, application deadline January 1; Spring, application deadline September 1; Programs have rolling admissions. PhD deadline is January 1; MA program deadline for Fall admission is March 1, for Spring admission September 1. EdS program has rolling admissions. *Fee:* $35. online application fee $35; paper application fee is $45.

Missouri, University of, St. Louis
Department of Psychology
Arts & Sciences
One University Boulevard
St. Louis, MO 63121
Telephone: (314) 516-5393
Fax: (314) 516-5392
E-mail: *geot@UMSL.EDU*
Web: *http://www.umsl.edu/divisions/artscience/psychology/*

Department Information:

1967. Chairperson: George T. Taylor, PhD. Number of faculty: total—full-time 25, part-time 2; women—full-time 13, part-time 1; total—minority—full-time 1.

Programs and Degrees Offered:

Listed in the following order: Program area, degree type (T if terminal Master's), number awarded 7/11–6/12. Clinical Psychology PhD (Doctor of Philosophy) 8, Industrial/Organizational Psychology PhD (Doctor of Philosophy) 3, Behavioral Neuroscience, no data.

APA Accreditation: Clinical PhD (Doctor of Philosophy).

Student Applications/Admissions:

Student Applications

Clinical Psychology PhD (Doctor of Philosophy)—Applications 2012–2013, 147. Total applicants accepted 2012–2013, 12. Number full-time enrolled (new admits only) 2012–2013, 6. Number part-time enrolled (new admits only) 2012–2013, 0. Total enrolled 2012–2013 full-time, 32. Total enrolled 2012–2013 part-time, 0. Openings 2013–2014, 6. The median number of years required for completion of a degree in 2012–2013 were 6. The number of students enrolled full- and part-time who were dismissed or voluntarily withdrew from this program area in 2012–2013 were 1. *Industrial/Organizational Psychology PhD (Doctor of Philosophy)*—Applications 2012–2013, 80. Total applicants accepted 2012–2013, 8. Number full-time enrolled (new admits only) 2012–2013, 4. Number part-time enrolled (new admits only) 2012–2013, 0. Total enrolled 2012–2013 full-time, 31. Total enrolled 2012–2013 part-time, 0. Openings 2013–2014, 5. The median number of years required for completion of a degree in 2012–2013 were 7. The number of students enrolled full- and part-time who were dismissed or voluntarily withdrew from this program area in 2012–2013 were 1. *Behavioral Neuroscience*—No data.

Scores: Entries appear in this order: required test or GPA, minimum score (if required), median score of students entering in 2012–2013. *Clinical Psychology PhD (Doctor of Philosophy)*: GRE-V no minimum stated, 600, GRE-Q no minimum stated, 675, GRE-Analytical no minimum stated, 5, overall undergraduate GPA no minimum stated, 3.8.

Other Criteria: (importance of criteria rated low, medium, or high): GRE scores—high, research experience—high, work experience—medium, extracurricular activity—low, clinically related public service—medium, GPA—high, letters of recommendation—high, interview—medium, statement of goals and objectives—high, undergraduate major in psychology—medium, Only the clinical and behavioral neuroscience programs have a formal in-person interview procedure. Importance of criteria varies by program.

Student Characteristics: The following represents characteristics of students in 2012–2013 in all graduate psychology programs in the department: Female—full-time 53, part-time 0; Male—full-time 19, part-time 0; African American/Black—full-time 1, part-time 0; Hispanic/Latino(a)—full-time 0, part-time 0; Asian/Pacific Islander—full-time 4, part-time 0; American Indian/Alaska Native—full-time 0, part-time 0; Caucasian/White—full-time 63, part-time 0; Multi-ethnic—full-time 4, part-time 0; students subject to the Americans With Disabilities Act—full-time 0, part-time 0; Unknown ethnicity—full-time 0, part-time 0; International students who hold an F-1 or J-1 Visa—full-time 0, part-time 0.

Financial Information/Assistance:

Tuition for Full-Time Study: *Master's:* State residents: $409 per credit hour; Nonstate residents: $1,008 per credit hour. *Doctoral:* State residents: $409 per credit hour; Nonstate residents: $1,008 per credit hour. Tuition is subject to change. Additional fees are assessed to students beyond the costs of tuition for the following: computer, parking, activities. See the following website for updates and changes in tuition costs: http://www.umsl.edu/cashiers/tuition-fees/index.html.

Financial Assistance:

First-Year Students: Teaching assistantships available for first year. Average amount paid per academic year: $10,500. Average number of hours worked per week: 20. Apply by January 15. Research assistantships available for first year. Average amount paid per academic year: $12,500. Average number of hours worked per week: 20. Apply by January 15. Fellowships and scholarships available for first year. Average amount paid per academic year: $4,000. Average number of hours worked per week: 0.

Advanced Students: Teaching assistantships available for advanced students. Average amount paid per academic year: $11,500. Average number of hours worked per week: 20. Apply by January 15. Research assistantships available for advanced students. Average amount paid per academic year: $13,500. Average number of hours worked per week: 20. Apply by January 15. Fellowships and scholarships available for advanced students. Average amount paid per academic year: $4,000. Average number of hours worked per week: 0.

Additional Information: Of all students currently enrolled full time, 80% benefited from one or more of the listed financial assistance programs.

Internships/Practica: Doctoral Degree (PhD Clinical Psychology): For those doctoral students for whom a professional psychology internship was required in this program prior to graduation, (4) students applied for an internship in 2011–2012, with (3) students obtaining an internship. Of those students who obtained an internship, (3) were paid internships. Of those students who obtained an internship, (2) students placed in APA/CPA accredited internships, (1) students placed in internships not APA/CPA accredited, but listed with the Association of Psychology Postdoctoral and Internship Programs (APPIC), (0) students placed in internships conforming to guidelines of the Council of Directors of School Psychology Programs (CDSPP), (0) students placed in internships that were not APA/CPA accredited, APPIC or CDSPP listed. Students (clinical) participate in practica in our Community Psychological Service (the psychology clinic), and a paid clinical clerkship, which may be in a community or university-based program. Advanced students in behavioral neuroscience have internship opportunities with research labs at local medical schools, Washington University and Saint Louis University.

Housing and Day Care: On-campus housing is available. See the following website for more information: http://www.umsl.edu/services/reslife/. On-campus day care facilities are available. See the following website for more information: http://www.umsl.edu/~kids/.

Employment of Department Graduates:

Master's Degree Graduates: Of those who graduated in the academic year 2011–2012, the following categories and numbers represent the postgraduate activities and employment of master's degree graduates: Enrolled in another graduate/professional program (1), enrolled in a postdoctoral residency/fellowship (n/a), employed in independent practice (n/a), employed in a hospital/medical center (3), total from the above (master's) (4).

Doctoral Degree Graduates: Of those who graduated in the academic year 2011–2012, the following categories and numbers represent the postgraduate activities and employment of doctoral degree graduates: Enrolled in a psychology doctoral program (n/a), enrolled in a postdoctoral residency/fellowship (5), employed in business or industry (3), total from the above (doctoral) (8).

Additional Information:

Orientation, Objectives, and Emphasis of Department: The orientation of the department emphasizes psychology as science yet also recognizes the important social responsibilities of psychology, especially in the clinical and applied areas. Emphasis of behavioral neuroscience is in neuropsychology, cognitive behaviors, psychophysiology and animal models of psychopathology, and behavioral neuropharmacology/endocrinology . The department offers a broad spectrum of high-quality programs at the undergraduate and graduate levels.

Special Facilities or Resources: The Department of Psychology is housed in Stadler Hall, and research laboratories and computers are conveniently located in the building. The psychological clinic (Community Psychological Service) is also contained within Stadler Hall. The Center for Trauma Recovery and Child Advocacy Center each have community clinics, which are housed on campus. Physical facilities include workshops and animal, social, and human experimental laboratories. A wide range of research equipment is available, including videotaping facilities, computer terminals, and personal computers.

Information for Students With Physical Disabilities: See the following website for more information: http://www.umsl.edu/services/disabled/.

Application Information:
Send to Graduate Admissions, University of Missouri-St. Louis, One University Boulevard, St. Louis, MO 63121-4499. Application available online. URL of online application: http://www.umsl.edu/divisions/graduate/admissions/application-form.html. Students are admitted in the Fall, application deadline December 15. Clinical program deadline: December 15. Behavioral Neuroscience deadline: January 15. Industrial/Organizational deadline: January 15. *Fee:* $35.

Saint Louis University
Department of Psychology
Arts & Sciences
3511 Laclede Avenue
St. Louis, MO
Telephone: (314) 977-2300
E-mail: *gfellerj@slu.edu*
Web: *http://www.slu.edu/x13122.xml*

Department Information:
1926. Chairperson: Jeffrey D. Gfeller, PhD. Number of faculty: total—full-time 28; women—full-time 13; total—minority—full-time 4, part-time 2; women minority—full-time 2, part-time 1; faculty subject to the Americans With Disabilities Act 1.

Programs and Degrees Offered:
Listed in the following order: Program area, degree type (T if terminal Master's), number awarded 7/11–6/12. Industrial/Organizational Psychology PhD (Doctor of Philosophy) 5, Clinical Psychology PhD (Doctor of Philosophy) 8, Experimental Psychology PhD (Doctor of Philosophy) 7.

APA Accreditation: Clinical PhD (Doctor of Philosophy). Student Outcome Data Website: http://www.slu.edu/department-of-psychology-home/graduate-programs/clinical-psychology/student-admission-outcomes-and-other-data.

Student Applications/Admissions:

Student Applications

Industrial/Organizational Psychology PhD (Doctor of Philosophy)—Applications 2012–2013, 42. Total applicants accepted 2012–2013, 8. Number full-time enrolled (new admits only) 2012–2013, 6. Total enrolled 2012–2013 full-time, 24. Openings 2013–2014, 4. The median number of years required for completion of a degree in 2012–2013 were 5. The number of students enrolled full- and part-time who were dismissed or voluntarily withdrew from this program area in 2012–2013 were 0. *Clinical Psychology PhD (Doctor of Philosophy)*—Applications 2012–2013, 165. Total applicants accepted 2012–2013, 11. Number full-time enrolled (new admits only) 2012–2013, 8. Total enrolled 2012–2013 full-time, 34. Openings 2013–2014, 8. The median number of years required for completion of a degree in 2012–2013 were 6. The number of students enrolled full- and part-time who were dismissed or voluntarily withdrew from this program area in 2012–2013 were 0. *Experimental Psychology PhD (Doctor of Philosophy)*—Applications 2012–2013, 62. Total applicants accepted 2012–2013, 10. Number full-time enrolled (new admits only) 2012–2013, 6. Total enrolled 2012–2013 full-time, 32. Openings 2013–2014, 6. The median number of years required for completion of a degree in 2012–2013 were 6. The number of students enrolled full- and part-time who were dismissed or voluntarily withdrew from this program area in 2012–2013 were 0.

Scores: Entries appear in this order: required test or GPA, minimum score (if required), median score of students entering in 2012–2013. *Industrial/Organizational Psychology PhD (Doctor of Philosophy)*: GRE-V 153, 158, GRE-Q 153, 163, GRE-Analytical 3.5, 4.5, overall undergraduate GPA 3.2, 3.7; *Clinical Psychology PhD (Doctor of Philosophy)*: GRE-V no minimum stated, 160, GRE-Q no minimum stated, 162, GRE-Analytical no minimum stated, 4.5, overall undergraduate GPA no minimum stated, 3.65, psychology GPA no minimum stated, 3.8; *Experimental Psychology PhD (Doctor of Philosophy)*: GRE-V no minimum stated, GRE-Q no minimum stated, GRE-Analytical no minimum stated, overall undergraduate GPA no minimum stated, psychology GPA no minimum stated.

Other Criteria: (importance of criteria rated low, medium, or high): GRE scores—medium, research experience—high, work experience—medium, extracurricular activity—low, clinically related public service—medium, GPA—high, letters of recommendation—medium, interview—high, statement of goals and objectives—high, ETS PPI—medium, undergraduate major in psychology—high, specific undergraduate psychology courses taken—medium, These criteria may vary for different program areas. The Clinical Psychology program highly recommends that applicants complete the ETS PPI.

Student Characteristics: The following represents characteristics of students in 2012–2013 in all graduate psychology programs in the department: Female—full-time 62, part-time 0; Male—full-time 28, part-time 0; African American/Black—full-time 9, part-time 0; Hispanic/Latino(a)—full-time 2, part-time 0; Asian/Pacific Islander—full-time 4, part-time 0; American Indian/Alaska Native—full-time 0, part-time 0; Caucasian/White—full-time 72, part-time 0; Multi-ethnic—full-time 3, part-time 0; students subject to the Americans With Disabilities Act—full-time 3, part-time 0; Unknown ethnicity—full-time 0, part-time 0; International students who hold an F-1 or J-1 Visa—full-time 2, part-time 0.

Financial Information/Assistance:

Tuition for Full-Time Study: *Doctoral:* State residents: $1,010 per credit hour; Nonstate residents: $1,010 per credit hour. Tuition is subject to change. Additional fees are assessed to students beyond the costs of tuition for the following: Student Graduate Association Fee, Student Union Fee. See the following website for updates and changes in tuition costs: http://www.slu.edu/x21887.xml.

Financial Assistance:

First-Year Students: Teaching assistantships available for first year. Average amount paid per academic year: $18,000. Average number of hours worked per week: 20. Apply by January 1. Research assistantships available for first year. Average amount paid per academic year: $20,000. Average number of hours worked per week: 20. Apply by January 1.

Advanced Students: Teaching assistantships available for advanced students. Average amount paid per academic year: $9,000. Average number of hours worked per week: 10. Apply by January 1. Research assistantships available for advanced students. Average amount paid per academic year: $9,000. Average number of hours worked per week: 10. Apply by January 1.

Additional Information: Of all students currently enrolled full time, 68% benefited from one or more of the listed financial assistance programs. Application and information available online at: http://www.slu.edu/graduate-admission-home/affording-graduate-education.

Internships/Practica: Doctoral Degree (PhD Clinical Psychology): For those doctoral students for whom a professional psychology internship was required in this program prior to graduation, (9) students applied for an internship in 2011–2012, with (9) students obtaining an internship. Of those students who obtained an internship, (9) were paid internships. Of those students who obtained an internship, (9) students placed in APA/CPA accredited internships, (0) students placed in internships not APA/CPA accredited, but listed with the Association of Psychology Postdoctoral and Internship Programs (APPIC), (0) students placed in internships conforming to guidelines of the Council of Directors of School Psychology Programs (CDSPP), (0) students placed in internships that were not APA/CPA accredited, APPIC or CDSPP listed. The Clinical program has established collaborative relationships with various medical centers, agencies, and private practitioners throughout the community to provide advanced practica and training in the science and practice of psychology.

Housing and Day Care: On-campus housing is available. See the following website for more information: http://www.slu.edu/reslife.xml. No on-campus day care facilities are available.

Employment of Department Graduates:

Master's Degree Graduates: Of those who graduated in the academic year 2011–2012, the following categories and numbers represent the postgraduate activities and employment of master's

degree graduates: Enrolled in a postdoctoral residency/fellowship (n/a), employed in independent practice (n/a), total from the above (master's) (0).

Doctoral Degree Graduates: Of those who graduated in the academic year 2011–2012, the following categories and numbers represent the postgraduate activities and employment of doctoral degree graduates: Enrolled in a psychology doctoral program (n/a), enrolled in a postdoctoral residency/fellowship (6), employed in an academic position at a university (4), employed in other positions at a higher education institution (2), employed in business or industry (2), employed in a hospital/medical center (4), other employment position (2), do not know (1), total from the above (doctoral) (21).

Additional Information:

Orientation, Objectives, and Emphasis of Department: Our mission is to educate students in the discipline of psychology and its applications. We encourage intellectual curiosity, critical thinking, and ethical responsibility in our teaching, research and its applications. Our commitment to value-based, holistic education and our enthusiasm for psychology is realized in the products of our research, in our graduates, and in service to others.

Special Facilities or Resources: The Clinical Program operates an on-campus Psychological Services Center, which serves as a primary site for supervised clinical experiences with children, adolescents, adults, couples and families. Resources available to Experimental students include animal housing, research suites for neuroscience and sleep research; and several laboratory suites for social, cognitive, and developmental research. In addition to space for laboratory research, the students in the Industrial/Organizational Program are involved with the Center for the Application of Behavioral Sciences. Housed within the department, this Center provides opportunities for training in organizational consulting and program evaluation in field settings.

Information for Students With Physical Disabilities: See the following website for more information: http://www.slu.edu/x24491.xml.

Application Information:
Send to Office of Admission, DuBourg Hall, Room 119, Saint Louis University, 1 North Grand Blvd., Saint Louis, MO 63103. Application available online. URL of online application: http://www.slu.edu/graduate-admission-home/apply-now. Students are admitted in the Fall, application deadline January 1. *Fee:* $55.

The School of Professional Psychology at Forest Institute
Clinical Psychology
2885 West Battlefield Road
Springfield, MO 65807
Telephone: (417) 823-3477
Fax: (417) 823-3442
E-mail: *admissions@forest.edu*
Web: *http://www.forest.edu*

Department Information:
1979. Vice President of Academic Affairs: Gerald Porter, PhD. Number of faculty: total—full-time 17, part-time 41; women—full-time 9, part-time 14; total—minority—full-time 2; women minority—full-time 1.

Programs and Degrees Offered:
Listed in the following order: Program area, degree type (T if terminal Master's), number awarded 7/11–6/12. Clinical Psychology MA/MS (Master of Arts/Science) (T) 18, Marriage and Family Therapy MA/MS (Master of Arts/Science) (T) 5, Applied Behavior Analysis MA/MS (Master of Arts/Science) (T) 0, Counseling Psychology MA/MS (Master of Arts/Science) (T) 9, Clinical Psychology PsyD (Doctor of Psychology) 33.

APA Accreditation: On Probation PsyD (Doctor of Psychology). Student Outcome Data Website: http://www.forest.edu/psyd/student-admissions—outcomes—other-data.aspx.

Student Applications/Admissions:
Student Applications

Clinical Psychology MA/MS (Master of Arts/Science)—Number full-time enrolled (new admits only) 2012–2013, 28. Total enrolled 2012–2013 full-time, 38. Total enrolled 2012–2013 part-time, 4. Openings 2013–2014, 15. The median number of years required for completion of a degree in 2012–2013 were 2. *Marriage and Family Therapy MA/MS (Master of Arts/Science)*—Number full-time enrolled (new admits only) 2012–2013, 2. Total enrolled 2012–2013 full-time, 4. Total enrolled 2012–2013 part-time, 5. Openings 2013–2014, 9. The median number of years required for completion of a degree in 2012–2013 were 3. *Applied Behavior Analysis MA/MS (Master of Arts/Science)*—Number full-time enrolled (new admits only) 2012–2013, 4. Number part-time enrolled (new admits only) 2012–2013, 0. Total enrolled 2012–2013 full-time, 6. Total enrolled 2012–2013 part-time, 3. Openings 2013–2014, 17. The median number of years required for completion of a degree in 2012–2013 were 2. *Counseling Psychology MA/MS (Master of Arts/Science)*—Number full-time enrolled (new admits only) 2012–2013, 14. Total enrolled 2012–2013 full-time, 14. Total enrolled 2012–2013 part-time, 3. Openings 2013–2014, 15. The median number of years required for completion of a degree in 2012–2013 were 2. *Clinical Psychology PsyD (Doctor of Psychology)*—Applications 2012–2013, 0. Total applicants accepted 2012–2013, 0. Number full-time enrolled (new admits only) 2012–2013, 15. Number part-time enrolled (new admits only) 2012–2013, 0. Total enrolled 2012–2013 full-time, 132. Total enrolled 2012–2013 part-time, 48. Openings 2013–2014, 14. The median number of years required for completion of a degree in 2012–2013 were 5. The number of students enrolled full- and part-time who were dismissed or voluntarily withdrew from this program area in 2012–2013 were 0.

Scores: Entries appear in this order: required test or GPA, minimum score (if required), median score of students entering in 2012–2013. *Clinical Psychology MA/MS (Master of Arts/Science):* overall undergraduate GPA no minimum stated; *Marriage and Family Therapy MA/MS (Master of Arts/Science):* GRE-V no minimum stated, GRE-Q no minimum stated, GRE-Analytical no minimum stated, overall undergraduate GPA no minimum stated; *Applied Behavior Analysis MA/MS (Master of Arts/Science):* GRE-V no minimum stated, GRE-Q no minimum stated, GRE-Analytical no minimum stated, overall undergraduate GPA no minimum stated; *Counseling Psychology MA/MS (Master of Arts/Science):* overall undergraduate GPA no minimum stated; *Clinical Psychology PsyD (Doctor of Psychology)*: GRE-V no minimum stated, GRE-Q no minimum stated, GRE-Analytical 4.0, overall undergraduate GPA 3.2, Masters GPA 3.5.

Other Criteria: (importance of criteria rated low, medium, or high): GRE scores—high, research experience—medium, work experience—medium, extracurricular activity—low, clinically related public service—medium, GPA—high, letters of recommendation—high, interview—high, statement of goals and objectives—high, undergraduate major in psychology—low, specific undergraduate psychology courses taken—high.

Student Characteristics: The following represents characteristics of students in 2012–2013 in all graduate psychology programs in the department: Female—full-time 135, part-time 44; Male—full-time 59, part-time 19; African American/Black—full-time 3, part-time 10; Hispanic/Latino(a)—full-time 1, part-time 3; Asian/Pacific Islander—full-time 8, part-time 2; American Indian/Alaska Native—full-time 5, part-time 4; Caucasian/White—full-time 168, part-time 41; Multi-ethnic—full-time 5, part-time 2; students subject to the Americans With Disabilities Act—full-time 17, part-time 9; Unknown ethnicity—full-time 4, part-time 1; International students who hold an F-1 or J-1 Visa—full-time 3, part-time 0.

Financial Information/Assistance:

Tuition for Full-Time Study: *Master's:* State residents: $525 per credit hour; Nonstate residents: $525 per credit hour. *Doctoral:* State residents: $760 per credit hour; Nonstate residents: $760 per credit hour. Tuition is subject to change. Additional fees are assessed to students beyond the costs of tuition for the following: Institutional per semester fee. Tuition costs vary by program. See the following website for updates and changes in tuition costs: http://www.forest.edu/ad-fi-tuition-fees.aspx.

Financial Assistance:

First-Year Students: Fellowships and scholarships available for first year. Apply by January 15.

Advanced Students: Teaching assistantships available for advanced students. Apply by June 1. Fellowships and scholarships available for advanced students. Apply by June 1.

Additional Information: Application and information available online at: http://www.forest.edu/ad-fin-options.aspx.

Internships/Practica: Doctoral Degree (PsyD Clinical Psychology): For those doctoral students for whom a professional psychology internship was required in this program prior to graduation, (31) students applied for an internship in 2011–2012, with (23) students obtaining an internship. Of those students who obtained an internship, (23) were paid internships. Of those students who obtained an internship, (6) students placed in APA/CPA accredited internships, (17) students placed in internships not APA/CPA accredited, but listed with the Association of Psychology Postdoctoral and Internship Programs (APPIC), (0) students placed in internships conforming to guidelines of the Council of Directors of School Psychology Programs (CDSPP), (0) students placed in internships that were not APA/CPA accredited, APPIC or CDSPP listed. Master's Degree (MA/MS Clinical Psychology): An internship experience, such as a final research project or "capstone" experience is required of graduates. Master's Degree (MA/MS Marriage and Family Therapy): An internship experience, such as a final research project or "capstone" experience is

required of graduates. Master's Degree (MA/MS Applied Behavior Analysis): An internship experience, such as a final research project or "capstone" experience is required of graduates. Master's Degree (MA/MS Counseling Psychology): An internship experience, such as a final research project or "capstone" experience is required of graduates. Doctoral Degree (PsyD Clinical Psychology): Doctoral students complete their practica in our school's mental health clinic, as well as in a variety of community based and government agencies (including medical, educational, and forensic settings) to obtain a minimum of 1200 hours of experience. In the fifth year of study, PsyD students are required to complete a one year clinical predoctoral internship that is accredited by APA/CPA, or is APPIC membered. Master's Degrees (MA in Clinical or Counseling Psychology): Practica for both terminal clinical master's and for terminal counseling master's students exist in mental health and human service agencies in Springfield, St. Louis, and their surrounding areas. The school currently approves and monitors over 25 practicum sites to assist master's students in completing a minimum of 450 practicum hours. (MA in Marriage & Family Therapy): Terminal MFT students complete no less than 500 hours of practicum under the supervision of an AAMFT supervisor at our school's mental health clinic and/or community agencies that focus on relationship focused therapy. (MS in Applied Behavior Analysis): Terminal ABA students complete 750 hours of practicum at pre-approved sites in experiences that have received approval from the BACB (Behavior Analyst Certification Board).

Housing and Day Care: On-campus housing is available. No on-campus day care facilities are available.

Employment of Department Graduates:

Master's Degree Graduates: Of those who graduated in the academic year 2011–2012, the following categories and numbers represent the postgraduate activities and employment of master's degree graduates: Enrolled in a postdoctoral residency/fellowship (n/a), employed in independent practice (n/a), total from the above (master's) (0).

Doctoral Degree Graduates: Of those who graduated in the academic year 2011–2012, the following categories and numbers represent the postgraduate activities and employment of doctoral degree graduates: Enrolled in a psychology doctoral program (n/a), total from the above (doctoral) (0).

Additional Information:

Orientation, Objectives, and Emphasis of Department: The design of the PsyD in Clinical Psychology program is based on the belief that a thorough understanding of the comprehensive body of psychological knowledge, skills, and attitudes is essential for professional practitioners. The acquisition of this broad-based understanding and these abilities requires that the curriculum cover a combination of didactic knowledge, skill training, and supervised clinical experience with faculty and supervisors who provide appropriate role models. The PsyD degree is designed for individuals seeking an educational and training program geared toward professional application. Students are prepared to offer professional services in diagnostic, therapeutic, consultative, and administrative settings. Research and investigation skills are complimented by an increased focus on the use of research findings and theoretical formulations. The field practicum and internship are supervised clinical experiences that are integrated with the academic coursework. The faculty represents a variety of theoretical orientations and is committed to the rigorous preparation of students to become competent providers of service as well as ethical contributing members of the professional community. The MA in Clinical Psychology program is intended to provide a comprehensive exposure to the scientific foundations of psychology, including theories, concepts, and empirical knowledge of human development and behavior. Masters programs are valuable to those who wish to increase their understanding of human behavior. These would include teachers, clergy, and training and personnel officers. While completion of a masters degree can provide a solid foundation for eventual pursuit of a doctorate, the purpose of these programs is to provide the necessary course work to obtain licensure at the master's level in most states.

Special Facilities or Resources: The main campus of Forest Institute is located in the heart of the Ozarks. The academic/administrative center provides students with a modern facility and state of the art learning technology. The Murney Clinic provides students with a captive training experience in an outpatient community mental health clinic equipped with advanced digital audio and video training technologies. Practicum training engages students in active learning to serve underserved populations. Students also provide practicum services throughout the rural Ozarks by partnering with homeless shelters, correctional facilities, public schools, FQHC's, and many other not-for-profit agencies. Our St. Louis site offers a flexible evening curriculum crafted with working professionals in mind. Offering the MACL, MSABA and MACP programs, students enrolled at the St. Louis site can complete the program, focusing on just two courses per semester or tackling as many as four at a time. Each course meets two nights per week for eight weeks during the Fall and Spring semesters and two nights per week during the Summer semesters.

Application Information:

Send to The School of Professional Psychology at Forest Institute, Office of Admissions, 2885 West Battlefield Road, Springfield, MO 65807. Application available online. URL of online application: http://www.forest.edu/ad-form-apply.aspx. Students are admitted in the Fall, application deadline January 15; Programs have rolling admissions. The PsyD program admits only in the fall. The Master's programs have rolling admissions. *Fee:* $50.

Washington University in St. Louis

Department of Psychology
One Brookings Drive, Box 1125
St. Louis, MO 63130
Telephone: (314) 935-6520
Fax: (314) 935-7588
E-mail: *mcclelland@wustl.edu*
Web: *http://psychweb.wustl.edu/*

Department Information:

1924. Chairperson: Randy J. Larsen. Number of faculty: total—full-time 30, part-time 2; women—full-time 11; total—minority—full-time 4; women minority—full-time 2.

Programs and Degrees Offered:

Listed in the following order: Program area, degree type (T if terminal Master's), number awarded 7/11–6/12. Clinical Psychology PhD (Doctor of Philosophy) 4, Aging and Development PhD (Doctor of Philosophy) 1, Behavior/Brain/Cognition PhD (Doctor of Philosophy) 3, Social/Personality Psychology PhD (Doctor of Philosophy) 1.

APA Accreditation: Clinical PhD (Doctor of Philosophy). Student Outcome Data Website: http://psychweb.wustl.edu/graduate/clinical-psychology/time-program-completion.

Student Applications/Admissions:

Student Applications

Clinical Psychology PhD (Doctor of Philosophy)—Applications 2012–2013, 238. Total applicants accepted 2012–2013, 4. Number full-time enrolled (new admits only) 2012–2013, 4. Number part-time enrolled (new admits only) 2012–2013, 0. Total enrolled 2012–2013 full-time, 29. Total enrolled 2012–2013 part-time, 0. Openings 2013–2014, 4. The median number of years required for completion of a degree in 2012–2013 were 6. The number of students enrolled full- and part-time who were dismissed or voluntarily withdrew from this program area in 2012–2013 were 1. *Aging and Development PhD (Doctor of Philosophy)*—Applications 2012–2013, 17. Total applicants accepted 2012–2013, 4. Number full-time enrolled (new admits only) 2012–2013, 3. Number part-time enrolled (new admits only) 2012–2013, 0. Total enrolled 2012–2013 full-time, 15. Total enrolled 2012–2013 part-time, 0. Openings 2013–2014, 2. The median number of years required for completion of a degree in 2012–2013 were 6. The number of students enrolled full- and part-time who were dismissed or voluntarily withdrew from this program area in 2012–2013 were 1. *Behavior/Brain/Cognition PhD (Doctor of Philosophy)*—Applications 2012–2013, 94. Total applicants accepted 2012–2013, 11. Number full-time enrolled (new admits only) 2012–2013, 5. Number part-time enrolled (new admits only) 2012–2013, 0. Total enrolled 2012–2013 full-time, 25. Total enrolled 2012–2013 part-time, 0. Openings 2013–2014, 5. The median number of years required for completion of a degree in 2012–2013 were 4. The number of students enrolled full- and part-time who were dismissed or voluntarily withdrew from this program area in 2012–2013 were 1. *Social/Personality Psychology PhD (Doctor of Philosophy)*—Applications 2012–2013, 36. Total applicants accepted 2012–2013, 4. Number full-time enrolled (new admits only) 2012–2013, 3. Number part-time enrolled (new admits only) 2012–2013, 0. Total enrolled 2012–2013 full-time, 13. Total enrolled 2012–2013 part-time, 0. Openings 2013–2014, 3. The median number of years required for completion of a degree in 2012–2013 were 6. The number of students enrolled full- and part-time who were dismissed or voluntarily withdrew from this program area in 2012–2013 were 0.

Scores: Entries appear in this order: required test or GPA, minimum score (if required), median score of students entering in 2012–2013. *Clinical Psychology PhD (Doctor of Philosophy):* GRE-V no minimum stated, GRE-Q no minimum stated, GRE-Analytical no minimum stated, overall undergraduate GPA no minimum stated; *Aging and Development PhD (Doctor of Philosophy):* GRE-V no minimum stated, GRE-Q no minimum stated, GRE-Analytical no minimum stated, overall undergraduate GPA no minimum stated; *Behavior/Brain/Cognition PhD (Doctor of Philosophy):* GRE-V no minimum stated, GRE-Q no minimum stated, GRE-Analytical no minimum stated, overall undergraduate GPA no minimum stated; *Social/Personality Psychology PhD (Doctor of Philosophy):* GRE-V no minimum stated, GRE-Q no minimum stated, GRE-Analytical no minimum stated, overall undergraduate GPA no minimum stated.

Other Criteria: (importance of criteria rated low, medium, or high): GRE scores—high, research experience—high, work experience—low, clinically related public service—low, GPA—high, letters of recommendation—high, interview—high, statement of goals and objectives—high, undergraduate major in psychology—medium, specific undergraduate psychology courses taken—high, Interview (by invitation only) is required for applicants prior to acceptance. Phone and/or Skype interviews are possible for applicants who live abroad. For additional information on admission requirements, go to http://psychweb.wustl.edu/graduate-alternative/admission-financial-aid.

Student Characteristics: The following represents characteristics of students in 2012–2013 in all graduate psychology programs in the department: Female—full-time 58, part-time 0; Male—full-time 24, part-time 0; African American/Black—full-time 5, part-time 0; Hispanic/Latino(a)—full-time 4, part-time 0; Asian/Pacific Islander—full-time 22, part-time 0; American Indian/Alaska Native—full-time 0, part-time 0; Caucasian/White—full-time 45, part-time 0; Multi-ethnic—full-time 0, part-time 0; students subject to the Americans With Disabilities Act—full-time 1, part-time 0; Unknown ethnicity—full-time 6, part-time 0; International students who hold an F-1 or J-1 Visa—full-time 13, part-time 0.

Financial Information/Assistance:

Tuition for Full-Time Study: *Doctoral:* State residents: per academic year $44,100; Nonstate residents: per academic year $44,100. Tuition is subject to change. See the following website for updates and changes in tuition costs: http://graduateschool.wustl.edu/prospective_students/financial-information/tuition-and-fees.

Financial Assistance:

First-Year Students: Research assistantships available for first year. Average amount paid per academic year: $20,650. Average number of hours worked per week: 10. Traineeships available for first year. Average number of hours worked per week: 0. Fellowships and scholarships available for first year. Average amount paid per academic year: $20,000. Average number of hours worked per week: 0. Apply by January 25.

Advanced Students: Teaching assistantships available for advanced students. Average amount paid per academic year: $20,650. Average number of hours worked per week: 10. Research assistantships available for advanced students. Average amount paid per academic year: $20,650. Average number of hours worked per week: 15. Traineeships available for advanced students. Average amount paid per academic year: $20,650. Average number of hours worked per week: 0. Fellowships and scholarships available for advanced students. Average amount paid per academic year: $20,650. Average number of hours worked per week: 0.

Additional Information: Of all students currently enrolled full time, 100% benefited from one or more of the listed financial assistance programs. Application and information available online at: http://graduateschool.wustl.edu/prospective_students/financial-information.

Internships/Practica: Doctoral Degree (PhD Clinical Psychology): For those doctoral students for whom a professional psychol-ogy internship was required in this program prior to graduation, (3) students applied for an internship in 2011–2012, with (3) students obtaining an internship. Of those students who obtained an internship, (3) were paid internships. Of those students who obtained an internship, (3) students placed in APA/CPA accredited internships, (0) students placed in internships not APA/CPA accredited, but listed with the Association of Psychology Postdoctoral and Internship Programs (APPIC), (0) students placed in internships conforming to guidelines of the Council of Directors of School Psychology Programs (CDSPP), (0) students placed in internships that were not APA/CPA accredited, APPIC or CDSPP listed.

Housing and Day Care: No on-campus housing is available. On-campus day care facilities are available. See the following website for more information: http://nurseryschool.wustl.edu/; http://childcare.wustl.edu/.

Employment of Department Graduates:

Master's Degree Graduates: Of those who graduated in the academic year 2011–2012, the following categories and numbers represent the postgraduate activities and employment of master's degree graduates: Enrolled in a postdoctoral residency/fellowship (n/a), employed in independent practice (n/a), total from the above (master's) (0).

Doctoral Degree Graduates: Of those who graduated in the academic year 2011–2012, the following categories and numbers represent the postgraduate activities and employment of doctoral degree graduates: Enrolled in a psychology doctoral program (n/a), enrolled in a postdoctoral residency/fellowship (7), employed in an academic position at a university (2), total from the above (doctoral) (9).

Additional Information:

Orientation, Objectives, and Emphasis of Department: The emphasis within the clinical program is on training clinical scientists and promoting an integration of science and practice. Its goal is to train students who will lead the search for knowledge regarding the assessment, understanding, and treatment of psychological disorders. In the experimental programs, the development of generalists with one or more areas of specialization is the department's orientation.

Special Facilities or Resources: The department's extensive facilities include animal, human psychophysiological, psychoacoustic, and clinical training laboratories; computer labs; closed circuit TV; and Neuroimaging (fMRI) and Image Analysis Laboratory.

Information for Students With Physical Disabilities: See the following website for more information: http://disability.wustl.edu/DisabilityResources.aspx.

Application Information:
Send to Meg McClelland, Graduate Program Coordinator, Washington University, Department of Psychology, Campus Box 1125, St. Louis, MO 63130-4899. Application available online. URL of online application: https://gsasapply.wustl.edu/apply/. Students are admitted in the Fall, application deadline December 15. *Fee:* $45. Candidate for a fee waiver must have attended an undergraduate institution within the United States and have received financial assistance. Fee wavier must be completed by a representative from the financial aid office at the undergraduate institution.

Montana State University Billings

Department of Psychology
College of Arts and Sciences
1500 North University Drive
Billings, MT 59101
Telephone: (406) 657-2242
Fax: (406) 657-2187
E-mail: kathy.sabe@msubillings.edu
Web: http://www.msubillings.edu/grad/Program-Psychology.htm

Department Information:
1967. Chairperson: Dr. Michael Havens. Number of faculty: total—full-time 5, part-time 2; women—full-time 1, part-time 2.

Programs and Degrees Offered:
Listed in the following order: Program area, degree type (T if terminal Master's), number awarded 7/11–6/12. Psychology MA/MS (Master of Arts/Science) (T) 4.

Student Applications/Admissions:
Student Applications
Psychology MA/MS (Master of Arts/Science)—Applications 2012–2013, 19. Total applicants accepted 2012–2013, 15. Number full-time enrolled (new admits only) 2012–2013, 7. Number part-time enrolled (new admits only) 2012–2013, 0. Total enrolled 2012–2013 full-time, 19. Total enrolled 2012–2013 part-time, 0. Openings 2013–2014, 10. The median number of years required for completion of a degree in 2012–2013 were 2. The number of students enrolled full- and part-time who were dismissed or voluntarily withdrew from this program area in 2012–2013 were 0.
Scores: Entries appear in this order: required test or GPA, minimum score (if required), median score of students entering in 2012–2013. *Psychology MA/MS (Master of Arts/Science):* GRE-V no minimum stated, 292, GRE-Q no minimum stated, 334, GRE-Analytical no minimum stated, 3.5, overall undergraduate GPA no minimum stated, 2.97.
Other Criteria: (importance of criteria rated low, medium, or high): GRE scores—medium, research experience—medium, work experience—low, extracurricular activity—low, clinically related public service—low, GPA—high, letters of recommendation—high, statement of goals and objectives—high, undergraduate major in psychology—medium, specific undergraduate psychology courses taken—medium. For additional information on admission requirements, go to http://www.msubillings.edu/grad/Admission.htm.

Student Characteristics: The following represents characteristics of students in 2012–2013 in all graduate psychology programs in the department: Female—full-time 12, part-time 0; Male—full-time 7, part-time 0; African American/Black—full-time 0, part-time 0; Hispanic/Latino(a)—full-time 0, part-time 0; Asian/Pacific Islander—full-time 0, part-time 0; American Indian/Alaska Native—full-time 1, part-time 0; Caucasian/White—full-time 18, part-time 0; Multi-ethnic—full-time 0, part-time 0; students subject to the Americans With Disabilities Act—full-time 0, part-time 0; Unknown ethnicity—full-time 0, part-time 0; International students who hold an F-1 or J-1 Visa—full-time 1, part-time 0.

Financial Information/Assistance:
Tuition for Full-Time Study: *Master's:* State residents: per academic year $4,980; Nonstate residents: per academic year $12,848. Tuition is subject to change. Additional fees are assessed to students beyond the costs of tuition for the following: online course fees and lab fees. See the following website for updates and changes in tuition costs: http://www.msubillings.edu/future/cost-GradStudies.htm.

Financial Assistance:
First-Year Students: Research assistantships available for first year.
Advanced Students: Teaching assistantships available for advanced students. Research assistantships available for advanced students.
Additional Information: Of all students currently enrolled full time, 50% benefited from one or more of the listed financial assistance programs. Application and information available online at: http://www.msubillings.edu/finaid/.

Internships/Practica: Our students do internships at several clinics around Billings, including two residential treatment facilities for children and adolescents and a prison prerelease center. Clinical psychologists in private practice also frequently take on our students as testing technicians. Students interested in a teaching career are offered the opportunity to teach undergraduate courses in our department.

Housing and Day Care: On-campus housing is available. See the following website for more information: http://www.msubillings.edu/reslife/. On-campus day care facilities are available. See the following website for more information: http://www.msubillings.edu/childcare/.

Employment of Department Graduates:
Master's Degree Graduates: Of those who graduated in the academic year 2011–2012, the following categories and numbers represent the postgraduate activities and employment of master's degree graduates: Enrolled in a psychology doctoral program (3), enrolled in a postdoctoral residency/fellowship (n/a), employed in independent practice (n/a), employed in a community mental health/counseling center (1), total from the above (master's) (4).
Doctoral Degree Graduates: Of those who graduated in the academic year 2011–2012, the following categories and numbers represent the postgraduate activities and employment of doctoral degree graduates: Enrolled in a psychology doctoral program (n/a), total from the above (doctoral) (0).

Additional Information:
Orientation, Objectives, and Emphasis of Department: Ours is a fairly small department with faculty members representing clinical, social, developmental, and physiological psychology. We have been successful in preparing students for doctoral training, mostly in clinical psychology programs. Some of our students have gone

on to successful careers as master's-level clinicians. In the last two years our program has been reenergized by successfully hiring two new faculty members.

Special Facilities or Resources: One faculty member is conducting research on nonpharmaceutical treatment of ADHD in residents of a prison prerelease center. Another is studying depression in ranch families. Students are participating in both of these projects. Our newest faculty member studies attachment styles and their relation to addiction and other maladaptive behaviors.

Information for Students With Physical Disabilities: See the following website for more information: http://www.msubillings.edu/dss/.

Application Information:
Send to Office of Graduate Studies. Application available online. URL of online application: https://www.applyweb.com/apply/msubillg/. Students are admitted in the Fall, application deadline March 12; Spring, application deadline November 1; Summer, application deadline February 20. Applications received by dates specified will be given priority, but late applications will be considered until classes are full. *Fee:* $40.

Montana, The University of
Department of Psychology
Arts and Sciences
143 Skaggs Building
Missoula, MT 59812-1584
Telephone: (406) 243-4521
Fax: (406) 243-6366
E-mail: *nabil.haddad@umontana.edu*
Web: *http://www.umt.edu/psych/*

Department Information:
1920. Chairperson: Nabil Haddad. Number of faculty: total—full-time 20, part-time 1; women—full-time 9, part-time 1; total—minority—full-time 2; women minority—full-time 2; faculty subject to the Americans With Disabilities Act 1.

Programs and Degrees Offered:
Listed in the following order: Program area, degree type (T if terminal Master's), number awarded 7/11–6/12. Clinical Psychology PhD (Doctor of Philosophy) 4, Developmental Psychology PhD (Doctor of Philosophy) 1, School Psychology EdS (School Psychology) 2, School Psychology PhD (Doctor of Philosophy) 0, Animal Behavior-Cognition PhD (Doctor of Philosophy) 0.

APA Accreditation: Clinical PhD (Doctor of Philosophy). Student Outcome Data Website: http://psychweb.psy.umt.edu/www/graduate_clinical_applicant.asp.

Student Applications/Admissions:
Student Applications
Clinical Psychology PhD (Doctor of Philosophy)—Applications 2012–2013, 208. Total applicants accepted 2012–2013, 5. Number full-time enrolled (new admits only) 2012–2013, 5. Number part-time enrolled (new admits only) 2012–2013, 0. Total enrolled 2012–2013 full-time, 21. Total enrolled 2012–

2013 part-time, 15. Openings 2013–2014, 6. The median number of years required for completion of a degree in 2012–2013 were 6. The number of students enrolled full- and part-time who were dismissed or voluntarily withdrew from this program area in 2012–2013 were 0. *Developmental Psychology PhD (Doctor of Philosophy)*—Applications 2012–2013, 5. Total applicants accepted 2012–2013, 1. Number full-time enrolled (new admits only) 2012–2013, 1. Number part-time enrolled (new admits only) 2012–2013, 0. Total enrolled 2012–2013 full-time, 1. Total enrolled 2012–2013 part-time, 1. Openings 2013–2014, 1. The median number of years required for completion of a degree in 2012–2013 were 4. The number of students enrolled full- and part-time who were dismissed or voluntarily withdrew from this program area in 2012–2013 were 0. *School Psychology EdS (School Psychology)*—Applications 2012–2013, 13. Total applicants accepted 2012–2013, 8. Number full-time enrolled (new admits only) 2012–2013, 6. Number part-time enrolled (new admits only) 2012–2013, 0. Total enrolled 2012–2013 full-time, 8. Total enrolled 2012–2013 part-time, 5. Openings 2013–2014, 4. The median number of years required for completion of a degree in 2012–2013 were 2. The number of students enrolled full- and part-time who were dismissed or voluntarily withdrew from this program area in 2012–2013 were 0. *School Psychology PhD (Doctor of Philosophy)*—Applications 2012–2013, 2. Total applicants accepted 2012–2013, 2. Number full-time enrolled (new admits only) 2012–2013, 2. Number part-time enrolled (new admits only) 2012–2013, 0. Total enrolled 2012–2013 full-time, 6. Total enrolled 2012–2013 part-time, 3. Openings 2013–2014, 2. The number of students enrolled full- and part-time who were dismissed or voluntarily withdrew from this program area in 2012–2013 were 0. *Animal Behavior-Cognition PhD (Doctor of Philosophy)*—Applications 2012–2013, 8. Total applicants accepted 2012–2013, 2. Number full-time enrolled (new admits only) 2012–2013, 1. Number part-time enrolled (new admits only) 2012–2013, 1. Total enrolled 2012–2013 full-time, 3. Total enrolled 2012–2013 part-time, 3. Openings 2013–2014, 2. The number of students enrolled full- and part-time who were dismissed or voluntarily withdrew from this program area in 2012–2013 were 0.

Scores: Entries appear in this order: required test or GPA, minimum score (if required), median score of students entering in 2012–2013. *Clinical Psychology PhD (Doctor of Philosophy):* GRE-V no minimum stated, GRE-Q no minimum stated, GRE-Analytical no minimum stated; *Developmental Psychology PhD (Doctor of Philosophy):* GRE-V no minimum stated, GRE-Q no minimum stated, GRE-Analytical no minimum stated, GRE-Subject (Psychology) no minimum stated; *School Psychology EdS (School Psychology):* GRE-V no minimum stated, GRE-Q no minimum stated, GRE-Analytical no minimum stated; *School Psychology PhD (Doctor of Philosophy):* GRE-V no minimum stated, GRE-Q no minimum stated, GRE-Analytical no minimum stated, overall undergraduate GPA no minimum stated; *Animal Behavior-Cognition PhD (Doctor of Philosophy):* GRE-V no minimum stated, GRE-Q no minimum stated, GRE-Analytical no minimum stated, GRE-Subject (Psychology) no minimum stated, overall undergraduate GPA no minimum stated.

Other Criteria: (importance of criteria rated low, medium, or high): GRE scores—high, research experience—medium, work experience—medium, extracurricular activity—low, clinically related public service—medium, GPA—medium, letters of recommendation—high, interview—high, statement of goals and objectives—high, undergraduate major in psychology—low, specific undergraduate psychology courses taken—low, Clinical service is a criterion for clinical program only. Clinical faculty place higher importance on the statement of goals and objectives and the interview (phone and/or live), and medium importance on GRE scores. For additional information on admission requirements, go to http://psychweb.psy.umt.edu/www/application.asp.

Student Characteristics: The following represents characteristics of students in 2012–2013 in all graduate psychology programs in the department: Female—full-time 27, part-time 20; Male—full-time 12, part-time 7; African American/Black—full-time 0, part-time 0; Hispanic/Latino(a)—full-time 1, part-time 2; Asian/Pacific Islander—full-time 1, part-time 1; American Indian/Alaska Native—full-time 5, part-time 2; Caucasian/White—full-time 31, part-time 17; Multi-ethnic—full-time 1, part-time 0; students subject to the Americans With Disabilities Act—full-time 0, part-time 0; Unknown ethnicity—full-time 0, part-time 5; International students who hold an F-1 or J-1 Visa—full-time 0, part-time 0.

Financial Information/Assistance:
Tuition for Full-Time Study: *Master's:* State residents: per academic year $5,176, $216 per credit hour; Nonstate residents: per academic year $16,594, $691 per credit hour. *Doctoral:* State residents: per academic year $5,848, $244 per credit hour; Nonstate residents: per academic year $16,784, $699 per credit hour. Tuition is subject to change. Additional fees are assessed to students beyond the costs of tuition for the following: registration, facilities, equip, tech, ASUM, campus rec, transportation etc. See the following website for updates and changes in tuition costs: http://www.umt.edu/bussrvcs/Students/default.aspx.

Financial Assistance:
First-Year Students: Teaching assistantships available for first year. Average amount paid per academic year: $14,800. Average number of hours worked per week: 15. Apply by December 1.
Advanced Students: Teaching assistantships available for advanced students. Average amount paid per academic year: $14,800. Average number of hours worked per week: 15. Apply by March 15. Research assistantships available for advanced students. Average amount paid per academic year: $14,800. Average number of hours worked per week: 15. Apply by March 15. Traineeships available for advanced students. Average amount paid per academic year: $14,800. Average number of hours worked per week: 15. Apply by March 15.
Additional Information: Of all students currently enrolled full time, 70% benefited from one or more of the listed financial assistance programs. Application and information available online at: http://www.umt.edu/grad/Financial_Information/default.php.

Internships/Practica: Doctoral Degree (PhD Clinical Psychology): For those doctoral students for whom a professional psychology internship was required in this program prior to graduation, (3) students applied for an internship in 2011–2012, with (3) students obtaining an internship. Of those students who obtained an internship, (3) were paid internships. Of those students who obtained an internship, (3) students placed in APA/CPA accredited internships, (0) students placed in internships not APA/CPA accredited, but listed with the Association of Psychology

Postdoctoral and Internship Programs (APPIC), (0) students placed in internships conforming to guidelines of the Council of Directors of School Psychology Programs (CDSPP), (0) students placed in internships that were not APA/CPA accredited, APPIC or CDSPP listed. Doctoral Degree (PhD School Psychology): For those doctoral students for whom a professional psychology internship was required in this program prior to graduation, (1) students applied for an internship in 2011–2012, with (1) students obtaining an internship. Of those students who obtained an internship, (1) were paid internships. Of those students who obtained an internship, (1) students placed in APA/CPA accredited internships, (0) students placed in internships not APA/CPA accredited, but listed with the Association of Psychology Postdoctoral and Internship Programs (APPIC), (0) students placed in internships conforming to guidelines of the Council of Directors of School Psychology Programs (CDSPP), (0) students placed in internships that were not APA/CPA accredited, APPIC or CDSPP listed.

Housing and Day Care: On-campus housing is available. See the following website for more information: http://www.umt.edu/reslife/. On-campus day care facilities are available. See the following website for more information: http://www.umt.edu/childcare.

Employment of Department Graduates:
Master's Degree Graduates: Of those who graduated in the academic year 2011–2012, the following categories and numbers represent the postgraduate activities and employment of master's degree graduates: Enrolled in a psychology doctoral program (1), enrolled in a postdoctoral residency/fellowship (n/a), employed in independent practice (n/a), employed in a professional position in a school system (1), total from the above (master's) (2).
Doctoral Degree Graduates: Of those who graduated in the academic year 2011–2012, the following categories and numbers represent the postgraduate activities and employment of doctoral degree graduates: Enrolled in a psychology doctoral program (n/a), enrolled in a postdoctoral residency/fellowship (3), employed in an academic position at a university (1), employed in a community mental health/counseling center (1), total from the above (doctoral) (5).

Additional Information:
Orientation, Objectives, and Emphasis of Department: The Clinical Psychology PhD program trains students in basic psychological science and clinical skills including assessment, diagnosis, and therapeutic interventions. The program is based on the scientist–practitioner model and a variety of theoretical orientations are represented and taught. The training is a balanced combination of coursework, practicum and research. Upon completion of the program, graduates are well prepared for professional careers as clinical psychologists in institutional, academic, and private settings. In addition to generalist training, two specialty emphases are also offered: child and family and neuropsychology. The Experimental Psychology PhD programs offer research specializations in the fields of animal behavior, cognition, developmental psychology, social psychology and quantitative psychology. Graduates have found placement in academic, research, and applied settings. The School Psychology program offers both doctoral (PhD) and specialist (EdS) level training based on the scientist-scholar-practitioner model and is aimed at professional preparation of school psychologists who are grounded thoroughly in the principles of human development, behavior and educational psy-

chology. Doctoral candidates are trained to assume leadership roles in academia, research and clinical/school practice. Specialist level candidates are trained to provide psychoeducational services on a systems and individual basis.

Special Facilities or Resources: The Department of Psychology is housed in a modern building. It has classrooms; offices; research laboratories for social, developmental, and learning experimentation; and colony rooms for small animals. A clinical psychology center serves as a meeting place for clinical classes, seminars, research groups, and clinical services.

Information for Students With Physical Disabilities: See the following website for more information: http://www.umt.edu/dss/.

Application Information:
Send to Graduate Admissions, Department of Psychology, The University of Montana, Skaggs Building 143, Missoula, MT 59812-1584. Application available online. URL of online application: http://www.applyweb.com/apply/uomont/menu.html. Students are admitted in the Fall, application deadline December 1. The December 1 deadline is a firm date for the Clinical program. Developmental, Animal Behavior/Cognition and School Psychology programs have rolling admissions. Priority will be given to complete application packets postmarked by December 1. *Fee:* $60.

Nebraska, University of, Lincoln

Department of Educational Psychology
College of Education and Human Sciences
114 Teachers College Hall
Lincoln, NE 68588-0345
Telephone: (402) 472-2223
Fax: (402) 472-8319
E-mail: *rdeayala@unlserve.unl.edu*
Web: *http://cehs.unl.edu/edpsych/*

Department Information:

1908. Chairperson: R.J. De Ayala. Number of faculty: total—full-time 22; women—full-time 8; total—minority—full-time 3; women minority—full-time 1.

Programs and Degrees Offered:

Listed in the following order: Program area, degree type (T if terminal Master's), number awarded 7/11–6/12. Cognition, Learning, and Development PhD (Doctor of Philosophy) 15, Counseling Psychology PhD (Doctor of Philosophy) 15, Quantitative, Qualitative, & Psychometric Methods PhD (Doctor of Philosophy) 5, School Psychology PhD (Doctor of Philosophy) 16.

APA Accreditation:

Counseling PhD (Doctor of Philosophy). Student Outcome Data Website: http://cehs.unl.edu/edpsych/graduate/copsych.shtml. School PhD (Doctor of Philosophy). Student Outcome Data Website: http://cehs.unl.edu/edpsych/graduate/schpsych.shtml.

Student Applications/Admissions:

Student Applications

Cognition, Learning, and Development PhD (Doctor of Philosophy)—Applications 2012–2013, 21. Total applicants accepted 2012–2013, 17. Number full-time enrolled (new admits only) 2012–2013, 11. Total enrolled 2012–2013 full-time, 49. Openings 2013–2014, 5. *Counseling Psychology PhD (Doctor of Philosophy)*—Applications 2012–2013, 86. Total applicants accepted 2012–2013, 23. Number full-time enrolled (new admits only) 2012–2013, 11. Total enrolled 2012–2013 full-time, 54. Openings 2013–2014, 6. *Quantitative, Qualitative, & Psychometric Methods PhD (Doctor of Philosophy)*—Applications 2012–2013, 15. Total applicants accepted 2012–2013, 11. Number full-time enrolled (new admits only) 2012–2013, 7. Total enrolled 2012–2013 full-time, 34. Total enrolled 2012–2013 part-time, 4. Openings 2013–2014, 5. *School Psychology PhD (Doctor of Philosophy)*—Applications 2012–2013, 44. Total applicants accepted 2012–2013, 11. Number full-time enrolled (new admits only) 2012–2013, 9. Total enrolled 2012–2013 full-time, 38. Total enrolled 2012–2013 part-time, 0. Openings 2013–2014, 8.

Scores: Entries appear in this order: required test or GPA, minimum score (if required), median score of students entering in 2012–2013. *Cognition, Learning, and Development PhD (Doctor of Philosophy)*: GRE-V no minimum stated, 153, GRE-Q no minimum stated, 151; *Counseling Psychology PhD (Doctor of Philosophy)*: GRE-V no minimum stated, 152, GRE-Q no minimum stated, 147; *Quantitative, Qualitative, & Psychometric*

Methods PhD (Doctor of Philosophy): GRE-V no minimum stated, 160, GRE-Q no minimum stated, 149; *School Psychology PhD (Doctor of Philosophy)*: GRE-V no minimum stated, 158, GRE-Q no minimum stated, 147.

Other Criteria: (importance of criteria rated low, medium, or high): GRE scores—high, research experience—high, work experience—high, extracurricular activity—medium, clinically related public service—high, GPA—high, letters of recommendation—high, interview—high, statement of goals and objectives—high. For additional information on admission requirements, go to http://cehs.unl.edu/edpsych/graduate/ProspectiveIndex.shtml.

Student Characteristics: The following represents characteristics of students in 2012–2013 in all graduate psychology programs in the department: Female—full-time 127, part-time 4; Male—full-time 48, part-time 0; African American/Black—full-time 9, part-time 0; Hispanic/Latino(a)—full-time 6, part-time 0; Asian/Pacific Islander—full-time 22, part-time 0; American Indian/Alaska Native—full-time 1, part-time 0; Caucasian/White—full-time 136, part-time 4; Multi-ethnic—full-time 1, part-time 0; students subject to the Americans With Disabilities Act—full-time 0, part-time 0; Unknown ethnicity—full-time 0, part-time 0; International students who hold an F-1 or J-1 Visa—full-time 13, part-time 0.

Financial Information/Assistance:

Tuition for Full-Time Study: *Master's:* State residents: $285 per credit hour; Nonstate residents: $768 per credit hour. *Doctoral:* State residents: $285 per credit hour; Nonstate residents: $768 per credit hour. Tuition is subject to change. Additional fees are assessed to students beyond the costs of tuition for the following: program & facilities fees, library & technology fees, dependent on courseload. See the following website for updates and changes in tuition costs: http://studentaccounts.unl.edu/tuitionfee.

Financial Assistance:

First-Year Students: Teaching assistantships available for first year. Average amount paid per academic year: $15,000. Average number of hours worked per week: 20. Research assistantships available for first year. Average amount paid per academic year: $15,000. Average number of hours worked per week: 20. Fellowships and scholarships available for first year. Average amount paid per academic year: $9,750. Average number of hours worked per week: 13.

Advanced Students: Teaching assistantships available for advanced students. Average number of hours worked per week: 20. Research assistantships available for advanced students. Average number of hours worked per week: 20. Fellowships and scholarships available for advanced students.

Additional Information: Of all students currently enrolled full time, 66% benefited from one or more of the listed financial assistance programs. Application and information available online at: http://cehs.unl.edu/edpsych/graduate/finaid.shtml.

Internships/Practica: Doctoral Degree (PhD Counseling Psychology): For those doctoral students for whom a professional psychology internship was required in this program prior to graduation,

(3) students applied for an internship in 2011–2012, with (3) students obtaining an internship. Of those students who obtained an internship, (3) were paid internships. Of those students who obtained an internship, (3) students placed in APA/CPA accredited internships, (0) students placed in internships not APA/CPA accredited, but listed with the Association of Psychology Postdoctoral and Internship Programs (APPIC), (0) students placed in internships conforming to guidelines of the Council of Directors of School Psychology Programs (CDSPP), (0) students placed in internships that were not APA/CPA accredited, APPIC or CDSPP listed. Doctoral Degree (PhD School Psychology): For those doctoral students for whom a professional psychology internship was required in this program prior to graduation, (8) students applied for an internship in 2011–2012, with (8) students obtaining an internship. Of those students who obtained an internship, (8) were paid internships. Of those students who obtained an internship, (8) students placed in APA/CPA accredited internships, (0) students placed in internships not APA/CPA accredited, but listed with the Association of Psychology Postdoctoral and Internship Programs (APPIC), (0) students placed in internships conforming to guidelines of the Council of Directors of School Psychology Programs (CDSPP), (0) students placed in internships that were not APA/CPA accredited, APPIC or CDSPP listed. The Counseling Psychology and School Psychology programs have sets of practicum courses wherein students provide direct and consultation services to students, staff and families in urban school settings. The Nebraska Internship Consortium in Professional Psychology is affiliated with the School Psychology program. Doctoral students in the QQPM program are encouraged to obtain internships.

Housing and Day Care: On-campus housing is available. See the following website for more information: http://housing.unl.edu/. On-campus day care facilities are available. See the following website for more information: http://childcare.unl.edu/.

Employment of Department Graduates:

Master's Degree Graduates: Of those who graduated in the academic year 2011–2012, the following categories and numbers represent the postgraduate activities and employment of master's degree graduates: Enrolled in a postdoctoral residency/fellowship (n/a), employed in independent practice (n/a), total from the above (master's) (0).

Doctoral Degree Graduates: Of those who graduated in the academic year 2011–2012, the following categories and numbers represent the postgraduate activities and employment of doctoral degree graduates: Enrolled in a psychology doctoral program (n/a), total from the above (doctoral) (0).

Additional Information:

Orientation, Objectives, and Emphasis of Department: Our objective is to develop applied behavioral scientists that are able to function in a variety of settings and roles ranging from educational settings to private practice. The department's broad base offers a diversity of orientations and role models for students.

Special Facilities or Resources: The department operated Counseling and School Psychology Clinic serves as a practicum site for the School Psychology and Counseling Psychology programs. In addition, the department's excellent contacts with the community promote access to practical experiences and research subject pools. The department contains the Buros Center for Testing and its comprehensive reference library of assessment devices. The department also is home to the Center for Instructional Innovation, which conducts research on teaching and learning, and the Nebraska Prevention Center for Alcohol and Drug Abuse, as well as connections with the Nebraska Research Center on Children, Youth, Families and Schools.

Information for Students With Physical Disabilities: See the following website for more information: http://www.unl.edu/ssd/.

Application Information:
Send to Attention: Allison Jones, Admissions Coordinator, Department of Educational Psychology, 114 Teachers College Hall, University of Nebraska-Lincoln, Lincoln, NE 68588. Application available online. URL of online application: http://cehs.unl.edu/edpsych/graduate/apply.shtml. Students are admitted in the Fall, application deadline December 1; Spring, application deadline October 1. School Psychology program deadline is December 1; Counseling Psychology program is December 5. Cognition, Learning, & Developmental considers applications for admission at October 1, January 15, & May 15 deadlines. Quantitative, Qualitative, & Psychometric Methods (QQPM) considers applications for admission at October 1 and January 15 deadline. *Fee:* $50. Written request for waiver of fee indicating need/justification for waiver or deferral of application fee.

Nebraska, University of, Lincoln
Department of Psychology
Arts & Sciences
238 Burnett Hall
Lincoln, NE 68588-0308
Telephone: (402) 472-3721
Fax: (402) 472-4637
E-mail: *jlongwell1@unl.edu*
Web: *http://psychology.unl.edu/*

Department Information:
1889. Chairperson: Rick A. Bevins. Number of faculty: total—full-time 25, part-time 4; women—full-time 8, part-time 1; total—minority—full-time 3; women minority—full-time 1.

Programs and Degrees Offered:
Listed in the following order: Program area, degree type (T if terminal Master's), number awarded 7/11–6/12. Clinical Psychology PhD (Doctor of Philosophy) 7, Cognitive & Quantitative Psychology PhD (Doctor of Philosophy) 0, Law and Psychology PhD (Doctor of Philosophy) 1, Neuroscience & Behavior PhD (Doctor of Philosophy) 0, Developmental Psychology PhD (Doctor of Philosophy) 1, Social/Personality Psychology PhD (Doctor of Philosophy) 1.

APA Accreditation: Clinical PhD (Doctor of Philosophy). Student Outcome Data Website: http://psychology.unl.edu/grad/clinical.shtml.

Student Applications/Admissions:
Student Applications
Clinical Psychology PhD (Doctor of Philosophy)—Applications 2012–2013, 308. Total applicants accepted 2012–2013, 14. Number full-time enrolled (new admits only) 2012–2013, 12.

Total enrolled 2012–2013 full-time, 60. Openings 2013–2014, 8. The median number of years required for completion of a degree in 2012–2013 were 6. The number of students enrolled full- and part-time who were dismissed or voluntarily withdrew from this program area in 2012–2013 were 0. *Cognitive & Quantitative Psychology PhD (Doctor of Philosophy)*—Applications 2012–2013, 15. Total applicants accepted 2012–2013, 0. Number full-time enrolled (new admits only) 2012–2013, 0. Number part-time enrolled (new admits only) 2012–2013, 0. Total enrolled 2012–2013 full-time, 7. Total enrolled 2012–2013 part-time, 0. Openings 2013–2014, 1. The number of students enrolled full- and part-time who were dismissed or voluntarily withdrew from this program area in 2012–2013 were 0. *Law and Psychology PhD (Doctor of Philosophy)*—Applications 2012–2013, 36. Total applicants accepted 2012–2013, 0. Number full-time enrolled (new admits only) 2012–2013, 0. Number part-time enrolled (new admits only) 2012–2013, 0. Total enrolled 2012–2013 full-time, 10. Total enrolled 2012–2013 part-time, 0. Openings 2013–2014, 2. The median number of years required for completion of a degree in 2012–2013 were 6. The number of students enrolled full- and part-time who were dismissed or voluntarily withdrew from this program area in 2012–2013 were 0. *Neuroscience & Behavior PhD (Doctor of Philosophy)*—Applications 2012–2013, 20. Total applicants accepted 2012–2013, 1. Number full-time enrolled (new admits only) 2012–2013, 1. Total enrolled 2012–2013 full-time, 12. Total enrolled 2012–2013 part-time, 0. Openings 2013–2014, 2. The number of students enrolled full- and part-time who were dismissed or voluntarily withdrew from this program area in 2012–2013 were 0. *Developmental Psychology PhD (Doctor of Philosophy)*—Applications 2012–2013, 11. Total applicants accepted 2012–2013, 3. Number full-time enrolled (new admits only) 2012–2013, 3. Number part-time enrolled (new admits only) 2012–2013, 0. Total enrolled 2012–2013 full-time, 18. Total enrolled 2012–2013 part-time, 0. Openings 2013–2014, 1. The median number of years required for completion of a degree in 2012–2013 were 5. The number of students enrolled full- and part-time who were dismissed or voluntarily withdrew from this program area in 2012–2013 were 0. *Social/Personality Psychology PhD (Doctor of Philosophy)*—Applications 2012–2013, 21. Total applicants accepted 2012–2013, 4. Number full-time enrolled (new admits only) 2012–2013, 4. Number part-time enrolled (new admits only) 2012–2013, 0. Total enrolled 2012–2013 full-time, 21. Total enrolled 2012–2013 part-time, 0. Openings 2013–2014, 2. The median number of years required for completion of a degree in 2012–2013 were 6. The number of students enrolled full- and part-time who were dismissed or voluntarily withdrew from this program area in 2012–2013 were 0.

Scores: Entries appear in this order: required test or GPA, minimum score (if required), median score of students entering in 2012–2013. *Clinical Psychology PhD (Doctor of Philosophy):* GRE-V no minimum stated, 606, GRE-Q no minimum stated, 722, GRE-Analytical no minimum stated, overall undergraduate GPA no minimum stated, 3.79, psychology GPA no minimum stated, Masters GPA no minimum stated; *Cognitive & Quantitative Psychology PhD (Doctor of Philosophy):* GRE-V no minimum stated, GRE-Q no minimum stated, GRE-Analytical no minimum stated, overall undergraduate GPA no minimum stated, psychology GPA no minimum stated, Masters GPA no minimum stated; *Law and Psychology PhD (Doctor of Philoso-*

phy): GRE-V no minimum stated, GRE-Q no minimum stated, GRE-Analytical no minimum stated, overall undergraduate GPA no minimum stated, psychology GPA no minimum stated, Masters GPA no minimum stated; *Neuroscience & Behavior PhD (Doctor of Philosophy):* GRE-V no minimum stated, GRE-Q no minimum stated, GRE-Analytical no minimum stated, overall undergraduate GPA no minimum stated, psychology GPA no minimum stated, Masters GPA no minimum stated; *Developmental Psychology PhD (Doctor of Philosophy):* GRE-V no minimum stated, GRE-Q no minimum stated, GRE-Analytical no minimum stated, overall undergraduate GPA no minimum stated, psychology GPA no minimum stated, Masters GPA no minimum stated; *Social/Personality Psychology PhD (Doctor of Philosophy):* GRE-V no minimum stated, GRE-Q no minimum stated, GRE-Analytical no minimum stated, overall undergraduate GPA no minimum stated, psychology GPA no minimum stated, Masters GPA no minimum stated.

Other Criteria: (importance of criteria rated low, medium, or high): GRE scores—medium, research experience—medium, work experience—medium, extracurricular activity—low, clinically related public service—medium, GPA—medium, letters of recommendation—high, interview—medium, statement of goals and objectives—medium, undergraduate major in psychology—low, specific undergraduate psychology courses taken—low. For additional information on admission requirements, go to http://psychology.unl.edu/grad/admission_requirements.shtml.

Student Characteristics: The following represents characteristics of students in 2012–2013 in all graduate psychology programs in the department: Female—full-time 89, part-time 0; Male—full-time 39, part-time 0; African American/Black—full-time 2, part-time 0; Hispanic/Latino(a)—full-time 17, part-time 0; Asian/Pacific Islander—full-time 7, part-time 0; American Indian/Alaska Native—full-time 0, part-time 0; Caucasian/White—full-time 100, part-time 0; Multi-ethnic—full-time 2, part-time 0; students subject to the Americans With Disabilities Act—full-time 0, part-time 0; Unknown ethnicity—full-time 0, part-time 0; International students who hold an F-1 or J-1 Visa—full-time 0, part-time 0.

Financial Information/Assistance:

Tuition for Full-Time Study: *Doctoral:* State residents: $285 per credit hour; Nonstate residents: $768 per credit hour. Tuition is subject to change. See the following website for updates and changes in tuition costs: http://studentaccounts.unl.edu/tuitionfee/12-13/rates/in-person.

Financial Assistance:

First-Year Students: Teaching assistantships available for first year. Average number of hours worked per week: 19. Research assistantships available for first year. Average number of hours worked per week: 19. Fellowships and scholarships available for first year. Average number of hours worked per week: 19.

Advanced Students: Teaching assistantships available for advanced students. Average number of hours worked per week: 19. Research assistantships available for advanced students. Average number of hours worked per week: 19. Fellowships and scholarships available for advanced students.

Additional Information: Of all students currently enrolled full time, 100% benefited from one or more of the listed financial

assistance programs. Application and information available online at: http://www.unl.edu/gradstudies/prospective/money.

Internships/Practica: Doctoral Degree (PhD Clinical Psychology): For those doctoral students for whom a professional psychology internship was required in this program prior to graduation, (9) students applied for an internship in 2011–2012, with (9) students obtaining an internship. Of those students who obtained an internship, (9) were paid internships. Of those students who obtained an internship, (9) students placed in APA/CPA accredited internships, (0) students placed in internships not APA/CPA accredited, but listed with the Association of Psychology Postdoctoral and Internship Programs (APPIC), (0) students placed in internships conforming to guidelines of the Council of Directors of School Psychology Programs (CDSPP), (0) students placed in internships that were not APA/CPA accredited, APPIC or CDSPP listed. The clinical program offers numerous internship opportunities for students. We have an excellent record of placements for our students at high-quality internship sites throughout North America and participate in the APPIC internship match process.

Housing and Day Care: On-campus housing is available. See the following website for more information: http://housing.unl.edu/. On-campus day care facilities are available. See the following website for more information: http://childcare.unl.edu/.

Employment of Department Graduates:

Master's Degree Graduates: Of those who graduated in the academic year 2011–2012, the following categories and numbers represent the postgraduate activities and employment of master's degree graduates: Enrolled in a postdoctoral residency/fellowship (n/a), employed in independent practice (n/a), total from the above (master's) (0).

Doctoral Degree Graduates: Of those who graduated in the academic year 2011–2012, the following categories and numbers represent the postgraduate activities and employment of doctoral degree graduates: Enrolled in a psychology doctoral program (n/a), total from the above (doctoral) (0).

Additional Information:

Orientation, Objectives, and Emphasis of Department: The Department of Psychology at the University of Nebraska-Lincoln offers PhD programs that emphasize the development of research and teaching excellence, collegial partnerships between students and faculty, and the cross-fertilization of ideas between specializations in the context of a rigorous, but flexible, training program. The goal of the clinical program is to produce broadly trained, scientifically-oriented psychologists who have skills in both research and professional activities. The cognitive, biopsychology, developmental, and social-personality programs all emphasize research training but also place equal importance upon training for college or university teaching and policy/applied careers. Students in the PhD/JD program take their first year in the Law College, and then concentrate on psychology plus law to graduate with a double doctorate.

Special Facilities or Resources: The department has a number of resources including the Ruth Staples Child Development Laboratory, the Center for Children, Families and the Law, the BUROS Mental Measurement Institute, the NEAR Center, the UNL Public Policy Center, and the Lincoln Regional Mental Health Center.

Information for Students With Physical Disabilities: See the following website for more information: http://www.unl.edu/ssd/.

Application Information:
Application available online. URL of online application: http://go.unl.edu/gradapp. Students are admitted in the Fall, application deadline December 15. *Fee:* $45.

Nebraska, University of, Omaha
Department of Psychology
Arts and Sciences
6001 Dodge Street
Omaha, NE 68182-0274
Telephone: (402) 554-2592
Fax: (402) 554-2556
E-mail: *josephbrown@unomaha.edu*
Web: *http://www.unomaha.edu/psych/*

Department Information:
Chairperson: Brigette Ryalls. Number of faculty: total—full-time 18; women—full-time 8; total—minority—full-time 2; women minority—full-time 1.

Programs and Degrees Offered:
Listed in the following order: Program area, degree type (T if terminal Master's), number awarded 7/11–6/12. Industrial/Organizational Psychology MA/MS (Master of Arts/Science) 0, School Psychology MA/MS (Master of Arts/Science) 0, Neuroscience & Behavior PhD (Doctor of Philosophy) 0, Developmental Psychology MA/MS (Master of Arts/Science) 0, Experimental Psychology MA/MS (Master of Arts/Science) 0, Developmental Psychology PhD (Doctor of Philosophy) 0, School Psychology EdS (School Psychology) 5, Industrial/Organizational Psychology MA/MS (Master of Arts/Science) (T) 4, Industrial/Organizational Psychology PhD (Doctor of Philosophy) 3, Neuroscience & Behavior MA/MS (Master of Arts/Science) 1, Applied Behavior Analysis MA/MS (Master of Arts/Science) (T) 0.

Student Applications/Admissions:
Student Applications
Industrial/Organizational Psychology MA/MS (Master of Arts/Science)—Applications 2012–2013, 21. Total applicants accepted 2012–2013, 9. Number full-time enrolled (new admits only) 2012–2013, 5. Number part-time enrolled (new admits only) 2012–2013, 0. Total enrolled 2012–2013 full-time, 21. Total enrolled 2012–2013 part-time, 0. Openings 2013–2014, 5. The median number of years required for completion of a degree in 2012–2013 were 2. The number of students enrolled full- and part-time who were dismissed or voluntarily withdrew from this program area in 2012–2013 were 0. *School Psychology MA/MS (Master of Arts/Science)*—Applications 2012–2013, 22. Total applicants accepted 2012–2013, 9. Number full-time enrolled (new admits only) 2012–2013, 3. Total enrolled 2012–2013 full-time, 15. Total enrolled 2012–2013 part-time, 0. Openings 2013–2014, 14. The median number of years required for completion of a degree in 2012–2013 were 2. The

number of students enrolled full- and part-time who were dismissed or voluntarily withdrew from this program area in 2012–2013 were 2. *Neuroscience & Behavior PhD (Doctor of Philosophy)*—Applications 2012–2013, 3. Total applicants accepted 2012–2013, 3. Number full-time enrolled (new admits only) 2012–2013, 1. Number part-time enrolled (new admits only) 2012–2013, 0. Total enrolled 2012–2013 full-time, 3. Total enrolled 2012–2013 part-time, 0. Openings 2013–2014, 4. The number of students enrolled full- and part-time who were dismissed or voluntarily withdrew from this program area in 2012–2013 were 0. *Developmental Psychology MA/MS (Master of Arts/Science)*—Applications 2012–2013, 10. Total applicants accepted 2012–2013, 2. Number full-time enrolled (new admits only) 2012–2013, 1. Total enrolled 2012–2013 full-time, 6. Total enrolled 2012–2013 part-time, 0. Openings 2013–2014, 4. The median number of years required for completion of a degree in 2012–2013 were 3. The number of students enrolled full- and part-time who were dismissed or voluntarily withdrew from this program area in 2012–2013 were 0. *Experimental Psychology MA/MS (Master of Arts/Science)*—Applications 2012–2013, 12. Total applicants accepted 2012–2013, 5. Number full-time enrolled (new admits only) 2012–2013, 1. Number part-time enrolled (new admits only) 2012–2013, 0. Total enrolled 2012–2013 full-time, 4. Total enrolled 2012–2013 part-time, 0. Openings 2013–2014, 2. The median number of years required for completion of a degree in 2012–2013 were 3. The number of students enrolled full- and part-time who were dismissed or voluntarily withdrew from this program area in 2012–2013 were 0. *Developmental Psychology PhD (Doctor of Philosophy)*—Applications 2012–2013, 2. Total applicants accepted 2012–2013, 1. Number full-time enrolled (new admits only) 2012–2013, 3. Number part-time enrolled (new admits only) 2012–2013, 0. Total enrolled 2012–2013 full-time, 6. Total enrolled 2012–2013 part-time, 0. Openings 2013–2014, 2. The number of students enrolled full- and part-time who were dismissed or voluntarily withdrew from this program area in 2012–2013 were 0. *School Psychology EdS (School Psychology)*—Applications 2012–2013, 6. Total applicants accepted 2012–2013, 6. Number full-time enrolled (new admits only) 2012–2013, 4. Number part-time enrolled (new admits only) 2012–2013, 0. Total enrolled 2012–2013 full-time, 7. Total enrolled 2012–2013 part-time, 0. Openings 2013–2014, 8. The median number of years required for completion of a degree in 2012–2013 were 4. The number of students enrolled full- and part-time who were dismissed or voluntarily withdrew from this program area in 2012–2013 were 0. *Industrial/Organizational Psychology MA/MS (Master of Arts/Science)*—Applications 2012–2013, 21. Total applicants accepted 2012–2013, 6. Number full-time enrolled (new admits only) 2012–2013, 5. Number part-time enrolled (new admits only) 2012–2013, 0. Total enrolled 2012–2013 full-time, 14. Total enrolled 2012–2013 part-time, 0. Openings 2013–2014, 6. The median number of years required for completion of a degree in 2012–2013 were 3. The number of students enrolled full- and part-time who were dismissed or voluntarily withdrew from this program area in 2012–2013 were 0. *Industrial/Organizational Psychology PhD (Doctor of Philosophy)*—Applications 2012–2013, 13. Total applicants accepted 2012–2013, 3. Number full-time enrolled (new admits only) 2012–2013, 1. Total enrolled 2012–2013 full-time, 15. Openings 2013–2014, 3. The number of students enrolled full- and part-time who were dismissed or voluntarily withdrew

from this program area in 2012–2013 were 0. *Neuroscience & Behavior MA/MS (Master of Arts/Science)*—Applications 2012–2013, 5. Total applicants accepted 2012–2013, 2. Number full-time enrolled (new admits only) 2012–2013, 1. Total enrolled 2012–2013 full-time, 8. Openings 2013–2014, 6. The median number of years required for completion of a degree in 2012–2013 were 3. The number of students enrolled full- and part-time who were dismissed or voluntarily withdrew from this program area in 2012–2013 were 0. *Applied Behavior Analysis MA/MS (Master of Arts/Science)*—Applications 2012–2013, 16. Total applicants accepted 2012–2013, 8. Number full-time enrolled (new admits only) 2012–2013, 4. Total enrolled 2012–2013 full-time, 12. Openings 2013–2014, 14. The median number of years required for completion of a degree in 2012–2013 were 2. The number of students enrolled full- and part-time who were dismissed or voluntarily withdrew from this program area in 2012–2013 were 3.

Scores: Entries appear in this order: required test or GPA, minimum score (if required), median score of students entering in 2012–2013. *Industrial/Organizational Psychology PhD (Doctor of Philosophy)*: GRE-V no minimum stated, GRE-Q no minimum stated; *Applied Behavior Analysis MA/MS (Master of Arts/Science)*: GRE-V no minimum stated, GRE-Q no minimum stated.

Other Criteria: (importance of criteria rated low, medium, or high): GRE scores—high, research experience—high, work experience—medium, extracurricular activity—medium, clinically related public service—low, GPA—high, letters of recommendation—high, interview—medium, statement of goals and objectives—high, undergraduate major in psychology—low. For additional information on admission requirements, go to http://www.unomaha.edu/psych/graduate.php.

Student Characteristics: The following represents characteristics of students in 2012–2013 in all graduate psychology programs in the department: Female—full-time 76, part-time 0; Male—full-time 35, part-time 0; African American/Black—full-time 2, part-time 0; Hispanic/Latino(a)—full-time 2, part-time 0; Asian/Pacific Islander—full-time 3, part-time 0; American Indian/Alaska Native—full-time 0, part-time 0; Caucasian/White—full-time 104, part-time 0; Multi-ethnic—full-time 0, part-time 0; students subject to the Americans With Disabilities Act—full-time 0, part-time 0; Unknown ethnicity—full-time 0, part-time 0; International students who hold an F-1 or J-1 Visa—full-time 2, part-time 0.

Financial Information/Assistance:

Tuition for Full-Time Study: *Master's:* State residents: $236 per credit hour; Nonstate residents: $622 per credit hour. *Doctoral:* State residents: $236 per credit hour; Nonstate residents: $622 per credit hour. Tuition is subject to change. See the following website for updates and changes in tuition costs: http://cashiering.unomaha.edu/tuition.php.

Financial Assistance:

First-Year Students: Teaching assistantships available for first year. Average amount paid per academic year: $11,921. Average number of hours worked per week: 20. Apply by January 5. Research assistantships available for first year. Average amount paid per academic year: $11,921. Average number of hours worked per week: 20. Apply by January 5. Fellowships and scholarships available for first year. Average amount paid per academic year:

$11,921. Average number of hours worked per week: 20. Apply by January 5.

Advanced Students: Teaching assistantships available for advanced students. Average amount paid per academic year: $11,921. Average number of hours worked per week: 20. Apply by January 5. Research assistantships available for advanced students. Average amount paid per academic year: $11,921. Average number of hours worked per week: 20. Apply by January 5. Fellowships and scholarships available for advanced students. Average amount paid per academic year: $11,921. Average number of hours worked per week: 20. Apply by January 5.

Additional Information: Of all students currently enrolled full time, 50% benefited from one or more of the listed financial assistance programs. Application and information available online at: http://www.unomaha.edu/graduate/assistantships.php.

Internships/Practica: An internship in school psychology is available and required within the EdS program leading to certification in the field of school psychology. Practica are also available (and for some degrees required) in industrial/organizational psychology and developmental psychology.

Housing and Day Care: On-campus housing is available. See the following website for more information: http://housing.unomaha.edu/index.php. On-campus day care facilities are available. See the following website for more information: http://mbsc.unomaha.edu/child.php.

Employment of Department Graduates:

Master's Degree Graduates: Of those who graduated in the academic year 2011–2012, the following categories and numbers represent the postgraduate activities and employment of master's degree graduates: Enrolled in a postdoctoral residency/fellowship (n/a), employed in independent practice (n/a), total from the above (master's) (0).

Doctoral Degree Graduates: Of those who graduated in the academic year 2011–2012, the following categories and numbers represent the postgraduate activities and employment of doctoral degree graduates: Enrolled in a psychology doctoral program (n/a), total from the above (doctoral) (0).

Additional Information:

Orientation, Objectives, and Emphasis of Department: The department is broadly eclectic, placing emphasis on theory, research, and application. The MA program is primarily for students who anticipate continuing their education at the PhD level. The MA degree may be completed in eight areas of psychology. The MS program is primarily for students who view the master's degree as terminal and who wish to emphasize application in the fields of educational-school or industrial/organizational psychology. These two areas may be emphasized within the MA program as well.

Special Facilities or Resources: The department maintains extensive laboratory facilities in a variety of experimental areas, both human and animal. The animal colony consists of rats, gerbils, mice, and golden lion tamarins. Up-to-date interactive computer facilities are readily available. The Center for Applied Psychological Services is a departmentally controlled, faculty-student consulting service that provides an opportunity to gain practical experience in industrial psychology and school psychology. The department maintains working relationships with the Children's Rehabilitation Institute, the Department of Pediatrics, the Department of Physiology, and the University of Nebraska Medical Center. In addition, contact exists with the Boys Town Institute, Boys Town Home, Henry Doorly Zoo, Union Pacific Railroad, and Mutual of Omaha.

Information for Students With Physical Disabilities: See the following website for more information: http://www.unomaha.edu/disability/.

Application Information:
Send to Graduate Studies Admissions, 6001 Dodge Street, EAB 203, Omaha, NE 68182-0274. Application available online. URL of online application: http://www.unomaha.edu/graduate/prospective/applyfor admission.php. Students are admitted in the Fall, application deadline January 5. *Fee:* $45.

Nevada, University of, Las Vegas

Department of Psychology
Liberal Arts
4505 South Maryland Parkway, Box 455030
Las Vegas, NV 89154-5030
Telephone: (702) 895-3305
Fax: (702) 895-0195
E-mail: *mark.ashcraft@unlv.edu*
Web: *http://psychology.unlv.edu*

Department Information:

1960. Chairperson: Mark H. Ashcraft. Number of faculty: total—full-time 23, part-time 21; women—full-time 10, part-time 14; total—minority—full-time 1, part-time 3; women minority—full-time 1, part-time 3; faculty subject to the Americans With Disabilities Act 1.

Programs and Degrees Offered:

Listed in the following order: Program area, degree type (T if terminal Master's), number awarded 7/11–6/12. Clinical Psychology PhD (Doctor of Philosophy) 9, Experimental Psychology PhD (Doctor of Philosophy) 8.

APA Accreditation: Clinical PhD (Doctor of Philosophy). Student Outcome Data Website: http://psychology.unlv.edu/performance.htm.

Student Applications/Admissions:

Student Applications

Clinical Psychology PhD (Doctor of Philosophy)—Applications 2012–2013, 75. Total applicants accepted 2012–2013, 9. Number full-time enrolled (new admits only) 2012–2013, 9. Number part-time enrolled (new admits only) 2012–2013, 0. Total enrolled 2012–2013 full-time, 39. Total enrolled 2012–2013 part-time, 0. Openings 2013–2014, 8. The median number of years required for completion of a degree in 2012–2013 were 6. The number of students enrolled full- and part-time who were dismissed or voluntarily withdrew from this program area in 2012–2013 were 0. *Experimental Psychology PhD (Doctor of Philosophy)*—Applications 2012–2013, 71. Total applicants accepted 2012–2013, 5. Number full-time enrolled (new admits only) 2012–2013, 4. Number part-time enrolled (new admits only) 2012–2013, 0. Total enrolled 2012–2013 full-time, 32. Total enrolled 2012–2013 part-time, 0. Openings 2013–2014, 8. The median number of years required for completion of a degree in 2012–2013 were 6. The number of students enrolled full- and part-time who were dismissed or voluntarily withdrew from this program area in 2012–2013 were 1.

Scores: Entries appear in this order: required test or GPA, minimum score (if required), median score of students entering in 2012–2013. *Clinical Psychology PhD (Doctor of Philosophy):* GRE-V 550, 575, GRE-Q 550, 723, overall undergraduate GPA 3.5, 3.69, psychology GPA 3.5, 3.81; *Experimental Psychology PhD (Doctor of Philosophy):* GRE-V 550, 550, GRE-Q 550, 655, overall undergraduate GPA 3.5, 3.61, psychology GPA 3.5, 3.75.

Other Criteria: (importance of criteria rated low, medium, or high): GRE scores—high, research experience—high, work experience—medium, extracurricular activity—low, clinically related public service—medium, GPA—high, letters of recommendation—high, interview—high, statement of goals and objectives—high, undergraduate major in psychology—high, specific undergraduate psychology courses taken—low, Our experimental program ranks clinically related public service as low.

Student Characteristics: The following represents characteristics of students in 2012–2013 in all graduate psychology programs in the department: Female—full-time 50, part-time 0; Male—full-time 25, part-time 0; African American/Black—full-time 2, part-time 0; Hispanic/Latino(a)—full-time 4, part-time 0; Asian/Pacific Islander—full-time 6, part-time 0; American Indian/Alaska Native—full-time 2, part-time 0; Caucasian/White—full-time 50, part-time 0; Multi-ethnic—full-time 6, part-time 0; students subject to the Americans With Disabilities Act—full-time 0, part-time 0; Unknown ethnicity—full-time 5, part-time 0; International students who hold an F-1 or J-1 Visa—full-time 4, part-time 0.

Financial Information/Assistance:

Tuition for Full-Time Study: *Doctoral:* State residents: per academic year $7,128; Nonstate residents: per academic year $18,937. Tuition is subject to change. Additional fees are assessed to students beyond the costs of tuition for the following: lab assessment materials for some courses. See the following website for updates and changes in tuition costs: http://cashiering.unlv.edu/tuition.html.

Financial Assistance:

First-Year Students: Teaching assistantships available for first year. Average amount paid per academic year: $15,000. Average number of hours worked per week: 20. Apply by January 15. Research assistantships available for first year. Average amount paid per academic year: $15,000. Average number of hours worked per week: 20. Apply by January 15.

Advanced Students: Teaching assistantships available for advanced students. Average amount paid per academic year: $12,000. Average number of hours worked per week: 20. Apply by March 1. Research assistantships available for advanced students. Average amount paid per academic year: $12,000. Average number of hours worked per week: 20. Apply by March 1. Fellowships and scholarships available for advanced students. Average amount paid per academic year: $15,000. Average number of hours worked per week: 20. Apply by March 1.

Additional Information: Of all students currently enrolled full time, 94% benefited from one or more of the listed financial assistance programs. Application and information available online at: http://graduatecollege.unlv.edu/financing/.

Internships/Practica: Doctoral Degree (PhD Clinical Psychology): For those doctoral students for whom a professional psychology internship was required in this program prior to graduation, (7) students applied for an internship in 2011–2012, with (7) students obtaining an internship. Of those students who obtained

an internship, (7) were paid internships. Of those students who obtained an internship, (6) students placed in APA/CPA accredited internships, (0) students placed in internships not APA/CPA accredited, but listed with the Association of Psychology Postdoctoral and Internship Programs (APPIC), (0) students placed in internships conforming to guidelines of the Council of Directors of School Psychology Programs (CDSPP), (1) students placed in internships that were not APA/CPA accredited, APPIC or CDSPP listed. Students work in various community practicum settings as part of their training experience.

Housing and Day Care: No on-campus housing is available. On-campus day care facilities are available. See the following website for more information: http://preschool.unlv.edu/.

Employment of Department Graduates:

Master's Degree Graduates: Of those who graduated in the academic year 2011–2012, the following categories and numbers represent the postgraduate activities and employment of master's degree graduates: Enrolled in a postdoctoral residency/fellowship (n/a), employed in independent practice (n/a), total from the above (master's) (0).

Doctoral Degree Graduates: Of those who graduated in the academic year 2011–2012, the following categories and numbers represent the postgraduate activities and employment of doctoral degree graduates: Enrolled in a psychology doctoral program (n/a), total from the above (doctoral) (0).

Additional Information:

Orientation, Objectives, and Emphasis of Department: The department has the following goals: generating new psychological knowledge through original scholarly research; disseminating psychological knowledge through scholarly articles, books, and other relevant media, and the development of professional conduct through mentorship and supervision of graduate and undergraduate students, and through effective teaching at the graduate and undergraduate levels; promoting self-exploration and self-awareness among students to develop an appreciation of diversity; creating a just, diverse, and humane working and learning environment; enhancing organizational climate, research, teaching/mentoring, and services related to multiculturalism and diversity; creating an effective and responsive administrative infrastructure to serve all stakeholders, including faculty, graduate and undergraduate students, other administrative units within the College and University, and the larger public; and serving the community by bringing faculty and student expertise to bear on important local and regional issues. The UNLV Experimental Psychology doctoral program is designed to prepare experimental psychologists for the rich opportunities that are presented by a changing employment picture. This program addresses the training needs of new psychologists in ways that traditional programs do not. Specifically, the program combines a strong focus on the major content areas of experimental psychology and methodology/statistics, while also providing opportunities to learn skills and conduct research that can be applied to real-world problems. In short, graduate training will produce experimental psychologists who can be employed in both academic and non-academic settings.

Special Facilities or Resources: The strongest resource of the UNLV Psychology Department is the many talents of its diverse faculty. Our graduate program is small enough to provide close personal interaction experiences for training, and yet we encourage students to demonstrate initiative and to undertake the major responsibility for their graduate learning experiences. Student research is encouraged within the department and throughout the university.

Information for Students With Physical Disabilities: See the following website for more information: http://drc.unlv.edu/.

Application Information:
Application available online. URL of online application: http://graduatecollege.unlv.edu/admissions/. Students are admitted in the Fall, application deadline December 1. *Fee:* $75.

Nevada, University of, Reno
Department of Psychology
Liberal Arts
1664 North Virginia Street / Mail Stop 0296
Reno, NV 89557
Telephone: (775) 784-6828
Fax: (775) 784-1126
E-mail: *vmf@unr.edu*
Web: *http://www.unr.edu/cla/psych/*

Department Information:
1920. Chairperson: Victoria M. Follette. Number of faculty: total—full-time 20; women—full-time 8; total—minority—full-time 2; women minority—full-time 2.

Programs and Degrees Offered:
Listed in the following order: Program area, degree type (T if terminal Master's), number awarded 7/11–6/12. Behavior Analysis PhD (Doctor of Philosophy) 12, Clinical Psychology PhD (Doctor of Philosophy) 1, Cognitive and Brain Sciences PhD (Doctor of Philosophy) 2.

APA Accreditation: Clinical PhD (Doctor of Philosophy).

Student Applications/Admissions:
Student Applications

Behavior Analysis PhD (Doctor of Philosophy)—Applications 2012–2013, 42. Total applicants accepted 2012–2013, 14. Number full-time enrolled (new admits only) 2012–2013, 14. Number part-time enrolled (new admits only) 2012–2013, 0. Total enrolled 2012–2013 full-time, 48. Total enrolled 2012–2013 part-time, 0. Openings 2013–2014, 10. The median number of years required for completion of a degree in 2012–2013 were 4. The number of students enrolled full- and part-time who were dismissed or voluntarily withdrew from this program area in 2012–2013 were 1. *Clinical Psychology PhD (Doctor of Philosophy)*—Applications 2012–2013, 114. Total applicants accepted 2012–2013, 8. Number full-time enrolled (new admits only) 2012–2013, 8. Number part-time enrolled (new admits only) 2012–2013, 0. Total enrolled 2012–2013 full-time, 46. Total enrolled 2012–2013 part-time, 0. The median number of years required for completion of a degree in 2012–2013 were 7. The number of students enrolled full- and part-time who were dismissed or voluntarily withdrew from this program area in 2012–2013 were 0. *Cognitive and Brain Sciences*

PhD (Doctor of Philosophy)—Applications 2012–2013, 16. Total applicants accepted 2012–2013, 10. Number full-time enrolled (new admits only) 2012–2013, 5. Number part-time enrolled (new admits only) 2012–2013, 0. Total enrolled 2012–2013 full-time, 23. Total enrolled 2012–2013 part-time, 0. Openings 2013–2014, 5. The median number of years required for completion of a degree in 2012–2013 were 6. The number of students enrolled full- and part-time who were dismissed or voluntarily withdrew from this program area in 2012–2013 were 2.

Scores: Entries appear in this order: required test or GPA, minimum score (if required), median score of students entering in 2012–2013. *Clinical Psychology PhD (Doctor of Philosophy):* GRE-V no minimum stated, GRE-Q no minimum stated, GRE-Subject (Psychology) no minimum stated, overall undergraduate GPA no minimum stated.

Other Criteria: (importance of criteria rated low, medium, or high): GRE scores—high, research experience—high, work experience—high, extracurricular activity—medium, clinically related public service—medium, GPA—high, letters of recommendation—high, interview—high, statement of goals and objectives—high, undergraduate major in psychology—low, specific undergraduate psychology courses taken—medium, Interview for admission in behavior analysis and clinical psychology is required. For additional information on admission requirements, go to http://www.unr.edu/cla/psych/graduate.html.

Student Characteristics: The following represents characteristics of students in 2012–2013 in all graduate psychology programs in the department: Female—full-time 68, part-time 0; Male—full-time 47, part-time 0; African American/Black—full-time 0, part-time 0; Hispanic/Latino(a)—full-time 7, part-time 0; Asian/Pacific Islander—full-time 15, part-time 0; American Indian/Alaska Native—full-time 0, part-time 0; Caucasian/White—full-time 89, part-time 0; Multi-ethnic—full-time 0, part-time 0; students subject to the Americans With Disabilities Act—full-time 0, part-time 0; Unknown ethnicity—full-time 4, part-time 0; International students who hold an F-1 or J-1 Visa—full-time 6, part-time 0.

Financial Information/Assistance:

Tuition for Full-Time Study: *Doctoral:* State residents: per academic year $11,088; Nonstate residents: per academic year $24,998. Tuition is subject to change. Additional fees are assessed to students beyond the costs of tuition for the following: health center (enrolled in six credits or more) $135.50. See the following website for updates and changes in tuition costs: http://www.unr.edu/tuition-and-fees.

Financial Assistance:

First-Year Students: Teaching assistantships available for first year. Average amount paid per academic year: $15,500. Average number of hours worked per week: 20. Research assistantships available for first year. Average amount paid per academic year: $15,500. Average number of hours worked per week: 20.

Advanced Students: Teaching assistantships available for advanced students. Average amount paid per academic year: $15,500. Average number of hours worked per week: 20. Research assistantships available for advanced students. Average amount paid per academic year: $15,500. Average number of hours worked per week: 20.

Additional Information: Of all students currently enrolled full time, 90% benefited from one or more of the listed financial assistance programs. Application and information available online at: http://www.unr.edu/grad/funding.

Internships/Practica: Doctoral Degree (PhD Clinical Psychology): For those doctoral students for whom a professional psychology internship was required in this program prior to graduation, (4) students applied for an internship in 2011–2012, with (3) students obtaining an internship. Of those students who obtained an internship, (3) were paid internships. Of those students who obtained an internship, (3) students placed in APA/CPA accredited internships, (0) students placed in internships not APA/CPA accredited, but listed with the Association of Psychology Postdoctoral and Internship Programs (APPIC), (0) students placed in internships conforming to guidelines of the Council of Directors of School Psychology Programs (CDSPP), (0) students placed in internships that were not APA/CPA accredited, APPIC or CDSPP listed. Clinical—Participation in clinical practica is required for students. From the last half of the first year through the third year, students see clients at the Psychological Service Center, an in-house clinic. During the fourth year, students are required to complete a 1000-hour practicum (externship) on campus or at agencies in the area. Finally, students are required to complete a 2000 hour, APA-approved internship during their final year.

Housing and Day Care: On-campus housing is available. See the following website for more information: http://www.reslife.unr.edu/. On-campus day care facilities are available. See the following website for more information: http://www.unr.edu/education/centers/cfrc/programs-and-services.

Employment of Department Graduates:

Master's Degree Graduates: Of those who graduated in the academic year 2011–2012, the following categories and numbers represent the postgraduate activities and employment of master's degree graduates: Enrolled in a postdoctoral residency/fellowship (n/a), employed in independent practice (n/a), total from the above (master's) (0).

Doctoral Degree Graduates: Of those who graduated in the academic year 2011–2012, the following categories and numbers represent the postgraduate activities and employment of doctoral degree graduates: Enrolled in a psychology doctoral program (n/a), enrolled in a postdoctoral residency/fellowship (4), employed in independent practice (1), employed in an academic position at a university (2), employed in business or industry (3), total from the above (doctoral) (10).

Additional Information:

Orientation, Objectives, and Emphasis of Department: The Cognitive and Brain Science (previously Experimental) program in psychology is research-oriented. The division offers specialized work in human cognition and cognitive neuroscience; learning, perception and psychophysics; and animal communication. The clinical program has a scientist–practitioner emphasis and offers skills in psychotherapy, assessment, evaluation, and community psychology. The behavior analysis program emphasizes applied behavior analysis, especially in institutional settings, and examines both the theoretical and applied ramifications of the behavioral programs.

Special Facilities or Resources: Cognitive and Brain Science—the program has active labs with facilities for research in visual perception, memory, cognition, and animal behavior and communication (including opportunities for research at the primate center at Central Washington University). Behavior Analysis—the program has a lab where students work with autistic children and developmentally disabled clients. Clinical—the primary academic/research facility of the program is the Psychological Service Center, an in-house training clinic that serves the community by offering services on a sliding fee basis.

Information for Students With Physical Disabilities: See the following website for more information: http://www.unr.edu/drc.

Application Information:
Send to Admissions, Psychology Department/296, University of Nevada, Reno, NV 89557. Application available online. URL of online application: http://www.unr.edu/grad/admissions/apply. Students are admitted in the Fall, application deadline January 1; Spring, application deadline November 1. For the Fall semester, the deadline for Clinical Psychology and Behavior Analysis is January 1, and February 1 for Cognitive and Brain Sciences. For the Spring semester, the deadline is November 1 for Cognitive and Brain Sciences only. *Fee:* $60. International applicants pay an application fee of $95.

Antioch University New England

Clinical Psychology
40 Avon Street
Keene, NH 03431-3516
Telephone: (603) 283-2183
Fax: (603) 357-1679
E-mail: *cpeterson@antioch.edu*
Web: *http://www.antiochne.edu/cp/*

Department Information:

1982. Chairperson: Kathi A. Borden, PhD. Number of faculty: total—full-time 11, part-time 23; women—full-time 5, part-time 11; total—minority—full-time 1; women minority—full-time 1.

Programs and Degrees Offered:

Listed in the following order: Program area, degree type (T if terminal Master's), number awarded 7/11–6/12. Clinical Psychology PsyD (Doctor of Psychology) 23.

APA Accreditation: Clinical PsyD (Doctor of Psychology). Student Outcome Data Website: http://www.antiochne.edu/cp/.

Student Applications/Admissions:

Student Applications

Clinical Psychology PsyD (Doctor of Psychology)—Applications 2012–2013, 87. Total applicants accepted 2012–2013, 49. Number full-time enrolled (new admits only) 2012–2013, 19. Number part-time enrolled (new admits only) 2012–2013, 0. Total enrolled 2012–2013 full-time, 157. Total enrolled 2012–2013 part-time, 3. Openings 2013–2014, 25. The median number of years required for completion of a degree in 2012–2013 were 6. The number of students enrolled full- and part-time who were dismissed or voluntarily withdrew from this program area in 2012–2013 were 1.

Scores: Entries appear in this order: required test or GPA, minimum score (if required), median score of students entering in 2012–2013. *Clinical Psychology PsyD (Doctor of Psychology):* GRE-V 500, 570, GRE-Q 500, 580, GRE-Analytical no minimum stated, 5, GRE-Subject (Psychology) 500, 590, overall undergraduate GPA 3.0, 3.41.

Other Criteria: (importance of criteria rated low, medium, or high): GRE scores—high, research experience—medium, work experience—medium, extracurricular activity—low, clinically related public service—medium, GPA—high, letters of recommendation—high, interview—high, statement of goals and objectives—high, undergraduate major in psychology—medium, specific undergraduate psychology courses taken—medium. For additional information on admission requirements, go to http://www.antiochne.edu/admissions/appprocess_psyd.cfm.

Student Characteristics: The following represents characteristics of students in 2012–2013 in all graduate psychology programs in the department: Female—full-time 124, part-time 3; Male—full-time 33, part-time 0; African American/Black—full-time 3, part-time 1; Hispanic/Latino(a)—full-time 3, part-time 0; Asian/Pa-

cific Islander—full-time 0, part-time 0; American Indian/Alaska Native—full-time 1, part-time 0; Caucasian/White—full-time 136, part-time 2; Multi-ethnic—full-time 0, part-time 0; students subject to the Americans With Disabilities Act—full-time 6, part-time 0; Unknown ethnicity—full-time 11, part-time 1; International students who hold an F-1 or J-1 Visa—full-time 3, part-time 0.

Financial Information/Assistance:

Tuition for Full-Time Study: *Doctoral:* State residents: per academic year $30,300; Nonstate residents: per academic year $30,300. Tuition is subject to change. Additional fees are assessed to students beyond the costs of tuition for the following: dissertation/continuation fee; internship fee. See the following website for updates and changes in tuition costs: http://www.antiochne.edu/financial/tuition_cp.cfm.

Financial Assistance:

First-Year Students: Teaching assistantships available for first year. Apply by March 1. Research assistantships available for first year. Average amount paid per academic year: $1,081. Average number of hours worked per week: 6. Apply by March 1. Fellowships and scholarships available for first year. Apply by March 1.

Advanced Students: Teaching assistantships available for advanced students. Average amount paid per academic year: $1,073. Average number of hours worked per week: 6. Apply by March 1. Research assistantships available for advanced students. Average amount paid per academic year: $2,531. Average number of hours worked per week: 6. Apply by March 1. Fellowships and scholarships available for advanced students. Average amount paid per academic year: $1,583. Apply by March 1.

Additional Information: Of all students currently enrolled full time, 18% benefited from one or more of the listed financial assistance programs. Application and information available online at: http://www.antiochne.edu/financial/.

Internships/Practica: Doctoral Degree (PsyD Clinical Psychology): For those doctoral students for whom a professional psychology internship was required in this program prior to graduation, (31) students applied for an internship in 2011–2012, with (25) students obtaining an internship. Of those students who obtained an internship, (22) were paid internships. Of those students who obtained an internship, (10) students placed in APA/CPA accredited internships, (8) students placed in internships not APA/CPA accredited, but listed with the Association of Psychology Postdoctoral and Internship Programs (APPIC), (0) students placed in internships conforming to guidelines of the Council of Directors of School Psychology Programs (CDSPP), (7) students placed in internships that were not APA/CPA accredited, APPIC or CDSPP listed. Students complete practica at agencies within driving distance around New England. About 11 students per year do practicum at the Antioch Family Therapy and Psychological Services Center (PSC), within the Department of Clinical Psychology. It functions as a mental health clinic providing a range of psychological services to residents from Keene and surrounding communities, and to Antioch New England students in departments other than Clinical Psychology. These services include individual psychotherapy, couple and family therapy, individual and family assessment, and various problem-specific psychoeducational groups and seminars. In addition, the PSC is actively involved in community outreach services; clinicians are encouraged to develop public psychoeducation and consultation activities, and to work in collaboration with other social service agencies for the purpose of ongoing community needs assessment and program development. A practicum at the PSC offers the student a unique opportunity for more concentrated interaction with core faculty—through supervision, training, and involvement in applied clinical and research projects of mutual interest. Specialized training opportunities exist for students interested in health psychology, family therapy, and assessment. Students seek internships through APPIC match.

Housing and Day Care: No on-campus housing is available. No on-campus day care facilities are available.

Employment of Department Graduates:

Master's Degree Graduates: Of those who graduated in the academic year 2011–2012, the following categories and numbers represent the postgraduate activities and employment of master's degree graduates: Enrolled in a postdoctoral residency/fellowship (n/a), employed in independent practice (n/a), total from the above (master's) (0).

Doctoral Degree Graduates: Of those who graduated in the academic year 2011–2012, the following categories and numbers represent the postgraduate activities and employment of doctoral degree graduates: Enrolled in a psychology doctoral program (n/a), enrolled in a postdoctoral residency/fellowship (9), employed in independent practice (4), employed in a professional position in a school system (1), employed in government agency (1), employed in a community mental health/counseling center (8), total from the above (doctoral) (23).

Additional Information:

Orientation, Objectives, and Emphasis of Department: Our practitioner-scholar program prepares clinicians to undertake multiple roles for the expanded world of future clinical psychology practice. Our graduates see clients; supervise other clinicians; consult, train, and teach; perform complex assessments; develop and administer programs; act as advocates to influence public policy; and conduct applied research such as evaluating treatment effectiveness, conducting needs assessments, and performing program evaluations. Our program includes broad training, offering a range of theoretical perspectives, a sound psychological knowledge base, and supervised practice. With a commitment to social responsibility, social justice, and diversity, we emphasize a social vision of clinical psychology, responsive to the needs of the larger society. We view research in clinical psychology as being rooted in solving professional and social problems, where science and practice are integrated and complementary. Preparation as local clinical scientists includes training in an array of methodologies and encourages students to explore their professional interests within the required dissertation and other research, elective course/concentration, and clinical opportunities. Our students

learn to engage in reflective practice with self-awareness and an understanding of the importance of all professional relationships. Our pedagogy brings together theory, research, and practice through integrative, reflective learning experiences which help students develop their professional voice.

Special Facilities or Resources: The Center for Research on Psychological Practice (CROPP) in the Department of Clinical Psychology serves both the department and the community. This center is designed to address particular emerging educational aspects of doctoral training in clinical psychology that are not regularly included within the usual professional psychology curriculum—those relevant to applied clinical research skills and the associated administrative, consultative, and policy-creation roles of doctoral level psychologists. Several specific areas of research are priorities for CROPP. These include program evaluation and quality assurance issues, such as needs assessment, outcome and satisfaction research, cost-benefit analysis, policy analysis, and other topics relevant to mental health service management; public welfare issues such as treatment access, utilization, and outcomes for underserved, rural, low socioeconomic, and minority populations; development of novel treatment and delivery systems; and methodological issues including the assessment and development of methods and measures appropriate for practice research. The research is done primarily in community service settings and entails collaboration with agencies and caregivers throughout the region. The development of this kind of research center, particularly within the context of a doctoral program in clinical psychology, has not, to our knowledge, been done elsewhere in the country. The Antioch University New England Multicultural Center for Research and Practice addresses the diverse array of emerging multicultural information which represents an enormous and unique opportunity to revolutionize and improve education, training, research, and human services, while addressing concerns of social justice. The Center has a particular focus on racial and ethnic minority and immigrant youth, adults, and families. It provides an excellent model of how the combination of research and practice can have a positive impact on communities across New England and beyond. The services of the Multicultural Center include social support for racial and ethnic minority peoples; individual and group multicultural interactions; workshops on multicultural awareness and acceptance; workshops on racism and stereotypes; consultation with professionals, educators, and businesses on multicultural applications and services; and coalition-building among disenfranchised groups. Its Web-based services include access to multicultural tests housed in the Center, resources of multicultural test titles and reviews, multicultural lecture notes, awareness exercises, documentation of processes and outcomes of multicultural service delivery, and a national multicultural course syllabus archive.

Information for Students With Physical Disabilities: See the following website for more information: http://www.antiochne.edu/sds/.

Application Information:

Send to Office of Doctoral Admissions, Antioch University New England, 40 Avon Street, Keene, NH, 03431-3552. Application available online. URL of online application: https://www.applyweb.com/apply/antiochne/menu.html. Students are admitted in the Fall, application deadline January 4. *Fee:* $75.

New Hampshire, University of
Department of Psychology
College of Liberal Arts
Conant Hall
Durham, NH 03824
Telephone: (603) 862-2360
Fax: (603) 862-4986
E-mail: *robin.scholefield@unh.edu*
Web: *http://www.unh.edu/psychology/*

Department Information:
1923. Chairperson: Robert G. Mair. Number of faculty: total—full-time 20; women—full-time 7; total—minority—full-time 1.

Programs and Degrees Offered:
Listed in the following order: Program area, degree type (T if terminal Master's), number awarded 7/11–6/12. Developmental Psychology PhD (Doctor of Philosophy) 0, Social/Personality Psychology PhD (Doctor of Philosophy) 1, Brain, Behavior and Cognition PhD (Doctor of Philosophy) 2.

Student Applications/Admissions:
Student Applications
Developmental Psychology PhD (Doctor of Philosophy)—Applications 2012–2013, 16. Total applicants accepted 2012–2013, 0. Number full-time enrolled (new admits only) 2012–2013, 0. Total enrolled 2012–2013 full-time, 5. Openings 2013–2014, 2. The median number of years required for completion of a degree in 2012–2013 were 5. The number of students enrolled full- and part-time who were dismissed or voluntarily withdrew from this program area in 2012–2013 were 1. *Social/Personality Psychology PhD (Doctor of Philosophy)*—Applications 2012–2013, 37. Total applicants accepted 2012–2013, 0. Number full-time enrolled (new admits only) 2012–2013, 0. Total enrolled 2012–2013 full-time, 11. Openings 2013–2014, 3. The median number of years required for completion of a degree in 2012–2013 were 5. The number of students enrolled full- and part-time who were dismissed or voluntarily withdrew from this program area in 2012–2013 were 0. *Brain, Behavior and Cognition PhD (Doctor of Philosophy)*—Applications 2012–2013, 36. Total applicants accepted 2012–2013, 1. Number full-time enrolled (new admits only) 2012–2013, 1. Number part-time enrolled (new admits only) 2012–2013, 0. Total enrolled 2012–2013 full-time, 8. Total enrolled 2012–2013 part-time, 0. Openings 2013–2014, 6. The median number of years required for completion of a degree in 2012–2013 were 5. The number of students enrolled full- and part-time who were dismissed or voluntarily withdrew from this program area in 2012–2013 were 2.
Scores: Entries appear in this order: required test or GPA, minimum score (if required), median score of students entering in 2012–2013. *Developmental Psychology PhD (Doctor of Philosophy)*: GRE-V no minimum stated, GRE-Q no minimum stated, GRE-Analytical no minimum stated, overall undergraduate GPA no minimum stated; *Social/Personality Psychology PhD (Doctor of Philosophy)*: GRE-V no minimum stated, GRE-Q no minimum stated, GRE-Analytical no minimum stated, overall undergraduate GPA no minimum stated; *Brain, Behavior and Cognition PhD (Doctor of Philosophy)*: GRE-V no minimum stated, GRE-Q no minimum stated, GRE-Analytical no minimum stated, overall undergraduate GPA no minimum stated.
Other Criteria: (importance of criteria rated low, medium, or high): GRE scores—high, research experience—high, work experience—low, extracurricular activity—low, GPA—high, letters of recommendation—high, interview—low, statement of goals and objectives—high, interests match program—high, undergraduate major in psychology—medium, specific undergraduate psychology courses taken—medium. For additional information on admission requirements, go to http://www.unh.edu/psychology/.

Student Characteristics: The following represents characteristics of students in 2012–2013 in all graduate psychology programs in the department: Female—full-time 17, part-time 0; Male—full-time 8, part-time 0; African American/Black—full-time 0, part-time 0; Hispanic/Latino(a)—full-time 0, part-time 0; Asian/Pacific Islander—full-time 0, part-time 0; American Indian/Alaska Native—full-time 0, part-time 0; Caucasian/White—full-time 24, part-time 0; Multi-ethnic—full-time 1, part-time 0; students subject to the Americans With Disabilities Act—full-time 0, part-time 0; Unknown ethnicity—full-time 0, part-time 0; International students who hold an F-1 or J-1 Visa—full-time 1, part-time 0.

Financial Information/Assistance:
Tuition for Full-Time Study: *Doctoral:* State residents: per academic year $13,500, $750 per credit hour; Nonstate residents: per academic year $25,940, $1,089 per credit hour. Tuition is subject to change. See the following website for updates and changes in tuition costs: http://www.unh.edu/business-services/tuitgrad.html.

Financial Assistance:
First-Year Students: Teaching assistantships available for first year. Average amount paid per academic year: $14,800. Average number of hours worked per week: 20.
Advanced Students: Teaching assistantships available for advanced students. Average amount paid per academic year: $16,800. Average number of hours worked per week: 20. Fellowships and scholarships available for advanced students. Average amount paid per academic year: $16,800.
Additional Information: Of all students currently enrolled full time, 100% benefited from one or more of the listed financial assistance programs. Application and information available online at: http://www.gradschool.unh.edu/grad_aid.php.

Housing and Day Care: On-campus housing is available. See the following website for more information: http://www.unh.edu/housing/gradhousing/. On-campus day care facilities are available. See the following website for more information: http://www.chhs.unh.edu/csdc/index.

Employment of Department Graduates:
Master's Degree Graduates: Of those who graduated in the academic year 2011–2012, the following categories and numbers represent the postgraduate activities and employment of master's degree graduates: Enrolled in a postdoctoral residency/fellowship (n/a), employed in independent practice (n/a), total from the above (master's) (0).
Doctoral Degree Graduates: Of those who graduated in the academic year 2011–2012, the following categories and numbers represent the postgraduate activities and employment of doctoral

degree graduates: Enrolled in a psychology doctoral program (n/a), employed in an academic position at a university (3), total from the above (doctoral) (3).

Additional Information:

Orientation, Objectives, and Emphasis of Department: All students receive tuition waivers and stipends for at least 4 years, in exchange for serving as graduate assistants in their early years and as teachers in their later years. Students can apply for research and summer funding. The program's basic goal is the preparation of doctoral students for academic careers. We focus on the development of psychologists who have broad knowledge of psychology, who can teach and communicate effectively, and who can carry out sound research. Specialties are offered in the following areas: Brain, Behavior and Cognition (behavioral and cognitive neuroscience, cognition, vision); Developmental Psychology; and Social/Personality Psychology. Besides completing academic courses, our program places a distinctive emphasis on preparing graduate students for future roles as faculty members in college or university settings. Students complete a year-long seminar and practicum in the teaching of psychology, which introduces them to the theory and practice of teaching, while they concurrently teach under the supervision of master-teachers. Students also gain experience in other faculty roles such as sponsoring undergraduate students' research and serving on committees. Students are involved in research activities throughout the program. After graduation, most students secure academic positions.

Special Facilities or Resources: The department occupies several buildings and offers research facilities, equipment, and resources in all of its areas of specialization. In addition, the department has up-to-date computing and related resources.

Information for Students With Physical Disabilities: See the following website for more information: http://www.unh.edu/disabilityservices/.

Application Information:
Send to Dean of the Graduate School, University of New Hampshire, Thompson Hall, Durham, NH 03824. Application available online. URL of online application: http://www.gradschool.unh.edu/apply.php. Students are admitted in the Fall, application deadline January 15. Review of applications begins January 15 and continues until the incoming class is filled. *Fee:* $65.

Rivier University
Psychology
420 South Main Street
Nashua, NH 03060
Telephone: (603) 897-8596
Fax: (603) 897-8805
E-mail: *eharwood@rivier.edu*
Web: *http://www.rivier.edu/admissions/graduate/academic-programs/default.aspx?id=17076*

Department Information:
1974. Department Coordinator: Elizabeth Harwood, PhD. Number of faculty: total—full-time 5, part-time 11; women—full-time 3, part-time 8; minority—part-time 1; women minority—part-time 1.

Programs and Degrees Offered:
Listed in the following order: Program area, degree type (T if terminal Master's), number awarded 7/11–6/12. Clinical Psychology MA/MS (Master of Arts/Science) (T) 4, Experimental Psychology MA/MS (Master of Arts/Science) (T) 2.

Student Applications/Admissions:
Student Applications

Clinical Psychology MA/MS (Master of Arts/Science)—Applications 2012–2013, 17. Total applicants accepted 2012–2013, 12. Number full-time enrolled (new admits only) 2012–2013, 11. Number part-time enrolled (new admits only) 2012–2013, 1. Total enrolled 2012–2013 full-time, 15. Total enrolled 2012–2013 part-time, 1. Openings 2013–2014, 15. The median number of years required for completion of a degree in 2012–2013 were 2. The number of students enrolled full- and part-time who were dismissed or voluntarily withdrew from this program area in 2012–2013 were 2. *Experimental Psychology MA/MS (Master of Arts/Science)*—Applications 2012–2013, 10. Total applicants accepted 2012–2013, 9. Number full-time enrolled (new admits only) 2012–2013, 8. Total enrolled 2012–2013 full-time, 10. Openings 2013–2014, 10. The median number of years required for completion of a degree in 2012–2013 were 2. The number of students enrolled full- and part-time who were dismissed or voluntarily withdrew from this program area in 2012–2013 were 0.

Scores: Entries appear in this order: required test or GPA, minimum score (if required), median score of students entering in 2012–2013. *Clinical Psychology MA/MS (Master of Arts/Science):* overall undergraduate GPA 3.0, last 2 years GPA 3.0, psychology GPA 3.0; *Experimental Psychology MA/MS (Master of Arts/Science):* overall undergraduate GPA 3.0, last 2 years GPA 3.0, psychology GPA 3.0.

Other Criteria: (importance of criteria rated low, medium, or high): research experience—low, work experience—low, extracurricular activity—low, clinically related public service—low, GPA—high, letters of recommendation—medium, interview—medium, statement of goals and objectives—high, fit to program—medium, undergraduate major in psychology—low, specific undergraduate psychology courses taken—medium.

Student Characteristics: The following represents characteristics of students in 2012–2013 in all graduate psychology programs in the department: Female—full-time 20, part-time 1; Male—full-time 5, part-time 0; Hispanic/Latino(a)—full-time 1, part-time 0; Caucasian/White—full-time 20, part-time 1; Multi-ethnic—full-time 1, part-time 0; students subject to the Americans With Disabilities Act—full-time 0, part-time 0; Unknown ethnicity—full-time 3, part-time 0; International students who hold an F-1 or J-1 Visa—full-time 0, part-time 0.

Financial Information/Assistance:
Tuition for Full-Time Study: Master's: State residents: $513 per credit hour; Nonstate residents: $513 per credit hour. Tuition is subject to change. See the following website for updates and changes in tuition costs: http://www.rivier.edu/bo/default.aspx?id=2467.

Financial Assistance:

First-Year Students: No information provided.

Advanced Students: Research assistantships available for advanced students. Average number of hours worked per week: 14.

Additional Information: Application and information available online at: http://www.rivier.edu/finaid/default.aspx?id=13038.

Internships/Practica: Master's Degree (MA/MS Clinical Psychology): An internship experience, such as a final research project or "capstone" experience is required of graduates. Master's Degree (MA/MS Experimental Psychology): An internship experience, such as a final research project or "capstone" experience is required of graduates. Graduate internships are arranged individually based on the student's prior experience and the learning opportunities provided at the internship setting. We currently have internship sites in a variety of settings and working with a variety of populations. These include working with children in schools, afterschool prevention programs and clinical child care facilities. Also available are internships with older adults in nursing homes, senior activity centers and assisted living facilities. Internships in juvenile justice settings as well as group homes for adolescents, in hospital settings for individuals with both chronic developmental disabilities and acquired brain injuries, day treatment programs for adults with developmental disabilities, and transitional living programs are other settings. Our connection with a longitudinal research study at Judge Baker Guidance in Boston, MA has provided a number of our students who are interested in research with opportunities to pursue that interest. Similar research opportunities are available through an annual statewide study of homelessness in New Hampshire.

Housing and Day Care: On-campus housing is available. See the following website for more information: http://www.rivier.edu/life/oncampus/default.aspx?id=1100. On-campus day care facilities are available. See the following website for more information: http://www.rivier.edu/ecc/default.aspx?id=2125.

Employment of Department Graduates:

Master's Degree Graduates: Of those who graduated in the academic year 2011–2012, the following categories and numbers represent the postgraduate activities and employment of master's degree graduates: Enrolled in another graduate/professional program (1), enrolled in a postdoctoral residency/fellowship (n/a), employed in independent practice (n/a), employed in an academic position at a 2-year/4-year college (1), employed in a community mental health/counseling center (1), employed in a hospital/medical center (1), do not know (2), total from the above (master's) (6).

Doctoral Degree Graduates: Of those who graduated in the academic year 2011–2012, the following categories and numbers represent the postgraduate activities and employment of doctoral degree graduates: Enrolled in a psychology doctoral program (n/a), total from the above (doctoral) (0).

Additional Information:

Orientation, Objectives, and Emphasis of Department: The Department of Psychology offers a Master of Science degree program in Experimental and Clinical Psychology. Both are day programs and may be completed on either a full-time or part-time basis. The vision of the programs is one of collegiality and mentorship. Students develop a sense of mutual support and identity under the guidance of a faculty mentor and gain practical research and/or clinical experience in the Behavioral Science Lab or Clinical Psychology internship program. As day programs that provide students with a dedicated space in support of their research and clinical training, Rivier's graduate programs help build a sense of camaraderie between graduate students and their professors and create an environment in which integrated learning is the shared responsibility of all. The master's programs put into practice the Boulder scientist–practitioner model of graduate psychology education by providing students with solid foundation in both the biopsychosocial basis of behavior and the methodological and quantitative skills acquired through research design, data collection, analysis, and evaluation. These skills will prepare students to progress to PhD or PsyD doctoral programs, teach in higher education on a part-time basis, or find employment in academic, business, governmental, or human service settings. These programs are ideal choices for individuals seeking master's-level training in psychology in order to become more competitive in the job market, expand career options, and develop earning potential not afforded by a baccalaureate degree alone.

Special Facilities or Resources: The psychology department has two dedicated facilities: the Behavioral Science Laboratory and the Clinical Psychology Laboratory. The Behavioral Science Laboratory (BSL) provides graduate students with access to the tools necessary for studying, characterizing and analyzing human behavior. The BSL has 6 computer stations (5 experimental and 1 researcher) equipped with state-of-the-art data acquisition and analysis software. The 400 sq. ft. facility also features reference texts on design and analysis, peer-reviewed psychology journals and a ten-foot modular conference table that facilitates interaction among graduate students and between students and faculty. The Clinical Psychology Laboratory includes a classroom, an observation room with a one-way mirror, and a research room with three computers for student use. In addition, the facility is equipped with audio/video recording capability, a wide screen television for video presentations, and a general use area where students may interact, study, or just relax. Much like the BSL, this facility is used for both educational and research purposes.

Information for Students With Physical Disabilities: See the following website for more information: http://www.rivier.edu/ds/default.aspx?id=74.

Application Information:
Send to Rivier University, Office of Admissions, 420 South Main Street, Nashua, NH 03060. Application available online. URL of online application: http://www.rivier.edu/admissions/graduate/. Programs have rolling admissions. *Fee:* $25.

Fairleigh Dickinson University, Metropolitan Campus

School of Psychology
University College: Arts-Sciences-Professional Studies
1000 River Road
Teaneck, NJ 07666
Telephone: (201) 692-2300
Fax: (201) 692-2304
E-mail: *dumont@fdu.edu*
Web: *http://view.fdu.edu/default.aspx?id=169*

Department Information:
1960. Director: Ron Dumont Ed.D., NCSP. Number of faculty: total—full-time 18, part-time 19; women—full-time 11, part-time 12.

Programs and Degrees Offered:
Listed in the following order: Program area, degree type (T if terminal Master's), number awarded 7/11–6/12. General/Theoretical Psychology MA/MS (Master of Arts/Science) (T) 8, Clinical Psychology PhD (Doctor of Philosophy) 10, School Psychology PsyD (Doctor of Psychology) 12, Psychopharmacology MA/MS (Master of Arts/Science) (T) 13, School Psychology MA/MS (Master of Arts/Science) (T) 10, Forensic Psychology MA/MS (Master of Arts/Science) (T) 9.

APA Accreditation: Clinical PhD (Doctor of Philosophy). Student Outcome Data Website: http://view.fdu.edu/default.aspx?id=6281.

Student Applications/Admissions:

Student Applications
General/Theoretical Psychology MA/MS (Master of Arts/Science)—Applications 2012–2013, 31. Total applicants accepted 2012–2013, 28. Number full-time enrolled (new admits only) 2012–2013, 8. Number part-time enrolled (new admits only) 2012–2013, 1. Total enrolled 2012–2013 full-time, 15. Total enrolled 2012–2013 part-time, 5. Openings 2013–2014, 12. The median number of years required for completion of a degree in 2012–2013 were 2. The number of students enrolled full- and part-time who were dismissed or voluntarily withdrew from this program area in 2012–2013 were 1. *Clinical Psychology PhD (Doctor of Philosophy)*—Applications 2012–2013, 242. Total applicants accepted 2012–2013, 21. Number full-time enrolled (new admits only) 2012–2013, 14. Number part-time enrolled (new admits only) 2012–2013, 0. Total enrolled 2012–2013 full-time, 81. Total enrolled 2012–2013 part-time, 0. Openings 2013–2014, 14. The median number of years required for completion of a degree in 2012–2013 were 5. The number of students enrolled full- and part-time who were dismissed or voluntarily withdrew from this program area in 2012–2013 were 1. *School Psychology PsyD (Doctor of Psychology)*—Applications 2012–2013, 54. Total applicants accepted 2012–2013, 15. Number full-time enrolled (new admits only) 2012–2013, 16. Number part-time enrolled (new admits only) 2012–2013, 0. Total enrolled 2012–2013 full-time, 64. Openings 2013–2014, 15. The median number of years required for

completion of a degree in 2012–2013 were 4. The number of students enrolled full- and part-time who were dismissed or voluntarily withdrew from this program area in 2012–2013 were 0. *Psychopharmacology MA/MS (Master of Arts/Science)*—Applications 2012–2013, 25. Total applicants accepted 2012–2013, 25. Number part-time enrolled (new admits only) 2012–2013, 20. Total enrolled 2012–2013 part-time, 45. Openings 2013–2014, 20. The median number of years required for completion of a degree in 2012–2013 were 2. The number of students enrolled full- and part-time who were dismissed or voluntarily withdrew from this program area in 2012–2013 were 3. *School Psychology MA/MS (Master of Arts/Science)*—Applications 2012–2013, 44. Total applicants accepted 2012–2013, 18. Number full-time enrolled (new admits only) 2012–2013, 10. Total enrolled 2012–2013 full-time, 41. Openings 2013–2014, 12. The median number of years required for completion of a degree in 2012–2013 were 3. The number of students enrolled full- and part-time who were dismissed or voluntarily withdrew from this program area in 2012–2013 were 1. *Forensic Psychology MA/MS (Master of Arts/Science)*—Applications 2012–2013, 80. Total applicants accepted 2012–2013, 25. Number full-time enrolled (new admits only) 2012–2013, 18. Number part-time enrolled (new admits only) 2012–2013, 0. Total enrolled 2012–2013 full-time, 30. Total enrolled 2012–2013 part-time, 0. Openings 2013–2014, 20. The median number of years required for completion of a degree in 2012–2013 were 2. The number of students enrolled full- and part-time who were dismissed or voluntarily withdrew from this program area in 2012–2013 were 0.

Scores: Entries appear in this order: required test or GPA, minimum score (if required), median score of students entering in 2012–2013. *General/Theoretical Psychology MA/MS (Master of Arts/Science)*: GRE-V no minimum stated, GRE-Q no minimum stated, GRE-Analytical no minimum stated, GRE-Subject (Psychology) no minimum stated; *Clinical Psychology PhD (Doctor of Philosophy)*: GRE-V no minimum stated, GRE-Q no minimum stated, GRE-Analytical no minimum stated, GRE-Subject (Psychology) no minimum stated; *Forensic Psychology MA/MS (Master of Arts/Science)*: GRE-V 500, GRE-Q 500, overall undergraduate GPA 3.0, 3.4.

Other Criteria: (importance of criteria rated low, medium, or high): GRE scores—medium, research experience—high, work experience—medium, extracurricular activity—medium, clinically related public service—high, GPA—medium, letters of recommendation—high, interview—high, statement of goals and objectives—high, These criteria are used for admission to PhD and PsyD programs. For PsyD program, research experience would be low and work experience would be medium-high.

Student Characteristics: The following represents characteristics of students in 2012–2013 in all graduate psychology programs in the department: Female—full-time 169, part-time 46; Male—full-time 51, part-time 24; African American/Black—full-time 0, part-time 0; Hispanic/Latino(a)—full-time 0, part-time 0; Asian/Pacific Islander—full-time 0, part-time 0; American Indian/Alaska Native—full-time 0, part-time 0; Caucasian/White—full-time 0, part-time 0; Multi-ethnic—full-time 0, part-time 0; students subject to the Americans With Disabilities Act—full-time 0, part-time 0; Unknown ethnicity—full-time 0, part-time 0; International students who hold an F-1 or J-1 Visa—full-time 0, part-time 0.

Financial Information/Assistance:

Tuition for Full-Time Study: *Master's:* State residents: $1,099 per credit hour; Nonstate residents: $1,099 per credit hour. *Doctoral:* State residents: per academic year $27,624; Nonstate residents: per academic year $27,624. Tuition is subject to change. Tuition costs vary by program. See the following website for updates and changes in tuition costs: http://view.fdu.edu/default.aspx?id=438. Higher tuition cost for this program: Clinical Psychology: $34200/academic year.

Financial Assistance:

First-Year Students: Research assistantships available for first year. Average amount paid per academic year: $17,100. Average number of hours worked per week: 8.

Advanced Students: Research assistantships available for advanced students. Average amount paid per academic year: $15,100. Average number of hours worked per week: 8.

Additional Information: Of all students currently enrolled full time, 33% benefited from one or more of the listed financial assistance programs. Application and information available online at: http://view.fdu.edu/default.aspx?id=398.

Internships/Practica: Doctoral Degree (PhD Clinical Psychology): For those doctoral students for whom a professional psychology internship was required in this program prior to graduation, (15) students applied for an internship in 2011–2012, with (13) students obtaining an internship. Of those students who obtained an internship, (12) were paid internships. Of those students who obtained an internship, (10) students placed in APA/CPA accredited internships, (3) students placed in internships not APA/CPA accredited, but listed with the Association of Psychology Postdoctoral and Internship Programs (APPIC), (0) students placed in internships conforming to guidelines of the Council of Directors of School Psychology Programs (CDSPP), (0) students placed in internships that were not APA/CPA accredited, APPIC or CDSPP listed. Doctoral Degree (PsyD School Psychology): For those doctoral students for whom a professional psychology internship was required in this program prior to graduation, (14) students applied for an internship in 2011–2012, with (14) students obtaining an internship. Of those students who obtained an internship, (14) were paid internships. Of those students who obtained an internship, (0) students placed in APA/CPA accredited internships, (0) students placed in internships not APA/CPA accredited, but listed with the Association of Psychology Postdoctoral and Internship Programs (APPIC), (0) students placed in internships conforming to guidelines of the Council of Directors of School Psychology Programs (CDSPP), (14) students placed in internships that were not APA/CPA accredited, APPIC or CDSPP listed. Master's Degree (MA/MS Psychopharmacology): An internship experience, such as a final research project or "capstone" experience is required of graduates. Master's Degree (MA/MS School Psychology): An internship experience, such as a final research project or "capstone" experience is required of

graduates. Master's Degree (MA/MS Forensic Psychology): An internship experience, such as a final research project or "capstone" experience is required of graduates. All PhD students are required to complete research and clinical practica during their first three years. Clinical practica may be completed on-campus at the University's Center for Psychological Services. Externships are required for the Forensic and School MA programs. PsyD students must complete a one-year internship.

Housing and Day Care: No on-campus housing is available. No on-campus day care facilities are available.

Employment of Department Graduates:

Master's Degree Graduates: Of those who graduated in the academic year 2011–2012, the following categories and numbers represent the postgraduate activities and employment of master's degree graduates: Enrolled in a postdoctoral residency/fellowship (n/a), employed in independent practice (n/a), total from the above (master's) (0).

Doctoral Degree Graduates: Of those who graduated in the academic year 2011–2012, the following categories and numbers represent the postgraduate activities and employment of doctoral degree graduates: Enrolled in a psychology doctoral program (n/a), total from the above (doctoral) (0).

Additional Information:

Orientation, Objectives, and Emphasis of Department: The orientation of the department is essentially based on the scientist–practitioner model. In terms of theoretical orientations, some faculty are dynamicists, some behaviorists, and some humanists, though there is a sense of eclecticism that pervades those who are practitioners. There is a considerable emphasis on empirical research as the preferred basis for developing a theoretical orientation.

Special Facilities or Resources: The department operates the Center for Psychological Services which provides students in the PhD and PsyD programs opportunities in therapy and assessment with adults, children, families, and couples. The department has research laboratories equipped for experiments with humans as well as with small animals. Equipment includes computer facilities (both micro- and mainframe), a four-channel physiograph, electrophysiological stimulating and recording equipment, operant equipment for programming and recording behavior, two- and four-channel tachistoscopes, various other sensory apparatuses, standard and computer-based EEG recorders, and equipment and supplies for psychopharmacological studies.

Information for Students With Physical Disabilities: See the following website for more information: http://view.fdu.edu/default.aspx?id=8683.

Application Information:

Send to School of Psychology (T-WH1-01), Fairleigh Dickinson University, 1000 River Road, Teaneck, NJ 07666. URL of online application: http://view.fdu.edu/default.aspx?id=1936. Students are admitted in the Fall, application deadline January 15; Spring, application deadline. Application deadline for Fall: January 15 for Clinical Psychology PhD; March 1 for School Psychology PsyD; March 15 for Master's degrees in School and Forensic Psychology. Spring admission is only for applicants to MA program in general/theoretical psychology. *Fee:* $40. Fee is $40 for doctoral programs and $35 for MA programs.

Georgian Court University (2012 data)
Department of Psychology and Graduate Programs in School
   Psychology and Clinical Mental Health Counseling
Arts & Sciences
900 Lakewood Avenue
Lakewood, NJ 08701
Telephone: (732) 987-2636
Fax: (732) 987-2090
E-mail: *field@georgian.edu*
Web: *http://www.georgian.edu/psychology/index.htm*

Department Information:
   1972. Chairperson: Susan E. O. Field. Number of faculty: total—full-time 13, part-time 18; women—full-time 6, part-time 13; faculty subject to the Americans With Disabilities Act 1.

Programs and Degrees Offered:
   Listed in the following order: Program area, degree type (T if terminal Master's), number awarded 7/11–6/12. Clinical Mental Health Counseling MA/MS (Master of Arts/Science) (T) 19, Applied Behavior Analysis MA/MS (Master of Arts/Science) (T) 0, School Psychology MA/MS (Master of Arts/Science) (T) 9.

Student Applications/Admissions:
   Student Applications
   Clinical Mental Health Counseling MA/MS (Master of Arts/Science)—Applications 2012–2013, 45. Total applicants accepted 2012–2013, 21. Number full-time enrolled (new admits only) 2012–2013, 12. Number part-time enrolled (new admits only) 2012–2013, 3. Total enrolled 2012–2013 full-time, 33. Total enrolled 2012–2013 part-time, 24. Openings 2013–2014, 20. The median number of years required for completion of a degree in 2012–2013 were 3. The number of students enrolled full- and part-time who were dismissed or voluntarily withdrew from this program area in 2012–2013 were 2. *Applied Behavior Analysis MA/MS (Master of Arts/Science)*—Applications 2012–2013, 35. Total applicants accepted 2012–2013, 33. Number full-time enrolled (new admits only) 2012–2013, 13. Number part-time enrolled (new admits only) 2012–2013, 20. Total enrolled 2012–2013 full-time, 13. Total enrolled 2012–2013 part-time, 20. Openings 2013–2014, 24. The number of students enrolled full- and part-time who were dismissed or voluntarily withdrew from this program area in 2012–2013 were 2. *School Psychology MA/MS (Master of Arts/Science)*—Applications 2012–2013, 40. Total applicants accepted 2012–2013, 13. Number full-time enrolled (new admits only) 2012–2013, 10. Number part-time enrolled (new admits only) 2012–2013, 1. Total enrolled 2012–2013 full-time, 28. Total enrolled 2012–2013 part-time, 17. Openings 2013–2014, 20. The median number of years required for completion of a degree in 2012–2013 were 4. The number of students enrolled full- and part-time who were dismissed or voluntarily withdrew from this program area in 2012–2013 were 2.

Scores: Entries appear in this order: required test or GPA, minimum score (if required), median score of students entering in 2012–2013. *Clinical Mental Health Counseling MA/MS (Master of Arts/Science):* overall undergraduate GPA 3.0, 3.27; *Applied Behavior Analysis MA/MS (Master of Arts/Science):* overall undergraduate GPA 3.0, 3.56; *School Psychology MA/MS (Master of Arts/Science):* overall undergraduate GPA 3.0, 3.47.
Other Criteria: (importance of criteria rated low, medium, or high): GRE scores—medium, research experience—low, work experience—low, extracurricular activity—low, clinically related public service—low, GPA—high, letters of recommendation—high, interview—high, statement of goals and objectives—medium, MAT or Praxis—medium, undergraduate major in psychology—medium, specific undergraduate psychology courses taken—high, School Psychology requires the MAT. ABA requires either MAT, Praxis, or GRE. Clinical Mental Health Counseling requires MAT or GRE. For additional information on admission requirements, go to http://www.georgian.edu/psychology/index.htm.

Student Characteristics: The following represents characteristics of students in 2012–2013 in all graduate psychology programs in the department: Female—full-time 72, part-time 58; Male—full-time 2, part-time 3; African American/Black—full-time 2, part-time 1; Hispanic/Latino(a)—full-time 3, part-time 2; Asian/Pacific Islander—full-time 1, part-time 1; American Indian/Alaska Native—full-time 0, part-time 0; Caucasian/White—full-time 63, part-time 51; Multi-ethnic—full-time 1, part-time 1; students subject to the Americans With Disabilities Act—full-time 0, part-time 0; Unknown ethnicity—full-time 4, part-time 5; International students who hold an F-1 or J-1 Visa—full-time 0, part-time 0.

Financial Information/Assistance:
Tuition for Full-Time Study: *Master's:* State residents: $745 per credit hour; Nonstate residents: $745 per credit hour. Tuition is subject to change. Additional fees are assessed to students beyond the costs of tuition for the following: Some courses include lab fees and/or assessment protocol fees. See the following website for updates and changes in tuition costs: http://www.georgian.edu/bursar/grad_costs.htm.

Financial Assistance:
   First-Year Students: No information provided.
   Advanced Students: Teaching assistantships available for advanced students. Average amount paid per academic year: $600. Average number of hours worked per week: 9.
   Additional Information: Of all students currently enrolled full time, 15% benefited from one or more of the listed financial assistance programs. Application and information available online at: http://www.georgian.edu/fa/graduates.htm.

Internships/Practica: Master's Degree (MA/MS Clinical Mental Health Counseling): An internship experience, such as a final research project or "capstone" experience is required of graduates. Master's Degree (MA/MS Applied Behavior Analysis): An internship experience, such as a final research project or "capstone" experience is required of graduates. Master's Degree (MA/MS School Psychology): An internship experience, such as a final research project or "capstone" experience is required of graduates. The School Psychology program includes a 300 clock-hour practicum and a 1200-hour, year-long externship in the public schools. The Clinical Mental Health Counseling program includes a 100 clock-hour practicum and a 600-hour, year-long internship with triadic supervision. The Applied Behavior Analysis program includes a 750-hour year-long internship.

Housing and Day Care: No on-campus housing is available. No on-campus day care facilities are available.

Employment of Department Graduates:

Master's Degree Graduates: Of those who graduated in the academic year 2011–2012, the following categories and numbers represent the postgraduate activities and employment of master's degree graduates: Enrolled in another graduate/professional program (19), enrolled in a postdoctoral residency/fellowship (n/a), employed in independent practice (n/a), employed in an academic position at a university (1), employed in a community mental health/counseling center (11), other employment position (10), do not know (8), total from the above (master's) (49).

Doctoral Degree Graduates: Of those who graduated in the academic year 2011–2012, the following categories and numbers represent the postgraduate activities and employment of doctoral degree graduates: Enrolled in a psychology doctoral program (n/a), total from the above (doctoral) (0).

Additional Information:

Orientation, Objectives, and Emphasis of Department: The graduate programs in Clinical Mental Health Counseling, School Psychology, and Applied Behavior Analysis reflect the University's mission and core values of respect, integrity, service, justice, and compassion. We are committed to preparing professionals to address the needs of individuals and their families, emphasizing issues of diversity and social justice. The program philosophy is to promote professional practice by developing competent, socially-conscious professionals capable of providing evidence-based services to individuals and organizations in the community.

Special Facilities or Resources: Our program has observation rooms for counseling practicum and a lab for experimental and group work. Internships and practica are typically served in community-based programs.

Information for Students With Physical Disabilities: See the following website for more information: http://www.georgian.edu/learningcenter/index.htm.

Application Information:

Send to Mr. Patrick Givens, Associate Director of Graduate Admissions, Georgian Court University, 900 Lakewood Avenue, Lakewood, NJ 08701. Application available online. URL of online application: http://www.georgian.edu/admissions/grad.htm. Students are admitted in the Fall, application deadline March 1; Programs have rolling admissions. ABA program has rolling admissions; programs in School Psychology and Clinical Mental Health Counseling admit students only in the fall. *Fee:* $40. Online applications have no application fee, and students who attend a graduate open house pay no application fee.

Kean University

Department of Psychology; Department of Advanced Studies in Psychology
Morris Avenue
Union, NJ 07083
Telephone: (908) 737-5870
Fax: (908) 737-5875
E-mail: *sbousque@kean.edu and fgardner@kean.edu*
Web: *http://www.kean.edu*

Department Information:

1969. Chairperson: Dr. Suzanne Bousquet; Dr. Frank Gardner. Number of faculty: total—full-time 18, part-time 60; women—full-time 13, part-time 40; total—minority—full-time 3, part-time 15; women minority—full-time 3, part-time 10; faculty subject to the Americans With Disabilities Act 1.

Programs and Degrees Offered:

Listed in the following order: Program area, degree type (T if terminal Master's), number awarded 7/11–6/12. Marriage and Family Therapy Diploma Other 7, Human Behavior and Organizational Psychology MA/MS (Master of Arts/Science) (T) 6, Psychological Services MA/MS (Master of Arts/Science) (T) 15, School Psychology Diploma Other 10, Educational Psychology MA/MS (Master of Arts/Science) 23, School and Clinical Psychology PsyD (Doctor of Psychology) 0.

Student Applications/Admissions:

Student Applications

Marriage and Family Therapy Diploma Other—Applications 2012–2013, 24. Total applicants accepted 2012–2013, 19. Number full-time enrolled (new admits only) 2012–2013, 15. Number part-time enrolled (new admits only) 2012–2013, 4. Total enrolled 2012–2013 full-time, 50. Total enrolled 2012–2013 part-time, 19. Openings 2013–2014, 12. The median number of years required for completion of a degree in 2012–2013 were 3. The number of students enrolled full- and part-time who were dismissed or voluntarily withdrew from this program area in 2012–2013 were 0. *Human Behavior and Organizational Psychology MA/MS (Master of Arts/Science)*—Total enrolled 2012–2013 full-time, 4. Total enrolled 2012–2013 part-time, 45. Openings 2013–2014, 20. The median number of years required for completion of a degree in 2012–2013 were 2. The number of students enrolled full- and part-time who were dismissed or voluntarily withdrew from this program area in 2012–2013 were 0. *Psychological Services MA/MS (Master of Arts/Science)*—Applications 2012–2013, 30. Total applicants accepted 2012–2013, 24. Number full-time enrolled (new admits only) 2012–2013, 20. Number part-time enrolled (new admits only) 2012–2013, 4. Total enrolled 2012–2013 full-time, 65. Total enrolled 2012–2013 part-time, 23. Openings 2013–2014, 28. The median number of years required for completion of a degree in 2012–2013 were 3. The number of students enrolled full- and part-time who were dismissed or voluntarily withdrew from this program area in 2012–2013 were 3. *School Psychology Diploma Other*—Number full-time enrolled (new admits only) 2012–2013, 12. Number part-time enrolled (new admits only) 2012–2013, 0. Total enrolled 2012–2013 full-time, 35. Total enrolled 2012–2013 part-time, 0. Openings 2013–2014, 12. The median number of years required for completion of a degree in 2012–2013 were 3. The number of students enrolled full- and part-time who were dismissed or voluntarily withdrew from this program area in 2012–2013 were 1. *Educational Psychology MA/MS (Master of Arts/Science)*—Total enrolled 2012–2013 full-time, 35. Total enrolled 2012–2013 part-time, 0. Openings 2013–2014, 12. The median number of years required for completion of a degree in 2012–2013 were 2. The number of students enrolled full- and part-time who were dismissed or voluntarily withdrew from this program area in 2012–2013 were 2. *School and Clinical Psychology PsyD (Doctor of Psychology)*—Applications 2012–2013, 40. Total applicants accepted 2012–2013, 12. Number full-time enrolled (new admits only) 2012–2013, 10. Number part-time enrolled (new admits only) 2012–2013, 0. Total enrolled 2012–2013 full-time, 40. Total enrolled 2012–2013 part-time, 0. Openings 2013–2014, 12. The number of students enrolled full- and part-time who were dismissed or voluntarily withdrew from this program area in 2012–2013 were 1.

Scores: Entries appear in this order: required test or GPA, minimum score (if required), median score of students entering in 2012–2013. *Marriage and Family Therapy Diploma Other:* GRE-V no minimum stated, GRE-Q no minimum stated, GRE-Analytical no minimum stated; *Human Behavior and Organizational Psychology MA/MS (Master of Arts/Science):* GRE-V no minimum stated, GRE-Q no minimum stated, GRE-Analytical no minimum stated, overall undergraduate GPA 3.0; *Psychological Services MA/MS (Master of Arts/Science):* GRE-V no minimum stated, GRE-Q no minimum stated, GRE-Analytical no minimum stated; *School Psychology Diploma Other:* GRE-V no minimum stated, GRE-Q no minimum stated, GRE-Analytical no minimum stated, overall undergraduate GPA 3.3, last 2 years GPA no minimum stated; *Educational Psychology MA/MS (Master of Arts/Science):* GRE-V 500, GRE-Q 500, GRE-Analytical 3, overall undergraduate GPA 3.3, last 2 years GPA no minimum stated; *School and Clinical Psychology PsyD (Doctor of Psychology):* GRE-V 550, GRE-Q 550, GRE-Analytical no minimum stated, GRE-Subject (Psychology) 550, overall undergraduate GPA 3.30, last 2 years GPA no minimum stated, Masters GPA 3.5.

Other Criteria: (importance of criteria rated low, medium, or high): GRE scores—low, research experience—low, work experience—medium, extracurricular activity—low, clinically related public service—high, GPA—high, letters of recommendation—high, interview—high, statement of goals and objectives—high, undergraduate major in psychology—high, specific undergraduate psychology courses taken—medium. For additional information on admission requirements, go to http://grad.kean.edu/content/application-requirements.

Student Characteristics: The following represents characteristics of students in 2012–2013 in all graduate psychology programs in the department: Female—full-time 101, part-time 27; Male—full-time 57, part-time 20; African American/Black—full-time 8, part-time 17; Hispanic/Latino(a)—full-time 10, part-time 11; Asian/Pacific Islander—full-time 5, part-time 4; American Indian/Alaska Native—full-time 0, part-time 0; Caucasian/White—full-time 84, part-time 65; Multi-ethnic—full-time 0, part-time 0; students subject to the Americans With Disabilities Act—full-time 0, part-time 0; Unknown ethnicity—full-time 0, part-time 5; International students who hold an F-1 or J-1 Visa—full-time 4, part-time 0.

Financial Information/Assistance:
Tuition for Full-Time Study: *Master's:* State residents: per academic year $11,748, $572 per credit hour; Nonstate residents: per academic year $15,922, $701 per credit hour. *Doctoral:* State residents: per academic year $15,466, $596 per credit hour; Nonstate residents: per academic year $19,260, $710 per credit hour. Tuition is subject to change. Additional fees are assessed to students beyond the costs of tuition for the following: Full-Time Clinic Fee/PsyD program is $500.00 per semester. See the following website for updates and changes in tuition costs: http://grad.kean.edu/tuition-and-fees.

Financial Assistance:
First-Year Students: Teaching assistantships available for first year. Average amount paid per academic year: $3,217. Average number of hours worked per week: 15. Apply by June 1.

Advanced Students: Teaching assistantships available for advanced students. Average amount paid per academic year: $3,217. Average number of hours worked per week: 15. Apply by June 1.

Additional Information: Of all students currently enrolled full time, 20% benefited from one or more of the listed financial assistance programs. Application and information available online at: http://grad.kean.edu/financialaid.

Internships/Practica: Doctoral Degree (PsyD School and Clinical Psychology): For those doctoral students for whom a professional psychology internship was required in this program prior to graduation, (9) students applied for an internship in 2011–2012, with (9) students obtaining an internship. Of those students who obtained an internship, (9) were paid internships. Of those students who obtained an internship, (8) students placed in APA/CPA accredited internships, (1) students placed in internships not APA/CPA accredited, but listed with the Association of Psychology Postdoctoral and Internship Programs (APPIC), (0) students placed in internships conforming to guidelines of the Council of Directors of School Psychology Programs (CDSPP), (0) students placed in internships that were not APA/CPA accredited, APPIC or CDSPP listed. Master's Degree (MA/MS Psychological Services): An internship experience, such as a final research project or "capstone" experience is required of graduates. Master's Degree (Other School Psychology Diploma): An internship experience, such as a final research project or "capstone" experience is required of graduates. Master's Degree (MA/MS Educational Psychology): An internship experience, such as a final research project or "capstone" experience is required of graduates. Internships/practica in a variety of settings are available for students in the professional diploma programs in school psychology and marriage and family therapy. Doctoral students obtain externships in both school and clinical settings.

Housing and Day Care: No on-campus housing is available. On-campus day care facilities are available. See the following website for more information: http://www.kean.edu/KU/Child-Care-Center.

Employment of Department Graduates:
Master's Degree Graduates: Of those who graduated in the academic year 2011–2012, the following categories and numbers represent the postgraduate activities and employment of master's degree graduates: Enrolled in a postdoctoral residency/fellowship

(n/a), employed in independent practice (n/a), total from the above (master's) (0).

Doctoral Degree Graduates: Of those who graduated in the academic year 2011–2012, the following categories and numbers represent the postgraduate activities and employment of doctoral degree graduates: Enrolled in a psychology doctoral program (n/a), total from the above (doctoral) (0).

Additional Information:

Orientation, Objectives, and Emphasis of Department: Our academic emphasis is eclectic. All classes are small, which facilitates the opportunity for personal growth.

Special Facilities or Resources: Special resources include computer facilities that are integrated with statistics, measurements, and professional psychology testing courses.

Information for Students With Physical Disabilities: See the following website for more information: http://www.kean.edu/KU/Disability-Services.

Application Information:
Application available online. URL of online application: http://apply.kean.edu/. Students are admitted in the Fall, application deadline January 2; Spring, application deadline November 1. For School Psychology, fall admission only with deadline of March 15. For PsyD, fall admission only with deadline of January 2. All other programs, fall and spring admissions. *Fee:* $75. $150 for international students.

Rider University (2012 data)
School Psychology Program
College of Liberal Arts, Education and Science
2083 Lawrenceville Road
Lawrenceville, NJ 08648
Telephone: (609) 896-5353
E-mail: *sdombrowski@rider.edu*
Web: *http://www.rider.edu/academics/colleges-schools/college-liberal-arts-education-science/school-education/graduate-progra-15*

Department Information:
1979. Program Director: Stefan C. Dombrowski, PhD. Number of faculty: total—full-time 6; women—full-time 3; total—minority—full-time 1; faculty subject to the Americans With Disabilities Act 1.

Programs and Degrees Offered:
Listed in the following order: Program area, degree type (T if terminal Master's), number awarded 7/11–6/12. School Psychology EdS (School Psychology) 7.

Student Applications/Admissions:
Student Applications
School Psychology EdS (School Psychology)—Applications 2012–2013, 42. Total applicants accepted 2012–2013, 16. Number full-time enrolled (new admits only) 2012–2013, 14. Total enrolled 2012–2013 full-time, 14. Openings 2013–2014, 12. The median number of years required for completion of a

degree in 2012–2013 were 3. The number of students enrolled full- and part-time who were dismissed or voluntarily withdrew from this program area in 2012–2013 were 1.

Scores: Entries appear in this order: required test or GPA, minimum score (if required), median score of students entering in 2012–2013. School Psychology EdS (School Psychology): GRE-V 144, 155, GRE-Q 144, 155, GRE-Analytical 3, 4, overall undergraduate GPA 2.75, 3.60, last 2 years GPA 2.75, 3.70.

Other Criteria: (importance of criteria rated low, medium, or high): GRE scores—medium, research experience—medium, work experience—medium, extracurricular activity—medium, GPA—medium, letters of recommendation—medium, interview—medium, statement of goals and objectives—medium.

Student Characteristics: The following represents characteristics of students in 2012–2013 in all graduate psychology programs in the department: Female—full-time 24, part-time 0; Male—full-time 6, part-time 0; African American/Black—full-time 1, part-time 0; Hispanic/Latino(a)—full-time 1, part-time 0; Asian/Pacific Islander—full-time 0, part-time 0; American Indian/Alaska Native—full-time 0, part-time 0; Caucasian/White—full-time 0, part-time 0; Multi-ethnic—full-time 0, part-time 0; students subject to the Americans With Disabilities Act—full-time 1, part-time 0; Unknown ethnicity—full-time 0, part-time 0; International students who hold an F-1 or J-1 Visa—full-time 0, part-time 0.

Financial Information/Assistance:
Tuition for Full-Time Study: *Master's:* State residents: $670 per credit hour; Nonstate residents: $670 per credit hour. Tuition is subject to change. Additional fees are assessed to students beyond the costs of tuition for the following: Technology fee of $35 per course. See the following website for updates and changes in tuition costs: http://www.rider.edu/offices-services/finaid/tuition-fees/graduate-tuition-fees.

Financial Assistance:
First-Year Students: Research assistantships available for first year. Average number of hours worked per week: 20.

Advanced Students: Research assistantships available for advanced students. Fellowships and scholarships available for advanced students. Average amount paid per academic year: $2,000.

Additional Information: Of all students currently enrolled full time, 60% benefited from one or more of the listed financial assistance programs. Application and information available online at: http://www.rider.edu/offices-services/finaid/scholarships-grants/graduate-scholarships.

Internships/Practica: Internship is a culminating experience consisting of 1200 clock hours. The internship occurs on a full-time basis over a period of one year or on a part-time basis over two consecutive years. Interns are expected to perform all of the roles and functions of a professional school psychologist. As the intern progresses in the experience, greater levels of independence in practice are expected. Internship sites are selected in conjunction with program faculty. NASP guidelines mandate that the 1200-hour internship must be completed under the following stipulations so as to assure a comprehensive experience: an intern shall work a minimum of 2.5 days per week over two consecutive years; a minimum of 600 hours must be completed in a school setting. Up to 600 hours may be served in a non-school setting that is related to the practice of school psychology. Internship is a collaboration between the university training program and the field site. Written guidelines for internship placement are submitted to prospective field supervisors. These guidelines stipulate program requirements concerning program, student, and field supervisor responsibilities. The field supervisor must have a minimum of three years of experience as a school psychologist and demonstrate a commitment to providing quality supervision. A letter of agreement including the field supervisor's name will be forwarded from the program to the appropriate site administrators and/or their designees in which adherence to these guidelines are indicated. The acceptance of this written agreement indicates the commitment of the field supervisor to adhere to program requirements. This agreement must be secured prior to the start of the internship. An intern in a school setting is to be provided on an average of at least 2 hours per week of field-based supervision by a certified school psychologist.

Housing and Day Care: On-campus housing is available. See the following website for more information: http://www.rider.edu/housing. No on-campus day care facilities are available.

Employment of Department Graduates:

Master's Degree Graduates: Of those who graduated in the academic year 2011–2012, the following categories and numbers represent the postgraduate activities and employment of master's degree graduates: Enrolled in a postdoctoral residency/fellowship (n/a), employed in independent practice (n/a), employed in a professional position in a school system (11), total from the above (master's) (11).

Doctoral Degree Graduates: Of those who graduated in the academic year 2011–2012, the following categories and numbers represent the postgraduate activities and employment of doctoral degree graduates: Enrolled in a psychology doctoral program (n/a), total from the above (doctoral) (0).

Additional Information:

Orientation, Objectives, and Emphasis of Department: The Rider University School Psychology program is dedicated to educating future school psychologists within a climate of scholarly inquiry and the context of a scientist–practitioner model of service delivery. Rider University's School Psychology program is fully approved by the National Association of School Psychologists (NASP), preparing students to become certified School Psychologists at the state and national level. The 67-credit degree program offers a blend of traditional and contemporary training and innovative practica that result in our graduates being actively recruited by employers. Problem-solving and data-based decision-making permeate all aspects of training with the ultimate goal of fostering the knowledge base, skill set, reflective practice, and professional commitment to improve the educational and mental health of children and adolescents in the schools. The program offers a highly-structured, developmental curriculum that builds upon preceding coursework and experience. Through a variety of theoretical, conceptual, and experiential pedagogical activities, students are prepared to provide a range of evidence-based services including consultation, psychological assessment, behavioral and academic intervention, prevention, counseling, and program planning/evaluation. Students also receive training in sensitively working with clients from diverse cultural and individual backgrounds. Complementing the program's philosophy, the fundamental goals of the program are to provide each graduate with the required skills, professionalism, and knowledge base to become

a productive member of the school psychology community, including: the ability to implement a problem-solving model supported by a solid understanding of the knowledge base and empirical literature of school psychology as well as legal, ethical, and professional standards of practice; the capacity to provide psychological services and educational consultation within diverse contexts where individual differences in ethnicity, socioeconomic status, culture, gender, sexual orientation, and abilities are appreciated; the ability to work collaboratively with educators, administrators, school counselors, families, and the community to provide a comprehensive range of educational and mental health services to children and adolescents; and the capacity to utilize data-based decision making and empirically supported prevention, assessment, and intervention strategies that result in a positive impact on youth, families, and the communities/schools that they serve. Professional knowledge and skills are developed across the ten domains of training and practice established by NASP. The acquisition of knowledge and skills is monitored and evaluated across the program via traditional assessment methods and performance-based outcomes representative of professional practice. Students also compile a portfolio to document and reflect upon their professional growth and to serve as evidence of competency across the domains of training and practice. The program is committed to providing a stimulating learning community that embraces and values the human and cultural diversity of its members and of society. The program is also committed to attracting and retaining students who are members of underrepresented groups. Therefore, individuals from diverse socioeconomic, ethnic, gender and sexual identities are strongly encouraged to apply. Within the program diversity is examined as a subject and is embedded as a topic across coursework. Students are expected to develop the dispositions, knowledge, and skills to work effectively with individuals of diverse needs (e.g., ethnic, cultural, SES, sexual orientation, gender identity, abilities, disabilities).

Information for Students With Physical Disabilities: See the following website for more information: http://www.rider.edu/academics/academic-support-services.

Application Information:
Send to Rider University, Office of Graduate Admission, 2083 Lawrenceville Road, Lawrenceville, NJ, 08648-3099. Application available online. URL of online application: http://www.rider.edu/admissions/graduate-admission/apply-now. Students are admitted in the Fall, application deadline February 1. *Fee:* $50.

Rowan University
Department of Psychology
College of Liberal Arts and Sciences
201 Mullica Hill Road
Glassboro, NJ 08028-1701
Telephone: (856) 256-4500, ext. 3757
Fax: (856) 256-4892
E-mail: *crawfordg@rowan.edu*
Web: *http://www.rowan.edu/colleges/csm/departments/psychology/maCounseling/index.html*

Department Information:
1969. Program Coordinator: Ginean Crawford, MFT, LPC, NCC, ACS. Number of faculty: total—full-time 15, part-time 4;

women—full-time 12, part-time 2; total—minority—full-time 1; women minority—full-time 1.

Programs and Degrees Offered:

Listed in the following order: Program area, degree type (T if terminal Master's), number awarded 7/11–6/12. Clinical Mental Health Counseling MA/MS (Master of Arts/Science) (T) 12, Mental Health Counseling Certificate Other 0.

Student Applications/Admissions:

Student Applications

Clinical Mental Health Counseling MA/MS (Master of Arts/Science)—Applications 2012–2013, 18. Total applicants accepted 2012–2013, 7. Number full-time enrolled (new admits only) 2012–2013, 6. Number part-time enrolled (new admits only) 2012–2013, 0. Total enrolled 2012–2013 full-time, 13. Total enrolled 2012–2013 part-time, 1. Openings 2013–2014, 8. The median number of years required for completion of a degree in 2012–2013 were 2. The number of students enrolled full- and part-time who were dismissed or voluntarily withdrew from this program area in 2012–2013 were 1. Mental Health Counseling Certificate Other—Applications 2012–2013, 5. Total applicants accepted 2012–2013, 5. Number full-time enrolled (new admits only) 2012–2013, 0. Number part-time enrolled (new admits only) 2012–2013, 0. Openings 2013–2014, 5. The median number of years required for completion of a degree in 2012–2013 were 2. The number of students enrolled full- and part-time who were dismissed or voluntarily withdrew from this program area in 2012–2013 were 0.

Scores: Entries appear in this order: required test or GPA, minimum score (if required), median score of students entering in 2012–2013. Clinical Mental Health Counseling MA/MS (Master of Arts/Science): GRE-V no minimum stated, GRE-Q no minimum stated, GRE-Analytical no minimum stated, overall undergraduate GPA 3.0; Mental Health Counseling Certificate Other: GRE-V no minimum stated, GRE-Q no minimum stated, GRE-Analytical no minimum stated, overall undergraduate GPA no minimum stated, last 2 years GPA no minimum stated, psychology GPA no minimum stated.

Other Criteria: (importance of criteria rated low, medium, or high): GRE scores—medium, research experience—medium, work experience—medium, extracurricular activity—low, clinically related public service—high, GPA—high, letters of recommendation—high, interview—high, statement of goals and objectives—high, undergraduate major in psychology—high, specific undergraduate psychology courses taken—medium. For additional information on admission requirements, go to http://www.rowancgce.com/science-math/ma-health-counseling.

Student Characteristics: The following represents characteristics of students in 2012–2013 in all graduate psychology programs in the department: Female—full-time 10, part-time 0; Male—full-time 3, part-time 1; African American/Black—full-time 0, part-time 1; Hispanic/Latino(a)—full-time 0, part-time 0; Asian/Pacific Islander—full-time 0, part-time 0; American Indian/Alaska Native—full-time 0, part-time 0; Caucasian/White—full-time 13, part-time 0; Multi-ethnic—full-time 0, part-time 0; students subject to the Americans With Disabilities Act—full-time 0, part-time 0; Unknown ethnicity—full-time 0, part-time 0; International students who hold an F-1 or J-1 Visa—full-time 0, part-time 0.

Financial Information/Assistance:

Tuition for Full-Time Study: Master's: State residents: $771 per credit hour; Nonstate residents: $771 per credit hour. Tuition is subject to change. See the following website for updates and changes in tuition costs: http://www.rowancgce.com/tuition.

Financial Assistance:

First-Year Students: No information provided.
Advanced Students: No information provided.
Additional Information: Of all students currently enrolled full time, 0% benefited from one or more of the listed financial assistance programs. Application and information available online at: http://www.rowancgce.com/aid.

Internships/Practica: Master's Degree (MA/MS Clinical Mental Health Counseling): An internship experience, such as a final research project or "capstone" experience is required of graduates. Practica are available in a wide range of mental health settings.

Housing and Day Care: On-campus housing is available. See the following website for more information: http://www.rowan.edu/studentaffairs/reslife/. On-campus day care facilities are available. See the following website for more information: http://www.rowan.edu/colleges/education/childcare/.

Employment of Department Graduates:

Master's Degree Graduates: Of those who graduated in the academic year 2011–2012, the following categories and numbers represent the postgraduate activities and employment of master's degree graduates: Enrolled in a postdoctoral residency/fellowship (n/a), employed in independent practice (n/a), employed in an academic position at a university (1), employed in a community mental health/counseling center (4), do not know (11), total from the above (master's) (16).

Doctoral Degree Graduates: Of those who graduated in the academic year 2011–2012, the following categories and numbers represent the postgraduate activities and employment of doctoral degree graduates: Enrolled in a psychology doctoral program (n/a), total from the above (doctoral) (0).

Additional Information:

Orientation, Objectives, and Emphasis of Department: The program is designed to be consistent with an evidence based practice model. This 60 credit Master's program prepares students to become mental health counselors and is designed to meet the coursework and practicum requirements of the National Board of Certified Counselors.

Information for Students With Physical Disabilities: See the following website for more information: http://www.rowan.edu/studentaffairs/asc/disabilityresources/.

Application Information:

Send to Rowan University, CGCE Admissions, James Hall, Room 3129, 201 Mullica Hill Road, Glassboro, NJ 08028-1701. Application available online. URL of online application: http://www.rowancgce.com/admissions/apply. Students are admitted in the Fall, application deadline February 15. The February 15th deadline is a soft deadline. We will continue to accept applications until we have selected a class. Fee: $65.

Rutgers—The State University of New Jersey
Department of Applied Psychology
Graduate School of Applied and Professional Psychology
152 Frelinghuysen Road, Busch Campus, Psychology Building
  Addition
Piscataway, NJ 08854
Telephone: (848) 445-3973
Fax: (732) 445-4888
E-mail: sgforman@rci.rutgers.edu
Web: http://gsappweb.rutgers.edu/programs/school/index.php

Department Information:
1974. Chairperson: Susan G. Forman, PhD. Number of faculty: total—full-time 8, part-time 4; women—full-time 5, part-time 2.

Programs and Degrees Offered:
Listed in the following order: Program area, degree type (T if terminal Master's), number awarded 7/11–6/12. School Psychology PsyD (Doctor of Psychology) 13.

APA Accreditation: School PsyD (Doctor of Psychology). Student Outcome Data Website: http://gsappweb.rutgers.edu/programs/school/.

Student Applications/Admissions:
Student Applications
School Psychology PsyD (Doctor of Psychology)—Applications 2012–2013, 91. Total applicants accepted 2012–2013, 30. Number full-time enrolled (new admits only) 2012–2013, 19. Total enrolled 2012–2013 full-time, 92. Openings 2013–2014, 18. The median number of years required for completion of a degree in 2012–2013 were 4. The number of students enrolled full- and part-time who were dismissed or voluntarily withdrew from this program area in 2012–2013 were 0.
Scores: Entries appear in this order: required test or GPA, minimum score (if required), median score of students entering in 2012–2013. School Psychology PsyD (Doctor of Psychology): GRE-V no minimum stated, 157, GRE-Q no minimum stated, 154, GRE-Analytical no minimum stated, 4.0, GRE-Subject (Psychology) no minimum stated, 660, overall undergraduate GPA no minimum stated, 3.72.
Other Criteria: (importance of criteria rated low, medium, or high): GRE scores—high, research experience—medium, work experience—high, extracurricular activity—medium, clinically related public service—high, GPA—high, letters of recommendation—high, interview—high, statement of goals and objectives—high, undergraduate major in psychology—medium, specific undergraduate psychology courses taken—high. For additional information on admission requirements, go to http://gsappweb.rutgers.edu/pstudents/admissions.php.

Student Characteristics: The following represents characteristics of students in 2012–2013 in all graduate psychology programs in the department: Female—full-time 78, part-time 0; Male—full-time 14, part-time 0; African American/Black—full-time 9, part-time 0; Hispanic/Latino(a)—full-time 5, part-time 0; Asian/Pacific Islander—full-time 4, part-time 0; American Indian/Alaska Native—part-time 0; Caucasian/White—full-time 74, part-time 0; Multi-ethnic—part-time 0; students subject to the Americans With Disabilities Act—full-time 0, part-time 0; Unknown ethnicity—full-time 0, part-time 0; International students who hold an F-1 or J-1 Visa—full-time 1, part-time 0.

Financial Information/Assistance:
Tuition for Full-Time Study: *Doctoral:* State residents: per academic year $18,528, $772 per credit hour; Nonstate residents: per academic year $29,928, $1,247 per credit hour. Tuition is subject to change. Additional fees are assessed to students beyond the costs of tuition for the following: campus fee, computer fee, and school fee.

Financial Assistance:
First-Year Students: Fellowships and scholarships available for first year. Average amount paid per academic year: $12,500.
Advanced Students: Teaching assistantships available for advanced students. Average amount paid per academic year: $23,000. Traineeships available for advanced students. Average amount paid per academic year: $12,000. Fellowships and scholarships available for advanced students. Average amount paid per academic year: $12,500.
Additional Information: Of all students currently enrolled full time, 25% benefited from one or more of the listed financial assistance programs. Application and information available online at: http://gradstudy.rutgers.edu/financial/financial-information.

Internships/Practica: Doctoral Degree (PsyD School Psychology): For those doctoral students for whom a professional psychology internship was required in this program prior to graduation, (16) students applied for an internship in 2011–2012, with (16) students obtaining an internship. Of those students who obtained an internship, (16) were paid internships. Of those students who obtained an internship, (0) students placed in APA/CPA accredited internships, (0) students placed in internships not APA/CPA accredited, but listed with the Association of Psychology Postdoctoral and Internship Programs (APPIC), (16) students placed in internships conforming to guidelines of the Council of Directors of School Psychology Programs (CDSPP), (0) students placed in internships that were not APA/CPA accredited, APPIC or CDSPP listed. A special component of the student's training is the integration of practicum experiences with didactic courses from the second semester of the first year throughout the remaining semesters of training. These experiences begin by introducing the student to the roles and functions of a school psychologist, the functioning of child study teams, and a variety of schooling issues. For three consecutive semesters, students spend a minimum of one day per week in a public school with a doctoral level school psychologist supervisor/mentor. During the fifth and sixth semester, students may elect a different practicum experience from their first based upon their interests. These practica are supervised by on-site doctoral school psychologists and by on-campus faculty. The courses, the practica, and the supervision comprise the planned scaffold for educating students. In addition, there are numerous opportunities for learning and practice through colloquia, symposia, informal discussions, faculty projects, the psychological clinic and the Center for Applied Psychology.

Housing and Day Care: On-campus housing is available. See the following website for more information: http://ruoncampus.rutgers.edu/living-at-rutgers/graduate-students. On-campus day care facilities are available. See the following website for more information: http://uhr.rutgers.edu/worklife-balance/family-programs/child-care-and-development-centers.

Employment of Department Graduates:

Master's Degree Graduates: Of those who graduated in the academic year 2011–2012, the following categories and numbers represent the postgraduate activities and employment of master's degree graduates: Enrolled in a postdoctoral residency/fellowship (n/a), employed in independent practice (n/a), total from the above (master's) (0).

Doctoral Degree Graduates: Of those who graduated in the academic year 2011–2012, the following categories and numbers represent the postgraduate activities and employment of doctoral degree graduates: Enrolled in a psychology doctoral program (n/a), employed in a professional position in a school system (13), total from the above (doctoral) (13).

Additional Information:

Orientation, Objectives, and Emphasis of Department: The department of applied psychology is a unit dedicated (1) to enhancement of mental health and learning of children, adolescents, and adults in schools and related educational settings, and (2) to development of organizations that allow schooling to occur in effective and efficient ways. Three interrelated dimensions serve to structure the department. An applied research dimension signifies the important weight placed on generating new knowledge; an education and training dimension reflects concern for development of high-level practitioners and leaders of school psychology; an organizational and community services dimension is targeted at providing schools and related educational settings with consultation and technical assistance in areas of instruction and learning. A continuum of instruction ranges from observation and assessment through intervention models that include supervised experience as an essential component of didactic instruction. Core faculty are augmented by senior psychologists whose major professional involvement is in the schools or organizational and community settings.

Special Facilities or Resources: There are two special facilities that are an integrated part of the training program. One is an on-site psychological clinic which serves the university and state communities. Assessment and intervention programs are offered. The other is the Center for Applied Psychology, a division of GSAPP that develops, implements, and evaluates projects involving faculty, students and others from the community. Included in these projects are the Eating Disorders Clinic, Foster Care Counseling, and a home-based intervention program for developmentally disabled individuals.

Information for Students With Physical Disabilities: See the following website for more information: http://disabilityservices.rutgers.edu/.

Application Information:
Send to Rutgers, The State University of New Jersey, Office of Graduate Admissions, 18 Bishop Place, New Brunswick, NJ 08901. Application available online. URL of online application: http://gradstudy.rutgers.edu/apply/overview. Students are admitted in the Fall, application deadline January 9. *Fee:* $65.

Rutgers—The State University of New Jersey
Department of Clinical Psychology
Graduate School of Applied and Professional Psychology
152 Frelinghuysen Road
Piscataway, NJ 08854
Telephone: (848) 445-3980
Fax: (732) 445-4888
E-mail: *bbry@rci.rutgers.edu*
Web: *http://gsappweb.rutgers.edu/programs/clinical/index.php*

Department Information:
1974. Chairperson: Brenna H. Bry. Number of faculty: total—full-time 18, part-time 9; women—full-time 10, part-time 6; total—minority—full-time 4; women minority—full-time 3; faculty subject to the Americans With Disabilities Act 1.

Programs and Degrees Offered:
Listed in the following order: Program area, degree type (T if terminal Master's), number awarded 7/11–6/12. Clinical Psychology PsyD (Doctor of Psychology) 16.

APA Accreditation: Clinical PsyD (Doctor of Psychology). Student Outcome Data Website: http://gsappweb.rutgers.edu/programs/clinical/index.php.

Student Applications/Admissions:
Student Applications

Clinical Psychology PsyD (Doctor of Psychology)—Applications 2012–2013, 472. Total applicants accepted 2012–2013, 28. Number full-time enrolled (new admits only) 2012–2013, 17. Number part-time enrolled (new admits only) 2012–2013, 0. Total enrolled 2012–2013 full-time, 111. Total enrolled 2012–2013 part-time, 0. Openings 2013–2014, 18. The median number of years required for completion of a degree in 2012–2013 were 6. The number of students enrolled full- and part-time who were dismissed or voluntarily withdrew from this program area in 2012–2013 were 0.

Scores: Entries appear in this order: required test or GPA, minimum score (if required), median score of students entering in 2012–2013. *Clinical Psychology PsyD (Doctor of Psychology):* GRE-V no minimum stated, 161, GRE-Q no minimum stated, 155, GRE-Analytical no minimum stated, GRE-Subject (Psychology) no minimum stated, 710, overall undergraduate GPA no minimum stated, 3.80.

Other Criteria: (importance of criteria rated low, medium, or high): GRE scores—medium, research experience—medium, work experience—high, extracurricular activity—high, clinically related public service—high, GPA—high, letters of recommendation—high, interview—high, statement of goals and objectives—high, undergraduate major in psychology—medium, specific undergraduate psychology courses taken—medium. For additional information on admission requirements, go to http://gsappweb.rutgers.edu/pstudents/admissions.php.

Student Characteristics: The following represents characteristics of students in 2012–2013 in all graduate psychology programs in the department: Female—full-time 70, part-time 0; Male—full-time 41, part-time 0; African American/Black—full-time 12, part-time 0; Hispanic/Latino(a)—full-time 15, part-time 0; Asian/Pacific Islander—full-time 12, part-time 0; American Indian/Alaska

Native—full-time 0, part-time 0; Caucasian/White—full-time 66, part-time 0; Multi-ethnic—part-time 0; students subject to the Americans With Disabilities Act—full-time 0, part-time 0; Unknown ethnicity—full-time 6, part-time 0; International students who hold an F-1 or J-1 Visa—full-time 4, part-time 0.

Financial Information/Assistance:

Tuition for Full-Time Study: *Doctoral:* State residents: per academic year $18,526, $772 per credit hour; Nonstate residents: per academic year $29,948, $1,247 per credit hour. Tuition is subject to change. Additional fees are assessed to students beyond the costs of tuition for the following: college fees and computer fees. See the following website for updates and changes in tuition costs: http://www.studentabc.rutgers.edu/tuition-and-fees.

Financial Assistance:

First-Year Students: Fellowships and scholarships available for first year. Average amount paid per academic year: $17,000.

Advanced Students: Teaching assistantships available for advanced students. Average amount paid per academic year: $25,969. Research assistantships available for advanced students. Average amount paid per academic year: $17,000. Traineeships available for advanced students. Average amount paid per academic year: $25,969. Fellowships and scholarships available for advanced students. Average amount paid per academic year: $15,000.

Additional Information: Of all students currently enrolled full time, 30% benefited from one or more of the listed financial assistance programs.

Internships/Practica: Doctoral Degree (PsyD Clinical Psychology): For those doctoral students for whom a professional psychology internship was required in this program prior to graduation, (13) students applied for an internship in 2011–2012, with (12) students obtaining an internship. Of those students who obtained an internship, (12) were paid internships. Of those students who obtained an internship, (10) students placed in APA/CPA accredited internships, (2) students placed in internships not APA/CPA accredited, but listed with the Association of Psychology Postdoctoral and Internship Programs (APPIC), (0) students placed in internships conforming to guidelines of the Council of Directors of School Psychology Programs (CDSPP), (0) students placed in internships that were not APA/CPA accredited, APPIC or CDSPP listed. The PsyD program provides a broadly based practicum program which is structured around the needs and interests of our students. Students can choose placements in hospitals which include a hospice program, neuropsych testing, and long and short term inpatient treatment programs for both adolescents and adults. They can choose to be placed in university-based specialty clinics, traditional community mental health centers, college counseling centers, and specialized schools for children (autism, learning disabled, emotionally disturbed). Students can be placed in public school based mental health clinics or in programs which provide service to at-risk youth, those with serious mental illness, and those with addictive disorders. Our programs are selected for their attention to supervision but also for their balance regarding gender, race and socio-economic levels.

Housing and Day Care: On-campus housing is available. See the following website for more information: http://ruoncampus.rutgers.edu/living-at-rutgers/graduate-students. On-campus day care facilities are available. See the following website for more information: http://uhr.rutgers.edu/worklife-balance/family-programs/child-care-and-development-centers.

Employment of Department Graduates:

Master's Degree Graduates: Of those who graduated in the academic year 2011–2012, the following categories and numbers represent the postgraduate activities and employment of master's degree graduates: Enrolled in a postdoctoral residency/fellowship (n/a), employed in independent practice (n/a), total from the above (master's) (0).

Doctoral Degree Graduates: Of those who graduated in the academic year 2011–2012, the following categories and numbers represent the postgraduate activities and employment of doctoral degree graduates: Enrolled in a psychology doctoral program (n/a), enrolled in a postdoctoral residency/fellowship (3), employed in independent practice (4), employed in an academic position at a university (2), employed in other positions at a higher education institution (1), employed in a community mental health/counseling center (4), employed in a hospital/medical center (6), total from the above (doctoral) (20).

Additional Information:

Orientation, Objectives, and Emphasis of Department: The PsyD program emphasizes pragmatic training in problem solving and planned change techniques. Didactic training in basic psychological principles is coupled with practical, graduate instruction in a range of assessment and intervention modes. The level of involvement becomes progressively more intense during the student's course of training. Most courses include (1) a seminar component oriented around case discussions and substantive theoretical issues of clinical import, (2) a practicum component during which students see clients in the intervention mode or problem area under study, and (3) a supervision component by which the student receives guidance from an experienced clinical instructor in a wide range of applied clinical settings. All three components are coordinated around a central conceptual issue, such as a mode of intervention or a clinical problem area. Instruction and supervision are offered by full-time faculty and senior psychologists whose primary professional involvement is in applied clinical settings throughout the state. In addition to required general core courses, students may emphasize training within any of three perspectives: psychodynamic, behavioral, or systems approaches. This last perspective focuses on family, organizational and community services.

Special Facilities or Resources: The Center for Applied Psychology at GSAPP is the focal point for the field experiences that are critical in the development of professional psychologists. The projects overseen by the Center are cornerstones of training for our students; the GSAPP Psychological Clinic, the Foster Care Counseling project, the Natural Setting Therapeutic Management program, the Anxiety Disorders Clinic, and our extensive network of practicum placements are all available to our students. Students are placed in community-based organizations where the recipients of the services we provide are often underserved. These placements include community mental health centers, hospitals, special schools, and other programs. All students are placed in a practicum setting for at least one full day per week during their years at GSAPP. All students see clients through our Clinic and receive one hour of individual supervision for each hour of therapy. The Clinic has specialty sub-clinics which will allow students to gain experience and supervision in specific treatment approaches working with faculty experts.

Information for Students With Physical Disabilities: See the following website for more information: http://disabilityservices.rutgers.edu/.

Application Information:
Send to Graduate and Professional Admissions, Rutgers, The State University of New Jersey, 18 Bishop Place, New Brunswick, NJ 08901-8530. Application available online. URL of online application: http://gradstudy.rutgers.edu/apply/overview. Students are admitted in the Fall, application deadline January 5. *Fee:* $75. Project 1000 - Fee waived.

Seton Hall University (2012 data)
Professional Psychology and Family Therapy
Education and Human Services
400 South Orange Avenue
South Orange, NJ 07079
Telephone: (973) 761-9451
Fax: (973) 275-2188
E-mail: *Laura.Palmer@shu.edu*
Web: *http://www.shu.edu/academics/education/professional-psychology/*

Department Information:
1965. Chairperson: Laura Palmer, PhD, ABPP. Number of faculty: total—full-time 12, part-time 1; women—full-time 7; total—minority—full-time 1; women minority—full-time 1.

Programs and Degrees Offered:
Listed in the following order: Program area, degree type (T if terminal Master's), number awarded 7/11–6/12. Counseling Psychology PhD (Doctor of Philosophy) 6, Counseling/Professional Counseling Ma/Eds MA/MS (Master of Arts/Science) (T) 17, Marriage and Family Therapy Eds Other 2, School and Community Psychology EdS (School Psychology) 7, Counseling/Professional Counseling (Online) MA/MS (Master of Arts/Science) (T) 27, Psychological Studies MA/MS (Master of Arts/Science) (T) 14, School Counseling (Online) MA/MS (Master of Arts/Science) (T) 32, School Counseling MA/MS (Master of Arts/Science) (T) 0, Counseling/Professional Counseling Eds (Online) Other 8, Marriage and Family Therapy MA/MS (Master of Arts/Science) (T) 5.

APA Accreditation: Counseling PhD (Doctor of Philosophy). Student Outcome Data Website: http://www.shu.edu/academics/education/phd-counseling-pscyhology/.

Student Applications/Admissions:
Student Applications
Counseling Psychology PhD (Doctor of Philosophy)—Applications 2012–2013, 130. Total applicants accepted 2012–2013, 8. Number full-time enrolled (new admits only) 2012–2013, 5. Number part-time enrolled (new admits only) 2012–2013, 0. Total enrolled 2012–2013 full-time, 29. Total enrolled 2012–2013 part-time, 0. Openings 2013–2014, 7. The median number of years required for completion of a degree in 2012–2013 were 5. The number of students enrolled full- and part-time who were dismissed or voluntarily withdrew from this program area in 2012–2013 were 0. *Counseling/Professional Counseling*

Ma/Eds MA/MS (Master of Arts/Science)—Applications 2012–2013, 60. Total applicants accepted 2012–2013, 12. Number full-time enrolled (new admits only) 2012–2013, 12. Number part-time enrolled (new admits only) 2012–2013, 0. Total enrolled 2012–2013 full-time, 33. Total enrolled 2012–2013 part-time, 0. Openings 2013–2014, 20. The median number of years required for completion of a degree in 2012–2013 were 4. The number of students enrolled full- and part-time who were dismissed or voluntarily withdrew from this program area in 2012–2013 were 1. *Marriage and Family Therapy Eds Other*—Total applicants accepted 2012–2013, 2. Number full-time enrolled (new admits only) 2012–2013, 2. Total enrolled 2012–2013 full-time, 6. Openings 2013–2014, 10. The number of students enrolled full- and part-time who were dismissed or voluntarily withdrew from this program area in 2012–2013 were 0. *School and Community Psychology EdS (School Psychology)*—Applications 2012–2013, 15. Total applicants accepted 2012–2013, 10. Number full-time enrolled (new admits only) 2012–2013, 10. Number part-time enrolled (new admits only) 2012–2013, 0. Total enrolled 2012–2013 full-time, 53. Total enrolled 2012–2013 part-time, 0. Openings 2013–2014, 10. The median number of years required for completion of a degree in 2012–2013 were 2. The number of students enrolled full- and part-time who were dismissed or voluntarily withdrew from this program area in 2012–2013 were 2. *Counseling/Professional Counseling (Online) MA/MS (Master of Arts/Science)*—Applications 2012–2013, 68. Total applicants accepted 2012–2013, 52. Number full-time enrolled (new admits only) 2012–2013, 27. Total enrolled 2012–2013 full-time, 117. Openings 2013–2014, 30. The median number of years required for completion of a degree in 2012–2013 were 2. The number of students enrolled full- and part-time who were dismissed or voluntarily withdrew from this program area in 2012–2013 were 3. *Psychological Studies MA/MS (Master of Arts/Science)*—Applications 2012–2013, 18. Total applicants accepted 2012–2013, 18. Number full-time enrolled (new admits only) 2012–2013, 10. Number part-time enrolled (new admits only) 2012–2013, 5. Total enrolled 2012–2013 full-time, 20. Total enrolled 2012–2013 part-time, 15. Openings 2013–2014, 15. The median number of years required for completion of a degree in 2012–2013 were 2. The number of students enrolled full- and part-time who were dismissed or voluntarily withdrew from this program area in 2012–2013 were 0. *School Counseling (Online) MA/MS (Master of Arts/Science)*—Applications 2012–2013, 70. Total applicants accepted 2012–2013, 59. Number full-time enrolled (new admits only) 2012–2013, 38. Total enrolled 2012–2013 full-time, 126. Openings 2013–2014, 30. The median number of years required for completion of a degree in 2012–2013 were 2. The number of students enrolled full- and part-time who were dismissed or voluntarily withdrew from this program area in 2012–2013 were 4. *School Counseling MA/MS (Master of Arts/Science)*—Applications 2012–2013, 8. Total applicants accepted 2012–2013, 6. Number full-time enrolled (new admits only) 2012–2013, 5. Number part-time enrolled (new admits only) 2012–2013, 1. Total enrolled 2012–2013 full-time, 10. Total enrolled 2012–2013 part-time, 1. Openings 2013–2014, 10. The number of students enrolled full- and part-time who were dismissed or voluntarily withdrew from this program area in 2012–2013 were 1. *Counseling/Professional Counseling Eds (Online) Other*—Applications 2012–2013, 8. Total applicants accepted 2012–2013, 8. Number full-time enrolled (new admits only) 2012–2013, 5. Total enrolled 2012–2013 full-time, 5. Openings 2013–2014, 24. The median number of years required for completion of a degree in 2012–2013 was 1. The number of students enrolled full- and part-time who were dismissed or voluntarily withdrew from this program area in 2012–2013 were 0. *Marriage and Family Therapy MA/MS (Master of Arts/Science)*—Total applicants accepted 2012–2013, 36. Number full-time enrolled (new admits only) 2012–2013, 36. Total enrolled 2012–2013 full-time, 31. Openings 2013–2014, 35. The number of students enrolled full- and part-time who were dismissed or voluntarily withdrew from this program area in 2012–2013 were 0.

Scores: Entries appear in this order: required test or GPA, minimum score (if required), median score of students entering in 2012–2013. *Counseling Psychology PhD (Doctor of Philosophy):* GRE-V 500, 490, GRE-Q 500, 570, overall undergraduate GPA 3.00, 3.60, Masters GPA 3.5, 3.76; *Counseling/Professional Counseling MA/EdS MA/MS (Master of Arts/Science):* GRE-V no minimum stated, GRE-Q no minimum stated, GRE-Analytical no minimum stated, overall undergraduate GPA no minimum stated, last 2 years GPA no minimum stated; *Marriage and Family Therapy EdS Other:* GRE-V no minimum stated, GRE-Q no minimum stated, GRE-Analytical no minimum stated, overall undergraduate GPA no minimum stated; *School and Community Psychology EdS (School Psychology):* GRE-V 450, GRE-Q 450, overall undergraduate GPA 3; *Counseling/Professional Counseling (Online) MA/MS (Master of Arts/Science):* GRE-V no minimum stated, GRE-Q no minimum stated, GRE-Analytical no minimum stated, overall undergraduate GPA 2.75, 3.24, last 2 years GPA 2.83, 3.66; *Psychological Studies MA/MS (Master of Arts/Science):* GRE-V no minimum stated, GRE-Q no minimum stated, GRE-Analytical no minimum stated, overall undergraduate GPA no minimum stated, last 2 years GPA no minimum stated; *School Counseling (Online) MA/MS (Master of Arts/Science):* GRE-V no minimum stated, GRE-Q no minimum stated, GRE-Analytical no minimum stated, overall undergraduate GPA 2.42, 3.75, last 2 years GPA 3.83, 3.75; *School Counseling MA/MS (Master of Arts/Science):* GRE-V no minimum stated, GRE-Q no minimum stated, GRE-Analytical no minimum stated, overall undergraduate GPA no minimum stated, last 2 years GPA no minimum stated; *Counseling/Professional Counseling EdS (Online) Other:* GRE-V no minimum stated, GRE-Q no minimum stated, GRE-Analytical no minimum stated, overall undergraduate GPA no minimum stated, last 2 years GPA 3.25, 3.92; *Marriage and Family Therapy MA/MS (Master of Arts/Science):* GRE-V no minimum stated, GRE-Q no minimum stated, GRE-Analytical no minimum stated.

Other Criteria: (importance of criteria rated low, medium, or high): GRE scores—high, research experience—high, work experience—medium, extracurricular activity—medium, clinically related public service—medium, GPA—high, letters of recommendation—high, interview—high, statement of goals and objectives—high, undergraduate major in psychology—medium, specific undergraduate psychology courses taken—low. For additional information on admission requirements, go to http://www.shu.edu/academics/education/graduate-programs.cfm.

Student Characteristics: The following represents characteristics of students in 2012–2013 in all graduate psychology programs in the department: Female—full-time 19, part-time 0; Male—full-time 10, part-time 0; African American/Black—full-time 4, part-time 0; Hispanic/Latino(a)—full-time 2, part-time 0; Asian/Pacific Islander—full-time 2, part-time 0; American Indian/Alaska Native—full-time 0, part-time 0; Caucasian/White—full-time 19, part-time 0; Multi-ethnic—full-time 2, part-time 0; students subject to the Americans With Disabilities Act—full-time 2, part-time 0; Unknown ethnicity—full-time 0, part-time 0; International students who hold an F-1 or J-1 Visa—full-time 0, part-time 0.

Financial Information/Assistance:

Tuition for Full-Time Study: *Master's:* State residents: $1,033 per credit hour; Nonstate residents: $1,033 per credit hour. *Doctoral:* State residents: $1,033 per credit hour; Nonstate residents: $1,033 per credit hour. Tuition is subject to change. Tuition costs vary by program. See the following website for updates and changes in tuition costs: http://www.shu.edu/applying/graduate/tuition-costs.cfm.

Financial Assistance:

First-Year Students: Research assistantships available for first year. Average amount paid per academic year: $4,500. Average number of hours worked per week: 20.

Advanced Students: Research assistantships available for advanced students. Average amount paid per academic year: $4,500. Average number of hours worked per week: 20. Fellowships and scholarships available for advanced students. Average amount paid per academic year: $5,000. Average number of hours worked per week: 8. Apply by June 1.

Additional Information: Of all students currently enrolled full time, 75% benefited from one or more of the listed financial assistance programs. Application and information available online at: http://www.shu.edu/applying/graduate/grad-finaid.cfm.

Internships/Practica: Doctoral Degree (PhD Counseling Psychology): For those doctoral students for whom a professional psychology internship was required in this program prior to graduation, (5) students applied for an internship in 2011–2012, with (5) students obtaining an internship. Of those students who obtained an internship, (5) were paid internships. Of those students who obtained an internship, (5) students placed in APA/CPA accredited internships, (0) students placed in internships not APA/CPA accredited, but listed with the Association of Psychology Postdoctoral and Internship Programs (APPIC), (0) students placed in internships conforming to guidelines of the Council of Directors of School Psychology Programs (CDSPP), (0) students placed in internships that were not APA/CPA accredited, APPIC or CDSPP listed. Master's Degree (MA/MS Counseling/Professional Counseling MA/EdS): An internship experience, such as a final research project or "capstone" experience is required of graduates. Master's Degree (MA/MS Counseling/Professional Counseling (Online)): An internship experience, such as a final research project or "capstone" experience is required of graduates. Master's Degree (MA/MS School Counseling (Online)): An internship experience, such as a final research project or "capstone" experience is required of graduates. Master's Degree (MA/MS School Counseling): An internship experience, such as a final research project or "capstone" experience is required of graduates. Master's Degree (MA/MS Marriage and Family Therapy): An internship experience, such as a final research project or "capstone" experience is required of graduates. The Marriage and Family students follow the standards of the Commission on Accreditation for Marriage and Family Therapy Education. The doctoral students adhere to Psychology guidelines. The students in all MA and EdS programs (except psychological studies) complete an internship/practicum sequence consistent with their professional training models.

Housing and Day Care: No on-campus housing is available. No on-campus day care facilities are available.

Employment of Department Graduates:
Master's Degree Graduates: Of those who graduated in the academic year 2011–2012, the following categories and numbers represent the postgraduate activities and employment of master's degree graduates: Enrolled in a psychology doctoral program (0), enrolled in another graduate/professional program (0), enrolled in a postdoctoral residency/fellowship (n/a), employed in independent practice (n/a), employed in an academic position at a university (0), employed in an academic position at a 2-year/4-year college (0), employed in other positions at a higher education institution (0), employed in a professional position in a school system (0), employed in business or industry (0), employed in government agency (0), employed in a community mental health/counseling center (0), employed in a hospital/medical center (0), still seeking employment (0), other employment position (0), total from the above (master's) (0).
Doctoral Degree Graduates: Of those who graduated in the academic year 2011–2012, the following categories and numbers represent the postgraduate activities and employment of doctoral degree graduates: Enrolled in a psychology doctoral program (n/a), enrolled in a postdoctoral residency/fellowship (1), employed in an academic position at a university (2), employed in an academic position at a 2-year/4-year college (0), employed in other positions at a higher education institution (1), employed in a professional position in a school system (0), employed in business or industry (0), employed in government agency (0), employed in a community mental health/counseling center (1), employed in a hospital/medical center (1), still seeking employment (0), other employment position (0), do not know (1), total from the above (doctoral) (7).

Additional Information:
Orientation, Objectives, and Emphasis of Department: The Marriage and Family program is based on a systemic orientation to family psychology and family therapy. The goals of Counseling Psychology encompass knowledge of the science of psychology and counseling psychology as a specialty, integration of research and practice, and commitment to ongoing professional development. Professional counselors are mental health practitioners trained to help individual clients and groups address common developmental challenges and transitions as well as more severe emotional difficulties. School psychology students learn to specialize in assessment and evaluations in schools. Programs listed as MA/EdS are combined programs in which students are afforded the opportunity to continue their studies without applying for the advanced degree.

Special Facilities or Resources: The department has individual counseling/assessment rooms, family and couple laboratories, and group therapy rooms, all of which are wired with audiovisual equipment with centralized viewing in a control room. There are rooms for data analysis as well. Seton Hall University has a beautiful campus located in twenty five miles west of New York City. Students attending on-campus programs have access to a broad range of clinical training sites, including but not limited to community based public and private schools, community mental health centers, large university teaching hospitals, college and university counseling centers, alcohol and drug rehabilitation centers, assisted living programs, therapeutic nurseries, prisons, programs serving military personnel and their families, and programs that provide couples and family therapy - to name a few. Additionally, students in the Counseling Psychology doctoral program benefit from two annual international training experiences, which take place in Trinidad and Tobago.

Information for Students With Physical Disabilities: See the following website for more information: http://www.shu.edu/offices/disability-support-services-index.cfm.

Application Information:
Send to Graduate Admissions College of Education and Human Services, Seton Hall University, 400 South Orange Avenue, South Orange, NJ 07079. Application available online. Students are admitted in the Spring, application deadline October 1, November 1; Fall, application deadline January 15. Counseling Psychology PhD (January 15), Counseling/ School Counseling MA/EdS (Spring: November 1 and Fall: June 1); School and Community Psychology EdS (Spring: October 1 and Fall: February 1), and all other programs rolling admissions. *Fee:* $50.

Seton Hall University (2012 data)
Psychology/Experimental Psychology
Arts and Sciences
400 South Orange Avenue
South Orange, NJ 07079
Telephone: (973) 761-9484
Fax: (973) 275-5829
E-mail: *psych@shu.edu*
Web: *http://www.shu.edu/academics/artsci/ms-psychology/index.cfm*

Department Information:
1952. Chairperson: Susan A. Nolan, PhD. Number of faculty: total—full-time 12, part-time 6; women—full-time 7, part-time 3; minority—part-time 1; women minority—part-time 1; faculty subject to the Americans With Disabilities Act 1.

Programs and Degrees Offered:
Listed in the following order: Program area, degree type (T if terminal Master's), number awarded 7/11–6/12. Experimental Psychology (Thesis Track) MA/MS (Master of Arts/Science) (T) 4, Experimental Psychology (Non-Thesis Track) MA/MS (Master of Arts/Science) (T) 0.

Student Applications/Admissions:
Student Applications
Experimental Psychology (Thesis Track) MA/MS (Master of Arts/Science)—Applications 2012–2013, 20. Total applicants accepted 2012–2013, 13. Number full-time enrolled (new admits only) 2012–2013, 9. Total enrolled 2012–2013 full-time, 22. Openings 2013–2014, 12. The median number of years required for completion of a degree in 2012–2013 were 2. *Experimental Psychology (Non-Thesis Track) MA/MS (Master of Arts/*

Science)—Applications 2012–2013, 3. Total applicants accepted 2012–2013, 3. Number full-time enrolled (new admits only) 2012–2013, 3. Total enrolled 2012–2013 full-time, 3. Openings 2013–2014, 5. The median number of years required for completion of a degree in 2012–2013 were 2. The number of students enrolled full- and part-time who were dismissed or voluntarily withdrew from this program area in 2012–2013 were 0.

Scores: Entries appear in this order: required test or GPA, minimum score (if required), median score of students entering in 2012–2013. *Experimental Psychology (Thesis Track) MA/MS (Master of Arts/Science):* GRE-V no minimum stated, GRE-Q no minimum stated, GRE-Analytical no minimum stated, overall undergraduate GPA 3.0; *Experimental Psychology (Non-thesis Track) MA/MS (Master of Arts/Science):* GRE-V no minimum stated, GRE-Q no minimum stated, GRE-Analytical no minimum stated, overall undergraduate GPA 3.0.

Other Criteria: (importance of criteria rated low, medium, or high): GRE scores—medium, research experience—high, work experience—low, extracurricular activity—medium, GPA—high, letters of recommendation—high, statement of goals and objectives—high, undergraduate major in psychology—low, specific undergraduate psychology courses taken—high, Please indicate Thesis or Non-Thesis track in materials and statements. If applying for a concentration in Behavioral Neuroscience track, demonstration of physiological, cognitive, learning types of courses is preferred. For additional information on admission requirements, go to http://www.shu.edu/academics/artsci/ms-psychology/index.cfm.

Student Characteristics: The following represents characteristics of students in 2012–2013 in all graduate psychology programs in the department: Female—full-time 16, part-time 0; Male—full-time 6, part-time 0; African American/Black—full-time 1, part-time 0; Hispanic/Latino(a)—part-time 0; Asian/Pacific Islander—full-time 2, part-time 0; American Indian/Alaska Native—full-time 0, part-time 0; Caucasian/White—full-time 18, part-time 0; Multi-ethnic—full-time 1, part-time 0; students subject to the Americans With Disabilities Act—full-time 1, part-time 0; Unknown ethnicity—full-time 0, part-time 0; International students who hold an F-1 or J-1 Visa—full-time 1, part-time 0.

Financial Information/Assistance:

Tuition for Full-Time Study: *Master's:* State residents: $1,033 per credit hour; . Tuition is subject to change. Additional fees are assessed to students beyond the costs of tuition for the following: University and Technology Fees, $305 per semester. See the following website for updates and changes in tuition costs: http://www.shu.edu/offices/bursar-tuition-and-fees.cfm#gradtuition.

Financial Assistance:

First-Year Students: Teaching assistantships available for first year. Average amount paid per academic year: $8,500. Average number of hours worked per week: 20. Research assistantships available for first year. Average amount paid per academic year: $5,200. Average number of hours worked per week: 20.

Advanced Students: Teaching assistantships available for advanced students. Average amount paid per academic year: $8,500. Average number of hours worked per week: 20. Research assistantships available for advanced students. Average amount paid per academic year: $5,200. Average number of hours worked per week: 20.

Additional Information: Of all students currently enrolled full time, 75% benefited from one or more of the listed financial assistance programs.

Internships/Practica: Master's Degree (MA/MS Experimental Psychology (Thesis Track)): An internship experience, such as a final research project or "capstone" experience is required of graduates. Master's Degree (MA/MS Experimental Psychology (Non-thesis Track)): An internship experience, such as a final research project or "capstone" experience is required of graduates.

Housing and Day Care: No on-campus housing is available. No on-campus day care facilities are available.

Employment of Department Graduates:

Master's Degree Graduates: Of those who graduated in the academic year 2011–2012, the following categories and numbers represent the postgraduate activities and employment of master's degree graduates: Enrolled in a psychology doctoral program (4), enrolled in a postdoctoral residency/fellowship (n/a), employed in independent practice (n/a), total from the above (master's) (4).

Doctoral Degree Graduates: Of those who graduated in the academic year 2011–2012, the following categories and numbers represent the postgraduate activities and employment of doctoral degree graduates: Enrolled in a psychology doctoral program (n/a), total from the above (doctoral) (0).

Additional Information:

Orientation, Objectives, and Emphasis of Department: The Department of Psychology offers the Master of Science (M.S.) in Experimental Psychology (with an optional concentration in Behavioral Neuroscience). The program is designed to train students in the scientific methods of psychology in preparation for involvement in basic research and teaching, as well as for work in applied settings (e.g. clinical psychology or industrial/organizational psychology). The M.S. degree program is designed specifically for students seeking to gain a solid foundation in empirical research for eventual entry into PhD programs in scientific psychology or for students desiring to explore the field. Students completing this program will be in a better position to apply for admission to doctoral programs in the field, including experimental psychology and neuroscience as well as doctoral degrees in scientist/practitioner programs in clinical or counseling psychology. Graduates may also go on to related areas of employment such as laboratory assistants, market researchers, science writers and community college instructors. The Experimental Psychology graduate program consists of 36 credits, typically completed in two years of full-time study (9 credits per semester). The courses include traditional areas of psychological science with an optional concentration in Behavioral Neuroscience (BNS). The Behavioral Neuroscience concentration represents courses that are most directly relevant to behavioral studies of brain functioning. The MS program offers two separate tracks for admission: a Thesis-track, in which students design, execute and defend before a committee an experimental research study, or a Non-thesis track, in which students complete a scientific literature review instead of conducting an original research experiment. In both tracks, students are paired with faculty members to gain immersive experience in laboratory research.

Special Facilities or Resources: A suite of nine 8' X 8' cubicles are available for graduate student use. An Animal Conditioning

Laboratory consists of eight test cubicles, each equipped with an operant chamber interfaced to an IBM Desktop computer. A five room Physiological Psychology Suite of approximately 400 square feet is used for surgical preparations, histology, and behavioral testing of rodents. Several mazes are also available for the study of learning and memory in rodents. The laboratories share access to two animal colony rooms for housing rodents. Research space for human experimental psychology investigations includes a corridor lined by eleven research cubicles each one approximately 90 square feet and a research participant reception area of approximately 200 square feet. Equipment for these cubicles includes desktop computers and associated equipment that allows them to function as laboratory control devices. Three of these machines have video capture cards permitting still frame capture and video-conferencing with Sony video camcorders. In addition, the department's Perceptual Laboratory consists of a three-room suite totaling 650 square feet. A one-way vision room is also available, as are additional suites for data collection.

Application Information:
Send to Office of the Provost, Attn: Graduate Admissions, Seton Hall University, 400 South Orange Avenue, South Orange, NJ 07079. Application available online. Students are admitted in the Fall, application deadline July 1. Strong applications submitted before April 1 have a greater chance of admittance and of receiving Graduate Assistantships. *Fee:* $50.

William Paterson University
Psychology/MA in Clinical and Counseling Psychology
Humanities & Social Sciences
300 Pompton Road
Wayne, NJ 07470
Telephone: (973) 720-3629
Fax: (973) 720-3392
E-mail: *Psychgrad@wpunj.edu*
Web: *http://www.wpunj.edu/cohss/departments/psychology/graduate.dot*

Department Information:
1999. Graduate Director: Bruce J. Diamond, PhD. Number of faculty: total—full-time 9; women—full-time 7; total—minority—full-time 2; women minority—full-time 2.

Programs and Degrees Offered:
Listed in the following order: Program area, degree type (T if terminal Master's), number awarded 7/11–6/12. Clinical and Counseling Psychology MA/MS (Master of Arts/Science) (T) 13.

Student Applications/Admissions:
Student Applications
Clinical and Counseling Psychology MA/MS *(Master of Arts/ Science)*—Applications 2012–2013, 107. Total applicants accepted 2012–2013, 30. Number full-time enrolled (new admits only) 2012–2013, 17. Number part-time enrolled (new admits only) 2012–2013, 0. Total enrolled 2012–2013 full-time, 26. Total enrolled 2012–2013 part-time, 2. Openings 2013–2014, 20. The median number of years required for completion of a degree in 2012–2013 were 2. The number of students enrolled full- and part-time who were dismissed or voluntarily withdrew from this program area in 2012–2013 were 0.
Scores: Entries appear in this order: required test or GPA, minimum score (if required), median score of students entering in 2012–2013. *Clinical and Counseling Psychology MA/MS (Master of Arts/Science):* GRE-V no minimum stated, GRE-Q no minimum stated, GRE-Analytical no minimum stated, overall undergraduate GPA 3.0.
Other Criteria: (importance of criteria rated low, medium, or high): GRE scores—high, research experience—medium, work experience—medium, extracurricular activity—medium, clinically related public service—high, GPA—high, letters of recommendation—high, interview—medium, statement of goals and objectives—high, undergraduate major in psychology—medium, specific undergraduate psychology courses taken—high. For additional information on admission requirements, go to http://www.wpunj.edu/cohss/departments/psychology/graduate.dot.

Student Characteristics: The following represents characteristics of students in 2012–2013 in all graduate psychology programs in the department: Female—full-time 18, part-time 2; Male—full-time 8, part-time 0; African American/Black—full-time 3, part-time 0; Hispanic/Latino(a)—full-time 3, part-time 0; Asian/Pacific Islander—full-time 0, part-time 0; American Indian/Alaska Native—full-time 0, part-time 0; Caucasian/White—full-time 15, part-time 1; Multi-ethnic—full-time 5, part-time 1; students subject to the Americans With Disabilities Act—full-time 0, part-time 0; Unknown ethnicity—full-time 0, part-time 0; International students who hold an F-1 or J-1 Visa—full-time 0, part-time 0.

Financial Information/Assistance:
Tuition for Full-Time Study: *Master's:* State residents: $637 per credit hour; Nonstate residents: $991 per credit hour. Tuition is subject to change. See the following website for updates and changes in tuition costs: http://www.wpunj.edu/studentaccounts/tuition-and-fees/graduate.dot.

Financial Assistance:
First-Year Students: Traineeships available for first year. Average amount paid per academic year: $6,000. Average number of hours worked per week: 20. Apply by April 1.
Advanced Students: Traineeships available for advanced students. Average amount paid per academic year: $6,000. Average number of hours worked per week: 20. Apply by April 1.
Additional Information: Of all students currently enrolled full time, 29% benefited from one or more of the listed financial assistance programs. Application and information available online at: http://www.wpunj.edu/admissions/graduate/finaid.dot.

Internships/Practica: Master's Degree (MA/MS Clinical and Counseling Psychology): An internship experience, such as a final research project or "capstone" experience is required of graduates. Graduates and interns have served in a wide variety of inpatient and outpatient settings including hospitals, community mental health clinics, wellness centers, health maintenance facilities, local, regional, national and international health care organizations, group homes, drug treatment facilities, rehabilitation centers, correctional facilities and gerontology programs. With appropriate licensing and/or under proper licensed supervision, graduates of our program are able to conduct assessments; provide clinical and health-related services to individuals, groups and families using appropriate diagnostic and intervention techniques; participate in institutional and organizational research and work on an elective basis with a variety of populations (e.g., chronic and acute diseases and disorders, children, adolescents, the elderly, the severely mentally ill, the neurologically impaired, substance abusers, and others).

Housing and Day Care: On-campus housing is available. See the following website for more information: http://www.wpunj.edu/reslife/. On-campus day care facilities are available. See the following website for more information: http://www.wpunj.edu/child-development/.

Employment of Department Graduates:

Master's Degree Graduates: Of those who graduated in the academic year 2011–2012, the following categories and numbers represent the postgraduate activities and employment of master's degree graduates: Enrolled in a psychology doctoral program (5), enrolled in a postdoctoral residency/fellowship (n/a), employed in independent practice (n/a), employed in an academic position at a 2-year/4-year college (3), employed in other positions at a higher education institution (1), employed in a community mental health/counseling center (5), total from the above (master's) (14).

Doctoral Degree Graduates: Of those who graduated in the academic year 2011–2012, the following categories and numbers represent the postgraduate activities and employment of doctoral degree graduates: Enrolled in a psychology doctoral program (n/a), total from the above (doctoral) (0).

Additional Information:

Orientation, Objectives, and Emphasis of Department: We train clinicians who are ethically, socially, and culturally sensitive; who are competitive in pursuing their career aspirations; and who are motivated to continue learning and developing their skills throughout their professional careers. Towards this end, the program: 1. Emphasizes the ethical responsibility of practitioners to be knowledgeable and up-to-date in their understanding of behavior, psychopathology, health-related behaviors, therapeutic applications, and evolving outcome research; 2. Encourages self-reflection and examination of one's sensitivities to social and cultural issues and limitations and the need to seek consultation, supervision or referral as appropriate. 2. Gives priority to the highest level of program and course content in teaching, clinical supervision and research and in supporting quality practicum experiences in order to enhance student learning and training. 3. Enhances knowledge and skills and emphasizes the importance of research, continuing education and informed interpretation of new research; 4. Stresses critical thinking, reflection, intellectual independence, scholarship and an appreciation for staying current with research; and 5. Requires a comprehensive project integrating empirical, theoretical, social, ethical, cultural, diagnostic and therapeutic issues or a research project that makes an original contribution to the literature. The department is currently developing a doctoral program in clinical psychology.

Special Facilities or Resources: The program recently moved into new and renovated space within Science Hall-East. The facility provides students and faculty with a Clinical Teaching Suite that includes training rooms equipped with state-of-the-art video recording and viewing capabilities. The new facilities also include a Testing and Media Instructional Room, research labs, teaching spaces, and a Graduate Study room, providing students ample space for research, learning and study. The program maintains a wide array of assessment instruments, videos and equipment which are available to faculty and students. The University has a modern library with numerous online databases, media and study areas. The University Commons is seconds away and provides a food mall, recreation area, ballrooms and informal leisure spaces and lounges. The campus is wireless and includes labs equipped with software applications for teaching, research and meeting student needs. The campus has an Instructional Research Technology Lab that helps support IT-related activities.

Information for Students With Physical Disabilities: See the following website for more information: http://www.wpunj.edu/disabilityservices/.

Application Information:
Send to Office of Graduate Studies, Morrison Hall, Room 102, William Paterson University, 300 Pompton Road, Wayne, NJ 07470. Application available online. URL of online application: http://www.wpunj.edu/admissions/graduate/apply-now.dot. Students are admitted in the Fall, application deadline May 1. *Fee:* $50. If you attend a Graduate Open House, the application fee is waived.

New Mexico State University
Counseling and Educational Psychology
College of Education
Box 30001 MSC 3CEP
Las Cruces, NM 88003-8001
Telephone: (575) 646-2121
Fax: (575) 646-8035
E-mail: *eadams@nmsu.edu*
Web: *http://education.nmsu.edu/cep/*

Department Information:

1905. Department Head: Jonathan Schwartz, PhD. Number of faculty: total—full-time 10, part-time 4; women—full-time 8, part-time 1; total—minority—full-time 6, part-time 1; women minority—full-time 6, part-time 1.

Programs and Degrees Offered:

Listed in the following order: Program area, degree type (T if terminal Master's), number awarded 7/11–6/12. Counseling and Guidance MA/MS (Master of Arts/Science) (T) 10, School Psychology EdS (School Psychology) 3, Counseling Psychology PhD (Doctor of Philosophy) 4.

APA Accreditation: Counseling PhD (Doctor of Philosophy). Student Outcome Data Website: http://education.nmsu.edu/cep/phd/index. html.

Student Applications/Admissions:

Student Applications

Counseling and Guidance MA/MS (Master of Arts/Science)—Applications 2012–2013, 45. Total applicants accepted 2012–2013, 13. Number full-time enrolled (new admits only) 2012–2013, 6. Number part-time enrolled (new admits only) 2012–2013, 7. Total enrolled 2012–2013 full-time, 15. Total enrolled 2012–2013 part-time, 15. Openings 2013–2014, 13. The median number of years required for completion of a degree in 2012–2013 were 2. The number of students enrolled full- and part-time who were dismissed or voluntarily withdrew from this program area in 2012–2013 were 1. *School Psychology EdS (School Psychology)*—Applications 2012–2013, 18. Total applicants accepted 2012–2013, 12. Number full-time enrolled (new admits only) 2012–2013, 6. Number part-time enrolled (new admits only) 2012–2013, 6. Total enrolled 2012–2013 full-time, 15. Total enrolled 2012–2013 part-time, 11. Openings 2013–2014, 12. The median number of years required for completion of a degree in 2012–2013 were 3. The number of students enrolled full- and part-time who were dismissed or voluntarily withdrew from this program area in 2012–2013 were 3. *Counseling Psychology PhD (Doctor of Philosophy)*—Applications 2012–2013, 100. Total applicants accepted 2012–2013, 6. Number full-time enrolled (new admits only) 2012–2013, 6. Number part-time enrolled (new admits only) 2012–2013, 0. Total enrolled 2012–2013 full-time, 30. Total enrolled 2012–2013 part-time, 6. Openings 2013–2014, 6. The median number of years required for completion of a degree in 2012–2013 were 5. The number of students enrolled full-

and part-time who were dismissed or voluntarily withdrew from this program area in 2012–2013 were 0.

Scores: Entries appear in this order: required test or GPA, minimum score (if required), median score of students entering in 2012–2013. *Counseling and Guidance MA/MS (Master of Arts/Science):* GRE-V no minimum stated, GRE-Q no minimum stated; *Counseling Psychology PhD (Doctor of Philosophy):* GRE-V no minimum stated, 500, GRE-Q no minimum stated, 500, GRE-Analytical no minimum stated, 4.0, overall undergraduate GPA no minimum stated, 3.7.

Other Criteria: (importance of criteria rated low, medium, or high): GRE scores—medium, research experience—high, work experience—medium, extracurricular activity—medium, clinically related public service—high, GPA—high, letters of recommendation—high, interview—high, statement of goals and objectives—high, writing sample—medium, undergraduate major in psychology—medium, specific undergraduate psychology courses taken—low. For additional information on admission requirements, go to http://education.nmsu.edu/cep/ index.html.

Student Characteristics: The following represents characteristics of students in 2012–2013 in all graduate psychology programs in the department: Female—full-time 49, part-time 26; Male—full-time 11, part-time 6; African American/Black—full-time 2, part-time 2; Hispanic/Latino(a)—full-time 20, part-time 12; Asian/ Pacific Islander—full-time 2, part-time 1; American Indian/ Alaska Native—full-time 1, part-time 1; Caucasian/White—full-time 29, part-time 16; Multi-ethnic—full-time 6, part-time 0; students subject to the Americans With Disabilities Act—full-time 0, part-time 0; Unknown ethnicity—full-time 0, part-time 0; International students who hold an F-1 or J-1 Visa—full-time 0, part-time 0.

Financial Information/Assistance:

Tuition for Full-Time Study: *Master's:* State residents: per academic year $6,308, $261 per credit hour; Nonstate residents: per academic year $18,720, $780 per credit hour. *Doctoral:* State residents: per academic year $6,308, $261 per credit hour; Nonstate residents: per academic year $18,720, $780 per credit hour. Tuition is subject to change. See the following website for updates and changes in tuition costs: http://www.nmsu.edu/~uar/ schcosts.htm.

Financial Assistance:

First-Year Students: Teaching assistantships available for first year. Average amount paid per academic year: $8,000. Average number of hours worked per week: 10. Fellowships and scholarships available for first year. Average amount paid per academic year: $4,500.

Advanced Students: Teaching assistantships available for advanced students. Average amount paid per academic year: $8,000. Average number of hours worked per week: 10. Fellowships and scholarships available for advanced students. Average amount paid per academic year: $4,500.

Additional Information: Of all students currently enrolled full time, 60% benefited from one or more of the listed financial assistance programs. Application and information available online at: http://gradschool.nmsu.edu/.

Internships/Practica: Doctoral Degree (PhD Counseling Psychology): For those doctoral students for whom a professional psychology internship was required in this program prior to graduation, (9) students applied for an internship in 2011–2012, with (9) students obtaining an internship. Of those students who obtained an internship, (9) were paid internships. Of those students who obtained an internship, (7) students placed in APA/CPA accredited internships, (0) students placed in internships not APA/CPA accredited, but listed with the Association of Psychology Postdoctoral and Internship Programs (APPIC), (0) students placed in internships conforming to guidelines of the Council of Directors of School Psychology Programs (CDSPP), (2) students placed in internships that were not APA/CPA accredited, APPIC or CDSPP listed. Master's Degree (MA/MS Counseling and Guidance): An internship experience, such as a final research project or "capstone" experience is required of graduates. Practicum placements include university counseling centers, public schools, a primary care setting, community mental health centers, hospitals, adolescent residential centers, the Department of Vocational Rehabilitation, military bases, substance abuse treatment centers, and nursing homes.

Housing and Day Care: On-campus housing is available. See the following website for more information: http://www.nmsu.edu/~housing/graduate/. On-campus day care facilities are available. See the following website for more information: http://education.nmsu.edu/ci/earlychildhood/mcvi.html.

Employment of Department Graduates:

Master's Degree Graduates: Of those who graduated in the academic year 2011–2012, the following categories and numbers represent the postgraduate activities and employment of master's degree graduates: Enrolled in a postdoctoral residency/fellowship (n/a), employed in independent practice (n/a), employed in a professional position in a school system (2), employed in a community mental health/counseling center (6), employed in a hospital/medical center (1), not seeking employment (1), total from the above (master's) (10).

Doctoral Degree Graduates: Of those who graduated in the academic year 2011–2012, the following categories and numbers represent the postgraduate activities and employment of doctoral degree graduates: Enrolled in a psychology doctoral program (n/a), enrolled in a postdoctoral residency/fellowship (1), employed in other positions at a higher education institution (1), employed in a hospital/medical center (1), not seeking employment (1), total from the above (doctoral) (4).

Additional Information:

Orientation, Objectives, and Emphasis of Department: The major thrust of the department is the preparation of professionals for licensure and positions in counseling psychology; mental health and school counseling; school psychology, and related areas. Three graduate degrees are available: (1) Doctor of Philosophy, (2) Masters of Arts, and (3) Specialist in Education. The PhD in Counseling Psychology, which is accredited by the American Psychological Association, is based on the scientist–practitioner model through which both research and service delivery skills are acquired. Graduates of the program are prepared to conduct research, provide service, teach, and supervise. Emphases in the Counseling Psychology program include cultural diversity, generalist training in a variety of modalities, supervision and behavioral health consultation. The Master of Arts in Counseling and Guidance prepares professional counselors to offer individual, family, and group counseling in schools, agencies, hospitals, and private practice. The curriculum covers human development; appraisal; diagnosis; treatment planning; and individual and professional issues. The School Psychology Program (EdS) prepares professionals for positions in public schools and other organizations which require advanced assessment, counseling, consultation and supervision skills. A major research project (thesis) is a degree requirement.

Special Facilities or Resources: The Counseling and School Psychology Training and Research Center is a training/service facility sponsored by the Department of Counseling and Educational Psychology which provides excellent opportunities for supervised counseling and supervision-of-supervision. Four rooms are available for videotaping, and have one-way mirrors, telephones, and microphone-speakers for live supervision of counseling and live supervision of supervision. The facility has a "state-of-the-art" bug in the ear system which helps facilitate live supervision for immediate feedback to the counselor in training. We also have extensive training with similar supervisory capabilities at the Family Medicine Center, a primary care center staffed by Family Medicine residents and Counseling Psychology students.

Information for Students With Physical Disabilities: See the following website for more information: http://www.nmsu.edu/~ssd/.

Application Information:
Application available online. URL of online application: http://prospective.nmsu.edu/graduate/apply/index.html. Students are admitted in the Fall, application deadline January 15; Summer, application deadline December 15. The PhD Program deadline is December 15 (students will begin the program in the summer). The EdS Program deadline is January 15. The MA Program deadline is February 1. *Fee:* $30. McNair scholars can have their fees waived.

New Mexico State University
Department of Psychology
College of Arts and Sciences
Department 3452, P.O. Box 30001
Las Cruces, NM 88003
Telephone: (575) 646-2502
Fax: (575) 646-6212
E-mail: *lmadson@nmsu.edu*
Web: *http://psych.nmsu.edu*

Department Information:
1950. Head: Dominic A. Simon. Number of faculty: total—full-time 13; women—full-time 3; faculty subject to the Americans With Disabilities Act 1.

Programs and Degrees Offered:

Listed in the following order: Program area, degree type (T if terminal Master's), number awarded 7/11–6/12. Cognitive Psychology PhD (Doctor of Philosophy) 1, Engineering PhD (Doctor of Philosophy) 0, Social Psychology PhD (Doctor of Philosophy) 2, General Experimental Psychology MA/MS (Master of Arts/Science) 10.

Student Applications/Admissions:

Student Applications

Cognitive Psychology PhD (Doctor of Philosophy)—Applications 2012–2013, 0. Total applicants accepted 2012–2013, 0. Number full-time enrolled (new admits only) 2012–2013, 0. Number part-time enrolled (new admits only) 2012–2013, 0. Total enrolled 2012–2013 full-time, 4. Total enrolled 2012–2013 part-time, 0. Openings 2013–2014, 2. The median number of years required for completion of a degree in 2012–2013 were 3. The number of students enrolled full- and part-time who were dismissed or voluntarily withdrew from this program area in 2012–2013 were 0. *Engineering PhD (Doctor of Philosophy)*—Applications 2012–2013, 2. Total applicants accepted 2012–2013, 0. Number full-time enrolled (new admits only) 2012–2013, 0. Number part-time enrolled (new admits only) 2012–2013, 0. Total enrolled 2012–2013 full-time, 1. Total enrolled 2012–2013 part-time, 0. Openings 2013–2014, 2. The number of students enrolled full- and part-time who were dismissed or voluntarily withdrew from this program area in 2012–2013 were 0. *Social Psychology PhD (Doctor of Philosophy)*—Applications 2012–2013, 7. Total applicants accepted 2012–2013, 3. Number full-time enrolled (new admits only) 2012–2013, 1. Number part-time enrolled (new admits only) 2012–2013, 0. Total enrolled 2012–2013 full-time, 11. Total enrolled 2012–2013 part-time, 0. Openings 2013–2014, 2. The median number of years required for completion of a degree in 2012–2013 were 3. The number of students enrolled full- and part-time who were dismissed or voluntarily withdrew from this program area in 2012–2013 were 0. *General Experimental Psychology MA/MS (Master of Arts/Science)*—Applications 2012–2013, 35. Total applicants accepted 2012–2013, 11. Number full-time enrolled (new admits only) 2012–2013, 7. Number part-time enrolled (new admits only) 2012–2013, 0. Total enrolled 2012–2013 full-time, 18. Total enrolled 2012–2013 part-time, 0. Openings 2013–2014, 4. The median number of years required for completion of a degree in 2012–2013 were 3. The number of students enrolled full- and part-time who were dismissed or voluntarily withdrew from this program area in 2012–2013 were 1.

Scores: Entries appear in this order: required test or GPA, minimum score (if required), median score of students entering in 2012–2013. *Cognitive Psychology PhD (Doctor of Philosophy):* GRE-V 157, GRE-Q 157, GRE-Analytical 4.5, overall undergraduate GPA 3.0, Masters GPA 3.0; *Engineering PhD (Doctor of Philosophy):* GRE-V 157, GRE-Q 157, GRE-Analytical 4.5, overall undergraduate GPA 3.0, Masters GPA 3.0; *Social Psychology PhD (Doctor of Philosophy):* GRE-V 157, GRE-Q 157, GRE-Analytical 4.5, overall undergraduate GPA 3.0, Masters GPA 3.0; *General Experimental Psychology MA/MS (Master of Arts/Science):* GRE-V 153, GRE-Q 149, GRE-Analytical 4.0, overall undergraduate GPA 3.0.

Other Criteria: (importance of criteria rated low, medium, or high): GRE scores—high, research experience—medium, work experience—low, GPA—high, letters of recommendation—high, interview—medium, statement of goals and objectives—high, applicant's interests—high, undergraduate major in psychology—medium, specific undergraduate psychology courses taken—medium. For additional information on admission requirements, go to http://psych.nmsu.edu/admissions.html.

Student Characteristics: The following represents characteristics of students in 2012–2013 in all graduate psychology programs in the department: Female—full-time 19, part-time 0; Male—full-time 15, part-time 0; African American/Black—full-time 1, part-time 0; Hispanic/Latino(a)—full-time 5, part-time 0; Asian/Pacific Islander—full-time 8, part-time 0; American Indian/Alaska Native—full-time 0, part-time 0; Caucasian/White—full-time 19, part-time 0; Multi-ethnic—full-time 1, part-time 0; students subject to the Americans With Disabilities Act—full-time 1, part-time 0; Unknown ethnicity—full-time 0, part-time 0; International students who hold an F-1 or J-1 Visa—full-time 8, part-time 0.

Financial Information/Assistance:

Tuition for Full-Time Study: *Master's:* State residents: per academic year $6,514, $271 per credit hour; Nonstate residents: per academic year $19,540, $814 per credit hour. *Doctoral:* State residents: per academic year $6,514, $271 per credit hour; Nonstate residents: per academic year $19,540, $814 per credit hour. Tuition is subject to change. Additional fees are assessed to students beyond the costs of tuition for the following: wellness fee, Associated Students of NMSU fee. See the following website for updates and changes in tuition costs: http://www.nmsu.edu/~uar/schcosts.htm.

Financial Assistance:

First-Year Students: Teaching assistantships available for first year. Average amount paid per academic year: $16,100. Average number of hours worked per week: 20. Apply by February 1. Research assistantships available for first year. Average amount paid per academic year: $16,100. Average number of hours worked per week: 20. Apply by February 1. Fellowships and scholarships available for first year. Apply by February 1.

Advanced Students: Teaching assistantships available for advanced students. Average amount paid per academic year: $16,700. Average number of hours worked per week: 20. Apply by February 1. Research assistantships available for advanced students. Average amount paid per academic year: $16,700. Average number of hours worked per week: 20. Apply by February 1. Fellowships and scholarships available for advanced students. Apply by February 1.

Additional Information: Of all students currently enrolled full time, 100% benefited from one or more of the listed financial assistance programs. Application and information available online at: http://gradschool.nmsu.edu/fellowships/.

Internships/Practica: For the PhD degree, students must either complete an internship of at least three month duration OR independently teach an undergraduate course. Many master's students in spend a summer or half-year as an intern in industry, but it is not required for the MA degree.

Housing and Day Care: On-campus housing is available. See the following website for more information: http://www.nmsu.edu/~housing/graduate/. On-campus day care facilities are available. See the following website for more information: http://education.nmsu.edu/ci/earlychildhood/mcvi.html.

Employment of Department Graduates:

Master's Degree Graduates: Of those who graduated in the academic year 2011–2012, the following categories and numbers represent the postgraduate activities and employment of master's degree graduates: Enrolled in a psychology doctoral program (3), enrolled in another graduate/professional program (4), enrolled in a postdoctoral residency/fellowship (n/a), employed in independent practice (n/a), employed in business or industry (3), total from the above (master's) (10).

Doctoral Degree Graduates: Of those who graduated in the academic year 2011–2012, the following categories and numbers represent the postgraduate activities and employment of doctoral degree graduates: Enrolled in a psychology doctoral program (n/a), employed in an academic position at a 2-year/4-year college (1), employed in business or industry (1), do not know (1), total from the above (doctoral) (3).

Additional Information:

Orientation, Objectives, and Emphasis of Department: The department offers an MA degree in general experimental psychology that allows an emphasis in cognitive, engineering, or social psychology. The PhD is offered in the major areas of cognitive, engineering, and social psychology. Students must earn an MA degree before being admitted to the doctoral program. All programs are experimentally oriented and have the distinctive characteristic of pursuing and extending basic research questions in applied settings.

Special Facilities or Resources: All faculty members have specialized laboratories with a wide variety of computer hardware and software. These include auditory perception and eye tracking labs used to study perceptual and cognitive issues, a biopsychology lab equipped to measure ERPs, an automation lab used to study human interactions with automated systems including unmanned aerial vehicles, and a developmental laboratory equipped with sophisticated equipment for recording, analyzing, and editing mother-infant interactions, etc.

Information for Students With Physical Disabilities: See the following website for more information: http://www.nmsu.edu/~ssd/.

Application Information:
Send to Chair of Graduate Committee, Department of Psychology, MSC 3452, New Mexico State University, Las Cruces, NM 88003-8001. Application available online. URL of online application: http://prospective.nmsu.edu/graduate/apply/. Students are admitted in the Fall, application deadline February 1. *Fee:* $40. Application fee of $50 for international applicants.

New Mexico, University of
Department of Psychology
Arts and Science
Logan Hall, MSC03 2220
Albuquerque, NM 87131-0001
Telephone: (505) 277-4121
Fax: (505) 277-1394
E-mail: *psych@unm.edu*
Web: *http://psych.unm.edu*

Department Information:
1960. Chairperson: Jane Ellen Smith. Number of faculty: total—full-time 24, part-time 3; women—full-time 8, part-time 3; total—minority—full-time 3, part-time 1; women minority—full-time 1, part-time 1.

Programs and Degrees Offered:
Listed in the following order: Program area, degree type (T if terminal Master's), number awarded 7/11–6/12. Clinical Psychology PhD (Doctor of Philosophy) 9, Developmental Psychology PhD (Doctor of Philosophy) 0, Evolutionary Psychology PhD (Doctor of Philosophy) 0, Cognition, Brain and Behavior PhD (Doctor of Philosophy) 5, Health Psychology PhD (Doctor of Philosophy) 0, Quantitative Methodology PhD (Doctor of Philosophy) 0.

APA Accreditation: Clinical PhD (Doctor of Philosophy). Student Outcome Data Website: http://psych.unm.edu/graduate-studies/Clinical-Applicant-Data.html.

Student Applications/Admissions:

Student Applications

Clinical Psychology PhD (Doctor of Philosophy)—Applications 2012–2013, 134. Total applicants accepted 2012–2013, 7. Number full-time enrolled (new admits only) 2012–2013, 7. Number part-time enrolled (new admits only) 2012–2013, 0. Total enrolled 2012–2013 full-time, 38. Total enrolled 2012–2013 part-time, 0. Openings 2013–2014, 6. The median number of years required for completion of a degree in 2012–2013 were 7. The number of students enrolled full- and part-time who were dismissed or voluntarily withdrew from this program area in 2012–2013 were 0. *Developmental Psychology PhD (Doctor of Philosophy)*—Applications 2012–2013, 1. Total applicants accepted 2012–2013, 0. Number full-time enrolled (new admits only) 2012–2013, 0. Number part-time enrolled (new admits only) 2012–2013, 0. Total enrolled 2012–2013 full-time, 3. Total enrolled 2012–2013 part-time, 0. The number of students enrolled full- and part-time who were dismissed or voluntarily withdrew from this program area in 2012–2013 were 0. *Evolutionary Psychology PhD (Doctor of Philosophy)*—Applications 2012–2013, 25. Total applicants accepted 2012–2013, 1. Number full-time enrolled (new admits only) 2012–2013, 0. Number part-time enrolled (new admits only) 2012–2013, 0. Total enrolled 2012–2013 full-time, 6. Total enrolled 2012–2013 part-time, 0. Openings 2013–2014, 2. The number of students enrolled full- and part-time who were dismissed or voluntarily withdrew from this program area in 2012–2013 were 0. *Cognition, Brain and Behavior PhD (Doctor of Philosophy)*—Applications 2012–2013, 23. Total applicants accepted 2012–2013, 9. Number full-time enrolled (new admits only)

537

2012–2013, 5. Number part-time enrolled (new admits only) 2012–2013, 0. Total enrolled 2012–2013 full-time, 25. Total enrolled 2012–2013 part-time, 0. Openings 2013–2014, 3. The median number of years required for completion of a degree in 2012–2013 were 8. The number of students enrolled full- and part-time who were dismissed or voluntarily withdrew from this program area in 2012–2013 were 0. *Health Psychology PhD (Doctor of Philosophy)*—Applications 2012–2013, 7. Total applicants accepted 2012–2013, 1. Number full-time enrolled (new admits only) 2012–2013, 0. Total enrolled 2012–2013 full-time, 1. The number of students enrolled full- and part-time who were dismissed or voluntarily withdrew from this program area in 2012–2013 were 0. *Quantitative Methodology PhD (Doctor of Philosophy)*—Applications 2012–2013, 0. Total enrolled 2012–2013 full-time, 4. The number of students enrolled full- and part-time who were dismissed or voluntarily withdrew from this program area in 2012–2013 were 0.

Scores: Entries appear in this order: required test or GPA, minimum score (if required), median score of students entering in 2012–2013. *Clinical Psychology PhD (Doctor of Philosophy)*: GRE-V no minimum stated, 570, GRE-Q no minimum stated, 662, GRE-Analytical no minimum stated, 4, GRE-Subject (Psychology) no minimum stated, 662; *Developmental Psychology PhD (Doctor of Philosophy)*: GRE-V no minimum stated, GRE-Q no minimum stated, GRE-Analytical no minimum stated, GRE-Subject (Psychology) no minimum stated; *Evolutionary Psychology PhD (Doctor of Philosophy)*: GRE-V no minimum stated, 600, GRE-Q no minimum stated, 703, GRE-Analytical no minimum stated, 4, GRE-Subject (Psychology) no minimum stated, 693; *Cognition, Brain and Behavior PhD (Doctor of Philosophy)*: GRE-V no minimum stated, 545, GRE-Q no minimum stated, 624, GRE-Analytical no minimum stated, 4, GRE-Subject (Psychology) no minimum stated, 652; *Health Psychology PhD (Doctor of Philosophy)*: GRE-V no minimum stated, 560, GRE-Q no minimum stated, 527, GRE-Analytical no minimum stated, 3.7, GRE-Subject (Psychology) no minimum stated, 639.

Other Criteria: (importance of criteria rated low, medium, or high): GRE scores—high, research experience—high, work experience—medium, extracurricular activity—medium, clinically related public service—medium, GPA—high, letters of recommendation—high, interview—high, statement of goals and objectives—high, undergraduate major in psychology—high, specific undergraduate psychology courses taken—high. For additional information on admission requirements, go to http://psych.unm.edu/graduate-studies/graduate-admissions.html.

Student Characteristics: The following represents characteristics of students in 2012–2013 in all graduate psychology programs in the department: Female—full-time 54, part-time 0; Male—full-time 23, part-time 0; African American/Black—full-time 0, part-time 0; Hispanic/Latino(a)—full-time 13, part-time 0; Asian/Pacific Islander—full-time 4, part-time 0; American Indian/Alaska Native—full-time 1, part-time 0; Caucasian/White—full-time 56, part-time 0; Multi-ethnic—full-time 1, part-time 0; students subject to the Americans With Disabilities Act—full-time 0, part-time 0; Unknown ethnicity—full-time 2, part-time 0; International students who hold an F-1 or J-1 Visa—full-time 2, part-time 0.

Financial Information/Assistance:
Tuition for Full-Time Study: *Doctoral:* State residents: $277 per credit hour; Nonstate residents: $886 per credit hour. Tuition is subject to change. Additional fees are assessed to students beyond the costs of tuition for the following: GPSA, course fees. See the following website for updates and changes in tuition costs: http://www.unm.edu/~bursar/tuitionrates.html.

Financial Assistance:
First-Year Students: Teaching assistantships available for first year. Average amount paid per academic year: $12,467. Average number of hours worked per week: 20. Apply by April 15. Research assistantships available for first year. Average amount paid per academic year: $12,467. Average number of hours worked per week: 20. Apply by April 15.

Advanced Students: Teaching assistantships available for advanced students. Average amount paid per academic year: $14,791. Average number of hours worked per week: 20. Apply by April 15. Research assistantships available for advanced students. Average amount paid per academic year: $14,791. Average number of hours worked per week: 20. Apply by April 15.

Additional Information: Of all students currently enrolled full time, 95% benefited from one or more of the listed financial assistance programs. Application and information available online at: http://ogs.unm.edu/resources/funding-resources/.

Internships/Practica: Doctoral Degree (PhD Clinical Psychology): For those doctoral students for whom a professional psychology internship was required in this program prior to graduation, (4) students applied for an internship in 2011–2012, with (4) students obtaining an internship. Of those students who obtained an internship, (4) were paid internships. Of those students who obtained an internship, (4) students placed in APA/CPA accredited internships, (0) students placed in internships not APA/CPA accredited, but listed with the Association of Psychology Postdoctoral and Internship Programs (APPIC), (0) students placed in internships conforming to guidelines of the Council of Directors of School Psychology Programs (CDSPP), (0) students placed in internships that were not APA/CPA accredited, APPIC or CDSPP listed. .

Housing and Day Care: On-campus housing is available. See the following website for more information: http://housing.unm.edu/. On-campus day care facilities are available. See the following website for more information: http://childcare.unm.edu/.

Employment of Department Graduates:
Master's Degree Graduates: Of those who graduated in the academic year 2011–2012, the following categories and numbers represent the postgraduate activities and employment of master's degree graduates: Enrolled in a postdoctoral residency/fellowship (n/a), employed in independent practice (n/a), total from the above (master's) (0).

Doctoral Degree Graduates: Of those who graduated in the academic year 2011–2012, the following categories and numbers represent the postgraduate activities and employment of doctoral degree graduates: Enrolled in a psychology doctoral program (n/a), total from the above (doctoral) (0).

Additional Information:
Orientation, Objectives, and Emphasis of Department: Founded in 1960, the doctoral program in psychology is based on the

premise that psychology, in all of its areas, is fundamentally an experimental discipline. For all students, the PhD is awarded in general experimental psychology, and students acquire a solid foundation in both scientific methodology and general psychology. Within this framework, students specialize in any of several competency areas. The well-trained psychologist, within this perspective, is one who combines competence in the general discipline of psychology with excellence in his or her chosen specialization.

Special Facilities or Resources: The department is housed in a building on the central campus. In addition to faculty and administrative offices and seminar rooms, the building is equipped for sophisticated research. There are soundproof chambers for conducting experiments, a variety of timing devices, computer terminals, and electromechanical measuring equipment. Laboratory facilities exist for research in human memory, learning, cognitive psychology, perception, information processing, attention, decision making, developmental, social, personality, neuropsychology, psychophysiology, and clinical psychology. The building also has a large animal research facility with primates and rodents.

The campus animal research facility is equipped for surgery and for delicate measurements of brain activities as well as for tests of physical, cognitive, and emotional responses. Microcomputers are widely used in individual faculty laboratories and in a graduate student computer room. The Department of Psychology Clinic opened in 1982 and offers diagnostic and therapeutic services to the Albuquerque community while providing an excellent training facility for clinical students. The department also recently opened a clinical neuroscience center that was funded by a $5 million NIH stimulus grant.

Information for Students With Physical Disabilities: See the following website for more information: http://as2.unm.edu/.

Application Information:
Send to Graduate Admissions Coordinator, Department of Psychology, MSC03 2220, 1 University of New Mexico, Albuquerque, NM 87131-0001. Application available online. URL of online application: http://www.unm.edu/apply/. Students are admitted in the Fall, application deadline December 15. The deadline for full financial consideration is December 15. We accept applications through May 1 ONLY IF positions remain. *Fee:* $50.

Adelphi University

The Derner Institute of Advanced Psychological Studies
158 Cambridge Avenue
Garden City, NY 11530
Telephone: (516) 877-4801
Fax: (516) 877-4805
E-mail: *ross@adelphi.edu*
Web: *http://derner.adelphi.edu/*

Department Information:

1952. Dean: Jacques P. Barber. Number of faculty: total—full-time 29, part-time 160; women—full-time 13, part-time 93; total—minority—full-time 5, part-time 15; women minority—full-time 4, part-time 10.

Programs and Degrees Offered:

Listed in the following order: Program area, degree type (T if terminal Master's), number awarded 7/11–6/12. Clinical Psychology PhD (Doctor of Philosophy) 26, Psychotherapy Postgraduate Certificate Other 10, Clinical Psychology Respecialization Respecialization Diploma 0, General Psychology MA/MS (Master of Arts/Science) (T) 40, School Psychology MA/MS (Master of Arts/Science) (T) 17, Mental Health Counseling MA/MS (Master of Arts/Science) (T) 12.

APA Accreditation: Clinical PhD (Doctor of Philosophy). Student Outcome Data Website: http://derner.adelphi.edu/phd-clinical-psychology-degree.php.

Student Applications/Admissions:

Student Applications

Clinical Psychology PhD (Doctor of Philosophy)—Applications 2012–2013, 235. Total applicants accepted 2012–2013, 47. Number full-time enrolled (new admits only) 2012–2013, 20. Total enrolled 2012–2013 full-time, 114. Total enrolled 2012–2013 part-time, 0. Openings 2013–2014, 20. The median number of years required for completion of a degree in 2012–2013 were 6. The number of students enrolled full- and part-time who were dismissed or voluntarily withdrew from this program area in 2012–2013 were 5. *Psychotherapy Postgraduate Certificate Other*—Applications 2012–2013, 25. Total applicants accepted 2012–2013, 20. Number full-time enrolled (new admits only) 2012–2013, 0. Number part-time enrolled (new admits only) 2012–2013, 12. Openings 2013–2014, 20. The median number of years required for completion of a degree in 2012–2013 were 2. The number of students enrolled full- and part-time who were dismissed or voluntarily withdrew from this program area in 2012–2013 were 2. *Clinical Psychology Respecialization Respecialization Diploma*—Applications 2012–2013, 2. Total applicants accepted 2012–2013, 0. Number full-time enrolled (new admits only) 2012–2013, 0. Number part-time enrolled (new admits only) 2012–2013, 0. Openings 2013–2014, 1. The number of students enrolled full- and part-time who were dismissed or voluntarily withdrew from this program area in 2012–2013 were 0. *General Psychology MA/MS (Master of Arts/Science)*—Applications 2012–2013, 114. Total appli-

cants accepted 2012–2013, 98. Number full-time enrolled (new admits only) 2012–2013, 40. Number part-time enrolled (new admits only) 2012–2013, 21. Total enrolled 2012–2013 full-time, 93. Total enrolled 2012–2013 part-time, 43. Openings 2013–2014, 100. The median number of years required for completion of a degree in 2012–2013 was 1. The number of students enrolled full- and part-time who were dismissed or voluntarily withdrew from this program area in 2012–2013 were 4. *School Psychology MA/MS (Master of Arts/Science)*—Applications 2012–2013, 53. Total applicants accepted 2012–2013, 32. Number full-time enrolled (new admits only) 2012–2013, 23. Number part-time enrolled (new admits only) 2012–2013, 0. Total enrolled 2012–2013 full-time, 60. Total enrolled 2012–2013 part-time, 2. Openings 2013–2014, 20. The median number of years required for completion of a degree in 2012–2013 were 3. The number of students enrolled full- and part-time who were dismissed or voluntarily withdrew from this program area in 2012–2013 were 2. *Mental Health Counseling MA/MS (Master of Arts/Science)*—Applications 2012–2013, 61. Total applicants accepted 2012–2013, 46. Number full-time enrolled (new admits only) 2012–2013, 14. Total enrolled 2012–2013 full-time, 27. Openings 2013–2014, 20. The median number of years required for completion of a degree in 2012–2013 were 2. The number of students enrolled full- and part-time who were dismissed or voluntarily withdrew from this program area in 2012–2013 were 1.

Scores: Entries appear in this order: required test or GPA, minimum score (if required), median score of students entering in 2012–2013. *Clinical Psychology PhD (Doctor of Philosophy):* GRE-V 550, 640, GRE-Q 550, 690, GRE-Subject (Psychology) 550, 700, overall undergraduate GPA 3.00, 3.54, Masters GPA 3.5, 3.8; *General Psychology MA/MS (Master of Arts/Science):* overall undergraduate GPA 3.00, 3.45; *School Psychology MA/MS (Master of Arts/Science):* overall undergraduate GPA 3.00, 3.52; *Mental Health Counseling MA/MS (Master of Arts/Science):* GRE-V 490, 550, GRE-Q 520, 590, GRE-Analytical 3.5, 4.0, overall undergraduate GPA 3.00, 3.52.

Other Criteria: (importance of criteria rated low, medium, or high): GRE scores—high, research experience—high, work experience—high, extracurricular activity—low, clinically related public service—high, GPA—high, letters of recommendation—high, interview—high, statement of goals and objectives—high, specific undergraduate psychology courses taken—high. For additional information on admission requirements, go to http://academics.adelphi.edu/derner-grad.php.

Student Characteristics: The following represents characteristics of students in 2012–2013 in all graduate psychology programs in the department: Female—full-time 192, part-time 54; Male—full-time 102, part-time 17; African American/Black—full-time 30, part-time 20; Hispanic/Latino(a)—full-time 8, part-time 6; Asian/Pacific Islander—full-time 13, part-time 3; American Indian/Alaska Native—full-time 0, part-time 0; Caucasian/White—full-time 243, part-time 42; Multi-ethnic—full-time 0, part-time 0; students subject to the Americans With Disabilities Act—full-time 0, part-time 0; Unknown ethnicity—full-time 0, part-time 0; International students who hold an F-1 or J-1 Visa—full-time 12, part-time 3.

Financial Information/Assistance:

Tuition for Full-Time Study: *Master's:* State residents: $1,030 per credit hour; Nonstate residents: $1,030 per credit hour. *Doctoral:* State residents: per academic year $38,000; Nonstate residents: per academic year $38,000. See the following website for updates and changes in tuition costs: http://ecampus.adelphi.edu/sfs/tuition_fees_grad.php.

Financial Assistance:

First-Year Students: Teaching assistantships available for first year. Average amount paid per academic year: $10,000. Average number of hours worked per week: 10. Apply by April 15. Research assistantships available for first year. Average amount paid per academic year: $10,000. Average number of hours worked per week: 10. Apply by April 15.

Advanced Students: Teaching assistantships available for advanced students. Average amount paid per academic year: $12,500. Average number of hours worked per week: 12. Apply by April 15. Research assistantships available for advanced students. Average amount paid per academic year: $12,500. Average number of hours worked per week: 12. Apply by April 15. Fellowships and scholarships available for advanced students. Average amount paid per academic year: $12,500. Apply by April 15.

Additional Information: Of all students currently enrolled full time, 70% benefited from one or more of the listed financial assistance programs. Application and information available online at: http://ecampus.adelphi.edu/sfs/graduate.php.

Internships/Practica: Doctoral Degree (PhD Clinical Psychology): For those doctoral students for whom a professional psychology internship was required in this program prior to graduation, (19) students applied for an internship in 2011–2012, with (18) students obtaining an internship. Of those students who obtained an internship, (15) were paid internships. Of those students who obtained an internship, (14) students placed in APA/CPA accredited internships, (1) students placed in internships not APA/CPA accredited, but listed with the Association of Psychology Postdoctoral and Internship Programs (APPIC), (0) students placed in internships conforming to guidelines of the Council of Directors of School Psychology Programs (CDSPP), (3) students placed in internships that were not APA/CPA accredited, APPIC or CDSPP listed. Doctoral Degree (Respecialization Diploma Clinical Psychology Respecialization): For those doctoral students for whom a professional psychology internship was required in this program prior to graduation, (1) students applied for an internship in 2011–2012, with (1) students obtaining an internship. Of those students who obtained an internship, (1) were paid internships. Of those students who obtained an internship, (0) students placed in APA/CPA accredited internships, (0) students placed in internships not APA/CPA accredited, but listed with the Association of Psychology Postdoctoral and Internship Programs (APPIC), (0) students placed in internships conforming to guidelines of the Council of Directors of School Psychology Programs (CDSPP), (1) students placed in internships that were not APA/CPA accredited, APPIC or CDSPP listed. Master's Degree (MA/MS School Psychology): An internship experience, such as a final research project or "capstone" experience is required of graduates. Master's Degree (MA/MS Mental Health Counseling): An internship experience, such as a final research project or "capstone" experience is required of graduates. For the doctoral program, students are assigned to the Psychological Services Clinic, the training facility of the PhD Program. Begin-

ning in the first year of the doctoral program, students are trained to perform intake evaluations. In the following years, students are trained to perform psychodiagnostic evaluations and psychotherapy. Students are also assigned to their first externship, usually a one-day-a-week experience, at full service mental health centers during their second year of training. They apply to a second, two-day-a-week externship during their third year. During their fifth year, students complete a one-year internship in clinical psychology. For the Postgraduate Programs, students are assigned to the Postdoctoral Psychotherapy Center, the training facility of the Postdoctoral Program.

Housing and Day Care: No on-campus housing is available. On-campus day care facilities are available. See the following website for more information: http://www.adelphi.edu/elc/.

Employment of Department Graduates:

Master's Degree Graduates: Of those who graduated in the academic year 2011–2012, the following categories and numbers represent the postgraduate activities and employment of master's degree graduates: Enrolled in a psychology doctoral program (21), enrolled in another graduate/professional program (12), enrolled in a postdoctoral residency/fellowship (n/a), employed in independent practice (n/a), employed in a professional position in a school system (12), employed in business or industry (5), employed in a community mental health/counseling center (7), employed in a hospital/medical center (7), do not know (5), total from the above (master's) (69).

Doctoral Degree Graduates: Of those who graduated in the academic year 2011–2012, the following categories and numbers represent the postgraduate activities and employment of doctoral degree graduates: Enrolled in a psychology doctoral program (n/a), enrolled in a postdoctoral residency/fellowship (7), employed in independent practice (1), employed in an academic position at a university (1), employed in other positions at a higher education institution (4), employed in a community mental health/counseling center (3), employed in a hospital/medical center (9), total from the above (doctoral) (25).

Additional Information:

Orientation, Objectives, and Emphasis of Department: The Derner Institute of Advanced Psychological Studies is the first university-based professional school of psychology. The orientation is psychodynamic and the model is scholar-practitioner. The doctoral program in clinical and the respecialization program are oriented toward community service and prepare the students for careers in clinical service; the postgraduate programs prepare graduates for the practice of psychoanalysis and psychotherapy. All doctoral programs offer supervised experience in research and theory. The clinical program consists of four years of coursework, which includes at least one day a week of supervised practice each year and a fifth-year full-time internship; the respecialization program consists of two years of coursework, including at least one day a week of supervised practice each year and a third-year full-time internship. There are several postdoctoral programs: the original program in psychoanalysis is still the best-known, and it consists of four years of seminars, case conferences, personal therapy, and supervised practice. There are also programs of shorter duration, including Child Psychotherapy, Group Psychotherapy, Marriage and Couples Therapy, and Psychodynamic School Psychology. The General MA program is a 36-credit program, and students often graduate in one year. A new MA program in School

Psychology was begun in Spring 2003; it is a three-year program, with a joint emphasis on didactic instruction and supervised practice. A new MA program in Mental Health Counseling, also with a joint emphasis on didactic instruction and supervised practice, was begun in Fall 2004.

Special Facilities or Resources: Facilities include videotape recording studios and perception, learning, developmental, cognition, and applied research laboratories. The Institute has close interaction with two health-related professional schools, the Adelphi School of Nursing and the Adelphi School of Social Work, and with affiliated community school and clinical facilities. The Institute maintains two major clinical facilities, the Adelphi University Psychological Services Center and the Postdoctoral Psychotherapy Center. An APA-accredited continuing education program brings a series of distinguished workshops to the campus.

Information for Students With Physical Disabilities: See the following website for more information: http://students.adelphi.edu/sa/dss/.

Application Information:

Application available online. URL of online application: http://admissions.adelphi.edu/onlineapp.php. Students are admitted in the Fall, application deadline December 5; Programs have rolling admissions. Applicants for the PhD program have a December 5 deadline. For School Psychology and Mental Health Counseling the deadline is March 1. MA in General Psychology program has rolling admissions. Postdoctoral applicants begin in Fall only, but have no application deadline. *Fee:* $50. Graduate admissions will waive application fee if a request for waiver is completed.

Alfred University
Division of Counseling and School Psychology
Graduate School
One Saxon Drive
Alfred, NY 14802-1205
Telephone: (607) 871-2212
Fax: (607) 871-3422
E-mail: *laubackc@alfred.edu*
Web: *http://www.alfred.edu/gradschool/school-psychology/*

Department Information:

1953. Director of School Psychology Program: Cris W. Lauback. Number of faculty: total—full-time 7, part-time 5; women—full-time 4, part-time 3; minority—part-time 1; women minority—part-time 1; faculty subject to the Americans With Disabilities Act 1.

Programs and Degrees Offered:

Listed in the following order: Program area, degree type (T if terminal Master's), number awarded 7/11–6/12. School Psychology PsyD (Doctor of Psychology) 7, School Psychology Specialist MA/MS (Master of Arts/Science) 13.

APA Accreditation: School PsyD (Doctor of Psychology). Student Outcome Data Website: http://www.alfred.edu/gradschool/school-psychology/psyd-specialization.cfm.

Student Applications/Admissions:
Student Applications

School Psychology PsyD (Doctor of Psychology)—Applications 2012–2013, 22. Total applicants accepted 2012–2013, 14. Number full-time enrolled (new admits only) 2012–2013, 5. Number part-time enrolled (new admits only) 2012–2013, 0. Total enrolled 2012–2013 full-time, 26. Total enrolled 2012–2013 part-time, 27. Openings 2013–2014, 7. The median number of years required for completion of a degree in 2012–2013 were 6. The number of students enrolled full- and part-time who were dismissed or voluntarily withdrew from this program area in 2012–2013 were 0. *School Psychology Specialist MA/MS (Master of Arts/Science)*—Applications 2012–2013, 24. Total applicants accepted 2012–2013, 17. Number full-time enrolled (new admits only) 2012–2013, 8. Number part-time enrolled (new admits only) 2012–2013, 0. Total enrolled 2012–2013 full-time, 20. Total enrolled 2012–2013 part-time, 0. Openings 2013–2014, 15. The median number of years required for completion of a degree in 2012–2013 were 3. The number of students enrolled full- and part-time who were dismissed or voluntarily withdrew from this program area in 2012–2013 were 0.

Scores: Entries appear in this order: required test or GPA, minimum score (if required), median score of students entering in 2012–2013. *School Psychology PsyD (Doctor of Psychology):* GRE-V no minimum stated, 155, GRE-Q no minimum stated, 148, GRE-Analytical no minimum stated, 4.3, overall undergraduate GPA no minimum stated, 3.32; *School Psychology Specialist MA/MS (Master of Arts/Science):* GRE-V no minimum stated, 147, GRE-Q no minimum stated, 148, GRE-Analytical no minimum stated, 3.75, overall undergraduate GPA no minimum stated, 3.6.

Other Criteria: (importance of criteria rated low, medium, or high): GRE scores—medium, research experience—medium, work experience—medium, extracurricular activity—medium, clinically related public service—low, GPA—high, letters of recommendation—high, interview—high, statement of goals and objectives—high, undergraduate major in psychology—medium, specific undergraduate psychology courses taken—high, The PsyD program places a higher emphasis on research experience as an undergraduate, and requires a statement of research interests. For additional information on admission requirements, go to http://www.alfred.edu/gradschool/school-psychology/applying.cfm.

Student Characteristics: The following represents characteristics of students in 2012–2013 in all graduate psychology programs in the department: Female—full-time 37, part-time 24; Male—full-time 9, part-time 3; African American/Black—full-time 5, part-time 1; Hispanic/Latino(a)—full-time 2, part-time 2; Asian/Pacific Islander—full-time 1, part-time 1; American Indian/Alaska Native—full-time 0, part-time 0; Caucasian/White—full-time 38, part-time 23; Multi-ethnic—full-time 0, part-time 0; students subject to the Americans With Disabilities Act—full-time 1, part-time 1; Unknown ethnicity—full-time 0, part-time 0; International students who hold an F-1 or J-1 Visa—full-time 0, part-time 0.

Financial Information/Assistance:
Tuition for Full-Time Study: *Master's:* State residents: per academic year $38,020, $810 per credit hour; Nonstate residents: per academic year $38,020, $810 per credit hour. *Doctoral:* State

residents: per academic year $38,020, $810 per credit hour; Non-state residents: per academic year $38,020, $810 per credit hour. Tuition is subject to change. Additional fees are assessed to students beyond the costs of tuition for the following: An activity fee and laboratory fee are charged. See the following website for updates and changes in tuition costs: http://www.alfred.edu/finaid/graduate/cost.cfm.

Financial Assistance:

First-Year Students: Research assistantships available for first year. Average amount paid per academic year: $19,010. Average number of hours worked per week: 7. Fellowships and scholarships available for first year. Average amount paid per academic year: $38,020. Average number of hours worked per week: 7.

Advanced Students: Teaching assistantships available for advanced students. Average amount paid per academic year: $19,010. Average number of hours worked per week: 7. Research assistantships available for advanced students. Average amount paid per academic year: $19,010. Average number of hours worked per week: 7. Fellowships and scholarships available for advanced students. Average amount paid per academic year: $38,020. Average number of hours worked per week: 15.

Additional Information: Of all students currently enrolled full time, 100% benefited from one or more of the listed financial assistance programs. Application and information available online at: http://www.alfred.edu/gradschool/school-psychology/grants.cfm.

Internships/Practica: Doctoral Degree (PsyD School Psychology): For those doctoral students for whom a professional psychology internship was required in this program prior to graduation, (4) students applied for an internship in 2011–2012, with (4) students obtaining an internship. Of those students who obtained an internship, (3) were paid internships. Of those students who obtained an internship, (0) students placed in APA/CPA accredited internships, (0) students placed in internships not APA/CPA accredited, but listed with the Association of Psychology Postdoctoral and Internship Programs (APPIC), (4) students placed in internships conforming to guidelines of the Council of Directors of School Psychology Programs (CDSPP), (0) students placed in internships that were not APA/CPA accredited, APPIC or CDSPP listed. Students obtaining the Specialists degree (MA/CAS) and doctoral degree (PsyD) may pursue internships any place in the United States. Most Specialist students choose sites at public schools across New York State and northern Pennsylvania; several obtain internships in Colorado, Maryland and Virginia. Doctoral students are required to complete a portion of their internship in a school setting, but many also choose sites and internship experiences in both school and clinical settings. A portion of doctoral students each year choose to intern at APPIC- and APA-accredited sites.

Housing and Day Care: No on-campus housing is available. No on-campus day care facilities are available.

Employment of Department Graduates:

Master's Degree Graduates: Of those who graduated in the academic year 2011–2012, the following categories and numbers represent the postgraduate activities and employment of master's degree graduates: Enrolled in a psychology doctoral program (2), enrolled in a postdoctoral residency/fellowship (n/a), employed in independent practice (n/a), employed in a professional position in a school system (18), total from the above (master's) (20).

Doctoral Degree Graduates: Of those who graduated in the academic year 2011–2012, the following categories and numbers represent the postgraduate activities and employment of doctoral degree graduates: Enrolled in a psychology doctoral program (n/a), employed in an academic position at a university (2), employed in a professional position in a school system (5), total from the above (doctoral) (7).

Additional Information:

Orientation, Objectives, and Emphasis of Department: The Alfred School Psychology programs emphasize a field-centered, systems-oriented, practitioner-scientist approach. The primary goal of the programs is the preparation of problem-solving psychologists with special concern for the application of psychological knowledge in a variety of child and family related settings. Students acquire knowledge in a wide variety of psychological theories and practices; skills are learned and then demonstrated in a number of different applied settings. They develop the personal characteristics and academic competencies necessary to work effectively with others in the identification, prevention and remediation of psychological and educational problems with children and adults. Training in school psychology at Alfred University offers extensive one-to-one contact between students and faculty members to encourage the personalized learning process. PsyD students are involved in field experience and research orientation from the first semester on. Training in the following areas is provided: knowledge base in psychology and education, assessment, intervention and remediation including counseling, play therapy and family work, consulting/training with teachers, administrators and parents, research methodology, program evaluation, and professional identification and functioning. Training at the doctoral level emphasizes applied research and the development of an area of specialization.

Special Facilities or Resources: Departmental resources include an extensive library of psychological and educational assessment tools, a media library of assessment and psychotherapy processes, as well as a library of psychotherapy and intervention materials. All first-year graduate students complete a year-long practicum in a school setting; second-year students complete a year-long practicum in our on-campus mental health clinic (Child and Family Services Center). The Center provides consultation, assessment, and psychotherapy services to children and families in the local community. The Center is a state of the art facility which utilizes group supervision in combination with digital recording of sessions and use of MacBooks to communicate with supervisors. Additionally, a graduate student workroom houses PCs and printers for student use which have necessary assessment scoring software; a student lounge is also available.

Information for Students With Physical Disabilities: See the following website for more information: http://www.alfred.edu/academics/disabled.cfm.

Application Information:
Send to Graduate Admissions, Alfred University, Saxon Drive, Alfred, NY 14802. Application available online. URL of online application: https://www.alfred.edu/admissions/gradapp/. Students are admitted in the Fall, application deadline January 15. Deadline for fall admission to the PsyD program is January 15; for the MA/CAS program the

deadline is February 1. Late applications are considered if places in the class still exist for qualified applicants. *Fee:* $60.

City University of New York: Brooklyn College

Department of Psychology
School of Natural and Behavioral Sciences
2900 Bedford Avenue
Brooklyn, NY 11210
Telephone: (718) 951-5601
Fax: (718) 951-4814
E-mail: *BenzionC@brooklyn.cuny.edu*
Web: *http://www.brooklyn.cuny.edu/web/academics/schools/ naturalsciences/graduate/psychology.php*

Department Information:

1935. Chairperson: Margaret-Ellen Pipe. Number of faculty: total—full-time 29; women—full-time 14; total—minority—full-time 2; women minority—full-time 1.

Programs and Degrees Offered:

Listed in the following order: Program area, degree type (T if terminal Master's), number awarded 7/11–6/12. Experimental Psychology MA/MS (Master of Arts/Science) (T) 15, Industrial/ Organizational Psychology MA/MS (Master of Arts/Science) (T) 39, Mental Health Counseling MA/MS (Master of Arts/Science) (T) 38.

Student Applications/Admissions:

Student Applications

Experimental Psychology MA/MS (Master of Arts/Science)—Applications 2012–2013, 64. Total applicants accepted 2012–2013, 20. Number full-time enrolled (new admits only) 2012–2013, 4. Number part-time enrolled (new admits only) 2012–2013, 16. Total enrolled 2012–2013 full-time, 8. Total enrolled 2012–2013 part-time, 36. Openings 2013–2014, 25. The median number of years required for completion of a degree in 2012–2013 were 3. The number of students enrolled full- and part-time who were dismissed or voluntarily withdrew from this program area in 2012–2013 were 0. *Industrial/Organizational Psychology MA/MS (Master of Arts/Science)*—Applications 2012–2013, 152. Total applicants accepted 2012–2013, 45. Number full-time enrolled (new admits only) 2012–2013, 9. Number part-time enrolled (new admits only) 2012–2013, 36. Total enrolled 2012–2013 full-time, 17. Total enrolled 2012–2013 part-time, 112. Openings 2013–2014, 50. The median number of years required for completion of a degree in 2012–2013 were 3. The number of students enrolled full- and part-time who were dismissed or voluntarily withdrew from this program area in 2012–2013 were 0. *Mental Health Counseling MA/MS (Master of Arts/Science)*—Applications 2012–2013, 140. Total applicants accepted 2012–2013, 40. Number full-time enrolled (new admits only) 2012–2013, 40. Number part-time enrolled (new admits only) 2012–2013, 0. Total enrolled 2012–2013 full-time, 80. Total enrolled 2012–2013 part-time, 0. Openings 2013–2014, 40. The median number of years required for completion of a degree in 2012–2013 were 2. The number of students enrolled full- and part-time who were dismissed or voluntarily withdrew from this program area in 2012–2013 were 1.

Scores: Entries appear in this order: required test or GPA, minimum score (if required), median score of students entering in 2012–2013. *Experimental Psychology MA/MS (Master of Arts/ Science):* overall undergraduate GPA 3.00; *Industrial/Organizational Psychology MA/MS (Master of Arts/Science):* overall undergraduate GPA 3.00; *Mental Health Counseling MA/MS (Master of Arts/Science):* overall undergraduate GPA 3.00.

Other Criteria: (importance of criteria rated low, medium, or high): GRE scores—medium, research experience—high, work experience—medium, extracurricular activity—low, clinically related public service—low, GPA—medium, letters of recommendation—high, interview—medium, statement of goals and objectives—high, undergraduate major in psychology—medium, specific undergraduate psychology courses taken—high, The MA program in Industrial and Organizational has a greater emphasis on applications of psychology. The MA in Experimental Psychology focuses on a strong background in research. Both these programs require that applicants offer 12 undergraduate credits in psychology with courses in statistics and in research methods. The MA program in Mental Health Counseling requires that applicants offer 15 credits, with a statistics course. The MA program in Mental Health Counseling has a greater emphasis on work, internship or volunteer experience in human services; research experience is less important. For additional information on admission requirements, go to http://www.brooklyn.cuny.edu/web/ academics/schools/naturalsciences/graduate/psychology/ programs.php.

Student Characteristics: The following represents characteristics of students in 2012–2013 in all graduate psychology programs in the department: Female—full-time 88, part-time 91; Male—full-time 51, part-time 49; African American/Black—full-time 23, part-time 22; Hispanic/Latino(a)—full-time 28, part-time 26; Asian/Pacific Islander—full-time 20, part-time 23; American Indian/Alaska Native—full-time 0, part-time 0; Caucasian/White—full-time 68, part-time 69; Multi-ethnic—full-time 0, part-time 0; students subject to the Americans With Disabilities Act—full-time 1, part-time 2; Unknown ethnicity—full-time 0, part-time 0; International students who hold an F-1 or J-1 Visa—full-time 13, part-time 0.

Financial Information/Assistance:

Tuition for Full-Time Study: *Master's:* State residents: per academic year $8,690, $365 per credit hour; Nonstate residents: $675 per credit hour. Tuition is subject to change. Additional fees are assessed to students beyond the costs of tuition for the following: student technology fee, student activity fee, CUNY consolidation fee. See the following website for updates and changes in tuition costs: http://www.brooklyn.cuny.edu/web/about/offices/bursar/ tuition/graduate.php.

Financial Assistance:

First-Year Students: Fellowships and scholarships available for first year. Apply by January 1.

Advanced Students: Fellowships and scholarships available for advanced students. Apply by February 1.

Additional Information: Application and information available online at: http://www.brooklyn.cuny.edu/web/about/administration/enrollment/financial/graduate.php.

Internships/Practica: Master's Degree (MA/MS Mental Health Counseling): An internship experience, such as a final research project or "capstone" experience is required of graduates. The MA program in Industrial and Organizational Psychology has an internship component that most students avail themselves of. It functions as both training and as an opportunity to experience the hands-on application of principles in a work setting. The MA program in Mental Health Counseling requires two semesters of pre-degree supervised practica and two semesters of internship. An additional 3000 hours of post-degree supervised internship is required for licensure.

Housing and Day Care: No on-campus housing is available. On-campus day care facilities are available. See the following website for more information: http://schooled.brooklyn.cuny.edu/ECC/ECC-index.htm.

Employment of Department Graduates:

Master's Degree Graduates: Of those who graduated in the academic year 2011–2012, the following categories and numbers represent the postgraduate activities and employment of master's degree graduates: Enrolled in a postdoctoral residency/fellowship (n/a), employed in independent practice (n/a), total from the above (master's) (0).

Doctoral Degree Graduates: Of those who graduated in the academic year 2011–2012, the following categories and numbers represent the postgraduate activities and employment of doctoral degree graduates: Enrolled in a psychology doctoral program (n/a), total from the above (doctoral) (0).

Additional Information:

Orientation, Objectives, and Emphasis of Department: The Industrial/Organizational Psychology MA program offers training in two tracks: Human Relations, with focus on the group, and Organizational Behavior, with focus on the organization. Graduates from both tracks are prepared for entry-level, executive positions in Human Resources and Personnel. The MA program in Mental Health Counseling provides experiential learning with counseling practicum experience in mental health settings, along with comprehensive course work that prepares students for practice in mental health counseling. Graduates are eligible to take the NYS licensing exam which permits private/independent practice of counseling. The Experimental Psychology program offers training for those aiming to go on to a doctoral program in Psychology, since the courses offered in this program are doctoral-level courses.

Special Facilities or Resources: There are over a dozen active laboratories in the department focusing on topics such as the physiology of taste and preference formation, children's acquisition of spatial knowledge, transactive knowledge in organizations, implicit learning in cognitive disorders, visual functions in Down syndrome, creativity and cognition in the arts, comparative psychology in cephalopods, amphibians, and crustaceans, hippocampal atrophy in early Alzheimer's disease, implicit impression formation, Darwinian models of mate selection, biomimetic robotics, neurodegeneration in the aged, and parent-child communication. All labs are well equipped and some are supported by grants from NSF, NIH, NASA, DARPA, and other organizations. Several faculty have appointments and working collaborations with research labs in city hospitals and medical schools with access to technologies such as fMRI.

Information for Students With Physical Disabilities: See the following website for more information: http://www.brooklyn.cuny.edu/web/about/offices/disability.php.

Application Information:
Send to Office of Graduate Admissions, Brooklyn College, 2900 Bedford Avenue, Brooklyn, NY 11210. Application available online. URL of online application: http://www.brooklyn.cuny.edu/web/admissions/graduate/apply.php. Students are admitted in the Fall, application deadline February 1; Spring, application deadline November 1. MA application for Mental Health Counseling is February 1. Deadline for all other MA programs for Fall is March 1. Spring admissions are for the Experimental MA program only. *Fee:* $125.

City University of New York: Brooklyn College

School Psychologist Graduate Program, School of Education
Brooklyn College
2900 Bedford Avenue, Room 1107 James
Brooklyn, NY 11210
Telephone: (718) 951-5876
Fax: (718) 951-4816
E-mail: *paulmc@brooklyn.cuny.edu*
Web: *http://www.brooklyn.cuny.edu/web/academics/schools/education/graduate/psychology.php*

Department Information:

1968. Program Coordinator: Paul McCabe. Number of faculty: total—full-time 6, part-time 9; women—full-time 4, part-time 5; total—minority—full-time 2, part-time 3; women minority—full-time 1, part-time 3.

Programs and Degrees Offered:

Listed in the following order: Program area, degree type (T if terminal Master's), number awarded 7/11–6/12. School Psychology MA/MS (Master of Arts/Science) 18, School Psychology (Bilingual) MA/MS (Master of Arts/Science) 3.

Student Applications/Admissions:

Student Applications

School Psychology MA/MS (Master of Arts/Science)—Applications 2012–2013, 145. Total applicants accepted 2012–2013, 32. Number full-time enrolled (new admits only) 2012–2013, 20. Number part-time enrolled (new admits only) 2012–2013, 12. Total enrolled 2012–2013 full-time, 58. Total enrolled 2012–2013 part-time, 34. Openings 2013–2014, 35. The median number of years required for completion of a degree in 2012–2013 were 3. The number of students enrolled full- and part-time who were dismissed or voluntarily withdrew from this program area in 2012–2013 were 0. *School Psychology (Bilingual) MA/MS (Master of Arts/Science)*—Applications 2012–2013, 25. Total applicants accepted 2012–2013, 8. Number full-time enrolled (new admits only) 2012–2013, 5. Number part-time enrolled (new admits only) 2012–2013, 3. Total enrolled 2012–2013 full-time, 5. Total enrolled 2012–2013 part-time, 3. Openings 2013–2014, 15. The median number of years required for completion of a degree in 2012–2013 were 3. The number of students enrolled full- and part-time who were dismissed or voluntarily withdrew from this program area in 2012–2013 were 0.

Scores: Entries appear in this order: required test or GPA, minimum score (if required), median score of students entering in 2012–2013. *School Psychology MA/MS (Master of Arts/Science):* overall undergraduate GPA 3.0, psychology GPA 3.0; *School Psychology (Bilingual) MA/MS (Master of Arts/Science):* overall undergraduate GPA 3.0, psychology GPA 3.0.

Other Criteria: (importance of criteria rated low, medium, or high): GRE scores—low, research experience—medium, work experience—high, extracurricular activity—medium, clinically related public service—high, GPA—high, letters of recommendation—high, interview—high, statement of goals and objectives—high, writing sample—high, undergraduate major in psychology—low, specific undergraduate psychology courses taken—low.

Student Characteristics: The following represents characteristics of students in 2012–2013 in all graduate psychology programs in the department: Female—full-time 39, part-time 45; Male—full-time 6, part-time 3; African American/Black—full-time 10, part-time 6; Hispanic/Latino(a)—full-time 10, part-time 6; Asian/Pacific Islander—full-time 1, part-time 4; American Indian/Alaska Native—full-time 0, part-time 0; Caucasian/White—full-time 24, part-time 32; Multi-ethnic—full-time 0, part-time 0; students subject to the Americans With Disabilities Act—full-time 0, part-time 0; Unknown ethnicity—full-time 0, part-time 0; International students who hold an F-1 or J-1 Visa—full-time 0, part-time 0.

Financial Information/Assistance:
Tuition for Full-Time Study: *Master's:* State residents: per academic year $8,690, $365 per credit hour; Nonstate residents: $675 per credit hour. Additional fees are assessed to students beyond the costs of tuition for the following: student technology fee. See the following website for updates and changes in tuition costs: http://www.brooklyn.cuny.edu/web/about/offices/bursar/tuition/graduate.php.

Financial Assistance:
First-Year Students: Fellowships and scholarships available for first year. Apply by March 15.

Advanced Students: Fellowships and scholarships available for advanced students. Apply by March 15.

Additional Information: Of all students currently enrolled full time, 10% benefited from one or more of the listed financial assistance programs. Application and information available online at: http://www.brooklyn.cuny.edu/web/about/administration/enrollment/financial/graduate.php.

Internships/Practica: Internships are available and coordinated through our program with various schools, both public and private, working with both the mainstream population, as well as special populations. In addition, internships are available in mental health clinics, agencies, and hospitals. Practica in assessment, intervention, consultation, and counseling are designed to reinforce students' course work.

Housing and Day Care: On-campus housing is available. See the following website for more information: http://www.1kenilworth.com/. On-campus day care facilities are available. See the following website for more information: http://depthome.brooklyn.cuny.edu/schooled/ECC/ECC-index.htm.

Employment of Department Graduates:
Master's Degree Graduates: Of those who graduated in the academic year 2011–2012, the following categories and numbers represent the postgraduate activities and employment of master's degree graduates: Enrolled in a psychology doctoral program (2), enrolled in a postdoctoral residency/fellowship (n/a), employed in independent practice (n/a), employed in a professional position in a school system (16), total from the above (master's) (18).

Doctoral Degree Graduates: Of those who graduated in the academic year 2011–2012, the following categories and numbers represent the postgraduate activities and employment of doctoral degree graduates: Enrolled in a psychology doctoral program (n/a), total from the above (doctoral) (0).

Additional Information:
Orientation, Objectives, and Emphasis of Department: The aim of the school psychologists' training program is to meet the community needs for professionally competent personnel to function in the schools as consultants on psychological aspects of learning and mental health. Students are prepared to make assessments of situations involving children, parents, and school personnel to achieve the more optimal functioning of children in the school setting. Coursework will prepare students in the areas of measurement and evaluation, personality understanding, educational objectives and procedures, curriculum development, and research. Students will also be trained to achieve greater integration between school and community. Elements of the program will provide students with opportunities for self-reflection, collaboration with other professionals and families, and engagement in issues of diversity and social justice.

Special Facilities or Resources: In addition to the use of the Brooklyn College library, students are welcome to use all the libraries at other colleges within the CUNY system. The School Psychology Program also has a small library of texts and journals for the students' use.

Information for Students With Physical Disabilities: See the following website for more information: http://www.brooklyn.cuny.edu/web/about/offices/disability.php.

Application Information:
Send to Brooklyn College, Admissions Office, 2900 Bedford Avenue, Brooklyn, NY 11210. Application available online. URL of online application: http://www.brooklyn.cuny.edu/web/admissions/graduate/apply.php. Students are admitted in the Fall, application deadline February 1. *Fee:* $125.

City University of New York: Graduate Center

Behavior Analysis Training Area
Queens College
65-30 Kissena Boulevard
Flushing, NY 11367
Telephone: (718) 997-3630
Fax: (718) 997-3257
E-mail: *bruce.brown@qc.cuny.edu*
Web: *http://www.gc.cuny.edu/Page-Elements/Academics-Research-Centers-Initiatives/Doctoral-Programs/Psychology/Training-Areas/Behavior-Analysis*

Department Information:

1967. Coordinator: Bruce L. Brown. Number of faculty: total—full-time 11; women—full-time 4; total—minority—full-time 1; women minority—full-time 1.

Programs and Degrees Offered:

Listed in the following order: Program area, degree type (T if terminal Master's), number awarded 7/11–6/12. Behavior Analysis PhD (Doctor of Philosophy) 10.

Student Applications/Admissions:

Student Applications

Behavior Analysis PhD (Doctor of Philosophy)—Applications 2012–2013, 16. Total applicants accepted 2012–2013, 5. Number full-time enrolled (new admits only) 2012–2013, 4. Number part-time enrolled (new admits only) 2012–2013, 0. Total enrolled 2012–2013 full-time, 32. Total enrolled 2012–2013 part-time, 0. Openings 2013–2014, 3. The median number of years required for completion of a degree in 2012–2013 were 7. The number of students enrolled full- and part-time who were dismissed or voluntarily withdrew from this program area in 2012–2013 were 1.

Other Criteria: (importance of criteria rated low, medium, or high): GRE scores—high, research experience—high, work experience—low, extracurricular activity—low, clinically related public service—low, GPA—high, letters of recommendation—high, interview—high, statement of goals and objectives—high, undergraduate major in psychology—medium, specific undergraduate psychology courses taken—high. For additional information on admission requirements, go to http://www.gc.cuny.edu/Prospective-Current-Students/Prospective-Students/Admission-Requirements.

Student Characteristics: The following represents characteristics of students in 2012–2013 in all graduate psychology programs in the department: Female—full-time 21, part-time 0; Male—full-time 11, part-time 0; African American/Black—full-time 1, part-time 0; Hispanic/Latino(a)—full-time 2, part-time 0; Asian/Pacific Islander—full-time 1, part-time 0; American Indian/Alaska Native—full-time 0, part-time 0; Caucasian/White—full-time 28, part-time 0; Multi-ethnic—full-time 0, part-time 0; students subject to the Americans With Disabilities Act—full-time 0, part-time 0; Unknown ethnicity—full-time 0, part-time 0; International students who hold an F-1 or J-1 Visa—full-time 2, part-time 0.

Financial Information/Assistance:

Tuition for Full-Time Study: *Doctoral:* State residents: per academic year $7,770; Nonstate residents: $755 per credit hour.

Tuition is subject to change. See the following website for updates and changes in tuition costs: http://www.gc.cuny.edu/Prospective-Current-Students/Current-Students/Tuition-Fees.

Financial Assistance:

First-Year Students: Fellowships and scholarships available for first year. Average amount paid per academic year: $18,000. Average number of hours worked per week: 20. Apply by December 1.

Advanced Students: Teaching assistantships available for advanced students. Average amount paid per academic year: $10,000. Average number of hours worked per week: 6.

Additional Information: Of all students currently enrolled full time, 78% benefited from one or more of the listed financial assistance programs. Application and information available online at: http://www.gc.cuny.edu/Prospective-Current-Students/New-Current-Students/Financial-Assistance.

Housing and Day Care: On-campus housing is available. See the following website for more information: http://www.qc.cuny.edu/StudentLife/TheSummit/. On-campus day care facilities are available. See the following website for more information: http://www.qc.cuny.edu/StudentLife/services/ChildDevelopment/.

Employment of Department Graduates:

Master's Degree Graduates: Of those who graduated in the academic year 2011–2012, the following categories and numbers represent the postgraduate activities and employment of master's degree graduates: Enrolled in a postdoctoral residency/fellowship (n/a), employed in independent practice (n/a), total from the above (master's) (0).

Doctoral Degree Graduates: Of those who graduated in the academic year 2011–2012, the following categories and numbers represent the postgraduate activities and employment of doctoral degree graduates: Enrolled in a psychology doctoral program (n/a), employed in an academic position at a university (1), total from the above (doctoral) (1).

Additional Information:

Orientation, Objectives, and Emphasis of Department: Behavior Analysis Training Area (BATA, formerly Learning Processes and Behavior Analysis) offers doctoral students in psychology training in the experimental analysis of human and animal behavior and in applied behavior analysis. Students and faculty investigate a wide spectrum of behavioral processes through lectures and experimental laboratory course work, advanced seminars, informal student-faculty discussions, practica, internships, and individual research projects. Faculty and students publish regularly in peer-reviewed journals and are strongly represented at major national and international conferences. Their current research interests include such topics as categorization and concept formation, language acquisition, affective behavior, behavioral assessment, human and animal timing, pattern recognition, stimulus control, behavioral community psychology, education and training of children with autism, and staff training in organizational settings. The BATA program is seeking reaccreditation in behavior analysis by the Association for Behavior Analysis, and licensure-qualification in New York State. The Behavior Analysis Certification Board, Inc. has approved a subset of the curriculum as a course sequence that meets the coursework requirements for eligibility to take the Board Certified Behavior Analyst Examination. Applicants will have to meet additional requirements to qualify.

Information for Students With Physical Disabilities: See the following website for more information: http://www.qc.cuny.edu/StudentLife/services/specialserv/.

Application Information:

Send to Office of Admissions, The Graduate School & University Center of the City University of New York, 365 Fifth Avenue, New York, NY 10016-4309. Application available online. URL of online application: http://www.gc.cuny.edu/Prospective-Current-Students/Prospective-Students/Application-Instructions-Forms. Students are admitted in the Fall, application deadline December 1. *Fee:* $125.

City University of New York: Graduate Center
Clinical Psychology with Emphasis in Neuropsychology
Queens College
65-30 Kissena Boulevard
Queens, NY 11367
Telephone: (718) 997-3630
Fax: (718) 997-3257
E-mail: *nancy.foldi@qc.cuny.edu*
Web: *http://www.gc.cuny.edu/Page-Elements/Academics-Research-Centers-Initiatives/Doctoral-Programs/Psychology/Training-Areas/Clinical-Queens*

Department Information:

1968. Director of Clinical Training: Nancy S. Foldi, PhD. Number of faculty: total—full-time 30, part-time 3; women—full-time 13, part-time 2; total—minority—full-time 5; women minority—full-time 2.

Programs and Degrees Offered:

Listed in the following order: Program area, degree type (T if terminal Master's), number awarded 7/11–6/12. Clinical Psychology: Neuropsychology PhD (Doctor of Philosophy) 4, Basic Neuropsychology PhD (Doctor of Philosophy) 0.

Student Applications/Admissions:
Student Applications

Clinical Psychology: Neuropsychology PhD (Doctor of Philosophy)—Applications 2012–2013, 57. Total applicants accepted 2012–2013, 11. Number full-time enrolled (new admits only) 2012–2013, 6. Total enrolled 2012–2013 full-time, 53. Openings 2013–2014, 8. The median number of years required for completion of a degree in 2012–2013 were 6. The number of students enrolled full- and part-time who were dismissed or voluntarily withdrew from this program area in 2012–2013 were 0. *Basic Neuropsychology PhD (Doctor of Philosophy)*—Applications 2012–2013, 20. Total applicants accepted 2012–2013, 8. Number full-time enrolled (new admits only) 2012–2013, 5. Total enrolled 2012–2013 full-time, 21. The median number of years required for completion of a degree in 2012–2013 were 4. The number of students enrolled full- and part-time who were dismissed or voluntarily withdrew from this program area in 2012–2013 were 0.

Scores: Entries appear in this order: required test or GPA, minimum score (if required), median score of students entering in 2012–2013. *Clinical Psychology: Neuropsychology PhD (Doctor of Philosophy):* GRE-V no minimum stated, GRE-Q no minimum stated, GRE-Analytical no minimum stated, overall undergraduate GPA no minimum stated, last 2 years GPA no minimum stated, psychology GPA no minimum stated, Masters GPA no minimum stated; *Basic Neuropsychology PhD (Doctor of Philosophy):* GRE-V no minimum stated, GRE-Q no minimum stated, GRE-Analytical no minimum stated, overall undergraduate GPA no minimum stated, psychology GPA no minimum stated, Masters GPA no minimum stated.

Other Criteria: (importance of criteria rated low, medium, or high): GRE scores—medium, research experience—high, work experience—low, extracurricular activity—low, clinically related public service—low, GPA—high, letters of recommendation—high, interview—high, statement of goals and objectives—high, undergraduate major in psychology—low. For additional information on admission requirements, go to http://www.gc.cuny.edu/Prospective-Current-Students/Prospective-Students/Admission-Requirements.

Student Characteristics: The following represents characteristics of students in 2012–2013 in all graduate psychology programs in the department: Female—full-time 56, part-time 0; Male—full-time 18, part-time 0; African American/Black—full-time 0, part-time 0; Hispanic/Latino(a)—full-time 2, part-time 0; Asian/Pacific Islander—full-time 2, part-time 0; American Indian/Alaska Native—full-time 0, part-time 0; Caucasian/White—full-time 0, part-time 0; Multi-ethnic—full-time 0, part-time 0; students subject to the Americans With Disabilities Act—full-time 0, part-time 0; Unknown ethnicity—full-time 0, part-time 0; International students who hold an F-1 or J-1 Visa—full-time 3, part-time 0.

Financial Information/Assistance:

Tuition for Full-Time Study: *Doctoral:* State residents: per academic year $6,580; Nonstate residents: $645 per credit hour. Tuition is subject to change. Additional fees are assessed to students beyond the costs of tuition for the following: student activity fee, student technology fee, student health fee.

Financial Assistance:

First-Year Students: Teaching assistantships available for first year. Average amount paid per academic year: $0. Average number of hours worked per week: 0. Research assistantships available for first year. Average amount paid per academic year: $0. Average number of hours worked per week: 0. Traineeships available for first year. Average amount paid per academic year: $0. Average number of hours worked per week: 0. Fellowships and scholarships available for first year. Average amount paid per academic year: $0. Average number of hours worked per week: 0.

Advanced Students: Teaching assistantships available for advanced students. Average number of hours worked per week: 0. Research assistantships available for advanced students. Average number of hours worked per week: 0. Fellowships and scholarships available for advanced students. Average number of hours worked per week: 0.

Additional Information: Of all students currently enrolled full time, 60% benefited from one or more of the listed financial assistance programs.

Internships/Practica: Doctoral Degree (PhD Clinical Psychology: Neuropsychology): For those doctoral students for whom a professional psychology internship was required in this program prior to graduation, (7) students applied for an internship in 2011–2012, with (7) students obtaining an internship. Of those students who obtained an internship, (5) were paid internships. Of those students who obtained an internship, (4) students placed in APA/CPA accredited internships, (3) students placed in internships not APA/CPA accredited, but listed with the Association of Psychology Postdoctoral and Internship Programs (APPIC), (0) students placed in internships conforming to guidelines of the Council of Directors of School Psychology Programs (CDSPP), (0) students placed in internships that were not APA/CPA accredited, APPIC or CDSPP listed. Clinical Track students experience at least three different clinical practica. Additionally, all clinical track students must complete a one year predoctoral internship.

Housing and Day Care: On-campus housing is available. See the following website for more information: http://www.thesummitatqc.com/. On-campus day care facilities are available. See the following website for more information: http://qcpages.qc.cuny.edu/qcchild/.

Employment of Department Graduates:

Master's Degree Graduates: Of those who graduated in the academic year 2011–2012, the following categories and numbers represent the postgraduate activities and employment of master's degree graduates: Enrolled in a postdoctoral residency/fellowship (n/a), employed in independent practice (n/a), total from the above (master's) (0).

Doctoral Degree Graduates: Of those who graduated in the academic year 2011–2012, the following categories and numbers represent the postgraduate activities and employment of doctoral degree graduates: Enrolled in a psychology doctoral program (n/a), enrolled in a postdoctoral residency/fellowship (10), employed in a hospital/medical center (2), total from the above (doctoral) (12).

Additional Information:

Orientation, Objectives, and Emphasis of Department: The Clinical Psychology PhD program is an academically-oriented PhD program with a core philosophy based on two premises. The first of these is that productive research, effective teaching, and responsible clinical practice are integrally interdependent. That is, effective teaching must include critical analysis of current research data, and clinical assessment and treatment procedures must be empirically validated. The second premise is that the understanding of impaired or disordered brain function in humans requires rigorous training in the neurosciences as well as in the traditional clinical topics. The program was designed to train professionals with competence in research and/or teaching of Clinical Psychology as well as in the area of brain-behavior relationships, and in the application of these competencies in clinical settings. The clinical program will require 90 credits (starting in 2013) including at least two years of practicum training. The program provides students the opportunity to acquire and apply the skills appropriate to the practice of clinical neuropsychology. Students receive training in the evidence-based treatment, and evaluation of psychological and neuropsychological function in various clinical populations, which may include children or adults, neurological, neurosurgical, rehabilitation medicine and psychiatric patients, as well as in the use of rehabilitative, psychotherapeutic, and remediative techniques. A full-year internship is required for graduation from the program.

Special Facilities or Resources: The Program has well equipped laboratories for clinical psychology, including individual faculty who focus on human research and faculty who focus on animal models. The campus runs the QC Psychology Clinic, which provides supervised training for students early in their career.

Application Information:
Send to Office of Admissions, The Graduate School & University Center of the City University of New York, 365 Fifth Avenue, New York, NY 10016-4309. Application available online. URL of online application: http://www.gc.cuny.edu/Prospective-Current-Students/Prospective-Students/Application-Instructions-Forms. Students are admitted in the Fall, application deadline December 1. *Fee:* $150.

City University of New York: Graduate School and University Center
PhD Program in Educational Psychology
365 Fifth Avenue
New York, NY 10016-4309
Telephone: (212) 817-8285
Fax: (212) 817-1516
E-mail: *mkelly@gc.cuny.edu*
Web: *http://www.gc.cuny.edu/educationalpsychology*

Department Information:
1969. Executive Officer: Mario Antonio Kelly. Number of faculty: total—full-time 6, part-time 5; women—full-time 2, part-time 3; total—minority—full-time 1, part-time 1.

Programs and Degrees Offered:
Listed in the following order: Program area, degree type (T if terminal Master's), number awarded 7/11–6/12. Educational Psychology PhD (Doctor of Philosophy) 19.

APA Accreditation: School PhD (Doctor of Philosophy). Student Outcome Data Website: http://www.gc.cuny.edu/Page-Elements/Academics-Research-Centers-Initiatives/Doctoral-Programs/Educational-Psychology/Program/School-Psychology.

Student Applications/Admissions:
Student Applications
Educational Psychology PhD (Doctor of Philosophy)—Applications 2012–2013, 114. Total applicants accepted 2012–2013, 13. Number full-time enrolled (new admits only) 2012–2013, 8. Number part-time enrolled (new admits only) 2012–2013, 1. Total enrolled 2012–2013 full-time, 86. Total enrolled 2012–2013 part-time, 6. Openings 2013–2014, 9. The number of students enrolled full- and part-time who were dismissed or voluntarily withdrew from this program area in 2012–2013 were 8.

Scores: Entries appear in this order: required test or GPA, minimum score (if required), median score of students entering in 2012–2013. *Educational Psychology PhD (Doctor of Philosophy):* GRE-V no minimum stated, GRE-Q no minimum stated. *Other Criteria:* (importance of criteria rated low, medium, or high): GRE scores—high, research experience—medium, work experience—medium, extracurricular activity—low, clinically related public service—low, GPA—medium, letters of recommendation—high, interview—high, statement of goals and objectives—high, undergraduate major in psychology—low, specific undergraduate psychology courses taken—low.

Student Characteristics: The following represents characteristics of students in 2012–2013 in all graduate psychology programs in the department: Female—full-time 69, part-time 5; Male—full-time 17, part-time 1; African American/Black—full-time 6, part-time 0; Hispanic/Latino(a)—full-time 4, part-time 0; Asian/Pacific Islander—part-time 1; American Indian/Alaska Native—full-time 0, part-time 0; Caucasian/White—full-time 73, part-time 0; Multi-ethnic—full-time 0, part-time 0; students subject to the Americans With Disabilities Act—full-time 0, part-time 0; Unknown ethnicity—full-time 3, part-time 5; International students who hold an F-1 or J-1 Visa—full-time 1, part-time 0.

Financial Information/Assistance:

Tuition for Full-Time Study: *Doctoral:* State residents: per academic year $8,200; Nonstate residents: $795 per credit hour. Additional fees are assessed to students beyond the costs of tuition for the following: student activities fee=$41.60/semester; technology fee=$100/semester. See the following website for updates and changes in tuition costs: http://www.gc.cuny.edu/Prospective-Current-Students/Current-Students/Tuition-Fees.

Financial Assistance:

First-Year Students: Research assistantships available for first year. Average amount paid per academic year: $8,200. Average number of hours worked per week: 5. Apply by January 15. Fellowships and scholarships available for first year. Average amount paid per academic year: $25,000. Average number of hours worked per week: 5. Apply by January 15.

Advanced Students: Teaching assistantships available for advanced students. Average amount paid per academic year: $5,000. Average number of hours worked per week: 5. Research assistantships available for advanced students. Average amount paid per academic year: $8,200. Average number of hours worked per week: 5. Fellowships and scholarships available for advanced students. Average amount paid per academic year: $25,000. Average number of hours worked per week: 5.

Additional Information: Of all students currently enrolled full time, 50% benefited from one or more of the listed financial assistance programs. Application and information available online at: http://www.gc.cuny.edu/Prospective-Current-Students/Current-Students/Financial-Assistance.

Internships/Practica: Doctoral Degree (PhD Educational Psychology): For those doctoral students for whom a professional psychology internship was required in this program prior to graduation, (4) students applied for an internship in 2011–2012, with (4) students obtaining an internship. Of those students who obtained an internship, (4) were paid internships. Of those students who obtained an internship, (0) students placed in APA/CPA accredited internships, (0) students placed in internships not APA/CPA accredited, but listed with the Association of Psychology Postdoctoral and Internship Programs (APPIC), (4) students placed in internships conforming to guidelines of the Council of Directors of School Psychology Programs (CDSPP), (0) students placed in internships that were not APA/CPA accredited, APPIC or CDSPP listed.

Housing and Day Care: On-campus housing is available. See the following website for more information: http://www.gc.cuny.edu/Prospective-Current-Students/Student-Life/Housing. On-campus day care facilities are available. See the following website for more information: http://www.gc.cuny.edu/Prospective-Current-Students/Student-Life/Resources.

Employment of Department Graduates:

Master's Degree Graduates: Of those who graduated in the academic year 2011–2012, the following categories and numbers represent the postgraduate activities and employment of master's degree graduates: Enrolled in a postdoctoral residency/fellowship (n/a), employed in independent practice (n/a), total from the above (master's) (0).

Doctoral Degree Graduates: Of those who graduated in the academic year 2011–2012, the following categories and numbers represent the postgraduate activities and employment of doctoral degree graduates: Enrolled in a psychology doctoral program (n/a), employed in other positions at a higher education institution (2), employed in a professional position in a school system (5), other employment position (1), total from the above (doctoral) (8).

Additional Information:

Orientation, Objectives, and Emphasis of Department: The PhD program in Educational Psychology is research oriented, preparing students for teaching, research, and program development in various educational settings such as universities, school systems, research institutions, community agencies, as well as in educational publishing, television, and in other agencies with training programs. Four areas of concentration are offered: quantitative methods in educational and psychological research, learning development and instruction, school psychology, and educational policy analysis.

Special Facilities or Resources: The Educational Psychology program is affiliated with a university based research institute, CASE (Center for Advanced Study in Education). CASE is heavily involved in the evaluation and implementation of various applied educational programs. Our faculty and students have worked as principal investigators and research assistants on CASE projects.

Application Information:
Send to Admissions Office, CUNY Graduate Center, 365 Fifth Avenue, New York, NY 10016-4309. Application available online. URL of online application: http://www.gc.cuny.edu/Prospective-Current-Students/Prospective-Students/Admission-Requirements. Students are admitted in the Fall, application deadline January 15. *Fee:* $125.

City University of New York: John Jay College of Criminal Justice

Department of Psychology
John Jay College of Criminal Justice, CUNY
524 West 59th Street, 10th Floor
New York, NY 10019
Telephone: (212) 237-8782
Fax: (212) 237-8742
E-mail: Jwulach@jjay.cuny.edu
Web: http://www.jjay.cuny.edu/departments/psychology/about_us.php

Department Information:

1976. Director, MA Program: James S. Wulach, PhD, J.D. Number of faculty: total—full-time 46, part-time 14; women—full-time 25, part-time 6; total—minority—full-time 12, part-time 4; women minority—full-time 5, part-time 2; faculty subject to the Americans With Disabilities Act 16.

Programs and Degrees Offered:

Listed in the following order: Program area, degree type (T if terminal Master's), number awarded 7/11–6/12. Forensic Psychology MA/MS (Master of Arts/Science) (T) 137, Forensic Mental Health Counseling MA/MS (Master of Arts/Science) (T) 0, Postgraduate Certificate in Forensic Psychology Other 0, Ma-Jd in Forensic Psychology & Law Other.

Student Applications/Admissions:

Student Applications

Forensic Psychology MA/MS (Master of Arts/Science)—Applications 2012–2013, 307. Total applicants accepted 2012–2013, 254. Number full-time enrolled (new admits only) 2012–2013, 117. Number part-time enrolled (new admits only) 2012–2013, 103. Total enrolled 2012–2013 full-time, 157. Total enrolled 2012–2013 part-time, 154. Openings 2013–2014, 115. The median number of years required for completion of a degree in 2012–2013 were 2. The number of students enrolled full- and part-time who were dismissed or voluntarily withdrew from this program area in 2012–2013 were 26. Forensic Mental Health Counseling MA/MS (Master of Arts/Science)—Applications 2012–2013, 156. Total applicants accepted 2012–2013, 124. Number full-time enrolled (new admits only) 2012–2013, 52. Number part-time enrolled (new admits only) 2012–2013, 72. Total enrolled 2012–2013 full-time, 52. Total enrolled 2012–2013 part-time, 72. Openings 2013–2014, 35. The number of students enrolled full- and part-time who were dismissed or voluntarily withdrew from this program area in 2012–2013 were 0. Postgraduate Certificate in Forensic Psychology Other—Applications 2012–2013, 10. Total applicants accepted 2012–2013, 6. Number full-time enrolled (new admits only) 2012–2013, 0. Number part-time enrolled (new admits only) 2012–2013, 5. Openings 2013–2014, 10. The median number of years required for completion of a degree in 2012–2013 were 2. The number of students enrolled full- and part-time who were dismissed or voluntarily withdrew from this program area in 2012–2013 were 1. Ma-Jd in Forensic Psychology & Law Other—Openings 2013–2014, 10.

Scores: Entries appear in this order: required test or GPA, minimum score (if required), median score of students entering in 2012–2013. Forensic Psychology MA/MS (Master of Arts/Science): GRE-V 145, GRE-Q 145, GRE-Analytical no minimum stated, overall undergraduate GPA 3.00, 3.20; Forensic Mental Health Counseling MA/MS (Master of Arts/Science): GRE-V no minimum stated, 145, GRE-Q no minimum stated, 145, GRE-Analytical no minimum stated, overall undergraduate GPA 3.00, 3.20; Postgraduate Certificate in Forensic Psychology Other: GRE-V 145, GRE-Q 145, overall undergraduate GPA 3.0, 3.2; MA-JD in Forensic Psychology & Law Other: GRE-V 145, GRE-Q 145, GRE-Analytical no minimum stated, overall undergraduate GPA 3.0.

Other Criteria: (importance of criteria rated low, medium, or high): GRE scores—high, research experience—low, work experience—low, GPA—high, letters of recommendation—medium, statement of goals and objectives—low, undergraduate major in psychology—medium, specific undergraduate psychology courses taken—high, MA Program: GPA & GRE Scores weighted most heavily. For additional information on admission requirements, go to http://www.jjay.cuny.edu/451.php.

Student Characteristics: The following represents characteristics of students in 2012–2013 in all graduate psychology programs in the department: Female—full-time 148, part-time 169; Male—full-time 61, part-time 62; African American/Black—full-time 14, part-time 35; Hispanic/Latino(a)—full-time 17, part-time 26; Asian/Pacific Islander—full-time 2, part-time 9; American Indian/Alaska Native—full-time 1, part-time 0; Caucasian/White—full-time 175, part-time 161; Multi-ethnic—full-time 0, part-time 0; Unknown ethnicity—full-time 0, part-time 0.

Financial Information/Assistance:

Tuition for Full-Time Study: Master's: State residents: per academic year $8,690, $365 per credit hour; Nonstate residents: $675 per credit hour. Tuition is subject to change. See the following website for updates and changes in tuition costs: http://www.jjay.cuny.edu/501.php.

Financial Assistance:

First-Year Students: No information provided.
Advanced Students: No information provided.
Additional Information: No information provided.

Internships/Practica: Master's Degree (MA/MS Forensic Psychology): An internship experience, such as a final research project or "capstone" experience is required of graduates. Master's Degree (MA/MS Forensic Mental Health Counseling): An internship experience, such as a final research project or "capstone" experience is required of graduates. (MA Program in Forensic Psychology): Most students complete a 300-hour externship in local forensic psychology settings, such as hospitals or prisons. (MA Program in Forensic Mental Health Counseling): Most students complete a 600-hour externship in local forensic psychology settings, such as hospitals or prisons.

Housing and Day Care: No on-campus housing is available. On-campus day care facilities are available. See the following website for more information: http://www.jjay.cuny.edu/5106.php.

Employment of Department Graduates:

Master's Degree Graduates: Of those who graduated in the academic year 2011–2012, the following categories and numbers represent the postgraduate activities and employment of master's

degree graduates: Enrolled in a postdoctoral residency/fellowship (n/a), employed in independent practice (n/a), total from the above (master's) (0).

Doctoral Degree Graduates: Of those who graduated in the academic year 2011–2012, the following categories and numbers represent the postgraduate activities and employment of doctoral degree graduates: Enrolled in a psychology doctoral program (n/a), total from the above (doctoral) (0).

Additional Information:

Orientation, Objectives, and Emphasis of Department: The 42-credit MA Program in Forensic Psychology program is designed to train students to provide professional MA-level services to, and within, the legal system—especially the criminal justice system; and to provide a background for psychology doctoral study in the future. In addition to offering (and requiring) traditional master's level clinical psychology courses, we offer specialized courses in psychology and the law; the psychology and treatment of juvenile and adult offenders and the victims of crime; forensic evaluation and testimony; jury research; eyewitness research; psychological profiles of homicidal offenders; psychology of terrorism; and forensic psychological research. There is a research track for advanced students to work on MA theses with professors. Courses are primarily offered in the afternoon and evening. Many of our full-time faculty members have postdoctoral psychological certifications; 6 are lawyers as well as psychologists; and many have extensive forensic experience as practitioners and/or researchers. Some of our graduates become MA psychologists within the criminal justice system, working with offenders, delinquents, and victims. Other graduates enhance their present careers in law enforcement, probation, or parole by completing the program. Many of our graduates continue their education in psychology doctoral programs, or in law. The MA Program in Forensic Mental Health Counseling is a new 60-credit program, sponsored by the Psychology Department, which has been approved by NY State as a "license eligible" program for NY Mental Health Counselors, with a forensic specialization. Coursework is similar to the MA Program in Forensic Psychology, with less emphasis on research, and more courses oriented towards becoming a NY licensed mental health counselor. The Postgraduate Certificate in Forensic Psychology is an 18 credit specialization, from courses within the MA Program in Forensic Psychology, for those who already have a graduate degree and wish to develop a forensic focus in one of these six areas: Psychological Assessment & Forensic Psychology; Family Violence & Victims; Forensic Counseling & Psychotherapy; Research in Forensic Psychology; Selected Topics; or Forensic Psychological Assessment & Testimony. The Joint MA-JD Program, with NY Law School is a four year accelerated program specializing in Forensic Psychology and Mental Health Disability Law.

Special Facilities or Resources: The department maintains affiliations with the major forensic psychology institutions in the New York metropolitan area. The Program is endowed for student-psychology research, in the Forensic Psychology Research Institute. In addition, the full academic resources and educational milieu of John Jay College of Criminal Justice, CUNY, are available to our students.

Information for Students With Physical Disabilities: See the following website for more information: http://www.jjay.cuny.edu/2023.php.

Application Information:
Send to Graduate Admissions, John Jay College of Criminal Justice, CUNY, 524 West 59th Street, New York, NY 10019. Application available online. URL of online application: http://www.jjay.cuny.edu/795.php. Students are admitted in the Fall, application deadline May 15; Spring, application deadline December 1. *Fee:* $125.

Columbia University
Department of Counseling and Clinical Psychology/ Program in Clinical Psychology
Teachers College
Box 303, 525 West 120th Street
New York, NY 10027-6696
Telephone: (212) 678-8127
Fax: (212) 678-3275
E-mail: *miville@tc.edu*
Web: *http://www.tc.edu/ccp*

Department Information:
1996. Chairperson: Marie Miville. Number of faculty: total—full-time 20, part-time 26; women—full-time 11, part-time 15; total—minority—full-time 7, part-time 2; women minority—full-time 4, part-time 1; faculty subject to the Americans With Disabilities Act 1.

Programs and Degrees Offered:
Listed in the following order: Program area, degree type (T if terminal Master's), number awarded 7/11–6/12. Clinical Psychology PhD (Doctor of Philosophy) 9, Applied Psychology MA/MS (Master of Arts/Science) (T) 82.

APA Accreditation: Clinical PhD (Doctor of Philosophy). Student Outcome Data Website: http://www.tc.edu/ccp/Clinical/.

Student Applications/Admissions:
Student Applications

Clinical Psychology PhD (Doctor of Philosophy)—Applications 2012–2013, 370. Total applicants accepted 2012–2013, 10. Number full-time enrolled (new admits only) 2012–2013, 9. Total enrolled 2012–2013 full-time, 26. Total enrolled 2012–2013 part-time, 16. Openings 2013–2014, 8. The median number of years required for completion of a degree in 2012–2013 were 6. The number of students enrolled full- and part-time who were dismissed or voluntarily withdrew from this program area in 2012–2013 were 0. *Applied Psychology MA/MS (Master of Arts/Science)*—Applications 2012–2013, 250. Total applicants accepted 2012–2013, 140. Number full-time enrolled (new admits only) 2012–2013, 98. Number part-time enrolled (new admits only) 2012–2013, 20. Total enrolled 2012–2013 full-time, 144. Total enrolled 2012–2013 part-time, 38. Openings 2013–2014, 95. The median number of years required for completion of a degree in 2012–2013 were 2. The number of students enrolled full- and part-time who were dismissed or voluntarily withdrew from this program area in 2012–2013 were 2.

Scores: Entries appear in this order: required test or GPA, minimum score (if required), median score of students entering in 2012–2013. *Clinical Psychology PhD (Doctor of Philosophy):* GRE-V 640, 670, GRE-Q 640, 680, GRE-Analytical no minimum stated, GRE-Subject (Psychology) 640, 680, overall undergraduate GPA no minimum stated, last 2 years GPA no minimum stated, psychology GPA no minimum stated; *Applied Psychology MA/MS (Master of Arts/Science):* GRE-V 500, 610, GRE-Q 500, 600, GRE-Analytical 500, 600, overall undergraduate GPA 2.5, 3.4.

Other Criteria: (importance of criteria rated low, medium, or high): GRE scores—high, research experience—high, work experience—high, extracurricular activity—medium, clinically related public service—medium, GPA—medium, letters of recommendation—high, interview—high, statement of goals and objectives—medium, undergraduate major in psychology—medium, specific undergraduate psychology courses taken—medium. For additional information on admission requirements, go to http://www.tc.edu/ccp.

Student Characteristics: The following represents characteristics of students in 2012–2013 in all graduate psychology programs in the department: Female—full-time 200, part-time 102; Male—full-time 89, part-time 50; African American/Black—full-time 21, part-time 10; Hispanic/Latino(a)—full-time 17, part-time 6; Asian/Pacific Islander—full-time 33, part-time 4; American Indian/Alaska Native—full-time 1, part-time 0; Caucasian/White—full-time 199, part-time 118; Multi-ethnic—full-time 14, part-time 2; students subject to the Americans With Disabilities Act—full-time 3, part-time 0; Unknown ethnicity—full-time 0, part-time 0; International students who hold an F-1 or J-1 Visa—full-time 3, part-time 0.

Financial Information/Assistance:

Tuition for Full-Time Study: *Master's:* State residents: $1,350 per credit hour; Nonstate residents: $1,350 per credit hour. *Doctoral:* State residents: $1,350 per credit hour; Nonstate residents: $1,350 per credit hour. Tuition is subject to change. See the following website for updates and changes in tuition costs: http://www.tc.edu/controller/students/.

Financial Assistance:

First-Year Students: Research assistantships available for first year. Average amount paid per academic year: $20,000. Average number of hours worked per week: 20. Apply by December 15. Fellowships and scholarships available for first year. Average amount paid per academic year: $20,000. Average number of hours worked per week: 20. Apply by December 15.

Advanced Students: Teaching assistantships available for advanced students. Average amount paid per academic year: $1,600. Average number of hours worked per week: 3. Research assistantships available for advanced students. Average amount paid per academic year: $20,000. Average number of hours worked per week: 20. Apply by December 15. Fellowships and scholarships available for advanced students. Average amount paid per academic year: $20,000. Average number of hours worked per week: 20.

Additional Information: Of all students currently enrolled full time, 70% benefited from one or more of the listed financial assistance programs. Application and information available online at: http://www.tc.columbia.edu/financialaid/.

Internships/Practica: Doctoral Degree (PhD Clinical Psychology): For those doctoral students for whom a professional psychology internship was required in this program prior to graduation, (8) students applied for an internship in 2011–2012, with (7) students obtaining an internship. Of those students who obtained an internship, (7) were paid internships. Of those students who obtained an internship, (7) students placed in APA/CPA accredited internships, (0) students placed in internships not APA/CPA accredited, but listed with the Association of Psychology Postdoctoral and Internship Programs (APPIC), (0) students placed in internships conforming to guidelines of the Council of Directors of School Psychology Programs (CDSPP), (0) students placed in internships that were not APA/CPA accredited, APPIC or CDSPP listed. Master's Degree (MA/MS Applied Psychology): An internship experience, such as a final research project or "capstone" experience is required of graduates. Master's students in the Department of Counseling and Clinical Psychology complete fieldwork appropriate to their track or area of interest in a variety of settings including schools, hospitals, diverse mental health clinics and rehabilitation centers. Doctoral students do externships in settings similar to the ones indicated above, in preparation for their required APA-approved internships. In addition, all PhD students as well as the MEd students engage in practicum experiences at the Center for Educational and Psychological Services at the College. The Center is a community resource that provides low-cost services for the public utilizing graduate students from several departments within the College. All students receive supervision provided by full-time and adjunct faculty. PhD students in the clinical and counseling programs complete a one-year (or equivalent) full-time internship.

Housing and Day Care: On-campus housing is available. See the following website for more information: http://www.tc.columbia.edu/housing/. On-campus day care facilities are available. See the following website for more information: http://www.tc.columbia.edu/centers/hollingworth/index.asp; http://www.tc.edu/ritagold/.

Employment of Department Graduates:

Master's Degree Graduates: Of those who graduated in the academic year 2011–2012, the following categories and numbers represent the postgraduate activities and employment of master's degree graduates: Enrolled in a psychology doctoral program (30), enrolled in a postdoctoral residency/fellowship (n/a), employed in independent practice (n/a), total from the above (master's) (30).

Doctoral Degree Graduates: Of those who graduated in the academic year 2011–2012, the following categories and numbers represent the postgraduate activities and employment of doctoral degree graduates: Enrolled in a psychology doctoral program (n/a), enrolled in a postdoctoral residency/fellowship (8), employed in independent practice (7), employed in an academic position at a university (4), employed in an academic position at a 2-year/4-year college (4), employed in other positions at a higher education institution (2), employed in a professional position in a school system (3), employed in business or industry (2), employed in government agency (1), employed in a community mental health/counseling center (2), employed in a hospital/medical center (4), still seeking employment (1), total from the above (doctoral) (38).

Additional Information:

Orientation, Objectives, and Emphasis of Department: This department prepares students to investigate and address the psychological needs of individuals, families, groups, organizations/institutions and communities. Counseling psychology focuses on normal and optimal development across the lifespan, with particular attention to expanding knowledge and skills in occupational choice and transitions, and multicultural and group counseling.

Clinical Psychology primarily uses a broad-based psychodynamic perspective to study and treat a variety of psychological and psychoeducational problems. In addition to sharing an interest and appreciation for the critical role of culture in development and adaptation, both programs highly value the teaching of clinical and research skills. Thus, students in this department are trained to become knowledgeable and proficient researchers, to provide psychological and educational leadership, and to be effective practitioners. Specifically, graduates from these programs seek positions in teaching, research, policy, administration, psychotherapy, and counseling.

Special Facilities or Resources: The College provides academic/research support in several ways. Students of the College have access to all the libraries of Columbia University. Of particular interest in addition to the Milbank Memorial Library here at Teachers College, are the Psychology Library on the main Columbia campus and the library at the School of Social Work. Technology has transformed most libraries to computer-oriented environments with immediate access to information. The Library not only provides the access but instruction to students so they may avail themselves of the new technology. The ERIC system as well as Inter-Library Loan are also available.

Information for Students With Physical Disabilities: See the following website for more information: http://www.tc.columbia.edu/administration/ossd/.

Application Information:

Send to Teachers College, Office of Admission, Thorndike Hall, 3rd Floor, 525 West 120th Street, New York, NY 10027-6696. Application available online. URL of online application: http://www.tc.edu/admissions/. Students are admitted in the Fall, application deadline December 15. The Doctoral application deadline is December 15th. For masters applications, all admissions materials must be received by April 15th for priority consideration or by July 15th for final consideration. *Fee:* $65. Waiver is available. Hardship verification is done via a letter from Financial Aid Officer at the applicant's previous academic institution.

Columbia University

Health and Behavior Studies/School Psychology
Teachers College
525 West 120th Street, Box 120
New York, NY 10027
Telephone: (212) 678-3942
Fax: (212) 678-4034
E-mail: *brassard@tc.edu*
Web: *http://www.tc.columbia.edu/hbs/schoolpsych/*

Department Information:

1996. Chairperson: Stephen Peverly. Number of faculty: total—full-time 5, part-time 11; women—full-time 3, part-time 9; total—minority—full-time 1, part-time 1; women minority—full-time 1, part-time 1; faculty subject to the Americans With Disabilities Act 1.

Programs and Degrees Offered:

Listed in the following order: Program area, degree type (T if terminal Master's), number awarded 7/11–6/12. School Psychol-ogy PhD (Doctor of Philosophy) 5, School Psychology MEd (Education) 19.

APA Accreditation: School PhD (Doctor of Philosophy). Student Outcome Data Website: http://www.tc.columbia.edu/hbs/SchoolPsych/.

Student Applications/Admissions:

Student Applications

School Psychology PhD (Doctor of Philosophy)—Applications 2012–2013, 68. Total applicants accepted 2012–2013, 5. Number full-time enrolled (new admits only) 2012–2013, 4. Number part-time enrolled (new admits only) 2012–2013, 0. Total enrolled 2012–2013 full-time, 20. Openings 2013–2014, 4. The median number of years required for completion of a degree in 2012–2013 were 8. The number of students enrolled full- and part-time who were dismissed or voluntarily withdrew from this program area in 2012–2013 were 0. *School Psychology MEd (Education)*—Applications 2012–2013, 83. Total applicants accepted 2012–2013, 40. Number full-time enrolled (new admits only) 2012–2013, 20. Number part-time enrolled (new admits only) 2012–2013, 0. Total enrolled 2012–2013 full-time, 64. Total enrolled 2012–2013 part-time, 2. Openings 2013–2014, 23. The median number of years required for completion of a degree in 2012–2013 were 3. The number of students enrolled full- and part-time who were dismissed or voluntarily withdrew from this program area in 2012–2013 were 1.

Scores: Entries appear in this order: required test or GPA, minimum score (if required), median score of students entering in 2012–2013. *School Psychology PhD (Doctor of Philosophy):* GRE-V 500, 570, GRE-Q 620, 720, GRE-Analytical 4.0, 5.0, overall undergraduate GPA 2.81, 3.55, Masters GPA no minimum stated; *School Psychology MEd (Education):* GRE-V 390, 515, GRE-Q 440, 630, GRE-Analytical 2.0, 4.5, overall undergraduate GPA 2.75, 3.52.

Other Criteria: (importance of criteria rated low, medium, or high): GRE scores—high, research experience—high, work experience—medium, extracurricular activity—medium, clinically related public service—medium, GPA—high, letters of recommendation—high, interview—high, statement of goals and objectives—high, undergraduate major in psychology—medium, Research is important for the PhD, not the EdM. For additional information on admission requirements, go to http://www.tc.edu/hbs/SchoolPsych.

Student Characteristics: The following represents characteristics of students in 2012–2013 in all graduate psychology programs in the department: Female—full-time 74, part-time 2; Male—full-time 7, part-time 1; African American/Black—full-time 3, part-time 0; Hispanic/Latino(a)—full-time 3, part-time 1; Asian/Pacific Islander—full-time 7, part-time 0; American Indian/Alaska Native—full-time 0, part-time 0; Caucasian/White—full-time 65, part-time 3; Multi-ethnic—full-time 0, part-time 0; students subject to the Americans With Disabilities Act—full-time 1, part-time 0; Unknown ethnicity—full-time 0, part-time 0; International students who hold an F-1 or J-1 Visa—full-time 5, part-time 0.

Financial Information/Assistance:

Tuition for Full-Time Study: *Master's:* State residents: $1,286 per credit hour; Nonstate residents: $1,286 per credit hour. *Doc-*

toral: State residents: $1,286 per credit hour; Nonstate residents: $1,286 per credit hour. Additional fees are assessed to students beyond the costs of tuition for the following: college fee, medical fee, research fee. See the following website for updates and changes in tuition costs: http://www.tc.columbia.edu/financialaid/.

Financial Assistance:

First-Year Students: Fellowships and scholarships available for first year. Average amount paid per academic year: $18,000.

Advanced Students: Teaching assistantships available for advanced students. Average amount paid per academic year: $14,116. Average number of hours worked per week: 13. Fellowships and scholarships available for advanced students. Average amount paid per academic year: $20,000.

Additional Information: Of all students currently enrolled full time, 25% benefited from one or more of the listed financial assistance programs. Application and information available online at: http://www.tc.columbia.edu/financialaid.

Internships/Practica: Doctoral Degree (PhD School Psychology): For those doctoral students for whom a professional psychology internship was required in this program prior to graduation, (4) students applied for an internship in 2011–2012, with (4) students obtaining an internship. Of those students who obtained an internship, (4) were paid internships. Of those students who obtained an internship, (4) students placed in APA/CPA accredited internships, (0) students placed in internships not APA/CPA accredited, but listed with the Association of Psychology Postdoctoral and Internship Programs (APPIC), (0) students placed in internships conforming to guidelines of the Council of Directors of School Psychology Programs (CDSPP), (0) students placed in internships that were not APA/CPA accredited, APPIC or CDSPP listed. First year—Two practica in our Dean Hope Center for Educational and Psychological Services: (1) Practicum in Assessment of Reading and School Subject Difficulties (Fall); (2) Practicum in Psychoeducational Assessment with Culturally Diverse Students (Spring). Second year—students engage in fieldwork (2 days/week over the academic year in one of our cooperating inner-city schools) and a practicum in psychoeducational groups (the groups are run within students' fieldwork sites). Third year—EdM students do a yearlong internship in the schools while PhD students have externship (2 days/week over an academic year; most students are required to do 2 externships: one in a school and one in a hospital or clinic); Fifth year for PhD students—internship (full calendar year; students must have an approved dissertation proposal before they begin to do the internship after completing most or all of their dissertation). Most students enter the APPIC match to obtain an internship.

Housing and Day Care: On-campus housing is available. See the following website for more information: http://www.tc.columbia.edu/housing/. On-campus day care facilities are available. See the following website for more information: htp://www.tc.columbia.edu/centers/ritagold/.

Employment of Department Graduates:

Master's Degree Graduates: Of those who graduated in the academic year 2011–2012, the following categories and numbers represent the postgraduate activities and employment of master's degree graduates: Enrolled in a postdoctoral residency/fellowship (n/a), employed in independent practice (n/a), employed in a professional position in a school system (16), other employment position (1), do not know (2), total from the above (master's) (19).

Doctoral Degree Graduates: Of those who graduated in the academic year 2011–2012, the following categories and numbers represent the postgraduate activities and employment of doctoral degree graduates: Enrolled in a psychology doctoral program (n/a), enrolled in a postdoctoral residency/fellowship (2), employed in a professional position in a school system (3), employed in business or industry (1), employed in a hospital/medical center (1), do not know (1), total from the above (doctoral) (8).

Additional Information:

Orientation, Objectives, and Emphasis of Department: The primary theoretical orientation of our program is cognitive and developmental with strong applications to instruction and mental health. We place a particularly strong emphasis on prevention and intervention in these areas. Throughout the curriculum, there is a balance between science and practice, and we ensure that all students are well grounded in the theory and methods of psychological science. Most students opt to go through the general curriculum. However, some have adopted a specialization in the deaf and hearing impaired.

Special Facilities or Resources: The School Psychology program has a) a state-of-the-art clinic and test library with a large student room for first year school psychology students, b) strong collaborative relationships with six inner-city schools that serve as fieldwork (practicum) sites for our master's and doctoral students in the second year, and c) it participates in the NYC metro-wide externship network for 3rd year (and sometimes 5th year) doctoral students.

Information for Students With Physical Disabilities: See the following website for more information: http://www.tc.columbia.edu/oasid/.

Application Information:
Send to Office of Admissions, Box 302, Teachers College, Columbia University, 525 West 120th Street, New York, NY 10027. Application available online. URL of online application: http://www.tc.columbia.edu/admissions/. Students are admitted in the Fall, application deadline December 15. *Fee:* $65.

Cornell University
Department of Human Development
The New York State College of Human Ecology
G77 Martha Van Rensselaer Hall
Ithaca, NY 14853-4401
Telephone: (607) 255-7620
Fax: (607) 255-9856
E-mail: *blb5@cornell.edu*
Web: *http://www.human.cornell.edu/hd/index.cfm*

Department Information:
1925. Chairperson: Charles Brainerd. Number of faculty: total—full-time 23; women—full-time 11; total—minority—full-time 4; women minority—full-time 2.

Programs and Degrees Offered:
Listed in the following order: Program area, degree type (T if terminal Master's), number awarded 7/11–6/12. Developmental Psychology PhD (Doctor of Philosophy) 6, Human Development and Family Studies PhD (Doctor of Philosophy) 0.

Student Applications/Admissions:
Student Applications

Developmental Psychology PhD (Doctor of Philosophy)—Applications 2012–2013, 61. Number full-time enrolled (new admits only) 2012–2013, 7. Number part-time enrolled (new admits only) 2012–2013, 0. Total enrolled 2012–2013 full-time, 38. Total enrolled 2012–2013 part-time, 0. Openings 2013–2014, 6. The median number of years required for completion of a degree in 2012–2013 were 5. The number of students enrolled full- and part-time who were dismissed or voluntarily withdrew from this program area in 2012–2013 were 0. *Human Development and Family Studies PhD (Doctor of Philosophy)*—Applications 2012–2013, 22. Total applicants accepted 2012–2013, 1. Number full-time enrolled (new admits only) 2012–2013, 0. Number part-time enrolled (new admits only) 2012–2013, 0. Openings 2013–2014, 1. The number of students enrolled full- and part-time who were dismissed or voluntarily withdrew from this program area in 2012–2013 were 0.

Other Criteria: (importance of criteria rated low, medium, or high): GRE scores—high, research experience—high, work experience—low, extracurricular activity—low, clinically related public service—low, GPA—high, letters of recommendation—high, interview—medium, statement of goals and objectives—high, undergraduate major in psychology—medium, specific undergraduate psychology courses taken—medium. For additional information on admission requirements, go to http://www.humec.cornell.edu/hd/graduate/admissions-funding.cfm.

Student Characteristics: The following represents characteristics of students in 2012–2013 in all graduate psychology programs in the department: Female—full-time 28, part-time 0; Male—full-time 10, part-time 0; African American/Black—full-time 3, part-time 0; Hispanic/Latino(a)—full-time 2, part-time 0; Asian/Pacific Islander—full-time 2, part-time 0; American Indian/Alaska Native—full-time 1, part-time 0; Caucasian/White—full-time 30, part-time 0; Multi-ethnic—full-time 0, part-time 0; students subject to the Americans With Disabilities Act—full-time 0, part-time 0; Unknown ethnicity—full-time 0, part-time 0; International students who hold an F-1 or J-1 Visa—full-time 10, part-time 0.

Financial Information/Assistance:
Tuition for Full-Time Study: *Doctoral:* State residents: per academic year $20,800; Nonstate residents: per academic year $20,800. Tuition is subject to change. See the following website for updates and changes in tuition costs: http://www.gradschool.cornell.edu/costs-and-funding/tuition-and-costs.

Financial Assistance:
First-Year Students: Teaching assistantships available for first year. Average amount paid per academic year: $23,470. Average number of hours worked per week: 15. Apply by January 1. Research assistantships available for first year. Average amount paid per academic year: $23,470. Average number of hours worked per week: 15. Apply by January 1. Fellowships and scholarships available for first year. Average amount paid per academic year: $23,470. Average number of hours worked per week: 0. Apply by January 1.

Advanced Students: Teaching assistantships available for advanced students. Average amount paid per academic year: $23,470. Average number of hours worked per week: 15. Apply by January 1. Research assistantships available for advanced students. Average amount paid per academic year: $23,470. Average number of hours worked per week: 15. Apply by January 1. Fellowships and scholarships available for advanced students. Average amount paid per academic year: $23,470. Average number of hours worked per week: 0. Apply by January 1.

Additional Information: Of all students currently enrolled full time, 100% benefited from one or more of the listed financial assistance programs. Application and information available online at: http://www.gradschool.cornell.edu/costs-and-funding.

Housing and Day Care: On-campus housing is available. See the following website for more information: http://living.sas.cornell.edu/. On-campus day care facilities are available. See the following website for more information: https://www.hr.cornell.edu/life/support/child_care_center.html.

Employment of Department Graduates:
Master's Degree Graduates: Of those who graduated in the academic year 2011–2012, the following categories and numbers represent the postgraduate activities and employment of master's degree graduates: Enrolled in a postdoctoral residency/fellowship (n/a), employed in independent practice (n/a), total from the above (master's) (0).

Doctoral Degree Graduates: Of those who graduated in the academic year 2011–2012, the following categories and numbers represent the postgraduate activities and employment of doctoral degree graduates: Enrolled in a psychology doctoral program (n/a), enrolled in a postdoctoral residency/fellowship (3), employed in an academic position at a university (3), total from the above (doctoral) (6).

Additional Information:
Orientation, Objectives, and Emphasis of Department: The graduate program trains researchers and prepares students for research and teaching careers in academic life, work in government agencies, and careers as researchers on projects carried out in a variety of public and private sectors. We offer training in six broad categories: Aging and Health; Cognitive Development; Group Disparities in Development; Human Behavioral Neuroscience; Law, Psychology, and Human Development; and Social and Personality Development. We do not offer training in counseling psychology, marriage counseling, or family therapy. The doctoral program in Human Development has 35 faculty; 23 are members of the Department of Human Development and 12 have primary appointments in the departments of Psychology, Design and Environmental Analysis, Policy Analysis and Management, the Law school, or in the Weill Cornell Medical College. The faculty includes psychologists and sociologists. There are approximately 35 graduate students in the program. The program offers two graduate degrees: the PhD and the MA

Special Facilities or Resources: The department houses a number of laboratories dedicated to individual projects as well as several non-dedicated laboratories and research rooms, including rooms with audio and visual recording capability. Dedicated space also houses fMRI facilities designed for testing humans. There are numerous opportunities for research collaboration with area schools, day care centers, after school programs, youth agencies, and senior housing and other centers. Several faculty in the department also have appointments and affiliations with the Bronfenbrenner Center for Translational Research, the Cornell Edward R. Roybal Center for Translational Research on Aging, Weill Cornell Medical College in New York City, the Cornell Population Program, and the Center for the Study of Inequality. The department also maintains graduate student computer facilities with statistical software and experimental management programs such as E-prime. A comprehensive, continually updated set of statistical analysis programs are available to all graduate students through the Cornell Institute for Social and Economic Research and free data management and analysis support is provided by the Cornell Statistical Consulting Unit.

Information for Students With Physical Disabilities: See the following website for more information: http://sds.cornell.edu/.

Application Information:
Application available online. URL of online application: http://www.gradschool.cornell.edu/admissions/applying/apply-now. Students are admitted in the Fall, application deadline January 1. *Fee:* $80. In cases of extreme financial need, a fee waiver will be considered. A letter of request for a waiver and documentation of need such as a letter from the college financial aid office needs to be submitted.

Cornell University
Graduate Field of Psychology
Arts & Sciences
211 Uris Hall
Ithaca, NY 14853-7601
Telephone: (607) 255-3834
Fax: (607) 255-8433
E-mail: *pac34@cornell.edu*
Web: *http://www.psych.cornell.edu/*

Department Information:
1885. Director of Graduate Studies: David J. Field. Number of faculty: total—full-time 22, part-time 2; women—full-time 8; total—minority—full-time 1; women minority—full-time 1.

Programs and Degrees Offered:
Listed in the following order: Program area, degree type (T if terminal Master's), number awarded 7/11–6/12. Behavioral and Evolutionary Neuroscience (Ben) PhD (Doctor of Philosophy) 1, Perception, Cognition and Development (Pcd) PhD (Doctor of Philosophy) 3, Social and Personality Psychology PhD (Doctor of Philosophy) 4.

Student Applications/Admissions:
Student Applications
Behavioral and Evolutionary Neuroscience (Ben) PhD (Doctor of Philosophy)—Applications 2012–2013, 18. Total applicants accepted 2012–2013, 2. Number full-time enrolled (new admits only) 2012–2013, 1. Total enrolled 2012–2013 full-time, 19. Total enrolled 2012–2013 part-time, 0. Openings 2013–2014, 2. The median number of years required for com-

pletion of a degree in 2012–2013 were 6. The number of students enrolled full- and part-time who were dismissed or voluntarily withdrew from this program area in 2012–2013 were 1. *Perception, Cognition and Development (Pcd) PhD (Doctor of Philosophy)*—Applications 2012–2013, 36. Total applicants accepted 2012–2013, 2. Number full-time enrolled (new admits only) 2012–2013, 3. Total enrolled 2012–2013 full-time, 17. Total enrolled 2012–2013 part-time, 0. Openings 2013–2014, 2. The median number of years required for completion of a degree in 2012–2013 were 5. The number of students enrolled full- and part-time who were dismissed or voluntarily withdrew from this program area in 2012–2013 were 1. *Social and Personality Psychology PhD (Doctor of Philosophy)*—Applications 2012–2013, 134. Total applicants accepted 2012–2013, 2. Number full-time enrolled (new admits only) 2012–2013, 1. Total enrolled 2012–2013 full-time, 13. Total enrolled 2012–2013 part-time, 0. Openings 2013–2014, 2. The median number of years required for completion of a degree in 2012–2013 were 5. The number of students enrolled full- and part-time who were dismissed or voluntarily withdrew from this program area in 2012–2013 were 0.

Other Criteria: (importance of criteria rated low, medium, or high): GRE scores—high, research experience—high, work experience—low, extracurricular activity—low, GPA—high, letters of recommendation—high, statement of goals and objectives—high. For additional information on admission requirements, go to http://www.psych.cornell.edu/grad_howto_apply.

Student Characteristics: The following represents characteristics of students in 2012–2013 in all graduate psychology programs in the department: Female—full-time 30, part-time 0; Male—full-time 19, part-time 0; African American/Black—full-time 0, part-time 0; Hispanic/Latino(a)—full-time 3, part-time 0; Asian/Pacific Islander—full-time 10, part-time 0; American Indian/Alaska Native—full-time 1, part-time 0; Caucasian/White—full-time 35, part-time 0; Multi-ethnic—full-time 0, part-time 0; students subject to the Americans With Disabilities Act—full-time 0, part-time 0; Unknown ethnicity—full-time 0, part-time 0; International students who hold an F-1 or J-1 Visa—full-time 9, part-time 0.

Financial Information/Assistance:
Tuition for Full-Time Study: *Doctoral:* State residents: per academic year $29,500; Nonstate residents: per academic year $29,500. Tuition is subject to change. See the following website for updates and changes in tuition costs: http://www.gradschool.cornell.edu/costs-and-funding/tuition-and-costs.

Financial Assistance:
First-Year Students: Teaching assistantships available for first year. Average amount paid per academic year: $23,470. Average number of hours worked per week: 20. Fellowships and scholarships available for first year. Average amount paid per academic year: $23,470.

Advanced Students: Teaching assistantships available for advanced students. Average amount paid per academic year: $23,470. Average number of hours worked per week: 20. Fellowships and scholarships available for advanced students. Average amount paid per academic year: $23,470.

Additional Information: Of all students currently enrolled full time, 100% benefited from one or more of the listed financial

assistance programs. Application and information available online at: http://www.gradschool.cornell.edu/costs-and-funding.

Housing and Day Care: On-campus housing is available. See the following website for more information: http://living.sas.cornell.edu/live/. On-campus day care facilities are available. See the following website for more information: https://www.hr.cornell.edu/life/support/child_care_center.html.

Employment of Department Graduates:
Master's Degree Graduates: Of those who graduated in the academic year 2011–2012, the following categories and numbers represent the postgraduate activities and employment of master's degree graduates: Enrolled in a postdoctoral residency/fellowship (n/a), employed in independent practice (n/a), total from the above (master's) (0).
Doctoral Degree Graduates: Of those who graduated in the academic year 2011–2012, the following categories and numbers represent the postgraduate activities and employment of doctoral degree graduates: Enrolled in a psychology doctoral program (n/a), enrolled in another graduate/professional program (1), enrolled in a postdoctoral residency/fellowship (5), employed in an academic position at a university (2), total from the above (doctoral) (8).

Additional Information:
Orientation, Objectives, and Emphasis of Department: The Psychology Department of the College of Arts and Sciences at Cornell has a faculty of 25 psychologists and is divided into three areas—perception, cognition and development (encompassing cognition, language, perception, and its developmental perspectives), behavioral and evolutionary neuroscience (focusing on hormones and behavior, neural development, and sensory systems), and social and personality psychology (social cognition, judgment, and decision making). We do not have clinical, community, or counseling programs. We have a strong research orientation, training our students to become professional academics or researchers. Our 39 students design their graduate programs under the supervision of their special committees. These committees consist of at least four members of the graduate faculty at Cornell; at least three are from within the department. The chair of the committee is a member of the Graduate Field of Psychology, which consists of the 26 members of our department plus 20 researchers in allied fields (human development, education, industrial and labor relations, and neurobiology and behavior). Two other committee members serve as minor members, one of whom can be outside the Graduate Field of Psychology, and the fourth member oversees breadth requirements.

Special Facilities or Resources: The three areas of our program each have laboratories associated with them. Each of the members of the perception, cognition and development program has a separate laboratory, fully equipped with state-of-the-art computer equipment. In addition, the program has several computer-based teaching laboratories. The Behavioral Evolutionary Neuroscience group each has separate labs and computers, and animal housing facilities where relevant, but they share much of the equipment and lab space. There is also a teaching lab associated with B.E.N.'s group labs. The social and personality psychologists all have their own individual labs, with state-of-the-art computer equipment, and ample space for a full range of behavioral experiments. Also available are a set of cubicles with networked computers, observa-

tion rooms with one-way mirrors, video observation cameras and recorders, and a fully-equipped ERP lab.

Information for Students With Physical Disabilities: See the following website for more information: http://sds.cornell.edu/.

Application Information:
Application available online. URL of online application: http://gradschool.cornell.edu/admissions/applying/apply-now. Students are admitted in the Fall, application deadline December 15. *Fee:* $70.

Fordham University
Department of Psychology
Arts and Sciences
441 East Fordham Road
Bronx, NY 10458
Telephone: (718) 817-3775
Fax: (718) 817-3785
E-mail: *schiaffino@fordham.edu*
Web: *http://www.fordham.edu/psychology/*

Department Information:
1933. Chairperson: Kathleen M. Schiaffino. Number of faculty: total—full-time 30; women—full-time 14; total—minority—full-time 6; women minority—full-time 4.

Programs and Degrees Offered:
Listed in the following order: Program area, degree type (T if terminal Master's), number awarded 7/11–6/12. Clinical Psychology PhD (Doctor of Philosophy) 12, Psychometrics and Quantitative Psychology PhD (Doctor of Philosophy) 5, Applied Developmental Psychology PhD (Doctor of Philosophy) 7, Applied Psychological Methods MA/MS (Master of Arts/Science) (T) 0.

APA Accreditation: Clinical PhD (Doctor of Philosophy).

Student Applications/Admissions:
Student Applications
Clinical Psychology PhD (Doctor of Philosophy)—Applications 2012–2013, 600. Total applicants accepted 2012–2013, 14. Number full-time enrolled (new admits only) 2012–2013, 10. Number part-time enrolled (new admits only) 2012–2013, 0. Total enrolled 2012–2013 full-time, 74. Total enrolled 2012–2013 part-time, 0. Openings 2013–2014, 10. The median number of years required for completion of a degree in 2012–2013 were 7. The number of students enrolled full- and part-time who were dismissed or voluntarily withdrew from this program area in 2012–2013 were 0. *Psychometrics and Quantitative Psychology PhD (Doctor of Philosophy)*—Applications 2012–2013, 10. Total applicants accepted 2012–2013, 5. Number full-time enrolled (new admits only) 2012–2013, 4. Number part-time enrolled (new admits only) 2012–2013, 0. Total enrolled 2012–2013 full-time, 22. Total enrolled 2012–2013 part-time, 0. Openings 2013–2014, 4. The median number of years required for completion of a degree in 2012–2013 were 5. The number of students enrolled full- and part-time who were dismissed or voluntarily withdrew from this program area in 2012–2013 were 0. *Applied Developmental Psychology PhD (Doc-*

tor of Philosophy)—Applications 2012–2013, 31. Total applicants accepted 2012–2013, 8. Number full-time enrolled (new admits only) 2012–2013, 4. Number part-time enrolled (new admits only) 2012–2013, 0. Total enrolled 2012–2013 full-time, 29. Total enrolled 2012–2013 part-time, 0. Openings 2013–2014, 4. The median number of years required for completion of a degree in 2012–2013 were 5. The number of students enrolled full- and part-time who were dismissed or voluntarily withdrew from this program area in 2012–2013 were 0. *Applied Psychological Methods MA/MS (Master of Arts/Science)*—Applications 2012–2013, 14. Total applicants accepted 2012–2013, 3. Number full-time enrolled (new admits only) 2012–2013, 3. Number part-time enrolled (new admits only) 2012–2013, 0. Total enrolled 2012–2013 full-time, 5. Total enrolled 2012–2013 part-time, 0. Openings 2013–2014, 5. The median number of years required for completion of a degree in 2012–2013 were 2. The number of students enrolled full- and part-time who were dismissed or voluntarily withdrew from this program area in 2012–2013 were 0.

Scores: Entries appear in this order: required test or GPA, minimum score (if required), median score of students entering in 2012–2013. *Clinical Psychology PhD (Doctor of Philosophy):* GRE-V 600, 660, GRE-Q 660, 710, GRE-Analytical 4.5, 5, overall undergraduate GPA 3.55; *Psychometrics and Quantitative Psychology PhD (Doctor of Philosophy):* GRE-V 480, 600, GRE-Q 590, 700, GRE-Analytical 4, 4, overall undergraduate GPA 3.39; *Applied Developmental Psychology PhD (Doctor of Philosophy):* GRE-V 570, 600, GRE-Q 570, 620, GRE-Analytical 5, 5, overall undergraduate GPA 3.64.

Other Criteria: (importance of criteria rated low, medium, or high): GRE scores—high, research experience—high, work experience—medium, extracurricular activity—medium, clinically related public service—medium, GPA—high, letters of recommendation—high, interview—high, statement of goals and objectives—high, undergraduate major in psychology—medium, specific undergraduate psychology courses taken—high.

Student Characteristics: The following represents characteristics of students in 2012–2013 in all graduate psychology programs in the department: Female—full-time 85, part-time 0; Male—full-time 45, part-time 0; African American/Black—full-time 15, part-time 0; Hispanic/Latino(a)—full-time 20, part-time 0; Asian/Pacific Islander—full-time 15, part-time 0; American Indian/Alaska Native—full-time 2, part-time 0; Caucasian/White—full-time 78, part-time 0; Multi-ethnic—full-time 0, part-time 0; students subject to the Americans With Disabilities Act—full-time 0, part-time 0; Unknown ethnicity—full-time 0, part-time 0; International students who hold an F-1 or J-1 Visa—full-time 15, part-time 0.

Financial Information/Assistance:

Tuition for Full-Time Study: *Master's:* State residents: $1,320 per credit hour; Nonstate residents: $1,320 per credit hour. *Doctoral:* State residents: $1,320 per credit hour; Nonstate residents: $1,320 per credit hour. Tuition is subject to change. See the following website for updates and changes in tuition costs: http://www.fordham.edu/tuition__financial_a/graduate_students/.

Financial Assistance:

First-Year Students: Teaching assistantships available for first year. Average amount paid per academic year: $21,800. Aver-

age number of hours worked per week: 15. Apply by December 9. Research assistantships available for first year. Average amount paid per academic year: $21,800. Average number of hours worked per week: 15. Apply by December 9. Fellowships and scholarships available for first year. Average amount paid per academic year: $24,000. Average number of hours worked per week: 0. Apply by December 9.

Advanced Students: Teaching assistantships available for advanced students. Average amount paid per academic year: $23,200. Average number of hours worked per week: 15. Apply by January 4. Research assistantships available for advanced students. Average amount paid per academic year: $23,200. Average number of hours worked per week: 15. Apply by January 4. Fellowships and scholarships available for advanced students. Average amount paid per academic year: $27,100. Average number of hours worked per week: 15. Apply by January 4.

Additional Information: Of all students currently enrolled full time, 100% benefited from one or more of the listed financial assistance programs. Application and information available online at: http://www.fordham.edu/tuition__financial_a/graduate_students/.

Internships/Practica: Doctoral Degree (PhD Clinical Psychology): For those doctoral students for whom a professional psychology internship was required in this program prior to graduation, (16) students applied for an internship in 2011–2012, with (14) students obtaining an internship. Of those students who obtained an internship, (14) were paid internships. Of those students who obtained an internship, (14) students placed in APA/CPA accredited internships, (0) students placed in internships not APA/CPA accredited, but listed with the Association of Psychology Postdoctoral and Internship Programs (APPIC), (0) students placed in internships conforming to guidelines of the Council of Directors of School Psychology Programs (CDSPP), (0) students placed in internships that were not APA/CPA accredited, APPIC or CDSPP listed. Master's Degree (MA/MS Applied Psychological Methods): An internship experience, such as a final research project or "capstone" experience is required of graduates. Internships in a variety of public and private facilities are available for students during and after coursework. Clinical requires an internship after the dissertation has been proposed. All four programs offer multiple one-semester externships in relevant settings.

Housing and Day Care: No on-campus housing is available. No on-campus day care facilities are available.

Employment of Department Graduates:

Master's Degree Graduates: Of those who graduated in the academic year 2011–2012, the following categories and numbers represent the postgraduate activities and employment of master's degree graduates: Enrolled in a postdoctoral residency/fellowship (n/a), employed in independent practice (n/a), total from the above (master's) (0).

Doctoral Degree Graduates: Of those who graduated in the academic year 2011–2012, the following categories and numbers represent the postgraduate activities and employment of doctoral degree graduates: Enrolled in a psychology doctoral program (n/a), enrolled in a postdoctoral residency/fellowship (7), employed in an academic position at a 2-year/4-year college (1), employed in other positions at a higher education institution (1), employed in business or industry (2), employed in government agency (3), employed in a community mental health/counseling center (1), employed in a hospital/medical center (3), do not know (2), total from the above (doctoral) (20).

Additional Information:

Orientation, Objectives, and Emphasis of Department: Clinical psychology prepares students for practice, research, and teaching in the clinical field as both professionals and scientists. Courses can be grouped under four major areas: clinical theory and methodology, research topics and methods, behavioral classification and assessment, and treatment approaches. Specializations include Family and Child, Health/Neuropsychology, and Forensics. There is a full-time, one-year internship. Applied Developmental Psychology (ADP) trains professionals who can conduct both basic and applied research in developmental processes across the lifespan and who can share their knowledge in academic and community-based settings. ADP focuses on the interplay between developmental processes and social contexts including design and evaluation of programs; consultation to public policy makers; development and evaluation of programs and materials directed at children and families; and parent and family education. The Psychometrics and Quantitative Psychology program focuses on the quantitative and research-oriented commonalities relevant to most of the behavioral sciences, and their applications in industry, education, and the health services. Students become familiar with statistics, psychological testing, use of computer systems, and other research techniques, as well as with the psychology of individual differences. The MS in Applied Psychological Methods provides training in research, psychometrics, data mining, and program evaluation to foster research and evaluation skills in individuals working in corporate and non-profit settings.

Special Facilities or Resources: The Clinical program takes advantage of a wide array of training sites and research sites in the New York City area (Bellevue, Sloan Kettering, Mt Sinai, AECOM, etc). The program also has its own clinical research site. Applied Developmental students and faculty conduct research and program evaluation with local schools and hospitals and the program is a member of a coalition of community service groups in the Northwest Bronx. A Bronx Community Center for Engaged Research has been developed to foster these activities. Psychometric students and faculty work closely with ETS and the College Board and also hospitals (Sloan Kettering, Mt. Sinai, etc) around measurement issues. The new MS in Applied Psychological Methods draws upon these same resources for the development of one semester capstone internships.

Information for Students With Physical Disabilities: See the following website for more information: http://www.fordham.edu/campus_resources/student_services/.

Application Information:

Send to Fordham University, Graduate Admissions Office, Keating 216, 441 East Fordham Rd, Bronx, NY 10458. Application available online. URL of online application: http://www.fordham.edu/admissions/index.asp. Students are admitted in the Fall, application deadline December 8. *Fee:* $70.

Fordham University

Division of Psychological and Educational Services
Graduate School of Education
113 West 60th Street, Room 1008
New York, NY 10023
Telephone: (212) 636-6460
Fax: (212) 636-6641
E-mail: *mjackson@fordham.edu*
Web: *http://www.fordham.edu/gse*

Department Information:

1927. Chairperson: Margo Jackson. Number of faculty: total—full-time 17, part-time 17; women—full-time 11, part-time 12; total—minority—full-time 6; women minority—full-time 5.

Programs and Degrees Offered:

Listed in the following order: Program area, degree type (T if terminal Master's), number awarded 7/11–6/12. Counseling Psychology PhD (Doctor of Philosophy) 10, School Psychology PhD (Doctor of Philosophy) 10, School Psychology Diploma Other 31, Bilingual School Psychology Diploma Other 2, School Counseling MEd (Education) 21, Mental Health Counseling MEd (Education) 24.

APA Accreditation: Counseling PhD (Doctor of Philosophy). School PhD (Doctor of Philosophy).

Student Applications/Admissions:

Student Applications

Counseling Psychology PhD (Doctor of Philosophy)—Applications 2012–2013, 159. Total applicants accepted 2012–2013, 25. Number full-time enrolled (new admits only) 2012–2013, 10. Number part-time enrolled (new admits only) 2012–2013, 1. Total enrolled 2012–2013 full-time, 26. Total enrolled 2012–2013 part-time, 24. Openings 2013–2014, 12. The median number of years required for completion of a degree in 2012–2013 were 6. The number of students enrolled full- and part-time who were dismissed or voluntarily withdrew from this program area in 2012–2013 were 0. *School Psychology PhD (Doctor of Philosophy)*—Applications 2012–2013, 91. Total applicants accepted 2012–2013, 37. Number full-time enrolled (new admits only) 2012–2013, 11. Number part-time enrolled (new admits only) 2012–2013, 4. Total enrolled 2012–2013 full-time, 34. Total enrolled 2012–2013 part-time, 39. Openings 2013–2014, 12. The median number of years required for completion of a degree in 2012–2013 were 8. The number of students enrolled full- and part-time who were dismissed or voluntarily withdrew from this program area in 2012–2013 were 0. *School Psychology Diploma Other*—Applications 2012–2013, 40. Total applicants accepted 2012–2013, 34. Number full-time enrolled (new admits only) 2012–2013, 18. Number part-time enrolled (new admits only) 2012–2013, 2. Total enrolled 2012–2013 full-time, 39. Total enrolled 2012–2013 part-time, 26. Openings 2013–2014, 25. The median number of years required for completion of a degree in 2012–2013 were 3. The number of students enrolled full- and part-time who were dismissed or voluntarily withdrew from this program area in 2012–2013 were 0. *Bilingual School Psychology Diploma Other*—Applications 2012–2013, 3. Total applicants accepted 2012–2013, 3. Number full-time enrolled (new admits only)

2012–2013, 2. Total enrolled 2012–2013 full-time, 7. Total enrolled 2012–2013 part-time, 8. Openings 2013–2014, 8. The median number of years required for completion of a degree in 2012–2013 were 3. The number of students enrolled full- and part-time who were dismissed or voluntarily withdrew from this program area in 2012–2013 were 0. *School Counseling MEd (Education)*—Applications 2012–2013, 92. Total applicants accepted 2012–2013, 68. Number full-time enrolled (new admits only) 2012–2013, 13. Number part-time enrolled (new admits only) 2012–2013, 4. Total enrolled 2012–2013 full-time, 29. Total enrolled 2012–2013 part-time, 10. Openings 2013–2014, 25. The median number of years required for completion of a degree in 2012–2013 were 2. The number of students enrolled full- and part-time who were dismissed or voluntarily withdrew from this program area in 2012–2013 were 0. *Mental Health Counseling MEd (Education)*—Applications 2012–2013, 135. Total applicants accepted 2012–2013, 76. Number full-time enrolled (new admits only) 2012–2013, 21. Number part-time enrolled (new admits only) 2012–2013, 3. Total enrolled 2012–2013 full-time, 28. Total enrolled 2012–2013 part-time, 5. Openings 2013–2014, 25. The median number of years required for completion of a degree in 2012–2013 were 2. The number of students enrolled full- and part-time who were dismissed or voluntarily withdrew from this program area in 2012–2013 were 0.

Scores: Entries appear in this order: required test or GPA, minimum score (if required), median score of students entering in 2012–2013. *Counseling Psychology PhD (Doctor of Philosophy)*: GRE-V no minimum stated, 160, GRE-Q no minimum stated, 154, overall undergraduate GPA 3.0, 3.58; *School Psychology PhD (Doctor of Philosophy)*: GRE-V no minimum stated, 154, GRE-Q no minimum stated, 154, GRE-Analytical no minimum stated, 4.8, overall undergraduate GPA no minimum stated, 3.49.

Other Criteria: (importance of criteria rated low, medium, or high): GRE scores—high, research experience—medium, work experience—medium, extracurricular activity—medium, clinically related public service—medium, GPA—high, letters of recommendation—high, interview—low, statement of goals and objectives—high, undergraduate major in psychology—low, specific undergraduate psychology courses taken—low.

Student Characteristics: The following represents characteristics of students in 2012–2013 in all graduate psychology programs in the department: Female—full-time 137, part-time 98; Male—full-time 26, part-time 14; African American/Black—full-time 19, part-time 7; Hispanic/Latino(a)—full-time 3, part-time 15; Asian/Pacific Islander—full-time 9, part-time 4; American Indian/Alaska Native—full-time 0, part-time 2; Caucasian/White—full-time 115, part-time 75; Multi-ethnic—full-time 0, part-time 0; students subject to the Americans With Disabilities Act—full-time 0, part-time 0; Unknown ethnicity—full-time 17, part-time 9; International students who hold an F-1 or J-1 Visa—full-time 4, part-time 4.

Financial Information/Assistance:
Tuition for Full-Time Study: *Master's:* State residents: $1,136 per credit hour; Nonstate residents: $1,136 per credit hour. *Doctoral:* State residents: $1,136 per credit hour; Nonstate residents: $1,136 per credit hour. Tuition is subject to change. See the following website for updates and changes in tuition costs: http://www.fordham.edu/tuition__financial_a/graduate_students/.

Financial Assistance:
First-Year Students: Research assistantships available for first year. Fellowships and scholarships available for first year.

Advanced Students: Research assistantships available for advanced students. Apply by February. Fellowships and scholarships available for advanced students.

Additional Information: Of all students currently enrolled full time, 60% benefited from one or more of the listed financial assistance programs. Application and information available online at: http://www.fordham.edu/tuition__financial_a/graduate_students/.

Internships/Practica: Doctoral Degree (PhD Counseling Psychology): For those doctoral students for whom a professional psychology internship was required in this program prior to graduation, (11) students applied for an internship in 2011–2012, with (11) students obtaining an internship. Of those students who obtained an internship, (9) were paid internships. Of those students who obtained an internship, (7) students placed in APA/CPA accredited internships, (2) students placed in internships not APA/CPA accredited, but listed with the Association of Psychology Postdoctoral and Internship Programs (APPIC), (0) students placed in internships conforming to guidelines of the Council of Directors of School Psychology Programs (CDSPP), (2) students placed in internships that were not APA/CPA accredited, APPIC or CDSPP listed. Doctoral Degree (PhD School Psychology): For those doctoral students for whom a professional psychology internship was required in this program prior to graduation, (5) students applied for an internship in 2011–2012, with (5) students obtaining an internship. Of those students who obtained an internship, (5) were paid internships. Of those students who obtained an internship, (0) students placed in APA/CPA accredited internships, (0) students placed in internships not APA/CPA accredited, but listed with the Association of Psychology Postdoctoral and Internship Programs (APPIC), (5) students placed in internships conforming to guidelines of the Council of Directors of School Psychology Programs (CDSPP), (0) students placed in internships that were not APA/CPA accredited, APPIC or CDSPP listed. Students complete practica, field experiences, externships and internships in a wide variety of sites throughout the metropolitan NYC area. Sites such as P-12 schools, hospitals, mental health agencies and clinics and college counseling centers all vary by setting, type and diversity of the population served.

Housing and Day Care: No on-campus housing is available. No on-campus day care facilities are available.

Employment of Department Graduates:
Master's Degree Graduates: Of those who graduated in the academic year 2011–2012, the following categories and numbers represent the postgraduate activities and employment of master's degree graduates: Enrolled in a psychology doctoral program (3), enrolled in a postdoctoral residency/fellowship (n/a), employed in independent practice (n/a), employed in a professional position in a school system (2), do not know (40), total from the above (master's) (45).

Doctoral Degree Graduates: Of those who graduated in the academic year 2011–2012, the following categories and numbers represent the postgraduate activities and employment of doctoral degree graduates: Enrolled in a psychology doctoral program (n/a), enrolled in a postdoctoral residency/fellowship (2), employed in an academic position at a university (2), employed in a community mental health/counseling center (1), employed in a hospital/medical center (2), do not know (3), total from the above (doctoral) (10).

Additional Information:

Orientation, Objectives, and Emphasis of Department: Prepares professionals for positions in PreK'12 schools, mental health settings; counseling services in higher education, adult education, business, industry, and independent psychological practice. Also provides advanced training for teachers and individuals interested in research or the development and evaluation of educational programs and materials.

Special Facilities or Resources: Fordham University's Graduate School of Education offers several higher learning and community based centers and institutes: The Center for Educational Partnerships, The Rosa A. Hagin School Consultation Center and Early Childhood Center, The Center for Catholic Leadership and Faith-Based Education, Center for Learning in Unsupervised Environment, Human Resilency, Advanced Placement Summer Institute and the Psychological Services Institute.

Information for Students With Physical Disabilities: See the following website for more information: http://www.fordham.edu/dss/.

Application Information:

Application available online. URL of online application: http://www.fordham.edu/admissions/. Students are admitted in the Fall, application deadline December 15; Summer, application deadline. Counseling Psychology PhD - December 15. School Psychology PhD and Professional Diploma - January 15. Counseling MSE's - March 1. *Fee:* $50.

Hofstra University

Department of Psychology
Hofstra College of Liberal Arts and Sciences
135 Hofstra University
Hempstead, NY 11549
Telephone: (516) 463-5624
Fax: (516) 463-6052
E-mail: *Charles.F.Levinthal@hofstra.edu*
Web: *http://www.hofstra.edu/Academics/Colleges/HCLAS/PSY/*

Department Information:

1948. Chairperson: Charles F. Levinthal, PhD. Number of faculty: total—full-time 30, part-time 21; women—full-time 12, part-time 8; total—minority—full-time 3, part-time 1; women minority—full-time 2, part-time 1; faculty subject to the Americans With Disabilities Act 1.

Programs and Degrees Offered:

Listed in the following order: Program area, degree type (T if terminal Master's), number awarded 7/11–6/12. Clinical Psychology PhD (Doctor of Philosophy) 14, Industrial/Organizational Psychology MA/MS (Master of Arts/Science) (T) 24, School-Community Psychology PsyD (Doctor of Psychology) 11, Applied Organizational Psychology PhD (Doctor of Philosophy) 5.

APA Accreditation: Clinical PhD (Doctor of Philosophy). Student Outcome Data Website: http://www.hofstra.edu/Academics/Colleges/HCLAS/PSY/phdcp/phdcp_admdata.html. School PsyD (Doctor of Psychology). Student Outcome Data Website: http://www.hofstra.edu/academics/colleges/hclas/psy/psydsc/psydsc_StudentAdmissions_Outcomes_OtherData.html.

Student Applications/Admissions:

Student Applications

Clinical Psychology PhD (Doctor of Philosophy)—Applications 2012–2013, 263. Total applicants accepted 2012–2013, 23. Number full-time enrolled (new admits only) 2012–2013, 14. Total enrolled 2012–2013 full-time, 82. Total enrolled 2012–2013 part-time, 0. Openings 2013–2014, 14. The median number of years required for completion of a degree in 2012–2013 were 6. The number of students enrolled full- and part-time who were dismissed or voluntarily withdrew from this program area in 2012–2013 were 0. *Industrial/Organizational Psychology MA/MS (Master of Arts/Science)*—Applications 2012–2013, 83. Total applicants accepted 2012–2013, 64. Number full-time enrolled (new admits only) 2012–2013, 22. Number part-time enrolled (new admits only) 2012–2013, 6. Total enrolled 2012–2013 full-time, 50. Total enrolled 2012–2013 part-time, 6. Openings 2013–2014, 25. The median number of years required for completion of a degree in 2012–2013 were 2. The number of students enrolled full- and part-time who were dismissed or voluntarily withdrew from this program area in 2012–2013 were 3. *School-Community Psychology PsyD (Doctor of Psychology)*—Applications 2012–2013, 100. Total applicants accepted 2012–2013, 29. Number full-time enrolled (new admits only) 2012–2013, 10. Number part-time enrolled (new admits only) 2012–2013, 2. Total enrolled 2012–2013 full-time, 44. Total enrolled 2012–2013 part-time, 8. Openings 2013–2014, 12. The median number of years required for completion of a degree in 2012–2013 were 5. The number of students enrolled full- and part-time who were dismissed or voluntarily withdrew from this program area in 2012–2013 were 1. *Applied Organizational Psychology PhD (Doctor of Philosophy)*—Applications 2012–2013, 29. Total applicants accepted 2012–2013, 20. Number full-time enrolled (new admits only) 2012–2013, 9. Number part-time enrolled (new admits only) 2012–2013, 0. Total enrolled 2012–2013 full-time, 34. Total enrolled 2012–2013 part-time, 0. Openings 2013–2014, 8. The median number of years required for completion of a degree in 2012–2013 were 4. The number of students enrolled full- and part-time who were dismissed or voluntarily withdrew from this program area in 2012–2013 were 0.

Scores: Entries appear in this order: required test or GPA, minimum score (if required), median score of students entering in 2012–2013. *Clinical Psychology PhD (Doctor of Philosophy):* GRE-V no minimum stated, 617, GRE-Q no minimum stated, 689, GRE-Analytical no minimum stated, GRE-Subject (Psychology) no minimum stated, 682, overall undergraduate GPA no minimum stated, 3.71, psychology GPA no minimum stated, Masters GPA no minimum stated; *Industrial/Organizational Psychology MA/MS (Master of Arts/Science):* GRE-V 500, 153, GRE-Q 500, 153, overall undergraduate GPA 3.00, 3.7; *School-Community Psychology PsyD (Doctor of Psychology):* GRE-V 153, GRE-Q 144, GRE-Analytical no minimum stated, GRE-Subject (Psychology) no minimum stated, 600, overall undergraduate GPA no minimum stated, 3.5; *Applied Organizational Psychology PhD (Doctor of Philosophy):* GRE-V

500, 500, GRE-Q 600, 600, GRE-Analytical no minimum stated, Masters GPA 3.0, 3.5.

Other Criteria: (importance of criteria rated low, medium, or high): GRE scores—high, research experience—high, work experience—medium, extracurricular activity—medium, clinically related public service—medium, GPA—high, letters of recommendation—medium, interview—high, statement of goals and objectives—medium, undergraduate major in psychology—medium, specific undergraduate psychology courses taken—medium, For Clinical PhD program: research experience high, especially professional presentations and publications, clinically related public service high, statement of goals and objectives high. For PsyD program: research experience low, clinically related public service medium, statement of goals and objectives medium. For PhD in Applied Organizational Psychology, a master's degree in one of the social sciences or in business is required. For additional information on admission requirements, go to http://www.hofstra.edu/Academics/Colleges/HCLAS/PSY/psy_proggrad.html.

Student Characteristics: The following represents characteristics of students in 2012–2013 in all graduate psychology programs in the department: Female—full-time 135, part-time 10; Male—full-time 75, part-time 4; African American/Black—full-time 11, part-time 1; Hispanic/Latino(a)—full-time 3, part-time 0; Asian/Pacific Islander—full-time 13, part-time 0; American Indian/Alaska Native—full-time 0, part-time 0; Caucasian/White—full-time 183, part-time 13; Multi-ethnic—full-time 0, part-time 0; students subject to the Americans With Disabilities Act—full-time 0, part-time 0; Unknown ethnicity—full-time 0, part-time 0; International students who hold an F-1 or J-1 Visa—full-time 5, part-time 0.

Financial Information/Assistance:

Tuition for Full-Time Study: *Master's:* State residents: $1,080 per credit hour; Nonstate residents: $1,080 per credit hour. *Doctoral:* State residents: per academic year $34,815, $1,080 per credit hour; Nonstate residents: per academic year $34,815, $1,080 per credit hour. Tuition is subject to change. Additional fees are assessed to students beyond the costs of tuition for the following: university, technology and activity fees. Tuition costs vary by program. See the following website for updates and changes in tuition costs: http://www.hofstra.edu/sfs/bursar/bursar_tuition.html.

Financial Assistance:

First-Year Students: Teaching assistantships available for first year. Average number of hours worked per week: 6. Research assistantships available for first year. Average number of hours worked per week: 5. Fellowships and scholarships available for first year.

Advanced Students: Teaching assistantships available for advanced students. Average number of hours worked per week: 6. Research assistantships available for advanced students. Average number of hours worked per week: 5. Fellowships and scholarships available for advanced students.

Additional Information: Of all students currently enrolled full time, 33% benefited from one or more of the listed financial assistance programs. Application and information available online at: http://www.hofstra.edu/Academics/grad/grad_fa_scholarships.html.

Internships/Practica: Doctoral Degree (PhD Clinical Psychology): For those doctoral students for whom a professional psychology internship was required in this program prior to graduation, (20) students applied for an internship in 2011–2012, with (15) students obtaining an internship. Of those students who obtained an internship, (14) were paid internships. Of those students who obtained an internship, (13) students placed in APA/CPA accredited internships, (0) students placed in internships not APA/CPA accredited, but listed with the Association of Psychology Postdoctoral and Internship Programs (APPIC), (0) students placed in internships conforming to guidelines of the Council of Directors of School Psychology Programs (CDSPP), (2) students placed in internships that were not APA/CPA accredited, APPIC or CDSPP listed. Doctoral Degree (PsyD School-Community Psychology): For those doctoral students for whom a professional psychology internship was required in this program prior to graduation, (16) students applied for an internship in 2011–2012, with (16) students obtaining an internship. Of those students who obtained an internship, (7) were paid internships. Of those students who obtained an internship, (0) students placed in APA/CPA accredited internships, (0) students placed in internships not APA/CPA accredited, but listed with the Association of Psychology Postdoctoral and Internship Programs (APPIC), (9) students placed in internships conforming to guidelines of the Council of Directors of School Psychology Programs (CDSPP), (7) students placed in internships that were not APA/CPA accredited, APPIC or CDSPP listed. Master's Degree (MA/MS Industrial/Organizational Psychology): An internship experience, such as a final research project or "capstone" experience is required of graduates. In the clinical PhD and PsyD programs students complete a series of practica in which assessment, testing, and interviewing skills are developed. PhD students complete various courses and role playing experiences in adult psychotherapy. PhD students are required to apply for internships using the APPIC national match process following the completion of all coursework and the defense of a dissertation proposal. PsyD students complete a diversified and extended internship over a two-year period. The students are first placed in a school (three days per week) and then in a community agency (3 days per week). In the PhD program in Applied Organizational Psychology, a major part of the student's training, including a paid internship, research courses, and doctoral dissertation, will involve projects in organizations. The internship provides practical experience working for an organization for approximately 20 hours per week, under the supervision of a manager designated by the organization and approved by the program faculty. All research projects, including the dissertation, must serve the educational needs of the students and advance scientific knowledge in the field of organizational psychology; they cannot only serve the interests of the organization. Dissertation research may be conducted in the laboratory, the organization, or both. In addition to sound scientific methodology, the dissertation must have both practical and theoretical significance. This integration of science and practice is a major objective of the program. MA students in Industrial/Organizational Psychology, during their second year of training, complete an internship in a business setting.

Housing and Day Care: On-campus housing is available. See the following website for more information: http://www.hofstra.edu/StudentAffairs/StudentServices/ResLife/. On-campus day care facilities are available. See the following website for more information: http://www.hofstra.edu/community/slzctr/slzctr_childcare.html.

Employment of Department Graduates:

Master's Degree Graduates: Of those who graduated in the academic year 2011–2012, the following categories and numbers represent the postgraduate activities and employment of master's degree graduates: Enrolled in a postdoctoral residency/fellowship (n/a), employed in independent practice (n/a), employed in an academic position at a university (2), employed in business or industry (13), do not know (9), total from the above (master's) (24).

Doctoral Degree Graduates: Of those who graduated in the academic year 2011–2012, the following categories and numbers represent the postgraduate activities and employment of doctoral degree graduates: Enrolled in a psychology doctoral program (n/a), enrolled in a postdoctoral residency/fellowship (3), employed in independent practice (2), employed in an academic position at a university (1), employed in an academic position at a 2-year/4-year college (1), employed in a professional position in a school system (6), employed in business or industry (6), employed in government agency (2), employed in a community mental health/counseling center (7), employed in a hospital/medical center (2), total from the above (doctoral) (30).

Additional Information:

Orientation, Objectives, and Emphasis of Department: The PhD program in Clinical Psychology is designed to provide doctoral students with assessment and therapeutic skill competence along with a solid scientific foundation in order to have careers working with the wide variety of psychopathology found among the mentally ill. The program employs a scientist–practitioner model of education. Program graduates have readily found employment in a wide variety of mental health clinics, group practices, and public and private agencies as well as hospitals and medical centers. Many have chosen academic paths by becoming college and university faculty members, medical school faculty, research scientists, expert consultants or editors for psychological publishers. The clinical psychology program is based upon cognitive-behavioral theory and represents the full psychotherapeutic spectrum of this orientation. The APA-accredited PsyD program in School-Community Psychology trains practitioners who are skilled in providing psychological services to children, families, and schools. Schools are viewed as being part of the larger community. Thus, in addition to being trained in a school-based, direct service model, emphasis is placed upon training students whose subject of study is the educational or community system in which children develop. PsyD students are trained as consultants who may be involved in educational and mental health program implementation and evaluation in settings such as the judicial system, the schools, personnel agencies, police departments, immigration centers, etc. Most graduates of the PsyD program are employed in schools. The PhD program in Applied Organizational Psychology prepares students for careers as psychologists in business, industry, government, and other private and public organizations. Graduates of this program are trained to apply scientific methods to the solutions of problems related to individual and group behavior in organizations. They are also capable of teaching and researching these topics in higher education settings. The program's overall approach is based on a scientist–practitioner model in which students are exposed to research methodology, factual content, theory, and the application of these skills and knowledge to the solution of practical problems in organizations. The MA program in Industrial/Organizational Psychology prepares students for careers in human resources, training, management, and organizational development. It provides a background in statistics, research design, social psychology, cognition and perception, and learning. The courses in I/O Psychology include selection, training, performance appraisal, worker motivation, and organization development. The curriculum is strengthened by an internship sequence which provides on-site supervised experience working on applied projects in business. The types of work that graduates perform include employee selection, management development, survey research, training, organizational development, performance appraisal, career development and program evaluation.

Special Facilities or Resources: A community services center, the Psychological Evaluation, Research and Counseling Clinic (PERCC), provides practicum experiences for students in the areas of assessment, intervention, and research. A laboratory, instrumented for videotaping, is equipped to handle research in areas of interviewing, communication, problem solving, psychotherapy, and team building. An outstanding library and a computer center are also available, as are many department microcomputers and videotape equipment. The student workroom has six computers for exclusive doctoral student use and all major software programs are available for student use.

Information for Students With Physical Disabilities: See the following website for more information: http://www.hofstra.edu/studentaffairs/stddis/.

Application Information:
Application available online. URL of online application: http://www.hofstra.edu/Academics/grad/grad_apply.html. Students are admitted in the Fall, application deadline December 15. Deadline for the PhD in Clinical Psychology is December 15. Deadline for the PsyD in School-Community Psychology is January 15. Deadline for the PhD in Applied Organizational Psychology is February 1. Applications for the MA in Industrial-Organizational Psychology are accepted on a rolling basis until the class is filled. *Fee:* $70. $75 for international student applicants.

Iona College
Department of Psychology/Masters of Arts in Psychology
715 North Avenue
New Rochelle, NY 10801
Telephone: (914) 637-7788
Fax: (914) 633-2528
E-mail: *agotlieb@iona.edu*
Web: *http://www.iona.edu/academic/artsscience/departments/Psychology*

Department Information:
1963. Chairperson: Paul Greene, PhD. Number of faculty: total—full-time 12, part-time 16; women—full-time 7, part-time 10; total—minority—full-time 3, part-time 2; women minority—full-time 2, part-time 2.

Programs and Degrees Offered:
Listed in the following order: Program area, degree type (T if terminal Master's), number awarded 7/11–6/12. School Psychol-

ogy MA/MS (Master of Arts/Science) (T) 16, Industrial-Organizational Psychology MA/MS (Master of Arts/Science) (T) 8, Mental Health Counseling MA/MS (Master of Arts/Science) (T) 14, General-Experimental Psychology MA/MS (Master of Arts/Science) (T) 4.

Student Applications/Admissions:

Student Applications

School Psychology MA/MS (Master of Arts/Science)—Applications 2012–2013, 44. Total applicants accepted 2012–2013, 42. Number full-time enrolled (new admits only) 2012–2013, 10. Number part-time enrolled (new admits only) 2012–2013, 5. Total enrolled 2012–2013 full-time, 25. Total enrolled 2012–2013 part-time, 21. Openings 2013–2014, 20. The median number of years required for completion of a degree in 2012–2013 were 2. The number of students enrolled full- and part-time who were dismissed or voluntarily withdrew from this program area in 2012–2013 were 1. Industrial-Organizational Psychology MA/MS (Master of Arts/Science)—Applications 2012–2013, 21. Total applicants accepted 2012–2013, 20. Number full-time enrolled (new admits only) 2012–2013, 3. Number part-time enrolled (new admits only) 2012–2013, 3. Total enrolled 2012–2013 full-time, 15. Total enrolled 2012–2013 part-time, 4. Openings 2013–2014, 20. The median number of years required for completion of a degree in 2012–2013 was 1. The number of students enrolled full- and part-time who were dismissed or voluntarily withdrew from this program area in 2012–2013 were 0. Mental Health Counseling MA/MS (Master of Arts/Science)—Applications 2012–2013, 27. Total applicants accepted 2012–2013, 22. Number full-time enrolled (new admits only) 2012–2013, 2. Number part-time enrolled (new admits only) 2012–2013, 2. Total enrolled 2012–2013 full-time, 23. Total enrolled 2012–2013 part-time, 8. Openings 2013–2014, 20. The median number of years required for completion of a degree in 2012–2013 were 3. The number of students enrolled full- and part-time who were dismissed or voluntarily withdrew from this program area in 2012–2013 were 2. General-Experimental Psychology MA/MS (Master of Arts/Science)—Applications 2012–2013, 5. Total applicants accepted 2012–2013, 5. Number full-time enrolled (new admits only) 2012–2013, 2. Number part-time enrolled (new admits only) 2012–2013, 0. Total enrolled 2012–2013 full-time, 6. Total enrolled 2012–2013 part-time, 0. Openings 2013–2014, 3. The median number of years required for completion of a degree in 2012–2013 were 2. The number of students enrolled full- and part-time who were dismissed or voluntarily withdrew from this program area in 2012–2013 were 0.

Scores: Entries appear in this order: required test or GPA, minimum score (if required), median score of students entering in 2012–2013. School Psychology MA/MS (Master of Arts/Science): overall undergraduate GPA 3.00, 3.18, psychology GPA 3.00; Industrial-Organizational Psychology MA/MS (Master of Arts/Science): overall undergraduate GPA 3.00, 3.17, psychology GPA 3.00; Mental Health Counseling MA/MS (Master of Arts/Science): overall undergraduate GPA 3.00, 3.84, psychology GPA 3.00; General-Experimental Psychology MA/MS (Master of Arts/Science): overall undergraduate GPA 3.00, 3.34, last 2 years GPA no minimum stated, psychology GPA 3.00.

Other Criteria: (importance of criteria rated low, medium, or high): research experience—medium, work experience—medium, extracurricular activity—medium, clinically related public service—medium, GPA—high, letters of recommendation—high, interview—low, undergraduate major in psychology—medium, specific undergraduate psychology courses taken—high. For additional information on admission requirements, go to http://www.iona.edu/ionagrad/programs/.

Student Characteristics: The following represents characteristics of students in 2012–2013 in all graduate psychology programs in the department: Female—full-time 58, part-time 29; Male—full-time 11, part-time 4; Caucasian/White—full-time 0, part-time 0; students subject to the Americans With Disabilities Act—full-time 0, part-time 0; Unknown ethnicity—full-time 0, part-time 0; International students who hold an F-1 or J-1 Visa—full-time 0, part-time 0.

Financial Information/Assistance:

Tuition for Full-Time Study: Master's: State residents: $912 per credit hour; Nonstate residents: $912 per credit hour. Additional fees are assessed to students beyond the costs of tuition for the following: program/student service fees - $225 per term. See the following website for updates and changes in tuition costs: http://www.iona.edu/admin/sfs/sa/tuition/.

Financial Assistance:

First-Year Students: Fellowships and scholarships available for first year. Average amount paid per academic year: $18,944.

Advanced Students: Fellowships and scholarships available for advanced students. Average amount paid per academic year: $18,944.

Additional Information: Of all students currently enrolled full time, 10% benefited from one or more of the listed financial assistance programs. Application and information available online at: http://www.iona.edu/ionagrad/financialaid/index.cfm.

Internships/Practica: Master's Degree (MA/MS School Psychology): An internship experience, such as a final research project or "capstone" experience is required of graduates. Master's Degree (MA/MS Industrial-Organizational Psychology): An internship experience, such as a final research project or "capstone" experience is required of graduates. Master's Degree (MA/MS Mental Health Counseling): An internship experience, such as a final research project or "capstone" experience is required of graduates. Master's Degree (MA/MS General-Experimental Psychology): An internship experience, such as a final research project or "capstone" experience is required of graduates. Students specializing in areas that may meet New York State requirements for employment, certification, or licensure, are required to take appropriate internship courses. While there is no guarantee that the student will get accepted by a site, the Department fully assists its students by providing instruction and personal guidance.

Housing and Day Care: No on-campus housing is available. No on-campus day care facilities are available.

Employment of Department Graduates:

Master's Degree Graduates: Of those who graduated in the academic year 2011–2012, the following categories and numbers represent the postgraduate activities and employment of master's degree graduates: Enrolled in a postdoctoral residency/fellowship (n/a), employed in independent practice (n/a), total from the above (master's) (0).

Doctoral Degree Graduates: Of those who graduated in the academic year 2011–2012, the following categories and numbers represent the postgraduate activities and employment of doctoral degree graduates: Enrolled in a psychology doctoral program (n/a), total from the above (doctoral) (0).

Additional Information:

Orientation, Objectives, and Emphasis of Department: The Psychology Department offers separate MA degrees in School Psychology, Mental Health Counseling, Industrial-Organizational psychology, and General-Experimental Psychology. All degree programs have been approved by the Education Department of New York State. The School Psychology program has been approved by NASP. The MA in Mental Health Counseling fulfills the academic requirements to take the licensing exam in New York. All programs have been designed for persons who are considering a career in psychology or who are en route to doctoral study in psychology, or are already employed in the field. The programs provide a balance of theoretical, methodological and practical expertise, as well as extensive training in written and oral expression. They are designed to provide pertinent new experiences, enhance knowledge in substantive areas, and facilitate maximum development of essential professional competencies and attitudes.

Special Facilities or Resources: The Department contains space dedicated to supporting research projects in specialties of psychology including social, perception, developmental, learning, treatment, and cognition. Extensive computer and software capabilities are available.

Application Information:

Send to Office of Graduate Admissions, School of Arts and Sciences, 715 North Avenue, New Rochelle, NY 10801. Application available online. URL of online application: http://www.iona.edu/admissions/applytoiona.cfm. Students are admitted in the Fall, application deadline February 15; Programs have rolling admissions. The School Psychology Program admits new students in the Fall Semester only, with a recommended application deadline of February 15. All other programs have rolling admissions. *Fee:* $50.

Long Island University
Department of Psychology
LIU Post
720 Northern Boulevard
Brookville, NY 11548
Telephone: (516) 299-2377
Fax: (516) 299-3105
E-mail: *gerald.lachter@liu.edu*
Web: *http://www.liu.edu/CWPost/Academics/Schools/CLAS/
Dept/Psychology.aspx*

Department Information:

1954. Chairperson: Gerald D. Lachter. Number of faculty: total—full-time 15, part-time 6; women—full-time 8, part-time 4; total—minority—full-time 1, part-time 1; women minority—part-time 1.

Programs and Degrees Offered:

Listed in the following order: Program area, degree type (T if terminal Master's), number awarded 7/11–6/12. Experimental Psy-

chology MA/MS (Master of Arts/Science) (T) 8, Clinical Psychology PsyD (Doctor of Psychology) 16, Advanced Certificate Applied Behavior Analysis Other 21.

APA Accreditation: Clinical PsyD (Doctor of Psychology). Student Outcome Data Website: http://www.liu.edu/CWPost/Academics/Schools/CLAS/Dept/Psychology/PsyD2/Student-Admiss.

Student Applications/Admissions:

Student Applications

Experimental Psychology MA/MS (Master of Arts/Science)—Applications 2012–2013, 28. Total applicants accepted 2012–2013, 7. Number full-time enrolled (new admits only) 2012–2013, 3. Total enrolled 2012–2013 full-time, 5. Openings 2013–2014, 10. The median number of years required for completion of a degree in 2012–2013 were 2. The number of students enrolled full- and part-time who were dismissed or voluntarily withdrew from this program area in 2012–2013 were 0. *Clinical Psychology PsyD (Doctor of Psychology)*—Applications 2012–2013, 295. Total applicants accepted 2012–2013, 43. Number full-time enrolled (new admits only) 2012–2013, 20. Total enrolled 2012–2013 full-time, 95. Openings 2013–2014, 20. The median number of years required for completion of a degree in 2012–2013 were 5. The number of students enrolled full- and part-time who were dismissed or voluntarily withdrew from this program area in 2012–2013 were 0. *Advanced Certificate Applied Behavior Analysis Other*—Applications 2012–2013, 38. Total applicants accepted 2012–2013, 28. Number part-time enrolled (new admits only) 2012–2013, 23. Total enrolled 2012–2013 part-time, 23. Openings 2013–2014, 20. The median number of years required for completion of a degree in 2012–2013 was 1. The number of students enrolled full- and part-time who were dismissed or voluntarily withdrew from this program area in 2012–2013 were 0.

Scores: Entries appear in this order: required test or GPA, minimum score (if required), median score of students entering in 2012–2013. *Experimental Psychology MA/MS (Master of Arts/Science):* GRE-V no minimum stated, GRE-Q no minimum stated, GRE-Analytical no minimum stated, overall undergraduate GPA no minimum stated, psychology GPA no minimum stated; *Clinical Psychology PsyD (Doctor of Psychology):* GRE-V no minimum stated, 162, GRE-Q no minimum stated, 155, GRE-Analytical no minimum stated, 5.0, GRE-Subject (Psychology) no minimum stated, 705, overall undergraduate GPA no minimum stated, psychology GPA no minimum stated.

Other Criteria: (importance of criteria rated low, medium, or high): GRE scores—medium, research experience—high, work experience—high, extracurricular activity—low, clinically related public service—high, GPA—high, letters of recommendation—high, interview—high, statement of goals and objectives—medium, undergraduate major in psychology—medium, specific undergraduate psychology courses taken—medium, Clinical experience not rated highly for MA program. Research experience rated highly for MA program.

Student Characteristics: The following represents characteristics of students in 2012–2013 in all graduate psychology programs in the department: Female—full-time 80, part-time 18; Male—full-time 25, part-time 4; African American/Black—full-time 4, part-time 2; Hispanic/Latino(a)—full-time 8, part-time 3; Asian/Pa-

cific Islander—full-time 3, part-time 0; American Indian/Alaska Native—full-time 0, part-time 0; Caucasian/White—full-time 80, part-time 17; Multi-ethnic—full-time 0, part-time 0; students subject to the Americans With Disabilities Act—full-time 0, part-time 0; Unknown ethnicity—full-time 10, part-time 0; International students who hold an F-1 or J-1 Visa—full-time 0, part-time 0.

Financial Information/Assistance:

Tuition for Full-Time Study: *Master's:* State residents: $1,068 per credit hour; Nonstate residents: $1,068 per credit hour. *Doctoral:* State residents: per academic year $44,000; Nonstate residents: per academic year $44,000. Tuition is subject to change. Additional fees are assessed to students beyond the costs of tuition for the following: $100/semester activity fee. See the following website for updates and changes in tuition costs: http://www.liu.edu/About/Administration/University-Departments/SFO/Tuition.aspx.

Financial Assistance:

First-Year Students: Teaching assistantships available for first year. Research assistantships available for first year. Fellowships and scholarships available for first year.

Advanced Students: Teaching assistantships available for advanced students. Research assistantships available for advanced students. Fellowships and scholarships available for advanced students.

Additional Information: Of all students currently enrolled full time, 75% benefited from one or more of the listed financial assistance programs. Application and information available online at: http://www.liu.edu/CWPost/Financial-Assistance/Basics.aspx.

Internships/Practica: Doctoral Degree (PsyD Clinical Psychology): For those doctoral students for whom a professional psychology internship was required in this program prior to graduation, (20) students applied for an internship in 2011–2012, with (20) students obtaining an internship. Of those students who obtained an internship, (20) were paid internships. Of those students who obtained an internship, (20) students placed in APA/CPA accredited internships, (0) students placed in internships not APA/CPA accredited, but listed with the Association of Psychology Postdoctoral and Internship Programs (APPIC), (0) students placed in internships conforming to guidelines of the Council of Directors of School Psychology Programs (CDSPP), (0) students placed in internships that were not APA/CPA accredited, APPIC or CDSPP listed. Master's Degree (MA/MS Experimental Psychology): An internship experience, such as a final research project or "capstone" experience is required of graduates. A wide range of internship and practicum placements are available.

Housing and Day Care: On-campus housing is available. See the following website for more information: http://www.liu.edu/CWPost/StudentLife/ResLife.aspx. No on-campus day care facilities are available.

Employment of Department Graduates:

Master's Degree Graduates: Of those who graduated in the academic year 2011–2012, the following categories and numbers represent the postgraduate activities and employment of master's degree graduates: Enrolled in a psychology doctoral program (2), enrolled in another graduate/professional program (2), enrolled

in a postdoctoral residency/fellowship (n/a), employed in independent practice (n/a), total from the above (master's) (4).

Doctoral Degree Graduates: Of those who graduated in the academic year 2011–2012, the following categories and numbers represent the postgraduate activities and employment of doctoral degree graduates: Enrolled in a psychology doctoral program (n/a), employed in a hospital/medical center (2), other employment position (10), total from the above (doctoral) (12).

Additional Information:

Orientation, Objectives, and Emphasis of Department: The Master's degree program gives students a broad background in Experimental Psychology. Faculty interests include Behavior Analysis, Cognition and Perception, and Neuroscience. The program is designed to prepare students for admission to doctoral programs, or to give them the skills necessary to obtain employment. The Clinical Psychology doctoral program at the C.W. Post Campus of Long Island University offers a Doctor of Psychology (PsyD) degree and has as its basic purpose the training of doctoral level clinical psychologists who will exhibit professional attitudes and apply current knowledge and practice skills for the prevention and alleviation of psychological problems. The program is also committed to training students who will provide services in public sector settings to traditionally underserved groups. While the mission is to broadly train clinical psychologists, the program also seeks to provide each student with special competencies in one of three areas: family violence, applied child, and serious and persistent mental illness. The program also provides its graduates with clinical and theoretical training in two major orientations — cognitive-behavioral and psychoanalytic. The Clinical Psychology Doctoral Program is fully accredited by the American Psychological Association. In 2009, the APA awarded the Program with accreditation until 2016, the longest possible period of accreditation. The program is also registered by the New York State Education Department and listed by the Association of State and Provincial Psychology Boards and the National Register of Health Service Providers in Psychology as a designated institution offering a doctoral program in psychology. The program is based on the practitioner-scholar model of clinical training.

Special Facilities or Resources: Laboratories exist for the study of animal and human learning, cognition and perception, and neuroscience. The PsyD program has its own Psychological Services Center that provides mental health services to the community as well as serving as a site for training students.

Information for Students With Physical Disabilities: See the following website for more information: http://www.liu.edu/CWPost/StudentLife/Services/LSC/DSS.

Application Information:

Send to Graduate Admissions, LIU Post, Brookville, NY 11548. Application available online. URL of online application: http://www.liu.edu/CWPost/Admissions/Graduate/Start/Apply. Students are admitted in the Fall, application deadline January 31; Programs have rolling admissions. January 31 for PsyD; June 1 for MA; August 1 for Advanced Certificate Program. *Fee:* $40.

Long Island University
Psychology/Clinical Psychology
Richard L. Conolly College
1 University Plaza
Brooklyn, NY 11201
Telephone: (718) 488-1164
Fax: (718) 488-1179
E-mail: *nicholas.papouchis@liu.edu*
Web: *http://www2.brooklyn.liu.edu/psych/psy_core.htm*

Department Information:

1967. Director, PhD Program in Clinical Psychology: Nicholas Papouchis. Number of faculty: total—full-time 16, part-time 6; women—full-time 6, part-time 3; total—minority—full-time 6; women minority—full-time 2; faculty subject to the Americans With Disabilities Act 1.

Programs and Degrees Offered:

Listed in the following order: Program area, degree type (T if terminal Master's), number awarded 7/11–6/12. Clinical Psychology PhD (Doctor of Philosophy) 16, General Psychology MA/MS (Master of Arts/Science) (T) 19.

APA Accreditation: Clinical PhD (Doctor of Philosophy). Student Outcome Data Website: http://liu.edu/Brooklyn/Academics/Schools/CLAS/Programs/Div3/Psychology/PhD-Psychology.

Student Applications/Admissions:

Student Applications

Clinical Psychology PhD (Doctor of Philosophy)—Applications 2012–2013, 237. Total applicants accepted 2012–2013, 25. Number full-time enrolled (new admits only) 2012–2013, 17. Number part-time enrolled (new admits only) 2012–2013, 0. Total enrolled 2012–2013 full-time, 95. Total enrolled 2012–2013 part-time, 9. Openings 2013–2014, 16. The median number of years required for completion of a degree in 2012–2013 were 6. The number of students enrolled full- and part-time who were dismissed or voluntarily withdrew from this program area in 2012–2013 were 1. *General Psychology MA/MS (Master of Arts/Science)*—Applications 2012–2013, 20. Total applicants accepted 2012–2013, 9. Number full-time enrolled (new admits only) 2012–2013, 6. Number part-time enrolled (new admits only) 2012–2013, 3. Total enrolled 2012–2013 full-time, 29. Total enrolled 2012–2013 part-time, 25. Openings 2013–2014, 20. The median number of years required for completion of a degree in 2012–2013 were 4. The number of students enrolled full- and part-time who were dismissed or voluntarily withdrew from this program area in 2012–2013 were 0.

Scores: Entries appear in this order: required test or GPA, minimum score (if required), median score of students entering in 2012–2013. *Clinical Psychology PhD (Doctor of Philosophy)*: GRE-V 575, 650, GRE-Q 575, 650, GRE-Analytical 4.0, 5.0, GRE-Subject (Psychology) 550, 660, overall undergraduate GPA 3.2, 3.5, last 2 years GPA 3.4, 3.5, psychology GPA 3.5, 3.75; *General Psychology MA/MS (Master of Arts/Science)*: overall undergraduate GPA 3.0.

Other Criteria: (importance of criteria rated low, medium, or high): GRE scores—high, research experience—high, work experience—high, extracurricular activity—low, clinically re-lated public service—medium, GPA—high, letters of recommendation—high, interview—high, statement of goals and objectives—high, publications and posters—medium, undergraduate major in psychology—medium, specific undergraduate psychology courses taken—medium, The above requirements are for the PhD Program in Clinical Psychology. Requirements for the MA Program include a GPA of 2.75, good letters of recommendation and a committment to pursue a scholarly foundation at the graduate level in psychology. For additional information on admission requirements, go to http://www2.brooklyn.liu.edu/psych/phdprogram/.

Student Characteristics: The following represents characteristics of students in 2012–2013 in all graduate psychology programs in the department: Female—full-time 97, part-time 25; Male—full-time 27, part-time 9; African American/Black—full-time 16, part-time 10; Hispanic/Latino(a)—full-time 16, part-time 9; Asian/Pacific Islander—full-time 12, part-time 6; American Indian/Alaska Native—full-time 0, part-time 0; Caucasian/White—full-time 80, part-time 9; Multi-ethnic—full-time 0, part-time 0; students subject to the Americans With Disabilities Act—full-time 0, part-time 0; Unknown ethnicity—full-time 0, part-time 0; International students who hold an F-1 or J-1 Visa—full-time 4, part-time 0.

Financial Information/Assistance:

Tuition for Full-Time Study: *Master's:* State residents: $1,068 per credit hour; Nonstate residents: $1,068 per credit hour. *Doctoral:* State residents: per academic year $44,444, $1,421 per credit hour; Nonstate residents: per academic year $44,444, $1,421 per credit hour. Tuition is subject to change. See the following website for updates and changes in tuition costs: http://www.liu.edu/SFS/Tuition/Tuition.

Financial Assistance:

First-Year Students: Research assistantships available for first year. Average amount paid per academic year: $1,250. Average number of hours worked per week: 10. Apply by April 15. Fellowships and scholarships available for first year. Average amount paid per academic year: $3,800. Average number of hours worked per week: 10. Apply by April 15.

Advanced Students: Teaching assistantships available for advanced students. Average amount paid per academic year: $2,400. Average number of hours worked per week: 10. Apply by April 15. Research assistantships available for advanced students. Average amount paid per academic year: $1,250. Average number of hours worked per week: 10. Apply by April 15. Fellowships and scholarships available for advanced students. Average amount paid per academic year: $3,800. Average number of hours worked per week: 10. Apply by April 15.

Additional Information: Of all students currently enrolled full time, 100% benefited from one or more of the listed financial assistance programs. Application and information available online at: http://www.liu.edu/Brooklyn/Financial-Services/Financial-Aid-Basics.

Internships/Practica: Doctoral Degree (PhD Clinical Psychology): For those doctoral students for whom a professional psychology internship was required in this program prior to graduation, (7) students applied for an internship in 2011–2012, with (6) students obtaining an internship. Of those students who obtained an internship, (6) were paid internships. Of those students who obtained an internship, (6) students placed in APA/CPA accredited internships, (0) students placed in internships not APA/CPA accredited, but listed with the Association of Psychology Postdoctoral and Internship Programs (APPIC), (0) students placed in internships conforming to guidelines of the Council of Directors of School Psychology Programs (CDSPP), (0) students placed in internships that were not APA/CPA accredited, APPIC or CDSPP listed. Students in the master's program have a variety of practica available to them. Doctoral practicum settings and internships in the New York City Metropolitan area are among the best in the country and offer training with a wide range of clinical patients and a number of specializations. Among these are child training, family training, neuropsychology and forensic training. Students in the PhD program regularly train in the best of these externship and practicum settings and over the three years from 2002 to 2005 doctoral students matched 100% with their internship choices. For 2005-2006 to 2010-2011 the percentage of doctoral students matching was 97%. This is an exceptional record of being accepted at the finest internship sites in the Northeast.

Housing and Day Care: On-campus housing is available. See the following website for more information: http://www.liu.edu/Brooklyn/StudentLife/ResLife/Grad-Apt.aspx. No on-campus day care facilities are available.

Employment of Department Graduates:
Master's Degree Graduates: Of those who graduated in the academic year 2011–2012, the following categories and numbers represent the postgraduate activities and employment of master's degree graduates: Enrolled in a psychology doctoral program (2), enrolled in a postdoctoral residency/fellowship (n/a), employed in independent practice (n/a), employed in a professional position in a school system (6), employed in government agency (3), employed in a community mental health/counseling center (3), employed in a hospital/medical center (3), other employment position (3), total from the above (master's) (20).
Doctoral Degree Graduates: Of those who graduated in the academic year 2011–2012, the following categories and numbers represent the postgraduate activities and employment of doctoral degree graduates: Enrolled in a psychology doctoral program (n/a), enrolled in a postdoctoral residency/fellowship (4), employed in an academic position at a university (1), employed in business or industry (1), employed in government agency (3), employed in a community mental health/counseling center (5), not seeking employment (2), total from the above (doctoral) (16).

Additional Information:
Orientation, Objectives, and Emphasis of Department: The PhD and master's programs are housed in an urban institution with a multicultural undergraduate student body. This diversity enriches the students' appreciation of the complexity of the clinical and theoretical issues relevant to work in psychology. The theoretical orientation of the clinical training sequence reflects the spectrum of psychodynamic approaches to treatment and familiarizes students with dialectical behavior therapy, cognitive-behavioral and family systems approaches as well. Clinical students are exposed, in a graded series of practicum experiences, to both short-term and longer term approaches to psychotherapy with the New York area's culturally diverse clinical populations. Students are also trained in a range of psychological assessment procedures including cognitive, projective, and neuropsychological testing. The

program also seeks to train clinical psychologists who are competent in research and grounded in the science of psychology. To this end, doctoral students receive extensive training in research design and statistics early in their coursework and complete a second-year research project prior to beginning their dissertation. The final goal and emphasis of the department and the PhD program is to enable students to develop a broad base of knowledge in clinical psychology. Doctoral students are provided with opportunities for clinical training with adults, children and adolescents, training in family therapy, group therapy and research training in a range of topics relevant to psychology.

Special Facilities or Resources: The Department of Psychology has the following facilities and resources: An on-site Psychological Services Center where clinical students' clinical work is carefully supervised by the doctoral faculty; an ongoing psychotherapy research group; research labs for the study of unconscious cognitive processes and personality and mood/anxiety disorders; training in child and adolescent clinical work at a number of New York area clinical training facilities; opportunity for specialized electives in neuropsychology; free access to computer training and computer facilities; and three full-tuition minority research fellowships for selected minority doctoral candidates. Finally, students in the PhD program have the spectrum of New York City's clinical and educational facilities available for them to be trained in.

Application Information:
Send to Long Island University, Brooklyn Campus, Admissions Processing Center, P.O. Box 810, Randolph, MA 02368-0810. Application available online. URL of online application: http://www.liu.edu/Brooklyn/Admissions/Graduate.aspx. Students are admitted in the Fall, application deadline January 5. For MA program, deadline is one month before the beginning of the semester. *Fee:* $40.

Marist College
Department of Psychology
Poughkeepsie, NY 12601
Telephone: (845) 575-3000
Fax: (845) 575-3965
E-mail: *james.regan@marist.edu*
Web: *http://www.marist.edu/sbs/graduate/*

Department Information:
1972. Graduate Program Director: James Regan, PhD. Number of faculty: total—full-time 16, part-time 34; women—full-time 6, part-time 20; total—minority—full-time 5, part-time 3; women minority—full-time 3, part-time 3.

Programs and Degrees Offered:
Listed in the following order: Program area, degree type (T if terminal Master's), number awarded 7/11–6/12. General Psychology MA/MS (Master of Arts/Science) (T) 12, School Psychology MA/MS (Master of Arts/Science) (T) 15, Mental Health Counseling MA/MS (Master of Arts/Science) (T) 15, Educational Psychology MA/MS (Master of Arts/Science) (T) 22.

Student Applications/Admissions:
Student Applications
General Psychology MA/MS (Master of Arts/Science)—Applications 2012–2013, 28. Total applicants accepted 2012–2013,

15. Number full-time enrolled (new admits only) 2012–2013, 15. Number part-time enrolled (new admits only) 2012–2013, 0. Total enrolled 2012–2013 full-time, 32. Total enrolled 2012–2013 part-time, 0. Openings 2013–2014, 20. The median number of years required for completion of a degree in 2012–2013 were 2. The number of students enrolled full- and part-time who were dismissed or voluntarily withdrew from this program area in 2012–2013 were 0. *School Psychology MA/MS (Master of Arts/Science)*—Applications 2012–2013, 41. Total applicants accepted 2012–2013, 35. Number full-time enrolled (new admits only) 2012–2013, 17. Number part-time enrolled (new admits only) 2012–2013, 0. Total enrolled 2012–2013 full-time, 46. Total enrolled 2012–2013 part-time, 0. Openings 2013–2014, 20. The median number of years required for completion of a degree in 2012–2013 were 3. The number of students enrolled full- and part-time who were dismissed or voluntarily withdrew from this program area in 2012–2013 were 2. *Mental Health Counseling MA/MS (Master of Arts/Science)*—Applications 2012–2013, 39. Total applicants accepted 2012–2013, 26. Number full-time enrolled (new admits only) 2012–2013, 20. Number part-time enrolled (new admits only) 2012–2013, 0. Total enrolled 2012–2013 full-time, 31. Total enrolled 2012–2013 part-time, 2. Openings 2013–2014, 20. The median number of years required for completion of a degree in 2012–2013 were 2. The number of students enrolled full- and part-time who were dismissed or voluntarily withdrew from this program area in 2012–2013 were 0. *Educational Psychology MA/MS (Master of Arts/Science)*—Applications 2012–2013, 40. Total applicants accepted 2012–2013, 33. Number full-time enrolled (new admits only) 2012–2013, 3. Number part-time enrolled (new admits only) 2012–2013, 30. Total enrolled 2012–2013 full-time, 50. Total enrolled 2012–2013 part-time, 36. Openings 2013–2014, 30. The median number of years required for completion of a degree in 2012–2013 were 2. The number of students enrolled full- and part-time who were dismissed or voluntarily withdrew from this program area in 2012–2013 were 0.

Scores: Entries appear in this order: required test or GPA, minimum score (if required), median score of students entering in 2012–2013. *General Psychology MA/MS (Master of Arts/Science):* overall undergraduate GPA 3.4, psychology GPA 3.4; *School Psychology MA/MS (Master of Arts/Science):* GRE-V no minimum stated, GRE-Q no minimum stated, overall undergraduate GPA 3.0; *Mental Health Counseling MA/MS (Master of Arts/Science):* GRE-V no minimum stated, 148, GRE-Q no minimum stated, 144., GRE-Analytical no minimum stated, 4.0, overall undergraduate GPA 3.0, 3.38, last 2 years GPA 3.0, psychology GPA 3.0; *Educational Psychology MA/MS (Master of Arts/Science):* overall undergraduate GPA 3.0.

Other Criteria: (importance of criteria rated low, medium, or high): GRE scores—low, research experience—low, work experience—medium, extracurricular activity—low, clinically related public service—medium, GPA—high, letters of recommendation—high, interview—high, statement of goals and objectives—low, undergraduate major in psychology—low, specific undergraduate psychology courses taken—low. For additional information on admission requirements, go to http://www.marist.edu/admission/graduate/deadlines.html.

Student Characteristics: The following represents characteristics of students in 2012–2013 in all graduate psychology programs in the department: Female—full-time 141, part-time 27; Male—full-time 18, part-time 11; African American/Black—full-time 8, part-time 7; Hispanic/Latino(a)—full-time 17, part-time 0; Asian/Pacific Islander—full-time 2, part-time 0; American Indian/Alaska Native—full-time 0, part-time 0; Caucasian/White—full-time 125, part-time 31; Multi-ethnic—full-time 7, part-time 0; students subject to the Americans With Disabilities Act—full-time 1, part-time 2; Unknown ethnicity—full-time 0, part-time 0; International students who hold an F-1 or J-1 Visa—full-time 0, part-time 0.

Financial Information/Assistance:

Tuition for Full-Time Study: *Master's:* State residents: per academic year $16,680, $720 per credit hour; Nonstate residents: per academic year $16,680, $720 per credit hour. Tuition is subject to change. Tuition costs vary by program. See the following website for updates and changes in tuition costs: http://www.marist.edu/financialaid/graduate/.

Financial Assistance:

First-Year Students: Research assistantships available for first year. Average amount paid per academic year: $4,500. Average number of hours worked per week: 10. Apply by April 15.

Advanced Students: Research assistantships available for advanced students. Average amount paid per academic year: $4,500. Average number of hours worked per week: 10. Apply by April 15.

Additional Information: Of all students currently enrolled full time, 60% benefited from one or more of the listed financial assistance programs. Application and information available online at: http://www.marist.edu/financialaid/graduate/.

Internships/Practica: Master's Degree (MA/MS General Psychology): An internship experience, such as a final research project or "capstone" experience is required of graduates. Master's Degree (MA/MS School Psychology): An internship experience, such as a final research project or "capstone" experience is required of graduates. Master's Degree (MA/MS Mental Health Counseling): An internship experience, such as a final research project or "capstone" experience is required of graduates. Master's Degree (MA/MS Educational Psychology): An internship experience, such as a final research project or "capstone" experience is required of graduates. The Mid-Hudson area has many public and private agencies dealing with mental health, developmental disabilities, criminal justice, and social services. In addition, numerous school districts participate with the school psychology program. Students choose their own placement site in consultation with their faculty supervisor.

Housing and Day Care: No on-campus housing is available. No on-campus day care facilities are available.

Employment of Department Graduates:

Master's Degree Graduates: Of those who graduated in the academic year 2011–2012, the following categories and numbers represent the postgraduate activities and employment of master's degree graduates: Enrolled in a psychology doctoral program (15), enrolled in another graduate/professional program (7), enrolled in a postdoctoral residency/fellowship (n/a), employed in independent practice (n/a), employed in an academic position at a 2-year/4-year college (3), employed in other positions at a higher education institution (3), employed in a professional position in a school system (22), employed in business or industry (2), employed in government agency (2), employed in a community mental health/counseling center (8), employed in a hospital/medical center (2), still seeking employment (2), total from the above (master's) (66).

Doctoral Degree Graduates: Of those who graduated in the academic year 2011–2012, the following categories and numbers represent the postgraduate activities and employment of doctoral degree graduates: Enrolled in a psychology doctoral program (n/a), total from the above (doctoral) (0).

Additional Information:

Orientation, Objectives, and Emphasis of Department: The Master of Arts program focuses on either mental health counseling or school psychology. The program goals include providing students with the relevant theory, skills, and practical experience that will enable them to perform competently in assessing individual differences, in counseling, and in planning and implementing effective individual, group, and systems-level interventions. Students interested in working in community settings will find a variety of opportunities for "hands-on" experience. The mental health counseling program fulfills the academic component for students who want to be licensed in New York State as Mental Health Counselors and the school psychology program leads to New York certification as a school psychologist.

Special Facilities or Resources: Interested students can assist in research at facilities such as the Nathan Kline Research Institute, The Center for Advanced Brain Imaging, The Marist Institute for Community Research, Dutchess County Department of Mental Hygiene and Public Health, and the Montrose and Castlepoint Veterans Hospitals.

Information for Students With Physical Disabilities: See the following website for more information: http://www.marist.edu/specialservices/.

Application Information:

Send to Director of Graduate Admissions, Marist College, Poughkeepsie, NY 12601. Application available online. URL of online application: http://www.marist.edu/admission/graduate/apply.html. Students are admitted in the Fall, application deadline April 15; Spring, application deadline December 1; Summer, application deadline April 1. Students considered after deadlines as space allows. *Fee:* $50.

New York University
Department of Applied Psychology
Steinhardt School of Culture, Education, & Human
    Development
246 Greene Street - Kimball Hall
New York, NY 10003
Telephone: (212) 998-5555
Fax: (212) 995-3654
E-mail: *applied.psychology@nyu.edu*
Web: *http://steinhardt.nyu.edu/appsych*

Department Information:
1990. Chairperson: Dr. LaRue Allen. Number of faculty: total—full-time 37, part-time 41; women—full-time 26, part-time 23;

total—minority—full-time 8, part-time 1; women minority—full-time 8, part-time 1; faculty subject to the Americans With Disabilities Act 4.

Programs and Degrees Offered:
Listed in the following order: Program area, degree type (T if terminal Master's), number awarded 7/11–6/12. Counseling and Guidance MA/MS (Master of Arts/Science) (T) 80, Counseling Psychology PhD (Doctor of Philosophy) 4, Psychological Development PhD (Doctor of Philosophy) 6, Educational Psychology MA/MS (Master of Arts/Science) (T) 5, Human Development and Social Intervention MA/MS (Master of Arts/Science) (T) 11, Psychology and Social Intervention PhD (Doctor of Philosophy) 0.

APA Accreditation: Counseling PhD (Doctor of Philosophy). Student Outcome Data Website: http://steinhardt.nyu.edu/appsych/phd/counseling_psychology/Students_Admissions_Outcomes_Other_Data.

Student Applications/Admissions:
Student Applications

Counseling and Guidance MA/MS (Master of Arts/Science)—Applications 2012–2013, 584. Total applicants accepted 2012–2013, 244. Number full-time enrolled (new admits only) 2012–2013, 85. Number part-time enrolled (new admits only) 2012–2013, 7. Total enrolled 2012–2013 full-time, 190. Total enrolled 2012–2013 part-time, 8. Openings 2013–2014, 105. The median number of years required for completion of a degree in 2012–2013 were 2. The number of students enrolled full- and part-time who were dismissed or voluntarily withdrew from this program area in 2012–2013 were 0. *Counseling Psychology PhD (Doctor of Philosophy)*—Applications 2012–2013, 215. Total applicants accepted 2012–2013, 3. Number full-time enrolled (new admits only) 2012–2013, 3. Number part-time enrolled (new admits only) 2012–2013, 0. Total enrolled 2012–2013 full-time, 32. Total enrolled 2012–2013 part-time, 0. Openings 2013–2014, 4. The median number of years required for completion of a degree in 2012–2013 were 8. The number of students enrolled full- and part-time who were dismissed or voluntarily withdrew from this program area in 2012–2013 were 0. *Psychological Development PhD (Doctor of Philosophy)*—Applications 2012–2013, 58. Total applicants accepted 2012–2013, 8. Number full-time enrolled (new admits only) 2012–2013, 4. Number part-time enrolled (new admits only) 2012–2013, 0. Total enrolled 2012–2013 full-time, 20. Total enrolled 2012–2013 part-time, 0. Openings 2013–2014, 3. The median number of years required for completion of a degree in 2012–2013 were 6. The number of students enrolled full- and part-time who were dismissed or voluntarily withdrew from this program area in 2012–2013 were 0. *Educational Psychology MA/MS (Master of Arts/Science)*—Applications 2012–2013, 0. Total applicants accepted 2012–2013, 0. Number full-time enrolled (new admits only) 2012–2013, 0. Number part-time enrolled (new admits only) 2012–2013, 0. The median number of years required for completion of a degree in 2012–2013 were 2. The number of students enrolled full- and part-time who were dismissed or voluntarily withdrew from this program area in 2012–2013 were 0. *Human Development and Social Intervention MA/MS (Master of Arts/Science)*—Applications 2012–2013, 103. Total applicants accepted 2012–2013, 78. Number full-time enrolled (new admits only) 2012–2013,

19. Number part-time enrolled (new admits only) 2012–2013, 0. Total enrolled 2012–2013 full-time, 47. Total enrolled 2012–2013 part-time, 0. Openings 2013–2014, 25. The median number of years required for completion of a degree in 2012–2013 were 2. The number of students enrolled full- and part-time who were dismissed or voluntarily withdrew from this program area in 2012–2013 were 0. *Psychology and Social Intervention PhD (Doctor of Philosophy)*—Applications 2012–2013, 70. Total applicants accepted 2012–2013, 2. Number full-time enrolled (new admits only) 2012–2013, 2. Number part-time enrolled (new admits only) 2012–2013, 0. Total enrolled 2012–2013 full-time, 12. Total enrolled 2012–2013 part-time, 0. Openings 2013–2014, 2. The number of students enrolled full- and part-time who were dismissed or voluntarily withdrew from this program area in 2012–2013 were 0.

Scores: Entries appear in this order: required test or GPA, minimum score (if required), median score of students entering in 2012–2013. *Counseling and Guidance MA/MS (Master of Arts/Science):* overall undergraduate GPA 3.0, 3.5, last 2 years GPA 3.0, 3.5; *Counseling Psychology PhD (Doctor of Philosophy):* GRE-V 550, 550, GRE-Q 550, 550, last 2 years GPA 3.0, 3.5, psychology GPA 3.0, 3.5; *Psychological Development PhD (Doctor of Philosophy):* GRE-V 550, 550, GRE-Q 550, 550, overall undergraduate GPA 3.0, 3.0, last 2 years GPA 3.5, 3.5; *Educational Psychology MA/MS (Master of Arts/Science):* overall undergraduate GPA 3.0, 3.5, last 2 years GPA 3.0, 3.5; *Human Development and Social Intervention MA/MS (Master of Arts/Science):* GRE-V no minimum stated, GRE-Q no minimum stated, overall undergraduate GPA 3.0, 3.5, last 2 years GPA 3.0, 3.5; *Psychology and Social Intervention PhD (Doctor of Philosophy):* GRE-V 550, 500, GRE-Q 550, 500, overall undergraduate GPA 3.0, 3.0, last 2 years GPA 3.5, 3.5.

Other Criteria: (importance of criteria rated low, medium, or high): GRE scores—medium, research experience—high, work experience—medium, extracurricular activity—medium, clinically related public service—medium, GPA—high, letters of recommendation—high, interview—high, statement of goals and objectives—high, undergraduate major in psychology—medium, The above criteria range from "medium" to "high" for admission into the doctoral programs. Master's programs primarily consider GPA, statement of goals and objectives, and letters of recommendation; interviews sometimes required for master's applicants.

Student Characteristics: The following represents characteristics of students in 2012–2013 in all graduate psychology programs in the department: Female—full-time 237, part-time 6; Male—full-time 52, part-time 2; African American/Black—full-time 41, part-time 1; Hispanic/Latino(a)—full-time 40, part-time 2; Asian/Pacific Islander—full-time 30, part-time 0; American Indian/Alaska Native—full-time 1, part-time 0; Caucasian/White—full-time 133, part-time 4; Multi-ethnic—full-time 7, part-time 0; students subject to the Americans With Disabilities Act—full-time 1, part-time 0; Unknown ethnicity—full-time 53, part-time 1; International students who hold an F-1 or J-1 Visa—full-time 42, part-time 0.

Financial Information/Assistance:
Tuition for Full-Time Study: *Master's:* State residents: per academic year $32,808, $1,367 per credit hour; Nonstate residents:

per academic year $32,808, $1,367 per credit hour. *Doctoral:* State residents: per academic year $32,808, $1,367 per credit hour; Nonstate residents: per academic year $32,808, $1,367 per credit hour. Tuition is subject to change. Additional fees are assessed to students beyond the costs of tuition for the following: registration fee for 1st credit- $432 and $63 per additional credit. See the following website for updates and changes in tuition costs: http://steinhardt.nyu.edu/graduate_admissions/tuition.

Financial Assistance:
First-Year Students: Research assistantships available for first year. Average amount paid per academic year: $25,060. Average number of hours worked per week: 20. Apply by December 1. Fellowships and scholarships available for first year. Average amount paid per academic year: $25,060. Apply by December 1.

Advanced Students: Research assistantships available for advanced students. Average amount paid per academic year: $25,060. Average number of hours worked per week: 20. Fellowships and scholarships available for advanced students. Average amount paid per academic year: $18,000.

Additional Information: Of all students currently enrolled full time, 100% benefited from one or more of the listed financial assistance programs. Application and information available online at: http://steinhardt.nyu.edu/financial_aid/.

Internships/Practica: Doctoral Degree (PhD Counseling Psychology): For those doctoral students for whom a professional psychology internship was required in this program prior to graduation, (2) students applied for an internship in 2011–2012, with (2) students obtaining an internship. Of those students who obtained an internship, (1) were paid internships. Of those students who obtained an internship, (1) students placed in APA/CPA accredited internships, (0) students placed in internships not APA/CPA accredited, but listed with the Association of Psychology Postdoctoral and Internship Programs (APPIC), (0) students placed in internships conforming to guidelines of the Council of Directors of School Psychology Programs (CDSPP), (1) students placed in internships that were not APA/CPA accredited, APPIC or CDSPP listed. Master's Degree (MA/MS Counseling and Guidance): An internship experience, such as a final research project or "capstone" experience is required of graduates. Available in the following areas: school and university counseling; counseling in community agencies, hospitals, and business; psychological development; measurement and evaluation.

Housing and Day Care: On-campus housing is available. See the following website for more information: http://www.nyu.edu/housing/. No on-campus day care facilities are available.

Employment of Department Graduates:
Master's Degree Graduates: Of those who graduated in the academic year 2011–2012, the following categories and numbers represent the postgraduate activities and employment of master's degree graduates: Enrolled in a postdoctoral residency/fellowship (n/a), employed in independent practice (n/a), total from the above (master's) (0).

Doctoral Degree Graduates: Of those who graduated in the academic year 2011–2012, the following categories and numbers represent the postgraduate activities and employment of doctoral degree graduates: Enrolled in a psychology doctoral program (n/a), total from the above (doctoral) (0).

Additional Information:

Orientation, Objectives, and Emphasis of Department: The cornerstone of our department is the marriage of theory and practice driven by the University's commitment to being a private university in the public service. To this end, the department's programs reflect both a concern for excellence in teaching and the opportunity to learn from involvement in community based data collection. Emphases and specific core requirements differ somewhat from program to program, but include a solid foundation in the basic psychological disciplines. Departmental faculty have ongoing research projects in many areas, including: cognition; language; social and emotional development; health and human development; applied measurement and research methods; working people's lives; spirituality; multicultural assessment; group and organizational dynamics; psychopathology and personality; sexual and gender identity; communication and creative expression; trauma and resilience; parenting; immigration.

Special Facilities or Resources: The Infancy Studies Laboratory conducts research in infant temperament, perceptual development, learning and attention, parenting views and child rearing styles. The Measurement Laboratory contains educational and psychological tests and reference books. PC computers are available for data analysis and word processing. The Institute for Human Development and Social Change aims to break new intellectual ground through its support for interdisciplinary research and training across, social, behavioral, health, and policy sciences. In the spirit of the common enterprise university, it brings together faculty, graduate students and undergraduate students from professional schools and the Faculty of Arts and Science. The Center for Research on Culture, Development and Education conducts longitudinal research on the pathways to educational success in early childhood and early adolescence, among New York City families of 5 ethnic groups. Center for Health, Identity, Behavior, & Prevention Studies (CHIBPS) conducts formative and intervention research on social and psychological factors that contribute to HIV transmission and the synergy between drug use, mental health, and HIV transmission. The Child and Family Policy Center conducts research, offers technical assistance and works to disseminate state-of-the field knowledge to bring children's healthy development and school success to the forefront of policymaking, program design, and practice.

Information for Students With Physical Disabilities: See the following website for more information: http://www.nyu.edu/csd/.

Application Information:

Send to Office of Graduate Admissions, The Steinhardt School of Education, Culture, and Human Development, New York University, 82 Washington Sq. East, Floor 3, New York, NY 10003. Application available online. URL of online application: http://steinhardt.nyu.edu/application/. Students are admitted in the Fall, application deadline December 15. Doctoral programs: December 15; Counseling MA programs: January 15. *Fee:* $75.

New York University, Graduate School of Arts and Science
Department of Psychology
6 Washington Place, Room 550
New York, NY 10003
Telephone: (212) 998-7900
Fax: (212) 995-4018
E-mail: *marc.skurski@nyu.edu*
Web: *http://www.psych.nyu.edu*

Department Information:
1950. Chairperson: Gregory L. Murphy. Number of faculty: total—full-time 41; women—full-time 14; total—minority—full-time 1; women minority—full-time 1.

Programs and Degrees Offered:
Listed in the following order: Program area, degree type (T if terminal Master's), number awarded 7/11–6/12. General Psychology MA/MS (Master of Arts/Science) (T) 63, Industrial/Organizational MA/MS (Master of Arts/Science) (T) 15, Cognition and Perception PhD (Doctor of Philosophy) 9, Social PhD (Doctor of Philosophy) 8.

Student Applications/Admissions:
Student Applications

General Psychology MA/MS (Master of Arts/Science)—Applications 2012–2013, 477. Total applicants accepted 2012–2013, 268. Number part-time enrolled (new admits only) 2012–2013, 76. Total enrolled 2012–2013 part-time, 205. *Industrial/Organizational MA/MS (Master of Arts/Science)*—Applications 2012–2013, 202. Total applicants accepted 2012–2013, 84. Number part-time enrolled (new admits only) 2012–2013, 24. Total enrolled 2012–2013 part-time, 63. *Cognition and Perception PhD (Doctor of Philosophy)*—Applications 2012–2013, 213. Total applicants accepted 2012–2013, 14. Number full-time enrolled (new admits only) 2012–2013, 7. Total enrolled 2012–2013 full-time, 42. The median number of years required for completion of a degree in 2012–2013 were 5. The number of students enrolled full- and part-time who were dismissed or voluntarily withdrew from this program area in 2012–2013 were 1. *Social PhD (Doctor of Philosophy)*—Applications 2012–2013, 259. Total applicants accepted 2012–2013, 13. Number full-time enrolled (new admits only) 2012–2013, 10. Total enrolled 2012–2013 full-time, 36. The median number of years required for completion of a degree in 2012–2013 were 6. The number of students enrolled full- and part-time who were dismissed or voluntarily withdrew from this program area in 2012–2013 were 0.

Other Criteria: (importance of criteria rated low, medium, or high): GRE scores—medium, research experience—high, work experience—low, extracurricular activity—low, clinically related public service—low, GPA—medium, letters of recommendation—high, statement of goals and objectives—high, These rankings are for the PhD only. For master's program, letters of recommendation and statement of goals and objectives have high importance; other criteria are low; no interviews are given. GRE/GPA varies by program.

Student Characteristics: The following represents characteristics of students in 2012–2013 in all graduate psychology programs in

the department: Female—full-time 47, part-time 175; Male—full-time 31, part-time 93; African American/Black—full-time 3, part-time 10; Hispanic/Latino(a)—full-time 1, part-time 17; Asian/Pacific Islander—full-time 10, part-time 29; American Indian/Alaska Native—part-time 1; Caucasian/White—full-time 46, part-time 128; Multi-ethnic—full-time 1, part-time 2; students subject to the Americans With Disabilities Act—full-time 0, part-time 0; Unknown ethnicity—full-time 17, part-time 81; International students who hold an F-1 or J-1 Visa—full-time 8, part-time 65.

Financial Information/Assistance:

Tuition for Full-Time Study: *Master's:* State residents: $1,437 per credit hour; Nonstate residents: $1,437 per credit hour. *Doctoral:* State residents: $1,437 per credit hour; Nonstate residents: $1,437 per credit hour. Tuition costs vary by program. See the following website for updates and changes in tuition costs: http://www.nyu.edu/bursar/.

Financial Assistance:

First-Year Students: Research assistantships available for first year. Average amount paid per academic year: $32,060. Average number of hours worked per week: 20. Apply by December 12. Traineeships available for first year. Fellowships and scholarships available for first year. Average amount paid per academic year: $32,060. Average number of hours worked per week: 20. Apply by December 12.

Advanced Students: Research assistantships available for advanced students. Average amount paid per academic year: $25,060. Average number of hours worked per week: 20. Traineeships available for advanced students. Fellowships and scholarships available for advanced students. Average amount paid per academic year: $25,060. Average number of hours worked per week: 20.

Additional Information: Of all students currently enrolled full time, 100% benefited from one or more of the listed financial assistance programs. Application and information available online at: http://gsas.nyu.edu/page/grad.financialaid.html.

Internships/Practica: Master's students may opt to take Fieldwork, which would enable them to obtain supervised experience in selected agencies, clinics, and industrial and non-profit organizations relevant to the career or academic objectives of the student.

Housing and Day Care: On-campus housing is available. See the following website for more information: http://www.nyu.edu/life/living-at-nyu.html. No on-campus day care facilities are available.

Employment of Department Graduates:

Master's Degree Graduates: Of those who graduated in the academic year 2011–2012, the following categories and numbers represent the postgraduate activities and employment of master's degree graduates: Enrolled in a postdoctoral residency/fellowship (n/a), employed in independent practice (n/a), total from the above (master's) (0).

Doctoral Degree Graduates: Of those who graduated in the academic year 2011–2012, the following categories and numbers represent the postgraduate activities and employment of doctoral degree graduates: Enrolled in a psychology doctoral program (n/a), total from the above (doctoral) (0).

Additional Information:

Orientation, Objectives, and Emphasis of Department: The doctoral programs emphasize research. The cognition-perception program has faculty whose research focuses on memory, emotion, psycholinguistics, categorization, cognitive neuroscience, visual perception and attention. The social program trains researchers in theory and methods for understanding individuals and groups in social and organizational contexts. Training is provided in subareas ranging from social cognition to motivation, personality, close relationships, groups and organizations. A doctoral concentration in developmental psychology emphasizes research training cutting across the traditional areas of psychology. Students may minor in quantitative psychology or in any of the above programs. The Master's program in General Psychology has the flexibility to suit students who wish to explore several areas of psychology to find the area that interests them most, as well as students who wish to shape their course of study to fit special interests and needs, including preparation for admission to a doctoral program. The Master's program in Industrial/Organizational Psychology is designed to prepare graduates to apply research and principles of human behavior to a variety of organizational settings, such as human resources departments and management consulting firms. The program can also be modified for students who are preparing for admission to doctoral programs in Industrial/Organizational and related fields. Students in the master's programs may opt for either full- or part-time status.

Special Facilities or Resources: The Department of Psychology maintains laboratories, classrooms, project rooms, and a magnetic resonance (MR) neuroimaging facility. Modern laboratories are continually improved through grants from foundations and federal agencies. The Center for Brain Imaging houses a research-dedicated 3 Tesla Siemens MR system for the use of faculty and students interested in research using functional brain imaging. The center includes faculty members from both the Department of Psychology and the Center for Neural Science, as well as individuals whose expertise is in MR physics and statistical methods for analysis. The Department also has an Magnetoencephalography (MEG) lab dedicated to Cognitive Neuroscience investigations, primarily of language but also of vision and other cognitive functions. Finally, the department maintains several computer classrooms and laboratories, and the University offers technical courses on emerging computational tools. Faculty laboratories are equipped with specialized computer equipment within each of the graduate programs. The department collaborates closely with the Center for Neural Science in maintaining a technical shop.

Information for Students With Physical Disabilities: See the following website for more information: http://www.nyu.edu/csd.

Application Information:

Application available online. URL of online application: http://gsas.nyu.edu/page/grad.admissionsapplication.html. Students are admitted in the Fall, application deadline December 12; Spring, application deadline October 1; Summer, application deadline February 1. PhD students admitted only in the Fall (application deadline December 12). Master's in General Psychology: Fall deadline: May 1; Spring deadline: October 15; Summer deadline: March 15. Master's in Industrial/Organizational Psychology: Fall deadline: February 1; Spring deadline: October 1; Summer deadline: February 1. *Fee:* $90.

Pace University

Department of Psychology
Dyson College of Arts and Sciences
One Pace Plaza
New York, NY 10038
Telephone: (212) 346-1506
Fax: (212) 346-1618
E-mail: *fdenmark@pace.edu*
Web: *http://www.pace.edu/dyson/academic-departments-and-programs/psychology—-nyc*

Department Information:
1961. Interim Chair: Florence Denmark. Number of faculty: total—full-time 14, part-time 48; women—full-time 11, part-time 31; total—minority—full-time 5, part-time 11; women minority—full-time 4, part-time 7.

Programs and Degrees Offered:
Listed in the following order: Program area, degree type (T if terminal Master's), number awarded 7/11–6/12. Psychology MA/MS (Master of Arts/Science) (T) 12, School-Clinical Child Psychology PsyD (Doctor of Psychology) 17, School Psychology EdS (School Psychology) 19.

APA Accreditation: Combination PsyD (Doctor of Psychology). Student Outcome Data Website: http://www.pace.edu/dyson/academic-departments-and-programs/psychology—-nyc/graduate-programs.

Student Applications/Admissions:
Student Applications
Psychology MA/MS (Master of Arts/Science)—Applications 2012–2013, 65. Total applicants accepted 2012–2013, 41. Number full-time enrolled (new admits only) 2012–2013, 11. Number part-time enrolled (new admits only) 2012–2013, 0. Total enrolled 2012–2013 full-time, 19. Total enrolled 2012–2013 part-time, 9. Openings 2013–2014, 25. The median number of years required for completion of a degree in 2012–2013 were 2. The number of students enrolled full- and part-time who were dismissed or voluntarily withdrew from this program area in 2012–2013 were 0. *School-Clinical Child Psychology PsyD (Doctor of Psychology)*—Applications 2012–2013, 243. Total applicants accepted 2012–2013, 54. Number full-time enrolled (new admits only) 2012–2013, 15. Number part-time enrolled (new admits only) 2012–2013, 0. Total enrolled 2012–2013 full-time, 118. Total enrolled 2012–2013 part-time, 17. Openings 2013–2014, 15. The median number of years required for completion of a degree in 2012–2013 were 6. The number of students enrolled full- and part-time who were dismissed or voluntarily withdrew from this program area in 2012–2013 were 2. *School Psychology EdS (School Psychology)*—Applications 2012–2013, 38. Total applicants accepted 2012–2013, 1. Openings 2013–2014, 2. The median number of years required for completion of a degree in 2012–2013 were 3. The number of students enrolled full- and part-time who were dismissed or voluntarily withdrew from this program area in 2012–2013 were 0.
Scores: Entries appear in this order: required test or GPA, minimum score (if required), median score of students entering in 2012–2013. *Psychology MA/MS (Master of Arts/Science)*: GRE-V no minimum stated, GRE-Q no minimum stated, over-

all undergraduate GPA no minimum stated; *School-Clinical Child Psychology PsyD (Doctor of Psychology)*: GRE-V no minimum stated, GRE-Q no minimum stated, overall undergraduate GPA no minimum stated; *School Psychology EdS (School Psychology)*: GRE-V no minimum stated, GRE-Q no minimum stated, overall undergraduate GPA no minimum stated.
Other Criteria: (importance of criteria rated low, medium, or high): GRE scores—high, research experience—medium, work experience—medium, extracurricular activity—low, clinically related public service—medium, GPA—high, letters of recommendation—high, interview—high, statement of goals and objectives—high, undergraduate major in psychology—medium, specific undergraduate psychology courses taken—low.

Student Characteristics: The following represents characteristics of students in 2012–2013 in all graduate psychology programs in the department: Female—full-time 99, part-time 16; Male—full-time 19, part-time 1; African American/Black—full-time 3, part-time 5; Hispanic/Latino(a)—full-time 4, part-time 6; Asian/Pacific Islander—full-time 6, part-time 5; American Indian/Alaska Native—full-time 1, part-time 0; Caucasian/White—full-time 57, part-time 51; Multi-ethnic—full-time 2, part-time 1; students subject to the Americans With Disabilities Act—full-time 2, part-time 0; Unknown ethnicity—full-time 3, part-time 1; International students who hold an F-1 or J-1 Visa—full-time 8, part-time 2.

Financial Information/Assistance:
Tuition for Full-Time Study: *Master's:* State residents: $1,024 per credit hour; Nonstate residents: $1,024 per credit hour. *Doctoral:* State residents: $1,024 per credit hour; Nonstate residents: $1,024 per credit hour. Tuition is subject to change. See the following website for updates and changes in tuition costs: http://www.pace.edu/prospectivestudents/graduate/tuition-fees.

Financial Assistance:
First-Year Students: Research assistantships available for first year. Average amount paid per academic year: $2,500. Average number of hours worked per week: 10. Apply by January 15. Fellowships and scholarships available for first year. Average amount paid per academic year: $5,000. Apply by January 15.
Advanced Students: Research assistantships available for advanced students. Average amount paid per academic year: $2,500. Average number of hours worked per week: 10. Apply by January 15. Fellowships and scholarships available for advanced students. Average amount paid per academic year: $5,000. Apply by January 15.
Additional Information: Of all students currently enrolled full time, 40% benefited from one or more of the listed financial assistance programs. Application and information available online at: http://www.pace.edu/prospectivestudents/graduate/financial-aid.

Internships/Practica: Doctoral Degree (PsyD School-Clinical Child Psychology): For those doctoral students for whom a professional psychology internship was required in this program prior to graduation, (21) students applied for an internship in 2011–2012, with (21) students obtaining an internship. Of those students who obtained an internship, (21) were paid internships. Of those students who obtained an internship, (11) students placed in APA/CPA accredited internships, (7) students placed in internships not APA/CPA accredited, but listed with the Association of Psychology Postdoctoral and Internship Programs (APPIC), (0) students placed in internships conforming to guidelines of the Council of Directors of School Psychology Programs (CDSPP), (3) students placed in internships that were not APA/CPA accredited, APPIC or CDSPP listed. Most school psychology and bilingual school psychology internships occur in the New York metropolitan region, including Long Island, Westchester County, and school districts throughout northern and central New Jersey. Doctoral internships are typically secured through the APPIC system; the doctoral program also utilizes CDSPP guidelines in approving internships. Doctoral students typically secure internships in the New York metropolitan region.

Housing and Day Care: On-campus housing is available. See the following website for more information: http://www.pace.edu/prospectivestudents/graduate/life-at-pace/housing-and-residential-life. No on-campus day care facilities are available.

Employment of Department Graduates:

Master's Degree Graduates: Of those who graduated in the academic year 2011–2012, the following categories and numbers represent the postgraduate activities and employment of master's degree graduates: Enrolled in a postdoctoral residency/fellowship (n/a), employed in independent practice (n/a), total from the above (master's) (0).

Doctoral Degree Graduates: Of those who graduated in the academic year 2011–2012, the following categories and numbers represent the postgraduate activities and employment of doctoral degree graduates: Enrolled in a psychology doctoral program (n/a), enrolled in a postdoctoral residency/fellowship (2), employed in independent practice (1), employed in other positions at a higher education institution (1), employed in a professional position in a school system (3), employed in a community mental health/counseling center (5), employed in a hospital/medical center (2), do not know (3), total from the above (doctoral) (17).

Additional Information:

Orientation, Objectives, and Emphasis of Department: Pace University's PsyD in School-Clinical Child Psychology program prepares professional psychologists as health service providers with expertise in school and clinical psychology. These professional psychologists will be prepared to develop, provide, supervise, and research a full range of evidence-based psychological services. They will be uniquely prepared to provide clinical and educational expertise and consultation within school and clinical settings in order to best serve children and families across a variety of systems of service delivery. The program utilizes a practitioner-scholar training model that prepares psychologists to provide direct and indirect services from a variety of theoretical perspectives, appreciate cultural and other forms of diversity, and function with the ethical guidelines provided by the American Psychological Association (APA) and the National Association of School Psychologists (NASP). The specific goals related to student learning in the PsyD program are to develop a stable professional identity, a scientific approach to knowledge generation and scientific foundations for evaluating practices, interventions, and programs, and development of ethical awareness. As a competency-based program, practitioner-scholars are trained in assessment and diagnosis, psychoeducational interventions, individual and group interventions aimed at alleviating suffering and promoting health and well-being, and carrying out consultation, evidence-based supervision, and applied research.

Special Facilities or Resources: The Psychology Department maintains the McShane Center for Psychological Services. This on-site training facility provides practicum training for students in the M.S.Ed., M.S.Ed. Bilingual, and PsyD programs. For example, training opportunities include biofeedback, interviewing, parent-infant observations, psychodiagnostics, and psychotherapy.

Information for Students With Physical Disabilities: See the following website for more information: http://www.pace.edu/counseling-center/resources-students-disabilities.

Application Information:
Send to Office of Graduate Admissions, Pace University, 1 Pace Plaza, New York, NY 10038. Application available online. URL of online application: http://www.pace.edu/prospectivestudents/apply-today. Students are admitted in the Fall, application deadline January 15; Spring, application deadline December 1; Summer, application deadline May 1. There is a January 15 deadline for MS Ed and PsyD programs; this is the only application date for these two programs. Fall deadline for MA is August 1, spring deadline for MA is December 1, and summer deadline for MA is May 1. *Fee:* $70.

Rensselaer Polytechnic Institute (2012 data)
Cognitive Science
110 8th Street, Carnegie Building, Room #108
Troy, NY 12180-3590
Telephone: (518) 276-6473
Fax: (518) 276-8268
E-mail: *osgane@rpi.edu*
Web: *http://www.cogsci.rpi.edu/*

Department Information:
2000. Head: Selmer Bringsjord. Number of faculty: total—full-time 21, part-time 5; women—full-time 3, part-time 1; total—minority—full-time 3; women minority—full-time 1.

Programs and Degrees Offered:
Listed in the following order: Program area, degree type (T if terminal Master's), number awarded 7/11–6/12. Cognitive Science PhD (Doctor of Philosophy) 3.

Student Applications/Admissions:
Student Applications
Cognitive Science PhD (Doctor of Philosophy)—Applications 2012–2013, 39. Total applicants accepted 2012–2013, 3. Number full-time enrolled (new admits only) 2012–2013, 2. Total enrolled 2012–2013 full-time, 21. Total enrolled 2012–2013 part-time, 1. Openings 2013–2014, 6.
Scores: Entries appear in this order: required test or GPA, minimum score (if required), median score of students entering in 2012–2013. *Cognitive Science PhD (Doctor of Philosophy):* GRE-V 550, 640, GRE-Q 550, 760, GRE-Analytical 4.0, 5.0, overall undergraduate GPA 3.0, 3.4.
Other Criteria: (importance of criteria rated low, medium, or high): GRE scores—high, research experience—high, work

experience—low, extracurricular activity—low, GPA—medium, letters of recommendation—high, interview—medium, statement of goals and objectives—high.

Student Characteristics: The following represents characteristics of students in 2012–2013 in all graduate psychology programs in the department: Female—full-time 5, part-time 1; Male—full-time 16, part-time 0; African American/Black—full-time 0, part-time 0; Hispanic/Latino(a)—full-time 2, part-time 0; Asian/Pacific Islander—full-time 2, part-time 1; American Indian/Alaska Native—full-time 0, part-time 0; Caucasian/White—full-time 17, part-time 0; Multi-ethnic—full-time 0, part-time 0; students subject to the Americans With Disabilities Act—full-time 0, part-time 0; Unknown ethnicity—full-time 0, part-time 0; International students who hold an F-1 or J-1 Visa—full-time 4, part-time 0.

Financial Information/Assistance:

Tuition for Full-Time Study: *Doctoral:* State residents: per academic year $41,600, $1,980 per credit hour; Nonstate residents: per academic year $41,600, $1,980 per credit hour. See the following website for updates and changes in tuition costs: http://gradoffice.rpi.edu/update.do?catcenterkey=17.

Financial Assistance:

First-Year Students: Teaching assistantships available for first year. Average amount paid per academic year: $17,500. Average number of hours worked per week: 20. Apply by January 15. Research assistantships available for first year. Average amount paid per academic year: $17,500. Average number of hours worked per week: 20. Apply by January 15. Fellowships and scholarships available for first year. Average amount paid per academic year: $23,500. Apply by January 15.

Advanced Students: No information provided.

Additional Information: Of all students currently enrolled full time, 100% benefited from one or more of the listed financial assistance programs. Application and information available online at: http://admissions.rpi.edu/graduate/index.html.

Housing and Day Care: On-campus housing is available. See the following website for more information: http://reslife.rpi.edu/setup.do. On-campus day care facilities are available. See the following website for more information: http://reslife.rpi.edu/update.do?artcenterkey=63.

Employment of Department Graduates:

Master's Degree Graduates: Of those who graduated in the academic year 2011–2012, the following categories and numbers represent the postgraduate activities and employment of master's degree graduates: Enrolled in a postdoctoral residency/fellowship (n/a), employed in independent practice (n/a), total from the above (master's) (0).

Doctoral Degree Graduates: Of those who graduated in the academic year 2011–2012, the following categories and numbers represent the postgraduate activities and employment of doctoral degree graduates: Enrolled in a psychology doctoral program (n/a), total from the above (doctoral) (0).

Additional Information:

Orientation, Objectives, and Emphasis of Department: The department is committed to the concept of integrated cognitive systems. Specifically, research and teaching falls into areas that together cover low- to high-level cognition, whether in minds or machines: reasoning (human and machine); computational cognitive modeling; cognitive engineering; perception and action.

Special Facilities or Resources: Modern research facilities, including the CogWorks Laboratory, Interactive and Distance Education Assessment (IDEA) Laboratory, Rensselaer Artificial Intelligence and Reasoning Laboratory (RAIR Lab), Perception and Action Lab (PandA Lab), Human-Level Intelligence Laboratory, the Cognitive Architecture Laboratory (CogArch Lab), and dedicated space in the Institute's new Social and Behavioral Research Laboratory, provide a new expression of the Department's interests in cognitive science that integrates the diverse research activities of the faculty in the Department.

Information for Students With Physical Disabilities: See the following website for more information: http://doso.rpi.edu/update.do?catcenterkey=5.

Application Information:
Send to Admissions, Rensselaer Polytechnic Institute, Troy, NY 12180. Application available online. URL of online application: http://admissions.rpi.edu/graduate/. Students are admitted in the Fall, application deadline January 15. *Fee:* $75.

Roberts Wesleyan College
Department of Psychology/Graduate Psychology Program
School of Liberal Arts & Sciences
2301 Westside Drive
Rochester, NY 14624-1997
Telephone: (585) 594-6011
Fax: (585) 594-6124
E-mail: *repass_cheryl@roberts.edu*
Web: *http://www.roberts.edu/gradpsych*

Department Information:
2002. Director, Graduate Psychology Programs: Cheryl L. Repass, PsyD, NCSP. Number of faculty: total—full-time 8; women—full-time 6.

Programs and Degrees Offered:
Listed in the following order: Program area, degree type (T if terminal Master's), number awarded 7/11–6/12. School Psychology MA/MS (Master of Arts/Science) (T) 13, School Counseling MA/MS (Master of Arts/Science) (T) 4.

Student Applications/Admissions:
Student Applications
School Psychology MA/MS (Master of Arts/Science)—Applications 2012–2013, 20. Total applicants accepted 2012–2013, 14. Number full-time enrolled (new admits only) 2012–2013, 8. Number part-time enrolled (new admits only) 2012–2013, 1. Total enrolled 2012–2013 full-time, 25. Total enrolled 2012–2013 part-time, 5. Openings 2013–2014, 15. The median number of years required for completion of a degree in 2012–2013 were 3. The number of students enrolled full- and part-time who were dismissed or voluntarily withdrew from this program area in 2012–2013 were 0. *School Counseling MA/MS (Master*

of Arts/Science)—Applications 2012–2013, 8. Total applicants accepted 2012–2013, 4. Number full-time enrolled (new admits only) 2012–2013, 4. Number part-time enrolled (new admits only) 2012–2013, 0. Total enrolled 2012–2013 full-time, 11. Total enrolled 2012–2013 part-time, 0. Openings 2013–2014, 15. The median number of years required for completion of a degree in 2012–2013 were 2. The number of students enrolled full- and part-time who were dismissed or voluntarily withdrew from this program area in 2012–2013 were 1.

Scores: Entries appear in this order: required test or GPA, minimum score (if required), median score of students entering in 2012–2013. *School Psychology MA/MS (Master of Arts/Science):* GRE-V no minimum stated, GRE-Q no minimum stated, GRE-Analytical no minimum stated, overall undergraduate GPA 3.0; *School Counseling MA/MS (Master of Arts/Science):* GRE-V no minimum stated, GRE-Q no minimum stated, GRE-Analytical no minimum stated, overall undergraduate GPA 3.0.

Other Criteria: (importance of criteria rated low, medium, or high): GRE scores—medium, work experience—medium, extracurricular activity—low, clinically related public service—low, GPA—high, letters of recommendation—high, interview—high, statement of goals and objectives—high, fit w/ college's mission—high, undergraduate major in psychology—low, specific undergraduate psychology courses taken—high, GRE Scores not required for School Counseling Program.

Student Characteristics: The following represents characteristics of students in 2012–2013 in all graduate psychology programs in the department: Female—full-time 28, part-time 5; Male—full-time 8, part-time 0; African American/Black—full-time 4, part-time 2; Hispanic/Latino(a)—full-time 0, part-time 0; Asian/Pacific Islander—full-time 1, part-time 0; American Indian/Alaska Native—full-time 1, part-time 0; Caucasian/White—full-time 32, part-time 4; Multi-ethnic—full-time 1, part-time 0; students subject to the Americans With Disabilities Act—full-time 0, part-time 0; Unknown ethnicity—full-time 0, part-time 1; International students who hold an F-1 or J-1 Visa—full-time 0, part-time 0.

Financial Information/Assistance:

Tuition for Full-Time Study: *Master's:* State residents: per academic year $18,300, $610 per credit hour; Nonstate residents: per academic year $18,300, $610 per credit hour. Tuition is subject to change. Additional fees are assessed to students beyond the costs of tuition for the following: One-time fees: student-$300; health-$110; PSY 522-$130; student association-$35. See the following website for updates and changes in tuition costs: http://www.roberts.edu/home/admissions/financial-aid/student-accounts-tuition/tuition.aspx.

Financial Assistance:

First-Year Students: Fellowships and scholarships available for first year. Average amount paid per academic year: $2,192.

Advanced Students: Teaching assistantships available for advanced students. Average amount paid per academic year: $900. Average number of hours worked per week: 8.

Additional Information: Of all students currently enrolled full time, 33% benefited from one or more of the listed financial assistance programs.

Internships/Practica: Master's Degree (MA/MS School Psychology): An internship experience, such as a final research project or "capstone" experience is required of graduates. Master's Degree (MA/MS School Counseling): An internship experience, such as a final research project or "capstone" experience is required of graduates. Students in school psychology complete a 1200-hour internship their third year which is typically paid by the school district in the form of a stipend. Out-of-state internships are also a possibility. These internships pay anywhere from 28K - 40K and are also contracted for 1200 hours. Students in school counseling secure local unpaid internships for 600 hours.

Housing and Day Care: On-campus housing is available. See the following website for more information: http://www.roberts.edu/home/student-life/student-life/residence-life.aspx. No on-campus day care facilities are available.

Employment of Department Graduates:

Master's Degree Graduates: Of those who graduated in the academic year 2011–2012, the following categories and numbers represent the postgraduate activities and employment of master's degree graduates: Enrolled in a postdoctoral residency/fellowship (n/a), employed in independent practice (n/a), employed in other positions at a higher education institution (1), employed in a professional position in a school system (12), employed in a community mental health/counseling center (1), still seeking employment (1), other employment position (2), total from the above (master's) (17).

Doctoral Degree Graduates: Of those who graduated in the academic year 2011–2012, the following categories and numbers represent the postgraduate activities and employment of doctoral degree graduates: Enrolled in a psychology doctoral program (n/a), total from the above (doctoral) (0).

Additional Information:

Orientation, Objectives, and Emphasis of Department: The mission of the School Psychology and School Counseling programs is to prepare students, in a Christian context, for effective, compassionate, professional practice. The programs aim to prepare students for exemplary service and leadership in private and public agencies/educational institutions, utilizing a scientist–practitioner approach, with special attention given to the Christian community, locally, nationally, and internationally.

Information for Students With Physical Disabilities: See the following website for more information: http://www.roberts.edu/home/student-life/student-life/learning-center.aspx.

Application Information:

Send to Department of Psychology, Graduate Admissions Office, Roberts Wesleyan College, 2301 Westside Drive, Rochester, NY 14624-1997. Application available online. URL of online application: http://www.roberts.edu/home/admissions/apply-now.aspx. Students are admitted in the Fall, application deadline February 1. After March 1, admissions will be handled on a rolling basis, as space in the program permits. *Fee:* $35. Application fee is waived for online applicants.

Sage Colleges, The (2012 data)
Department of Psychology
65 First Street
Troy, NY 12180
Telephone: (518) 244-2221
Fax: (518) 244-4564
E-mail: jennis@sage.edu
Web: http://www.sage.edu/

Department Information:

Chairperson: Dr. Sybillyn Jennings. Number of faculty: total—full-time 10, part-time 9; women—full-time 9, part-time 4.

Programs and Degrees Offered:

Listed in the following order: Program area, degree type (T if terminal Master's), number awarded 7/11–6/12. Community Psychology MA/MS (Master of Arts/Science) (T) 4, Counseling and Community Psychology MA/MS (Master of Arts/Science) (T) 11, Forensic Mental Health Certificate Other 3.

Student Applications/Admissions:

Student Applications

Community Psychology MA/MS (Master of Arts/Science)—Applications 2012–2013, 3. Total applicants accepted 2012–2013, 2. Number full-time enrolled (new admits only) 2012–2013, 0. Number part-time enrolled (new admits only) 2012–2013, 2. Openings 2013–2014, 20. The median number of years required for completion of a degree in 2012–2013 were 2. The number of students enrolled full- and part-time who were dismissed or voluntarily withdrew from this program area in 2012–2013 were 0. *Counseling and Community Psychology MA/MS (Master of Arts/Science)*—Applications 2012–2013, 29. Total applicants accepted 2012–2013, 24. Number part-time enrolled (new admits only) 2012–2013, 13. Total enrolled 2012–2013 part-time, 62. Openings 2013–2014, 25. The median number of years required for completion of a degree in 2012–2013 were 4. The number of students enrolled full- and part-time who were dismissed or voluntarily withdrew from this program area in 2012–2013 were 2. *Forensic Mental Health Certificate Other*—Applications 2012–2013, 14. Total applicants accepted 2012–2013, 12. Number part-time enrolled (new admits only) 2012–2013, 9. Total enrolled 2012–2013 part-time, 16. Openings 2013–2014, 8. The median number of years required for completion of a degree in 2012–2013 were 4. The number of students enrolled full- and part-time who were dismissed or voluntarily withdrew from this program area in 2012–2013 were 2.

Scores: Entries appear in this order: required test or GPA, minimum score (if required), median score of students entering in 2012–2013. *Counseling and Community Psychology MA/MS (Master of Arts/Science):* overall undergraduate GPA 3.0.

Other Criteria: (importance of criteria rated low, medium, or high): research experience—low, work experience—high, extracurricular activity—low, clinically related public service—medium, GPA—high, letters of recommendation—high, interview—high, statement of goals and objectives—high, undergraduate major in psychology—medium, specific undergraduate psychology courses taken—high, Certificate in Forensic Mental Health: undergraduate degree in social sciences.

Student Characteristics: The following represents characteristics of students in 2012–2013 in all graduate psychology programs in the department: Female—part-time 89; Male—part-time 5; African American/Black—full-time 0, part-time 11; Hispanic/Latino(a)—full-time 0, part-time 5; Asian/Pacific Islander—full-time 0, part-time 1; American Indian/Alaska Native—full-time 0, part-time 0; Caucasian/White—full-time 0, part-time 76; Multi-ethnic—full-time 0, part-time 1; students subject to the Americans With Disabilities Act—full-time 0, part-time 0; Unknown ethnicity—full-time 0, part-time 0; International students who hold an F-1 or J-1 Visa—full-time 0, part-time 0.

Financial Information/Assistance:

Tuition for Full-Time Study: *Master's:* State residents: $635 per credit hour; Nonstate residents: $635 per credit hour. Tuition is subject to change.

Financial Assistance:

First-Year Students: Research assistantships available for first year. Average amount paid per academic year: $2,000. Average number of hours worked per week: 10. Apply by June 1.

Advanced Students: Teaching assistantships available for advanced students. Average amount paid per academic year: $2,000. Average number of hours worked per week: 10. Apply by June 1. Research assistantships available for advanced students. Average amount paid per academic year: $2,000. Average number of hours worked per week: 10. Apply by June 1.

Additional Information: Of all students currently enrolled full time, 25% benefited from one or more of the listed financial assistance programs.

Internships/Practica: Master's Degree (MA/MS Community Psychology): An internship experience, such as a final research project or "capstone" experience is required of graduates. Master's Degree (MA/MS Counseling and Community Psychology): An internship experience, such as a final research project or "capstone" experience is required of graduates. As part of each degree, all students are required to complete an internship (direct services) and/or externship (not direct services) placement, depending upon the selected area of concentration. Internships comprise one year counseling placements in a setting appropriate to the student's interests; externships are one semester projects in a setting of the student's choice.

Housing and Day Care: On-campus housing is available. No on-campus day care facilities are available.

Employment of Department Graduates:

Master's Degree Graduates: Of those who graduated in the academic year 2011–2012, the following categories and numbers represent the postgraduate activities and employment of master's degree graduates: Enrolled in a psychology doctoral program (0), enrolled in another graduate/professional program (1), enrolled in a postdoctoral residency/fellowship (n/a), employed in independent practice (n/a), employed in an academic position at a university (0), employed in an academic position at a 2-year/4-year college (0), employed in a community mental health/counseling center (5), other employment position (4), do not know (10), total from the above (master's) (20).

Doctoral Degree Graduates: Of those who graduated in the academic year 2011–2012, the following categories and numbers represent the postgraduate activities and employment of doctoral

degree graduates: Enrolled in a psychology doctoral program (n/a), total from the above (doctoral) (0).

Additional Information:

Orientation, Objectives, and Emphasis of Department: Our two degrees (MA in Community Psychology, and MA in Counseling/ Community Psychology) provide students with the academic and skills training to become practitioners at the master's level. The programs range in credits from 42 to 60, depending on degree. The emphasis is on developing and strengthening student skills for application (whether individual or systems level) in the context of strong theoretical foundations. Graduates of MA in Counseling/ Community Psychology are eligible to sit for licensure as a mental health counselor in New York State.

Special Facilities or Resources: In addition to the faculty resources one would assume at the master's level, a particular advantage for psychology programs at Sage Graduate School is our prime location in the Capital District area of New York State. The geographic size, population density, and availability of widely varied populations make possible a wide variety of experiences.

Application Information:

Send to Graduate Admissions, The Sage Colleges, 45 Ferry Street, Troy, New York 12180. Application available online. URL of online application: www.sage.edu/sgs. Students are admitted in the Fall, application deadline April 1; Summer, application deadline April 1; Programs have rolling admissions. Community Psychology: rolling admissions. Counseling/Community Psychology: April 1st for Summer and Fall-priority deadline Forensic Mental Health Certificate: April 1st for Summer and Fall-priority deadline. *Fee:* $40.

St. John's University (2012 data)
Psychology
St. John's College of Arts & Sciences
8000 Utopia Parkway
Queens, NY 11439
Telephone: (718) 990-6368
Fax: (718) 990-6705
E-mail: *digiuser@stjohns.edu*
Web: *http://www.stjohns.edu/academics/graduate/liberalarts/departments/psychology*

Department Information:

1958. Chairperson: Raymond DiGiuseppe, PhD. Number of faculty: total—full-time 36, part-time 33; women—full-time 18, part-time 18; total—minority—full-time 8, part-time 4; women minority—full-time 5, part-time 3; faculty subject to the Americans With Disabilities Act 1.

Programs and Degrees Offered:

Listed in the following order: Program area, degree type (T if terminal Master's), number awarded 7/11–6/12. Clinical Psychology PhD (Doctor of Philosophy) 10, School Psychology PsyD (Doctor of Psychology) 25, School Psychology MA/MS (Master of Arts/Science) (T) 12, General Experimental Psychology MA/ MS (Master of Arts/Science) (T) 8.

APA Accreditation: Clinical PhD (Doctor of Philosophy). Student Outcome Data Website: http://www.stjohns.edu/academics/graduate/liberalarts/departments/psychology/programs/phd_cp. School PsyD (Doctor of Psychology). Student Outcome Data Website: http://www.stjohns.edu/academics/graduate/liberalarts/departments/psychology/programs/psyd_sp/data.stj.

Student Applications/Admissions:

Student Applications

Clinical Psychology PhD (Doctor of Philosophy)—Applications 2012–2013, 380. Total applicants accepted 2012–2013, 10. Number full-time enrolled (new admits only) 2012–2013, 10. Number part-time enrolled (new admits only) 2012–2013, 0. Total enrolled 2012–2013 full-time, 71. Total enrolled 2012–2013 part-time, 0. Openings 2013–2014, 10. The median number of years required for completion of a degree in 2012–2013 were 6. The number of students enrolled full- and part-time who were dismissed or voluntarily withdrew from this program area in 2012–2013 were 0. *School Psychology PsyD (Doctor of Psychology)*—Applications 2012–2013, 134. Total applicants accepted 2012–2013, 18. Number full-time enrolled (new admits only) 2012–2013, 18. Number part-time enrolled (new admits only) 2012–2013, 0. Openings 2013–2014, 18. The median number of years required for completion of a degree in 2012–2013 were 6. The number of students enrolled full- and part-time who were dismissed or voluntarily withdrew from this program area in 2012–2013 were 0. *School Psychology MA/MS (Master of Arts/Science)*—Applications 2012–2013, 52. Total applicants accepted 2012–2013, 13. Number full-time enrolled (new admits only) 2012–2013, 13. Number part-time enrolled (new admits only) 2012–2013, 0. Openings 2013–2014, 16. The median number of years required for completion of a degree in 2012–2013 were 3. The number of students enrolled full- and part-time who were dismissed or voluntarily withdrew from this program area in 2012–2013 were 0. *General Experimental Psychology MA/MS (Master of Arts/Science)*—Applications 2012–2013, 41. Total applicants accepted 2012–2013, 11. Number full-time enrolled (new admits only) 2012–2013, 5. Number part-time enrolled (new admits only) 2012–2013, 6. Total enrolled 2012–2013 full-time, 11. Total enrolled 2012–2013 part-time, 12. Openings 2013–2014, 14. The median number of years required for completion of a degree in 2012–2013 were 2. The number of students enrolled full- and part-time who were dismissed or voluntarily withdrew from this program area in 2012–2013 were 0.

Scores: Entries appear in this order: required test or GPA, minimum score (if required), median score of students entering in 2012–2013. *Clinical Psychology PhD (Doctor of Philosophy):* GRE-V 600, 640, GRE-Q 600, 705, GRE-Analytical 4, 4.7, GRE-Subject (Psychology) 600, 722, overall undergraduate GPA 3.3, 3.74, psychology GPA 3.3, 3.84; *School Psychology PsyD (Doctor of Psychology):* GRE-V 500, 540, GRE-Q 510, 635, GRE-Analytical 4.35, 4.5, GRE-Subject (Psychology) 550, 630, overall undergraduate GPA 3.2, 3.5, psychology GPA 3.3, 3.5; *School Psychology MA/MS (Master of Arts/Science):* GRE-V 450, 501, GRE-Q 500, 550, GRE-Analytical 3, 3.75, GRE-Subject (Psychology) 500, 620, overall undergraduate GPA 3.0, 3.3, psychology GPA 3.0, 3.5; *General Experimental Psychology MA/MS (Master of Arts/Science):* overall undergraduate GPA 3.00, 3.3, last 2 years GPA no minimum stated, psychology GPA 3.00, 3.4.

Other Criteria: (importance of criteria rated low, medium, or high): GRE scores—high, research experience—high, work experience—medium, extracurricular activity—low, clinically related public service—high, GPA—high, letters of recommendation—medium, interview—high, statement of goals and objectives—high, Samples of writing—high, undergraduate major in psychology—medium, specific undergraduate psychology courses taken—high, Clinical/professional experience is not relevant for the MA program in General Experimental Psychology. Research experience is less relevant for the MS program in School Psychology. For additional information on admission requirements, go to http://www.stjohns.edu/admission/graduate/graduate.stj.

Student Characteristics: The following represents characteristics of students in 2012–2013 in all graduate psychology programs in the department: Female—full-time 163, part-time 31; Male—full-time 25, part-time 9; African American/Black—full-time 0, part-time 0; Hispanic/Latino(a)—full-time 0, part-time 0; Asian/Pacific Islander—full-time 0, part-time 0; American Indian/Alaska Native—full-time 0, part-time 0; Caucasian/White—full-time 0, part-time 0; Multi-ethnic—full-time 0, part-time 0; students subject to the Americans With Disabilities Act—full-time 0, part-time 0; Unknown ethnicity—full-time 0, part-time 0; International students who hold an F-1 or J-1 Visa—full-time 0, part-time 0.

Financial Information/Assistance:

Tuition for Full-Time Study: *Master's:* State residents: $1,000 per credit hour; Nonstate residents: $1,000 per credit hour. *Doctoral:* State residents: $1,070 per credit hour; Nonstate residents: per academic year $12,240, $1,020 per credit hour. Tuition is subject to change. Tuition costs vary by program. See the following website for updates and changes in tuition costs: http://www.stjohns.edu/services/financial/bursar/tuition/. Higher tuition cost for this program: Clinical Psychology - $1200.00 per credit hour.

Financial Assistance:

First-Year Students: Teaching assistantships available for first year. Average amount paid per academic year: $8,000. Average number of hours worked per week: 18. Apply by January 15. Research assistantships available for first year. Average amount paid per academic year: $8,000. Average number of hours worked per week: 18. Fellowships and scholarships available for first year. Average amount paid per academic year: $8,000. Average number of hours worked per week: 18. Apply by January 15.

Advanced Students: Teaching assistantships available for advanced students. Average amount paid per academic year: $8,000. Average number of hours worked per week: 18. Apply by January 15. Research assistantships available for advanced students. Average amount paid per academic year: $8,000. Average number of hours worked per week: 18. Fellowships and scholarships available for advanced students. Average amount paid per academic year: $8,000. Average number of hours worked per week: 18. Apply by January 15.

Additional Information: Application and information available online at: http://www.stjohns.edu/academics/provost/scholarships.

Internships/Practica: Doctoral Degree (PhD Clinical Psychology): For those doctoral students for whom a professional psychology internship was required in this program prior to graduation, (10) students applied for an internship in 2011–2012, with (10) students obtaining an internship. Of those students who obtained an internship, (10) were paid internships. Of those students who obtained an internship, (8) students placed in APA/CPA accredited internships, (1) students placed in internships not APA/CPA accredited, but listed with the Association of Psychology Postdoctoral and Internship Programs (APPIC), (0) students placed in internships conforming to guidelines of the Council of Directors of School Psychology Programs (CDSPP), (1) students placed in internships that were not APA/CPA accredited, APPIC or CDSPP listed. Doctoral Degree (PsyD School Psychology): For those doctoral students for whom a professional psychology internship was required in this program prior to graduation, (18) students applied for an internship in 2011–2012, with (18) students obtaining an internship. Of those students who obtained an internship, (16) were paid internships. Of those students who obtained an internship, (1) students placed in APA/CPA accredited internships, (0) students placed in internships not APA/CPA accredited, but listed with the Association of Psychology Postdoctoral and Internship Programs (APPIC), (17) students placed in internships conforming to guidelines of the Council of Directors of School Psychology Programs (CDSPP), (0) students placed in internships that were not APA/CPA accredited, APPIC or CDSPP listed. Master's Degree (MA/MS School Psychology): An internship experience, such as a final research project or "capstone" experience is required of graduates. The department relationships with hospitals, clinics, agencies, and schools throughout the New York Region for externships and internships.

Housing and Day Care: On-campus housing is available. See the following website for more information: http://www.stjohns.edu/admission/graduate/housing.stj. No on-campus day care facilities are available.

Employment of Department Graduates:

Master's Degree Graduates: Of those who graduated in the academic year 2011–2012, the following categories and numbers represent the postgraduate activities and employment of master's degree graduates: Enrolled in another graduate/professional program (0), enrolled in a postdoctoral residency/fellowship (n/a), employed in independent practice (n/a), employed in an academic position at a university (0), employed in an academic position at a 2-year/4-year college (0), not seeking employment (0), do not know (0), total from the above (master's) (0).

Doctoral Degree Graduates: Of those who graduated in the academic year 2011–2012, the following categories and numbers represent the postgraduate activities and employment of doctoral degree graduates: Enrolled in a psychology doctoral program (n/a), enrolled in another graduate/professional program (0), employed in an academic position at a university (0), not seeking employment (0), do not know (0), total from the above (doctoral) (0).

Additional Information:

Orientation, Objectives, and Emphasis of Department: The Psychology Department exemplifies the mission of the university as described in the Mission Statement of St. John's University. The department is committed to academic excellence, operates in accordance with accepted ethical principles and with respect for individual rights and dignity, is committed to service to the community, and demonstrates through its research, teaching, and clinical training an appreciation of the importance of cultural diversity.

Special Facilities or Resources: The department operates a training clinc, The Center for Psychological Services, for the the Clinical Psychology and School Psychology programs.

Information for Students With Physical Disabilities: See the following website for more information: http://www.stjohns.edu/campus/handbook/chapter6/disabilities.stj.

Application Information:

Send to St. John's University, Office of Graduate Admission, 8000 Utopia Parkway, Newman Hall, Room 106, Queens, NY 11439. Send support material to: Graduate Admission Processing Service Center, St. John's University, P.O. Box 811, Randolph, MA 02368-0811. Application available online. URL of online application: http://www.stjohns.edu/admission/graduate/apply. Programs have rolling admissions. PhD in Clinical Psychology - Fall and PsyD in School Psychology - January 15. MS in School Psychology - March 15. MA in General/Experimental Psychology - Rolling Fee: $70.

State University of New York at New Paltz

Department of Psychology/Counseling Graduate Program
JFT 314, 600 Hawk Drive
New Paltz, NY 12561-2440
Telephone: (845) 257-3467
Fax: (845) 257-3474
E-mail: *gradpsych@newpaltz.edu,*
   counsgradprogram@newpaltz.edu
Web: *http://www.newpaltz.edu/psychology/graduate*

Department Information:

1969. Chairperson: Glenn Geher. Number of faculty: total—full-time 17, part-time 12; women—full-time 9, part-time 10; total—minority—full-time 5, part-time 2; women minority—full-time 2, part-time 2.

Programs and Degrees Offered:

Listed in the following order: Program area, degree type (T if terminal Master's), number awarded 7/11–6/12. Psychology MA/MS (Master of Arts/Science) (T) 3, Mental Health Counseling MA/MS (Master of Arts/Science) (T) 7, School Counseling MA/MS (Master of Arts/Science) (T) 5, Mental Health Counseling Respecialization Diploma.

Student Applications/Admissions:

Student Applications

Psychology MA/MS (Master of Arts/Science)—Applications 2012–2013, 37. Total applicants accepted 2012–2013, 22. Total enrolled 2012–2013 full-time, 13. Total enrolled 2012–2013 part-time, 3. Openings 2013–2014, 9. The number of students enrolled full- and part-time who were dismissed or voluntarily withdrew from this program area in 2012–2013 were 0. *Mental Health Counseling MA/MS (Master of Arts/Science)*—Applications 2012–2013, 31. Number full-time enrolled (new admits only) 2012–2013, 11. Number part-time enrolled (new admits only) 2012–2013, 3. Total enrolled 2012–2013 full-time, 27. Total enrolled 2012–2013 part-time, 6. Openings 2013–2014, 12. *School Counseling MA/MS (Master of Arts/Science)*—Applications 2012–2013, 28. Number full-time enrolled (new admits only) 2012–2013, 10. Number part-

time enrolled (new admits only) 2012–2013, 3. Total enrolled 2012–2013 full-time, 23. Total enrolled 2012–2013 part-time, 6. Openings 2013–2014, 12. The number of students enrolled full- and part-time who were dismissed or voluntarily withdrew from this program area in 2012–2013 were 0. *Mental Health Counseling Respecialization Diploma*—

Scores: Entries appear in this order: required test or GPA, minimum score (if required), median score of students entering in 2012–2013. *Psychology MA/MS (Master of Arts/Science)*: GRE-V no minimum stated, GRE-Q no minimum stated, GRE-Analytical no minimum stated, overall undergraduate GPA 3.0, psychology GPA 3.0; *Mental Health Counseling MA/MS (Master of Arts/Science)*: GRE-V no minimum stated, GRE-Q no minimum stated, GRE-Analytical no minimum stated, overall undergraduate GPA 3.0; *School Counseling MA/MS (Master of Arts/Science)*: GRE-V no minimum stated, GRE-Q no minimum stated, GRE-Analytical no minimum stated, overall undergraduate GPA 3.0.

Other Criteria: (importance of criteria rated low, medium, or high): GRE scores—medium, research experience—high, work experience—medium, extracurricular activity—medium, clinically related public service—high, GPA—high, letters of recommendation—high, interview—medium, statement of goals and objectives—high, writing ability—high, undergraduate major in psychology—low, specific undergraduate psychology courses taken—medium, Admissions criteria are weighted differently for the counseling and psychology programs. Work experience and clinically related public service are low in importance for the MA Psychology program, while research experience is only medium for counseling. The Advanced Certificate in Mental Health Counseling does not require GRE scores, but the other programs all do. For additional information on admission requirements, go to http://www.newpaltz.edu/psychology/graduate/.

Student Characteristics: The following represents characteristics of students in 2012–2013 in all graduate psychology programs in the department: Female—full-time 47, part-time 12; Male—full-time 16, part-time 3; Caucasian/White—full-time 0, part-time 0; Unknown ethnicity—full-time 0, part-time 0.

Financial Information/Assistance:

Tuition for Full-Time Study: *Master's:* State residents: per academic year $8,370, $349 per credit hour; Nonstate residents: per academic year $13,250, $552 per credit hour. Tuition is subject to change. See the following website for updates and changes in tuition costs: http://www.newpaltz.edu/financialaid/tuition.cfm.

Financial Assistance:

First-Year Students: Teaching assistantships available for first year. Average amount paid per academic year: $5,000. Average number of hours worked per week: 20. Research assistantships available for first year. Traineeships available for first year. Fellowships and scholarships available for first year. Average number of hours worked per week: 10.

Advanced Students: Teaching assistantships available for advanced students. Average amount paid per academic year: $5,000. Average number of hours worked per week: 20. Research assistantships available for advanced students. Fellowships and scholarships available for advanced students.

Additional Information: Of all students currently enrolled full time, 30% benefited from one or more of the listed financial assistance programs. Application and information available online at: http://www.newpaltz.edu/financialaid.

Internships/Practica: Master's Degree (MA/MS Psychology): An internship experience, such as a final research project or "capstone" experience is required of graduates. Master's Degree (MA/MS Mental Health Counseling): An internship experience, such as a final research project or "capstone" experience is required of graduates. Master's Degree (MA/MS School Counseling): An internship experience, such as a final research project or "capstone" experience is required of graduates. All students in the mental health counseling program complete a practicum at the college counseling center and the career advising center. Additional internship opportunities are available with regional public and private mental health agencies. In addition to practicum and internship requirements, mental health counseling students complete a curriculum of mental health counseling coursework. The program is registered with New York State as a program meeting the educational requirements for mental health counseling licensure. All students in the school counseling program must complete a practicum and an internship experience at one of several area school districts. The practicum and internship may be completed within an elementary, middle, or high school setting. Students will have the option of completing the practicum and internship within the same school/school district or to change the school, school district, and/or grade level to gain a wide range of experience.

Housing and Day Care: On-campus housing is available. See the following website for more information: http://www.newpaltz.edu/reslife/. On-campus day care facilities are available. See the following website for more information: http://www.newpaltz.edu/childrenscenter/.

Employment of Department Graduates:
Master's Degree Graduates: Of those who graduated in the academic year 2011–2012, the following categories and numbers represent the postgraduate activities and employment of master's degree graduates: Enrolled in a psychology doctoral program (5), enrolled in a postdoctoral residency/fellowship (n/a), employed in independent practice (n/a), employed in a professional position in a school system (2), employed in a community mental health/counseling center (4), do not know (2), total from the above (master's) (13).
Doctoral Degree Graduates: Of those who graduated in the academic year 2011–2012, the following categories and numbers represent the postgraduate activities and employment of doctoral degree graduates: Enrolled in a psychology doctoral program (n/a), total from the above (doctoral) (0).

Additional Information:
Orientation, Objectives, and Emphasis of Department: Founded in 1828, America's 99th oldest university is an exciting blend of tradition and vision, providing students with the skills and knowledge needed to meet the challenges of the 21st century. SUNY New Paltz offers graduate training in psychology and mental health counseling. The 36-credit MA in psychology program offers general graduate training in psychology. The program provides students with the opportunity to select electives in a variety of fields including social, experimental, and organizational psychology as well as counseling. The program may serve as preparation for entry into a doctoral program or as additional training for those who plan to enter or are already involved in applied areas of psychology. The 48-credit MS in mental health counseling program serves both students looking to become licensed as mental health counselors and those seeking to eventually proceed into doctoral training programs. Degree requirements cover a core curriculum and specialization courses. Three fieldwork courses provide hands-on mental health counseling training experiences under supervision of licensed professionals. The program is registered with the State Education Department as meeting the educational requirements necessary for mental health counseling licensure in New York, making this a very marketable degree.

Special Facilities or Resources: Laboratory facilities and equipment (computers, videotaping equipment) are available to support student and faculty research in a variety of research areas. The department also maintains links to local and community organizations for research opportunities. In addition, the department has a computer lab for research and instruction with Internet access. All graduate students have access to word processing, SPSS, and the world-wide Web through the campus computer network.

Information for Students With Physical Disabilities: See the following website for more information: http://www.newpaltz.edu/drc.

Application Information:
Send to The Graduate School, SUNY New Paltz, 1 Hawk Drive, New Paltz, NY 12561-2443. Application available online. URL of online application: http://www.newpaltz.edu/graduate/steps.html. Students are admitted in the Fall, application deadline February 1; Spring, application deadline November 15. The counseling programs request applications be submitted by February 1; applications received after that date will be reviewed as long as openings in the fall class remain. The MA Psychology program begins reviewing fall applications February 15 and spring applications November 15. Advanced Certificate in Mental Health Counseling and MA Psychology accept applications for both spring and fall admission; MS in Mental Health Counseling and School Counseling only accept applications for fall admission. *Fee:* $50.

State University of New York, Binghamton University

Psychology
Arts and Sciences
P.O. Box 6000
Binghamton, NY 13902-6000
Telephone: (607) 777-2334
Fax: (607) 777-4890
E-mail: rmiller@binghamton.edu
Web: http://www2.binghamton.edu/psychology/

Department Information:
1965. Chairperson: Peter Gerhardstein. Number of faculty: total—full-time 33, part-time 7; women—full-time 15, part-time 3; total—minority—full-time 2; women minority—full-time 2.

Programs and Degrees Offered:
Listed in the following order: Program area, degree type (T if terminal Master's), number awarded 7/11–6/12. Behavioral Neu-

roscience PhD (Doctor of Philosophy) 3, Clinical Psychology PhD (Doctor of Philosophy) 5, Cognitive Psychology PhD (Doctor of Philosophy) 2.

APA Accreditation: Clinical PhD (Doctor of Philosophy). Student Outcome Data Website: http://www2.binghamton.edu/psychology/graduate/clinical-psychology/applicant-data.html.

Student Applications/Admissions:

Student Applications

Behavioral Neuroscience PhD (Doctor of Philosophy)—Applications 2012–2013, 54. Total applicants accepted 2012–2013, 16. Number full-time enrolled (new admits only) 2012–2013, 9. Number part-time enrolled (new admits only) 2012–2013, 0. Total enrolled 2012–2013 full-time, 28. Total enrolled 2012–2013 part-time, 0. Openings 2013–2014, 6. The median number of years required for completion of a degree in 2012–2013 were 6. The number of students enrolled full- and part-time who were dismissed or voluntarily withdrew from this program area in 2012–2013 were 1. *Clinical Psychology PhD (Doctor of Philosophy)*—Applications 2012–2013, 263. Total applicants accepted 2012–2013, 8. Number full-time enrolled (new admits only) 2012–2013, 5. Number part-time enrolled (new admits only) 2012–2013, 0. Total enrolled 2012–2013 full-time, 41. Total enrolled 2012–2013 part-time, 0. Openings 2013–2014, 8. The median number of years required for completion of a degree in 2012–2013 were 6. The number of students enrolled full- and part-time who were dismissed or voluntarily withdrew from this program area in 2012–2013 were 1. *Cognitive Psychology PhD (Doctor of Philosophy)*—Applications 2012–2013, 34. Total applicants accepted 2012–2013, 4. Number full-time enrolled (new admits only) 2012–2013, 4. Number part-time enrolled (new admits only) 2012–2013, 0. Total enrolled 2012–2013 full-time, 17. Total enrolled 2012–2013 part-time, 0. Openings 2013–2014, 5. The median number of years required for completion of a degree in 2012–2013 were 6. The number of students enrolled full- and part-time who were dismissed or voluntarily withdrew from this program area in 2012–2013 were 1.

Scores: Entries appear in this order: required test or GPA, minimum score (if required), median score of students entering in 2012–2013. *Behavioral Neuroscience PhD (Doctor of Philosophy)*: GRE-V no minimum stated, GRE-Q no minimum stated, GRE-Analytical no minimum stated, overall undergraduate GPA no minimum stated; *Clinical Psychology PhD (Doctor of Philosophy)*: GRE-V no minimum stated, GRE-Q no minimum stated, GRE-Analytical no minimum stated, overall undergraduate GPA no minimum stated; *Cognitive Psychology PhD (Doctor of Philosophy)*: GRE-V no minimum stated, GRE-Q no minimum stated, GRE-Analytical no minimum stated, overall undergraduate GPA no minimum stated.

Other Criteria: (importance of criteria rated low, medium, or high): GRE scores—high, research experience—high, work experience—medium, extracurricular activity—low, clinically related public service—medium, GPA—high, letters of recommendation—high, interview—high, statement of goals and objectives—high, undergraduate major in psychology—low, specific undergraduate psychology courses taken—medium. For additional information on admission requirements, go to http://www2.binghamton.edu/psychology/graduate/admission.html.

Student Characteristics: The following represents characteristics of students in 2012–2013 in all graduate psychology programs in the department: Female—full-time 56, part-time 0; Male—full-time 30, part-time 0; African American/Black—full-time 5, part-time 0; Hispanic/Latino(a)—full-time 4, part-time 0; Asian/Pacific Islander—full-time 1, part-time 0; American Indian/Alaska Native—full-time 0, part-time 0; Caucasian/White—full-time 76, part-time 0; Multi-ethnic—full-time 0, part-time 0; students subject to the Americans With Disabilities Act—full-time 0, part-time 0; Unknown ethnicity—full-time 0, part-time 0; International students who hold an F-1 or J-1 Visa—full-time 1, part-time 0.

Financial Information/Assistance:

Tuition for Full-Time Study: *Doctoral:* State residents: per academic year $8,870, $370 per credit hour; Nonstate residents: per academic year $15,160, $632 per credit hour. Tuition is subject to change. See the following website for updates and changes in tuition costs: http://www2.binghamton.edu/student-accounts/.

Financial Assistance:

First-Year Students: Teaching assistantships available for first year. Average amount paid per academic year: $16,500. Average number of hours worked per week: 10. Research assistantships available for first year. Average amount paid per academic year: $16,500. Fellowships and scholarships available for first year. Average amount paid per academic year: $16,500.

Advanced Students: Teaching assistantships available for advanced students. Average amount paid per academic year: $16,500. Average number of hours worked per week: 10. Research assistantships available for advanced students. Average amount paid per academic year: $16,500. Fellowships and scholarships available for advanced students. Average amount paid per academic year: $16,500.

Additional Information: Of all students currently enrolled full time, 97% benefited from one or more of the listed financial assistance programs. Application and information available online at: http://www2.binghamton.edu/grad-school/prospective-students/cost-aid-funding/.

Internships/Practica: Doctoral Degree (PhD Clinical Psychology): For those doctoral students for whom a professional psychology internship was required in this program prior to graduation, (7) students applied for an internship in 2011–2012, with (7) students obtaining an internship. Of those students who obtained an internship, (7) were paid internships. Of those students who obtained an internship, (7) students placed in APA/CPA accredited internships, (0) students placed in internships not APA/CPA accredited, but listed with the Association of Psychology Postdoctoral and Internship Programs (APPIC), (0) students placed in internships conforming to guidelines of the Council of Directors of School Psychology Programs (CDSPP), (0) students placed in internships that were not APA/CPA accredited, APPIC or CDSPP listed. Students in the clinical area are required to complete two practica — a psychotherapy practicum and a community practicum. The psychotherapy practicum is conducted in the department clinic under the supervision of a faculty member and generally involves the joint treatment of a variety of problems across a broad range of ages and diagnoses. The community practicum consists of supervised clinical activity and/or research at one of a wide range of local agencies, hospitals, and clinics. Students in cognitive psychology are invited—but not required—to complete a research-related practicum in industry. Past internships included training at GE, IBM, Microsoft, Lockheed Martin, and others.

Housing and Day Care: No on-campus housing is available. On-campus day care facilities are available. See the following website for more information: http://www2.binghamton.edu/campus-pre-school/.

Employment of Department Graduates:

Master's Degree Graduates: Of those who graduated in the academic year 2011–2012, the following categories and numbers represent the postgraduate activities and employment of master's degree graduates: Enrolled in a postdoctoral residency/fellowship (n/a), employed in independent practice (n/a), total from the above (master's) (0).

Doctoral Degree Graduates: Of those who graduated in the academic year 2011–2012, the following categories and numbers represent the postgraduate activities and employment of doctoral degree graduates: Enrolled in a psychology doctoral program (n/a), enrolled in a postdoctoral residency/fellowship (6), employed in an academic position at a university (3), employed in government agency (1), total from the above (doctoral) (10).

Additional Information:

Orientation, Objectives, and Emphasis of Department: The psychology department emphasizes basic and applied research in its three areas of specialization: clinical psychology, cognitive psychology, and behavioral neuroscience. The goal of our APA-accredited clinical program is to develop scientists and practitioners. By virtue of ongoing research involvement, students are expected to contribute to knowledge about psychopathology, assessment, and treatment. Our cognitive program has two major research emphases, one focused on learning and memory and the other focused on perception and language (in both the visual and auditory domains). Researchers in this area also work in industrial settings and collaborate with local industry. Our behavioral neuroscience program emphasizes the study of neural and hormonal bases of normal and abnormal behavior and their developmental antecedents in preclinical animal models.

Special Facilities or Resources: All faculty have state-of-the-art, spacious laboratories. The clinical program supports an active in-house mental health clinic. Members of the cognitive area have access to sophisticated systems for the manipulation of auditory and visual stimuli and the online measurement of evoked response potentials, eyetracking, and cognitive processes. Members of the behavioral neurosciences area share multi-user histology, micro-neuroimaging, and neurochemistry laboratories. A new building for animal research has recently been completed.

Information for Students With Physical Disabilities: See the following website for more information: http://www2.binghamton.edu/ssd/.

Application Information:

Application available online. URL of online application: http://www2.binghamton.edu/grad-school/prospective-students/apply.html. Students are admitted in the Fall, application deadline December 15. Deadline for Behavioral Neuroscience and Clinical programs is December 15. Deadline for Cognitive Psychology program is January 3. *Fee:* $75.

State University of New York, College at Plattsburgh
Psychology Department
Beaumont Hall, 101 Broad Street
Plattsburgh, NY 12901
Telephone: (518) 564-3076
Fax: (518) 564-3397
E-mail: *renee.bator@plattsburgh.edu*
Web: *http://www.plattsburgh.edu/academics/psychology*

Department Information:
1970. Chairperson: Drs. Morales and Dunham, Co-Chairs. Number of faculty: total—full-time 13, part-time 5; women—full-time 6, part-time 4; total—minority—full-time 1, part-time 1; women minority—part-time 1.

Programs and Degrees Offered:
Listed in the following order: Program area, degree type (T if terminal Master's), number awarded 7/11–6/12. School Psychology MA/MS (Master of Arts/Science) (T) 11.

Student Applications/Admissions:
Student Applications

School Psychology MA/MS (Master of Arts/Science)—Applications 2012–2013, 30. Total applicants accepted 2012–2013, 9. Number full-time enrolled (new admits only) 2012–2013, 8. Number part-time enrolled (new admits only) 2012–2013, 0. Total enrolled 2012–2013 full-time, 28. Total enrolled 2012–2013 part-time, 0. Openings 2013–2014, 10. The median number of years required for completion of a degree in 2012–2013 were 3. The number of students enrolled full- and part-time who were dismissed or voluntarily withdrew from this program area in 2012–2013 were 1.

Scores: Entries appear in this order: required test or GPA, minimum score (if required), median score of students entering in 2012–2013. *School Psychology MA/MS (Master of Arts/Science):* overall undergraduate GPA 3.0.

Other Criteria: (importance of criteria rated low, medium, or high): GRE scores—low, research experience—medium, work experience—high, extracurricular activity—medium, clinically related public service—high, GPA—high, letters of recommendation—medium, interview—medium, statement of goals and objectives—high, undergraduate major in psychology—medium, specific undergraduate psychology courses taken—high. For additional information on admission requirements, go to http://www.plattsburgh.edu/academics/psychology/graduateprogram/graduateadmissions.php.

Student Characteristics: The following represents characteristics of students in 2012–2013 in all graduate psychology programs in the department: Female—full-time 23, part-time 0; Male—full-time 5, part-time 0; African American/Black—full-time 2, part-time 0; Hispanic/Latino(a)—full-time 2, part-time 0; Asian/Pacific Islander—full-time 0, part-time 0; American Indian/Alaska Native—full-time 0, part-time 0; Caucasian/White—full-time 21, part-time 0; Multi-ethnic—full-time 1, part-time 0; students subject to the Americans With Disabilities Act—full-time 0, part-time 0; Unknown ethnicity—full-time 2, part-time 0; International students who hold an F-1 or J-1 Visa—full-time 1, part-time 0.

Financial Information/Assistance:

Tuition for Full-Time Study: *Master's:* State residents: per academic year $9,370; Nonstate residents: per academic year $16,680. Tuition is subject to change. See the following website for updates and changes in tuition costs: http://www.plattsburgh.edu/studentlife/studentaccounts/summary.php.

Financial Assistance:

First-Year Students: Research assistantships available for first year. Average amount paid per academic year: $4,600. Average number of hours worked per week: 10. Apply by February 15. Traineeships available for first year. Average amount paid per academic year: $5,000. Average number of hours worked per week: 15. Apply by February 15.

Advanced Students: Research assistantships available for advanced students. Average amount paid per academic year: $4,600. Average number of hours worked per week: 10. Apply by February 15. Traineeships available for advanced students. Average amount paid per academic year: $5,000. Average number of hours worked per week: 15. Apply by February 15.

Additional Information: Of all students currently enrolled full time, 20% benefited from one or more of the listed financial assistance programs. Application and information available online at: http://www.plattsburgh.edu/offices/admin/financialaid/.

Internships/Practica: Master's Degree (MA/MS School Psychology): An internship experience, such as a final research project or "capstone" experience is required of graduates. During the third and final year of graduate study, students are placed within school districts on a full-time basis. School districts sometimes offer a stipend under contractual agreement with the graduate student and the University. Stipends range from $7,000 to $14,000. Relocating to a school district in order to receive a stipend might be necessary.

Housing and Day Care: On-campus housing is available. See the following website for more information: http://www.plattsburgh.edu/studentlife/housing/. On-campus day care facilities are available. See the following website for more information: http://www.plattsburgh.edu/offices/buildings/childcare.php.

Employment of Department Graduates:

Master's Degree Graduates: Of those who graduated in the academic year 2011–2012, the following categories and numbers represent the postgraduate activities and employment of master's degree graduates: Enrolled in a postdoctoral residency/fellowship (n/a), employed in independent practice (n/a), employed in a professional position in a school system (7), do not know (4), total from the above (master's) (11).

Doctoral Degree Graduates: Of those who graduated in the academic year 2011–2012, the following categories and numbers represent the postgraduate activities and employment of doctoral degree graduates: Enrolled in a psychology doctoral program (n/a), total from the above (doctoral) (0).

Additional Information:

Orientation, Objectives, and Emphasis of Department: The curriculum is a three-year, 70 hour MA program in psychology. The program offers coursework in psychological theories and skill development and applied experiences in area schools and community agencies. The goal of the program is to enable students to work effectively with individuals and groups and to act as psychological resources in schools and the community. A unique feature of the program is that many courses, beginning in the first semester, combine theory and research with practicum experiences in school and clinical work. Students develop competencies in personality, research methods, psychological assessment, behavior modification, individual and group psychotherapy, and community mental health. An important aspect of graduate training is the internship served the third year of graduate study at area schools. The Psychology Department and the agencies involved provide extensive supervision of students' work.

Special Facilities or Resources: All students participate in off-site practicum experiences in local schools. The Neuropsychology Clinic and Psychoeducational Services center provide some graduate students with on-site practicum experiences. The Nexus program (an after school program for children diagnosed with Autism Spectrum Disorders) provides some graduate students with on-site practicum experiences.

Information for Students With Physical Disabilities: See the following website for more information: http://www.plattsburgh.edu/offices/support/sss/.

Application Information:

Send to Graduate Admissions, Kehoe Hall, SUNY-Plattsburgh, 101 Broad Street, Plattsburgh, NY 12901. Application available online. URL of online application: http://www.plattsburgh.edu/admissions/graduate/apply.php. Students are admitted in the Fall, application deadline February 15. *Fee:* $100.

State University of New York, University of Albany

Educational and Counseling Psychology
School of Education
1400 Washington Avenue
Albany, NY 12222
Telephone: (518) 442-5050
Fax: (518) 442-4953
E-mail: *ecpyinfo@albany.edu*
Web: *http://www.albany.edu/education/edpsych.php*

Department Information:

1963. Chairperson: Kevin P. Quinn. Number of faculty: total—full-time 21, part-time 10; women—full-time 12, part-time 4; total—minority—full-time 4; women minority—full-time 1.

Programs and Degrees Offered:

Listed in the following order: Program area, degree type (T if terminal Master's), number awarded 7/11–6/12. Counseling Psychology PhD (Doctor of Philosophy) 9, Educational Psychology MA/MS (Master of Arts/Science) 6, School Psychology Certificate Other 3, Mental Health Counseling MA/MS (Master of Arts/Science) (T) 28, Educational Psychology PhD (Doctor of Philosophy) 4, School Psychology PsyD (Doctor of Psychology) 6.

APA Accreditation: Counseling PhD (Doctor of Philosophy). Student Outcome Data Website: http://www.albany.edu/counseling_psych//doc/program/program_statistics.html. School PsyD (Doctor of Psychology). Student Outcome Data Website: http://www.albany.edu/schoolpsych/programs_psyd.shtml.

Student Applications/Admissions:

Student Applications

Counseling Psychology PhD (Doctor of Philosophy)—Applications 2012–2013, 130. Total applicants accepted 2012–2013, 7. Number full-time enrolled (new admits only) 2012–2013, 7. Number part-time enrolled (new admits only) 2012–2013, 0. Total enrolled 2012–2013 full-time, 43. Total enrolled 2012–2013 part-time, 1. Openings 2013–2014, 4. The median number of years required for completion of a degree in 2012–2013 were 6. The number of students enrolled full- and part-time who were dismissed or voluntarily withdrew from this program area in 2012–2013 were 1. *Educational Psychology MA/MS (Master of Arts/Science)*—Applications 2012–2013, 36. Total applicants accepted 2012–2013, 25. Number full-time enrolled (new admits only) 2012–2013, 7. Number part-time enrolled (new admits only) 2012–2013, 1. Total enrolled 2012–2013 full-time, 12. Total enrolled 2012–2013 part-time, 6. Openings 2013–2014, 30. The median number of years required for completion of a degree in 2012–2013 were 2. The number of students enrolled full- and part-time who were dismissed or voluntarily withdrew from this program area in 2012–2013 were 0. *School Psychology Certificate Other*—Applications 2012–2013, 34. Total applicants accepted 2012–2013, 20. Number full-time enrolled (new admits only) 2012–2013, 13. Total enrolled 2012–2013 full-time, 27. Openings 2013–2014, 10. The median number of years required for completion of a degree in 2012–2013 were 3. The number of students enrolled full- and part-time who were dismissed or voluntarily withdrew from this program area in 2012–2013 were 2. *Mental Health Counseling MA/MS (Master of Arts/Science)*—Applications 2012–2013, 64. Total applicants accepted 2012–2013, 53. Number full-time enrolled (new admits only) 2012–2013, 26. Number part-time enrolled (new admits only) 2012–2013, 2. Total enrolled 2012–2013 full-time, 56. Total enrolled 2012–2013 part-time, 4. Openings 2013–2014, 30. The median number of years required for completion of a degree in 2012–2013 were 2. The number of students enrolled full- and part-time who were dismissed or voluntarily withdrew from this program area in 2012–2013 were 3. *Educational Psychology PhD (Doctor of Philosophy)*—Applications 2012–2013, 41. Total applicants accepted 2012–2013, 22. Number full-time enrolled (new admits only) 2012–2013, 9. Number part-time enrolled (new admits only) 2012–2013, 4. Total enrolled 2012–2013 full-time, 37. Total enrolled 2012–2013 part-time, 14. Openings 2013–2014, 10. The median number of years required for completion of a degree in 2012–2013 were 6. The number of students enrolled full- and part-time who were dismissed or voluntarily withdrew from this program area in 2012–2013 were 0. *School Psychology PsyD (Doctor of Psychology)*—Applications 2012–2013, 42. Total applicants accepted 2012–2013, 10. Number full-time enrolled (new admits only) 2012–2013, 4. Number part-time enrolled (new admits only) 2012–2013, 0. Total enrolled 2012–2013 full-time, 26. Total enrolled 2012–2013 part-time, 0. Openings 2013–2014, 5. The median number of years required for completion of a degree in 2012–2013 were 5. The number of students enrolled full- and part-time who were dismissed or voluntarily withdrew from this program area in 2012–2013 were 1.

Scores: Entries appear in this order: required test or GPA, minimum score (if required), median score of students entering in 2012–2013. *Counseling Psychology PhD (Doctor of Philosophy):* GRE-V no minimum stated, 640, GRE-Q no minimum stated, 650, GRE-Analytical no minimum stated, 4.5, overall undergraduate GPA no minimum stated, 3.54, psychology GPA no minimum stated; *Educational Psychology MA/MS (Master of Arts/Science):* overall undergraduate GPA 3.0; *School Psychology Certificate Other:* GRE-V no minimum stated, 520, GRE-Q no minimum stated, 620, GRE-Analytical no minimum stated, 4.5, overall undergraduate GPA 3.0, 3.6; *Mental Health Counseling MA/MS (Master of Arts/Science):* GRE-V no minimum stated, 550, GRE-Q no minimum stated, 550, GRE-Analytical no minimum stated, overall undergraduate GPA no minimum stated, 3.5, psychology GPA no minimum stated, 3.7; *Educational Psychology PhD (Doctor of Philosophy):* GRE-V no minimum stated, 560, GRE-Q no minimum stated, 600, overall undergraduate GPA no minimum stated, Masters GPA no minimum stated; *School Psychology PsyD (Doctor of Psychology):* GRE-V 500, 530, GRE-Q 500, 670, GRE-Analytical no minimum stated, 4, overall undergraduate GPA 3.0, 3.69.

Other Criteria: (importance of criteria rated low, medium, or high): GRE scores—high, research experience—high, work experience—medium, extracurricular activity—low, clinically related public service—low, GPA—high, letters of recommendation—medium, interview—medium, statement of goals and objectives—high, undergraduate major in psychology—medium, specific undergraduate psychology courses taken—medium, The counseling psychology PhD and school psychology PsyD programs do require interviews, whereas the educational psychology PhD program does not. Undergraduate psychology major is not a high priority for the educational psychology PhD. Applicants for the MS in educational psychology do not need to submit GREs. Research experience is not required for the master's in mental health counseling or for the CAS in school psychology. For additional information on admission requirements, go to http://www.albany.edu/education/edpsych.php.

Student Characteristics: The following represents characteristics of students in 2012–2013 in all graduate psychology programs in the department: Female—full-time 163, part-time 20; Male—full-time 38, part-time 5; African American/Black—full-time 12, part-time 0; Hispanic/Latino(a)—full-time 12, part-time 1; Asian/Pacific Islander—full-time 27, part-time 4; American Indian/Alaska Native—full-time 0, part-time 0; Caucasian/White—full-time 149, part-time 20; Multi-ethnic—full-time 0, part-time 0; students subject to the Americans With Disabilities Act—full-time 1, part-time 0; Unknown ethnicity—full-time 1, part-time 0; International students who hold an F-1 or J-1 Visa—full-time 20, part-time 3.

Financial Information/Assistance:

Tuition for Full-Time Study: *Master's:* State residents: per academic year $9,864, $411 per credit hour; Nonstate residents: per academic year $18,360, $765 per credit hour. *Doctoral:* State residents: per academic year $9,864, $411 per credit hour; Nonstate residents: per academic year $18,360, $765 per credit hour. Tuition is subject to change. Additional fees are assessed to students beyond the costs of tuition for the following: university fee, student activity fee, comprehensive fee, grad student organization fee. See the following website for updates and changes in tuition costs: http://www.albany.edu/studentaccounts/costs_grad.php.

Financial Assistance:

First-Year Students: Research assistantships available for first year. Average amount paid per academic year: $13,000.

Advanced Students: Teaching assistantships available for advanced students. Average amount paid per academic year: $13,000. Research assistantships available for advanced students. Average amount paid per academic year: $13,000. Traineeships available for advanced students. Fellowships and scholarships available for advanced students. Average amount paid per academic year: $13,000.

Additional Information: Application and information available online at: http://www.albany.edu/education/funding.php.

Internships/Practica: Doctoral Degree (PhD Counseling Psychology): For those doctoral students for whom a professional psychology internship was required in this program prior to graduation, (8) students applied for an internship in 2011–2012, with (8) students obtaining an internship. Of those students who obtained an internship, (8) were paid internships. Of those students who obtained an internship, (8) students placed in APA/CPA accredited internships, (0) students placed in internships not APA/CPA accredited, but listed with the Association of Psychology Postdoctoral and Internship Programs (APPIC), (0) students placed in internships conforming to guidelines of the Council of Directors of School Psychology Programs (CDSPP), (0) students placed in internships that were not APA/CPA accredited, APPIC or CDSPP listed. Doctoral Degree (PsyD School Psychology): For those doctoral students for whom a professional psychology internship was required in this program prior to graduation, (3) students applied for an internship in 2011–2012, with (3) students obtaining an internship. Of those students who obtained an internship, (3) were paid internships. Of those students who obtained an internship, (0) students placed in APA/CPA accredited internships, (1) students placed in internships not APA/CPA accredited, but listed with the Association of Psychology Postdoctoral and Internship Programs (APPIC), (2) students placed in internships conforming to guidelines of the Council of Directors of School Psychology Programs (CDSPP), (0) students placed in internships that were not APA/CPA accredited, APPIC or CDSPP listed. Master's Degree (MA/MS Mental Health Counseling): An internship experience, such as a final research project or "capstone" experience is required of graduates. In counseling psychology, PhD students take beginning and advanced practica and practica in specialized procedures. The initial, year-long practicum is taken at the University-operated Psychological Services Center, a training facility for graduate students in the counseling and clinical psychology programs. Opportunities for advanced practica are community based, and include outpatient and inpatient therapy and assessment in hospitals (private and VA), college counseling centers, community mental health centers, and residential treatment settings for youth. Our doctoral students have been highly successful in obtaining their preferred APA-accredited internships. Master's students in mental health counseling take practica in community agencies and hospitals. Both PsyD and Certificate of Advanced Study students in school psychology complete school-based practica. Students obtain supervised experience in assessment, individual and group counseling, classroom interventions, and consultation. Doctoral students in school psychology complete additional field training experiences in local schools and agencies to reinforce basic skills and to develop additional expertise in consultation, prevention, and systems issues. Certificate students complete a one-year, full-time internship in a public school system to develop and reinforce basic skill competencies needed for future employment.

Housing and Day Care: On-campus housing is available. See the following website for more information: http://www.albany.edu/housing/index.shtml. On-campus day care facilities are available. See the following website for more information: http://www.campuschildrenscenter.com/.

Employment of Department Graduates:

Master's Degree Graduates: Of those who graduated in the academic year 2011–2012, the following categories and numbers represent the postgraduate activities and employment of master's degree graduates: Enrolled in a psychology doctoral program (3), enrolled in another graduate/professional program (1), enrolled in a postdoctoral residency/fellowship (n/a), employed in independent practice (n/a), employed in a professional position in a school system (2), employed in government agency (3), employed in a community mental health/counseling center (15), still seeking employment (4), total from the above (master's) (28).

Doctoral Degree Graduates: Of those who graduated in the academic year 2011–2012, the following categories and numbers represent the postgraduate activities and employment of doctoral degree graduates: Enrolled in a psychology doctoral program (n/a), enrolled in a postdoctoral residency/fellowship (1), employed in independent practice (1), employed in an academic position at a university (2), employed in an academic position at a 2-year/4-year college (1), employed in other positions at a higher education institution (4), employed in a hospital/medical center (3), still seeking employment (1), other employment position (1), total from the above (doctoral) (14).

Additional Information:

Orientation, Objectives, and Emphasis of Department: The master's program in mental health counseling and the certificate of advanced study program in school psychology are practitioner-focused, leading to certification/licensure in NY State. In the APA-accredited school psychology and counseling psychology doctoral programs, practice and science are viewed as complementary and interdependent, implemented through coursework in psychological foundations, research methods, intervention theory and assessment, and by research and practice opportunities via assistantships, professional development activities, practica, and specialized coursework. Our generalist training emphasizes normal development and theory and methods related to prevention and remediation of intra- and interpersonal human concerns. We have many opportunities to explore issues of individual and multicultural diversity, to learn a variety of theoretical orientations, to pursue a range of research topics and methods, to study with a multicultural array of colleagues, to work with diverse client populations in multiple work settings, and to engage in varied professional roles. The master's program in educational psychology and methodology focuses on research-based knowledge of human development, learning and individual differences, and the development of skills and understanding of research methods and statistics. An important role of this program is to provide introductory graduate work in psychology and education.

Special Facilities or Resources: Our fee-for-service community training clinic, the Psychological Services Center, is directed by a licensed psychologist. Second-year doctoral students in counseling psychology are supervised by licensed faculty using live and recorded video monitoring. Advanced doctoral students may have clinical assistantships at the Center, where they gain additional experience in psychodiagnostic assessment and psychotherapy.

One unique aspect of the program in Counseling Psychology is the opportunity for PhD students who are reasonably fluent in Spanish to participate in an exchange program with a family therapy graduate training program in northwestern Spain (Galicia). The Division of School Psychology maintains ongoing training partnerships with a number of local school districts and community agencies. Faculty in the Educational Psychology and Methodology Division are associated with two centers that provide students with opportunities to gain experience to supplement their coursework. The Child Research and Study Center undertakes research into the acquisition and remediation of reading skills, and consults with schools and parents regarding children's school-related difficulties. The Evaluation Consortium contracts to evaluate a wide variety of programs provided by schools and agencies.

Information for Students With Physical Disabilities: See the following website for more information: http://www.albany.edu/disability/.

Application Information:
Send to Office of Graduate Studies, University at Albany, 1400 Washington Avenue, Albany, NY 12222. Application available online. URL of online application: http://www.albany.edu/graduate/online_app.php. Students are admitted in the Fall, application deadline December 1. For school psychology, the application deadlines are as follows: Certificate of Advanced Study January 30, PsyD January 2. For educational psychology, the master's is rolling admission, whereas the PhD deadline is January 15. For counseling psychology, the master's deadline is December 15, and the PhD deadline is December 1. *Fee:* $75.

Stony Brook University
Department of Psychology
Stony Brook, NY 11794-2500
Telephone: (631) 632-7855
Fax: (631) 632-7876
E-mail: *marilynn.wollmuth@stonybrook.edu*
Web: *http://www.psychology.sunysb.edu*

Department Information:
1961. Chairperson: Daniel Klein. Number of faculty: total—full-time 29; women—full-time 14; total—minority—full-time 3; women minority—full-time 2.

Programs and Degrees Offered:
Listed in the following order: Program area, degree type (T if terminal Master's), number awarded 7/11–6/12. Integrative Neuroscience PhD (Doctor of Philosophy) 2, Clinical Psychology PhD (Doctor of Philosophy) 5, Cognitive Science PhD (Doctor of Philosophy) 4, Social/Health Psychology PhD (Doctor of Philosophy) 6, General Psychology MA/MS (Master of Arts/Science) 11.

APA Accreditation: Clinical PhD (Doctor of Philosophy). Student Outcome Data Website: http://www.psychology.sunysb.edu/psychology/index.php?graduate/areasofstudy/clinical.

Student Applications/Admissions:
Student Applications
Integrative Neuroscience PhD (Doctor of Philosophy)—Applications 2012–2013, 30. Total applicants accepted 2012–2013, 2. Number full-time enrolled (new admits only) 2012–2013, 2. Total enrolled 2012–2013 full-time, 14. Openings 2013–2014, 3. The median number of years required for completion of a degree in 2012–2013 were 5. The number of students enrolled full- and part-time who were dismissed or voluntarily withdrew from this program area in 2012–2013 were 0. *Clinical Psychology PhD (Doctor of Philosophy)*—Applications 2012–2013, 274. Total applicants accepted 2012–2013, 10. Number full-time enrolled (new admits only) 2012–2013, 3. Total enrolled 2012–2013 full-time, 29. Openings 2013–2014, 5. The median number of years required for completion of a degree in 2012–2013 were 6. The number of students enrolled full- and part-time who were dismissed or voluntarily withdrew from this program area in 2012–2013 were 0. *Cognitive Science PhD (Doctor of Philosophy)*—Applications 2012–2013, 46. Total applicants accepted 2012–2013, 10. Number full-time enrolled (new admits only) 2012–2013, 5. Total enrolled 2012–2013 full-time, 21. Openings 2013–2014, 5. The median number of years required for completion of a degree in 2012–2013 were 5. The number of students enrolled full- and part-time who were dismissed or voluntarily withdrew from this program area in 2012–2013 were 0. *Social/Health Psychology PhD (Doctor of Philosophy)*—Applications 2012–2013, 84. Total applicants accepted 2012–2013, 5. Number full-time enrolled (new admits only) 2012–2013, 5. Total enrolled 2012–2013 full-time, 16. Openings 2013–2014, 4. The median number of years required for completion of a degree in 2012–2013 were 5. The number of students enrolled full- and part-time who were dismissed or voluntarily withdrew from this program area in 2012–2013 were 0. *General Psychology MA/MS (Master of Arts/Science)*—Applications 2012–2013, 115. Total applicants accepted 2012–2013, 31. Number full-time enrolled (new admits only) 2012–2013, 15. Total enrolled 2012–2013 full-time, 15. Openings 2013–2014, 18. The median number of years required for completion of a degree in 2012–2013 was 1. The number of students enrolled full- and part-time who were dismissed or voluntarily withdrew from this program area in 2012–2013 were 0.

Scores: Entries appear in this order: required test or GPA, minimum score (if required), median score of students entering in 2012–2013. *Integrative Neuroscience PhD (Doctor of Philosophy)*: GRE-V no minimum stated, GRE-Q no minimum stated, GRE-Analytical no minimum stated; *Clinical Psychology PhD (Doctor of Philosophy)*: GRE-V no minimum stated, 633, GRE-Q no minimum stated, 740, GRE-Analytical no minimum stated, 4.07, overall undergraduate GPA no minimum stated, 3.5; *Cognitive Science PhD (Doctor of Philosophy)*: GRE-V no minimum stated, GRE-Q no minimum stated; *Social/Health Psychology PhD (Doctor of Philosophy)*: GRE-V no minimum stated, GRE-Q no minimum stated, GRE-Analytical no minimum stated.

Other Criteria: (importance of criteria rated low, medium, or high): GRE scores—high, research experience—high, work experience—low, extracurricular activity—low, clinically related public service—low, GPA—medium, letters of recommendation—high, interview—medium, statement of goals and objectives—high. For additional information on admission requirements, go to http://www.psychology.sunysb.edu/psychology/index.php?graduate/prospectivestudents.

Student Characteristics: The following represents characteristics of students in 2012–2013 in all graduate psychology programs in the department: Female—full-time 65, part-time 0; Male—full-time 27, part-time 0; African American/Black—full-time 2, part-time 0; Hispanic/Latino(a)—full-time 3, part-time 0; Asian/Pacific Islander—full-time 9, part-time 0; American Indian/Alaska Native—full-time 0, part-time 0; Caucasian/White—full-time 56, part-time 0; Multi-ethnic—part-time 0; students subject to the Americans With Disabilities Act—full-time 0, part-time 0; Unknown ethnicity—full-time 0, part-time 0; International students who hold an F-1 or J-1 Visa—full-time 8, part-time 0.

Financial Information/Assistance:

Tuition for Full-Time Study: *Master's:* State residents: per academic year $9,370, $390 per credit hour; Nonstate residents: per academic year $16,680, $695 per credit hour. *Doctoral:* State residents: per academic year $9,370, $390 per credit hour; Nonstate residents: per academic year $16,680, $695 per credit hour. Tuition is subject to change. See the following website for updates and changes in tuition costs: http://www.stonybrook.edu/bursar/tuition/tuition-and-fee-rates.shtml.

Financial Assistance:

First-Year Students: Teaching assistantships available for first year. Average amount paid per academic year: $17,145. Average number of hours worked per week: 20. Apply by December 15. Research assistantships available for first year. Average amount paid per academic year: $17,145. Average number of hours worked per week: 20. Apply by December 15. Fellowships and scholarships available for first year. Average amount paid per academic year: $22,145. Average number of hours worked per week: 20. Apply by December 15.

Advanced Students: Teaching assistantships available for advanced students. Average amount paid per academic year: $17,145. Average number of hours worked per week: 20. Research assistantships available for advanced students. Average amount paid per academic year: $17,145. Average number of hours worked per week: 20. Fellowships and scholarships available for advanced students. Average amount paid per academic year: $2,340. Average number of hours worked per week: 20.

Additional Information: Of all students currently enrolled full time, 100% benefited from one or more of the listed financial assistance programs. Application and information available online at: http://www.psychology.sunysb.edu/psychology/index.php?graduate/prospectivestudents/financialinformation.

Internships/Practica: Doctoral Degree (PhD Clinical Psychology): For those doctoral students for whom a professional psychology internship was required in this program prior to graduation, (6) students applied for an internship in 2011–2012, with (6) students obtaining an internship. Of those students who obtained an internship, (6) were paid internships. Of those students who obtained an internship, (4) students placed in APA/CPA accredited internships, (2) students placed in internships not APA/CPA accredited, but listed with the Association of Psychology Postdoctoral and Internship Programs (APPIC), (0) students placed in internships conforming to guidelines of the Council of Directors of School Psychology Programs (CDSPP), (0) students placed in internships that were not APA/CPA accredited, APPIC or CDSPP listed.

Housing and Day Care: On-campus housing is available. See the following website for more information: http://www.studentaffairs.stonybrook.edu/res/index.aspx. On-campus day care facilities are available. See the following website for more information: http://www.stonybrook.edu/childcare/.

Employment of Department Graduates:

Master's Degree Graduates: Of those who graduated in the academic year 2011–2012, the following categories and numbers represent the postgraduate activities and employment of master's degree graduates: Enrolled in a postdoctoral residency/fellowship (n/a), employed in independent practice (n/a), total from the above (master's) (0).

Doctoral Degree Graduates: Of those who graduated in the academic year 2011–2012, the following categories and numbers represent the postgraduate activities and employment of doctoral degree graduates: Enrolled in a psychology doctoral program (n/a), enrolled in a postdoctoral residency/fellowship (7), employed in an academic position at a university (7), employed in other positions at a higher education institution (1), still seeking employment (1), total from the above (doctoral) (16).

Additional Information:

Orientation, Objectives, and Emphasis of Department: In all areas, the primary emphasis is on research training through research advisement and apprenticeship. Students are encouraged to become involved in ongoing research immediately and to engage in independent research when sufficient skills and knowledge permit, with the goal of becoming active and original contributors. As the first behavioral clinical curriculum in the country, Stony Brook has served as a model for a number of other behaviorally oriented clinical programs and continues to be a leader in that field. Research in the experimental area focuses on human perception and cognition and now includes visual cognition, psycholinguistics, memory, attention, and perception. The biopsychology research of core faculty spans the fields of behavioral neuroscience, molecular biology, cognitive neuroscience and affective neuroscience. Students obtain a broad foundation in neuroscience while developing expertise in a focused research program. Research in social and health psychology includes the study of close relationships in adults and children; prejudice, racism, and stereotyping; and the representation and processing of social experience, motivation, and self-regulation.

Special Facilities or Resources: Besides faculty laboratories for human, animal, and physiological research, and electronics and machine shops, other campus facilities for research and graduate training include: Psychological Center, the training, research, and service unit for clinical psychology; Point of Woods Laboratory School with a special education class for elementary students; University Preschool with children from 18 months to 5 years of age; University Marital Therapy Clinic; and Suffolk Child Development Center, a private school for autistic, retarded, aphasic, and developmentally delayed children. Clinical neuropsychology uses affiliations with the University Health Sciences Center, local schools, an agency for the mentally retarded, and a Veterans Administration hospital. Departmental CRT terminals and 12 additional terminals and two printers in the division's Social Science Data Laboratory are used with campus computers.

Information for Students With Physical Disabilities: See the following website for more information: http://studentaffairs. stonybrook.edu/dss/.

Application Information:
Send to Graduate Office, Department of Psychology, Stony Brook University, Stony Brook, NY 11794-2500. Application available online. URL of online application: https://app.applyyourself.com/?id= sunysb-gs. Students are admitted in the Fall, application deadline December 15. *Fee:* $100.

Syracuse University
Department of Psychology
Arts & Sciences
430 Huntington Hall, 150 Marshall Street
Syracuse, NY 13244-2340
Telephone: (315) 443-2354
Fax: (315) 443-4085
E-mail: *pvanable@syr.edu*
Web: *http://psychology.syr.edu/*

Department Information:
1952. Chairperson: Peter A. Vanable. Number of faculty: total—full-time 25; women—full-time 10; total—minority—full-time 2; women minority—full-time 2.

Programs and Degrees Offered:
Listed in the following order: Program area, degree type (T if terminal Master's), number awarded 7/11–6/12. Clinical Psychology PhD (Doctor of Philosophy) 2, Experimental Psychology PhD (Doctor of Philosophy) 0, School Psychology PhD (Doctor of Philosophy) 1, Social Psychology PhD (Doctor of Philosophy) 0.

APA Accreditation: Clinical PhD (Doctor of Philosophy). Student Outcome Data Website: http://psychology.syr.edu/graduate/Clinical. html. School PhD (Doctor of Philosophy). Student Outcome Data Website: http://psychology.syr.edu/graduate/School_Psychology_ Program.html.

Student Applications/Admissions:
Student Applications
Clinical Psychology PhD (Doctor of Philosophy)—Applications 2012–2013, 110. Total applicants accepted 2012–2013, 10. Number full-time enrolled (new admits only) 2012–2013, 6. Number part-time enrolled (new admits only) 2012–2013, 0. Total enrolled 2012–2013 full-time, 31. Total enrolled 2012–2013 part-time, 0. Openings 2013–2014, 5. The median number of years required for completion of a degree in 2012–2013 were 7. The number of students enrolled full- and part-time who were dismissed or voluntarily withdrew from this program area in 2012–2013 were 1. *Experimental Psychology PhD (Doctor of Philosophy)*—Applications 2012–2013, 20. Total applicants accepted 2012–2013, 2. Number full-time enrolled (new admits only) 2012–2013, 2. Number part-time enrolled (new admits only) 2012–2013, 0. Total enrolled 2012–2013 full-time, 7. Total enrolled 2012–2013 part-time, 0. Openings 2013–2014, 2. The median number of years required for completion of a degree in 2012–2013 were 5. The number of students enrolled full- and part-time who were dismissed or

voluntarily withdrew from this program area in 2012–2013 were 0. *School Psychology PhD (Doctor of Philosophy)*—Applications 2012–2013, 37. Total applicants accepted 2012–2013, 4. Number full-time enrolled (new admits only) 2012–2013, 4. Number part-time enrolled (new admits only) 2012–2013, 0. Total enrolled 2012–2013 full-time, 17. Total enrolled 2012–2013 part-time, 0. Openings 2013–2014, 4. The median number of years required for completion of a degree in 2012–2013 were 5. The number of students enrolled full- and part-time who were dismissed or voluntarily withdrew from this program area in 2012–2013 were 0. *Social Psychology PhD (Doctor of Philosophy)*—Applications 2012–2013, 0. Total applicants accepted 2012–2013, 0. Number full-time enrolled (new admits only) 2012–2013, 0. Number part-time enrolled (new admits only) 2012–2013, 0. Total enrolled 2012–2013 full-time, 6. Total enrolled 2012–2013 part-time, 0. The median number of years required for completion of a degree in 2012–2013 were 5. The number of students enrolled full- and part-time who were dismissed or voluntarily withdrew from this program area in 2012–2013 were 0.

Scores: Entries appear in this order: required test or GPA, minimum score (if required), median score of students entering in 2012–2013. *Clinical Psychology PhD (Doctor of Philosophy)*: GRE-V 155, 160, GRE-Q 153, 156, GRE-Analytical 4.5, 5, overall undergraduate GPA 3.58, 3.65; *Experimental Psychology PhD (Doctor of Philosophy)*: GRE-V 152, 156, GRE-Q 147, 151, GRE-Analytical 3.4, 4.8, overall undergraduate GPA 3.4, 3.70; *School Psychology PhD (Doctor of Philosophy)*: GRE-V 151, 153, GRE-Q 151, 152, GRE-Analytical 4.0, 4.0, overall undergraduate GPA 3.4, 3.64; *Social Psychology PhD (Doctor of Philosophy)*: GRE-V no minimum stated, GRE-Q no minimum stated, GRE-Analytical no minimum stated, overall undergraduate GPA no minimum stated.

Other Criteria: (importance of criteria rated low, medium, or high): GRE scores—high, research experience—high, work experience—medium, extracurricular activity—low, clinically related public service—medium, GPA—high, letters of recommendation—high, interview—high, statement of goals and objectives—high, undergraduate major in psychology—medium, Interview requirements vary from program to program. For additional information on admission requirements, go to http://psychology.syr.edu/graduate/index.html.

Student Characteristics: The following represents characteristics of students in 2012–2013 in all graduate psychology programs in the department: Female—full-time 42, part-time 0; Male—full-time 12, part-time 0; African American/Black—full-time 1, part-time 0; Hispanic/Latino(a)—full-time 1, part-time 0; Asian/Pacific Islander—full-time 5, part-time 0; American Indian/Alaska Native—full-time 0, part-time 0; Caucasian/White—full-time 46, part-time 0; Multi-ethnic—full-time 1, part-time 0; students subject to the Americans With Disabilities Act—full-time 0, part-time 0; Unknown ethnicity—full-time 0, part-time 0; International students who hold an F-1 or J-1 Visa—full-time 6, part-time 0.

Financial Information/Assistance:
Tuition for Full-Time Study: *Doctoral:* State residents: per academic year $29,976, $1,249 per credit hour; Nonstate residents: per academic year $29,976, $1,249 per credit hour. Tuition is subject to change. See the following website for updates and

changes in tuition costs: http://www.syr.edu/financialaid/costofattendance/.

Financial Assistance:

First-Year Students: Teaching assistantships available for first year. Average amount paid per academic year: $14,000. Average number of hours worked per week: 20. Apply by January 1. Research assistantships available for first year. Average amount paid per academic year: $14,000. Average number of hours worked per week: 20. Apply by January 1. Fellowships and scholarships available for first year. Average amount paid per academic year: $23,135. Average number of hours worked per week: 0. Apply by January 1.

Advanced Students: Teaching assistantships available for advanced students. Average amount paid per academic year: $14,000. Average number of hours worked per week: 20. Research assistantships available for advanced students. Average amount paid per academic year: $14,000. Average number of hours worked per week: 20. Traineeships available for advanced students. Average amount paid per academic year: $14,000. Average number of hours worked per week: 20. Fellowships and scholarships available for advanced students. Average amount paid per academic year: $23,135. Average number of hours worked per week: 0.

Additional Information: Of all students currently enrolled full time, 100% benefited from one or more of the listed financial assistance programs. Application and information available online at: http://www.syr.edu/financialaid/index.html.

Internships/Practica: Doctoral Degree (PhD Clinical Psychology): For those doctoral students for whom a professional psychology internship was required in this program prior to graduation, (1) students applied for an internship in 2011–2012, with (1) students obtaining an internship. Of those students who obtained an internship, (1) were paid internships. Of those students who obtained an internship, (1) students placed in APA/CPA accredited internships, (0) students placed in internships not APA/CPA accredited, but listed with the Association of Psychology Postdoctoral and Internship Programs (APPIC), (0) students placed in internships conforming to guidelines of the Council of Directors of School Psychology Programs (CDSPP), (0) students placed in internships that were not APA/CPA accredited, APPIC or CDSPP listed. Doctoral Degree (PhD School Psychology): For those doctoral students for whom a professional psychology internship was required in this program prior to graduation, (2) students applied for an internship in 2011–2012, with (2) students obtaining an internship. Of those students who obtained an internship, (2) were paid internships. Of those students who obtained an internship, (1) students placed in APA/CPA accredited internships, (0) students placed in internships not APA/CPA accredited, but listed with the Association of Psychology Postdoctoral and Internship Programs (APPIC), (1) students placed in internships conforming to guidelines of the Council of Directors of School Psychology Programs (CDSPP), (0) students placed in internships that were not APA/CPA accredited, APPIC or CDSPP listed. Students in the clinical and school psychology training programs have appropriate internship and practicum experiences available in hospitals, schools, and other community and University settings. Following completion of their coursework, clinical students complete APA-approved internships as part of their required program of study.

Housing and Day Care: On-campus housing is available. See the following website for more information: http://housingmealplans.

syr.edu. On-campus day care facilities are available. See the following website for more information: http://falk.syr.edu/ChildFamilyStudies/BMW.aspx; http://eeccc.syr.edu/.

Employment of Department Graduates:

Master's Degree Graduates: Of those who graduated in the academic year 2011–2012, the following categories and numbers represent the postgraduate activities and employment of master's degree graduates: Enrolled in a postdoctoral residency/fellowship (n/a), employed in independent practice (n/a), total from the above (master's) (0).

Doctoral Degree Graduates: Of those who graduated in the academic year 2011–2012, the following categories and numbers represent the postgraduate activities and employment of doctoral degree graduates: Enrolled in a psychology doctoral program (n/a), total from the above (doctoral) (0).

Additional Information:

Orientation, Objectives, and Emphasis of Department: Our goal is to train high caliber scientists in psychology. Students work closely with a faculty advisor whose research interests are similar to the student's (one can change to a new advisor, however, if one's research interests change). Our APA-approved programs in clinical and school psychology are based on the Boulder scientist–practitioner model. There are four thematic foci in the department: Cognitive Aging; Health and Behavior; the Scholarship of the Causes, Consequences, and Remediation of Social Challenges; and the Psychology of Children in Home and School. Students can gain exposure to research in coping with chronic illness, HIV prevention, memory processes in older adults, school based intervention, substance abuse, stigma and group processes, to name a few. A second goal is training future teachers of psychology. Students typically engage in several semesters of teaching, beginning with sections of introductory psychology and moving on to teach more specialized courses. Entering students participate in the University's "Future Professoriate Program," a teaching practicum nationally known for helping new graduate students enter the profession. Other teaching opportunities are available in the department's Allport Project, which involves undergraduates in faculty research activities. As part of this program, graduate students may offer supervised but essentially independent seminars for undergraduates in their specialty area. Students enrolled in the clinical and school psychology programs gain clinical experience through our university-based psychological services center and placement in area schools and hospitals.

Special Facilities or Resources: The Department of Psychology is housed in Huntington Hall, an historic building that has been remodeled to provide offices and seminar rooms, as well as laboratories for the study of cognition, social psychology, behavioral medicine, family interaction, and group processes. Labs and offices are equipped with microcomputers for data collection and analysis. A separate wing houses the department's Psychological Services Center, which offers facilities for clinical and school psychology practicum training and research. In addition, the Department has two facilities on campus and two facilities off campus that provide additional lab space. Other facilities are available through faculty collaborations with researchers at the Upstate Medical University, which is adjacent to Huntington Hall. The Department and its Center for Health and Behavior support two full-time computer technicians.

Information for Students With Physical Disabilities: See the following website for more information: http://disabilityservices.syr.edu/.

Application Information:
Send to Graduate School, Suite 303, Bowne Hall, Syracuse University, Syracuse, NY 13244-1200. Application available online. URL of online application: http://www.syr.edu/gradschool/em/future_howtoapply.html. Students are admitted in the Fall, application deadline January 1. *Fee:* $75.

The College at Brockport, State University of New York

Department of Psychology
350 New Campus Drive
Brockport, NY 14420
Telephone: (585) 395-2488
Fax: (585) 395-2116
E-mail: *psychdpt@brockport.edu*
Web: *http://www.brockport.edu/psh/grad/*

Department Information:
1965. Chairperson: Melissa M. Brown. Number of faculty: total—full-time 13, part-time 2; women—full-time 10, part-time 1.

Programs and Degrees Offered:
Listed in the following order: Program area, degree type (T if terminal Master's), number awarded 7/11–6/12. Clinical Psychology — Applied Emphasis MA/MS (Master of Arts/Science) (T) 7, Clinical Psychology — Research Emphasis MA/MS (Master of Arts/Science) (T), General Psychology — Research Emphasis MA/MS (Master of Arts/Science) (T).

Student Applications/Admissions:
Student Applications
Clinical Psychology — Applied Emphasis MA/MS (Master of Arts/Science)—Applications 2012–2013, 19. Total applicants accepted 2012–2013, 5. Number full-time enrolled (new admits only) 2012–2013, 5. Total enrolled 2012–2013 full-time, 14. Total enrolled 2012–2013 part-time, 2. Openings 2013–2014, 8. The median number of years required for completion of a degree in 2012–2013 were 2. The number of students enrolled full- and part-time who were dismissed or voluntarily withdrew from this program area in 2012–2013 were 0. *Clinical Psychology — Research Emphasis MA/MS (Master of Arts/Science)*—Openings 2013–2014, 8. *General Psychology — Research Emphasis MA/MS (Master of Arts/Science)*—Openings 2013–2014, 8.
Scores: Entries appear in this order: required test or GPA, minimum score (if required), median score of students entering in 2012–2013. *Clinical Psychology — Applied Emphasis MA/MS (Master of Arts/Science):* GRE-V no minimum stated, GRE-Q no minimum stated, GRE-Analytical no minimum stated, overall undergraduate GPA no minimum stated, last 2 years GPA no minimum stated, psychology GPA no minimum stated; *Clinical Psychology — Research Emphasis MA/MS (Master of Arts/Science):* GRE-V no minimum stated, GRE-Q no minimum stated, GRE-Analytical no minimum stated, overall undergraduate GPA no minimum stated, last 2 years GPA no minimum stated, psychology GPA no minimum stated; *General Psychology — Research Emphasis MA/MS (Master of Arts/Science):* GRE-V no minimum stated, GRE-Q no minimum stated, GRE-Analytical no minimum stated, overall undergraduate GPA no minimum stated, last 2 years GPA no minimum stated, psychology GPA no minimum stated.
Other Criteria: (importance of criteria rated low, medium, or high): GRE scores—medium, research experience—medium, work experience—medium, clinically related public service—medium, GPA—high, letters of recommendation—high, interview—high, statement of goals and objectives—high, undergraduate major in psychology—medium, specific undergraduate psychology courses taken—low. For additional information on admission requirements, go to http://www.brockport.edu/psh/grad/admission.html.

Student Characteristics: The following represents characteristics of students in 2012–2013 in all graduate psychology programs in the department: Female—full-time 9, part-time 2; Male—full-time 1, part-time 2; African American/Black—full-time 0, part-time 0; Hispanic/Latino(a)—full-time 0, part-time 0; Asian/Pacific Islander—full-time 1, part-time 0; American Indian/Alaska Native—full-time 0, part-time 0; Caucasian/White—full-time 9, part-time 4; Multi-ethnic—full-time 0, part-time 0; students subject to the Americans With Disabilities Act—full-time 0, part-time 0; Unknown ethnicity—full-time 0, part-time 0; International students who hold an F-1 or J-1 Visa—full-time 0, part-time 0.

Financial Information/Assistance:
Tuition for Full-Time Study: *Master's:* State residents: per academic year $9,370; Nonstate residents: per academic year $16,680. Tuition is subject to change. See the following website for updates and changes in tuition costs: http://www.brockport.edu/finaid/cost_of_attendance.html.

Financial Assistance:
First-Year Students: Teaching assistantships available for first year. Average amount paid per academic year: $6,000. Average number of hours worked per week: 20. Apply by April 1.
Advanced Students: Teaching assistantships available for advanced students. Average amount paid per academic year: $6,000. Average number of hours worked per week: 20. Apply by April 1.
Additional Information: Of all students currently enrolled full time, 14% benefited from one or more of the listed financial assistance programs. Application and information available online at: http://www.brockport.edu/graduate/prospective/.

Internships/Practica: Master's Degree (MA/MS Clinical Psychology — Applied Emphasis): An internship experience, such as a final research project or "capstone" experience is required of graduates. Master's Degree (MA/MS Clinical Psychology — Research Emphasis): An internship experience, such as a final research project or "capstone" experience is required of graduates. Master's Degree (MA/MS General Psychology — Research Emphasis): An internship experience, such as a final research project or "capstone" experience is required of graduates. Practical experience is available in nearly 50 human service agencies in western New York, including the college counseling center, VA and academic medical centers, and state and local mental health, developmental disability/autism centers, and other community service agencies. Each practicum placement is developed individually, based on the specific student and agency involved. Each practicum is supervised by an agency staff member as well as a faculty member from the Department of Psychology. Students must successfully complete all required coursework before beginning the practicum.

Housing and Day Care: No on-campus housing is available. On-campus day care facilities are available. See the following website for more information: http://www.brockport.edu/bccc/.

Employment of Department Graduates:

Master's Degree Graduates: Of those who graduated in the academic year 2011–2012, the following categories and numbers represent the postgraduate activities and employment of master's degree graduates: Enrolled in a psychology doctoral program (2), enrolled in a postdoctoral residency/fellowship (n/a), employed in independent practice (n/a), employed in a hospital/medical center (1), do not know (5), total from the above (master's) (8).

Doctoral Degree Graduates: Of those who graduated in the academic year 2011–2012, the following categories and numbers represent the postgraduate activities and employment of doctoral degree graduates: Enrolled in a psychology doctoral program (n/a), total from the above (doctoral) (0).

Additional Information:

Orientation, Objectives, and Emphasis of Department: The MA in Psychology program provides promising students with challenging and engaging graduate-level educational experiences. Its three tracks are customized to help students meet their personal academic goals, such as becoming more competitive for admission into doctoral programs or securing master's-level positions in human services and the mental health fields. In the clinically-focused track, students are trained as scientists and practitioners, concerned with the application of psychological principles to the treatment and prevention of behavior disorders. Courses provide theoretical and practical training in contemporary methods of assessment, behavioral and cognitive-behavioral clinical intervention, and program evaluation. In the research-intensive tracks, students deepen their core knowledge of psychology and show their ability to thrive amongst other talented students in graduate study. Moreover, students work closely with their individual faculty mentors to sharpen their research skills and generate scholarly products. In this way, these tracks can be a springboard to doctoral-level study in clinical or non-clinical fields. One of our program's greatest strengths is its emphasis in methods of observation, intervention, and research with behavior disorders and developmental disabilities, but students will be able to explore research opportunities with faculty members with expertise in many different areas of psychology.

Special Facilities or Resources: The department has facilities for research in the biobehavioral sciences, as well as sensory-perceptual, clinical, developmental, and personality psychology topics; and assessment/intervention training. Laboratory space, computer equipment, and an extensive file of psychological assessment instruments are also available.

Information for Students With Physical Disabilities: See the following website for more information: http://www.brockport.edu/osd/.

Application Information:
Send to The Graduate School, The College at Brockport, 350 New Campus Drive, Brockport, NY 14420-2914. Application available online. URL of online application: http://www.brockport.edu/bounce/webapp. Students are admitted in the Fall, application deadline April 1. *Fee:* $50.

The New School for Social Research
Department of Psychology
80 Fifth Avenue, 7th Floor
New York, NY 10011
Telephone: (212) 229-5727
Fax: (212) 989-0846
E-mail: *gfpsych@newschool.edu*
Web: *http://www.newschool.edu/nssr/psychology/*

Department Information:
1936. Chairperson: Jeremy Safran PhD & Emanuele Castano PhD. Number of faculty: total—full-time 17, part-time 1; women—full-time 6, part-time 1; total—minority—full-time 3; women minority—full-time 1.

Programs and Degrees Offered:
Listed in the following order: Program area, degree type (T if terminal Master's), number awarded 7/11–6/12. Clinical Psychology PhD (Doctor of Philosophy) 13, Cognitive, Social, Developmental Psychology (Csd) PhD (Doctor of Philosophy) 5, General Psychology MA/MS (Master of Arts/Science) (T) 69.

APA Accreditation: Clinical PhD (Doctor of Philosophy). Student Outcome Data Website: http://www.newschool.edu/nssr/subpage.aspx?id=9888.

Student Applications/Admissions:

Student Applications

Clinical Psychology PhD (Doctor of Philosophy)—Applications 2012–2013, 33. Total applicants accepted 2012–2013, 16. Number full-time enrolled (new admits only) 2012–2013, 16. Number part-time enrolled (new admits only) 2012–2013, 0. Total enrolled 2012–2013 full-time, 91. Total enrolled 2012–2013 part-time, 0. Openings 2013–2014, 15. The median number of years required for completion of a degree in 2012–2013 were 6. The number of students enrolled full- and part-time who were dismissed or voluntarily withdrew from this program area in 2012–2013 were 0. *Cognitive, Social, Developmental Psychology (Csd) PhD (Doctor of Philosophy)*—Applications 2012–2013, 5. Total applicants accepted 2012–2013, 5. Number full-time enrolled (new admits only) 2012–2013, 5. Number part-time enrolled (new admits only) 2012–2013, 0. Total enrolled 2012–2013 full-time, 31. Total enrolled 2012–2013 part-time, 0. Openings 2013–2014, 10. The median number of years required for completion of a degree in 2012–2013 were 5. The number of students enrolled full- and part-time who were dismissed or voluntarily withdrew from this program area in 2012–2013 were 0. *General Psychology MA/MS (Master of Arts/Science)*—Applications 2012–2013, 264. Total applicants accepted 2012–2013, 218. Number full-time enrolled (new admits only) 2012–2013, 82. Number part-time enrolled (new admits only) 2012–2013, 26. Total enrolled 2012–2013 full-time, 119. Total enrolled 2012–2013 part-time, 86. Openings 2013–2014, 80. The median number of years required for completion of a degree in 2012–2013 were 2. The number of students enrolled full- and part-time who were dismissed or voluntarily withdrew from this program area in 2012–2013 were 4.

Scores: Entries appear in this order: required test or GPA, minimum score (if required), median score of students entering in 2012–2013. *Clinical Psychology PhD (Doctor of Philosophy):* Masters GPA 3.5; *Cognitive, Social, Developmental Psychology (CSD) PhD (Doctor of Philosophy):* Masters GPA 3.5; *General Psychology MA/MS (Master of Arts/Science):* GRE-V 290, 555, GRE-Q 470, 630.

Other Criteria: (importance of criteria rated low, medium, or high): GRE scores—medium, research experience—medium, work experience—high, extracurricular activity—medium, clinically related public service—medium, GPA—high, letters of recommendation—high, statement of goals and objectives—high, writing sample—high, undergraduate major in psychology—medium, specific undergraduate psychology courses taken—medium, Only Master's students at The New School for Social Research are eligible to apply to our PhD programs. Outside applicants with previous graduate credit must apply first to the MA program at The New School for Social Research, then once they complete 12 credits of course work here, they may transfer credits from a previous degree. For additional information on admission requirements, go to http://www.newschool.edu/nssr/psychology/.

Student Characteristics: The following represents characteristics of students in 2012–2013 in all graduate psychology programs in the department: Female—full-time 201, part-time 45; Male—full-time 40, part-time 41; African American/Black—full-time 13, part-time 5; Hispanic/Latino(a)—full-time 25, part-time 6; Asian/Pacific Islander—full-time 4, part-time 8; American Indian/Alaska Native—full-time 0, part-time 1; Caucasian/White—full-time 151, part-time 57; Multi-ethnic—full-time 21, part-time 4; students subject to the Americans With Disabilities Act—full-time 1, part-time 0; Unknown ethnicity—full-time 27, part-time 5; International students who hold an F-1 or J-1 Visa—full-time 30, part-time 4.

Financial Information/Assistance:

Tuition for Full-Time Study: *Master's:* State residents: $1,755 per credit hour; Nonstate residents: $1,720 per credit hour. *Doctoral:* State residents: per academic year $31,590, $1,755 per credit hour; Nonstate residents: per academic year $31,590, $1,755 per credit hour. Tuition is subject to change. Additional fees are assessed to students beyond the costs of tuition for the following: university service fee. See the following website for updates and changes in tuition costs: http://www.newschool.edu/student-services/registrar/tuition/2013-2014/social-research/.

Financial Assistance:

First-Year Students: Fellowships and scholarships available for first year. Average amount paid per academic year: $7,800. Apply by December 15.

Advanced Students: Teaching assistantships available for advanced students. Average amount paid per academic year: $8,250. Average number of hours worked per week: 10. Apply by March 1. Research assistantships available for advanced students. Average amount paid per academic year: $6,000. Average number of hours worked per week: 15. Apply by March 1. Fellowships and scholarships available for advanced students. Average amount paid per academic year: $9,660. Apply by March 1.

Additional Information: Of all students currently enrolled full time, 56% benefited from one or more of the listed financial assistance programs. Application and information available online at: http://www.newschool.edu/student-services/student-financial-services/.

Internships/Practica: Doctoral Degree (PhD Clinical Psychology): For those doctoral students for whom a professional psychology internship was required in this program prior to graduation, (12) students applied for an internship in 2011–2012, with (11) students obtaining an internship. Of those students who obtained an internship, (10) were paid internships. Of those students who obtained an internship, (9) students placed in APA/CPA accredited internships, (1) students placed in internships not APA/CPA accredited, but listed with the Association of Psychology Postdoctoral and Internship Programs (APPIC), (0) students placed in internships conforming to guidelines of the Council of Directors of School Psychology Programs (CDSPP), (1) students placed in internships that were not APA/CPA accredited, APPIC or CDSPP listed. Depending on their research areas, students pursuing general psychology can gain internship and work experience in a range of applied settings, including industry research labs and non-profit organizations. Master's level psychology students who are interested in applying to the Clinical PhD program are strongly encouraged to pursue volunteer clinical positions available at local hospitals or institutes. First-year doctoral students in the clinical program participate in an integrated program designed to help them develop as scientist–practitioners. The practicum is based at Beth Israel Medical Center and involves supervised psychotherapy and Structured Clinical Interview for DSM-V (SCID) training within the Brief Psychotherapy Research Program established at Beth Israel. Students also spend 4 hours per week on an inpatient rotation, co-leading groups and attending relevant unit meetings. Clinical supervision is provided by The New School faculty and by Beth Israel staff psychologists and psychiatrists. This experience provides strong preparation for the 16-20 hour per week externships in their second and third years of PhD level study at approved, affiliated sites. After completing their dissertation proposals, all Clinical PhD students are required to complete an APA-accredited predoctoral internship. During the internship application process, students receive administrative and academic support services from the Director of Clinical Training, Assistant Director of Clinical Training and the Director of Clinical Student Affairs.

Housing and Day Care: On-campus housing is available. See the following website for more information: http://www.newschool.edu/student-services/student-housing/residences/graduate-housing/. No on-campus day care facilities are available.

Employment of Department Graduates:

Master's Degree Graduates: Of those who graduated in the academic year 2011–2012, the following categories and numbers represent the postgraduate activities and employment of master's degree graduates: Enrolled in a postdoctoral residency/fellowship (n/a), employed in independent practice (n/a), total from the above (master's) (0).

Doctoral Degree Graduates: Of those who graduated in the academic year 2011–2012, the following categories and numbers represent the postgraduate activities and employment of doctoral degree graduates: Enrolled in a psychology doctoral program (n/a), enrolled in another graduate/professional program (2), enrolled in a postdoctoral residency/fellowship (9), employed in independent practice (1), employed in a community mental health/counseling center (3), employed in a hospital/medical center (7), total from the above (doctoral) (22).

Additional Information:

Orientation, Objectives, and Emphasis of Department: The Psychology Department provides a broad theoretical background emphasizing the scientific study of human behavior. The master's program accommodates both full- and part-time students, with courses in cognitive, developmental, social, and clinical psychology. All MA students design and carry out original individual research projects. At the PhD level, students may specialize either in research psychology or in clinical psychology. The doctoral program reflects an apprenticeship model in which students work closely with individual faculty on collaborative research. Admission to doctoral candidacy is based on students' academic performance in our master's program, interviews with faculty, a personal essay, and passing the psychology comprehensive examination. There is a strong emphasis on cultural psychology as a framework for understanding basic psychological theories, and on approaching psychology in ways that are sensitive to socio-cultural diversity. Students enrolled in the Ph.D program in Cognitive, Social, and Developmental Psychology (CSD) are prepared for careers in academics as well as in applied settings. Within the clinical psychology doctoral program, there is a strong emphasis on both theory and research. Clinical students have opportunities to gain clinical experience and are prepared as scientist–practitioners equally at home in clinical, research, and teaching settings. The Clinical Psychology Doctoral program is APA-accredited and accepts 16 new students annually.

Special Facilities or Resources: All students may participate in collaborative research projects with faculty in labs that feature equipment and software dedicated to the particular research carried out by department members. Students have library access not only at New School social science libraries but also at NYU's Bobst library, the Cooper Union Library, and other libraries within a New York consortium. Various state-of-the-art computing facilities are also available. For clinical PhD students, the New School-Beth Israel Center for Clinical Training and Research provides unusually broad training in outpatient clinics, inpatient units, and clinical research programs. First year clinical PhD students have access to the Psychology library at Beth Israel Medical Center, perform intake evaluations on Beth Israel's psychiatry outpatient clinic and provide group therapy on adult inpatient units. They also attend psychiatry grand rounds and training seminars on child abuse and assault prevention. Second and third-year clinical students may continue work at Beth Israel Medical Center conducting therapy through the Brief Psychotherapy Research Project. Psychotherapy sessions are videotaped with patients' consent, and students review these sessions in supervision with Beth Israel supervising psychologists. Cases are also discussed in externship seminars with New School faculty.

Information for Students With Physical Disabilities: See the following website for more information: http://www.newschool. edu/student-services/student-disability-services/.

Application Information:
Send to Office of Admission, New School for Social Research, 72 Fifth Avenue, 3rd Floor, New York, NY 10011. Application available online. URL of online application: http://www.newschool.edu/ admission/apply-online/. Students are admitted in the Fall, application deadline January 15; Spring, application deadline November 15; Programs have rolling admissions. Spring - November 15th priority deadline. Applications will be accepted on a rolling basis thereafter. Fall - January 15th priority deadline. Applications will be accepted on a rolling basis thereafter. *Fee:* $50.

University at Albany, State University of New York
Department of Psychology
College of Arts and Sciences
1400 Washington Avenue
Albany, NY 12222
Telephone: (518) 442-4820
Fax: (518) 442-4867
E-mail: *psychology@albany.edu*
Web: *http://www.albany.edu/psychology*

Department Information:

1950. Chairperson: Jeanette Altarriba. Number of faculty: total—full-time 29; women—full-time 12; total—minority—full-time 5; women minority—full-time 4.

Programs and Degrees Offered:

Listed in the following order: Program area, degree type (T if terminal Master's), number awarded 7/11–6/12. Behavioral Neuroscience PhD (Doctor of Philosophy) 3, Clinical Psychology PhD (Doctor of Philosophy) 11, Cognitive Psychology PhD (Doctor of Philosophy) 0, Industrial/Organizational Psychology PhD (Doctor of Philosophy) 1, Social/Personality Psychology PhD (Doctor of Philosophy) 1, Industrial/Organizational Psychology MA/MS (Master of Arts/Science) (T) 3.

APA Accreditation: Clinical PhD (Doctor of Philosophy). Student Outcome Data Website: http://www.albany.edu/psychology/clinical_psychology.php.

Student Applications/Admissions:
Student Applications

Behavioral Neuroscience PhD (Doctor of Philosophy)—Applications 2012–2013, 25. Total applicants accepted 2012–2013, 2. Number full-time enrolled (new admits only) 2012–2013, 2. Number part-time enrolled (new admits only) 2012–2013, 0. Total enrolled 2012–2013 full-time, 13. Total enrolled 2012–2013 part-time, 0. Openings 2013–2014, 3. The median number of years required for completion of a degree in 2012–2013 were 6. The number of students enrolled full- and part-time who were dismissed or voluntarily withdrew from this program area in 2012–2013 were 0. *Clinical Psychology PhD (Doctor of Philosophy)*—Applications 2012–2013, 194. Total applicants accepted 2012–2013, 8. Number full-time enrolled (new admits only) 2012–2013, 6. Number part-time enrolled (new admits only) 2012–2013, 0. Total enrolled 2012–2013 full-time, 38. Total enrolled 2012–2013 part-time, 0. Openings 2013–2014, 6. The median number of years required for completion of a degree in 2012–2013 were 7. The number of students enrolled full- and part-time who were dismissed or voluntarily withdrew from this program area in 2012–2013 were 0. *Cognitive Psychology PhD (Doctor of Philosophy)*—Applications 2012–2013, 22. Total applicants accepted 2012–2013, 10. Number full-time enrolled (new admits only) 2012–2013, 5. Number part-time enrolled (new admits only) 2012–2013, 0. Total enrolled 2012–2013 full-time, 12. Total enrolled 2012–2013 part-time, 0. Openings 2013–2014, 1. The number of students enrolled full- and part-time who were dismissed or voluntarily withdrew from this program area in 2012–2013 were 0. *Industrial/Organizational Psychology PhD (Doctor of Philosophy)*—Applications 2012–2013, 36. Total applicants accepted 2012–2013, 8. Number full-time enrolled (new admits only) 2012–2013, 4. Number part-time enrolled (new admits only) 2012–2013, 0. Total enrolled 2012–2013 full-time, 15. Total enrolled 2012–2013 part-time, 0. Openings 2013–2014, 3. The median number of years required for completion of a degree in 2012–2013 were 10. The number of students enrolled full- and part-time who were dismissed or voluntarily withdrew from this program area in 2012–2013 were 0. *Social/Personality Psychology PhD (Doctor of Philosophy)*—Applications 2012–2013, 29. Total applicants accepted 2012–2013, 6. Number full-time enrolled (new admits only) 2012–2013, 2. Number part-time enrolled (new admits only) 2012–2013, 0. Total enrolled 2012–2013 full-time, 14. Total enrolled 2012–2013 part-time, 0. Openings 2013–2014, 2. The median number of years required for completion of a degree in 2012–2013 were 5. The number of students enrolled full- and part-time who were dismissed or voluntarily withdrew from this program area in 2012–2013 were 0. *Industrial/Organizational Psychology MA/MS (Master of Arts/Science)*—Applications 2012–2013, 49. Total applicants accepted 2012–2013, 13. Number full-time enrolled (new admits only) 2012–2013, 6. Number part-time enrolled (new admits only) 2012–2013, 0. Total enrolled 2012–2013 full-time, 9. Total enrolled 2012–2013 part-time, 0. Openings 2013–2014, 3. The median number of years required for completion of a degree in 2012–2013 were 2. The number of students enrolled full- and part-time who were dismissed or voluntarily withdrew from this program area in 2012–2013 were 0.

Scores: Entries appear in this order: required test or GPA, minimum score (if required), median score of students entering in 2012–2013. *Clinical Psychology PhD (Doctor of Philosophy):* GRE-V no minimum stated, 645, GRE-Q no minimum stated, 677, GRE-Subject (Psychology) no minimum stated, 679, overall undergraduate GPA no minimum stated, 3.48, psychology GPA no minimum stated, 3.69; *Cognitive Psychology PhD (Doctor of Philosophy):* GRE-V no minimum stated, 600, GRE-Q no minimum stated, 646, overall undergraduate GPA no minimum stated, 3.5; *Industrial/Organizational Psychology PhD (Doctor of Philosophy):* GRE-V no minimum stated, 570, GRE-Q no minimum stated, 674, overall undergraduate GPA no minimum stated, 3.56; *Social/Personality Psychology PhD (Doctor of Philosophy):* GRE-V no minimum stated, 660, GRE-Q no minimum stated, 715, overall undergraduate GPA no minimum stated, 3.6.

Other Criteria: (importance of criteria rated low, medium, or high): GRE scores—high, research experience—high, work experience—low, extracurricular activity—low, clinically related public service—medium, GPA—high, letters of recommendation—high, interview—high, statement of goals and objectives—high, undergraduate major in psychology—me-

dium, specific undergraduate psychology courses taken—medium, The interview process and clinically related service are relevant for the clinical psychology program only. For additional information on admission requirements, go to http://www.albany.edu/psychology/how_to_apply.php.

Student Characteristics: The following represents characteristics of students in 2012–2013 in all graduate psychology programs in the department: Female—full-time 66, part-time 0; Male—full-time 35, part-time 0; African American/Black—full-time 3, part-time 0; Hispanic/Latino(a)—full-time 6, part-time 0; Asian/Pacific Islander—full-time 10, part-time 0; American Indian/Alaska Native—full-time 0, part-time 0; Caucasian/White—full-time 75, part-time 0; Multi-ethnic—full-time 6, part-time 0; students subject to the Americans With Disabilities Act—full-time 0, part-time 0; Unknown ethnicity—full-time 1, part-time 0; International students who hold an F-1 or J-1 Visa—full-time 6, part-time 0.

Financial Information/Assistance:

Tuition for Full-Time Study: *Master's:* State residents: per academic year $9,370, $390 per credit hour; Nonstate residents: per academic year $16,680, $695 per credit hour. *Doctoral:* State residents: per academic year $9,370, $390 per credit hour; Nonstate residents: per academic year $16,680, $695 per credit hour. Tuition is subject to change. Additional fees are assessed to students beyond the costs of tuition for the following: university fee, comprehensive service fee, grad student organization fee. See the following website for updates and changes in tuition costs: http://www.albany.edu/studentaccounts/costs.php.

Financial Assistance:

First-Year Students: Teaching assistantships available for first year. Average amount paid per academic year: $14,000. Average number of hours worked per week: 20.

Advanced Students: Teaching assistantships available for advanced students. Average amount paid per academic year: $14,000. Average number of hours worked per week: 20.

Additional Information: Of all students currently enrolled full time, 44% benefited from one or more of the listed financial assistance programs. Application and information available online at: http://www.albany.edu/gradstudies/grad_costs.php.

Internships/Practica: Doctoral Degree (PhD Clinical Psychology): For those doctoral students for whom a professional psychology internship was required in this program prior to graduation, (10) students applied for an internship in 2011–2012, with (9) students obtaining an internship. Of those students who obtained an internship, (9) were paid internships. Of those students who obtained an internship, (6) students placed in APA/CPA accredited internships, (2) students placed in internships not APA/CPA accredited, but listed with the Association of Psychology Postdoctoral and Internship Programs (APPIC), (0) students placed in internships conforming to guidelines of the Council of Directors of School Psychology Programs (CDSPP), (1) students placed in internships that were not APA/CPA accredited, APPIC or CDSPP listed. Master's Degree (MA/MS Industrial/Organizational Psychology): An internship experience, such as a final research project or "capstone" experience is required of graduates. During the second year of our doctoral program in Clinical Psychology, students are placed at the Psychological Services Center, a University operated center that serves the general population of the city of Albany. During this placement students are supervised by members of the Clinical faculty. In their third year, students are required to participate in a community-based practicum. These practica include placements in community mental health centers, VA inpatient and outpatient centers, inpatient and outpatient clinics in community hospitals and rehabilitation centers, residential facilities for youth, and the University's counseling center. Students may also elect to participate in an additional community-based practicum experience during their 4th year of training. Students are encouraged to attend APA accredited internships during their 5th year of study. Our students have attended internships in a variety of settings including children's hospitals, psychiatric hospitals, VA hospitals, university affiliated medical centers, general hospitals, and rehabilitation centers. Practicum and internship placements for doctoral students in the Industrial/Organizational Psychology specialization are possible with a number of local and national corporations and government agencies.

Housing and Day Care: On-campus housing is available. See the following website for more information: http://www.albany.edu/housing/. On-campus day care facilities are available. See the following website for more information: http://www.albany.edu/ukids/.

Employment of Department Graduates:
  Master's Degree Graduates: Of those who graduated in the academic year 2011–2012, the following categories and numbers represent the postgraduate activities and employment of master's degree graduates: Enrolled in a postdoctoral residency/fellowship (n/a), employed in independent practice (n/a), total from the above (master's) (0).
  Doctoral Degree Graduates: Of those who graduated in the academic year 2011–2012, the following categories and numbers represent the postgraduate activities and employment of doctoral degree graduates: Enrolled in a psychology doctoral program (n/a), enrolled in a postdoctoral residency/fellowship (2), employed in independent practice (3), employed in an academic position at a university (7), employed in a professional position in a school system (1), employed in a community mental health/counseling center (1), employed in a hospital/medical center (1), do not know (1), total from the above (doctoral) (16).

Additional Information:
  Orientation, Objectives, and Emphasis of Department: All facets of the graduate program reflect a commitment to the empirical tradition in psychology. Thus, involvement in research is stressed in all areas of study. Students begin an apprentice relationship with faculty members upon entry into the department and are expected to remain actively involved in research throughout their graduate careers. A major goal of the department is to train individuals who will make research contributions to the field. Admission is offered in five areas: behavioral neuroscience, clinical, cognitive, industrial/organizational, and social-personality. All areas of concentration train students for careers as teachers and research scientists. In addition, the social, clinical, and industrial/organizational areas prepare students for careers in applied settings. The orientation of the clinical program emphasizes cognitive and behavioral approaches.

  Special Facilities or Resources: Resources and facilities include university- and grant-funded student stipends, plus stipends from other campus sources; a state-of-the-art animal facility and research laboratories in the Life Sciences Building; several human research laboratories; grant-supported research and treatment clinics; the Psychological Services Center for practicum training; and a variety of research equipment.

  Information for Students With Physical Disabilities: See the following website for more information: http://www.albany.edu/disability/.

Application Information:
Send to The Office of Graduate Admissions, University Administration Building 121, 1400 Washington Avenue, Albany, NY 12222. Application available online. URL of online application: http://www.albany.edu/graduate/online_app.php. Students are admitted in the Fall, application deadline December 1. PhD programs - December 1 for clinical psychology; January 15 for all other PhD programs. I/O MA program - March 1. *Fee:* $75. University guidelines permit waiver of this required fee only for those applicants who can evidence prior or current participation in a qualifying educational opportunity program, including but not limited to Project 1000, EOP, HEOP or similar specially targeted higher education opportunity programs.

University at Buffalo, State University of New York
Department of Counseling, School, and Educational
  Psychology
Graduate School of Education
409 Baldy Hall
Buffalo, NY 14260-1000
Telephone: (716) 645-2484
Fax: (716) 645-6616
E-mail: *nmyers@buffalo.edu*
Web: *http://gse.buffalo.edu/csep*

Department Information:
  1949. Chairperson: Timothy P. Janikowski. Number of faculty: total—full-time 19, part-time 1; women—full-time 10; total—minority—full-time 5; women minority—full-time 2.

Programs and Degrees Offered:
  Listed in the following order: Program area, degree type (T if terminal Master's), number awarded 7/11–6/12. Counselor Education PhD (Doctor of Philosophy) 1, Educational Psychology PhD (Doctor of Philosophy) 2, Rehabilitation Counseling MA/MS (Master of Arts/Science) (T) 21, School Counseling MEd (Education) 19, Counseling/School Psychology PhD (Doctor of Philosophy) 9, Educational Psychology MA/MS (Master of Arts/Science) (T) 3, School Psychology MA/MS (Master of Arts/Science) (T) 10, Mental Health Counseling MA/MS (Master of Arts/Science) (T) 11, Certificate in School Counseling Other 10, Certificate in Mental Health Counseling Other 0.

APA Accreditation: Combination PhD (Doctor of Philosophy). Student Outcome Data Website: http://gse.buffalo.edu/programs/cpsp/outcomes.

Student Applications/Admissions:
  Student Applications
    Counselor Education PhD (Doctor of Philosophy)—Applications 2012–2013, 16. Total applicants accepted 2012–2013, 3. Num-

ber full-time enrolled (new admits only) 2012–2013, 0. Number part-time enrolled (new admits only) 2012–2013, 3. Total enrolled 2012–2013 full-time, 4. Total enrolled 2012–2013 part-time, 17. Openings 2013–2014, 3. The median number of years required for completion of a degree in 2012–2013 were 6. The number of students enrolled full- and part-time who were dismissed or voluntarily withdrew from this program area in 2012–2013 were 1. *Educational Psychology PhD (Doctor of Philosophy)*—Applications 2012–2013, 15. Total applicants accepted 2012–2013, 2. Number full-time enrolled (new admits only) 2012–2013, 2. Number part-time enrolled (new admits only) 2012–2013, 0. Total enrolled 2012–2013 full-time, 8. Total enrolled 2012–2013 part-time, 2. Openings 2013–2014, 3. The median number of years required for completion of a degree in 2012–2013 were 5. The number of students enrolled full- and part-time who were dismissed or voluntarily withdrew from this program area in 2012–2013 were 0. *Rehabilitation Counseling MA/MS (Master of Arts/Science)*—Applications 2012–2013, 107. Total applicants accepted 2012–2013, 46. Number full-time enrolled (new admits only) 2012–2013, 14. Number part-time enrolled (new admits only) 2012–2013, 32. Total enrolled 2012–2013 full-time, 18. Total enrolled 2012–2013 part-time, 68. Openings 2013–2014, 45. The median number of years required for completion of a degree in 2012–2013 were 2. The number of students enrolled full- and part-time who were dismissed or voluntarily withdrew from this program area in 2012–2013 were 0. *School Counseling MEd (Education)*—Applications 2012–2013, 36. Total applicants accepted 2012–2013, 18. Number full-time enrolled (new admits only) 2012–2013, 16. Number part-time enrolled (new admits only) 2012–2013, 2. Total enrolled 2012–2013 full-time, 15. Total enrolled 2012–2013 part-time, 2. Openings 2013–2014, 25. The median number of years required for completion of a degree in 2012–2013 was 1. The number of students enrolled full- and part-time who were dismissed or voluntarily withdrew from this program area in 2012–2013 were 1. *Counseling/School Psychology PhD (Doctor of Philosophy)*—Applications 2012–2013, 86. Total applicants accepted 2012–2013, 8. Number full-time enrolled (new admits only) 2012–2013, 8. Number part-time enrolled (new admits only) 2012–2013, 0. Total enrolled 2012–2013 full-time, 47. Total enrolled 2012–2013 part-time, 0. Openings 2013–2014, 8. The median number of years required for completion of a degree in 2012–2013 were 5. The number of students enrolled full- and part-time who were dismissed or voluntarily withdrew from this program area in 2012–2013 were 0. *Educational Psychology MA/MS (Master of Arts/Science)*—Applications 2012–2013, 30. Total applicants accepted 2012–2013, 5. Number full-time enrolled (new admits only) 2012–2013, 5. Number part-time enrolled (new admits only) 2012–2013, 0. Total enrolled 2012–2013 full-time, 7. Total enrolled 2012–2013 part-time, 3. Openings 2013–2014, 4. The median number of years required for completion of a degree in 2012–2013 were 2. The number of students enrolled full- and part-time who were dismissed or voluntarily withdrew from this program area in 2012–2013 were 0. *School Psychology MA/MS (Master of Arts/Science)*—Applications 2012–2013, 48. Total applicants accepted 2012–2013, 11. Number full-time enrolled (new admits only) 2012–2013, 11. Number part-time enrolled (new admits only) 2012–2013, 0. Total enrolled 2012–2013 full-time, 29. Total enrolled 2012–2013 part-time, 0. Openings 2013–2014, 10. The median number of years required for

completion of a degree in 2012–2013 were 3. The number of students enrolled full- and part-time who were dismissed or voluntarily withdrew from this program area in 2012–2013 were 0. *Mental Health Counseling MA/MS (Master of Arts/Science)*—Applications 2012–2013, 67. Total applicants accepted 2012–2013, 14. Number full-time enrolled (new admits only) 2012–2013, 14. Number part-time enrolled (new admits only) 2012–2013, 0. Total enrolled 2012–2013 full-time, 26. Total enrolled 2012–2013 part-time, 2. Openings 2013–2014, 15. The median number of years required for completion of a degree in 2012–2013 were 2. The number of students enrolled full- and part-time who were dismissed or voluntarily withdrew from this program area in 2012–2013 were 0. *Certificate in School Counseling Other*—Applications 2012–2013, 17. Total applicants accepted 2012–2013, 17. Number full-time enrolled (new admits only) 2012–2013, 8. Number part-time enrolled (new admits only) 2012–2013, 9. Total enrolled 2012–2013 full-time, 9. Total enrolled 2012–2013 part-time, 9. Openings 2013–2014, 15. The median number of years required for completion of a degree in 2012–2013 was 1. The number of students enrolled full- and part-time who were dismissed or voluntarily withdrew from this program area in 2012–2013 were 0. *Certificate in Mental Health Counseling Other*—Applications 2012–2013, 28. Total applicants accepted 2012–2013, 20. Number full-time enrolled (new admits only) 2012–2013, 1. Number part-time enrolled (new admits only) 2012–2013, 20. Total enrolled 2012–2013 full-time, 1. Total enrolled 2012–2013 part-time, 20. Openings 2013–2014, 15. The median number of years required for completion of a degree in 2012–2013 were 2. The number of students enrolled full- and part-time who were dismissed or voluntarily withdrew from this program area in 2012–2013 were 3.

Scores: Entries appear in this order: required test or GPA, minimum score (if required), median score of students entering in 2012–2013. *Counselor Education PhD (Doctor of Philosophy)*: GRE-V 140, 147, GRE-Q 140, 141, GRE-Analytical 4.0, 4.5, overall undergraduate GPA 3.0, 3.2, Masters GPA 3.0, 3.75; *Educational Psychology PhD (Doctor of Philosophy)*: GRE-V no minimum stated, 150, GRE-Q no minimum stated, 154, GRE-Analytical no minimum stated, 3.5, overall undergraduate GPA no minimum stated, 3.69, Masters GPA 3.0; *Rehabilitation Counseling MA/MS (Master of Arts/Science)*: overall undergraduate GPA 3.0, 3.26; *School Counseling MEd (Education)*: GRE-V no minimum stated, 139, GRE-Q no minimum stated, 139, GRE-Analytical no minimum stated, 3.5, overall undergraduate GPA 3.0, 3.23; *Counseling/School Psychology PhD (Doctor of Philosophy)*: GRE-V no minimum stated, 150, GRE-Q no minimum stated, 151, GRE-Analytical no minimum stated, 4.5, overall undergraduate GPA 3.0, 3.61; *Educational Psychology MA/MS (Master of Arts/Science)*: GRE-V no minimum stated, 147, GRE-Q no minimum stated, 151, GRE-Analytical no minimum stated, 3.5, overall undergraduate GPA 3.0, 3.53; *School Psychology MA/MS (Master of Arts/Science)*: GRE-V no minimum stated, 151, GRE-Q no minimum stated, 151, GRE-Analytical 3.0, 4.5, overall undergraduate GPA 3.0, 3.58; *Mental Health Counseling MA/MS (Master of Arts/Science)*: GRE-V no minimum stated, 150, GRE-Q no minimum stated, 146, GRE-Analytical no minimum stated, 4.0, overall undergraduate GPA 3.0, 3.54.

Other Criteria: (importance of criteria rated low, medium, or high): GRE scores—high, research experience—medium, work experience—low, extracurricular activity—low, clinically related public service—medium, GPA—high, letters of recommendation—medium, interview—high, statement of goals and objectives—high, undergraduate major in psychology—medium, specific undergraduate psychology courses taken—low, Not all programs conduct personal interviews. For additional information on admission requirements, go to http://gse.buffalo.edu/apply.

Student Characteristics: The following represents characteristics of students in 2012–2013 in all graduate psychology programs in the department: Female—full-time 132, part-time 102; Male—full-time 32, part-time 21; African American/Black—full-time 13, part-time 14; Hispanic/Latino(a)—full-time 9, part-time 4; Asian/Pacific Islander—full-time 18, part-time 2; American Indian/Alaska Native—full-time 2, part-time 1; Caucasian/White—full-time 114, part-time 94; Multi-ethnic—full-time 2, part-time 0; students subject to the Americans With Disabilities Act—full-time 0, part-time 0; Unknown ethnicity—full-time 6, part-time 8; International students who hold an F-1 or J-1 Visa—full-time 15, part-time 6.

Financial Information/Assistance:
Tuition for Full-Time Study: *Master's:* State residents: per academic year $9,370, $390 per credit hour; Nonstate residents: per academic year $16,680, $695 per credit hour. *Doctoral:* State residents: per academic year $9,370, $390 per credit hour; Nonstate residents: per academic year $16,680, $695 per credit hour. Tuition is subject to change. See the following website for updates and changes in tuition costs: http://studentaccounts.buffalo.edu/tuition/index.php.

Financial Assistance:
First-Year Students: Research assistantships available for first year. Average amount paid per academic year: $9,000. Average number of hours worked per week: 20. Apply by April 15.
Advanced Students: Research assistantships available for advanced students. Average amount paid per academic year: $9,000. Average number of hours worked per week: 20. Apply by April 15.
Additional Information: Of all students currently enrolled full time, 7% benefited from one or more of the listed financial assistance programs. Application and information available online at: http://gse.buffalo.edu/admissions/fin-aid.

Internships/Practica: Doctoral Degree (PhD Counseling/School Psychology): For those doctoral students for whom a professional psychology internship was required in this program prior to graduation, (9) students applied for an internship in 2011–2012, with (8) students obtaining an internship. Of those students who obtained an internship, (6) were paid internships. Of those students who obtained an internship, (8) students placed in APA/CPA accredited internships, (0) students placed in internships not APA/CPA accredited, but listed with the Association of Psychology Postdoctoral and Internship Programs (APPIC), (0) students placed in internships conforming to guidelines of the Council of Directors of School Psychology Programs (CDSPP), (0) students placed in internships that were not APA/CPA accredited, APPIC or CDSPP listed. Master's Degree (MA/MS Rehabilitation Counseling): An internship experience, such as a final research project or "capstone" experience is required of graduates. Master's Degree (MA/MS Educational Psychology): An internship experience, such as a final research project or "capstone" experience is re-

quired of graduates. Master's Degree (MA/MS School Psychology): An internship experience, such as a final research project or "capstone" experience is required of graduates. Master's Degree (MA/MS Mental Health Counseling): An internship experience, such as a final research project or "capstone" experience is required of graduates. Practica and internships available at area schools, community agencies, and hospitals. Experience with death and end of life issues, forensics, persons with disabilities, and assessment is available.

Housing and Day Care: On-campus housing is available. See the following website for more information: http://www.student-affairs.buffalo.edu/housing/apartments.php. On-campus day care facilities are available. See the following website for more information: http://www.ubccc.buffalo.edu/; http://ecrc.buffalo.edu/.

Employment of Department Graduates:
Master's Degree Graduates: Of those who graduated in the academic year 2011–2012, the following categories and numbers represent the postgraduate activities and employment of master's degree graduates: Enrolled in a psychology doctoral program (3), enrolled in another graduate/professional program (5), enrolled in a postdoctoral residency/fellowship (n/a), employed in independent practice (n/a), employed in other positions at a higher education institution (1), employed in a professional position in a school system (11), employed in business or industry (1), employed in government agency (5), employed in a community mental health/counseling center (14), employed in a hospital/medical center (5), still seeking employment (9), not seeking employment (1), other employment position (3), do not know (5), total from the above (master's) (63).
Doctoral Degree Graduates: Of those who graduated in the academic year 2011–2012, the following categories and numbers represent the postgraduate activities and employment of doctoral degree graduates: Enrolled in a psychology doctoral program (n/a), enrolled in a postdoctoral residency/fellowship (2), employed in independent practice (2), employed in a professional position in a school system (1), employed in business or industry (1), employed in government agency (1), employed in a community mental health/counseling center (1), employed in a hospital/medical center (1), still seeking employment (1), total from the above (doctoral) (10).

Additional Information:
Orientation, Objectives, and Emphasis of Department: Departmental emphasis is on research based counseling with adults, college students, adolescents, children, and persons with disabilities. Doctoral programs follow the scientist–practitioner model. Some focus on preparing college faculty. Increased integration of counseling, school, and educational psychology programs is developing. Field experience and research experience are continuous through the programs.

Special Facilities or Resources: Department offers training experiences in a wide variety of schools, agencies, and colleges in both urban and suburban settings.

Information for Students With Physical Disabilities: See the following website for more information: http://www.buffalo.edu/accessibility/.

Application Information:

Send to Office of Graduate Admissions, Graduate School of Education, 366 Baldy Hall, University at Buffalo, The State University of New York, Buffalo, NY 14260-1000. Application available online. URL of online application: http://gse.buffalo.edu/apply. Students are admitted in the Fall, application deadline December 1. Counseling/School Psychology: December 1 application deadline for fall admission; Counselor Education, Mental Health Counseling, and Rehabilitation Counseling: March 1 application deadline for fall admission; School Counseling and School Psychology: February 1 application deadline for fall admission; Educational Psychology has rolling admissions and applications are considered for both fall and spring admission. *Fee:* $50.

University at Buffalo, State University of New York
Department of Psychology
College of Arts and Sciences
206 Park Hall
Buffalo, NY 14260-4110
Telephone: (716) 645-3651
Fax: (716) 645-3801
E-mail: *ccolder@buffalo.edu*
Web: *http://www.psychology.buffalo.edu*

Department Information:

1921. Chairperson: Stephen T. Tiffany. Number of faculty: total—full-time 26, part-time 20; women—full-time 8, part-time 12; total—minority—full-time 2, part-time 3; women minority—full-time 1, part-time 1.

Programs and Degrees Offered:

Listed in the following order: Program area, degree type (T if terminal Master's), number awarded 7/11–6/12. Behavioral Neuroscience PhD (Doctor of Philosophy) 1, Clinical Psychology PhD (Doctor of Philosophy) 5, Cognitive Psychology PhD (Doctor of Philosophy) 2, Social-Personality Psychology PhD (Doctor of Philosophy) 0, General Psychology MA/MS (Master of Arts/Science) (T) 13.

APA Accreditation: Clinical PhD (Doctor of Philosophy). Student Outcome Data Website: http://www.psychology.buffalo.edu/graduate/phd/clinical/more/admissions/.

Student Applications/Admissions:

Student Applications

Behavioral Neuroscience PhD (Doctor of Philosophy)—Applications 2012–2013, 11. Total applicants accepted 2012–2013, 2. Number full-time enrolled (new admits only) 2012–2013, 1. Number part-time enrolled (new admits only) 2012–2013, 0. Total enrolled 2012–2013 full-time, 8. Total enrolled 2012–2013 part-time, 0. Openings 2013–2014, 5. The median number of years required for completion of a degree in 2012–2013 were 5. The number of students enrolled full- and part-time who were dismissed or voluntarily withdrew from this program area in 2012–2013 were 0. *Clinical Psychology PhD (Doctor of Philosophy)*—Applications 2012–2013, 148. Total applicants accepted 2012–2013, 6. Number full-time enrolled (new admits only) 2012–2013, 4. Number part-time enrolled (new admits only) 2012–2013, 0. Total enrolled 2012–2013 full-time, 34. Total enrolled 2012–2013 part-time, 0. Openings 2013–2014, 6. The median number of years required for completion of a degree in 2012–2013 were 7. The number of students enrolled full- and part-time who were dismissed or voluntarily withdrew from this program area in 2012–2013 were 0. *Cognitive Psychology PhD (Doctor of Philosophy)*—Applications 2012–2013, 24. Total applicants accepted 2012–2013, 8. Number full-time enrolled (new admits only) 2012–2013, 2. Total enrolled 2012–2013 full-time, 16. Total enrolled 2012–2013 part-time, 0. Openings 2013–2014, 7. The median number of years required for completion of a degree in 2012–2013 were 5. The number of students enrolled full- and part-time who were dismissed or voluntarily withdrew from this program area in 2012–2013 were 0. *Social-Personality Psychology PhD (Doctor of Philosophy)*—Applications 2012–2013, 25. Total applicants accepted 2012–2013, 3. Number full-time enrolled (new admits only) 2012–2013, 1. Total enrolled 2012–2013 full-time, 12. Total enrolled 2012–2013 part-time, 0. Openings 2013–2014, 5. The median number of years required for completion of a degree in 2012–2013 were 5. The number of students enrolled full- and part-time who were dismissed or voluntarily withdrew from this program area in 2012–2013 were 0. *General Psychology MA/MS (Master of Arts/Science)*—Applications 2012–2013, 144. Total applicants accepted 2012–2013, 17. Number full-time enrolled (new admits only) 2012–2013, 10. Number part-time enrolled (new admits only) 2012–2013, 2. Total enrolled 2012–2013 full-time, 19. Total enrolled 2012–2013 part-time, 10. Openings 2013–2014, 20. The median number of years required for completion of a degree in 2012–2013 were 2. The number of students enrolled full- and part-time who were dismissed or voluntarily withdrew from this program area in 2012–2013 were 0.

Scores: Entries appear in this order: required test or GPA, minimum score (if required), median score of students entering in 2012–2013. *Behavioral Neuroscience PhD (Doctor of Philosophy):* GRE-V no minimum stated, 158, GRE-Q no minimum stated, 148, GRE-Analytical no minimum stated, 4.0, overall undergraduate GPA 3.0, 3.75; *Clinical Psychology PhD (Doctor of Philosophy):* GRE-V no minimum stated, 160, GRE-Q no minimum stated, 154, GRE-Analytical no minimum stated, 4.5, overall undergraduate GPA 3.0, 3.7; *Cognitive Psychology PhD (Doctor of Philosophy):* GRE-V no minimum stated, 158, GRE-Q no minimum stated, 155, GRE-Analytical no minimum stated, 4.5, overall undergraduate GPA no minimum stated, 3.66; *Social-Personality Psychology PhD (Doctor of Philosophy):* GRE-V no minimum stated, 161, GRE-Q no minimum stated, 155, GRE-Analytical no minimum stated, 5.0, overall undergraduate GPA 3.0, 3.85; *General Psychology MA/MS (Master of Arts/Science):* GRE-V no minimum stated, 155, GRE-Q no minimum stated, 150, GRE-Analytical no minimum stated, 4.0, overall undergraduate GPA 3.0, 3.52.

Other Criteria: (importance of criteria rated low, medium, or high): GRE scores—medium, research experience—high, work experience—low, extracurricular activity—low, clinically related public service—medium, GPA—high, letters of recommendation—high, interview—medium, statement of goals and objectives—high, undergraduate major in psychology—low, specific undergraduate psychology courses taken—low, Interview for clinical only. For additional information on admission requirements, go to http://www.psychology.buffalo.edu/graduate/phd/apply/.

Student Characteristics: The following represents characteristics of students in 2012–2013 in all graduate psychology programs in the department: Female—full-time 59, part-time 3; Male—full-time 30, part-time 7; African American/Black—full-time 0, part-time 1; Hispanic/Latino(a)—full-time 9, part-time 0; Asian/Pacific Islander—full-time 7, part-time 1; American Indian/Alaska Native—full-time 2, part-time 0; Caucasian/White—full-time 71, part-time 8; Multi-ethnic—full-time 0, part-time 0; students subject to the Americans With Disabilities Act—full-time 0, part-time 0; Unknown ethnicity—full-time 0, part-time 0; International students who hold an F-1 or J-1 Visa—full-time 8, part-time 0.

Financial Information/Assistance:

Tuition for Full-Time Study: *Master's:* State residents: per academic year $9,370, $390 per credit hour; Nonstate residents: per academic year $16,680, $695 per credit hour. *Doctoral:* State residents: per academic year $9,370, $390 per credit hour; Nonstate residents: per academic year $16,680, $695 per credit hour. Tuition is subject to change. Additional fees are assessed to students beyond the costs of tuition for the following: comprehensive and activity fees. See the following website for updates and changes in tuition costs: http://studentaccounts.buffalo.edu/tuition/.

Financial Assistance:

First-Year Students: Teaching assistantships available for first year. Average amount paid per academic year: $13,500. Average number of hours worked per week: 20. Research assistantships available for first year. Average amount paid per academic year: $13,500. Average number of hours worked per week: 20. Fellowships and scholarships available for first year. Average amount paid per academic year: $13,500.

Advanced Students: Teaching assistantships available for advanced students. Average amount paid per academic year: $13,800. Average number of hours worked per week: 20. Research assistantships available for advanced students. Average amount paid per academic year: $13,800. Average number of hours worked per week: 20. Fellowships and scholarships available for advanced students. Average amount paid per academic year: $13,500.

Additional Information: Of all students currently enrolled full time, 70% benefited from one or more of the listed financial assistance programs.

Internships/Practica: Doctoral Degree (PhD Clinical Psychology): For those doctoral students for whom a professional psychology internship was required in this program prior to graduation, (4) students applied for an internship in 2011–2012, with (3) students obtaining an internship. Of those students who obtained an internship, (3) were paid internships. Of those students who obtained an internship, (3) students placed in APA/CPA accredited internships, (0) students placed in internships not APA/CPA accredited, but listed with the Association of Psychology Postdoctoral and Internship Programs (APPIC), (0) students placed in internships conforming to guidelines of the Council of Directors of School Psychology Programs (CDSPP), (0) students placed in internships that were not APA/CPA accredited, APPIC or CDSPP listed. Several clinical practica are offered each year for students in the doctoral program in Clinical Psychology and for other doctoral students with permission of the instructor. In addition, there is a summer practicum focused on treatment of children with attention deficit/hyperactivity disorder.

Housing and Day Care: On-campus housing is available. See the following website for more information: http://www.grad.buffalo.edu/life/housing.php. On-campus day care facilities are available. See the following website for more information: http://www.ubccc.buffalo.edu/.

Employment of Department Graduates:

Master's Degree Graduates: Of those who graduated in the academic year 2011–2012, the following categories and numbers represent the postgraduate activities and employment of master's degree graduates: Enrolled in a psychology doctoral program (9), enrolled in another graduate/professional program (2), enrolled in a postdoctoral residency/fellowship (n/a), employed in independent practice (n/a), employed in business or industry (1), do not know (1), total from the above (master's) (13).

Doctoral Degree Graduates: Of those who graduated in the academic year 2011–2012, the following categories and numbers represent the postgraduate activities and employment of doctoral degree graduates: Enrolled in a psychology doctoral program (n/a), enrolled in a postdoctoral residency/fellowship (3), employed in an academic position at a university (1), employed in an academic position at a 2-year/4-year college (1), employed in a hospital/medical center (3), total from the above (doctoral) (8).

Additional Information:

Orientation, Objectives, and Emphasis of Department: The Department of Psychology offers doctoral degrees in Behavioral Neuroscience, Clinical Psychology, Cognitive Psychology, and Social-Personality Psychology and a Master's degree in psychology with several specializations. The department has as its defining characteristic and distinguishing mission the conduct and communication of research and scholarship that contributes to the scientific understanding of psychology and the provision of high-quality graduate education and training. The department is dedicated to offering state-of-the-art education and training to its graduate students to prepare them to become leading researchers and to assume important positions in academic institutions or professional practice. We offer students a learning environment that is exciting and challenging, one that will allow them to follow their interests and fully develop their research skills. The research emphasis in the doctoral program in Behavioral Neuroscience is on the neural, endocrine, and molecular bases of behavior. Areas of specialization in Clinical Psychology include adult mood and anxiety disorders, relationship dysfunction, behavioral medicine, attention deficit/hyperactivity disorder, and child and adolescent aggression and substance abuse. The program in Cognitive Psychology focuses on the processes underlying perception, attention, memory, spoken and written language comprehension, language acquisition, categorization, problem solving, and thinking. Faculty research interests in the Social-Personality program include close relationships, social cognition, self-concept, and self-esteem.

Special Facilities or Resources: The Department of Psychology has specialized research facilities for the study of language comprehension, auditory and speech perception, memory, categorization, animal cognition, visual perception, attention, social interaction, small group processes, animal surgery research, behavior therapy, human psychophysiology and biofeedback, and neurochemical and electrophysiological investigations into the physiological bases of behavior. Many of these laboratories are computer-based. The department also has ample facilities for individual and group therapy, marriage counseling, and therapeutic work with children.

One-way vision screens and videotape equipment are available for observation and supervision. Internships are available through the department's Psychological Services Center. Excellent facilities are available for working with animals. Students have liberal access to the University's computing services on the North Campus.

Information for Students With Physical Disabilities: See the following website for more information: http://www.student-affairs.buffalo.edu/ods/.

Application Information:
Send to Director of Graduate Admissions, Department of Psychology, University at Buffalo—The State University of New York, Park Hall Room 210, Buffalo, NY 14260-4110. Application available online. URL of online application: https://www.gradmit.buffalo.edu. Students are admitted in the Fall, application deadline December 1. MA application deadline for fall enrollment is March 1. *Fee:* $75. Fee is waived for McNair Scholar, Project 1000, EOP, HEOP or SEEK.

Yeshiva University
Ferkauf Graduate School of Psychology
Albert Einstein College of Medicine
1300 Morris Park Avenue
Bronx, NY 10461-1602
Telephone: (718) 430-3850
Fax: (718) 430-3960
E-mail: *michael.gill@einstein.yu.edu*
Web: *http://www.yu.edu/ferkauf*

Department Information:
1957. Dean: Lawrence J. Siegel, PhD, ABPP. Number of faculty: total—full-time 30, part-time 28; women—full-time 14, part-time 17; total—minority—full-time 5, part-time 6; women minority—full-time 3, part-time 4; faculty subject to the Americans With Disabilities Act 1.

Programs and Degrees Offered:
Listed in the following order: Program area, degree type (T if terminal Master's), number awarded 7/11–6/12. Clinical Psychology PsyD (Doctor of Psychology) 20, School/Clinical Child Psychology PsyD (Doctor of Psychology) 21, Mental Health Counseling MA/MS (Master of Arts/Science) (T) 10, Clinical Health Psychology PhD (Doctor of Philosophy) 13.

APA Accreditation: Clinical PsyD (Doctor of Psychology). Student Outcome Data Website: http://www.yu.edu/ferkauf/clinical-psychology/. Combination PsyD (Doctor of Psychology). Student Outcome Data Website: http://www.yu.edu/ferkauf/school-clinical-child-psychology/. Clinical PhD (Doctor of Philosophy). Student Outcome Data Website: http://www.yu.edu/ferkauf/clinical-psychology-health-emphasis/about/.

Student Applications/Admissions:
Student Applications
Clinical Psychology PsyD (Doctor of Psychology)—Applications 2012–2013, 350. Total applicants accepted 2012–2013, 80. Number full-time enrolled (new admits only) 2012–2013, 21.

Total enrolled 2012–2013 full-time, 111. Total enrolled 2012–2013 part-time, 12. Openings 2013–2014, 21. The median number of years required for completion of a degree in 2012–2013 were 5. The number of students enrolled full- and part-time who were dismissed or voluntarily withdrew from this program area in 2012–2013 were 1. *School/Clinical Child Psychology PsyD (Doctor of Psychology)*—Applications 2012–2013, 220. Total applicants accepted 2012–2013, 43. Number full-time enrolled (new admits only) 2012–2013, 24. Total enrolled 2012–2013 full-time, 101. Total enrolled 2012–2013 part-time, 9. Openings 2013–2014, 20. The median number of years required for completion of a degree in 2012–2013 were 5. The number of students enrolled full- and part-time who were dismissed or voluntarily withdrew from this program area in 2012–2013 were 1. *Mental Health Counseling MA/MS (Master of Arts/Science)*—Applications 2012–2013, 300. Total applicants accepted 2012–2013, 111. Number full-time enrolled (new admits only) 2012–2013, 18. Number part-time enrolled (new admits only) 2012–2013, 2. Total enrolled 2012–2013 full-time, 36. Total enrolled 2012–2013 part-time, 2. Openings 2013–2014, 20. The median number of years required for completion of a degree in 2012–2013 were 2. The number of students enrolled full- and part-time who were dismissed or voluntarily withdrew from this program area in 2012–2013 were 0. *Clinical Health Psychology PhD (Doctor of Philosophy)*—Applications 2012–2013, 120. Total applicants accepted 2012–2013, 55. Number full-time enrolled (new admits only) 2012–2013, 15. Number part-time enrolled (new admits only) 2012–2013, 4. Total enrolled 2012–2013 full-time, 83. Total enrolled 2012–2013 part-time, 11. Openings 2013–2014, 14. The median number of years required for completion of a degree in 2012–2013 were 5. The number of students enrolled full- and part-time who were dismissed or voluntarily withdrew from this program area in 2012–2013 were 1.

Scores: Entries appear in this order: required test or GPA, minimum score (if required), median score of students entering in 2012–2013. *Clinical Psychology PsyD (Doctor of Psychology):* GRE-V no minimum stated, GRE-Q no minimum stated, overall undergraduate GPA no minimum stated, psychology GPA no minimum stated; *School/Clinical Child Psychology PsyD (Doctor of Psychology):* GRE-V no minimum stated, GRE-Q no minimum stated, overall undergraduate GPA no minimum stated, psychology GPA no minimum stated; *Mental Health Counseling MA/MS (Master of Arts/Science):* GRE-V no minimum stated, GRE-Q no minimum stated, overall undergraduate GPA no minimum stated, psychology GPA no minimum stated; *Clinical Health Psychology PhD (Doctor of Philosophy):* GRE-V no minimum stated, GRE-Q no minimum stated, overall undergraduate GPA no minimum stated, psychology GPA no minimum stated.

Other Criteria: (importance of criteria rated low, medium, or high): GRE scores—high, research experience—high, work experience—high, extracurricular activity—high, clinically related public service—high, GPA—high, letters of recommendation—high, interview—high, statement of goals and objectives—high, undergraduate major in psychology—medium, specific undergraduate psychology courses taken—medium. For additional information on admission requirements, go to http://yu.edu/Admissions/Graduate/Ferkauf/.

Student Characteristics: The following represents characteristics of students in 2012–2013 in all graduate psychology programs in

the department: Female—full-time 244, part-time 19; Male—full-time 87, part-time 15; African American/Black—full-time 11, part-time 0; Hispanic/Latino(a)—full-time 21, part-time 2; Asian/Pacific Islander—full-time 10, part-time 3; American Indian/Alaska Native—full-time 0, part-time 0; Caucasian/White—full-time 284, part-time 27; Multi-ethnic—full-time 4, part-time 1; students subject to the Americans With Disabilities Act—full-time 1, part-time 1; Unknown ethnicity—full-time 1, part-time 1; International students who hold an F-1 or J-1 Visa—full-time 10, part-time 3.

Financial Information/Assistance:

Tuition for Full-Time Study: *Master's:* State residents: per academic year $32,710, $1,495 per credit hour; Nonstate residents: per academic year $32,710, $1,495 per credit hour. *Doctoral:* State residents: per academic year $32,710, $1,495 per credit hour; Nonstate residents: per academic year $32,710, $1,495 per credit hour. Tuition is subject to change. Additional fees are assessed to students beyond the costs of tuition for the following: student activities fee; materials fee; registration fee. See the following website for updates and changes in tuition costs: http://yu.edu/admissions/graduate/ferkauf/finance/.

Financial Assistance:

First-Year Students: Teaching assistantships available for first year. Average amount paid per academic year: $4,000. Average number of hours worked per week: 10. Research assistantships available for first year. Average amount paid per academic year: $2,000. Average number of hours worked per week: 20. Traineeships available for first year. Average amount paid per academic year: $15,000. Average number of hours worked per week: 20. Fellowships and scholarships available for first year. Average amount paid per academic year: $20,000. Average number of hours worked per week: 0.

Advanced Students: Teaching assistantships available for advanced students. Average amount paid per academic year: $4,000. Average number of hours worked per week: 10. Research assistantships available for advanced students. Average amount paid per academic year: $10,000. Average number of hours worked per week: 20. Traineeships available for advanced students. Average amount paid per academic year: $15,000. Average number of hours worked per week: 20. Fellowships and scholarships available for advanced students. Average amount paid per academic year: $20,000. Average number of hours worked per week: 0.

Additional Information: Of all students currently enrolled full time, 70% benefited from one or more of the listed financial assistance programs. Application and information available online at: http://yu.edu/admissions/graduate/ferkauf/finance/.

Internships/Practica: Doctoral Degree (PsyD Clinical Psychology): For those doctoral students for whom a professional psychology internship was required in this program prior to graduation, (25) students applied for an internship in 2011–2012, with (25) students obtaining an internship. Of those students who obtained an internship, (25) were paid internships. Of those students who obtained an internship, (23) students placed in APA/CPA accredited internships, (2) students placed in internships not APA/CPA accredited, but listed with the Association of Psychology Postdoctoral and Internship Programs (APPIC), (0) students placed in internships conforming to guidelines of the Council of Directors of School Psychology Programs (CDSPP), (0) students placed in internships that were not APA/CPA accredited, APPIC

or CDSPP listed. Doctoral Degree (PsyD School/Clinical Child Psychology): For those doctoral students for whom a professional psychology internship was required in this program prior to graduation, (15) students applied for an internship in 2011–2012, with (15) students obtaining an internship. Of those students who obtained an internship, (13) were paid internships. Of those students who obtained an internship, (9) students placed in APA/CPA accredited internships, (0) students placed in internships not APA/CPA accredited, but listed with the Association of Psychology Postdoctoral and Internship Programs (APPIC), (1) students placed in internships conforming to guidelines of the Council of Directors of School Psychology Programs (CDSPP), (5) students placed in internships that were not APA/CPA accredited, APPIC or CDSPP listed. Doctoral Degree (PhD Clinical Health Psychology): For those doctoral students for whom a professional psychology internship was required in this program prior to graduation, (13) students applied for an internship in 2011–2012, with (13) students obtaining an internship. Of those students who obtained an internship, (11) were paid internships. Of those students who obtained an internship, (10) students placed in APA/CPA accredited internships, (2) students placed in internships not APA/CPA accredited, but listed with the Association of Psychology Postdoctoral and Internship Programs (APPIC), (0) students placed in internships conforming to guidelines of the Council of Directors of School Psychology Programs (CDSPP), (1) students placed in internships that were not APA/CPA accredited, APPIC or CDSPP listed. Master's Degree (MA/MS Mental Health Counseling): An internship experience, such as a final research project or "capstone" experience is required of graduates.

Housing and Day Care: No on-campus housing is available. On-campus day care facilities are available.

Employment of Department Graduates:

Master's Degree Graduates: Of those who graduated in the academic year 2011–2012, the following categories and numbers represent the postgraduate activities and employment of master's degree graduates: Enrolled in a psychology doctoral program (25), enrolled in another graduate/professional program (5), enrolled in a postdoctoral residency/fellowship (n/a), employed in independent practice (n/a), do not know (5), total from the above (master's) (35).

Doctoral Degree Graduates: Of those who graduated in the academic year 2011–2012, the following categories and numbers represent the postgraduate activities and employment of doctoral degree graduates: Enrolled in a psychology doctoral program (n/a), enrolled in a postdoctoral residency/fellowship (3), employed in independent practice (7), employed in an academic position at a university (2), employed in an academic position at a 2-year/4-year college (2), employed in other positions at a higher education institution (1), employed in a professional position in a school system (15), employed in business or industry (3), employed in a community mental health/counseling center (11), employed in a hospital/medical center (20), still seeking employment (1), other employment position (2), do not know (1), total from the above (doctoral) (68).

Additional Information:

Orientation, Objectives, and Emphasis of Department: The objective of the Ferkauf Graduate School of Psychology is to promote a balance between the scientific-research orientation and the practitioner model. The Clinical Psychology (Health Emphasis) program places greater emphasis upon applied and basic research, whereas the Clinical and School-Clinical Child Psychology programs focus on the scientist–practitioner model with integrated clinical research and supervised practicum experiences. Further, Ferkauf offers PhD and PsyD degrees placing emphasis on research in the former and on application in the latter. A comprehensive theoretical orientation is offered with a psychodynamic focus and an applied behavioral emphasis. In all specialty areas, and at all levels of training, there is a strong commitment to the foundations of psychology, and a core of basic courses is required in all programs. Collaborations with the major NYC health and hospital institutions and schools are well established for all programs.

Special Facilities or Resources: All psychology programs offer practicum experience through Ferkauf's Center for Psychological and Psychoeducational Services. The Center provides a wide range of evaluation, remediation, and therapeutic services for children, adolescents, and adults in the neighboring communities, in addition to consultation services directly to the local schools. Ferkauf is located on Yeshiva University's campus of the Albert Einstein College of Medicine which has led to the development of cooperative programs and activities with various disciplines in medicine as well as added training opportunities for students at the various service delivery agencies affiliated with the medical college.

Information for Students With Physical Disabilities: See the following website for more information: http://yu.edu/student-life/resources-and-services/disability-services.

Application Information:
Send to Director of Admissions, Ferkauf Graduate School of Psychology, 1300 Morris Park Avenue, Bronx, NY 10461. Application available online. URL of online application: http://yu.edu/Admissions/Graduate/Ferkauf/. Students are admitted in the Fall, application deadline January 1. Clinical PsyD - January 1; Clinical (Health emphasis) PhD - January 15; School/Clinical Child PsyD - February 1; Mental Health Counseling Psychology MA - February 15. *Fee:* $50.

Appalachian State University

Department of Psychology
Arts and Science
Smith-Wright Hall
Boone, NC 28608
Telephone: (828) 262-2272
Fax: (828) 262-2974
E-mail: *dennistonjc@appstate.edu*
Web: *http://www.psych.appstate.edu*

Department Information:

1966. Chairperson: James C. Denniston. Number of faculty: total—full-time 36, part-time 2; women—full-time 14, part-time 1.

Programs and Degrees Offered:

Listed in the following order: Program area, degree type (T if terminal Master's), number awarded 7/11–6/12. General Experimental Psychology MA/MS (Master of Arts/Science) (T) 5, Industrial/Organizational-Hr Management MA/MS (Master of Arts/Science) (T) 7, Clinical Health Psychology MA/MS (Master of Arts/Science) (T) 7, School Psychology EdS (School Psychology) 7.

Student Applications/Admissions:

Student Applications

General Experimental Psychology MA/MS (Master of Arts/Science)—Applications 2012–2013, 46. Total applicants accepted 2012–2013, 10. Number full-time enrolled (new admits only) 2012–2013, 6. Number part-time enrolled (new admits only) 2012–2013, 0. Total enrolled 2012–2013 full-time, 14. Total enrolled 2012–2013 part-time, 0. Openings 2013–2014, 6. The median number of years required for completion of a degree in 2012–2013 were 3. *Industrial/Organizational-Hr Management MA/MS (Master of Arts/Science)*—Applications 2012–2013, 131. Total applicants accepted 2012–2013, 18. Number full-time enrolled (new admits only) 2012–2013, 9. Number part-time enrolled (new admits only) 2012–2013, 0. Total enrolled 2012–2013 full-time, 19. Total enrolled 2012–2013 part-time, 0. Openings 2013–2014, 8. The median number of years required for completion of a degree in 2012–2013 were 2. The number of students enrolled full- and part-time who were dismissed or voluntarily withdrew from this program area in 2012–2013 were 0. *Clinical Health Psychology MA/MS (Master of Arts/Science)*—Applications 2012–2013, 155. Total applicants accepted 2012–2013, 11. Number full-time enrolled (new admits only) 2012–2013, 9. Total enrolled 2012–2013 full-time, 18. Total enrolled 2012–2013 part-time, 5. Openings 2013–2014, 9. The median number of years required for completion of a degree in 2012–2013 were 3. The number of students enrolled full- and part-time who were dismissed or voluntarily withdrew from this program area in 2012–2013 were 2. *School Psychology EdS (School Psychology)*—Applications 2012–2013, 87. Total applicants accepted 2012–2013, 11. Number full-time enrolled (new admits only) 2012–2013, 8. Number part-time enrolled (new admits only) 2012–2013, 0. Total enrolled 2012–2013 full-time, 19. Total enrolled 2012–

2013 part-time, 0. Openings 2013–2014, 9. The median number of years required for completion of a degree in 2012–2013 were 3. The number of students enrolled full- and part-time who were dismissed or voluntarily withdrew from this program area in 2012–2013 were 3.

Scores: Entries appear in this order: required test or GPA, minimum score (if required), median score of students entering in 2012–2013. *General Experimental Psychology MA/MS (Master of Arts/Science)*: GRE-V 143, 155, GRE-Q 143, 146, GRE-Analytical 3.0, 3.8, overall undergraduate GPA 3.0, 3.3; *Industrial/Organizational-HR Management MA/MS (Master of Arts/Science)*: GRE-V 150, 155, GRE-Q 147, 156, GRE-Analytical 3.5, 4.0, overall undergraduate GPA 3.4, 3.6; *Clinical Health Psychology MA/MS (Master of Arts/Science)*: GRE-V 155, 157, GRE-Q 147, 151, GRE-Analytical 3.0, 4.5, overall undergraduate GPA 3.2, 3.7; *School Psychology EdS (School Psychology)*: GRE-V 146, 154, GRE-Q 143, 150, GRE-Analytical 3.5, 4.0, overall undergraduate GPA 3.0, 3.5.

Other Criteria: (importance of criteria rated low, medium, or high): GRE scores—high, research experience—medium, work experience—low, extracurricular activity—low, clinically related public service—low, GPA—high, letters of recommendation—medium, interview—high, statement of goals and objectives—high, undergraduate major in psychology—medium, specific undergraduate psychology courses taken—medium, An interview is not required for Industrial/Organizational or Experimental Psychology. Interviews are given high importance for the Clinical Health and School Psychology programs. For additional information on admission requirements, go to http://www.psych.appstate.edu/gradprograms.html.

Student Characteristics: The following represents characteristics of students in 2012–2013 in all graduate psychology programs in the department: Female—full-time 54, part-time 4; Male—full-time 16, part-time 1; African American/Black—full-time 1, part-time 0; Hispanic/Latino(a)—full-time 0, part-time 0; Asian/Pacific Islander—full-time 1, part-time 0; American Indian/Alaska Native—full-time 0, part-time 0; Caucasian/White—full-time 68, part-time 5; Multi-ethnic—full-time 0, part-time 0; students subject to the Americans With Disabilities Act—full-time 0, part-time 0; Unknown ethnicity—full-time 0, part-time 0; International students who hold an F-1 or J-1 Visa—full-time 2, part-time 0.

Financial Information/Assistance:

Tuition for Full-Time Study: *Master's:* State residents: per academic year $6,065; Nonstate residents: per academic year $17,877. Tuition is subject to change. See the following website for updates and changes in tuition costs: http://studentaccounts.appstate.edu/tuition-and-fees.

Financial Assistance:

First-Year Students: Teaching assistantships available for first year. Average amount paid per academic year: $5,000. Average number of hours worked per week: 10. Research assistantships available for first year. Average amount paid per academic year: $7,500. Average number of hours worked per week: 15. Fellow-

ships and scholarships available for first year. Average amount paid per academic year: $11,000. Average number of hours worked per week: 20.

Advanced Students: Teaching assistantships available for advanced students. Average amount paid per academic year: $8,000. Average number of hours worked per week: 20. Research assistantships available for advanced students. Average amount paid per academic year: $7,500. Average number of hours worked per week: 15.

Additional Information: Of all students currently enrolled full time, 97% benefited from one or more of the listed financial assistance programs. Application and information available online at: http://www.graduate.appstate.edu/admissions/.

Internships/Practica: Master's Degree (MA/MS General Experimental Psychology): An internship experience, such as a final research project or "capstone" experience is required of graduates. Master's Degree (MA/MS Industrial/Organizational-HR Management): An internship experience, such as a final research project or "capstone" experience is required of graduates. Master's Degree (MA/MS Clinical Health Psychology): An internship experience, such as a final research project or "capstone" experience is required of graduates. Clinical Health students complete two semester-long practica. These are often at the University Counseling Center, the Psychology AD/HD Clinic, or at two other regional mental health institutes. Students complete a 1,000-hour internship at a medical or mental health setting. School students complete two semester-long practica in public schools and a 1200-hour internship, half of which must be in a public school setting. Industrial/Organizational-Human Resources Management students have the option of completing a 450-hour internship in human resources or organizational development.

Housing and Day Care: No on-campus housing is available. On-campus day care facilities are available. See the following website for more information: http://lucybrock.appstate.edu/ AND http://childdevelopment.appstate.edu/.

Employment of Department Graduates:

Master's Degree Graduates: Of those who graduated in the academic year 2011–2012, the following categories and numbers represent the postgraduate activities and employment of master's degree graduates: Enrolled in a psychology doctoral program (6), enrolled in a postdoctoral residency/fellowship (n/a), employed in independent practice (n/a), employed in other positions at a higher education institution (1), employed in a professional position in a school system (7), employed in business or industry (6), employed in government agency (1), employed in a community mental health/counseling center (4), do not know (1), total from the above (master's) (26).

Doctoral Degree Graduates: Of those who graduated in the academic year 2011–2012, the following categories and numbers represent the postgraduate activities and employment of doctoral degree graduates: Enrolled in a psychology doctoral program (n/a), total from the above (doctoral) (0).

Additional Information:

Orientation, Objectives, and Emphasis of Department: The department is student oriented, with a Program Director for each graduate program and a Graduate Programs Coordinator. The General-Experimental program is primarily predoctoral for experimental psychology, but one can structure an applied orientation.

The Clinical Health program trains professionals for master's level licensure as LPAs and applied practice in mental health and medical settings or for doctoral study in clinical psychology. The School Psychology program is NCATE/NASP accredited and offers the master's and specialist degree. The Industrial/Organizational-Human Resource Management program integrates with the Department of Management in the College of Business and trains professionals to work in business, industry, and government.

Special Facilities or Resources: Biofeedback facilities, student computer laboratory, neuroscience laboratory, an animal operant conditioning laboratory, and a Psychology Clinic at the Institute for Health & Human Services are available.

Information for Students With Physical Disabilities: See the following website for more information: http://www.ods.appstate.edu.

Application Information:
Send to The Dean, Cratis D. Williams Graduate School, John E. Thomas Building, Appalachian State University, Boone NC 28608. Application available online. URL of online application: http://www.graduate.appstate.edu/admissions/. Students are admitted in the Fall, application deadline December 20. Clinical Health has a December 20 deadline, School Psychology program has a February 1 deadline, and I/O-HRM and General Experimental programs have March 1 application deadlines. *Fee:* $55.

Duke University
Department of Psychology and Neuroscience
229 Psychology/Sociology Building, P.O. Box 90085
9 Flowers Drive
Durham, NC 27708
Telephone: (919) 660-5715
Fax: (919) 660-5726
E-mail: *morrell@duke.edu*
Web: *http://psychandneuro.duke.edu/*

Department Information:
1948. Chairperson: Dr. Harris Cooper. Number of faculty: total—full-time 39, part-time 14; women—full-time 15, part-time 4; total—minority—full-time 5; women minority—full-time 2.

Programs and Degrees Offered:
Listed in the following order: Program area, degree type (T if terminal Master's), number awarded 7/11–6/12. Developmental Psychology PhD (Doctor of Philosophy) 1, Social Psychology PhD (Doctor of Philosophy) 1, Clinical Psychology PhD (Doctor of Philosophy) 8, Systems & Integrative Neuroscience PhD (Doctor of Philosophy) 0, Cognition & Cognitive Neuroscience PhD (Doctor of Philosophy) 2, Jd/Ma Social and Health Sciences MA/MS (Master of Arts/Science) (T) 2.

APA Accreditation: Clinical PhD (Doctor of Philosophy). Student Outcome Data Website: http://psychandneuro.duke.edu/graduate/training/clinical.

Student Applications/Admissions:

Student Applications

Developmental Psychology PhD (Doctor of Philosophy)—Applications 2012–2013, 47. Total applicants accepted 2012–2013, 2. Number full-time enrolled (new admits only) 2012–2013, 1. Number part-time enrolled (new admits only) 2012–2013, 0. Total enrolled 2012–2013 full-time, 12. Total enrolled 2012–2013 part-time, 0. Openings 2013–2014, 4. The median number of years required for completion of a degree in 2012–2013 were 5. *Social Psychology PhD (Doctor of Philosophy)*—Applications 2012–2013, 73. Total applicants accepted 2012–2013, 2. Number full-time enrolled (new admits only) 2012–2013, 2. Number part-time enrolled (new admits only) 2012–2013, 0. Total enrolled 2012–2013 full-time, 12. Total enrolled 2012–2013 part-time, 0. Openings 2013–2014, 3. The median number of years required for completion of a degree in 2012–2013 were 9. The number of students enrolled full- and part-time who were dismissed or voluntarily withdrew from this program area in 2012–2013 were 0. *Clinical Psychology PhD (Doctor of Philosophy)*—Applications 2012–2013, 316. Total applicants accepted 2012–2013, 7. Number full-time enrolled (new admits only) 2012–2013, 4. Number part-time enrolled (new admits only) 2012–2013, 0. Total enrolled 2012–2013 full-time, 35. Total enrolled 2012–2013 part-time, 0. Openings 2013–2014, 4. The median number of years required for completion of a degree in 2012–2013 were 7. The number of students enrolled full- and part-time who were dismissed or voluntarily withdrew from this program area in 2012–2013 were 1. *Systems & Integrative Neuroscience PhD (Doctor of Philosophy)*—Applications 2012–2013, 25. Total applicants accepted 2012–2013, 2. Number full-time enrolled (new admits only) 2012–2013, 2. Number part-time enrolled (new admits only) 2012–2013, 0. Total enrolled 2012–2013 full-time, 10. Total enrolled 2012–2013 part-time, 0. Openings 2013–2014, 2. The number of students enrolled full- and part-time who were dismissed or voluntarily withdrew from this program area in 2012–2013 were 0. *Cognition & Cognitive Neuroscience PhD (Doctor of Philosophy)*—Applications 2012–2013, 126. Total applicants accepted 2012–2013, 3. Number full-time enrolled (new admits only) 2012–2013, 2. Number part-time enrolled (new admits only) 2012–2013, 0. Total enrolled 2012–2013 full-time, 30. Total enrolled 2012–2013 part-time, 0. Openings 2013–2014, 3. The median number of years required for completion of a degree in 2012–2013 were 6. The number of students enrolled full- and part-time who were dismissed or voluntarily withdrew from this program area in 2012–2013 were 0. *Jd/Ma Social and Health Sciences MA/MS (Master of Arts/Science)*—Applications 2012–2013, 1. Total applicants accepted 2012–2013, 1. Number full-time enrolled (new admits only) 2012–2013, 0. Number part-time enrolled (new admits only) 2012–2013, 1. Openings 2013–2014, 2. The median number of years required for completion of a degree in 2012–2013 were 3.

Scores: Entries appear in this order: required test or GPA, minimum score (if required), median score of students entering in 2012–2013. *Developmental Psychology PhD (Doctor of Philosophy)*: GRE-V no minimum stated, 620, GRE-Q no minimum stated, 740, GRE-Analytical no minimum stated, 4.9, overall undergraduate GPA no minimum stated, 3.63; *Social Psychology PhD (Doctor of Philosophy)*: GRE-V no minimum stated, 650, GRE-Q no minimum stated, 720, GRE-Analytical no minimum stated, 4.5, overall undergraduate GPA no minimum

stated, 3.8; *Clinical Psychology PhD (Doctor of Philosophy)*: GRE-V no minimum stated, 668, GRE-Q no minimum stated, 710, GRE-Analytical no minimum stated, 5.1, overall undergraduate GPA no minimum stated, 3.7; *Systems & Integrative Neuroscience PhD (Doctor of Philosophy)*: GRE-V no minimum stated, 610, GRE-Q no minimum stated, 610, GRE-Analytical no minimum stated, 5.0, overall undergraduate GPA no minimum stated, 4.0; *Cognition & Cognitive Neuroscience PhD (Doctor of Philosophy)*: GRE-V no minimum stated, 650, GRE-Q no minimum stated, 690, GRE-Analytical no minimum stated, 4.75, overall undergraduate GPA no minimum stated, 3.7.

Other Criteria: (importance of criteria rated low, medium, or high): GRE scores—high, research experience—high, work experience—high, extracurricular activity—low, clinically related public service—medium, GPA—high, letters of recommendation—high, interview—high, statement of goals and objectives—high, specific undergraduate psychology courses taken—medium, Clinically Related Public Service is not required for Developmental, Social, Cognitive, or Neuro. For additional information on admission requirements, go to http://psychandneuro.duke.edu/graduate/apply.

Student Characteristics: The following represents characteristics of students in 2012–2013 in all graduate psychology programs in the department: Female—full-time 73, part-time 2; Male—full-time 26, part-time 1; African American/Black—full-time 6, part-time 0; Hispanic/Latino(a)—full-time 6, part-time 0; Asian/Pacific Islander—full-time 10, part-time 0; American Indian/Alaska Native—full-time 1, part-time 0; Caucasian/White—full-time 75, part-time 3; Multi-ethnic—full-time 0, part-time 0; students subject to the Americans With Disabilities Act—full-time 0, part-time 0; Unknown ethnicity—full-time 1, part-time 0; International students who hold an F-1 or J-1 Visa—full-time 10, part-time 0.

Financial Information/Assistance:

Tuition for Full-Time Study: *Doctoral:* State residents: per academic year $44,000; Nonstate residents: per academic year $44,000. Tuition is subject to change. Additional fees are assessed to students beyond the costs of tuition for the following: activity, health, and recreation fees. See the following website for updates and changes in tuition costs: http://gradschool.duke.edu/financial_support/coa/.

Financial Assistance:

First-Year Students: Teaching assistantships available for first year. Average amount paid per academic year: $21,580. Average number of hours worked per week: 19. Apply by December 1. Research assistantships available for first year. Average amount paid per academic year: $21,580. Average number of hours worked per week: 19. Apply by December 1. Fellowships and scholarships available for first year. Average amount paid per academic year: $21,580. Apply by December 1.

Advanced Students: Teaching assistantships available for advanced students. Average amount paid per academic year: $21,580. Average number of hours worked per week: 19. Apply by December 1. Research assistantships available for advanced students. Average amount paid per academic year: $21,580. Average number of hours worked per week: 19. Apply by December 1. Fellowships and scholarships available for advanced students. Average amount paid per academic year: $21,580. Apply by December 1.

Additional Information: Of all students currently enrolled full time, 99% benefited from one or more of the listed financial assistance programs. Application and information available online at: http://gradschool.duke.edu/financial_support/.

Internships/Practica: Doctoral Degree (PhD Clinical Psychology): For those doctoral students for whom a professional psychology internship was required in this program prior to graduation, (3) students applied for an internship in 2011–2012, with (3) students obtaining an internship. Of those students who obtained an internship, (3) were paid internships. Of those students who obtained an internship, (3) students placed in APA/CPA accredited internships, (0) students placed in internships not APA/CPA accredited, but listed with the Association of Psychology Postdoctoral and Internship Programs (APPIC), (0) students placed in internships conforming to guidelines of the Council of Directors of School Psychology Programs (CDSPP), (0) students placed in internships that were not APA/CPA accredited, APPIC or CDSPP listed. Doctoral students in our clinical program receive experience in our own departmental clinic as well as a great number of local institutions and medical center facilities.

Housing and Day Care: On-campus housing is available. See the following website for more information: http://studentaffairs.duke.edu/hdrl/graduate-professional-students. On-campus day care facilities are available. See the following website for more information: http://www.hr.duke.edu/benefits/family/care/onsite/.

Employment of Department Graduates:

Master's Degree Graduates: Of those who graduated in the academic year 2011–2012, the following categories and numbers represent the postgraduate activities and employment of master's degree graduates: Enrolled in a postdoctoral residency/fellowship (n/a), employed in independent practice (n/a), total from the above (master's) (0).

Doctoral Degree Graduates: Of those who graduated in the academic year 2011–2012, the following categories and numbers represent the postgraduate activities and employment of doctoral degree graduates: Enrolled in a psychology doctoral program (n/a), enrolled in a postdoctoral residency/fellowship (5), employed in an academic position at a university (2), employed in an academic position at a 2-year/4-year college (3), employed in a hospital/medical center (1), not seeking employment (1), total from the above (doctoral) (12).

Additional Information:

Orientation, Objectives, and Emphasis of Department: The department features a strong mentor-oriented training program with areas of specialization in clinical health, adult and child psychology, as well as programs in developmental and social psychology. Emphasis is placed on informal interaction among faculty and students; seminars and small groups of faculty and graduate students meet regularly.

Special Facilities or Resources: The department has collaborative ties with the Center for Child and Family Policy, the Center for Cognitive Neuroscience, the Center for the Study of Aging and Human Development, the Fuqua School of Business, Medical Psychology, the Center for Aging and Human Development, the Center for Child and Family Policy, and the Carolina Consortium on Human Development and UNC-Duke Collaborative Graduate Certificate Program in Developmental Psychology. State-of-the-art facilities, including specially equipped laboratories and clinics, are available for student use. These include computational facilities for word processing, data analysis, and experimental programming.

Information for Students With Physical Disabilities: See the following website for more information: http://www.access.duke.edu/.

Application Information:
Send to The Graduate School, 2127 Campus Drive, Box 90065, Durham, NC 27708. Application available online. URL of online application: http://gradschool.duke.edu/admissions/requirements/online_ap.php. Students are admitted in the Fall, application deadline December 1. Clinical deadline is December 1; deadline for all other programs is December 8. *Fee:* $75.

East Carolina University
Department of Psychology
Arts & Sciences
104 Rawl
Greenville, NC 27858-4353
Telephone: (252) 328-6800
Fax: (252) 328-6283
E-mail: *bakerr@ecu.edu*
Web: *http://www.ecu.edu/psyc*

Department Information:
1959. Interim Chair: Susan McCammon. Number of faculty: total—full-time 37, part-time 14; women—full-time 19, part-time 7; total—minority—full-time 6; women minority—full-time 5.

Programs and Degrees Offered:
Listed in the following order: Program area, degree type (T if terminal Master's), number awarded 7/11–6/12. School Psychology MA/MS (Master of Arts/Science) (T) 5, Industrial/Organizational Psychology MA/MS (Master of Arts/Science) (T) 8, Clinical Health Psychology PhD (Doctor of Philosophy) 0, Pediatric School Psychology PhD (Doctor of Philosophy) 2, Occupational Health Psychology PhD (Doctor of Philosophy) 0.

APA Accreditation: Clinical PhD (Doctor of Philosophy). Student Outcome Data Website: http://www.ecu.edu/cs-cas/psyc/Clinical-Health-About.cfm.

Student Applications/Admissions:
Student Applications
School Psychology MA/MS (Master of Arts/Science)—Applications 2012–2013, 41. Total applicants accepted 2012–2013, 13. Number full-time enrolled (new admits only) 2012–2013, 7. Number part-time enrolled (new admits only) 2012–2013, 0. Total enrolled 2012–2013 full-time, 20. Total enrolled 2012–2013 part-time, 0. Openings 2013–2014, 7. The median number of years required for completion of a degree in 2012–2013 were 3. The number of students enrolled full- and part-time who were dismissed or voluntarily withdrew from this program area in 2012–2013 were 0. *Industrial/Organizational Psychology MA/MS (Master of Arts/Science)*—Applications 2012–2013,

74. Total applicants accepted 2012–2013, 19. Number full-time enrolled (new admits only) 2012–2013, 8. Number part-time enrolled (new admits only) 2012–2013, 0. Total enrolled 2012–2013 full-time, 19. Total enrolled 2012–2013 part-time, 0. Openings 2013–2014, 10. The median number of years required for completion of a degree in 2012–2013 were 2. The number of students enrolled full- and part-time who were dismissed or voluntarily withdrew from this program area in 2012–2013 were 0. *Clinical Health Psychology PhD (Doctor of Philosophy)*—Applications 2012–2013, 55. Total applicants accepted 2012–2013, 6. Number full-time enrolled (new admits only) 2012–2013, 6. Number part-time enrolled (new admits only) 2012–2013, 0. Total enrolled 2012–2013 full-time, 23. Total enrolled 2012–2013 part-time, 0. Openings 2013–2014, 5. The median number of years required for completion of a degree in 2012–2013 were 5. The number of students enrolled full- and part-time who were dismissed or voluntarily withdrew from this program area in 2012–2013 were 0. *Pediatric School Psychology PhD (Doctor of Philosophy)*—Applications 2012–2013, 20. Total applicants accepted 2012–2013, 3. Number full-time enrolled (new admits only) 2012–2013, 3. Number part-time enrolled (new admits only) 2012–2013, 0. Total enrolled 2012–2013 full-time, 13. Total enrolled 2012–2013 part-time, 0. Openings 2013–2014, 3. The median number of years required for completion of a degree in 2012–2013 were 4. The number of students enrolled full- and part-time who were dismissed or voluntarily withdrew from this program area in 2012–2013 were 1. *Occupational Health Psychology PhD (Doctor of Philosophy)*—Applications 2012–2013, 0. Total applicants accepted 2012–2013, 0. Number full-time enrolled (new admits only) 2012–2013, 0. Number part-time enrolled (new admits only) 2012–2013, 0. Openings 2013–2014, 3. The number of students enrolled full- and part-time who were dismissed or voluntarily withdrew from this program area in 2012–2013 were 0.

Scores: Entries appear in this order: required test or GPA, minimum score (if required), median score of students entering in 2012–2013. *School Psychology MA/MS (Master of Arts/Science):* GRE-V no minimum stated, 153, GRE-Q no minimum stated, 151, GRE-Analytical no minimum stated, 4.0, overall undergraduate GPA no minimum stated, 3.67; *Industrial/Organizational Psychology MA/MS (Master of Arts/Science):* GRE-V no minimum stated, 154, GRE-Q no minimum stated, 152, overall undergraduate GPA 3.0, 3.52; *Clinical Health Psychology PhD (Doctor of Philosophy):* GRE-V no minimum stated, 154, GRE-Q no minimum stated, 152, GRE-Analytical no minimum stated, 4.0, overall undergraduate GPA no minimum stated, 3.71; *Pediatric School Psychology PhD (Doctor of Philosophy):* GRE-V no minimum stated, 156, GRE-Q no minimum stated, 163, GRE-Analytical no minimum stated, 4.5; *Occupational Health Psychology PhD (Doctor of Philosophy):* GRE-V no minimum stated, GRE-Q no minimum stated, GRE-Analytical no minimum stated.

Other Criteria: (importance of criteria rated low, medium, or high): GRE scores—high, research experience—high, work experience—medium, extracurricular activity—low, clinically related public service—medium, GPA—high, letters of recommendation—high, interview—high, statement of goals and objectives—high, undergraduate major in psychology—high, specific undergraduate psychology courses taken—medium, .

Student Characteristics: The following represents characteristics of students in 2012–2013 in all graduate psychology programs in the department: Female—full-time 53, part-time 0; Male—full-time 22, part-time 0; African American/Black—full-time 3, part-time 2; Hispanic/Latino(a)—full-time 0, part-time 0; Asian/Pacific Islander—full-time 1, part-time 1; American Indian/Alaska Native—full-time 0, part-time 0; Caucasian/White—full-time 62, part-time 6; Multi-ethnic—full-time 0, part-time 0; students subject to the Americans With Disabilities Act—full-time 0, part-time 0; Unknown ethnicity—full-time 0, part-time 0; International students who hold an F-1 or J-1 Visa—full-time 0, part-time 0.

Financial Information/Assistance:

Tuition for Full-Time Study: *Master's:* State residents: per academic year $4,009; Nonstate residents: per academic year $15,840. *Doctoral:* State residents: per academic year $4,009; Nonstate residents: per academic year $15,840. Tuition is subject to change. Additional fees are assessed to students beyond the costs of tuition for the following: university fees, health service fee, educational/technology fee. See the following website for updates and changes in tuition costs: http://www.ecu.edu/cashier/tufee.cfm.

Financial Assistance:

First-Year Students: Research assistantships available for first year. Average amount paid per academic year: $4,500. Average number of hours worked per week: 10. Apply by February 1.

Advanced Students: Teaching assistantships available for advanced students. Average amount paid per academic year: $15,000. Average number of hours worked per week: 20. Apply by December 1. Research assistantships available for advanced students. Average amount paid per academic year: $15,000. Average number of hours worked per week: 20. Apply by December 1. Fellowships and scholarships available for advanced students. Average amount paid per academic year: $3,000. Average number of hours worked per week: 0. Apply by February 15.

Additional Information: Of all students currently enrolled full time, 81% benefited from one or more of the listed financial assistance programs. Application and information available online at: http://www.ecu.edu/cs-acad/gradschool/funding.cfm.

Internships/Practica: Doctoral Degree (PhD Clinical Health Psychology): For those doctoral students for whom a professional psychology internship was required in this program prior to graduation, (3) students applied for an internship in 2011–2012, with (2) students obtaining an internship. Of those students who obtained an internship, (2) were paid internships. Of those students who obtained an internship, (2) students placed in APA/CPA accredited internships, (0) students placed in internships not APA/CPA accredited, but listed with the Association of Psychology Postdoctoral and Internship Programs (APPIC), (0) students placed in internships conforming to guidelines of the Council of Directors of School Psychology Programs (CDSPP), (0) students placed in internships that were not APA/CPA accredited, APPIC or CDSPP listed. Doctoral Degree (PhD Pediatric School Psychology): For those doctoral students for whom a professional psychology internship was required in this program prior to graduation, (4) students applied for an internship in 2011–2012, with (4) students obtaining an internship. Of those students who obtained an internship, (4) were paid internships. Of those students who obtained an internship, (0) students placed in APA/CPA accredited internships, (1) students placed in internships not APA/

CPA accredited, but listed with the Association of Psychology Postdoctoral and Internship Programs (APPIC), (3) students placed in internships conforming to guidelines of the Council of Directors of School Psychology Programs (CDSPP), (0) students placed in internships that were not APA/CPA accredited, APPIC or CDSPP listed. Master's Degree (MA/MS School Psychology): An internship experience, such as a final research project or "capstone" experience is required of graduates. Master's Degree (MA/MS Industrial/Organizational Psychology): An internship experience, such as a final research project or "capstone" experience is required of graduates. Doctoral Internships for CHP and PSP are sought primarily via APPIC. Some School Psychology doctoral students choose internships within public school systems. Doctoral practica include placements in the Brody School of Medicine Cardiac Psychology, Family Medicine, and Psychiatry Clinics; Vidant Medical Center Rehabilitation, Behavioral Health, and NICU Follow-up Clinics; Veterans Administration Outpatient Clinic; General Adult Neuropsychology Clinic; Cherry Psychiatric Hospital; school-based mental health services (Greene/Rocky Mt. County Schools); Pitt County Schools Trans-disciplinary Play-based Assessment Teams; and ECU Psychological Assessment and Specialty Services (PASS; in-house clinic): Adult Healthy Weight Clinic, Pediatric Healthy Weight Clinic, Women's Health Psychology Clinic, and Pediatric Behavioral Health Clinic. Specialist-level School Psychology students have practica and internships in various public school systems across the state and region. I/O Master's students completing their first year of training are required to complete a 400-hour internship in various organizational/health/business settings.

Housing and Day Care: On-campus housing is available. See the following website for more information: http://www.ecu.edu/campusliving/. On-campus day care facilities are available. See the following website for more information: http://www.ecu.edu/che/cdfr/cdl.html.

Employment of Department Graduates:
   Master's Degree Graduates: Of those who graduated in the academic year 2011–2012, the following categories and numbers represent the postgraduate activities and employment of master's degree graduates: Enrolled in a psychology doctoral program (1), enrolled in a postdoctoral residency/fellowship (n/a), employed in independent practice (n/a), employed in a professional position in a school system (5), employed in business or industry (7), total from the above (master's) (13).
   Doctoral Degree Graduates: Of those who graduated in the academic year 2011–2012, the following categories and numbers represent the postgraduate activities and employment of doctoral degree graduates: Enrolled in a psychology doctoral program (n/a), employed in a professional position in a school system (2), employed in a hospital/medical center (1), total from the above (doctoral) (3).

Additional Information:
   Orientation, Objectives, and Emphasis of Department: ECU Psychology provides distinctive educational experiences with exemplary teaching, scholarship, and service. We prepare students for careers in health care, education and business, and provide leadership within the field through cutting-edge research and prominent national roles. Graduate Programs in the Department include: School Psychology MA/CAS (NASP-approved); MA in Industrial/Organizational psychology; and PhD in Health Psychol-

ogy with three separate and specific concentrations ' Clinical Health Psychology (CHP), Pediatric School Psychology (PSP), & Occupational Health Psychology (OHP). Last year, CHP obtained full accreditation by American Psychological Association (APA). The clinical program espouses a scientist–practitioner model with a health emphasis, training graduates to work within primary care teams, hospitals, health organizations, etc., and academic settings. PSP prepares students to advance school psychology through original research and to professionally apply health psychology principles to school psychology practices across a three-tier model of service delivery. PSP will seek APA accreditation as a School program. Students from CHP and PSP are eligible for licensure as Licensed Psychologists and Health Services Providers by NC Board of Psychology; PSP graduates are also eligible for school-level licensure. OHP trains occupational health professionals to improve the quality of working life and enhance the safety, health and well-being of workers across occupations.

Special Facilities or Resources: The department has a student lounge dedicated to Graduate Students, interview and testing facilities, the PASS Clinic, and an animal laboratory. The school program works closely with community schools and mental health agencies. The doctoral health psychology program works closely with the Brody School of Medicine, family care practices, state health agencies, as well as with the Sleep Disorders Center, the Heart Center, pediatric specialty clinic and psychiatric medicine.

Information for Students With Physical Disabilities: See the following website for more information: http://www.ecu.edu/cs-studentlife/dss/.

Application Information:
Send to East Carolina University Graduate School, 131 Ragsdale Hall, Greenville, NC 27858-4353. Application available online. URL of online application: http://www.ecu.edu/gradschool. Students are admitted in the Fall, application deadline December 1. Deadline for all PhD programs is December 1. Deadline for all Master's programs is February 1. *Fee:* $70. Application fee waived for McNair Scholars.

East Carolina University
Medical Family Therapy
College of Human Ecology
112 Redditt House
Greenville, NC 27858
Telephone: (252) 737-2042
Fax: (252) 328-5418
E-mail: *lamsona@ecu.edu*
Web: *http://www.ecu.edu/che/cdfr/phdmft.html*

Department Information:
   2004. Program Director: Dr. Angela Lamson. Number of faculty: total—full-time 6; women—full-time 2; total—minority—full-time 1.

Programs and Degrees Offered:
   Listed in the following order: Program area, degree type (T if terminal Master's), number awarded 7/11–6/12. Medical Family Therapy PhD (Doctor of Philosophy).

Student Applications/Admissions:

Student Applications

Medical Family Therapy PhD (Doctor of Philosophy)—Number full-time enrolled (new admits only) 2012–2013, 2. Number part-time enrolled (new admits only) 2012–2013, 0. Total enrolled 2012–2013 full-time, 9. Total enrolled 2012–2013 part-time, 2.

Scores: Entries appear in this order: required test or GPA, minimum score (if required), median score of students entering in 2012–2013. Medical Family Therapy PhD (Doctor of Philosophy): GRE-V no minimum stated, GRE-Q no minimum stated, GRE-Analytical no minimum stated, overall undergraduate GPA 2.75, Masters GPA 3.0.

Other Criteria: (importance of criteria rated low, medium, or high): GRE scores—high, research experience—high, work experience—medium, extracurricular activity—low, clinically related public service—medium, GPA—high, letters of recommendation—high, interview—high, statement of goals and objectives—high, undergraduate major in psychology—low. For additional information on admission requirements, go to http://www.ecu.edu/che/cdfr/phdmft.html.

Student Characteristics: The following represents characteristics of students in 2012–2013 in all graduate psychology programs in the department: Female—full-time 6, part-time 2; Male—full-time 3, part-time 0; African American/Black—full-time 0, part-time 0; Hispanic/Latino(a)—full-time 0, part-time 0; Asian/Pacific Islander—full-time 0, part-time 0; American Indian/Alaska Native—full-time 1, part-time 0; Caucasian/White—full-time 8, part-time 2; Multi-ethnic—full-time 0, part-time 0; students subject to the Americans With Disabilities Act—full-time 0, part-time 0; Unknown ethnicity—full-time 0, part-time 0; International students who hold an F-1 or J-1 Visa—full-time 0, part-time 0.

Financial Information/Assistance:

Tuition for Full-Time Study: Doctoral: State residents: per academic year $7,114, $444 per credit hour; Nonstate residents: per academic year $28,702, $1,793 per credit hour. Tuition is subject to change. See the following website for updates and changes in tuition costs: http://www.ecu.edu/cashier/tufee.cfm.

Financial Assistance:

First-Year Students: Teaching assistantships available for first year. Average amount paid per academic year: $26,000. Average number of hours worked per week: 20. Apply by March 15. Research assistantships available for first year. Average amount paid per academic year: $26,000. Average number of hours worked per week: 20. Apply by March 15.

Advanced Students: Teaching assistantships available for advanced students. Average amount paid per academic year: $26,000. Average number of hours worked per week: 20. Apply by March 15. Research assistantships available for advanced students. Average amount paid per academic year: $26,000. Average number of hours worked per week: 20. Apply by March 15.

Additional Information: Of all students currently enrolled full time, 100% benefited from one or more of the listed financial assistance programs. Application and information available online at: http://www.ecu.edu/financial/.

Internships/Practica: Each doctoral student is required to complete an internship lasting a minimum of 9 months in duration. The internship must meet the site requirements and those set forth by the program and in agreement with the MFT educational guidelines. The ECU MedFT program further requires that each internship site be situated in a medical context or in a context where students will have access to working with medical populations (research and/or clinical).

Housing and Day Care: No on-campus housing is available. On-campus day care facilities are available. See the following website for more information: http://www.ecu.edu/che/cdfr/cdl.html.

Employment of Department Graduates:

Master's Degree Graduates: Of those who graduated in the academic year 2011–2012, the following categories and numbers represent the postgraduate activities and employment of master's degree graduates: Enrolled in a postdoctoral residency/fellowship (n/a), employed in independent practice (n/a), total from the above (master's) (0).

Doctoral Degree Graduates: Of those who graduated in the academic year 2011–2012, the following categories and numbers represent the postgraduate activities and employment of doctoral degree graduates: Enrolled in a psychology doctoral program (n/a), employed in an academic position at a university (1), employed in a community mental health/counseling center (2), total from the above (doctoral) (3).

Additional Information:

Orientation, Objectives, and Emphasis of Department: The mission of the doctoral program in Medical Family Therapy (MedFT) is to advance students' learning in the areas of research, theory, clinical practice, leadership, supervision, and teaching in order to prepare and qualify them to pursue employment as researchers, educators, administrators, and/or clinicians in the field of medical family therapy.

Special Facilities or Resources: In August of 2011, the Redditt House: Medical Family Therapy Research Academy opened and serves as a research and training site for faculty and MedFT students to further strengthen the capacity for unique research training opportunities. The ECU Family Therapy Clinic opened in 1991 and serves as a training facility for our MFT and MedFT students. The clinic offers a way for faculty to provide co-therapy with Master's and doctoral-level therapists and is also a great location for supervision of students in the program.

Information for Students With Physical Disabilities: See the following website for more information: http://www.ecu.edu/dss.

Application Information:

Send to ECU Graduate School, 131 Ragsdale, Greenville, NC 27858-4353. Application available online. URL of online application: http://www.ecu.edu/gradschool/. Students are admitted in the Fall, application deadline January 1. Fee: $60.

North Carolina State University

Department of Psychology
College of Humanities and Social Sciences
640 Poe Hall, Box 7650
Raleigh, NC 27695-7650
Telephone: (919) 515-2251
Fax: (919) 515-1716
E-mail: *psych@ncsu.edu*
Web: *http://psychology.chass.ncsu.edu/*

Department Information:

1938. Department Head: Douglas J. Gillan. Number of faculty: total—full-time 26, part-time 3; women—full-time 9, part-time 1; total—minority—full-time 2.

Programs and Degrees Offered:

Listed in the following order: Program area, degree type (T if terminal Master's), number awarded 7/11–6/12. Human Factors & Ergonomics PhD (Doctor of Philosophy) 1, Lifespan Developmental Psychology PhD (Doctor of Philosophy) 3, Industrial/Organizational Psychology PhD (Doctor of Philosophy) 3, Public Interest PhD (Doctor of Philosophy) 4, School Psychology PhD (Doctor of Philosophy) 8.

APA Accreditation: School PhD (Doctor of Philosophy). Student Outcome Data Website: http://psychology.chass.ncsu.edu/pss/.php.

Student Applications/Admissions:

Student Applications

Human Factors & Ergonomics PhD (Doctor of Philosophy)— Applications 2012–2013, 41. Total applicants accepted 2012–2013, 10. Number full-time enrolled (new admits only) 2012–2013, 5. Number part-time enrolled (new admits only) 2012–2013, 0. Total enrolled 2012–2013 full-time, 19. Total enrolled 2012–2013 part-time, 10. Openings 2013–2014, 5. The median number of years required for completion of a degree in 2012–2013 were 7. The number of students enrolled full- and part-time who were dismissed or voluntarily withdrew from this program area in 2012–2013 were 0. *Lifespan Developmental Psychology PhD (Doctor of Philosophy)*—Applications 2012–2013, 40. Total applicants accepted 2012–2013, 6. Number full-time enrolled (new admits only) 2012–2013, 4. Number part-time enrolled (new admits only) 2012–2013, 0. Total enrolled 2012–2013 full-time, 18. Total enrolled 2012–2013 part-time, 2. Openings 2013–2014, 5. The median number of years required for completion of a degree in 2012–2013 were 6. The number of students enrolled full- and part-time who were dismissed or voluntarily withdrew from this program area in 2012–2013 were 1. *Industrial/Organizational Psychology PhD (Doctor of Philosophy)*—Applications 2012–2013, 86. Total applicants accepted 2012–2013, 8. Number full-time enrolled (new admits only) 2012–2013, 4. Number part-time enrolled (new admits only) 2012–2013, 0. Total enrolled 2012–2013 full-time, 18. Total enrolled 2012–2013 part-time, 11. Openings 2013–2014, 5. The median number of years required for completion of a degree in 2012–2013 were 5. The number of students enrolled full- and part-time who were dismissed or voluntarily withdrew from this program area in 2012–2013 were 0. *Public Interest PhD (Doctor of Philosophy)*—Applications 2012–2013, 35. Total applicants accepted 2012–2013,

16. Number full-time enrolled (new admits only) 2012–2013, 6. Number part-time enrolled (new admits only) 2012–2013, 0. Total enrolled 2012–2013 full-time, 14. Total enrolled 2012–2013 part-time, 11. Openings 2013–2014, 5. The median number of years required for completion of a degree in 2012–2013 were 8. The number of students enrolled full- and part-time who were dismissed or voluntarily withdrew from this program area in 2012–2013 were 1. *School Psychology PhD (Doctor of Philosophy)*—Applications 2012–2013, 56. Total applicants accepted 2012–2013, 6. Number full-time enrolled (new admits only) 2012–2013, 3. Number part-time enrolled (new admits only) 2012–2013, 0. Total enrolled 2012–2013 full-time, 11. Total enrolled 2012–2013 part-time, 5. Openings 2013–2014, 5. The median number of years required for completion of a degree in 2012–2013 were 8. The number of students enrolled full- and part-time who were dismissed or voluntarily withdrew from this program area in 2012–2013 were 0.

Scores: Entries appear in this order: required test or GPA, minimum score (if required), median score of students entering in 2012–2013. *Human Factors & Ergonomics PhD (Doctor of Philosophy):* GRE-V 150, GRE-Q 150, GRE-Analytical 4.0, overall undergraduate GPA 3.0, last 2 years GPA 3.0, psychology GPA 3.0; *Lifespan Developmental Psychology PhD (Doctor of Philosophy):* GRE-V 150, GRE-Q 150, GRE-Analytical 4, overall undergraduate GPA 3.0, last 2 years GPA 3.0, psychology GPA 3.0; *Industrial/Organizational Psychology PhD (Doctor of Philosophy):* GRE-V 150, GRE-Q 150, GRE-Analytical 4, overall undergraduate GPA 3.0, last 2 years GPA 3.0, psychology GPA 3.0; *Public Interest PhD (Doctor of Philosophy):* GRE-V 150, GRE-Q 150, GRE-Analytical 4, overall undergraduate GPA 3.0, last 2 years GPA 3.0, psychology GPA 3.0; *School Psychology PhD (Doctor of Philosophy):* GRE-V 150, GRE-Q 150, GRE-Analytical 4, overall undergraduate GPA 3.0, last 2 years GPA 3.0, psychology GPA 3.0.

Other Criteria: (importance of criteria rated low, medium, or high): GRE scores—high, research experience—high, work experience—medium, extracurricular activity—low, clinically related public service—low, GPA—high, letters of recommendation—high, interview—medium, statement of goals and objectives—high, research interests—high, undergraduate major in psychology—medium, specific undergraduate psychology courses taken—high, Psychology in the Public Interest gives greater weight to work experience and public service than do other program areas. Human Factors and Ergonomics has a special interest in math and non-psychology-science backgrounds of applicants. For additional information on admission requirements, go to http://psychology.chass.ncsu.edu/graduate/admissions.php.

Student Characteristics: The following represents characteristics of students in 2012–2013 in all graduate psychology programs in the department: Female—full-time 53, part-time 26; Male—full-time 27, part-time 13; African American/Black—full-time 7, part-time 5; Hispanic/Latino(a)—full-time 0, part-time 0; Asian/Pacific Islander—full-time 8, part-time 2; American Indian/Alaska Native—full-time 1, part-time 0; Caucasian/White—full-time 57, part-time 30; Multi-ethnic—full-time 7, part-time 2; students subject to the Americans With Disabilities Act—full-time 1, part-time 0; Unknown ethnicity—full-time 0, part-time 0; International students who hold an F-1 or J-1 Visa—full-time 5, part-time 1.

Financial Information/Assistance:

Tuition for Full-Time Study: *Doctoral:* State residents: per academic year $6,883; Nonstate residents: per academic year $18,930. Tuition is subject to change. Additional fees are assessed to students beyond the costs of tuition for the following: A required fee of $1,025.28 per semester is also assessed. See the following website for updates and changes in tuition costs: http://www.fis.ncsu.edu/cashier/tuition/.

Financial Assistance:

First-Year Students: Teaching assistantships available for first year. Average amount paid per academic year: $14,000. Average number of hours worked per week: 20. Research assistantships available for first year. Average amount paid per academic year: $14,000. Average number of hours worked per week: 20.

Advanced Students: Teaching assistantships available for advanced students. Average amount paid per academic year: $14,000. Average number of hours worked per week: 20. Research assistantships available for advanced students. Average amount paid per academic year: $14,000. Average number of hours worked per week: 20.

Additional Information: Of all students currently enrolled full time, 50% benefited from one or more of the listed financial assistance programs. Application and information available online at: http://www.ncsu.edu/grad/financial-support/.

Internships/Practica: Doctoral Degree (PhD School Psychology): For those doctoral students for whom a professional psychology internship was required in this program prior to graduation, (7) students applied for an internship in 2011–2012, with (7) students obtaining an internship. Of those students who obtained an internship, (3) were paid internships. Of those students who obtained an internship, (1) students placed in APA/CPA accredited internships, (1) students placed in internships not APA/CPA accredited, but listed with the Association of Psychology Postdoctoral and Internship Programs (APPIC), (5) students placed in internships conforming to guidelines of the Council of Directors of School Psychology Programs (CDSPP), (0) students placed in internships that were not APA/CPA accredited, APPIC or CDSPP listed. Practica and internships are required for both master's and doctoral students in the School Psychology program. These include supervised experiences in assessment, consultation, intervention, research, and professional school psychology in a wide variety of school-related settings. Students in Human Factors and Ergonomics are also expected to obtain employment for at least one summer/semester in one of the many suitable companies located in the Research Triangle area.

Housing and Day Care: On-campus housing is available. See the following website for more information: http://www.ncsu.edu/housing/. On-campus day care facilities are available. See the following website for more information: http://www.ncsu.edu/human_resources/benefits/Childcare/index.php.

Employment of Department Graduates:

Master's Degree Graduates: Of those who graduated in the academic year 2011–2012, the following categories and numbers represent the postgraduate activities and employment of master's degree graduates: Enrolled in a postdoctoral residency/fellowship (n/a), employed in independent practice (n/a), total from the above (master's) (0).

Doctoral Degree Graduates: Of those who graduated in the academic year 2011–2012, the following categories and numbers represent the postgraduate activities and employment of doctoral degree graduates: Enrolled in a psychology doctoral program (n/a), enrolled in a postdoctoral residency/fellowship (3), employed in independent practice (1), employed in an academic position at a university (1), employed in other positions at a higher education institution (3), employed in a professional position in a school system (4), employed in business or industry (2), employed in a community mental health/counseling center (1), employed in a hospital/medical center (3), still seeking employment (1), total from the above (doctoral) (19).

Additional Information:

Orientation, Objectives, and Emphasis of Department: The department trains in the scientist–practitioner model. Students are expected to become knowledgeable about both research and application within their area of study. There are five specialty areas with different emphases. Lifespan Developmental Psychology stresses a balance of conceptual, research-analytical, and application skills and encompasses social and cognitive development from infancy to old age. Human Factors and Ergonomics emphasizes the cognitive/perceptual aspects of human factors, including research on visual displays, visual/auditory spatial judgments, ergonomics for older adults and the effective information transfer for complex systems. This track has a cooperative relationship with the Ergonomics/Biomechanics Program in Industrial & Systems Engineering. The Psychology in the Public Interest program (formerly known as Human Resource Development/Community Psychology) is a problem-oriented program dealing with research and professional issues in communities and social systems. Industrial-Organizational (I-O) students may concentrate in areas such as performance appraisal, selection, training, job analysis, work motivation, organizational theory/development and the interface of technology with I-O issues. School Psychology develops behavioral scientists who apply psychological knowledge and techniques in school and family settings to help students, parents, and teachers.

Special Facilities or Resources: The department is housed primarily on two floors of a modern building. Teaching Assistants share office space; Research Assistants have space within faculty research areas. All programs have appropriate laboratory space and facilities. These include specialized lab facilities: Audition Laboratory, Cognitive-Development Laboratory, Ergonomics and Aging Laboratory, Human-Computer Interaction Laboratory, Social Development Laboratory, and Visual Performance Laboratory. Ergonomics, Public Interest, I/O, and School students may have opportunities to work in state government, industry, schools, and community agencies to gain practical and research experience. As the surrounding region continues to develop, more opportunities appear each year. Students are, however, required to maintain continuous registration and carry an adequate course load each semester. Students are permitted to enroll in courses at the University of North Carolina-Chapel Hill and at Duke University, as if the courses were offered on their home campus. Beyond basic research, statistics, and program/departmental course requirements, students have considerable flexibility in developing individually-tailored plans of study.

Information for Students With Physical Disabilities: See the following website for more information: http://dso.dasa.ncsu.edu/.

Application Information:

Application available online. URL of online application: http://www2.acs.ncsu.edu/grad/applygrad.htm. Students are admitted in the Fall, application deadline December 15. The program in School Psychology sets its deadline at December 15; deadline for all other programs is January 5. *Fee:* $75. $75 for U.S. citizens and permanent residents; $85 for international applicants. McNair Scholars, or other U.S. citizens with significant financial restrictions, may request waiver of the application fee.

North Carolina, University of, Chapel Hill

Department of Psychology
Arts and Sciences
CB #3270
Chapel Hill, NC 27599-3270
Telephone: (919) 962-4153
Fax: (919) 962-2537
E-mail: *terrigault@unc.edu*
Web: *http://psychology.unc.edu/*

Department Information:

1921. Chairperson: Donald T. Lysle. Number of faculty: total—full-time 56, part-time 5; women—full-time 31, part-time 4; total—minority—full-time 6; women minority—full-time 5.

Programs and Degrees Offered:

Listed in the following order: Program area, degree type (T if terminal Master's), number awarded 7/11–6/12. Behavioral Neuroscience PhD (Doctor of Philosophy) 3, Quantitative PhD (Doctor of Philosophy) 1, Social PhD (Doctor of Philosophy) 1, Clinical PhD (Doctor of Philosophy) 4, Cognitive PhD (Doctor of Philosophy) 4, Developmental PhD (Doctor of Philosophy) 4.

APA Accreditation: Clinical PhD (Doctor of Philosophy). Student Outcome Data Website: http://clinicalpsych.unc.edu/graduate-program/student-admissions-outcomes-and-other-data.

Student Applications/Admissions:

Student Applications

Behavioral Neuroscience PhD (Doctor of Philosophy)—Applications 2012–2013, 58. Total applicants accepted 2012–2013, 6. Number full-time enrolled (new admits only) 2012–2013, 4. Number part-time enrolled (new admits only) 2012–2013, 0. Total enrolled 2012–2013 full-time, 16. Total enrolled 2012–2013 part-time, 0. Openings 2013–2014, 4. The median number of years required for completion of a degree in 2012–2013 were 6. The number of students enrolled full- and part-time who were dismissed or voluntarily withdrew from this program area in 2012–2013 were 0. *Quantitative PhD (Doctor of Philosophy)*—Applications 2012–2013, 47. Total applicants accepted 2012–2013, 3. Number full-time enrolled (new admits only) 2012–2013, 1. Total enrolled 2012–2013 full-time, 15. Total enrolled 2012–2013 part-time, 0. Openings 2013–2014, 3. The median number of years required for completion of a degree in 2012–2013 were 5. The number of students enrolled full- and part-time who were dismissed or voluntarily withdrew from this program area in 2012–2013 were 0. *Social PhD (Doctor of Philosophy)*—Applications 2012–2013, 127. Total applicants accepted 2012–2013, 5. Number full-time enrolled (new

admits only) 2012–2013, 4. Total enrolled 2012–2013 full-time, 17. Total enrolled 2012–2013 part-time, 0. Openings 2013–2014, 4. The median number of years required for completion of a degree in 2012–2013 were 5. The number of students enrolled full- and part-time who were dismissed or voluntarily withdrew from this program area in 2012–2013 were 0. *Clinical PhD (Doctor of Philosophy)*—Applications 2012–2013, 634. Total applicants accepted 2012–2013, 13. Number full-time enrolled (new admits only) 2012–2013, 7. Number part-time enrolled (new admits only) 2012–2013, 0. Total enrolled 2012–2013 full-time, 51. Total enrolled 2012–2013 part-time, 0. Openings 2013–2014, 8. The median number of years required for completion of a degree in 2012–2013 were 6. *Cognitive PhD (Doctor of Philosophy)*—Applications 2012–2013, 55. Total applicants accepted 2012–2013, 4. Number full-time enrolled (new admits only) 2012–2013, 1. Number part-time enrolled (new admits only) 2012–2013, 0. Total enrolled 2012–2013 full-time, 14. Openings 2013–2014, 4. The median number of years required for completion of a degree in 2012–2013 were 5. The number of students enrolled full- and part-time who were dismissed or voluntarily withdrew from this program area in 2012–2013 were 0. *Developmental PhD (Doctor of Philosophy)*—Applications 2012–2013, 62. Total applicants accepted 2012–2013, 7. Number full-time enrolled (new admits only) 2012–2013, 5. Number part-time enrolled (new admits only) 2012–2013, 0. Total enrolled 2012–2013 full-time, 19. Total enrolled 2012–2013 part-time, 0. Openings 2013–2014, 4. The median number of years required for completion of a degree in 2012–2013 were 6. The number of students enrolled full- and part-time who were dismissed or voluntarily withdrew from this program area in 2012–2013 were 0.

Scores: Entries appear in this order: required test or GPA, minimum score (if required), median score of students entering in 2012–2013. *Behavioral Neuroscience PhD (Doctor of Philosophy):* GRE-V 500, 545, GRE-Q 500, 675, overall undergraduate GPA 3.0, 3.35; *Quantitative PhD (Doctor of Philosophy):* GRE-V 500, 635, GRE-Q 500, 735, overall undergraduate GPA 3.0, 3.75; *Social PhD (Doctor of Philosophy):* GRE-V 500, 705, GRE-Q 500, 750, overall undergraduate GPA 3.0, 3.88; *Clinical PhD (Doctor of Philosophy):* GRE-V 500, 650, GRE-Q 500, 750, overall undergraduate GPA 3.0, 3.76; *Cognitive PhD (Doctor of Philosophy):* GRE-V 500, 610, GRE-Q 500, 720, overall undergraduate GPA 3.0, 3.65; *Developmental PhD (Doctor of Philosophy):* GRE-V 500, 570, GRE-Q 500, 670, overall undergraduate GPA 3.0, 3.66.

Other Criteria: (importance of criteria rated low, medium, or high): GRE scores—high, research experience—high, work experience—medium, clinically related public service—medium, GPA—high, letters of recommendation—high, interview—medium, statement of goals and objectives—high, undergraduate major in psychology—medium, specific undergraduate psychology courses taken—medium. For additional information on admission requirements, go to http://psychology.unc.edu/graduate-studies/admissions-process.

Student Characteristics: The following represents characteristics of students in 2012–2013 in all graduate psychology programs in the department: Female—full-time 90, part-time 0; Male—full-time 42, part-time 0; African American/Black—full-time 11, part-time 0; Hispanic/Latino(a)—full-time 4, part-time 0; Asian/Pacific Islander—full-time 8, part-time 0; American Indian/Alaska

Native—full-time 0, part-time 0; Caucasian/White—full-time 96, part-time 0; Multi-ethnic—full-time 5, part-time 0; students subject to the Americans With Disabilities Act—full-time 0, part-time 0; Unknown ethnicity—full-time 8, part-time 0; International students who hold an F-1 or J-1 Visa—full-time 7, part-time 0.

Financial Information/Assistance:

Tuition for Full-Time Study: *Doctoral:* State residents: per academic year $7,834; Nonstate residents: per academic year $23,924. Tuition is subject to change. Additional fees are assessed to students beyond the costs of tuition for the following: student fees are currently $928 per semester, subject to legislative change. See the following website for updates and changes in tuition costs: http://finance.unc.edu/saur/student-account-services/tuition-and-fees/.

Financial Assistance:

First-Year Students: Teaching assistantships available for first year. Average amount paid per academic year: $16,500. Average number of hours worked per week: 15. Research assistantships available for first year. Average amount paid per academic year: $16,500. Average number of hours worked per week: 15. Traineeships available for first year. Average amount paid per academic year: $22,032. Fellowships and scholarships available for first year. Average amount paid per academic year: $20,000.

Advanced Students: Teaching assistantships available for advanced students. Average amount paid per academic year: $17,400. Average number of hours worked per week: 15. Research assistantships available for advanced students. Average amount paid per academic year: $20,000. Average number of hours worked per week: 15. Traineeships available for advanced students. Average amount paid per academic year: $22,032. Fellowships and scholarships available for advanced students. Average amount paid per academic year: $20,000.

Additional Information: Of all students currently enrolled full time, 95% benefited from one or more of the listed financial assistance programs.

Internships/Practica: Doctoral Degree (PhD Clinical): For those doctoral students for whom a professional psychology internship was required in this program prior to graduation, (15) students applied for an internship in 2011–2012, with (15) students obtaining an internship. Of those students who obtained an internship, (15) were paid internships. Of those students who obtained an internship, (15) students placed in APA/CPA accredited internships, (0) students placed in internships not APA/CPA accredited, but listed with the Association of Psychology Postdoctoral and Internship Programs (APPIC), (0) students placed in internships conforming to guidelines of the Council of Directors of School Psychology Programs (CDSPP), (0) students placed in internships that were not APA/CPA accredited, APPIC or CDSPP listed. Students within the doctoral program in clinical psychology engage in a wide range of clinical practicum activities beginning in the first year of doctoral study. A variety of sites are included in our practicum arrangements. One of these sites is the University of North Carolina Medical School, which includes opportunities in a number of areas including child, family, adolescent, and adults. There are also specialized opportunities at that site to work with children with developmental disabilities and college students in a university counseling setting. Students also receive training at Central Regional Hospital, a state psychiatric hospital; opportunities there range from child, adolescent, adult, and geriatric patients. Overall, Central Regional Hospital emphasizes treatment of more disturbed individuals, but opportunities are available as well for outpatient treatment. Third, students are involved in our Psychology Department Psychological Services Clinic, our in-house outpatient treatment facility. Students work with a wide variety of clients within that context, with specialized opportunities in anxiety disorders and marital therapy. Among other sites, students provide consultation to the local school system, to the Orange-Person-Chatham Mental Health Center, and a variety of other sites that are arranged on an as needed basis.

Housing and Day Care: On-campus housing is available. See the following website for more information: http://housing.unc.edu/. No on-campus day care facilities are available.

Employment of Department Graduates:

Master's Degree Graduates: Of those who graduated in the academic year 2011–2012, the following categories and numbers represent the postgraduate activities and employment of master's degree graduates: Enrolled in a postdoctoral residency/fellowship (n/a), employed in independent practice (n/a), total from the above (master's) (0).

Doctoral Degree Graduates: Of those who graduated in the academic year 2011–2012, the following categories and numbers represent the postgraduate activities and employment of doctoral degree graduates: Enrolled in a psychology doctoral program (n/a), enrolled in a postdoctoral residency/fellowship (7), employed in an academic position at a university (1), employed in an academic position at a 2-year/4-year college (3), employed in other positions at a higher education institution (1), employed in business or industry (1), employed in government agency (2), still seeking employment (1), not seeking employment (1), total from the above (doctoral) (17).

Additional Information:

Orientation, Objectives, and Emphasis of Department: Each graduate training program is designed to acquaint students with the theoretical and research content of their specialty and to train them in the research and teaching skills needed to make contributions to science and society. In addition, certain programs (for example, the clinical program) include an emphasis on the development of competence in appropriate professional skills. Faculty members maintain a balance of commitment to research, teaching and service.

Special Facilities or Resources: Affiliated clinical and research facilities are: the Psychological Services Clinic, Psychology Department; Central Regional Hospital, Butner, NC; North Carolina Memorial Hospital, Chapel Hill; Murdoch Developmental Center, Butner; Center for Developmental Science, Chapel Hill; VA Hospital, Durham; Frank Porter Graham Child Development Center, Chapel Hill; Carolina Population Center, Chapel Hill; North Carolina Highway Safety Research Center, Chapel Hill; L.L. Thurstone Psychometric Laboratory, Chapel Hill; the Positive Emotions and Psychophysiology Laboratory, Chapel Hill; the Odum Institute for Research in Social Sciences, Chapel Hill; Neurobiology Curriculum, University of North Carolina; Research Laboratories of the U.S. Environmental Protection Agency, Research Triangle Park; and TEACCH Division, North Carolina Memorial Hospital, specializing in the treatment and education of victims of autism and related disorders of communication.

Information for Students With Physical Disabilities: See the following website for more information: http://accessibility.unc.edu/.

Application Information:
Application available online. URL of online application: https://app.applyyourself.com/?id=unc-ch. Students are admitted in the Fall, application deadline December 11. *Fee:* $78.

North Carolina, University of, Charlotte
Department of Psychology
Liberal Arts and Sciences
9201 University City Boulevard
Charlotte, NC 28223-0001
Telephone: (704) 687-1315
Fax: (704) 687-1317
E-mail: *rtedesch@uncc.edu*
Web: *http://psych.uncc.edu/*

Department Information:
1960. Graduate Coordinator: Dr. Richard Tedeschi. Number of faculty: total—full-time 34, part-time 10; women—full-time 18, part-time 4; total—minority—full-time 2; women minority—full-time 2.

Programs and Degrees Offered:
Listed in the following order: Program area, degree type (T if terminal Master's), number awarded 7/11–6/12. Psychology MA/MS (Master of Arts/Science) (T) 4, Industrial/Organizational MA/MS (Master of Arts/Science) (T) 6, Organizational Science PhD (Doctor of Philosophy) 6, Health Psychology PhD (Doctor of Philosophy) 2.

Student Applications/Admissions:
Student Applications
Psychology MA/MS (Master of Arts/Science)—Applications 2012–2013, 130. Total applicants accepted 2012–2013, 8. Number full-time enrolled (new admits only) 2012–2013, 5. Number part-time enrolled (new admits only) 2012–2013, 0. Total enrolled 2012–2013 full-time, 15. Total enrolled 2012–2013 part-time, 2. Openings 2013–2014, 5. The median number of years required for completion of a degree in 2012–2013 were 2. The number of students enrolled full- and part-time who were dismissed or voluntarily withdrew from this program area in 2012–2013 were 1. *Industrial/Organizational MA/MS (Master of Arts/Science)*—Applications 2012–2013, 0. Total applicants accepted 2012–2013, 0. Number full-time enrolled (new admits only) 2012–2013, 0. Number part-time enrolled (new admits only) 2012–2013, 0. The median number of years required for completion of a degree in 2012–2013 were 2. The number of students enrolled full- and part-time who were dismissed or voluntarily withdrew from this program area in 2012–2013 were 0. *Organizational Science PhD (Doctor of Philosophy)*—Applications 2012–2013, 70. Total applicants accepted 2012–2013, 7. Number full-time enrolled (new admits only) 2012–2013, 5. Total enrolled 2012–2013 full-time, 20.

Total enrolled 2012–2013 part-time, 2. Openings 2013–2014, 5. The median number of years required for completion of a degree in 2012–2013 were 4. The number of students enrolled full- and part-time who were dismissed or voluntarily withdrew from this program area in 2012–2013 were 0. *Health Psychology PhD (Doctor of Philosophy)*—Applications 2012–2013, 88. Total applicants accepted 2012–2013, 12. Number full-time enrolled (new admits only) 2012–2013, 8. Number part-time enrolled (new admits only) 2012–2013, 0. Total enrolled 2012–2013 full-time, 28. Total enrolled 2012–2013 part-time, 5. Openings 2013–2014, 10. The median number of years required for completion of a degree in 2012–2013 were 5. The number of students enrolled full- and part-time who were dismissed or voluntarily withdrew from this program area in 2012–2013 were 0.

Scores: Entries appear in this order: required test or GPA, minimum score (if required), median score of students entering in 2012–2013. *Psychology MA/MS (Master of Arts/Science):* GRE-V 150, 159, GRE-Q 150, 155, overall undergraduate GPA 3.0, 3.4, psychology GPA 3.0, 3.4; *Industrial/Organizational MA/MS (Master of Arts/Science):* GRE-V no minimum stated, 550, GRE-Q no minimum stated, 655, overall undergraduate GPA 3.0, 3.70; *Organizational Science PhD (Doctor of Philosophy):* GRE-V 500, 630, GRE-Q 500, 670, GRE-Analytical no minimum stated, overall undergraduate GPA 3.0; *Health Psychology PhD (Doctor of Philosophy):* GRE-V 500, 576, GRE-Q 500, 670, GRE-Analytical 4.0, 4.0, overall undergraduate GPA 3.0, 3.5, psychology GPA 3.0, 3.5.

Other Criteria: (importance of criteria rated low, medium, or high): GRE scores—high, research experience—high, work experience—medium, extracurricular activity—low, clinically related public service—medium, GPA—high, letters of recommendation—high, interview—medium, statement of goals and objectives—high, undergraduate major in psychology—medium, specific undergraduate psychology courses taken—medium, Health Psychology: Clinical work important for clinical emphasis; community work important for community emphasis of the Health Psychology Program. Industrial/Organizational: GRE Scores-high, Research Experience-medium, Work Experience-medium, Extracurricular Activity-low, Clinically Related Public Service-low, GPA-high, Letters of Recommendation-high, Interview-none, Statement of Goals and Objectives-high, Undergraduate major in psychology-medium, Specific undergraduate psychology courses taken-medium, other-none. Organizational Science: GRE Scores-high, Research Experience-high, Work Experience-low, Extracurricular Activity-low, Clinically Related Public Service-none, GPA-high, Letters of Recommendation-high, Interview-none, Statement of Goals and Objectives-high, Undergraduate major in psychology-none, Specific undergraduate psychology courses taken-none, other-interest in interdisciplinary education.

Student Characteristics: The following represents characteristics of students in 2012–2013 in all graduate psychology programs in the department: Female—full-time 51, part-time 13; Male—full-time 15, part-time 2; African American/Black—full-time 5, part-time 0; Hispanic/Latino(a)—full-time 1, part-time 0; Asian/Pacific Islander—full-time 3, part-time 0; American Indian/Alaska Native—full-time 0, part-time 0; Caucasian/White—full-time 57, part-time 15; Multi-ethnic—full-time 0, part-time 0; students subject to the Americans With Disabilities Act—full-time 0, part-

time 0; Unknown ethnicity—full-time 0, part-time 0; International students who hold an F-1 or J-1 Visa—full-time 1, part-time 0.

Financial Information/Assistance:

Tuition for Full-Time Study: *Master's:* State residents: per academic year $6,348; Nonstate residents: per academic year $18,636. *Doctoral:* State residents: per academic year $6,348; Nonstate residents: per academic year $18,636. Tuition is subject to change. See the following website for updates and changes in tuition costs: http://finance.uncc.edu/controllers-office/student-accounts/tuition-and-fees.

Financial Assistance:

First-Year Students: Teaching assistantships available for first year. Average amount paid per academic year: $9,000. Average number of hours worked per week: 20. Apply by March 1. Research assistantships available for first year. Average amount paid per academic year: $8,500. Average number of hours worked per week: 20. Apply by March 1. Fellowships and scholarships available for first year. Average amount paid per academic year: $2,150. Apply by March 1.

Advanced Students: Teaching assistantships available for advanced students. Average amount paid per academic year: $9,000. Average number of hours worked per week: 20. Research assistantships available for advanced students. Average amount paid per academic year: $8,500. Average number of hours worked per week: 20.

Additional Information: Of all students currently enrolled full time, 60% benefited from one or more of the listed financial assistance programs. Application and information available online at: http://finaid.uncc.edu/graduate-student-information.

Internships/Practica: Doctoral Degree (PhD Health Psychology): For those doctoral students for whom a professional psychology internship was required in this program prior to graduation, (4) students applied for an internship in 2011–2012, with (4) students obtaining an internship. Of those students who obtained an internship, (2) were paid internships. Of those students who obtained an internship, (3) students placed in APA/CPA accredited internships, (1) students placed in internships not APA/CPA accredited, but listed with the Association of Psychology Postdoctoral and Internship Programs (APPIC), (0) students placed in internships conforming to guidelines of the Council of Directors of School Psychology Programs (CDSPP), (0) students placed in internships that were not APA/CPA accredited, APPIC or CDSPP listed. Master's Degree (MA/MS Psychology): An internship experience, such as a final research project or "capstone" experience is required of graduates. Master's Degree (MA/MS Industrial/Organizational): An internship experience, such as a final research project or "capstone" experience is required of graduates. Psychology: Students are required to enroll in 2 semesters of practicum, working 22 hrs/week in community agencies such as mental health centers, prisons, hospitals, and non-profit organizations. Industrial/Organizational: An extensive practicum component utilizes the Charlotte area as the setting for applied experience. All students must complete 3 hours of projects in I/O Psychology and they are strongly encouraged to take 6 hours.

Housing and Day Care: On-campus housing is available. See the following website for more information: http://housing.uncc.edu/. No on-campus day care facilities are available.

Employment of Department Graduates:

Master's Degree Graduates: Of those who graduated in the academic year 2011–2012, the following categories and numbers represent the postgraduate activities and employment of master's degree graduates: Enrolled in a postdoctoral residency/fellowship (n/a), employed in independent practice (n/a), employed in other positions at a higher education institution (1), employed in business or industry (5), total from the above (master's) (6).

Doctoral Degree Graduates: Of those who graduated in the academic year 2011–2012, the following categories and numbers represent the postgraduate activities and employment of doctoral degree graduates: Enrolled in a psychology doctoral program (n/a), enrolled in a postdoctoral residency/fellowship (1), employed in independent practice (2), total from the above (doctoral) (3).

Additional Information:

Orientation, Objectives, and Emphasis of Department: The objective of the master's degree program is to train psychologists in the knowledge and skills necessary to address problems encountered in industry, organizations, and the community. The program has an applied emphasis. Graduates of the program are eligible to apply for licensing in North Carolina as psychological associates. Although our goals emphasize application of psychological principles in organizational, clinical, and community settings, the rigorous program allows students to prepare themselves well for further education in psychology.

Special Facilities or Resources: The psychology department is housed in a modern classroom office building that provides offices, demonstration rooms, a workshop, and specialty laboratories for research. Facilities include a computerized laboratory with 37 microcomputers; many small testing, training, and interview rooms with one-way mirrors for direct observation; audio intercommunications; and closed circuit television. There is extensive audio and video equipment available as well as a research trailer, tachistoscopes, programming and timing equipment, and microcomputers. The psychometric laboratory contains an extensive inventory of current tests of intelligence, personality, and interest, as well as calculators and microcomputers for testing, test score evaluation and data analysis. A well-equipped physiological laboratory is available for work including human electrophysiology.

Information for Students With Physical Disabilities: See the following website for more information: http://ds.uncc.edu/.

Application Information:

Send to Graduate Admissions, UNC-Charlotte, 9201 University City Blvd., Charlotte, NC 28223. Application available online. URL of online application: https://app.applyyourself.com/?id=uncc-cob. Students are admitted in the Fall, application deadline December 1. January 15 is the deadline for Industrial/Organizational program. March 1 is the deadline for Clinical/Community MA program. December 1 is the deadline for Health PhD program. *Fee:* $35.

North Carolina, University of, Wilmington
Psychology
Arts and Sciences
601 South College Road
Wilmington, NC 28403-5612
Telephone: (910) 962-3370
Fax: (910) 962-7010
E-mail: *myersb@uncw.edu*
Web: *http://www.uncw.edu/psy/*

Department Information:
1972. Chairperson: Richard Ogle, PhD. Number of faculty: total—full-time 34; women—full-time 19; total—minority—full-time 4; women minority—full-time 3; faculty subject to the Americans With Disabilities Act 1.

Programs and Degrees Offered:
Listed in the following order: Program area, degree type (T if terminal Master's), number awarded 7/11–6/12. General Psychology MA/MS (Master of Arts/Science) (T) 14, Applied Behavior Analysis MA/MS (Master of Arts/Science) (T) 2, Substance Abuse Treatment MA/MS (Master of Arts/Science) (T) 3.

Student Applications/Admissions:
Student Applications
General Psychology MA/MS (Master of Arts/Science)—Applications 2012–2013, 73. Total applicants accepted 2012–2013, 24. Number full-time enrolled (new admits only) 2012–2013, 20. Number part-time enrolled (new admits only) 2012–2013, 0. Total enrolled 2012–2013 full-time, 31. Total enrolled 2012–2013 part-time, 2. Openings 2013–2014, 18. The median number of years required for completion of a degree in 2012–2013 were 2. The number of students enrolled full- and part-time who were dismissed or voluntarily withdrew from this program area in 2012–2013 were 0. *Applied Behavior Analysis MA/MS (Master of Arts/Science)*—Applications 2012–2013, 51. Total applicants accepted 2012–2013, 10. Number full-time enrolled (new admits only) 2012–2013, 6. Number part-time enrolled (new admits only) 2012–2013, 0. Total enrolled 2012–2013 full-time, 18. Total enrolled 2012–2013 part-time, 0. Openings 2013–2014, 8. The median number of years required for completion of a degree in 2012–2013 were 2. The number of students enrolled full- and part-time who were dismissed or voluntarily withdrew from this program area in 2012–2013 were 0. *Substance Abuse Treatment MA/MS (Master of Arts/Science)*—Applications 2012–2013, 26. Total applicants accepted 2012–2013, 8. Number full-time enrolled (new admits only) 2012–2013, 6. Number part-time enrolled (new admits only) 2012–2013, 0. Total enrolled 2012–2013 full-time, 17. Total enrolled 2012–2013 part-time, 1. Openings 2013–2014, 6. The median number of years required for completion of a degree in 2012–2013 were 2. The number of students enrolled full- and part-time who were dismissed or voluntarily withdrew from this program area in 2012–2013 were 2.
Scores: Entries appear in this order: required test or GPA, minimum score (if required), median score of students entering in 2012–2013. *General Psychology MA/MS (Master of Arts/Science)*: GRE-V no minimum stated, 154, GRE-Q no minimum stated, 150, GRE-Analytical no minimum stated, 4.5,

overall undergraduate GPA no minimum stated, last 2 years GPA no minimum stated, 3.62; *Applied Behavior Analysis MA/MS (Master of Arts/Science)*: GRE-V no minimum stated, 153, GRE-Q no minimum stated, 149, GRE-Analytical no minimum stated, 4.5, overall undergraduate GPA no minimum stated, last 2 years GPA no minimum stated, 3.68; *Substance Abuse Treatment MA/MS (Master of Arts/Science)*: GRE-V no minimum stated, 153, GRE-Q no minimum stated, 149, GRE-Analytical no minimum stated, 4, overall undergraduate GPA no minimum stated, last 2 years GPA no minimum stated, 3.62.
Other Criteria: (importance of criteria rated low, medium, or high): GRE scores—high, research experience—high, work experience—low, extracurricular activity—low, clinically related public service—medium, GPA—high, letters of recommendation—high, interview—high, statement of goals and objectives—high, undergraduate major in psychology—medium, specific undergraduate psychology courses taken—high, In the Substance Abuse Treatment Psychology concentration, clinically related public service may be given more weight, since this concentration emphasizes the development of clinical as well as research skills. In the Applied Behavior Analysis concentration, previous experience—volunteer or paid— with people with disabilities is very important. Coursework in learning and principles of behavior change are also highly desirable. For additional information on admission requirements, go to http://www.uncw.edu/psy/grad/grad-application.html.

Student Characteristics: The following represents characteristics of students in 2012–2013 in all graduate psychology programs in the department: Female—full-time 55, part-time 1; Male—full-time 10, part-time 2; African American/Black—full-time 1, part-time 0; Hispanic/Latino(a)—full-time 2, part-time 0; Asian/Pacific Islander—full-time 1, part-time 0; American Indian/Alaska Native—full-time 1, part-time 0; Caucasian/White—full-time 60, part-time 3; Multi-ethnic—full-time 0, part-time 0; students subject to the Americans With Disabilities Act—full-time 0, part-time 0; Unknown ethnicity—full-time 0, part-time 0; International students who hold an F-1 or J-1 Visa—full-time 1, part-time 0.

Financial Information/Assistance:
Tuition for Full-Time Study: *Master's:* State residents: per academic year $6,335; Nonstate residents: per academic year $18,237. Tuition is subject to change. See the following website for updates and changes in tuition costs: http://www.uncw.edu/studentaccounts/tuition_fees.html.

Financial Assistance:
First-Year Students: Teaching assistantships available for first year. Average amount paid per academic year: $11,000. Average number of hours worked per week: 20. Apply by January 15. Research assistantships available for first year. Average amount paid per academic year: $11,000. Average number of hours worked per week: 20. Apply by January 15. Traineeships available for first year. Apply by January 15.
Advanced Students: Teaching assistantships available for advanced students. Average amount paid per academic year: $11,000. Average number of hours worked per week: 20. Apply by January 15. Research assistantships available for advanced students. Average amount paid per academic year: $11,000. Average number of hours worked per week: 20. Apply by January

15. Fellowships and scholarships available for advanced students. Average number of hours worked per week: 0.

Additional Information: Of all students currently enrolled full time, 75% benefited from one or more of the listed financial assistance programs. Application and information available online at: http://www.uncw.edu/psy/grad/grad-financial.html.

Internships/Practica: Master's Degree (MA/MS Applied Behavior Analysis): An internship experience, such as a final research project or "capstone" experience is required of graduates. Master's Degree (MA/MS Substance Abuse Treatment): An internship experience, such as a final research project or "capstone" experience is required of graduates. In the Substance Abuse Treatment Psychology concentration and the Applied Behavior Analysis concentration, students are prepared for work with dual diagnosis clients or with developmentally disabled clients through the completion of a required practicum and internship. The required internship and practicum consist of at least 1500 hours total of supervised experience working with substance abuse, autism, mental retardation and other psychological and behavioral problems. Training sites include: community mental health centers, correctional institutions, university counseling centers, inpatient and outpatient substance abuse treatment centers and residential centers for autistic and mentally retarded individuals.

Housing and Day Care: On-campus housing is available. See the following website for more information: http://www.uncw.edu/stuaff/housing/. No on-campus day care facilities are available.

Employment of Department Graduates:

Master's Degree Graduates: Of those who graduated in the academic year 2011–2012, the following categories and numbers represent the postgraduate activities and employment of master's degree graduates: Enrolled in a psychology doctoral program (8), enrolled in a postdoctoral residency/fellowship (n/a), employed in independent practice (n/a), employed in other positions at a higher education institution (1), employed in business or industry (3), employed in government agency (1), employed in a community mental health/counseling center (5), other employment position (1), total from the above (master's) (19).

Doctoral Degree Graduates: Of those who graduated in the academic year 2011–2012, the following categories and numbers represent the postgraduate activities and employment of doctoral degree graduates: Enrolled in a psychology doctoral program (n/a), total from the above (doctoral) (0).

Additional Information:

Orientation, Objectives, and Emphasis of Department: The department is committed to fostering an understanding of psychological research and practice and emphasizes the importance of faculty as student mentors. Research methodology and application are emphasized for all students regardless of concentration. Students in the General Psychology concentration are prepared to continue to the PhD in a variety of content areas. Students completing the clinical concentration in Substance Abuse Treatment are prepared to work with dual diagnosis clients in mental health clinics and other public service agencies. The clinical Applied Behavior Analysis concentration prepares students for work primarily with autistic and mentally retarded individuals.

The SATP and ABA graduates meet all academic requirements to apply for North Carolina state licensure as a Psychological Associate and either North Carolina State certification as a Licensed Clinical Addictions Specialist (SATP concentration) or National Board Certification as a Behavior Analyst (BCBA concentration).

Special Facilities or Resources: Special facilities or resources include research laboratories (behavioral pharmacology, human, and animal). All students have access to word processing software, SAS, and SPSS on the university computer system. The Psychology Department occupies a new 80,000 square foot building with research laboratories for 32 faculty and their students.

Information for Students With Physical Disabilities: See the following website for more information: http://www.uncw.edu/disability/.

Application Information:
Send to Graduate School, University of North Carolina Wilmington, 601 South College Road, Wilmington, NC 28403-5955. Application available online. URL of online application: http://www.uncw.edu/gradschool/admissions.html. Students are admitted in the Fall, application deadline January 15. *Fee:* $60. Fee waived for McNair Scholars and Active Duty Military.

Wake Forest University
Department of Psychology
Arts & Sciences
P.O. Box 7778
Winston-Salem, NC 27109
Telephone: (336) 758-5424
Fax: (336) 758-4733
E-mail: FurrRM@wfu.edu
Web: http://college.wfu.edu/psychology/

Department Information:
1958. Chairperson: Dale Dagenbach. Number of faculty: total—full-time 21, part-time 7; women—full-time 7, part-time 4; total—minority—full-time 3, part-time 1; women minority—full-time 1, part-time 1.

Programs and Degrees Offered:
Listed in the following order: Program area, degree type (T if terminal Master's), number awarded 7/11–6/12. General Psychology MA/MS (Master of Arts/Science) (T) 9.

Student Applications/Admissions:
Student Applications
General Psychology MA/MS (Master of Arts/Science)—Applications 2012–2013, 149. Total applicants accepted 2012–2013, 16. Number full-time enrolled (new admits only) 2012–2013, 16. Number part-time enrolled (new admits only) 2012–2013, 0. Total enrolled 2012–2013 full-time, 29. Total enrolled 2012–2013 part-time, 0. Openings 2013–2014, 13. The median number of years required for completion of a degree in 2012–2013 were 2. The number of students enrolled full- and part-time who were dismissed or voluntarily withdrew from this program area in 2012–2013 were 0.

Scores: Entries appear in this order: required test or GPA, minimum score (if required), median score of students entering in 2012–2013. *General Psychology MA/MS (Master of Arts/Science):* GRE-V no minimum stated, 161, GRE-Q no minimum stated, 156, GRE-Analytical no minimum stated, overall undergraduate GPA no minimum stated, 3.60, last 2 years GPA no minimum stated, psychology GPA no minimum stated.

Other Criteria: (importance of criteria rated low, medium, or high): GRE scores—medium, research experience—high, GPA—high, letters of recommendation—high, statement of goals and objectives—medium, undergraduate major in psychology—low, specific undergraduate psychology courses taken—medium. For additional information on admission requirements, go to http://college.wfu.edu/psychology/graduate-program/.

Student Characteristics: The following represents characteristics of students in 2012–2013 in all graduate psychology programs in the department: Female—full-time 18, part-time 0; Male—full-time 11, part-time 0; African American/Black—full-time 1, part-time 0; Hispanic/Latino(a)—full-time 0, part-time 0; Asian/Pacific Islander—full-time 0, part-time 0; American Indian/Alaska Native—full-time 0, part-time 0; Caucasian/White—full-time 22, part-time 0; Multi-ethnic—full-time 6, part-time 0; students subject to the Americans With Disabilities Act—full-time 0, part-time 0; Unknown ethnicity—full-time 0, part-time 0; International students who hold an F-1 or J-1 Visa—full-time 0, part-time 0.

Financial Information/Assistance:

Tuition for Full-Time Study: *Master's:* State residents: per academic year $33,174, $1,181 per credit hour; Nonstate residents: per academic year $33,174, $1,181 per credit hour. Tuition is subject to change. See the following website for updates and changes in tuition costs: http://graduate.wfu.edu/admissions/costofstudy.html.

Financial Assistance:

First-Year Students: Teaching assistantships available for first year. Average amount paid per academic year: $9,000. Average number of hours worked per week: 15. Apply by January 15. Research assistantships available for first year. Average amount paid per academic year: $9,000. Average number of hours worked per week: 15. Apply by January 15. Fellowships and scholarships available for first year.

Advanced Students: Teaching assistantships available for advanced students. Average amount paid per academic year: $9,000. Average number of hours worked per week: 15. Apply by January 15. Research assistantships available for advanced students. Average amount paid per academic year: $9,000. Average number of hours worked per week: 15. Apply by January 15. Fellowships and scholarships available for advanced students.

Additional Information: Of all students currently enrolled full time, 100% benefited from one or more of the listed financial assistance programs. Application and information available online at: http://graduate.wfu.edu/admissions/costofstudy.html.

Internships/Practica: Master's Degree (MA/MS General Psychology): An internship experience, such as a final research project or "capstone" experience is required of graduates.

Housing and Day Care: No on-campus housing is available. No on-campus day care facilities are available.

Employment of Department Graduates:

Master's Degree Graduates: Of those who graduated in the academic year 2011–2012, the following categories and numbers represent the postgraduate activities and employment of master's degree graduates: Enrolled in a psychology doctoral program (4), enrolled in a postdoctoral residency/fellowship (n/a), employed in independent practice (n/a), employed in other positions at a higher education institution (1), do not know (4), total from the above (master's) (9).

Doctoral Degree Graduates: Of those who graduated in the academic year 2011–2012, the following categories and numbers represent the postgraduate activities and employment of doctoral degree graduates: Enrolled in a psychology doctoral program (n/a), total from the above (doctoral) (0).

Additional Information:

Orientation, Objectives, and Emphasis of Department: The department aims to provide rigorous master's level training, with an emphasis on mastery of theory, research methodology, and content in the basic areas of psychology. This is a general, research-oriented MA program for capable students, most of whom will continue to the PhD.

Special Facilities or Resources: The Department of Psychology occupies a beautiful and spacious building that is equipped with state-of-the-art teaching and laboratory facilities. Learning resources include in-class multimedia instruction equipment, departmental mini- and microcomputers, departmental and university libraries, and information technology centers. Ample research space is available, including social, developmental, cognitive, perception, physiological, and animal behavior laboratories. Office space is available for graduate students. The department has links with the Wake Forest University School of Medicine (e.g., Neuroscience) which can provide opportunities for students. All students work closely with individual faculty on research during both years (2:1 student/faculty ratio). Wake Forest University offers the academic and technological resources, facilities, and Division I athletic programs, music, theater, and art associated with a larger university, with the individual attention that a smaller university can provide.

Information for Students With Physical Disabilities: See the following website for more information: http://lac.wfu.edu/disability-services/.

Application Information:
Send to Dean of the Graduate School, Wake Forest University, 1834 Wake Forest Road, Room 6, Reynolda Hall, P.O. Box 7487 Reynolda Station, Winston-Salem, NC 27109-7487. Application available online. URL of online application: http://graduate.wfu.edu/admissions/. Students are admitted in the Fall, application deadline January 15. *Fee:* $75. Upon request to the Graduate School, application fee can be waived for reasons of financial hardship or by participation in some programs.

Western Carolina University (2012 data)

Department of Psychology
College of Education and Allied Professions
91 Killian Building Lane
Cullowhee, NC 28723
Telephone: (828) 227-7361
Fax: (828) 227-7005
E-mail: *psychology@wcu.edu*
Web: *http://www.wcu.edu/3064.asp*

Department Information:

1930. Department Head: David M. McCord, PhD. Number of faculty: total—full-time 21, part-time 4; women—full-time 12, part-time 1; total—minority—full-time 2; women minority—full-time 1; faculty subject to the Americans With Disabilities Act 1.

Programs and Degrees Offered:

Listed in the following order: Program area, degree type (T if terminal Master's), number awarded 7/11–6/12. Clinical Psychology MA/MS (Master of Arts/Science) (T) 8, General-Experimental Psychology MA/MS (Master of Arts/Science) (T) 3, Specialist in School Psychology Other 6.

Student Applications/Admissions:

Student Applications

Clinical Psychology MA/MS (Master of Arts/Science)—Applications 2012–2013, 50. Total applicants accepted 2012–2013, 8. Number full-time enrolled (new admits only) 2012–2013, 8. Number part-time enrolled (new admits only) 2012–2013, 0. Total enrolled 2012–2013 full-time, 15. Total enrolled 2012–2013 part-time, 0. Openings 2013–2014, 9. The median number of years required for completion of a degree in 2012–2013 were 2. The number of students enrolled full- and part-time who were dismissed or voluntarily withdrew from this program area in 2012–2013 were 1. *General-Experimental Psychology MA/MS (Master of Arts/Science)*—Applications 2012–2013, 8. Total applicants accepted 2012–2013, 3. Number full-time enrolled (new admits only) 2012–2013, 3. Number part-time enrolled (new admits only) 2012–2013, 0. Total enrolled 2012–2013 full-time, 6. Total enrolled 2012–2013 part-time, 0. Openings 2013–2014, 4. The median number of years required for completion of a degree in 2012–2013 were 2. The number of students enrolled full- and part-time who were dismissed or voluntarily withdrew from this program area in 2012–2013 were 0. *Specialist in School Psychology Other*—Applications 2012–2013, 25. Total applicants accepted 2012–2013, 6. Number full-time enrolled (new admits only) 2012–2013, 6. Number part-time enrolled (new admits only) 2012–2013, 0. Total enrolled 2012–2013 full-time, 15. Total enrolled 2012–2013 part-time, 0. Openings 2013–2014, 9. The median number of years required for completion of a degree in 2012–2013 were 3. The number of students enrolled full- and part-time who were dismissed or voluntarily withdrew from this program area in 2012–2013 were 2.

Scores: Entries appear in this order: required test or GPA, minimum score (if required), median score of students entering in 2012–2013. *Clinical Psychology MA/MS (Master of Arts/ Science):* GRE-V no minimum stated, GRE-Q no minimum stated, GRE-Analytical no minimum stated, last 2 years GPA 3.0; *General-Experimental Psychology MA/MS (Master of Arts/*

Science): GRE-V no minimum stated, GRE-Q no minimum stated, GRE-Analytical no minimum stated, overall undergraduate GPA no minimum stated, last 2 years GPA 3.0; *Specialist in School Psychology Other:* GRE-V no minimum stated, GRE-Q no minimum stated, GRE-Analytical no minimum stated, overall undergraduate GPA no minimum stated, last 2 years GPA 3.0.

Other Criteria: (importance of criteria rated low, medium, or high): GRE scores—high, research experience—high, work experience—medium, extracurricular activity—medium, clinically related public service—medium, GPA—high, letters of recommendation—high, interview—high, statement of goals and objectives—medium, undergraduate major in psychology—high, specific undergraduate psychology courses taken—medium. For additional information on admission requirements, go to http://www.wcu.edu/6839.asp.

Student Characteristics: The following represents characteristics of students in 2012–2013 in all graduate psychology programs in the department: Female—full-time 0, part-time 0; Male—full-time 0, part-time 0; African American/Black—full-time 0, part-time 0; Hispanic/Latino(a)—full-time 0, part-time 0; Asian/Pacific Islander—full-time 2, part-time 0; American Indian/Alaska Native—full-time 0, part-time 0; Caucasian/White—full-time 33, part-time 0; Multi-ethnic—full-time 0, part-time 0; students subject to the Americans With Disabilities Act—full-time 0, part-time 0; Unknown ethnicity—full-time 0, part-time 0; International students who hold an F-1 or J-1 Visa—full-time 1, part-time 0.

Financial Information/Assistance:

Tuition for Full-Time Study: *Master's:* State residents: per academic year $7,088; Nonstate residents: per academic year $16,673. Tuition is subject to change. See the following website for updates and changes in tuition costs: http://www.wcu.edu/13093.asp.

Financial Assistance:

First-Year Students: No information provided.

Advanced Students: No information provided.

Additional Information: Of all students currently enrolled full time, 90% benefited from one or more of the listed financial assistance programs. Application and information available online at: http://www.wcu.edu/253.asp.

Internships/Practica: Master's Degree (MA/MS Clinical Psychology): An internship experience, such as a final research project or "capstone" experience is required of graduates. Master's Degree (MA/MS General-Experimental Psychology): An internship experience, such as a final research project or "capstone" experience is required of graduates. School psychology students complete practicum and internship requirements in public schools. Clinical psychology students may choose from a variety of practicum sites, including the university counseling center, the Asheville VA Hospital, Jackson Psychological Services (outpatient), Skyland Care Center (geriatric/Alzheimer's), and various Asheville-area service provider settings.

Housing and Day Care: On-campus housing is available. See the following website for more information: http://www.wcu.edu/152. asp. On-campus day care facilities are available. See the following website for more information: http://www.wcu.edu/7252.asp.

Employment of Department Graduates:

Master's Degree Graduates: Of those who graduated in the academic year 2011–2012, the following categories and numbers represent the postgraduate activities and employment of master's degree graduates: Enrolled in a psychology doctoral program (5), enrolled in a postdoctoral residency/fellowship (n/a), employed in independent practice (n/a), employed in an academic position at a university (1), employed in a professional position in a school system (5), employed in a community mental health/counseling center (2), total from the above (master's) (13).

Doctoral Degree Graduates: Of those who graduated in the academic year 2011–2012, the following categories and numbers represent the postgraduate activities and employment of doctoral degree graduates: Enrolled in a psychology doctoral program (n/a), total from the above (doctoral) (0).

Additional Information:

Orientation, Objectives, and Emphasis of Department: The Department of Psychology provides the state, region, and university with a center of scholarship in the psychological sciences. The most important expression of this scholarship occurs through (1) effective teaching in the undergraduate and graduate degree programs in psychology, (2) service courses for programs in education and other areas of study, and (3) general education courses open to all undergraduates.

Special Facilities or Resources: The department is very research-oriented, with ample laboratory space, computer facilities, a new Tobii eye tracking device, and very accessible faculty. All incoming clinical and general-experimental students are paired with a research advisor prior to arrival, with the goal of a project in data collection by October. All students are expected to complete at least one or two research projects in addition to their own master's thesis.

Information for Students With Physical Disabilities: See the following website for more information: http://www.wcu.edu/12789.asp.

Application Information:

Send to Graduate School Western Carolina University Cullowhee, NC 28723. Application available online. URL of online application: http://www.wcu.edu/43.asp. Students are admitted in the Fall, application deadline March 1.

North Dakota State University
Department of Psychology
Science and Mathematics
232 Minard Hall
Fargo, ND 58105
Telephone: (701) 231-8622
Fax: (701) 231-8426
E-mail: *NDSU.psych@ndsu.edu*
Web: *http://www.ndsu.edu/psychology/*

Department Information:
1965. Chairperson: James Council. Number of faculty: total—full-time 22, part-time 6; women—full-time 6, part-time 4.

Programs and Degrees Offered:
Listed in the following order: Program area, degree type (T if terminal Master's), number awarded 7/11–6/12. Cognitive and Visual Neuroscience PhD (Doctor of Philosophy) 1, Health/Social Psychology PhD (Doctor of Philosophy) 3, Psychological Clinical Science PhD (Doctor of Philosophy) 0.

Student Applications/Admissions:
Student Applications
Cognitive and Visual Neuroscience PhD (Doctor of Philosophy)—Applications 2012–2013, 15. Total applicants accepted 2012–2013, 3. Number full-time enrolled (new admits only) 2012–2013, 2. Total enrolled 2012–2013 full-time, 6. Openings 2013–2014, 3. The median number of years required for completion of a degree in 2012–2013 were 4. The number of students enrolled full- and part-time who were dismissed or voluntarily withdrew from this program area in 2012–2013 were 0. *Health/Social Psychology PhD (Doctor of Philosophy)*—Applications 2012–2013, 26. Total applicants accepted 2012–2013, 3. Number full-time enrolled (new admits only) 2012–2013, 2. Total enrolled 2012–2013 full-time, 7. Total enrolled 2012–2013 part-time, 1. Openings 2013–2014, 2. The median number of years required for completion of a degree in 2012–2013 were 4. The number of students enrolled full- and part-time who were dismissed or voluntarily withdrew from this program area in 2012–2013 were 1. *Psychological Clinical Science PhD (Doctor of Philosophy)*—Applications 2012–2013, 20. Total applicants accepted 2012–2013, 7. Number full-time enrolled (new admits only) 2012–2013, 3. Total enrolled 2012–2013 full-time, 5. Openings 2013–2014, 4. The number of students enrolled full- and part-time who were dismissed or voluntarily withdrew from this program area in 2012–2013 were 0.
Scores: Entries appear in this order: required test or GPA, minimum score (if required), median score of students entering in 2012–2013. *Psychological Clinical Science PhD (Doctor of Philosophy)*: GRE-V no minimum stated, GRE-Q no minimum stated, overall undergraduate GPA 3.0.
Other Criteria: (importance of criteria rated low, medium, or high): GRE scores—high, research experience—high, extracurricular activity—low, GPA—high, letters of recommendation—high, statement of goals and objectives—high, under-graduate major in psychology—medium, specific undergraduate psychology courses taken—medium. For additional information on admission requirements, go to http://www.ndsu.edu/psychology/graduate_programs/application_procedures/.

Student Characteristics: The following represents characteristics of students in 2012–2013 in all graduate psychology programs in the department: Female—full-time 8, part-time 1; Male—full-time 13, part-time 1; African American/Black—full-time 0, part-time 0; Hispanic/Latino(a)—full-time 2, part-time 0; Asian/Pacific Islander—full-time 4, part-time 0; American Indian/Alaska Native—full-time 0, part-time 0; Caucasian/White—full-time 15, part-time 2; Multi-ethnic—full-time 0, part-time 0; students subject to the Americans With Disabilities Act—full-time 0, part-time 0; Unknown ethnicity—full-time 0, part-time 0; International students who hold an F-1 or J-1 Visa—part-time 0.

Financial Information/Assistance:
Tuition for Full-Time Study: *Doctoral:* State residents: per academic year $6,400, $274 per credit hour; Nonstate residents: per academic year $17,569, $732 per credit hour. Additional fees are assessed to students beyond the costs of tuition for the following: student fees cover cost of wellness center, technology access, athletic events. See the following website for updates and changes in tuition costs: http://www.ndsu.edu/bisonconnection/accounts/tuition/.

Financial Assistance:
First-Year Students: Teaching assistantships available for first year. Average amount paid per academic year: $16,000. Average number of hours worked per week: 20. Apply by February 1. Research assistantships available for first year. Average amount paid per academic year: $16,000. Average number of hours worked per week: 20. Apply by February 1.

Advanced Students: Teaching assistantships available for advanced students. Average amount paid per academic year: $16,000. Average number of hours worked per week: 20. Apply by February 1. Research assistantships available for advanced students. Average amount paid per academic year: $16,000. Average number of hours worked per week: 20. Apply by February 1. Fellowships and scholarships available for advanced students. Average amount paid per academic year: $16,000. Average number of hours worked per week: 20. Apply by February 1.

Additional Information: Of all students currently enrolled full time, 100% benefited from one or more of the listed financial assistance programs. Application and information available online at: http://www.ndsu.edu/bisonconnection/finaid/.

Internships/Practica: Doctoral Degree (PhD Psychological Clinical Science): For those doctoral students for whom a professional psychology internship was required in this program prior to graduation, (0) students applied for an internship in 2011–2012, with (0) students obtaining an internship. Of those students who obtained an internship, (0) were paid internships. Of those students who obtained an internship, (0) students placed in APA/CPA accredited internships, (0) students placed in internships not APA/CPA accredited, but listed with the Association of Psychology Postdoctoral and Internship Programs (APPIC), (0) students placed in internships conforming to guidelines of the Council of Directors of School Psychology Programs (CDSPP), (0) students placed in internships that were not APA/CPA accredited, APPIC or CDSPP listed. Research practica are available for doctoral students who wish to develop applied research skills and experiences. Sites include a private foundation for research on addictions and eating disorders, a nationally prominent organization for clinical drug trials, a chronic pain treatment program, a community mental health center, and several sites devoted to survey research.

Housing and Day Care: On-campus housing is available. See the following website for more information: http://www.ndsu.edu/reslife/. On-campus day care facilities are available. See the following website for more information: http://www.ndsu.edu/childcenter/.

Employment of Department Graduates:
Master's Degree Graduates: Of those who graduated in the academic year 2011–2012, the following categories and numbers represent the postgraduate activities and employment of master's degree graduates: Enrolled in a postdoctoral residency/fellowship (n/a), employed in independent practice (n/a), total from the above (master's) (0).
Doctoral Degree Graduates: Of those who graduated in the academic year 2011–2012, the following categories and numbers represent the postgraduate activities and employment of doctoral degree graduates: Enrolled in a psychology doctoral program (n/a), employed in an academic position at a 2-year/4-year college (2), employed in other positions at a higher education institution (1), total from the above (doctoral) (3).

Additional Information:
Orientation, Objectives, and Emphasis of Department: Our strong research tradition has earned us a reputation as one of the best small psychology departments in the nation. PhD training is designed to produce graduates with records in research and teaching, which will make them highly competitive for employment in both traditional academic and nontraditional government and private sector settings. Our programs are based on a mentoring model, in which students work closely with specific faculty members who match their research interests.

Special Facilities or Resources: The department has state-of-the-art facilities for research in electrophysiology (including EEG), vision, and cognition, as well as ample space for other research projects. A center for research on virtual reality, multi-sensory integration, and driving simulation is very active. As the largest population center in the region, Fargo-Moorhead serves as a center for medical services for a large geographic area. There are 3 major hospitals (including a VA), a medical school Department of Neuroscience, a psychiatric hospital, a neuroscience research institute, and a private pharmaceutical research institute, which offer opportunities for collaboration. NDSU also has a Research and Technology Park which may offer research experiences involving advanced technology.

Information for Students With Physical Disabilities: See the following website for more information: http://www.ndsu.edu/disabilityservices/.

Application Information:
Send to NDSU Graduate School, NDSU Dept. 2820, P.O. Box 6050, Fargo, ND 58108. Application available online. URL of online application: http://www.ndsu.edu/gradschool/. Students are admitted in the Fall, application deadline February 1. Application deadline for the Psychological Clinical Science program is February 1; deadline is February 15 for other programs. Applications arriving after deadlines will be considered until positions are filled. *Fee:* $35.

North Dakota State University
Developmental Science
Human Development and Education
NDSU Dept. 2615, P.O. Box 6050
Fargo, ND 58108-6050
Telephone: (701) 231-8268
Fax: (701) 231-9645
E-mail: *jim.deal@ndsu.edu*
Web: *http://www.ndsu.edu/hdfs/developmental_science_phd/*

Department Information:
Chairperson: Jim Deal. Number of faculty: total—full-time 9; women—full-time 6.

Programs and Degrees Offered:
Listed in the following order: Program area, degree type (T if terminal Master's), number awarded 7/11–6/12. Developmental Science PhD (Doctor of Philosophy) 0.

Student Applications/Admissions:
Student Applications
Developmental Science PhD (Doctor of Philosophy)—Applications 2012–2013, 6. Total applicants accepted 2012–2013, 5. Number full-time enrolled (new admits only) 2012–2013, 3. Number part-time enrolled (new admits only) 2012–2013, 0. Total enrolled 2012–2013 full-time, 4. Total enrolled 2012–2013 part-time, 0. Openings 2013–2014, 5. The number of students enrolled full- and part-time who were dismissed or voluntarily withdrew from this program area in 2012–2013 were 0.
Scores: Entries appear in this order: required test or GPA, minimum score (if required), median score of students entering in 2012–2013. *Developmental Science PhD (Doctor of Philosophy):* GRE-V 155, GRE-Q 155, overall undergraduate GPA 3.0, Masters GPA 3.5.
Other Criteria: (importance of criteria rated low, medium, or high): GRE scores—high, research experience—high, work experience—low, extracurricular activity—medium, GPA—high, letters of recommendation—high, interview—low, statement of goals and objectives—high, research interest match—medium, undergraduate major in psychology—low, specific undergraduate psychology courses taken—medium. For additional information on admission requirements, go to http://www.ndsu.edu/hdfs/developmental_science_phd/application_process/.

Student Characteristics: The following represents characteristics of students in 2012–2013 in all graduate psychology programs in the department: Female—full-time 3, part-time 0; Male—full-time 1, part-time 0; African American/Black—full-time 1, part-

time 0; Hispanic/Latino(a)—full-time 0, part-time 0; Asian/Pacific Islander—full-time 0, part-time 0; American Indian/Alaska Native—full-time 0, part-time 0; Caucasian/White—full-time 3, part-time 0; Multi-ethnic—full-time 0, part-time 0; students subject to the Americans With Disabilities Act—full-time 0, part-time 0; Unknown ethnicity—full-time 0, part-time 0; International students who hold an F-1 or J-1 Visa—full-time 1, part-time 0.

Financial Information/Assistance:

Tuition for Full-Time Study: *Doctoral:* State residents: per academic year $6,580, $274 per credit hour; Nonstate residents: per academic year $17,569, $732 per credit hour. Tuition is subject to change. See the following website for updates and changes in tuition costs: http://www.ndsu.edu/bisonconnection/accounts/tuition/.

Financial Assistance:

First-Year Students: Teaching assistantships available for first year. Average amount paid per academic year: $10,000. Average number of hours worked per week: 13. Apply by February 1. Research assistantships available for first year. Average amount paid per academic year: $10,000. Average number of hours worked per week: 13. Apply by February 1.

Advanced Students: Teaching assistantships available for advanced students. Average amount paid per academic year: $10,000. Average number of hours worked per week: 13. Apply by February 1. Research assistantships available for advanced students. Average amount paid per academic year: $10,000. Average number of hours worked per week: 13. Apply by February 1.

Additional Information: Of all students currently enrolled full time, 100% benefited from one or more of the listed financial assistance programs. Application and information available online at: http://www.ndsu.edu/hdfs/developmental_science_phd/funding_opportunities/.

Housing and Day Care: On-campus housing is available. See the following website for more information: http://www.ndsu.edu/reslife/. On-campus day care facilities are available. See the following website for more information: http://www.ndsu.edu/wellness/information/.

Employment of Department Graduates:

Master's Degree Graduates: Of those who graduated in the academic year 2011–2012, the following categories and numbers represent the postgraduate activities and employment of master's degree graduates: Enrolled in a postdoctoral residency/fellowship (n/a), employed in independent practice (n/a), total from the above (master's) (0).

Doctoral Degree Graduates: Of those who graduated in the academic year 2011–2012, the following categories and numbers represent the postgraduate activities and employment of doctoral degree graduates: Enrolled in a psychology doctoral program (n/a), total from the above (doctoral) (0).

Additional Information:

Orientation, Objectives, and Emphasis of Department: The Developmental Science program combines elements of Developmental Psychology and Human Development by integrating the biological, cognitive, and socioemotional underpinnings of lifespan development and incorporating familial, social, institutional and cultural contexts. Developmental Science stands in contrast to more traditional fields by incorporating diverse disciplinary perspectives into a cohesive framework. The doctoral curriculum incorporates a substantial research apprenticeship that requires students to participate in presenting and publishing research above and beyond their theses and dissertations. This requirement serves to build students' scholarly records and employability, and graduates of the program will be well-positioned to become leaders of this emerging field.

Special Facilities or Resources: The department maintains a lab equipped with a one-way mirror and state of the art video equipment for observational research. We utilize Noldus' The Observer software for the collection, analysis, and presentation of observational data.

Information for Students With Physical Disabilities: See the following website for more information: http://www.ndsu.edu/disabilityservices/.

Application Information:
Send to Joel Hektner, Graduate Coordinator. Application available online. URL of online application: http://www.ndsu.edu/gradschool/prospective_students/. Students are admitted in the Fall, application deadline February 1. Applications accepted after deadline if program is not full. *Fee:* $35.

North Dakota, University of
Counseling Psychology and Community Services
Education and Human Development
231 Centennial Drive, Stop 8255
Grand Forks, ND 58202-8255
Telephone: (701) 777-2729
Fax: (701) 777-3184
E-mail: *cindy.juntunen@email.und.edu*
Web: *http://education.und.edu/counseling-psychology-and-community-services/*

Department Information:
1963. Chairperson: Kara Wettersten. Number of faculty: total—full-time 9, part-time 2; women—full-time 5, part-time 1; total—minority—full-time 2; women minority—full-time 1.

Programs and Degrees Offered:
Listed in the following order: Program area, degree type (T if terminal Master's), number awarded 7/11–6/12. Counseling Psychology PhD (Doctor of Philosophy) 6, Counseling MA/MS (Master of Arts/Science) (T).

APA Accreditation: Counseling PhD (Doctor of Philosophy). Student Outcome Data Website: http://education.und.edu/counseling-psychology-and-community-services/phd.cfm.

Student Applications/Admissions:
Student Applications
Counseling Psychology PhD (Doctor of Philosophy)—Applications 2012–2013, 59. Total applicants accepted 2012–2013, 9. Number full-time enrolled (new admits only) 2012–2013, 7. Number part-time enrolled (new admits only) 2012–2013, 0.

Total enrolled 2012–2013 full-time, 34. Total enrolled 2012–2013 part-time, 4. Openings 2013–2014, 7. The median number of years required for completion of a degree in 2012–2013 were 5. The number of students enrolled full- and part-time who were dismissed or voluntarily withdrew from this program area in 2012–2013 were 1. *Counseling MA/MS (Master of Arts/Science)*—Number full-time enrolled (new admits only) 2012–2013, 11. Number part-time enrolled (new admits only) 2012–2013, 20. Total enrolled 2012–2013 full-time, 34. Total enrolled 2012–2013 part-time, 49. Openings 2013–2014, 40. The number of students enrolled full- and part-time who were dismissed or voluntarily withdrew from this program area in 2012–2013 were 2.

Scores: Entries appear in this order: required test or GPA, minimum score (if required), median score of students entering in 2012–2013. *Counseling Psychology PhD (Doctor of Philosophy)*: GRE-V no minimum stated, 540, GRE-Q no minimum stated, 600, GRE-Analytical no minimum stated, 4.5, overall undergraduate GPA 2.75, 3.67, last 2 years GPA 2.75, 3.85, psychology GPA 2.75, 3.75; *Counseling MA/MS (Master of Arts/Science)*: overall undergraduate GPA 2.75, last 2 years GPA 2.75.

Other Criteria: (importance of criteria rated low, medium, or high): GRE scores—medium, research experience—high, work experience—medium, extracurricular activity—medium, clinically related public service—medium, GPA—high, letters of recommendation—high, interview—high, statement of goals and objectives—high, undergraduate major in psychology—medium, specific undergraduate psychology courses taken—medium, GRE is required for PhD; MAT is required for MA degree. For additional information on admission requirements, go to http://education.und.edu/counseling-psychology-and-community-services/phd-adm-req.cfm.

Student Characteristics: The following represents characteristics of students in 2012–2013 in all graduate psychology programs in the department: Female—full-time 49, part-time 43; Male—full-time 19, part-time 10; African American/Black—full-time 1, part-time 1; Hispanic/Latino(a)—full-time 2, part-time 1; Asian/Pacific Islander—full-time 2, part-time 0; American Indian/Alaska Native—full-time 5, part-time 4; Caucasian/White—full-time 56, part-time 47; Multi-ethnic—full-time 2, part-time 0; students subject to the Americans With Disabilities Act—full-time 2, part-time 2; Unknown ethnicity—full-time 0, part-time 0; International students who hold an F-1 or J-1 Visa—full-time 6, part-time 0.

Financial Information/Assistance:

Tuition for Full-Time Study: *Master's:* State residents: per academic year $7,531, $314 per credit hour; Nonstate residents: per academic year $17,938, $747 per credit hour. *Doctoral:* State residents: per academic year $7,531, $314 per credit hour; Nonstate residents: per academic year $17,938, $747 per credit hour. Tuition is subject to change. Additional fees are assessed to students beyond the costs of tuition for the following: technology, university services, system services, course fees for practicum and assessment. See the following website for updates and changes in tuition costs: http://und.edu/finance-operations/student-account-services/tuition-rates.cfm.

Financial Assistance:

First-Year Students: Teaching assistantships available for first year. Average amount paid per academic year: $8,060. Aver-

age number of hours worked per week: 10. Apply by April 15. Research assistantships available for first year. Average amount paid per academic year: $8,060. Average number of hours worked per week: 10. Apply by April 15. Traineeships available for first year. Average amount paid per academic year: $15,885. Average number of hours worked per week: 20. Apply by April 15.

Advanced Students: Teaching assistantships available for advanced students. Average amount paid per academic year: $8,060. Average number of hours worked per week: 10. Apply by April 15. Research assistantships available for advanced students. Average amount paid per academic year: $8,060. Average number of hours worked per week: 10. Apply by April 15. Traineeships available for advanced students. Average amount paid per academic year: $15,885. Average number of hours worked per week: 20. Apply by April 15.

Additional Information: Of all students currently enrolled full time, 65% benefited from one or more of the listed financial assistance programs. Application and information available online at: http://graduateschool.und.edu/graduate-students/financial-assistance/index.cfm.

Internships/Practica: Doctoral Degree (PhD Counseling Psychology): For those doctoral students for whom a professional psychology internship was required in this program prior to graduation, (8) students applied for an internship in 2011–2012, with (7) students obtaining an internship. Of those students who obtained an internship, (7) were paid internships. Of those students who obtained an internship, (7) students placed in APA/CPA accredited internships, (0) students placed in internships not APA/CPA accredited, but listed with the Association of Psychology Postdoctoral and Internship Programs (APPIC), (0) students placed in internships conforming to guidelines of the Council of Directors of School Psychology Programs (CDSPP), (0) students placed in internships that were not APA/CPA accredited, APPIC or CDSPP listed. Master's Degree (MA/MS Counseling): An internship experience, such as a final research project or "capstone" experience is required of graduates. We have Practicum Training Partners at a wide range of sites. Students in both the MA and PhD programs are placed in several university counseling centers and community mental health agencies in Grand Forks and the surrounding region. Several doctoral practicum placements are available in hospital, medical, and integrated care settings. We also have doctoral placements with the Grand Forks Air Force Base and two correctional centers. Most practicum placements are located within an hour's drive of Grand Forks, although a few sites require greater travel commitment. The program has a focused effort on rural behavioral health, providing opportunities for rural practicum placements. Doctoral students are required to establish a written Practicum Training Plan with their advisors during their first year of study, in order to make the best use of practicum toward their ultimate career goals.

Housing and Day Care: On-campus housing is available. See the following website for more information: http://und.edu/student-life/housing/. On-campus day care facilities are available. See the following website for more information: http://und.edu/centers/childrens/.

Employment of Department Graduates:

Master's Degree Graduates: Of those who graduated in the academic year 2011–2012, the following categories and numbers represent the postgraduate activities and employment of master's

degree graduates: Enrolled in a psychology doctoral program (5), enrolled in a postdoctoral residency/fellowship (n/a), employed in independent practice (n/a), employed in other positions at a higher education institution (1), employed in a professional position in a school system (1), employed in a community mental health/counseling center (5), not seeking employment (1), do not know (4), total from the above (master's) (17).

Doctoral Degree Graduates: Of those who graduated in the academic year 2011–2012, the following categories and numbers represent the postgraduate activities and employment of doctoral degree graduates: Enrolled in a psychology doctoral program (n/a), enrolled in a postdoctoral residency/fellowship (1), employed in an academic position at a university (1), employed in other positions at a higher education institution (2), employed in a community mental health/counseling center (1), employed in a hospital/medical center (1), total from the above (doctoral) (6).

Additional Information:

Orientation, Objectives, and Emphasis of Department: The Department's graduate programs consist of the PhD in Counseling Psychology and the MA in Counseling. The PhD program is accredited by the American Psychological Association and provides generalist training as a scientist–practitioner. The overarching goal of the PhD program in Counseling Psychology is to prepare entry level counseling psychologists who are well-trained and competent in both the practice and science of the profession. This is achieved through six training goals that are anchored in the foundational and functional competencies of professional psychology. The MA Program has 4 emphases: Community Agency Counseling, Rehabilitation Counseling, Addictions Counseling, all offered on campus, and School Counseling, offered online. The School Counseling emphasis is accredited by the National Council for the Accreditation of Teacher Education. Both programs emphasize multicultural competence and an emphasis on social justice and advocacy.

Special Facilities or Resources: The department has office space for doctoral students, observation labs for practicing counseling and assessment skills, and access to significant research space. The college in which the department is housed (Education and Human Development) completed a major renovation and expansion in September 2011, so new state-of-the-art classrooms and meeting rooms are readily available. The department has established numerous community partnerships to support training opportunities for graduate students. On campus, these relationships often support student access to additional Graduate Service Assistantships that support their training experiences. The doctoral program has excellent opportunities for student support, including assistantship positions, tuition waivers, and grant-funded traineeships.

Information for Students With Physical Disabilities: See the following website for more information: http://www.und.edu/dept/dss/.

Application Information:
Send to The Graduate School at UND. Application available online. URL of online application: http://graduateschool.und.edu/mygradspace.cfm. Students are admitted in the Fall, application deadline December 1; Spring, application deadline November 1; Summer, application deadline February 1. PhD in Counseling Psychology - December 1 deadline for Fall admission (it is possible to begin in Summer). MA program in School Counseling (online) - November 1 deadline for January admission. MA program in Counseling (mental health, addictions, rehabilitation; on-campus) - February 1 for Summer or Fall admission. *Fee:* $35. Application fees are waived for McNair scholars.

North Dakota, University of (2012 data)
Department of Psychology
Arts and Science
P.O. Box 8380
Grand Forks, ND 58202-8380
Telephone: (701) 777-3451
Fax: (701) 777-3454
E-mail: *alan.king@email.und.edu*
Web: *http://www.und.edu/dept/psych/*

Department Information:
1921. Chairperson: Mark Grabe. Number of faculty: total—full-time 23; women—full-time 8; total—minority—full-time 1; faculty subject to the Americans With Disabilities Act 1.

Programs and Degrees Offered:
Listed in the following order: Program area, degree type (T if terminal Master's), number awarded 7/11–6/12. Clinical Psychology PhD (Doctor of Philosophy) 8, General Experimental Psychology PhD (Doctor of Philosophy) 1, Forensic Psychology (M.S.) MA/MS (Master of Arts/Science) (T) 3, Forensic Psychology (MA - Online) MA/MS (Master of Arts/Science) (T) 23.

APA Accreditation: Clinical PhD (Doctor of Philosophy). Student Outcome Data Website: http://arts-sciences.und.edu/psychology/clinical.

Student Applications/Admissions:
Student Applications

Clinical Psychology PhD (Doctor of Philosophy)—Applications 2012–2013, 80. Total applicants accepted 2012–2013, 7. Number full-time enrolled (new admits only) 2012–2013, 7. Number part-time enrolled (new admits only) 2012–2013, 0. Total enrolled 2012–2013 full-time, 43. Total enrolled 2012–2013 part-time, 0. Openings 2013–2014, 8. The median number of years required for completion of a degree in 2012–2013 were 5. The number of students enrolled full- and part-time who were dismissed or voluntarily withdrew from this program area in 2012–2013 were 1. *General Experimental Psychology PhD (Doctor of Philosophy)*—Applications 2012–2013, 7. Total applicants accepted 2012–2013, 6. Number full-time enrolled (new admits only) 2012–2013, 3. Number part-time enrolled (new admits only) 2012–2013, 0. Total enrolled 2012–2013 full-time, 8. Total enrolled 2012–2013 part-time, 0. Openings 2013–2014, 3. The median number of years required for completion of a degree in 2012–2013 were 5. The number of students enrolled full- and part-time who were dismissed or voluntarily withdrew from this program area in 2012–2013 were 0. *Forensic Psychology (M.S.) MA/MS (Master of Arts/Science)*—Applications 2012–2013, 17. Total applicants accepted 2012–2013, 4. Number full-time enrolled (new admits only) 2012–2013, 4. Total enrolled 2012–2013 full-time, 6. Openings 2013–2014, 3. The median number of years required for completion of a degree in 2012–2013 were 2. The number of students enrolled full- and part-time who were dismissed or voluntarily withdrew from this program area in 2012–2013 were 0. *Forensic Psychology (MA - Online) MA/MS (Master of Arts/Science)*—Applications 2012–2013, 135. Total applicants accepted 2012–2013, 45. Number full-time enrolled (new admits only) 2012–2013, 45. Total enrolled 2012–2013 full-time, 132. Openings 2013–2014, 40. The median number of years required for completion of a degree in 2012–2013 were 2. The number of students enrolled full- and part-time who were dismissed or voluntarily withdrew from this program area in 2012–2013 were 6.

Scores: Entries appear in this order: required test or GPA, minimum score (if required), median score of students entering in 2012–2013. *Clinical Psychology PhD (Doctor of Philosophy)*: GRE-V no minimum stated, 557, GRE-Q no minimum stated, 679, GRE-Analytical 2.5, 4.4, GRE-Subject (Psychology) no minimum stated, 693, overall undergraduate GPA 3.2, 3.83, last 2 years GPA no minimum stated, 3.92, Masters GPA no minimum stated, 4.00; *General Experimental Psychology PhD (Doctor of Philosophy)*: GRE-V no minimum stated, GRE-Q no minimum stated, GRE-Analytical 2.5, GRE-Subject (Psychology) no minimum stated, overall undergraduate GPA 3.2, last 2 years GPA no minimum stated, Masters GPA no minimum stated; *Forensic Psychology (M.S.) MA/MS (Master of Arts/Science)*: GRE-V no minimum stated, GRE-Q no minimum stated, GRE-Analytical 2.5, GRE-Subject (Psychology) no minimum stated, overall undergraduate GPA 3.2, last 2 years GPA no minimum stated; *Forensic Psychology (MA - Online) MA/MS (Master of Arts/Science)*: overall undergraduate GPA 3.2, last 2 years GPA no minimum stated.

Other Criteria: (importance of criteria rated low, medium, or high): GRE scores—high, research experience—high, work experience—medium, extracurricular activity—low, clinically related public service—medium, GPA—high, letters of recommendation—medium, interview—high, statement of goals and objectives—high, undergraduate major in psychology—medium, specific undergraduate psychology courses taken—medium.

Student Characteristics: The following represents characteristics of students in 2012–2013 in all graduate psychology programs in the department: Female—full-time 56, part-time 0; Male—full-time 9, part-time 0; African American/Black—full-time 1, part-time 0; Hispanic/Latino(a)—full-time 0, part-time 0; Asian/Pacific Islander—full-time 1, part-time 0; American Indian/Alaska Native—full-time 9, part-time 0; Caucasian/White—full-time 54, part-time 0; Multi-ethnic—full-time 0, part-time 0; students subject to the Americans With Disabilities Act—full-time 0, part-time 0; Unknown ethnicity—full-time 0, part-time 0; International students who hold an F-1 or J-1 Visa—full-time 2, part-time 0.

Financial Information/Assistance:

Tuition for Full-Time Study: *Master's:* State residents: per academic year $7,565, $298 per credit hour; Nonstate residents: per academic year $17,810, $706 per credit hour. *Doctoral:* State residents: per academic year $7,565, $298 per credit hour; Nonstate residents: per academic year $17,810, $706 per credit hour. Tuition is subject to change.

Financial Assistance:

First-Year Students: Teaching assistantships available for first year. Average amount paid per academic year: $11,241. Average number of hours worked per week: 15. Apply by none.

Advanced Students: Teaching assistantships available for advanced students. Average amount paid per academic year: $15,581. Average number of hours worked per week: 15. Apply by none.

Additional Information: Of all students currently enrolled full time, 100% benefited from one or more of the listed financial assistance programs.

Internships/Practica: Doctoral Degree (PhD Clinical Psychology): For those doctoral students for whom a professional psychology internship was required in this program prior to graduation, (7) students applied for an internship in 2011–2012, with (4) students obtaining an internship. Of those students who obtained an internship, (4) were paid internships. Of those students who obtained an internship, (3) students placed in APA/CPA accredited internships, (1) students placed in internships not APA/CPA accredited, but listed with the Association of Psychology Postdoctoral and Internship Programs (APPIC), (0) students placed in internships conforming to guidelines of the Council of Directors of School Psychology Programs (CDSPP), (0) students placed in internships that were not APA/CPA accredited, APPIC or CDSPP listed. Master's Degree (MA/MS Forensic Psychology (MA - Online)): An internship experience, such as a final research project or "capstone" experience is required of graduates. Psychological Services Center (PSC). Each year you will be assigned to one of the four PSC supervision teams. These teams are primarily supervised by program faculty, and students typically plan to work with as many different PSC supervisors as possible during their time in the program. You will be assigned to a team during your first year, but in subsequent years your preferences will be taken into consideration during team assignments. This process usually occurs late in the Spring semester. PSC teams typically consist of one or two students from each class. Student responsibilities, duties, and opportunities will vary from team to team. The clinical curriculum provides requirements regarding the number of Clinical Practice (PSY 580) credit hours in which you should enroll each semester.   External Placements. The clinical program also maintains agreements with over a dozen institutions within and beyond the Grand Forks community to provide more extensive training opportunities. Upper-level students compete for these positions in April and May of each year. Clinical students typically complete two full years (one full year at 16-20 hrs/wk) of external placement prior to internship. Our rate of success in attaining accredited or APPIC-member internships on match day has been 31/35 over the past five years (89%).

Housing and Day Care: On-campus housing is available. On-campus day care facilities are available.

Employment of Department Graduates:

Master's Degree Graduates: Of those who graduated in the academic year 2011–2012, the following categories and numbers represent the postgraduate activities and employment of master's degree graduates: Enrolled in a postdoctoral residency/fellowship (n/a), employed in independent practice (n/a), total from the above (master's) (0).

Doctoral Degree Graduates: Of those who graduated in the academic year 2011–2012, the following categories and numbers represent the postgraduate activities and employment of doctoral degree graduates: Enrolled in a psychology doctoral program (n/a), enrolled in a postdoctoral residency/fellowship (1), employed in an academic position at a university (2), employed in other positions at a higher education institution (1), employed in a community mental health/counseling center (5), total from the above (doctoral) (9).

Additional Information:

Orientation, Objectives, and Emphasis of Department: The Psychology Department has a multidimensional mission to provide quality undergraduate and graduate education, student advisement at both the baccalaureate and post-baccalaureate levels, teacher education for graduate students pursuing higher education positions, and a high level of faculty and student scholarship. The department also commits to efforts to enhance mental health care service delivery in underserved populations by underrepresented emerging professionals via our Indians in Psychology Doctoral Education (INPSYDE) clinical training program. We maintain large graduate training commitments to our clinical PhD (n = 43), experimental PhD (n = 8), forensic M.S. (n = 6), and forensic MA (n = 132) students. The department presently has 23 full-time faculty positions. Students are admitted into one of four different training tracks in the Department of Psychology: Clinical PhD program, General-Experimental PhD program, Forensic M.S. program, or Forensic MA distance program. The department awards a MA degree in general psychology after completion of the thesis (and remaining curriculum requirements) for students enrolled in one of our two PhD programs. UND does not offer a terminal master's degree in clinical or general experimental psychology. The department's graduate programs are designed for residential students who are enrolled full-time (part-time students are not admitted). The PhD programs are scientifically-oriented and offer intensive training in the scholarly research and applied aspects of their areas. They are designed to produce respected scholars in the field as manifested in the generation of high quality research which is disseminated in lecturing, writing, and presentations. We also expect students to apply scientific findings in their respective area of specialization and to integrate scientific and applied activities as a method of further enhancing the quality of each.

Special Facilities or Resources: The Psychology Department is housed in Corwin-Larimore Hall, a four-story building remodeled to provide a facility for study and research. The department was also fortunate to occupy about a third of the Northern Plains Center for Behavioral Research Building next to Corwin-Larimore and the Nursing College. This four-story building is provides additional research space for a number of our faculty as well as our INPSYDE program. The department also utilizes space in Montgomery Hall across the street to house our Psychological Services Center (PSC) which serves as a community training clinic for the clinical psychology PhD program.

Information for Students With Physical Disabilities: See the following website for more information: http://www.und.edu/dept/psych/clinicaladmission.html.

Application Information:
Send to Graduate School University of North Dakota, Box 8178, Grand Forks, ND 58202. Application available online. Students are admitted in the Fall, application deadline January 15. *Fee:* $35.

Akron, University of

Department of Counseling/Collaborative Program in Counseling Psychology
The College of Education
27 South Forge Street
Akron, OH 44325-5007
Telephone: (330) 972-7777
Fax: (330) 972-5292
E-mail: *kj25@uakron.edu*
Web: *http://www.uakron.edu/education/academic-programs/counseling/*

Department Information:

1968. Chairperson: Dr. Karin Jordan. Number of faculty: total—full-time 9, part-time 4; women—full-time 6, part-time 3; total—minority—full-time 3; women minority—full-time 1.

Programs and Degrees Offered:

Listed in the following order: Program area, degree type (T if terminal Master's), number awarded 7/11–6/12. Collaborative Program in Counseling Psychology PhD (Doctor of Philosophy) 4.

APA Accreditation: Counseling PhD (Doctor of Philosophy). Student Outcome Data Website: http://www.uakron.edu/psychology/academics/cpcp/program-outcome-data.dot.

Student Applications/Admissions:

Student Applications

Collaborative Program in Counseling Psychology PhD (Doctor of Philosophy)—Applications 2012–2013, 39. Total applicants accepted 2012–2013, 4. Number full-time enrolled (new admits only) 2012–2013, 4. Number part-time enrolled (new admits only) 2012–2013, 0. Total enrolled 2012–2013 full-time, 11. Total enrolled 2012–2013 part-time, 14. Openings 2013–2014, 4. The median number of years required for completion of a degree in 2012–2013 were 7. The number of students enrolled full- and part-time who were dismissed or voluntarily withdrew from this program area in 2012–2013 were 0.

Scores: Entries appear in this order: required test or GPA, minimum score (if required), median score of students entering in 2012–2013. *Collaborative Program in Counseling Psychology PhD (Doctor of Philosophy):* GRE-V 550, GRE-Q 550, GRE-Subject (Psychology) no minimum stated, overall undergraduate GPA 2.75, last 2 years GPA 3.0, Masters GPA 3.25.

Other Criteria: (importance of criteria rated low, medium, or high): GRE scores—high, research experience—high, work experience—medium, extracurricular activity—low, clinically related public service—low, GPA—high, letters of recommendation—high, interview—high, statement of goals and objectives—high. For additional information on admission requirements, go to http://www.uakron.edu/psychology/academics/cpcp/admissions/index.dot.

Student Characteristics: The following represents characteristics of students in 2012–2013 in all graduate psychology programs in the department: Female—full-time 16, part-time 7; Male—full-time 4, part-time 4; African American/Black—full-time 2, part-time 0; Hispanic/Latino(a)—full-time 1, part-time 0; Asian/Pacific Islander—full-time 1, part-time 0; American Indian/Alaska Native—full-time 0, part-time 0; Caucasian/White—full-time 17, part-time 0; Multi-ethnic—full-time 0, part-time 0; students subject to the Americans With Disabilities Act—full-time 0, part-time 1; Unknown ethnicity—full-time 0, part-time 0; International students who hold an F-1 or J-1 Visa—full-time 0, part-time 0.

Financial Information/Assistance:

Tuition for Full-Time Study: *Doctoral:* State residents: $404 per credit hour; Nonstate residents: $727 per credit hour. Tuition is subject to change. See the following website for updates and changes in tuition costs: http://www.uakron.edu/student-accounts/costs/.

Financial Assistance:

First-Year Students: Teaching assistantships available for first year. Average amount paid per academic year: $10,500. Average number of hours worked per week: 20. Apply by April 15. Research assistantships available for first year. Average amount paid per academic year: $10,500. Average number of hours worked per week: 20. Apply by April 15.

Advanced Students: Teaching assistantships available for advanced students. Average amount paid per academic year: $10,500. Average number of hours worked per week: 20. Apply by April 15. Research assistantships available for advanced students. Average amount paid per academic year: $10,500. Average number of hours worked per week: 20. Apply by April 15.

Additional Information: Of all students currently enrolled full time, 92% benefited from one or more of the listed financial assistance programs. Application and information available online at: http://www.uakron.edu/gradsch/financial-assistance/.

Internships/Practica: Doctoral Degree (PhD Collaborative Program in Counseling Psychology): For those doctoral students for whom a professional psychology internship was required in this program prior to graduation, (4) students applied for an internship in 2011–2012, with (3) students obtaining an internship. Of those students who obtained an internship, (3) were paid internships. Of those students who obtained an internship, (3) students placed in APA/CPA accredited internships, (0) students placed in internships not APA/CPA accredited, but listed with the Association of Psychology Postdoctoral and Internship Programs (APPIC), (0) students placed in internships conforming to guidelines of the Council of Directors of School Psychology Programs (CDSPP), (0) students placed in internships that were not APA/CPA accredited, APPIC or CDSPP listed. Practica are offered in the department's clinic, the counseling center on campus, and a broad range of settings in the community.

Housing and Day Care: On-campus housing is available. See the following website for more information: http://www.uakron.edu/reslife/. On-campus day care facilities are available. See the following website for more information: http://www.uakron.edu/education/community-engagement/ccd/index.dot.

Employment of Department Graduates:

Master's Degree Graduates: Of those who graduated in the academic year 2011–2012, the following categories and numbers represent the postgraduate activities and employment of master's degree graduates: Enrolled in a postdoctoral residency/fellowship (n/a), employed in independent practice (n/a), total from the above (master's) (0).

Doctoral Degree Graduates: Of those who graduated in the academic year 2011–2012, the following categories and numbers represent the postgraduate activities and employment of doctoral degree graduates: Enrolled in a psychology doctoral program (n/a), enrolled in a postdoctoral residency/fellowship (2), employed in other positions at a higher education institution (1), employed in a community mental health/counseling center (1), total from the above (doctoral) (4).

Additional Information:

Orientation, Objectives, and Emphasis of Department: The department subscribes to a scientist–practitioner model of training. Its objective is to provide a core of courses in general psychology and courses in the specialty of counseling psychology. The emphasis is on preparation for teaching, research, and practice career paths.

Special Facilities or Resources: The department has its own computer lab and houses the College of Education Clinic for Individual and Family Counseling.

Information for Students With Physical Disabilities: See the following website for more information: http://www.uakron.edu/access/.

Application Information:
Send to The Graduate School, Polsky Building, Room 469, The University of Akron, Akron, OH 44325-2101. Application available online. URL of online application: http://www.uakron.edu/gradsch/apply-online/docdegr.dot. Students are admitted in the Fall, application deadline December 1. Prospective students with Master's degrees in a related field should indicate that they are applying to the Collaborative Program in Counseling Psychology (PhD) through the Department of Counseling. Prospective students with Bachelor's degrees should indicate that they are applying to the Collaborative Program in Counseling Psychology (MA/PhD) through the Department of Psychology. *Fee:* $40.

Akron, University of
Department of Psychology
Buchtel College of Arts and Sciences
College of Arts & Sciences Building, 290 East Buchtel Avenue
Akron, OH 44325-4301
Telephone: (330) 972-7280
Fax: (330) 972-5174
E-mail: *plevy@uakron.edu*
Web: *http://www.uakron.edu/psychology*

Department Information:
1921. Chairperson: Paul E. Levy. Number of faculty: total—full-time 18; women—full-time 9; total—minority—full-time 2; women minority—full-time 2.

Programs and Degrees Offered:
Listed in the following order: Program area, degree type (T if terminal Master's), number awarded 7/11–6/12. Counseling Psychology PhD (Doctor of Philosophy) 3, Applied Cognitive Aging PhD (Doctor of Philosophy) 1, Industrial/Organizational Psychology MA/MS (Master of Arts/Science) (T) 4, Industrial/Organizational Psychology PhD (Doctor of Philosophy) 1, Adult Development and Aging PhD (Doctor of Philosophy) 0.

APA Accreditation: Counseling PhD (Doctor of Philosophy). Student Outcome Data Website: http://www.uakron.edu/psychology/academics/cpcp/program-outcome-data.dot.

Student Applications/Admissions:
Student Applications

Counseling Psychology PhD (Doctor of Philosophy)—Applications 2012–2013, 59. Total applicants accepted 2012–2013, 9. Number full-time enrolled (new admits only) 2012–2013, 5. Number part-time enrolled (new admits only) 2012–2013, 0. Total enrolled 2012–2013 full-time, 23. Total enrolled 2012–2013 part-time, 9. Openings 2013–2014, 6. The median number of years required for completion of a degree in 2012–2013 were 7. The number of students enrolled full- and part-time who were dismissed or voluntarily withdrew from this program area in 2012–2013 were 0. *Applied Cognitive Aging PhD (Doctor of Philosophy)*—Applications 2012–2013, 0. Total applicants accepted 2012–2013, 0. Number full-time enrolled (new admits only) 2012–2013, 0. Number part-time enrolled (new admits only) 2012–2013, 0. The median number of years required for completion of a degree in 2012–2013 were 10. The number of students enrolled full- and part-time who were dismissed or voluntarily withdrew from this program area in 2012–2013 were 0. *Industrial/Organizational Psychology MA/MS (Master of Arts/Science)*—Applications 2012–2013, 48. Total applicants accepted 2012–2013, 4. Number full-time enrolled (new admits only) 2012–2013, 5. Number part-time enrolled (new admits only) 2012–2013, 0. Total enrolled 2012–2013 full-time, 10. Total enrolled 2012–2013 part-time, 0. Openings 2013–2014, 4. The median number of years required for completion of a degree in 2012–2013 were 2. The number of students enrolled full- and part-time who were dismissed or voluntarily withdrew from this program area in 2012–2013 were 0. *Industrial/Organizational Psychology PhD (Doctor of Philosophy)*—Applications 2012–2013, 89. Total applicants accepted 2012–2013, 8. Number full-time enrolled (new admits only) 2012–2013, 5. Number part-time enrolled (new admits only) 2012–2013, 0. Total enrolled 2012–2013 full-time, 28. Total enrolled 2012–2013 part-time, 15. Openings 2013–2014, 6. The median number of years required for completion of a degree in 2012–2013 were 5. The number of students enrolled full- and part-time who were dismissed or voluntarily withdrew from this program area in 2012–2013 were 0. *Adult Development and Aging PhD (Doctor of Philosophy)*—Applications 2012–2013, 11. Total applicants accepted 2012–2013, 2. Number full-time enrolled (new admits only) 2012–2013, 2. Number part-time enrolled (new admits only) 2012–2013, 0. Total enrolled 2012–2013 full-time, 8. Total enrolled 2012–2013 part-time, 0. Openings 2013–2014, 3. The number of students enrolled full- and part-time who were dismissed or voluntarily withdrew from this program area in 2012–2013 were 0.

Scores: Entries appear in this order: required test or GPA, minimum score (if required), median score of students entering

in 2012–2013. *Counseling Psychology PhD (Doctor of Philosophy)*: GRE-V 151, 159, GRE-Q 144, 155, GRE-Analytical 3.5, 4.5, overall undergraduate GPA 2.90, 3.74, psychology GPA no minimum stated; *Industrial/Organizational Psychology MA/MS (Master of Arts/Science)*: GRE-V 153, 158, GRE-Q 146, 148, GRE-Analytical 4.0, 4.5, overall undergraduate GPA 3.83, 3.88, psychology GPA no minimum stated; *Industrial/Organizational Psychology PhD (Doctor of Philosophy)*: GRE-V 153, 157, GRE-Q 150, 156, GRE-Analytical 3.5, 4.0, overall undergraduate GPA 3.73, 3.83, psychology GPA no minimum stated; *Adult Development and Aging PhD (Doctor of Philosophy)*: GRE-V 151, 156, GRE-Q 152, 160, GRE-Analytical 4.0, 4.7, overall undergraduate GPA 3.05, 3.21, psychology GPA no minimum stated.

Other Criteria: (importance of criteria rated low, medium, or high): GRE scores—high, research experience—high, work experience—low, extracurricular activity—low, clinically related public service—low, GPA—high, letters of recommendation—medium, interview—medium, statement of goals and objectives—high, On campus interviews and telephone interviews are used as a selection criterion only in the Counseling Psychology program. I/O program does telephone screening of those that it intends to accept.

Student Characteristics: The following represents characteristics of students in 2012–2013 in all graduate psychology programs in the department: Female—full-time 47, part-time 20; Male—full-time 22, part-time 4; African American/Black—full-time 4, part-time 2; Hispanic/Latino(a)—full-time 3, part-time 2; Asian/Pacific Islander—full-time 3, part-time 2; American Indian/Alaska Native—full-time 0, part-time 0; Caucasian/White—full-time 59, part-time 18; Multi-ethnic—full-time 0, part-time 0; students subject to the Americans With Disabilities Act—full-time 0, part-time 0; Unknown ethnicity—full-time 0, part-time 0; International students who hold an F-1 or J-1 Visa—full-time 3, part-time 0.

Financial Information/Assistance:

Tuition for Full-Time Study: *Master's:* State residents: per academic year $12,958, $438 per credit hour; Nonstate residents: per academic year $21,606, $727 per credit hour. *Doctoral:* State residents: per academic year $12,958, $438 per credit hour; Nonstate residents: per academic year $21,606, $727 per credit hour. Tuition is subject to change. See the following website for updates and changes in tuition costs: http://www.uakron.edu/admissions/graduate/tuition__fees.dot.

Financial Assistance:

First-Year Students: Teaching assistantships available for first year. Average amount paid per academic year: $11,500. Average number of hours worked per week: 20. Apply by December 1. Fellowships and scholarships available for first year. Average amount paid per academic year: $0. Average number of hours worked per week: 0. Apply by December 1.

Advanced Students: Teaching assistantships available for advanced students. Average amount paid per academic year: $12,500. Average number of hours worked per week: 20. Apply by April 15. Research assistantships available for advanced students. Average amount paid per academic year: $12,500. Average number of hours worked per week: 20. Apply by April 15.

Additional Information: Of all students currently enrolled full time, 100% benefited from one or more of the listed financial

assistance programs. Application and information available online at: http://www.uakron.edu/gradsch/financial-assistance/.

Internships/Practica: Doctoral Degree (PhD Counseling Psychology): For those doctoral students for whom a professional psychology internship was required in this program prior to graduation, (5) students applied for an internship in 2011–2012, with (5) students obtaining an internship. Of those students who obtained an internship, (5) were paid internships. Of those students who obtained an internship, (5) students placed in APA/CPA accredited internships, (0) students placed in internships not APA/CPA accredited, but listed with the Association of Psychology Postdoctoral and Internship Programs (APPIC), (0) students placed in internships conforming to guidelines of the Council of Directors of School Psychology Programs (CDSPP), (0) students placed in internships that were not APA/CPA accredited, APPIC or CDSPP listed. Practica are offered in the department's own Counseling Training Clinic and Center for Organizational Research. Students also have access to a wide variety of community-based practica in industrial and public settings, hospitals, the University's Counseling Testing and Careers Center, and community mental health centers.

Housing and Day Care: On-campus housing is available. See the following website for more information: http://www.uakron.edu/reslife. On-campus day care facilities are available. See the following website for more information: http://www.uakron.edu/education/community-engagement/ccd.

Employment of Department Graduates:

Master's Degree Graduates: Of those who graduated in the academic year 2011–2012, the following categories and numbers represent the postgraduate activities and employment of master's degree graduates: Enrolled in a postdoctoral residency/fellowship (n/a), employed in independent practice (n/a), employed in business or industry (4), total from the above (master's) (4).

Doctoral Degree Graduates: Of those who graduated in the academic year 2011–2012, the following categories and numbers represent the postgraduate activities and employment of doctoral degree graduates: Enrolled in a psychology doctoral program (n/a), enrolled in a postdoctoral residency/fellowship (1), employed in an academic position at a 2-year/4-year college (1), employed in other positions at a higher education institution (1), employed in business or industry (1), employed in government agency (1), total from the above (doctoral) (5).

Additional Information:

Orientation, Objectives, and Emphasis of Department: The department's goals are to: (1) increase and diffuse psychological knowledge by advancing the discipline both as a science and as a means of promoting human welfare; (2) promote psychology in all its branches in the broadest and most liberal manner; (3) encourage research in psychology; and (4) advance high standards of education, achievement, professional ethics and conduct. The department subscribes to a scientist–practitioner model of training. Graduate students take a common set of courses in foundational areas of psychology in addition to their specialty coursework, with study in the specialty area beginning early in graduate training. The emphasis is on preparation for teaching as well as for research, industrial, or mental health services career paths. Industrial/organizational, gerontological, and counseling psychology are the specialty emphases at the MA and PhD level.

Special Facilities or Resources: To enhance research and instruction, we maintain a number of psychological research laboratories designed for individual and group studies, and equipped with computers, one-way viewing mirrors, video equipment, etc. Over 60 computers are available to faculty and students for word processing, statistical analysis, classroom instruction, e-mail correspondence, and web access. A programmer/technician provides full-time support for the hardware and software in the department and writes custom software for experimental control, stimulus display, and data collection. We maintain an in-house library of teaching resources for graduate teaching assistants, as well as a test library with over 100 tests and manuals for assessment of a broad range of constructs. We are affiliated with the university's Institute for Life-Span Development and Gerontology and the Center for the History of Psychology.

Information for Students With Physical Disabilities: See the following website for more information: http://www.uakron.edu/access.

Application Information:
Send to Graduate School, The University of Akron, Polsky Building, Room 469, Akron, OH 44325-2101. Application available online. URL of online application: http://www.uakron.edu/admissions/graduate/. Students are admitted in the Fall, application deadline December 1. Counseling Deadline: December 1. I/O and ADA Deadline: January 15. *Fee:* $40. International application fee is $60.

Bowling Green State University
Department of Psychology
Bowling Green, OH 43403
Telephone: (419) 372-2306
Fax: (419) 372-6013
E-mail: *pwatson@bgsu.edu*
Web: *http://www.bgsu.edu/departments/psych/*

Department Information:
1947. Chairperson: Michael Zickar. Number of faculty: total—full-time 27; women—full-time 9; total—minority—full-time 2.

Programs and Degrees Offered:
Listed in the following order: Program area, degree type (T if terminal Master's), number awarded 7/11–6/12. Clinical Psychology PhD (Doctor of Philosophy) 7, Developmental Psychology PhD (Doctor of Philosophy) 1, Neural & Cognitive Sciences PhD (Doctor of Philosophy) 1, Industrial/Organizational Psychology PhD (Doctor of Philosophy) 3.

APA Accreditation: Clinical PhD (Doctor of Philosophy). Student Outcome Data Website: http://www.bgsu.edu/departments/psych/page36679.html.

Student Applications/Admissions:
Student Applications
Clinical Psychology PhD (Doctor of Philosophy)—Applications 2012–2013, 211. Total applicants accepted 2012–2013, 10. Number full-time enrolled (new admits only) 2012–2013, 9. Number part-time enrolled (new admits only) 2012–2013, 0.

Total enrolled 2012–2013 full-time, 61. Total enrolled 2012–2013 part-time, 0. Openings 2013–2014, 10. The median number of years required for completion of a degree in 2012–2013 were 6. The number of students enrolled full- and part-time who were dismissed or voluntarily withdrew from this program area in 2012–2013 were 1. *Developmental Psychology PhD (Doctor of Philosophy)*—Applications 2012–2013, 5. Total applicants accepted 2012–2013, 1. Number full-time enrolled (new admits only) 2012–2013, 1. Number part-time enrolled (new admits only) 2012–2013, 0. Total enrolled 2012–2013 full-time, 7. Total enrolled 2012–2013 part-time, 0. Openings 2013–2014, 3. The median number of years required for completion of a degree in 2012–2013 were 5. The number of students enrolled full- and part-time who were dismissed or voluntarily withdrew from this program area in 2012–2013 were 0. *Neural & Cognitive Sciences PhD (Doctor of Philosophy)*—Applications 2012–2013, 24. Total applicants accepted 2012–2013, 7. Number full-time enrolled (new admits only) 2012–2013, 6. Total enrolled 2012–2013 full-time, 13. Openings 2013–2014, 5. The median number of years required for completion of a degree in 2012–2013 were 6. The number of students enrolled full- and part-time who were dismissed or voluntarily withdrew from this program area in 2012–2013 were 3. *Industrial/Organizational Psychology PhD (Doctor of Philosophy)*—Applications 2012–2013, 107. Total applicants accepted 2012–2013, 13. Number full-time enrolled (new admits only) 2012–2013, 6. Total enrolled 2012–2013 full-time, 26. Openings 2013–2014, 5. The median number of years required for completion of a degree in 2012–2013 were 6. The number of students enrolled full- and part-time who were dismissed or voluntarily withdrew from this program area in 2012–2013 were 1.

Scores: Entries appear in this order: required test or GPA, minimum score (if required), median score of students entering in 2012–2013. *Clinical Psychology PhD (Doctor of Philosophy):* GRE-V no minimum stated, GRE-Q no minimum stated, overall undergraduate GPA no minimum stated, 3.59; *Developmental Psychology PhD (Doctor of Philosophy):* GRE-V no minimum stated, GRE-Q no minimum stated, overall undergraduate GPA no minimum stated, 3.75; *Neural & Cognitive Sciences PhD (Doctor of Philosophy):* GRE-V no minimum stated, GRE-Q no minimum stated, overall undergraduate GPA no minimum stated, 3.71; *Industrial/Organizational Psychology PhD (Doctor of Philosophy):* GRE-V no minimum stated, GRE-Q no minimum stated, overall undergraduate GPA no minimum stated, 3.48.

Other Criteria: (importance of criteria rated low, medium, or high): GRE scores—high, research experience—high, work experience—medium, extracurricular activity—medium, clinically related public service—high, GPA—high, letters of recommendation—high, interview—high, statement of goals and objectives—high, Clinically related public service and interview are high for Clinical program only. For additional information on admission requirements, go to http://www.bgsu.edu/departments/psych/page31038.html.

Student Characteristics: The following represents characteristics of students in 2012–2013 in all graduate psychology programs in the department: Female—full-time 75, part-time 0; Male—full-time 32, part-time 0; African American/Black—full-time 2, part-time 0; Hispanic/Latino(a)—full-time 1, part-time 0; Asian/Pacific Islander—full-time 12, part-time 0; American Indian/Alaska

Native—full-time 1, part-time 0; Caucasian/White—full-time 79, part-time 0; Multi-ethnic—full-time 0, part-time 0; students subject to the Americans With Disabilities Act—full-time 0, part-time 0; Unknown ethnicity—full-time 12, part-time 0; International students who hold an F-1 or J-1 Visa—full-time 9, part-time 0.

Financial Information/Assistance:

Tuition for Full-Time Study: *Doctoral:* State residents: per academic year $11,632, $485 per credit hour; Nonstate residents: per academic year $18,940, $790 per credit hour. Tuition is subject to change. See the following website for updates and changes in tuition costs: http://www.bgsu.edu/offices/bursar/index.html.

Financial Assistance:

First-Year Students: Teaching assistantships available for first year. Average amount paid per academic year: $12,500. Average number of hours worked per week: 20. Apply by December 15. Research assistantships available for first year. Average amount paid per academic year: $12,500. Average number of hours worked per week: 20. Apply by December 15.

Advanced Students: Teaching assistantships available for advanced students. Average amount paid per academic year: $12,500. Average number of hours worked per week: 20. Apply by December 15. Research assistantships available for advanced students. Average amount paid per academic year: $12,500. Average number of hours worked per week: 20. Apply by December 15. Traineeships available for advanced students. Average amount paid per academic year: $12,500. Average number of hours worked per week: 20. Apply by December 15. Fellowships and scholarships available for advanced students. Average amount paid per academic year: $12,500. Average number of hours worked per week: 0. Apply by March.

Additional Information: Of all students currently enrolled full time, 99% benefited from one or more of the listed financial assistance programs.

Internships/Practica: Doctoral Degree (PhD Clinical Psychology): For those doctoral students for whom a professional psychology internship was required in this program prior to graduation, (12) students applied for an internship in 2011–2012, with (10) students obtaining an internship. Of those students who obtained an internship, (10) were paid internships. Of those students who obtained an internship, (10) students placed in APA/CPA accredited internships, (0) students placed in internships not APA/CPA accredited, but listed with the Association of Psychology Postdoctoral and Internship Programs (APPIC), (0) students placed in internships conforming to guidelines of the Council of Directors of School Psychology Programs (CDSPP), (0) students placed in internships that were not APA/CPA accredited, APPIC or CDSPP listed. In their beginning years, clinical students are placed on Basic Clinical Skills practicum teams through the Department's Psychological Services Center (PSC) that provide experience with a broad range of clients and clinical problems. Students focus on the application of such basic clinical skills as psychological assessment and interventions, the integration of science and practice, case conceptualization, clinical judgment and decision-making and report writing. In their second year students begin receiving in-house training in psychotherapy through the PSC. As clinical students progress through the program they are placed on Advanced Clinical Skills teams that involve them in current projects providing "hands-on" experience

with the integration of research and practice as it applies to individuals, health/behavioral medicine, the community, or special populations (e.g., children, problem drinkers). More advanced clinical students are provided practicum opportunities consistent with their interest through a number of outside placements, such as community mental health centers, a nearby medical college, the university counseling center and health service, an inpatient child and adolescent facility, hospital-based rehabilitation centers, treatment centers for children and families, and programs for individuals with severe mental disabilities and emotional disorders. Industrial/Organizational students are strongly encouraged to apply for a formal internship after completion of their Master's project. Although such experiences are encouraged and typically followed, internships are not required of I/O students for completion of the doctoral degree. Other experiences through coursework activities and Institute for Psychological Research and Application (IPRA) projects can collectively serve the same function as an internship.

Housing and Day Care: No on-campus housing is available. No on-campus day care facilities are available.

Employment of Department Graduates:

Master's Degree Graduates: Of those who graduated in the academic year 2011–2012, the following categories and numbers represent the postgraduate activities and employment of master's degree graduates: Enrolled in a postdoctoral residency/fellowship (n/a), employed in independent practice (n/a), total from the above (master's) (0).

Doctoral Degree Graduates: Of those who graduated in the academic year 2011–2012, the following categories and numbers represent the postgraduate activities and employment of doctoral degree graduates: Enrolled in a psychology doctoral program (n/a), total from the above (doctoral) (0).

Additional Information:

Orientation, Objectives, and Emphasis of Department: The primary goal of the PhD program is the development of scientists capable of advancing psychological knowledge. The program is characterized by both an emphasis on extensive academic training in general psychology and an early and continuing commitment to research. Although each graduate student will seek an area in which to develop his or her own expertise, students will be expected to be knowledgeable about many areas and will be encouraged to pursue interests that cross conventional specialty lines. The program is research-oriented. Each student normally works in close association with a sponsor or chairperson whose special competence matches the student's interest, but students are free to pursue research interests with any faculty member and in any area(s) they choose. Both basic and applied research are well represented within the department. The clinical program has concentrations in clinical child, behavioral medicine, and community, as well as general clinical.

Special Facilities or Resources: The department is located in the psychology building with excellent facilities for all forms of research. The building houses all faculty and graduate students. The department operates a community-oriented Psychological Services Center and the Institute for Psychological Research and Application. The department operates its own computer facility with terminals to the mainframe computer available in the building, as well as a microcomputer facility.

Information for Students With Physical Disabilities: See the following website for more information: http://www.bgsu.edu/offices/sa/disability/.

Application Information:
Application available online. URL of online application: http://www.bgsu.edu/gradcoll/page24959.html. Students are admitted in the Fall, application deadline December 15th. December 15th deadline for Clinical and January 1st deadline for Industrial/Organizational, Developmental, Neural & Cognitive. *Fee:* $45. International application fee is $75.

Cincinnati, University of
Department of Psychology
Arts and Sciences
4130 Edwards One
Cincinnati, OH 45221-0376
Telephone: (513) 556-5577
Fax: (513) 556-4168
E-mail: *Kloosa@ucmail.uc.edu*
Web: *http://www.artsci.uc.edu/psychology/*

Department Information:
1901. Head: Heidi Kloos, PhD. Number of faculty: total—full-time 21, part-time 10; women—full-time 14, part-time 3; total—minority—full-time 6, part-time 1; women minority—full-time 5, part-time 1.

Programs and Degrees Offered:
Listed in the following order: Program area, degree type (T if terminal Master's), number awarded 7/11–6/12. Clinical Psychology PhD (Doctor of Philosophy) 4, Experimental Psychology PhD (Doctor of Philosophy) 4.

APA Accreditation: Clinical PhD (Doctor of Philosophy). Student Outcome Data Website: http://www.artsci.uc.edu/collegedepts/psychology/grad/phd/.

Student Applications/Admissions:
Student Applications
Clinical Psychology PhD (Doctor of Philosophy)—Applications 2012–2013, 245. Total applicants accepted 2012–2013, 8. Number full-time enrolled (new admits only) 2012–2013, 6. Number part-time enrolled (new admits only) 2012–2013, 0. Total enrolled 2012–2013 full-time, 25. Total enrolled 2012–2013 part-time, 16. Openings 2013–2014, 6. The median number of years required for completion of a degree in 2012–2013 were 6. The number of students enrolled full- and part-time who were dismissed or voluntarily withdrew from this program area in 2012–2013 were 2. *Experimental Psychology PhD (Doctor of Philosophy)*—Applications 2012–2013, 40. Total applicants accepted 2012–2013, 10. Number full-time enrolled (new admits only) 2012–2013, 7. Number part-time enrolled (new admits only) 2012–2013, 0. Total enrolled 2012–2013 full-time, 24. Total enrolled 2012–2013 part-time, 8. Openings 2013–2014, 8. The median number of years required for completion of a degree in 2012–2013 were 5. The number of students enrolled full- and part-time who were dismissed or

voluntarily withdrew from this program area in 2012–2013 were 1.

Scores: Entries appear in this order: required test or GPA, minimum score (if required), median score of students entering in 2012–2013. *Clinical Psychology PhD (Doctor of Philosophy):* GRE-V 154, 157, GRE-Q 143, 153, GRE-Analytical 4, 4.5, overall undergraduate GPA 3.22, 3.65; *Experimental Psychology PhD (Doctor of Philosophy):* GRE-V 146, 160, GRE-Q 142, 155, GRE-Analytical 3.5, 4.5, overall undergraduate GPA 3.08, 3.56.

Other Criteria: (importance of criteria rated low, medium, or high): GRE scores—medium, research experience—high, work experience—high, extracurricular activity—low, clinically related public service—medium, GPA—medium, letters of recommendation—high, interview—high, statement of goals and objectives—high, fit w/ faculty mentor—high, undergraduate major in psychology—medium, specific undergraduate psychology courses taken—high, Clinically related public service is only considered strongly for students applying for clinical training. For additional information on admission requirements, go to http://www.artsci.uc.edu/collegedepts/psychology/grad/phd/appinfo.aspx.

Student Characteristics: The following represents characteristics of students in 2012–2013 in all graduate psychology programs in the department: Female—full-time 49, part-time 24; Male—full-time 17, part-time 7; African American/Black—full-time 9, part-time 2; Hispanic/Latino(a)—full-time 4, part-time 4; Asian/Pacific Islander—full-time 0, part-time 2; American Indian/Alaska Native—full-time 0, part-time 0; Caucasian/White—full-time 36, part-time 16; Multi-ethnic—full-time 0, part-time 0; students subject to the Americans With Disabilities Act—full-time 2, part-time 0; Unknown ethnicity—full-time 0, part-time 0; International students who hold an F-1 or J-1 Visa—full-time 7, part-time 0.

Financial Information/Assistance:
Tuition for Full-Time Study: *Doctoral:* State residents: per academic year $13,822, $627 per credit hour; Nonstate residents: per academic year $25,336, $774 per credit hour. Tuition is subject to change. Additional fees are assessed to students beyond the costs of tuition for the following: computer fees & insurance. See the following website for updates and changes in tuition costs: http://www.uc.edu/af/bursar/fees.html.

Financial Assistance:
First-Year Students: Teaching assistantships available for first year. Research assistantships available for first year. Fellowships and scholarships available for first year.

Advanced Students: Teaching assistantships available for advanced students. Research assistantships available for advanced students. Traineeships available for advanced students. Fellowships and scholarships available for advanced students.

Additional Information: Of all students currently enrolled full time, 100% benefited from one or more of the listed financial assistance programs. Application and information available online at: http://financialaid.uc.edu/gradstudents.html.

Internships/Practica: Doctoral Degree (PhD Clinical Psychology): For those doctoral students for whom a professional psychology internship was required in this program prior to graduation, (8) students applied for an internship in 2011–2012, with (7) students obtaining an internship. Of those students who obtained an internship, (7) were paid internships. Of those students who obtained an internship, (7) students placed in APA/CPA accredited internships, (0) students placed in internships not APA/CPA accredited, but listed with the Association of Psychology Postdoctoral and Internship Programs (APPIC), (0) students placed in internships conforming to guidelines of the Council of Directors of School Psychology Programs (CDSPP), (0) students placed in internships that were not APA/CPA accredited, APPIC or CDSPP listed. All clinical students in years three and four typically perform a paid, 20-hour/week clinical (or clinical research) training placement at an external site in the Greater Cincinnati area. Often these placements are at the University of Cincinnati Medical Center, the Cincinnati Children's Hospital Medical Center, or a variety of community agencies. If students need a fifth year of support prior to beginning an APA-accredited clinical internship, we can generally arrange a clinical training opportunity, although priority for placements goes to students in years 1 through 4. While most of our experimental students do their paid training assignments within the department, there are also paid external training slots available for some of our students in private industry or with the federal government.

Housing and Day Care: No on-campus housing is available. On-campus day care facilities are available. See the following website for more information: http://www.uc.edu/elc.html; http://cech.uc.edu/centers/arlitt.html.

Employment of Department Graduates:
Master's Degree Graduates: Of those who graduated in the academic year 2011–2012, the following categories and numbers represent the postgraduate activities and employment of master's degree graduates: Enrolled in a postdoctoral residency/fellowship (n/a), employed in independent practice (n/a), total from the above (master's) (0).
Doctoral Degree Graduates: Of those who graduated in the academic year 2011–2012, the following categories and numbers represent the postgraduate activities and employment of doctoral degree graduates: Enrolled in a psychology doctoral program (n/a), enrolled in a postdoctoral residency/fellowship (4), employed in an academic position at a university (2), employed in government agency (1), employed in a hospital/medical center (1), total from the above (doctoral) (8).

Additional Information:
Orientation, Objectives, and Emphasis of Department: The University of Cincinnati offers the PhD in Psychology, including an APA-accredited training program in Clinical Psychology. Clinical students must specify a specialty training area, which may include health, neuropsychology or general training. For students who are seeking an Experimental degree, we offer training primarily in Cognition, Action and Perception; Human Factors and Experimental Neuropsychology. The doctoral program is limited to full-time students who show outstanding promise. Students are admitted to the doctoral program to work with a faculty research mentor. Faculty mentors are responsible for ensuring that students are actively engaged in doing research from the very start of their graduate school career, and that this work leads successfully to a master's thesis and a dissertation.

Special Facilities or Resources: The department's clinical program has close ties to the UC College of Medicine, Cincinnati Children's Hospital Medical Center, and a wide range of community agencies. The experimental program has close collaborations with the UC College of Medicine, the College of Engineering, and agencies including Wright Patterson Air Force Base and NIOSH.

Information for Students With Physical Disabilities: See the following website for more information: http://www.uc.edu/aess/disability.html.

Application Information:
Send to Graduate Secretary, Department of Psychology, University of Cincinnati, P.O. Box 210376, Cincinnati, OH 45221-0376. Application available online. URL of online application: http://grad.uc.edu/admissions.html. Students are admitted in the Fall, application deadline December 6. *Fee:* $70.

Cincinnati, University of
School Psychology
Education, Criminal Justice, and Human Services
P.O. Box 210068
Cincinnati, OH 45221-0068
Telephone: (513) 556-3342
Fax: (513) 556-3898
E-mail: *renee.hawkins@uc.edu*
Web: *http://cech.uc.edu/programs/school_psychology.html*

Department Information:
1983. School Director: Janet Graden. Number of faculty: total—full-time 5, part-time 1; women—full-time 3.

Programs and Degrees Offered:
Listed in the following order: Program area, degree type (T if terminal Master's), number awarded 7/11–6/12. School Psychology PhD (Doctor of Philosophy) 2, School Psychology EdS (School Psychology) 11.

Student Applications/Admissions:
Student Applications
School Psychology PhD (Doctor of Philosophy)—Applications 2012–2013, 12. Total applicants accepted 2012–2013, 7. Number full-time enrolled (new admits only) 2012–2013, 4. Number part-time enrolled (new admits only) 2012–2013, 0. Total enrolled 2012–2013 full-time, 11. Total enrolled 2012–2013 part-time, 9. Openings 2013–2014, 4. The median number of years required for completion of a degree in 2012–2013 were 7. The number of students enrolled full- and part-time who were dismissed or voluntarily withdrew from this program area in 2012–2013 were 0. *School Psychology EdS (School Psychology)*—Applications 2012–2013, 46. Total applicants accepted 2012–2013, 19. Number full-time enrolled (new admits only) 2012–2013, 12. Number part-time enrolled (new admits only) 2012–2013, 0. Total enrolled 2012–2013 full-time, 24. Total enrolled 2012–2013 part-time, 10. Openings 2013–2014, 12. The median number of years required for completion of a degree in 2012–2013 were 3. The number of students enrolled full- and part-time who were dismissed or voluntarily withdrew from this program area in 2012–2013 were 1.

Scores: Entries appear in this order: required test or GPA, minimum score (if required), median score of students entering in 2012–2013. *School Psychology PhD (Doctor of Philosophy):* GRE-V no minimum stated, 157, GRE-Q no minimum stated, 151, GRE-Analytical no minimum stated, 4.5, overall undergraduate GPA no minimum stated, 3.53, last 2 years GPA no minimum stated, 3.83, psychology GPA no minimum stated, 3.81; *School Psychology EdS (School Psychology):* GRE-V no minimum stated, 154, GRE-Q no minimum stated, 147, GRE-Analytical no minimum stated, 4.5, overall undergraduate GPA no minimum stated, 3.68, last 2 years GPA no minimum stated, 3.73, psychology GPA no minimum stated, 3.71.

Other Criteria: (importance of criteria rated low, medium, or high): GRE scores—high, research experience—medium, work experience—medium, extracurricular activity—medium, clinically related public service—high, GPA—high, letters of recommendation—high, interview—high, statement of goals and objectives—high, undergraduate major in psychology—medium, specific undergraduate psychology courses taken—medium, Specific, focused goals aligned with doctoral study (including research) are expected for doctoral applicants. For additional information on admission requirements, go to http://cech.uc.edu/programs/school_psychology/future_students/the-admissions-process.html.

Student Characteristics: The following represents characteristics of students in 2012–2013 in all graduate psychology programs in the department: Female—full-time 32, part-time 16; Male—full-time 3, part-time 3; African American/Black—full-time 1, part-time 1; Hispanic/Latino(a)—full-time 0, part-time 0; Asian/Pacific Islander—full-time 0, part-time 0; American Indian/Alaska Native—full-time 0, part-time 0; Caucasian/White—full-time 34, part-time 18; Multi-ethnic—full-time 0, part-time 0; students subject to the Americans With Disabilities Act—full-time 0, part-time 0; Unknown ethnicity—full-time 0, part-time 0; International students who hold an F-1 or J-1 Visa—full-time 0, part-time 0.

Financial Information/Assistance:

Tuition for Full-Time Study: *Master's:* State residents: per academic year $14,182, $710 per credit hour; Nonstate residents: per academic year $25,696, $1,285 per credit hour. *Doctoral:* State residents: per academic year $14,182, $710 per credit hour; Nonstate residents: per academic year $25,696, $1,285 per credit hour. Tuition is subject to change. See the following website for updates and changes in tuition costs: http://www.uc.edu/af/bursar/fees.html.

Financial Assistance:

First-Year Students: Research assistantships available for first year. Average amount paid per academic year: $11,115. Average number of hours worked per week: 20. Fellowships and scholarships available for first year. Average amount paid per academic year: $10,000.

Advanced Students: Teaching assistantships available for advanced students. Average amount paid per academic year: $11,115. Average number of hours worked per week: 20. Research assistantships available for advanced students. Average amount paid per academic year: $11,115. Average number of hours worked per week: 20. Traineeships available for advanced students. Average amount paid per academic year: $25,000. Fellowships and scholarships available for advanced students. Average amount paid per academic year: $15,000. Average number of hours worked per week: 0.

Additional Information: Of all students currently enrolled full time, 100% benefited from one or more of the listed financial assistance programs. Application and information available online at: http://cech.uc.edu/programs/school_psychology/future_students/financial_assistance_information.html.

Internships/Practica: Doctoral Degree (PhD School Psychology): For those doctoral students for whom a professional psychology internship was required in this program prior to graduation, (3) students applied for an internship in 2011–2012, with (3) students obtaining an internship. Of those students who obtained an internship, (3) were paid internships. Of those students who obtained an internship, (0) students placed in APA/CPA accredited internships, (0) students placed in internships not APA/CPA accredited, but listed with the Association of Psychology Postdoctoral and Internship Programs (APPIC), (3) students placed in internships conforming to guidelines of the Council of Directors of School Psychology Programs (CDSPP), (0) students placed in internships that were not APA/CPA accredited, APPIC or CDSPP listed. All students, specialist and doctoral level, complete extensive practica prior to internship in field settings that include local school districts and educational agencies. In the first year, students are placed in schools (urban settings, K-12) to learn about schooling, educational issues, effective instruction, and roles and responsibilities of various personnel. Field experiences also occur to support foundation skills in applied behavior analysis and academic and behavioral intervention. Doctoral students also participate as research team members in schools in Years 1 through 3. Throughout the second year, students are enrolled in an integrated practicum experience, in which students obtain extensive supervised experience in delivery of services from a consultative, intervention-based tiered service delivery model. Students collaborate to design, implement, and evaluate prevention and intervention plans in the practicum, incorporating elements of their learning from across course work. In addition, they complete field experiences in behavioral counseling and functional assessment. Third year doctoral students completed advanced field-based work in research and facilitating systems change. Specialist-level students complete a 10-month, 1500 hour school-based internship. These internships are arranged through the program and are paid. In the internship, students provide a full range of comprehensive school psychological services, with supervision from a licensed school psychologist and from university faculty. Doctoral students complete an advanced field experience in Year 3, participating in leadership, staff development, supervision, and research activities. Doctoral students complete a 1500 hour internship consistent with CDSPP, APA, and NASP internship requirements.

Housing and Day Care: On-campus housing is available. See the following website for more information: http://www.uc.edu/uchousing/graduate_housing.html. On-campus day care facilities are available. See the following website for more information: http://www.uc.edu/elc.html; http://cech.uc.edu/centers/arlitt.html.

Employment of Department Graduates:

Master's Degree Graduates: Of those who graduated in the academic year 2011–2012, the following categories and numbers represent the postgraduate activities and employment of master's

degree graduates: Enrolled in a postdoctoral residency/fellowship (n/a), employed in independent practice (n/a), employed in a professional position in a school system (10), total from the above (master's) (10).

Doctoral Degree Graduates: Of those who graduated in the academic year 2011–2012, the following categories and numbers represent the postgraduate activities and employment of doctoral degree graduates: Enrolled in a psychology doctoral program (n/a), employed in a professional position in a school system (2), total from the above (doctoral) (2).

Additional Information:

Orientation, Objectives, and Emphasis of Department: The School Psychology program at the University of Cincinnati is dedicated to preparing highly competent professional school psychologists, at the specialist (EdS) and doctoral (PhD) levels, according to the scientist–practitioner model. The program builds on foundations in psychology and education, and fosters a special sensitivity to cultural diversity of all people and respect for the uniqueness and human dignity of each person. The program emphasizes the delivery of school psychological services within a tiered service delivery model (prevention to targeted intervention) using a collaborative consultation model from an ecological / behavioral orientation. Students learn to view problems from an ecological / systems perspective focusing on child, family, school and community and to provide comprehensive intervention-based services utilizing data-based decision making to design, implement, and evaluate strategies for preventing and resolving learning and adjustment problem situations across a tiered service delivery model. A child advocacy perspective, built on a scientist–practitioner foundation, provides a framework for guiding decisions and practices to support positive outcomes for all children. Both theoretical and empirical bases of professional practice are emphasized and a diverse range of practical experiences are provided throughout all preparation (preschool to high school, in urban, suburban, and rural settings). The program is noted for its intervention emphasis, focusing on data-based decision making across all tiers of service delivery (prevention/school-wide intervention, target and supplemental intervention, and intensive, individualized intervention). In addition to these program themes, training at the doctoral level emphasizes advanced research and evaluation training, leadership supervision and systems-level change facilitation. Doctoral students participate as research team members in schools in Years 1 through 3 prior to leading pre-dissertation and dissertation studies.

Special Facilities or Resources: The program has access to excellent field-based training and research partnerships through collaborative relationships with several local school districts, educational agencies, and Head Start programs. Research facilities include statistical consultation for students, a college evaluation services center, and support for student research through college-sponsored mentoring grants.

Information for Students With Physical Disabilities: See the following website for more information: http://www.uc.edu/aess/disability.html.

Application Information:

Application available online. URL of online application: http://grad.uc.edu/admissions.html. Students are admitted in the Fall, application deadline January 15. *Fee:* $45.

Cleveland State University
Counseling Psychology
Education and Human Services
2121 Euclid Avenue
Cleveland, OH 44115
Telephone: (216) 687-4697
Fax: (216) 875-9697
E-mail: *w.pruett-butler@csuohio.edu*
Web: *http://www.csuohio.edu/cehs/departments/DOC/cp_doc.html*

Department Information:

1986. Director of Training: Donna Schultheiss. Number of faculty: total—full-time 9; women—full-time 5; total—minority—full-time 2; women minority—full-time 1.

Programs and Degrees Offered:

Listed in the following order: Program area, degree type (T if terminal Master's), number awarded 7/11–6/12. Counseling Psychology PhD (Doctor of Philosophy) 1, Clinical Mental Health Counseling MEd (Education) 12, School Counseling MEd (Education) 34.

APA Accreditation: Counseling PhD (Doctor of Philosophy). Student Outcome Data Website: http://www.csuohio.edu/cehs/departments/DOC/cp_doc.html.

Student Applications/Admissions:
Student Applications

Counseling Psychology PhD (Doctor of Philosophy)—Applications 2012–2013, 21. Total applicants accepted 2012–2013, 9. Number full-time enrolled (new admits only) 2012–2013, 2. Number part-time enrolled (new admits only) 2012–2013, 0. Total enrolled 2012–2013 full-time, 30. Total enrolled 2012–2013 part-time, 0. Openings 2013–2014, 7. The median number of years required for completion of a degree in 2012–2013 were 6. The number of students enrolled full- and part-time who were dismissed or voluntarily withdrew from this program area in 2012–2013 were 0. *Clinical Mental Health Counseling MEd (Education)*—Applications 2012–2013, 69. Total applicants accepted 2012–2013, 47. Number full-time enrolled (new admits only) 2012–2013, 12. Number part-time enrolled (new admits only) 2012–2013, 12. Total enrolled 2012–2013 full-time, 29. Total enrolled 2012–2013 part-time, 11. Openings 2013–2014, 60. The median number of years required for completion of a degree in 2012–2013 were 5. The number of students enrolled full- and part-time who were dismissed or voluntarily withdrew from this program area in 2012–2013 were 0. *School Counseling MEd (Education)*—Applications 2012–2013, 45. Total applicants accepted 2012–2013, 23. Number full-time enrolled (new admits only) 2012–2013, 1. Number part-time enrolled (new admits only) 2012–2013, 6. Total enrolled 2012–2013 full-time, 3. Total enrolled 2012–2013 part-time, 10. Openings 2013–2014, 60. The median number of years required for completion of a degree in 2012–2013 were 3. The number of students enrolled full- and part-time who were dismissed or voluntarily withdrew from this program area in 2012–2013 were 0.

Scores: Entries appear in this order: required test or GPA, minimum score (if required), median score of students entering

in 2012–2013. *Counseling Psychology PhD (Doctor of Philosophy)*: GRE-V no minimum stated, 151, GRE-Q no minimum stated, 147, overall undergraduate GPA 2.85, 3.59, Masters GPA no minimum stated, 3.84; *Clinical Mental Health Counseling MEd (Education)*: GRE-V no minimum stated, 150, GRE-Q no minimum stated, 144, overall undergraduate GPA no minimum stated; *School Counseling MEd (Education)*: GRE-V no minimum stated, 149, GRE-Q no minimum stated, 142, GRE-Analytical no minimum stated, overall undergraduate GPA no minimum stated.

Other Criteria: (importance of criteria rated low, medium, or high): GRE scores—high, research experience—high, work experience—medium, extracurricular activity—low, clinically related public service—medium, GPA—high, letters of recommendation—high, interview—high, statement of goals and objectives—high, undergraduate major in psychology—low, specific undergraduate psychology courses taken—low, Criteria vary for masters programs. For additional information on admission requirements, go to http://www.csuohio.edu/cehs/departments/DOC/cp_doc.html.

Student Characteristics: The following represents characteristics of students in 2012–2013 in all graduate psychology programs in the department: Female—full-time 48, part-time 0; Male—full-time 14, part-time 21; African American/Black—full-time 8, part-time 24; Hispanic/Latino(a)—full-time 4, part-time 2; Asian/Pacific Islander—full-time 1, part-time 2; American Indian/Alaska Native—full-time 0, part-time 0; Caucasian/White—full-time 46, part-time 68; Multi-ethnic—full-time 0, part-time 1; students subject to the Americans With Disabilities Act—full-time 0, part-time 0; Unknown ethnicity—full-time 2, part-time 7; International students who hold an F-1 or J-1 Visa—full-time 2, part-time 0.

Financial Information/Assistance:

Tuition for Full-Time Study: *Master's:* State residents: per academic year $13,279, $510 per credit hour; Nonstate residents: per academic year $24,979, $960 per credit hour. *Doctoral:* State residents: per academic year $13,279, $510 per credit hour; Nonstate residents: per academic year $17,959, $690 per credit hour. Tuition is subject to change. See the following website for updates and changes in tuition costs: http://www.csuohio.edu/offices/treasuryservices/tuition/.

Financial Assistance:

First-Year Students: Teaching assistantships available for first year. Average amount paid per academic year: $11,800. Average number of hours worked per week: 20. Apply by April 15. Research assistantships available for first year. Average amount paid per academic year: $5,900. Average number of hours worked per week: 10. Apply by April 15.

Advanced Students: Teaching assistantships available for advanced students. Average amount paid per academic year: $11,800. Average number of hours worked per week: 20. Apply by April 15. Research assistantships available for advanced students. Average amount paid per academic year: $5,900. Average number of hours worked per week: 10. Apply by April 15.

Additional Information: Application and information available online at: http://mycsu.csuohio.edu/gradcollege/students/graduateassistant/index.html.

Internships/Practica: Doctoral Degree (PhD Counseling Psychology): For those doctoral students for whom a professional psychol-

ogy internship was required in this program prior to graduation, (8) students applied for an internship in 2011–2012, with (6) students obtaining an internship. Of those students who obtained an internship, (4) were paid internships. Of those students who obtained an internship, (4) students placed in APA/CPA accredited internships, (0) students placed in internships not APA/CPA accredited, but listed with the Association of Psychology Postdoctoral and Internship Programs (APPIC), (0) students placed in internships conforming to guidelines of the Council of Directors of School Psychology Programs (CDSPP), (2) students placed in internships that were not APA/CPA accredited, APPIC or CDSPP listed. Consistent with the program's focus on serving diverse urban populations, all practicum sites are situated in Northeast Ohio, and most are located in the heart of the greater Cleveland area. Our sites include mental health agencies, hospitals, residential centers, schools, and college counseling centers. As such, students have a rich opportunity to gain exposure to clients from a variety of backgrounds. This also ensures that students have ample opportunity to be trained across the spectrum of functioning and a wide continuum of roles, including testing, treatment, community outreach and prevention.

Housing and Day Care: On-campus housing is available. See the following website for more information: http://www.csuohio.edu/services/reslife/. On-campus day care facilities are available. See the following website for more information: http://www.csuohio.edu/services/childcare/.

Employment of Department Graduates:

Master's Degree Graduates: Of those who graduated in the academic year 2011–2012, the following categories and numbers represent the postgraduate activities and employment of master's degree graduates: Enrolled in a postdoctoral residency/fellowship (n/a), employed in independent practice (n/a), total from the above (master's) (0).

Doctoral Degree Graduates: Of those who graduated in the academic year 2011–2012, the following categories and numbers represent the postgraduate activities and employment of doctoral degree graduates: Enrolled in a psychology doctoral program (n/a), enrolled in a postdoctoral residency/fellowship (1), employed in a community mental health/counseling center (1), employed in a hospital/medical center (1), total from the above (doctoral) (3).

Additional Information:

Orientation, Objectives, and Emphasis of Department: The Counseling Psychology Program at Cleveland State University is based on a scientist–practitioner model of training and practice. The program emphasizes counseling psychology as a scientific discipline that is based in the tradition of studying individual differences and the social and cultural context of human behavior. It provides extensive study of multicultural aspects of human behavior with particular emphasis on the impact of urban environments. Its mission is to educate counseling psychologists with strong professional identification with the discipline and with the knowledge, skills, and attitudes to work effectively with diverse populations of clients. In the tradition of counseling psychology, the program's mission is also to educate students who are skilled not only to intervene with clients experiencing psychological dysfunction, but also to facilitate healthy development. Its training model is largely interdisciplinary, integrating knowledge in urban studies, educational psychology, organizational development, and educational policy with core content in research design, foundations of psychology, and counseling psychology courses. Counseling psychology students are enrolled in Urban Education courses with doctoral students in related disciplines in several courses to foster an interdisciplinary understanding of human behavior in urban contexts.

Information for Students With Physical Disabilities: See the following website for more information: http://www.csuohio.edu/offices/disability/.

Application Information:

Send to Campus411 All-in-1, Main Classroom 116, 1899 East 22nd Street, Cleveland, OH 44115-2214. Application available online. URL of online application: http://www.csuohio.edu/gradcollege/admissions/degree.html. Students are admitted in the Fall, application deadline January 15; Programs have rolling admissions. Doctoral applications for Counseling Psychology accepted January 15 only. *Fee:* $30.

Cleveland State University

Department of Psychology
College of Sciences and Health Professions
2121 Euclid Avenue
Cleveland, OH 44115
Telephone: (216) 687-2544
Fax: (216) 687-9294
E-mail: *k.mcnamara@csuohio.edu*
Web: *http://www.csuohio.edu/sciences/dept/psychology/*

Department Information:

1968. Chairperson: Kathy McNamara. Number of faculty: total—full-time 16, part-time 13; women—full-time 7, part-time 8; total—minority—full-time 2, part-time 4; women minority—full-time 2, part-time 3.

Programs and Degrees Offered:

Listed in the following order: Program area, degree type (T if terminal Master's), number awarded 7/11–6/12. Clinical Psychology MA/MS (Master of Arts/Science) (T), Adult Development and Aging PhD (Doctor of Philosophy), Specialist in School Psychology Other, Experimental Research MA/MS (Master of Arts/Science) (T), Consumer and Industrial Research MA/MS (Master of Arts/Science) (T), Diversity Management MA/MS (Master of Arts/Science).

Student Applications/Admissions:

Student Applications

Clinical Psychology MA/MS (Master of Arts/Science)—Applications 2012–2013, 87. Total applicants accepted 2012–2013, 12. Number full-time enrolled (new admits only) 2012–2013, 12. Total enrolled 2012–2013 full-time, 27. *Adult Development and Aging PhD (Doctor of Philosophy)—Specialist in School Psychology Other*—Applications 2012–2013, 55. Total applicants accepted 2012–2013, 11. Number full-time enrolled (new admits only) 2012–2013, 11. Total enrolled 2012–2013 full-time, 36. *Experimental Research MA/MS (Master of Arts/Science)*—Applications 2012–2013, 29. Total applicants accepted 2012–2013, 8. Number full-time enrolled (new admits only) 2012–2013, 8. Total enrolled 2012–2013 full-time, 12. *Consumer and Industrial Research MA/MS (Master of Arts/Science)*—

Applications 2012–2013, 19. Total applicants accepted 2012–2013, 5. Number full-time enrolled (new admits only) 2012–2013, 5. Total enrolled 2012–2013 full-time, 11. *Diversity Management MA/MS (Master of Arts/Science)*—Applications 2012–2013, 22. Total applicants accepted 2012–2013, 14. Number full-time enrolled (new admits only) 2012–2013, 14. Total enrolled 2012–2013 full-time, 26. Openings 2013–2014, 20. The number of students enrolled full- and part-time who were dismissed or voluntarily withdrew from this program area in 2012–2013 were 3.

Scores: Entries appear in this order: required test or GPA, minimum score (if required), median score of students entering in 2012–2013. *Clinical Psychology MA/MS (Master of Arts/Science):* GRE-V 500, 460, GRE-Q 500, 560, GRE-Analytical 4.0, 4.0, overall undergraduate GPA 3.0, 3.4; *Adult Development and Aging PhD (Doctor of Philosophy):* GRE-V 550, 550, GRE-Q 500, 590, GRE-Analytical 4.0, 4.5, GRE-Subject (Psychology) 550, 640, overall undergraduate GPA 3.25, 3.8; *Specialist in School Psychology Other:* GRE-V 500, 450, GRE-Q 500, 540, GRE-Analytical 4.0, 3.5, overall undergraduate GPA 2.75, 3.3; *Experimental Research MA/MS (Master of Arts/Science):* GRE-V 500, 500, GRE-Q 500, 540, GRE-Analytical 4.0, 3.5; *Consumer and Industrial Research MA/MS (Master of Arts/Science):* GRE-V 500, 500, GRE-Q 500, 560, GRE-Analytical 4.0, 4.0.

Other Criteria: (importance of criteria rated low, medium, or high): GRE scores—high, research experience—high, work experience—medium, clinically related public service—low, GPA—high, letters of recommendation—high, interview—high, statement of goals and objectives—high, undergraduate major in psychology—medium, specific undergraduate psychology courses taken—medium. For additional information on admission requirements, go to http://www.csuohio.edu/sciences/dept/psychology/graduate/.

Student Characteristics: The following represents characteristics of students in 2012–2013 in all graduate psychology programs in the department: Female—full-time 68, part-time 0; Male—full-time 17, part-time 0; African American/Black—full-time 4, part-time 0; Hispanic/Latino(a)—full-time 1, part-time 0; Asian/Pacific Islander—full-time 0, part-time 0; American Indian/Alaska Native—full-time 0, part-time 0; Caucasian/White—full-time 80, part-time 0; Multi-ethnic—full-time 0, part-time 0; students subject to the Americans With Disabilities Act—full-time 1, part-time 0; Unknown ethnicity—full-time 0, part-time 0; International students who hold an F-1 or J-1 Visa—part-time 0.

Financial Information/Assistance:

Tuition for Full-Time Study: *Master's:* State residents: $510 per credit hour; Nonstate residents: $988 per credit hour. *Doctoral:* State residents: $510 per credit hour; Nonstate residents: $710 per credit hour. Additional fees are assessed to students beyond the costs of tuition for the following: online courses; lab fees for some courses. See the following website for updates and changes in tuition costs: http://www.csuohio.edu/offices/treasuryservices/tuition/. Higher tuition cost for this program: Diversity Management.

Financial Assistance:

First-Year Students: Teaching assistantships available for first year. Average amount paid per academic year: $2,400. Average number of hours worked per week: 10. Research assistantships available for first year. Average amount paid per academic year: $2,400. Average number of hours worked per week: 10.

Advanced Students: Teaching assistantships available for advanced students. Average amount paid per academic year: $15,500. Average number of hours worked per week: 20. Research assistantships available for advanced students. Average amount paid per academic year: $15,500. Average number of hours worked per week: 20.

Additional Information: Application and information available online at: http://www.csuohio.edu/sciences/dept/psychology/graduate/assistantship.html.

Internships/Practica: Master's Degree (MA/MS Clinical Psychology): An internship experience, such as a final research project or "capstone" experience is required of graduates. Master's Degree (MA/MS Experimental Research): An internship experience, such as a final research project or "capstone" experience is required of graduates. Clinical students and third-year School Psychology students complete a 20-hour/40-hour per week internship (respectively) as part of the degree requirements. Consumer and Industrial Research program students are encouraged to apply for paid internships in business settings to earn hands-on consulting or research experience. Practica during the two-year curriculum are integrated into coursework.

Housing and Day Care: On-campus housing is available. See the following website for more information: http://www.csuohio.edu/services/reslife/. On-campus day care facilities are available. See the following website for more information: http://www.csuohio.edu/services/childcare/.

Employment of Department Graduates:

Master's Degree Graduates: Of those who graduated in the academic year 2011–2012, the following categories and numbers represent the postgraduate activities and employment of master's degree graduates: Enrolled in a postdoctoral residency/fellowship (n/a), employed in independent practice (n/a), total from the above (master's) (0).

Doctoral Degree Graduates: Of those who graduated in the academic year 2011–2012, the following categories and numbers represent the postgraduate activities and employment of doctoral degree graduates: Enrolled in a psychology doctoral program (n/a), total from the above (doctoral) (0).

Additional Information:

Orientation, Objectives, and Emphasis of Department: Departmental faculty provide significant breadth across the entire discipline as well as considerable depth in professional and applied areas. The Clinical program is a CAMPP-approved program. It emphasizes theory, principles, and application, which prepares students for more advanced training (PhD, PsyD, EdD) or for jobs requiring psychological service in clinical, community, and educational settings. Orientations include psychodynamic, cognitive, and behavioral viewpoints in assessment and individual, group, family, and community intervention. The School program is NASP-accredited. A post-MA year fulfills requirements for the Psychology Specialist degree. The primary goals of the Experimental Research program are to train students to conduct scientific research in a chosen area of psychology and to prepare students for further graduate work in psychology or for employment in research settings and institutions. The Consumer/Industrial Research program prepares students to apply psychological concepts

and research techniques in business and in institutional settings. It combines advanced quantitative research with hands-on experience involving problems and issues encountered in industrial and service organizations. The department also jointly operates a PhD program in Adult Development and Aging with the University of Akron. Upon completion of the program, students will be able to teach, carry out research, and serve as community consultants on the cognitive, motor, perceptual, and social functioning of adults throughout their life span.

Information for Students With Physical Disabilities: See the following website for more information: http://www.csuohio.edu/offices/disability/.

Application Information:
Send to Cleveland State University, Graduate Admissions, 2121 Euclid Avenue, Cleveland, OH 44115. Application available online. URL of online application: http://www.csuohio.edu/gradcollege/admissions/degree.html. Students are admitted in the Fall, application deadline February 15. *Fee:* $30.

Dayton, University of
Department of Counselor Education & Human Services/School Psychology
School of Education and Allied Professions
300 College Park Avenue
Dayton, OH 45469-0530
Telephone: (937) 229-3644
Fax: (937) 229-1055
E-mail: *sdavies1@udayton.edu*
Web: *http://www.udayton.edu/education/edc/programs/school_psychology.php*

Department Information:
1978. Chairperson: Molly Schaller, PhD. Number of faculty: total—full-time 12, part-time 3; women—full-time 8, part-time 3; total—minority—full-time 1.

Programs and Degrees Offered:
Listed in the following order: Program area, degree type (T if terminal Master's), number awarded 7/11–6/12. School Psychology EdS (School Psychology) 12.

Student Applications/Admissions:
Student Applications
School Psychology EdS (School Psychology)—Applications 2012–2013, 46. Total applicants accepted 2012–2013, 10. Number full-time enrolled (new admits only) 2012–2013, 9. Number part-time enrolled (new admits only) 2012–2013, 1. Total enrolled 2012–2013 full-time, 26. Total enrolled 2012–2013 part-time, 7. Openings 2013–2014, 12. The median number of years required for completion of a degree in 2012–2013 were 3. The number of students enrolled full- and part-time who were dismissed or voluntarily withdrew from this program area in 2012–2013 were 3.

Scores: Entries appear in this order: required test or GPA, minimum score (if required), median score of students entering in 2012–2013. School Psychology EdS (School Psychology): GRE-V no minimum stated, GRE-Q no minimum stated, GRE-

Analytical no minimum stated, overall undergraduate GPA 2.75.

Other Criteria: (importance of criteria rated low, medium, or high): GRE scores—medium, research experience—medium, work experience—medium, extracurricular activity—low, clinically related public service—low, GPA—medium, letters of recommendation—medium, interview—high, statement of goals and objectives—medium, undergraduate major in psychology—medium, specific undergraduate psychology courses taken—medium. For additional information on admission requirements, go to http://www.udayton.edu/learn/graduate/education/major_school_psychology.php.

Student Characteristics: The following represents characteristics of students in 2012–2013 in all graduate psychology programs in the department: Female—full-time 22, part-time 5; Male—full-time 4, part-time 2; African American/Black—full-time 0, part-time 1; Hispanic/Latino(a)—full-time 0, part-time 0; Asian/Pacific Islander—full-time 0, part-time 0; American Indian/Alaska Native—full-time 0, part-time 0; Caucasian/White—full-time 26, part-time 6; Multi-ethnic—full-time 0, part-time 0; students subject to the Americans With Disabilities Act—full-time 0, part-time 0; Unknown ethnicity—full-time 0, part-time 0; International students who hold an F-1 or J-1 Visa—full-time 0, part-time 0.

Financial Information/Assistance:
Tuition for Full-Time Study: *Master's:* State residents: $541 per credit hour; Nonstate residents: $541 per credit hour. Tuition is subject to change. Additional fees are assessed to students beyond the costs of tuition for the following: $25.00 University Fee. See the following website for updates and changes in tuition costs: http://www.udayton.edu/bursar/tuitionfees/. Higher tuition cost for this program: Educational Specialist degree after completing Masters is $649.00 per credit hour.

Financial Assistance:
First-Year Students: Research assistantships available for first year. Average amount paid per academic year: $8,550. Average number of hours worked per week: 20. Apply by January 9.

Advanced Students: Research assistantships available for advanced students. Average amount paid per academic year: $9,200. Average number of hours worked per week: 20. Apply by January 9. Fellowships and scholarships available for advanced students. Average amount paid per academic year: $22,000.

Additional Information: Of all students currently enrolled full time, 60% benefited from one or more of the listed financial assistance programs. Application and information available online at: http://www.udayton.edu/flyersfirst/financialaid/grad/.

Internships/Practica: The practicum experience provides supervised opportunities to hone skills required in professional practice. This experience also includes a complementary course individually based on setting and field experience. The culminating internship provides an opportunity to develop professionally under the guidance of professionals. The paid internship is completed on a full-time basis for one year in a school district supervised by qualified school psychologists.

Housing and Day Care: On-campus housing is available. See the following website for more information: http://www.udayton.edu/studev/housing/current/graduate_options.php. On-campus day care facilities are available. See the following website for more information: http://www.udayton.edu/education/cel/bombeckcenter/.

Employment of Department Graduates:
Master's Degree Graduates: Of those who graduated in the academic year 2011–2012, the following categories and numbers represent the postgraduate activities and employment of master's degree graduates: Enrolled in a postdoctoral residency/fellowship (n/a), employed in independent practice (n/a), employed in a professional position in a school system (8), total from the above (master's) (8).

Doctoral Degree Graduates: Of those who graduated in the academic year 2011–2012, the following categories and numbers represent the postgraduate activities and employment of doctoral degree graduates: Enrolled in a psychology doctoral program (n/a), total from the above (doctoral) (0).

Additional Information:
Orientation, Objectives, and Emphasis of Department: The school psychology program is comprehensive, integrated, and sequential. Courses reflect the most current advances in the field of school psychology and education with a commitment to the implementation and integration of the most current technology applications. This program is structured so course content blends effectively with field experience.

Special Facilities or Resources: We are pleased to have new facilities housing graduate classes. The River Campus, located at 1700 South Patterson Boulevard, welcomes graduate students in Counselor Education and Educational Leadership. This beautiful facility has a wide range of interactive classroom space as well as high tech observation labs for Master's-level counseling students.

Information for Students With Physical Disabilities: See the following website for more information: http://www.udayton.edu/ltc/learningresources/.

Application Information:
Send to University of Dayton, Graduate Admissions, 300 College Park Avenue, Dayton, OH 45469-1670. Application available online. URL of online application: https://gradadmission.udayton.edu/application/app_login.asp. Students are admitted in the Fall, application deadline January 10. *Fee:* $0.

Dayton, University of
Department of Psychology
300 College Park Avenue
Dayton, OH 45469-1430
Telephone: (937) 229-2713
Fax: (937) 229-3900
E-mail: *cphelps1@udayton.edu*
Web: *http://www.udayton.edu/artssciences/psychology/index.php*

Department Information:
1937. Chairperson: Carolyn Roecker Phelps. Number of faculty: total—full-time 20, part-time 6; women—full-time 8, part-time 3; total—minority—full-time 3.

Programs and Degrees Offered:

Listed in the following order: Program area, degree type (T if terminal Master's), number awarded 7/11–6/12. Clinical Psychology MA/MS (Master of Arts/Science) (T) 7, General Psychology MA/MS (Master of Arts/Science) (T) 1, Cognitive-Human Factors Psychology MA/MS (Master of Arts/Science) (T) 0.

Student Applications/Admissions:

Student Applications

Clinical Psychology MA/MS (Master of Arts/Science)—Applications 2012–2013, 71. Total applicants accepted 2012–2013, 8. Number full-time enrolled (new admits only) 2012–2013, 8. Number part-time enrolled (new admits only) 2012–2013, 0. Total enrolled 2012–2013 full-time, 16. Total enrolled 2012–2013 part-time, 0. Openings 2013–2014, 8. The median number of years required for completion of a degree in 2012–2013 were 3. The number of students enrolled full- and part-time who were dismissed or voluntarily withdrew from this program area in 2012–2013 were 1. *General Psychology MA/MS (Master of Arts/Science)*—Applications 2012–2013, 25. Total applicants accepted 2012–2013, 4. Number full-time enrolled (new admits only) 2012–2013, 3. Number part-time enrolled (new admits only) 2012–2013, 0. Total enrolled 2012–2013 full-time, 9. Total enrolled 2012–2013 part-time, 0. Openings 2013–2014, 5. The median number of years required for completion of a degree in 2012–2013 were 3. The number of students enrolled full- and part-time who were dismissed or voluntarily withdrew from this program area in 2012–2013 were 0. *Cognitive-Human Factors Psychology MA/MS (Master of Arts/Science)*—Applications 2012–2013, 0. Total applicants accepted 2012–2013, 0.

Scores: Entries appear in this order: required test or GPA, minimum score (if required), median score of students entering in 2012–2013. *Clinical Psychology MA/MS (Master of Arts/Science):* GRE-V no minimum stated, GRE-Q no minimum stated, GRE-Analytical no minimum stated, overall undergraduate GPA no minimum stated, psychology GPA no minimum stated; *General Psychology MA/MS (Master of Arts/Science):* GRE-V no minimum stated, GRE-Q no minimum stated, GRE-Analytical no minimum stated, overall undergraduate GPA no minimum stated, psychology GPA no minimum stated.

Other Criteria: (importance of criteria rated low, medium, or high): GRE scores—high, research experience—high, work experience—medium, extracurricular activity—low, clinically related public service—low, GPA—high, letters of recommendation—high, statement of goals and objectives—high, undergraduate major in psychology—medium, specific undergraduate psychology courses taken—high.

Student Characteristics: The following represents characteristics of students in 2012–2013 in all graduate psychology programs in the department: Female—full-time 18, part-time 0; Male—full-time 7, part-time 0; African American/Black—full-time 2, part-time 0; Hispanic/Latino(a)—full-time 0, part-time 0; Asian/Pacific Islander—full-time 0, part-time 0; American Indian/Alaska Native—full-time 0, part-time 0; Caucasian/White—full-time 23, part-time 0; Multi-ethnic—full-time 0, part-time 0; students subject to the Americans With Disabilities Act—full-time 0, part-time 0; Unknown ethnicity—full-time 0, part-time 0; International students who hold an F-1 or J-1 Visa—full-time 0, part-time 0.

Financial Information/Assistance:

Tuition for Full-Time Study: *Master's:* State residents: $788 per credit hour; Nonstate residents: $788 per credit hour. Tuition is subject to change. See the following website for updates and changes in tuition costs: http://www.udayton.edu/bursar/tuitionfees/index.php.

Financial Assistance:

First-Year Students: Teaching assistantships available for first year. Average amount paid per academic year: $10,818. Average number of hours worked per week: 20. Apply by March 1. Research assistantships available for first year. Average amount paid per academic year: $10,818. Average number of hours worked per week: 20. Apply by March 1. Traineeships available for first year. Average amount paid per academic year: $6,000. Average number of hours worked per week: 17. Apply by March 1.

Advanced Students: Teaching assistantships available for advanced students. Average amount paid per academic year: $10,818. Average number of hours worked per week: 20. Apply by March 1. Research assistantships available for advanced students. Average amount paid per academic year: $10,818. Average number of hours worked per week: 20. Apply by March 1. Traineeships available for advanced students. Average amount paid per academic year: $6,000. Average number of hours worked per week: 17. Apply by March 1.

Additional Information: Of all students currently enrolled full time, 88% benefited from one or more of the listed financial assistance programs. Application and information available online at: http://www.udayton.edu/flyersfirst/financialaid/grad/index.php.

Internships/Practica: Master's Degree (MA/MS Clinical Psychology): An internship experience, such as a final research project or "capstone" experience is required of graduates. Master's Degree (MA/MS General Psychology): An internship experience, such as a final research project or "capstone" experience is required of graduates. Master's Degree (MA/MS Cognitive-Human Factors Psychology): An internship experience, such as a final research project or "capstone" experience is required of graduates. A limited number of paid traineeship placements at local mental health agencies are available for both first and second year clinical students. These traineeships satisfy the programs's practicum requirements and include partial tuition remission. The human factors practicum is required of all program students and enables the student to gain practical experience working for governmental agencies or industrial firms during the summer between their first and second years.

Housing and Day Care: No on-campus housing is available. On-campus day care facilities are available. See the following website for more information: http://www.udayton.edu/education/cel/bombeckcenter/.

Employment of Department Graduates:

Master's Degree Graduates: Of those who graduated in the academic year 2011–2012, the following categories and numbers represent the postgraduate activities and employment of master's degree graduates: Enrolled in a psychology doctoral program (4), enrolled in a postdoctoral residency/fellowship (n/a), employed in independent practice (n/a), employed in a hospital/medical center (1), do not know (1), total from the above (master's) (6).

Doctoral Degree Graduates: Of those who graduated in the academic year 2011–2012, the following categories and numbers represent the postgraduate activities and employment of doctoral degree graduates: Enrolled in a psychology doctoral program (n/a), total from the above (doctoral) (0).

Additional Information:

Orientation, Objectives, and Emphasis of Department: The Department of Psychology offers graduate programs leading to the MA degree in clinical and general psychology. Emphasis is placed on integrating theory and literature with appropriate applied experience and on competence in the development of relevant research. This is the product of individual supervision and a low student-to-faculty ratio. The aim of the department is to prepare the student for doctoral training or employment at the MA level in an applied/community setting, in research, or in teaching. A recent survey has shown that over 86% of our MA graduates who applied for doctoral programs in the last 6 years were accepted. Also, 98% of our MA graduates seeking employment have found jobs in psychologically related areas.

Special Facilities or Resources: Laboratory and computer facilities are available to support student and faculty research. These include computer-based facilities for research in cognitive science, human factors, social psychology, and clinical psychology as well as a state-of-the-art Information Science Research Laboratory for multidisciplinary research in human-computer interaction. In additon, research opportunities are available through the University's Research Institute, the Fitz Center for Leadership in Community, and local community agencies.

Information for Students With Physical Disabilities: See the following website for more information: http://www.udayton.edu/ltc/learningresources/index.php.

Application Information:
Application available online. URL of online application: http://gradadmission.udayton.edu/application. Students are admitted in the Fall, application deadline March 1. *Fee:* $0.

Kent State University
Department of Psychology
College of Arts and Sciences
P.O. Box 5190
Kent, OH 44242-0001
Telephone: (330) 672-2166
Fax: (330) 672-3786
E-mail: *gradpsyc@kent.edu*
Web: *http://www.kent.edu/cas/psychology/index.cfm*

Department Information:
1936. Chairperson: Maria Zaragoza, PhD. Number of faculty: total—full-time 32; women—full-time 18; total—minority—full-time 4; women minority—full-time 4; faculty subject to the Americans With Disabilities Act 2.

Programs and Degrees Offered:
Listed in the following order: Program area, degree type (T if terminal Master's), number awarded 7/11–6/12. Clinical Psychol-

ogy PhD (Doctor of Philosophy) 13, Experimental Psychology PhD (Doctor of Philosophy) 3.

APA Accreditation: Clinical PhD (Doctor of Philosophy). Student Outcome Data Website: http://www.kent.edu/CAS/Psychology/graduate/trainingareas/clinical/index.cfm.

Student Applications/Admissions:
Student Applications

Clinical Psychology PhD (Doctor of Philosophy)—Applications 2012–2013, 356. Total applicants accepted 2012–2013, 12. Number full-time enrolled (new admits only) 2012–2013, 12. Number part-time enrolled (new admits only) 2012–2013, 0. Total enrolled 2012–2013 full-time, 64. Total enrolled 2012–2013 part-time, 0. Openings 2013–2014, 9. The median number of years required for completion of a degree in 2012–2013 were 6. The number of students enrolled full- and part-time who were dismissed or voluntarily withdrew from this program area in 2012–2013 were 1. *Experimental Psychology PhD (Doctor of Philosophy)*—Applications 2012–2013, 80. Total applicants accepted 2012–2013, 8. Number full-time enrolled (new admits only) 2012–2013, 6. Number part-time enrolled (new admits only) 2012–2013, 0. Total enrolled 2012–2013 full-time, 35. Total enrolled 2012–2013 part-time, 0. Openings 2013–2014, 8. The median number of years required for completion of a degree in 2012–2013 were 6. The number of students enrolled full- and part-time who were dismissed or voluntarily withdrew from this program area in 2012–2013 were 2.

Scores: Entries appear in this order: required test or GPA, minimum score (if required), median score of students entering in 2012–2013. *Clinical Psychology PhD (Doctor of Philosophy):* GRE-V no minimum stated, 157, GRE-Q no minimum stated, 154, overall undergraduate GPA 3.0, 3.68, last 2 years GPA 3.0; *Experimental Psychology PhD (Doctor of Philosophy):* GRE-V no minimum stated, 154, GRE-Q no minimum stated, 155, overall undergraduate GPA 3.0, 4.5, last 2 years GPA 3.0.

Other Criteria: (importance of criteria rated low, medium, or high): GRE scores—high, research experience—high, work experience—low, extracurricular activity—low, clinically related public service—low, GPA—high, letters of recommendation—high, interview—high, statement of goals and objectives—high, undergraduate major in psychology—high, specific undergraduate psychology courses taken—medium. For additional information on admission requirements, go to http://www.kent.edu/CAS/Psychology/futurestudents/graduate-apply.cfm.

Student Characteristics: The following represents characteristics of students in 2012–2013 in all graduate psychology programs in the department: Female—full-time 65, part-time 0; Male—full-time 34, part-time 0; African American/Black—full-time 2, part-time 0; Hispanic/Latino(a)—full-time 3, part-time 0; Asian/Pacific Islander—full-time 2, part-time 0; American Indian/Alaska Native—full-time 0, part-time 0; Caucasian/White—full-time 88, part-time 0; Multi-ethnic—full-time 0, part-time 0; students subject to the Americans With Disabilities Act—full-time 0, part-time 0; Unknown ethnicity—full-time 0, part-time 0; International students who hold an F-1 or J-1 Visa—full-time 4, part-time 0.

Financial Information/Assistance:

Tuition for Full-Time Study: *Doctoral:* State residents: $397 per credit hour; Nonstate residents: $739 per credit hour. Tuition is subject to change. See the following website for updates and changes in tuition costs: http://www.kent.edu/bursar/termdetail/tuition-fee-schedules.cfm.

Financial Assistance:

First-Year Students: Teaching assistantships available for first year. Average amount paid per academic year: $15,429. Average number of hours worked per week: 20. Apply by December 15. Research assistantships available for first year. Average amount paid per academic year: $15,429. Average number of hours worked per week: 20. Apply by December 15.

Advanced Students: Teaching assistantships available for advanced students. Average amount paid per academic year: $15,429. Average number of hours worked per week: 20. Research assistantships available for advanced students. Average amount paid per academic year: $15,429. Average number of hours worked per week: 20. Fellowships and scholarships available for advanced students.

Additional Information: Of all students currently enrolled full time, 99% benefited from one or more of the listed financial assistance programs. Application and information available online at: http://www.kent.edu/graduatestudies/prospectivestudents/financial-aid.cfm.

Internships/Practica: Doctoral Degree (PhD Clinical Psychology): For those doctoral students for whom a professional psychology internship was required in this program prior to graduation, (14) students applied for an internship in 2011–2012, with (14) students obtaining an internship. Of those students who obtained an internship, (14) were paid internships. Of those students who obtained an internship, (14) students placed in APA/CPA accredited internships, (0) students placed in internships not APA/CPA accredited, but listed with the Association of Psychology Postdoctoral and Internship Programs (APPIC), (0) students placed in internships conforming to guidelines of the Council of Directors of School Psychology Programs (CDSPP), (0) students placed in internships that were not APA/CPA accredited, APPIC or CDSPP listed. Two semesters of didactic practica and five semesters of clinical practica in the Department's Psychological Clinic are required. Clinical students also must complete a minimum of 1000 hours of supervised clinical experience at local placement sites and a 2000 hour supervised clinical internship in an internship program accredited by the American Psychological Association (these are competitive internships).

Housing and Day Care: On-campus housing is available. See the following website for more information: https://www.kent.edu/housing/prospectiveresidents/. On-campus day care facilities are available. See the following website for more information: http://www.kent.edu/ehhs/cdc/.

Employment of Department Graduates:

Master's Degree Graduates: Of those who graduated in the academic year 2011–2012, the following categories and numbers represent the postgraduate activities and employment of master's degree graduates: Enrolled in a postdoctoral residency/fellowship (n/a), employed in independent practice (n/a), total from the above (master's) (0).

Doctoral Degree Graduates: Of those who graduated in the academic year 2011–2012, the following categories and numbers represent the postgraduate activities and employment of doctoral degree graduates: Enrolled in a psychology doctoral program (n/a), enrolled in a postdoctoral residency/fellowship (6), employed in independent practice (1), employed in an academic position at a university (1), employed in an academic position at a 2-year/4-year college (4), employed in other positions at a higher education institution (2), employed in a hospital/medical center (2), do not know (1), total from the above (doctoral) (17).

Additional Information:

Orientation, Objectives, and Emphasis of Department: The programs' objectives are to train those who can contribute through research, teaching, service, innovation, and administration. Graduate students in clinical psychology may specialize in adult psychopathology, assessment, child clinical and adolescent, neuropsychology, or health. Graduate students in experimental psychology may specialize in behavioral neuroscience, cognitive, developmental, health, or social psychology. Students in both programs may obtain a minor in Quantitative Methods. A common program of basic core courses is required of all students. Training facilities and laboratories are freely available to graduate students.

Special Facilities or Resources: The Department has well-equipped laboratories available for human and animal research. Research opportunities also are available in various mental health and hospital settings in the area. Clinical training opportunities are available in the Psychological Clinic, which is staffed by clinical faculty and graduate students. The Applied Psychology Center supports research focused on psychological problems of social significance.

Information for Students With Physical Disabilities: See the following website for more information: http://www.kent.edu/sas/.

Application Information:

Send to Division of Graduate Studies, Cartwright Hall, 650 Hilltop Drive, Kent State University, Kent, OH 44242. Application available online. URL of online application: http://www.kent.edu/admissions/apply/graduate/. Students are admitted in the Fall, application deadline December 15. *Fee:* $30.

Kent State University

School Psychology Program
College of Education, Health, and Human Services
150 Terrace Drive, School of LDES, 405 White Hall
Kent, OH 44242
Telephone: (330) 672-2294
Fax: (330) 672-2512
E-mail: *fsansost@kent.edu*
Web: *http://www.kent.edu/ehhs/spsy/index.cfm*

Department Information:

1964. School Director: Dr. Mary Dellman-Jenkins. Number of faculty: total—full-time 4, part-time 4; women—full-time 1, part-time 3; total—minority—full-time 1; women minority—full-time 1.

Programs and Degrees Offered:
Listed in the following order: Program area, degree type (T if terminal Master's), number awarded 7/11–6/12. School Psychology PhD (Doctor of Philosophy) 1, School Psychology EdS (School Psychology) 14.

APA Accreditation: School PhD (Doctor of Philosophy). Student Outcome Data Website: http://www.kent.edu/ehhs/spsy/m-ed-ph-d-program.cfm.

Student Applications/Admissions:
Student Applications
School Psychology PhD (Doctor of Philosophy)—Applications 2012–2013, 14. Total applicants accepted 2012–2013, 5. Number full-time enrolled (new admits only) 2012–2013, 1. Number part-time enrolled (new admits only) 2012–2013, 0. Total enrolled 2012–2013 full-time, 6. Total enrolled 2012–2013 part-time, 5. Openings 2013–2014, 4. The median number of years required for completion of a degree in 2012–2013 were 7. The number of students enrolled full- and part-time who were dismissed or voluntarily withdrew from this program area in 2012–2013 were 0. School Psychology EdS (School Psychology)—Applications 2012–2013, 37. Total applicants accepted 2012–2013, 25. Number full-time enrolled (new admits only) 2012–2013, 15. Number part-time enrolled (new admits only) 2012–2013, 0. Total enrolled 2012–2013 full-time, 49. Total enrolled 2012–2013 part-time, 0. Openings 2013–2014, 18. The median number of years required for completion of a degree in 2012–2013 were 3. The number of students enrolled full- and part-time who were dismissed or voluntarily withdrew from this program area in 2012–2013 were 2.

Scores: Entries appear in this order: required test or GPA, minimum score (if required), median score of students entering in 2012–2013. School Psychology PhD (Doctor of Philosophy): GRE-V no minimum stated, GRE-Q no minimum stated, GRE-Analytical no minimum stated, overall undergraduate GPA 3.0; School Psychology EdS (School Psychology): GRE-V no minimum stated, GRE-Q no minimum stated, GRE-Analytical no minimum stated, overall undergraduate GPA 3.0.

Other Criteria: (importance of criteria rated low, medium, or high): GRE scores—high, research experience—high, work experience—medium, extracurricular activity—medium, clinically related public service—medium, GPA—high, letters of recommendation—high, interview—high, statement of goals and objectives—high. For additional information on admission requirements, go to http://www.kent.edu/ehhs/ldes/spsy/admissions.cfm.

Student Characteristics: The following represents characteristics of students in 2012–2013 in all graduate psychology programs in the department: Female—full-time 53, part-time 4; Male—full-time 2, part-time 1; African American/Black—full-time 0, part-time 0; Hispanic/Latino(a)—full-time 1, part-time 1; Asian/Pacific Islander—full-time 0, part-time 0; American Indian/Alaska Native—full-time 0, part-time 0; Caucasian/White—full-time 53, part-time 4; Multi-ethnic—full-time 1, part-time 0; Unknown ethnicity—full-time 0, part-time 0; International students who hold an F-1 or J-1 Visa—full-time 0, part-time 0.

Financial Information/Assistance:
Tuition for Full-Time Study: *Master's:* State residents: per academic year $10,290, $468 per credit hour; Nonstate residents: per academic year $17,806, $738 per credit hour. *Doctoral:* State residents: per academic year $10,920, $468 per credit hour; Nonstate residents: per academic year $17,806, $738 per credit hour. Tuition is subject to change. Additional fees are assessed to students beyond the costs of tuition for the following: Some courses (e.g., assessment) require minimal additional materials fees. See the following website for updates and changes in tuition costs: http://www.kent.edu/bursar/termdetail/tuition-fee-schedules.cfm.

Financial Assistance:
First-Year Students: Teaching assistantships available for first year. Average amount paid per academic year: $8,500. Average number of hours worked per week: 20. Research assistantships available for first year. Average amount paid per academic year: $8,500. Average number of hours worked per week: 20.

Advanced Students: Teaching assistantships available for advanced students. Average amount paid per academic year: $12,000. Average number of hours worked per week: 20. Research assistantships available for advanced students. Average amount paid per academic year: $12,000. Average number of hours worked per week: 20.

Additional Information: Application and information available online at: http://www.kent.edu/graduatestudies/prospectivestudents/financial-aid.cfm.

Internships/Practica: Doctoral Degree (PhD School Psychology): For those doctoral students for whom a professional psychology internship was required in this program prior to graduation, (1) students applied for an internship in 2011–2012, with (1) students obtaining an internship. Of those students who obtained an internship, (1) were paid internships. Of those students who obtained an internship, (0) students placed in APA/CPA accredited internships, (1) students placed in internships not APA/CPA accredited, but listed with the Association of Psychology Postdoctoral and Internship Programs (APPIC), (0) students placed in internships conforming to guidelines of the Council of Directors of School Psychology Programs (CDSPP), (0) students placed in internships that were not APA/CPA accredited, APPIC or CDSPP listed. Practica occur in educational and mental health settings that are chosen to provide: (a) comprehensive experiences that complement previous and current preparation; (b) appropriate supervision and mentorship; and (c) applied experiences to address individual and program objectives. EdS students take two years of practica prior to internship. Doctoral students participate in multiple years of practica. Both the Specialist and Doctoral internships in school psychology follow the completion of all course work and practica. Specialist level internships are full-time for an academic year, and must occur in school settings. If completed in Ohio, the internship must conform to the Ohio Internship in School Psychology Guidelines. These internships have historically been state-supported, and students receive a generous training stipend. A variety of approved settings may be appropriate for the doctoral internship, including educational settings, hospitals, and mental health centers.

Housing and Day Care: On-campus housing is available. See the following website for more information: http://www.kent.edu/housing/index.cfm. On-campus day care facilities are available. See the following website for more information: http://www.kent.edu/ehhs/cdc/index.cfm.

Employment of Department Graduates:

Master's Degree Graduates: Of those who graduated in the academic year 2011–2012, the following categories and numbers represent the postgraduate activities and employment of master's degree graduates: Enrolled in a postdoctoral residency/fellowship (n/a), employed in independent practice (n/a), employed in a professional position in a school system (14), total from the above (master's) (14).

Doctoral Degree Graduates: Of those who graduated in the academic year 2011–2012, the following categories and numbers represent the postgraduate activities and employment of doctoral degree graduates: Enrolled in a psychology doctoral program (n/a), employed in a professional position in a school system (1), total from the above (doctoral) (1).

Additional Information:

Orientation, Objectives, and Emphasis of Department: The KSU school psychology program embraces a preventive mental health model as a context for the study of psychological and educational principles that influence the adjustment of individuals and systems. A commitment to using the science of psychology to promote human welfare is emphasized. In addition, recognizing the pluralistic nature of our society, the program is committed to fostering in its students sensitivity to, appreciation for, and understanding of all individual differences. The program emphasizes the provision of services to individual schools and children, in addition to attaining a functional understanding of systems-consultation and the ability to promote and implement primary and secondary prevention programs to optimize adjustment. The KSU doctoral (PhD) program in school psychology adheres to a scientist–practitioner model of training, which conceptualizes school psychologists as data-oriented problem-solvers and transmitters of psychological knowledge and skill. Since the doctoral program's emphasis is on the application of psychology in applied educational and mental health settings, students are required to demonstrate competence in the substantive content areas of psychological and educational theory and practice. Other related areas outside the school psychology core include coursework in the biological, cognitive/perceptual, social, developmental, and historical/systems bases of behavior, as well as in the areas of curriculum and instruction, educational foundations, and research.

Special Facilities or Resources: The Center for Disability Studies provides interdisciplinary research support for faculty and graduate students engaged in research on disability issues. The Child Development Center, an early childhood model laboratory school, provides opportunities for faculty and student research and practice. The Family Child Learning Center, which offers early intervention services to infants and toddlers with disabilities and their families, offers a training location for grant-funded school psychology students and for faculty research. The Bureau of Educational Research provides a source of support for students who are engaged in research activities, including data entry and analysis.

Information for Students With Physical Disabilities: See the following website for more information: http://www.kent.edu/sas/index.cfm.

Application Information:
Send to Kent State University, Division of Graduate Studies, 650 Hilltop Drive, Cartwright Hall, Kent, Ohio 44242. Application available online. URL of online application: http://www.kent.edu/admissions/apply/graduate/index.cfm. Students are admitted in the Fall, application deadline June 15; Spring, application deadline October 15; Summer, application deadline January 10. The preferred admission cycle is the January 10 deadline in order to begin the program in June (Summer). *Fee:* $30.

Marietta College
Department of Psychology
215 Fifth Street
Marietta, OH 45750
Telephone: (740) 376-4762
Fax: (740) 376-4459
E-mail: *sibickym@marietta.edu*
Web: *http://www.marietta.edu/departments/Psychology/*

Department Information:
1926. Director of the Master of Arts Program in General Psychology: Mark E. Sibicky. Number of faculty: total—full-time 5; women—full-time 2.

Programs and Degrees Offered:
Listed in the following order: Program area, degree type (T if terminal Master's), number awarded 7/11–6/12. General Psychology MA/MS (Master of Arts/Science) (T) 1.

Student Applications/Admissions:
Student Applications

General Psychology MA/MS (Master of Arts/Science)—Applications 2012–2013, 9. Total applicants accepted 2012–2013, 7. Number full-time enrolled (new admits only) 2012–2013, 6. Number part-time enrolled (new admits only) 2012–2013, 0. Total enrolled 2012–2013 full-time, 12. Total enrolled 2012–2013 part-time, 0. Openings 2013–2014, 10. The median number of years required for completion of a degree in 2012–2013 were 2. The number of students enrolled full- and part-time who were dismissed or voluntarily withdrew from this program area in 2012–2013 were 1.

Scores: Entries appear in this order: required test or GPA, minimum score (if required), median score of students entering in 2012–2013. *General Psychology MA/MS (Master of Arts/Science):* GRE-V no minimum stated, GRE-Q no minimum stated, GRE-Analytical no minimum stated, overall undergraduate GPA 3.0, psychology GPA 3.0.

Other Criteria: (importance of criteria rated low, medium, or high): GRE scores—medium, research experience—low, work experience—low, extracurricular activity—low, clinically related public service—low, GPA—medium, letters of recommendation—high, statement of goals and objectives—high, undergraduate major in psychology—medium, specific undergraduate psychology courses taken—high. For additional information on admission requirements, go to http://www.marietta.edu/Academics/graduate_degrees/Master_of_Arts_in_Psychology.html.

Student Characteristics: The following represents characteristics of students in 2012–2013 in all graduate psychology programs in the department: Female—full-time 9, part-time 0; Male—full-time 3, part-time 0; African American/Black—full-time 0, part-

time 0; Hispanic/Latino(a)—full-time 0, part-time 0; Asian/Pacific Islander—full-time 0, part-time 0; American Indian/Alaska Native—full-time 0, part-time 0; Caucasian/White—full-time 12, part-time 0; Multi-ethnic—full-time 0, part-time 0; students subject to the Americans With Disabilities Act—full-time 0, part-time 0; Unknown ethnicity—full-time 0, part-time 0; International students who hold an F-1 or J-1 Visa—full-time 0, part-time 0.

Financial Information/Assistance:

Tuition for Full-Time Study: *Master's:* State residents: $700 per credit hour; Nonstate residents: $700 per credit hour. Tuition is subject to change.

Financial Assistance:

First-Year Students: Teaching assistantships available for first year. Average amount paid per academic year: $4,000. Average number of hours worked per week: 15. Apply by April 1. Research assistantships available for first year. Average amount paid per academic year: $4,000. Average number of hours worked per week: 15. Apply by April 1.

Advanced Students: Teaching assistantships available for advanced students. Average amount paid per academic year: $4,000. Average number of hours worked per week: 15. Apply by April 1. Research assistantships available for advanced students. Average amount paid per academic year: $4,000. Average number of hours worked per week: 15. Apply by April 1.

Additional Information: Of all students currently enrolled full time, 35% benefited from one or more of the listed financial assistance programs.

Internships/Practica: Master's Degree (MA/MS General Psychology): An internship experience, such as a final research project or "capstone" experience is required of graduates. Students select two three-credit electives in an applied professional practicum experience. The practicum is designed to provide students with an applied experience relating to their career interests in psychology. Students choose electives from the following areas: The Teaching of Psychology - designed to train students to be effective instructors of psychology; Supervised Internship - internships in the area of clinical, developmental, or applied psychology (e.g. business/law); Directed Independent Research - students pursue their own research interests under the direction of a faculty member.

Housing and Day Care: No on-campus housing is available. No on-campus day care facilities are available.

Employment of Department Graduates:

Master's Degree Graduates: Of those who graduated in the academic year 2011–2012, the following categories and numbers represent the postgraduate activities and employment of master's degree graduates: Enrolled in a postdoctoral residency/fellowship (n/a), employed in independent practice (n/a), employed in a community mental health/counseling center (1), total from the above (master's) (1).

Doctoral Degree Graduates: Of those who graduated in the academic year 2011–2012, the following categories and numbers represent the postgraduate activities and employment of doctoral degree graduates: Enrolled in a psychology doctoral program (n/a), total from the above (doctoral) (0).

Additional Information:

Orientation, Objectives, and Emphasis of Department: The Psychology Department at Marietta College offers a two-year Master of Arts Degree in General Psychology. The program is designed to give students a strong graduate level foundation in psychology so students may pursue further education in psychology at the PhD level or to aid students in securing employment in a field related to psychology. The orientation of the department faculty is that psychology is a science, and that psychological research and knowledge can be applied to improving people's lives. The two year program consists of 24 core content hours in psychology, six hours of applied practicum electives in an area of professional psychology (e.g., clinical internship, developmental internship, teaching of psychology), and six hours of supervised thesis research. The program offers the opportunity for students to pursue research interests in clinical, social, developmental, cognitive, or biological psychology. Faculty have high expectations for students' academic performance, yet are committed to mentoring students and helping students achieve their educational and professional goals.

Special Facilities or Resources: The Psychology Department at Marietta College has a newly remodeled human research laboratory equipped with research cubicles, video equipment, one-way observational windows, and specialized cognitive and physiological equipment and software. Students may apply for graduate research and conference travel funds. Other facilities include a graduate seminar room, graduate student office and student lounge.

Information for Students With Physical Disabilities: See the following website for more information: http://www.marietta.edu/Academics/resources/ARC/disability.html.

Application Information:

Send to Office of Admissions, Master of Arts in Psychology, Marietta College, 215 Fifth Street, Marietta, Ohio 45750. Application available online. URL of online application: http://www.marietta.edu/Academics/graduate_degrees/Master_of_Arts_in_Psychology.html. Students are admitted in the Fall, application deadline April 1. *Fee:* $25.

Miami University of Ohio
Department of Psychology
90 North Patterson Avenue
Oxford, OH 45056
Telephone: (513) 529-2400
Fax: (513) 529-2420
E-mail: *hugenbk@miamioh.edu*
Web: *http://www.units.muohio.edu/psychology/*

Department Information:

1888. Chairperson: Leonard S. Mark. Number of faculty: total—full-time 37, part-time 2; women—full-time 23; total—minority—full-time 3; women minority—full-time 2.

Programs and Degrees Offered:

Listed in the following order: Program area, degree type (T if terminal Master's), number awarded 7/11–6/12. Clinical Psychol-

ogy PhD (Doctor of Philosophy) 5, Brain and Cognitive Science PhD (Doctor of Philosophy) 3, Social Psychology PhD (Doctor of Philosophy) 3.

APA Accreditation: Clinical PhD (Doctor of Philosophy). Student Outcome Data Website: http://www.units.muohio.edu/psychology/research-areas/clinical/student-admissions-outcomes-and-other-data.

Student Applications/Admissions:

Student Applications

Clinical Psychology PhD (Doctor of Philosophy)—Applications 2012–2013, 155. Total applicants accepted 2012–2013, 6. Number full-time enrolled (new admits only) 2012–2013, 6. Number part-time enrolled (new admits only) 2012–2013, 0. Total enrolled 2012–2013 full-time, 39. Total enrolled 2012–2013 part-time, 0. Openings 2013–2014, 6. The median number of years required for completion of a degree in 2012–2013 were 7. The number of students enrolled full- and part-time who were dismissed or voluntarily withdrew from this program area in 2012–2013 were 0. *Brain and Cognitive Science PhD (Doctor of Philosophy)*—Applications 2012–2013, 33. Total applicants accepted 2012–2013, 4. Number full-time enrolled (new admits only) 2012–2013, 4. Number part-time enrolled (new admits only) 2012–2013, 0. Total enrolled 2012–2013 full-time, 23. Total enrolled 2012–2013 part-time, 0. Openings 2013–2014, 3. The median number of years required for completion of a degree in 2012–2013 were 5. *Social Psychology PhD (Doctor of Philosophy)*—Applications 2012–2013, 54. Total applicants accepted 2012–2013, 2. Number full-time enrolled (new admits only) 2012–2013, 2. Number part-time enrolled (new admits only) 2012–2013, 0. Total enrolled 2012–2013 full-time, 14. Total enrolled 2012–2013 part-time, 0. Openings 2013–2014, 3. The median number of years required for completion of a degree in 2012–2013 were 6. The number of students enrolled full- and part-time who were dismissed or voluntarily withdrew from this program area in 2012–2013 were 0.

Scores: Entries appear in this order: required test or GPA, minimum score (if required), median score of students entering in 2012–2013. *Brain and Cognitive Science PhD (Doctor of Philosophy):* GRE-V 152, 160, GRE-Q 154, 162, GRE-Analytical 3.5, 3.75, overall undergraduate GPA 3.15, 3.59; *Social Psychology PhD (Doctor of Philosophy):* GRE-V 157, 160, GRE-Q 155, 161, GRE-Analytical 4.5, 4.75, overall undergraduate GPA 3.45, 3.51.

Other Criteria: (importance of criteria rated low, medium, or high): GRE scores—medium, research experience—high, work experience—low, extracurricular activity—medium, clinically related public service—medium, GPA—high, letters of recommendation—high, interview—medium, statement of goals and objectives—high, undergraduate major in psychology—low, specific undergraduate psychology courses taken—medium, Only Clinical program employs an interview; Social and Brain/Cognitive areas offer an "Open House/Visit" day for students offered admission. For additional information on admission requirements, go to http://www.units.muohio.edu/psychology/graduate/graduate-admission.

Student Characteristics: The following represents characteristics of students in 2012–2013 in all graduate psychology programs in the department: Female—full-time 48, part-time 0; Male—full-time 28, part-time 0; African American/Black—full-time 3, part-time 0; Hispanic/Latino(a)—full-time 1, part-time 0; Asian/Pacific Islander—full-time 11, part-time 0; American Indian/Alaska Native—full-time 1, part-time 0; Caucasian/White—full-time 59, part-time 0; Multi-ethnic—full-time 1, part-time 0; students subject to the Americans With Disabilities Act—full-time 1, part-time 0; Unknown ethnicity—full-time 0, part-time 0; International students who hold an F-1 or J-1 Visa—full-time 8, part-time 0.

Financial Information/Assistance:

Tuition for Full-Time Study: *Doctoral:* State residents: per academic year $12,864, $715 per credit hour; Nonstate residents: per academic year $27,483, $1,526 per credit hour. Tuition is subject to change. See the following website for updates and changes in tuition costs: http://www.units.muohio.edu/bur/fees/oxfees_grad_08-09_later.php.

Financial Assistance:

First-Year Students: Teaching assistantships available for first year. Average amount paid per academic year: $20,619. Average number of hours worked per week: 20. Apply by December 1. Research assistantships available for first year. Average amount paid per academic year: $15,392. Average number of hours worked per week: 20. Apply by December 1.

Advanced Students: Teaching assistantships available for advanced students. Average amount paid per academic year: $20,619. Average number of hours worked per week: 20. Research assistantships available for advanced students. Average amount paid per academic year: $15,392. Average number of hours worked per week: 20. Fellowships and scholarships available for advanced students. Average amount paid per academic year: $20,619. Average number of hours worked per week: 20.

Additional Information: Of all students currently enrolled full time, 100% benefited from one or more of the listed financial assistance programs. Application and information available online at: http://www.units.muohio.edu/psychology/graduate/graduate-admission/application-details.

Internships/Practica: Doctoral Degree (PhD Clinical Psychology): For those doctoral students for whom a professional psychology internship was required in this program prior to graduation, (5) students applied for an internship in 2011–2012, with (5) students obtaining an internship. Of those students who obtained an internship, (5) were paid internships. Of those students who obtained an internship, (5) students placed in APA/CPA accredited internships, (0) students placed in internships not APA/CPA accredited, but listed with the Association of Psychology Postdoctoral and Internship Programs (APPIC), (0) students placed in internships conforming to guidelines of the Council of Directors of School Psychology Programs (CDSPP), (0) students placed in internships that were not APA/CPA accredited, APPIC or CDSPP listed. There are opportunities for students to engage in practica and internships as well as conduct applied research. Traineeships for advanced clinical students are available in a wide range of settings including community mental health centers, hospitals, and school systems.

Housing and Day Care: On-campus housing is available. See the following website for more information: http://www.hdg.muohio.edu/Housing/. On-campus day care facilities are available. See the following website for more information: http://www.miniuniversity.net/.

Employment of Department Graduates:

Master's Degree Graduates: Of those who graduated in the academic year 2011–2012, the following categories and numbers represent the postgraduate activities and employment of master's degree graduates: Enrolled in a postdoctoral residency/fellowship (n/a), employed in independent practice (n/a), total from the above (master's) (0).

Doctoral Degree Graduates: Of those who graduated in the academic year 2011–2012, the following categories and numbers represent the postgraduate activities and employment of doctoral degree graduates: Enrolled in a psychology doctoral program (n/a), enrolled in a postdoctoral residency/fellowship (3), employed in an academic position at a university (2), employed in an academic position at a 2-year/4-year college (2), employed in a community mental health/counseling center (2), total from the above (doctoral) (9).

Additional Information:

Orientation, Objectives, and Emphasis of Department: The goal of the department is to provide an environment in which students thrive intellectually. We strive for a balance between enough structure to gauge student progress and provide grounding in the breadth of psychology and enough freedom for students to design programs optimal to their own professional goals. The department provides training and experience in research, teaching, and application of psychology. The department offers basic and applied research orientations in all programs. The clinical program emphasizes a theory-research-practicum combination, so that graduates will be able to function in a variety of academic and service settings. The objective of the department is to produce skilled, informed, and enthusiastic psychologists, capable of contributing to their field in a variety of ways.

Special Facilities or Resources: The department has laboratories dedicated to the study of social cognition, group processes and social interaction as well as cognitive processes including higher-order cognition, decision-making, perception, spatial cognition, and motor control. Two laboratories use virtual environments to study spatial cognition and posture, and one of these has created one of the largest virtual environments in the world. Two biological psychology laboratories offer advanced facilities for neurological recording, drug delivery, and pharmacological and histological analyses. The Center for Human Psychophysiology offers access to EEG and other psychophysiological measurement tools. The Center for Psychological Inquiry facilitates undergraduate research. The Psychology Clinic includes group and child therapy rooms, individual assessment and therapy rooms, a test library, conference room, and offices for the clinic director and a full-time secretary. Clinical services are offered in a training or research context to university students and the Oxford community, including a school-based mental health program. Research with children is facilitated by a good relationship with local public school systems and childcare facilities. Access to clinical populations is available through the Psychology Clinic and through cooperative arrangements with nearby mental health centers. Several faculty are engaged in community action projects related to mental health needs in local communities.

Information for Students With Physical Disabilities: See the following website for more information: http://www.units.miamioh.edu/oeeo/odr/.

Application Information:
Send to The Graduate School, 102 Roudebush, Miami University, Oxford, Ohio 45056. Application available online. URL of online application: http://wwwmiamimuohioedu/graduate-studies/admission/ Students are admitted in the Fall, application deadline December 1. December 1 for Clinical applicants. January 1 for Social & Brain & Cognitive applicants. *Fee:* $50.

Ohio State University (2012 data)
School of Physical Activity and Educational Services
Education
100A PAES Building, 305 West 17th Avenue
Columbus, OH 43210
Telephone: (614) 292-5909
Fax: (614) 292-4255
E-mail: *joseph.21@osu.edu*
Web: *http://ehe.osu.edu*

Department Information:
1996. Director: Jim Kinder. Number of faculty: total—full-time 3; women—full-time 3; total—minority—full-time 2; women minority—full-time 2.

Programs and Degrees Offered:
Listed in the following order: Program area, degree type (T if terminal Master's), number awarded 7/11–6/12. School Psychology MA/MS (Master of Arts/Science) 16, School Psychology PhD (Doctor of Philosophy) 6.

Student Applications/Admissions:
Student Applications

School Psychology MA/MS (Master of Arts/Science)—Applications 2012–2013, 89. Total applicants accepted 2012–2013, 12. Number full-time enrolled (new admits only) 2012–2013, 11. Total enrolled 2012–2013 full-time, 14. Total enrolled 2012–2013 part-time, 0. Openings 2013–2014, 10. The median number of years required for completion of a degree in 2012–2013 were 3. The number of students enrolled full- and part-time who were dismissed or voluntarily withdrew from this program area in 2012–2013 were 1. *School Psychology PhD (Doctor of Philosophy)*—Applications 2012–2013, 15. Total applicants accepted 2012–2013, 5. Number full-time enrolled (new admits only) 2012–2013, 2. Total enrolled 2012–2013 full-time, 19. Openings 2013–2014, 5. The median number of years required for completion of a degree in 2012–2013 were 5. The number of students enrolled full- and part-time who were dismissed or voluntarily withdrew from this program area in 2012–2013 were 0.

Scores: Entries appear in this order: required test or GPA, minimum score (if required), median score of students entering in 2012–2013. *School Psychology MA/MS (Master of Arts/Science):* GRE-V 500, GRE-Q 500, overall undergraduate GPA 3.0; *School Psychology PhD (Doctor of Philosophy):* GRE-V no minimum stated, GRE-Q no minimum stated, overall undergraduate GPA 3.0.

Other Criteria: (importance of criteria rated low, medium, or high): GRE scores—high, research experience—high, work experience—medium, extracurricular activity—medium, clinically related public service—medium, GPA—high, letters of recommendation—high, interview—high, statement of goals and objectives—high, undergraduate major in psychology—medium, specific undergraduate psychology courses taken—medium.

Student Characteristics: The following represents characteristics of students in 2012–2013 in all graduate psychology programs in the department: Female—full-time 27, part-time 0; Male—full-time 6, part-time 0; African American/Black—full-time 4, part-time 0; Hispanic/Latino(a)—full-time 3, part-time 0; Asian/Pacific Islander—full-time 0, part-time 0; American Indian/Alaska Native—full-time 0, part-time 0; Caucasian/White—full-time 0, part-time 0; Multi-ethnic—full-time 0, part-time 0; students subject to the Americans With Disabilities Act—full-time 1, part-time 0; Unknown ethnicity—full-time 0, part-time 0; International students who hold an F-1 or J-1 Visa—full-time 0, part-time 0.

Financial Information/Assistance:
Tuition for Full-Time Study: *Master's:* State residents: per academic year $9,000; Nonstate residents: per academic year $21,000. *Doctoral:* State residents: per academic year $9,000; Nonstate residents: per academic year $21,000. Tuition is subject to change.

Financial Assistance:
First-Year Students: Fellowships and scholarships available for first year. Average amount paid per academic year: $10,000. Apply by January 1.
Advanced Students: Fellowships and scholarships available for advanced students. Average amount paid per academic year: $10,000. Apply by January 1.
Additional Information: Of all students currently enrolled full time, 40% benefited from one or more of the listed financial assistance programs.

Internships/Practica: Doctoral Degree (PhD School Psychology): For those doctoral students for whom a professional psychology internship was required in this program prior to graduation, (1) students applied for an internship in 2011–2012, with (1) students obtaining an internship. Of those students who obtained an internship, (1) were paid internships. Of those students who obtained an internship, (0) students placed in APA/CPA accredited internships, (0) students placed in internships not APA/CPA accredited, but listed with the Association of Psychology Postdoctoral and Internship Programs (APPIC), (0) students placed in internships conforming to guidelines of the Council of Directors of School Psychology Programs (CDSPP), (1) students placed in internships that were not APA/CPA accredited, APPIC or CDSPP listed. Master's Degree (MA/MS School Psychology): An internship experience, such as a final research project or "capstone" experience is required of graduates. Master's students are engaged in practica during their two years of study. All students gain experience in an urban school district as well as either a rural or suburban setting. Students are involved in a 9-month school-based internship in the Central Ohio area. Internships are paid.

Housing and Day Care: On-campus housing is available. On-campus day care facilities are available. See the following website for more information: http://hr.osu.edu/childcare/index.aspx.

Employment of Department Graduates:
Master's Degree Graduates: Of those who graduated in the academic year 2011–2012, the following categories and numbers represent the postgraduate activities and employment of master's degree graduates: Enrolled in a postdoctoral residency/fellowship (n/a), employed in independent practice (n/a), employed in an academic position at a 2-year/4-year college (1), employed in a professional position in a school system (10), total from the above (master's) (11).
Doctoral Degree Graduates: Of those who graduated in the academic year 2011–2012, the following categories and numbers represent the postgraduate activities and employment of doctoral degree graduates: Enrolled in a psychology doctoral program (n/a), total from the above (doctoral) (0).

Additional Information:
Orientation, Objectives, and Emphasis of Department: The Counselor Education, Rehabilitation Services, and School Psychology Section in the School of Physical Activity and Educational Services emphasizes the preparation of individuals who can function in human services settings such as public and private schools and universities, social agencies, state and federal government agencies, business and industry, hospitals and health care facilities, and rehabilitation agencies. Emphasizing primary prevention, the program will help students, learners, and clients achieve optimal levels of human functioning and advocate for organizations and systems that promote optimal levels of human functioning. Students in the program may undertake course work to emphasize one or more of the three areas: (a) counselor education; (b) rehabilitation services; or (c) school psychology.

Special Facilities or Resources: The School of Physical Activities and Educational Services moved into a new building Spring of 2007. The Counselor Education and School Psychology Programs have a state of the art clinic facility.

Application Information:
Send to School of Physical Activity and Educational Services, Student Services and Academic Programs, 100A PAES Building, 305 West 17th Avenue, Columbus, OH 43210. Students are admitted in the Fall, application deadline December 15. *Fee:* $40.

Ohio State University, The
Department of Psychology
College of Social and Behavioral Sciences
225 Psychology Building, 1835 Neil Avenue
Columbus, OH 43210
Telephone: (614) 292-4112
Fax: (614) 688-8261
E-mail: *basey.3@osu.edu*
Web: *http://www.psy.ohio-state.edu*

Department Information:
1907. Chairperson: Richard E. Petty, PhD. Number of faculty: total—full-time 55, part-time 24; women—full-time 15, part-time 15; total—minority—full-time 7, part-time 2; women minority—full-time 2, part-time 1.

Programs and Degrees Offered:

Listed in the following order: Program area, degree type (T if terminal Master's), number awarded 7/11–6/12. Clinical Psychology PhD (Doctor of Philosophy) 6, Cognitive Psychology PhD (Doctor of Philosophy) 1, Developmental Psychology PhD (Doctor of Philosophy) 0, Intellectual and Developmental Disabilities PhD (Doctor of Philosophy) 1, Behavioral Neuroscience PhD (Doctor of Philosophy) 1, Quantitative Psychology PhD (Doctor of Philosophy) 5, Social Psychology PhD (Doctor of Philosophy) 5.

APA Accreditation: Clinical PhD (Doctor of Philosophy). Student Outcome Data Website: http://www.psy.ohio-state.edu/programs/clinical/applicant.php.

Student Applications/Admissions:

Student Applications

Clinical Psychology PhD (Doctor of Philosophy)—Applications 2012–2013, 200. Total applicants accepted 2012–2013, 22. Number full-time enrolled (new admits only) 2012–2013, 12. Number part-time enrolled (new admits only) 2012–2013, 0. Total enrolled 2012–2013 full-time, 55. Total enrolled 2012–2013 part-time, 0. Openings 2013–2014, 13. The median number of years required for completion of a degree in 2012–2013 were 6. The number of students enrolled full- and part-time who were dismissed or voluntarily withdrew from this program area in 2012–2013 were 0. *Cognitive Psychology PhD (Doctor of Philosophy)*—Applications 2012–2013, 45. Total applicants accepted 2012–2013, 10. Number full-time enrolled (new admits only) 2012–2013, 4. Number part-time enrolled (new admits only) 2012–2013, 0. Total enrolled 2012–2013 full-time, 18. Total enrolled 2012–2013 part-time, 0. Openings 2013–2014, 16. The median number of years required for completion of a degree in 2012–2013 were 5. The number of students enrolled full- and part-time who were dismissed or voluntarily withdrew from this program area in 2012–2013 were 2. *Developmental Psychology PhD (Doctor of Philosophy)*—Applications 2012–2013, 28. Total applicants accepted 2012–2013, 6. Number full-time enrolled (new admits only) 2012–2013, 2. Number part-time enrolled (new admits only) 2012–2013, 0. Total enrolled 2012–2013 full-time, 10. Total enrolled 2012–2013 part-time, 0. Openings 2013–2014, 7. The median number of years required for completion of a degree in 2012–2013 were 7. The number of students enrolled full- and part-time who were dismissed or voluntarily withdrew from this program area in 2012–2013 were 2. *Intellectual and Developmental Disabilities PhD (Doctor of Philosophy)*—Applications 2012–2013, 31. Total applicants accepted 2012–2013, 3. Number full-time enrolled (new admits only) 2012–2013, 0. Number part-time enrolled (new admits only) 2012–2013, 0. Total enrolled 2012–2013 full-time, 10. Total enrolled 2012–2013 part-time, 0. Openings 2013–2014, 3. The median number of years required for completion of a degree in 2012–2013 were 6. The number of students enrolled full- and part-time who were dismissed or voluntarily withdrew from this program area in 2012–2013 were 0. *Behavioral Neuroscience PhD (Doctor of Philosophy)*—Applications 2012–2013, 30. Total applicants accepted 2012–2013, 1. Number full-time enrolled (new admits only) 2012–2013, 1. Number part-time enrolled (new admits only) 2012–2013, 0. Total enrolled 2012–2013 full-time, 8. Total enrolled 2012–2013 part-time, 0. Openings 2013–2014, 1. The median number of years required for com-

pletion of a degree in 2012–2013 were 7. The number of students enrolled full- and part-time who were dismissed or voluntarily withdrew from this program area in 2012–2013 were 0. *Quantitative Psychology PhD (Doctor of Philosophy)*—Applications 2012–2013, 28. Total applicants accepted 2012–2013, 5. Number full-time enrolled (new admits only) 2012–2013, 3. Number part-time enrolled (new admits only) 2012–2013, 0. Total enrolled 2012–2013 full-time, 19. Total enrolled 2012–2013 part-time, 0. Openings 2013–2014, 5. The median number of years required for completion of a degree in 2012–2013 were 5. The number of students enrolled full- and part-time who were dismissed or voluntarily withdrew from this program area in 2012–2013 were 3. *Social Psychology PhD (Doctor of Philosophy)*—Applications 2012–2013, 117. Total applicants accepted 2012–2013, 8. Number full-time enrolled (new admits only) 2012–2013, 5. Number part-time enrolled (new admits only) 2012–2013, 0. Total enrolled 2012–2013 full-time, 30. Total enrolled 2012–2013 part-time, 0. Openings 2013–2014, 10. The median number of years required for completion of a degree in 2012–2013 were 6. The number of students enrolled full- and part-time who were dismissed or voluntarily withdrew from this program area in 2012–2013 were 1.

Scores: Entries appear in this order: required test or GPA, minimum score (if required), median score of students entering in 2012–2013. *Clinical Psychology PhD (Doctor of Philosophy)*: GRE-V no minimum stated, GRE-Q no minimum stated, GRE-Analytical no minimum stated, 4.75, overall undergraduate GPA 3.0, 3.83; *Cognitive Psychology PhD (Doctor of Philosophy)*: GRE-V no minimum stated, GRE-Q no minimum stated, GRE-Analytical no minimum stated, 4.0, overall undergraduate GPA 3.0, 3.83; *Developmental Psychology PhD (Doctor of Philosophy)*: GRE-V no minimum stated, GRE-Q no minimum stated, GRE-Analytical no minimum stated, 4.5, overall undergraduate GPA 3.0, 3.9; *Intellectual and Developmental Disabilities PhD (Doctor of Philosophy)*: GRE-V no minimum stated, GRE-Q no minimum stated, GRE-Analytical no minimum stated, 5, overall undergraduate GPA 3.0, 3.9; *Behavioral Neuroscience PhD (Doctor of Philosophy)*: GRE-V no minimum stated, GRE-Q no minimum stated, GRE-Analytical no minimum stated, 4.5, overall undergraduate GPA 3.0, 3.62; *Quantitative Psychology PhD (Doctor of Philosophy)*: GRE-V no minimum stated, GRE-Q no minimum stated, GRE-Analytical no minimum stated, 3.75, overall undergraduate GPA 3.0, 3.8; *Social Psychology PhD (Doctor of Philosophy)*: GRE-V no minimum stated, GRE-Q no minimum stated, GRE-Analytical no minimum stated, 5, overall undergraduate GPA 3.0, 3.79.

Other Criteria: (importance of criteria rated low, medium, or high): GRE scores—high, research experience—high, work experience—low, extracurricular activity—low, clinically related public service—low, GPA—high, letters of recommendation—high, interview—medium, statement of goals and objectives—medium, undergraduate major in psychology—low, Clinical area ranks Interview as High. For additional information on admission requirements, go to http://www.psy.ohio-state.edu/graduate/application.php.

Student Characteristics: The following represents characteristics of students in 2012–2013 in all graduate psychology programs in the department: Female—full-time 93, part-time 0; Male—full-time 57, part-time 0; African American/Black—full-time 8, part-time 0; Hispanic/Latino(a)—full-time 10, part-time 0; Asian/Pa-

cific Islander—full-time 21, part-time 0; American Indian/Alaska Native—full-time 0, part-time 0; Caucasian/White—full-time 100, part-time 0; Multi-ethnic—full-time 5, part-time 0; students subject to the Americans With Disabilities Act—full-time 2, part-time 0; Unknown ethnicity—full-time 6, part-time 0; International students who hold an F-1 or J-1 Visa—full-time 21, part-time 0.

Financial Information/Assistance:

Tuition for Full-Time Study: *Doctoral:* State residents: per academic year $12,000, $792 per credit hour; Nonstate residents: per academic year $29,513, $1,874 per credit hour. Tuition is subject to change. See the following website for updates and changes in tuition costs: http://registrar.osu.edu/feetables/mainfeetables.asp.

Financial Assistance:

First-Year Students: Teaching assistantships available for first year. Average amount paid per academic year: $14,400. Average number of hours worked per week: 20. Apply by December 1. Research assistantships available for first year. Average amount paid per academic year: $14,400. Average number of hours worked per week: 20. Apply by December 1. Fellowships and scholarships available for first year. Average amount paid per academic year: $20,220. Average number of hours worked per week: 0. Apply by December 1.

Advanced Students: Teaching assistantships available for advanced students. Average amount paid per academic year: $16,200. Average number of hours worked per week: 20. Apply by December 1. Research assistantships available for advanced students. Average amount paid per academic year: $16,200. Average number of hours worked per week: 20. Apply by December 1. Traineeships available for advanced students. Average amount paid per academic year: $16,200. Average number of hours worked per week: 20. Apply by December 1. Fellowships and scholarships available for advanced students. Average amount paid per academic year: $24,000. Average number of hours worked per week: 0.

Additional Information: Of all students currently enrolled full time, 100% benefited from one or more of the listed financial assistance programs. Application and information available online at: http://www.psy.ohio-state.edu/graduate/.

Internships/Practica: Doctoral Degree (PhD Clinical Psychology): For those doctoral students for whom a professional psychology internship was required in this program prior to graduation, (12) students applied for an internship in 2011–2012, with (12) students obtaining an internship. Of those students who obtained an internship, (12) were paid internships. Of those students who obtained an internship, (12) students placed in APA/CPA accredited internships, (0) students placed in internships not APA/CPA accredited, but listed with the Association of Psychology Postdoctoral and Internship Programs (APPIC), (0) students placed in internships conforming to guidelines of the Council of Directors of School Psychology Programs (CDSPP), (0) students placed in internships that were not APA/CPA accredited, APPIC or CDSPP listed. Doctoral Degree (PhD Intellectual and Developmental Disabilities): For those doctoral students for whom a professional psychology internship was required in this program prior to graduation, (0) students applied for an internship in 2011–2012, with (0) students obtaining an internship. Of those students

who obtained an internship, (0) were paid internships. Of those students who obtained an internship, (0) students placed in APA/CPA accredited internships, (0) students placed in internships not APA/CPA accredited, but listed with the Association of Psychology Postdoctoral and Internship Programs (APPIC), (0) students placed in internships conforming to guidelines of the Council of Directors of School Psychology Programs (CDSPP), (0) students placed in internships that were not APA/CPA accredited, APPIC or CDSPP listed. For students in the clinical training program, initial practica are conducted at the in-house Psychological Services Center (PSC), supervised by core clinical faculty. Following one year of in-house training, students progress to advanced clinical experiences at program-approved externship sites throughout the community, where students gain clinical assessment and treatment experiences in a variety of settings consistent with the program's three training tracks: Adult Psychopathology, Health Psychology, and Child-Clinical Psychology. Advanced students also have the opportunity to continue treating clients in the in-house PSC while receiving supervision from adjunct faculty in the community. Additionally, all students must complete a one-year full-time internship in clinical psychology prior to the awarding of the doctoral degree.

Housing and Day Care: On-campus housing is available. See the following website for more information: http://urds.osu.edu/housing/graduate-professional-housing/. On-campus day care facilities are available. See the following website for more information: http://hr.osu.edu/childcare/.

Employment of Department Graduates:

Master's Degree Graduates: Of those who graduated in the academic year 2011–2012, the following categories and numbers represent the postgraduate activities and employment of master's degree graduates: Enrolled in a postdoctoral residency/fellowship (n/a), employed in independent practice (n/a), total from the above (master's) (0).

Doctoral Degree Graduates: Of those who graduated in the academic year 2011–2012, the following categories and numbers represent the postgraduate activities and employment of doctoral degree graduates: Enrolled in a psychology doctoral program (n/a), enrolled in a postdoctoral residency/fellowship (10), employed in an academic position at a university (3), employed in other positions at a higher education institution (1), employed in business or industry (3), employed in government agency (1), total from the above (doctoral) (18).

Additional Information:

Orientation, Objectives, and Emphasis of Department: The department is comprehensive in nature, with PhD programs in nearly all the major fields of study in psychology. The programs all strive to educate psychological scientists, and there is consequently a strong emphasis on research training in the doctoral programs, even in the applied areas. Our objective is to prepare theoretically sophisticated psychologists who leave us with effective skills to build upon in their later careers and with the ability to grow as psychology develops as a science and profession.

Special Facilities or Resources: There are several research labs specializing in the various programs of the OSU psychology department. In addition, since The Ohio State University is a well-known and well-established research institution, there are several non-department labs located throughout the campus that would be of possible interest to psychology graduate students.

Information for Students With Physical Disabilities: See the following website for more information: http://www.ods.ohio-state.edu/.

Application Information:
Application available online. URL of online application: https://www. applyweb.com/apply/osugrad/index.html. Students are admitted in the Fall, application deadline December 1. *Fee:* $40. International applications $50.

Ohio University
Department of Psychology
Arts and Sciences
200 Porter Hall
Athens, OH 45701-2979
Telephone: (740) 593-1707
Fax: (740) 593-0579
E-mail: *carlsonb@ohio.edu*
Web: *http://www.ohioupsychology.com/*

Department Information:
1922. Chairperson: Bruce Carlson, PhD. Number of faculty: to-tal—full-time 24; women—full-time 8; total—minority—full-time 4; women minority—full-time 2; faculty subject to the Americans With Disabilities Act 1.

Programs and Degrees Offered:
Listed in the following order: Program area, degree type (T if terminal Master's), number awarded 7/11–6/12. Clinical Psychology PhD (Doctor of Philosophy) 7, Industrial/Organizational Psychology PhD (Doctor of Philosophy) 1, Social Psychology PhD (Doctor of Philosophy) 1, Cognitive Psychology PhD (Doctor of Philosophy) 0, Health Psychology PhD (Doctor of Philosophy) 0, Applied Quantitative Psychology PhD (Doctor of Philosophy) 0.

APA Accreditation: Clinical PhD (Doctor of Philosophy). Student Outcome Data Website: http://www.ohioupsychology.com/program_statistics.html.

Student Applications/Admissions:
Student Applications
Clinical Psychology PhD (Doctor of Philosophy)—Applications 2012–2013, 149. Total applicants accepted 2012–2013, 9. Number full-time enrolled (new admits only) 2012–2013, 9. Total enrolled 2012–2013 full-time, 47. Openings 2013–2014, 9. The median number of years required for completion of a degree in 2012–2013 were 5. The number of students enrolled full- and part-time who were dismissed or voluntarily withdrew from this program area in 2012–2013 were 0. *Industrial/Organizational Psychology PhD (Doctor of Philosophy)*—Applications 2012–2013, 35. Total applicants accepted 2012–2013, 1. Number full-time enrolled (new admits only) 2012–2013, 1. Total enrolled 2012–2013 full-time, 12. Total enrolled 2012–2013

part-time, 0. Openings 2013–2014, 3. The median number of years required for completion of a degree in 2012–2013 were 8. The number of students enrolled full- and part-time who were dismissed or voluntarily withdrew from this program area in 2012–2013 were 0. *Social Psychology PhD (Doctor of Philosophy)*—Applications 2012–2013, 41. Total applicants accepted 2012–2013, 1. Number full-time enrolled (new admits only) 2012–2013, 1. Total enrolled 2012–2013 full-time, 11. Openings 2013–2014, 3. The median number of years required for completion of a degree in 2012–2013 were 6. The number of students enrolled full- and part-time who were dismissed or voluntarily withdrew from this program area in 2012–2013 were 0. *Cognitive Psychology PhD (Doctor of Philosophy)*—Applications 2012–2013, 10. Total applicants accepted 2012–2013, 0. Number full-time enrolled (new admits only) 2012–2013, 0. Total enrolled 2012–2013 full-time, 5. Openings 2013–2014, 2. The number of students enrolled full- and part-time who were dismissed or voluntarily withdrew from this program area in 2012–2013 were 0. *Health Psychology PhD (Doctor of Philosophy)*—Applications 2012–2013, 18. Total applicants accepted 2012–2013, 2. Number full-time enrolled (new admits only) 2012–2013, 2. Total enrolled 2012–2013 full-time, 8. Openings 2013–2014, 2. The number of students enrolled full- and part-time who were dismissed or voluntarily withdrew from this program area in 2012–2013 were 0. *Applied Quantitative Psychology PhD (Doctor of Philosophy)*—Applications 2012–2013, 3. Total applicants accepted 2012–2013, 1. Number full-time enrolled (new admits only) 2012–2013, 1. Total enrolled 2012–2013 full-time, 4. Openings 2013–2014, 2. The number of students enrolled full- and part-time who were dismissed or voluntarily withdrew from this program area in 2012–2013 were 0.

Scores: Entries appear in this order: required test or GPA, minimum score (if required), median score of students entering in 2012–2013. *Clinical Psychology PhD (Doctor of Philosophy):* GRE-V no minimum stated, 157, GRE-Q no minimum stated, 161, overall undergraduate GPA no minimum stated, 3.62; *Health Psychology PhD (Doctor of Philosophy):* GRE-V no minimum stated, 158, GRE-Q no minimum stated, 154.

Other Criteria: (importance of criteria rated low, medium, or high): GRE scores—high, research experience—high, work experience—low, extracurricular activity—low, clinically related public service—medium, GPA—high, letters of recommendation—high, interview—medium, statement of goals and objectives—medium, undergraduate major in psychology—low, specific undergraduate psychology courses taken—low. For additional information on admission requirements, go to http://www.ohioupsychology.com/Graduate-Admissions.html.

Student Characteristics: The following represents characteristics of students in 2012–2013 in all graduate psychology programs in the department: Female—full-time 60, part-time 0; Male—full-time 27, part-time 0; African American/Black—full-time 3, part-time 0; Hispanic/Latino(a)—full-time 1, part-time 0; Asian/Pacific Islander—full-time 9, part-time 0; American Indian/Alaska Native—full-time 0, part-time 0; Caucasian/White—full-time 74, part-time 0; Multi-ethnic—full-time 0, part-time 0; students subject to the Americans With Disabilities Act—full-time 0, part-time 0; Unknown ethnicity—full-time 0, part-time 0; International students who hold an F-1 or J-1 Visa—full-time 12, part-time 0.

Financial Information/Assistance:

Tuition for Full-Time Study: *Doctoral:* State residents: per academic year $8,518; Nonstate residents: per academic year $16,510. Tuition is subject to change. Additional fees are assessed to students beyond the costs of tuition for the following: general, technology, medical (optional), and legal (optional) fees. See the following website for updates and changes in tuition costs: http://www.ohio.edu/graduate/tuition.cfm.

Financial Assistance:

First-Year Students: Teaching assistantships available for first year. Average amount paid per academic year: $14,200. Average number of hours worked per week: 15. Research assistantships available for first year. Average amount paid per academic year: $14,200. Average number of hours worked per week: 15. Fellowships and scholarships available for first year. Average amount paid per academic year: $18,200. Average number of hours worked per week: 12.

Advanced Students: Teaching assistantships available for advanced students. Average amount paid per academic year: $14,200. Average number of hours worked per week: 15. Research assistantships available for advanced students. Average amount paid per academic year: $14,200. Average number of hours worked per week: 15. Traineeships available for advanced students. Average amount paid per academic year: $14,200. Average number of hours worked per week: 15. Fellowships and scholarships available for advanced students. Average amount paid per academic year: $14,200. Average number of hours worked per week: 12.

Additional Information: Of all students currently enrolled full time, 100% benefited from one or more of the listed financial assistance programs. Application and information available online at: http://www.ohioupsychology.com/Graduate-Admissions-Financial-Aid.html.

Internships/Practica: Doctoral Degree (PhD Clinical Psychology): For those doctoral students for whom a professional psychology internship was required in this program prior to graduation, (9) students applied for an internship in 2011–2012, with (9) students obtaining an internship. Of those students who obtained an internship, (9) were paid internships. Of those students who obtained an internship, (9) students placed in APA/CPA accredited internships, (0) students placed in internships not APA/CPA accredited, but listed with the Association of Psychology Postdoctoral and Internship Programs (APPIC), (0) students placed in internships conforming to guidelines of the Council of Directors of School Psychology Programs (CDSPP), (0) students placed in internships that were not APA/CPA accredited, APPIC or CDSPP listed. Clinical doctoral interns are placed in APA-approved, one-year internships throughout the country. Supervised training in clinical skills is provided for all clinical students in area mental health agencies, clinics, and the departmental psychology clinic. Such training is in addition to traineeships and internships. Supervised practicum experience is provided for organizational students in area industries and organizations.

Housing and Day Care: On-campus housing is available. See the following website for more information: http://www.ohio.edu/graduate/newadmit/housing.cfm. On-campus day care facilities are available. See the following website for more information: http://www.ohio.edu/childdevcenter/.

Employment of Department Graduates:

Master's Degree Graduates: Of those who graduated in the academic year 2011–2012, the following categories and numbers represent the postgraduate activities and employment of master's degree graduates: Enrolled in a postdoctoral residency/fellowship (n/a), employed in independent practice (n/a), total from the above (master's) (0).

Doctoral Degree Graduates: Of those who graduated in the academic year 2011–2012, the following categories and numbers represent the postgraduate activities and employment of doctoral degree graduates: Enrolled in a psychology doctoral program (n/a), enrolled in a postdoctoral residency/fellowship (3), employed in an academic position at a university (3), employed in business or industry (2), employed in government agency (1), total from the above (doctoral) (9).

Additional Information:

Orientation, Objectives, and Emphasis of Department: The clinical doctoral program is a scientist/practitioner program, offering balanced training in research and clinical skills. Practicum training is offered in intellectual and personality assessment. Therapy sequences are offered in health psychology, individual and group psychotherapy, behavior modification, and child psychology. Traineeships are available at the university counseling center and area mental health agencies and clinics. The department has a psychology training clinic. The doctoral program in experimental psychology provides intensive training in scholarly and research activities, preparing the student for positions in academic and research settings. The department offers an applied quantitative psychology track. This track offers advanced training in quantitative methods to graduate students who are concurrently studying in one of the other experimental or clinical psychology programs. Besides the usual coursework in psychology, students who select this track receive extensive training in mathematics, computer science, and statistics.

Special Facilities or Resources: A new addition to Porter Hall, where the Department of Psychology is housed, was completed in the Fall of 2008. This addition contains numerous research labs equipped for a wide variety of human research activities, including psychophysiology, cognitive, social, and health. The department has its own clinic, which is used to train clinical doctoral students. Two computer laboratories in the Psychology Department, one with 30 computers and one with 4 computers, are also available for student research. All computer services, except for printing, are free of charge. Ohio University recently awarded the Psychology Department selective investment funds, which represent a major increase in funding for the department.

Information for Students With Physical Disabilities: See the following website for more information: http://www.ohio.edu/disabilities/.

Application Information:

Application available online. URL of online application: http://www.ohio.edu/graduate/apply/index.cfm. Students are admitted in the Fall, application deadline December 1. *Fee:* $50. The fee is waived or deferred with a statement of need from the financial aid office of the applicant's college.

Toledo, University of
Department of Psychology
Language, Literature & Social Science
MS#948
Toledo, OH 43606
Telephone: (419) 530-2717
Fax: (419) 530-8479
E-mail: *jjasper@utnet.utoledo.edu*
Web: *http://www.utoledo.edu/psychology/*

Department Information:
1913. Chairperson: Dr. J.D. Jasper. Number of faculty: total—full-time 20, part-time 2; women—full-time 7, part-time 1; total—minority—full-time 3; women minority—full-time 2.

Programs and Degrees Offered:
Listed in the following order: Program area, degree type (T if terminal Master's), number awarded 7/11–6/12. Experimental Psychology PhD (Doctor of Philosophy) 5, Clinical Psychology PhD (Doctor of Philosophy) 5.

APA Accreditation: Clinical PhD (Doctor of Philosophy). Student Outcome Data Website: http://psychology.utoledo.edu/showpage. asp?name=statistics.

Student Applications/Admissions:
Student Applications
Experimental Psychology PhD (Doctor of Philosophy)—Applications 2012–2013, 32. Total applicants accepted 2012–2013, 8. Number full-time enrolled (new admits only) 2012–2013, 5. Number part-time enrolled (new admits only) 2012–2013, 0. Total enrolled 2012–2013 full-time, 21. Total enrolled 2012–2013 part-time, 0. Openings 2013–2014, 5. The median number of years required for completion of a degree in 2012–2013 were 5. The number of students enrolled full- and part-time who were dismissed or voluntarily withdrew from this program area in 2012–2013 were 0. *Clinical Psychology PhD (Doctor of Philosophy)*—Applications 2012–2013, 118. Total applicants accepted 2012–2013, 6. Number full-time enrolled (new admits only) 2012–2013, 4. Number part-time enrolled (new admits only) 2012–2013, 0. Total enrolled 2012–2013 full-time, 28. Total enrolled 2012–2013 part-time, 0. Openings 2013–2014, 6. The median number of years required for completion of a degree in 2012–2013 were 5. The number of students enrolled full- and part-time who were dismissed or voluntarily withdrew from this program area in 2012–2013 were 1.

Scores: Entries appear in this order: required test or GPA, minimum score (if required), median score of students entering in 2012–2013. *Experimental Psychology PhD (Doctor of Philosophy):* GRE-V 140, 155, GRE-Q 140, 152, GRE-Analytical 3.0, 4.25; *Clinical Psychology PhD (Doctor of Philosophy):* GRE-V 153, GRE-Q 145, GRE-Analytical 4, 4.5, overall undergraduate GPA 3.00, 3.72.

Other Criteria: (importance of criteria rated low, medium, or high): GRE scores—high, research experience—high, work experience—medium, extracurricular activity—medium, clinically related public service—low, GPA—high, letters of recommendation—high, interview—medium, statement of goals and objectives—high, undergraduate major in psychology—medium, specific undergraduate psychology courses taken—low. For additional information on admission requirements, go to http://psychology.utoledo.edu/showpage.asp?name=admission_clinic.

Student Characteristics: The following represents characteristics of students in 2012–2013 in all graduate psychology programs in the department: Female—full-time 32, part-time 0; Male—full-time 17, part-time 0; African American/Black—full-time 0, part-time 0; Hispanic/Latino(a)—full-time 2, part-time 0; Asian/Pacific Islander—full-time 4, part-time 0; American Indian/Alaska Native—full-time 0, part-time 0; Caucasian/White—full-time 43, part-time 0; Multi-ethnic—full-time 0, part-time 0; students subject to the Americans With Disabilities Act—full-time 0, part-time 0; Unknown ethnicity—full-time 0, part-time 0; International students who hold an F-1 or J-1 Visa—full-time 6, part-time 0.

Financial Information/Assistance:
Tuition for Full-Time Study: *Doctoral:* State residents: per academic year $12,594; Nonstate residents: per academic year $22,828. Tuition is subject to change.

Financial Assistance:
First-Year Students: Teaching assistantships available for first year. Average amount paid per academic year: $13,000. Average number of hours worked per week: 20. Research assistantships available for first year. Average amount paid per academic year: $13,000. Average number of hours worked per week: 20.

Advanced Students: Teaching assistantships available for advanced students. Average amount paid per academic year: $15,000. Average number of hours worked per week: 20. Research assistantships available for advanced students. Average amount paid per academic year: $15,000. Average number of hours worked per week: 20. Traineeships available for advanced students. Average amount paid per academic year: $15,000. Average number of hours worked per week: 20.

Additional Information: Of all students currently enrolled full time, 100% benefited from one or more of the listed financial assistance programs. Application and information available online at: http://psychology.utoledo.edu/showpage.asp?name=financial_support_experimental.

Internships/Practica: Doctoral Degree (PhD Clinical Psychology): For those doctoral students for whom a professional psychology internship was required in this program prior to graduation, (4) students applied for an internship in 2011–2012, with (3) students obtaining an internship. Of those students who obtained an internship, (3) were paid internships. Of those students who obtained an internship, (3) students placed in APA/CPA accredited internships, (0) students placed in internships not APA/CPA accredited, but listed with the Association of Psychology Postdoctoral and Internship Programs (APPIC), (0) students placed in internships conforming to guidelines of the Council of Directors of School Psychology Programs (CDSPP), (0) students placed in internships that were not APA/CPA accredited, APPIC or CDSPP listed.

Housing and Day Care: On-campus housing is available. See the following website for more information: http://www.utoledo.edu/studentaffairs/reslife/index/index.html. On-campus day care facilities are available. See the following website for more information:

http://www.utoledo.edu/centers/earlylearn/; http://www.utoledo.edu/studentaffairs/appletree/.

Employment of Department Graduates:
Master's Degree Graduates: Of those who graduated in the academic year 2011–2012, the following categories and numbers represent the postgraduate activities and employment of master's degree graduates: Enrolled in a postdoctoral residency/fellowship (n/a), employed in independent practice (n/a), total from the above (master's) (0).
Doctoral Degree Graduates: Of those who graduated in the academic year 2011–2012, the following categories and numbers represent the postgraduate activities and employment of doctoral degree graduates: Enrolled in a psychology doctoral program (n/a), enrolled in a postdoctoral residency/fellowship (4), employed in an academic position at a 2-year/4-year college (2), total from the above (doctoral) (6).

Additional Information:
Orientation, Objectives, and Emphasis of Department: Our department features an APA accredited Clinical Psychology PhD program as well as an Experimental Psychology PhD program, offering specializations in Social Psychology, Developmental Psychology, Cognitive Psychology, and Behavioral Neuroscience and Learning. Although these programs differ in many respects, the purpose of both programs is to provide superior training in psychological research methods, statistical procedures, clinical practice, and theoretical comprehension. Our doctoral training emphasizes the inculcation of scientific attitudes with regard to (a) the gathering and evaluation of information, (b) the solving of basic and applied research problems, and in the clinical area, and (c) clinical assessment and psychotherapy.

Information for Students With Physical Disabilities: See the following website for more information: http://www.utoledo.edu/success/academicaccess/index.html.

Application Information:
Send to Graduate School, University of Toledo, Toledo, OH 43606. Application available online. URL of online application: http://www.utoledo.edu/graduate/prospectivestudents/admission/guidelines.html. Students are admitted in the Fall, application deadline December 1. Clinical Area due December 1; Experimental Area due January 15. *Fee:* $45.

Wright State University
Department of Psychology
College of Science and Mathematics
335 Fawcett Hall, 3640 Colonel Glenn Highway
Dayton, OH 45435-0001
Telephone: (937) 775-3348
Fax: (937) 775-3347
E-mail: *debra.steele-johnson@wright.edu*
Web: *http://www.wright.edu/cosm/departments/psychology/*

Department Information:
1979. Chairperson: Debra Steele-Johnson. Number of faculty: total—full-time 26, part-time 26; women—full-time 9, part-time 13; total—minority—full-time 2, part-time 2; women minority—

full-time 1, part-time 1; faculty subject to the Americans With Disabilities Act 1.

Programs and Degrees Offered:
Listed in the following order: Program area, degree type (T if terminal Master's), number awarded 7/11–6/12. Industrial/Organizational Psychology PhD (Doctor of Philosophy) 2, Human Factors PhD (Doctor of Philosophy) 1.

Student Applications/Admissions:
Student Applications
Industrial/Organizational Psychology PhD (Doctor of Philosophy)—Applications 2012–2013, 42. Total applicants accepted 2012–2013, 4. Number full-time enrolled (new admits only) 2012–2013, 4. Number part-time enrolled (new admits only) 2012–2013, 0. Total enrolled 2012–2013 full-time, 23. Total enrolled 2012–2013 part-time, 20. Openings 2013–2014, 4. The median number of years required for completion of a degree in 2012–2013 were 5. The number of students enrolled full- and part-time who were dismissed or voluntarily withdrew from this program area in 2012–2013 were 0. *Human Factors PhD (Doctor of Philosophy)*—Applications 2012–2013, 14. Total applicants accepted 2012–2013, 6. Number full-time enrolled (new admits only) 2012–2013, 6. Number part-time enrolled (new admits only) 2012–2013, 0. Total enrolled 2012–2013 full-time, 31. Total enrolled 2012–2013 part-time, 6. Openings 2013–2014, 4. The median number of years required for completion of a degree in 2012–2013 were 7. The number of students enrolled full- and part-time who were dismissed or voluntarily withdrew from this program area in 2012–2013 were 0.
Scores: Entries appear in this order: required test or GPA, minimum score (if required), median score of students entering in 2012–2013. *Industrial/Organizational Psychology PhD (Doctor of Philosophy):* GRE-V no minimum stated, GRE-Q no minimum stated, GRE-Analytical no minimum stated, overall undergraduate GPA no minimum stated; *Human Factors PhD (Doctor of Philosophy):* GRE-V no minimum stated, GRE-Q no minimum stated, GRE-Analytical no minimum stated, overall undergraduate GPA no minimum stated.
Other Criteria: (importance of criteria rated low, medium, or high): GRE scores—high, research experience—high, work experience—medium, extracurricular activity—low, GPA—high, letters of recommendation—high, interview—medium, statement of goals and objectives—high. For additional information on admission requirements, go to http://www.wright.edu/cosm/departments/psychology/graduate/howtoapply.html.

Student Characteristics: The following represents characteristics of students in 2012–2013 in all graduate psychology programs in the department: Female—full-time 24, part-time 2; Male—full-time 31, part-time 3; African American/Black—full-time 2, part-time 0; Hispanic/Latino(a)—full-time 2, part-time 1; Asian/Pacific Islander—full-time 5, part-time 0; American Indian/Alaska Native—full-time 0, part-time 0; Caucasian/White—full-time 44, part-time 4; Multi-ethnic—full-time 0, part-time 0; students subject to the Americans With Disabilities Act—full-time 1, part-time 0; Unknown ethnicity—full-time 2, part-time 0; International students who hold an F-1 or J-1 Visa—full-time 0, part-time 0.

Financial Information/Assistance:

Tuition for Full-Time Study: *Doctoral:* State residents: per academic year $12,240, $564 per credit hour; Nonstate residents: per academic year $20,738, $961 per credit hour. Tuition is subject to change. See the following website for updates and changes in tuition costs: http://www.wright.edu/bursar/tuition-fees.

Financial Assistance:

First-Year Students: Teaching assistantships available for first year. Average amount paid per academic year: $12,793. Average number of hours worked per week: 20. Apply by January 1. Research assistantships available for first year. Average amount paid per academic year: $12,793. Average number of hours worked per week: 20. Apply by January 1. Fellowships and scholarships available for first year. Average amount paid per academic year: $13,000. Average number of hours worked per week: 20. Apply by January 1.

Advanced Students: Teaching assistantships available for advanced students. Average amount paid per academic year: $12,793. Average number of hours worked per week: 20. Apply by January 1. Research assistantships available for advanced students. Average amount paid per academic year: $12,793. Average number of hours worked per week: 20. Apply by January 1.

Additional Information: Of all students currently enrolled full time, 100% benefited from one or more of the listed financial assistance programs. Application and information available online at: http://www.wright.edu/graduate-school/admissions/graduate-assistantships.

Internships/Practica: Students participate in internships and practica with local businesses and Wright Patterson Air Force Base. Students working at the base can receive support.

Housing and Day Care: No on-campus housing is available. On-campus day care facilities are available. See the following website for more information: http://www.miniuniversity.net/Wright-State-University.asp.

Employment of Department Graduates:

Master's Degree Graduates: Of those who graduated in the academic year 2011–2012, the following categories and numbers represent the postgraduate activities and employment of master's degree graduates: Enrolled in a postdoctoral residency/fellowship (n/a), employed in independent practice (n/a), total from the above (master's) (0).

Doctoral Degree Graduates: Of those who graduated in the academic year 2011–2012, the following categories and numbers represent the postgraduate activities and employment of doctoral degree graduates: Enrolled in a psychology doctoral program (n/a), total from the above (doctoral) (0).

Additional Information:

Orientation, Objectives, and Emphasis of Department: The Department offers MS and PhD degrees in Human Factors and Industrial/Organizational Psychology. Students specialize in one of these areas, but the program is designed to foster an understanding of both areas and the importance of considering both aspects in the design of industrial, aerospace, health care, or other systems.

The program prepares students for careers in research, teaching, design and practice in government, consulting, business, or industry. It includes course work, research training, and experience with system design and applications. Students work closely with faculty beginning early in the program. Human factors, including cognitive engineering, deals with the characteristics of human beings that are applicable to the design of systems and devices of all kinds while industrial/organizational deals with individual or group behaviors in work settings (macrosystem variables). The department has a critical mass of students and faculty in these areas and is unique because its focus on applied psychology does not include students in clinical psychology. Both majors are strengthened by being located in the Dayton, Ohio metropolitan region, which is a rapidly developing high technology sector, a major human factors and cognitive engineering research and development center, and a region of considerable industrial and corporate strength.

Special Facilities or Resources: The Department of Psychology has modern state-of-the-art research laboratories, well-equipped teaching laboratories, and office space for faculty and graduate assistants. Specialized equipment in dedicated research laboratories supports research on sensory processes, motor control, spatial orientation, human-computer interaction and display design, flight simulation, cultural cognition, naturalistic decision making, memory, aging, expertise, teamwork, assessment, training, and stress in the workplace. In addition, faculty and student share a number of individual and group testing rooms. Computer facilities include over 350 UNIX workstations, PCs, and Macintoshes. The Department works cooperatively with research laboratories, research and development organizations, and corporations in the region. These include facilities for virtual environment generation, including 3-D visual displays, 3-D auditory displays, and tactile/haptic displays. The Virtual Environment Research, Interactive Technology, and Simulation (VERITAS) facility, which is owned and operated by Wright State University but housed at Wright Patterson Air Force Base, is unique in the world. The facility includes a room-size display that surrounds the user with interactive 3-D auditory and visual images. The Department of Psychology has a Memorandum of Agreement with the U.S. Air Force Research Laboratory that facilitates utilization of its sophisticated behavioral laboratories such as flight simulators and the Auditory Localization Facility. The Air Force Research Laboratory supports multi-nation research on complex cognition. The department has two well-equipped laboratories for the study of the performance and training for complex team tasks.

Information for Students With Physical Disabilities: See the following website for more information: http://www.wright.edu/dis_services.

Application Information:

Send to School of Graduate Studies, Wright State University, E344 Student Union, 3640 Colonel Glenn Highway, Dayton, OH 45435-0001. Application available online. URL of online application: http://www.wright.edu/graduate-school/admissions/apply-now. Students are admitted in the Fall, application deadline January 1. *Fee:* $40.

Wright State University

School of Professional Psychology
3640 Colonel Glenn Highway
Dayton, OH 45435-0001
Telephone: (937) 775-3490
Fax: (937) 775-3434
E-mail: *lapearllogan.winfrey@wright.edu*
Web: *http://psychology.wright.edu/*

Department Information:
1979. Dean and Professor: Larry C. James, PhD, ABPP. Number of faculty: total—full-time 16, part-time 7; women—full-time 9, part-time 3; total—minority—full-time 6; women minority—full-time 3; faculty subject to the Americans With Disabilities Act 2.

Programs and Degrees Offered:
Listed in the following order: Program area, degree type (T if terminal Master's), number awarded 7/11–6/12. Clinical Psychology PsyD (Doctor of Psychology) 18.

APA Accreditation: Clinical PsyD (Doctor of Psychology). Student Outcome Data Website: http://psychology.wright.edu/about-sopp/education-outcomes.

Student Applications/Admissions:
Student Applications
Clinical Psychology PsyD (Doctor of Psychology)—Applications 2012–2013, 183. Total applicants accepted 2012–2013, 19. Number full-time enrolled (new admits only) 2012–2013, 19. Number part-time enrolled (new admits only) 2012–2013, 0. Total enrolled 2012–2013 full-time, 95. Total enrolled 2012–2013 part-time, 14. Openings 2013–2014, 30. The median number of years required for completion of a degree in 2012–2013 were 5. The number of students enrolled full- and part-time who were dismissed or voluntarily withdrew from this program area in 2012–2013 were 1.
Scores: Entries appear in this order: required test or GPA, minimum score (if required), median score of students entering in 2012–2013. *Clinical Psychology PsyD (Doctor of Psychology):* GRE-V 152, GRE-Q 148, GRE-Analytical 4.1, GRE-Subject (Psychology) 559, overall undergraduate GPA 3.41, psychology GPA 3.65.
Other Criteria: (importance of criteria rated low, medium, or high): GRE scores—medium, research experience—low, work experience—medium, extracurricular activity—medium, clinically related public service—high, GPA—high, letters of recommendation—high, interview—high, statement of goals and objectives—high, resume—high, undergraduate major in psychology—medium, specific undergraduate psychology courses taken—high. For additional information on admission requirements, go to http://psychology.wright.edu/admissions/admission-and-application.

Student Characteristics: The following represents characteristics of students in 2012–2013 in all graduate psychology programs in the department: Female—full-time 72, part-time 12; Male—full-time 23, part-time 2; African American/Black—full-time 15, part-time 2; Hispanic/Latino(a)—full-time 4, part-time 1; Asian/Pacific Islander—full-time 5, part-time 1; American Indian/Alaska Native—full-time 1, part-time 0; Caucasian/White—full-time 66, part-time 10; Multi-ethnic—full-time 4, part-time 0; students subject to the Americans With Disabilities Act—full-time 3, part-time 0; Unknown ethnicity—full-time 0, part-time 0; International students who hold an F-1 or J-1 Visa—full-time 3, part-time 1.

Financial Information/Assistance:
Tuition for Full-Time Study: *Doctoral:* State residents: per academic year $21,552, $665 per credit hour; Nonstate residents: per academic year $34,440, $1,064 per credit hour. Tuition is subject to change. See the following website for updates and changes in tuition costs: http://www.wright.edu/bursar/tuition-fees.

Financial Assistance:
First-Year Students: Fellowships and scholarships available for first year. Average amount paid per academic year: $7,000.
Advanced Students: Traineeships available for advanced students. Average amount paid per academic year: $5,500. Average number of hours worked per week: 16. Fellowships and scholarships available for advanced students. Average amount paid per academic year: $8,889.
Additional Information: Of all students currently enrolled full time, 84% benefited from one or more of the listed financial assistance programs.

Internships/Practica: Doctoral Degree (PsyD Clinical Psychology): For those doctoral students for whom a professional psychology internship was required in this program prior to graduation, (23) students applied for an internship in 2011–2012, with (21) students obtaining an internship. Of those students who obtained an internship, (21) were paid internships. Of those students who obtained an internship, (20) students placed in APA/CPA accredited internships, (1) students placed in internships not APA/CPA accredited, but listed with the Association of Psychology Postdoctoral and Internship Programs (APPIC), (0) students placed in internships conforming to guidelines of the Council of Directors of School Psychology Programs (CDSPP), (0) students placed in internships that were not APA/CPA accredited, APPIC or CDSPP listed. SOPP runs an APA-accredited internship program which has five slots annually; selections are made competitively from a national pool of students. SOPP students are eligible to apply for this internship program. Most SOPP students are matched with internship programs outside the local area. SOPP students have a strong match rate with APA-accredited internship programs across the country. During years 2, 3, and 4 of the doctoral program, students are assigned to year-long practicum placements for 2 days (16-20 hours) per week. Most practicum placements carry a stipend of $5,500 for a 12-month period. Approximately half the practicum placements are in the two clinical/teaching facilities operated by the school. These include Counseling and Wellness Services on WSU's campus, which provides psychological services for the university's student body, and the Ellis Human Development Institute, which is located in Dayton, Ohio and provides a broad range of psychological services and special treatment programs developed in response to the needs of the Dayton community. The remaining practicum placements are located in a broad array of service settings located primarily in Dayton and southwestern Ohio. These practicum settings include public agencies, correctional settings, hospitals, health and mental health clinics, etc.

Housing and Day Care: On-campus housing is available. See the following website for more information: http://www.wright.edu/

students/housing/. On-campus day care facilities are available. See the following website for more information: http://miniuniversity. net/Wright-State-University.asp.

Employment of Department Graduates:

Master's Degree Graduates: Of those who graduated in the academic year 2011–2012, the following categories and numbers represent the postgraduate activities and employment of master's degree graduates: Enrolled in a postdoctoral residency/fellowship (n/a), employed in independent practice (n/a), total from the above (master's) (0).

Doctoral Degree Graduates: Of those who graduated in the academic year 2011–2012, the following categories and numbers represent the postgraduate activities and employment of doctoral degree graduates: Enrolled in a psychology doctoral program (n/a), enrolled in a postdoctoral residency/fellowship (2), employed in independent practice (2), employed in an academic position at a university (1), employed in other positions at a higher education institution (2), employed in government agency (3), employed in a community mental health/counseling center (2), employed in a hospital/medical center (1), still seeking employment (2), do not know (3), total from the above (doctoral) (18).

Additional Information:

Orientation, Objectives, and Emphasis of Department: The School of Professional Psychology is committed to a practitioner model of professional education that educates students at the doctoral level for the eclectic, general practice of psychology. As a part of its educational mission, the school emphasizes cultural and other aspects of diversity in the composition of its student body, faculty, staff and curriculum. The curriculum is organized around seven core competency areas that are fundamental to the practice of psychology currently and in the future, including diversity, research and evaluation, assessment, intervention, relationship, management-supervision, and consultation-education. In years 1 and 2, the curriculum is designed around foundation coursework and the development of basic competencies. Years 3 and 4 are devoted to the development of advanced competency levels. Year 5 is dedicated to a predoctoral internship.

Special Facilities or Resources: The program operates two large clinical service centers that are designed to accommodate academic teaching, clinical training, clinical program development and research. Counseling and Wellness Services is located in the Student Union along with other student health and wellness services. This service center provides assessment and group/individual therapy services to the university student body which numbers approximately 18,000. Opportunities are available for trainees to participate in crisis intervention, prevention programs, outreach to residence halls, and multidisciplinary training with medical and nursing students. The second service center, the Ellis Human Development Institute, is located in an urban, primarily African-American section of Dayton. The Ellis Human Development Institute provides assessment and group/individual therapy to children, adolescents and adults from the Dayton community. Several special treatment programs provide unique opportunities for trainees. These include violence prevention programs for minority adolescents, treatment programs addressing perpetrators and victims of domestic violence, and an assessment/intervention program for persons with dementia. Both service centers house trainee and faculty offices and computers for student use in research and training activities; both facilities are equipped with state-of-the-art equipment for videotaped and live clinical supervision.

Information for Students With Physical Disabilities: See the following website for more information: http://www.wright.edu/ students/dis_services/.

Application Information:

Send to Office of Admissions/Alumni Relations, School of Professional Psychology, 110 Health Sciences Building, Wright State University, 3640 Colonel Glenn Hwy., Dayton, OH 45435-0001. Application available online. URL of online application: https://app.applyyourself. com/?id=ws-psych. Students are admitted in the Fall, application deadline January 1. *Fee:* $50. Application fee can be waived if applicant provides data of financial hardship.

Xavier University
Department of Psychology
College of Social Sciences, Health and Education
Elet Hall
Cincinnati, OH 45207-6511
Telephone: (513) 745-3533
Fax: (513) 745-3327
E-mail: *stukenb@xavier.edu*
Web: *http://www.xavier.edu/psychology-grad*

Department Information:

1962. Chairperson: Karl W. Stukenberg, PhD, ABPP. Number of faculty: total—full-time 15, part-time 11; women—full-time 9, part-time 6; total—minority—full-time 2, part-time 3; women minority—full-time 2, part-time 3.

Programs and Degrees Offered:

Listed in the following order: Program area, degree type (T if terminal Master's), number awarded 7/11–6/12. Clinical Psychology PsyD (Doctor of Psychology) 11, Experimental Psychology MA/MS (Master of Arts/Science) (T) 0, Industrial/Organizational Psychology MA/MS (Master of Arts/Science) (T) 3.

APA Accreditation: Clinical PsyD (Doctor of Psychology). Student Outcome Data Website: http://www.xavier.edu/psychology-doctorate/ Information-for-Prospective-and-Current-Students.cfm.

Student Applications/Admissions:

Student Applications

Clinical Psychology PsyD (Doctor of Psychology)—Applications 2012–2013, 202. Total applicants accepted 2012–2013, 35. Number full-time enrolled (new admits only) 2012–2013, 16. Number part-time enrolled (new admits only) 2012–2013, 0. Total enrolled 2012–2013 full-time, 83. Total enrolled 2012–2013 part-time, 12. Openings 2013–2014, 16. The median number of years required for completion of a degree in 2012–2013 were 5. The number of students enrolled full- and part-time who were dismissed or voluntarily withdrew from this program area in 2012–2013 were 0. *Experimental Psychology MA/MS (Master of Arts/Science)*—Applications 2012–2013, 13. Total applicants accepted 2012–2013, 0. Number full-time enrolled (new admits only) 2012–2013, 0. Number part-time enrolled (new admits only) 2012–2013, 0. The number of students enrolled full- and part-time who were dismissed or voluntarily withdrew from this program area in 2012–2013 were 0. *Industrial/Organizational Psychology MA/MS (Master of Arts/Science)*—Applications 2012–2013, 73. Total applicants accepted 2012–2013, 23. Number full-time enrolled (new admits only) 2012–2013, 13. Number part-time enrolled (new admits only) 2012–2013, 0. Total enrolled 2012–2013 full-time, 21. Total enrolled 2012–2013 part-time, 6. Openings 2013–2014, 10. The median number of years required for completion of a degree in 2012–2013 were 2.

Scores: Entries appear in this order: required test or GPA, minimum score (if required), median score of students entering in 2012–2013. *Clinical Psychology PsyD (Doctor of Psychology):* GRE-V no minimum stated, GRE-Q no minimum stated, GRE-Analytical no minimum stated, overall undergraduate GPA 3.0, psychology GPA 3.0; *Experimental Psychology MA/MS (Master of Arts/Science):* GRE-V no minimum stated, GRE-Q no minimum stated, GRE-Analytical no minimum stated, overall undergraduate GPA 3.0, psychology GPA 3.0; *Industrial/Organizational Psychology MA/MS (Master of Arts/Science):* GRE-V no minimum stated, GRE-Q no minimum stated, GRE-Analytical no minimum stated, overall undergraduate GPA 3.0, psychology GPA 3.0.

Other Criteria: (importance of criteria rated low, medium, or high): GRE scores—high, research experience—medium, work experience—medium, extracurricular activity—low, clinically related public service—medium, GPA—high, letters of recommendation—high, interview—low, statement of goals and objectives—high, undergraduate major in psychology—medium, specific undergraduate psychology courses taken—low, The graduate programs require a tests and measurements course that, if the student has not completed, he or she can take it on the web the summer before matriculating. The I-O program requires an undergraduate Industrial-Organizational Psychology course. If the student has not completed, he or she can take it during the summer or take a proficiency exam. For additional information on admission requirements, go to http://www.xavier.edu/psychology-doctorate/admission.cfm.

Student Characteristics: The following represents characteristics of students in 2012–2013 in all graduate psychology programs in the department: Female—full-time 79, part-time 12; Male—full-time 25, part-time 6; African American/Black—full-time 1, part-time 3; Hispanic/Latino(a)—full-time 3, part-time 0; Asian/Pacific Islander—full-time 5, part-time 0; American Indian/Alaska Native—full-time 0, part-time 0; Caucasian/White—full-time 95, part-time 15; Multi-ethnic—full-time 0, part-time 0; students subject to the Americans With Disabilities Act—full-time 0, part-time 0; Unknown ethnicity—full-time 0, part-time 0; International students who hold an F-1 or J-1 Visa—full-time 0, part-time 0.

Financial Information/Assistance:
Tuition for Full-Time Study: *Master's:* State residents: $594 per credit hour; Nonstate residents: $594 per credit hour. *Doctoral:* State residents: $752 per credit hour; Nonstate residents: $752 per credit hour. Additional fees are assessed to students beyond the costs of tuition for the following: assessment course materials, diversity course fee, APAGS dues, liability insurance fee and software. Tuition costs vary by program. See the following website for updates and changes in tuition costs: http://www.xavier.edu/financial-aid/tuition.cfm?type=grad.

Financial Assistance:
First-Year Students: Teaching assistantships available for first year. Average number of hours worked per week: 20. Apply by December 15. Research assistantships available for first year. Average number of hours worked per week: 10. Apply by December 15. Fellowships and scholarships available for first year. Apply by December 15.

Advanced Students: Teaching assistantships available for advanced students. Average number of hours worked per week: 10. Apply by March 1. Traineeships available for advanced students. Apply by March 1. Fellowships and scholarships available for advanced students. Apply by March 1.

Additional Information: Application and information available online at: http://www.xavier.edu/financial-aid/graduate-students/.

Internships/Practica: Doctoral Degree (PsyD Clinical Psychology): For those doctoral students for whom a professional psychology internship was required in this program prior to graduation, (18) students applied for an internship in 2011–2012, with (13) students obtaining an internship. Of those students who obtained an internship, (13) were paid internships. Of those students who obtained an internship, (12) students placed in APA/CPA accredited internships, (0) students placed in internships not APA/CPA accredited, but listed with the Association of Psychology Postdoctoral and Internship Programs (APPIC), (0) students placed in internships conforming to guidelines of the Council of Directors of School Psychology Programs (CDSPP), (1) students placed in internships that were not APA/CPA accredited, APPIC or CDSPP listed. Master's Degree (MA/MS Industrial/Organizational Psychology): An internship experience, such as a final research project or "capstone" experience is required of graduates. In an urban setting, the university has established relationships with a number of private and public agencies, businesses, hospitals, and mental health care centers. PsyD students are given the opportunity to work with underserved populations within the three ares of interest in our PsyD program— child/adolescent, older adults and severe mental illness. MA in I-O students work in settings where we have established relationships for internships.

Housing and Day Care: No on-campus housing is available. No on-campus day care facilities are available.

Employment of Department Graduates:
Master's Degree Graduates: Of those who graduated in the academic year 2011–2012, the following categories and numbers represent the postgraduate activities and employment of master's degree graduates: Enrolled in a postdoctoral residency/fellowship (n/a), employed in independent practice (n/a), other employment position (3), total from the above (master's) (3).
Doctoral Degree Graduates: Of those who graduated in the academic year 2011–2012, the following categories and numbers represent the postgraduate activities and employment of doctoral degree graduates: Enrolled in a psychology doctoral program (n/a), enrolled in a postdoctoral residency/fellowship (7), employed in independent practice (1), employed in a professional position in a school system (1), employed in government agency (2), employed in a community mental health/counseling center (1), total from the above (doctoral) (12).

Additional Information:

Orientation, Objectives, and Emphasis of Department: Both the master's and doctoral programs provide students with the knowledge and range of skills necessary to provide psychological services in today's changing professional climate. Our objective for the master's students is to prepare them for immediate employment or entry into a doctoral program in their field. Our objective for the doctoral program is to prepare students to serve as clinical psychologists in their communities. The basic philosophy of the PsyD program is to educate skilled practitioners who have a solid appreciation of the role of science in all aspects of professional activity. It is based on a practitioner-scientist model of training.

Special Facilities or Resources: The department has an affiliation with the Psychological Services Center on campus, which provides psychological services to both the university population and the Greater Cincinnati community. The Center provides the opportunity for training, service, and research. There are opportunities to work in various other areas (e.g., student development) in the university. The department also has established contact with care providers in the community, which provides the opportunity to learn the delivery of service and research that occurs in such organizations.

Information for Students With Physical Disabilities: See the following website for more information: http://www.xavier.edu/lac/student-disability-services.cfm.

Application Information:
Send to Assistant Director Enrollment and Student Services, Psychology Department, Xavier University, 3800 Victory Parkway, Cincinnati, OH 45207-6511. Application available online. URL of online application: http://www.xavier.edu/graduate-admission/. Students are admitted in the Fall, application deadline December 15. February 1 deadline for master's applicants. *Fee:* $35.

Central Oklahoma, University of

Department of Psychology
College of Education & Professional Studies
100 North University Drive
Edmond, OK 73034
Telephone: (405) 974-5707
Fax: (405) 974-3865
E-mail: *mhamlin@uco.edu*
Web: *http://www.uco.edu/ceps/dept/psy/psychology-ma.asp*

Department Information:
 1968. Chairperson: Mark Hamlin. Number of faculty: total—full-time 16, part-time 8; women—full-time 9, part-time 6; total—minority—full-time 4; women minority—full-time 3.

Programs and Degrees Offered:
 Listed in the following order: Program area, degree type (T if terminal Master's), number awarded 7/11–6/12. Counseling Psychology MA/MS (Master of Arts/Science) (T) 4, General Psychology MA/MS (Master of Arts/Science) (T) 10, Experimental Psychology MA/MS (Master of Arts/Science) 8, School Psychology MA/MS (Master of Arts/Science) (T) 5, Forensic Psychology MA/MS (Master of Arts/Science) 0.

Student Applications/Admissions:
 Student Applications
 Counseling Psychology MA/MS (Master of Arts/Science)—Applications 2012–2013, 43. Total applicants accepted 2012–2013, 19. Number full-time enrolled (new admits only) 2012–2013, 14. Number part-time enrolled (new admits only) 2012–2013, 0. Total enrolled 2012–2013 full-time, 30. Total enrolled 2012–2013 part-time, 13. Openings 2013–2014, 20. The median number of years required for completion of a degree in 2012–2013 were 3. The number of students enrolled full- and part-time who were dismissed or voluntarily withdrew from this program area in 2012–2013 were 3. *General Psychology MA/MS (Master of Arts/Science)*—Applications 2012–2013, 16. Total applicants accepted 2012–2013, 9. Number full-time enrolled (new admits only) 2012–2013, 6. Number part-time enrolled (new admits only) 2012–2013, 3. Total enrolled 2012–2013 full-time, 10. Openings 2013–2014, 10. The median number of years required for completion of a degree in 2012–2013 were 2. The number of students enrolled full- and part-time who were dismissed or voluntarily withdrew from this program area in 2012–2013 were 1. *Experimental Psychology MA/MS (Master of Arts/Science)*—Applications 2012–2013, 9. Total applicants accepted 2012–2013, 6. Number full-time enrolled (new admits only) 2012–2013, 6. Number part-time enrolled (new admits only) 2012–2013, 0. Total enrolled 2012–2013 full-time, 16. Total enrolled 2012–2013 part-time, 4. Openings 2013–2014, 10. The median number of years required for completion of a degree in 2012–2013 were 2. The number of students enrolled full- and part-time who were dismissed or voluntarily withdrew from this program area in 2012–2013 were 2. *School Psychology MA/MS (Master of Arts/Science)*—Applications 2012–2013, 11. Total applicants ac-cepted 2012–2013, 11. Number full-time enrolled (new admits only) 2012–2013, 3. Number part-time enrolled (new admits only) 2012–2013, 4. Total enrolled 2012–2013 full-time, 7. Total enrolled 2012–2013 part-time, 8. Openings 2013–2014, 10. The median number of years required for completion of a degree in 2012–2013 were 3. The number of students enrolled full- and part-time who were dismissed or voluntarily withdrew from this program area in 2012–2013 were 4. *Forensic Psychology MA/MS (Master of Arts/Science)*—Applications 2012–2013, 11. Total applicants accepted 2012–2013, 11. Number full-time enrolled (new admits only) 2012–2013, 11. Total enrolled 2012–2013 full-time, 11. Openings 2013–2014, 3. The median number of years required for completion of a degree in 2012–2013 were 2. The number of students enrolled full- and part-time who were dismissed or voluntarily withdrew from this program area in 2012–2013 were 0.

Scores: Entries appear in this order: required test or GPA, minimum score (if required), median score of students entering in 2012–2013. *Counseling Psychology MA/MS (Master of Arts/Science):* GRE-V 290, 298, GRE-Q no minimum stated, GRE-Analytical 3.5, 3.70, overall undergraduate GPA 3.00, 3.30; *General Psychology MA/MS (Master of Arts/Science):* GRE-V 290, 244, GRE-Q no minimum stated, GRE-Analytical 3.5, 3.71, overall undergraduate GPA 2.75, 3.23; *Experimental Psychology MA/MS (Master of Arts/Science):* GRE-V 290, 301, GRE-Q no minimum stated, GRE-Analytical 3.5, 4.13, overall undergraduate GPA 2.75, 3.50; *School Psychology MA/MS (Master of Arts/Science):* GRE-V 290, 294, GRE-Q no minimum stated, GRE-Analytical 3.5, 4.15, overall undergraduate GPA 3.00, 3.27; *Forensic Psychology MA/MS (Master of Arts/Science):* GRE-V 290, 294, GRE-Q no minimum stated, GRE-Analytical 3.5, 3.70, overall undergraduate GPA 3.00, 3.44.

Other Criteria: (importance of criteria rated low, medium, or high): GRE scores—medium, research experience—high, work experience—medium, extracurricular activity—medium, clinically related public service—high, GPA—high, letters of recommendation—high, interview—low, statement of goals and objectives—low, undergraduate major in psychology—medium, specific undergraduate psychology courses taken—high, . For additional information on admission requirements, go to http://www.uco.edu/ceps/dept/psy/psychology-ma.asp.

Student Characteristics: The following represents characteristics of students in 2012–2013 in all graduate psychology programs in the department: Female—full-time 40, part-time 15; Male—full-time 34, part-time 10; African American/Black—full-time 14, part-time 5; Hispanic/Latino(a)—full-time 7, part-time 3; Asian/Pacific Islander—full-time 6, part-time 2; American Indian/Alaska Native—full-time 2, part-time 0; Caucasian/White—full-time 45, part-time 15; Multi-ethnic—full-time 0, part-time 0; students subject to the Americans With Disabilities Act—full-time 0, part-time 1; Unknown ethnicity—full-time 0, part-time 0; International students who hold an F-1 or J-1 Visa—full-time 0, part-time 0.

Financial Information/Assistance:
 Tuition for Full-Time Study: *Master's:* State residents: $195 per credit hour; Nonstate residents: $490 per credit hour. Tuition is

subject to change. See the following website for updates and changes in tuition costs: http://www.uco.edu/em/registrar/tuitionandfees.asp.

Financial Assistance:
First-Year Students: Teaching assistantships available for first year. Average amount paid per academic year: $3,640. Average number of hours worked per week: 10. Apply by May. Research assistantships available for first year. Average amount paid per academic year: $1,690. Average number of hours worked per week: 5. Apply by March.

Advanced Students: Teaching assistantships available for advanced students. Average amount paid per academic year: $3,640. Average number of hours worked per week: 10. Apply by May. Research assistantships available for advanced students. Average amount paid per academic year: $1,690. Average number of hours worked per week: 5. Apply by March.

Additional Information: Of all students currently enrolled full time, 20% benefited from one or more of the listed financial assistance programs. Application and information available online at: http://www.uco.edu/graduate/financial/index.asp.

Internships/Practica: Master's Degree (MA/MS Counseling Psychology): An internship experience, such as a final research project or "capstone" experience is required of graduates. Master's Degree (MA/MS General Psychology): An internship experience, such as a final research project or "capstone" experience is required of graduates. Master's Degree (MA/MS School Psychology): An internship experience, such as a final research project or "capstone" experience is required of graduates. Internships/Practica: MA Counseling, General, Experimental, Forensic and School - practica are available in teaching and research. MA Counseling - 2 separate practica are required where students initially work in our departmental clinic and then are placed off-campus in community mental health clinics in our area. MA School - 3 separate practica are required. After graduation, a one year post graduate internship is required at a pre-approved clinic or school location.

Housing and Day Care: On-campus housing is available. See the following website for more information: http://www.uco.edu/administration/housing/. No on-campus day care facilities are available.

Employment of Department Graduates:
Master's Degree Graduates: Of those who graduated in the academic year 2011–2012, the following categories and numbers represent the postgraduate activities and employment of master's degree graduates: Enrolled in a postdoctoral residency/fellowship (n/a), employed in independent practice (n/a), total from the above (master's) (0).
Doctoral Degree Graduates: Of those who graduated in the academic year 2011–2012, the following categories and numbers represent the postgraduate activities and employment of doctoral degree graduates: Enrolled in a psychology doctoral program (n/a), total from the above (doctoral) (0).

Additional Information:
Orientation, Objectives, and Emphasis of Department: Excellent training to pursue doctoral work with the General experimental option - or Licensed Professional Counselor (LPC), or Licensed Behavioral Practitioner (LPB) with the Counseling Psychology

Option. School Psychometry offered with the School Psychology option. Option for Board Certified Behavioral Analysis certification.

Special Facilities or Resources: The department has excellent computer facilities. It has counseling clinic facilities in our Psychology Center with audio/visual equipment to train students in community counseling. We have a Learning & Behavior Clinic off-site for testing and training. There is a Cognitive Research Laboratory that includes shared research space with two psychophysiological units capable of collecting EEG, EMG, and cardiovascular data, a unit to collect eye tracking data, and several data collection software packages for the precise presentation of experimental stimuli.

Information for Students With Physical Disabilities: See the following website for more information: http://www.uco.edu/student-affairs/dss/index.asp.

Application Information:
Send to Dean of the Graduate College, 100 North University Drive, University of Central OK, Edmond, OK 73034. Application available online. URL of online application: http://www.uco.edu/graduate/admissions/index.asp. Students are admitted in the Fall, application deadline January 1; Programs have rolling admissions. The deadline is for the Forensic, Counseling and School Psychology option only. Experimental and General are open enrollment. *Fee:* $50.

Oklahoma City University
MEd in Applied Behavioral Studies: Professional Counseling
Petree College of Arts & Sciences (Dept of Education)
2501 North Blackwelder
Oklahoma City, OK 73106
Telephone: (405) 208-5387
Fax: (405) 208-6012
E-mail: *bfarha@okcu.edu*
Web: *http://www.okcu.edu/petree/education/counseling.aspx*

Department Information:
1970. Professor & Director: Bryan Farha. Number of faculty: total—full-time 3, part-time 3; women—full-time 1, part-time 2; total—minority—full-time 1, part-time 1; women minority—part-time 1.

Programs and Degrees Offered:
Listed in the following order: Program area, degree type (T if terminal Master's), number awarded 7/11–6/12. Applied Behavioral Studies:Professional Counseling MEd (Education).

Student Applications/Admissions:
Student Applications
Applied Behavioral Studies:Professional Counseling MEd (Education)—Total enrolled 2012–2013 full-time, 31. Total enrolled 2012–2013 part-time, 9.
Scores: Entries appear in this order: required test or GPA, minimum score (if required), median score of students entering in 2012–2013. *Applied Behavioral Studies:Professional Counseling MEd (Education):* overall undergraduate GPA 3.0.

Other Criteria: (importance of criteria rated low, medium, or high): GPA—high, letters of recommendation—high, interview—high, statement of goals and objectives—high, effective English ability—medium, undergraduate major in psychology—low, specific undergraduate psychology courses taken—low. For additional information on admission requirements, go to http://www.okcu.edu/petree/education/counseling.aspx.

Student Characteristics: The following represents characteristics of students in 2012–2013 in all graduate psychology programs in the department: Female—full-time 25, part-time 6; Male—full-time 6, part-time 3; African American/Black—full-time 4, part-time 0; Hispanic/Latino(a)—full-time 2, part-time 0; Asian/Pacific Islander—full-time 1, part-time 0; American Indian/Alaska Native—full-time 1, part-time 0; Caucasian/White—full-time 23, part-time 7; Multi-ethnic—full-time 0, part-time 2; students subject to the Americans With Disabilities Act—full-time 0, part-time 0; Unknown ethnicity—full-time 0, part-time 0; International students who hold an F-1 or J-1 Visa—full-time 3, part-time 0.

Financial Information/Assistance:

Tuition for Full-Time Study: *Master's:* State residents: $936 per credit hour; Nonstate residents: $936 per credit hour. Tuition is subject to change. See the following website for updates and changes in tuition costs: http://www.okcu.edu/financialaid/tuition/graduate/.

Financial Assistance:

First-Year Students: No information provided.
Advanced Students: No information provided.
Additional Information: Application and information available online at: http://www.okcu.edu/financialaid/.

Housing and Day Care: On-campus housing is available. See the following website for more information: http://www.okcu.edu/students/reslife/manor.aspx. No on-campus day care facilities are available.

Employment of Department Graduates:

Master's Degree Graduates: Of those who graduated in the academic year 2011–2012, the following categories and numbers represent the postgraduate activities and employment of master's degree graduates: Enrolled in a postdoctoral residency/fellowship (n/a), employed in independent practice (n/a), total from the above (master's) (0).

Doctoral Degree Graduates: Of those who graduated in the academic year 2011–2012, the following categories and numbers represent the postgraduate activities and employment of doctoral degree graduates: Enrolled in a psychology doctoral program (n/a), total from the above (doctoral) (0).

Additional Information:

Orientation, Objectives, and Emphasis of Department: The Petree College offers the Master of Education (MEd) degree in Applied Behavioral Studies: Professional Counseling in the Division of Education & Professional Studies (Department of Education). The program is designed to train students to become professional counselors and render services to individuals, groups, and families experiencing normal adjustment difficulties of a personal, social, or career nature in settings such as community counseling centers, mental health clinics, youth & guidance centers, human service agencies, drug and alcohol treatment facilities, university counseling centers, abuse shelters, religious counseling centers, and private practice (once licensed). Students are encouraged to secure internships in settings consistent with their specific areas of professional interest. To attain the professional counseling concentration, students must accrue at least 60 credit hours, including field experience. The sequenced mental health program of study is designed to meet the Oklahoma State Department of Health's academic requirements to become a Licensed Professional Counselor (LPC).

Information for Students With Physical Disabilities: See the following website for more information: http://www.okcu.edu/students/health/disability/.

Application Information:
Send to Oklahoma City University, Office of Admission, 2501 North Blackwelder, Oklahoma City, OK 73106. Application available online. URL of online application: http://www.okcu.edu/admission/graduate/apply.aspx. Students are admitted in the Fall; Programs have rolling admissions. We admit students for spring as well, but the program is designed for fall admission, so while spring admission is possible, it will not speed up graduation since there are prerequisites and the student would be out of sequence to begin study. *Fee:* $50.

Oklahoma State University
Department of Psychology
Arts & Sciences
116 North Murray Hall
Stillwater, OK 74078-3064
Telephone: (405) 744-6027
Fax: (405) 744-8067
E-mail: *larry.mullins@okstate.edu*
Web: *http://psychology.okstate.edu*

Department Information:
1920. Head: Larry L. Mullins. Number of faculty: total—full-time 23; women—full-time 9; total—minority—full-time 5; women minority—full-time 2.

Programs and Degrees Offered:
Listed in the following order: Program area, degree type (T if terminal Master's), number awarded 7/11–6/12. Clinical Psychology PhD (Doctor of Philosophy) 6, Lifespan Developmental Psychology PhD (Doctor of Philosophy) 2.

APA Accreditation: Clinical PhD (Doctor of Philosophy). Student Outcome Data Website: http://psychology.okstate.edu/graduate-programs/clinical-psychology-program.

Student Applications/Admissions:

Student Applications

Clinical Psychology PhD (Doctor of Philosophy)—Applications 2012–2013, 155. Total applicants accepted 2012–2013, 9. Number full-time enrolled (new admits only) 2012–2013, 6. Number part-time enrolled (new admits only) 2012–2013, 0. Total enrolled 2012–2013 full-time, 35. Total enrolled 2012–2013 part-time, 0. Openings 2013–2014, 7. The median number of years required for completion of a degree in 2012–2013 were 6. The number of students enrolled full- and part-time who were dismissed or voluntarily withdrew from this program area in 2012–2013 were 0. Lifespan Developmental Psychology PhD (Doctor of Philosophy)—Applications 2012–2013, 11. Total applicants accepted 2012–2013, 1. Number full-time enrolled (new admits only) 2012–2013, 0. Number part-time enrolled (new admits only) 2012–2013, 0. Total enrolled 2012–2013 full-time, 22. Total enrolled 2012–2013 part-time, 0. Openings 2013–2014, 4. The median number of years required for completion of a degree in 2012–2013 were 6. The number of students enrolled full- and part-time who were dismissed or voluntarily withdrew from this program area in 2012–2013 were 0.

Scores: Entries appear in this order: required test or GPA, minimum score (if required), median score of students entering in 2012–2013. Clinical Psychology PhD (Doctor of Philosophy): GRE-V no minimum stated, 161, GRE-Q no minimum stated, 150, GRE-Analytical no minimum stated, overall undergraduate GPA no minimum stated, 3.57, last 2 years GPA no minimum stated, psychology GPA no minimum stated; Lifespan Developmental Psychology PhD (Doctor of Philosophy): GRE-V no minimum stated, GRE-Q no minimum stated, GRE-Analytical no minimum stated, overall undergraduate GPA no minimum stated, last 2 years GPA no minimum stated, psychology GPA no minimum stated.

Other Criteria: (importance of criteria rated low, medium, or high): GRE scores—high, research experience—high, work experience—low, extracurricular activity—low, clinically related public service—low, GPA—high, letters of recommendation—high, interview—high, statement of goals and objectives—high, specific undergraduate psychology courses taken—high. For additional information on admission requirements, go to http://psychology.okstate.edu/graduate-programs.

Student Characteristics: The following represents characteristics of students in 2012–2013 in all graduate psychology programs in the department: Female—full-time 40, part-time 0; Male—full-time 17, part-time 0; African American/Black—full-time 1, part-time 0; Hispanic/Latino(a)—full-time 5, part-time 0; Asian/Pacific Islander—full-time 0, part-time 0; American Indian/Alaska Native—full-time 6, part-time 0; Caucasian/White—full-time 45, part-time 0; Multi-ethnic—full-time 0, part-time 0; students subject to the Americans With Disabilities Act—full-time 1, part-time 0; Unknown ethnicity—full-time 0, part-time 0; International students who hold an F-1 or J-1 Visa—full-time 1, part-time 0.

Financial Information/Assistance:

Tuition for Full-Time Study: Doctoral: State residents: $178 per credit hour; Nonstate residents: $709 per credit hour. Tuition is subject to change. Additional fees are assessed to students beyond the costs of tuition for the following: Health services, activities, technology. See the following website for updates and changes in tuition costs: http://bursar.okstate.edu/tuitionestimate.asp.

Financial Assistance:

First-Year Students: Teaching assistantships available for first year. Average amount paid per academic year: $10,800. Average number of hours worked per week: 20. Research assistantships available for first year. Average amount paid per academic year: $10,800. Average number of hours worked per week: 20. Traineeships available for first year. Average amount paid per academic year: $18,000. Average number of hours worked per week: 0. Fellowships and scholarships available for first year. Average amount paid per academic year: $3,000. Average number of hours worked per week: 0.

Advanced Students: Teaching assistantships available for advanced students. Average amount paid per academic year: $12,726. Average number of hours worked per week: 20. Research assistantships available for advanced students. Average amount paid per academic year: $12,726. Average number of hours worked per week: 20. Traineeships available for advanced students. Average amount paid per academic year: $18,000. Average number of hours worked per week: 0. Fellowships and scholarships available for advanced students. Average number of hours worked per week: 0.

Additional Information: Of all students currently enrolled full time, 100% benefited from one or more of the listed financial assistance programs.

Internships/Practica: Doctoral Degree (PhD Clinical Psychology): For those doctoral students for whom a professional psychology internship was required in this program prior to graduation, (7) students applied for an internship in 2011–2012, with (7) students obtaining an internship. Of those students who obtained an internship, (7) were paid internships. Of those students who obtained an internship, (7) students placed in APA/CPA accredited internships, (0) students placed in internships not APA/CPA accredited, but listed with the Association of Psychology Postdoctoral and Internship Programs (APPIC), (0) students placed in internships conforming to guidelines of the Council of Directors of School Psychology Programs (CDSPP), (0) students placed in internships that were not APA/CPA accredited, APPIC or CDSPP listed. For clinical students, the first 2 years of practicum experience are through our on-site clinic. Advanced students are eligible to participate in external supervised practica at affiliated agencies.

Housing and Day Care: On-campus housing is available. See the following website for more information: http://www.reslife.okstate.edu. No on-campus day care facilities are available.

Employment of Department Graduates:

Master's Degree Graduates: Of those who graduated in the academic year 2011–2012, the following categories and numbers represent the postgraduate activities and employment of master's degree graduates: Enrolled in a postdoctoral residency/fellowship (n/a), employed in independent practice (n/a), total from the above (master's) (0).

Doctoral Degree Graduates: Of those who graduated in the academic year 2011–2012, the following categories and numbers represent the postgraduate activities and employment of doctoral degree graduates: Enrolled in a psychology doctoral program (n/a), enrolled in a postdoctoral residency/fellowship (3), employed in an academic position at a university (4), employed in an academic position at a 2-year/4-year college (1), employed in a hospital/medical center (1), total from the above (doctoral) (9).

Additional Information:

Orientation, Objectives, and Emphasis of Department: The doctoral program in clinical psychology is based on the scientist–practitioner model. The program emphasizes the development of knowledge and skills in basic psychology, clinical theory, assessment and treatment procedures, and research. Practica, coursework, and internships are selected to enhance the student's interests. Students are expected, through additional coursework, specialized practica, and research, to develop a subspecialty in general clinical, clinical child, or health psychology. The program in Lifespan Developmental Psychology is a true lifespan program that has three primary goals: instruction in content areas of developmental psychology, training in research methodology and quantitative analysis, and preparation for teaching and/or research on applied topics. Students with interests in animal behavior, personality, psycholinguistics, social psychology, and quantitative methods are also encouraged to apply.

Special Facilities or Resources: The Department of Psychology is located in North Murray Hall near the center of the OSU campus. All students are provided office space that they share with 2-4 others. Offices are equipped with personal computers with access to SPSS, MS Office, the Internet, and printers. Wireless internet access is available in North Murray Hall. Every student is also provided a free email account. Graduate students also share a common room with a refrigerator, microwave oven, 2 additional computers with Adobe Professional, and a color printer. In addition, the Department of Psychology maintains a 24-station computer lab for student research, teaching, and other endeavors. The department operates the Psychological Services Center, an on-campus facility for clinical work and research. The center has equipment and facilities to accommodate a number of specialized services and functions, including videotaping, direct observation of clinical work using one-way mirrors, and direct supervision through telephones placed in therapy rooms. The department maintains liaisons with many off-campus organizations and agencies which provide the student with access to special populations for research as well as clinical activities. The department offers a variety of support services through the Psychology Diversified Students Program and the Psychology Graduate Students Association. Students are provided preadmission and postadmission assistance.

Information for Students With Physical Disabilities: See the following website for more information: http://sds.okstate.edu/.

Application Information:

Send to Department Head, Department of Psychology, OSU, 116 North Murray Hall, Stillwater, OK 74078-3064. Application available online. URL of online application: http://gradcollege.okstate.edu/apply/. Students are admitted in the Fall, application deadline December 1. December 1 deadline for Clinical Psychology; December 15 for Lifespan Developmental Psychology. *Fee:* $50.

Oklahoma State University (2012 data)
School of Applied Health and Educational Psychology
College of Education
434 Willard Hall
Stillwater, OK 74078
Telephone: (405) 744-6040
Fax: (405) 744-6756
E-mail: *john.romans@okstate.edu*
Web: *http://www.okstate.edu/education*

Department Information:

1997. School Head: Dr. John S.C. Romans, PhD Number of faculty: total—full-time 38, part-time 31; women—full-time 18, part-time 18; total—minority—full-time 5; women minority—full-time 3.

Programs and Degrees Offered:

Listed in the following order: Program area, degree type (T if terminal Master's), number awarded 7/11–6/12. Counseling Psychology PhD (Doctor of Philosophy) 8, School Psychology PhD (Doctor of Philosophy) 8, School Psychology EdS (School Psychology) 8, Educational Psychology PhD (Doctor of Philosophy) 3.

APA Accreditation: Counseling PhD (Doctor of Philosophy). Student Outcome Data Website: http://education.okstate.edu/student-admissions-outcomes-and-other-data. School PhD (Doctor of Philosophy). Student Outcome Data Website: http://education.okstate.edu/academic-units/school-of-applied-health-a-educational-psychology/school-psychology.

Student Applications/Admissions:

Student Applications

Counseling Psychology PhD (Doctor of Philosophy)—Applications 2012–2013, 67. Total applicants accepted 2012–2013, 8. Number full-time enrolled (new admits only) 2012–2013, 8. Number part-time enrolled (new admits only) 2012–2013, 0. Total enrolled 2012–2013 full-time, 34. Total enrolled 2012–2013 part-time, 7. Openings 2013–2014, 8. The median number of years required for completion of a degree in 2012–2013 were 5. The number of students enrolled full- and part-time who were dismissed or voluntarily withdrew from this program area in 2012–2013 were 0. *School Psychology PhD (Doctor of Philosophy)*—Applications 2012–2013, 35. Total applicants accepted 2012–2013, 8. Number full-time enrolled (new admits only) 2012–2013, 8. Number part-time enrolled (new admits only) 2012–2013, 0. Total enrolled 2012–2013 full-time, 32. Total enrolled 2012–2013 part-time, 6. Openings 2013–2014, 8. The median number of years required for completion of a degree in 2012–2013 were 5. The number of students enrolled full- and part-time who were dismissed or voluntarily withdrew from this program area in 2012–2013 were 0. *School Psychology EdS (School Psychology)*—Applications 2012–2013, 26. Total applicants accepted 2012–2013, 8. Number full-time enrolled (new admits only) 2012–2013, 8. Number part-time enrolled (new admits only) 2012–2013, 0. Total enrolled 2012–2013 full-time, 24. Total enrolled 2012–2013 part-time, 0. Openings 2013–2014, 8. The median number of years required for completion of a degree in 2012–2013 were 4. *Educational Psychology PhD (Doctor of Philosophy)*—Applications 2012–2013, 15. Total applicants accepted 2012–2013, 9. Number full-time enrolled (new admits only) 2012–2013, 3. Number part-time enrolled (new admits only) 2012–2013, 6. Total enrolled 2012–2013 full-time, 6. Total enrolled 2012–2013 part-time, 18. Openings 2013–2014, 6. The median number of years required for completion of a degree in 2012–2013 were 5. The number of students enrolled full- and part-time who were dismissed or voluntarily withdrew from this program area in 2012–2013 were 1.

Other Criteria: (importance of criteria rated low, medium, or high): GRE scores—high, research experience—high, work experience—medium, extracurricular activity—medium, clinically related public service—medium, GPA—high, letters of recommendation—high, interview—high, statement of goals and objectives—high, School Psychology: work experience and clinically related public service low, letters and interview are high. Statement of Goals-High.

Student Characteristics: The following represents characteristics of students in 2012–2013 in all graduate psychology programs in the department: Female—full-time 55, part-time 17; Male—full-time 41, part-time 14; African American/Black—full-time 5, part-time 2; Hispanic/Latino(a)—full-time 6, part-time 3; Asian/Pacific Islander—full-time 4, part-time 0; American Indian/Alaska Native—full-time 1, part-time 1; Caucasian/White—full-time 78, part-time 21; Multi-ethnic—full-time 2, part-time 4; students subject to the Americans With Disabilities Act—full-time 0, part-time 0; Unknown ethnicity—full-time 0, part-time 0; International students who hold an F-1 or J-1 Visa—full-time 0, part-time 0.

Financial Information/Assistance:

Tuition for Full-Time Study: *Master's:* State residents: per academic year $2,664, $168 per credit hour; Nonstate residents: per academic year $9,985, $667 per credit hour. *Doctoral:* State residents: per academic year $2,664, $168 per credit hour; Nonstate residents: per academic year $9,985, $667 per credit hour. Tuition is subject to change. See the following website for updates and changes in tuition costs: http://bursar.okstate.edu/tuition.html.

Financial Assistance:

First-Year Students: Teaching assistantships available for first year. Average amount paid per academic year: $4,005. Average number of hours worked per week: 10. Apply by April 15. Research assistantships available for first year. Average amount paid per academic year: $8,010. Average number of hours worked per week: 20. Apply by April 15. Traineeships available for first year.

Advanced Students: Teaching assistantships available for advanced students. Average amount paid per academic year: $4,635. Average number of hours worked per week: 10. Apply by April 15. Research assistantships available for advanced students. Average amount paid per academic year: $4,635. Average number of hours worked per week: 10. Apply by April 15. Traineeships available for advanced students. Average amount paid per academic year: $9,270. Average number of hours worked per week: 20. Fellowships and scholarships available for advanced students. Average amount paid per academic year: $250.

Additional Information: Of all students currently enrolled full time, 87% benefited from one or more of the listed financial assistance programs.

Internships/Practica: Doctoral Degree (PhD Counseling Psychology): For those doctoral students for whom a professional psychology internship was required in this program prior to graduation, (8) students applied for an internship in 2011–2012, with (8) students obtaining an internship. Of those students who obtained an internship, (8) were paid internships. Of those students who obtained an internship, (8) students placed in APA/CPA accredited internships, (0) students placed in internships not APA/CPA accredited, but listed with the Association of Psychology Postdoctoral and Internship Programs (APPIC), (0) students placed in internships conforming to guidelines of the Council of Directors of School Psychology Programs (CDSPP), (0) students placed in internships that were not APA/CPA accredited, APPIC or CDSPP listed. Doctoral Degree (PhD School Psychology): For those doctoral students for whom a professional psychology internship was required in this program prior to graduation, (8) students applied for an internship in 2011–2012, with (8) students obtaining an internship. Of those students who obtained an internship, (8) were paid internships. Of those students who obtained an internship, (8) students placed in APA/CPA accredited internships, (0) students placed in internships not APA/CPA accredited, but listed with the Association of Psychology Postdoctoral and Internship Programs (APPIC), (0) students placed in internships conforming to guidelines of the Council of Directors of School Psychology Programs (CDSPP), (0) students placed in internships that were not APA/CPA accredited, APPIC or CDSPP listed. Internships - Multiple settings for internship experiences are available nationally on a competitive basis, faculty must approve site selection. Students have obtained internships in a wide variety of settings (i.e., health centers, hospital settings). Internships must meet established standards for predoctoral internships in counseling psychology. Practicum - Practica are available at on-campus agencies, including a university counseling service, a mental health clinic at the student hospital, a career information center, and a marriage and family counseling service. Several off-campus placements are within a 75 mile radius of Stillwater, particularly in and around Tulsa and Oklahoma City, and sites include a stipend. School Psychology PhD students are required to compete for internship through APPIC. There has been 100% match for school psychology students. School Psychology EdS students complete the internship in approved public school settings. Practica are completed in public school settings and in the School Psychology Center.

Housing and Day Care: On-campus housing is available. See the following website for more information: www.reslife.okstate.edu. No on-campus day care facilities are available.

Employment of Department Graduates:

Master's Degree Graduates: Of those who graduated in the academic year 2011–2012, the following categories and numbers represent the postgraduate activities and employment of master's degree graduates: Enrolled in a psychology doctoral program (0), enrolled in a postdoctoral residency/fellowship (n/a), employed in independent practice (n/a), total from the above (master's) (0).

Doctoral Degree Graduates: Of those who graduated in the academic year 2011–2012, the following categories and numbers represent the postgraduate activities and employment of doctoral degree graduates: Enrolled in a psychology doctoral program (n/a), employed in independent practice (2), employed in an academic position at a university (1), employed in other positions at a higher education institution (1), employed in a professional position in a school system (2), employed in government agency (2), employed in a community mental health/counseling center (2), employed in a hospital/medical center (1), total from the above (doctoral) (11).

Additional Information:
Orientation, Objectives, and Emphasis of Department: Counseling Psychology—The orientation of the Counseling Psychology program is consistent both with the historical development of counseling psychology and with the current roles and functions of counseling psychology. We give major emphasis to prevention/developmental/educational interventions, and to remediation of problems that arise in the normal development of relatively well functioning people. The focus on prevention and developmental change brings us to seek knowledge and skills related to facilitation of growth, such as training in education, consultation, environmental change and self-help. It is the focus upon the assets, skills and strengths, and possibilities for further development of persons that is most reflective of the general philosophical orientation, of counseling psychology and of this program. The School Psychology program is based on the scientist–practitioner model, which emphasizes the application of the scientific knowledge base and methodological rigor in the delivery of school psychology services and in conducting research. Training in the scientist–practitioner model at OSU is for the purpose of developing a Science-Based Learner Success (SBLS) orientation in our students. Our philosophy is that all children and youth have the right to be successful and school psychologists are important agents who assist children, families, and others to be successful. Success refers not only to accomplishment of immediate goals but also to long range goals of adulthood such as contributing to society, social integration, meaningful work, and maximizing personal potential. The SBLS orientation focuses on prevention and intervention services related to children's psychoeducational and mental health and wellness. School Specialist and Doctoral programs are also approved by the National Association of School Psychologists. Educational Psychology is concerned with all aspects of psychology that are relevant to education, in particular, focal areas in the professions of Human Development, Education of the Gifted and Talented, and Instructional Psychology. The goal of the Educational Psychology program is to bring together theory and research from psychology and related disciplines in order to facilitate healthy human development and effective learning and teaching in any educational setting. The program is designed to prepare graduates to teach in college or university settings, public education, and/or to do research in university, business, and government settings.

Special Facilities or Resources: Community/School Services, Counseling Psychology Clinic and the School Psychology Clinic.

Information for Students With Physical Disabilities: See the following website for more information: http://www.okstate.edu/ucs/stdis/index.html.

Application Information:
Send to College of Education, Graduate Studies Records, Oklahoma State University, 325 Willard, Stillwater, OK 74078. Application available online. URL of online application: http://gradcollege.okstate.edu/apply/default.htm. Students are admitted in the Spring, application deadline See below. Counseling Psychology application deadlines: PhD: December 1, Master's: March 15 & October 15 School Psychol-

ogy application deadline: PhD: February 1 Educational Psychology application deadline: PhD: February 1, Master's: Rolling Educational Specialist application deadline: March 1, Applications completed after these deadlines might prevent your acceptance. *Fee:* $40. The international application fee is $75.

Oklahoma, University of
Department of Educational Psychology
The Jeannine Rainbolt College of Education
820 Van Vleet Oval, Room 321
Norman, OK 73019-2041
Telephone: (405) 325-5974
Fax: (405) 325-6655
E-mail: *edpsych@ou.edu*
Web: *http://www.ou.edu/content/education/departments/edpy.html*

Department Information:
1986. Chairperson: Dr. Xun Ge. Number of faculty: total—full-time 24, part-time 2; women—full-time 16, part-time 1; total—minority—full-time 5; women minority—full-time 4.

Programs and Degrees Offered:
Listed in the following order: Program area, degree type (T if terminal Master's), number awarded 7/11–6/12. Counseling Psychology PhD (Doctor of Philosophy) 9, Community Counseling MEd (Education) 11, Instructional Psychology and Technology MEd (Education) 1, Instructional Psychology and Technology PhD (Doctor of Philosophy) 1, Special Education MEd (Education) 1, Special Education PhD (Doctor of Philosophy) 2.

APA Accreditation: Counseling PhD (Doctor of Philosophy). Student Outcome Data Website: http://www.ou.edu/content/education/departments/edpy/programs/counseling-psychology/program-outcomes.html.

Student Applications/Admissions:
Student Applications
Counseling Psychology PhD (Doctor of Philosophy)—Applications 2012–2013, 67. Total applicants accepted 2012–2013, 7. Number full-time enrolled (new admits only) 2012–2013, 3. Number part-time enrolled (new admits only) 2012–2013, 1. Total enrolled 2012–2013 full-time, 24. Total enrolled 2012–2013 part-time, 23. Openings 2013–2014, 8. The median number of years required for completion of a degree in 2012–2013 were 5. The number of students enrolled full- and part-time who were dismissed or voluntarily withdrew from this program area in 2012–2013 were 0. *Community Counseling MEd (Education)*—Applications 2012–2013, 39. Total applicants accepted 2012–2013, 14. Number full-time enrolled (new admits only) 2012–2013, 14. Number part-time enrolled (new admits only) 2012–2013, 0. Total enrolled 2012–2013 full-time, 33. Total enrolled 2012–2013 part-time, 2. Openings 2013–2014, 15. The median number of years required for completion of a degree in 2012–2013 were 2. The number of students enrolled full- and part-time who were dismissed or voluntarily withdrew from this program area in 2012–2013 were 3. *Instructional Psychology and Technology MEd (Education)*—Applications 2012–2013, 25. Total applicants accepted 2012–2013, 19.

Number full-time enrolled (new admits only) 2012–2013, 5. Number part-time enrolled (new admits only) 2012–2013, 9. Total enrolled 2012–2013 full-time, 9. Total enrolled 2012–2013 part-time, 28. Openings 2013–2014, 15. The median number of years required for completion of a degree in 2012–2013 were 2. The number of students enrolled full- and part-time who were dismissed or voluntarily withdrew from this program area in 2012–2013 were 0. *Instructional Psychology and Technology PhD (Doctor of Philosophy)*—Applications 2012–2013, 22. Total applicants accepted 2012–2013, 5. Number full-time enrolled (new admits only) 2012–2013, 1. Number part-time enrolled (new admits only) 2012–2013, 0. Total enrolled 2012–2013 full-time, 2. Total enrolled 2012–2013 part-time, 13. Openings 2013–2014, 5. The median number of years required for completion of a degree in 2012–2013 were 2. The number of students enrolled full- and part-time who were dismissed or voluntarily withdrew from this program area in 2012–2013 were 0. *Special Education MEd (Education)*—Applications 2012–2013, 25. Total applicants accepted 2012–2013, 19. Number full-time enrolled (new admits only) 2012–2013, 7. Number part-time enrolled (new admits only) 2012–2013, 7. Total enrolled 2012–2013 full-time, 11. Total enrolled 2012–2013 part-time, 15. Openings 2013–2014, 15. The median number of years required for completion of a degree in 2012–2013 were 4. The number of students enrolled full- and part-time who were dismissed or voluntarily withdrew from this program area in 2012–2013 were 1. *Special Education PhD (Doctor of Philosophy)*—Applications 2012–2013, 10. Total applicants accepted 2012–2013, 2. Number full-time enrolled (new admits only) 2012–2013, 1. Number part-time enrolled (new admits only) 2012–2013, 0. Total enrolled 2012–2013 full-time, 3. Total enrolled 2012–2013 part-time, 14. Openings 2013–2014, 5. The median number of years required for completion of a degree in 2012–2013 were 6. The number of students enrolled full- and part-time who were dismissed or voluntarily withdrew from this program area in 2012–2013 were 2.

Scores: Entries appear in this order: required test or GPA, minimum score (if required), median score of students entering in 2012–2013. *Counseling Psychology PhD (Doctor of Philosophy):* GRE-V no minimum stated, 508, GRE-Q no minimum stated, 644, last 2 years GPA 3.0, 3.73, psychology GPA no minimum stated; *Community Counseling MEd (Education):* GRE-V no minimum stated, 461, GRE-Q no minimum stated, 581, GRE-Analytical no minimum stated, 4.11, last 2 years GPA 3.0, 3.51; *Instructional Psychology and Technology MEd (Education):* last 2 years GPA 3.0, 3.42; *Instructional Psychology and Technology PhD (Doctor of Philosophy):* GRE-V no minimum stated, 553, GRE-Q no minimum stated, 569, last 2 years GPA 3.0, 3.89; *Special Education MEd (Education):* last 2 years GPA 3.0, 3.47; *Special Education PhD (Doctor of Philosophy):* GRE-V no minimum stated, 148, GRE-Q no minimum stated, 148, last 2 years GPA 3.0, 3.96.

Other Criteria: (importance of criteria rated low, medium, or high): GRE scores—medium, research experience—medium, work experience—medium, extracurricular activity—medium, clinically related public service—medium, GPA—medium, letters of recommendation—medium, interview—high, statement of goals and objectives—medium, undergraduate major in psychology—medium, The Instructional Psychology and Technology programs do not require interviews for all applicants. However, the Admissions Committee may require some students to interview in order to make final decisions regarding admission. For additional information on admission requirements, go to http://www.ou.edu/content/education/departments/edpy/admission.html.

Student Characteristics: The following represents characteristics of students in 2012–2013 in all graduate psychology programs in the department: Female—full-time 59, part-time 64; Male—full-time 23, part-time 31; African American/Black—full-time 7, part-time 8; Hispanic/Latino(a)—full-time 7, part-time 3; Asian/Pacific Islander—full-time 6, part-time 6; American Indian/Alaska Native—full-time 4, part-time 5; Caucasian/White—full-time 48, part-time 65; Multi-ethnic—full-time 4, part-time 3; students subject to the Americans With Disabilities Act—full-time 1, part-time 0; Unknown ethnicity—full-time 6, part-time 5; International students who hold an F-1 or J-1 Visa—full-time 13, part-time 5.

Financial Information/Assistance:

Tuition for Full-Time Study: *Master's:* State residents: per academic year $3,153, $175 per credit hour; Nonstate residents: per academic year $11,750, $652 per credit hour. *Doctoral:* State residents: per academic year $3,153, $175 per credit hour; Nonstate residents: per academic year $11,750, $652 per credit hour. Tuition is subject to change. Additional fees are assessed to students beyond the costs of tuition for the following: university services, course materials, and technology. Tuition costs vary by program. See the following website for updates and changes in tuition costs: https://www.ou.edu/content/bursar/tuition_fees.html.

Financial Assistance:

First-Year Students: Teaching assistantships available for first year. Average amount paid per academic year: $10,197. Average number of hours worked per week: 20. Research assistantships available for first year. Average amount paid per academic year: $10,197. Average number of hours worked per week: 20. Fellowships and scholarships available for first year. Average amount paid per academic year: $15,197. Average number of hours worked per week: 20.

Advanced Students: Teaching assistantships available for advanced students. Average amount paid per academic year: $10,197. Average number of hours worked per week: 20. Research assistantships available for advanced students. Average amount paid per academic year: $10,197. Average number of hours worked per week: 20. Fellowships and scholarships available for advanced students. Average amount paid per academic year: $15,197. Average number of hours worked per week: 20.

Additional Information: Of all students currently enrolled full time, 41% benefited from one or more of the listed financial assistance programs. Application and information available online at: http://www.ou.edu/content/gradweb/aud/current/funding.html.

Internships/Practica: Doctoral Degree (PhD Counseling Psychology): For those doctoral students for whom a professional psychology internship was required in this program prior to graduation, (8) students applied for an internship in 2011–2012, with (7) students obtaining an internship. Of those students who obtained an internship, (7) were paid internships. Of those students who obtained an internship, (7) students placed in APA/CPA accredited internships, (0) students placed in internships not APA/

CPA accredited, but listed with the Association of Psychology Postdoctoral and Internship Programs (APPIC), (0) students placed in internships conforming to guidelines of the Council of Directors of School Psychology Programs (CDSPP), (0) students placed in internships that were not APA/CPA accredited, APPIC or CDSPP listed. Master's: Numerous hospitals and clinics in the local area. Doctoral: Students choose from APA-accredited sites (two in the local area and others across the nation).

Housing and Day Care: On-campus housing is available. See the following website for more information: http://www.housing.ou.edu. On-campus day care facilities are available.

Employment of Department Graduates:

Master's Degree Graduates: Of those who graduated in the academic year 2011–2012, the following categories and numbers represent the postgraduate activities and employment of master's degree graduates: Enrolled in a psychology doctoral program (5), enrolled in a postdoctoral residency/fellowship (n/a), employed in independent practice (n/a), employed in a professional position in a school system (2), employed in business or industry (1), employed in government agency (1), employed in a community mental health/counseling center (1), do not know (11), total from the above (master's) (21).

Doctoral Degree Graduates: Of those who graduated in the academic year 2011–2012, the following categories and numbers represent the postgraduate activities and employment of doctoral degree graduates: Enrolled in a psychology doctoral program (n/a), employed in independent practice (2), employed in an academic position at a university (5), employed in other positions at a higher education institution (2), employed in a professional position in a school system (1), still seeking employment (1), not seeking employment (1), do not know (1), total from the above (doctoral) (13).

Additional Information:

Orientation, Objectives, and Emphasis of Department: The department is committed to developing and disseminating new knowledge through research and scholarly activity, delivering quality instruction and professional training, and pursuing research and training opportunities at the junctures of the disciplines within the department.

Special Facilities or Resources: The Counseling Psychology Clinic is a community-based training site for our students. The clientele reflects diverse diagnostic classifications with some cultural diversity. Couples, children, and families make up a large proportion of the population served by the clinic.

Information for Students With Physical Disabilities: See the following website for more information: http://drc.ou.edu/.

Application Information:
Send to Graduate Programs Officer, Dept. of Educational Psychology, University of Oklahoma, 820 Van Vleet Oval, Room 321, Norman, OK 73019-2041. Application available online. URL of online application: http://www.ou.edu/admissions/home.html. Students are admitted in the Fall, application deadline January 10; Spring, application deadline October 1. Deadline for Counseling PhD is January 10; Community Counseling MEd is January 31. Deadlines for Instructional Psychology & Technology MEd: Spring - October 15; Fall - March 15 and July 1; PhD: February 1. Special Education PhD March 1; MEd - Spring - October 1; Fall - March 1. *Fee:* $40.

Oklahoma, University of
Department of Psychology
Arts and Sciences
455 West Lindsey
Norman, OK 73019-2007
Telephone: (405) 325-4511
Fax: (405) 325-4737
E-mail: *kpaine@ou.edu*
Web: *http://www.ou.edu/cas/psychology/*

Department Information:
1928. Chairperson: Jorge Mendoza. Number of faculty: total—full-time 24, part-time 4; women—full-time 10, part-time 2; total—minority—full-time 5; women minority—full-time 2.

Programs and Degrees Offered:
Listed in the following order: Program area, degree type (T if terminal Master's), number awarded 7/11–6/12. Industrial/Organizational Psychology MA/MS (Master of Arts/Science) (T) 1, Social Psychology PhD (Doctor of Philosophy) 2, Cognitive Psychology PhD (Doctor of Philosophy) 3, Experimental Personality PhD (Doctor of Philosophy) 1, Industrial/Organizational Psychology PhD (Doctor of Philosophy) 7, Quantitative/Measurement PhD (Doctor of Philosophy) 1, Developmental PhD (Doctor of Philosophy) 2.

Student Applications/Admissions:

Student Applications

Industrial/Organizational Psychology MA/MS (Master of Arts/Science)—Applications 2012–2013, 3. Total applicants accepted 2012–2013, 1. Number full-time enrolled (new admits only) 2012–2013, 0. Number part-time enrolled (new admits only) 2012–2013, 0. Total enrolled 2012–2013 full-time, 1. Total enrolled 2012–2013 part-time, 0. Openings 2013–2014, 2. The median number of years required for completion of a degree in 2012–2013 were 3. *Social Psychology PhD (Doctor of Philosophy)*—Applications 2012–2013, 21. Total applicants accepted 2012–2013, 0. Number full-time enrolled (new admits only) 2012–2013, 0. Number part-time enrolled (new admits only) 2012–2013, 0. Total enrolled 2012–2013 full-time, 10. Total enrolled 2012–2013 part-time, 0. Openings 2013–2014, 3. The median number of years required for completion of a degree in 2012–2013 were 5. The number of students enrolled full- and part-time who were dismissed or voluntarily withdrew from this program area in 2012–2013 were 0. *Cognitive Psychology PhD (Doctor of Philosophy)*—Applications 2012–2013, 16. Total applicants accepted 2012–2013, 7. Number full-time enrolled (new admits only) 2012–2013, 5. Number part-time enrolled (new admits only) 2012–2013, 0. Total enrolled 2012–2013 full-time, 14. Total enrolled 2012–2013 part-time, 0. Openings 2013–2014, 4. The median number of years required for completion of a degree in 2012–2013 were 5. The number of students enrolled full- and part-time who were dismissed or voluntarily withdrew from this program area in 2012–2013 were 0. *Experimental Personality PhD (Doctor of Philosophy)*—Applications 2012–2013, 4. Total applicants accepted 2012–2013, 0. Number full-time enrolled (new admits only) 2012–2013, 0. Number part-time enrolled (new admits only) 2012–2013, 0. Total enrolled 2012–2013 full-time, 2. Total enrolled 2012–2013 part-time, 0. Openings 2013–2014, 2. The median number of years required for completion of a degree in 2012–2013 were 5. The number of students enrolled full- and part-time who were dismissed or voluntarily withdrew from this program area in 2012–2013 were 0. *Industrial/Organizational Psychology PhD (Doctor of Philosophy)*—Applications 2012–2013, 46. Total applicants accepted 2012–2013, 6. Number full-time enrolled (new admits only) 2012–2013, 5. Number part-time enrolled (new admits only) 2012–2013, 0. Total enrolled 2012–2013 full-time, 29. Openings 2013–2014, 8. The median number of years required for completion of a degree in 2012–2013 were 5. The number of students enrolled full- and part-time who were dismissed or voluntarily withdrew from this program area in 2012–2013 were 0. *Quantitative/Measurement PhD (Doctor of Philosophy)*—Applications 2012–2013, 11. Total applicants accepted 2012–2013, 0. Number full-time enrolled (new admits only) 2012–2013, 0. Total enrolled 2012–2013 full-time, 8. Total enrolled 2012–2013 part-time, 0. Openings 2013–2014, 3. The median number of years required for completion of a degree in 2012–2013 were 5. The number of students enrolled full- and part-time who were dismissed or voluntarily withdrew from this program area in 2012–2013 were 0. *Developmental PhD (Doctor of Philosophy)*—Applications 2012–2013, 10. Total applicants accepted 2012–2013, 1. Number full-time enrolled (new admits only) 2012–2013, 1. Total enrolled 2012–2013 full-time, 4. Openings 2013–2014, 2. The median number of years required for completion of a degree in 2012–2013 were 5. The number of students enrolled full- and part-time who were dismissed or voluntarily withdrew from this program area in 2012–2013 were 0.

Scores: Entries appear in this order: required test or GPA, minimum score (if required), median score of students entering in 2012–2013. *Industrial/Organizational Psychology MA/MS (Master of Arts/Science):* GRE-V no minimum stated, 158, GRE-Q no minimum stated, 156, GRE-Analytical no minimum stated, 4.8, overall undergraduate GPA 3.0, 3.6, last 2 years GPA 3.0, 3.7; *Social Psychology PhD (Doctor of Philosophy):* GRE-V no minimum stated, 158, GRE-Q no minimum stated, 156, GRE-Analytical no minimum stated, 4.8, overall undergraduate GPA 3.0, 3.8, last 2 years GPA 3.0, 3.8; *Cognitive Psychology PhD (Doctor of Philosophy):* GRE-V no minimum stated, 158, GRE-Q no minimum stated, 156, GRE-Analytical no minimum stated, 5.0, overall undergraduate GPA 3.0, 3.6, last 2 years GPA 3.0, 3.8, Masters GPA 3.0, 3.8; *Experimental Personality PhD (Doctor of Philosophy):* GRE-V no minimum stated, 158, GRE-Q no minimum stated, 156, GRE-Analytical no minimum stated, 4.8, overall undergraduate GPA 3.0, 3.7, last 2 years GPA 3.0, 3.9; *Industrial/Organizational Psychology PhD (Doctor of Philosophy):* GRE-V no minimum stated, 158, GRE-Q no minimum stated, 157, GRE-Analytical no minimum stated, 4.8, overall undergraduate GPA 3.0, 3.7, last 2 years GPA 3.0, 3.8; *Quantitative/Measurement PhD (Doctor of Philosophy):* GRE-V no minimum stated, 158, GRE-Q no minimum stated, 157, GRE-Analytical no minimum stated, 4.6, overall undergraduate GPA 3.0, 3.6, last 2 years GPA 3.0, 3.9; *Developmental PhD (Doctor of Philosophy):* GRE-V no minimum stated, 158, GRE-Q no minimum stated, 156, GRE-

Analytical no minimum stated, 4.8, overall undergraduate GPA 3.0, 3.7, last 2 years GPA 3.0, 3.8.

Other Criteria: (importance of criteria rated low, medium, or high): GRE scores—high, research experience—high, work experience—low, extracurricular activity—low, GPA—high, letters of recommendation—high, interview—low, statement of goals and objectives—high, undergraduate major in psychology—low, specific undergraduate psychology courses taken—medium, Work experience is more important to the I/O program. For additional information on admission requirements, go to http://www.ou.edu/cas/psychology/Graduate/GradAdmReq.html.

Student Characteristics: The following represents characteristics of students in 2012–2013 in all graduate psychology programs in the department: Female—full-time 32, part-time 0; Male—full-time 36, part-time 0; African American/Black—full-time 2, part-time 0; Hispanic/Latino(a)—full-time 5, part-time 0; Asian/Pacific Islander—full-time 8, part-time 0; American Indian/Alaska Native—full-time 2, part-time 0; Caucasian/White—full-time 51, part-time 0; Multi-ethnic—full-time 0, part-time 0; students subject to the Americans With Disabilities Act—full-time 0, part-time 0; Unknown ethnicity—full-time 0, part-time 0; International students who hold an F-1 or J-1 Visa—full-time 7, part-time 0.

Financial Information/Assistance:

Tuition for Full-Time Study: *Master's:* State residents: $178 per credit hour; Nonstate residents: $652 per credit hour. *Doctoral:* State residents: $178 per credit hour; Nonstate residents: $652 per credit hour. Tuition is subject to change. See the following website for updates and changes in tuition costs: https://www.ou.edu/content/bursar/tuition_fees.html.

Financial Assistance:

First-Year Students: Teaching assistantships available for first year. Average amount paid per academic year: $12,587. Average number of hours worked per week: 20. Apply by January 1. Research assistantships available for first year. Average amount paid per academic year: $12,587. Average number of hours worked per week: 20. Apply by January 1. Fellowships and scholarships available for first year. Average amount paid per academic year: $19,587. Average number of hours worked per week: 20.

Advanced Students: Teaching assistantships available for advanced students. Average amount paid per academic year: $13,530. Average number of hours worked per week: 20. Research assistantships available for advanced students. Average amount paid per academic year: $13,530. Average number of hours worked per week: 20.

Additional Information: Of all students currently enrolled full time, 95% benefited from one or more of the listed financial assistance programs. Application and information available online at: http://www.ou.edu/cas/psychology/Graduate/Support.html.

Housing and Day Care: On-campus housing is available. See the following website for more information: http://www.housing.ou.edu/. On-campus day care facilities are available.

Employment of Department Graduates:

Master's Degree Graduates: Of those who graduated in the academic year 2011–2012, the following categories and numbers represent the postgraduate activities and employment of master's

degree graduates: Enrolled in a postdoctoral residency/fellowship (n/a), employed in independent practice (n/a), total from the above (master's) (0).

Doctoral Degree Graduates: Of those who graduated in the academic year 2011–2012, the following categories and numbers represent the postgraduate activities and employment of doctoral degree graduates: Enrolled in a psychology doctoral program (n/a), employed in an academic position at a university (1), employed in an academic position at a 2-year/4-year college (2), employed in business or industry (7), employed in government agency (2), do not know (4), total from the above (doctoral) (16).

Additional Information:

Orientation, Objectives, and Emphasis of Department: All programs are highly research oriented within the broad framework of experimental psychology. The department aims to produce creative and productive psychologists to function in academic and research settings, and toward this end emphasizes early and continuing involvement in research. Achievement of orientation and objectives is demonstrated by the excellent placement record of doctoral graduates, and by the department's recent rating as ninth in the nation in percent of publishing faculty. An excellent program in Quantitative Methods in Psychology is an especially attractive feature of the quality graduate training offered.

Special Facilities or Resources: The department offers modern research facilities with microprocessor-controlled laboratories, instrumentation shops with a full-time engineer, a small animal colony, a university computing center, a departmental computing center for graduate students, and graduate offices located near faculty and departmental offices.

Information for Students With Physical Disabilities: See the following website for more information: http://www.ou.edu/drc/home.html.

Application Information:
Send to Graduate Admissions Committee, Department of Psychology, University of Oklahoma, 455 West Lindsey, Room 705, Norman, OK 73019-2007. Application available online. URL of online application: http://www.ou.edu/cas/psychology/Graduate/GradAppinfo.html. Students are admitted in the Fall, application deadline January 1. *Fee:* $40. Fee is $90 for international students.

Tulsa, University of
Department of Psychology
Henry Kendall College of Arts and Sciences
800 South Tucker Drive
Tulsa, OK 74104-3189
Telephone: (918) 631-2248
Fax: (918) 631-2833
E-mail: *sandra-barney@utulsa.edu*
Web: *http://www.cas.utulsa.edu/psych*

Department Information:
1926. Chairperson: Dr. Judy Berry. Number of faculty: total—full-time 13, part-time 6; women—full-time 7, part-time 5; total—minority—full-time 1; women minority—full-time 1.

Programs and Degrees Offered:
Listed in the following order: Program area, degree type (T if terminal Master's), number awarded 7/11–6/12. Industrial/Organizational Psychology PhD (Doctor of Philosophy) 2, Industrial/Organizational Psychology MA/MS (Master of Arts/Science) (T) 7, Clinical Psychology MA/MS (Master of Arts/Science) (T) 3, Clinical Psychology PhD (Doctor of Philosophy) 4, Clinical Psychology Ma/Jd MA/MS (Master of Arts/Science) (T) 0, Industrial/Organizational Psychology Ma/Jd MA/MS (Master of Arts/Science) 0.

APA Accreditation: Clinical PhD (Doctor of Philosophy).

Student Applications/Admissions:
Student Applications
Industrial/Organizational Psychology PhD (Doctor of Philosophy)—Applications 2012–2013, 39. Total applicants accepted 2012–2013, 5. Number full-time enrolled (new admits only) 2012–2013, 3. Number part-time enrolled (new admits only) 2012–2013, 0. Total enrolled 2012–2013 full-time, 11. Total enrolled 2012–2013 part-time, 0. Openings 2013–2014, 3. The median number of years required for completion of a degree in 2012–2013 were 6. The number of students enrolled full- and part-time who were dismissed or voluntarily withdrew from this program area in 2012–2013 were 1. *Industrial/Organizational Psychology MA/MS (Master of Arts/Science)*—Applications 2012–2013, 42. Total applicants accepted 2012–2013, 14. Number full-time enrolled (new admits only) 2012–2013, 13. Number part-time enrolled (new admits only) 2012–2013, 0. Total enrolled 2012–2013 full-time, 20. Total enrolled 2012–2013 part-time, 0. Openings 2013–2014, 10. The median number of years required for completion of a degree in 2012–2013 were 2. The number of students enrolled full- and part-time who were dismissed or voluntarily withdrew from this program area in 2012–2013 were 0. *Clinical Psychology MA/MS (Master of Arts/Science)*—Applications 2012–2013, 8. Total applicants accepted 2012–2013, 3. Number full-time enrolled (new admits only) 2012–2013, 3. Total enrolled 2012–2013 full-time, 6. Total enrolled 2012–2013 part-time, 0. Openings 2013–2014, 3. The median number of years required for completion of a degree in 2012–2013 were 2. The number of students enrolled full- and part-time who were dismissed or voluntarily withdrew from this program area in 2012–2013 were 0. *Clinical Psychology PhD (Doctor of Philosophy)*—Applications 2012–2013, 128. Total applicants accepted 2012–2013, 9. Number full-time enrolled (new admits only) 2012–2013, 6. Number part-time enrolled (new admits only) 2012–2013, 0. Total enrolled 2012–2013 full-time, 35. Total enrolled 2012–2013 part-time, 0. Openings 2013–2014, 5. The median number of years required for completion of a degree in 2012–2013 were 6. The number of students enrolled full- and part-time who were dismissed or voluntarily withdrew from this program area in 2012–2013 were 0. *Clinical Psychology Ma/Jd MA/MS (Master of Arts/Science)*—Applications 2012–2013, 3. Total applicants accepted 2012–2013, 1. Number full-time enrolled (new admits only) 2012–2013, 0. Number part-time enrolled (new admits only) 2012–2013, 0. Openings 2013–2014, 1. The median number of years required for completion of a degree in 2012–2013 were 5. The number of students enrolled full- and part-time who were dismissed or voluntarily withdrew from this program area in 2012–2013 were 0. *Industrial/Organizational Psychology Ma/Jd MA/MS (Master of Arts/*

Science)—Applications 2012–2013, 2. Total applicants accepted 2012–2013, 1. Number full-time enrolled (new admits only) 2012–2013, 1. Number part-time enrolled (new admits only) 2012–2013, 0. Total enrolled 2012–2013 full-time, 1. Total enrolled 2012–2013 part-time, 0. Openings 2013–2014, 1. The median number of years required for completion of a degree in 2012–2013 were 5. The number of students enrolled full- and part-time who were dismissed or voluntarily withdrew from this program area in 2012–2013 were 0.

Scores: Entries appear in this order: required test or GPA, minimum score (if required), median score of students entering in 2012–2013. *Industrial/Organizational Psychology PhD (Doctor of Philosophy):* GRE-V no minimum stated, 156, GRE-Q no minimum stated, 149, GRE-Analytical no minimum stated, 4.75, overall undergraduate GPA 3.0, 3.85; *Industrial/Organizational Psychology MA/MS (Master of Arts/Science):* GRE-V no minimum stated, 154, GRE-Q no minimum stated, 150, GRE-Analytical no minimum stated, 4.5, overall undergraduate GPA 3.0, 3.7; *Clinical Psychology MA/MS (Master of Arts/Science):* GRE-V no minimum stated, 153, GRE-Q no minimum stated, 152, GRE-Analytical no minimum stated, 4.5, overall undergraduate GPA 3.0, 3.7; *Clinical Psychology PhD (Doctor of Philosophy):* GRE-V no minimum stated, 154, GRE-Q no minimum stated, 153, GRE-Analytical no minimum stated, 4.5, overall undergraduate GPA 3.0, 3.7, Masters GPA no minimum stated, 3.8; *Clinical Psychology MA/JD MA/MS (Master of Arts/Science):* GRE-V no minimum stated, 153, GRE-Q no minimum stated, 150, GRE-Analytical no minimum stated, 5.0, overall undergraduate GPA 3.0, 3.6; *Industrial/Organizational Psychology MA/JD MA/MS (Master of Arts/Science):* GRE-V no minimum stated, 160, GRE-Q no minimum stated, 153, GRE-Analytical no minimum stated, 4.5, overall undergraduate GPA 3.0, 3.6.

Other Criteria: (importance of criteria rated low, medium, or high): GRE scores—high, research experience—high, work experience—low, extracurricular activity—low, clinically related public service—medium, GPA—high, letters of recommendation—high, interview—high, statement of goals and objectives—high, quality of undergrad inst—medium, undergraduate major in psychology—medium, specific undergraduate psychology courses taken—medium, Resume or CV required for clinical program applicants. Interview for clinical PhD only.

Student Characteristics: The following represents characteristics of students in 2012–2013 in all graduate psychology programs in the department: Female—full-time 52, part-time 0; Male—full-time 21, part-time 0; African American/Black—full-time 1, part-time 0; Hispanic/Latino(a)—full-time 2, part-time 0; Asian/Pacific Islander—full-time 4, part-time 0; American Indian/Alaska Native—full-time 0, part-time 0; Caucasian/White—full-time 62, part-time 0; Multi-ethnic—full-time 0, part-time 0; students subject to the Americans With Disabilities Act—full-time 0, part-time 0; Unknown ethnicity—full-time 4, part-time 0; International students who hold an F-1 or J-1 Visa—full-time 3, part-time 0.

Financial Information/Assistance:
Tuition for Full-Time Study: *Master's:* State residents: $1,086 per credit hour; Nonstate residents: $1,086 per credit hour. *Doctoral:* State residents: $1,086 per credit hour; Nonstate residents: $1,086 per credit hour. Tuition is subject to change. Additional fees are assessed to students beyond the costs of tuition for the following: student association fee - $60; community fee - $100/sem. See the following website for updates and changes in tuition costs: http://www.utulsa.edu/academics/colleges/Graduate-School/About-the-School.aspx.

Financial Assistance:
First-Year Students: Teaching assistantships available for first year. Average amount paid per academic year: $13,236. Average number of hours worked per week: 20. Apply by February 1. Research assistantships available for first year. Average amount paid per academic year: $13,236. Average number of hours worked per week: 20. Apply by February 1. Fellowships and scholarships available for first year. Average number of hours worked per week: 20.

Advanced Students: Teaching assistantships available for advanced students. Average amount paid per academic year: $13,236. Average number of hours worked per week: 20. Apply by February 1. Research assistantships available for advanced students. Average amount paid per academic year: $13,236. Average number of hours worked per week: 20. Apply by February 1. Fellowships and scholarships available for advanced students. Average number of hours worked per week: 20.

Additional Information: Of all students currently enrolled full time, 70% benefited from one or more of the listed financial assistance programs. Application and information available online at: http://www.utulsa.edu/academics/colleges/Graduate-School/Graduate-Financial-Assistance.aspx.

Internships/Practica: Doctoral Degree (PhD Clinical Psychology): For those doctoral students for whom a professional psychology internship was required in this program prior to graduation, (6) students applied for an internship in 2011–2012, with (5) students obtaining an internship. Of those students who obtained an internship, (4) were paid internships. Of those students who obtained an internship, (5) students placed in APA/CPA accredited internships, (0) students placed in internships not APA/CPA accredited, but listed with the Association of Psychology Postdoctoral and Internship Programs (APPIC), (0) students placed in internships conforming to guidelines of the Council of Directors of School Psychology Programs (CDSPP), (0) students placed in internships that were not APA/CPA accredited, APPIC or CDSPP listed. Master's Degree (MA/MS Industrial/Organizational Psychology): An internship experience, such as a final research project or "capstone" experience is required of graduates. In the clinical program, supervised applied training begins early in the program. Practicum experiences occur primarily in community settings, utilizing the wide variety of agencies with which the department has relationships and allowing the student to interact with various mental health professionals. Placements include the university health center, community mental health centers, hospitals, community service agencies, and private practice groups. Attempts are made to allow students to choose practicum activities that are most consistent with their professional goals, although it is recognized that a diversity of experiences can provide a strong foundation for professional development. Practicum activities are supervised by an on-site professional, and the practicum experience is organized and monitored by the Coordinator of Practicum Training in conjunction with the Clinical Program Committee.

Housing and Day Care: On-campus housing is available. See the following website for more information: http://www.utulsa.edu/

student-life/Living-and-Dining-on-Campus.aspx. On-campus day care facilities are available. See the following website for more information: http://www.kindercare.com/our-centers/tulsa/ok/000859/.

Employment of Department Graduates:

Master's Degree Graduates: Of those who graduated in the academic year 2011–2012, the following categories and numbers represent the postgraduate activities and employment of master's degree graduates: Enrolled in a psychology doctoral program (2), enrolled in another graduate/professional program (1), enrolled in a postdoctoral residency/fellowship (n/a), employed in independent practice (n/a), employed in business or industry (5), employed in a community mental health/counseling center (1), still seeking employment (1), total from the above (master's) (10).

Doctoral Degree Graduates: Of those who graduated in the academic year 2011–2012, the following categories and numbers represent the postgraduate activities and employment of doctoral degree graduates: Enrolled in a psychology doctoral program (n/a), enrolled in a postdoctoral residency/fellowship (3), employed in business or industry (2), employed in government agency (1), total from the above (doctoral) (6).

Additional Information:

Orientation, Objectives, and Emphasis of Department: Our graduate programs in applied psychology are central to the departmental mission, which is: to generate new psychological knowledge to help individuals, organizations, and communities make decisions and solve problems; to offer a future-oriented, intellectually challenging, and socially relevant curriculum; and to equip students to make a difference through their work by providing them with an extensive knowledge base as well as the analytical and practical skills needed to apply knowledge wisely. Our programs train students to do what applied psychologists actually do in today's society. The programs in I/O psychology emphasize personnel psychology and organizational development, theory and behavior, with a special focus on individual assessment. The doctoral program in clinical psychology develops scientist–practitioners using the following training components. First, coursework is distributed across clinical core, general psychology, methodology core, and elective offerings. Second, research mentoring is experienced in the precandidacy and dissertation projects. Third, procedural knowledge is developed in clinical practicum and internship training. Fourth, declarative knowledge is developed through comprehensive written and oral examinations covering general psychological knowledge and methods, and clinical psychology.

Special Facilities or Resources: The Department of Psychology is located in Lorton Hall, a building located near the center of the TU campus. The building contains faculty offices, classrooms, offices for graduate students on assistantships, a graduate student lounge, research space, and clinical training space. McFarlin Library, a two-minute walk from Lorton Hall, contains more than three million items and more than 6,000 periodical subscriptions. The library's catalogue is computerized and is accessible from terminals across campus. Computer searches of the major information databases in psychology are available to students at no charge. Major computer application suites and statistical packages (e.g., SPSS) are available for word processing, data analyses, test interpretation, and other tasks. The university has several computer labs with a variety of hardware configurations and software packages for student use. Visiting scholars and professionals often join the graduate faculty in presenting special courses, workshops, and seminars. Each year, colloquium speakers offer opinions, ideas, and research on topics of current interest in psychology.

Information for Students With Physical Disabilities: See the following website for more information: http://www.utulsa.edu/student-life/Center-for-Student-Academic-Support/.

Application Information:

Send to Graduate School, University of Tulsa, 800 South Tucker Drive, Tulsa, OK 74104. Application available online. URL of online application: https://secureweb.utulsa.edu/graduate/application/. Students are admitted in the Fall, application deadline December 1. For the Clinical psychology program, the application due date is December 1. For the Industrial/Organizational psychology program, the application due date is December 15. *Fee:* $40. Application fee is waived for McNair scholars.

George Fox University (2012 data)
Graduate Department of Clinical Psychology
School of Behavioral and Health Sciences
414 North Meridian Street # V104
Newberg, OR 97132-2697
Telephone: (503) 554-2370
Fax: (503) 554-2371
E-mail: *psyd@georgefox.edu*
Web: *http://psyd.georgefox.edu*

Department Information:
1981. Chairperson: Mary Peterson. Number of faculty: total—full-time 10, part-time 6; women—full-time 4, part-time 2; total—minority—full-time 2.

Programs and Degrees Offered:
Listed in the following order: Program area, degree type (T if terminal Master's), number awarded 7/11–6/12. Clinical Psychology PsyD (Doctor of Psychology) 16.

APA Accreditation: Clinical PsyD (Doctor of Psychology). Student Outcome Data Website: http://www.georgefox.edu/psyd.

Student Applications/Admissions:
Student Applications
Clinical Psychology PsyD (Doctor of Psychology)—Applications 2012–2013, 95. Total applicants accepted 2012–2013, 40. Number full-time enrolled (new admits only) 2012–2013, 25. Number part-time enrolled (new admits only) 2012–2013, 0. Total enrolled 2012–2013 full-time, 100. Total enrolled 2012–2013 part-time, 7. Openings 2013–2014, 22. The median number of years required for completion of a degree in 2012–2013 were 5. The number of students enrolled full- and part-time who were dismissed or voluntarily withdrew from this program area in 2012–2013 were 1.
Scores: Entries appear in this order: required test or GPA, minimum score (if required), median score of students entering in 2012–2013. *Clinical Psychology PsyD (Doctor of Psychology):* GRE-V 450, 480, GRE-Q 500, 590, overall undergraduate GPA 3.0, 3.4.
Other Criteria: (importance of criteria rated low, medium, or high): GRE scores—high, research experience—low, work experience—medium, extracurricular activity—low, clinically related public service—medium, GPA—high, letters of recommendation—high, interview—high, statement of goals and objectives—high, Christian worldview—high, undergraduate major in psychology—medium, specific undergraduate psychology courses taken—low. For additional information on admission requirements, go to http://www.georgefox.edu/psyd/admission/index.html.

Student Characteristics: The following represents characteristics of students in 2012–2013 in all graduate psychology programs in the department: Female—full-time 68, part-time 6; Male—full-time 32, part-time 1; African American/Black—full-time 2, part-time 0; Hispanic/Latino(a)—full-time 7, part-time 0; Asian/Pacific Islander—full-time 4, part-time 0; American Indian/Alaska Native—full-time 3, part-time 1; Caucasian/White—full-time 80, part-time 6; Multi-ethnic—full-time 2, part-time 0; students subject to the Americans With Disabilities Act—full-time 1, part-time 0; Unknown ethnicity—full-time 2, part-time 0; International students who hold an F-1 or J-1 Visa—full-time 1, part-time 0.

Financial Information/Assistance:
Tuition for Full-Time Study: *Doctoral:* State residents: $760 per credit hour; Nonstate residents: $760 per credit hour. Tuition is subject to change. Additional fees are assessed to students beyond the costs of tuition for the following: Student activity and health fees. See the following website for updates and changes in tuition costs: http://www.georgefox.edu/psyd/admission/scholarships.html.

Financial Assistance:
First-Year Students: Fellowships and scholarships available for first year. Average amount paid per academic year: $4,000. Average number of hours worked per week: 0. Apply by March 30.
Advanced Students: Teaching assistantships available for advanced students. Average amount paid per academic year: $3,000. Average number of hours worked per week: 5. Research assistantships available for advanced students. Average amount paid per academic year: $2,100. Average number of hours worked per week: 5. Fellowships and scholarships available for advanced students. Average amount paid per academic year: $4,000. Average number of hours worked per week: 0. Apply by March 30.
Additional Information: Of all students currently enrolled full time, 40% benefited from one or more of the listed financial assistance programs. Application and information available online at: http://www.georgefox.edu/offices/sfs/grad/financial-aid/.

Internships/Practica: Doctoral Degree (PsyD Clinical Psychology): For those doctoral students for whom a professional psychology internship was required in this program prior to graduation, (15) students applied for an internship in 2011–2012, with (15) students obtaining an internship. Of those students who obtained an internship, (14) were paid internships. Of those students who obtained an internship, (9) students placed in APA/CPA accredited internships, (5) students placed in internships not APA/CPA accredited, but listed with the Association of Psychology Postdoctoral and Internship Programs (APPIC), (0) students placed in internships conforming to guidelines of the Council of Directors of School Psychology Programs (CDSPP), (1) students placed in internships that were not APA/CPA accredited, APPIC or CDSPP listed. Students are required to complete four years of practicum (minimum of 1500 hours) in a variety of settings in the greater Portland metropolitan area. Practicum settings include hospitals, primary care medical settings, community mental health agencies, drug and alcohol programs, schools, and prisons. Inpatient and out-patient experiences are available. All practicum experience is gained under the careful supervision of licensed psychologists at the practicum sites. Additionally, students receive weekly clinical oversight on campus by core faculty. Students apply for internships within the system developed by the Association of Psychology Postdoctoral and Internship Centers (APPIC).

Students complete a one-year full-time internship (2000 hours) at an approved internship site during their fifth year in the program. Usually, 90% of applicants obtain an APA- and/or APPIC-approved internship sites.

Housing and Day Care: No on-campus housing is available. No on-campus day care facilities are available.

Employment of Department Graduates:
Master's Degree Graduates: Of those who graduated in the academic year 2011–2012, the following categories and numbers represent the postgraduate activities and employment of master's degree graduates: Enrolled in a postdoctoral residency/fellowship (n/a), employed in independent practice (n/a), total from the above (master's) (0).
Doctoral Degree Graduates: Of those who graduated in the academic year 2011–2012, the following categories and numbers represent the postgraduate activities and employment of doctoral degree graduates: Enrolled in a psychology doctoral program (n/a), enrolled in a postdoctoral residency/fellowship (15), not seeking employment (1), total from the above (doctoral) (16).

Additional Information:
Orientation, Objectives, and Emphasis of Department: The goal of the Graduate Department of Clinical Psychology (GDCP) is to prepare professional psychologists who are competent to provide psychological services in a wide variety of clinical settings, who are knowledgeable in critical evaluation and application of psychological research, and who are committed to the highest standards of professional ethics. The central distinctive feature of the program is the integration of a Christian worldview and the science of psychology at philosophical, practical and personal levels. Graduates are trained broadly but also as specialists in meeting the unique psychological needs of the Christian community and others who wish a spiritual dimension to be included in their treatment. Other distinctive aspects of the program include close mentoring using clinical and research team models and an option for training emphases in Assessment, Rural and Health Psychology. Graduates are prepared for licensure as clinical psychologists. Alumni of the GDCP are licensed in numerous states throughout the U.S. They engage in practice in a variety of settings, including independent and group practice, hospitals, community mental health clinics, government, corrections, public health agencies, and church and para-church organizations. Graduates also teach in a variety of settings, including colleges and seminaries.

Personal Behavior Statement: http://www.georgefox.edu/psyd/about/beliefs.html.

Special Facilities or Resources: High-speed microcomputers, laser printers, and complete statistical (SPSS PC+) and graphics software are provided in a computer lab. The Murdock Learning Resource Center provides library support for the psychology program. The library has excellent access to materials important to contemporary clinical and empirical work in most areas of clinical psychology. In addition, the library receives more than 140 periodicals in psychology and related disciplines, most available electronically. Students also have online access to major computerized databases through library services, including PsycInfo, DIALOG, ERIC, and many others. In addition to full-text access to many psychology journals, George Fox University maintains coopera-tive arrangements with other local educational institutions, providing psychology students with a full range of user services, including interlibrary loans and direct borrowing privileges. A full range of traditional campus facilities are also available such as athletic, arts outlets, student lounge and meal service. A newly remodeled building is the campus location for the PsyD program. The new quarters include all PsyD classrooms, faculty offices, student lounge area, computer lab, cafe, conference rooms, clinical demonstration and videotaping rooms, and student parking.

Information for Students With Physical Disabilities: See the following website for more information: http://www.georgefox.edu/arc/.

Application Information:
Send to Adina McConaughey, Graduate Admissions, George Fox University, 414 North Meridian Street # 6149, Newberg, OR 97132. Application available online. URL of online application: https://www.applyweb.com/apply/gfu/menu.html. Students are admitted in the Fall, application deadline January 15. Early Notification deadline is November 15. Special circumstances for delayed or late applications will be considered. Strong applicants will be considered after deadline on a space-available basis. We accept alternate applications throughout the year. *Fee:* $40. Fee waiver for McNairs Scholars and Act Six Leadership & Scholars.

Oregon, University of
Counseling Psychology
College of Education
5251 University of Oregon
Eugene, OR 97403-5251
Telephone: (541) 346-2456
Fax: (541) 346-6778
E-mail: *cpsy@uoregon.edu*
Web: *http://education.uoregon.edu/cpsy*

Department Information:
1954. Area Head: Lauren Lindstrom. Number of faculty: total—full-time 6, part-time 2; women—full-time 5, part-time 2; total—minority—full-time 2, part-time 1; women minority—full-time 2, part-time 1.

Programs and Degrees Offered:
Listed in the following order: Program area, degree type (T if terminal Master's), number awarded 7/11–6/12. Counseling Psychology PhD (Doctor of Philosophy) 7.

APA Accreditation: Counseling PhD (Doctor of Philosophy). Student Outcome Data Website: https://education.uoregon.edu/cpsy.

Student Applications/Admissions:
Student Applications
Counseling Psychology PhD (Doctor of Philosophy)—Applications 2012–2013, 204. Total applicants accepted 2012–2013, 9. Number full-time enrolled (new admits only) 2012–2013, 8. Number part-time enrolled (new admits only) 2012–2013, 0. Total enrolled 2012–2013 full-time, 41. Total enrolled 2012–2013 part-time, 0. Openings 2013–2014, 8. The median num-

ber of years required for completion of a degree in 2012–2013 were 6. The number of students enrolled full- and part-time who were dismissed or voluntarily withdrew from this program area in 2012–2013 were 0.

Scores: Entries appear in this order: required test or GPA, minimum score (if required), median score of students entering in 2012–2013. *Counseling Psychology PhD (Doctor of Philosophy):* GRE-V no minimum stated, 573, GRE-Q no minimum stated, 572, GRE-Analytical no minimum stated, 4.5, overall undergraduate GPA no minimum stated, 3.58.

Other Criteria: (importance of criteria rated low, medium, or high): GRE scores—medium, research experience—high, work experience—high, extracurricular activity—medium, clinically related public service—medium, GPA—high, letters of recommendation—high, interview—high, statement of goals and objectives—high, second language skills—low, undergraduate major in psychology—medium, specific undergraduate psychology courses taken—medium. For additional information on admission requirements, go to https://education.uoregon.edu/counseling-psychology/admissions.

Student Characteristics: The following represents characteristics of students in 2012–2013 in all graduate psychology programs in the department: Female—full-time 37, part-time 0; Male—full-time 4, part-time 0; African American/Black—full-time 2, part-time 0; Hispanic/Latino(a)—full-time 8, part-time 0; Asian/Pacific Islander—full-time 7, part-time 0; American Indian/Alaska Native—full-time 0, part-time 0; Caucasian/White—full-time 21, part-time 0; Multi-ethnic—full-time 2, part-time 0; students subject to the Americans With Disabilities Act—full-time 1, part-time 0; Unknown ethnicity—full-time 1, part-time 0; International students who hold an F-1 or J-1 Visa—full-time 0, part-time 0.

Financial Information/Assistance:

Tuition for Full-Time Study: *Doctoral:* State residents: per academic year $17,586, $490 per credit hour; Nonstate residents: per academic year $23,904, $774 per credit hour. Tuition is subject to change. Additional fees are assessed to students beyond the costs of tuition for the following: practicum courses have a $60 fee. Tuition costs vary by program. See the following website for updates and changes in tuition costs: http://registrar.uoregon.edu/costs.

Financial Assistance:

First-Year Students: Teaching assistantships available for first year. Average amount paid per academic year: $24,540. Average number of hours worked per week: 13. Apply by March. Fellowships and scholarships available for first year. Average amount paid per academic year: $3,000. Average number of hours worked per week: 0. Apply by February.

Advanced Students: Teaching assistantships available for advanced students. Average amount paid per academic year: $28,491. Average number of hours worked per week: 13. Apply by March. Fellowships and scholarships available for advanced students. Average amount paid per academic year: $3,000. Average number of hours worked per week: 0. Apply by February.

Additional Information: Of all students currently enrolled full time, 100% benefited from one or more of the listed financial assistance programs. Application and information available online at: https://education.uoregon.edu/counseling-psychology/student-funding.

Internships/Practica: Doctoral Degree (PhD Counseling Psychology): For those doctoral students for whom a professional psychology internship was required in this program prior to graduation, (5) students applied for an internship in 2011–2012, with (5) students obtaining an internship. Of those students who obtained an internship, (5) were paid internships. Of those students who obtained an internship, (5) students placed in APA/CPA accredited internships, (0) students placed in internships not APA/CPA accredited, but listed with the Association of Psychology Postdoctoral and Internship Programs (APPIC), (0) students placed in internships conforming to guidelines of the Council of Directors of School Psychology Programs (CDSPP), (0) students placed in internships that were not APA/CPA accredited, APPIC or CDSPP listed. All students are required to participate in one year of both adult and child/family practica. Numerous externship opportunities exist throughout the community.

Housing and Day Care: On-campus housing is available. See the following website for more information: http://housing.uoregon.edu/. On-campus day care facilities are available. See the following website for more information: http://hr.uoregon.edu/content/child-care-campus.

Employment of Department Graduates:

Master's Degree Graduates: Of those who graduated in the academic year 2011–2012, the following categories and numbers represent the postgraduate activities and employment of master's degree graduates: Enrolled in a postdoctoral residency/fellowship (n/a), employed in independent practice (n/a), total from the above (master's) (0).

Doctoral Degree Graduates: Of those who graduated in the academic year 2011–2012, the following categories and numbers represent the postgraduate activities and employment of doctoral degree graduates: Enrolled in a psychology doctoral program (n/a), enrolled in a postdoctoral residency/fellowship (2), employed in independent practice (1), employed in a community mental health/counseling center (2), employed in a hospital/medical center (1), do not know (1), total from the above (doctoral) (7).

Additional Information:

Orientation, Objectives, and Emphasis of Department: Accredited by the American Psychological Association (APA) since 1955, the UO doctoral program in Counseling Psychology emphasizes an ecological model of training, research, and practice. Students focus research and training in prevention and treatment relevant to work with children, adolescents, families, and adults. The ecological model holds that human behavior occurs within a context of multiple interacting systems, influenced by unique social, historical, political, and cultural factors. Students in the CPSY program are trained to view assessment, intervention, and research within the contexts of these systems. Development of multicultural competencies is emphasized throughout the curriculum.

Special Facilities or Resources: Students work cooperatively in research areas at Oregon Social Learning Center, the Oregon Research Institute and the Child and Family Center.

Information for Students With Physical Disabilities: See the following website for more information: http://aec.uoregon.edu/.

Application Information:
Send to Student Coordinator, Counseling Psychology, 5251 University of Oregon, Eugene, OR, 97403-5251. Application available online. URL of online application: https://gradweb.uoregon.edu/online_app/application/guidelines1.asp. Students are admitted in the Fall, application deadline December 15. *Fee:* $50. Contact UO Graduate School Admissions regarding conditions for waiver or deferral of fee.

Oregon, University of
Department of Psychology
College of Arts and Sciences
1227 University of Oregon
Eugene, OR 97403-1227
Telephone: (541) 346-5060
Fax: (541) 346-4911
E-mail: *gradsec@psych.uoregon.edu*
Web: *http://psychweb.uoregon.edu*

Department Information:
1895. Department Head: Louis J. Moses, PhD. Number of faculty: total—full-time 28, part-time 1; women—full-time 9; total—minority—full-time 6; women minority—full-time 1.

Programs and Degrees Offered:
Listed in the following order: Program area, degree type (T if terminal Master's), number awarded 7/11–6/12. Clinical Psychology PhD (Doctor of Philosophy) 2, Cognitive/ Neuroscience/ Systems PhD (Doctor of Philosophy) 5, Developmental Psychology PhD (Doctor of Philosophy) 4, Individualized Master's MA/MS (Master of Arts/Science) (T) 8, Social/Personality Psychology PhD (Doctor of Philosophy) 2.

APA Accreditation: Clinical PhD (Doctor of Philosophy). Student Outcome Data Website: http://psychweb.uoregon.edu/graduates/intellectualcommunities/clinical.

Student Applications/Admissions:
Student Applications
Clinical Psychology PhD (Doctor of Philosophy)—Applications 2012–2013, 245. Total applicants accepted 2012–2013, 6. Number full-time enrolled (new admits only) 2012–2013, 4. Total enrolled 2012–2013 full-time, 20. Total enrolled 2012–2013 part-time, 2. Openings 2013–2014, 4. The number of students enrolled full- and part-time who were dismissed or voluntarily withdrew from this program area in 2012–2013 were 1. *Cognitive/ Neuroscience/Systems PhD (Doctor of Philosophy)*—Applications 2012–2013, 103. Total applicants accepted 2012–2013, 7. Number full-time enrolled (new admits only) 2012–2013, 5. Total enrolled 2012–2013 full-time, 19. Openings 2013–2014, 2. The number of students enrolled full- and part-time who were dismissed or voluntarily withdrew from this program area in 2012–2013 were 0. *Developmental Psychology PhD (Doctor of Philosophy)*—Applications 2012–2013, 44. Total applicants accepted 2012–2013, 4. Number full-time enrolled (new admits only) 2012–2013, 3. Total enrolled 2012–2013 full-time, 13. Total enrolled 2012–2013 part-time, 1. Openings 2013–2014, 2. *Individualized Master's MA/MS (Master of Arts/Science)*—Applications 2012–2013, 28. Total applicants accepted 2012–2013, 12. Number full-time enrolled (new admits only) 2012–2013, 12. Total enrolled 2012–2013 full-time, 23. Openings 2013–2014, 10. *Social/Personality Psychology PhD (Doctor of Philosophy)*—Applications 2012–2013, 101. Total applicants accepted 2012–2013, 8. Number full-time enrolled (new admits only) 2012–2013, 6. Total enrolled 2012–2013 full-time, 20. Openings 2013–2014, 2.

Scores: Entries appear in this order: required test or GPA, minimum score (if required), median score of students entering in 2012–2013. *Clinical Psychology PhD (Doctor of Philosophy):* GRE-V no minimum stated, 162, GRE-Q no minimum stated, 155, GRE-Analytical no minimum stated, 5.3, overall undergraduate GPA no minimum stated, 3.74, last 2 years GPA no minimum stated, psychology GPA no minimum stated; *Cognitive/ Neuroscience/Systems PhD (Doctor of Philosophy):* GRE-V no minimum stated, GRE-Q no minimum stated, GRE-Analytical no minimum stated, overall undergraduate GPA no minimum stated, last 2 years GPA no minimum stated, psychology GPA no minimum stated; *Developmental Psychology PhD (Doctor of Philosophy):* GRE-V no minimum stated, GRE-Q no minimum stated, GRE-Analytical no minimum stated, overall undergraduate GPA no minimum stated, last 2 years GPA no minimum stated, psychology GPA no minimum stated; *Individualized Master's MA/MS (Master of Arts/Science):* GRE-V no minimum stated, GRE-Q no minimum stated, GRE-Analytical no minimum stated, overall undergraduate GPA no minimum stated, last 2 years GPA no minimum stated, psychology GPA no minimum stated; *Social/Personality Psychology PhD (Doctor of Philosophy):* GRE-V no minimum stated, GRE-Q no minimum stated, GRE-Analytical no minimum stated, overall undergraduate GPA no minimum stated, last 2 years GPA no minimum stated, psychology GPA no minimum stated.

Other Criteria: (importance of criteria rated low, medium, or high): GRE scores—high, research experience—high, work experience—low, extracurricular activity—low, clinically related public service—medium, GPA—high, letters of recommendation—high, interview—high, statement of goals and objectives—high, Please check with department regarding interviews. For additional information on admission requirements, go to http://psychweb.uoregon.edu/graduates/doctoralprogram/applicationprocedures.

Student Characteristics: The following represents characteristics of students in 2012–2013 in all graduate psychology programs in the department: Female—full-time 62, part-time 3; Male—full-time 33, part-time 0; African American/Black—full-time 1, part-time 0; Hispanic/Latino(a)—full-time 4, part-time 0; Asian/Pacific Islander—full-time 9, part-time 1; American Indian/Alaska Native—full-time 0, part-time 0; Caucasian/White—full-time 65, part-time 2; Multi-ethnic—full-time 1, part-time 0; students subject to the Americans With Disabilities Act—full-time 0, part-time 0; Unknown ethnicity—full-time 15, part-time 0; International students who hold an F-1 or J-1 Visa—full-time 9, part-time 0.

Financial Information/Assistance:
Tuition for Full-Time Study: *Master's:* State residents: $490 per credit hour; Nonstate residents: $774 per credit hour. *Doctoral:* State residents: per academic year $14,529, $490 per credit hour; Nonstate residents: per academic year $22,197, $774 per credit hour. Tuition is subject to change. See the following website

for updates and changes in tuition costs: http://registrar.uoregon. edu/costs.

Financial Assistance:

First-Year Students: Teaching assistantships available for first year. Research assistantships available for first year. Fellowships and scholarships available for first year.

Advanced Students: Teaching assistantships available for advanced students. Research assistantships available for advanced students. Fellowships and scholarships available for advanced students.

Additional Information: Of all students currently enrolled full time, 95% benefited from one or more of the listed financial assistance programs. Application and information available online at: http://gradschool.uoregon.edu/funding-awards.

Internships/Practica: Doctoral Degree (PhD Clinical Psychology): For those doctoral students for whom a professional psychology internship was required in this program prior to graduation, (3) students applied for an internship in 2011–2012, with (2) students obtaining an internship. Of those students who obtained an internship, (2) were paid internships. Of those students who obtained an internship, (2) students placed in APA/CPA accredited internships, (0) students placed in internships not APA/CPA accredited, but listed with the Association of Psychology Postdoctoral and Internship Programs (APPIC), (0) students placed in internships conforming to guidelines of the Council of Directors of School Psychology Programs (CDSPP), (0) students placed in internships that were not APA/CPA accredited, APPIC or CDSPP listed. Master's Degree (MA/MS Individualized Master's): An internship experience, such as a final research project or "capstone" experience is required of graduates.

Housing and Day Care: On-campus housing is available. See the following website for more information: http://housing.uoregon. edu/. On-campus day care facilities are available. See the following website for more information: http://hr.uoregon.edu/content/ child-care-campus.

Employment of Department Graduates:

Master's Degree Graduates: Of those who graduated in the academic year 2011–2012, the following categories and numbers represent the postgraduate activities and employment of master's degree graduates: Enrolled in a postdoctoral residency/fellowship (n/a), employed in independent practice (n/a), total from the above (master's) (0).

Doctoral Degree Graduates: Of those who graduated in the academic year 2011–2012, the following categories and numbers represent the postgraduate activities and employment of doctoral degree graduates: Enrolled in a psychology doctoral program (n/a), total from the above (doctoral) (0).

Additional Information:

Orientation, Objectives, and Emphasis of Department: The course of study is tailored largely to the student's particular needs. There are minimal formal requirements for the doctorate, which include three course sequences (contemporary issues in psychology, statistics, and a first-year research practicum); a supporting area requirement, consisting of at least two graduate-level, graded courses, and a major project, such as a paper or teaching an original course; a major preliminary examination; and, of course, the doctoral dissertation. Clinical students engage in several prac-

tica beginning in the first year. All programs require and are organized to facilitate student research from the first year.

Special Facilities or Resources: Straub Hall houses the psychology clinic, equipment for psychophysiological research, specialized facilities for research in child and social psychology, and experimental laboratories for human research. Numerous microcomputers are available for research and teaching. A short distance from the main psychology building are well-equipped animal labs for research in physiological psychology. Graduate students and faculty participate in interdisciplinary programs in cognitive science, neuroscience, and developmental psychopathology. Local nonprofit research groups including Oregon Research Institute, Oregon Social Learning Center and Decision Research provide unusual auspices and opportunities for students.

Information for Students With Physical Disabilities: See the following website for more information: http://ds.uoregon.edu/.

Application Information:
Send to Graduate Secretary, Department of Psychology, 1227 University of Oregon, Eugene, OR 97403-1227. Application available online. URL of online application: https://gradweb.uoregon.edu/online_app/ application/guidelines1.asp. Students are admitted in the Fall, application deadline December 1. Individualized master's deadline for fall admission is May 15. *Fee:* $50.

Pacific University
School of Professional Psychology
College of Health Professions
Pacific University, 190 SE 8th Avenue, Suite 260
Hillsboro, OR 97123
Telephone: (503) 352-7277
Fax: (503) 352-7320
E-mail: *millerco@pacificu.edu*
Web: *http://www.pacificu.edu/spp/*

Department Information:
1979. Dean: Christiane Brems. Number of faculty: total—full-time 22, part-time 19; women—full-time 16, part-time 12; total—minority—full-time 4; women minority—full-time 4; faculty subject to the Americans With Disabilities Act 1.

Programs and Degrees Offered:
Listed in the following order: Program area, degree type (T if terminal Master's), number awarded 7/11–6/12. Clinical Psychology PsyD (Doctor of Psychology) 40, Counseling Psychology MA/MS (Master of Arts/Science) (T) 44, Clinical Psychology PhD (Doctor of Philosophy) 0.

APA Accreditation: Clinical PsyD (Doctor of Psychology). Student Outcome Data Website: http://www.pacificu.edu/spp/program_stats. cfm.

Student Applications/Admissions:
Student Applications
Clinical Psychology PsyD (Doctor of Psychology)—Applications 2012–2013, 240. Total applicants accepted 2012–2013, 104.

Number full-time enrolled (new admits only) 2012–2013, 55. Number part-time enrolled (new admits only) 2012–2013, 0. Total enrolled 2012–2013 full-time, 199. Total enrolled 2012–2013 part-time, 75. Openings 2013–2014, 55. The median number of years required for completion of a degree in 2012–2013 were 6. The number of students enrolled full- and part-time who were dismissed or voluntarily withdrew from this program area in 2012–2013 were 12. *Counseling Psychology MA/MS (Master of Arts/Science)*—Applications 2012–2013, 120. Total applicants accepted 2012–2013, 70. Number full-time enrolled (new admits only) 2012–2013, 43. Number part-time enrolled (new admits only) 2012–2013, 1. Total enrolled 2012–2013 full-time, 85. Total enrolled 2012–2013 part-time, 2. Openings 2013–2014, 44. The median number of years required for completion of a degree in 2012–2013 were 2. The number of students enrolled full- and part-time who were dismissed or voluntarily withdrew from this program area in 2012–2013 were 6. *Clinical Psychology PhD (Doctor of Philosophy)*—Applications 2012–2013, 0. Total applicants accepted 2012–2013, 0. Number full-time enrolled (new admits only) 2012–2013, 0. Number part-time enrolled (new admits only) 2012–2013, 0. Openings 2013–2014, 7. The number of students enrolled full- and part-time who were dismissed or voluntarily withdrew from this program area in 2012–2013 were 0. *Scores:* Entries appear in this order: required test or GPA, minimum score (if required), median score of students entering in 2012–2013. *Clinical Psychology PsyD (Doctor of Psychology):* GRE-V no minimum stated, 523, GRE-Q no minimum stated, 609, GRE-Analytical no minimum stated, 4.3, overall undergraduate GPA no minimum stated, 3.5, Masters GPA no minimum stated, 3.8; *Clinical Psychology PhD (Doctor of Philosophy):* GRE-V no minimum stated, GRE-Q no minimum stated, GRE-Analytical no minimum stated, overall undergraduate GPA 3.3, Masters GPA no minimum stated.
Other Criteria: (importance of criteria rated low, medium, or high): GRE scores—medium, research experience—medium, work experience—medium, extracurricular activity—low, clinically related public service—low, GPA—medium, letters of recommendation—high, interview—high, statement of goals and objectives—high, undergraduate major in psychology—medium, specific undergraduate psychology courses taken—medium, GRE scores required for PsyD and PhD programs only. For additional information on admission requirements, go to http://www.pacificu.edu/spp/admissions/.

Student Characteristics: The following represents characteristics of students in 2012–2013 in all graduate psychology programs in the department: Female—full-time 199, part-time 75; Male—full-time 85, part-time 2; African American/Black—full-time 5, part-time 0; Hispanic/Latino(a)—full-time 7, part-time 5; Asian/Pacific Islander—full-time 8, part-time 2; American Indian/Alaska Native—full-time 1, part-time 1; Caucasian/White—full-time 220, part-time 55; Multi-ethnic—full-time 2, part-time 1; students subject to the Americans With Disabilities Act—full-time 22, part-time 4; Unknown ethnicity—full-time 41, part-time 13; International students who hold an F-1 or J-1 Visa—full-time 3, part-time 3.

Financial Information/Assistance:
Tuition for Full-Time Study: *Master's:* State residents: per academic year $21,855, $889 per credit hour; Nonstate residents: per academic year $21,855, $889 per credit hour. *Doctoral:* State residents: per academic year $29,871, $905 per credit hour; Nonstate residents: per academic year $29,871, $905 per credit hour. Tuition is subject to change. Tuition costs vary by program.

Financial Assistance:
First-Year Students: Fellowships and scholarships available for first year. Average amount paid per academic year: $3,000. Average number of hours worked per week: 7. Apply by January 14.
Advanced Students: Teaching assistantships available for advanced students. Average amount paid per academic year: $3,600. Average number of hours worked per week: 7. Apply by April 1. Fellowships and scholarships available for advanced students. Average amount paid per academic year: $3,000. Apply by April 1.
Additional Information: Of all students currently enrolled full time, 36% benefited from one or more of the listed financial assistance programs. Application and information available online at: http://wwwpacificuedu/spp/admissions/clinical/financialaidcfm

Internships/Practica: Doctoral Degree (PsyD Clinical Psychology): For those doctoral students for whom a professional psychology internship was required in this program prior to graduation, (61) students applied for an internship in 2011–2012, with (50) students obtaining an internship. Of those students who obtained an internship, (50) were paid internships. Of those students who obtained an internship, (28) students placed in APA/CPA accredited internships, (22) students placed in internships not APA/CPA accredited, but listed with the Association of Psychology Postdoctoral and Internship Programs (APPIC), (0) students placed in internships conforming to guidelines of the Council of Directors of School Psychology Programs (CDSPP), (0) students placed in internships that were not APA/CPA accredited, APPIC or CDSPP listed. Master's Degree (MA/MS Counseling Psychology): An internship experience, such as a final research project or "capstone" experience is required of graduates. Each student is required to complete 6 terms (two years) of practicum. Training entails integration of theoretical knowledge through its application in clinical practice. The experience includes supervised practice in the application of professional psychological competencies with a range of client populations, age groups, and clinical problems. PsyD clinical students complete their two years of required practicum while they are taking courses in the program. The practicum experience includes a minimum of 500 training hours per year, of which approximately one-third to one-half are in direct service, one-fourth in supervisory and training activities, and the remainder in administrative/clerical duties related to the above. The practicum experience typically involves approximately 16 hours per week of supervised experience in a clinical setting, and affords the student the opportunity to integrate theoretical knowledge, research, and clinical skills. Many students gain some practicum experience at the program's own training clinic, and other community sites in the Portland area are also available, allowing for exposure to varied sites and populations. Depending upon availability of site, students also may participate in additional, non-required clinical training experiences for credit. The Pacific Psychology Clinic operates an APPIC member/APA-approved internship program. There are three intern positions. MA in Counseling Psychology students complete 700 hours (15 credits, 3 terms) of internship in their second year. Students who elect to complete the yearlong sequence of organizational behavior courses also complete a 100 hour OB practicum in addition.

Housing and Day Care: No on-campus housing is available. No on-campus day care facilities are available.

Employment of Department Graduates:

Master's Degree Graduates: Of those who graduated in the academic year 2011–2012, the following categories and numbers represent the postgraduate activities and employment of master's degree graduates: Enrolled in a postdoctoral residency/fellowship (n/a), employed in independent practice (n/a), total from the above (master's) (0).

Doctoral Degree Graduates: Of those who graduated in the academic year 2011–2012, the following categories and numbers represent the postgraduate activities and employment of doctoral degree graduates: Enrolled in a psychology doctoral program (n/a), enrolled in a postdoctoral residency/fellowship (5), employed in independent practice (3), employed in other positions at a higher education institution (4), employed in government agency (2), employed in a community mental health/counseling center (3), employed in a hospital/medical center (4), other employment position (2), do not know (21), total from the above (doctoral) (44).

Additional Information:

Orientation, Objectives, and Emphasis of Department: The School of Professional Psychology prepares students for mastery and success in a rapidly evolving, demanding profession. Professional psychology and counseling require a solid grounding in the science of psychology, a keen sense of ethics, strong interpersonal and research skills, and the ability to work in a variety of professional roles with clients from a diverse range of backgrounds. The curriculum is designed to build and integrate these components of professional practice. The School offers two colloquia each year featuring nationally-known presenters. The School emphasizes community involvement and flexible, diversity-appropriate, practical applications of scientific psychology. The clinical psychology program follows a practitioner-scholar model of professional education, with coursework reflecting the latest empirical findings in the field. We present students with a broad range of theoretical perspectives and expose them to assessment, intervention, research/evaluation, consultation/education, and management/supervision. The counseling psychology program emphasizes the local clinical scientist model. The use of the latest and best scientific findings is a mainstay of our professional training. The faculty encourage students to use the scientific method and an empirical approach with each client.

Special Facilities or Resources: The School maintains the Pacific Psychology Clinic, a training clinic at two sites. The Hillsboro clinic is located on the Health Professions Campus in Hillsboro, and provides services in both Spanish and English. The Portland clinic is located in downtown Portland. These clinics offer a wide range of psychological services to the community.

Information for Students With Physical Disabilities: See the following website for more information: http://www.pacificu.edu/studentlife/lss/index.cfm.

Application Information:
Send to Pacific University, Graduate and Professional Programs Office of Admissions, 190 Southeast 8th Avenue, Ste 181, Hillsboro, OR 97123. Application available online. URL of online application: https://www.applyweb.com/apply/pup/index.html. Students are admitted in the Fall, application deadline January 23. Deadline for MA in Counseling Psychology: February 15. Deadline for PhD in Clinical Psychology: February 8. *Fee:* $40.

Portland State University
Psychology Department
College of Liberal Arts & Sciences
P.O. Box 751
Portland, OR 97207-0751
Telephone: (503) 725-3923
Fax: (503) 725-3904
E-mail: *cdmohr@pdx.edu*
Web: *http://www.pdx.edu/psy/*

Department Information:
1955. Chairperson: Sherwin Davidson, Ph. D. Number of faculty: total—full-time 18; women—full-time 8; total—minority—full-time 3; women minority—full-time 1.

Programs and Degrees Offered:
Listed in the following order: Program area, degree type (T if terminal Master's), number awarded 7/11–6/12. Applied Developmental PhD (Doctor of Philosophy) 0, Applied Social & Community PhD (Doctor of Philosophy) 4, Industrial/Organizational PhD (Doctor of Philosophy) 3.

Student Applications/Admissions:

Student Applications

Applied Developmental PhD (Doctor of Philosophy)—Applications 2012–2013, 29. Total applicants accepted 2012–2013, 2. Number full-time enrolled (new admits only) 2012–2013, 2. Total enrolled 2012–2013 full-time, 13. Total enrolled 2012–2013 part-time, 0. Openings 2013–2014, 4. The median number of years required for completion of a degree in 2012–2013 were 6. The number of students enrolled full- and part-time who were dismissed or voluntarily withdrew from this program area in 2012–2013 were 0. *Applied Social & Community PhD (Doctor of Philosophy)*—Applications 2012–2013, 51. Total applicants accepted 2012–2013, 3. Number full-time enrolled (new admits only) 2012–2013, 3. Number part-time enrolled (new admits only) 2012–2013, 0. Total enrolled 2012–2013 full-time, 21. Total enrolled 2012–2013 part-time, 0. Openings 2013–2014, 4. The median number of years required for completion of a degree in 2012–2013 were 6. The number of students enrolled full- and part-time who were dismissed or voluntarily withdrew from this program area in 2012–2013 were 1. *Industrial/Organizational PhD (Doctor of Philosophy)*—Applications 2012–2013, 70. Total applicants accepted 2012–2013, 3. Number full-time enrolled (new admits only) 2012–2013, 3. Number part-time enrolled (new admits only) 2012–2013, 0. Total enrolled 2012–2013 full-time, 21. Total enrolled 2012–2013 part-time, 0. Openings 2013–2014, 6. The median number of years required for completion of a degree in 2012–2013 were 5. The number of students enrolled full- and part-time who were dismissed or voluntarily withdrew from this program area in 2012–2013 were 0.

Scores: Entries appear in this order: required test or GPA, minimum score (if required), median score of students entering in 2012–2013. *Applied Developmental PhD (Doctor of Philosophy):* GRE-V no minimum stated, 160, GRE-Q no minimum stated, 156, GRE-Analytical no minimum stated, 4.5, overall undergraduate GPA 3.25, 3.90, last 2 years GPA no minimum stated; *Applied Social & Community PhD (Doctor of Philosophy):* GRE-V no minimum stated, 160, GRE-Q no minimum stated, 156, GRE-Analytical no minimum stated, 4.5, overall undergraduate GPA 3.25, 3.90, last 2 years GPA no minimum stated; *Industrial/Organizational PhD (Doctor of Philosophy):* GRE-V no minimum stated, 160, GRE-Q no minimum stated, 156, GRE-Analytical no minimum stated, 4.5, overall undergraduate GPA 3.25, 3.90, last 2 years GPA no minimum stated.
Other Criteria: (importance of criteria rated low, medium, or high): GRE scores—high, research experience—high, work experience—medium, extracurricular activity—medium, clinically related public service—low, GPA—high, letters of recommendation—high, statement of goals and objectives—high, undergraduate major in psychology—medium, specific undergraduate psychology courses taken—medium. For additional information on admission requirements, go to http://www.pdx.edu/psy/application-instructions.

Student Characteristics: The following represents characteristics of students in 2012–2013 in all graduate psychology programs in the department: Female—full-time 41, part-time 0; Male—full-time 14, part-time 0; African American/Black—full-time 0, part-time 0; Hispanic/Latino(a)—full-time 0, part-time 0; Asian/Pacific Islander—full-time 0, part-time 0; American Indian/Alaska Native—full-time 0, part-time 0; Caucasian/White—full-time 0, part-time 0; Multi-ethnic—full-time 0, part-time 0; students subject to the Americans With Disabilities Act—full-time 0, part-time 0; Unknown ethnicity—full-time 55, part-time 0; International students who hold an F-1 or J-1 Visa—full-time 0, part-time 0.

Financial Information/Assistance:
Tuition for Full-Time Study: *Master's:* State residents: per academic year $9,504, $352 per credit hour; Nonstate residents: per academic year $14,634, $542 per credit hour. *Doctoral:* State residents: per academic year $9,504, $352 per credit hour; Nonstate residents: per academic year $14,634, $542 per credit hour. Tuition is subject to change. Additional fees are assessed to students beyond the costs of tuition for the following: health services, building, campus recreation. See the following website for updates and changes in tuition costs: http://www.pdx.edu/financial-services/tuition-fees.

Financial Assistance:
First-Year Students: Teaching assistantships available for first year. Average amount paid per academic year: $10,800. Average number of hours worked per week: 19. Research assistantships available for first year. Average amount paid per academic year: $10,800. Average number of hours worked per week: 19. Fellowships and scholarships available for first year. Average amount paid per academic year: $10,800. Average number of hours worked per week: 19.
Advanced Students: Teaching assistantships available for advanced students. Average amount paid per academic year: $12,250. Average number of hours worked per week: 19. Research assistantships available for advanced students. Average amount paid per academic year: $12,250. Average number of hours worked per week: 19. Fellowships and scholarships available for advanced students. Average amount paid per academic year: $12,250. Average number of hours worked per week: 19.

Additional Information: Of all students currently enrolled full time, 100% benefited from one or more of the listed financial assistance programs. Application and information available online at: http://www.pdx.edu/psy/funding-possibilities.

Internships/Practica: The university is located in downtown Portland, the major metropolitan area in the state of Oregon. Consequently, internships are readily available in a variety of applied settings. Placements are also available through the ongoing research activities of the faculty.

Housing and Day Care: On-campus housing is available. See the following website for more information: http://www.pdx.edu/housing/. On-campus day care facilities are available. See the following website for more information: http://www.hgcdc.pdx.edu/.

Employment of Department Graduates:
Master's Degree Graduates: Of those who graduated in the academic year 2011–2012, the following categories and numbers represent the postgraduate activities and employment of master's degree graduates: Enrolled in a psychology doctoral program (8), enrolled in a postdoctoral residency/fellowship (n/a), employed in independent practice (n/a), total from the above (master's) (8).
Doctoral Degree Graduates: Of those who graduated in the academic year 2011–2012, the following categories and numbers represent the postgraduate activities and employment of doctoral degree graduates: Enrolled in a psychology doctoral program (n/a), enrolled in a postdoctoral residency/fellowship (2), employed in an academic position at a university (1), employed in business or industry (2), employed in government agency (1), not seeking employment (1), total from the above (doctoral) (7).

Additional Information:
Orientation, Objectives, and Emphasis of Department: Students are given a broad background in applied psychology, which prepares them for careers in academics, research, or various applied settings, such as governmental agencies, manufacturing and service industries, health organizations and labor organizations. Doctoral students major in one specialty area and minor in a second (e.g., research methods, Occupational Health Psychology). Major areas include Applied Developmental Psychology, focusing on how knowledge and research regarding human development can be used to help solve real-world problems. The major focus is Developmental Science and Education, with special attention to the development of motivation, mindfulness, self and identity, and coping in the context of relationships with parents, teachers, and peers. Industrial/Organizational (I/O) Psychology concerns the application of psychological theories, research methods, and intervention strategies to workplace issues, with a goal of helping organizations to be highly productive while ensuring that their workers are able to lead physically and psychologically healthy work lives. The Applied Social and Community area faculty/students share an interest in urban health and community well-being, which includes work promoting mental and physical health, as well as healthy social outcomes and remediating negative influences like discrimination. Graduate students in the area specialize in either the Applied Social or Community Psychology track.

Special Facilities or Resources: The Department of Psychology's location in the heart of downtown Portland offers unique academic and research opportunities in the service of the department's applied mission. Strong collaborative relationships with local industry, organizations, and community agencies offer venues for course related projects, faculty research initiatives, practicum placements, and required student research. A number of University-based resources also enhance our students' skills and experiences. For example, the University's writing center allows faculty and students to hone technical writing skills. The Instructional Development Support Center provides training in computer and media-based applications to foster improved teaching and more sophisticated research approaches.

Information for Students With Physical Disabilities: See the following website for more information: http://www.drc.pdx.edu.

Application Information:
Send to Portland State University, Department of Psychology, P.O. Box 751, Portland, OR 97207-0751. Application available online. URL of online application: http://www.pdx.edu/admissions/graduate-applicant. Students are admitted in the Fall, application deadline December 15. *Fee:* $50.

Southern Oregon University
Master in Mental Health Counseling
1250 Siskiyou Boulevard
Ashland, OR 97520
Telephone: (541)552-6947
Fax: (541)552-6988
E-mail: MHC@sou.edu
Web: http://www.sou.edu/psychology/mhc/

Department Information:
2000. Chairperson: Daniel DeNeui, PhD. Number of faculty: total—full-time 6; women—full-time 3.

Programs and Degrees Offered:
Listed in the following order: Program area, degree type (T if terminal Master's), number awarded 7/11–6/12. Mental Health Counseling MA/MS (Master of Arts/Science) (T) 21.

Student Applications/Admissions:
Student Applications
Mental Health Counseling MA/MS (Master of Arts/Science)—Applications 2012–2013, 70. Total applicants accepted 2012–2013, 22. Number full-time enrolled (new admits only) 2012–2013, 22. Number part-time enrolled (new admits only) 2012–2013, 0. Total enrolled 2012–2013 full-time, 46. Total enrolled 2012–2013 part-time, 0. Openings 2013–2014, 22. The median number of years required for completion of a degree in 2012–2013 were 2. The number of students enrolled full- and part-time who were dismissed or voluntarily withdrew from this program area in 2012–2013 were 2.
Scores: Entries appear in this order: required test or GPA, minimum score (if required), median score of students entering in 2012–2013. Mental Health Counseling MA/MS (Master of Arts/Science): GRE-V 150, GRE-Q 150, GRE-Analytical 3.0,

overall undergraduate GPA 3.0, last 2 years GPA 3.0, psychology GPA 3.0.
Other Criteria: (importance of criteria rated low, medium, or high): GRE scores—high, research experience—low, work experience—low, extracurricular activity—low, clinically related public service—low, GPA—high, letters of recommendation—high, statement of goals and objectives—high, specific undergraduate psychology courses taken—high. For additional information on admission requirements, go to http://www.sou.edu/psychology/mhc/requirements.html.

Student Characteristics: The following represents characteristics of students in 2012–2013 in all graduate psychology programs in the department: Female—full-time 36, part-time 0; Male—full-time 10, part-time 0; African American/Black—full-time 1, part-time 0; Hispanic/Latino(a)—full-time 3, part-time 0; Asian/Pacific Islander—full-time 2, part-time 0; American Indian/Alaska Native—full-time 2, part-time 0; Caucasian/White—full-time 29, part-time 0; Multi-ethnic—full-time 2, part-time 0; students subject to the Americans With Disabilities Act—full-time 1, part-time 0; Unknown ethnicity—full-time 7, part-time 0; International students who hold an F-1 or J-1 Visa—full-time 2, part-time 0.

Financial Information/Assistance:
Tuition for Full-Time Study: *Master's:* State residents: per academic year $21,944; Nonstate residents: per academic year $26,984. Tuition is subject to change. See the following website for updates and changes in tuition costs: http://sou.edu/enrollment/tuitionandfees.html.

Financial Assistance:
First-Year Students: Teaching assistantships available for first year. Average amount paid per academic year: $4,500. Average number of hours worked per week: 12.
Advanced Students: Teaching assistantships available for advanced students. Average amount paid per academic year: $4,500. Average number of hours worked per week: 12.
Additional Information: Of all students currently enrolled full time, 2% benefited from one or more of the listed financial assistance programs. Application and information available online at: http://sou.edu/enrollment/financial-aid/.

Internships/Practica: Master's Degree (MA/MS Mental Health Counseling): An internship experience, such as a final research project or "capstone" experience is required of graduates. The Mental Health Counseling program requires on-campus practica during the first year of courses. Internship placement in the community for students in the second year is required to help fulfill state license requirements.

Housing and Day Care: On-campus housing is available. See the following website for more information: http://www.sou.edu/housing/. On-campus day care facilities are available. See the following website for more information: http://www.sou.edu/scc/.

Employment of Department Graduates:
Master's Degree Graduates: Of those who graduated in the academic year 2011–2012, the following categories and numbers represent the postgraduate activities and employment of master's degree graduates: Enrolled in a psychology doctoral program (1), enrolled in a postdoctoral residency/fellowship (n/a), employed

in independent practice (n/a), employed in government agency (2), employed in a community mental health/counseling center (17), not seeking employment (1), total from the above (master's) (21).

Doctoral Degree Graduates: Of those who graduated in the academic year 2011–2012, the following categories and numbers represent the postgraduate activities and employment of doctoral degree graduates: Enrolled in a psychology doctoral program (n/a), total from the above (doctoral) (0).

Additional Information:

Orientation, Objectives, and Emphasis of Department: The principle objective of the Master's degree in Mental Health Counseling is to provide professional training in the application of psychological principles and methodologies in order to increase functioning and service delivery in public and private agencies, organizations, and communities. The Mental Health Counseling program is based on a common integrated core of courses. The central goal of this core is to train master's-level practitioners who are grounded in professional ethics and values, well-versed in the empirical nature of their professions, and sensitive to and supportive of the increasing multicultural diversity of our communities. The Mental Health Counseling program is accredited by the Council for Accreditation of Counseling and Related Educational Programs (CACREP). This program is also recognized by the Oregon Board of Licensed Professional Counselors and Therapists (OBLPCT) as meeting the educational requirements for application for licensure at a Licensed Professional Counselor.

Information for Students With Physical Disabilities: See the following website for more information: http://www.sou.edu/access/dss/.

Application Information:

Send to Master in Mental Health Counseling, Southern Oregon University, 1250 Siskiyou Boulevard, Ashland, OR 97520. Application available online. URL of online application: http://www.sou.edu/admissions/graduate/gr-apply.html. Students are admitted in the Fall, application deadline February 15. *Fee:* $50.

Bucknell University

Department of Psychology
203 O'Leary Center
Lewisburg, PA 17837
Telephone: (570) 577-1200
Fax: (570) 577-7007
E-mail: *jwade@bucknell.edu*
Web: *http://www.bucknell.edu/Psychology.xml*

Department Information:

Chairperson: T. Joel Wade, PhD. Number of faculty: total—full-time 14; women—full-time 5; total—minority—full-time 1.

Programs and Degrees Offered:

Listed in the following order: Program area, degree type (T if terminal Master's), number awarded 7/11–6/12. General/Experimental Psychology MA/MS (Master of Arts/Science) (T) 1.

Student Applications/Admissions:

Student Applications

General/Experimental Psychology MA/MS (Master of Arts/Science)—Applications 2012–2013, 12. Total applicants accepted 2012–2013, 3. Number full-time enrolled (new admits only) 2012–2013, 3. Total enrolled 2012–2013 full-time, 4. Openings 2013–2014, 2. The median number of years required for completion of a degree in 2012–2013 were 2. The number of students enrolled full- and part-time who were dismissed or voluntarily withdrew from this program area in 2012–2013 were 0.

Scores: Entries appear in this order: required test or GPA, minimum score (if required), median score of students entering in 2012–2013. *General/Experimental Psychology MA/MS (Master of Arts/Science):* GRE-V no minimum stated, GRE-Q no minimum stated, GRE-Analytical no minimum stated, GRE-Subject (Psychology) no minimum stated, overall undergraduate GPA 3.0.

Other Criteria: (importance of criteria rated low, medium, or high): GRE scores—medium, research experience—medium, work experience—low, extracurricular activity—low, clinically related public service—low, GPA—medium, letters of recommendation—high, statement of goals and objectives—high, undergraduate major in psychology—low, specific undergraduate psychology courses taken—medium. For additional information on admission requirements, go to http://www.bucknell.edu/x1752.xml.

Student Characteristics: The following represents characteristics of students in 2012–2013 in all graduate psychology programs in the department: Female—full-time 2, part-time 0; Male—full-time 2, part-time 0; African American/Black—full-time 0, part-time 0; Hispanic/Latino(a)—full-time 0, part-time 0; Asian/Pacific Islander—full-time 0, part-time 0; American Indian/Alaska Native—full-time 0, part-time 0; Caucasian/White—full-time 4, part-time 0; Multi-ethnic—full-time 0, part-time 0; students subject to the Americans With Disabilities Act—full-time 0, part-time 0; Unknown ethnicity—full-time 0, part-time 0; International students who hold an F-1 or J-1 Visa—full-time 0, part-time 0.

Financial Information/Assistance:

Tuition for Full-Time Study: *Master's:* State residents: $1,156 per credit hour; Nonstate residents: $1,156 per credit hour. See the following website for updates and changes in tuition costs: http://www.bucknell.edu/x1781.xml.

Financial Assistance:

First-Year Students: Teaching assistantships available for first year.

Advanced Students: Teaching assistantships available for advanced students.

Additional Information: Of all students currently enrolled full time, 100% benefited from one or more of the listed financial assistance programs. Application and information available online at: http://www.bucknell.edu/x1781.xml.

Internships/Practica: Master's Degree (MA/MS General/Experimental Psychology): An internship experience, such as a final research project or "capstone" experience is required of graduates. Practica can be arranged in local clinical settings.

Housing and Day Care: No on-campus housing is available. On-campus day care facilities are available. See the following website for more information: http://www.sunflowercc.org/.

Employment of Department Graduates:

Master's Degree Graduates: Of those who graduated in the academic year 2011–2012, the following categories and numbers represent the postgraduate activities and employment of master's degree graduates: Enrolled in a postdoctoral residency/fellowship (n/a), employed in independent practice (n/a), total from the above (master's) (0).

Doctoral Degree Graduates: Of those who graduated in the academic year 2011–2012, the following categories and numbers represent the postgraduate activities and employment of doctoral degree graduates: Enrolled in a psychology doctoral program (n/a), total from the above (doctoral) (0).

Additional Information:

Orientation, Objectives, and Emphasis of Department: The objective of our M.S. program in general/experimental psychology is to provide additional coursework and closely mentored research experience to students who have completed an undergraduate degree and who wish to go on to pursue doctoral-level training in psychology.

Special Facilities or Resources: All department faculty have research lab suites. There are also facilities for animal research.

Information for Students With Physical Disabilities: See the following website for more information: http://www.bucknell.edu/x7056.xml.

Application Information:

Send to Graduate Studies, 228 Marts Hall, Bucknell University, Lewisburg, PA 17837. Application available online. URL of online application: http://www.bucknell.edu/x1751.xml. Students are admitted in the Fall, application deadline February 1. *Fee:* $25.

Carnegie Mellon University
Department of Psychology
Humanities and Social Sciences
Baker Hall 332D
Pittsburgh, PA 15213
Telephone: (412) 268-6026
Fax: (412) 268-2798
E-mail: *donahoe@andrew.cmu.edu*
Web: *http://www.psy.cmu.edu/*

Department Information:

1948. Head: Michael Scheier. Number of faculty: total—full-time 27, part-time 1; women—full-time 10; total—minority—full-time 1; women minority—full-time 1.

Programs and Degrees Offered:

Listed in the following order: Program area, degree type (T if terminal Master's), number awarded 7/11–6/12. Cognitive/Cognitive Neuroscience PhD (Doctor of Philosophy) 3, Developmental Psychology PhD (Doctor of Philosophy) 1, Social/Health/Personality Psychology PhD (Doctor of Philosophy) 0, Psychology and Behavioral Decision Research PhD (Doctor of Philosophy) 0.

Student Applications/Admissions:

Student Applications

Cognitive/Cognitive Neuroscience PhD (Doctor of Philosophy)—Applications 2012–2013, 85. Total applicants accepted 2012–2013, 5. Number full-time enrolled (new admits only) 2012–2013, 1. Number part-time enrolled (new admits only) 2012–2013, 0. Total enrolled 2012–2013 full-time, 15. Total enrolled 2012–2013 part-time, 0. Openings 2013–2014, 9. The median number of years required for completion of a degree in 2012–2013 were 5. The number of students enrolled full- and part-time who were dismissed or voluntarily withdrew from this program area in 2012–2013 were 0. *Developmental Psychology PhD (Doctor of Philosophy)*—Applications 2012–2013, 15. Total applicants accepted 2012–2013, 3. Number full-time enrolled (new admits only) 2012–2013, 2. Number part-time enrolled (new admits only) 2012–2013, 0. Total enrolled 2012–2013 full-time, 6. Total enrolled 2012–2013 part-time, 0. Openings 2013–2014, 1. The median number of years required for completion of a degree in 2012–2013 were 5. The number of students enrolled full- and part-time who were dismissed or voluntarily withdrew from this program area in 2012–2013 were 0. *Social/Health/Personality Psychology PhD (Doctor of Philosophy)*—Applications 2012–2013, 51. Total applicants accepted 2012–2013, 3. Number full-time enrolled (new admits only) 2012–2013, 2. Number part-time enrolled (new admits only) 2012–2013, 0. Total enrolled 2012–2013 full-time, 7. Total enrolled 2012–2013 part-time, 0. Openings 2013–2014, 2. The median number of years required for completion of a degree in 2012–2013 were 5. The number of students enrolled full- and part-time who were dismissed or voluntarily withdrew from this program area in 2012–2013 were 0. *Psychology and Behavioral Decision Research PhD (Doctor of Philosophy)*—Applications 2012–2013, 0. Total applicants

accepted 2012–2013, 0. Number full-time enrolled (new admits only) 2012–2013, 0. Number part-time enrolled (new admits only) 2012–2013, 0. The number of students enrolled full- and part-time who were dismissed or voluntarily withdrew from this program area in 2012–2013 were 0.

Scores: Entries appear in this order: required test or GPA, minimum score (if required), median score of students entering in 2012–2013. *Cognitive/Cognitive Neuroscience PhD (Doctor of Philosophy):* GRE-V 160, GRE-Q 148, overall undergraduate GPA 3.7; *Developmental Psychology PhD (Doctor of Philosophy):* GRE-V 160, GRE-Q 148, overall undergraduate GPA 3.7; *Social/Health/Personality Psychology PhD (Doctor of Philosophy):* GRE-V 160, GRE-Q 148, overall undergraduate GPA 3.7; *Psychology and Behavioral Decision Research PhD (Doctor of Philosophy):* GRE-V 160, GRE-Q 148, overall undergraduate GPA 3.7.

Other Criteria: (importance of criteria rated low, medium, or high): GRE scores—high, research experience—high, work experience—low, GPA—high, letters of recommendation—high, interview—high, statement of goals and objectives—high, undergraduate major in psychology—medium, specific undergraduate psychology courses taken—medium. For additional information on admission requirements, go to http://www.psy.cmu.edu/grad_program/applyonline.html.

Student Characteristics: The following represents characteristics of students in 2012–2013 in all graduate psychology programs in the department: Female—full-time 20, part-time 0; Male—full-time 8, part-time 0; African American/Black—full-time 1, part-time 0; Hispanic/Latino(a)—full-time 0, part-time 0; Asian/Pacific Islander—full-time 2, part-time 0; American Indian/Alaska Native—full-time 1, part-time 0; Caucasian/White—full-time 18, part-time 0; Multi-ethnic—full-time 0, part-time 0; students subject to the Americans With Disabilities Act—full-time 0, part-time 0; Unknown ethnicity—full-time 6, part-time 0; International students who hold an F-1 or J-1 Visa—full-time 5, part-time 0.

Financial Information/Assistance:

Tuition for Full-Time Study: *Doctoral:* State residents: per academic year $38,556; Nonstate residents: per academic year $38,556. Tuition is subject to change. See the following website for updates and changes in tuition costs: http://www.cmu.edu/hub/tuition/graduate/index.html.

Financial Assistance:

First-Year Students: Fellowships and scholarships available for first year. Average amount paid per academic year: $22,032.

Advanced Students: Fellowships and scholarships available for advanced students. Average amount paid per academic year: $22,032.

Additional Information: Of all students currently enrolled full time, 100% benefited from one or more of the listed financial assistance programs. Application and information available online at: http://www.psy.cmu.edu/grad_program/applying.html.

Housing and Day Care: No on-campus housing is available. On-campus day care facilities are available. See the following website for more information: http://www.cmu.edu/cyert-center/.

Employment of Department Graduates:

Master's Degree Graduates: Of those who graduated in the academic year 2011–2012, the following categories and numbers

represent the postgraduate activities and employment of master's degree graduates: Enrolled in a postdoctoral residency/fellowship (n/a), employed in independent practice (n/a), total from the above (master's) (0).

Doctoral Degree Graduates: Of those who graduated in the academic year 2011–2012, the following categories and numbers represent the postgraduate activities and employment of doctoral degree graduates: Enrolled in a psychology doctoral program (n/a), enrolled in a postdoctoral residency/fellowship (4), total from the above (doctoral) (4).

Additional Information:

Orientation, Objectives, and Emphasis of Department: The department offers doctoral programs in the areas of cognitive psychology, cognitive neuroscience, social-personality psychology, and developmental psychology. Because the graduate program is small, the student's course of study can be tailored to meet individual needs and interests. Further, students have many opportunities to work closely with faculty members on research projects of mutual interest. Carnegie Mellon University has a strong tradition of interdisciplinary research, and it is easy for students to interact with faculty and students from other graduate programs on campus. Many of our students take courses or engage in research with people from the Departments of Computer Science, Statistics, Social Science, English, Philosophy, and the Graduate School of Industrial Administration.

Information for Students With Physical Disabilities: See the following website for more information: http://www.cmu.edu/hr/eos/disability/index.html.

Application Information:
Send to Graduate Program Coordinator, Department of Psychology, Carnegie Mellon University, Pittsburgh, PA 15213. Application available online. URL of online application: http://www.psy.cmu.edu/grad_program/applyonline.html. Students are admitted in the Fall, application deadline November 28. *Fee:* $45.

Carnegie Mellon University
Organizational Behavior and Theory
Tepper School of Business
5000 Forbes Avenue
Pittsburgh, PA 15213
Telephone: (412) 268-1319
Fax: (412) 268-2810
E-mail: *lrapp@andrew.cmu.edu*
Web: *http://www.tepper.cmu.edu/doctoral-program/fields-of-study/organizational-behavior-and-theory/*

Department Information:
OB PhD Coordinator: Mark Fichman. Number of faculty: total—full-time 10; women—full-time 7; total—minority—full-time 1; women minority—full-time 1.

Programs and Degrees Offered:
Listed in the following order: Program area, degree type (T if terminal Master's), number awarded 7/11–6/12. Organizational Behavior and Theory PhD (Doctor of Philosophy) 3.

Student Applications/Admissions:
Student Applications

Organizational Behavior and Theory PhD (Doctor of Philosophy)—Applications 2012–2013, 194. Total applicants accepted 2012–2013, 2. Number full-time enrolled (new admits only) 2012–2013, 2. Total enrolled 2012–2013 full-time, 11. Openings 2013–2014, 2. The number of students enrolled full- and part-time who were dismissed or voluntarily withdrew from this program area in 2012–2013 were 0.

Scores: Entries appear in this order: required test or GPA, minimum score (if required), median score of students entering in 2012–2013. *Organizational Behavior and Theory PhD (Doctor of Philosophy):* GRE-V no minimum stated, GRE-Q no minimum stated.

Other Criteria: (importance of criteria rated low, medium, or high): GRE scores—high, research experience—medium, GPA—high, letters of recommendation—high, statement of goals and objectives—high. For additional information on admission requirements, go to http://www.tepper.cmu.edu/doctoral-program/application-procedures/.

Student Characteristics: The following represents characteristics of students in 2012–2013 in all graduate psychology programs in the department: Female—full-time 7, part-time 0; Male—full-time 4, part-time 0; African American/Black—full-time 1, part-time 0; Hispanic/Latino(a)—full-time 0, part-time 0; Asian/Pacific Islander—full-time 5, part-time 0; American Indian/Alaska Native—full-time 0, part-time 0; Caucasian/White—full-time 5, part-time 0; Multi-ethnic—full-time 0, part-time 0; students subject to the Americans With Disabilities Act—full-time 0, part-time 0; Unknown ethnicity—full-time 0, part-time 0; International students who hold an F-1 or J-1 Visa—full-time 6, part-time 0.

Financial Information/Assistance:
Tuition for Full-Time Study: *Doctoral:* State residents: per academic year $54,158; Nonstate residents: per academic year $54,158. Additional fees are assessed to students beyond the costs of tuition for the following: student activity fee, technology fee, Port Authority fee. See the following website for updates and changes in tuition costs: http://www.tepper.cmu.edu/current-students/current-graduate-students/financial-aid/index.aspx.

Financial Assistance:
First-Year Students: Fellowships and scholarships available for first year. Average amount paid per academic year: $30,000. Apply by January 15.

Advanced Students: Teaching assistantships available for advanced students. Research assistantships available for advanced students. Fellowships and scholarships available for advanced students. Average amount paid per academic year: $30,000.

Additional Information: Of all students currently enrolled full time, 100% benefited from one or more of the listed financial assistance programs. Application and information available online at: http://www.tepper.cmu.edu/current-students/current-doctoral/financial-aid/index.aspx.

Housing and Day Care: No on-campus housing is available. No on-campus day care facilities are available.

Employment of Department Graduates:
Master's Degree Graduates: Of those who graduated in the academic year 2011–2012, the following categories and numbers

represent the postgraduate activities and employment of master's degree graduates: Enrolled in a postdoctoral residency/fellowship (n/a), employed in independent practice (n/a), total from the above (master's) (0).

Doctoral Degree Graduates: Of those who graduated in the academic year 2011–2012, the following categories and numbers represent the postgraduate activities and employment of doctoral degree graduates: Enrolled in a psychology doctoral program (n/a), enrolled in a postdoctoral residency/fellowship (1), employed in an academic position at a 2-year/4-year college (1), still seeking employment (1), total from the above (doctoral) (3).

Additional Information:

Orientation, Objectives, and Emphasis of Department: The goal of the doctoral program in Organizational Behavior and Theory at the Tepper School of Business is to produce scientists who will make significant research contributions to our understanding of the structure and functioning of organizations. To achieve this goal the student is placed in a learning environment where a unique set of quantitative and discipline-based skills can be acquired. The opportunities for interdisciplinary work at Tepper provide new avenues for approaching organizational problems. The program attempts to combine structure and flexibility. Structure is achieved by identifying a set of core areas in which the student should become competent. These are quantitative methods, design and measurement, organization theory, and a selected specialty area. Flexibility in the program is achieved by having students and their advisers work out a combination of learning activities consistent with the students' interests and needs. Courses, participation in research projects, summer papers, and special tutorials with individual faculty are some of these learning activities.

Information for Students With Physical Disabilities: See the following website for more information: http://www.cmu.edu/hr/eos/disability/.

Application Information:
Send to Doctoral Program Applications, 247 Posner Hall, Tepper School of Business, Carnegie Mellon University, Pittsburgh, PA 15213-3890. Application available online. URL of online application: https://app.applyyourself.com/?id=cmu-phd. Students are admitted in the Fall, application deadline January 15. *Fee:* $70.

Chestnut Hill College
Department of Professional Psychology
9601 Germantown Avenue
Philadelphia, PA 19118-2693
Telephone: (215) 248-7077
Fax: (215) 753-3619
E-mail: *profpsyc@chc.edu*
Web: *http://www.chc.edu/psyd*

Department Information:
1987. Chairperson: Cheryll Rothery, PsyD, ABPP. Number of faculty: total—full-time 13, part-time 25; women—full-time 7,

part-time 13; total—minority—full-time 4, part-time 3; women minority—full-time 4, part-time 2.

Programs and Degrees Offered:
Listed in the following order: Program area, degree type (T if terminal Master's), number awarded 7/11–6/12. Clinical Psychology PsyD (Doctor of Psychology) 19, Clinical and Counseling Psychology MA/MS (Master of Arts/Science) (T) 54.

APA Accreditation: Clinical PsyD (Doctor of Psychology). Student Outcome Data Website: http://www.chc.edu/psyd/data.

Student Applications/Admissions:

Student Applications

Clinical Psychology PsyD (Doctor of Psychology)—Applications 2012–2013, 167. Total applicants accepted 2012–2013, 45. Number full-time enrolled (new admits only) 2012–2013, 20. Number part-time enrolled (new admits only) 2012–2013, 0. Total enrolled 2012–2013 full-time, 111. Total enrolled 2012–2013 part-time, 12. Openings 2013–2014, 20. The median number of years required for completion of a degree in 2012–2013 were 6. The number of students enrolled full- and part-time who were dismissed or voluntarily withdrew from this program area in 2012–2013 were 1. *Clinical and Counseling Psychology MA/MS (Master of Arts/Science)*—Applications 2012–2013, 164. Total applicants accepted 2012–2013, 151. Number full-time enrolled (new admits only) 2012–2013, 22. Number part-time enrolled (new admits only) 2012–2013, 32. Total enrolled 2012–2013 full-time, 117. Total enrolled 2012–2013 part-time, 230. The median number of years required for completion of a degree in 2012–2013 were 3.

Scores: Entries appear in this order: required test or GPA, minimum score (if required), median score of students entering in 2012–2013. *Clinical Psychology PsyD (Doctor of Psychology):* GRE-V no minimum stated, 501, GRE-Q no minimum stated, 563, GRE-Analytical no minimum stated, 4.18, overall undergraduate GPA no minimum stated, 3.44.

Other Criteria: (importance of criteria rated low, medium, or high): GRE scores—high, research experience—low, work experience—low, extracurricular activity—low, clinically related public service—low, GPA—high, letters of recommendation—high, interview—high, statement of goals and objectives—high, writing ability—high, undergraduate major in psychology—medium, specific undergraduate psychology courses taken—high, Writing ability is a criterion for the PsyD program. Applicants to the PsyD program must have completed at least four undergraduate courses in psychology including General Psychology, Abnormal Psychology and Statistics. For additional information on admission requirements, go to http://www.chc.edu/psyd/admissions.

Student Characteristics: The following represents characteristics of students in 2012–2013 in all graduate psychology programs in the department: Female—full-time 195, part-time 214; Male—full-time 47, part-time 57; African American/Black—full-time 16, part-time 33; Hispanic/Latino(a)—full-time 9, part-time 14; Asian/Pacific Islander—full-time 8, part-time 5; American Indian/Alaska Native—full-time 0, part-time 0; Caucasian/White—full-time 162, part-time 147; Multi-ethnic—full-time 5, part-time

2; students subject to the Americans With Disabilities Act—full-time 12, part-time 1; Unknown ethnicity—full-time 38, part-time 65; International students who hold an F-1 or J-1 Visa—full-time 4, part-time 5.

Financial Information/Assistance:

Tuition for Full-Time Study: *Master's:* State residents: $650 per credit hour; Nonstate residents: $650 per credit hour. *Doctoral:* State residents: $920 per credit hour; Nonstate residents: $920 per credit hour. Tuition is subject to change. See the following website for updates and changes in tuition costs: http://www.chc.edu/Graduate/Admissions/Graduate_Tuition_and_Fees/.

Financial Assistance:

First-Year Students: Research assistantships available for first year. Average number of hours worked per week: 12.

Advanced Students: Teaching assistantships available for advanced students. Average number of hours worked per week: 12. Research assistantships available for advanced students. Average number of hours worked per week: 12.

Additional Information: Of all students currently enrolled full time, 12% benefited from one or more of the listed financial assistance programs. Application and information available online at: http://www.chc.edu/Graduate/Financial_Aid/.

Internships/Practica: Doctoral Degree (PsyD Clinical Psychology): For those doctoral students for whom a professional psychology internship was required in this program prior to graduation, (21) students applied for an internship in 2011–2012, with (20) students obtaining an internship. Of those students who obtained an internship, (20) were paid internships. Of those students who obtained an internship, (9) students placed in APA/CPA accredited internships, (11) students placed in internships not APA/CPA accredited, but listed with the Association of Psychology Postdoctoral and Internship Programs (APPIC), (0) students placed in internships conforming to guidelines of the Council of Directors of School Psychology Programs (CDSPP), (0) students placed in internships that were not APA/CPA accredited, APPIC or CDSPP listed. Master's Degree (MA/MS Clinical and Counseling Psychology): An internship experience, such as a final research project or "capstone" experience is required of graduates. Students in the master's program must complete three semesters of practicum. Students in the doctoral program are required to complete three years of practicum (one of which may be waived if the student completed a practicum prior to admission as part of their master's program) and a full-time internship. Doctoral students have the option of completing an APA-accredited, APPIC, or other program approved internship. At the present time, there are over 50 mental health facilities that the program has approved as sites for practica and internships. Two faculty members are dedicated to assisting students in securing the most appropriate site for their practicum and internship experiences.

Housing and Day Care: No on-campus housing is available. No on-campus day care facilities are available.

Employment of Department Graduates:

Master's Degree Graduates: Of those who graduated in the academic year 2011–2012, the following categories and numbers represent the postgraduate activities and employment of master's degree graduates: Enrolled in a postdoctoral residency/fellowship (n/a), employed in independent practice (n/a), total from the above (master's) (0).

Doctoral Degree Graduates: Of those who graduated in the academic year 2011–2012, the following categories and numbers represent the postgraduate activities and employment of doctoral degree graduates: Enrolled in a psychology doctoral program (n/a), enrolled in a postdoctoral residency/fellowship (8), employed in an academic position at a 2-year/4-year college (1), employed in other positions at a higher education institution (2), employed in a professional position in a school system (1), employed in a community mental health/counseling center (6), employed in a hospital/medical center (1), total from the above (doctoral) (19).

Additional Information:

Orientation, Objectives, and Emphasis of Department: The theoretical base of the Department of Professional Psychology at Chestnut Hill College is a complementary blend of psychodynamic and systems theories. The insights of psychodynamic theory, including modern object relations theory, serve as a method for understanding the individual. Likewise, the perspective of systems theory addresses ways individuals, families and communities influence one another. This synergistic blend of psychodynamic and systems theories promotes a holistic understanding of human behavior within family and social contexts. Structured sequence of mentoring and advising is designed to enable the student to complete the dissertation in a step-by-step manner prior to internship.

Special Facilities or Resources: All classrooms are fully equipped for multi-media presentations, and many classrooms have SmartBoard technology. Observation rooms are available for recording and observing clinical sessions. An extensive library of psychological testing equipment is available for student use. The college is part of a library consortium that increases available lending privileges offered to each student. Doctoral students have free interlibrary loan privileges. Students have access to statistical software and test scoring/interpretation software. Advanced doctoral students may teach a master's level course under the direct supervision of a faculty member.

Information for Students With Physical Disabilities: See the following website for more information: http://www.chc.edu/disability.

Application Information:
Send to Director of Graduate Admissions, Chestnut Hill College, 9601 Germantown Avenue, Philadelphia, PA 19118-2693. Students are admitted in the Fall, application deadline January 15; Programs have rolling admissions. All students in the PsyD Program begin classes in the fall semester. Students in the terminal master's program may begin classes in the fall, spring or summer semester. Master's program has rolling admissions. The PsyD Program accepts applicants to Year I on a rolling admission basis until the entering class is filled. All applicants whose applications are complete by January 15th will be notified of their status by April 1st. The application deadline for Year II is January 15th. *Fee:* $85. PsyD application fee is $85, Master's application fee is $55.

Drexel University

Department of Psychology
College of Arts and Sciences
MS 626, 245 North 15th Street
Philadelphia, PA 19102
Telephone: (215) 762-7249
Fax: (215) 762-8625
E-mail: *james.herbert@drexel.edu*
Web: *http://www.drexel.edu/psychology/*

Department Information:

2002. Chairperson: James Herbert. Number of faculty: total—full-time 29, part-time 7; women—full-time 14, part-time 7; total—minority—full-time 2, part-time 2; women minority—full-time 1, part-time 2.

Programs and Degrees Offered:

Listed in the following order: Program area, degree type (T if terminal Master's), number awarded 7/11–6/12. Clinical Psychology PhD (Doctor of Philosophy) 9, Ms in Psychology MA/MS (Master of Arts/Science) (T) 10, Law-Psychology PhD (Doctor of Philosophy) 3, Applied Cognitive and Brain Sciences PhD (Doctor of Philosophy) 0.

APA Accreditation: Clinical PhD (Doctor of Philosophy). Student Outcome Data Website: http://www.drexel.edu/psychology/academics/graduate/clinical/data/. Clinical PhD (Doctor of Philosophy).

Student Applications/Admissions:

Student Applications

Clinical Psychology PhD (Doctor of Philosophy)—Applications 2012–2013, 605. Total applicants accepted 2012–2013, 9. Number full-time enrolled (new admits only) 2012–2013, 9. Number part-time enrolled (new admits only) 2012–2013, 0. Total enrolled 2012–2013 full-time, 48. Total enrolled 2012–2013 part-time, 0. Openings 2013–2014, 10. The median number of years required for completion of a degree in 2012–2013 were 5. The number of students enrolled full- and part-time who were dismissed or voluntarily withdrew from this program area in 2012–2013 were 0. *Ms in Psychology MA/MS (Master of Arts/Science)*—Applications 2012–2013, 38. Total applicants accepted 2012–2013, 9. Number full-time enrolled (new admits only) 2012–2013, 9. Total enrolled 2012–2013 full-time, 21. Openings 2013–2014, 10. The median number of years required for completion of a degree in 2012–2013 were 2. The number of students enrolled full- and part-time who were dismissed or voluntarily withdrew from this program area in 2012–2013 were 0. *Law-Psychology PhD (Doctor of Philosophy)*—Applications 2012–2013, 22. Total applicants accepted 2012–2013, 2. Number full-time enrolled (new admits only) 2012–2013, 2. Total enrolled 2012–2013 full-time, 13. Openings 2013–2014, 2. The median number of years required for completion of a degree in 2012–2013 were 7. The number of students enrolled full- and part-time who were dismissed or voluntarily withdrew from this program area in 2012–2013 were 0. *Applied Cognitive and Brain Sciences PhD (Doctor of Philosophy)*—Applications 2012–2013, 25. Total applicants accepted 2012–2013, 3. Number full-time enrolled (new admits only) 2012–2013, 3. Number part-time enrolled (new admits only) 2012–2013, 0. Total enrolled 2012–2013 full-time, 3.

Total enrolled 2012–2013 part-time, 0. Openings 2013–2014, 2. The number of students enrolled full- and part-time who were dismissed or voluntarily withdrew from this program area in 2012–2013 were 1.

Scores: Entries appear in this order: required test or GPA, minimum score (if required), median score of students entering in 2012–2013. *Clinical Psychology PhD (Doctor of Philosophy):* GRE-V 600, 670, GRE-Q 600, 690, GRE-Subject (Psychology) 600, 690, overall undergraduate GPA 3.4, 3.7, last 2 years GPA 3.5, 3.8, psychology GPA 3.5, 3.8; *MS in Psychology MA/MS (Master of Arts/Science):* GRE-V 500, 570, GRE-Q 500, 600, GRE-Subject (Psychology) 500, 620, overall undergraduate GPA 3.0, 3.4, last 2 years GPA 3.2, 3.6, psychology GPA 3.2, 3.6; *Law-Psychology PhD (Doctor of Philosophy):* GRE-V 600, 710, GRE-Q 600, 700, GRE-Subject (Psychology) 600, overall undergraduate GPA 3.2, 3.6, last 2 years GPA 3.4, 3.8, psychology GPA 3.5, 3.8; *Applied Cognitive and Brain Sciences PhD (Doctor of Philosophy):* GRE-V 600, GRE-Q 600, GRE-Subject (Psychology) 600, overall undergraduate GPA 3.2, last 2 years GPA 3.4, psychology GPA 3.5.

Other Criteria: (importance of criteria rated low, medium, or high): GRE scores—high, research experience—high, work experience—low, extracurricular activity—low, clinically related public service—medium, GPA—high, letters of recommendation—high, interview—high, statement of goals and objectives—high, fit with faculty mentor—high, undergraduate major in psychology—medium, specific undergraduate psychology courses taken—medium, Research experience is weighted less heavily for applicants for the MS program. For additional information on admission requirements, go to http://www.drexel.edu/psychology/academics/graduate/.

Student Characteristics: The following represents characteristics of students in 2012–2013 in all graduate psychology programs in the department: Female—full-time 72, part-time 0; Male—full-time 13, part-time 0; African American/Black—full-time 3, part-time 0; Hispanic/Latino(a)—full-time 3, part-time 0; Asian/Pacific Islander—full-time 2, part-time 0; American Indian/Alaska Native—full-time 0, part-time 0; Caucasian/White—full-time 77, part-time 0; Multi-ethnic—full-time 0, part-time 0; students subject to the Americans With Disabilities Act—full-time 4, part-time 0; Unknown ethnicity—full-time 0, part-time 0; International students who hold an F-1 or J-1 Visa—full-time 1, part-time 0.

Financial Information/Assistance:

Tuition for Full-Time Study: *Master's:* State residents: $1,040 per credit hour; Nonstate residents: $1,040 per credit hour. *Doctoral:* State residents: $1,040 per credit hour; Nonstate residents: $1,040 per credit hour. Tuition is subject to change. Additional fees are assessed to students beyond the costs of tuition for the following: General fee of $260 per quarter. See the following website for updates and changes in tuition costs: http://drexel.edu/grad/financing/tuition/.

Financial Assistance:

First-Year Students: Teaching assistantships available for first year. Average amount paid per academic year: $13,000. Average number of hours worked per week: 15. Research assistantships available for first year. Average amount paid per academic year: $15,000. Average number of hours worked per week: 15. Fellow-

ships and scholarships available for first year. Average amount paid per academic year: $5,000.

Advanced Students: Research assistantships available for advanced students. Average amount paid per academic year: $15,000. Average number of hours worked per week: 10. Traineeships available for advanced students. Average amount paid per academic year: $13,000. Average number of hours worked per week: 20. Fellowships and scholarships available for advanced students. Average amount paid per academic year: $5,000.

Additional Information: Of all students currently enrolled full time, 80% benefited from one or more of the listed financial assistance programs. Application and information available online at: http://www.drexel.edu/psychology/academics/graduate/.

Internships/Practica: Doctoral Degree (PhD Clinical Psychology): For those doctoral students for whom a professional psychology internship was required in this program prior to graduation, (12) students applied for an internship in 2011–2012, with (11) students obtaining an internship. Of those students who obtained an internship, (11) were paid internships. Of those students who obtained an internship, (11) students placed in APA/CPA accredited internships, (0) students placed in internships not APA/CPA accredited, but listed with the Association of Psychology Postdoctoral and Internship Programs (APPIC), (0) students placed in internships conforming to guidelines of the Council of Directors of School Psychology Programs (CDSPP), (0) students placed in internships that were not APA/CPA accredited, APPIC or CDSPP listed. Doctoral Degree (PhD Law-Psychology): For those doctoral students for whom a professional psychology internship was required in this program prior to graduation, (3) students applied for an internship in 2011–2012, with (3) students obtaining an internship. Of those students who obtained an internship, (3) were paid internships. Of those students who obtained an internship, (3) students placed in APA/CPA accredited internships, (0) students placed in internships not APA/CPA accredited, but listed with the Association of Psychology Postdoctoral and Internship Programs (APPIC), (0) students placed in internships conforming to guidelines of the Council of Directors of School Psychology Programs (CDSPP), (0) students placed in internships that were not APA/CPA accredited, APPIC or CDSPP listed. Master's Degree (MA/MS MS in Psychology): An internship experience, such as a final research project or "capstone" experience is required of graduates. On-campus practicum sites include the Forensic Clinic, the Heart Failure/Cardiac Transplant Center, the Anxiety Treatment and Research Center, and the Laboratory for Innovations in Health-Related Behavior Change. Off-campus practicum sites include a variety of in-/outpatient psychiatric units, University of Pennsylvania Center for the Treatment and Study of Anxiety, University of Pennsylvania Center for Weight and Eating Disorders, Children's Hospital of Philadelphia and approximately sixty other practicum sites.

Housing and Day Care: On-campus housing is available. See the following website for more information: http://www.drexel.edu/dbs/universityHousing/graduateHousing/. No on-campus day care facilities are available.

Employment of Department Graduates:

Master's Degree Graduates: Of those who graduated in the academic year 2011–2012, the following categories and numbers represent the postgraduate activities and employment of master's degree graduates: Enrolled in a psychology doctoral program (5),

enrolled in a postdoctoral residency/fellowship (n/a), employed in independent practice (n/a), employed in government agency (1), employed in a hospital/medical center (1), still seeking employment (1), other employment position (1), do not know (1), total from the above (master's) (10).

Doctoral Degree Graduates: Of those who graduated in the academic year 2011–2012, the following categories and numbers represent the postgraduate activities and employment of doctoral degree graduates: Enrolled in a psychology doctoral program (n/a), enrolled in a postdoctoral residency/fellowship (5), employed in an academic position at a university (1), employed in an academic position at a 2-year/4-year college (1), employed in other positions at a higher education institution (1), other employment position (1), total from the above (doctoral) (9).

Additional Information:

Orientation, Objectives, and Emphasis of Department: The Drexel University Department of Psychology has doctoral programs based heavily upon a scientist–practitioner model of training in clinical psychology and has been designed to place emphasis on both components, but somewhat greater emphasis on research. The theoretical orientation is based largely on Social Learning Theory, in which students gain proficiency in the theory and practice of broad-spectrum behavioral approaches to assessment and intervention. The clinical PhD program offers concentrations in health psychology, neuropsychology, and forensic psychology. The new program in Applied Cognitive and Brain Sciences is focused primarily on cognitive psychology and cognitive neuroscience, although the research emphasis is of an applied nature. The MS program (non-clinical) is designed to provide students with research skills in preparation for application for doctoral training, or employment with researchers in academia, industry, or public sector settings.

Special Facilities or Resources: Drexel has a major tertiary care medical center that provides exceptional opportunities in health-related areas for psychology. In addition, a Division of Behavioral Neurobiology and the University Neurobiology program, as well as the University Neurosciences program, provide opportunities for learning and collaboration on research at neuropharmacologic and neurophysiologic levels to complement our neuropsychological training. We are surrounded by a wealth of top-notch medical centers including the University of Pennsylvania, Children's Hospital of Philadelphia, Jefferson University Hospitals, and Temple University.

Information for Students With Physical Disabilities: See the following website for more information: http://www.drexel.edu/oed/disabilityResources/.

Application Information:
Send to Graduate Admission, Drexel University, 3141 Chestnut Street, Suite 212, Philadelphia, PA 19104. Application available online. URL of online application: http://www.drexel.edu/psychology/academics/graduate/. Students are admitted in the Fall, application deadline December 1. Deadline for MS is February 1, for all other programs it is December 1. *Fee:* $0. $50 if applying via hardcopy rather than online.

Duquesne University

Department of Counseling, Psychology and Special Education,
School Psychology Program
School of Education
G3 Canevin Hall
Pittsburgh, PA 15282
Telephone: (412) 396-1058
Fax: (412) 396-1340
E-mail: *czwalgaa@duq.edu*
Web: *http://www.duq.edu/academics/schools/education/*
graduate-programs-education/school-psychology-graduate-
programs

Department Information:

1969. Program Director: Ara J. Schmitt, PhD. Number of faculty: total—full-time 6, part-time 2; women—full-time 4; total—minority—full-time 1.

Programs and Degrees Offered:

Listed in the following order: Program area, degree type (T if terminal Master's), number awarded 7/11–6/12. Child Psychology MEd (Education) 17, School Psychology Certificate Other 1, School Psychology PhD (Doctor of Philosophy) 10, School Psychology PsyD (Doctor of Psychology) 0.

APA Accreditation: School PhD (Doctor of Philosophy).

Student Applications/Admissions:

Student Applications

Child Psychology MEd (Education)—Applications 2012–2013, 16. Total applicants accepted 2012–2013, 16. Number full-time enrolled (new admits only) 2012–2013, 10. Number part-time enrolled (new admits only) 2012–2013, 0. Total enrolled 2012–2013 full-time, 27. Total enrolled 2012–2013 part-time, 0. Openings 2013–2014, 15. The median number of years required for completion of a degree in 2012–2013 were 2. The number of students enrolled full- and part-time who were dismissed or voluntarily withdrew from this program area in 2012–2013 were 0. *School Psychology Certificate Other*—Applications 2012–2013, 16. Total applicants accepted 2012–2013, 2. Number full-time enrolled (new admits only) 2012–2013, 2. Number part-time enrolled (new admits only) 2012–2013, 0. Total enrolled 2012–2013 full-time, 3. Total enrolled 2012–2013 part-time, 0. The median number of years required for completion of a degree in 2012–2013 were 3. The number of students enrolled full- and part-time who were dismissed or voluntarily withdrew from this program area in 2012–2013 were 0. *School Psychology PhD (Doctor of Philosophy)*—Applications 2012–2013, 44. Total applicants accepted 2012–2013, 21. Number full-time enrolled (new admits only) 2012–2013, 7. Number part-time enrolled (new admits only) 2012–2013, 0. Total enrolled 2012–2013 full-time, 25. Total enrolled 2012–2013 part-time, 17. Openings 2013–2014, 6. The median number of years required for completion of a degree in 2012–2013 were 5. The number of students enrolled full- and part-time who were dismissed or voluntarily withdrew from this program area in 2012–2013 were 1. *School Psychology PsyD (Doctor of Psychology)*—Applications 2012–2013, 20. Total applicants accepted 2012–2013, 31. Number full-time enrolled (new admits only) 2012–2013, 14. Number part-time enrolled (new

admits only) 2012–2013, 0. Total enrolled 2012–2013 full-time, 33. Total enrolled 2012–2013 part-time, 2. Openings 2013–2014, 16. The median number of years required for completion of a degree in 2012–2013 were 4. The number of students enrolled full- and part-time who were dismissed or voluntarily withdrew from this program area in 2012–2013 were 1.

Scores: Entries appear in this order: required test or GPA, minimum score (if required), median score of students entering in 2012–2013. *Child Psychology MEd (Education):* overall undergraduate GPA 3.0; *School Psychology Certificate Other:* GRE-V no minimum stated, 500, GRE-Q no minimum stated, 640, GRE-Analytical no minimum stated, 4.0, overall undergraduate GPA no minimum stated, 3.16; *School Psychology PhD (Doctor of Philosophy):* GRE-V no minimum stated, 500, GRE-Q no minimum stated, 580, GRE-Analytical no minimum stated, 4.0, overall undergraduate GPA no minimum stated, 3.5; *School Psychology PsyD (Doctor of Psychology):* GRE-V no minimum stated, 500, GRE-Q no minimum stated, 560, GRE-Analytical no minimum stated, 4.0, overall undergraduate GPA no minimum stated, 3.5.

Other Criteria: (importance of criteria rated low, medium, or high): GRE scores—high, research experience—medium, work experience—medium, extracurricular activity—low, clinically related public service—low, GPA—high, letters of recommendation—medium, interview—high, statement of goals and objectives—high, undergraduate major in psychology—low, specific undergraduate psychology courses taken—low. For additional information on admission requirements, go to http://www.duq.edu/schoolpsych.

Student Characteristics: The following represents characteristics of students in 2012–2013 in all graduate psychology programs in the department: Female—full-time 77, part-time 16; Male—full-time 11, part-time 3; African American/Black—full-time 3, part-time 2; Hispanic/Latino(a)—full-time 0, part-time 1; Asian/Pacific Islander—full-time 1, part-time 0; American Indian/Alaska Native—full-time 0, part-time 0; Caucasian/White—full-time 80, part-time 16; Multi-ethnic—full-time 4, part-time 0; students subject to the Americans With Disabilities Act—full-time 0, part-time 0; Unknown ethnicity—full-time 0, part-time 0; International students who hold an F-1 or J-1 Visa—full-time 2, part-time 0.

Financial Information/Assistance:

Tuition for Full-Time Study: *Master's:* State residents: per academic year $31,740, $1,058 per credit hour; Nonstate residents: per academic year $31,740, $1,058 per credit hour. *Doctoral:* State residents: per academic year $31,740, $1,058 per credit hour; Nonstate residents: per academic year $31,740, $1,058 per credit hour. Tuition is subject to change. See the following website for updates and changes in tuition costs: http://www.duq.edu/admissions-and-aid/tuition/graduate-tuition-rates.

Financial Assistance:

First-Year Students: Research assistantships available for first year. Average number of hours worked per week: 20. Apply by March 1.

Advanced Students: Research assistantships available for advanced students. Average number of hours worked per week: 20. Apply by March 1.

Additional Information: Of all students currently enrolled full time, 5% benefited from one or more of the listed financial assistance programs. Application and information available online at: http://www.duq.edu/financial-aid/.

Internships/Practica: Doctoral Degree (PhD School Psychology): For those doctoral students for whom a professional psychology internship was required in this program prior to graduation, (3) students applied for an internship in 2011–2012, with (3) students obtaining an internship. Of those students who obtained an internship, (3) were paid internships. Of those students who obtained an internship, (1) students placed in APA/CPA accredited internships, (0) students placed in internships not APA/CPA accredited, but listed with the Association of Psychology Postdoctoral and Internship Programs (APPIC), (2) students placed in internships conforming to guidelines of the Council of Directors of School Psychology Programs (CDSPP), (0) students placed in internships that were not APA/CPA accredited, APPIC or CDSPP listed. Doctoral Degree (PsyD School Psychology): For those doctoral students for whom a professional psychology internship was required in this program prior to graduation, (9) students applied for an internship in 2011–2012, with (9) students obtaining an internship. Of those students who obtained an internship, (9) were paid internships. Of those students who obtained an internship, (0) students placed in APA/CPA accredited internships, (0) students placed in internships not APA/CPA accredited, but listed with the Association of Psychology Postdoctoral and Internship Programs (APPIC), (9) students placed in internships conforming to guidelines of the Council of Directors of School Psychology Programs (CDSPP), (0) students placed in internships that were not APA/CPA accredited, APPIC or CDSPP listed. Certification Program requires 2 Practica and 1 Internship; Doctoral Programs require 2 Practica, 1 Doctoral Practicum and 1 Internship.

Housing and Day Care: On-campus housing is available. See the following website for more information: http://www.duq.edu/residence-life/. On-campus day care facilities are available. See the following website for more information: http://www.duq.edu/work-at-du/benefits/other-benefits/campus-services/child-care-services.

Employment of Department Graduates:
Master's Degree Graduates: Of those who graduated in the academic year 2011–2012, the following categories and numbers represent the postgraduate activities and employment of master's degree graduates: Enrolled in a postdoctoral residency/fellowship (n/a), employed in independent practice (n/a), total from the above (master's) (0).
Doctoral Degree Graduates: Of those who graduated in the academic year 2011–2012, the following categories and numbers represent the postgraduate activities and employment of doctoral degree graduates: Enrolled in a psychology doctoral program (n/a), total from the above (doctoral) (0).

Additional Information:
Orientation, Objectives, and Emphasis of Department: The Duquesne University School Psychology program, guided by the belief that all children can learn, is dedicated to providing both breadth and depth of professional training in a theoretically-integrated, research-based learning environment. The program prepares ethical practitioners, scientists and scholars who are life-long learners committed to enhancing the well-being of youth, their families, and the systems that serve them. The program achieves this by engaging in scholarly activities that advance the field of school psychology, maintaining a modern curriculum that employs aspects of multiculturalism and diversity, examining emerging trends in the profession, conducting continuous outcome assessment for program improvement, and providing support to our graduates.

Special Facilities or Resources: The program has a curriculum library of current psychological and educational tests for training and research purposes.

Information for Students With Physical Disabilities: See the following website for more information: http://www.duq.edu/special-students/.

Application Information:
Send to Dr. Ara J. Schmitt, School Psychology Program, G3B Canevin Hall, Pittsburgh, PA 15282. Application available online. URL of online application: http://www.duq.edu/apply/grad/education. Students are admitted in the Fall, application deadline January 15; Programs have rolling admissions. Master's program has rolling admissions. *Fee:* $50. The $50 fee is waived if application is completed online.

Duquesne University
Department of Psychology
McAnulty College and Graduate School of Liberal Arts
600 Forbes Avenue
Pittsburgh, PA 15282
Telephone: (412) 396-6520
Fax: (412) 396-1368
E-mail: *psychology@duq.edu*
Web: *http://www.duq.edu/academics/schools/liberal-arts/graduate-school/programs/clinical-psychology*

Department Information:
1959. Chairperson: Leswin Laubscher, PhD. Number of faculty: total—full-time 13; women—full-time 5; total—minority—full-time 1.

Programs and Degrees Offered:
Listed in the following order: Program area, degree type (T if terminal Master's), number awarded 7/11–6/12. Clinical Psychology PhD (Doctor of Philosophy) 8.

APA Accreditation: Clinical PhD (Doctor of Philosophy). Student Outcome Data Website: http://www.duq.edu/academics/schools/liberal-arts/graduate-school/programs/clinical-psychology.

Student Applications/Admissions:
Student Applications
Clinical Psychology PhD (Doctor of Philosophy)—Applications 2012–2013, 99. Total applicants accepted 2012–2013, 7. Number full-time enrolled (new admits only) 2012–2013, 7. Number part-time enrolled (new admits only) 2012–2013, 0. Total enrolled 2012–2013 full-time, 49. Total enrolled 2012–2013 part-time, 0. Openings 2013–2014, 7. The median number of

years required for completion of a degree in 2012–2013 were 7. The number of students enrolled full- and part-time who were dismissed or voluntarily withdrew from this program area in 2012–2013 were 1.

Scores: Entries appear in this order: required test or GPA, minimum score (if required), median score of students entering in 2012–2013. *Clinical Psychology PhD (Doctor of Philosophy):* GRE-V no minimum stated, GRE-Q no minimum stated, GRE-Analytical no minimum stated.

Other Criteria: (importance of criteria rated low, medium, or high): GRE scores—medium, research experience—medium, work experience—medium, extracurricular activity—medium, clinically related public service—medium, GPA—medium, letters of recommendation—high, interview—high, statement of goals and objectives—high. For additional information on admission requirements, go to http://www.duq.edu/academics/schools/liberal-arts/graduate-school/programs/clinical-psychology/apply.

Student Characteristics: The following represents characteristics of students in 2012–2013 in all graduate psychology programs in the department: Female—full-time 25, part-time 0; Male—full-time 24, part-time 0; African American/Black—full-time 1, part-time 0; Hispanic/Latino(a)—full-time 1, part-time 0; Asian/Pacific Islander—full-time 6, part-time 0; American Indian/Alaska Native—full-time 0, part-time 0; Caucasian/White—full-time 38, part-time 0; Multi-ethnic—full-time 3, part-time 0; students subject to the Americans With Disabilities Act—full-time 1, part-time 0; Unknown ethnicity—full-time 0, part-time 0; International students who hold an F-1 or J-1 Visa—full-time 8, part-time 0.

Financial Information/Assistance:

Tuition for Full-Time Study: *Doctoral:* State residents: $966 per credit hour; Nonstate residents: $966 per credit hour. Tuition is subject to change. See the following website for updates and changes in tuition costs: http://www.duq.edu/admissions-and-aid/tuition/graduate-tuition-rates.

Financial Assistance:

First-Year Students: Research assistantships available for first year. Average amount paid per academic year: $17,000. Average number of hours worked per week: 15. Apply by December 15.

Advanced Students: Teaching assistantships available for advanced students. Average amount paid per academic year: $17,000. Average number of hours worked per week: 15. Apply by December 15. Research assistantships available for advanced students. Average amount paid per academic year: $17,000. Average number of hours worked per week: 15. Apply by December 15.

Additional Information: Of all students currently enrolled full time, 100% benefited from one or more of the listed financial assistance programs. Application and information available online at: http://www.duq.edu/admissions-and-aid/financial-aid.

Internships/Practica: Doctoral Degree (PhD Clinical Psychology): For those doctoral students for whom a professional psychology internship was required in this program prior to graduation, (5) students applied for an internship in 2011–2012, with (5) students obtaining an internship. Of those students who obtained an internship, (5) were paid internships. Of those students who obtained an internship, (5) students placed in APA/CPA accredited internships, (0) students placed in internships not APA/

CPA accredited, but listed with the Association of Psychology Postdoctoral and Internship Programs (APPIC), (0) students placed in internships conforming to guidelines of the Council of Directors of School Psychology Programs (CDSPP), (0) students placed in internships that were not APA/CPA accredited, APPIC or CDSPP listed. The Duquesne University Psychology Clinic, which serves more than 70 clients weekly, is the primary training facility for the doctoral students. All services, including assessment and psychotherapy for Duquesne University students, employees, and members of the greater Pittsburgh communities, are provided by the doctoral students. Licensed clinical faculty members and selected licensed adjunct faculty psychologists in the community are involved in the supervision of all doctoral students. The first four years of the doctoral program typically involve case work at the Clinic. Additionally, students attend at least one academic year of external practicum placement in settings such as hospitals, university counseling centers, and VA centers. External practica are typically completed during the third year of the program. A second year of external practicum training, taken in the fourth year, is strongly recommended.

Housing and Day Care: On-campus housing is available. See the following website for more information: http://www.duq.edu/life-at-duquesne/housing. On-campus day care facilities are available. See the following website for more information: http://www.duq.edu/work-at-du/benefits/other-benefits/campus-services/child-care-services.

Employment of Department Graduates:

Master's Degree Graduates: Of those who graduated in the academic year 2011–2012, the following categories and numbers represent the postgraduate activities and employment of master's degree graduates: Enrolled in a postdoctoral residency/fellowship (n/a), employed in independent practice (n/a), total from the above (master's) (0).

Doctoral Degree Graduates: Of those who graduated in the academic year 2011–2012, the following categories and numbers represent the postgraduate activities and employment of doctoral degree graduates: Enrolled in a psychology doctoral program (n/a), total from the above (doctoral) (0).

Additional Information:

Orientation, Objectives, and Emphasis of Department: Internationally recognized for over three decades, the Psychology Department at Duquesne University engages in the systematic and rigorous articulation of psychology as a human science. The Department understands psychology as a positive response to the challenges of the 21st century ' one that includes existentialism, phenomenology, hermeneutics, psychoanalysis and depth psychology, humanistic psychology, feminism, critical theory, and post-structuralism, and a sensitivity to the diverse cultural contexts within which this response may find expression. Psychology as a human science pursues collaborative, qualitative research methods that pay special attention to what is particular to human beings and their worlds. Accordingly, the Department educates psychologists who are sensitive to the multiple meanings of human life, and who work toward the liberation and well-being of persons individually as well as in community.

Special Facilities or Resources: The psychology clinic provides the opportunity for supervised training in personal counseling and for research in the field of counseling and psychotherapy. Field placements are available in clinical psychology. The Silverman Center is a research center containing a comprehensive collection of world literature in phenomenology.

Information for Students With Physical Disabilities: See the following website for more information: http://www.duq.edu/life-at-duquesne/student-services/.

Application Information:
Send to Duquesne University, McAnulty College and Graduate School of Liberals Arts, Graduate Office, 600 Forbes Avenue, Pittsburgh, PA 15282. Application available online. URL of online application: http://www.duq.edu/academics/schools/liberal-arts/graduate-school/apply-to-duquesne. Students are admitted in the Fall, application deadline December 15. *Fee:* $0. There is no fee to apply online.

Geneva College
Master of Arts in Counseling
3200 College Avenue
Beaver Falls, PA 15010
Telephone: (724) 847-6697
Fax: (724) 847-6101
E-mail: *counseling@geneva.edu*
Web: *http://www.geneva.edu/page/grad_counseling*

Department Information:
1987. MA in Counseling Program Director: Carol B. Luce, PhD. Number of faculty: total—full-time 5, part-time 6; women—full-time 2, part-time 2; faculty subject to the Americans With Disabilities Act 1.

Programs and Degrees Offered:
Listed in the following order: Program area, degree type (T if terminal Master's), number awarded 7/11–6/12. Marriage and Family Counseling MA/MS (Master of Arts/Science) (T) 4, Clinical Mental Health Counseling MA/MS (Master of Arts/Science) (T) 4, School Counseling MA/MS (Master of Arts/Science) (T) 4.

Student Applications/Admissions:
Student Applications
Marriage and Family Counseling MA/MS (Master of Arts/Science)—Applications 2012–2013, 35. Total applicants accepted 2012–2013, 26. Number full-time enrolled (new admits only) 2012–2013, 6. Number part-time enrolled (new admits only) 2012–2013, 11. Total enrolled 2012–2013 full-time, 14. Total enrolled 2012–2013 part-time, 19. Openings 2013–2014, 12. The median number of years required for completion of a degree in 2012–2013 were 2. The number of students enrolled full- and part-time who were dismissed or voluntarily withdrew from this program area in 2012–2013 were 1. *Clinical Mental Health Counseling MA/MS (Master of Arts/Science)*—Applications 2012–2013, 56. Total applicants accepted 2012–2013, 39. Number full-time enrolled (new admits only) 2012–2013, 22. Number part-time enrolled (new admits only) 2012–2013, 7. Total enrolled 2012–2013 full-time, 25. Total enrolled 2012–2013 part-time, 14. Openings 2013–2014, 12. The median number of years required for completion of a degree in 2012–2013 were 3. The number of students enrolled full- and part-time who were dismissed or voluntarily withdrew from

this program area in 2012–2013 were 2. *School Counseling MA/MS (Master of Arts/Science)*—Applications 2012–2013, 12. Total applicants accepted 2012–2013, 8. Number full-time enrolled (new admits only) 2012–2013, 5. Number part-time enrolled (new admits only) 2012–2013, 2. Total enrolled 2012–2013 full-time, 14. Total enrolled 2012–2013 part-time, 5. Openings 2013–2014, 6. The median number of years required for completion of a degree in 2012–2013 were 2. The number of students enrolled full- and part-time who were dismissed or voluntarily withdrew from this program area in 2012–2013 were 0.

Scores: Entries appear in this order: required test or GPA, minimum score (if required), median score of students entering in 2012–2013. *Marriage and Family Counseling MA/MS (Master of Arts/Science):* overall undergraduate GPA 3.3; *Clinical Mental Health Counseling MA/MS (Master of Arts/Science):* overall undergraduate GPA 3.3; *School Counseling MA/MS (Master of Arts/Science):* overall undergraduate GPA 3.3.

Other Criteria: (importance of criteria rated low, medium, or high): research experience—low, work experience—medium, extracurricular activity—medium, clinically related public service—medium, GPA—medium, letters of recommendation—high, interview—medium, statement of goals and objectives—high, specific undergraduate psychology courses taken—medium, Undergrad courses should include 12 credits in psychology, counseling, sociology or classes in a related field. Successful completion of an undergraduate statistics class is highly recommended but not mandatory. For additional information on admission requirements, go to http://www.geneva.edu/object/counseling_admissions.

Student Characteristics: The following represents characteristics of students in 2012–2013 in all graduate psychology programs in the department: Female—full-time 38, part-time 27; Male—full-time 15, part-time 11; African American/Black—full-time 4, part-time 5; Hispanic/Latino(a)—full-time 0, part-time 0; Asian/Pacific Islander—full-time 0, part-time 0; American Indian/Alaska Native—full-time 0, part-time 0; Caucasian/White—full-time 49, part-time 33; Multi-ethnic—full-time 0, part-time 0; students subject to the Americans With Disabilities Act—full-time 0, part-time 0; Unknown ethnicity—full-time 0, part-time 0; International students who hold an F-1 or J-1 Visa—full-time 0, part-time 0.

Financial Information/Assistance:
Tuition for Full-Time Study: *Master's:* State residents: $640 per credit hour; Nonstate residents: $640 per credit hour. Tuition is subject to change. See the following website for updates and changes in tuition costs: https://www.geneva.edu/page/tuition_costs.

Financial Assistance:
First-Year Students: Research assistantships available for first year. Average amount paid per academic year: $500. Average number of hours worked per week: 3. Fellowships and scholarships available for first year. Average amount paid per academic year: $5,120. Average number of hours worked per week: 20. Apply by May 1.

Advanced Students: Teaching assistantships available for advanced students. Average amount paid per academic year: $1,600. Average number of hours worked per week: 6. Apply by July. Research assistantships available for advanced students.

Average amount paid per academic year: $500. Average number of hours worked per week: 3. Fellowships and scholarships available for advanced students. Average amount paid per academic year: $15,360. Average number of hours worked per week: 20. Apply by May 1.

Additional Information: Of all students currently enrolled full time, 20% benefited from one or more of the listed financial assistance programs. Application and information available online at: http://www.geneva.edu/object/counseling_grad_assistantships.

Internships/Practica: Master's Degree (MA/MS Marriage and Family Counseling): An internship experience, such as a final research project or "capstone" experience is required of graduates. Master's Degree (MA/MS Clinical Mental Health Counseling): An internship experience, such as a final research project or "capstone" experience is required of graduates. Master's Degree (MA/MS School Counseling): An internship experience, such as a final research project or "capstone" experience is required of graduates. A practicum and internship program is in place. This practicum and internship experience is in line with the CACREP standards for master's level counseling programs. Practica are 100 hours in length with individual and group supervision and direct client contact. Marriage and family internships are 600 hours in length with direct client contact included; mental health internships are 900 hours in length with direct client contact hours included; school internships are 600 hours in length with 300 hours on the elementary level and 300 hours on the secondary level. All internships will involve site placements typically in the Beaver County and Pittsburgh area, supervision via qualified master's and/or doctoral prepared practitioners, and onsite as well as college supervision. Practica and internships are arranged by the faculty coordinators.

Housing and Day Care: No on-campus housing is available. No on-campus day care facilities are available.

Employment of Department Graduates:
Master's Degree Graduates: Of those who graduated in the academic year 2011–2012, the following categories and numbers represent the postgraduate activities and employment of master's degree graduates: Enrolled in another graduate/professional program (1), enrolled in a postdoctoral residency/fellowship (n/a), employed in independent practice (n/a), employed in a professional position in a school system (1), employed in a community mental health/counseling center (8), employed in a hospital/medical center (1), not seeking employment (1), total from the above (master's) (12).
Doctoral Degree Graduates: Of those who graduated in the academic year 2011–2012, the following categories and numbers represent the postgraduate activities and employment of doctoral degree graduates: Enrolled in a psychology doctoral program (n/a), total from the above (doctoral) (0).

Additional Information:
Orientation, Objectives, and Emphasis of Department: The philosophies of counseling in the MA in Counseling Program at Geneva College are embedded in a Christian view of human nature and God's created world. A growing body of research literature affirms that Christian faith establishes a basis for healthy personality development, interpersonal relations, and mental health. A multidimensional holistic view of persons examines the interweaving of physical, emotional, social, cognitive, behavioral, and spiritual aspects of life. Integrative psychotherapeutic conceptualizations based on this multidimensionality promote healing and change. Counseling students and faculty engage in Christian spiritual growth, thus modeling adherence to the faith and values they profess and facilitating academic learning, counseling, effectiveness, and ability to consult in the larger church community and beyond. The MA in Counseling Program at Geneva College provides academic training in the development of knowledge, skills, and personal awareness pertinent to the counseling profession and encourages students to integrate Christian faith and Biblical knowledge with the training and practice of counseling. The program is designed so that post-baccalaureate students who complete this degree and acquire the required postgraduate supervised experience in the practice of counseling will be eligible to become Licensed Professional Counselors.

Special Facilities or Resources: Beaver Falls Main Campus: Department facilities include a computer lab and a modern clinical counseling facility. The computer lab is equipped with WordPerfect for Windows, SPSS for Windows, and various experimental and clinical software resources. The lab is also connected to the Internet. MA in Counseling program is also offered at the RLA building in Cranberry Township, PA. The entire facility is Technology-Based with all classrooms and all other rooms equipped with wireless internet access, LCD projector, laptop, screen, microphones and speakers. Staffing and IT help are always available.

Information for Students With Physical Disabilities: See the following website for more information: https://www.geneva.edu/page/access_disability_serv.

Application Information:
Send to MA in Counseling Program Manager, Geneva College, 3200 College Avenue, Beaver Falls, PA 15010. Application available online. URL of online application: http://www.geneva.edu/object/counseling_onlineapp. Students are admitted in the Programs have rolling admissions. *Fee:* $50. Application fee is waived for online application. For the hard copy application, the fee may be waived at the discretion of the Program Manager.

Immaculata University
Department of Graduate Psychology
College of Graduate Studies
Box 500, Loyola Hall
Immaculata, PA 19345
Telephone: (610) 647-4400 Ext. 3509
Fax: (610) 647-2324
E-mail: *jyalof@immaculata.edu*
Web: *http://www.immaculata.edu/academics/departments/graduate_psychology*

Department Information:
1983. Chairperson: Jed Yalof. Number of faculty: total—full-time 13, part-time 25; women—full-time 10, part-time 14; total—minority—full-time 2, part-time 2; women minority—full-time 2, part-time 1.

Programs and Degrees Offered:
Listed in the following order: Program area, degree type (T if terminal Master's), number awarded 7/11–6/12. Clinical Psychol-

ogy PsyD (Doctor of Psychology) 8, Counseling Psychology MA/MS (Master of Arts/Science) (T) 31, Elementary School Counseling MA/MS (Master of Arts/Science) (T) 1, School Psychology MA/MS (Master of Arts/Science) (T) 4, Secondary School Counseling MA/MS (Master of Arts/Science) 7, School Psychology Certification Other 1, Elementary/Secondary Counseling MA/MS (Master of Arts/Science) 3.

APA Accreditation: Clinical PsyD (Doctor of Psychology). Student Outcome Data Website: http://www.immaculata.edu/academics/departments/graduatepsychology/outcomes.

Student Applications/Admissions:

Student Applications

Clinical Psychology PsyD (Doctor of Psychology)—Applications 2012–2013, 129. Total applicants accepted 2012–2013, 54. Number full-time enrolled (new admits only) 2012–2013, 24. Total enrolled 2012–2013 full-time, 112. Total enrolled 2012–2013 part-time, 52. Openings 2013–2014, 25. The median number of years required for completion of a degree in 2012–2013 were 6. The number of students enrolled full- and part-time who were dismissed or voluntarily withdrew from this program area in 2012–2013 were 2. Counseling Psychology MA/MS (Master of Arts/Science)—Applications 2012–2013, 94. Total applicants accepted 2012–2013, 69. Number full-time enrolled (new admits only) 2012–2013, 42. Total enrolled 2012–2013 full-time, 33. Total enrolled 2012–2013 part-time, 121. The number of students enrolled full- and part-time who were dismissed or voluntarily withdrew from this program area in 2012–2013 were 6. Elementary School Counseling MA/MS (Master of Arts/Science)—Total enrolled 2012–2013 full-time, 1. Total enrolled 2012–2013 part-time, 0. The number of students enrolled full- and part-time who were dismissed or voluntarily withdrew from this program area in 2012–2013 were 0. School Psychology MA/MS (Master of Arts/Science)—Total enrolled 2012–2013 full-time, 14. Total enrolled 2012–2013 part-time, 10. The number of students enrolled full- and part-time who were dismissed or voluntarily withdrew from this program area in 2012–2013 were 0. Secondary School Counseling MA/MS (Master of Arts/Science)—Total enrolled 2012–2013 full-time, 2. Total enrolled 2012–2013 part-time, 3. The number of students enrolled full- and part-time who were dismissed or voluntarily withdrew from this program area in 2012–2013 were 0. School Psychology Certification Other—Total enrolled 2012–2013 full-time, 2. Total enrolled 2012–2013 part-time, 0. The number of students enrolled full- and part-time who were dismissed or voluntarily withdrew from this program area in 2012–2013 were 0. Elementary/Secondary Counseling MA/MS (Master of Arts/Science)—Total enrolled 2012–2013 full-time, 3. Total enrolled 2012–2013 part-time, 17. The number of students enrolled full- and part-time who were dismissed or voluntarily withdrew from this program area in 2012–2013 were 0.

Other Criteria: (importance of criteria rated low, medium, or high): GRE scores—high, GPA—high, letters of recommendation—medium, interview—high, statement of goals and objectives—medium. For additional information on admission requirements, go to http://www.immaculata.edu/admissions/graduate/requirements.

Student Characteristics: The following represents characteristics of students in 2012–2013 in all graduate psychology programs in

the department: Female—full-time 131, part-time 158; Male—full-time 36, part-time 45; African American/Black—full-time 12, part-time 19; Hispanic/Latino(a)—full-time 12, part-time 5; Asian/Pacific Islander—full-time 1, part-time 5; American Indian/Alaska Native—full-time 1, part-time 0; Caucasian/White—full-time 123, part-time 160; Multi-ethnic—full-time 3, part-time 1; students subject to the Americans With Disabilities Act—full-time 0, part-time 0; Unknown ethnicity—full-time 14, part-time 14; International students who hold an F-1 or J-1 Visa—full-time 0, part-time 0.

Financial Information/Assistance:

Tuition for Full-Time Study: *Master's:* State residents: $620 per credit hour; Nonstate residents: $620 per credit hour. *Doctoral:* State residents: $850 per credit hour; Nonstate residents: $850 per credit hour. Tuition is subject to change. See the following website for updates and changes in tuition costs: http://www.immaculata.edu/admissions/graduate/tuition_fees.

Financial Assistance:

First-Year Students: No information provided.

Advanced Students: Traineeships available for advanced students. Average amount paid per academic year: $28,900. Apply by May. Fellowships and scholarships available for advanced students. Average amount paid per academic year: $5,100. Apply by April.

Additional Information: Application and information available online at: http://www.immaculata.edu/admissions/graduate/finaid.

Internships/Practica: Doctoral Degree (PsyD Clinical Psychology): For those doctoral students for whom a professional psychology internship was required in this program prior to graduation, (35) students applied for an internship in 2011–2012, with (35) students obtaining an internship. Of those students who obtained an internship, (35) were paid internships. Of those students who obtained an internship, (9) students placed in APA/CPA accredited internships, (26) students placed in internships not APA/CPA accredited, but listed with the Association of Psychology Postdoctoral and Internship Programs (APPIC), (0) students placed in internships conforming to guidelines of the Council of Directors of School Psychology Programs (CDSPP), (0) students placed in internships that were not APA/CPA accredited, APPIC or CDSPP listed. Doctoral Degree (Other School Psychology Certification): For those doctoral students for whom a professional psychology internship was required in this program prior to graduation, (0) students applied for an internship in 2011–2012, with (0) students obtaining an internship. Of those students who obtained an internship, (0) were paid internships. Of those students who obtained an internship, (0) students placed in APA/CPA accredited internships, (0) students placed in internships not APA/CPA accredited, but listed with the Association of Psychology Postdoctoral and Internship Programs (APPIC), (0) students placed in internships conforming to guidelines of the Council of Directors of School Psychology Programs (CDSPP), (0) students placed in internships that were not APA/CPA accredited, APPIC or CDSPP listed. Master's Degree (MA/MS Counseling Psychology): An internship experience, such as a final research project or "capstone" experience is required of graduates. Master's Degree (MA/MS Elementary School Counseling): An internship experience, such as a final research project or "capstone" experience is required of graduates. Master's Degree (MA/MS School Psychology): An internship experience, such as a final research project or "capstone" experience is required of graduates. The Graduate Psychology Department places counseling psychology, school psychology, and clinical psychology students at sites throughout the Philadelphia and tri-county area and with supervisors with qualifications specific to student and program requirements. The department has an APPIC-member consortium for predoctoral internship training to which its students are required to apply, in addition to applying to APA-accredited sites and other APPIC internships both locally and nationally. Clinical doctoral students complete diagnostic and therapy placements prior to internship. Elective field placements are available and encouraged for clinical psychology doctoral students. Students entering the PsyD program with a BA or equivalent are required to complete a field placement early in their program of study as one of their electives and work toward the MA in Clinical Psychology as part of earning the PsyD. Students work with either the Master's field site coordinator or doctoral field site and predoctoral internship coordinator to identify prospective field placements for their different programs of study.

Housing and Day Care: On-campus housing is available. See the following website for more information: http://www.immaculata. edu/ResidenceLifeandHousing. No on-campus day care facilities are available.

Employment of Department Graduates:

Master's Degree Graduates: Of those who graduated in the academic year 2011–2012, the following categories and numbers represent the postgraduate activities and employment of master's degree graduates: Enrolled in a postdoctoral residency/fellowship (n/a), employed in independent practice (n/a), total from the above (master's) (0).

Doctoral Degree Graduates: Of those who graduated in the academic year 2011–2012, the following categories and numbers represent the postgraduate activities and employment of doctoral degree graduates: Enrolled in a psychology doctoral program (n/a), total from the above (doctoral) (0).

Additional Information:

Orientation, Objectives, and Emphasis of Department: At the master's level, the department's orientation is the professional preparation of the master's counselor in relation to counselor licensure in PA. The department also prepares students for elementary school counseling, secondary school counseling, combined elementary and secondary school counseling, and school psychology certification. There are also certification only programs for students with the MA degree; these programs are lower enrollment. In all cases, training emphasizes knowledge, skill and competency through classroom, practicum and internship. The department's orientation is the preparation of doctoral-level clinical psychologists within the practitioner-scholar model of professional psychology. This preparation entails a generalist curriculum emphasizing theory, therapy, diagnostics and clinical training, with doctoral dissertation research aligned with a practitioner model. Students entering with a bachelor's degree or non-psychology MA degree or equivalency can earn a MA degree in Clinical Psychology. Traineeships and scholarships are competitive and for MA and PsyD level students. There is also a Professional Development Award to support student attendance at conferences at which they present academic research and/or papers.

Special Facilities or Resources: The college has a comprehensive center for academic computing and modern technology available for student computer needs and utilization. The Gabrielle Library was opened in 1993 and houses journals and texts and has online search available to students.

Information for Students With Physical Disabilities: See the following website for more information: http://www.immaculata. edu/academics/academic_success/accommodations.

Application Information:
Send to Assistant Dean, College of Graduate Studies, Immaculata University, 1145 King Road, Box 500, Immaculata, PA 19345. Application available online. URL of online application: http://www. immaculata.edu/admissions/graduate/applications. Students are admitted in the Fall, application deadline January 15. PsyD Clinical: January 15 application deadline for Summer or Fall admission. All other programs have rolling admissions. *Fee:* $75. Application fee is $50 for master's, $75 for doctoral program.

Indiana University of Pennsylvania
Department of Psychology - Clinical Psychology Doctoral
    Program
Natural Sciences and Mathematics
1020 Oakland Avenue, 201 Uhler Hall
Indiana, PA 15705-1064
Telephone: (724) 357-4519
Fax: (724) 357-4087
E-mail: *David.LaPorte@iup.edu*
Web: *http://www.iup.edu/psychology/psyd*

Department Information:
1984. Chairperson: Raymond Pavloski, PhD. Number of faculty: total—full-time 28, part-time 4; women—full-time 17, part-time 4; total—minority—full-time 2; women minority—full-time 1.

Programs and Degrees Offered:
Listed in the following order: Program area, degree type (T if terminal Master's), number awarded 7/11–6/12. Clinical Psychology PsyD (Doctor of Psychology) 10.

APA Accreditation: Clinical PsyD (Doctor of Psychology). Student Outcome Data Website: http://www.iup.edu/psychology/psyd/default. aspx.

Student Applications/Admissions:
Student Applications
Clinical Psychology PsyD (Doctor of Psychology)—Applications 2012–2013, 123. Total applicants accepted 2012–2013, 32. Number full-time enrolled (new admits only) 2012–2013, 15. Number part-time enrolled (new admits only) 2012–2013, 0. Total enrolled 2012–2013 full-time, 70. Total enrolled 2012–2013 part-time, 3. Openings 2013–2014, 15. The median number of years required for completion of a degree in 2012–2013 were 5. The number of students enrolled full- and part-time who were dismissed or voluntarily withdrew from this program area in 2012–2013 were 0.
Scores: Entries appear in this order: required test or GPA, minimum score (if required), median score of students entering

in 2012–2013. *Clinical Psychology PsyD (Doctor of Psychology)*: GRE-V 500, 605, GRE-Q 500, 667, overall undergraduate GPA 3.0, 3.69, last 2 years GPA no minimum stated, psychology GPA no minimum stated, Masters GPA no minimum stated.

Other Criteria: (importance of criteria rated low, medium, or high): GRE scores—high, research experience—medium, work experience—medium, extracurricular activity—low, clinically related public service—high, GPA—high, letters of recommendation—high, interview—high, statement of goals and objectives—high, undergraduate major in psychology—medium, specific undergraduate psychology courses taken—medium. For additional information on admission requirements, go to http://www.iup.edu/page.aspx?id=47457.

Student Characteristics: The following represents characteristics of students in 2012–2013 in all graduate psychology programs in the department: Female—full-time 55, part-time 2; Male—full-time 15, part-time 1; African American/Black—full-time 0, part-time 0; Hispanic/Latino(a)—full-time 1, part-time 0; Asian/Pacific Islander—full-time 4, part-time 0; American Indian/Alaska Native—full-time 0, part-time 0; Caucasian/White—full-time 64, part-time 6; Multi-ethnic—full-time 1, part-time 0; students subject to the Americans With Disabilities Act—full-time 1, part-time 0; Unknown ethnicity—full-time 0, part-time 0; International students who hold an F-1 or J-1 Visa—full-time 3, part-time 0.

Financial Information/Assistance:

Tuition for Full-Time Study: *Doctoral:* State residents: per academic year $14,448, $451 per credit hour; Nonstate residents: per academic year $21,688, $677 per credit hour. Tuition is subject to change. Additional fees are assessed to students beyond the costs of tuition for the following: technology, activity, instructional, registration, wellness, transportation, student services. See the following website for updates and changes in tuition costs: http://www.iup.edu/page.aspx?id=17303.

Financial Assistance:

First-Year Students: No information provided.

Advanced Students: Teaching assistantships available for advanced students. Average amount paid per academic year: $22,398. Average number of hours worked per week: 20. Apply by May 11. Research assistantships available for advanced students. Average amount paid per academic year: $3,265. Average number of hours worked per week: 10. Apply by April 1. Traineeships available for advanced students. Average amount paid per academic year: $6,530. Average number of hours worked per week: 20. Apply by February 1.

Additional Information: Of all students currently enrolled full time, 88% benefited from one or more of the listed financial assistance programs. Application and information available online at: http://www.iup.edu/upper.aspx?id=4733.

Internships/Practica: Doctoral Degree (PsyD Clinical Psychology): For those doctoral students for whom a professional psychology internship was required in this program prior to graduation, (11) students applied for an internship in 2011–2012, with (8) students obtaining an internship. Of those students who obtained an internship, (8) were paid internships. Of those students who obtained an internship, (7) students placed in APA/CPA accredited internships, (0) students placed in internships not APA/ CPA accredited, but listed with the Association of Psychology Postdoctoral and Internship Programs (APPIC), (0) students placed in internships conforming to guidelines of the Council of Directors of School Psychology Programs (CDSPP), (1) students placed in internships that were not APA/CPA accredited, APPIC or CDSPP listed. Students begin clinical experiences in the first year through course-based practica. During the second and later years, students enroll in the department-sponsored Center for Applied Psychology (CAP) training clinics, performing both therapy and assessment. Training in the CAP clinics is supplemented with required external practica, currently available in approximately 40 different sites.

Housing and Day Care: On-campus housing is available. See the following website for more information: http://www.iup.edu/ housing/default.aspx. On-campus day care facilities are available. See the following website for more information: http://www. indikids.org/locations/university.php.

Employment of Department Graduates:

Master's Degree Graduates: Of those who graduated in the academic year 2011–2012, the following categories and numbers represent the postgraduate activities and employment of master's degree graduates: Enrolled in a postdoctoral residency/fellowship (n/a), employed in independent practice (n/a), total from the above (master's) (0).

Doctoral Degree Graduates: Of those who graduated in the academic year 2011–2012, the following categories and numbers represent the postgraduate activities and employment of doctoral degree graduates: Enrolled in a psychology doctoral program (n/a), enrolled in a postdoctoral residency/fellowship (5), employed in independent practice (1), employed in government agency (2), employed in a community mental health/counseling center (2), total from the above (doctoral) (10).

Additional Information:

Orientation, Objectives, and Emphasis of Department: The Psychology Department offers a Doctor of Psychology degree in Clinical Psychology (PsyD) that places emphasis upon professional applications of psychology based on the local clinical scientist model and on a solid grounding in the scientific knowledge base of psychology. Training follows a generalist model with opportunities to develop advanced competencies through courses and special practica. The core curriculum consists of seven areas including elective coursework. Heavy emphasis is placed on integrating psychological knowledge with treatment, evaluation, consultation and service delivery program design. The program is designed to meet the academic requirements of licensure and provide the background to assume responsibilities in appropriate professional settings. Current areas of interest that allow students to begin pre-specialization include: forensic, child clinical, behavioral medicine, clinical neuropsychology, and college counseling.

Special Facilities or Resources: The Department of Psychology includes two 16-computer laboratories, a graduate student computer lab, individual research space with recording capabilities, seminar rooms and a graduate student lounge. Each graduate student office is provided with computer access to the department server and the Internet. The facilities for the CAP include 12 treatment rooms as well as one seminar room, all connected with a master recording system. The CAP also houses computer facilities for test administration and scoring.

Information for Students With Physical Disabilities: See the following website for more information: http://www.iup.edu/disabilitysupport/default.aspx.

Application Information:
Send to School of Graduate Studies and Research, Indiana University of Pennsylvania, Stright Hall, Room 101, 210 South Tenth Street, Indiana, PA 15705-1048. Application available online. URL of online application: http://www.iup.edu/admissions/graduate/howto/default.aspx. Students are admitted in the Fall, application deadline December 15. *Fee:* $50.

La Salle University
Counseling and Family Therapy Master's Programs
1900 West Olney Avenue
Philadelphia, PA 19141
Telephone: (215) 951-1767
Fax: (215) 991-3585
E-mail: *tonrey@lasalle.edu*
Web: *http://www.lasalle.edu/grad/index.php?section=clinical&page=index*

Department Information:
1948. Director, Counseling and Family Therapy Master's Programs: Donna A. Tonrey, PsyD, LMFT, LPC. Number of faculty: total—full-time 20, part-time 33; women—full-time 12, part-time 18; total—minority—full-time 2, part-time 4; women minority—full-time 1, part-time 3.

Programs and Degrees Offered:
Listed in the following order: Program area, degree type (T if terminal Master's), number awarded 7/11–6/12. Counseling and Family Therapy MA/MS (Master of Arts/Science) (T) 105.

Student Applications/Admissions:
Student Applications
Counseling and Family Therapy MA/MS (Master of Arts/Science)—Applications 2012–2013, 400. Total applicants accepted 2012–2013, 225. Number full-time enrolled (new admits only) 2012–2013, 32. Number part-time enrolled (new admits only) 2012–2013, 109. Total enrolled 2012–2013 full-time, 31. Total enrolled 2012–2013 part-time, 330. Openings 2013–2014, 200. The median number of years required for completion of a degree in 2012–2013 were 4. The number of students enrolled full- and part-time who were dismissed or voluntarily withdrew from this program area in 2012–2013 were 5.
Scores: Entries appear in this order: required test or GPA, minimum score (if required), median score of students entering in 2012–2013. *Counseling and Family Therapy MA/MS (Master of Arts/Science):* overall undergraduate GPA 3.0, 3.5.
Other Criteria: (importance of criteria rated low, medium, or high): GRE scores—medium, research experience—medium, work experience—medium, extracurricular activity—medium, clinically related public service—medium, GPA—high, letters of recommendation—high, statement of goals and objectives—high, undergraduate major in psychology—medium, specific undergraduate psychology courses taken—medium. For additional information on admission requirements, go to

http://www.lasalle.edu/grad/index.php?section=clinical&group=professional&page=admission.

Student Characteristics: The following represents characteristics of students in 2012–2013 in all graduate psychology programs in the department: Female—full-time 26, part-time 237; Male—full-time 5, part-time 93; African American/Black—full-time 4, part-time 45; Hispanic/Latino(a)—full-time 1, part-time 10; Asian/Pacific Islander—full-time 0, part-time 10; American Indian/Alaska Native—full-time 0, part-time 0; Caucasian/White—full-time 24, part-time 226; Multi-ethnic—full-time 1, part-time 1; students subject to the Americans With Disabilities Act—full-time 1, part-time 0; Unknown ethnicity—full-time 1, part-time 38; International students who hold an F-1 or J-1 Visa—full-time 4, part-time 0.

Financial Information/Assistance:
Tuition for Full-Time Study: *Master's:* State residents: $700 per credit hour; Nonstate residents: $700 per credit hour. Tuition is subject to change. Additional fees are assessed to students beyond the costs of tuition for the following: $100.00 General University Fee, Technology Fee $100.00 per semester. See the following website for updates and changes in tuition costs: http://www.lasalle.edu/grad/index.php?section=clinical&page=tuition.

Financial Assistance:
First-Year Students: Fellowships and scholarships available for first year. Average amount paid per academic year: $2,500.
Advanced Students: Research assistantships available for advanced students. Average amount paid per academic year: $1,500. Average number of hours worked per week: 10. Traineeships available for advanced students.
Additional Information: Of all students currently enrolled full time, 25% benefited from one or more of the listed financial assistance programs. Application and information available online at: http://www.lasalle.edu/grad/index.php?section=clinical&page=financialaid.

Internships/Practica: Master's Degree (MA/MS Counseling and Family Therapy): An internship experience, such as a final research project or "capstone" experience is required of graduates. 75 Students are placed in sites, located throughout the Tri-State area. The internship placements are specific to the areas of concentrations and supervised by professionals highly qualified in particular realms of expertise.

Housing and Day Care: On-campus housing is available. See the following website for more information: http://www.lasalle.edu/students/dean/admin/housing/gradhousing.htm. On-campus day care facilities are available. See the following website for more information: http://buildingblocksatlasalle.com/.

Employment of Department Graduates:
Master's Degree Graduates: Of those who graduated in the academic year 2011–2012, the following categories and numbers represent the postgraduate activities and employment of master's degree graduates: Enrolled in a postdoctoral residency/fellowship (n/a), employed in independent practice (n/a), total from the above (master's) (0).
Doctoral Degree Graduates: Of those who graduated in the academic year 2011–2012, the following categories and numbers represent the postgraduate activities and employment of doctoral

degree graduates: Enrolled in a psychology doctoral program (n/a), total from the above (doctoral) (0).

Additional Information:

Orientation, Objectives, and Emphasis of Department: Three areas of concentration are available within the program: Professional Clinical Counseling, Marriage and Family therapy, and Industrial/Organizational Management and Human Resources. The program stresses skills training and clinical preparation for these concentrations, including preparation for Licensed Professional Counselor or Licensed Marriage and Family Therapist. It also prepares students for doctoral studies. The program is based on a holistic view of the person, which stresses the integration of the psychological, systemic, cultural, and spiritual dimensions of experience.

Application Information:

Send to Graduate Enrollment, Box 826, LaSalle University, 1900 West Olney Avenue, Philadelphia, PA 19141. Application available online. URL of online application: http://www.lasalle.edu/grad/index.php?section—ain&page=apply. Students are admitted in the Fall, application deadline August 1; Spring, application deadline December 1; Summer, application deadline April 1; Programs have rolling admissions. International student applications should be complete at least two months prior to the dates listed above. *Fee:* $35. Fee Waived for On-Line Application (which is recommended).

Lehigh University
Department of Education and Human Services
Education
Mountain Top Campus, 111 Research Drive
Bethlehem, PA 18015
Telephone: (610) 758-3241
Fax: (610) 758-6223
E-mail: *gjd3@lehigh.edu*
Web: *http://www.lehigh.edu/education/*

Department Information:

1995. Chairperson: George DuPaul. Number of faculty: total—full-time 30; women—full-time 18; total—minority—full-time 7; women minority—full-time 4.

Programs and Degrees Offered:

Listed in the following order: Program area, degree type (T if terminal Master's), number awarded 7/11–6/12. Counseling Psychology PhD (Doctor of Philosophy) 7, Counseling and Human Services MEd (Education) 10, Elementary School Counseling MEd (Education) 4, School Psychology PhD (Doctor of Philosophy) 6, Secondary School Counseling MEd (Education) 2, School Psychology EdS (School Psychology) 5, International Counseling MEd (Education) 27.

APA Accreditation: Counseling PhD (Doctor of Philosophy). Student Outcome Data Website: http://coe.lehigh.edu/academics/degrees/cp-phd. School PhD (Doctor of Philosophy). Student Outcome Data Website: http://coe.lehigh.edu/academics/degrees/phdschpsych.

Student Applications/Admissions:
Student Applications

Counseling Psychology PhD (Doctor of Philosophy)—Applications 2012–2013, 110. Total applicants accepted 2012–2013, 4. Number full-time enrolled (new admits only) 2012–2013, 4. Number part-time enrolled (new admits only) 2012–2013, 0. Total enrolled 2012–2013 full-time, 28. Total enrolled 2012–2013 part-time, 0. Openings 2013–2014, 6. The median number of years required for completion of a degree in 2012–2013 were 6. The number of students enrolled full- and part-time who were dismissed or voluntarily withdrew from this program area in 2012–2013 were 1. *Counseling and Human Services MEd (Education)*—Applications 2012–2013, 85. Total applicants accepted 2012–2013, 26. Number full-time enrolled (new admits only) 2012–2013, 8. Number part-time enrolled (new admits only) 2012–2013, 5. Total enrolled 2012–2013 full-time, 15. Total enrolled 2012–2013 part-time, 8. Openings 2013–2014, 40. The median number of years required for completion of a degree in 2012–2013 were 2. The number of students enrolled full- and part-time who were dismissed or voluntarily withdrew from this program area in 2012–2013 were 0. *Elementary School Counseling MEd (Education)*—Applications 2012–2013, 8. Total applicants accepted 2012–2013, 5. Number full-time enrolled (new admits only) 2012–2013, 0. Number part-time enrolled (new admits only) 2012–2013, 4. Total enrolled 2012–2013 full-time, 4. Total enrolled 2012–2013 part-time, 5. Openings 2013–2014, 10. The median number of years required for completion of a degree in 2012–2013 were 2. The number of students enrolled full- and part-time who were dismissed or voluntarily withdrew from this program area in 2012–2013 were 0. *School Psychology PhD (Doctor of Philosophy)*—Applications 2012–2013, 40. Total applicants accepted 2012–2013, 10. Number full-time enrolled (new admits only) 2012–2013, 3. Number part-time enrolled (new admits only) 2012–2013, 0. Total enrolled 2012–2013 full-time, 32. Total enrolled 2012–2013 part-time, 0. Openings 2013–2014, 5. The median number of years required for completion of a degree in 2012–2013 were 8. The number of students enrolled full- and part-time who were dismissed or voluntarily withdrew from this program area in 2012–2013 were 0. *Secondary School Counseling MEd (Education)*—Applications 2012–2013, 13. Total applicants accepted 2012–2013, 6. Number full-time enrolled (new admits only) 2012–2013, 5. Number part-time enrolled (new admits only) 2012–2013, 1. Total enrolled 2012–2013 full-time, 11. Total enrolled 2012–2013 part-time, 5. Openings 2013–2014, 6. The median number of years required for completion of a degree in 2012–2013 were 2. The number of students enrolled full- and part-time who were dismissed or voluntarily withdrew from this program area in 2012–2013 were 0. *School Psychology EdS (School Psychology)*—Applications 2012–2013, 33. Total applicants accepted 2012–2013, 8. Number full-time enrolled (new admits only) 2012–2013, 3. Number part-time enrolled (new admits only) 2012–2013, 0. Total enrolled 2012–2013 full-time, 11. Openings 2013–2014, 5. The median number of years required for completion of a degree in 2012–2013 were 3. The number of students enrolled full- and part-time who were dismissed or voluntarily withdrew from this program area in 2012–2013 were 0. *International Counseling MEd (Education)*—Applications 2012–2013, 21. Total applicants accepted 2012–2013, 10. Number full-time enrolled (new admits only) 2012–2013, 0. Number part-time enrolled (new admits only) 2012–2013,

11. Openings 2013–2014, 30. The median number of years required for completion of a degree in 2012–2013 were 3. The number of students enrolled full- and part-time who were dismissed or voluntarily withdrew from this program area in 2012–2013 were 0.

Scores: Entries appear in this order: required test or GPA, minimum score (if required), median score of students entering in 2012–2013. *Counseling Psychology PhD (Doctor of Philosophy):* GRE-V no minimum stated, 560, GRE-Q no minimum stated, 690, overall undergraduate GPA no minimum stated, 3.72; *Counseling and Human Services MEd (Education):* overall undergraduate GPA 3.0; *Elementary School Counseling MEd (Education):* overall undergraduate GPA 3.0; *School Psychology PhD (Doctor of Philosophy):* GRE-V 480, 570, GRE-Q 560, 690, GRE-Analytical 4.0, 5.0, overall undergraduate GPA 3.00, 3.78; *Secondary School Counseling MEd (Education):* overall undergraduate GPA 3.0; *School Psychology EdS (School Psychology):* GRE-V 470, 615, GRE-Q 420, 540, GRE-Analytical 4.0, 5.0, overall undergraduate GPA 3.72, 3.77; *International Counseling MEd (Education):* overall undergraduate GPA 3.0.

Other Criteria: (importance of criteria rated low, medium, or high): GRE scores—medium, research experience—high, work experience—medium, extracurricular activity—medium, clinically related public service—medium, GPA—high, letters of recommendation—medium, interview—medium, statement of goals and objectives—high, additional statements—high, undergraduate major in psychology—medium, specific undergraduate psychology courses taken—medium, School psychology requires 3 statements focused on 1) professional or research interests, 2) related experiences, and 3) experiences with diverse populations.

Student Characteristics: The following represents characteristics of students in 2012–2013 in all graduate psychology programs in the department: Female—full-time 84, part-time 40; Male—full-time 17, part-time 12; African American/Black—full-time 9, part-time 0; Hispanic/Latino(a)—full-time 7, part-time 0; Asian/Pacific Islander—full-time 8, part-time 0; American Indian/Alaska Native—full-time 0, part-time 0; Caucasian/White—full-time 76, part-time 18; Multi-ethnic—full-time 1, part-time 0; students subject to the Americans With Disabilities Act—full-time 0, part-time 0; Unknown ethnicity—full-time 0, part-time 34; International students who hold an F-1 or J-1 Visa—full-time 2, part-time 0.

Financial Information/Assistance:

Tuition for Full-Time Study: *Master's:* State residents: $550 per credit hour; Nonstate residents: $550 per credit hour. *Doctoral:* State residents: $550 per credit hour; Nonstate residents: $550 per credit hour. Tuition is subject to change. See the following website for updates and changes in tuition costs: http://www.lehigh.edu/~inburs/gr_fee_schedule.html.

Financial Assistance:

First-Year Students: Research assistantships available for first year. Average amount paid per academic year: $16,000. Average number of hours worked per week: 20. Apply by January 1. Traineeships available for first year. Average amount paid per academic year: $16,000. Average number of hours worked per week: 20. Apply by January 1. Fellowships and scholarships available for first year. Average amount paid per academic year: $26,000. Average number of hours worked per week: 20.

Advanced Students: Research assistantships available for advanced students. Average amount paid per academic year: $16,000. Average number of hours worked per week: 20. Traineeships available for advanced students. Average amount paid per academic year: $16,000. Average number of hours worked per week: 20. Fellowships and scholarships available for advanced students. Average amount paid per academic year: $26,000. Average number of hours worked per week: 20.

Additional Information: Of all students currently enrolled full time, 80% benefited from one or more of the listed financial assistance programs. Application and information available online at: http://coe.lehigh.edu/admissions/financial-aid.

Internships/Practica: Doctoral Degree (PhD Counseling Psychology): For those doctoral students for whom a professional psychology internship was required in this program prior to graduation, (2) students applied for an internship in 2011–2012, with (2) students obtaining an internship. Of those students who obtained an internship, (2) were paid internships. Of those students who obtained an internship, (0) students placed in APA/CPA accredited internships, (2) students placed in internships not APA/CPA accredited, but listed with the Association of Psychology Postdoctoral and Internship Programs (APPIC), (0) students placed in internships conforming to guidelines of the Council of Directors of School Psychology Programs (CDSPP), (0) students placed in internships that were not APA/CPA accredited, APPIC or CDSPP listed. Doctoral Degree (PhD School Psychology): For those doctoral students for whom a professional psychology internship was required in this program prior to graduation, (4) students applied for an internship in 2011–2012, with (4) students obtaining an internship. Of those students who obtained an internship, (4) were paid internships. Of those students who obtained an internship, (0) students placed in APA/CPA accredited internships, (0) students placed in internships not APA/CPA accredited, but listed with the Association of Psychology Postdoctoral and Internship Programs (APPIC), (4) students placed in internships conforming to guidelines of the Council of Directors of School Psychology Programs (CDSPP), (0) students placed in internships that were not APA/CPA accredited, APPIC or CDSPP listed. The Counseling Psychology program maintains contracts with a variety of practicum settings. Training in individual, group, couples, and family counseling is readily available. Students receive at least two hours of individual and two hours group supervision per week. Many sites provide additional training on specific issues in counseling. The Counseling Psychology programs have established a partnership with a local urban school district to provide enhanced in-school psychological services in elementary and middle schools. The School Psychology program also has established partnerships with local schools and health agencies for student practica. Third and fourth year doctoral students complete practica two days per week that provides hours toward state certification.

Housing and Day Care: On-campus housing is available. See the following website for more information: http://www4.lehigh.edu/housing/graduate. On-campus day care facilities are available. See the following website for more information: http://www.lehigh.edu/~inluccc.

Employment of Department Graduates:

Master's Degree Graduates: Of those who graduated in the academic year 2011–2012, the following categories and numbers

represent the postgraduate activities and employment of master's degree graduates: Enrolled in a postdoctoral residency/fellowship (n/a), employed in independent practice (n/a), employed in a professional position in a school system (6), total from the above (master's) (6).

Doctoral Degree Graduates: Of those who graduated in the academic year 2011–2012, the following categories and numbers represent the postgraduate activities and employment of doctoral degree graduates: Enrolled in a psychology doctoral program (n/a), enrolled in a postdoctoral residency/fellowship (8), employed in independent practice (1), employed in an academic position at a university (1), employed in other positions at a higher education institution (3), employed in a professional position in a school system (2), other employment position (4), total from the above (doctoral) (19).

Additional Information:

Orientation, Objectives, and Emphasis of Department: The College of Education offers degree programs in counseling and school psychology. The program in school psychology offers training at both educational specialist (NASP-approved) and doctoral (PhD) levels (NASP-approved and APA-accredited). Within the PhD program, subspecializations in Health/Pediatric School Psychology and in Students At-Risk for Disabilities are offered. The program at all levels is systems and behaviorally oriented, emphasizing collaborative problem-solving based research, consultation, behavioral assessment and intervention in the implementation of school psychology services. The program in counseling psychology emphasizes a scientist–practitioner model and trains professional psychologists for employment in educational, industrial, and community settings. The counseling psychology program also offers training at the master's level. The training program emphasizes diversity and multicultural perspectives throughout the curriculum.

Special Facilities or Resources: The school psychology program has a number of research and training projects that are focused on students with behavior and cognitive disabilities. The department has the Center for Promoting Research to Practice, a unit that houses several major research grants involved in bringing known research findings into school and community settings. The department also has university-affiliated training and research programs that provide living arrangements and day treatment programs for adults with developmental disabilities. The department also operates a laboratory school (Centennial School) for children and adolescents with emotional disturbance. All facilities are integrated into the training of students primarily in the school psychology programs. The counseling psychology program has a lab for videotaping and editing. Both programs have established partnerships with urban school districts. School psychology has established practicum placements in local hospitals and with the Children's Hospital of Philadelphia as part of the pediatric school psychology subspecialization track.

Information for Students With Physical Disabilities: See the following website for more information: http://www.lehigh.edu/~inacsup/disabilities/.

Application Information:
Send to Ms. Donna Johnson, College of Education, Lehigh University, 111 Research Drive, Bethlehem, PA 18015. Application available online. URL of online application: http://www.cas.lehigh.edu/lugradapp/. Students are admitted in the Fall, application deadline January 1. Deadline for Counseling Psychology and School Psychology doctoral programs as well as the School Psychology EdS program is January 1. Deadline for Counseling Master's programs is March 1. *Fee:* $65. Fee is waived if applicant attends the College's Open House.

Lehigh University
Department of Psychology
Arts and Sciences
17 Memorial Drive East
Bethlehem, PA 18015
Telephone: (610) 758-3630
Fax: (610) 758-6277
E-mail: m.gill@lehigh.edu
Web: http://cas.lehigh.edu/CASWeb/default.aspx?id=1398

Department Information:
1931. Chairperson: Ageliki Nicolopoulou. Number of faculty: total—full-time 15, part-time 1; women—full-time 9.

Programs and Degrees Offered:
Listed in the following order: Program area, degree type (T if terminal Master's), number awarded 7/11–6/12. Human Cognition and Development PhD (Doctor of Philosophy) 8.

Student Applications/Admissions:

Student Applications

Human Cognition and Development PhD (Doctor of Philosophy)— Applications 2012–2013, 65. Number full-time enrolled (new admits only) 2012–2013, 8. Number part-time enrolled (new admits only) 2012–2013, 0. Total enrolled 2012–2013 full-time, 19. Total enrolled 2012–2013 part-time, 0. The median number of years required for completion of a degree in 2012–2013 were 5. The number of students enrolled full- and part-time who were dismissed or voluntarily withdrew from this program area in 2012–2013 were 1.

Other Criteria: (importance of criteria rated low, medium, or high): GRE scores—medium, research experience—high, work experience—low, GPA—medium, letters of recommendation—high, interview—medium, statement of goals and objectives—high, undergraduate major in psychology—medium, specific undergraduate psychology courses taken—low.

Student Characteristics: The following represents characteristics of students in 2012–2013 in all graduate psychology programs in the department: Female—full-time 17, part-time 0; Male—full-time 2, part-time 0; African American/Black—full-time 0, part-time 0; Hispanic/Latino(a)—full-time 0, part-time 0; Asian/Pacific Islander—full-time 5, part-time 0; American Indian/Alaska Native—full-time 0, part-time 0; Caucasian/White—full-time 14, part-time 0; Multi-ethnic—full-time 0, part-time 0; students subject to the Americans With Disabilities Act—full-time 0, part-time 0; Unknown ethnicity—full-time 0, part-time 0; International students who hold an F-1 or J-1 Visa—full-time 4, part-time 0.

Financial Information/Assistance:
Tuition for Full-Time Study: *Doctoral:* State residents: $1,260 per credit hour; Nonstate residents: $1,260 per credit hour. Tu-

ition is subject to change. See the following website for updates and changes in tuition costs: http://www.lehigh.edu/~inburs/gr_fee_schedule.html.

Financial Assistance:

First-Year Students: Teaching assistantships available for first year. Average amount paid per academic year: $18,900. Average number of hours worked per week: 15. Apply by January 1. Research assistantships available for first year. Average amount paid per academic year: $18,900. Average number of hours worked per week: 15. Apply by January 1. Fellowships and scholarships available for first year. Average amount paid per academic year: $22,000. Average number of hours worked per week: 0. Apply by January 1.

Advanced Students: Teaching assistantships available for advanced students. Average amount paid per academic year: $19,400. Average number of hours worked per week: 15. Research assistantships available for advanced students. Average amount paid per academic year: $19,400. Average number of hours worked per week: 15. Fellowships and scholarships available for advanced students. Average amount paid per academic year: $22,000. Average number of hours worked per week: 0.

Additional Information: Of all students currently enrolled full time, 100% benefited from one or more of the listed financial assistance programs. Application and information available online at: http://cas.cas2.lehigh.edu/content/financial-aid.

Housing and Day Care: On-campus housing is available. See the following website for more information: http://www4.lehigh.edu/housing/graduate. On-campus day care facilities are available. See the following website for more information: http://www.lehigh.edu/~inluccc/.

Employment of Department Graduates:

Master's Degree Graduates: Of those who graduated in the academic year 2011–2012, the following categories and numbers represent the postgraduate activities and employment of master's degree graduates: Enrolled in a psychology doctoral program (3), enrolled in another graduate/professional program (2), enrolled in a postdoctoral residency/fellowship (n/a), employed in independent practice (n/a), total from the above (master's) (5).

Doctoral Degree Graduates: Of those who graduated in the academic year 2011–2012, the following categories and numbers represent the postgraduate activities and employment of doctoral degree graduates: Enrolled in a psychology doctoral program (n/a), enrolled in a postdoctoral residency/fellowship (3), total from the above (doctoral) (3).

Additional Information:

Orientation, Objectives, and Emphasis of Department: The Doctoral Program in Psychology is a research-intensive program that combines focus with flexibility. Focus is provided by the program emphasis on Human Cognition and Development and by a core curriculum. Flexibility is provided by the ability to tailor a research specialization in an area of Cognition and Language, Developmental Psychology, or Social Cognition and Personality. Graduate students define an area of specialization through their selection of graduate seminars and through their research experiences. All students are actively engaged in research throughout their residence in the program, and they work in collaboration with faculty members and student colleagues. Departmental faculty conduct research on basic cognitive, linguistic, and social-cognitive processes, and the development of these processes across the lifespan. In addition to research within the psychology department, the psychology faculty and students partake in interdisciplinary endeavors with researchers from other university departments and programs, including the Cognitive Science program.

Special Facilities or Resources: The department's well-equipped laboratories provide an excellent setting for research. The department has extensive facilities available for graduate student research, including a child study center, and cognitive, developmental, and social laboratories. Lehigh has a sophisticated network system that connects all campus computers and servers and provides easy access to the Internet.

Information for Students With Physical Disabilities: See the following website for more information: http://www.lehigh.edu/~inacsup/disabilities/.

Application Information:
Send to Graduate Programs Office, Lehigh University, 9 West Packer Avenue, Bethlehem, PA 18015-3075. Application available online. URL of online application: https://cas.lehigh.edu/LUGradApp/. Students are admitted in the Fall, application deadline January 1. *Fee:* $75. Application fee waived for those who attend College of Arts and Sciences Open House for Prospective Graduate Students (typically in the fall).

Millersville University
Department of Psychology
Byerly Hall
Millersville, PA 17551
Telephone: (717) 872-3093
Fax: (717) 871-2480
E-mail: *claudia.haferkamp@millersville.edu*
Web: *http://www.millersville.edu/psychology/*

Department Information:
1967. Chairperson: Helena Tuleya-Payne. Number of faculty: total—full-time 16, part-time 5; women—full-time 12, part-time 4; total—minority—full-time 4; women minority—full-time 4.

Programs and Degrees Offered:
Listed in the following order: Program area, degree type (T if terminal Master's), number awarded 7/11–6/12. Clinical Psychology MA/MS (Master of Arts/Science) (T) 15, School Counseling MEd (Education) 13, School Psychology MA/MS (Master of Arts/Science) 16, Supervision Of School Guidance MEd (Education) 0, Supervision Of School Psychology MA/MS (Master of Arts/Science) 0.

Student Applications/Admissions:
Student Applications
Clinical Psychology MA/MS (Master of Arts/Science)—Applications 2012–2013, 66. Total applicants accepted 2012–2013, 43. Number full-time enrolled (new admits only) 2012–2013,

15. Number part-time enrolled (new admits only) 2012–2013, 7. Total enrolled 2012–2013 full-time, 41. Total enrolled 2012–2013 part-time, 20. Openings 2013–2014, 40. The median number of years required for completion of a degree in 2012–2013 were 3. The number of students enrolled full- and part-time who were dismissed or voluntarily withdrew from this program area in 2012–2013 were 0. *School Counseling MEd (Education)*—Applications 2012–2013, 22. Total applicants accepted 2012–2013, 20. Number full-time enrolled (new admits only) 2012–2013, 2. Number part-time enrolled (new admits only) 2012–2013, 5. Total enrolled 2012–2013 full-time, 5. Total enrolled 2012–2013 part-time, 38. Openings 2013–2014, 25. The median number of years required for completion of a degree in 2012–2013 were 3. The number of students enrolled full- and part-time who were dismissed or voluntarily withdrew from this program area in 2012–2013 were 0. *School Psychology MA/MS (Master of Arts/Science)*—Applications 2012–2013, 36. Total applicants accepted 2012–2013, 27. Number full-time enrolled (new admits only) 2012–2013, 9. Number part-time enrolled (new admits only) 2012–2013, 2. Total enrolled 2012–2013 full-time, 23. Total enrolled 2012–2013 part-time, 19. Openings 2013–2014, 30. The median number of years required for completion of a degree in 2012–2013 were 3. The number of students enrolled full- and part-time who were dismissed or voluntarily withdrew from this program area in 2012–2013 were 0. *Supervision Of School Guidance MEd (Education)*—Applications 2012–2013, 1. Total applicants accepted 2012–2013, 1. Number full-time enrolled (new admits only) 2012–2013, 0. Number part-time enrolled (new admits only) 2012–2013, 0. Openings 2013–2014, 5. The median number of years required for completion of a degree in 2012–2013 was 1. *Supervision Of School Psychology MA/MS (Master of Arts/Science)*—Applications 2012–2013, 0. Total applicants accepted 2012–2013, 0. Number full-time enrolled (new admits only) 2012–2013, 0. Number part-time enrolled (new admits only) 2012–2013, 0. Openings 2013–2014, 5.

Scores: Entries appear in this order: required test or GPA, minimum score (if required), median score of students entering in 2012–2013. *Clinical Psychology MA/MS (Master of Arts/Science):* GRE-V 147, GRE-Q 148, GRE-Analytical 3.5, overall undergraduate GPA 2.75; *School Counseling MEd (Education):* GRE-V 147, GRE-Q 148, GRE-Analytical 3.5, overall undergraduate GPA 2.75; *School Psychology MA/MS (Master of Arts/Science):* GRE-V 147, GRE-Q 148, GRE-Analytical 3.5, overall undergraduate GPA 2.75.

Other Criteria: (importance of criteria rated low, medium, or high): GRE scores—medium, research experience—medium, work experience—high, extracurricular activity—low, clinically related public service—high, GPA—high, letters of recommendation—high, interview—high, statement of goals and objectives—high, writing sample—medium, undergraduate major in psychology—high, specific undergraduate psychology courses taken—high, The School Counseling M.Ed program requires applicants to have 6 credits of Psychology courses and 6 credits of education courses. Persons who did not major in Psychology as undegraduates must complete 18 credits of undergraduate Psychology coursework before applying to either the School Psychology or Clinical Psychology programs.

Student Characteristics: The following represents characteristics of students in 2012–2013 in all graduate psychology programs in the department: Female—full-time 53, part-time 60; Male—full-time 16, part-time 17; African American/Black—full-time 4, part-time 3; Hispanic/Latino(a)—full-time 2, part-time 2; Asian/Pacific Islander—full-time 5, part-time 1; American Indian/Alaska Native—full-time 0, part-time 0; Caucasian/White—full-time 58, part-time 71; Multi-ethnic—full-time 0, part-time 0; students subject to the Americans With Disabilities Act—full-time 0, part-time 0; Unknown ethnicity—full-time 0, part-time 0; International students who hold an F-1 or J-1 Visa—full-time 1, part-time 1.

Financial Information/Assistance:

Tuition for Full-Time Study: *Master's:* State residents: $548 per credit hour; Nonstate residents: $773 per credit hour. Tuition is subject to change. Additional fees are assessed to students beyond the costs of tuition for the following: general fee (supports student organizations) and technology fee. See the following website for updates and changes in tuition costs: http://www.millersville.edu/bursar/gradcosts.php.

Financial Assistance:

First-Year Students: Research assistantships available for first year. Average amount paid per academic year: $5,000. Average number of hours worked per week: 20.

Advanced Students: Research assistantships available for advanced students. Average amount paid per academic year: $5,400.

Additional Information: Of all students currently enrolled full time, 30% benefited from one or more of the listed financial assistance programs. Application and information available online at: http://www.millersville.edu/graduate/admissions/financial-support.php.

Internships/Practica: Master's Degree (MA/MS Clinical Psychology): An internship experience, such as a final research project or "capstone" experience is required of graduates. Field experiences are required of all students in clinical, school counseling, and school psychology programs. Students in the Certification Program in School Psychology are required to complete a full-time internship over one academic year (minimum 1200 hours). Students in the Clinical program complete a 600 hour internship in inpatient or outpatient mental health settings. Students in School Counseling complete their practica as counselors working in K-12 schools.

Housing and Day Care: No on-campus housing is available. No on-campus day care facilities are available.

Employment of Department Graduates:

Master's Degree Graduates: Of those who graduated in the academic year 2011–2012, the following categories and numbers represent the postgraduate activities and employment of master's degree graduates: Enrolled in a postdoctoral residency/fellowship (n/a), employed in independent practice (n/a), total from the above (master's) (0).

Doctoral Degree Graduates: Of those who graduated in the academic year 2011–2012, the following categories and numbers represent the postgraduate activities and employment of doctoral degree graduates: Enrolled in a psychology doctoral program (n/a), total from the above (doctoral) (0).

Additional Information:

Orientation, Objectives, and Emphasis of Department: All programs emphasize theory, research skills, and applied practical experience combined with a high degree of self-awareness and interpersonal relationship skills. The MS program in Clinical Psychology prepares clinicians with skills in psychological assessment/diagnosis, and an eclectic/cognitive-behavioral repertoire of skills in individual, group and family therapy. Graduates may obtain licensure as "professional counselors" and work in a wide range of inpatient and outpatient mental health settings with children and adults. The Certification Program in School Psychology is accredited by the National Association of School Psychologists (NASP) and prepares students for entry level positions as school psychologists. Knowledge about the educational process, psychological and emotional growth, and data-based decision-making are central to the training program. The MEd and Certification in School Counseling programs prepare students as school counselors for grades K-12. Operating under a prevention/intervention and solution-focused model, students develop into professionals who are responsive to the needs of the school setting.

Special Facilities or Resources: A microcomputer lab with access to the mainframe is available in the department. Millersville's campus is fully wireless. The Department has a clinic with observation and digital recording facilities. Ganser Library houses approximately half a million books and provides access to nearly 3500 periodical titles. The research and information needs of faculty, staff, and students, are met by subject specialists who provide extensive reference service within the library, at off-site locations, and electronically. Scholarly research is supported by a comprehensive and well-developed library collection that is continuously being augmented by the most current resources available, in print and electronic formats. The Library belongs to several state-wide and regional library consortia that allows for resource sharing, reciprocal borrowing, and collaborative purchasing.

Information for Students With Physical Disabilities: See the following website for more information: http://www.millersville.edu/learningservices/.

Application Information:
Send to Graduate Studies Office, Millersville University, P.O. Box 1002, Millersville, PA 17551-0302. Application available online. URL of online application: http://www.millersville.edu/admissions/graduate/apply/index.php. Students are admitted in the Fall, application deadline January 15; Spring, application deadline October 1. Applicants whose applications are not fully complete by the deadline may apply for "nondegree status" which will permit the applicant to enroll in a graduate core course if space permits. If the applicant is later admitted to a graduate program, a max of 9 nondegree credits may be applied to the graduate program. Summer applicants may also apply for nondegree status and take graduate classes while awaiting their interviews in either summer or fall. *Fee:* $40.

Penn State Harrisburg
Psychology Program
777 West Harrisburg Pike
Middletown, PA 17057-4898
Telephone: (717) 948-6063
Fax: (717) 948-6519
E-mail: *dvo@psu.edu*
Web: *http://hbg.psu.edu/departments/bsed/psy/*

Department Information:
1992. Program Coordinator: Thomas G. Bowers. Number of faculty: total—full-time 12; women—full-time 9.

Programs and Degrees Offered:
Listed in the following order: Program area, degree type (T if terminal Master's), number awarded 7/11–6/12. Applied Clinical Psychology MA/MS (Master of Arts/Science) (T) 8, Applied Psychological Research MA/MS (Master of Arts/Science) (T) 2.

Student Applications/Admissions:
Student Applications
Applied Clinical Psychology MA/MS (Master of Arts/Science)—Applications 2012–2013, 60. Total applicants accepted 2012–2013, 25. Number full-time enrolled (new admits only) 2012–2013, 13. Number part-time enrolled (new admits only) 2012–2013, 2. Total enrolled 2012–2013 full-time, 34. Total enrolled 2012–2013 part-time, 26. Openings 2013–2014, 15. The median number of years required for completion of a degree in 2012–2013 were 4. The number of students enrolled full- and part-time who were dismissed or voluntarily withdrew from this program area in 2012–2013 were 0. *Applied Psychological Research MA/MS (Master of Arts/Science)*—Applications 2012–2013, 10. Total applicants accepted 2012–2013, 4. Number full-time enrolled (new admits only) 2012–2013, 2. Number part-time enrolled (new admits only) 2012–2013, 0. Total enrolled 2012–2013 full-time, 4. Total enrolled 2012–2013 part-time, 5. Openings 2013–2014, 5. The median number of years required for completion of a degree in 2012–2013 were 3. The number of students enrolled full- and part-time who were dismissed or voluntarily withdrew from this program area in 2012–2013 were 0.

Scores: Entries appear in this order: required test or GPA, minimum score (if required), median score of students entering in 2012–2013. *Applied Clinical Psychology MA/MS (Master of Arts/Science)*: GRE-V 146, GRE-Q 146, GRE-Analytical 3.5, last 2 years GPA 3.00; *Applied Psychological Research MA/MS (Master of Arts/Science)*: GRE-V 146, GRE-Q 146, GRE-Analytical 3.5, last 2 years GPA 3.00.

Other Criteria: (importance of criteria rated low, medium, or high): GRE scores—high, research experience—medium, work experience—low, extracurricular activity—low, clinically related public service—low, GPA—high, letters of recommendation—high, interview—high, statement of goals and objectives—high, undergraduate major in psychology—low, specific undergraduate psychology courses taken—high. For additional information on admission requirements, go to http://hbg.psu.edu/Programs/Graduate/MastersDegrees.php.

Student Characteristics: The following represents characteristics of students in 2012–2013 in all graduate psychology programs in

the department: Female—full-time 31, part-time 23; Male—full-time 7, part-time 8; African American/Black—full-time 0, part-time 1; Hispanic/Latino(a)—full-time 0, part-time 1; Asian/Pacific Islander—full-time 2, part-time 0; American Indian/Alaska Native—full-time 0, part-time 0; Caucasian/White—full-time 30, part-time 29; Multi-ethnic—full-time 0, part-time 0; students subject to the Americans With Disabilities Act—full-time 0, part-time 0; Unknown ethnicity—full-time 6, part-time 0; International students who hold an F-1 or J-1 Visa—full-time 2, part-time 1.

Financial Information/Assistance:

Tuition for Full-Time Study: *Master's*: State residents: per academic year $16,364, $682 per credit hour; Nonstate residents: per academic year $28,642, $1,193 per credit hour. Tuition is subject to change. See the following website for updates and changes in tuition costs: http://tuition.psu.edu/tuitiondynamic/TuitionAndFees.aspx.

Financial Assistance:

First-Year Students: Research assistantships available for first year. Average amount paid per academic year: $15,000. Average number of hours worked per week: 20. Apply by February 1. Fellowships and scholarships available for first year. Average amount paid per academic year: $15,000. Average number of hours worked per week: 20. Apply by February 1.

Advanced Students: Fellowships and scholarships available for advanced students.

Additional Information: Of all students currently enrolled full time, 10% benefited from one or more of the listed financial assistance programs. Application and information available online at: http://harrisburg.psu.edu/financial-aid/financial-aid-for-graduate-students.

Internships/Practica: Master's Degree (MA/MS Applied Clinical Psychology): An internship experience, such as a final research project or "capstone" experience is required of graduates. Master's Degree (MA/MS Applied Psychological Research): An internship experience, such as a final research project or "capstone" experience is required of graduates. Students in the Applied Clinical Psychology program are required to complete 7 credits of supervised clinical internship. Students in the Applied Psychological Research program are required to complete 6 credits of research in collaboration with the program faculty.

Housing and Day Care: On-campus housing is available. See the following website for more information: http://www.hfs.psu.edu/harrisburg/housing/. On-campus day care facilities are available. See the following website for more information: http://harrisburg.psu.edu/places/childcare-center.

Employment of Department Graduates:

Master's Degree Graduates: Of those who graduated in the academic year 2011–2012, the following categories and numbers represent the postgraduate activities and employment of master's degree graduates: Enrolled in a postdoctoral residency/fellowship (n/a), employed in independent practice (n/a), total from the above (master's) (0).

Doctoral Degree Graduates: Of those who graduated in the academic year 2011–2012, the following categories and numbers represent the postgraduate activities and employment of doctoral degree graduates: Enrolled in a psychology doctoral program (n/a), total from the above (doctoral) (0).

Additional Information:

Orientation, Objectives, and Emphasis of Department: The Applied Clinical Psychology program prepares students to work as mental health professionals in a variety of settings and is intended to provide the academic training necessary for graduates to apply for master's-level licensing for mental health professionals in the Commonwealth of Pennsylvania. The overall model emphasizes the scientific bases of behavior, including biological, social, and individual difference factors. The training model is health-oriented rather than pathology-oriented and emphasizes the development of helping skills, including both assessment and intervention. The Applied Psychological Research program focuses on the development of research skills within the context of scientific training in psychology. The program is designed to meet the needs of students who plan careers in research or administration within human services or similar organizations, who plan to conduct research in other settings, or who plan to pursue doctoral study. Students can select electives and research experiences to reflect their individual interests in consultation with their advisor.

Special Facilities or Resources: Most students avail themselves of the resources in community hospitals, residential, and outpatient institutions for hands-on clinical and research experience. The department maintains an on-campus research facility which is available for use by graduate students working with faculty on research projects.

Information for Students With Physical Disabilities: See the following website for more information: http://harrisburg.psu.edu/disability-services.

Application Information:

Send to Graduate Admissions, Penn State Harrisburg, 777 West Harrisburg Pike, Middletown, PA 17057-4898. Application available online. URL of online application: http://harrisburg.psu.edu/admissions/graduate-admissions. Students are admitted in the Fall, application deadline April 30. January 10 application deadline for University fellowships and assistantships. We review applications on a rolling basis. Early applications are encouraged for full consideration for financial aid. *Fee*: $65.

Pennsylvania State University
Department of Human Development and Family Studies
College of Health and Human Development
315 HHD East
University Park, PA 16802
Telephone: (814) 863-8000
Fax: (814) 863-7963
E-mail: *mjs6@psu.edu*
Web: *http://www.hhdev.psu.edu/hdfs/graduate*

Department Information:

1974. Professor in Charge of Graduate Program: Eva Lefkowitz. Number of faculty: total—full-time 35; women—full-time 18; total—minority—full-time 4; women minority—full-time 4.

Programs and Degrees Offered:

Listed in the following order: Program area, degree type (T if terminal Master's), number awarded 7/11–6/12. Human Development and Family Studies PhD (Doctor of Philosophy) 14.

Student Applications/Admissions:

Student Applications

Human Development and Family Studies PhD (Doctor of Philosophy)—Applications 2012–2013, 101. Total applicants accepted 2012–2013, 25. Number full-time enrolled (new admits only) 2012–2013, 13. Number part-time enrolled (new admits only) 2012–2013, 0. Total enrolled 2012–2013 full-time, 69. Total enrolled 2012–2013 part-time, 0. Openings 2013–2014, 15. The median number of years required for completion of a degree in 2012–2013 were 5. The number of students enrolled full- and part-time who were dismissed or voluntarily withdrew from this program area in 2012–2013 were 0.

Scores: Entries appear in this order: required test or GPA, minimum score (if required), median score of students entering in 2012–2013. *Human Development and Family Studies PhD (Doctor of Philosophy):* GRE-V no minimum stated, 160, GRE-Q no minimum stated, 148, GRE-Analytical no minimum stated, 5, overall undergraduate GPA no minimum stated, last 2 years GPA no minimum stated.

Other Criteria: (importance of criteria rated low, medium, or high): GRE scores—high, research experience—high, work experience—low, extracurricular activity—low, GPA—high, letters of recommendation—high, interview—low, statement of goals and objectives—high, writing sample—high. For additional information on admission requirements, go to http://www.hhdev.psu.edu/hdfs/graduate/apply.

Student Characteristics: The following represents characteristics of students in 2012–2013 in all graduate psychology programs in the department: Female—full-time 60, part-time 0; Male—full-time 9, part-time 0; African American/Black—full-time 2, part-time 0; Hispanic/Latino(a)—full-time 2, part-time 0; Asian/Pacific Islander—full-time 19, part-time 0; American Indian/Alaska Native—full-time 0, part-time 0; Caucasian/White—full-time 46, part-time 0; Multi-ethnic—full-time 0, part-time 0; students subject to the Americans With Disabilities Act—full-time 0, part-time 0; Unknown ethnicity—full-time 0, part-time 0; International students who hold an F-1 or J-1 Visa—full-time 14, part-time 0.

Financial Information/Assistance:

Tuition for Full-Time Study: *Doctoral:* State residents: per academic year $17,177, $716 per credit hour; Nonstate residents: per academic year $29,656, $1,236 per credit hour. Tuition is subject to change. See the following website for updates and changes in tuition costs: http://tuition.psu.edu.

Financial Assistance:

First-Year Students: Teaching assistantships available for first year. Average amount paid per academic year: $16,425. Average number of hours worked per week: 20. Apply by January 15. Research assistantships available for first year. Average amount paid per academic year: $16,425. Average number of hours worked per week: 20. Apply by January 15. Fellowships and scholarships available for first year. Average amount paid per academic year: $17,270. Average number of hours worked per week: 10. Apply by January 15.

Advanced Students: Teaching assistantships available for advanced students. Average amount paid per academic year: $16,425. Average number of hours worked per week: 20. Research assistantships available for advanced students. Average amount paid per academic year: $16,425. Average number of hours worked per week: 20. Fellowships and scholarships available for advanced students. Average amount paid per academic year: $17,955.

Additional Information: Of all students currently enrolled full time, 100% benefited from one or more of the listed financial assistance programs. Application and information available online at: http://www.hhdev.psu.edu/hdfs/graduate/aid.

Housing and Day Care: On-campus housing is available. See the following website for more information: http://www.housing.psu.edu/housing/housing/graduate-and-family-housing/index.cfm. On-campus day care facilities are available. See the following website for more information: http://childcare.psu.edu/.

Employment of Department Graduates:

Master's Degree Graduates: Of those who graduated in the academic year 2011–2012, the following categories and numbers represent the postgraduate activities and employment of master's degree graduates: Enrolled in a postdoctoral residency/fellowship (n/a), employed in independent practice (n/a), total from the above (master's) (0).

Doctoral Degree Graduates: Of those who graduated in the academic year 2011–2012, the following categories and numbers represent the postgraduate activities and employment of doctoral degree graduates: Enrolled in a psychology doctoral program (n/a), enrolled in a postdoctoral residency/fellowship (8), employed in an academic position at a university (1), employed in other positions at a higher education institution (1), employed in a hospital/medical center (1), still seeking employment (3), total from the above (doctoral) (14).

Additional Information:

Orientation, Objectives, and Emphasis of Department: The basic objectives of the human development and family studies (HDFS) program are the following: to expand knowledge about the development and functioning of individuals, small groups, and families; to improve methods for studying processes of human development and change; and to create and disseminate improved techniques and strategies for enhancing individual and family functioning, helping people learn to cope more effectively with problems of living, and preventing normal life problems from becoming serious difficulties. The program takes a life-span perspective, recognizing that the most important aspects of development and types of life tasks and situations vary from infancy and childhood through maturity and old age, as well as through the life cycle of the family, and that each phase of development is a precursor to the next. There is a firm commitment to an interdisciplinary and multiprofessional approach to these objectives and to the development of competence in applying rigorous methods of empirical inquiry. All students are expected to acquire a broad interdisciplinary base of knowledge and to develop competence in depth in one of four primary program areas: family development, individual development, human development intervention, or methodology.

Special Facilities or Resources: Several additional facilities are associated with the College of Health and Human Development that provide significant resources to our Department, in terms of graduate training opportunities and student funding. These include the Child Development Laboratory and Bennett Family Center, which are high quality early child care programs providing care to children from early infancy through kindergarten. Each unit has observational rooms for the study of individual and group behavior of children and adults. Our students also avail themselves of the resources provided by several College-based centers, including the Prevention Research Center for the Promotion of Human Development, the Methodology Center, the Methodology Consulting Center, the Center for Childhood Obesity, and the Center for Healthy Aging. All of these centers are directed by HDFS faculty and provide a variety of funding and training opportunities for our graduate students. The Centers are direct outgrowths of our program's four core areas: Individual Development, Prevention/ Intervention, Methodology, and Family Development.

Information for Students With Physical Disabilities: See the following website for more information: http://equity.psu.edu/ods.

Application Information:
Send to Graduate Admissions c/o Mary Jo Spicer, Penn State University, Department of Human Development and Family Studies, S211 Henderson Building, University Park, PA 16802. Application available online. URL of online application: http://www.gradsch.psu.edu/portal/. Students are admitted in the Fall, application deadline January 15. *Fee:* $65.

Pennsylvania State University

Department of Psychology
140 Moore Building
University Park, PA 16802-3104
Telephone: (814) 863-1721
Fax: (814) 863-7002
E-mail: *sbg4@psu.edu*
Web: *http://psych.la.psu.edu*

Department Information:
1933. Professor and Head: Melvin M. Mark. Number of faculty: total—full-time 72, part-time 3; women—full-time 36, part-time 2; total—minority—full-time 11; women minority—full-time 7.

Programs and Degrees Offered:
Listed in the following order: Program area, degree type (T if terminal Master's), number awarded 7/11–6/12. Clinical Psychology PhD (Doctor of Philosophy) 7, Clinical Child Psychology PhD (Doctor of Philosophy) 6, Cognitive Psychology PhD (Doctor of Philosophy) 0, Developmental Psychology PhD (Doctor of Philosophy) 2, Industrial/Organizational Psychology PhD (Doctor of Philosophy) 3, Social Psychology PhD (Doctor of Philosophy) 2.

APA Accreditation: Clinical PhD (Doctor of Philosophy). Student Outcome Data Website: http://psych.la.psu.edu/graduate/programAreas/clinicalProgram.html.

Student Applications/Admissions:
Student Applications
Clinical Psychology PhD (Doctor of Philosophy)—Applications 2012–2013, 297. Total applicants accepted 2012–2013, 6.

Number full-time enrolled (new admits only) 2012–2013, 6. Total enrolled 2012–2013 full-time, 24. Total enrolled 2012–2013 part-time, 2. Openings 2013–2014, 6. The median number of years required for completion of a degree in 2012–2013 were 7. The number of students enrolled full- and part-time who were dismissed or voluntarily withdrew from this program area in 2012–2013 were 0. *Clinical Child Psychology PhD (Doctor of Philosophy)*—Applications 2012–2013, 211. Total applicants accepted 2012–2013, 5. Number full-time enrolled (new admits only) 2012–2013, 5. Total enrolled 2012–2013 full-time, 17. Openings 2013–2014, 5. The median number of years required for completion of a degree in 2012–2013 were 7. The number of students enrolled full- and part-time who were dismissed or voluntarily withdrew from this program area in 2012–2013 were 1. *Cognitive Psychology PhD (Doctor of Philosophy)*—Applications 2012–2013, 54. Total applicants accepted 2012–2013, 5. Number full-time enrolled (new admits only) 2012–2013, 5. Total enrolled 2012–2013 full-time, 15. Total enrolled 2012–2013 part-time, 1. Openings 2013–2014, 5. The number of students enrolled full- and part-time who were dismissed or voluntarily withdrew from this program area in 2012–2013 were 1. *Developmental Psychology PhD (Doctor of Philosophy)*—Applications 2012–2013, 38. Total applicants accepted 2012–2013, 5. Number full-time enrolled (new admits only) 2012–2013, 5. Total enrolled 2012–2013 full-time, 11. Total enrolled 2012–2013 part-time, 0. Openings 2013–2014, 5. The median number of years required for completion of a degree in 2012–2013 were 4. The number of students enrolled full- and part-time who were dismissed or voluntarily withdrew from this program area in 2012–2013 were 0. *Industrial/Organizational Psychology PhD (Doctor of Philosophy)*—Applications 2012–2013, 152. Total applicants accepted 2012–2013, 6. Number full-time enrolled (new admits only) 2012–2013, 6. Total enrolled 2012–2013 full-time, 22. Total enrolled 2012–2013 part-time, 0. Openings 2013–2014, 4. The median number of years required for completion of a degree in 2012–2013 were 4. The number of students enrolled full- and part-time who were dismissed or voluntarily withdrew from this program area in 2012–2013 were 0. *Social Psychology PhD (Doctor of Philosophy)*—Applications 2012–2013, 85. Total applicants accepted 2012–2013, 5. Number full-time enrolled (new admits only) 2012–2013, 5. Total enrolled 2012–2013 full-time, 10. Total enrolled 2012–2013 part-time, 1. Openings 2013–2014, 5. The median number of years required for completion of a degree in 2012–2013 were 6. The number of students enrolled full- and part-time who were dismissed or voluntarily withdrew from this program area in 2012–2013 were 1.

Scores: Entries appear in this order: required test or GPA, minimum score (if required), median score of students entering in 2012–2013. *Clinical Psychology PhD (Doctor of Philosophy):* GRE-V no minimum stated, GRE-Q no minimum stated; *Clinical Child Psychology PhD (Doctor of Philosophy):* GRE-V no minimum stated, GRE-Q no minimum stated.

Other Criteria: (importance of criteria rated low, medium, or high): GRE scores—high, research experience—high, work experience—medium, extracurricular activity—low, clinically related public service—medium, GPA—high, letters of recommendation—high, interview—high, statement of goals and objectives—high, undergraduate major in psychology—medium, specific undergraduate psychology courses taken—medium, Clinical weighs work, clinical experience, and interviews heavily; other areas do not weight these factors strongly. For additional information on admission requirements, go to http://psych.la.psu.edu/graduate/howToApply.html.

Student Characteristics: The following represents characteristics of students in 2012–2013 in all graduate psychology programs in the department: Female—full-time 84, part-time 2; Male—full-time 45, part-time 0; African American/Black—full-time 6, part-time 0; Hispanic/Latino(a)—full-time 8, part-time 0; Asian/Pacific Islander—full-time 17, part-time 1; American Indian/Alaska Native—full-time 0, part-time 0; Caucasian/White—full-time 100, part-time 1; Multi-ethnic—full-time 0, part-time 0; students subject to the Americans With Disabilities Act—full-time 0, part-time 0; Unknown ethnicity—full-time 2, part-time 0; International students who hold an F-1 or J-1 Visa—full-time 12, part-time 0.

Financial Information/Assistance:

Tuition for Full-Time Study: *Doctoral:* State residents: per academic year $17,670; Nonstate residents: per academic year $30,374. Tuition is subject to change. See the following website for updates and changes in tuition costs: http://tuition.psu.edu/.

Financial Assistance:

First-Year Students: Teaching assistantships available for first year. Average amount paid per academic year: $16,920. Average number of hours worked per week: 20. Apply by December 1. Research assistantships available for first year. Average amount paid per academic year: $16,920. Average number of hours worked per week: 20. Apply by December 1. Fellowships and scholarships available for first year. Average amount paid per academic year: $21,000. Average number of hours worked per week: 0. Apply by December 1.

Advanced Students: Teaching assistantships available for advanced students. Average amount paid per academic year: $16,920. Average number of hours worked per week: 20. Research assistantships available for advanced students. Average amount paid per academic year: $16,920. Average number of hours worked per week: 20. Fellowships and scholarships available for advanced students. Average amount paid per academic year: $21,000. Average number of hours worked per week: 0.

Additional Information: Of all students currently enrolled full time, 90% benefited from one or more of the listed financial assistance programs. Application and information available online at: http://psych.la.psu.edu/graduate/funding-students.html.

Internships/Practica: Doctoral Degree (PhD Clinical Psychology): For those doctoral students for whom a professional psychology internship was required in this program prior to graduation, (7) students applied for an internship in 2011–2012, with (7) students obtaining an internship. Of those students who obtained an internship, (7) were paid internships. Of those students who obtained an internship, (7) students placed in APA/CPA accredited internships, (0) students placed in internships not APA/CPA accredited, but listed with the Association of Psychology Postdoctoral and Internship Programs (APPIC), (0) students placed in internships conforming to guidelines of the Council of Directors of School Psychology Programs (CDSPP), (0) students placed in internships that were not APA/CPA accredited, APPIC or CDSPP listed. Doctoral Degree (PhD Clinical Child Psychology): For those doctoral students for whom a professional psychology internship was required in this program prior to graduation,

(1) students applied for an internship in 2011–2012, with (1) students obtaining an internship. Of those students who obtained an internship, (1) were paid internships. Of those students who obtained an internship, (1) students placed in APA/CPA accredited internships, (0) students placed in internships not APA/CPA accredited, but listed with the Association of Psychology Postdoctoral and Internship Programs (APPIC), (0) students placed in internships conforming to guidelines of the Council of Directors of School Psychology Programs (CDSPP), (0) students placed in internships that were not APA/CPA accredited, APPIC or CDSPP listed.

Housing and Day Care: On-campus housing is available. See the following website for more information: http://www.hfs.psu.edu/housing/housing/graduate-and-family-housing/index.cfm. On-campus day care facilities are available. See the following website for more information: http://childcare.psu.edu/.

Employment of Department Graduates:

Master's Degree Graduates: Of those who graduated in the academic year 2011–2012, the following categories and numbers represent the postgraduate activities and employment of master's degree graduates: Enrolled in a postdoctoral residency/fellowship (n/a), employed in independent practice (n/a), total from the above (master's) (0).

Doctoral Degree Graduates: Of those who graduated in the academic year 2011–2012, the following categories and numbers represent the postgraduate activities and employment of doctoral degree graduates: Enrolled in a psychology doctoral program (n/a), enrolled in a postdoctoral residency/fellowship (9), employed in an academic position at a university (6), employed in business or industry (2), other employment position (1), total from the above (doctoral) (18).

Additional Information:

Orientation, Objectives, and Emphasis of Department: Graduate study in psychology at Penn State is characterized by highly flexible, individualized programs leading to the PhD in Psychology. Each student is associated with one of the five program areas offered in the department: clinical (including child clinical); cognitive; developmental; industrial/organizational; and social. Students in any program area may combine their program of study with a specialization in behavioral neuroscience by choosing appropriate courses and seminars. Students choosing this specialization may pursue the integration of neuroscience methods and theories by applying these approaches to research topics within their program areas. Within each area, certain courses are usually suggested for all students. The details of a student's program, however, are worked out on an individual basis with a faculty advisor. A major specialization and breadth outside the major are required. The major is selected from among the six specialty areas of the department listed above; breadth requirements are flexible and individualized to career goals. Depending upon the individual student's particular program of study, graduates may be employed in academic departments, research institutes, industry, governmental agencies, or various service delivery settings.

Special Facilities or Resources: The department has clinical, learning-cognition, perception, physiological, psychophysiology, developmental and social laboratories; microcomputer laboratories; access to the University's mainframe and electronic communication system (e-mail and Internet) and computer laboratories; clinical practica in local mental health centers and hospitals in addition to the department's Psychological Clinic, which functions as a mental health center for the catchment area of central Pennsylvania; industrial/organizational practica in industrial and government organizations; developmental practica and research opportunities in day care and preschool settings. A number of centers or institutes are housed within, or affiliated with the department, including a new Child Study Center.

Information for Students With Physical Disabilities: See the following website for more information: http://equity.psu.edu/ods.

Application Information:

Send to Graduate Admissions, Department of Psychology, Penn State University, 132 Moore Building, University Park, PA 16802. Application available online. URL of online application: http://www.gradsch. psu.edu/prospective/apply.html. Students are admitted in the Fall, application deadline December 1. *Fee:* $65.

Pennsylvania, University of
Applied Psychology-Human Development Division
Graduate School of Education
3700 Walnut Street
Philadelphia, PA 19104-6216
Telephone: (215) 898-4176
Fax: (215) 573-2115
E-mail: *rhambeau@gse.upenn.edu*
Web: *http://www.gse.upenn.edu/aphd/*

Department Information:

1975. Chairperson: Michael J. Nakkula, Ed.D. Number of faculty: total—full-time 10, part-time 20; women—full-time 5, part-time 12; total—minority—full-time 4, part-time 10; women minority—full-time 2, part-time 4.

Programs and Degrees Offered:

Listed in the following order: Program area, degree type (T if terminal Master's), number awarded 7/11–6/12. Counseling and Psychological Services MEd (Education) 54, Interdisciplinary Studies in Human Development MA/MS (Master of Arts/Science) 11, Interdisciplinary Studies in Human Development PhD (Doctor of Philosophy) 7, Professional Counseling and Psychology Other 12, School Counseling Certification Other 0, School & Mental Health Counseling MEd (Education) 19.

Student Applications/Admissions:
Student Applications

Counseling and Psychological Services MEd (Education)—Applications 2012–2013, 252. Total applicants accepted 2012–2013, 118. Number full-time enrolled (new admits only) 2012–2013, 36. Number part-time enrolled (new admits only) 2012–2013, 9. Total enrolled 2012–2013 full-time, 110. Total enrolled 2012–2013 part-time, 8. Openings 2013–2014, 35. The median number of years required for completion of a degree in 2012–2013 was 1. The number of students enrolled full- and part-time who were dismissed or voluntarily withdrew from this program area in 2012–2013 were 0. *Interdisciplinary Studies in Human Development MA/MS (Master of Arts/Science)*—Applications 2012–2013, 80. Total applicants accepted

2012–2013, 68. Number full-time enrolled (new admits only) 2012–2013, 17. Number part-time enrolled (new admits only) 2012–2013, 2. Total enrolled 2012–2013 full-time, 17. Total enrolled 2012–2013 part-time, 13. Openings 2013–2014, 25. The median number of years required for completion of a degree in 2012–2013 was 1. *Interdisciplinary Studies in Human Development PhD (Doctor of Philosophy)*—Applications 2012–2013, 80. Total applicants accepted 2012–2013, 68. Number full-time enrolled (new admits only) 2012–2013, 1. Number part-time enrolled (new admits only) 2012–2013, 0. Total enrolled 2012–2013 full-time, 9. Total enrolled 2012–2013 part-time, 0. Openings 2013–2014, 4. The median number of years required for completion of a degree in 2012–2013 were 5. *Professional Counseling and Psychology Other*—Applications 2012–2013, 27. Total applicants accepted 2012–2013, 27. Number full-time enrolled (new admits only) 2012–2013, 10. Number part-time enrolled (new admits only) 2012–2013, 3. Total enrolled 2012–2013 full-time, 10. Total enrolled 2012–2013 part-time, 3. Openings 2013–2014, 25. The median number of years required for completion of a degree in 2012–2013 were 2. The number of students enrolled full- and part-time who were dismissed or voluntarily withdrew from this program area in 2012–2013 were 0. *School Counseling Certification Other*—Applications 2012–2013, 13. Total applicants accepted 2012–2013, 12. Number full-time enrolled (new admits only) 2012–2013, 12. Number part-time enrolled (new admits only) 2012–2013, 0. Total enrolled 2012–2013 full-time, 12. Total enrolled 2012–2013 part-time, 0. Openings 2013–2014, 20. The median number of years required for completion of a degree in 2012–2013 were 2. *School & Mental Health Counseling MEd (Education)*—Applications 2012–2013, 40. Total applicants accepted 2012–2013, 35. Number full-time enrolled (new admits only) 2012–2013, 55. Number part-time enrolled (new admits only) 2012–2013, 0. Total enrolled 2012–2013 full-time, 55. Total enrolled 2012–2013 part-time, 0. Openings 2013–2014, 35. The median number of years required for completion of a degree in 2012–2013 were 2. The number of students enrolled full- and part-time who were dismissed or voluntarily withdrew from this program area in 2012–2013 were 1.

Scores: Entries appear in this order: required test or GPA, minimum score (if required), median score of students entering in 2012–2013. *Counseling and Psychological Services MEd (Education):* GRE-V no minimum stated, GRE-Q no minimum stated, GRE-Analytical no minimum stated; *Interdisciplinary Studies in Human Development MA/MS (Master of Arts/Science):* GRE-V no minimum stated, GRE-Q no minimum stated, GRE-Analytical no minimum stated; *Interdisciplinary Studies in Human Development PhD (Doctor of Philosophy):* GRE-V no minimum stated, GRE-Q no minimum stated, GRE-Analytical no minimum stated, GRE-Subject (Psychology) no minimum stated; *Professional Counseling and Psychology Other:* GRE-V no minimum stated, GRE-Q no minimum stated, GRE-Analytical no minimum stated; *School Counseling Certification Other:* GRE-V no minimum stated, GRE-Q no minimum stated, GRE-Analytical no minimum stated.

Other Criteria: (importance of criteria rated low, medium, or high): GRE scores—high, research experience—medium, work experience—medium, extracurricular activity—medium, clinically related public service—medium, GPA—high, letters of recommendation—high, interview—high, statement of goals and objectives—high, undergraduate major in psychology—medium, specific undergraduate psychology courses taken—medium. For additional information on admission requirements, go to http://www.gse.upenn.edu/admissions_financial/instructions.

Student Characteristics: The following represents characteristics of students in 2012–2013 in all graduate psychology programs in the department: Female—full-time 110, part-time 17; Male—full-time 14, part-time 3; African American/Black—full-time 19, part-time 1; Hispanic/Latino(a)—full-time 7, part-time 0; Asian/Pacific Islander—full-time 16, part-time 7; American Indian/Alaska Native—full-time 0, part-time 0; Caucasian/White—full-time 72, part-time 12; Multi-ethnic—full-time 6, part-time 0; students subject to the Americans With Disabilities Act—full-time 4, part-time 0; Unknown ethnicity—full-time 4, part-time 0; International students who hold an F-1 or J-1 Visa—full-time 8, part-time 3.

Financial Information/Assistance:

Tuition for Full-Time Study: *Master's:* State residents: per academic year $39,914; Nonstate residents: per academic year $39,914. *Doctoral:* State residents: per academic year $28,768; Nonstate residents: per academic year $28,768. Tuition costs vary by program. See the following website for updates and changes in tuition costs: http://www.gse.upenn.edu/admissions_financial/tuition.

Financial Assistance:

First-Year Students: Teaching assistantships available for first year. Average number of hours worked per week: 20. Apply by December 15. Research assistantships available for first year. Average number of hours worked per week: 20. Apply by December 15. Fellowships and scholarships available for first year. Average number of hours worked per week: 20. Apply by December 15.

Advanced Students: Teaching assistantships available for advanced students. Average number of hours worked per week: 20. Research assistantships available for advanced students. Average number of hours worked per week: 20. Fellowships and scholarships available for advanced students. Average number of hours worked per week: 20.

Additional Information: Of all students currently enrolled full time, 85% benefited from one or more of the listed financial assistance programs. Application and information available online at: http://www.gse.upenn.edu/admissions_financial/finaid.

Internships/Practica: Masters students in Counseling and Psychological Services engage in supervised practica for 8 hours a week for two semesters. Placements include schools, community colleges, career services, clinics, and community agencies. MPhil students are required to complete a supervised two-semester, 20-hour per week internship. The Executive Program in School and Mental Health Counseling is an executive-style master's-degree program for working educators and professionals interested in working as school counselors or Licensed Professional Counselors. The program requires a practicum and an internship.

Housing and Day Care: On-campus housing is available. See the following website for more information: http://www.business-services.upenn.edu/housing/. On-campus day care facilities are available. See the following website for more information: http://cms.business-services.upenn.edu/childcare/.

Employment of Department Graduates:

Master's Degree Graduates: Of those who graduated in the academic year 2011–2012, the following categories and numbers represent the postgraduate activities and employment of master's degree graduates: Enrolled in a postdoctoral residency/fellowship (n/a), employed in independent practice (n/a), employed in an academic position at a university (5), employed in a professional position in a school system (3), employed in business or industry (4), total from the above (master's) (12).

Doctoral Degree Graduates: Of those who graduated in the academic year 2011–2012, the following categories and numbers represent the postgraduate activities and employment of doctoral degree graduates: Enrolled in a psychology doctoral program (n/a), total from the above (doctoral) (0).

Additional Information:

Orientation, Objectives, and Emphasis of Department: Our programs provide a foundation in the core concepts of applied psychology: intervention, prevention, assessment, learning/development, and applied practice and/or research, for careers in counseling, mental health, teaching, and research in various settings. The one-year Counseling and Psychological Services (CAPS) master's program prepares students in the foundations of providing supportive services. The MPhil program in Professional Counseling and Psychology is a continuation for current CAPS students. The Executive Program in School & Mental Health Counseling (SMHC) enables students with full time careers to earn their degree in two years through one-weekend-a-month and one-week-in-summer sessions. The MPhil and SMHC programs prepare students for guidance counseling certification and/or licensure as a professional counselor. The Interdisciplinary Studies in Human Development PhD and MSEd programs combine the study of social, emotional, cognitive, and physical aspects of human development that are focused on urban populations, considered within eco-cultural contexts, and relevant to social policies. Students create a specialized program of study of human development across the lifespan. Career interests: traditional academic appointment; youth programming /services; urban/ethnic studies; adult development/learning; corporate human resources development; international programming (e.g., work with NGOs); foundation administration/program development; collaborative efforts/health care facilities.

Special Facilities or Resources: Penn GSE houses state-of-the-art computer labs and classrooms, student lounges, and offers wireless access. Many opportunities exist for students to participate in the Faculty's new and ongoing research that address issues of local, national and international populations.

Information for Students With Physical Disabilities: See the following website for more information: http://www.vpul.upenn.edu/lrc/sds/.

Application Information:

Send to Admissions Office, Graduate School of Education, University of Pennsylvania, 3700 Walnut Street, Philadelphia, PA 19104-6216. Application available online. URL of online application: http://www.gse.upenn.edu/admissions_financial. Students are admitted in the Fall, application deadline December 15; Programs have rolling admissions. Deadline for applications to the PhD program in Interdisciplinary Studies in Human Development is December 15. Executive Program in School and Mental Health Counseling MSEd deadline is June

15. Counseling and Psychological Services, MSEd, Interdisciplinary Studies in Human Development MSEd and Professional Counseling and Psychology MPhil applications are accepted on a rolling basis for Fall Admission only. *Fee:* $0.

Pennsylvania, University of

Department of Psychology
3720 Walnut Street
Philadelphia, PA 19104
Telephone: (215) 898-7300
Fax: (215) 898-7301
E-mail: *grad_coordinator@psych.upenn.edu*
Web: *http://psychology.sas.upenn.edu/graduate*

Department Information:

1887. Chairperson: Dr. Robert DeRubeis. Number of faculty: total—full-time 31; women—full-time 12; total—minority—full-time 2; women minority—full-time 2.

Programs and Degrees Offered:

Listed in the following order: Program area, degree type (T if terminal Master's), number awarded 7/11–6/12. Psychology PhD (Doctor of Philosophy) 5, Clinical Psychology PhD (Doctor of Philosophy) 2.

APA Accreditation: Clinical PhD (Doctor of Philosophy). Student Outcome Data Website: http://psychology.sas.upenn.edu/graduate/resareas/cppp.

Student Applications/Admissions:

Student Applications

Psychology PhD (Doctor of Philosophy)—Applications 2012–2013, 310. Total applicants accepted 2012–2013, 20. Number full-time enrolled (new admits only) 2012–2013, 12. Total enrolled 2012–2013 full-time, 41. Openings 2013–2014, 6. The median number of years required for completion of a degree in 2012–2013 were 5. The number of students enrolled full- and part-time who were dismissed or voluntarily withdrew from this program area in 2012–2013 were 2. *Clinical Psychology PhD (Doctor of Philosophy)*—Applications 2012–2013, 444. Total applicants accepted 2012–2013, 8. Number full-time enrolled (new admits only) 2012–2013, 5. Number part-time enrolled (new admits only) 2012–2013, 0. Total enrolled 2012–2013 full-time, 19. Total enrolled 2012–2013 part-time, 0. Openings 2013–2014, 4. The median number of years required for completion of a degree in 2012–2013 were 6. The number of students enrolled full- and part-time who were dismissed or voluntarily withdrew from this program area in 2012–2013 were 0.

Scores: Entries appear in this order: required test or GPA, minimum score (if required), median score of students entering in 2012–2013. *Psychology PhD (Doctor of Philosophy):* GRE-V no minimum stated, 165, GRE-Q no minimum stated, 159, GRE-Analytical no minimum stated, 5.0, overall undergraduate GPA no minimum stated, 3.8; *Clinical Psychology PhD (Doctor of Philosophy):* GRE-V no minimum stated, 730, GRE-Q no minimum stated, 750, GRE-Analytical no minimum stated, overall undergraduate GPA no minimum stated, 3.87.

Other Criteria: (importance of criteria rated low, medium, or high): GRE scores—medium, research experience—high, work experience—low, clinically related public service—low, GPA—medium, letters of recommendation—high, interview—medium, statement of goals and objectives—high, specific undergraduate psychology courses taken—low. For additional information on admission requirements, go to http://psychology.sas.upenn.edu/graduate/applicants.

Student Characteristics: The following represents characteristics of students in 2012–2013 in all graduate psychology programs in the department: Female—full-time 42, part-time 0; Male—full-time 18, part-time 0; African American/Black—full-time 0, part-time 0; Hispanic/Latino(a)—full-time 2, part-time 0; Asian/Pacific Islander—full-time 8, part-time 0; American Indian/Alaska Native—full-time 0, part-time 0; Caucasian/White—full-time 46, part-time 0; Multi-ethnic—full-time 4, part-time 0; students subject to the Americans With Disabilities Act—full-time 0, part-time 0; Unknown ethnicity—full-time 0, part-time 0; International students who hold an F-1 or J-1 Visa—full-time 12, part-time 0.

Financial Information/Assistance:

Financial Assistance:

First-Year Students: Traineeships available for first year. Apply by December 15. Fellowships and scholarships available for first year. Apply by December 15.

Advanced Students: Teaching assistantships available for advanced students. Apply by December 15. Research assistantships available for advanced students. Apply by December 15. Traineeships available for advanced students. Apply by December 15. Fellowships and scholarships available for advanced students. Apply by December 15.

Additional Information: Of all students currently enrolled full time, 100% benefited from one or more of the listed financial assistance programs. Application and information available online at: http://psychology.sas.upenn.edu/graduate/applicants.

Internships/Practica: Doctoral Degree (PhD Clinical Psychology): For those doctoral students for whom a professional psychology internship was required in this program prior to graduation, (2) students applied for an internship in 2011–2012, with (2) students obtaining an internship. Of those students who obtained an internship, (2) were paid internships. Of those students who obtained an internship, (2) students placed in APA/CPA accredited internships, (0) students placed in internships not APA/CPA accredited, but listed with the Association of Psychology Postdoctoral and Internship Programs (APPIC), (0) students placed in internships conforming to guidelines of the Council of Directors of School Psychology Programs (CDSPP), (0) students placed in internships that were not APA/CPA accredited, APPIC or CDSPP listed. Because of the wealth of opportunities for clinical training in the Philadelphia area, Penn does not run an in-house psychological services clinic. Rather, Penn's clinical students have the opportunity to participate in practica at local hospitals, clinics and research facilities staffed and run by world-renowned clinical scientists. The Associate Director of Clinical Training helps students decide which practicum experiences best suit the student's needs and interests, and arranges for placements at the appropriate sites.

Housing and Day Care: On-campus housing is available. See the following website for more information: http://www.upenn.edu/

housing. On-campus day care facilities are available. See the following website for more information: http://www.upenn.edu/childcare/.

Employment of Department Graduates:

Master's Degree Graduates: Of those who graduated in the academic year 2011–2012, the following categories and numbers represent the postgraduate activities and employment of master's degree graduates: Enrolled in a postdoctoral residency/fellowship (n/a), employed in independent practice (n/a), total from the above (master's) (0).

Doctoral Degree Graduates: Of those who graduated in the academic year 2011–2012, the following categories and numbers represent the postgraduate activities and employment of doctoral degree graduates: Enrolled in a psychology doctoral program (n/a), enrolled in a postdoctoral residency/fellowship (4), employed in an academic position at a university (1), employed in a professional position in a school system (1), employed in business or industry (1), total from the above (doctoral) (7).

Additional Information:

Orientation, Objectives, and Emphasis of Department: The Department of Psychology at the University of Pennsylvania offers curricular and research opportunities for the study of sensation, perception, cognition, cognitive neuroscience, decision-making, language, learning, motivation, emotion, motor control, psychopathology, and social processes. Biological, cultural, developmental, comparative, experimental, and mathematical approaches to these areas are used in ongoing teaching and research. The department has an APA-accredited clinical program that is designed to prepare students for research careers in interventions, psychopathology and personality. The interests of the faculty and students in the department cover the entire field of research-oriented psychology. Still, the Department of Psychology at Pennsylvania functions as a single unit whose guiding principle is scientific excellence. Students are admitted to the department. The primary determinant of acceptance is academic promise rather than specific area of interest. Faculty join together from different subdisciplines for teaching and research purposes so that students become conversant with issues in a number of different areas. A high level of interaction among department members (students and faculty), within and across disciplines, helps generate both a shared set of interests in the theoretical, historical, and philosophical foundations of psychology and active collaboration in research projects. The first-year program is divided between courses that introduce various areas of psychology and a focused research experience. A deep involvement in research continues throughout the graduate program, and is supplemented by participation in seminars, the weekly departmental colloquium, teaching, and general intellectual give and take.

Special Facilities or Resources: The department has facilities for functional magnetic resonance imaging, transcranial magnetic stimulation, high density electroencephalograhy and magneto encephalography, high speed computing capabilities, and high frequency electrophysiology recording. In addition, the department supports a fully equipped wood, metal, and electronics shop. Also readily available for research in the near environs of the department are 4 major University-affiliated hospitals, urban public and private schools.

Information for Students With Physical Disabilities: See the following website for more information: http://www.vpul.upenn.edu/lrc/sds/index.html.

Application Information:

Send to Graduate School of Arts and Sciences, 3401 Walnut Street, Suite 322A, Philadelphia, PA 19104. Application available online. URL of online application: https://app.applyyourself.com/?id=upenn-g. Students are admitted in the Fall, application deadline December 15. *Fee:* $80.

Philadelphia College of Osteopathic Medicine
Psychology Department
4190 City Avenue
Philadelphia, PA 19131-1693
Telephone: (215) 871-6442
Fax: (215) 871-6458
E-mail: *RobertD@pcom.edu*
Web: *http://www.pcom.edu*

Department Information:

1995. Chairperson: Robert A. DiTomasso, PhD, ABPP. Number of faculty: total—full-time 19, part-time 81; women—full-time 12, part-time 50; total—minority—full-time 3, part-time 13; women minority—full-time 1, part-time 7.

Programs and Degrees Offered:

Listed in the following order: Program area, degree type (T if terminal Master's), number awarded 7/11–6/12. Psychology Cags Other 10, Counseling & Clinical Health Psychology MA/MS (Master of Arts/Science) (T) 28, Clinical Psychology Respecialization Diploma 1, Clinical Psychology PsyD (Doctor of Psychology) 27, Organizational Development and Leadership - Pa MA/MS (Master of Arts/Science) (T) 11, School Psychology MA/MS (Master of Arts/Science) (T) 18, School Psychology EdS (School Psychology) 21, School Psychology PsyD (Doctor of Psychology) 21, School Psychology Respecialization Diploma 0, Clinical Health Psychology Certificate Other 0, Clinical Neuropsychology Certificate Other 1, Organizational Development and Leadership - Ga MA/MS (Master of Arts/Science) (T) 0.

APA Accreditation: Clinical PsyD (Doctor of Psychology). Student Outcome Data Website: http://www.pcom.edu/Academic_Programs/aca_psych/PsyD_in_Clinical_Psychology/APA_Disclosure_Statements.html.

Student Applications/Admissions:

Student Applications

Psychology Cags Other—Applications 2012–2013, 16. Total applicants accepted 2012–2013, 11. Number full-time enrolled (new admits only) 2012–2013, 11. Total enrolled 2012–2013 full-time, 11. Openings 2013–2014, 15. The median number of years required for completion of a degree in 2012–2013 was 1. The number of students enrolled full- and part-time who were dismissed or voluntarily withdrew from this program area in 2012–2013 were 0. *Counseling & Clinical Health Psychology MA/MS (Master of Arts/Science)*—Applications 2012–2013, 140. Total applicants accepted 2012–2013, 60. Number full-time enrolled (new admits only) 2012–2013, 35. Number part-time enrolled (new admits only) 2012–2013, 3. Total enrolled 2012–2013 full-time, 61. Total enrolled 2012–2013 part-time, 13. Openings 2013–2014, 32. The median number of years required for completion of a degree in 2012–2013 were 2. The number of students enrolled full- and part-time who were dismissed or voluntarily withdrew from this program area in 2012–2013 were 2. *Clinical Psychology Respecialization Diploma*—Applications 2012–2013, 2. Total applicants accepted 2012–2013, 0. Number full-time enrolled (new admits only) 2012–2013, 0. Number part-time enrolled (new admits only) 2012–2013, 0. Openings 2013–2014, 2. The median number of years required for completion of a degree in 2012–2013 were 5. The number of students enrolled full- and part-time who were dismissed or voluntarily withdrew from this program area in 2012–2013 were 0. *Clinical Psychology PsyD (Doctor of Psychology)*—Number full-time enrolled (new admits only) 2012–2013, 29. Number part-time enrolled (new admits only) 2012–2013, 0. Total enrolled 2012–2013 full-time, 136. Total enrolled 2012–2013 part-time, 0. Openings 2013–2014, 28. The median number of years required for completion of a degree in 2012–2013 were 5. The number of students enrolled full- and part-time who were dismissed or voluntarily withdrew from this program area in 2012–2013 were 0. *Organizational Development and Leadership - Pa MA/MS (Master of Arts/Science)*—Applications 2012–2013, 32. Total applicants accepted 2012–2013, 22. Number full-time enrolled (new admits only) 2012–2013, 10. Number part-time enrolled (new admits only) 2012–2013, 7. Total enrolled 2012–2013 full-time, 30. Total enrolled 2012–2013 part-time, 22. Openings 2013–2014, 35. The median number of years required for completion of a degree in 2012–2013 were 2. The number of students enrolled full- and part-time who were dismissed or voluntarily withdrew from this program area in 2012–2013 were 1. *School Psychology MA/MS (Master of Arts/Science)*—Applications 2012–2013, 38. Total applicants accepted 2012–2013, 30. Number full-time enrolled (new admits only) 2012–2013, 17. Number part-time enrolled (new admits only) 2012–2013, 0. Total enrolled 2012–2013 full-time, 17. Total enrolled 2012–2013 part-time, 0. Openings 2013–2014, 20. The median number of years required for completion of a degree in 2012–2013 was 1. The number of students enrolled full- and part-time who were dismissed or voluntarily withdrew from this program area in 2012–2013 were 1. *School Psychology EdS (School Psychology)*—Applications 2012–2013, 23. Total applicants accepted 2012–2013, 20. Number full-time enrolled (new admits only) 2012–2013, 18. Number part-time enrolled (new admits only) 2012–2013, 0. Total enrolled 2012–2013 full-time, 51. Total enrolled 2012–2013 part-time, 0. Openings 2013–2014, 20. The median number of years required for completion of a degree in 2012–2013 were 3. The number of students enrolled full- and part-time who were dismissed or voluntarily withdrew from this program area in 2012–2013 were 0. *School Psychology PsyD (Doctor of Psychology)*—Applications 2012–2013, 33. Total applicants accepted 2012–2013, 29. Number full-time enrolled (new admits only) 2012–2013, 20. Number part-time enrolled (new admits only) 2012–2013, 0. Total enrolled 2012–2013 full-time, 65. Total enrolled 2012–2013 part-time, 0. Openings 2013–2014, 15. The median number of years required for

completion of a degree in 2012–2013 were 4. The number of students enrolled full- and part-time who were dismissed or voluntarily withdrew from this program area in 2012–2013 were 0. *School Psychology Respecialization Diploma*—Applications 2012–2013, 0. Total applicants accepted 2012–2013, 0. Number full-time enrolled (new admits only) 2012–2013, 0. Number part-time enrolled (new admits only) 2012–2013, 0. Openings 2013–2014, 3. The median number of years required for completion of a degree in 2012–2013 were 2. The number of students enrolled full- and part-time who were dismissed or voluntarily withdrew from this program area in 2012–2013 were 0. *Clinical Health Psychology Certificate Other*—Applications 2012–2013, 1. Total applicants accepted 2012–2013, 1. Number full-time enrolled (new admits only) 2012–2013, 1. Number part-time enrolled (new admits only) 2012–2013, 0. Total enrolled 2012–2013 full-time, 1. Total enrolled 2012–2013 part-time, 0. Openings 2013–2014, 6. The median number of years required for completion of a degree in 2012–2013 was 1. The number of students enrolled full- and part-time who were dismissed or voluntarily withdrew from this program area in 2012–2013 were 0. *Clinical Neuropsychology Certificate Other*—Applications 2012–2013, 1. Total applicants accepted 2012–2013, 1. Number full-time enrolled (new admits only) 2012–2013, 0. Number part-time enrolled (new admits only) 2012–2013, 1. Openings 2013–2014, 6. The median number of years required for completion of a degree in 2012–2013 was 1. The number of students enrolled full- and part-time who were dismissed or voluntarily withdrew from this program area in 2012–2013 were 0. *Organizational Development and Leadership - Ga MA/MS (Master of Arts/Science)*—Applications 2012–2013, 9. Total applicants accepted 2012–2013, 7. Number full-time enrolled (new admits only) 2012–2013, 4. Number part-time enrolled (new admits only) 2012–2013, 1. Total enrolled 2012–2013 full-time, 18. Total enrolled 2012–2013 part-time, 6. Openings 2013–2014, 30. The number of students enrolled full- and part-time who were dismissed or voluntarily withdrew from this program area in 2012–2013 were 0.

Scores: Entries appear in this order: required test or GPA, minimum score (if required), median score of students entering in 2012–2013. *Psychology CAGS Other:* overall undergraduate GPA 3.0; *Counseling & Clinical Health Psychology MA/MS (Master of Arts/Science):* overall undergraduate GPA 3.0, 3.36; *Clinical Psychology Respecialization Diploma:* overall undergraduate GPA 3.0; *Clinical Psychology PsyD (Doctor of Psychology):* overall undergraduate GPA 3.0, 3.49, Masters GPA 3.3, 3.8; *Organizational Development and Leadership - PA MA/MS (Master of Arts/Science):* overall undergraduate GPA 3.0, 3.13; *School Psychology MA/MS (Master of Arts/Science):* overall undergraduate GPA 3.0, 3.36; *School Psychology EdS (School Psychology):* overall undergraduate GPA 3.0, 3.24; *School Psychology PsyD (Doctor of Psychology):* overall undergraduate GPA 3.0, Masters GPA 3.0; *School Psychology Respecialization Diploma:* overall undergraduate GPA no minimum stated; *Clinical Health Psychology Certificate Other:* overall undergraduate GPA no minimum stated; *Clinical Neuropsychology Certificate Other:* overall undergraduate GPA 3.0; *Organizational Development and Leadership - GA MA/MS (Master of Arts/Science):* overall undergraduate GPA 3.0.

Other Criteria: (importance of criteria rated low, medium, or high): GRE scores—medium, research experience—low, work experience—high, extracurricular activity—medium, clinically related public service—high, GPA—high, letters of recommendation—high, interview—high, statement of goals and objectives—high, graded writing sample—high, undergraduate major in psychology—medium, specific undergraduate psychology courses taken—medium, Work experience is weighted medium as an admission criterion for the MS in School Psychology, MS in Counseling & Clinical Health Psychology, and CAGS programs. Work experience is weighted high as an admissions criterion for the MS in ODL, EdS and PsyD programs. In addition, a master's degree in psychology or a related field is required for admissions to the Clinical PsyD program. For additional information on admission requirements, go to http://www.pcom.edu/Admissions/adm_app_process/adm_app_process.html.

Student Characteristics: The following represents characteristics of students in 2012–2013 in all graduate psychology programs in the department: Female—full-time 302, part-time 32; Male—full-time 88, part-time 10; African American/Black—full-time 67, part-time 8; Hispanic/Latino(a)—full-time 9, part-time 2; Asian/Pacific Islander—full-time 15, part-time 2; American Indian/Alaska Native—full-time 2, part-time 0; Caucasian/White—full-time 283, part-time 29; Multi-ethnic—full-time 10, part-time 0; students subject to the Americans With Disabilities Act—full-time 4, part-time 0; Unknown ethnicity—full-time 4, part-time 1; International students who hold an F-1 or J-1 Visa—full-time 3, part-time 0.

Financial Information/Assistance:

Tuition for Full-Time Study: *Master's:* State residents: $739 per credit hour; Nonstate residents: $739 per credit hour. *Doctoral:* State residents: $1,019 per credit hour; Nonstate residents: $1,019 per credit hour. Tuition is subject to change. Additional fees are assessed to students beyond the costs of tuition for the following: Comprehensive fee (each term): $181. Tuition costs vary by program. See the following website for updates and changes in tuition costs: http://www.pcom.edu/Administration/Administrative_Departments/Bursar_s_Office/do_tuition.html. Higher tuition cost for this program: EdS: $799/credit hour; MS in ODL: $731/credit hour.

Financial Assistance:

First-Year Students: Research assistantships available for first year. Average amount paid per academic year: $6,000. Average number of hours worked per week: 12. Fellowships and scholarships available for first year. Average amount paid per academic year: $1,000.

Advanced Students: Teaching assistantships available for advanced students. Average amount paid per academic year: $1,500. Average number of hours worked per week: 5. Research assistantships available for advanced students. Average amount paid per academic year: $7,200. Average number of hours worked per week: 12. Fellowships and scholarships available for advanced students. Average amount paid per academic year: $2,400. Average number of hours worked per week: 5.

Additional Information: Of all students currently enrolled full time, 8% benefited from one or more of the listed financial assistance programs. Application and information available online at: http://www.pcom.edu/Financial_Aid/Financial_Aid.html.

Internships/Practica: Doctoral Degree (PsyD Clinical Psychology): For those doctoral students for whom a professional psychology internship was required in this program prior to graduation, (18) students applied for an internship in 2011–2012, with (17) students obtaining an internship. Of those students who obtained an internship, (17) were paid internships. Of those students who obtained an internship, (7) students placed in APA/CPA accredited internships, (10) students placed in internships not APA/CPA accredited, but listed with the Association of Psychology Postdoctoral and Internship Programs (APPIC), (0) students placed in internships conforming to guidelines of the Council of Directors of School Psychology Programs (CDSPP), (0) students placed in internships that were not APA/CPA accredited, APPIC or CDSPP listed. Doctoral Degree (PsyD School Psychology): For those doctoral students for whom a professional psychology internship was required in this program prior to graduation, (12) students applied for an internship in 2011–2012, with (11) students obtaining an internship. Of those students who obtained an internship, (11) were paid internships. Of those students who obtained an internship, (1) students placed in APA/CPA accredited internships, (0) students placed in internships not APA/CPA accredited, but listed with the Association of Psychology Postdoctoral and Internship Programs (APPIC), (10) students placed in internships conforming to guidelines of the Council of Directors of School Psychology Programs (CDSPP), (0) students placed in internships that were not APA/CPA accredited, APPIC or CDSPP listed. Master's Degree (MA/MS Organizational Development and Leadership - PA): An internship experience, such as a final research project or "capstone" experience is required of graduates. Practica are fieldwork experiences completed by master's level and doctoral students at a PCOM approved clinical training site. The minimum weekly hour requirements vary from program to program. Practicum sites are committed to excellence in the training of professionals, and provide extensive supervision and formative clinical experiences. They offer a wide range of training, including the use of empirically supported interventions, brief treatment models, cognitive behavioral therapy, and treatment of psychological/medical problems. Students engage in evaluation, psychological testing (PsyD only), psychotherapy, and professional clinical work. Practica include seminars taught by faculty that provide a place for students to discuss their experiences and help them integrate coursework with on-site training. Students participate in pratica at the Psychology Department's Center for Brief Therapy, a multi-faceted clinical training center, as well as sites including community agencies, hospitals, university counseling centers, prisons, schools, and specialized treatment centers. The department has a broad network of practicum sites in Pennsylvania, New Jersey, Maryland, and Delaware. Students apply for internships through the APPIC matching program.

Housing and Day Care: No on-campus housing is available. No on-campus day care facilities are available.

Employment of Department Graduates:

Master's Degree Graduates: Of those who graduated in the academic year 2011–2012, the following categories and numbers represent the postgraduate activities and employment of master's degree graduates: Enrolled in a psychology doctoral program (7), enrolled in another graduate/professional program (16), enrolled in a postdoctoral residency/fellowship (n/a), employed in independent practice (n/a), employed in business or industry (6), employed in government agency (4), employed in a community mental health/counseling center (19), employed in a hospital/medical center (4), other employment position (1), total from the above (master's) (57).

Doctoral Degree Graduates: Of those who graduated in the academic year 2011–2012, the following categories and numbers represent the postgraduate activities and employment of doctoral degree graduates: Enrolled in a psychology doctoral program (n/a), enrolled in a postdoctoral residency/fellowship (10), employed in a professional position in a school system (22), employed in a community mental health/counseling center (14), employed in a hospital/medical center (2), total from the above (doctoral) (48).

Additional Information:

Orientation, Objectives, and Emphasis of Department: The mission of the Department of Psychology at PCOM is to prepare highly-skilled, compassionate psychologists and master's level psychological specialists to provide empirically-based, active, focused, and collaborative assessments and treatments with sensitivity to cultural and ethnic diversity and the underserved. Grounded in the cognitive-behavioral tradition, the graduate programs in psychology train practitioner-scholars to offer assessment, intervention, consultation, management, and leadership as local clinical scientists, and to engage in scholarly activities, advocacy, and life-long learning in the field of psychology.

Special Facilities or Resources: The academic facilities at PCOM include state-of-the-art amphitheaters and classroom facilities, computer laboratories with extensive software including PsycLIT and SPSS, a recently renovated library that includes sophisticated online resources, and the HealthNet teleconferencing system. The Center for Brief Therapy, a mental health clinic housed in the Department of Psychology, provides multi-faceted clinical training and research opportunities for students. PCOM also has three neighborhood health care centers in Philadelphia and one in LaPorte Pennsylvania.

Information for Students With Physical Disabilities: See the following website for more information: http://www.pcom.edu/Student_Life/Student_Affairs_Main/Academic_Personal.html.

Application Information:
Send to Philadelphia College of Osteopathic Medicine, Department of Admissions, 4170 City Avenue, Philadelphia, PA 19131. Application available online. URL of online application: http://www.pcom.edu/General_Information/apply_now.html. Students are admitted in the Fall, application deadline; Spring, application deadline; Summer, application deadline; Programs have rolling admissions. The PsyD in Clinical Psychology, EdS in School Psychology, and MS in Counseling & Clinical Health Psychology programs admit students for the fall term only. The MS and PsyD in School Psychology programs admit students for the summer term only. The MS in ODL program admits students for the fall and spring terms only. The CAGS program admits students during all terms. There are no official deadlines; applications will be reviewed until the incoming class is filled. Students are encouraged to apply early. *Fee:* $50.

Pittsburgh, University of
Department of Psychology in Education
School of Education
5930 Posvar Hall
Pittsburgh, PA 15260
Telephone: (412) 648-7036
Fax: (412) 624-7231
E-mail: *johnson@pitt.edu*
Web: *http://www.education.pitt.edu/AcademicDepartments/PsychologyinEducation.aspx*

Department Information:
1986. Chairperson: Carl Johnson. Number of faculty: total—full-time 10; women—full-time 6; total—minority—full-time 1.

Programs and Degrees Offered:
Listed in the following order: Program area, degree type (T if terminal Master's), number awarded 7/11–6/12. Applied Developmental Psychology MA/MS (Master of Arts/Science) (T) 31, Applied Developmental Psychology PhD (Doctor of Philosophy) 1.

Student Applications/Admissions:
Student Applications
Applied Developmental Psychology MA/MS (Master of Arts/Science)—Applications 2012–2013, 86. Total applicants accepted 2012–2013, 55. Number full-time enrolled (new admits only) 2012–2013, 18. Number part-time enrolled (new admits only) 2012–2013, 11. Total enrolled 2012–2013 full-time, 35. Total enrolled 2012–2013 part-time, 34. Openings 2013–2014, 40. The median number of years required for completion of a degree in 2012–2013 were 2. *Applied Developmental Psychology PhD (Doctor of Philosophy)*—Applications 2012–2013, 24. Total applicants accepted 2012–2013, 5. Number full-time enrolled (new admits only) 2012–2013, 3. Number part-time enrolled (new admits only) 2012–2013, 0. Total enrolled 2012–2013 full-time, 17. Total enrolled 2012–2013 part-time, 3. Openings 2013–2014, 6. The median number of years required for completion of a degree in 2012–2013 were 6.
Scores: Entries appear in this order: required test or GPA, minimum score (if required), median score of students entering in 2012–2013. *Applied Developmental Psychology PhD (Doctor of Philosophy):* GRE-V no minimum stated, GRE-Q no minimum stated, GRE-Analytical no minimum stated.
Other Criteria: (importance of criteria rated low, medium, or high): GRE scores—medium, research experience—medium, work experience—medium, extracurricular activity—low, clinically related public service—medium, GPA—medium, letters of recommendation—medium, statement of goals and objectives—high, specific undergraduate psychology courses taken—high.

Student Characteristics: The following represents characteristics of students in 2012–2013 in all graduate psychology programs in the department: Female—full-time 47, part-time 29; Male—full-time 4, part-time 8; African American/Black—full-time 4, part-time 4; Hispanic/Latino(a)—full-time 3, part-time 1; Asian/Pacific Islander—full-time 12, part-time 1; American Indian/Alaska Native—full-time 0, part-time 0; Caucasian/White—full-time 31, part-time 30; students subject to the Americans With Disabilities

Act—full-time 0, part-time 0; Unknown ethnicity—full-time 1, part-time 1; International students who hold an F-1 or J-1 Visa—full-time 10, part-time 0.

Financial Information/Assistance:

Tuition for Full-Time Study: *Master's:* State residents: per academic year $19,336, $782 per credit hour; Nonstate residents: per academic year $31,658, $1,295 per credit hour. *Doctoral:* State residents: per academic year $19,336, $782 per credit hour; Nonstate residents: per academic year $31,658, $1,295 per credit hour. Tuition is subject to change. See the following website for updates and changes in tuition costs: http://www.education.pitt.edu/FutureStudents/TuitionFinancialAid.aspx.

Financial Assistance:

First-Year Students: Teaching assistantships available for first year. Average amount paid per academic year: $8,230. Average number of hours worked per week: 10. Research assistantships available for first year. Average amount paid per academic year: $16,460. Average number of hours worked per week: 20.

Advanced Students: Teaching assistantships available for advanced students. Average amount paid per academic year: $8,230. Average number of hours worked per week: 10. Research assistantships available for advanced students. Average amount paid per academic year: $16,460. Average number of hours worked per week: 20.

Additional Information: Of all students currently enrolled full time, 20% benefited from one or more of the listed financial assistance programs. Application and information available online at: http://www.education.pitt.edu/FutureStudents/TuitionFinancialAid.aspx.

Internships/Practica:

The Applied Developmental Program maintains extensive connections with community organizations that provide opportunities for internships in programs that serve children, youth and families in many different capacities.

Housing and Day Care: No on-campus housing is available. On-campus day care facilities are available. See the following website for more information: http://www.childdevelopment.pitt.edu/.

Employment of Department Graduates:

Master's Degree Graduates: Of those who graduated in the academic year 2011–2012, the following categories and numbers represent the postgraduate activities and employment of master's degree graduates: Enrolled in a psychology doctoral program (4), enrolled in another graduate/professional program (2), enrolled in a postdoctoral residency/fellowship (n/a), employed in independent practice (n/a), employed in other positions at a higher education institution (2), employed in a professional position in a school system (3), employed in government agency (1), employed in a community mental health/counseling center (9), employed in a hospital/medical center (4), still seeking employment (1), total from the above (master's) (26).

Doctoral Degree Graduates: Of those who graduated in the academic year 2011–2012, the following categories and numbers represent the postgraduate activities and employment of doctoral degree graduates: Enrolled in a psychology doctoral program (n/a), enrolled in a postdoctoral residency/fellowship (1), employed in an academic position at a university (2), employed in a community mental health/counseling center (1), total from the above (doctoral) (4).

Additional Information:

Orientation, Objectives, and Emphasis of Department: The Master of Science Degree in Applied Developmental Psychology emphasizes the integration of knowledge of human development with the skills and expertise essential for developing, implementing and evaluating effective programs for children, youth and families. Graduates of the program pursue professional careers as program administrators and child development specialists in areas such as teaching, research and professional practice.

Special Facilities or Resources: The Applied Developmental Program is closely allied with several leading research, policy and service organizations in the University including the Learning Policy Center, the Office of Child Development, and the University, Community, Leaders, and Individuals with Disabilities Center.

Information for Students With Physical Disabilities: See the following website for more information: http://www.studentaffairs.pitt.edu/drswelcome.

Application Information:

Send to University of Pittsburgh School of Education, Student Service Center, 5500 Wesley W. Posvar Hall, Pittsburgh, PA 15260. Application available online. URL of online application: https://app.applyyourself.com/?id=up-ed. Students are admitted in the Fall, application deadline March 1. Applications after the deadline are seriously considered if all the places are not filled. *Fee:* $50.

Pittsburgh, University of
Psychology
Kenneth P. Dietrich School of Arts and Sciences
3129 Sennott Square, 210 South Bouquet Street
Pittsburgh, PA 15260
Telephone: (412) 624-4502
Fax: (412) 624-4428
E-mail: *psygrad@pitt.edu*
Web: *http://www.psychology.pitt.edu*

Department Information:

1904. Chairperson: Daniel Shaw. Number of faculty: total—full-time 40, part-time 8; women—full-time 17, part-time 4; total—minority—full-time 1; women minority—full-time 1.

Programs and Degrees Offered:

Listed in the following order: Program area, degree type (T if terminal Master's), number awarded 7/11–6/12. Clinical Psychology PhD (Doctor of Philosophy) 6, Cognitive Psychology PhD (Doctor of Philosophy) 6, Developmental Psychology PhD (Doctor of Philosophy) 1, Biological and Health Psychology PhD (Doctor of Philosophy) 0, Individualized PhD (Doctor of Philosophy) 0, Social Psychology PhD (Doctor of Philosophy) 1.

APA Accreditation: Clinical PhD (Doctor of Philosophy). Student Outcome Data Website: http://www.psychology.pitt.edu/graduate/clinical/index.php.

Student Applications/Admissions:

Student Applications

Clinical Psychology PhD (Doctor of Philosophy)—Applications 2012–2013, 292. Total applicants accepted 2012–2013, 9. Number full-time enrolled (new admits only) 2012–2013, 9. Total enrolled 2012–2013 full-time, 53. Total enrolled 2012–2013 part-time, 0. Openings 2013–2014, 5. The median number of years required for completion of a degree in 2012–2013 were 8. The number of students enrolled full- and part-time who were dismissed or voluntarily withdrew from this program area in 2012–2013 were 0. *Cognitive Psychology PhD (Doctor of Philosophy)*—Applications 2012–2013, 83. Total applicants accepted 2012–2013, 7. Number full-time enrolled (new admits only) 2012–2013, 7. Total enrolled 2012–2013 full-time, 31. Total enrolled 2012–2013 part-time, 0. Openings 2013–2014, 4. The median number of years required for completion of a degree in 2012–2013 were 7. The number of students enrolled full- and part-time who were dismissed or voluntarily withdrew from this program area in 2012–2013 were 0. *Developmental Psychology PhD (Doctor of Philosophy)*— Applications 2012–2013, 32. Total applicants accepted 2012–2013, 3. Number full-time enrolled (new admits only) 2012–2013, 3. Total enrolled 2012–2013 full-time, 10. Total enrolled 2012–2013 part-time, 0. Openings 2013–2014, 2. The median number of years required for completion of a degree in 2012–2013 were 7. The number of students enrolled full- and part-time who were dismissed or voluntarily withdrew from this program area in 2012–2013 were 0. *Biological and Health Psychology PhD (Doctor of Philosophy)*—Applications 2012–2013, 28. Total applicants accepted 2012–2013, 1. Number full-time enrolled (new admits only) 2012–2013, 1. Total enrolled 2012–2013 full-time, 6. Openings 2013–2014, 3. The number of students enrolled full- and part-time who were dismissed or voluntarily withdrew from this program area in 2012–2013 were 1. *Individualized PhD (Doctor of Philosophy)*—Total applicants accepted 2012–2013, 0. Number full-time enrolled (new admits only) 2012–2013, 0. Total enrolled 2012–2013 full-time, 1. Total enrolled 2012–2013 part-time, 0. Openings 2013–2014, 1. The number of students enrolled full- and part-time who were dismissed or voluntarily withdrew from this program area in 2012–2013 were 0. *Social Psychology PhD (Doctor of Philosophy)*—Applications 2012–2013, 27. Total applicants accepted 2012–2013, 1. Number full-time enrolled (new admits only) 2012–2013, 1. Total enrolled 2012–2013 full-time, 5. Total enrolled 2012–2013 part-time, 0. Openings 2013–2014, 1. The median number of years required for completion of a degree in 2012–2013 were 7. The number of students enrolled full- and part-time who were dismissed or voluntarily withdrew from this program area in 2012–2013 were 0.

Scores: Entries appear in this order: required test or GPA, minimum score (if required), median score of students entering in 2012–2013. *Clinical Psychology PhD (Doctor of Philosophy)*: GRE-V no minimum stated, GRE-Q no minimum stated, overall undergraduate GPA 3.0.

Other Criteria: (importance of criteria rated low, medium, or high): GRE scores—high, research experience—high, work experience—medium, extracurricular activity—low, clinically related public service—low, GPA—high, letters of recommendation—high, interview—high, statement of goals and objectives—medium. For additional information on admission re-

quirements, go to http://www.psychology.pitt.edu/graduate/apply.php.

Student Characteristics: The following represents characteristics of students in 2012–2013 in all graduate psychology programs in the department: Female—full-time 87, part-time 0; Male—full-time 19, part-time 0; African American/Black—full-time 5, part-time 0; Hispanic/Latino(a)—full-time 3, part-time 0; Asian/Pacific Islander—full-time 17, part-time 0; American Indian/Alaska Native—full-time 0, part-time 0; Caucasian/White—full-time 81, part-time 0; Multi-ethnic—full-time 0, part-time 0; students subject to the Americans With Disabilities Act—full-time 1, part-time 0; Unknown ethnicity—full-time 0, part-time 0; International students who hold an F-1 or J-1 Visa—full-time 10, part-time 0.

Financial Information/Assistance:

Tuition for Full-Time Study: *Doctoral:* State residents: per academic year $19,336, $782 per credit hour; Nonstate residents: per academic year $31,658, $1,295 per credit hour. Tuition is subject to change. See the following website for updates and changes in tuition costs: http://www.ir.pitt.edu/tuition/tuitionrates.php.

Financial Assistance:

First-Year Students: Teaching assistantships available for first year. Average amount paid per academic year: $16,300. Average number of hours worked per week: 20. Apply by December 1. Research assistantships available for first year. Average amount paid per academic year: $15,270. Average number of hours worked per week: 20. Apply by December 1. Traineeships available for first year. Average amount paid per academic year: $20,000. Apply by December 1. Fellowships and scholarships available for first year. Average amount paid per academic year: $19,450. Apply by December 1.

Advanced Students: Teaching assistantships available for advanced students. Average amount paid per academic year: $16,930. Average number of hours worked per week: 20. Research assistantships available for advanced students. Average amount paid per academic year: $15,900. Average number of hours worked per week: 20. Traineeships available for advanced students. Average amount paid per academic year: $20,000. Fellowships and scholarships available for advanced students. Average amount paid per academic year: $19,610.

Additional Information: Of all students currently enrolled full time, 100% benefited from one or more of the listed financial assistance programs. Application and information available online at: http://www.psychology.pitt.edu/graduate/financial-support.php

Internships/Practica: Doctoral Degree (PhD Clinical Psychology): For those doctoral students for whom a professional psychology internship was required in this program prior to graduation, (9) students applied for an internship in 2011–2012, with (9) students obtaining an internship. Of those students who obtained an internship, (9) were paid internships. Of those students who obtained an internship, (9) students placed in APA/CPA accredited internships, (0) students placed in internships not APA/CPA accredited, but listed with the Association of Psychology Postdoctoral and Internship Programs (APPIC), (0) students placed in internships conforming to guidelines of the Council of Directors of School Psychology Programs (CDSPP), (0) students placed in internships that were not APA/CPA accredited, APPIC or CDSPP listed. .

Housing and Day Care: No on-campus housing is available. On-campus day care facilities are available. See the following website for more information: http://www.ucdc.pitt.edu/.

Employment of Department Graduates:

Master's Degree Graduates: Of those who graduated in the academic year 2011–2012, the following categories and numbers represent the postgraduate activities and employment of master's degree graduates: Enrolled in a postdoctoral residency/fellowship (n/a), employed in independent practice (n/a), total from the above (master's) (0).

Doctoral Degree Graduates: Of those who graduated in the academic year 2011–2012, the following categories and numbers represent the postgraduate activities and employment of doctoral degree graduates: Enrolled in a psychology doctoral program (n/a), enrolled in a postdoctoral residency/fellowship (8), employed in an academic position at a university (2), employed in business or industry (1), employed in a community mental health/counseling center (1), do not know (2), total from the above (doctoral) (14).

Additional Information:

Orientation, Objectives, and Emphasis of Department: Basic research training is emphasized, and most projects involve research with important practical implications. The graduate programs include Clinical Psychology, Cognitive Psychology and Cognitive Neuroscience, Developmental Psychology, Biological and Health Psychology, Social Psychology, and joint programs in Clinical-Developmental and Clinical-Health Psychology. Some examples of training opportunities are projects on infant socialization, cognitive, language and social development of children, psychological stress on the cardiovascular and immune systems, nicotine and alcohol use, decision making in groups, stereotyping, reading processes, school and non-school learning, and brain models of attention and reading. Seminars are small (5–12 students), and close working relationships are encouraged with faculty, especially the student's advisor. Excellent relationships with other departments and schools offer unusually flexible opportunities to carry out interdisciplinary work and gain access to scholars in the Pittsburgh community. All students are expected to teach at least one course, and carry out an original research dissertation. Financial support is available for students through teaching, research, and fellowships.

Special Facilities or Resources: The facilities of the department include experimental laboratories, extensive computer facilities, a small-groups laboratory, the Clinical Psychology Center, and the laboratories of the Learning Research and Development Center. These services offer the advanced graduate student opportunities for supervised practicum and research experiences. The department also maintains cooperative arrangements with many organizations in Pittsburgh engaged in various kinds of psychological work. These include the Brain Imaging Research Center, Children's Hospital, Pittsburgh Cancer Institute, the Western Psychiatric Institute and Clinic, and several local agencies of the Veterans Administration Medical Centers. Collaboration with these organizations consists of part-time instruction by the staffs of these agencies, the sharing of laboratory and clinical facilities, and the appointment in those organizations of graduate students in psychology as clinical or research assistants.

Information for Students With Physical Disabilities: See the following website for more information: http://www.drs.pitt.edu/.

Application Information:
Application available online. URL of online application: https://app.applyyourself.com/?id=up-as. Students are admitted in the Fall, application deadline December 1. *Fee:* $50. Fees deferred for McNair Scholars.

Saint Joseph's University
Department of Psychology
5600 City Avenue
Philadelphia, PA 19131-1395
Telephone: (610) 660-1800
Fax: (610) 660-1819
E-mail: *jmindell@sju.edu*
Web: *http://www.sju.edu/int/academics/cas/grad/psychology/*

Department Information:
1960. Director, Graduate Psychology Program: Jodi A. Mindell, PhD Number of faculty: total—full-time 11; women—full-time 6; total—minority—full-time 1; women minority—full-time 1.

Programs and Degrees Offered:
Listed in the following order: Program area, degree type (T if terminal Master's), number awarded 7/11–6/12. Experimental Psychology MA/MS (Master of Arts/Science) (T) 20.

Student Applications/Admissions:

Student Applications

Experimental Psychology MA/MS (Master of Arts/Science)—Applications 2012–2013, 80. Total applicants accepted 2012–2013, 23. Number full-time enrolled (new admits only) 2012–2013, 23. Total enrolled 2012–2013 full-time, 37. Total enrolled 2012–2013 part-time, 0. Openings 2013–2014, 20. The median number of years required for completion of a degree in 2012–2013 were 2. The number of students enrolled full- and part-time who were dismissed or voluntarily withdrew from this program area in 2012–2013 were 1.

Scores: Entries appear in this order: required test or GPA, minimum score (if required), median score of students entering in 2012–2013. *Experimental Psychology MA/MS (Master of Arts/Science):* GRE-V no minimum stated, GRE-Q no minimum stated, overall undergraduate GPA no minimum stated.

Other Criteria: (importance of criteria rated low, medium, or high): GRE scores—medium, research experience—high, work experience—low, extracurricular activity—medium, clinically related public service—low, GPA—high, letters of recommendation—high, statement of goals and objectives—medium, undergraduate major in psychology—medium, specific undergraduate psychology courses taken—high. For additional information on admission requirements, go to http://www.sju.edu/int/academics/cas/grad/psychology/admission.

Student Characteristics: The following represents characteristics of students in 2012–2013 in all graduate psychology programs in the department: Female—full-time 28, part-time 0; Male—full-time 9, part-time 0; African American/Black—full-time 2, part-time 0; Hispanic/Latino(a)—full-time 0, part-time 0; Asian/Pacific Islander—full-time 2, part-time 0; American Indian/Alaska Native—full-time 0, part-time 0; Caucasian/White—full-time 33, part-time 0; Multi-ethnic—full-time 0, part-time 0; students subject to the Americans With Disabilities Act—full-time 0, part-

time 0; Unknown ethnicity—full-time 0, part-time 0; International students who hold an F-1 or J-1 Visa—full-time 0, part-time 0.

Financial Information/Assistance:
Tuition for Full-Time Study: *Master's:* State residents: $823 per credit hour; Nonstate residents: $823 per credit hour. Tuition is subject to change. See the following website for updates and changes in tuition costs: http://www.sju.edu/int/academics/cas/grad/tuition.html.

Financial Assistance:
First-Year Students: No information provided.
Advanced Students: Teaching assistantships available for advanced students. Average amount paid per academic year: $7,200. Average number of hours worked per week: 20. Research assistantships available for advanced students. Average amount paid per academic year: $7,200. Average number of hours worked per week: 20.
Additional Information: Of all students currently enrolled full time, 30% benefited from one or more of the listed financial assistance programs. Application and information available online at: http://www.sju.edu/int/academics/cas/grad/finaid.html.

Internships/Practica: Master's Degree (MA/MS Experimental Psychology): An internship experience, such as a final research project or "capstone" experience is required of graduates.

Housing and Day Care: No on-campus housing is available. On-campus day care facilities are available. Children's School at St. John's in Bala Cynwyd, PA.

Employment of Department Graduates:
Master's Degree Graduates: Of those who graduated in the academic year 2011–2012, the following categories and numbers represent the postgraduate activities and employment of master's degree graduates: Enrolled in a psychology doctoral program (3), enrolled in a postdoctoral residency/fellowship (n/a), employed in independent practice (n/a), employed in business or industry (7), employed in a hospital/medical center (8), total from the above (master's) (18).
Doctoral Degree Graduates: Of those who graduated in the academic year 2011–2012, the following categories and numbers represent the postgraduate activities and employment of doctoral degree graduates: Enrolled in a psychology doctoral program (n/a), total from the above (doctoral) (0).

Additional Information:
Orientation, Objectives, and Emphasis of Department: The Saint Joseph's University graduate program in Experimental Psychology is designed to provide students with a solid grounding in the scientific study of psychology. Graduates of the program will have a firm foundation in the scientific method and the skills with which to pursue the scientific study of psychological questions. The program offers a traditional and academically oriented 48-credit curriculum, which requires a qualifying comprehensive examination and an empirical thesis project. The program is designed for successful completion over two academic years. The Saint Joseph's University psychology graduate program has been constructed to complement the strengths and interests of the present psychology faculty and facilities and to reflect the current state of the discipline of psychology. The curriculum is composed of three major components: an 8-credit common core required of all students; 24 credits of content based courses; and a 16-credit research component in which students complete the comprehensive examination and research thesis.

Special Facilities or Resources: All psychology faculty have equipped and active research laboratories in which graduate students pursue independent research projects for completion of their thesis requirement. Support facilities for graduate-level research and education are impressive. A vivarium, certifiable by the United States Public Health Service, for the housing of animal subjects is in operation and is fully staffed. For research involving human subjects, the department coordinates a subject pool consisting of approximately 300 subjects per semester. Additionally, the Psychology Department at Saint Joseph's operates PsyNet, a state-of-the-art Macintosh-AppleShare local area network which is attached to a campus-wide computer network through an Ethernet connection. PsyNet consists of 35 Macintosh computers and peripherals for all faculty and staff plus fileservers and laser printers. Two student computer classrooms/laboratories which include an additional 20 computers are also available within the department. PsyNet software includes various word processing, statistical, spreadsheet, database, graphics, and simulation packages.

Information for Students With Physical Disabilities: See the following website for more information: http://www.sju.edu/int/studentlife/studentresources/sess/ssd/.

Application Information:
Send to Graduate Admissions Office, Saint Joseph's University, 5600 City Avenue, Philadelphia, PA 19131-1395. Application available online. URL of online application: http://www.sju.edu/information/application-process-0. Students are admitted in the Fall, application deadline March 1. *Fee:* $35. Waived for attendees of online open house.

Seton Hill University
Graduate & Adult Studies/Marriage & Family Therapy MA
1 Seton Drive
Greensburg, PA 15301
Telephone: (724) 838-4208
Fax: (724) 830-1891
E-mail: *Gadmit@setonhill.edu*
Web: *http://www.setonhill.edu/academics/graduate_programs/marriage_and_family_therapy*

Department Information:
2008. Program Director: Dr. Rebecca Harvey. Number of faculty: total—full-time 2, part-time 10; women—full-time 1, part-time 8; total—minority—full-time 1.

Programs and Degrees Offered:
Listed in the following order: Program area, degree type (T if terminal Master's), number awarded 7/11–6/12. Marriage and Family Therapy MA/MS (Master of Arts/Science) (T) 14.

Student Applications/Admissions:
Student Applications
Marriage and Family Therapy MA/MS (Master of Arts/Science)— Applications 2012–2013, 89. Total applicants accepted 2012–

723

2013, 29. Openings 2013–2014, 20. The median number of years required for completion of a degree in 2012–2013 were 2. *Other Criteria:* (importance of criteria rated low, medium, or high): work experience—medium, extracurricular activity—medium, clinically related public service—medium, GPA—medium, letters of recommendation—medium, interview—high, statement of goals and objectives—medium, undergraduate major in psychology—low, specific undergraduate psychology courses taken—low. For additional information on admission requirements, go to http://www.setonhill.edu/admissions/graduate_admissions/admission_requirements.

Student Characteristics: The following represents characteristics of students in 2012–2013 in all graduate psychology programs in the department: Female—full-time 25, part-time 9; Male—full-time 5, part-time 2; African American/Black—full-time 3, part-time 1; Hispanic/Latino(a)—full-time 0, part-time 0; Asian/Pacific Islander—full-time 1, part-time 0; American Indian/Alaska Native—full-time 0, part-time 0; Caucasian/White—full-time 26, part-time 9; Multi-ethnic—full-time 0, part-time 1; students subject to the Americans With Disabilities Act—full-time 0, part-time 0; Unknown ethnicity—full-time 0, part-time 0; International students who hold an F-1 or J-1 Visa—full-time 1, part-time 0.

Financial Information/Assistance:
Tuition for Full-Time Study: *Master's:* State residents: $790 per credit hour; Nonstate residents: $790 per credit hour. Tuition is subject to change. See the following website for updates and changes in tuition costs: http://www.setonhill.edu/admissions/tuition_and_financial_aid/graduate_programs/tuition_fees.

Financial Assistance:
First-Year Students: Fellowships and scholarships available for first year.
Advanced Students: Fellowships and scholarships available for advanced students.
Additional Information: Of all students currently enrolled full time, 95% benefited from one or more of the listed financial assistance programs. Application and information available online at: http://www.setonhill.edu/admissions/tuition_and_financial_aid/graduate_programs/financial_aid.

Housing and Day Care: On-campus housing is available. See the following website for more information: http://www.setonhill.edu/campuslife/housing_and_dining/. No on-campus day care facilities are available.

Employment of Department Graduates:
Master's Degree Graduates: Of those who graduated in the academic year 2011–2012, the following categories and numbers represent the postgraduate activities and employment of master's degree graduates: Enrolled in a postdoctoral residency/fellowship (n/a), employed in independent practice (n/a), employed in a community mental health/counseling center (12), other employment position (2), total from the above (master's) (14).
Doctoral Degree Graduates: Of those who graduated in the academic year 2011–2012, the following categories and numbers represent the postgraduate activities and employment of doctoral degree graduates: Enrolled in a psychology doctoral program (n/a), total from the above (doctoral) (0).

Additional Information:
Orientation, Objectives, and Emphasis of Department: The objectives of the Master of Arts in Marriage and Family Therapy program are to ensure that students are: educated in family systems theory in general, and to the wide variety of specific family systems theories and therapies; trained to think and act systematically, which includes recognizing the connections that exist between micro-level and macro-level processes; sensitized to issues of power and the ways in which structured inequalities shape family processes and human relationships; taught effective skills and techniques for clinical assessment and intervention; exposed to the latest advances in MFT research and how to critically digest, evaluate, and utilize research in their clinical practice; educated about the landscape of the current mental health delivery system and how the MFT profession is located within that environment; informed of the ethical and legal standards of the profession; encouraged to develop critical thinking skills; encouraged to develop a heightened sense of self-awareness through reflection; and provided with sufficient supervised practical experience to develop a unique style of family therapy practice.

Special Facilities or Resources: The Seton Hill Center for Family Therapy is a community-based mental health center and training site in downtown Greensburg, PA. Therapy services are provided by the advanced graduate students in Seton Hill's Marriage and Family Therapy program, under the mentorship of experienced clinicians on the faculty at Seton Hill. This new facility uses advanced technology and modern design to provide community members with affordable mental health services. Our Center allows our students to gain practical experience in caring for clients in a supportive learning environment.

Information for Students With Physical Disabilities: See the following website for more information: http://www.setonhill.edu/campuslife/student_support/disability_services.

Application Information:
Send to Office of Graduate and Adult Studies, Seton Hill University, 1 Seton Drive, Greensburg, PA 15601. Application available online. URL of online application: https://apply.setonhill.edu/. Students are admitted in the Fall, application deadline March 15; Spring, application deadline December 1; Summer, application deadline March 15; Programs have rolling admissions. Deadlines are recommended, not hard. *Fee:* $35. Application free online.

Temple University
Department of Psychology
College of Liberal Arts
1701 North 13th Street, Room 668
Philadelphia, PA 19122-6085
Telephone: (215) 204-7321
Fax: (215) 204-5539
E-mail: *marsha.weinraub@temple.edu*
Web: *http://www.temple.edu/psychology*

Department Information:
1924. Chairperson: Marsha Weinraub. Number of faculty: total—full-time 36; women—full-time 17; total—minority—full-time 3; women minority—full-time 2.

Programs and Degrees Offered:
Listed in the following order: Program area, degree type (T if terminal Master's), number awarded 7/11–6/12. Clinical Psychology PhD (Doctor of Philosophy) 7, Developmental Psychology PhD (Doctor of Philosophy) 2, Brain and Cognitive Sciences PhD (Doctor of Philosophy) 5, Social Psychology PhD (Doctor of Philosophy) 3, Developmental Psychopathology PhD (Doctor of Philosophy) 0, Neuroscience PhD (Doctor of Philosophy).

APA Accreditation: Clinical PhD (Doctor of Philosophy). Student Outcome Data Website: http://www.temple.edu/psychology/clinical/index.htm.

Student Applications/Admissions:
Student Applications
Clinical Psychology PhD (Doctor of Philosophy)—Applications 2012–2013, 400. Total applicants accepted 2012–2013, 11. Number full-time enrolled (new admits only) 2012–2013, 12. Total enrolled 2012–2013 full-time, 61. Total enrolled 2012–2013 part-time, 0. Openings 2013–2014, 12. The median number of years required for completion of a degree in 2012–2013 were 6. The number of students enrolled full- and part-time who were dismissed or voluntarily withdrew from this program area in 2012–2013 were 0. *Developmental Psychology PhD (Doctor of Philosophy)*—Applications 2012–2013, 55. Total applicants accepted 2012–2013, 10. Number full-time enrolled (new admits only) 2012–2013, 5. Total enrolled 2012–2013 full-time, 12. Total enrolled 2012–2013 part-time, 0. Openings 2013–2014, 5. The median number of years required for completion of a degree in 2012–2013 were 5. The number of students enrolled full- and part-time who were dismissed or voluntarily withdrew from this program area in 2012–2013 were 1. *Brain and Cognitive Sciences PhD (Doctor of Philosophy)*—Applications 2012–2013, 52. Total applicants accepted 2012–2013, 5. Number full-time enrolled (new admits only) 2012–2013, 5. Total enrolled 2012–2013 full-time, 23. Total enrolled 2012–2013 part-time, 0. Openings 2013–2014, 5. The median number of years required for completion of a degree in 2012–2013 were 5. The number of students enrolled full- and part-time who were dismissed or voluntarily withdrew from this program area in 2012–2013 were 2. *Social Psychology PhD (Doctor of Philosophy)*—Applications 2012–2013, 47. Total applicants accepted 2012–2013, 2. Number full-time enrolled (new admits only) 2012–2013, 2. Total enrolled 2012–2013 full-time, 7. Total enrolled 2012–2013 part-time, 0. Openings 2013–2014, 2. The median number of years required for completion of a degree in 2012–2013 were 5. The number of students enrolled full- and part-time who were dismissed or voluntarily withdrew from this program area in 2012–2013 were 0. *Developmental Psychopathology PhD (Doctor of Philosophy)*—Applications 2012–2013, 25. Total applicants accepted 2012–2013, 4. Number full-time enrolled (new admits only) 2012–2013, 2. Total enrolled 2012–2013 full-time, 4. Total enrolled 2012–2013 part-time, 0. Openings 2013–2014, 2. *Neuroscience PhD (Doctor of Philosophy)*—Openings 2013–2014, 3.

Scores: Entries appear in this order: required test or GPA, minimum score (if required), median score of students entering in 2012–2013. *Clinical Psychology PhD (Doctor of Philosophy):* GRE-V no minimum stated, 640, GRE-Q no minimum stated, 710, GRE-Analytical no minimum stated, overall undergraduate GPA no minimum stated, 3.68, psychology GPA no mini-

mum stated; *Developmental Psychology PhD (Doctor of Philosophy):* GRE-V no minimum stated, GRE-Q no minimum stated, GRE-Analytical no minimum stated, overall undergraduate GPA no minimum stated, psychology GPA no minimum stated; *Brain and Cognitive Sciences PhD (Doctor of Philosophy):* GRE-V no minimum stated, GRE-Q no minimum stated, GRE-Analytical no minimum stated, overall undergraduate GPA no minimum stated, psychology GPA no minimum stated; *Social Psychology PhD (Doctor of Philosophy):* GRE-V no minimum stated, GRE-Q no minimum stated, GRE-Analytical no minimum stated, overall undergraduate GPA no minimum stated, psychology GPA no minimum stated; *Developmental Psychopathology PhD (Doctor of Philosophy):* GRE-V no minimum stated, GRE-Q no minimum stated, GRE-Analytical no minimum stated, overall undergraduate GPA no minimum stated; *Neuroscience PhD (Doctor of Philosophy):* GRE-V no minimum stated, GRE-Q no minimum stated, GRE-Analytical no minimum stated, overall undergraduate GPA no minimum stated, psychology GPA no minimum stated.

Other Criteria: (importance of criteria rated low, medium, or high): GRE scores—high, research experience—high, work experience—low, extracurricular activity—low, clinically related public service—low, GPA—high, letters of recommendation—high, interview—high, statement of goals and objectives—high, undergraduate major in psychology—low, specific undergraduate psychology courses taken—medium. For additional information on admission requirements, go to http://www.temple.edu/psychology/graduate/applications/requirements/.

Student Characteristics: The following represents characteristics of students in 2012–2013 in all graduate psychology programs in the department: Female—full-time 56, part-time 0; Male—full-time 33, part-time 0; African American/Black—full-time 4, part-time 0; Hispanic/Latino(a)—full-time 0, part-time 0; Asian/Pacific Islander—full-time 5, part-time 0; American Indian/Alaska Native—full-time 0, part-time 0; Caucasian/White—full-time 0, part-time 0; Multi-ethnic—full-time 0, part-time 0; students subject to the Americans With Disabilities Act—full-time 0, part-time 0; Unknown ethnicity—full-time 0, part-time 0; International students who hold an F-1 or J-1 Visa—full-time 0, part-time 0.

Financial Information/Assistance:
Tuition for Full-Time Study: *Doctoral:* State residents: $687 per credit hour; Nonstate residents: $981 per credit hour. Tuition is subject to change. See the following website for updates and changes in tuition costs: http://www.temple.edu/grad/admissions/tuition_fees.htm.

Financial Assistance:
First-Year Students: Teaching assistantships available for first year. Average amount paid per academic year: $16,690. Average number of hours worked per week: 20. Research assistantships available for first year. Average amount paid per academic year: $16,690. Average number of hours worked per week: 20. Fellowships and scholarships available for first year. Average amount paid per academic year: $22,000. Average number of hours worked per week: 0.

Advanced Students: Teaching assistantships available for advanced students. Average amount paid per academic year: $16,690. Average number of hours worked per week: 20. Research

assistantships available for advanced students. Average amount paid per academic year: $16,690. Average number of hours worked per week: 20. Fellowships and scholarships available for advanced students. Average amount paid per academic year: $22,000. Average number of hours worked per week: 0.

Additional Information: Of all students currently enrolled full time, 100% benefited from one or more of the listed financial assistance programs. Application and information available online at: http://www.temple.edu/psychology/graduate/applications/financial/.

Internships/Practica: Doctoral Degree (PhD Clinical Psychology): For those doctoral students for whom a professional psychology internship was required in this program prior to graduation, (10) students applied for an internship in 2011–2012, with (10) students obtaining an internship. Of those students who obtained an internship, (10) were paid internships. Of those students who obtained an internship, (10) students placed in APA/CPA accredited internships, (0) students placed in internships not APA/CPA accredited, but listed with the Association of Psychology Postdoctoral and Internship Programs (APPIC), (0) students placed in internships conforming to guidelines of the Council of Directors of School Psychology Programs (CDSPP), (0) students placed in internships that were not APA/CPA accredited, APPIC or CDSPP listed. Clinical students complete a 2,000-hour predoctoral internship at an agency or hospital typically in the Philadelphia metropolitan area.

Housing and Day Care: On-campus housing is available. See the following website for more information: http://www.temple.edu/studentaffairs/housing/. No on-campus day care facilities are available.

Employment of Department Graduates:

Master's Degree Graduates: Of those who graduated in the academic year 2011–2012, the following categories and numbers represent the postgraduate activities and employment of master's degree graduates: Enrolled in a postdoctoral residency/fellowship (n/a), employed in independent practice (n/a), total from the above (master's) (0).

Doctoral Degree Graduates: Of those who graduated in the academic year 2011–2012, the following categories and numbers represent the postgraduate activities and employment of doctoral degree graduates: Enrolled in a psychology doctoral program (n/a), enrolled in a postdoctoral residency/fellowship (2), employed in an academic position at a 2-year/4-year college (1), total from the above (doctoral) (3).

Additional Information:

Orientation, Objectives, and Emphasis of Department: The psychology department offers graduate training in: brain and cognitive sciences; clinical; developmental; developmental psychopathology; neuroscience; and social decision making and emotions. All doctoral programs are designed to prepare students for teaching in universities and colleges, conducting research in field and laboratory settings, and providing consultation in applied settings. The clinical program trains scientist–practitioners and provides students with research and clinical experience.

Special Facilities or Resources: The psychology department occupies eight floors of a high-rise building. The physical resources housed in the building include the Psychological Services Center (an in-house mental health facility where clinical students obtain practicum experience in psychotherapy), extensive laboratory space for human research, a human electrophysiology lab, an infant behavior lab, numerous observation rooms with one-way mirrors, audiovisual equipment (including mobile video equipment), and excellent computer facilities, including numerous micro- and minicomputers.

Information for Students With Physical Disabilities: See the following website for more information: http://www.temple.edu/studentaffairs/disability/.

Application Information:
Send to Graduate Administrator. Application available online. URL of online application: http://wwwtempleedu/apply/common/appcheckasp Students are admitted in the Fall, application deadline December 1. *Fee:* $65.

Villanova University
Department of Psychology
800 Lancaster Avenue
Villanova, PA 19085
Telephone: (610) 519-4720
Fax: (610) 519-4269
E-mail: *psychologyinformation@villanova.edu*
Web: *http://www1.villanova.edu/villanova/artsci/psychology.html*

Department Information:
1959. Chairperson: Thomas Toppino. Number of faculty: total—full-time 16, part-time 6; women—full-time 6, part-time 3; total—minority—full-time 1, part-time 1; women minority—part-time 1.

Programs and Degrees Offered:
Listed in the following order: Program area, degree type (T if terminal Master's), number awarded 7/11–6/12. General Psychology MA/MS (Master of Arts/Science) (T) 18.

Student Applications/Admissions:
Student Applications
General Psychology MA/MS (Master of Arts/Science)—Applications 2012–2013, 140. Total applicants accepted 2012–2013, 39. Number full-time enrolled (new admits only) 2012–2013, 18. Total enrolled 2012–2013 full-time, 37. Total enrolled 2012–2013 part-time, 0. Openings 2013–2014, 21. The median number of years required for completion of a degree in 2012–2013 were 2. The number of students enrolled full- and part-time who were dismissed or voluntarily withdrew from this program area in 2012–2013 were 0.

Scores: Entries appear in this order: required test or GPA, minimum score (if required), median score of students entering in 2012–2013. General Psychology MA/MS (Master of Arts/Science): GRE-V no minimum stated, 570, GRE-Q no minimum stated, 670, GRE-Analytical no minimum stated, 4.7, overall undergraduate GPA no minimum stated, 3.7, psychology GPA no minimum stated, 3.8.

Other Criteria: (importance of criteria rated low, medium, or high): GRE scores—high, research experience—medium, work experience—low, extracurricular activity—low, clinically related public service—low, GPA—high, letters of recommendation—high, interview—medium, statement of goals and objectives—medium, undergraduate major in psychology—medium, specific undergraduate psychology courses taken—high. For additional information on admission requirements, go to http://www1.villanova.edu/villanova/artsci/psychology/graduate/prospective/admission.html.

Student Characteristics: The following represents characteristics of students in 2012–2013 in all graduate psychology programs in the department: Female—full-time 23, part-time 0; Male—full-time 21, part-time 0; African American/Black—full-time 0, part-time 0; Hispanic/Latino(a)—full-time 4, part-time 0; Asian/Pacific Islander—full-time 2, part-time 0; American Indian/Alaska Native—full-time 0, part-time 0; Caucasian/White—full-time 38, part-time 0; Multi-ethnic—full-time 0, part-time 0; students subject to the Americans With Disabilities Act—full-time 0, part-time 0; Unknown ethnicity—full-time 0, part-time 0; International students who hold an F-1 or J-1 Visa—full-time 1, part-time 0.

Financial Information/Assistance:

Tuition for Full-Time Study: *Master's:* State residents: $700 per credit hour; Nonstate residents: $700 per credit hour. Tuition is subject to change. See the following website for updates and changes in tuition costs: http://www1.villanova.edu/villanova/finance/bursar/tuition/gradrates.html.

Financial Assistance:

First-Year Students: Research assistantships available for first year. Average amount paid per academic year: $14,680. Average number of hours worked per week: 20. Apply by March 1. Traineeships available for first year. Average amount paid per academic year: $7,340. Average number of hours worked per week: 14. Apply by March 1. Fellowships and scholarships available for first year. Average number of hours worked per week: 7. Apply by March 1.

Advanced Students: Research assistantships available for advanced students. Average amount paid per academic year: $14,680. Average number of hours worked per week: 20. Apply by March 1. Traineeships available for advanced students. Average amount paid per academic year: $7,340. Average number of hours worked per week: 14. Apply by March 1. Fellowships and scholarships available for advanced students. Average number of hours worked per week: 7. Apply by March 1.

Additional Information: Of all students currently enrolled full time, 55% benefited from one or more of the listed financial assistance programs. Application and information available online at: http://www1.villanova.edu/villanova/artsci/graduate/financing/cost.html.

Internships/Practica: Master's Degree (MA/MS General Psychology): An internship experience, such as a final research project or "capstone" experience is required of graduates.

Housing and Day Care: No on-campus housing is available. No on-campus day care facilities are available.

Employment of Department Graduates:

Master's Degree Graduates: Of those who graduated in the academic year 2011–2012, the following categories and numbers represent the postgraduate activities and employment of master's degree graduates: Enrolled in a psychology doctoral program (8), enrolled in another graduate/professional program (1), enrolled in a postdoctoral residency/fellowship (n/a), employed in independent practice (n/a), employed in business or industry (2), employed in a community mental health/counseling center (2), still seeking employment (2), do not know (1), total from the above (master's) (16).

Doctoral Degree Graduates: Of those who graduated in the academic year 2011–2012, the following categories and numbers represent the postgraduate activities and employment of doctoral degree graduates: Enrolled in a psychology doctoral program (n/a), total from the above (doctoral) (0).

Additional Information:

Orientation, Objectives, and Emphasis of Department: The department offers a program of study leading to the Master of Science in psychology. Individually tailored to meet each student's career interests and needs, the program provides a solid foundation in psychology with special emphasis on preparation for doctoral work. All incoming students are required to take a seminar in the foundations of research and a statistics course. All students also take laboratory courses in Cognition & Learning and Biopsychology. Depending upon the student's interest, he or she selects four elective courses from a reasonably broad range of course offerings such as psychopathology, psychological testing, developmental psychology, social psychology, personality, theories of psychotherapy, behavior modification, special topics, and individual research. During the second year, student efforts are concentrated on the thesis project, which is an intensive empirically-based project, done under the supervision of a faculty mentor. The student/faculty ratio approaches 2:1, allowing close interaction, careful advisement, and individual attention. The department has an active, research-oriented faculty.

Special Facilities or Resources: In addition to office space for faculty and all graduate assistants, the department has approximately 5800 square feet available for research. Equipment of particular interest to the graduate student includes: electronic and computer-controlled tachistoscopes; animal conditioning chambers; cognitive/computer labs; complete facilities for surgery and histology, including stereotaxic equipment for brain implantation; environmental chambers and rooms equipped for observation and automated recording of animal behavior; radial mazes; well-equipped vision labs; one-way vision rooms; audio/video recording and playback facilities; facilities for the design and development of experiments; and computer-based teaching labs. University computing facilities are all networked, with hundreds of remote terminals available.

Information for Students With Physical Disabilities: See the following website for more information: http://www1.villanova.edu/villanova/studentlife/disabilityservices.html.

Application Information:
Send to Dean, Graduate School, Villanova University, 800 Lancaster Avenue, Villanova, PA 19085. Application available online. URL of online application: http://www1.villanova.edu/villanova/artsci/graduate/application.html. Students are admitted in the Fall, application deadline March 1. Strong applications received by March 1 have a better chance of acceptance. Completed applications must be received by March 1 to ensure full consideration for financial aid. We may accept applications up until August 1 if there is space available. *Fee:* $50.

West Chester University of Pennsylvania

Department of Psychology
West Chester, PA 19383
Telephone: (610) 436-2945
Fax: (610) 436-2846
E-mail: *vjohnson@wcupa.edu*
Web: *http://www.wcupa.edu/_academics/sch_cas.psy/*

Department Information:

1967. Chairperson: Loretta Rieser-Danner. Number of faculty: total—full-time 22; women—full-time 14; total—minority—full-time 2; women minority—full-time 1.

Programs and Degrees Offered:

Listed in the following order: Program area, degree type (T if terminal Master's), number awarded 7/11–6/12. Clinical Psychology MA/MS (Master of Arts/Science) (T) 18, General Psychology MA/MS (Master of Arts/Science) (T) 1, Industrial/Organizational Psychology MA/MS (Master of Arts/Science) (T) 10.

Student Applications/Admissions:

Student Applications

Clinical Psychology MA/MS (Master of Arts/Science)—Applications 2012–2013, 96. Total applicants accepted 2012–2013, 55. Number full-time enrolled (new admits only) 2012–2013, 24. Number part-time enrolled (new admits only) 2012–2013, 0. Total enrolled 2012–2013 full-time, 61. Openings 2013–2014, 20. The median number of years required for completion of a degree in 2012–2013 were 2. The number of students enrolled full- and part-time who were dismissed or voluntarily withdrew from this program area in 2012–2013 were 0. *General Psychology MA/MS (Master of Arts/Science)*—Applications 2012–2013, 18. Total applicants accepted 2012–2013, 8. Number full-time enrolled (new admits only) 2012–2013, 5. Total enrolled 2012–2013 full-time, 10. Openings 2013–2014, 6. The median number of years required for completion of a degree in 2012–2013 were 2. The number of students enrolled full- and part-time who were dismissed or voluntarily withdrew from this program area in 2012–2013 were 0. *Industrial/Organizational Psychology MA/MS (Master of Arts/Science)*—Applications 2012–2013, 27. Total applicants accepted 2012–2013, 17. Number full-time enrolled (new admits only) 2012–2013, 4. Number part-time enrolled (new admits only) 2012–2013, 1. Total enrolled 2012–2013 full-time, 21. Total enrolled 2012–2013 part-time, 1. Openings 2013–2014, 15. The median number of years required for completion of a degree in 2012–2013 were 2.

Scores: Entries appear in this order: required test or GPA, minimum score (if required), median score of students entering in 2012–2013. *Clinical Psychology MA/MS (Master of Arts/Science):* GRE-V 153, GRE-Q 144, overall undergraduate GPA 3.0, 3.42, psychology GPA 3.25, 3.5; *General Psychology MA/MS (Master of Arts/Science):* GRE-V 500, GRE-Q 500, overall undergraduate GPA 3.0, psychology GPA 3.25; *Industrial/Organizational Psychology MA/MS (Master of Arts/Science):* GRE-V no minimum stated, 490, GRE-Q no minimum stated, 535, overall undergraduate GPA 3.0, 3.4, psychology GPA 3.25, 3.56.

Other Criteria: (importance of criteria rated low, medium, or high): GRE scores—high, research experience—medium, work experience—medium, extracurricular activity—medium, clinically related public service—medium, GPA—high, letters of recommendation—high, statement of goals and objectives—high, undergraduate major in psychology—low, specific undergraduate psychology courses taken—medium. For additional information on admission requirements, go to http://www.wcupa.edu/_academics/sch_cas.psy/gradadmissions.asp.

Student Characteristics: The following represents characteristics of students in 2012–2013 in all graduate psychology programs in the department: Female—full-time 64, part-time 1; Male—full-time 28, part-time 0; African American/Black—full-time 5, part-time 0; Hispanic/Latino(a)—full-time 3, part-time 0; Asian/Pacific Islander—full-time 5, part-time 0; American Indian/Alaska Native—full-time 1, part-time 0; Caucasian/White—full-time 78, part-time 1; Multi-ethnic—full-time 0, part-time 0; students subject to the Americans With Disabilities Act—full-time 0, part-time 0; Unknown ethnicity—full-time 0, part-time 0; International students who hold an F-1 or J-1 Visa—full-time 3, part-time 0.

Financial Information/Assistance:

Tuition for Full-Time Study: *Master's:* State residents: per academic year $7,220, $429 per credit hour; Nonstate residents: per academic year $11,592, $644 per credit hour. Tuition is subject to change. Additional fees are assessed to students beyond the costs of tuition for the following: general fee for full-time students: $105.05 per credit hour in-state and $115.05 for out-of-state. Tuition costs vary by program. See the following website for updates and changes in tuition costs: http://www.wcupa.edu/_information/afa/Fiscal/Bursar/tuition.asp. Higher tuition cost for this program: Clinical program = 12 credits per semester ($10,296 in state; $15,456 out of state).

Financial Assistance:

First-Year Students: Research assistantships available for first year. Average amount paid per academic year: $2,500. Average number of hours worked per week: 10. Apply by March 1.

Advanced Students: Research assistantships available for advanced students. Average amount paid per academic year: $2,500. Average number of hours worked per week: 10. Apply by March 1.

Additional Information: Of all students currently enrolled full time, 10% benefited from one or more of the listed financial assistance programs. Application and information available online at: http://www.wcupa.edu/_SERVICES/FIN_AID/.

Internships/Practica: Master's Degree (MA/MS Clinical Psychology): An internship experience, such as a final research project or "capstone" experience is required of graduates. Master's Degree (MA/MS General Psychology): An internship experience, such as a final research project or "capstone" experience is required of graduates. Master's Degree (MA/MS Industrial/Organizational Psychology): An internship experience, such as a final research project or "capstone" experience is required of graduates.

Clinical students are required to complete 6 credit hours of practicum and internship in a mental health setting. I/O students are required to complete a 3 credit hour internship in business or industry.

Housing and Day Care: No on-campus housing is available. No on-campus day care facilities are available.

Employment of Department Graduates:

Master's Degree Graduates: Of those who graduated in the academic year 2011–2012, the following categories and numbers represent the postgraduate activities and employment of master's degree graduates: Enrolled in a postdoctoral residency/fellowship (n/a), employed in independent practice (n/a), total from the above (master's) (0).

Doctoral Degree Graduates: Of those who graduated in the academic year 2011–2012, the following categories and numbers represent the postgraduate activities and employment of doctoral degree graduates: Enrolled in a psychology doctoral program (n/a), total from the above (doctoral) (0).

Additional Information:

Orientation, Objectives, and Emphasis of Department: The concentration in clinical psychology is designed for students who wish to work in applied settings such as community mental health facilities, hospitals, counseling centers, and other social and rehabilitation agencies, or who wish to continue their education at the doctoral level. Students with the latter goal in mind are strongly encouraged to engage in research in the course of their master's degree training by participating in faculty members' ongoing research programs or conducting their own research under faculty supervision for research report or thesis credit. The industrial/organizational concentration is appropriate for students interested in employment in business or industry, or for those who wish to continue their education at the doctoral level in a related area. A 3-credit internship and 3- to 6-credit research report or thesis are required. With careful selection of electives, internship placement, and research focus, students are able to develop specialization in human factors, personnel evaluation and placement, or group and organizational processes. The concentration in general psychology, in addition to exposing students to the major traditional subject matter of psychology, also provides the opportunity to explore particular areas of psychology in depth through the appropriate selection of elective coursework and research. The general concentration is appropriate for students interested in continuing their education at the doctoral level, as well as those interested in employment, particularly in research positions, upon the receipt of their master's degree.

Special Facilities or Resources: The department has laboratory space and equipment to support a variety of animal and human research.

Information for Students With Physical Disabilities: See the following website for more information: http://www.wcupa.edu/ussss/ossd/.

Application Information:

Send to Office of Graduate Studies and Sponsored Research, West Chester University, West Chester, PA 19383. Application available online. URL of online application: https://www.applyweb.com/apply/wcgrad/menu.html. Students are admitted in the Fall, application deadline March 1. Late applications will be reviewed if space remains in the program. *Fee:* $35.

Widener University
Institute for Graduate Clinical Psychology
School of Human Service Professions
One University Place
Chester, PA 19013
Telephone: (610) 499-1206
Fax: (610) 499-4625
E-mail: *graduate.psychology@widener.edu*
Web: *http://www.widener.edu/igcp/*

Department Information:
1970. Associate Dean and Director: Sanjay R. Nath, PhD. Number of faculty: total—full-time 15, part-time 14; women—full-time 6, part-time 6; total—minority—full-time 1, part-time 6.

Programs and Degrees Offered:
Listed in the following order: Program area, degree type (T if terminal Master's), number awarded 7/11–6/12. Clinical Psychology PsyD (Doctor of Psychology) 28.

APA Accreditation: Clinical PsyD (Doctor of Psychology). Student Outcome Data Website: http://www.widener.edu/academics/schools/shsp/psyd/studentadmissionsandotherdata.aspx.

Student Applications/Admissions:
Student Applications
Clinical Psychology PsyD (Doctor of Psychology)—Applications 2012–2013, 304. Total applicants accepted 2012–2013, 55. Number full-time enrolled (new admits only) 2012–2013, 43. Number part-time enrolled (new admits only) 2012–2013, 0. Total enrolled 2012–2013 full-time, 174. Total enrolled 2012–2013 part-time, 12. Openings 2013–2014, 32. The median number of years required for completion of a degree in 2012–2013 were 5. The number of students enrolled full- and part-time who were dismissed or voluntarily withdrew from this program area in 2012–2013 were 1.

Scores: Entries appear in this order: required test or GPA, minimum score (if required), median score of students entering in 2012–2013. *Clinical Psychology PsyD (Doctor of Psychology):* GRE-V 156, GRE-Q 156, GRE-Analytical 4.5, overall undergraduate GPA 3.2.

Other Criteria: (importance of criteria rated low, medium, or high): GRE scores—high, work experience—medium, extracurricular activity—medium, clinically related public service—medium, GPA—high, letters of recommendation—high, interview—high, statement of goals and objectives—high, specific undergraduate psychology courses taken—low, An undergraduate major in psychology is not required for admission; however, some basic psychology courses are required before enrollment (statistics, research design/experimental psychology, abnormal psychology/psychopathology). We encourage applications from individuals from various disciplines and with a wide range of experiences. For additional information on admission requirements, go to http://www.widener.edu/academics/schools/shsp/psyd/admission/default.aspx.

Student Characteristics: The following represents characteristics of students in 2012–2013 in all graduate psychology programs in the department: Female—full-time 136, part-time 7; Male—full-time 38, part-time 5; African American/Black—full-time 9, part-time 2; Hispanic/Latino(a)—full-time 13, part-time 0; Asian/Pacific Islander—full-time 12, part-time 1; American Indian/Alaska Native—full-time 1, part-time 0; Caucasian/White—full-time 133, part-time 9; Multi-ethnic—full-time 4, part-time 0; students subject to the Americans With Disabilities Act—full-time 2, part-time 0; Unknown ethnicity—full-time 2, part-time 0; International students who hold an F-1 or J-1 Visa—full-time 6, part-time 0.

Financial Information/Assistance:

Tuition for Full-Time Study: *Doctoral:* State residents: per academic year $26,116; Nonstate residents: per academic year $26,116. Tuition is subject to change. See the following website for updates and changes in tuition costs: http://www.widener.edu/admissions/graduate/tuition.aspx.

Financial Assistance:

First-Year Students: Fellowships and scholarships available for first year. Average amount paid per academic year: $17,759. Average number of hours worked per week: 0. Apply by March 1.

Advanced Students: No information provided.

Additional Information: Of all students currently enrolled full time, 33% benefited from one or more of the listed financial assistance programs. Application and information available online at: http://www.widener.edu/admissions/graduate/financial_aid/default.aspx.

Internships/Practica: Doctoral Degree (PsyD Clinical Psychology): For those doctoral students for whom a professional psychology internship was required in this program prior to graduation, (67) students applied for an internship in 2011–2012, with (67) students obtaining an internship. Of those students who obtained an internship, (67) were paid internships. Of those students who obtained an internship, (67) students placed in APA/CPA accredited internships, (0) students placed in internships not APA/CPA accredited, but listed with the Association of Psychology Postdoctoral and Internship Programs (APPIC), (0) students placed in internships conforming to guidelines of the Council of Directors of School Psychology Programs (CDSPP), (0) students placed in internships that were not APA/CPA accredited, APPIC or CDSPP listed. The program has an exclusively affiliated internship that is a half-time over a two-year period. The APA-accredited internship is housed at Widener University, but placements are within a 50-mile radius of the campus. 100% of fourth- and fifth-year students are placed.

Housing and Day Care: On-campus housing is available. See the following website for more information: http://www.widener.edu/campus_life/living/housing/. On-campus day care facilities are available. See the following website for more information: http://cdc.widener.edu/.

Employment of Department Graduates:

Master's Degree Graduates: Of those who graduated in the academic year 2011–2012, the following categories and numbers represent the postgraduate activities and employment of master's degree graduates: Enrolled in a postdoctoral residency/fellowship (n/a), employed in independent practice (n/a), total from the above (master's) (0).

Doctoral Degree Graduates: Of those who graduated in the academic year 2011–2012, the following categories and numbers represent the postgraduate activities and employment of doctoral degree graduates: Enrolled in a psychology doctoral program (n/a), enrolled in a postdoctoral residency/fellowship (5), employed in independent practice (2), employed in an academic position at a university (1), employed in other positions at a higher education institution (2), employed in a professional position in a school system (3), employed in business or industry (2), employed in government agency (4), employed in a community mental health/counseling center (7), employed in a hospital/medical center (3), total from the above (doctoral) (29).

Additional Information:

Orientation, Objectives, and Emphasis of Department: The PsyD program retains the basic skills and knowledge traditional to clinical psychology, such as psychodiagnostic testing and psychotherapy, while simultaneously exposing the individual to new ideas and practices in the field. The law-psychology (JD/PsyD) program presumes that every law and court decision is in part based upon psychological assumptions about how people act and how their actions can be controlled. It is designed to train lawyer-clinical psychologists to identify and evaluate these assumptions and apply their psychological knowledge to improve the law, legal process, and legal system. Students earn a law degree from the Widener University School of Law, and a doctorate in psychology from Widener's Institute for Graduate Clinical Psychology. The PsyD/MBA program is based on the premise that health care organizations as well as the mental health and health care fields at large are in need of well-trained leaders and advocates who integrate psychological and business-organizational knowledge.

Special Facilities or Resources: One of the hallmarks of our program is the variety of internship and practicum opportunities available to students, all of which are within driving distance of the university. A corollary resource is the availability of practicing clinicians to teach in the program, a factor that provides breadth, relevance, and enrichment to the curriculum. Widener University is situated near Philadelphia and in the middle of the Eastern corridor between New York and Washington, DC. As a result, our students enjoy a rich diversity of educational resources, field experiences, and employment opportunities.

Information for Students With Physical Disabilities: See the following website for more information: http://www.widener.edu/academics/support/disabilities/default.aspx.

Application Information:
Send to Widener University, Attn: Clinical Psychology Admissions, One University Place, Chester, PA 19013. Application available online. URL of online application: http://www.widener.edu/admissions/graduate/. Students are admitted in the Fall, application deadline December 15. *Fee:* $50.

Widener University (2012 data)
Law-Psychology (JD-PsyD) Graduate Training Program
Institute for Graduate Clinical Psychology & School of Law
One University Place
Chester, PA 19013-5792
Telephone: (610) 499-1206
Fax: (610) 499-4625
E-mail: *aelwork@widener.edu*
Web: *http://www.widener.edu/jdpsyd*

Department Information:
1989. Director - (within Institute for Graduate Clinical Psycholog: Amiram Elwork, PhD. Number of faculty: total—full-time 13, part-time 15; women—full-time 5, part-time 10; total—minority—full-time 2, part-time 4; women minority—full-time 1, part-time 2.

Programs and Degrees Offered:
Listed in the following order: Program area, degree type (T if terminal Master's), number awarded 7/11–6/12. Law-Psychology (Jd/ Psyd) Other 2.

Student Applications/Admissions:
Student Applications
Law-Psychology (Jd/ Psyd) Other—Applications 2012–2013, 8. Total applicants accepted 2012–2013, 2. Number full-time enrolled (new admits only) 2012–2013, 2. Total enrolled 2012–2013 full-time, 10. Total enrolled 2012–2013 part-time, 0. Openings 2013–2014, 3. The median number of years required for completion of a degree in 2012–2013 were 6. The number of students enrolled full- and part-time who were dismissed or voluntarily withdrew from this program area in 2012–2013 were 0.

Scores: Entries appear in this order: required test or GPA, minimum score (if required), median score of students entering in 2012–2013. *Law-Psychology (JD/ PsyD) Other:* GRE-V no minimum stated, GRE-Q no minimum stated, GRE-Analytical no minimum stated, overall undergraduate GPA no minimum stated, last 2 years GPA no minimum stated, psychology GPA no minimum stated.

Other Criteria: (importance of criteria rated low, medium, or high): GRE scores—high, research experience—low, work experience—medium, extracurricular activity—medium, clinically related public service—medium, GPA—high, letters of recommendation—medium, interview—high, statement of goals and objectives—high, LSAT—high, undergraduate major in psychology—medium, specific undergraduate psychology courses taken—medium.

Student Characteristics: The following represents characteristics of students in 2012–2013 in all graduate psychology programs in the department: Female—full-time 5, part-time 0; Male—full-time 5, part-time 0; African American/Black—full-time 0, part-time 0; Hispanic/Latino(a)—full-time 0, part-time 0; Asian/Pacific Islander—full-time 0, part-time 0; American Indian/Alaska Native—full-time 1, part-time 0; Caucasian/White—full-time 7, part-time 0; Multi-ethnic—full-time 0, part-time 0; students subject to the Americans With Disabilities Act—full-time 0, part-time 0; Unknown ethnicity—full-time 2, part-time 0; International students who hold an F-1 or J-1 Visa—full-time 0, part-time 0.

Financial Information/Assistance:
Tuition for Full-Time Study: *Doctoral:* State residents: per academic year $28,500; Nonstate residents: per academic year $28,500. Tuition is subject to change.

Financial Assistance:
First-Year Students: Fellowships and scholarships available for first year. Average amount paid per academic year: $0. Average number of hours worked per week: 0.

Advanced Students: Traineeships available for advanced students. Average amount paid per academic year: $0. Average number of hours worked per week: 0. Fellowships and scholarships available for advanced students. Average amount paid per academic year: $0. Average number of hours worked per week: 0.

Additional Information: Of all students currently enrolled full time, 100% benefited from one or more of the listed financial assistance programs.

Internships/Practica: Students are in field placements during five of the six years of training. During two of the first three years, students are assigned to clinical psychology practica. These are introductory experiences designed to acquaint the students with a variety of settings in which they can develop fundamental psychological skills in testing/assessment and psychotherapy/intervention. Fourth year field experiences are in a legal setting (law firm, court, legal agency), where they are given an opportunity to practice their legal skills. Fifth and sixth year experiences are internship rotations that allow students the opportunity to sharpen their clinical and forensic psychology skills. Widener's APA accredited integrated clinical internship with its various rotations (including forensic rotations) is highly unusual. In most programs, students participate in internships that are independent of their graduate programs. Our internship is embedded in the program. While continuing to take their coursework, students complete their internship rotations over a two-year period at various clinical sites affiliated with Widener. This allows for better integration between coursework and practical experience and relieves the student of the inconveniences associated with finding a separate internship and/or relocating.

Housing and Day Care: On-campus housing is available. On-campus day care facilities are available.

Employment of Department Graduates:
Master's Degree Graduates: Of those who graduated in the academic year 2011–2012, the following categories and numbers represent the postgraduate activities and employment of master's degree graduates: Enrolled in a psychology doctoral program (0), enrolled in another graduate/professional program (0), enrolled in a postdoctoral residency/fellowship (n/a), employed in independent practice (n/a), employed in an academic position at a university (0), employed in an academic position at a 2-year/4-year college (0), employed in other positions at a higher education institution (0), employed in a professional position in a school system (0), employed in business or industry (0), employed in government agency (0), employed in a community mental health/counseling center (0), employed in a hospital/medical center (0), still seeking employment (0), other employment position (0), total from the above (master's) (0).

Doctoral Degree Graduates: Of those who graduated in the academic year 2011–2012, the following categories and numbers represent the postgraduate activities and employment of doctoral degree graduates: Enrolled in a psychology doctoral program (n/a), enrolled in a postdoctoral residency/fellowship (0), employed in independent practice (0), employed in an academic position at a university (0), employed in an academic position at a 2-year/4-year college (0), employed in other positions at a higher education institution (0), employed in a professional position in a school system (0), employed in business or industry (0), employed in government agency (0), employed in a community mental health/counseling center (0), employed in a hospital/medical center (0), still seeking employment (0), other employment position (0), total from the above (doctoral) (0).

Additional Information:

Orientation, Objectives, and Emphasis of Department: Widener University's Law-Psychology Graduate Program is based on the idea that many legal issues involve underlying psychological questions. It trains graduates to combine their knowledge of psychology and law and bring fresh insights to the process of understanding, evaluating and correcting important psycholegal problems. While a large portion of the curriculum is similar to that required of all students in the PsyD and JD programs, it includes a number of courses and requirements (e.g., dissertation) designed specifically to help students acquire an integration of psychology and law and to develop specialized skills. In addition, students are given opportunities to put their integrated skills into practice within their field placements. Students develop special expertise on many issues at the interface of law and clinical psychology and are prepared to play diverse roles in society, including lawyer, forensic psychologist, professor, consultant, administrator, policy maker, judge, l6egislator, etc. This 6-year program offers several benefits: (1) It allows students to pursue clinical psychology and law simultaneously. (2) It saves students the equivalent of two years of tuition and time. (3) It trains graduates to integrate the two fields conceptually and offers them a significant way of differentiating themselves in the job market.

Special Facilities or Resources: Widener University is situated near Philadelphia and in the middle of the eastern corridor between New York and Washington, DC As a result, our students enjoy a rich diversity of educational resources, field experiences, and employment opportunities.

Application Information:
Send to Law-Psychology Graduate Program, Admissions Institute for Graduate Clinical Psychology, One University Place, Chester, PA 19013-5792. Application available online. URL of online application: http://www.widener.edu/jdpsyd. Students are admitted in the Fall, application deadline February 1. *Fee:* $0.

Brown University

Department of Cognitive, Linguistic, and Psychological
  Sciences
190 Thayer St
Providence, RI 02912
Telephone: (401) 863-2727
Fax: (401) 863-2255
E-mail: *CLPS@brown.edu*
Web: *http://brown.edu/Departments/CLPS*

Department Information:

1891. Chairperson: William Heindel. Number of faculty: total—full-time 29; women—full-time 11; total—minority—full-time 1; women minority—full-time 1.

Programs and Degrees Offered:

Listed in the following order: Program area, degree type (T if terminal Master's), number awarded 7/11–6/12. Psychology PhD (Doctor of Philosophy) 2, Cognitive Science PhD (Doctor of Philosophy) 4, Linguistics PhD (Doctor of Philosophy) 0.

Student Applications/Admissions:

Student Applications

Psychology PhD (Doctor of Philosophy)—Applications 2012–2013, 115. Total applicants accepted 2012–2013, 4. Number full-time enrolled (new admits only) 2012–2013, 4. Number part-time enrolled (new admits only) 2012–2013, 0. Total enrolled 2012–2013 full-time, 16. Total enrolled 2012–2013 part-time, 0. Openings 2013–2014, 3. The median number of years required for completion of a degree in 2012–2013 were 5. The number of students enrolled full- and part-time who were dismissed or voluntarily withdrew from this program area in 2012–2013 were 0. *Cognitive Science PhD (Doctor of Philosophy)*—Applications 2012–2013, 118. Total applicants accepted 2012–2013, 14. Number full-time enrolled (new admits only) 2012–2013, 6. Number part-time enrolled (new admits only) 2012–2013, 0. Total enrolled 2012–2013 full-time, 25. Total enrolled 2012–2013 part-time, 2. Openings 2013–2014, 6. The median number of years required for completion of a degree in 2012–2013 were 5. The number of students enrolled full- and part-time who were dismissed or voluntarily withdrew from this program area in 2012–2013 were 0. *Linguistics PhD (Doctor of Philosophy)*—Applications 2012–2013, 28. Total applicants accepted 2012–2013, 1. Number full-time enrolled (new admits only) 2012–2013, 1. Number part-time enrolled (new admits only) 2012–2013, 0. Total enrolled 2012–2013 full-time, 1. Total enrolled 2012–2013 part-time, 0. Openings 2013–2014, 1. The median number of years required for completion of a degree in 2012–2013 were 5. The number of students enrolled full- and part-time who were dismissed or voluntarily withdrew from this program area in 2012–2013 were 0.

Scores: Entries appear in this order: required test or GPA, minimum score (if required), median score of students entering in 2012–2013. *Psychology PhD (Doctor of Philosophy):* GRE-V no minimum stated, GRE-Q no minimum stated, GRE-Analytical no minimum stated; *Cognitive Science PhD (Doctor of Philosophy):* GRE-V no minimum stated, GRE-Q no minimum stated, GRE-Analytical no minimum stated; *Linguistics PhD (Doctor of Philosophy):* GRE-V no minimum stated, GRE-Q no minimum stated, GRE-Analytical no minimum stated.

Other Criteria: (importance of criteria rated low, medium, or high): GRE scores—high, research experience—high, work experience—low, extracurricular activity—low, GPA—high, letters of recommendation—high, interview—high, statement of goals and objectives—high, undergraduate major in psychology—low, specific undergraduate psychology courses taken—low, For each of the three programs (psychology, cognitive science, linguistics), somewhat different prior course work is expected.

Student Characteristics: The following represents characteristics of students in 2012–2013 in all graduate psychology programs in the department: Female—full-time 18, part-time 0; Male—full-time 24, part-time 2; African American/Black—full-time 1, part-time 0; Hispanic/Latino(a)—full-time 4, part-time 0; Asian/Pacific Islander—full-time 1, part-time 0; American Indian/Alaska Native—part-time 0; Caucasian/White—full-time 18, part-time 2; Multi-ethnic—full-time 0, part-time 0; students subject to the Americans With Disabilities Act—full-time 0, part-time 0; Unknown ethnicity—full-time 18, part-time 0; International students who hold an F-1 or J-1 Visa—full-time 18, part-time 0.

Financial Information/Assistance:

Tuition for Full-Time Study: *Doctoral:* State residents: per academic year $42,808; Nonstate residents: per academic year $42,808. Tuition is subject to change. See the following website for updates and changes in tuition costs: http://www.brown.edu/Administration/Financial_Services/Bursar/GraduateStudents.html.

Financial Assistance:

First-Year Students: Fellowships and scholarships available for first year. Average amount paid per academic year: $26,250.

Advanced Students: Teaching assistantships available for advanced students. Average amount paid per academic year: $26,250. Research assistantships available for advanced students. Average amount paid per academic year: $26,250. Fellowships and scholarships available for advanced students. Average amount paid per academic year: $26,250.

Additional Information: Of all students currently enrolled full time, 100% benefited from one or more of the listed financial assistance programs. Application and information available online at: http://www.brown.edu/academics/gradschool/financing-support/phd-funding.

Housing and Day Care: On-campus housing is available. See the following website for more information: http://reslife.brown.edu/graduate_students/oncampus.html. No on-campus day care facilities are available.

Employment of Department Graduates:

Master's Degree Graduates: Of those who graduated in the academic year 2011–2012, the following categories and numbers

represent the postgraduate activities and employment of master's degree graduates: Enrolled in a postdoctoral residency/fellowship (n/a), employed in independent practice (n/a), total from the above (master's) (0).

Doctoral Degree Graduates: Of those who graduated in the academic year 2011–2012, the following categories and numbers represent the postgraduate activities and employment of doctoral degree graduates: Enrolled in a psychology doctoral program (n/a), enrolled in a postdoctoral residency/fellowship (4), employed in an academic position at a university (2), total from the above (doctoral) (6).

Additional Information:

Orientation, Objectives, and Emphasis of Department: Brown University's Department of Cognitive, Linguistic, and Psychological Sciences is a unique interdisciplinary department that offers PhD programs in three fields: Cognitive Science, Linguistics, and Psychology. Graduate students are admitted to the Department as a whole and select a specific PhD program by the end of their first year. Given the interdisciplinary collaborations among faculty in the department, graduate students are able to carry out coursework and research in many areas and from many methodological perspectives. Students are encouraged to compose advising committees with faculty from the different programs to be exposed to multiple approaches and traditions.

Special Facilities or Resources: Ambulatory virtual reality systems; wide-area motion tracking system; high-performance parallel supercomputer; 3.0T MRI system; 64-channel Event Related Potential (ERP) system, multiple eye-trackers; speech and phonetics labs; gait laboratory; high-performance 3-D graphics work stations; animal behavior and communication laboratories; infant and child testing facilities; computerized testing labs; dyadic and group social interaction AV recording facilities.

Information for Students With Physical Disabilities: See the following website for more information: http://www.brown.edu/Student_Services/Office_of_Student_Life/dss/.

Application Information:

Application available online. URL of online application: https://www.applyweb.com/browng/. Students are admitted in the Fall, application deadline December 15. *Fee:* $75.

Rhode Island College
Psychology Department
Faculty of Arts & Sciences
600 Mt. Pleasant Avenue HM 311
Providence, RI 02908
Telephone: (401) 456-8015
Fax: (401) 456-8751
E-mail: *psychgradprgm@ric.edu*
Web: *http://www.ric.edu/graduateStudies*

Department Information:

Director, Graduate Programs in Psychology: Christine A. Marco, PhD. Number of faculty: total—full-time 18; women—full-time 9; total—minority—full-time 1; women minority—full-time 1; faculty subject to the Americans With Disabilities Act 1.

Programs and Degrees Offered:

Listed in the following order: Program area, degree type (T if terminal Master's), number awarded 7/11–6/12. Psychology MA/MS (Master of Arts/Science) (T) 3, Health Psychology Certificate Other.

Student Applications/Admissions:
Student Applications

Psychology MA/MS (Master of Arts/Science)—Applications 2012–2013, 17. Total applicants accepted 2012–2013, 7. Number full-time enrolled (new admits only) 2012–2013, 2. Number part-time enrolled (new admits only) 2012–2013, 2. Total enrolled 2012–2013 full-time, 5. Total enrolled 2012–2013 part-time, 6. Openings 2013–2014, 15. The median number of years required for completion of a degree in 2012–2013 were 2. The number of students enrolled full- and part-time who were dismissed or voluntarily withdrew from this program area in 2012–2013 were 0. *Health Psychology Certificate Other*—Applications 2012–2013, 3. Total applicants accepted 2012–2013, 2. Number part-time enrolled (new admits only) 2012–2013, 1. Total enrolled 2012–2013 part-time, 1. Openings 2013–2014, 10.

Scores: Entries appear in this order: required test or GPA, minimum score (if required), median score of students entering in 2012–2013. *Psychology MA/MS (Master of Arts/Science):* GRE-V no minimum stated, GRE-Q no minimum stated, overall undergraduate GPA 3.0, last 2 years GPA 3.0, psychology GPA 3.0; *Health Psychology Certificate Other:* overall undergraduate GPA 3.0, last 2 years GPA 3.0, psychology GPA 3.0.
Other Criteria: (importance of criteria rated low, medium, or high): GRE scores—high, research experience—medium, work experience—low, extracurricular activity—low, GPA—high, letters of recommendation—high, interview—high, statement of goals and objectives—high, undergraduate major in psychology—medium, specific undergraduate psychology courses taken—high. For additional information on admission requirements, go to http://www.ric.edu/psychology/psychMa.php.

Student Characteristics: The following represents characteristics of students in 2012–2013 in all graduate psychology programs in the department: Female—full-time 4, part-time 7; Male—full-time 1, part-time 0; African American/Black—full-time 0, part-time 0; Hispanic/Latino(a)—full-time 0, part-time 0; Asian/Pacific Islander—full-time 0, part-time 0; American Indian/Alaska Native—full-time 0, part-time 0; Caucasian/White—full-time 0, part-time 0; Multi-ethnic—full-time 0, part-time 0; students subject to the Americans With Disabilities Act—full-time 0, part-time 0; Unknown ethnicity—full-time 5, part-time 7; International students who hold an F-1 or J-1 Visa—full-time 0, part-time 0.

Financial Information/Assistance:
Tuition for Full-Time Study: *Master's:* State residents: $372 per credit hour; Nonstate residents: $724 per credit hour. Tuition is subject to change. See the following website for updates and changes in tuition costs: http://www.ric.edu/bursar/tuition.php. Higher tuition cost for this program: MA and CT students living within a 50-mile radius receive a discounted tuition rate.

Financial Assistance:
First-Year Students: Teaching assistantships available for first year. Average amount paid per academic year: $3,000. Aver-

age number of hours worked per week: 20. Apply by March 1. Fellowships and scholarships available for first year. Average amount paid per academic year: $1,000. Apply by March 1.

Advanced Students: Teaching assistantships available for advanced students. Average amount paid per academic year: $3,000. Apply by March 1.

Additional Information: Of all students currently enrolled full time, 20% benefited from one or more of the listed financial assistance programs. Application and information available online at: http://www.ric.edu/financialAid/graduate2.php.

Internships/Practica: Master's Degree (MA/MS Psychology): An internship experience, such as a final research project or "capstone" experience is required of graduates.

Housing and Day Care: No on-campus housing is available. On-campus day care facilities are available. See the following website for more information: http://www.riccoop.org/.

Employment of Department Graduates:
Master's Degree Graduates: Of those who graduated in the academic year 2011–2012, the following categories and numbers represent the postgraduate activities and employment of master's degree graduates: Enrolled in a postdoctoral residency/fellowship (n/a), employed in independent practice (n/a), total from the above (master's) (0).
Doctoral Degree Graduates: Of those who graduated in the academic year 2011–2012, the following categories and numbers represent the postgraduate activities and employment of doctoral degree graduates: Enrolled in a psychology doctoral program (n/a), total from the above (doctoral) (0).

Additional Information:
Orientation, Objectives, and Emphasis of Department: The overall mission of the graduate programs in psychology at Rhode Island College is to provide an education in the science of human behavior. The Certificate of Graduate Studies (C.G.S.) in Health Psychology program requires 16 credits of post-baccalaureate coursework in research methods, statistics, health psychology, stress management, epidemiology & health statistics, and public health science, which can be used in a variety of health-related employment settings. The Master of Arts (MA) in Psychology degree is designed to prepare students for doctoral study. Students in the Masters program complete 30 credits of coursework in research methods, statistics, personality, cognitive, developmental, social psychology, plus electives. All students in the Masters program are required to complete an independent research project and a comprehensive exam. The psychology department faculty at Rhode Island College have ongoing research interests in the areas of intergroup relations, family violence, chemical dependency, gambling disorders, health psychology, language development, moral development, and neuroscience.

Special Facilities or Resources: Research laboratories include areas of social psychology, developmental psychology, health psychology, neuroscience, and language development.

Information for Students With Physical Disabilities: See the following website for more information: http://www.ric.edu/disabilityservices/.

Application Information:
Send to Graduate Program Admissions, c/o Dean of the Faculty of Arts and Sciences, 150 Gaige Hall, Rhode Island College, 600 Mt. Pleasant Avenue, Providence, RI 02908. Application available online. URL of online application: http://www.ric.edu/facultyArtsSciences/graduate_requirements.php. Students are admitted in the Fall, application deadline March 1; Spring, application deadline November 1. Applications received after these deadlines will be considered for admission on a space-available basis. Applicants who are also applying for assistantships or scholarships must meet the March 1 deadline. *Fee:* $50.

Rhode Island, University of
Department of Psychology
Arts and Sciences
142 Flagg Road
Kingston, RI 02881
Telephone: (401) 874-2193
Fax: (401) 874-2157
E-mail: *sbrady@uri.edu*
Web: *http://www.uri.edu/artsci/psy*

Department Information:
1961. Interim Chairperson: Susan Brady. Number of faculty: total—full-time 26; women—full-time 12; total—minority—full-time 2; women minority—full-time 2.

Programs and Degrees Offered:
Listed in the following order: Program area, degree type (T if terminal Master's), number awarded 7/11–6/12. School Psychology MA/MS (Master of Arts/Science) (T) 4, Clinical Psychology PhD (Doctor of Philosophy) 5, School Psychology PhD (Doctor of Philosophy) 4, Behavioral Science PhD (Doctor of Philosophy) 3.

APA Accreditation: Clinical PhD (Doctor of Philosophy). Student Outcome Data Website: http://www.uri.edu/artsci/psy/clinical_stats. School PhD (Doctor of Philosophy). Student Outcome Data Website: http://www.uri.edu/artsci/psy/school_prospectivestudent.

Student Applications/Admissions:
Student Applications
School Psychology MA/MS (Master of Arts/Science)—Applications 2012–2013, 34. Total applicants accepted 2012–2013, 7. Number full-time enrolled (new admits only) 2012–2013, 4. Number part-time enrolled (new admits only) 2012–2013, 0. Total enrolled 2012–2013 full-time, 13. Total enrolled 2012–2013 part-time, 0. Openings 2013–2014, 6. The median number of years required for completion of a degree in 2012–2013 were 3. The number of students enrolled full- and part-time who were dismissed or voluntarily withdrew from this program area in 2012–2013 were 0. *Clinical Psychology PhD (Doctor of Philosophy)*—Applications 2012–2013, 277. Total applicants accepted 2012–2013, 11. Number full-time enrolled (new admits only) 2012–2013, 5. Number part-time enrolled (new admits only) 2012–2013, 0. Total enrolled 2012–2013 full-time, 39. Total enrolled 2012–2013 part-time, 0. Openings 2013–2014, 6. The median number of years required for completion of a degree in 2012–2013 were 6. The number of students enrolled full- and part-time who were dismissed or

voluntarily withdrew from this program area in 2012–2013 were 0. *School Psychology PhD (Doctor of Philosophy)*—Applications 2012–2013, 45. Total applicants accepted 2012–2013, 15. Number full-time enrolled (new admits only) 2012–2013, 10. Number part-time enrolled (new admits only) 2012–2013, 0. Total enrolled 2012–2013 full-time, 31. Total enrolled 2012–2013 part-time, 0. Openings 2013–2014, 6. The median number of years required for completion of a degree in 2012–2013 were 6. The number of students enrolled full- and part-time who were dismissed or voluntarily withdrew from this program area in 2012–2013 were 1. *Behavioral Science PhD (Doctor of Philosophy)*—Applications 2012–2013, 28. Total applicants accepted 2012–2013, 11. Number full-time enrolled (new admits only) 2012–2013, 7. Number part-time enrolled (new admits only) 2012–2013, 0. Total enrolled 2012–2013 full-time, 38. Total enrolled 2012–2013 part-time, 0. Openings 2013–2014, 6. The median number of years required for completion of a degree in 2012–2013 were 4. The number of students enrolled full- and part-time who were dismissed or voluntarily withdrew from this program area in 2012–2013 were 0.

Scores: Entries appear in this order: required test or GPA, minimum score (if required), median score of students entering in 2012–2013. *School Psychology MA/MS (Master of Arts/Science):* GRE-V no minimum stated, 500, GRE-Q no minimum stated, 520, GRE-Analytical no minimum stated, 4, overall undergraduate GPA no minimum stated, 3.25; *Clinical Psychology PhD (Doctor of Philosophy):* GRE-V no minimum stated, 157, GRE-Q no minimum stated, 155, overall undergraduate GPA no minimum stated, 3.52; *School Psychology PhD (Doctor of Philosophy):* GRE-V no minimum stated, 550, GRE-Q no minimum stated, 600, GRE-Analytical no minimum stated, 4.5, overall undergraduate GPA no minimum stated, 3.50; *Behavioral Science PhD (Doctor of Philosophy):* GRE-V no minimum stated, 490, GRE-Q no minimum stated, 705, overall undergraduate GPA no minimum stated, 3.56.

Other Criteria: (importance of criteria rated low, medium, or high): GRE scores—medium, research experience—high, work experience—medium, extracurricular activity—low, clinically related public service—medium, GPA—high, letters of recommendation—high, interview—high, statement of goals and objectives—high, program match—high, undergraduate major in psychology—medium, specific undergraduate psychology courses taken—medium, Importance of criteria varies by program. Behavioral Science: High emphasis on research interest and experience; no required interview; we also consider GPA, GRE, focus and quality of personal statement, teaching experience, multicultural interests, reference letters, and program-applicant fit. Clinical Program: Factors we look at are: GRE, GPA, program/applicant match, research experience, letters of recommendation, and overall evaluation. Interview required. School Program: Academic aptitude (GRE + GPA); quality of personal statement; research and applied experience; letters of recommendation; fit between applicant goals and program offerings. For additional information on admission requirements, go to http://www.uri.edu/artsci/psy/all_admissions.

Student Characteristics: The following represents characteristics of students in 2012–2013 in all graduate psychology programs in the department: Female—full-time 93, part-time 0; Male—full-time 28, part-time 0; African American/Black—full-time 18, part-time 0; Hispanic/Latino(a)—full-time 15, part-time 0; Asian/Pacific Islander—full-time 9, part-time 0; American Indian/Alaska Native—full-time 1, part-time 0; Caucasian/White—full-time 77, part-time 0; Multi-ethnic—full-time 1, part-time 0; students subject to the Americans With Disabilities Act—full-time 1, part-time 0; Unknown ethnicity—full-time 0, part-time 0; International students who hold an F-1 or J-1 Visa—full-time 10, part-time 0.

Financial Information/Assistance:

Tuition for Full-Time Study: *Master's:* State residents: per academic year $11,532, $641 per credit hour; Nonstate residents: per academic year $23,606, $1,311 per credit hour. *Doctoral:* State residents: per academic year $11,532, $641 per credit hour; Nonstate residents: per academic year $23,606, $1,311 per credit hour. Tuition is subject to change. Additional fees are assessed to students beyond the costs of tuition for the following: health services, student services, technology, registration. See the following website for updates and changes in tuition costs: http://www.uri.edu/es/acadinfo/acadyear/tuition.html.

Financial Assistance:

First-Year Students: Teaching assistantships available for first year. Average amount paid per academic year: $15,344. Average number of hours worked per week: 20. Apply by April 1. Research assistantships available for first year. Average amount paid per academic year: $15,344. Average number of hours worked per week: 20. Fellowships and scholarships available for first year. Average amount paid per academic year: $15,344. Average number of hours worked per week: 0. Apply by March 4.

Advanced Students: Teaching assistantships available for advanced students. Average amount paid per academic year: $16,028. Average number of hours worked per week: 20. Apply by April 1. Research assistantships available for advanced students. Average amount paid per academic year: $16,028. Average number of hours worked per week: 20. Fellowships and scholarships available for advanced students. Average amount paid per academic year: $16,028. Average number of hours worked per week: 0. Apply by March 4.

Additional Information: Of all students currently enrolled full time, 62% benefited from one or more of the listed financial assistance programs. Application and information available online at: http://www.uri.edu/gsadmis/Financial_Support.htm.

Internships/Practica: Doctoral Degree (PhD Clinical Psychology): For those doctoral students for whom a professional psychology internship was required in this program prior to graduation, (8) students applied for an internship in 2011–2012, with (7) students obtaining an internship. Of those students who obtained an internship, (7) were paid internships. Of those students who obtained an internship, (6) students placed in APA/CPA accredited internships, (0) students placed in internships not APA/CPA accredited, but listed with the Association of Psychology Postdoctoral and Internship Programs (APPIC), (0) students placed in internships conforming to guidelines of the Council of Directors of School Psychology Programs (CDSPP), (1) students placed in internships that were not APA/CPA accredited, APPIC or CDSPP listed. Doctoral Degree (PhD School Psychology): For those doctoral students for whom a professional psychology internship was required in this program prior to graduation, (5) students applied for an internship in 2011–2012, with (5) students obtaining an internship. Of those students who obtained an internship, (5) were paid internships. Of those students who obtained an internship, (0) students placed in APA/CPA accredited internships, (0) students placed in internships not APA/CPA accredited, but listed with the Association of Psychology Postdoctoral and Internship Programs (APPIC), (5) students placed in internships conforming to guidelines of the Council of Directors of School Psychology Programs (CDSPP), (0) students placed in internships that were not APA/CPA accredited, APPIC or CDSPP listed. Master's Degree (MA/MS School Psychology): An internship experience, such as a final research project or "capstone" experience is required of graduates. The Clinical Psychology program has an excellent record of matching students to internship placements. Our students attend top New England and national internship programs. School Psychology students who choose to apply for APPIC internships have had similar success in internship placements. The Clinical program requires 5 semesters of practicum placement in our on-campus training clinic in cognitive behavioral therapy, family therapy, interpersonal process therapy, and multicultural therapy. Students also receive training in working with ethnically diverse clients. From the third year on, clinical students are placed in off campus externships that include training in areas such as neuropsychological assessment, structured diagnostic interviewing, psychotherapy, university counseling, and pediatric psychology. School students complete school- based practica in years 1 and 2 of the program. The masters students complete an internship in year 3. The doctoral students take advanced practica in years 3 and 4 in school settings, as well as in a variety of other child and adolescent service delivery settings (e.g., pediatric hospital). In year 5, the doctoral students in the School Psychology program complete a year long internship. The School program adheres to the Internship guidelines of the Council of Directors of School Psychology Programs.

Housing and Day Care: On-campus housing is available. See the following website for more information: http://housing.uri.edu/info/graduate-housing.php. On-campus day care facilities are available. See the following website for more information: http://www.uri.edu/hss/hdf/cdc/hdfcdckingston.htm.

Employment of Department Graduates:
Master's Degree Graduates: Of those who graduated in the academic year 2011–2012, the following categories and numbers represent the postgraduate activities and employment of master's degree graduates: Enrolled in a postdoctoral residency/fellowship (n/a), employed in independent practice (n/a), employed in a professional position in a school system (3), total from the above (master's) (3).
Doctoral Degree Graduates: Of those who graduated in the academic year 2011–2012, the following categories and numbers represent the postgraduate activities and employment of doctoral degree graduates: Enrolled in a psychology doctoral program (n/a), enrolled in a postdoctoral residency/fellowship (5), employed in independent practice (1), employed in an academic position at a university (2), employed in other positions at a higher education institution (2), employed in a professional position in a school system (1), employed in business or industry (1), employed in government agency (1), employed in a community mental health/counseling center (1), total from the above (doctoral) (14).

Additional Information:
Orientation, Objectives, and Emphasis of Department: Both the Clinical and School Psychology programs of the URI Psychology Department identify as scientist practitioner programs and both are accredited by the American Psychological Association. The Behavioral Science program has an applied quantitative emphasis. The department has a strong commitment to diversity and multicultural competence. There is a lively interaction among the programs and access to training in advanced statistical and methodological approaches. The research and professional interests of the faculty fall into these interest areas: (1) health psychology with an emphasis on health promotion/disease prevention; (2) research methodology; (3) gender, diversity, and multicultural psychology; (4) family, child, and developmental psychology; (5) neuropsychology and (6) school psychology practice. Graduates of our programs have developed diverse careers in academia, government service, schools, private industry, the nonprofit sector, and private consulting and practice.

Special Facilities or Resources: The Department operates an on-campus training facility, the Psychological Consultation Center, where students train under direct faculty supervision for professional practice service roles with individual clients, families, and children. The department is closely allied with the Cancer Prevention Research Center, one of the nation's leading centers for behavioral health promotion and disease prevention. Students also participate in research and training activities with the Department's Community Research and Services Team, the URI Family Resource Partnership, the Feinstein Hunger Center, as well as with several training partnerships with medical centers and community mental health service agencies.

Information for Students With Physical Disabilities: See the following website for more information: http://www.uri.edu/disability/dss/.

Application Information:
Application available online. URL of online application: http://www.uri.edu/gsadmis/gs_apply.html. Students are admitted in the Fall, application deadline December 1. Deadlines: Clinical - December 1; School - December 15; Behavioral Science - January 6. *Fee:* $65.

Roger Williams University (2012 data)
Department of Psychology
Arts and Sciences
One Old Ferry Road
Bristol, RI 02809-2921
Telephone: (401) 254-3509
Fax: (401) 254-3286
E-mail: *dwhitworth@rwu.edu*
Web: *http://www.rwu.edu*

Department Information:
1969. Chairperson: Laura Turner, PhD. Number of faculty: total—full-time 13, part-time 10; women—full-time 7, part-time 7; total—minority—full-time 3, part-time 1; women minority—full-time 1, part-time 1.

Programs and Degrees Offered:
Listed in the following order: Program area, degree type (T if terminal Master's), number awarded 7/11–6/12. Forensic Psychology MA/MS (Master of Arts/Science) (T) 16.

Student Applications/Admissions:

Student Applications

Forensic Psychology MA/MS (Master of Arts/Science)—Applications 2012–2013, 78. Total applicants accepted 2012–2013, 20. Number full-time enrolled (new admits only) 2012–2013, 14. Number part-time enrolled (new admits only) 2012–2013, 0. Total enrolled 2012–2013 full-time, 30. Total enrolled 2012–2013 part-time, 0. Openings 2013–2014, 20. The median number of years required for completion of a degree in 2012–2013 were 2. The number of students enrolled full- and part-time who were dismissed or voluntarily withdrew from this program area in 2012–2013 were 0.

Scores: Entries appear in this order: required test or GPA, minimum score (if required), median score of students entering in 2012–2013. *Forensic Psychology MA/MS (Master of Arts/Science):* GRE-V 500, 509, GRE-Q 500, 533, overall undergraduate GPA 3.0, 3.46.

Other Criteria: (importance of criteria rated low, medium, or high): GRE scores—high, research experience—high, work experience—medium, extracurricular activity—low, clinically related public service—medium, GPA—high, letters of recommendation—high, statement of goals and objectives—high, undergraduate major in psychology—medium, specific undergraduate psychology courses taken—high.

Student Characteristics: The following represents characteristics of students in 2012–2013 in all graduate psychology programs in the department: Female—full-time 27, part-time 0; Male—full-time 3, part-time 0; African American/Black—full-time 2, part-time 0; Hispanic/Latino(a)—full-time 2, part-time 0; Asian/Pacific Islander—full-time 0, part-time 0; American Indian/Alaska Native—full-time 0, part-time 0; Caucasian/White—full-time 12, part-time 0; Multi-ethnic—full-time 0, part-time 0; students subject to the Americans With Disabilities Act—full-time 0, part-time 0; Unknown ethnicity—full-time 0, part-time 0; International students who hold an F-1 or J-1 Visa—full-time 2, part-time 0.

Financial Information/Assistance:

Tuition for Full-Time Study: *Master's:* State residents: per academic year $16,104, $671 per credit hour; Nonstate residents: per academic year $16,104, $671 per credit hour. Tuition is subject to change.

Financial Assistance:

First-Year Students: Research assistantships available for first year. Average amount paid per academic year: $1,000. Apply by March 15. Fellowships and scholarships available for first year. Average amount paid per academic year: $1,500. Apply by March 15.

Advanced Students: Research assistantships available for advanced students. Average amount paid per academic year: $1,000. Fellowships and scholarships available for advanced students. Average amount paid per academic year: $1,500.

Additional Information: Of all students currently enrolled full time, 70% benefited from one or more of the listed financial assistance programs. Application and information available online at: http://www.rwu.edu/admission/financialaid/.

Internships/Practica: The clincial training program for the Master of Arts in Forensic Psychology at Roger Williams University offers a wide range of practicum placement sites in Massachusetts and Rhode Island with opportunities to clinically work with a diversity of forensic populations. We currently have practicum placements within adult and juvenile correctional settings, adult inpatient forensic hospitals and state hospitals, juvenile court clinics, juvenile treatment programs, state and federal correctional programs for the evaluation and treatment of adult sex offenders, community mental health programs, and outpatient substance abuse programs. There are also a few research practicum placements available. Students receive comprehensive training and clinical supervision on-site from practicing forensic psychologists and forensic mental health practitioners in the assessment and treatment of forensic mental health patients and clients. The focus of the clinical practicum placements is to provide the student with an opportunity to apply clinical skills and techniques learned in clinical course work. Students are encouraged to examine case studies, training issues, ethical dilemmas and conflicts within their continued course work on campus. The practicum placements function as a vital place for students to form professional relationships in the field and to network with allied forensic mental health professionals, a key to later opportunities for employment in the forensic mental health field. Practicum placements also provide a valuable enhancement of a student's application for continued graduate education toward a doctorate in psychology.

Housing and Day Care: On-campus housing is available. See the following website for more information: www.rwu.edu/studentlife/residencelife/universityhousing/. No on-campus day care facilities are available.

Employment of Department Graduates:

Master's Degree Graduates: Of those who graduated in the academic year 2011–2012, the following categories and numbers represent the postgraduate activities and employment of master's degree graduates: Enrolled in a psychology doctoral program (4), enrolled in another graduate/professional program (0), enrolled in a postdoctoral residency/fellowship (n/a), employed in independent practice (n/a), employed in a community mental health/counseling center (7), employed in a hospital/medical center (5), total from the above (master's) (16).

Doctoral Degree Graduates: Of those who graduated in the academic year 2011–2012, the following categories and numbers represent the postgraduate activities and employment of doctoral degree graduates: Enrolled in a psychology doctoral program (n/a), total from the above (doctoral) (0).

Additional Information:

Orientation, Objectives, and Emphasis of Department: The Psychology Department strives to provide assessment and treatment skills for students interested in employment in a forensic setting or further training at the doctoral level. Faculty members work closely with students to help them develop an understanding and appreciation of the role of psychologists in legal proceedings and the law. Students are prepared to apply these skills to the problems of community and of the larger society. The department stresses tolerance for the views of others and an appreciation of the value of diversity. Other departmental objectives include preparing students to evaluate published research and think critically about their own ideas and the ideas of others.

Application Information:

Send to Office of Graduate Admission, One Old Ferry Road, Bristol, RI 02809. Application available online. URL of online application: http://www.rwu.edu/admission/grad/apply.htm. Students are admitted in the Fall, application deadline March 15. *Fee:* $50.

Citadel, The
Department of Psychology
171 Moultrie Street
Charleston, SC 29409
Telephone: (843) 953-5320
Fax: (843) 953-6797
E-mail: *steve.nida@citadel.edu*
Web: *http://www.citadel.edu/*

Department Information:
1976. Department Head: Steve A. Nida. Number of faculty: total—full-time 12, part-time 8; women—full-time 4, part-time 5; total—minority—full-time 1; faculty subject to the Americans With Disabilities Act 1.

Programs and Degrees Offered:
Listed in the following order: Program area, degree type (T if terminal Master's), number awarded 7/11–6/12. School Psychology EdS (School Psychology) 12, Clinical Counseling Psychology MA/MS (Master of Arts/Science) (T) 10.

Student Applications/Admissions:
Student Applications
School Psychology EdS (School Psychology)—Applications 2012–2013, 25. Total applicants accepted 2012–2013, 19. Number full-time enrolled (new admits only) 2012–2013, 14. Number part-time enrolled (new admits only) 2012–2013, 1. Total enrolled 2012–2013 full-time, 36. Total enrolled 2012–2013 part-time, 2. Openings 2013–2014, 12. The median number of years required for completion of a degree in 2012–2013 were 3. The number of students enrolled full- and part-time who were dismissed or voluntarily withdrew from this program area in 2012–2013 were 0. *Clinical Counseling Psychology MA/MS (Master of Arts/Science)*—Applications 2012–2013, 65. Total applicants accepted 2012–2013, 44. Number full-time enrolled (new admits only) 2012–2013, 27. Number part-time enrolled (new admits only) 2012–2013, 3. Total enrolled 2012–2013 full-time, 67. Total enrolled 2012–2013 part-time, 1. Openings 2013–2014, 40. The median number of years required for completion of a degree in 2012–2013 were 3. The number of students enrolled full- and part-time who were dismissed or voluntarily withdrew from this program area in 2012–2013 were 10.

Scores: Entries appear in this order: required test or GPA, minimum score (if required), median score of students entering in 2012–2013. *School Psychology EdS (School Psychology)*: GRE-V 153, 151, GRE-Q 144, 146, overall undergraduate GPA 3.00, 3.39; *Clinical Counseling Psychology MA/MS (Master of Arts/Science)*: GRE-V 153, GRE-Q 144, overall undergraduate GPA 3.00, 3.08.

Other Criteria: (importance of criteria rated low, medium, or high): GRE scores—high, research experience—medium, work experience—medium, extracurricular activity—low, clinically related public service—medium, GPA—high, letters of recommendation—high, interview—high, statement of goals and objectives—high, undergraduate major in psychology—low.

Student Characteristics: The following represents characteristics of students in 2012–2013 in all graduate psychology programs in the department: Female—full-time 97, part-time 2; Male—full-time 6, part-time 1; African American/Black—full-time 10, part-time 1; Hispanic/Latino(a)—full-time 0, part-time 0; Asian/Pacific Islander—full-time 1, part-time 0; American Indian/Alaska Native—full-time 0, part-time 0; Caucasian/White—full-time 92, part-time 2; Multi-ethnic—full-time 0, part-time 0; students subject to the Americans With Disabilities Act—full-time 4, part-time 1; Unknown ethnicity—full-time 0, part-time 0; International students who hold an F-1 or J-1 Visa—full-time 1, part-time 0.

Financial Information/Assistance:
Tuition for Full-Time Study: *Master's:* State residents: $510 per credit hour; Nonstate residents: $840 per credit hour. Tuition is subject to change. Additional fees are assessed to students beyond the costs of tuition for the following: lab fees in some courses. See the following website for updates and changes in tuition costs: http://www.citadel.edu/root/graduatecollege-fees.

Financial Assistance:
First-Year Students: Teaching assistantships available for first year. Average amount paid per academic year: $7,000. Average number of hours worked per week: 20. Research assistantships available for first year. Average amount paid per academic year: $7,000. Average number of hours worked per week: 20.

Advanced Students: Teaching assistantships available for advanced students. Average amount paid per academic year: $7,000. Average number of hours worked per week: 20. Research assistantships available for advanced students. Average amount paid per academic year: $7,000. Average number of hours worked per week: 20.

Additional Information: Of all students currently enrolled full time, 25% benefited from one or more of the listed financial assistance programs. Application and information available online at: http://www.citadel.edu/root/financial-aid-cgc.

Internships/Practica: Master's Degree (MA/MS Clinical Counseling Psychology): An internship experience, such as a final research project or "capstone" experience is required of graduates. The EdS program in School Psychology requires two practica where students provide services in the public school systems (40 and 125 hours, respectively) and a 1200-hour internship (some are paid), at least 600 of which involve direct services within the public school system. The MA in Clinical Counseling Psychology requires one practicum (150 hours) and one internship (600 hours) where students provide clinical/counseling services in public mental health/substance abuse treatment facilities. These are unpaid field experiences.

Housing and Day Care: No on-campus housing is available. No on-campus day care facilities are available.

Employment of Department Graduates:

Master's Degree Graduates: Of those who graduated in the academic year 2011–2012, the following categories and numbers represent the postgraduate activities and employment of master's degree graduates: Enrolled in a postdoctoral residency/fellowship (n/a), employed in independent practice (n/a), employed in a professional position in a school system (11), employed in government agency (1), employed in a community mental health/counseling center (11), employed in a hospital/medical center (6), still seeking employment (3), other employment position (2), do not know (2), total from the above (master's) (36).

Doctoral Degree Graduates: Of those who graduated in the academic year 2011–2012, the following categories and numbers represent the postgraduate activities and employment of doctoral degree graduates: Enrolled in a psychology doctoral program (n/a), total from the above (doctoral) (0).

Additional Information:

Orientation, Objectives, and Emphasis of Department: The School Psychology program is based on the scientist–practitioner model and emphasizes the school psychologist as a data-based problem-solver who applies psychological principles, knowledge and skill to processes and problems of education and schooling. Students are trained to provide a range of psychological assessment, consultation, intervention, prevention, program development and evaluation services with the goal of maximizing student learning and development. The School Psychology program has been accredited by the National Association of School Psychologists (NASP) since 1988. Students in the Master of Arts in Psychology: Clinical Counseling program are prepared to become scholarly practitioners of psychosocial counseling in community agencies, including college counseling centers, hospitals, mental health centers, and social services agencies. The program's model blends didactic and experience-based training to facilitate students' ability to utilize an empirical approach to assessment, goal development, intervention, and evaluation of services for a wide range of individuals and families experiencing a variety of psychosocial difficulties. The program is accredited by the Master's in Psychology Accreditation Council and is a member of the Council of Applied Master's Programs in Psychology.

Special Facilities or Resources: The Citadel's Department of Psychology enjoys a strong working relationship with the area school districts and agencies which provide mental health/substance abuse services. In addition, the nearby Medical University of South Carolina provides internship opportunities.

Information for Students With Physical Disabilities: See the following website for more information: http://www.citadel.edu/root/asc-disability-services.

Application Information:
Send to College of Graduate and Professional Studies, The Citadel, 171 Moultrie Street, Charleston, SC 29409. Application available online. URL of online application: http://www.citadel.edu/root/ graduatecollege-apply/graduate. Students are admitted in the Fall, application deadline March 15. *Fee:* $30.

Clemson University
Department of Psychology
418 Brackett Hall
Clemson, SC 29634-1355
Telephone: (864) 656-3210
Fax: (864) 656-0358
E-mail: *rsincla@clemson.edu*
Web: *http://www.clemson.edu/psych/*

Department Information:
1976. Chairperson: Patrick Raymark. Number of faculty: total—full-time 24; women—full-time 5; total—minority—full-time 3.

Programs and Degrees Offered:
Listed in the following order: Program area, degree type (T if terminal Master's), number awarded 7/11–6/12. Human Factors PhD (Doctor of Philosophy) 2, Industrial/Organizational PhD (Doctor of Philosophy) 2.

Student Applications/Admissions:

Student Applications

Human Factors PhD (Doctor of Philosophy)—Applications 2012–2013, 50. Total applicants accepted 2012–2013, 4. Number full-time enrolled (new admits only) 2012–2013, 3. Number part-time enrolled (new admits only) 2012–2013, 0. Total enrolled 2012–2013 full-time, 17. Total enrolled 2012–2013 part-time, 2. Openings 2013–2014, 6. The number of students enrolled full- and part-time who were dismissed or voluntarily withdrew from this program area in 2012–2013 were 0. *Industrial/Organizational PhD (Doctor of Philosophy)*—Applications 2012–2013, 140. Total applicants accepted 2012–2013, 3. Number full-time enrolled (new admits only) 2012–2013, 3. Number part-time enrolled (new admits only) 2012–2013, 0. Total enrolled 2012–2013 full-time, 18. Total enrolled 2012–2013 part-time, 2. Openings 2013–2014, 6. The number of students enrolled full- and part-time who were dismissed or voluntarily withdrew from this program area in 2012–2013 were 0.

Scores: Entries appear in this order: required test or GPA, minimum score (if required), median score of students entering in 2012–2013. *Human Factors PhD (Doctor of Philosophy):* GRE-V no minimum stated, 540, GRE-Q no minimum stated, 650, GRE-Analytical no minimum stated, 4, overall undergraduate GPA no minimum stated, 3.5; *Industrial/Organizational PhD (Doctor of Philosophy):* GRE-V no minimum stated, 560, GRE-Q no minimum stated, 610, GRE-Analytical no minimum stated, 4.5, overall undergraduate GPA no minimum stated, 3.7.

Other Criteria: (importance of criteria rated low, medium, or high): GRE scores—high, research experience—high, work experience—medium, extracurricular activity—low, GPA—high, letters of recommendation—high, interview—medium, statement of goals and objectives—high, undergraduate major in psychology—medium, specific undergraduate psychology courses taken—low. For additional information on admission requirements, go to http://www.clemson.edu/psych/grad/apply/.

Student Characteristics: The following represents characteristics of students in 2012–2013 in all graduate psychology programs in the department: Female—full-time 23, part-time 0; Male—full-time 9, part-time 0; African American/Black—full-time 1, part-time 0; Hispanic/Latino(a)—full-time 1, part-time 0; Asian/Pacific Islander—full-time 0, part-time 0; American Indian/Alaska Native—full-time 0, part-time 0; Caucasian/White—full-time 30, part-time 0; Multi-ethnic—full-time 0, part-time 0; students subject to the Americans With Disabilities Act—full-time 0, part-time 0; Unknown ethnicity—full-time 0, part-time 0; International students who hold an F-1 or J-1 Visa—full-time 1, part-time 0.

Financial Information/Assistance:

Tuition for Full-Time Study: *Master's:* State residents: per academic year $4,814; Nonstate residents: per academic year $9,588. *Doctoral:* State residents: per academic year $4,814; Nonstate residents: per academic year $9,588. Tuition is subject to change. See the following website for updates and changes in tuition costs: http://grad.clemson.edu/programs/tuition.php.

Financial Assistance:

First-Year Students: Teaching assistantships available for first year. Average amount paid per academic year: $12,000. Average number of hours worked per week: 20. Apply by January 15. Research assistantships available for first year. Average amount paid per academic year: $12,000. Average number of hours worked per week: 20. Apply by January 15. Fellowships and scholarships available for first year. Average amount paid per academic year: $7,000. Average number of hours worked per week: 0. Apply by January 15.

Advanced Students: Teaching assistantships available for advanced students. Average amount paid per academic year: $14,000. Average number of hours worked per week: 20. Apply by January 15. Research assistantships available for advanced students. Average amount paid per academic year: $14,000. Average number of hours worked per week: 20. Apply by January 15. Fellowships and scholarships available for advanced students. Average amount paid per academic year: $7,000. Average number of hours worked per week: 0. Apply by January 15.

Additional Information: Of all students currently enrolled full time, 95% benefited from one or more of the listed financial assistance programs.

Internships/Practica: Students typically complete internships or other applied experiences beginning in their second year of the program. The location, content, and length of these experiences vary but nearly all are paid positions.

Housing and Day Care: On-campus housing is available. See the following website for more information: http://www.clemson.edu/campus-life/housing/. No on-campus day care facilities are available.

Employment of Department Graduates:

Master's Degree Graduates: Of those who graduated in the academic year 2011–2012, the following categories and numbers represent the postgraduate activities and employment of master's degree graduates: Enrolled in a psychology doctoral program (2), enrolled in a postdoctoral residency/fellowship (n/a), employed in independent practice (n/a), employed in business or industry (3), total from the above (master's) (5).

Doctoral Degree Graduates: Of those who graduated in the academic year 2011–2012, the following categories and numbers represent the postgraduate activities and employment of doctoral degree graduates: Enrolled in a psychology doctoral program (n/a), employed in an academic position at a university (2), other employment position (1), total from the above (doctoral) (3).

Additional Information:

Orientation, Objectives, and Emphasis of Department: The faculty of the Psychology Department are committed to excellence in teaching and research. The primary goals of the Master of Science program are to provide students with an essential core of knowledge in applied psychology and to develop applied research skills. The program is specifically designed to provide the student with the requisite theoretical foundations, skills in quantitative techniques and experimental design, and the practical problem-solving skills necessary to address real world problems in industry, business, and government. The emphasis is on the direct application of acquired training upon completion of the program. All of our graduate programs have a heavy out of the classroom research component with a required empirical thesis. The PhD programs prepare the student to generate and use knowledge in accordance with the scientist–practitioner model. In addition to the traditional areas of study in Industrial-Organizational Psychology and Human Factors (Engineering) Psychology, a new emphasis area in Occupational Health Psychology has been added to both the MS and PhD degree programs.

Special Facilities or Resources: The Psychology Department is housed on 4 floors of Brackett Hall. Students have access to several laboratories, including a Process Control Simulator Lab, Task Performance Lab, Psychophysiology Research Lab, Sleep Research Lab, Perception & Action Lab, Motion Sciences & Uncoupled Motion Simulation Lab, Visual Performance Lab, Driving Simulator Lab, Usability Testing Lab, Personnel Selection and Performance Appraisal Lab, I-O Research Lab, I-O Quant Lab, Social Psychology Lab, Residential Research Facility, Cognitive Aging & Technology Lab, as well as Virtual Reality and Robotics & Teleoperation facilities. To date, nearly 100% of our graduates have either gained employment in their chosen field or have been accepted into PhD programs (in many cases they have had one or more job offers before the completion of their degree). Our Human Factors program is one of only eight Psychology programs accredited by the Human Factors and Ergonomics Society.

Information for Students With Physical Disabilities: See the following website for more information: http://www.clemson.edu/campus-life/campus-services/sds/.

Application Information:
Application available online. URL of online application: http://www.grad.clemson.edu/admission/. Students are admitted in the Fall, application deadline January 15. *Fee:* $75.

Francis Marion University

Department of Psychology
P.O. Box 100547
Florence, SC 29502
Telephone: (843) 661-1641
Fax: (843) 661-1628
E-mail: *jhester@fmarion.edu*
Web: *http://fmupsychology.com/graduate-studies/*

Department Information:

1970. Chairperson: John R. Hester, PhD. Number of faculty: total—full-time 10, part-time 11; women—full-time 4, part-time 10; minority—part-time 1.

Programs and Degrees Offered:

Listed in the following order: Program area, degree type (T if terminal Master's), number awarded 7/11–6/12. Clinical/Counseling Psychology MA/MS (Master of Arts/Science) (T) 6, Specialist in School Psychology Other 5.

Student Applications/Admissions:

Student Applications

Clinical/Counseling Psychology MA/MS (Master of Arts/Science)—Applications 2012–2013, 26. Total applicants accepted 2012–2013, 14. Number full-time enrolled (new admits only) 2012–2013, 9. Total enrolled 2012–2013 full-time, 19. Total enrolled 2012–2013 part-time, 1. Openings 2013–2014, 12. The median number of years required for completion of a degree in 2012–2013 were 2. The number of students enrolled full- and part-time who were dismissed or voluntarily withdrew from this program area in 2012–2013 were 0. *Specialist in School Psychology Other*—Applications 2012–2013, 17. Total applicants accepted 2012–2013, 11. Number full-time enrolled (new admits only) 2012–2013, 6. Number part-time enrolled (new admits only) 2012–2013, 0. Total enrolled 2012–2013 full-time, 22. Total enrolled 2012–2013 part-time, 0. Openings 2013–2014, 8. The median number of years required for completion of a degree in 2012–2013 were 3. The number of students enrolled full- and part-time who were dismissed or voluntarily withdrew from this program area in 2012–2013 were 0.

Scores: Entries appear in this order: required test or GPA, minimum score (if required), median score of students entering in 2012–2013. *Clinical/Counseling Psychology MA/MS (Master of Arts/Science):* GRE-V 145, GRE-Q 145, GRE-Analytical 4.0, overall undergraduate GPA 3.0, psychology GPA 3.0; *Specialist in School Psychology Other:* GRE-V 145, GRE-Q 145, GRE-Analytical 4.0, overall undergraduate GPA 3.0, psychology GPA 3.0.

Other Criteria: (importance of criteria rated low, medium, or high): GRE scores—high, research experience—medium, work experience—medium, extracurricular activity—low, clinically related public service—medium, GPA—high, letters of recommendation—high, statement of goals and objectives—high, specific undergraduate psychology courses taken—medium. For additional information on admission requirements, go to http://fmupsychology.com/graduate-studies/admissions/.

Student Characteristics: The following represents characteristics of students in 2012–2013 in all graduate psychology programs in the department: Female—full-time 44, part-time 1; Male—full-time 4, part-time 0; African American/Black—full-time 7, part-time 1; Hispanic/Latino(a)—full-time 0, part-time 0; Asian/Pacific Islander—full-time 0, part-time 0; American Indian/Alaska Native—full-time 1, part-time 0; Caucasian/White—full-time 40, part-time 0; Multi-ethnic—full-time 0, part-time 0; students subject to the Americans With Disabilities Act—full-time 0, part-time 0; Unknown ethnicity—full-time 0, part-time 0; International students who hold an F-1 or J-1 Visa—full-time 2, part-time 0.

Financial Information/Assistance:

Tuition for Full-Time Study: *Master's:* State residents: per academic year $8,908, $445 per credit hour; Nonstate residents: per academic year $17,816, $890 per credit hour. Tuition is subject to change. See the following website for updates and changes in tuition costs: http://www.fmarion.edu/about/fees/.

Financial Assistance:

First-Year Students: Teaching assistantships available for first year. Average amount paid per academic year: $8,000. Average number of hours worked per week: 20. Research assistantships available for first year. Average amount paid per academic year: $7,000. Average number of hours worked per week: 20. Fellowships and scholarships available for first year. Average amount paid per academic year: $500.

Advanced Students: Teaching assistantships available for advanced students. Average amount paid per academic year: $8,000. Average number of hours worked per week: 20. Research assistantships available for advanced students. Average amount paid per academic year: $7,000. Average number of hours worked per week: 20. Fellowships and scholarships available for advanced students. Average amount paid per academic year: $500.

Additional Information: Of all students currently enrolled full time, 91% benefited from one or more of the listed financial assistance programs. Application and information available online at: http://fmupsychology.com/graduate-studies/financial-resources/.

Internships/Practica: Master's Degree (MA/MS Clinical/Counseling Psychology): An internship experience, such as a final research project or "capstone" experience is required of graduates. Master's Degree (Other Specialist in School Psychology): An internship experience, such as a final research project or "capstone" experience is required of graduates. Internships occur in a variety of community settings. Typically Clinical/Counseling students complete a full-time six month internship in state human service agencies. The School Psychology internship is a full-time experience as a school psychologist during a Fall and Spring semester. All interns develop a broad array of skills under supervision.

Housing and Day Care: On-campus housing is available. See the following website for more information: http://www.fmuhousing.com/. On-campus day care facilities are available. See the following website for more information: http://www.centerforthechild.org/.

Employment of Department Graduates:

Master's Degree Graduates: Of those who graduated in the academic year 2011–2012, the following categories and numbers

represent the postgraduate activities and employment of master's degree graduates: Enrolled in a postdoctoral residency/fellowship (n/a), employed in independent practice (n/a), total from the above (master's) (0).

Doctoral Degree Graduates: Of those who graduated in the academic year 2011–2012, the following categories and numbers represent the postgraduate activities and employment of doctoral degree graduates: Enrolled in a psychology doctoral program (n/a), total from the above (doctoral) (0).

Additional Information:

Orientation, Objectives, and Emphasis of Department: The primary purpose of the program is to prepare professionals for employment in human services agencies, schools, or similar settings. The program also provides for the continuing education of those individuals currently employed in the helping professions and prepares students for further graduate study.

Special Facilities or Resources: The department has excellent laboratory facilities on campus including a computer laboratory. Regional human services facilities, community agencies, and school districts are accessible off campus. In addition, the Richardson Center for the Child is located on campus and provides opportunities for observation as well as training of graduate students.

Information for Students With Physical Disabilities: See the following website for more information: http://www.fmarion.edu/students/disabilityservices.

Application Information:
Send to Graduate Office, Francis Marion University, P.O. Box 100547, Florence, SC 29502-0547. Application available online. URL of online application: http://www.fmarion.edu/academics/GraduatePrograms. Students are admitted in the Fall, application deadline February 15; Spring, application deadline October 15. The School Psychology option only has Fall admissions. *Fee:* $32.

South Carolina, University of (2012 data)
Department of Psychology
College of Arts and Sciences
1512 Pendleton Street
Columbia, SC 29208
Telephone: (803) 777-4137
Fax: (803) 777-9558
E-mail: *martibrown@sc.edu*
Web: *http://www.psych.sc.edu*

Department Information:
1912. Professor & Department Chair: John Henderson. Number of faculty: total—full-time 45, part-time 9; women—full-time 23, part-time 6; total—minority—full-time 6, part-time 1; women minority—full-time 6, part-time 1.

Programs and Degrees Offered:
Listed in the following order: Program area, degree type (T if terminal Master's), number awarded 7/11–6/12. Clinical-Community Psychology PhD (Doctor of Philosophy) 4, Experimental Psychology PhD (Doctor of Philosophy) 1, School Psychology PhD (Doctor of Philosophy) 7.

APA Accreditation: Clinical PhD (Doctor of Philosophy). School PhD (Doctor of Philosophy).

Student Applications/Admissions:

Student Applications
Clinical-Community Psychology PhD (Doctor of Philosophy)— Applications 2012–2013, 117. Total applicants accepted 2012–2013, 8. Number full-time enrolled (new admits only) 2012–2013, 3. Number part-time enrolled (new admits only) 2012–2013, 0. Total enrolled 2012–2013 full-time, 43. Total enrolled 2012–2013 part-time, 6. Openings 2013–2014, 6. The median number of years required for completion of a degree in 2012–2013 were 6. The number of students enrolled full- and part-time who were dismissed or voluntarily withdrew from this program area in 2012–2013 were 0. *Experimental Psychology PhD (Doctor of Philosophy)*—Applications 2012–2013, 43. Total applicants accepted 2012–2013, 13. Number full-time enrolled (new admits only) 2012–2013, 6. Number part-time enrolled (new admits only) 2012–2013, 0. Total enrolled 2012–2013 full-time, 26. Total enrolled 2012–2013 part-time, 1. Openings 2013–2014, 6. The median number of years required for completion of a degree in 2012–2013 were 6. The number of students enrolled full- and part-time who were dismissed or voluntarily withdrew from this program area in 2012–2013 were 1. *School Psychology PhD (Doctor of Philosophy)*—Applications 2012–2013, 37. Total applicants accepted 2012–2013, 6. Number full-time enrolled (new admits only) 2012–2013, 5. Number part-time enrolled (new admits only) 2012–2013, 0. Total enrolled 2012–2013 full-time, 19. Total enrolled 2012–2013 part-time, 1. Openings 2013–2014, 6. The median number of years required for completion of a degree in 2012–2013 were 5. The number of students enrolled full- and part-time who were dismissed or voluntarily withdrew from this program area in 2012–2013 were 0.

Scores: Entries appear in this order: required test or GPA, minimum score (if required), median score of students entering in 2012–2013. *Clinical-Community Psychology PhD (Doctor of Philosophy):* GRE-V no minimum stated, 590, GRE-Q no minimum stated, 640, GRE-Analytical no minimum stated, 4.5, GRE-Subject (Psychology) no minimum stated, 700, overall undergraduate GPA no minimum stated, 3.65, last 2 years GPA no minimum stated, 3.79, psychology GPA no minimum stated, 3.66; *Experimental Psychology PhD (Doctor of Philosophy):* GRE-V no minimum stated, 625, GRE-Q no minimum stated, 705, GRE-Analytical no minimum stated, 4.5, overall undergraduate GPA no minimum stated, 3.68, last 2 years GPA no minimum stated; *School Psychology PhD (Doctor of Philosophy):* GRE-V no minimum stated, 505, GRE-Q no minimum stated, 675, GRE-Analytical no minimum stated, 4.3, overall undergraduate GPA no minimum stated, 3.79, last 2 years GPA no minimum stated, psychology GPA no minimum stated.

Other Criteria: (importance of criteria rated low, medium, or high): GRE scores—medium, research experience—high, work experience—medium, extracurricular activity—medium, clinically related public service—medium, GPA—high, letters of recommendation—high, interview—high, statement of goals and objectives—high, undergraduate major in psychology—medium, specific undergraduate psychology courses taken—medium, Criteria vary for different programs. For additional information on admission requirements, go to http://www.psych.sc.edu.

Student Characteristics: The following represents characteristics of students in 2012–2013 in all graduate psychology programs in the department: Female—full-time 59, part-time 7; Male—full-time 29, part-time 1; African American/Black—full-time 10, part-time 0; Hispanic/Latino(a)—full-time 3, part-time 0; Asian/Pacific Islander—full-time 1, part-time 1; American Indian/Alaska Native—full-time 0, part-time 0; Caucasian/White—full-time 60, part-time 6; Multi-ethnic—full-time 1, part-time 0; students subject to the Americans With Disabilities Act—full-time 2, part-time 0; Unknown ethnicity—full-time 7, part-time 1; International students who hold an F-1 or J-1 Visa—full-time 6, part-time 0.

Financial Information/Assistance:
Tuition for Full-Time Study: *Doctoral:* State residents: per academic year $10,916, $455 per credit hour; Nonstate residents: per academic year $11,722, $977 per credit hour. Tuition is subject to change. Additional fees are assessed to students beyond the costs of tuition for the following: one time matriculation fee, technology & lab fees, intl student fees & taxes, health insur. See the following website for updates and changes in tuition costs: http://www.sc.edu/bursar/fees.shtml.

Financial Assistance:
First-Year Students: Teaching assistantships available for first year. Average amount paid per academic year: $15,750. Average number of hours worked per week: 20. Research assistantships available for first year. Average amount paid per academic year: $15,750. Average number of hours worked per week: 20. Traineeships available for first year. Fellowships and scholarships available for first year.
Advanced Students: Teaching assistantships available for advanced students. Average amount paid per academic year: $15,750. Average number of hours worked per week: 20. Research assistantships available for advanced students. Average amount paid per academic year: $15,750. Average number of hours worked per week: 20. Traineeships available for advanced students. Fellowships and scholarships available for advanced students.
Additional Information: Of all students currently enrolled full time, 100% benefited from one or more of the listed financial assistance programs. Application and information available online at: http://gradschool.sc.edu.

Internships/Practica: Doctoral Degree (PhD Clinical-Community Psychology): For those doctoral students for whom a professional psychology internship was required in this program prior to graduation, (7) students applied for an internship in 2011–2012, with (7) students obtaining an internship. Of those students who obtained an internship, (7) were paid internships. Of those students who obtained an internship, (5) students placed in APA/CPA accredited internships, (0) students placed in internships not APA/CPA accredited, but listed with the Association of Psychology Postdoctoral and Internship Programs (APPIC), (0) students placed in internships conforming to guidelines of the Council of Directors of School Psychology Programs (CDSPP), (2) students placed in internships that were not APA/CPA accredited, APPIC or CDSPP listed. Doctoral Degree (PhD School Psychology): For those doctoral students for whom a professional

psychology internship was required in this program prior to graduation, (3) students applied for an internship in 2011–2012, with (3) students obtaining an internship. Of those students who obtained an internship, (3) were paid internships. Of those students who obtained an internship, (2) students placed in APA/CPA accredited internships, (0) students placed in internships not APA/CPA accredited, but listed with the Association of Psychology Postdoctoral and Internship Programs (APPIC), (1) students placed in internships conforming to guidelines of the Council of Directors of School Psychology Programs (CDSPP), (0) students placed in internships that were not APA/CPA accredited, APPIC or CDSPP listed. Students in school psychology and clinical-community psychology complete at least one year of half-time placement in a community service agency expanding their experience with a diverse client population and multidisciplinary service providers.

Housing and Day Care: On-campus housing is available. See the following website for more information: http://www.housing.sc.edu/famgrad.html. On-campus day care facilities are available. See the following website for more information: http://www.sc.edu/childrenscenter/usccdc.shtml.

Employment of Department Graduates:
Master's Degree Graduates: Of those who graduated in the academic year 2011–2012, the following categories and numbers represent the postgraduate activities and employment of master's degree graduates: Enrolled in a psychology doctoral program (7), enrolled in a postdoctoral residency/fellowship (n/a), employed in independent practice (n/a), employed in other positions at a higher education institution (1), total from the above (master's) (8).
Doctoral Degree Graduates: Of those who graduated in the academic year 2011–2012, the following categories and numbers represent the postgraduate activities and employment of doctoral degree graduates: Enrolled in a psychology doctoral program (n/a), enrolled in another graduate/professional program (0), enrolled in a postdoctoral residency/fellowship (2), employed in independent practice (1), employed in an academic position at a university (3), employed in a professional position in a school system (3), employed in business or industry (1), employed in a hospital/medical center (2), other employment position (0), total from the above (doctoral) (12).

Additional Information:
Orientation, Objectives, and Emphasis of Department: The department has interdisciplinary research emphases in quantitative methods, developmental cognitive neuroscience/neurodevelopmental disorders, prevention science, reading and language, and ethnic minority health and mental health. Students in the experimental program can pursue research interests in behavioral neuroscience, cognitive neuroscience, cognitive, developmental, and quantitative psychology built on broad scientific training in experimental psychology. The school psychology program includes emphases in child assessment, individual and group consultation, educational research, and professional roles. In clinical-community, there is a wide latitude of choices: assessment, psychotherapy and behavioral interventions, community psychology, and consultation. Regular clinical-community training includes both adults and children, with an option of special emphasis on children or community settings.

Special Facilities or Resources: The special facilities and resources of the department include the university-directed psychological service center, the medical school, the VA hospital, the department-directed outpatient psychological services center, mental health centers and other educational and mental health service settings. Other laboratories include Behavioral Pharmacology Lab; Behavioral Neuroscience Lab with high density EEG and MRI; Developmental Sensory Neuroscience Lab; Experimental and Cognitive Processes Lab; Infant Attention Lab; Judgment and Decision Making Lab; and Attention and Perception Lab. We are actively involved in community agencies, the psychiatric training institution, and the psychopharmacology laboratory.

Information for Students With Physical Disabilities: See the following website for more information: http://www.sa.sc.edu/sds/.

Application Information:
Application available online. URL of online application: http://www.gradschool.sc.edu/apply.htm. Students are admitted in the Fall, application deadline December 1. The application deadline for fall admission in Clinical-Community Psychology and School Psychology is December 1 and for Experimental Psychology is January 1. *Fee:* $50.

South Carolina, University of, Aiken
Psychology
471 University Parkway
Aiken, SC 29801
Telephone: (803) 641-3358
Fax: (803) 641-3726
E-mail: *jstafford@usca.edu*
Web: *http://web.usca.edu/psychology/programs-and-courses/master-of-science.dot*

Department Information:
Chairperson: Ed Callen. Number of faculty: total—full-time 9, part-time 2; women—full-time 8.

Programs and Degrees Offered:
Listed in the following order: Program area, degree type (T if terminal Master's), number awarded 7/11–6/12. Applied Clinical Psychology MA/MS (Master of Arts/Science) (T) 1.

Student Applications/Admissions:
Student Applications
Applied Clinical Psychology MA/MS (Master of Arts/Science)—Applications 2012–2013, 52. Total applicants accepted 2012–2013, 26. Number full-time enrolled (new admits only) 2012–2013, 14. Number part-time enrolled (new admits only) 2012–2013, 0. Total enrolled 2012–2013 full-time, 24. Total enrolled 2012–2013 part-time, 8. Openings 2013–2014, 13. The median number of years required for completion of a degree in 2012–2013 were 2. The number of students enrolled full- and part-time who were dismissed or voluntarily withdrew from this program area in 2012–2013 were 0.
Scores: Entries appear in this order: required test or GPA, minimum score (if required), median score of students entering in 2012–2013. *Applied Clinical Psychology MA/MS (Master of Arts/Science):* GRE-V 148, 155, GRE-Q 136, 146, GRE-Ana-

lytical 3.0, 4.0, overall undergraduate GPA 2.9, 3.5, psychology GPA 3.1, 3.6.
Other Criteria: (importance of criteria rated low, medium, or high): GRE scores—high, research experience—medium, work experience—low, extracurricular activity—low, clinically related public service—low, GPA—high, letters of recommendation—high, interview—medium, statement of goals and objectives—medium, conference presentations—medium, undergraduate major in psychology—medium, specific undergraduate psychology courses taken—medium. For additional information on admission requirements, go to http://web.usca.edu/psychology/programs-and-courses/master-of-science.dot.

Student Characteristics: The following represents characteristics of students in 2012–2013 in all graduate psychology programs in the department: Female—full-time 19, part-time 7; Male—full-time 5, part-time 1; African American/Black—full-time 0, part-time 1; Hispanic/Latino(a)—full-time 0, part-time 1; Asian/Pacific Islander—full-time 1, part-time 0; American Indian/Alaska Native—full-time 0, part-time 0; Caucasian/White—full-time 22, part-time 6; Multi-ethnic—full-time 1, part-time 0; students subject to the Americans With Disabilities Act—full-time 1, part-time 0; Unknown ethnicity—full-time 0, part-time 0; International students who hold an F-1 or J-1 Visa—full-time 0, part-time 0.

Financial Information/Assistance:
Tuition for Full-Time Study: *Master's:* State residents: per academic year $11,272; Nonstate residents: per academic year $24,196. Tuition is subject to change. See the following website for updates and changes in tuition costs: http://web.usca.edu/admissions/cost_attendance.dot.

Financial Assistance:
First-Year Students: Teaching assistantships available for first year. Average amount paid per academic year: $5,000. Average number of hours worked per week: 15. Apply by June 1. Traineeships available for first year. Average amount paid per academic year: $5,000. Average number of hours worked per week: 15. Apply by June 1.

Advanced Students: Teaching assistantships available for advanced students. Average amount paid per academic year: $5,000. Average number of hours worked per week: 15. Apply by June 1. Traineeships available for advanced students. Average amount paid per academic year: $5,000. Average number of hours worked per week: 15. Apply by June 1.

Additional Information: Of all students currently enrolled full time, 88% benefited from one or more of the listed financial assistance programs. Application and information available online at: http://web.usca.edu/psychology/graduate-assistantships.dot.

Internships/Practica: Master's Degree (MA/MS Applied Clinical Psychology): An internship experience, such as a final research project or "capstone" experience is required of graduates. Most students have paid assistantships in which they work in an agency in the community. The assistantships for first year students are in settings such as the school system and developmental centers while second year students are in agencies such as psychiatric hospitals or child advocacy centers, conducting assessments and/or providing psychotherapy. In addition, we have a training clinic in our department where advanced graduate students conduct individual and group therapy with children and adults and various types of psychological evaluations. Each student is required to take a minimum of two semesters of practicum in which they receive training in the clinic.

Housing and Day Care: On-campus housing is available. See the following website for more information: http://web.usca.edu/housing/. On-campus day care facilities are available. See the following website for more information: http://web.usca.edu/childrens-center/.

Employment of Department Graduates:

Master's Degree Graduates: Of those who graduated in the academic year 2011–2012, the following categories and numbers represent the postgraduate activities and employment of master's degree graduates: Enrolled in a postdoctoral residency/fellowship (n/a), employed in independent practice (n/a), total from the above (master's) (0).

Doctoral Degree Graduates: Of those who graduated in the academic year 2011–2012, the following categories and numbers represent the postgraduate activities and employment of doctoral degree graduates: Enrolled in a psychology doctoral program (n/a), total from the above (doctoral) (0).

Additional Information:

Orientation, Objectives, and Emphasis of Department: Our program provides graduate study and clinical experience in preparation for careers in applied clinical and counseling settings and as a foundation for students interested in pursuing advanced doctoral studies. Students enrolled in this program are expected to pursue a plan of study to assure increased professional competence and breadth of knowledge in the field of clinical and counseling psychology. The degree objectives are designed to enable the student to: understand principles of psychology and how they are applied; understand a diversity of theoretical perspectives; interpret and apply statistical and research techniques; understand professional, legal and ethical principles as they pertain to professional conduct and responsibility; and understand and develop skills in assessment procedures and intervention strategies. Our program is an approved member of the Council of Applied Master's Programs in Psychology (CAMPP). Since the development of the degree program, a strong emphasis has been placed on the need to train students within the tradition of the scientist–practitioner guidelines espoused by CAMPP. It is the belief of faculty that the master's-level practitioner is well-served by participation in this process and that the critical-thinking skills so essential to sound clinical decision-making is enhanced through research experience. Our program received full accreditation from the Master's in Psychology and Counseling Accreditation Council (MPCAC) in 2004. The mission of MPCAC is to accredit academic programs in psychology, which promote training in the scientific practice of professional psychology at the master's level. Accreditation reflects a commitment to science-based training, with goals of enhancing services to the consumer and the public at large.

Information for Students With Physical Disabilities: See the following website for more information: http://web.usca.edu/ds/index.dot.

Application Information:
Send to Karen Morris, Coordinator Graduate Studies, USCA Graduate Office, 471 University Parkway, Aiken, SC 29801. Application available online. URL of online application: http://web.usca.edu/applynow/.

Students are admitted in the Fall, application deadline April 1. Applications will be accepted until all slots are filled. *Fee:* $45.

Winthrop University
Department of Psychology
Arts and Sciences
135 Kinard
Rock Hill, SC 29733
Telephone: (803) 323-2117
Fax: (803) 323-2371
E-mail: *prusj@winthrop.edu*
Web: *http://www.winthrop.edu/psychology/*

Department Information:
1923. Chairperson: Dr. Joe Prus. Number of faculty: total—full-time 15, part-time 5; women—full-time 8, part-time 4; total—minority—full-time 2, part-time 1; women minority—full-time 2, part-time 1.

Programs and Degrees Offered:
Listed in the following order: Program area, degree type (T if terminal Master's), number awarded 7/11–6/12. School Psychology EdS (School Psychology) 10.

Student Applications/Admissions:

Student Applications

School Psychology EdS (School Psychology)—Applications 2012–2013, 53. Total applicants accepted 2012–2013, 10. Number full-time enrolled (new admits only) 2012–2013, 9. Number part-time enrolled (new admits only) 2012–2013, 0. Total enrolled 2012–2013 full-time, 28. Total enrolled 2012–2013 part-time, 0. Openings 2013–2014, 10. The median number of years required for completion of a degree in 2012–2013 were 3. The number of students enrolled full- and part-time who were dismissed or voluntarily withdrew from this program area in 2012–2013 were 1.

Scores: Entries appear in this order: required test or GPA, minimum score (if required), median score of students entering in 2012–2013. *School Psychology EdS (School Psychology):* GRE-V no minimum stated, 155, GRE-Q no minimum stated, 148, GRE-Analytical no minimum stated, 4, overall undergraduate GPA no minimum stated, 3.6, last 2 years GPA no minimum stated, 3.7, psychology GPA no minimum stated, 3.7.

Other Criteria: (importance of criteria rated low, medium, or high): GRE scores—medium, research experience—low, work experience—medium, extracurricular activity—low, clinically related public service—medium, GPA—high, letters of recommendation—medium, interview—high, statement of goals and objectives—medium, experience with children—high, undergraduate major in psychology—medium, specific undergraduate psychology courses taken—medium. For additional information on admission requirements, go to http://www.winthrop.edu/cas/psychology/default-grad.aspx?id=26690.

Student Characteristics: The following represents characteristics of students in 2012–2013 in all graduate psychology programs in the department: Female—full-time 28, part-time 0; Male—full-time 0, part-time 0; African American/Black—full-time 3, part-time 0; Hispanic/Latino(a)—full-time 1, part-time 0; Asian/Pa-

cific Islander—full-time 1, part-time 0; American Indian/Alaska Native—full-time 0, part-time 0; Caucasian/White—full-time 23, part-time 0; Multi-ethnic—full-time 0, part-time 0; students subject to the Americans With Disabilities Act—full-time 0, part-time 0; Unknown ethnicity—full-time 0, part-time 0; International students who hold an F-1 or J-1 Visa—full-time 0, part-time 0.

Financial Information/Assistance:

Tuition for Full-Time Study: *Master's:* State residents: per academic year $13,026, $543 per credit hour; Nonstate residents: per academic year $23,452, $980 per credit hour. Tuition is subject to change. Additional fees are assessed to students beyond the costs of tuition for the following: small lab fees in assessment courses. See the following website for updates and changes in tuition costs: http://www.winthrop.edu/graduateschool/default. aspx?id=3397.

Financial Assistance:

First-Year Students: Teaching assistantships available for first year. Average amount paid per academic year: $3,600. Average number of hours worked per week: 20. Apply by April 15. Research assistantships available for first year. Average amount paid per academic year: $3,600. Average number of hours worked per week: 20. Apply by April 15. Fellowships and scholarships available for first year. Average amount paid per academic year: $1,000. Apply by April 15.

Advanced Students: Traineeships available for advanced students. Average amount paid per academic year: $4,500. Average number of hours worked per week: 15.

Additional Information: Of all students currently enrolled full time, 93% benefited from one or more of the listed financial assistance programs. Application and information available online at: http://www.winthrop.edu/graduateschool/default.aspx?id= 4497.

Internships/Practica: The program provides paid traineeships during the second year and internships during the third year in area school districts and agencies. Rural, suburban, and urban field settings include diverse student/client populations. The internship includes a full range of school psychological services. Each intern receives supervision from both a faculty member and a field-based, credentialed supervisor.

Housing and Day Care: On-campus housing is available. See the following website for more information: http://www.winthrop.edu/ reslife/default.aspx. On-campus day care facilities are available. See the following website for more information: http://www. winthrop.edu/macfeat/.

Employment of Department Graduates:

Master's Degree Graduates: Of those who graduated in the academic year 2011–2012, the following categories and numbers represent the postgraduate activities and employment of master's degree graduates: Enrolled in a postdoctoral residency/fellowship (n/a), employed in independent practice (n/a), employed in a professional position in a school system (10), total from the above (master's) (10).

Doctoral Degree Graduates: Of those who graduated in the academic year 2011–2012, the following categories and numbers represent the postgraduate activities and employment of doctoral degree graduates: Enrolled in a psychology doctoral program (n/a), total from the above (doctoral) (0).

Additional Information:

Orientation, Objectives, and Emphasis of Department: The Winthrop School Psychology Program is designed to prepare practitioners who are competent to provide a full range of school psychological services, including consultation, academic and behavioral intervention, psychoeducational assessment, research and evaluation, and counseling. The three-year, full-time program leading to both MS and Specialist in School Psychology degrees qualifies graduates for state and national certification as a school psychologist pending attainment of a passing score on the Praxis II exam in school psychology (the program has a 100% pass rate for the past five years and an excellent record of its graduates finding employment). The program emphasizes evidenced-based psychological and psychoeducational methods. Students are prepared to work with diverse clients from birth to adulthood, and with families, teachers, and others in the schools and community. The program includes an applied, competency-based approach to training that progresses sequentially from foundations and practicum courses to a 450-hour traineeship to a 1200-hour internship, and affords maximum individualized supervision. Program faculty represent considerable ethnic and experiential diversity. All have advanced degrees and credentials in school psychology, are active in the profession at local, state, and national levels, and view teaching and supervision as their primary roles. Faculty encourage a collaborative approach to learning and close cooperation and support among students.

Special Facilities or Resources: Winthrop University is a state-supported institution of about 6,000 students which provides students with access to a state-of-the-art health center, campus center, university library, and a variety of other resources. Access to such department resources as a graduate student workroom, computer lab, and school psychology mini-library and assessment resource center is also available. Winthrop's 418-acre campus is located in the greater Charlotte, NC area, which includes a great variety of resources which may be of personal or professional interest to graduate students in school psychology.

Information for Students With Physical Disabilities: See the following website for more information: http://www.winthrop.edu/ disabilities/.

Application Information:

Send to The Graduate School, Winthrop University, Rock Hill, SC 29733. Application available online. URL of online application: http:// www.winthrop.edu/graduateschool/. Students are admitted in the Fall, application deadline January 15. *Fee:* $50. Application fee may be waived by program director in cases of financial hardship. Application fee waived for McNair Scholars.

South Dakota, University of
Department of Psychology
414 East Clark Street
Vermillion, SD 57069
Telephone: (605) 677-5351
Fax: (605) 677-3195
E-mail: *Randy.Quevillon@usd.edu*
Web: *http://www.usd.edu/arts-and-sciences/psychology/*

Department Information:
1926. Chairperson: Randal Quevillon. Number of faculty: total—full-time 15, part-time 1; women—full-time 7; total—minority—full-time 3; women minority—full-time 2.

Programs and Degrees Offered:
Listed in the following order: Program area, degree type (T if terminal Master's), number awarded 7/11–6/12. Clinical Psychology PhD (Doctor of Philosophy) 9, Human Factors PhD (Doctor of Philosophy) 0.

APA Accreditation: Clinical PhD (Doctor of Philosophy). Student Outcome Data Website: http://www.usd.edu/arts-and-sciences/psychology/clinical-psychology/student-admissions-outcomes-data.cfm.

Student Applications/Admissions:
Student Applications
Clinical Psychology PhD (Doctor of Philosophy)—Applications 2012–2013, 108. Total applicants accepted 2012–2013, 9. Number full-time enrolled (new admits only) 2012–2013, 6. Number part-time enrolled (new admits only) 2012–2013, 0. Total enrolled 2012–2013 full-time, 34. Total enrolled 2012–2013 part-time, 0. Openings 2013–2014, 6. The median number of years required for completion of a degree in 2012–2013 were 7. The number of students enrolled full- and part-time who were dismissed or voluntarily withdrew from this program area in 2012–2013 were 0. *Human Factors PhD (Doctor of Philosophy)*—Applications 2012–2013, 6. Total applicants accepted 2012–2013, 4. Number full-time enrolled (new admits only) 2012–2013, 3. Total enrolled 2012–2013 full-time, 8. Total enrolled 2012–2013 part-time, 0. Openings 2013–2014, 3. The median number of years required for completion of a degree in 2012–2013 were 6. The number of students enrolled full- and part-time who were dismissed or voluntarily withdrew from this program area in 2012–2013 were 0.
Scores: Entries appear in this order: required test or GPA, minimum score (if required), median score of students entering in 2012–2013. *Clinical Psychology PhD (Doctor of Philosophy):* GRE-V no minimum stated, 154, GRE-Q no minimum stated, 151, GRE-Analytical no minimum stated, overall undergraduate GPA no minimum stated, 3.57; *Human Factors PhD (Doctor of Philosophy):* GRE-V no minimum stated, GRE-Q no minimum stated, overall undergraduate GPA 3.0.
Other Criteria: (importance of criteria rated low, medium, or high): GRE scores—medium, research experience—high, work experience—medium, extracurricular activity—medium,

clinically related public service—medium, GPA—medium, letters of recommendation—high, interview—high, statement of goals and objectives—medium, match with program—high, Applicant's responses to the Supplemental Application questions are highly weighted in the Clinical program admissions process. The Clinical program requires an interview and the Human Factors program does not. For additional information on admission requirements, go to http://www.usd.edu/arts-and-sciences/psychology/graduate.cfm.

Student Characteristics: The following represents characteristics of students in 2012–2013 in all graduate psychology programs in the department: Female—full-time 24, part-time 0; Male—full-time 21, part-time 0; African American/Black—full-time 1, part-time 0; Hispanic/Latino(a)—full-time 0, part-time 0; Asian/Pacific Islander—full-time 5, part-time 0; American Indian/Alaska Native—full-time 2, part-time 0; Caucasian/White—full-time 37, part-time 0; Multi-ethnic—full-time 0, part-time 0; students subject to the Americans With Disabilities Act—full-time 0, part-time 0; Unknown ethnicity—full-time 0, part-time 0; International students who hold an F-1 or J-1 Visa—full-time 3, part-time 0.

Financial Information/Assistance:
Tuition for Full-Time Study: *Doctoral:* State residents: $196 per credit hour; Nonstate residents: $416 per credit hour. Tuition is subject to change. See the following website for updates and changes in tuition costs: http://www.usd.edu/arts-and-sciences/psychology/clinical-psychology/tuition-fees-expenses.cfm.

Financial Assistance:
First-Year Students: Teaching assistantships available for first year. Average amount paid per academic year: $6,500. Average number of hours worked per week: 16. Research assistantships available for first year. Average amount paid per academic year: $6,500. Average number of hours worked per week: 16. Fellowships and scholarships available for first year. Average amount paid per academic year: $9,000. Average number of hours worked per week: 16.
Advanced Students: Teaching assistantships available for advanced students. Average amount paid per academic year: $6,500. Average number of hours worked per week: 16. Research assistantships available for advanced students. Average amount paid per academic year: $8,000. Average number of hours worked per week: 16. Traineeships available for advanced students. Average amount paid per academic year: $10,000. Average number of hours worked per week: 16. Fellowships and scholarships available for advanced students. Average amount paid per academic year: $10,000. Average number of hours worked per week: 16.
Additional Information: Of all students currently enrolled full time, 100% benefited from one or more of the listed financial assistance programs. Application and information available online at: http://www.usd.edu/financial-aid/financial-aid-for-graduate-students.cfm.

Internships/Practica: Doctoral Degree (PhD Clinical Psychology): For those doctoral students for whom a professional psychology internship was required in this program prior to graduation,

(6) students applied for an internship in 2011–2012, with (6) students obtaining an internship. Of those students who obtained an internship, (6) were paid internships. Of those students who obtained an internship, (6) students placed in APA/CPA accredited internships, (0) students placed in internships not APA/CPA accredited, but listed with the Association of Psychology Postdoctoral and Internship Programs (APPIC), (0) students placed in internships conforming to guidelines of the Council of Directors of School Psychology Programs (CDSPP), (0) students placed in internships that were not APA/CPA accredited, APPIC or CDSPP listed. Several internships are available in Human Factors: placements with IBM, Lockheed, Hewlett-Packard, and Intel have been recent examples. In Clinical, a twelve month internship is required in the final year, and we are proud of the record our students have achieved in obtaining top placements. We also have available a series of paid clinical placements. In addition, many graduate courses include practicum components, and clinical students are placed on practicum teams through the Psychological Services Center each semester.

Housing and Day Care: On-campus housing is available. See the following website for more information: http://www.usd.edu/campus-life/student-services/university-housing/. On-campus day care facilities are available. See the following website for more information: http://www.usd.edu/campus-life/childcare/.

Employment of Department Graduates:

Master's Degree Graduates: Of those who graduated in the academic year 2011–2012, the following categories and numbers represent the postgraduate activities and employment of master's degree graduates: Enrolled in a postdoctoral residency/fellowship (n/a), employed in independent practice (n/a), total from the above (master's) (0).

Doctoral Degree Graduates: Of those who graduated in the academic year 2011–2012, the following categories and numbers represent the postgraduate activities and employment of doctoral degree graduates: Enrolled in a psychology doctoral program (n/a), employed in an academic position at a university (2), employed in government agency (1), employed in a community mental health/counseling center (6), total from the above (doctoral) (9).

Additional Information:

Orientation, Objectives, and Emphasis of Department: The department seeks to develop scholars who can contribute to the expansion of psychological information. The major goals of the theoretically eclectic program in clinical psychology are to increase students' knowledge of and identification with psychology as a method of inquiry about human behavior and to provide students with the theory, skills, and experience to function in a professional, research, or academic capacity. Training is provided

in traditional areas as well as disaster psychology, rural community psychology, cross-cultural issues (particularly work with American Indian populations), program evaluation, neuropsychology, family therapy, and women's issues. The experience thus provided serves to broaden professional competencies and increase the versatility of the program's graduates. The overall mission of Human Factors psychology is to improve living and working through knowledge of the abilities and limitations of the person part of human-machine or socio-technical systems. The program's goal is to train doctoral-level professionals qualified to do research in industry, government, and universities. As an element of their training, all graduate students conduct empirical investigations. In recent years, the Human Factors Laboratory has supported studies of information processing, human-computer interfaces, motor performance, program evaluation and testing, traffic safety, transportation systems, and the effects of chemical agents and stress on human efficiency.

Special Facilities or Resources: Available to all psychology graduate students are computer lab facilities including word processing and statistical analysis software. Microcomputers are also easily accessible within the department for personal computing and research purposes. Much general purpose, highly adaptable research equipment is available to both Clinical and Human Factors students. The Human Factors Laboratory is particularly well-equipped for experimentation within the specialty areas of current interest to associated faculty. The Department houses the Disaster Mental Health Institute, a South Dakota Board of Regents Center of Excellence, which provides unique research and service opportunities for graduate students as well as specialized coursework and assistantships. The Psychological Services Center, which supplies clinical services for both University students and the general public, accepts referrals from physicians, schools, and other community and state agencies. The Center has offices equipped for a variety of diagnostic and therapeutic activities, including neuropsychological work. The Department's students take full advantage of training and experience available at local, state, and regional mental health facilities.

Information for Students With Physical Disabilities: See the following website for more information: http://www.usd.edu/academics/disability-services/index.cfm.

Application Information:

Send to Dean, Graduate School, University of South Dakota, 414 East Clark Street, Vermilion, SD 57069-2390. Application available online. URL of online application: http://www.usd.edu/graduate-school/apply.cfm. Students are admitted in the Fall, application deadline January 5. Clinical Program due January 5, Human Factors Program due February 15. *Fee:* $35.

Austin Peay State University

Department of Psychology
601 College Street
Clarksville, TN 37044
Telephone: (931) 221-7232
Fax: (931) 221-6267
E-mail: *fungs@apsu.edu*
Web: *http://www.apsu.edu/psychology/*

Department Information:
1968. Chairperson: Dr. Samuel Fung. Number of faculty: total—full-time 16, part-time 8; women—full-time 8, part-time 7; total—minority—full-time 3, part-time 1; women minority—full-time 2, part-time 1.

Programs and Degrees Offered:
Listed in the following order: Program area, degree type (T if terminal Master's), number awarded 7/11–6/12. Mental Health Counseling MA/MS (Master of Arts/Science) (T) 10, Industrial/Organizational Psychology MA/MS (Master of Arts/Science) (T) 6, School Counseling MA/MS (Master of Arts/Science) (T) 4.

Student Applications/Admissions:
Student Applications
Mental Health Counseling MA/MS (Master of Arts/Science)—Applications 2012–2013, 40. Total applicants accepted 2012–2013, 21. Number full-time enrolled (new admits only) 2012–2013, 21. Total enrolled 2012–2013 full-time, 21. Openings 2013–2014, 10. The number of students enrolled full- and part-time who were dismissed or voluntarily withdrew from this program area in 2012–2013 were 0. *Industrial/Organizational Psychology MA/MS (Master of Arts/Science)*—Applications 2012–2013, 44. Total applicants accepted 2012–2013, 12. Number full-time enrolled (new admits only) 2012–2013, 13. Total enrolled 2012–2013 full-time, 35. Openings 2013–2014, 15. The number of students enrolled full- and part-time who were dismissed or voluntarily withdrew from this program area in 2012–2013 were 0. *School Counseling MA/MS (Master of Arts/Science)*—Applications 2012–2013, 28. Total applicants accepted 2012–2013, 11. Number full-time enrolled (new admits only) 2012–2013, 11. Total enrolled 2012–2013 full-time, 33. Openings 2013–2014, 10.
Scores: Entries appear in this order: required test or GPA, minimum score (if required), median score of students entering in 2012–2013. *Mental Health Counseling MA/MS (Master of Arts/Science):* GRE-V 350, GRE-Q 350, overall undergraduate GPA 3.0; *Industrial/Organizational Psychology MA/MS (Master of Arts/Science):* GRE-V 350, GRE-Q 350, overall undergraduate GPA 3.0; *School Counseling MA/MS (Master of Arts/Science):* GRE-V 350, GRE-Q 350, overall undergraduate GPA 3.0.
Other Criteria: (importance of criteria rated low, medium, or high): GRE scores—medium, research experience—low, GPA—medium, letters of recommendation—high, statement of goals and objectives—high, undergraduate major in psychology—high, specific undergraduate psychology courses taken—medium. For additional information on admission requirements, go to http://www.apsu.edu/psychology/grad.

Student Characteristics: The following represents characteristics of students in 2012–2013 in all graduate psychology programs in the department: Female—full-time 0, part-time 0; Male—full-time 0, part-time 0; African American/Black—full-time 0, part-time 0; Hispanic/Latino(a)—full-time 0, part-time 0; Asian/Pacific Islander—full-time 0, part-time 0; American Indian/Alaska Native—full-time 0, part-time 0; Caucasian/White—full-time 0, part-time 0; Multi-ethnic—full-time 0, part-time 0; students subject to the Americans With Disabilities Act—full-time 0, part-time 0; Unknown ethnicity—full-time 0, part-time 0; International students who hold an F-1 or J-1 Visa—full-time 0, part-time 0.

Financial Information/Assistance:
Tuition for Full-Time Study: *Master's:* State residents: per academic year $6,600, $364 per credit hour; Nonstate residents: per academic year $18,180, $1,010 per credit hour. Tuition is subject to change. Additional fees are assessed to students beyond the costs of tuition for the following: technology access fee, general access fee. See the following website for updates and changes in tuition costs: http://www.apsu.edu/bursar/tuition.

Financial Assistance:
First-Year Students: Teaching assistantships available for first year. Average number of hours worked per week: 20.
Advanced Students: Teaching assistantships available for advanced students.
Additional Information: Of all students currently enrolled full time, 11% benefited from one or more of the listed financial assistance programs. Application and information available online at: http://www.apsu.edu/financialaid/.

Internships/Practica: Master's Degree (MA/MS Mental Health Counseling): An internship experience, such as a final research project or "capstone" experience is required of graduates. Master's Degree (MA/MS Industrial/Organizational Psychology): An internship experience, such as a final research project or "capstone" experience is required of graduates. Master's Degree (MA/MS School Counseling): An internship experience, such as a final research project or "capstone" experience is required of graduates. There are some paid internships available at the present. A variety of unpaid internships are available in mental health agencies, schools, or community agencies.

Housing and Day Care: On-campus housing is available. See the following website for more information: http://www.apsu.edu/housing/Halls/emerald_hill. On-campus day care facilities are available. See the following website for more information: http://www.apsu.edu/clc/.

Employment of Department Graduates:

Master's Degree Graduates: Of those who graduated in the academic year 2011–2012, the following categories and numbers represent the postgraduate activities and employment of master's degree graduates: Enrolled in a postdoctoral residency/fellowship (n/a), employed in independent practice (n/a), total from the above (master's) (0).

Doctoral Degree Graduates: Of those who graduated in the academic year 2011–2012, the following categories and numbers represent the postgraduate activities and employment of doctoral degree graduates: Enrolled in a psychology doctoral program (n/a), total from the above (doctoral) (0).

Additional Information:

Orientation, Objectives, and Emphasis of Department: The programs in the department are based on the concept that both a strong foundation in theoretical principles and the development of skills in the application of these principles and techniques is necessary in the training of psychologists or counselors. The Master of Arts (MA) in Industrial/Organizational Psychology is an online degree program. The program educates students to design, develop, implement, and evaluate psychologically-based human resources and interventions in organizations. The Master of Science (M.S.) in Counseling Program has two concentrations: Community Counseling and School Counseling. The community counseling concentration prepares students to work in a variety of community agency settings and/or eventual private practice. Students completing this concentration will have met the educational requirements for licensure in Tennessee as a Licensed Professional Counselor with Mental Health Service provider status. The school counseling program is designed to prepare graduates for school counseling positions at elementary, middle/junior high and high school levels. Graduates will meet the current licensing requirements for the Tennessee Board of Education.

Special Facilities or Resources: The Department of Psychology has a variety of facilities to provide learning and research opportunities. Rooms equipped with one-way observation windows, video and other monitoring equipment are available for counseling, testing and human research. The department has arranged for internship and practicum experiences with a variety of community agencies. Laboratories for vision, infant development, animal learning, and behavioral physiology are available for faculty and student research. The department has numerous microcomputers connected to the University's high-speed fiber-optic network for data collection, analysis, and the preparation of manuscripts.

Information for Students With Physical Disabilities: See the following website for more information: http://www.apsu.edu/disability/.

Application Information:

Send to Office of Graduate Admissions, Austin Peay State University, P.O. Box 4458, Clarksville, TN 37044. Application available online. URL of online application: http://www.apsu.edu/Admissions/apply. Students are admitted in the Fall, application deadline March 1. We begin to review applications beginning March 1, but continue to accept applications and admit students until program capacity is reached. *Fee:* $25.

East Tennessee State University

Department of Psychology
College of Arts & Sciences
Box 70649 (Psychology)
Johnson City, TN 37614-0649
Telephone: (423) 439-4424
Fax: (423) 439-5695
E-mail: *dixonw@etsu.edu*
Web: *http://www.etsu.edu/cas/psychology*

Department Information:

1966. Chairperson: Wallace E. Dixon, Jr. Number of faculty: total—full-time 18, part-time 2; women—full-time 7, part-time 2.

Programs and Degrees Offered:

Listed in the following order: Program area, degree type (T if terminal Master's), number awarded 7/11–6/12. Clinical Psychology PhD (Doctor of Philosophy) 2, Experimental Psychology PhD (Doctor of Philosophy) 0.

APA Accreditation: Clinical PhD (Doctor of Philosophy). Student Outcome Data Website: http://www.etsu.edu/cas/psychology/programs/clinicalphd.aspx.

Student Applications/Admissions:

Student Applications

Clinical Psychology PhD (Doctor of Philosophy)—Applications 2012–2013, 59. Total applicants accepted 2012–2013, 4. Number full-time enrolled (new admits only) 2012–2013, 4. Number part-time enrolled (new admits only) 2012–2013, 0. Total enrolled 2012–2013 full-time, 24. Total enrolled 2012–2013 part-time, 0. Openings 2013–2014, 6. The median number of years required for completion of a degree in 2012–2013 were 5. The number of students enrolled full- and part-time who were dismissed or voluntarily withdrew from this program area in 2012–2013 were 1. *Experimental Psychology PhD (Doctor of Philosophy)*—Number full-time enrolled (new admits only) 2012–2013, 8. Number part-time enrolled (new admits only) 2012–2013, 0. Total enrolled 2012–2013 full-time, 8. Total enrolled 2012–2013 part-time, 0.

Scores: Entries appear in this order: required test or GPA, minimum score (if required), median score of students entering in 2012–2013. *Clinical Psychology PhD (Doctor of Philosophy):* GRE-V no minimum stated, 570, GRE-Q no minimum stated, 610, GRE-Analytical no minimum stated, 4, overall undergraduate GPA no minimum stated, 3.7; *Experimental Psychology PhD (Doctor of Philosophy):* GRE-V no minimum stated, GRE-Q no minimum stated, overall undergraduate GPA 3.0.

Other Criteria: (importance of criteria rated low, medium, or high): GRE scores—high, research experience—high, work experience—medium, extracurricular activity—low, clinically related public service—low, GPA—high, letters of recommendation—high, interview—medium, statement of goals and objectives—high, undergraduate major in psychology—high, specific undergraduate psychology courses taken—medium, The Experimental PhD concentration may or may not have in-person interviews. Interviews are often conducted over the telephone. Clinically Related Public Service is also not considered for the Experimental concentration. For additional information on admission requirements, go to http://www.etsu.edu/cas/psychology.

Student Characteristics: The following represents characteristics of students in 2012–2013 in all graduate psychology programs in the department: Female—full-time 21, part-time 0; Male—full-time 11, part-time 0; African American/Black—full-time 1, part-time 0; Hispanic/Latino(a)—full-time 0, part-time 0; Asian/Pacific Islander—full-time 0, part-time 0; American Indian/Alaska Native—full-time 1, part-time 0; Caucasian/White—full-time 30, part-time 0; Multi-ethnic—full-time 0, part-time 0; students subject to the Americans With Disabilities Act—full-time 1, part-time 0; Unknown ethnicity—full-time 0, part-time 0; International students who hold an F-1 or J-1 Visa—full-time 0, part-time 0.

Financial Information/Assistance:
Tuition for Full-Time Study: *Master's:* State residents: per academic year $8,713, $413 per credit hour; Nonstate residents: per academic year $22,373, $1,034 per credit hour. *Doctoral:* State residents: per academic year $8,713, $413 per credit hour; Nonstate residents: per academic year $22,373, $1,034 per credit hour. Tuition is subject to change. See the following website for updates and changes in tuition costs: http://www.etsu.edu/fa/fs/bursar/.

Financial Assistance:
First-Year Students: Research assistantships available for first year. Average amount paid per academic year: $12,000. Average number of hours worked per week: 20. Apply by December 31.
Advanced Students: Traineeships available for advanced students. Average amount paid per academic year: $12,000. Average number of hours worked per week: 20. Apply by December 31.
Additional Information: Of all students currently enrolled full time, 100% benefited from one or more of the listed financial assistance programs. Application and information available online at: http://www.etsu.edu/gradstud/GATS_FAQ.aspx.

Internships/Practica: Doctoral Degree (PhD Clinical Psychology): For those doctoral students for whom a professional psychology internship was required in this program prior to graduation, (4) students applied for an internship in 2011–2012, with (2) students obtaining an internship. Of those students who obtained an internship, (2) were paid internships. Of those students who obtained an internship, (1) students placed in APA/CPA accredited internships, (1) students placed in internships not APA/CPA accredited, but listed with the Association of Psychology Postdoctoral and Internship Programs (APPIC), (0) students placed in internships conforming to guidelines of the Council of Directors of School Psychology Programs (CDSPP), (0) students placed in internships that were not APA/CPA accredited, APPIC or CDSPP listed. Clinical: Internships and practica in assessment and therapy are available to students enrolled in the clinical psychology program. They are conducted in the area mental health, behavioral health and primary care facilities under the joint supervision of departmental faculty and adjunct faculty located in the facilities. Students also participate in intensive clinical training in the department's training clinic. Experimental: Beginning with the second year, experimental students will participate in supervised teaching experiences. They will complete a course in teaching of psychology then enroll in teaching practica as a part of both masters level and doctoral level training. Masters students will be responsible for teaching one hour laboratory sections of courses. Doctoral students will be teacher of record for 3- or 4-hour undergraduate courses.

Housing and Day Care: On-campus housing is available. See the following website for more information: http://www.etsu.edu/students/housing/. On-campus day care facilities are available. See the following website for more information: http://www.etsu.edu/students/acts/students/childcareservices.aspx.

Employment of Department Graduates:
Master's Degree Graduates: Of those who graduated in the academic year 2011–2012, the following categories and numbers represent the postgraduate activities and employment of master's degree graduates: Enrolled in a postdoctoral residency/fellowship (n/a), employed in independent practice (n/a), total from the above (master's) (0).
Doctoral Degree Graduates: Of those who graduated in the academic year 2011–2012, the following categories and numbers represent the postgraduate activities and employment of doctoral degree graduates: Enrolled in a psychology doctoral program (n/a), enrolled in another graduate/professional program (1), employed in a community mental health/counseling center (1), total from the above (doctoral) (2).

Additional Information:
Orientation, Objectives, and Emphasis of Department: The Department of Psychology, College of Arts and Sciences, offers a Doctor of Philosophy in Psychology with Concentrations in Clinical and Experimental Psychology. The clinical psychology concentration provides students with training in clinical psychology with an emphasis in integrated rural primary care psychology. The experimental psychology concentration trains students in the application of basic and applied research with a translational focus, and prepares them for future faculty positions through instruction in teaching, grant writing, and the development of long-term, programmatic research.

Special Facilities or Resources: The psychology department maintains behavioral neuroscience, social psychology, developmental psychology, and clinical psychology laboratory facilities. All laboratories are used for undergraduate and graduate instructional research and for student and faculty research.

Information for Students With Physical Disabilities: See the following website for more information: http://www.etsu.edu/students/disable/.

Application Information:
Send to School of Graduate Studies, East Tennessee State University, P.O. Box 70720, Johnson City, TN 37614-1710. Application available online. URL of online application: http://www.etsu.edu/gradstud/ApplyNow.aspx. Students are admitted in the Fall, application deadline December 31. The Clinical concentration deadline is December 31; the Experimental concentration is January 15. Students are normally admitted only in the Fall term. *Fee:* $25.

Memphis, University of

Department of Counseling, Educational Psychology and
  Research, Program in Counseling Psychology
Education
100 Ball Building
Memphis, TN 38152
Telephone: (901) 678-2841
Fax: (901) 678-5114
E-mail: *slease@memphis.edu*
Web: *http://www.memphis.edu/cepr/counseling-psychology.htm*

Department Information:

1972. Chairperson: Douglas Strohmer. Number of faculty: total—full-time 28; women—full-time 14; total—minority—full-time 6; women minority—full-time 3; faculty subject to the Americans With Disabilities Act 2.

Programs and Degrees Offered:

Listed in the following order: Program area, degree type (T if terminal Master's), number awarded 7/11–6/12. Counseling Psychology PhD (Doctor of Philosophy) 5.

APA Accreditation: Counseling PhD (Doctor of Philosophy). Student Outcome Data Website: http://www.memphis.edu/cepr/counseling-psychology-information.htm.

Student Applications/Admissions:

Student Applications

Counseling Psychology PhD (Doctor of Philosophy)—Applications 2012–2013, 70. Total applicants accepted 2012–2013, 16. Number full-time enrolled (new admits only) 2012–2013, 8. Number part-time enrolled (new admits only) 2012–2013, 0. Total enrolled 2012–2013 full-time, 34. Total enrolled 2012–2013 part-time, 5. Openings 2013–2014, 8. The median number of years required for completion of a degree in 2012–2013 were 4. The number of students enrolled full- and part-time who were dismissed or voluntarily withdrew from this program area in 2012–2013 were 1.

Scores: Entries appear in this order: required test or GPA, minimum score (if required), median score of students entering in 2012–2013. *Counseling Psychology PhD (Doctor of Philosophy):* GRE-V 500, 550, GRE-Q 500, 590, GRE-Analytical 4, 4.5, Masters GPA 3.5, 3.94.

Other Criteria: (importance of criteria rated low, medium, or high): GRE scores—high, research experience—medium, work experience—medium, clinically related public service—low, GPA—high, letters of recommendation—high, interview—medium, statement of goals and objectives—high, fit w/ program philosophy—high. For additional information on admission requirements, go to http://www.memphis.edu/cepr/counseling-psychology.htm.

Student Characteristics: The following represents characteristics of students in 2012–2013 in all graduate psychology programs in the department: Female—full-time 22, part-time 2; Male—full-time 12, part-time 3; African American/Black—full-time 3, part-time 0; Hispanic/Latino(a)—full-time 0, part-time 0; Asian/Pacific Islander—full-time 1, part-time 0; American Indian/Alaska Native—full-time 1, part-time 0; Caucasian/White—full-time 28, part-time 5; Multi-ethnic—full-time 1, part-time 0; students subject to the Americans With Disabilities Act—full-time 2, part-time 0; Unknown ethnicity—full-time 0, part-time 0; International students who hold an F-1 or J-1 Visa—full-time 2, part-time 1.

Financial Information/Assistance:

Tuition for Full-Time Study: *Doctoral:* State residents: per academic year $15,550, $509 per credit hour; Nonstate residents: per academic year $30,197, $1,130 per credit hour. Tuition is subject to change. See the following website for updates and changes in tuition costs: http://bf.memphis.edu/finance/bursar/feepayment.php.

Financial Assistance:

First-Year Students: Teaching assistantships available for first year. Average amount paid per academic year: $6,000. Average number of hours worked per week: 20. Apply by April 1. Research assistantships available for first year. Average amount paid per academic year: $6,000. Average number of hours worked per week: 20. Apply by April 1. Fellowships and scholarships available for first year.

Advanced Students: Teaching assistantships available for advanced students. Average amount paid per academic year: $6,000. Average number of hours worked per week: 20. Apply by April 1. Research assistantships available for advanced students. Average amount paid per academic year: $6,000. Average number of hours worked per week: 20. Apply by April 1. Fellowships and scholarships available for advanced students. Average amount paid per academic year: $10,000. Average number of hours worked per week: 20.

Additional Information: Of all students currently enrolled full time, 100% benefited from one or more of the listed financial assistance programs. Application and information available online at: http://www.memphis.edu/gradschool/ga_awards_fellowships/gainfo.php.

Internships/Practica: Doctoral Degree (PhD Counseling Psychology): For those doctoral students for whom a professional psychology internship was required in this program prior to graduation, (9) students applied for an internship in 2011–2012, with (7) students obtaining an internship. Of those students who obtained an internship, (7) were paid internships. Of those students who obtained an internship, (7) students placed in APA/CPA accredited internships, (0) students placed in internships not APA/CPA accredited, but listed with the Association of Psychology Postdoctoral and Internship Programs (APPIC), (0) students placed in internships conforming to guidelines of the Council of Directors of School Psychology Programs (CDSPP), (0) students placed in internships that were not APA/CPA accredited, APPIC or CDSPP listed. Doctoral students complete a minimum of two practica during their three years of coursework; many students complete up to five practica. The department has an extensive network of relationships with community agencies for providing practicum placements for students. These placements include: university and college counseling centers, VAs/hospitals, community mental health centers, private practice, pediatric neuroassessment, and correctional services.

Housing and Day Care: On-campus housing is available. See the following website for more information: http://www.memphis.edu/reslife/. On-campus day care facilities are available. See the following website for more information: http://www.memphis.edu/childcareweb/.

Employment of Department Graduates:

Master's Degree Graduates: Of those who graduated in the academic year 2011–2012, the following categories and numbers represent the postgraduate activities and employment of master's degree graduates: Enrolled in a postdoctoral residency/fellowship (n/a), employed in independent practice (n/a), total from the above (master's) (0).

Doctoral Degree Graduates: Of those who graduated in the academic year 2011–2012, the following categories and numbers represent the postgraduate activities and employment of doctoral degree graduates: Enrolled in a psychology doctoral program (n/a), enrolled in a postdoctoral residency/fellowship (1), employed in independent practice (2), employed in government agency (1), not seeking employment (1), total from the above (doctoral) (5).

Additional Information:

Orientation, Objectives, and Emphasis of Department: The PhD in Counseling Psychology at The University of Memphis is designed to train generalist psychologists who promote human development in the areas of mental health, career development, emotional and social learning, and decision-making in a rapidly changing global environment. Training is grounded in the scientist–practitioner training model (equal emphasis on science and practice) and emphasizes multicultural competency and responsibility and commitment to human welfare. Didactic and experiential activities are designed to anchor students firmly within the discipline of psychology. The program emphasizes research, development, prevention, and remediation in the context of social justice as vehicles for helping individuals, families, and groups achieve competence and a sense of well-being. The department has a strong commitment to training professionals to work with diverse populations in urban settings. Within the context of the University mission, students are expected to develop the critical thinking skills necessary for lifelong learning and to contribute to the global community. Students are expected to acquire: (1) an identity as a counseling psychologist; (2) a knowledge foundation in psychology, research, counseling, psychological evaluation, and professional standards; and (3) competencies in research, practice, and teaching. The program is individualized to meet the student's goals. Graduates are prepared for positions in various settings, including counseling centers, mental health centers, hospitals, private practice, or academia.

Special Facilities or Resources: Department faculty have research teams that provide opportunities for faculty and students to collaborate on research and consultation products. Many students are also involved in cross-disciplinary research with Psychology and Women's Studies faculty. Students have graduate assistant training opportunities with approved community agencies.

Information for Students With Physical Disabilities: See the following website for more information: http://www.memphis.edu/sds/.

Application Information:
Send to Suzanne Lease, Counseling Psychology Admissions, 100 Ball Building, The University of Memphis, Memphis, TN 38152. Application available online. URL of online application: http://memphis.edu/gradschool/admproc.php. Students are admitted in the Fall, application deadline December 5. *Fee:* $35. The fee is $60 for international students.

Memphis, University of
Department of Psychology
College of Arts and Sciences
202 Psychology Building
Memphis, TN 38152-3230
Telephone: (901) 678-2145
Fax: (901) 678-2579
E-mail: *dconnabl@memphis.edu*
Web: *http://www.memphis.edu/psychology*

Department Information:
1957. Chairperson: Frank Andrasik. Number of faculty: total—full-time 31, part-time 6; women—full-time 9, part-time 2; total—minority—full-time 2, part-time 1; women minority—full-time 1, part-time 1; faculty subject to the Americans With Disabilities Act 1.

Programs and Degrees Offered:
Listed in the following order: Program area, degree type (T if terminal Master's), number awarded 7/11–6/12. Clinical Psychology PhD (Doctor of Philosophy) 5, School Psychology MA/MS (Master of Arts/Science) (T) 9, General Psychology MA/MS (Master of Arts/Science) (T) 5, School Psychology PhD (Doctor of Philosophy) 4, Experimental Psychology PhD (Doctor of Philosophy) 8.

APA Accreditation: Clinical PhD (Doctor of Philosophy). Student Outcome Data Website: http://www.memphis.edu/psychology/graduate/Clinical/clinical_data.php.

Student Applications/Admissions:

Student Applications

Clinical Psychology PhD (Doctor of Philosophy)—Applications 2012–2013, 230. Total applicants accepted 2012–2013, 6. Number full-time enrolled (new admits only) 2012–2013, 6. Number part-time enrolled (new admits only) 2012–2013, 0. Total enrolled 2012–2013 full-time, 42. Total enrolled 2012–2013 part-time, 0. Openings 2013–2014, 9. The median number of years required for completion of a degree in 2012–2013 were 6. The number of students enrolled full- and part-time who were dismissed or voluntarily withdrew from this program area in 2012–2013 were 0. *School Psychology MA/MS (Master of Arts/Science)*—Applications 2012–2013, 17. Total applicants accepted 2012–2013, 4. Number full-time enrolled (new admits only) 2012–2013, 4. Number part-time enrolled (new admits only) 2012–2013, 0. Total enrolled 2012–2013 full-time, 19. Total enrolled 2012–2013 part-time, 0. Openings 2013–2014, 10. The median number of years required for completion of a degree in 2012–2013 were 3. The number of students enrolled full- and part-time who were dismissed or voluntarily withdrew from this program area in 2012–2013 were 0. *General Psychology MA/MS (Master of Arts/Science)*—Applications 2012–2013, 51. Total applicants accepted 2012–2013, 18. Number full-time enrolled (new admits only) 2012–2013, 18. Total enrolled 2012–2013 full-time, 33. Total enrolled 2012–2013 part-time, 4. Openings 2013–2014, 12. The median number of years required for completion of a degree in 2012–2013 were 3. The number of students enrolled full- and part-time who were dismissed or voluntarily withdrew from this program area in 2012–2013 were 0. *School Psychology PhD (Doctor of Philosophy)*—Applications 2012–2013, 8. Total applicants accepted 2012–2013, 0. Number full-time enrolled (new admits only) 2012–2013, 4. Number part-time enrolled (new admits only) 2012–2013, 0. Total enrolled 2012–2013 full-time, 9. Total enrolled 2012–2013 part-time, 0. Openings 2013–2014, 4. The median number of years required for completion of a degree in 2012–2013 were 5. The number of students enrolled full- and part-time who were dismissed or voluntarily withdrew from this program area in 2012–2013 were 0. *Experimental Psychology PhD (Doctor of Philosophy)*— Applications 2012–2013, 31. Total applicants accepted 2012–2013, 4. Number full-time enrolled (new admits only) 2012–2013, 4. Number part-time enrolled (new admits only) 2012–2013, 0. Total enrolled 2012–2013 full-time, 32. Total enrolled 2012–2013 part-time, 0. Openings 2013–2014, 4. The median number of years required for completion of a degree in 2012–2013 were 5. The number of students enrolled full- and part-time who were dismissed or voluntarily withdrew from this program area in 2012–2013 were 0.

Scores: Entries appear in this order: required test or GPA, minimum score (if required), median score of students entering in 2012–2013. *Clinical Psychology PhD (Doctor of Philosophy):* GRE-V no minimum stated, 600, GRE-Q no minimum stated, 690, GRE-Analytical no minimum stated, overall undergraduate GPA no minimum stated, 3.76; *General Psychology MA/MS (Master of Arts/Science):* GRE-V no minimum stated, 153, GRE-Q no minimum stated, 146; *School Psychology PhD (Doctor of Philosophy):* GRE-V no minimum stated, 156, GRE-Q no minimum stated, 148, overall undergraduate GPA no minimum stated, 3.63; *Experimental Psychology PhD (Doctor of Philosophy):* GRE-V no minimum stated, 154, GRE-Q no minimum stated, 147, overall undergraduate GPA no minimum stated, 3.5.

Other Criteria: (importance of criteria rated low, medium, or high): GRE scores—high, research experience—high, work experience—medium, extracurricular activity—low, clinically related public service—low, GPA—high, letters of recommendation—high, interview—medium, statement of goals and objectives—high, undergraduate major in psychology—high, specific undergraduate psychology courses taken—medium. For additional information on admission requirements, go to http://www.memphis.edu/psychology/graduate/Apply/index.php.

Student Characteristics: The following represents characteristics of students in 2012–2013 in all graduate psychology programs in the department: Female—full-time 92, part-time 2; Male—full-time 43, part-time 2; African American/Black—full-time 9, part-time 3; Hispanic/Latino(a)—full-time 3, part-time 0; Asian/Pacific Islander—full-time 10, part-time 0; American Indian/Alaska Native—full-time 0, part-time 0; Caucasian/White—full-time 112, part-time 1; Multi-ethnic—full-time 1, part-time 0; students subject to the Americans With Disabilities Act—full-time 0, part-time 0; Unknown ethnicity—full-time 0, part-time 0; International students who hold an F-1 or J-1 Visa—full-time 4, part-time 0.

Financial Information/Assistance:
Tuition for Full-Time Study: *Master's:* State residents: per academic year $10,310, $509 per credit hour; Nonstate residents: per academic year $23,230, $1,130 per credit hour. *Doctoral:* State residents: per academic year $10,310, $509 per credit hour; Nonstate residents: per academic year $23,230, $1,130 per credit hour. Tuition is subject to change. See the following website for updates and changes in tuition costs: http://bf.memphis.edu/finance/bursar/.

Financial Assistance:
First-Year Students: Teaching assistantships available for first year. Average amount paid per academic year: $13,000. Average number of hours worked per week: 20. Research assistantships available for first year. Average amount paid per academic year: $13,000. Average number of hours worked per week: 20.

Advanced Students: Teaching assistantships available for advanced students. Average amount paid per academic year: $14,000. Average number of hours worked per week: 20. Research assistantships available for advanced students. Average amount paid per academic year: $14,000. Average number of hours worked per week: 20. Traineeships available for advanced students. Average amount paid per academic year: $14,000. Average number of hours worked per week: 20.

Additional Information: Of all students currently enrolled full time, 65% benefited from one or more of the listed financial assistance programs.

Internships/Practica: Doctoral Degree (PhD Clinical Psychology): For those doctoral students for whom a professional psychology internship was required in this program prior to graduation, (7) students applied for an internship in 2011–2012, with (7) students obtaining an internship. Of those students who obtained an internship, (7) were paid internships. Of those students who obtained an internship, (7) students placed in APA/CPA accredited internships, (0) students placed in internships not APA/CPA accredited, but listed with the Association of Psychology Postdoctoral and Internship Programs (APPIC), (0) students placed in internships conforming to guidelines of the Council of Directors of School Psychology Programs (CDSPP), (0) students placed in internships that were not APA/CPA accredited, APPIC or CDSPP listed. Doctoral Degree (PhD School Psychology): For those doctoral students for whom a professional psychology internship was required in this program prior to graduation, (2) students applied for an internship in 2011–2012, with (1) students obtaining an internship. Of those students who obtained an internship, (1) were paid internships. Of those students who obtained an internship, (1) students placed in APA/CPA accredited internships, (0) students placed in internships not APA/CPA accredited, but listed with the Association of Psychology Postdoctoral and Internship Programs (APPIC), (0) students placed in internships conforming to guidelines of the Council of Directors of School Psychology Programs (CDSPP), (0) students placed in internships that were not APA/CPA accredited, APPIC or CDSPP listed. Master's Degree (MA/MS General Psychology): An internship experience, such as a final research project or "capstone" experience is required of graduates. The department has an extensive network of relationships with local agencies for providing practicum experiences for students. Doctoral clinical students work 20 hours per week at one of these practicum sites for a minimum of one year. Our clinical placement sites include facilities such as a multidisciplinary diagnostic center for children with developmental disabilities, a local psychiatric hospital, our student health clinic, a federal prison, several psychologists' practices, and the world famous St. Jude Children's Research Hospital. In addition, our students often engage in short-term training on a volunteer basis at the Memphis VA Medical Center and a number of other community agencies. Students also complete two years of paid research assistantships in a faculty member's lab or on one of the various clinical grants operating in the department. All students can use these sites for other forms of practicum experience and research as the need arises. The department has no in-house internships. Clinical students complete internships during the fifth or sixth year at sites nationwide.

Housing and Day Care: On-campus housing is available. See the following website for more information: http://www.memphis.edu/reslife/. On-campus day care facilities are available. See the following website for more information: http://www.memphis.edu/childcareweb/.

Employment of Department Graduates:

Master's Degree Graduates: Of those who graduated in the academic year 2011–2012, the following categories and numbers represent the postgraduate activities and employment of master's degree graduates: Enrolled in a psychology doctoral program (4), enrolled in another graduate/professional program (8), enrolled in a postdoctoral residency/fellowship (n/a), employed in independent practice (n/a), employed in business or industry (2), do not know (5), total from the above (master's) (19).

Doctoral Degree Graduates: Of those who graduated in the academic year 2011–2012, the following categories and numbers represent the postgraduate activities and employment of doctoral degree graduates: Enrolled in a psychology doctoral program (n/a), enrolled in a postdoctoral residency/fellowship (2), employed in an academic position at a university (1), employed in an academic position at a 2-year/4-year college (1), employed in other positions at a higher education institution (1), employed in a professional position in a school system (5), employed in business or industry (1), employed in a community mental health/counseling center (2), do not know (2), total from the above (doctoral) (15).

Additional Information:

Orientation, Objectives, and Emphasis of Department: The department philosophy emphasizes the training of experimentally sophisticated research scientists and practitioners. All programs have a strong research emphasis. Professional training is based upon a research foundation and students are exposed to a broad range of theoretical perspectives. Diversity of professional training activities and collaborative research activities is emphasized. Students are afforded maximum freedom to pursue their own interests and tailor programs to their needs. All PhD and master's programs are serviced by six research areas within the department: Clinical Health Psychology, Behavioral Neuroscience, Child and Family Studies, Cognitive and Social Processes, Industrial/Organizational and Applied Psychology, and Psychopathology/Psychotherapy.

Special Facilities or Resources: The department as a whole has a strong research orientation, ranking high among psychology departments across the nation in total research and development expenditures. The department is housed in a modern, well-equipped barrier-free building, providing offices and laboratory space for all students. The department includes the Center for Applied Psychological Research (CAPR), the Institute for Intelli-

gent Systems (IIS), and the Psychological Services Center (PSC). The CAPR is a state-sponsored center of excellence that has provided the department with approximately $1 million per year for the past 20 years. The IIS is an interdisciplinary enterprise comprised of researchers and students from the fields of cognitive psychology, computer science, mathematics, physics, neuroscience, education, linguistics, philosophy, anthropology, engineering, and business. The Psychological Services Center is a fee-for-service outpatient mental health clinic located in the psychology building. In this clinic doctoral students receive intensive supervision as they learn to provide a wide range of assessment and intervention services. In addition, the PSC provides an invaluable resource for the conduct of a variety of research projects. The clients are referred from the greater Memphis area.

Information for Students With Physical Disabilities: See the following website for more information: http://www.memphis.edu/sds/.

Application Information:
Send to Graduate Admissions, Department of Psychology, 202 Psychology Building, University of Memphis, Memphis, TN 38152. Application available online. URL of online application: http://www.memphis.edu/gradschool/admproc.php. Students are admitted in the Fall, application deadline. The application deadline for clinical PhD program is December 5. The application deadline for all other PhD programs is January 15. The application deadline for the master's program in General Psychology is May 15. The application deadline for the MA/EdS in School Psychology is June 15. *Fee:* $35. The application fee for the graduate school is $35 for domestic students and $60 for international students.

Middle Tennessee State University
Department of Psychology
Education and Behavioral Science
Box 87
Murfreesboro, TN 37132
Telephone: (615) 898-2706
Fax: (615) 898-5027
E-mail: *gschmidt@mtsu.edu*
Web: *http://www.mtsu.edu/psychology/*

Department Information:
1967. Interim Chairperson: Dr. Greg Schmidt. Number of faculty: total—full-time 42, part-time 16; women—full-time 18, part-time 10; total—minority—full-time 4, part-time 1; women minority—full-time 2.

Programs and Degrees Offered:
Listed in the following order: Program area, degree type (T if terminal Master's), number awarded 7/11–6/12. Clinical Psychology MA/MS (Master of Arts/Science) (T) 9, Experimental Psychology MA/MS (Master of Arts/Science) (T) 4, Industrial/Organizational Psychology MA/MS (Master of Arts/Science) (T) 17, Quantitative Psychology MA/MS (Master of Arts/Science) (T) 4, School Psychology EdS (School Psychology) 8.

Student Applications/Admissions:

Student Applications

Clinical Psychology MA/MS (Master of Arts/Science)—Applications 2012–2013, 42. Total applicants accepted 2012–2013, 26. Number full-time enrolled (new admits only) 2012–2013, 10. Number part-time enrolled (new admits only) 2012–2013, 0. Total enrolled 2012–2013 full-time, 25. Total enrolled 2012–2013 part-time, 8. Openings 2013–2014, 14. The median number of years required for completion of a degree in 2012–2013 were 3. The number of students enrolled full- and part-time who were dismissed or voluntarily withdrew from this program area in 2012–2013 were 0. *Experimental Psychology MA/MS (Master of Arts/Science)*—Applications 2012–2013, 28. Total applicants accepted 2012–2013, 7. Number full-time enrolled (new admits only) 2012–2013, 5. Total enrolled 2012–2013 full-time, 16. Total enrolled 2012–2013 part-time, 2. Openings 2013–2014, 8. The median number of years required for completion of a degree in 2012–2013 were 2. The number of students enrolled full- and part-time who were dismissed or voluntarily withdrew from this program area in 2012–2013 were 0. *Industrial/Organizational Psychology MA/MS (Master of Arts/Science)*—Applications 2012–2013, 60. Total applicants accepted 2012–2013, 20. Number full-time enrolled (new admits only) 2012–2013, 12. Number part-time enrolled (new admits only) 2012–2013, 0. Total enrolled 2012–2013 full-time, 27. Total enrolled 2012–2013 part-time, 0. Openings 2013–2014, 12. The median number of years required for completion of a degree in 2012–2013 were 2. The number of students enrolled full- and part-time who were dismissed or voluntarily withdrew from this program area in 2012–2013 were 0. *Quantitative Psychology MA/MS (Master of Arts/Science)*—Applications 2012–2013, 9. Total applicants accepted 2012–2013, 6. Number full-time enrolled (new admits only) 2012–2013, 5. Total enrolled 2012–2013 full-time, 9. Total enrolled 2012–2013 part-time, 3. Openings 2013–2014, 6. The median number of years required for completion of a degree in 2012–2013 were 2. The number of students enrolled full- and part-time who were dismissed or voluntarily withdrew from this program area in 2012–2013 were 1. *School Psychology EdS (School Psychology)*—Applications 2012–2013, 30. Total applicants accepted 2012–2013, 25. Number full-time enrolled (new admits only) 2012–2013, 11. Number part-time enrolled (new admits only) 2012–2013, 1. Total enrolled 2012–2013 full-time, 29. Total enrolled 2012–2013 part-time, 2. Openings 2013–2014, 12. The median number of years required for completion of a degree in 2012–2013 were 3. The number of students enrolled full- and part-time who were dismissed or voluntarily withdrew from this program area in 2012–2013 were 0.

Scores: Entries appear in this order: required test or GPA, minimum score (if required), median score of students entering in 2012–2013. *Clinical Psychology MA/MS (Master of Arts/Science)*: GRE-V 146, 154, GRE-Q 145, 152, GRE-Analytical 3.5, 4, overall undergraduate GPA 2.92, 3.46; *Experimental Psychology MA/MS (Master of Arts/Science)*: GRE-V 146, 150, GRE-Q 145, 150, overall undergraduate GPA 3.00, 3.2; *Quantitative Psychology MA/MS (Master of Arts/Science)*: GRE-V no minimum stated, 470, GRE-Q no minimum stated, 630, GRE-Analytical no minimum stated, 4, overall undergraduate GPA 3.0; *School Psychology EdS (School Psychology)*: GRE-V 450, 510, GRE-Q 450, 530, GRE-Analytical no minimum stated, 4.1, overall undergraduate GPA no minimum stated.

Other Criteria: (importance of criteria rated low, medium, or high): GRE scores—high, research experience—medium, work experience—medium, extracurricular activity—low, clinically related public service—medium, GPA—high, letters of recommendation—high, interview—low, statement of goals and objectives—high, undergraduate major in psychology—medium, specific undergraduate psychology courses taken—medium, Statement of Goals & Objectives for Industrial/Organizational, Experimental & School Psychology only.

Student Characteristics: The following represents characteristics of students in 2012–2013 in all graduate psychology programs in the department: Female—full-time 144, part-time 0; Male—full-time 38, part-time 0; African American/Black—full-time 7, part-time 0; Hispanic/Latino(a)—full-time 1, part-time 0; Asian/Pacific Islander—full-time 7, part-time 0; American Indian/Alaska Native—full-time 1, part-time 0; Caucasian/White—full-time 165, part-time 0; Multi-ethnic—full-time 0, part-time 0; students subject to the Americans With Disabilities Act—full-time 0, part-time 0; Unknown ethnicity—full-time 1, part-time 0; International students who hold an F-1 or J-1 Visa—full-time 7, part-time 0.

Financial Information/Assistance:

Tuition for Full-Time Study: *Master's:* State residents: per academic year $8,900, $445 per credit hour; Nonstate residents: per academic year $20,940, $1,047 per credit hour. Tuition is subject to change. See the following website for updates and changes in tuition costs: http://www.mtsu.edu/bursar/rates_main.php.

Financial Assistance:

First-Year Students: Research assistantships available for first year. Average amount paid per academic year: $3,000. Average number of hours worked per week: 10.

Advanced Students: Research assistantships available for advanced students. Average amount paid per academic year: $3,000. Average number of hours worked per week: 10.

Additional Information: Of all students currently enrolled full time, 20% benefited from one or more of the listed financial assistance programs. Application and information available online at: http://www.mtsu.edu/graduate/student/gtas.php.

Internships/Practica: Master's Degree (MA/MS Clinical Psychology): An internship experience, such as a final research project or "capstone" experience is required of graduates. Master's Degree (MA/MS Experimental Psychology): An internship experience, such as a final research project or "capstone" experience is required of graduates. Master's Degree (MA/MS Industrial/Organizational Psychology): An internship experience, such as a final research project or "capstone" experience is required of graduates. Master's Degree (MA/MS Quantitative Psychology): An internship experience, such as a final research project or "capstone" experience is required of graduates. Field placements are available in a variety of mental health facilities, inpatient facilities, the VA hospital, drug abuse facilities, K-12 school settings, and industry and government sites.

Housing and Day Care: On-campus housing is available. See the following website for more information: http://www.mtsu.edu/housing/. On-campus day care facilities are available. See the following website for more information: http://www.mtsu.edu/pcsw/childcare_Dir/childcare.php.

Employment of Department Graduates:

Master's Degree Graduates: Of those who graduated in the academic year 2011–2012, the following categories and numbers represent the postgraduate activities and employment of master's degree graduates: Enrolled in a psychology doctoral program (2), enrolled in a postdoctoral residency/fellowship (n/a), employed in independent practice (n/a), employed in an academic position at a 2-year/4-year college (1), employed in a professional position in a school system (8), employed in business or industry (16), total from the above (master's) (27).

Doctoral Degree Graduates: Of those who graduated in the academic year 2011–2012, the following categories and numbers represent the postgraduate activities and employment of doctoral degree graduates: Enrolled in a psychology doctoral program (n/a), total from the above (doctoral) (0).

Additional Information:

Orientation, Objectives, and Emphasis of Department: We have an applied department with research and service priorities. A strong academic program is available for students seeking to improve their backgrounds in core areas of psychology for admission to doctoral programs. Applied programs lead to certification and/or licensure in school psychology, school counseling, and clinical. Industrial/Organizational program nationally acclaimed.

Information for Students With Physical Disabilities: See the following website for more information: http://www.mtsu.edu/dssemail/.

Application Information:

Send to Office of Graduate Studies, Cope Administration Building, 114, Middle Tennessee State University, Murfreesboro, TN 37132. Application available online. URL of online application: http://www.mtsu.edu/graduate/apply.php. Students are admitted in the Fall, application deadline March 1; Spring, application deadline October 1. *Fee:* $35.

Tennessee, University of, Chattanooga

Department of Psychology
College of Arts and Sciences
350 Holt Hall
Chattanooga, TN 37403
Telephone: (423) 425-4262
Fax: (423) 425-4284
E-mail: *boleary@utc.edu*
Web: *http://www.utc.edu/Academic/Psychology/*

Department Information:

1969. Department Head: Brian J. O'Leary. Number of faculty: total—full-time 13, part-time 6; women—full-time 3, part-time 3.

Programs and Degrees Offered:

Listed in the following order: Program area, degree type (T if terminal Master's), number awarded 7/11–6/12. Industrial-Organizational Psychology MA/MS (Master of Arts/Science) (T) 19, Research MA/MS (Master of Arts/Science) (T) 5.

Student Applications/Admissions:

Student Applications

Industrial-Organizational Psychology MA/MS (Master of Arts/Science)—Applications 2012–2013, 70. Total applicants accepted 2012–2013, 30. Number full-time enrolled (new admits only) 2012–2013, 13. Total enrolled 2012–2013 full-time, 30. Total enrolled 2012–2013 part-time, 0. Openings 2013–2014, 15. The median number of years required for completion of a degree in 2012–2013 were 2. The number of students enrolled full- and part-time who were dismissed or voluntarily withdrew from this program area in 2012–2013 were 3. *Research MA/MS (Master of Arts/Science)*—Applications 2012–2013, 15. Total applicants accepted 2012–2013, 10. Number full-time enrolled (new admits only) 2012–2013, 6. Total enrolled 2012–2013 full-time, 16. Total enrolled 2012–2013 part-time, 0. Openings 2013–2014, 5. The median number of years required for completion of a degree in 2012–2013 were 2. The number of students enrolled full- and part-time who were dismissed or voluntarily withdrew from this program area in 2012–2013 were 0.

Scores: Entries appear in this order: required test or GPA, minimum score (if required), median score of students entering in 2012–2013. *Industrial-Organizational Psychology MA/MS (Master of Arts/Science):* GRE-V no minimum stated, GRE-Q no minimum stated, GRE-Analytical no minimum stated, overall undergraduate GPA no minimum stated; *Research MA/MS (Master of Arts/Science):* GRE-V no minimum stated, GRE-Q no minimum stated, GRE-Analytical no minimum stated, overall undergraduate GPA no minimum stated, last 2 years GPA no minimum stated, psychology GPA no minimum stated.

Other Criteria: (importance of criteria rated low, medium, or high): GRE scores—high, research experience—medium, work experience—low, extracurricular activity—low, clinically related public service—low, GPA—high, letters of recommendation—medium, interview—low, statement of goals and objectives—medium, undergraduate major in psychology—medium, specific undergraduate psychology courses taken—low, Admission to the Research program requires sponsorship of a faculty member, highly values research experience and an undergraduate major in psychology. Admission to the I/O program requires a psychology or social science research methods and statistics course. For additional information on admission requirements, go to http://www.utc.edu/Academic/Industrial-OrganizationalPsychology/Admissions.php.

Student Characteristics: The following represents characteristics of students in 2012–2013 in all graduate psychology programs in the department: Female—full-time 26, part-time 0; Male—full-time 20, part-time 0; African American/Black—full-time 2, part-time 0; Hispanic/Latino(a)—full-time 1, part-time 0; Asian/Pacific Islander—full-time 1, part-time 0; American Indian/Alaska Native—full-time 0, part-time 0; Caucasian/White—full-time 42, part-time 0; Multi-ethnic—full-time 0, part-time 0; students subject to the Americans With Disabilities Act—full-time 0, part-time 0; Unknown ethnicity—full-time 0, part-time 0; International students who hold an F-1 or J-1 Visa—full-time 1, part-time 0.

Financial Information/Assistance:

Tuition for Full-Time Study: *Master's:* State residents: per academic year $8,350; Nonstate residents: per academic year $22,696.

Tuition is subject to change. See the following website for updates and changes in tuition costs: http://www.utc.edu/Administration/Bursar/fees.php.

Financial Assistance:

First-Year Students: Teaching assistantships available for first year. Average amount paid per academic year: $2,000. Average number of hours worked per week: 5. Apply by August 20. Research assistantships available for first year. Average amount paid per academic year: $2,750. Average number of hours worked per week: 10. Apply by July 1.

Advanced Students: Teaching assistantships available for advanced students. Average amount paid per academic year: $2,000. Average number of hours worked per week: 5. Apply by August 20. Research assistantships available for advanced students. Average amount paid per academic year: $2,750. Average number of hours worked per week: 10. Apply by July 1.

Additional Information: Of all students currently enrolled full time, 50% benefited from one or more of the listed financial assistance programs. Application and information available online at: http://www.utc.edu/Administration/FinancialAid/gradstudents.php.

Internships/Practica: Master's Degree (MA/MS Industrial-Organizational Psychology): An internship experience, such as a final research project or "capstone" experience is required of graduates. Master's Degree (MA/MS Research): An internship experience, such as a final research project or "capstone" experience is required of graduates. The integration of course work and practice throughout the students' graduate academic program is essential to prepare I/O students for applied professional careers. To achieve this end, I/O students become involved in a variety of real life work organization activities through completion of a practicum program. They are encouraged to start this practicum after their second semester of academic work. Six semester hours of practicum credit are required (involving at least 300 hours of actual work time), and an additional three semester hours may be taken as a part of the elective portion of the program. The practicum is carried out in private and public work organizations in which the students engage in a wide variety of projects under the guidance of field supervisors, coordinated by the I/O faculty.

Housing and Day Care: On-campus housing is available. See the following website for more information: http://housing.utc.edu/. On-campus day care facilities are available. See the following website for more information: http://www.utc.edu/utccc/.

Employment of Department Graduates:

Master's Degree Graduates: Of those who graduated in the academic year 2011–2012, the following categories and numbers represent the postgraduate activities and employment of master's degree graduates: Enrolled in a psychology doctoral program (5), enrolled in a postdoctoral residency/fellowship (n/a), employed in independent practice (n/a), employed in business or industry (10), other employment position (5), do not know (5), total from the above (master's) (25).

Doctoral Degree Graduates: Of those who graduated in the academic year 2011–2012, the following categories and numbers represent the postgraduate activities and employment of doctoral degree graduates: Enrolled in a psychology doctoral program (n/a), total from the above (doctoral) (0).

Additional Information:

Orientation, Objectives, and Emphasis of Department: The goal of the I/O program is to provide students with the training necessary to pursue a variety of I/O related fields. These include, but are not limited to, positions in human resources, industrial/organizational consulting, training, and organization development. The I/O program can be used as a preparation for the pursuit of doctoral training in I/O related fields of study. The curriculum is organized around specific core knowledge domains particular to I/O psychology. The industrial domain includes content such as job analysis, selection, and training. The organizational domain includes content such as work motivation, attitudes, leadership, organizational development, and group processes. The third domain, research methodology, includes experimental design and univariate and multivariate statistical analysis. The research program is designed primarily to prepare students to pursue doctoral level training. Students work in an apprenticeship model with faculty to develop strong design and analysis skills.

Special Facilities or Resources: Center for Applied Social Research conducts surveys and other applied research in the community. We have a close relationship with SHRM Chattanooga, the local SHRM chapter, and with several local work organizations.

Information for Students With Physical Disabilities: See the following website for more information: http://www.utc.edu/Administration/OfficeForStudentsWithDisabilities/.

Application Information:
Send to The Graduate School, The University of Tennessee at Chattanooga, Department 5305, 615 McCallie Avenue, Chattanooga, TN 37403. Application available online. URL of online application: http://www.utc.edu/Administration/GraduateSchool/. Students are admitted in the Fall, application deadline March 15. Students may be admitted if they apply after the March deadline if space permits. *Fee:* $30. $35 for international students.

Tennessee, University of, Knoxville
Department of Educational Psychology and Counseling
Education, Health, and Human Sciences
525 Jane and David Bailey Education Complex
Knoxville, TN 37996-3452
Telephone: (865) 974-8145
Fax: (865) 974-0135
E-mail: *mccallum@utk.edu*
Web: *http://web.utk.edu/~edpsych/*

Department Information:
1956. Head: R. Steve McCallum. Number of faculty: total—full-time 25, part-time 4; women—full-time 12; total—minority—full-time 2; women minority—full-time 1.

Programs and Degrees Offered:
Listed in the following order: Program area, degree type (T if terminal Master's), number awarded 7/11–6/12. Education MA/MS (Master of Arts/Science) (T) 5, Counselor Education PhD (Doctor of Philosophy) 3, School Psychology PhD (Doctor of Philosophy) 5, Educational Psychology and Research PhD (Doc-

tor of Philosophy) 6, Counseling MA/MS (Master of Arts/Science) (T) 22, Education PhD (Doctor of Philosophy) 5.

APA Accreditation: School PhD (Doctor of Philosophy). Student Outcome Data Website: http://web.utk.edu/~edpsych/school_psychology/default.html.

Student Applications/Admissions:

Student Applications

Education MA/MS (Master of Arts/Science)—Applications 2012–2013, 12. Total applicants accepted 2012–2013, 7. Number full-time enrolled (new admits only) 2012–2013, 7. Total enrolled 2012–2013 full-time, 22. Openings 2013–2014, 9. The median number of years required for completion of a degree in 2012–2013 were 2. The number of students enrolled full- and part-time who were dismissed or voluntarily withdrew from this program area in 2012–2013 were 2. *Counselor Education PhD (Doctor of Philosophy)*—Applications 2012–2013, 15. Total applicants accepted 2012–2013, 8. Number full-time enrolled (new admits only) 2012–2013, 5. Total enrolled 2012–2013 full-time, 18. Openings 2013–2014, 7. The median number of years required for completion of a degree in 2012–2013 were 3. The number of students enrolled full- and part-time who were dismissed or voluntarily withdrew from this program area in 2012–2013 were 1. *School Psychology PhD (Doctor of Philosophy)*—Applications 2012–2013, 46. Total applicants accepted 2012–2013, 7. Number full-time enrolled (new admits only) 2012–2013, 7. Total enrolled 2012–2013 full-time, 32. Openings 2013–2014, 7. The median number of years required for completion of a degree in 2012–2013 were 5. The number of students enrolled full- and part-time who were dismissed or voluntarily withdrew from this program area in 2012–2013 were 1. *Educational Psychology and Research PhD (Doctor of Philosophy)*—Applications 2012–2013, 14. Total applicants accepted 2012–2013, 8. Number full-time enrolled (new admits only) 2012–2013, 7. Total enrolled 2012–2013 full-time, 41. Openings 2013–2014, 10. The median number of years required for completion of a degree in 2012–2013 were 4. The number of students enrolled full- and part-time who were dismissed or voluntarily withdrew from this program area in 2012–2013 were 0. *Counseling MA/MS (Master of Arts/Science)*—Applications 2012–2013, 100. Total applicants accepted 2012–2013, 30. Number full-time enrolled (new admits only) 2012–2013, 15. Total enrolled 2012–2013 full-time, 30. Openings 2013–2014, 15. The median number of years required for completion of a degree in 2012–2013 were 2. The number of students enrolled full- and part-time who were dismissed or voluntarily withdrew from this program area in 2012–2013 were 2. *Education PhD (Doctor of Philosophy)*—Applications 2012–2013, 11. Total applicants accepted 2012–2013, 7. Number full-time enrolled (new admits only) 2012–2013, 5. Total enrolled 2012–2013 full-time, 40. Openings 2013–2014, 7. The median number of years required for completion of a degree in 2012–2013 were 3. The number of students enrolled full- and part-time who were dismissed or voluntarily withdrew from this program area in 2012–2013 were 1.

Scores: Entries appear in this order: required test or GPA, minimum score (if required), median score of students entering in 2012–2013. *Education MA/MS (Master of Arts/Science):* GRE-V no minimum stated, GRE-Q no minimum stated, GRE-Analytical no minimum stated, overall undergraduate GPA no minimum stated, last 2 years GPA no minimum stated; *Counselor Education PhD (Doctor of Philosophy):* GRE-V 500, 540, GRE-Q 450, 510, GRE-Analytical 4.0, 4.5, overall undergraduate GPA 3.4, last 2 years GPA 3.70, Masters GPA no minimum stated; *School Psychology PhD (Doctor of Philosophy):* GRE-V 500, 530, GRE-Q 500, 510, GRE-Analytical 4.0, 4.6, overall undergraduate GPA no minimum stated, last 2 years GPA no minimum stated, Masters GPA no minimum stated; *Educational Psychology and Research PhD (Doctor of Philosophy):* GRE-V 500, GRE-Q 500, GRE-Analytical 4.0, overall undergraduate GPA no minimum stated, last 2 years GPA no minimum stated, Masters GPA no minimum stated; *Counseling MA/MS (Master of Arts/Science):* GRE-V no minimum stated, GRE-Q no minimum stated, GRE-Analytical 4.0, 4.5, overall undergraduate GPA 3.2, 3.6, last 2 years GPA 3.2; *Education PhD (Doctor of Philosophy):* GRE-V 500, 510, GRE-Q 500, overall undergraduate GPA no minimum stated.

Other Criteria: (importance of criteria rated low, medium, or high): GRE scores—medium, research experience—low, work experience—low, extracurricular activity—medium, clinically related public service—medium, GPA—high, letters of recommendation—high, interview—high, statement of goals and objectives—medium, undergraduate major in psychology—low. For additional information on admission requirements, go to http://web.utk.edu/~edpsych/admissions_US.html.

Student Characteristics: The following represents characteristics of students in 2012–2013 in all graduate psychology programs in the department: Female—full-time 110, part-time 8; Male—full-time 73, part-time 2; African American/Black—full-time 7, part-time 0; Hispanic/Latino(a)—full-time 3, part-time 0; Asian/Pacific Islander—full-time 5, part-time 0; American Indian/Alaska Native—full-time 0, part-time 0; Caucasian/White—full-time 168, part-time 0; Multi-ethnic—full-time 0, part-time 0; students subject to the Americans With Disabilities Act—full-time 2, part-time 0; Unknown ethnicity—full-time 0, part-time 0; International students who hold an F-1 or J-1 Visa—full-time 6, part-time 0.

Financial Information/Assistance:

Tuition for Full-Time Study: *Master's:* State residents: per academic year $10,280, $563 per credit hour; Nonstate residents: per academic year $18,188, $1,591 per credit hour. *Doctoral:* State residents: per academic year $10,280, $563 per credit hour; Nonstate residents: per academic year $18,188, $1,591 per credit hour. Tuition is subject to change. See the following website for updates and changes in tuition costs: http://web.utk.edu/~bursar/tuition.html.

Financial Assistance:

First-Year Students: Teaching assistantships available for first year. Average amount paid per academic year: $6,000. Average number of hours worked per week: 10. Apply by January 31. Research assistantships available for first year. Average amount paid per academic year: $5,000. Average number of hours worked per week: 10. Apply by January 31. Fellowships and scholarships available for first year. Average amount paid per academic year: $5,000.

Advanced Students: Teaching assistantships available for advanced students. Average amount paid per academic year: $6,000. Average number of hours worked per week: 10. Apply by January 31. Research assistantships available for advanced students. Average amount paid per academic year: $5,000. Average number of hours worked per week: 10. Apply by January 31. Fellowships and scholarships available for advanced students. Average amount paid per academic year: $5,000.

Additional Information: Of all students currently enrolled full time, 25% benefited from one or more of the listed financial assistance programs. Application and information available online at: http://web.utk.edu/~edpsych/assistantships.html.

Internships/Practica: Doctoral Degree (PhD School Psychology): For those doctoral students for whom a professional psychology internship was required in this program prior to graduation, (5) students applied for an internship in 2011–2012, with (5) students obtaining an internship. Of those students who obtained an internship, (4) were paid internships. Of those students who obtained an internship, (4) students placed in APA/CPA accredited internships, (0) students placed in internships not APA/CPA accredited, but listed with the Association of Psychology Postdoctoral and Internship Programs (APPIC), (1) students placed in internships conforming to guidelines of the Council of Directors of School Psychology Programs (CDSPP), (0) students placed in internships that were not APA/CPA accredited, APPIC or CDSPP listed. Master's Degree (MA/MS Counseling): An internship experience, such as a final research project or "capstone" experience is required of graduates. Assessment, counseling, and consultation practica are required of all school psychology/counseling students. In addition, a 1,500-hour internship is required for EdS students and a 2000-hour internship is required for PhD students. The Department is a member of an APA-approved internship consortium.

Housing and Day Care: On-campus housing is available. See the following website for more information: http://uthousing.utk.edu/tnliving/. On-campus day care facilities are available. See the following website for more information: http://elc.utk.edu/.

Employment of Department Graduates:

Master's Degree Graduates: Of those who graduated in the academic year 2011–2012, the following categories and numbers represent the postgraduate activities and employment of master's degree graduates: Enrolled in a psychology doctoral program (5), enrolled in a postdoctoral residency/fellowship (n/a), employed in independent practice (n/a), total from the above (master's) (5).

Doctoral Degree Graduates: Of those who graduated in the academic year 2011–2012, the following categories and numbers represent the postgraduate activities and employment of doctoral degree graduates: Enrolled in a psychology doctoral program (n/a), enrolled in another graduate/professional program (5), employed in independent practice (2), employed in an academic position at a university (4), employed in an academic position at a 2-year/4-year college (4), employed in other positions at a higher education institution (3), employed in a professional position in a school system (10), employed in business or industry (5), employed in government agency (3), employed in a community mental health/counseling center (8), employed in a hospital/medical center (6), other employment position (6), total from the above (doctoral) (56).

Additional Information:

Orientation, Objectives, and Emphasis of Department: Members of the Educational Psychology and Counseling Department envision playing an instrumental role in the creation of contextually linked learning environments that promote and enhance success for all learners. We expect these environments to exemplify a spirit of collaboration and cooperation, respect for diversity, concern for mental and physical health, positive attitudes toward constructive and meaningful change, and a commitment to lifelong learning. Faculty and students in the Psychoeducational Studies Unit are expected to model the behaviors and reflect the values that are necessary to achieve this vision. The Psychoeducational Studies Unit will provide national leadership in creating learning environments that: (1) foster psychological health, (2) address authentic educational needs, and (3) promote lifelong learning. Unit faculty and students will draw upon a growing body of knowledge about the psychology, biology, and social/cultural contexts of learning in promoting systematic change that leads to the enhancement of the learner. Specifically, the Unit will seek opportunities in a diversity of contexts for learners to apply information-based problem solving, engage in critical thinking, provide counseling services, and implement the structures and processes necessary for effective collaboration.

Information for Students With Physical Disabilities: See the following website for more information: http://ods.utk.edu/.

Application Information:
Send to Graduate School, University of Tennessee, 111 Student Services, Knoxville, TN 37996-3452. Application available online. URL of online application: http://graduateadmissions.utk.edu/apply.shtml. Students are admitted in the Fall, application deadline December 10; Spring, application deadline October 15. Program deadline is December 10 for Counselor Education and Learning Environments and Educational Studies programs, January 8 for Counseling program, and January 15 for School Psychology PhD program. *Fee:* $35.

Tennessee, University of, Knoxville
Department of Psychology
Arts & Sciences
312 Austin Peay Building
Knoxville, TN 37996-0900
Telephone: (865) 974-3328
Fax: (865) 974-3330
E-mail: *cjogle@utk.edu*
Web: *http://psychology.utk.edu/*

Department Information:
1957. Department Head: Deborah P. Welsh, PhD. Number of faculty: total—full-time 33, part-time 14; women—full-time 13, part-time 3; total—minority—full-time 2; women minority—full-time 2.

Programs and Degrees Offered:
Listed in the following order: Program area, degree type (T if terminal Master's), number awarded 7/11–6/12. Clinical Psychology PhD (Doctor of Philosophy) 8, Experimental Psychology MA/MS (Master of Arts/Science) (T) 3, Counseling Psychology PhD (Doctor of Philosophy) 4, Experimental Psychology PhD (Doctor of Philosophy) 3.

APA Accreditation: Clinical PhD (Doctor of Philosophy). Student Outcome Data Website: http://web.utk.edu/~clinical/future-stats.

shtml. Counseling PhD (Doctor of Philosophy). Student Outcome Data Website: http://psychology.utk.edu/gradstudy/counseling/program_data.shtml.

Student Applications/Admissions:

Student Applications

Clinical Psychology PhD (Doctor of Philosophy)—Applications 2012–2013, 233. Total applicants accepted 2012–2013, 7. Number full-time enrolled (new admits only) 2012–2013, 7. Total enrolled 2012–2013 full-time, 45. Total enrolled 2012–2013 part-time, 0. Openings 2013–2014, 7. The median number of years required for completion of a degree in 2012–2013 were 6. The number of students enrolled full- and part-time who were dismissed or voluntarily withdrew from this program area in 2012–2013 were 0. Experimental Psychology MA/MS (Master of Arts/Science)—Applications 2012–2013, 34. Total applicants accepted 2012–2013, 3. Number full-time enrolled (new admits only) 2012–2013, 3. Total enrolled 2012–2013 full-time, 10. Total enrolled 2012–2013 part-time, 0. Openings 2013–2014, 4. The median number of years required for completion of a degree in 2012–2013 were 2. The number of students enrolled full- and part-time who were dismissed or voluntarily withdrew from this program area in 2012–2013 were 0. Counseling Psychology PhD (Doctor of Philosophy)—Applications 2012–2013, 140. Total applicants accepted 2012–2013, 6. Number full-time enrolled (new admits only) 2012–2013, 6. Total enrolled 2012–2013 full-time, 33. Openings 2013–2014, 7. The median number of years required for completion of a degree in 2012–2013 were 5. The number of students enrolled full- and part-time who were dismissed or voluntarily withdrew from this program area in 2012–2013 were 0. Experimental Psychology PhD (Doctor of Philosophy)—Applications 2012–2013, 67. Total applicants accepted 2012–2013, 4. Number full-time enrolled (new admits only) 2012–2013, 4. Total enrolled 2012–2013 full-time, 36. Openings 2013–2014, 7. The median number of years required for completion of a degree in 2012–2013 were 5. The number of students enrolled full- and part-time who were dismissed or voluntarily withdrew from this program area in 2012–2013 were 0.

Scores: Entries appear in this order: required test or GPA, minimum score (if required), median score of students entering in 2012–2013. Clinical Psychology PhD (Doctor of Philosophy): GRE-V 156, 161, GRE-Q 151, 154, overall undergraduate GPA 3.68, 3.82; Experimental Psychology MA/MS (Master of Arts/Science): GRE-V no minimum stated, 470, GRE-Q no minimum stated, 560, overall undergraduate GPA no minimum stated, 3.80; Counseling Psychology PhD (Doctor of Philosophy): GRE-V 410, 629, GRE-Q 440, 671, overall undergraduate GPA 3.0, 3.75; Experimental Psychology PhD (Doctor of Philosophy): GRE-V no minimum stated, 547, GRE-Q no minimum stated, 625, overall undergraduate GPA no minimum stated, 3.58.

Other Criteria: (importance of criteria rated low, medium, or high): GRE scores—medium, research experience—high, work experience—low, extracurricular activity—low, clinically related public service—low, GPA—high, letters of recommendation—high, interview—high, statement of goals and objectives—high, fit with program—high, undergraduate major in psychology—low, specific undergraduate psychology courses taken—low. For additional information on admission

requirements, go to http://psychology.utk.edu/gradstudy/admissions.shtml.

Student Characteristics: The following represents characteristics of students in 2012–2013 in all graduate psychology programs in the department: Female—full-time 89, part-time 0; Male—full-time 30, part-time 0; African American/Black—full-time 7, part-time 0; Hispanic/Latino(a)—full-time 2, part-time 0; Asian/Pacific Islander—full-time 11, part-time 0; American Indian/Alaska Native—full-time 3, part-time 0; Caucasian/White—full-time 87, part-time 0; Multi-ethnic—full-time 2, part-time 0; students subject to the Americans With Disabilities Act—full-time 0, part-time 0; Unknown ethnicity—full-time 7, part-time 0; International students who hold an F-1 or J-1 Visa—full-time 8, part-time 0.

Financial Information/Assistance:

Tuition for Full-Time Study: Master's: State residents: per academic year $10,280, $501 per credit hour; Nonstate residents: per academic year $28,768, $1,512 per credit hour. Doctoral: State residents: per academic year $10,280, $501 per credit hour; Nonstate residents: per academic year $28,768, $1,512 per credit hour. Tuition is subject to change. See the following website for updates and changes in tuition costs: http://web.utk.edu/~bursar/.

Financial Assistance:

First-Year Students: Research assistantships available for first year. Average amount paid per academic year: $14,270. Average number of hours worked per week: 20.

Advanced Students: Teaching assistantships available for advanced students. Research assistantships available for advanced students. Fellowships and scholarships available for advanced students.

Additional Information: Of all students currently enrolled full time, 100% benefited from one or more of the listed financial assistance programs.

Internships/Practica: Doctoral Degree (PhD Clinical Psychology): For those doctoral students for whom a professional psychology internship was required in this program prior to graduation, (4) students applied for an internship in 2011–2012, with (3) students obtaining an internship. Of those students who obtained an internship, (3) were paid internships. Of those students who obtained an internship, (3) students placed in APA/CPA accredited internships, (0) students placed in internships not APA/CPA accredited, but listed with the Association of Psychology Postdoctoral and Internship Programs (APPIC), (0) students placed in internships conforming to guidelines of the Council of Directors of School Psychology Programs (CDSPP), (0) students placed in internships that were not APA/CPA accredited, APPIC or CDSPP listed. Doctoral Degree (PhD Counseling Psychology): For those doctoral students for whom a professional psychology internship was required in this program prior to graduation, (6) students applied for an internship in 2011–2012, with (6) students obtaining an internship. Of those students who obtained an internship, (6) were paid internships. Of those students who obtained an internship, (6) students placed in APA/CPA accredited internships, (0) students placed in internships not APA/CPA accredited, but listed with the Association of Psychology Postdoctoral and Internship Programs (APPIC), (0) students placed in internships conforming to guidelines of the Council of Directors of School Psychology Programs (CDSPP), (0) students placed in internships that were not APA/CPA accredited, APPIC or CDSPP listed. Master's Degree (MA/MS Experimental Psychology): An internship experience, such as a final research project or "capstone" experience is required of graduates. All Clinical students are required to participate in two 12-month practica, one in our Departmental Psychological Clinic and the other in a community mental health facility. Both practica are supervised by doctoral degreed clinical psychologists, and the clientele are children, adolescents, and adults who seek help for their emotional and behavioral problems. In addition, Clinical and Counseling students are required to serve a one-year internship.

Housing and Day Care: On-campus housing is available. See the following website for more information: http://uthousing.utk.edu/tnliving/future/graduate.shtml. On-campus day care facilities are available. See the following website for more information: http://elc.utk.edu/.

Employment of Department Graduates:

Master's Degree Graduates: Of those who graduated in the academic year 2011–2012, the following categories and numbers represent the postgraduate activities and employment of master's degree graduates: Enrolled in a psychology doctoral program (1), enrolled in a postdoctoral residency/fellowship (n/a), employed in independent practice (n/a), do not know (2), total from the above (master's) (3).

Doctoral Degree Graduates: Of those who graduated in the academic year 2011–2012, the following categories and numbers represent the postgraduate activities and employment of doctoral degree graduates: Enrolled in a psychology doctoral program (n/a), enrolled in a postdoctoral residency/fellowship (1), employed in an academic position at a 2-year/4-year college (1), do not know (1), total from the above (doctoral) (3).

Additional Information:

Orientation, Objectives, and Emphasis of Department: The graduate faculty maintain active research programs in cognition, developmental, ethology, gender, health, organizational, personality, phenomenology, psychobiology, psychometrics, sensation/perception, and social psychology. The MA program is appropriate for students wanting a master's degree as part of progress toward a doctorate, or for those who wish to complement a degree in a different field. The Experimental PhD program prepares students for academic/research careers and for careers involving the application of psychological principles as practitioners in industrial, forensic, organizational, and community settings. Areas of concentration include applied psychology, child development, cognition, and consciousness, health psychology, phenomenology, and social/personality. The Clinical PhD program combines psychodynamic and research components, requiring exposure to a wide range of theoretical views and technical practices. Minors available are child development, health psychology, and social psychology. In order to foster appropriate breadth and interdisciplinary training, some cognate work outside the department of psychology is required of all doctoral students. The Counseling program is designed to enable students to become behavioral scientists, skilled in psychological research and its application. Students are trained to provide services to a wide variety of clients in numerous settings. Program objectives are to train doctoral-level counseling psychologists who have knowledge of, and competence in, (a) the foundation and discipline of psychology, (b) social science research and methodology, and (c) specific therapeutic and inter-

vention skills related to being a counseling psychologist. We follow a Scientist-Practitioner-Advocate Training Model and also have a two-year Social Justice practicum sequence.

Special Facilities or Resources: Facilities include computer support in equipment and staff, human and animal laboratories, a psychology clinic for training and research, and a new university library with expanded serials holdings.

Information for Students With Physical Disabilities: See the following website for more information: http://ods.utk.edu/.

Application Information:
Application available online. URL of online application: http://graduateadmissions.utk.edu/apply.shtml. Students are admitted in the Fall, application deadline December 1. Deadline for PhD programs is December 1; for Master's program it is March 1. *Fee:* $60.

Vanderbilt University
Human & Organizational Development
Peabody College of Education & Human Development
Peabody #90, 230 Appleton Place
Nashville, TN 37203-5721
Telephone: (615) 322-8484
Fax: (615) 343-2661
E-mail: *sherrie.a.lane@vanderbilt.edu*
Web: *http://peabody.vanderbilt.edu/departments/hod/index.php*

Department Information:
1999. Chairperson: Beth Shinn. Number of faculty: total—full-time 30, part-time 10; women—full-time 19, part-time 7; total—minority—full-time 5; women minority—full-time 3.

Programs and Degrees Offered:
Listed in the following order: Program area, degree type (T if terminal Master's), number awarded 7/11–6/12. Human Development Counseling MEd (Education) 28, Community Research & Action PhD (Doctor of Philosophy) 2, Community Development and Action MEd (Education) 15.

Student Applications/Admissions:
Student Applications
Human Development Counseling MEd (Education)—Applications 2012–2013, 186. Total applicants accepted 2012–2013, 31. Number full-time enrolled (new admits only) 2012–2013, 30. Number part-time enrolled (new admits only) 2012–2013, 0. Total enrolled 2012–2013 full-time, 63. Total enrolled 2012–2013 part-time, 0. Openings 2013–2014, 35. The median number of years required for completion of a degree in 2012–2013 was 1. The number of students enrolled full- and part-time who were dismissed or voluntarily withdrew from this program area in 2012–2013 were 0. *Community Research & Action PhD (Doctor of Philosophy)*—Applications 2012–2013, 156. Total applicants accepted 2012–2013, 6. Number full-time enrolled (new admits only) 2012–2013, 4. Number part-time enrolled (new admits only) 2012–2013, 0. Total enrolled 2012–2013 full-time, 34. Total enrolled 2012–2013 part-time, 0. Openings 2013–2014, 6. The median number of years re-

quired for completion of a degree in 2012–2013 were 2. *Community Development and Action MEd (Education)*—Applications 2012–2013, 66. Total applicants accepted 2012–2013, 32. Number full-time enrolled (new admits only) 2012–2013, 12. Total enrolled 2012–2013 full-time, 26. Total enrolled 2012–2013 part-time, 0. Openings 2013–2014, 30. The median number of years required for completion of a degree in 2012–2013 was 1. The number of students enrolled full- and part-time who were dismissed or voluntarily withdrew from this program area in 2012–2013 were 0.

Scores: Entries appear in this order: required test or GPA, minimum score (if required), median score of students entering in 2012–2013. *Human Development Counseling MEd (Education):* GRE-V 500, 556, GRE-Q 500, 590, GRE-Analytical 3.5, 4.5, overall undergraduate GPA 3.0, 3.8; *Community Research & Action PhD (Doctor of Philosophy):* GRE-V no minimum stated, 640, GRE-Q no minimum stated, 710, GRE-Analytical 4.5, 5.0, overall undergraduate GPA 3.3, 3.6, Masters GPA 3.6, 3.75; *Community Development and Action MEd (Education):* GRE-V 500, 559, GRE-Q 500, 600, GRE-Analytical 3.5, 4.4, overall undergraduate GPA 3.0, 3.15.

Other Criteria: (importance of criteria rated low, medium, or high): GRE scores—high, research experience—medium, work experience—low, extracurricular activity—low, clinically related public service—medium, GPA—high, letters of recommendation—high, interview—high, statement of goals and objectives—high, writing samples—high, undergraduate major in psychology—low, specific undergraduate psychology courses taken—low, Research experience less important for Master's programs than for the PhD program. Clinically related public service helpful for all programs. Additional writing samples are requested for the application to the PhD program. For additional information on admission requirements, go to http://peabody.vanderbilt.edu/departments/hod/graduate-programs/.

Student Characteristics: The following represents characteristics of students in 2012–2013 in all graduate psychology programs in the department: Female—full-time 93, part-time 0; Male—full-time 30, part-time 0; African American/Black—full-time 15, part-time 0; Hispanic/Latino(a)—full-time 4, part-time 0; Asian/Pacific Islander—full-time 9, part-time 0; American Indian/Alaska Native—full-time 0, part-time 0; Caucasian/White—full-time 90, part-time 0; Multi-ethnic—full-time 0, part-time 0; students subject to the Americans With Disabilities Act—full-time 0, part-time 0; Unknown ethnicity—full-time 5, part-time 0; International students who hold an F-1 or J-1 Visa—full-time 0, part-time 0.

Financial Information/Assistance:
Tuition for Full-Time Study: *Master's:* State residents: per academic year $28,920, $1,265 per credit hour; Nonstate residents: per academic year $28,920, $1,265 per credit hour. *Doctoral:* State residents: per academic year $33,678, $1,871 per credit hour; Nonstate residents: per academic year $33,678, $1,871 per credit hour. Tuition is subject to change. Additional fees are assessed to students beyond the costs of tuition for the following: student health insurance, student activities and recreation, library fees. Tuition costs vary by program. See the following website for updates and changes in tuition costs: http://www.vanderbilt.edu/stuaccts/.

Financial Assistance:
First-Year Students: Teaching assistantships available for first year. Average amount paid per academic year: $11,385. Average number of hours worked per week: 10. Apply by February 1. Research assistantships available for first year. Average amount paid per academic year: $11,385. Average number of hours worked per week: 10. Apply by February 1. Fellowships and scholarships available for first year. Average amount paid per academic year: $22,770. Average number of hours worked per week: 20. Apply by February 1.

Advanced Students: Teaching assistantships available for advanced students. Average amount paid per academic year: $14,000. Average number of hours worked per week: 10. Apply by February 1. Research assistantships available for advanced students. Average amount paid per academic year: $14,000. Average number of hours worked per week: 10. Apply by February 1. Fellowships and scholarships available for advanced students. Average amount paid per academic year: $24,000. Average number of hours worked per week: 20. Apply by February 1.

Additional Information: Of all students currently enrolled full time, 60% benefited from one or more of the listed financial assistance programs. Application and information available online at: http://www.vanderbilt.edu/financialaid/.

Internships/Practica: The CDA and CRA programs require a 15-week internship. Possible sites include: Mayor's Office/Metro Council/Planning Commission; local community development organization; regional planning or civic design center; youth development center; healthcare corporation; neighborhood health clinic; alcohol and drug treatment center; welfare or housing agency; state health and human service agencies; Vanderbilt Institute for Public Policy Studies (Centers for Mental Health Policy, Evaluation Research and Methodology, Child and Family Policy, Crime and Justice Policy, Environmental Management Studies, Health Policy, Psychotherapy Research and Policy, State and Local Policy). The HDC Program requires a one-year internship that provides opportunities to apply knowledge and skills primarily in the areas of: social service agencies; mental health centers; schools (K-12); employee assistance programs; and other human services delivery programs.

Housing and Day Care: No on-campus housing is available. On-campus day care facilities are available. See the following website for more information: http://healthandwellness.vanderbilt.edu/child-family-center/.

Employment of Department Graduates:
Master's Degree Graduates: Of those who graduated in the academic year 2011–2012, the following categories and numbers represent the postgraduate activities and employment of master's degree graduates: Enrolled in a postdoctoral residency/fellowship (n/a), employed in independent practice (n/a), employed in a professional position in a school system (13), employed in business or industry (12), employed in government agency (3), employed in a community mental health/counseling center (13), total from the above (master's) (41).

Doctoral Degree Graduates: Of those who graduated in the academic year 2011–2012, the following categories and numbers represent the postgraduate activities and employment of doctoral degree graduates: Enrolled in a psychology doctoral program (n/a), enrolled in a postdoctoral residency/fellowship (1), employed in an academic position at a university (1), employed in government agency (1), total from the above (doctoral) (3).

Additional Information:

Orientation, Objectives, and Emphasis of Department: Although the vast majority of faculty in the department are psychologists, our orientation is interdisciplinary. There are three graduate programs, all oriented to helping diverse communities and individuals identify and develop their strengths: a long-standing Master's in Human Development Counseling (HDC), a Master's in Community Development & Action (CDA), and a PhD in Community Research & Action (CRA, with a terminal master's degree included). The latter two started in 2001. The HDC Program prepares students to meet the psychological needs of the normally developing population, who sometimes require professional help. Through a humanistic training model and a two-year curriculum, students develop a strong theoretical grounding in life-span human development, and school or community counseling. The CDA program is for those who desire training for program administration/evaluation work in public or private, international or domestic, community service, planning, or development organizations. The Doctoral Degree in Community Research and Action is designed to train action-researchers for academic or program/policy-related careers in applied community studies: i.e., community psychology, community development, prevention, community health/mental health, organizational change, and ethics. Coursework in qualitative and quantitative methods and evaluation research is required. The program builds on the one in Community Psychology previously in the Department of Psychology and Human Development and reflects the move in the field to become interdisciplinary.

Special Facilities or Resources: Peabody College has its own library, several computer centers, and nationally known research centers, including the Learning Sciences Institute and the Kennedy Center for Research on Human Development, mental retardation and other disabilities. Also on the beautiful and historic Peabody campus is the Vanderbilt Institute for Public Policy Studies (Centers for Mental Health Policy, Evaluation Research and Methodology, Child and Family Policy, Crime and Justice Policy, Environmental Management Studies, Health Policy, Psychotherapy Research and Policy, State and Local Policy). Our department has its own center, the Center for Community Studies. Located in Nashville, the Tennessee state capital, opportunities abound for research and internships in state and local health and human service agencies and schools.

Information for Students With Physical Disabilities: See the following website for more information: http://www.vanderbilt.edu/ead/.

Application Information:

Send to Office of Graduate Admissions, Peabody College at Vanderbilt University, 230 Appleton Place, Peabody #227, Nashville, TN 37203-5721. Application available online. URL of online application: http://peabody.vanderbilt.edu/degrees-programs/masters-edd-programs/apply_for_masters_or_edd/apply_for_admission.php. Students are admitted in the Fall, application deadline December 1; Spring, application deadline November 1. The deadline for the PhD program in Community Research and Action is December 1, and the deadline for the MEd in Human Development Counseling is December 31. The Community Development & Action MEd Program has a rolling

admissions process and also admits for the spring semester. November 1 is the preferred deadline for spring admissions. *Fee:* $40. Application fee is waived when applying online.

Vanderbilt University
Psychological Sciences
111 21st Avenue South or Peabody College #512, 230
  Appleton Place
Nashville, TN 37240
Telephone: (615) 322-2874
Fax: (615) 343-8449
E-mail: *lydia.dumas@vanderbilt.edu or*
  ally.armstead@vanderbilt.edu
Web: *http://www.vanderbilt.edu/psychological_sciences/*

Department Information:

1925. Chairperson: Andrew J. Tomarken & David Cole. Number of faculty: total—full-time 73, part-time 9; women—full-time 31, part-time 6; total—minority—full-time 4; women minority—full-time 2; faculty subject to the Americans With Disabilities Act 1.

Programs and Degrees Offered:

Listed in the following order: Program area, degree type (T if terminal Master's), number awarded 7/11–6/12. Neuroscience PhD (Doctor of Philosophy) 1, Clinical Science PhD (Doctor of Philosophy) 7, Cognition and Cognitive Neuroscience PhD (Doctor of Philosophy) 6, Developmental Science PhD (Doctor of Philosophy) 1, Quantitative Methods and Evaluation PhD (Doctor of Philosophy) 3.

APA Accreditation: Clinical PhD (Doctor of Philosophy). Student Outcome Data Website: http://www.vanderbilt.edu/psychological_sciences/graduate/programs/clinical.php.

Student Applications/Admissions:

Student Applications

Neuroscience PhD (Doctor of Philosophy)—Applications 2012–2013, 83. Total applicants accepted 2012–2013, 3. Number full-time enrolled (new admits only) 2012–2013, 2. Number part-time enrolled (new admits only) 2012–2013, 0. Total enrolled 2012–2013 full-time, 12. Total enrolled 2012–2013 part-time, 0. Openings 2013–2014, 4. The median number of years required for completion of a degree in 2012–2013 were 4. The number of students enrolled full- and part-time who were dismissed or voluntarily withdrew from this program area in 2012–2013 were 0. *Clinical Science PhD (Doctor of Philosophy)*—Applications 2012–2013, 398. Total applicants accepted 2012–2013, 10. Number full-time enrolled (new admits only) 2012–2013, 4. Number part-time enrolled (new admits only) 2012–2013, 0. Total enrolled 2012–2013 full-time, 34. Total enrolled 2012–2013 part-time, 0. Openings 2013–2014, 16. The median number of years required for completion of a degree in 2012–2013 were 7. The number of students enrolled full- and part-time who were dismissed or voluntarily withdrew from this program area in 2012–2013 were 0. *Cognition and Cognitive Neuroscience PhD (Doctor of Philosophy)*—Applications 2012–2013, 149. Total applicants accepted 2012–2013, 8. Number full-time enrolled (new admits only) 2012–2013, 4. Total enrolled 2012–2013 full-time, 27. Openings 2013–

2014, 10. The median number of years required for completion of a degree in 2012–2013 were 6. The number of students enrolled full- and part-time who were dismissed or voluntarily withdrew from this program area in 2012–2013 were 0. *Developmental Science PhD (Doctor of Philosophy)*—Applications 2012–2013, 61. Total applicants accepted 2012–2013, 3. Number full-time enrolled (new admits only) 2012–2013, 3. Total enrolled 2012–2013 full-time, 10. Openings 2013–2014, 3. The median number of years required for completion of a degree in 2012–2013 were 5. The number of students enrolled full- and part-time who were dismissed or voluntarily withdrew from this program area in 2012–2013 were 0. *Quantitative Methods and Evaluation PhD (Doctor of Philosophy)*—Applications 2012–2013, 59. Total applicants accepted 2012–2013, 5. Number full-time enrolled (new admits only) 2012–2013, 1. Total enrolled 2012–2013 full-time, 4. Openings 2013–2014, 5. The median number of years required for completion of a degree in 2012–2013 were 6. The number of students enrolled full- and part-time who were dismissed or voluntarily withdrew from this program area in 2012–2013 were 0.

Scores: Entries appear in this order: required test or GPA, minimum score (if required), median score of students entering in 2012–2013. *Neuroscience PhD (Doctor of Philosophy)*: GRE-V no minimum stated, 162, GRE-Q no minimum stated, 167, overall undergraduate GPA no minimum stated, 3.56, psychology GPA no minimum stated, 3.78; *Clinical Science PhD (Doctor of Philosophy)*: GRE-V no minimum stated, 164, GRE-Q no minimum stated, 156, overall undergraduate GPA no minimum stated, 3.74, psychology GPA no minimum stated, 3.85; *Cognition and Cognitive Neuroscience PhD (Doctor of Philosophy)*: GRE-V no minimum stated, 161, GRE-Q no minimum stated, 161, overall undergraduate GPA no minimum stated, 3.69, psychology GPA no minimum stated, 3.66; *Developmental Science PhD (Doctor of Philosophy)*: GRE-V no minimum stated, 165, GRE-Q no minimum stated, 156, overall undergraduate GPA no minimum stated, 3.58, psychology GPA no minimum stated, 3.75; *Quantitative Methods and Evaluation PhD (Doctor of Philosophy)*: GRE-V no minimum stated, 162, GRE-Q no minimum stated, 159, overall undergraduate GPA no minimum stated, 3.77, psychology GPA no minimum stated, 3.8.

Other Criteria: (importance of criteria rated low, medium, or high): GRE scores—high, research experience—high, work experience—low, extracurricular activity—low, clinically related public service—low, GPA—high, letters of recommendation—high, interview—high, statement of goals and objectives—high, undergraduate major in psychology—low, specific undergraduate psychology courses taken—low. For additional information on admission requirements, go to http://www.vanderbilt.edu/psychological_sciences/graduate/prospective/index.php.

Student Characteristics: The following represents characteristics of students in 2012–2013 in all graduate psychology programs in the department: Female—full-time 62, part-time 0; Male—full-time 25, part-time 0; African American/Black—full-time 3, part-time 0; Hispanic/Latino(a)—full-time 1, part-time 0; Asian/Pacific Islander—full-time 17, part-time 0; American Indian/Alaska Native—full-time 0, part-time 0; Caucasian/White—full-time 62, part-time 0; Multi-ethnic—full-time 0, part-time 0; students subject to the Americans With Disabilities Act—full-time 0, part-time 0; Unknown ethnicity—full-time 4, part-time 0; International students who hold an F-1 or J-1 Visa—full-time 17, part-time 0.

Financial Information/Assistance:

Tuition for Full-Time Study: *Doctoral:* State residents: per academic year $41,088, $1,712 per credit hour; Nonstate residents: per academic year $41,088, $1,712 per credit hour. Tuition is subject to change. Additional fees are assessed to students beyond the costs of tuition for the following: student activity and recreation fees.

Financial Assistance:

First-Year Students: Teaching assistantships available for first year. Average amount paid per academic year: $22,200. Average number of hours worked per week: 20. Apply by December 1. Research assistantships available for first year. Average amount paid per academic year: $22,200. Average number of hours worked per week: 20. Apply by December 1. Fellowships and scholarships available for first year. Average amount paid per academic year: $22,200. Average number of hours worked per week: 20. Apply by December 1.

Advanced Students: Teaching assistantships available for advanced students. Average amount paid per academic year: $22,200. Average number of hours worked per week: 20. Apply by December 1. Research assistantships available for advanced students. Average amount paid per academic year: $22,200. Average number of hours worked per week: 20. Apply by December 1. Traineeships available for advanced students. Average amount paid per academic year: $22,032. Average number of hours worked per week: 20. Apply by December 1. Fellowships and scholarships available for advanced students. Average amount paid per academic year: $22,200. Average number of hours worked per week: 20. Apply by December 1.

Additional Information: Of all students currently enrolled full time, 100% benefited from one or more of the listed financial assistance programs. Application and information available online at: http://www.vanderbilt.edu/psychological_sciences/graduate/prospective/aid.php.

Internships/Practica: Doctoral Degree (PhD Clinical Science): For those doctoral students for whom a professional psychology internship was required in this program prior to graduation, (9) students applied for an internship in 2011–2012, with (7) students obtaining an internship. Of those students who obtained an internship, (7) were paid internships. Of those students who obtained an internship, (7) students placed in APA/CPA accredited internships, (0) students placed in internships not APA/CPA accredited, but listed with the Association of Psychology Postdoctoral and Internship Programs (APPIC), (0) students placed in internships conforming to guidelines of the Council of Directors of School Psychology Programs (CDSPP), (0) students placed in internships that were not APA/CPA accredited, APPIC or CDSPP listed. We offer up to two dozen different placements for students to do their practica. These include two VA Medical Centers, VU Child and Adolescent Psychiatric Hospital, VU Diabetes Center, VU Psychological and Counseling Center, Mobile Crisis Response Service, public school systems, State Prison, and mental health facilities for both children and adults.

Housing and Day Care: No on-campus housing is available. On-campus day care facilities are available. See the following website for more information: http://healthandwellness.vanderbilt.edu/child-family-center/child-care-center/.

Employment of Department Graduates:

Master's Degree Graduates: Of those who graduated in the academic year 2011–2012, the following categories and numbers represent the postgraduate activities and employment of master's degree graduates: Enrolled in a postdoctoral residency/fellowship (n/a), employed in independent practice (n/a), total from the above (master's) (0).

Doctoral Degree Graduates: Of those who graduated in the academic year 2011–2012, the following categories and numbers represent the postgraduate activities and employment of doctoral degree graduates: Enrolled in a psychology doctoral program (n/a), enrolled in a postdoctoral residency/fellowship (6), do not know (1), total from the above (doctoral) (7).

Additional Information:

Orientation, Objectives, and Emphasis of Department: The doctoral program in Psychological Sciences is offered jointly by the Department of Psychology in the College of Arts and Science and the Department of Psychology and Human Development in the Peabody College at Vanderbilt University. The program focuses on psychological theory and original empirical research. Students are admitted to work toward the PhD in these areas: Clinical Science, Cognition and Cognitive Neuroscience, Developmental Science, Neuroscience, or Quantitative Methods and Evaluation. A major goal is the placement of students in academic settings. The curriculum is designed to: (a) familiarize students with major areas of psychology; (b) provide specialized training in at least one of the five specific areas; and (c) provide students flexibility to enroll in classes consistent with their research interests. Students take core courses in quantitative methods and their substantive area, enroll in advanced seminars, and attend weekly area group colloquia. In addition to coursework, we expect students to be continually involved in research throughout their tenure in our program. We use a one-on-one mentoring model as a primary though not exclusive means of advising for the acquisition of scientific skills by students.

Special Facilities or Resources: Psychological Sciences is housed in Wilson Hall, Jesup Psychological Laboratory, and Hobbs Laboratory of Human Development. We have state-of-the-art laboratories for carrying out basic research with humans and animals that include computer stimulus presentation and response collection capabilities, computers for data analysis and computational modeling, and specialized research equipment (including eyetracking environments, virtual reality, and custom experimental hardware and electronics). Research with humans, including both adults and children, and including those with brain damage and mental illness, is conducted in laboratories at Wilson, Hobbs and at laboratories in the Kennedy Center and the Vanderbilt Medical Center. Wilson Hall contains an AAALAC-accredited animal care facility with dedicated and experienced staff to support husbandry, enrichment, and surgery for species used in basic research. Faculty members have their own dedicated laboratory space for conducting clinical, cognitive and cognitive neuroscience, developmental, neuroscience, and quantitative research. Research in Psychological Sciences is enhanced by a number of Research Centers that support a variety of shared research equipment and services: Advanced Computing Center for Research and Education, Center for Integrative and Cognitive Neuroscience, Institute for Imaging Science, Kennedy Center, Learning Sciences Institute and Vanderbilt Vision Research Center.

Information for Students With Physical Disabilities: See the following website for more information: http://www.vanderbilt.edu/ead/ds_about.html.

Application Information:
Send to Psychological Sciences Program, Vanderbilt University, GPC #324, 230 Appleton Place, Nashville, TN 37203-5721. Application available online. URL of online application: https://graduateapplications.vanderbilt.edu/. Students are admitted in the Fall, application deadline December 1. *Fee:* $0. Application fee waived for online applications.

Angelo State University

Department of Psychology, Sociology, and Social Work
College of Health and Human Services
2601 West Avenue North
San Angelo, TX 76909
Telephone: (325) 942-2068
Fax: (325) 942-2290
E-mail: *Bill.Davidson@angelo.edu*
Web: *http://www.angelo.edu/dept/psychology_sociology/*

Department Information:

1983. Department Head: William B. Davidson. Number of faculty: total—full-time 15, part-time 12; women—full-time 7, part-time 8; total—minority—full-time 2, part-time 1; women minority—full-time 2.

Programs and Degrees Offered:

Listed in the following order: Program area, degree type (T if terminal Master's), number awarded 7/11–6/12. Counseling Psychology MA/MS (Master of Arts/Science) (T) 6, Applied Psychology MA/MS (Master of Arts/Science) (T) 2, Industrial/Organizational Psychology MA/MS (Master of Arts/Science) (T) 7.

Student Applications/Admissions:

Student Applications

Counseling Psychology MA/MS (Master of Arts/Science)—Applications 2012–2013, 44. Total applicants accepted 2012–2013, 32. Number full-time enrolled (new admits only) 2012–2013, 21. Number part-time enrolled (new admits only) 2012–2013, 11. Total enrolled 2012–2013 full-time, 48. Total enrolled 2012–2013 part-time, 4. Openings 2013–2014, 10. The median number of years required for completion of a degree in 2012–2013 were 2. The number of students enrolled full- and part-time who were dismissed or voluntarily withdrew from this program area in 2012–2013 were 7. *Applied Psychology MA/MS (Master of Arts/Science)*—Applications 2012–2013, 33. Total applicants accepted 2012–2013, 25. Number full-time enrolled (new admits only) 2012–2013, 12. Number part-time enrolled (new admits only) 2012–2013, 5. Total enrolled 2012–2013 full-time, 20. Total enrolled 2012–2013 part-time, 8. Openings 2013–2014, 10. The median number of years required for completion of a degree in 2012–2013 were 2. The number of students enrolled full- and part-time who were dismissed or voluntarily withdrew from this program area in 2012–2013 were 3. *Industrial/Organizational Psychology MA/MS (Master of Arts/Science)*—Applications 2012–2013, 17. Total applicants accepted 2012–2013, 15. Number full-time enrolled (new admits only) 2012–2013, 15. Number part-time enrolled (new admits only) 2012–2013, 0. Total enrolled 2012–2013 full-time, 18. Total enrolled 2012–2013 part-time, 0. Openings

2013–2014, 10. The median number of years required for completion of a degree in 2012–2013 were 2. The number of students enrolled full- and part-time who were dismissed or voluntarily withdrew from this program area in 2012–2013 were 2.

Scores: Entries appear in this order: required test or GPA, minimum score (if required), median score of students entering in 2012–2013. *Industrial/Organizational Psychology MA/MS (Master of Arts/Science):* GRE-V no minimum stated, 480, GRE-Q no minimum stated, 580, GRE-Analytical no minimum stated, 4.1, overall undergraduate GPA 3.0, 3.3, psychology GPA 3.25.

Other Criteria: (importance of criteria rated low, medium, or high): GRE scores—high, research experience—low, work experience—low, GPA—high, letters of recommendation—medium, statement of goals and objectives—medium, undergraduate major in psychology—low, specific undergraduate psychology courses taken—low. For additional information on admission requirements, go to http://www.angelo.edu/dept/psychology_sociology/grad_program/.

Student Characteristics: The following represents characteristics of students in 2012–2013 in all graduate psychology programs in the department: Female—full-time 64, part-time 9; Male—full-time 22, part-time 3; African American/Black—full-time 3, part-time 1; Hispanic/Latino(a)—full-time 14, part-time 1; Asian/Pacific Islander—full-time 1, part-time 0; American Indian/Alaska Native—full-time 0, part-time 0; Caucasian/White—full-time 68, part-time 9; Multi-ethnic—full-time 0, part-time 0; students subject to the Americans With Disabilities Act—full-time 0, part-time 0; Unknown ethnicity—full-time 0, part-time 1; International students who hold an F-1 or J-1 Visa—full-time 0, part-time 0.

Financial Information/Assistance:

Tuition for Full-Time Study: *Master's:* State residents: per academic year $5,340, $608 per credit hour; Nonstate residents: per academic year $10,920, $918 per credit hour. Tuition is subject to change. See the following website for updates and changes in tuition costs: http://www.angelo.edu/services/controller/sa_tuition&fees.php.

Financial Assistance:

First-Year Students: Research assistantships available for first year. Average amount paid per academic year: $7,490. Average number of hours worked per week: 17. Apply by April 15. Fellowships and scholarships available for first year. Average amount paid per academic year: $2,300. Apply by March 1.

Advanced Students: Teaching assistantships available for advanced students. Average amount paid per academic year: $11,095. Average number of hours worked per week: 20. Apply by April 15. Research assistantships available for advanced students. Average amount paid per academic year: $7,490. Average number of hours worked per week: 17. Apply by April 15. Fellowships and scholarships available for advanced students. Average amount paid per academic year: $2,300. Apply by March 1.

Additional Information: Of all students currently enrolled full time, 36% benefited from one or more of the listed financial assistance programs. Application and information available online at: http://www.angelo.edu/dept/psychology_sociology/grad_program/employment.php.

Internships/Practica: Practicum opportunities are available in many local public and private mental health facilities and also in local corporate entities.

Housing and Day Care: On-campus housing is available. See the following website for more information: http://www.angelo.edu/dept/residential_programs/. No on-campus day care facilities are available.

Employment of Department Graduates:

Master's Degree Graduates: Of those who graduated in the academic year 2011–2012, the following categories and numbers represent the postgraduate activities and employment of master's degree graduates: Enrolled in a postdoctoral residency/fellowship (n/a), employed in independent practice (n/a), total from the above (master's) (0).

Doctoral Degree Graduates: Of those who graduated in the academic year 2011–2012, the following categories and numbers represent the postgraduate activities and employment of doctoral degree graduates: Enrolled in a psychology doctoral program (n/a), total from the above (doctoral) (0).

Additional Information:

Orientation, Objectives, and Emphasis of Department: The department emphasizes personalized training, small class sizes, and a balance between research skills and practitioner skills. We offer the Applied Psychology program completely online.

Special Facilities or Resources: The department is equipped with state-of-the-art psychology and computer laboratories. Training also occurs in local agencies and hospitals, private companies and university administration offices.

Information for Students With Physical Disabilities: See the following website for more information: http://www.angelo.edu/services/student_life/disability.html.

Application Information:

Send to Office of the Graduate Dean, Angelo State University, ASU Station #11025, San Angelo, TX 76909-1025. Application available online. URL of online application: http://www.angelo.edu/dept/grad_school/admission_info/applynow.php. Students are admitted in the Fall, application deadline July 15; Spring, application deadline December 1; Summer, application deadline April 30. Summer I Application Deadline is April 30, Summer II Application Deadline is May 31. **Fee:** $40.

Baylor University

Department of Psychology and Neuroscience, PhD Program in Psychology
Arts and Sciences
One Bear Place 97334
Waco, TX 76798-7334
Telephone: (254) 710-2961
Fax: (254) 710-3033
E-mail: *Wade_Rowatt@baylor.edu*
Web: *http://www.baylor.edu/psychologyneuroscience*

Department Information:

1950. Chairperson: J.L. Diaz-Granados, PhD. Number of faculty: total—full-time 21; women—full-time 6; total—minority—full-time 5; women minority—full-time 2.

Programs and Degrees Offered:

Listed in the following order: Program area, degree type (T if terminal Master's), number awarded 7/11–6/12. Clinical Psychology PsyD (Doctor of Psychology) 9, Psychology PhD (Doctor of Philosophy) 1.

APA Accreditation: Clinical PsyD (Doctor of Psychology). Student Outcome Data Website: http://wwwbayloredu/psychologyneuroscience/indexphp?id=72649.

Student Applications/Admissions:

Student Applications

Clinical Psychology PsyD (Doctor of Psychology)—Applications 2012–2013, 190. Total applicants accepted 2012–2013, 6. Number full-time enrolled (new admits only) 2012–2013, 6. Total enrolled 2012–2013 full-time, 32. Total enrolled 2012–2013 part-time, 0. Openings 2013–2014, 7. The median number of years required for completion of a degree in 2012–2013 were 5. The number of students enrolled full- and part-time who were dismissed or voluntarily withdrew from this program area in 2012–2013 were 0. *Psychology PhD (Doctor of Philosophy)*—Applications 2012–2013, 82. Total applicants accepted 2012–2013, 7. Number full-time enrolled (new admits only) 2012–2013, 3. Total enrolled 2012–2013 full-time, 19. Openings 2013–2014, 6. The median number of years required for completion of a degree in 2012–2013 were 5. The number of students enrolled full- and part-time who were dismissed or voluntarily withdrew from this program area in 2012–2013 were 1.

Scores: Entries appear in this order: required test or GPA, minimum score (if required), median score of students entering in 2012–2013. *Clinical Psychology PsyD (Doctor of Psychology)*: GRE-V 587, GRE-Q 587, overall undergraduate GPA 3.5, psychology GPA 3.0; *Psychology PhD (Doctor of Philosophy)*: GRE-V 500, GRE-Q 500.

Other Criteria: (importance of criteria rated low, medium, or high): GRE scores—high, research experience—high, work experience—medium, extracurricular activity—medium, clinically related public service—medium, GPA—high, letters of recommendation—high, interview—high, statement of goals and objectives—medium, undergraduate major in psychology—low.

Student Characteristics: The following represents characteristics of students in 2012–2013 in all graduate psychology programs in the department: Female—full-time 35, part-time 0; Male—full-time 17, part-time 0; African American/Black—full-time 1, part-time 0; Hispanic/Latino(a)—full-time 4, part-time 0; Asian/Pacific Islander—full-time 7, part-time 0; American Indian/Alaska Native—full-time 0, part-time 0; Caucasian/White—full-time 42, part-time 0; Multi-ethnic—full-time 0, part-time 0; students subject to the Americans With Disabilities Act—full-time 0, part-time 0; Unknown ethnicity—full-time 0, part-time 0; International students who hold an F-1 or J-1 Visa—full-time 2, part-time 0.

Financial Information/Assistance:

Tuition for Full-Time Study: *Doctoral:* State residents: $1,274 per credit hour; Nonstate residents: $1,274 per credit hour. Tuition is subject to change. Additional fees are assessed to students beyond the costs of tuition for the following: General Student Fee, 12 hours or more per semester ($1,107). See the following website for updates and changes in tuition costs: http://www.baylor.edu/graduate/index.php?id=42277.

Financial Assistance:

First-Year Students: Teaching assistantships available for first year. Average amount paid per academic year: $20,000. Average number of hours worked per week: 20. Apply by January 2. Research assistantships available for first year. Average amount paid per academic year: $20,000. Average number of hours worked per week: 20. Apply by January 2. Traineeships available for first year. Average amount paid per academic year: $20,000. Average number of hours worked per week: 20. Apply by January 2. Fellowships and scholarships available for first year.

Advanced Students: Teaching assistantships available for advanced students. Average amount paid per academic year: $20,000. Average number of hours worked per week: 20. Apply by January 2. Research assistantships available for advanced students. Average amount paid per academic year: $20,000. Average number of hours worked per week: 20. Apply by January 2. Traineeships available for advanced students. Average amount paid per academic year: $20,000. Average number of hours worked per week: 20. Apply by January 2. Fellowships and scholarships available for advanced students.

Additional Information: Of all students currently enrolled full time, 100% benefited from one or more of the listed financial assistance programs. Application and information available online at: http://www.baylor.edu/psychologyneuroscience/.

Internships/Practica: Doctoral Degree (PsyD Clinical Psychology): For those doctoral students for whom a professional psychology internship was required in this program prior to graduation, (4) students applied for an internship in 2011–2012, with (3) students obtaining an internship. Of those students who obtained an internship, (3) were paid internships. Of those students who obtained an internship, (3) students placed in APA/CPA accredited internships, (0) students placed in internships not APA/CPA accredited, but listed with the Association of Psychology Postdoctoral and Internship Programs (APPIC), (0) students placed in internships conforming to guidelines of the Council of Directors of School Psychology Programs (CDSPP), (0) students placed in internships that were not APA/CPA accredited, APPIC or CDSPP listed. The PsyD Program incorporates an extensive practicum program with placements available in 16 community agencies and treatment facilities. Of our graduates over the last 11 years, 105 of 107 have obtained APA-accredited internships.

Housing and Day Care: No on-campus housing is available. On-campus day care facilities are available. See the following website for more information: http://www.baylor.edu/pipercdc/.

Employment of Department Graduates:

Master's Degree Graduates: Of those who graduated in the academic year 2011–2012, the following categories and numbers represent the postgraduate activities and employment of master's degree graduates: Enrolled in a postdoctoral residency/fellowship (n/a), employed in independent practice (n/a), total from the above (master's) (0).

Doctoral Degree Graduates: Of those who graduated in the academic year 2011–2012, the following categories and numbers represent the postgraduate activities and employment of doctoral degree graduates: Enrolled in a psychology doctoral program (n/a), employed in independent practice (6), employed in an academic position at a university (2), employed in an academic position at a 2-year/4-year college (1), employed in government agency (4), employed in a community mental health/counseling center (2), employed in a hospital/medical center (2), total from the above (doctoral) (17).

Additional Information:

Orientation, Objectives, and Emphasis of Department: The department offers a broad range of courses in the areas of clinical psychology, behavioral neuroscience, social psychology and general experimental psychology. The Doctor of Psychology (PsyD) program has the longest history of accreditation by the American Psychological Association. The PsyD program emphasizes a professional-scholar model with a goal of developing competencies based on current research and scholarship in clinical psychology. Extensive practicum experience is integrated with concurrent coursework. A formal dissertation involving applied clinical research is also required. The goal of Baylor's PsyD program is to develop professional psychologists with the conceptual and clinical competencies necessary to deliver psychological services in a manner that is effective and responsive to individual and societal needs both now and in the future. The doctoral program in Psychology (PhD) has three training tracks: Behavioral Neuroscience, Social Psychology and General Experimental. Doctoral students are expected to acquire sufficient knowledge and expertise to permit them to work as independent scholars at the frontier of their field upon graduation. Extensive training is provided in laboratory research and experimental design for social psychology and behavioral neuroscience students. The Doctor of Philosophy (PhD) degree is ultimately awarded to those individuals who have attained a high level of scholarship in a selected field through independent study, research, and creative thought.

Special Facilities or Resources: The department has a number of well-equipped research laboratories. PhD program: Computer-controlled programmable laboratory in memory and cognition; complete facilities for research on animal learning and behavior (including animal colony); developmental psychobiology laboratory, with facilities for behavioral and pharmacological research, including teratological studies; inhalation chambers for administration of ethanol (and other substances). Single-subject brain-recording (EEG) and electron microscopy facilities are available. The Department also houses a community clinic that facilitates the clinical training and related research activities for PsyD students.

Information for Students With Physical Disabilities: See the following website for more information: http://www.baylor.edu/oala/.

Application Information:

Send to Baylor University; Graduate Admissions; One Bear Place 97264; Waco, TX 76798. Application available online. URL of online application: http://www.baylor.edu/graduate/index.php?id=42273. Students are admitted in the Fall, application deadline January 15; Summer, application deadline January 2. Psychology (PhD), January 15; only accept applications for Fall admission. Clinical Psychology (PsyD), January 2; only accept applications for Summer admission. *Fee:* $50.

Baylor University

Educational Psychology
Education
One Bear Place #97301
Waco, TX 76798-7301
Telephone: (254) 710-3112
Fax: (254) 710-3265
E-mail: *Marley_Watkins@baylor.edu*
Web: *http://www.baylor.edu/soe/edp/*

Department Information:

1967. Chairperson: Marley Watkins, PhD, ABPP. Number of faculty: total—full-time 11, part-time 4; women—full-time 6, part-time 3; total—minority—full-time 1; women minority—full-time 1.

Programs and Degrees Offered:

Listed in the following order: Program area, degree type (T if terminal Master's), number awarded 7/11–6/12. School Psychology EdS (School Psychology) 6, Educational Psychology PhD (Doctor of Philosophy) 3.

Student Applications/Admissions:

Student Applications

School Psychology EdS (School Psychology)—Applications 2012–2013, 20. Total applicants accepted 2012–2013, 9. Number full-time enrolled (new admits only) 2012–2013, 7. Number part-time enrolled (new admits only) 2012–2013, 0. Total enrolled 2012–2013 full-time, 21. Total enrolled 2012–2013 part-time, 0. Openings 2013–2014, 7. The median number of years required for completion of a degree in 2012–2013 were 3. The number of students enrolled full- and part-time who were dismissed or voluntarily withdrew from this program area in 2012–2013 were 2. *Educational Psychology PhD (Doctor of Philosophy)*—Applications 2012–2013, 7. Total applicants accepted 2012–2013, 5. Number full-time enrolled (new admits only) 2012–2013, 5. Number part-time enrolled (new admits only) 2012–2013, 0. Total enrolled 2012–2013 full-time, 12. Total enrolled 2012–2013 part-time, 13. Openings 2013–2014, 5. The median number of years required for completion of a degree in 2012–2013 were 6. The number of students enrolled full- and part-time who were dismissed or voluntarily withdrew from this program area in 2012–2013 were 1.

Scores: Entries appear in this order: required test or GPA, minimum score (if required), median score of students entering in 2012–2013. *School Psychology EdS (School Psychology)*: GRE-V no minimum stated, 157, GRE-Q no minimum stated, 151, GRE-Analytical no minimum stated, overall undergraduate GPA 3.0, 3.7, last 2 years GPA 3.0; *Educational Psychology PhD (Doctor of Philosophy)*: GRE-V no minimum stated, 154, GRE-Q no minimum stated, 151, GRE-Analytical no minimum stated, overall undergraduate GPA 3.0, 3.4, Masters GPA 3.5, 3.8.

Other Criteria: (importance of criteria rated low, medium, or high): GRE scores—high, research experience—medium, work experience—low, extracurricular activity—low, clinically related public service—low, GPA—high, letters of recommendation—high, interview—medium, statement of goals and objectives—high, undergraduate major in psychology—medium, specific undergraduate psychology courses taken—low, EdS program is most interested in GRE, GPA, and clinical experience whereas PhD program is most interested in GRE, GPA, and research experience/promise. For additional information on admission requirements, go to http://www.baylor.edu/soe/edp/.

Student Characteristics: The following represents characteristics of students in 2012–2013 in all graduate psychology programs in the department: Female—full-time 28, part-time 13; Male—full-time 5, part-time 0; African American/Black—full-time 3, part-time 2; Hispanic/Latino(a)—full-time 3, part-time 0; Asian/Pacific Islander—full-time 4, part-time 1; American Indian/Alaska Native—full-time 0, part-time 0; Caucasian/White—full-time 23, part-time 9; Multi-ethnic—full-time 0, part-time 1; students subject to the Americans With Disabilities Act—full-time 0, part-time 0; Unknown ethnicity—full-time 0, part-time 0; International students who hold an F-1 or J-1 Visa—full-time 2, part-time 0.

Financial Information/Assistance:

Tuition for Full-Time Study: *Master's:* State residents: per academic year $25,390, $1,274 per credit hour; Nonstate residents: per academic year $25,390, $1,274 per credit hour. *Doctoral:* State residents: per academic year $25,390, $1,274 per credit hour; Nonstate residents: per academic year $25,390, $1,274 per credit hour. Tuition is subject to change. See the following website for updates and changes in tuition costs: http://www.baylor.edu/sfs/index.php?id=93956.

Financial Assistance:

First-Year Students: Teaching assistantships available for first year. Average number of hours worked per week: 15. Apply by February 1. Research assistantships available for first year. Average number of hours worked per week: 15. Apply by February 1. Fellowships and scholarships available for first year. Average number of hours worked per week: 0. Apply by February 1.

Advanced Students: Teaching assistantships available for advanced students. Average number of hours worked per week: 15. Apply by February 1. Research assistantships available for advanced students. Average number of hours worked per week: 15. Apply by February 1. Fellowships and scholarships available for advanced students. Average number of hours worked per week: 0. Apply by February 1.

Additional Information: Of all students currently enrolled full time, 99% benefited from one or more of the listed financial assistance programs. Application and information available online at: http://www.baylor.edu/soe/edp/index.php?id=65337.

Internships/Practica: School psychology students engage in practica in local schools and the Baylor Autism Resource Center during their second year. Their third and final year consists of an internship in public schools.

Housing and Day Care: On-campus housing is available. See the following website for more information: http://www.baylor.edu/graduate/index.php?id=42516. On-campus day care facilities are available. See the following website for more information: http://www.baylor.edu/pipercdc/.

Employment of Department Graduates:

Master's Degree Graduates: Of those who graduated in the academic year 2011–2012, the following categories and numbers represent the postgraduate activities and employment of master's degree graduates: Enrolled in a postdoctoral residency/fellowship (n/a), employed in independent practice (n/a), employed in a professional position in a school system (6), total from the above (master's) (6).

Doctoral Degree Graduates: Of those who graduated in the academic year 2011–2012, the following categories and numbers represent the postgraduate activities and employment of doctoral degree graduates: Enrolled in a psychology doctoral program (n/a), employed in an academic position at a university (1), employed in other positions at a higher education institution (2), total from the above (doctoral) (3).

Additional Information:

Orientation, Objectives, and Emphasis of Department: The PhD program in Educational Psychology affords graduate students the opportunity to select a specialization in Exceptionalities, Learning and Development, or Measurement. The EdS program in School Psychology prepares students to apply a scientist–practitioner model in their work with school-age children as well as with parents, teachers, and administrators. Students receive extensive experience within the Baylor Autism Resource Center. This program is approved by the National Association of School Psychologists (NASP). The applied behavior analysis (ABA) specialization is designed for students who are interested in behavior management such as working with people with developmental disabilities (e.g., autism spectrum disorders).

Special Facilities or Resources: Baylor Autism Resource Center: research, teaching, and services to children with autism and their families. The Psychometric Laboratory supports the faculty and students at Baylor University and other academic institutions in the development, application, and analysis of measurement in educational/psychological research.

Information for Students With Physical Disabilities: See the following website for more information: http://www.baylor.edu/oala/.

Application Information:

Send to Baylor University, Department of Educational Psychology, Attn: Admissions, One Bear Place #97301, Waco, TX 76798-7301. Application available online. URL of online application: http://www.baylor.edu/graduate/index.php?id=42508. Students are admitted in the Fall, application deadline February 1. *Fee:* $50.

Houston, University of
Department of Educational Psychology
College of Education
491 Farish Hall
Houston, TX 77204-5029
Telephone: (713) 743-5043
Fax: (713) 743-4996
E-mail: *tkubiszyn@uh.edu*
Web: *http://www.coe.uh.edu/academic-departments/epsy/index.php*

Department Information:

1980. Chairperson: Dr. Thomas Kubiszyn. Number of faculty: total—full-time 22, part-time 3; women—full-time 13, part-time 1; total—minority—full-time 9, part-time 1; women minority—full-time 6.

Programs and Degrees Offered:

Listed in the following order: Program area, degree type (T if terminal Master's), number awarded 7/11–6/12. Counseling Psychology PhD (Doctor of Philosophy) 8, Educational Psychology & Individual Differences PhD (Doctor of Philosophy) 2, Counseling MEd (Education) 60, Educational Psychology MEd (Education) 9, School Psychology PhD (Doctor of Philosophy) 2.

APA Accreditation: Counseling PhD (Doctor of Philosophy). Student Outcome Data Website: http://www.coe.uh.edu/academic-programs/counseling-psychology-ph/apa.php. School PhD (Doctor of Philosophy). Student Outcome Data Website: http://www.coe.uh.edu/academic-programs/school-psychology/apa.php.

Student Applications/Admissions:

Student Applications

Counseling Psychology PhD (Doctor of Philosophy)—Applications 2012–2013, 122. Total applicants accepted 2012–2013, 9. Number full-time enrolled (new admits only) 2012–2013, 10. Number part-time enrolled (new admits only) 2012–2013, 0. Total enrolled 2012–2013 full-time, 32. Total enrolled 2012–2013 part-time, 12. Openings 2013–2014, 9. The median number of years required for completion of a degree in 2012–2013 were 5. The number of students enrolled full- and part-time who were dismissed or voluntarily withdrew from this program area in 2012–2013 were 0. *Educational Psychology & Individual Differences PhD (Doctor of Philosophy)*—Applications 2012–2013, 23. Total applicants accepted 2012–2013, 12. Number full-time enrolled (new admits only) 2012–2013, 10. Number part-time enrolled (new admits only) 2012–2013, 0.

Total enrolled 2012–2013 full-time, 21. Total enrolled 2012–2013 part-time, 14. Openings 2013–2014, 11. The median number of years required for completion of a degree in 2012–2013 were 4. The number of students enrolled full- and part-time who were dismissed or voluntarily withdrew from this program area in 2012–2013 were 2. *Counseling MEd (Education)*—Applications 2012–2013, 91. Total applicants accepted 2012–2013, 58. Number full-time enrolled (new admits only) 2012–2013, 13. Number part-time enrolled (new admits only) 2012–2013, 3. Total enrolled 2012–2013 full-time, 52. Total enrolled 2012–2013 part-time, 40. Openings 2013–2014, 60. The median number of years required for completion of a degree in 2012–2013 were 2. The number of students enrolled full- and part-time who were dismissed or voluntarily withdrew from this program area in 2012–2013 were 1. *Educational Psychology MEd (Education)*—Applications 2012–2013, 25. Total applicants accepted 2012–2013, 12. Number full-time enrolled (new admits only) 2012–2013, 3. Number part-time enrolled (new admits only) 2012–2013, 0. Total enrolled 2012–2013 full-time, 9. Total enrolled 2012–2013 part-time, 11. Openings 2013–2014, 5. The median number of years required for completion of a degree in 2012–2013 were 2. The number of students enrolled full- and part-time who were dismissed or voluntarily withdrew from this program area in 2012–2013 were 1. *School Psychology PhD (Doctor of Philosophy)*—Applications 2012–2013, 26. Total applicants accepted 2012–2013, 6. Number full-time enrolled (new admits only) 2012–2013, 5. Total enrolled 2012–2013 full-time, 27. Total enrolled 2012–2013 part-time, 0. Openings 2013–2014, 6. The median number of years required for completion of a degree in 2012–2013 were 4. The number of students enrolled full- and part-time who were dismissed or voluntarily withdrew from this program area in 2012–2013 were 0.

Scores: Entries appear in this order: required test or GPA, minimum score (if required), median score of students entering in 2012–2013. *Counseling Psychology PhD (Doctor of Philosophy)*: GRE-V no minimum stated, GRE-Q no minimum stated, GRE-Analytical no minimum stated, overall undergraduate GPA no minimum stated; *Educational Psychology & Individual Differences PhD (Doctor of Philosophy)*: GRE-V no minimum stated, GRE-Q no minimum stated, GRE-Analytical no minimum stated; *Counseling MEd (Education)*: GRE-V no minimum stated, GRE-Q no minimum stated, GRE-Analytical no minimum stated, overall undergraduate GPA no minimum stated; *Educational Psychology MEd (Education)*: GRE-V no minimum stated, GRE-Q no minimum stated, GRE-Analytical no minimum stated, overall undergraduate GPA no minimum stated; *School Psychology PhD (Doctor of Philosophy)*: GRE-V no minimum stated, GRE-Q no minimum stated, GRE-Analytical no minimum stated, overall undergraduate GPA no minimum stated.

Other Criteria: (importance of criteria rated low, medium, or high): GRE scores—high, research experience—high, work experience—medium, extracurricular activity—high, clinically related public service—medium, GPA—high, letters of recommendation—high, interview—high, statement of goals and objectives—high, undergraduate major in psychology—medium, specific undergraduate psychology courses taken—medium, PhD programs emphasize research experience and research interests more than do the master's programs.

Student Characteristics: The following represents characteristics of students in 2012–2013 in all graduate psychology programs in the department: Female—full-time 120, part-time 70; Male—full-time 17, part-time 10; African American/Black—full-time 17, part-time 8; Hispanic/Latino(a)—full-time 11, part-time 19; Asian/Pacific Islander—full-time 26, part-time 4; American Indian/Alaska Native—full-time 0, part-time 0; Caucasian/White—full-time 80, part-time 48; Multi-ethnic—full-time 0, part-time 0; students subject to the Americans With Disabilities Act—full-time 1, part-time 0; Unknown ethnicity—full-time 3, part-time 1; International students who hold an F-1 or J-1 Visa—full-time 0, part-time 0.

Financial Information/Assistance:

Tuition for Full-Time Study: *Master's:* State residents: per academic year $9,000, $370 per credit hour; Nonstate residents: per academic year $20,160, $721 per credit hour. *Doctoral:* State residents: per academic year $9,000, $379 per credit hour; Nonstate residents: per academic year $20,160, $730 per credit hour. Tuition is subject to change. See the following website for updates and changes in tuition costs: http://www.uh.edu/financial/graduate/tuition-fees/tuition/index.php.

Financial Assistance:

First-Year Students: Teaching assistantships available for first year. Average amount paid per academic year: $12,732. Average number of hours worked per week: 20. Apply by April 15. Research assistantships available for first year. Average amount paid per academic year: $12,732. Average number of hours worked per week: 20. Apply by April 15. Fellowships and scholarships available for first year. Average amount paid per academic year: $3,000. Apply by March 1.

Advanced Students: Teaching assistantships available for advanced students. Average amount paid per academic year: $15,132. Average number of hours worked per week: 20. Apply by April 15. Research assistantships available for advanced students. Average amount paid per academic year: $15,132. Average number of hours worked per week: 20. Apply by April 15.

Additional Information: Of all students currently enrolled full time, 50% benefited from one or more of the listed financial assistance programs. Application and information available online at: http://www.coe.uh.edu/future-students/fin_aid_scholarships/index.php.

Internships/Practica: Doctoral Degree (PhD Counseling Psychology): For those doctoral students for whom a professional psychology internship was required in this program prior to graduation, (11) students applied for an internship in 2011–2012, with (8) students obtaining an internship. Of those students who obtained an internship, (8) were paid internships. Of those students who obtained an internship, (6) students placed in APA/CPA accredited internships, (2) students placed in internships not APA/CPA accredited, but listed with the Association of Psychology Postdoctoral and Internship Programs (APPIC), (0) students placed in internships conforming to guidelines of the Council of Directors of School Psychology Programs (CDSPP), (0) students placed in internships that were not APA/CPA accredited, APPIC or CDSPP listed. Doctoral Degree (PhD School Psychology):

For those doctoral students for whom a professional psychology internship was required in this program prior to graduation, (2) students applied for an internship in 2011–2012, with (2) students obtaining an internship. Of those students who obtained an internship, (2) were paid internships. Of those students who obtained an internship, (1) students placed in APA/CPA accredited internships, (0) students placed in internships not APA/CPA accredited, but listed with the Association of Psychology Postdoctoral and Internship Programs (APPIC), (1) students placed in internships conforming to guidelines of the Council of Directors of School Psychology Programs (CDSPP), (0) students placed in internships that were not APA/CPA accredited, APPIC or CDSPP listed. All counseling psychology doctoral students and counseling master's students participate in supervised practica at numerous sites throughout the Houston area. Examples of the types of sites at which students have completed practica include veteran's and children's hospitals, counseling centers and school districts. In addition, doctoral counseling psychology students are required to complete a one year, full-time internship approved by the faculty. These sites range widely in orientation, focus and geographic location. All school psychology doctoral students must complete two years of advanced practicum (half-time) as well as a one year, full-time predoctoral internship. Practica are arranged for students, and are available at various sites around the Houston area, including school districts, Texas Children's Hospital, M.D. Anderson Children's Cancer Hospital, Harris County Juvenile Probation, Harris County Children's Psychiatric Center, and the Mental Retardation and Autism Unit of the Harris County Mental Health and Mental Retardation Department. Internship sites are available in a variety of settings in the Houston area and around the country.

Housing and Day Care: On-campus housing is available. See the following website for more information: http://www.housing.uh.edu/. On-campus day care facilities are available. See the following website for more information: http://www.uh.edu/clc/.

Employment of Department Graduates:
Master's Degree Graduates: Of those who graduated in the academic year 2011–2012, the following categories and numbers represent the postgraduate activities and employment of master's degree graduates: Enrolled in a postdoctoral residency/fellowship (n/a), employed in independent practice (n/a), total from the above (master's) (0).

Doctoral Degree Graduates: Of those who graduated in the academic year 2011–2012, the following categories and numbers represent the postgraduate activities and employment of doctoral degree graduates: Enrolled in a psychology doctoral program (n/a), enrolled in a postdoctoral residency/fellowship (4), employed in independent practice (3), employed in an academic position at a university (1), employed in other positions at a higher education institution (1), employed in a professional position in a school system (4), employed in a community mental health/counseling center (1), employed in a hospital/medical center (2), total from the above (doctoral) (16).

Additional Information:
Orientation, Objectives, and Emphasis of Department: Graduates of the Educational Psychology Department have made significant contributions to many university faculties, state and national boards, in private practice, in government agencies, and in leadership roles in public and private schools. Students choose the Educational Psychology Department in order to study with our nationally recognized faculty and to participate in innovative research in one of the most diverse research institutions in the country. The Counseling Psychology PhD program (accredited by the American Psychological Association) prepares highly skilled scientist–practitioners. Counseling psychologists can assume several roles in a variety of settings including personal, educational and career counseling services; college and university teaching; research; and consultation to organizations concerned with psychological and interpersonal development. The PhD program in School Psychology (accredited by the American Psychological Association and approved by the National Association of School Psychologists) also prepares professional psychologists in the scientist–practitioner tradition. Graduates are trained to assume leadership, direct service and consultative roles and careers in public and private PK-12 schools, health and mental health related settings, colleges and universities, research institutions, and in independent practice. The Educational Psychology and Individual Differences PhD program is dedicated to the advancement and application of knowledge relevant to human learning, development, health education, psychological functioning, and higher education administration. Graduates pursue careers as faculty members, researchers, administrators, and other leadership positions in a variety of organizations. The Master's of Education (MEd) in Counseling program prepares counselors to assume positions in education and mental health settings, such as public schools, junior colleges, university counseling and advisement centers, and community mental health agencies. The major objective of the Masters of Education (MEd) program is to offer students preparation in psychological theories and their application to teaching and learning in school and other educational settings, and research, measurement, and evaluation.

Special Facilities or Resources: Located in the heart of a highly diverse metropolitan area with almost 5 million inhabitants, the Department has access to a wealth of community research facilities and resources (e.g., 56 school districts, a range of community-based mental health and specialty clinics and agencies, a large VA Hospital, 20 hospitals within the Texas Medical Center). Within the College of Education, the Center for Information Technology in Education (CITE) Laboratory provides faculty, staff, and students with computing and multimedia environments, technology resources, and timely service-oriented user support. Several faculty have active funded and unfunded research teams that provide students with a range of research options, often in collaboration with major facilities (i.e., medical facilities, schools, community/state organizations) in the Houston community.

Information for Students With Physical Disabilities: See the following website for more information: http://www.uh.edu/csd/.

Application Information:
Send to Graduate Admissions, Dept. of Educational Psychology, University of Houston, 491 Farish Hall, Houston, TX 77204-5029. Application available online. URL of online application: http://www.coe.uh.edu/future-students/how-to-apply/graduate. Students are admitted in the Fall, application deadline December 1; Spring, application deadline September 15. Application deadline for Counseling Psychology PhD and School Psychology PhD is December 1. Deadline for PhD in Educational Psychology and Individual Differences is February 1. Counseling MEd deadlines are January 15 (fall) and September 15

(spring); Educational Psychology MEd is March 1 (fall) and October 1 (spring). *Fee:* $45.

Houston, University of
Department of Psychology
College of Liberal Arts and Social Sciences
126 Heyne Building
Houston, TX 77204-5022
Telephone: (713) 743-8508
Fax: (713) 743-8588
E-mail: *ptolar@uh.edu*
Web: *http://www.psychology.uh.edu*

Department Information:

1939. Chairperson: David J. Francis. Number of faculty: total—full-time 34; women—full-time 15; total—minority—full-time 7; women minority—full-time 6.

Programs and Degrees Offered:

Listed in the following order: Program area, degree type (T if terminal Master's), number awarded 7/11–6/12. Clinical Psychology PhD (Doctor of Philosophy) 12, Industrial/Organizational Psychology PhD (Doctor of Philosophy) 3, Social Psychology PhD (Doctor of Philosophy) 1, Developmental Psychology PhD (Doctor of Philosophy) 1.

APA Accreditation:

Clinical PhD (Doctor of Philosophy). Student Outcome Data Website: http://www.uh.edu/class/psychology/clinical-psych/about/index.php.

Student Applications/Admissions:

Student Applications

Clinical Psychology PhD (Doctor of Philosophy)—Applications 2012–2013, 427. Total applicants accepted 2012–2013, 25. Number full-time enrolled (new admits only) 2012–2013, 13. Number part-time enrolled (new admits only) 2012–2013, 0. Total enrolled 2012–2013 full-time, 74. Total enrolled 2012–2013 part-time, 0. Openings 2013–2014, 12. The median number of years required for completion of a degree in 2012–2013 were 6. The number of students enrolled full- and part-time who were dismissed or voluntarily withdrew from this program area in 2012–2013 were 2. *Industrial/Organizational Psychology PhD (Doctor of Philosophy)*—Applications 2012–2013, 91. Total applicants accepted 2012–2013, 15. Number full-time enrolled (new admits only) 2012–2013, 8. Number part-time enrolled (new admits only) 2012–2013, 0. Total enrolled 2012–2013 full-time, 24. Total enrolled 2012–2013 part-time, 0. Openings 2013–2014, 6. The median number of years required for completion of a degree in 2012–2013 were 7. The number of students enrolled full- and part-time who were dismissed or voluntarily withdrew from this program area in 2012–2013 were 0. *Social Psychology PhD (Doctor of Philosophy)*—Applications 2012–2013, 64. Total applicants accepted 2012–2013, 2. Number full-time enrolled (new admits only) 2012–2013, 2. Number part-time enrolled (new admits only) 2012–2013, 0. Total enrolled 2012–2013 full-time, 17. Total enrolled 2012–2013 part-time, 0. Openings 2013–2014, 4. The median number of years required for completion of a degree in 2012–2013 were 6. The number of students enrolled full-

and part-time who were dismissed or voluntarily withdrew from this program area in 2012–2013 were 1. *Developmental Psychology PhD (Doctor of Philosophy)*—Applications 2012–2013, 30. Total applicants accepted 2012–2013, 9. Number full-time enrolled (new admits only) 2012–2013, 5. Total enrolled 2012–2013 full-time, 20. Openings 2013–2014, 4. The median number of years required for completion of a degree in 2012–2013 were 6. The number of students enrolled full- and part-time who were dismissed or voluntarily withdrew from this program area in 2012–2013 were 1.

Scores: Entries appear in this order: required test or GPA, minimum score (if required), median score of students entering in 2012–2013. *Clinical Psychology PhD (Doctor of Philosophy):* GRE-V no minimum stated, GRE-Q no minimum stated, GRE-Analytical no minimum stated, overall undergraduate GPA no minimum stated, psychology GPA no minimum stated; *Industrial/Organizational Psychology PhD (Doctor of Philosophy):* GRE-V no minimum stated, GRE-Q no minimum stated, GRE-Analytical no minimum stated, overall undergraduate GPA no minimum stated, psychology GPA no minimum stated; *Social Psychology PhD (Doctor of Philosophy):* GRE-V no minimum stated, GRE-Q no minimum stated, GRE-Analytical no minimum stated, overall undergraduate GPA no minimum stated, psychology GPA no minimum stated; *Developmental Psychology PhD (Doctor of Philosophy):* GRE-V no minimum stated, GRE-Q no minimum stated, GRE-Analytical no minimum stated, overall undergraduate GPA no minimum stated, psychology GPA no minimum stated.

Other Criteria: (importance of criteria rated low, medium, or high): GRE scores—medium, research experience—high, work experience—medium, extracurricular activity—medium, clinically related public service—medium, GPA—medium, letters of recommendation—high, interview—high, statement of goals and objectives—high. For additional information on admission requirements, go to http://www.uh.edu/class/psychology/graduate/admissions/.

Student Characteristics: The following represents characteristics of students in 2012–2013 in all graduate psychology programs in the department: Female—full-time 104, part-time 0; Male—full-time 31, part-time 0; African American/Black—full-time 8, part-time 0; Hispanic/Latino(a)—full-time 9, part-time 0; Asian/Pacific Islander—full-time 13, part-time 0; American Indian/Alaska Native—full-time 0, part-time 0; Caucasian/White—full-time 104, part-time 0; Multi-ethnic—full-time 1, part-time 0; students subject to the Americans With Disabilities Act—full-time 0, part-time 0; Unknown ethnicity—full-time 0, part-time 0; International students who hold an F-1 or J-1 Visa—full-time 14, part-time 0.

Financial Information/Assistance:

Tuition for Full-Time Study: *Doctoral:* State residents: per academic year $8,640, $320 per credit hour; Nonstate residents: per academic year $18,117, $671 per credit hour. Tuition is subject to change. See the following website for updates and changes in tuition costs: http://www.uh.edu/financial/graduate/tuition-fees/index.php.

Financial Assistance:

First-Year Students: Teaching assistantships available for first year. Average amount paid per academic year: $11,580. Average number of hours worked per week: 20. Research assistantships

available for first year. Average amount paid per academic year: $14,400. Average number of hours worked per week: 20. Fellowships and scholarships available for first year. Average amount paid per academic year: $2,500.

Advanced Students: Teaching assistantships available for advanced students. Average amount paid per academic year: $13,200. Average number of hours worked per week: 20. Research assistantships available for advanced students. Average amount paid per academic year: $16,800. Average number of hours worked per week: 20. Fellowships and scholarships available for advanced students. Average amount paid per academic year: $2,500.

Additional Information: Of all students currently enrolled full time, 95% benefited from one or more of the listed financial assistance programs. Application and information available online at: http://www.uh.edu/financial/graduate/index.php.

Internships/Practica: Doctoral Degree (PhD Clinical Psychology): For those doctoral students for whom a professional psychology internship was required in this program prior to graduation, (14) students applied for an internship in 2011–2012, with (14) students obtaining an internship. Of those students who obtained an internship, (14) were paid internships. Of those students who obtained an internship, (14) students placed in APA/CPA accredited internships, (0) students placed in internships not APA/CPA accredited, but listed with the Association of Psychology Postdoctoral and Internship Programs (APPIC), (0) students placed in internships conforming to guidelines of the Council of Directors of School Psychology Programs (CDSPP), (0) students placed in internships that were not APA/CPA accredited, APPIC or CDSPP listed. Internships are available for advanced students at a number of sites that include private industry, medical centers, state hospitals, and private practices.

Housing and Day Care: On-campus housing is available. See the following website for more information: http://housing.uh.edu/. On-campus day care facilities are available. See the following website for more information: http://www.uh.edu/clc/.

Employment of Department Graduates:

Master's Degree Graduates: Of those who graduated in the academic year 2011–2012, the following categories and numbers represent the postgraduate activities and employment of master's degree graduates: Enrolled in a postdoctoral residency/fellowship (n/a), employed in independent practice (n/a), total from the above (master's) (0).

Doctoral Degree Graduates: Of those who graduated in the academic year 2011–2012, the following categories and numbers represent the postgraduate activities and employment of doctoral degree graduates: Enrolled in a psychology doctoral program (n/a), total from the above (doctoral) (0).

Additional Information:

Orientation, Objectives, and Emphasis of Department: Clinical offers APA-approved training in research, assessment, intervention, and consultation related to complex human problems, including behavioral problems having a neurological basis. Industrial/organizational offers broad training in industrial/organizational psychology with options for specialization in either

the personnel or organizational subfields. Social emphasizes research careers in behavioral and preventive medicine; interpersonal interaction processes, with an emphasis on close relationships and motivation; and social cognition. Developmental focuses on experimental research in developmental cognitive neuroscience, including perception, speech, language, reading, attention, decision-making, memory, and emotion, using imaging, electrophysiological, and neurochemical techniques in human and animal models.

Special Facilities or Resources: The facilities of the department are comparable to those of any major department in a large university. A variety of community settings are available for applied research in all areas of specialization. Specialized laboratories have modern equipment for research in family and couple interaction, biofeedback, personnel interviewing, electrophysiology, and animal studies, as well as access to an fMRI scanner. Several research and clinical practica are available within the community and at several hospitals (the Texas Medical Center is one of the largest in the world).

Information for Students With Physical Disabilities: See the following website for more information: http://www.uh.edu/csd/.

Application Information:
Send to Academic Affairs Office, Department of Psychology, 126 Heyne Building, University of Houston, Houston, TX 77204-5022. Application available online. URL of online application: http://www.uh.edu/admissions/apply/graduate/. Students are admitted in the Fall, application deadline December 1. Deadline for Clinical and Developmental is December 1. Deadline for I/O and Social is January 15. *Fee:* $40.

Lamar University-Beaumont
Department of Psychology
Arts & Sciences
P.O. Box 10036
Beaumont, TX 77710
Telephone: (409) 880-8285
Fax: (409) 880-1779
E-mail: *RASMITH@lamar.edu*
Web: *http://dept.lamar.edu/psychology/*

Department Information:
1964. Chairperson: Randolph A. Smith. Number of faculty: total—full-time 9, part-time 3; women—full-time 6; total—minority—full-time 1, part-time 1; women minority—full-time 1.

Programs and Degrees Offered:
Listed in the following order: Program area, degree type (T if terminal Master's), number awarded 7/11–6/12. Applied Psychology MA/MS (Master of Arts/Science) (T) 5.

Student Applications/Admissions:
Student Applications
Applied Psychology MA/MS (Master of Arts/Science)—Applications 2012–2013, 20. Total applicants accepted 2012–2013, 15. Number full-time enrolled (new admits only) 2012–2013,

10. Number part-time enrolled (new admits only) 2012–2013, 0. Total enrolled 2012–2013 full-time, 21. Total enrolled 2012–2013 part-time, 5. Openings 2013–2014, 15. The median number of years required for completion of a degree in 2012–2013 were 2. The number of students enrolled full- and part-time who were dismissed or voluntarily withdrew from this program area in 2012–2013 were 1.

Scores: Entries appear in this order: required test or GPA, minimum score (if required), median score of students entering in 2012–2013. *Applied Psychology MA/MS (Master of Arts/Science):* GRE-V 150, GRE-Q 150, overall undergraduate GPA 3.0, 3.2.

Other Criteria: (importance of criteria rated low, medium, or high): GRE scores—high, research experience—medium, work experience—low, extracurricular activity—low, clinically related public service—low, GPA—high, letters of recommendation—low, statement of goals and objectives—low, undergraduate major in psychology—low, specific undergraduate psychology courses taken—high. For additional information on admission requirements, go to http://dept.lamar.edu/psychology/grad.html.

Student Characteristics: The following represents characteristics of students in 2012–2013 in all graduate psychology programs in the department: Female—full-time 16, part-time 4; Male—full-time 5, part-time 1; African American/Black—full-time 2, part-time 0; Hispanic/Latino(a)—full-time 4, part-time 0; Asian/Pacific Islander—full-time 1, part-time 0; American Indian/Alaska Native—full-time 0, part-time 0; Caucasian/White—full-time 14, part-time 5; Multi-ethnic—full-time 0, part-time 0; students subject to the Americans With Disabilities Act—full-time 1, part-time 0; Unknown ethnicity—full-time 0, part-time 0; International students who hold an F-1 or J-1 Visa—full-time 1, part-time 0.

Financial Information/Assistance:
Tuition for Full-Time Study: *Master's:* State residents: $308 per credit hour; Nonstate residents: $662 per credit hour. Tuition is subject to change. Additional fees are assessed to students beyond the costs of tuition for the following: health center, technology, library, student services. See the following website for updates and changes in tuition costs: http://students.lamar.edu/paying-for-school/tuition-and-fees.html.

Financial Assistance:
First-Year Students: Teaching assistantships available for first year. Average amount paid per academic year: $3,000. Average number of hours worked per week: 20. Fellowships and scholarships available for first year. Average amount paid per academic year: $1,000.

Advanced Students: Teaching assistantships available for advanced students. Average amount paid per academic year: $3,000. Average number of hours worked per week: 20. Fellowships and scholarships available for advanced students. Average amount paid per academic year: $1,000.

Additional Information: Of all students currently enrolled full time, 90% benefited from one or more of the listed financial assistance programs. Application and information available online at: http://financialaid.lamar.edu/index.html.

Internships/Practica: A variety of community health settings provide useful practicum experiences for Community-Clinical students in child, adolescent and adult counseling and assessment. There is also a clinic in the Psychology Department where students practice counseling under supervision. Practicum experiences for the Industrial/Organizational students place them in a variety of organizational and industrial work environments.

Housing and Day Care: On-campus housing is available. See the following website for more information: http://beacardinal.lamar.edu/housing/. No on-campus day care facilities are available.

Employment of Department Graduates:
Master's Degree Graduates: Of those who graduated in the academic year 2011–2012, the following categories and numbers represent the postgraduate activities and employment of master's degree graduates: Enrolled in a psychology doctoral program (2), enrolled in a postdoctoral residency/fellowship (n/a), employed in independent practice (n/a), employed in other positions at a higher education institution (1), employed in a community mental health/counseling center (2), do not know (2), total from the above (master's) (7).

Doctoral Degree Graduates: Of those who graduated in the academic year 2011–2012, the following categories and numbers represent the postgraduate activities and employment of doctoral degree graduates: Enrolled in a psychology doctoral program (n/a), total from the above (doctoral) (0).

Additional Information:
Orientation, Objectives, and Emphasis of Department: The Department of Psychology offers a program of study leading to the Master of Science degree in Applied Psychology. It is designed to prepare professional personnel for employment in business, industry, or community mental health agencies. The track in Community-Clinical Psychology includes training in assessment and therapy techniques for individuals, groups, and families. The track in Industrial/Organizational Psychology integrates the traditional areas of industrial psychology with the more contemporary areas of organizational development and analysis. Both tracks also prepare graduates for entry to doctoral programs.

Special Facilities or Resources: The Department currently maintains a psychological clinic that is used for training and research. It is available to both the student population as well as those in the surrounding community. The department also has a computer lab and research space.

Information for Students With Physical Disabilities: See the following website for more information: http://dept.lamar.edu/sfswd/.

Application Information:
Application available online. URL of online application: http://beacardinal.lamar.edu/how-to-apply/graduate.html. Students are admitted in the Fall, application deadline March 15. *Fee:* $30.

Midwestern State University

Department of Psychology
Prothro-Yeager College of Humanities & Social Sciences
3410 Taft Boulevard
Wichita Falls, TX 76308
Telephone: (940) 397-4340
Fax: (940) 397-4682
E-mail: *david.carlston@mwsu.edu*
Web: *http://libarts.mwsu.edu/psychology/ma/*

Department Information:

1975. Psychology Graduate Coordinator: Dave Carlston. Number of faculty: total—full-time 5; women—full-time 1; total—minority—full-time 1; women minority—full-time 1.

Programs and Degrees Offered:

Listed in the following order: Program area, degree type (T if terminal Master's), number awarded 7/11–6/12. Clinical/Counseling Psychology MA/MS (Master of Arts/Science) (T) 9.

Student Applications/Admissions:

Student Applications

Clinical/Counseling Psychology MA/MS (Master of Arts/Science)—Applications 2012–2013, 18. Total applicants accepted 2012–2013, 8. Number full-time enrolled (new admits only) 2012–2013, 8. Number part-time enrolled (new admits only) 2012–2013, 0. Total enrolled 2012–2013 full-time, 17. Total enrolled 2012–2013 part-time, 0. Openings 2013–2014, 8. The median number of years required for completion of a degree in 2012–2013 were 2. The number of students enrolled full- and part-time who were dismissed or voluntarily withdrew from this program area in 2012–2013 were 0.

Scores: Entries appear in this order: required test or GPA, minimum score (if required), median score of students entering in 2012–2013. *Clinical/Counseling Psychology MA/MS (Master of Arts/Science):* GRE-V no minimum stated, GRE-Q no minimum stated, GRE-Analytical no minimum stated, overall undergraduate GPA no minimum stated, last 2 years GPA no minimum stated, psychology GPA no minimum stated.

Other Criteria: (importance of criteria rated low, medium, or high): GRE scores—high, research experience—medium, work experience—medium, extracurricular activity—low, clinically related public service—medium, GPA—high, letters of recommendation—high, statement of goals and objectives—high, undergraduate major in psychology—medium, specific undergraduate psychology courses taken—medium. For additional information on admission requirements, go to http://libarts.mwsu.edu/psychology/ma/Admissions.asp?LL=1490.

Student Characteristics: The following represents characteristics of students in 2012–2013 in all graduate psychology programs in the department: Female—full-time 14, part-time 0; Male—full-time 3, part-time 0; African American/Black—full-time 0, part-time 0; Hispanic/Latino(a)—full-time 0, part-time 0; Asian/Pacific Islander—full-time 1, part-time 0; American Indian/Alaska Native—full-time 0, part-time 0; Caucasian/White—full-time 16, part-time 0; Multi-ethnic—full-time 0, part-time 0; students subject to the Americans With Disabilities Act—full-time 0, part-time 0; Unknown ethnicity—full-time 0, part-time 0; International students who hold an F-1 or J-1 Visa—full-time 1, part-time 0.

Financial Information/Assistance:

Tuition for Full-Time Study: *Master's:* State residents: per academic year $9,330; Nonstate residents: per academic year $10,300. Tuition is subject to change. See the following website for updates and changes in tuition costs: http://www.mwsu.edu/busoffice/tuitionandfeerates.asp?LL=1183.

Financial Assistance:

First-Year Students: Research assistantships available for first year. Average amount paid per academic year: $3,750. Average number of hours worked per week: 5. Apply by July 1. Fellowships and scholarships available for first year. Average amount paid per academic year: $1,000. Average number of hours worked per week: 0. Apply by July 1.

Advanced Students: Teaching assistantships available for advanced students. Average amount paid per academic year: $3,750. Average number of hours worked per week: 5. Apply by July 1. Research assistantships available for advanced students. Average amount paid per academic year: $3,750. Average number of hours worked per week: 5. Apply by July 1. Fellowships and scholarships available for advanced students. Average amount paid per academic year: $1,000. Average number of hours worked per week: 0. Apply by July 1.

Additional Information: Of all students currently enrolled full time, 100% benefited from one or more of the listed financial assistance programs. Application and information available online at: http://academics.mwsu.edu/graduateschool/scholarships.asp.

Internships/Practica: Master's Degree (MA/MS Clinical/Counseling Psychology): An internship experience, such as a final research project or "capstone" experience is required of graduates. Students completing the clinical/counseling program complete 9 credit hours of practicum for a total of 450 clock-hours of work and study in an applied clinical/counseling setting. Students have completed practica at First Step, Inc. (a battered women's shelter), Taft Counseling Center (non-profit, outpatient service provider), the North Texas State Hospital (adult, child, and forensic units), Rose Street Mental Health (for-profit outpatient service provider), Hospice of Wichita Falls, and with a variety of other licensed psychologists in the community.

Housing and Day Care: On-campus housing is available. See the following website for more information: http://housing.mwsu.edu/. No on-campus day care facilities are available.

Employment of Department Graduates:

Master's Degree Graduates: Of those who graduated in the academic year 2011–2012, the following categories and numbers represent the postgraduate activities and employment of master's degree graduates: Enrolled in a psychology doctoral program (1), enrolled in another graduate/professional program (1), enrolled in a postdoctoral residency/fellowship (n/a), employed in independent practice (n/a), employed in a community mental health/counseling center (3), do not know (4), total from the above (master's) (9).

Doctoral Degree Graduates: Of those who graduated in the academic year 2011–2012, the following categories and numbers represent the postgraduate activities and employment of doctoral

degree graduates: Enrolled in a psychology doctoral program (n/a), total from the above (doctoral) (0).

Additional Information:

Orientation, Objectives, and Emphasis of Department: The clinical/counseling psychology graduate program is available in either a 50-hour or 60-hour curriculum option and is designed to lead to certification as a Licensed Professional Counselor (LPC) or Licensed Psychological Associate (LPA). Students may pursue thesis or non-thesis options. Although our emphasis is on training the master's level practitioner, we actively encourage our students to pursue doctoral training, and we see the training we provide as a first step toward that goal.

Special Facilities or Resources: Midwestern State University is located near two state hospitals, a regional community mental health and mental retardation treatment center, and two private psychiatric hospitals. A newly remodeled clinic and computer lab are available for student use, and Graduate Research and Teaching Assistants are provided with office space.

Information for Students With Physical Disabilities: See the following website for more information: http://students.mwsu.edu/disability/.

Application Information:

Send to Dr. David Carlston, Graduate Coordinator. Department of Psychology, Midwestern State University, 3410 Taft, Wichita Falls, TX 76308. Application available online. URL of online application: http://admissions.mwsu.edu/apply.asp. Students are admitted in the Fall, application deadline July 1; Spring, application deadline November 15. *Fee:* $35.

North Texas, University of
Department of Psychology
1155 Union Circle #311280
Denton, TX 76203-5017
Telephone: (940) 565-2671
Fax: (940) 565-4682
E-mail: *Apply.Psychology@unt.edu*
Web: *http://psychology.unt.edu/*

Department Information:

Chairperson: Dr. Vicki Campbell. Number of faculty: total—full-time 33, part-time 11; women—full-time 12, part-time 9; total—minority—full-time 3; faculty subject to the Americans With Disabilities Act 2.

Programs and Degrees Offered:

Listed in the following order: Program area, degree type (T if terminal Master's), number awarded 7/11–6/12. Clinical Psychology PhD (Doctor of Philosophy) 4, Counseling Psychology PhD (Doctor of Philosophy) 8, Clinical Health Psychology & Behavorial Medicine PhD (Doctor of Philosophy) 5, Experimental Psychology PhD (Doctor of Philosophy) 2.

APA Accreditation: Clinical PhD (Doctor of Philosophy). Student Outcome Data Website: http://psychology.unt.edu/graduate-programs/clinical-psychology/student-disclosure-information. Counseling PhD (Doctor of Philosophy). Student Outcome Data Website: http://psychology.unt.edu/graduate-programs/counseling-psychology/student-disclosure-information. Clinical PhD (Doctor of Philosophy). Student Outcome Data Website: http://psychology.unt.edu/graduate-programs/clinical-health-psychology-consortium/student-disclosure-information.

Student Applications/Admissions:
Student Applications

Clinical Psychology PhD (Doctor of Philosophy)—Applications 2012–2013, 166. Total applicants accepted 2012–2013, 12. Number full-time enrolled (new admits only) 2012–2013, 8. Total enrolled 2012–2013 full-time, 48. Openings 2013–2014, 8. The median number of years required for completion of a degree in 2012–2013 were 6. The number of students enrolled full- and part-time who were dismissed or voluntarily withdrew from this program area in 2012–2013 were 1. *Counseling Psychology PhD (Doctor of Philosophy)*—Applications 2012–2013, 197. Total applicants accepted 2012–2013, 9. Number full-time enrolled (new admits only) 2012–2013, 9. Total enrolled 2012–2013 full-time, 55. Openings 2013–2014, 8. The median number of years required for completion of a degree in 2012–2013 were 6. The number of students enrolled full- and part-time who were dismissed or voluntarily withdrew from this program area in 2012–2013 were 2. *Clinical Health Psychology & Behavorial Medicine PhD (Doctor of Philosophy)*—Applications 2012–2013, 43. Total applicants accepted 2012–2013, 5. Number full-time enrolled (new admits only) 2012–2013, 5. Number part-time enrolled (new admits only) 2012–2013, 0. Total enrolled 2012–2013 full-time, 32. Total enrolled 2012–2013 part-time, 0. Openings 2013–2014, 3. The median number of years required for completion of a degree in 2012–2013 were 7. The number of students enrolled full- and part-time who were dismissed or voluntarily withdrew from this program area in 2012–2013 were 1. *Experimental Psychology PhD (Doctor of Philosophy)*—Applications 2012–2013, 13. Total applicants accepted 2012–2013, 1. Number full-time enrolled (new admits only) 2012–2013, 1. Total enrolled 2012–2013 full-time, 10. Openings 2013–2014, 4. The median number of years required for completion of a degree in 2012–2013 were 5. The number of students enrolled full- and part-time who were dismissed or voluntarily withdrew from this program area in 2012–2013 were 0.

Scores: Entries appear in this order: required test or GPA, minimum score (if required), median score of students entering in 2012–2013. *Clinical Psychology PhD (Doctor of Philosophy):* GRE-V no minimum stated, 600, GRE-Q no minimum stated, 645, overall undergraduate GPA 3.00, 3.59, last 2 years GPA 3.50, psychology GPA 3.50; *Counseling Psychology PhD (Doctor of Philosophy):* GRE-V no minimum stated, 574, GRE-Q no minimum stated, 649, overall undergraduate GPA 3.00, 3.50, last 2 years GPA 3.50, psychology GPA 3.50; *Clinical Health Psychology & Behavorial Medicine PhD (Doctor of Philosophy):* GRE-V no minimum stated, 470, GRE-Q no minimum stated, 630, overall undergraduate GPA 3.00, 3.56, last 2 years GPA 3.50, 3.75, psychology GPA 3.50, 3.70; *Experimental Psychology PhD (Doctor of Philosophy):* GRE-V no minimum stated, GRE-Q no minimum stated, overall undergraduate GPA 3.00, last 2 years GPA 3.50, psychology GPA 3.50.

Other Criteria: (importance of criteria rated low, medium, or high): GRE scores—medium, research experience—high, work experience—medium, extracurricular activity—medium, GPA—high, letters of recommendation—high, interview—high, statement of goals and objectives—high, undergraduate major in psychology—high, specific undergraduate psychology courses taken—high. For additional information on admission requirements, go to http://psychology.unt.edu/graduate-applications.

Student Characteristics: The following represents characteristics of students in 2012–2013 in all graduate psychology programs in the department: Female—full-time 127, part-time 0; Male—full-time 44, part-time 0; African American/Black—full-time 7, part-time 0; Hispanic/Latino(a)—full-time 8, part-time 0; Asian/Pacific Islander—full-time 9, part-time 0; American Indian/Alaska Native—full-time 0, part-time 0; Caucasian/White—full-time 89, part-time 0; Multi-ethnic—full-time 0, part-time 0; students subject to the Americans With Disabilities Act—full-time 0, part-time 0; Unknown ethnicity—full-time 58, part-time 0; International students who hold an F-1 or J-1 Visa—full-time 7, part-time 0.

Financial Information/Assistance:

Tuition for Full-Time Study: *Doctoral:* State residents: per academic year $10,900; Nonstate residents: per academic year $23,536. Tuition is subject to change. See the following website for updates and changes in tuition costs: http://financialaid.unt.edu/costs.

Financial Assistance:

First-Year Students: Teaching assistantships available for first year. Average amount paid per academic year: $13,138. Average number of hours worked per week: 20. Apply by July 15. Research assistantships available for first year. Average amount paid per academic year: $13,138. Average number of hours worked per week: 20. Apply by July 15. Fellowships and scholarships available for first year. Average amount paid per academic year: $13,138. Average number of hours worked per week: 20. Apply by July 15.

Advanced Students: Teaching assistantships available for advanced students. Average amount paid per academic year: $15,457. Average number of hours worked per week: 20. Apply by July 15. Research assistantships available for advanced students. Average amount paid per academic year: $15,457. Average number of hours worked per week: 20. Apply by July 15. Fellowships and scholarships available for advanced students. Average amount paid per academic year: $15,457. Average number of hours worked per week: 20. Apply by July 15.

Additional Information: Of all students currently enrolled full time, 56% benefited from one or more of the listed financial assistance programs.

Internships/Practica: Doctoral Degree (PhD Clinical Psychology): For those doctoral students for whom a professional psychology internship was required in this program prior to graduation, (11) students applied for an internship in 2011–2012, with (11) students obtaining an internship. Of those students who obtained an internship, (11) were paid internships. Of those students who obtained an internship, (10) students placed in APA/CPA accredited internships, (1) students placed in internships not APA/CPA accredited, but listed with the Association of Psychology Postdoctoral and Internship Programs (APPIC), (0) students placed in internships conforming to guidelines of the Council of

Directors of School Psychology Programs (CDSPP), (0) students placed in internships that were not APA/CPA accredited, APPIC or CDSPP listed. Doctoral Degree (PhD Counseling Psychology): For those doctoral students for whom a professional psychology internship was required in this program prior to graduation, (8) students applied for an internship in 2011–2012, with (8) students obtaining an internship. Of those students who obtained an internship, (8) were paid internships. Of those students who obtained an internship, (8) students placed in APA/CPA accredited internships, (0) students placed in internships not APA/CPA accredited, but listed with the Association of Psychology Postdoctoral and Internship Programs (APPIC), (0) students placed in internships conforming to guidelines of the Council of Directors of School Psychology Programs (CDSPP), (0) students placed in internships that were not APA/CPA accredited, APPIC or CDSPP listed. Doctoral Degree (PhD Clinical Health Psychology & Behavorial Medicine): For those doctoral students for whom a professional psychology internship was required in this program prior to graduation, (6) students applied for an internship in 2011–2012, with (3) students obtaining an internship. Of those students who obtained an internship, (3) were paid internships. Of those students who obtained an internship, (2) students placed in APA/CPA accredited internships, (1) students placed in internships not APA/CPA accredited, but listed with the Association of Psychology Postdoctoral and Internship Programs (APPIC), (0) students placed in internships conforming to guidelines of the Council of Directors of School Psychology Programs (CDSPP), (0) students placed in internships that were not APA/CPA accredited, APPIC or CDSPP listed. .

Housing and Day Care: On-campus housing is available. See the following website for more information: http://reslife.unt.edu/. No on-campus day care facilities are available.

Employment of Department Graduates:

Master's Degree Graduates: Of those who graduated in the academic year 2011–2012, the following categories and numbers represent the postgraduate activities and employment of master's degree graduates: Enrolled in a postdoctoral residency/fellowship (n/a), employed in independent practice (n/a), total from the above (master's) (0).

Doctoral Degree Graduates: Of those who graduated in the academic year 2011–2012, the following categories and numbers represent the postgraduate activities and employment of doctoral degree graduates: Enrolled in a psychology doctoral program (n/a), enrolled in a postdoctoral residency/fellowship (5), employed in independent practice (1), employed in an academic position at a university (1), employed in an academic position at a 2-year/4-year college (1), employed in business or industry (1), employed in a community mental health/counseling center (5), employed in a hospital/medical center (4), total from the above (doctoral) (18).

Additional Information:

Orientation, Objectives, and Emphasis of Department: Our department adopts the scientist–practitioner model, fostering an appreciation of psychology as a science and as a profession. We embrace a multiplicity of theoretical viewpoints and research interests. Students are involved in graded research and/or clinical practicum experiences by integrating experiential with didactic instruction. Experimental Psychology provides a highly individualized program for the student interested in study and research in one of several specialized areas. Clinical and Counseling Psychology programs support the development of a well-rounded professional psychologist. These purposes include a thorough grounding in scientific methodology and an orientation to the profession, development of competency in psychological assessment and evaluation, and training in various psychotherapeutic and counseling techniques and skills. Clinical Psychology: Health and Behavioral Medicine involves a joint program with UNT Health Science Center, which emphasizes mind-body interaction as students focus on the matrix of biopsychosocial and environmental processes in understanding etiological and diagnostic factors of illness, prevention, and recovery in order to meet the holistic needs of the individual.

Special Facilities or Resources: The Psychology Clinic provides professional training, scientific research, and community service. Teams of licensed psychologists and doctoral students in the APA-accredited Clinical, Counseling, and Clinical Health and Behavior Medicine PhD programs provide therapy and psychological testing to adults, adolescents, children, couples, and families and address problems ranging from everyday stress and relationship issues to more serious problems like depression, anxiety, bi-polar disorder, ADHD, and chronic medical conditions. Research and service activities of the Clinic involve members of the entire department. The Center for Sport Psychology and Performance Excellence (CSPPE) provides interdisciplinary training for students in psychology and kinesiology who are interested in specializing in sport psychology. Through the Center, students work with Psychology and KHPR faculty in coursework, research, and applied experiences. The Center for Psychosocial Health Research is an interdisciplinary center that conducts research on wellness in a chronic illness context. Research focuses on exploring stigma and forgiveness as a stressor and coping strategy for people living with HIV/AIDS and for the LGBT community. The Sleep and Health research lab focuses on the epidemiology of sleep and health and explores the role insomnia plays as a risk factor for psychological and medical disorders in various populations.

Information for Students With Physical Disabilities: See the following website for more information: http://www.unt.edu/oda/.

Application Information:
Application available online. URL of online application: http://tsgs.unt.edu/apply. Students are admitted in the Fall, application deadline December 1; Programs have rolling admissions. Experimental Psychology admits year-round. *Fee:* $60. McNair and Project 1000.

Our Lady of the Lake University
Psychology
School of Professional Studies
411 SW 24th Street
San Antonio, TX 78207
Telephone: (210) 431-3914
Fax: (210) 431-3927
E-mail: *jbiever@ollusa.edu*
Web: *http://www.ollusa.edu*

Department Information:
1983. Chairperson: Joan Biever, PhD. Number of faculty: total—full-time 12, part-time 12; women—full-time 9, part-time 10;

total—minority—full-time 6, part-time 8; women minority—full-time 4, part-time 4.

Programs and Degrees Offered:
Listed in the following order: Program area, degree type (T if terminal Master's), number awarded 7/11–6/12. Counseling Psychology PsyD (Doctor of Psychology) 2, School Psychology MA/MS (Master of Arts/Science) (T) 11, Family and Individual Psychotherapy MA/MS (Master of Arts/Science) (T) 0.

APA Accreditation: Counseling PsyD (Doctor of Psychology). Student Outcome Data Website: http://www.ollusa.edu/s/1190/ollu.aspx?sid=1190&gid=1&pgid=6689.

Student Applications/Admissions:
Student Applications

Counseling Psychology PsyD (Doctor of Psychology)—Applications 2012–2013, 20. Total applicants accepted 2012–2013, 6. Number full-time enrolled (new admits only) 2012–2013, 6. Number part-time enrolled (new admits only) 2012–2013, 0. Total enrolled 2012–2013 full-time, 48. Total enrolled 2012–2013 part-time, 0. Openings 2013–2014, 6. The median number of years required for completion of a degree in 2012–2013 were 6. The number of students enrolled full- and part-time who were dismissed or voluntarily withdrew from this program area in 2012–2013 were 0. *School Psychology MA/MS (Master of Arts/Science)*—Applications 2012–2013, 6. Total applicants accepted 2012–2013, 4. Number full-time enrolled (new admits only) 2012–2013, 4. Number part-time enrolled (new admits only) 2012–2013, 0. Total enrolled 2012–2013 full-time, 29. Total enrolled 2012–2013 part-time, 0. Openings 2013–2014, 10. The median number of years required for completion of a degree in 2012–2013 were 2. The number of students enrolled full- and part-time who were dismissed or voluntarily withdrew from this program area in 2012–2013 were 0. *Family and Individual Psychotherapy MA/MS (Master of Arts/Science)*—Applications 2012–2013, 44. Total applicants accepted 2012–2013, 22. Number full-time enrolled (new admits only) 2012–2013, 22. Total enrolled 2012–2013 full-time, 51. Openings 2013–2014, 20. The median number of years required for completion of a degree in 2012–2013 were 2. The number of students enrolled full- and part-time who were dismissed or voluntarily withdrew from this program area in 2012–2013 were 0.

Scores: Entries appear in this order: required test or GPA, minimum score (if required), median score of students entering in 2012–2013. *Counseling Psychology PsyD (Doctor of Psychology):* GRE-V no minimum stated, GRE-Q no minimum stated, GRE-Analytical no minimum stated, GRE-Subject (Psychology) 520, overall undergraduate GPA 2.5, last 2 years GPA 3.0, psychology GPA 3.0, Masters GPA 3.5; *School Psychology MA/MS (Master of Arts/Science):* GRE-V no minimum stated, GRE-Q no minimum stated; *Family and Individual Psychotherapy MA/MS (Master of Arts/Science):* GRE-V no minimum stated, 470, GRE-Q no minimum stated, 520, overall undergraduate GPA 2.5, last 2 years GPA 3.0.

Other Criteria: (importance of criteria rated low, medium, or high): GRE scores—medium, research experience—low, work experience—high, extracurricular activity—low, clinically related public service—medium, GPA—high, letters of recommendation—high, interview—high, statement of goals and objectives—high.

Student Characteristics: The following represents characteristics of students in 2012–2013 in all graduate psychology programs in the department: Female—full-time 120, part-time 0; Male—full-time 8, part-time 0; African American/Black—full-time 3, part-time 0; Hispanic/Latino(a)—full-time 52, part-time 0; Asian/Pacific Islander—full-time 1, part-time 0; American Indian/Alaska Native—full-time 0, part-time 0; Caucasian/White—full-time 37, part-time 0; Multi-ethnic—full-time 1, part-time 0; students subject to the Americans With Disabilities Act—full-time 0, part-time 0; Unknown ethnicity—full-time 14, part-time 0; International students who hold an F-1 or J-1 Visa—full-time 4, part-time 0.

Financial Information/Assistance:

Tuition for Full-Time Study: *Master's:* State residents: $745 per credit hour; Nonstate residents: $745 per credit hour. *Doctoral:* State residents: $840 per credit hour; Nonstate residents: $840 per credit hour. Tuition is subject to change. See the following website for updates and changes in tuition costs: http://www.ollusa.edu/s/1190/ollu-form.aspx?sid=346&gid=1&pgid=909.

Financial Assistance:

First-Year Students: Teaching assistantships available for first year. Average amount paid per academic year: $5,000. Average number of hours worked per week: 6. Research assistantships available for first year. Average amount paid per academic year: $8,400. Average number of hours worked per week: 10. Fellowships and scholarships available for first year. Average amount paid per academic year: $21,605. Average number of hours worked per week: 0.

Advanced Students: Teaching assistantships available for advanced students. Average amount paid per academic year: $5,000. Average number of hours worked per week: 6. Research assistantships available for advanced students. Average amount paid per academic year: $22,680. Average number of hours worked per week: 10. Fellowships and scholarships available for advanced students. Average amount paid per academic year: $33,000.

Additional Information: Of all students currently enrolled full time, 20% benefited from one or more of the listed financial assistance programs.

Internships/Practica: Doctoral Degree (PsyD Counseling Psychology): For those doctoral students for whom a professional psychology internship was required in this program prior to graduation, (11) students applied for an internship in 2011–2012, with (8) students obtaining an internship. Of those students who obtained an internship, (8) were paid internships. Of those students who obtained an internship, (7) students placed in APA/CPA accredited internships, (1) students placed in internships not APA/CPA accredited, but listed with the Association of Psychology Postdoctoral and Internship Programs (APPIC), (0) students placed in internships conforming to guidelines of the Council of Directors of School Psychology Programs (CDSPP), (0) students placed in internships that were not APA/CPA accredited, APPIC or CDSPP listed. Master's Degree (MA/MS School Psychology): An internship experience, such as a final research project or "capstone" experience is required of graduates. The psychology department operates a training clinic, the Community Counseling Service (CCS), which serves as the initial practicum site for all master's and doctoral students. At the CCS, practicum students work in teams of up to six students under the live supervision of psychology faculty. The CCS is located in and serves a low-income, predominantly Mexican-American community. Supervision of Spanish-language psychotherapy is available. A variety of off-campus sites are available to students in their second and subsequent semesters of practica. Students are placed at off-campus sites according to their career interests and training needs. Available practicum sites include public and private schools, hospitals, and community agencies.

Housing and Day Care: On-campus housing is available. See the following website for more information: http://www.ollusa.edu/housing. No on-campus day care facilities are available.

Employment of Department Graduates:

Master's Degree Graduates: Of those who graduated in the academic year 2011–2012, the following categories and numbers represent the postgraduate activities and employment of master's degree graduates: Enrolled in a postdoctoral residency/fellowship (n/a), employed in independent practice (n/a), total from the above (master's) (0).

Doctoral Degree Graduates: Of those who graduated in the academic year 2011–2012, the following categories and numbers represent the postgraduate activities and employment of doctoral degree graduates: Enrolled in a psychology doctoral program (n/a), enrolled in a postdoctoral residency/fellowship (2), employed in independent practice (20), employed in a professional position in a school system (2), employed in a community mental health/counseling center (2), employed in a hospital/medical center (5), total from the above (doctoral) (31).

Additional Information:

Orientation, Objectives, and Emphasis of Department: Graduate psychology programs at OLLU adhere to the practitioner-scholar model of training and emphasize brief, systemic approaches to psychotherapy. Postmodern and multicultural perspectives are infused throughout the curriculum, including practica. A certificate in psychological services for Spanish-speaking populations is available.

Special Facilities or Resources: The department's training clinic serves as both a training and research facility. Research facilities are also available in the building which houses the psychology department.

Information for Students With Physical Disabilities: See the following website for more information: http://www.ollusa.edu/s/1190/ollu.aspx?sid=1190&gid=1&pgid=4619.

Application Information:

Send to Graduate Admissions Office, Our Lady of the Lake University, 411 Southwest 24th Street, San Antonio, TX 78207. Application available online. URL of online application: http://admissions.ollusa.edu/s/1190/ollu.aspx?sid=1190&gid=1&pgid=257. Students are admitted in the Fall, application deadline January 15. January 15 for PsyD program; March 1 for MS programs. *Fee:* $25.

Rice University
Department of Psychology
6100 Main Street - MS 25
Houston, TX 77005
Telephone: (713) 348-4856
Fax: (713) 348-5221
E-mail: *psyc@rice.edu*
Web: *http://psychology.rice.edu/*

Department Information:
1966. Chairperson: Jim Dannemiller. Number of faculty: total—full-time 17; women—full-time 8; total—minority—full-time 1.

Programs and Degrees Offered:
Listed in the following order: Program area, degree type (T if terminal Master's), number awarded 7/11–6/12. Industrial/Organizational Psychology PhD (Doctor of Philosophy) 2, Cognitive Psychology PhD (Doctor of Philosophy) 0, Human-Computer Interaction/Human Factors PhD (Doctor of Philosophy) 2, Training PhD (Doctor of Philosophy) 2, Cognitive Neuroscience PhD (Doctor of Philosophy) 2.

Student Applications/Admissions:
Student Applications
Industrial/Organizational Psychology PhD (Doctor of Philosophy)—Applications 2012–2013, 91. Total applicants accepted 2012–2013, 5. Number full-time enrolled (new admits only) 2012–2013, 3. Total enrolled 2012–2013 full-time, 13. Openings 2013–2014, 4. The median number of years required for completion of a degree in 2012–2013 were 5. The number of students enrolled full- and part-time who were dismissed or voluntarily withdrew from this program area in 2012–2013 were 0. *Cognitive Psychology PhD (Doctor of Philosophy)*—Applications 2012–2013, 12. Total applicants accepted 2012–2013, 0. Number full-time enrolled (new admits only) 2012–2013, 0. Number part-time enrolled (new admits only) 2012–2013, 0. Total enrolled 2012–2013 full-time, 2. Total enrolled 2012–2013 part-time, 0. Openings 2013–2014, 3. The median number of years required for completion of a degree in 2012–2013 were 5. The number of students enrolled full- and part-time who were dismissed or voluntarily withdrew from this program area in 2012–2013 were 1. *Human-Computer Interaction/Human Factors PhD (Doctor of Philosophy)*—Applications 2012–2013, 18. Total applicants accepted 2012–2013, 1. Number full-time enrolled (new admits only) 2012–2013, 0. Number part-time enrolled (new admits only) 2012–2013, 0. Total enrolled 2012–2013 full-time, 9. Total enrolled 2012–2013 part-time, 0. Openings 2013–2014, 3. The median number of years required for completion of a degree in 2012–2013 were 6. The number of students enrolled full- and part-time who were dismissed or voluntarily withdrew from this program area in 2012–2013 were 0. *Training PhD (Doctor of Philosophy)*—Applications 2012–2013, 2. Total applicants accepted 2012–2013, 0. Number full-time enrolled (new admits only) 2012–2013, 0. Number part-time enrolled (new admits only) 2012–2013, 0. Openings 2013–2014, 1. The median number of years required for completion of a degree in 2012–2013 were 6. The number of students enrolled full- and part-time who were dismissed or voluntarily withdrew from this program area in 2012–2013 were 0. *Cognitive Neuroscience PhD (Doctor of Philosophy)*—Applications 2012–2013, 16. Total applicants accepted 2012–2013, 1. Number full-time enrolled (new admits only) 2012–2013, 1. Total enrolled 2012–2013 full-time, 13. Openings 2013–2014, 3. The median number of years required for completion of a degree in 2012–2013 were 6. The number of students enrolled full- and part-time who were dismissed or voluntarily withdrew from this program area in 2012–2013 were 0.

Scores: Entries appear in this order: required test or GPA, minimum score (if required), median score of students entering in 2012–2013. *Industrial/Organizational Psychology PhD (Doctor of Philosophy)*: GRE-V no minimum stated, 620, GRE-Q no minimum stated, 720, GRE-Analytical no minimum stated, 4.0, overall undergraduate GPA no minimum stated, 3.91; *Cognitive Psychology PhD (Doctor of Philosophy)*: GRE-V no minimum stated, 520, GRE-Q no minimum stated, 720, GRE-Analytical no minimum stated, 4.0, overall undergraduate GPA no minimum stated, 3.65; *Human-Computer Interaction/Human Factors PhD (Doctor of Philosophy)*: GRE-V no minimum stated, 580, GRE-Q no minimum stated, 660, GRE-Analytical no minimum stated, 5.0, overall undergraduate GPA no minimum stated, 3.5; *Training PhD (Doctor of Philosophy)*: GRE-V no minimum stated, GRE-Q no minimum stated, GRE-Analytical no minimum stated, overall undergraduate GPA no minimum stated; *Cognitive Neuroscience PhD (Doctor of Philosophy)*: GRE-V no minimum stated, 680, GRE-Q no minimum stated, 790, GRE-Analytical no minimum stated, 4.0, overall undergraduate GPA no minimum stated, 3.66.

Other Criteria: (importance of criteria rated low, medium, or high): GRE scores—high, research experience—high, work experience—low, extracurricular activity—low, GPA—high, letters of recommendation—high, statement of goals and objectives—high, faculty-applicant fit—high, undergraduate major in psychology—medium, specific undergraduate psychology courses taken—medium. For additional information on admission requirements, go to http://psychology.rice.edu/Content.aspx?id=70.

Student Characteristics: The following represents characteristics of students in 2012–2013 in all graduate psychology programs in the department: Female—full-time 27, part-time 0; Male—full-time 10, part-time 0; African American/Black—full-time 4, part-time 0; Hispanic/Latino(a)—full-time 3, part-time 0; Asian/Pacific Islander—full-time 10, part-time 0; American Indian/Alaska Native—full-time 0, part-time 0; Caucasian/White—full-time 18, part-time 0; Multi-ethnic—full-time 0, part-time 0; students subject to the Americans With Disabilities Act—full-time 0, part-time 0; Unknown ethnicity—full-time 2, part-time 0; International students who hold an F-1 or J-1 Visa—full-time 11, part-time 0.

Financial Information/Assistance:
Tuition for Full-Time Study: *Doctoral:* State residents: per academic year $36,610; Nonstate residents: per academic year $36,610. Tuition is subject to change. Additional fees are assessed to students beyond the costs of tuition for the following: health insurance, student health services, student organizations. See the

following website for updates and changes in tuition costs: http://students.rice.edu/students/Tuition_Fees.aspx.

Financial Assistance:

First-Year Students: Research assistantships available for first year. Average amount paid per academic year: $18,500. Average number of hours worked per week: 18. Apply by January 15. Fellowships and scholarships available for first year. Average amount paid per academic year: $18,500. Average number of hours worked per week: 0. Apply by January 15.

Advanced Students: Research assistantships available for advanced students. Average amount paid per academic year: $18,500. Average number of hours worked per week: 18. Apply by January 15. Fellowships and scholarships available for advanced students. Average amount paid per academic year: $18,500. Average number of hours worked per week: 0. Apply by January 15.

Additional Information: Of all students currently enrolled full time, 97% benefited from one or more of the listed financial assistance programs. Application and information available online at: http://psychology.rice.edu/Content.aspx?id=71.

Internships/Practica: Graduate students beyond their third year have the opportunity to work in internships in the Houston area. Although not required, many of our students have internships at local organizations including NASA, the Texas Medical Center, Hewlett Packard, and a variety of consulting firms. Other students work in summer internships around the country.

Housing and Day Care: On-campus housing is available. See the following website for more information: http://campushousing.rice.edu/graduate. No on-campus day care facilities are available.

Employment of Department Graduates:

Master's Degree Graduates: Of those who graduated in the academic year 2011–2012, the following categories and numbers represent the postgraduate activities and employment of master's degree graduates: Enrolled in a postdoctoral residency/fellowship (n/a), employed in independent practice (n/a), total from the above (master's) (0).

Doctoral Degree Graduates: Of those who graduated in the academic year 2011–2012, the following categories and numbers represent the postgraduate activities and employment of doctoral degree graduates: Enrolled in a psychology doctoral program (n/a), enrolled in a postdoctoral residency/fellowship (3), employed in an academic position at a university (2), employed in business or industry (2), employed in government agency (1), total from the above (doctoral) (8).

Additional Information:

Orientation, Objectives, and Emphasis of Department: The Rice program emphasizes training in basic and applied research and in the skills necessary to conduct research. The content areas to which this emphasis is applied are cognitive psychology (including cognitive neuroscience), industrial/organizational, and human-computer interaction. We believe that training in research and research skills generalizes very broadly to the kinds of tasks that professional psychologists will be asked to perform both in the university laboratory and in addressing such diverse applied questions as organizational management, system design, and program evaluation. Students in the cognitive neuroscience program are encouraged to participate in courses and research opportunities available from our joint program in neuroscience with Baylor College of Medicine. Students in the other areas are encouraged to develop research interests that combine content areas across the department. Industrial/organizational and human factors psychologists, for example, might collaborate on research dealing with organizational communication via email. Cognitive and industrial/organizational psychologists might investigate cognitive processes underlying performance appraisal; and human factors and cognitive psychologists might collaborate on studies of risk perception and the perceptual and attentional properties of computer displays. Although some of our students prefer to devote their energies to laboratory research in preparation for academic positions in basic areas, many students take advantage of the opportunities we provide for "real world" experience. The department arranges internships or practica in a wide variety of settings for interested advanced students.

Special Facilities or Resources: Graduate students in the Rice Psychology programs benefit from their access to a large and vital Houston business community, NASA, and over 40 teaching and research centers in the Texas Medical Center. Within the department, graduate students in all programs have ready access to a variety of powerful Macintosh and Windows-based computers that more than meet the needs of students for data collection, simulation, instruction, word processing, and computation. The department contains facilities for the study of dyadic and small group interaction, social judgment, decision making, and computer-interface design. In addition to the facilities physically located in the Psychology Department, Rice University has a state-of-the-art computer laboratory for research in the social sciences that has been constructed with support from the National Science Foundation. The cognitive neuroscience area has benefited from the recent acquisition of a transcranial magnetic stimulation (TMS) device for investigating brain function, two eye-tracking devices, a Silicon Graphics workstation for neuroimaging data analysis and 3D rendering of brains from MRI scans, and a dense-sensor array (128 channel) event-related potential (ERP) recording system that allows the detailed description of neural systems. Collaborations with institutions in the nearby Texas Medical Center provide access to functional neuroimaging facilities, which include the new Houston Neuroimaging Laboratory at Baylor College of Medicine that has two 3T research-dedicated scanners.

Information for Students With Physical Disabilities: See the following website for more information: http://dss.rice.edu/.

Application Information:
Send to Graduate Admissions, Psychology Department, MS-25, Rice University, 6100 Main Street, Houston, TX 77005. Application available online. URL of online application: https://psycgradapps.rice.edu/. Students are admitted in the Fall, application deadline January 15. *Fee:* $85.

Sam Houston State University

Department of Psychology
Humanities and Social Sciences
Box 2447
Huntsville, TX 77341-2447
Telephone: (936) 294-1174
Fax: (936) 294-3798
E-mail: *psychology@shsu.edu*
Web: *http://www.shsu.edu/~psy_www/*

Department Information:
1970. Chairperson: Christopher Wilson. Number of faculty: total—full-time 20, part-time 3; women—full-time 6, part-time 1; total—minority—full-time 3; women minority—full-time 1.

Programs and Degrees Offered:
Listed in the following order: Program area, degree type (T if terminal Master's), number awarded 7/11–6/12. Clinical Psychology MA/MS (Master of Arts/Science) (T) 16, General Psychology MA/MS (Master of Arts/Science) (T) 3, Specialist in School Psychology Other 8, Clinical Psychology (Forensic Emphasis) PhD (Doctor of Philosophy) 6.

APA Accreditation: Clinical PhD (Doctor of Philosophy). Student Outcome Data Website: http://www.shsu.edu/~clinpsy/.

Student Applications/Admissions:
Student Applications
Clinical Psychology MA/MS (Master of Arts/Science)—Applications 2012–2013, 88. Total applicants accepted 2012–2013, 16. Number full-time enrolled (new admits only) 2012–2013, 15. Number part-time enrolled (new admits only) 2012–2013, 0. Total enrolled 2012–2013 full-time, 34. Total enrolled 2012–2013 part-time, 0. Openings 2013–2014, 16. The median number of years required for completion of a degree in 2012–2013 were 2. The number of students enrolled full- and part-time who were dismissed or voluntarily withdrew from this program area in 2012–2013 were 0. *General Psychology MA/MS (Master of Arts/Science)*—Applications 2012–2013, 26. Total applicants accepted 2012–2013, 10. Number full-time enrolled (new admits only) 2012–2013, 10. Number part-time enrolled (new admits only) 2012–2013, 0. Total enrolled 2012–2013 full-time, 14. Total enrolled 2012–2013 part-time, 0. Openings 2013–2014, 15. The median number of years required for completion of a degree in 2012–2013 were 2. The number of students enrolled full- and part-time who were dismissed or voluntarily withdrew from this program area in 2012–2013 were 0. *Specialist in School Psychology Other*—Applications 2012–2013, 17. Total applicants accepted 2012–2013, 10. Number full-time enrolled (new admits only) 2012–2013, 8. Number part-time enrolled (new admits only) 2012–2013, 0. Total enrolled 2012–2013 full-time, 29. Total enrolled 2012–2013 part-time, 0. Openings 2013–2014, 12. The median number of years required for completion of a degree in 2012–2013 were 3. The number of students enrolled full- and part-time who were dismissed or voluntarily withdrew from this program area in 2012–2013 were 1. *Clinical Psychology (Forensic Emphasis) PhD (Doctor of Philosophy)*—Applications 2012–2013, 169. Total applicants accepted 2012–2013, 13. Number full-time enrolled (new admits only) 2012–2013, 9. Number part-time

enrolled (new admits only) 2012–2013, 0. Total enrolled 2012–2013 full-time, 51. Total enrolled 2012–2013 part-time, 0. Openings 2013–2014, 9. The median number of years required for completion of a degree in 2012–2013 were 6. The number of students enrolled full- and part-time who were dismissed or voluntarily withdrew from this program area in 2012–2013 were 1.

Scores: Entries appear in this order: required test or GPA, minimum score (if required), median score of students entering in 2012–2013. *Clinical Psychology MA/MS (Master of Arts/Science)*: GRE-V 400, 581, GRE-Q 450, 633, overall undergraduate GPA 3.00, 3.71; *General Psychology MA/MS (Master of Arts/Science)*: GRE-V 400, 496, GRE-Q 450, 647, overall undergraduate GPA 3.00, 3.66; *Specialist in School Psychology Other*: GRE-V 400, 471, GRE-Q 450, 536, overall undergraduate GPA 3.00, 3.50; *Clinical Psychology (Forensic Emphasis) PhD (Doctor of Philosophy)*: GRE-V no minimum stated, 579, GRE-Q no minimum stated, 641, GRE-Analytical no minimum stated, overall undergraduate GPA no minimum stated, 3.65.

Other Criteria: (importance of criteria rated low, medium, or high): GRE scores—high, research experience—high, work experience—low, extracurricular activity—low, clinically related public service—medium, GPA—high, letters of recommendation—high, interview—high, statement of goals and objectives—high, fit with the program—high, undergraduate major in psychology—medium, specific undergraduate psychology courses taken—medium, No interview is required for admission to our Master's programs. For additional information on admission requirements, go to http://www.shsu.edu/~psy_www/GradProgram.html.

Student Characteristics: The following represents characteristics of students in 2012–2013 in all graduate psychology programs in the department: Female—full-time 104, part-time 0; Male—full-time 24, part-time 0; African American/Black—full-time 6, part-time 0; Hispanic/Latino(a)—full-time 12, part-time 0; Asian/Pacific Islander—full-time 10, part-time 0; American Indian/Alaska Native—full-time 1, part-time 0; Caucasian/White—full-time 99, part-time 0; Multi-ethnic—full-time 0, part-time 0; students subject to the Americans With Disabilities Act—full-time 0, part-time 0; Unknown ethnicity—full-time 0, part-time 0; International students who hold an F-1 or J-1 Visa—full-time 0, part-time 0.

Financial Information/Assistance:
Tuition for Full-Time Study: *Master's:* State residents: per academic year $5,112, $213 per credit hour; Nonstate residents: per academic year $12,552, $523 per credit hour. *Doctoral:* State residents: per academic year $5,112, $213 per credit hour; Nonstate residents: per academic year $12,552, $523 per credit hour. Tuition is subject to change. Additional fees are assessed to students beyond the costs of tuition for the following: student service, student center, computer use, library, advisement, and records. See the following website for updates and changes in tuition costs: http://www.shsu.edu/~csh_www/financial.html.

Financial Assistance:
First-Year Students: Teaching assistantships available for first year. Average amount paid per academic year: $16,000. Average number of hours worked per week: 20. Research assistantships available for first year. Average amount paid per academic year:

$16,000. Average number of hours worked per week: 20. Fellowships and scholarships available for first year. Average amount paid per academic year: $10,000.

Advanced Students: Teaching assistantships available for advanced students. Average amount paid per academic year: $16,000. Average number of hours worked per week: 20. Research assistantships available for advanced students. Average amount paid per academic year: $16,000. Average number of hours worked per week: 20. Traineeships available for advanced students. Average amount paid per academic year: $16,000. Average number of hours worked per week: 20. Fellowships and scholarships available for advanced students. Average amount paid per academic year: $16,000.

Additional Information: Of all students currently enrolled full time, 100% benefited from one or more of the listed financial assistance programs.

Internships/Practica: Doctoral Degree (PhD Clinical Psychology (Forensic Emphasis)): For those doctoral students for whom a professional psychology internship was required in this program prior to graduation, (8) students applied for an internship in 2011–2012, with (8) students obtaining an internship. Of those students who obtained an internship, (8) were paid internships. Of those students who obtained an internship, (8) students placed in APA/CPA accredited internships, (0) students placed in internships not APA/CPA accredited, but listed with the Association of Psychology Postdoctoral and Internship Programs (APPIC), (0) students placed in internships conforming to guidelines of the Council of Directors of School Psychology Programs (CDSPP), (0) students placed in internships that were not APA/CPA accredited, APPIC or CDSPP listed. Master's Degree (MA/MS Clinical Psychology): An internship experience, such as a final research project or "capstone" experience is required of graduates. Master's Degree (Other Specialist in School Psychology): An internship experience, such as a final research project or "capstone" experience is required of graduates. We offer a variety of internships and practica for each of the applied tracks. Students in the School psychology program complete a one-year internship in schools. There are a variety of practicum placements for students in the Clinical psychology master's program, including the University Counseling Center, area community mental health centers, and the psychological services centers of the Texas Department of Criminal Justice (TDCJ). Students in the clinical doctoral program are assigned to a variety of practica, including Ben Taub General Hospital in Houston, ADAPT Counseling, various private facilities and practices, probation departments, and The Institute for Rehabilitation and Research (neuropsychology). These students also work at our on-campus Psychological Services Center, which provides both general mental health services (e.g., individual psychotherapy, couples counseling, psychological assessment), and forensic services (e.g., treatment programs for offender populations and evaluations for the courts).

Housing and Day Care: On-campus housing is available. See the following website for more information: http://www.shsu.edu/~hou_www/. No on-campus day care facilities are available.

Employment of Department Graduates:

Master's Degree Graduates: Of those who graduated in the academic year 2011–2012, the following categories and numbers represent the postgraduate activities and employment of master's degree graduates: Enrolled in a postdoctoral residency/fellowship (n/a), employed in independent practice (n/a), total from the above (master's) (0).

Doctoral Degree Graduates: Of those who graduated in the academic year 2011–2012, the following categories and numbers represent the postgraduate activities and employment of doctoral degree graduates: Enrolled in a psychology doctoral program (n/a), employed in an academic position at a university (1), employed in an academic position at a 2-year/4-year college (1), employed in government agency (2), employed in a community mental health/counseling center (1), employed in a hospital/medical center (3), total from the above (doctoral) (8).

Additional Information:

Orientation, Objectives, and Emphasis of Department: The Clinical and School Master's programs are applied training programs that develop effective Master's-level practitioners. Students in these programs receive extensive and eclectic training in both psychotherapy and psychometrics and conclude their training with extensive supervised practicum experience. Graduates can seek licensure as psychological associates through Texas State Board of Examiners of Psychologists. Graduates of the School program can seek national certification from National Association of School Psychologists and licensure as specialists in school psychology in Texas. Other licensures within the state of Texas such as professional counselor's licensure may be available with additional course work. The General track involves broader exposure to psychology's core disciplines and allows the student more elective flexibility to craft an individual specialty. The focus within the General Program is on developing research skills. Graduates of all three programs often progress to doctoral training here or elsewhere. Our clinical doctoral program is a scientist–practitioner program that provides broad and general training in clinical psychology with an emphasis on forensic psychology and the training of legally informed clinicians. In addition to extensive training in general psychological assessment and treatment, students help to conduct a variety of forensic evaluations for the courts (e.g., risk assessment, competence, and sanity evaluations). Students will have the basic preparation they need to pursue postdoctoral specialty training and conduct legally-relevant clinical psychology research.

Special Facilities or Resources: The department enjoys ample testing and observation space, including a live animal facility. The university's computing facilities offer extensive access to personal computers complete with the latest software. The area provides access to a wide variety of clinical and research populations. These include persons housed in medical and mental health facilities located in the Texas Medical Center, as well as juvenile and adult offender populations.

Information for Students With Physical Disabilities: See the following website for more information: http://www.shsu.edu/~counsel/sswd.html.

Application Information:
Send to Office of Graduate Studies, Sam Houston State University, P.O. Box 2478, Huntsville, TX 77341-2478. Application available online. URL of online application: http://www.shsu.edu/~grs_www/. Students are admitted in the Fall, application deadline December 15. December 15 is the deadline for the doctoral program, February 15 for the Master's programs. *Fee:* $45.

Southern Methodist University

Department of Psychology
Dedman College
6116 North Central Expressway, Suite 1300, P.O. Box 750442
Dallas, TX 75206-0442
Telephone: (214) 768-4924
Fax: (214) 768-3910
E-mail: *aconner@smu.edu*
Web: *http://www.smu.edu/psychology/*

Department Information:

1925. Chairperson: Ernest Jouriles, PhD. Number of faculty: total—full-time 15; women—full-time 6.

Programs and Degrees Offered:

Listed in the following order: Program area, degree type (T if terminal Master's), number awarded 7/11–6/12. Clinical Psychology PhD (Doctor of Philosophy) 1.

APA Accreditation: Clinical PhD (Doctor of Philosophy). Student Outcome Data Website: http://smu.edu/psychology/html/graduateStudentStats.html.

Student Applications/Admissions:

Student Applications

Clinical Psychology PhD (Doctor of Philosophy)—Applications 2012–2013, 126. Total applicants accepted 2012–2013, 8. Number full-time enrolled (new admits only) 2012–2013, 4. Total enrolled 2012–2013 full-time, 28. Openings 2013–2014, 5. The median number of years required for completion of a degree in 2012–2013 were 6. The number of students enrolled full- and part-time who were dismissed or voluntarily withdrew from this program area in 2012–2013 were 0.

Scores: Entries appear in this order: required test or GPA, minimum score (if required), median score of students entering in 2012–2013. *Clinical Psychology PhD (Doctor of Philosophy)*: GRE-V 500, 575, GRE-Q 500, 690, GRE-Analytical 4.5, 4.5, overall undergraduate GPA 3.0, 3.4, Masters GPA no minimum stated.

Other Criteria: (importance of criteria rated low, medium, or high): GRE scores—high, research experience—high, work experience—low, extracurricular activity—low, clinically related public service—medium, GPA—high, letters of recommendation—high, interview—high, statement of goals and objectives—high, research interests—high, undergraduate major in psychology—low, specific undergraduate psychology courses taken—medium.

Student Characteristics: The following represents characteristics of students in 2012–2013 in all graduate psychology programs in the department: Female—full-time 25, part-time 0; Male—full-time 3, part-time 0; African American/Black—full-time 1, part-time 0; Hispanic/Latino(a)—full-time 1, part-time 0; Asian/Pacific Islander—full-time 1, part-time 0; American Indian/Alaska Native—full-time 1, part-time 0; Caucasian/White—full-time 23, part-time 0; Multi-ethnic—full-time 1, part-time 0; students subject to the Americans With Disabilities Act—full-time 0, part-time 0; Unknown ethnicity—full-time 0, part-time 0; International students who hold an F-1 or J-1 Visa—full-time 1, part-time 0.

Financial Information/Assistance:

Tuition for Full-Time Study: *Doctoral:* State residents: per academic year $32,958, $1,831 per credit hour; Nonstate residents: per academic year $32,958, $1,831 per credit hour. Tuition is subject to change. See the following website for updates and changes in tuition costs: http://smu.edu/bursar/GR_tuitionfees.asp.

Financial Assistance:

First-Year Students: Teaching assistantships available for first year. Average amount paid per academic year: $16,000. Average number of hours worked per week: 20. Apply by December 1.

Advanced Students: Teaching assistantships available for advanced students. Average amount paid per academic year: $16,000. Average number of hours worked per week: 20. Apply by June 1.

Additional Information: Of all students currently enrolled full time, 100% benefited from one or more of the listed financial assistance programs. Application and information available online at: http://smu.edu/psychology/html/graduateStudentSupport.html.

Internships/Practica: Doctoral Degree (PhD Clinical Psychology): For those doctoral students for whom a professional psychology internship was required in this program prior to graduation, (6) students applied for an internship in 2011–2012, with (5) students obtaining an internship. Of those students who obtained an internship, (5) were paid internships. Of those students who obtained an internship, (4) students placed in APA/CPA accredited internships, (1) students placed in internships not APA/CPA accredited, but listed with the Association of Psychology Postdoctoral and Internship Programs (APPIC), (0) students placed in internships conforming to guidelines of the Council of Directors of School Psychology Programs (CDSPP), (0) students placed in internships that were not APA/CPA accredited, APPIC or CDSPP listed. Internal practica include Assessment, Dating Violence Prevention, Social Anxiety Disorders Treatment, and Project Support (which involves parent training and family support for victims of domestic violence). External practica include a variety of supervised experiences in correctional facilities, hospitals, wellness centers, counseling centers, and couples/family therapy settings.

Housing and Day Care: On-campus housing is available. See the following website for more information: http://smu.edu/housing/. On-campus day care facilities are available. See the following website for more information: http://smu.edu/childcare/.

Employment of Department Graduates:

Master's Degree Graduates: Of those who graduated in the academic year 2011–2012, the following categories and numbers represent the postgraduate activities and employment of master's degree graduates: Enrolled in a postdoctoral residency/fellowship (n/a), employed in independent practice (n/a), total from the above (master's) (0).

Doctoral Degree Graduates: Of those who graduated in the academic year 2011–2012, the following categories and numbers represent the postgraduate activities and employment of doctoral degree graduates: Enrolled in a psychology doctoral program (n/a), not seeking employment (1), total from the above (doctoral) (1).

Additional Information:

Orientation, Objectives, and Emphasis of Department: The mission of SMU's 70 hour doctoral program in clinical psychology is to train psychologists whose professional activities are based on scientific knowledge and methods. The program integrates rigorous research training with state-of-the-art, evidence-based clinical training. Thus, our program emphasizes the development of conceptual and research skills as well as scientifically-based clinical practice skills. The overarching goal is for our graduates to use empirical methods to advance psychological knowledge and whose approach to clinical phenomena is consistent with scientific evidence.

Special Facilities or Resources: The department houses a Family Research Center and has a number of well-equipped laboratories for research on various topics in clinical psychology.

Information for Students With Physical Disabilities: See the following website for more information: http://smu.edu/alec/dass.asp.

Application Information:
Send to The Office of Graduate Studies, Southern Methodist University, PO Box 750240, Dallas, TX 75275-0240. Application available online. URL of online application: http://smu.edu/graduate/apply.asp. Students are admitted in the Fall, application deadline December 1. *Fee:* $75.

Stephen F. Austin State University

Department of Psychology
Liberal and Applied Arts
Box 13046, SFA Station
Nacogdoches, TX 75962
Telephone: (936) 468-4402
Fax: (936) 468-4015
E-mail: *graduatepsychology@sfasu.edu*
Web: *http://www.sfasu.edu/sfapsych/114.asp*

Department Information:
1962. Interim Chair: Dr. Jerry Williams. Number of faculty: total—full-time 11, part-time 2; women—full-time 6, part-time 1; total—minority—full-time 3; women minority—full-time 1.

Programs and Degrees Offered:
Listed in the following order: Program area, degree type (T if terminal Master's), number awarded 7/11–6/12. General Psychology MA/MS (Master of Arts/Science) (T) 9.

Student Applications/Admissions:
Student Applications

General Psychology MA/MS (Master of Arts/Science)—Applications 2012–2013, 20. Total applicants accepted 2012–2013, 12. Number full-time enrolled (new admits only) 2012–2013, 5. Number part-time enrolled (new admits only) 2012–2013, 1. Total enrolled 2012–2013 full-time, 9. Total enrolled 2012–2013 part-time, 1. Openings 2013–2014, 15. The median number of years required for completion of a degree in 2012–2013 was 1. The number of students enrolled full- and part-time who were dismissed or voluntarily withdrew from this program area in 2012–2013 were 0.

Scores: Entries appear in this order: required test or GPA, minimum score (if required), median score of students entering in 2012–2013. *General Psychology MA/MS (Master of Arts/Science):* GRE-V no minimum stated, GRE-Q no minimum stated, overall undergraduate GPA 3.0.

Other Criteria: (importance of criteria rated low, medium, or high): GRE scores—medium, research experience—medium, work experience—low, extracurricular activity—low, clinically related public service—low, GPA—high, letters of recommendation—medium, statement of goals and objectives—medium, undergraduate major in psychology—low, specific undergraduate psychology courses taken—medium. For additional information on admission requirements, go to http://www.sfasu.edu/sfapsych/113.asp.

Student Characteristics: The following represents characteristics of students in 2012–2013 in all graduate psychology programs in the department: Female—full-time 11, part-time 2; Male—full-time 6, part-time 0; African American/Black—full-time 2, part-time 0; Hispanic/Latino(a)—full-time 1, part-time 1; Asian/Pacific Islander—full-time 1, part-time 0; American Indian/Alaska Native—full-time 0, part-time 0; Caucasian/White—full-time 5, part-time 0; Multi-ethnic—full-time 1, part-time 0; students subject to the Americans With Disabilities Act—full-time 0, part-time 0; Unknown ethnicity—full-time 0, part-time 0; International students who hold an F-1 or J-1 Visa—full-time 0, part-time 0.

Financial Information/Assistance:
Tuition for Full-Time Study: *Master's:* State residents: per academic year $4,536, $126 per credit hour; Nonstate residents: per academic year $14,472, $402 per credit hour. Tuition is subject to change. Additional fees are assessed to students beyond the costs of tuition for the following: student service, student center, library, publication, recreation center use. See the following website for updates and changes in tuition costs: http://www.sfasu.edu/controller/businessoffice/students/rate_tables.asp.

Financial Assistance:
First-Year Students: Teaching assistantships available for first year. Average amount paid per academic year: $9,225. Average number of hours worked per week: 20. Apply by May 15. Research assistantships available for first year. Average amount paid per academic year: $9,225. Average number of hours worked per week: 20. Apply by May 15.

Advanced Students: Teaching assistantships available for advanced students. Average amount paid per academic year: $9,225. Average number of hours worked per week: 20. Research assistantships available for advanced students. Average amount paid per academic year: $9,225. Average number of hours worked per week: 20.

Additional Information: Of all students currently enrolled full time, 62% benefited from one or more of the listed financial assistance programs. Application and information available online at: http://www.sfasu.edu/graduate/104.asp.

Housing and Day Care: On-campus housing is available. See the following website for more information: http://www.sfasu.edu/reslife/102.asp. On-campus day care facilities are available. See the following website for more information: http://www.sfasu.edu/echl/.

Employment of Department Graduates:

Master's Degree Graduates: Of those who graduated in the academic year 2011–2012, the following categories and numbers represent the postgraduate activities and employment of master's degree graduates: Enrolled in a psychology doctoral program (5), enrolled in another graduate/professional program (2), enrolled in a postdoctoral residency/fellowship (n/a), employed in independent practice (n/a), employed in an academic position at a university (2), employed in an academic position at a 2-year/4-year college (2), employed in business or industry (1), total from the above (master's) (12).

Doctoral Degree Graduates: Of those who graduated in the academic year 2011–2012, the following categories and numbers represent the postgraduate activities and employment of doctoral degree graduates: Enrolled in a psychology doctoral program (n/a), total from the above (doctoral) (0).

Additional Information:

Orientation, Objectives, and Emphasis of Department: The primary goal of this one-year, 36-hour, General Psychology MA program is to prepare students for admission to doctoral training programs in psychology by enabling them to earn graduate course credit and gain valuable research and teaching experience. Our degree program would also be of interest to persons who would like to earn an MA in psychology as a means of furthering their professional goals (e.g., by augmenting their research skills), even if those goals have no explicit connection to psychology. This is a non-thesis master's program. However, students can elect to continue for a second year in order to conduct a formal thesis research project. Students interested in a career in teaching psychology have the option of enrolling in a Teaching Seminar; excellent performance in this course could lead to an opportunity to teach a freshman-level course, should the student elect to remain in the program for a second year. Applications for Fall, Spring, and Summer admission will be considered.

Special Facilities or Resources: The department's facilities occupy more than 20,000 square feet. An extensive research suite and other research spaces permit data collection either with individual participants or groups. The spaces include 50 PC microcomputers for various programs in the department. There are also laboratories for human research in sensory psychophysics, learning, cognition, social, developmental, personality, and industrial/organizational psychology. Supplemental technical assistance from facilities in other departments on campus is available. All department classrooms are supplied with multimedia equipment. The department has an instructional computing laboratory consisting of 21 networked PC microcomputers and extensive supporting hardware and software for computing across the psychology curriculum. Most laboratory areas, classrooms, and graduate assistant offices contain both PC and Macintosh microcomputers, many of which are networked and support research and instruction.

Information for Students With Physical Disabilities: See the following website for more information: http://www.sfasu.edu/disabilityservices/.

Application Information:
Send to Graduate Program Coordinator, Department of Psychology, Stephen F. Austin State University, Box 13046, SFA Station, Nacogdoches, TX 75962. Application available online. URL of online application: http://www.sfasu.edu/graduate/101.asp. Students are admitted in the Fall, application deadline July 15; Spring, application deadline November 15; Summer, application deadline April 15. The earlier the submission, the greater the likelihood of receiving an assistantship. *Fee:* $25.

Texas A&M International University
Department of Psychology and Communication
College of Arts and Sciences
5201 University Boulevard
Laredo, TX 78041-1900
Telephone: (956) 326-2475
Fax: (956) 326-2474
E-mail: *bonnie.rudolph@tamiu.edu*
Web: *http://www.tamiu.edu/coas/psy*

Department Information:
1994. Director of Master's Program in Counseling Psychology: Bonnie A. Rudolph. Number of faculty: total—full-time 5; women—full-time 3; total—minority—full-time 2; women minority—full-time 1.

Programs and Degrees Offered:
Listed in the following order: Program area, degree type (T if terminal Master's), number awarded 7/11–6/12. Counseling Psychology MA/MS (Master of Arts/Science) (T) 20, Psychology MA/MS (Master of Arts/Science) (T) 2.

Student Applications/Admissions:
Student Applications
Counseling Psychology MA/MS (Master of Arts/Science)—Applications 2012–2013, 43. Total applicants accepted 2012–2013, 13. Number full-time enrolled (new admits only) 2012–2013, 13. Total enrolled 2012–2013 full-time, 43. Openings 2013–2014, 6. The median number of years required for completion of a degree in 2012–2013 were 2. The number of students enrolled full- and part-time who were dismissed or voluntarily withdrew from this program area in 2012–2013 were 2. *Psychology MA/MS (Master of Arts/Science)*—Applications 2012–2013, 6. Total applicants accepted 2012–2013, 6. Number full-time enrolled (new admits only) 2012–2013, 6. Total enrolled 2012–2013 full-time, 6. Openings 2013–2014, 6. The median number of years required for completion of a degree in 2012–2013 were 2. The number of students enrolled full- and part-time who were dismissed or voluntarily withdrew from this program area in 2012–2013 were 0.

Scores: Entries appear in this order: required test or GPA, minimum score (if required), median score of students entering in 2012–2013. *Counseling Psychology MA/MS (Master of Arts/Science):* last 2 years GPA 3.00, psychology GPA 3.00.

Other Criteria: (importance of criteria rated low, medium, or high): GRE scores—high, research experience—medium, work experience—medium, extracurricular activity—medium, clinically related public service—high, GPA—medium, letters of recommendation—medium, interview—high, statement of goals and objectives—medium, specific undergraduate psychology courses taken—high, The Masters in Counseling Psychology requires 4 undergraduate courses be completed with a B average across them. They are abnormal, personality, research methods and theories and principles of testing. For additional information on admission requirements, go to http://www.tamiu.edu/coas/psy/Degrees.shtml.

Student Characteristics: The following represents characteristics of students in 2012–2013 in all graduate psychology programs in the department: Female—full-time 36, part-time 0; Male—full-time 13, part-time 0; African American/Black—full-time 1, part-time 0; Hispanic/Latino(a)—full-time 45, part-time 0; Asian/Pacific Islander—full-time 0, part-time 0; American Indian/Alaska Native—full-time 0, part-time 0; Caucasian/White—full-time 3, part-time 0; Multi-ethnic—full-time 0, part-time 0; students subject to the Americans With Disabilities Act—full-time 0, part-time 0; Unknown ethnicity—full-time 0, part-time 0; International students who hold an F-1 or J-1 Visa—full-time 0, part-time 0.

Financial Information/Assistance:

Tuition for Full-Time Study: *Master's:* State residents: per academic year $5,250, $200 per credit hour; Nonstate residents: per academic year $11,559, $425 per credit hour. Tuition is subject to change. See the following website for updates and changes in tuition costs: http://www.tamiu.edu/adminis/comptroler/cashiers.shtml.

Financial Assistance:

First-Year Students: Teaching assistantships available for first year. Average amount paid per academic year: $18,000. Average number of hours worked per week: 20. Apply by April 1. Fellowships and scholarships available for first year. Average amount paid per academic year: $9,000. Average number of hours worked per week: 10. Apply by April 1.

Advanced Students: Research assistantships available for advanced students. Average amount paid per academic year: $17,000. Average number of hours worked per week: 15. Apply by May 15.

Additional Information: Of all students currently enrolled full time, 15% benefited from one or more of the listed financial assistance programs. Application and information available online at: http://www.tamiu.edu/gradschool/fellowships.shtml.

Internships/Practica: Master's Degree (MA/MS Counseling Psychology): An internship experience, such as a final research project or "capstone" experience is required of graduates. Master's Degree (MA/MS Psychology): An internship experience, such as a final research project or "capstone" experience is required of graduates. The practicum and internships offer unique training opportunities to prepare competent counselors. Competence exercises include alliance and outcome measurement as well as session process analyses, in addition to more conventional training in documentation and treatment planning. Practicum and internships consist of working at settings such as college counseling centers, forensic settings, drug and alcohol counseling/prevention agencies, domestic violence/battered women shelters, child advocacy centers, and professional counseling clinics. On-site supervisors provide thirty-minute supervision sessions. Psychologists on campus provide an additional 2.5 hours of supervision in individual, triadic, and group formats. Peer feedback and group cohesiveness are also vital parts of training. All graduates complete Practicum and Counseling Internship I. Students who choose the non-thesis (clinical) track also complete Internship II. The clinical track provides a total of 3 semesters of practical experience in counseling (600 hours), a minimum of which is 240 hours of face-to-face counseling activities.

Housing and Day Care: On-campus housing is available. See the following website for more information: http://www.tamiu.edu/housing/housing.shtml. No on-campus day care facilities are available.

Employment of Department Graduates:

Master's Degree Graduates: Of those who graduated in the academic year 2011–2012, the following categories and numbers represent the postgraduate activities and employment of master's degree graduates: Enrolled in a postdoctoral residency/fellowship (n/a), employed in independent practice (n/a), employed in an academic position at a university (2), employed in an academic position at a 2-year/4-year college (1), employed in other positions at a higher education institution (1), employed in a professional position in a school system (1), employed in a community mental health/counseling center (2), total from the above (master's) (7).
Doctoral Degree Graduates: Of those who graduated in the academic year 2011–2012, the following categories and numbers represent the postgraduate activities and employment of doctoral degree graduates: Enrolled in a psychology doctoral program (n/a), total from the above (doctoral) (0).

Additional Information:

Orientation, Objectives, and Emphasis of Department: The Master of Arts in Counseling Psychology provides training for counselors with strong foundations in eclectic, humanistic, multicultural and community perspectives. Students in our international campus and community are self-reflective active learners. The excellent student-faculty ratio (average class=11) provides extra attention for its students to identify and achieve their own individual goals. There is an advisory board composed of student and faculty representatives as well as community leaders, which strives to expand the counseling program to improve the quality of life in South Texas. Students complete courses in counseling theories, techniques, and attitudes, multicultural counseling, human development, psychopathology, ethical and legal issues, group counseling, career counseling, assessment, and statistical research design. Electives include coursework in crisis counseling, brief collaborative therapy, community interventions, play therapy, elderly mental health, Latino mental health, alcohol and drug counseling, and bilingualism. Faculty are specialists in brief collaborative therapy, crisis intervention, psycholinguistics, memory, multicultural counseling, psychotherapy research, and counselor professional development. Graduates are eligible to sit for the Licensed Professional Counselor (LPC-Texas) Examination. Students can select a thesis track if they are interested in research and further study at the doctoral level. Our program meets every recommendation of the Multicultural Competency Checklist. The new MS in Psychology is designed to prepare the student for PhD work. The focus of preparation is methodology and research.

Special Facilities or Resources: The international flavor of the University and Texas/Mexico border community provides a rich milieu for multicultural and community counseling exploration and education. This is one of the program's greatest resources.

Texas A&M International is one of the fastest growing university communities in the United States. Additionally, an off-campus community-counseling center, The Texas A&M International University Community Stress Center, offers free bilingual counseling and psycho-educational services. At this center, student-counselors complete practica and internships in direct and indirect community and client interventions with faculty supervision. The Master of Arts in Counseling Psychology (MACP) Program works closely with Career Services, Student Counseling, and Academic Support and Enrichment to provide training and employment opportunities for student-counselors. A departmental computer lab exists that is currently used for cognitive and language research. It is equipped for detailed analysis of research in memory, cognition, psycholinguistics, bilingualism, as well as other research. A Counseling/Research lab is equipped with digital and video recording, internet video conferencing and standard computer programs. It is available for student use in recording counseling sessions and conducting research.

Information for Students With Physical Disabilities: See the following website for more information: http://www.tamiu.edu/wellness/disability.shtml.

Application Information:

Send to Texas A&M International University, Office of Graduate Studies & Research, 5201 University Boulevard, Laredo, TX 78041-1900. Application available online. URL of online application: http://www.tamiu.edu/gradschool/. Students are admitted in the Fall, application deadline April 30; Spring, application deadline November 30; Summer, application deadline April 30. *Fee:* $35. $25.00 late fee if submitted after the deadline.

Texas A&M University

Educational Psychology
College of Education & Human Development
704 Harrington Tower, MS 4225
College Station, TX 77843-4225
Telephone: (979) 845-1831
Fax: (979) 862-1256
E-mail: *v-willson@tamu.edu*
Web: *http://epsy.tamu.edu/*

Department Information:

Department Head: Victor Willson. Number of faculty: total—full-time 40, part-time 1; women—full-time 24, part-time 1; total—minority—full-time 17; women minority—full-time 11.

Programs and Degrees Offered:

Listed in the following order: Program area, degree type (T if terminal Master's), number awarded 7/11–6/12. School Psychology PhD (Doctor of Philosophy) 9, Counseling Psychology PhD (Doctor of Philosophy) 7, Educational Psychology PhD (Doctor of Philosophy) 16.

APA Accreditation: School PhD (Doctor of Philosophy). Student Outcome Data Website: http://epsy.tamu.edu/articles/student_admissions__outcomes_and_other_data. Counseling PhD (Doctor of Philosophy). Student Outcome Data Website: http://cpsy.tamu.edu/program_statistics/.

Student Applications/Admissions:

Student Applications

School Psychology PhD (Doctor of Philosophy)—Applications 2012–2013, 37. Total applicants accepted 2012–2013, 22. Number full-time enrolled (new admits only) 2012–2013, 8. Number part-time enrolled (new admits only) 2012–2013, 0. Total enrolled 2012–2013 full-time, 34. Total enrolled 2012–2013 part-time, 8. Openings 2013–2014, 10. The median number of years required for completion of a degree in 2012–2013 were 5. The number of students enrolled full- and part-time who were dismissed or voluntarily withdrew from this program area in 2012–2013 were 4. *Counseling Psychology PhD (Doctor of Philosophy)*—Applications 2012–2013, 76. Total applicants accepted 2012–2013, 18. Number full-time enrolled (new admits only) 2012–2013, 6. Total enrolled 2012–2013 full-time, 31. Total enrolled 2012–2013 part-time, 7. Openings 2013–2014, 8. The median number of years required for completion of a degree in 2012–2013 were 6. The number of students enrolled full- and part-time who were dismissed or voluntarily withdrew from this program area in 2012–2013 were 0. *Educational Psychology PhD (Doctor of Philosophy)*—Applications 2012–2013, 41. Total applicants accepted 2012–2013, 26. Number full-time enrolled (new admits only) 2012–2013, 13. Number part-time enrolled (new admits only) 2012–2013, 3. Total enrolled 2012–2013 full-time, 71. Total enrolled 2012–2013 part-time, 107. Openings 2013–2014, 18. The median number of years required for completion of a degree in 2012–2013 were 6. The number of students enrolled full- and part-time who were dismissed or voluntarily withdrew from this program area in 2012–2013 were 0.

Scores: Entries appear in this order: required test or GPA, minimum score (if required), median score of students entering in 2012–2013. *School Psychology PhD (Doctor of Philosophy):* GRE-V no minimum stated, GRE-Q no minimum stated, GRE-Subject (Psychology) no minimum stated, overall undergraduate GPA no minimum stated; *Counseling Psychology PhD (Doctor of Philosophy):* GRE-V no minimum stated, GRE-Q no minimum stated; *Educational Psychology PhD (Doctor of Philosophy):* GRE-V no minimum stated, GRE-Q no minimum stated, GRE-Analytical no minimum stated.

Other Criteria: (importance of criteria rated low, medium, or high): GRE scores—medium, research experience—high, work experience—medium, extracurricular activity—medium, clinically related public service—high, GPA—medium, letters of recommendation—high, interview—high, statement of goals and objectives—high, fit with program—high, undergraduate major in psychology—low, specific undergraduate psychology courses taken—low. For additional information on admission requirements, go to http://epsy.tamu.edu/articles/graduate_admissions.

Student Characteristics: The following represents characteristics of students in 2012–2013 in all graduate psychology programs in the department: Female—full-time 112, part-time 100; Male—full-time 24, part-time 22; African American/Black—full-time 11, part-time 9; Hispanic/Latino(a)—full-time 24, part-time 33; Asian/Pacific Islander—full-time 50, part-time 7; American Indian/Alaska Native—full-time 0, part-time 0; Caucasian/White—full-time 51, part-time 73; Multi-ethnic—full-time 0, part-time 0; students subject to the Americans With Disabilities Act—full-time 1, part-time 0; Unknown ethnicity—full-time 0, part-time

0; International students who hold an F-1 or J-1 Visa—full-time 42, part-time 3.

Financial Information/Assistance:

Tuition for Full-Time Study: *Doctoral:* State residents: per academic year $4,077, $226 per credit hour; Nonstate residents: per academic year $12,000, $577 per credit hour. Tuition is subject to change. Tuition costs vary by program. See the following website for updates and changes in tuition costs: http://sbs.tamu.edu/accounts-billing/tuition-fees/cost-attendance/.

Financial Assistance:

First-Year Students: Research assistantships available for first year. Average amount paid per academic year: $18,000. Average number of hours worked per week: 20. Fellowships and scholarships available for first year. Average amount paid per academic year: $25,000. Average number of hours worked per week: 20. Apply by December 1.

Advanced Students: Teaching assistantships available for advanced students. Average amount paid per academic year: $15,000. Average number of hours worked per week: 20. Research assistantships available for advanced students. Average amount paid per academic year: $18,000. Average number of hours worked per week: 20. Fellowships and scholarships available for advanced students. Average amount paid per academic year: $20,000. Average number of hours worked per week: 20.

Additional Information: Of all students currently enrolled full time, 70% benefited from one or more of the listed financial assistance programs. Application and information available online at: http://epsy.tamu.edu/articles/assistantships.

Internships/Practica: Doctoral Degree (PhD School Psychology): For those doctoral students for whom a professional psychology internship was required in this program prior to graduation, (8) students applied for an internship in 2011–2012, with (5) students obtaining an internship. Of those students who obtained an internship, (5) were paid internships. Of those students who obtained an internship, (5) students placed in APA/CPA accredited internships, (0) students placed in internships not APA/CPA accredited, but listed with the Association of Psychology Postdoctoral and Internship Programs (APPIC), (0) students placed in internships conforming to guidelines of the Council of Directors of School Psychology Programs (CDSPP), (0) students placed in internships that were not APA/CPA accredited, APPIC or CDSPP listed. Doctoral Degree (PhD Counseling Psychology): For those doctoral students for whom a professional psychology internship was required in this program prior to graduation, (4) students applied for an internship in 2011–2012, with (3) students obtaining an internship. Of those students who obtained an internship, (3) were paid internships. Of those students who obtained an internship, (3) students placed in APA/CPA accredited internships, (0) students placed in internships not APA/CPA accredited, but listed with the Association of Psychology Postdoctoral and Internship Programs (APPIC), (0) students placed in internships conforming to guidelines of the Council of Directors of School Psychology Programs (CDSPP), (0) students placed in internships that were not APA/CPA accredited, APPIC or CDSPP listed. Students in School Psychology and Counseling Psychology participate in the APPIC match program.

Housing and Day Care: On-campus housing is available. See the following website for more information: http://reslife.tamu.edu/.

On-campus day care facilities are available. See the following website for more information: http://childrens-center.tamu.edu/.

Employment of Department Graduates:

Master's Degree Graduates: Of those who graduated in the academic year 2011–2012, the following categories and numbers represent the postgraduate activities and employment of master's degree graduates: Enrolled in a postdoctoral residency/fellowship (n/a), employed in independent practice (n/a), total from the above (master's) (0).

Doctoral Degree Graduates: Of those who graduated in the academic year 2011–2012, the following categories and numbers represent the postgraduate activities and employment of doctoral degree graduates: Enrolled in a psychology doctoral program (n/a), employed in an academic position at a university (5), employed in other positions at a higher education institution (9), employed in a professional position in a school system (12), employed in government agency (2), do not know (5), total from the above (doctoral) (33).

Additional Information:

Orientation, Objectives, and Emphasis of Department: We are among the top-ranked Educational Psychology departments in the nation. We are committed to making a difference through excellence in our research, education and community outreach activities.

Special Facilities or Resources: Education Research Evaluation Laboratory (EREL) and Counseling and Assessment Clinic (CAC) on campus and in Bryan, TX.

Information for Students With Physical Disabilities: See the following website for more information: http://disability.tamu.edu/.

Application Information:

Application available online. URL of online application: http://admissions.tamu.edu/graduate/. Students are admitted in the Fall, application deadline December 1. *Fee:* $50. $90.00 for international applicants.

Texas A&M University—Commerce
Department of Psychology, Counseling and Special Education
College of Education and Human Services
Binnion Hall
Commerce, TX 75429
Telephone: (903) 886-5200
Fax: (903) 886-5510
E-mail: *Jennifer.Schroeder@tamuc.edu*
Web: *http://www.tamuc.edu/academics/colleges/educationHumanServices/departments/psychologyCounselingSpecialEducation/*

Department Information:

1962. Interim Department Head: Dr. Jennifer Schroeder. Number of faculty: total—full-time 34; women—full-time 17; total—minority—full-time 9; women minority—full-time 5.

Programs and Degrees Offered:

Listed in the following order: Program area, degree type (T if terminal Master's), number awarded 7/11–6/12. Educational Psychology PhD (Doctor of Philosophy) 5, School Psychology EdS (School Psychology) 12, Applied Psychology MA/MS (Master of Arts/Science) (T) 5, General Experimental Psychology MA/MS (Master of Arts/Science) (T) 9.

Student Applications/Admissions:

Student Applications

Educational Psychology PhD (Doctor of Philosophy)—Applications 2012–2013, 20. Total applicants accepted 2012–2013, 6. Number full-time enrolled (new admits only) 2012–2013, 4. Number part-time enrolled (new admits only) 2012–2013, 2. Total enrolled 2012–2013 full-time, 21. Total enrolled 2012–2013 part-time, 15. Openings 2013–2014, 10. The median number of years required for completion of a degree in 2012–2013 were 9. The number of students enrolled full- and part-time who were dismissed or voluntarily withdrew from this program area in 2012–2013 were 0. School Psychology EdS (School Psychology)—Applications 2012–2013, 20. Total applicants accepted 2012–2013, 4. Number full-time enrolled (new admits only) 2012–2013, 3. Number part-time enrolled (new admits only) 2012–2013, 3. Total enrolled 2012–2013 full-time, 15. Total enrolled 2012–2013 part-time, 15. Openings 2013–2014, 10. The median number of years required for completion of a degree in 2012–2013 were 4. The number of students enrolled full- and part-time who were dismissed or voluntarily withdrew from this program area in 2012–2013 were 4. Applied Psychology MA/MS (Master of Arts/Science)—Applications 2012–2013, 8. Total applicants accepted 2012–2013, 7. Number full-time enrolled (new admits only) 2012–2013, 7. Number part-time enrolled (new admits only) 2012–2013, 0. Total enrolled 2012–2013 full-time, 18. Total enrolled 2012–2013 part-time, 20. Openings 2013–2014, 10. The median number of years required for completion of a degree in 2012–2013 were 2. The number of students enrolled full- and part-time who were dismissed or voluntarily withdrew from this program area in 2012–2013 were 1. General Experimental Psychology MA/MS (Master of Arts/Science)—Applications 2012–2013, 6. Total applicants accepted 2012–2013, 6. Number full-time enrolled (new admits only) 2012–2013, 6. Number part-time enrolled (new admits only) 2012–2013, 0. Total enrolled 2012–2013 full-time, 16. Total enrolled 2012–2013 part-time, 0. Openings 2013–2014, 10. The median number of years required for completion of a degree in 2012–2013 were 3. The number of students enrolled full- and part-time who were dismissed or voluntarily withdrew from this program area in 2012–2013 were 1.

Scores: Entries appear in this order: required test or GPA, minimum score (if required), median score of students entering in 2012–2013. Educational Psychology PhD (Doctor of Philosophy): GRE-V no minimum stated, 153, GRE-Q no minimum stated, 146, GRE-Analytical no minimum stated, 4.5; School Psychology EdS (School Psychology): GRE-V no minimum stated, GRE-Q no minimum stated; Applied Psychology MA/MS (Master of Arts/Science): GRE-V no minimum stated, GRE-Q no minimum stated, overall undergraduate GPA no minimum stated; General Experimental Psychology MA/MS (Master of Arts/Science): GRE-V no minimum stated, 153, GRE-Q no minimum stated, 550, GRE-Analytical no minimum stated, 4.5.

Other Criteria: (importance of criteria rated low, medium, or high): GRE scores—medium, research experience—medium, work experience—medium, GPA—medium, letters of recommendation—medium, statement of goals and objectives—high, undergraduate major in psychology—low, Greater importance would be assigned to prior research experience, graduate education, and publications/scholarly activity for the doctoral program.

Student Characteristics: The following represents characteristics of students in 2012–2013 in all graduate psychology programs in the department: Female—full-time 45, part-time 38; Male—full-time 25, part-time 12; African American/Black—full-time 9, part-time 6; Hispanic/Latino(a)—full-time 3, part-time 1; Asian/Pacific Islander—full-time 1, part-time 0; American Indian/Alaska Native—full-time 0, part-time 0; Caucasian/White—full-time 57, part-time 43; Multi-ethnic—full-time 0, part-time 0; students subject to the Americans With Disabilities Act—full-time 1, part-time 0; Unknown ethnicity—full-time 0, part-time 0; International students who hold an F-1 or J-1 Visa—full-time 6, part-time 0.

Financial Information/Assistance:

Tuition for Full-Time Study: Master's: State residents: $402 per credit hour; Nonstate residents: $753 per credit hour. Doctoral: State residents: $402 per credit hour; Nonstate residents: $753 per credit hour. Tuition is subject to change. See the following website for updates and changes in tuition costs: http://web.tamuc.edu/admissions/tuitionCosts/default.aspx.

Financial Assistance:

First-Year Students: Teaching assistantships available for first year. Average amount paid per academic year: $8,000. Average number of hours worked per week: 20. Research assistantships available for first year. Average amount paid per academic year: $8,000. Average number of hours worked per week: 20. Fellowships and scholarships available for first year. Average amount paid per academic year: $1,000.

Advanced Students: Teaching assistantships available for advanced students. Average amount paid per academic year: $10,000. Average number of hours worked per week: 20. Research assistantships available for advanced students. Average amount paid per academic year: $10,000. Average number of hours worked per week: 20. Fellowships and scholarships available for advanced students. Average amount paid per academic year: $1,000.

Additional Information: Of all students currently enrolled full time, 10% benefited from one or more of the listed financial assistance programs. Application and information available online at: http://web.tamuc.edu/academics/graduateSchool/funding/default.aspx.

Internships/Practica: Master's Degree (EdS School Psychology): An internship experience, such as a final research project or "capstone" experience is required of graduates. There are on-site university clinic practica for school and applied programs. The school psychology program requires a 1200-hour internship in the public schools.

Housing and Day Care: On-campus housing is available. See the following website for more information: http://www.tamuc.edu/studentLife/housing/default.aspx. On-campus day care facilities are available. See the following website for more information:

http://www.tamuc.edu/studentLife/campusServices/childrensLearningCenter/.

Employment of Department Graduates:

Master's Degree Graduates: Of those who graduated in the academic year 2011–2012, the following categories and numbers represent the postgraduate activities and employment of master's degree graduates: Enrolled in a psychology doctoral program (1), enrolled in another graduate/professional program (1), enrolled in a postdoctoral residency/fellowship (n/a), employed in independent practice (n/a), employed in a professional position in a school system (7), employed in government agency (1), employed in a community mental health/counseling center (1), employed in a hospital/medical center (1), total from the above (master's) (12).

Doctoral Degree Graduates: Of those who graduated in the academic year 2011–2012, the following categories and numbers represent the postgraduate activities and employment of doctoral degree graduates: Enrolled in a psychology doctoral program (n/a), employed in an academic position at a university (3), employed in business or industry (1), employed in government agency (1), total from the above (doctoral) (5).

Additional Information:

Orientation, Objectives, and Emphasis of Department: The focus of the educational psychology program is human interventions (direct and indirect), statistics and research design, and cognition and instruction. Students will acquire an in-depth knowledge of human learning and cognition, instructional strategies, and research and evaluation. This emphasis will prepare students to integrate knowledge of human cognition and instructional practice across a variety of occupational, educational and content matter domains, with emphasis on applications of learning technologies. The same is true of our Master's program in General/Experimental Psychology, which a student earns as part of our 90-hour doctoral programs. Or, students can enroll in the Master's program as a terminal degree. This is a 36-hour program that can either emphasize research (with a required empirical thesis) or not. The applied master's program is fully accredited by the Interorganizational Board of Accreditation for Master's in Psychology Programs (IBAMPP). The applied master's program is designed to prepare students to meet the requirements for certification as an associate psychologist in the State of Texas. Associate psychologists are employed in a variety of governmental and private organizations, such as mental health centers, clinics, and hospitals. The school psychology program has been approved by the National Association of School Psychologists (NASP) and includes coursework in psychological foundations, educational foundations, assessment, professional school psychology, practica and an internship.

Special Facilities or Resources: Multimedia Instructional Lab, multimedia classrooms, on-site Integrated University Clinic, research partnerships with business industry, Center for excellence-learning technologies, support for online learning, Cognitive Developmental Lab, Cognitive Science Lab, Cognition Lab, Health Psychology Lab, Social Cognition Lab, and School Psychology Resource Center.

Application Information:

Send to Graduate School, P.O. Box 3011, Texas A&M—Commerce, Commerce, TX 75429-3011. Application available online. URL of online application: http://web.tamuc.edu/academics/graduateSchool/applyOnline.aspx. Students are admitted in the Fall, application deadline April 15; Spring, application deadline November 15; Programs have rolling admissions. The deadlines for the Educational Psychology PhD program and School Psychology Specialist program are April 15 for fall admission and November 15 for spring admission. The Master's programs have rolling admissions. *Fee:* $50.

Texas Christian University

Department of Psychology
College of Science and Engineering
TCU Box 298920
Fort Worth, TX 76129
Telephone: (817) 257-7410
Fax: (817) 257-7681
E-mail: *c.lord@tcu.edu*
Web: *http://www.psy.tcu.edu/gradpro.html*

Department Information:

1959. Chairperson: Mauricio Papini. Number of faculty: total—full-time 15; women—full-time 7.

Programs and Degrees Offered:

Listed in the following order: Program area, degree type (T if terminal Master's), number awarded 7/11–6/12. Experimental Psychology PhD (Doctor of Philosophy) 4.

Student Applications/Admissions:

Student Applications

Experimental Psychology PhD (Doctor of Philosophy)—Applications 2012–2013, 40. Total applicants accepted 2012–2013, 10. Number full-time enrolled (new admits only) 2012–2013, 5. Number part-time enrolled (new admits only) 2012–2013, 0. Total enrolled 2012–2013 full-time, 29. Total enrolled 2012–2013 part-time, 0. Openings 2013–2014, 4. The median number of years required for completion of a degree in 2012–2013 were 5. The number of students enrolled full- and part-time who were dismissed or voluntarily withdrew from this program area in 2012–2013 were 0.

Scores: Entries appear in this order: required test or GPA, minimum score (if required), median score of students entering in 2012–2013. *Experimental Psychology PhD (Doctor of Philosophy):* GRE-V 420, 540, GRE-Q 510, 600, GRE-Analytical 3.0, 4.5, overall undergraduate GPA 3.4, 3.7, last 2 years GPA 3.2, 3.6, psychology GPA 3.3, 3.7.

Other Criteria: (importance of criteria rated low, medium, or high): GRE scores—low, research experience—high, GPA—medium, letters of recommendation—high, statement of goals and objectives—high, undergraduate major in psychology—low, specific undergraduate psychology courses taken—low. For additional information on admission requirements, go to http://www.psy.tcu.edu/gradpro.html.

Student Characteristics: The following represents characteristics of students in 2012–2013 in all graduate psychology programs in the department: Female—full-time 15, part-time 0; Male—full-time 14, part-time 0; African American/Black—full-time 0, part-time 0; Hispanic/Latino(a)—full-time 1, part-time 0; Asian/Pacific Islander—full-time 3, part-time 0; American Indian/Alaska Native—full-time 0, part-time 0; Caucasian/White—full-time 25, part-time 0; Multi-ethnic—full-time 0, part-time 0; students subject to the Americans With Disabilities Act—full-time 0, part-time 0; Unknown ethnicity—full-time 0, part-time 0; International students who hold an F-1 or J-1 Visa—full-time 3, part-time 0.

Financial Information/Assistance:

Tuition for Full-Time Study: *Doctoral:* State residents: $1,215 per credit hour; Nonstate residents: $1,215 per credit hour. See the following website for updates and changes in tuition costs: http://www.graduate.tcu.edu/default.asp?d=page&pid=sp146.

Financial Assistance:

First-Year Students: Fellowships and scholarships available for first year. Average amount paid per academic year: $0. Average number of hours worked per week: 0.

Advanced Students: Teaching assistantships available for advanced students. Average amount paid per academic year: $18,500. Average number of hours worked per week: 20. Apply by January 31.

Additional Information: Of all students currently enrolled full time, 90% benefited from one or more of the listed financial assistance programs. Application and information available online at: http://www.graduate.tcu.edu/default.asp?d=page&pid=sp147.

Housing and Day Care: No on-campus housing is available. No on-campus day care facilities are available.

Employment of Department Graduates:

Master's Degree Graduates: Of those who graduated in the academic year 2011–2012, the following categories and numbers represent the postgraduate activities and employment of master's degree graduates: Enrolled in a postdoctoral residency/fellowship (n/a), employed in independent practice (n/a), total from the above (master's) (0).

Doctoral Degree Graduates: Of those who graduated in the academic year 2011–2012, the following categories and numbers represent the postgraduate activities and employment of doctoral degree graduates: Enrolled in a psychology doctoral program (n/a), employed in an academic position at a university (1), employed in other positions at a higher education institution (2), employed in business or industry (1), still seeking employment (1), total from the above (doctoral) (5).

Additional Information:

Orientation, Objectives, and Emphasis of Department: The psychology graduate program at Texas Christian University leads to a PhD in general experimental psychology. We do not accept applicants who seek only a terminal master's degree, nor applicants who prefer to specialize in clinical, counseling, or other applied areas. The program is primarily a basic research degree. Within this degree, the student may study diverse areas of interest with emphasis possible in the following: learning-comparative, developmental-cognition, social psychology, and behavioral neuroscience. The environment is stimulating, informal, and conducive to close student-faculty relations. All 12 research faculty have productive research labs and are excited about mentoring PhD students.

Special Facilities or Resources: Assuming that physical proximity is conducive to more interdisciplinary work of substance, TCU has located all its science-related activities in or near the Science

Research Center, dedicated in 1971. The Department of Psychology occupies two floors of the center's Winton-Scott Hall. The university library, containing over one million volumes, is located next to the science facilities. About 140 periodicals of psychological interest are available, plus online access to almost all journals. Full-time personnel skilled in electronics, glass blowing, woodworking, and metalworking aid in construction and maintenance of special equipment or instruments. TCU has 10 open computer labs equipped with Windows-based PCs and Macintosh computers (over 100 Windows-based machines and 39 Mac-based machines). All of the labs provide full Internet access and laser printing. Additionally, some of the labs have scanners, zip drives, CD burners, and web cams. The Psychology department also has a computer lab with 6 Windows-based PCs, all of which are connected to the Internet, and a networked laser printer. Additionally, all of the research laboratories in the department have networked computers. From the various labs, students have access to a variety of software including SPSS, SAS, SYSTAT, and Microsoft Office. Also, the University provides e-mail accounts and storage space on the University server.

Information for Students With Physical Disabilities: See the following website for more information: http://www.acs.tcu.edu/disability_services.asp.

Application Information:
Send to Gary Boehm, Coordinator of Graduate Studies, TCU Box 298920, Fort Worth, TX 76129. Application available online. URL of online application: http://www.psy.tcu.edu/gradpro.html. Students are admitted in the Fall, application deadline January 31. *Fee:* $60. No application fee for International Students.

Texas Southwestern Medical Center, The University of
Division of Psychology, Graduate Program in Clinical Psychology
5323 Harry Hines Boulevard
Dallas, TX 75390-9044
Telephone: (214) 648-5277
Fax: (214) 648-5297
E-mail: *beth.kennard@utsouthwestern.edu*
Web: *http://www.utsouthwestern.edu/graduateschool/clinicalpsychology.html*

Department Information:
1956. Chairperson: C. Munro Cullum, PhD. Number of faculty: total—full-time 83; women—full-time 40; total—minority—full-time 10; women minority—full-time 6; faculty subject to the Americans With Disabilities Act 3.

Programs and Degrees Offered:
Listed in the following order: Program area, degree type (T if terminal Master's), number awarded 7/11–6/12. Clinical Psychology PhD (Doctor of Philosophy) 12.

APA Accreditation: Clinical PhD (Doctor of Philosophy). Student Outcome Data Website: http://www.utsouthwestern.edu/education/graduate-school/programs/phd-degrees/clinical-psychology/training-outcomes.html.

Student Applications/Admissions:

Student Applications

Clinical Psychology PhD (Doctor of Philosophy)—Applications 2012–2013, 211. Total applicants accepted 2012–2013, 12. Number full-time enrolled (new admits only) 2012–2013, 10. Total enrolled 2012–2013 full-time, 35. Total enrolled 2012–2013 part-time, 0. Openings 2013–2014, 10. The median number of years required for completion of a degree in 2012–2013 were 4. The number of students enrolled full- and part-time who were dismissed or voluntarily withdrew from this program area in 2012–2013 were 1.

Scores: Entries appear in this order: required test or GPA, minimum score (if required), median score of students entering in 2012–2013. Clinical Psychology PhD (Doctor of Philosophy): GRE-V 500, GRE-Q 500, overall undergraduate GPA no minimum stated, 3.72.

Other Criteria: (importance of criteria rated low, medium, or high): GRE scores—high, research experience—high, work experience—high, extracurricular activity—low, clinically related public service—medium, GPA—high, letters of recommendation—high, interview—high, statement of goals and objectives—high, undergraduate major in psychology—medium, specific undergraduate psychology courses taken—medium. For additional information on admission requirements, go to http://www.utsouthwestern.edu/education/graduate-school/programs/phd-degrees/clinical-psychology/.

Student Characteristics: The following represents characteristics of students in 2012–2013 in all graduate psychology programs in the department: Female—full-time 23, part-time 0; Male—full-time 12, part-time 0; African American/Black—full-time 3, part-time 0; Hispanic/Latino(a)—full-time 2, part-time 0; Asian/Pacific Islander—full-time 5, part-time 0; American Indian/Alaska Native—full-time 0, part-time 0; Caucasian/White—full-time 25, part-time 0; Multi-ethnic—full-time 0, part-time 0; students subject to the Americans With Disabilities Act—full-time 1, part-time 0; Unknown ethnicity—full-time 0, part-time 0; International students who hold an F-1 or J-1 Visa—full-time 1, part-time 0.

Financial Information/Assistance:

Tuition for Full-Time Study: Doctoral: State residents: per academic year $5,084; Nonstate residents: per academic year $12,524. Tuition is subject to change. See the following website for updates and changes in tuition costs: http://www.utsouthwestern.edu/about-us/administrative-offices/financial-aid/.

Financial Assistance:

First-Year Students: Teaching assistantships available for first year. Apply by December 1. Research assistantships available for first year. Apply by December 1.

Advanced Students: Teaching assistantships available for advanced students. Research assistantships available for advanced students. Average number of hours worked per week: 20. Traineeships available for advanced students. Average number of hours worked per week: 20.

Additional Information: Of all students currently enrolled full time, 77% benefited from one or more of the listed financial assistance programs.

Internships/Practica: Doctoral Degree (PhD Clinical Psychology): For those doctoral students for whom a professional psychol-ogy internship was required in this program prior to graduation, (6) students applied for an internship in 2011–2012, with (6) students obtaining an internship. Of those students who obtained an internship, (6) were paid internships. Of those students who obtained an internship, (6) students placed in APA/CPA accredited internships, (0) students placed in internships not APA/CPA accredited, but listed with the Association of Psychology Postdoctoral and Internship Programs (APPIC), (0) students placed in internships conforming to guidelines of the Council of Directors of School Psychology Programs (CDSPP), (0) students placed in internships that were not APA/CPA accredited, APPIC or CDSPP listed. The program provides more than 1000 hours of clinical practica, followed by an APA-accredited captive internship. These clinical experiences are closely supervised. In order to achieve the goal of broad professional preparation, students will have a number of different clinical placements over the course of their practicum and internship assignments. These assignments are carried out at UT Southwestern facilities, agencies, regional medical centers, area schools, community agencies, university counseling centers, and rehabilitation institutes. These clinical training sites include the following: Parkland Memorial Hospital [PMH]; Neuropsychology Service [UTSWMC]; McDermott Pain Management Center [UTSWMC]; Children's Medical Center [CMC]; the Mental Health Service of Southern Methodist University; Student Counseling Center at the University of Texas at Arlington; Dallas County Juvenile Department; Baylor University Medical Center; Scottish Rite Hospital for Children; and Johnson County Adult Probation Services.

Housing and Day Care: On-campus housing is available. See the following website for more information: http://www.utsouthwestern.edu/education/student-services/housing/. On-campus day care facilities are available. See the following website for more information: http://www.utsouthwestern.edu/education/student-services/child-care.html.

Employment of Department Graduates:

Master's Degree Graduates: Of those who graduated in the academic year 2011–2012, the following categories and numbers represent the postgraduate activities and employment of master's degree graduates: Enrolled in a postdoctoral residency/fellowship (n/a), employed in independent practice (n/a), total from the above (master's) (0).

Doctoral Degree Graduates: Of those who graduated in the academic year 2011–2012, the following categories and numbers represent the postgraduate activities and employment of doctoral degree graduates: Enrolled in a psychology doctoral program (n/a), enrolled in a postdoctoral residency/fellowship (7), employed in independent practice (2), employed in a community mental health/counseling center (3), total from the above (doctoral) (12).

Additional Information:

Orientation, Objectives, and Emphasis of Department: The Graduate Program in Clinical Psychology is a four-year doctoral program with an affiliated predoctoral internship program in clinical psychology, which is separately accredited by the APA. The program provides a combination of experiences in both clinical and research settings reflecting our basic training philosophy, which is a clinician-researcher model. Our specific objectives include offering the student the opportunity to acquire, experience, or develop the following: 1. A closely knit integration between basic psychological knowledge (both theoretical and empirical) and responsible professional services; 2. A wide variety of supervised and broadly conceived clinical and consulting experiences; 3. A sensitivity to professional responsibilities in the context of significant social needs; 4. An understanding of research principles, methodology, and skill in formulating, designing, and implementing psychological research; and 5. A competence and confidence in the role of psychology in multidisciplinary settings.

Special Facilities or Resources: UT Southwestern has a number of laboratories and clinical settings investigating the brain/behavior relationship, as well as many projects focusing on the psychosocial aspects of various medical and psychiatric disorders. Disorders studied include affective illness, anxiety, schizophrenia, sleepwake dysfunctions, and medical conditions such as Alzheimer's disease, epilepsy, temporomandibular disorder, cystic fibrosis, and organ transplantation. Notable examples of comprehensive clinical research programs at UT Southwestern include the following: an affective disorders research program; a child psychiatry research program; a sleep disorders research laboratory; an Alzheimer's Disease Center; a neuropsychology laboratory; a pain management program; a schizophrenia research program that includes translational research; and research programs in basic neuroscience.

Application Information:
Application available online. URL of online application: http://www. utsouthwestern.edu/gradapp. Students are admitted in the Fall, application deadline December 1. *Fee:* $0.

Texas State University—San Marcos
Psychology Department/Master of Arts in Psychological
 Research
College of Liberal Arts
601 University Drive
San Marcos, TX 78666-4616
Telephone: (512) 245-2526
Fax: (512) 245-3153
E-mail: *psychology@txstate.edu*
Web: *http://www.psych.txstate.edu*

Department Information:
 1969. Chairperson: William L. Kelemen, PhD. Number of faculty: total—full-time 30, part-time 5; women—full-time 18, part-time 1; total—minority—full-time 4, part-time 1; women minority—full-time 3.

Programs and Degrees Offered:
 Listed in the following order: Program area, degree type (T if terminal Master's), number awarded 7/11–6/12. Health Psychology MA/MS (Master of Arts/Science) (T) 20, Psychological Research MA/MS (Master of Arts/Science) (T) 0.

Student Applications/Admissions:
 Student Applications
  Health Psychology MA/MS *(Master of Arts/Science)*—Applications 2012–2013, 0. Total applicants accepted 2012–2013, 0. Number full-time enrolled (new admits only) 2012–2013, 0. Number part-time enrolled (new admits only) 2012–2013, 0. Total enrolled 2012–2013 full-time, 20. Total enrolled 2012–

2013 part-time, 11. The median number of years required for completion of a degree in 2012–2013 were 2. The number of students enrolled full- and part-time who were dismissed or voluntarily withdrew from this program area in 2012–2013 were 0. *Psychological Research MA/MS (Master of Arts/Science)*—Applications 2012–2013, 0. Total applicants accepted 2012–2013, 0. Number full-time enrolled (new admits only) 2012–2013, 0. Number part-time enrolled (new admits only) 2012–2013, 0. Openings 2013–2014, 15. The number of students enrolled full- and part-time who were dismissed or voluntarily withdrew from this program area in 2012–2013 were 0.
 Scores: Entries appear in this order: required test or GPA, minimum score (if required), median score of students entering in 2012–2013. *Health Psychology MA/MS (Master of Arts/Science):* GRE-V no minimum stated, GRE-Q no minimum stated, last 2 years GPA 3.0; *Psychological Research MA/MS (Master of Arts/Science):* GRE-V no minimum stated, GRE-Q no minimum stated, overall undergraduate GPA 3.0.
 Other Criteria: (importance of criteria rated low, medium, or high): GRE scores—medium, research experience—medium, work experience—low, extracurricular activity—low, clinically related public service—low, GPA—high, letters of recommendation—high, statement of goals and objectives—high, undergraduate major in psychology—medium, specific undergraduate psychology courses taken—high. For additional information on admission requirements, go to http://www.psych. txstate.edu/degrees-programs/graduate/mapr.html.

Student Characteristics: The following represents characteristics of students in 2012–2013 in all graduate psychology programs in the department: Female—full-time 15, part-time 6; Male—full-time 5, part-time 5; African American/Black—full-time 1, part-time 1; Hispanic/Latino(a)—full-time 3, part-time 2; Asian/Pacific Islander—full-time 1, part-time 0; American Indian/Alaska Native—full-time 0, part-time 0; Caucasian/White—full-time 14, part-time 7; Multi-ethnic—full-time 0, part-time 0; students subject to the Americans With Disabilities Act—full-time 0, part-time 0; Unknown ethnicity—full-time 1, part-time 1; International students who hold an F-1 or J-1 Visa—full-time 0, part-time 0.

Financial Information/Assistance:
 Tuition for Full-Time Study: *Master's:* State residents: per academic year $6,546; Nonstate residents: per academic year $12,863. Tuition is subject to change. See the following website for updates and changes in tuition costs: http://www.sbs.txstate.edu/billing. html.

Financial Assistance:
 First-Year Students: Teaching assistantships available for first year. Average amount paid per academic year: $10,152. Average number of hours worked per week: 20. Apply by June 15. Research assistantships available for first year. Average amount paid per academic year: $10,152. Average number of hours worked per week: 20. Apply by June 15.
 Advanced Students: Teaching assistantships available for advanced students. Average amount paid per academic year: $10,404. Average number of hours worked per week: 20. Apply by June 15. Research assistantships available for advanced students. Average amount paid per academic year: $10,404. Average number of hours worked per week: 20. Apply by June 15.

Additional Information: Of all students currently enrolled full time, 80% benefited from one or more of the listed financial assistance programs. Application and information available online at: http://www.finaid.txstate.edu/graduate.html.

Internships/Practica: Master's Degree (MA/MS Health Psychology): An internship experience, such as a final research project or "capstone" experience is required of graduates. Master's Degree (MA/MS Psychological Research): An internship experience, such as a final research project or "capstone" experience is required of graduates.

Housing and Day Care: On-campus housing is available. See the following website for more information: http://www.reslife.txstate.edu. On-campus day care facilities are available. See the following website for more information: http://www.fcs.txstate.edu/cdc/.

Employment of Department Graduates:

Master's Degree Graduates: Of those who graduated in the academic year 2011–2012, the following categories and numbers represent the postgraduate activities and employment of master's degree graduates: Enrolled in a psychology doctoral program (3), enrolled in another graduate/professional program (2), enrolled in a postdoctoral residency/fellowship (n/a), employed in independent practice (n/a), employed in business or industry (1), employed in a community mental health/counseling center (4), still seeking employment (1), other employment position (3), do not know (6), total from the above (master's) (20).

Doctoral Degree Graduates: Of those who graduated in the academic year 2011–2012, the following categories and numbers represent the postgraduate activities and employment of doctoral degree graduates: Enrolled in a psychology doctoral program (n/a), total from the above (doctoral) (0).

Additional Information:

Orientation, Objectives, and Emphasis of Department: The goal of the Master's program in Psychological Research at Texas State University-San Marcos is to foster competence in the methodological foundations and conduct of psychological research across a wide variety of settings. Students will gain expertise regarding the impact of biological, social, emotional, cognitive, and behavioral factors on psychological phenomena. Focus is placed on learning interpersonal/research skills and statistical competencies relevant to the responsible and ethical conduct of both basic and applied psychological research. This program is appropriate for individuals wishing to work in basic and applied research settings or intending to pursue a doctoral degree in Psychology. The program requires completion of 38 student credit hours, which includes 6 credit hours for completion of a thesis.

Special Facilities or Resources: The Psychology Department at Texas State University is housed in an LEED-certified building completed in June 2012. Research facilities include electrophysiology labs, behavioral testing labs, an event-related potentials (ERP) lab, a sleep lab, a salivary analysis lab, an eye-tracking lab, a portable transcranial laser doppler lab, interpersonal interaction labs, and group survey and computer testing labs.

Information for Students With Physical Disabilities: See the following website for more information: http://www.ods.txstate.edu/.

Application Information:
Send to The Graduate College, Texas State University, 601 University Drive, San Marcos, TX 78666-4605. Application available online. URL of online application: http://www.gradcollege.txstate.edu/. Students are admitted in the Fall, application deadline June 15. *Fee:* $40.

Texas Tech University
Department of Psychology
Arts & Sciences
Box 42051
Lubbock, TX 79409-2051
Telephone: (806) 742-3711, ext. 222
Fax: (806) 742-0818
E-mail: *kay.hill@ttu.edu*
Web: *http://www.depts.ttu.edu/psy/*

Department Information:
1950. Chairperson: Lee M. Cohen, PhD. Number of faculty: total—full-time 31; women—full-time 13; total—minority—full-time 2; faculty subject to the Americans With Disabilities Act 1.

Programs and Degrees Offered:
Listed in the following order: Program area, degree type (T if terminal Master's), number awarded 7/11–6/12. Clinical Psychology PhD (Doctor of Philosophy) 6, Applied Cognitive Psychology PhD (Doctor of Philosophy) 2, Counseling Psychology PhD (Doctor of Philosophy) 8, General Experimental Psychology PhD (Doctor of Philosophy) 1, Human Factors PhD (Doctor of Philosophy) 2, Social Psychology PhD (Doctor of Philosophy) 4.

APA Accreditation: Clinical PhD (Doctor of Philosophy). Student Outcome Data Website: http://www.depts.ttu.edu/psy/graduate_programs/clinical/overview.php. Counseling PhD (Doctor of Philosophy). Student Outcome Data Website: http://www.depts.ttu.edu/psy/graduate_programs/counseling/overview.php.

Student Applications/Admissions:

Student Applications

Clinical Psychology PhD (Doctor of Philosophy)—Applications 2012–2013, 110. Total applicants accepted 2012–2013, 9. Number full-time enrolled (new admits only) 2012–2013, 9. Number part-time enrolled (new admits only) 2012–2013, 0. Total enrolled 2012–2013 full-time, 45. Total enrolled 2012–2013 part-time, 0. Openings 2013–2014, 9. The median number of years required for completion of a degree in 2012–2013 were 6. The number of students enrolled full- and part-time who were dismissed or voluntarily withdrew from this program area in 2012–2013 were 0. *Applied Cognitive Psychology PhD (Doctor of Philosophy)*—Applications 2012–2013, 12. Total applicants accepted 2012–2013, 3. Number full-time enrolled (new admits only) 2012–2013, 3. Number part-time enrolled (new admits only) 2012–2013, 0. Total enrolled 2012–2013 full-time, 9. Total enrolled 2012–2013 part-time, 1. Openings 2013–2014, 4. The median number of years required for completion of a degree in 2012–2013 were 5. The number of students enrolled full- and part-time who were dismissed or voluntarily withdrew from this program area in 2012–2013 were 0. *Counseling Psychology PhD (Doctor of Philosophy)*—Applications 2012–2013, 70. Total applicants accepted 2012–

2013, 9. Number full-time enrolled (new admits only) 2012–2013, 8. Number part-time enrolled (new admits only) 2012–2013, 0. Total enrolled 2012–2013 full-time, 43. Total enrolled 2012–2013 part-time, 0. Openings 2013–2014, 8. The median number of years required for completion of a degree in 2012–2013 were 6. The number of students enrolled full- and part-time who were dismissed or voluntarily withdrew from this program area in 2012–2013 were 0. *General Experimental Psychology PhD (Doctor of Philosophy)*—Applications 2012–2013, 3. Total applicants accepted 2012–2013, 1. Number full-time enrolled (new admits only) 2012–2013, 1. Number part-time enrolled (new admits only) 2012–2013, 0. Total enrolled 2012–2013 full-time, 2. Total enrolled 2012–2013 part-time, 1. Openings 2013–2014, 1. The median number of years required for completion of a degree in 2012–2013 were 5. The number of students enrolled full- and part-time who were dismissed or voluntarily withdrew from this program area in 2012–2013 were 0. *Human Factors PhD (Doctor of Philosophy)*—Applications 2012–2013, 28. Total applicants accepted 2012–2013, 4. Number full-time enrolled (new admits only) 2012–2013, 4. Number part-time enrolled (new admits only) 2012–2013, 0. Total enrolled 2012–2013 full-time, 15. Total enrolled 2012–2013 part-time, 1. Openings 2013–2014, 4. The median number of years required for completion of a degree in 2012–2013 were 5. The number of students enrolled full- and part-time who were dismissed or voluntarily withdrew from this program area in 2012–2013 were 0. *Social Psychology PhD (Doctor of Philosophy)*—Applications 2012–2013, 24. Total applicants accepted 2012–2013, 4. Number full-time enrolled (new admits only) 2012–2013, 4. Number part-time enrolled (new admits only) 2012–2013, 0. Total enrolled 2012–2013 full-time, 16. Total enrolled 2012–2013 part-time, 1. Openings 2013–2014, 4. The median number of years required for completion of a degree in 2012–2013 were 5. The number of students enrolled full- and part-time who were dismissed or voluntarily withdrew from this program area in 2012–2013 were 0.

Scores: Entries appear in this order: required test or GPA, minimum score (if required), median score of students entering in 2012–2013. *Clinical Psychology PhD (Doctor of Philosophy):* GRE-V no minimum stated, 157, GRE-Q no minimum stated, 151, GRE-Analytical no minimum stated, 4; *Applied Cognitive Psychology PhD (Doctor of Philosophy):* GRE-V no minimum stated, 160, GRE-Q no minimum stated, 149, GRE-Analytical no minimum stated, 4; *Counseling Psychology PhD (Doctor of Philosophy):* GRE-V no minimum stated, 156, GRE-Q no minimum stated, 146, GRE-Analytical no minimum stated, 4; *General Experimental Psychology PhD (Doctor of Philosophy):* GRE-V no minimum stated, 147, GRE-Q no minimum stated, 148, GRE-Analytical no minimum stated, 4; *Human Factors PhD (Doctor of Philosophy):* GRE-V no minimum stated, 155, GRE-Q no minimum stated, 150, GRE-Analytical no minimum stated, 4, overall undergraduate GPA no minimum stated, 3.60; *Social Psychology PhD (Doctor of Philosophy):* GRE-V no minimum stated, 160, GRE-Q no minimum stated, 152.

Other Criteria: (importance of criteria rated low, medium, or high): GRE scores—medium, research experience—high, work experience—medium, extracurricular activity—low, clinically related public service—medium, GPA—medium, letters of recommendation—high, interview—high, statement of goals and objectives—high, undergraduate major in psychology—low, specific undergraduate psychology courses taken—

medium, Work experience for experimental-low, counseling-medium, clinical-high; extracurricular activity for experimental-low, counseling-medium, clinical-medium; interview for clinical-high, counseling-high, experimental-medium. Interviews usually held in late January or early February. For additional information on admission requirements, go to http://www.depts.ttu.edu/psy/graduate_programs/how_to_apply.php.

Student Characteristics: The following represents characteristics of students in 2012–2013 in all graduate psychology programs in the department: Female—full-time 94, part-time 2; Male—full-time 36, part-time 2; African American/Black—full-time 11, part-time 0; Hispanic/Latino(a)—full-time 26, part-time 0; Asian/Pacific Islander—full-time 9, part-time 0; American Indian/Alaska Native—full-time 0, part-time 0; Caucasian/White—full-time 74, part-time 0; Multi-ethnic—full-time 2, part-time 0; students subject to the Americans With Disabilities Act—full-time 1, part-time 0; Unknown ethnicity—full-time 8, part-time 4; International students who hold an F-1 or J-1 Visa—full-time 3, part-time 0.

Financial Information/Assistance:

Tuition for Full-Time Study: *Doctoral:* State residents: per academic year $6,069; Nonstate residents: per academic year $14,485. Tuition is subject to change. See the following website for updates and changes in tuition costs: http://www.depts.ttu.edu/studentbusinessservices/tuitionandfees/tuitiongrids.php.

Financial Assistance:

First-Year Students: Teaching assistantships available for first year. Average amount paid per academic year: $10,549. Average number of hours worked per week: 20. Research assistantships available for first year. Average amount paid per academic year: $10,549. Average number of hours worked per week: 20. Fellowships and scholarships available for first year. Average amount paid per academic year: $1,000. Average number of hours worked per week: 0.

Advanced Students: Teaching assistantships available for advanced students. Average amount paid per academic year: $12,462. Average number of hours worked per week: 20. Research assistantships available for advanced students. Average amount paid per academic year: $12,462. Average number of hours worked per week: 20. Fellowships and scholarships available for advanced students. Average amount paid per academic year: $1,000. Average number of hours worked per week: 0.

Additional Information: Of all students currently enrolled full time, 98% benefited from one or more of the listed financial assistance programs. Application and information available online at: http://www.depts.ttu.edu/financialaid/.

Internships/Practica: Doctoral Degree (PhD Clinical Psychology): For those doctoral students for whom a professional psychology internship was required in this program prior to graduation, (3) students applied for an internship in 2011–2012, with (3) students obtaining an internship. Of those students who obtained an internship, (3) were paid internships. Of those students who obtained an internship, (3) students placed in APA/CPA accredited internships, (0) students placed in internships not APA/CPA accredited, but listed with the Association of Psychology Postdoctoral and Internship Programs (APPIC), (0) students placed in internships conforming to guidelines of the Council of Directors of School Psychology Programs (CDSPP), (0) students placed in internships that were not APA/CPA accredited, APPIC or CDSPP listed. Doctoral Degree (PhD Counseling Psychology): For those doctoral students for whom a professional psychology internship was required in this program prior to graduation, (7) students applied for an internship in 2011–2012, with (6) students obtaining an internship. Of those students who obtained an internship, (6) were paid internships. Of those students who obtained an internship, (6) students placed in APA/CPA accredited internships, (0) students placed in internships not APA/CPA accredited, but listed with the Association of Psychology Postdoctoral and Internship Programs (APPIC), (0) students placed in internships conforming to guidelines of the Council of Directors of School Psychology Programs (CDSPP), (0) students placed in internships that were not APA/CPA accredited, APPIC or CDSPP listed. Practica are available in our Psychology Clinic and the Texas Tech University Counseling Center. Paid practica are available in the community. Such placements include a psychiatric prison, the departments of Family Medicine, Oncology, Pediatric Oncology, Internal Medicine, and Neuropsychiatry in the TTU Health Sciences Center, StarCare (CMHC), a community child psychology practice, a community neuropsychology practice, and conducting assessments at the state school and with local psychologists.

Housing and Day Care: On-campus housing is available. See the following website for more information: http://housing.ttu.edu/. On-campus day care facilities are available. See the following website for more information: http://www.depts.ttu.edu/hs/cdrc/.

Employment of Department Graduates:

Master's Degree Graduates: Of those who graduated in the academic year 2011–2012, the following categories and numbers represent the postgraduate activities and employment of master's degree graduates: Enrolled in a postdoctoral residency/fellowship (n/a), employed in independent practice (n/a), total from the above (master's) (0).

Doctoral Degree Graduates: Of those who graduated in the academic year 2011–2012, the following categories and numbers represent the postgraduate activities and employment of doctoral degree graduates: Enrolled in a psychology doctoral program (n/a), employed in independent practice (2), employed in an academic position at a university (5), employed in an academic position at a 2-year/4-year college (3), employed in business or industry (1), employed in government agency (5), employed in a community mental health/counseling center (4), employed in a hospital/medical center (2), do not know (2), total from the above (doctoral) (24).

Additional Information:

Orientation, Objectives, and Emphasis of Department: The clinical program adheres to a basic scientist–practitioner model with equal emphasis given to these components of clinical training. The program strives to develop student competencies in the following areas: psychotherapy and other major patterns of psychological treatment, clinical research, psychodiagnostic assessment, psychopathology, personality, and general psychology. The doctoral specialization in counseling psychology is also firmly committed to a concept of balanced scientist–practitioner training and is designed to foster the development of competence in basic psychology, counseling and psychotherapy, psychological assessment, psychological research, and professional ethics. Programs in experimental psychology (cognitive/applied cognitive, social,

human factors) encompass a variety of research interests, both basic and applied. Students in these programs are exposed to the data, methods and theories and a wide variety of basic areas of psychology while at the same time developing a commitment to an area of special interest through research with a faculty mentor. Collaborative work across departmental programs is encouraged, and the department also collaborates with colleagues in management, industrial engineering, neuroscience, neuropsychiatry, the TTU Neuroimaging Institute (fMRI), and the TTU Health Sciences Center.

Special Facilities or Resources: The department is housed in its own four-story building (plus a basement, for 5 floors total), which includes a large, well-equipped psychology clinic for practicum training, numerous laboratories equipped for human research activities, and sufficient student workspace and offices. The university maintains constantly expanding computing support systems that can be accessed from computers in the psychology building. The Psychology Department has a number of microcomputers and software available for student use. The university enjoys an unusually good relationship with the local metropolitan community of over 250,000 residents. Major medical facilities, a private psychiatric hospital, a psychiatric prison and a state school for the developmentally disabled are located within the city, and APA-accredited internship training is available in the TTU Student Counseling Center.

Information for Students With Physical Disabilities: See the following website for more information: http://www.depts.ttu.edu/students/sds/.

Application Information:
Send to Texas Tech University, Admissions, Psychology Department, Box 42051, Lubbock, TX 79409-2051. Application available online. URL of online application: http://www.depts.ttu.edu/gradschool/admissions/apply.php. Students are admitted in the Fall, application deadline December 1. Deadlines for application: Clinical: December 1, Counseling: December 1, Experimental: January 15. *Fee:* $60.

Texas Tech University
Educational Psychology and Leadership/Educational Psychology
College of Education
Box 41071
Lubbock, TX 79409-1071
Telephone: (806) 834-2486
Fax: (806) 742-2179
E-mail: *kamau.siwatu@ttu.edu*
Web: *http://www.educ.ttu.edu*

Department Information:
1963. Program Coordinator: Kamau Oginga Siwatu, PhD. Number of faculty: total—full-time 8; women—full-time 2; total—minority—full-time 4.

Programs and Degrees Offered:
Listed in the following order: Program area, degree type (T if terminal Master's), number awarded 7/11–6/12. Educational Psy-

chology MEd (Education) 5, Educational Psychology PhD (Doctor of Philosophy) 1.

Student Applications/Admissions:

Student Applications

Educational Psychology MEd (Education)—Applications 2012–2013, 5. Total applicants accepted 2012–2013, 5. Number full-time enrolled (new admits only) 2012–2013, 0. Total enrolled 2012–2013 full-time, 1. Openings 2013–2014, 15. The median number of years required for completion of a degree in 2012–2013 were 2. The number of students enrolled full- and part-time who were dismissed or voluntarily withdrew from this program area in 2012–2013 were 0. *Educational Psychology PhD (Doctor of Philosophy)*—Applications 2012–2013, 10. Total applicants accepted 2012–2013, 8. Number full-time enrolled (new admits only) 2012–2013, 5. Total enrolled 2012–2013 full-time, 40. Openings 2013–2014, 10. The median number of years required for completion of a degree in 2012–2013 were 7. The number of students enrolled full- and part-time who were dismissed or voluntarily withdrew from this program area in 2012–2013 were 0.

Scores: Entries appear in this order: required test or GPA, minimum score (if required), median score of students entering in 2012–2013. *Educational Psychology MEd (Education):* GRE-V no minimum stated, GRE-Q no minimum stated, GRE-Analytical no minimum stated; *Educational Psychology PhD (Doctor of Philosophy):* GRE-V no minimum stated, GRE-Q no minimum stated, GRE-Analytical no minimum stated.

Other Criteria: (importance of criteria rated low, medium, or high): GRE scores—low, research experience—high, work experience—medium, extracurricular activity—medium, clinically related public service—low, GPA—medium, letters of recommendation—high, interview—medium, statement of goals and objectives—high. For additional information on admission requirements, go to http://cms.educ.ttu.edu/academic-programs/psychology-and-leadership/educational-psychology/default.

Student Characteristics: The following represents characteristics of students in 2012–2013 in all graduate psychology programs in the department: Female—full-time 32, part-time 0; Male—full-time 9, part-time 0; African American/Black—full-time 3, part-time 0; Hispanic/Latino(a)—full-time 3, part-time 0; Asian/Pacific Islander—full-time 9, part-time 0; American Indian/Alaska Native—full-time 0, part-time 0; Caucasian/White—full-time 26, part-time 0; Multi-ethnic—full-time 0, part-time 0; students subject to the Americans With Disabilities Act—full-time 0, part-time 0; Unknown ethnicity—full-time 0, part-time 0; International students who hold an F-1 or J-1 Visa—full-time 1, part-time 0.

Financial Information/Assistance:

Tuition for Full-Time Study: *Master's:* State residents: per academic year $5,100, $252 per credit hour; Nonstate residents: per academic year $11,748, $604 per credit hour. *Doctoral:* State residents: per academic year $5,100, $252 per credit hour; Nonstate residents: per academic year $11,748, $604 per credit hour. Tuition is subject to change. See the following website for updates and changes in tuition costs: http://www.depts.ttu.edu/studentbusinessservices/.

Financial Assistance:

First-Year Students: Teaching assistantships available for first year. Average amount paid per academic year: $11,000. Average number of hours worked per week: 20. Apply by February 1. Research assistantships available for first year. Average amount paid per academic year: $11,000. Average number of hours worked per week: 20. Apply by February 1. Fellowships and scholarships available for first year. Average amount paid per academic year: $23,000. Average number of hours worked per week: 20. Apply by February 1.

Advanced Students: Teaching assistantships available for advanced students. Average amount paid per academic year: $11,000. Average number of hours worked per week: 20. Apply by February 1. Research assistantships available for advanced students. Average amount paid per academic year: $11,000. Average number of hours worked per week: 20. Apply by February 1. Fellowships and scholarships available for advanced students. Average amount paid per academic year: $11,000. Average number of hours worked per week: 20. Apply by February 1.

Additional Information: Of all students currently enrolled full time, 85% benefited from one or more of the listed financial assistance programs. Application and information available online at: http://www.depts.ttu.edu/gradschool/funding/.

Internships/Practica: Doctoral students are typically allowed to team teach with faculty who have graduate status. They may also teach an undergraduate course in educational psychology. School Psychology students are eligible for practicum experiences across multiple school districts and the Burkhart Center for Autism Education and Research.

Housing and Day Care: On-campus housing is available. See the following website for more information: http://housing.ttu.edu/. On-campus day care facilities are available. See the following website for more information: http://www.depts.ttu.edu/hs/cdrc/index.php.

Employment of Department Graduates:

Master's Degree Graduates: Of those who graduated in the academic year 2011–2012, the following categories and numbers represent the postgraduate activities and employment of master's degree graduates: Enrolled in a psychology doctoral program (4), enrolled in a postdoctoral residency/fellowship (n/a), employed in independent practice (n/a), other employment position (1), total from the above (master's) (5).

Doctoral Degree Graduates: Of those who graduated in the academic year 2011–2012, the following categories and numbers represent the postgraduate activities and employment of doctoral degree graduates: Enrolled in a psychology doctoral program (n/a), employed in an academic position at a 2-year/4-year college (1), total from the above (doctoral) (1).

Additional Information:

Orientation, Objectives, and Emphasis of Department: Educational Psychology is an academic program in the Department of Educational Psychology and Leadership. The program equips students with a comprehensive knowledge of learning, motivation, development, and educational foundations. Additionally, students learn to apply quantitative and qualitative research skills in a manner that promotes educational improvement while valuing diversity. Thus, educational psychology attracts students from various educational and professional backgrounds including education; psychology; human sciences; business; sports sciences; and health sciences. Students may seek either a Doctoral (PhD) or Master's degree (MEd) in Educational Psychology. The doctoral program emphasizes research and teaching and prepares students for career positions in academia. Additionally, Educational Psychology prepares students for careers in educational research and measurement, such as those found in universities (e.g., institutional research), government agencies, and testing companies. However, students may also choose a practitioner-oriented emphasis or specialization, such as school psychology or sport psychology, by crafting an individualized, interdisciplinary degree plan. The master's program is designed to provide students with content knowledge that facilitates the application of research in educational psychology to educational settings. Teachers are especially encouraged to select the applied master's degree plan that is designed to prepare highly effective, culturally sensitive educators.

Special Facilities or Resources: Educational Psychology students have access to focused research teams that facilitate inquiry through the support of data collection, availability of specialized statistical software, and consultation. School Psychology students have the opportunity to work with the Burkhart Center for Autism Education and Research.

Information for Students With Physical Disabilities: See the following website for more information: http://www.depts.ttu.edu/ studentaffairs/sds/.

Application Information:
Send to Office of Graduate Admissions, Texas Tech University, P.O. Box 41030, Lubbock, TX 79409-1070. Application available online. URL of online application: http://www.depts.ttu.edu/gradschool/ admissions/apply.php. Programs have rolling admissions. Application should be complete at least three months prior to the date of intended enrollment. *Fee:* $60.

Texas Woman's University
Department of Psychology and Philosophy
Arts & Sciences
P.O. Box 425470
Denton, TX 76204
Telephone: (940) 898-2303
Fax: (940) 898-2301
E-mail: *dmiller@twu.edu*
Web: *http://www.twu.edu/psychology-philosophy/*

Department Information:
1942. Chairperson: Daniel C. Miller, PhD, ABPP. Number of faculty: total—full-time 16; women—full-time 10; total—minority—full-time 1.

Programs and Degrees Offered:
Listed in the following order: Program area, degree type (T if terminal Master's), number awarded 7/11–6/12. Counseling Psychology PhD (Doctor of Philosophy) 10, School Psychology PhD (Doctor of Philosophy) 3, Counseling MA/MS (Master of Arts/ Science) (T) 11, School Psychology EdS (School Psychology) 6.

APA Accreditation: Counseling PhD (Doctor of Philosophy). Student Outcome Data Website: http://www.twu.edu/psychology-philosophy/ counseling-psychology-phd-data.asp. School PhD (Doctor of Philosophy). Student Outcome Data Website: http://www.twu.edu/ psychology-philosophy/school-psychology-phd-data.asp.

Student Applications/Admissions:
Student Applications
Counseling Psychology PhD (Doctor of Philosophy)—Applications 2012–2013, 84. Total applicants accepted 2012–2013, 6. Number full-time enrolled (new admits only) 2012–2013, 6. Number part-time enrolled (new admits only) 2012–2013, 0. Total enrolled 2012–2013 full-time, 48. Total enrolled 2012–2013 part-time, 0. Openings 2013–2014, 6. The median number of years required for completion of a degree in 2012–2013 were 6. The number of students enrolled full- and part-time who were dismissed or voluntarily withdrew from this program area in 2012–2013 were 0. *School Psychology PhD (Doctor of Philosophy)*—Applications 2012–2013, 20. Total applicants accepted 2012–2013, 7. Number full-time enrolled (new admits only) 2012–2013, 6. Number part-time enrolled (new admits only) 2012–2013, 0. Total enrolled 2012–2013 full-time, 27. Total enrolled 2012–2013 part-time, 6. Openings 2013–2014, 7. The median number of years required for completion of a degree in 2012–2013 were 4. The number of students enrolled full- and part-time who were dismissed or voluntarily withdrew from this program area in 2012–2013 were 0. *Counseling MA/ MS (Master of Arts/Science)*—Applications 2012–2013, 60. Total applicants accepted 2012–2013, 10. Number full-time enrolled (new admits only) 2012–2013, 9. Number part-time enrolled (new admits only) 2012–2013, 0. Total enrolled 2012–2013 full-time, 27. Total enrolled 2012–2013 part-time, 1. Openings 2013–2014, 10. The median number of years required for completion of a degree in 2012–2013 were 3. The number of students enrolled full- and part-time who were dismissed or voluntarily withdrew from this program area in 2012–2013 were 1. *School Psychology EdS (School Psychology)*— Applications 2012–2013, 21. Total applicants accepted 2012– 2013, 4. Number full-time enrolled (new admits only) 2012– 2013, 4. Number part-time enrolled (new admits only) 2012– 2013, 0. Total enrolled 2012–2013 full-time, 16. Total enrolled 2012–2013 part-time, 0. Openings 2013–2014, 15. The median number of years required for completion of a degree in 2012– 2013 were 3. The number of students enrolled full- and part-time who were dismissed or voluntarily withdrew from this program area in 2012–2013 were 0.

Scores: Entries appear in this order: required test or GPA, minimum score (if required), median score of students entering in 2012–2013. *Counseling Psychology PhD (Doctor of Philosophy):* GRE-V 153, GRE-Q 144, GRE-Analytical 3.5, 4.5, overall undergraduate GPA 3.5, 3.64, Masters GPA 3.5, 3.78; *School Psychology PhD (Doctor of Philosophy):* GRE-V 149, 149, GRE-Q 149, 149, GRE-Analytical 3.5, 3.5, overall undergraduate GPA 3.0, 3.54, last 2 years GPA 3.5, 3.6, psychology GPA 3.5, 3.6, Masters GPA 3.5, 3.85; *Counseling MA/MS (Master of Arts/Science):* GRE-V 153, GRE-Q 144, GRE-Analytical 4.0, overall undergraduate GPA 3.5, last 2 years GPA 3.0, psychology GPA 3.5; *School Psychology EdS (School Psychology):* GRE-V 360, 457, GRE-Q 380, 540, psychology GPA 2.5, 2.89.

Other Criteria: (importance of criteria rated low, medium, or high): GRE scores—medium, research experience—medium, work experience—high, extracurricular activity—medium, clinically related public service—medium, GPA—high, letters of recommendation—high, interview—high, statement of goals and objectives—high, writing skills—high. For additional information on admission requirements, go to http://www.twu.edu/psychology-philosophy/default.asp.

Student Characteristics: The following represents characteristics of students in 2012–2013 in all graduate psychology programs in the department: Female—full-time 102, part-time 10; Male—full-time 12, part-time 0; African American/Black—full-time 12, part-time 0; Hispanic/Latino(a)—full-time 10, part-time 1; Asian/Pacific Islander—full-time 8, part-time 1; American Indian/Alaska Native—full-time 1, part-time 0; Caucasian/White—full-time 90, part-time 2; Multi-ethnic—full-time 2, part-time 0; students subject to the Americans With Disabilities Act—full-time 2, part-time 0; Unknown ethnicity—full-time 0, part-time 0; International students who hold an F-1 or J-1 Visa—full-time 0, part-time 0.

Financial Information/Assistance:

Tuition for Full-Time Study: *Master's:* State residents: per academic year $6,722, $216 per credit hour; Nonstate residents: per academic year $17,603, $567 per credit hour. *Doctoral:* State residents: per academic year $6,722, $216 per credit hour; Nonstate residents: per academic year $17,603, $567 per credit hour. Tuition is subject to change. Additional fees are assessed to students beyond the costs of tuition for the following: Library fee, student union fee. See the following website for updates and changes in tuition costs: http://www.twu.edu/bursar/.

Financial Assistance:

First-Year Students: Teaching assistantships available for first year. Average amount paid per academic year: $11,808. Average number of hours worked per week: 20. Research assistantships available for first year.

Advanced Students: Teaching assistantships available for advanced students. Average amount paid per academic year: $11,808. Average number of hours worked per week: 20. Research assistantships available for advanced students.

Additional Information: Of all students currently enrolled full time, 20% benefited from one or more of the listed financial assistance programs. Application and information available online at: http://www.twu.edu/psychology-philosophy/program-costs.asp.

Internships/Practica: Doctoral Degree (PhD Counseling Psychology): For those doctoral students for whom a professional psychology internship was required in this program prior to graduation, (7) students applied for an internship in 2011–2012, with (7) students obtaining an internship. Of those students who obtained an internship, (7) were paid internships. Of those students who obtained an internship, (4) students placed in APA/CPA accredited internships, (3) students placed in internships not APA/CPA accredited, but listed with the Association of Psychology Postdoctoral and Internship Programs (APPIC), (0) students placed in internships conforming to guidelines of the Council of Directors of School Psychology Programs (CDSPP), (0) students placed in internships that were not APA/CPA accredited, APPIC or CDSPP listed. Doctoral Degree (PhD School Psychology): For those doctoral students for whom a professional psychology internship was required in this program prior to graduation, (4) students applied for an internship in 2011–2012, with (4) students

obtaining an internship. Of those students who obtained an internship, (4) were paid internships. Of those students who obtained an internship, (2) students placed in APA/CPA accredited internships, (0) students placed in internships not APA/CPA accredited, but listed with the Association of Psychology Postdoctoral and Internship Programs (APPIC), (2) students placed in internships conforming to guidelines of the Council of Directors of School Psychology Programs (CDSPP), (0) students placed in internships that were not APA/CPA accredited, APPIC or CDSPP listed. Master's Degree (MA/MS Counseling): An internship experience, such as a final research project or "capstone" experience is required of graduates. There are numerous placements in the Dallas-Fort Worth metropolitan area. Doctoral students are expected to use the APPIC Directory for internship placement.

Housing and Day Care: On-campus housing is available. See the following website for more information: http://www.twu.edu/housing/. No on-campus day care facilities are available.

Employment of Department Graduates:

Master's Degree Graduates: Of those who graduated in the academic year 2011–2012, the following categories and numbers represent the postgraduate activities and employment of master's degree graduates: Enrolled in a psychology doctoral program (0), enrolled in another graduate/professional program (0), enrolled in a postdoctoral residency/fellowship (n/a), employed in independent practice (n/a), employed in an academic position at a university (0), employed in other positions at a higher education institution (1), employed in a professional position in a school system (7), employed in a community mental health/counseling center (8), employed in a hospital/medical center (1), not seeking employment (1), do not know (0), total from the above (master's) (18).

Doctoral Degree Graduates: Of those who graduated in the academic year 2011–2012, the following categories and numbers represent the postgraduate activities and employment of doctoral degree graduates: Enrolled in a psychology doctoral program (n/a), enrolled in another graduate/professional program (0), enrolled in a postdoctoral residency/fellowship (0), employed in independent practice (4), employed in an academic position at a university (0), employed in an academic position at a 2-year/4-year college (1), employed in other positions at a higher education institution (3), employed in a professional position in a school system (4), employed in business or industry (0), employed in government agency (1), employed in a community mental health/counseling center (1), employed in a hospital/medical center (0), still seeking employment (0), not seeking employment (0), other employment position (0), do not know (0), total from the above (doctoral) (14).

Additional Information:

Orientation, Objectives, and Emphasis of Department: Both the APA-accredited Counseling Psychology doctoral program and the Counseling Psychology master's program prepare students in the practitioner-scientist model for counseling practice with particular emphasis on family systems, gender issues, assessment, and psychotherapeutic work with individuals and families in their contextual systems. The model provides clear training in both practice and science, but emphasizes practice, practice that is informed by science. The programs' philosophy, curricula, faculty, and students, situated within the unique context of the TWU mission, attempt to create an atmosphere that is supportive, open, and flexible. Graduate training in school psychology at the master's level provides a program emphasizing direct service to school settings. Specific competencies and areas of specialization stressed in coursework and field-based training include child development, psychopathology, theories and principles of learning, behavioral intervention and prevention strategies, diagnostic assessment, and evaluation techniques. The APA-accredited school psychology doctoral program focuses on applied preparation and training experiences in professional school psychology. It prepares students in skills required in direct-to-client services (for example, diagnostic assessment and evaluation skills, therapeutic and intervention techniques, and competencies in the application of learning principles). This program also provides training and supervised experiences in the consultation model, emphasizing such competencies as systems and organizational analysis, supervision of programs and services, diagnostic team leadership, grant proposal writing, in-service education, and general coordination of school-based services in a consultative capacity.

Special Facilities or Resources: The University Counseling Center is an APA-approved internship site.

Information for Students With Physical Disabilities: See the following website for more information: http://www.twu.edu/dss/.

Application Information:
Send to Admissions Coordinator, Department of Psychology and Philosophy, Texas Woman's University, P.O. Box 425470, Denton, TX 76204-5470. Application available online. URL of online application: http://www.twu.edu/admissions/graduate.asp. Students are admitted in the Fall, application deadline December 15. December 15 for PhD Counseling Program, February 1 for all other programs. *Fee:* $50.

Texas, University of, Arlington
Department of Psychology
College of Science
Department of Psychology, UTA Box 19528
Arlington, TX 76019-0528
Telephone: (817) 272-2281
Fax: (817) 272-2364
E-mail: *fuchs@uta.edu*
Web: *http://www.uta.edu/psychology*

Department Information:
1959. Interim Chair: Perry Fuchs. Number of faculty: total—full-time 18, part-time 1; women—full-time 8; total—minority—full-time 5; women minority—full-time 3.

Programs and Degrees Offered:
Listed in the following order: Program area, degree type (T if terminal Master's), number awarded 7/11–6/12. Industrial/Organizational Psychology MA/MS (Master of Arts/Science) (T) 5, Health Psychology PhD (Doctor of Philosophy) 3, Experimental Psychology PhD (Doctor of Philosophy) 1.

Student Applications/Admissions:
Student Applications
Industrial/Organizational Psychology MA/MS (Master of Arts/Science)—Applications 2012–2013, 46. Total applicants ac-

cepted 2012–2013, 15. Number full-time enrolled (new admits only) 2012–2013, 15. Number part-time enrolled (new admits only) 2012–2013, 0. Total enrolled 2012–2013 full-time, 24. Total enrolled 2012–2013 part-time, 1. Openings 2013–2014, 12. The median number of years required for completion of a degree in 2012–2013 were 3. The number of students enrolled full- and part-time who were dismissed or voluntarily withdrew from this program area in 2012–2013 were 3. *Health Psychology PhD (Doctor of Philosophy)*—Applications 2012–2013, 36. Total applicants accepted 2012–2013, 7. Number full-time enrolled (new admits only) 2012–2013, 6. Number part-time enrolled (new admits only) 2012–2013, 0. Total enrolled 2012–2013 full-time, 25. Total enrolled 2012–2013 part-time, 2. Openings 2013–2014, 5. The median number of years required for completion of a degree in 2012–2013 were 6. The number of students enrolled full- and part-time who were dismissed or voluntarily withdrew from this program area in 2012–2013 were 2. *Experimental Psychology PhD (Doctor of Philosophy)*—Applications 2012–2013, 38. Total applicants accepted 2012–2013, 0. Number full-time enrolled (new admits only) 2012–2013, 0. Number part-time enrolled (new admits only) 2012–2013, 0. Total enrolled 2012–2013 full-time, 18. Total enrolled 2012–2013 part-time, 7. Openings 2013–2014, 4. The median number of years required for completion of a degree in 2012–2013 were 6. The number of students enrolled full- and part-time who were dismissed or voluntarily withdrew from this program area in 2012–2013 were 1.

Scores: Entries appear in this order: required test or GPA, minimum score (if required), median score of students entering in 2012–2013. *Industrial/Organizational Psychology MA/MS (Master of Arts/Science):* GRE-V no minimum stated, 152, GRE-Q no minimum stated, 153, GRE-Analytical no minimum stated, 3.57, overall undergraduate GPA no minimum stated, 3.53; *Health Psychology PhD (Doctor of Philosophy):* GRE-V no minimum stated, 157, GRE-Q no minimum stated, 151, GRE-Analytical no minimum stated, 3.9, overall undergraduate GPA no minimum stated, 3.56; *Experimental Psychology PhD (Doctor of Philosophy):* GRE-V no minimum stated, GRE-Q no minimum stated, GRE-Analytical no minimum stated, overall undergraduate GPA no minimum stated.

Other Criteria: (importance of criteria rated low, medium, or high): GRE scores—medium, research experience—high, extracurricular activity—low, clinically related public service—low, GPA—medium, letters of recommendation—high, statement of goals and objectives—high, undergraduate major in psychology—low, specific undergraduate psychology courses taken—medium. For additional information on admission requirements, go to http://www.uta.edu/psychology/Admissions.html.

Student Characteristics: The following represents characteristics of students in 2012–2013 in all graduate psychology programs in the department: Female—full-time 45, part-time 8; Male—full-time 24, part-time 1; African American/Black—full-time 3, part-time 1; Hispanic/Latino(a)—full-time 1, part-time 0; Asian/Pacific Islander—full-time 8, part-time 0; American Indian/Alaska Native—full-time 1, part-time 0; Caucasian/White—full-time 45, part-time 6; Multi-ethnic—full-time 0, part-time 0; students subject to the Americans With Disabilities Act—full-time 0, part-time 0; Unknown ethnicity—full-time 11, part-time 2; International students who hold an F-1 or J-1 Visa—full-time 12, part-time 0.

Financial Information/Assistance:

Tuition for Full-Time Study: *Master's:* State residents: per academic year $8,000; Nonstate residents: per academic year $16,370. *Doctoral:* State residents: per academic year $8,000; Nonstate residents: per academic year $16,370. Tuition is subject to change. See the following website for updates and changes in tuition costs: http://policy.uta.edu/UtaSfs/Application?cmd=feedescr.

Financial Assistance:

First-Year Students: Teaching assistantships available for first year. Average amount paid per academic year: $18,000. Average number of hours worked per week: 20. Research assistantships available for first year. Average amount paid per academic year: $18,000. Average number of hours worked per week: 20. Fellowships and scholarships available for first year. Average amount paid per academic year: $1,000.

Advanced Students: Teaching assistantships available for advanced students. Average amount paid per academic year: $18,000. Average number of hours worked per week: 20. Research assistantships available for advanced students. Average amount paid per academic year: $18,000. Average number of hours worked per week: 20. Fellowships and scholarships available for advanced students. Average amount paid per academic year: $1,000.

Additional Information: Of all students currently enrolled full time, 53% benefited from one or more of the listed financial assistance programs. Application and information available online at: http://grad.pci.uta.edu/students/finances/.

Internships/Practica: Master's Degree (MA/MS Industrial/Organizational Psychology): An internship experience, such as a final research project or "capstone" experience is required of graduates. The Arlington-Dallas-Fort Worth area is a major center of business and industrial growth in Texas and offers diverse practical opportunities in consulting firms, corporations, government and private agencies, as well as health and health care agencies, social agencies and the like.

Housing and Day Care: On-campus housing is available. See the following website for more information: http://www.uta.edu/housing/. On-campus day care facilities are available. See the following website for more information: http://www.ywcafortworth.com/web/our-programs/early-childhood-programs/child-development-programs/arlington-child-development-center/.

Employment of Department Graduates:

Master's Degree Graduates: Of those who graduated in the academic year 2011–2012, the following categories and numbers represent the postgraduate activities and employment of master's degree graduates: Enrolled in a postdoctoral residency/fellowship (n/a), employed in independent practice (n/a), total from the above (master's) (0).

Doctoral Degree Graduates: Of those who graduated in the academic year 2011–2012, the following categories and numbers represent the postgraduate activities and employment of doctoral degree graduates: Enrolled in a psychology doctoral program (n/a), employed in other positions at a higher education institution (2), employed in business or industry (3), employed in a hospital/medical center (1), do not know (3), total from the above (doctoral) (9).

Additional Information:

Orientation, Objectives, and Emphasis of Department: The objective of graduate work in psychology is to educate the student in the methods and basic content of the discipline and to provide an apprenticeship in the execution of creative research in laboratory and/or field settings. The graduate programs provide comprehensive interdisciplinary training in Experimental Psychology, Health Psychology/Neuroscience, and Industrial/Organizational Psychology. All students in the graduate program are broadly trained in statistical and experimental design. The concentration in Experimental Psychology is designed to form a basis for the doctoral program but is open to those seeking a terminal master's degree. The experimental program trains students to be research scientists in areas of interest that include animal behavior, animal learning, cognitive, developmental, evolutionary, neuroscience, quantitative, and social/personality psychology. The concentration in Health Psychology/Neuroscience is designed to train researchers in health and behavior, working at the cutting edge of interdisciplinary, biomedical, and biobehavioral investigation in areas such as pain, stress, psychoimmunology, cancer, and aging. The Master of Science in Industrial/Organizational Psychology combines rigorous course work in experimental design, quantitative methods, and management with practicum experience enabling students to perform effectively in the workplace.

Special Facilities or Resources: Each faculty member who is active in research in the Psychology Department is fortunate to have ample space. The department has approximately 18,000 total square feet of research space; 7,000 square feet for human subject research and 11,000 square feet for animal research. Graduate students work in faculty labs and use their research facilities. The department is able to utilize modern audiovisual technology in the classroom and is equipped with computer facilities for graduate research. Graduate students have in-office network connections as well as computer access in research laboratories and departmental computer labs. In addition to the departmental computer labs, OIT provides students with access to over 500 computers in 9 computer labs across campus. Each computer lab is equipped with high-end PC and/or Macintosh computers, an abundant array of office and general productivity software, as well as discipline specific software, laser printing, and broadband Internet access. The University Libraries include the Central Library, the Architecture and Fine Arts Library, and the Science and Engineering Library. Library resources include a full array of modern technological access to print electronic information, Internet access and an extensive interlibrary loan network in addition to the 2,430,000 books, periodicals, documents, technical reports, etc. on hand.

Information for Students With Physical Disabilities: See the following website for more information: http://www.uta.edu/disability/.

Application Information:

Send to Department of Psychology, Box 19528, The University of Texas at Arlington, Arlington, TX 76019-0528. Application available online. URL of online application: http://grad.pci.uta.edu/prospective/apply/howto/. Students are admitted in the Fall, application deadline February 1. *Fee:* $40. Application fee for international students is $70.

Texas, University of, Austin
Department of Educational Psychology
College of Education
1912 Speedway, Stop D5800
Austin, TX 78712-1296
Telephone: (512) 471-4155
Fax: (512) 471-1288
E-mail: *vstockwell@austin.utexas.edu*
Web: *http://www.edb.utexas.edu/education/departments/edp/*

Department Information:

1923. Chairperson: Cindy I. Carlson. Number of faculty: total—full-time 26, part-time 4; women—full-time 17, part-time 1; total—minority—full-time 5, part-time 2; women minority—full-time 4; faculty subject to the Americans With Disabilities Act 1.

Programs and Degrees Offered:

Listed in the following order: Program area, degree type (T if terminal Master's), number awarded 7/11–6/12. Counseling Psychology PhD (Doctor of Philosophy) 7, Quantitative Methods PhD (Doctor of Philosophy) 2, School Psychology PhD (Doctor of Philosophy) 8, Ma/Med - Human Dev., Culture, & Learning Sciences Other 4, Ma/Med - Counselor Education Other 9, Ma/Med - Quantitative Methods Other 3, Human Development, Culture, & Learning Sciences PhD (Doctor of Philosophy) 11.

APA Accreditation: Counseling PhD (Doctor of Philosophy). Student Outcome Data Website: http://www.edb.utexas.edu/education/departments/edp/doctoral/cp/about/apa_statistics/. School PhD (Doctor of Philosophy). Student Outcome Data Website: http://www.edb.utexas.edu/education/departments/edp/doctoral/sp/about/apa_stats/.

Student Applications/Admissions:

Student Applications

Counseling Psychology PhD (Doctor of Philosophy)—Applications 2012–2013, 164. Total applicants accepted 2012–2013, 11. Number full-time enrolled (new admits only) 2012–2013, 5. Number part-time enrolled (new admits only) 2012–2013, 0. Total enrolled 2012–2013 full-time, 33. Total enrolled 2012–2013 part-time, 19. Openings 2013–2014, 10. The median number of years required for completion of a degree in 2012–2013 were 6. The number of students enrolled full- and part-time who were dismissed or voluntarily withdrew from this program area in 2012–2013 were 2. *Quantitative Methods PhD (Doctor of Philosophy)*—Applications 2012–2013, 16. Total applicants accepted 2012–2013, 7. Number full-time enrolled (new admits only) 2012–2013, 2. Number part-time enrolled (new admits only) 2012–2013, 0. Total enrolled 2012–2013 full-time, 19. Total enrolled 2012–2013 part-time, 3. Openings 2013–2014, 10. The median number of years required for completion of a degree in 2012–2013 were 4. The number of students enrolled full- and part-time who were dismissed or voluntarily withdrew from this program area in 2012–2013 were 0. *School Psychology PhD (Doctor of Philosophy)*—Applications 2012–2013, 58. Total applicants accepted 2012–2013, 13. Number full-time enrolled (new admits only) 2012–2013, 8. Number part-time enrolled (new admits only) 2012–2013, 0.

Total enrolled 2012–2013 full-time, 43. Total enrolled 2012–2013 part-time, 14. Openings 2013–2014, 10. The median number of years required for completion of a degree in 2012–2013 were 6. The number of students enrolled full- and part-time who were dismissed or voluntarily withdrew from this program area in 2012–2013 were 1. *Ma/Med - Human Dev., Culture, & Learning Sciences*—Applications 2012–2013, 45. Total applicants accepted 2012–2013, 30. Number full-time enrolled (new admits only) 2012–2013, 8. Number part-time enrolled (new admits only) 2012–2013, 1. Total enrolled 2012–2013 full-time, 12. Total enrolled 2012–2013 part-time, 3. Openings 2013–2014, 15. The median number of years required for completion of a degree in 2012–2013 were 2. The number of students enrolled full- and part-time who were dismissed or voluntarily withdrew from this program area in 2012–2013 were 0. *Ma/Med - Counselor Education*—Applications 2012–2013, 48. Total applicants accepted 2012–2013, 27. Number full-time enrolled (new admits only) 2012–2013, 18. Number part-time enrolled (new admits only) 2012–2013, 3. Total enrolled 2012–2013 full-time, 30. Total enrolled 2012–2013 part-time, 11. Openings 2013–2014, 25. The median number of years required for completion of a degree in 2012–2013 was 1. The number of students enrolled full- and part-time who were dismissed or voluntarily withdrew from this program area in 2012–2013 were 0. *Ma/Med - Quantitative Methods*—Applications 2012–2013, 20. Total applicants accepted 2012–2013, 16. Number full-time enrolled (new admits only) 2012–2013, 11. Number part-time enrolled (new admits only) 2012–2013, 1. Total enrolled 2012–2013 full-time, 14. Total enrolled 2012–2013 part-time, 1. Openings 2013–2014, 20. The median number of years required for completion of a degree in 2012–2013 were 2. The number of students enrolled full- and part-time who were dismissed or voluntarily withdrew from this program area in 2012–2013 were 0. *Human Development, Culture, & Learning Sciences PhD (Doctor of Philosophy)*—Applications 2012–2013, 41. Total applicants accepted 2012–2013, 14. Number full-time enrolled (new admits only) 2012–2013, 9. Number part-time enrolled (new admits only) 2012–2013, 0. Total enrolled 2012–2013 full-time, 35. Total enrolled 2012–2013 part-time, 8. Openings 2013–2014, 7. The median number of years required for completion of a degree in 2012–2013 were 6. The number of students enrolled full- and part-time who were dismissed or voluntarily withdrew from this program area in 2012–2013 were 0.

Scores: Entries appear in this order: required test or GPA, minimum score (if required), median score of students entering in 2012–2013. *Counseling Psychology PhD (Doctor of Philosophy):* GRE-V no minimum stated, 680, GRE-Q no minimum stated, 670, GRE-Analytical no minimum stated, 5, last 2 years GPA no minimum stated, 3.82; *Quantitative Methods PhD (Doctor of Philosophy):* GRE-V no minimum stated, 535, GRE-Q no minimum stated, 763, GRE-Analytical no minimum stated, 3.5, last 2 years GPA no minimum stated, 3.63; *School Psychology PhD (Doctor of Philosophy):* GRE-V no minimum stated, 598, GRE-Q no minimum stated, 730, GRE-Analytical no minimum stated, 4, last 2 years GPA no minimum stated, 3.63; *MA/MEd - Human Dev., Culture, & Learning Sciences Other:* GRE-V no minimum stated, 590, GRE-Q no minimum stated, 705, GRE-Analytical no minimum stated, 4, last 2 years GPA no minimum stated, 3.65; *MA/MEd - Counselor Education:* GRE-V no minimum stated, 465, GRE-Q no minimum stated, 630, GRE-Analytical no minimum stated, 4.0, last 2 years GPA no minimum stated, 3.64; MA/ MEd - *Quantitative Methods*: GRE-V no minimum stated, 523, GRE-Q no minimum stated, 740, GRE-Analytical no minimum stated, 3, last 2 years GPA no minimum stated, 3.17; *Human Development, Culture, & Learning Sciences PhD (Doctor of Philosophy)*: GRE-V no minimum stated, 610, GRE-Q no minimum stated, 720, GRE-Analytical no minimum stated, 4, last 2 years GPA no minimum stated, 3.70.

Other Criteria: (importance of criteria rated low, medium, or high): GRE scores—high, research experience—medium, work experience—medium, extracurricular activity—medium, clinically related public service—medium, GPA—high, letters of recommendation—high, interview—medium, statement of goals and objectives—high, undergraduate major in psychology—low, specific undergraduate psychology courses taken— low, Different areas may consider criteria somewhat differently. For additional information on admission requirements, go to http://www.edb.utexas.edu/education/departments/edp/ prospective/.

Student Characteristics: The following represents characteristics of students in 2012–2013 in all graduate psychology programs in the department: Female—full-time 140, part-time 47; Male—full-time 46, part-time 12; African American/Black—full-time 15, part-time 1; Hispanic/Latino(a)—full-time 23, part-time 8; Asian/ Pacific Islander—full-time 19, part-time 6; American Indian/ Alaska Native—full-time 2, part-time 1; Caucasian/White—full-time 124, part-time 29; Multi-ethnic—full-time 0, part-time 0; students subject to the Americans With Disabilities Act—full-time 2, part-time 0; Unknown ethnicity—full-time 0, part-time 0; International students who hold an F-1 or J-1 Visa—full-time 13, part-time 2.

Financial Information/Assistance:

Tuition for Full-Time Study: *Master's*: State residents: $467 per credit hour; Nonstate residents: $908 per credit hour. *Doctoral*: State residents: $467 per credit hour; Nonstate residents: $908 per credit hour. Tuition is subject to change. See the following website for updates and changes in tuition costs: http://www. utexas.edu/business/accounting/sar/t_f_rates.html.

Financial Assistance:

First-Year Students: Teaching assistantships available for first year. Average amount paid per academic year: $12,849. Average number of hours worked per week: 20. Apply by April 1. Research assistantships available for first year. Average amount paid per academic year: $14,000. Average number of hours worked per week: 20. Apply by April 1. Fellowships and scholarships available for first year. Average amount paid per academic year: $1,500. Average number of hours worked per week: 0. Apply by December 1.

Advanced Students: Teaching assistantships available for advanced students. Average amount paid per academic year: $12,849. Average number of hours worked per week: 20. Apply by April 1. Research assistantships available for advanced students. Average amount paid per academic year: $14,000. Average number of hours worked per week: 20. Apply by April 1. Fellowships and scholarships available for advanced students. Average amount paid per academic year: $1,500. Average number of hours worked per week: 0. Apply by December 1.

Additional Information: Of all students currently enrolled full time, 70% benefited from one or more of the listed financial assistance programs. Application and information available online at: http://www.edb.utexas.edu/education/departments/edp/admissions/financial/.

Internships/Practica: Doctoral Degree (PhD Counseling Psychology): For those doctoral students for whom a professional psychology internship was required in this program prior to graduation, (8) students applied for an internship in 2011–2012, with (8) students obtaining an internship. Of those students who obtained an internship, (8) were paid internships. Of those students who obtained an internship, (7) students placed in APA/CPA accredited internships, (0) students placed in internships not APA/ CPA accredited, but listed with the Association of Psychology Postdoctoral and Internship Programs (APPIC), (0) students placed in internships conforming to guidelines of the Council of Directors of School Psychology Programs (CDSPP), (1) students placed in internships that were not APA/CPA accredited, APPIC or CDSPP listed. Doctoral Degree (PhD School Psychology): For those doctoral students for whom a professional psychology internship was required in this program prior to graduation, (7) students applied for an internship in 2011–2012, with (7) students obtaining an internship. Of those students who obtained an internship, (7) were paid internships. Of those students who obtained an internship, (7) students placed in APA/CPA accredited internships, (0) students placed in internships not APA/CPA accredited, but listed with the Association of Psychology Postdoctoral and Internship Programs (APPIC), (0) students placed in internships conforming to guidelines of the Council of Directors of School Psychology Programs (CDSPP), (0) students placed in internships that were not APA/CPA accredited, APPIC or CDSPP listed. Master's Degree (MA/MEd - Human Dev., Culture, & Learning Sciences): An internship experience, such as a final research project or "capstone" experience is required of graduates. In the Counseling Psychology program, internships are generally available in APA-approved counseling and mental health centers, other university counseling centers, and community/hospital settings that provide in-depth supervision. In the School Psychology program, internship sites are often in APA-approved school systems and hospital/community settings that have an educational component. Other programs coordinate a variety of practicum settings to provide both research and applied experiences.

Housing and Day Care: On-campus housing is available. See the following website for more information: http://www.utexas.edu/ student/housing/. On-campus day care facilities are available. See the following website for more information: http://www.utexas. edu/childcenter/.

Employment of Department Graduates:

Master's Degree Graduates: Of those who graduated in the academic year 2011–2012, the following categories and numbers represent the postgraduate activities and employment of master's degree graduates: Enrolled in a psychology doctoral program (4), enrolled in another graduate/professional program (1), enrolled in a postdoctoral residency/fellowship (n/a), employed in independent practice (n/a), employed in other positions at a higher education institution (2), employed in a professional position in a school system (3), employed in business or industry (1), employed in a community mental health/counseling center (1), still seeking employment (1), other employment position (2), do not know (1), total from the above (master's) (16).

Doctoral Degree Graduates: Of those who graduated in the academic year 2011–2012, the following categories and numbers represent the postgraduate activities and employment of doctoral degree graduates: Enrolled in a psychology doctoral program (n/a), enrolled in a postdoctoral residency/fellowship (15), employed in independent practice (1), employed in an academic position at a university (3), employed in an academic position at a 2-year/4-year college (1), employed in other positions at a higher education institution (3), employed in a professional position in a school system (1), employed in business or industry (1), employed in a community mental health/counseling center (2), other employment position (1), total from the above (doctoral) (28).

Additional Information:

Orientation, Objectives, and Emphasis of Department: Training in educational psychology relates human behavior to the educational process as it occurs in the home, in peer groups, in nursery school through graduate school, in business and industry, in the military, in institutions for persons with physical or mental disabilities, and in myriad other settings. In so doing, it includes study in the following areas: the biological bases of behavior; history and systems of psychology and of education; the psychology of learning, motivation, cognition, and instruction; developmental, social, and personality psychology; psychological and educational measurement, statistics, evaluation, and research methodology; the professional areas of school psychology and counseling psychology; and general academic educational psychology.

Special Facilities or Resources: The University of Texas at Austin has the fifth largest academic library in the United States and also provides online access to hundreds of electronic databases. Our department also has access, through our college's Learning Technology Center, to several microcomputer and multimedia laboratories, technical assistance, resource materials, and audiovisual equipment and services. Academic computing facilities are extensive, ranging from mainframes to microcomputers. Additional resources include several university-wide centers with which our faculty are associated, including UT's Counseling and Mental Health Center.

Information for Students With Physical Disabilities: See the following website for more information: http://ddce.utexas.edu/disability/.

Application Information:
Application available online. URL of online application: http://www.utexas.edu/ogs/admissions/howtous.html. Students are admitted in the Fall, application deadline December 1; Summer, application deadline February 10. The deadline for Counseling Psychology and School Psychology is December 1. The priority deadline for other PhD areas is January 10 (although students who want to be considered for fellowships should have completed applications by January 1). The priority deadline for the master's specializations is February 10 for summer or fall admissions. Fee: $65. Fee may be waived, at the discretion of Graduate Admissions (GIAC), in cases of demonstrated financial need.

Texas, University of, Austin
Department of Human Development and Family Sciences
College of Natural Sciences
108 East Dean Keeton Street, Stop A2702
Austin, TX 78712-0141
Telephone: (512) 475-8065
Fax: (512) 475-8662
E-mail: he-hdfgrad@utlists.utexas.edu
Web: http://he.utexas.edu/hdfs/graduate-program

Department Information:
1962. Chairperson: Deborah Jacobvitz, PhD. Number of faculty: total—full-time 14; women—full-time 10; total—minority—full-time 1; women minority—full-time 1.

Programs and Degrees Offered:
Listed in the following order: Program area, degree type (T if terminal Master's), number awarded 7/11–6/12. Human Development & Family Sciences PhD (Doctor of Philosophy) 7.

Student Applications/Admissions:
Student Applications

Human Development & Family Sciences PhD (Doctor of Philosophy)—Applications 2012–2013, 32. Total applicants accepted 2012–2013, 9. Number full-time enrolled (new admits only) 2012–2013, 5. Total enrolled 2012–2013 full-time, 34. Total enrolled 2012–2013 part-time, 2. Openings 2013–2014, 10. The median number of years required for completion of a degree in 2012–2013 were 5. The number of students enrolled full- and part-time who were dismissed or voluntarily withdrew from this program area in 2012–2013 were 1.

Scores: Entries appear in this order: required test or GPA, minimum score (if required), median score of students entering in 2012–2013. Human Development & Family Sciences PhD (Doctor of Philosophy): GRE-V no minimum stated, GRE-Q no minimum stated, GRE-Analytical no minimum stated, overall undergraduate GPA no minimum stated, last 2 years GPA 3.0, Masters GPA no minimum stated.

Other Criteria: (importance of criteria rated low, medium, or high): GRE scores—high, research experience—high, work experience—low, extracurricular activity—low, clinically related public service—medium, GPA—high, letters of recommendation—high, interview—high, statement of goals and objectives—high, undergraduate major in psychology—low, specific undergraduate psychology courses taken—low. For additional information on admission requirements, go to http://he.utexas.edu/hdfs/graduate-program/application-process.

Student Characteristics: The following represents characteristics of students in 2012–2013 in all graduate psychology programs in the department: Female—full-time 27, part-time 1; Male—full-time 7, part-time 1; African American/Black—full-time 1, part-time 0; Hispanic/Latino(a)—full-time 1, part-time 0; Asian/Pacific Islander—full-time 7, part-time 1; American Indian/Alaska Native—full-time 0, part-time 0; Caucasian/White—full-time 25, part-time 1; Multi-ethnic—full-time 0, part-time 0; students subject to the Americans With Disabilities Act—full-time 0, part-

time 0; Unknown ethnicity—full-time 0, part-time 0; International students who hold an F-1 or J-1 Visa—full-time 10, part-time 1.

Financial Information/Assistance:

Tuition for Full-Time Study: *Doctoral:* State residents: per academic year $8,350; Nonstate residents: per academic year $16,454. Tuition is subject to change. See the following website for updates and changes in tuition costs: http://www.utexas.edu/tuition/costs.html.

Financial Assistance:

First-Year Students: Teaching assistantships available for first year. Average amount paid per academic year: $16,550. Average number of hours worked per week: 20. Apply by December 1. Research assistantships available for first year. Average amount paid per academic year: $16,718. Average number of hours worked per week: 20. Apply by December 1. Fellowships and scholarships available for first year. Average amount paid per academic year: $18,000. Average number of hours worked per week: 20. Apply by December 1.

Advanced Students: Teaching assistantships available for advanced students. Average amount paid per academic year: $17,610. Average number of hours worked per week: 20. Apply by December 1. Research assistantships available for advanced students. Average amount paid per academic year: $17,788. Average number of hours worked per week: 20. Apply by December 1. Fellowships and scholarships available for advanced students. Average amount paid per academic year: $18,000. Average number of hours worked per week: 20. Apply by December 1.

Additional Information: Of all students currently enrolled full time, 94% benefited from one or more of the listed financial assistance programs. Application and information available online at: http://he.utexas.edu/hdfs/graduate-program/departmental-support.

Housing and Day Care: On-campus housing is available. See the following website for more information: http://www.utexas.edu/student/housing/index.php. On-campus day care facilities are available. See the following website for more information: http://www.utexas.edu/childcenter/.

Employment of Department Graduates:

Master's Degree Graduates: Of those who graduated in the academic year 2011–2012, the following categories and numbers represent the postgraduate activities and employment of master's degree graduates: Enrolled in a postdoctoral residency/fellowship (n/a), employed in independent practice (n/a), total from the above (master's) (0).

Doctoral Degree Graduates: Of those who graduated in the academic year 2011–2012, the following categories and numbers represent the postgraduate activities and employment of doctoral degree graduates: Enrolled in a psychology doctoral program (n/a), employed in an academic position at a university (2), employed in other positions at a higher education institution (1), employed in business or industry (4), total from the above (doctoral) (7).

Additional Information:

Orientation, Objectives, and Emphasis of Department: The program leading to the PhD in Human Development and Family Sciences is designed to prepare individuals for research, teaching, and administrative positions in colleges and universities and for positions in research, government, and other public and private settings. The focus of the program is research concerning the interplay between individual development and family relationships. Development of the individual is considered within the context of the family, peer group, community, and culture. The family is studied as a system of relationships, with attention given to roles, communication, conflict resolution and negotiation, socialization, and family members' perceptions and emotions during interactions with one another. The program emphasizes the investigation of the family and other social processes that contribute to competence and optimal development in individuals from birth to maturity and on how such competencies, once developed, are reflected in interpersonal relationships and family interactions.

Special Facilities or Resources: The graduate program is housed in the Sarah and Charles Seay building, supporting wireless internet service with access to the university's extensive library collection and statistical software packages, and a computer lab reserved for graduate student research. The Seay building contains a number of facilities for data collection, including five rooms in which children, couples, or families can be observed unobtrusively behind a one-way mirror in an observation booth. In addition to the departmental resources, the multicultural population of Austin constitutes a rich resource for both research and practicum experiences. The library, computation center, and support services of the University of Texas at Austin are among the best in the nation. Free services available to students include the Learning Skills Center, Career Choice Information Center, and Counseling Center. The Priscilla Pond Flawn Child and Family Laboratory at The University of Texas at Austin is a part of the Department of Human Development and Family Sciences (HDFS) in the School of Human Ecology. Licensed by the State of Texas and accredited by the National Association for the Education of Young Children (NAEYC), the Child and Family Laboratory provides a high quality early childhood experience to children ages 18 months through 6 years of age. In partnership with HDFS, the Child and Family Laboratory provides educational and training opportunities for our University students through observation and interaction in the classrooms and supports research in human development and family relationships. We also serve as a model of best practice in early care and child growth and development through advocacy and outreach.

Information for Students With Physical Disabilities: See the following website for more information: http://ddce.utexas.edu/disability/.

Application Information:

Send to Graduate Coordinator, The University of Texas at Austin, Department of Human Development and Family Sciences, 108 East Dean Keeton Street, Stop A2702, Austin, TX 78712. Application available online. URL of online application: http://www.utexas.edu/ogs/admissions/howtous.html. Students are admitted in the Fall, application deadline December 1. *Fee:* $50.

Texas, University of, Austin

Department of Psychology
College of Liberal Arts
108 East Dean Keeton, A8000
Austin, TX 78712
Telephone: (512) 471-6398
Fax: (512) 471-0760
E-mail: *kterry@austin.utexas.edu*
Web: *http://www.utexas.edu/cola/depts/psychology/*

Department Information:

1910. Chairperson: James Pennebaker. Number of faculty: total—full-time 52; women—full-time 22; total—minority—full-time 7; women minority—full-time 3.

Programs and Degrees Offered:

Listed in the following order: Program area, degree type (T if terminal Master's), number awarded 7/11–6/12. Behavioral Neuroscience PhD (Doctor of Philosophy) 1, Clinical Psychology PhD (Doctor of Philosophy) 5, Developmental Psychology PhD (Doctor of Philosophy) 2, Individual Differences and Evolutionary Psychology PhD (Doctor of Philosophy) 2, Social and Personality Psychology PhD (Doctor of Philosophy) 6, Cognitive Systems PhD (Doctor of Philosophy) 3, Perceptual Systems PhD (Doctor of Philosophy) 2.

APA Accreditation: Clinical PhD (Doctor of Philosophy). Student Outcome Data Website: http://www.utexas.edu/cola/depts/psychology/areas-of-study/clinical/statistics.php.

Student Applications/Admissions:

Student Applications

Behavioral Neuroscience PhD (Doctor of Philosophy)—Applications 2012–2013, 45. Total applicants accepted 2012–2013, 7. Number full-time enrolled (new admits only) 2012–2013, 4. Total enrolled 2012–2013 full-time, 18. Total enrolled 2012–2013 part-time, 0. Openings 2013–2014, 3. The median number of years required for completion of a degree in 2012–2013 were 6. The number of students enrolled full- and part-time who were dismissed or voluntarily withdrew from this program area in 2012–2013 were 0. *Clinical Psychology PhD (Doctor of Philosophy)*—Applications 2012–2013, 293. Total applicants accepted 2012–2013, 12. Number full-time enrolled (new admits only) 2012–2013, 6. Total enrolled 2012–2013 full-time, 27. Total enrolled 2012–2013 part-time, 0. Openings 2013–2014, 10. The median number of years required for completion of a degree in 2012–2013 were 6. The number of students enrolled full- and part-time who were dismissed or voluntarily withdrew from this program area in 2012–2013 were 0. *Developmental Psychology PhD (Doctor of Philosophy)*—Applications 2012–2013, 35. Total applicants accepted 2012–2013, 3. Number full-time enrolled (new admits only) 2012–2013, 1. Total enrolled 2012–2013 full-time, 12. Total enrolled 2012–2013 part-time, 0. Openings 2013–2014, 4. The median number of years required for completion of a degree in 2012–2013 were 6. The number of students enrolled full- and part-time who were dismissed or voluntarily withdrew from this program area in 2012–2013 were 0. *Individual Differences and Evolutionary Psychology PhD (Doctor of Philosophy)*—Applications 2012–2013, 20. Total applicants accepted 2012–2013,

0. Number full-time enrolled (new admits only) 2012–2013, 0. Total enrolled 2012–2013 full-time, 6. Total enrolled 2012–2013 part-time, 0. The median number of years required for completion of a degree in 2012–2013 were 6. The number of students enrolled full- and part-time who were dismissed or voluntarily withdrew from this program area in 2012–2013 were 0. *Social and Personality Psychology PhD (Doctor of Philosophy)*—Applications 2012–2013, 131. Total applicants accepted 2012–2013, 10. Number full-time enrolled (new admits only) 2012–2013, 3. Total enrolled 2012–2013 full-time, 15. Total enrolled 2012–2013 part-time, 0. Openings 2013–2014, 4. The median number of years required for completion of a degree in 2012–2013 were 5. The number of students enrolled full- and part-time who were dismissed or voluntarily withdrew from this program area in 2012–2013 were 0. *Cognitive Systems PhD (Doctor of Philosophy)*—Applications 2012–2013, 63. Total applicants accepted 2012–2013, 8. Number full-time enrolled (new admits only) 2012–2013, 6. Total enrolled 2012–2013 full-time, 16. Openings 2013–2014, 3. The median number of years required for completion of a degree in 2012–2013 were 6. The number of students enrolled full- and part-time who were dismissed or voluntarily withdrew from this program area in 2012–2013 were 0. *Perceptual Systems PhD (Doctor of Philosophy)*—Applications 2012–2013, 12. Total applicants accepted 2012–2013, 4. Number full-time enrolled (new admits only) 2012–2013, 0. Total enrolled 2012–2013 full-time, 5. Openings 2013–2014, 2. The median number of years required for completion of a degree in 2012–2013 were 6. The number of students enrolled full- and part-time who were dismissed or voluntarily withdrew from this program area in 2012–2013 were 0.

Scores: Entries appear in this order: required test or GPA, minimum score (if required), median score of students entering in 2012–2013. *Behavioral Neuroscience PhD (Doctor of Philosophy):* GRE-V no minimum stated, 522, GRE-Q no minimum stated, 680, GRE-Analytical no minimum stated, 4.5, last 2 years GPA no minimum stated, 3.45; *Clinical Psychology PhD (Doctor of Philosophy):* GRE-V no minimum stated, 647, GRE-Q no minimum stated, 727, GRE-Analytical no minimum stated, 4.5, last 2 years GPA no minimum stated, 3.87; *Developmental Psychology PhD (Doctor of Philosophy):* GRE-V no minimum stated, 640, GRE-Q no minimum stated, 667, GRE-Analytical no minimum stated, 5.3, last 2 years GPA no minimum stated, 3.87; *Individual Differences and Evolutionary Psychology PhD (Doctor of Philosophy):* GRE-V no minimum stated, 685, GRE-Q no minimum stated, 760, GRE-Analytical no minimum stated, 43.5, last 2 years GPA no minimum stated, 3.95; *Social and Personality Psychology PhD (Doctor of Philosophy):* GRE-V no minimum stated, 630, GRE-Q no minimum stated, 720, GRE-Analytical no minimum stated, 4.50, last 2 years GPA no minimum stated, 3.80, Masters GPA no minimum stated; *Cognitive Systems PhD (Doctor of Philosophy):* GRE-V no minimum stated, 580, GRE-Q no minimum stated, 735, GRE-Analytical no minimum stated, 4.5, last 2 years GPA no minimum stated, 3.93; *Perceptual Systems PhD (Doctor of Philosophy):* GRE-V no minimum stated, 550, GRE-Q no minimum stated, 760, GRE-Analytical no minimum stated, 4.05, last 2 years GPA no minimum stated, 3.32.

Other Criteria: (importance of criteria rated low, medium, or high): GRE scores—high, research experience—high, work experience—medium, extracurricular activity—low, clinically related public service—medium, GPA—high, letters of recommendation—high, interview—high, statement of goals and objectives—high, undergraduate major in psychology—high, specific undergraduate psychology courses taken—high, Other areas would not consider Clinical experience. For additional information on admission requirements, go to http://www.utexas.edu/cola/depts/psychology/graduate/admissions/.

Student Characteristics: The following represents characteristics of students in 2012–2013 in all graduate psychology programs in the department: Female—full-time 62, part-time 0; Male—full-time 37, part-time 0; African American/Black—full-time 3, part-time 0; Hispanic/Latino(a)—full-time 13, part-time 0; Asian/Pacific Islander—full-time 4, part-time 0; American Indian/Alaska Native—full-time 1, part-time 0; Caucasian/White—full-time 72, part-time 0; Multi-ethnic—full-time 0, part-time 0; students subject to the Americans With Disabilities Act—full-time 1, part-time 0; Unknown ethnicity—full-time 6, part-time 0; International students who hold an F-1 or J-1 Visa—full-time 6, part-time 0.

Financial Information/Assistance:
Tuition for Full-Time Study: *Doctoral:* State residents: per academic year $9,551; Nonstate residents: per academic year $15,851. Tuition is subject to change. See the following website for updates and changes in tuition costs: http://www.utexas.edu/business/accounting/sar/t_f_rates.html.

Financial Assistance:
First-Year Students: Teaching assistantships available for first year. Average amount paid per academic year: $15,346. Average number of hours worked per week: 20. Research assistantships available for first year. Average amount paid per academic year: $15,346. Average number of hours worked per week: 20. Fellowships and scholarships available for first year. Average amount paid per academic year: $24,000.

Advanced Students: Teaching assistantships available for advanced students. Average amount paid per academic year: $19,905. Average number of hours worked per week: 20. Research assistantships available for advanced students. Average amount paid per academic year: $16,905. Average number of hours worked per week: 20. Fellowships and scholarships available for advanced students. Average amount paid per academic year: $25,000.

Additional Information: Of all students currently enrolled full time, 100% benefited from one or more of the listed financial assistance programs. Application and information available online at: http://www.utexas.edu/cola/depts/psychology/graduate/admissions/financial.php.

Internships/Practica: Doctoral Degree (PhD Clinical Psychology): For those doctoral students for whom a professional psychology internship was required in this program prior to graduation, (5) students applied for an internship in 2011–2012, with (5) students obtaining an internship. Of those students who obtained an internship, (5) were paid internships. Of those students who obtained an internship, (5) students placed in APA/CPA accredited internships, (0) students placed in internships not APA/CPA accredited, but listed with the Association of Psychology Postdoctoral and Internship Programs (APPIC), (0) students placed in internships conforming to guidelines of the Council of Directors of School Psychology Programs (CDSPP), (0) students placed in internships that were not APA/CPA accredited, APPIC or CDSPP listed. Clinical students participate in practica at agencies in the Austin area, including the Austin State Hospital, Austin Child Guidance Center, Brown Schools, and the UT Counseling-Psychological Services Center. Most students select an internship at nationally recognized clinical settings such as the Langley Porter Neuropsychiatric Institute, or the University of California at San Diego Psychological Internship Consortium. Local settings are also available.

Housing and Day Care: No on-campus housing is available. On-campus day care facilities are available. See the following website for more information: http://www.utexas.edu/childcenter/.

Employment of Department Graduates:
Master's Degree Graduates: Of those who graduated in the academic year 2011–2012, the following categories and numbers represent the postgraduate activities and employment of master's degree graduates: Enrolled in a postdoctoral residency/fellowship (n/a), employed in independent practice (n/a), total from the above (master's) (0).
Doctoral Degree Graduates: Of those who graduated in the academic year 2011–2012, the following categories and numbers represent the postgraduate activities and employment of doctoral degree graduates: Enrolled in a psychology doctoral program (n/a), enrolled in a postdoctoral residency/fellowship (16), employed in an academic position at a university (2), employed in business or industry (3), employed in government agency (1), still seeking employment (1), total from the above (doctoral) (23).

Additional Information:
Orientation, Objectives, and Emphasis of Department: The major goal of graduate training in the Department of Psychology is to aid in developing the competence and professional commitment that are essential to scholarly contributions in the field of psychology. All students, upon completing the program, are expected to be well informed about general psychology, well qualified to conduct independent research, and prepared to teach in their area of interest. Within certain specialized areas, they will be prepared for professional practice. The program culminates in the PhD degree, and it is designed for the person committed to psychological research and an academic career. All of the graduate study areas have a strong academic research emphasis. All of the areas also recognize the necessity of developing knowledge and skills for applied research positions and, in the clinical area, for professional competence.

Special Facilities or Resources: The Department of Psychology moved into the Seay Building in May of 2002. This building houses seminar rooms, offices, and research laboratories. The research space includes small rooms for individual testing and larger rooms for group experiments. Some rooms have adjacent observation rooms. An anechoic testing chamber is available for auditory research. All of the departmental laboratories have computers associated with them. Departmental computers are available for student use. Facilities for research with children include the Children's Research Laboratory with numerous experimental suites. The facilities of the Animal Resource Center support research with animals. The support resources of the department include two well-equipped shops with full-time technicians and staff for computer assistance. The support resources of the university include the Computation Center, one of the finest academic computation facilities in the United States, and the Perry-Castaneda Library, one of the largest academic libraries in the country.

Faculty members in the Department of Psychology are affiliated with the Center for Perceptual Systems, the Institute for Cognitive Science, and the Institute for Neuroscience.

Information for Students With Physical Disabilities: See the following website for more information: http://ddce.utexas.edu/disability/.

Application Information:
Send to The University of Texas at Austin, Graduate and International Admissions Center, P.O. Box 7608, Austin, TX 78713-7608. Application available online. URL of online application: http://www.applytexas.org. Students are admitted in the Fall, application deadline December 1. *Fee:* $65. McNair Scholars will have application fee waived. International students pay a $90 application fee.

Texas, University of, Dallas
Psychological Sciences
School of Behavioral and Brain Sciences
800 West Campbell Road, GR 41
Richardson, TX 75080-3021
Telephone: (972) 883-2355
Fax: (972) 883-2491
E-mail: *mary.felipe@utdallas.edu;*
  adrienne.barnett@utdallas.edu
Web: *http://www.utdallas.edu/bbs/*

Department Information:
1976. Program Heads: Dr. Melanie Spence and Dr. Marion Underwood. Number of faculty: total—full-time 30; women—full-time 17; total—minority—full-time 5; women minority—full-time 2.

Programs and Degrees Offered:
Listed in the following order: Program area, degree type (T if terminal Master's), number awarded 7/11–6/12. Psychological Sciences PhD (Doctor of Philosophy) 5, Psychological Sciences MA/MS (Master of Arts/Science) (T) 3.

Student Applications/Admissions:
Student Applications
Psychological Sciences PhD (Doctor of Philosophy)—Applications 2012–2013, 39. Total applicants accepted 2012–2013, 5. Number full-time enrolled (new admits only) 2012–2013, 5. Number part-time enrolled (new admits only) 2012–2013, 0. Total enrolled 2012–2013 full-time, 20. Total enrolled 2012–2013 part-time, 6. Openings 2013–2014, 5. The median number of years required for completion of a degree in 2012–2013 were 6. The number of students enrolled full- and part-time who were dismissed or voluntarily withdrew from this program area in 2012–2013 were 0. *Psychological Sciences MA/MS (Master of Arts/Science)*—Applications 2012–2013, 38. Total applicants accepted 2012–2013, 15. Number full-time enrolled (new admits only) 2012–2013, 13. Number part-time enrolled (new admits only) 2012–2013, 0. Total enrolled 2012–2013 full-time, 20. Total enrolled 2012–2013 part-time, 0. Openings 2013–2014, 15. The median number of years required for completion of a degree in 2012–2013 were 2. The number of students enrolled full- and part-time who were dismissed or

voluntarily withdrew from this program area in 2012–2013 were 1.

Scores: Entries appear in this order: required test or GPA, minimum score (if required), median score of students entering in 2012–2013. *Psychological Sciences PhD (Doctor of Philosophy):* GRE-V 153, GRE-Q 152, overall undergraduate GPA 3.0; *Psychological Sciences MA/MS (Master of Arts/Science):* GRE-V 153, GRE-Q 144, overall undergraduate GPA 3.0.

Other Criteria: (importance of criteria rated low, medium, or high): GRE scores—high, research experience—high, work experience—medium, extracurricular activity—medium, GPA—high, letters of recommendation—high, interview—medium, statement of goals and objectives—high, fit w/ faculty mentor—high, undergraduate major in psychology—high, specific undergraduate psychology courses taken—high. For additional information on admission requirements, go to http://www.utdallas.edu/bbs/psysciphd/prospective.html.

Student Characteristics: The following represents characteristics of students in 2012–2013 in all graduate psychology programs in the department: Female—full-time 25, part-time 4; Male—full-time 15, part-time 2; African American/Black—full-time 1, part-time 1; Hispanic/Latino(a)—full-time 5, part-time 2; Asian/Pacific Islander—full-time 10, part-time 0; American Indian/Alaska Native—full-time 1, part-time 0; Caucasian/White—full-time 23, part-time 3; Multi-ethnic—full-time 0, part-time 0; students subject to the Americans With Disabilities Act—full-time 0, part-time 0; Unknown ethnicity—full-time 0, part-time 0; International students who hold an F-1 or J-1 Visa—full-time 8, part-time 0.

Financial Information/Assistance:
Tuition for Full-Time Study: *Master's:* State residents: per academic year $13,134; Nonstate residents: per academic year $23,766. *Doctoral:* State residents: per academic year $13,134; Nonstate residents: per academic year $23,766. Tuition is subject to change. See the following website for updates and changes in tuition costs: http://www.utdallas.edu/bursar/tuition/tables/.

Financial Assistance:
First-Year Students: Teaching assistantships available for first year. Average amount paid per academic year: $19,800. Average number of hours worked per week: 20. Apply by December 1. Research assistantships available for first year. Average amount paid per academic year: $19,800. Average number of hours worked per week: 20. Apply by December 1.

Advanced Students: Teaching assistantships available for advanced students. Average amount paid per academic year: $19,800. Average number of hours worked per week: 20. Apply by December 1. Research assistantships available for advanced students. Average amount paid per academic year: $19,800. Average number of hours worked per week: 20. Apply by December 1.

Additional Information: Of all students currently enrolled full time, 79% benefited from one or more of the listed financial assistance programs. Application and information available online at: http://www.utdallas.edu/student/finaid/.

Internships/Practica: Master's Degree (MA/MS Psychological Sciences): An internship experience, such as a final research project or "capstone" experience is required of graduates. Students in the MS program have the opportunity to gain applied experiences through the internship program in the School of Behavioral and Brain Sciences, which facilitates networking with a variety of community agencies and programs.

Housing and Day Care: On-campus housing is available. See the following website for more information: http://www.utdallas.edu/housing/uv/. No on-campus day care facilities are available.

Employment of Department Graduates:

Master's Degree Graduates: Of those who graduated in the academic year 2011–2012, the following categories and numbers represent the postgraduate activities and employment of master's degree graduates: Enrolled in a psychology doctoral program (3), enrolled in a postdoctoral residency/fellowship (n/a), employed in independent practice (n/a), not seeking employment (1), total from the above (master's) (4).

Doctoral Degree Graduates: Of those who graduated in the academic year 2011–2012, the following categories and numbers represent the postgraduate activities and employment of doctoral degree graduates: Enrolled in a psychology doctoral program (n/a), enrolled in a postdoctoral residency/fellowship (1), employed in an academic position at a university (3), not seeking employment (1), total from the above (doctoral) (5).

Additional Information:

Orientation, Objectives, and Emphasis of Department: The Psychological Sciences PhD program is an experimental psychology program that prepares students for leadership roles in research and teaching. Students benefit from the high quality of faculty research, small classes and seminars, extensive professional development, and a rich array of interdisciplinary opportunities within the School of Behavioral and Brain Sciences. Students can major in developmental psychology, cognitive psychology, or social/personality psychology. From the start of training, students are actively engaged in research laboratories with a faculty mentor. The research requirements include a qualifying thesis research project and a dissertation research project. Students are expected to complete the program coursework and research requirements in four years. Professional development is facilitated through School colloquia, regular brown bag series, presentations at professional meetings, and guidance in the development of teaching skills. The Master of Science program, which began in Fall 2008, provides advanced training to prepare serious student scholars for nationally prominent doctoral programs in clinical and experimental psychology. This research-focused program requires active involvement with a research mentor and at least one laboratory throughout the two-year training. Students complete advanced coursework and have the opportunity to gain applied experiences through the internship program. The program does not provide clinical training or lead to licensure as a counselor or psychologist. The M.S. curriculum offers opportunities for specialization in the following core fields: developmental, cognitive, social and personality, or neuroscience. Masters students take mostly doctoral-level coursework. This program is designed for full-time students; most courses are offered during the day.

Special Facilities or Resources: The Psychological Sciences program is a part of the U.T. Dallas School of Behavioral and Brain Sciences, which offers exceptional research facilities, including an on-site laboratory preschool, infant research labs, and video observation laboratories. The Psychological Sciences faculty has strong expertise in development from infancy through the lifespan, social relationships at all stages of life, and cognition and

neuroscience, including an emerging emphasis on brain imaging. Many of the Psychological Sciences faculty work collaboratively across our doctoral programs in Cognition and Neuroscience, Communication Sciences and Disorders, and Audiology. The doctoral programs are complemented by four research centers: the Center for Brain Health, the Callier Center, the Center for Children and Families, and the Center for Vital Longevity.

Information for Students With Physical Disabilities: See the following website for more information: http://www.utdallas.edu/studentaccess/.

Application Information:

Send to The University of Texas at Dallas, Admission and Enrollment Services, 800 West Campbell Road, Richardson, TX 75080-3021. Application available online. URL of online application: http://www.utdallas.edu/gradapp/. Students are admitted in the Fall, application deadline December 1. MS Program Application Deadline: February 15. *Fee:* $50.

Texas, University of, El Paso

Department of Psychology
500 West University Avenue
El Paso, TX 79968-0553
Telephone: (915) 747-5551
Fax: (915) 747-6553
E-mail: *tvcooper@utep.edu*
Web: *http://academics.utep.edu/Default.aspx?tabid=6423*

Department Information:

1965. Chairperson: Edward Castaneda. Number of faculty: total—full-time 18, part-time 8; women—full-time 5, part-time 2; total—minority—full-time 5, part-time 1; women minority—full-time 1.

Programs and Degrees Offered:

Listed in the following order: Program area, degree type (T if terminal Master's), number awarded 7/11–6/12. Clinical Psychology MA/MS (Master of Arts/Science) (T) 3, Psychology PhD (Doctor of Philosophy) 9.

Student Applications/Admissions:

Student Applications

Clinical Psychology MA/MS (Master of Arts/Science)—Applications 2012–2013, 17. Total applicants accepted 2012–2013, 11. Number full-time enrolled (new admits only) 2012–2013, 6. Number part-time enrolled (new admits only) 2012–2013, 0. Total enrolled 2012–2013 full-time, 9. Total enrolled 2012–2013 part-time, 2. Openings 2013–2014, 5. The median number of years required for completion of a degree in 2012–2013 were 3. The number of students enrolled full- and part-time who were dismissed or voluntarily withdrew from this program area in 2012–2013 were 0. *Psychology PhD (Doctor of Philosophy)*—Applications 2012–2013, 47. Total applicants accepted 2012–2013, 22. Number full-time enrolled (new admits only) 2012–2013, 10. Number part-time enrolled (new admits only) 2012–2013, 0. Total enrolled 2012–2013 full-time, 31. Total enrolled 2012–2013 part-time, 7. Openings 2013–2014, 12. The median number of years required for completion of a degree in 2012–2013 were 6. The number of students enrolled full- and part-time who were dismissed or voluntarily withdrew from this program area in 2012–2013 were 0.

Scores: Entries appear in this order: required test or GPA, minimum score (if required), median score of students entering in 2012–2013. *Clinical Psychology MA/MS (Master of Arts/ Science):* GRE-V no minimum stated, GRE-Q no minimum stated, overall undergraduate GPA no minimum stated, 3.69; *Psychology PhD (Doctor of Philosophy):* GRE-V no minimum stated, GRE-Q no minimum stated, overall undergraduate GPA no minimum stated.

Other Criteria: (importance of criteria rated low, medium, or high): GRE scores—high, research experience—high, work experience—low, extracurricular activity—low, clinically related public service—low, GPA—high, letters of recommendation—high, statement of goals and objectives—high, undergraduate major in psychology—medium, Applicants who did not major or minor in psychology need to take several leveling courses before their application will be considered competitive. For additional information on admission requirements, go to http://academics.utep.edu/Default.aspx?tabid=26650.

Student Characteristics: The following represents characteristics of students in 2012–2013 in all graduate psychology programs in the department: Female—full-time 33, part-time 5; Male—full-time 12, part-time 8; African American/Black—full-time 0, part-time 0; Hispanic/Latino(a)—full-time 22, part-time 5; Asian/Pacific Islander—full-time 1, part-time 1; American Indian/Alaska Native—full-time 0, part-time 0; Caucasian/White—full-time 17, part-time 5; Multi-ethnic—full-time 0, part-time 1; students subject to the Americans With Disabilities Act—full-time 0, part-time 0; Unknown ethnicity—full-time 0, part-time 0; International students who hold an F-1 or J-1 Visa—full-time 4, part-time 1.

Financial Information/Assistance:

Tuition for Full-Time Study: *Master's:* State residents: per academic year $5,486; Nonstate residents: per academic year $11,804. *Doctoral:* State residents: per academic year $5,486; Nonstate residents: per academic year $11,804. Tuition is subject to change. See the following website for updates and changes in tuition costs: http://academics.utep.edu/Default.aspx?tabid=47747.

Financial Assistance:

First-Year Students: Teaching assistantships available for first year. Average amount paid per academic year: $15,000. Average number of hours worked per week: 20. Apply by December 15. Research assistantships available for first year. Average amount paid per academic year: $15,000. Average number of hours worked per week: 20. Apply by December 15.

Advanced Students: Teaching assistantships available for advanced students. Average amount paid per academic year: $15,000. Average number of hours worked per week: 20. Apply by December 15. Research assistantships available for advanced students. Average amount paid per academic year: $15,000. Average number of hours worked per week: 20. Apply by December 15.

Additional Information: Of all students currently enrolled full time, 100% benefited from one or more of the listed financial assistance programs. Application and information available online at: http://graduate.utep.edu/scholarships.html.

Internships/Practica: Master's Degree (MA/MS Clinical Psychology): An internship experience, such as a final research project or "capstone" experience is required of graduates. The Clinical MA program requires three hours of internship.

Housing and Day Care: On-campus housing is available. See the following website for more information: http://sa.utep.edu/housing/. On-campus day care facilities are available. See the following website for more information: http://sa.utep.edu/childcare/.

Employment of Department Graduates:

Master's Degree Graduates: Of those who graduated in the academic year 2011–2012, the following categories and numbers represent the postgraduate activities and employment of master's degree graduates: Enrolled in a psychology doctoral program (1), enrolled in a postdoctoral residency/fellowship (n/a), employed in independent practice (n/a), employed in other positions at a higher education institution (1), total from the above (master's) (2).

Doctoral Degree Graduates: Of those who graduated in the academic year 2011–2012, the following categories and numbers represent the postgraduate activities and employment of doctoral degree graduates: Enrolled in a psychology doctoral program (n/a), enrolled in a postdoctoral residency/fellowship (1), employed in an academic position at a university (2), employed in an academic position at a 2-year/4-year college (1), employed in other positions at a higher education institution (1), employed in government agency (1), total from the above (doctoral) (6).

Additional Information:

Orientation, Objectives, and Emphasis of Department: The PhD program is designed to train research psychologists and offers four areas of concentration: (1) Health (2) Legal, (3) Language Acquisition and Bilingualism, and (4) Social, Cognitive, & Neuroscience. The clinical MA program is designed as a terminal master's degree and emphasizes all applied skills in psychological assessment and treatment. Three tracks exist within the clinical MA program: the PhD preparation track, the Psychological Associate preparation track, and the Licensed Professional Counselor preparation track. Special focus is directed toward bilingual, bicultural issues.

Special Facilities or Resources: The Psychology Department occupies a three story, 24000 square foot, building that contains state-of-the-art equipment for investigating a wide range of cognitive, behavioral, and neuro-chemical processes and phenomena. Laboratories contain virtual reality equipment for studies of aggression, reaction time equipment for studies of stereotyping and language processing, EEG equipment for studies of attitudes, stereotypes, and deception, picture morphing equipment for studies of eyewitness identification, and eye-tracking equipment for studies of cognitive processes that guide bilingual reading. Neuroscience labs contain neurochemistry equipment for quantifying brain neurotransmitter levels, and behavioral equipment for assessing addictive behavior, anxiety-like properties, memory function, and fine motor movements. The neuroscience space also contains a recently renovated animal vivarium. Additional labs contain sound-proofed interview rooms equipped with covert digital audio-video recording devices, carbon monoxide monitors for assessing short term smoking status, blood alcohol level monitors for studies of intoxication, and psychophysiological instruments for monitoring heart rate, eye blinks, the startle reflex, and inhibitory control. The Psychology Department has also established numerous community-based participatory research projects. Off-campus sites include clinics, schools, hospitals, medical centers, and a large military base, as well as other community settings in a bi-cultural environment.

Information for Students With Physical Disabilities: See the following website for more information: http://sa.utep.edu/cass/.

Application Information:

Send to Graduate School, Academic Services Building, Room 223, University of Texas at El Paso, 500 West University Avenue, El Paso, TX 79968-0566. Application available online. URL of online application: http://graduate.utep.edu/prospective.html. Students are admitted in the Fall, application deadline December 15. *Fee:* $45. The fee for Mexican applicants is $45; the fee for all other international applicants is $80.

Texas, University of, Pan American
Department of Psychology
College of Social and Behavioral Sciences
1201 West University Drive, SBSC 358
Edinburg, TX 78541
Telephone: (956) 665-3329
Fax: (956) 665-3333
E-mail: *pgasquoine@utpa.edu*
Web: *http://www.utpa.edu/psychology*

Department Information:

1972. Department Chair; Graduate Program Director: Philip Gasquoine, PhD. Number of faculty: total—full-time 8; women—full-time 3; total—minority—full-time 5; women minority—full-time 3.

Programs and Degrees Offered:

Listed in the following order: Program area, degree type (T if terminal Master's), number awarded 7/11–6/12. Clinical Psychology MA/MS (Master of Arts/Science) (T) 15, Experimental Psychology MA/MS (Master of Arts/Science) (T) 9, Certificate in Bcba Other 3.

Student Applications/Admissions:

Student Applications

Clinical Psychology MA/MS (Master of Arts/Science)—Applications 2012–2013, 51. Total applicants accepted 2012–2013, 17. Number full-time enrolled (new admits only) 2012–2013, 17. Number part-time enrolled (new admits only) 2012–2013, 0. Total enrolled 2012–2013 full-time, 38. Total enrolled 2012–2013 part-time, 2. Openings 2013–2014, 20. The median number of years required for completion of a degree in 2012–2013 were 2. The number of students enrolled full- and part-time who were dismissed or voluntarily withdrew from this program area in 2012–2013 were 3. *Experimental Psychology MA/MS (Master of Arts/Science)*—Applications 2012–2013, 9. Total applicants accepted 2012–2013, 6. Number full-time enrolled (new admits only) 2012–2013, 6. Number part-time enrolled (new admits only) 2012–2013, 0. Total enrolled 2012–2013 full-time, 12. Total enrolled 2012–2013 part-time, 0. Openings 2013–2014, 6. The median number of years required for completion of a degree in 2012–2013 were 2. The

number of students enrolled full- and part-time who were dismissed or voluntarily withdrew from this program area in 2012–2013 were 1. *Certificate in Bcba Other*—Applications 2012–2013, 12. Total applicants accepted 2012–2013, 9. Number full-time enrolled (new admits only) 2012–2013, 7. Number part-time enrolled (new admits only) 2012–2013, 1. Total enrolled 2012–2013 full-time, 7. Total enrolled 2012–2013 part-time, 1. Openings 2013–2014, 10. The median number of years required for completion of a degree in 2012–2013 were 2. The number of students enrolled full- and part-time who were dismissed or voluntarily withdrew from this program area in 2012–2013 were 1.

Scores: Entries appear in this order: required test or GPA, minimum score (if required), median score of students entering in 2012–2013. *Clinical Psychology MA/MS (Master of Arts/Science):* GRE-V no minimum stated, GRE-Q no minimum stated, overall undergraduate GPA 3.0; *Experimental Psychology MA/MS (Master of Arts/Science):* GRE-V no minimum stated, GRE-Q no minimum stated, overall undergraduate GPA 3.0; *Certificate in BCBA Other:* GRE-V no minimum stated, GRE-Q no minimum stated, overall undergraduate GPA 3.0.

Other Criteria: (importance of criteria rated low, medium, or high): GRE scores—medium, research experience—medium, work experience—medium, extracurricular activity—low, clinically related public service—low, GPA—high, letters of recommendation—high, statement of goals and objectives—medium, undergraduate major in psychology—medium, specific undergraduate psychology courses taken—medium. For additional information on admission requirements, go to http://portal.utpa.edu/utpa_main/daa_home/csbs_home/psy_anth_home/psy_grad_app_procedure.

Student Characteristics: The following represents characteristics of students in 2012–2013 in all graduate psychology programs in the department: Female—full-time 41, part-time 1; Male—full-time 7, part-time 1; African American/Black—full-time 0, part-time 0; Hispanic/Latino(a)—full-time 43, part-time 1; Asian/Pacific Islander—full-time 0, part-time 0; American Indian/Alaska Native—full-time 0, part-time 0; Caucasian/White—full-time 5, part-time 1; Multi-ethnic—full-time 0, part-time 0; students subject to the Americans With Disabilities Act—full-time 0, part-time 0; Unknown ethnicity—full-time 0, part-time 0; International students who hold an F-1 or J-1 Visa—full-time 0, part-time 0.

Financial Information/Assistance:

Tuition for Full-Time Study: *Master's:* State residents: per academic year $5,489, $277 per credit hour; Nonstate residents: per academic year $12,509, $554 per credit hour. Tuition is subject to change. Additional fees are assessed to students beyond the costs of tuition for the following: $75 course fee per semester. See the following website for updates and changes in tuition costs: http://portal.utpa.edu/utpa_main/dess_home/finaid_home/students_home/students_tuition/tuition_coa.

Financial Assistance:

First-Year Students: Teaching assistantships available for first year. Average amount paid per academic year: $5,000. Average number of hours worked per week: 19. Research assistantships available for first year. Average amount paid per academic year: $10,000. Average number of hours worked per week: 19.

Advanced Students: Teaching assistantships available for advanced students. Average amount paid per academic year: $5,000. Average number of hours worked per week: 19. Research assistantships available for advanced students. Average amount paid per academic year: $10,000. Average number of hours worked per week: 19.

Additional Information: Of all students currently enrolled full time, 12% benefited from one or more of the listed financial assistance programs. Application and information available online at: http://portal.utpa.edu/utpa_main/dess_home/finaid_home.

Internships/Practica: Master's Degree (MA/MS Clinical Psychology): An internship experience, such as a final research project or "capstone" experience is required of graduates. Master's Degree (MA/MS Experimental Psychology): An internship experience, such as a final research project or "capstone" experience is required of graduates. Internships in clinical psychology are for 480 clock hours, at least 100 of which must involve direct patient contact. Internship sites include independent licensed psychologists, public and private mental health clinics and hospitals. Practica for the BCBA certificate allow for completion of hours to become eligible to sit for the national certification exam. BCBA practicum sites include public not-for-profit agencies that serve severely disabled children and some independent home placements.

Housing and Day Care: On-campus housing is available. See the following website for more information: http://www.utpa.edu/reslife. On-campus day care facilities are available. See the following website for more information: http://portal.utpa.edu/utpa_main/dess_home/childcare_home.

Employment of Department Graduates:
Master's Degree Graduates: Of those who graduated in the academic year 2011–2012, the following categories and numbers represent the postgraduate activities and employment of master's degree graduates: Enrolled in a postdoctoral residency/fellowship (n/a), employed in independent practice (n/a), total from the above (master's) (0).
Doctoral Degree Graduates: Of those who graduated in the academic year 2011–2012, the following categories and numbers represent the postgraduate activities and employment of doctoral degree graduates: Enrolled in a psychology doctoral program (n/a), total from the above (doctoral) (0).

Additional Information:
Orientation, Objectives, and Emphasis of Department: The Masters degree in Clinical Psychology is designed to provide research-based assessment and intervention strategies, skills training, diagnostic assessment skills, clinical experience, and supervision of professional practices in the field of applied psychology. The program is designed to fulfill academic requirements for taking the Texas State Board Exam as a Licensed Psychological Associate (LPA) and/or a Licensed Professional Counselor (LPC). There are thesis and non-thesis tracks. For the Masters degree in Experimental Psychology all students must complete a thesis as this degree is designed to prepare students for admission to research PhD programs. The certificate in BCBA satisfies all requirements (including practicum hours) for taking the national Board Certification exam as a Behavior Analyst.

Information for Students With Physical Disabilities: See the following website for more information: http://portal.utpa.edu/utpa_main/dess_home/dos_home/disability_home.

Application Information:
Send to Office of Graduate Studies, Administration Building Room 116, University of Texas - Pan American, 1201 West University Drive, Edinburg, TX 78541. Application available online. URL of online application: https://apply.embark.com/grad/utpa. Students are admitted in the Fall, application deadline June 15. *Fee:* $50.

Texas, University of, San Antonio
Department of Educational Psychology
College of Education and Human Development
501 West Cesar East Chavez Boulevard
San Antonio, TX 78207
Telephone: (210) 458-2650
Fax: (210) 458-2019
E-mail: *Teresa.Pena@utsa.edu*
Web: *http://education.utsa.edu/educational_psychology/welcome/*

Department Information:
2009. Chairperson: Dr. Norma Guerra. Number of faculty: total—full-time 11; women—full-time 8; total—minority—full-time 5; women minority—full-time 5.

Programs and Degrees Offered:
Listed in the following order: Program area, degree type (T if terminal Master's), number awarded 7/11–6/12. School Psychology MA/MS (Master of Arts/Science) (T) 0.

Student Applications/Admissions:
Student Applications
School Psychology MA/MS (Master of Arts/Science)—Applications 2012–2013, 73. Total applicants accepted 2012–2013, 44. Number full-time enrolled (new admits only) 2012–2013, 31. Number part-time enrolled (new admits only) 2012–2013, 13. Total enrolled 2012–2013 full-time, 64. Total enrolled 2012–2013 part-time, 23. The median number of years required for completion of a degree in 2012–2013 were 4. The number of students enrolled full- and part-time who were dismissed or voluntarily withdrew from this program area in 2012–2013 were 5.

Scores: Entries appear in this order: required test or GPA, minimum score (if required), median score of students entering in 2012–2013. *School Psychology MA/MS (Master of Arts/Science):* GRE-V no minimum stated, 425, GRE-Q no minimum stated, 455, GRE-Analytical 3.0, 3.8, last 2 years GPA 3.0, 3.2.
Other Criteria: (importance of criteria rated low, medium, or high): GRE scores—medium, research experience—low, work experience—low, clinically related public service—low, GPA—high, letters of recommendation—medium, statement of goals and objectives—medium, undergraduate major in psychology—medium. For additional information on admission requirements, go to http://education.utsa.edu/educational_psychology/master_of_arts_in_school_psychology/.

Student Characteristics: The following represents characteristics of students in 2012–2013 in all graduate psychology programs in the department: Female—full-time 56, part-time 19; Male—full-time 8, part-time 4; African American/Black—full-time 4, part-time 2; Hispanic/Latino(a)—full-time 29, part-time 11; Asian/Pacific Islander—full-time 0, part-time 1; American Indian/Alaska Native—full-time 0, part-time 0; Caucasian/White—full-time 27, part-time 9; Multi-ethnic—full-time 3, part-time 0; students subject to the Americans With Disabilities Act—full-time 0, part-time 0; Unknown ethnicity—full-time 1, part-time 0; International students who hold an F-1 or J-1 Visa—full-time 0, part-time 0.

Financial Information/Assistance:

Tuition for Full-Time Study: *Master's:* State residents: per academic year $6,634; Nonstate residents: per academic year $19,270. Tuition is subject to change. Additional fees are assessed to students beyond the costs of tuition for the following: university required fees, school psychology support fee. See the following website for updates and changes in tuition costs: http://graduateschool.utsa.edu/funding/graduate-tuition-and-fees/.

Financial Assistance:

First-Year Students: Research assistantships available for first year. Average amount paid per academic year: $8,208. Average number of hours worked per week: 19.

Advanced Students: Research assistantships available for advanced students. Average amount paid per academic year: $8,208. Average number of hours worked per week: 19.

Additional Information: Of all students currently enrolled full time, 10% benefited from one or more of the listed financial assistance programs. Application and information available online at: http://graduateschool.utsa.edu/funding/.

Internships/Practica: Master's Degree (MA/MS School Psychology): An internship experience, such as a final research project or "capstone" experience is required of graduates. Practicum and internship are culminating, field-based experiences in which knowledge and skills acquired in coursework are applied in professional settings. San Antonio has the advantage of being in the center of a number of urban, suburban, and rural school districts. Surrounding areas offer additional practicum and internship opportunities. The practicum is taken across two semesters, typically during the second year for students on the full-time track. Practicum sites must be approved by program faculty in order to ensure that the site will provide the appropriate learning experiences (e.g., assessment, consultation, counseling) and supervision. The practicum must consist of at least 150 clock hours per semester (total = 300 hours over the course of two semesters). Practicum students will be supervised by site supervisors and university faculty. The internship is taken across two semesters, typically during the third year for students on the full-time track. The internship must consist of at least 1200 clock hours of experience (600 clock hours per semester over the course of two semesters). The internship is a full-time commitment and internship sites must be approved by program faculty in order to ensure that appropriate experiences and supervision will be provided.

Housing and Day Care: On-campus housing is available. See the following website for more information: http://utsa.edu/housing/. On-campus day care facilities are available. See the following website for more information: http://www.utsa.edu/cdc/.

Employment of Department Graduates:

Master's Degree Graduates: Of those who graduated in the academic year 2011–2012, the following categories and numbers represent the postgraduate activities and employment of master's degree graduates: Enrolled in a postdoctoral residency/fellowship (n/a), employed in independent practice (n/a), total from the above (master's) (0).

Doctoral Degree Graduates: Of those who graduated in the academic year 2011–2012, the following categories and numbers represent the postgraduate activities and employment of doctoral degree graduates: Enrolled in a psychology doctoral program (n/a), total from the above (doctoral) (0).

Additional Information:

Orientation, Objectives, and Emphasis of Department: The mission of the Department of Educational Psychology is to promote the development and application of scientific knowledge. To do so, our faculty members are committed to: producing high-quality, innovative research and scholarship; providing effective and culturally inclusive instructional technologies to prepare practitioners and researchers to use the tools, resources, and strategies necessary to improve the educational experience of all learners; preparing culturally competent scientist–practitioners and researchers to effectively contribute to the applied psychological development and well-being of children and adolescents; providing responsive educational and psychological services to the local community, schools, and beyond; and engaging in participatory and leadership roles in local, national, and international institutions and organizations.

Special Facilities or Resources: The Psychological Assessment and Consultation Center (PACC) is an important learning resource for students. Located in Durango Building, the PACC houses all of the assessment instruments used in the psychological assessment courses, and also contains resources to facilitate students' learning such as computers with scoring and interpretive software programs, training rooms where students can practice test administration, equipment for recording practice administrations, and a library that includes references related to assessment, in addition to multimedia materials related to intervention, consultation, psychopathology, and research/statistics. Faculty in the Department of Educational Psychology also use the PACC for research meetings and supervision of clinical activities. Finally, the PACC provides a space to facilitate the provision of community services such as parent consultation.

Information for Students With Physical Disabilities: See the following website for more information: http://utsa.edu/disability/.

Application Information:
Send to The University of Texas at San Antonio, Attn: The Graduate School, One UTSA Circle, San Antonio, TX 78249. Application available online. URL of online application: http://graduateschool.utsa.edu/. Students are admitted in the Fall, application deadline July 1; Spring, application deadline November 1; Summer, application deadline April 1. International Applicants: Deadline for Fall is April 1; for Spring is September 1, and for Summer is March 1. *Fee:* $45.

Texas, University of, Tyler

Department of Psychology and Counseling
3900 University Boulevard
Tyler, TX 75799
Telephone: (903) 566-7130
Fax: (903) 565-5923
E-mail: *cbarke@uttyler.edu*
Web: *http://www.uttyler.edu/psychology/*

Department Information:
1973. Chairperson: Charles Barké. Number of faculty: total—full-time 15, part-time 6; women—full-time 7, part-time 4; total—minority—full-time 2; women minority—full-time 1.

Programs and Degrees Offered:
Listed in the following order: Program area, degree type (T if terminal Master's), number awarded 7/11–6/12. Clinical Mental Health Counseling MA/MS (Master of Arts/Science) (T) 12, School Counseling MA/MS (Master of Arts/Science) (T) 5, Clinical Psychology MA/MS (Master of Arts/Science) (T) 12.

Student Applications/Admissions:
Student Applications
Clinical Mental Health Counseling MA/MS (Master of Arts/Science)—Total applicants accepted 2012–2013, 52. Number full-time enrolled (new admits only) 2012–2013, 21. Number part-time enrolled (new admits only) 2012–2013, 7. Total enrolled 2012–2013 full-time, 52. Total enrolled 2012–2013 part-time, 23. Openings 2013–2014, 40. The median number of years required for completion of a degree in 2012–2013 were 2. *School Counseling MA/MS (Master of Arts/Science)*—Applications 2012–2013, 40. Total applicants accepted 2012–2013, 31. Number full-time enrolled (new admits only) 2012–2013, 1. Number part-time enrolled (new admits only) 2012–2013, 23. Total enrolled 2012–2013 full-time, 3. Total enrolled 2012–2013 part-time, 35. Openings 2013–2014, 35. The median number of years required for completion of a degree in 2012–2013 were 2. The number of students enrolled full- and part-time who were dismissed or voluntarily withdrew from this program area in 2012–2013 were 4. *Clinical Psychology MA/MS (Master of Arts/Science)*—Applications 2012–2013, 79. Total applicants accepted 2012–2013, 56. Number full-time enrolled (new admits only) 2012–2013, 25. Number part-time enrolled (new admits only) 2012–2013, 6. Total enrolled 2012–2013 full-time, 46. Total enrolled 2012–2013 part-time, 26. Openings 2013–2014, 35. The median number of years required for completion of a degree in 2012–2013 were 2. The number of students enrolled full- and part-time who were dismissed or voluntarily withdrew from this program area in 2012–2013 were 4.
Scores: Entries appear in this order: required test or GPA, minimum score (if required), median score of students entering in 2012–2013. *Clinical Mental Health Counseling MA/MS (Master of Arts/Science):* GRE-V no minimum stated, GRE-Q no minimum stated, overall undergraduate GPA 2.75; *School Counseling MA/MS (Master of Arts/Science):* GRE-V no minimum stated, GRE-Q no minimum stated, overall undergraduate GPA 2.75; *Clinical Psychology MA/MS (Master of Arts/Science):* GRE-V no minimum stated, GRE-Q no minimum stated, overall undergraduate GPA 2.75, last 2 years GPA 3.00.

Other Criteria: (importance of criteria rated low, medium, or high): GRE scores—medium, research experience—low, work experience—low, extracurricular activity—low, clinically related public service—medium, GPA—high, letters of recommendation—high, statement of goals and objectives—medium, undergraduate major in psychology—medium, specific undergraduate psychology courses taken—medium. For additional information on admission requirements, go to http://www.uttyler.edu/psychology/graduate/admission-requirements.php.

Student Characteristics: The following represents characteristics of students in 2012–2013 in all graduate psychology programs in the department: Female—full-time 79, part-time 64; Male—full-time 22, part-time 20; African American/Black—full-time 3, part-time 1; Hispanic/Latino(a)—full-time 8, part-time 5; Asian/Pacific Islander—full-time 2, part-time 2; American Indian/Alaska Native—full-time 0, part-time 0; Caucasian/White—full-time 88, part-time 76; Multi-ethnic—full-time 0, part-time 0; students subject to the Americans With Disabilities Act—full-time 0, part-time 0; Unknown ethnicity—full-time 0, part-time 0; International students who hold an F-1 or J-1 Visa—full-time 0, part-time 0.

Financial Information/Assistance:
Tuition for Full-Time Study: *Master's:* State residents: per academic year $5,986; Nonstate residents: per academic year $12,304. Tuition is subject to change. Additional fees are assessed to students beyond the costs of tuition for the following: Required fees: $11/credit Student Service Fee. See the following website for updates and changes in tuition costs: http://www.uttyler.edu/graduate/calculator.php.

Financial Assistance:
First-Year Students: Research assistantships available for first year. Average number of hours worked per week: 10. Fellowships and scholarships available for first year. Average amount paid per academic year: $1,000.
Advanced Students: Teaching assistantships available for advanced students. Average amount paid per academic year: $2,500. Average number of hours worked per week: 10. Research assistantships available for advanced students. Average amount paid per academic year: $5,000. Average number of hours worked per week: 20. Fellowships and scholarships available for advanced students. Average amount paid per academic year: $1,000.
Additional Information: Of all students currently enrolled full time, 30% benefited from one or more of the listed financial assistance programs. Application and information available online at: http://www.uttyler.edu/graduate/fin/.

Internships/Practica: Master's Degree (MA/MS Clinical Mental Health Counseling): An internship experience, such as a final research project or "capstone" experience is required of graduates. Master's Degree (MA/MS School Counseling): An internship experience, such as a final research project or "capstone" experience is required of graduates. Master's Degree (MA/MS Clinical Psychology): An internship experience, such as a final research project or "capstone" experience is required of graduates. Available practicum sites include nearby private psychiatric hospitals, MHMR facilities, children's therapy facilities, crisis centers and safe houses for abused women, neuropsychology rehabilitation hospitals, prisons, and schools, as well as our own community counseling center.

Housing and Day Care: On-campus housing is available. See the following website for more information: http://www.uttyler.edu/housing/. No on-campus day care facilities are available.

Employment of Department Graduates:

Master's Degree Graduates: Of those who graduated in the academic year 2011–2012, the following categories and numbers represent the postgraduate activities and employment of master's degree graduates: Enrolled in a psychology doctoral program (4), enrolled in a postdoctoral residency/fellowship (n/a), employed in independent practice (n/a), employed in an academic position at a 2-year/4-year college (2), employed in a professional position in a school system (8), employed in a community mental health/counseling center (5), still seeking employment (5), do not know (5), total from the above (master's) (29).

Doctoral Degree Graduates: Of those who graduated in the academic year 2011–2012, the following categories and numbers represent the postgraduate activities and employment of doctoral degree graduates: Enrolled in a psychology doctoral program (n/a), total from the above (doctoral) (0).

Additional Information:

Orientation, Objectives, and Emphasis of Department: The purpose of our program is to prepare competent, applied practitioners at the master's level. The curriculum is very practical, stressing clinical assessment and intervention, and hands-on experience in relevant areas. Our students have been very successful in finding employment in mental health settings and in gaining admission to clinical and counseling psychology doctoral programs. Special opportunities are provided for training in clinical neuropsychological assessment and psychopharmacology, for training in marital and family counseling, school counseling or for training to become a licensed specialist in school psychology.

Special Facilities or Resources: We have on campus counseling/clinical labs, an on campus Clinic and a Community Clinic, all used for training graduate students in our program. We also have research labs for use by faculty and their graduate students.

Information for Students With Physical Disabilities: See the following website for more information: http://www2.uttyler.edu/disabilityservices/index.php.

Application Information:
Send to Psychology Graduate Coordinator, Department of Psychology, University of Texas at Tyler, 3900 University Boulevard, Tyler, TX 75799. Application available online. URL of online application: http://www.uttyler.edu/graduate/gradadmissions/. Programs have rolling admissions. *Fee:* $40.

Brigham Young University (2012 data)
Department of Counseling Psychology and Special Education
David O. McKay School of Education
340 MCKB
Provo, UT 84602
Telephone: (801) 422-3857
Fax: (801) 422-0198
E-mail: aaron_jackson@byu.edu
Web: http://education.byu.edu/cpse/

Department Information:
1969. Chairperson: Tim Smith. Number of faculty: total—full-time 7, part-time 5; women—full-time 3, part-time 1; minority—part-time 1.

Programs and Degrees Offered:
Listed in the following order: Program area, degree type (T if terminal Master's), number awarded 7/11–6/12. School Psychology EdS (School Psychology) 12, Counseling Psychology PhD (Doctor of Philosophy) 6.

APA Accreditation: Counseling PhD (Doctor of Philosophy). Student Outcome Data Website: http://education.byu.edu/cpse/phd/informed_decisions.html.

Student Applications/Admissions:
Student Applications
School Psychology EdS (School Psychology)—Applications 2012–2013, 34. Total applicants accepted 2012–2013, 12. Number full-time enrolled (new admits only) 2012–2013, 12. Total enrolled 2012–2013 full-time, 34. Openings 2013–2014, 12. The median number of years required for completion of a degree in 2012–2013 were 3. The number of students enrolled full- and part-time who were dismissed or voluntarily withdrew from this program area in 2012–2013 were 1. *Counseling Psychology PhD (Doctor of Philosophy)*—Applications 2012–2013, 43. Total applicants accepted 2012–2013, 6. Number full-time enrolled (new admits only) 2012–2013, 6. Number part-time enrolled (new admits only) 2012–2013, 0. Total enrolled 2012–2013 full-time, 30. Openings 2013–2014, 6. The median number of years required for completion of a degree in 2012–2013 were 5. The number of students enrolled full- and part-time who were dismissed or voluntarily withdrew from this program area in 2012–2013 were 0.
Scores: Entries appear in this order: required test or GPA, minimum score (if required), median score of students entering in 2012–2013. *School Psychology EdS (School Psychology):* GRE-V no minimum stated, GRE-Q no minimum stated, GRE-Analytical no minimum stated, last 2 years GPA no minimum stated; *Counseling Psychology PhD (Doctor of Philosophy):* GRE-V no minimum stated, 554, GRE-Q no minimum stated, 651, GRE-Analytical no minimum stated, 4.3, overall undergraduate GPA no minimum stated, last 2 years GPA no minimum stated, 3.72.

Other Criteria: (importance of criteria rated low, medium, or high): GRE scores—medium, research experience—medium, work experience—medium, extracurricular activity—low, clinically related public service—medium, GPA—high, letters of recommendation—medium, interview—high, statement of goals and objectives—high, undergraduate major in psychology—low, specific undergraduate psychology courses taken—medium.

Student Characteristics: The following represents characteristics of students in 2012–2013 in all graduate psychology programs in the department: Female—full-time 37, part-time 10; Male—full-time 23, part-time 11; African American/Black—full-time 1, part-time 0; Hispanic/Latino(a)—full-time 2, part-time 0; Asian/Pacific Islander—full-time 5, part-time 0; American Indian/Alaska Native—full-time 1, part-time 0; Caucasian/White—full-time 52, part-time 0; Multi-ethnic—full-time 0, part-time 0; students subject to the Americans With Disabilities Act—full-time 0, part-time 0; Unknown ethnicity—full-time 0, part-time 0; International students who hold an F-1 or J-1 Visa—full-time 2, part-time 0.

Financial Information/Assistance:
Tuition for Full-Time Study: *Master's:* State residents: per academic year $7,438, $331 per credit hour; Nonstate residents: per academic year $14,875, $662 per credit hour. *Doctoral:* State residents: per academic year $7,438, $331 per credit hour; Nonstate residents: per academic year $14,875, $662 per credit hour. Tuition is subject to change.

Financial Assistance:
First-Year Students: Teaching assistantships available for first year. Average amount paid per academic year: $7,800. Average number of hours worked per week: 15. Research assistantships available for first year. Average amount paid per academic year: $7,800. Average number of hours worked per week: 15. Fellowships and scholarships available for first year. Average amount paid per academic year: $1,200.
Advanced Students: Teaching assistantships available for advanced students. Average amount paid per academic year: $8,600. Average number of hours worked per week: 15. Research assistantships available for advanced students. Average amount paid per academic year: $8,600. Average number of hours worked per week: 15. Fellowships and scholarships available for advanced students. Average amount paid per academic year: $1,200.
Additional Information: Of all students currently enrolled full time, 100% benefited from one or more of the listed financial assistance programs.

Internships/Practica: Doctoral Degree (PhD Counseling Psychology): For those doctoral students for whom a professional psychology internship was required in this program prior to graduation, (5) students applied for an internship in 2011–2012, with (5) students obtaining an internship. Of those students who obtained an internship, (5) were paid internships. Of those students who obtained an internship, (4) students placed in APA/CPA accredited internships, (1) students placed in internships not APA/CPA accredited, but listed with the Association of Psychology Postdoctoral and Internship Programs (APPIC), (0) students placed in internships conforming to guidelines of the Council of Directors of School Psychology Programs (CDSPP), (0) students placed in internships that were not APA/CPA accredited, APPIC or CDSPP listed. Master's students complete practica for 5 hours per week during the first and second years of study and a full-time internship (5/8 of teacher pay) the third year. Doctoral students admitted at the bachelor's level complete 2 semesters of introductory practicum. All doctoral students complete 4 semesters of practicum in BYU's counseling center. They also complete 1 teaching practicum, and 2 community-based practica. A full-year internship is required. Assistance is given for placements.

Housing and Day Care: On-campus housing is available. See the following website for more information: http://housing.byu.edu/. No on-campus day care facilities are available.

Employment of Department Graduates:

Master's Degree Graduates: Of those who graduated in the academic year 2011–2012, the following categories and numbers represent the postgraduate activities and employment of master's degree graduates: Enrolled in a postdoctoral residency/fellowship (n/a), employed in independent practice (n/a), total from the above (master's) (0).

Doctoral Degree Graduates: Of those who graduated in the academic year 2011–2012, the following categories and numbers represent the postgraduate activities and employment of doctoral degree graduates: Enrolled in a psychology doctoral program (n/a), employed in independent practice (1), employed in other positions at a higher education institution (4), total from the above (doctoral) (5).

Additional Information:

Orientation, Objectives, and Emphasis of Department: The Department of Counseling Psychology and Special Education offers master's programs in Special Education, an EdS degree in School Psychology, and a PhD program in Counseling Psychology. The School Psychology program prepares students for certification as school psychologists. The Counseling Psychology program prepares individuals for licensure as psychologists. The program is both broad-based and specific in nature; that is, one is expected to take certain courses that could be required for licensure or for certification and graduation, but the program encourages students to take coursework in varied disciplines such as marriage and family therapy, organizational behavior, and other fields allied with psychology and education. The focus of the School Psychology EdS program is to prepare graduates for K-12 school settings. The doctoral program prepares counseling psychologists to work in counseling centers, academic positions, and other mental health settings.

Personal Behavior Statement: https://honorcode.byu.edu/.

Special Facilities or Resources: The department has a Counseling Psychology Center with five individual counseling rooms and one large group room available for the observation and videotaping of students in counseling and assessment. These are assigned specifically to the department, while an abundance of other media-related facilities for the teaching and learning experience are available on campus as well as off campus. The department also provides spacious study and work carrels. The Counseling and Career Center has eight offices for practicum students. All of these offices have videotaping capabilities and are equipped for live supervision.

Information for Students With Physical Disabilities: See the following website for more information: https://uac.byu.edu/.

Application Information:
Send to Office of Graduate Studies, B-356 ASB, BYU, Provo, UT 84602. Application available online. URL of online application: http://www.byu.edu/gradstudies/. Students are admitted in the Fall, application deadline January 15. *Fee:* $50.

Brigham Young University

Department of Psychology
Family, Home & Social Sciences
1001 SWKT
Provo, UT 84602-5543
Telephone: (801) 422-4287
Fax: (801) 422-0602
E-mail: *lisa_norton@byu.edu*
Web: *http://psychology.byu.edu*

Department Information:
1921. Chairperson: Dawson W. Hedges. Number of faculty: total—full-time 32, part-time 8; women—full-time 5, part-time 5; total—minority—full-time 1; women minority—full-time 1.

Programs and Degrees Offered:
Listed in the following order: Program area, degree type (T if terminal Master's), number awarded 7/11–6/12. General Psychology PhD (Doctor of Philosophy) 3, Clinical Psychology PhD (Doctor of Philosophy) 8.

APA Accreditation: Clinical PhD (Doctor of Philosophy). Student Outcome Data Website: https://psychology.byu.edu/Pages/Graduate/Clinical/Outcomes.aspx.

Student Applications/Admissions:
Student Applications
General Psychology PhD (Doctor of Philosophy)—Applications 2012–2013, 24. Total applicants accepted 2012–2013, 7. Number full-time enrolled (new admits only) 2012–2013, 4. Total enrolled 2012–2013 full-time, 15. Openings 2013–2014, 8. The median number of years required for completion of a degree in 2012–2013 were 4. The number of students enrolled full- and part-time who were dismissed or voluntarily withdrew from this program area in 2012–2013 were 0. *Clinical Psychology PhD (Doctor of Philosophy)*—Applications 2012–2013, 70. Total applicants accepted 2012–2013, 10. Number full-time enrolled (new admits only) 2012–2013, 8. Total enrolled 2012–2013 full-time, 47. Openings 2013–2014, 8. The median number of years required for completion of a degree in 2012–2013

were 5. The number of students enrolled full- and part-time who were dismissed or voluntarily withdrew from this program area in 2012–2013 were 0.

Scores: Entries appear in this order: required test or GPA, minimum score (if required), median score of students entering in 2012–2013. *General Psychology PhD (Doctor of Philosophy):* GRE-V no minimum stated, 159, GRE-Q no minimum stated, 155, GRE-Analytical no minimum stated, 4.8, last 2 years GPA no minimum stated, 3.85, Masters GPA no minimum stated; *Clinical Psychology PhD (Doctor of Philosophy):* GRE-V no minimum stated, 158, GRE-Q no minimum stated, 153, GRE-Analytical no minimum stated, 4.25, overall undergraduate GPA no minimum stated, last 2 years GPA 3.0, 3.76.

Other Criteria: (importance of criteria rated low, medium, or high): GRE scores—high, research experience—high, work experience—medium, extracurricular activity—low, clinically related public service—medium, GPA—high, letters of recommendation—high, interview—high, statement of goals and objectives—high, undergraduate major in psychology—medium, specific undergraduate psychology courses taken—medium, 1. "Clinically Related Public Service": Relevant to Clinical PhD applicants only. 2. "Undergraduate Major in Psychology" and "Specific Undergraduate Psychology Courses Taken": Students may have completed courses in other departments which would be considered equivalent to having taken certain psychology courses. For additional information on admission requirements, go to https://psychology.byu.edu/Pages/Graduate/Clinical/Admissions.aspx.

Student Characteristics: The following represents characteristics of students in 2012–2013 in all graduate psychology programs in the department: Female—full-time 28, part-time 0; Male—full-time 34, part-time 0; African American/Black—full-time 2, part-time 0; Hispanic/Latino(a)—full-time 3, part-time 0; Asian/Pacific Islander—full-time 5, part-time 0; American Indian/Alaska Native—full-time 1, part-time 0; Caucasian/White—full-time 51, part-time 0; Multi-ethnic—full-time 0, part-time 0; students subject to the Americans With Disabilities Act—full-time 1, part-time 0; Unknown ethnicity—full-time 0, part-time 0; International students who hold an F-1 or J-1 Visa—full-time 3, part-time 0.

Financial Information/Assistance:

Tuition for Full-Time Study: *Master's:* State residents: per academic year $5,950, $331 per credit hour; Nonstate residents: per academic year $11,900, $662 per credit hour. *Doctoral:* State residents: per academic year $5,950, $331 per credit hour; Nonstate residents: per academic year $11,900, $662 per credit hour. Tuition is subject to change.

Financial Assistance:

First-Year Students: Teaching assistantships available for first year. Average amount paid per academic year: $11,000. Average number of hours worked per week: 15. Research assistantships available for first year. Average amount paid per academic year: $11,000. Average number of hours worked per week: 15.

Advanced Students: Teaching assistantships available for advanced students. Average amount paid per academic year: $11,500. Average number of hours worked per week: 15. Research assistantships available for advanced students. Average amount paid per academic year: $11,500. Average number of hours worked per week: 15. Traineeships available for advanced students. Aver-

age amount paid per academic year: $14,000. Average number of hours worked per week: 20.

Additional Information: Of all students currently enrolled full time, 100% benefited from one or more of the listed financial assistance programs.

Internships/Practica: Doctoral Degree (PhD Clinical Psychology): For those doctoral students for whom a professional psychology internship was required in this program prior to graduation, (11) students applied for an internship in 2011–2012, with (10) students obtaining an internship. Of those students who obtained an internship, (10) were paid internships. Of those students who obtained an internship, (9) students placed in APA/CPA accredited internships, (1) students placed in internships not APA/CPA accredited, but listed with the Association of Psychology Postdoctoral and Internship Programs (APPIC), (0) students placed in internships conforming to guidelines of the Council of Directors of School Psychology Programs (CDSPP), (0) students placed in internships that were not APA/CPA accredited, APPIC or CDSPP listed. Students in the General PhD program have the opportunity for internships in a wide variety of community settings, ranging from mental health to business. Clinical PhD students complete three types of practica: 1) BYU Comprehensive Clinic Integrative Practicum: Students see clients from the community in their first three years under the supervision of full-time clinical faculty. The clinic is a unique interdisciplinary training and research facility housing state-of-the-art audiovisual and computer resources for BYU's Clinical Psychology, Marriage and Family Therapy, Social Work, and Communication Disorders programs. 2) Clerkships: Students are required to complete two unpaid clerkships of 60 hours each. The clerkships allow students to work with different service agencies dealing with different focus groups: examples include prison, state hospital, residential treatment centers, private practice with a variety of age groups and presenting problems, developmentally disabled/autistic classrooms, and rehabilitation centers. 3) Externships: The clinical program arranges reimbursed training placements for students in over 25 community agencies where students are supervised by onsite licensed professionals, who typically hold affiliate appointments in the Psychology Department. These opportunities provide an excellent foundation for the integration of classroom experiences with practical work applications.

Housing and Day Care: On-campus housing is available. See the following website for more information: http://housing.byu.edu/. No on-campus day care facilities are available.

Employment of Department Graduates:

Master's Degree Graduates: Of those who graduated in the academic year 2011–2012, the following categories and numbers represent the postgraduate activities and employment of master's degree graduates: Enrolled in a postdoctoral residency/fellowship (n/a), employed in independent practice (n/a), total from the above (master's) (0).

Doctoral Degree Graduates: Of those who graduated in the academic year 2011–2012, the following categories and numbers represent the postgraduate activities and employment of doctoral degree graduates: Enrolled in a psychology doctoral program (n/a), enrolled in another graduate/professional program (1), enrolled in a postdoctoral residency/fellowship (2), employed in an academic position at a university (2), employed in an academic position at a 2-year/4-year college (1), employed in other positions at a higher education institution (3), employed in government agency (1), employed in a community mental health/counseling center (1), total from the above (doctoral) (11).

Additional Information:

Orientation, Objectives, and Emphasis of Department: The mission of the Psychology Department is to discover, disseminate, and apply principles of psychology within a scholarly framework that is compatible with the values and purposes of Brigham Young University and its sponsor. Two degrees are offered: General Psychology PhD (emphasis areas in Applied Social Psychology, Developmental Psychology, and Behavioral Neuroscience) and Clinical Psychology PhD. For the General PhD, students complete a common core of course work during the first three semesters. By the end of the second year, students in both PhD programs complete the requirements for a second-year project. The philosophy of the clinical psychology program adheres to the scientist-professional model. Training focuses on academic and research competence as well as on theory and practicum experiences necessary to develop strong clinical skills. The program is eclectic in its theoretical approach, drawing from a wide range of orientations in an attempt to give broad exposure to a diversity of traditional and innovative approaches. If they wish, students may elect to complete an emphasis in 1) Child, Adolescent, and Family, 2) Clinical Neuropsychology, or 3) Clinical Research.

Personal Behavior Statement: While the university is sponsored by the LDS (Mormon) Church, non-LDS students are welcome and considered without bias. The university does expect that all students, regardless of religion, maintain the behavioral standards of the university. These include high standards of honor, integrity, and morality; graciousness in personal behavior; and abstinence from such things as tobacco, alcohol, and the nonmedical use of drugs. The text of this agreement can be viewed at http://honorcode.byu.edu.

Special Facilities or Resources: 1) 3 Tesla MRI Research Facility: This new scanner is capable of doing functional MRI and DT, enabling collaborative projects across disciplines. 2) Comprehensive Clinic: The university maintains a large clinic for training and research purposes, serving 200-250 clients each week. 3) Computer Facilities: Extensive computer facilities are available throughout the department, college, and university. 4) Neuroimaging and Behavior Laboratory: Research and training in the area of neuroimaging and cognitive neuroscience are facilitated by a laboratory consisting of multiple computers, video, data storage, and printer workstations. These are supported by software that allows for the capture, processing, isolation, and imaging output of specific areas of the brain from MRI and CT images and from metabolic imaging studies.

Information for Students With Physical Disabilities: See the following website for more information: http://uac.byu.edu.

Application Information:

Application available online. URL of online application: https://www.byu.edu/gradstudies/admissions/applynow.php. Students are admitted in the Fall, application deadline December 15. *Fee:* $50.

Utah State University

Department of Psychology
Education and Human Services
2810 Old Main Hill
Logan, UT 84322-2810
Telephone: (435) 797-1460
Fax: (435) 797-1448
E-mail: *psychology@usu.edu*
Web: *http://psychology.usu.edu*

Department Information:

1938. Chairperson: Gretchen Peacock, PhD. Number of faculty: total—full-time 25, part-time 1; women—full-time 13, part-time 1; total—minority—full-time 4, part-time 1; women minority—full-time 4, part-time 1.

Programs and Degrees Offered:

Listed in the following order: Program area, degree type (T if terminal Master's), number awarded 7/11–6/12. Combined Clinical/Counseling/School Psychology PhD (Doctor of Philosophy) 3, Experimental and Applied Psychological Science PhD (Doctor of Philosophy) 4, School Psychology EdS (School Psychology) 3, School Counseling MA/MS (Master of Arts/Science) (T) 58.

APA Accreditation: Combination PhD (Doctor of Philosophy). Student Outcome Data Website: http://psychology.usu.edu/Graduate-Programs/Combined-Program-in-Clinical-Counseling-School-Psychology-PhD/Student-admissions-outcomes-and-other-data/.

Student Applications/Admissions:

Student Applications

Combined Clinical/Counseling/School Psychology PhD (Doctor of Philosophy)—Applications 2012–2013, 127. Total applicants accepted 2012–2013, 10. Number full-time enrolled (new admits only) 2012–2013, 7. Number part-time enrolled (new admits only) 2012–2013, 0. Total enrolled 2012–2013 full-time, 37. Total enrolled 2012–2013 part-time, 0. Openings 2013–2014, 8. The median number of years required for completion of a degree in 2012–2013 were 7. The number of students enrolled full- and part-time who were dismissed or voluntarily withdrew from this program area in 2012–2013 were 1. *Experimental and Applied Psychological Science PhD (Doctor of Philosophy)*—Applications 2012–2013, 30. Total applicants accepted 2012–2013, 6. Number full-time enrolled (new admits only) 2012–2013, 4. Number part-time enrolled (new admits only) 2012–2013, 0. Total enrolled 2012–2013 full-time, 22. Total enrolled 2012–2013 part-time, 0. Openings 2013–2014, 8. The number of students enrolled full- and part-time who were dismissed or voluntarily withdrew from this program area in 2012–2013 were 1. *School Psychology EdS (School Psychology)*—Applications 2012–2013, 17. Total applicants accepted 2012–2013, 7. Number full-time enrolled (new admits only) 2012–2013, 5. Total enrolled 2012–2013 full-time, 17. Openings 2013–2014, 5. The median number of years required for completion of a degree in 2012–2013 were 4. The number of students enrolled full- and part-time who were dismissed or voluntarily withdrew from this program area in 2012–2013 were 0. *School Counseling MA/MS (Master of Arts/Science)*—Applications 2012–2013, 60. Total applicants accepted 2012–2013, 34. Number part-time enrolled (new admits only) 2012–2013, 31. Total enrolled 2012–2013 part-time, 103. Openings 2013–2014, 55. The median number of years required for completion of a degree in 2012–2013 were 3. The number of students enrolled full- and part-time who were dismissed or voluntarily withdrew from this program area in 2012–2013 were 0.

Scores: Entries appear in this order: required test or GPA, minimum score (if required), median score of students entering in 2012–2013. *Combined Clinical/Counseling/School Psychology PhD (Doctor of Philosophy):* GRE-V no minimum stated, 160, GRE-Q no minimum stated, 154, GRE-Analytical no minimum stated, overall undergraduate GPA no minimum stated, last 2 years GPA no minimum stated, 3.81; *Experimental and Applied Psychological Science PhD (Doctor of Philosophy):* GRE-V no minimum stated, GRE-Q no minimum stated, GRE-Analytical no minimum stated, overall undergraduate GPA no minimum stated, last 2 years GPA no minimum stated; *School Psychology EdS (School Psychology):* GRE-V no minimum stated, GRE-Q no minimum stated, GRE-Analytical no minimum stated, overall undergraduate GPA no minimum stated, last 2 years GPA no minimum stated; *School Counseling MA/MS (Master of Arts/Science):* overall undergraduate GPA no minimum stated, last 2 years GPA no minimum stated.

Other Criteria: (importance of criteria rated low, medium, or high): GRE scores—medium, research experience—medium, work experience—medium, extracurricular activity—low, clinically related public service—medium, GPA—high, letters of recommendation—medium, interview—medium, statement of goals and objectives—high, undergraduate major in psychology—medium, specific undergraduate psychology courses taken—medium, The different graduate programs weight the above criteria in different ways. For example, research experience is much more important for the two PhD programs. For additional information on admission requirements, go to http://psychology.usu.edu/.

Student Characteristics: The following represents characteristics of students in 2012–2013 in all graduate psychology programs in the department: Female—full-time 45, part-time 78; Male—full-time 31, part-time 25; African American/Black—full-time 3, part-time 0; Hispanic/Latino(a)—full-time 6, part-time 4; Asian/Pacific Islander—full-time 2, part-time 1; American Indian/Alaska Native—full-time 2, part-time 0; Caucasian/White—full-time 57, part-time 96; Multi-ethnic—full-time 4, part-time 2; students subject to the Americans With Disabilities Act—full-time 0, part-time 0; Unknown ethnicity—full-time 2, part-time 0; International students who hold an F-1 or J-1 Visa—full-time 0, part-time 0.

Financial Information/Assistance:

Tuition for Full-Time Study: *Master's:* State residents: per academic year $5,516; Nonstate residents: per academic year $18,711. *Doctoral:* State residents: per academic year $5,516; Nonstate residents: per academic year $18,711. Tuition is subject to change. Additional fees are assessed to students beyond the costs of tuition for the following: various student fees amount to approximately $1000 per year (including insurance). See the following website for updates and changes in tuition costs: http://www.usu.edu/registrar/htm/tuition/.

Financial Assistance:

First-Year Students: Teaching assistantships available for first year. Average amount paid per academic year: $10,000. Aver-

age number of hours worked per week: 20. Research assistantships available for first year. Average amount paid per academic year: $10,000. Average number of hours worked per week: 20. Fellowships and scholarships available for first year. Average amount paid per academic year: $20,000.

Advanced Students: Teaching assistantships available for advanced students. Average amount paid per academic year: $10,000. Average number of hours worked per week: 20. Apply by March 1. Research assistantships available for advanced students. Average amount paid per academic year: $10,000. Average number of hours worked per week: 20.

Additional Information: Of all students currently enrolled full time, 100% benefited from one or more of the listed financial assistance programs. Application and information available online at: http://rgs.usu.edu/graduateschool/htm/finances.

Internships/Practica: Doctoral Degree (PhD Combined Clinical/Counseling/School Psychology): For those doctoral students for whom a professional psychology internship was required in this program prior to graduation, (6) students applied for an internship in 2011–2012, with (6) students obtaining an internship. Of those students who obtained an internship, (6) were paid internships. Of those students who obtained an internship, (5) students placed in APA/CPA accredited internships, (1) students placed in internships not APA/CPA accredited, but listed with the Association of Psychology Postdoctoral and Internship Programs (APPIC), (0) students placed in internships conforming to guidelines of the Council of Directors of School Psychology Programs (CDSPP), (0) students placed in internships that were not APA/CPA accredited, APPIC or CDSPP listed. Master's Degree (EdS School Psychology): An internship experience, such as a final research project or "capstone" experience is required of graduates. Master's Degree (MA/MS School Counseling): An internship experience, such as a final research project or "capstone" experience is required of graduates. Students in the Combined PhD program are placed in a variety of sites for practicum training including community mental health centers, the USU Counseling Center, the Center for Persons with Disabilities (a University Center for Excellence in Developmental Disabilities), residential eating disorders treatment facility, and medical facilities in the area. Students from the Combined program accept internships across the country. Students in the School Psychology and School Counseling programs completed practica and internships in school districts. Internship experiences can be in Utah or completed out-of-state.

Housing and Day Care: On-campus housing is available. See the following website for more information: http://www.usu.edu/housing. On-campus day care facilities are available. See the following website for more information: http://www.usu.edu/fchd/earlyCare/.

Employment of Department Graduates:

Master's Degree Graduates: Of those who graduated in the academic year 2011–2012, the following categories and numbers represent the postgraduate activities and employment of master's degree graduates: Enrolled in a postdoctoral residency/fellowship (n/a), employed in independent practice (n/a), employed in other positions at a higher education institution (6), employed in a professional position in a school system (38), employed in business or industry (1), employed in government agency (3), employed in a community mental health/counseling center (1), still seeking employment (5), not seeking employment (4), do not know (3), total from the above (master's) (61).

Doctoral Degree Graduates: Of those who graduated in the academic year 2011–2012, the following categories and numbers represent the postgraduate activities and employment of doctoral degree graduates: Enrolled in a psychology doctoral program (n/a), enrolled in a postdoctoral residency/fellowship (2), employed in independent practice (1), employed in an academic position at a university (1), employed in other positions at a higher education institution (2), employed in government agency (1), total from the above (doctoral) (7).

Additional Information:

Orientation, Objectives, and Emphasis of Department: The Utah State University Department of Psychology offers two graduate PhD specializations. The Experimental and Applied Psychological Sciences program offers training in a number of areas including behavior analysis, sociobehavioral epidemiology, and cognition. The Combined clinical/counseling/school psychology program offers integrated training across clinical, counseling, and school psychology (accredited by the American Psychological Association since 1975). Emphasis areas within this program include: child/school psychology, rural/multicultural psychology, and health/neuropsychology. The department also offers an EdS program in School Psychology and a MS program in School Counseling. The School Counseling program is part-time, distance-based program. The two graduate PhD programs share a common core of doctoral courses intended to provide an advanced overview of several major areas of psychology. All doctoral programs offer extensive training within their specific areas; however, the common core is designed to ensure that no student will complete the PhD without being exposed to the diverse theoretical and methodological perspectives in the field of psychology. The common core also provides students the opportunity to become aware of the scholarly interests of faculty members in all programs, thus broadening students' choices of faculty advisors and dissertation chairpersons. Tuition awards are available to PhD students for the majority of their doctoral program courses.

Special Facilities or Resources: Students in the School Psychology and Combined programs benefit from the department's Psychology Community Clinic. In addition, the department has cooperative relations with other campus and off-campus facilities that provide excellent settings for student training, including area school districts, the USU Center for Persons with Disabilities, and the USU Counseling Center. Students in the EAPS program may work in animal (rat and pigeon) labs of their faculty supervisors.

Information for Students With Physical Disabilities: See the following website for more information: http://www.usu.edu/drc/.

Application Information:
Send to Utah State University, School of Graduate Studies, Logan, UT 84322-0900. Application available online. URL of online application: https://rgs.usu.edu/gradguide/htm/apply. Students are admitted in the Fall, application deadline December 15. PhD Combined Clinical/Counseling/School Psychology Program and PhD Experimental and Applied Psychological Science deadlines are December 15, EdS School Psychology deadline is February 1, and MS School Counseling deadline is May 1. *Fee:* $55.

Utah, University of (2012 data)
Department of Educational Psychology, Counseling Psychology and School Psychology Programs
College of Education
1705 East Campus Center Drive, Room 113
Salt Lake City, UT 84112-9255
Telephone: (801) 581-7148
Fax: (801) 581-5566
E-mail: *linda.bredin@utah.edu*
Web: *http://www.ed.utah.edu/edps/*

Department Information:
1949. Chairperson: Elaine Clark. Number of faculty: total—full-time 21, part-time 1; women—full-time 10, part-time 1; total—minority—full-time 3; women minority—full-time 1.

Programs and Degrees Offered:
Listed in the following order: Program area, degree type (T if terminal Master's), number awarded 7/11–6/12. Counseling Psychology PhD (Doctor of Philosophy) 4, School Psychology PhD (Doctor of Philosophy) 3, Learning Sciences PhD (Doctor of Philosophy) 1, Instructional Design and Educational Technology MA/MS (Master of Arts/Science) 12, Professional Counseling MEd (Education) 6, School Counseling MEd (Education) 12, Statistics MA/MS (Master of Arts/Science) (T) 1, Reading and Literacy PhD (Doctor of Philosophy) 8, Reading and Literacy MEd (Education) 4, School Psychology MA/MS (Master of Arts/Science) 1, Elementary Education MEd (Education) 10.

APA Accreditation: Counseling PhD (Doctor of Philosophy). School PhD (Doctor of Philosophy).

Student Applications/Admissions:
Student Applications

Counseling Psychology PhD (Doctor of Philosophy)—Applications 2012–2013, 88. Total applicants accepted 2012–2013, 4. Number full-time enrolled (new admits only) 2012–2013, 4. Number part-time enrolled (new admits only) 2012–2013, 4. Total enrolled 2012–2013 full-time, 41. Total enrolled 2012–2013 part-time, 1. Openings 2013–2014, 6. The median number of years required for completion of a degree in 2012–2013 were 6. The number of students enrolled full- and part-time who were dismissed or voluntarily withdrew from this program area in 2012–2013 were 2. *School Psychology PhD (Doctor of Philosophy)*—Applications 2012–2013, 22. Total applicants accepted 2012–2013, 7. Number full-time enrolled (new admits only) 2012–2013, 7. Number part-time enrolled (new admits only) 2012–2013, 0. Total enrolled 2012–2013 full-time, 33. Total enrolled 2012–2013 part-time, 1. Openings 2013–2014, 8. The median number of years required for completion of a degree in 2012–2013 were 6. The number of students enrolled full- and part-time who were dismissed or voluntarily withdrew from this program area in 2012–2013 were 0. *Learning Sciences PhD (Doctor of Philosophy)*—Applications 2012–2013, 4. Total applicants accepted 2012–2013, 3. Number full-time enrolled (new admits only) 2012–2013, 3. Number part-time enrolled (new admits only) 2012–2013, 3. Total enrolled 2012–2013 full-time, 12. Total enrolled 2012–2013 part-time, 1. Openings 2013–2014, 5. The median number of years required for completion of a degree in 2012–2013 were 6. The number of students enrolled full- and part-time who were dismissed or voluntarily withdrew from this program area in 2012–2013 were 1. *Instructional Design and Educational Technology MA/MS (Master of Arts/Science)*—Applications 2012–2013, 22. Total applicants accepted 2012–2013, 18. Number full-time enrolled (new admits only) 2012–2013, 13. Number part-time enrolled (new admits only) 2012–2013, 18. Total enrolled 2012–2013 full-time, 51. Total enrolled 2012–2013 part-time, 0. Openings 2013–2014, 20. The median number of years required for completion of a degree in 2012–2013 were 2. The number of students enrolled full- and part-time who were dismissed or voluntarily withdrew from this program area in 2012–2013 were 2. *Professional Counseling MEd (Education)*—Applications 2012–2013, 46. Total applicants accepted 2012–2013, 12. Number full-time enrolled (new admits only) 2012–2013, 12. Total enrolled 2012–2013 full-time, 16. Openings 2013–2014, 12. The median number of years required for completion of a degree in 2012–2013 were 2. The number of students enrolled full- and part-time who were dismissed or voluntarily withdrew from this program area in 2012–2013 were 0. *School Counseling MEd (Education)*—Applications 2012–2013, 39. Total applicants accepted 2012–2013, 14. Number full-time enrolled (new admits only) 2012–2013, 14. Number part-time enrolled (new admits only) 2012–2013, 0. Total enrolled 2012–2013 full-time, 40. Total enrolled 2012–2013 part-time, 1. Openings 2013–2014, 20. The median number of years required for completion of a degree in 2012–2013 were 2. The number of students enrolled full- and part-time who were dismissed or voluntarily withdrew from this program area in 2012–2013 were 6. *Statistics MA/MS (Master of Arts/Science)*—Applications 2012–2013, 4. Total applicants accepted 2012–2013, 3. Number full-time enrolled (new admits only) 2012–2013, 3. Number part-time enrolled (new admits only) 2012–2013, 0. Total enrolled 2012–2013 full-time, 6. Total enrolled 2012–2013 part-time, 0. Openings 2013–2014, 3. The median number of years required for completion of a degree in 2012–2013 were 2. The number of students enrolled full- and part-time who were dismissed or voluntarily withdrew from this program area in 2012–2013 were 1. *Reading and Literacy PhD (Doctor of Philosophy)*—Applications 2012–2013, 2. Total applicants accepted 2012–2013, 2. Number full-time enrolled (new admits only) 2012–2013, 2. Total enrolled 2012–2013 full-time, 15. Openings 2013–2014, 4. The median number of years required for completion of a degree in 2012–2013 were 7. The number of students enrolled full- and part-time who were dismissed or voluntarily withdrew from this program area in 2012–2013 were 0. *Reading and Literacy MEd (Education)*—Applications 2012–2013, 21. Total applicants accepted 2012–2013, 21. Number full-time enrolled (new admits only) 2012–2013, 21. Total enrolled 2012–2013 full-time, 32. Openings 2013–2014, 30. The median number of years required for completion of a degree in 2012–2013 were 2. The number of students enrolled full- and part-time who were dismissed or voluntarily withdrew from this program area in 2012–2013 were 3. *School Psychology MA/MS (Master of Arts/Science)*—Applications 2012–2013, 20. Total applicants accepted 2012–2013, 4. Number full-time enrolled (new admits only) 2012–2013, 4. Total enrolled 2012–2013 full-time, 20. Openings 2013–2014, 6. The median number of years required for completion of a degree in 2012–2013 were 6. The number of students enrolled full- and part-time who were dismissed or voluntarily withdrew from this program area

in 2012–2013 were 0. *Elementary Education MEd (Education)*—Applications 2012–2013, 5. Total applicants accepted 2012–2013, 5. Number full-time enrolled (new admits only) 2012–2013, 2. Total enrolled 2012–2013 full-time, 25. Openings 2013–2014, 8. The median number of years required for completion of a degree in 2012–2013 were 2. The number of students enrolled full- and part-time who were dismissed or voluntarily withdrew from this program area in 2012–2013 were 0.

Scores: Entries appear in this order: required test or GPA, minimum score (if required), median score of students entering in 2012–2013. *Counseling Psychology PhD (Doctor of Philosophy):* GRE-V 430, 460, GRE-Q 560, 635, GRE-Analytical 4.0, 4.25, overall undergraduate GPA 3.51, 3.54; *School Psychology PhD (Doctor of Philosophy):* GRE-V 450, 520, GRE-Q 490, 630, GRE-Analytical 4.0, 4.5, overall undergraduate GPA 3.1, 3.5; *Learning Sciences PhD (Doctor of Philosophy):* GRE-V 440, 535, GRE-Q 490, 540, GRE-Analytical 3.0, 4.3, overall undergraduate GPA 2.87, 3.65; *Instructional Design and Educational Technology MA/MS (Master of Arts/Science):* overall undergraduate GPA 2.2, 3.58; *Professional Counseling MEd (Education):* GRE-V 500, 580, GRE-Q 500, 590, GRE-Analytical 3.0, 4.0, overall undergraduate GPA 3.0, 3.52; *School Counseling MEd (Education):* GRE-V 330, 500, GRE-Q 340, 540, GRE-Analytical 2.5, 4.0, overall undergraduate GPA 2.9, 3.44; *Statistics MA/MS (Master of Arts/Science):* GRE-V 460, 500, GRE-Q 630, 660, GRE-Analytical 3.5, 3.5, overall undergraduate GPA 3.29, 3.40; *Reading and Literacy PhD (Doctor of Philosophy):* GRE-V 500, GRE-Q 500, GRE-Analytical 3.0, 4.5, overall undergraduate GPA 3.13, 3.27; *Reading and Literacy MEd (Education):* GRE-Analytical 3.0, 4.5, overall undergraduate GPA no minimum stated; *School Psychology MA/MS (Master of Arts/Science):* GRE-V 470, 580, GRE-Q 460, 570, GRE-Analytical 4.5, 4.75, overall undergraduate GPA 3.42, 3.91; *Elementary Education MEd (Education):* GRE-Analytical 4.0, 4.5, overall undergraduate GPA 3.0, 3.26.

Other Criteria: (importance of criteria rated low, medium, or high): GRE scores—high, research experience—high, work experience—high, extracurricular activity—medium, clinically related public service—medium, GPA—high, letters of recommendation—high, interview—high, statement of goals and objectives—high, undergraduate major in psychology—medium, Each program reviews and rates its own applicants. For additional information on admission requirements, go to http://www.ed.utah.edu/edps/.

Student Characteristics: The following represents characteristics of students in 2012–2013 in all graduate psychology programs in the department: Female—full-time 172, part-time 0; Male—full-time 61, part-time 0; African American/Black—full-time 2, part-time 0; Hispanic/Latino(a)—full-time 16, part-time 0; Asian/Pacific Islander—full-time 9, part-time 0; American Indian/Alaska Native—full-time 4, part-time 0; Caucasian/White—full-time 149, part-time 66; Multi-ethnic—full-time 5, part-time 0; students subject to the Americans With Disabilities Act—full-time 0, part-time 0; Unknown ethnicity—full-time 48, part-time 0; International students who hold an F-1 or J-1 Visa—full-time 7, part-time 0.

Financial Information/Assistance:

Tuition for Full-Time Study: *Master's:* State residents: per academic year $5,066, $1,027 per credit hour; Nonstate residents:

per academic year $17,654, $2,957 per credit hour. *Doctoral:* State residents: per academic year $5,066, $1,027 per credit hour; Non-state residents: per academic year $17,654, $2,957 per credit hour. Tuition is subject to change. Additional fees are assessed to students beyond the costs of tuition for the following: mandatory University fees, some special course fees for materials.

Financial Assistance:

First-Year Students: Teaching assistantships available for first year. Average amount paid per academic year: $12,000. Average number of hours worked per week: 20. Apply by April. Research assistantships available for first year. Average amount paid per academic year: $12,000. Average number of hours worked per week: 20.

Advanced Students: Teaching assistantships available for advanced students. Average amount paid per academic year: $12,000. Average number of hours worked per week: 20. Apply by April. Research assistantships available for advanced students. Average amount paid per academic year: $12,000. Average number of hours worked per week: 20. Traineeships available for advanced students. Fellowships and scholarships available for advanced students. Average amount paid per academic year: $12,000. Average number of hours worked per week: 20. Apply by March.

Additional Information: Of all students currently enrolled full time, 25% benefited from one or more of the listed financial assistance programs.

Internships/Practica: Doctoral Degree (PhD Counseling Psychology): For those doctoral students for whom a professional psychology internship was required in this program prior to graduation, (1) students applied for an internship in 2011–2012, with (1) students obtaining an internship. Of those students who obtained an internship, (1) were paid internships. Of those students who obtained an internship, (0) students placed in APA/CPA accredited internships, (1) students placed in internships not APA/CPA accredited, but listed with the Association of Psychology Postdoctoral and Internship Programs (APPIC), (0) students placed in internships conforming to guidelines of the Council of Directors of School Psychology Programs (CDSPP), (0) students placed in internships that were not APA/CPA accredited, APPIC or CDSPP listed. Doctoral Degree (PhD School Psychology): For those doctoral students for whom a professional psychology internship was required in this program prior to graduation, (5) students applied for an internship in 2011–2012, with (5) students obtaining an internship. Of those students who obtained an internship, (5) were paid internships. Of those students who obtained an internship, (1) students placed in APA/CPA accredited internships, (0) students placed in internships not APA/CPA accredited, but listed with the Association of Psychology Postdoctoral and Internship Programs (APPIC), (4) students placed in internships conforming to guidelines of the Council of Directors of School Psychology Programs (CDSPP), (0) students placed in internships that were not APA/CPA accredited, APPIC or CDSPP listed. Master's Degree (Med Professional Counseling): An internship experience, such as a final research project or "capstone" experience is required of graduates. Practica for Counseling Psychology doctoral students vary and include such settings as University of Utah Counseling Center and other campus services; community mental health settings; hospital settings; and private practice. Pre-doctoral internships are typically taken nationally in university counseling centers, community mental health settings, veterans hospitals, and specialty settings. School Psychology practica initially focus on participation in an on campus clinic and gradually move into field based settings appropriate to the field of school psychology. Specialized practica also allow for supervised experiences in early childhood settings, "stand alone" community based clinics, and specialized treatment programs. Pre-doctoral Internships are completed in local school districts or in other approved settings.

Housing and Day Care: On-campus housing is available. See the following website for more information: Housing and Residential Education: http://www.housing.utah.edu. On-campus day care facilities are available. See the following website for more information: Child Care Coordinating Office: http://www.childcare.utah.edu/.

Employment of Department Graduates:

Master's Degree Graduates: Of those who graduated in the academic year 2011–2012, the following categories and numbers represent the postgraduate activities and employment of master's degree graduates: Enrolled in a postdoctoral residency/fellowship (n/a), employed in independent practice (n/a), employed in an academic position at a 2-year/4-year college (0), employed in other positions at a higher education institution (0), employed in a professional position in a school system (4), employed in business or industry (0), employed in a community mental health/counseling center (8), employed in a hospital/medical center (0), not seeking employment (2), other employment position (1), do not know (57), total from the above (master's) (72).

Doctoral Degree Graduates: Of those who graduated in the academic year 2011–2012, the following categories and numbers represent the postgraduate activities and employment of doctoral degree graduates: Enrolled in a psychology doctoral program (n/a), employed in an academic position at a university (5), employed in an academic position at a 2-year/4-year college (0), employed in other positions at a higher education institution (3), employed in a professional position in a school system (2), employed in business or industry (0), employed in government agency (0), employed in a community mental health/counseling center (1), employed in a hospital/medical center (0), not seeking employment (0), other employment position (0), do not know (8), total from the above (doctoral) (19).

Additional Information:

Orientation, Objectives, and Emphasis of Department: The Department of Educational Psychology at the University of Utah is characterized by an emphasis on the application of behavioral sciences to educational and psychological processes. The department is organized into 4 program areas: Counseling and Counseling Psychology (MS, MEd, PhD); School Psychology (MS, MEd, PhD); Reading and Literacy (MEd and PhD); and Learning Sciences with four subprograms: Learning and Cognition (PhD), a master's level (MEd) program in Instructional Design and Educational Technology (IDET), and two interdepartmental programs, one that leads to a Master's in Statistics (MSTAT) and the other that leads to a master's (MEd) in Elementary Education . The basic master's level programming includes one to two years of academic work (and in some cases an additional year of internship). Doctoral programs include Counseling Psychology (APA accredited since 1957), School Psychology (APA accredited since 1986), and Learning Sciences (the Learning and Cognition area). The emphasis of the department is on the application of psychological principles in educational and human service settings. In addition, doctoral programs represent a scientist–practitioner model with considerable emphasis on the development of research as well as professional skills.

Special Facilities or Resources: A variety of research and training opportunities are available to students through relationships the department has developed with various university and community facilities. Included are the University Counseling Center, medical center, computer center, and the adjacent regional Veterans Administration Medical Center. Community facilities include local school districts, community mental health centers, children's hospital, general hospitals, child guidance clinics, and various state social service agencies. The department maintains its own statistics laboratory. Students have access to computer stations and use of college computer network.

Application Information:

Send to Admissions, University of Utah, Department of Educational Psychology, 1705 East Campus Center Drive, Room 113, Salt Lake City, Utah 84112-9255. Application available online. URL of online application: http://ed.utah.edu. Students are admitted in the Fall, application deadline December 15. IDET and Learning Sciences — rolling Reading and Literacy MEd — 1 November and 1 April. Reading and Literacy PhD — 1 April. Elementary Education MEd — February 1, November 1. *Fee:* $55.

Utah, University of
Department of Psychology
Social & Behavioral Science
380 South 1530 East, Room 502
Salt Lake City, UT 84112
Telephone: (801) 581-6124
Fax: (801) 581-5841
E-mail: *nancy.seegmiller@psych.utah.edu*
Web: *http://www.psych.utah.edu*

Department Information:

1925. Chairperson: Cynthia A. Berg. Number of faculty: total—full-time 27, part-time 2; women—full-time 15; total—minority—full-time 5; women minority—full-time 2.

Programs and Degrees Offered:

Listed in the following order: Program area, degree type (T if terminal Master's), number awarded 7/11–6/12. Clinical Psychology PhD (Doctor of Philosophy) 4, Cognition and Neuroscience PhD (Doctor of Philosophy) 1, Developmental Psychology PhD (Doctor of Philosophy) 1, Social Psychology PhD (Doctor of Philosophy) 2.

APA Accreditation: Clinical PhD (Doctor of Philosophy). Student Outcome Data Website: http://www.psych.utah.edu/graduate/clinical.php.

Student Applications/Admissions:
Student Applications

Clinical Psychology PhD (Doctor of Philosophy)—Applications 2012–2013, 287. Total applicants accepted 2012–2013, 7.

Number full-time enrolled (new admits only) 2012–2013, 7. Number part-time enrolled (new admits only) 2012–2013, 0. Total enrolled 2012–2013 full-time, 30. Total enrolled 2012–2013 part-time, 6. Openings 2013–2014, 6. The median number of years required for completion of a degree in 2012–2013 were 7. The number of students enrolled full- and part-time who were dismissed or voluntarily withdrew from this program area in 2012–2013 were 1. *Cognition and Neuroscience PhD (Doctor of Philosophy)*—Applications 2012–2013, 37. Total applicants accepted 2012–2013, 3. Number full-time enrolled (new admits only) 2012–2013, 0. Number part-time enrolled (new admits only) 2012–2013, 0. Total enrolled 2012–2013 full-time, 10. Total enrolled 2012–2013 part-time, 0. Openings 2013–2014, 4. The median number of years required for completion of a degree in 2012–2013 were 4. The number of students enrolled full- and part-time who were dismissed or voluntarily withdrew from this program area in 2012–2013 were 0. *Developmental Psychology PhD (Doctor of Philosophy)*—Applications 2012–2013, 39. Total applicants accepted 2012–2013, 4. Number full-time enrolled (new admits only) 2012–2013, 0. Number part-time enrolled (new admits only) 2012–2013, 0. Total enrolled 2012–2013 full-time, 6. Total enrolled 2012–2013 part-time, 0. Openings 2013–2014, 3. The median number of years required for completion of a degree in 2012–2013 were 7. The number of students enrolled full- and part-time who were dismissed or voluntarily withdrew from this program area in 2012–2013 were 0. *Social Psychology PhD (Doctor of Philosophy)*—Applications 2012–2013, 47. Total applicants accepted 2012–2013, 4. Number full-time enrolled (new admits only) 2012–2013, 2. Number part-time enrolled (new admits only) 2012–2013, 0. Total enrolled 2012–2013 full-time, 12. Total enrolled 2012–2013 part-time, 0. Openings 2013–2014, 3. The median number of years required for completion of a degree in 2012–2013 were 6. The number of students enrolled full- and part-time who were dismissed or voluntarily withdrew from this program area in 2012–2013 were 0.

Other Criteria: (importance of criteria rated low, medium, or high): GRE scores—medium, research experience—high, work experience—medium, extracurricular activity—medium, clinically related public service—medium, GPA—medium, letters of recommendation—high, interview—high, statement of goals and objectives—high, undergraduate major in psychology—medium, specific undergraduate psychology courses taken—medium. For additional information on admission requirements, go to http://www.psych.utah.edu/graduate/apply.php.

Student Characteristics: The following represents characteristics of students in 2012–2013 in all graduate psychology programs in the department: Female—full-time 43, part-time 4; Male—full-time 15, part-time 2; African American/Black—full-time 1, part-time 0; Hispanic/Latino(a)—full-time 0, part-time 1; Asian/Pacific Islander—full-time 4, part-time 0; American Indian/Alaska Native—full-time 0, part-time 0; Caucasian/White—full-time 52, part-time 5; Multi-ethnic—full-time 0, part-time 0; students subject to the Americans With Disabilities Act—full-time 0, part-time 0; Unknown ethnicity—full-time 1, part-time 0; International students who hold an F-1 or J-1 Visa—full-time 4, part-time 0.

Financial Information/Assistance:

Tuition for Full-Time Study: *Doctoral:* State residents: per academic year $7,140; Nonstate residents: per academic year $22,900. Tuition is subject to change. See the following website for updates and changes in tuition costs: http://fbs.admin.utah.edu/income/tuition/.

Financial Assistance:

First-Year Students: Teaching assistantships available for first year. Average amount paid per academic year: $14,000. Average number of hours worked per week: 20. Research assistantships available for first year. Average amount paid per academic year: $14,000. Average number of hours worked per week: 20. Fellowships and scholarships available for first year. Average amount paid per academic year: $14,000.

Advanced Students: Teaching assistantships available for advanced students. Average amount paid per academic year: $14,000. Average number of hours worked per week: 20. Research assistantships available for advanced students. Average amount paid per academic year: $14,000. Average number of hours worked per week: 20. Fellowships and scholarships available for advanced students. Average amount paid per academic year: $15,000.

Additional Information: Of all students currently enrolled full time, 95% benefited from one or more of the listed financial assistance programs. Application and information available online at: http://www.psych.utah.edu/graduate/funding.php.

Internships/Practica: Doctoral Degree (PhD Clinical Psychology): For those doctoral students for whom a professional psychology internship was required in this program prior to graduation, (4) students applied for an internship in 2011–2012, with (4) students obtaining an internship. Of those students who obtained an internship, (4) were paid internships. Of those students who obtained an internship, (4) students placed in APA/CPA accredited internships, (0) students placed in internships not APA/CPA accredited, but listed with the Association of Psychology Postdoctoral and Internship Programs (APPIC), (0) students placed in internships conforming to guidelines of the Council of Directors of School Psychology Programs (CDSPP), (0) students placed in internships that were not APA/CPA accredited, APPIC or CDSPP listed. Extensive clinical training experiences are available through close ties with facilities in the community. A sample of these include the Veteran's Administration Hospital, The University Medical Center, Primary Children's Hospital, the Children's Behavioral Therapy Unit, the Juvenile Detention Center, The University Neuropsychiatric Institute, the University Counseling Center, and local community health centers. There are four APA-approved internships in the local community.

Housing and Day Care: On-campus housing is available. See the following website for more information: http://housing.utah.edu/. On-campus day care facilities are available. See the following website for more information: http://childcare.utah.edu/.

Employment of Department Graduates:

Master's Degree Graduates: Of those who graduated in the academic year 2011–2012, the following categories and numbers represent the postgraduate activities and employment of master's degree graduates: Enrolled in a postdoctoral residency/fellowship (n/a), employed in independent practice (n/a), total from the above (master's) (0).

Doctoral Degree Graduates: Of those who graduated in the academic year 2011–2012, the following categories and numbers represent the postgraduate activities and employment of doctoral degree graduates: Enrolled in a psychology doctoral program (n/a), enrolled in a postdoctoral residency/fellowship (4), employed in an academic position at a university (1), employed in an academic position at a 2-year/4-year college (2), employed in a hospital/medical center (1), total from the above (doctoral) (8).

Additional Information:

Orientation, Objectives, and Emphasis of Department: We offer comprehensive training in psychology, including Clinical (general, child-family, health, & neuropsychology emphases), Developmental, Cognitive and Neural Science, and Social. Students generally receive support throughout their training. Students are selected for area programs with individual faculty advisers. They do research in their areas, and clinical students also receive applied training. Graduates accept jobs in academic departments, research centers, and applied settings.

Special Facilities or Resources: Special facilities include the Early Childhood Education Center and 3 on-campus hospitals.

Information for Students With Physical Disabilities: See the following website for more information: http://disability.utah.edu/.

Application Information:
Send to Graduate Admissions Secretary, Psychology Department, 380 South 1530 East, Room 502, Salt Lake City, UT 84112. Application available online. URL of online application: http://www.psych.utah.edu/graduate/apply.php. Students are admitted in the Fall, application deadline December 15. *Fee:* $55.

Goddard College

MA Psychology & Clinical Mental Health Counseling Program
123 Pitkin Road
Plainfield, VT 05667
Telephone: (802) 454-8311, (800) 468-4888
Fax: (802) 454-1029
E-mail: *Steven.James@goddard.edu*
Web: *http://www.goddard.edu/ma-psychology-and-counseling*

Department Information:

1988. Chairperson: Steven E. James, PhD Number of faculty: total—full-time 2, part-time 6; women—full-time 1, part-time 5; total—minority—full-time 1, part-time 3; women minority—part-time 3.

Programs and Degrees Offered:

Listed in the following order: Program area, degree type (T if terminal Master's), number awarded 7/11–6/12. Clinical Mental Health Counseling MA/MS (Master of Arts/Science) (T) 15, Psychology MA/MS (Master of Arts/Science) (T) 1.

Student Applications/Admissions:

Student Applications

Clinical Mental Health Counseling MA/MS (Master of Arts/Science)—Applications 2012–2013, 52. Total applicants accepted 2012–2013, 28. Number full-time enrolled (new admits only) 2012–2013, 22. Number part-time enrolled (new admits only) 2012–2013, 5. Total enrolled 2012–2013 full-time, 54. Total enrolled 2012–2013 part-time, 10. Openings 2013–2014, 30. The median number of years required for completion of a degree in 2012–2013 were 2. The number of students enrolled full- and part-time who were dismissed or voluntarily withdrew from this program area in 2012–2013 were 3. *Psychology MA/MS (Master of Arts/Science)*—Applications 2012–2013, 3. Total applicants accepted 2012–2013, 3. Number full-time enrolled (new admits only) 2012–2013, 0. Number part-time enrolled (new admits only) 2012–2013, 0. Openings 2013–2014, 2. The median number of years required for completion of a degree in 2012–2013 were 2. The number of students enrolled full- and part-time who were dismissed or voluntarily withdrew from this program area in 2012–2013 were 0.

Other Criteria: (importance of criteria rated low, medium, or high): research experience—low, work experience—high, extracurricular activity—medium, clinically related public service—high, GPA—medium, letters of recommendation—high, interview—low, statement of goals and objectives—high, iconoclastic intent—high, undergraduate major in psychology—high, specific undergraduate psychology courses taken—medium.

Student Characteristics: The following represents characteristics of students in 2012–2013 in all graduate psychology programs in the department: Female—full-time 37, part-time 8; Male—full-time 17, part-time 3; African American/Black—full-time 1, part-time 0; Hispanic/Latino(a)—full-time 1, part-time 0; Asian/Pacific Islander—full-time 0, part-time 0; American Indian/Alaska Native—full-time 0, part-time 0; Caucasian/White—full-time 30, part-time 11; Multi-ethnic—full-time 2, part-time 0; students subject to the Americans With Disabilities Act—full-time 3, part-time 0; Unknown ethnicity—full-time 20, part-time 0; International students who hold an F-1 or J-1 Visa—full-time 1, part-time 0.

Financial Information/Assistance:

Tuition for Full-Time Study: *Master's:* State residents: per academic year $15,000, $625 per credit hour; Nonstate residents: per academic year $15,000, $625 per credit hour. Tuition is subject to change. See the following website for updates and changes in tuition costs: http://www.goddard.edu/admissions/tuition-and-fees.

Financial Assistance:

First-Year Students: Fellowships and scholarships available for first year. Average amount paid per academic year: $1,445. Average number of hours worked per week: 0.

Advanced Students: Traineeships available for advanced students. Average amount paid per academic year: $1,000. Fellowships and scholarships available for advanced students. Average amount paid per academic year: $1,445. Average number of hours worked per week: 0.

Additional Information: Of all students currently enrolled full time, 0% benefited from one or more of the listed financial assistance programs. Application and information available online at: http://www.goddard.edu/admissions-financial-aid/financial-aid.

Internships/Practica: Master's Degree (MA/MS Clinical Mental Health Counseling): An internship experience, such as a final research project or "capstone" experience is required of graduates. Master's Degree (MA/MS Psychology): An internship experience, such as a final research project or "capstone" experience is required of graduates. Students are required to complete a minimum of 600 hours of supervised practicum during the program. This practicum takes place at a location convenient to the student that has been reviewed and evaluated by the program faculty as appropriate to the student's plan of study, providing appropriate licensed supervision and offering direct counseling experience. Students propose sites at which they would like to work to the faculty for review and approval.

Housing and Day Care: On-campus housing is available. No on-campus day care facilities are available.

Employment of Department Graduates:

Master's Degree Graduates: Of those who graduated in the academic year 2011–2012, the following categories and numbers represent the postgraduate activities and employment of master's degree graduates: Enrolled in a psychology doctoral program (4), enrolled in a postdoctoral residency/fellowship (n/a), employed in independent practice (n/a), employed in an academic position at a university (1), employed in a professional position in a school system (1), employed in business or industry (2), employed in government agency (1), employed in a community mental health/counseling center (2), employed in a hospital/medical center (1), not seeking employment (1), other employment position (1), total from the above (master's) (14).

Doctoral Degree Graduates: Of those who graduated in the academic year 2011–2012, the following categories and numbers represent the postgraduate activities and employment of doctoral degree graduates: Enrolled in a psychology doctoral program (n/a), total from the above (doctoral) (0).

Additional Information:

Orientation, Objectives, and Emphasis of Department: Graduate study in Psychology & Counseling consists of a unique combination of intensive campus residencies and directed, independent study off campus. Students design their own emphasis of study or enter into the defined concentrations in organizational development or sexual orientation studies. The primary goal of the program is to develop skills in individual, family and/or community psychology, grounded in theory and research, personal experience and self-knowledge, and relevant to current social complexities. While pursuing their own specialized interests, students gain mastery in the broad range of subjects necessary for the effective and ethical practice of counseling. Study begins each semester with a week-long residency at the college, a time of planning for the ensuing semester and attending seminars. Returning home, the student begins implementation of the detailed study plan based upon the student's particular interests and needs. Through appropriate design of their study plan, students may meet the educational requirements for master's level licensure or certification in their state. The program is approved by the Council of Applied Master's Programs in Psychology.

Application Information:

Send to Admissions Office, Goddard College, 123 Pitkin Road, Plainfield, VT 05667. Application available online. URL of online application: https://admissions.goddard.edu/application/apply. Students are admitted in the Fall, application deadline September 23; Spring, application deadline March 4. *Fee:* $40. Waiver by written petition.

Saint Michael's College
Psychology Department/Graduate Program in Clinical
 Psychology
Saint Michael's College
One Winooski Park
Colchester, VT 05439
Telephone: (802) 654-2206
Fax: (802) 654-2478
E-mail: *rmiller@smcvt.edu*
Web: *http://www.smcvt.edu/graduate/psych/*

Department Information:

1984. Director: Ronald B. Miller. Number of faculty: total—full-time 6, part-time 8; women—full-time 3, part-time 6.

Programs and Degrees Offered:

Listed in the following order: Program area, degree type (T if terminal Master's), number awarded 7/11–6/12. Clinical Psychology MA/MS (Master of Arts/Science) (T) 16.

Student Applications/Admissions:
Student Applications

Clinical Psychology MA/MS (Master of Arts/Science)—Applications 2012–2013, 35. Total applicants accepted 2012–2013, 21. Number full-time enrolled (new admits only) 2012–2013, 6. Number part-time enrolled (new admits only) 2012–2013, 9. Total enrolled 2012–2013 full-time, 26. Total enrolled 2012–2013 part-time, 30. Openings 2013–2014, 17. The median number of years required for completion of a degree in 2012–2013 were 3. The number of students enrolled full- and part-time who were dismissed or voluntarily withdrew from this program area in 2012–2013 were 2.

Scores: Entries appear in this order: required test or GPA, minimum score (if required), median score of students entering in 2012–2013. *Clinical Psychology MA/MS (Master of Arts/Science):* overall undergraduate GPA 3.0, psychology GPA 3.25.

Other Criteria: (importance of criteria rated low, medium, or high): research experience—low, work experience—high, extracurricular activity—medium, clinically related public service—high, GPA—high, letters of recommendation—high, interview—high, statement of goals and objectives—high, undergraduate major in psychology—medium, specific undergraduate psychology courses taken—high.

Student Characteristics: The following represents characteristics of students in 2012–2013 in all graduate psychology programs in the department: Female—full-time 18, part-time 18; Male—full-time 10, part-time 10; African American/Black—full-time 0, part-time 1; Hispanic/Latino(a)—full-time 2, part-time 0; Asian/Pacific Islander—full-time 2, part-time 0; American Indian/Alaska Native—full-time 1, part-time 0; Caucasian/White—full-time 24, part-time 26; Multi-ethnic—full-time 0, part-time 0; students subject to the Americans With Disabilities Act—full-time 0, part-time 0; Unknown ethnicity—full-time 0, part-time 0; International students who hold an F-1 or J-1 Visa—part-time 0.

Financial Information/Assistance:

Tuition for Full-Time Study: *Master's:* State residents: $570 per credit hour; Nonstate residents: $570 per credit hour. Tuition is subject to change. See the following website for updates and changes in tuition costs: http://www.smcvt.edu/Admissions/Financial-Aid-and-Tuition.aspx.

Financial Assistance:

First-Year Students: Teaching assistantships available for first year. Average number of hours worked per week: 20. Apply by July 1.

Advanced Students: No information provided.

Additional Information: Of all students currently enrolled full time, 5% benefited from one or more of the listed financial assistance programs. Application and information available online at: http://www.smcvt.edu/Admissions/Financial-Aid-and-Tuition.aspx.

Internships/Practica: Master's Degree (MA/MS Clinical Psychology): An internship experience, such as a final research project or "capstone" experience is required of graduates. We have practicum and internship sites in the following settings: schools, college counseling centers, teaching hospitals, correctional centers, Visiting Nurses Association, community mental health outpatient and residential offices, drug and alcohol treatment center, adolescent day treatment program.

Housing and Day Care: No on-campus housing is available. On-campus day care facilities are available. See the following website for more information: http://www.smcvt.edu/On-Campus/Offices-and-Services/Early-Learning-Center.aspx.

Employment of Department Graduates:

Master's Degree Graduates: Of those who graduated in the academic year 2011–2012, the following categories and numbers represent the postgraduate activities and employment of master's degree graduates: Enrolled in a psychology doctoral program (1), enrolled in a postdoctoral residency/fellowship (n/a), employed in independent practice (n/a), employed in an academic position at a 2-year/4-year college (1), employed in a professional position in a school system (1), employed in a community mental health/counseling center (12), employed in a hospital/medical center (1), total from the above (master's) (16).

Doctoral Degree Graduates: Of those who graduated in the academic year 2011–2012, the following categories and numbers represent the postgraduate activities and employment of doctoral degree graduates: Enrolled in a psychology doctoral program (n/a), total from the above (doctoral) (0).

Additional Information:

Orientation, Objectives, and Emphasis of Department: The focus of the MA program in clinical psychology is on the integration of theory, research, and practice in the preparation of professional psychologists. Our goal is to provide an educational milieu that respects the individual educational goals of the student and fosters intellectual, personal, and professional development. The program is eclectic in orientation and the faculty offer a diversity of interests, orientations, and experiences within the framework of our curriculum. We see ourselves as preparing students for professional practice in community agencies, schools, hospitals, and public and private clinics. Cross-registration in courses offered by the college's other master's degree programs in education, administration, and theology is available for those wishing an interdisciplinary emphasis. The curriculum is also designed with two further objectives in mind: (1) the preparation of students for state licensing examinations, and (2) further doctoral study in professional psychology at another institution. All classes are held in the evening, permitting full- or part-time study. The program seeks to integrate a psychodynamic understanding of the therapeutic relationship with humanistic values and a social systems perspective.

Special Facilities or Resources: St. Michael's College offers the graduate student a faculty committed to teaching and professional training in a non-bureaucratic learning environment. All clinical courses are taught by highly experienced clinical practitioners who serve as part-time faculty. The full-time faculty teach core courses in general, developmental, and social psychology, as well as research methods. The college has excellent computing facilities for the support of social science research.

Application Information:
Send to Graduate Admission, Saint Michael's College, One Winooski Park Box 286, Colchester, VT 05439. Application available online. URL of online application: http://www.smcvt.edu/Graduate-Programs/Prospective-Students/Graduate-Admission.aspx. Students are admit-

ted in the Fall, application deadline July 1; Spring, application deadline December 1. Fall enrollment is recommended, and applications for Fall are encouraged by July 1, in order to be eligible for Teaching Assistant position. *Fee:* $40.

Union Institute & University
Graduate Psychology
3 University Way, Suite 3
Brattleboro, VT 05301
Telephone: (802) 257-9411
Fax: (802) 257-0682
E-mail: *william.lax@myunion.edu*
Web: *http://www.myunion.edu/Home.aspx*

Department Information:
2001. Dean: William Lax, PhD. Number of faculty: total—full-time 8, part-time 19; women—full-time 4, part-time 7; total—minority—full-time 3, part-time 1; women minority—full-time 2.

Programs and Degrees Offered:
Listed in the following order: Program area, degree type (T if terminal Master's), number awarded 7/11–6/12. Clinical Psychology PsyD (Doctor of Psychology) 3, Counseling and Psychology MA/MS (Master of Arts/Science) (T) 22.

Student Applications/Admissions:

Student Applications

Clinical Psychology PsyD (Doctor of Psychology)—Applications 2012–2013, 28. Total applicants accepted 2012–2013, 10. Number full-time enrolled (new admits only) 2012–2013, 9. Total enrolled 2012–2013 full-time, 49. Total enrolled 2012–2013 part-time, 3. Openings 2013–2014, 24. The median number of years required for completion of a degree in 2012–2013 were 5. The number of students enrolled full- and part-time who were dismissed or voluntarily withdrew from this program area in 2012–2013 were 0. *Counseling and Psychology MA/MS (Master of Arts/Science)*—Applications 2012–2013, 35. Total applicants accepted 2012–2013, 28. Number full-time enrolled (new admits only) 2012–2013, 22. Number part-time enrolled (new admits only) 2012–2013, 0. Total enrolled 2012–2013 full-time, 48. Openings 2013–2014, 24. The median number of years required for completion of a degree in 2012–2013 were 2. The number of students enrolled full- and part-time who were dismissed or voluntarily withdrew from this program area in 2012–2013 were 0.

Scores: Entries appear in this order: required test or GPA, minimum score (if required), median score of students entering in 2012–2013. *Clinical Psychology PsyD (Doctor of Psychology):* overall undergraduate GPA 3.0, 3.29, Masters GPA 3.0, 3.67; *Counseling and Psychology MA/MS (Master of Arts/Science):* overall undergraduate GPA no minimum stated, last 2 years GPA no minimum stated, psychology GPA no minimum stated.

Other Criteria: (importance of criteria rated low, medium, or high): research experience—medium, work experience—medium, extracurricular activity—medium, clinically related public service—high, GPA—high, letters of recommendation—high, interview—high, statement of goals and objectives—high, undergraduate major in psychology—medium, specific undergraduate psychology courses taken—medium, Admission to the PsyD program requires an on-site interview and a writing sample completed during the interview day. The MAP does not require an interview.

Student Characteristics: The following represents characteristics of students in 2012–2013 in all graduate psychology programs in the department: Female—full-time 47, part-time 2; Male—full-time 50, part-time 1; African American/Black—full-time 4, part-time 1; Hispanic/Latino(a)—full-time 8, part-time 0; Asian/Pacific Islander—full-time 1, part-time 0; American Indian/Alaska Native—full-time 1, part-time 0; Caucasian/White—full-time 82, part-time 2; Multi-ethnic—full-time 0, part-time 0; students subject to the Americans With Disabilities Act—full-time 6, part-time 0; Unknown ethnicity—full-time 1, part-time 0; International students who hold an F-1 or J-1 Visa—full-time 0, part-time 0.

Financial Information/Assistance:

Tuition for Full-Time Study: *Master's:* State residents: $778 per credit hour; Nonstate residents: $778 per credit hour. *Doctoral:* State residents: $888 per credit hour; Nonstate residents: $888 per credit hour. Tuition is subject to change. Additional fees are assessed to students beyond the costs of tuition for the following: technology fee: $60 per term. Tuition costs vary by program. See the following website for updates and changes in tuition costs: http://www.myunion.edu/Admissions/TuitionPaymentOptions/ProgramCosts.aspx.

Financial Assistance:

First-Year Students: No information provided.

Advanced Students: Research assistantships available for advanced students. Average amount paid per academic year: $10,000. Average number of hours worked per week: 15. Apply by October 15. Fellowships and scholarships available for advanced students. Average amount paid per academic year: $50,000. Apply by October 15.

Additional Information: Of all students currently enrolled full time, 69% benefited from one or more of the listed financial assistance programs. Application and information available online at: http://www.myunion.edu/Offices/FinancialAid.aspx.

Internships/Practica: Doctoral Degree (PsyD Clinical Psychology): For those doctoral students for whom a professional psychology internship was required in this program prior to graduation, (12) students applied for an internship in 2011–2012, with (10) students obtaining an internship. Of those students who obtained an internship, (9) were paid internships. Of those students who obtained an internship, (1) students placed in APA/CPA accredited internships, (0) students placed in internships not APA/CPA accredited, but listed with the Association of Psychology Postdoctoral and Internship Programs (APPIC), (0) students placed in internships conforming to guidelines of the Council of Directors of School Psychology Programs (CDSPP), (9) students placed in internships that were not APA/CPA accredited, APPIC or CDSPP listed. Master's Degree (MA/MS Counseling and Psychology): An internship experience, such as a final research project or "capstone" experience is required of graduates. All programs require practicum and/or internship training. All PsyD students are required to successfully complete practicum (600-800 hours per year for two years) and internship (2000 hours) training. Students need to be at a practicum placement located within a

five-hour radius of their cohort center (either Brattleboro, VT or Cincinnati, OH). The practicum must include at least two hours per week of face-to-face supervision by a licensed psychologist and cannot be one's job. The internship should be appropriate both to our program's training model and to the learner's individual goals. The Director of Clinical Training assists in the application processes. Whenever possible, the internship will be at a site accredited by APA or listed with APPIC. For internship sites not listed by APPIC or accredited by APA, the Director of Clinical Training will formalize agreements with these sites to ensure that the internship meets APPIC guidelines. MAP students must complete an internship. The program conducts internship supervision workshops during residencies to help students regarding their internship experiences. The Associate Program Director is also available to assist in placements.

Housing and Day Care: No on-campus housing is available. No on-campus day care facilities are available.

Employment of Department Graduates:

Master's Degree Graduates: Of those who graduated in the academic year 2011–2012, the following categories and numbers represent the postgraduate activities and employment of master's degree graduates: Enrolled in a postdoctoral residency/fellowship (n/a), employed in independent practice (n/a), total from the above (master's) (0).

Doctoral Degree Graduates: Of those who graduated in the academic year 2011–2012, the following categories and numbers represent the postgraduate activities and employment of doctoral degree graduates: Enrolled in a psychology doctoral program (n/a), enrolled in a postdoctoral residency/fellowship (3), total from the above (doctoral) (3).

Additional Information:

Orientation, Objectives, and Emphasis of Department: The PsyD program utilizes a distributed learning model to provide academic coursework in clinical psychology. The distributed learning model includes traditional classroom based courses along with online courses. Courses are offered in an organized, sequential manner, with each semester and year building upon prior learning experiences. In addition to courses, students engage in supervised clinical training experiences, as well as completing a Clinical Review and Dissertation. In the first year of the program, students attend courses on-campus (either Cincinnati, OH or Brattleboro, VT) every other weekend during the term. In years two and three, students attend classes one weekend a month. In years one through three, all students attend two week-long Academic Meetings, held in Brattleboro, VT in the fall and in Cincinnati, OH in the spring. The MAP program provides training in counseling psychology and strives to enhance and disseminate the science of psychology, emphasizing the professional development of its graduate students. Students attend three academic residencies in Brattleboro, VT or Cincinnati, OH, one each term and participate in hybrid and online classes. The MAP also offers a Certificate in Alcohol and Drug Counseling embedded in the degree program.

Special Facilities or Resources: The PsyD program supports its Center for Clinical Mindfulness and Meditation (CCMM) and is an APA-approved sponsor of continuing education for psychologists. The CCMM is designed to serve the international community as a resource to develop and foster the research and clinical applications of mindfulness and meditation, and to provide information, resources, networking, and training for clinicians, researchers, students and the general public on mindfulness and other forms of meditation. Students are strongly supported by the faculty in their professional development and encouraged to conduct research, present and publish their work. Students have opportunities to be involved in faculty research and have presented, sometimes along with faculty, at regional and national conferences. Faculty have a broad range of research interests, consistent with the program's goals and training model. These areas include, but are not limited to: working with under-served populations, cultural competence and diversity, child and family psychology, school-based services, Native American cultures, neuropsychology, family psychology, narrative therapy, supervision and organizational consultation, and forensic assessments.

Information for Students With Physical Disabilities: See the following website for more information: http://www.myunion.edu/About/Policies/ADAUniversityPolicy.aspx.

Application Information:
Send to Diane Robinson, MEd, 3 University Way, Suite 3, Brattleboro, VT 05301. Application available online. URL of online application: http://apply.myunion.edu/. Students are admitted in the Fall, application deadline January 15; Winter, application deadline December 1; Spring, application deadline March 1; Programs have rolling admissions. The PsyD program has an ongoing admissions review, with the first review beginning on January 15. The PsyD has a single entry in September. The MAP has three entry dates: Fall, Winter and Spring/Summer terms. *Fee:* $50.

Vermont, University of
Department of Psychology
Arts and Sciences
2 Colchester Avenue, John Dewey Hall
Burlington, VT 05405-0134
Telephone: (802) 656-2670
Fax: (802) 656-8783
E-mail: *psychology@uvm.edu*
Web: *http://www.uvm.edu/psychology*

Department Information:
1937. Chairperson: William Falls, PhD. Number of faculty: total—full-time 25, part-time 7; women—full-time 14, part-time 5; total—minority—full-time 3, part-time 1; women minority—full-time 1, part-time 1; faculty subject to the Americans With Disabilities Act 1.

Programs and Degrees Offered:
Listed in the following order: Program area, degree type (T if terminal Master's), number awarded 7/11–6/12. General/Experimental Psychology PhD (Doctor of Philosophy) 3, Clinical Psychology PhD (Doctor of Philosophy) 3.

APA Accreditation: Clinical PhD (Doctor of Philosophy). Student Outcome Data Website: http://www.uvm.edu/psychology/graduate/?Page=clinical/clinical_applicant_data.html&SM=clinicalsubmenu.html.

Student Applications/Admissions:
Student Applications
General/Experimental Psychology PhD (Doctor of Philosophy)—Applications 2012–2013, 56. Total applicants accepted 2012–2013, 2. Number full-time enrolled (new admits only) 2012–2013, 2. Number part-time enrolled (new admits only) 2012–2013, 0. Total enrolled 2012–2013 full-time, 24. Total enrolled 2012–2013 part-time, 0. Openings 2013–2014, 6. The median number of years required for completion of a degree in 2012–2013 were 7. The number of students enrolled full- and part-time who were dismissed or voluntarily withdrew from this program area in 2012–2013 were 0. *Clinical Psychology PhD (Doctor of Philosophy)*—Applications 2012–2013, 219. Total applicants accepted 2012–2013, 5. Number full-time enrolled (new admits only) 2012–2013, 5. Number part-time enrolled (new admits only) 2012–2013, 0. Total enrolled 2012–2013 full-time, 28. Total enrolled 2012–2013 part-time, 0. Openings 2013–2014, 5. The median number of years required for completion of a degree in 2012–2013 were 8. The number of students enrolled full- and part-time who were dismissed or voluntarily withdrew from this program area in 2012–2013 were 0.

Scores: Entries appear in this order: required test or GPA, minimum score (if required), median score of students entering in 2012–2013. *General/Experimental Psychology PhD (Doctor of Philosophy):* GRE-V 510, 560, GRE-Q 430, 680, overall undergraduate GPA 3.49, 3.68; *Clinical Psychology PhD (Doctor of Philosophy):* GRE-V 560, 760, GRE-Q 690, 730, overall undergraduate GPA 3.45, 3.51.

Other Criteria: (importance of criteria rated low, medium, or high): GRE scores—high, research experience—high, work experience—medium, extracurricular activity—low, clinically related public service—medium, GPA—high, letters of recommendation—high, interview—high, statement of goals and objectives—high, undergraduate major in psychology—high, specific undergraduate psychology courses taken—medium, Clinically related public service is of importance for clinical program only. For additional information on admission requirements, go to http://www.uvm.edu/psychology/graduate/?Page=application.html&SM=applicationsubmenu.html.

Student Characteristics: The following represents characteristics of students in 2012–2013 in all graduate psychology programs in the department: Female—full-time 35, part-time 0; Male—full-time 17, part-time 0; African American/Black—full-time 1, part-time 0; Hispanic/Latino(a)—full-time 1, part-time 0; Asian/Pacific Islander—full-time 2, part-time 0; American Indian/Alaska Native—full-time 1, part-time 0; Caucasian/White—full-time 47, part-time 0; Multi-ethnic—full-time 0, part-time 0; students subject to the Americans With Disabilities Act—full-time 0, part-time 0; Unknown ethnicity—full-time 0, part-time 0; International students who hold an F-1 or J-1 Visa—full-time 2, part-time 0.

Financial Information/Assistance:
Tuition for Full-Time Study: *Doctoral:* State residents: $589 per credit hour; Nonstate residents: $1,444 per credit hour. Tuition is subject to change. See the following website for updates and changes in tuition costs: http://www.uvm.edu/~stdfinsv/?Page=graduate-tuition.html&SM=tuitionsubmenu.html.

Financial Assistance:

First-Year Students: Teaching assistantships available for first year. Average amount paid per academic year: $17,000. Average number of hours worked per week: 20. Research assistantships available for first year. Average amount paid per academic year: $28,000. Average number of hours worked per week: 20. Traineeships available for first year. Average amount paid per academic year: $21,600. Average number of hours worked per week: 20. Fellowships and scholarships available for first year. Average amount paid per academic year: $17,000. Average number of hours worked per week: 10.

Advanced Students: Teaching assistantships available for advanced students. Average amount paid per academic year: $17,000. Average number of hours worked per week: 20. Research assistantships available for advanced students. Average amount paid per academic year: $28,000. Average number of hours worked per week: 20. Traineeships available for advanced students. Average amount paid per academic year: $21,600. Average number of hours worked per week: 20.

Additional Information: Of all students currently enrolled full time, 100% benefited from one or more of the listed financial assistance programs. Application and information available online at: http://www.uvm.edu/psychology/graduate/?Page=graduate_student_support.html&SM=programwidesubmenu.html.

Internships/Practica: Doctoral Degree (PhD Clinical Psychology): For those doctoral students for whom a professional psychology internship was required in this program prior to graduation, (5) students applied for an internship in 2011–2012, with (5) students obtaining an internship. Of those students who obtained an internship, (5) were paid internships. Of those students who obtained an internship, (4) students placed in APA/CPA accredited internships, (1) students placed in internships not APA/CPA accredited, but listed with the Association of Psychology Postdoctoral and Internship Programs (APPIC), (0) students placed in internships conforming to guidelines of the Council of Directors of School Psychology Programs (CDSPP), (0) students placed in internships that were not APA/CPA accredited, APPIC or CDSPP listed. Multiple clinical practica are available, including outpatient and inpatient adult assessment and psychotherapy, outpatient child and adolescent assessment and psychotherapy, community mental health centers, and medical centers/hospitals. All practica are funded for 20 hours per week.

Housing and Day Care: On-campus housing is available. See the following website for more information: http://reslife.uvm.edu/. On-campus day care facilities are available. See the following website for more information: http://www.uvm.edu/~ccc/.

Employment of Department Graduates:

Master's Degree Graduates: Of those who graduated in the academic year 2011–2012, the following categories and numbers represent the postgraduate activities and employment of master's degree graduates: Enrolled in a postdoctoral residency/fellowship (n/a), employed in independent practice (n/a), total from the above (master's) (0).

Doctoral Degree Graduates: Of those who graduated in the academic year 2011–2012, the following categories and numbers represent the postgraduate activities and employment of doctoral degree graduates: Enrolled in a psychology doctoral program (n/a), enrolled in a postdoctoral residency/fellowship (3), employed in an academic position at a university (2), employed in government agency (1), total from the above (doctoral) (6).

Additional Information:

Orientation, Objectives, and Emphasis of Department: The clinical psychology program is based upon a scientist–practitioner model and is designed to develop competent professional psychologists who can function in applied academic or research positions. Training stresses early placement in a variety of nearby clinical facilities and simultaneous research training relevant to clinical problems. Clinical orientations are primarily cognitive-behavioral. The general/experimental program admits students in three broad specialty areas: (1) basic and applied developmental and social psychology that includes research on ways in which people simultaneously influence and are influenced by social situations and cultural contexts; (2) biobehavioral psychology that focuses on behavioral and neurobiological approaches to learning, memory, emotion, and drug abuse; and (3) human behavioral pharmacology and substance abuse treatment. Students must fulfill general/experimental program requirements as well as requirements for the specialty area in which they are accepted. Applicants should be as specific as possible about their program interest areas.

Special Facilities or Resources: The department has excellent laboratories in behavioral neuroscience, group dynamics, developmental, human psychophysiology, and general human testing. Excellent computer facilities and an in-house psychology clinic with clinical research equipment are available.

Information for Students With Physical Disabilities: See the following website for more information: http://www.uvm.edu/access/.

Application Information:
Send to Graduate College, Admissions Office, 330 Waterman Building, University of Vermont, Burlington, VT 05405-0160. Application available online. URL of online application: https://www.applyweb.com/apply/uvmg/menu.html. Students are admitted in the Fall, application deadline December 1. Deadline is December 1 for Clinical program and January 2 for General/Experimental program. *Fee:* $40. Possibility of waiver for minority applicants.

American School of Professional Psychology at Argosy University/Washington, DC

Clinical Psychology
American School of Professional Psychology
1550 Wilson Boulevard, Suite 600
Arlington, VA 22209
Telephone: (703) 526-5800
Fax: (571) 480-7402
E-mail: *rbarrett@argosy.edu*
Web: *http://www.argosy.edu*

Department Information:
1994. Chair, Clinical Psychology Programs: Robert F. Barrett, PhD. Number of faculty: total—full-time 24, part-time 4; women—full-time 16, part-time 2; total—minority—full-time 5, part-time 1; women minority—full-time 3, part-time 1.

Programs and Degrees Offered:
Listed in the following order: Program area, degree type (T if terminal Master's), number awarded 7/11–6/12. Clinical Psychology PsyD (Doctor of Psychology) 79, Clinical Psychology MA/MS (Master of Arts/Science) (T) 12.

APA Accreditation: Clinical PsyD (Doctor of Psychology). Student Outcome Data Website: http://www.argosy.edu/clinical-psychology/washington-dc-virginia/psyd-programs-doctorate-degree-88712.aspx.

Student Applications/Admissions:
Student Applications
Clinical Psychology PsyD (Doctor of Psychology)—Applications 2012–2013, 173. Total applicants accepted 2012–2013, 56. Number full-time enrolled (new admits only) 2012–2013, 47. Number part-time enrolled (new admits only) 2012–2013, 7. Total enrolled 2012–2013 full-time, 341. Total enrolled 2012–2013 part-time, 10. Openings 2013–2014, 70. The median number of years required for completion of a degree in 2012–2013 were 5. The number of students enrolled full- and part-time who were dismissed or voluntarily withdrew from this program area in 2012–2013 were 9. *Clinical Psychology MA/MS (Master of Arts/Science)*—Applications 2012–2013, 27. Total applicants accepted 2012–2013, 5. Number full-time enrolled (new admits only) 2012–2013, 5. Number part-time enrolled (new admits only) 2012–2013, 1. Total enrolled 2012–2013 full-time, 7. Total enrolled 2012–2013 part-time, 3. Openings 2013–2014, 20. The median number of years required for completion of a degree in 2012–2013 were 2. The number of students enrolled full- and part-time who were dismissed or voluntarily withdrew from this program area in 2012–2013 were 0.
Scores: Entries appear in this order: required test or GPA, minimum score (if required), median score of students entering in 2012–2013. *Clinical Psychology PsyD (Doctor of Psychology):* GRE-V no minimum stated, GRE-Q no minimum stated, overall undergraduate GPA 3.25, Masters GPA 3.50; *Clinical Psychology MA/MS (Master of Arts/Science):* GRE-V no minimum

stated, GRE-Q no minimum stated, overall undergraduate GPA 3.0.
Other Criteria: (importance of criteria rated low, medium, or high): GRE scores—medium, research experience—low, work experience—low, extracurricular activity—low, clinically related public service—medium, GPA—high, letters of recommendation—high, interview—high, statement of goals and objectives—high, undergraduate major in psychology—medium, specific undergraduate psychology courses taken—high, Clinical experience is less important for applicants to MA program. For additional information on admission requirements, go to http://www.argosy.edu/admissions/Default.aspx.

Student Characteristics: The following represents characteristics of students in 2012–2013 in all graduate psychology programs in the department: Female—full-time 281, part-time 10; Male—full-time 67, part-time 3; African American/Black—full-time 66, part-time 6; Hispanic/Latino(a)—full-time 30, part-time 0; Asian/Pacific Islander—full-time 25, part-time 0; American Indian/Alaska Native—full-time 1, part-time 0; Caucasian/White—full-time 209, part-time 6; Multi-ethnic—full-time 6, part-time 0; students subject to the Americans With Disabilities Act—full-time 13, part-time 0; Unknown ethnicity—full-time 11, part-time 1; International students who hold an F-1 or J-1 Visa—full-time 20, part-time 0.

Financial Information/Assistance:
Tuition for Full-Time Study: *Master's:* State residents: per academic year $32,536, $1,162 per credit hour; Nonstate residents: per academic year $32,536, $1,162 per credit hour. *Doctoral:* State residents: per academic year $32,536, $1,162 per credit hour; Nonstate residents: per academic year $32,536, $1,162 per credit hour. Tuition is subject to change. See the following website for updates and changes in tuition costs: http://www.argosy.edu/admissions/Default.aspx.

Financial Assistance:
First-Year Students: Fellowships and scholarships available for first year. Average amount paid per academic year: $1,000.
Advanced Students: Teaching assistantships available for advanced students. Average amount paid per academic year: $2,137. Average number of hours worked per week: 5. Research assistantships available for advanced students. Average amount paid per academic year: $2,850. Average number of hours worked per week: 4. Fellowships and scholarships available for advanced students. Average amount paid per academic year: $2,850. Average number of hours worked per week: 8.
Additional Information: Of all students currently enrolled full time, 26% benefited from one or more of the listed financial assistance programs. Application and information available online at: http://www.argosy.edu/financial-aid/Default.aspx.

Internships/Practica: Doctoral Degree (PsyD Clinical Psychology): For those doctoral students for whom a professional psychology internship was required in this program prior to graduation, (65) students applied for an internship in 2011–2012, with (59) students obtaining an internship. Of those students who obtained an internship, (59) were paid internships. Of those students who obtained an internship, (27) students placed in APA/CPA accredited internships, (31) students placed in internships not APA/CPA accredited, but listed with the Association of Psychology Postdoctoral and Internship Programs (APPIC), (0) students placed in internships conforming to guidelines of the Council of Directors of School Psychology Programs (CDSPP), (1) students placed in internships that were not APA/CPA accredited, APPIC or CDSPP listed. Master's Degree (MA/MS Clinical Psychology): An internship experience, such as a final research project or "capstone" experience is required of graduates. Practicum training is designed to give students the opportunity to work under supervision with a clinical population within a mental health delivery system. Students learn to apply their theoretical knowledge; implement, develop, and assess the efficacy of clinical techniques; and develop the professional attitudes important for the identity of a professional psychologist. Doctoral students complete two training practicum sequences (600 hours each) focusing on assessment or psychotherapy skills or integrating the two. Master's students are required to complete one practicum (600 hours). All doctoral students are required to complete a one year (12 month) internship as a condition for graduation. This intensive and supervised contact with clients is essential for giving greater breadth and depth to the student's overall academic experience. Typically, students will begin the internship during their fourth or fifth year, depending on the student's progress through the curriculum.

Housing and Day Care: No on-campus housing is available. No on-campus day care facilities are available.

Employment of Department Graduates:

Master's Degree Graduates: Of those who graduated in the academic year 2011–2012, the following categories and numbers represent the postgraduate activities and employment of master's degree graduates: Enrolled in a psychology doctoral program (8), enrolled in a postdoctoral residency/fellowship (n/a), employed in independent practice (n/a), other employment position (3), do not know (1), total from the above (master's) (12).

Doctoral Degree Graduates: Of those who graduated in the academic year 2011–2012, the following categories and numbers represent the postgraduate activities and employment of doctoral degree graduates: Enrolled in a psychology doctoral program (n/a), enrolled in a postdoctoral residency/fellowship (67), employed in independent practice (3), employed in an academic position at a university (3), employed in a community mental health/counseling center (1), other employment position (4), do not know (1), total from the above (doctoral) (79).

Additional Information:

Orientation, Objectives, and Emphasis of Department: The doctoral program in clinical psychology (PsyD) is designed to educate and train students to function effectively in diverse professional roles. The program emphasizes the development of attitudes, knowledge, and skills essential in the formation of professional psychologists who are committed to the ethical provision of quality services. The school offers a broad-based curriculum, providing a meaningful integration of diverse theoretical perspectives, scholarship, and practice. The program offers concentrations in forensic psychology, health and neuropsychology, child and family, and diversity. Opportunities are available for students to develop expertise in a number of areas including the provision of services to specific populations such as children and families; theoretical perspectives such as cognitive-behavioral, family systems, psycho-

dynamic, and client centered; and areas of application such as forensics and health psychology. The Master's degree (MA) in clinical psychology is designed to meet the needs of both those students seeking a terminal degree for work in the mental health field and those who eventually plan to pursue a doctoral degree. The program provides a solid core of basic psychology, as well as a strong clinical orientation with an emphasis in psychological assessment.

Special Facilities or Resources: Argosy University is conveniently located minutes from downtown Washington, DC. The on-site library has developed a focused psychology collection consisting of reference titles and books, journals, diagnostic assessment instruments, and audiovisual equipment. There are two computer labs and students have full access to both computerized literature searches and electronic text of most journals. In addition, students have access to the rich library resources of the Washington, DC area including the National Library of Medicine and the Library of Congress.

Application Information:
Send to Admissions Department, Argosy University/Washington, DC, 1550 Wilson Boulevard, Suite 600, Arlington, VA 22209. Application available online. URL of online application: http://www.argosy.edu/admissions/Default.aspx. Students are admitted in the Fall, application deadline January 15. Application must be completed by January 15th to qualify for the April 1st decision. *Fee:* $50.

College of William and Mary
Department of Psychology/Predoctoral MA Program
P.O. Box 8795
Williamsburg, VA 23187-8795
Telephone: (757) 221-3870
Fax: (757) 221-3896
E-mail: *tlcoates@wm.edu*
Web: *http://www.wm.edu/as/psychology/*

Department Information:
1946. Chairperson: Janice L. Zeman, PhD. Number of faculty: total—full-time 21, part-time 10; women—full-time 8, part-time 5.

Programs and Degrees Offered:
Listed in the following order: Program area, degree type (T if terminal Master's), number awarded 7/11–6/12. General Psychology MA/MS (Master of Arts/Science) (T) 6.

Student Applications/Admissions:
Student Applications
General Psychology MA/MS (Master of Arts/Science)—Applications 2012–2013, 134. Total applicants accepted 2012–2013, 8. Number full-time enrolled (new admits only) 2012–2013, 8. Number part-time enrolled (new admits only) 2012–2013, 0. Total enrolled 2012–2013 full-time, 17. Total enrolled 2012–2013 part-time, 0. Openings 2013–2014, 8. The median number of years required for completion of a degree in 2012–2013 were 2. The number of students enrolled full- and part-time who were dismissed or voluntarily withdrew from this program area in 2012–2013 were 0.

Scores: Entries appear in this order: required test or GPA, minimum score (if required), median score of students entering in 2012–2013. *General Psychology MA/MS (Master of Arts/Science):* GRE-V no minimum stated, 600, GRE-Q no minimum stated, 670, GRE-Analytical no minimum stated.

Other Criteria: (importance of criteria rated low, medium, or high): GRE scores—medium, research experience—high, work experience—medium, extracurricular activity—low, clinically related public service—low, GPA—medium, letters of recommendation—high, statement of goals and objectives—high, specific undergraduate psychology courses taken—high. For additional information on admission requirements, go to http://www.wm.edu/as/psychology/gradprogram/maprogram/maadmissionreqs/.

Student Characteristics: The following represents characteristics of students in 2012–2013 in all graduate psychology programs in the department: Female—full-time 10, part-time 0; Male—full-time 7, part-time 0; African American/Black—full-time 0, part-time 0; Hispanic/Latino(a)—full-time 0, part-time 0; Asian/Pacific Islander—full-time 2, part-time 0; American Indian/Alaska Native—full-time 0, part-time 0; Caucasian/White—full-time 14, part-time 0; Multi-ethnic—full-time 0, part-time 0; students subject to the Americans With Disabilities Act—full-time 0, part-time 0; Unknown ethnicity—full-time 1, part-time 0; International students who hold an F-1 or J-1 Visa—full-time 0, part-time 0.

Financial Information/Assistance:

Tuition for Full-Time Study: *Master's:* State residents: per academic year $11,404, $385 per credit hour; Nonstate residents: per academic year $25,790, $1,000 per credit hour. Tuition is subject to change. See the following website for updates and changes in tuition costs: http://www.wm.edu/admission/financialaid/tuition/.

Financial Assistance:

First-Year Students: Teaching assistantships available for first year. Average amount paid per academic year: $11,000. Average number of hours worked per week: 20. Apply by February 15. Research assistantships available for first year. Average amount paid per academic year: $11,000. Average number of hours worked per week: 20. Apply by February 15.

Advanced Students: Teaching assistantships available for advanced students. Average amount paid per academic year: $11,000. Average number of hours worked per week: 20. Apply by February 15. Research assistantships available for advanced students. Average amount paid per academic year: $11,000. Average number of hours worked per week: 20. Apply by February 15.

Additional Information: Of all students currently enrolled full time, 100% benefited from one or more of the listed financial assistance programs. Application and information available online at: http://www.wm.edu/admission/financialaid/.

Internships/Practica: Master's Degree (MA/MS General Psychology): An internship experience, such as a final research project or "capstone" experience is required of graduates.

Housing and Day Care: On-campus housing is available. See the following website for more information: http://www.wm.edu/offices/residencelife/oncampus/residencehalls/graduate/index.php. On-campus day care facilities are available. See the following website for more information: http://www.wm.edu/offices/auxiliary/wccc/.

Employment of Department Graduates:

Master's Degree Graduates: Of those who graduated in the academic year 2011–2012, the following categories and numbers represent the postgraduate activities and employment of master's degree graduates: Enrolled in a psychology doctoral program (4), enrolled in another graduate/professional program (1), enrolled in a postdoctoral residency/fellowship (n/a), employed in independent practice (n/a), employed in other positions at a higher education institution (1), total from the above (master's) (6).

Doctoral Degree Graduates: Of those who graduated in the academic year 2011–2012, the following categories and numbers represent the postgraduate activities and employment of doctoral degree graduates: Enrolled in a psychology doctoral program (n/a), total from the above (doctoral) (0).

Additional Information:

Orientation, Objectives, and Emphasis of Department: The general psychology MA program is designed to prepare students for admission to PhD programs. Students are not admitted if they are not planning to further their education. There is a heavy research emphasis throughout both years of the program.

Special Facilities or Resources: Our faculty members develop and work with the MA students to design, conduct, and analyze research data. These studies are often published in professional journals. Subjects accessible for research include individuals from the community, college students, and rats.

Information for Students With Physical Disabilities: See the following website for more information: http://www.wm.edu/offices/deanofstudents/services/disabilityservices/.

Application Information:

Send to Director of Graduate Studies, Psychology Department, The College of William and Mary, P.O. Box 8795, Williamsburg, VA 23187-8795. Application available online. URL of online application: http://www.applyweb.com/apply/wmgrad/. Students are admitted in the Fall, application deadline February 15. *Fee:* $45.

George Mason University

Department of Psychology
Humanities and Social Sciences
4400 University Drive, MSN 3F5
Fairfax, VA 22030-4444
Telephone: (703) 993-1342
Fax: (703) 993-1359
E-mail: *dwiggin3@gmu.edu*
Web: *http://psychology.gmu.edu/*

Department Information:

1966. Chairperson: Robert Smith. Number of faculty: total—full-time 48, part-time 23; women—full-time 22, part-time 13; total—minority—full-time 4; women minority—full-time 4.

Programs and Degrees Offered:

Listed in the following order: Program area, degree type (T if terminal Master's), number awarded 7/11–6/12. Clinical Psychology PhD (Doctor of Philosophy) 11, Industrial/Organizational Psychology PhD (Doctor of Philosophy) 9, Human Factors and Applied Cognition PhD (Doctor of Philosophy) 43, Applied Developmental Psychology PhD (Doctor of Philosophy) 9, School Psychology MA/MS (Master of Arts/Science) (T) 11, Industrial/Organizational Psychology MA/MS (Master of Arts/Science) (T) 9, Human Factors and Applied Cognition MA/MS (Master of Arts/Science) (T) 20, Applied Developmental Psychology MA/MS (Master of Arts/Science) (T) 15, Cognitive and Behavioral Neuroscience MA/MS (Master of Arts/Science) (T) 8, Cognitive and Behavioral Neuroscience PhD (Doctor of Philosophy) 1.

APA Accreditation:

Clinical PhD (Doctor of Philosophy). Student Outcome Data Website: http://psychology.gmu.edu/graduate/clinical/clinical-psychology-program-statistics/stats.

Student Applications/Admissions:

Student Applications

Clinical Psychology PhD (Doctor of Philosophy)—Applications 2012–2013, 274. Total applicants accepted 2012–2013, 10. Number full-time enrolled (new admits only) 2012–2013, 6. Number part-time enrolled (new admits only) 2012–2013, 0. Total enrolled 2012–2013 full-time, 33. Total enrolled 2012–2013 part-time, 1. Openings 2013–2014, 7. The median number of years required for completion of a degree in 2012–2013 were 6. The number of students enrolled full- and part-time who were dismissed or voluntarily withdrew from this program area in 2012–2013 were 2. *Industrial/Organizational Psychology PhD (Doctor of Philosophy)*—Applications 2012–2013, 111. Total applicants accepted 2012–2013, 12. Number full-time enrolled (new admits only) 2012–2013, 5. Number part-time enrolled (new admits only) 2012–2013, 0. Total enrolled 2012–2013 full-time, 15. Total enrolled 2012–2013 part-time, 16. Openings 2013–2014, 6. The median number of years required for completion of a degree in 2012–2013 were 7. The number of students enrolled full- and part-time who were dismissed or voluntarily withdrew from this program area in 2012–2013 were 0. *Human Factors and Applied Cognition PhD (Doctor of Philosophy)*—Applications 2012–2013, 38. Total applicants accepted 2012–2013, 8. Number full-time enrolled (new admits only) 2012–2013, 7. Number part-time enrolled (new admits only) 2012–2013, 0. Total enrolled 2012–2013 full-time, 22. Total enrolled 2012–2013 part-time, 6. Openings 2013–2014, 5. The median number of years required for completion of a degree in 2012–2013 were 7. The number of students enrolled full- and part-time who were dismissed or voluntarily withdrew from this program area in 2012–2013 were 0. *Applied Developmental Psychology PhD (Doctor of Philosophy)*—Applications 2012–2013, 37. Total applicants accepted 2012–2013, 13. Number full-time enrolled (new admits only) 2012–2013, 7. Number part-time enrolled (new admits only) 2012–2013, 0. Total enrolled 2012–2013 full-time, 17. Total enrolled 2012–2013 part-time, 3. Openings 2013–2014, 6. The median number of years required for completion of a degree in 2012–2013 were 5. The number of students enrolled

full- and part-time who were dismissed or voluntarily withdrew from this program area in 2012–2013 were 0. *School Psychology MA/MS (Master of Arts/Science)*—Applications 2012–2013, 49. Total applicants accepted 2012–2013, 13. Number full-time enrolled (new admits only) 2012–2013, 7. Number part-time enrolled (new admits only) 2012–2013, 0. Total enrolled 2012–2013 full-time, 15. Total enrolled 2012–2013 part-time, 1. Openings 2013–2014, 9. The median number of years required for completion of a degree in 2012–2013 were 3. The number of students enrolled full- and part-time who were dismissed or voluntarily withdrew from this program area in 2012–2013 were 0. *Industrial/Organizational Psychology MA/MS (Master of Arts/Science)*—Applications 2012–2013, 130. Total applicants accepted 2012–2013, 24. Number full-time enrolled (new admits only) 2012–2013, 3. Number part-time enrolled (new admits only) 2012–2013, 6. Total enrolled 2012–2013 full-time, 5. Total enrolled 2012–2013 part-time, 14. Openings 2013–2014, 10. The median number of years required for completion of a degree in 2012–2013 were 2. The number of students enrolled full- and part-time who were dismissed or voluntarily withdrew from this program area in 2012–2013 were 0. *Human Factors and Applied Cognition MA/MS (Master of Arts/Science)*—Applications 2012–2013, 44. Total applicants accepted 2012–2013, 17. Number full-time enrolled (new admits only) 2012–2013, 5. Number part-time enrolled (new admits only) 2012–2013, 4. Total enrolled 2012–2013 full-time, 11. Total enrolled 2012–2013 part-time, 22. Openings 2013–2014, 14. The median number of years required for completion of a degree in 2012–2013 were 2. The number of students enrolled full- and part-time who were dismissed or voluntarily withdrew from this program area in 2012–2013 were 1. *Applied Developmental Psychology MA/MS (Master of Arts/Science)*—Applications 2012–2013, 55. Total applicants accepted 2012–2013, 16. Number full-time enrolled (new admits only) 2012–2013, 6. Number part-time enrolled (new admits only) 2012–2013, 4. Total enrolled 2012–2013 full-time, 9. Total enrolled 2012–2013 part-time, 9. Openings 2013–2014, 10. The median number of years required for completion of a degree in 2012–2013 were 2. The number of students enrolled full- and part-time who were dismissed or voluntarily withdrew from this program area in 2012–2013 were 0. *Cognitive and Behavioral Neuroscience MA/MS (Master of Arts/Science)*—Applications 2012–2013, 43. Total applicants accepted 2012–2013, 9. Number full-time enrolled (new admits only) 2012–2013, 2. Number part-time enrolled (new admits only) 2012–2013, 3. Total enrolled 2012–2013 full-time, 3. Total enrolled 2012–2013 part-time, 9. Openings 2013–2014, 4. The median number of years required for completion of a degree in 2012–2013 were 7. The number of students enrolled full- and part-time who were dismissed or voluntarily withdrew from this program area in 2012–2013 were 1. *Cognitive and Behavioral Neuroscience PhD (Doctor of Philosophy)*—Applications 2012–2013, 23. Total applicants accepted 2012–2013, 3. Number full-time enrolled (new admits only) 2012–2013, 0. Number part-time enrolled (new admits only) 2012–2013, 3. Total enrolled 2012–2013 full-time, 5. Total enrolled 2012–2013 part-time, 7. Openings 2013–2014, 2. The median number of years required for completion of a degree in 2012–2013 were 8. The number of students enrolled full- and part-time who were dismissed or voluntarily withdrew from this program area in 2012–2013 were 0.

Scores: Entries appear in this order: required test or GPA, minimum score (if required), median score of students entering in 2012–2013. *Clinical Psychology PhD (Doctor of Philosophy):* GRE-V no minimum stated, 164, GRE-Q no minimum stated, 159, overall undergraduate GPA no minimum stated, 3.85, last 2 years GPA 3.25, psychology GPA 3.25; *Industrial/Organizational Psychology PhD (Doctor of Philosophy):* GRE-V no minimum stated, GRE-Q no minimum stated, GRE-Analytical no minimum stated, overall undergraduate GPA no minimum stated, last 2 years GPA 3.0, psychology GPA 3.25; *Human Factors and Applied Cognition PhD (Doctor of Philosophy):* GRE-V no minimum stated, GRE-Q no minimum stated, GRE-Analytical no minimum stated, last 2 years GPA 3.0, psychology GPA 3.25; *Applied Developmental Psychology PhD (Doctor of Philosophy):* GRE-V no minimum stated, GRE-Q no minimum stated, GRE-Analytical no minimum stated, psychology GPA 3.25, Masters GPA 3.25; *School Psychology MA/MS (Master of Arts/Science):* GRE-V no minimum stated, GRE-Q no minimum stated, overall undergraduate GPA no minimum stated, last 2 years GPA 3.0, psychology GPA 3.25; *Industrial/Organizational Psychology MA/MS (Master of Arts/Science):* GRE-V no minimum stated, GRE-Q no minimum stated, overall undergraduate GPA no minimum stated, last 2 years GPA 3.0, psychology GPA 3.25; *Human Factors and Applied Cognition MA/MS (Master of Arts/Science):* GRE-V no minimum stated, GRE-Q no minimum stated, last 2 years GPA 3.0, psychology GPA 3.25; *Applied Developmental Psychology MA/MS (Master of Arts/Science):* GRE-V no minimum stated, GRE-Q no minimum stated, GRE-Analytical no minimum stated, last 2 years GPA 3.0, psychology GPA 3.25; *Cognitive and Behavioral Neuroscience MA/MS (Master of Arts/Science):* GRE-V no minimum stated, GRE-Q no minimum stated, GRE-Analytical no minimum stated, last 2 years GPA 3.0, psychology GPA 3.25; *Cognitive and Behavioral Neuroscience PhD (Doctor of Philosophy):* GRE-V no minimum stated, GRE-Q no minimum stated, GRE-Analytical no minimum stated, last 2 years GPA 3.0, psychology GPA 3.25.

Other Criteria: (importance of criteria rated low, medium, or high): GRE scores—high, research experience—medium, work experience—medium, extracurricular activity—low, clinically related public service—medium, GPA—high, letters of recommendation—high, interview—high, statement of goals and objectives—high, undergraduate major in psychology—medium, specific undergraduate psychology courses taken—high, The Clinical and School programs interview a select group by invitation only. The Cognitive and Behavioral Neuroscience, Developmental, Human Factors/Applied Cognition, and Industrial/Organizational programs do not require an interview but hold an Open House for selected students to attend. Clinical and Applied Developmental PhD are required to submit the PhD Departmental Form where they select two faculty they wish to work with. This is strongly recommended but not required for other concentrations. For additional information on admission requirements, go to http://psychology.gmu.edu/.

Student Characteristics: The following represents characteristics of students in 2012–2013 in all graduate psychology programs in the department: Female—full-time 87, part-time 42; Male—full-time 48, part-time 46; African American/Black—full-time 4, part-time 2; Hispanic/Latino(a)—full-time 3, part-time 8; Asian/Pacific Islander—full-time 14, part-time 7; American Indian/Alaska Native—full-time 0, part-time 0; Caucasian/White—full-time 94, part-time 59; Multi-ethnic—full-time 5, part-time 3; students subject to the Americans With Disabilities Act—full-time 0, part-time 0; Unknown ethnicity—full-time 15, part-time 9; International students who hold an F-1 or J-1 Visa—full-time 9, part-time 0.

Financial Information/Assistance:

Tuition for Full-Time Study: *Master's:* State residents: per academic year $9,920, $478 per credit hour; Nonstate residents: per academic year $24,603, $1,142 per credit hour. *Doctoral:* State residents: per academic year $9,920, $478 per credit hour; Nonstate residents: per academic year $24,603, $1,142 per credit hour. Tuition is subject to change. See the following website for updates and changes in tuition costs: http://studentaccounts.gmu.edu/.

Financial Assistance:

First-Year Students: Teaching assistantships available for first year. Average amount paid per academic year: $16,600. Apply by January 1. Research assistantships available for first year. Average amount paid per academic year: $16,600. Apply by January 1. Fellowships and scholarships available for first year. Average amount paid per academic year: $1,000. Apply by January 1.

Advanced Students: Teaching assistantships available for advanced students. Average amount paid per academic year: $16,000. Apply by February 15. Research assistantships available for advanced students. Average amount paid per academic year: $16,000. Apply by February 15.

Additional Information: Of all students currently enrolled full time, 60% benefited from one or more of the listed financial assistance programs. Application and information available online at: http://chss.gmu.edu/graduate/college-information-funding.

Internships/Practica: Doctoral Degree (PhD Clinical Psychology): For those doctoral students for whom a professional psychology internship was required in this program prior to graduation, (7) students applied for an internship in 2011–2012, with (7) students obtaining an internship. Of those students who obtained an internship, (7) were paid internships. Of those students who obtained an internship, (6) students placed in APA/CPA accredited internships, (0) students placed in internships not APA/CPA accredited, but listed with the Association of Psychology Postdoctoral and Internship Programs (APPIC), (0) students placed in internships conforming to guidelines of the Council of Directors of School Psychology Programs (CDSPP), (1) students placed in internships that were not APA/CPA accredited, APPIC or CDSPP listed. Master's Degree (MA/MS School Psychology): An internship experience, such as a final research project or "capstone" experience is required of graduates. Master's Degree (MA/MS Cognitive and Behavioral Neuroscience): An internship experience, such as a final research project or "capstone" experience is required of graduates. All programs either require or offer practicum placements in a wide variety of settings, including mental health treatment facilities, medical facilities, schools, government agencies, the military, and businesses and organizations.

Housing and Day Care: On-campus housing is available. See the following website for more information: http://housing.gmu.edu/graduate/. On-campus day care facilities are available. See the following website for more information: http://www.gmu.edu/depts/cdc/.

Employment of Department Graduates:

Master's Degree Graduates: Of those who graduated in the academic year 2011–2012, the following categories and numbers represent the postgraduate activities and employment of master's degree graduates: Enrolled in a postdoctoral residency/fellowship (n/a), employed in independent practice (n/a), total from the above (master's) (0).

Doctoral Degree Graduates: Of those who graduated in the academic year 2011–2012, the following categories and numbers represent the postgraduate activities and employment of doctoral degree graduates: Enrolled in a psychology doctoral program (n/a), total from the above (doctoral) (0).

Additional Information:

Orientation, Objectives, and Emphasis of Department: All graduate programs emphasize both basic research and the application of research to solving problems in families, schools, industry, government, and health care settings.

Special Facilities or Resources: The Developmental research area includes individual test rooms, a family interaction room, and a number of faculty research areas; some of the test rooms are equipped with video and computers. Cognitive and Behavioral Neuroscience includes a rodent colony, modern facilities for behavior testing (including drug self-administration), a Neurolucida system for neuroanatomical evaluation, and extensive histological capability. Cognitive and Behavioral Neuroscience also has collaborative relationships with the Center for Biomedical Genomics and Informatics for gene microarray work, and the Krasnow Institute for Advanced Study for neuroanatomy, neurophysiology, and neural modeling work. The Human Factors/Applied Cognitive labs include numerous workstations for computer display and data collection, several eyetrackers, several simulators (including a cockpit simulator) and human electrophysiology; a Near Infrared Imaging System is planned for the very near future. Industrial/Organizational research space includes laboratory space for work on groups, teamwork, and leadership. Clinical facilities include a professional Clinic, and research/interview space in faculty labs. The Center for Cognitive Development, housed in the same building as the Clinic, works with local school systems, and the School and Clinical programs, on issues related to child development. Some students use nearby resources for research, such as the National Institutes of Health.

Information for Students With Physical Disabilities: See the following website for more information: http://www.gmu.edu/depts/unilife/ods/.

Application Information:

Application available online. URL of online application: http://admissions.gmu.edu/grad/applynow/. Students are admitted in the Fall, application deadline December 1. December 1 for Clinical PhD; Applied Developmental PhD; December 15 for Industrial/Organizational PhD; January 1 for Cognitive and Behavioral Neurosciences PhD; Human Factors/Applied Cognition PhD; January 15 for School MA; February 1 for all other MA programs. *Fee:* $65.

George Mason University

Division of Educational Psychology, Research Methods & Ed Policy
College of Education and Human Development
4400 University Drive, MS 6D2
Fairfax, VA 22030
Telephone: (703) 993-3679
Fax: (703) 993-3678
E-mail: *khowe1@gmu.edu*
Web: *http://gse.gmu.edu/programs/edpsych/*

Department Information:

Division Director: Dr. Anastasia Kitsantas. Number of faculty: total—full-time 11; women—full-time 6; total—minority—full-time 1; faculty subject to the Americans With Disabilities Act 2.

Programs and Degrees Offered:

Listed in the following order: Program area, degree type (T if terminal Master's), number awarded 7/11–6/12. Educational Psychology MA/MS (Master of Arts/Science) (T), Data-Driven Decision-Making Certificate Other, Educational Psychology PhD (Doctor of Philosophy).

Student Applications/Admissions:

Student Applications

Educational Psychology MA/MS (Master of Arts/Science)—Data-Driven Decision-Making Certificate Other—Educational Psychology PhD (Doctor of Philosophy)—

Scores: Entries appear in this order: required test or GPA, minimum score (if required), median score of students entering in 2012–2013. *Educational Psychology MA/MS (Master of Arts/Science)*: GRE-V no minimum stated, GRE-Q no minimum stated, GRE-Analytical no minimum stated, overall undergraduate GPA 3.0, last 2 years GPA 3.0; *Educational Psychology PhD (Doctor of Philosophy)*: GRE-V no minimum stated, GRE-Q no minimum stated, GRE-Analytical no minimum stated.

Other Criteria: (importance of criteria rated low, medium, or high): For additional information on admission requirements, go to http://gse.gmu.edu/programs/edpsych/admissions/.

Student Characteristics: The following represents characteristics of students in 2012–2013 in all graduate psychology programs in the department: Female—full-time 11, part-time 60; Male—full-time 5, part-time 6; African American/Black—full-time 0, part-time 0; Hispanic/Latino(a)—full-time 0, part-time 0; Asian/Pacific Islander—full-time 0, part-time 0; American Indian/Alaska Native—full-time 0, part-time 0; Caucasian/White—full-time 0, part-time 0; Multi-ethnic—full-time 0, part-time 0; students subject to the Americans With Disabilities Act—full-time 0, part-time 0; Unknown ethnicity—full-time 0, part-time 0; International students who hold an F-1 or J-1 Visa—full-time 0, part-time 0.

Financial Information/Assistance:

Tuition for Full-Time Study: *Master's:* State residents: $461 per credit hour; Nonstate residents: $1,100 per credit hour. *Doctoral:* State residents: $461 per credit hour; Nonstate residents: $1,100 per credit hour. Tuition is subject to change. Tuition costs vary by program. See the following website for updates and changes in tuition costs: http://studentaccounts.gmu.edu/tuition.html.

Financial Assistance:

First-Year Students: No information provided.

Advanced Students: No information provided.

Additional Information: Application and information available online at: http://cehd.gmu.edu/financialaid/.

Internships/Practica: Master's Degree (MA/MS Educational Psychology): An internship experience, such as a final research project or "capstone" experience is required of graduates.

Housing and Day Care: No on-campus housing is available. On-campus day care facilities are available. See the following website for more information: http://www.gmu.edu/depts/cdc/.

Employment of Department Graduates:

Master's Degree Graduates: Of those who graduated in the academic year 2011–2012, the following categories and numbers represent the postgraduate activities and employment of master's degree graduates: Enrolled in a postdoctoral residency/fellowship (n/a), employed in independent practice (n/a), total from the above (master's) (0).

Doctoral Degree Graduates: Of those who graduated in the academic year 2011–2012, the following categories and numbers represent the postgraduate activities and employment of doctoral degree graduates: Enrolled in a psychology doctoral program (n/a), total from the above (doctoral) (0).

Additional Information:

Orientation, Objectives, and Emphasis of Department: The Educational Psychology Program is designed to offer individuals the opportunity to apply principles of learning, cognition and motivation to vital problems in the area of education; develop a solid understanding of research, assessment, and evaluation methodologies; and develop an analytical and scholarly approach to critically assessing theoretical perspectives, research, and practice within and across content domains. Our doctoral program is individualized, interdisciplinary, and experiential. Students, with the guidance of faculty advisors, plan their own programs to meet self-defined goals. To accomplish these goals, students engage in a variety of intensive courses, independent studies, seminars, and internships of a highly practical nature. Success in the program requires a high degree of personal initiative, self-directed learning, and commitment to inquiry as a style of personal and professional growth.

Information for Students With Physical Disabilities: See the following website for more information: http://ods.gmu.edu.

Application Information:

Send to George Mason University, CEHD Admissions, Thompson Hall, Room 2700, 4400 University Drive, MS 4D1, Fairfax, VA 22030. Application available online. URL of online application: http://admissions.gmu.edu/ApplyNow/. Students are admitted in the Fall, application deadline April 1; Spring, application deadline November 1; Programs have rolling admissions. *Fee:* $75.

Institute for the Psychological Sciences
Department of Psychology
2001 Jefferson Davis Highway, Suite 511
Arlington, VA 22202
Telephone: (703) 416-1441
E-mail: *wnordling@ipsciences.edu*
Web: *http://ipsciences.edu/*

Department Information:
1999. Chairperson: William Nordling, PhD. Number of faculty: total—full-time 11, part-time 3; women—full-time 4; total—minority—full-time 1; women minority—full-time 1; faculty subject to the Americans With Disabilities Act 1.

Programs and Degrees Offered:
Listed in the following order: Program area, degree type (T if terminal Master's), number awarded 7/11–6/12. Clinical Psychology MA/MS (Master of Arts/Science) (T) 26, General Psychology MA/MS (Master of Arts/Science) (T) 0, Clinical Psychology PsyD (Doctor of Psychology) 2.

Student Applications/Admissions:
Student Applications
Clinical Psychology MA/MS (Master of Arts/Science)—Applications 2012–2013, 62. Total applicants accepted 2012–2013, 49. Number full-time enrolled (new admits only) 2012–2013, 22. Number part-time enrolled (new admits only) 2012–2013, 0. Total enrolled 2012–2013 full-time, 44. Total enrolled 2012–2013 part-time, 3. Openings 2013–2014, 35. The median number of years required for completion of a degree in 2012–2013 were 2. The number of students enrolled full- and part-time who were dismissed or voluntarily withdrew from this program area in 2012–2013 were 3. *General Psychology MA/MS (Master of Arts/Science)*—Applications 2012–2013, 0. Total applicants accepted 2012–2013, 0. Number full-time enrolled (new admits only) 2012–2013, 0. Openings 2013–2014, 10. The median number of years required for completion of a degree in 2012–2013 were 2. The number of students enrolled full- and part-time who were dismissed or voluntarily withdrew from this program area in 2012–2013 were 0. *Clinical Psychology PsyD (Doctor of Psychology)*—Applications 2012–2013, 18. Total applicants accepted 2012–2013, 8. Number full-time enrolled (new admits only) 2012–2013, 8. Total enrolled 2012–2013 full-time, 36. Total enrolled 2012–2013 part-time, 1. Openings 2013–2014, 8. The median number of years required for completion of a degree in 2012–2013 were 4. The number of students enrolled full- and part-time who were dismissed or voluntarily withdrew from this program area in 2012–2013 were 1.

Scores: Entries appear in this order: required test or GPA, minimum score (if required), median score of students entering in 2012–2013. *Clinical Psychology MA/MS (Master of Arts/Science):* overall undergraduate GPA 3.0, last 2 years GPA 3.0, psychology GPA 3.0; *General Psychology MA/MS (Master of Arts/Science):* overall undergraduate GPA 3.0, last 2 years GPA 3.0, psychology GPA 3.0; *Clinical Psychology PsyD (Doctor of Psychology):* GRE-V no minimum stated, GRE-Q no minimum stated, overall undergraduate GPA 3.0, last 2 years GPA 3.0, psychology GPA 3.0, Masters GPA 3.5.

Other Criteria: (importance of criteria rated low, medium, or high): GRE scores—medium, research experience—medium, work experience—high, extracurricular activity—medium, clinically related public service—low, GPA—high, letters of recommendation—medium, interview—high, statement of goals and objectives—high, undergraduate major in psychology—low, specific undergraduate psychology courses taken—medium, Clinical suitability not applicable for M.S. Program in General Psychology. For additional information on admission requirements, go to http://ipsciences.edu/admission-requirements-process/.

Student Characteristics: The following represents characteristics of students in 2012–2013 in all graduate psychology programs in the department: Female—full-time 56, part-time 1; Male—full-time 28, part-time 1; African American/Black—full-time 1, part-time 0; Hispanic/Latino(a)—full-time 5, part-time 1; Asian/Pacific Islander—full-time 1, part-time 0; American Indian/Alaska Native—full-time 0, part-time 0; Caucasian/White—full-time 63, part-time 1; Multi-ethnic—full-time 3, part-time 0; students subject to the Americans With Disabilities Act—full-time 0, part-time 0; Unknown ethnicity—full-time 1, part-time 0; International students who hold an F-1 or J-1 Visa—full-time 10, part-time 0.

Financial Information/Assistance:

Tuition for Full-Time Study: *Master's:* State residents: per academic year $20,520, $855 per credit hour; Nonstate residents: per academic year $20,520, $855 per credit hour. *Doctoral:* State residents: per academic year $20,760, $865 per credit hour; Nonstate residents: per academic year $20,760, $865 per credit hour. Tuition is subject to change. Additional fees are assessed to students beyond the costs of tuition for the following: library, student activities. Tuition costs vary by program. See the following website for updates and changes in tuition costs: http://ipsciences.edu/prospective-studentsfinancing-your-education-cost-of-attendance/. Higher tuition cost for this program: PsyD.

Financial Assistance:

First-Year Students: Research assistantships available for first year. Average amount paid per academic year: $5,000. Average number of hours worked per week: 10. Apply by March 1. Fellowships and scholarships available for first year. Average amount paid per academic year: $5,000. Average number of hours worked per week: 0. Apply by March 1.

Advanced Students: Teaching assistantships available for advanced students. Average amount paid per academic year: $7,500. Average number of hours worked per week: 10. Apply by March 1. Research assistantships available for advanced students. Average amount paid per academic year: $5,000. Average number of hours worked per week: 9. Apply by March 1. Traineeships available for advanced students. Average amount paid per academic year: $7,500. Average number of hours worked per week: 10. Apply by March 1. Fellowships and scholarships available for advanced students. Average amount paid per academic year: $6,030. Average number of hours worked per week: 0. Apply by March 1.

Additional Information: Of all students currently enrolled full time, 42% benefited from one or more of the listed financial assistance programs.

Internships/Practica: Doctoral Degree (PsyD Clinical Psychology): For those doctoral students for whom a professional psychology internship was required in this program prior to graduation, (8) students applied for an internship in 2011–2012, with (8) students obtaining an internship. Of those students who obtained an internship, (8) were paid internships. Of those students who obtained an internship, (3) students placed in APA/CPA accredited internships, (2) students placed in internships not APA/CPA accredited, but listed with the Association of Psychology Postdoctoral and Internship Programs (APPIC), (0) students placed in internships conforming to guidelines of the Council of Directors of School Psychology Programs (CDSPP), (3) students placed in internships that were not APA/CPA accredited, APPIC or CDSPP listed. Master's Degree (MA/MS Clinical Psychology): An internship experience, such as a final research project or "capstone" experience is required of graduates. Master's Degree (MA/MS General Psychology): An internship experience, such as a final research project or "capstone" experience is required of graduates. In their third year of training, PsyD students participate in a yearlong practicum in the IPS Training Clinic. PsyD students in their fourth year of training and M.S. students in an optional third year of training have access to a wide variety of externship/practicum sites given that the Institute is located in the Washington DC Metro Area.

Housing and Day Care: No on-campus housing is available. No on-campus day care facilities are available.

Employment of Department Graduates:

Master's Degree Graduates: Of those who graduated in the academic year 2011–2012, the following categories and numbers represent the postgraduate activities and employment of master's degree graduates: Enrolled in a psychology doctoral program (8), enrolled in a postdoctoral residency/fellowship (n/a), employed in independent practice (n/a), employed in a professional position in a school system (1), employed in a community mental health/counseling center (3), other employment position (3), total from the above (master's) (15).

Doctoral Degree Graduates: Of those who graduated in the academic year 2011–2012, the following categories and numbers represent the postgraduate activities and employment of doctoral degree graduates: Enrolled in a psychology doctoral program (n/a), employed in other positions at a higher education institution (2), total from the above (doctoral) (2).

Additional Information:

Orientation, Objectives, and Emphasis of Department: The Department adopts a practitioner-scholar model of training and education of psychologists. In doing so the degree programs form the students who can practice scientific psychology integrated with a Catholic worldview.

Special Facilities or Resources: The Washington DC Metro Area is an environment rich in educational and cultural resources for students. In addition to the IPS Library, students have access to the libraries of other universities and centers of learning within the area. The IPS also has a chapel and a chaplain who provides students with opportunities for spiritual development.

Application Information:

Send to The Institute for the Psychological Sciences, Attn: Admissions, 2001 Jefferson Davis Highway, Suite 511, Arlington, VA 22202. Students are admitted in the Fall, application deadline February 1. Fall MS Admission Deadline: February 1. Space permitting, applications will be accepted for the M.S. programs until May 31. MS Early Decision: December 20. Fall PsyD deadline: November 1. *Fee:* $55. Application fee is waived for applications completed by December 20.

Marymount University

Department of Forensic Psychology
School of Education and Human Services
2807 North Glebe Road
Arlington, VA 22207
Telephone: (703) 284-5705
Fax: (703) 284-5708
E-mail: *grad.admissions@marymount.edu*
Web: *http://marymount.edu/academics/programs/forensicPsych*

Department Information:

1999. Chairperson: Dr. Jason Doll. Number of faculty: total—full-time 5, part-time 12; women—full-time 3, part-time 5; minority—part-time 2.

Programs and Degrees Offered:

Listed in the following order: Program area, degree type (T if terminal Master's), number awarded 7/11–6/12. Forensic Psychology MA/MS (Master of Arts/Science) (T) 82.

Student Applications/Admissions:

Student Applications

Forensic Psychology MA/MS (Master of Arts/Science)—Applications 2012–2013, 213. Total applicants accepted 2012–2013, 139. Number full-time enrolled (new admits only) 2012–2013, 67. Number part-time enrolled (new admits only) 2012–2013, 8. Total enrolled 2012–2013 full-time, 131. Total enrolled 2012–2013 part-time, 44. Openings 2013–2014, 90. The median number of years required for completion of a degree in 2012–2013 were 2. The number of students enrolled full- and part-time who were dismissed or voluntarily withdrew from this program area in 2012–2013 were 1.

Scores: Entries appear in this order: required test or GPA, minimum score (if required), median score of students entering in 2012–2013. *Forensic Psychology MA/MS (Master of Arts/Science):* GRE-V 150, 152, GRE-Q 141, 148, GRE-Analytical 4.0, 4.25, overall undergraduate GPA 3.00, 3.45.

Other Criteria: (importance of criteria rated low, medium, or high): GRE scores—high, research experience—medium, work experience—medium, extracurricular activity—medium, clinically related public service—low, GPA—high, letters of recommendation—medium, statement of goals and objectives—high, undergraduate major in psychology—low, specific undergraduate psychology courses taken—low. For additional information on admission requirements, go to http://marymount.edu/academics/programs/forensicPsych/admission.aspx.

Student Characteristics: The following represents characteristics of students in 2012–2013 in all graduate psychology programs in the department: Female—full-time 121, part-time 36; Male—full-time 10, part-time 8; African American/Black—full-time 7, part-time 2; Hispanic/Latino(a)—full-time 8, part-time 1; Asian/Pacific Islander—full-time 2, part-time 0; American Indian/Alaska Native—full-time 2, part-time 0; Caucasian/White—full-time

102, part-time 35; Multi-ethnic—full-time 2, part-time 2; students subject to the Americans With Disabilities Act—full-time 0, part-time 0; Unknown ethnicity—full-time 8, part-time 4; International students who hold an F-1 or J-1 Visa—full-time 3, part-time 0.

Financial Information/Assistance:

Tuition for Full-Time Study: Master's: State residents: $850 per credit hour; Nonstate residents: $850 per credit hour. Tuition is subject to change. Additional fees are assessed to students beyond the costs of tuition for the following: $8.25/credit hr-tech fee; New graduate student fee $190 (one-time); $75 internship application fee. See the following website for updates and changes in tuition costs: http://www.marymount.edu/studentAccts/tuition.aspx.

Financial Assistance:

First-Year Students: Research assistantships available for first year. Average amount paid per academic year: $3,750. Average number of hours worked per week: 20.

Advanced Students: Research assistantships available for advanced students. Average amount paid per academic year: $3,750. Average number of hours worked per week: 20.

Additional Information: Application and information available online at: http://www.marymount.edu/financialAid/graduate.

Internships/Practica: Master's Degree (MA/MS Forensic Psychology): An internship experience, such as a final research project or "capstone" experience is required of graduates. Forensic psychology students may choose an internship in a wide variety of settings, including local and state correctional facilities, local community mental health treatment centers, victim witness programs, domestic violence programs and shelters, national and local mental health advocacy organizations, child welfare agencies and advocacy organizations, adult services agencies (serving incapacitated and incompetent adults), juvenile court services, state and local law enforcement, federal law enforcement, intelligence and justice agencies, and any and all areas in which psychological expertise and psychological services would be applied in a legal setting (criminal, civil, and juvenile justice).

Housing and Day Care: On-campus housing is available. See the following website for more information: http://www.marymount.edu/studentLife/livingCampus/housing/grad. No on-campus day care facilities are available.

Employment of Department Graduates:

Master's Degree Graduates: Of those who graduated in the academic year 2011–2012, the following categories and numbers represent the postgraduate activities and employment of master's degree graduates: Enrolled in a postdoctoral residency/fellowship (n/a), employed in independent practice (n/a), total from the above (master's) (0).

Doctoral Degree Graduates: Of those who graduated in the academic year 2011–2012, the following categories and numbers represent the postgraduate activities and employment of doctoral degree graduates: Enrolled in a psychology doctoral program (n/a), total from the above (doctoral) (0).

Additional Information:

Orientation, Objectives, and Emphasis of Department: The Department of Forensic Psychology offers a Master of Arts in Forensic

Psychology. This degree provides graduates with the skills and knowledge they need to provide effective, high quality services in a variety of forensic settings. These settings include probation and parole, victim assistance, intelligence, corrections, law enforcement, and other arenas within the juvenile, civil, and criminal justice systems. To accomplish this goal, the program balances the acquisition of traditional psychological knowledge and skills with a specialized understanding of the justice system.

Special Facilities or Resources: The location of Marymount in suburban Washington provides our students with a large number of opportunities for internships and employment in the area, especially with federal agencies. The university is a member of the Washington Consortium of College and Universities, which gives students access to the library facilities and classes of most of the major universities in the area. Also, approximately every other summer, students have the opportunity to learn about and experience forensic psychology in the English justice system via a collaborative relationship with the Forensic Psychology Program at London Metropolitan University.

Information for Students With Physical Disabilities: See the following website for more information: http://www.marymount. edu/studentLife/services/disability.

Application Information:
Send to Office of Graduate Admissions, Marymount University, 2807 North Glebe Road, Arlington, VA 22207. Application available online. URL of online application: http://www.marymount.edu/ admissions/graduate/applying. Students are admitted in the Fall, application deadline February 16. *Fee:* $40.

Old Dominion University
Department of Psychology
College of Sciences
Mills Godwin Building—Room 250
Norfolk, VA 23529-0267
Telephone: (757) 683-4439
Fax: (757) 683-5087
E-mail: *bwinstea@odu.edu*
Web: *http://sci.odu.edu/psychology/*

Department Information:
1954. Chairperson: Barbara Winstead. Number of faculty: total—full-time 26, part-time 8; women—full-time 11, part-time 7; total—minority—full-time 3, part-time 1; women minority—full-time 2, part-time 1.

Programs and Degrees Offered:
Listed in the following order: Program area, degree type (T if terminal Master's), number awarded 7/11–6/12. General Psychology MA/MS (Master of Arts/Science) (T) 3, Industrial/Organizational Psychology PhD (Doctor of Philosophy) 0, Human Factors PhD (Doctor of Philosophy) 1, Applied Experimental Psychology PhD (Doctor of Philosophy) 4.

Student Applications/Admissions:
Student Applications
General Psychology MA/MS (Master of Arts/Science)—Applications 2012–2013, 66. Total applicants accepted 2012–2013,

9. Number full-time enrolled (new admits only) 2012–2013, 8. Total enrolled 2012–2013 full-time, 24. Total enrolled 2012–2013 part-time, 0. Openings 2013–2014, 10. The median number of years required for completion of a degree in 2012–2013 were 2. The number of students enrolled full- and part-time who were dismissed or voluntarily withdrew from this program area in 2012–2013 were 4. *Industrial/Organizational Psychology PhD (Doctor of Philosophy)*—Applications 2012–2013, 34. Total applicants accepted 2012–2013, 4. Number full-time enrolled (new admits only) 2012–2013, 2. Total enrolled 2012–2013 full-time, 19. Total enrolled 2012–2013 part-time, 0. Openings 2013–2014, 4. The median number of years required for completion of a degree in 2012–2013 were 5. The number of students enrolled full- and part-time who were dismissed or voluntarily withdrew from this program area in 2012–2013 were 1. *Human Factors PhD (Doctor of Philosophy)*—Applications 2012–2013, 23. Total applicants accepted 2012–2013, 6. Number full-time enrolled (new admits only) 2012–2013, 4. Total enrolled 2012–2013 full-time, 19. Total enrolled 2012–2013 part-time, 0. Openings 2013–2014, 4. The median number of years required for completion of a degree in 2012–2013 were 7. The number of students enrolled full- and part-time who were dismissed or voluntarily withdrew from this program area in 2012–2013 were 0. *Applied Experimental Psychology PhD (Doctor of Philosophy)*—Applications 2012–2013, 17. Total applicants accepted 2012–2013, 6. Number full-time enrolled (new admits only) 2012–2013, 4. Total enrolled 2012–2013 full-time, 16. Openings 2013–2014, 4. The median number of years required for completion of a degree in 2012–2013 were 5. The number of students enrolled full- and part-time who were dismissed or voluntarily withdrew from this program area in 2012–2013 were 0.

Scores: Entries appear in this order: required test or GPA, minimum score (if required), median score of students entering in 2012–2013. *General Psychology MA/MS (Master of Arts/ Science):* GRE-V no minimum stated, 155, GRE-Q no minimum stated, 148, GRE-Analytical no minimum stated, 4.00, overall undergraduate GPA no minimum stated, 3.65; *Industrial/Organizational Psychology PhD (Doctor of Philosophy):* GRE-V no minimum stated, 158, GRE-Q no minimum stated, 156, GRE-Analytical no minimum stated, 4.75, overall undergraduate GPA no minimum stated, 3.41; *Human Factors PhD (Doctor of Philosophy):* GRE-V no minimum stated, 157, GRE-Q no minimum stated, 149, GRE-Analytical no minimum stated, 4.5, overall undergraduate GPA no minimum stated, 3.50; *Applied Experimental Psychology PhD (Doctor of Philosophy):* GRE-V no minimum stated, 154, GRE-Q no minimum stated, 155, GRE-Analytical no minimum stated, 3.5, overall undergraduate GPA no minimum stated, 3.89.

Other Criteria: (importance of criteria rated low, medium, or high): GRE scores—high, research experience—high, work experience—medium, extracurricular activity—medium, clinically related public service—low, GPA—high, letters of recommendation—high, interview—high, statement of goals and objectives—medium, undergraduate major in psychology—medium, specific undergraduate psychology courses taken—medium. For additional information on admission requirements, go to http://sci.odu.edu/psychology/.

Student Characteristics: The following represents characteristics of students in 2012–2013 in all graduate psychology programs in the department: Female—full-time 48, part-time 0; Male—full-

time 30, part-time 0; African American/Black—full-time 3, part-time 0; Hispanic/Latino(a)—full-time 3, part-time 0; Asian/Pacific Islander—full-time 3, part-time 0; American Indian/Alaska Native—full-time 0, part-time 0; Caucasian/White—full-time 69, part-time 0; Multi-ethnic—full-time 0, part-time 0; students subject to the Americans With Disabilities Act—full-time 0, part-time 0; Unknown ethnicity—full-time 0, part-time 0; International students who hold an F-1 or J-1 Visa—full-time 4, part-time 0.

Financial Information/Assistance:
Tuition for Full-Time Study: *Master's:* State residents: $393 per credit hour; Nonstate residents: $997 per credit hour. *Doctoral:* State residents: $393 per credit hour; Nonstate residents: $997 per credit hour. Tuition is subject to change. See the following website for updates and changes in tuition costs: http://ww2.odu. edu/af/finance/students/tuition_rates/.

Financial Assistance:
First-Year Students: Teaching assistantships available for first year. Average amount paid per academic year: $15,000. Average number of hours worked per week: 20. Apply by January 5. Research assistantships available for first year. Average amount paid per academic year: $15,000. Average number of hours worked per week: 20. Apply by January 5. Fellowships and scholarships available for first year. Average amount paid per academic year: $18,000. Apply by January 5.
Advanced Students: Teaching assistantships available for advanced students. Average amount paid per academic year: $15,000. Average number of hours worked per week: 20. Research assistantships available for advanced students. Average amount paid per academic year: $15,000. Average number of hours worked per week: 20. Fellowships and scholarships available for advanced students. Average amount paid per academic year: $18,000.
Additional Information: Of all students currently enrolled full time, 80% benefited from one or more of the listed financial assistance programs. Application and information available online at: http://ww2.odu.edu/af/finaid/graduate_student/.

Internships/Practica: Internships are highly encouraged for those enrolled in all three PhD programs and are available at local businesses, hospitals, and military and government agencies, as well as out-of-state. Practicum and internship experiences are also available for all graduate students.

Housing and Day Care: On-campus housing is available. See the following website for more information: http://www.odu.edu/housing. On-campus day care facilities are available. See the following website for more information: http://www.odu.edu/life/community-services/child-care.

Employment of Department Graduates:
Master's Degree Graduates: Of those who graduated in the academic year 2011–2012, the following categories and numbers represent the postgraduate activities and employment of master's degree graduates: Enrolled in a psychology doctoral program (2), enrolled in a postdoctoral residency/fellowship (n/a), employed in independent practice (n/a), employed in business or industry (1), total from the above (master's) (3).
Doctoral Degree Graduates: Of those who graduated in the academic year 2011–2012, the following categories and numbers represent the postgraduate activities and employment of doctoral degree graduates: Enrolled in a psychology doctoral program (n/a), enrolled in another graduate/professional program (2), employed in an academic position at a university (2), employed in government agency (1), total from the above (doctoral) (5).

Additional Information:
Orientation, Objectives, and Emphasis of Department: The department offers PhD programs in Applied Experimental, Human Factors, and Industrial/Organizational Psychology. Concentrations within Applied Experimental include health, community, substance use and abuse, developmental, cognition, memory, and quantitative. Concentrations within Human Factors include medical modeling and simulation, aviation, decision support systems, human-computer interaction, cognitive and behavioral reactions to alarms and alerts, and cognitive and behavioral responses to mild motion (sopite syndrome). Concentrations within Industrial/Organizational include organizational (e.g., leadership, career development, work-family interface, organizational change and development, positive organizations, international and cross-cultural perspectives, and occupational health) and personnel (e.g, game-based training, self-development, training using social media, technology in research and human resource management). The programs are designed to provide in-depth training in applied experimental, human factors, or industrial/organizational psychology and specialized training in an area of concentration. A program of graduate study leading to the degree of Master of Science with a concentration in general experimental psychology is also offered by the department. The department participates in the Virginia Consortium Program in Clinical Psychology which, in collaboration with Eastern Virginia Medical School, and Norfolk State University, offers the PhD in Clinical Psychology.

Special Facilities or Resources: The department has a Human Computer Interaction and Usability Analysis lab, a driving simulator, eyetrack recording equipment, a Bar Lab, a Technology iN Training (TNT) lab, computer labs for data collection, and other research facilities. A close collaboration with the Virginia Modeling, Analysis and Simulation Center provides students with opportunities to engage in command and control simulation, surgical simulation, and virtual reality research. The psychology faculty and graduate students also maintain active collaborations with NASA Langley Research Center, Eastern Virginia Medical School, Children's Hospital of the King's Daughters, Norfolk State University and community and government groups, such as Virginia Department of Motor Vehicles, Department of Public Health, and Newport News Shipbuilding. Field research is facilitated by strong connections to industry and a large alumni network.

Information for Students With Physical Disabilities: See the following website for more information: http://studentaffairs.odu.edu/educationalaccessibility/.

Application Information:
Send to Old Dominion University, Office of Graduate Admissions, 105 Rollins Hall, Norfolk, VA 23529-0050. Application available online. URL of online application: http://www.odu.edu/admission/apply/graduate. Students are admitted in the Fall, application deadline January 5. January 5 for PhD, May 15 for MS. *Fee:* $50.

Radford University

Department of Psychology
Humanities and Behavioral Sciences
P.O. Box 6946
Radford, VA 24142-6946
Telephone: (540) 831-5361
Fax: (540) 831-6113
E-mail: *hlips@radford.edu*
Web: *http://www.radford.edu/content/chbs/home/
    psychology.html*

Department Information:

1937. Chairperson: Hilary M. Lips. Number of faculty: total—full-time 23, part-time 4; women—full-time 11, part-time 3.

Programs and Degrees Offered:

Listed in the following order: Program area, degree type (T if terminal Master's), number awarded 7/11–6/12. Counseling Psychology PsyD (Doctor of Psychology) 3, Clinical Counseling Psychology MA/MS (Master of Arts/Science) (T) 7, Experimental Psychology MA/MS (Master of Arts/Science) (T) 6, Industrial/Organizational Psychology MA/MS (Master of Arts/Science) (T) 7, School Psychology EdS (School Psychology) 11.

APA Accreditation: Counseling PsyD (Doctor of Psychology). Student Outcome Data Website: http://www.radford.edu/content/chbs/home/psychology/programs/counseling/Student-Admissions-Outcomes-and-Other-Data.html.

Student Applications/Admissions:

Student Applications

Counseling Psychology PsyD (Doctor of Psychology)—Applications 2012–2013, 10. Total applicants accepted 2012–2013, 4. Number full-time enrolled (new admits only) 2012–2013, 3. Total enrolled 2012–2013 full-time, 14. Total enrolled 2012–2013 part-time, 0. Openings 2013–2014, 4. The number of students enrolled full- and part-time who were dismissed or voluntarily withdrew from this program area in 2012–2013 were 1. *Clinical Counseling Psychology MA/MS (Master of Arts/Science)*—Applications 2012–2013, 52. Total applicants accepted 2012–2013, 20. Number full-time enrolled (new admits only) 2012–2013, 7. Number part-time enrolled (new admits only) 2012–2013, 0. Total enrolled 2012–2013 full-time, 14. Total enrolled 2012–2013 part-time, 0. Openings 2013–2014, 8. The median number of years required for completion of a degree in 2012–2013 were 2. The number of students enrolled full- and part-time who were dismissed or voluntarily withdrew from this program area in 2012–2013 were 0. *Experimental Psychology MA/MS (Master of Arts/Science)*—Applications 2012–2013, 12. Total applicants accepted 2012–2013, 8. Number full-time enrolled (new admits only) 2012–2013, 3. Number part-time enrolled (new admits only) 2012–2013, 0. Total enrolled 2012–2013 full-time, 9. Total enrolled 2012–2013 part-time, 0. Openings 2013–2014, 8. The median number of years required for completion of a degree in 2012–2013 were 2. The number of students enrolled full- and part-time who were dismissed or voluntarily withdrew from this program area in 2012–2013 were 0. *Industrial/Organizational Psychology MA/MS (Master of Arts/Science)*—Applications 2012–2013, 45. Total applicants accepted 2012–2013, 28. Number full-time

enrolled (new admits only) 2012–2013, 10. Total enrolled 2012–2013 full-time, 21. Total enrolled 2012–2013 part-time, 0. Openings 2013–2014, 12. The median number of years required for completion of a degree in 2012–2013 were 2. The number of students enrolled full- and part-time who were dismissed or voluntarily withdrew from this program area in 2012–2013 were 0. *School Psychology EdS (School Psychology)*—Applications 2012–2013, 34. Total applicants accepted 2012–2013, 26. Number full-time enrolled (new admits only) 2012–2013, 8. Number part-time enrolled (new admits only) 2012–2013, 0. Total enrolled 2012–2013 full-time, 19. Total enrolled 2012–2013 part-time, 0. Openings 2013–2014, 12. The median number of years required for completion of a degree in 2012–2013 were 3. The number of students enrolled full- and part-time who were dismissed or voluntarily withdrew from this program area in 2012–2013 were 0.

Scores: Entries appear in this order: required test or GPA, minimum score (if required), median score of students entering in 2012–2013. *Counseling Psychology PsyD (Doctor of Psychology):* GRE-V no minimum stated, 156, GRE-Q no minimum stated, 149, overall undergraduate GPA no minimum stated, 3.24, Masters GPA no minimum stated, 3.78; *Clinical Counseling Psychology MA/MS (Master of Arts/Science):* GRE-V no minimum stated, 154, GRE-Q no minimum stated, 150, overall undergraduate GPA no minimum stated, 3.60; *Experimental Psychology MA/MS (Master of Arts/Science):* GRE-V no minimum stated, 152, GRE-Q no minimum stated, 146, overall undergraduate GPA no minimum stated, 3.53; *Industrial/Organizational Psychology MA/MS (Master of Arts/Science):* GRE-V no minimum stated, 151, GRE-Q no minimum stated, 151, overall undergraduate GPA no minimum stated, 3.44; *School Psychology EdS (School Psychology):* GRE-V no minimum stated, 149, GRE-Q no minimum stated, 147, overall undergraduate GPA no minimum stated, 3.58.

Other Criteria: (importance of criteria rated low, medium, or high): GRE scores—medium, research experience—high, work experience—medium, extracurricular activity—medium, clinically related public service—high, GPA—high, letters of recommendation—high, interview—high, statement of goals and objectives—medium, undergraduate major in psychology—medium, specific undergraduate psychology courses taken—low, Interview required for doctoral program but not for masters' programs. For additional information on admission requirements, go to http://www.radford.edu/content/chbs/home/psychology/programs.html.

Student Characteristics: The following represents characteristics of students in 2012–2013 in all graduate psychology programs in the department: Female—full-time 62, part-time 0; Male—full-time 15, part-time 0; African American/Black—full-time 3, part-time 0; Hispanic/Latino(a)—full-time 1, part-time 0; Asian/Pacific Islander—full-time 2, part-time 0; American Indian/Alaska Native—full-time 0, part-time 0; Caucasian/White—full-time 71, part-time 0; Multi-ethnic—full-time 0, part-time 0; students subject to the Americans With Disabilities Act—full-time 0, part-time 0; Unknown ethnicity—full-time 0, part-time 0; International students who hold an F-1 or J-1 Visa—full-time 0, part-time 0.

Financial Information/Assistance:

Tuition for Full-Time Study: *Master's:* State residents: per academic year $7,038, $391 per credit hour; Nonstate residents: per

847

academic year $13,806, $767 per credit hour. Tuition is subject to change. Additional fees are assessed to students beyond the costs of tuition for the following: The numbers above include both fees and tuition. Tuition costs vary by program. See the following website for updates and changes in tuition costs: http://stuacct.asp.radford.edu/acad_fees/costs.aspx.

Financial Assistance:
First-Year Students: Teaching assistantships available for first year. Average amount paid per academic year: $10,000. Average number of hours worked per week: 20. Apply by March 1. Research assistantships available for first year. Average amount paid per academic year: $4,500. Average number of hours worked per week: 10. Apply by March 1. Traineeships available for first year. Average amount paid per academic year: $13,500. Average number of hours worked per week: 20. Fellowships and scholarships available for first year. Average amount paid per academic year: $1,000. Apply by March 1.

Advanced Students: Teaching assistantships available for advanced students. Average amount paid per academic year: $10,000. Average number of hours worked per week: 20. Apply by February 15. Research assistantships available for advanced students. Average amount paid per academic year: $4,500. Average number of hours worked per week: 10. Apply by February 15. Traineeships available for advanced students. Average amount paid per academic year: $13,500. Average number of hours worked per week: 20. Fellowships and scholarships available for advanced students. Average amount paid per academic year: $600. Apply by April 1.

Additional Information: Of all students currently enrolled full time, 60% benefited from one or more of the listed financial assistance programs. Application and information available online at: http://www.radford.edu/content/grad/home/cost/assistantships.html.

Internships/Practica: Doctoral Degree (PsyD Counseling Psychology): For those doctoral students for whom a professional psychology internship was required in this program prior to graduation, (4) students applied for an internship in 2011–2012, with (3) students obtaining an internship. Of those students who obtained an internship, (3) were paid internships. Of those students who obtained an internship, (3) students placed in APA/CPA accredited internships, (0) students placed in internships not APA/CPA accredited, but listed with the Association of Psychology Postdoctoral and Internship Programs (APPIC), (0) students placed in internships conforming to guidelines of the Council of Directors of School Psychology Programs (CDSPP), (0) students placed in internships that were not APA/CPA accredited, APPIC or CDSPP listed. Master's Degree (MA/MS Clinical Counseling Psychology): An internship experience, such as a final research project or "capstone" experience is required of graduates. Master's Degree (MA/MS Experimental Psychology): An internship experience, such as a final research project or "capstone" experience is required of graduates. Master's Degree (MA/MS Industrial/Organizational Psychology): An internship experience, such as a final research project or "capstone" experience is required of graduates. Internships and/or practica are required for all programs.

Housing and Day Care: On-campus housing is available. See the following website for more information: http://www.radford.edu/content/student-affairs/home/residential-life.html. No on-campus day care facilities are available.

Employment of Department Graduates:
Master's Degree Graduates: Of those who graduated in the academic year 2011–2012, the following categories and numbers represent the postgraduate activities and employment of master's degree graduates: Enrolled in a psychology doctoral program (3), enrolled in another graduate/professional program (2), enrolled in a postdoctoral residency/fellowship (n/a), employed in independent practice (n/a), employed in other positions at a higher education institution (3), employed in a professional position in a school system (7), employed in business or industry (7), employed in a community mental health/counseling center (1), not seeking employment (3), other employment position (2), total from the above (master's) (28).

Doctoral Degree Graduates: Of those who graduated in the academic year 2011–2012, the following categories and numbers represent the postgraduate activities and employment of doctoral degree graduates: Enrolled in a psychology doctoral program (n/a), employed in a community mental health/counseling center (3), total from the above (doctoral) (3).

Additional Information:
Orientation, Objectives, and Emphasis of Department: The department aims to train psychologists who are well versed in both the theoretical and applied aspects of the discipline. The emphasis of the department is eclectic: school, clinical-counseling, experimental, industrial/organizational and counseling options are available at the graduate level. The School program is an Ed.S program that also provides preparation for certification and licensing as a school psychologist in Virginia. The Psy.D program in Counseling Psychology, with an emphasis on rural mental health, started in the Fall of 2008, and was accredited by APA in 2012.

Special Facilities or Resources: We have computer laboratories and some research space for use by graduate students. We have good animal lab facilities. The department has established a center for gender studies and laboratory for brain research.

Application Information:
Send to College of Graduate and Professional Studies, P.O. Box 6928, Radford University, Radford, VA 24142. Application available online. URL of online application: http://www.radford.edu/content/grad/home/admissions/apply.html. Students are admitted in the Fall, application deadline December 15. Deadline for the PsyD program is December 15; for the EdS in School Psychology and MA programs the deadline is February 15. *Fee:* $50.

Regent University
Doctoral Program in Clinical Psychology
School of Psychology & Counseling
1000 Regent University Drive
Virginia Beach, VA 23464
Telephone: (757) 352-4296
Fax: (757) 352-4304
E-mail: *jennrip@regent.edu*
Web: *http://www.regent.edu/psyd*

Department Information:
1996. Chairperson: Jennifer S. Ripley, PhD. Number of faculty: total—full-time 9, part-time 6; women—full-time 5, part-time

2; total—minority—full-time 3; women minority—full-time 3; faculty subject to the Americans With Disabilities Act 1.

Programs and Degrees Offered:

Listed in the following order: Program area, degree type (T if terminal Master's), number awarded 7/11–6/12. Clinical Psychology PsyD (Doctor of Psychology) 23.

APA Accreditation: Clinical PsyD (Doctor of Psychology). Student Outcome Data Website: http://www.regent.edu/acad/schcou/aboutus/prog_eval/psyd/index.html.

Student Applications/Admissions:

Student Applications

Clinical Psychology PsyD (Doctor of Psychology)—Applications 2012–2013, 122. Total applicants accepted 2012–2013, 34. Number full-time enrolled (new admits only) 2012–2013, 18. Number part-time enrolled (new admits only) 2012–2013, 0. Total enrolled 2012–2013 full-time, 102. Total enrolled 2012–2013 part-time, 0. Openings 2013–2014, 18. The median number of years required for completion of a degree in 2012–2013 were 6. The number of students enrolled full- and part-time who were dismissed or voluntarily withdrew from this program area in 2012–2013 were 6.

Scores: Entries appear in this order: required test or GPA, minimum score (if required), median score of students entering in 2012–2013. *Clinical Psychology PsyD (Doctor of Psychology):* GRE-V no minimum stated, GRE-Q no minimum stated, GRE-Analytical no minimum stated, overall undergraduate GPA 3.0.

Other Criteria: (importance of criteria rated low, medium, or high): GRE scores—high, research experience—medium, work experience—medium, extracurricular activity—medium, clinically related public service—medium, GPA—high, letters of recommendation—medium, interview—high, statement of goals and objectives—medium, leadership experiences—medium, undergraduate major in psychology—medium, specific undergraduate psychology courses taken—medium, Whole person review is used with an emphasis on academic and interpersonal skills and personal qualities and experiences to add to the learning environment. For additional information on admission requirements, go to http://www.regent.edu/acad/schcou/admissions/adm_psy.htm.

Student Characteristics: The following represents characteristics of students in 2012–2013 in all graduate psychology programs in the department: Female—full-time 70, part-time 0; Male—full-time 32, part-time 0; African American/Black—full-time 18, part-time 0; Hispanic/Latino(a)—full-time 3, part-time 0; Asian/Pacific Islander—full-time 2, part-time 0; American Indian/Alaska Native—full-time 0, part-time 0; Caucasian/White—full-time 75, part-time 0; Multi-ethnic—full-time 4, part-time 0; students subject to the Americans With Disabilities Act—full-time 4, part-time 0; Unknown ethnicity—full-time 0, part-time 0; International students who hold an F-1 or J-1 Visa—full-time 4, part-time 0.

Financial Information/Assistance:

Tuition for Full-Time Study: *Doctoral:* State residents: per academic year $25,670, $780 per credit hour; Nonstate residents: per academic year $25,670, $780 per credit hour. Tuition is subject to change. Additional fees are assessed to students beyond the costs of tuition for the following: $200 Technology; $20 Council of Graduate Students; $10 Academic Services. See the following website for updates and changes in tuition costs: http://www.regent.edu/acad/schcou/admissions/financial/cost_of_attendance.htm.

Financial Assistance:

First-Year Students: Fellowships and scholarships available for first year. Average amount paid per academic year: $4,861. Apply by December 15.

Advanced Students: Teaching assistantships available for advanced students. Average amount paid per academic year: $7,500. Average number of hours worked per week: 12. Apply by April 1. Research assistantships available for advanced students. Average amount paid per academic year: $7,500. Average number of hours worked per week: 12. Apply by April 1. Fellowships and scholarships available for advanced students. Average amount paid per academic year: $5,525. Apply by April 1.

Additional Information: Of all students currently enrolled full time, 100% benefited from one or more of the listed financial assistance programs. Application and information available online at: http://www.regent.edu/acad/schcou/admissions/financial/.

Internships/Practica: Doctoral Degree (PsyD Clinical Psychology): For those doctoral students for whom a professional psychology internship was required in this program prior to graduation, (24) students applied for an internship in 2011–2012, with (17) students obtaining an internship. Of those students who obtained an internship, (17) were paid internships. Of those students who obtained an internship, (13) students placed in APA/CPA accredited internships, (3) students placed in internships not APA/CPA accredited, but listed with the Association of Psychology Postdoctoral and Internship Programs (APPIC), (0) students placed in internships conforming to guidelines of the Council of Directors of School Psychology Programs (CDSPP), (1) students placed in internships that were not APA/CPA accredited, APPIC or CDSPP listed. All PsyD students complete a three semester placement in the campus training clinic, the Psychological Services Center, during their second year. A three semester practicum placement is completed during the third year at any of a wide variety of community practicum sites such as military and VA clinics, inpatient brain injury units, psychiatric hospitals, group practices, community mental health agencies, outpatient practices, or correctional settings.

Housing and Day Care: On-campus housing is available. See the following website for more information: http://www.regent.edu/campus/housing/. No on-campus day care facilities are available.

Employment of Department Graduates:

Master's Degree Graduates: Of those who graduated in the academic year 2011–2012, the following categories and numbers represent the postgraduate activities and employment of master's degree graduates: Enrolled in a postdoctoral residency/fellowship (n/a), employed in independent practice (n/a), total from the above (master's) (0).

Doctoral Degree Graduates: Of those who graduated in the academic year 2011–2012, the following categories and numbers represent the postgraduate activities and employment of doctoral degree graduates: Enrolled in a psychology doctoral program (n/a), enrolled in a postdoctoral residency/fellowship (5), employed in independent practice (3), employed in other positions at a higher education institution (1), employed in a hospital/medical center (6), do not know (3), total from the above (doctoral) (18).

Additional Information:

Orientation, Objectives, and Emphasis of Department: The Doctoral Program in Clinical Psychology adopts a practitioner-scholar model of clinical training within an educational context committed to the integration of scientific psychology and a Christian worldview. The clinical training is broad and general, however marital and family therapy, consulting psychology, clinical child psychology, forensic psychology, and health psychology are emphases among the faculty and in the curriculum.

Personal Behavior Statement: http://www.regent.edu/acad/schedu/pdfs/appl_community_life.pdf.

Special Facilities or Resources: Regent is located in Virginia Beach, Virginia which is part of Tidewater, the largest urban area in Virginia. There are numerous community resources for practica. The campus also houses the Psychological Services Center, our doctoral training clinic that provides services to the campus and surrounding community. The PSC includes state of the art technology for videotaping and observation of clinical activities.

Information for Students With Physical Disabilities: See the following website for more information: http://www.regent.edu/admin/stusrv/student_life/disabilities.cfm.

Application Information:
Send to Enrollment Support Services, 1000 Regent University Drive, LIB 102; Virginia Beach, VA 23464. Application available online. URL of online application: http://www.regent.edu/admissions/application.html. Students are admitted in the Fall, application deadline December 15. *Fee:* $50.

Virginia Commonwealth University
Department of Psychology
Humanities and Sciences
806 West Franklin Street, Box 842018
Richmond, VA 23284-2018
Telephone: (804) 828-1193
Fax: (804) 828-2237
E-mail: *wkliewer@vcu.edu*
Web: *http://www.psychology.vcu.edu/*

Department Information:
1969. Chairperson: Wendy Kliewer. Number of faculty: total—full-time 41; women—full-time 22; total—minority—full-time 8; women minority—full-time 6; faculty subject to the Americans With Disabilities Act 1.

Programs and Degrees Offered:
Listed in the following order: Program area, degree type (T if terminal Master's), number awarded 7/11–6/12. Clinical Psychology PhD (Doctor of Philosophy) 8, Counseling Psychology PhD (Doctor of Philosophy) 8, Social Psychology PhD (Doctor of Philosophy) 5, Biopsychology PhD (Doctor of Philosophy) 2, Developmental Psychology PhD (Doctor of Philosophy) 1, Health Psychology PhD (Doctor of Philosophy) 0.

APA Accreditation: Clinical PhD (Doctor of Philosophy). Student Outcome Data Website: http://www.psychology.vcu.edu/clinical/index.shtml. Counseling PhD (Doctor of Philosophy). Student Outcome Data Website: http://www.psychology.vcu.edu/counseling/program.shtml.

Student Applications/Admissions:

Student Applications

Clinical Psychology PhD (Doctor of Philosophy)—Applications 2012–2013, 231. Total applicants accepted 2012–2013, 8. Number full-time enrolled (new admits only) 2012–2013, 8. Number part-time enrolled (new admits only) 2012–2013, 0. Total enrolled 2012–2013 full-time, 53. Total enrolled 2012–2013 part-time, 0. Openings 2013–2014, 8. The median number of years required for completion of a degree in 2012–2013 were 6. The number of students enrolled full- and part-time who were dismissed or voluntarily withdrew from this program area in 2012–2013 were 0. *Counseling Psychology PhD (Doctor of Philosophy)*—Applications 2012–2013, 187. Total applicants accepted 2012–2013, 4. Number full-time enrolled (new admits only) 2012–2013, 4. Total enrolled 2012–2013 full-time, 33. Openings 2013–2014, 4. The median number of years required for completion of a degree in 2012–2013 were 6. The number of students enrolled full- and part-time who were dismissed or voluntarily withdrew from this program area in 2012–2013 were 1. *Social Psychology PhD (Doctor of Philosophy)*—Applications 2012–2013, 31. Total applicants accepted 2012–2013, 2. Number full-time enrolled (new admits only) 2012–2013, 2. Number part-time enrolled (new admits only) 2012–2013, 0. Total enrolled 2012–2013 full-time, 9. Total enrolled 2012–2013 part-time, 0. Openings 2013–2014, 2. The median number of years required for completion of a degree in 2012–2013 were 5. The number of students enrolled full- and part-time who were dismissed or voluntarily withdrew from this program area in 2012–2013 were 0. *Biopsychology PhD (Doctor of Philosophy)*—Applications 2012–2013, 15. Total applicants accepted 2012–2013, 0. Number full-time enrolled (new admits only) 2012–2013, 0. Number part-time enrolled (new admits only) 2012–2013, 0. Total enrolled 2012–2013 full-time, 5. Total enrolled 2012–2013 part-time, 0. The median number of years required for completion of a degree in 2012–2013 were 5. The number of students enrolled full- and part-time who were dismissed or voluntarily withdrew from this program area in 2012–2013 were 0. *Developmental Psychology PhD (Doctor of Philosophy)*—Applications 2012–2013, 20. Total applicants accepted 2012–2013, 2. Number full-time enrolled (new admits only) 2012–2013, 2. Number part-time enrolled (new admits only) 2012–2013, 0. Total enrolled 2012–2013 full-time, 12. Total enrolled 2012–2013 part-time, 0. Openings 2013–2014, 2. The median number of years required for completion of a degree in 2012–2013 were 6. The number of students enrolled full- and part-time who were dismissed or voluntarily withdrew from this program area in 2012–2013 were 1. *Health Psychology PhD (Doctor of Philosophy)*—Applications 2012–2013, 39. Total applicants accepted 2012–2013, 3. Number full-time enrolled (new admits only) 2012–2013, 3. Number part-time enrolled (new admits only) 2012–2013, 0. Total enrolled 2012–2013 full-time, 8. Total enrolled 2012–2013 part-time, 0. Openings 2013–2014, 4. The number of students enrolled full- and part-time who were dismissed or voluntarily withdrew from this program area in 2012–2013 were 0.

Scores: Entries appear in this order: required test or GPA, minimum score (if required), median score of students entering in 2012–2013. *Clinical Psychology PhD (Doctor of Philosophy)*: GRE-V no minimum stated, 159, GRE-Q no minimum stated, 154, GRE-Analytical no minimum stated, overall undergraduate GPA no minimum stated, 3.38, last 2 years GPA no minimum stated, psychology GPA no minimum stated; *Counseling Psychology PhD (Doctor of Philosophy)*: GRE-V no minimum stated, 610, GRE-Q no minimum stated, 686, GRE-Analytical no minimum stated, overall undergraduate GPA no minimum stated, 3.80, last 2 years GPA no minimum stated, psychology GPA no minimum stated; *Social Psychology PhD (Doctor of Philosophy)*: GRE-V no minimum stated, GRE-Q no minimum stated, GRE-Analytical no minimum stated, overall undergraduate GPA no minimum stated, last 2 years GPA no minimum stated, psychology GPA no minimum stated; *Biopsychology PhD (Doctor of Philosophy)*: GRE-V no minimum stated, GRE-Q no minimum stated, GRE-Analytical no minimum stated, overall undergraduate GPA no minimum stated, last 2 years GPA no minimum stated, psychology GPA no minimum stated; *Developmental Psychology PhD (Doctor of Philosophy)*: GRE-V no minimum stated, GRE-Q no minimum stated, GRE-Analytical no minimum stated, overall undergraduate GPA no minimum stated, last 2 years GPA no minimum stated, psychology GPA no minimum stated; *Health Psychology PhD (Doctor of Philosophy)*: GRE-V no minimum stated, GRE-Q no minimum stated, GRE-Analytical no minimum stated, overall undergraduate GPA no minimum stated, last 2 years GPA no minimum stated, psychology GPA no minimum stated.

Other Criteria: (importance of criteria rated low, medium, or high): GRE scores—high, research experience—high, work experience—high, extracurricular activity—medium, clinically related public service—medium, GPA—high, letters of recommendation—high, interview—medium, statement of goals and objectives—medium, undergraduate major in psychology—medium, specific undergraduate psychology courses taken—medium, All programs emphasize research experience, GPA, letters of recommendation, and GREs. The clinical and counseling programs emphasize match between student interests and faculty interests more than the experimental programs. Clinical and counseling programs also emphasize importance of clinically related experiences. For additional information on admission requirements, go to http://www.psychology.vcu.edu/graduate/prospective/index.shtml.

Student Characteristics: The following represents characteristics of students in 2012–2013 in all graduate psychology programs in the department: Female—full-time 93, part-time 0; Male—full-time 27, part-time 0; African American/Black—full-time 17, part-time 0; Hispanic/Latino(a)—full-time 13, part-time 0; Asian/Pacific Islander—full-time 5, part-time 0; American Indian/Alaska Native—full-time 0, part-time 0; Caucasian/White—full-time 85, part-time 0; Multi-ethnic—full-time 0, part-time 0; students subject to the Americans With Disabilities Act—full-time 0, part-time 0; Unknown ethnicity—full-time 0, part-time 0; International students who hold an F-1 or J-1 Visa—full-time 3, part-time 0.

Financial Information/Assistance:

Tuition for Full-Time Study: *Doctoral*: State residents: per academic year $7,863, $436 per credit hour; Nonstate residents: per academic year $16,762, $931 per credit hour. Tuition is subject to change. See the following website for updates and changes in tuition costs: http://www.enrollment.vcu.edu/accounting/tuition_fees.html.

Financial Assistance:

First-Year Students: Teaching assistantships available for first year. Average amount paid per academic year: $13,500. Average number of hours worked per week: 20. Research assistantships available for first year. Average amount paid per academic year: $13,500. Average number of hours worked per week: 20. Fellowships and scholarships available for first year.

Advanced Students: Teaching assistantships available for advanced students. Average amount paid per academic year: $13,500. Average number of hours worked per week: 20. Research assistantships available for advanced students. Average amount paid per academic year: $13,500. Average number of hours worked per week: 20. Fellowships and scholarships available for advanced students.

Additional Information: Of all students currently enrolled full time, 96% benefited from one or more of the listed financial assistance programs. Application and information available online at: http://www.enrollment.vcu.edu/finaid/.

Internships/Practica: Doctoral Degree (PhD Clinical Psychology): For those doctoral students for whom a professional psychology internship was required in this program prior to graduation, (10) students applied for an internship in 2011–2012, with (10) students obtaining an internship. Of those students who obtained an internship, (10) were paid internships. Of those students who obtained an internship, (10) students placed in APA/CPA accredited internships, (0) students placed in internships not APA/CPA accredited, but listed with the Association of Psychology Postdoctoral and Internship Programs (APPIC), (0) students placed in internships conforming to guidelines of the Council of Directors of School Psychology Programs (CDSPP), (0) students placed in internships that were not APA/CPA accredited, APPIC or CDSPP listed. Doctoral Degree (PhD Counseling Psychology): For those doctoral students for whom a professional psychology internship was required in this program prior to graduation, (9) students applied for an internship in 2011–2012, with (9) students obtaining an internship. Of those students who obtained an internship, (9) were paid internships. Of those students who obtained an internship, (8) students placed in APA/CPA accredited internships, (0) students placed in internships not APA/CPA accredited, but listed with the Association of Psychology Postdoctoral and Internship Programs (APPIC), (0) students placed in internships conforming to guidelines of the Council of Directors of School Psychology Programs (CDSPP), (1) students placed in internships that were not APA/CPA accredited, APPIC or CDSPP listed. Practicum (external) and internship required for clinical and counseling programs. Sites range from the following: VA hospitals, federal prisons, counseling centers, medical campus opportunities, Children's Hospitals, and juvenile facilities.

Housing and Day Care: On-campus housing is available. See the following website for more information: http://www.housing.vcu.edu/. On-campus day care facilities are available. See the following website for more information: http://www.hr.vcu.edu/wellness/childcare.html.

Employment of Department Graduates:

Master's Degree Graduates: Of those who graduated in the academic year 2011–2012, the following categories and numbers represent the postgraduate activities and employment of master's degree graduates: Enrolled in a postdoctoral residency/fellowship (n/a), employed in independent practice (n/a), total from the above (master's) (0).

Doctoral Degree Graduates: Of those who graduated in the academic year 2011–2012, the following categories and numbers represent the postgraduate activities and employment of doctoral degree graduates: Enrolled in a psychology doctoral program (n/a), enrolled in a postdoctoral residency/fellowship (15), employed in independent practice (1), employed in an academic position at a university (5), employed in an academic position at a 2-year/4-year college (1), employed in a hospital/medical center (1), do not know (1), total from the above (doctoral) (24).

Additional Information:

Orientation, Objectives, and Emphasis of Department: The graduate programs in psychology are designed to provide a core education in the basic science of psychology and to enable students to develop skills specific to their area of interest. Students are educated first as psychologists, and are then helped to develop competence in a more specialized area relevant to their scholarly and professional objectives. In addition to formal research requirements for the thesis and dissertation, students in the graduate programs are encouraged to conduct independent research, participate in research teams, or collaborate with faculty conducting research on an ongoing basis. The clinical and counseling psychology programs strongly emphasize the scientist–practitioner model. Students in the clinical program may elect to develop specialized competency in one of several different tracks, including behavior therapy/cognitive behavior therapy, behavioral medicine, clinical child, and adult psychotherapy process. The counseling psychology program prepares students to function in a variety of research and applied settings and to work with people experiencing a broad range of emotional, social, or behavioral problems. The experimental program stresses the acquisition of experimental skills as well as advanced training in one of four specialty areas: biopsychology, developmental psychology, health psychology, and social psychology.

Special Facilities or Resources: The department maintains laboratories for research in the areas of health, biopsychology, developmental, social, psychophysiology, behavioral assessment, and psychotherapy process. The department also operates the Center for Psychological Services and Development, which provides mental health services for clients referred from throughout the Richmond metropolitan area. Students in the clinical and counseling programs complete practica in the Center and in a variety of off-campus practicum facilities located in the community. Cooperation with a variety of programs and departments on the University's medical campus, the Medical College of Virginia, is extensive for both research and training.

Information for Students With Physical Disabilities: See the following website for more information: http://www.students.vcu.edu/dss/.

Application Information:

Send to Virginia Commonwealth University, Graduate School, Moseley House, 1001 Grove Avenue, P.O. Box 843051, Richmond, VA 23284-3051. Application available online. URL of online application: http://www.graduate.vcu.edu/admission/prospective/apply.html. Students are admitted in the Fall, application deadline December 1. Deadlines are December 1st for Clinical and Counseling Psychology, December 15th for Social Psychology, and January 10th for Health Psychology, Developmental Psychology, and Biopsychology. *Fee:* $50.

Virginia Consortium Program in Clinical Psychology
Program in Clinical Psychology
EVMS, NSU & ODU
Norfolk State University, 700 Park Avenue, MCAR-410
Norfolk, VA 23504
Telephone: (757) 451-7733
Fax: (757) 823-8919
E-mail: *exoneill@odu.edu*
Web: *http://www.sci.odu.edu/vcpcp/*

Department Information:

1978. Director of Clinical Training: Michael L. Stutts, PhD. Number of faculty: total—full-time 22; women—full-time 12; total—minority—full-time 6; women minority—full-time 6.

Programs and Degrees Offered:

Listed in the following order: Program area, degree type (T if terminal Master's), number awarded 7/11–6/12. Virginia Consortium Program in Clinical Psychology PsyD (Doctor of Psychology) 7.

APA Accreditation: Clinical PsyD (Doctor of Psychology). Student Outcome Data Website: http://www.sci.odu.edu/vcpcp/apa_required_tables.shtml.

Student Applications/Admissions:

Student Applications

Virginia Consortium Program in Clinical Psychology PsyD (Doctor of Psychology)—Applications 2012–2013, 143. Total applicants accepted 2012–2013, 12. Number full-time enrolled (new admits only) 2012–2013, 6. Number part-time enrolled (new admits only) 2012–2013, 0. Total enrolled 2012–2013 full-time, 41. Total enrolled 2012–2013 part-time, 0. Openings 2013–2014, 6. The median number of years required for completion of a degree in 2012–2013 were 5. The number of students enrolled full- and part-time who were dismissed or voluntarily withdrew from this program area in 2012–2013 were 0.

Scores: Entries appear in this order: required test or GPA, minimum score (if required), median score of students entering in 2012–2013. *Virginia Consortium Program in Clinical Psychology PsyD (Doctor of Psychology):* GRE-V no minimum stated, 570, GRE-Q no minimum stated, 550, GRE-Analytical no minimum stated, 4.5, overall undergraduate GPA 2.5, 3.84, last 2 years GPA 3.0, psychology GPA 3.0, Masters GPA 3.0.

Other Criteria: (importance of criteria rated low, medium, or high): GRE scores—medium, research experience—medium, work experience—medium, extracurricular activity—low, clinically related public service—medium, GPA—medium, letters of recommendation—medium, interview—high, statement of goals and objectives—high, undergraduate major in psychology—medium, specific undergraduate psychology courses taken—medium. For additional information on admission requirements, go to http://www.sci.odu.edu/vcpcp/application/admission.shtml.

Student Characteristics: The following represents characteristics of students in 2012–2013 in all graduate psychology programs in the department: Female—full-time 34, part-time 0; Male—full-time 7, part-time 0; African American/Black—full-time 6, part-time 0; Hispanic/Latino(a)—full-time 6, part-time 0; Asian/Pacific Islander—full-time 3, part-time 0; American Indian/Alaska Native—full-time 0, part-time 0; Caucasian/White—full-time 26, part-time 0; Multi-ethnic—full-time 0, part-time 0; students subject to the Americans With Disabilities Act—full-time 0, part-time 0; Unknown ethnicity—full-time 0, part-time 0; International students who hold an F-1 or J-1 Visa—full-time 1, part-time 0.

Financial Information/Assistance:

Tuition for Full-Time Study: *Doctoral:* State residents: per academic year $15,000; Nonstate residents: per academic year $15,000. Tuition is subject to change. Additional fees are assessed to students beyond the costs of tuition for the following: Dissertation binding & microfilming; a $150 graduation fee. See the following website for updates and changes in tuition costs: http://www.sci.odu.edu/vcpcp/application/financial_aid.shtml.

Financial Assistance:

First-Year Students: Teaching assistantships available for first year. Average amount paid per academic year: $12,000. Average number of hours worked per week: 15. Apply by December 1. Research assistantships available for first year. Average amount paid per academic year: $7,000. Average number of hours worked per week: 10. Apply by December 1.

Advanced Students: Teaching assistantships available for advanced students. Average amount paid per academic year: $12,000. Average number of hours worked per week: 20. Apply by March 15. Research assistantships available for advanced students. Average amount paid per academic year: $7,000. Average number of hours worked per week: 8. Apply by March 15. Traineeships available for advanced students. Average amount paid per academic year: $8,000. Average number of hours worked per week: 20. Apply by March 15.

Additional Information: Of all students currently enrolled full time, 94% benefited from one or more of the listed financial assistance programs. Application and information available online at: http://www.sci.odu.edu/vcpcp/application/financial_aid.shtml.

Internships/Practica: Doctoral Degree (PsyD Virginia Consortium Program in Clinical Psychology): For those doctoral students for whom a professional psychology internship was required in this program prior to graduation, (9) students applied for an internship in 2011–2012, with (9) students obtaining an internship. Of those students who obtained an internship, (9) were paid internships. Of those students who obtained an internship, (8) students placed in APA/CPA accredited internships, (1) students placed in internships not APA/CPA accredited, but listed with the Association of Psychology Postdoctoral and Internship Programs (APPIC), (0) students placed in internships conforming to guidelines of the Council of Directors of School Psychology Programs (CDSPP), (0) students placed in internships that were not APA/CPA accredited, APPIC or CDSPP listed. Practicum training is offered in a variety of diverse settings: mental health centers, medical hospitals, children's residential treatment facilities, public school systems, university counseling centers, social services clinics, private practices, and rehabilitation units. Settings include inpatient, partial hospitalization, residential, and outpatient. Populations include children, adolescents, adults, and the elderly from most socioeconomic levels and ethnic groups. Services include most forms of assessment; individual, group, and family intervention modalities, and consultative and other indirect services. Placements are arranged to ensure that each student is exposed to several settings and populations.

Housing and Day Care: On-campus housing is available. No on-campus day care facilities are available.

Employment of Department Graduates:

Master's Degree Graduates: Of those who graduated in the academic year 2011–2012, the following categories and numbers represent the postgraduate activities and employment of master's degree graduates: Enrolled in a postdoctoral residency/fellowship (n/a), employed in independent practice (n/a), total from the above (master's) (0).

Doctoral Degree Graduates: Of those who graduated in the academic year 2011–2012, the following categories and numbers represent the postgraduate activities and employment of doctoral degree graduates: Enrolled in a psychology doctoral program (n/a), enrolled in a postdoctoral residency/fellowship (3), employed in an academic position at a university (2), employed in a community mental health/counseling center (1), employed in a hospital/medical center (1), total from the above (doctoral) (7).

Additional Information:

Orientation, Objectives, and Emphasis of Department: The Virginia Consortium is a single, unified 4+ 1 clinical psychology program co-sponsored by three institutions: Eastern Virginia Medical School, Norfolk State University, and Old Dominion University. It is in transition from a PsyD degree-granting program to a PhD degree-granting program. Its mission is to produce practicing clinical psychologists who are competent in individual and cultural diversity, educated in the basic subjects and methods of psychological science, capable of critically assimilating and generating new knowledge, proficient in the delivery and evaluation of clinical services, and able to assume leadership positions in health service delivery organizations. The curriculum is generalist in content and in theoretical orientation. Knowledge acquired in the classroom is applied in an orderly sequence of supervised practica providing exposure to multiple settings, populations, and intervention modalities. Practicum objectives are integrated with the goals of classroom education to facilitate systematic and cumulative acquisition of clinical skills. In Year 3, the student pursues individual interests by integrating individualized coursework with advanced practica and a clinical dissertation. In Year 4, the student continues advanced practica and competes for a full-time clinical internship to be taken in Year 5. Dissertation defense is expected, though not required, to occur prior to internship.

Special Facilities or Resources: Students are considered full-time in all three sponsoring schools. This permits access to: three libraries with several computerized literature search databases and 400 periodicals in psychology; three computing centers; multiple health services; and a variety of athletic facilities. Research may be conducted at practicum placement facilities.

Information for Students With Physical Disabilities: See the following website for more information: http://www.sci.odu.edu/vcpcp/schools.shtml.

Application Information:
Send to Virginia Consortium Program in Clinical Psychology, NSU/McDemmond Center for Applied Research-Room 410, Norfolk, VA 23504. Application available online. URL of online application: http://www.sci.odu.edu/vcpcp/application/application.shtml. Students are admitted in the Fall, application deadline December 1. *Fee:* $65.

Virginia Polytechnic Institute and State University
Department of Psychology
College of Science
109 Williams Hall
Blacksburg, VA 24061
Telephone: (540) 231-6581
Fax: (540) 231-3652
E-mail: *jdunsmor@vt.edu*
Web: *http://www.psyc.vt.edu/*

Department Information:
1965. Chairperson: Robert S. Stephens. Number of faculty: total—full-time 32; women—full-time 11; total—minority—full-time 3; women minority—full-time 2.

Programs and Degrees Offered:
Listed in the following order: Program area, degree type (T if terminal Master's), number awarded 7/11–6/12. Clinical Psychology PhD (Doctor of Philosophy) 7, Industrial/Organizational Psychology PhD (Doctor of Philosophy) 1, Developmental and Biological Psychology PhD (Doctor of Philosophy) 3.

APA Accreditation: Clinical PhD (Doctor of Philosophy). Student Outcome Data Website: http://www.psyc.vt.edu/graduate/clinical/.

Student Applications/Admissions:
Student Applications
Clinical Psychology PhD (Doctor of Philosophy)—Applications 2012–2013, 192. Total applicants accepted 2012–2013, 12. Number full-time enrolled (new admits only) 2012–2013, 8. Number part-time enrolled (new admits only) 2012–2013, 0. Total enrolled 2012–2013 full-time, 44. Total enrolled 2012–2013 part-time, 0. Openings 2013–2014, 6. The median number of years required for completion of a degree in 2012–2013 were 6. The number of students enrolled full- and part-time who were dismissed or voluntarily withdrew from this program area in 2012–2013 were 1. *Industrial/Organizational Psychology PhD (Doctor of Philosophy)*—Applications 2012–2013, 65. Total applicants accepted 2012–2013, 6. Number full-time enrolled (new admits only) 2012–2013, 4. Number part-time enrolled (new admits only) 2012–2013, 0. Total enrolled 2012–2013 full-time, 17. Openings 2013–2014, 4. The median number of years required for completion of a degree in 2012–2013 were 4. The number of students enrolled full- and part-time who were dismissed or voluntarily withdrew from this program area in 2012–2013 were 0. *Developmental and Biological Psychology PhD (Doctor of Philosophy)*—Applications 2012–2013, 54. Total applicants accepted 2012–2013, 7. Number full-time enrolled (new admits only) 2012–2013, 6. Number part-time enrolled (new admits only) 2012–2013, 0. Total enrolled 2012–2013 full-time, 23. Openings 2013–2014, 6. The median number of years required for completion of a degree in 2012–2013 were 5. The number of students enrolled full- and part-time who were dismissed or voluntarily withdrew from this program area in 2012–2013 were 0.

Scores: Entries appear in this order: required test or GPA, minimum score (if required), median score of students entering in 2012–2013. *Clinical Psychology PhD (Doctor of Philosophy):* GRE-V no minimum stated, 628, GRE-Q no minimum stated, 745, GRE-Analytical no minimum stated, overall undergraduate GPA no minimum stated, 3.73; *Industrial/Organizational Psychology PhD (Doctor of Philosophy):* GRE-V no minimum stated, GRE-Q no minimum stated, GRE-Analytical no minimum stated; *Developmental and Biological Psychology PhD (Doctor of Philosophy):* GRE-V no minimum stated, GRE-Q no minimum stated, GRE-Analytical no minimum stated.

Other Criteria: (importance of criteria rated low, medium, or high): GRE scores—high, research experience—high, work experience—low, clinically related public service—medium, GPA—high, letters of recommendation—high, interview—medium, statement of goals and objectives—medium, undergraduate major in psychology—low, specific undergraduate psychology courses taken—low, Congruence of applicant's goals with program objectives and faculty research - high. For additional information on admission requirements, go to http://www.psyc.vt.edu/graduate/.

Student Characteristics: The following represents characteristics of students in 2012–2013 in all graduate psychology programs in the department: Female—full-time 57, part-time 0; Male—full-time 27, part-time 0; African American/Black—full-time 6, part-time 0; Hispanic/Latino(a)—full-time 2, part-time 0; Asian/Pacific Islander—full-time 12, part-time 0; American Indian/Alaska Native—full-time 0, part-time 0; Caucasian/White—full-time 64, part-time 0; Multi-ethnic—full-time 0, part-time 0; students subject to the Americans With Disabilities Act—full-time 0, part-time 0; Unknown ethnicity—full-time 0, part-time 0; International students who hold an F-1 or J-1 Visa—full-time 8, part-time 0.

Financial Information/Assistance:
Tuition for Full-Time Study: *Doctoral:* State residents: per academic year $10,677, $593 per credit hour; Nonstate residents: per academic year $20,926, $1,162 per credit hour. Tuition is subject to change. Additional fees are assessed to students beyond the costs of tuition for the following: Comprehensive fees: VA Resident - $868/sem; Non-VA Resident - $1,170/sem. See the following website for updates and changes in tuition costs: http://www.bursar.vt.edu/tuition/.

Financial Assistance:

First-Year Students: Teaching assistantships available for first year. Average amount paid per academic year: $14,390. Average number of hours worked per week: 20. Research assistantships available for first year. Average amount paid per academic year: $16,092. Average number of hours worked per week: 20.

Advanced Students: Teaching assistantships available for advanced students. Average amount paid per academic year: $15,244. Average number of hours worked per week: 20. Research assistantships available for advanced students. Average amount paid per academic year: $16,089. Average number of hours worked per week: 20.

Additional Information: Of all students currently enrolled full time, 97% benefited from one or more of the listed financial assistance programs. Application and information available online at: http://www.psyc.vt.edu/graduate.

Internships/Practica: Doctoral Degree (PhD Clinical Psychology): For those doctoral students for whom a professional psychology internship was required in this program prior to graduation, (12) students applied for an internship in 2011–2012, with (9) students obtaining an internship. Of those students who obtained an internship, (9) were paid internships. Of those students who obtained an internship, (9) students placed in APA/CPA accredited internships, (0) students placed in internships not APA/CPA accredited, but listed with the Association of Psychology Postdoctoral and Internship Programs (APPIC), (0) students placed in internships conforming to guidelines of the Council of Directors of School Psychology Programs (CDSPP), (0) students placed in internships that were not APA/CPA accredited, APPIC or CDSPP listed. Students in Clinical psychology complete practica in department-run, off-campus clinics serving adults and children from the community. They also complete an externship in one of a variety of local agency and hospital settings. They also are required to complete a predoctoral clinical internship as part of the PhD. Students in Industrial/Organizational psychology are encouraged to pursue summer internships.

Housing and Day Care: On-campus housing is available. See the following website for more information: http://www.housing.vt.edu. No on-campus day care facilities are available.

Employment of Department Graduates:

Master's Degree Graduates: Of those who graduated in the academic year 2011–2012, the following categories and numbers represent the postgraduate activities and employment of master's degree graduates: Enrolled in a postdoctoral residency/fellowship (n/a), employed in independent practice (n/a), total from the above (master's) (0).

Doctoral Degree Graduates: Of those who graduated in the academic year 2011–2012, the following categories and numbers represent the postgraduate activities and employment of doctoral degree graduates: Enrolled in a psychology doctoral program (n/a), enrolled in a postdoctoral residency/fellowship (6), employed in an academic position at a university (2), employed in an academic position at a 2-year/4-year college (1), employed in other positions at a higher education institution (1), employed in business or industry (2), employed in a community mental health/counseling center (1), employed in a hospital/medical center (1), not seeking employment (1), total from the above (doctoral) (15).

Additional Information:

Orientation, Objectives, and Emphasis of Department: The graduate programs are designed to ensure that students receive excellent preparation in research methods and psychological theory in order to be successful in either academic or applied settings. Training and experience in the teaching of psychology is available. The Clinical Psychology program is based on the clinical scientist model and emphasizes research methods and theory in understanding, preventing, and treating health and mental health problems in adults and children. Clinical concentrations include child, adult, and health psychology. The Industrial/Organizational Psychology program prepares students for research and teaching positions as well as for the solution of individual, group, and organizational problems in applied work settings. Psychometrics, research design, and statistics are emphasized. The Developmental and Biological Psychology program trains students in experimental psychology with a focus on preparing psychologists for teaching and research settings. Students may concentrate their studies in developmental or psychobiological research areas or both.

Special Facilities or Resources: The Psychological Services Center and Child Study Center are located off-campus and provide the foundation for practicum and research training in Clinical Psychology. The Center for Research in Health Behavior is also located off-campus and is primarily involved in prevention research supported by the National Institutes of Health. Virginia Tech Community Partners is another off-campus research facility, located in downtown Roanoke. Faculty, students, and staff benefit from Virginia Tech's state-of-the-art communications system that links every dormitory room, laboratory, office, and classroom to computing capabilities, audio and video data, and the World Wide Web. The entire campus has easy access to supercomputers across the country, worldwide libraries and data systems. Department resources also include two state-of-the-art laboratories that are dedicated to undergraduate and graduate teaching and research. The psychophysiological laboratory includes eight computer workstations, five EEG/Evoked Potential work stations (32 channel Neuroscan; Neurosearch-24), eye tracker equipment, Coulbourn physiological units, and extensive perception equipment. The other computer laboratory includes 25 computer workstations with cognitive and neurophysiological experiments, SAS and SPSS statistical packages, Bilog and Multilog programs. Graduate students also have ready access to PC and Macintosh computers for word processing and Internet access.

Information for Students With Physical Disabilities: See the following website for more information: http://www.ssd.vt.edu/.

Application Information:
Send to Graduate Admissions Coordinator, 109 Williams Hall, Department of Psychology 0436, Virginia Tech, Blacksburg, VA 24061. Application available online. URL of online application: https://www.applyweb.com/apply/vtechg/index.html. Students are admitted in the Fall, application deadline December 5. Application deadline for Clinical program is December 5; for Developmental and Biological Psychology and Industrial/Organizational Psychology is January 5. *Fee:* $65.

University of
ograms in Clinical and School Psychology
School of Education
.O. Box 400267
Charlottesville, VA 22904-4267
Telephone: (434) 924-7472
Fax: (434) 924-1433
E-mail: *rer5r@virginia.edu*
Web: *http://curry.virginia.edu/academics/areas-of-study/clinical-school-psychology*

Department Information:

1976. Director: Ronald E. Reeve. Number of faculty: total—full-time 6, part-time 4; women—full-time 2, part-time 3; total—minority—full-time 1, part-time 1; women minority—part-time 1.

Programs and Degrees Offered:

Listed in the following order: Program area, degree type (T if terminal Master's), number awarded 7/11–6/12. Curry Program in Clinical and School Psychology PhD (Doctor of Philosophy) 7.

APA Accreditation: Clinical PhD (Doctor of Philosophy). Student Outcome Data Website: http://curry.virginiahttp://curry.virginia.edu/academics/degrees/doctor-of-philosophy/ph.d.-in-clinical-and-school-psychology/admission-outcomes.

Student Applications/Admissions:

Student Applications

Curry Program in Clinical and School Psychology PhD (Doctor of Philosophy)—Applications 2012–2013, 141. Total applicants accepted 2012–2013, 12. Number full-time enrolled (new admits only) 2012–2013, 6. Number part-time enrolled (new admits only) 2012–2013, 0. Total enrolled 2012–2013 full-time, 27. Total enrolled 2012–2013 part-time, 0. Openings 2013–2014, 6. The median number of years required for completion of a degree in 2012–2013 were 5. The number of students enrolled full- and part-time who were dismissed or voluntarily withdrew from this program area in 2012–2013 were 0.

Scores: Entries appear in this order: required test or GPA, minimum score (if required), median score of students entering in 2012–2013. *Curry Program in Clinical and School Psychology PhD (Doctor of Philosophy):* GRE-V no minimum stated, 610, GRE-Q no minimum stated, 670, GRE-Analytical no minimum stated, overall undergraduate GPA no minimum stated, 3.6.

Other Criteria: (importance of criteria rated low, medium, or high): GRE scores—medium, research experience—medium, work experience—medium, extracurricular activity—low, clinically related public service—medium, GPA—high, letters of recommendation—high, interview—high, statement of goals and objectives—high, undergraduate major in psychology—medium, specific undergraduate psychology courses taken—medium. For additional information on admission requirements, go to http://curry.virginia.edu/academics/areas-of-study/clinical-school-psychology.

Student Characteristics: The following represents characteristics of students in 2012–2013 in all graduate psychology programs in the department: Female—full-time 25, part-time 0; Male—full-time 2, part-time 0; African American/Black—full-time 3, part-time 0; Hispanic/Latino(a)—full-time 0, part-time 0; Asian/Pacific Islander—full-time 1, part-time 0; American Indian/Alaska Native—full-time 0, part-time 0; Caucasian/White—full-time 23, part-time 0; Multi-ethnic—full-time 0, part-time 0; students subject to the Americans With Disabilities Act—full-time 0, part-time 0; Unknown ethnicity—full-time 0, part-time 0; International students who hold an F-1 or J-1 Visa—full-time 0, part-time 0.

Financial Information/Assistance:

Tuition for Full-Time Study: *Doctoral:* State residents: per academic year $15,682; Nonstate residents: per academic year $25,688. See the following website for updates and changes in tuition costs: http://www.virginia.edu/studentaccounts/tuition_and_fee.html.

Financial Assistance:

First-Year Students: Teaching assistantships available for first year. Average amount paid per academic year: $2,000. Average number of hours worked per week: 10. Apply by March 1. Research assistantships available for first year. Average amount paid per academic year: $5,000. Average number of hours worked per week: 10. Apply by March 1. Fellowships and scholarships available for first year. Average amount paid per academic year: $14,000. Average number of hours worked per week: 10. Apply by March 1.

Advanced Students: Teaching assistantships available for advanced students. Average amount paid per academic year: $2,000. Average number of hours worked per week: 8. Apply by March 1. Research assistantships available for advanced students. Average amount paid per academic year: $5,000. Average number of hours worked per week: 8. Apply by March 1. Fellowships and scholarships available for advanced students. Average amount paid per academic year: $14,000. Average number of hours worked per week: 8. Apply by March 1.

Additional Information: Of all students currently enrolled full time, 100% benefited from one or more of the listed financial assistance programs.

Internships/Practica: Doctoral Degree (PhD Curry Program in Clinical and School Psychology): For those doctoral students for whom a professional psychology internship was required in this program prior to graduation, (5) students applied for an internship in 2011–2012, with (4) students obtaining an internship. Of those students who obtained an internship, (4) were paid internships. Of those students who obtained an internship, (4) students placed in APA/CPA accredited internships, (0) students placed in internships not APA/CPA accredited, but listed with the Association of Psychology Postdoctoral and Internship Programs (APPIC), (0) students placed in internships conforming to guidelines of the Council of Directors of School Psychology Programs (CDSPP), (0) students placed in internships that were not APA/CPA accredited, APPIC or CDSPP listed. Students undertake external clinical practica and school internships in area public and private schools, state mental hospitals/residential treatment centers for children or adults, a regional medically affiliated children's rehabilitation center, a family stress clinic, a federal correctional facility, and other mental health settings in the university and community. During the fifth year of training, students complete a full-time one-year internship in clinical psychology.

Housing and Day Care: On-campus housing is available. See the following website for more information: http://www.virginia.edu/housing/. On-campus day care facilities are available. See the following website for more information: http://www.virginia.edu/childdevelopmentcenter/.

Employment of Department Graduates:

Master's Degree Graduates: Of those who graduated in the academic year 2011–2012, the following categories and numbers represent the postgraduate activities and employment of master's degree graduates: Enrolled in a postdoctoral residency/fellowship (n/a), employed in independent practice (n/a), total from the above (master's) (0).

Doctoral Degree Graduates: Of those who graduated in the academic year 2011–2012, the following categories and numbers represent the postgraduate activities and employment of doctoral degree graduates: Enrolled in a psychology doctoral program (n/a), enrolled in a postdoctoral residency/fellowship (7), total from the above (doctoral) (7).

Additional Information:

Orientation, Objectives, and Emphasis of Department: The primary goal of the training program in the Curry Programs in Clinical and School Psychology is to produce clinical and school psychologists who will make substantial contributions to the field in a variety of professional and scientific roles. The majority of graduates seek leadership positions in settings such as medical centers, schools, and mental health agencies, while others pursue academic and research careers. All students complete a common core of coursework and practica in both basic science and professional skills. Students have the opportunity for specialized training and research in concentration areas such as family therapy, forensic psychology, and school interventions, among others. The predominant theoretical and practice orientations of the faculty are cognitive behavioral, psychodynamic, and family systems. All students are expected to develop clinical and research skills, and the integration of clinical, classroom, and research experiences is emphasized. Many students in the PhD program pursue training in both clinical and school psychology through the clinical-school track.

Special Facilities or Resources: The Curry Program operates a comprehensive psychological clinic, the Center for Clinical Psychology Services, serving families, couples, and individuals of all ages and diverse backgrounds, within the Sheila Johnson Center for Human Services (SJC). The new Sheila Johnson Center is well equipped for live and videotaped supervision and conveniently located in the new Bavaro Hall, with faculty and student offices nearby. In addition, the Program has close working relationships with numerous community agencies, schools, clinics, and hospitals that permit training and research in many different mental health and educational settings. Our students have research and consultation opportunities with numerous projects, including the Center for Positive Youth Development, Young Women Leaders Program, Virginia Youth Violence Project, Center for the Advanced Study of Teaching and Learning, and the Prisoners and Their Families Project. The Curry School of Education is a national leader in instructional technology, with outstanding computing facilities and technology support, smart classrooms, and its own library. Students enjoy easy access to the extensive University of Virginia Library system, which includes a collection of nearly 5 million volumes and has state-of-the-art electronic library resources.

Information for Students With Physical Disabilities: See the following website for more information: http://www.virginia.edu/accessibility/.

Application Information:
Send to Admissions Office, Curry School of Education, P.O. Box 400261, University of Virginia, Charlottesville, VA 22904-4261. Application available online. URL of online application: http://curry.virginia.edu/academics/admissions/information. Students are admitted in the Fall, application deadline January 5. *Fee:* $60.

Virginia, University of
Department of Psychology
102 Gilmer Hall, P.O. Box 400400
Charlottesville, VA 22904-4400
Telephone: (434) 982-4750
Fax: (434) 982-4766
E-mail: *psychology@virginia.edu*
Web: *http://avillage.web.virginia.edu/psych/*

Department Information:
1929. Chairperson: David L. Hill. Number of faculty: total—full-time 34; women—full-time 9; total—minority—full-time 7; women minority—full-time 1.

Programs and Degrees Offered:
Listed in the following order: Program area, degree type (T if terminal Master's), number awarded 7/11–6/12. Clinical Psychology PhD (Doctor of Philosophy) 5, Cognitive Psychology PhD (Doctor of Philosophy) 2, Community Psychology PhD (Doctor of Philosophy) 1, Developmental Psychology PhD (Doctor of Philosophy) 1, Quantitative Psychology PhD (Doctor of Philosophy) 1, Social Psychology PhD (Doctor of Philosophy) 3, Sensory and Systems Neuroscience PhD (Doctor of Philosophy) 1.

APA Accreditation: Clinical PhD (Doctor of Philosophy). Student Outcome Data Website: http://avillage.web.virginia.edu/Psych/ResearchAreas/Clinical.

Student Applications/Admissions:
Student Applications
Clinical Psychology PhD (Doctor of Philosophy)—Applications 2012–2013, 308. Total applicants accepted 2012–2013, 6. Number full-time enrolled (new admits only) 2012–2013, 4. Number part-time enrolled (new admits only) 2012–2013, 0. Total enrolled 2012–2013 full-time, 27. Total enrolled 2012–2013 part-time, 0. Openings 2013–2014, 5. The median number of years required for completion of a degree in 2012–2013 were 6. The number of students enrolled full- and part-time who were dismissed or voluntarily withdrew from this program area in 2012–2013 were 0. *Cognitive Psychology PhD (Doctor of Philosophy)*—Applications 2012–2013, 52. Total applicants accepted 2012–2013, 4. Number full-time enrolled (new admits only) 2012–2013, 2. Number part-time enrolled (new admits only) 2012–2013, 0. Total enrolled 2012–2013 full-

time, 12. Total enrolled 2012–2013 part-time, 0. Openings 2013–2014, 3. The median number of years required for completion of a degree in 2012–2013 were 6. The number of students enrolled full- and part-time who were dismissed or voluntarily withdrew from this program area in 2012–2013 were 0. *Community Psychology PhD (Doctor of Philosophy)*—Applications 2012–2013, 27. Total applicants accepted 2012–2013, 2. Number full-time enrolled (new admits only) 2012–2013, 1. Number part-time enrolled (new admits only) 2012–2013, 0. Total enrolled 2012–2013 full-time, 10. Total enrolled 2012–2013 part-time, 0. Openings 2013–2014, 2. The median number of years required for completion of a degree in 2012–2013 were 5. The number of students enrolled full- and part-time who were dismissed or voluntarily withdrew from this program area in 2012–2013 were 0. *Developmental Psychology PhD (Doctor of Philosophy)*—Applications 2012–2013, 55. Total applicants accepted 2012–2013, 4. Number full-time enrolled (new admits only) 2012–2013, 2. Number part-time enrolled (new admits only) 2012–2013, 0. Total enrolled 2012–2013 full-time, 10. Total enrolled 2012–2013 part-time, 0. Openings 2013–2014, 2. The median number of years required for completion of a degree in 2012–2013 were 6. The number of students enrolled full- and part-time who were dismissed or voluntarily withdrew from this program area in 2012–2013 were 0. *Quantitative Psychology PhD (Doctor of Philosophy)*—Applications 2012–2013, 20. Total applicants accepted 2012–2013, 3. Number full-time enrolled (new admits only) 2012–2013, 1. Number part-time enrolled (new admits only) 2012–2013, 0. Total enrolled 2012–2013 full-time, 8. Total enrolled 2012–2013 part-time, 0. Openings 2013–2014, 3. The median number of years required for completion of a degree in 2012–2013 were 4. The number of students enrolled full- and part-time who were dismissed or voluntarily withdrew from this program area in 2012–2013 were 0. *Social Psychology PhD (Doctor of Philosophy)*—Applications 2012–2013, 162. Total applicants accepted 2012–2013, 6. Number full-time enrolled (new admits only) 2012–2013, 2. Number part-time enrolled (new admits only) 2012–2013, 0. Total enrolled 2012–2013 full-time, 18. Total enrolled 2012–2013 part-time, 0. Openings 2013–2014, 3. The median number of years required for completion of a degree in 2012–2013 were 6. The number of students enrolled full- and part-time who were dismissed or voluntarily withdrew from this program area in 2012–2013 were 0. *Sensory and Systems Neuroscience PhD (Doctor of Philosophy)*—Applications 2012–2013, 27. Total applicants accepted 2012–2013, 3. Number full-time enrolled (new admits only) 2012–2013, 1. Number part-time enrolled (new admits only) 2012–2013, 0. Total enrolled 2012–2013 full-time, 4. Total enrolled 2012–2013 part-time, 0. The median number of years required for completion of a degree in 2012–2013 were 8. The number of students enrolled full- and part-time who were dismissed or voluntarily withdrew from this program area in 2012–2013 were 0.

Scores: Entries appear in this order: required test or GPA, minimum score (if required), median score of students entering in 2012–2013. *Clinical Psychology PhD (Doctor of Philosophy):* GRE-V no minimum stated, GRE-Q no minimum stated, GRE-Analytical no minimum stated, overall undergraduate GPA no minimum stated, last 2 years GPA no minimum stated, psychology GPA no minimum stated, Masters GPA no minimum stated; *Cognitive Psychology PhD (Doctor of Philosophy):* GRE-V no minimum stated, GRE-Q no minimum

stated, GRE-Analytical no minimum stated, overall undergraduate GPA no minimum stated, last 2 years GPA no minimum stated, psychology GPA no minimum stated, Masters GPA no minimum stated; *Community Psychology PhD (Doctor of Philosophy):* GRE-V no minimum stated, GRE-Q no minimum stated, GRE-Analytical no minimum stated, overall undergraduate GPA no minimum stated, last 2 years GPA no minimum stated, psychology GPA no minimum stated, Masters GPA no minimum stated; *Developmental Psychology PhD (Doctor of Philosophy):* GRE-V no minimum stated, GRE-Q no minimum stated, GRE-Analytical no minimum stated, overall undergraduate GPA no minimum stated, last 2 years GPA no minimum stated, psychology GPA no minimum stated, Masters GPA no minimum stated; *Quantitative Psychology PhD (Doctor of Philosophy):* GRE-V no minimum stated, GRE-Q no minimum stated, GRE-Analytical no minimum stated, overall undergraduate GPA no minimum stated, last 2 years GPA no minimum stated, psychology GPA no minimum stated, Masters GPA no minimum stated; *Social Psychology PhD (Doctor of Philosophy):* GRE-V no minimum stated, GRE-Q no minimum stated, GRE-Analytical no minimum stated, overall undergraduate GPA no minimum stated, last 2 years GPA no minimum stated, psychology GPA no minimum stated, Masters GPA no minimum stated; *Sensory and Systems Neuroscience PhD (Doctor of Philosophy):* GRE-V no minimum stated, GRE-Q no minimum stated, GRE-Analytical no minimum stated, overall undergraduate GPA no minimum stated, last 2 years GPA no minimum stated, psychology GPA no minimum stated, Masters GPA no minimum stated.

Other Criteria: (importance of criteria rated low, medium, or high): GRE scores—medium, research experience—high, work experience—medium, extracurricular activity—low, clinically related public service—low, GPA—high, letters of recommendation—high, interview—medium, statement of goals and objectives—high, Publications and presentations at conferences are valued as actual work experience in an area related to the degree sought. For additional information on admission requirements, go to http://avillage.web.virginia.edu/Psych/Graduates/admissions.

Student Characteristics: The following represents characteristics of students in 2012–2013 in all graduate psychology programs in the department: Female—full-time 61, part-time 0; Male—full-time 28, part-time 0; African American/Black—full-time 5, part-time 0; Hispanic/Latino(a)—full-time 0, part-time 0; Asian/Pacific Islander—full-time 14, part-time 0; American Indian/Alaska Native—full-time 0, part-time 0; Caucasian/White—full-time 66, part-time 0; Multi-ethnic—full-time 4, part-time 0; students subject to the Americans With Disabilities Act—full-time 0, part-time 0; Unknown ethnicity—full-time 0, part-time 0; International students who hold an F-1 or J-1 Visa—full-time 12, part-time 0.

Financial Information/Assistance:

Tuition for Full-Time Study: *Doctoral:* State residents: per academic year $15,672; Nonstate residents: per academic year $25,678. Tuition is subject to change. See the following website for updates and changes in tuition costs: http://www.virginia.edu/studentaccounts/tuition_and_fee.html.

Financial Assistance:

First-Year Students: Teaching assistantships available for first year. Average amount paid per academic year: $9,250. Aver-

age number of hours worked per week: 10. Research assistantships available for first year. Average amount paid per academic year: $17,000. Average number of hours worked per week: 20. Fellowships and scholarships available for first year. Average amount paid per academic year: $10,750. Average number of hours worked per week: 0.

Advanced Students: Teaching assistantships available for advanced students. Average amount paid per academic year: $9,250. Average number of hours worked per week: 10. Research assistantships available for advanced students. Average amount paid per academic year: $17,000. Average number of hours worked per week: 20. Fellowships and scholarships available for advanced students. Average amount paid per academic year: $6,750. Average number of hours worked per week: 0.

Additional Information: Of all students currently enrolled full time, 100% benefited from one or more of the listed financial assistance programs. Application and information available online at: http://avillage.web.virginia.edu/Psych/Graduates/finaid.

Internships/Practica: Doctoral Degree (PhD Clinical Psychology): For those doctoral students for whom a professional psychology internship was required in this program prior to graduation, (3) students applied for an internship in 2011–2012, with (3) students obtaining an internship. Of those students who obtained an internship, (3) were paid internships. Of those students who obtained an internship, (3) students placed in APA/CPA accredited internships, (0) students placed in internships not APA/CPA accredited, but listed with the Association of Psychology Postdoctoral and Internship Programs (APPIC), (0) students placed in internships conforming to guidelines of the Council of Directors of School Psychology Programs (CDSPP), (0) students placed in internships that were not APA/CPA accredited, APPIC or CDSPP listed. For clinical program: Multiple practica at University Hospital, State Mental Hospital for children and adults, Kluge Children's Center; Community Mental Health Center; Law and Psychiatry Unit; Department Clinic and other places as connections and student interest suggest.

Housing and Day Care: On-campus housing is available. See the following website for more information: http://www.virginia.edu/housing/grad.php. On-campus day care facilities are available. See the following website for more information: http://www.virginia.edu/childdevelopmentcenter/.

Employment of Department Graduates:

Master's Degree Graduates: Of those who graduated in the academic year 2011–2012, the following categories and numbers represent the postgraduate activities and employment of master's degree graduates: Enrolled in a postdoctoral residency/fellowship (n/a), employed in independent practice (n/a), total from the above (master's) (0).

Doctoral Degree Graduates: Of those who graduated in the academic year 2011–2012, the following categories and numbers represent the postgraduate activities and employment of doctoral degree graduates: Enrolled in a psychology doctoral program (n/a), enrolled in a postdoctoral residency/fellowship (13), employed in an academic position at a university (1), do not know (3), total from the above (doctoral) (17).

Additional Information:

Orientation, Objectives, and Emphasis of Department: The department emphasizes research on a wide spectrum of psychological issues with clinical, developmental, social, cognitive, sensory and systems neuroscience, quantitative, and community specialties. In addition, new tracks are being developed, such as social ecology and development, law and psychology, family, and minority issues.

Special Facilities or Resources: The department has in excess of 50,000 square feet for offices, laboratories, seminar rooms, and classrooms. Special facilities include rooms for psychophysical investigations, a suite of rooms devoted to developmental, clinical, and social laboratories, and specialized research facilities for the study of animal behavior and psychobiology. Sound-attenuated rooms, electrically shielded rooms, numerous one-way vision rooms, surgery and vivarium rooms, and a darkroom are all available. There is also a library for psychology and biology housed in the same building. There are ample computer facilities. All labs are connected to a local area network and a university-wide local area network. This allows the labs to connect to other available University machines such as IBM RS/6000 unix machines.

Information for Students With Physical Disabilities: See the following website for more information: http://www.virginia.edu/studenthealth/lnec.html.

Application Information:
Send to Dean of the Graduate School, The University of Virginia, P.O. Box 400775, 437 Cabell Hall, Charlottesville, VA 22904-4775. Application available online. URL of online application: http://gsas.virginia.edu/admission. Students are admitted in the Fall, application deadline December 15. *Fee:* $60.

Antioch University, Seattle

PsyD in Psychology
School of Applied Psychology, Counseling and Family Therapy
2326 6th Avenue
Seattle, WA 98121-1814
Telephone: (206) 268-4828
Fax: (206) 441-3307
E-mail: *mwieneke@antioch.edu*
Web: *http://www.antiochseattle.edu/academics/psyd-clinical-psychology-2/*

Department Information:

2004. Chairperson: Mary Wieneke, PhD. Number of faculty: total—full-time 9, part-time 16; women—full-time 6, part-time 7; total—minority—full-time 2, part-time 2; women minority—full-time 2, part-time 1.

Programs and Degrees Offered:

Listed in the following order: Program area, degree type (T if terminal Master's), number awarded 7/11–6/12. Clinical Psychology PsyD (Doctor of Psychology) 8.

Student Applications/Admissions:

Student Applications

Clinical Psychology PsyD (Doctor of Psychology)—Applications 2012–2013, 65. Total applicants accepted 2012–2013, 34. Number full-time enrolled (new admits only) 2012–2013, 18. Number part-time enrolled (new admits only) 2012–2013, 4. Total enrolled 2012–2013 full-time, 50. Total enrolled 2012–2013 part-time, 69. Openings 2013–2014, 27. The median number of years required for completion of a degree in 2012–2013 were 6. The number of students enrolled full- and part-time who were dismissed or voluntarily withdrew from this program area in 2012–2013 were 4.

Scores: Entries appear in this order: required test or GPA, minimum score (if required), median score of students entering in 2012–2013. *Clinical Psychology PsyD (Doctor of Psychology):* overall undergraduate GPA no minimum stated, last 2 years GPA no minimum stated, psychology GPA no minimum stated, Masters GPA no minimum stated.

Other Criteria: (importance of criteria rated low, medium, or high): GRE scores—medium, research experience—medium, work experience—medium, extracurricular activity—medium, clinically related public service—medium, GPA—medium, letters of recommendation—high, interview—high, statement of goals and objectives—high, undergraduate major in psychology—medium, specific undergraduate psychology courses taken—high. For additional information on admission requirements, go to http://www.antiochseattle.edu/admissions/requirements-and-deadlines/psy-d-psychology/.

Student Characteristics: The following represents characteristics of students in 2012–2013 in all graduate psychology programs in the department: Female—full-time 38, part-time 61; Male—full-time 12, part-time 15; African American/Black—full-time 7, part-time 2; Hispanic/Latino(a)—full-time 2, part-time 8; Asian/Pacific Islander—full-time 2, part-time 2; American Indian/Alaska Native—full-time 0, part-time 3; Caucasian/White—full-time 26, part-time 42; Multi-ethnic—full-time 3, part-time 6; students subject to the Americans With Disabilities Act—full-time 3, part-time 0; Unknown ethnicity—full-time 13, part-time 3; International students who hold an F-1 or J-1 Visa—full-time 0, part-time 4.

Financial Information/Assistance:

Tuition for Full-Time Study: *Doctoral:* State residents: per academic year $28,120, $766 per credit hour; Nonstate residents: per academic year $28,120, $766 per credit hour. Tuition is subject to change. Additional fees are assessed to students beyond the costs of tuition for the following: quarterly student service fee, fees for assessment labs and technology fee. See the following website for updates and changes in tuition costs: http://www.antiochseattle.edu/financial-aid-2/tuition-and-fees/.

Financial Assistance:

First-Year Students: Fellowships and scholarships available for first year. Average amount paid per academic year: $15,200. Average number of hours worked per week: 15. Apply by June 15.

Advanced Students: Teaching assistantships available for advanced students. Research assistantships available for advanced students. Fellowships and scholarships available for advanced students. Average amount paid per academic year: $15,200. Average number of hours worked per week: 15.

Additional Information: Of all students currently enrolled full time, 10% benefited from one or more of the listed financial assistance programs. Application and information available online at: http://www.antiochseattle.edu/financial-aid-2/.

Internships/Practica: Doctoral Degree (PsyD Clinical Psychology): For those doctoral students for whom a professional psychology internship was required in this program prior to graduation, (17) students applied for an internship in 2011–2012, with (17) students obtaining an internship. Of those students who obtained an internship, (1) were paid internships. Of those students who obtained an internship, (0) students placed in APA/CPA accredited internships, (3) students placed in internships not APA/CPA accredited, but listed with the Association of Psychology Postdoctoral and Internship Programs (APPIC), (0) students placed in internships conforming to guidelines of the Council of Directors of School Psychology Programs (CDSPP), (14) students placed in internships that were not APA/CPA accredited, APPIC or CDSPP listed. Throughout their experience, Antioch University Seattle students have the opportunity to develop their clinical, applied research, and assessment skills. There is an emphasis on multicultural competency and social justice is woven into the practical training experiences and placements. Practicum, preinternship, and internship placements may include working in the Antioch University Seattle Clinic and/or a variety of community engagements. Supervision and mentoring are provided by licensed professionals and licensed psychologists. Currently there are opportunities for placement in forensic, clinical child, clinical adult, therapeutic school, neuropsychology assessment, rehabilitation, college counseling centers, community mental health, and health psychology mental health sites. Collaborative relationships with community sites are nurtured to provide ongoing opportunities for dynamic involvement in psychological services provision, applied research, and psychological assessment opportunities. These practical training experiences culminate in the predoctoral internship, which is a full-time year or half-time two-year placement for advanced training in a particular setting in professional psychology. Local predoctoral internship placements are available. In addition, AUS participates in the Association of Psychology Postdoctoral and Internship Center's (APPIC) internship match program and students will have the opportunity to apply for internships nationally through this program.

Housing and Day Care: No on-campus housing is available. No on-campus day care facilities are available.

Employment of Department Graduates:

Master's Degree Graduates: Of those who graduated in the academic year 2011–2012, the following categories and numbers represent the postgraduate activities and employment of master's degree graduates: Enrolled in a postdoctoral residency/fellowship (n/a), employed in independent practice (n/a), total from the above (master's) (0).

Doctoral Degree Graduates: Of those who graduated in the academic year 2011–2012, the following categories and numbers represent the postgraduate activities and employment of doctoral degree graduates: Enrolled in a psychology doctoral program (n/a), enrolled in a postdoctoral residency/fellowship (1), employed in independent practice (7), employed in an academic position at a university (3), employed in an academic position at a 2-year/4-year college (1), employed in other positions at a higher education institution (1), employed in government agency (1), employed in a community mental health/counseling center (1), employed in a hospital/medical center (2), do not know (1), total from the above (doctoral) (18).

Additional Information:

Orientation, Objectives, and Emphasis of Department: Antioch University Seattle's PsyD program in clinical psychology prepares students for professional careers in psychology. The mission of Antioch University Seattle is to educate students to engage in lifelong reflective learning within the context of social change agency in this ever-changing world. The program follows the practitioner/scholar model with equal emphasis on practice and research. Antioch invites and supports students to follow their passion, personally and professionally, to promote health, education, social justice, and human welfare. The program offers flexibility in the curriculum to enable adult learners to progress either full time or part time through their graduate studies after completing the first year of full time studies. The curriculum includes foundational courses as well as an ability to select concentrations while providing treatment through the on-site AUS mental health clinic and/or community placements. AUS concentrations provide our students with a spectrum of theoretical perspectives and practical experiences along with stimulating professional seminars. The faculty are experienced teachers, clinicians, researchers, and social advocates; many are well-known in both state-wide

and national psychology organizations. Faculty members bring a balance of traditional and contemporary perspectives in the field of clinical psychology, educating students to become informed and effective practitioners and scholars.

Special Facilities or Resources: Antioch University Seattle offers opportunities to pursue clinical practice and assessment, as well as academic and research enterprises in our on-site sliding-scale community clinic. Students who are closely supervised provide high quality psychological services to various populations. AUS Clinic offers high quality psychological services including counseling and testing to the Seattle community in a safe and supportive setting. In addition, AUS has arrangements with local specialty treatment facilities so our students can gain experience with additional populations and treatment modalities. Our students also are encouraged to work closely with faculty on cutting edge research on issues of social justice and social change. For example, working on a multi-disciplinary research team with a nationally renowned expert for the Study of War Stress Injuries dedicated to the study, identification, and elimination of contributing factors responsible for cyclic failure in meeting the military mental health needs of the warrior class. Students are an integral part of departmental and university-wide committees, which helps prepare them for future careers in administration, research, therapy, academia, public policy, and higher education. There are several different opportunities for students to join research teams with faculty and community based research teams of their interests.

Information for Students With Physical Disabilities: See the following website for more information: http://www. antiochseattle.edu/disability-support-services/.

Application Information:
Send to Admissions Office, 2326 6th Avenue, Seattle, WA 98121-1814. Application available online. URL of online application: http:// www.antiochseattle.edu/admissions/. Students are admitted in the Fall, application deadline January 15. *Fee:* $50 for online applications and a $75 fee for paper applications.

Central Washington University
Department of Psychology
College of the Sciences
400 East University Way
Ellensburg, WA 98926-7575
Telephone: (509) 963-2381
Fax: (509) 963-2307
E-mail: *steins@cwu.edu*
Web: *http://www.cwu.edu/psychology/*

Department Information:
1965. Chairperson: Stephanie Stein. Number of faculty: total—full-time 20, part-time 13; women—full-time 10, part-time 6.

Programs and Degrees Offered:
Listed in the following order: Program area, degree type (T if terminal Master's), number awarded 7/11–6/12. Mental Health Counseling MA/MS (Master of Arts/Science) (T) 11, Experimental Psychology MA/MS (Master of Arts/Science) (T) 9, School

Psychology EdS (School Psychology) 7, Experimental Psychology (Aba Specialization) MA/MS (Master of Arts/Science) (T) 1.

Student Applications/Admissions:

Student Applications

Mental Health Counseling MA/MS (Master of Arts/Science)—Applications 2012–2013, 59. Total applicants accepted 2012–2013, 9. Number full-time enrolled (new admits only) 2012–2013, 9. Number part-time enrolled (new admits only) 2012–2013, 0. Total enrolled 2012–2013 full-time, 23. Total enrolled 2012–2013 part-time, 2. Openings 2013–2014, 10. The median number of years required for completion of a degree in 2012–2013 were 2. The number of students enrolled full- and part-time who were dismissed or voluntarily withdrew from this program area in 2012–2013 were 1. Experimental Psychology MA/MS (Master of Arts/Science)—Applications 2012–2013, 24. Total applicants accepted 2012–2013, 5. Number full-time enrolled (new admits only) 2012–2013, 5. Number part-time enrolled (new admits only) 2012–2013, 0. Total enrolled 2012–2013 full-time, 19. Total enrolled 2012–2013 part-time, 2. Openings 2013–2014, 10. The median number of years required for completion of a degree in 2012–2013 were 2. The number of students enrolled full- and part-time who were dismissed or voluntarily withdrew from this program area in 2012–2013 were 1. School Psychology EdS (School Psychology)—Applications 2012–2013, 29. Total applicants accepted 2012–2013, 11. Number full-time enrolled (new admits only) 2012–2013, 8. Number part-time enrolled (new admits only) 2012–2013, 0. Total enrolled 2012–2013 full-time, 24. Openings 2013–2014, 10. The median number of years required for completion of a degree in 2012–2013 were 3. The number of students enrolled full- and part-time who were dismissed or voluntarily withdrew from this program area in 2012–2013 were 2. Experimental Psychology (Aba Specialization) MA/MS (Master of Arts/Science)—Applications 2012–2013, 6. Total applicants accepted 2012–2013, 4. Number full-time enrolled (new admits only) 2012–2013, 4. Number part-time enrolled (new admits only) 2012–2013, 0. Total enrolled 2012–2013 full-time, 4. Total enrolled 2012–2013 part-time, 0. Openings 2013–2014, 6. The median number of years required for completion of a degree in 2012–2013 were 3. The number of students enrolled full- and part-time who were dismissed or voluntarily withdrew from this program area in 2012–2013 were 0.

Scores: Entries appear in this order: required test or GPA, minimum score (if required), median score of students entering in 2012–2013. Mental Health Counseling MA/MS (Master of Arts/Science): GRE-V 150, 152, GRE-Q 141, 150; Experimental Psychology MA/MS (Master of Arts/Science): GRE-V no minimum stated, GRE-Q no minimum stated; School Psychology EdS (School Psychology): GRE-V no minimum stated, GRE-Q no minimum stated, last 2 years GPA 3.00; Experimental Psychology (ABA Specialization) MA/MS (Master of Arts/Science): GRE-V no minimum stated, GRE-Q no minimum stated.

Other Criteria: (importance of criteria rated low, medium, or high): GRE scores—medium, research experience—medium, work experience—medium, extracurricular activity—low, clinically related public service—medium, GPA—high, letters of recommendation—high, statement of goals and objectives—high, undergraduate major in psychology—medium, specific undergraduate psychology courses taken—medium.

Student Characteristics: The following represents characteristics of students in 2012–2013 in all graduate psychology programs in the department: Female—full-time 47, part-time 6; Male—full-time 25, part-time 3; African American/Black—full-time 3, part-time 0; Hispanic/Latino(a)—full-time 3, part-time 0; Asian/Pacific Islander—full-time 2, part-time 0; American Indian/Alaska Native—full-time 1, part-time 0; Caucasian/White—full-time 59, part-time 9; Multi-ethnic—full-time 13, part-time 0; students subject to the Americans With Disabilities Act—full-time 0, part-time 0; Unknown ethnicity—full-time 0, part-time 0; International students who hold an F-1 or J-1 Visa—full-time 1, part-time 0.

Financial Information/Assistance:

Tuition for Full-Time Study: Master's: State residents: per academic year $8,382, $279 per credit hour; Nonstate residents: per academic year $18,717, $623 per credit hour. Tuition is subject to change. See the following website for updates and changes in tuition costs: http://www.cwu.edu/registrar/tuition.

Financial Assistance:

First-Year Students: Teaching assistantships available for first year. Average amount paid per academic year: $16,489. Average number of hours worked per week: 20. Apply by February 1. Research assistantships available for first year. Average amount paid per academic year: $16,489. Average number of hours worked per week: 20. Apply by February 1.

Advanced Students: Teaching assistantships available for advanced students. Average amount paid per academic year: $16,489. Average number of hours worked per week: 20. Apply by February 1. Research assistantships available for advanced students. Average amount paid per academic year: $16,489. Average number of hours worked per week: 20. Apply by February 1.

Additional Information: Of all students currently enrolled full time, 28% benefited from one or more of the listed financial assistance programs. Application and information available online at: http://www.cwu.edu/masters/graduate-student-funding.

Internships/Practica: Master's Degree (MA/MS Mental Health Counseling): An internship experience, such as a final research project or "capstone" experience is required of graduates. Master's Degree (MA/MS Experimental Psychology): An internship experience, such as a final research project or "capstone" experience is required of graduates. Master's Degree (MA/MS Experimental Psychology (ABA Specialization)): An internship experience, such as a final research project or "capstone" experience is required of graduates. The Mental Health Counseling Psychology program requires four quarters of practica and a 900 hour internship. School Counseling program requires four quarters of practica and a 400 hour internship. School Psychology program requires two quarters of practica and a one-year internship. Recent school psychology internships have been paid positions. Practica in applied experimental psychology are offered. Students enrolled in the Experimental Psychology-Applied Behavior Analysis specialization are required to complete 1500 hours of supervised practicum (as required by the Behavior Analysis Certification Board) in partial fulfillment of the requirements to sit for the Board Certified Behavior Analyst certification exam.

Housing and Day Care: On-campus housing is available. See the following website for more information: http://www.cwu.edu/housing/. On-campus day care facilities are available. See the following website for more information: http://www.cwu.edu/early-learning/.

Employment of Department Graduates:

Master's Degree Graduates: Of those who graduated in the academic year 2011–2012, the following categories and numbers represent the postgraduate activities and employment of master's degree graduates: Enrolled in a postdoctoral residency/fellowship (n/a), employed in independent practice (n/a), employed in an academic position at a university (1), employed in a professional position in a school system (15), employed in government agency (4), employed in a community mental health/counseling center (2), do not know (1), total from the above (master's) (23).

Doctoral Degree Graduates: Of those who graduated in the academic year 2011–2012, the following categories and numbers represent the postgraduate activities and employment of doctoral degree graduates: Enrolled in a psychology doctoral program (n/a), total from the above (doctoral) (0).

Additional Information:

Orientation, Objectives, and Emphasis of Department: Central Washington University's graduate program in psychology prepares students for professional employment in a variety of settings, including mental health agencies, public schools, community colleges, and business or industry. We also prepare students for successful completion of doctoral degree programs in psychology. The programs include extensive supervision in practicum and internship settings and research partnerships with faculty mentors. Our School Psychology program is NASP approved. Our Mental Health Counseling program is CACREP accredited. The educational requirements of the Animal Behavior Society's Associate Applied Animal Behaviorist Certificate can be met by completing the MS Experimental degree program with an appropriate selection of core and elective courses. Additionally, a specialization in Applied Behavior Analysis is offered through the MS Experimental degree program. Completion of this track will allow individuals to sit for the Board Certified Behavior Analyst certification exam.

Special Facilities or Resources: Our facilities include an on-site community counseling and psychological assessment center for training in counseling and testing; animal research laboratories, including a laboratory for the study of language learning in chimpanzees; a human behavior laboratory; a computer lab; and a complete mechanical and electrical instrumentation services center.

Information for Students With Physical Disabilities: See the following website for more information: http://www.cwu.edu/disability-support/.

Application Information:

Send to Office of Graduate Studies, Central Washington University, 400 East University Way, Ellensburg, WA 98926-7510. Application available online. URL of online application: https://app.applyyourself.com/?id=cwugrad. Students are admitted in the Fall, application deadline February 1. *Fee:* $50. Application fee may be waived by demonstration of financial need.

Eastern Washington University

Department of Psychology
College of Social and Behavioral Sciences and Social Work
135 Martin Hall
Cheney, WA 99004-6325
Telephone: (509) 359-2827
Fax: (509) 359-4366
E-mail: *psychology@ewu.edu*
Web: *http://www.ewu.edu/psychology/*

Department Information:

1934. Chairperson: Jonathan W. Anderson, PhD. Number of faculty: total—full-time 37; women—full-time 11; total—minority—full-time 2; women minority—full-time 2; faculty subject to the Americans With Disabilities Act 1.

Programs and Degrees Offered:

Listed in the following order: Program area, degree type (T if terminal Master's), number awarded 7/11–6/12. Psychology MA/MS (Master of Arts/Science) (T) 10, School Psychology EdS (School Psychology) 9, School Psychology Certificate Other 1, Applied Psychology MA/MS (Master of Arts/Science) (T) 24.

Student Applications/Admissions:

Student Applications

Psychology MA/MS (Master of Arts/Science)—Applications 2012–2013, 60. Total applicants accepted 2012–2013, 18. Number full-time enrolled (new admits only) 2012–2013, 14. Number part-time enrolled (new admits only) 2012–2013, 0. Total enrolled 2012–2013 full-time, 23. Total enrolled 2012–2013 part-time, 0. Openings 2013–2014, 12. The median number of years required for completion of a degree in 2012–2013 were 2. The number of students enrolled full- and part-time who were dismissed or voluntarily withdrew from this program area in 2012–2013 were 1. *School Psychology EdS (School Psychology)*—Applications 2012–2013, 30. Total applicants accepted 2012–2013, 14. Number full-time enrolled (new admits only) 2012–2013, 13. Total enrolled 2012–2013 full-time, 36. Openings 2013–2014, 14. The median number of years required for completion of a degree in 2012–2013 were 3. The number of students enrolled full- and part-time who were dismissed or voluntarily withdrew from this program area in 2012–2013 were 0. *School Psychology Certificate Other*—Applications 2012–2013, 18. Total applicants accepted 2012–2013, 16. Number full-time enrolled (new admits only) 2012–2013, 13. Number part-time enrolled (new admits only) 2012–2013, 0. Total enrolled 2012–2013 full-time, 22. Openings 2013–2014, 15. The median number of years required for completion of a degree in 2012–2013 were 2. The number of students enrolled full- and part-time who were dismissed or voluntarily withdrew from this program area in 2012–2013 were 4. *Applied Psychology MA/MS (Master of Arts/Science)*—Applications 2012–2013, 79. Total applicants accepted 2012–2013, 18. Number full-time enrolled (new admits only) 2012–2013, 18. Total enrolled 2012–2013 full-time, 44. Openings 2013–2014, 24. The median number of years required for completion of a degree in 2012–2013 were 2. The number of students enrolled full- and part-time who were dismissed or voluntarily withdrew from this program area in 2012–2013 were 1.

Scores: Entries appear in this order: required test or GPA, minimum score (if required), median score of students entering in 2012–2013. *Psychology MA/MS (Master of Arts/Science):* GRE-V no minimum stated, GRE-Q no minimum stated, GRE-Analytical no minimum stated, last 2 years GPA 3.00; *School Psychology EdS (School Psychology):* GRE-V no minimum stated, GRE-Q no minimum stated, GRE-Analytical no minimum stated, last 2 years GPA 3.00; *Applied Psychology MA/MS (Master of Arts/Science):* GRE-V no minimum stated, GRE-Q no minimum stated, GRE-Analytical no minimum stated, overall undergraduate GPA no minimum stated, last 2 years GPA 3.00, psychology GPA no minimum stated.

Other Criteria: (importance of criteria rated low, medium, or high): GRE scores—medium, research experience—medium, work experience—medium, extracurricular activity—medium, clinically related public service—medium, GPA—medium, letters of recommendation—medium, interview—medium, statement of goals and objectives—medium, undergraduate major in psychology—medium, specific undergraduate psychology courses taken—medium, The Certificate Program in School Psychology places heavy emphasis on letters of intent, the interview, and Master's GPA. The fit of the Master's Degree training for transition to a career in School Psychology is considered important. The School Psychology EdS Degree program places heavy emphasis on the letter of intent (statement of purpose) and the interview. We are interested in candidates who have investigated the field and can speak to their preparation for training in school psychology. The MS in Applied Psychology program places emphasis on background experiences and the interview process. We are interested in candidates who demonstrate the characteristics to be skilled clinicians. The MS in Psychology program places equal weight on the letter of intent, letters of reference, GPA, GRE scores, and other relevant experiences (e.g., research, work history). This program is interested in candidates who seek a scientist-practitioner model of training. For additional information on admission requirements, go to http://www.ewu.edu/csbssw/programs/psychology.xml.

Student Characteristics: The following represents characteristics of students in 2012–2013 in all graduate psychology programs in the department: Female—full-time 80, part-time 0; Male—full-time 45, part-time 0; African American/Black—full-time 0, part-time 0; Hispanic/Latino(a)—full-time 4, part-time 0; Asian/Pacific Islander—full-time 2, part-time 0; American Indian/Alaska Native—full-time 1, part-time 0; Caucasian/White—full-time 117, part-time 0; Multi-ethnic—full-time 1, part-time 0; students subject to the Americans With Disabilities Act—full-time 1, part-time 0; Unknown ethnicity—full-time 0, part-time 0; International students who hold an F-1 or J-1 Visa—full-time 0, part-time 0.

Financial Information/Assistance:
Tuition for Full-Time Study: *Master's:* State residents: per academic year $7,371; Nonstate residents: per academic year $22,450. Tuition is subject to change. Tuition costs vary by program. See the following website for updates and changes in tuition costs: http://access.ewu.edu/student-financial-services/cost-and-fees/tuition-rates.xml. Higher tuition cost for this program: Post-Master's Certificate in School Psychology.

Financial Assistance:
First-Year Students: Teaching assistantships available for first year. Average number of hours worked per week: 19. Apply by March 1. Research assistantships available for first year. Average number of hours worked per week: 19. Apply by March 1. Fellowships and scholarships available for first year. Apply by March 1.

Advanced Students: Teaching assistantships available for advanced students. Average number of hours worked per week: 19. Apply by March 1. Research assistantships available for advanced students. Average number of hours worked per week: 19. Apply by March 1. Fellowships and scholarships available for advanced students. Apply by March 1.

Additional Information: Of all students currently enrolled full time, 50% benefited from one or more of the listed financial assistance programs. Application and information available online at: http://www.ewu.edu/grad/graduate-assistantships-and-tuition-waivers.xml.

Internships/Practica: Master's Degree (MA/MS Psychology): An internship experience, such as a final research project or "capstone" experience is required of graduates. Master's Degree (EdS School Psychology): An internship experience, such as a final research project or "capstone" experience is required of graduates. Master's Degree (MA/MS Applied Psychology): An internship experience, such as a final research project or "capstone" experience is required of graduates. Available internships and practica are available in a wide variety of places. This allows students to gain experience working with different age ranges (i.e., children to older adults) in different environments (i.e., prison to community mental health agencies) with a variety of psychiatric conditions.

Housing and Day Care: On-campus housing is available. See the following website for more information: http://access.ewu.edu/UniversityApartments.xml. On-campus day care facilities are available. See the following website for more information: http://www.ewu.edu/about/administration/student-affairs/ewu-childrens-center.xml.

Employment of Department Graduates:
Master's Degree Graduates: Of those who graduated in the academic year 2011–2012, the following categories and numbers represent the postgraduate activities and employment of master's degree graduates: Enrolled in a postdoctoral residency/fellowship (n/a), employed in independent practice (n/a), total from the above (master's) (0).

Doctoral Degree Graduates: Of those who graduated in the academic year 2011–2012, the following categories and numbers represent the postgraduate activities and employment of doctoral degree graduates: Enrolled in a psychology doctoral program (n/a), total from the above (doctoral) (0).

Additional Information:
Orientation, Objectives, and Emphasis of Department: Master's level graduate study in psychology provides the student with advanced preparation for practice in the field or for entering doctoral-level programs in psychology. Five graduate programs are offered by the department of Psychology: an MS in Psychology, Experimental emphasis; MS in Psychology, Clinical emphasis; MS in Applied Psychology, Mental Health emphasis; MS in Applied Psychology, School Counseling emphasis. We also offer a certifi-

cate program in School Psychology: Post-Master's Certificate in School Psychology.

Special Facilities or Resources: Students are provided an office.

Information for Students With Physical Disabilities: See the following website for more information: http://access.ewu.edu/disability-support-services.xml.

Application Information:
Send to Eastern Washington University, Department of Psychology, Cheney, WA 99004. Application available online. URL of online application: http://www.ewu.edu/grad/programs.xml. Students are admitted in the Fall, application deadline January 15. MS in Applied Psychology deadline: February 1. MS in Psychology and EdS in School Psychology early consideration deadline: January 15, deadline: March 1. Post-Master's Certificate in School Psychology deadline: March 1. *Fee:* $50.

Gonzaga University
Department of Counselor Education
School of Education
501 East Boone Avenue
Spokane, WA 99258-0025
Telephone: (509) 313-3512
Fax: (509) 313-5964
E-mail: *young@gonzaga.edu*
Web: *http://www.gonzaga.edu/Academics/Colleges-and-Schools/School-of-Education/Majors-Programs/Counselor-Education/*

Department Information:
1960. Chairperson: Mark Young. Number of faculty: total—full-time 5, part-time 9; women—full-time 2, part-time 6; total—minority—full-time 1, part-time 2; women minority—full-time 1, part-time 1.

Programs and Degrees Offered:
Listed in the following order: Program area, degree type (T if terminal Master's), number awarded 7/11–6/12. School Counseling MA/MS (Master of Arts/Science) (T) 10, Community Counseling MA/MS (Master of Arts/Science) (T) 15, Marriage and Family Counseling MA/MS (Master of Arts/Science) (T) 9, Master Of Counseling Other 20.

Student Applications/Admissions:
Student Applications
School Counseling MA/MS (Master of Arts/Science)—Applications 2012–2013, 40. Total applicants accepted 2012–2013, 10. Number full-time enrolled (new admits only) 2012–2013, 10. Number part-time enrolled (new admits only) 2012–2013, 3. Total enrolled 2012–2013 full-time, 20. Total enrolled 2012–2013 part-time, 4. Openings 2013–2014, 10. The median number of years required for completion of a degree in 2012–2013 were 2. The number of students enrolled full- and part-time who were dismissed or voluntarily withdrew from this program area in 2012–2013 were 2. *Community Counseling MA/MS (Master of Arts/Science)*—Applications 2012–2013,

80. Total applicants accepted 2012–2013, 25. Number full-time enrolled (new admits only) 2012–2013, 20. Number part-time enrolled (new admits only) 2012–2013, 3. Total enrolled 2012–2013 full-time, 43. Total enrolled 2012–2013 part-time, 5. Openings 2013–2014, 20. The median number of years required for completion of a degree in 2012–2013 were 2. The number of students enrolled full- and part-time who were dismissed or voluntarily withdrew from this program area in 2012–2013 were 2. *Marriage and Family Counseling MA/MS (Master of Arts/Science)*—Applications 2012–2013, 35. Total applicants accepted 2012–2013, 10. Number full-time enrolled (new admits only) 2012–2013, 9. Number part-time enrolled (new admits only) 2012–2013, 3. Total enrolled 2012–2013 full-time, 21. Total enrolled 2012–2013 part-time, 3. Openings 2013–2014, 10. The median number of years required for completion of a degree in 2012–2013 were 2. The number of students enrolled full- and part-time who were dismissed or voluntarily withdrew from this program area in 2012–2013 were 1. *Master Of Counseling Other*—Applications 2012–2013, 65. Total applicants accepted 2012–2013, 22. Number full-time enrolled (new admits only) 2012–2013, 22. Number part-time enrolled (new admits only) 2012–2013, 0. Total enrolled 2012–2013 full-time, 49. Total enrolled 2012–2013 part-time, 0. Openings 2013–2014, 20. The median number of years required for completion of a degree in 2012–2013 were 2. The number of students enrolled full- and part-time who were dismissed or voluntarily withdrew from this program area in 2012–2013 were 2.

Scores: Entries appear in this order: required test or GPA, minimum score (if required), median score of students entering in 2012–2013. *School Counseling MA/MS (Master of Arts/Science):* overall undergraduate GPA 3.0; *Community Counseling MA/MS (Master of Arts/Science):* overall undergraduate GPA 3.0; *Marriage and Family Counseling MA/MS (Master of Arts/Science):* overall undergraduate GPA 3.0; *Master of Counseling Other:* overall undergraduate GPA 3.0.

Other Criteria: (importance of criteria rated low, medium, or high): GRE scores—low, work experience—medium, extracurricular activity—medium, clinically related public service—medium, GPA—medium, letters of recommendation—high, interview—high, statement of goals and objectives—high, emotional intelligence—high, undergraduate major in psychology—low, specific undergraduate psychology courses taken—low.

Student Characteristics: The following represents characteristics of students in 2012–2013 in all graduate psychology programs in the department: Female—full-time 81, part-time 1; Male—full-time 21, part-time 12; African American/Black—full-time 2, part-time 0; Hispanic/Latino(a)—full-time 3, part-time 1; Asian/Pacific Islander—full-time 1, part-time 0; American Indian/Alaska Native—full-time 2, part-time 0; Caucasian/White—full-time 80, part-time 12; Multi-ethnic—full-time 3, part-time 0; students subject to the Americans With Disabilities Act—full-time 4, part-time 1; Unknown ethnicity—full-time 19, part-time 0; International students who hold an F-1 or J-1 Visa—full-time 1, part-time 0.

Financial Information/Assistance:
Tuition for Full-Time Study: *Master's:* State residents: $805 per credit hour; Nonstate residents: $805 per credit hour. Tuition is subject to change. Tuition costs vary by program. See the following

website for updates and changes in tuition costs: http://www.gonzaga.edu/studentaccounts.

Financial Assistance:

First-Year Students: Teaching assistantships available for first year. Average amount paid per academic year: $3,200. Average number of hours worked per week: 6. Apply by May 1. Research assistantships available for first year. Average amount paid per academic year: $3,200. Average number of hours worked per week: 6. Apply by May 1.

Advanced Students: Teaching assistantships available for advanced students. Average amount paid per academic year: $3,200. Average number of hours worked per week: 6. Apply by May 1. Research assistantships available for advanced students. Average amount paid per academic year: $3,200. Average number of hours worked per week: 6. Apply by May 1.

Additional Information: Of all students currently enrolled full time, 35% benefited from one or more of the listed financial assistance programs.

Internships/Practica: Master's Degree (MA/MS School Counseling): An internship experience, such as a final research project or "capstone" experience is required of graduates. Master's Degree (MA/MS Community Counseling): An internship experience, such as a final research project or "capstone" experience is required of graduates. Master's Degree (MA/MS Marriage and Family Counseling): An internship experience, such as a final research project or "capstone" experience is required of graduates. Students complete a 100-hour practicum and a 600-hour internship at a site chosen by the student to meet his or her professional interests. School track students currently are placed in schools at elementary, junior high, high school, and alternative settings. Agency track students are placed at sites including but not limited to geriatric, hospital, community mental health, adolescent, marriage and family, child, community college, career, and life-skills settings. A strong reputation within our community has enabled students to select quality placements in diverse settings of the student's choosing.

Housing and Day Care: On-campus housing is available. See the following website for more information: http://www.gonzaga.edu/Student-Life/Residence-Life-and-Dining-Services/On-Campus-Living/. No on-campus day care facilities are available.

Employment of Department Graduates:

Master's Degree Graduates: Of those who graduated in the academic year 2011–2012, the following categories and numbers represent the postgraduate activities and employment of master's degree graduates: Enrolled in a psychology doctoral program (3), enrolled in another graduate/professional program (1), enrolled in a postdoctoral residency/fellowship (n/a), employed in independent practice (n/a), employed in an academic position at a 2-year/4-year college (1), employed in other positions at a higher education institution (2), employed in a professional position in a school system (10), employed in business or industry (1), employed in government agency (1), employed in a community mental health/counseling center (12), employed in a hospital/medical center (1), still seeking employment (1), other employment position (3), total from the above (master's) (36).

Doctoral Degree Graduates: Of those who graduated in the academic year 2011–2012, the following categories and numbers represent the postgraduate activities and employment of doctoral degree graduates: Enrolled in a psychology doctoral program (n/a), total from the above (doctoral) (0).

Additional Information:

Orientation, Objectives, and Emphasis of Department: The philosophical theme running throughout the university is humanism. A realistic, balanced attitude is a necessary prerequisite for assisting others professionally. Careful selection of students helps to insure the inclusion of healthy individuals with the highest potential for success, as does faculty modeling, encouragement of trust, and communication of clear expectations. Indicators of counselor success are demonstration of skills and conflict resolution, consistent interpersonal behaviors, recognition of strengths and weaknesses, a clear grasp of goals, and self-knowledge of one's impact on others, as well as strong academic performance. Acquisition of counseling competence comes through both personal and professional growth. Immersion in an intensive course of study with a closely linked group of peers encourages open and honest processing, which in turn contributes to personal growth. The department believes that students must possess insight and awareness, and clarity about the boundaries between their personal issues and those of the client. Students training to become professionals must be treated as professionals. Faculty practice collegiality with students, maintain high standards of performance, and furnish an atmosphere of professionalism. Students share cases, exchanging professional advice and input. In addition to the presentation of major theories of counseling, students must develop a personal theory of counseling and demonstrate competence in its use. Faculty are humanistic, but eclectic, disseminating information about effective techniques without imposing any one approach on the students. Students are closely observed in the classroom, practicum and internship and receive critical monitoring and evaluation from faculty, field supervisor, and peers. All three programs are CACREP accredited. The Community Counseling Program is now titled Clinical Mental Health Counseling beginning in 2013. Our theme statement is "We are practitioners who are intentional in the development of relationships that honor the strengths of all individuals and the promotion of transformational growth."

Special Facilities or Resources: The Department of Counselor Education is proud to offer a modern and complete clinic training center, with four practicum rooms, a departmental library, and conference room. The clinic has two-way glass, and is equipped with audio-video technological equipment which can be operated in the clinic room by either the student (for taping and reviewing personal work) or by any department faculty member from faculty offices (for viewing and/or taping).

Application Information:

Send to Graduate Admissions, School of Education, Gonzaga University, 502 East Boone, Spokane, WA 99258-0025. Application available online. URL of online application: http://www.gonzaga.edu/Admissions/Graduate/Apply/default.asp. Students are admitted in the Fall, application deadline March 1. We have two application deadlines. The first, January 15th, is for early admittance. The second, March 1st, is regular admittance. *Fee:* $50.

Puget Sound, University of

School of Education
1500 North Warner #1051
Tacoma, WA 98416
Telephone: (253) 879-3344
Fax: (253) 879-3926
E-mail: *kirchner@pugetsound.edu*
Web: *http://www.pugetsound.edu/academics/departments-and-programs/graduate/school-of-education/med/*

Department Information:

1961. Director: Grace L. Kirchner. Number of faculty: total—full-time 2, part-time 3; women—full-time 2.

Programs and Degrees Offered:

Listed in the following order: Program area, degree type (T if terminal Master's), number awarded 7/11–6/12. School Counseling MEd (Education) 7, Mental Health Counseling MEd (Education) 5.

Student Applications/Admissions:

Student Applications

School Counseling MEd (Education)—Applications 2012–2013, 14. Total applicants accepted 2012–2013, 13. Number full-time enrolled (new admits only) 2012–2013, 7. Number part-time enrolled (new admits only) 2012–2013, 3. Total enrolled 2012–2013 full-time, 22. Total enrolled 2012–2013 part-time, 3. Openings 2013–2014, 12. The median number of years required for completion of a degree in 2012–2013 were 2. The number of students enrolled full- and part-time who were dismissed or voluntarily withdrew from this program area in 2012–2013 were 0. *Mental Health Counseling MEd (Education)*—Applications 2012–2013, 11. Total applicants accepted 2012–2013, 5. Number full-time enrolled (new admits only) 2012–2013, 2. Number part-time enrolled (new admits only) 2012–2013, 2. Total enrolled 2012–2013 full-time, 3. Total enrolled 2012–2013 part-time, 2. Openings 2013–2014, 6. The median number of years required for completion of a degree in 2012–2013 were 2. The number of students enrolled full- and part-time who were dismissed or voluntarily withdrew from this program area in 2012–2013 were 0.

Scores: Entries appear in this order: required test or GPA, minimum score (if required), median score of students entering in 2012–2013. *School Counseling MEd (Education):* GRE-V no minimum stated, GRE-Q no minimum stated, GRE-Analytical no minimum stated, overall undergraduate GPA no minimum stated; *Mental Health Counseling MEd (Education):* GRE-V no minimum stated, GRE-Q no minimum stated, GRE-Analytical no minimum stated, overall undergraduate GPA no minimum stated.

Other Criteria: (importance of criteria rated low, medium, or high): GRE scores—medium, research experience—low, work experience—medium, extracurricular activity—low, clinically related public service—medium, GPA—medium, letters of recommendation—medium, interview—high, statement of goals and objectives—medium. For additional information on admission requirements, go to http://www.pugetsound.edu/admission/apply/graduate-students/education/.

Student Characteristics: The following represents characteristics of students in 2012–2013 in all graduate psychology programs in the department: Female—full-time 12, part-time 11; Male—full-time 2, part-time 0; African American/Black—full-time 0, part-time 1; Hispanic/Latino(a)—full-time 0, part-time 2; Asian/Pacific Islander—full-time 0, part-time 1; American Indian/Alaska Native—full-time 0, part-time 0; Caucasian/White—full-time 11, part-time 6; Multi-ethnic—full-time 2, part-time 1; students subject to the Americans With Disabilities Act—full-time 0, part-time 0; Unknown ethnicity—full-time 1, part-time 0; International students who hold an F-1 or J-1 Visa—full-time 0, part-time 0.

Financial Information/Assistance:

Tuition for Full-Time Study: *Master's:* State residents: $820 per credit hour; Nonstate residents: $820 per credit hour. Tuition is subject to change. See the following website for updates and changes in tuition costs: http://www.pugetsound.edu/admission/financing-your-education/graduate-students/master-of-education/.

Financial Assistance:

First-Year Students: Traineeships available for first year. Average amount paid per academic year: $13,000. Average number of hours worked per week: 18.

Advanced Students: Traineeships available for advanced students. Average amount paid per academic year: $13,000. Average number of hours worked per week: 18.

Additional Information: Application and information available online at: http://www.pugetsound.edu/admission/financing-your-education/.

Internships/Practica: We require a 400-hour internship in a school or agency setting. Prior to the internship, students participate in an on-campus practicum course held once a week for 12 weeks.

Housing and Day Care: No on-campus housing is available. No on-campus day care facilities are available.

Employment of Department Graduates:

Master's Degree Graduates: Of those who graduated in the academic year 2011–2012, the following categories and numbers represent the postgraduate activities and employment of master's degree graduates: Enrolled in a psychology doctoral program (1), enrolled in a postdoctoral residency/fellowship (n/a), employed in independent practice (n/a), employed in an academic position at a 2-year/4-year college (1), employed in a professional position in a school system (4), employed in a community mental health/counseling center (2), still seeking employment (1), not seeking employment (1), other employment position (1), do not know (1), total from the above (master's) (12).

Doctoral Degree Graduates: Of those who graduated in the academic year 2011–2012, the following categories and numbers represent the postgraduate activities and employment of doctoral degree graduates: Enrolled in a psychology doctoral program (n/a), total from the above (doctoral) (0).

Additional Information:

Orientation, Objectives, and Emphasis of Department: We are housed in the School of Education and our primary mission is to train school counselors; however, many of our graduates find employment in social service settings.

Information for Students With Physical Disabilities: See the following website for more information: http://www.pugetsound.edu/academics/academic-resources/disability-services/.

Application Information:

Send to Office of Admission, 1500 North Warner Street, CMB 1062, Tacoma, WA 98416-1062. Application available online. URL of online application: http://www.pugetsound.edu/admission/apply/graduate-students/education/education-application/. Students are admitted in the Fall, application deadline March 1. *Fee:* $60.

Seattle Pacific University
Clinical Psychology Department
School of Psychology, Family and Community
3307 Third Avenue, West
Seattle, WA 98119
Telephone: (206) 281-2839
Fax: (206) 281-2695
E-mail: *clinicalpsyc@spu.edu*
Web: *http://spu.edu/depts/spfc/*

Department Information:

1995. Chairperson: Jay R. Skidmore, PhD. Number of faculty: total—full-time 8, part-time 6; women—full-time 4, part-time 4; total—minority—full-time 1.

Programs and Degrees Offered:

Listed in the following order: Program area, degree type (T if terminal Master's), number awarded 7/11–6/12. Clinical Psychology PhD (Doctor of Philosophy) 15.

APA Accreditation: Clinical PhD (Doctor of Philosophy). Student Outcome Data Website: http://spu.edu/depts/spfc/clinicalpsych/index.asp.

Student Applications/Admissions:

Student Applications

Clinical Psychology PhD (Doctor of Philosophy)—Applications 2012–2013, 147. Total applicants accepted 2012–2013, 22. Number full-time enrolled (new admits only) 2012–2013, 11. Number part-time enrolled (new admits only) 2012–2013, 0. Total enrolled 2012–2013 full-time, 68. Total enrolled 2012–2013 part-time, 0. Openings 2013–2014, 16. The median number of years required for completion of a degree in 2012–2013 were 5. The number of students enrolled full- and part-time who were dismissed or voluntarily withdrew from this program area in 2012–2013 were 1.

Scores: Entries appear in this order: required test or GPA, minimum score (if required), median score of students entering in 2012–2013. *Clinical Psychology PhD (Doctor of Philosophy):* GRE-V no minimum stated, 156, GRE-Q no minimum stated, 152, overall undergraduate GPA no minimum stated, 3.62.

Other Criteria: (importance of criteria rated low, medium, or high): GRE scores—high, research experience—high, work experience—medium, extracurricular activity—medium, clinically related public service—high, GPA—high, letters of recommendation—high, interview—high, statement of goals and objectives—high, match with faculty—high, undergraduate major in psychology—high, specific undergraduate psychology courses taken—medium. For additional information on admission requirements, go to http://spu.edu/depts/spfc/clinicalpsych/prospective/admissions.asp.

Student Characteristics: The following represents characteristics of students in 2012–2013 in all graduate psychology programs in the department: Female—full-time 61, part-time 0; Male—full-time 11, part-time 0; African American/Black—full-time 0, part-time 0; Hispanic/Latino(a)—full-time 2, part-time 0; Asian/Pacific Islander—full-time 7, part-time 0; American Indian/Alaska Native—full-time 1, part-time 0; Caucasian/White—full-time 58, part-time 0; Multi-ethnic—full-time 2, part-time 0; students subject to the Americans With Disabilities Act—full-time 0, part-time 0; Unknown ethnicity—full-time 2, part-time 0; International students who hold an F-1 or J-1 Visa—full-time 0, part-time 0.

Financial Information/Assistance:

Tuition for Full-Time Study: *Doctoral:* State residents: per academic year $35,592, $673 per credit hour; Nonstate residents: per academic year $35,592, $673 per credit hour. Tuition is subject to change. See the following website for updates and changes in tuition costs: http://spu.edu/depts/sfs/StudentAccounts/Costs/index.asp.

Financial Assistance:

First-Year Students: Fellowships and scholarships available for first year. Average amount paid per academic year: $5,000.

Advanced Students: Teaching assistantships available for advanced students. Average amount paid per academic year: $8,000. Average number of hours worked per week: 15. Research assistantships available for advanced students. Average amount paid per academic year: $4,000. Average number of hours worked per week: 8. Fellowships and scholarships available for advanced students. Average amount paid per academic year: $8,000.

Additional Information: Of all students currently enrolled full time, 50% benefited from one or more of the listed financial assistance programs. Application and information available online at: http://www.spu.edu/depts/sfs/.

Internships/Practica: Doctoral Degree (PhD Clinical Psychology): For those doctoral students for whom a professional psychology internship was required in this program prior to graduation, (12) students applied for an internship in 2011–2012, with (12) students obtaining an internship. Of those students who obtained an internship, (12) were paid internships. Of those students who obtained an internship, (12) students placed in APA/CPA accredited internships, (0) students placed in internships not APA/CPA accredited, but listed with the Association of Psychology Postdoctoral and Internship Programs (APPIC), (0) students placed in internships conforming to guidelines of the Council of Directors of School Psychology Programs (CDSPP), (0) students placed in internships that were not APA/CPA accredited, APPIC or CDSPP listed. Clinical training requirements include two one-year practicum placements during the 3rd and 4th years of the program (part-time, averaging 16 hours/week, resulting in average total practicum experience of approximately 1200 hours), as well as a full-time one-year (2000 hours) clinical psychology internship during the 5th year of the PhD program. Practicum placements are external to the university in a variety of mental health centers, hospitals, medical/dental clinics, and rehabilitation facilities in the greater Puget Sound area. Students apply for their internship in the APPIC Match and each year most obtain placements at competitive mental health and medical centers around the country. Theoretical models and orientations among the faculty include cognitive behavioral, psychodynamic, interpersonal, family systems, and humanistic approaches. Faculty tend to integrate more than one perspective in theories, teaching and professional practices. We incorporate and contribute to evidence-based research, and expect our students to utilize clinical science as well as theory in their clinical work.

Housing and Day Care: On-campus housing is available. See the following website for more information: http://www.spu.edu/depts/reslife/. On-campus day care facilities are available.

Employment of Department Graduates:

Master's Degree Graduates: Of those who graduated in the academic year 2011–2012, the following categories and numbers represent the postgraduate activities and employment of master's degree graduates: Enrolled in a postdoctoral residency/fellowship (n/a), employed in independent practice (n/a), total from the above (master's) (0).

Doctoral Degree Graduates: Of those who graduated in the academic year 2011–2012, the following categories and numbers represent the postgraduate activities and employment of doctoral degree graduates: Enrolled in a psychology doctoral program (n/a), enrolled in a postdoctoral residency/fellowship (8), employed in an academic position at a university (1), employed in government agency (2), employed in a community mental health/counseling center (1), employed in a hospital/medical center (4), total from the above (doctoral) (16).

Additional Information:

Orientation, Objectives, and Emphasis of Department: The Clinical Psychology PhD Program at SPU is designed to provide training in professional psychology in accordance with the Local Clinical Scientist (LCS) model of doctoral education, described in the article, The local clinical scientist: a bridge between science and practice published in American Psychologist (Stricker & Trierweiler, 1995). The Local Clinical Scientist extends the scientific and professional ideals in the original Boulder Scientist-Practitioner (BSP) model of clinical psychology (Raimy, 1950). At the same time, we try to encompass broader concepts of science and more explicitly integrate the art of clinical practice. We also endorse the core competencies outlined by the National Council of Schools and Programs of Professional Psychology (NCSPP), and are committed to helping students achieve mastery of the core competencies of clinical skills. Our doctoral program typically requires four years of graduate coursework, during which clinical practicum training as well as dissertation research are also completed, followed by a one-year full-time internship (elsewhere) in the fifth year. We are an APA-accredited program in clinical psychology, and also a "designated doctoral program" with

ASPPB/NR, which verifies our curriculum meets the educational requirements for licensing psychologists in the United States.

Special Facilities or Resources: The School maintains a fully-equipped suite of psychology research laboratories, including a psycho-physiological lab, child-developmental lab, and social psychology lab. The University's newly-opened Science Building has wet labs, animal learning facilities, and a psycho-physiological demonstration classroom. The Department is housed in Marston Hall, which was completely renovated for us in 2001. The University Library is a 4-story structure with conference rooms, private study rooms and group meeting rooms. The library contains approximately 10,000 volumes relevant to the field of psychology, including books, media, a test file, and over 500 journals available either in paper, microfilm, and full-text online. In addition to traditional inter-library loan services, Seattle Pacific University is a member of the Orbis Cascade Alliance, a consortium of 26 public and private academic libraries in Washington and Oregon which provides access to a combined collection of over 22 million volumes of books and other materials. Students have access to several computer labs on campus, which have SPSS installed. Student are given an SPU e-mail account and have 24/7 access to our online Blackboard where program forms, syllabi, schedules, etc. are posted for students to download.

Information for Students With Physical Disabilities: See the following website for more information: http://www.spu.edu/depts/cfl/dss/index.asp.

Application Information:
Send to Graduate Center, Seattle Pacific University. Application available online. URL of online application: https://app.applyyourself.com/?id=spu-grad. Students are admitted in the Fall, application deadline December 15. Fee: $75.

Seattle University
Graduate Psychology Program
Arts and Sciences
901 12th Avenue, P.O. Box 222000
Seattle, WA 98122-1090
Telephone: (206) 296-5400
Fax: (206) 296-2141
E-mail: krycka@seattleu.edu
Web: http://www.seattleu.edu/artsci/map/default.aspx

Department Information:
1981. Director, Graduate Program: Kevin Krycka, PsyD. Number of faculty: total—full-time 5, part-time 5; women—full-time 2, part-time 2.

Programs and Degrees Offered:
Listed in the following order: Program area, degree type (T if terminal Master's), number awarded 7/11–6/12. Existential-Phenomenological Psychology MA/MS (Master of Arts/Science) (T) 22.

Student Applications/Admissions:
Student Applications
Existential-Phenomenological Psychology MA/MS (Master of Arts/Science)—Applications 2012–2013, 77. Total applicants ac-

cepted 2012–2013, 29. Number full-time enrolled (new admits only) 2012–2013, 22. Number part-time enrolled (new admits only) 2012–2013, 1. Total enrolled 2012–2013 full-time, 44. Total enrolled 2012–2013 part-time, 3. Openings 2013–2014, 22. The median number of years required for completion of a degree in 2012–2013 were 2. The number of students enrolled full- and part-time who were dismissed or voluntarily withdrew from this program area in 2012–2013 were 3.

Scores: Entries appear in this order: required test or GPA, minimum score (if required), median score of students entering in 2012–2013. *Existential-Phenomenological Psychology MA/MS (Master of Arts/Science):* overall undergraduate GPA 3.0.

Other Criteria: (importance of criteria rated low, medium, or high): research experience—low, work experience—medium, extracurricular activity—medium, clinically related public service—high, GPA—high, letters of recommendation—high, interview—high, statement of goals and objectives—medium, bio/writing sample—high, undergraduate major in psychology—medium, specific undergraduate psychology courses taken—high. For additional information on admission requirements, go to http://www.seattleu.edu/artsci/map/Inner.aspx?id=19170.

Student Characteristics: The following represents characteristics of students in 2012–2013 in all graduate psychology programs in the department: Female—full-time 38, part-time 3; Male—full-time 6, part-time 0; African American/Black—full-time 0, part-time 1; Hispanic/Latino(a)—full-time 2, part-time 0; Asian/Pacific Islander—full-time 4, part-time 0; American Indian/Alaska Native—full-time 0, part-time 0; Caucasian/White—full-time 32, part-time 2; Multi-ethnic—full-time 6, part-time 0; students subject to the Americans With Disabilities Act—full-time 0, part-time 0; Unknown ethnicity—full-time 0, part-time 0; International students who hold an F-1 or J-1 Visa—full-time 2, part-time 0.

Financial Information/Assistance:

Tuition for Full-Time Study: *Master's:* State residents: per academic year $22,680, $630 per credit hour; Nonstate residents: per academic year $22,680, $630 per credit hour. Tuition is subject to change. See the following website for updates and changes in tuition costs: http://www.seattleu.edu/graduate-admissions/finances/tuition/.

Financial Assistance:

First-Year Students: Research assistantships available for first year. Average amount paid per academic year: $11,000. Average number of hours worked per week: 20. Apply by June 15. Fellowships and scholarships available for first year. Average amount paid per academic year: $2,500. Apply by January 15.

Advanced Students: Research assistantships available for advanced students. Average amount paid per academic year: $9,000. Average number of hours worked per week: 20. Apply by June 15. Fellowships and scholarships available for advanced students. Average amount paid per academic year: $2,500. Apply by January 15.

Additional Information: Of all students currently enrolled full time, 40% benefited from one or more of the listed financial assistance programs. Application and information available online at: http://www.seattleu.edu/graduate-admissions/finances/.

Internships/Practica: Master's Degree (MA/MS Existential-Phenomenological Psychology): An internship experience, such as a final research project or "capstone" experience is required of graduates. A variety of supervised internships (typically about 20 hrs/week during second year) in a wide variety of community agencies, hospitals, shelters and clinics.

Housing and Day Care: On-campus housing is available. See the following website for more information: http://www.seattleu.edu/housing/. No on-campus day care facilities are available.

Employment of Department Graduates:

Master's Degree Graduates: Of those who graduated in the academic year 2011–2012, the following categories and numbers represent the postgraduate activities and employment of master's degree graduates: Enrolled in a psychology doctoral program (4), enrolled in a postdoctoral residency/fellowship (n/a), employed in independent practice (n/a), employed in a professional position in a school system (5), employed in a community mental health/counseling center (22), still seeking employment (15), other employment position (2), total from the above (master's) (48).

Doctoral Degree Graduates: Of those who graduated in the academic year 2011–2012, the following categories and numbers represent the postgraduate activities and employment of doctoral degree graduates: Enrolled in a psychology doctoral program (n/a), total from the above (doctoral) (0).

Additional Information:

Orientation, Objectives, and Emphasis of Department: With an emphasis on existential-phenomenological psychology, this master's degree is designed to offer an interdisciplinary program focusing on the qualitative, experiential study of psychological events in the context of the person's life. By laying the foundations for a therapeutic attitude, the program prepares students for entrance into the helping professions or for further study of the psychological world. It is humanistic in that it intends to deepen the appreciation for the human condition by rigorous reflection on immediate psychological experiences and on the wisdom accumulated by the long tradition of the humanities. It is phenomenological in that it develops an attitude of openness and wonder toward psychological reality without holding theoretical prejudgments. It is therapeutic in that it focuses on the psychological conditions that help people deal with the difficulties of life.

Special Facilities or Resources: The program has a tradition of involving selected students in qualitative research projects.

Information for Students With Physical Disabilities: See the following website for more information: http://www.seattleu.edu/sas/DisabilityServices/.

Application Information:
Send to Graduate Admissions Office, Seattle University, P.O. Box 222000, Seattle, WA 98122-1090. Application available online. URL of online application: http://www.seattleu.edu/graduate-admissions/apply/. Students are admitted in the Fall, application deadline January 15. *Fee:* $55.

Walla Walla University

School of Education and Psychology
204 South College Avenue
College Place, WA 99324
Telephone: (509) 527-2211
Fax: (509) 527-2248
E-mail: *lee.stough@wallawalla.edu*
Web: *http://www.wallawalla.edu/counseling*

Department Information:
1965. Dean: Julian Melgosa. Number of faculty: total—full-time 4, part-time 1; women—full-time 1; total—minority—full-time 2.

Programs and Degrees Offered:
Listed in the following order: Program area, degree type (T if terminal Master's), number awarded 7/11–6/12. Counseling Psychology MA/MS (Master of Arts/Science) (T) 5.

Student Applications/Admissions:
Student Applications
Counseling Psychology MA/MS (Master of Arts/Science)—Applications 2012–2013, 16. Total applicants accepted 2012–2013, 14. Number full-time enrolled (new admits only) 2012–2013, 12. Total enrolled 2012–2013 full-time, 22. Openings 2013–2014, 12. The median number of years required for completion of a degree in 2012–2013 were 2. The number of students enrolled full- and part-time who were dismissed or voluntarily withdrew from this program area in 2012–2013 were 4.
Scores: Entries appear in this order: required test or GPA, minimum score (if required), median score of students entering in 2012–2013. *Counseling Psychology MA/MS (Master of Arts/Science):* GRE-V no minimum stated, 150, GRE-Q no minimum stated, 145, GRE-Analytical no minimum stated, 3.5, overall undergraduate GPA 2.75, 3.4.
Other Criteria: (importance of criteria rated low, medium, or high): GRE scores—medium, research experience—low, work experience—medium, extracurricular activity—low, clinically related public service—medium, GPA—high, letters of recommendation—high, interview—high, statement of goals and objectives—high, undergraduate major in psychology—low, specific undergraduate psychology courses taken—low. For additional information on admission requirements, go to http://www.wallawalla.edu/index.php?id=7586.

Student Characteristics: The following represents characteristics of students in 2012–2013 in all graduate psychology programs in the department: Female—full-time 12, part-time 0; Male—full-time 10, part-time 0; African American/Black—full-time 1, part-time 0; Hispanic/Latino(a)—full-time 1, part-time 0; Asian/Pacific Islander—full-time 1, part-time 0; American Indian/Alaska Native—full-time 0, part-time 0; Caucasian/White—full-time 17, part-time 0; Multi-ethnic—full-time 2, part-time 0; students subject to the Americans With Disabilities Act—full-time 0, part-time 0; Unknown ethnicity—full-time 0, part-time 0; International students who hold an F-1 or J-1 Visa—full-time 0, part-time 0.

Financial Information/Assistance:
Tuition for Full-Time Study: *Master's:* State residents: $550 per credit hour; Nonstate residents: $550 per credit hour. Tuition is subject to change. See the following website for updates and changes in tuition costs: http://www.wallawalla.edu/attend-wwu/student-financial-services/estimated-expenses/.

Financial Assistance:
First-Year Students: Fellowships and scholarships available for first year. Average amount paid per academic year: $2,340. Average number of hours worked per week: 0.
Advanced Students: Fellowships and scholarships available for advanced students. Average amount paid per academic year: $2,340. Average number of hours worked per week: 0.
Additional Information: Of all students currently enrolled full time, 100% benefited from one or more of the listed financial assistance programs. Application and information available online at: http://www.wallawalla.edu/index.php?id=7585.

Internships/Practica: Master's Degree (MA/MS Counseling Psychology): An internship experience, such as a final research project or "capstone" experience is required of graduates. The School of Education and Psychology operates a free counseling center for the community on site. The counseling center is comprised of four private counseling rooms and a group room that are equipped with one-way mirrors and video-cameras. During the second year of their program, students begin working in the center and have the opportunity to develop their clinical skills counseling individuals, couples, and families presenting with a variety of concerns. Program faculty provide individual and group supervision in either live or video formats on a regular basis. After successfully completing the supervised practica, students complete a 600-800 hour internship at an approved site in the community. The School has developed relationships with various agencies where students will receive quality internship experiences that fit their interests.

Housing and Day Care: On-campus housing is available. See the following website for more information: http://www.wallawalla.edu/life-at-wwu/student-life/student-housing/. On-campus day care facilities are available. See the following website for more information: https://www.wallawalla.edu/2949.

Employment of Department Graduates:
Master's Degree Graduates: Of those who graduated in the academic year 2011–2012, the following categories and numbers represent the postgraduate activities and employment of master's degree graduates: Enrolled in a psychology doctoral program (1), enrolled in a postdoctoral residency/fellowship (n/a), employed in independent practice (n/a), employed in an academic position at a university (1), employed in a community mental health/counseling center (3), total from the above (master's) (5).
Doctoral Degree Graduates: Of those who graduated in the academic year 2011–2012, the following categories and numbers represent the postgraduate activities and employment of doctoral degree graduates: Enrolled in a psychology doctoral program (n/a), total from the above (doctoral) (0).

Additional Information:
Orientation, Objectives, and Emphasis of Department: The School of Education and Psychology offers thesis and non-thesis Master of Arts degrees in counseling psychology. Our program is designed to foster the development of both the art and science of therapy through rigorous study, reflection, and clinical supervision. Students are expected to attain a broad range of competence

in the core areas in counseling psychology including human development and learning, individual and group counseling, career development, assessment, ethics, research, and statistics. Faculty present an integrative approach to treatment that focuses on the development of therapeutic presence and the application of core principles, core processes, and a variety of strategies for working with emotion, cognition, behavior, and interpersonal and systemic factors. Students acquire a range of clinical skills they can use in working with diverse clients and learn to apply theory to practice through supervised practicum and internship experiences. In a supportive, yet challenging environment, students are encouraged to build upon life experiences and personal strengths, and take advantage of the opportunities to expand their awareness of self and others. If students desire, faculty assist them in the development and application of a philosophy of Christian service. All graduates are prepared to take the National Counselor's Exam and to become Licensed Mental Health Counselors, or to continue their training in doctoral programs.

Special Facilities or Resources: The School of Education and Psychology operates a free counseling center for the community where ongoing outcome research is being conducted. An enriched preschool program for children ages 3-5 is located in the on-site child development center.

Information for Students With Physical Disabilities: See the following website for more information: http://www.wallawalla.edu/resources/student-support-services/.

Application Information:
Send to Graduate Studies, Walla Walla University, 204 South College Avenue, College Place, WA 99324. Application available online. URL of online application: http://www.wallawalla.edu/academics/graduate/application. Students are admitted in the Fall, application deadline Rolling. Qualified students are admitted throughout the spring and summer until the cohort is full. *Fee:* $50.

Washington State University
Educational Leadership and Counseling Psychology
Education
P.O. Box 642136
Pullman, WA 99164-2136
Telephone: (509) 335-9195
Fax: (509) 335-2097
E-mail: *jasievers@wsu.edu*
Web: *http://education.wsu.edu/graduate/specializations/counselingpsych*

Department Information:
1940. Chairperson: Dr. Kelly Ward. Number of faculty: total—full-time 13; women—full-time 7; total—minority—full-time 4; women minority—full-time 2.

Programs and Degrees Offered:
Listed in the following order: Program area, degree type (T if terminal Master's), number awarded 7/11–6/12. Counseling Psychology PhD (Doctor of Philosophy) 8, Educational Psychology PhD (Doctor of Philosophy) 2, Counseling MA/MS (Master of Arts/Science) (T) 30, Educational Psychology MEd (Education) 0.

APA Accreditation: Counseling PhD (Doctor of Philosophy). Student Outcome Data Website: http://education.wsu.edu/graduate/specializations/counselingpsych/phd/.

Student Applications/Admissions:
Student Applications
Counseling Psychology PhD (Doctor of Philosophy)—Applications 2012–2013, 97. Total applicants accepted 2012–2013, 19. Number full-time enrolled (new admits only) 2012–2013, 8. Total enrolled 2012–2013 full-time, 27. Total enrolled 2012–2013 part-time, 11. Openings 2013–2014, 7. The median number of years required for completion of a degree in 2012–2013 were 6. The number of students enrolled full- and part-time who were dismissed or voluntarily withdrew from this program area in 2012–2013 were 2. *Educational Psychology PhD (Doctor of Philosophy)*—Applications 2012–2013, 19. Total applicants accepted 2012–2013, 8. Number full-time enrolled (new admits only) 2012–2013, 1. Number part-time enrolled (new admits only) 2012–2013, 0. Total enrolled 2012–2013 full-time, 10. Total enrolled 2012–2013 part-time, 1. Openings 2013–2014, 7. The median number of years required for completion of a degree in 2012–2013 were 4. The number of students enrolled full- and part-time who were dismissed or voluntarily withdrew from this program area in 2012–2013 were 0. *Counseling MA/MS (Master of Arts/Science)*—Applications 2012–2013, 29. Total applicants accepted 2012–2013, 23. Number full-time enrolled (new admits only) 2012–2013, 12. Number part-time enrolled (new admits only) 2012–2013, 0. Total enrolled 2012–2013 full-time, 32. Total enrolled 2012–2013 part-time, 11. Openings 2013–2014, 12. The median number of years required for completion of a degree in 2012–2013 were 2. The number of students enrolled full- and part-time who were dismissed or voluntarily withdrew from this program area in 2012–2013 were 0. *Educational Psychology MEd (Education)*—Applications 2012–2013, 11. Total applicants accepted 2012–2013, 3. Number full-time enrolled (new admits only) 2012–2013, 1. Number part-time enrolled (new admits only) 2012–2013, 0. Total enrolled 2012–2013 full-time, 4. Total enrolled 2012–2013 part-time, 1. Openings 2013–2014, 3. The median number of years required for completion of a degree in 2012–2013 were 2. The number of students enrolled full- and part-time who were dismissed or voluntarily withdrew from this program area in 2012–2013 were 0.
Scores: Entries appear in this order: required test or GPA, minimum score (if required), median score of students entering in 2012–2013. *Counseling Psychology PhD (Doctor of Philosophy):* GRE-V no minimum stated, 152, GRE-Q no minimum stated, 146, overall undergraduate GPA no minimum stated, 3.57; *Educational Psychology PhD (Doctor of Philosophy):* GRE-V no minimum stated, 150, GRE-Q no minimum stated, 160; *Counseling MA/MS (Master of Arts/Science):* GRE-V no minimum stated, 152, GRE-Q no minimum stated, 145, GRE-Analytical no minimum stated, 3.5, overall undergraduate GPA no minimum stated, 3.52; *Educational Psychology MEd (Education):* GRE-V no minimum stated, 151, GRE-Q no minimum stated, 145.
Other Criteria: (importance of criteria rated low, medium, or high): GRE scores—medium, research experience—medium,

work experience—medium, extracurricular activity—medium, clinically related public service—medium, GPA—high, letters of recommendation—high, statement of goals and objectives—high.

Student Characteristics: The following represents characteristics of students in 2012–2013 in all graduate psychology programs in the department: Female—full-time 51, part-time 20; Male—full-time 22, part-time 4; African American/Black—full-time 4, part-time 1; Hispanic/Latino(a)—full-time 16, part-time 7; Asian/Pacific Islander—full-time 12, part-time 4; American Indian/Alaska Native—full-time 1, part-time 0; Caucasian/White—full-time 28, part-time 12; Multi-ethnic—full-time 1, part-time 0; students subject to the Americans With Disabilities Act—full-time 1, part-time 0; Unknown ethnicity—full-time 5, part-time 0; International students who hold an F-1 or J-1 Visa—full-time 6, part-time 0.

Financial Information/Assistance:

Tuition for Full-Time Study: *Master's:* State residents: per academic year $11,736, $587 per credit hour; Nonstate residents: per academic year $25,168, $1,258 per credit hour. *Doctoral:* State residents: per academic year $11,736, $587 per credit hour; Nonstate residents: per academic year $25,168, $1,258 per credit hour. Tuition is subject to change. See the following website for updates and changes in tuition costs: http://www.finaid.wsu.edu/coa.html.

Financial Assistance:

First-Year Students: Teaching assistantships available for first year. Average amount paid per academic year: $12,865. Average number of hours worked per week: 20. Research assistantships available for first year. Average amount paid per academic year: $12,865. Average number of hours worked per week: 20. Fellowships and scholarships available for first year.

Advanced Students: Teaching assistantships available for advanced students. Average amount paid per academic year: $13,653. Average number of hours worked per week: 20. Research assistantships available for advanced students. Average amount paid per academic year: $13,653. Average number of hours worked per week: 20. Fellowships and scholarships available for advanced students.

Additional Information: Of all students currently enrolled full time, 75% benefited from one or more of the listed financial assistance programs. Application and information available online at: http://www.gradschool.wsu.edu/FutureStudents/Finance/.

Internships/Practica: Doctoral Degree (PhD Counseling Psychology): For those doctoral students for whom a professional psychology internship was required in this program prior to graduation, (8) students applied for an internship in 2011–2012, with (7) students obtaining an internship. Of those students who obtained an internship, (7) were paid internships. Of those students who obtained an internship, (5) students placed in APA/CPA accredited internships, (1) students placed in internships not APA/CPA accredited, but listed with the Association of Psychology Postdoctoral and Internship Programs (APPIC), (0) students placed in internships conforming to guidelines of the Council of Directors of School Psychology Programs (CDSPP), (1) students placed in internships that were not APA/CPA accredited, APPIC or CDSPP listed. Master's Degree (MA/MS Counseling): An internship experience, such as a final research project or "capstone" experience is required of graduates.

Housing and Day Care: On-campus housing is available. See the following website for more information: http://housing.wsu.edu/. On-campus day care facilities are available. See the following website for more information: http://childrenscenter.wsu.edu/.

Employment of Department Graduates:

Master's Degree Graduates: Of those who graduated in the academic year 2011–2012, the following categories and numbers represent the postgraduate activities and employment of master's degree graduates: Enrolled in a postdoctoral residency/fellowship (n/a), employed in independent practice (n/a), employed in a hospital/medical center (3), do not know (31), total from the above (master's) (34).

Doctoral Degree Graduates: Of those who graduated in the academic year 2011–2012, the following categories and numbers represent the postgraduate activities and employment of doctoral degree graduates: Enrolled in a psychology doctoral program (n/a), employed in other positions at a higher education institution (2), do not know (5), total from the above (doctoral) (7).

Additional Information:

Orientation, Objectives, and Emphasis of Department: The doctoral program in counseling psychology subscribes to the scientist–practitioner model of doctoral training. That is, while graduates are prepared to function as counseling psychologists in a variety of academic and service delivery settings, the common thread of all training is a balance of applied, theoretical, and scientific components in the practice of professional psychology. The emphasis of the program is on the facilitation of psychological growth and development, stressing the interaction of individual, environmental and socio-cultural factors in the treatment of psychological problems, as well as the promotion of health through better self-management and self-renewal.

Special Facilities or Resources: The Attentional Processes and Hypnosis Lab is a nine room complex equipped with state of the art computerized brain activity (EEG) mapping equipment, a jet transport flight simulator, a Restricted Environmental Stimulation Therapy (REST) dry flotation chamber, a standard sound attenuated REST chamber, and a full array of intercommunications, observation, and psychophysiological monitoring equipment. The Learning and Performance Research Center is a service and research center providing educational and social services agencies in Washington State and beyond with assessment and program evaluation assistance. The Culture and Personality Laboratory is the base for multinational studies on culture and personality, drawing on cross-cultural and indigenous perspectives. We also have a Counseling Laboratory Classroom (Room 223) for lab skills and assessment training activities which includes one-way mirrors/observation capabilities, and individual rooms for counseling skills training and demonstration purposes. The Pacific Northwest Center for Mestizo and Indigenous Research and Outreach (Room 121) focuses on the generation, transmission, and application of knowledge to serve the needs of Latino/Mestizo and Native/Indigenous communities in the Pacific Northwest.

Information for Students With Physical Disabilities: See the following website for more information: http://drc.wsu.edu/.

Application Information:
Send to College of Education, Office of Graduate Studies, 252 Cleveland Hall, P.O. Box 642114, Pullman, WA 99164-2114. Application

available online. URL of online application: http://www.gradschool.
wsu.edu/FutureStudents/Apply. Students are admitted in the Fall, application
deadline January 10. *Fee: $75.*

Washington, University of
Department of Psychology
Arts & Sciences
Box 351525
Seattle, WA 98195-1525
Telephone: (206) 543-8687
Fax: (206) 685-3157
E-mail: *mizumori@u.washington.edu*
Web: *http://web.psych.washington.edu/*

Department Information:
1917. Chairperson: Sheri J.Y. Mizumori, PhD. Number of faculty:
total—full-time 43, part-time 4; women—full-time 18, part-time
3; total—minority—full-time 9; women minority—full-time 2.

Programs and Degrees Offered:
Listed in the following order: Program area, degree type (T if
terminal Master's), number awarded 7/11–6/12. Animal Behavior
PhD (Doctor of Philosophy) 1, Clinical Psychology PhD (Doctor
of Philosophy) 4, Child Clinical PhD (Doctor of Philosophy) 2,
Cognition and Perception PhD (Doctor of Philosophy) 3, Developmental Psychology PhD (Doctor of Philosophy) 1, Behavioral
Neuroscience PhD (Doctor of Philosophy) 1, Social and Personality Psychology PhD (Doctor of Philosophy) 2, Quantitative Psychology PhD (Doctor of Philosophy) 0.

APA Accreditation: Clinical PhD (Doctor of Philosophy). Student
Outcome Data Website: http://web.psych.washington.edu/psych.php#
p=236.

Student Applications/Admissions:
Student Applications
Animal Behavior PhD (Doctor of Philosophy)—Applications
2012–2013, 33. Total applicants accepted 2012–2013, 4. Number full-time enrolled (new admits only) 2012–2013, 3. Number part-time enrolled (new admits only) 2012–2013, 0. Total
enrolled 2012–2013 full-time, 10. Total enrolled 2012–2013
part-time, 1. Openings 2013–2014, 2. The median number of
years required for completion of a degree in 2012–2013 were
5. The number of students enrolled full- and part-time who
were dismissed or voluntarily withdrew from this program area
in 2012–2013 were 0. *Clinical Psychology PhD (Doctor of Philosophy)*—Applications 2012–2013, 379. Total applicants accepted 2012–2013, 5. Number full-time enrolled (new admits
only) 2012–2013, 5. Number part-time enrolled (new admits
only) 2012–2013, 0. Total enrolled 2012–2013 full-time, 29.
Total enrolled 2012–2013 part-time, 6. Openings 2013–2014,
5. The median number of years required for completion of a
degree in 2012–2013 were 8. The number of students enrolled
full- and part-time who were dismissed or voluntarily withdrew
from this program area in 2012–2013 were 0. *Child Clinical
PhD (Doctor of Philosophy)*—Applications 2012–2013, 290.
Total applicants accepted 2012–2013, 8. Number full-time
enrolled (new admits only) 2012–2013, 4. Number part-time
enrolled (new admits only) 2012–2013, 0. Total enrolled

2012–2013 full-time, 20. Total enrolled 2012–2013 part-time,
6. Openings 2013–2014, 3. The median number of years required for completion of a degree in 2012–2013 were 7. The
number of students enrolled full- and part-time who were
dismissed or voluntarily withdrew from this program area in
2012–2013 were 0. *Cognition and Perception PhD (Doctor of
Philosophy)*—Applications 2012–2013, 79. Total applicants accepted 2012–2013, 5. Number full-time enrolled (new admits
only) 2012–2013, 2. Number part-time enrolled (new admits
only) 2012–2013, 0. Total enrolled 2012–2013 full-time, 11.
Total enrolled 2012–2013 part-time, 5. Openings 2013–2014,
3. The median number of years required for completion of a
degree in 2012–2013 were 5. The number of students enrolled
full- and part-time who were dismissed or voluntarily withdrew
from this program area in 2012–2013 were 0. *Developmental
Psychology PhD (Doctor of Philosophy)*—Applications 2012–
2013, 43. Total applicants accepted 2012–2013, 6. Number
full-time enrolled (new admits only) 2012–2013, 1. Number
part-time enrolled (new admits only) 2012–2013, 0. Total
enrolled 2012–2013 full-time, 5. Total enrolled 2012–2013
part-time, 3. Openings 2013–2014, 2. The median number of
years required for completion of a degree in 2012–2013 were
6. The number of students enrolled full- and part-time who
were dismissed or voluntarily withdrew from this program area
in 2012–2013 were 0. *Behavioral Neuroscience PhD (Doctor
of Philosophy)*—Applications 2012–2013, 23. Total applicants
accepted 2012–2013, 3. Number full-time enrolled (new
admits only) 2012–2013, 1. Number part-time enrolled (new
admits only) 2012–2013, 0. Total enrolled 2012–2013 full-
time, 10. Total enrolled 2012–2013 part-time, 2. Openings
2013–2014, 1. The median number of years required for completion of a degree in 2012–2013 were 5. The number of
students enrolled full- and part-time who were dismissed or
voluntarily withdrew from this program area in 2012–2013
were 1. *Social and Personality Psychology PhD (Doctor of Philosophy)*—Applications 2012–2013, 135. Total applicants accepted 2012–2013, 5. Number full-time enrolled (new admits
only) 2012–2013, 4. Number part-time enrolled (new admits
only) 2012–2013, 0. Total enrolled 2012–2013 full-time, 10.
Total enrolled 2012–2013 part-time, 3. Openings 2013–2014,
1. The median number of years required for completion of a
degree in 2012–2013 were 7. The number of students enrolled
full- and part-time who were dismissed or voluntarily withdrew
from this program area in 2012–2013 were 0. *Quantitative
Psychology PhD (Doctor of Philosophy)*—Applications 2012–
2013, 7. Total applicants accepted 2012–2013, 12. Number
full-time enrolled (new admits only) 2012–2013, 1. Total enrolled 2012–2013 full-time, 2. The number of students enrolled
full- and part-time who were dismissed or voluntarily withdrew
from this program area in 2012–2013 were 0.
Scores: Entries appear in this order: required test or GPA,
minimum score (if required), median score of students entering
in 2012–2013. *Animal Behavior PhD (Doctor of Philosophy):*
GRE-V no minimum stated, GRE-Q no minimum stated, overall undergraduate GPA no minimum stated, last 2 years GPA
no minimum stated; *Clinical Psychology PhD (Doctor of Philosophy):* GRE-V no minimum stated, GRE-Q no minimum stated,
overall undergraduate GPA no minimum stated, 3.78, last 2
years GPA no minimum stated; *Child Clinical PhD (Doctor of
Philosophy):* GRE-V no minimum stated, GRE-Q no minimum
stated, overall undergraduate GPA no minimum stated, last
2 years GPA no minimum stated; *Cognition and Perception PhD*

(*Doctor of Philosophy*): GRE-V no minimum stated, GRE-Q no minimum stated, overall undergraduate GPA no minimum stated, last 2 years GPA no minimum stated; *Developmental Psychology PhD (Doctor of Philosophy)*: GRE-V no minimum stated, GRE-Q no minimum stated, overall undergraduate GPA no minimum stated, last 2 years GPA no minimum stated; *Behavioral Neuroscience PhD (Doctor of Philosophy)*: GRE-V no minimum stated, GRE-Q no minimum stated, overall undergraduate GPA no minimum stated, last 2 years GPA no minimum stated; *Social and Personality Psychology PhD (Doctor of Philosophy)*: GRE-V no minimum stated, GRE-Q no minimum stated, overall undergraduate GPA no minimum stated, last 2 years GPA no minimum stated; *Quantitative Psychology PhD (Doctor of Philosophy)*: GRE-V no minimum stated, GRE-Q no minimum stated, overall undergraduate GPA no minimum stated, last 2 years GPA no minimum stated.

Other Criteria: (importance of criteria rated low, medium, or high): GRE scores—high, research experience—high, work experience—medium, extracurricular activity—low, clinically related public service—low, GPA—medium, letters of recommendation—high, interview—high, statement of goals and objectives—high, Individual areas evaluate applications differently, but all require a strong background in research and/or statistics. For additional information on admission requirements, go to http://web.psych.washington.edu/psych.php#p=137.

Student Characteristics: The following represents characteristics of students in 2012–2013 in all graduate psychology programs in the department: Female—full-time 67, part-time 16; Male—full-time 30, part-time 10; African American/Black—full-time 2, part-time 0; Hispanic/Latino(a)—full-time 4, part-time 0; Asian/Pacific Islander—full-time 22, part-time 5; American Indian/Alaska Native—full-time 0, part-time 0; Caucasian/White—full-time 67, part-time 20; Multi-ethnic—full-time 2, part-time 1; students subject to the Americans With Disabilities Act—full-time 1, part-time 0; Unknown ethnicity—full-time 0, part-time 0; International students who hold an F-1 or J-1 Visa—full-time 4, part-time 2.

Financial Information/Assistance:

Tuition for Full-Time Study: *Doctoral:* State residents: per academic year $14,358; Nonstate residents: per academic year $26,768. Tuition is subject to change. See the following website for updates and changes in tuition costs: http://opb.washington.edu/content/tuition-and-required-fees.

Financial Assistance:

First-Year Students: Teaching assistantships available for first year. Average amount paid per academic year: $15,669. Average number of hours worked per week: 20. Research assistantships available for first year. Average amount paid per academic year: $15,669. Average number of hours worked per week: 20. Traineeships available for first year. Average amount paid per academic year: $15,669. Average number of hours worked per week: 20.

Advanced Students: Teaching assistantships available for advanced students. Average amount paid per academic year: $16,848. Average number of hours worked per week: 20. Research assistantships available for advanced students. Average amount paid per academic year: $16,848. Average number of hours worked per week: 20. Traineeships available for advanced students. Average amount paid per academic year: $16,848. Average number of hours worked per week: 20.

Additional Information: Of all students currently enrolled full time, 95% benefited from one or more of the listed financial assistance programs.

Internships/Practica: Doctoral Degree (PhD Clinical Psychology): For those doctoral students for whom a professional psychology internship was required in this program prior to graduation, (4) students applied for an internship in 2011–2012, with (3) students obtaining an internship. Of those students who obtained an internship, (3) were paid internships. Of those students who obtained an internship, (3) students placed in APA/CPA accredited internships, (0) students placed in internships not APA/CPA accredited, but listed with the Association of Psychology Postdoctoral and Internship Programs (APPIC), (0) students placed in internships conforming to guidelines of the Council of Directors of School Psychology Programs (CDSPP), (0) students placed in internships that were not APA/CPA accredited, APPIC or CDSPP listed. Doctoral Degree (PhD Child Clinical): For those doctoral students for whom a professional psychology internship was required in this program prior to graduation, (4) students applied for an internship in 2011–2012, with (3) students obtaining an internship. Of those students who obtained an internship, (3) were paid internships. Of those students who obtained an internship, (3) students placed in APA/CPA accredited internships, (0) students placed in internships not APA/CPA accredited, but listed with the Association of Psychology Postdoctoral and Internship Programs (APPIC), (0) students placed in internships conforming to guidelines of the Council of Directors of School Psychology Programs (CDSPP), (0) students placed in internships that were not APA/CPA accredited, APPIC or CDSPP listed. A variety of local and national predoctoral internships are available in clinical psychology.

Housing and Day Care: On-campus housing is available. See the following website for more information: https://www.hfs.washington.edu/housing/Default.aspx?id=184. On-campus day care facilities are available. See the following website for more information: http://www.washington.edu/admin/hr/benefits/worklife/childcare/children-centers.html.

Employment of Department Graduates:

Master's Degree Graduates: Of those who graduated in the academic year 2011–2012, the following categories and numbers represent the postgraduate activities and employment of master's degree graduates: Enrolled in a postdoctoral residency/fellowship (n/a), employed in independent practice (n/a), total from the above (master's) (0).

Doctoral Degree Graduates: Of those who graduated in the academic year 2011–2012, the following categories and numbers represent the postgraduate activities and employment of doctoral degree graduates: Enrolled in a psychology doctoral program (n/a), enrolled in a postdoctoral residency/fellowship (6), employed in independent practice (1), employed in an academic position at a university (1), employed in business or industry (3), employed in a community mental health/counseling center (1), employed in a hospital/medical center (1), do not know (1), total from the above (doctoral) (14).

Additional Information:

Orientation, Objectives, and Emphasis of Department: The program is committed to research-oriented scientific psychology. No degree programs are available in counseling or humanistic psychology. The clinical program emphasizes both clinical and research competencies and has areas of specialization in child clinical, and subspecialties in behavioral medicine, health psychology, and community psychology. Diversity science and quantitative psychology minors are now available to students in our program.

Special Facilities or Resources: University and urban settings provide many resources, including the University of Washington Medical Center, UW Autism Center, Addictive Behaviors Research Center, Psychological Services and Training Center, Behavioral Research & Therapy Clinics, Institute for Learning and Brain Sciences, UW Center for Anxiety and Traumatic Stress, Washington National Primate Research Center, Children's Hospital and Regional Medical Center; nearby Veterans Administration facilities, and Sound Mental Health.

Information for Students With Physical Disabilities: See the following website for more information: http://www.washington.edu/admin/dso/.

Application Information:

Send to Graduate Selections Committee, Department of Psychology, Box 351525, University of Washington, Seattle, WA 98195-1525. Application available online. URL of online application: https://www.grad.uw.edu/applForAdmiss/. Students are admitted in the Fall, application deadline December 15. *Fee:* $75. Fee waivers are available to current McNair Scholars and PPIA Fellows who have sent documentation to the Graduate School prior to requesting the fee waiver. Fee waivers are also available to applicants who qualify for need-based waivers (need-based applicants must have earned income under the appropriate State of Washington family or individual income limits in the most recent tax year preceding the application). Fee waiver requests must be submitted in the online application after all steps of the application have been completed and at least 7 calendar days prior to December 15—late requests will automatically be denied.

Marshall University
Department of Psychology
Liberal Arts
One John Marshall Drive
Huntington, WV 25755-2672
Telephone: (304) 696-6446
Fax: (304) 696-2784
E-mail: *mewaldt@marshall.edu*
Web: *http://www.marshall.edu/wpmu/psych*

Department Information:
1960. Chairperson: Steven Mewaldt. Number of faculty: total—full-time 19, part-time 2; women—full-time 8, part-time 1; total—minority—full-time 1.

Programs and Degrees Offered:
Listed in the following order: Program area, degree type (T if terminal Master's), number awarded 7/11–6/12. Clinical Psychology PsyD (Doctor of Psychology) 10, Psychology MA/MS (Master of Arts/Science) (T) 25.

APA Accreditation: Clinical PsyD (Doctor of Psychology). Student Outcome Data Website: http://www.marshall.edu/wpmu/psych/programs/psyd-program/.

Student Applications/Admissions:
Student Applications
Clinical Psychology PsyD (Doctor of Psychology)—Applications 2012–2013, 60. Total applicants accepted 2012–2013, 11. Number full-time enrolled (new admits only) 2012–2013, 11. Number part-time enrolled (new admits only) 2012–2013, 0. Total enrolled 2012–2013 full-time, 39. Total enrolled 2012–2013 part-time, 6. Openings 2013–2014, 10. The median number of years required for completion of a degree in 2012–2013 were 5. The number of students enrolled full- and part-time who were dismissed or voluntarily withdrew from this program area in 2012–2013 were 0. *Psychology MA/MS (Master of Arts/Science)*—Applications 2012–2013, 44. Total applicants accepted 2012–2013, 28. Number full-time enrolled (new admits only) 2012–2013, 18. Number part-time enrolled (new admits only) 2012–2013, 7. Total enrolled 2012–2013 full-time, 31. Total enrolled 2012–2013 part-time, 30. Openings 2013–2014, 25. The median number of years required for completion of a degree in 2012–2013 were 2. The number of students enrolled full- and part-time who were dismissed or voluntarily withdrew from this program area in 2012–2013 were 2.
Scores: Entries appear in this order: required test or GPA, minimum score (if required), median score of students entering in 2012–2013. *Clinical Psychology PsyD (Doctor of Psychology):* GRE-V 150, 154, GRE-Q 141, 153, overall undergraduate GPA no minimum stated, 3.6; *Psychology MA/MS (Master of Arts/Science):* GRE-V 150, GRE-Q 141, GRE-Analytical no minimum stated, overall undergraduate GPA 3.0.

Other Criteria: (importance of criteria rated low, medium, or high): GRE scores—medium, research experience—medium, work experience—medium, extracurricular activity—medium, clinically related public service—medium, GPA—high, letters of recommendation—medium, interview—medium, statement of goals and objectives—high, undergraduate major in psychology—medium, specific undergraduate psychology courses taken—high, MA program admission is based primarily on GPA and GRE scores; PsyD program considers these, plus statement of professional goals, clinical and research experience, commitment to and understanding of rural psychological service delivery, and letters of recommendation. An interview may be required of PsyD applicants and applicants to the clinical emphasis of the MA program. We accept PsyD students via two routes- those with Master's degrees in psychology and those who are just begining their graduate education. Criteria are similar, but weightings are a bit different for each; professional experience and demonstrated experience with rural issues are weighted more heavily in our post-MA pool.

Student Characteristics: The following represents characteristics of students in 2012–2013 in all graduate psychology programs in the department: Female—full-time 52, part-time 25; Male—full-time 18, part-time 11; African American/Black—full-time 4, part-time 0; Hispanic/Latino(a)—full-time 1, part-time 0; Asian/Pacific Islander—full-time 0, part-time 0; American Indian/Alaska Native—full-time 1, part-time 0; Caucasian/White—full-time 64, part-time 36; Multi-ethnic—full-time 0, part-time 0; students subject to the Americans With Disabilities Act—full-time 0, part-time 0; Unknown ethnicity—full-time 0, part-time 0; International students who hold an F-1 or J-1 Visa—full-time 3, part-time 0.

Financial Information/Assistance:
Tuition for Full-Time Study: *Master's:* State residents: per academic year $6,230, $346 per credit hour; Nonstate residents: per academic year $15,000, $855 per credit hour. *Doctoral:* State residents: per academic year $8,366, $466 per credit hour; Nonstate residents: per academic year $18,272, $1,015 per credit hour. Tuition is subject to change. Tuition costs vary by program. See the following website for updates and changes in tuition costs: http://www.marshall.edu/wpmu/bursar.

Financial Assistance:
First-Year Students: Teaching assistantships available for first year. Average amount paid per academic year: $3,000. Average number of hours worked per week: 10. Research assistantships available for first year. Average amount paid per academic year: $3,000. Average number of hours worked per week: 10.

Advanced Students: Teaching assistantships available for advanced students. Average amount paid per academic year: $3,000. Average number of hours worked per week: 10. Apply by April 15. Research assistantships available for advanced students.

Average amount paid per academic year: $3,000. Average number of hours worked per week: 10. Traineeships available for advanced students. Average amount paid per academic year: $3,000. Average number of hours worked per week: 10.

Additional Information: Of all students currently enrolled full time, 80% benefited from one or more of the listed financial assistance programs. Application and information available online at: http://www.marshall.edu/wpmu/sfa/.

Internships/Practica: Doctoral Degree (PsyD Clinical Psychology): For those doctoral students for whom a professional psychology internship was required in this program prior to graduation, (9) students applied for an internship in 2011–2012, with (8) students obtaining an internship. Of those students who obtained an internship, (8) were paid internships. Of those students who obtained an internship, (7) students placed in APA/CPA accredited internships, (0) students placed in internships not APA/CPA accredited, but listed with the Association of Psychology Postdoctoral and Internship Programs (APPIC), (0) students placed in internships conforming to guidelines of the Council of Directors of School Psychology Programs (CDSPP), (1) students placed in internships that were not APA/CPA accredited, APPIC or CDSPP listed. PsyD program: 2nd year students work in department's clinic in Huntington; 3rd year students work at variety of sites in the Huntington community, 4th year students work at rural placements. Some are in collaboration with primary medical facilities; some may require an overnight stay. Students must complete a full-year, full-time or 2 year, part-time predoctoral internship in order to graduate. Clinical MA: Practicum students work in Marshall's community clinic in Dunbar, WV; master's level interns work in area mental health agencies. MA level students interested in I/O have access to a variety of business and organizational field placements.

Housing and Day Care: On-campus housing is available. See the following website for more information: http://www.marshall.edu/housing/. On-campus day care facilities are available. See the following website for more information: http://www.marshall.edu/cda/.

Employment of Department Graduates:
Master's Degree Graduates: Of those who graduated in the academic year 2011–2012, the following categories and numbers represent the postgraduate activities and employment of master's degree graduates: Enrolled in a psychology doctoral program (1), enrolled in another graduate/professional program (2), enrolled in a postdoctoral residency/fellowship (n/a), employed in independent practice (n/a), employed in an academic position at a 2-year/4-year college (1), employed in business or industry (1), employed in government agency (1), employed in a community mental health/counseling center (4), do not know (15), total from the above (master's) (25).
Doctoral Degree Graduates: Of those who graduated in the academic year 2011–2012, the following categories and numbers represent the postgraduate activities and employment of doctoral degree graduates: Enrolled in a psychology doctoral program (n/a), enrolled in a postdoctoral residency/fellowship (2), employed in independent practice (4), employed in other positions at a higher education institution (1), employed in a community mental health/counseling center (1), employed in a hospital/medical center (2), total from the above (doctoral) (10).

Additional Information:
Orientation, Objectives, and Emphasis of Department: Our PsyD program in Clinical Psychology (offered on our Huntington WV campus) accepted its first students in Fall 2002 and we received APA accreditation in the spring of 2006. The program was re-accredited in 2011. The program is also recognized as a designated program by the National Register/ASPPC Designation project. The program's emphasis is on preparing scholar-practitioners for rural/underserved populations in Appalachia and other rural areas. Particular foci of the doctoral program include understanding the needs and challenges of working in rural communities, preparing doctoral level psychologists to work within these communities, and provision of services to those areas through the training program itself. A wide range of theoretical perspectives are represented in our faculty. The MA program can be individualized to address a variety of academic and professional objectives for students. There is an "area of emphasis" available in clinical psychology (based in our S. Charleston, WV campus) which prepares students for entry level clinical work at the MA level. Students can also take coursework, do research and obtain field placements in interest areas such as I/O psychology and a variety of disciplinary areas such as developmental, cognitive, social, etc. The Psychology MA program is a popular foundation program for students intending to complete Marshall's EdS program in School Psychology in the Graduate College of Education and Human Services.

Special Facilities or Resources: Departmental and university computer facilities are available to students for clinical work and for research projects in all programs. Online library resources are excellent. Through department clinics, clinical students are afforded the opportunity to work, under supervision, with clients from the community and university. Placements for PsyD students are available at nearby community mental health centers, state hospitals, and the VA as well as at a variety of more rural sites for advanced training. MA level students interested in I/O have access to a variety of business and organizational field placements. Faculty have a variety of active, ongoing research projects available for student collaboration.

Information for Students With Physical Disabilities: See the following website for more information: http://www.marshall.edu/wpmu/disabled/.

Application Information:
Send to Admissions Office, Marshall University Graduate College, 100 Angus Peyton Drive, S., Charleston, WV 25303-1600. Application available online. URL of online application: http://www.marshall.edu/graduate/admissions/how-to-apply-for-admission/. Students are admitted in the Fall, application deadline December 1; Programs have rolling admissions. December 1 deadline for PsyD program (all new PsyD students start in subsequent Fall semester); MA program has ongoing review of applicants; new MA students can begin in any semester. MA applicants for clinical emphasis program must apply by March 15 and will begin in the subsequent Fall semester. *Fee:* $40.

West Virginia University

Department of Counseling, Rehabilitation Counseling and
  Counseling Psychology
Education and Human Services
502 Allen Hall, P.O. Box 6122
Morgantown, WV 26506-6122
Telephone: (304) 293-2227
Fax: (304) 293-4082
E-mail: *James.Bartee@mail.wvu.edu*
Web: *http://counseling.wvu.edu*

Department Information:

1948. Chairperson: Jeffrey A. Daniels. Number of faculty: total—full-time 11; women—full-time 7.

Programs and Degrees Offered:

Listed in the following order: Program area, degree type (T if terminal Master's), number awarded 7/11–6/12. Counseling Psychology PhD (Doctor of Philosophy) 3.

APA Accreditation: Counseling PhD (Doctor of Philosophy). Student Outcome Data Website: http://counseling.wvu.edu/counseling_psychology/future_students.

Student Applications/Admissions:

Student Applications

Counseling Psychology PhD (Doctor of Philosophy)—Applications 2012–2013, 0. Total applicants accepted 2012–2013, 0. Number full-time enrolled (new admits only) 2012–2013, 0. Number part-time enrolled (new admits only) 2012–2013, 0. Total enrolled 2012–2013 full-time, 24. Total enrolled 2012–2013 part-time, 10. Openings 2013–2014, 6. The median number of years required for completion of a degree in 2012–2013 were 6. The number of students enrolled full- and part-time who were dismissed or voluntarily withdrew from this program area in 2012–2013 were 1.

Scores: Entries appear in this order: required test or GPA, minimum score (if required), median score of students entering in 2012–2013. *Counseling Psychology PhD (Doctor of Philosophy):* GRE-V 500, GRE-Q 500, GRE-Analytical no minimum stated, Masters GPA 3.5.

Other Criteria: (importance of criteria rated low, medium, or high): GRE scores—medium, research experience—medium, work experience—high, extracurricular activity—medium, clinically related public service—medium, GPA—medium, letters of recommendation—high, interview—high, statement of goals and objectives—high, Goodness of fit—high, undergraduate major in psychology—low, specific undergraduate psychology courses taken—low. For additional information on admission requirements, go to http://counseling.wvu.edu/counseling_psychology/future_students/admissions.

Student Characteristics: The following represents characteristics of students in 2012–2013 in all graduate psychology programs in the department: Female—full-time 16, part-time 5; Male—full-time 8, part-time 5; African American/Black—full-time 2, part-time 0; Hispanic/Latino(a)—full-time 0, part-time 0; Asian/Pacific Islander—full-time 1, part-time 0; American Indian/Alaska Native—full-time 0, part-time 0; Caucasian/White—full-time 21, part-time 10; Multi-ethnic—full-time 0, part-time 0; students subject to the Americans With Disabilities Act—full-time 0, part-time 0; Unknown ethnicity—full-time 0, part-time 0; International students who hold an F-1 or J-1 Visa—full-time 1, part-time 0.

Financial Information/Assistance:

Tuition for Full-Time Study: *Doctoral:* State residents: per academic year $7,300, $405 per credit hour; Nonstate residents: per academic year $20,244, $1,124 per credit hour. Tuition is subject to change. Additional fees are assessed to students beyond the costs of tuition for the following: mandatory fees per semester - $834 for in-state and $957 for out-of-state. See the following website for updates and changes in tuition costs: http://financialaid.wvu.edu/tuition-cost-information.

Financial Assistance:

First-Year Students: Teaching assistantships available for first year. Average amount paid per academic year: $12,000. Average number of hours worked per week: 20. Research assistantships available for first year. Average amount paid per academic year: $12,000. Average number of hours worked per week: 20. Fellowships and scholarships available for first year. Average amount paid per academic year: $18,000. Average number of hours worked per week: 0.

Advanced Students: Teaching assistantships available for advanced students. Average amount paid per academic year: $12,000. Average number of hours worked per week: 20. Research assistantships available for advanced students. Average amount paid per academic year: $12,000. Average number of hours worked per week: 20. Fellowships and scholarships available for advanced students. Average amount paid per academic year: $18,000. Average number of hours worked per week: 0.

Additional Information: Of all students currently enrolled full time, 88% benefited from one or more of the listed financial assistance programs. Application and information available online at: http://counseling.wvu.edu/home/financial_aid.

Internships/Practica: Doctoral Degree (PhD Counseling Psychology): For those doctoral students for whom a professional psychology internship was required in this program prior to graduation, (8) students applied for an internship in 2011–2012, with (7) students obtaining an internship. Of those students who obtained an internship, (7) were paid internships. Of those students who obtained an internship, (6) students placed in APA/CPA accredited internships, (0) students placed in internships not APA/CPA accredited, but listed with the Association of Psychology Postdoctoral and Internship Programs (APPIC), (0) students placed in internships conforming to guidelines of the Council of Directors of School Psychology Programs (CDSPP), (1) students placed in internships that were not APA/CPA accredited, APPIC or CDSPP listed. The doctoral program offers a variety of opportunities for practicum training. Some of the placement sites include:

the federal prison system, mental health agencies, employee assistant programs, private practices, VAMCs, local school systems, university counseling center, and others. We have been successful in matching interns with programs in college counseling centers, VAMCs, hospitals/clinics, community mental health centers and consortia, and child and adolescent guidance/treatment centers.

Housing and Day Care: On-campus housing is available. See the following website for more information: http://housing.wvu.edu/. On-campus day care facilities are available. See the following website for more information: http://childlearningcenter.wvu. edu/.

Employment of Department Graduates:

Master's Degree Graduates: Of those who graduated in the academic year 2011–2012, the following categories and numbers represent the postgraduate activities and employment of master's degree graduates: Enrolled in a postdoctoral residency/fellowship (n/a), employed in independent practice (n/a), total from the above (master's) (0).

Doctoral Degree Graduates: Of those who graduated in the academic year 2011–2012, the following categories and numbers represent the postgraduate activities and employment of doctoral degree graduates: Enrolled in a psychology doctoral program (n/a), employed in other positions at a higher education institution (1), employed in a community mental health/counseling center (2), total from the above (doctoral) (3).

Additional Information:

Orientation, Objectives, and Emphasis of Department: The department faculty represent a variety of theoretical orientations. The objective of the department is to train professionals primarily to serve clients with intact personalities, but who may be experiencing difficulties related to personal adjustment, interpersonal relationships, developmental problems, crises, academic or career stress, or decisions. The employment settings for our graduates typically include college and university counseling and testing services, community mental health agencies, clinics, hospitals, schools, rehabilitation centers, correctional centers, the United States Armed Services, and private practice.

Special Facilities or Resources: Facilities include an extensive medical center, including video equipment and computer terminals; training and observation rooms; and practicum and internship sites in a variety of settings for master's and doctoral students as described above.

Information for Students With Physical Disabilities: See the following website for more information: http://disabilityservices. wvu.edu/.

Application Information:
Send to Admissions Coordinator, Department of Counseling, Rehabilitation Counseling and Counseling Psychology, West Virginia University, P.O. Box 6122, Morgantown, WV 25606-6122. Application available online. URL of online application: http://counseling.wvu.edu/ counseling_psychology/future_students/admissions. Students are admitted in the Fall, application deadline December 1. *Fee:* $60.

West Virginia University
Department of Psychology
Eberly College of Arts and Sciences
P.O. Box 6040
Morgantown, WV 26506-6040
Telephone: (304) 293-2001, ext. 31628
Fax: (304) 293-6606
E-mail: *PsychGradAdmissions@mail.wvu.edu*
Web: *http://psychology.wvu.edu*

Department Information:
1929. Chairperson: Tracy Morris. Number of faculty: total—full-time 24; women—full-time 15.

Programs and Degrees Offered:
Listed in the following order: Program area, degree type (T if terminal Master's), number awarded 7/11–6/12. Lifespan Developmental Psychology PhD (Doctor of Philosophy) 4, Behavior Analysis PhD (Doctor of Philosophy) 3, Clinical Psychology PhD (Doctor of Philosophy) 8, Clinical Psychology MA/MS (Master of Arts/Science) (T) 1, Behavioral Neuroscience PhD (Doctor of Philosophy) 0.

APA Accreditation: Clinical PhD (Doctor of Philosophy). Student Outcome Data Website: http://psychology.wvu.edu/future_students/ graduate_programs/doctoral_programs/ph_d__in_clinical_psychology/ student_data.

Student Applications/Admissions:

Student Applications
Lifespan Developmental Psychology PhD (Doctor of Philosophy)— Applications 2012–2013, 23. Total applicants accepted 2012–2013, 4. Number full-time enrolled (new admits only) 2012–2013, 4. Number part-time enrolled (new admits only) 2012–2013, 0. Total enrolled 2012–2013 full-time, 19. Total enrolled 2012–2013 part-time, 0. Openings 2013–2014, 5. The median number of years required for completion of a degree in 2012–2013 were 5. The number of students enrolled full- and part-time who were dismissed or voluntarily withdrew from this program area in 2012–2013 were 1. *Behavior Analysis PhD (Doctor of Philosophy)—*Applications 2012–2013, 38. Total applicants accepted 2012–2013, 5. Number full-time enrolled (new admits only) 2012–2013, 5. Number part-time enrolled (new admits only) 2012–2013, 0. Total enrolled 2012–2013 full-time, 16. Total enrolled 2012–2013 part-time, 0. Openings 2013–2014, 5. The median number of years required for completion of a degree in 2012–2013 were 5. The number of students enrolled full- and part-time who were dismissed or voluntarily withdrew from this program area in 2012–2013 were 0. *Clinical Psychology PhD (Doctor of Philosophy)—*Applications 2012–2013, 142. Total applicants accepted 2012–2013, 6. Number full-time enrolled (new admits only) 2012–2013, 6. Number part-time enrolled (new admits only) 2012–2013, 0. Total enrolled 2012–2013 full-time, 40. Total enrolled 2012–2013 part-time, 0. Openings 2013–2014, 8. The median number of years required for completion of a degree in 2012–2013 were 5. The number of students enrolled full- and part-time who were dismissed or voluntarily withdrew from this program area in 2012–2013 were 1. *Clinical Psychology MA/ MS (Master of Arts/Science)—*Applications 2012–2013, 38.

Total applicants accepted 2012–2013, 1. Number full-time enrolled (new admits only) 2012–2013, 1. Number part-time enrolled (new admits only) 2012–2013, 0. Total enrolled 2012–2013 full-time, 2. Total enrolled 2012–2013 part-time, 0. Openings 2013–2014, 2. The median number of years required for completion of a degree in 2012–2013 were 2. The number of students enrolled full- and part-time who were dismissed or voluntarily withdrew from this program area in 2012–2013 were 0. *Behavioral Neuroscience PhD (Doctor of Philosophy)*—Applications 2012–2013, 19. Total applicants accepted 2012–2013, 4. Number full-time enrolled (new admits only) 2012–2013, 4. Number part-time enrolled (new admits only) 2012–2013, 0. Total enrolled 2012–2013 full-time, 6. Total enrolled 2012–2013 part-time, 0. Openings 2013–2014, 5. The median number of years required for completion of a degree in 2012–2013 were 4. The number of students enrolled full- and part-time who were dismissed or voluntarily withdrew from this program area in 2012–2013 were 0.

Scores: Entries appear in this order: required test or GPA, minimum score (if required), median score of students entering in 2012–2013. *Lifespan Developmental Psychology PhD (Doctor of Philosophy)*: GRE-V 500, 480, GRE-Q 500, 640, GRE-Analytical no minimum stated, 3.5, overall undergraduate GPA 3.00, 3.64, last 2 years GPA no minimum stated, psychology GPA no minimum stated; *Behavior Analysis PhD (Doctor of Philosophy)*: GRE-V 500, 560, GRE-Q 500, 655, GRE-Analytical no minimum stated, 4.5, overall undergraduate GPA 3.00, 3.64, last 2 years GPA no minimum stated, psychology GPA no minimum stated; *Clinical Psychology PhD (Doctor of Philosophy)*: GRE-V 500, 590, GRE-Q 500, 630, GRE-Analytical no minimum stated, 4.7, GRE-Subject (Psychology) no minimum stated, 635, overall undergraduate GPA 3.00, 3.72, last 2 years GPA no minimum stated, psychology GPA no minimum stated; *Clinical Psychology MA/MS (Master of Arts/Science)*: GRE-V 500, GRE-Q 500, GRE-Analytical no minimum stated, GRE-Subject (Psychology) no minimum stated, overall undergraduate GPA 3.00, last 2 years GPA no minimum stated, psychology GPA no minimum stated; *Behavioral Neuroscience PhD (Doctor of Philosophy)*: GRE-V 500, 575, GRE-Q 500, 725, GRE-Analytical no minimum stated, 5.0, overall undergraduate GPA 3.00, 3.81, last 2 years GPA no minimum stated, psychology GPA no minimum stated.

Other Criteria: (importance of criteria rated low, medium, or high): GRE scores—high, research experience—high, work experience—medium, extracurricular activity—medium, clinically related public service—medium, GPA—high, letters of recommendation—high, interview—high, statement of goals and objectives—high, specific undergraduate psychology courses taken—medium, Match between faculty and student interests is of high importance. Only clinical programs give high value to clinically related public service. Research experience is of medium importance for the Master's program. For additional information on admission requirements, go to http://psychology.wvu.edu/future_students/graduate_programs.

Student Characteristics: The following represents characteristics of students in 2012–2013 in all graduate psychology programs in the department: Female—full-time 62, part-time 0; Male—full-time 21, part-time 0; African American/Black—full-time 2, part-time 0; Hispanic/Latino(a)—full-time 1, part-time 0; Asian/Pacific Islander—full-time 4, part-time 0; American Indian/Alaska Native—full-time 1, part-time 0; Caucasian/White—full-time 71,

part-time 0; Multi-ethnic—full-time 1, part-time 0; students subject to the Americans With Disabilities Act—full-time 0, part-time 0; Unknown ethnicity—full-time 3, part-time 0; International students who hold an F-1 or J-1 Visa—full-time 5, part-time 0.

Financial Information/Assistance:

Tuition for Full-Time Study: *Master's:* State residents: per academic year $7,040, $391 per credit hour; Nonstate residents: per academic year $19,854, $1,102 per credit hour. *Doctoral:* State residents: per academic year $7,040, $391 per credit hour; Nonstate residents: per academic year $19,854, $1,102 per credit hour. Tuition is subject to change. See the following website for updates and changes in tuition costs: http://financialservices.wvu.edu/.

Financial Assistance:

First-Year Students: Teaching assistantships available for first year. Average amount paid per academic year: $12,400. Average number of hours worked per week: 20. Apply by December 15. Research assistantships available for first year. Average amount paid per academic year: $12,400. Average number of hours worked per week: 20. Apply by December 15. Traineeships available for first year. Average amount paid per academic year: $12,400. Average number of hours worked per week: 20. Apply by December 15. Fellowships and scholarships available for first year. Average amount paid per academic year: $17,500. Average number of hours worked per week: 0. Apply by December 15.

Advanced Students: Teaching assistantships available for advanced students. Average amount paid per academic year: $12,400. Average number of hours worked per week: 20. Apply by December 15. Research assistantships available for advanced students. Average amount paid per academic year: $12,400. Average number of hours worked per week: 20. Apply by December 15. Traineeships available for advanced students. Average amount paid per academic year: $12,400. Average number of hours worked per week: 20. Apply by December 15. Fellowships and scholarships available for advanced students. Average amount paid per academic year: $17,500. Average number of hours worked per week: 0. Apply by December 15.

Additional Information: Of all students currently enrolled full time, 93% benefited from one or more of the listed financial assistance programs. Application and information available online at: http://grad.wvu.edu/financial_assistance/.

Internships/Practica: Doctoral Degree (PhD Clinical Psychology): For those doctoral students for whom a professional psychology internship was required in this program prior to graduation, (7) students applied for an internship in 2011–2012, with (5) students obtaining an internship. Of those students who obtained an internship, (5) were paid internships. Of those students who obtained an internship, (5) students placed in APA/CPA accredited internships, (0) students placed in internships not APA/CPA accredited, but listed with the Association of Psychology Postdoctoral and Internship Programs (APPIC), (0) students placed in internships conforming to guidelines of the Council of Directors of School Psychology Programs (CDSPP), (0) students placed in internships that were not APA/CPA accredited, APPIC or CDSPP listed. Master's Degree (MA/MS Clinical Psychology): An internship experience, such as a final research project or "capstone" experience is required of graduates. Paid clinical placements at out-of-department sites are available for doctoral clinical students who have earned master's degrees. These out-of-department practicum sites include WVU Carruth Counseling Center, "Kennedy" Federal Correctional Institution, Hopemont Hospital, Sharpe Hospital, the Robert C. Byrd Health Sciences Center, a private practice, various behavioral/community mental health agencies, and children and youth services agencies. These sites are located in Morgantown and across the state and region. Stipends for practicum range from $13,000 to $16,000, require 16 hours of work per week, and virtually all last 12 months.

Housing and Day Care: On-campus housing is available. See the following website for more information: http://housing.wvu.edu/. On-campus day care facilities are available. See the following website for more information: http://childlearningcenter.wvu. edu/.

Employment of Department Graduates:

Master's Degree Graduates: Of those who graduated in the academic year 2011–2012, the following categories and numbers represent the postgraduate activities and employment of master's degree graduates: Enrolled in a postdoctoral residency/fellowship (n/a), employed in independent practice (n/a), total from the above (master's) (0).

Doctoral Degree Graduates: Of those who graduated in the academic year 2011–2012, the following categories and numbers represent the postgraduate activities and employment of doctoral degree graduates: Enrolled in a psychology doctoral program (n/a), total from the above (doctoral) (0).

Additional Information:

Orientation, Objectives, and Emphasis of Department: The Psychology Department offers the Doctor of Philosophy degree in Behavior Analysis, Behavioral Neuroscience, Life-Span Developmental, Clinical Child, and Clinical Psychology, and a terminal Professional Master's degree in Clinical Psychology. The Department employs a junior colleague model of training, in which graduate students participate fully in research, teaching, and service activities. The Behavior Analysis doctoral program trains students in basic research, theory, and applications of behavioral psychology. These three areas of study are integrated in the Behavior Analysis curriculum; however, a student may emphasize either basic or applied research. The Life-Span Developmental program emphasizes cognitive and social/personality development across the life span. It combines breadth of exposure across a variety of perspectives on the life span with depth and rigor in research training and the opportunity to specialize in an age period such as infancy, childhood, adolescence, or adulthood and old age. The

Master's and PhD Clinical programs have a behavioral/cognitive behavioral orientation. The Clinical Doctoral programs train scientist–practitioners who function effectively in academic, medical center, or clinical applied settings. Specializations in developmental psychology, behavior analysis, and clinical health psychology are available. The Clinical Professional Master's Program is designed to train practitioners with a terminal Master's degree to work with adults in rural areas.

Special Facilities or Resources: The Department is housed in the Life Sciences Building, which has modern animal research quarters for work with rats, pigeons, and other species. There are several computer-based laboratories and other laboratories for studies of learning in humans and animals, behavioral pharmacology, and neurosciences. There are additional facilities for human research in learning, cognition, small group processes, developmental psychology, social behavior, and psychophysiology. Clinical practicum opportunities are available through the Department's Quin Curtis Center for Psychological Service, Training, and Research, as well as in numerous mental health agencies throughout the state. Videotaping and direct observation equipment and facilities are available. The West Virginia University Medical Center provides facilities for research and training in such departments and areas as behavioral medicine and psychiatry, pediatrics, neurology, and dentistry. Local preschools and public schools have been cooperative in providing access to children and facilities for child development research; local businesses and other agencies offer sites for practice and research in applied behavior analysis, local senior centers and homes provide access to older adult populations, and the University's Center on Aging-Education Unit and Center for Women's Studies facilitate research related to their purviews. The University maintains an extensive network of computer facilities, and the Department provides an office and a computer for every graduate student.

Information for Students With Physical Disabilities: See the following website for more information: http://disabilityservices. wvu.edu/.

Application Information:

Send to Departmental Admissions Committee, Department of Psychology, West Virginia University, P.O. Box 6040, Morgantown, WV 26506-6040. Application available online. URL of online application: http://grad.wvu.edu/. Students are admitted in the Fall, application deadline December 15. Professional MA in Clinical Psychology deadline is March 1. *Fee:* $60.

Marquette University

Counselor Education and Counseling Psychology
College of Education
561 North 15th Street, 150 Schroeder Complex
Milwaukee, WI 53233
Telephone: (414) 288-5790
Fax: (414) 288-6100
E-mail: *alan.burkard@marquette.edu*
Web: *http://www.marquette.edu/education/grad/cecp.shtml*

Department Information:
1996. Chairperson: Alan W. Burkard. Number of faculty: total—full-time 8; women—full-time 4; total—minority—full-time 1; women minority—full-time 1.

Programs and Degrees Offered:
Listed in the following order: Program area, degree type (T if terminal Master's), number awarded 7/11–6/12. Counseling MA/MS (Master of Arts/Science) (T) 35, Counseling Psychology PhD (Doctor of Philosophy) 9.

APA Accreditation: Counseling PhD (Doctor of Philosophy). Student Outcome Data Website: http://www.marquette.edu/education/grad/cecp_doctorate_disclosure.shtml.

Student Applications/Admissions:
Student Applications
Counseling MA/MS (Master of Arts/Science)—Applications 2012–2013, 117. Total applicants accepted 2012–2013, 28. Number full-time enrolled (new admits only) 2012–2013, 28. Number part-time enrolled (new admits only) 2012–2013, 0. Total enrolled 2012–2013 full-time, 66. Total enrolled 2012–2013 part-time, 4. Openings 2013–2014, 27. The median number of years required for completion of a degree in 2012–2013 were 2. The number of students enrolled full- and part-time who were dismissed or voluntarily withdrew from this program area in 2012–2013 were 2. *Counseling Psychology PhD (Doctor of Philosophy)*—Applications 2012–2013, 64. Total applicants accepted 2012–2013, 4. Number full-time enrolled (new admits only) 2012–2013, 4. Number part-time enrolled (new admits only) 2012–2013, 0. Total enrolled 2012–2013 full-time, 16. Total enrolled 2012–2013 part-time, 5. Openings 2013–2014, 4. The median number of years required for completion of a degree in 2012–2013 were 6. The number of students enrolled full- and part-time who were dismissed or voluntarily withdrew from this program area in 2012–2013 were 0.
Scores: Entries appear in this order: required test or GPA, minimum score (if required), median score of students entering in 2012–2013. *Counseling MA/MS (Master of Arts/Science):* GRE-V no minimum stated, 550, GRE-Q no minimum stated, 670, GRE-Analytical no minimum stated, 4.5, overall undergraduate GPA no minimum stated, 3.47; *Counseling Psychology PhD (Doctor of Philosophy):* GRE-V no minimum stated, 580, GRE-Q no minimum stated, 670, GRE-Analytical no mini-

mum stated, 4.5, overall undergraduate GPA no minimum stated, 3.55, Masters GPA no minimum stated, 3.92.
Other Criteria: (importance of criteria rated low, medium, or high): GRE scores—high, research experience—high, work experience—medium, extracurricular activity—medium, clinically related public service—medium, GPA—high, letters of recommendation—high, interview—high, statement of goals and objectives—high, undergraduate major in psychology—medium, specific undergraduate psychology courses taken—medium, Research experience is much more important for admission into our PhD program than it is for our master's programs. For additional information on admission requirements, go to http://www.marquette.edu/education/grad/cecp.shtml.

Student Characteristics: The following represents characteristics of students in 2012–2013 in all graduate psychology programs in the department: Female—full-time 62, part-time 6; Male—full-time 20, part-time 3; African American/Black—full-time 5, part-time 0; Hispanic/Latino(a)—full-time 3, part-time 1; Asian/Pacific Islander—full-time 2, part-time 1; American Indian/Alaska Native—full-time 0, part-time 0; Caucasian/White—full-time 63, part-time 5; Multi-ethnic—full-time 2, part-time 1; students subject to the Americans With Disabilities Act—full-time 3, part-time 1; Unknown ethnicity—full-time 7, part-time 1; International students who hold an F-1 or J-1 Visa—full-time 3, part-time 0.

Financial Information/Assistance:
Tuition for Full-Time Study: *Master's:* State residents: $735 per credit hour; Nonstate residents: $735 per credit hour. *Doctoral:* State residents: $735 per credit hour; Nonstate residents: $735 per credit hour. See the following website for updates and changes in tuition costs: http://www.marquette.edu/about/studenttuition.shtml.

Financial Assistance:
First-Year Students: Research assistantships available for first year. Average amount paid per academic year: $6,700. Average number of hours worked per week: 10. Apply by February 15. Fellowships and scholarships available for first year. Average amount paid per academic year: $6,700. Average number of hours worked per week: 0. Apply by February 15.
Advanced Students: Research assistantships available for advanced students. Average amount paid per academic year: $6,700. Average number of hours worked per week: 10. Apply by February 15. Fellowships and scholarships available for advanced students. Average amount paid per academic year: $13,000. Average number of hours worked per week: 0.
Additional Information: Of all students currently enrolled full time, 100% benefited from one or more of the listed financial assistance programs. Application and information available online at: http://www.marquette.edu/grad/finaid_index.shtml.

Internships/Practica: Doctoral Degree (PhD Counseling Psychology): For those doctoral students for whom a professional psychology internship was required in this program prior to graduation, (6) students applied for an internship in 2011–2012, with (6) students obtaining an internship. Of those students who obtained an internship, (6) were paid internships. Of those students who obtained an internship, (5) students placed in APA/CPA accredited internships, (1) students placed in internships not APA/CPA accredited, but listed with the Association of Psychology Postdoctoral and Internship Programs (APPIC), (0) students placed in internships conforming to guidelines of the Council of Directors of School Psychology Programs (CDSPP), (0) students placed in internships that were not APA/CPA accredited, APPIC or CDSPP listed. Master's Degree (MA/MS Counseling): An internship experience, such as a final research project or "capstone" experience is required of graduates. We work with a wide range of inpatient and outpatient agencies and educational institutions serving a broad range of clients, from children to seniors and from relatively minor adjustment issues to serious psychopathology. We currently work with approximately 60 agencies and schools and continually try to find additional sites offering superior clinical experience and supervision.

Housing and Day Care: On-campus housing is available. See the following website for more information: http://www.marquette.edu/orl/. On-campus day care facilities are available. See the following website for more information: http://www.marquette.edu/child-care-center/.

Employment of Department Graduates:

Master's Degree Graduates: Of those who graduated in the academic year 2011–2012, the following categories and numbers represent the postgraduate activities and employment of master's degree graduates: Enrolled in a psychology doctoral program (1), enrolled in another graduate/professional program (1), enrolled in a postdoctoral residency/fellowship (n/a), employed in independent practice (n/a), employed in a professional position in a school system (7), employed in business or industry (7), employed in a community mental health/counseling center (10), employed in a hospital/medical center (3), do not know (6), total from the above (master's) (35).

Doctoral Degree Graduates: Of those who graduated in the academic year 2011–2012, the following categories and numbers represent the postgraduate activities and employment of doctoral degree graduates: Enrolled in a psychology doctoral program (n/a), enrolled in a postdoctoral residency/fellowship (2), employed in an academic position at a university (2), employed in an academic position at a 2-year/4-year college (1), employed in other positions at a higher education institution (1), employed in a professional position in a school system (1), employed in government agency (2), employed in a community mental health/counseling center (1), employed in a hospital/medical center (3), total from the above (doctoral) (13).

Additional Information:

Orientation, Objectives, and Emphasis of Department: Our Master's in Counseling and PhD in Counseling Psychology programs are based on a comprehensive biopsychosocial approach to understanding human behavior. We believe that a sensitivity to biological, psychological, social, multicultural, and developmental influences on behavior increases students' effectiveness both as practitioners and as researchers. We use a generalist approach that includes broad preparation in the diverse areas needed to practice competently as psychological scientists and practitioners in today's health care systems. The master's programs in counseling include specializations in school counseling and clinical men-

tal health counseling, with optional specializations in addictions counseling and child/adolescent counseling. The doctoral program in counseling psychology is accredited by APA.

Special Facilities or Resources: Our faculty, and Marquette University as a whole, are committed to offering high quality education. Our coursework, practica, research activities, and other training opportunities are all designed to provide current and comprehensive preparation. Our student body is small, so students receive substantial individual attention. We are also committed to developing students' competencies to work with diverse multicultural groups, and we welcome applications from individuals with diverse backgrounds. The full-time faculty are engaged in a variety of research projects with which students may become involved. Our close affiliation with the Behavior Clinic, a community-based facility focusing on children 0-5 years of age and their parents, provides counseling and research opportunities for our students.

Information for Students With Physical Disabilities: See the following website for more information: http://www.marquette.edu/disability-services/.

Application Information:
Send to Graduate School, P.O. Box 1881, Milwaukee, WI 53201. Application available online. URL of online application: http://www.marquette.edu/grad/apply/. Students are admitted in the Fall, application deadline December 1. The application deadline for the PhD program is December 1, and February 1 for the master's programs. *Fee:* $50.

Marquette University
Department of Psychology
Arts and Sciences
P.O. Box 1881
Milwaukee, WI 53201-1881
Telephone: (414) 288-7218
Fax: (414) 288-5333
E-mail: *john.grych@marquette.edu*
Web: *http://www.marquette.edu/psyc*

Department Information:
1952. Chairperson: John Grych. Number of faculty: total—full-time 17; women—full-time 7; total—minority—full-time 3; women minority—full-time 1.

Programs and Degrees Offered:
Listed in the following order: Program area, degree type (T if terminal Master's), number awarded 7/11–6/12. Clinical Psychology PhD (Doctor of Philosophy) 6.

APA Accreditation: Clinical PhD (Doctor of Philosophy). Student Outcome Data Website: http://www.marquette.edu/psyc/graduate.shtml.

Student Applications/Admissions:
Student Applications
Clinical Psychology PhD (Doctor of Philosophy)—Applications 2012–2013, 220. Total applicants accepted 2012–2013, 9.

Number full-time enrolled (new admits only) 2012–2013, 5. Number part-time enrolled (new admits only) 2012–2013, 0. Total enrolled 2012–2013 full-time, 41. Openings 2013–2014, 5. The median number of years required for completion of a degree in 2012–2013 were 7. The number of students enrolled full- and part-time who were dismissed or voluntarily withdrew from this program area in 2012–2013 were 0.

Scores: Entries appear in this order: required test or GPA, minimum score (if required), median score of students entering in 2012–2013. *Clinical Psychology PhD (Doctor of Philosophy):* GRE-V no minimum stated, 580, GRE-Q no minimum stated, 690, GRE-Analytical no minimum stated, 4.5, overall undergraduate GPA no minimum stated, 3.62.

Other Criteria: (importance of criteria rated low, medium, or high): GRE scores—medium, research experience—high, work experience—low, clinically related public service—medium, GPA—medium, letters of recommendation—high, interview—high, statement of goals and objectives—high, undergraduate major in psychology—medium, specific undergraduate psychology courses taken—medium. For additional information on admission requirements, go to http://www.marquette.edu/psyc/graduate_apply.shtml.

Student Characteristics: The following represents characteristics of students in 2012–2013 in all graduate psychology programs in the department: Female—full-time 33, part-time 0; Male—full-time 8, part-time 0; African American/Black—full-time 1, part-time 0; Hispanic/Latino(a)—full-time 3, part-time 0; Asian/Pacific Islander—full-time 2, part-time 0; American Indian/Alaska Native—full-time 0, part-time 0; Caucasian/White—full-time 35, part-time 0; Multi-ethnic—full-time 0, part-time 0; students subject to the Americans With Disabilities Act—full-time 0, part-time 0; Unknown ethnicity—full-time 0, part-time 0; International students who hold an F-1 or J-1 Visa—full-time 1, part-time 0.

Financial Information/Assistance:

Tuition for Full-Time Study: *Doctoral:* State residents: $1,025 per credit hour; Nonstate residents: $1,025 per credit hour. Tuition is subject to change. See the following website for updates and changes in tuition costs: http://www.marquette.edu/about/studenttuition.shtml.

Financial Assistance:

First-Year Students: Teaching assistantships available for first year. Average amount paid per academic year: $15,336. Average number of hours worked per week: 20. Apply by December 15. Research assistantships available for first year. Average amount paid per academic year: $15,336. Average number of hours worked per week: 20. Apply by December 15. Fellowships and scholarships available for first year. Average amount paid per academic year: $16,000. Average number of hours worked per week: 0. Apply by December 15.

Advanced Students: Teaching assistantships available for advanced students. Average amount paid per academic year: $14,850. Average number of hours worked per week: 20. Apply by November 15. Research assistantships available for advanced students. Average amount paid per academic year: $14,850. Average number of hours worked per week: 20. Apply by November 15. Traineeships available for advanced students. Average amount paid per academic year: $7,700. Average number of hours worked per week: 9. Apply by April 1. Fellowships and scholarships avail-

able for advanced students. Average amount paid per academic year: $17,500. Average number of hours worked per week: 0. Apply by December 1.

Additional Information: Of all students currently enrolled full time, 80% benefited from one or more of the listed financial assistance programs. Application and information available online at: http://www.marquette.edu/psyc/graduate_finaid.shtml.

Internships/Practica: Doctoral Degree (PhD Clinical Psychology): For those doctoral students for whom a professional psychology internship was required in this program prior to graduation, (7) students applied for an internship in 2011–2012, with (7) students obtaining an internship. Of those students who obtained an internship, (7) were paid internships. Of those students who obtained an internship, (7) students placed in APA/CPA accredited internships, (0) students placed in internships not APA/CPA accredited, but listed with the Association of Psychology Postdoctoral and Internship Programs (APPIC), (0) students placed in internships conforming to guidelines of the Council of Directors of School Psychology Programs (CDSPP), (0) students placed in internships that were not APA/CPA accredited, APPIC or CDSPP listed. Doctoral students obtain supervised clinical experience throughout their training. Practica are offered in the Department's training clinic (the Center for Psychological Services), a local academic medical center, a VA hospital, and in community agencies. The Department's training clinic provides assessment and intervention services to members of the general community under the supervision of licensed clinical faculty members. Students have averaged 750 hours in the clinic, and typically acquire 1,500 to 2,000 hours in pre-internship practicum experiences. Marquette University's urban location provides a wealth of training opportunities in the community. Recent practicum experiences have included placements in agencies that provided training in neuropsychological assessment, geropsychology, behavioral medicine, pediatric health, and family therapy. Doctoral students are required to complete a 2,000 hour internship. To date, students have completed APA-approved internships in settings located throughout the United States.

Housing and Day Care: On-campus housing is available. See the following website for more information: http://www.marquette.edu/orl/. On-campus day care facilities are available. See the following website for more information: http://www.marquette.edu/child-care-center/.

Employment of Department Graduates:

Master's Degree Graduates: Of those who graduated in the academic year 2011–2012, the following categories and numbers represent the postgraduate activities and employment of master's degree graduates: Enrolled in a postdoctoral residency/fellowship (n/a), employed in independent practice (n/a), total from the above (master's) (0).

Doctoral Degree Graduates: Of those who graduated in the academic year 2011–2012, the following categories and numbers represent the postgraduate activities and employment of doctoral degree graduates: Enrolled in a psychology doctoral program (n/a), enrolled in a postdoctoral residency/fellowship (4), employed in a hospital/medical center (2), total from the above (doctoral) (6).

Additional Information:

Orientation, Objectives, and Emphasis of Department: The Clinical Psychology program offers courses and training leading to the degree of Doctor of Philosophy (PhD) in Clinical Psychology. All doctoral students earn a Master of Science degree as they progress toward the doctoral degree. The doctoral program is approved by the American Psychological Association to train scientist-professionals. Students receive a solid foundation in the scientific study of psychology and in empirically-based intervention. Training in statistics, measurement, and research methods ensures competence in conducting empirical research and in critically evaluating one's own and others' clinical and empirical work. Students become competent in professional practice skills such as assessment, interventions, and consultation. Supervised clinical experiences are planned throughout the curriculum. Graduates of the doctoral program are prepared for employment as academics, researchers, clinical psychologists, consultants, teachers, and administrators.

Special Facilities or Resources: The department is located in completely refurbished and modern quarters that include a psychology clinic, an undergraduate teaching laboratory, and ample space for both faculty and student research. A full range of computer services is available at no charge to students. Located in a large metropolitan area, Marquette University is within easy commuting distance to a variety of hospitals and agencies in which training and research opportunities may be available.

Information for Students With Physical Disabilities: See the following website for more information: http://www.marquette.edu/disability-services/.

Application Information:
Send to Graduate School, 305 Holthusen Hall, Marquette University, 1324 West Wisconsin Avenue, Milwaukee, WI 53201-1881. Application available online. URL of online application: http://www.marquette.edu/grad/apply/. Students are admitted in the Fall, application deadline December 1. *Fee:* $50. Waived for evidence of financial need.

Wisconsin School of Professional Psychology
Professional School
9120 West Hampton Avenue, Suite 212
Milwaukee, WI 53225
Telephone: (414) 464-9777
Fax: (414) 358-5590
E-mail: *kathleenrusch@sbcglobal.net*
Web: *http://www.wspp.edu*

Department Information:
1980. President: Kathleen M. Rusch, PhD Number of faculty: total—full-time 7, part-time 24; women—full-time 4, part-time 10; minority—part-time 2; women minority—part-time 1.

Programs and Degrees Offered:
Listed in the following order: Program area, degree type (T if terminal Master's), number awarded 7/11–6/12. Clinical Psychology PsyD (Doctor of Psychology) 5.

APA Accreditation: Clinical PsyD (Doctor of Psychology). Student Outcome Data Website: http://wspp.edu/whywspp/wacompl.

Student Applications/Admissions:
Student Applications
Clinical Psychology PsyD (Doctor of Psychology)—Applications 2012–2013, 46. Total applicants accepted 2012–2013, 17. Number full-time enrolled (new admits only) 2012–2013, 13. Number part-time enrolled (new admits only) 2012–2013, 2. Total enrolled 2012–2013 full-time, 39. Total enrolled 2012–2013 part-time, 50. Openings 2013–2014, 15. The median number of years required for completion of a degree in 2012–2013 were 6. The number of students enrolled full- and part-time who were dismissed or voluntarily withdrew from this program area in 2012–2013 were 1.

Scores: Entries appear in this order: required test or GPA, minimum score (if required), median score of students entering in 2012–2013. *Clinical Psychology PsyD (Doctor of Psychology):* GRE-V 500, 500, GRE-Q 500, 500, GRE-Analytical 4.5, 4.5, overall undergraduate GPA 3.0, 3.0, last 2 years GPA no minimum stated, psychology GPA 3.5, 3.5, Masters GPA 3.75, 3.75.

Other Criteria: (importance of criteria rated low, medium, or high): GRE scores—medium, research experience—low, work experience—high, extracurricular activity—medium, clinically related public service—high, GPA—medium, letters of recommendation—high, interview—high, statement of goals and objectives—high, essay—high, undergraduate major in psychology—medium, specific undergraduate psychology courses taken—high. For additional information on admission requirements, go to http://wspp.edu/admissions.

Student Characteristics: The following represents characteristics of students in 2012–2013 in all graduate psychology programs in the department: Female—full-time 28, part-time 40; Male—full-time 11, part-time 10; African American/Black—full-time 0, part-time 1; Hispanic/Latino(a)—full-time 1, part-time 1; Asian/Pacific Islander—full-time 2, part-time 2; American Indian/Alaska Native—full-time 1, part-time 0; Caucasian/White—full-time 35, part-time 46; Multi-ethnic—full-time 0, part-time 0; students subject to the Americans With Disabilities Act—full-time 1, part-time 1; Unknown ethnicity—full-time 0, part-time 0; International students who hold an F-1 or J-1 Visa—full-time 0, part-time 0.

Financial Information/Assistance:
Tuition for Full-Time Study: *Doctoral:* State residents: per academic year $31,550, $825 per credit hour; Nonstate residents: per academic year $31,550, $825 per credit hour. Tuition is subject to change. Additional fees are assessed to students beyond the costs of tuition for the following: $50 materials fee for all assessment courses; $50 tech fee per semester.

Financial Assistance:
First-Year Students: Teaching assistantships available for first year. Fellowships and scholarships available for first year. Average amount paid per academic year: $3,000. Average number of hours worked per week: 0. Apply by February 15.

Advanced Students: Teaching assistantships available for advanced students. Average number of hours worked per week: 15. Apply by February 15. Traineeships available for advanced students. Average number of hours worked per week: 12. Fellowships and scholarships available for advanced students. Average amount paid per academic year: $1,000. Average number of hours worked per week: 0. Apply by February 15.

Additional Information: Of all students currently enrolled full time, 4% benefited from one or more of the listed financial assistance programs. Application and information available online at: http://wspp.edu/student-support/financial-aid.

Internships/Practica: Doctoral Degree (PsyD Clinical Psychology): For those doctoral students for whom a professional psychology internship was required in this program prior to graduation, (8) students applied for an internship in 2011–2012, with (8) students obtaining an internship. Of those students who obtained an internship, (8) were paid internships. Of those students who obtained an internship, (5) students placed in APA/CPA accredited internships, (3) students placed in internships not APA/CPA accredited, but listed with the Association of Psychology Postdoctoral and Internship Programs (APPIC), (0) students placed in internships conforming to guidelines of the Council of Directors of School Psychology Programs (CDSPP), (0) students placed in internships that were not APA/CPA accredited, APPIC or CDSPP listed. WSPP has an on-site training clinic, the Psychology Center, which is designed to serve two purposes: to provide supervised training to students and to provide quality clinical services to an inner-city, multicultural, disadvantaged population. The Center also maintains contracts and affiliations with a number of local service agencies to provide on-site services. Regardless of whether on- or off-site, all practica are supervised by WSPP faculty to ensure quality of supervision and communication with our DCT. Some 40 supervisors, all licensed and most National Register listed, are readily available. For assessment practica, WSPP maintains a library of psychological tests available for student use free of charge. Thus, all students are guaranteed ample practicum opportunities (the program requires 2,000 hours) without having to search for sites or supervisors. This high level of clinical training has led to our very high internship placement rate to date.

Housing and Day Care: No on-campus housing is available. No on-campus day care facilities are available.

Employment of Department Graduates:
Master's Degree Graduates: Of those who graduated in the academic year 2011–2012, the following categories and numbers represent the postgraduate activities and employment of master's degree graduates: Enrolled in a postdoctoral residency/fellowship (n/a), employed in independent practice (n/a), total from the above (master's) (0).
Doctoral Degree Graduates: Of those who graduated in the academic year 2011–2012, the following categories and numbers represent the postgraduate activities and employment of doctoral degree graduates: Enrolled in a psychology doctoral program (n/a), employed in government agency (1), employed in a community mental health/counseling center (3), employed in a hospital/medical center (1), total from the above (doctoral) (5).

Additional Information:
Orientation, Objectives, and Emphasis of Department: The Wisconsin School of Professional Psychology has as its goal the provision of a doctoral level education that emphasizes the acquisition of the traditional skills which defined the professional in the past, while staying open to new developments as they emerge. Our APA-accredited program balances theoretical and practical coursework, taking its impetus from the American Psychological Association's Vail Conference. The school's curriculum was developed in accordance with APA norms and is continually evaluated to ensure compliance with the requirements of that body. WSPP trains students toward competence in the following areas: self-awareness, assessment, research and evaluation, ethics and professional standards, management and supervision, relationship, intervention, respect for diversity, consultation, social responsibility and community service. In its training philosophy, the school emphasizes clarity of verbal expression in written and oral communication, the development of clinical acumen, and an appreciation of the link between scientific data and clinical practice. Our program's small size and large faculty create abundant opportunities for mentorship with practicing psychologists in an apprentice-like setting.

Special Facilities or Resources: The Wisconsin School of Professional Psychology maintains a Training Clinic which includes facilities for research and practicum work associated with clinical courses. The Training Center houses an outpatient mental health clinic which serves a primarily inner-city, culturally diverse population, as well as provides opportunities for supervised experience with a wide range of clinical problems and populations. The center offers services to the community on a sliding fee basis. Supervision is provided by faculty.

Application Information:
Send to Wisconsin School of Professional Psychology, 9120 West Hampton Avenue, Milwaukee, WI 53225. Students are admitted in the Fall, application deadline January 15; Spring, application deadline October 15. *Fee:* $75.

Wisconsin, University of, Eau Claire
Department of Psychology
Arts and Sciences
University of Wisconsin-Eau Claire
Eau Claire, WI 54702
Telephone: (715) 836-5733
Fax: (715) 836-2214
E-mail: *tusingm@uwec.edu*
Web: *http://www.uwec.edu/Psyc/graduate/index.htm*

Department Information:
1965. Acting Chair: Kate Lang. Number of faculty: total—full-time 18, part-time 3; women—full-time 9, part-time 3.

Programs and Degrees Offered:
Listed in the following order: Program area, degree type (T if terminal Master's), number awarded 7/11–6/12. School Psychology EdS (School Psychology) 7.

Student Applications/Admissions:
Student Applications
School Psychology EdS (School Psychology)—Number full-time enrolled (new admits only) 2012–2013, 10. Number part-time enrolled (new admits only) 2012–2013, 1. Total enrolled 2012–2013 full-time, 20. Total enrolled 2012–2013 part-time, 2. Openings 2013–2014, 8. The median number of years required for completion of a degree in 2012–2013 were 3. The number of students enrolled full- and part-time who were

dismissed or voluntarily withdrew from this program area in 2012–2013 were 0.

Scores: Entries appear in this order: required test or GPA, minimum score (if required), median score of students entering in 2012–2013. *School Psychology EdS (School Psychology):* GRE-V 400, 460, overall undergraduate GPA 3.0, 3.61.

Other Criteria: (importance of criteria rated low, medium, or high): GRE scores—high, research experience—medium, work experience—medium, extracurricular activity—medium, clinically related public service—medium, GPA—high, letters of recommendation—high, interview—high, statement of goals and objectives—high. For additional information on admission requirements, go to http://www.uwec.edu/Psyc/graduate/UWECSchoolPsychAdmissions.htm.

Student Characteristics: The following represents characteristics of students in 2012–2013 in all graduate psychology programs in the department: Female—full-time 18, part-time 2; Male—full-time 2, part-time 0; African American/Black—full-time 0, part-time 0; Hispanic/Latino(a)—full-time 1, part-time 0; Asian/Pacific Islander—full-time 0, part-time 0; American Indian/Alaska Native—full-time 0, part-time 0; Caucasian/White—full-time 19, part-time 2; Multi-ethnic—full-time 0, part-time 0; students subject to the Americans With Disabilities Act—full-time 0, part-time 0; Unknown ethnicity—full-time 0, part-time 0; International students who hold an F-1 or J-1 Visa—full-time 0, part-time 0.

Financial Information/Assistance:
Tuition for Full-Time Study: *Master's:* State residents: per academic year $8,484, $432 per credit hour; Nonstate residents: per academic year $18,290, $975 per credit hour. Tuition is subject to change. See the following website for updates and changes in tuition costs: http://www.uwec.edu/finaid/costs/index.htm.

Financial Assistance:
First-Year Students: Teaching assistantships available for first year. Average amount paid per academic year: $7,013. Average number of hours worked per week: 13. Apply by March 1. Fellowships and scholarships available for first year. Average amount paid per academic year: $500. Apply by March 1.

Advanced Students: Teaching assistantships available for advanced students. Average amount paid per academic year: $7,013. Average number of hours worked per week: 13. Apply by March 1. Fellowships and scholarships available for advanced students. Average amount paid per academic year: $500. Apply by March 1.

Additional Information: Of all students currently enrolled full time, 80% benefited from one or more of the listed financial assistance programs. Application and information available online at: http://www.uwec.edu/admissions/graduate/fininfo.htm.

Internships/Practica: Internships are required for the Educational Specialist degree and comprise the third year of training. Students must complete a year of full-time practice as school psychologists under the supervision of an appropriately credentialed school psychologist. Students may enroll in the internship upon completion of all requirements except the thesis.

Housing and Day Care: No on-campus housing is available. On-campus day care facilities are available. See the following website for more information: http://www.uwec.edu/children/index.htm.

Employment of Department Graduates:
Master's Degree Graduates: Of those who graduated in the academic year 2011–2012, the following categories and numbers represent the postgraduate activities and employment of master's degree graduates: Enrolled in a postdoctoral residency/fellowship (n/a), employed in independent practice (n/a), employed in a professional position in a school system (4), total from the above (master's) (4).

Doctoral Degree Graduates: Of those who graduated in the academic year 2011–2012, the following categories and numbers represent the postgraduate activities and employment of doctoral degree graduates: Enrolled in a psychology doctoral program (n/a), total from the above (doctoral) (0).

Additional Information:
Orientation, Objectives, and Emphasis of Department: The School Psychology program is offered by the Department of Psychology in cooperation with the College of Education and Human Services. The School Psychology program is based on the scientist–practitioner model. As scientists, students develop a strong data- and research-based orientation as problem solvers in the practice of school psychology. As practitioners, students develop a high level of competence in skills required of school psychologists: assessment, intervention, and evaluation at the individual, group, and systems levels. Two values guide all aspects of the school psychologist's activities and the training program: 1) sensitivity to and respect for individual differences and diversity; and 2) high standards of ethical and professional conduct. The program has two unique features: the Human Development Center and an ongoing collaborative relationship with the Lac du Flambeau American Indian community.

Special Facilities or Resources: Extensive on-campus and field site training opportunities are available. Two interdisciplinary clinics—The Human Development Center (Psychology-School Psychology; Special Education-Learning Disabilities and Early Childhood; Communication Sciences and Disorders; and Elementary Education-Reading) and the Psychological Services Center (Psychology-School Psychology and Nursing)—provide on-campus training in diagnostics and intervention services. Area schools, residential facilities for developmentally disabled, emotionally disturbed youth and adults, and clinics offer an extensive array of additional supervised training settings. In addition, the program has a continuing collaborative relationship with the Lac du Flambeau American Indian community which offers opportunities for short-term or semester-long practica.

Information for Students With Physical Disabilities: See the following website for more information: http://www.uwec.edu/SSD/.

Application Information:
Send to Office of Admissions, UW-Eau Claire, Eau Claire, WI 54702-4004. Application available online. URL of online application: http://www.uwec.edu/graduate/index.htm. Students are admitted in the Fall, application deadline March 1. *Fee:* $56.

Wisconsin, University of, La Crosse
Department of Psychology/School Psychology
College of Liberal Studies
1725 State Street, 347 Graff Main Hall
La Crosse, WI 54601
Telephone: (608) 785-8441
Fax: (608) 785-8443
E-mail: *rdixon@uwlax.edu*
Web: *http://www.uwlax.edu/schoolpsych/*

Department Information:
1967. Chairperson: Betsy L. Morgan. Number of faculty: total—full-time 20, part-time 12; women—full-time 14, part-time 5; total—minority—full-time 1, part-time 1; women minority—full-time 1.

Programs and Degrees Offered:
Listed in the following order: Program area, degree type (T if terminal Master's), number awarded 7/11–6/12. School Psychology EdS (School Psychology) 13.

Student Applications/Admissions:
Student Applications
School Psychology EdS (School Psychology)—Applications 2012–2013, 52. Total applicants accepted 2012–2013, 18. Number full-time enrolled (new admits only) 2012–2013, 7. Total enrolled 2012–2013 full-time, 19. Total enrolled 2012–2013 part-time, 13. Openings 2013–2014, 12. The median number of years required for completion of a degree in 2012–2013 were 3. The number of students enrolled full- and part-time who were dismissed or voluntarily withdrew from this program area in 2012–2013 were 0.

Scores: Entries appear in this order: required test or GPA, minimum score (if required), median score of students entering in 2012–2013. *School Psychology EdS (School Psychology):* GRE-V no minimum stated, 149, GRE-Q no minimum stated, 145, GRE-Analytical no minimum stated, 4.0, overall undergraduate GPA no minimum stated, 3.48, last 2 years GPA no minimum stated, 3.59, psychology GPA no minimum stated, 3.58.

Other Criteria: (importance of criteria rated low, medium, or high): GRE scores—medium, research experience—medium, work experience—medium, extracurricular activity—medium, clinically related public service—high, GPA—high, letters of recommendation—high, interview—high, statement of goals and objectives—high, Personal Potential Index—high, undergraduate major in psychology—low, specific undergraduate psychology courses taken—low. For additional information on admission requirements, go to http://www.uwlax.edu/schoolpsych/How to Apply.htm.

Student Characteristics: The following represents characteristics of students in 2012–2013 in all graduate psychology programs in the department: Female—full-time 16, part-time 10; Male—full-time 3, part-time 3; African American/Black—full-time 1, part-time 0; Hispanic/Latino(a)—full-time 0, part-time 0; Asian/Pacific Islander—full-time 0, part-time 1; American Indian/Alaska Native—full-time 0, part-time 0; Caucasian/White—full-time 18, part-time 12; Multi-ethnic—full-time 0, part-time 0; students subject to the Americans With Disabilities Act—full-time 0, part-time 0; Unknown ethnicity—full-time 0, part-time 0; International students who hold an F-1 or J-1 Visa—full-time 0, part-time 0.

Financial Information/Assistance:
Tuition for Full-Time Study: *Master's:* State residents: per academic year $8,760, $487 per credit hour; Nonstate residents: per academic year $17,892, $994 per credit hour. Tuition is subject to change. Additional fees are assessed to students beyond the costs of tuition for the following: Special fees may be assessed for certain courses for supplemental materials and/or equipment. See the following website for updates and changes in tuition costs: http://www.uwlax.edu/cashiers/tuitionfeeschedule.htm.

Financial Assistance:
First-Year Students: Research assistantships available for first year. Average amount paid per academic year: $4,454. Average number of hours worked per week: 9. Apply by March 1.

Advanced Students: Research assistantships available for advanced students. Average amount paid per academic year: $4,454. Average number of hours worked per week: 9. Apply by March 1.

Additional Information: Of all students currently enrolled full time, 32% benefited from one or more of the listed financial assistance programs. Application and information available online at: http://www.uwlax.edu/schoolpsych/Graduate-Assistantships.htm.

Internships/Practica: The School Psychology program prepares graduate students for certification as School Psychologists through academic coursework, 700 hours of supervised school practica, and a one year, 1200-hour school internship. Graduate students are placed in local schools as early and intensively as possible. During their second, third and fourth semesters students spend two days per week working in local schools under the direct supervision of experienced school psychologists. During these school practica, students develop professional skills in assessment, consultation, intervention, counseling, and case management. Many of the core courses require projects which are completed in the schools during practica.

Housing and Day Care: On-campus housing is available. See the following website for more information: http://www.uwlax.edu/ResLife/. On-campus day care facilities are available. See the following website for more information: http://www.uwlax.edu/childcare/.

Employment of Department Graduates:
Master's Degree Graduates: Of those who graduated in the academic year 2011–2012, the following categories and numbers represent the postgraduate activities and employment of master's degree graduates: Enrolled in a postdoctoral residency/fellowship (n/a), employed in independent practice (n/a), employed in a professional position in a school system (11), total from the above (master's) (11).

Doctoral Degree Graduates: Of those who graduated in the academic year 2011–2012, the following categories and numbers represent the postgraduate activities and employment of doctoral degree graduates: Enrolled in a psychology doctoral program (n/a), total from the above (doctoral) (0).

Additional Information:

Orientation, Objectives, and Emphasis of Department: The emphasis of this program is to train school psychologists who are effective teacher, parent and school consultants. The program also emphasizes a pupil services model which addresses the educational and mental health needs of all children. The School Psychology knowledge base includes areas of Professional School Psychology, Educational Psychology, Psychological Foundations, Educational Foundations, and Mental Health. To provide psychological services in education, graduates of the School Psychology program must also have considerable knowledge of curriculum, special education and pupil services. Graduates of the program are employed in public schools or educational agencies which serve public schools.

Special Facilities or Resources: Extensive fieldwork in local schools is a key to professional training. Faculty work closely with field supervisors and observe student performance in the field.

Information for Students With Physical Disabilities: See the following website for more information: http://www.uwlax.edu/drs/.

Application Information:

Send to School Psychology Admissions, 347 Graff Main Hall, University of Wisconsin-La Crosse, 1725 State Street, La Crosse, WI 54601. Application available online. URL of online application: http://www.uwlax.edu/admissions/html/gradmis.htm. Students are admitted in the Fall, application deadline January 31. *Fee:* $56.

Wisconsin, University of, Madison

Department of Counseling Psychology, Counseling Psychology Program
School of Education
335 Education Building - 1000 Bascom Mall
Madison, WI 53706-1326
Telephone: (608) 262-4807
Fax: (608) 265-3347
E-mail: *counpsych@education.wisc.edu*
Web: *http://counselingpsych.education.wisc.edu/*

Department Information:

1964. Chairperson: Alberta M. Gloria. Number of faculty: total—full-time 9, part-time 1; women—full-time 3, part-time 1; total—minority—full-time 5; women minority—full-time 2; faculty subject to the Americans With Disabilities Act 1.

Programs and Degrees Offered:

Listed in the following order: Program area, degree type (T if terminal Master's), number awarded 7/11–6/12. Counseling MA/MS (Master of Arts/Science) (T) 15, Counseling Psychology PhD (Doctor of Philosophy) 9.

APA Accreditation: Counseling PhD (Doctor of Philosophy). Student Outcome Data Website: http://counselingpsych.education.wisc.edu/cp/phd-program/phd-program-outcomes.

Student Applications/Admissions:

Student Applications

Counseling MA/MS (Master of Arts/Science)—Applications 2012–2013, 224. Total applicants accepted 2012–2013, 33. Number full-time enrolled (new admits only) 2012–2013, 11. Number part-time enrolled (new admits only) 2012–2013, 2. Total enrolled 2012–2013 full-time, 25. Total enrolled 2012–2013 part-time, 9. Openings 2013–2014, 14. The median number of years required for completion of a degree in 2012–2013 were 2. The number of students enrolled full- and part-time who were dismissed or voluntarily withdrew from this program area in 2012–2013 were 0. *Counseling Psychology PhD (Doctor of Philosophy)*—Applications 2012–2013, 154. Total applicants accepted 2012–2013, 8. Number full-time enrolled (new admits only) 2012–2013, 7. Number part-time enrolled (new admits only) 2012–2013, 0. Total enrolled 2012–2013 full-time, 38. Total enrolled 2012–2013 part-time, 5. Openings 2013–2014, 8. The median number of years required for completion of a degree in 2012–2013 were 6. The number of students enrolled full- and part-time who were dismissed or voluntarily withdrew from this program area in 2012–2013 were 2.

Scores: Entries appear in this order: required test or GPA, minimum score (if required), median score of students entering in 2012–2013. *Counseling MA/MS (Master of Arts/Science):* GRE-V no minimum stated, GRE-Q no minimum stated, GRE-Analytical no minimum stated, last 2 years GPA 3.0; *Counseling Psychology PhD (Doctor of Philosophy):* GRE-V no minimum stated, GRE-Q no minimum stated, GRE-Analytical no minimum stated, last 2 years GPA 3.0.

Other Criteria: (importance of criteria rated low, medium, or high): GRE scores—medium, research experience—high, work experience—medium, extracurricular activity—high, clinically related public service—high, GPA—medium, letters of recommendation—high, interview—high, statement of goals and objectives—high, undergraduate major in psychology—high, specific undergraduate psychology courses taken—medium. The information above applies to our Counseling Psychology PhD program applicants. For Counseling MS applicants, all criteria remain the same except: research experience is low, extracurricular activity is medium, an interview may not be required, undergraduate major in psychology is medium and specific undergraduate psychology courses taken is high.

Student Characteristics: The following represents characteristics of students in 2012–2013 in all graduate psychology programs in the department: Female—full-time 43, part-time 6; Male—full-time 20, part-time 8; African American/Black—full-time 5, part-time 2; Hispanic/Latino(a)—full-time 15, part-time 2; Asian/Pacific Islander—full-time 13, part-time 0; American Indian/Alaska Native—full-time 1, part-time 3; Caucasian/White—full-time 28, part-time 7; Multi-ethnic—full-time 1, part-time 0; students subject to the Americans With Disabilities Act—full-time 0, part-time 0; Unknown ethnicity—full-time 0, part-time 0; International students who hold an F-1 or J-1 Visa—full-time 7, part-time 0.

Financial Information/Assistance:

Tuition for Full-Time Study: *Master's:* State residents: per academic year $11,838, $742 per credit hour; Nonstate residents: per academic year $25,165, $1,575 per credit hour. *Doctoral:* State residents: per academic year $11,838, $742 per credit hour; Nonstate residents: per academic year $25,165, $1,575 per credit hour. Tuition is subject to change. Additional fees are assessed to students beyond the costs of tuition for the following: Some courses carry an additional course fee of $50 or $200. See the following website for updates and changes in tuition costs: http://registrar.wisc.edu/tuition_&_fees.htm.

Financial Assistance:

First-Year Students: Teaching assistantships available for first year. Average amount paid per academic year: $14,000. Average number of hours worked per week: 13. Research assistantships available for first year. Average amount paid per academic year: $14,000. Average number of hours worked per week: 13. Fellowships and scholarships available for first year. Average amount paid per academic year: $14,000. Average number of hours worked per week: 13.

Advanced Students: Teaching assistantships available for advanced students. Average amount paid per academic year: $14,000. Average number of hours worked per week: 13. Research assistantships available for advanced students. Average amount paid per academic year: $14,000. Average number of hours worked per week: 13. Fellowships and scholarships available for advanced students. Average amount paid per academic year: $14,000. Average number of hours worked per week: 13.

Additional Information: Of all students currently enrolled full time, 35% benefited from one or more of the listed financial assistance programs. Application and information available online at: http://counselingpsych.education.wisc.edu/cp/phd-program/funding.

Internships/Practica: Doctoral Degree (PhD Counseling Psychology): For those doctoral students for whom a professional psychology internship was required in this program prior to graduation, (8) students applied for an internship in 2011–2012, with (8) students obtaining an internship. Of those students who obtained an internship, (8) were paid internships. Of those students who obtained an internship, (7) students placed in APA/CPA accredited internships, (1) students placed in internships not APA/CPA accredited, but listed with the Association of Psychology Postdoctoral and Internship Programs (APPIC), (0) students placed in internships conforming to guidelines of the Council of Directors of School Psychology Programs (CDSPP), (0) students placed in internships that were not APA/CPA accredited, APPIC or CDSPP listed. Master's Degree (MA/MS Counseling): An internship experience, such as a final research project or "capstone" experience is required of graduates. Both master's and doctoral students are required to take at least two semesters of practica. For doctoral students (and some master's students), local sites include Dane County Community Mental Health Agency, Mendota Mental Health Institute, University of Wisconsin Counseling and Consultation Services, Veteran's Administration Hospital, and Family Therapy, Inc. The majority of practicum placements are in the Madison area but some are placed in nearby metropolitan areas in Wisconsin such as Milwaukee and Green Bay, as well as in rural communities served by regional mental health clinics.

Housing and Day Care: On-campus housing is available. See the following website for more information: http://www.housing.wisc.edu/universityapartments. On-campus day care facilities are available. See the following website for more information: http://occfr.wisc.edu/child_care.htm.

Employment of Department Graduates:

Master's Degree Graduates: Of those who graduated in the academic year 2011–2012, the following categories and numbers represent the postgraduate activities and employment of master's degree graduates: Enrolled in a psychology doctoral program (1), enrolled in a postdoctoral residency/fellowship (n/a), employed in independent practice (n/a), employed in other positions at a higher education institution (2), employed in a professional position in a school system (5), employed in business or industry (1), employed in government agency (2), employed in a community mental health/counseling center (3), do not know (1), total from the above (master's) (15).

Doctoral Degree Graduates: Of those who graduated in the academic year 2011–2012, the following categories and numbers represent the postgraduate activities and employment of doctoral degree graduates: Enrolled in a psychology doctoral program (n/a), enrolled in a postdoctoral residency/fellowship (6), employed in an academic position at a university (2), employed in a community mental health/counseling center (1), total from the above (doctoral) (9).

Additional Information:

Orientation, Objectives, and Emphasis of Department: The master's and doctoral programs are intended to provide a closely integrated didactic experimental curriculum for the preparation of counseling professionals. The master's degree strongly emphasizes service delivery, and its practicum/internship components reflect that emphasis. The doctoral degree emphasizes the integration of counseling and psychological theory and practice with substantive development of research skills in the domains encompassed by counseling psychology. The PhD program in counseling psychology is APA-accredited utilizing the scientist–practitioner model. Students are prepared for academic, service-delivery, research, and administrative positions in professional psychology. The Department infuses principles of multiculturalism throughout the curriculum.

Special Facilities or Resources: The department possesses excellent computer facilities including multimedia production. Also, two counseling psychologists employed at the University Counseling Service are adjunct professors in the department and provide us with on-going linkage with that service for practica and internships. We also have very up-to-date computer software assessment resources. The department, together with the departments of Educational Psychology, Rehabilitation Psychology and Special Education, currently utilize an interdisciplinary training center that provides professional training practices.

Information for Students With Physical Disabilities: See the following website for more information: http://www.mcburney.wisc.edu/.

Application Information:
Send to Department of Counseling Psychology, Graduate Admissions, UW-Madison, 335 Education Building - 1000 Bascom Mall, Madison, WI, 53706-1326. Application available online. URL of online application: https://www.gradsch.wisc.edu/eapp/eapp.pl. Students are admitted in the Fall, application deadline December 1. The application deadline for PhD applicants is December 1. The application deadline for MS applicants is January 15. *Fee:* $56.

Wisconsin, University of, Madison (2012 data)
Department of Educational Psychology, School Psychology
  Program
1025 West Johnson Street
Madison, WI 53706-1796
Telephone: (608) 262-3432
Fax: (608) 262-0843
E-mail: *edpsych@wisc.edu*
Web: *http://www.education.wisc.edu/edpsych/index.html*

Department Information:
1960. Chairperson: Charles W. Kalish. Number of faculty: total—full-time 18; women—full-time 7; total—minority—full-time 1; women minority—full-time 1.

Programs and Degrees Offered:
Listed in the following order: Program area, degree type (T if terminal Master's), number awarded 7/11–6/12. School Psychology PhD (Doctor of Philosophy) 3, Quantitative Psychology PhD (Doctor of Philosophy) 2, Learning Science PhD (Doctor of Philosophy) 1, Human Development PhD (Doctor of Philosophy) 1.

APA Accreditation: School PhD (Doctor of Philosophy).

Student Applications/Admissions:
Student Applications
School Psychology PhD (Doctor of Philosophy)—Applications 2012–2013, 105. Total applicants accepted 2012–2013, 26. Number full-time enrolled (new admits only) 2012–2013, 7. Number part-time enrolled (new admits only) 2012–2013, 0. Total enrolled 2012–2013 full-time, 28. Total enrolled 2012–2013 part-time, 8. Openings 2013–2014, 8. The median number of years required for completion of a degree in 2012–2013 were 6. The number of students enrolled full- and part-time who were dismissed or voluntarily withdrew from this program area in 2012–2013 were 1. *Quantitative Psychology PhD (Doctor of Philosophy)*—Applications 2012–2013, 22. Total applicants accepted 2012–2013, 8. Number full-time enrolled (new admits only) 2012–2013, 3. Total enrolled 2012–2013 full-time, 7. Total enrolled 2012–2013 part-time, 4. Openings 2013–2014, 10. The median number of years required for completion of a degree in 2012–2013 were 6. The number of students enrolled full- and part-time who were dismissed or voluntarily withdrew from this program area in 2012–2013 were 0. *Learning Science PhD (Doctor of Philosophy)*—Applications 2012–2013, 24. Total applicants accepted 2012–2013, 4. Number full-time enrolled (new admits only) 2012–2013, 2. Number part-time enrolled (new admits only) 2012–2013, 0. Total enrolled 2012–2013 full-time, 8. Total enrolled 2012–2013 part-time, 11. Openings 2013–2014, 4. The median number of years required for completion of a degree in 2012–2013 were 8. The number of students enrolled full- and part-time who were dismissed or voluntarily withdrew from this program area in 2012–2013 were 0. *Human Development PhD (Doctor of Philosophy)*—Applications 2012–2013, 34. Total applicants

accepted 2012–2013, 17. Number full-time enrolled (new admits only) 2012–2013, 4. Number part-time enrolled (new admits only) 2012–2013, 0. Total enrolled 2012–2013 full-time, 9. Total enrolled 2012–2013 part-time, 9. Openings 2013–2014, 10. The median number of years required for completion of a degree in 2012–2013 were 3. The number of students enrolled full- and part-time who were dismissed or voluntarily withdrew from this program area in 2012–2013 were 0.
Scores: Entries appear in this order: required test or GPA, minimum score (if required), median score of students entering in 2012–2013. *School Psychology PhD (Doctor of Philosophy):* overall undergraduate GPA 3.0, 3.56; *Quantitative Psychology PhD (Doctor of Philosophy):* GRE-V no minimum stated, 559, GRE-Q no minimum stated, 738, overall undergraduate GPA 3.0, 3.72; *Learning Science PhD (Doctor of Philosophy):* GRE-V no minimum stated, 570, GRE-Q no minimum stated, 665, overall undergraduate GPA 3.0, 3.59; *Human Development PhD (Doctor of Philosophy):* GRE-V no minimum stated, 535, GRE-Q no minimum stated, 733, overall undergraduate GPA 3.0, 3.64.
Other Criteria: (importance of criteria rated low, medium, or high): GRE scores—medium, research experience—medium, work experience—medium, extracurricular activity—low, clinically related public service—medium, GPA—medium, letters of recommendation—high, interview—high, statement of goals and objectives—high, undergraduate major in psychology—medium, specific undergraduate psychology courses taken—low.

Student Characteristics: The following represents characteristics of students in 2012–2013 in all graduate psychology programs in the department: Female—full-time 45, part-time 23; Male—full-time 7, part-time 9; African American/Black—full-time 1, part-time 1; Hispanic/Latino(a)—full-time 3, part-time 1; Asian/Pacific Islander—full-time 0, part-time 0; American Indian/Alaska Native—full-time 1, part-time 0; Caucasian/White—full-time 52, part-time 7; Multi-ethnic—full-time 0, part-time 0; students subject to the Americans With Disabilities Act—full-time 0, part-time 0; Unknown ethnicity—full-time 10, part-time 8; International students who hold an F-1 or J-1 Visa—full-time 9, part-time 7.

Financial Information/Assistance:
Tuition for Full-Time Study: *Master's:* State residents: per academic year $11,375, $713 per credit hour; Nonstate residents: per academic year $25,133, $1,573 per credit hour. *Doctoral:* State residents: per academic year $11,375, $713 per credit hour; Nonstate residents: per academic year $25,133, $1,573 per credit hour. Tuition is subject to change. See the following website for updates and changes in tuition costs: http://www.registrar.wisc.edu/.

Financial Assistance:
First-Year Students: Teaching assistantships available for first year. Average amount paid per academic year: $14,087. Average number of hours worked per week: 20. Apply by December 1. Research assistantships available for first year. Average amount

paid per academic year: $16,506. Average number of hours worked per week: 20. Apply by December 1. Traineeships available for first year. Apply by December 1. Fellowships and scholarships available for first year. Average amount paid per academic year: $18,756. Average number of hours worked per week: 0. Apply by December 1.

Advanced Students: Teaching assistantships available for advanced students. Average amount paid per academic year: $16,264. Average number of hours worked per week: 20. Apply by December 1. Research assistantships available for advanced students. Average amount paid per academic year: $16,506. Average number of hours worked per week: 20. Apply by December 1. Traineeships available for advanced students. Apply by December 1. Fellowships and scholarships available for advanced students. Average amount paid per academic year: $18,756. Average number of hours worked per week: 0. Apply by December 1.

Additional Information: Of all students currently enrolled full time, 76% benefited from one or more of the listed financial assistance programs. Application and information available online at: www.wisc.edu/grad.

Internships/Practica: Doctoral Degree (PhD School Psychology): For those doctoral students for whom a professional psychology internship was required in this program prior to graduation, (7) students applied for an internship in 2011–2012, with (7) students obtaining an internship. Of those students who obtained an internship, (7) were paid internships. Of those students who obtained an internship, (0) students placed in APA/CPA accredited internships, (7) students placed in internships not APA/CPA accredited, but listed with the Association of Psychology Postdoctoral and Internship Programs (APPIC), (0) students placed in internships conforming to guidelines of the Council of Directors of School Psychology Programs (CDSPP), (0) students placed in internships that were not APA/CPA accredited, APPIC or CDSPP listed. The School Psychology Program admits students interested in obtaining a PhD. Students working toward this goal complete a two-semester clinical practicum experience during year two (300-hour minimum) and a two-semester field practicum during year three which provides a minimum of 600 clock hours of supervised practice at approved field sites. This practicum experience is provided by the department. After the master's, students are required to complete either an APA approved internship or establish one of their own in a school (public or private), clinic, or hospital that is approved by the program to complete their PhD requirements. It requires a full-time experience (minimum of 2000 hours) for the academic (or calendar) year or half-time for 2 consecutive academic years. The Wisconsin Internship Consortium in Professional School Psychology (WICPSP) is also administered through the School Psychology Program. The primary focus of the predoctoral internship program is to provide advanced training for graduate students from a wide variety of cooperating sites where an internship is provided over several rotations. This internship is implemented according to Ethical Principles of Psychologists (APA, 1992), and the criteria published by the National Register of Health Service Providers and the National Association of School Psychologists are also followed. Criteria endorsed by the Council of Directors of School Psychology are also met.

Housing and Day Care: On-campus housing is available. See the following website for more information: http://www.housing.wisc.edu. On-campus day care facilities are available.

Employment of Department Graduates:
Master's Degree Graduates: Of those who graduated in the academic year 2011–2012, the following categories and numbers represent the postgraduate activities and employment of master's degree graduates: Enrolled in a psychology doctoral program (3), enrolled in a postdoctoral residency/fellowship (n/a), employed in independent practice (n/a), total from the above (master's) (3).
Doctoral Degree Graduates: Of those who graduated in the academic year 2011–2012, the following categories and numbers represent the postgraduate activities and employment of doctoral degree graduates: Enrolled in a psychology doctoral program (n/a), enrolled in another graduate/professional program (0), enrolled in a postdoctoral residency/fellowship (0), employed in independent practice (0), employed in an academic position at a university (0), employed in an academic position at a 2-year/4-year college (0), employed in other positions at a higher education institution (0), employed in a professional position in a school system (3), employed in business or industry (0), employed in government agency (0), employed in a community mental health/counseling center (0), employed in a hospital/medical center (0), still seeking employment (0), not seeking employment (0), other employment position (0), do not know (0), total from the above (doctoral) (3).

Additional Information:
Orientation, Objectives, and Emphasis of Department: The School Psychology program, within the Department of Educational Psychology, prepares professional psychologists to use knowledge of the behavioral sciences in ways that enhance the learning and adjustment of both normal and exceptional children, their families, and their teachers. A balanced emphasis is placed on developing competencies necessary for functioning in both applied settings such as schools and community agencies, and in research positions in institutions of higher education. The program focus is the study of psychological and educational principles which influence the adjustment of individuals from birth to 21 years. Students are required to demonstrate competencies in the substantive content areas of psychological and educational theory and practice.

Special Facilities or Resources: The Educational and Psychological Training Center serves advanced graduate students in educational psychology. It provides diagnostic and treatment services for children and adolescents experiencing a variety of learning and behavior problems. The Laboratory of Experimental Design provides assistance to students and faculty in the design and analysis of research. Members of the laboratory include graduate students and faculty in the quantitative area.

Application Information:
Send to Graduate Admissions Coordinator, Educational Psychology, 1025 West Johnson Street, Madison, WI 53706-1796. Application available online. URL of online application: www.wisc.edu/grad. Students are admitted in the Fall, application deadline December 1. *Fee:* $56.

Wisconsin, University of, Madison
Department of Psychology
College of Letters and Science
W. J. Brogden Psychology Building, 1202 West Johnson
  Street
Madison, WI 53706
Telephone: (608) 262-2079
Fax: (608) 262-4029
E-mail: *gradinfo@psych.wisc.edu*
Web: *http://psych.wisc.edu/*

Department Information:
1888. Chairperson: Patricia G. Devine. Number of faculty: total—full-time 34; women—full-time 18; total—minority—full-time 3; women minority—full-time 3.

Programs and Degrees Offered:
Listed in the following order: Program area, degree type (T if terminal Master's), number awarded 7/11–6/12. Biology Of Brain & Behavior PhD (Doctor of Philosophy) 1, Clinical Psychology PhD (Doctor of Philosophy) 6, Cognitive and Cognitive Neurosciences PhD (Doctor of Philosophy) 3, Developmental Psychology PhD (Doctor of Philosophy) 2, Social Psychology and Personality PhD (Doctor of Philosophy) 0, Individualized Graduate Major PhD (Doctor of Philosophy) 2, Perception PhD (Doctor of Philosophy) 0.

APA Accreditation: Clinical PhD (Doctor of Philosophy). Student Outcome Data Website: http://glial.psych.wisc.edu/index.php/psychgradprospective/psychgradabout/172.

Student Applications/Admissions:
Student Applications
Biology Of Brain & Behavior PhD (Doctor of Philosophy)—Applications 2012–2013, 29. Total applicants accepted 2012–2013, 3. Number full-time enrolled (new admits only) 2012–2013, 1. Number part-time enrolled (new admits only) 2012–2013, 0. Total enrolled 2012–2013 full-time, 7. Total enrolled 2012–2013 part-time, 0. The median number of years required for completion of a degree in 2012–2013 were 6. The number of students enrolled full- and part-time who were dismissed or voluntarily withdrew from this program area in 2012–2013 were 0. *Clinical Psychology PhD (Doctor of Philosophy)*—Applications 2012–2013, 251. Total applicants accepted 2012–2013, 5. Number full-time enrolled (new admits only) 2012–2013, 1. Number part-time enrolled (new admits only) 2012–2013, 0. Total enrolled 2012–2013 full-time, 23. Total enrolled 2012–2013 part-time, 0. The median number of years required for completion of a degree in 2012–2013 were 7. The number of students enrolled full- and part-time who were dismissed or voluntarily withdrew from this program area in 2012–2013 were 0. *Cognitive and Cognitive Neurosciences PhD (Doctor of Philosophy)*—Applications 2012–2013, 56. Total applicants accepted 2012–2013, 3. Number full-time enrolled (new admits only) 2012–2013, 1. Number part-time enrolled (new admits only) 2012–2013, 0. Total enrolled 2012–2013 full-time, 12. Total enrolled 2012–2013 part-time, 0. The median number of years required for completion of a degree in 2012–2013 were 7. *Developmental Psychology PhD (Doctor of Philosophy)*—Applications 2012–2013, 48. Total applicants accepted 2012–

2013, 5. Number full-time enrolled (new admits only) 2012–2013, 1. Total enrolled 2012–2013 full-time, 7. The median number of years required for completion of a degree in 2012–2013 were 6. The number of students enrolled full- and part-time who were dismissed or voluntarily withdrew from this program area in 2012–2013 were 0. *Social Psychology and Personality PhD (Doctor of Philosophy)*—Applications 2012–2013, 56. Total applicants accepted 2012–2013, 5. Number full-time enrolled (new admits only) 2012–2013, 2. Number part-time enrolled (new admits only) 2012–2013, 0. Total enrolled 2012–2013 full-time, 11. Total enrolled 2012–2013 part-time, 0. The median number of years required for completion of a degree in 2012–2013 were 6. The number of students enrolled full- and part-time who were dismissed or voluntarily withdrew from this program area in 2012–2013 were 0. *Individualized Graduate Major PhD (Doctor of Philosophy)*—Applications 2012–2013, 21. Total applicants accepted 2012–2013, 3. Number full-time enrolled (new admits only) 2012–2013, 3. Number part-time enrolled (new admits only) 2012–2013, 0. Total enrolled 2012–2013 full-time, 15. Total enrolled 2012–2013 part-time, 0. The median number of years required for completion of a degree in 2012–2013 were 6. The number of students enrolled full- and part-time who were dismissed or voluntarily withdrew from this program area in 2012–2013 were 0. *Perception PhD (Doctor of Philosophy)*—Applications 2012–2013, 0. Total applicants accepted 2012–2013, 0. Number full-time enrolled (new admits only) 2012–2013, 0. Number part-time enrolled (new admits only) 2012–2013, 0. Total enrolled 2012–2013 full-time, 1. Total enrolled 2012–2013 part-time, 0. The number of students enrolled full- and part-time who were dismissed or voluntarily withdrew from this program area in 2012–2013 were 0.

Scores: Entries appear in this order: required test or GPA, minimum score (if required), median score of students entering in 2012–2013. *Biology of Brain & Behavior PhD (Doctor of Philosophy)*: GRE-V no minimum stated, GRE-Q no minimum stated, GRE-Analytical no minimum stated, overall undergraduate GPA 3.0, last 2 years GPA 3.0; *Clinical Psychology PhD (Doctor of Philosophy)*: GRE-V no minimum stated, GRE-Q no minimum stated, GRE-Analytical no minimum stated, overall undergraduate GPA 3.0, last 2 years GPA 3.0; *Cognitive and Cognitive Neurosciences PhD (Doctor of Philosophy)*: GRE-V no minimum stated, GRE-Q no minimum stated, GRE-Analytical no minimum stated, overall undergraduate GPA 3.0, last 2 years GPA 3.0; *Developmental Psychology PhD (Doctor of Philosophy)*: GRE-V no minimum stated, GRE-Q no minimum stated, GRE-Analytical no minimum stated, overall undergraduate GPA 3.0, last 2 years GPA 3.0; *Social Psychology and Personality PhD (Doctor of Philosophy)*: GRE-V no minimum stated, GRE-Q no minimum stated, GRE-Analytical no minimum stated, overall undergraduate GPA 3.0, last 2 years GPA 3.0; *Individualized Graduate Major PhD (Doctor of Philosophy)*: GRE-V no minimum stated, GRE-Q no minimum stated, GRE-Analytical no minimum stated, overall undergraduate GPA 3.0, last 2 years GPA 3.0; *Perception PhD (Doctor of Philosophy)*: GRE-V no minimum stated, GRE-Q no minimum stated, GRE-Analytical no minimum stated, overall undergraduate GPA 3.0, last 2 years GPA 3.0.

Other Criteria: (importance of criteria rated low, medium, or high): GRE scores—high, research experience—high, GPA—high, letters of recommendation—high, interview—high, statement of goals and objectives—high, undergraduate major in psychology—low, specific undergraduate psychology courses taken—low. For additional information on admission requirements, go to http://glial.psych.wisc.edu/index.php/psychgradprospective.

Student Characteristics: The following represents characteristics of students in 2012–2013 in all graduate psychology programs in the department: Female—full-time 47, part-time 0; Male—full-time 29, part-time 0; African American/Black—full-time 3, part-time 0; Hispanic/Latino(a)—full-time 1, part-time 0; Asian/Pacific Islander—full-time 7, part-time 0; American Indian/Alaska Native—full-time 1, part-time 0; Caucasian/White—full-time 55, part-time 0; Multi-ethnic—full-time 0, part-time 0; students subject to the Americans With Disabilities Act—full-time 0, part-time 0; Unknown ethnicity—full-time 9, part-time 0; International students who hold an F-1 or J-1 Visa—full-time 9, part-time 0.

Financial Information/Assistance:

Tuition for Full-Time Study: *Doctoral:* State residents: per academic year $11,838; Nonstate residents: per academic year $25,164. Tuition is subject to change. See the following website for updates and changes in tuition costs: http://registrar.wisc.edu/tuition_&_fees.htm.

Financial Assistance:

First-Year Students: Teaching assistantships available for first year. Average amount paid per academic year: $14,088. Average number of hours worked per week: 20. Apply by December 1. Research assistantships available for first year. Average amount paid per academic year: $16,668. Average number of hours worked per week: 20. Apply by December 1. Traineeships available for first year. Average amount paid per academic year: $21,180. Average number of hours worked per week: 20. Apply by December 1. Fellowships and scholarships available for first year. Average amount paid per academic year: $18,567. Average number of hours worked per week: 0. Apply by December 1.

Advanced Students: Teaching assistantships available for advanced students. Average amount paid per academic year: $16,264. Average number of hours worked per week: 20. Research assistantships available for advanced students. Average amount paid per academic year: $16,668. Average number of hours worked per week: 20. Traineeships available for advanced students. Average amount paid per academic year: $21,180. Average number of hours worked per week: 20. Fellowships and scholarships available for advanced students. Average amount paid per academic year: $12,375. Average number of hours worked per week: 0.

Additional Information: Of all students currently enrolled full time, 100% benefited from one or more of the listed financial assistance programs. Application and information available online at: http://info.gradsch.wisc.edu/education/funding/index.html.

Internships/Practica: Doctoral Degree (PhD Clinical Psychology): For those doctoral students for whom a professional psychology internship was required in this program prior to graduation, (6) students applied for an internship in 2011–2012, with (6) students obtaining an internship. Of those students who obtained an internship, (6) were paid internships. Of those students who obtained an internship, (6) students placed in APA/CPA accredited internships, (0) students placed in internships not APA/CPA accredited, but listed with the Association of Psychology Postdoctoral and Internship Programs (APPIC), (0) students

placed in internships conforming to guidelines of the Council of Directors of School Psychology Programs (CDSPP), (0) students placed in internships that were not APA/CPA accredited, APPIC or CDSPP listed. Clinical psychology graduate students are required to complete a minimum of 400 hours of practicum experience, of which at least 150 hours are in direct service experience and at least 75 hours are in formally scheduled supervision. Each student will complete a 160-hour clerkship at a preapproved site which is designed to expose students to diverse clinical populations and the practice of clinical psychology in an applied setting. Also, a one-year internship is required.

Housing and Day Care: On-campus housing is available. See the following website for more information: http://www.housing.wisc.edu/universityapartments. On-campus day care facilities are available. See the following website for more information: http://occfr.wisc.edu/child_care.htm.

Employment of Department Graduates:

Master's Degree Graduates: Of those who graduated in the academic year 2011–2012, the following categories and numbers represent the postgraduate activities and employment of master's degree graduates: Enrolled in a postdoctoral residency/fellowship (n/a), employed in independent practice (n/a), total from the above (master's) (0).

Doctoral Degree Graduates: Of those who graduated in the academic year 2011–2012, the following categories and numbers represent the postgraduate activities and employment of doctoral degree graduates: Enrolled in a psychology doctoral program (n/a), total from the above (doctoral) (0).

Additional Information:

Orientation, Objectives, and Emphasis of Department: The psychology PhD program is characterized by the following goals: emphasis both on extensive academic training in general psychology and on intensive research training in the student's particular area of concentration, a wide offering of content courses and seminars permitting the student considerable freedom in working out a program of study in collaboration with the major professor, and early and continuing commitment to research. Students are expected to become competent scholars and creative scientists in their own areas of concentration.

Special Facilities or Resources: The department has an extraordinary array of research facilities. Virtually all laboratories are fully computer controlled, and the department's general-purpose facilities are freely available to all graduate students. The Brogden Building and the Harlow Primate Laboratory have special facilities for housing animals, as well as for behavioral, pharmacological, anatomical, immunological, and physiological studies. We are well-equipped for studies of visual, auditory, and language perception and other areas of cognitive psychology. In addition, the Psychology Department Research and Training Clinic is housed in the Brogden Building. Many of the faculty and graduate students are affiliated with the Institute of Aging, the Waisman Center on Mental Retardation and Human Development, the Wisconsin Regional Primate Research Center, the Health Emotions Center, the Neuroscience Training Program, the Keck Neuroimaging Center, the Hearing Training Program, the Institute for Research on Poverty, the NSF National Consortium on Violence Research, and the Women's Studies Research Center. There are strong ties to the departments of Anatomy, Anthropology, Communicative Disorders, Educational Psychology, Entomology, Immunology, Industrial Engineering, Ophthalmology, Psychiatry, Sociology, Wildlife Ecology, Zoology, the Mass Communication Research Center, the Institute for Research on Poverty, and the Survey Research Laboratory.

Information for Students With Physical Disabilities: See the following website for more information: http://www.mcburney.wisc.edu/.

Application Information:
Send to Graduate Admissions, Department of Psychology, University of Wisconsin, 1202 West Johnson Street, Madison, WI 53706. Application available online. URL of online application: https://www.gradsch.wisc.edu/eapp/eapp.pl. Students are admitted in the Fall, application deadline December 1. *Fee:* $56.

Wisconsin, University of, Madison (2012 data)
Human Development & Family Studies
School of Human Ecology
4198 Nancy Nicolas Hall, 1300 Linden Drive
Madison, WI 53706
Telephone: (608) 263-2381
Fax: (608) 265-6048
E-mail: *hdfs@mail.sohe.wisc.edu*
Web: *http://www.sohe.wisc.edu/hdfs/*

Department Information:
1903. Chairperson: Julie Poehlmann. Number of faculty: total—full-time 11, part-time 1; women—full-time 8, part-time 1; total—minority—full-time 2; women minority—full-time 2.

Programs and Degrees Offered:
Listed in the following order: Program area, degree type (T if terminal Master's), number awarded 7/11–6/12. Human Development & Family Studies MA/MS (Master of Arts/Science) 4, Human Development & Family Studies PhD (Doctor of Philosophy) 5.

Student Applications/Admissions:
Student Applications
Human Development & Family Studies MA/MS (Master of Arts/Science)—Applications 2012–2013, 10. Total applicants accepted 2012–2013, 5. Number full-time enrolled (new admits only) 2012–2013, 3. Number part-time enrolled (new admits only) 2012–2013, 0. Total enrolled 2012–2013 full-time, 4. Total enrolled 2012–2013 part-time, 0. Openings 2013–2014, 5. The median number of years required for completion of a degree in 2012–2013 were 4. The number of students enrolled full- and part-time who were dismissed or voluntarily withdrew from this program area in 2012–2013 were 0. *Human Development & Family Studies PhD (Doctor of Philosophy)*—Applications 2012–2013, 46. Total applicants accepted 2012–2013, 19. Number full-time enrolled (new admits only) 2012–2013, 4. Number part-time enrolled (new admits only) 2012–2013, 0. Total enrolled 2012–2013 full-time, 18. Openings 2013–2014, 5. The median number of years required for completion of a degree in 2012–2013 were 6. The number of students

enrolled full- and part-time who were dismissed or voluntarily withdrew from this program area in 2012–2013 were 0.
Scores: Entries appear in this order: required test or GPA, minimum score (if required), median score of students entering in 2012–2013. *Human Development & Family Studies MA/MS (Master of Arts/Science):* GRE-V no minimum stated, 512, GRE-Q no minimum stated, 570, GRE-Analytical no minimum stated, 3.9, overall undergraduate GPA 3.0, 3.38; *Human Development & Family Studies PhD (Doctor of Philosophy):* GRE-V no minimum stated, 571, GRE-Q no minimum stated, 668, GRE-Analytical no minimum stated, 4.4, overall undergraduate GPA 3.0, 3.70.
Other Criteria: (importance of criteria rated low, medium, or high): GRE scores—medium, research experience—medium, work experience—low, GPA—high, letters of recommendation—high, statement of goals and objectives—high, Fit w/ faculty interests—high. For additional information on admission requirements, go to http://www.grad.wisc.edu/education/admissions/index.html.

Student Characteristics: The following represents characteristics of students in 2012–2013 in all graduate psychology programs in the department: Female—full-time 20, part-time 0; Male—full-time 2, part-time 0; African American/Black—full-time 1, part-time 0; Hispanic/Latino(a)—full-time 1, part-time 0; Asian/Pacific Islander—full-time 1, part-time 0; American Indian/Alaska Native—full-time 1, part-time 0; Caucasian/White—full-time 18, part-time 0; Multi-ethnic—full-time 0, part-time 0; students subject to the Americans With Disabilities Act—full-time 0, part-time 0; Unknown ethnicity—full-time 0, part-time 0; International students who hold an F-1 or J-1 Visa—full-time 5, part-time 0.

Financial Information/Assistance:
Tuition for Full-Time Study: *Master's:* State residents: per academic year $10,941, $685 per credit hour; Nonstate residents: per academic year $25,108, $1,571 per credit hour. *Doctoral:* State residents: per academic year $10,941, $685 per credit hour; Nonstate residents: per academic year $25,108, $1,571 per credit hour. Tuition is subject to change. See the following website for updates and changes in tuition costs: http://registrar.wisc.edu/tuition_&_fees.htm.

Financial Assistance:
First-Year Students: Teaching assistantships available for first year. Average amount paid per academic year: $9,392. Average number of hours worked per week: 13. Fellowships and scholarships available for first year.
Advanced Students: Teaching assistantships available for advanced students. Average amount paid per academic year: $10,843. Average number of hours worked per week: 13. Research assistantships available for advanced students. Average number of hours worked per week: 13. Fellowships and scholarships available for advanced students.
Additional Information: Of all students currently enrolled full time, 95% benefited from one or more of the listed financial assistance programs. Application and information available online at: http://www.grad.wisc.edu/education/funding/index.h.

Housing and Day Care: On-campus housing is available. See the following website for more information: http://www.housing.wisc.

edu/. On-campus day care facilities are available. See the following website for more information: http://occfr.wisc.edu.

Employment of Department Graduates:

Master's Degree Graduates: Of those who graduated in the academic year 2011–2012, the following categories and numbers represent the postgraduate activities and employment of master's degree graduates: Enrolled in a psychology doctoral program (3), enrolled in a postdoctoral residency/fellowship (n/a), employed in independent practice (n/a), do not know (1), total from the above (master's) (4).

Doctoral Degree Graduates: Of those who graduated in the academic year 2011–2012, the following categories and numbers represent the postgraduate activities and employment of doctoral degree graduates: Enrolled in a psychology doctoral program (n/a), employed in an academic position at a 2-year/4-year college (1), employed in other positions at a higher education institution (1), employed in government agency (1), do not know (2), total from the above (doctoral) (5).

Additional Information:

Orientation, Objectives, and Emphasis of Department: The UW Human Development and Family Studies Graduate Program provides opportunities for advanced study and research on human development and families across the life span. Two assumptions are basic to the philosophy and organization of the program. First, we can only understand individual development within its social context, and families are an essential component of this context. Second, we can only understand families within their larger social context—historical change, social class, ethnicity, and public policy. The program offers courses on development in infancy, childhood, adolescence, adulthood, and old age. Other courses focus on family relationships, process, and diversity. The faculty bring the perspectives of many different disciplines and methodologies to their work. Faculty and students never lose sight, however, of the connections among human development, family life, and the broader sociohistorical context.

Special Facilities or Resources: Because the department has joint faculty in UW-Extension, students often work in the community doing community based research and outreach projects. Departmental faculty have affiliated appointments with research centers and other programs on campus, which students have access to. The Family Interaction Lab in the department provides a naturalistic, home-like setting for unobtrusive videotaping of interactions. A control room is located adjacent to the interaction room for camera control, taping, editing, dubbing and coding of videotapes. The department is also affiliated with the Center for Excellence in Family Studies.

Information for Students With Physical Disabilities: See the following website for more information: http://www.mcburney. wisc.edu/services/.

Application Information:
Send to Graduate Admissions, Human Development & Family Studies Graduate Program, University of Wisconsin—Madison, 4198 Nancy Nicolas Hall, 1300 Linden Drive, Madison, WI 53706. Application available online. URL of online application: https://www.gradsch.wisc. edu/eapp/eapp.pl. Students are admitted in the Fall, application deadline early January *Fee:* $56.

Wisconsin, University of, Milwaukee
Department of Psychology
College of Letters and Science
P.O. Box 413
Milwaukee, WI 53201-0413
Telephone: (414) 229-7228
Fax: (414) 229-5219
E-mail: *suelima@uwm.edu*
Web: *http://www4.uwm.edu/letsci/psychology/*

Department Information:
1956. Chairperson: W. Hobart Davies. Number of faculty: total—full-time 28; women—full-time 10; total—minority—full-time 2.

Programs and Degrees Offered:
Listed in the following order: Program area, degree type (T if terminal Master's), number awarded 7/11–6/12. Experimental Behavior Analysis MA/MS (Master of Arts/Science) (T) 0, Experimental Health Psychology MA/MS (Master of Arts/Science) (T) 2, Experimental PhD (Doctor of Philosophy) 4, Clinical Psychology PhD (Doctor of Philosophy) 6.

APA Accreditation: Clinical PhD (Doctor of Philosophy). Student Outcome Data Website: http://www4.uwm.edu/letsci/psychology/ graduate/phdprograms/clinical/index.cfm.

Student Applications/Admissions:

Student Applications

Experimental Behavior Analysis MA/MS (Master of Arts/Science)—Applications 2012–2013, 20. Total applicants accepted 2012–2013, 4. Number full-time enrolled (new admits only) 2012–2013, 4. Number part-time enrolled (new admits only) 2012–2013, 0. Total enrolled 2012–2013 full-time, 10. Total enrolled 2012–2013 part-time, 0. Openings 2013–2014, 6. The number of students enrolled full- and part-time who were dismissed or voluntarily withdrew from this program area in 2012–2013 were 0. *Experimental Health Psychology MA/MS (Master of Arts/Science)*—Applications 2012–2013, 20. Total applicants accepted 2012–2013, 4. Number full-time enrolled (new admits only) 2012–2013, 4. Number part-time enrolled (new admits only) 2012–2013, 0. Total enrolled 2012–2013 full-time, 4. Total enrolled 2012–2013 part-time, 0. Openings 2013–2014, 5. The median number of years required for completion of a degree in 2012–2013 were 2. The number of students enrolled full- and part-time who were dismissed or voluntarily withdrew from this program area in 2012–2013 were 0. *Experimental PhD (Doctor of Philosophy)*—Applications 2012–2013, 49. Total applicants accepted 2012–2013, 8. Number full-time enrolled (new admits only) 2012–2013, 8. Number part-time enrolled (new admits only) 2012–2013, 0. Total enrolled 2012–2013 full-time, 35. Total enrolled 2012–2013 part-time, 0. Openings 2013–2014, 6. The median number of years required for completion of a degree in 2012–2013 were 6. The number of students enrolled full- and part-time who were dismissed or voluntarily withdrew from this program area in 2012–2013 were 0. *Clinical Psychology PhD (Doctor of Philosophy)*—Applications 2012–2013, 205. Total applicants accepted 2012–2013, 11. Number full-time enrolled (new admits only) 2012–2013, 7. Number part-time enrolled (new admits only) 2012–2013, 0. Total enrolled 2012–2013 full-time, 39.

Total enrolled 2012–2013 part-time, 0. Openings 2013–2014, 6. The median number of years required for completion of a degree in 2012–2013 were 6. The number of students enrolled full- and part-time who were dismissed or voluntarily withdrew from this program area in 2012–2013 were 0.

Scores: Entries appear in this order: required test or GPA, minimum score (if required), median score of students entering in 2012–2013. *Experimental Behavior Analysis MA/MS (Master of Arts/Science):* GRE-V no minimum stated, GRE-Q no minimum stated, GRE-Analytical no minimum stated, overall undergraduate GPA 3.00, last 2 years GPA no minimum stated, psychology GPA no minimum stated; *Experimental Health Psychology MA/MS (Master of Arts/Science):* GRE-V no minimum stated, GRE-Q no minimum stated, GRE-Analytical no minimum stated, overall undergraduate GPA 3.00, last 2 years GPA no minimum stated, psychology GPA no minimum stated; *Experimental PhD (Doctor of Philosophy):* GRE-V no minimum stated, 155, GRE-Q no minimum stated, 152, GRE-Analytical no minimum stated, 4.75, overall undergraduate GPA 3.00, 3.46, last 2 years GPA no minimum stated, psychology GPA no minimum stated; *Clinical Psychology PhD (Doctor of Philosophy):* GRE-V no minimum stated, 161, GRE-Q no minimum stated, 157, GRE-Analytical no minimum stated, 5.0, overall undergraduate GPA 3.00, 3.65, last 2 years GPA no minimum stated, psychology GPA no minimum stated.

Other Criteria: (importance of criteria rated low, medium, or high): GRE scores—high, research experience—high, work experience—low, extracurricular activity—low, clinically related public service—medium, GPA—high, letters of recommendation—high, interview—high, statement of goals and objectives—high, undergraduate major in psychology—medium, specific undergraduate psychology courses taken—medium, Currently, an interview isn't required for admission to the PhD Program in Experimental Psychology, but an interview is required for admission to the PhD Program in Clinical Psychology. For additional information on admission requirements, go to http://www4.uwm.edu/letsci/psychology/graduate/gradapp.cfm.

Student Characteristics: The following represents characteristics of students in 2012–2013 in all graduate psychology programs in the department: Female—full-time 59, part-time 0; Male—full-time 29, part-time 0; African American/Black—full-time 1, part-time 0; Hispanic/Latino(a)—full-time 5, part-time 0; Asian/Pacific Islander—full-time 8, part-time 0; American Indian/Alaska Native—full-time 0, part-time 0; Caucasian/White—full-time 74, part-time 0; Multi-ethnic—full-time 0, part-time 0; students subject to the Americans With Disabilities Act—full-time 0, part-time 0; Unknown ethnicity—full-time 0, part-time 0; International students who hold an F-1 or J-1 Visa—full-time 7, part-time 0.

Financial Information/Assistance:

Tuition for Full-Time Study: *Master's:* State residents: per academic year $10,482, $978 per credit hour; Nonstate residents: per academic year $23,948, $1,757 per credit hour. *Doctoral:* State residents: per academic year $10,482, $978 per credit hour; Nonstate residents: per academic year $23,948, $1,757 per credit hour. Tuition is subject to change. Additional fees are assessed to students beyond the costs of tuition for the following: additional student fees vary from $490 to $812 per year. See the following website for updates and changes in tuition costs: http://www4.uwm.edu/bfs/depts/bursar/tuition-rate-schedules.cfm.

Financial Assistance:

First-Year Students: Teaching assistantships available for first year. Average amount paid per academic year: $11,605. Average number of hours worked per week: 20. Apply by December 1. Research assistantships available for first year. Average amount paid per academic year: $17,000. Average number of hours worked per week: 20. Apply by December 1. Fellowships and scholarships available for first year. Average amount paid per academic year: $14,000. Average number of hours worked per week: 0. Apply by December 1.

Advanced Students: Teaching assistantships available for advanced students. Average amount paid per academic year: $13,453. Average number of hours worked per week: 20. Apply by December 1. Research assistantships available for advanced students. Average amount paid per academic year: $17,000. Average number of hours worked per week: 20. Apply by December 1. Fellowships and scholarships available for advanced students. Average amount paid per academic year: $14,000. Average number of hours worked per week: 0. Apply by December 1.

Additional Information: Of all students currently enrolled full time, 84% benefited from one or more of the listed financial assistance programs.

Internships/Practica: Doctoral Degree (PhD Clinical Psychology): For those doctoral students for whom a professional psychology internship was required in this program prior to graduation, (5) students applied for an internship in 2011–2012, with (5) students obtaining an internship. Of those students who obtained an internship, (5) were paid internships. Of those students who obtained an internship, (5) students placed in APA/CPA accredited internships, (0) students placed in internships not APA/CPA accredited, but listed with the Association of Psychology Postdoctoral and Internship Programs (APPIC), (0) students placed in internships conforming to guidelines of the Council of Directors of School Psychology Programs (CDSPP), (0) students placed in internships that were not APA/CPA accredited, APPIC or CDSPP listed. Master's Degree (MA/MS Experimental Behavior Analysis): An internship experience, such as a final research project or "capstone" experience is required of graduates. Master's Degree (MA/MS Experimental Health Psychology): An internship experience, such as a final research project or "capstone" experience is required of graduates. The clinical PhD program requires practica and an extramural internship at an APA-accredited site. The doctoral major in Behavior Analysis and the master's program in Behavior Analysis require practica. Numerous training sites in the greater Milwaukee area are used for practica, providing students with excellent training.

Housing and Day Care: On-campus housing is available. See the following website for more information: http://www4.uwm.edu/housing/. On-campus day care facilities are available. See the following website for more information: http://www4.uwm.edu/children/.

Employment of Department Graduates:

Master's Degree Graduates: Of those who graduated in the academic year 2011–2012, the following categories and numbers represent the postgraduate activities and employment of master's degree graduates: Enrolled in a psychology doctoral program (1), enrolled in a postdoctoral residency/fellowship (n/a), employed in independent practice (n/a), employed in business or industry (1), total from the above (master's) (2).

Doctoral Degree Graduates: Of those who graduated in the academic year 2011–2012, the following categories and numbers represent the postgraduate activities and employment of doctoral degree graduates: Enrolled in a psychology doctoral program (n/a), enrolled in a postdoctoral residency/fellowship (9), employed in an academic position at a university (1), total from the above (doctoral) (10).

Additional Information:

Orientation, Objectives, and Emphasis of Department: The department has an APA-accredited PhD program in clinical psychology (which includes earning the MS), a PhD program in experimental psychology (which includes earning the MS), and terminal MS programs in experimental health psychology and experimental behavior analysis. The experimental PhD program offers specializations in neuroscience, behavior analysis, and health psychology. The Behavior Analysis Certification Board, Inc® has approved our behavior analysis curriculum as meeting the requirements for eligibility to take the Board Certified Behavior Analyst Examination® to become BCBA's. Our PhD program in clinical psychology is a member of The Academy of Psychological Clinical Science; membership is based on a thorough peer review process. Our membership indicates our commitment to excellence in scientific training, and to using clinical science as the foundation for designing, implementing, and evaluating assessment and intervention procedures. All students in our department are directly involved in research under the direction of their major professor. Most students in the clinical and experimental doctoral programs are funded via teaching assistantships (or, sometimes, research assistantships or project assistantships), which require approximately 20 hours of work per week.

Special Facilities or Resources: The department moved to a completely remodeled building in 1985, which contains a separate research laboratory for each member of the faculty and specifically designed quarters for teaching laboratory courses. Special construction, air conditioning, and ventilation were included in the teaching and research laboratories to accommodate work with animal subjects and human participants. There is also a mechanical and woodworking shop and an electronics shop, supervised by a full-time technician. The department training clinic is housed in a separate wing of the building with its own offices, clerical staff, research space, clinic rooms, and full-time director.

Information for Students With Physical Disabilities: See the following website for more information: http://www4.uwm.edu/sac/.

Application Information:
Send to Chairperson, Graduate Admissions Committee, Department of Psychology, P.O. Box 413, Milwaukee, WI 53201-0413. Application available online. URL of online application: http://www.graduateschool.uwm.edu/students/prospective/apply/. Students are admitted in the Fall, application deadline December 1. The application deadline is December 1 for the PhD program in Clinical Psychology, and December 31 for the other programs. *Fee:* $56. Application fee for foreign students is $96.

Wisconsin, University of, Milwaukee
Educational Psychology
Education
2400 East Hartford IP0413
Milwaukee, WI 53211
Telephone: (414) 229-4767
Fax: (414) 229-4939
E-mail: *nadya@uwm.edu*
Web: *http://www4.uwm.edu/soe/academics/ed_psych/*

Department Information:
1965. Chairperson: Nadya A. Fouad. Number of faculty: total—full-time 17; women—full-time 11; total—minority—full-time 10; women minority—full-time 8.

Programs and Degrees Offered:
Listed in the following order: Program area, degree type (T if terminal Master's), number awarded 7/11–6/12. Counseling MA/MS (Master of Arts/Science) 43, School Psychology EdS (School Psychology) 13, Learning and Development MA/MS (Master of Arts/Science) (T) 2, Counseling Psychology PhD (Doctor of Philosophy) 8, School Psychology PhD (Doctor of Philosophy) 2, Learning and Development PhD (Doctor of Philosophy) 1, Educational Statistics and Measurement MA/MS (Master of Arts/Science) 12, Educational Statistics and Measurement PhD (Doctor of Philosophy) 0.

APA Accreditation: Counseling PhD (Doctor of Philosophy). Student Outcome Data Website: http://www4.uwm.edu/soe/academics/ed_psych/counseling_psych/. School PhD (Doctor of Philosophy). Student Outcome Data Website: http://www4.uwm.edu/soe/academics/ed_psych/school_psych/.

Student Applications/Admissions:

Student Applications

Counseling MA/MS (Master of Arts/Science)—Applications 2012–2013, 136. Total applicants accepted 2012–2013, 99. Number full-time enrolled (new admits only) 2012–2013, 36. Number part-time enrolled (new admits only) 2012–2013, 11. Total enrolled 2012–2013 full-time, 84. Total enrolled 2012–2013 part-time, 40. Openings 2013–2014, 60. The median number of years required for completion of a degree in 2012–2013 were 4. The number of students enrolled full- and part-time who were dismissed or voluntarily withdrew from this program area in 2012–2013 were 0. *School Psychology EdS (School Psychology)*—Applications 2012–2013, 50. Total applicants accepted 2012–2013, 17. Number full-time enrolled (new admits only) 2012–2013, 10. Number part-time enrolled (new admits only) 2012–2013, 0. Total enrolled 2012–2013 full-time, 20. Total enrolled 2012–2013 part-time, 0. Openings 2013–2014, 10. The median number of years required for completion of a degree in 2012–2013 were 3. The number of students enrolled full- and part-time who were dismissed or voluntarily withdrew from this program area in 2012–2013 were 0. *Learning and Development MA/MS (Master of Arts/Science)*—Applications 2012–2013, 10. Total applicants accepted 2012–2013, 3. Number part-time enrolled (new admits only) 2012–2013, 2. Total enrolled 2012–2013 full-time, 2. Total enrolled 2012–2013 part-time, 5. Openings 2013–2014, 3. The median number of years required for completion of a degree in 2012–2013 were 2. The number of students enrolled full- and part-time who were dismissed or voluntarily withdrew from this program area in 2012–2013 were 0. *Counseling Psychology PhD (Doctor of Philosophy)*—Applications 2012–2013, 48. Total applicants accepted 2012–2013, 8. Number full-time enrolled (new admits only) 2012–2013, 6. Number part-time enrolled (new admits only) 2012–2013, 0. Total enrolled 2012–2013 full-time, 25. Total enrolled 2012–2013 part-time, 1. Openings 2013–2014, 7. The median number of years required for completion of a degree in 2012–2013 were 5. The number of students enrolled full- and part-time who were dismissed or voluntarily withdrew from this program area in 2012–2013 were 1. *School Psychology PhD (Doctor of Philosophy)*—Applications 2012–2013, 7. Total applicants accepted 2012–2013, 3. Number full-time enrolled (new admits only) 2012–2013, 2. Number part-time enrolled (new admits only) 2012–2013, 0. Total enrolled 2012–2013 full-time, 19. Total enrolled 2012–2013 part-time, 1. Openings 2013–2014, 5. The median number of years required for completion of a degree in 2012–2013 were 5. The number of students enrolled full- and part-time who were dismissed or voluntarily withdrew from this program area in 2012–2013 were 0. *Learning and Development PhD (Doctor of Philosophy)*—Applications 2012–2013, 6. Total applicants accepted 2012–2013, 3. Number full-time enrolled (new admits only) 2012–2013, 1. Number part-time enrolled (new admits only) 2012–2013, 2. Total enrolled 2012–2013 full-time, 2. Total enrolled 2012–2013 part-time, 4. Openings 2013–2014, 3. The median number of years required for completion of a degree in 2012–2013 were 4. The number of students enrolled full- and part-time who were dismissed or voluntarily withdrew from this program area in 2012–2013 were 0. *Educational Statistics and Measurement MA/MS (Master of Arts/Science)*—Applications 2012–2013, 15. Total applicants accepted 2012–2013, 6. Number full-time enrolled (new admits only) 2012–2013, 4. Total enrolled 2012–2013 full-time, 5. Openings 2013–2014, 5. The median number of years required for completion of a degree in 2012–2013 were 2. *Educational Statistics and Measurement PhD (Doctor of Philosophy)*—Applications 2012–2013, 5. Total applicants accepted 2012–2013, 3. Number full-time enrolled (new admits only) 2012–2013, 1. Total enrolled 2012–2013 full-time, 8. Total enrolled 2012–2013 part-time, 3. Openings 2013–2014, 3.

Scores: Entries appear in this order: required test or GPA, minimum score (if required), median score of students entering in 2012–2013. *Counseling MA/MS (Master of Arts/Science):* overall undergraduate GPA 3.0, last 2 years GPA 3.0; *School Psychology EdS (School Psychology):* overall undergraduate GPA 3.0, last 2 years GPA 3.0; *Learning and Development MA/MS (Master of Arts/Science):* overall undergraduate GPA 3.0, last 2 years GPA 3.0, psychology GPA no minimum stated; *Counseling Psychology PhD (Doctor of Philosophy):* GRE-V no minimum stated, GRE-Q no minimum stated, GRE-Analytical no minimum stated, overall undergraduate GPA no minimum stated; *School Psychology PhD (Doctor of Philosophy):* GRE-V no minimum stated, GRE-Q no minimum stated, GRE-Analytical no minimum stated, overall undergraduate GPA

3.0, last 2 years GPA 3.0, Masters GPA 3.0; *Learning and Development PhD (Doctor of Philosophy):* GRE-V no minimum stated, GRE-Q no minimum stated, GRE-Analytical no minimum stated, overall undergraduate GPA 3.0, last 2 years GPA 3.0, Masters GPA 3.0; *Educational Statistics and Measurement MA/MS (Master of Arts/Science):* GRE-V no minimum stated, GRE-Q no minimum stated, GRE-Analytical no minimum stated, overall undergraduate GPA 3.5, last 2 years GPA 3.5; *Educational Statistics and Measurement PhD (Doctor of Philosophy):* GRE-V no minimum stated, GRE-Q no minimum stated, GRE-Analytical no minimum stated, overall undergraduate GPA 3.5, last 2 years GPA 3.5, Masters GPA 3.5.

Other Criteria: (importance of criteria rated low, medium, or high): GRE scores—high, research experience—medium, work experience—low, GPA—medium, letters of recommendation—high, statement of goals and objectives—high, research interests—high, undergraduate major in psychology—low, specific undergraduate psychology courses taken—low, Clinical experience is not required for the Educational Statistics and Measurement or Learning and Development programs.

Student Characteristics: The following represents characteristics of students in 2012–2013 in all graduate psychology programs in the department: Female—full-time 132, part-time 44; Male—full-time 39, part-time 15; African American/Black—full-time 7, part-time 7; Hispanic/Latino(a)—full-time 3, part-time 3; Asian/Pacific Islander—full-time 9, part-time 1; American Indian/Alaska Native—full-time 1, part-time 1; Caucasian/White—full-time 133, part-time 43; Multi-ethnic—full-time 13, part-time 3; Unknown ethnicity—full-time 1, part-time 0; International students who hold an F-1 or J-1 Visa—full-time 4, part-time 1.

Financial Information/Assistance:

Tuition for Full-Time Study: *Master's:* State residents: per academic year $11,482, $717 per credit hour; Nonstate residents: per academic year $23,947, $1,496 per credit hour. *Doctoral:* State residents: per academic year $11,482, $717 per credit hour; Nonstate residents: per academic year $23,947, $1,496 per credit hour. Tuition is subject to change. Additional fees are assessed to students beyond the costs of tuition for the following: assessment courses have additional course fees. See the following website for updates and changes in tuition costs: http://www4.uwm.edu/bfs/depts/bursar/tuition.cfm.

Financial Assistance:

First-Year Students: Teaching assistantships available for first year. Average amount paid per academic year: $13,455. Average number of hours worked per week: 20. Research assistantships available for first year. Average amount paid per academic year: $15,000. Average number of hours worked per week: 20. Fellowships and scholarships available for first year. Average amount paid per academic year: $13,455. Average number of hours worked per week: 20.

Advanced Students: Teaching assistantships available for advanced students. Average amount paid per academic year: $16,268. Average number of hours worked per week: 20. Research assistantships available for advanced students. Average amount paid per academic year: $15,000. Average number of hours worked per week: 20. Fellowships and scholarships available for advanced students. Average amount paid per academic year: $16,268. Average number of hours worked per week: 0.

Additional Information: Of all students currently enrolled full time, 65% benefited from one or more of the listed financial assistance programs. Application and information available online at: http://www4.uwm.edu/soe/departments/ed_psychology/financial_assistance.cfm.

Internships/Practica: Doctoral Degree (PhD Counseling Psychology): For those doctoral students for whom a professional psychology internship was required in this program prior to graduation, (4) students applied for an internship in 2011–2012, with (4) students obtaining an internship. Of those students who obtained an internship, (4) were paid internships. Of those students who obtained an internship, (2) students placed in APA/CPA accredited internships, (1) students placed in internships not APA/CPA accredited, but listed with the Association of Psychology Postdoctoral and Internship Programs (APPIC), (0) students placed in internships conforming to guidelines of the Council of Directors of School Psychology Programs (CDSPP), (1) students placed in internships that were not APA/CPA accredited, APPIC or CDSPP listed. Doctoral Degree (PhD School Psychology): For those doctoral students for whom a professional psychology internship was required in this program prior to graduation, (4) students applied for an internship in 2011–2012, with (4) students obtaining an internship. Of those students who obtained an internship, (4) were paid internships. Of those students who obtained an internship, (2) students placed in APA/CPA accredited internships, (1) students placed in internships not APA/CPA accredited, but listed with the Association of Psychology Postdoctoral and Internship Programs (APPIC), (0) students placed in internships conforming to guidelines of the Council of Directors of School Psychology Programs (CDSPP), (1) students placed in internships that were not APA/CPA accredited, APPIC or CDSPP listed. Students are placed in a variety of educational, business, and community settings as part of their graduate training. Students in the Educational and Statistical Measurements doctoral program will have the opportunity to gain experience as research assistants in research design, evaluation, scale development, psycho-metrics, and statistical consulting in the Consulting Office for Research and Evaluation (CORE).

Housing and Day Care: On-campus housing is available. See the following website for more information: http://www4.uwm.edu/housing/. On-campus day care facilities are available. See the following website for more information: http://www4.uwm.edu/children/.

Employment of Department Graduates:

Master's Degree Graduates: Of those who graduated in the academic year 2011–2012, the following categories and numbers represent the postgraduate activities and employment of master's degree graduates: Enrolled in a psychology doctoral program (4), enrolled in another graduate/professional program (1), enrolled in a postdoctoral residency/fellowship (n/a), employed in independent practice (n/a), employed in a professional position in a school system (10), not seeking employment (1), total from the above (master's) (16).

Doctoral Degree Graduates: Of those who graduated in the academic year 2011–2012, the following categories and numbers represent the postgraduate activities and employment of doctoral degree graduates: Enrolled in a psychology doctoral program (n/a), enrolled in a postdoctoral residency/fellowship (3), employed in independent practice (3), employed in an academic position at a university (2), employed in a professional position in a school system (2), employed in government agency (1), employed in a community mental health/counseling center (1), employed in a hospital/medical center (3), other employment position (1), do not know (1), total from the above (doctoral) (17).

Additional Information:

Orientation, Objectives, and Emphasis of Department: The department has one MS program with majors in Community Counseling, School Counseling, School Psychology (also EdS), Research Methodology, as well as Learning and Development. The PhD program in Educational Psychology includes Educational and Statistical Measurement, Learning & Development, School Psychology and Counseling Psychology. The PhD programs in School Psychology and Counseling Psychology, follow the model of training outlined by the American Psychological Association. The programs are based on the scientist–practitioner model, in which students are trained as psychological scientists with specializations in school or counseling psychology. Our department has strong, multicultural perspectives within each of the programs, with an emphasis on the contextual factors in student's work, and both provide unique training in the psychological, social, and educational needs of multi-ethnic populations within an urban psychosocial context. Students gain the knowledge, skills, and attitudes to work in a heterogeneous environment. Students are prepared to work in academic, service delivery, research and administrative positions.

Special Facilities or Resources: The department possesses excellent computer facilities. The department enjoys a strong collaborative relationship with the Department of Psychology, working together in an on-campus psychology clinic. We also have strong linkages to urban community and school partners, which provide students with a diverse set of research and practice opportunities.

Information for Students With Physical Disabilities: See the following website for more information: http://www4.uwm.edu/sac/.

Application Information:
Send to Application Chair, Department of Educational Psychology, UW–Milwaukee, P.O. Box 413, Milwaukee, WI 53201. Application available online. URL of online application: http://www.graduateschool.uwm.edu/students/prospective/apply/. Students are admitted in the Fall, application deadline December 1; Spring, application deadline September 1. Deadlines: School/Community Counseling: MS - March 1. Counseling Psychology: PhD - December 1. Educational Statistics and Measurement: MS and PhD - December 15. Learning and Development: MS and PhD - January 15 for fall admission and September 15 for spring admission. School Psychology: EdS - January 3. School Psychology: PhD - December 10. *Fee:* $56. An additional $40 is required for applicants who have non-U.S. college work.

Wisconsin, University of, Oshkosh

Psychology
800 Algoma Boulevard, CF 29
Oshkosh, WI 54901
Telephone: (920) 424-2302
Fax: (920) 424-1204
E-mail: *hongp@uwosh.edu*
Web: *http://www.uwosh.edu/psychology*

Department Information:

1959. Chairperson: Dr. David Lishner. Number of faculty: total—full-time 10, part-time 6; women—full-time 5, part-time 4; total—minority—full-time 4; women minority—full-time 3.

Programs and Degrees Offered:

Listed in the following order: Program area, degree type (T if terminal Master's), number awarded 7/11–6/12. Cognitive and Affective Science MA/MS (Master of Arts/Science) (T) 10.

Student Applications/Admissions:

Student Applications

Cognitive and Affective Science MA/MS (Master of Arts/Science)—Applications 2012–2013, 9. Total applicants accepted 2012–2013, 8. Number full-time enrolled (new admits only) 2012–2013, 8. Total enrolled 2012–2013 full-time, 16. Openings 2013–2014, 10. The median number of years required for completion of a degree in 2012–2013 were 2. The number of students enrolled full- and part-time who were dismissed or voluntarily withdrew from this program area in 2012–2013 were 1.

Scores: Entries appear in this order: required test or GPA, minimum score (if required), median score of students entering in 2012–2013. *Cognitive and Affective Science MA/MS (Master of Arts/Science):* GRE-V no minimum stated, GRE-Q no minimum stated, GRE-Analytical no minimum stated, overall undergraduate GPA 2.75, last 2 years GPA no minimum stated. *Other Criteria:* (importance of criteria rated low, medium, or high): GRE scores—medium, research experience—medium, work experience—low, extracurricular activity—low, GPA—medium, letters of recommendation—medium, statement of goals and objectives—medium, undergraduate major in psychology—low, specific undergraduate psychology courses taken—medium. For additional information on admission requirements, go to http://www.uwosh.edu/psychology/graduate-studies/apply.

Student Characteristics: The following represents characteristics of students in 2012–2013 in all graduate psychology programs in the department: Female—full-time 8, part-time 0; Male—full-time 8, part-time 0; African American/Black—full-time 0, part-time 0; Hispanic/Latino(a)—full-time 0, part-time 0; Asian/Pacific Islander—full-time 1, part-time 0; American Indian/Alaska Native—full-time 0, part-time 0; Caucasian/White—full-time 15, part-time 0; Multi-ethnic—full-time 0, part-time 0; students subject to the Americans With Disabilities Act—full-time 0, part-time 0; Unknown ethnicity—full-time 0, part-time 0; International students who hold an F-1 or J-1 Visa—full-time 1, part-time 0.

Financial Information/Assistance:

Tuition for Full-Time Study: *Master's:* State residents: per academic year $8,280, $460 per credit hour; Nonstate residents: per academic year $17,730, $985 per credit hour. Tuition is subject to change. See the following website for updates and changes in tuition costs: http://www.uwosh.edu/fin_aid/costs.

Financial Assistance:

First-Year Students: Research assistantships available for first year. Average amount paid per academic year: $4,000. Average number of hours worked per week: 10. Apply by May 1.

Advanced Students: Research assistantships available for advanced students. Average amount paid per academic year: $4,000. Average number of hours worked per week: 10. Apply by May 1.

Additional Information: Of all students currently enrolled full time, 100% benefited from one or more of the listed financial assistance programs. Application and information available online at: http://www.uwosh.edu/fin_aid/graduate-students.

Internships/Practica: Master's Degree (MA/MS Cognitive and Affective Science): An internship experience, such as a final research project or "capstone" experience is required of graduates.

Housing and Day Care: On-campus housing is available. See the following website for more information: http://www.housing.uwosh.edu/. On-campus day care facilities are available. See the following website for more information: http://www.uwosh.edu/childrens_center/.

Employment of Department Graduates:

Master's Degree Graduates: Of those who graduated in the academic year 2011–2012, the following categories and numbers represent the postgraduate activities and employment of master's degree graduates: Enrolled in a psychology doctoral program (4), enrolled in another graduate/professional program (2), enrolled in a postdoctoral residency/fellowship (n/a), employed in independent practice (n/a), employed in business or industry (5), total from the above (master's) (11).

Doctoral Degree Graduates: Of those who graduated in the academic year 2011–2012, the following categories and numbers represent the postgraduate activities and employment of doctoral degree graduates: Enrolled in a psychology doctoral program (n/a), total from the above (doctoral) (0).

Additional Information:

Orientation, Objectives, and Emphasis of Department: The goals of the Master of Science program in Cognitive and Affective Science are: expose students to various approaches of the study of psychology, such as social, clinical, biological, cognitive, health, and developmental; apply the methodological approaches used in collaborative research and covered in coursework; offer foundational courses in scientific methodology and quantitative analysis, as well as content seminars that examine behavior within a cognitive and affective framework; and create research-scholars with an intellectual and experiential background that will allow them to effectively pursue their future professional objectives.

Special Facilities or Resources: Animal colony; Human physiology & neurology lab (EEG).

Information for Students With Physical Disabilities: See the following website for more information: http://www.uwosh.edu/deanofstudents/disability-services.

Application Information:
Send to UW Oshkosh Graduate Studies, Dempsey 337, 800 Algoma Boulevard, Oshkosh, WI 54901. Application available online. URL of online application: http://www.uwosh.edu/gradstudies/admissions. Students are admitted in the Fall, application deadline June 1. *Fee:* $25.

Wisconsin, University of, Stout
Psychology Department/Master of Science in Applied
  Psychology (MSAP)
College of Education, Health and Human Sciences
Harvey Hall 237
Menomonie, WI 54751-0790
Telephone: (715) 232-2478
Fax: (715) 232-5303
E-mail: *molinem@uwstout.edu*
Web: *http://www.uwstout.edu/programs/msap/index.cfm*

Department Information:
1982. Chairperson: Dr. Kristina Gorbatenko-Roth. Number of faculty: total—full-time 16, part-time 6; women—full-time 15, part-time 2; total—minority—full-time 1; women minority—full-time 1.

Programs and Degrees Offered:
Listed in the following order: Program area, degree type (T if terminal Master's), number awarded 7/11–6/12. Applied Psychology MA/MS (Master of Arts/Science) (T) 21.

Student Applications/Admissions:
Student Applications
Applied Psychology MA/MS (Master of Arts/Science)—Applications 2012–2013, 30. Total applicants accepted 2012–2013, 15. Number full-time enrolled (new admits only) 2012–2013, 15. Number part-time enrolled (new admits only) 2012–2013, 0. Total enrolled 2012–2013 full-time, 36. Total enrolled 2012–2013 part-time, 0. Openings 2013–2014, 20. The median number of years required for completion of a degree in 2012–2013 were 2. The number of students enrolled full- and part-time who were dismissed or voluntarily withdrew from this program area in 2012–2013 were 1.
Scores: Entries appear in this order: required test or GPA, minimum score (if required), median score of students entering in 2012–2013. *Applied Psychology MA/MS (Master of Arts/Science):* overall undergraduate GPA 3.0, 3.5.
Other Criteria: (importance of criteria rated low, medium, or high): GRE scores—medium, research experience—high, work experience—high, extracurricular activity—medium, clinically related public service—low, GPA—high, letters of recommendation—high, statement of goals and objectives—high, applied experience/resume—high, undergraduate major in psychology—low, specific undergraduate psychology courses taken—high. For additional information on admission requirements, go to http://www.uwstout.edu/programs/msap/applying.cfm.

Student Characteristics: The following represents characteristics of students in 2012–2013 in all graduate psychology programs in the department: Female—full-time 7, part-time 0; Male—full-time 8, part-time 0; African American/Black—full-time 0, part-time 0; Hispanic/Latino(a)—full-time 1, part-time 0; Asian/Pacific Islander—full-time 2, part-time 0; American Indian/Alaska Native—full-time 0, part-time 0; Caucasian/White—full-time 33, part-time 0; Multi-ethnic—full-time 0, part-time 0; students subject to the Americans With Disabilities Act—full-time 0, part-time 0; Unknown ethnicity—full-time 0, part-time 0; International students who hold an F-1 or J-1 Visa—full-time 2, part-time 0.

Financial Information/Assistance:
Tuition for Full-Time Study: *Master's:* State residents: per academic year $8,428, $418 per credit hour; Nonstate residents: per academic year $16,181, $829 per credit hour. Tuition is subject to change. Additional fees are assessed to students beyond the costs of tuition for the following: SPSS and other computer software required; to be purchased by student. See the following website for updates and changes in tuition costs: http://www.uwstout.edu/stubus/tuitionrate.cfm.

Financial Assistance:
First-Year Students: Teaching assistantships available for first year. Average amount paid per academic year: $4,103. Average number of hours worked per week: 8. Traineeships available for first year. Average amount paid per academic year: $4,103. Average number of hours worked per week: 8. Fellowships and scholarships available for first year. Apply by January 15.
Advanced Students: Teaching assistantships available for advanced students. Average amount paid per academic year: $4,103. Average number of hours worked per week: 8. Traineeships available for advanced students. Fellowships and scholarships available for advanced students. Apply by January 15.
Additional Information: Of all students currently enrolled full time, 66% benefited from one or more of the listed financial assistance programs. Application and information available online at: http://www.uwstout.edu/grad/prospect/finance.cfm.

Internships/Practica: Master's Degree (MA/MS Applied Psychology): An internship experience, such as a final research project or "capstone" experience is required of graduates. MSAP students are required to do a practicum in external consulting and a 240 hour internship. Students are encouraged to seek out placement sites early in their program work. 85% of MSAP courses involve 'hands-on' applied learning typically through group projects.

Housing and Day Care: On-campus housing is available. See the following website for more information: http://www.uwstout.edu/housing/. On-campus day care facilities are available. See the following website for more information: http://www.uwstout.edu/soe/cfsc/index.cfm.

Employment of Department Graduates:
Master's Degree Graduates: Of those who graduated in the academic year 2011–2012, the following categories and numbers represent the postgraduate activities and employment of master's degree graduates: Enrolled in a postdoctoral residency/fellowship (n/a), employed in independent practice (n/a), employed in other positions at a higher education institution (1), employed in busi-

ness or industry (4), employed in a hospital/medical center (2), total from the above (master's) (7).

Doctoral Degree Graduates: Of those who graduated in the academic year 2011–2012, the following categories and numbers represent the postgraduate activities and employment of doctoral degree graduates: Enrolled in a psychology doctoral program (n/a), total from the above (doctoral) (0).

Additional Information:

Orientation, Objectives, and Emphasis of Department: The MS in Applied Psychology (MSAP) is a two-year program designed around a core of psychological theories, principles, and research methods. The program emphasizes experiential learning, as over 85% of the required courses involve applied projects. Students choose from among three concentration areas: industrial/organizational psychology, evaluation research, and health promotion & disease prevention. Dual concentrations are typical. The MSAP program is designed to provide students with the knowledge, experience, skills, and abilities to apply theories and methods to the identification of and solution to a variety of 21st century, real-world problems in business and industry, health care, and non-profit organizations. A majority of classes incorporate real-world, hands-on learning opportunities that involve extensive group work and communication with external stakeholders. Numerous opportunities exist outside of formal courses for additional applied experience.

Special Facilities or Resources: The university has numerous consulting relationships with local and regional businesses and industries, health related organizations, governmental agencies, and non-profit organizations. MSAP students utilize the latest multimedia hardware and software to perform both quantitative and qualitative analyses. Several facilities and labs within the College of Education, Health and Human Services and the Psychology Department have received lab modernization funds.

Information for Students With Physical Disabilities: See the following website for more information: http://www.uwstout.edu/services/disability/.

Application Information:

Send to Dr. Susan Staggs, Program Director, M.S. Applied Psychology, Psychology Department, University of Wisconsin-Stout, Menomonie, WI 54751-0790. Application available online. URL of online application: http://www.uwstout.edu/grad/prospect/apply.cfm. Students are admitted in the Fall, application deadline February 1. Applications are accepted past the deadline, space permitting. *Fee:* $56. $106 for International students.

Wyoming, University of

Department of Psychology
Arts and Sciences
Dept. 3415, 1000 East University Avenue
Laramie, WY 82071
Telephone: (307) 766-6303
Fax: (307) 766-2926
E-mail: cpepper@uwyo.edu
Web: http://www.uwyo.edu/psychology

Department Information:

1909. Chairperson: Carolyn Pepper. Number of faculty: total—full-time 17; women—full-time 8; total—minority—full-time 2; women minority—full-time 1.

Programs and Degrees Offered:

Listed in the following order: Program area, degree type (T if terminal Master's), number awarded 7/11–6/12. Clinical Psychology PhD (Doctor of Philosophy) 4, Psychology and Law PhD (Doctor of Philosophy) 1, Social Psychology PhD (Doctor of Philosophy) 0, Cognition/Cognitive Development PhD (Doctor of Philosophy) 0.

APA Accreditation: Clinical PhD (Doctor of Philosophy). Student Outcome Data Website: http://www.uwyo.edu/psychology/graduate/clinical psychology.html.

Student Applications/Admissions:

Student Applications

Clinical Psychology PhD (Doctor of Philosophy)—Applications 2012–2013, 123. Total applicants accepted 2012–2013, 8. Number full-time enrolled (new admits only) 2012–2013, 5. Total enrolled 2012–2013 full-time, 29. Total enrolled 2012–2013 part-time, 0. Openings 2013–2014, 5. The median number of years required for completion of a degree in 2012–2013 were 7. The number of students enrolled full- and part-time who were dismissed or voluntarily withdrew from this program area in 2012–2013 were 0. *Psychology and Law PhD (Doctor of Philosophy)*—Applications 2012–2013, 5. Total applicants accepted 2012–2013, 2. Number full-time enrolled (new admits only) 2012–2013, 1. Total enrolled 2012–2013 full-time, 3. Openings 2013–2014, 1. The median number of years required for completion of a degree in 2012–2013 were 5. The number of students enrolled full- and part-time who were dismissed or voluntarily withdrew from this program area in 2012–2013 were 1. *Social Psychology PhD (Doctor of Philosophy)*—Applications 2012–2013, 17. Total applicants accepted 2012–2013, 2. Number full-time enrolled (new admits only) 2012–2013, 1. Total enrolled 2012–2013 full-time, 4. Openings 2013–2014, 1. The number of students enrolled full- and part-time who were dismissed or voluntarily withdrew from this program area in 2012–2013 were 0. *Cognition/Cognitive Development PhD (Doctor of Philosophy)*—Applications 2012–2013, 12. Total applicants accepted 2012–2013, 2. Number full-time enrolled (new admits only) 2012–2013, 1. Number part-time enrolled (new admits only) 2012–2013, 0. Total

enrolled 2012–2013 full-time, 1. Total enrolled 2012–2013 part-time, 0. Openings 2013–2014, 2. The number of students enrolled full- and part-time who were dismissed or voluntarily withdrew from this program area in 2012–2013 were 0.

Scores: Entries appear in this order: required test or GPA, minimum score (if required), median score of students entering in 2012–2013. *Clinical Psychology PhD (Doctor of Philosophy):* GRE-V no minimum stated, 152, GRE-Q no minimum stated, 152, GRE-Analytical no minimum stated, 5.0, overall undergraduate GPA no minimum stated, 3.61, last 2 years GPA no minimum stated, psychology GPA no minimum stated, 3.77, Masters GPA no minimum stated, 4.0; *Psychology and Law PhD (Doctor of Philosophy):* GRE-V no minimum stated, 157, GRE-Q no minimum stated, 152, GRE-Analytical no minimum stated, 5.0, overall undergraduate GPA no minimum stated, 3.7, last 2 years GPA no minimum stated, psychology GPA no minimum stated, 3.7, Masters GPA no minimum stated, 3.8; *Social Psychology PhD (Doctor of Philosophy):* GRE-V no minimum stated, 160, GRE-Q no minimum stated, 149, GRE-Analytical no minimum stated, 4.0, overall undergraduate GPA no minimum stated, 3.92, last 2 years GPA no minimum stated, psychology GPA no minimum stated, 3.96; *Cognition/Cognitive Development PhD (Doctor of Philosophy):* GRE-V no minimum stated, 152, GRE-Q no minimum stated, 154, GRE-Analytical no minimum stated, 4.0, GRE-Subject (Psychology) no minimum stated, overall undergraduate GPA no minimum stated, 3.3, last 2 years GPA no minimum stated, psychology GPA no minimum stated, 3.6, Masters GPA no minimum stated, 3.9.

Other Criteria: (importance of criteria rated low, medium, or high): GRE scores—high, research experience—high, work experience—low, extracurricular activity—low, clinically related public service—medium, GPA—medium, letters of recommendation—high, interview—high, statement of goals and objectives—high, undergraduate major in psychology—medium, specific undergraduate psychology courses taken—medium, Work Experience is relevant to the Clinical Program only. For additional information on admission requirements, go to http://www.uwyo.edu/psychology/graduate/graduate application process.html.

Student Characteristics: The following represents characteristics of students in 2012–2013 in all graduate psychology programs in the department: Female—full-time 26, part-time 0; Male—full-time 11, part-time 0; African American/Black—full-time 0, part-time 0; Hispanic/Latino(a)—full-time 2, part-time 0; Asian/Pacific Islander—full-time 4, part-time 0; American Indian/Alaska Native—full-time 1, part-time 0; Caucasian/White—full-time 21, part-time 0; Multi-ethnic—full-time 0, part-time 0; students subject to the Americans With Disabilities Act—full-time 0, part-time 0; Unknown ethnicity—full-time 9, part-time 0; International students who hold an F-1 or J-1 Visa—full-time 2, part-time 0.

Financial Information/Assistance:

Tuition for Full-Time Study: *Doctoral:* State residents: per academic year $4,944, $206 per credit hour; Nonstate residents: per academic year $13,824, $576 per credit hour. Tuition is subject to change. See the following website for updates and changes in tuition costs: http://www.uwyo.edu/fsbo/accounts-receivable/.

Financial Assistance:

First-Year Students: Teaching assistantships available for first year. Average amount paid per academic year: $11,349. Average number of hours worked per week: 20. Research assistantships available for first year. Average amount paid per academic year: $11,349. Average number of hours worked per week: 20.

Advanced Students: Teaching assistantships available for advanced students. Average amount paid per academic year: $15,795. Average number of hours worked per week: 20. Research assistantships available for advanced students. Average amount paid per academic year: $15,795. Average number of hours worked per week: 20.

Additional Information: Of all students currently enrolled full time, 100% benefited from one or more of the listed financial assistance programs. Application and information available online at: http://www.uwyo.edu/psychology/graduate/financial assistance.html.

Internships/Practica: Doctoral Degree (PhD Clinical Psychology): For those doctoral students for whom a professional psychology internship was required in this program prior to graduation, (6) students applied for an internship in 2011–2012, with (6) students obtaining an internship. Of those students who obtained an internship, (6) were paid internships. Of those students who obtained an internship, (6) students placed in APA/CPA accredited internships, (0) students placed in internships not APA/CPA accredited, but listed with the Association of Psychology Postdoctoral and Internship Programs (APPIC), (0) students placed in internships conforming to guidelines of the Council of Directors of School Psychology Programs (CDSPP), (0) students placed in internships that were not APA/CPA accredited, APPIC or CDSPP listed. Given Wyoming's large geographic area (approximately 100,000 square miles) and small population (approximately 500,000), we arrange practica and clerkships for Clinical students in various settings throughout the state. Clerkships are typically conducted in the summer for extended periods of time. Practica and clerkships include a variety of clinical populations such as children, adolescents, adults, and elderly people. They occur in a range of placements including outpatient mental health centers, inpatient hospitals, VA Medical Centers and residential programs. Specialty experiences include forensic evaluation, substance abuse training, and parent training.

Housing and Day Care: On-campus housing is available. See the following website for more information: http://www.uwyo.edu/reslife-dining/. On-campus day care facilities are available. See the following website for more information: http://www.uwyo.edu/ecec/.

Employment of Department Graduates:

Master's Degree Graduates: Of those who graduated in the academic year 2011–2012, the following categories and numbers represent the postgraduate activities and employment of master's degree graduates: Enrolled in a postdoctoral residency/fellowship (n/a), employed in independent practice (n/a), total from the above (master's) (0).

Doctoral Degree Graduates: Of those who graduated in the academic year 2011–2012, the following categories and numbers represent the postgraduate activities and employment of doctoral degree graduates: Enrolled in a psychology doctoral program (n/a), enrolled in a postdoctoral residency/fellowship (3), employed in independent practice (1), total from the above (doctoral) (4).

Additional Information:

Orientation, Objectives, and Emphasis of Department: The University of Wyoming is the only four-year university in the state of Wyoming. The psychology department has a broad undergraduate teaching mission and has one of the largest number of majors in the College of Arts and Sciences. The graduate curriculum provides breadth of training in psychology and permits specialization in various content areas. The Clinical Psychology PhD Program is based on the scientist–practitioner model. The goal of the clinical program is to provide students with the knowledge base and broad conceptual skills necessary for professional practice and/or research in a variety of settings. The PhD programs in Social Psychology, Cognitive/Cognitive Development, and Psychology & Law provide students with broad training that can be used in a variety of academic and applied settings. All programs contain opportunities for both applied and basic research training. Research collaboration across all programs is encouraged.

Special Facilities or Resources: The department has approximately 24,000 square feet of laboratory, office, and clinic space in a science complex with direct access to the university's science library and various computer labs. Faculty laboratories range from wet laboratories designed for the biological aspects of human behavior to labs designed to assess mock jurors and jury decision-making. The Psychology Clinic has ample space for individual or small group assessment and treatment. These facilities also have observation mirrors and digital recording capability.

Information for Students With Physical Disabilities: See the following website for more information: http://www.uwyo.edu/udss/.

Application Information:

Send to Graduate Admissions Committee, Department of Psychology, University of Wyoming, Department 3415, 1000 East University Avenue, Laramie, WY 82071. Application available online. URL of online application: http://www.uwyo.edu/uwgrad/prospective/applying/. Students are admitted in the Fall, application deadline January 15. *Fee:* $50.

Acadia University

Department of Psychology
18 University Avenue
Wolfville, NS B4P 2R6
Telephone: (902) 585-1301
Fax: (902) 585-1078
E-mail: *peter.horvath@acadiau.ca*
Web: *http://www.psychology.acadiau.ca*

Department Information:

1926. Head: Dr. Peter McLeod. Number of faculty: total—full-time 11; women—full-time 6; total—minority—full-time 1.

Programs and Degrees Offered:

Listed in the following order: Program area, degree type (T if terminal Master's), number awarded 7/11–6/12. Clinical Psychology MA/MS (Master of Arts/Science) (T) 4.

Student Applications/Admissions:

Student Applications

Clinical Psychology MA/MS (Master of Arts/Science)—Applications 2012–2013, 38. Total applicants accepted 2012–2013, 5. Number full-time enrolled (new admits only) 2012–2013, 5. Total enrolled 2012–2013 full-time, 10. Openings 2013–2014, 5. The median number of years required for completion of a degree in 2012–2013 were 2. The number of students enrolled full- and part-time who were dismissed or voluntarily withdrew from this program area in 2012–2013 were 0.

Scores: Entries appear in this order: required test or GPA, minimum score (if required), median score of students entering in 2012–2013. *Clinical Psychology MA/MS (Master of Arts/Science):* GRE-V 500, GRE-Q 500, GRE-Analytical 4.0, overall undergraduate GPA 3.0, last 2 years GPA 3.0, psychology GPA 3.0.

Other Criteria: (importance of criteria rated low, medium, or high): GRE scores—high, research experience—high, work experience—medium, extracurricular activity—medium, clinically related public service—medium, GPA—high, letters of recommendation—high, interview—high, statement of goals and objectives—high, undergraduate major in psychology—high. For additional information on admission requirements, go to http://psychology.acadiau.ca/Graduate.html.

Student Characteristics: The following represents characteristics of students in 2012–2013 in all graduate psychology programs in the department: Female—full-time 10, part-time 0; Male—full-time 0, part-time 0; African American/Black—full-time 0, part-time 0; Hispanic/Latino(a)—full-time 0, part-time 0; Asian/Pacific Islander—full-time 0, part-time 0; American Indian/Alaska Native—full-time 0, part-time 0; Caucasian/White—full-time 10, part-time 0; Multi-ethnic—full-time 0, part-time 0; students subject to the Americans With Disabilities Act—full-time 0, part-time 0; Unknown ethnicity—full-time 0, part-time 0; International students who hold an F-1 or J-1 Visa—full-time 0, part-time 0.

Financial Information/Assistance:

Tuition for Full-Time Study: *Master's:* State residents: per academic year $3,634; Nonstate residents: per academic year $4,656. Tuition is subject to change. See the following website for updates and changes in tuition costs: http://gradstudies.acadiau.ca/fees.html.

Financial Assistance:

First-Year Students: Teaching assistantships available for first year. Average amount paid per academic year: $9,000. Average number of hours worked per week: 10. Apply by February 1. Research assistantships available for first year. Average amount paid per academic year: $12,000.

Advanced Students: Teaching assistantships available for advanced students. Average amount paid per academic year: $8,000. Average number of hours worked per week: 10.

Additional Information: Of all students currently enrolled full time, 100% benefited from one or more of the listed financial assistance programs. Application and information available online at: http://gradstudies.acadiau.ca/StudentFunding.html.

Internships/Practica: Master's Degree (MA/MS Clinical Psychology): An internship experience, such as a final research project or "capstone" experience is required of graduates. Two 250-hour internships are mandatory in intervention and assessment.

Housing and Day Care: On-campus housing is available. See the following website for more information: http://residencelife.acadiau.ca/. No on-campus day care facilities are available.

Employment of Department Graduates:

Master's Degree Graduates: Of those who graduated in the academic year 2011–2012, the following categories and numbers represent the postgraduate activities and employment of master's degree graduates: Enrolled in another graduate/professional program (2), enrolled in a postdoctoral residency/fellowship (n/a), employed in independent practice (n/a), employed in a community mental health/counseling center (1), employed in a hospital/medical center (1), total from the above (master's) (4).

Doctoral Degree Graduates: Of those who graduated in the academic year 2011–2012, the following categories and numbers represent the postgraduate activities and employment of doctoral degree graduates: Enrolled in a psychology doctoral program (n/a), total from the above (doctoral) (0).

Additional Information:

Orientation, Objectives, and Emphasis of Department: The department's principle objective is to train MSc students in clinical psychology. The department's orientation is eclectic although there is an emphasis on cognitive-behavioural approaches to problems in psychology. Our curriculum is highly respected, and graduates going on to doctoral programs elsewhere have had recognition of their master's level coursework from Acadia. We are registered with CAMPP.

Special Facilities or Resources: The department is part of the cooperative clinical PhD program of Dalhousie University.

Information for Students With Physical Disabilities: See the following website for more information: http://disabilityaccess. acadiau.ca.

Application Information:

Send to Office of Research and Graduate Studies, Acadia University, Wolfville, NS, B4P 2R6. Application available online. URL of online application: http://gradstudies.acadiau.ca/GradAdmissions.html. Students are admitted in the Fall, application deadline February 1. *Fee:* $50. Note: All dollar amounts specified in this entry are Canadian dollars.

Alberta, University of
Department of Psychology
P217 Biological Sciences Building
Edmonton, AB T6G 2E9
Telephone: (708) 492-5216
Fax: (708) 492-1768
E-mail: *jeff.bisanz@ualberta.ca*
Web: *http://www.psych.ualberta.ca*

Department Information:

1961. Chairperson: Jeffrey Bisanz. Number of faculty: total—full-time 31; women—full-time 9; total—minority—full-time 3; women minority—full-time 1.

Programs and Degrees Offered:

Listed in the following order: Program area, degree type (T if terminal Master's), number awarded 7/11–6/12. Psychology MA/MS (Master of Arts/Science) 5, Psychology PhD (Doctor of Philosophy) 4.

Student Applications/Admissions:

Student Applications

Psychology MA/MS (Master of Arts/Science)—Applications 2012–2013, 41. Total applicants accepted 2012–2013, 13. Number full-time enrolled (new admits only) 2012–2013, 8. Total enrolled 2012–2013 full-time, 19. *Psychology PhD (Doctor of Philosophy)*—Applications 2012–2013, 28. Total applicants accepted 2012–2013, 9. Number full-time enrolled (new admits only) 2012–2013, 4. Total enrolled 2012–2013 full-time, 29.

Scores: Entries appear in this order: required test or GPA, minimum score (if required), median score of students entering in 2012–2013. *Psychology MA/MS (Master of Arts/Science):* GRE-V no minimum stated, GRE-Q no minimum stated, GRE-Analytical no minimum stated, overall undergraduate GPA no minimum stated, last 2 years GPA no minimum stated; *Psychology PhD (Doctor of Philosophy):* GRE-V no minimum stated, GRE-Q no minimum stated, GRE-Analytical no minimum stated, overall undergraduate GPA no minimum stated, last 2 years GPA no minimum stated, Masters GPA no minimum stated.

Other Criteria: (importance of criteria rated low, medium, or high): GRE scores—high, research experience—high, work experience—low, extracurricular activity—low, GPA—high,

letters of recommendation—high, statement of goals and objectives—high, undergraduate major in psychology—medium, specific undergraduate psychology courses taken—medium. For additional information on admission requirements, go to http://www.psych.ualberta.ca/graduate/appinfo.php.

Student Characteristics: The following represents characteristics of students in 2012–2013 in all graduate psychology programs in the department: Female—full-time 30, part-time 0; Male—full-time 18, part-time 0; Caucasian/White—full-time 0, part-time 0; students subject to the Americans With Disabilities Act—full-time 0, part-time 0; Unknown ethnicity—full-time 0, part-time 0; International students who hold an F-1 or J-1 Visa—full-time 0, part-time 0.

Financial Information/Assistance:

Tuition for Full-Time Study: *Master's:* State residents: per academic year $5,252; Nonstate residents: per academic year $8,022. *Doctoral:* State residents: per academic year $5,252; Nonstate residents: per academic year $8,022. Tuition is subject to change. See the following website for updates and changes in tuition costs: http://www.gradstudies.ualberta.ca/regfees/.

Financial Assistance:

First-Year Students: Teaching assistantships available for first year. Average amount paid per academic year: $23,250. Average number of hours worked per week: 12. Apply by January 15. Research assistantships available for first year. Average amount paid per academic year: $23,250. Average number of hours worked per week: 12. Apply by January 15.

Advanced Students: Teaching assistantships available for advanced students. Average amount paid per academic year: $23,877. Average number of hours worked per week: 12. Apply by January 15. Research assistantships available for advanced students. Average amount paid per academic year: $23,877. Average number of hours worked per week: 12. Apply by January 15.

Additional Information: Of all students currently enrolled full time, 95% benefited from one or more of the listed financial assistance programs. Application and information available online at: http://www.psych.ualberta.ca/graduate/finsupport.php.

Housing and Day Care: On-campus housing is available. See the following website for more information: http://www.residence. ualberta.ca/. On-campus day care facilities are available. See the following website for more information: http://www.asinfo. ualberta.ca/AffiliatedChildCare.

Employment of Department Graduates:

Master's Degree Graduates: Of those who graduated in the academic year 2011–2012, the following categories and numbers represent the postgraduate activities and employment of master's degree graduates: Enrolled in a psychology doctoral program (4), enrolled in a postdoctoral residency/fellowship (n/a), employed in independent practice (n/a), do not know (1), total from the above (master's) (5).

Doctoral Degree Graduates: Of those who graduated in the academic year 2011–2012, the following categories and numbers represent the postgraduate activities and employment of doctoral degree graduates: Enrolled in a psychology doctoral program (n/a),

enrolled in a postdoctoral residency/fellowship (1), employed in an academic position at a 2-year/4-year college (2), employed in a government agency (1), total from the above (doctoral) (4).

Additional Information:

Orientation, Objectives, and Emphasis of Department: The goal of the graduate program is to train competent and independent researchers who will make significant contributions to the discipline of psychology. The program entails early and sustained involvement in research and ensures that students attain expertise in focal and related domains. The program offers training that leads to degrees in a range of research areas, including: Behaviour, Systems and Cognitive Neuroscience; Cognition; Comparative Cognition and Behaviour; Developmental Science; and Social and Cultural Psychology. Recent PhD graduates from the Department have successfully found positions in universities and colleges, branches of government, and industry. A reasonably close match between the research interests of prospective students and faculty members is essential because the program involves apprenticeship-style training. Although many faculty members conduct research on problems that have practical and social significance, we do not have programs in clinical, counseling, or industrial/organizational psychology.

Special Facilities or Resources: The department maintains a number of specialized support facilities for staff and student use including an electronics shop, labs for teaching and research use, and an instructional technology lab to support teaching. In addition, the department maintains a psychology reading room. Department computing resources include approximately 300 computers used in research and a further 40 computers used for administration and instructional needs. All staff and student computers have network capability on the department and campus networks. Technical assistance for research, teaching, and administrative needs is provided by department technical staff. For research services, the department maintains a fully equipped electronics shop staffed by technicians who design, build, and maintain custom laboratory equipment and data acquisition devices for laboratory applications. The shop contains a variety of professional equipment for electronics and fabrication work and stocks supplies for research and equipment needs. Technical staff also provide a full range of assistance with equipment selection and ordering, equipment repair, and new equipment configuration and setup. Other resources include the University Teaching and Learning Program, which improves the teaching skills of graduate students through workshops and practica, and the Community-University Partnership, which facilitates community- and school-based research.

Information for Students With Physical Disabilities: See the following website for more information: http://www.uofaweb.ualberta.ca/SSDS/.

Application Information:

Send to Graduate Program Assistant, Department of Psychology, P-217D Biological Sciences, University of Alberta, Edmonton, AB Canada T6G 2E9. Application available online. URL of online application: http://www.gradstudies.ualberta.ca/apply/. Students are admitted in the Fall, application deadline January 15. *Fee:* $100. Note: All dollar amounts specified in this entry are Canadian dollars.

British Columbia, University of

Department of Psychology
2136 West Mall, Kenny Psychology Building
Vancouver, BC V6T 1Z4
Telephone: (604) 822-3144
Fax: (604) 822-6923
E-mail: *gradsec@psych.ubc.ca*
Web: *http://www.psych.ubc.ca*

Department Information:

1951. Head: Alan Kingstone. Number of faculty: total—full-time 49, part-time 27; women—full-time 23, part-time 16.

Programs and Degrees Offered:

Listed in the following order: Program area, degree type (T if terminal Master's), number awarded 7/11–6/12. Behavioral Neuroscience PhD (Doctor of Philosophy) 3, Clinical Psychology PhD (Doctor of Philosophy) 2, Developmental Psychology PhD (Doctor of Philosophy) 1, Cognitive Science PhD (Doctor of Philosophy) 0, Social/Personality Psychology PhD (Doctor of Philosophy) 2, Quantitative Methods PhD (Doctor of Philosophy) 0, Health Psychology PhD (Doctor of Philosophy) 0.

APA Accreditation: Clinical PhD (Doctor of Philosophy). Student Outcome Data Website: http://www.psych.ubc.ca/grad-pgm/areasspec.psy?contid=101306171911.

CPA Accreditation: Clinical PhD (Doctor of Philosophy).

Student Applications/Admissions:

Student Applications

Behavioral Neuroscience PhD (Doctor of Philosophy)—Applications 2012–2013, 19. Total applicants accepted 2012–2013, 4. Number full-time enrolled (new admits only) 2012–2013, 2. Number part-time enrolled (new admits only) 2012–2013, 0. Total enrolled 2012–2013 full-time, 8. Total enrolled 2012–2013 part-time, 0. Openings 2013–2014, 6. The median number of years required for completion of a degree in 2012–2013 were 6. The number of students enrolled full- and part-time who were dismissed or voluntarily withdrew from this program area in 2012–2013 were 1. *Clinical Psychology PhD (Doctor of Philosophy)*—Applications 2012–2013, 156. Total applicants accepted 2012–2013, 7. Number full-time enrolled (new admits only) 2012–2013, 6. Number part-time enrolled (new admits only) 2012–2013, 0. Total enrolled 2012–2013 full-time, 33. Total enrolled 2012–2013 part-time, 0. Openings 2013–2014, 6. The median number of years required for completion of a degree in 2012–2013 were 7. The number of students enrolled full- and part-time who were dismissed or voluntarily withdrew from this program area in 2012–2013 were 0. *Developmental Psychology PhD (Doctor of Philosophy)*—Applications 2012–2013, 33. Total applicants accepted 2012–2013, 3. Number full-time enrolled (new admits only) 2012–2013, 2. Number part-time enrolled (new admits only) 2012–2013, 0. Total enrolled 2012–2013 full-time, 8. Total enrolled 2012–2013 part-time, 0. Openings 2013–2014, 6. The median number of years required for completion of a degree in 2012–2013 were 6. The number of students enrolled full- and part-time who were dismissed or voluntarily withdrew from this program area in 2012–2013 were 0. *Cognitive Science PhD*

(*Doctor of Philosophy*)—Applications 2012–2013, 33. Total applicants accepted 2012–2013, 2. Number full-time enrolled (new admits only) 2012–2013, 1. Number part-time enrolled (new admits only) 2012–2013, 0. Total enrolled 2012–2013 full-time, 21. Total enrolled 2012–2013 part-time, 0. Openings 2013–2014, 6. The number of students enrolled full- and part-time who were dismissed or voluntarily withdrew from this program area in 2012–2013 were 1. *Social/Personality Psychology PhD (Doctor of Philosophy)*—Applications 2012–2013, 65. Total applicants accepted 2012–2013, 6. Number full-time enrolled (new admits only) 2012–2013, 1. Number part-time enrolled (new admits only) 2012–2013, 0. Total enrolled 2012–2013 full-time, 23. Total enrolled 2012–2013 part-time, 0. Openings 2013–2014, 6. The median number of years required for completion of a degree in 2012–2013 were 5. The number of students enrolled full- and part-time who were dismissed or voluntarily withdrew from this program area in 2012–2013 were 0. *Quantitative Methods PhD (Doctor of Philosophy)*—Applications 2012–2013, 5. Total applicants accepted 2012–2013, 0. Number full-time enrolled (new admits only) 2012–2013, 0. Number part-time enrolled (new admits only) 2012–2013, 0. Total enrolled 2012–2013 full-time, 1. Total enrolled 2012–2013 part-time, 0. Openings 2013–2014, 4. The number of students enrolled full- and part-time who were dismissed or voluntarily withdrew from this program area in 2012–2013 were 1. *Health Psychology PhD (Doctor of Philosophy)*—Applications 2012–2013, 18. Total applicants accepted 2012–2013, 3. Number full-time enrolled (new admits only) 2012–2013, 2. Number part-time enrolled (new admits only) 2012–2013, 0. Total enrolled 2012–2013 full-time, 4. Total enrolled 2012–2013 part-time, 0. Openings 2013–2014, 6. The number of students enrolled full- and part-time who were dismissed or voluntarily withdrew from this program area in 2012–2013 were 3.

Scores: Entries appear in this order: required test or GPA, minimum score (if required), median score of students entering in 2012–2013. *Behavioral Neuroscience PhD (Doctor of Philosophy)*: GRE-V 96, 97, GRE-Q 84, 90, GRE-Analytical 56, 71, last 2 years GPA 90, 93; *Clinical Psychology PhD (Doctor of Philosophy)*: GRE-V no minimum stated, GRE-Q no minimum stated, GRE-Analytical no minimum stated, last 2 years GPA 85, 92; *Developmental Psychology PhD (Doctor of Philosophy)*: GRE-V 77, 88, GRE-Q 87, 87, GRE-Analytical 74, 75, last 2 years GPA 100, 100; *Cognitive Science PhD (Doctor of Philosophy)*: GRE-V no minimum stated, GRE-Q no minimum stated, GRE-Analytical no minimum stated, last 2 years GPA no minimum stated; *Social/Personality Psychology PhD (Doctor of Philosophy)*: GRE-V no minimum stated, GRE-Q no minimum stated, GRE-Analytical no minimum stated, last 2 years GPA no minimum stated; *Quantitative Methods PhD (Doctor of Philosophy)*: GRE-V no minimum stated, GRE-Q no minimum stated, GRE-Analytical no minimum stated, last 2 years GPA no minimum stated; *Health Psychology PhD (Doctor of Philosophy)*: GRE-V 89, 95, GRE-Q 72, 72, GRE-Analytical 87, 87, last 2 years GPA 95, 97.

Other Criteria: (importance of criteria rated low, medium, or high): GRE scores—medium, research experience—high, clinically related public service—low, GPA—high, letters of recommendation—high, interview—medium, statement of goals and objectives—high, undergraduate major in psychology—high, specific undergraduate psychology courses taken—medium. For additional information on admission require-

ments, go to http://www.psych.ubc.ca/grad-pgm/admissions.psy.

Student Characteristics: The following represents characteristics of students in 2012–2013 in all graduate psychology programs in the department: Female—full-time 67, part-time 0; Male—full-time 31, part-time 0; African American/Black—full-time 0, part-time 0; Hispanic/Latino(a)—full-time 0, part-time 0; Asian/Pacific Islander—full-time 0, part-time 0; American Indian/Alaska Native—full-time 0, part-time 0; Caucasian/White—full-time 0, part-time 0; Multi-ethnic—full-time 0, part-time 0; students subject to the Americans With Disabilities Act—full-time 0, part-time 0; Unknown ethnicity—full-time 98, part-time 0; International students who hold an F-1 or J-1 Visa—full-time 0, part-time 0.

Financial Information/Assistance:

Tuition for Full-Time Study: *Master's:* State residents: per academic year $4,350; Nonstate residents: per academic year $4,350. *Doctoral:* State residents: per academic year $4,350; Nonstate residents: per academic year $4,350. Tuition is subject to change. See the following website for updates and changes in tuition costs: http://www.grad.ubc.ca/prospective-students/tuition-fees-cost-living/graduate-tuition-fees.

Financial Assistance:

First-Year Students: Teaching assistantships available for first year. Average amount paid per academic year: $10,914. Average number of hours worked per week: 12. Apply by December 15. Research assistantships available for first year. Average amount paid per academic year: $5,000. Apply by December 15. Fellowships and scholarships available for first -year. Average amount paid per academic year: $17,500. Apply by December 15.

Advanced Students: Teaching assistantships available for advanced students. Average amount paid per academic year: $11,342. Average number of hours worked per week: 12. Apply by December 15. Research assistantships available for advanced students. Average amount paid per academic year: $5,000. Apply by December 15. Fellowships and scholarships available for advanced students. Average amount paid per academic year: $16,000. Apply by September 15.

Additional Information: Of all students currently enrolled full time, 100% benefited from one or more of the listed financial assistance programs. Application and information available online at: http://www.psych.ubc.ca/grad-pgm/awadsapps.psy.

Internships/Practica: Doctoral Degree (PhD Clinical Psychology): For those doctoral students for whom a professional psychology internship was required in this program prior to graduation, (4) students applied for an internship in 2011–2012, with (2) students obtaining an internship. Of those students who obtained an internship, (2) were paid internships. Of those students who obtained an internship, (2) students placed in APA/CPA accredited internships, (0) students placed in internships not APA/CPA accredited, but listed with the Association of Psychology Postdoctoral and Internship Programs (APPIC), (0) students placed in internships conforming to guidelines of the Council of Directors of School Psychology Programs (CDSPP), (0) students placed in internships that were not APA/CPA accredited, APPIC or CDSPP listed. Clinical students are required to do two years of practicum in our psychology training clinic as well as community-based practica. A CPA- or APA-accredited psychology internship is required for the PhD in clinical psychology.

Housing and Day Care: On-campus housing is available. See the following website for more information: http://www.grad.ubc.ca/campus-community/residential-graduate-colleges. On-campus day care facilities are available. See the following website for more information: http://www.childcare.ubc.ca/.

Employment of Department Graduates:

Master's Degree Graduates: Of those who graduated in the academic year 2011–2012, the following categories and numbers represent the postgraduate activities and employment of master's degree graduates: Enrolled in a psychology doctoral program (20), enrolled in a postdoctoral residency/fellowship (n/a), employed in independent practice (n/a), employed in other positions at a higher education institution (1), employed in business or industry (1), total from the above (master's) (22).

Doctoral Degree Graduates: Of those who graduated in the academic year 2011–2012, the following categories and numbers represent the postgraduate activities and employment of doctoral degree graduates: Enrolled in a psychology doctoral program (n/a), enrolled in a postdoctoral residency/fellowship (1), employed in independent practice (1), employed in an academic position at a university (4), do not know (1), total from the above (doctoral) (7).

Additional Information:

Orientation, Objectives, and Emphasis of Department: The department is organized into seven subject content areas with which faculty and graduate students are affiliated. Graduate training emphasizes a high degree of research competence and, from the beginning of the program, students are involved in increasingly independent research activities.

Special Facilities or Resources: The department is housed in an attractive building of about 90,000 square feet, designed for psychological research. The department has well-equipped research facilities including a psychology clinic, observation galleries, and animal, psychophysiological, perceptual, cognitive, and social/personality laboratories.

Information for Students With Physical Disabilities: See the following website for more information: http://www.students.ubc.ca/access/disability-services/.

Application Information:

Send to Graduate Secretary, Department of Psychology, University of British Columbia, Vancouver, BC, Canada V6T 1Z4. Application available online. URL of online application: http://www.grad.ubc.ca/apply/online/. Students are admitted in the Fall, application deadline December 15. *Fee:* $93. The application fee for international applicants is $153. The application fee is waived for international applicants whose correspondence address is located in one of the world's 50 least developed countries, as declared by the United Nations. Note: All dollar amounts specified in this entry are Canadian dollars.

Calgary, University of
Department of Psychology
2500 University Drive, Northwest
Calgary, AB T2N 1N4
Telephone: (403) 220-5561
Fax: (403) 282-8249
E-mail: *psycgrad@ucalgary.ca*
Web: *http://www.psyc.ucalgary.ca/*

Department Information:
1964. Head: Dr. David Hodgins. Number of faculty: total—full-time 29; women—full-time 11; total—minority—full-time 2; women minority—full-time 1.

Programs and Degrees Offered:
Listed in the following order: Program area, degree type (T if terminal Master's), number awarded 7/11–6/12. Psychology PhD (Doctor of Philosophy) 6, Clinical Psychology PhD (Doctor of Philosophy) 13.

CPA Accreditation: Clinical PhD (Doctor of Philosophy).

Student Applications/Admissions:
Student Applications
Psychology PhD (Doctor of Philosophy)—Applications 2012–2013, 45. Total applicants accepted 2012–2013, 11. Number full-time enrolled (new admits only) 2012–2013, 11. Total enrolled 2012–2013 full-time, 46. Total enrolled 2012–2013 part-time, 0. Openings 2013–2014, 10. The median number of years required for completion of a degree in 2012–2013 were 4. The number of students enrolled full- and part-time who were dismissed or voluntarily withdrew from this program area in 2012–2013 were 0. *Clinical Psychology PhD (Doctor of Philosophy)*—Applications 2012–2013, 82. Total applicants accepted 2012–2013, 6. Number full-time enrolled (new admits only) 2012–2013, 6. Total enrolled 2012–2013 full-time, 38. Total enrolled 2012–2013 part-time, 0. Openings 2013–2014, 6. The median number of years required for completion of a degree in 2012–2013 were 4. The number of students enrolled full- and part-time who were dismissed or voluntarily withdrew from this program area in 2012–2013 were 0.

Scores: Entries appear in this order: required test or GPA, minimum score (if required), median score of students entering in 2012–2013. *Psychology PhD (Doctor of Philosophy)*: GRE-V no minimum stated, GRE-Q no minimum stated, GRE-Analytical no minimum stated, overall undergraduate GPA 3.0, last 2 years GPA 3.4, Masters GPA 3.4; *Clinical Psychology PhD (Doctor of Philosophy)*: GRE-V no minimum stated, GRE-Q no minimum stated, GRE-Analytical no minimum stated, overall undergraduate GPA 3.0, last 2 years GPA 3.6, Masters GPA 3.6.

Other Criteria: (importance of criteria rated low, medium, or high): GRE scores—medium, research experience—high, work experience—medium, extracurricular activity—low, clinically related public service—medium, GPA—high, letters of recommendation—high, interview—medium, statement of goals and objectives—medium, research proposal—medium, undergraduate major in psychology—high, specific undergraduate psychology courses taken—high. For additional information on admission requirements, go to https://psychology.ucalgary.ca/graduate-program.

Student Characteristics: The following represents characteristics of students in 2012–2013 in all graduate psychology programs in the department: Female—full-time 58, part-time 0; Male—full-time 26, part-time 0; African American/Black—full-time 0, part-time 0; Hispanic/Latino(a)—full-time 0, part-time 0; Asian/Pacific Islander—full-time 10, part-time 0; American Indian/Alaska Native—full-time 0, part-time 0; Caucasian/White—full-time 70, part-time 0; Multi-ethnic—full-time 0, part-time 0; students subject to the Americans With Disabilities Act—full-time 0, part-time 0; Unknown ethnicity—full-time 4, part-time 0; International students who hold an F-1 or J-1 Visa—full-time 4, part-time 0.

Financial Information/Assistance:

Tuition for Full-Time Study: *Master's:* State residents: per academic year $5,540; Nonstate residents: per academic year $12,570. *Doctoral:* State residents: per academic year $5,540; Nonstate residents: per academic year $12,570. Tuition is subject to change. See the following website for updates and changes in tuition costs: http://grad.ucalgary.ca/prospective/tuition.

Financial Assistance:

First-Year Students: Teaching assistantships available for first year. Average amount paid per academic year: $16,232. Average number of hours worked per week: 12. Fellowships and scholarships available for first -year. Average amount paid per academic year: $4,086.

Advanced Students: Teaching assistantships available for advanced students. Average amount paid per academic year: $16,232. Average number of hours worked per week: 12. Fellowships and scholarships available for advanced students. Average amount paid per academic year: $4,086.

Additional Information: Of all students currently enrolled full time, 100% benefited from one or more of the listed financial assistance programs. Application and information available online at: http://grad.ucalgary.ca/awards.

Internships/Practica: Doctoral Degree (PhD Clinical Psychology): For those doctoral students for whom a professional psychology internship was required in this program prior to graduation, (5) students applied for an internship in 2011–2012, with (5) students obtaining an internship. Of those students who obtained an internship, (5) were paid internships. Of those students who obtained an internship, (5) students placed in APA/CPA accredited internships, (0) students placed in internships not APA/CPA accredited, but listed with the Association of Psychology Postdoctoral and Internship Programs (APPIC), (0) students placed in internships conforming to guidelines of the Council of Directors of School Psychology Programs (CDSPP), (0) students placed in internships that were not APA/CPA accredited, APPIC or CDSPP listed. Practica are available at several settings, including Alberta Health Services and other community services.

Housing and Day Care: On-campus housing is available. See the following website for more information: http://www.ucalgary.ca/residence/. On-campus day care facilities are available. See the following website for more information: http://www.ucalgary.ca/uccc/.

Employment of Department Graduates:

Master's Degree Graduates: Of those who graduated in the academic year 2011–2012, the following categories and numbers represent the postgraduate activities and employment of master's degree graduates: Enrolled in a postdoctoral residency/fellowship (n/a), employed in independent practice (n/a), total from the above (master's) (0).

Doctoral Degree Graduates: Of those who graduated in the academic year 2011–2012, the following categories and numbers represent the postgraduate activities and employment of doctoral degree graduates: Enrolled in a psychology doctoral program (n/a), enrolled in a postdoctoral residency/fellowship (2), employed in an academic position at a university (1), employed in business or industry (1), employed in a hospital/medical center (5), total from the above (doctoral) (9).

Additional Information:

Orientation, Objectives, and Emphasis of Department: This is a research-oriented department with a strong focus on applied problems. We offer both a clinical psychology and a psychology program. Specific research programs in psychology include: Brain and Cognitive Science, Industrial/Organizational Psychology, and Social and Theoretical Psychology.

Information for Students With Physical Disabilities: See the following website for more information: http://www.ucalgary.ca/drc/.

Application Information:

Send to Graduate Programs Administrator, Department of Psychology, 2500 University Drive Northwest, University of Calgary, Calgary, AB T2N 1N4 Canada. Application available online. URL of online application: https://iac01.ucalgary.ca/StudentAdmission/default.aspx. Students are admitted in the Fall, application deadline January 1; Winter, application deadline October 1. The deadline for the Clinical Psychology program is January 1, and the deadline for the Psychology Graduate Program is January 1 for September start and October 1 for January start. *Fee:* $100. International student application fee is $130 Canadian. Note: All dollar amounts specified in this entry are Canadian dollars.

Carleton University
Department of Psychology
Faculty of Arts and Social Sciences
1125 Colonel By Drive
Ottawa, ON K1S 5B6
Telephone: (613) 520-4017
Fax: (613) 520-3667
E-mail: *Gradpsychology@carleton.ca*
Web: *http://www.carleton.ca/psychology/*

Department Information:

1953. Chairperson: Anne Bowker. Number of faculty: total—full-time 39; women—full-time 21.

Programs and Degrees Offered:

Listed in the following order: Program area, degree type (T if terminal Master's), number awarded 7/11–6/12. Psychology MA/

MS (Master of Arts/Science) (T) 33, Psychology PhD (Doctor of Philosophy) 11.

Student Applications/Admissions:

Student Applications

Psychology MA/MS (Master of Arts/Science)—Applications 2012–2013, 161. Total applicants accepted 2012–2013, 39. Number full-time enrolled (new admits only) 2012–2013, 27. Number part-time enrolled (new admits only) 2012–2013, 0. Total enrolled 2012–2013 full-time, 81. Total enrolled 2012–2013 part-time, 3. Openings 2013–2014, 35. The median number of years required for completion of a degree in 2012–2013 were 2. The number of students enrolled full- and part-time who were dismissed or voluntarily withdrew from this program area in 2012–2013 were 4. *Psychology PhD (Doctor of Philosophy)*—Applications 2012–2013, 47. Total applicants accepted 2012–2013, 16. Number full-time enrolled (new admits only) 2012–2013, 14. Number part-time enrolled (new admits only) 2012–2013, 1. Total enrolled 2012–2013 full-time, 64. Total enrolled 2012–2013 part-time, 8. Openings 2013–2014, 14. The median number of years required for completion of a degree in 2012–2013 were 5. The number of students enrolled full- and part-time who were dismissed or voluntarily withdrew from this program area in 2012–2013 were 3.

Scores: Entries appear in this order: required test or GPA, minimum score (if required), median score of students entering in 2012–2013. *Psychology MA/MS (Master of Arts/Science):* overall undergraduate GPA 70, 79, last 2 years GPA 72, 80, psychology GPA 79, 85; *Psychology PhD (Doctor of Philosophy):* last 2 years GPA 80, 80, psychology GPA 80, 85, Masters GPA 80, 90.

Other Criteria: (importance of criteria rated low, medium, or high): research experience—high, work experience—medium, extracurricular activity—medium, GPA—high, letters of recommendation—high, interview—low, statement of goals and objectives—high, undergraduate major in psychology—high, specific undergraduate psychology courses taken—high. For additional information on admission requirements, go to http://www2.carleton.ca/psychology/graduate-studies/graduate/.

Student Characteristics: The following represents characteristics of students in 2012–2013 in all graduate psychology programs in the department: Female—full-time 113, part-time 7; Male—full-time 32, part-time 4; African American/Black—full-time 0, part-time 0; Hispanic/Latino(a)—full-time 0, part-time 0; Asian/Pacific Islander—full-time 2, part-time 0; American Indian/Alaska Native—full-time 0, part-time 0; Caucasian/White—full-time 143, part-time 11; Multi-ethnic—full-time 0, part-time 0; students subject to the Americans With Disabilities Act—full-time 0, part-time 0; Unknown ethnicity—full-time 0, part-time 0; International students who hold an F-1 or J-1 Visa—full-time 2, part-time 0.

Financial Information/Assistance:

Tuition for Full-Time Study: *Master's:* State residents: per academic year $8,732; Nonstate residents: per academic year $18,600. *Doctoral:* State residents: per academic year $8,732; Nonstate residents: per academic year $18,600. Tuition is subject to change. See the following website for updates and changes in tuition costs: http://www5.carleton.ca/financialservices/student-accounts-receivable/tuition-fees/.

Financial Assistance:

First-Year Students: Teaching assistantships available for first year. Average amount paid per academic year: $10,129. Average number of hours worked per week: 10. Apply by January 15. Research assistantships available for first year. Average amount paid per academic year: $3,000. Apply by January 15. Fellowships and scholarships available for first -year. Average amount paid per academic year: $5,000. Apply by January 15.

Advanced Students: Teaching assistantships available for advanced students. Average amount paid per academic year: $10,129. Average number of hours worked per week: 10. Apply by January 15. Research assistantships available for advanced students. Average amount paid per academic year: $3,500. Apply by January 15. Fellowships and scholarships available for advanced students. Average amount paid per academic year: $8,000. Apply by January 15.

Additional Information: Of all students currently enrolled full time, 90% benefited from one or more of the listed financial assistance programs. Application and information available online at: http://www2.carleton.ca/psychology/graduate-studies/scholarships-and-awards/.

Housing and Day Care: On-campus housing is available. See the following website for more information: http://housing.carleton.ca/. On-campus day care facilities are available. See the following website for more information: http://www.cbccc.ca/.

Employment of Department Graduates:

Master's Degree Graduates: Of those who graduated in the academic year 2011–2012, the following categories and numbers represent the postgraduate activities and employment of master's degree graduates: Enrolled in a psychology doctoral program (15), enrolled in a postdoctoral residency/fellowship (n/a), employed in independent practice (n/a), employed in an academic position at a 2-year/4-year college (1), employed in a professional position in a school system (1), employed in business or industry (1), employed in a government agency (12), employed in a community mental health/counseling center (1), other employment position (2), total from the above (master's) (33).

Doctoral Degree Graduates: Of those who graduated in the academic year 2011–2012, the following categories and numbers represent the postgraduate activities and employment of doctoral degree graduates: Enrolled in a psychology doctoral program (n/a), enrolled in a postdoctoral residency/fellowship (1), employed in an academic position at a university (4), employed in a government agency (5), employed in a community mental health/counseling center (1), total from the above (doctoral) (11).

Additional Information:

Orientation, Objectives, and Emphasis of Department: The program is strongly research-oriented, although practical courses such as quantitative methods, testing and behavior modification are available. This degree however does not offer training in applied areas (e.g. clinical, educational, counseling psychology, etc).

Information for Students With Physical Disabilities: See the following website for more information: http://www1.carleton.ca/pmc/.

Application Information:

Send to Graduate Studies Administrator, B-557 Loeb Building, 1125 Colonel By Drive, Ottawa, ON K1S 5B6. Application available online.

URL of online application: http://graduate.carleton.ca/apply-online/. Students are admitted in the Fall, application deadline January 15; Winter, application deadline November 1. *Fee*: $100. Note: All dollar amounts specified in this entry are Canadian dollars.

Concordia University
Department of Psychology
Faculty of Arts and Science
7141 Sherbrooke Street West
Montreal, QC H4B 1R6
Telephone: (514) 848-2424
Fax: (514) 848-4545
E-mail: *Shirley.Black@concordia.ca*
Web: *http://www.psychology.concordia.ca*

Department Information:
1963. Chairperson: Jean-Roch Laurence, PhD. Number of faculty: total—full-time 47, part-time 22; women—full-time 19, part-time 7; total—minority—full-time 1, part-time 1; women minority—full-time 1.

Programs and Degrees Offered:
Listed in the following order: Program area, degree type (T if terminal Master's), number awarded 7/11–6/12. Research and Clinical Training PhD (Doctor of Philosophy) 14, Research PhD (Doctor of Philosophy) 7.

APA Accreditation: Clinical PhD (Doctor of Philosophy). Student Outcome Data Website: http://psychology.concordia.ca/graduateprograms/programoptions/.

CPA Accreditation: Clinical PhD (Doctor of Philosophy).

Student Applications/Admissions:
Student Applications
Research and Clinical Training PhD (Doctor of Philosophy)—Applications 2012–2013, 218. Total applicants accepted 2012–2013, 13. Number full-time enrolled (new admits only) 2012–2013, 11. Number part-time enrolled (new admits only) 2012–2013, 0. Total enrolled 2012–2013 full-time, 75. Total enrolled 2012–2013 part-time, 0. Openings 2013–2014, 11. The median number of years required for completion of a degree in 2012–2013 were 6. The number of students enrolled full- and part-time who were dismissed or voluntarily withdrew from this program area in 2012–2013 were 2. *Research PhD (Doctor of Philosophy)*—Applications 2012–2013, 55. Total applicants accepted 2012–2013, 12. Number full-time enrolled (new admits only) 2012–2013, 11. Number part-time enrolled (new admits only) 2012–2013, 1. Total enrolled 2012–2013 full-time, 55. Total enrolled 2012–2013 part-time, 1. Openings 2013–2014, 10. The median number of years required for completion of a degree in 2012–2013 were 6. The number of students enrolled full- and part-time who were dismissed or voluntarily withdrew from this program area in 2012–2013 were 0.
Other Criteria: (importance of criteria rated low, medium, or high): GRE scores—low, research experience—high, work experience—medium, extracurricular activity—low, clinically related public service—medium, GPA—medium, letters of recommendation—high, interview—medium, statement of goals and objectives—high, undergraduate major in psychology—high, specific undergraduate psychology courses taken—medium, Research Option does not require clinically related service. Thesis Supervisor is required for admission to graduate program. For additional information on admission requirements, go to http://psychology.concordia.ca/graduateprograms/applyingtopsychology/graduateapplication/.

Student Characteristics: The following represents characteristics of students in 2012–2013 in all graduate psychology programs in the department: Female—full-time 95, part-time 0; Male—full-time 35, part-time 1; African American/Black—full-time 1, part-time 0; Hispanic/Latino(a)—full-time 7, part-time 0; Asian/Pacific Islander—full-time 9, part-time 0; American Indian/Alaska Native—full-time 0, part-time 0; Caucasian/White—full-time 110, part-time 1; Multi-ethnic—full-time 3, part-time 0; students subject to the Americans With Disabilities Act—full-time 0, part-time 0; Unknown ethnicity—full-time 0, part-time 0; International students who hold an F-1 or J-1 Visa—full-time 11, part-time 0.

Financial Information/Assistance:
Tuition for Full-Time Study: *Master's:* State residents: per academic year $2,439; Nonstate residents: per academic year $16,467. *Doctoral:* State residents: per academic year $2,439; Nonstate residents: per academic year $14,785. Tuition is subject to change. Tuition costs vary by program. See the following website for updates and changes in tuition costs: http://www.concordia.ca/admissions/tuition-and-fees/graduate/.

Financial Assistance:
First-Year Students: Teaching assistantships available for first year. Average amount paid per academic year: $6,074. Average number of hours worked per week: 10. Apply by August 1. Research assistantships available for first year. Average amount paid per academic year: $11,646. Average number of hours worked per week: 10. Fellowships and scholarships available for first - year. Average amount paid per academic year: $20,000. Apply by October.

Advanced Students: Teaching assistantships available for advanced students. Average amount paid per academic year: $6,074. Average number of hours worked per week: 10. Apply by August 1. Research assistantships available for advanced students. Average amount paid per academic year: $7,971. Average number of hours worked per week: 10. Fellowships and scholarships available for advanced students. Average amount paid per academic year: $21,200. Apply by October.

Additional Information: Of all students currently enrolled full time, 74% benefited from one or more of the listed financial assistance programs. Application and information available online at: http://graduatestudies.concordia.ca/prospectivestudents/funding/.

Internships/Practica: Doctoral Degree (PhD Research and Clinical Training): For those doctoral students for whom a professional psychology internship was required in this program prior to graduation, (12) students applied for an internship in 2011–2012, with (7) students obtaining an internship. Of those students who obtained an internship, (5) were paid internships. Of those students who obtained an internship, (5) students placed in APA/CPA accredited internships, (0) students placed in internships not

APA/CPA accredited, but listed with the Association of Psychology Postdoctoral and Internship Programs (APPIC), (0) students placed in internships conforming to guidelines of the Council of Directors of School Psychology Programs (CDSPP), (2) students placed in internships that were not APA/CPA accredited, APPIC or CDSPP listed. Clinical students complete a variety of practica and internships while in program residence. All clinical students receive extensive practicum experience in psychotherapy and assessment in our on-campus training clinic, the Applied Psychology Center (APC). APC clients are seen by graduate students under the supervision of clinical faculty. The types of services offered by the APC reflect the interests of clinical supervisors and students, and may include individual, family, or marital psychotherapy, behavior therapy for sexual or phobic difficulties, and treatment of child disorders. During the summer of their second year, students also complete a full-time practicum at a mental health facility in the Montreal area. During their final year in the program, students complete their full-time, predoctoral clinical internships. Recent students have undertaken predoctoral internships at a variety of mental health facilities across Canada and the United States. All students are encouraged to seek internship positions in settings accredited by either the Canadian or American Psychological Associations.

Housing and Day Care: On-campus housing is available. See the following website for more information: http://residence. concordia.ca/. On-campus day care facilities are available. See the following website for more information: http://deanofstudents. concordia.ca/childcare/.

Employment of Department Graduates:
Master's Degree Graduates: Of those who graduated in the academic year 2011–2012, the following categories and numbers represent the postgraduate activities and employment of master's degree graduates: Enrolled in a postdoctoral residency/fellowship (n/a), employed in independent practice (n/a), total from the above (master's) (0).
Doctoral Degree Graduates: Of those who graduated in the academic year 2011–2012, the following categories and numbers represent the postgraduate activities and employment of doctoral degree graduates: Enrolled in a psychology doctoral program (n/a), enrolled in a postdoctoral residency/fellowship (1), employed in independent practice (3), employed in a community mental health/counseling center (2), employed in a hospital/medical center (5), do not know (3), total from the above (doctoral) (14).

Additional Information:
Orientation, Objectives, and Emphasis of Department: Graduate education in both experimental and clinical psychology is strongly research-oriented and intended for students who are planning to complete the PhD degree. The research program for all students is based on an apprentice-type model. An outstanding feature of graduate education at Concordia is that students pursuing only research studies and students pursuing research and clinical studies may conduct their research in the laboratory of any faculty member. A wide variety of contemporary research areas are represented, ranging from behavioral neurobiology, to cognitive and developmental science, to applied interventions with humans. Research findings from numerous areas are integrated in an effort to solve problems associated with appetitive motivation and drug dependence, memory and aging, human cognition and development, developmental psychobiology, adult and child

psychopathology, and sexual dysfunctions, to name several examples. Clinical training is based on the scientist–practitioner model. That is, clinical students meet the same research requirements as other students, and receive extensive professional training in the delivery of psychological services. Students may choose to specialize their clinical training with children or adults.

Special Facilities or Resources: The department has extensive animal and human research facilities that are supported by provincial, federal, and U.S. granting agencies as well as various internal and private sector funds. Research laboratories are well equipped. The department also contains two research centers that are jointly funded by the Government of Quebec and the University, the Center for Studies in Behavioral Neurobiology, and the Center for Research in Human Development. Both centers coordinate multidisciplinary research programs, provide state-of-the-art laboratory equipment, and sponsor colloquia by specialists from other universities in North America and abroad. All graduate students benefit from activities supported by the research centers.

Information for Students With Physical Disabilities: See the following website for more information: http://supportservices. concordia.ca/disabilities.

Application Information:
Send to Concordia University, Graduate Admissions Application Centre, P.O. Box 2002, Station H, Montréal, Québec H3G 2V4, Canada. Application available online. URL of online application: https:// connect2.concordia.ca/concordia/. Students are admitted in the Fall, application deadline December 15. *Fee:* $100. Note: All dollar amounts specified in this entry are Canadian dollars.

Dalhousie University
Department of Psychology
Life Sciences Centre
Halifax, NS B3H 4R2
Telephone: (902) 494-7804
Fax: (902) 494-6585
E-mail: *Ray.Klein@dal.ca*
Web: *http://www.psychology.dal.ca/*

Department Information:
1863. Chairperson: Ray Klein. Number of faculty: total—full-time 32, part-time 6; women—full-time 13, part-time 3.

Programs and Degrees Offered:
Listed in the following order: Program area, degree type (T if terminal Master's), number awarded 7/11–6/12. Clinical Psychology PhD (Doctor of Philosophy) 5, Experimental-Animal PhD (Doctor of Philosophy) 0, Experimental—Human PhD (Doctor of Philosophy) 0, Neuroscience MA/MS (Master of Arts/Science) 2, Experimental—Animal MA/MS (Master of Arts/Science) 0, Neuroscience PhD (Doctor of Philosophy) 2, Experimental—Human MA/MS (Master of Arts/Science) 2.

CPA Accreditation: Clinical PhD (Doctor of Philosophy).

Student Applications/Admissions:

Student Applications

Clinical Psychology PhD (Doctor of Philosophy)—Applications 2012–2013, 120. Total applicants accepted 2012–2013, 7. Number full-time enrolled (new admits only) 2012–2013, 7. Number part-time enrolled (new admits only) 2012–2013, 0. Total enrolled 2012–2013 full-time, 40. Total enrolled 2012–2013 part-time, 0. Openings 2013–2014, 6. The median number of years required for completion of a degree in 2012–2013 were 5. The number of students enrolled full- and part-time who were dismissed or voluntarily withdrew from this program area in 2012–2013 were 0. *Experimental-Animal PhD (Doctor of Philosophy)*—Applications 2012–2013, 1. Total applicants accepted 2012–2013, 1. Number full-time enrolled (new admits only) 2012–2013, 1. Number part-time enrolled (new admits only) 2012–2013, 0. Total enrolled 2012–2013 full-time, 1. Total enrolled 2012–2013 part-time, 0. Openings 2013–2014, 6. The median number of years required for completion of a degree in 2012–2013 were 5. The number of students enrolled full- and part-time who were dismissed or voluntarily withdrew from this program area in 2012–2013 were 0. *Experimental—Human PhD (Doctor of Philosophy)*—Applications 2012–2013, 2. Total applicants accepted 2012–2013, 2. Number full-time enrolled (new admits only) 2012–2013, 2. Number part-time enrolled (new admits only) 2012–2013, 0. Total enrolled 2012–2013 full-time, 13. Total enrolled 2012–2013 part-time, 0. Openings 2013–2014, 6. The median number of years required for completion of a degree in 2012–2013 were 5. The number of students enrolled full- and part-time who were dismissed or voluntarily withdrew from this program area in 2012–2013 were 0. *Neuroscience MA/MS (Master of Arts/Science)*—Applications 2012–2013, 5. Total applicants accepted 2012–2013, 2. Number full-time enrolled (new admits only) 2012–2013, 2. Number part-time enrolled (new admits only) 2012–2013, 0. Total enrolled 2012–2013 full-time, 5. Total enrolled 2012–2013 part-time, 0. Openings 2013–2014, 6. The median number of years required for completion of a degree in 2012–2013 were 2. The number of students enrolled full- and part-time who were dismissed or voluntarily withdrew from this program area in 2012–2013 were 0. *Experimental—Animal MA/MS (Master of Arts/Science)*—Applications 2012–2013, 14. Total applicants accepted 2012–2013, 0. Number full-time enrolled (new admits only) 2012–2013, 0. Number part-time enrolled (new admits only) 2012–2013, 0. Openings 2013–2014, 6. The median number of years required for completion of a degree in 2012–2013 were 2. The number of students enrolled full- and part-time who were dismissed or voluntarily withdrew from this program area in 2012–2013 were 0. *Neuroscience PhD (Doctor of Philosophy)*—Applications 2012–2013, 3. Total applicants accepted 2012–2013, 3. Number full-time enrolled (new admits only) 2012–2013, 3. Number part-time enrolled (new admits only) 2012–2013, 0. Total enrolled 2012–2013 full-time, 7. Total enrolled 2012–2013 part-time, 0. Openings 2013–2014, 6. The median number of years required for completion of a degree in 2012–2013 were 5. The number of students enrolled full- and part-time who were dismissed or voluntarily withdrew from this program area in 2012–2013 were 0. *Experimental—Human MA/MS (Master of Arts/Science)*—Applications 2012–2013, 14. Total applicants accepted 2012–2013, 1. Number full-time enrolled (new admits only) 2012–2013, 1. Number part-time enrolled (new admits only) 2012–2013, 0. Total enrolled 2012–2013 full-time, 5. Total enrolled 2012–2013 part-time, 0. Openings 2013–2014, 6. The median number of years required for completion of a degree in 2012–2013 were 2. The number of students enrolled full- and part-time who were dismissed or voluntarily withdrew from this program area in 2012–2013 were 0.

Scores: Entries appear in this order: required test or GPA, minimum score (if required), median score of students entering in 2012–2013. *Clinical Psychology PhD (Doctor of Philosophy):* GRE-V no minimum stated, GRE-Q no minimum stated, GRE-Analytical no minimum stated, GRE-Subject (Psychology) no minimum stated, overall undergraduate GPA no minimum stated, psychology GPA no minimum stated; *Experimental-Animal PhD (Doctor of Philosophy):* GRE-V no minimum stated, GRE-Q no minimum stated, GRE-Analytical no minimum stated, overall undergraduate GPA no minimum stated, psychology GPA no minimum stated; *Experimental—Human PhD (Doctor of Philosophy):* GRE-V no minimum stated, GRE-Q no minimum stated, GRE-Analytical no minimum stated, overall undergraduate GPA no minimum stated, psychology GPA no minimum stated; *Neuroscience MA/MS (Master of Arts/Science):* overall undergraduate GPA no minimum stated, psychology GPA no minimum stated; *Experimental—Animal MA/MS (Master of Arts/Science):* GRE-V no minimum stated, GRE-Q no minimum stated, GRE-Analytical no minimum stated, overall undergraduate GPA no minimum stated, psychology GPA no minimum stated; *Neuroscience PhD (Doctor of Philosophy):* overall undergraduate GPA no minimum stated, psychology GPA no minimum stated; *Experimental—Human MA/MS (Master of Arts/Science):* GRE-V no minimum stated, GRE-Q no minimum stated, GRE-Analytical no minimum stated, overall undergraduate GPA no minimum stated, psychology GPA no minimum stated.

Other Criteria: (importance of criteria rated low, medium, or high): GRE scores—medium, research experience—high, work experience—low, extracurricular activity—low, clinically related public service—low, GPA—high, letters of recommendation—high, interview—medium, statement of goals and objectives—high, willing supervisor—high, undergraduate major in psychology—high, specific undergraduate psychology courses taken—low, Clinically related public service is high for clinical program. For additional information on admission requirements, go to http://psychology.dal.ca/Programs/.

Student Characteristics: The following represents characteristics of students in 2012–2013 in all graduate psychology programs in the department: Female—full-time 47, part-time 0; Male—full-time 24, part-time 0; African American/Black—full-time 0, part-time 0; Hispanic/Latino(a)—full-time 0, part-time 0; Asian/Pacific Islander—full-time 1, part-time 0; American Indian/Alaska Native—full-time 0, part-time 0; Caucasian/White—full-time 69, part-time 0; Multi-ethnic—full-time 0, part-time 0; students subject to the Americans With Disabilities Act—full-time 0, part-time 0; Unknown ethnicity—full-time 1, part-time 0; International students who hold an F-1 or J-1 Visa—full-time 1, part-time 0.

Financial Information/Assistance:

Tuition for Full-Time Study: *Master's:* State residents: per academic year $8,891; Nonstate residents: per academic year $14,396. *Doctoral:* State residents: per academic year $9,236; Nonstate residents: per academic year $14,741. Tuition is subject to change.

See the following website for updates and changes in tuition costs: http://www.dal.ca/admissions/money_matters/tuition_fees_costs.html.

Financial Assistance:

First-Year Students: Teaching assistantships available for first year. Average amount paid per academic year: $2,795. Average number of hours worked per week: 10. Fellowships and scholarships available for first -year. Average amount paid per academic year: $18,000.

Advanced Students: Teaching assistantships available for advanced students. Average amount paid per academic year: $2,795. Average number of hours worked per week: 10. Fellowships and scholarships available for advanced students. Average amount paid per academic year: $18,300.

Additional Information: Of all students currently enrolled full time, 100% benefited from one or more of the listed financial assistance programs.

Internships/Practica: Doctoral Degree (PhD Clinical Psychology): For those doctoral students for whom a professional psychology internship was required in this program prior to graduation, (2) students applied for an internship in 2011–2012, with (2) students obtaining an internship. Of those students who obtained an internship, (2) were paid internships. Of those students who obtained an internship, (2) students placed in APA/CPA accredited internships, (0) students placed in internships not APA/CPA accredited, but listed with the Association of Psychology Postdoctoral and Internship Programs (APPIC), (0) students placed in internships conforming to guidelines of the Council of Directors of School Psychology Programs (CDSPP), (0) students placed in internships that were not APA/CPA accredited, APPIC or CDSPP listed. Practicum training is integrated into the Clinical Psychology PhD curriculum, to complement knowledge and skills developed through coursework, to provide opportunities to master specific assessment and intervention techniques, and to ensure that students meet expectations with regard to core competencies. Brief practica are incorporated into a number of the core clinical courses; however, the majority of practicum hours are accumulated through community placements, under the supervision of registered psychologists. Dalhousie is situated in close proximity to a variety of excellent health care facilities, including the IWK Health Centre, the QEII Health Centre, the Nova Scotia Hospital, the Canadian Forces Hospital at CFB Stadacona, and the East Coast Forensic Hospital. Under the guidance of the Field Placement Coordinator, students select and complete a program of practicum placements designed to meet their individual training needs. Students are required to complete a minimum of 600 hours of formal practicum training, but it is recognized that additional practicum hours (for a total of about 1000-1200 hours) are often necessary to ensure a competitive internship application.

Housing and Day Care: On-campus housing is available. See the following website for more information: http://www.dal.ca/campus_life/residence_housing/residence.html. On-campus day care facilities are available. See the following website for more information: http://ucc.dal.ca/.

Employment of Department Graduates:

Master's Degree Graduates: Of those who graduated in the academic year 2011–2012, the following categories and numbers represent the postgraduate activities and employment of master's degree graduates: Enrolled in a psychology doctoral program (6), enrolled in a postdoctoral residency/fellowship (n/a), employed in independent practice (n/a), total from the above (master's) (6).

Doctoral Degree Graduates: Of those who graduated in the academic year 2011–2012, the following categories and numbers represent the postgraduate activities and employment of doctoral degree graduates: Enrolled in a psychology doctoral program (n/a), employed in an academic position at a university (3), employed in a hospital/medical center (5), total from the above (doctoral) (8).

Additional Information:

Orientation, Objectives, and Emphasis of Department: The Department of Psychology offers graduate training leading to MSc and PhD degrees in psychology and in psychology/neuroscience, and to a PhD in clinical psychology. Our graduate programs emphasize training for research. They are best described as apprenticeship programs in which students work closely with a faculty member who has agreed to supervise the student's research. Compared with many other graduate programs, we place less emphasis on course work and greater emphasis on research, scholarship, and independent thinking. The graduate program in psychology/neuroscience is coordinated by the Psychology Department and an interdisciplinary Neuroscience Program Committee with representation from the Departments of Anatomy, Biochemistry, Pharmacology, Physiology and Biophysics, and Psychology. Master's level students in psychology and psychology/neuroscience are expected to advance into the corresponding PhD programs. We do not have a terminal Master's program. The PhD program in clinical psychology is cooperatively administered by the Psychology Department and the Clinical Program Committee with representation from Acadia University, Dalhousie University, Mount Saint Vincent University, Saint Mary's University, and professional psychologists from the teaching hospitals. It is a fast-track PhD Program in which students entering from the bachelor's degree are first registered in an MSc and then fast-tracked into the PhD before the end of their first year, without completing a master's thesis or obtaining a master's degree. Students admitted with a master's degree in Psychology or a closely related field are eligible for direct-entry into the Clinical PhD. Students with a master's degree in Clinical Psychology may be eligible for advanced standing within the program; those with a non-clinical Master's degree may receive course exemptions. Advanced standing and course exemptions are evaluated on a case-by-case basis in consultation with the Clinical Director of Training. The clinical program is a structured five-year program which follows the scientist–practitioner model. During the first four years of the clinical psychology program, students complete required courses, conduct supervised and thesis research, and gain clinical experience through field placements. In the fifth year, students are placed in a full-year clinical internship.

Special Facilities or Resources: The Department of Psychology is located in the Life Sciences Centre which also contains the departments of biology, earth sciences, and oceanography. The psychology building contains very extensive laboratory areas, some with circulating sea-water aquaria, and is designed for research with a range of animal groups (humans, cats, birds, fish, invertebrates) using a range of research techniques in behavior, electrophysiology, neuroanatomy, immunocytochemistry, neurogenetics, and so forth. The department also houses an electronics and woodworking shop, an animal care facility, a surgical facility, a computer lab for word processing, communications, and access to a mainframe; specific neuroscience facilities are in close proximity to hospitals.

Information for Students With Physical Disabilities: See the following website for more information: http://studentaccessibility.dal.ca/.

Application Information:

Send to Graduate Program Secretary, Psychology Department, Dalhousie University, Halifax, NS B3H 4R2. Application available online. URL of online application: http://www.dal.ca/admissions/apply/applying_as_a_graduate_student.html. Students are admitted in the Fall, application deadline January 1. *Fee:* $70. Note: All dollar amounts specified in this entry are Canadian dollars.

Guelph, University of
Department of Psychology
College of Social and Applied Human Sciences
4th Floor MacKinnon Extension
Guelph, ON N1G 2W1
Telephone: (519) 824-4120 ext. 53508
Fax: (519) 837-8629
E-mail: *evans@psy.uoguelph.ca*
Web: *http://www.uoguelph.ca/psychology/*

Department Information:

1966. Chairperson: Mary Ann Evans. Number of faculty: total—full-time 33; women—full-time 14; total—minority—full-time 4; women minority—full-time 2.

Programs and Degrees Offered:

Listed in the following order: Program area, degree type (T if terminal Master's), number awarded 7/11–6/12. Neuroscience and Applied Cognitive Science PhD (Doctor of Philosophy) 5, Industrial/Organizational PhD (Doctor of Philosophy) 2, Applied Social PhD (Doctor of Philosophy) 3, Clinical Psychology:Applied Developmental Emphasis PhD (Doctor of Philosophy) 5, Neuroscience and Applied Cognitive Science MA/MS (Master of Arts/Science) 2, Applied Social MA/MS (Master of Arts/Science) 0, Clinical Psychology:Applied Developmental Emphasis MA/MS (Master of Arts/Science) 6, Industrial/Organizational MA/MS (Master of Arts/Science) 3.

CPA Accreditation: Clinical PhD (Doctor of Philosophy).

Student Applications/Admissions:

Student Applications

Neuroscience and Applied Cognitive Science PhD (Doctor of Philosophy)—Applications 2012–2013, 5. Total applicants accepted 2012–2013, 0. Number full-time enrolled (new admits only) 2012–2013, 0. Number part-time enrolled (new admits only) 2012–2013, 0. Total enrolled 2012–2013 full-time, 12. Total enrolled 2012–2013 part-time, 2. Openings 2013–2014, 4. The median number of years required for completion of a degree in 2012–2013 were 4. The number of students enrolled full- and part-time who were dismissed or voluntarily withdrew from this program area in 2012–2013 were 0. *Industrial/Organi-*

zational PhD (Doctor of Philosophy)—Applications 2012–2013, 3. Total applicants accepted 2012–2013, 2. Number full-time enrolled (new admits only) 2012–2013, 2. Number part-time enrolled (new admits only) 2012–2013, 0. Total enrolled 2012–2013 full-time, 7. Total enrolled 2012–2013 part-time, 0. Openings 2013–2014, 5. The median number of years required for completion of a degree in 2012–2013 were 4. The number of students enrolled full- and part-time who were dismissed or voluntarily withdrew from this program area in 2012–2013 were 0. *Applied Social PhD (Doctor of Philosophy)*—Applications 2012–2013, 8. Total applicants accepted 2012–2013, 4. Number full-time enrolled (new admits only) 2012–2013, 1. Number part-time enrolled (new admits only) 2012–2013, 0. Total enrolled 2012–2013 full-time, 10. Total enrolled 2012–2013 part-time, 1. Openings 2013–2014, 2. The median number of years required for completion of a degree in 2012–2013 were 4. The number of students enrolled full- and part-time who were dismissed or voluntarily withdrew from this program area in 2012–2013 were 0. *Clinical Psychology:Applied Developmental Emphasis PhD (Doctor of Philosophy)*—Applications 2012–2013, 9. Total applicants accepted 2012–2013, 7. Number full-time enrolled (new admits only) 2012–2013, 7. Number part-time enrolled (new admits only) 2012–2013, 0. Total enrolled 2012–2013 full-time, 27. Total enrolled 2012–2013 part-time, 6. Openings 2013–2014, 8. The median number of years required for completion of a degree in 2012–2013 were 5. The number of students enrolled full- and part-time who were dismissed or voluntarily withdrew from this program area in 2012–2013 were 0. *Neuroscience and Applied Cognitive Science MA/MS (Master of Arts/Science)*—Applications 2012–2013, 20. Total applicants accepted 2012–2013, 8. Number full-time enrolled (new admits only) 2012–2013, 8. Number part-time enrolled (new admits only) 2012–2013, 0. Total enrolled 2012–2013 full-time, 13. Total enrolled 2012–2013 part-time, 1. Openings 2013–2014, 4. The median number of years required for completion of a degree in 2012–2013 were 2. The number of students enrolled full- and part-time who were dismissed or voluntarily withdrew from this program area in 2012–2013 were 1. *Applied Social MA/MS (Master of Arts/Science)*—Applications 2012–2013, 7. Total applicants accepted 2012–2013, 6. Number full-time enrolled (new admits only) 2012–2013, 6. Number part-time enrolled (new admits only) 2012–2013, 0. Total enrolled 2012–2013 full-time, 8. Total enrolled 2012–2013 part-time, 0. Openings 2013–2014, 4. The number of students enrolled full- and part-time who were dismissed or voluntarily withdrew from this program area in 2012–2013 were 0. *Clinical Psychology:Applied Developmental Emphasis MA/MS (Master of Arts/Science)*—Applications 2012–2013, 81. Total applicants accepted 2012–2013, 5. Number full-time enrolled (new admits only) 2012–2013, 5. Number part-time enrolled (new admits only) 2012–2013, 0. Total enrolled 2012–2013 full-time, 13. Total enrolled 2012–2013 part-time, 1. Openings 2013–2014, 4. The median number of years required for completion of a degree in 2012–2013 were 2. The number of students enrolled full- and part-time who were dismissed or voluntarily withdrew from this program area in 2012–2013 were 0. *Industrial/Organizational MA/MS (Master of Arts/Science)*—Applications 2012–2013, 14. Total applicants accepted 2012–2013, 6. Number full-time enrolled (new admits only) 2012–2013, 6. Number part-time enrolled (new admits only) 2012–2013, 0. Total enrolled 2012–2013 full-time, 11. Total enrolled 2012–2013 part-time, 0. Openings

2013–2014, 1. The median number of years required for completion of a degree in 2012–2013 were 2. The number of students enrolled full- and part-time who were dismissed or voluntarily withdrew from this program area in 2012–2013 were 0.

Scores: Entries appear in this order: required test or GPA, minimum score (if required), median score of students entering in 2012–2013. *Neuroscience and Applied Cognitive Science PhD (Doctor of Philosophy):* psychology GPA no minimum stated, Masters GPA no minimum stated; *Industrial/Organizational PhD (Doctor of Philosophy):* GRE-V no minimum stated, GRE-Q no minimum stated, GRE-Analytical no minimum stated, GRE-Subject (Psychology) no minimum stated, overall undergraduate GPA no minimum stated, last 2 years GPA no minimum stated, psychology GPA no minimum stated, Masters GPA no minimum stated; *Applied Social PhD (Doctor of Philosophy):* last 2 years GPA no minimum stated, psychology GPA no minimum stated, Masters GPA no minimum stated; *Clinical Psychology:Applied Developmental Emphasis PhD (Doctor of Philosophy):* GRE-V no minimum stated, 558, GRE-Q no minimum stated, 658, GRE-Analytical no minimum stated, 5.7, GRE-Subject (Psychology) no minimum stated, 669, last 2 years GPA no minimum stated, 84, psychology GPA no minimum stated, 84, Masters GPA no minimum stated, 86; *Neuroscience and Applied Cognitive Science MA/MS (Master of Arts/Science):* last 2 years GPA no minimum stated, psychology GPA no minimum stated; *Applied Social MA/MS (Master of Arts/Science):* GRE-V no minimum stated, GRE-Q no minimum stated, GRE-Analytical no minimum stated, GRE-Subject (Psychology) no minimum stated, last 2 years GPA no minimum stated, psychology GPA no minimum stated; *Clinical Psychology:Applied Developmental Emphasis MA/MS (Master of Arts/Science):* GRE-V no minimum stated, GRE-Q no minimum stated, GRE-Analytical no minimum stated, GRE-Subject (Psychology) no minimum stated, last 2 years GPA no minimum stated, psychology GPA no minimum stated; *Industrial/Organizational MA/MS (Master of Arts/Science):* GRE-V no minimum stated, GRE-Q no minimum stated, GRE-Analytical no minimum stated, GRE-Subject (Psychology) no minimum stated, overall undergraduate GPA no minimum stated, last 2 years GPA no minimum stated, psychology GPA no minimum stated.

Other Criteria: (importance of criteria rated low, medium, or high): GRE scores—high, research experience—high, work experience—medium, extracurricular activity—low, clinically related public service—low, GPA—high, letters of recommendation—high, interview—high, statement of goals and objectives—high, undergraduate major in psychology—high, specific undergraduate psychology courses taken—medium, The field of Neuroscience and Applied Cognitive Science accepts applications from candidates with degrees in allied fields. For additional information on admission requirements, go to http://www.uoguelph.ca/psychology/page.cfm?id=697.

Student Characteristics: The following represents characteristics of students in 2012–2013 in all graduate psychology programs in the department: Female—full-time 71, part-time 11; Male—full-time 30, part-time 0; African American/Black—full-time 3, part-time 1; Hispanic/Latino(a)—full-time 0, part-time 0; Asian/Pacific Islander—full-time 2, part-time 0; American Indian/Alaska Native—full-time 0, part-time 0; Caucasian/White—full-time 96, part-time 10; Multi-ethnic—part-time 0; students subject to the Americans With Disabilities Act—full-time 0, part-time 0; Unknown ethnicity—full-time 0, part-time 0; International students who hold an F-1 or J-1 Visa—full-time 4, part-time 0.

Financial Information/Assistance:

Tuition for Full-Time Study: *Master's:* State residents: per academic year $8,274; Nonstate residents: per academic year $18,402. *Doctoral:* State residents: per academic year $8,274; Nonstate residents: per academic year $18,402. Tuition is subject to change. See the following website for updates and changes in tuition costs: https://www.uoguelph.ca/graduatestudies/finance.

Financial Assistance:

First-Year Students: Teaching assistantships available for first year. Average amount paid per academic year: $11,055. Average number of hours worked per week: 10. Research assistantships available for first year. Average amount paid per academic year: $5,000. Fellowships and scholarships available for first -year. Average amount paid per academic year: $2,500.

Advanced Students: Teaching assistantships available for advanced students. Average amount paid per academic year: $11,055. Average number of hours worked per week: 10. Research assistantships available for advanced students. Average amount paid per academic year: $5,000. Fellowships and scholarships available for advanced students. Average amount paid per academic year: $5,000.

Additional Information: Of all students currently enrolled full time, 100% benefited from one or more of the listed financial assistance programs.

Internships/Practica: Doctoral Degree (PhD Clinical Psychology:Applied Developmental Emphasis): For those doctoral students for whom a professional psychology internship was required in this program prior to graduation, (8) students applied for an internship in 2011–2012, with (8) students obtaining an internship. Of those students who obtained an internship, (6) were paid internships. Of those students who obtained an internship, (8) students placed in APA/CPA accredited internships, (0) students placed in internships not APA/CPA accredited, but listed with the Association of Psychology Postdoctoral and Internship Programs (APPIC), (0) students placed in internships conforming to guidelines of the Council of Directors of School Psychology Programs (CDSPP), (0) students placed in internships that were not APA/CPA accredited, APPIC or CDSPP listed. Clinical Psychology: Applied Developmental Emphasis students work two days per week for one semester with the psychological services staff at local public school boards. During a later semester, they are placed two days a week for two semesters in a service facility for atypical children. In addition they complete practica at the Department's in-house training clinic, the Centre for Psychological Services. All 3 students who applied for internship placements to begin Fall '13 gained an accredited internship placement of their first choice. Applied Social Psychology students select practica in settings that include community health facilities, correctional and medical treatment settings, and private consulting firms. Industrial/Organizational and Applied Cognitive Science practica take place in industrial, governmental, and military settings.

Housing and Day Care: On-campus housing is available. See the following website for more information: http://www.housing. uoguelph.ca/page.cfm. On-campus day care facilities are available.

See the following website for more information: http://www.uoguelph.ca/studentaffairs/childcare/home/index.shtml.

Employment of Department Graduates:

Master's Degree Graduates: Of those who graduated in the academic year 2011–2012, the following categories and numbers represent the postgraduate activities and employment of master's degree graduates: Enrolled in a psychology doctoral program (8), enrolled in a postdoctoral residency/fellowship (n/a), employed in independent practice (n/a), employed in business or industry (1), other employment position (2), total from the above (master's) (11).

Doctoral Degree Graduates: Of those who graduated in the academic year 2011–2012, the following categories and numbers represent the postgraduate activities and employment of doctoral degree graduates: Enrolled in a psychology doctoral program (n/a), enrolled in a postdoctoral residency/fellowship (3), employed in an academic position at a university (3), employed in a professional position in a school system (2), employed in a government agency (2), employed in a community mental health/counseling center (2), employed in a hospital/medical center (1), other employment position (2), total from the above (doctoral) (15).

Additional Information:

Orientation, Objectives, and Emphasis of Department: The Department of Psychology offers graduate programs leading to a Master of Arts and a Doctor of Philosophy in three fields: Applied Social Psychology, Clinical Psychology: Applied Developmental Emphasis, and Industrial/Organizational Psychology. The three fields follow a scientist–practitioner model and provide training in both research and professional skills. The graduate program in Neuroscience and Applied Cognitive Science leads to an MSc. Collaborative MSc and PhD programs in Toxicology with the Department of Chemistry and Neuroscience with the Department of Biomedical Science are available. All fields provide a firm grounding in theory and research in relevant content areas. The PhD Clinical program is accredited by the Canadian Psychological Association.

Special Facilities or Resources: Faculty offices and laboratories are located mainly in the MacKinnon Building and Blackwood Hall. Graduate students have office space in Blackwood Hall and the MacKinnon Building. The department is well supported with computer facilities. These include a microcomputer laboratory and extensive microcomputer support for research, teaching, data analysis, and word processing. Facilities for animal research include a fully equipped surgery room and physiological recording equipment. For research with human subjects, the department possesses portable video-recording equipment, observation rooms and experimental chambers. All of these facilities are supplemented by excellent workshop and technical support. The Centre for Psychological Services is a non-profit organization associated with the Department of Psychology at the University of Guelph. The Centre provides high quality psychological services at a reasonable cost, working with families and the community. The Centre is involved in training students in Clinical Psychology: Applied Developmental Emphasis and offers workshops and presentations to professionals in the community. Consulting experience is available via coursework to Industrial/Organizational Psychology students, allowing them to apply the knowledge gained in their courses.

Information for Students With Physical Disabilities: See the following website for more information: http://www.uoguelph.ca/csd/.

Application Information:

Send to Graduate Secretary, Department of Psychology, University of Guelph, Guelph, Ontario N1G 2W1, Canada. Application available online. URL of online application: http://horizon.ouac.on.ca/guelph/grad/. Students are admitted in the Fall, application deadline December 15. Applications for Applied Social Psychology and Clinical Psychology: Applied Developmental Emphasis are due on December 15. Applications for Industrial/Organizational Psychology and Neuroscience and Applied Cognitive Science are due on January 15. *Fee:* $100. Note: All dollar amounts specified in this entry are Canadian dollars.

Manitoba, University of
Psychology
P514 Duff Roblin Building
Winnipeg, MB R3T 2N2
Telephone: (204) 474-6377
Fax: (204) 474-7917
E-mail: *Psyc_Grad_Office@umanitoba.ca*
Web: *http://www.umanitoba.ca/psychology*

Department Information:

1947. Head: Todd A. Mondor. Number of faculty: total—full-time 36, part-time 5; women—full-time 14, part-time 1.

Programs and Degrees Offered:

Listed in the following order: Program area, degree type (T if terminal Master's), number awarded 7/11–6/12. Applied Behaviour Analysis PhD (Doctor of Philosophy) 4, Brain and Cognitive Sciences PhD (Doctor of Philosophy) 4, Clinical Psychology PhD (Doctor of Philosophy) 8, Developmental Psychology PhD (Doctor of Philosophy) 1, Methodology PhD (Doctor of Philosophy) 1, Social/Personality Psychology PhD (Doctor of Philosophy) 2, School Psychology MA/MS (Master of Arts/Science) (T) 0.

CPA Accreditation: Clinical PhD (Doctor of Philosophy).

Student Applications/Admissions:

Student Applications

Applied Behaviour Analysis PhD (Doctor of Philosophy)—Applications 2012–2013, 6. Total applicants accepted 2012–2013, 4. Number full-time enrolled (new admits only) 2012–2013, 3. Number part-time enrolled (new admits only) 2012–2013, 0. Total enrolled 2012–2013 full-time, 18. Total enrolled 2012–2013 part-time, 0. Openings 2013–2014, 4. The median number of years required for completion of a degree in 2012–2013 were 5. The number of students enrolled full- and part-time who were dismissed or voluntarily withdrew from this program area in 2012–2013 were 0. *Brain and Cognitive Sciences PhD (Doctor of Philosophy)*—Applications 2012–2013, 7. Total applicants accepted 2012–2013, 6. Number full-time enrolled (new admits only) 2012–2013, 3. Number part-time enrolled (new admits only) 2012–2013, 0. Total enrolled 2012–2013 full-time, 20. Total enrolled 2012–2013 part-time, 0. Openings 2013–2014, 4. The median number of years required for completion of a degree in 2012–2013 were 3. The number of students enrolled full- and part-time who were dismissed or voluntarily withdrew from this program area in 2012–2013 were 0. *Clinical Psychology PhD (Doctor of Philosophy)*—Applications 2012–2013, 54. Total applicants accepted 2012–2013, 8. Number full-time enrolled (new admits only) 2012–2013, 6. Number part-time enrolled (new admits only) 2012–2013, 0. Total enrolled 2012–2013 full-time, 53. Total enrolled 2012–2013 part-time, 0. Openings 2013–2014, 5. The median number of years required for completion of a degree in 2012–2013 were 6. The number of students enrolled full- and part-time who were dismissed or voluntarily withdrew from this program area in 2012–2013 were 1. *Developmental Psychology PhD (Doctor of Philosophy)*—Applications 2012–2013, 2. Total applicants accepted 2012–2013, 0. Number full-time enrolled (new admits only) 2012–2013, 0. Number part-time enrolled (new admits only) 2012–2013, 0. Total enrolled 2012–2013 full-time, 5. Total enrolled 2012–2013 part-time, 0. Openings 2013–2014, 2. The median number of years required for completion of a degree in 2012–2013 were 2. The number of students enrolled full- and part-time who were dismissed or voluntarily withdrew from this program area in 2012–2013 were 0. *Methodology PhD (Doctor of Philosophy)*—Applications 2012–2013, 1. Total applicants accepted 2012–2013, 1. Number full-time enrolled (new admits only) 2012–2013, 0. Number part-time enrolled (new admits only) 2012–2013, 0. Openings 2013–2014, 3. The median number of years required for completion of a degree in 2012–2013 were 2. The number of students enrolled full- and part-time who were dismissed or voluntarily withdrew from this program area in 2012–2013 were 0. *Social/Personality Psychology PhD (Doctor of Philosophy)*—Applications 2012–2013, 12. Total applicants accepted 2012–2013, 4. Number full-time enrolled (new admits only) 2012–2013, 2. Number part-time enrolled (new admits only) 2012–2013, 0. Total enrolled 2012–2013 full-time, 12. Total enrolled 2012–2013 part-time, 0. Openings 2013–2014, 4. The median number of years required for completion of a degree in 2012–2013 were 4. The number of students enrolled full- and part-time who were dismissed or voluntarily withdrew from this program area in 2012–2013 were 0. *School Psychology MA/MS (Master of Arts/Science)*—Applications 2012–2013, 25. Total applicants accepted 2012–2013, 11. Number full-time enrolled (new admits only) 2012–2013, 9. Number part-time enrolled (new admits only) 2012–2013, 0. Total enrolled 2012–2013 full-time, 18. Total enrolled 2012–2013 part-time, 0. Openings 2013–2014, 8. The median number of years required for completion of a degree in 2012–2013 were 2. The number of students enrolled full- and part-time who were dismissed or voluntarily withdrew from this program area in 2012–2013 were 0.

Scores: Entries appear in this order: required test or GPA, minimum score (if required), median score of students entering in 2012–2013. *Applied Behaviour Analysis PhD (Doctor of Philosophy):* GRE-V 156, 157, GRE-Q 145, 152, GRE-Analytical 3.5, 4.0, last 2 years GPA 3.56, 3.57; *Brain and Cognitive Sciences PhD (Doctor of Philosophy):* GRE-V 150, 156, GRE-Q 144, 154, GRE-Analytical 4.0, 5.5, last 2 years GPA 3.58, 4.04; *Clinical Psychology PhD (Doctor of Philosophy):* GRE-V 158, 161, GRE-Q 148, 162, GRE-Analytical 4.5, 4.5, last 2 years GPA 4.01, 4.1; *Developmental Psychology PhD (Doctor of Philosophy):* GRE-V no minimum stated, GRE-Q no minimum stated, GRE-Analytical no minimum stated, last 2 years GPA no minimum stated; *Methodology PhD (Doctor of Philosophy):*

GRE-V no minimum stated, GRE-Q no minimum stated, GRE-Analytical no minimum stated, last 2 years GPA no minimum stated; *Social/Personality Psychology PhD (Doctor of Philosophy):* GRE-V 148, 156, GRE-Q 148, 150, GRE-Analytical 4.5, 4.5, last 2 years GPA 4.16, 4.23; *School Psychology MA/MS (Master of Arts/Science):* GRE-V 149, 156, GRE-Q 145, 155, GRE-Analytical 4, 5, last 2 years GPA 3.67, 4.07. *Other Criteria:* (importance of criteria rated low, medium, or high): GRE scores—high, research experience—high, work experience—medium, extracurricular activity—low, clinically related public service—medium, GPA—high, letters of recommendation—medium, interview—low, statement of goals and objectives—low, undergraduate major in psychology—high, specific undergraduate psychology courses taken—medium. For additional information on admission requirements, go to http://www.umanitoba.ca/faculties/arts/departments/psychology/graduate/admissions.php.

Student Characteristics: The following represents characteristics of students in 2012–2013 in all graduate psychology programs in the department: Female—full-time 98, part-time 0; Male—full-time 28, part-time 0; African American/Black—full-time 0, part-time 0; Hispanic/Latino(a)—full-time 0, part-time 0; Asian/Pacific Islander—full-time 0, part-time 0; American Indian/Alaska Native—full-time 0, part-time 0; Caucasian/White—full-time 0, part-time 0; Multi-ethnic—full-time 0, part-time 0; students subject to the Americans With Disabilities Act—full-time 0, part-time 0; Unknown ethnicity—full-time 0, part-time 0; International students who hold an F-1 or J-1 Visa—full-time 0, part-time 0.

Financial Information/Assistance:

Tuition for Full-Time Study: *Master's:* State residents: per academic year $4,283; Nonstate residents: per academic year $8,566. *Doctoral:* State residents: per academic year $4,283; Nonstate residents: per academic year $8,566. Tuition is subject to change. See the following website for updates and changes in tuition costs: http://umanitoba.ca/student/records/fees/988.html.

Financial Assistance:

First-Year Students: Teaching assistantships available for first year. Average number of hours worked per week: 12. Research assistantships available for first year. Fellowships and scholarships available for first -year.

Advanced Students: Teaching assistantships available for advanced students. Average number of hours worked per week: 12. Research assistantships available for advanced students. Fellowships and scholarships available for advanced students.

Additional Information: Of all students currently enrolled full time, 60% benefited from one or more of the listed financial assistance programs. Application and information available online at: http://www.umanitoba.ca/faculties/arts/departments/psychology/graduate/financial.html.

Internships/Practica: Doctoral Degree (PhD Clinical Psychology): For those doctoral students for whom a professional psychology internship was required in this program prior to graduation, (7) students applied for an internship in 2011–2012, with (3) students obtaining an internship. Of those students who obtained an internship, (2) were paid internships. Of those students who obtained an internship, (2) students placed in APA/CPA accredited internships, (0) students placed in internships not APA/

CPA accredited, but listed with the Association of Psychology Postdoctoral and Internship Programs (APPIC), (0) students placed in internships conforming to guidelines of the Council of Directors of School Psychology Programs (CDSPP), (1) students placed in internships that were not APA/CPA accredited, APPIC or CDSPP listed. Clinical students have access to practica at our Psychological Service Center. A limited number of practica within the community are available for senior graduate students. However, the department does not offer an internship program.

Housing and Day Care: On-campus housing is available. See the following website for more information: http://umanitoba.ca/student/housing/. On-campus day care facilities are available. See the following website for more information: http://umanitoba.ca/student/resource/playcare/.

Employment of Department Graduates:

Master's Degree Graduates: Of those who graduated in the academic year 2011–2012, the following categories and numbers represent the postgraduate activities and employment of master's degree graduates: Enrolled in a psychology doctoral program (6), enrolled in another graduate/professional program (1), enrolled in a postdoctoral residency/fellowship (n/a), employed in independent practice (n/a), employed in a community mental health/counseling center (2), other employment position (4), total from the above (master's) (13).

Doctoral Degree Graduates: Of those who graduated in the academic year 2011–2012, the following categories and numbers represent the postgraduate activities and employment of doctoral degree graduates: Enrolled in a psychology doctoral program (n/a), enrolled in another graduate/professional program (1), enrolled in a postdoctoral residency/fellowship (1), employed in independent practice (2), employed in a community mental health/counseling center (1), employed in a hospital/medical center (2), total from the above (doctoral) (7).

Additional Information:

Orientation, Objectives, and Emphasis of Department: The primary purpose of our program is to provide training in several specialized areas of psychology for individuals desiring to advance their level of knowledge, their research skills, and their applied capabilities. The MA program is designed to provide a broad foundation, as well as specialized skills, in the scientific approach to psychology. The PhD program provides a higher degree of specialization coupled with more intensive training in research and application. Specialized areas of training within the department include applied behavioral analysis, brain and cognitive sciences, clinical, developmental, methodology, school, and social/personality.

Special Facilities or Resources: Basic research facilities are housed in over 100 dedicated research rooms. We host a large computer lab maintained by a crew of three excellent computer technicians, integrated animal care facilities under the supervision of three dedicated animal care technicians, and a field station at which avian behavior may be studied. These resources are augmented by collaborative relationships we have with other university departments, local hospitals, St. Amant Centre, and the National Research Council: Institute for Biodiagnostics.

Information for Students With Physical Disabilities: See the following website for more information: http://umanitoba.ca/student/resource/disability_services/.

Application Information:
Send to Faculty of Graduate Studies, 500 University Centre, University of Manitoba, Winnipeg, MB R3T 2N2. Application available online. URL of online application: http://umanitoba.ca/faculties/graduate_studies/admissions/index.html. Students are admitted in the Fall, application deadline December 15. *Fee:* $100. Note: All dollar amounts specified in this entry are Canadian dollars.

McGill University
Department of Educational and Counselling Psychology
Faculty of Education, Room 614
3700 McTavish Street
Montreal, QC H3A 1Y2
Telephone: (514) 398-4242
Fax: (514) 398-6968
E-mail: *samantha.ryan@mcgill.ca*
Web: *http://www.mcgill.ca/edu-ecp*

Department Information:
1965. Chairperson: Jeff Derevensky. Number of faculty: total—full-time 26; women—full-time 13.

Programs and Degrees Offered:
Listed in the following order: Program area, degree type (T if terminal Master's), number awarded 7/11–6/12. Counselling Psychology PhD (Doctor of Philosophy) 4, Educational Psychology PhD (Doctor of Philosophy) 4, School/Applied Child Psychology PhD (Doctor of Philosophy) 3.

APA Accreditation: Counseling PhD (Doctor of Philosophy). Student Outcome Data Website: http://www.mcgill.ca/edu-ecp/programs/counsellingpsych/phd/details. School PhD (Doctor of Philosophy). Student Outcome Data Website: http://www.mcgill.ca/edu-ecp/programs/schoolpsych/phd/outcomes.

CPA Accreditation: Counseling PhD (Doctor of Philosophy).

Student Applications/Admissions:
Student Applications
Counselling Psychology PhD (Doctor of Philosophy)—Applications 2012–2013, 33. Total applicants accepted 2012–2013, 9. Number full-time enrolled (new admits only) 2012–2013, 11. Number part-time enrolled (new admits only) 2012–2013, 0. Total enrolled 2012–2013 full-time, 41. Total enrolled 2012–2013 part-time, 0. Openings 2013–2014, 10. The median number of years required for completion of a degree in 2012–2013 were 7. The number of students enrolled full- and part-time who were dismissed or voluntarily withdrew from this program area in 2012–2013 were 0. *Educational Psychology PhD (Doctor of Philosophy)*—Applications 2012–2013, 23. Total applicants accepted 2012–2013, 9. Number full-time enrolled

(new admits only) 2012–2013, 9. Total enrolled 2012–2013 full-time, 43. Openings 2013–2014, 10. The median number of years required for completion of a degree in 2012–2013 were 8. The number of students enrolled full- and part-time who were dismissed or voluntarily withdrew from this program area in 2012–2013 were 0. *School/Applied Child Psychology PhD (Doctor of Philosophy)*—Applications 2012–2013, 20. Total applicants accepted 2012–2013, 8. Number full-time enrolled (new admits only) 2012–2013, 8. Number part-time enrolled (new admits only) 2012–2013, 0. Total enrolled 2012–2013 full-time, 48. Total enrolled 2012–2013 part-time, 0. Openings 2013–2014, 8. The median number of years required for completion of a degree in 2012–2013 were 6. The number of students enrolled full- and part-time who were dismissed or voluntarily withdrew from this program area in 2012–2013 were 0.

Scores: Entries appear in this order: required test or GPA, minimum score (if required), median score of students entering in 2012–2013. *Counselling Psychology PhD (Doctor of Philosophy):* last 2 years GPA 3.2; *Educational Psychology PhD (Doctor of Philosophy):* overall undergraduate GPA 3.00; *School/Applied Child Psychology PhD (Doctor of Philosophy):* GRE-V no minimum stated, GRE-Q no minimum stated, GRE-Analytical no minimum stated, GRE-Subject (Psychology) no minimum stated, overall undergraduate GPA 3.00.

Other Criteria: (importance of criteria rated low, medium, or high): GRE scores—medium, research experience—high, work experience—high, extracurricular activity—high, clinically related public service—medium, GPA—high, letters of recommendation—high, interview—medium, statement of goals and objectives—high, undergraduate major in psychology—high, specific undergraduate psychology courses taken—medium, Relative weight of these criteria varies across program areas. For additional information on admission requirements, go to http://www.mcgill.ca/edu-ecp/prospective.

Student Characteristics: The following represents characteristics of students in 2012–2013 in all graduate psychology programs in the department: Female—full-time 227, part-time 72; Male—full-time 38, part-time 6; African American/Black—full-time 0, part-time 0; Hispanic/Latino(a)—full-time 0, part-time 0; Asian/Pacific Islander—full-time 0, part-time 0; American Indian/Alaska Native—full-time 0, part-time 0; Caucasian/White—full-time 0, part-time 0; Multi-ethnic—full-time 0, part-time 0; students subject to the Americans With Disabilities Act—full-time 0, part-time 0; Unknown ethnicity—full-time 0, part-time 0; International students who hold an F-1 or J-1 Visa—full-time 0, part-time 0.

Financial Information/Assistance:

Tuition for Full-Time Study: *Doctoral:* State residents: per academic year $3,763; Nonstate residents: per academic year $15,250. Tuition is subject to change. Tuition costs vary by program. See the following website for updates and changes in tuition costs: http://www.mcgill.ca/student-accounts/tuition-fees/tuition-and-fees.

Financial Assistance:

First-Year Students: Research assistantships available for first year. Average amount paid per academic year: $5,000. Fellowships and scholarships available for first -year. Average amount paid per academic year: $5,000.

Advanced Students: Teaching assistantships available for advanced students. Average amount paid per academic year: $2,000. Average number of hours worked per week: 3. Research assistantships available for advanced students. Average amount paid per academic year: $8,000. Average number of hours worked per week: 10. Fellowships and scholarships available for advanced students.

Additional Information: Of all students currently enrolled full time, 50% benefited from one or more of the listed financial assistance programs. Application and information available online at: http://www.mcgill.ca/edu-ecp/students/finances.

Internships/Practica: Doctoral Degree (PhD Counselling Psychology): For those doctoral students for whom a professional psychology internship was required in this program prior to graduation, (4) students applied for an internship in 2011–2012, with (4) students obtaining an internship. Of those students who obtained an internship, (3) were paid internships. Of those students who obtained an internship, (3) students placed in APA/CPA accredited internships, (0) students placed in internships not APA/CPA accredited, but listed with the Association of Psychology Postdoctoral and Internship Programs (APPIC), (0) students placed in internships conforming to guidelines of the Council of Directors of School Psychology Programs (CDSPP), (1) students placed in internships that were not APA/CPA accredited, APPIC or CDSPP listed. Doctoral Degree (PhD School/Applied Child Psychology): For those doctoral students for whom a professional psychology internship was required in this program prior to graduation, (4) students applied for an internship in 2011–2012, with (4) students obtaining an internship. Of those students who obtained an internship, (0) were paid internships. Of those students who obtained an internship, (0) students placed in APA/CPA accredited internships, (0) students placed in internships not APA/CPA accredited, but listed with the Association of Psychology Postdoctoral and Internship Programs (APPIC), (4) students placed in internships conforming to guidelines of the Council of Directors of School Psychology Programs (CDSPP), (0) students placed in internships that were not APA/CPA accredited, APPIC or CDSPP listed. All students in the professional psychology programs are required to complete internships. According to the program option these may be in mental health facilities, community social service agencies, schools, psychoeducational clinics, etc. In some internships, more than one setting is advised or required. New internship opportunities are regularly added, and students are welcome to seek out those which may especially suit their needs, subject to program approval.

Housing and Day Care: On-campus housing is available. See the following website for more information: http://www.mcgill.ca/students/housing/. On-campus day care facilities are available. See the following website for more information: http://www.mcgill.ca/daycare/.

Employment of Department Graduates:

Master's Degree Graduates: Of those who graduated in the academic year 2011–2012, the following categories and numbers represent the postgraduate activities and employment of master's degree graduates: Enrolled in a postdoctoral residency/fellowship (n/a), employed in independent practice (n/a), total from the above (master's) (0).

Doctoral Degree Graduates: Of those who graduated in the academic year 2011–2012, the following categories and numbers represent the postgraduate activities and employment of doctoral degree graduates: Enrolled in a psychology doctoral program (n/a), total from the above (doctoral) (0).

Additional Information:

Orientation, Objectives, and Emphasis of Department: There are five broad areas of major graduate-level specialization: Counseling Psychology, Human Development, Learning Sciences, Health Professions Education and School/Applied Child Psychology. A substantial base in research methods and statistics is provided and adjusted to students' entering competence. Graduate students in professional school psychology normally enter the Master's progam and are considered for transfer to the PhD (if that is their goal) after 2 years for a further 4 to 5 years of training. Graduate studies directed toward research, academic, and leadership careers follow a similar enrollment pattern except that the program normally requires one year less at the doctoral level. Students are welcome to take selected courses in other departments and at other Quebec universities.

Special Facilities or Resources: The Department has the following facilities/laboratories: Supporting Active Learning and Technological Innovation in Science Education (SALTISE), Health Psychology Research Group, CORE (Coping and Resilience) Research Team, Canadian Early Intervention Research Team, Teaching and Learning Services, Laboratory for the Study of Metacognition and Advanced Learning Technologies (SMART Lab), International Centre for Youth Gambling Problems, Health Research Team, McGill Youth Study Team (MYST), Higher Education Research Group, Talwar Child Development Research Lab, Neuroscience Lab for Research and Education in Developmental Disorders, Perceptual Neuroscience Laboratory for Autism & Development (PN Lab), McGill Psychotherapy Process Research Group (MPPRG), High Ability and Inquiry Research Group (HAIR), SPARC (Social Policy, Advocacy, Research, Community), Self-Injury Outreach & Support, Resilience, Pediatric Psychology, & Neurogenetic Connections Lab (The Connections Lab), Achievement Motivation and Emotion (AME) Research Group, Advanced Technologies for Learning in Authentic Settings (ATLAS), Psychoeducational and Counselling Clinic, Assessment Materials Resource Centre, and educational computer labs.

Information for Students With Physical Disabilities: See the following website for more information: http://www.mcgill.ca/osd/.

Application Information:
Send to Alexander Nowak, Graduate Program Advisor, Professional Psychology Graduate Programs (Counselling Psychology and School/Applied Child Psychology); Geri Norton, Graduate Program Coordinator, Professional Educational Psychology Graduate Programs (Educational Psychology). Application available online. URL of online application: http://www.mcgill.ca/gradapplicants/apply. Students are admitted in the Fall, application deadline December 15. School/Applied Child Psych Deadline - January 15; Counselling Psychology - December 15; Educational Psychology - January 15. Special circumstances may be examined on an individual basis. *Fee:* $100. Note: All dollar amounts specified in this entry are Canadian dollars.

McGill University
Department of Psychology
1205 Avenue Docteur Penfield
Montreal, QC H3A 1B1
Telephone: (514) 398-6124
Fax: (514) 398-4896
E-mail: *giovanna.locascio@mcgill.ca*
Web: *http://www.psych.mcgill.ca*

Department Information:
1922. Chairperson: David Zuroff. Number of faculty: total—full-time 37, part-time 6; women—full-time 17, part-time 3.

Programs and Degrees Offered:
Listed in the following order: Program area, degree type (T if terminal Master's), number awarded 7/11–6/12. Clinical Psychology PhD (Doctor of Philosophy) 12, Experimental Psychology PhD (Doctor of Philosophy) 11.

APA Accreditation: Clinical PhD (Doctor of Philosophy). Student Outcome Data Website: http://www.psych.mcgill.ca/grad/program/data.htm.

CPA Accreditation: Clinical PhD (Doctor of Philosophy).

Student Applications/Admissions:
Student Applications

Clinical Psychology PhD (Doctor of Philosophy)—Applications 2012–2013, 154. Total applicants accepted 2012–2013, 7. Number full-time enrolled (new admits only) 2012–2013, 7. Number part-time enrolled (new admits only) 2012–2013, 0. Total enrolled 2012–2013 full-time, 44. Total enrolled 2012–2013 part-time, 0. Openings 2013–2014, 8. The median number of years required for completion of a degree in 2012–2013 were 6. The number of students enrolled full- and part-time who were dismissed or voluntarily withdrew from this program area in 2012–2013 were 0. *Experimental Psychology PhD (Doctor of Philosophy)*—Applications 2012–2013, 92. Total applicants accepted 2012–2013, 9. Number full-time enrolled (new admits only) 2012–2013, 8. Number part-time enrolled (new admits only) 2012–2013, 0. Total enrolled 2012–2013 full-time, 54. Total enrolled 2012–2013 part-time, 0. Openings 2013–2014, 15. The median number of years required for completion of a degree in 2012–2013 were 5. The number of students enrolled full- and part-time who were dismissed or voluntarily withdrew from this program area in 2012–2013 were 0.

Scores: Entries appear in this order: required test or GPA, minimum score (if required), median score of students entering in 2012–2013. *Clinical Psychology PhD (Doctor of Philosophy):* GRE-V no minimum stated, GRE-Q no minimum stated, GRE-Analytical no minimum stated, GRE-Subject (Psychology) no minimum stated, overall undergraduate GPA 3.3, last 2 years GPA no minimum stated, psychology GPA no minimum stated, Masters GPA no minimum stated; *Experimental Psychology PhD (Doctor of Philosophy):* GRE-V no minimum stated, GRE-Q no minimum stated, GRE-Analytical no minimum stated, GRE-Subject (Psychology) no minimum stated, overall undergraduate GPA no minimum stated, last 2 years

GPA no minimum stated, psychology GPA no minimum stated, Masters GPA no minimum stated.

Other Criteria: (importance of criteria rated low, medium, or high): GRE scores—high, research experience—high, work experience—medium, extracurricular activity—low, clinically related public service—medium, GPA—high, letters of recommendation—high, interview—medium, statement of goals and objectives—high, undergraduate major in psychology—high, specific undergraduate psychology courses taken—high. For additional information on admission requirements, go to http://www.psych.mcgill.ca/grad/program/application_admission.htm.

Student Characteristics: The following represents characteristics of students in 2012–2013 in all graduate psychology programs in the department: Female—full-time 78, part-time 0; Male—full-time 30, part-time 0; African American/Black—full-time 0, part-time 0; Hispanic/Latino(a)—full-time 0, part-time 0; Asian/Pacific Islander—full-time 0, part-time 0; American Indian/Alaska Native—full-time 0, part-time 0; Caucasian/White—full-time 0, part-time 0; Multi-ethnic—full-time 0, part-time 0; students subject to the Americans With Disabilities Act—full-time 0, part-time 0; Unknown ethnicity—full-time 0, part-time 0; International students who hold an F-1 or J-1 Visa—full-time 0, part-time 0.

Financial Information/Assistance:

Tuition for Full-Time Study: *Doctoral:* State residents: per academic year $3,800; Nonstate residents: per academic year $3,800. Tuition is subject to change. See the following website for updates and changes in tuition costs: http://www.mcgill.ca/student-accounts/fees/grad/. Higher tuition cost for this program: for international students tuition is $15300/year.

Financial Assistance:

First-Year Students: Teaching assistantships available for first year. Fellowships and scholarships available for first -year.

Advanced Students: Teaching assistantships available for advanced students. Fellowships and scholarships available for advanced students.

Additional Information: Of all students currently enrolled full time, 100% benefited from one or more of the listed financial assistance programs. Application and information available online at: http://www.psych.mcgill.ca/grad/program/financial_matters.htm.

Internships/Practica: Doctoral Degree (PhD Clinical Psychology): For those doctoral students for whom a professional psychology internship was required in this program prior to graduation, (15) students applied for an internship in 2011–2012, with (15) students obtaining an internship. Of those students who obtained an internship, (15) were paid internships. Of those students who obtained an internship, (15) students placed in APA/CPA accredited internships, (0) students placed in internships not APA/CPA accredited, but listed with the Association of Psychology Postdoctoral and Internship Programs (APPIC), (0) students placed in internships conforming to guidelines of the Council of Directors of School Psychology Programs (CDSPP), (0) students placed in internships that were not APA/CPA accredited, APPIC or CDSPP listed. The majority of students in our clinical program complete their internships within Montreal, especially at McGill-affiliated hospitals. These include three large and two small general hospitals, a large psychiatric hospital, and a large children's hospital, where a wide range of assessment and treatment skills can be acquired. Specialized, advanced training is provided at other institutions in the areas of neuropsychology, hearing impairments, orthopedic disabilities, and rehabilitation. One advantage of having a local internship is that it facilitates the integration of the student's clinical and research activities. In addition, the department is able to monitor the quality of the training at the placements. All placements have active, ongoing commitments to research. Students have also completed internships at a wide variety of settings in other parts of Canada, the United States, and Europe. Settings outside Montreal must meet with staff approval.

Housing and Day Care: On-campus housing is available. See the following website for more information: http://www.mcgill.ca/students/housing/. On-campus day care facilities are available. See the following website for more information: http://www.mcgill.ca/daycare/.

Employment of Department Graduates:

Master's Degree Graduates: Of those who graduated in the academic year 2011–2012, the following categories and numbers represent the postgraduate activities and employment of master's degree graduates: Enrolled in a postdoctoral residency/fellowship (n/a), employed in independent practice (n/a), total from the above (master's) (0).

Doctoral Degree Graduates: Of those who graduated in the academic year 2011–2012, the following categories and numbers represent the postgraduate activities and employment of doctoral degree graduates: Enrolled in a psychology doctoral program (n/a), enrolled in a postdoctoral residency/fellowship (10), employed in independent practice (1), employed in a hospital/medical center (5), do not know (1), total from the above (doctoral) (17).

Additional Information:

Orientation, Objectives, and Emphasis of Department: McGill University's Department of Psychology offers graduate work leading to the PhD degree. The program in experimental psychology includes the areas of cognitive science (perception, learning, and language), developmental, social, personality, quantitative, and behavioral neuroscience. A program in clinical psychology is also offered. The basic purpose of the graduate program is to provide the student with an environment in which he or she is free to develop skills and expertise that will serve during a professional career in teaching, research, or clinical service as a psychologist. Individually conceived and conducted research in the student's area of interest is the single most important activity of all graduate students in the department.

Information for Students With Physical Disabilities: See the following website for more information: http://www.mcgill.ca/osd/.

Application Information:
Application available online. URL of online application: http://www.mcgill.ca/gradapplicants/apply/process. Students are admitted in the Fall, application deadline December 1. *Fee:* $100. Note: All dollar amounts specified in this entry are Canadian dollars.

New Brunswick, University of
Department of Psychology
P.O. Box 4400
Fredericton, NB E3B 5A3
Telephone: (506) 453-4707
Fax: (506) 447-3063
E-mail: *carmen@unb.ca*
Web: *http://www.unb.ca/fredericton/arts/departments/*
  psychology/

Department Information:
1966. Chairperson: E. Sandra Byers. Number of faculty: total—full-time 14; women—full-time 8; total—minority—full-time 1; women minority—full-time 1.

Programs and Degrees Offered:
Listed in the following order: Program area, degree type (T if terminal Master's), number awarded 7/11–6/12. Clinical Psychology PhD (Doctor of Philosophy) 2, Experimental Psychology PhD (Doctor of Philosophy) 1.

CPA Accreditation: Clinical PhD (Doctor of Philosophy).

Student Applications/Admissions:
Student Applications
Clinical Psychology PhD (Doctor of Philosophy)—Applications 2012–2013, 74. Total applicants accepted 2012–2013, 12. Number full-time enrolled (new admits only) 2012–2013, 2. Number part-time enrolled (new admits only) 2012–2013, 0. Total enrolled 2012–2013 full-time, 30. Total enrolled 2012–2013 part-time, 1. Openings 2013–2014, 6. The median number of years required for completion of a degree in 2012–2013 were 7. The number of students enrolled full- and part-time who were dismissed or voluntarily withdrew from this program area in 2012–2013 were 0. *Experimental Psychology PhD (Doctor of Philosophy)*—Applications 2012–2013, 8. Total applicants accepted 2012–2013, 3. Number full-time enrolled (new admits only) 2012–2013, 2. Number part-time enrolled (new admits only) 2012–2013, 0. Total enrolled 2012–2013 full-time, 9. Total enrolled 2012–2013 part-time, 1. Openings 2013–2014, 6. The median number of years required for completion of a degree in 2012–2013 were 7. The number of students enrolled full- and part-time who were dismissed or voluntarily withdrew from this program area in 2012–2013 were 1.
Scores: Entries appear in this order: required test or GPA, minimum score (if required), median score of students entering in 2012–2013. *Clinical Psychology PhD (Doctor of Philosophy):* GRE-V no minimum stated, GRE-Q no minimum stated, GRE-Analytical no minimum stated, overall undergraduate GPA 3.7; *Experimental Psychology PhD (Doctor of Philosophy):* GRE-V no minimum stated, GRE-Q no minimum stated, GRE-Analytical no minimum stated, overall undergraduate GPA 3.7.
Other Criteria: (importance of criteria rated low, medium, or high): GRE scores—medium, research experience—high, work experience—medium, extracurricular activity—low, clinically related public service—low, GPA—high, letters of recommendation—high, interview—high, statement of goals and objectives—high, undergraduate major in psychology—high, specific undergraduate psychology courses taken—medium, More emphasis is placed on research experience for students admitted to the Experimental program. A telephone interview is required for applicants to both of our programs. For additional information on admission requirements, go to http://www.unb.ca/fredericton/arts/graduate/psychology/admissions.html.

Student Characteristics: The following represents characteristics of students in 2012–2013 in all graduate psychology programs in the department: Female—full-time 34, part-time 2; Male—full-time 5, part-time 0; African American/Black—full-time 0, part-time 0; Hispanic/Latino(a)—full-time 1, part-time 0; Asian/Pacific Islander—full-time 1, part-time 0; American Indian/Alaska Native—full-time 0, part-time 0; Caucasian/White—full-time 37, part-time 2; Multi-ethnic—full-time 0, part-time 0; students subject to the Americans With Disabilities Act—full-time 0, part-time 0; Unknown ethnicity—full-time 0, part-time 0; International students who hold an F-1 or J-1 Visa—full-time 3, part-time 0.

Financial Information/Assistance:
Tuition for Full-Time Study: *Doctoral:* State residents: per academic year $7,067; Nonstate residents: per academic year $12,033. Tuition is subject to change. See the following website for updates and changes in tuition costs: http://www.unb.ca/moneymatters/tuitionandfees/index.html.

Financial Assistance:
First-Year Students: Teaching assistantships available for first year. Average amount paid per academic year: $4,719. Average number of hours worked per week: 6. Apply by January 15. Fellowships and scholarships available for first -year. Average amount paid per academic year: $9,500. Apply by January 15.
Advanced Students: Teaching assistantships available for advanced students. Average amount paid per academic year: $4,927. Average number of hours worked per week: 6. Apply by January 15. Fellowships and scholarships available for advanced students. Average amount paid per academic year: $12,000. Apply by January 15.
Additional Information: Of all students currently enrolled full time, 22% benefited from one or more of the listed financial assistance programs. Application and information available online at: http://www.unb.ca/gradstudies/aid/index.html.

Internships/Practica: Doctoral Degree (PhD Clinical Psychology): For those doctoral students for whom a professional psychology internship was required in this program prior to graduation, (4) students applied for an internship in 2011–2012, with (3) students obtaining an internship. Of those students who obtained an internship, (3) were paid internships. Of those students who obtained an internship, (2) students placed in APA/CPA accredited internships, (1) students placed in internships not APA/CPA accredited, but listed with the Association of Psychology Postdoctoral and Internship Programs (APPIC), (0) students placed in internships conforming to guidelines of the Council of Directors of School Psychology Programs (CDSPP), (0) students placed in internships that were not APA/CPA accredited, APPIC or CDSPP listed. Students in the Clinical program have completed practica in the following types of local agencies: mental health clinic, general hospital, university counseling services, psychiatric hospital, or school system.

Housing and Day Care: On-campus housing is available. See the following website for more information: http://www.unb.ca/fredericton/residence/. On-campus day care facilities are available. See the following website for more information: http://www.unb.ca/chdc/index.html.

Employment of Department Graduates:

Master's Degree Graduates: Of those who graduated in the academic year 2011–2012, the following categories and numbers represent the postgraduate activities and employment of master's degree graduates: Enrolled in a postdoctoral residency/fellowship (n/a), employed in independent practice (n/a), employed in other positions at a higher education institution (1), total from the above (master's) (1).

Doctoral Degree Graduates: Of those who graduated in the academic year 2011–2012, the following categories and numbers represent the postgraduate activities and employment of doctoral degree graduates: Enrolled in a psychology doctoral program (n/a), employed in an academic position at a university (1), employed in a community mental health/counseling center (1), employed in a hospital/medical center (1), total from the above (doctoral) (3).

Additional Information:

Orientation, Objectives, and Emphasis of Department: The Department of Psychology offers an integrated MA/PhD degree designed to provide extensive specialized study in either Clinical or Experimental Psychology. The Clinical program provides graduates with both sufficient skills in assessment, treatment, and outcome evaluation to initiate careers in service settings under appropriate supervision, and with the knowledge and training needed for an academic career. The Experimental program emphasizes individual training and the development of skills to equally prepare the student for a research-oriented career in academic or applied settings.

Special Facilities or Resources: The department occupies Keirstead Hall, which is well supplied with research equipment. The facilities include laboratories for research in human learning, cognition, perception, development, physiology and neuropsychology; a direct line to the computer center; space for research and teaching in clinical, community, behavior therapy, biofeedback, and other areas of applied or clinical psychology. On campus, there also is a wellness (community) clinic and a counselling (students) centre, whose respective directors and some staff are Licensed Psychologists, and where students can complete supervised practica.

Information for Students With Physical Disabilities: See the following website for more information: http://www.unb.ca/aboutunb/accessibility/.

Application Information:
Application available online. URL of online application: http://www.unb.ca/gradstudies/admissions/index.html. Students are admitted in the Fall, application deadline January 15. *Fee:* $50. The School of Graduate Studies offers "fee waivers" to selected applicants on the basis of academic merit. Note: All dollar amounts specified in this entry are Canadian dollars.

Ottawa, University of
School of Psychology
Faculty of Social Sciences
Vanier Hall, 136 Jean-Jacques Lussier
Ottawa, ON K1N 6N5
Telephone: (613) 562-5800 X4197
Fax: (613) 562-5147
E-mail: *mcote@uottawa.ca*
Web: *http://www.socialsciences.uottawa.ca/psy/eng/index.asp*

Department Information:
1941. Director and Associate Dean: Luc Pelletier. Number of faculty: total—full-time 51, part-time 50; women—full-time 21, part-time 32.

Programs and Degrees Offered:
Listed in the following order: Program area, degree type (T if terminal Master's), number awarded 7/11–6/12. Clinical Psychology PhD (Doctor of Philosophy) 11, Experimental Psychology PhD (Doctor of Philosophy) 8.

CPA Accreditation: Clinical PhD (Doctor of Philosophy).

Student Applications/Admissions:
Student Applications

Clinical Psychology PhD (Doctor of Philosophy)—Applications 2012–2013, 208. Total applicants accepted 2012–2013, 19. Number full-time enrolled (new admits only) 2012–2013, 15. Number part-time enrolled (new admits only) 2012–2013, 0. Total enrolled 2012–2013 full-time, 102. Total enrolled 2012–2013 part-time, 11. Openings 2013–2014, 15. The median number of years required for completion of a degree in 2012–2013 were 6. The number of students enrolled full- and part-time who were dismissed or voluntarily withdrew from this program area in 2012–2013 were 0. *Experimental Psychology PhD (Doctor of Philosophy)*—Applications 2012–2013, 55. Total applicants accepted 2012–2013, 22. Number full-time enrolled (new admits only) 2012–2013, 17. Number part-time enrolled (new admits only) 2012–2013, 0. Total enrolled 2012–2013 full-time, 76. Total enrolled 2012–2013 part-time, 3. Openings 2013–2014, 15. The median number of years required for completion of a degree in 2012–2013 were 6. The number of students enrolled full- and part-time who were dismissed or voluntarily withdrew from this program area in 2012–2013 were 1.

Scores: Entries appear in this order: required test or GPA, minimum score (if required), median score of students entering in 2012–2013. *Clinical Psychology PhD (Doctor of Philosophy):* last 2 years GPA 8.0, 9.0; *Experimental Psychology PhD (Doctor of Philosophy):* last 2 years GPA 8.0, 8.8.

Other Criteria: (importance of criteria rated low, medium, or high): research experience—high, work experience—low, extracurricular activity—low, clinically related public service—medium, GPA—high, letters of recommendation—high, statement of goals and objectives—high, undergraduate major in psychology—high, specific undergraduate psychology courses taken—high. For additional information on admission requirements, go to www.etudesup.uottawa.ca/default.aspx?tabid=1727&monControl=Admission&ProgId=579.

Student Characteristics: The following represents characteristics of students in 2012–2013 in all graduate psychology programs in the department: Female—full-time 151, part-time 12; Male—full-time 27, part-time 2; African American/Black—full-time 3, part-time 0; Hispanic/Latino(a)—full-time 1, part-time 0; Asian/Pacific Islander—full-time 16, part-time 0; American Indian/Alaska Native—full-time 0, part-time 0; Caucasian/White—full-time 155, part-time 14; Multi-ethnic—full-time 1, part-time 0; students subject to the Americans With Disabilities Act—full-time 0, part-time 0; Unknown ethnicity—full-time 2, part-time 0; International students who hold an F-1 or J-1 Visa—full-time 4, part-time 0.

Financial Information/Assistance:

Tuition for Full-Time Study: *Doctoral:* State residents: per academic year $6,899; Nonstate residents: per academic year $16,124. Tuition is subject to change. See the following website for updates and changes in tuition costs: http://www.registrar.uottawa.ca/Default.aspx?tabid=4168.

Financial Assistance:

First-Year Students: Teaching assistantships available for first year. Average amount paid per academic year: $10,335. Average number of hours worked per week: 10. Apply by June. Research assistantships available for first year. Average amount paid per academic year: $10,335. Average number of hours worked per week: 10. Apply by June. Fellowships and scholarships available for first -year. Average amount paid per academic year: $9,000. Apply by March.

Advanced Students: Teaching assistantships available for advanced students. Average amount paid per academic year: $10,335. Average number of hours worked per week: 10. Apply by June. Research assistantships available for advanced students. Average amount paid per academic year: $10,335. Average number of hours worked per week: 10. Apply by June. Traineeships available for advanced students. Average amount paid per academic year: $28,000. Apply by October. Fellowships and scholarships available for advanced students. Average amount paid per academic year: $9,000. Apply by October.

Additional Information: Of all students currently enrolled full time, 95% benefited from one or more of the listed financial assistance programs. Application and information available online at: http://www.grad.uottawa.ca/Default.aspx?tabid=1458.

Internships/Practica: Doctoral Degree (PhD Clinical Psychology): For those doctoral students for whom a professional psychology internship was required in this program prior to graduation, (13) students applied for an internship in 2011–2012, with (13) students obtaining an internship. Of those students who obtained an internship, (13) were paid internships. Of those students who obtained an internship, (13) students placed in APA/CPA accredited internships, (0) students placed in internships not APA/CPA accredited, but listed with the Association of Psychology Postdoctoral and Internship Programs (APPIC), (0) students placed in internships conforming to guidelines of the Council of Directors of School Psychology Programs (CDSPP), (0) students placed in internships that were not APA/CPA accredited, APPIC or CDSPP listed. Internships, required of all clinical program students, take place in accredited external settings in Canada and the USA as well as in local, approved training units. There is one internal training unit: the Centre for Psychological Services which also offers practicum training as well as an accredited internship. There are twenty-one external units providing practicum training: Brockville General Hospital, Canadian Forces Health Services, Catholic School Board of Eastern Ontario, Center for the Treatment of Sexual Abuse and Childhood Trauma, Centre Hospitalier Pierre Janet, Children's Hospital of Eastern Ontario, Centre psycho-social de Vanier, Conseil des écoles catholiques de langue française, Crossroads Children's Centre, Emerging Minds, Montfort Hospital, Ottawa-Carleton Detention Centre, Ottawa Mindfulness Clinic, Royal Ottawa Health Care Group - Brockville, Royal Ottawa Health Care Group - Ottawa, Santé Familiale de Clarence-Rockland, The Children's Aid Society of Ottawa-Carleton, The Ottawa Hospital, The Rehabilitation Centre, Ottawa Children's Treatment Center, and Western Quebec School Board.

Housing and Day Care: On-campus housing is available. See the following website for more information: http://www.residence.uottawa.ca/en/index.html. On-campus day care facilities are available. See the following website for more information: http://gbccc.ca/.

Employment of Department Graduates:

Master's Degree Graduates: Of those who graduated in the academic year 2011–2012, the following categories and numbers represent the postgraduate activities and employment of master's degree graduates: Enrolled in a postdoctoral residency/fellowship (n/a), employed in independent practice (n/a), total from the above (master's) (0).

Doctoral Degree Graduates: Of those who graduated in the academic year 2011–2012, the following categories and numbers represent the postgraduate activities and employment of doctoral degree graduates: Enrolled in a psychology doctoral program (n/a), enrolled in a postdoctoral residency/fellowship (1), employed in a professional position in a school system (1), employed in a community mental health/counseling center (4), employed in a hospital/medical center (4), total from the above (doctoral) (11).

Additional Information:

Orientation, Objectives, and Emphasis of Department: The objective of the program in Experimental Psychology is to train researchers in one or more of the following areas - neuro-imaging, psychopharmacology, psychoneuroendocrinology, psychophysiology, human and animal cognition, perception, learning, language, sleep and dreams, social, cognitive and emotional development, personality, intergroup relations, motivation, and the social psychology of health, sports and work. Students interested in behavioral neuroscience and its sub-disciplines may also enroll in the Behavioural Neurosciences Specialization Program, which is a collaborative program coordinated by the University of Ottawa and Carleton University. The objective of the clinical psychology program is to provide doctoral training in the area of clinical psychology and prepare students to work with adults, children, and youth. Professional training includes cognitive-behavioral, experiential, interpersonal, and community consultation approaches. Thesis supervisors within the clinical program have special expertise in areas such as social development mental health problems throughout the lifespan, depression, assessment, psychotherapy, marital therapy, family psychology, community psychology, health psychology, genetically based developmental disorders, human sexuality, cross-cultural psychology, and program evaluation. Clinical students may also elect to choose a thesis supervisor from the Experimental program or adjunct professors/

clinical professors who are members of the Faculty of Graduate and Postdoctoral Studies.

Special Facilities or Resources: The School of Psychology clinical training unit, the Centre for Psychological Services, offers assessment and treatment for adults, youth, families and couples. The Centre for Research on Educational and Community Services provides program evaluation and consultation services to local social services agencies.

Information for Students With Physical Disabilities: See the following website for more information: http://www.sass.uottawa.ca/welcome.php.

Application Information:
Send to Faculty of Social Sciences, 120 University, Social Sciences Hall, Room 3021, Ottawa, ON, K1N 6N5, Canada. Application available online. URL of online application: http://www.grad.uottawa.ca/default.aspx?tabid=1624. Students are admitted in the Fall, application deadline December 15. Experimental program - January 10. Fee: $100. Note: All dollar amounts specified in this entry are Canadian dollars.

Queen's University
Department of Psychology
Humphrey Hall, 62 Arch Street
Kingston, ON K7L 3N6
Telephone: (613) 533-2872
Fax: (613) 533-2499
E-mail: psychead@queensu.ca
Web: http://www.queensu.ca/psychology/index.html

Department Information:
1949. Chairperson: Dr. Rick Beninger. Number of faculty: total—full-time 32; women—full-time 18; total—minority—full-time 3; women minority—full-time 3.

Programs and Degrees Offered:
Listed in the following order: Program area, degree type (T if terminal Master's), number awarded 7/11–6/12. Brain, Behavior, and Cognitive Science PhD (Doctor of Philosophy) 2, Clinical Psychology PhD (Doctor of Philosophy) 4, Social-Personality Psychology PhD (Doctor of Philosophy) 6, Developmental Psychology PhD (Doctor of Philosophy) 1, Brain, Behavior, and Cognitive Science MA/MS (Master of Arts/Science) 2, Clinical Psychology MA/MS (Master of Arts/Science) 1, Developmental Psychology MA/MS (Master of Arts/Science) 2, Social-Personality Psychology MA/MS (Master of Arts/Science) 4.

CPA Accreditation: Clinical PhD (Doctor of Philosophy).

Student Applications/Admissions:
Student Applications
Brain, Behavior, and Cognitive Science PhD (Doctor of Philosophy)—Applications 2012–2013, 4. Total applicants accepted 2012–2013, 2. Number full-time enrolled (new admits only) 2012–2013, 2. Number part-time enrolled (new admits only) 2012–2013, 0. Total enrolled 2012–2013 full-time, 9. Total enrolled 2012–2013 part-time, 0. Openings 2013–2014, 4. The

median number of years required for completion of a degree in 2012–2013 were 5. The number of students enrolled full- and part-time who were dismissed or voluntarily withdrew from this program area in 2012–2013 were 0. Clinical Psychology PhD (Doctor of Philosophy)—Applications 2012–2013, 11. Total applicants accepted 2012–2013, 4. Number full-time enrolled (new admits only) 2012–2013, 4. Number part-time enrolled (new admits only) 2012–2013, 0. Total enrolled 2012–2013 full-time, 21. Total enrolled 2012–2013 part-time, 1. Openings 2013–2014, 10. The median number of years required for completion of a degree in 2012–2013 were 6. The number of students enrolled full- and part-time who were dismissed or voluntarily withdrew from this program area in 2012–2013 were 0. Social-Personality Psychology PhD (Doctor of Philosophy)—Applications 2012–2013, 3. Total applicants accepted 2012–2013, 1. Number full-time enrolled (new admits only) 2012–2013, 1. Number part-time enrolled (new admits only) 2012–2013, 0. Total enrolled 2012–2013 full-time, 9. Total enrolled 2012–2013 part-time, 0. Openings 2013–2014, 3. The median number of years required for completion of a degree in 2012–2013 were 4. The number of students enrolled full- and part-time who were dismissed or voluntarily withdrew from this program area in 2012–2013 were 1. Developmental Psychology PhD (Doctor of Philosophy)—Applications 2012–2013, 6. Total applicants accepted 2012–2013, 2. Number full-time enrolled (new admits only) 2012–2013, 0. Number part-time enrolled (new admits only) 2012–2013, 0. Total enrolled 2012–2013 full-time, 6. Total enrolled 2012–2013 part-time, 0. Openings 2013–2014, 1. The median number of years required for completion of a degree in 2012–2013 were 7. The number of students enrolled full- and part-time who were dismissed or voluntarily withdrew from this program area in 2012–2013 were 0. Brain, Behavior, and Cognitive Science MA/MS (Master of Arts/Science)—Applications 2012–2013, 8. Total applicants accepted 2012–2013, 4. Number full-time enrolled (new admits only) 2012–2013, 3. Number part-time enrolled (new admits only) 2012–2013, 0. Total enrolled 2012–2013 full-time, 6. Total enrolled 2012–2013 part-time, 0. Openings 2013–2014, 4. The median number of years required for completion of a degree in 2012–2013 were 2. The number of students enrolled full- and part-time who were dismissed or voluntarily withdrew from this program area in 2012–2013 were 0. Clinical Psychology MA/MS (Master of Arts/Science)—Applications 2012–2013, 130. Total applicants accepted 2012–2013, 12. Number full-time enrolled (new admits only) 2012–2013, 3. Number part-time enrolled (new admits only) 2012–2013, 0. Total enrolled 2012–2013 full-time, 12. Total enrolled 2012–2013 part-time, 0. Openings 2013–2014, 9. The median number of years required for completion of a degree in 2012–2013 were 2. The number of students enrolled full- and part-time who were dismissed or voluntarily withdrew from this program area in 2012–2013 were 0. Developmental Psychology MA/MS (Master of Arts/Science)—Applications 2012–2013, 7. Total applicants accepted 2012–2013, 4. Number full-time enrolled (new admits only) 2012–2013, 2. Number part-time enrolled (new admits only) 2012–2013, 0. Total enrolled 2012–2013 full-time, 3. Total enrolled 2012–2013 part-time, 0. Openings 2013–2014, 4. The median number of years required for completion of a degree in 2012–2013 were 2. The number of students enrolled full- and part-time who were dismissed or voluntarily withdrew from this program area in 2012–2013 were 0. Social-Personality

Psychology MA/MS (Master of Arts/Science)—Applications 2012–2013, 7. Total applicants accepted 2012–2013, 3. Number full-time enrolled (new admits only) 2012–2013, 2. Number part-time enrolled (new admits only) 2012–2013, 0. Total enrolled 2012–2013 full-time, 4. Total enrolled 2012–2013 part-time, 0. Openings 2013–2014, 4. The median number of years required for completion of a degree in 2012–2013 were 2. The number of students enrolled full- and part-time who were dismissed or voluntarily withdrew from this program area in 2012–2013 were 0.

Scores: Entries appear in this order: required test or GPA, minimum score (if required), median score of students entering in 2012–2013. *Brain, Behavior, and Cognitive Science PhD (Doctor of Philosophy):* GRE-V no minimum stated, 584, GRE-Q no minimum stated, 704, GRE-Analytical no minimum stated, 5.3, GRE-Subject (Psychology) no minimum stated, 749, last 2 years GPA no minimum stated, psychology GPA no minimum stated, Masters GPA no minimum stated; *Clinical Psychology PhD (Doctor of Philosophy):* GRE-V no minimum stated, 584, GRE-Q no minimum stated, 704, GRE-Analytical no minimum stated, 5.3, GRE-Subject (Psychology) no minimum stated, 749, last 2 years GPA no minimum stated, psychology GPA no minimum stated, Masters GPA no minimum stated; *Social-Personality Psychology PhD (Doctor of Philosophy):* GRE-V no minimum stated, 584, GRE-Q no minimum stated, 704, GRE-Analytical no minimum stated, 5.3, GRE-Subject (Psychology) no minimum stated, 749, overall undergraduate GPA no minimum stated, last 2 years GPA no minimum stated, psychology GPA no minimum stated, Masters GPA no minimum stated; *Developmental Psychology PhD (Doctor of Philosophy):* GRE-V no minimum stated, 584, GRE-Q no minimum stated, 704, GRE-Analytical no minimum stated, 5.3, GRE-Subject (Psychology) no minimum stated, 749, overall undergraduate GPA no minimum stated, last 2 years GPA no minimum stated, psychology GPA no minimum stated, Masters GPA no minimum stated; *Brain, Behavior, and Cognitive Science MA/MS (Master of Arts/Science):* GRE-V no minimum stated, 584, GRE-Q no minimum stated, 704, GRE-Analytical no minimum stated, 5.3, GRE-Subject (Psychology) no minimum stated, 749, overall undergraduate GPA no minimum stated, last 2 years GPA no minimum stated; *Clinical Psychology MA/MS (Master of Arts/Science):* GRE-V no minimum stated, 584, GRE-Q no minimum stated, 704, GRE-Analytical no minimum stated, 5.3, GRE-Subject (Psychology) no minimum stated, 749, overall undergraduate GPA no minimum stated, last 2 years GPA no minimum stated, psychology GPA no minimum stated; *Developmental Psychology MA/MS (Master of Arts/Science):* GRE-V no minimum stated, 584, GRE-Q no minimum stated, 704, GRE-Analytical no minimum stated, 5.3, GRE-Subject (Psychology) no minimum stated, 749, overall undergraduate GPA no minimum stated, last 2 years GPA no minimum stated; *Social-Personality Psychology MA/MS (Master of Arts/Science):* GRE-V no minimum stated, 584, GRE-Q no minimum stated, 704, GRE-Analytical no minimum stated, 5.3, GRE-Subject (Psychology) no minimum stated, 749, overall undergraduate GPA no minimum stated, last 2 years GPA no minimum stated.

Other Criteria: (importance of criteria rated low, medium, or high): GRE scores—high, research experience—medium, work experience—low, extracurricular activity—low, clinically related public service—low, GPA—high, letters of recommendation—high, statement of goals and objectives—high,

supervisor availability—high, undergraduate major in psychology—high, specific undergraduate psychology courses taken—high. For additional information on admission requirements, go to http://www.queensu.ca/psychology/Graduate/Prospective-Students.html.

Student Characteristics: The following represents characteristics of students in 2012–2013 in all graduate psychology programs in the department: Female—full-time 65, part-time 3; Male—full-time 22, part-time 0; African American/Black—full-time 0, part-time 0; Hispanic/Latino(a)—full-time 0, part-time 0; Asian/Pacific Islander—full-time 9, part-time 0; American Indian/Alaska Native—full-time 1, part-time 0; Caucasian/White—full-time 65, part-time 3; Multi-ethnic—full-time 3, part-time 0; students subject to the Americans With Disabilities Act—full-time 0, part-time 0; Unknown ethnicity—full-time 5, part-time 0; International students who hold an F-1 or J-1 Visa—full-time 5, part-time 0.

Financial Information/Assistance:

Tuition for Full-Time Study: *Master's:* State residents: per academic year $7,313; Nonstate residents: per academic year $14,105. *Doctoral:* State residents: per academic year $7,313; Nonstate residents: per academic year $14,105. Tuition is subject to change. See the following website for updates and changes in tuition costs: http://www.queensu.ca/registrar/currentstudents/fees.html.

Financial Assistance:

First-Year Students: Teaching assistantships available for first year. Average amount paid per academic year: $7,879. Average number of hours worked per week: 10. Fellowships and scholarships available for first-year. Average amount paid per academic year: $20,000. Average number of hours worked per week: 0.

Advanced Students: Teaching assistantships available for advanced students. Average amount paid per academic year: $7,879. Average number of hours worked per week: 10. Fellowships and scholarships available for advanced students. Average amount paid per academic year: $20,000. Average number of hours worked per week: 0.

Additional Information: Of all students currently enrolled full time, 60% benefited from one or more of the listed financial assistance programs. Application and information available online at: http://www.queensu.ca/psychology/Graduate/Funding-Opportunities.html.

Internships/Practica: Doctoral Degree (PhD Clinical Psychology): For those doctoral students for whom a professional psychology internship was required in this program prior to graduation, (5) students applied for an internship in 2011–2012, with (4) students obtaining an internship. Of those students who obtained an internship, (4) were paid internships. Of those students who obtained an internship, (4) students placed in APA/CPA accredited internships, (0) students placed in internships not APA/CPA accredited, but listed with the Association of Psychology Postdoctoral and Internship Programs (APPIC), (0) students placed in internships conforming to guidelines of the Council of Directors of School Psychology Programs (CDSPP), (0) students placed in internships that were not APA/CPA accredited, APPIC or CDSPP listed. Clinical program students must complete a predoctoral internship in an approved setting under the primary supervision of a registered Psychologist. Students are expected to seek placement in a CPA/APA-approved site.

Housing and Day Care: On-campus housing is available. See the following website for more information: http://residences.housing. queensu.ca/. On-campus day care facilities are available. See the following website for more information: http://www.queensu.ca/ daycare/index.html.

Employment of Department Graduates:

Master's Degree Graduates: Of those who graduated in the academic year 2011–2012, the following categories and numbers represent the postgraduate activities and employment of master's degree graduates: Enrolled in a psychology doctoral program (10), enrolled in a postdoctoral residency/fellowship (n/a), employed in independent practice (n/a), do not know (1), total from the above (master's) (11).

Doctoral Degree Graduates: Of those who graduated in the academic year 2011–2012, the following categories and numbers represent the postgraduate activities and employment of doctoral degree graduates: Enrolled in a psychology doctoral program (n/a), total from the above (doctoral) (0).

Additional Information:

Orientation, Objectives, and Emphasis of Department: All programs stress empirical research. The Brain, Behavior, and Cognitive Science program, the Developmental program, and the Social-Personality program emphasize research skills and scholarship, preparing students for either academic positions or for research positions in government, industry, and the like. The Clinical program is based on a scientist–practitioner model of training that emphasizes the integration of research and clinical skills in the understanding, assessment, treatment, and prevention of psychological problems.

Special Facilities or Resources: Extensive computer and laboratory facilities are available to graduate students for research and clinical experience.

Information for Students With Physical Disabilities: See the following website for more information: http://www.queensu.ca/ hcds/ds/index.html.

Application Information:

Send to The Registrar, School of Graduate Studies and Research, Gordon Hall, Queen's University, Kingston, ON Canada K7L 3N6. Application available online. URL of online application: http://www. queensu.ca/sgs/forstudents/application.html. Students are admitted in the Fall, application deadline December 1. *Fee:* $105. Note: All dollar amounts specified in this entry are Canadian dollars.

Regina, University of
Department of Psychology
3737 Wascana Parkway
Regina, SK S4S 0A2
Telephone: (306) 585-4157
Fax: (306) 585-4772
E-mail: *richard.maclennan@uregina.ca*
Web: *http://www.uregina.ca/arts/psychology/*

Department Information:
1965. Department Head: Richard MacLennan. Number of faculty: total—full-time 19; women—full-time 8.

Programs and Degrees Offered:
Listed in the following order: Program area, degree type (T if terminal Master's), number awarded 7/11–6/12. Clinical Psychology MA/MS (Master of Arts/Science) (T) 6, Experimental and Applied Psychology MA/MS (Master of Arts/Science) (T) 0, Experimental and Applied Psychology PhD (Doctor of Philosophy) 0, Clinical Psychology PhD (Doctor of Philosophy) 3.

CPA Accreditation: Clinical PhD (Doctor of Philosophy).

Student Applications/Admissions:
Student Applications

Clinical Psychology MA/MS (Master of Arts/Science)—Applications 2012–2013, 46. Total applicants accepted 2012–2013, 5. Number full-time enrolled (new admits only) 2012–2013, 5. Number part-time enrolled (new admits only) 2012–2013, 0. Total enrolled 2012–2013 full-time, 12. Total enrolled 2012–2013 part-time, 0. Openings 2013–2014, 5. The median number of years required for completion of a degree in 2012–2013 were 2. The number of students enrolled full- and part-time who were dismissed or voluntarily withdrew from this program area in 2012–2013 were 0. *Experimental and Applied Psychology MA/MS (Master of Arts/Science)*—Applications 2012–2013, 7. Total applicants accepted 2012–2013, 0. Number full-time enrolled (new admits only) 2012–2013, 0. Number part-time enrolled (new admits only) 2012–2013, 0. Total enrolled 2012–2013 full-time, 6. Total enrolled 2012–2013 part-time, 0. Openings 2013–2014, 4. The median number of years required for completion of a degree in 2012–2013 were 2. The number of students enrolled full- and part-time who were dismissed or voluntarily withdrew from this program area in 2012–2013 were 1. *Experimental and Applied Psychology PhD (Doctor of Philosophy)*—Applications 2012–2013, 8. Total applicants accepted 2012–2013, 0. Number full-time enrolled (new admits only) 2012–2013, 0. Number part-time enrolled (new admits only) 2012–2013, 0. Total enrolled 2012–2013 full-time, 9. Total enrolled 2012–2013 part-time, 0. Openings 2013–2014, 4. The median number of years required for completion of a degree in 2012–2013 were 4. The number of students enrolled full- and part-time who were dismissed or voluntarily withdrew from this program area in 2012–2013 were 2. *Clinical Psychology PhD (Doctor of Philosophy)*—Applications 2012–2013, 8. Total applicants accepted 2012–2013, 0. Number full-time enrolled (new admits only) 2012–2013, 0. Number part-time enrolled (new admits only) 2012–2013, 0. Total enrolled 2012–2013 full-time, 32. Total enrolled 2012–2013 part-time, 0. Openings 2013–2014, 5. The median number of years required for completion of a degree in 2012–2013 were 4. The number of students enrolled full- and part-time who were dismissed or voluntarily withdrew from this program area in 2012–2013 were 1.

Scores: Entries appear in this order: required test or GPA, minimum score (if required), median score of students entering in 2012–2013. *Clinical Psychology MA/MS (Master of Arts/ Science):* GRE-V no minimum stated, GRE-Q no minimum stated, GRE-Analytical no minimum stated, GRE-Subject (Psychology) no minimum stated, overall undergraduate GPA no minimum stated; *Experimental and Applied Psychology MA/MS (Master of Arts/Science):* GRE-V no minimum stated, GRE-Q no minimum stated, GRE-Analytical no minimum stated, GRE-Subject (Psychology) no minimum stated, overall undergraduate GPA no minimum stated; *Experimental and Applied*

Psychology PhD (Doctor of Philosophy): GRE-V no minimum stated, GRE-Q no minimum stated, GRE-Analytical no minimum stated, GRE-Subject (Psychology) no minimum stated, overall undergraduate GPA no minimum stated; *Clinical Psychology PhD (Doctor of Philosophy)*: GRE-V no minimum stated, GRE-Q no minimum stated, GRE-Analytical no minimum stated, GRE-Subject (Psychology) no minimum stated, overall undergraduate GPA no minimum stated.

Other Criteria: (importance of criteria rated low, medium, or high): GRE scores—high, research experience—medium, work experience—low, extracurricular activity—low, clinically related public service—medium, GPA—high, letters of recommendation—high, statement of goals and objectives—high, undergraduate major in psychology—high, specific undergraduate psychology courses taken—low.

Student Characteristics: The following represents characteristics of students in 2012–2013 in all graduate psychology programs in the department: Female—full-time 44, part-time 0; Male—full-time 15, part-time 0; African American/Black—full-time 0, part-time 0; Hispanic/Latino(a)—full-time 0, part-time 0; Asian/Pacific Islander—full-time 1, part-time 0; American Indian/Alaska Native—full-time 2, part-time 0; Caucasian/White—full-time 48, part-time 0; Multi-ethnic—full-time 0, part-time 0; students subject to the Americans With Disabilities Act—full-time 1, part-time 0; Unknown ethnicity—full-time 8, part-time 0; International students who hold an F-1 or J-1 Visa—full-time 1, part-time 0.

Financial Information/Assistance:

Tuition for Full-Time Study: *Master's:* State residents: per academic year $4,363, $312 per credit hour; Nonstate residents: per academic year $6,763. *Doctoral:* State residents: per academic year $4,685; Nonstate residents: per academic year $7,085. Tuition is subject to change. See the following website for updates and changes in tuition costs: http://www.uregina.ca/gradstudies/current-students/tuition.html.

Financial Assistance:

First-Year Students: Teaching assistantships available for first year. Average amount paid per academic year: $2,356. Average number of hours worked per week: 7. Apply by June 15. Research assistantships available for first year. Average amount paid per academic year: $5,500. Average number of hours worked per week: 7. Apply by February 28. Fellowships and scholarships available for first -year. Average amount paid per academic year: $6,000. Average number of hours worked per week: 0. Apply by June 15.

Advanced Students: Teaching assistantships available for advanced students. Average amount paid per academic year: $2,469. Average number of hours worked per week: 7. Apply by June 15. Research assistantships available for advanced students. Average amount paid per academic year: $6,000. Average number of hours worked per week: 7. Apply by February 28. Fellowships and scholarships available for advanced students. Average amount paid per academic year: $7,000. Average number of hours worked per week: 0. Apply by June 15.

Additional Information: Of all students currently enrolled full time, 60% benefited from one or more of the listed financial assistance programs. Application and information available online at: http://www.uregina.ca/gradstudies/scholarships/.

Internships/Practica: Doctoral Degree (PhD Clinical Psychology): For those doctoral students for whom a professional psychology internship was required in this program prior to graduation, (5) students applied for an internship in 2011–2012, with (4) students obtaining an internship. Of those students who obtained an internship, (4) were paid internships. Of those students who obtained an internship, (4) students placed in APA/CPA accredited internships, (0) students placed in internships not APA/CPA accredited, but listed with the Association of Psychology Postdoctoral and Internship Programs (APPIC), (0) students placed in internships conforming to guidelines of the Council of Directors of School Psychology Programs (CDSPP), (0) students placed in internships that were not APA/CPA accredited, APPIC or CDSPP listed. Master's Degree (MA/MS Clinical Psychology): An internship experience, such as a final research project or "capstone" experience is required of graduates. Master's Degree (MA/MS Experimental and Applied Psychology): An internship experience, such as a final research project or "capstone" experience is required of graduates. A wide array of community resources are available and well utilized in providing practicum and internship training. The department cannot guarantee placement in these facilities.

Housing and Day Care: On-campus housing is available. See the following website for more information: http://www.uregina.ca/student/residence/. On-campus day care facilities are available. See the following website for more information: http://www.uregina.ca/hr/careers/realize/daycare.html.

Employment of Department Graduates:

Master's Degree Graduates: Of those who graduated in the academic year 2011–2012, the following categories and numbers represent the postgraduate activities and employment of master's degree graduates: Enrolled in a psychology doctoral program (4), enrolled in a postdoctoral residency/fellowship (n/a), employed in independent practice (n/a), employed in a community mental health/counseling center (1), employed in a hospital/medical center (1), total from the above (master's) (6).

Doctoral Degree Graduates: Of those who graduated in the academic year 2011–2012, the following categories and numbers represent the postgraduate activities and employment of doctoral degree graduates: Enrolled in a psychology doctoral program (n/a), employed in an academic position at a university (2), do not know (1), total from the above (doctoral) (3).

Additional Information:

Orientation, Objectives, and Emphasis of Department: Teaching and research are oriented toward clinical, social, and applied approaches. The majority of graduate students are in clinical psychology. Faculty orientation is eclectic. Cognitive behavioral and humanistic approaches are represented. Neuropsychology is also well represented.

Special Facilities or Resources: The department has clinical/counselling rooms for research purposes, a small testing library, permanent space for faculty research, observation rooms and computer labs.

Information for Students With Physical Disabilities: See the following website for more information: http://www.uregina.ca/student/accessibility/.

Application Information:
Send to Dean, Faculty of Graduate Studies and Research, University of Regina, 3737 Wascana Parkway, Regina, SK S4S 0A2. Application available online. URL of online application: http://www.uregina.ca/gradstudies/prospective-students/index.html. Students are admitted in the Fall, application deadline January 15. *Fee:* $100. Note: All dollar amounts specified in this entry are Canadian dollars.

Ryerson University
Department of Psychology
350 Victoria Street
Toronto, ON M5B 2K3
Telephone: (416) 979-5000
Fax: (416) 979-5273
E-mail: *mdionne@psych.ryerson.ca*
Web: *http://www.ryerson.ca/psychology/*

Department Information:
1974. Chairperson: Dr. Martin Antony. Number of faculty: total—full-time 33; women—full-time 21; total—minority—full-time 3; women minority—full-time 3.

Programs and Degrees Offered:
Listed in the following order: Program area, degree type (T if terminal Master's), number awarded 7/11–6/12. Clinical Psychology MA/MS (Master of Arts/Science) 9, Psychological Science MA/MS (Master of Arts/Science) 7, Clinical Psychology PhD (Doctor of Philosophy) 0, Psychological Science PhD (Doctor of Philosophy) 0.

CPA Accreditation: Clinical PhD (Doctor of Philosophy).

Student Applications/Admissions:
Student Applications
Clinical Psychology MA/MS (Master of Arts/Science)—Applications 2012–2013, 239. Total applicants accepted 2012–2013, 9. Number full-time enrolled (new admits only) 2012–2013, 9. Number part-time enrolled (new admits only) 2012–2013, 0. Total enrolled 2012–2013 full-time, 16. Total enrolled 2012–2013 part-time, 0. Openings 2013–2014, 8. The median number of years required for completion of a degree in 2012–2013 were 2. The number of students enrolled full- and part-time who were dismissed or voluntarily withdrew from this program area in 2012–2013 were 0. *Psychological Science MA/MS (Master of Arts/Science)*—Applications 2012–2013, 26. Total applicants accepted 2012–2013, 6. Number full-time enrolled (new admits only) 2012–2013, 6. Number part-time enrolled (new admits only) 2012–2013, 0. Total enrolled 2012–2013 full-time, 15. Total enrolled 2012–2013 part-time, 0. Openings 2013–2014, 8. The median number of years required for completion of a degree in 2012–2013 were 2. The number of students enrolled full- and part-time who were dismissed or voluntarily withdrew from this program area in 2012–2013 were 0. *Clinical Psychology PhD (Doctor of Philosophy)*—Applications 2012–2013, 17. Total applicants accepted 2012–2013, 11. Number full-time enrolled (new admits only) 2012–2013, 11. Number part-time enrolled (new admits only) 2012–2013, 0. Total enrolled 2012–2013 full-time, 44. Total enrolled 2012–2013 part-time, 0. Openings 2013–2014, 8. The number

of students enrolled full- and part-time who were dismissed or voluntarily withdrew from this program area in 2012–2013 were 0. *Psychological Science PhD (Doctor of Philosophy)*—Applications 2012–2013, 12. Total applicants accepted 2012–2013, 4. Number full-time enrolled (new admits only) 2012–2013, 4. Number part-time enrolled (new admits only) 2012–2013, 0. Total enrolled 2012–2013 full-time, 21. Total enrolled 2012–2013 part-time, 0. Openings 2013–2014, 8. The median number of years required for completion of a degree in 2012–2013 were 3. The number of students enrolled full- and part-time who were dismissed or voluntarily withdrew from this program area in 2012–2013 were 0.

Scores: Entries appear in this order: required test or GPA, minimum score (if required), median score of students entering in 2012–2013. *Clinical Psychology PhD (Doctor of Philosophy):* GRE-V no minimum stated, GRE-Q no minimum stated.

Other Criteria: (importance of criteria rated low, medium, or high): GRE scores—medium, research experience—high, work experience—medium, extracurricular activity—low, clinically related public service—low, GPA—high, letters of recommendation—high, interview—high, statement of goals and objectives—high, undergraduate major in psychology—medium, specific undergraduate psychology courses taken—medium, Undergraduate major in psychology is strongly recommended for both fields, and is especially important for the clinical psychology field. For additional information on admission requirements, go to http://www.ryerson.ca/psychology/graduate/future/admissions/.

Student Characteristics: The following represents characteristics of students in 2012–2013 in all graduate psychology programs in the department: Female—full-time 82, part-time 0; Male—full-time 14, part-time 0; African American/Black—full-time 0, part-time 0; Hispanic/Latino(a)—full-time 1, part-time 0; Asian/Pacific Islander—full-time 14, part-time 0; American Indian/Alaska Native—full-time 0, part-time 0; Caucasian/White—full-time 81, part-time 0; Multi-ethnic—full-time 0, part-time 0; students subject to the Americans With Disabilities Act—full-time 0, part-time 0; Unknown ethnicity—full-time 0, part-time 0; International students who hold an F-1 or J-1 Visa—full-time 0, part-time 0.

Financial Information/Assistance:
Tuition for Full-Time Study: *Master's:* State residents: per academic year $10,227; Nonstate residents: per academic year $19,675. *Doctoral:* State residents: per academic year $9,455; Nonstate residents: per academic year $19,675. Tuition is subject to change. See the following website for updates and changes in tuition costs: http://www.ryerson.ca/graduate/fees/.

Financial Assistance:
First-Year Students: Teaching assistantships available for first year. Average amount paid per academic year: $10,398. Average number of hours worked per week: 10. Research assistantships available for first year. Average amount paid per academic year: $10,398. Average number of hours worked per week: 10. Fellowships and scholarships available for first -year. Average amount paid per academic year: $8,000. Average number of hours worked per week: 0.

Advanced Students: Teaching assistantships available for advanced students. Average amount paid per academic year: $11,230. Average number of hours worked per week: 10. Research

assistantships available for advanced students. Average amount paid per academic year: $11,230. Average number of hours worked per week: 10. Fellowships and scholarships available for advanced students. Average amount paid per academic year: $8,000. Average number of hours worked per week: 0.

Additional Information: Of all students currently enrolled full time, 78% benefited from one or more of the listed financial assistance programs. Application and information available online at: http://www.ryerson.ca/psychology/graduate/current/finances/.

Internships/Practica: Doctoral Degree (PhD Clinical Psychology): For those doctoral students for whom a professional psychology internship was required in this program prior to graduation, (4) students applied for an internship in 2011–2012, with (4) students obtaining an internship. Of those students who obtained an internship, (4) were paid internships. Of those students who obtained an internship, (4) students placed in APA/CPA accredited internships, (0) students placed in internships not APA/CPA accredited, but listed with the Association of Psychology Postdoctoral and Internship Programs (APPIC), (0) students placed in internships conforming to guidelines of the Council of Directors of School Psychology Programs (CDSPP), (0) students placed in internships that were not APA/CPA accredited, APPIC or CDSPP listed. Practicum placements are available to our Clinical Psychology students at our Clinical Psychology Training Clinic, housed within a family practice clinic of St. Michael's Hospital. Practicum placements at the Clinic provide Clinical Psychology students with the opportunity to gain experience serving a wide range of clients in a hospital-based, interprofessional setting. Our Clinical Psychology students have also been successful at securing practicum placements at top training centres, including Baycrest, Bellwood Health Services, the Centre for Addiction and Mental Health, Hamilton Health Sciences, Humber River Regional Hospital, North York General Hospital, St. Joseph's Healthcare Hamilton, Toronto General Hospital, Ryerson Centre for Student Development and Counselling, St. Michael's Hospital, Toronto Rehabilitation Institute, and others. With a focus on breadth and depth training in research methodology, possible practicum placements for the Psychological Science students include both internal sites such as the research labs of faculty in the Ryerson Department of Psychology as well as external sites such as the Centre for Addiction and Mental Health, Defense Research and Development Canada, Health Canada, Hospital for Sick Children, MultiHealth Systems (MHS), Rotman Research Institute, and Transport Canada.

Housing and Day Care: No on-campus housing is available. On-campus day care facilities are available. See the following website for more information: http://www.ryerson.ca/ece/researchlabs/elc/.

Employment of Department Graduates:
   Master's Degree Graduates: Of those who graduated in the academic year 2011–2012, the following categories and numbers represent the postgraduate activities and employment of master's degree graduates: Enrolled in a psychology doctoral program (15), enrolled in a postdoctoral residency/fellowship (n/a), employed in independent practice (n/a), employed in business or industry (1), total from the above (master's) (16).
   Doctoral Degree Graduates: Of those who graduated in the academic year 2011–2012, the following categories and numbers represent the postgraduate activities and employment of doctoral

degree graduates: Enrolled in a psychology doctoral program (n/a), total from the above (doctoral) (0).

Additional Information:
   Orientation, Objectives, and Emphasis of Department: Launched in the fall of 2007, our program offers students opportunities to study in either Clinical Psychology (accredited by the Canadian Psychological Association in May 2012) or Psychological Science. The Psychological Science stream offers opportunities to specialize in research areas that include cognition and perception; neuroscience; history, culture, and individual differences; social, community, and forensic psychology; and developmental psychology. The graduate program in Psychology offers an innovative curriculum that is anchored in research training. Trained at some of the top universities in Canada, the United States, and around the world, the core faculty (including 26 hired since 2005) bring a rigorous and student-centered approach to scientific and clinical training. Based in a department known for excellence in training, the program takes advantage of its downtown Toronto location, with proximity to major sites for practicum training and clinical research, and offers students access to world-class training opportunities.

Special Facilities or Resources: The Department has developed a state-of-the-art Psychology Research and Training Centre lab facility that includes over 15,000 square feet of research space, and our new Institute for Stress, Health, and Wellbeing provides training in and access to research equipment for psychology graduate students to study stress. The Clinical Psychology Training Clinic, housed within a family practice clinic of St. Michael's Hospital, provides a unique opportunity for graduate students to gain experience serving a wide range of clients in a hospital-based, interprofessional setting; the Clinic is a state-of-the-art facility, designed according to the latest medical infrastructure standards. These new spaces have been built from the ground up to serve the research and training needs of our psychology graduate students and faculty.

Information for Students With Physical Disabilities: See the following website for more information: http://www.ryerson.ca/studentservices/accesscentre/.

Application Information:
Application available online. URL of online application: http://horizon.ouac.on.ca/ryerson/grad. Students are admitted in the Fall, application deadline December 6. *Fee:* $110. Note: All dollar amounts specified in this entry are Canadian dollars.

Saint Mary's University
Department of Psychology
923 Robie Street
Halifax, NS B3H 3C3
Telephone: (902) 420-5846
Fax: (902) 496-8287
E-mail: *vic.catano@smu.ca*
Web: *http://www.smu.ca/academic/science/psych/*

Department Information:
   1966. Chairperson: Victor Catano. Number of faculty: total—full-time 20, part-time 25; women—full-time 9, part-time 10.

Programs and Degrees Offered:

Listed in the following order: Program area, degree type (T if terminal Master's), number awarded 7/11–6/12. Industrial/Organizational Psychology MA/MS (Master of Arts/Science) (T) 6, Industrial/Organizational Psychology PhD (Doctor of Philosophy) 3.

Student Applications/Admissions:

Student Applications

Industrial/Organizational Psychology MA/MS (Master of Arts/Science)—Applications 2012–2013, 20. Total applicants accepted 2012–2013, 8. Number full-time enrolled (new admits only) 2012–2013, 8. Number part-time enrolled (new admits only) 2012–2013, 0. Total enrolled 2012–2013 full-time, 12. Total enrolled 2012–2013 part-time, 1. Openings 2013–2014, 5. The median number of years required for completion of a degree in 2012–2013 were 2. The number of students enrolled full- and part-time who were dismissed or voluntarily withdrew from this program area in 2012–2013 were 1. Industrial/Organizational Psychology PhD (Doctor of Philosophy)—Applications 2012–2013, 6. Total applicants accepted 2012–2013, 3. Number full-time enrolled (new admits only) 2012–2013, 3. Number part-time enrolled (new admits only) 2012–2013, 0. Total enrolled 2012–2013 full-time, 9. Total enrolled 2012–2013 part-time, 4. Openings 2013–2014, 3. The median number of years required for completion of a degree in 2012–2013 were 5. The number of students enrolled full- and part-time who were dismissed or voluntarily withdrew from this program area in 2012–2013 were 0.

Scores: Entries appear in this order: required test or GPA, minimum score (if required), median score of students entering in 2012–2013. Industrial/Organizational Psychology MA/MS (Master of Arts/Science): GRE-V no minimum stated, GRE-Q no minimum stated, GRE-Analytical no minimum stated, overall undergraduate GPA no minimum stated; Industrial/Organizational Psychology PhD (Doctor of Philosophy): GRE-V no minimum stated, GRE-Q no minimum stated, GRE-Analytical no minimum stated, overall undergraduate GPA no minimum stated, Masters GPA no minimum stated.

Other Criteria: (importance of criteria rated low, medium, or high): GRE scores—high, research experience—high, work experience—low, extracurricular activity—low, GPA—high, letters of recommendation—medium, statement of goals and objectives—high, Honours degree—high, undergraduate major in psychology—high, specific undergraduate psychology courses taken—low. For additional information on admission requirements, go to http://www.smu.ca/academic/science/psych/grad_info.html.

Student Characteristics: The following represents characteristics of students in 2012–2013 in all graduate psychology programs in the department: Female—full-time 16, part-time 3; Male—full-time 5, part-time 2; African American/Black—full-time 0, part-time 0; Hispanic/Latino(a)—full-time 0, part-time 0; Asian/Pacific Islander—full-time 1, part-time 0; American Indian/Alaska Native—full-time 0, part-time 0; Caucasian/White—full-time 18, part-time 10; Multi-ethnic—full-time 1, part-time 0; students subject to the Americans With Disabilities Act—full-time 0, part-time 0; Unknown ethnicity—full-time 0, part-time 0; International students who hold an F-1 or J-1 Visa—full-time 1, part-time 0.

Financial Information/Assistance:

Tuition for Full-Time Study: Master's: State residents: per academic year $3,925; Nonstate residents: per academic year $7,549. Doctoral: State residents: per academic year $5,305; Nonstate residents: per academic year $7,721. Tuition is subject to change. See the following website for updates and changes in tuition costs: http://www.smu.ca/servicecentre/ttn_undergrad.html.

Financial Assistance:

First-Year Students: Teaching assistantships available for first year. Average amount paid per academic year: $5,000. Average number of hours worked per week: 13. Apply by February 1. Research assistantships available for first year. Average amount paid per academic year: $7,500. Average number of hours worked per week: 10. Traineeships available for first year. Average amount paid per academic year: $8,000. Fellowships and scholarships available for first -year. Average amount paid per academic year: $7,500. Average number of hours worked per week: 0. Apply by February 1.

Advanced Students: Teaching assistantships available for advanced students. Average amount paid per academic year: $5,000. Average number of hours worked per week: 13. Apply by June 1. Research assistantships available for advanced students. Average amount paid per academic year: $7,500. Average number of hours worked per week: 10. Traineeships available for advanced students. Fellowships and scholarships available for advanced students. Average amount paid per academic year: $15,000. Average number of hours worked per week: 0. Apply by June 1.

Additional Information: Of all students currently enrolled full time, 90% benefited from one or more of the listed financial assistance programs. Application and information available online at: http://www.smu.ca/academic/science/psych/grad_info.html.

Internships/Practica: Master's Degree (MA/MS Industrial/Organizational Psychology): An internship experience, such as a final research project or "capstone" experience is required of graduates. Master's students are required to complete a supervised, full-time, paid internship (minimum of 500 hours) in the summer following their first year or part-time during their second year. Placements are available in a variety of government agencies, human resource departments, research agencies, and private consulting firms. Salaries range from $7,000 to $14,000 for the four months.

Housing and Day Care: On-campus housing is available. See the following website for more information: http://www.smu.ca/administration/resoffic/family.html. On-campus day care facilities are available. See the following website for more information: http://www.smu.ca/administration/studentservices/daycare.html.

Employment of Department Graduates:

Master's Degree Graduates: Of those who graduated in the academic year 2011–2012, the following categories and numbers represent the postgraduate activities and employment of master's degree graduates: Enrolled in a psychology doctoral program (2), enrolled in a postdoctoral residency/fellowship (n/a), employed in independent practice (n/a), employed in business or industry (2), employed in a government agency (5), total from the above (master's) (9).

Doctoral Degree Graduates: Of those who graduated in the academic year 2011–2012, the following categories and numbers represent the postgraduate activities and employment of doctoral

degree graduates: Enrolled in a psychology doctoral program (n/a), total from the above (doctoral) (0).

Additional Information:

Orientation, Objectives, and Emphasis of Department: Master's students will acquire a background in theory and research that is consistent with the scientist–practitioner model, preparing themselves for employment and/or continued graduate education. Full-time students normally require two years to complete the program. Part-time students may take two to four years longer. Master's students are normally provided with financial support for two years. PhD students will acquire a background in theory and research that is consistent with the scientist–practitioner model, preparing them for an academic career or a career in consulting and/or industry. Full-time students normally require three years to complete the program. PhD students are normally provided with financial support for three years.

Special Facilities or Resources: General research laboratories, graduate computer lab, small-group research space, graduate student offices, and a tests and measurements library that includes psychological test batteries are available. Support systems include audiovisual equipment, computer facilities, and a technical workshop. Students may be involved in the CN Centre for Occupational Health & Safety, as well as the Centre for Leadership Excellence.

Information for Students With Physical Disabilities: See the following website for more information: http://www.smu.ca/administration/atlcentre/welcome.html.

Application Information:

Send to Faculty of Graduate Studies & Research, Saint Mary's University, Halifax, Nova Scotia, Canada B3H 3C3. Students are admitted in the Fall, application deadline February 1. *Fee:* $70. Note: All dollar amounts specified in this entry are Canadian dollars.

Saskatchewan, University of
Department of Psychology
Arts and Science
9 Campus Drive
Saskatoon, SK S7N 5A5
Telephone: (306) 966-6657
Fax: (306) 966-6630
E-mail: *psychology.gradadvising@usask.ca*
Web: *http://www.artsandscience.usask.ca/psychology/*

Department Information:

1946. Head: Dr. Lorin Elias. Number of faculty: total—full-time 22, part-time 2; women—full-time 7, part-time 2.

Programs and Degrees Offered:

Listed in the following order: Program area, degree type (T if terminal Master's), number awarded 7/11–6/12. Clinical Psychology PhD (Doctor of Philosophy) 6, Applied Social Psychology PhD (Doctor of Philosophy) 7, Cognition and Neuroscience PhD (Doctor of Philosophy) 5, Culture and Human Development PhD (Doctor of Philosophy) 0.

APA Accreditation: Clinical PhD (Doctor of Philosophy).

CPA Accreditation: Clinical PhD (Doctor of Philosophy).

Student Applications/Admissions:

Student Applications

Clinical Psychology PhD (Doctor of Philosophy)—Applications 2012–2013, 62. Total applicants accepted 2012–2013, 5. Number full-time enrolled (new admits only) 2012–2013, 5. Number part-time enrolled (new admits only) 2012–2013, 0. Total enrolled 2012–2013 full-time, 39. Total enrolled 2012–2013 part-time, 0. Openings 2013–2014, 6. The median number of years required for completion of a degree in 2012–2013 were 7. The number of students enrolled full- and part-time who were dismissed or voluntarily withdrew from this program area in 2012–2013 were 0. *Applied Social Psychology PhD (Doctor of Philosophy)*—Applications 2012–2013, 16. Total applicants accepted 2012–2013, 3. Number full-time enrolled (new admits only) 2012–2013, 3. Number part-time enrolled (new admits only) 2012–2013, 0. Total enrolled 2012–2013 full-time, 14. Total enrolled 2012–2013 part-time, 0. Openings 2013–2014, 3. The median number of years required for completion of a degree in 2012–2013 were 5. The number of students enrolled full- and part-time who were dismissed or voluntarily withdrew from this program area in 2012–2013 were 0. *Cognition and Neuroscience PhD (Doctor of Philosophy)*—Applications 2012–2013, 5. Total applicants accepted 2012–2013, 0. Number full-time enrolled (new admits only) 2012–2013, 0. Number part-time enrolled (new admits only) 2012–2013, 0. Total enrolled 2012–2013 full-time, 13. Total enrolled 2012–2013 part-time, 0. Openings 2013–2014, 5. The median number of years required for completion of a degree in 2012–2013 were 5. The number of students enrolled full- and part-time who were dismissed or voluntarily withdrew from this program area in 2012–2013 were 0. *Culture and Human Development PhD (Doctor of Philosophy)*—Applications 2012–2013, 13. Total applicants accepted 2012–2013, 2. Number full-time enrolled (new admits only) 2012–2013, 2. Total enrolled 2012–2013 full-time, 13. Openings 2013–2014, 3. The median number of years required for completion of a degree in 2012–2013 were 4. The number of students enrolled full- and part-time who were dismissed or voluntarily withdrew from this program area in 2012–2013 were 0.

Scores: Entries appear in this order: required test or GPA, minimum score (if required), median score of students entering in 2012–2013. *Clinical Psychology PhD (Doctor of Philosophy):* GRE-V no minimum stated, GRE-Q no minimum stated, GRE-Analytical no minimum stated, GRE-Subject (Psychology) no minimum stated, overall undergraduate GPA 80, 85, last 2 years GPA 80, 85, psychology GPA 80, 85, Masters GPA 80, 85; *Applied Social Psychology PhD (Doctor of Philosophy):* last 2 years GPA 80, psychology GPA 80, Masters GPA 80; *Cognition and Neuroscience PhD (Doctor of Philosophy):* last 2 years GPA 80, psychology GPA 80, Masters GPA 80; *Culture and Human Development PhD (Doctor of Philosophy):* last 2 years GPA 80, psychology GPA 80.

Other Criteria: (importance of criteria rated low, medium, or high): GRE scores—medium, research experience—high, work experience—medium, extracurricular activity—low, clinically related public service—low, GPA—high, letters of recommendation—high, interview—high, statement of goals and objectives—high, undergraduate major in psychology—

high, specific undergraduate psychology courses taken—medium, GRE scores are ONLY required for the Clinical Program and the Applied Social Psychology (ASP) if you are in international applicant. For additional information on admission requirements, go to http://artsandscience.usask.ca/psychology/graduates/applying.php.

Student Characteristics: The following represents characteristics of students in 2012–2013 in all graduate psychology programs in the department: Female—full-time 62, part-time 0; Male—full-time 18, part-time 0; African American/Black—full-time 0, part-time 0; Hispanic/Latino(a)—full-time 0, part-time 0; Asian/Pacific Islander—full-time 0, part-time 0; American Indian/Alaska Native—full-time 0, part-time 0; Caucasian/White—full-time 0, part-time 0; Multi-ethnic—full-time 0, part-time 0; students subject to the Americans With Disabilities Act—full-time 0, part-time 0; Unknown ethnicity—full-time 0, part-time 0; International students who hold an F-1 or J-1 Visa—full-time 3, part-time 0.

Financial Information/Assistance:
Tuition for Full-Time Study: *Doctoral:* State residents: per academic year $3,447; Nonstate residents: per academic year $5,170. Tuition is subject to change. See the following website for updates and changes in tuition costs: http://students.usask.ca/current/paying/tuition.php?t=Graduate.

Financial Assistance:
First-Year Students: Teaching assistantships available for first year. Average amount paid per academic year: $16,000. Average number of hours worked per week: 10. Fellowships and scholarships available for first -year. Average amount paid per academic year: $18,000. Average number of hours worked per week: 5.

Advanced Students: Teaching assistantships available for advanced students. Average amount paid per academic year: $16,000. Average number of hours worked per week: 10. Fellowships and scholarships available for advanced students. Average amount paid per academic year: $20,000. Average number of hours worked per week: 5.

Additional Information: Of all students currently enrolled full time, 80% benefited from one or more of the listed financial assistance programs. Application and information available online at: http://www.usask.ca/cgsr/funding/index.php.

Internships/Practica: Doctoral Degree (PhD Clinical Psychology): For those doctoral students for whom a professional psychology internship was required in this program prior to graduation, (7) students applied for an internship in 2011–2012, with (6) students obtaining an internship. Of those students who obtained an internship, (6) were paid internships. Of those students who obtained an internship, (6) students placed in APA/CPA accredited internships, (0) students placed in internships not APA/CPA accredited, but listed with the Association of Psychology Postdoctoral and Internship Programs (APPIC), (0) students placed in internships conforming to guidelines of the Council of Directors of School Psychology Programs (CDSPP), (0) students placed in internships that were not APA/CPA accredited, APPIC or CDSPP listed. Full-time internships and practicum training concurrent with coursework are required at the MA and PhD levels in both clinical and applied social programs. In the clinical program, four-month MA internship placements are available at a number of hospital and outpatient clinics throughout the

province. At the PhD level, 12-month internships have been arranged in larger clinical settings with diversified client populations in Canada and the United States. The applied social program requires four-month applied research internships at both the MA and PhD levels. Practicum and internship placements are arranged in a wide variety of government, institutional, and business settings.

Housing and Day Care: On-campus housing is available. See the following website for more information: http://www.usask.ca/residence/. On-campus day care facilities are available. See the following website for more information: http://www.ussu.ca/childcarecentre/index.shtml.

Employment of Department Graduates:
Master's Degree Graduates: Of those who graduated in the academic year 2011–2012, the following categories and numbers represent the postgraduate activities and employment of master's degree graduates: Enrolled in a postdoctoral residency/fellowship (n/a), employed in independent practice (n/a), total from the above (master's) (0).

Doctoral Degree Graduates: Of those who graduated in the academic year 2011–2012, the following categories and numbers represent the postgraduate activities and employment of doctoral degree graduates: Enrolled in a psychology doctoral program (n/a), total from the above (doctoral) (0).

Additional Information:
Orientation, Objectives, and Emphasis of Department: All graduate programs are small and highly selective. The clinical program focuses on PhD training, based on a scientist–practitioner model with an eclectic theoretical perspective. The goal is to train people who will be able to function in a wide variety of community, agency, academic, and research settings. The applied social program attempts to train people at the MA and PhD level for researcher consultant positions in applied (MA) or academic (PhD) settings. Areas of concentration include program development and evaluation, group processes, and organizational development. The cognition and neuroscience programs are individually structured, admitting a few students to work with active research supervisors, most frequently in behavioral neuroscience, neuropsychology, cognitive psychology or culture and development.

Special Facilities or Resources: The Department has a Psychological Services Centre, an animal lab, and a cognitive science lab with access to fMRI facilities. There are also numerous microcomputers, excellent mainframe computer facilities, and a good research library. The Women's Studies Research Unit promotes scholarly research by, for, and about women, providing a source of support for all women studying, teaching, researching, and working on campus.

Information for Students With Physical Disabilities: See the following website for more information: http://students.usask.ca/current/disability/.

Application Information:
Send to Graduate Program Coordinator, University of Saskatchewan, Department of Psychology, 9 Campus Drive, Saskatoon, SK Canada S7N 5A5. Application available online. URL of online application: http://artsandscience.usask.ca/psychology/graduates/applying.php. Students are admitted in the Fall, application deadline December 15.

Fee: $75. Note: All dollar amounts specified in this entry are Canadian dollars.

Simon Fraser University

Department of Psychology
8888 University Drive
Burnaby, BC V5A 1S6
Telephone: (778) 782-3354
Fax: (778) 782-3427
E-mail: *turner@sfu.ca*
Web: *http://www.psyc.sfu.ca/*

Department Information:
1965. Chairperson: Neil Watson. Number of faculty: total—full-time 41; women—full-time 14.

Programs and Degrees Offered:
Listed in the following order: Program area, degree type (T if terminal Master's), number awarded 7/11–6/12. Clinical Psychology PhD (Doctor of Philosophy) 7, Psychology Graduate Program PhD (Doctor of Philosophy) 3.

APA Accreditation: Clinical PhD (Doctor of Philosophy). Student Outcome Data Website: http://www.psyc.sfu.ca/grad/index.php?topic= clin_progstats.

CPA Accreditation: Clinical PhD (Doctor of Philosophy).

Student Applications/Admissions:
Student Applications

Clinical Psychology PhD (Doctor of Philosophy)—Applications 2012–2013, 139. Total applicants accepted 2012–2013, 14. Number full-time enrolled (new admits only) 2012–2013, 8. Total enrolled 2012–2013 full-time, 70. Openings 2013–2014, 8. The median number of years required for completion of a degree in 2012–2013 were 5. The number of students enrolled full- and part-time who were dismissed or voluntarily withdrew from this program area in 2012–2013 were 0. *Psychology Graduate Program PhD (Doctor of Philosophy)*—Applications 2012–2013, 52. Total applicants accepted 2012–2013, 9. Number full-time enrolled (new admits only) 2012–2013, 8. Total enrolled 2012–2013 full-time, 46. Openings 2013–2014, 8. The median number of years required for completion of a degree in 2012–2013 were 5. The number of students enrolled full- and part-time who were dismissed or voluntarily withdrew from this program area in 2012–2013 were 0.

Scores: Entries appear in this order: required test or GPA, minimum score (if required), median score of students entering in 2012–2013. *Clinical Psychology PhD (Doctor of Philosophy):* GRE-V no minimum stated, 161, GRE-Q no minimum stated, 690, GRE-Analytical no minimum stated, 4.5, GRE-Subject (Psychology) no minimum stated, 745, overall undergraduate GPA no minimum stated, 3.97; *Psychology Graduate Program PhD (Doctor of Philosophy):* GRE-V no minimum stated, 590, GRE-Q no minimum stated, 675, GRE-Analytical no minimum stated, 4.5, overall undergraduate GPA no minimum stated, 3.72.

Other Criteria: (importance of criteria rated low, medium, or high): GRE scores—high, research experience—high, work experience—low, extracurricular activity—low, clinically related public service—low, GPA—high, letters of recommendation—high, interview—high, statement of goals and objectives—high, undergraduate major in psychology—high, specific undergraduate psychology courses taken—medium, Interview is more relevant to admission to clinical program. For additional information on admission requirements, go to http://www.psyc.sfu.ca/grad/index.php?topic=applications.

Student Characteristics: The following represents characteristics of students in 2012–2013 in all graduate psychology programs in the department: Female—full-time 84, part-time 0; Male—full-time 32, part-time 0; African American/Black—full-time 0, part-time 0; Hispanic/Latino(a)—full-time 0, part-time 0; Asian/Pacific Islander—full-time 0, part-time 0; American Indian/Alaska Native—full-time 0, part-time 0; Caucasian/White—full-time 0, part-time 0; Multi-ethnic—full-time 0, part-time 0; students subject to the Americans With Disabilities Act—full-time 0, part-time 0; Unknown ethnicity—full-time 0, part-time 0; International students who hold an F-1 or J-1 Visa—full-time 0, part-time 0.

Financial Information/Assistance:
Tuition for Full-Time Study: *Master's:* State residents: per academic year $4,985; Nonstate residents: per academic year $4,985. *Doctoral:* State residents: per academic year $4,985; Nonstate residents: per academic year $4,985. Tuition is subject to change. See the following website for updates and changes in tuition costs: http://www.sfu.ca/dean-gradstudies/future/tuition-and-fees.html.

Financial Assistance:
First-Year Students: Teaching assistantships available for first year. Average amount paid per academic year: $16,422. Average number of hours worked per week: 15. Research assistantships available for first year. Fellowships and scholarships available for first -year. Average amount paid per academic year: $6,250. Apply by March 15.

Advanced Students: Teaching assistantships available for advanced students. Average amount paid per academic year: $19,764. Average number of hours worked per week: 15. Research assistantships available for advanced students. Fellowships and scholarships available for advanced students. Average amount paid per academic year: $6,250. Apply by March 15.

Additional Information: Of all students currently enrolled full time, 100% benefited from one or more of the listed financial assistance programs. Application and information available online at: http://www.psyc.sfu.ca/grad.

Internships/Practica: Doctoral Degree (PhD Clinical Psychology): For those doctoral students for whom a professional psychology internship was required in this program prior to graduation, (10) students applied for an internship in 2011–2012, with (8) students obtaining an internship. Of those students who obtained an internship, (8) were paid internships. Of those students who obtained an internship, (8) students placed in APA/CPA accredited internships, (0) students placed in internships not APA/CPA accredited, but listed with the Association of Psychology Postdoctoral and Internship Programs (APPIC), (0) students placed in internships conforming to guidelines of the Council of Directors of School Psychology Programs (CDSPP), (0) students placed in internships that were not APA/CPA accredited, APPIC or CDSPP listed. Students in the Clinical program are required to complete an MA practicum and a PhD internship. The practica are coordinated by the Director of Clinical Training, and take place primarily in local multi-disciplinary community settings under the overall supervision of psychology personnel. Internships are all external to the program.

Housing and Day Care: On-campus housing is available. See the following website for more information: http://students.sfu. ca/residences/. On-campus day care facilities are available. See the following website for more information: http://www.sfu.ca/ childcare-society/.

Employment of Department Graduates:

Master's Degree Graduates: Of those who graduated in the academic year 2011–2012, the following categories and numbers represent the postgraduate activities and employment of master's degree graduates: Enrolled in a postdoctoral residency/fellowship (n/a), employed in independent practice (n/a), total from the above (master's) (0).

Doctoral Degree Graduates: Of those who graduated in the academic year 2011–2012, the following categories and numbers represent the postgraduate activities and employment of doctoral degree graduates: Enrolled in a psychology doctoral program (n/a), enrolled in a postdoctoral residency/fellowship (7), employed in independent practice (2), employed in an academic position at a 2-year/4-year college (1), employed in a hospital/medical center (1), total from the above (doctoral) (11).

Additional Information:

Orientation, Objectives, and Emphasis of Department: The department has a mainstream, empirical orientation. The department offers graduate work leading to master's and doctoral degrees in psychology or clinical psychology. Within the Psychology Graduate Program, all graduate students work on topics from one of the following research areas: clinical science; cognitive and neural sciences; developmental psychology; law and forensic psychology; social psychology; or history, quantitative and theoretical psychology. The Clinical Psychology Program subscribes to the scientist–practitioner model, and offers training in one of the following tracks: Clinical General, Clinical Child, Clinical Forensic, and Clinical Neuropsychology. In cooperation with the University of British Columbia, Law and Forensic Psychology students are allowed leave from one university to complete degree requirements in the other, in order to obtain both PhD and LL.B. degrees.

Special Facilities or Resources: The Psychology Department has numerous technical resources available to its members. A Microcomputer Lab houses 18 workstations running Windows XP and hosts a variety of statistical packages (SPSS, SAS, Lisrel, MathCAD, Systat), productivity packages (Microsoft Office, Acrobat, Write-N-Cite), Internet packages (Firefox, Thunderbird, secure file transfer programs), and other utility programs. While the University provides central e-mail service, the Department provides in-house file storage, printing, scanning, photocopying and teleconferencing resources. One conference room with an LCD projector and workstation is available for presentations (colloquia, thesis defences, etc.). Other portable multimedia equipment include LCD projectors, VCRs, and audio recording devices. Students normally receive office space in the research laboratories of their supervisors. Most faculty labs have computers and printers for graduate and honours students. Neuroscience labs for animal studies are equipped for physiological and behavioral research, as

well as advanced microscopy and image analysis. The department's array of technical and information technologies are managed and maintained by a five-member IT staff. The Clinical Program operates a separate training clinic with a full-time Director, Office Coordinator, and is staffed by clinical students. It has an extensive test library, audio/video recording capabilities, and presentation projection facilities. The library has excellent resources including online databases in psychology; inter-library loans of books and journals are readily accessible.

Information for Students With Physical Disabilities: See the following website for more information: http://students.sfu.ca/ disabilityaccess.html.

Application Information:
Send to Anita Turner, Graduate Program Assistant, Psychology Department, Simon Fraser University, 8888 University Drive, Burnaby, BC V5A 1S6. Application available online. URL of online application: https://go.sfu.ca/goprd/gradapplication.html. Students are admitted in the Fall, application deadline December 2. *Fee:* $90. Note: All dollar amounts specified in this entry are Canadian dollars.

Toronto, University of
Department of Psychology
100 Saint George Street
Toronto, ON M5S 3G3
Telephone: (416) 978-3404
Fax: (416) 976-4811
E-mail: *grad@psych.utoronto.ca*
Web: *http://www.psych.utoronto.ca*

Department Information:
1891. Graduate Chair: Morris Moscovitch. Number of faculty: total—full-time 75, part-time 44; women—full-time 29, part-time 17.

Programs and Degrees Offered:
Listed in the following order: Program area, degree type (T if terminal Master's), number awarded 7/11–6/12. Behavioral Neuroscience MA/MS (Master of Arts/Science) 3, Behavioral Neuroscience PhD (Doctor of Philosophy) 3, Cognition/Perception MA/MS (Master of Arts/Science) 14, Cognition/Perception PhD (Doctor of Philosophy) 8, Developmental Psychology MA/MS (Master of Arts/Science) 2, Social/Personality/Abnormal MA/MS (Master of Arts/Science) 8, Developmental Psychology PhD (Doctor of Philosophy) 1, Social/Personality/Abnormal PhD (Doctor of Philosophy) 5.

Student Applications/Admissions:
Student Applications
Behavioral Neuroscience MA/MS (Master of Arts/Science)—Applications 2012–2013, 20. Total applicants accepted 2012–2013, 6. Number full-time enrolled (new admits only) 2012–2013, 4. Total enrolled 2012–2013 full-time, 4. Openings 2013–2014, 10. The median number of years required for completion of a degree in 2012–2013 was 1. The number of students enrolled full- and part-time who were dismissed or voluntarily withdrew from this program area in 2012–2013 were 0. *Behavioral Neuroscience PhD (Doctor of Philosophy)*—

Applications 2012–2013, 2. Total enrolled 2012–2013 full-time, 25. Openings 2013–2014, 10. The median number of years required for completion of a degree in 2012–2013 were 5. The number of students enrolled full- and part-time who were dismissed or voluntarily withdrew from this program area in 2012–2013 were 0. *Cognition/Perception MA/MS (Master of Arts/Science)*—Applications 2012–2013, 62. Total applicants accepted 2012–2013, 19. Number full-time enrolled (new admits only) 2012–2013, 11. Total enrolled 2012–2013 full-time, 11. Openings 2013–2014, 10. The median number of years required for completion of a degree in 2012–2013 was 1. The number of students enrolled full- and part-time who were dismissed or voluntarily withdrew from this program area in 2012–2013 were 0. *Cognition/Perception PhD (Doctor of Philosophy)*—Applications 2012–2013, 12. Total applicants accepted 2012–2013, 3. Number full-time enrolled (new admits only) 2012–2013, 1. Total enrolled 2012–2013 full-time, 52. Openings 2013–2014, 10. The median number of years required for completion of a degree in 2012–2013 were 5. The number of students enrolled full- and part-time who were dismissed or voluntarily withdrew from this program area in 2012–2013 were 0. *Developmental Psychology MA/MS (Master of Arts/Science)*—Applications 2012–2013, 29. Total applicants accepted 2012–2013, 7. Number full-time enrolled (new admits only) 2012–2013, 5. Total enrolled 2012–2013 full-time, 5. Total enrolled 2012–2013 part-time, 1. Openings 2013–2014, 10. The median number of years required for completion of a degree in 2012–2013 was 1. The number of students enrolled full- and part-time who were dismissed or voluntarily withdrew from this program area in 2012–2013 were 0. *Social/Personality/Abnormal MA/MS (Master of Arts/Science)*—Applications 2012–2013, 102. Total applicants accepted 2012–2013, 11. Number full-time enrolled (new admits only) 2012–2013, 9. Total enrolled 2012–2013 full-time, 9. Openings 2013–2014, 10. The median number of years required for completion of a degree in 2012–2013 was 1. *Developmental Psychology PhD (Doctor of Philosophy)*—Applications 2012–2013, 3. Total applicants accepted 2012–2013, 0. Number full-time enrolled (new admits only) 2012–2013, 0. Total enrolled 2012–2013 full-time, 15. Openings 2013–2014, 10. The median number of years required for completion of a degree in 2012–2013 were 9. The number of students enrolled full- and part-time who were dismissed or voluntarily withdrew from this program area in 2012–2013 were 0. *Social/Personality/Abnormal PhD (Doctor of Philosophy)*—Applications 2012–2013, 25. Total applicants accepted 2012–2013, 3. Number full-time enrolled (new admits only) 2012–2013, 3. Total enrolled 2012–2013 full-time, 28. Openings 2013–2014, 10. The median number of years required for completion of a degree in 2012–2013 were 4. The number of students enrolled full- and part-time who were dismissed or voluntarily withdrew from this program area in 2012–2013 were 0.
Scores: Entries appear in this order: required test or GPA, minimum score (if required), median score of students entering in 2012–2013. *Behavioral Neuroscience MA/MS (Master of Arts/Science):* GRE-V no minimum stated, 158, GRE-Q no minimum stated, 158, GRE-Analytical no minimum stated, 4.5, last 2 years GPA 3.7, 4; *Behavioral Neuroscience PhD (Doctor of Philosophy):* GRE-V no minimum stated, 158, GRE-Q no minimum stated, 158, GRE-Analytical no minimum stated, 4.5, last 2 years GPA 3.7, 4, Masters GPA 3.7, 3.7; *Cognition/Perception MA/MS (Master of Arts/Science):* GRE-V no mini-

mum stated, 158, GRE-Q no minimum stated, 155, GRE-Analytical no minimum stated, 4.5, last 2 years GPA 3.7, 4; *Cognition/Perception PhD (Doctor of Philosophy):* GRE-V no minimum stated, 158, GRE-Q no minimum stated, 155, GRE-Analytical no minimum stated, 4.5, last 2 years GPA 3.7, 4, Masters GPA 3.7, 3.7; *Developmental Psychology MA/MS (Master of Arts/Science):* GRE-V no minimum stated, 162, GRE-Q no minimum stated, 153, GRE-Analytical no minimum stated, 5, last 2 years GPA 3.7, 4; *Social/Personality/Abnormal MA/MS (Master of Arts/Science):* GRE-V no minimum stated, 161, GRE-Q no minimum stated, 155, GRE-Analytical no minimum stated, 4.5, last 2 years GPA 3.7, 4; *Developmental Psychology PhD (Doctor of Philosophy):* GRE-V no minimum stated, 162, GRE-Q no minimum stated, 153, GRE-Analytical no minimum stated, 5, last 2 years GPA 3.7, 4, Masters GPA 3.7, 4; *Social/Personality/Abnormal PhD (Doctor of Philosophy):* GRE-V no minimum stated, 161, GRE-Q no minimum stated, 155, GRE-Analytical no minimum stated, 4.5, last 2 years GPA 3.7, 4, Masters GPA 3.7, 4.
Other Criteria: (importance of criteria rated low, medium, or high): GRE scores—high, research experience—high, work experience—low, extracurricular activity—low, GPA—high, letters of recommendation—high, interview—high, statement of goals and objectives—high, undergraduate major in psychology—medium, specific undergraduate psychology courses taken—medium. For additional information on admission requirements, go to http://home.psych.utoronto.ca/graduate/grad_admission.htm.

Student Characteristics: The following represents characteristics of students in 2012–2013 in all graduate psychology programs in the department: Female—full-time 94, part-time 1; Male—full-time 55, part-time 0; African American/Black—full-time 0, part-time 0; Hispanic/Latino(a)—full-time 0, part-time 0; Asian/Pacific Islander—full-time 0, part-time 0; American Indian/Alaska Native—full-time 0, part-time 0; Caucasian/White—full-time 0, part-time 0; Multi-ethnic—full-time 0, part-time 0; students subject to the Americans With Disabilities Act—full-time 0, part-time 0; Unknown ethnicity—full-time 149, part-time 1; International students who hold an F-1 or J-1 Visa—full-time 0, part-time 0.

Financial Information/Assistance:
Tuition for Full-Time Study: *Master's:* State residents: per academic year $8,402; Nonstate residents: per academic year $18,128. *Doctoral:* State residents: per academic year $8,402; Nonstate residents: per academic year $18,128. Tuition is subject to change. See the following website for updates and changes in tuition costs: http://www.provost.utoronto.ca/link/students.htm.

Financial Assistance:
First-Year Students: Teaching assistantships available for first year. Average amount paid per academic year: $8,490. Average number of hours worked per week: 10. Apply by June 1. Traineeships available for first year. Average amount paid per academic year: $6,000. Apply by December 15. Fellowships and scholarships available for first -year. Average amount paid per academic year: $9,412. Apply by December 15.

Advanced Students: Teaching assistantships available for advanced students. Average amount paid per academic year: $8,490. Average number of hours worked per week: 10. Apply by June 1. Traineeships available for advanced students. Average amount paid per academic year: $6,000. Apply by December 15. Fellowships and scholarships available for advanced students. Average amount paid per academic year: $9,412. Apply by December 15.

Additional Information: Of all students currently enrolled full time, 100% benefited from one or more of the listed financial assistance programs. Application and information available online at: http://wwwgradschoolutorontoca/fees-financial-supporthtm

Housing and Day Care: On-campus housing is available. See the following website for more information: http://www.housing.utoronto.ca/. On-campus day care facilities are available. See the following website for more information: http://www.familycare.utoronto.ca/child_care/childcare.html.

Employment of Department Graduates:

Master's Degree Graduates: Of those who graduated in the academic year 2011–2012, the following categories and numbers represent the postgraduate activities and employment of master's degree graduates: Enrolled in a psychology doctoral program (27), enrolled in a postdoctoral residency/fellowship (n/a), employed in independent practice (n/a), total from the above (master's) (27). *Doctoral Degree Graduates:* Of those who graduated in the academic year 2011–2012, the following categories and numbers represent the postgraduate activities and employment of doctoral degree graduates: Enrolled in a psychology doctoral program (n/a), enrolled in a postdoctoral residency/fellowship (6), employed in an academic position at a university (2), employed in a government agency (1), employed in a hospital/medical center (1), do not know (7), total from the above (doctoral) (17).

Additional Information:

Orientation, Objectives, and Emphasis of Department: The purpose of graduate training at the University of Toronto is to prepare students for careers in teaching and research. Teaching and research apprenticeships, therefore, constitute a large portion of such training. Research training is supplemented by courses and seminars. In some cases the courses are designed to provide up-to-date fundamental background information in psychology. The bulk of instruction, however, takes place in informal seminars; these provide an opportunity for the discussion of theoretical issues, the formulation of research problems, and the review of current developments in specific research areas. In the past, most of our graduates have entered academic careers. More recently, graduates have also taken research and managerial positions in research institutes, hospitals, government agencies, and industrial corporations.

Special Facilities or Resources: The department has modern laboratories at the St. George, Mississauga, and Scarborough campuses, as well as a fully equipped electronic workshop. Students have access to an extensive computer system including the university's central computer, the department's Sun computer, and many advanced microcomputers. The department has close ties to several medical hospitals, as well as the Rotman Research Institute of Baycrest Centre and the Centre for Addiction and Mental Health.

Information for Students With Physical Disabilities: See the following website for more information: http://www.accessibility.utoronto.ca/index.htm.

Application Information:
Send to Graduate Studies, Department of Psychology, University of Toronto, 100 St. George Street, Toronto, Ontario, Canada M5S 3G3. Application available online. URL of online application: https://apply.sgs.utoronto.ca/. Students are admitted in the Fall, application deadline December 1. *Fee:* $110. Note: All dollar amounts specified in this entry are Canadian dollars.

Victoria, University of
Department of Psychology
P.O. Box 1700 STN CSC
Victoria, BC V8W 2Y2
Telephone: (250) 721-7525
Fax: (250) 721-8929
E-mail: *psychgrd@uvic.ca*
Web: *http://www.web.uvic.ca/psyc/graduate/*

Department Information:
1963. Chairperson: Elizabeth Brimacombe. Number of faculty: total—full-time 31; women—full-time 13; total—minority—full-time 2.

Programs and Degrees Offered:
Listed in the following order: Program area, degree type (T if terminal Master's), number awarded 7/11–6/12. Cognition and Brain Science PhD (Doctor of Philosophy) 2, Experimental Neuropsychology PhD (Doctor of Philosophy) 4, Social Psychology PhD (Doctor of Philosophy) 2, Lifespan Development and Aging PhD (Doctor of Philosophy) 7, Clinical Psychology PhD (Doctor of Philosophy) 9, Individualized PhD (Doctor of Philosophy) 2.

APA Accreditation: Clinical PhD (Doctor of Philosophy). Student Outcome Data Website: http://web.uvic.ca/psyc/graduate/clinical_psychology.php.

CPA Accreditation: Clinical PhD (Doctor of Philosophy).

Student Applications/Admissions:
Student Applications

Cognition and Brain Science PhD (Doctor of Philosophy)—Applications 2012–2013, 24. Total applicants accepted 2012–2013, 1. Number full-time enrolled (new admits only) 2012–2013, 1. Total enrolled 2012–2013 full-time, 9. Total enrolled 2012–2013 part-time, 0. Openings 2013–2014, 3. The median number of years required for completion of a degree in 2012–2013 were 5. The number of students enrolled full- and part-time who were dismissed or voluntarily withdrew from this program area in 2012–2013 were 0. *Experimental Neuropsychology PhD (Doctor of Philosophy)*—Applications 2012–2013, 3. Total applicants accepted 2012–2013, 0. Number full-time enrolled (new admits only) 2012–2013, 0. Total enrolled 2012–2013 full-time, 3. Total enrolled 2012–2013 part-time, 0. Openings 2013–2014, 2. The median number of years required for completion of a degree in 2012–2013 were 5. The number of students enrolled full- and part-time who were dismissed or voluntarily withdrew from this program area in 2012–2013 were 0. *Social Psychology PhD (Doctor of Philosophy)*—Applications 2012–2013, 15. Total applicants accepted 2012–2013, 0. Number full-time enrolled (new admits only) 2012–2013, 4. Total enrolled 2012–2013 full-time, 7. Total enrolled 2012–2013 part-time, 0. Openings 2013–2014, 3. The median number of years required for completion of a degree in 2012–2013 were 5. The number of students enrolled full- and part-time who were dismissed or voluntarily withdrew from this program area in 2012–2013 were 0. *Lifespan Development and Aging PhD (Doctor of Philosophy)*—Applications 2012–2013, 7. Total applicants accepted 2012–2013, 4. Number full-time enrolled (new admits only) 2012–2013, 4. Total enrolled 2012–2013 full-time, 8. Openings 2013–2014, 4. The median number of years required for completion of a degree in 2012–2013 were 5. The number of students enrolled full- and part-time who were dismissed or voluntarily withdrew from this program area in 2012–2013 were 0. *Clinical Psychology PhD (Doctor of Philosophy)*—Applications 2012–2013, 140. Total applicants accepted 2012–2013, 7. Number full-time enrolled (new admits only) 2012–2013, 7. Total enrolled 2012–2013 full-time, 43. Openings 2013–2014, 8. The median number of years required for completion of a degree in 2012–2013 were 7. *Individualized PhD (Doctor of Philosophy)*—Applications 2012–2013, 6. Total applicants accepted 2012–2013, 0. Total enrolled 2012–2013 full-time, 9. Openings 2013–2014, 3. The median number of years required for completion of a degree in 2012–2013 were 6. **Scores:** Entries appear in this order: required test or GPA, minimum score (if required), median score of students entering in 2012–2013. *Cognition and Brain Science PhD (Doctor of Philosophy)*: GRE-V no minimum stated, GRE-Q no minimum stated, GRE-Analytical no minimum stated; *Experimental Neuropsychology PhD (Doctor of Philosophy)*: GRE-V no minimum stated, GRE-Q no minimum stated, GRE-Analytical no minimum stated; *Social Psychology PhD (Doctor of Philosophy)*: GRE-V no minimum stated, GRE-Q no minimum stated, GRE-Analytical no minimum stated, GRE-Subject (Psychology) no minimum stated; *Lifespan Development and Aging PhD (Doctor of Philosophy)*: GRE-V no minimum stated, GRE-Q no minimum stated, GRE-Analytical no minimum stated, GRE-Subject (Psychology) no minimum stated; *Clinical Psychology PhD (Doctor of Philosophy)*: GRE-V no minimum stated, GRE-Q no minimum stated, GRE-Analytical no minimum stated, overall undergraduate GPA no minimum stated, 3.72; *Individualized PhD (Doctor of Philosophy)*: GRE-V no minimum stated, GRE-Q no minimum stated, GRE-Analytical no minimum stated. **Other Criteria:** (importance of criteria rated low, medium, or high): GRE scores—high, research experience—high, work experience—medium, extracurricular activity—medium, clinically related public service—medium, GPA—high, letters of recommendation—high, interview—high, statement of goals and objectives—high, undergraduate major in psychology—high, specific undergraduate psychology courses taken—high, Group interview required for Clinical Programs only. For additional information on admission requirements, go to http://web.uvic.ca/psyc/graduate/admissions.php.

Student Characteristics: The following represents characteristics of students in 2012–2013 in all graduate psychology programs in the department: Female—full-time 60, part-time 0; Male—full-time 19, part-time 0; African American/Black—full-time 0, part-

time 0; Hispanic/Latino(a)—full-time 0, part-time 0; Asian/Pacific Islander—part-time 0; American Indian/Alaska Native—full-time 0, part-time 0; Caucasian/White—full-time 0, part-time 0; Multi-ethnic—part-time 0; students subject to the Americans With Disabilities Act—full-time 0, part-time 0; Unknown ethnicity—full-time 0, part-time 0; International students who hold an F-1 or J-1 Visa—full-time 0, part-time 0.

Financial Information/Assistance:
Tuition for Full-Time Study: *Doctoral:* State residents: per academic year $5,148; Nonstate residents: per academic year $6,126. Tuition is subject to change. See the following website for updates and changes in tuition costs: http://web.finance.uvic.ca/tuition/fees.php.

Financial Assistance:
First-Year Students: Teaching assistantships available for first year. Average amount paid per academic year: $2,350. Average number of hours worked per week: 10. Research assistantships available for first year. Average amount paid per academic year: $3,500. Fellowships and scholarships available for first -year. Average amount paid per academic year: $10,000.

Advanced Students: Teaching assistantships available for advanced students. Average amount paid per academic year: $4,700. Average number of hours worked per week: 20. Research assistantships available for advanced students. Average amount paid per academic year: $6,000. Fellowships and scholarships available for advanced students. Average amount paid per academic year: $15,000.

Additional Information: Of all students currently enrolled full time, 95% benefited from one or more of the listed financial assistance programs. Application and information available online at: http://registrar.uvic.ca/safa/index.html.

Internships/Practica: Doctoral Degree (PhD Clinical Psychology): For those doctoral students for whom a professional psychology internship was required in this program prior to graduation, (2) students applied for an internship in 2011–2012, with (2) students obtaining an internship. Of those students who obtained an internship, (2) were paid internships. Of those students who obtained an internship, (2) students placed in APA/CPA accredited internships, (0) students placed in internships not APA/CPA accredited, but listed with the Association of Psychology Postdoctoral and Internship Programs (APPIC), (0) students placed in internships conforming to guidelines of the Council of Directors of School Psychology Programs (CDSPP), (0) students placed in internships that were not APA/CPA accredited, APPIC or CDSPP listed. Internships and practica for students in the clinical program are arranged through the clinical program.

Housing and Day Care: On-campus housing is available. See the following website for more information: http://housing.uvic.ca/. On-campus day care facilities are available. See the following website for more information: http://www.uvic.ca/services/childcare/.

Employment of Department Graduates:
Master's Degree Graduates: Of those who graduated in the academic year 2011–2012, the following categories and numbers represent the postgraduate activities and employment of master's degree graduates: Enrolled in a postdoctoral residency/fellowship

(n/a), employed in independent practice (n/a), total from the above (master's) (0).

Doctoral Degree Graduates: Of those who graduated in the academic year 2011–2012, the following categories and numbers represent the postgraduate activities and employment of doctoral degree graduates: Enrolled in a psychology doctoral program (n/a), enrolled in a postdoctoral residency/fellowship (3), employed in a government agency (1), employed in a hospital/medical center (1), total from the above (doctoral) (5).

Additional Information:

Orientation, Objectives, and Emphasis of Department: The graduate program in psychology emphasizes the training of research competence, and, in the case of neuropsychology and lifespan, the acquisition of clinical skills. The department's orientation is strongly empirical, and students are expected to develop mastery of appropriate methods and design as well as of specific content areas of psychology. The program is directed toward the PhD degree, although students must obtain a master's degree as part of the normal requirements. Formal programs of study, involving a coordinated sequence of courses, are offered for both experimental and clinical neuropsychology (up to but not including a clinical internship), lifespan development, clinical lifespan development, social psychology, and cognition and brain sciences. Individual programs of study may be designed according to the interests of individual students and faculty members in such areas as addictions, consumer and industrial psychology, environmental psychology, experimental and applied behavior analysis, psychopathology, and human psychophysiology.

Special Facilities or Resources: Fully equipped facilities include a psychology clinic operating as an out-patient service and teaching clinic; large observation rooms with audio and video recording equipment for the study of group interaction and other social processes; microcomputer-based cognition laboratories; experimental rooms with one-way mirrors; electrophysiological recording rooms; and specialized labs for the study of visual and auditory perception. We have a Brain and Cognition Laboratory featuring two state-of-the-art event-related potential (ERP) systems. We recently began conducting functional magnetic resonance imaging (fMRI) research at nearby Royal Jubilee Hospital. The Department enjoys good community contact with local hospitals (general, rehabilitation, and extended care), schools, and private and government agencies, which provide sites for both research and practicum experiences.

Information for Students With Physical Disabilities: See the following website for more information: http://rcsd.uvic.ca/.

Application Information:
Send to Graduate Admissions and Records, University of Victoria, P.O. Box 1700 STN CSC, Victoria, BC V8W 2Y2, Canada. Application available online. URL of online application: http://www.uvic.ca/graduatestudies/admissions/admissions/apply/index.php. Students are admitted in the Fall, application deadline December 1. *Fee:* $110. $135 CAD if any post-secondary transcripts come from institutions outside of Canada. Note: All dollar amounts specified in this entry are Canadian dollars.

Waterloo, University of
Department of Psychology
200 University Avenue West
Waterloo, ON N2L 3G1
Telephone: (519) 888-4567
Fax: (519) 746-8631
E-mail: *cmacleod@uwaterloo.ca*
Web: *http://www.psychology.uwaterloo.ca/*

Department Information:
1963. Chairperson: Colin MacLeod. Number of faculty: total—full-time 39, part-time 1; women—full-time 17, part-time 1.

Programs and Degrees Offered:
Listed in the following order: Program area, degree type (T if terminal Master's), number awarded 7/11–6/12. Industrial/Organizational Psychology PhD (Doctor of Philosophy) 1, Social Psychology PhD (Doctor of Philosophy) 5, Cognitive Psychology PhD (Doctor of Philosophy) 6, Cognitive Neuroscience PhD (Doctor of Philosophy) 1, Clinical Psychology PhD (Doctor of Philosophy) 2, Developmental Psychology PhD (Doctor of Philosophy) 1, Industrial/Organizational Psychology MA/MS (Master of Arts/Science) (T) 3, Developmental Psychology MA/MS (Master of Arts/Science) (T) 2.

APA Accreditation: Clinical PhD (Doctor of Philosophy). Student Outcome Data Website: http://www.psychology.uwaterloo.ca/gradprog/programs/phd/clinical/index.html.

CPA Accreditation: Clinical PhD (Doctor of Philosophy).

Student Applications/Admissions:
Student Applications
Industrial/Organizational Psychology PhD (Doctor of Philosophy)—Applications 2012–2013, 13. Total applicants accepted 2012–2013, 6. Number full-time enrolled (new admits only) 2012–2013, 3. Total enrolled 2012–2013 full-time, 15. Total enrolled 2012–2013 part-time, 0. Openings 2013–2014, 8. *Social Psychology PhD (Doctor of Philosophy)*—Applications 2012–2013, 26. Total applicants accepted 2012–2013, 7. Number full-time enrolled (new admits only) 2012–2013, 4. Total enrolled 2012–2013 full-time, 15. Openings 2013–2014, 5. *Cognitive Psychology PhD (Doctor of Philosophy)*—Applications 2012–2013, 11. Total applicants accepted 2012–2013, 5. Number full-time enrolled (new admits only) 2012–2013, 4. Total enrolled 2012–2013 full-time, 14. Total enrolled 2012–2013 part-time, 0. Openings 2013–2014, 5. *Cognitive Neuroscience PhD (Doctor of Philosophy)*—Applications 2012–2013, 32. Total applicants accepted 2012–2013, 6. Number full-time enrolled (new admits only) 2012–2013, 5. Total enrolled 2012–2013 full-time, 21. Total enrolled 2012–2013 part-time, 2. Openings 2013–2014, 6. *Clinical Psychology PhD (Doctor of Philosophy)*—Applications 2012–2013, 143. Total applicants accepted 2012–2013, 7. Number full-time enrolled (new admits only) 2012–2013, 5. Total enrolled 2012–2013 full-time, 23. Total enrolled 2012–2013 part-time, 9. Openings

2013–2014, 8. *Developmental Psychology PhD (Doctor of Philosophy)*—Applications 2012–2013, 18. Total applicants accepted 2012–2013, 3. Number full-time enrolled (new admits only) 2012–2013, 2. Total enrolled 2012–2013 full-time, 7. Total enrolled 2012–2013 part-time, 0. Openings 2013–2014, 5. *Industrial/Organizational Psychology MA/MS (Master of Arts/Science)*—Applications 2012–2013, 42. Total applicants accepted 2012–2013, 1. Number full-time enrolled (new admits only) 2012–2013, 0. Total enrolled 2012–2013 full-time, 3. Total enrolled 2012–2013 part-time, 0. Openings 2013–2014, 4. *Developmental Psychology MA/MS (Master of Arts/Science)*—Applications 2012–2013, 11. Total applicants accepted 2012–2013, 3. Number full-time enrolled (new admits only) 2012–2013, 3. Total enrolled 2012–2013 full-time, 3. Openings 2013–2014, 5.

Scores: Entries appear in this order: required test or GPA, minimum score (if required), median score of students entering in 2012–2013. *Industrial/Organizational Psychology PhD (Doctor of Philosophy)*: GRE-V no minimum stated, GRE-Q no minimum stated, GRE-Analytical no minimum stated, last 2 years GPA no minimum stated, Masters GPA no minimum stated; *Social Psychology PhD (Doctor of Philosophy)*: GRE-V no minimum stated, GRE-Q no minimum stated, GRE-Analytical no minimum stated, last 2 years GPA no minimum stated, Masters GPA no minimum stated; *Cognitive Psychology PhD (Doctor of Philosophy)*: GRE-V no minimum stated, GRE-Q no minimum stated, GRE-Analytical no minimum stated, last 2 years GPA no minimum stated, Masters GPA no minimum stated; *Cognitive Neuroscience PhD (Doctor of Philosophy)*: GRE-V no minimum stated, GRE-Q no minimum stated, GRE-Analytical no minimum stated, last 2 years GPA no minimum stated, Masters GPA no minimum stated; *Clinical Psychology PhD (Doctor of Philosophy)*: GRE-V no minimum stated, GRE-Q no minimum stated, GRE-Analytical no minimum stated, last 2 years GPA no minimum stated, psychology GPA no minimum stated, Masters GPA no minimum stated; *Developmental Psychology PhD (Doctor of Philosophy)*: GRE-V no minimum stated, GRE-Q no minimum stated, GRE-Analytical no minimum stated, last 2 years GPA no minimum stated, Masters GPA no minimum stated; *Industrial/Organizational Psychology MA/MS (Master of Arts/Science)*: GRE-V no minimum stated, GRE-Q no minimum stated, GRE-Analytical no minimum stated, last 2 years GPA no minimum stated; *Developmental Psychology MA/MS (Master of Arts/Science)*: last 2 years GPA no minimum stated.

Other Criteria: (importance of criteria rated low, medium, or high): GRE scores—high, research experience—medium, work experience—low, clinically related public service—medium, GPA—high, letters of recommendation—high, interview—medium, statement of goals and objectives—medium, undergraduate major in psychology—high, specific undergraduate psychology courses taken—medium. For additional information on admission requirements, go to http://www.psychology.uwaterloo.ca/gradprog/admission/index.html.

Student Characteristics: The following represents characteristics of students in 2012–2013 in all graduate psychology programs in the department: Female—full-time 63, part-time 9; Male—full-time 38, part-time 2; African American/Black—full-time 0, part-time 0; Hispanic/Latino(a)—full-time 0, part-time 0; Asian/Pacific Islander—full-time 0, part-time 0; American Indian/Alaska Native—full-time 0, part-time 0; Caucasian/White—full-time 0, part-time 0; Multi-ethnic—full-time 0, part-time 0; students subject to the Americans With Disabilities Act—full-time 0, part-time 0; Unknown ethnicity—full-time 0, part-time 0; International students who hold an F-1 or J-1 Visa—full-time 0, part-time 0.

Financial Information/Assistance:
Tuition for Full-Time Study: *Master's:* State residents: per academic year $8,082; Nonstate residents: per academic year $18,918. *Doctoral:* State residents: per academic year $8,082; Nonstate residents: per academic year $18,918. Tuition is subject to change. See the following website for updates and changes in tuition costs: https://uwaterloo.ca/finance/student-accounts/tuition-fee-schedules.

Financial Assistance:
First-Year Students: Teaching assistantships available for first year. Research assistantships available for first year. Fellowships and scholarships available for first -year.

Advanced Students: Teaching assistantships available for advanced students. Research assistantships available for advanced students. Fellowships and scholarships available for advanced students.

Additional Information: Of all students currently enrolled full time, 100% benefited from one or more of the listed financial assistance programs. Application and information available online at: http://psychology.uwaterloo.ca/gradprog/financial.html.

Internships/Practica: Doctoral Degree (PhD Clinical Psychology): For those doctoral students for whom a professional psychology internship was required in this program prior to graduation, (5) students applied for an internship in 2011–2012, with (3) students obtaining an internship. Of those students who obtained an internship, (3) were paid internships. Of those students who obtained an internship, (3) students placed in APA/CPA accredited internships, (0) students placed in internships not APA/CPA accredited, but listed with the Association of Psychology Postdoctoral and Internship Programs (APPIC), (0) students placed in internships conforming to guidelines of the Council of Directors of School Psychology Programs (CDSPP), (0) students placed in internships that were not APA/CPA accredited, APPIC or CDSPP listed. Master's Degree (MA/MS Industrial/Organizational Psychology): An internship experience, such as a final research project or "capstone" experience is required of graduates. Master's Degree (MA/MS Developmental Psychology): An internship experience, such as a final research project or "capstone" experience is required of graduates. The Applied Master's program requires a 4-month supervised internship. The Clinical program requires a 4-month practicum during the program of study and a 12-month internship at the conclusion of the academic program. Most practicum placements are with local hospitals, schools or industries.

Housing and Day Care: On-campus housing is available. See the following website for more information: http://uwaterloo.ca/housing/. On-campus day care facilities are available. See the following website for more information: https://uwaterloo.ca/human-resources/family-support-services-programs/child-care-centres-campus.

Employment of Department Graduates:

Master's Degree Graduates: Of those who graduated in the academic year 2011–2012, the following categories and numbers represent the postgraduate activities and employment of master's degree graduates: Enrolled in a psychology doctoral program (1), enrolled in another graduate/professional program (1), enrolled in a postdoctoral residency/fellowship (n/a), employed in independent practice (n/a), employed in business or industry (1), still seeking employment (1), other employment position (1), total from the above (master's) (5).

Doctoral Degree Graduates: Of those who graduated in the academic year 2011–2012, the following categories and numbers represent the postgraduate activities and employment of doctoral degree graduates: Enrolled in a psychology doctoral program (n/a), enrolled in another graduate/professional program (1), enrolled in a postdoctoral residency/fellowship (8), employed in independent practice (3), employed in an academic position at a university (2), employed in business or industry (1), other employment position (1), total from the above (doctoral) (16).

Additional Information:

Orientation, Objectives, and Emphasis of Department: There is a strong emphasis on research in all six divisions of the PhD program, and MASc students are prepared for careers in applied psychology in a variety of areas. Students are involved either through participation in ongoing faculty research or through development of their own ideas; course work is intended to provide students with general knowledge and intensive preparation in their area of concentration. For some of the programs, the blending of theory and practice is experienced in internship and practicum arrangements.

Special Facilities or Resources: Within a large 4-story building, extensive laboratory facilities are available for animal and human research. Additional educational and resource centers operate in conjunction with academic and research programs. Research requiring special populations is often carried out at community institutions under the supervision of faculty members. Considerable investment has been made to technical services including excellent computer facilities and consulting personnel who are available for student research and courses.

Information for Students With Physical Disabilities: See the following website for more information: http://uwaterloo.ca/disability-services/.

Application Information:

Send to Graduate Studies Office, University of Waterloo, 200 University Avenue West, Waterloo, ON N2L 3G1. Application available online. URL of online application: http://uwaterloo.ca/graduate-studies/application-admission/apply-online. Students are admitted in the Fall, application deadline December 15. *Fee:* $100. Note: All dollar amounts specified in this entry are Canadian dollars.

Wilfrid Laurier University
Department of Psychology
75 University Avenue, West
Waterloo, ON N2L 3C5
Telephone: (519) 884-1970, Ext. 3371
Fax: (519) 746-7605
E-mail: *rsharkey@wlu.ca*
Web: *http://www.wlu.ca/science/psychology*

Department Information:

1956. Chairperson: Dr. Rudy Eikelboom. Number of faculty: total—full-time 35, part-time 18; women—full-time 11, part-time 11; total—minority—full-time 2, part-time 2; women minority—full-time 1, part-time 1.

Programs and Degrees Offered:

Listed in the following order: Program area, degree type (T if terminal Master's), number awarded 7/11–6/12. Behavioural Neuroscience MA/MS (Master of Arts/Science) (T) 2, Cognitive Neuroscience MA/MS (Master of Arts/Science) (T) 4, Community Psychology MA/MS (Master of Arts/Science) 5, Social Psychology MA/MS (Master of Arts/Science) (T) 2, Developmental Psychology MA/MS (Master of Arts/Science) 5, Behavioural Neuroscience PhD (Doctor of Philosophy) 0, Cognitive Neuroscience PhD (Doctor of Philosophy) 0, Community Psychology PhD (Doctor of Philosophy) 3, Developmental Psychology PhD (Doctor of Philosophy) 2, Social Psychology PhD (Doctor of Philosophy) 3.

Student Applications/Admissions:

Student Applications

Behavioural Neuroscience MA/MS (Master of Arts/Science)—Applications 2012–2013, 13. Total applicants accepted 2012–2013, 3. Number full-time enrolled (new admits only) 2012–2013, 3. Number part-time enrolled (new admits only) 2012–2013, 0. Total enrolled 2012–2013 full-time, 13. Total enrolled 2012–2013 part-time, 0. Openings 2013–2014, 5. The median number of years required for completion of a degree in 2012–2013 were 2. The number of students enrolled full- and part-time who were dismissed or voluntarily withdrew from this program area in 2012–2013 were 0. *Cognitive Neuroscience MA/MS (Master of Arts/Science)*—Applications 2012–2013, 11. Total applicants accepted 2012–2013, 3. Number full-time enrolled (new admits only) 2012–2013, 3. Number part-time enrolled (new admits only) 2012–2013, 0. Total enrolled 2012–2013 full-time, 7. Total enrolled 2012–2013 part-time, 0. Openings 2013–2014, 5. The median number of years required for completion of a degree in 2012–2013 were 2. The number of students enrolled full- and part-time who were dismissed or voluntarily withdrew from this program area in 2012–2013 were 0. *Community Psychology MA/MS (Master of Arts/Science)*—Applications 2012–2013, 26. Total applicants accepted 2012–2013, 5. Number full-time enrolled (new admits only) 2012–2013, 5. Number part-time enrolled (new admits only) 2012–2013, 0. Total enrolled 2012–2013 full-time, 16. Total enrolled 2012–2013 part-time, 2. Openings 2013–2014, 5. The median number of years required for completion of a degree in 2012–2013 were 3. The number of students enrolled full- and part-time who were dismissed or voluntarily withdrew from this program area in 2012–2013 were 0. *Social Psychology MA/MS (Master of Arts/Science)*—Applications 2012–2013, 26. Total applicants accepted 2012–2013, 0. Number full-time enrolled (new admits only) 2012–2013, 0. Number part-time enrolled (new admits only) 2012–2013, 0. Total enrolled 2012–2013 full-time, 8. Total enrolled 2012–2013 part-time, 0. Openings 2013–2014, 5. The median number of years required for completion of a degree in 2012–2013 were 2. The number of students enrolled full- and part-time who were dismissed or voluntarily withdrew from this program area in 2012–2013 were 0. *Developmental Psychology MA/MS (Master of Arts/Science)*—Applications 2012–2013, 25. Total applicants accepted 2012–2013, 7. Number full-time enrolled (new admits only) 2012–2013, 7. Total enrolled 2012–2013 full-time, 13. Openings 2013–2014, 5. The median number of years required for completion of a degree in 2012–2013 were 2. The number of students enrolled full- and part-time who were dismissed or voluntarily withdrew from this program area in 2012–2013 were 1. *Behavioural Neuroscience PhD (Doctor of Philosophy)*—Applications 2012–2013, 4. Total applicants accepted 2012–2013, 2. Number full-time enrolled (new admits only) 2012–2013, 2. Total enrolled 2012–2013 full-time, 4. Openings 2013–2014, 3. The number of students enrolled full- and part-time who were dismissed or voluntarily withdrew from this program area in 2012–2013 were 0. *Cognitive Neuroscience PhD (Doctor of Philosophy)*—Applications 2012–2013, 2. Total applicants accepted 2012–2013, 2. Number full-time enrolled (new admits only) 2012–2013, 2. Number part-time enrolled (new admits only) 2012–2013, 0. Total enrolled 2012–2013 full-time, 6. Total enrolled 2012–2013 part-time, 0. Openings 2013–2014, 3. The number of students enrolled full- and part-time who were dismissed or voluntarily withdrew from this program area in 2012–2013 were 0. *Community Psychology PhD (Doctor of Philosophy)*—Applications 2012–2013, 11. Total applicants accepted 2012–2013, 3. Number full-time enrolled (new admits only) 2012–2013, 4. Number part-time enrolled (new admits only) 2012–2013, 0. Total enrolled 2012–2013 full-time, 10. Total enrolled 2012–2013 part-time, 0. Openings 2013–2014, 3. The median number of years required for completion of a degree in 2012–2013 were 5. The number of students enrolled full- and part-time who were dismissed or voluntarily withdrew from this program area in 2012–2013 were 0. *Developmental Psychology PhD (Doctor of Philosophy)*—Applications 2012–2013, 6. Total applicants accepted 2012–2013, 3. Number full-time enrolled (new admits only) 2012–2013, 3. Number part-time enrolled (new admits only) 2012–2013, 0. Total enrolled 2012–2013 full-time, 13. Total enrolled 2012–2013 part-time, 1. Openings 2013–2014, 3. The median number of years required for completion of a degree in 2012–2013 were 4. The number of students enrolled full- and part-time who were dismissed or voluntarily withdrew from this program area in 2012–2013 were 0. *Social Psychology PhD (Doctor of Philosophy)*—Applications 2012–2013, 12. Total applicants accepted 2012–2013, 4. Number full-time enrolled (new admits only) 2012–2013, 4. Number part-time enrolled (new admits only) 2012–2013, 0. Total enrolled 2012–2013 full-time, 9. Total enrolled 2012–2013 part-time, 0. Openings 2013–2014, 3. The median number of years required for completion of a degree in 2012–2013 were 4. The number of students enrolled full- and part-time who were dismissed or voluntarily withdrew from this program area in 2012–2013 were 0.

Other Criteria: (importance of criteria rated low, medium, or high): research experience—medium, work experience—low, extracurricular activity—low, clinically related public service—low, GPA—high, letters of recommendation—high, interview—medium, statement of goals and objectives—high. For additional information on admission requirements, go to http://www.wlu.ca/page.php?grp_id=44&p=15351.

Student Characteristics: The following represents characteristics of students in 2012–2013 in all graduate psychology programs in the department: Female—full-time 69, part-time 3; Male—full-time 30, part-time 0; African American/Black—full-time 0, part-time 0; Hispanic/Latino(a)—full-time 0, part-time 0; Asian/Pacific Islander—full-time 8, part-time 0; American Indian/Alaska Native—full-time 1, part-time 0; Caucasian/White—full-time 90, part-time 3; Multi-ethnic—full-time 0, part-time 0; students subject to the Americans With Disabilities Act—full-time 0, part-time 0; Unknown ethnicity—full-time 0, part-time 0; International students who hold an F-1 or J-1 Visa—full-time 1, part-time 0.

Financial Information/Assistance:
Tuition for Full-Time Study: *Master's:* State residents: per academic year $7,547; Nonstate residents: per academic year $16,965. *Doctoral:* State residents: per academic year $7,547; Nonstate residents: per academic year $16,965. Tuition is subject to change. See the following website for updates and changes in tuition costs: http://www.wlu.ca/page.php?grp_id=36&p=654.

Financial Assistance:
   First-Year Students: No information provided.
   Advanced Students: No information provided.
   Additional Information: Of all students currently enrolled full time, 0% benefited from one or more of the listed financial assistance programs. Application and information available online at: http://www.wlu.ca/page.php?grp_id=36&p=9135.

Housing and Day Care: On-campus housing is available. See the following website for more information: http://waterloo.mylaurier.ca/residence/info/home.htm. On-campus day care facilities are available. See the following website for more information: http://www.wlu.ca/calendars/section.php?cal=1&s=188&sp=632&ss=676&y=23.

Employment of Department Graduates:
   Master's Degree Graduates: Of those who graduated in the academic year 2011–2012, the following categories and numbers represent the postgraduate activities and employment of master's degree graduates: Enrolled in a postdoctoral residency/fellowship (n/a), employed in independent practice (n/a), total from the above (master's) (0).
   Doctoral Degree Graduates: Of those who graduated in the academic year 2011–2012, the following categories and numbers represent the postgraduate activities and employment of doctoral degree graduates: Enrolled in a psychology doctoral program (n/a), total from the above (doctoral) (0).

Additional Information:
Orientation, Objectives, and Emphasis of Department: Graduate students can obtain an MA, MSc or PhD in one of the five fields of: 1) Behavioural Neuroscience, 2) Cognitive Neuroscience, 3) Community Psychology, 4) Social, and 5) Develop-

mental. The objective of the MA, MSc and PhD programs in the fields of Behavioural, Cognitive, Social and Developmental Psychology is to develop competence in designing, conducting, and evaluating research in the fields of Behavioural, Cognitive, Social and Developmental Psychology. Five half-credit courses and a thesis constitute the degree requirements in these MA/MSc programs. The purpose of these programs is to prepare students for doctoral studies, or for employment in an environment requiring research skills. Students in good standing can be considered for admission to the PhD programs in these area, which involve 7 half-credit courses, 2 comprehensive papers and a dissertation. In the field of Community Psychology, the objective is to train scientist–practitioners with skills in community collaboration. Students receive training in theory, research, and practice that will enable them to analyze the implications of social change for the delivery of community services. Six half-credit courses and a thesis are required for the MA degree. Students who complete this program are prepared for either doctoral level training or for employment in community research and service settings. Students in good standing can be considered for admission to the PhD program in this area, which involves 6 half-credit courses, 2 comprehensive papers and a dissertation.

Special Facilities or Resources: The department has free unlimited access to the university computers, microprocessors, extensive electromechanical equipment, full-time electronics research associate, full-time field supervisor, and access to a wide variety of field settings for research and consultation.

Information for Students With Physical Disabilities: See the following website for more information: http://waterloo.mylaurier.ca/accessible/info/home.htm.

Application Information:
Send to Rita Sharkey, Graduate Program Assistant, Psychology Department, Wilfrid Laurier University, 75 University Avenue West, Waterloo, ON N2L 3C5. Application available online. URL of online application: http://www.wlu.ca/page.php?grp_id=36&p=635. Students are admitted in the Fall, application deadline January 15. *Fee:* $100. Note: All dollar amounts specified in this entry are Canadian dollars.

Windsor, University of
Psychology
Faculty of Arts and Social Sciences
401 Sunset Avenue
Windsor, ON N9B 3P4
Telephone: (519) 253-3000, x 2232
Fax: (519) 973-7021
E-mail: *ckwantes@uwindsor.ca*
Web: *http://www.uwindsor.ca/psychology*

Department Information:
1944. Acting Head: Catherine Kwantes. Number of faculty: total—full-time 28; women—full-time 17; total—minority—full-time 2.

Programs and Degrees Offered:
Listed in the following order: Program area, degree type (T if terminal Master's), number awarded 7/11–6/12. Applied Social

Psychology PhD (Doctor of Philosophy) 1, Clinical Psychology PhD (Doctor of Philosophy) 12.

APA Accreditation: Clinical PhD (Doctor of Philosophy). Student Outcome Data Website: http://www.uwindsor.ca/psychology/admissionsoutcome-data.

CPA Accreditation: Clinical PhD (Doctor of Philosophy).

Student Applications/Admissions:
Student Applications
Applied Social Psychology PhD (Doctor of Philosophy)—Applications 2012–2013, 14. Total applicants accepted 2012–2013, 8. Number full-time enrolled (new admits only) 2012–2013, 3. Number part-time enrolled (new admits only) 2012–2013, 0. Total enrolled 2012–2013 full-time, 29. Total enrolled 2012–2013 part-time, 0. Openings 2013–2014, 4. The median number of years required for completion of a degree in 2012–2013 were 6. The number of students enrolled full- and part-time who were dismissed or voluntarily withdrew from this program area in 2012–2013 were 3. *Clinical Psychology PhD (Doctor of Philosophy)*—Applications 2012–2013, 125. Total applicants accepted 2012–2013, 18. Number full-time enrolled (new admits only) 2012–2013, 11. Number part-time enrolled (new admits only) 2012–2013, 0. Total enrolled 2012–2013 full-time, 90. Total enrolled 2012–2013 part-time, 0. Openings 2013–2014, 10. The median number of years required for completion of a degree in 2012–2013 were 7. The number of students enrolled full- and part-time who were dismissed or voluntarily withdrew from this program area in 2012–2013 were 1.
Scores: Entries appear in this order: required test or GPA, minimum score (if required), median score of students entering in 2012–2013. *Applied Social Psychology PhD (Doctor of Philosophy):* GRE-V no minimum stated, GRE-Q no minimum stated, GRE-Analytical no minimum stated, GRE-Subject (Psychology) no minimum stated, overall undergraduate GPA no minimum stated, last 2 years GPA no minimum stated, psychology GPA no minimum stated; *Clinical Psychology PhD (Doctor of Philosophy):* GRE-V no minimum stated, GRE-Q no minimum stated, GRE-Analytical no minimum stated, overall undergraduate GPA no minimum stated, last 2 years GPA no minimum stated, Masters GPA no minimum stated.
Other Criteria: (importance of criteria rated low, medium, or high): GRE scores—high, research experience—medium, work experience—low, extracurricular activity—low, clinically related public service—medium, GPA—high, letters of recommendation—high, interview—high, statement of goals and objectives—medium, honours thesis—high, undergraduate major in psychology—high, specific undergraduate psychology courses taken—high. For additional information on admission requirements, go to http://www.uwindsor.ca/psychology/admissions-and-application-procedures.

Student Characteristics: The following represents characteristics of students in 2012–2013 in all graduate psychology programs in the department: Female—full-time 98, part-time 0; Male—full-time 21, part-time 0; African American/Black—full-time 0, part-time 0; Hispanic/Latino(a)—full-time 0, part-time 0; Asian/Pacific Islander—full-time 0, part-time 0; American Indian/Alaska Native—full-time 0, part-time 0; Caucasian/White—full-time 0, part-time 0; Multi-ethnic—full-time 0, part-time 0; students subject to the Americans With Disabilities Act—full-time 0, part-time 0; Unknown ethnicity—full-time 0, part-time 0; International students who hold an F-1 or J-1 Visa—full-time 7, part-time 0.

Financial Information/Assistance:

Tuition for Full-Time Study: *Doctoral:* State residents: per academic year $7,666; Nonstate residents: per academic year $17,325. Tuition is subject to change. See the following website for updates and changes in tuition costs: http://web2.uwindsor.ca/finance/fee-estimator/.

Financial Assistance:

First-Year Students: Teaching assistantships available for first year. Average amount paid per academic year: $9,822. Average number of hours worked per week: 10. Apply by December 1. Research assistantships available for first year. Average number of hours worked per week: 10. Fellowships and scholarships available for first -year. Average amount paid per academic year: $5,500. Apply by December 1.

Advanced Students: Teaching assistantships available for advanced students. Average amount paid per academic year: $10,945. Average number of hours worked per week: 10. Apply by December 1. Research assistantships available for advanced students. Average number of hours worked per week: 10. Fellowships and scholarships available for advanced students. Average amount paid per academic year: $6,000. Apply by December 1.

Additional Information: Of all students currently enrolled full time, 90% benefited from one or more of the listed financial assistance programs.

Internships/Practica: Doctoral Degree (PhD Clinical Psychology): For those doctoral students for whom a professional psychology internship was required in this program prior to graduation, (19) students applied for an internship in 2011–2012, with (17) students obtaining an internship. Of those students who obtained an internship, (16) were paid internships. Of those students who obtained an internship, (12) students placed in APA/CPA accredited internships, (1) students placed in internships not APA/CPA accredited, but listed with the Association of Psychology Postdoctoral and Internship Programs (APPIC), (0) students placed in internships conforming to guidelines of the Council of Directors of School Psychology Programs (CDSPP), (4) students placed in internships that were not APA/CPA accredited, APPIC or CDSPP listed. A wide variety of clinical practica are available in the Windsor-Detroit area, and clinical students obtain additional summer practicum positions across the country. Students are placed in predoctoral internships throughout Canada and the U.S. Applied Social students obtain practica and internships in business and industry, community and health-related agencies.

Housing and Day Care: On-campus housing is available. See the following website for more information: http://www.uwindsor.ca/residence. No on-campus day care facilities are available.

Employment of Department Graduates:

Master's Degree Graduates: Of those who graduated in the academic year 2011–2012, the following categories and numbers represent the postgraduate activities and employment of master's degree graduates: Enrolled in a postdoctoral residency/fellowship (n/a), employed in independent practice (n/a), total from the above (master's) (0).

Doctoral Degree Graduates: Of those who graduated in the academic year 2011–2012, the following categories and numbers represent the postgraduate activities and employment of doctoral degree graduates: Enrolled in a psychology doctoral program (n/a), enrolled in a postdoctoral residency/fellowship (2), employed in independent practice (2), employed in business or industry (1), employed in a community mental health/counseling center (3), employed in a hospital/medical center (5), total from the above (doctoral) (13).

Additional Information:

Orientation, Objectives, and Emphasis of Department: The mission of the graduate programs in the Department of Psychology is to provide graduate students with a foundation of theory, research, and practice to enable them to conduct research and/or apply psychology in a variety of settings including universities, private practice, schools, health/medical organizations, social service agencies, businesses, and basic/applied research firms. Graduate offerings are divided into two areas: clinical and applied social. Students applying for the clinical program apply directly into specialty tracks of adult clinical, child clinical, or clinical neuropsychology. Each of the areas combines theoretical, substantive, and methodological coursework with a variety of applied training experiences.

Special Facilities or Resources: The Department of Psychology's PhD program is unique in that all areas of specialization (Applied Social, Clinical Neuropsychology, Adult Clinical and Child Clinical) have an applied focus. Applied training and research resources include the Psychological Services & Research Centre, the Child Study Centre, the Emotion-Cognition Research Laboratory, Health Research Centre for the Study of Violence against Women, Health & Well-being Laboratory, the Student Counselling Centre, and the Psycholinguistics and Neurolinguistics Laboratory. There are faculty-student research groups in the areas of eating disorders, trauma and psychotherapy, problem gambling, computer-mediated communication, feminist research, emotional competence, culture and diversity, health psychology, neuro-psychoanalysis, aging, forgiveness, applied memory, multicultural and counselling research, and autism. The department is affiliated with the Summit Centre for Preschool Children with Autism. The university campus has wireless computer access throughout. Researchers have access to a participant pool and web-based participant recruitment as well as systems that allow for web-based data collection.

Information for Students With Physical Disabilities: See the following website for more information: http://www.uwindsor.ca/disability/.

Application Information:
Send to Office of the Registrar, Graduate Studies Division, University of Windsor, 401 Sunset Avenue, Windsor, Ontario, Canada N9B 3P4. Application available online. URL of online application: http://www.uwindsor.ca/registrar/how-to-apply-0. Students are admitted in the Fall, application deadline December 1. *Fee:* $105. Note: All dollar amounts specified in this entry are Canadian dollars.

York University

Graduate Program in Psychology
4700 Keele Street, Room 297, Behavioural Science Building
Toronto, ON M3J 1P3
Telephone: (416) 736-5290
Fax: (416) 736-5814
E-mail: *dmccann@yorku.ca*
Web: *http://www.yorku.ca/gradpsyc/index.html*

Department Information:

1963. Director, Graduate Program in Psychology: Dr. Doug McCann. Number of faculty: total—full-time 82; women—full-time 42.

Programs and Degrees Offered:

Listed in the following order: Program area, degree type (T if terminal Master's), number awarded 7/11–6/12. Brain, Behaviour and Cognitive Sciences PhD (Doctor of Philosophy) 12, Clinical PhD (Doctor of Philosophy) 14, Clinical-Developmental PhD (Doctor of Philosophy) 18, Developmental Science PhD (Doctor of Philosophy) 8, History and Theory Of Psychology PhD (Doctor of Philosophy) 3, Social and Personality Psychology PhD (Doctor of Philosophy) 6, Quantitative Methods PhD (Doctor of Philosophy) 0.

APA Accreditation:

Clinical PhD (Doctor of Philosophy). Student Outcome Data Website: http://www.yorku.ca/gradpsyc/field2/prospective_students.html.

CPA Accreditation:

Clinical PhD (Doctor of Philosophy). Clinical PhD (Doctor of Philosophy).

Student Applications/Admissions:

Student Applications

Brain, Behaviour and Cognitive Sciences PhD (Doctor of Philosophy)—Applications 2012–2013, 27. Total applicants accepted 2012–2013, 12. Number full-time enrolled (new admits only) 2012–2013, 12. Number part-time enrolled (new admits only) 2012–2013, 0. Total enrolled 2012–2013 full-time, 36. Total enrolled 2012–2013 part-time, 2. Openings 2013–2014, 9. The median number of years required for completion of a degree in 2012–2013 were 6. The number of students enrolled full- and part-time who were dismissed or voluntarily withdrew from this program area in 2012–2013 were 3. *Clinical PhD (Doctor of Philosophy)*—Applications 2012–2013, 170. Total applicants accepted 2012–2013, 11. Number full-time enrolled (new admits only) 2012–2013, 11. Number part-time enrolled (new admits only) 2012–2013, 0. Total enrolled 2012–2013 full-time, 55. Total enrolled 2012–2013 part-time, 11. Openings 2013–2014, 7. The median number of years required for completion of a degree in 2012–2013 were 6. The number of students enrolled full- and part-time who were dismissed or voluntarily withdrew from this program area in 2012–2013 were 3. *Clinical-Developmental PhD (Doctor of Philosophy)*—Applications 2012–2013, 119. Total applicants accepted 2012–2013, 8. Number full-time enrolled (new admits only) 2012–2013, 8. Number part-time enrolled (new admits only) 2012–2013, 0. Total enrolled 2012–2013 full-time. 63. Total enrolled 2012–2013 part-time, 9. Openings 2013–2014, 9. The median number of years required for completion of a degree

in 2012–2013 were 6. The number of students enrolled full- and part-time who were dismissed or voluntarily withdrew from this program area in 2012–2013 were 2. *Developmental Science PhD (Doctor of Philosophy)*—Applications 2012–2013, 17. Total applicants accepted 2012–2013, 2. Number full-time enrolled (new admits only) 2012–2013, 2. Number part-time enrolled (new admits only) 2012–2013, 0. Total enrolled 2012–2013 full-time, 17. Total enrolled 2012–2013 part-time, 2. Openings 2013–2014, 6. The median number of years required for completion of a degree in 2012–2013 were 6. The number of students enrolled full- and part-time who were dismissed or voluntarily withdrew from this program area in 2012–2013 were 1. *History and Theory Of Psychology PhD (Doctor of Philosophy)*—Applications 2012–2013, 7. Total applicants accepted 2012–2013, 3. Number full-time enrolled (new admits only) 2012–2013, 3. Number part-time enrolled (new admits only) 2012–2013, 0. Total enrolled 2012–2013 full-time, 16. Total enrolled 2012–2013 part-time, 2. Openings 2013–2014, 2. The median number of years required for completion of a degree in 2012–2013 were 6. The number of students enrolled full- and part-time who were dismissed or voluntarily withdrew from this program area in 2012–2013 were 0. *Social and Personality Psychology PhD (Doctor of Philosophy)*—Applications 2012–2013, 53. Total applicants accepted 2012–2013, 2. Number full-time enrolled (new admits only) 2012–2013, 2. Number part-time enrolled (new admits only) 2012–2013, 0. Total enrolled 2012–2013 full-time, 20. Total enrolled 2012–2013 part-time, 3. Openings 2013–2014, 5. The median number of years required for completion of a degree in 2012–2013 were 6. The number of students enrolled full- and part-time who were dismissed or voluntarily withdrew from this program area in 2012–2013 were 1. *Quantitative Methods PhD (Doctor of Philosophy)*—Applications 2012–2013, 6. Total applicants accepted 2012–2013, 0. Number full-time enrolled (new admits only) 2012–2013, 0. Number part-time enrolled (new admits only) 2012–2013, 0. Total enrolled 2012–2013 full-time, 8. Total enrolled 2012–2013 part-time, 0. Openings 2013–2014, 2. The median number of years required for completion of a degree in 2012–2013 were 6. The number of students enrolled full- and part-time who were dismissed or voluntarily withdrew from this program area in 2012–2013 were 0.

Scores: Entries appear in this order: required test or GPA, minimum score (if required), median score of students entering in 2012–2013. *Brain, Behaviour and Cognitive Sciences PhD (Doctor of Philosophy):* GRE-V no minimum stated, GRE-Q no minimum stated, GRE-Analytical no minimum stated, last 2 years GPA no minimum stated, Masters GPA no minimum stated; *Clinical PhD (Doctor of Philosophy):* GRE-V no minimum stated, GRE-Q no minimum stated, GRE-Analytical no minimum stated, GRE-Subject (Psychology) no minimum stated, last 2 years GPA no minimum stated, Masters GPA no minimum stated; *Clinical-Developmental PhD (Doctor of Philosophy):* GRE-V no minimum stated, GRE-Q no minimum stated, GRE-Analytical no minimum stated, GRE-Subject (Psychology) no minimum stated, last 2 years GPA no minimum stated, Masters GPA no minimum stated; *Developmental Science PhD (Doctor of Philosophy):* GRE-V no minimum stated, GRE-Q no minimum stated, GRE-Analytical no minimum stated, last 2 years GPA no minimum stated, Masters GPA no minimum stated; *History and Theory of Psychology PhD (Doctor of Philosophy):* GRE-V no minimum stated, GRE-Q no minimum stated, GRE-Analytical no minimum stated, last 2 years GPA no minimum stated, Masters GPA no minimum stated; *Social and Personality Psychology PhD (Doctor of Philosophy)*: GRE-V no minimum stated, GRE-Q no minimum stated, GRE-Analytical no minimum stated, last 2 years GPA no minimum stated, Masters GPA no minimum stated; *Quantitative Methods PhD (Doctor of Philosophy)*: GRE-V no minimum stated, GRE-Q no minimum stated, GRE-Analytical no minimum stated, last 2 years GPA no minimum stated, Masters GPA no minimum stated.

Other Criteria: (importance of criteria rated low, medium, or high): GRE scores—high, research experience—high, work experience—medium, clinically related public service—low, GPA—high, letters of recommendation—high, statement of goals and objectives—medium, undergraduate major in psychology—medium, specific undergraduate psychology courses taken—low, The non-Clinical Areas place no weight on clinically related public service. For additional information on admission requirements, go to http://www.yorku.ca/gradpsyc/howtoapply.html.

Student Characteristics: The following represents characteristics of students in 2012–2013 in all graduate psychology programs in the department: Female—full-time 178, part-time 26; Male—full-time 37, part-time 3; African American/Black—full-time 0, part-time 0; Hispanic/Latino(a)—full-time 0, part-time 0; Asian/Pacific Islander—full-time 0, part-time 0; American Indian/Alaska Native—full-time 0, part-time 0; Caucasian/White—full-time 0, part-time 0; Multi-ethnic—full-time 0, part-time 0; students subject to the Americans With Disabilities Act—full-time 0, part-time 0; Unknown ethnicity—full-time 0, part-time 0; International students who hold an F-1 or J-1 Visa—full-time 0, part-time 0.

Financial Information/Assistance:

Tuition for Full-Time Study: *Doctoral:* State residents: per academic year $5,544; Nonstate residents: per academic year $12,033. Tuition is subject to change. See the following website for updates and changes in tuition costs: http://sfs.yorku.ca/fees/courses/index.php.

Financial Assistance:

First-Year Students: Teaching assistantships available for first year. Average amount paid per academic year: $8,905. Average number of hours worked per week: 10. Research assistantships available for first year. Average amount paid per academic year: $6,000. Average number of hours worked per week: 10. Traineeships available for first year. Fellowships and scholarships available for first -year. Average amount paid per academic year: $6,000.

Advanced Students: Teaching assistantships available for advanced students. Average amount paid per academic year: $16,041. Average number of hours worked per week: 10. Research assistantships available for advanced students. Average amount paid per academic year: $10,000. Average number of hours worked per week: 10. Fellowships and scholarships available for advanced students.

Additional Information: Of all students currently enrolled full time, 100% benefited from one or more of the listed financial assistance programs. Application and information available online at: http://futurestudents.yorku.ca/graduate/fees_and_funding.

Internships/Practica: Doctoral Degree (PhD Clinical): For those doctoral students for whom a professional psychology internship was required in this program prior to graduation, (8) students applied for an internship in 2011–2012, with (7) students obtaining an internship. Of those students who obtained an internship, (7) were paid internships. Of those students who obtained an internship, (5) students placed in APA/CPA accredited internships, (0) students placed in internships not APA/CPA accredited, but listed with the Association of Psychology Postdoctoral and Internship Programs (APPIC), (0) students placed in internships conforming to guidelines of the Council of Directors of School Psychology Programs (CDSPP), (2) students placed in internships that were not APA/CPA accredited, APPIC or CDSPP listed. Doctoral Degree (PhD Clinical-Developmental): For those doctoral students for whom a professional psychology internship was required in this program prior to graduation, (6) students applied for an internship in 2011–2012, with (5) students obtaining an internship. Of those students who obtained an internship, (4) were paid internships. Of those students who obtained an internship, (4) students placed in APA/CPA accredited internships, (1) students placed in internships not APA/CPA accredited, but listed with the Association of Psychology Postdoctoral and Internship Programs (APPIC), (0) students placed in internships conforming to guidelines of the Council of Directors of School Psychology Programs (CDSPP), (0) students placed in internships that were not APA/CPA accredited, APPIC or CDSPP listed. Doctoral internships are available; practicum work is done on a half-time basis during the academic year and, when possible, full-time during the summer. Research practica, and a clinical practicum as part of the Clinical Area's programme, are done on campus. Clinical internships are available in the York University Psychology Clinic (newly opened) and a variety of hospitals, clinics, and counseling centers in the city and elsewhere.

Housing and Day Care: On-campus housing is available. See the following website for more information: http://studenthousing.info.yorku.ca/yorkapts/. On-campus day care facilities are available. See the following website for more information: http://daycare.info.yorku.ca/; http://www.yorku.ca/children/.

Employment of Department Graduates:

Master's Degree Graduates: Of those who graduated in the academic year 2011–2012, the following categories and numbers represent the postgraduate activities and employment of master's degree graduates: Enrolled in a postdoctoral residency/fellowship (n/a), employed in independent practice (n/a), total from the above (master's) (0).

Doctoral Degree Graduates: Of those who graduated in the academic year 2011–2012, the following categories and numbers represent the postgraduate activities and employment of doctoral degree graduates: Enrolled in a psychology doctoral program (n/a), enrolled in a postdoctoral residency/fellowship (3), employed in independent practice (4), employed in a professional position in a school system (2), employed in business or industry (1), employed in a government agency (3), employed in a hospital/medical center (3), do not know (9), total from the above (doctoral) (25).

Additional Information:

Orientation, Objectives, and Emphasis of Department: Strength and depth are emphasized in the areas of brain, behaviour and cognitive science (learning, perception, physiological, psychometrics); clinical; clinical-development; developmental cognitive processes; history and theory; quantitative methods; and social-personality. The department prepares students as researchers and practitioners in a given area. Most students admitted to the MA are accepted on the assumption that they will continue into PhD studies.

Special Facilities or Resources: The department has a vivarium; substantial computing facilities; audiovisual equipment including VCRs; and observational laboratories with two-way mirrors.

Information for Students With Physical Disabilities: See the following website for more information: http://ds.info.yorku.ca/.

Application Information:
Send to Office of Graduate Admissions, P.O. Box GA2300, York University, 4700 Keele Street, Toronto, Ontario M3J 1P3, Canada. Application available online. URL of online application: http://futurestudents.yorku.ca/graduate/apply_now. Students are admitted in the Fall, application deadline December 11. *Fee:* $100. Note: All dollar amounts specified in this entry are Canadian dollars.

Oklahoma City University (MEd)
Oklahoma, University of (MEd)
University at Buffalo, State University of New York (MA/MS—terminal, Other)
Valparaiso University (MA/MS—terminal)
Vanderbilt University (MEd)
Washington State University (MA/MS—terminal)
Wisconsin, University of, Milwaukee (MA/MS)

Community Psychology
Alaska, University of, Fairbanks/Anchorage (PhD)
California, University of, Berkeley (PhD)
Central Connecticut State University (MA/MS—terminal)
DePaul University (PhD)
George Mason University (PhD)
George Washington University (PhD)
Georgia State University (PhD)
Hawaii, University of, Manoa (PhD)
Hofstra University (PsyD)
Illinois, University of, Chicago (PhD)
Illinois, University of, Urbana–Champaign (PhD)
Lamar University-Beaumont (MA/MS—terminal)
Maryland, University of, Baltimore County (PhD)
Massachusetts, University of, Lowell (MA/MS—terminal)
Metropolitan State University (MA/MS—terminal)
Michigan State University (PhD)
New Haven, University of (MA/MS)
New York University (MA/MS—terminal)
North Carolina State University (PhD)
North Carolina, University of, Charlotte (MA/MS—terminal)
Portland State University (PhD)
Sage Colleges, The (MA/MS—terminal)
Seton Hall University (EdS)
South Carolina, University of (PhD)
Texas A&M International University (MA/MS—terminal)
Vanderbilt University (MEd, PhD)
Virginia, University of (PhD)
Wayne State University (MA/MS—terminal)
West Virginia University (MA/MS—terminal)
Western Illinois University (MA/MS—terminal)
Wichita State University (PhD)
Wilfrid Laurier University (MA/MS, PhD)

Comparative Psychology
York University (PhD)

Consulting Psychology
Alliant International University: Fresno (MA/MS—terminal), PsyD)
Alliant International University: Los Angeles (MA/MS—terminal, PhD)
Alliant International University: San Diego (MA/MS—terminal, PhD)
Alliant International University: San Francisco (MA/MS—terminal, PhD)

New Haven, University of (MA/MS—terminal)
The Chicago School of Professional Psychology (PsyD)
Wayne State University (MA/MS—terminal, PhD)

Counseling Psychology
Adelphi University (MA/MS—terminal)
Akron, University of (PhD)
Alaska Pacific University (MA/MS—terminal, PsyD)
Alliant International University: San Francisco (MA/MS—terminal)
Angelo State University (MA/MS—terminal)
Argosy University/Orange County (EdD, MA/MS—terminal)
Arizona State University (PhD)
Assumption College (MA/MS—terminal)
Auburn University (PhD)
Augusta State University (MA/MS—terminal)
Ball State University (MA/MS—terminal, PhD)
Baltimore, University of (MA/MS—terminal, Other)
Boston College (PhD)
Brenau University (MA/MS—terminal)
Brigham Young University (PhD)
California Lutheran University (MA/MS—terminal)
Central Arkansas, University of (MA/MS—terminal, PhD)
Central Oklahoma, University of (MA/MS—terminal)
Central Washington University (MA/MS—terminal)
Chestnut Hill College (MA/MS—terminal)
Citadel, The (MA/MS—terminal)
Cleveland State University (PhD)
Colorado State University (PhD)
Denver, University of (MA/MS—terminal, PhD)
Florida International University (MA/MS—terminal)
Florida State University (MA/MS—terminal, PhD)
Florida, University of (PhD)
Fordham University (PhD)
Francis Marion University (MA/MS—terminal)
Frostburg State University (MA/MS—terminal)
Georgia State University (PhD)
Georgia, University of (PhD)
Goddard College (MA/MS—terminal)
Houston, University of (MEd, PhD)
Humboldt State University (MA/MS—terminal)
Illinois State University (MA/MS—terminal)
Illinois, University of, Urbana–Champaign (PhD)
Immaculata University (MA/MS—terminal)
Indiana State University (MA/MS, PhD)
Indiana University (PhD)
Iowa State University (PhD)

Iowa, University of (PhD)
Kansas, University of (MA/MS—terminal, PhD)
Kentucky, University of (EdS, MA/MS, PhD)
Lehigh University (MEd, PhD)
Louisiana State University Shreveport (MA/MS—terminal)
Louisville, University of (PhD)
Loyola University Maryland (MA/MS—terminal)
Loyola University of Chicago (PhD)
Marquette University (PhD)
Maryland, University of (PhD)
Massachusetts School of Professional Psychology (MA/MS, MA/MS—terminal)
Massachusetts, University of, Boston (PhD)
McGill University (PhD)
Memphis, University of (PhD)
Miami, University of (MA/MS—terminal, PhD)
Midwestern State University (MA/MS—terminal)
Millersville University (MA/MS—terminal)
Minnesota, University of (MA/MS—terminal, PhD)
Missouri, University of, Columbia (EdS, MEd, PhD)
Missouri, University of, Kansas City (PhD)
Morehead State University (MA/MS—terminal)
Nebraska, University of, Lincoln (PhD)
New Mexico State University (PhD)
New York University (PhD)
North Dakota, University of (PhD)
North Texas, University of (PhD)
Northeastern University (MA/MS—terminal, PhD)
Northern Arizona University (PhD)
Northern Colorado, University of (PhD)
Northwestern University (MA/MS—terminal)
Oklahoma State University (PhD)
Oklahoma, University of (PhD)
Oregon, University of (PhD)
Our Lady of the Lake University (PsyD)
Pacific University (MA/MS—terminal)
Palo Alto University (MA/MS—terminal)
Pennsylvania, University of (Other)
Philadelphia College of Osteopathic Medicine (MA/MS—terminal, Other)
Puget Sound, University of (MEd)
Purdue University (PhD)
Radford University (MA/MS—terminal, PsyD)
Roosevelt University (MA/MS—terminal)
Rosalind Franklin University of Medicine and Science (MA/MS—terminal)
Sage Colleges, The (MA/MS—terminal, Other)
Saint Francis, University of (MA/MS, MA/MS—terminal, MEd, Other)
Saint Mary's University of Minnesota (MA/MS—terminal)
Santa Clara University (MA/MS—terminal)
Seton Hall University (PhD)
South Alabama, University of (PhD)

Southern Illinois University Carbondale (PhD)
Southern Oregon University (MA/MS—terminal)
St. Thomas, University of (MA/MS—terminal, PsyD)
State University of New York, University of Albany (PhD)
Tennessee, University of, Knoxville (PhD)
Texas A&M International University (MA/MS—terminal)
Texas A&M University (PhD)
Texas Tech University (PhD)
Texas Woman's University (MA/MS—terminal, PhD)
Texas, University of, Austin (PhD)
The Chicago School of Professional Psychology (MA/MS—terminal, PhD)
The School of Professional Psychology at Forest Institute (MA/MS—terminal)
Towson University (MA/MS—terminal)
Union Institute & University (MA/MS—terminal)
University at Buffalo, State University of New York (PhD)
Utah, University of (MEd, PhD)
Valparaiso University (MA/MS—terminal)
Virginia Commonwealth University (PhD)
Walden University (PhD)
Walla Walla University (MA/MS—terminal)
Washington State University (PhD)
Wayne State University (MA/MS—terminal)
West Georgia, University of (MA/MS—terminal)
West Virginia University (PhD)
Western Michigan University (MA/MS—terminal, PhD)
William Paterson University (MA/MS—terminal)
Wisconsin, University of, Madison (MA/MS—terminal, PhD)
Wisconsin, University of, Milwaukee (PhD)
Yeshiva University (MA/MS—terminal)

D

Developmental Psychology
Akron, University of (PhD)
Alabama, University of (PhD)
Arizona State University (PhD)
Boston College (MA/MS, PhD)
Boston University (PhD)
Bowling Green State University (PhD)
British Columbia, University of (PhD)
California, University of, Berkeley (PhD)
California, University of, Davis (MA/MS—terminal, PhD)
California, University of, Los Angeles (PhD)
California, University of, Merced (PhD)
California, University of, Riverside (PhD)
California, University of, Santa Cruz (PhD)
Carnegie Mellon University (PhD)
Chicago, University of (PhD)

Claremont Graduate University (MA/MS—terminal, PhD)
Cleveland State University (PhD)
Connecticut, University of (PhD)
Cornell University (PhD)
Denver, University of (PhD)
DePaul University (PhD)
Duke University (PhD)
Florida International University (PhD)
Florida State University (PhD)
Florida, University of (PhD)
Fordham University (MA/MS—terminal, PhD)
George Mason University (MA/MS—terminal, PhD)
Georgetown University (PhD)
Georgia State University (PhD)
Guelph, University of (MA/MS, PhD)
Harvard University (PhD)
Hawaii, University of, Manoa (PhD)
Houston, University of (PhD)
Humboldt State University (MA/MS—terminal)
Illinois State University (MA/MS—terminal)
Illinois, University of, Urbana–Champaign (PhD)
Illinois, University of, Urbana–Champaign (PhD)
Indiana University (MA/MS, PhD)
Iowa, University of (PhD)
Johns Hopkins University (PhD)
Kansas, University of (PhD)
Louisiana State University (PhD)
Louisville, University of (PhD)
Loyola University of Chicago (PhD)
Maine, University of (PhD)
Manitoba, University of (PhD)
Maryland, University of (PhD)
Maryland, University of, Baltimore County (PhD)
Massachusetts, University of (PhD)
Miami, University of (PhD)
Michigan, University of (PhD)
Millersville University (MA/MS, MEd)
Minnesota, University of (PhD)
Missouri, University of (PhD)
Montana, The University of (PhD)
Nebraska, University of, Lincoln (PhD)
Nebraska, University of, Omaha (MA/MS, PhD)
New Hampshire, University of (PhD)
New Mexico, University of (PhD)
New Orleans, University of (PhD)
New York University (PhD)
North Carolina State University (PhD)
North Carolina, University of, Chapel Hill (PhD)
North Dakota State University (PhD)
Northern Illinois University (PhD)
Northwestern University (PhD)
Notre Dame, University of (PhD)
Ohio State University, The (PhD)
Oklahoma State University (PhD)
Oklahoma, University of (PhD)
Oregon, University of (PhD)
Pennsylvania State University (PhD)
Pennsylvania, University of (MA/MS, PhD)

Pittsburgh, University of (MA/MS—terminal, PhD)
Portland State University (PhD)
Purdue University (PhD)
Queen's University (MA/MS, PhD)
Saint Louis University (PhD)
San Diego State University (MA/MS)
San Francisco State University (MA/MS—terminal)
Saskatchewan, University of (PhD)
Southern California, University of (PhD)
Stanford University (PhD)
Temple University (PhD)
Texas, University of, Austin (Other, PhD)
Texas, University of, Dallas (MA/MS—terminal, PhD)
The New School for Social Research (PhD)
Toronto, University of (MA/MS, PhD)
Tulane University (PhD)
Utah, University of (PhD)
Vanderbilt University (PhD)
Victoria, University of (PhD)
Virginia Commonwealth University (PhD)
Virginia Polytechnic Institute and State University (PhD)
Virginia, University of (PhD)
Washington University in St. Louis (PhD)
Washington, University of (PhD)
Waterloo, University of (MA/MS—terminal, PhD)
West Virginia University (PhD)
Western Kentucky University (MA/MS)
Wilfrid Laurier University (MA/MS, PhD)
Wisconsin, University of, Madison (PhD)
Wisconsin, University of, Milwaukee (MA/MS—terminal, PhD)
Wyoming, University of (PhD)
Yale University (PhD)
York University (PhD)

E

Educational Psychology
Alliant International University: Irvine (MA/MS—terminal, PsyD)
Alliant International University: Los Angeles (MA/MS—terminal, PsyD)
Alliant International University: San Diego (MA/MS—terminal, PsyD)
Alliant International University: San Francisco (MA/MS—terminal, PsyD)
American International College (EdD, MA/MS)
Ball State University (PhD)
Baylor University (PhD)
Boston College (MA/MS, PhD)
City University of New York: Graduate School and University Center (PhD)
Denver, University of (MA/MS—terminal)
George Mason University (MA/MS—terminal, Other, PhD)
Hawaii, University of (MEd, PhD)
Houston, University of (MEd, PhD)
Illinois, University of, Chicago (MEd, PhD)
Indiana University (MA/MS, PhD)
Iowa, University of (PhD)
Kansas, University of (EdS, MEd, PhD)

Kean University (MA/MS)
Kentucky, University of (MA/MS—terminal, PhD)
Marist College (MA/MS—terminal)
Maryland, University of (PhD)
Massachusetts School of Professional Psychology (MA/MS—terminal)
McGill University (PhD)
Michigan, University of (PhD)
Mississippi State University (MA/MS—terminal)
Missouri, University of, Columbia (MA/MS—terminal, MEd, PhD)
New York University (MA/MS—terminal)
Oklahoma State University (PhD)
Oklahoma, University of (MEd, PhD)
State University of New York, University of Albany (MA/MS, PhD)
Tennessee, University of, Knoxville (MA/MS—terminal, PhD)
Texas A&M International University (MA/MS—terminal)
Texas A&M University (PhD)
Texas A&M University—Commerce (PhD)
Texas Tech University (MEd, PhD)
Texas, University of, Austin (Other)
University at Buffalo, State University of New York (MA/MS—terminal, PhD)
Utah, University of (MA/MS, MA/MS—terminal, MEd, PhD)
Walden University (PhD)
Washington State University (MEd, PhD)
Wayne State University (PhD)
Wisconsin, University of, Madison (PhD)
Wisconsin, University of, Milwaukee (PhD)

Environmental Psychology
Texas State University-San Marcos (MA/MS—terminal)
Victoria, University of (PhD)

Experimental Psychology (Applied)
Akron, University of (PhD)
Alabama, University of, at Huntsville (MA/MS—terminal)
Alberta, University of (MA/MS, PhD)
Angelo State University (MA/MS—terminal)
Appalachian State University (MA/MS—terminal)
Auburn University (MA/MS—terminal, PhD)
Augusta State University (MA/MS—terminal)
California State University, Fresno (MA/MS—terminal)
California State University, Long Beach (MA/MS—terminal)
Central Florida, University of (PhD)
Central Michigan University (PhD)
Central Washington University (MA/MS—terminal)
Clemson University (PhD)
Cleveland State University (MA/MS—terminal)
DePaul University (PhD)
East Tennessee State University (PhD)
Florida International University (PhD)

Florida, University of (PhD)
Fordham University (PhD)
Fort Hays State University (MA/MS—terminal)
Hawaii, University of, Manoa (PhD)
Idaho, University of (MA/MS—terminal)
Kent State University (PhD)
Louisiana, University of, Lafayette (MA/MS—terminal)
Louisiana, University of, Monroe (MA/MS—terminal)
Marietta College (MA/MS—terminal)
Memphis, University of (PhD)
Mississippi State University (MA/MS—terminal)
Missouri State University (MA/MS—terminal)
Nebraska, University of, Omaha (MA/MS)
New Mexico State University (MA/MS, PhD)
North Carolina, University of, Wilmington (MA/MS—terminal)
North Texas, University of (PhD)
Oklahoma, University of (PhD)
Old Dominion University (PhD)
Penn State Harrisburg (MA/MS—terminal)
Pennsylvania, University of (PhD)
Regina, University of (MA/MS—terminal, PhD)
Rice University (PhD)
Ryerson University (MA/MS, PhD)
Saint Joseph's University (MA/MS—terminal)
Simon Fraser University (PhD)
Southeastern Louisiana University (MA/MS—terminal)
Tennessee, University of, Chattanooga (MA/MS—terminal)
Toledo, University of (PhD)
University at Albany, State University of New York (PhD)
West Virginia University (PhD)
Wichita State University (PhD)

Experimental Psychology (General)
Alabama, University of, at Huntsville (MA/MS—terminal)
American University (MA/MS—terminal)
Appalachian State University (MA/MS—terminal)
Arkansas, University of (PhD)
Augusta State University (MA/MS—terminal)
Brandeis University (MA/MS—terminal)
Brown University (PhD)
Bucknell University (MA/MS—terminal)
California State University, Fresno (MA/MS—terminal)
California State University, Fullerton (MA/MS—terminal)
California State University, Long Beach (MA/MS—terminal)
California State University, Northridge (MA/MS—terminal)
California State University, San Marcos (MA/MS—terminal)
California, University of, San Diego (PhD)
Carnegie Mellon University (PhD)

Central Connecticut State University (MA/MS—terminal)
Central Michigan University (MA/MS—terminal)
Central Missouri, University of (MA/MS—terminal)
Central Oklahoma, University of (MA/MS)
Central Washington University (MA/MS—terminal)
Chicago, University of (PhD)
City University of New York: Brooklyn College (MA/MS—terminal)
Claremont Graduate University (PhD)
College of William and Mary (MA/MS—terminal)
Colorado, University of, Colorado Springs (MA/MS—terminal)
Dalhousie University (MA/MS, PhD)
DePaul University (MA/MS—terminal)
Eastern Kentucky University (MA/MS—terminal)
Eastern Michigan University (MA/MS—terminal)
Eastern Washington University (MA/MS—terminal)
Emporia State University (MA/MS—terminal)
Florida Atlantic University (MA/MS—terminal, PhD)
Fort Hays State University (MA/MS—terminal)
Georgia Southern University (MA/MS—terminal)
Hartford, University of (MA/MS—terminal)
Harvard University (PhD)
Idaho State University (PhD)
Idaho, University of (MA/MS—terminal)
Iona College (MA/MS—terminal)
Kentucky, University of (PhD)
Long Island University (MA/MS—terminal)
Louisiana, University of, Lafayette (MA/MS—terminal)
Louisiana, University of, Monroe (MA/MS—terminal)
Maine, University of (MA/MS)
Marietta College (MA/MS—terminal)
Marist College (MA/MS—terminal)
Massachusetts, University of, Dartmouth (MA/MS—terminal)
McGill University (PhD)
Memphis, University of (MA/MS—terminal)
Miami, University of (MA/MS—terminal)
Middle Tennessee State University (MA/MS—terminal)
Mississippi State University (MA/MS—terminal)
Mississippi, University of (PhD)
Missouri State University (MA/MS—terminal)
Missouri, University of, Kansas City (PhD)
Montana State University Billings (MA/MS—terminal)
Montana, The University of (PhD)
Morehead State University (MA/MS—terminal)
Nebraska, University of, Lincoln (PhD)
New Brunswick, University of (PhD)

New Mexico State University (MA/MS)
New York University, Graduate School of Arts and Science (PhD)
North Carolina, University of, Wilmington (MA/MS—terminal)
North Dakota, University of (PhD)
North Florida, University of (MA/MS—terminal)
Northern Arizona University (MA/MS—terminal)
Northern Michigan University (MA/MS—terminal)
Nova Southeastern University (MA/MS—terminal)
Oakland University (MA/MS—terminal, PhD)
Oklahoma, University of (MA/MS—terminal, PhD)
Old Dominion University (MA/MS—terminal)
Ottawa, University of (PhD)
Pace University (MA/MS—terminal)
Palo Alto University (MA/MS—terminal)
Pennsylvania, University of (PhD)
Pepperdine University (MA/MS)
Pittsburg State University (MA/MS—terminal)
Purdue University (PhD)
Queen's University (MA/MS, PhD)
Radford University (MA/MS—terminal)
Rhode Island College (MA/MS—terminal)
Rivier University (MA/MS—terminal)
Ryerson University (MA/MS, PhD)
Saint Joseph's University (MA/MS—terminal)
Sam Houston State University (MA/MS—terminal)
San Francisco State University (MA/MS—terminal)
San Jose State University (MA/MS—terminal)
Seton Hall University (MA/MS—terminal)
South Alabama, University of (MA/MS—terminal)
Southeastern Louisiana University (MA/MS—terminal)
Southern Connecticut State University (MA/MS—terminal)
St. John's University (MA/MS—terminal)
State University of New York at New Paltz (MA/MS—terminal)
Stephen F. Austin State University (MA/MS—terminal)
Stony Brook University (MA/MS, PhD)
Syracuse University (PhD)
Tennessee, University of, Knoxville (MA/MS—terminal, PhD)
Texas A&M International University (MA/MS—terminal)
Texas A&M University—Commerce (MA/MS—terminal)
Texas State University—San Marcos (MA/MS—terminal)
Texas Tech University (PhD)
Texas, University of, Arlington (PhD)
Texas, University of, Pan American (MA/MS—terminal)

The College at Brockport, State University of New York (MA/MS—terminal)
The New School for Social Research (MA/MS—terminal)
Towson University (MA/MS—terminal)
Tufts University (PhD)
University at Buffalo, State University of New York (MA/MS—terminal)
Utah State University (PhD)
Utah, University of (PhD)
Vermont, University of (PhD)
Victoria, University of (PhD)
Villanova University (MA/MS—terminal)
Wake Forest University (MA/MS—terminal)
Wayne State University (PhD)
West Chester University of Pennsylvania (MA/MS—terminal)
West Florida, The University of (MA/MS—terminal)
Western Carolina University (MA/MS—terminal)
Western Illinois University (MA/MS—terminal)
Wisconsin, University of, Madison (PhD)
Wisconsin, University of, Oshkosh (MA/MS—terminal)
Xavier University (MA/MS—terminal)

F

Family Psychology
Alliant International University: San Diego (PhD), PsyD, Respecialization Diploma)
Antioch University Santa Barbara (PsyD)
Argosy University/Orange County (EdD)
Arizona State University (PhD)
Azusa Pacific University (PsyD)
Fuller Theological Seminary (PsyD)
North Carolina State University (PhD)
Seattle Pacific University (PhD)
Seton Hill University (MA/MS—terminal)
The Chicago School of Professional Psychology (MA/MS—terminal, PsyD)
Wayne State University (MA/MS—terminal)

Forensic Psychology
Alliant International University: Los Angeles (PsyD)
Alliant International University: Sacramento (PsyD)
Alliant International University: San Diego (PsyD)
American International College (MA/MS—terminal)
Argosy University/Orange County (MA/MS—terminal)
Arizona State University (PhD)
Arizona, The University of (PhD)
Carleton University (MA/MS—terminal, PhD)
Central Oklahoma, University of (MA/MS)
City University of New York: John Jay College of Criminal Justice (MA/MS—terminal, Other)
Denver, University of (MA/MS—terminal)

Drexel University (PhD)
Fairleigh Dickinson University, Metropolitan Campus (MA/MS—terminal)
Florida International University (PhD)
George Washington University (MA/MS—terminal)
Louisiana, University of, Monroe (MA/MS—terminal)
Marymount University (MA/MS—terminal)
Massachusetts School of Professional Psychology (MA/MS—terminal)
Massachusetts, University of, Boston (MA/MS—terminal)
Missouri State University (MA/MS—terminal, Other)
Nebraska, University of, Lincoln (PhD)
North Dakota, University of (MA/MS—terminal)
Palo Alto University (MA/MS—terminal)
Roger Williams University (MA/MS—terminal)
Sage Colleges, The (Other)
Sam Houston State University (PhD)
Saskatchewan, University of (PhD)
The Chicago School of Professional Psychology (MA/MS—terminal, Other, PsyD)
Tulsa, University of (MA/MS—terminal)
Widener University (Other)
Wisconsin School of Professional Psychology (PsyD)
Wyoming, University of (PhD)

G

Gender Psychology
Hawaii, University of, Manoa (PhD)
Texas Woman's University (MA/MS—terminal, PhD)

General Psychology (Theory, History, and Philosophy)
Adelphi University (MA/MS—terminal)
Angelo State University (MA/MS—terminal)
Boston University (MA/MS—terminal)
Brandeis University (MA/MS—terminal)
Central Missouri, University of (MA/MS—terminal)
Central Oklahoma, University of (MA/MS—terminal)
Dayton, University of (MA/MS—terminal)
DePaul University (MA/MS—terminal)
Drexel University (MA/MS—terminal)
Eastern Kentucky University (MA/MS—terminal)
Fairleigh Dickinson University, Metropolitan Campus (MA/MS—terminal)
Goddard College (MA/MS—terminal)
Institute for the Psychological Sciences (MA/MS—terminal)
Long Island University (MA/MS—terminal)
Marist College (MA/MS—terminal)
Marshall University (MA/MS—terminal)

Memphis, University of (MA/MS—terminal)
Mount St. Mary's College (MA/MS—terminal)
New York University, Graduate School of Arts and Science (MA/MS—terminal)
North Florida, University of (MA/MS—terminal)
Northcentral University (MA/MS, PhD)
Northern Arizona University (MA/MS—terminal)
Northern Iowa, University of (MA/MS)
Nova Southeastern University (MA/MS—terminal)
Pace University (MA/MS—terminal)
Palo Alto University (MA/MS—terminal)
Pittsburg State University (MA/MS—terminal)
Saint Francis, University of (MA/MS—terminal)
Sam Houston State University (MA/MS—terminal)
Seton Hall University (MA/MS—terminal)
Simon Fraser University (PhD)
Southern Connecticut State University (MA/MS—terminal)
State University of New York at New Paltz (MA/MS—terminal)
Stephen F. Austin State University (MA/MS—terminal)
Stony Brook University (MA/MS)
The Chicago School of Professional Psychology (MA/MS—terminal, PsyD)
University at Buffalo, State University of New York (MA/MS—terminal)
West Chester University of Pennsylvania (MA/MS—terminal)
West Florida, The University of (MA/MS—terminal)
Western Carolina University (MA/MS—terminal)
York University (PhD)

Geropsychology
Akron, University of (PhD)
Cleveland State University (PhD)
Colorado, University of, Colorado Springs (PhD)
Florida, University of (PhD)
North Carolina State University (PhD)
Washington University in St. Louis (PhD)
West Virginia University (PhD)
Yeshiva University (PsyD)

H

Health Psychology
Alabama, University of, at Birmingham (PhD)
Alliant International University: Fresno (PhD)
Appalachian State University (MA/MS—terminal)
British Columbia, University of (PhD)
California State University, Dominguez Hills (MA/MS—terminal)
California, University of, Irvine (PhD)

California, University of, Los Angeles (PhD)
California, University of, Merced (PhD)
California, University of, Riverside (PhD)
Carnegie Mellon University (PhD)
Central Connecticut State University (MA/MS—terminal)
Claremont Graduate University (MA/MS—terminal)
Clemson University (PhD)
Colorado, University of, Denver (PhD)
Connecticut, University of (PhD)
Duke University (MA/MS—terminal, PhD)
East Carolina University (PhD)
George Fox University (PsyD)
George Washington University (PhD)
Guelph, University of (MA/MS, PhD)
Houston, University of (PhD)
Indiana University-Purdue University Indianapolis (PhD)
Indianapolis, University of (PsyD)
Iowa, University of (PhD)
Kansas State University (Other)
Kansas, University of (PhD)
Kentucky, University of (PhD)
Memphis, University of (PhD)
Mercer University School of Medicine (PhD)
Michigan, University of, Dearborn (MA/MS—terminal)
Missouri, University of, Kansas City (PhD)
New Mexico State University (PhD)
New Mexico, University of (PhD)
North Carolina State University (PhD)
North Carolina, University of, Charlotte (PhD)
North Dakota State University (PhD)
North Texas, University of (PhD)
Northern Arizona University (MA/MS—terminal)
Northwestern University Feinberg School of Medicine (PhD)
Ohio State University, The (PhD)
Ohio University (PhD)
Old Dominion University (PhD)
Penn State Harrisburg (MA/MS—terminal)
Philadelphia College of Osteopathic Medicine (Other)
Pittsburgh, University of (PhD)
Rhode Island College (Other)
Rhode Island, University of (PhD)
Rosalind Franklin University of Medicine and Science (PhD)
Southern California, University of, Keck School of Medicine (PhD)
Stony Brook University (PhD)
Syracuse University (PhD)
Texas State University—San Marcos (MA/MS—terminal)
Texas, University of, Arlington (PhD)
Uniformed Services University of the Health Sciences (PhD)
Utah, University of (PhD)
Virginia Commonwealth University (PhD)
Walden University (PhD)
Wisconsin, University of, Milwaukee (MA/MS—terminal, PhD)

Wisconsin, University of, Stout (MA/MS—terminal)
Yale University (PhD)
Yeshiva University (PhD)

Human Development and Family Studies
Arizona State University (PhD)
Cornell University (PhD)
Illinois, University of, Urbana–Champaign (PhD)
Iowa State University (MA/MS—terminal, PhD)
Pennsylvania State University (PhD)
Texas, University of, Austin (PhD)
Wisconsin, University of, Madison (MA/MS, PhD)

Human Factors
Arizona State University (MA/MS—terminal)
California State University, Long Beach (MA/MS—terminal)
Central Florida, University of (PhD)
Cincinnati, University of (PhD)
Clemson University (PhD)
Dayton, University of (MA/MS—terminal)
George Mason University (MA/MS—terminal, PhD)
Georgia Institute of Technology (PhD)
Idaho, University of (MA/MS—terminal)
Kansas State University (PhD)
Missouri Western State University (MA/MS—terminal)
New Mexico State University (PhD)
North Carolina State University (PhD)
Old Dominion University (PhD)
Rice University (PhD)
South Dakota, University of (PhD)
Texas Tech University (PhD)
Wichita State University (PhD)
Wright State University (PhD)

Humanistic Psychology
West Georgia, University of (MA/MS—terminal)

I

Industrial/Organizational Psychology
Akron, University of (MA/MS—terminal)
Alabama, University of, at Huntsville (MA/MS—terminal)
Alliant International University: Fresno (MA/MS—terminal, PsyD)
Alliant International University: Los Angeles (MA/MS—terminal, PhD)
Alliant International University: San Diego (MA/MS—terminal, PhD)
Alliant International University: San Francisco (MA/MS—terminal, PhD)
Angelo State University (MA/MS—terminal)
Appalachian State University (MA/MS—terminal)
Auburn University (PhD)
Austin Peay State University (MA/MS—terminal)

Baltimore, University of (MA/MS—terminal)
Bowling Green State University (PhD)
Calgary, University of (PhD)
California State University, Long Beach (MA/MS—terminal)
California State University, Sacramento (MA/MS—terminal)
Carnegie Mellon University (PhD)
Central Florida, University of (MA/MS—terminal, PhD)
Central Michigan University (MA/MS—terminal, PhD)
City University of New York: Brooklyn College (MA/MS—terminal)
Claremont Graduate University (MA/MS—terminal, PhD)
Clemson University (PhD)
Cleveland State University (MA/MS—terminal)
Colorado State University (PhD)
Connecticut, University of (PhD)
DePaul University (PhD)
Detroit Mercy, University of (MA/MS—terminal)
East Carolina University (MA/MS—terminal, PhD)
Eastern Kentucky University (MA/MS—terminal)
Emporia State University (MA/MS—terminal)
Florida Institute of Technology (MA/MS—terminal, PhD)
Florida International University (PhD)
George Mason University (MA/MS—terminal, PhD)
George Washington University (PhD)
Georgia Institute of Technology (PhD)
Georgia, University of (PhD)
Golden Gate University (MA/MS—terminal)
Guelph, University of (MA/MS, PhD)
Hartford, University of (MA/MS—terminal)
Hofstra University (MA/MS—terminal, PhD)
Houston, University of (PhD)
Illinois Institute of Technology (MA/MS—terminal, PhD)
Illinois State University (MA/MS—terminal)
Illinois, University of, Urbana–Champaign (MA/MS—terminal, PhD)
Indiana University-Purdue University Indianapolis (MA/MS—terminal)
Iona College (MA/MS—terminal)
Kansas State University (MA/MS—terminal, Other, PhD)
Kean University (MA/MS—terminal)
Lamar University-Beaumont (MA/MS—terminal)
Louisiana State University (PhD)
Maryland, University of (PhD)
Massachusetts School of Professional Psychology (MA/MS—terminal, PsyD)
Michigan State University (PhD)
Middle Tennessee State University (MA/MS—terminal)

Minnesota State University—Mankato (MA/MS—terminal)
Minnesota, University of (PhD)
Missouri State University (MA/MS—terminal)
Missouri, University of, St. Louis (PhD)
Nebraska, University of, Omaha (MA/MS, MA/MS—terminal, PhD)
New Haven, University of (MA/MS—terminal)
New York University, Graduate School of Arts and Science (MA/MS—terminal)
North Carolina State University (PhD)
North Carolina, University of, Charlotte (MA/MS—terminal, PhD)
Northern Arizona University (MEd)
Northern Illinois University (PhD)
Northern Kentucky University (MA/MS—terminal)
Northern Michigan University (MA/MS—terminal)
Ohio University (PhD)
Oklahoma, University of (MA/MS—terminal, PhD)
Old Dominion University (PhD)
Pennsylvania State University (PhD)
Philadelphia College of Osteopathic Medicine (MA/MS—terminal)
Portland State University (PhD)
Purdue University (PhD)
Radford University (MA/MS—terminal)
Rice University (PhD)
Roosevelt University (MA/MS—terminal, PhD)
Saint Louis University (PhD)
Saint Mary's University (MA/MS—terminal, PhD)
Salem State University (MA/MS—terminal)
San Diego State University (MA/MS—terminal)
San Francisco State University (MA/MS—terminal)
San Jose State University (MA/MS—terminal)
South Florida, University of (PhD)
Southeastern Louisiana University (MA/MS—terminal)
Southern Illinois University Carbondale (PhD)
Southern Illinois University Edwardsville (MA/MS—terminal)
St. Cloud State University (MA/MS—terminal)
Tennessee, University of, Chattanooga (MA/MS—terminal)
Texas, University of, Arlington (MA/MS—terminal)
The Chicago School of Professional Psychology (MA/MS—terminal, Other, PhD, PsyD)
Towson University (MA/MS)
Tulsa, University of (MA/MS, MA/MS—terminal, PhD)
University at Albany, State University of New York (MA/MS—terminal, PhD)
Virginia Polytechnic Institute and State University (PhD)

Walden University (PhD)
Waterloo, University of (MA/MS—terminal, PhD)
Wayne State University (MA/MS—terminal, PhD)
West Chester University of Pennsylvania (MA/MS—terminal)
West Florida, The University of (MA/MS—terminal)
Western Kentucky University (MA/MS—terminal)
Windsor, University of (PhD)
Wisconsin, University of, Stout (MA/MS—terminal)
Wright State University (PhD)
Xavier University (MA/MS—terminal)

M

Marriage and Family Therapy
Alliant International University: Irvine (MA/MS—terminal), PsyD)
Alliant International University: Los Angeles (MA/MS—terminal, PsyD)
Alliant International University: Sacramento (MA/MS—terminal, PsyD)
Alliant International University: San Diego (MA/MS—terminal, PsyD)
Alliant International University: San Francisco (MA/MS—terminal)
Argosy University/Orange County (MA/MS—terminal)
Azusa Pacific University (MA/MS—terminal)
California Lutheran University (MA/MS—terminal)
California Polytechnic State University (MA/MS—terminal)
California State Polytechnic University-Pomona (MA/MS—terminal)
East Carolina University (PhD)
Geneva College (MA/MS—terminal)
Golden Gate University (MA/MS—terminal)
Gonzaga University (MA/MS—terminal)
John F. Kennedy University (MA/MS—terminal)
Kean University (Other)
La Salle University (MA/MS—terminal)
Massachusetts School of Professional Psychology (MA/MS—terminal)
Massachusetts, University of, Boston (MA/MS—terminal)
Miami, University of (MA/MS—terminal)
Mount St. Mary's College (MA/MS—terminal)
Our Lady of the Lake University (MA/MS—terminal)
Palo Alto University (MA/MS—terminal)
Pepperdine University (MA/MS)
Saint Mary's University of Minnesota (MA/MS—terminal, Other)
Salem State University (MA/MS—terminal)
Seton Hall University (MA/MS—terminal, Other)
Seton Hill University (MA/MS—terminal)

Sonoma State University (MA/MS—terminal)

Texas, University of, Tyler (MA/MS—terminal)

The Chicago School of Professional Psychology (MA/MS—terminal, PsyD)

The School of Professional Psychology at Forest Institute (MA/MS—terminal)

Wheaton College (MA/MS—terminal)

Mental Health Counseling

Adelphi University (MA/MS—terminal)

Arizona State University (Other)

Austin Peay State University (MA/MS—terminal)

Barry University (MA/MS—terminal)

Boston College (MA/MS—terminal)

Bridgewater State University (MA/MS—terminal)

Central Washington University (MA/MS—terminal)

City University of New York: Brooklyn College (MA/MS—terminal)

City University of New York: John Jay College of Criminal Justice (MA/MS—terminal)

Cleveland State University (MEd)

Eastern Washington University (MA/MS—terminal)

Florida State University (MA/MS—terminal)

Fordham University (MEd)

Geneva College (MA/MS—terminal)

Georgia State University (MA/MS—terminal)

Georgian Court University (MA/MS—terminal)

Goddard College (MA/MS—terminal)

Indiana State University (MA/MS)

Indianapolis, University of (MA/MS—terminal)

Iona College (MA/MS—terminal)

Kean University (MA/MS—terminal)

La Salle University (MA/MS—terminal)

Lewis University (MA/MS—terminal)

Loyola University of Chicago (EdS)

Marist College (MA/MS—terminal)

Marquette University (MA/MS—terminal)

Massachusetts School of Professional Psychology (MA/MS—terminal)

Massachusetts, University of, Boston (MA/MS—terminal)

Miami, University of (MA/MS—terminal)

Missouri, University of, Kansas City (EdS, MA/MS—terminal)

New Mexico State University (MA/MS—terminal)

New York University (MA/MS—terminal)

North Dakota, University of (MA/MS—terminal)

Northeastern University (MA/MS—terminal)

Nova Southeastern University (MA/MS—terminal)

Palo Alto University (MA/MS—terminal)

Pennsylvania, University of (MEd)

Pittsburg State University (MA/MS—terminal)

Puget Sound, University of (MEd)

Rosalind Franklin University of Medicine and Science (MA/MS—terminal)

Rowan University (MA/MS—terminal, Other)

Saint Francis, University of (MA/MS—terminal)

Salem State University (MA/MS—terminal)

Seton Hall University (MA/MS—terminal, Other)

Sonoma State University (MA/MS—terminal)

State University of New York at New Paltz (MA/MS—terminal, Respecialization Diploma)

State University of New York, University of Albany (MA/MS—terminal)

Suffolk University (MA/MS—terminal)

Tennessee, University of, Knoxville (MA/MS—terminal, PhD)

Texas, University of, Tyler (MA/MS—terminal)

University at Buffalo, State University of New York (MA/MS—terminal, Other)

West Florida, The University of (MA/MS—terminal)

Wheaton College (MA/MS—terminal)

Yeshiva University (MA/MS—terminal)

Multicultural Psychology

Alliant International University: Los Angeles (PhD), PsyD)

Alliant International University: San Francisco (PhD, PsyD, Respecialization Diploma)

Cleveland State University (MA/MS)

Denver, University of (PsyD)

Fordham University (Other)

Hawaii, University of, Manoa (PhD)

John F. Kennedy University (PsyD)

Massachusetts, University of, Lowell (MA/MS—terminal)

New Mexico State University (EdS)

Pennsylvania, University of (PhD)

Seton Hall University (PhD)

Tennessee, University of, Knoxville (MA/MS—terminal)

The Chicago School of Professional Psychology (PhD)

Utah State University (PhD)

N

Neuropsychology

Arizona, The University of (PhD)

Boston University (PhD)

Brigham Young University (PhD)

Chicago, University of (PhD)

Cincinnati, University of (PhD)

Colorado State University (PhD)

Concordia University (PhD)

Connecticut, University of (PhD)

Drexel University (PhD)

Duke University (PhD)

Fuller Theological Seminary (PhD)

Georgia Institute of Technology (PhD)

Georgia State University (PhD)

Houston, University of (PhD)

Idaho, University of (PhD)

Michigan State University (PhD)

New Mexico, University of (PhD)

North Carolina, University of, Chapel Hill (PhD)

Philadelphia College of Osteopathic Medicine (Other)

Purdue University (PhD)

Saint Louis University (PhD)

South Florida, University of (PhD)

Temple University (PhD)

Texas, University of, Tyler (MA/MS—terminal)

Tulsa, University of (PhD)

Utah, University of (PhD)

Victoria, University of (PhD)

Virginia Consortium Program in Clinical Psychology (PsyD)

Wayne State University (PhD)

Yale University (PhD)

Neuroscience

Alabama, University of, at Birmingham (PhD)

American University (PhD)

Arizona State University (PhD)

Arizona, The University of (PhD)

Baylor University (PhD)

Boston College (PhD)

Bowling Green State University (PhD)

Brigham Young University (PhD)

British Columbia, University of (PhD)

California, University of, Berkeley (PhD)

California, University of, Irvine (PhD)

California, University of, Los Angeles (PhD)

California, University of, Riverside (PhD)

Colorado, University of, Boulder (PhD)

Concordia University (PhD)

Connecticut, University of (PhD)

Cornell University (PhD)

Dalhousie University (MA/MS, PhD)

Delaware, University of (PhD)

Denver, University of (PhD)

Drexel University (PhD)

Duke University (PhD)

Emory University (PhD)

Florida State University (PhD)

Florida, University of (PhD)

George Mason University (MA/MS—terminal, PhD)

George Washington University (PhD)

Georgetown University (PhD)

Guelph, University of (MA/MS, PhD)

Hawaii, University of, Manoa (PhD)

Idaho, University of (PhD)

Illinois, University of, Urbana–Champaign (PhD)

Indiana University (PhD)

Indiana University–Purdue University Indianapolis (PhD)

Iowa, University of (PhD)

Johns Hopkins University (PhD)

Kansas State University (PhD)

Kansas, University of (PhD)

Manitoba, University of (PhD)

Penn State Harrisburg (MA/MS—terminal)
Purdue University (PhD)
Rhode Island, University of (PhD)
South Carolina, University of (PhD)
Southern California, University of (PhD)
Tennessee, University of, Knoxville (PhD)
Texas, University of, Austin (Other, PhD)
Utah, University of (MA/MS—terminal, PhD)
Vanderbilt University (PhD)
Virginia, University of (PhD)
Washington, University of (PhD)
Wisconsin, University of, Madison (PhD)
Wisconsin, University of, Milwaukee (MA/MS, PhD)
York University (PhD)

R

Rehabilitation Psychology
Ball State University (MA/MS—terminal)
Illinois Institute of Technology (MA/MS—terminal, PhD)
Saint Francis, University of (MA/MS—terminal)
University at Buffalo, State University of New York (MA/MS—terminal)

S

School Counseling
Austin Peay State University (MA/MS—terminal)
Boston College (MA/MS—terminal)
Cleveland State University (MEd)
Eastern Washington University (MA/MS—terminal)
Fordham University (MEd)
Geneva College (MA/MS—terminal)
Georgia State University (MEd)
Gonzaga University (MA/MS—terminal, Other)
Houston, University of (MEd)
Immaculata University (MA/MS, MA/MS—terminal)
Lehigh University (MEd)
Lewis University (MA/MS—terminal)
Loyola University of Chicago (MEd)
Massachusetts, University of, Boston (MA/MS—terminal)
Millersville University (MEd)
Missouri, University of, Kansas City (EdS)
New York University (MA/MS—terminal)
North Dakota, University of (MA/MS—terminal)
Northeastern University (MA/MS—terminal)
Northern Arizona University (MEd)
Nova Southeastern University (MA/MS—terminal)
Pennsylvania, University of (MEd, Other)
Pittsburg State University (MA/MS—terminal)
Puget Sound, University of (MEd)
Roberts Wesleyan College (MA/MS—terminal)
Saint Francis, University of (MEd)

Seton Hall University (MA/MS—terminal)
Sonoma State University (MA/MS—terminal)
State University of New York at New Paltz (MA/MS—terminal)
Suffolk University (MA/MS—terminal)
Tennessee, University of, Knoxville (MA/MS—terminal, PhD)
Texas, University of, Austin (Other)
Texas, University of, Tyler (MA/MS—terminal)
University at Buffalo, State University of New York (MEd, Other)
Utah State University (MA/MS—terminal)
Utah, University of (MEd)
Vanderbilt University (MEd)
Wisconsin, University of, Milwaukee (MA/MS)

School Psychology
Adelphi University (MA/MS—terminal)
Alfred University (MA/MS, PsyD)
Alliant International University: Irvine (MA/MS—terminal, PsyD)
Alliant International University: Los Angeles (MA/MS—terminal, PsyD)
Alliant International University: San Diego (MA/MS—terminal, PsyD)
Alliant International University: San Francisco (MA/MS—terminal, PsyD)
American International College (EdD)
Appalachian State University (EdS)
Ball State University (EdS, PhD)
Baylor University (EdS)
Brigham Young University (EdS)
California State University, Fresno (EdS)
California, University of, Berkeley (PhD)
California, University of, Santa Barbara (MEd, PhD)
Central Arkansas, University of (MA/MS—terminal, PhD)
Central Michigan University (Other, PhD)
Central Oklahoma, University of (MA/MS—terminal)
Central Washington University (EdS)
Cincinnati, University of (EdS, PhD)
Citadel, The (EdS)
City University of New York: Brooklyn College (MA/MS)
City University of New York: Graduate School and University Center (PhD)
Cleveland State University (Other)
Columbia University (MEd, PhD)
Connecticut, University of (MA/MS, PhD)
Dayton, University of (EdS)
Denver, University of (EdS, PhD)
Detroit Mercy, University of (Other)
Duquesne University (Other, PhD, PsyD)
East Carolina University (MA/MS—terminal, PhD)
Eastern Illinois University (Other)
Eastern Kentucky University (EdS)
Eastern Washington University (EdS, Other)
Emporia State University (EdS)
Fairleigh Dickinson University, Metropolitan Campus (MA/MS—terminal, PsyD)

Florida State University (EdS, PhD)
Fordham University (Other, PhD)
Fort Hays State University (EdS, MA/MS—terminal)
Francis Marion University (Other)
Gallaudet University (Other)
George Mason University (MA/MS—terminal)
Georgia State University (EdS, PhD)
Georgia, University of (PhD)
Georgian Court University (MA/MS—terminal)
Hartford, University of (MA/MS—terminal)
Hofstra University (PsyD)
Houston, University of (PhD)
Humboldt State University (MA/MS—terminal)
Illinois State University (Other, PhD)
Immaculata University (MA/MS—terminal, Other)
Indiana State University (EdS, MEd, PhD)
Indiana University (EdS, PhD)
Iona College (MA/MS—terminal)
Iowa, University of (PhD)
Kansas, University of (EdS, PhD)
Kean University (Other, PsyD)
Kent State University (EdS, PhD)
Kentucky, University of (EdS, PhD)
Lehigh University (EdS, PhD)
Louisiana State University (PhD)
Louisiana State University Shreveport (Other)
Manitoba, University of (MA/MS—terminal)
Marist College (MA/MS—terminal)
Maryland, University of (PhD)
Massachusetts School of Professional Psychology (MA/MS—terminal, PsyD)
Massachusetts, University of, Boston (EdS, PhD)
McGill University (PhD)
Memphis, University of (MA/MS—terminal, PhD)
Michigan State University (PhD)
Middle Tennessee State University (EdS)
Millersville University (MA/MS)
Minnesota State University—Mankato (PsyD)
Minnesota State University—Moorhead (EdS)
Minnesota, University of (EdS, PhD)
Mississippi State University (EdS, PhD)
Missouri, University of, Columbia (EdS, MA/MS, PhD)
Montana, The University of (EdS, PhD)
Nebraska, University of, Lincoln (PhD)
Nebraska, University of, Omaha (EdS, MA/MS)
New Mexico State University (EdS)
North Carolina State University (PhD)
Northeastern University (EdS, MA/MS—terminal, PhD)
Northern Arizona University (EdS, PhD)
Northern Colorado, University of (EdS, PhD)
Northern Illinois University (PhD)
Nova Southeastern University (Other, PsyD)